A SHAKESPEAREAN GENEALOGY

This chart reflects Shakespeare's history plays and is thus not historically accurate. Many descendants of Henry II and Edward III are omitted. On occasion, Shakespeare combined or simply invented historical figures. These deviations from fact are explained in the notes.

In the chart, the names of Kings and Queens are printed in capitals, and the dates of their reigns are printed in bold. The names of characters appearing in the plays are underlined.

Henry
d. 1183

Edward, Prince of
Wales 1330–1376

RICHARD II
1367–1400
(1377–99)

William of
Hatfield

Lionel, Duke of
Clarence 1338–1368

Philippa
m. Edmund
Mortimer, Earl
of March

RICHARD I
1157–1199
(1189–99)

Philip Faulconbridge*
(Richard Plantagenet)

John of Gaunt,
Duke of Lancaster
1340–1399
m. Blanche of
Lancaster
m. Constance of
Castile
m. Katherine
Swynford

HENRY IV
1367–1413
(1399–1413)

Thomas Beaufort,
Duke of Exeter
1377–1427

Henry Beaufort,
Bishop of Winchester
1375–1447

John Beaufort,
Earl of Somerset
1372–1409

Joan Beaufort
m. Ralph Neville,
Earl of
Westmoreland

HENRY II
1133–1189
(1154–89)
m. Eleanor
of Aquitaine
d. 1204

Geoffrey, d. 1186
m. Constance
of Brittany

Arthur
1187–1203

JOHN 1167–1216
(1199–1216)

HENRY III
1207–1272
(1216–72)

EDWARD I
1239–1307
(1272–1307)

EDWARD II
1284–1327
(1307–27)

Edmund of Langley,
Duke of York
1341–1402

Edward, Duke of
Aumerle d. 1415

Richard, Earl
of Cambridge
d. 1415 m. Anne
Mortimer (above)

EDWARD III
1312–1377
(1327–77)
m. Philippa of
Hainault

Thomas of
Woodstock, Duke of
Gloucester 1355–1397

Anne

Eleanor
m. Alfonso VIII,
King of Castile

Blanche, d. 1252
m. Louis VIII
of France

William of
Windsor

*Philip Faulconbridge, the bastard son of Richard I, had no historical existence. Such a character appears in the play *The Life and Death of King John* and is referred to in passing in Holinshed's *Chronicles*.

† In the character of Edmund Mortimer, Shakespeare combines two historical figures. The Edmund Mortimer who married Catrin, daughter of Owain Glyndŵr, was the grandson of Lionel, Duke of Clarence, and the younger brother of Roger, Earl of March. He died in 1409. Shakespeare combines him with his nephew, the Edmund Mortimer recognized by Richard II as his heir (d. 1424). This second Edmund was the brother of Anne Mortimer and the uncle of Richard Plantagenet.

‡ The character of the Duke of Somerset combines Henry Beaufort with his younger brother Edmund (d. 1471), who succeeded him as Duke.

THE NORTON
SHAKESPEARE

BASED ON THE OXFORD EDITION

Volume 2
Later Plays

*The original Oxford Text on which this
edition is based was prepared by*

Stanley Wells
Gary Taylor
General Editors

John Jowett
William Montgomery

The Norton Shakespeare, Second Edition, is based on *William Shakespeare: The Complete Works*,
Second Edition, and is published by arrangement with Oxford University Press,
with additional material from W. W. Norton & Company, Inc.

THE NORTON
SHAKESPEARE

Based on the Oxford Edition

Volume 2
Later Plays

Stephen Greenblatt, *General Editor*
HARVARD UNIVERSITY

Walter Cohen
CORNELL UNIVERSITY

Jean E. Howard
COLUMBIA UNIVERSITY

Katharine Eisaman Maus
UNIVERSITY OF VIRGINIA

With an Essay on the Shakespearean stage
by Andrew Gurr

W · W · NORTON & COMPANY · NEW YORK · LONDON

W. W. Norton & Company has been independent since its founding in 1923, when William Warder Norton and Mary D. Herter Norton first published lectures delivered at the People's Institute, the adult education division of New York City's Cooper Union. The Nortons soon expanded their program beyond the Institute, publishing books by celebrated academics from America and abroad. By mid-century, the two major pillars of Norton's publishing program—trade books and college texts—were firmly established. In the 1950s, the Norton family transferred control of the company to its employees, and today—with a staff of four hundred and a comparable number of trade, college, and professional titles published each year—W. W. Norton & Company stands as the largest and oldest publishing house owned wholly by its employees.

Editor: Julia Reidhead
Manuscript editor: Carol Flechner
Electronic media editor: Eileen Connell
Editorial assistant: Rivka Genesen
Production manager: Diane O'Connor
Photo research: Rivka Genesen
Interior design: Antonina Krass
Managing editor, College: Marian Johnson

The Library of Congress has cataloged the one-volume edition as follows:

Shakespeare, William, 1564–1616.
The Norton Shakespeare / Stephen Greenblatt, general editor ; Walter Cohen, Jean E. Howard, Katharine Eisaman Maus [editors] ; with an essay on the Shakespearean stage by Andrew Gurr. — 2nd ed.
p. cm.
"Based on the Oxford edition."
Includes bibliographical references and index.
ISBN 978-0-393-92991-1
I. Greenblatt, Stephen 1943– II. Cohen, Walter, 1949– III. Howard Jean E. (Jean Elizabeth), 1948– IV. Maus, Katharine Eisaman, 1955– V. Gurr, Andrew.
VI. Title.
PR2754.G74 2008
822.3'3—dc22
2007046599

W. W. Norton & Company, Inc., 500 Fifth Avenue, New York, NY 10110
www.wwnorton.com

ISBN 978-0-393-93145-7

W. W. Norton & Company Ltd., Castle House, 75/76 Wells Street, London W1T 3QT

2 3 4 5 6 7 8 9 0

Contents

GENERAL INTRODUCTION   1

Stephen Greenblatt

LATER PLAYS   101

v

Appendices 1553

Contents by Genre

Comedies

Histories

Tragedies

Romances

Lost Plays

Contents by Genre

Comedies

Histories

Tragedies

Romances

Lost Plays

Illustrations

Preface

Shakespeare's principal medium, the drama, was thoroughly collaborative, and it involved as well continual efforts at revision and renewal. It seems appropriate, then, that this edition of his works is itself the result of sustained collaboration and revision. Two lists of editors' names on the title-page spread hint at the collaboration that has brought to fruition the *Norton Shakespeare*. But the title page does not tell the full history of this project. The text on which the *Norton Shakespeare* is based was published in both modern-spelling and original-spelling versions by Oxford University Press, in 1986. Under the general editorship of Stanley Wells and Gary Taylor, the Oxford text was a thorough rethinking of the entire body of Shakespeare's works, the most far-reaching and innovative revision of the traditional canon in centuries. When many classroom instructors who wanted to introduce their students to the works of Shakespeare through a modern text expressed a need for the pedagogical apparatus they have come to expect in an edition oriented toward students, Norton negotiated with Oxford to assemble an editorial team of its own to prepare the necessary teaching materials around the existing Oxford text. Hence ensued a collaboration of two publishers and two editorial teams.

To what extent is this the *Norton Shakespeare* and to what extent the Oxford text? Introductions (both the General Introduction and those to individual plays and poems), footnotes, glosses, bibliographies, genealogies, annals, maps, documents, and illustrations have all been the responsibility of the Norton team. Andrew Gurr's much-admired essay on the London theater in Shakespeare's time, specially commissioned for the *Norton Shakespeare,* has been moved in this second edition to the front matter.

The textual notes and variants derive for the most part from the work of the Oxford team, especially as represented in *William Shakespeare: A Textual Companion* (Oxford University Press, 1987), a remarkably comprehensive explanation of editorial decisions that is herewith strongly recommended to instructors as a valuable companion to this volume. Several of the textual notes—those to *The First Part of Henry the Sixth,* Various Poems, *The Two Noble Kinsmen, The Merry Wives of Windsor, Troilus and Cressida,* The Sonnets and "A Lover's Complaint"—have been substantially updated in the current edition, and all Textual Variants are now gathered in an appendix.

The Oxford text is widely available and already well known to scholars. A few words here may help clarify the extent of our fidelity to that text and the nature of the collaboration that has brought about this volume. The Oxford editors have profited from the massive and sustained attention accorded their edition by Shakespeare scholars across the globe, and of course they have continued to participate actively in the ongoing scholarly discussion about the nature of Shakespeare's text. In the reprintings of the Oxford volumes and in various articles over the past years, the Oxford editors have made a number of refinements of the edition they originally published. Such changes have been incorporated silently here. A small number of other changes made by the Norton team, however, were not part of the Oxford editors' design and were only accepted by them after we reached, through lengthy consultation, a mutual understanding about the nature, purpose, and intended audience of this volume. In all such changes, our main concern was for the classroom; we wished to make fully and clearly available the scholarly innovation and freshness of the Oxford text, while at the same time making certain that this was a superbly useful teaching text. It is a pleasure here to record, on behalf of the Norton team, our gratitude for the personal and professional generosity of the Oxford editors in offering advice and entertaining arguments in our common goal of providing the best student Shakespeare for our times. The Norton changes to the Oxford text are various, but in only a few instances are they major. The following brief notes are sufficient to summarize all of these changes, which are also indicated in appropriate play introductions, footnotes, or textual notes.

1. The Oxford editors, along with other scholars, have strenuously argued—in both the Oxford text and elsewhere—that the now-familiar text of *King Lear*, so nearly omnipresent in our classrooms as to seem unquestionably authoritative but in reality dating from the work of Alexander Pope (1723) and Lewis Theobald (1733), represents a wrongheaded conflation of two distinct versions of the play: Shakespeare's original creation as printed in the 1608 Quarto and his substantial revision as printed in the First Folio (1623). The Oxford text, therefore, prints both *The History of King Lear* and *The Tragedy of King Lear*. Norton follows suit, but where Oxford presents these two texts sequentially, we print them on facing pages. While each version may be read independently, and to ensure this we have provided glosses and footnotes for each, the substantial points of difference between the two are immediately apparent and available for comparison. But even many who agree with the scholarly argument for the two texts of *Lear* nevertheless favor making available a conflated text, the text on which innumerable performances of the play have been based and on which a huge body of literary criticism has been written. With the reluctant acquiescence, therefore, of the Oxford editors, we have included a conflated *Lear*, a text that has no part in the Oxford canon and that has been edited by Barbara K. Lewalski of Harvard University rather than by Gary Taylor, the editor of the Oxford *Lears*.

The Norton Shakespeare, then, includes three separate texts of *King Lear*. The reader can compare them, understand the role of editors in constructing the texts we now call Shakespeare's, explore in considerable detail the kinds of decisions that playwrights, editors, and printers make and remake, witness firsthand the historical transformation of what might at first glance seem fixed and unchanging. The *Norton Shakespeare* offers extraordinary access to this supremely brilliant, difficult, compelling play.

2. Among several other plays, *Hamlet* offers similar grounds for objections to the traditional conflation, but both the economics of publishing and the realities of bookbinding—not to mention our recognition of the limited time in the typical undergraduate syllabus—preclude our offering three (or even four) *Hamlets* to match three *Lears*. What we have provided in this edition is a convenient selection of parallel passages that will enable teachers to convey some of the complex, often enigmatic issues, at once stylistic and conceptual, raised by the different texts of the play.

The Oxford text of *Hamlet* was based upon the Folio text, with an appended list of Additional Passages from the Second Quarto (Q2). These additional readings total more than two hundred lines, a significant number, among which are lines that have come to seem very much part of the play as widely received, even if we may doubt that they belong with all the others in any single one of Shakespeare's *Hamlets*. The Norton team, while following the Oxford text, has moved the Q2 passages from the appendix to the body of the play. But in doing so, we have not wanted once again to produce a conflated text. We have therefore indented the Q2 passages, printed them in a different typeface, and numbered them in such a way as to make clear their provenance. Those who wish to read the Folio version of *Hamlet* can thus simply skip over the indented Q2 passages, while at the same time it is possible for readers to see clearly the place that the Q2 passages occupy. We have adopted a similar strategy with several other plays: passages printed in Oxford in appendices are generally printed here in the play texts, though clearly demarcated and not conflated. In the case of *The Taming of the Shrew* and the related quarto text, *The Taming of a Shrew*, however, we have followed Oxford's procedure and left the quarto passages in an appendix, since we believe the texts reflect two distinct plays rather than a revision of one. We have similarly reproduced Oxford's brief appendices to A *Midsummer Night's Dream* and *Henry V,* enabling readers to consider alternative revisions of certain passages.

3. For reasons understood by every Shakespearean (and rehearsed at some length in this volume), the Oxford editors chose to restore the name "Sir John Oldcastle" to the character much better known as Falstaff in *1 Henry IV.* (They made comparable changes in the names of the characters known as Bardolph and Peto.) But for reasons understood by everyone who has presented this play to undergraduates or sampled the centuries of enthusiastic criticism, the Norton editors, with the Oxford editors' gracious agreement, have for this classroom edition opted for the familiar name "Falstaff" (and those of his boon companions), properly noting the change and its significance in the play's introduction.

4. The Oxford editors chose not to differentiate between those stage directions that appeared in the early editions up to and including the Folio and those that have been added by subsequent editors. Instead, in *A Textual Companion* they include separate lists of the original stage directions. These lists are not readily available to readers of the Norton text, whose editors opted instead to bracket all stage directions that derive from editions published after the Folio. Readers can thus easily see which stage directions derive from texts that may bear at least some relation to performances in Shakespeare's time, if not to Shakespeare's own authorship. The Norton policy is more fully explained in the General Introduction.

5. The Oxford editors have newly prepared complete texts of the multiauthored *King Edward III* and *Sir Thomas More*, in which Shakespeare may have had a hand as collaborator. The texts are available online at wwnorton.com/shakespeare. In addition, the *Norton Shakespeare,* Second Edition, continues to print, with a revised introduction, notes, and glosses, passages from *Sir Thomas More* that appear in the surviving manuscript to be in Shakespeare's own handwriting, and we include for the first time an introduction and bibliography to *King Edward III.*

The collaboration with Oxford was obviously essential to the creation of the *Norton Shakespeare*. But in preparing this Second Edition and making it something fresh and engaging, the critically important collaboration has been with the thousands of people who have used the book. Many of these, teachers and students alike, have generously offered helpful suggestions along with praise. Guided by their responses, as well as by recent developments in Shakespeare scholarship, we determined to look afresh at every detail and to make a wide range of changes. The General Introduction and the individual play introductions have been substantially revised, in some cases wholly rewritten, to make them clearer and more accessible. Textual notes throughout have been updated in response to new findings, and there are hundreds of new and fine-tuned notes and glosses, designed to make this edition an even better tool for learning and pleasure. The General Bibliography has been reorganized and extensively updated, with 7 new sections and over 350 new entries. The Selected Bibliographies, too, have been updated as well as newly annotated. A new introduction provides an illuminating guide to the array of maps, three of them archival and three new, showing places important to Shakespeare's plays. The genealogies have been revised, as has been the text/contexts Timeline. New annotated film lists, including over 50 films, now follow the play introductions. Instructors who emphasize films in their courses may wish to assign *Shakespeare and Film: A Norton Guide* by Samuel Crowl, available packaged with the *Norton Shakespeare*. Finally, in response to many requests, we are making the *Norton Shakespeare* available in three different formats: the familiar one-volume clothbound edition, new two-volume chronological splits (*Early Plays and Poems* and *Later Plays*), and four genre paperbacks, each with a new introduction.

With the Second Edition of the *Norton Shakespeare,* the publisher expands its extensive online resource, Norton Literature Online (wwnorton.com/literature). Students who activate the free password in each new copy of the book gain access to an array of general resources, among them a glossary of literary terms, advice on writing about literature and using MLA documentation style, an author portrait gallery, more than 100 maps, and over 90 minutes of recorded readings and musical selections, among them 80 songs by Shakespeare. With their passwords, students also gain access to a site specifically developed to support the *Norton Shakespeare* (wwnorton.com/shakespeare). Based on content prepared by Mark Rose, University of California, Santa Barbara, this Web site invites students to explore six of the most widely taught plays—*The Merchant of Venice, 1 Henry IV, Hamlet, Othello, King Lear,* and *The Tempest*—through different contextual lenses. For each of these plays, the Web site provides materials on the elements of theater, sources, stage history, and critical receptions, as well as the complete Oxford text. Audio clips and stills from classic productions, etchings, photographs, and costume-design illustrations help students appreciate performance aspects of the plays. The student Web site also includes the redesigned "Shakespearean Chronicle, 1558–1616," an illustrated timeline that interweaves three kinds of chronologies illuminating Shakespeare's life and times. As noted above, a password-protected section of the Web site also includes the complete texts of *The Book of Sir Thomas More* and *The Reign of King Edward the Third,* prepared by the editors of the *Oxford Shakespeare.*

The creation of this edition has drawn heavily on the resources, experience, and skill of its remarkable publisher, the independent, employee-owned company W. W. Norton. Our principal guide has been our brilliant editor Julia Reidhead, whose calm intelligence, common sense, and steady focus have been essential in enabling us to reach our goal. With this Second Edition, we were blessed with the characteristically thoughtful oversight of Marian Johnson, managing editor, college department; scrupulous manuscript editing by Carol Flechner; and the assistance of an extraordinary group of Norton staffers: editorial assistant Rivka Genesen, who, among many other things, coordinated the art program; production manager Diane O'Connor; designer Antonina Krass; editor of the *Norton Shakespeare* Web site Eileen Connell; and proofreaders Paula Noonan and Ann Warren.

The *Norton Shakespeare* editors have, in addition, had the valuable—indeed, indispensable—support of a host of undergraduate and graduate research assistants, colleagues, friends, and family. Even a partial listing of those to whom we owe our heartfelt thanks is very long, but we are all fortunate enough to live in congenial and supportive environments, and the edition has been part of our lives for a long time. We owe special thanks for sustained dedication and learning to our principal assistants: Tiffany Alkan, Lianne Habinek, and Emily Peterson. Particular thanks are due to Noah Heringman for his work on the texts assembled in the documents section and for the prefatory notes and comments on those texts; to Philip Schwyzer for preparing the genealogies and the glossary and for conceiving and preparing the (now online) "Shakespearean Chronicle"; and to Holger Schott Syme for reconceiving and extensively updating the General Bibliography. In addition, we are deeply grateful to Ezra Feldman, Francesca Mari, Douglas McQueen-Thomson, Jeffrey Patterson, and Benjamin Woodring. All of these companions, and many more besides, have helped us find in this long collective enterprise what the "Dedicatorie Epistle" to the First Folio promises to its readers: delight. We make the same promise to the readers of our edition and invite them to continue the great Shakespearean collaboration.

STEPHEN GREENBLATT
WALTER COHEN
JEAN E. HOWARD
KATHARINE EISAMAN MAUS

Acknowledgments

Among our many critics, advisers, and friends, the following were of special help in providing critiques for particular plays or of the project as a whole: Janet Adelman (University of California, Berkeley), Joel Altman (University of California, Berkeley), Rebecca Bach (University of Alabama at Birmingham), John Baxter (Dalhousie University), Edward I. Berry (University of Victoria), Timothy Billings (Middlebury College), Bruce Boehrer (Florida State University), Barbara Bono (University at Buffalo, SUNY), Gordon M. Braden (University of Virginia), Douglas Brooks (Texas A&M University), Stephen Buhler (University of Nebraska—Lincoln), Richard Burt (University of Florida), Joseph F. Ceccio (University of Akron), Julie Crawford (Columbia University), Christy Desmet (University of Georgia), Heather Dubrow (University of Wisconsin—Madison), Laurie Ellinghausen (University of Missouri—Kansas City), Chris Fitter (Rutgers, State University of New Jersey), Susan Fraiman (University of Virginia), Daniel Gil (University of Oregon), Miriam Gilbert (University of Iowa), Suzanne Gossett (Loyola University), Elizabeth Hanson (Queen's University), Jim Harner (Texas A&M University), Jonathan Gil Harris (George Washington University), Don Hedrick (Kansas State University), Roze Hentschell (Colorado State University), Clifford Huffman (Stony Brook University, SUNY), John Huntington (University of Illinois at Chicago), Sujata Iyengar (University of Georgia), Kimberly Johnson (Brigham Young University), Coppélia Kahn (Brown University), Sean Keilen (University of Pennsylvania), Theodore B. Leinwand (University of Maryland), Zachary Lesser (University of Pennsylvania), Naomi Liebler (Montclair State University), Joyce MacDonald (University of Kentucky), Leah Marcus (Vanderbilt University), Mark Matheson (University of Utah), Robert Matz (George Mason University), Kristen McDermott (Central Michigan University), Ted McGee (University of Waterloo), Scott McMillin (late of Cornell University), Gordon McMullan (King's College London), John Moore (Pennsylvania State University), Carol Neely (University of Illinois at Urbana-Champaign), Lori Newcomb (University of Illinois at Urbana-Champaign), Karen Newman (New York University), Hillary Nunn (University of Akron), Thomas G. Olsen (SUNY at New Paltz), Jim O'Rourke (Florida State University), Paul Parrish (Texas A&M University), Michael Payne (Bucknell University), Rebecca J. Perederin (University of Virginia), Curtis Perry (Arizona State University), Susan Phillips (Northwestern University), Tanya Pollard (Brooklyn College, CUNY), Kristen Poole (University of Delaware), Arnold Preussner (Truman State University), Phyllis Rackin (University of Pennsylvania), Peter L. Rudnytsky (University of Florida), Benjamin Saunders (University of Oregon), Barbara Sebek (Colorado State University), Tracey Sedinger (University of Northern Colorado), Jyotsna Singh (Michigan State University), Andrew Stott (University at Buffalo, SUNY), Garrett Sullivan (Pennsylvania State University), Ramie Targoff (Brandeis University), Henry Turner (University of Wisconsin—Madison), Martine van Elk (California State University, Long Beach), William N. West (University of Colorado at Boulder), Linda Woodbridge (Pennsylvania State University), Lingui Yang (Texas A&M University).

General Introduction

by

STEPHEN GREENBLATT

"He was not of an age, but for all time!"

The celebration of Shakespeare's genius, eloquently initiated by his friend and rival Ben Jonson, has over the centuries become an institutionalized rite of civility. The person who does not love Shakespeare has made, the rite implies, an incomplete adjustment not simply to a particular culture—English culture of the late sixteenth and early seventeenth centuries—but to "culture" as a whole, the dense network of constraints and entitlements, dreams and practices that links us to nature. Indeed, so absolute is Shakespeare's achievement that he has himself come to seem like great creating nature: the common bond of humankind, the principle of hope, the symbol of the imagination's power to transcend time-bound beliefs and assumptions, peculiar historical circumstances, and specific artistic conventions.

The near-worship that Shakespeare inspires is one of the salient facts about his art. But we must at the same time acknowledge that this art is the product of peculiar historical circumstances and specific conventions, four centuries distant from our own. The acknowledgment is important because Shakespeare the working dramatist did not typically lay claim to the transcendent, visionary truths attributed to him by his most fervent admirers; his characters more modestly say, in the words of the magician Prospero, that their project was "to please" (*The Tempest,* Epilogue, line 13). The starting point, and perhaps the ending point as well, in any encounter with Shakespeare is simply to enjoy him, to savor his imaginative richness, to take pleasure in his infinite delight in language.

"If then you do not like him," Shakespeare's first editors wrote in 1623, "surely you are in some manifest danger not to understand him." Over the years, accommodations have been devised to make liking Shakespeare easier for everyone. When the stage sank to melodrama and light opera, Shakespeare—in suitably revised texts—was there. When the populace had a craving for hippodrama, plays performed entirely on horseback, *Hamlet* was dutifully rewritten and mounted. When audiences went mad for realism, live frogs croaked in productions of *A Midsummer Night's Dream.* When the stage was stripped bare and given over to stark exhibitions of sadistic cruelty, Shakespeare was our contemporary. And when the theater itself had lost some of its cultural centrality, Shakespeare moved effortlessly to Hollywood and the soundstages of the BBC.

This virtually universal appeal is one of the most astonishing features of the Shakespeare phenomenon: plays that were performed before glittering courts thrive in junior-high-school auditoriums; enemies set on destroying one another laugh at the same jokes and weep at the same catastrophes; some of the richest and most complex English verse ever written migrates with spectacular success into German and Italian, Hindi, Swahili, and Japanese. Is there a single, stable, continuous object that underlies all of these migrations and metamorphoses? Certainly not. The global diffusion and long life of Shakespeare's works depend on their extraordinary malleability, their protean capacity to elude definition and escape secure possession. At the same time, they are not without identifiable shared features: across centuries and continents, family resemblances link many of the wildly diverse manifestations of plays such as *Romeo and Juliet, Hamlet,* and *Twelfth Night.* And if there is no clear limit or end point, there is a reasonably clear beginning: the

1

England of the late sixteenth and early seventeenth centuries, when the plays and poems collected in this volume made their first appearance.

An art virtually without end or limit but with an identifiable, localized, historical origin: Shakespeare's achievement defies the facile opposition between transcendent and time-bound. It is not necessary to choose between an account of Shakespeare as the scion of a particular culture and an account of him as a universal genius who created works that continually renew themselves across national and generational boundaries. On the contrary: crucial clues to understanding his art's remarkable power to soar beyond its originary time and place lie in the very soil from which that art sprang.

Shakespeare's World

Life and Death

Life expectancy at birth in early modern England was exceedingly low by our standards: under thirty years old, compared with over seventy today. Infant mortality rates were extraordinarily high, and it is estimated that in the poorer parishes of London only about half the children survived to the age of fifteen, while the children of aristocrats fared only a little better. In such circumstances, some parents must have developed a certain detachment—one of Shakespeare's contemporaries writes of losing "some three or four children"—but there are many expressions of intense grief, so that we cannot assume that the frequency of death hardened people to loss or made it routine.

Still, the spectacle of death, along with that other great threshold experience, birth, must have been far more familiar to Shakespeare and his contemporaries than to ourselves. There was no equivalent in early modern England to our hospitals, and most births and deaths occurred at home. Physical means for the alleviation of pain and suffering were extremely limited—alcohol might dull the terror, but it was hardly an effective anesthetic—and medical treatment was generally both expensive and worthless, more likely to intensify suffering than to lead to a cure. This was a world without a concept of antiseptics, with little actual understanding of disease, with few effective ways of treating earaches or venereal disease, let alone the more terrible instances of what Shakespeare calls "the thousand natural shocks that flesh is heir to."

The worst of these shocks was the bubonic plague, which repeatedly ravaged England, and particularly English towns, until the third quarter of the seventeenth century. The plague was terrifyingly sudden in its onset, rapid in its spread, and almost invariably lethal. Physicians were helpless in the face of the epidemic, though they prescribed amulets,

Bill recording plague deaths in London, 1609.

preservatives, and sweet-smelling substances (on the theory that the plague was carried by noxious vapors). In the plague-ridden year of 1564, the year of Shakespeare's birth, some 254 people died in Stratford-upon-Avon, out of a total population of 800. The year before, some 20,000 Londoners are thought to have died; in 1593, almost 15,000; in 1603, 36,000, or over a sixth of the city's inhabitants. The social effects of these horrible visitations were severe: looting, violence, and despair, along with an intensification of the age's perennial poverty, unemployment, and food shortages. The London plague regulations of 1583, reissued with modifications in later epidemics, ordered that the infected and their households be locked in their homes for a month; that the streets be kept clean; that vagrants be expelled; and that funerals and plays be restricted or banned entirely.

The plague, then, had a direct and immediate impact on Shakespeare's own profession. City officials kept records of the weekly number of plague deaths; when these surpassed a certain number, the theaters were peremptorily closed. The basic idea was not only to prevent contagion but also to avoid making an angry God still angrier with the spectacle of idleness. While restricting public assemblies may in fact have slowed the epidemic, other public policies in times of plague, such as killing the cats and dogs, may have made matters worse (since the disease, as we now know, was spread not by these animals but by the fleas that bred on the black rats that infested the poorer neighborhoods). Moreover, the playing companies, driven out of London by the closing of the theaters, may have carried plague to the provincial towns.

Even in good times, when the plague was dormant and the weather favorable for farming, the food supply in England was precarious. A few successive bad harvests, such as occurred in the mid-1590s, could cause serious hardship, even starvation. Not surprisingly, the poor bore the brunt of the burden: inflation, low wages, and rent increases left large numbers of people with very little cushion against disaster. Further, at its best, the diet of most people seems to have been seriously deficient. The lower classes then, as throughout most of history, subsisted on one or two foodstuffs, usually low in protein. The upper classes disdained green vegetables and milk and gorged themselves on meat. Illnesses that we now trace to vitamin deficiencies were rampant. Some, but not much, relief from pain was provided by the beer that Elizabethans, including children, drank almost incessantly. (Home brewing aside, enough beer was sold in England for every man, woman, and child to have consumed 40 gallons a year.)

Wealth

Despite rampant disease, the population of England in Shakespeare's lifetime was steadily growing, from approximately 3,060,000 in 1564 to 4,060,000 in 1600 and 4,510,000 in 1616. Though the death rate was more than twice what it is in England today, the birthrate was almost three times the current figure. London's population in particular soared, from 60,000 in 1520 to 120,000 in 1550, 200,000 in 1600, and 375,000 half a century later, making it the largest and fastest-growing city not only in England but in all of Europe. Every year in the first half of the seventeenth century, about 10,000 people migrated to London from other parts of England—wages in London tended to be around 50 percent higher than in the rest of the country—and it is estimated that one in eight English people lived in London at some point in their lives. The economic viability of Shakespeare's profession was closely linked to this extraordinary demographic boom: between 1567 and 1642, a theater historian has calculated, the London playhouses were paid close to 50 million visits.

As these visits to the theater indicate, in the capital city and elsewhere a substantial number of English men and women, despite hardships that were never very distant, had money to spend. After the disorder and dynastic wars of the fifteenth century, England in the sixteenth and early seventeenth centuries was for the most part a nation at peace, and with peace came a measure of enterprise and prosperity: the landowning classes busied themselves building great houses, planting orchards and hop gardens, draining marshlands, bringing untilled "wastes" under cultivation. The artisans and laborers who actually accomplished these tasks, although they were generally paid very little, often managed to accumulate something, as did the small freeholding farmers, the yeomen, who are repeatedly celebrated in the period as the backbone of English national independence and well-being. William Harrison's *Description of England* (1577) lovingly itemizes the yeoman's precious possessions: "fair garnish of pewter on his cupboard, with so much more odd vessel going about the house, three or four featherbeds, so many coverlets and carpets of tapestry, a silver salt[cellar], a bowl for wine (if not a whole nest) and a dozen of spoons." There are comparable accounts of the hard-earned acquisitions of the city dwellers—masters and apprentices in small workshops, shipbuilders, wool merchants, clothmakers, chandlers, tradesmen, shopkeepers, along with lawyers, apothecaries, schoolteachers, scriveners, and the like—whose pennies from time to time enriched the coffers of the players.

The chief source of England's wealth in the sixteenth century was its textile industry, an industry that depended on a steady supply of wool. In *The Winter's Tale*, Shakespeare provides a warm, richly comic portrayal of a rural sheepshearing festival, but the increasingly intensive production of wool had in reality its grim side. When a character in Thomas More's *Utopia* (1516) complains that "the sheep are eating the people," he is referring to the practice of enclosure: throughout the sixteenth and early seventeenth centuries, many acres of croplands once farmed in common by rural communities were enclosed with fences by wealthy landowners and turned into pasturage. The ensuing misery, displacement, and food shortages led to repeated riots, some of them violent and bloody, along with a series of government proclamations, but the process of enclosure was not reversed.

The economic stakes were high, and not only for the domestic market. In 1565, woolen cloth alone made up more than three-fourths of England's exports. (The remainder consisted mostly of other textiles and raw wool, with some trade in lead, tin, grain, and skins.) The Company of Merchant Adventurers carried cloth to distant ports on the Baltic and Mediterranean, establishing links with Russia and Morocco (each took about 2 percent of London's cloth in 1597–98). English lead and tin, as well as fabrics, were sold in Tuscany and Turkey, and merchants found a market for Newcastle coal on the island of Malta. In the latter half of the century, London, which handled more than 85 percent of all exports, regularly shipped abroad more than 100,000 woolen cloths a year at a value of at least £750,000. This figure does not include the increasingly important and profitable trade in so-called New Draperies, including textiles that went by such exotic names as bombazines, calamancoes, damazellas, damizes, mockadoes, and virgenatoes. When the Earl of Kent in *King Lear* insults Oswald as a "filthy worsted-stocking knave" (2.2.14–15) or when the aristocratic Biron in *Love's Labour's Lost* declares that he will give up "taffeta phrases, silken terms precise, / Three-piled hyperboles" and woo henceforth "in russet yeas, and honest kersey noes" (5.2.406–07, 413), Shakespeare is assuming that a substantial portion of his audience will be alert to the social significance of fabric.

There is amusing confirmation of this alertness from an unexpected source: the report of a visit made to the Fortune playhouse in London in 1614 by a foreigner, Father Orazio Busino, the chaplain of the Venetian embassy. Father Busino neglected to mention the name of the play he saw, but like many foreigners, he was powerfully struck by the presence of gorgeously dressed women in the audience. In Venice, there was a special gallery for courtesans, but socially respectable women would not have been permitted to attend plays, as they could in England. In London, not only could middle- and upper-class women go to the theater, but they could also wear masks and mingle freely with male spectators and women of ill repute. The bemused cleric was uncertain about the ambiguous social situation in which he found himself:

> These theatres are frequented by a number of respectable and handsome ladies, who come freely and seat themselves among the men without the slightest hesitation. On the evening in question his Excellency and the Secretary were pleased to play me a trick by placing me amongst a bevy of young women. Scarcely was I seated ere a very

elegant dame, but in a mask, came and placed herself beside me. . . . She asked me for my address both in French and English; and, on my turning a deaf ear, she determined to honour me by showing me some fine diamonds on her fingers, repeatedly taking off not fewer than three gloves, which were worn one over the other. . . . This lady's bodice was of yellow satin richly embroidered, her petticoat of gold tissue with stripes, her robe of red velvet with a raised pile, lined with yellow muslin with broad stripes of pure gold. She wore an apron of point lace of various patterns: her head-tire was highly perfumed, and the collar of white satin beneath the delicately-wrought ruff struck me as extremely pretty.

Father Busino may have turned a deaf ear on this "elegant dame" but not a blind eye: his description of her dress is worthy of a fashion designer and conveys something of the virtual clothes cult that prevailed in England in the late sixteenth and early seventeenth centuries, a cult whose major shrine, outside the royal court, was the theater.

Imports, Patents, and Monopolies

England produced some luxury goods, but the clothing on the backs of the most fashionable theatergoers was likely to have come from abroad. By the late sixteenth century, the English were importing substantial quantities of silks, satins, velvets, embroidery, gold and silver lace, and other costly items to satisfy the extravagant tastes of the elite and of those who aspired to dress like the elite. The government tried to put a check on the sartorial ambitions of the upwardly mobile by passing sumptuary laws—that is, laws restricting to the ranks of the aristocracy the right to wear certain of the most precious fabrics. But the very existence of these laws, in practice almost impossible to enforce, only reveals the scope and significance of the perceived problem.

Sumptuary laws were in part a conservative attempt to protect the existing social order from upstarts. Social mobility was not widely viewed as a positive virtue, and moralists repeatedly urged people to stay in their place. Conspicuous consumption that was tolerated, even admired, in the aristocratic elite was denounced as sinful and monstrous in less exalted social circles. English authorities were also deeply concerned throughout the period about the effects of a taste for luxury goods on the balance of trade. One of the principal English imports was wine: the "sherris" whose virtues Falstaff extols in 2 *Henry IV* came from Xeres in Spain; the malmsey in which poor Clarence is drowned in *Richard III* was probably made in Greece or in the Canary Islands (from whence came Sir Toby Belch's "cup of canary" in *Twelfth Night*); and the "flagon of rhenish" that Yorick in *Hamlet* had once poured on the Gravedigger's head came from the Rhine region of Germany. Other imports included canvas, linen, fish, olive oil, sugar, molasses, dates, oranges and lemons, figs, raisins, almonds, capers, indigo, ostrich feathers, and that increasingly popular drug from the New World, tobacco.

Joint-stock companies were established to import goods for the burgeoning English market. The Merchant Venturers of the city of Bristol (established in 1552) handled great shipments of Spanish sack, the light, dry wine that largely displaced the vintages of Bordeaux and Burgundy when trade with France was disrupted by war. The Muscovy Company (established in 1555) traded English cloth and manufactured goods for Russian furs, oil, and beeswax. The Venice Company and the Turkey Company—uniting in 1593 to form the wealthy Levant Company—brought silk and spices home from Aleppo and carpets from Istanbul. The East India Company (founded in 1600), with its agent at Bantam in Java, brought pepper, cloves, nutmeg, and other spices from east Asia, along with indigo, cotton textiles, sugar, and saltpeter from India. English privateers "imported" American products, especially sugar, fish, and hides, in huge quantities, along with more precious cargoes. In 1592, a privateering expedition principally funded by Sir Walter Ralegh captured a huge Portuguese carrack (sailing ship), the *Madre de Dios,* in the Azores and brought it back to Dartmouth. The ship, the largest that had ever entered any English port, held 536 tons of pepper, cloves, cinnamon, cochineal, mace, civet, musk, ambergris,

Cannoneer. From *Edward Webbe, . . . His Travailes* (1590).

and nutmeg, as well as jewels, gold, ebony, carpets, and silks. Before order could be established, the English seamen began to pillage this immensely rich prize, and witnesses said they could smell the spices on all the streets around the harbor. Such piratical expeditions were rarely officially sanctioned by the state, but the queen had in fact privately invested £1,800, for which she received about £80,000.

In the years of war with Spain, 1586–1604, the goods captured by the privateers annually amounted to 10 to 15 percent of the total value of England's imports. But organized theft alone could not solve England's balance-of-trade problems. Statesmen were particularly worried that the nation's natural wealth was slipping away in exchange for unnecessary things. In his *Discourse of the Commonweal* (1549), the prominent humanist Sir Thomas Smith exclaims against the importation of such trifles as mirrors, paper, laces, gloves, pins, inkhorns, tennis balls, puppets, and playing cards. And more than a century later, the same fear that England was trading its riches for trifles and wasting away in idleness was expressed by the Bristol merchant John Cary. The solution, Cary argues in "An Essay on the State of England in Relation to Its Trade" (1695), is to expand productive domestic employment. "People are or may be the Wealth of a Nation," he writes, "yet it must be where you find Employment for them, else they are a Burden to it, as the Idle Drone is maintained by the Industry of the laborious Bee, so are all those who live by their Dependence on others, as Players, Ale-House Keepers, Common Fiddlers, and such like, but more particularly Beggars, who never set themselves to work."

Stage players, all too typically associated here with vagabonds and other idle drones, could have replied in their defense that they not only labored in their vocation but also exported their skills abroad: English acting companies routinely traveled overseas and performed as far away as Bohemia. But their labor was not regarded as a productive contribution to the national wealth, and plays were in truth no solution to the trade imbalances that worried authorities.

The government attempted to stem the flow of gold overseas by establishing a patent system initially designed to encourage skilled foreigners to settle in England by granting them exclusive rights to produce particular wares by a patented method. Patents were granted for such things as the making of hard white soap (1561), ovens and furnaces (1563), window glass (1567), sailcloths (1574), drinking glasses (1574), sulphur, brimstone, and oil (1577), armor and horse harness (1587), starch (1588), white writing paper made from rags (1589), aqua vitae and vinegar (1594), playing cards (1598), and mathematical instruments (1598).

Although their ostensible purpose was to increase the wealth of England, encourage technical innovation, and provide employment for the poor, the effect of patents was often the enrichment of a few and the hounding of poor competitors by wealthy monopolists, a group that soon extended well beyond foreign-born entrepreneurs to the favorites of the monarch who vied for the huge profits to be made. "If I had a monopoly out" on folly, the Fool in *King Lear* protests, glancing at the "lords and great men" around him, "they would have part on't." The passage appears only in the quarto version of the play (*History of King Lear* 4.135–36); it may have been cut for political reasons from the Folio. For the issue of monopolies provoked bitter criticism and parliamentary debate for decades. In 1601, Elizabeth was prevailed upon to revoke a number of the most hated monopolies, including aqua vitae and vinegar, bottles, brushes, fish livers, the coarse sailcloth known as poldavis and mildernix, pots, salt, and starch. The whole system was revoked during the reign of James I by an act of Parliament.

Haves and Have-Nots

When in the 1560s Elizabeth's ambassador to France, the humanist Sir Thomas Smith, wrote a description of England, he saw the commonwealth as divided into four sorts of people: "gentlemen, citizens, yeomen artificers, and laborers." At the forefront of the class of gentlemen was the monarch, followed by a very small group of nobles—dukes, marquesses, earls, viscounts, and barons—who either inherited their exalted titles, as the eldest male heirs of their families, or were granted them by the monarch. Under Elizabeth, this aristocratic peerage numbered between 50 and 60 individuals; James's promotions increased the number to nearer 130. Strictly speaking, Smith notes, the younger sons of the nobility were only entitled to be called "esquires," but in common speech they were also called "lords."

Below this tiny cadre of aristocrats in the social hierarchy of gentry were the knights, a title of honor conferred by the monarch, and below them were the "simple gentlemen." Who was a gentleman? According to Smith, "whoever studieth the laws of the realm, who studieth in the universities, who professeth liberal sciences, and to be short, who can live idly and without manual labor, and will bear the port, charge and countenance of a gentleman, he shall be called master . . . and shall be taken for a gentleman." To "live idly and without manual labor": where in Spain, for example, the crucial mark of a gentleman was "blood," in England it was "idleness," in the sense of sufficient income to afford an education and to maintain a social position without having to work with one's hands.

For Smith, the class of gentlemen was far and away the most important in the kingdom. Below were two groups that had at least some social standing and claim to authority: the citizens, or burgesses, those who held positions of importance and responsibility in their cities, and yeomen, farmers with land and a measure of economic independence. At the bottom of the social order was what Smith calls "the fourth sort of men which do not rule." The great mass of ordinary people have, Smith writes, "no voice nor authority in our commonwealth, and no account is made of them but only to be ruled." Still, even they can bear some responsibility, he notes, since they serve on juries and are named to such positions as churchwarden and constable.

In everyday practice, as modern social historians have observed, the English tended to divide the population not into four distinct classes but into two: a very small empowered group—the "richer" or "wiser" or "better" sort—and all the rest who were without much social standing or power, the "poorer" or "ruder" or "meaner" sort. References to the "middle sort of people" remain relatively rare until after Shakespeare's lifetime; these people are absorbed into the rulers or the ruled, depending on speaker and context.

The source of wealth for most of the ruling class, and the essential measure of social status, was landownership, and changes to the social structure in the sixteenth and seventeenth centuries were largely driven by the land market. The property that passed into private hands as the Tudors and early Stuarts sold off confiscated monastic estates and then their own crown lands for ready cash amounted to nearly a quarter of all the land in England. At the same time, the buying and selling of private estates was on the rise throughout the period. Land was bought up not only by established landowners seeking to enlarge their estates but by successful merchants, manufacturers, and urban professionals; even if the taint of vulgar moneymaking lingered around such figures, their heirs would be taken for true gentlemen. The rate of turnover in landownership was great; in many counties, well over half the gentle families in 1640 had appeared since the end of the fifteenth century. The class that Smith called "simple gentlemen" was expanding rapidly: in the fifteenth century, they had held no more than a quarter of the land in the country; but by the later seventeenth century, they controlled almost half. Over the same period, the land held by the great aristocratic magnates held steady at 15 to 20 percent of the total.

Riot and Disorder

London was a violent place in the first half of Shakespeare's career. There were thirty-five riots in the city in the years 1581–1602, twelve of them in the volatile month of June 1595. These included protests against the deeply unpopular lord mayor Sir John Spencer, attempts to release prisoners, anti-alien riots, and incidents of "popular market regulation." There is an unforgettable depiction of a popular uprising in *Coriolanus*, along with many other glimpses in Shakespeare's works, including John Cade's grotesque rebellion in *The First Part of the Contention (2 Henry VI)*, the plebeian violence in *Julius Caesar*, and Laertes' "riotous head" in *Hamlet*.

The London rioters were mostly drawn from the large mass of poor and discontented apprentices who typically chose as their scapegoats foreigners, prostitutes, and gentlemen's servingmen. Theaters were very often the site of the social confrontations that sparked disorder. For two days running in June 1584, disputes between apprentices and gentlemen triggered riots outside the Curtain Theatre involving up to a thousand participants. On one occasion, a gentleman was said to have exclaimed that "the apprentice was but a rascal, and some there were little better than rogues that took upon them the name of gentlemen, and said the prentices were but the scum of the world." These occasions culminated in attacks by the apprentices on London's law schools, the Inns of Court.

The most notorious and predictable incidents of disorder came on Shrove Tuesday (the Tuesday before the beginning of Lent), a traditional day of misrule when apprentices ran riot. Shrove Tuesday disturbances involved attacks by mobs of young men on the brothels of the South Bank, in the vicinity of the Globe and other public theaters. The city authorities took precautions to keep these disturbances from getting completely out of control but evidently did not regard them as serious threats to public order.

Of much greater concern throughout the Tudor and early Stuart years were the frequent incidents of rural rioting against the enclosure of commons and wasteland by local landlords (and, in the royal forests, by the crown). This form of popular protest was at its height during Shakespeare's career: in the years 1590–1610, the frequency of anti-enclosure rioting doubled from what it had been earlier in Elizabeth's reign.

Although they often became violent, anti-enclosure riots were usually directed not against individuals but against property. Villagers—sometimes several hundred, often fewer than a dozen—gathered to tear down newly planted hedges. The event often took place in a carnival atmosphere, with songs and drinking, that did not prevent the participants from acting with a good deal of political canniness and forethought. Especially in the Jacobean period, it was common for participants to establish a common fund for legal defense before commencing their assault on the hedges. Women were frequently involved, and on a number of occasions wives alone participated in the destruction of the enclosure, since there was a widespread, though erroneous, belief that married women acting without the knowledge of their husbands were immune from prosecution. In fact, the powerful Court of Star Chamber consistently ruled that both the wives and their husbands should be punished.

Peddler. From Jost Amman, *The Book of Trades* (1568).

Although Stratford was never the scene of serious rioting, enclosure controversies there turned violent more than once in Shakespeare's lifetime. In January 1601, Shakespeare's friend Richard Quiney and others leveled the hedges of Sir Edward Greville, lord of Stratford manor. Quiney was elected bailiff of Stratford in September of that year but did not live to enjoy the office for long. He died from a blow to the head struck by one of Greville's men in a tavern brawl. Greville, responsible for the administration of justice, neglected to punish the murderer.

There was further violence in January 1615, when William Combe's men threw to the ground two local aldermen who were filling in a ditch by which Combe was enclosing common fields near Stratford. The task of filling in the offending ditch was completed the next day by the women and children of Stratford. Combe's enclosure scheme was eventually stopped in the courts. Although he owned land whose value would have been affected by this controversy, Shakespeare took no active role in it, since he had previously come to a private settlement with the enclosers insuring him against personal loss.

Most incidents of rural rioting were small, localized affairs, and with good reason: when confined to the village community, riot was a misdemeanor; when it spread outward to include multiple communities, it became treason, punishable by death. The greatest of the anti-enclosure riots, those in which hundreds of individuals from a large area participated, commonly took place on the eve of full-scale regional rebellions. The largest of these disturbances, Kett's Rebellion, involved some 16,000 peasants, artisans, and townspeople who rose up in 1549 under the leadership of a Norfolk tanner and landowner, Robert Kett, to protest economic exploitation. The agrarian revolts in Shakespeare's lifetime were on a much smaller scale. In the abortive Oxfordshire Rebellion of 1596, a carpenter named Bartholomew Steere attempted to organize a rising against enclosing gentlemen. The optimistic Steere promised his followers that "it was but a month's work to overrun England" and informed them "that the commons long since in Spain did rise and kill all gentlemen . . . and since that time have lived merrily there." Steere expected several hundred men to join him on Enslow Hill on November 21, 1596, for the start of the rising; no more than twenty showed up. They were captured, imprisoned, and tortured. Several were executed, but Steere apparently cheated the hangman by dying in prison.

Rebellions, most often triggered by hunger and oppression, continued into the reign of James I. The Midland Revolt of 1607, which may be reflected in *Coriolanus*, consisted of a string of agrarian risings in the counties of Northamptonshire, Warwickshire, and Leicestershire, involving assemblies of up to 5,000 rebels in various places. The best known of their leaders was John Reynolds, called "Captain Powch" because of the pouch he wore, whose magical contents were supposed to defend the rebels from harm. (According to the chronicler Edmund Howes, when Reynolds was captured and the pouch opened, it contained "only a piece of green cheese.") The rebels, who were called by themselves and others both "Levelers" and "Diggers," insisted that they had no quarrel with the king but only sought an end to injurious enclosures. But Robert Wilkinson, who preached a sermon against the leaders at their trial, credited them with the intention to "level all states as they leveled banks and ditches." Most of the rebels got off relatively lightly, but, along with other ringleaders, Captain Powch was executed.

The Legal Status of Women

Even though England was ruled for over forty years by a powerful woman, the great majority of women in the kingdom had very restricted social, economic, and legal standing. To be sure, a tiny number of influential aristocratic women, such as the formidable Countess of Shrewsbury, Bess of Hardwick, wielded considerable power. But, these rare exceptions aside, women were denied any rightful claim to institutional authority or personal autonomy. When Sir Thomas Smith thinks of how he should describe his country's social order, he declares that "we do reject women, as those whom nature hath made to keep home and to nourish their family and children, and not to meddle with matters abroad, nor to bear office in a city or commonwealth."

Then, with a kind of glance over his shoulder, he makes an exception of those few for whom "the blood is respected, not the age nor the sex": for example, the queen.

English women were not under the full range of crushing constraints that afflicted women in some countries in Europe. Foreign visitors were struck by their relative freedom, as shown, for example, by the fact that respectable women could venture unchaperoned into the streets and attend the theater. Single women, whether widowed or unmarried, could, if they were of full age, inherit and administer land, make a will, sign a contract, possess property, sue and be sued, without a male guardian or proxy. But married women had no such rights under the common law.

Early modern writings about women and the family constantly return to a political model of domination and submission, in which the father justly rules over wife and children as the monarch rules over the state. This conception of a woman's role conveniently ignores the fact that a *majority* of the adult women at any time in Shakespeare's England were not married. They were either widows or spinsters (a term that was not yet pejorative), and thus for the most part managing their own affairs. Even within marriage, women typically had more control over certain spheres than moralizing writers on the family cared to admit. For example, village wives oversaw the production of eggs, cheese, and beer, and sold these goods in the market. As seamstresses, pawnbrokers, secondhand clothing dealers, peddlers, and the like—activities not controlled by the all-male guilds—women managed to acquire some economic power of their own, and, of course, they participated as well in the unregulated, black-market economy of the age and in the underworld of thievery and prostitution.

Women were not in practice as bereft of property as, according to English common law, they should have been. Demographic studies indicate that the inheritance system called primogeniture, the orderly transmission of property from father to eldest male heir, was more often an unfulfilled wish than a reality. Some 40 percent of marriages failed to produce a son, and in such circumstances fathers often left their land to their daughters, rather than to brothers, nephews, or male cousins. In many families, the father died before his male heir was old enough to inherit property, leaving the land, at least temporarily, in the hands of the mother. And while they were less likely than their brothers to inherit land ("real property"), daughters normally inherited a substantial share of their father's personal property (cash and movables).

In fact, the legal restrictions upon women, though severe in Shakespeare's time, actually worsened in subsequent decades. The English common law, the system of law based on court decisions rather than on codified written laws, was significantly less egalitarian in its approach to wives and daughters than were alternative legal codes (manorial, civil, and ecclesiastical) still in place in the late sixteenth century. The eventual triumph of common law stripped women of many traditional rights, slowly driving them out of economically productive trades and businesses.

Limited though it was, the economic freedom of Elizabethan and Jacobean women far exceeded their political and social freedom—the opportunity to receive a grammar-school or university education, to hold office in church or state, to have a voice in public debates, or even simply to speak their mind fully and openly in ordinary conversation. Women who asserted their views too vigorously risked being perceived as shrewish and labeled "scolds." Both urban and rural communities had a horror of scolds. In the Elizabethan period, such women came to be regarded as a threat to public order, to be dealt with by the local authorities. The preferred methods of correction included public humiliation—of the sort Katherine endures in *The Taming of the Shrew*—and such physical abuse as slapping, bridling, and soaking by means of a contraption called the "cucking stool" (or "ducking stool"). This latter punishment originated in the Middle Ages, but its use spread in the sixteenth century, when it became almost exclusively a punishment for women. From 1560 onward, cucking stools were built or renovated in many English provincial towns; between 1560 and 1600, the contraptions were installed by rivers or ponds in Norwich, Bridport, Shrewsbury, Kingston-upon-Thames, Marlborough, Devizes, Clitheroe, Thornbury, and Great Yarmouth.

Such punishment was usually intensified by a procession through the town to the sound of "rough music," the banging together of pots and pans. The same cruel festivity accompanied the "carting" or "riding" of those accused of being whores. In some parts of the country, villagers also took the law into their own hands, publicly shaming women who married men much younger than themselves or who beat or otherwise domineered over their husbands. One characteristic form of these charivaris, or rituals of shaming, was known in the West Country as the Skimmington Ride. Villagers would rouse the offending couple from bed with rough music and stage a raucous pageant in which a man, holding a distaff, would ride backward on a donkey, while his "wife" (another man dressed as a woman) struck him with a ladle. In these cases, the collective ridicule and indignation was evidently directed at least as much at the henpecked husband as at his transgressive wife.

Women and Print

Books published for a female audience surged in popularity in the late sixteenth century, reflecting an increase in female literacy. (It is striking how many of Shakespeare's women are shown reading.) This increase is probably linked to a Protestant longing for direct access to the Scriptures, and the new books marketed specifically for women included devotional manuals and works of religious instruction. But there were also practical guides to such subjects as female education (for example, Giovanni Bruto's *Necessarie, Fit, and Convenient Education of a Young Gentlewoman*, 1598), midwifery (James Guillemeau's *Child-birth; or, The Happy Delivery of Women*, 1612), needlework (Federico di Vinciolo's *New and Singular Patternes and Workes of Linnen*, 1591), cooking (Thomas Dawson's *The Good Husewifes Jewell*, 1587), gardening (Pierre Erondelle's *The French Garden for English Ladyes and Gentlewomen to Walke In*, 1605), and married life (Patrick Hannay's *A Happy Husband; or, Directions for a Maide to Choose Her Mate*, 1619). As the authors' names suggest, many of these works were translations, and almost all were written by men.

Starting in the 1570s, writers and their publishers increasingly addressed works of recreational literature (romance, fiction, and poetry) partially or even exclusively to women. Some books, such as Robert Greene's *Mamillia, a Mirrour or Looking-Glasse for the Ladies of Englande* (1583), directly specified in the title their desired audience. Others, such as Sir Philip Sidney's influential and popular romance *Arcadia* (1590–93), solicited female readership in their dedicatory epistles. The ranks of Sidney's followers eventually included his own niece, Mary Wroth, whose romance *Urania* was published in 1621.

In the literature of Shakespeare's time, women readers were not only wooed but also frequently railed at, in a continuation of a popular polemical genre that had long inspired heated charges and countercharges. Both sides in the polemic generally agreed that it was the duty of women to be chaste, dutiful, shamefast, and silent; the argument was whether women fulfilled or fell short of this proper role. Ironically, then, a modern reader is more likely to find inspiring accounts of courageous women not in the books written in defense of female virtue but in attacks on those who refused to be silent and obedient.

The most famous English skirmish in this controversy took place in a rash of pamphlets at the end of Shakespeare's life. Joseph Swetnam's crude *Araignment of Lewd, Idle, Froward, and Unconstant Women* (1615) provoked three fierce responses attributed to women: Rachel Speght's *A Mouzell [Muzzle] for Melastomus*, Ester Sowernam's *Ester Hath Hang'd Haman*, and Constantia Munda's *Worming of a Mad Dogge*, all 1617. There was also an anonymous play, *Swetnam, the Woman-hater, Arraigned by Women* (1618), in which Swetnam, depicted as a braggart and a lecher, is put on trial by women and made to recant his misogynistic lies.

Prior to the Swetnam controversy, only one English woman, "Jane Anger," had published a defense of women (*Jane Anger, Her Protection for Women*, 1589). Learned women writers in the sixteenth century tended not to become involved in public debate but rather to undertake a project to which it was difficult for even obdurately chauvinistic

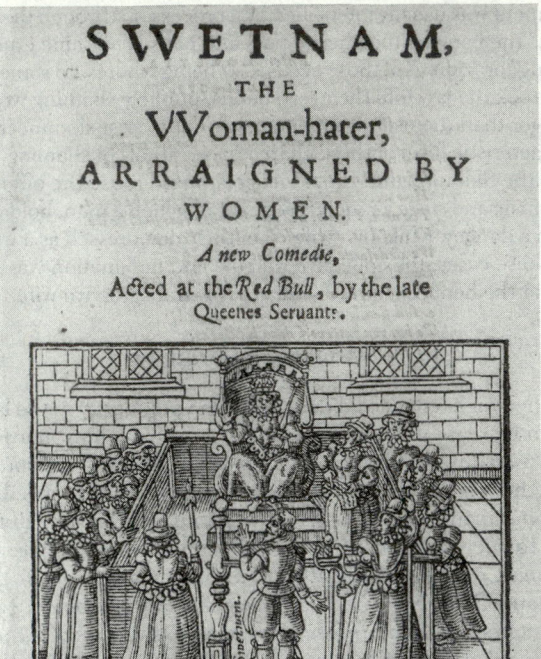

SWETNAM,

THE
Woman-hater,
ARRAIGNED BY
WOMEN.

A new Comedie,

Acted at the *Red Bull*, by the late
Queenes Seruants.

LONDON,
Printed for *Richard Meighen*, and are to be sold at his Shops
at Saint *Clements* Church, ouer-against *Essex* House, and
at *Westminster* Hall, 1620.

Title page of *Swetnam, the Woman-hater, Arraigned by Women* (1620), a play written in response to Joseph Swetnam's *The Araignment of Lewd, Idle, Froward and Unconstant Women* (1615); the woodcut depicts the trial of Swetnam in Act 4.

males to object: the translation of devotional literature into English. Thomas More's daughter Margaret More Roper translated Erasmus (*A Devout Treatise upon the Pater Noster*, 1524); Francis Bacon's mother, Anne Cooke Bacon, translated Bishop John Jewel (*An Apologie or Answere in Defence of the Churche of Englande*, 1564); Anne Locke Prowse, a friend of John Knox, translated the *Sermons of John Calvin* in 1560; and Mary Sidney, Countess of Pembroke, completed the metrical version of the Psalms that her brother Sir Philip Sidney had begun. Elizabeth Tudor (the future queen) herself translated, at the age of eleven, Marguerite de Navarre's *Miroir de l'âme pécheresse* (*The Glass of the Sinful Soul*, 1544). The translation was dedicated to her stepmother, Catherine Parr, herself the author of a frequently reprinted book of prayers.

There was in the sixteenth and early seventeenth centuries a social stigma attached to print. Far from celebrating publication, authors, and particularly female authors, often apologized for exposing themselves to the public gaze. Nonetheless, a number of women ventured beyond pious translations circulated in manuscript. Some, including Elizabeth Tyrwhitt, Anne Dowriche, Isabella Whitney, Mary Sidney, and Aemilia Lanyer, composed and published their own poems. Aemilia Lanyer's *Salve Deus Rex Judaeorum*, published in 1611, is a poem in praise of virtuous women, from Eve and the Virgin Mary to her noble patron, the Countess of Cumberland. "A Description of Cookeham," appended to the poem, may be the first English-country-house poem.

The first Tudor woman to translate a play was the learned Jane Lumley, who composed an English version of Euripides' *Iphigenia at Aulis* (c. 1550). The first known original play in English by a woman was by Elizabeth Cary, Viscountess Falkland, whose *Tragedie of Mariam, the Faire Queene of Jewry* was published in 1613. This remarkable play, which was not intended to be performed, includes speeches in defense of women's equality, though the most powerful of these is spoken by the villainous Salome, who schemes to divorce her husband and marry her lover. Cary, who bore eleven children, herself had a deeply troubled marriage, which effectively came to an end in 1625, when, defying her husband's staunchly Protestant family, she openly converted to Catholicism. Her biography was written by one of her four daughters, all of whom became nuns.

Henry VIII and the English Reformation

There had long been serious ideological and institutional tensions in the religious life of England, but officially, at least, England in the early sixteenth century had a single religion, Catholicism, whose acknowledged head was the pope in Rome. In 1517, drawing upon long-standing currents of dissent, Martin Luther, an Augustinian monk and professor of theology at the University of Wittenberg, challenged the authority of the pope and attacked several key doctrines of the Catholic Church. According to Luther, the Church, with its elaborate hierarchical structure centered in Rome, its rich monasteries and convents, and its enormous political influence, had become hopelessly corrupt, a conspiracy of venal priests who manipulated popular superstitions to enrich themselves and amass worldly power. Luther began by vehemently attacking the sale of indulgences—certificates promising the remission of punishments to be suffered in the afterlife by souls sent to purgatory to expiate their sins. These indulgences were a fraud, he argued; purgatory itself had no foundation in the Bible, which in his view was the only legitimate source of religious truth. Christians would be saved not by scrupulously following the ritual practices fostered by the Catholic Church—observing fast days, reciting the ancient Latin prayers, endowing chantries to say prayers for the dead, and so on—but by faith and faith alone.

This challenge, which came to be known as the Reformation, spread and gathered force, especially in northern Europe, where major leaders like the Swiss pastor Huldrych Zwingli and the French theologian John Calvin established institutional structures and elaborated various and sometimes conflicting doctrinal principles. Calvin, whose thought came to be particularly influential in England, emphasized the obligation of governments to implement God's will in the world. He advanced too the doctrine of predestination, by which, as he put it, "God adopts some to hope of life and sentences others to eternal death." God's "secret election" of the saved made Calvin uncomfortable, but his study of the Scriptures had led him to conclude that "only a small number, out of an incalculable multitude, should obtain salvation." It might seem that such a conclusion would lead to passivity or even despair, but for Calvin predestination was a mystery bound up with faith, confidence, and an active engagement in the fashioning of a Christian community.

The Reformation had a direct and powerful impact on those territories, especially in northern Europe, where it gained control. Monasteries were sacked, their possessions seized by princes or sold off to the highest bidder; the monks and nuns, expelled from their cloisters, were encouraged to break their vows of chastity and find spouses, as Luther and his wife, a former nun, had done. In the great cathedrals and in hundreds of smaller churches and chapels, the elaborate altarpieces, bejeweled crucifixes, crystal reliquaries holding the bones of saints, and venerated statues and paintings were attacked as "idols" and often defaced or destroyed. Protestant congregations continued, for the most part, to celebrate the most sacred Christian ritual, the Eucharist, or Lord's Supper, but they did so in a profoundly different spirit from that of the Catholic Church—more as commemoration than as miracle—and they now prayed not in the ancient liturgical Latin but in the vernacular.

"The Pope as Antichrist riding the Beast of the Apocalypse." From *Fierie Tryall of God's Saints* (1611; author unknown).

The Reformation was at first vigorously resisted in England. Indeed, with the support of his ardently Catholic chancellor, Thomas More, Henry VIII personally wrote (or at least lent his name to) a vehement, often scatological attack on Luther's character and views, an attack for which the pope granted him the honorific title "Defender of the Faith." Protestant writings, including translations of the Scriptures into English, were seized by officials of the church and state and burned. Protestants who made their views known were persecuted, driven to flee the country, or arrested, put on trial, and burned at the stake. But the situation changed drastically and decisively when in 1527 Henry decided to seek a divorce from his first wife, Catherine of Aragon, in order to marry Anne Boleyn.

Catherine had given birth to six children, but since only a daughter, Mary, survived infancy, Henry did not have the son he craved. Then as now, the Catholic Church did not ordinarily grant divorce, but Henry's lawyers argued on technical grounds that the marriage was invalid (and, therefore, by extension, that Mary was illegitimate and hence unable to inherit the throne). Matters of this kind were far less doctrinal than diplomatic: Catherine, the daughter of Ferdinand of Aragon and Isabella of Castile, had powerful allies in Rome, and the pope ruled against Henry's petition for a divorce. A series of momentous events followed, as England lurched away from the Church of Rome. In 1531, Henry charged the entire clergy of England with having usurped royal authority in the administration of canon law (the ecclesiastical law that governed faith, discipline, and morals, including such matters as divorce). Under extreme pressure, including the threat of mass confiscations and imprisonment, the Convocation of the English Clergy begged for pardon, made a donation to the royal coffers of over £100,000, and admitted that the king was "supreme head of the English Church and clergy" (modified by the rider "as far as the law of Christ allows"). On May 15 of the next year, the convocation submitted to the demand that the king be the final arbiter of canon law; on the next day, Thomas More resigned his post.

In 1533, Henry's marriage to Catherine was officially declared null and void, and on June 1 Anne Boleyn was crowned queen (a coronation Shakespeare depicts in his late play *All Is True*). The king was promptly excommunicated by the pope, Clement VII. In the following year, the parliamentary Act of Succession confirmed the effects of the divorce and required an oath from all adult male subjects confirming the new dynastic settlement. Thomas More and John Fisher, Bishop of Rochester, were among the small number who refused. The Act of Supremacy, passed later in the year, formally declared the king to be "Supreme Head of the Church in England" and again required an oath to this effect. In 1535 and 1536, further acts made it treasonous to refuse the oath of royal supremacy or, as More had tried to do, to remain silent. The first victims were three Carthusian monks who rejected the oath—"How could the king, a layman," said one of them, "be Head of the Church of England?"—and in May 1535, they were duly hanged, drawn, and quartered. A few weeks later, Fisher and More were convicted and beheaded. Between 1536 and 1539, the monasteries were suppressed and their vast wealth seized by the crown.

Royal defiance of the authority of Rome was a key element in the Reformation but did not by itself constitute the establishment of Protestantism in England. On the contrary, in the same year that Fisher and More were martyred for their adherence to Roman Catholicism, twenty-five Protestants, members of a sect known as Anabaptists, were burned for heresy on a single day. Through most of his reign, Henry remained an equal-opportunity persecutor, ruthless to Catholics loyal to Rome and hostile to some of those who espoused Reformation ideas, though many of these ideas gradually established themselves on English soil.

Even when Henry was eager to do so, it proved impossible to eradicate Protestantism, as it would later prove impossible for his successors to eradicate Catholicism. In large part this tenacity arose from the passionate, often suicidal heroism of men and women who felt that their souls' salvation depended on the precise character of their Christianity. It arose, too, from a mid-fifteenth-century technological innovation that made it almost impossible to suppress unwelcome ideas: the printing press. Early Protestants quickly grasped that with a few clandestine presses they could defy the Catholic authorities and flood the country with their texts. "How many printing presses there be in the world," wrote the Protestant polemicist John Foxe, "so many blockhouses there be against the high castle" of the pope in Rome, "so that either the pope must abolish knowledge and printing or printing at length will root him out." By the century's end, it was the Catholics who were using the clandestine press to propagate their beliefs in the face of Protestant persecution.

The greatest insurrection of the Tudor age was not over food, taxation, or land but over religion. On Sunday, October 1, 1536, stirred up by their vicar, the traditionalist parishioners of Louth in Lincolnshire, in the north of England, rose up in defiance of the ecclesiastical visitation sent to enforce royal supremacy. The rapidly spreading rebellion, which became known as the Pilgrimage of Grace, was led by the lawyer Robert Aske. The city of Lincoln fell to the rebels on October 6, and though it was soon retaken by royal forces, the rebels seized cities and fortifications throughout Yorkshire, Durham, Northumberland, Cumberland, Westmoreland, and northern Lancashire. Carlisle, Newcastle, and a few castles were all that were left to the king in the north. The Pilgrims soon numbered 40,000, led by some of the region's leading noblemen. The Duke of Norfolk, representing the crown, was forced to negotiate a truce, with a promise to support the rebels' demands that the king restore the monasteries, shore up the regional economy, suppress heresy, and dismiss his evil advisers.

The Pilgrims kept the peace for the rest of 1536, on the naive assumption that their demands would be met. But Henry moved suddenly early in 1537 to impose order and capture the ringleaders; 130 people, including lords, knights, heads of religious houses, and, of course, Robert Aske, were executed.

In 1549, two years after the death of Henry VIII, the west and the north of England were the sites of further unsuccessful risings for the restoration of Catholicism. The Western Rising is striking for its blend of Catholic universalism and intense regionalism among people who did not yet regard themselves as English. One of the rebels' articles, protesting against the imposition of the English Bible and religious service, declares, "We the Cornish men (whereof certain of us understand no English) utterly refuse this new English." The rebels besieged but failed to take the city of Exeter. As with almost all Tudor rebellions, the number of those executed in the aftermath of the failed rising was far greater than those killed in actual hostilities.

Henry VIII's Children: Edward, Mary, and Elizabeth

Upon Henry's death in 1547, his ten-year-old son, Edward VI, came to the throne, with his maternal uncle Edward Seymour named as Lord Protector and Duke of Somerset. Both Edward and his uncle were staunch Protestants, and reformers hastened to transform the English Church accordingly. During Edward's reign, Archbishop Thomas Cranmer formulated the forty-two articles of religion that became the core of Anglican orthodoxy and wrote the first Book of Common Prayer, which was officially adopted in 1549 as the basis of English worship services.

Somerset fell from power in 1549 and was replaced as Lord Protector by John Dudley, later Duke of Northumberland. When Edward fell seriously ill, probably of tuberculosis, Northumberland persuaded him to sign a will depriving his half sisters, Mary (the daughter of Catherine of Aragon) and Elizabeth (the daughter of Anne Boleyn), of their claim to royal succession. The Lord Protector was scheming to have his daughter-in-law, the Protestant Lady Jane Grey, a granddaughter of Henry VII, ascend to the throne. But when Edward died in 1553, Mary marshaled support, quickly secured the crown from Lady Jane (who had been titular queen for nine days), and had Lady Jane executed, along with her husband and Northumberland.

Queen Mary immediately took steps to return her kingdom to Roman Catholicism. Even though she was unable to get Parliament to agree to restore church lands seized under Henry VIII, she restored the Catholic Mass, once again affirmed the authority of the pope, and put down a rebellion that sought to depose her. Seconded by her ardently Catholic husband, Philip II, King of Spain, she initiated a series of religious persecutions that earned her (from her enemies) the name "Bloody Mary." Hundreds of Protestants took refuge abroad in cities such as Calvin's Geneva; almost three hundred less fortunate Protestants were condemned as heretics and burned at the stake.

The Family of Henry VIII: An Allegory of the Tudor Succession. By Lucas de Heere (c. 1572). Henry, in the middle, is flanked by Mary to his right, and Edward and Elizabeth to his left.

Mary died childless in 1558, and her younger half sister Elizabeth became queen. Elizabeth's succession had been by no means assured. For if Protestants regarded Henry VIII's marriage to Catherine as invalid and hence deemed Mary illegitimate, so Catholics regarded his marriage to Anne Boleyn as invalid and deemed Elizabeth illegitimate. Henry VIII himself seemed to support both views, since only three years after divorcing Catherine, he beheaded Anne Boleyn on charges of treason and adultery, and urged Parliament to invalidate the marriage. Moreover, though during her sister's reign Elizabeth outwardly complied with the official Catholic religious observance, Mary and her advisers were deeply suspicious, and the young princess's life was in grave danger. Poised and circumspect, Elizabeth warily evaded the traps that were set for her. As she ascended the throne, her actions were scrutinized for some indication of the country's future course. During her coronation procession, when a girl in an allegorical pageant presented her with a Bible in English translation—banned under Mary's reign—Elizabeth kissed the book, held it up reverently, and laid it to her breast; when the abbot and monks of Westminster Abbey came to greet her in broad daylight with candles (a symbol of Catholic devotion) in their hands, she briskly dismissed them with the telling words "Away with those torches! we can see well enough." England had returned to the Reformation.

Many English men and women, of all classes, remained loyal to the old Catholic faith, but English authorities under Elizabeth moved steadily, if cautiously, toward ensuring at least an outward conformity to the official Protestant settlement. Recusants, those who refused to attend regular Sunday services in their parish churches, were fined heavily. Anyone who wished to receive a university degree, to be ordained as a priest in the Church of England, or to be named as an officer of the state had to swear an oath to the royal supremacy. Commissioners were sent throughout the land to confirm that religious services were following the officially approved liturgy and to investigate any reported backsliding into Catholic practice or, alternatively, any attempts to introduce more radical reforms than the queen and her bishops had chosen to embrace. For the Protestant exiles who streamed back were eager not only to undo the damage Mary had done but to carry the Reformation much further. They sought to dismantle the church hierarchy, to purge the calendar of folk customs deemed pagan and the church service of ritual practices deemed superstitious, to dress the clergy in simple garb, and, at the extreme edge, to smash "idolatrous" statues, crucifixes, and altarpieces. Throughout her long reign, however, Elizabeth herself remained cautiously conservative and determined to hold in check what she regarded as the religious zealotry of Catholics, on the one side, and Puritans, on the other.

Shakespeare's plays tap into the ongoing confessional tensions: "Sometimes," Maria in *Twelfth Night* says of the sober, festivity-hating steward Malvolio, "he is a kind of puritan" (2.3.125). But they tend to avoid the risks of direct engagement: "The dev'l a puritan that he is, or anything constantly," Maria adds a moment later, "but a time-pleaser, an affectioned ass" (2.3.131–32). *The Winter's Tale* features a statue that comes to life—exactly the kind of magical image that Protestant polemicists excoriated as Catholic superstition and idolatry—but the play is set in pre-Christian world of the Delphic oracle. And as if this careful distancing might not be enough, the play's ruler goes out of his way to pronounce the wonder legitimate: "If this be magic, let it be an art / Lawful as eating" (5.3.110–11).

In the space of a single lifetime, England had gone officially from Roman Catholicism, to Catholicism under the supreme headship of the English king, to a guarded Protestantism, to a more radical Protestantism, to a renewed and aggressive Roman Catholicism, and finally to Protestantism again. Each of these shifts was accompanied by danger, persecution, and death. It was enough to make some people wary. Or skeptical. Or extremely agile.

The English Bible

Luther had undertaken a fundamental critique of the Catholic Church's sacramental system, a critique founded on the twin principles of salvation by faith alone (*sola fide*) and the absolute primacy of the Bible (*sola scriptura*). *Sola fide* contrasted faith with "works," by which was meant primarily the whole elaborate system of rituals sanctified, conducted, or directed by the priests. Protestants proposed to modify or reinterpret many of these rituals or, as with the rituals associated with purgatory, to abolish them altogether. *Sola scriptura* required direct lay access to the Bible, which meant in practice the widespread availability of vernacular translations. The Roman Catholic Church had not always and everywhere opposed such translations, but it generally preferred that the populace encounter the Scriptures through the interpretations of the priests, trained to read the Latin translation known as the Vulgate. In times of great conflict, this preference for clerical mediation hardened into outright prohibition of vernacular translation and into persecution and book burning.

Zealous Protestants set out, in the teeth of fierce opposition, to put the Bible into the hands of the laity. A remarkable translation of the New Testament, by an English Lutheran named William Tyndale, was printed on the Continent and smuggled into England in 1525; Tyndale's translation of the Pentateuch, the first five books of the Hebrew Bible, followed in 1530. Many copies of these translations were seized and burned, as was the translator himself, but the printing press made it extremely difficult for authorities to eradicate books for which there was a passionate demand. The English Bible was a force that could not be suppressed, and it became, in its various forms, the single most important book of the sixteenth century.

Tyndale's translation was completed by an associate, Miles Coverdale, whose rendering of the Psalms proved to be particularly influential. Their joint labor was the basis for the Great Bible (1539), the first authorized version of the Bible in English, a copy of which was ordered to be placed in every church in the kingdom. With the accession of Edward VI, many editions of the Bible followed, but the process was sharply reversed when Mary came to the throne in 1553. Along with people condemned as heretics, English Bibles were burned in great bonfires.

Marian persecution was indirectly responsible for what would become the most popular as well as most scholarly English Bible, the translation known as the Geneva Bible, prepared, with extensive, learned, and often fiercely polemical marginal notes, by English exiles in Calvin's Geneva and widely diffused in England after Elizabeth came to the throne. In addition, Elizabethan church authorities ordered a careful revision of the Great Bible, and this version, known as the Bishops' Bible, was the one read in the churches. The success of the Geneva Bible in particular prompted those Elizabethan Catholics who now in turn found themselves in exile to bring out a vernacular translation of their own in order to counter the Protestant readings and glosses. This Catholic translation, known as the Rheims Bible, may have been known to Shakespeare, but he seems to have been far better acquainted with the Geneva Bible, and he would also have repeatedly heard the Bishops' Bible read aloud. Scholars have identified over three hundred references to the Bible in Shakespeare's work; in one version or another, the Scriptures had a powerful impact on his imagination.

A Female Monarch in a Male World

In the last year of Mary's reign, 1558, the Scottish Calvinist minister John Knox thundered against what he called "the monstrous regiment of women." When the Protestant Elizabeth came to the throne the following year, Knox and his religious brethren were less inclined to denounce female rulers, but in England as elsewhere in Europe there remained a widespread conviction that women were unsuited to wield power over men. Many men seem to have regarded the capacity for rational thought as exclusively male; women, they assumed, were led only by their passions. While gentlemen mastered the arts of rhetoric and warfare, gentlewomen were expected to display the virtues of silence and good housekeeping. Among upper-class males, the will to dominate others was acceptable and, indeed, admired; the same will in women was condemned as a grotesque and dangerous aberration.

One of the Armada portraits (c. 1588). Note Elizabeth's hand on the globe.

Apologists for the queen countered these prejudices by appealing to historical precedent and legal theory. History offered inspiring examples of just female rulers, notably Deborah, the biblical prophetess who judged Israel. In the legal sphere, crown lawyers advanced the theory of "the king's two bodies." As England's crowned head, Elizabeth's person was mystically divided between her mortal "body natural" and the immortal "body politic." While the queen's natural body was inevitably subject to the failings of human flesh, the body politic was timeless and perfect. In political terms, therefore, Elizabeth's sex was a matter of no consequence, a thing indifferent.

Elizabeth, who had received a fine humanist education and an extended, dangerous lesson in the art of survival, made it immediately clear that she intended to rule in more than name only. She assembled a group of trustworthy advisers, foremost among them William Cecil (later named Lord Burghley, also known as Burleigh), but she insisted on making many of the crucial decisions herself. Like many Renaissance monarchs, Elizabeth was drawn to the idea of royal absolutism, the theory that ultimate power was properly concentrated in her person and, indeed, that God had appointed her to be His deputy in the kingdom. Opposition to her rule, in this view, was not only a political act but also a kind of impiety, a blasphemous grudging against the will of God. Apologists for absolutism contended that God commands obedience even to manifestly wicked rulers whom He has sent to punish the sinfulness of humankind. Such arguments were routinely made in speeches and political tracts and from the pulpits of churches, where they were incorporated into the *First* and *Second Book of Homilies,* which clergymen were required to read out to their congregations.

In reality, Elizabeth's power was not absolute. The government had a network of spies, informers, and agents provocateurs, but it lacked a standing army, a national police force, an efficient system of communication, and an extensive bureaucracy. Above all, the queen had limited financial resources and needed to turn periodically to an independent and often recalcitrant Parliament, which by long tradition had the sole right to levy taxes and to grant subsidies. Members of the House of Commons were elected from their boroughs, not appointed by the monarch, and although the queen had considerable influence over their decisions, she could by no means dictate policy. Under these constraints, Elizabeth ruled through a combination of adroit political maneuvering and imperious command, all the while enhancing her authority in the eyes of both court and country by means of an extraordinary cult of love.

"We all loved her," Elizabeth's godson Sir John Harington wrote, with just a touch of irony, a few years after the queen's death, "for she said she loved us." Ambassadors, courtiers, and parliamentarians all submitted to Elizabeth's cult of love, in which the queen's gender was transformed from a potential liability into a significant asset. Those who approached her generally did so on their knees and were expected to address her with extravagant compliments fashioned from the period's most passionate love poetry; she in turn spoke, when it suited her to do so, in the language of love poetry. The court moved in an atmosphere of romance, with music, dancing, plays, and the elaborate, fancy-dress entertainments called masques. The queen adorned herself in gorgeous clothes and rich jewels. When she went on one of her summer "progresses," ceremonial journeys through her land, she looked like an exotic, sacred image in a religious cult of love, and her noble hosts virtually bankrupted themselves to lavish upon her the costliest pleasures. England's leading artists, such as the poet Edmund Spenser and the painter Nicholas Hilliard, enlisted themselves in the celebration of Elizabeth's mystery, likening her to the goddesses and queens of mythology: Diana, Astraea, Gloriana. Her cult drew its power from cultural discourses that ranged from the secular (her courtiers could pine for her as a cruel Petrarchan mistress) to the sacred (the veneration that under Catholicism had been due to the Virgin Mary could now be directed toward England's semidivine queen).

There was a sober, even grim, aspect to these poetical fantasies: Elizabeth was brilliant at playing one dangerous faction off another, now turning her gracious smiles on one favorite, now honoring his hated rival, now suddenly looking elsewhere and raising an obscure upstart to royal favor. And when she was disobeyed or when she felt that her prerogatives had been challenged, she was capable of an anger that, as Harington put it, "left no doubtings whose daughter she was." Thus, when Sir Walter Ralegh, one of the queen's glittering favorites, married without her knowledge or consent, he found himself promptly imprisoned in the Tower of London. And when the Protestant polemicist John Stubbs ventured to publish a pamphlet stridently denouncing the queen's proposed marriage to the French Catholic Duke of Alençon, Stubbs and his publisher were arrested and had their right hands chopped off. (After receiving the blow, the now prudent Stubbs lifted his hat with his remaining hand and cried, "God save the Queen!")

The queen's marriage negotiations were a particularly fraught issue. When she came to the throne at twenty-five years old, speculation about a suitable match, already widespread, intensified and remained for decades at a fever pitch, for the stakes were high. If Elizabeth died childless, the Tudor line would come to an end. The nearest heir was her cousin Mary, Queen of Scots, a Catholic whose claim was supported by France and by the papacy, and whose penchant for sexual and political intrigue confirmed the worst fears of English Protestants. The obvious way to avert the nightmare was for Elizabeth to marry and produce an heir, and the pressure upon her to do so was intense.

More than the royal succession hinged on the question of the queen's marriage; Elizabeth's perceived eligibility was a vital factor in the complex machinations of international diplomacy. A dynastic marriage between the Queen of England and a foreign ruler would forge an alliance powerful enough to alter the balance of power in Europe. The English court hosted a steady stream of ambassadors from kings and princes eager to win the hand of the royal maiden, and Elizabeth, who prided herself on speaking fluent French and Italian (and on reading Latin and Greek), played her romantic part with exemplary skill, sighing and spinning the negotiations out for months and even years.

Most probably, she never meant to marry any of her numerous foreign (and domestic) suitors. Such a decisive act would have meant the end of her independence, as well as the end of the marriage game by which she played one power off against another. One day she would seem to be on the verge of accepting a proposal; the next, she would vow never to forsake her virginity. "She is a Princess," the French ambassador remarked, "who can act any part she pleases."

The Kingdom in Danger

Beset by Catholic and Protestant extremists, Elizabeth contrived to forge a moderate compromise that enabled her realm to avert the massacres and civil wars that poisoned France and other countries on the Continent. But menace was never far off, and there were constant fears of conspiracy, rebellion, and assassination. Many of the fears swirled around Mary, Queen of Scots, who had been driven from her own kingdom in 1568 by a powerful faction of rebellious nobles and had taken refuge in England. Her presence, under a kind of house arrest, was the source of intense anxiety and helped generate continual rumors of plots. Some of these plots were real enough, others imaginary, still others traps set in motion by the secret agents of the government's intelligence service under the direction of Sir Francis Walsingham. The situation worsened greatly after the St. Bartholomew's Day Massacre of Protestants (Huguenots) in France (August 24, 1572), after Spanish imperial armies invaded the Netherlands in order to stamp out Protestant rebels, and after the assassination there of Europe's other major Protestant leader, William of Orange (1584).

The queen's life seemed to be in even greater danger after Pope Gregory XIII's proclamation in 1580 that the assassination of the great heretic Elizabeth (who had been excommunicated a decade before) would not constitute a mortal sin. The immediate effect of the proclamation was to make existence more difficult for English Catholics, most of whom were loyal to the queen but who fell under grave suspicion. Suspicion was intensified by the clandestine presence of English Jesuits, trained at seminaries abroad and smuggled back into England to serve the Roman Catholic cause. When Elizabeth's spymaster Walsingham unearthed an assassination plot in the correspondence between the Queen of Scots and the Catholic Anthony Babington, the wretched Mary's fate was sealed. After vacillating, a very reluctant Elizabeth signed the death warrant in February 1587, and her cousin was beheaded.

The long-anticipated military confrontation with Catholic Spain was now unavoidable. Elizabeth learned that Philip II, her former brother-in-law and onetime suitor, was preparing to send an enormous fleet against her island realm. It was to sail to the Netherlands, where a Spanish army would be waiting to embark and invade England. Barring its way was England's small fleet of well-armed and highly maneuverable fighting vessels, backed up by ships from the merchant navy. The Invincible Armada reached English waters in July 1588, only to be routed in one of the most famous and decisive naval battles in European history. Then, in what many viewed as an act of God on behalf of Protestant England, the Spanish fleet was dispersed and all but destroyed by violent storms.

As England braced itself to withstand the invasion that never came, Elizabeth appeared in person to review a detachment of soldiers assembled at Tilbury. Dressed in a white gown and a silver breastplate, she declared that though some among her councillors had urged her not to appear before a large crowd of armed men, she would never fail to trust the loyalty of her faithful and loving subjects. Nor did she fear the Spanish armies. "I know I have the body of a weak and feeble woman," Elizabeth declared, "but I have the heart and stomach of a king, and of England too." In this celebrated speech, Elizabeth displayed many of her most memorable qualities: her self-consciously histrionic command of grand public occasion, her subtle blending of magniloquent rhetoric and the language of love, her strategic appropriation of traditionally masculine qualities, and her great personal courage. "We princes," she once remarked, "are set on stages in the sight and view of all the world."

The English and Otherness

Shakespeare's London had a large population of resident aliens, mainly artisans and merchants and their families, from Portugal, Italy, Spain, Germany, and, above all, France and the Netherlands. Many of these people were Protestant refugees, and they were accorded some legal and economic protection by the government. But they were not always welcome by the local populace. Throughout the sixteenth century, London was the site of repeated demonstrations and, on occasion, bloody riots against the communities of foreign artisans, who were accused of taking jobs away from Englishmen. There was widespread hostility as well toward the Welsh, the Scots, and especially the Irish, whom the English had for centuries been struggling unsuccessfully to subdue. The kings of England claimed to be rulers of Ireland, but in reality they effectively controlled only a small area known as the Pale, extending north from Dublin. The great majority of the Irish people remained stubbornly Catholic and, despite endlessly reiterated English repression, burning of villages, destruction of crops, and massacres, incorrigibly independent.

Shakespeare's *Henry V* (1598–99) seems to invite the audience to celebrate the conjoined heroism of English, Welsh, Scots, and Irish soldiers all fighting together as a "band of brothers" against the French. But such a way of imagining the national community must be set against the tensions and conflicting interests that often set these brothers at each other's throats. As Shakespeare's King Henry realizes, a feared or hated foreign enemy helps at least to mask these tensions, and, indeed, in the face of the Spanish Armada, even the bitter gulf between Catholic and Protestant Englishmen seemed to narrow significantly. But the patriotic alliance was only temporary.

Another way of partially masking the sharp differences in language, belief, and custom among the peoples of the British Isles was to group these people together in contrast to the Jews. Medieval England's Jewish population, the recurrent object of persecution, extortion, and massacre, had been officially expelled by King Edward I in 1290, but Elizabethan England harbored a tiny number of Jews or Jewish converts to

A Jewish man poisoning a well. From Pierre Boaistuau, *Certaine Secrete Wonders of Nature* (1569).

Christianity who were treated with suspicion and hostility. One of these was Elizabeth's own physician, Roderigo Lopez, who was tried in 1594 for an alleged plot to poison the queen. Convicted and condemned to the hideous execution reserved for traitors, Lopez went to his death, in the words of the Elizabethan historian William Camden, "affirming that he loved the Queen as well as he loved Jesus Christ; which coming from a man of the Jewish profession moved no small laughter in the standers-by." It is difficult to gauge the meaning here of the phrase "the Jewish profession," used to describe a man who never, as far as we know, professed Judaism, just as it is difficult to gauge the meaning of the crowd's cruel laughter.

Elizabethans appear to have been fascinated by Jews and Judaism but uncertain whether the terms referred to a people, a foreign nation, a set of strange practices, a living faith, a defunct religion, a villainous conspiracy, or a messianic inheritance. Protestant Reformers brooded deeply on the Hebraic origins of Christianity; government officials ordered the arrest of those "suspected to be Jews"; villagers paid pennies to itinerant fortune-tellers who claimed to be descended from Abraham or masters of cabalistic mysteries; and London playgoers, perhaps including some who laughed at Lopez on the scaffold, enjoyed the spectacle of the downfall of the wicked Barabas in Christopher Marlowe's *Jew of Malta* (c. 1592) and the forced conversion of Shylock in Shakespeare's *Merchant of Venice* (1596–97). Few if any of Shakespeare's contemporaries would have encountered on English soil Jews who openly practiced their religion, though England probably harbored a small number of so-called Marranos, Spanish or Portuguese Jews who had officially converted to Christianity but secretly continued to observe Jewish practices. Jews were not officially permitted to resettle in England until the middle of the seventeenth century, and even then their legal status was ambiguous.

Shakespeare's England also had a small African population whose skin color was the subject of pseudoscientific speculation and theological debate. Some Elizabethans believed that Africans' blackness resulted from the climate of the regions in which they lived, where, as one traveler put it, they were "so scorched and vexed with the heat of the sun, that in many places they curse it when it riseth." Others held that blackness was a curse inherited from their forefather Chus, the son of Ham, who had, according to Genesis, wickedly exposed the nakedness of the drunken Noah. George Best, a proponent of this theory of inherited skin color, reported that "I myself have seen an Ethiopian as black as coal brought into England, who taking a fair English woman to wife, begat a son in all respects as black as the father was, although England were his native country, and an English woman his mother: whereby it seemeth this blackness proceedeth rather of some natural infection of that man."

As the word "infection" suggests, Elizabethans frequently regarded blackness as a physical defect, though the blacks who lived in England and Scotland throughout the sixteenth century were also treated as exotic curiosities. At his marriage to Anne of Denmark, James I entertained his bride and her family by commanding four naked black youths to dance before him in the snow. (The youths died of exposure shortly afterward.) In 1594, in the festivities celebrating the baptism of James's son, a "Black-Moor" entered pulling an elaborately decorated chariot that was, in the original plan, supposed to be drawn in by a lion. There was a black trumpeter in the courts of Henry VII and Henry VIII, while Elizabeth had at least two black servants, one an entertainer and the other a page. Africans became increasingly popular as servants in aristocratic and gentle households in the last decades of the sixteenth century.

Man with head beneath his shoulders. From a Spanish edition of Sir John Mandeville's *Travels*. See *Othello* 1.3.144–45: "and men whose heads / Do grow beneath their shoulders." Such men were occasionally reported by medieval travelers to the East.

An Indian dance. From Thomas Hariot, *A Briefe and True Report of the New Found Land of Virginia* (1590 ed.).

Some of these Africans were almost certainly slaves, though the legal status of slavery in England was ambiguous. In Cartwright's case (1569), the court ruled "that England was too Pure an Air for Slaves to breathe in," but there is evidence that black slaves were owned in Elizabethan and Jacobean England. Moreover, by the mid-sixteenth century, the English had become involved in the profitable trade that carried African slaves to the New World. In 1562, John Hawkins embarked on his first slaving voyage, transporting some three hundred blacks from the Guinea coast to Hispaniola, where they were sold for £10,000. Elizabeth is reported to have said of this venture that it was "detestable, and would call down the Vengeance of Heaven upon the Undertakers." Nevertheless, she invested in Hawkins's subsequent voyages and loaned him ships.

English men and women of the sixteenth century experienced an unprecedented increase in knowledge of the world beyond their island, for a number of reasons. Religious persecution compelled both Catholics and Protestants to live abroad; wealthy gentlemen (and, in at least a few cases, ladies) traveled in France and Italy to view the famous cultural monuments; merchants published accounts of distant lands such as Turkey, Morocco, and Russia; and military and trading ventures took English ships to still more distant shores. In 1496, a Venetian tradesman living in Bristol, John Cabot, was granted a license by Henry VII to sail on a voyage of exploration; with his son Sebastian, he discovered Newfoundland and Nova Scotia. Remarkable feats of seamanship and recon-naissance soon followed: on his ship the *Golden Hind,* Sir Francis Drake circumnavigated the globe in 1579 and laid claim to California on behalf of the queen; a few years later, a ship commanded by Thomas Cavendish also completed a circumnavigation. Sir Mar-tin Frobisher explored bleak Baffin Island in search of a Northwest Passage to the Ori-ent; Sir John Davis explored the west coast of Greenland and discovered the Falkland Islands off the coast of Argentina; Sir Walter Ralegh ventured up the Orinoco Delta, in what is now Venezuela, in search of the mythical land of El Dorado. Accounts of these and other exploits were collected by a clergyman and promoter of empire, Richard Hak-luyt, and published as *The Principal Navigations* (1589; expanded edition 1599).

"To seek new worlds for gold, for praise, for glory," as Ralegh characterized such enter-prises, was not for the faint of heart: Drake, Cavendish, Frobisher, and Hawkins all died at sea, as did huge numbers of those who sailed under their command. Elizabethans sen-sible enough to stay at home could do more than read written accounts of their fellow countrymen's far-reaching voyages. Expeditions brought back native plants (including, most famously, tobacco), animals, cultural artifacts, and, on occasion, samples of the native peoples themselves, most often seized against their will. There were exhibitions in London of a kidnapped Eskimo with his kayak and of Virginians with their canoes. Most of these miserable captives, violently uprooted and vulnerable to European diseases, quickly perished, but even in death they were evidently valuable property: when the En-glish will not give one small coin "to relieve a lame beggar," one of the characters in *The Tempest* wryly remarks, "they will lay out ten to see a dead Indian" (2.2.30–31).

Perhaps most nations learn to define what they are by defining what they are not. This negative self-definition is, in any case, what Elizabethans seemed constantly to be doing, in travel books, sermons, political speeches, civic pageants, public exhibitions, and the-atrical spectacles of otherness. The extraordinary variety of these exercises (which include public executions and urban riots, as well as more benign forms of curiosity) sug-gests that the boundaries of national identity were by no means clear and unequivocal. Even peoples whom English writers routinely, viciously stigmatize as irreducibly alien—Italians, Indians, Turks, and Jews—have a surprising instability in the Elizabethan imag-ination and may appear for brief, intense moments as powerful models to be admired and emulated before they resume their place as emblems of despised otherness.

James I and the Union of the Crowns

Though under great pressure to do so, the aging Elizabeth steadfastly refused to name her successor. It became increasingly apparent, however, that it would be James Stuart, the son of Mary, Queen of Scots, and by the time Elizabeth's health began to fail, several of her principal advisers, including her chief minister, Robert Cecil, had been for several years in secret correspondence with him in Edinburgh. Crowned King James VI of Scotland in 1567 when he was but one year old, Mary's son had been raised as a Protestant by his powerful guardians, and in 1589 he married a Protestant princess, Anne of Denmark. When Elizabeth died on March 24, 1603, English officials reported that on her deathbed the queen had named James to succeed her.

Upon his accession, James—now styled James VI of Scotland and James I of England—made plain his intention to unite his two kingdoms. As he told Parliament in 1604, "What God hath conjoined then, let no man separate. I am the husband, and all of the whole isle is my lawful wife; I am the head and it is my body; I am the shep-herd and it is my flock." But the flock was less perfectly united than James optimisti-cally envisioned: English and Scottish were sharply distinct identities, as were Welsh and Cornish and other peoples who were incorporated, with varying degrees of will-ingness, into the realm.

Fearing that to change the name of the kingdom would invalidate all laws and insti-tutions established under the name of England, a fear that was partly real and partly a cover for anti-Scots prejudice, Parliament balked at James's desire to be called "King of

Funeral procession of Queen Elizabeth. From a watercolor sketch by an unknown artist (1603).

Great Britain" and resisted the unionist legislation that would have made Great Britain a legal reality. Although the English initially rejoiced at the peaceful transition from Elizabeth to her successor, there was a rising tide of resentment against James's advancement of Scots friends and his creation of new knighthoods. Lower down the social ladder, English and Scots occasionally clashed violently on the streets: in July 1603, James issued a proclamation against Scottish "insolencies," and in April 1604, he ordered the arrest of "swaggerers" waylaying Scots in London. The ensuing years did not bring the amity and docile obedience for which James hoped, and, though the navy now flew the Union Jack, combining the Scottish cross of St. Andrew and the English cross of St. George, the unification of the kingdoms remained throughout his reign an unfulfilled ambition.

Unfulfilled as well were James's lifelong dreams of ruling as an absolute monarch. Crown lawyers throughout Europe had long argued that a King, by virtue of his power to make law, must necessarily be above law. But in England, sovereignty was identified not with the King alone or with the people alone but with the "King in Parliament." Against his absolutist ambitions, James faced the crucial power to raise taxes that was vested not in the monarch but in the elected members of the Parliament. He faced as well a theory of republicanism that traced it roots back to ancient Rome and that prided itself on its steadfast and, if necessary, violent resistance to tyranny. Shakespeare's fascination with monarchy is apparent throughout his work, but in his Roman plays in particular, as well as in his long poem *The Rape of Lucrece*, he manifests an intense imaginative interest in the idea of a republic.

The Jacobean Court

With James as with Elizabeth, the royal court was the center of diplomacy, ambition, intrigue, and an intense jockeying for social position. As always in monarchies, proximity to the king's person was a central mark of favor, so that access to the royal bedchamber was one of the highest aims of the powerful, scheming lords who followed James from his sprawling London palace at Whitehall to the hunting lodges and country estates to which he loved to retreat. A coveted office, in the Jacobean as in the Tudor court, was the Groom of the Stool, the person who supervised the disposal of the king's wastes. The officeholder was close to the king at one of his most exposed and vulnerable moments, and enjoyed the further privilege of sleeping on a pallet at the foot of the royal bed and putting on the royal undershirt. Another, slightly less privileged official, the Gentleman of the Robes, dressed the king in his doublet and outer garments.

The royal lifestyle was increasingly expensive. Unlike Elizabeth, James had to maintain separate households for his queen and for the heir apparent, Prince Henry. (Upon Henry's death at the age of eighteen in 1612, his younger brother, Prince Charles, became heir, eventually succeeding his father in 1625.) James was also extremely generous to his friends, amassing his own huge debts in the course of paying off theirs. As early as 1605, he told his principal adviser that "it is a horror to me to think of the height of my place, the greatness of my debts, and the smallness of my means." This smallness notwithstanding, James continued to lavish gifts upon handsome favorites such as the Earl of Somerset, Robert Carr, and the Duke of Buckingham, George Villiers.

The attachment James formed for these favorites was highly romantic. "God so love me," the king wrote to Buckingham, "as I desire only to live in the world for your sake, and that I had rather live banished in any part of the earth with you than live a sorrowful widow's life without you." Such sentiments, not surprisingly, gave rise to widespread rumors of homosexual activities at court. The rumors are certainly plausible, even though the surviving evidence of same-sex relationships, at court or elsewhere, is extremely difficult to interpret. A statute of 1533 made "the detestable and abominable vice of buggery committed with mankind or beast" a felony punishable by death. (English law declined to recognize or criminalize lesbian acts.) The effect of the draconian laws against buggery and sodomy seems to have been to reduce actual prosecutions to the barest minimum: for the next hundred years, there are no known cases of trials resulting in a death sentence for homosexual activity alone. If the legal record is, therefore, unreliable as an index of the extent of homosexual relations, the literary record (including, most famously, the majority of Shakespeare's sonnets) is equally opaque. Any poetic avowal of male-male love may simply be a formal expression of affection based on classical models, or, alternatively, it may be an expression of passionate physical and spiritual love. The interpretive difficulty is compounded by the absence in the period of any clear reference to a homosexual "identity," even though there are many references to same-sex acts and feelings. What is clear is that male friendships at the court of James and elsewhere were suffused with a potential eroticism, at once delightful and threatening, that subsequent periods policed more anxiously.

In addition to the extravagant expenditures on his favorites, James was also the patron of ever more

James I. By John De Critz the Elder (c. 1606).

Two Young Men. By Crispin van den Broeck (c. 1590).

elaborate feasts and masques. Shakespeare's work provides a small glimpse of these in *The Tempest,* with its exotic banquet and its "majestic vision" of mythological goddesses and dancing nymphs and reapers. The actual Jacobean court masques, designed by the great architect, painter, and engineer Inigo Jones, were spectacular, fantastic, technically ingenious, and staggeringly costly celebrations of regal magnificence. With their exquisite costumes and their elegant blend of music, dancing, and poetry, the masques, generally performed by the noble lords and ladies of the court, were deliberately ephemeral exercises in conspicuous expenditure and consumption: by tradition, at the end of the performance, the private audience would rush forward and tear to pieces the gorgeous scenery. And although masques were enormously sophisticated entertainments, often on rather esoteric allegorical themes, they could on occasion collapse into grotesque excess. In a letter of 1606, Sir John Harington describes a masque in honor of the visiting Danish king in which the participants, no doubt toasting their royal majesties, had had too much to drink. A lady playing the part of the Queen of Sheba attempted to present precious gifts, "but, forgetting the steps arising to the canopy, overset her caskets into his Danish Majesty's lap. . . . His Majesty then got up and would dance with the Queen of Sheba; but he fell down and humbled himself before her, and was carried to an inner chamber and laid on a bed." Meanwhile, Harington writes, the masque continued with a pageant of Faith, Hope, and Charity, but Charity could barely keep her balance, while Hope and Faith "were both sick and spewing in the lower hall." This was, we can hope, not a typical occasion.

While the English seem initially to have welcomed James's free-spending ways as a change from the relative parsimoniousness of Queen Elizabeth, they were dismayed by its consequences. Elizabeth had died owing £400,000. In 1608, the royal debt had risen to £1,400,000 and was increasing by £140,000 a year. The money to pay off this debt, or at least to keep it under control, was raised by various means. These included customs farming (leasing the right to collect customs duties to private individuals); the highly unpopular impositions (duties on the import of nonnecessities, such as spices, silks, and currants); the sale of crown lands; the sale of baronetcies; and appeals to an increasingly grudging and recalcitrant Parliament. In 1614, Parliament demanded an end to impositions before it would relieve the king and was angrily dissolved without completing its business.

James's Religious Policy and the Persecution of Witches

Before his accession to the English throne, the king had made known his view of Puritans, the general name for a variety of Protestant sects that were agitating for a radical reform of the Church, the overthrow of its conservative hierarchy of bishops, and the rejection of a large number of traditional rituals and practices. In a book he wrote, *Basilikon Doron* (1599), James denounced "brainsick and heady preachers" who were prepared "to let King, people, law and all be trod underfoot." Yet he was not entirely unwilling to consider religious reforms. In religion, as in foreign policy, he was above all concerned to maintain peace.

On his way south to claim the throne of England in 1603, James was presented with the Millenary Petition (signed by 1,000 ministers), which urged him as "our physician" to heal the disease of lingering "popish" ceremonies. He responded by calling a conference on the ceremonies of the Church of England, which duly took place at Hampton Court Palace in January 1604. The delegates who spoke for reform were moderates, and there was little in the outcome to satisfy Puritans. Nevertheless, while the Church of England continued to cling to such remnants of the Catholic past as wedding rings, square caps, bishops, and Christmas, the conference did produce some reform in the area of ecclesiastical discipline. It also authorized a new English translation of the Bible, known as the King James Bible, which was printed in 1611, too late to have been extensively used by Shakespeare. Along with Shakespeare's works, the King James Bible has probably had the profoundest influence on the subsequent history of English literature.

Having arranged this compromise, James saw his main task as ensuring conformity. He promulgated the 1604 Canons (the first definitive code of canon law since the Reformation), which required all ministers to subscribe to three articles. The first affirmed royal supremacy; the second confirmed that there was nothing in the Book of Common Prayer "contrary to the Word of God" and required ministers to use only the authorized

The "swimming" of a suspected witch (1615).

services; the third asserted that the central tenets of the Church of England were "agreeable to the Word of God." There were strong objections to the second and third articles from those of Puritan leanings inside and outside the House of Commons. In the end, many ministers refused to conform or subscribe to the articles, but only about 90 of them, or 1 percent of the clergy, were deprived of their livings. In its theology and composition, the Church of England was little changed from what it had been under Elizabeth. In hindsight, what is most striking are the ominous signs of growing religious divisions that would by the 1640s burst forth in civil war and the execution of James's son Charles.

James seems to have taken seriously the official claims to the sacredness of kingship, and he certainly took seriously his own theories of religion and politics, which he had printed for the edification of his people. He was convinced that Satan, perpetually warring against God and His representatives on earth, was continually plotting against him. James thought, moreover, that he possessed special insight into Satan's wicked agents, the witches, and in 1597, while King of Scotland, he published his *Daemonology*, a learned exposition of their malign threat to his godly rule. Hundreds of witches, he believed, were involved in a 1590 conspiracy to kill him by raising storms at sea when he was sailing home from Denmark with his new bride.

In the 1590s, Scotland embarked on a virulent witch craze of the kind that had since the fifteenth century repeatedly afflicted France, Switzerland, and Germany, where many thousands of women (and a much smaller number of men) were caught in a nightmarish web of wild accusations. Tortured into lurid confessions of infant cannibalism, night flying, and sexual intercourse with the devil at huge, orgiastic "witches' Sabbaths," the victims had little chance to defend themselves and were routinely burned at the stake.

In England, too, there were witchcraft prosecutions, but on a much smaller scale and with significant differences in the nature of the accusations and the judicial procedures. Witch trials began in England in the 1540s; statutes against witchcraft were enacted in 1542, 1563, and 1604. English law did not allow judicial torture, stipulated lesser punishments in cases of "white magic," and mandated jury trials. Juries acquitted more than half of the defendants in witchcraft trials; in Essex, where the judicial records are particularly extensive, some 24 percent of those accused were executed, while the remainder of those convicted were pilloried and imprisoned or sentenced and reprieved. The accused were generally charged with *maleficium*, an evil deed—usually harming neighbors, causing destructive storms, or killing farm animals—but not with worshipping Satan.

After 1603, when James came to the English throne, he somewhat moderated his enthusiasm for the judicial murder of witches, for the most part defenseless, poor women resented by their neighbors. Although he did nothing to mitigate the ferocity of the ongoing witch hunts in his native Scotland, he did not try to institute Scottish-style persecutions and trials in his new realm. This relative waning of persecutorial eagerness principally reflects the differences between England and Scotland, but it may also bespeak some small, nascent skepticism on James's part about the quality of evidence brought against the accused and about the reliability of the "confessions" extracted from them. It is sobering to reflect that plays like Shakespeare's *Macbeth* (1606), Thomas Middleton's *Witch* (before 1616), and Thomas Dekker, John Ford, and William Rowley's *Witch of Edmonton* (1621) seem to be less the allies of skepticism than the exploiters of fear.

The Playing Field

Cosmic Spectacles

The first permanent, freestanding public theaters in England date only from Shakespeare's own lifetime: a London playhouse, the Red Lion, is mentioned in 1567, and James Burbage's playhouse, The Theatre, was built in 1576. (The innovative use of these new stages, crucial to a full understanding of Shakespeare's achievement, is, in this volume, the subject of a separate essay by the theater historian Andrew Gurr, pages 79–99.) But it is misleading to identify English drama exclusively with these specially constructed playhouses, for in fact there was a rich and vital theatrical tradition in England stretching back for centuries. Many towns in late medieval England were the sites of annual festivals that mounted elaborate cycles of plays depicting the great biblical stories, from the creation of the world to Christ's Passion and its miraculous aftermath. Most of these plays have been lost, but the surviving cycles, such as those from York, are magnificent and complex works of art. They are sometimes called "mystery plays," either because they were performed by the guilds of various crafts (known as "mysteries") or, more likely, because they represented the mysteries of the faith. The cycles were most often performed on the annual feast day instituted in the early fourteenth century in honor of the Corpus Christi, the sacrament of the Lord's Supper, which is perhaps the greatest of these religious mysteries.

The Feast of Corpus Christi, celebrated on the Thursday following Trinity Sunday, helped give the play cycles their extraordinary cultural resonance, but it also contributed to their downfall. For along with the specifically liturgical plays traditionally performed by religious confraternities and the "saints' plays," which depicted miraculous events in the lives of individual holy men and women, the mystery cycles were closely identified with the Catholic Church. Protestant authorities in the sixteenth century, eager to eradicate all remnants of popular Catholic piety, moved to suppress the annual procession of the Host, with its gorgeous banners, pageant carts, and cycle of visionary plays. In 1548, the Feast of Corpus Christi was abolished. Towns that continued to perform the mysteries were under increasing pressure to abandon them. It is sometimes said that the cycles were already dying out from neglect, but recent research has shown that many towns and their guilds were extremely reluctant to give them up. Desperate offers to strip away any traces of Catholic doctrine and to submit the play scripts to the authorities for their approval met with unbending opposition from the government. In 1576, the courts gave York permission to perform its cycle but only if

> in the said play no pageant be used or set forth wherein the Majesty of God the Father, God the Son, or God the Holy Ghost or the administration of either the Sacraments of baptism or of the Lord's Supper be counterfeited or represented, or anything played which tend to the maintenance of superstition and idolatry or which be contrary to the laws of God . . . or of the realm.

Such "permission" was tantamount to an outright ban. The local officials in the city of Norwich, proud of their St. George and the Dragon play, asked if they could at least parade the dragon costume through the streets, but even this modest request was refused. It is likely that as a young man Shakespeare had seen some of these plays: when Hamlet says of a noisy, strutting theatrical performance that it "out-Herods Herod," he is alluding to the famously bombastic role of Herod of Jewry in the mystery plays. But by the century's end, the cycles were no longer performed.

Early English theater was by no means restricted to these civic and religious festivals. Payments to professional and amateur performers appear in early records of towns and aristocratic households, although the terms—"ministralli," "histriones," "mimi," "lusores," and so forth—are not used with great consistency and make it difficult to distinguish among minstrels, jugglers, stage players, and other entertainers. Performers acted in town halls and the halls of guilds and aristocratic mansions, on scaffolds erected in town squares and marketplaces, on pageant wagons in the streets, and in inn yards. By the fifteenth century and probably earlier, there were organized companies of players traveling under noble patronage. Such companies earned a living providing amusement, while enhancing the prestige of the patron.

A description of a provincial performance in the late sixteenth century, written by one R. Willis, provides a glimpse of what seems to have been the usual procedure:

> In the City of Gloucester the manner is (as I think it is in other like corporations) that when the Players of Interludes come to town, they first attend the Mayor to

Panorama of London, showing two theaters, both round and both flying flags: a flying flag indicated that a performance was in progress. The Globe is in the foreground, and the Beargarden or Hope is to the left.

inform him what nobleman's servant they are, and so to get licence for their public playing; and if the Mayor like the Actors, or would show respect to their Lord and Master, he appoints them to play their first play before himself and the Aldermen and common Council of the City and that is called the Mayor's play, where everyone that will come in without money, the Mayor giving the players a reward as he thinks fit to show respect unto them.

In addition to their take from this "first play," the players would almost certainly have supplemented their income by performing in halls and inn yards, where they could pass the hat after the performance or even on some occasions charge an admission fee. It was no doubt a precarious existence.

The "Interludes" mentioned in Willis's description of the Gloucester performances are likely plays that were, in effect, staged dialogues on religious, moral, and political themes. Such works could, like the mysteries, be associated with Catholicism, but they were also used in the sixteenth century to convey polemical Protestant messages, and they reached outside the religious sphere to address secular concerns as well. Henry Medwall's *Fulgens and Lucrece* (c. 1490–1501), for example, pits a wealthy but dissolute nobleman against a virtuous public servant of humble origins, while John Heywood's *Play of the Weather* (c. 1525–33) stages a debate among social rivals, including a gentleman, a merchant, a forest ranger, and two millers. The structure of such plays reflects the training in argumentation that students received in Tudor schools and, in particular, the sustained practice in examining all sides of a difficult question. Some of Shakespeare's amazing ability to look at critical issues from multiple perspectives may be traced back to this practice and the dramatic interludes it helped to inspire.

Another major form of theater that flourished in England in the fifteenth century and continued on into the sixteenth was the morality play. Like the mysteries, moralities addressed questions of the ultimate fate of the soul. They did so, however, not by rehearsing scriptural stories but by dramatizing allegories of spiritual struggle. Typically, a person named Human or Mankind or Youth is faced with a choice between a pious life in the company of such associates as Mercy, Discretion, and Good Deeds and a dissolute life among riotous companions like Lust or Mischief. Plays like *Mankind* (c. 1465–70) and *Everyman* (c. 1495) show how powerful these unpromising-sounding dramas could be, in part because of the extraordinary comic vitality of the evil character, or Vice, and in part because of the poignancy and terror of an individual's encounter with death. Shakespeare clearly grasped this power. The hunchbacked Duke of Gloucester in *Richard III* gleefully likens himself to "the formal Vice, Iniquity." And when Othello wavers between Desdemona and Iago (himself a Vice figure), his anguished dilemma echoes the fateful choice repeatedly faced by the troubled, vulnerable protagonists of the moralities.

If such plays sound a bit like sermons, it is because they were. Clerics and actors shared some of the same rhetorical skills. It would be misleading to regard churchgoing and playgoing as comparable entertainments, but in attacking the stage, ministers often seemed to regard the professional players as dangerous rivals. The players themselves were generally too discreet to rise to the challenge; it would have been foolhardy to present the theater as the Church's direct competitor. Yet in its moral intensity and its command of impassioned language, the stage frequently emulates and outdoes the pulpit.

Music and Dance

Playacting took its place alongside other forms of public expression and entertainment as well. Perhaps the most important, from the perspective of the theater, were music and dance, since these were directly and repeatedly incorporated into plays. Many plays, comedies and tragedies alike, include occasions that call upon the characters to dance: hence Beatrice and Benedick join the other masked guests at the dance in *Much Ado About Nothing*; in *Twelfth Night,* the befuddled Sir Andrew, at the instigation of the drunken Sir Toby Belch, displays his skill, such as it is, in capering; Romeo and Juliet first see each other at the Capulet ball; the witches dance in a ring around the hideous caldron and perform an "antic round" to cheer Macbeth's spirits; and, in one of Shakespeare's strangest and most wonderful scenes, the drunken Antony in *Antony and Cleopatra* joins hands with Caesar, Enobarbus, Pompey, and others to dance "the Egyptian Bacchanals."

Moreover, virtually all plays in the period, including Shakespeare's, apparently ended with a dance. Brushing off the theatrical gore and changing their expressions from woe to pleasure, the actors in plays like *Hamlet* and *King Lear* would presumably have received the audience's applause and then bid for a second round of applause by performing a stately pavane or a lively jig. Indeed, jigs, with their comical leaping dance steps often accompanied by scurrilous ballads, became so popular that they drew not only large crowds but also official disapproval. A court order of 1612 complained about the "cutpurses and other lewd and ill-disposed persons" who flocked to the theater at the end of every play to be entertained by "lewd jigs, songs, and dances." The players were warned to suppress these disreputable entertainments on pain of imprisonment.

The displays of dancing onstage clearly reflected a widespread popular interest in dancing outside the walls of the playhouse as well. Renaissance intellectuals conjured up visions of the universe as a great cosmic dance, poets figured relations between men and women in terms of popular dance steps, stern moralists denounced dancing as an incitement to filthy lewdness, and, perhaps as significant, men of all classes evidently spent a great deal of time worrying about how shapely their legs looked in tights and how gracefully they could leap. Shakespeare assumes that his audience will be quite familiar with a variety of dances. "For hear me, Hero," Beatrice tells her friend, "wooing, wedding, and repenting is as a Scotch jig, a measure, and a cinquepace" (2.1.60–61). Her speech dwells on the comparison a bit, teasing out its implications, but it still does not make much sense if you do not already know something about the dances and perhaps occasionally venture to perform them yourself.

Closely linked to dancing and even more central to the stage was music, both instrumental and vocal. In the early sixteenth century, the Reformation had been disastrous for sacred music: many church organs were destroyed, choir schools were closed, the glorious polyphonal liturgies sung in the monasteries were suppressed. But by the latter part of the century, new perspectives were reinvigorating English music. Latin Masses were reset in English, and tunes were written for newly translated, metrical psalms. More important for the theater, styles of secular music were developed that emphasized music's link to humanist eloquence, its ability to heighten and to rival rhetorically powerful texts.

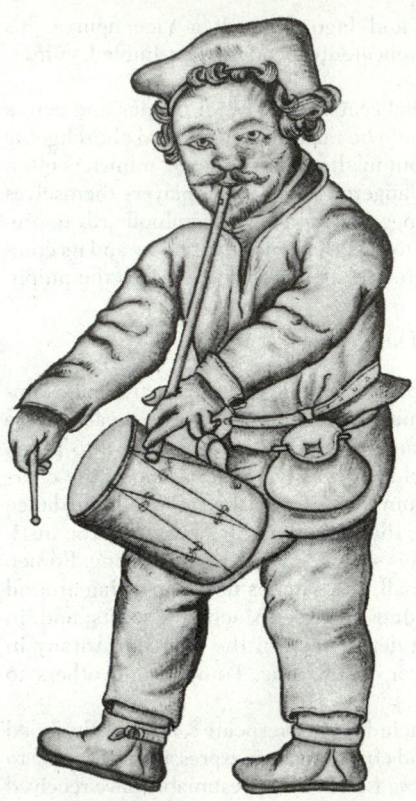

Richard Tarlton. Tarlton was the lead comedian of the Queen's Company from 1583, the year of its founding, until 1588, when he died.

This link is particularly evident in vocal music, at which Elizabethan composers excelled. Renowned composers William Byrd, Thomas Morley, John Dowland, and others wrote a rich profusion of madrigals (part songs for two to eight voices unaccompanied) and ayres (songs for solo voice, generally accompanied by the lute). These works, along with hymns, popular ballads, rounds, catches, and other forms of song, enjoyed immense popularity, not only in the royal court, where musical skill was regarded as an important accomplishment, and in aristocratic households, where professional musicians were employed as entertainers, but also in less exalted social circles. In his *Plaine and Easie Introduction to Practicall Musicke* (1597), Morley tells a story of social humiliation at a failure to perform that suggests that a well-educated Elizabethan was expected to be able to sing at sight. Even if this is an exaggeration in the interest of book sales, there is evidence of impressively widespread musical literacy, reflected in a splendid array of music for the lute, viol, recorder, harp, and virginal, as well as the marvelous vocal music.

Whether it is the aristocratic Orsino luxuriating in the dying fall of an exquisite melody or bully Bottom craving "the tongs and the bones," Shakespeare's characters frequently call for music. They also repeatedly give voice to the age's conviction that there was a deep relation between musical harmony and the harmonies of the well-ordered individual and state. "The man that hath no music in himself," warns Lorenzo in *The Merchant of Venice,* "nor is not moved with concord of sweet sounds,/Is fit for treasons, stratagems, and spoils" (5.1.82–84). This conviction, in turn, reflects a still deeper link between musical harmony and the divinely created harmony of the cosmos. When Ulysses, in *Troilus and Cressida,* wishes to convey the image of universal chaos, he speaks of the untuning of a string (1.3.109).

The playing companies must have regularly employed trained musicians, and many actors (like the actor who in playing Pandarus in *Troilus and Cressida* is supposed to accompany himself on the lute) must have possessed musical skill. Unfortunately, we possess the original settings for very few of Shakespeare's songs, possibly because many of them may have been set to popular tunes of the time that everyone knew and no one bothered to write down.

Alternative Entertainments

Plays, music, and dancing were by no means the only shows in town. There were jousts, tournaments, royal entries, religious processions, pageants in honor of newly installed civic officials or ambassadors arriving from abroad; wedding masques, court masques, and costumed entertainments known as "disguisings" or "mummings"; juggling acts, fortune-tellers, exhibitions of swordsmanship, mountebanks, folk healers, storytellers, magic shows; bearbaiting, bullbaiting, cockfighting, and other blood sports; folk festivals such as Maying, the Feast of Fools, Carnival, and Whitsun Ales. For several years, Elizabethan Londoners were delighted by a trained animal—Banks's Horse—that could, it was thought, do arithmetic and answer questions. And there was always the grim but compelling spectacle of public shaming, mutilation, and execution.

Most English towns had stocks and whipping posts. Drunks, fraudulent merchants, adulterers, and quarrelers could be placed in carts or mounted backward on asses and paraded through the streets for crowds to jeer and throw refuse at. Women accused of being scolds could be publicly muzzled by an iron device called a "brank" or tied to a cucking stool and dunked in the river. Convicted criminals could have their ears cut off, their noses slit, their foreheads branded. Public beheadings (generally reserved for the elite) and hangings were common. In the worst cases, felons were sentenced to be "hanged by the neck, and being alive cut down, and your privy members to be cut off, and your bowels to be taken out of your belly and there burned, you being alive."

Shakespeare occasionally takes note of these alternative entertainments: at the end of *Macbeth,* for example, with his enemies closing in on him, the doomed tyrant declares, "They have tied me to a stake. I cannot fly,/But bear-like I must fight the course" (5.7.1–2). The audience is reminded then that it is witnessing the human equivalent of a popular spectacle—a bear chained to a stake and attacked by fierce dogs—that they could have paid to watch at an arena near the Globe. And when, a few moments later, Macduff enters carrying Macbeth's head, the audience is seeing the theatrical equivalent of the execution of criminals and traitors that they could have also watched in the flesh, as it were, nearby. In a different key, the audiences who paid to see *A Midsummer Night's Dream* or *The Winter's Tale* got to enjoy the comic spectacle of a Maying and a Whitsun Pastoral, while the spectators of *The Tempest* could gawk at what the Folio list of characters calls a "salvage and deformed slave" and to enjoy an aristocratic magician's wedding masque in honor of his daughter.

An Elizabethan hanging.

The Enemies of the Stage

In 1624, a touring company of players arrived in Norwich and requested permission to perform. Permission was denied, but the municipal authorities, "in regard of the honorable respect which this City beareth to the right honorable the Lord Chamberlain," gave the players 20 shillings to get out of town. Throughout the sixteenth and early seventeenth centuries, there are many similar records of civic officials prohibiting performances and then, to appease a powerful patron, paying the actors to take their skills elsewhere. As early as the 1570s, there is evidence that the London authorities, while mindful of the players' influential protectors, were energetically trying to drive the theater out of the city.

Why should what we now regard as one of the undisputed glories of the age have aroused so much hostility? One answer, curiously enough, is traffic: plays drew large audiences—the public theaters could accommodate thousands—and residents objected to the crowds, the noise, and the crush of carriages. Other, more serious concerns were public health and crime. It was thought that numerous diseases, including the dreaded bubonic plague, were spread by noxious odors, and the packed playhouses were obvious breeding grounds for infection. (Patrons often tried to protect themselves by sniffing nosegays or stuffing cloves into their nostrils.) The large crowds drew pickpockets and other scoundrels. On one memorable afternoon, a pickpocket was caught in the act and tied for the duration of the play to one of the posts that held up the canopy above the stage.

Syphilis victim in a tub. Frontispiece to the play *Cornelianum Dolium* (1638), possibly authored by Thomas Randolph. The tub inscription translates as "I sit on the throne of love, I suffer in the tub," and the banner as "Farewell O sexual pleasures and lusts."

The theater was, moreover, a well-known haunt of prostitutes and, it was alleged, a place where innocent maids were seduced and respectable matrons corrupted. It was darkly rumored that "chambers and secret places" adjoined the theater galleries, and in any case, taverns, disreputable inns, and whorehouses were close at hand.

There were other charges as well. Plays were performed in the afternoon and, therefore, drew people, especially the young, away from their work. They were schools of idleness, luring apprentices from their trades, law students from their studies, housewives from their kitchens, and potentially pious souls from the sober meditations to which they might otherwise devote themselves. Wasting their time and money on disreputable shows, citizens exposed themselves to sexual provocation and outright political sedition. Even when the content of plays was morally exemplary—and, of course, few plays were so gratifyingly high-minded—the theater itself, in the eyes of most mayors and aldermen, was inherently disorderly.

The attack on the stage by civic officials was echoed and intensified by many of the age's moralists and religious leaders, especially those associated with Puritanism. While English Protestants earlier in the sixteenth century had attempted to counter the Catholic mystery cycles and saints' plays by mounting their own doctrinally correct dramas, by the century's end a fairly widespread consensus, even among those mildly sympathetic toward the theater, held that the stage and the pulpit were in tension with one another. After 1591, a ban on Sunday performances was strictly enforced, and in 1606, Parliament passed an act imposing a fine of £10 on any person who shall "in any stage-play, interlude, show, May-game, or pageant, jestingly or profanely speak or use the holy name of God, or of Christ Jesus, or of the Holy Ghost, or of the Trinity (which are not to be spoken but with fear and reverence)." If changes in the printed texts are a reliable indication, the players seem to have complied at least to some degree with the ruling. The Folio (1623) text of *Richard III*, for example, omits the Quarto's (1597) four uses of "zounds" (for "God's wounds"), along with a mention of "Christ's dear blood shed for our grievous sins"; "God's my judge" in *The Merchant of Venice* becomes "well I know"; "By Jesu" in *Henry V* becomes a very proper "I say"; and in all the plays, "God" from time to time metamorphoses to "Jove."

But for some of the theater's more extreme critics, these modest expurgations were tiny bandages on a gaping wound. In his huge book *Histriomastix* (1633), William Prynne regurgitates half a century of frenzied attacks on the "sinful, heathenish, lewd, ungodly Spectacles." In the eyes of Prynne and his fellow antitheatricalists, stage plays were part of a demonic tangle of obscene practices proliferating like a cancer in the body of society. It is "manifest to all men's judgments," he writes, that

> effeminate mixed dancing, dicing, stage-plays, lascivious pictures, wanton fashions, face-painting, health-drinking, long hair, love-locks, periwigs, women's curling, powdering and cutting of their hair, bonfires, New-year's gifts, May-games, amorous pastorals, lascivious effeminate music, excessive laughter, luxurious disorderly Christmas-keeping, mummeries . . . [are] wicked, unchristian pastimes.

Given the anxious emphasis on effeminacy, it is not surprising that denunciations of this kind obsessively focused on the use of boy actors to play the female parts. The enemies of the stage charged that theatrical transvestism excited illicit sexual desires, both heterosexual and homosexual.

Since cross-dressing violated a biblical prohibition (Deuteronomy 22:5), religious antitheatricalists attacked it as wicked regardless of its erotic charge; indeed, they often seemed to consider any act of impersonation as inherently wicked. In their view, the theater itself was Satan's domain. Thus a Cambridge scholar, John Greene, reports the sad fate of "a Christian woman" who went to the theater to see a play: "She entered in well and sound, but she returned and came forth possessed of the devil. Whereupon certain godly brethren demanded Satan how he durst be so bold, as to enter into her a Christian. Whereto he answered, that *he found her in his own house,* and therefore took possession of her as his own" (italic in original). When the "godly brethren" came to power in the mid-seventeenth century, with the overthrow of Charles I, they saw to it that the playhouses, temporarily shut down in 1642 at the onset of the Civil War, remained closed. The theater did not resume until the restoration of the monarchy in 1660.

Faced with enemies among civic officials and religious leaders, Elizabethan and Jacobean playing companies relied on the protection of their powerful patrons. As the liveried servants of aristocrats or of the monarch, the players could refute the charge that they were mere vagabonds, and they claimed, as a convenient legal fiction, that their public performances were necessary rehearsals in anticipation of those occasions when they would be called upon to entertain their noble masters. But harassment by the mayor and aldermen continued unabated, and the players were forced to build their theaters outside the immediate jurisdiction of the city authorities, either in the suburbs or in the areas known as the "liberties." A liberty was a piece of land within the City of London itself that was not directly subject to the authority of the lord mayor. The most significant of these from the point of view of the theater was the area near St. Paul's Cathedral called "the Blackfriars," where, until the dissolution of the monasteries in 1538, there had been a

Dominican monastery. It was here that in 1608 Shakespeare's company, then called the King's Men, built the indoor playhouse in which they performed during the winter months, reserving the open-air Globe in the suburb of Southwark for their summer performances.

Censorship and Regulation

In addition to those authorities who campaigned to shut down the theater, there were others whose task was to oversee, regulate, and censor it. Given the outright hostility of the former, the latter may have seemed to the London players equivocal allies rather than enemies. After all, plays that passed the censor were at least licensed to be performed and hence conceded to have some limited legitimacy. In April 1559, at the very start of her reign, Queen Elizabeth drafted a proposal that for the first time envisaged a system for the prior review and regulation of plays throughout her kingdom:

> The Queen's Majesty doth straightly forbid all manner interludes to be played either openly or privately, except the same be notified beforehand, and licensed within any city or town corporate, by the mayor or other chief officers of the same, and within any shire, by such as shall be lieutenants for the Queen's Majesty in the same shire, or by two of the Justices of Peace inhabiting within that part of the shire where any shall be played. . . . And for instruction to every of the said officers, her Majesty doth likewise charge every of them, as they will answer: that they permit none to be played wherein either matters of religion or of the governance of the estate of the commonweal shall be handled or treated upon, but by men of authority, learning and wisdom, nor to be handled before any audience, but of grave and discreet persons.

This proposal, which may not have been formally enacted, makes an important distinction between those who are entitled to address sensitive issues of religion and politics—authors "of authority, learning and wisdom" addressing audiences "of grave and discreet persons"—and those who are forbidden to do so.

The London public theater, with its playwrights who were the sons of glovers, shoemakers, and bricklayers and its audiences in which the privileged classes mingled with rowdy apprentices, masked women, and servants, was clearly not a place to which the government wished to grant freedom of expression. In 1581, the Master of the Revels, an official in the lord chamberlain's department whose role had hitherto been to provide entertainment at court, was given an expanded commission. Sir Edmund Tilney, the functionary who held the office, was authorized

> to warn, command, and appoint in all places within this our Realm of England, as well within franchises and liberties as without, all and every player or players with their playmakers, either belonging to any nobleman or otherwise . . . to appear before him with all such plays, tragedies, comedies, or shows as they shall in readiness or mean to set forth, and them to recite before our said Servant or his sufficient deputy, whom we ordain, appoint, and authorize by these presents of all such shows, plays, players, and playmakers, together with their playing places, to order and reform, authorize and put down, as shall be thought meet or unmeet unto himself or his said deputy in that behalf.

What emerged from this commission was in effect a national system of regulation and censorship. One of its consequences was to restrict virtually all licensed theater to the handful of authorized London-based playing companies. These companies would have to submit their plays for official scrutiny, but in return they received implicit, and on occasion explicit, protection against the continued fierce opposition of the local authorities. Plays reviewed and allowed by the Master of the Revels had been deemed fit to be performed before the monarch; how could mere aldermen legitimately claim that such plays should be banned as seditious?

The key question, of course, is how carefully the Master of the Revels scrutinized the plays brought before him either to hear or, more often from the 1590s onward, to peruse. What was Tilney, who served in the office until his death in 1610, or his successor, Sir George Buc, who served from 1610 to 1621, looking for? What did they insist be cut before they would release what was known as the "allowed copy," the only version licensed for performance? Unfortunately, the office books of the Master of the Revels in Shakespeare's time have been lost; what survives is a handful of scripts on which Tilney, Buc, and their assistants jotted their instructions. These suggest that the readings were rather painstaking, with careful attention paid to possible religious, political, and diplomatic repercussions. References, directly or strongly implied, to any living Christian prince or any important English nobleman, gentleman, or government official were particularly sensitive and likely to be struck. Renaissance political life was highly personalized; people in power were exceptionally alert to insult and zealously patrolled the boundaries of their prestige and reputation.

Moreover, the censors knew that audiences and readers were quite adept at applying theatrical representations distanced in time and space to their own world. At a time of riots against resident foreigners, Tilney read *Sir Thomas More,* a play in which Shakespeare probably had a hand, and instructed the players to cut scenes that, even though they were set in 1517, might have had an uncomfortable contemporary resonance. "Leave out the insurrection wholly," Tilney's note reads, "and the cause thereof and begin with Sir Thomas More at the Mayor's sessions, with a report afterwards of his good service done being sheriff of London upon a mutiny against the Lombards only by a short report and not otherwise at your own perils. E. Tilney." Of course, as Tilney knew perfectly well, most plays succeed precisely by mirroring, if only obliquely, their own times, but this particular reflection evidently seemed to him too dangerous or provocative.

The topical significance of a play depends in large measure on the particular moment in which it is performed and on certain features of the performance—for example, a striking resemblance between one of the characters and a well-known public figure—that the script itself will not necessarily disclose to us at this great distance or even to the censor at the time. Hence the Master of the Revels noted angrily of one play performed in 1632 that "there were diverse personated so naturally, both of lords and others of the court, that I took it ill." Hence, too, a play that was deemed allowable when it was first written and performed could return, like a nightmare, to haunt a different place and time. The most famous instance of such a return involves Shakespeare, for on the day before the Earl of Essex's attempted coup against Queen Elizabeth in 1601, someone paid the Lord Chamberlain's Men (the name of Shakespeare's company at the time) 40 shillings to revive their old play about the deposition and murder of Richard II. "I am Richard II," the queen declared. "Know ye not that?" However distressed she was by this performance, the queen significantly did not take out her wrath on the players: neither the playwright nor his company was punished, nor was the Master of the Revels criticized for allowing the play in the first place. It was Essex and several of his key supporters who lost their heads.

Evidence suggests that the Master of the Revels often regarded himself not as the strict censor of the theater but as its friendly guardian, charged with averting catastrophes. He was a bureaucrat concerned less with subversive ideas per se than with potential trouble. That is, there is no record of a dramatist being called to account for his heterodox beliefs; rather, plays were censored if they risked offending influential people, including important foreign allies, or if they threatened to cause public disorder by exacerbating religious or other controversies. The distinction is not a stable one, but it helps to explain the intellectual boldness, power, and freedom of a censored theater in a society in which the perceived enemies of the state were treated mercilessly. Shakespeare could have Lear articulate a searing indictment of social injustice—

> Robes and furred gowns hide all. Plate sin with gold,
> And the strong lance of justice hurtless breaks;
> Arm it in rags, a pygmy's straw does pierce it.
>
> (4.5.155–57)

—and evidently neither the Master of the Revels nor the courtiers in their robes and furred gowns protested. But when the Spanish ambassador complained about Thomas Middleton's anti-Spanish allegory *A Game at Chess*, performed at the Globe in 1624, the whole theater was shut down, the players were arrested, and the king professed to be furious at his official for licensing the play in the first place and allowing it to be performed for nine consecutive days.

In addition to the system for the licensing of plays for performance, there was also a system for the licensing of plays for publication. At the start of Shakespeare's career, such press licensing was the responsibility of the Court of High Commission, headed by the Archbishop of Canterbury and the Bishop of London. Their deputies, a panel of junior clerics, were supposed to review the manuscripts, granting licenses to those worthy of publication and rejecting any they deemed "heretical, seditious, or unseemly for Christian ears." Without a license, the Stationers' Company, the guild of the book trade, was not supposed to register a manuscript for publication. In practice, as various complaints and attempts to close loopholes attest, some playbooks were printed without a license. In 1607, the system was significantly revised when Sir George Buc began to license plays for the press. When Buc succeeded to the post of Master of the Revels in 1610, the powers to license plays for the stage and the page were vested in one man.

Theatrical Innovations

The theater continued to flourish under this system of regulation after Shakespeare's death; by the 1630s, as many as five playhouses were operating daily in London. When the theater reemerged after the eighteen-year hiatus imposed by Puritan rule, it quickly resumed its cultural importance, but not without a number of significant changes. Major innovations in staging resulted principally from Continental influences on the English artists who accompanied the court of Charles II into exile in France, where they supplied it with masques and other theatrical entertainments.

The institutional conditions and business practices of the two companies chartered by Charles after the Restoration in 1660 also differed from those of Shakespeare's theater. In place of the more collective practice of Shakespeare's company, the Restoration theaters were controlled by celebrated actor-managers who not only assigned themselves starring roles, in both comedy and tragedy, but also assumed sole responsibility for many business decisions, including the setting of their colleagues' salaries. At the same time, the power of the actor-manager, great as it was, was limited by the new importance of outside capital. No longer was the theater, with all of its properties from script to costumes, owned by the "sharers"—that is, by those actors who held shares in the joint-stock company. Instead, entrepreneurs would raise capital for increasingly fantastic sets and stage machinery that could cost as much as £3,000, an astronomical sum, for a single production. This investment, in turn, not only influenced the kinds of new plays written for the theater but helped to transform old plays that were revived, including Shakespeare's.

In his diary entry for August 24, 1661, Samuel Pepys notes that he has been "to the Opera, and there saw Hamlet, Prince of Denmark, done with scenes very well, but above all, Betterton did the prince's part beyond imagination." This is Thomas Betterton's first review, as it were, and it is typical of the enthusiasm he would inspire throughout his fifty-year career on the London stage. Pepys's brief and scattered remarks on the plays he voraciously attended in the 1660s are precious because they are among the few records from the period of concrete and immediate responses to theatrical performances. Modern readers might miss the significance of Pepys's phrase "done with scenes": this production of *Hamlet* was only the third play to use the movable sets first introduced to England by its producer, William Davenant. The central historical fact that makes the productions of this period so exciting is that public theater had been banned altogether for eighteen years until the Restoration of Charles II.

A brief discussion of theatrical developments in the Restoration period will enable us at least to glance longingly at a vast subject that lies outside the scope of this introduction: the rich performance history that extends from Shakespeare's time to our own, involving tens of thousands of productions and adaptations for theater, opera, Broadway musicals, and, of course, films. The scale of this history is vast in space as well as time: as early as 1607, there is a record of a *Hamlet* performed on board an English ship, HMS *Dragon*, off the coast of Sierra Leone, and troupes of English actors performed in the late sixteenth and early seventeenth centuries as far afield as Poland and Bohemia.

William Davenant, who claimed to be Shakespeare's bastard son, had become an expert on stage scenery while producing masques at the court of Charles I, and when the theaters reopened, he set to work on converting an indoor tennis court into a new kind of theater. He designed a broad open platform like that of the Elizabethan stage, but he replaced the relatively shallow space for "discoveries" (tableaux set up in an opening at the center of the stage, revealed by drawing back a curtain) and the "tiring-house" (the players' dressing room) behind this space with one expanded interior, framed by a proscenium arch, in which scenes could be displayed. These elaborately painted scenes could be moved on and off, using grooves on the floor. The perspectival effect for a spectator of one central painted panel with two "wings" on either side was that of three sides of a room. This effect anticipated that of the familiar "picture frame" stage, developed fully in the nineteenth century, and began a subtle shift in theater away from the elaborate verbal descriptions that are so central to Shakespeare and toward the evocative visual poetry of the set designer's art.

Another convention of Shakespeare's stage, the use of boy actors for female roles, gave way to the more complete illusion of women playing women's parts. The king issued a decree in 1662 forcefully permitting, if not requiring, the use of actresses. The royal decree is couched in the language of social and moral reform: the introduction of actresses will require the "reformation" of scurrilous and profane passages in plays, and this, in turn, will help forestall some of the objections that shut the theaters down in 1642. In reality, male theater audiences, composed of a narrower range of courtiers and aristocrats than in Shakespeare's time, met this intended reform with the assumption that the new actresses were fair game sexually; most actresses (with the partial exception of those who married male members of their troupes) were regarded as, or actually became, whores. But despite the social stigma and the fact that their salaries were predictably lower than those of their male counterparts, the stage saw some formidable female stars by the 1680s.

The first recorded appearance of an actress was that of a Desdemona in December 1660. Betterton's Ophelia in 1661 was Mary Saunderson (c. 1637–1712), who became Mrs. Betterton a year later. The most famous Ophelia of the period was Susanna Mountfort, who appeared in that role for the first time at the age of fifteen in 1705. The performance by Mountfort that became legendary occurred in 1720, after a disappointment in love, or so it was said, had driven her mad. Hearing that *Hamlet* was being performed, Mountfort escaped from her keepers and reached the theater, where she concealed herself until the scene in which Ophelia enters in her state of insanity. At this point, Mountfort rushed onto the stage and, in the words of a contemporary, "was in truth Ophelia herself, to the amazement of the performers and the astonishment of the audience."

That the character Ophelia became increasingly and decisively identified with the mad scene owes something to this occurrence, but it is also a consequence of the text used for Restoration performances of *Hamlet*. Having received the performance rights to a good number of Shakespeare's plays, Davenant altered them for the stage in the 1660s, and many of these acting versions remained in use for generations. In the case of *Hamlet*, neither Davenant nor his successors did what they so often did with other plays by Shakespeare—that is, alter the plot radically and interpolate other material. But many of the lines were cut or "improved." The cuts included most of Ophelia's sane speeches, such as her spirited retort to Laertes' moralizing; what remained made her part almost entirely an emblem of "female love melancholy."

Thomas Betterton (1635–1710), the prototype of the actor-manager, who would be the dominant figure in Shakespeare interpretation and in the theater generally through

The Spanish Tragedie:

OR,

Hieronimo is mad againe.

Containing the lamentable end of *Don Horatio*, and
Belimperia ; with the pittifull death of *Hieronimo*.

Newly corrected, amended, and enlarged with new
Additions of the *Painters* part, and others, as
it hath of late been diuers times acted.

LONDON,
Printed by W. White, for I. White and T. Langley,
and are to be sold at their Shop ouer against the
Sarazens head without New-gate. 1615.

Title page of Thomas Kyd's *Spanish Tragedie*
(1615). The first known edition dates from 1592.

the nineteenth century, made Hamlet his premier role. A contemporary who saw his last performance in the part (at the age of seventy-four, a rather old Prince of Denmark) wrote that to *read* Shakespeare's play was to encounter "dry, incoherent, & broken sentences," but that to see Betterton was to "prove" that the play was written "correctly." Spectators especially admired his reaction to the Ghost's appearance in the Queen's bedchamber: "his Countenance . . . thro' the violent and sudden Emotions of Amazement and Horror, turn[ed] instantly on the Sight of his fathers Spirit, as pale as his Neckcloath, when every Article of his Body seem's affected with a Tremor inexpressible." A piece of stage business in this scene, Betterton's upsetting his chair on the Ghost's entrance, became so thoroughly identified with the part that later productions were censured if the actor left it out. This business could very well have been handed down from Richard Burbage, the star of Shakespeare's original production, for Davenant, who had coached Betterton in the role, had known the performances of Joseph Taylor, who had succeeded Burbage in it. It is strangely gratifying to notice that Hamlets on stage and screen still occasionally upset their chairs.

Shakespeare's Life and Art

Playwrights, even hugely successful playwrights, were not ordinarily the objects of popular curiosity in early modern England, and few personal documents survive from Shakespeare's life of the kind that usually give the biographies of artists their appeal: no diary, no letters, private or public, no accounts of his childhood, almost no contemporary gossip, no scandals. Shakespeare's exact contemporary, the great playwright Christopher Marlowe, lived a mere twenty-nine years—he was murdered in 1593—but he left behind tantalizing glimpses of himself in police documents, the memos of high-ranking government officials, and detailed denunciations by sinister double agents. Ben Jonson recorded his opinions and his reading in a remarkable published notebook, *Timber; or, Discoveries Made upon Men and Matter,* and he also shared his views of the world (including some criticisms of his fellow playwright Shakespeare) with a Scottish poet, William Drummond of Hawthornden, who had the wit to jot them down for posterity. From Shakespeare, there is nothing comparable, not even a book with his name scribbled on the cover and a few marginal notes such as we have for Jonson, let alone working notebooks.

Yet Elizabethan England was a record-keeping society, and centuries of archival labor have turned up a substantial number of traces of its greatest playwright and his family. By themselves the traces would have relatively little interest, but in the light of Shakespeare's plays and poems, they have come to seem like precious relics and manage to achieve a considerable resonance.

Shakespeare's Family

William Shakespeare's grandfather Richard farmed land by the village of Snitterfield, near the small, pleasant market town of Stratford-upon-Avon, about 96 miles northwest of London. The playwright's father, John, moved in the mid-sixteenth century to Stratford, where he became a successful glover, landowner, moneylender, and dealer in wool and other agricultural goods. In or about 1557, he married Mary Arden, the daughter of a prosperous and well-connected farmer from the same area, Robert Arden of Wilmcote.

John Shakespeare was evidently highly esteemed by his fellow townspeople, for he held a series of important posts in local government. In 1556, he was appointed ale taster, an office reserved for "able persons and discreet," in 1558 was sworn in as a constable, and in 1561 was elected as one of the town's fourteen burgesses. As burgess, John served as one of the two chamberlains, responsible for administering borough property and revenues. In 1567, he was elected bailiff, Stratford's highest elective office and the equivalent of mayor. Although John Shakespeare signed all official documents with a cross or other sign, it is likely, but not certain, that he knew how to read and write. Mary, who also signed documents only with her mark, is less likely to have been literate.

According to the parish registers, which recorded baptisms and burials, the Shakespeares had eight children, four daughters and four sons, beginning with a daughter Joan born in 1558. A second daughter, Margaret, was born in December 1562 and died a few months later. William Shakespeare ("Gulielmus, filius Johannes Shakespeare"), their first son, was baptized on April 26, 1564. Since there was usually a few days' lapse between birth and baptism, it is conventional to celebrate Shakespeare's birthday on April 23, which happens to coincide with the feast of St. George, England's patron saint, and with the day of Shakespeare's death fifty-two years later.

William Shakespeare had three younger brothers, Gilbert, Richard, and Edmund, and two younger sisters, Joan and Anne. (It was often the custom to recycle a name, so the firstborn Joan must have died before the birth in 1569 of another daughter

"Southeast Prospect of Stratford-upon-Avon, 1746." From *The Gentleman's Magazine* (December 1792).

christened Joan, the only one of the girls to survive childhood.) Gilbert, who died in his forty-fifth year in 1612, is described in legal records as a Stratford haberdasher; Edmund followed William to London and became a professional actor, but evidently of no particular repute. He was only twenty-eight when he died in 1607 and was given an expensive funeral, perhaps paid for by his successful older brother.

At the high point of his public career, John Shakespeare, the father of this substantial family, applied to the Herald's College for a coat of arms, which would have marked his (and his family's) elevation from the ranks of substantial middle-class citizenry to that of the gentry. But the application went nowhere, for soon after he initiated what would have been a costly petitioning process, John apparently fell on hard times. The decline must have begun when William was still living at home, a boy of twelve or thirteen. From 1576 onward, John Shakespeare stopped attending council meetings. He became caught up in costly lawsuits, started mortgaging his land, and incurred substantial debts. In 1586, he was finally replaced on the council; in 1592, he was one of nine Stratford men listed as absenting themselves from church out of fear of being arrested for debt.

The reason for the reversal in John Shakespeare's fortunes is unknown. Some have speculated that it may have stemmed from adherence to Catholicism, since those who remained loyal to the old faith were subject to increasingly vigorous and costly discrimination. But if John Shakespeare was a Catholic, as seems quite possible, it would not necessarily explain his decline, since other Catholics (and Puritans) in Elizabethan Stratford and elsewhere managed to hold on to their offices. In any case, his fall from prosperity and local power, whatever its cause, was not absolute. In 1601, the last year of his life, his name was included among those qualified to speak on behalf of Stratford's rights. And he was by that time entitled to bear a coat of arms, for in 1596, some twenty years after the application to the Herald's office had been initiated, it was successfully renewed. There is no record of who paid for the bureaucratic procedures that made the grant possible, but it is likely to have been John's oldest son William, by that time a highly successful London playwright.

Education

Stratford was a small provincial town, but it had long been the site of an excellent free school, originally established by the Church in the thirteenth century. The main purpose of such schools in the Middle Ages had been to train prospective clerics; since many aristocrats could neither read nor write, literacy by itself conferred no special distinction and was not routinely viewed as desirable. But the situation began to change markedly in the sixteenth century. Protestantism placed a far greater emphasis upon lay literacy: for the sake of salvation, it was crucially important to be intimately acquainted with the Holy Book, and printing made that book readily available. Schools became less strictly bound up with training for the Church and more linked to the general acquisition of "literature," in the sense both of literacy and of cultural knowledge. In keeping with this new emphasis on reading and with humanist educational reform, the school was reorganized during the reign of Edward VI (1547–53). School records from the period have not survived, but it is almost certain that William Shakespeare attended the King's New School, as it was renamed in Edward's honor.

Scholars have painstakingly reconstructed the curriculum of schools of this kind and have even turned up the names and rather impressive credentials of the schoolmasters who taught there when Shakespeare was a student. (Shakespeare's principal teacher was Thomas Jenkins, an Oxford graduate, who received £20 a year and a rent-free house.) A child's education in Elizabethan England began at age four or five with two years at what was called the "petty school," attached to the main grammar school. The little scholars carried a "hornbook," a sheet of paper or parchment framed in wood and covered, for protection, with a transparent layer of horn. On the paper was written

The Cholmondeley sisters, c. 1600–10. This striking image brings to mind Shakespeare's fascination with twinship, both identical (notably in *The Comedy of Errors*) and fraternal (in *Twelfth Night*).

the alphabet and the Lord's Prayer, which were reproduced as well in the slightly more advanced *ABC with the Catechism,* a combination primer and rudimentary religious guide.

After students demonstrated some ability to read, the boys could go on, at about age seven, to the grammar school. Shakespeare's images of the experience are not particularly cheerful. In his famous account of the Seven Ages of Man, Jaques in *As You Like It* describes

> the whining schoolboy with his satchel
> And shining morning face, creeping like snail
> Unwillingly to school.
>
> (2.7.144–46)

The schoolboy would have crept quite early: the day began at 6:00 A.M. in summer and 7:00 A.M. in winter and continued until 5:00 P.M., with very few breaks or holidays.

At the core of the curriculum was the study of Latin, the mastery of which was in effect a prolonged male puberty rite involving much discipline and pain as well as pleasure. A late sixteenth-century Dutchman (whose name fittingly was Batty) proposed that God had created the human buttocks so that they could be severely beaten without risking permanent injury. Such thoughts dominated the pedagogy of the age, so that even an able young scholar, as we might imagine Shakespeare to have been, could scarcely have escaped recurrent flogging.

Shakespeare evidently reaped some rewards for the miseries he probably endured: his works are laced with echoes of many of the great Latin texts taught in grammar schools. One of his earliest comedies, *The Comedy of Errors,* is a brilliant variation on a theme by the Roman playwright Plautus, whom Elizabethan schoolchildren often performed as well as read; and one of his earliest tragedies, *Titus Andronicus,* is heavily indebted to Seneca. These are among the most visible of the classical influences that are often more subtly and pervasively interfused in Shakespeare's works. He seems to have had a particular fondness for *Aesop's Fables,* Apuleius's *Golden Ass,* and above all Ovid's *Metamorphoses.* His learned contemporary Ben Jonson remarked that Shakespeare had "small Latin and less Greek," but from this distance what is striking is not the limits of Shakespeare's learning but rather the unpretentious ease, intelligence, and gusto with which he draws upon what he must have first encountered as laborious study.

Traces of a Life

In November 1582, William Shakespeare, at the age of eighteen, married twenty-six-year-old Anne Hathaway, who came from the village of Shottery, near Stratford. Their first daughter, Susanna, was baptized six months later. This circumstance, along with the fact that Anne was eight years Will's senior, has given rise to a mountain of speculation, all the more lurid precisely because there is no further evidence. Shakespeare depicts in several plays situations in which marriage is precipitated by a pregnancy, but he also registers, in *Measure for Measure* (1.2.125ff.), the Elizabethan belief that a "true contract" of marriage could be legitimately made and then consummated simply by the mutual vows of the couple in the presence of witnesses.

On February 2, 1585, the twins Hamnet and Judith Shakespeare were baptized in Stratford. Hamnet died at the age of eleven, when his father was already living for much of the year in London as a successful playwright. These are Shakespeare's only known children, although the playwright and impresario William Davenant in the mid-seventeenth century claimed to be his bastard son. Since people did not ordinarily advertise their illegitimacy, the claim, though impossible to verify, at least suggests the unusual strength of the Shakespeare's posthumous reputation.

William Shakespeare's father, John, died in 1601; his mother died seven years later. They would have had the satisfaction of witnessing their eldest son's prosperity, and not only from a distance, for in 1597 William purchased New Place, the second largest house in Stratford. In 1607, the playwright's daughter Susanna married a successful and well-known physician, John Hall. The next year, the Halls had a daughter, Elizabeth, Shakespeare's first grandchild. In 1616, the year of Shakespeare's death, his daughter Judith married a vintner, Thomas Quiney, with whom she had three children. Shakespeare's widow, Anne, died in 1623, at the age of sixty-seven. His first-born, Susanna, died at the age of sixty-six in 1649, the year that King Charles I was beheaded by the parliamentary army. Judith lived through Cromwell's Protectorate and on to the Restoration of the monarchy; she died in February 1662, at the age of seventy-seven. By the end of the century, the line of Shakespeare's direct heirs was extinct.

Patient digging in the archives has turned up other traces of Shakespeare's life as a family man and a man of means: assessments, small fines, real-estate deeds, minor actions in court to collect debts. In addition to his fine Stratford house and a large garden and cottage facing it, Shakespeare bought substantial parcels of land in the vicinity. When in *The Tempest* the wedding celebration conjures up a vision of "barns and garners never empty," Shakespeare could have been glancing at what the legal documents record as his own "tithes of corn, grain, blade, and hay" in the fields near Stratford. At some point after 1610, Shakespeare seems to have begun to shift his attention from the London stage to his Stratford properties, although the term "retirement" implies a more decisive and definitive break than appears to have been the case. By 1613, when the Globe Theatre burned down during a performance of *All Is True (Henry VIII)*, Shakespeare was probably residing for the most part in Stratford, but he retained his financial interest in the rebuilt playhouse and probably continued to have some links to his theatrical colleagues. Still, by this point, his career as a playwright was substantially over. Legal documents from his last years show his main concern to be the protection of his real-estate interests in Stratford.

Half a century after Shakespeare's death, a Stratford vicar and physician, John Ward, noted in his diary that Shakespeare and his fellow poets Michael Drayton and Ben Jonson "had a merry meeting, and it seems drank too hard, for Shakespeare died of a fever there contracted." It is not inconceivable that Shakespeare's last illness was somehow linked, if only coincidentally, to the festivities on the occasion of the wedding in February 1616 of his daughter Judith (who was still alive when Ward made his diary entry). In any case, on March 25, 1616, Shakespeare revised his will, and on April 23 he died. Two days later, he was buried in the chancel of Holy Trinity Church beneath a stone bearing an epitaph he is said to have devised:

> Good friend for Jesus' sake forbear,
> To dig the dust enclosed here:
> Blest be the man that spares these stones,
> And curst be he that moves my bones.

The verses are hardly among Shakespeare's finest, but they seem to have been effective: though bones were routinely dug up to make room for others—a fate imagined with unforgettable intensity in the graveyard scene in *Hamlet*—his own remains were undisturbed. Like other vestiges of sixteenth- and early seventeenth-century Stratford, Shakespeare's grave has for centuries been the object of a tourist industry that borders on a religious cult.

Shakespeare's will has been examined with an intensity befitting this cult; every provision and formulaic phrase, no matter how minor or conventional, has borne a heavy weight of interpretation, none more so than the bequest to his wife, Anne, of only "my second-best bed." Scholars have pointed out that Anne would in any case have been provided for by custom and that the terms are not necessarily a deliberate slight, but the absence of the customary words "my loving wife" or "my well-beloved wife" is difficult to ignore.

Portrait of the Playwright as Young Provincial

The great problem with the surviving traces of Shakespeare's life is not that they are few but that they are dull. Christopher Marlowe was a double or triple agent, accused of brawling, sodomy, and atheism. Ben Jonson, who somehow clambered up from bricklayer's apprentice to classical scholar, served in the army in Flanders, killed a fellow actor in a duel, converted to Catholicism in prison in 1598, and returned to the Church of England in 1610. Provincial real-estate investments and the second-best bed cannot compete with such adventurous lives. Indeed, the relative ordinariness of Shakespeare's social background and life has contributed to a persistent current of speculation that the glover's son from Stratford-upon-Avon was not in fact the author of the plays attributed to him.

The anti-Stratfordians, as those who deny Shakespeare's authorship are sometimes called, almost always propose as the real author someone who came from a higher social class and received a more prestigious education. Francis Bacon, the Earl of Oxford, the Earl of Southampton, even Queen Elizabeth, have been advanced, among many others, as glamorous candidates for the role of clandestine playwright. Several famous people, including Mark Twain and Sigmund Freud, have espoused these theories, though very few scholars have joined them. Since Shakespeare was quite well-known in his own time as the author of the plays that bear his name, there would need to have been an extraordinary conspiracy to conceal the identity of the real master who (the theory goes) disdained to appear in the vulgarity of print or on the public stage. Like many conspiracy theories, the extreme implausibility of this one only seems to increase the fervent conviction of its advocates.

To the charge that a middle-class author from a small town could not have imagined the lives of kings and nobles, one can respond by citing the exceptional qualities that Ben Jonson praised in Shakespeare: "excellent *Phantsie*; brave notions, and gentle expressions." Even in ordinary mortals, the human imagination is a strange faculty; in Shakespeare, it seems to have been uncannily powerful, working its mysterious, transforming effects on everything it touched. His imagination was intensely engaged by what he found in books. He seems throughout his life to have been an intense, voracious reader, and it is fascinating to witness his creative encounters with Raphael Holinshed's *Chronicles of England, Scotlande, and Irelande*, Plutarch's *Lives of the Noble Grecians and Romans*, Ovid's *Metamorphoses*, Montaigne's *Essays*, and the Bible, to name only some of his favorite books. But books were clearly not the only objects of Shakespeare's attention; like most artists, he drew upon the whole range of his life experiences.

To integrate some of the probable circumstances of Shakespeare's early years with the particular shape of the theatrical imagination associated with his name, let us indulge briefly in the biographical daydreams that modern scholarship is supposed to have rendered forever obsolete. The vignettes that follow are conjectural, but they may suggest ways in which his life as we know it found its way into his art.

1. the gown of office

Shakespeare was a very young boy—not quite four years old—when the Stratford council elected his father, John, to a year's term as bailiff (the equivalent of mayor). The office, the town's highest, was attended with considerable ceremony. The bailiff and his deputy were entitled to appear in public in furred gowns, attended by leather-clad sergeants bearing maces before them. On Rogation Days (three days of prayer for the harvest, before Ascension Day), they would solemnly pace out the parish boundaries, and they would similarly walk in processions on market and fair days. On Sundays, the sergeants would accompany the bailiff to church, where he would sit with his wife in a front pew, and he would have a comparable seat of honor at sermons in the Guild Chapel.

Public deference was a matter of law as well as custom: any inhabitant who spoke disrespectfully to the bailiff or other town officer was subject to the penalty of three days and three nights in the stocks. Newcomers who sought employment—notably including traveling players who hoped to stage performances—were obliged to obtain the bailiff's permission. In the year that John Shakespeare held office, two such professional playing companies arrived in Stratford. They must have proceeded to the bailiff's house on Henley Street and presented the letters of recommendation, with wax seals, that showed that they were not vagabonds. They would have spoken with more than ordinary deference, since it was the bailiff who would decide whether they would be sent packing or—as was the case—allowed to post their bills announcing the performances. The first of these performances was usually free to all comers. The bailiff would have been expected to attend, for it was his privilege to determine the level of the reward to be paid out of the city coffers; he would, presumably, have been given one of the best seats in the guildhall, where a special stage had been erected. It is impossible to know whether John Shakespeare took his family to these plays, but his little boy would certainly have been aware of what was happening.

On a precocious child (or even, for that matter, on an ordinary child), the effect of his father's office and the elaborate rituals that attended it would be at least threefold. First, the ceremony would convey irresistibly the power of clothes (the gown of office) and of symbols (the mace) to transform identity as if by magic. Second, it would invest the father with immense power, distinction, and importance, awakening what we may call a lifelong dream of high station. And third, pulling slightly against this dream, it would provoke an odd feeling that the father's clothes do not fit, a perception that the office is not the same as the man, and an intimate, firsthand knowledge that when the robes are put off, their wearer is inevitably glimpsed in a far different, less exalted light.

2. progresses and elections

This second biographical fantasy, slightly less plausible than the first but still quite likely, involves a somewhat older child witnessing two characteristic forms of Elizabethan political ceremony, both of which were well known in the provinces. Queen Elizabeth was fond of going on what were known as "progresses," triumphant ceremonial journeys around her kingdom. Let us imagine that the young Shakespeare—say, in 1574, when he was ten years old—went with his kinsfolk or friends to Warwick, some 8 miles distant, to witness a progress. He would thus have participated as a spectator in an elaborate celebration of charismatic power: the courtiers in their gorgeous clothes, the nervous local officials bedecked in velvets and silks, and at the center, carried in a special litter like a painted idol, the bejeweled queen. Let us imagine further that in addition to being struck by the overwhelming force of this charisma, the boy was struck, too, by the way this force depended paradoxically on a sense that the queen was after all quite human. Elizabeth was in fact fond of calling attention to this peculiar tension between near-divinization and human ordinariness. For example, on this occasion at Warwick (and what follows really happened), after the trembling Recorder, presumably a local civil official of high standing, had made his official welcoming speech, Elizabeth offered her hand to him to be kissed: "Come hither, little Recorder," she said. "It was told me that you would be afraid to look upon me or to speak boldly; but you were not so afraid of me as I was of you; and I now thank you for putting me in mind of my duty." Of course, the charm of this royal "confession" of nervousness depends on its manifest implausibility: it is, in effect, a theatrical performance of humility by someone with immense confidence in her own histrionic power.

A royal progress was not the only form of spectacular political activity that Shakespeare might well have seen in the 1570s; it is still more likely that he would have witnessed parliamentary elections, particularly since his father was qualified to vote. In 1571, 1572, 1575, and 1578, there were shire elections conducted in nearby Warwick, elections that would certainly have attracted well over a thousand voters. These were often memorable events: large crowds came together; there was usually heavy drinking and carnivalesque festivity; and, at the same time, there was enacted, in a very different register from that of the monarchy, a ritual of empowerment. The people, those entitled to vote by virtue of meeting the property and residence requirements, chose their own representatives by giving their votes—their voices—to candidates for office. Here, legislative sovereignty was conferred not by God but by the consent of the community, a consent marked by shouts and applause.

Recent cultural historians have been so fascinated by the evident links between the spectacles of the absolutist monarchy and the theater that they have largely ignored the significance of this alternative public arena, one that generated intense excitement throughout the country. A child who was a spectator at a parliamentary election in the 1570s might well have found the occasion enormously compelling. It is striking, in any case, how often the adult Shakespeare returns to scenes of acclamation and mass consent, and striking, too, how much the theater depends on the soliciting of popular voices.

3. EXORCISMS

A third and final fantasy is even more speculative than the second and involves a controversial claim, which has long been hotly debated— that Shakespeare either was a secret Catholic or was at least raised in a Roman Catholic household in a time of official suspicion and persecution of recusancy. A late seventeenth-century Anglican clergyman, Richard Davies, jotted down in some notes on Shakespeare that "he died a papist." In a modern biographical study, E. A. J. Honigmann convincingly linked several of the schoolmasters who taught in Stratford at the time that Shakespeare would have been a pupil to a network of Catholic families in Lancashire with whom one "William Shakeshafte," possibly a young schoolmaster or player, was connected in the late 1570s or early 1580s.

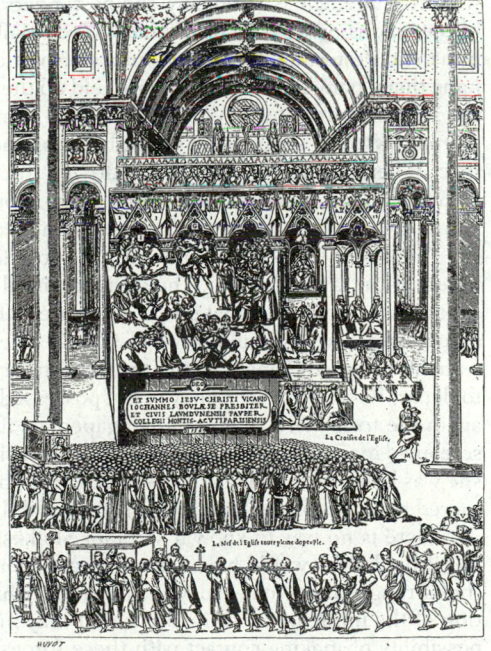

Exorcism: Nicole Aubry in the cathedral at Laon, 1566.

Catholics in Elizabethan England were not free to practice their religion—any more than Protestants, in Catholic countries, were free to practice theirs—and the beleaguered faithful, beset with spies, came together only at great risk to confess and receive Communion from clandestine priests. Under the circumstances, although a substantial portion of the population may have retained a residual inward loyalty to the traditional faith, the vast majority fell away from outward Catholic practice. After all, the churches, great and small, were now the places of Protestant worship; the innumerable local saints' shrines and pilgrimage sites had been systematically destroyed; the monasteries and convents had been abolished, their property bestowed on royal favorites or sold at bargain prices to local magnates. Seeking a spectacular way to demonstrate the enduring spiritual power and authenticity of the Roman Church, the embattled Counter-Reformers turned to an ancient ritual: exorcism. Devils who possessed the souls of troubled men and women had once been exorcised in public, but now the healing rite had to be conducted in secret, in a barn in a remote village, perhaps, or in the attic of the secluded house of a Catholic loyalist. The danger for those who presided was enormous—brutal interrogation, torture, and an unspeakably horrible execution was the usual fate of the missionary priests who were caught—but the vivid demonstration of the Church's triumph over evil was sufficiently compelling to warrant the risk. For despite the lynx-eyed alertness of the Protestant authorities, Catholics staged a surprising number of clandestine exorcisms, many of which drew substantial crowds.

Accepting for the moment that William Shakespeare was raised in the recusant faith of his father and mother, let us imagine that one day in the early 1580s the young man attended an exorcism of which he had learned through the secret network of the faithful. Here, based on an eyewitness account of such an occasion recently transcribed by Gerard Kilroy, is what he is likely to have seen. At the center of a large room, emptied of other furniture in order to accommodate the many observers, stood a bed. A young woman sat on the bed, and a priest, in clerical vestments, stood over her, preaching a sermon. As he spoke, the woman began to writhe and scream. At first the screams, uttered by a deep voice that could not have been the woman's although it came from her mouth, were not intelligible. Gradually, the bystanders began to make out some of the words, blasphemous oaths—"God's wounds! God's nails!"—followed by menaces, spoken as if by a rabid Protestant: "Popish priests, popish priests, to prison with them and hang them, hang them, hang them." The exorcist held up the Eucharist over the writhing woman, and the screams intensified. "Who are you?" he demanded. "I am Modu," the voice replied. "Depart, Modu!" shouted the priest, bringing the consecrated wafer closer to the demoniac. When that did not succeed in driving the devil out, the priest advanced a chafing dish of fire and brimstone, provoking more shouting and cursing, and then displayed a painting of the Blessed Virgin. "I will not behold or see her," screamed the demonic voice.

The longer the scene continued, the more there was confirmation of the contested tenets of the Catholic faith. The devil admitted that the Virgin Mary was a particularly efficacious intercessor, that purgatory existed, that the wafer, consecrated by the priest, actually was the body and blood of Christ. The devil also revealed that all Protestants were his followers. Finally, under the irresistible force of spiritual compulsion, he agreed to depart forever from the body of the possessed. The departure was difficult: again and again the tormented young woman gaped, as if her mouth were being torn open. She screamed in pain, rose up only to be cast down violently by invisible hands, cried out that she was being drowned, and called upon Jesus and his mother to save her. Only when a sacred relic was placed directly on her flesh did the devil finally leave her.

There is no way to know if William Shakespeare actually witnessed such a scene, but if he did, he would have carried away several indelible impressions: an awareness that strange, alien voices may speak from within ordinary, familiar bodies; an intimation of the immense, cosmic forces that may impinge upon human life; a belief in the possibility of making contact with these forces and compelling them to speak. These are, after all, the foundation stones of great tragedy.

Many years later, Shakespeare brooded about demonic possession when he was writing his greatest tragedy about the presence of evil in the world, *King Lear*. "This is the foul fiend Flibbertigibbet," shouts the madman, Poor Tom; "The Prince of Darkness is a gentleman. Modo he's called, and Mahu" (3.4.103, 127–28). But Poor Tom in that play is faking it; he is actually the noble Edgar, who has disguised himself as a madman in order to escape persecution. Did Shakespeare as a teenager already think that the whole compelling event, in all of its metaphysical weirdness, was a powerful theatrical fraud, a piece of pious propaganda? Perhaps. But if so, he also clearly understood that evil exists, that persecution is real, and that illusion has an irresistible force.

These imaginary portraits of the playwright as a young provincial introduce us to several of the root conditions of the Elizabethan theater. Biographical fantasies, though entirely speculative and playful, are useful in part because some people have found it difficult to conceive how Shakespeare, with his provincial roots and his restricted range of experience, could have so rapidly and completely mastered the central imaginative themes of his times. Moreover, it is sometimes difficult to grasp how seeming abstractions such as market society, monarchical state, and theological doctrine were actually experienced directly by peculiar, distinct individuals. Shakespeare's plays were social and collective events, but they also bore the stamp of a particular artist, one endowed with a remarkable capacity to craft lifelike illusions (what Jonson called "excellent *Phantsie*"), a daring willingness to articulate an original vision ("brave notions"), and a loving command, at once precise and generous, of language ("gentle expressions"). These plays are stitched together from shared cultural experiences, inherited dramatic devices, and the pungent vernacular of the day, but we should not lose sight of the extent to which they articulate an intensely personal vision, a bold shaping of the available materials. Four centuries of feverish biographical speculation, much of it foolish, bears witness to a basic intuition: the richness of these plays, their inexhaustible openness, is the consequence not only of the auspicious collective conditions of the culture but also of someone's exceptional skill, inventiveness, and courage at taking those conditions and making of them something rich and strange.

The Theater of the Nation

What precisely are the collective conditions highlighted by these vignettes? First, the growth of Stratford-upon-Avon, the bustling market town of which John Shakespeare was bailiff, is a small version of a momentous sixteenth-century development that made Shakespeare's career possible: the making of an urban "public." That development obviously depended on adequate numbers; the period experienced a rapid and still unexplained growth in population. With it came an expansion and elaboration of market relations: markets became less periodic, more continuous, and more abstract—centered, that is, not on the familiar materiality of goods but on the liquidity of capital and goods. In practical terms, this meant that it was possible to conceive of the theater not only as festive entertainment for special events—lord mayor's pageants, visiting princes, seasonal festivals, and the like—but as a permanent, year-round business venture. The venture relied on ticket sales—it was an innovation of this period to have money advanced in the expectation of pleasure rather than offered to servants afterward as a reward—and counted on habitual playgoing with a concomitant demand for new plays from competing theater companies: "But that's all one, our play is done," sings Feste at the end of *Twelfth Night* and adds a glance toward the next afternoon's proceeds: "And we'll strive to please you every day" (5.1.394–95).

Second, the royal progress is an instance of what the anthropologist Clifford Geertz has called the Theater State, a state that manifests its power and meaning in exemplary public performances. Professional companies of players, like the one Shakespeare belonged to, understood well that they existed in relation to this Theater State and would, if they were fortunate, be called upon to serve it. Unlike Ben Jonson, Shakespeare did not, as far as we know, write royal entertainments on commission, but his plays were frequently performed before Queen Elizabeth and then before King James and Queen Anne, along with their courtiers and privileged guests. There are many fascinating glimpses of these performances, including a letter from Walter Cope to Robert Cecil, early in James's reign. "Burbage is come," Cope writes, referring to the leading actor of Shakespeare's company, "and says there is no new play that the queen hath not seen, but they have revived an old one, called *Love's Labours Lost,* which for wit and mirth he says will please her exceedingly. And this is appointed to be played tomorrow night at my Lord of Southampton's." Not only would such theatrical performances have given great pleasure—evidently, the queen had already exhausted the company's new offerings—but they conferred prestige upon those who commanded them and those in whose honor they were mounted.

Monarchical power in the period was deeply allied to spectacular manifestations of the ruler's glory and disciplinary authority. The symbology of power depended on regal magnificence, reward, punishment, and pardon, all of which were heavily theatricalized. Indeed, the conspicuous public display does not simply serve the interests of power; on many occasions in the period, power seemed to exist in order to make pageantry possible, as if the nation's identity were only fully realized in theatrical performance. It would be easy to exaggerate this perception: the subjects of Queen Elizabeth and King James were acutely aware of the distinction between shadow and substance. But they were fascinated by the political magic through which shadows could be taken for substantial realities, and the ruling elite was largely complicit in the formation and celebration of a charismatic absolutism. At the same time, the claims of the monarch who professes herself or himself to be not the representative of the nation but its embodiment were set against the counterclaims of the House of Commons. And this institution, too, as we have glimpsed, had its own theatrical rituals, centered on the crowd whose shouts of approval, in heavily stage-managed elections, chose the individuals who would stand for the polity and participate in deliberations held in a hall whose resemblance to a theater did not escape contemporary notice.

Third, illicit exorcism points both to the theatricality of much religious ritual in the late Middle Ages and the Renaissance and to the heightened possibility of secularization. English Protestant authorities banned the medieval mystery plays, along with pilgrimages and other rituals associated with holy shrines and sacred images, but playing companies could satisfy at least some of the popular longings and appropriate aspects of the social energy no longer allowed a theological outlet. That is, official attacks on certain Catholic practices made it more possible for the public theater to appropriate and exploit their allure. Hence, for example, the plays that celebrated the solemn miracle of the Catholic Mass were banned, along with the most elaborate church vestments, but in *The Winter's Tale* Dion can speak in awe of what he witnessed at Apollo's temple:

> I shall report,
> For most it caught me, the celestial habits—
> Methinks I so should term them—and the reverence
> Of the grave wearers. O, the sacrifice—
> How ceremonious, solemn, and unearthly
> It was i'th' off'ring!
>
> (3.1.3–8)

And at the play's end, the statue of the innocent mother breathes, comes to life, and embraces her child.

The theater in Shakespeare's time, then, is intimately bound up with all three crucial cultural formations: the market society, the theater state, and the Church. But it is important to note that the institution is not *identified* with any of them. The theater may be a market phenomenon, but it is repeatedly and bitterly attacked as the enemy of diligent, sober, productive economic activity. Civic authorities generally regarded the theater as a pestilential nuisance, a parasite on the body of the commonwealth, a temptation to students, apprentices, housewives, even respectable merchants to leave their serious business and lapse into idleness and waste. That waste, it might be argued, could be partially recuperated if it went for the glorification of a guild or the entertainment of an important dignitary, but the only group regularly profiting from the theater were the players and their disreputable associates.

For his part, Shakespeare made a handsome profit from the commodification of theatrical entertainment, but he seems never to have written "city comedy"—plays set in London and more or less explicitly concerned with market relations—and his characters express deep reservations about the power of money and commerce: "That smooth-faced gentleman, tickling commodity," Philip the Bastard observes in *King John,* "wins of all, / Of kings, of beggars, old men, young men, maids" (2.1.574, 570–71). We could argue that the smooth-faced gentleman is none other than Shakespeare himself, for his drama famously mingles kings and clowns, princesses and panderers. But the mingling is set against a romantic current of social conservatism: in *Twelfth Night,* the aristocratic heiress Olivia falls in love with someone who appears far beneath her in wealth and social station, but it is revealed that he (and his sister Viola) are of noble blood; in *The Winter's Tale,* Leontes' daughter Perdita is raised as a shepherdess, but her noble nature shines through her humble upbringing, and she marries the Prince of Bohemia; the strange island maiden with whom Ferdinand, son of the King of Naples, falls madly in love in *The Tempest* turns out to be the daughter of the rightful Duke of Milan. Shakespeare pushes against this conservative logic in *All's Well That Ends Well,* but the noble young Bertram violently resists the unequal match thrust upon him by the King, and the play's mood is notoriously uneasy.

Similarly, Shakespeare's theater may have been patronized and protected by the monarchy—after 1603, his company received a royal patent and was known as the King's Men—but it was by no means identical in its interests or its ethos. To be sure, *Richard III* and *Macbeth* incorporate aspects of royal propaganda, but given the realities of censorship, Shakespeare's plays, and the period's drama as a whole, are surprisingly independent and complex in their political vision. There is, in any case, a certain inherent tension between kings and player kings: Elizabeth and James may both have likened themselves to actors onstage, but they were loath to admit their dependence on the applause and money, freely given or freely withheld, of the audience. The charismatic monarch insists that the sacredness of authority resides in the body of the ruler, not in a costume that may be worn and then discarded by an actor. Kings are not *representations* of power—or do not admit that they are—but claim to be the thing itself. The government institution that was actually based on the idea of representation, Parliament, had theatrical elements, as we have seen, but it significantly excluded any audience from its deliberations. And Shakespeare's oblique portraits of parliamentary representatives, the tribunes Sicinius Velutus and Junius Brutus in *Coriolanus,* are anything but flattering.

Finally, the theater drew significant energy from the liturgy and rituals of the late medieval Church, but as Shakespeare's contemporaries widely remarked, the playhouse and the Church were scarcely natural allies. Not only did the theater represent a potential competitor to worship services, and not only did ministers rail against prostitution and other vices associated with playgoing, but theatrical representation itself, even when ostensibly pious, seemed to many to empty out whatever it presented, turning substance into mere show. The theater could and did use the period's deep currents of religious feeling, but it had to do so carefully and with an awareness of conflicting interests.

Shakespeare Comes to London

How did Shakespeare decide to turn his prodigious talents to the stage? When did he make his way to London? How did he get his start? To these and similar questions we have a mountain of speculation but no secure answers. There is not a single surviving record of Shakespeare's existence from 1585, when his twins were baptized in Stratford church, until 1592, when a rival London playwright made an envious remark about him. In the late seventeenth century, the delightfully eccentric collector of gossip John Aubrey was informed that prior to moving to London the young Shakespeare had been a schoolteacher in the country. Aubrey also recorded a story that Shakespeare had been a rather unusual apprentice butcher: "When he killed a calf, he would do it in a high style, and make a speech."

These and other legends, including one that has Shakespeare whipped for poaching game, fill the void until the unmistakable reference in Robert Greene's *Groats-Worth of Witte, Bought with a Million of Repentance* (1592). An inspired hack writer with a university education, a penchant for self-dramatization, a taste for wild living, and a strong streak of resentment, Greene, in his early thirties, was dying in poverty when he penned his last farewell, piously urging his fellow dramatists Christopher Marlowe, Thomas Nashe, and George Peele to abandon the wicked stage before they were brought low, as he had been, by a new arrival: "For there is an upstart crow, beautified with our feathers, that with his 'Tiger's heart wrapped in player's hide' supposes he is as well able to bombast out a blank verse as the best of you, and, being an absolute *Johannes Factotum*, is in his own conceit the only Shake-scene in a country." If "Shake-scene" is not enough to identify the object of his attack, Greene parodies a line from Shakespeare's early play *Richard Duke of York* (*3 Henry VI*): "O tiger's heart wrapped in a woman's hide!" (1.4.138). Greene is accusing Shakespeare of being an upstart, a plagiarist, an egomaniacal jack-of-all-trades—and, above all perhaps, a popular success.

By 1592, then, Shakespeare had already arrived on the highly competitive London theatrical scene. He was successful enough to be attacked by Greene and, a few months later, defended by Henry Chettle, another hack writer who had seen Greene's manuscript through the press (or, some scholars speculate, had written the attack himself and passed it off as the dying Greene's). Chettle expresses his regret that he did not suppress Greene's diatribe and spare Shakespeare "because myself have seen his demeanor no less civil than he excellent in the quality he professes." Besides, Chettle adds, "divers of worship have reported his uprightness of dealing, which argues his honesty and his facetious [polished] grace in writing that approves his art." "Divers of worship": not only was Shakespeare established as an accomplished writer and actor, but he evidently had aroused the attention and the approbation of several socially prominent people. In Elizabethan England, aristocratic patronage, with the money, protection, and prestige it alone could provide, was probably a professional writer's most important asset.

This patronage, or at least Shakespeare's quest for it, is most visible in the dedications in 1593 and 1594 of his narrative poems *Venus and Adonis* and *The Rape of Lucrece* to the young nobleman Henry Wriothesley, Earl of Southampton. It may be glimpsed as well, perhaps, in the sonnets, with their extraordinary adoration of the fair youth, though the identity of that youth has never been determined. What return Shakespeare got for his exquisite offerings is likewise unknown. We do know that among wits and gallants, the narrative poems won Shakespeare a fine reputation as an immensely stylish and accomplished poet. An amateur play performed at Cambridge University at the end of the sixteenth century, *The Return from Parnassus*, makes fun of this vogue, as a foolish character effusively declares, "I'll worship sweet Mr. Shakespeare, and to honour him will lay his *Venus and Adonis* under my pillow." Many readers at the time may have done so: the poem went through sixteen editions before 1640, more than any other work by Shakespeare.

Patronage was crucially important not only for individual artists but also for the actors, playwrights, and investors who pooled their resources to form professional theater companies. The public playhouses had enemies, especially among civic and religious authorities, who wished greatly to curb performances or to ban them altogether. An act of 1572 included players among those classified as vagabonds, threatening them, therefore, with the horrible punishments meted out to those regarded as economic parasites. The players' escape route was to be nominally enrolled as the servants of high-ranking noblemen. The legal fiction was that their public performances were a kind of rehearsal for the command performances before the patron or the monarch.

When Shakespeare came to London, presumably in the late 1580s, there were more than a dozen of these companies operating under the patronage of various aristocrats.

We do not know for which of these companies, several of which had toured in Stratford, he originally worked, nor whether he began, as legend has it, as a prompter's assistant and then graduated to acting and playwriting. Shakespeare is listed among the actors in Ben Jonson's *Every Man in His Humour* (performed in 1598) and *Sejanus* (performed in 1603), but we do not know for certain what roles he played, nor are there records of any of his other performances. Tradition has it that he played Adam in *As You Like It* and the Ghost in *Hamlet,* but he was clearly not one of the leading actors of the day.

By the 1590s, the number of playing companies in London had been considerably reduced, in part through competition and in part through legislative restriction. (In 1572, knights and gentry lost the privilege of patronizing a troupe of actors; in 1598, justices of the peace lost the power to authorize performances.) By the early years of the seventeenth century, there were usually only three companies competing against one another in any season, along with two children's companies, which were often successful at drawing audiences away from the public playhouses. Shakespeare may initially have been associated with the Earl of Leicester's company or with the company of Ferdinando Stanley, Lord Strange; both groups included actors with whom Shakespeare was later linked. Or he may have belonged to the Earl of Pembroke's Men, since

there is evidence that they performed *The Taming of a Shrew* and a version of *Richard Duke of York (3 Henry VI)*. At any event, by 1594, Shakespeare was a member of the Lord Chamberlain's Men, for his name, along with those of Will Kemp (or Kempe) and Richard Burbage, appears on a record of those "servants to the Lord Chamberlain" paid for performance at the royal palace at Greenwich on December 26 and 28. Shakespeare stayed with this company, which during the reign of King James received royal patronage and became the King's Men, for the rest of his career.

Many playwrights in Shakespeare's time worked freelance, moving from company to company as opportunities arose, collaborating on projects, adding scenes to old plays, scrambling from one enterprise to another. But certain playwrights, among them the most successful, wrote for a single company, often agreeing contractually to give that company exclusive rights to their theatrical works. Shakespeare seems to have followed such a pattern. For the Lord Chamberlain's Men, he wrote an average of two plays per year. His company initially performed in The Theatre, a playhouse built in 1576 by an entrepreneurial carpenter, James Burbage, the father of the actor Richard, who was to perform many of

Edward Alleyn (1566–1626). Artist unknown. Alleyn was the great tragic actor of the Lord Admiral's Men (the principal rival to Shakespeare's company). He was famous especially for playing the great Marlovian heroes.

Shakespeare's greatest roles. When in 1597 their lease on this playhouse expired, the Lord Chamberlain's Men passed through a difficult and legally perilous time, but they formed a joint-stock company, raising sufficient capital to lease a site and put up a splendid new playhouse in the suburb of Southwark, on the south bank of the Thames. This playhouse, the Globe, opened in 1599. Shakespeare is listed in the legal agreement as one of the principal investors; and when the company began to use Blackfriars as their indoor playhouse around 1609, he was a major shareholder in that theater as well. The Lord Chamberlain's Men, later the King's Men, dominated the theater scene, and the shares were quite valuable. Then as now, the theater was an extremely risky enterprise—most of those who wrote plays and performed in them made pathetically little money—but Shakespeare was a notable exception. The fine house in Stratford and the coat of arms he succeeded in acquiring were among the fruits of his multiple mastery, as actor, playwright, and investor in the London stage.

The Shakespearean Trajectory

Even though Shakespeare's England was in many ways a record-keeping society, no reliable record survives that details the performances, year by year, in the London theaters. Every play had to be licensed by a government official, the Master of the Revels, but the records kept by the relevant officials from 1579 to 1621, Sir Edmund Tilney and Sir George Buc, have not survived. A major theatrical entrepreneur, Philip Henslowe, kept a careful account of his expenditures, including what he paid for the scripts he commissioned, but unfortunately Henslowe's main business was with the Rose and the Fortune theaters and not with the playhouses at which Shakespeare's company performed. A comparable ledger must have been kept by the shareholders of the Lord Chamberlain's Men, but it has not survived. Shakespeare himself apparently did not undertake to preserve for posterity the sum of his writings, let alone to clarify the chronology of his works or specify which plays he wrote alone and which with collaborators.

The principal source for Shakespeare's works is the 1623 Folio volume of *Mr. William Shakespeares Comedies, Histories, & Tragedies*. Most scholars believe that the editors were careful to include only those plays for which they knew Shakespeare to be the main author. Their edition does not, however, include any of Shakespeare's nondramatic poems, and it omits two plays in which Shakespeare is now thought to have had a significant hand, *Pericles, Prince of Tyre* and *The Two Noble Kinsmen*, along with his probable contribution to the multiauthored *Sir Thomas More*. (A number of other plays were attributed to Shakespeare, both before and after his death, but scholars have not generally accepted any of these into the established canon.) Moreover, the Folio edition does not print the plays in chronological order, nor does it attempt to establish a chronology. We do not know how much time would normally have elapsed between the writing of a play and its first performance, nor, with

IF YOV KNOW NOT ME,
You know no body.
OR,
The troubles of Queene ELIZABETH.

LONDON.
Printed by *B.A.* and *T.F.* for *Nathanaell Butter.* 1 6 3 2.

Title page of Thomas Heywood's *If You Know Not Me, You Know No Body; or, The Troubles of Queene Elizabeth* (1632 ed.).

a few exceptions, do we know with any certainty the month or even the year of the first performance of any of Shakespeare's plays. The quarto editions of those plays that were published during Shakespeare's lifetime obviously establish a date by which we know a given play had been written, but they give us little more than an end point, because there was likely to be a substantial though indeterminate gap between the first performance of a play and its publication.

With enormous patience and ingenuity, however, scholars have gradually assembled a considerable archive of evidence, both external and internal, for dating the composition of the plays. Besides actual publication, the external evidence includes explicit reference to a play, a record of its performance, or (as in the case of Greene's attack on the "upstart crow") the quoting of a line, though all of these can be maddeningly ambiguous. The most important single piece of external evidence appears in 1598 in *Palladis Tamia*, a long book of jumbled reflections by Francis Meres that includes a survey of the contemporary literary scene. Meres finds that "the sweet, witty soul of Ovid lives in melliflous and honey-tongued Shakespeare, witness his *Venus and Adonis*, his *Lucrece*, his sugered Sonnets among his private friends, etc." Meres goes on to list Shakespeare's accomplishments as a playwright as well:

> As Plautus and Seneca are accounted the best for Comedy and Tragedy among the Latins: so Shakespeare among the English is the most excellent in both kinds for the stage; for Comedy, witness his *Gentlemen of Verona*, his *Errors*, his *Love labors lost*, his *Love labours won*, his *Midsummers night dream*, & his *Merchant of Venice*: for Tragedy his *Richard the 2*, *Richard the 3*, *Henry the 4*, *King John*, *Titus Andronicus* and his *Romeo and Juliet*.

Meres thus provides a date by which twelve of Shakespeare's plays had definitely appeared (including one, *Love's Labour's Won*, that appears to have been lost or that we know by a different title). Unfortunately, Meres provides no clues about the order of appearance of these plays, and there are no other comparable lists.

Faced with the limitations of the external evidence, scholars have turned to a bewildering array of internal evidence, ranging from datable sources and topical allusions on the one hand to evolving stylistic features (ratio of verse to prose, percentage of rhyme to blank verse, colloquialisms, use of extended similes, and the like) on the other. Thus, for example, a cluster of plays with a high percentage of rhymed verse may follow closely upon Shakespeare's writing of the rhymed poems *Venus and Adonis* and *The Rape of Lucrece* and, therefore, be datable to 1594–95. Similarly, vocabulary overlap probably indicates proximity in composition, so if four or five plays share relatively "rare" vocabulary, it is likely that they were written in roughly the same period. Again, there seems to be a pattern in Shakespeare's use of colloquialisms, with a steady increase from *As You Like It* (1599–1600) to *Coriolanus* (1608), followed in the late romances by a retreat from the colloquial.

More sophisticated computer analysis should provide further guidance in the future, even though the precise order of the plays, still very much in dispute, is never likely to be settled to universal satisfaction. Still, certain broad patterns are now widely accepted. These patterns can be readily grasped in the *Norton Shakespeare*, which presents the plays in the chronological order proposed by the Oxford editors.

Shakespeare began his career, probably in the early 1590s, by writing both comedies and history plays. The attack by Greene suggests that he made his mark with the series of theatrically vital but rather crude plays based on the foreign and domestic broils that erupted during the unhappy reign of the Lancastrian Henry VI. Modern readers and audiences are more likely to find the first sustained evidence of unusual power in *Richard III* (c. 1592), a play that combines a brilliantly conceived central character, a dazzling command of histrionic rhetoric, and an overarching moral vision of English history.

At virtually the same time that he was setting his stamp on the genre of the history play, Shakespeare was writing his first—or first surviving—comedies. Here, there are even fewer signs than in the histories of an apprenticeship: *The Comedy of Errors,* one of his early efforts in this genre, already displays a rare command of the resources of comedy: mistaken identity, madcap confusion, and the threat of disaster, giving way in the end to reconciliation, recovery, and love. Shakespeare's other comedies from the early 1590s, *The Taming of the Shrew, The Two Gentlemen of Verona,* and *Love's Labour's Lost,* are no less remarkable for their sophisticated variations on familiar comic themes, their inexhaustible rhetorical inventiveness, and their poignant intimation, in the midst of festive celebration, of loss.

Successful as are these early histories and comedies, and indicative of an extraordinary theatrical talent, Shakespeare's achievement in the later 1590s would still have been all but impossible to foresee. Starting with *A Midsummer Night's Dream* (c. 1595), Shakespeare wrote an unprecedented series of romantic comedies—*The Merchant of Venice, The Merry Wives of Windsor, Much Ado About Nothing, As You Like It,* and *Twelfth Night* (c. 1602)—whose poetic richness and emotional complexity remain unmatched. In the same period, he wrote a sequence of profoundly searching and ambitious history plays—*Richard II, 1* and *2 Henry IV,* and *Henry V*—which together explore the death throes of feudal England and the birth of the modern nation-state ruled by a charismatic monarch. Both the comedies and histories of this period are marked by their capaciousness, their ability to absorb characters who press up against the outermost boundaries of the genre: the comedy *Merchant of Venice* somehow contains the figure, at once nightmarish and poignant, of Shylock, while the *Henry IV* plays, with their somber vision of crisis in the family and the state, bring to the stage one of England's greatest comic characters, Falstaff.

If in the mid to late 1590s Shakespeare reached the summit of his art in two major genres, he also manifested a lively interest in a third. As early as 1593, he wrote the crudely violent tragedy *Titus Andronicus,* the first of several plays on themes from Roman history, and a year or two later, in *Richard II,* he created in the protagonist a figure who achieves by the play's close the stature of a tragic hero. In the same year that Shakespeare wrote the wonderfully farcical "Pyramus and Thisbe" scene in *A Midsummer Night's Dream,* he probably also wrote the deeply tragic realization of the same story in *Romeo and Juliet.* But once again, the lyric anguish of *Romeo and Juliet* and the tormented self-revelation of *Richard II,* extraordinary as they are, could not have led anyone to predict the next phase of Shakespeare's career, the great tragic dramas that poured forth in the early years of the seventeenth century: *Hamlet, Othello, King Lear, Macbeth, Antony and Cleopatra,* and *Coriolanus.* These plays, written from 1601 to 1607, seem to mark a major shift in sensibility, an existential and metaphysical darkening that many readers think must have originated in a deep personal anguish, perhaps caused by the death of Shakespeare's father, John, in 1601.

Whatever the truth of these speculations—and we have no direct, personal testimony either to support or to undermine them—there appears to have occurred in the same period a shift as well in Shakespeare's comic sensibility. The comedies written between 1601 and 1604, *Troilus and Cressida, All's Well That Ends Well,* and *Measure for Measure,* are sufficiently different from the earlier comedies—more biting in tone, more uneasy with comic conventions, more ruthlessly questioning of the values of the characters and the resolutions of the plots—to have led many twentieth-century scholars to classify them as "problem plays" or "dark comedies." This category has recently begun to fall out of favor, since Shakespeare criticism is perfectly happy to demonstrate that *all* of the plays are "problem plays." But there is another group of plays, among the last Shakespeare wrote, that continue to constitute a distinct category. *Pericles, Cymbeline, The Winter's Tale,* and *The Tempest,* written between 1608 and 1611, when the playwright had developed a remarkably fluid, dreamlike sense of plot and a poetic style that could veer, apparently effortlessly, from the tortured to the ineffably sweet, are known as the "romances." These plays share an interest in the moral and emotional life less of the adolescents who dominate the earlier comedies than of their parents. The romances are deeply concerned with patterns of loss and recovery, suffering and redemption, despair and renewal. They have seemed to many critics to constitute a deliberate conclusion to a career that began in histories and comedies and passed through the dark and tormented tragedies.

One effect of the practice of printing Shakespeare's plays in a reconstructed chronological order, as this edition does, is to produce a kind of authorial plot, a progress from youthful exuberance and a heroic grappling with history, through psychological anguish and radical doubt, to a mature serenity built upon an understanding of loss. The ordering of Shakespeare's "complete works" in this way reconstitutes the figure of the author as the beloved hero of his own, lived romance. There are numerous reasons to treat this romance with considerable skepticism: the precise order of the plays remains in dispute, the obsessions of the earliest plays crisscross with those of the last, the drama is a collaborative art form, and the relation between authorial consciousness and theatrical representation is murky. Yet a longing to identify Shakespeare's personal trajectory, to chart his psychic and spiritual as well as professional progress, is all but irresistible.

The Fetishism of Dress

Whatever the personal resonance of Shakespeare's own life, his art is deeply enmeshed in the collective hopes, fears, and fantasies of his time. For example, throughout his plays, Shakespeare draws heavily upon his culture's investment in costume, symbols of authority, visible signs of status—the fetishism of dress he must have witnessed from early childhood. Disguise in his drama is often assumed to be incredibly effective: when Henry V borrows a cloak, when Portia dresses in a jurist's robes, when Viola puts on a young man's suit, it is as if each has become unrecognizable, as if identity resided in clothing. At the end of *Twelfth Night*, even though Viola's true identity has been disclosed, Orsino continues to call her Cesario; he will do so, he says, until she resumes her maid's garments, for only then will she be transformed into a woman:

> Cesario, come—
> For so you shall be while you are a man;
> But when in other habits you are seen,
> Orsino's mistress, and his fancy's queen.
> (5.1.372–75)

The pinnacle of this fetishism of costume is the royal crown, for whose identity-conferring power men are willing to die, but the principle is everywhere from the filthy blanket that transforms Edgar into Poor Tom to the coxcomb that is the badge of the licensed fool. Antonio, wishing to express his utter contempt, spits on Shylocks' "Jewish gaberdine," as if the clothing were the essence of the man; Kent, pouring insults on the loathsome Oswald, calls him a "filthy worsted-stocking knave"; and innocent Innogen, learning that her husband has ordered her murder, thinks of herself as an expensive cast-off dress, destined to be ripped at the seams:

> Poor I am stale, a garment out of fashion,
> And for I am richer than to hang by th' walls
> I must be ripped. To pieces with me!
> (*Cymbeline* 3.4.50–52)

What can be said, thought, felt, in this culture seems deeply dependent on the clothes one wears—clothes that one is, in effect, *permitted* or *compelled* to wear, since there is little freedom in dress. Shakespearean drama occasionally represents something like such freedom: after all, Viola in *Twelfth Night* chooses to put off her "maiden weeds," as does Rosalind, who declares, "We'll have a swashing and a martial outside" (*As You Like It* 1.3.114). But these choices are characteristically made under the pressure of desperate circumstances, here shipwreck and exile. Part of the charm of Shakespeare's heroines is their ability to transform distress into an opportunity for self-fashioning, but the plays often suggest that there is less autonomy than meets the eye. What looks like an escape from cultural determinism may be only a deeper form of constraint. We may take, as an allegorical emblem of this constraint, the transformation of the beggar Christopher Sly into a nobleman in the playful Induction to *The Taming of the Shrew.* The transformation seems to suggest that you are free to make of yourself whatever you choose to be—the play begins with the drunken Sly indignantly claiming the dignity of his pedigree ("Look in the Chronicles" [Induction 1.3–4])—but in fact he is only the subject of the mischievous lord's experiment, designed to demonstrate the interwovenness of clothing and identity. "What think you," the lord asks his huntsman,

> if he were conveyed to bed,
> Wrapped in sweet clothes, rings put upon his fingers,
> A most delicious banquet by his bed,
> And brave attendants near him when he wakes—
> Would not the beggar then forget himself?

To which the huntsman replies, in words that underscore the powerlessness of the drunken beggar, "Believe me, lord, I think he cannot choose" (Induction 1.33–38).

Petruccio's taming of Katherine is similarly constructed around an imposition of identity, an imposition closely bound up with the right to wear certain articles of clothing. When the haberdasher arrives with a fashionable lady's hat, Petruccio refuses it over his wife's vehement objections: "This doth fit the time, / And gentlewomen wear such caps as these." "When you are gentle," Petruccio replies, "you shall have one, too, / And not till then" (4.3.69–72). At the play's close, Petruccio demonstrates his authority by commanding his tamed wife to throw down her cap: "Off with that bauble, throw it underfoot" (5.2.126). Here as elsewhere in Shakespeare, acts of robing and disrobing are intensely charged, a charge that culminates in the trappings of monarchy. When Richard II, in a scene that was probably censored from the stage as well as the printed text during the reign of Elizabeth, is divested of his crown and scepter, he experiences the loss as the eradication of his name, the symbolic melting away of his identity:

> Alack the heavy day,
> That I have worn so many winters out
> And know not now what name to call myself!
> O, that I were a mockery king of snow,
> Standing before the sun of Bolingbroke
> To melt myself away in water-drops!
>   (4.1.247–52)

When Lear tears off his regal "lendings" in order to reduce himself to the nakedness of the Bedlam beggar, he is expressing not only his radical loss of social identity but the breakdown of his psychic order as well, expressing, therefore, his reduction to the condition of the "poor bare forked animal" that is the primal condition of undifferentiated existence. And when Cleopatra determines to kill herself in order to escape public humiliation in Rome, she magnificently affirms her essential being by arraying herself as she had once done to encounter Antony:

> Show me, my women, like a queen. Go fetch
> My best attires. I am again for Cydnus
> To meet Mark Antony.
>   (5.2.223–25)

Such scenes are a remarkable intensification of the everyday symbolic practice of Renaissance English culture, its characteristically deep and knowing commitment to illusion: "I know perfectly well that the woman in her crown and jewels and gorgeous gown is an aging, irascible, and fallible mortal—she herself virtually admits as much—yet I profess that she is the Virgin Queen, timelessly beautiful, wise, and just." Shakespeare understood how close this willed illusion was to the spirit of the theater, to the actors' ability to work on what the chorus in *Henry V* calls the "imaginary forces" of the audience. But there is throughout Shakespeare's works a counterintuition that, while it does not exactly overturn this illusion, renders it poignant, vulnerable, fraught. The "masculine usurp'd attire" that is donned by Viola, Rosalind, Portia, Jessica, and other Shakespeare heroines alters what they can say and do, reveals important aspects of their character, and changes their destiny, but it is, all the same, not theirs and not all of who they are. They have, the plays insist, natures that are neither transformed nor altogether concealed by their dress: "Pray God defend me," exclaims the frightened Viola. "A little thing would make me tell them how much I lack of a man" (*Twelfth Night* 3.4.268–69).

The Paradoxes of Identity

The gap between costume and identity is not simply a matter of what women supposedly lack; virtually all of Shakespeare's major characters, men and women, convey the sense of both a *self-division* and an *inward expansion*. The belief in a complex inward realm beyond costumes and status is a striking inversion of the clothes cult: we know perfectly well that the characters have no inner lives apart from what we see on the stage, and yet we believe that they continue to exist when we do not see them, that they exist apart from their represented words and actions, that they have hidden dimensions. How is this conviction aroused and sustained? In part, it is the effect of what the characters themselves say: "My grief lies all within," Richard II tells Bolingbroke,

> And these external manner of laments
> Are merely shadows to the unseen grief
> That swells with silence in the tortured soul.
> (4.1.285–88)

Similarly, Hamlet, dismissing the significance of his outward garments, declares, "I have that within which passeth show— / These but the trappings and the suits of woe" (1.2.85–86). And the distinction between inward and outward is reinforced throughout this play and elsewhere by an unprecedented use of the aside and the soliloquy.

The soliloquy is a continual reminder in Shakespeare that the inner life is by no means transparent to one's surrounding world. Prince Hal seems open and easy with his mates in Eastcheap, but he has a hidden reservoir of disgust:

> I know you all, and will a while uphold
> The unyoked humour of your idleness.
> Yet herein will I imitate the sun,
> Who doth permit the base contagious clouds
> To smother up his beauty from the world,
> That when he please again to be himself,
> Being wanted he may be more wondered at
> By breaking through the foul and ugly mists
> Of vapours that did seem to strangle him.
> (*1 Henry IV* 1.2.173–81)

"When he please again to be himself": the line implies that identity is a matter of free choice—you decide how much of yourself you wish to disclose—but Shakespeare employs other devices that suggest more elusive and intractable layers of inwardness. There is a peculiar, recurrent lack of fit between costume and character, in fools as in princes, that is not simply a matter of disguise and disclosure. If Hal's true identity is partially "smothered" in the tavern, it is not completely revealed either in his soldier's armor or in his royal robes, nor do his asides reach the bedrock of unimpeachable self-understanding.

Identity in Shakespeare repeatedly slips away from the characters themselves, as it does from Richard II after the deposition scene and from Lear after he has given away his land and from Macbeth after he has gained the crown. The slippage does not mean that they retreat into silence; rather, they embark on an experimental, difficult fashioning of themselves and the world, most often through role-playing. "I cannot do it," says the deposed and imprisoned Richard II. "Yet I'll hammer it out" (5.5.5). This could serve as the motto for many Shakespearean characters: Viola becomes Cesario, Rosalind calls herself Ganymede, Kent becomes Caius, Edgar presents himself as Poor Tom, Hamlet plays the madman that he has partly become, Hal pretends that he is his father and a highwayman and Hotspur and even himself. Even in comedy, these ventures into alternate identities are rarely matters of choice; in tragedy, they are always undertaken under pressure and compulsion. And often enough it is not a matter of role-playing at all, but of a drastic transformation whose extreme emblem is the harrowing madness of Lear and of Leontes.

There is a moment in *Richard II* in which the deposed King asks for a mirror and then, after musing on his reflection, throws it to the ground. The shattering of the glass serves to remind us not only of the fragility of identity in Shakespeare but of its characteristic appearance in fragmentary mirror images. The plays continually generate alternative reflections, identities that intersect with, underscore, echo, or otherwise set off that of the principal character. Hence, Desdemona and Iago are not only important figures in Othello's world, they also seem to embody partially realized aspects of himself; Falstaff and Hotspur play a comparable role in relation to Prince Hal, Fortinbras and Horatio in relation to Hamlet, Gloucester and the Fool in relation to Lear, and so forth. In many of these plays, the complementary and contrasting characters figure in subplots, subtly interwoven with the play's main plot and illuminating its concerns. The note so conspicuously sounded by Fortinbras at the close of *Hamlet*—what the hero might have been, "had he been put on"—is heard repeatedly in Shakespeare and contributes to the overwhelming intensity, poignancy, and complexity of the characters. This is a world in which outward appearance is everything and nothing, in which individuation is at once sharply etched and continually blurred, in which the victims of fate are haunted by the ghosts of the possible, in which everything is simultaneously as it must be and as it need not have been.

Are these antinomies signs of a struggle between contradictory and irreconcilable perspectives in Shakespeare? In certain plays—notably, *Measure for Measure, All's Well That Ends Well, Coriolanus,* and *Troilus and Cressida*—the tension seems both high and entirely unresolved. But Shakespearean contradictions are more often reminiscent of the capacious spirit of Montaigne, who refused any systematic order that would betray his sense of reality. Thus, individual characters are immensely important in Shakespeare—he is justly celebrated for his unmatched skill in the invention of particular dramatic identities, marked with distinct speech patterns, manifested in social status, and confirmed by costume and gesture—but the principle of individuation is not the rock on which his theatrical art is founded. After the masks are stripped away, the pretenses exposed, the claims of the ego shattered, there is a mysterious remainder; as the shamed but irrepressible Paroles declares in *All's Well That Ends Well,* "Simply the thing I am / Shall make me live" (4.3.310–11). Again and again, the audience is made to sense a deeper energy, a source of power that at once discharges itself in individual characters and seems to sweep right through them.

The Poet of Nature

In *The Birth of Tragedy,* Nietzsche called a comparable source of energy that he found in Greek tragedy "Dionysos." But the god's name, conjuring up Bacchic frenzy, does not seem appropriate to Shakespeare. In the late seventeenth and eighteenth centuries, it was more plausibly called Nature: "The world must be peopled," says the delightful Benedick in *Much Ado About Nothing* (2.3.213–14), and there are frequent invocations elsewhere of the happy, generative power that brings couples together—

> Jack shall have Jill,
> Naught shall go ill,
> the man shall have his mare again, and all shall be well.
> (*A Midsummer Night's Dream* 3.3.45–47)

—and the melancholy, destructive power that brings all living things to the grave: "Golden lads and girls all must, / As chimney-sweepers, come to dust" (*Cymbeline* 4.2.263–64).

But the celebration of Shakespeare as a poet of nature—often coupled with an inane celebration of his supposedly "natural" (that is, untutored) genius—has its distinct limitations. For Shakespearean art brilliantly interrogates the "natural," refusing to take for granted precisely what the celebrants think is most secure. His comedies are endlessly inventive in showing that love is not simply natural: the playful hint of bestiality in the line quoted above, "the man shall have his mare again" (from a play in which the Queen of the Fairies falls in love with an ass-headed laborer), lightly unsettles the boundaries between the natural and the perverse. These boundaries are called into question throughout Shakespeare's work, from the cross-dressing and erotic crosscurrents that deliciously complicate the lives of the characters in *Twelfth Night* and *As You Like It* to the terrifying violence that wells up from the heart of the family in *King Lear* or from the sweet intimacy of sexual desire in *Othello*. Even the boundary between life and death is not secure, as the ghosts in *Julius Caesar, Hamlet,* and *Macbeth* attest, while the principle of natural death (given its most eloquent articulation by old Hamlet's murderer, Claudius!) is repeatedly tainted and disrupted.

Disrupted, too, is the idea of order that constantly makes its claim, most insistently in the history plays. Scholars have observed the presence in Shakespeare's works of the so-called Tudor myth—the ideological justification of the ruling dynasty as a restoration of national order after a cycle of tragic violence. The violence, Tudor apologists claimed, was divine punishment unleashed after the deposition of the anointed king, Richard II, for God will not tolerate violations of the sanctified order. Traces of this propaganda certainly exist in the histories—Shakespeare may, for all we know, have personally subscribed to its premises—but a closer scrutiny of his plays has disclosed so many ironic reservations and qualifications and subversions as to call into question any straightforward adherence to a political line. The plays manifest a profound fascination with the monarchy and with the ambitions of the aristocracy, but the fascination is never simply endorsement. There is always at least the hint of a slippage between the great figures, whether admirable or monstrous, who stand at the pinnacle of authority and the vast, miscellaneous mass of soldiers, scriveners, ostlers, poets, whores, gardeners, thieves, weavers, shepherds, country gentlemen, sturdy beggars, and the like who make up the commonwealth. And the idea of order, though eloquently articulated (most memorably by Ulysses in *Troilus and Cressida*), is always shadowed by a relentless spirit of irony.

The Play of Language

If neither the individual nor nature nor order will serve, can we find a single comprehensive name for the underlying force in Shakespeare's work? Certainly not. The work is too protean and capacious. But much of the energy that surges through this astonishing body of plays and poems is closely linked to the power of language. Shakespeare was the supreme product of a rhetorical culture, a culture steeped in the arts of persuasion and verbal expressiveness. In 1512, the great Dutch humanist Erasmus published a work called *De copia verborum* that taught its readers how to cultivate "copiousness," verbal richness, in discourse. (Erasmus obligingly provides, as a sample, a list of 144 different ways of saying "Thank you for your letter.") Recommended modes of variation include putting the subject of an argument into fictional form, as well as the use of synonym, substitution, paraphrase, metaphor, metonymy, synecdoche, hyperbole, diminution, and a host of other figures of speech. To change emotional tone, he suggests trying *ironia, interrogatio, admiratio, dubitatio, abominatio*—the possibilities seem infinite.

In Renaissance England, certain syntactic forms or patterns of words known as "figures" (also called "schemes") were shaped and repeated in order to confer beauty or heighten expressive power. Figures were usually known by their Greek and Latin names, though in an Elizabethan rhetorical manual, *The Arte of English Poesie,* George Puttenham made a valiant if short-lived attempt to give them English equivalents, such as "*Hyperbole,* or the Overreacher," "*Ironia,* or the Dry Mock," and "*Ploce,* or the Doubler." Those who received a grammar-school education throughout Europe at almost any point between the Roman Empire and the eighteenth century probably knew by heart the names of up to one hundred such figures, just as they knew by heart their multiplication tables. According to one scholar's count, Shakespeare knew and made use of about two hundred.

As certain grotesquely inflated Renaissance texts attest, lessons from *De copia verborum* and similar rhetorical guides could encourage mere prolixity and verbal self-display. But even though he shared his culture's delight in rhetorical complexity, Shakespeare always understood how to swoop from baroque sophistication to breathtaking simplicity. Moreover, he grasped early in his career how to use figures of speech, tone, and rhythm not only to provide emphasis and elegant variety but also to articulate the inner lives of his characters. Take, for example, these lines from *Othello,* where, as scholars have noted, Shakespeare deftly combines four common rhetorical figures—*anaphora, parison, isocolon,* and *epistrophe*—to depict with painful vividness Othello's psychological torment:

> By the world,
> I think my wife be honest, and think she is not.
> I think that thou art just, and think thou art not.
> I'll have some proof.

> (3.3.388–91)

Anaphora is simply the repetition of a word at the beginning of a sequence of sentences or clauses ("I/I"). *Parison* is the correspondence of word to word within adjacent sentences or clauses, either by direct repetition ("think/think") or by the matching of noun with noun, verb with verb ("wife/thou"; "be/art"). *Isocolon* gives exactly the same length to corresponding clauses ("and think she is not/and think thou art not"), and *epistrophe* is the mirror image of *anaphora* in that it is the repetition of a word at the end of a sequence of sentences or clauses ("not/not"). Do we need to know the Greek names for these figures in order to grasp the effectiveness of Othello's lines? Of course not. But Shakespeare and his contemporaries, convinced that rhetoric provided the most natural and powerful means by which feelings could be conveyed to readers and listeners, were trained in an analytical language that helped at once to promote and to account for this effectiveness. In his 1593 edition of *The Garden of Eloquence,* Henry Peacham remarks that *epistrophe* "serveth to leave a word of importance in the end of a sentence, that it may the longer hold the sound in the mind of the hearer," and in *Directions for Speech and Style* (c. 1599), John Hoskins notes that *anaphora* "beats upon one thing to cause the quicker feeling in the audience."

Shakespeare also shared with his contemporaries a keen understanding of the ways that rhetorical devices could be used not only to express powerful feelings but to hide them: after all, the artist who created Othello also created Iago, Richard III, and Lady Macbeth. He could deftly skewer the rhetorical affectations of Polonius in *Hamlet* or the pedant Holophernes in *Love's Labour's Lost.* He could deploy stylistic variations to mark the boundaries not of different individuals but of different social realms; in *A Midsummer Night's Dream,* for example, the blank verse of Duke Theseus is played off against the rhymed couplets of the well-born young lovers, and both in turn contrast with the prose spoken by the artisans. At the same time that he thus marks boundaries between both individuals and groups, Shakespeare shows a remarkable ability to establish unifying patterns of imagery that knit together the diverse strands of his plot and suggest subtle links among characters who may be scarcely aware of how much they share with one another.

One of the hidden links in Shakespeare's own works is the frequent use he makes of a somewhat unusual rhetorical figure called *hendiadys*. An example from the Roman poet Virgil is the phrase *pateris libamus et auro*, "we drink from cups and gold" (*Georgics* 2.192). Rather than serving as an adjective or a dependent noun, as in "golden cups" or "cups of gold," the word "gold" serves as a substantive joined to another substantive, "cups," by a conjunction, "and." Shakespeare uses the figure over three hundred times in all, and since it does not appear in ancient or medieval lists of tropes and schemes and is treated only briefly by English rhetoricians, he may have come upon it directly in Virgil. *Hendiadys* literally means "one through two," though Shakespeare's versions often make us quickly, perhaps only subliminally, aware of the complexity of what ordinarily passes for straightforward perceptions. When Othello, in his suicide speech, invokes the memory of "a malignant and a turbaned Turk," the figure of speech at once associates enmity with cultural difference and keeps them slightly apart. And when Macbeth speaks of his "strange and self-abuse," the *hendiadys* seems briefly to hold both "strange" and "self" up for scrutiny. It would be foolish to make too much of any single feature in Shakespeare's varied and diverse creative achievement, and yet this curious rhetorical scheme has something of the quality of a fingerprint.

But all of his immense rhetorical gifts, though rich, beautiful, and supremely useful, do not adequately convey Shakespeare's relation to language, which is less strictly functional than a total immersion in the arts of persuasion may imply. An Erasmian admiration for copiousness cannot fully explain Shakespeare's astonishing vocabulary of some 25,000 words. (His closest rival among the great English poets of the period was John Milton, with about 12,000 words, and most major writers, let alone ordinary people, have much smaller vocabularies.) This immense word hoard, it is worth noting, was not the result of scanning a dictionary; in the late sixteenth century, there were no English dictionaries of the kind to which we are now accustomed. Shakespeare seems to have absorbed new words from virtually every discursive realm he ever encountered, and he experimented boldly and tirelessly with them. These experiments were facilitated by the very fact that dictionaries as we know them did not exist and by a flexibility in grammar, orthography, and diction that the more orderly, regularized English of the later seventeenth and eighteenth centuries suppressed.

Owing in part to the number of dialects in London, pronunciation was variable, and there were many opportunities for phonetic association between words: the words "bear," "barn," "bier," "bourne," "born," and "barne" could all sound like one another. Homonyms were given greater scope by the fact that the same word could be spelled so many different ways—Christopher Marlowe's name appears in the records as Marlowe, Marloe, Marlen, Marlyne, Merlin, Marley, Marlye, Morley, and Morle—and by the fact that a word's grammatical function could easily shift, from noun to verb, verb to adjective, and so forth. Since grammar and punctuation did not insist on relations of coordination and subordination, loose, nonsyntactic sentences were common, and etymologies were used to forge surprising or playful relations between distant words.

It would seem inherently risky for a popular playwright to employ a vocabulary so far in excess of what most mortals could possibly possess, but Shakespeare evidently counted on his audience's linguistic curiosity and adventurousness, just as he counted on its general and broad-based rhetorical competence. He was also usually careful to provide a context that in effect explained or translated his more arcane terms. For example, when Macbeth reflects with horror on his murderous hands, he shudderingly imagines that even the sea could not wash away the blood; on the contrary, his bloodstained hand, he says, "will rather / The multitudinous seas incarnadine." The meaning of the unfamiliar word "incarnadine" is explained by the next line: "Making the green one red" (2.2.59–61).

What is most striking is not the abstruseness or novelty of Shakespeare's language but its extraordinary vitality, a quality that the playwright seemed to pursue with a kind of passionate recklessness. Perhaps Samuel Johnson was looking in the right direction when he complained that the "quibble," or pun, was "the fatal Cleopatra for which

[Shakespeare] lost the world, and was content to lose it." For the power that continually discharges itself throughout the plays, at once constituting and unsettling everything it touches, is the polymorphous power of language, language that seems both costume and that which lies beneath the costume, personal identity and that which challenges the merely personal, nature and that which enables us to name nature and thereby distance ourselves from it.

Shakespeare's language has an overpowering exuberance and generosity that often resembles the experience of love. Consider, for example, Oberon's description in *A Midsummer Night's Dream* of the moment when he saw Cupid shoot his arrow at the fair vestal: "Thou rememb'rest," he asks Puck,

> Since once I sat upon a promontory
> And heard a mermaid on a dolphin's back
> Uttering such dulcet and harmonious breath
> That the rude sea grew civil at her song
> And certain stars shot madly from their spheres
> To hear the sea-maid's music?
>
> (2.1.148–54)

Here, Oberon's composition of place, lightly alluding to a classical emblem, is infused with a fantastically lush verbal brilliance. This brilliance, the result of masterful alliterative and rhythmical technique, seems gratuitous—that is, it does not advance the plot, but rather exhibits a capacity for display and self-delight that extends from the fairies to the playwright who has created them. The rich music of Oberon's words imitates the "dulcet and harmonious breath" he is intent on recalling, breath that has, in his account, an oddly contradictory effect: it is at once a principle of order, so that the rude sea is becalmed like a lower-class mob made civil by a skilled orator, and a principle of disorder, so that celestial bodies in their fixed spheres are thrown into mad confusion. And this contradictory effect, so intimately bound up with an inexplicable, supererogatory, and intensely erotic verbal magic, is a key to *A Midsummer Night's Dream,* with its exquisite blend of confusion and discipline, lunacy and hierarchical ceremony.

The fairies in this comedy seem to embody a pervasive sense found throughout Shakespeare's work that there is something uncanny about language, something that is not quite human, at least in the conventional and circumscribed sense of the human that dominates waking experience. In the comedies, this intuition is alarming but ultimately benign: Oberon and his followers trip through the great house at the play's close, blessing the bridebeds and warding off the nightmares that lurk in marriage and parenthood. But there is in Shakespeare an alternative, darker vision of the uncanniness of language, a vision also embodied in creatures that test the limits of the human—not the fairies of *A Midsummer Night's Dream* but the weird sisters of *Macbeth.* When in the tragedy's opening scene the witches chant "Fair is foul, and foul is fair" (1.1.10), they unsettle through the simplest and most radical act of linguistic equation (x is y) the fundamental antinomies through which a moral order is established. And when Macbeth appears onstage a few minutes later, his first words unconsciously echo what we have just heard from the witches' mouths: "So foul and fair a day I have not seen" (1.3.36). What is the meaning of this linguistic "unconscious"? On the face of things, Macbeth presumably means only that the day of fair victory is also a day of foul weather, but the fact that he echoes the witches (something that we hear but that he cannot know) intimates an occult link between them, even before their direct encounter. It is difficult, perhaps impossible, to specify exactly what this link signifies—generations of emboldened critics have tried without notable success—but we can at least affirm that its secret lair is in the play's language, like a half-buried pun whose full articulation will entail the murder of Duncan, the ravaging of his kingdom, and Macbeth's own destruction.

Macbeth is haunted by half-buried puns, equivocations, and ambiguous grammatical constructions known as amphibologies. They manifest themselves most obviously in the words of the witches, from the opening exchanges to the fraudulent assurances that deceive Macbeth at the close, but they are also present in his most intimate and private reflections, as in his tortured broodings about his proposed act of treason:

> If it were done when 'tis done, then 'twere well
> It were done quickly. If th'assassination
> Could trammel up the consequence, and catch
> With his surcease success: that but this blow
> Might be the be-all and the end-all, here,
> But here upon this bank and shoal of time,
> We'd jump the life to come.
>
> (1.7.1–7)

The dream is to reach a secure and decisive end, to catch as in a net (hence "trammel up") all of the slippery, unforeseen, and uncontrollable consequences of regicide, to hobble time as one might hobble a horse (another sense of "trammel up"), to stop the flow ("success") of events, to be, as Macbeth later puts it, "settled." But Macbeth's words themselves slip away from the closure he seeks; they slide into one another, trip over themselves, twist and double back and swerve into precisely the sickening uncertainties their speaker most wishes to avoid. And if we sense a barely discernible note of comedy in Macbeth's tortured language, a discordant playing with the senses of the word "done" and the hint of a childish tongue twister in the phrase "catch / With his surcease success," we are in touch with a dark pleasure to which Shakespeare was all his life addicted.

Look again at the couplet from *Cymbeline*: "Golden lads and girls all must, / As chimney-sweepers, come to dust."

The playwright who insinuated a pun into the solemn dirge is the same playwright whose tragic heroine in *Antony and Cleopatra*, pulling the bleeding body of her dying lover into the pyramid, says, "Our strength is all gone into heaviness" (4.16.34). He is the playwright whose Juliet, finding herself alone on the stage, says, "My dismal scene I needs must act alone" (*Romeo and Juliet* 4.3.19), and the playwright who can follow the long, wrenching periodic sentence that Othello speaks, just before he stabs himself, with the remark "O bloody period!" (5.2.366). The point is not merely the presence of puns in the midst of tragedy (as there are stabs of pain in the midst of Shakespearean comedy); it is rather the streak of wildness that they so deliberately disclose, the sublimely indecorous linguistic energy of which Shakespeare was at once the towering master and the most obedient, worshipful servant.

The Dream of the Master Text

Shakespeare and the Printed Book

Ben Jonson's famous tribute to Shakespeare—"He was not of an age, but for all time!"—comes in one of the dedicatory poems to the 1623 First Folio of *Mr. William Shakespeares Comedies, Histories, & Tragedies*. This large, handsome volume, the first collection of Shakespeare's plays, was not, as far as we know, the product of the playwright's own design. We do not even know if he would have approved of the Folio's division of each play into five acts or its organization of the plays into three loose generic categories. Several of the plays grouped among the histories—*Richard Duke of York* (3 *Henry VI*), *Richard II,* and *Richard III*—had been printed separately during Shakespeare's lifetime as tragedies; one of the most famous of his tragedies had appeared as *The History of King Lear*. The Folio editors evidently decided to group together as "histories" only those plays which dealt with English history after the Norman Conquest; hence, *King Lear,* set in ancient Britain, appears with the "tragedies," and so, too, despite its happy ending, does *Cymbeline, King of Britain*. One play, *Troilus and Cressida,* was printed first as a "history," then printed in a second version with a preface that describes it as a "comedy," and then printed in the Folio as a "tragedy." As a fitting

Sixteenth-century printing shop. Engraving by Jan van der Straet. From *Nova Reperta* (1580).

emblem of the confusion, *Troilus and Cressida* does not appear in the Folio title page: apparently included only at the last minute, it was placed, unpaginated, after the last of the histories and the first of the tragedies. Modern readers, who remain perplexed by its genre, may take some consolation from the fact that for Shakespeare and his contemporaries generic boundaries were not hard and fast.

Published seven years after the playwright's death, the Folio was printed by the London printers William and Isaac Jaggard, who were joined in this expensive venture by Edward Blount, John Smethwicke, and William Aspley. It was edited by two of Shakespeare's old friends and fellow actors, John Heminges and Henry Condell, who claimed to be using "True Originall Copies" in the author's own hand. (None of these copies has survived, or, more cautiously, none has to date been found.) Eighteen plays included in the First Folio had already appeared individually in print in the small-format and relatively inexpensive texts called "Quartos" (or, in one case, the still smaller format called "Octavo"); to these, Heminges and Condell added eighteen others never before published: *All's Well That Ends Well, Antony and Cleopatra, As You Like It, The Comedy of Errors, Coriolanus, Cymbeline, All Is True (Henry VIII), Julius Caesar, King John, Macbeth, Measure for Measure, The Taming of the Shrew, The Tempest, Timon of Athens, Twelfth Night, The Two Gentlemen of Verona, The Winter's Tale,* and *1 Henry VI.** None of the

---

*This sketch simplifies several complex questions such as the status of the 1594 Quarto called *The Taming of a Shrew,* sufficiently distinct from the similarly titled Folio text as to constitute for many editors a different play.

plays included in the Folio has dropped out of the generally accepted canon of Shakespeare's works, and only two plays not included in the volume (*Pericles* and *The Two Noble Kinsmen*) have been allowed to join this select company, along with the nondramatic poems. Of the latter, *Venus and Adonis* (1593) and *The Rape of Lucrece* (1594) first appeared during Shakespeare's lifetime in Quartos with dedications from the author to the Earl of Southampton. *Shakespeare's Sonnets* (1609) were apparently printed without his authorization, as were his poems in a collection called *The Passionate Pilgrim* (1599).

Over the centuries, there have been many attempts to discover and authenticate additional works partly or entirely written by Shakespeare. An interesting case has been made for sections of a history play entitled *King Edward the Third* and for some small traces in the eighteenth-century tragicomedy *The Double Falsehood*, allegedly based on a manuscript of the lost Shakespearean play *Cardenio*. *The Norton Shakespeare* includes a poem, "Shall I die?" whose original inclusion in the 1988 *Oxford Shakespeare* provoked vigorous debate and much skepticism. Still more skepticism greeted the attribution to Shakespeare of a long poem called "A Funeral Elegy," printed in an appendix to *The Norton Shakespeare*'s first edition and now dropped in the wake of widespread consensus that the attribution was false. In the future, other claimants will no doubt come forward, but, with the very few additions already noted, the Folio will always remain the foundation of Shakespeare's dramatic canon.

The plays were the property of the theatrical company in which Shakespeare was a shareholder. It was not normally in the interest of such companies to have their scripts circulating in print, at least while the plays were actively in repertory: players evidently feared competition from rival companies and thought that reading might dampen playgoing. Plays were generally sold only when the theaters were temporarily closed by plague, or when the company was in need of capital (four of Shakespeare's plays were published in 1600, presumably to raise money to pay the debts incurred in building the new Globe), or when a play had grown too old to revive profitably. There is no evidence that Shakespeare himself disagreed with this professional caution, no sign that he wished to see his plays in print. Unlike Ben Jonson, who took the radical step of rewriting his own plays for publication in the 1616 folio of his *Works*, Shakespeare evidently was not interested in constituting his plays as a canon. If in the sonnets he imagines his verse achieving a symbolic immortality, this dream apparently did not extend to his plays, at least through the medium of print.

Moreover, there is no evidence that Shakespeare had an interest in asserting authorial rights over his scripts or that he or any other working English playwright had a public "standing," legal or otherwise, from which to do so. (Jonson was ridiculed for his presumption.) There is no indication whatever that he could, for example, veto changes in his scripts or block interpolated scenes or withdraw a play from production if a particular interpretation, addition, or revision did not please him. To be sure, in his advice to the players, Hamlet urges that those who play the clowns "speak no more than is set down for them," but—apart from the question of whether the Prince speaks for the playwright—the play within the play in *Hamlet* is precisely an instance of a script altered to suit a particular occasion. It seems likely that Shakespeare would have routinely accepted the possibility of such alterations. Moreover, he would of necessity have routinely accepted the possibility, and in certain cases the virtual inevitability, of cuts in order to stage his plays in the two to two and one-half hours that was the normal performing time. There is an imaginative generosity in many of Shakespeare's scripts, as if he were deliberately offering his fellow actors more than they could use on any one occasion and, hence, giving them abundant materials with which to reconceive and revivify each play again and again as they or their audiences liked it. The Elizabethan theater, like most theater in our own time, was a collaborative enterprise, and the collaboration almost certainly extended to decisions about selection, trimming, shifts of emphasis, and minor or major revision.

For many years, it was thought that Shakespeare himself did little or no revising. Some recent editors—above all the editors of the *Oxford Shakespeare*, whose texts the

Norton presents—have argued persuasively that there are many signs of authorial revision, even wholesale rewriting. But there is no sign that Shakespeare sought through such revision to bring each of his plays to its "perfect," "final" form. On the contrary, many of the revisions seem to indicate that the scripts remained open texts, that the playwright and his company expected to add, cut, and rewrite as the occasion demanded.

Ralph Waldo Emerson once compared Shakespeare and his contemporary Francis Bacon in terms of the relative "finish" of their work. All of Bacon's work, wrote Emerson, "lies along the ground, a vast unfinished city." Each of Shakespeare's dramas, by contrast, "is perfect, hath an immortal integrity. To make Bacon's work complete, he must live to the end of the world." Recent scholarship suggests that Shakespeare was more like Bacon than Emerson thought. Neither the Folio nor the quarto texts of Shakespeare's plays bear the seal of final authorial intention, the mark of decisive closure that has served, at least ideally, as the guarantee of textual authenticity. We want to believe, as we read the text, "This is the play as Shakespeare himself wanted it read," but there is no license for such a reassuring sentiment. To be "not of an age, but for all time" means in Shakespeare's case not that the plays have achieved a static perfection, but that they are creatively, inexhaustibly unfinished.

That we have been so eager to link certain admired scripts to a single known playwright is closely related to changes in the status of artists in the Renaissance, changes that led to a heightened interest in the hand of the individual creator. Like medieval painting, medieval drama gives us few clues as to the particular individuals who fashioned the objects we admire. We know something about the places in which these objects were made, the circumstances that enabled their creation, the spaces in which they were placed, but relatively little about the particular artists themselves. It is easy to imagine a wealthy patron or a civic authority in the late Middle Ages commissioning a play on a particular subject (appropriate, for example, to a seasonal ritual, a religious observance, or a political festivity) and specifying the date, place, and length of the performance, the number of actors, even the costumes to be used, but it is more difficult to imagine him specifying a particular playwright and still less insisting that the entire play be written by this dramatist alone. Only with the Renaissance do we find a growing insistence on the name of the maker, the signature that heightens the value and even the meaning of the work by implying that it is the emanation of a single, distinct shaping consciousness.

In the case of Renaissance painting, we know that this signature does not necessarily mean that every stroke was made by the master. Some of the work, possibly the greater part of it, may have been done by assistants, with only the faces and a few finishing touches from the hand of the illustrious artist to whom the work is confidently attributed. As the skill of individual masters became more explicitly valued, contracts began to specify how much was to come from the brush of the principal painter. Consider, for example, the Italian painter Luca Signorelli's contract of 1499 for frescoes in Orvieto Cathedral:

> The said master Luca is bound and promises to paint [1] all the figures to be done on the said vault, and [2] especially the faces and all the parts of the figures from the middle of each figure upwards, and [3] that no painting should be done on it without Luca himself being present. . . . And it is agreed [4] that all the mixing of colours should be done by the said master Luca himself.

Such a contract at once reflects a serious cash interest in the characteristic achievement of a particular artist and a conviction that this achievement is compatible with the presence of other hands, provided those hands are subordinate, in the finished work. For paintings on a smaller scale, it was more possible to commission an exclusive performance. Thus, the contract for a small altarpiece by Signorelli's great teacher, Piero della Francesca, specifies that "no painter may put his hand to the brush other than Piero himself."

There is no record of any comparable concern for exclusivity in the English theater. Unfortunately, the contracts that Shakespeare and his fellow dramatists almost certainly signed have not, with one significant exception, survived. But plays written for the professional theater are by their nature an even more explicitly collective art form than paintings; they depend for their full realization on the collaboration of others, and that collaboration may well extend to the fashioning of the script. It seems that some authors may simply have been responsible for providing plots that others then dramatized; still others were hired to "mend" old plays or to supply prologues, epilogues, or songs. A particular playwright's name came to be attached to a certain identifiable style—a characteristic set of plot devices, a marked rhetorical range, a tonality of character—but this name may refer in effect more to a certain product associated with a particular playing company than to the individual artist who may or may not have written most of the script. The one contract whose details do survive, that entered into by Richard Brome and the actors and owners of the Salisbury Court Theatre in 1635, does not stipulate that Brome's plays must be written by him alone or even that he must be responsible for a certain specifiable proportion of each script. Rather, it specifies that the playwright "should not nor would write any play or any part of a play to any other players or playhouse, but apply all his study and endeavors therein for the benefit of the said company of the said playhouse." The Salisbury Court players want rights to everything Brome writes for the stage; the issue is not that the plays associated with his name be exclusively *his* but rather that he be exclusively *theirs*.

Recent textual scholarship, then, has been moving steadily away from a conception of Shakespeare's plays as direct, unmediated emanations from the mind of the author and toward a conception of them as working scripts, composed and continually reshaped as part of a collaborative commercial enterprise in competition with other, similar enterprises. One consequence has been the progressive weakening of the idea of the solitary, inspired genius, in the sense fashioned by Romanticism and figured splendidly in the statue of Shakespeare in the public gardens in Germany's Weimar, the city of Goethe and Schiller: the poet, with his sensitive, expressive face and high domed forehead sitting alone and brooding, a skull at his feet, a long-stemmed rose in his crotch. In place of this projection of German Romanticism, we have now a playwright and sometime actor who is also (to his considerable financial advantage) a major shareholder in the company—the Lord Chamberlain's Men, later the King's Men—to which he loyally supplies for most of his career an average of two plays per year.

These developments are salutary insofar as they direct attention to the actual conditions in which the textual traces that the Folio calls Shakespeare's "Comedies, Histories, & Tragedies" came to be produced, reproduced, consumed, revised, and transmitted to future generations. They highlight elements that Shakespeare shared with his contemporaries, and they insistently remind us that we are encountering scripts written primarily for the stage and not for the study. They make us more attentive to such matters as business cycles, plague rolls, the cost of costumes, government censorship, and urban topography and less concerned with the elusive and enigmatic details of the poet's biography—his supposed youthful escapades and erotic yearnings and psychological crises.

All well and good. But the fact remains that in 1623, seven years after the playwright's death, Heminges and Condell thought they could sell copies of their expensive collection of Shakespeare's plays—"What euer you do," they urge their readers, "buy"—by insisting that their texts were "as he conceiued them." This means that potential readers in the early seventeenth century were already interested in Shakespeare's "conceits"—his "wit," his imagination, and his creative power—and were willing to assign a high value to the products of his particular, identifiable skill, one distinguishable from that of his company and of his rival playwrights. After all, Jonson's tribute praises Shakespeare not as the playwright of the incomparable King's Men but as the equal of Aeschylus, Sophocles, and Euripides. And if we now see Shakespeare's dramaturgy in the context of his contemporaries and of a collective artistic practice, readers continue to have little difficulty recognizing that most of the plays attached to his name tower over those of his rivals.

From Foul to Fair: The Making of the Printed Play

What exactly is a printed play by Shakespeare? Is it like a novel or a poem? Is it like the libretto or the score of an opera? Is it the trace of an absent event? Is it the blueprint of an imaginary structure that will never be completed? Is it a record of what transpired in the mind of a man long dead? We might say cautiously that it is a mechanically reproduced version of what Shakespeare wrote, but unfortunately, with the possible (and disputed) exception of a small fragment from a collaboratively written play called *Sir Thomas More*, virtually nothing Shakespeare actually wrote in his own hand survives. We might propose that it is a printed version of the script that an Elizabethan actor would have held in his hands during rehearsals, but here, too, no such script of a Shakespeare play survives; and besides, Elizabethan actors were evidently not given the whole play to read. To reduce the expense of copying and the risk of unauthorized reproduction, each actor received only his own part, along with the cue lines. (Shakespeare uses this fact to delicious comic effect in *A Midsummer Night's Dream* 3.1.80–88.) Nonetheless, the play certainly existed as a whole, either in the author's original manuscript or in the copy prepared for the government censor or for the company's prompter or stage manager, so we might imagine the text we hold in our hands as a printed copy of one of these manuscripts. But since no contemporary manuscript survives of any of Shakespeare's plays, we cannot verify this hypothesis. And even if we could, we would not have resolved the question of the precise relation of the printed text either to the playwright's imagination or to the theatrical performance by the company to which he belonged.

All of Shakespeare's plays must have begun their textual careers in the form of "foul papers," drafts presumably covered with revisions, crossings-out, and general "blotting." To be sure, Heminges and Condell remark that so great was the playwright's facility that they "have scarce received from him a blot in his papers." This was, however, a routine and conventional compliment in the period. The same claim, made for the playwright John Fletcher in an edition published in 1647, is clearly contradicted by the survival of Fletcher's far-from-unblotted manuscripts. It is safe to assume that, since Shakespeare was human, his manuscripts contained their share of second and third thoughts scribbled in the margins and between the lines. Once complete, this authorial draft would usually have to be written out again, either by the playwright or by a professional scribe employed by the theater company, as "fair copy."

In the hands of the theater company, the fair copy (or sometimes, it seems, the foul papers themselves) would be annotated and transformed into "the book of the play" or the "playbook" (what we would now call a "promptbook"). Shakespeare's authorial draft presumably contained a certain number of stage directions, though these may have been sketchy and inconsistent. The promptbook clarified these and added others, noted theatrical properties and sound effects, and on occasion cut the full text to meet the necessities of performance. The promptbook was presented to the Master of the Revels for licensing, and it incorporated any changes upon which the master insisted. As the editors of the *Oxford Shakespeare* put it, the difference between foul papers and promptbook is the difference between "the text in an as yet individual, private form" and "a socialized text."

But the fact remains that for Shakespeare's plays, we have neither foul papers nor fair copies nor promptbooks. We have only the earliest printed editions of these texts in numerous individual quartos and in the First Folio. (Quartos are so called because each sheet of paper was folded twice, making four leaves or eight pages front and back; folio sheets were folded once, making two leaves or four pages front and back.) From clues embedded in these "substantive" texts—substantive because (with the exception of *The Two Noble Kinsmen*) they date from Shakespeare's own lifetime or from the collected works edited by his associates using, or claiming to use, his own manuscripts—editors attempt to reconstruct each play's journey from manuscript to print. Different plays took very different journeys.

Of the thirty-six plays included in the First Folio, eighteen had previously appeared in quarto editions, some of these in more than one printing. Generations of editors have distinguished between "good Quartos," presumably prepared from the author's own draft or from a scribal transcript of the play (fair copy), and "bad Quartos." The latter category, first formulated as such by A. W. Pollard in 1909, includes, by widespread but not universal agreement, the 1594 version of *The First Part of the Contention* (*2 Henry VI*), the 1595 *Richard Duke of York* (*3 Henry VI*), the 1597 *Richard the Third*, the 1597 *Romeo and Juliet*, the 1600 *Henry the Fifth*, the 1602 *Merry Wives of Windsor*, the 1603 *Hamlet*, and *Pericles* (1609). Some editors also regard the 1591 *Troublesome Reign of King John*, the 1594 *Taming of a Shrew*, and the 1608 *King Lear* as bad Quartos, but others have strenuously argued that these are distinct rather than faulty texts, and the whole concept of the bad Quarto has come under increasingly critical scrutiny. The criteria for distinguishing between "good" and "bad" texts are imprecise, and the evaluative terms seem to raise as many questions as they answer. Nevertheless, the striking mistakes, omissions, repetitions, and anomalies in a number of the Quartos require some explanation beyond the ordinary fallibility of scribes and printers.

The explanation most often proposed for suspect Quartos is that they are the products of "memorial reconstruction." The hypothesis, first advanced in 1910 by W. W. Greg, is that a series of features found in what seem to be particularly flawed texts may be traced to the derivation of the copy from the memory of one or more of the actors. Elizabethan actors, Greg observed, often found themselves away from the London theaters—for example, on tour in the provinces during plague periods—and may not on those occasions have had access to the promptbooks they would ordinarily have used. In such circumstances, those in the company who remembered a play may have written down or dictated the text, as best they could, perhaps adapting it for provincial performance. Moreover, unscrupulous actors may have sold such texts to enterprising printers eager to turn a quick profit.

Memorially reconstructed texts tend to be much shorter than those prepared from foul papers or fair copy; they frequently paraphrase or garble lines, drop or misplace speeches and whole scenes, and on occasion fill in the gaps with scraps from other plays. In several cases, scholars think they can detect which roles the rogue actors played, since these parts (and the scenes in which they appear) are reproduced with greater accuracy than the rest of the play. Typically, these roles are minor ones, since the leading parts would be played by actors with a greater stake in the overall financial interest of the company and, hence, less inclination to violate its policy. Thus, for example, editors speculate that the bad Quarto of *Hamlet* (Q1) was provided by the actor playing Marcellus (and doubling as Lucianus). What is often impossible to determine is whether particular differences between a bad Quarto and a good Quarto or Folio text result from the actor's faulty memory or from changes introduced in performance, possibly with the playwright's own consent, or from both. Shakespearean bad Quartos ceased to appear after 1609, perhaps as a result of greater scrutiny by the Master of the Revels, who after 1606 was responsible for licensing plays for publication as well as performance.

The syndicate that prepared the Folio had access to the manuscripts of the King's Men. In addition to the previously published editions of eighteen plays, they made use of scribal transcripts (fair copies), promptbooks, and (more rarely) foul papers. The indefatigable labors of generations of bibliographers, antiquaries, and textual scholars have recovered an extraordinary fund of information about the personnel, finances, organizational structure, and material practices of Elizabethan and Jacobean printing houses, including the names and idiosyncrasies of particular compositors who calculated the page length, set the type, and printed the sheets of the Folio. This impressive scholarship has for the most part intensified respect for the seriousness with which the Folio was prepared and printed, and where the Folio is defective, it has provided plausible readings from the Quartos or proposed emendations to approximate what Shakespeare is likely to have written. But it has not succeeded, despite all its heroic efforts, in transforming the Folio, or any other text, into an unobstructed, clear window into Shakespeare's mind.

The dream of the master text is a dream of transparency. The words on the page should ideally give the reader unmediated access to the astonishing forge of imaginative power that was the mind of the dramatist. Those words welled up from the genius of the great artist, and if the world were not an imperfect place, they would have been set down exactly as he conceived them and transmitted to each of us as a precious inheritance. Such is the vision—at its core closely related to the preservation of the holy text in the great scriptural religions—that has driven many of the great editors who have for centuries produced successive editions of Shakespeare's works. The vision was not yet fully formed in the First Folio, for Heminges and Condell still felt obliged to apologize to their noble patrons for dedicating to them a collection of mere "trifles." But by the eighteenth century, there were no longer any ritual apologies for Shakespeare; instead, there was a growing recognition not only of the supreme artistic importance of his works but also of the uncertain, conflicting, and in some cases corrupt state of the surviving texts. Every conceivable step, it was thought, must be undertaken to correct mistakes, strip away corruptions, return the texts to their pure and unsullied form, and make this form perfectly accessible to readers.

Paradoxically, this feverishly renewed, demanding, and passionate editorial project has produced the very opposite of the transparency that was the dream of the master text. The careful weighing of alternative readings, the production of a textual apparatus, the writing of notes and glosses, the modernizing and regularizing of spelling and punctuation, the insertion of scene divisions, the complex calculation of the process of textual transmission from foul papers to print, the equally complex calculation of the effects that censorship, government regulation, and, above all, theatrical performance had on the surviving documents all make inescapably apparent the fact that we do not have and never will have any direct, unmediated access to Shakespeare's imagination. Every Shakespeare text, from the first that was published to the most recent, has been edited: it has come into print by means of a tangled social process and inevitably exists at some remove from the author.

Heminges and Condell, who knew the author and had access to at least some of his manuscripts, lament the fact that Shakespeare did not live "to have set forth and overseen his own writings." And even had he done so—or, alternatively, even if a cache of his manuscripts were discovered in a Warwickshire attic tomorrow—all of the editorial problems would not be solved, nor would all of the levels of mediation be swept away. Certainly, the entire textual landscape would change. But the written word has strange powers: it seems to hold on to something of the very life of the person who has written it, but it also seems to pry that life loose from the writer, exposing it to vagaries of history and chance independent of those to which the writer was personally subject. Moreover, with the passing of centuries, the language itself and the whole frame of reference within which language and symbols are understood have decisively changed. The most learned modern scholar still lives at a huge experiential remove from Shakespeare's world and, even holding a precious copy of the First Folio in hand, cannot escape having to read across a vast chasm of time what is, after all, an edited text. The rest of us cannot so much as indulge in the fantasy of direct access: our eyes inevitably wander to the glosses and the explanatory notes.

The Oxford Shakespeare

The shattering of the dream of the master text is no cause for despair, nor should it lead us to throw our hands up and declare that one text is as good as another. What it does is to encourage the reader to be actively interested in the editorial principles that underlie the particular edition that he or she is using. It is said that the great artist Brueghel once told a nosy connoisseur who had come to his studio, "Keep your nose out of my paintings; the smell of the paint will poison you." In the case of Shakespeare, it is increasingly important to bring one's nose close to the page, as it were, and sniff the ink. More precisely, it is important to understand the rationale for the choices that the editors have made.

The text of the *Norton Shakespeare* is, with very few changes, that published by the Oxford University Press in 1988 and, in a second edition, in 2005. The *Oxford Shakespeare* was the extraordinary achievement of a team of editors, Stanley Wells, Gary Taylor, John Jowett, and William Montgomery, with Wells and Taylor serving as the general editors. The Oxford editors approached their task with a clear understanding that, as we have seen, all previous texts have been mediated by agents other than Shakespeare; however, they regard this mediation not as a melancholy obstacle intervening between the reader and the "true" Shakespearean text but rather as a constitutive element of this text. The art of the playwright is thoroughly dependent on the craft of go-betweens.

Shakespeare's plays were not written to be circulated in manuscript or printed form among readers. They were written to be performed by the players and, as the preface to the Quarto *Troilus and Cressida* indelicately puts it, "clapper-clawed with the palms of the vulgar." The public was, thus, never meant to be in a direct relationship with the author but in a "triangular relationship" in which the players gave voice and gesture to the author's words. As we have seen, Shakespeare was the master of the unfinished, the perpetually open. And even if we narrow our gaze and try to find only what Shakespeare himself might have regarded as a textual resting point, a place to stop and go on to another play, we have, the Oxford editors point out, a complex task. For whatever Shakespeare wrote was meant from the start to be supplemented by an invisible "paratext" consisting of words spoken by Shakespeare to the actors and by the actors to each other concerning emphasis, stage business, tone, pacing, possible cuts, and so forth. To the extent that this paratext was ever written down, it was recorded in the promptbook. Therefore, in contrast to standard editorial practice, the Oxford editors prefer, when there is a choice, copy based on the promptbook to copy based on the author's own draft. They choose the text immersed in history—that is, in the theatrical embodiment for which it was intended by its author—over the text unstained by the messy, collaborative demands of the playhouse. The closest we can get to Shakespeare's "final" version of a play—understanding that for him as for us there is no true "finality" in a theatrical text—is the latest version of that play performed by his company during his professional life—that is, during the time in which he could still oversee and participate in any cuts and revisions.

This choice does not mean that the Oxford editors are turning away from the very idea of Shakespeare as author. On the contrary, Wells and Taylor are deeply committed to establishing a text that comes as close as possible to the plays as Shakespeare wrote them, but they are profoundly attentive to the fact that he wrote them as a member of a company of players, a company in which he was a shareholder and an actor as well as a writer. "Writing" for the theater, at least for Shakespeare, is not simply a matter of setting words to paper and letting the pages drift away; it is a social process as well as an individual act. The Oxford editors acknowledge that some aspects of this social process may have been frustrating to Shakespeare: he may, for example, have been forced on occasion to cut lines and even whole scenes to which he was attached, or his fellow players may have insisted that they could not successfully perform what he had written, compelling him to make changes he did not welcome. But compromise and collaboration are part of what it means to be in the theater, and Wells and Taylor return again and again to the recognition that Shakespeare was, supremely, a man of the theater.

Is there a tension between the Oxford editors' preference for the performed, fully socialized text and their continued commitment to recovering the text as Shakespeare himself intended it? Yes. The tension is most visible in their determination to strip away textual changes arising from circumstances, such as government censorship, over which Shakespeare had no control. ("We have, wherever possible," they write, put "profanities back in Shakespeare's mouth.") It can be glimpsed as well in the editors' belief, almost a leap of faith, that there was little revision of Shakespeare's plays in his company's revivals between the time of his death and the publication of the Folio. But the tension is mainly a creative one, for it forces them (and, therefore, us) to attend to the playwright's unique imaginative power as well as his social and historical entanglements.

The Oxford editors took a radical stance on a second major issue: the question of authorial revision. Previous editors had generally accepted the fact that Shakespeare practiced revision within individual manuscripts—that is, while he was still in the act of writing a particular play—but they generally rejected the notion that he undertook substantial revisions from one version of a play to another (and, hence, from one manuscript to another). Wells and Taylor point out that six major works (*Hamlet, Othello, 2 Henry IV, King Lear, Richard II,* and *Troilus and Cressida*) survive in two independent substantive sources, both apparently authoritative, with hundreds of significant variant readings. Previous editors have generally sought to deny authority to one edition or another ("faced with two sheep," the Oxford editors observe wryly, "it is all too easy to insist that one *must* be a goat") or have conflated the two versions into a single text in an attempt to reconstruct the ideal, definitive, complete, and perfect version that they imagine Shakespeare must have reached for each of his plays. But if one doubts that Shakespeare ever conceived of his plays as closed, finished entities, if one recalls that he wrote them for the living repertory of the commercial playing company to which he belonged, then the whole concept of the single, authoritative text of each play loses its force. In a startling departure from the editorial tradition, the *Oxford Shakespeare* printed two distinct versions of *King Lear,* quarto and Folio, and the editors glanced longingly at the impractical but alluring possibility of including two texts of *Hamlet, Othello,* and *Troilus.*

The *Oxford Shakespeare* was published in both old-spelling and modern-spelling editions. The former, the first of its kind ever published, raised some reviewers' eyebrows because the project, a critical edition rather than a facsimile, required the modern editors to invent plausible Elizabethan spellings for their emendations and to add stage directions. The modern-spelling edition, which is the basis for Norton's text, is noteworthy for taking the principles of modernization further than they had generally been taken. Gone are such words as "murther," "mushrump," "vild," and "porpentine," which confer on many modern-spelling editions a certain cozy, Olde-English quaintness; Oxford replaces them with "murder," "mushroom," "vile," and "porcupine."

The inclusion of two texts of *King Lear* aroused considerable controversy when the *Oxford Shakespeare* first appeared, although by now the arguments for doing so have received widespread, though not unanimous, scholarly support. Other features remain controversial: "Ancients" Pistol and Iago have been modernized to "Ensigns"; *Henry VIII* has reverted to its performance title *All Is True;* demonic spirits in *Macbeth* sing lyrics written by Thomas Middleton. The white-hot intensity of the debates triggered by the *Oxford Shakespeare*'s editorial choices casts an interesting light on the place of Shakespeare not only in the culture at large but in the psyches of millions of individuals: any alteration, however minor, in a deeply familiar and beloved text, even an alteration based on thoughtful and highly plausible scholarly principles, arouses genuine anxiety. The anxiety in this case was intensified not only by the boldness of certain crucial emendations but also by the fact that the editors' explanations, arguments, and justifications for all their decisions were printed in a separate, massive volume, *William Shakespeare: A Textual Companion.* This formidable, dense volume is an astonishing monument to the seriousness, scholarly rigor, and immense labor of the Oxford editors. Anyone who is interested in pursuing why Shakespeare's words appear as they do in the current edition, anyone who wishes insight into the editors' detailed reasons for making the thousands of decisions required by a project of this kind, should consult the *Textual Companion.*

The Norton Shakespeare

The primary task that the editors of the *Norton Shakespeare* set themselves was to present the modern-spelling Oxford *Complete Works* in a way that would make the text more accessible to modern readers. The *Oxford Shakespeare* prints little more than the text itself: along with one-page introductions to the individual works, it contains a short general introduction, a list of contemporary allusions to Shakespeare, and a brief glossary. But while it is possible to enjoy a Shakespeare play on stage or screen without any assistance beyond the actors' own art, many readers at least since the eighteenth century have found it far more difficult to understand and to savor the texts without some more substantial commentary.

In addition to writing introductions, textual notes, and brief bibliographies for each of the works, the Norton editors provide glosses and footnotes designed to facilitate comprehension. Such is the staggering richness of Shakespeare's language that it is tempting to gloss everything. But there is a law of diminishing returns: too much explanatory whispering at the margins makes it difficult to enjoy what the reader has come for in the first place. Our general policy is to gloss only those words that cannot be found in an ordinary dictionary or whose meanings have altered out of recognition. The glosses attempt to be simple and straightforward, giving multiple meanings for words only when the meanings are essential for making sense of the passages in which they appear. We try not to gloss the same word over and over—it becomes distracting to be told three times on a single page that "an" means "if"—but we also assume that the reader does not have a perfect memory, so after an interval we will gloss the same word again.

Marginal glosses generally refer to a single word or a short phrase. The footnotes paraphrase longer units or provide other kinds of information, such as complex plays on words, significant allusions, textual cruxes, historical and cultural contexts. Here, too, however, we have tried to check the impulse to annotate so heavily that the reader is distracted from the pleasure of the text, and we have avoided notes that provide interpretation, as distinct from information.

Following the works, the Norton editors have provided lists of textual variants. These are variants from the control text only—that is, they do not record all of the variants in all of the substantive texts, nor do they record all of the myriad shifts of meaning that may arise from modernization of spelling and repunctuation. Readers who wish to pursue these interesting, if complex, topics are encouraged to consult the *Textual Companion,* along with the old-spelling *Oxford Shakespeare,* the Norton facsimile of the First Folio, and the quarto facsimiles published by the University of California Press. The *Norton Shakespeare* does provide a convenient list for each play of the different ways the same characters are designated in the speech prefixes in the substantive texts. These variants (for example, Lady Capulet in *Romeo and Juliet* is called, variously, "Lady," "Mother," "Wife," "Old Woman," etc.) often cast an interesting light on the ways a particular character is conceived. Variants as they appear in this edition, as well as their line numbers, are printed in boldface; each is followed by the corresponding reading in the control text, and sometimes the source from which the variant is taken. Further information on readings in substantive texts is given in brackets.

Stage directions pose a complex set of problems for the editors of a one-volume Shakespeare. The printing conventions for the stage directions in sixteenth- and seventeenth-century plays were different from those of our own time. Often all of the entrances for a particular scene are grouped together at the beginning, even though some of the characters clearly do not enter until later; placement in any case seems at times haphazard or simply incorrect. There are moments when the stage directions seem to provide stunning insight into the staging of the plays in Shakespeare's time, other moments when they are absent or misleading. It is difficult to gauge how much the stage directions in the substantive editions reflect Shakespeare's own words or at least decisions. It would seem that he was often relatively careless about them, understanding perhaps that these decisions in any precise sense would be the first to be made and unmade by different productions.

The Oxford editors, like virtually all modern editors, necessarily altered and supplemented the stage directions in their control texts. They decided to mark certain of the stage directions with a special sign to indicate a dubious action or placement, but they did not distinguish between the stage directions that came from the substantive texts and those added in later texts, from the seventeenth century to the present. They referred readers instead to the *Textual Companion,* which provides lists of the exact wording of the stage directions in the substantive texts.

The editors of the *Norton Shakespeare* share a sense of the limitations of the early stage directions and share as well some skepticism about how many of these should be attributed even indirectly to Shakespeare. Hence, we do not routinely differentiate between quarto and Folio stage directions; we do so only when we think it is a significant point. But there is, it seems to us, a real interest in knowing which stage directions come from those editions of the plays published up to the 1623 Folio (and including *The Two Noble Kinsmen,* published shortly thereafter) and which were added when the editors were no longer in contact with Shakespeare's presence or his manuscripts. Therefore, we have placed brackets around all stage directions that were added after the First Folio. Unbracketed stage directions, then, all derive from editions up through the Folio.

The *Norton Shakespeare* has made several other significant departures from the Oxford text. The Oxford editors note that when *1 Henry IV* was first performed, probably in 1596, the character we know as Sir John Falstaff was called Sir John Oldcastle. But in the wake of protests from Oldcastle's descendants, one of whom, William Brooke, tenth Baron Cobham, was Elizabeth I's lord chamberlain, Shakespeare changed the name to "Falstaff" (and probably for similar reasons changed the names of Falstaff's companions, Russell and Harvey, to "Bardolph" and "Peto"). Consistent with their decision not to honor changes that Shakespeare was *compelled* to make by censorship or other forms of pressure, the Oxford editors changed the names back to their initial form. But this decision is a problem for several reasons. It draws perhaps too sharp a distinction between those things that Shakespeare did under social pressure and those he did of his own accord. More seriously, it pulls against the principle of a text that represents the latest performance version of a play during Shakespeare's lifetime: after all, even the earliest quarto title page advertises "the humorous conceits of Sir John Falstaff." And, of course, it asks the reader to ignore completely and radically centuries of response—elaboration, fascination, and love—all focused passionately on Sir John Falstaff. The response is not a modern phenomenon: it began with Shakespeare, who developed the character as Sir John Falstaff in *2 Henry IV* and *The Merry Wives of Windsor.* Norton thus restores the more familiar names.

Another major departure from the Oxford text is Norton's printing of the so-called Additional Passages, especially in *Hamlet.* Consistent with their decision not to conflate quarto and Folio texts, the Oxford editors adhere to their control text for *Hamlet,* the Folio, and print those passages that appear only in the Second Quarto in an appendix at the end of the play. As explained at length in the Textual Note to the play, the Norton editors decided not to follow this course, but instead chose a different way of demarcating the quarto and Folio texts (inserting the quarto passages, indented, in the body of the text), one that makes it easier to see how the quarto passages functioned in a version of the play that Shakespeare also authored.

The *Norton Shakespeare* follows Oxford in printing separate quarto and Folio texts of *King Lear,* to which we have added a conflated version of the play so that readers will have the opportunity to assess for themselves the effects of the traditional editorial practice. Moreover, we have departed from Oxford in printing the quarto and Folio texts of the plays on facing pages, so that their differences can be readily weighed. In the hundreds of changes, some trivial and other momentous, it is possible to glimpse, across what Prospero calls "the dark backward and abysm of time," a thrilling sight: Shakespeare at work.

The Shakespearean Stage
by

ANDREW GURR

Publication by Performance

The curt exchange between the sentries in the first six lines of *Hamlet* tells us that it is very late at night ("'Tis now struck twelve") and that "'tis bitter cold." This opening was staged originally at the Globe in London in broad daylight, at 2 o'clock probably on a hot summer's afternoon. The words required the audience, half of them standing on three sides of the stage platform and all of them as visible to one another as the players were, to imagine themselves watching a scene quite the opposite of what they could see and feel around them. The original mode of staging for a Shakespearean play was utterly different from the cinematic realism we are used to now, where the screen gives us close-ups on a simulacrum of reality, an even more privileged view of the actors' facial twitches than we get in ordinary life. Eloquence then was in words, not facial expressions.

The playgoers of Shakespeare's time knew the plays in forms at which we can only now guess. It is a severe loss. Shakespeare's own primary concept of his plays was as stories "personated" onstage, not as words on a page. He himself never bothered to get his playscripts into print, and more than half of them were not published until seven years after his death, in the First Folio of his plays published as a memorial to him in 1623. His fellow playwright Francis Beaumont called the printing of plays "a second publication"; the first was their showing onstage. Print recorded a set of scripts, written for the original players to teach them what they should speak in the ensemble of the play in production. The only technology then available to record the performances was the written word. If video recordings had existed at that time, our understanding of Shakespeare would be vastly different from what it is today.

Since the texts were composed only to be a record of the words the players were to memorize, we now have to infer how the plays were originally staged largely by guess-work. Shakespeare was himself a player and shareholder in his acting company, and he expected to be present at rehearsals. Consequently, the stage directions in his scripts are distinctly skimpy compared with some of those provided by his fellow playwrights. He was cursory even in noting entrances and exits, let alone how he expected his company to stage the more complex spectacles, such as heaving Antony up to Cleopatra on her monument. There are sometimes hints in the stage directions and more frequently in the words used to describe some of the actions, and knowing what the design of the theater was like is a help as well. Knowing more about how Shakespeare expected his plays to be staged can transform how we think about them. But gaining such knowledge is no easy matter. One of the few certainties is that Shakespeare's plays in modern performance are even more different from the originals than modern printed editions are from the first much-thumbed manuscripts.

The Shakespearean Mindset

The general mindset of the original playgoers, the patterns of thinking and expectation that Tudor culture imposed on Shakespeare's audiences, is not really difficult to identify.

79

It is less easy, though, to pin it down in the sort of detail that tells us what the original concept of staging the plays would have been like. We know that all the original playgoers paid for the privilege of attending the plays and committed themselves willingly to suspend their disbelief in what they were to see. They knew as we do that they were paying to be entertained by fictions. Beyond that, we need reminding today that going to open-air performances in daylight in Shakespeare's time meant being constantly aware that one was in a theater, a place designed to offer illusions. On the one hand, this consciousness of oneself and where one was meant that the players had to do more to hold attention than is needed now, when audiences have nothing but the stage to look at and armchairs to sit in. On the other hand, it made everyone more receptive to extratheatrical tricks, such as Hamlet's reference to "this distracted globe," or Polonius's claim in the same play to have taken the part of Julius Caesar at the university and been killed by Brutus. The regular playgoers at the Globe who recognized Polonius as the man who had played Caesar in Shakespeare's play of the year before, and who recognized Hamlet as the man who had played Brutus, would laugh at this theatrical in-joke. But two scenes later, when Hamlet kills Polonius, they would think of it again, in a different light.

Features of the original mindset such as these are readily identifiable. For others, though, we need to look further, into the design of the theaters and into the staging traditions that they housed and that Shakespeare exploited. Invisibility has a part to play in *A Midsummer Night's Dream* that we can easily underrate, for instance. Invisibility onstage is a theatrical in-joke, an obvious privileging of the audience, which is allowed to see what the characters onstage can't. The impresario Philip Henslowe's inventory of costumes used at the Rose theater in 1597, which lists "a robe for to go invisible," indicates a fictional device that openly expects the willing suspension of the audience's disbelief. In *A Midsummer Night's Dream,* the ostensible invisibility of all the visible fairies emphasizes the theatricality of the whole presentation while pandering to the audience's self-indulgent superiority, the feeling that it knows what is going on better than any character, whether he be Bottom or even Duke Theseus. That prepares us for the mockery of stage realism we get later, in the mechanicals' play in Act 5, and even for the doubt we as willing audience might feel over Theseus's own skepticism about the dangers of imagination that he voices in his speech at the beginning of Act 5.

More to the point, though, it throws into question our readiness to be an audience, since we have ourselves been indulging in just the games of suspending disbelief that the play staged by the mechanicals enters into so unsuccessfully. When Theseus disputes with Hippolyta about the credibility of the lovers' story, he voices the very skepticism—about the lover, the lunatic, and the poet—that any sensible realist in the audience would have been feeling for most of the previous three acts in the forest. The play starts and ends at the court in broad daylight, while the scenes of midsummer madness take place at night in a forest. At the early amphitheaters, all the plays were staged in broad daylight, between 2 and 5 o'clock in the afternoon, and without any persuasive scenery: the two stage posts served as trees onstage. So the play, moving as it does from daylight realism to nocturnal fantasy and back again, with a last challenge to credulity in the mechanicals' burlesque of how to stage a play, has already thoroughly challenged the willing suspension of the viewers' disbelief. *A Midsummer Night's Dream* is a play about nocturnal dreams and fictions that are accepted as truths in broad daylight. It was only a small extension of this game to have the women's parts played by boys, as well as plots in which the girls dressed as boys, to the point where in *As You Like It* Rosalind was played by a boy playing a girl pretending to be a boy playing a girl.

The Shakespeare plays were written for a new and unique kind of playhouse, the Elizabethan amphitheater, which had a distinctive design quite different from modern theaters. Elizabethans knew what the standard features in their theaters stood for, and Shakespeare drew on that knowledge for the staging of his plays. The physical features of the playhouses were a potent element in the ways that the plays were designed for the Elizabethan mindset. When Richard III, the archdeceiver and playactor, appears "aloft between two Bishops" to claim the crown in *Richard III* 3.7, his placing on the stage balcony literally above the crowd on the stage would, even without the accompanying priests, have signified his ironic claim to a social and moral superiority that ought to have matched his elevation. When Richard II comes down from the wall of Flint Castle to the "base court" in *Richard II* 3.3, Elizabethans would have seen his descent as a withdrawal from power and status. These theaters were still new when Shakespeare started to write for them, and their novelty meant that the plays were written more tightly to fit their specific design than the plays of later years, when theatergoing had become a more routine social activity and different kinds of theater were available.

London Playgoing and the Law

This heightened sense of theatricality, or "metatheater," in Shakespearean audiences was far from the only difference in their mindset from that of all modern audiences. Regular playgoing in London only started in the 1570s, and through Shakespeare's earlier years it was always a perilous and precarious activity. The Lord Mayor of London and the mayors of most of England's larger towns hated playgoing and tried to suppress it whenever and wherever it appeared. Playgoing was exciting not only because it was new but because it was dangerous. The hostility of so many authorities to plays meant that they were seen almost automatically as subversive of authority. Paradoxically, the first London companies were only able to establish themselves in London through the active support of Queen Elizabeth and her Privy Council, which tried hard, in the face of constant complaints from the Lord Mayor, to ensure that the best companies would be on hand every Christmas to entertain the Queen's leisure hours. Popular support for playgoing depended on royal protection for the leading companies.

London was by far the largest city in England. Within a few years of Shakespeare's death, it became the largest in Europe. It was generally an orderly place to live, especially in the city itself. Even in the suburbs, where the poorer people had to live, there were not many of the riots and other disorders that preachers always associated with the brothels, animal-baiting arenas, and playhouses clustering there. The reputation that the playhouses gained for promoting riots was not well justified. Any crowd of people was seen by the authorities as a potential riot, and playhouses regularly drew some of the largest crowds that London had yet seen. The city's government was not designed to control large crowds of people. There was no paid police force, and the Lord Mayor was held responsible by the Privy Council, the Queen's governing committee, for any disorders that did occur. So the city authorities found that playgoing challenged their control over their people.

The rapid growth of London did not help the situation. Officially, the city was governed by the Lord Mayor and his council. But he had authority only inside the city, and London now spread through a large suburban area in the adjacent counties of Middlesex to the north and Surrey across the river to the south. Because the court and the national government were housed in London, the Privy Council often intervened in city affairs in its own interests, as well as when orders were needed that covered broader zones than the city itself. The periodic outbreaks of bubonic plague were one clear instance of such a need, because the plague took no notice of parish or city boundaries. The intrusion of the professional companies to play in London provided another. In the early years, they were chronic travelers, and London was simply one of many stopovers. But the Queen enjoyed seeing plays at Christmas, and her council accordingly supported the best companies so that they could perform for her. It protected the playing companies against the hatred of successive Lord Mayors, except when a national emergency such as a plague epidemic erupted. The Privy Council took control then by ordering the 126 parishes in and around London to list all deaths from plague separately from ordinary deaths. Each Thursday, the parish totals were added together. When the total number of deaths from plague in these lists rose above 30 in any one week, the Privy Council closed all places of public assembly. This meant especially the playhouses, which created by far the largest gatherings. When the theaters were closed, the playing companies had to revert to their traditional practice of going on tour to play in the towns through the country, provided that the news of plague did not precede them.

Plague was not the only reason for the government to lay its controlling hand on the companies. From the time the post was inaugurated in 1578, the Master of the Revels controlled all playing. He was executive officer to the Lord Chamberlain, the Privy Council officer responsible for the annual season of royal entertainment and thus, by extension, for the professional playing companies. The Master of the Revels licensed each company and censored its plays. He was expected to cut out any references to religion or affairs of state, and he tried to prevent other offenses by banning the depiction of any living person onstage. After 1594, he issued licenses to the approved London playhouses, too. Later still, the printing of any playbook was allowed only if he gave authority for it. The companies had to accept this tight control because the government was its only protector against the hostile municipal authorities, who included not only the Lord Mayor of London but also the mayors of most of the major towns in the country.

Most mayors had the commercial interest of keeping local employees at work to justify their hostility to playgoing. But across the country, the hostility went much deeper. A large proportion of the population disliked the very idea of playacting. Their reasons, ostensibly religious, were that for actors to pretend to be characters they were unlike in life was a deception and that for boys to dress as women was contrary to what the Bible said. Somewhere beneath this was a more basic fear of pretense and deceit, of people not acting honestly. It put actors into the same category as con men, cheats, and thieves. That was probably one reason why companies of boys acting men's parts were thought rather more tolerable than men pretending to be other kinds of men. The deception involved in boys playing men was more transparent than when men played characters other than themselves. There was also a strong Puritan suspicion about shows of any kind, which looked too much like the Catholic ceremonial that the new Church of England had renounced. Playgoing found much better favor on the Catholic side of English society than on the Puritan side. Different preachers took different positions over the new phenomenon of playgoing. But few would speak in its favor, and most of them openly disapproved of it. Playgoing was an idle pastime, and the devil finds work for idle hands.

In the 1590s, when *Romeo and Juliet* and Shakespeare's histories and early comedies were exciting audiences, only two playhouses and two companies were officially approved by the Queen's Privy Council for the entertainment of London's citizens. The other main forms of paid entertainment were bear- and bullbaiting, which were much harder on the performers than was playing and so could be staged less frequently. The hostility to plays meant that the right to perform was confined to only a few of the most outstanding companies. These few companies were in competition with one another, and this led to a rapid growth in the quality of their offerings. But playacting was always a marginal activity. Paying to enter a specially built theater in order to see professional companies perform plays was still a new phenomenon, and it still met with great opposition from the London authorities. The open-air theaters like the Globe were built out in the suburbs. London as a city had no centrally located playhouses until after the civil war and the restoration of the monarchy, in 1661. And even playing in the city's suburbs, where they were free from the Lord Mayor's control, the companies had to work under the control of the Privy Council. All the great amphitheaters were built either in Middlesex or in Surrey. At the height of their success, in the years after Shakespeare's death, the Privy Council never licensed more than four or five playhouses in London.

Playgoing in London was viewed even by the playgoers as an idle occupation. The largest numbers who went to the Globe were apprentices and artisans taking time off from work, often surreptitiously, and law students from the Inns of Court doing the same. These fugitives were linked with the wealthier kind of idler, "gallants" or rich gentlemen and other men of property, along with soldiers and sailors on leave from the wars, people visiting London from the country on business or pleasure (usually both), and above all the women of London. Women were not expected to be literate, but one did not need to be able to read and write to enjoy hearing and seeing a play. A respectable woman had to make sure she was escorted by a man. He might be a husband or a friend, or her page if she was rich, or her husband's apprentice if she was a middle-class citizen. She might have a mask on, part of standard women's wear outdoors to protect the face against the weather and to assert modesty—and perhaps anonymity. Market women (applewives and fishwives) went to plays in groups. Whores were expected to be there looking for business, especially from the gallants, but they usually had male escorts, too.

The social range of playgoers at the two playhouses approved for use in 1594 was almost complete, stretching from the aristocracy to the poorest workmen and boys. Many people disapproved of plays, but at peak times up to 25,000 a week flocked to see the variety of plays being offered. Prices for playgoing remained much the same throughout the decades up to 1642, when the parliamentary government that was fighting the King closed all the theaters for eighteen years. Until then, one could get standing room at an amphitheater for 1 penny (¹⁄₂₄₀th of a modern pound, roughly 1 cent),

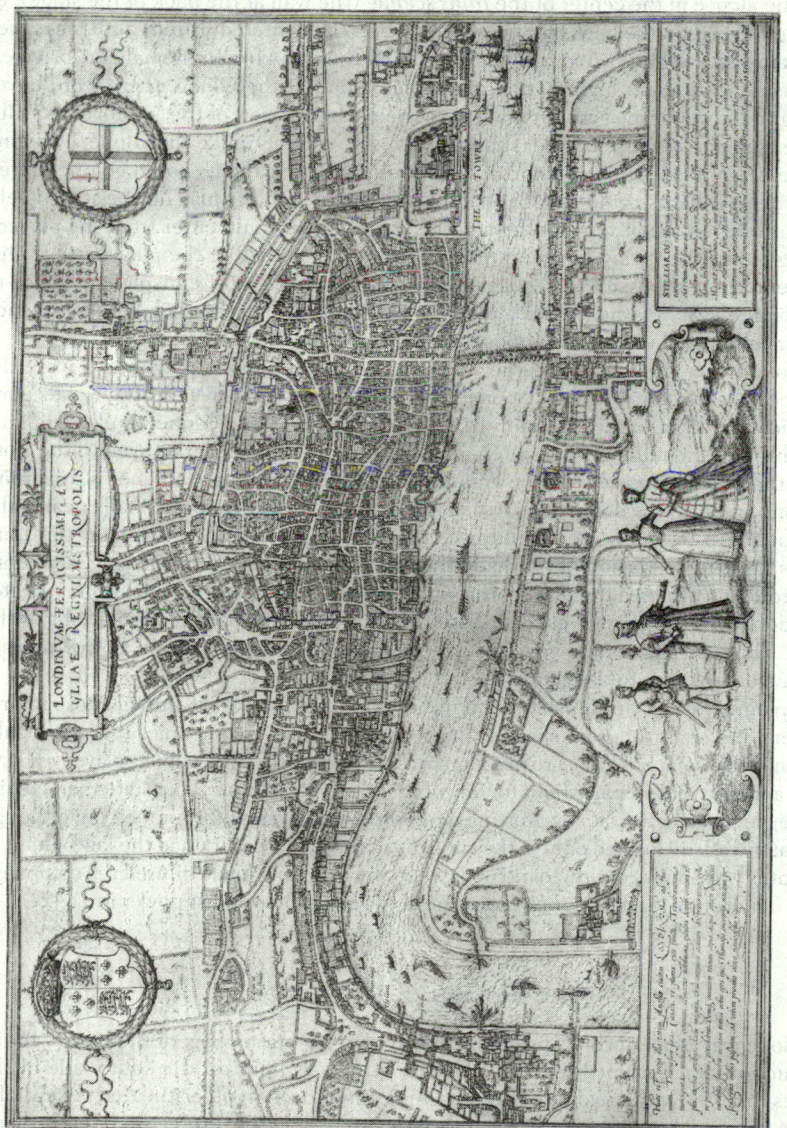

The city of London and its suburbs in 1572.

or a seat on a bench in the roofed galleries for twopence. A seat in a lord's room cost sixpence, which was not much less than a day's wage for a skilled artisan in 1600. The smaller roofed theaters that opened in 1599 were much more expensive. They were called "private" theaters to distinguish them from the "public" open-air amphitheaters, although the claim to privacy was mainly a convenient fiction to escape the controls imposed on the "public" theaters. At the Blackfriars hall theater, sixpence only gained you a seat in the topmost gallery, while a seat in the pit near the stage cost three times that amount and a seat in a box five times, or half a skilled worker's weekly wage.

It was not only the plays and players that were the sights at the playhouses. The richest lords and gallants went to be seen as much as they went to see. At the Globe, the costliest rooms were positioned alongside the balcony "above," over the stage. They were called "lords' rooms," and the playgoers who chose to sit there had a limited view of what went on beneath them. They saw no "discoveries," for instance, such as Portia's three caskets in *The Merchant of Venice,* which were uncovered underneath them inside the alcove in the center of the *frons scenae* (the wall at the back of the stage), or anything other than the backs of the players when they entered. But as audience, they were themselves highly visible, and that was what they paid for. In the hall, or "private," playhouses, with much higher admission prices than at the Globe, there were boxes flanking the stage for the gentry, which gave them a better view of the "discoveries." But at these "select" (because costlier) hall playhouses, where, unlike the Globe, everyone had a seat, some of the most colorful and exhibitionistic gallants could go one better. Up to fifteen gallants could pay for a stool to sit and watch the play on the stage itself, sitting in front of the boxes that flanked the stage. Each would enter from the players' dressing room (the "tiring-house") with his stool in hand before the play started. This gave them the best possible view of the play and easily the most conspicuous place in the audience's eye. Playgoing was a public occasion in which the visibility of audience members allowed them to play almost as large a part as the players.

Through the 1590s, the only permanent and custom-made playhouses were the large open-air theaters. Paying sixpence for a ferry across the river, as the richer playgoers did, or walking across London Bridge to the Rose or the Globe, or else trudging north through the mud of Shoreditch and Finsbury Fields or Clerkenwell to the Theatre or the Fortune in order to see a play, did not have great appeal when it was raining. Consequently, the companies were always trying to secure roofed halls nearer the city center. Up to 1594, they could use city inns, especially in winter, but the Lord Mayor's hostility to playing never made them reliable places for performing. Two constant problems troubled the players throughout these first years of professional theater in London: the city officials' chronic hatred of plays and the periodic visitations of the plague, which always led the government to close the theaters as soon as the number of plague deaths rose to dangerously high levels.

Playgoing was not firmly established in London until the Privy Council chose to protect it in 1594 and to approve specific playhouses for the two companies that it officially sanctioned. By then, Shakespeare had already made his mark. He became a player, a shareholder, and the resident playwright for one of these two companies. That status gained him a privileged place in the rapidly growing new world of playgoing. From then on, although his theater was still located only in the suburbs of the city, his work had the law behind it. That status was amply confirmed in 1603, when the new King made himself the company's patron. The King's Men held their status until the King himself lost power in 1642.

The Design of the Globe

The Globe was Shakespeare's principal playhouse. He put up part of the money for its construction and designed his best plays for it. It was built on the south side of the Thames in 1599, fashioned out of the framing timbers of an older theater. Essentially, it was a polygonal scaffold of twenty bays or sections, nearly 100 feet in outside diameter, making a circle of three levels of galleries that rose to more than 30 feet high, with wooden bench seating and cushions for those who could afford them. This surrounded an open "yard," into which the stage projected.

The yard was over 70 feet in diameter. Nearly half the audience stood on their feet to watch the play from inside this yard, closest to the stage platform. The stage extended out nearly to the middle of the yard, so the actors could stand in the center of the crowd. The uncertain privilege of having standing room in the open air around the stage platform could be bought with the minimal price for admission, 1 penny (about a cent). It had the advantage of proximity to the stage and the players; its disadvantage was keeping you on your feet for the two or three hours of the play, as well as leaving you subject to the weather. If you wanted a seat, or if it rained and you wanted shelter, you paid twice as much to sit in the three ranks of roofed galleries that circled behind the crowd standing in the yard. With some squeezing, the theater could hold over 3,000 people. It was an open-air theater because that gave it a larger capacity than a roofed hall. The drawback of its being open to the weather was more than outweighed by the gain in daylight that shone on stage and spectators alike.

The stage was a great square platform as much as 40 feet wide. It had over it a canopied roof, or "heavens," to protect the players and their expensive costumes from rain. This canopy was held up by two pillars rising through the stage. The stage platform was about 5 feet high and without any protective rails, so that the eyes of the audience in the yard were at the level of the players' feet. At the back of the stage, a wall—the *frons scenae*—stretched across the front of the players' tiring-house, the attiring or dressing room. It had a door on each flank and a wider curtained space in the center, which was used for major entrances and occasionally for set-piece scenes. Above these entry doors was a gallery or balcony, most of which was partitioned into rooms for the wealthiest spectators. A central room "above" was sometimes used in staging: for example, as Juliet's balcony, as the place for Richard III to stand between the bish-

The second Globe, from Wenceslaus Hollar's engraving of the "Long View" of London (1647). The two captions saying "The Globe" and "Beere bayting h." were accidentally transposed in the original. The Globe is the round structure in the center of the picture.

A photograph of the interior framework of the "new" Globe, on the south bank of the Thames in London, showing the general dimensions of the yard and the surrounding galleries.

ops, as the wall of Flint Castle in *Richard II,* and as the wall over the city gates of Harfleur in *Henry V.* After 1608, when Shakespeare's company acquired the Blackfriars consort of musicians, this central gallery room was turned into a curtained-off music room that could double as an "above" when required. Fewer than half of Shakespeare's plays need an "above."

The Original Staging Techniques

Shakespearean staging was emblematic. The "heavens" that covered the stage was the colorful feature from which gods descended to the earth of the stage platform. When Jupiter made his appearance in *Cymbeline,* in clouds of "sulphurous breath" provided by fireworks, he was mounted on an eagle being lowered through a trapdoor in the heavens. The other trapdoor, set in the stage platform itself, symbolized the opposite, a gateway to hell. The large stage trap was the place where the Gravedigger came to work at the beginning of Act 5 of *Hamlet.* It was the cell where Malvolio was imprisoned in *Twelfth Night.* The Shakespearean mindset accepted such conventions automatically.

Shakespeare inherited from Marlowe a tradition of using the stage trap as the dreaded hell's mouth. Barabbas plunges into it in *The Jew of Malta,* and the demons drag the screaming Faustus down it at the end of *Dr. Faustus.* Hell was not a fiction taken lightly by Elizabethans. Edward Alleyn, by far the most famous player of Faustus in the 1590s, wore a cross on his breast while he played the part, as insurance—just in case the fiction turned serious. Tracking the Elizabethan mindset about the stage trapdoor can give us a few warnings of what we might overlook when we come fresh to the plays today.

In the original staging of *Hamlet* at the Globe, the stage trap had two functions. Besides serving as Ophelia's grave, it was the distinctive entry point, not used by any other character, for the Ghost in Act 1. When he tells his son that he is "for the day confined to fast in fires," the first audiences would have already taken the point that he

The Globe as reconstructed in Southwark near the original site in London.

had come up from the underworld. His voice comes from under the stage, telling the soldiers to swear the oath of secrecy that Hamlet lays upon them. The connection between that original entry by the Ghost through the trap and the trap's later use for Ophelia is one we might easily miss. At the start of Act 5, the macabre discussion between the Gravediggers about whether she committed suicide and is, therefore, con-

The *frons scenae* of the new Globe.

A gesture using the language of hats, as shown by the man attending the brothers Browne.

signed to hell gets its sharpest edge from the association of the trap, here the grave being dug for her, with the Ghost's purgatorial fires. More to the point, though, Hamlet, as he eavesdrops on the curtailed burial ceremony, makes the same connection when he discovers that it is the body of Ophelia being so neglectfully interred. He remembers the other apparition that came up through the trap and springs forward in a grotesque parody of the Ghost, crying, "This is I, Hamlet the Dane!" It is a melodramatic claim to be acting a new role, that of his father the dead King. The first audiences would have remembered the ghost of dead King Hamlet using the stage trap at this point more readily than we do now. Hamlet's private knowledge of the Ghost and the trapdoor sets him, as so often happens in the play, at odds with his audience. Consequently, centuries of editors, like the characters onstage, have misread this claim as a declaration that young Hamlet ought to be King.

Since his own name is Hamlet, and since he alone could have made the connection between the Ghost and the trapdoor, he was all too likely to be misunderstood. In the next scene, Osric certainly shows that he understands Hamlet's graveside claim that he is his father's ghost to be a claim that he should now be King of Denmark. That explains why Osric insists on keeping his hat in his hand when he comes to invite Hamlet to duel with Laertes. With equals, an Elizabethan gentleman would doff his hat in greeting and then put it back on. Only in the presence of your master, or as a courtier in the presence of the King, did you keep it in your hand. Osric is trying tactfully to acknowledge what he thinks is Hamlet's lunatic claim to be King. He missed the private connection that Hamlet had made with the trapdoor and his father's ghost. Tudor body language, with its wordless gestures and signals that defined human relations, was an aspect of social life so widely understood that it needed no stage direction. The language of hats was a part of the Shakespearean mindset that we now have to register in footnotes.

Other signifiers are necessarily more elusive. We might take heart from the range of the comments made in *Much Ado About Nothing* 4.1 when Hero is accused and is seen to go red. Each of the viewers—Claudio, Leonato, and Friar Francis—gives a different reading (or "noting") of her blush. Different mindsets lead to visual indicators being read in different ways. Each reading tells as much about the observer as about the thing observed. We might add that since the blush is commented on so extensively, Shakespeare must have been concerned to save the boy playing Hero from the necessity of holding his breath long enough to produce the right visual effect.

Costume was a vital element in the plays, a mute and instant signifier of the scene. If a character entered carrying a candle and dressed in a gown with a nightcap on his head, he had evidently just been roused from bed. Characters who entered wearing cloaks and riding boots and possibly holding a whip had just ended a long journey. York,

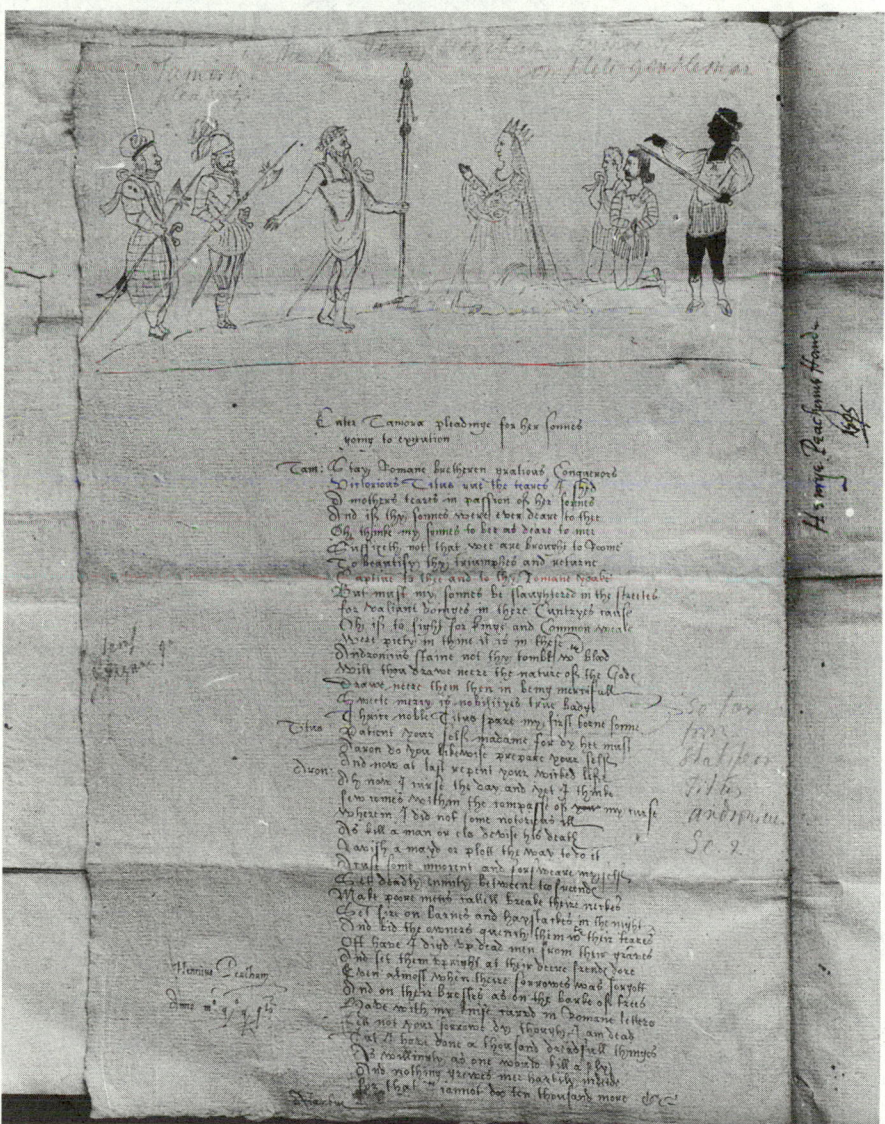

A sketch by Henry Peacham of an early staging of *Titus Andronicus* by Shakespeare's company (1595). Note the attempt at a Roman costume for Titus but not for his soldiers, who carry Tudor halberds, and note Aaron's makeup and wig.

entering in *Richard II* with a gorget (a metal neck plate, the "signs of war about his agèd neck" [2.2.74]), was preparing for battle. Even the women's wigs that the boys wore could be used to indicate the wearer's state of mind. Hair worn loose and unbound meant madness, whether in *Hamlet*'s Ophelia or *Troilus*'s Cassandra.

Comparable audience expectations could be roused by other visual features. Characters with faces blackened and wigs of curly black wool were recognized as Moors,

Johannes de Witt's drawing of the Swan Theatre in 1596, showing two boys playing women greeted by a chamberlain.

alien and dangerous non-Christians. Aaron the Moor in *Titus Andronicus* and the Prince of Morocco in *The Merchant of Venice* acquire that character as soon as they come in view. Othello, by Iago's report and by his own first appearance, takes on the same stereotype. By contrast, Iago is dressed like a simple and honest soldier. Only in the course of Act 1 does it become apparent that it is Othello who is the honest soldier, Iago the un-Christian alien. The play neatly reverses the visual stereotypes of Elizabethan staging. Twentieth-century playgoers miss most of these signals and the ways that the original players used them to show the discrepancy between outward appearance and inner person. As King Lear said, robes and furred gowns hide all.

For *The Merchant of Venice,* Shylock wore his "Jewish gabardine" and may also have put on a false nose, as Alleyn was said to have done for the title role in *The Jew of Malta.* Other national characteristics were noted by features of dress, such as the Irish "strait strossers" (tight trousers) that Macmorris would have worn in *Henry V.* The dress of the women in the plays, who were usually played by boys with unbroken voices, was always a special expense. The records kept by Philip Henslowe, owner of the Rose playhouse and impresario for the rival company to Shakespeare's, show that he paid the author less for the script of *A Woman Killed with Kindness* than he paid the costumer for the heroine's gown.

Women's clothing and the decorums and signals that women's costume contained were very different from those of men and men's clothing. Men frequently used their hats, doffing them to signal friendship and holding them in their hands while speaking to anyone in authority over them. Women's hats were fixed to their heads and were rarely if ever taken off in public. The forms and the language of women's clothes reflected the silent modesty and the quiet voices that men thought proper for women. Women had other devices to signal with, including handkerchiefs, fans, and face masks, and the boys playing the women's parts in the theaters exploited such accessories to the full. A lady out of doors commonly wore a mask to protect her complexion. When Othello is quizzing Emilia in 4.2 about his wife's behavior while she spoke to Cassio, he asks Emilia, who should have been chaperoning her mistress, whether Desdemona had not sent her away "to fetch her fan, her gloves, her mask, nor nothing?" There is little doubt that the boys would have routinely worn masks when they played gentlewomen onstage, and not just at the masked balls in *Romeo and Juliet, Love's Labour's Lost,* and *Much Ado About Nothing.*

Other features of the original staging stemmed from the actor–audience relationship, which differs radically in daylight, when both parties can see one another, from what we are used to in modern, darkened, theaters. An eavesdropping scene onstage, for instance, works rather on the same basis as the "invisible" fairies in *A Midsummer Night's Dream,* where the audience agrees to share the pretense. At the Globe, it also entailed adopting the eavesdropper's perspective. In *Much Ado,* the two games of eavesdropping played on Benedick and Beatrice are chiefly done around the two stage posts. In these scenes, the posts that held up the stage cover, or "heavens," near what we now think of as the front of the stage were round, like the whole auditorium, and their function was to allow things to be seen equally by all of the audience, wherever people might be standing or sitting. Members of the audience, sitting in the surrounding galleries or standing around the stage itself at the Globe or its predecessors, had the two tall painted pillars in their sight all the time, wherever they were in the playhouse. And since the audience was in a complete circle all around the stage, if the stage posts were used for concealment there was always a large proportion of the audience who could see the player trying to hide behind a post. It was a three-dimensional game in which the audience might find itself behind any of the game players, victims or eavesdroppers, complicit in either role.

The first of *Much Ado's* eavesdropping scenes, 2.3, starts as usual in Shakespeare with a verbal indication of the locality. Benedick tells his boy, "Bring it hither to me in the orchard." So we don't need stage trees to tell us where we are supposed to be. He later hides "in the arbour" to listen to what Don Pedro and the others have set for him; this means concealing himself behind a stage post, closer to the audience than the playactors who are talking about him. Don Pedro asks, "See you where Benedick hath hid himself?" a self-contradiction that confirms the game. When it is Beatrice's turn in her arbor scene, 3.1, she slips into a "bower" behind "this alley," which again signals a retreat behind the prominent stage post. These games are played with both of the eavesdroppers hiding behind the post at the stage edge, while the others do their talking at center stage between the two posts.

Such games of eavesdropping, using the same bits of the stage structure, make a strong visual contrast with all that goes on at what we two-dimensional thinkers, used to the pictorial staging of the cinema, call the "back" of the stage, or upstage—where, for instance, the Friar starts the broken-off wedding and where Claudio and Don Pedro later figure at Leonato's monument. These events are more distant from the audience, less obviously comic and intimate. The close proximity of players to audience in such activities as eavesdropping strongly influenced the audience's feeling of kinship with the different groupings of players.

A multitude of other staging differences can be identified. Quite apart from the fact that the language idioms were more familiar to the playgoers at the original Globe than they are now, all playgoers in 1600, many of them illiterate, were practiced listeners. The speed of speech, even in blank verse, was markedly higher then than the recitation of Shakespeare is today. The original performances of *Hamlet,* if the Folio version reflects what was usually acted, would have run for not much more than two and a half hours (the time quoted by Ben Jonson for a play as long as *Hamlet*), compared with the more than four hours that the full Folio or 1605 quarto text with at least one intermission would take today. Quicker speaking, quicker stage action, no intermissions, and the audience's ability to grasp the language more quickly meant that the plays galloped along. The story, not the verse, carried the thrust of the action. Occasional set speeches, like Hamlet's soliloquies or Gaunt's "sceptred isle" speech in *Richard II,* would be heard, familiar as they already were to many in the audience, like a solo aria in a modern opera. In theory if not in practice, the business of hearing, as "audience" (from the Latin *audire,* "to hear"), was more important than the business of seeing, as "spectators" (from the Latin *spectare,* "to see"). The visual aspects of acting, like scenic staging, are inherently two-dimensional and do not work well when the audience completely surrounds the actors. Most of Shakespeare's fellow writers, notably Jonson, understandably set a higher priority on the audience's hearing their verse than on their seeing what the players did with the lines. The poets wanted listeners, although the players did try to cater to the viewers. Yet for all the games with magic tricks and devils spouting fireworks that were part of the Shakespearean staging tradition, spectacle was a limited resource on the scene-free Elizabethan stage. Shakespeare in this was a poet more than a player. Even in his last and most richly staged plays—*Cymbeline, The Winter's Tale,* and *The Tempest*—he made notably less use of such "spectacles" than did his contemporaries.

One piece of internal evidence about the original staging is Hamlet's advice to the visiting players. In 3.2, before they stage the *Mousetrap* play that he has rewritten for them, he lectures them on what a noble student of the theater then considered to be good acting. He objects first to overacting and second to the clown who ad libs with his own jokes and does not keep to the script. How far this may have been Shakespeare's own view it is impossible to say. Hamlet is an amateur lecturing professionals about how they should do their job. His views are what we would expect an amateur playwright with a liking for plays that are "caviar to the general" to hold. His objections to the clown are noteworthy, because once the original performances ended, the clown would conclude the afternoon's entertainment with a comic song-and-dance jig. Thomas Platter, a young German-speaking Swiss student, went to the Globe in 1599 to see *Julius Caesar.* He reported back home that

> on 21 September after lunch I and my party crossed the river, and there in the playhouse with the thatched roof witnessed an excellent performance of the tragedy of the first emperor Julius Caesar with a cast of about fifteen people. When the play

The hall screen in the Middle Temple Hall, built in 1574. Shakespeare's company staged *Twelfth Night* in this hall in February 1602.

was over they danced marvellously and gracefully together as their custom is, two dressed as men and two as women.[1]

The script for one jig survives, probably played by Will Kemp, who was the Shakespeare company clown until he left just before *Hamlet* came to the Globe. Its story is a bawdy knockabout tale of different men trying to seduce a shopkeeper's wife in rhyming couplets, hiding in a chest from her husband, and beating one another up. There is nothing to say what the audience reaction to such a jig might have been after they had seen a performance of *Julius Caesar* or *Hamlet*. It is possible that the Globe players stopped offering that kind of coda when they acquired the clown who played Feste in *Twelfth Night* in 1601. The song with which Feste ends that play might have become an alternative form of closure, replacing the traditional bawdy jig.

Vigorous and rapid staging was inevitable when the half of the audience closest to the stage had to stand throughout the performance. Shakespeare's plays were distinctive among the other plays of the time for their reliance on verbal sparkle over scenes of battle and physical movement, but even the soliloquies raced along. There was little occasion for long pauses and emoting. Dumb shows, like the players' prelude to the *Mousetrap* play in *Hamlet*, were the nearest that the players came to silent acting. There were no intermissions—apples, nuts, and drink were peddled in the auditorium throughout the performance—and the only "comfort stations" were, for the men, the nearest blank wall; for the women, whatever convenient pots or bottles they might be carrying under their long skirts.

Nor were there any pauses to change scenes. There was no static scenery apart from an emblematic candle to signify a night scene, a bed "thrust out" onto the stage, or the canopied chair of state on which the ruler or judge sat for court scenes. Usually any

1. *Thomas Platter's Travels in England* (1599), rendered into English from the German, and with introductory matter by Clare Williams (London: Cape, 1937), p. 166.

special locality would be signaled in the first words of a new scene, but unlocalized scenes were routine. Each scene ended when all the characters left the stage and another set entered. No act breaks appear in the plays before *The Tempest*. *Henry V* marked each act with a Chorus, but even he entered on the heels of the characters from the previous scene. Blue-coated stagehands were a visibly invisible presence onstage. They would draw back the central hangings on the *frons scenae* for a discovery scene, carry on the chair of state on its dais for courtroom scenes, or push out the bed with Desdemona on it for the last act of *Othello*. They served the stage like the house servants with whom the nobility peopled every room in their great houses, silent machines ready to spring into action when needed.

There has been a great deal of speculation about the tiring-house front at the rear of the stage platform: did it look more like an indoor set or an outdoor one, like the hall screen of a great house or palace or like a housefront exterior? In fact, it could easily be either. The upper level of the *frons*, the balconied "above," might equally represent a musicians' gallery, like those in the main hall of a great house, or a city wall under which the central discovery space served as the city gates, as it did for York in *Richard Duke of York* (*3 Henry VI*) 4.8, or *Henry V*'s Harfleur (3.3.78). The "above" could equally be an indoor gallery or an outdoor balcony. The appearance of the stage was everything and nothing, depending on what the play required. Players and playwrights expected the audience members to use their imagination, as they had to with the opening lines of *Hamlet*, or, as the Prologue to *Henry V* put it, to "piece out our imperfections with your thoughts."

Shakespeare's Companies and Their Playhouses

Shakespeare's plays were written for a variety of staging conditions. Until 1594, when he joined a new company under the patronage of the Lord Chamberlain, the Queen's officer responsible for licensing playing companies, poets had written their plays for any kind of playhouse. The Queen's Men, the largest and best company of the 1580s, is on record as playing at the Bell, the Bel Savage, and the Bull inns inside the city, and at the Theatre and the Curtain playhouses in the suburbs. Early in 1594, it completed this sweep of all the available London venues by playing at the Rose. But in that year, the system of playing changed. The Lord Mayor had always objected to players using the city's inns, and in May 1594 he succeeded in securing the Lord Chamberlain's agreement to a total ban. From then on, only the specially built playhouses in the suburbs were available for plays.

The Queen's Men had been set up in 1583, drawn from all the then-existing major companies with the best players. This larger and favored group at first monopolized playing in London. But it was in decline by the early 1590s, and the shortage of companies to perform for the Queen at Christmas led the Lord Chamberlain and his son-in-law, the Lord Admiral, to set up two new companies in its place as a duopoly in May 1594. Shakespeare became a "sharer," or partner, in one of these companies. As part of the same new establishment, his company, the Lord Chamberlain's Men, was allocated the Theatre to perform in, while its partner company in the duopoly, the Lord Admiral's Men, was assigned to the Rose. This was the first time any playing company secured a playhouse officially authorized for its use alone.

The Theatre, originally built in 1576 by James Burbage, father of the leading player of the Lord Chamberlain's company, was in Shoreditch, a suburb to the north of the city. The Rose, built in 1587 by Philip Henslowe, father-in-law of the Lord Admiral's leading player, Edward Alleyn, was in the suburb of Southwark, on the south bank of the Thames. Henslowe's business papers, his accounts, some lists of costumes and other resources, and his "diary," a day-by-day listing of each day's takings and the plays that brought the money in, have survived for the period from 1592 until well into the next decade. Together they provide an invaluable record of how one of the two major companies of the later 1590s, the only rival to Shakespeare's company, operated through these years.[2] Some of Shakespeare's earlier plays, written before he joined the Lord Chamberlain's Men, including *1 Henry VI* and *Titus Andronicus*, were performed at the Rose. After May 1594, the new company acquired all of his early plays; every Shakespeare play through the next three years was written for the Theatre. Its familiarity supplied one sort of resource to the playwright. But the repertory system laid heavy demands on the company.

Henslowe's papers give a remarkable record of the company repertory for these years. Each afternoon, the same team of fifteen or so players would stage a different play. With only two companies operating in London, the demand was for constant change. No play at the Rose was staged more than four or five times in any month, and it was normal to stage a different play on each of the six afternoons of each week that they performed. A new play would be introduced roughly every three weeks—after three weeks of transcribing and learning the new parts; preparing the promptbook, costumes, and properties; and rehearsing in the mornings—while each afternoon, whichever of the established plays had been advertised around town on the playbills would be put on. The leading players had to memorize on average as many as eight hundred lines for each afternoon. Richard Burbage, who played the first Hamlet in 1601, probably had to play Richard III, Orlando in *As You Like It*, and Hamlet on successive afternoons while at the same time learning the part of Duke Orsino and rehearsing the new *Twelfth Night*—and still holding at least a dozen other parts in his head for the rest of the month's program. In the evenings, he might be called on to take the company to perform a different play at court or at a nobleman's house in the Strand. The best companies made a lot of money, but not without constant effort.

The companies were formed rather like guilds, controlled by their leading "sharers." Each senior player shared the company's profits and losses equally with his fellows. Most of the plays have seven or eight major speaking parts for the men, plus two for the boys playing the women. A normal London company had eight or ten sharers, who collectively chose the repertory of plays to be performed, bought the playbooks from the poets, and put up the money for the main company resource of playbooks and costumes (not to mention the wagon and horses for touring when plague forced the London theaters to close). Shakespeare made most of his fortune from his "share," first in his company and later in its two playhouses.

As a playhouse landlord, Henslowe took half of the takings from the galleries each afternoon for his rent, while the players shared all the yard takings and the other half of the gallery money. From their takings, the sharers paid hired hands to take the walk-on parts and to work as stagehands, musicians, bookkeeper or prompter, and "gatherers" at the different entry gates. The leading players also kept the boys who played the women's parts, housing and feeding them as "apprentices" in an imitation of the London livery companies and trades, which ran apprenticeships to train boys to become skilled artisans, or "journeymen." City apprenticeships ran for seven years from the age of seventeen, but the boy players began much younger, because unbroken voices were needed. They graduated to become adult players at an age when the city apprentices were only beginning their training. Most of the "extras," apart from the playing boys, would be left in London whenever the company had to go on tour.

Because the professional companies of the kind that Shakespeare joined all started as traveling groups rather than as companies settled at a single playhouse in London, the years up to 1594 yielded plays that could be staged anywhere. The company might be summoned to play at court, at private houses, or at the halls of the Inns of Court as readily as at inns or innyards or the custom-built theaters themselves. They traveled the country with their plays, using the great halls of country houses, or town guildhalls and local inns, wherever the town they visited allowed them. Consequently, the plays could not demand elaborate resources for staging. In this highly mobile tradition of traveling

---

2. See *Henslowe's Diary*, ed. R. A. Foakes (Cambridge, Eng.: Cambridge University Press, 1961).

companies, they were written in the expectation of the same basic but minimal features being available at each venue. Besides the stage platform itself, the basic features appear to have been two entry doors, usually a trap in the stage floor, a pair of stage pillars, sometimes a discovery space, and very occasionally a heavens with descent machinery. Apart from these fixtures, properties such as chairs and a table, a canopied throne on a dais, and sometimes a bed were also in regular use, though in a pinch these could be as mobile as the players themselves. The only essential traveling properties were players, playbooks, and costumes.

Once the two authorized companies settled permanently at the Theatre and the Rose in 1594, they slowly lost some of this mobility. The demands of versatility and readiness to make rapid changes now had to be switched from the venues to the plays themselves. A traveling company needed very few plays, since the locations and audiences were always changing. When the venues became fixed, it was the plays that had to keep changing. The Henslowe papers record that the Lord Admiral's Men staged an amazingly varied repertory of plays at the Rose. Shakespeare's company must have been equally versatile. The practice of giving popular plays long runs did not begin until the 1630s, by which time the number of London playhouses had grown to as many as five, all offering their plays each afternoon. Shakespeare's company in London had only the one peer from 1594 until 1600; and only two from then until 1608, aside from the once-weekly plays by the two boy companies, the "little eyases" mentioned in *Hamlet*, that started with the new century.

From May 1594 to April 1597 at the Theatre, in addition to all his earlier plays that he brought to his new company, Shakespeare gave them possibly *Romeo and Juliet* and *King John*, and certainly *Richard II, A Midsummer Night's Dream, 1 Henry IV*, and *The Merchant of Venice*. But then they ran into deep trouble, because they lost the Theatre. In April 1597, its original twenty-one-year lease expired, and the landlord, who disliked plays, refused to let them renew it. Anticipating this, the company's impresario, James Burbage, had built a new theater for them, a roofed place in the Blackfriars near St. Paul's Cathedral. The Blackfriars precinct was a "liberty," free from the Lord Mayor's jurisdiction. But the plan proved a disaster. The rich residents of Blackfriars objected, and the Privy Council stopped the theater from opening. From April 1597, Shakespeare's company had to rent the Curtain, an old neighbor of their now-silent Theatre, and it was there that the next four of Shakespeare's plays—*2 Henry IV, Much Ado About Nothing, The Merry Wives of Windsor*, and probably *Henry V*—were first staged.

In December 1598, losing hope of a new lease for the old Theatre, the Burbage sons had it pulled down and quietly transported its massive framing timbers across the Thames to make the scaffold for the Globe on the river's south bank, near the Rose. Most of their capital was sunk irretrievably into the Blackfriars theater, and they could afford only half the cost of rebuilding. So they raised money as best they could. Some of the company's more popular playbooks were sold to printers, including *Romeo and Juliet, Richard III, Richard II*, and *1 Henry IV*. More to the point, the Burbage brothers raised capital for the building by cutting in five of the leading players, including Shakespeare, and asking them to put up the other half of its cost. The Globe, its skeleton taken from the old Theatre, thus became the first playhouse to be owned by its players, and, within the limits set by the old frame, the first one built to their own design.

For this theater, one-eighth of which he personally owned, Shakespeare wrote his greatest plays: *Julius Caesar, As You Like It, Hamlet, Twelfth Night, Othello, All's Well That Ends Well, Measure for Measure, King Lear, Macbeth, Pericles, Antony and Cleopatra, Coriolanus, Cymbeline, The Winter's Tale*, and most likely *Troilus and Cressida* and *Timon of Athens*. As the first playhouse to be owned by the players who expected to use it, its fittings must have satisfied all the basic needs of Shakespearean staging. At one time or another, the company staged every one of Shakespeare's plays there.

In 1600, a company consisting entirely of boys started using the Blackfriars playhouse that Richard Burbage's father had tried to open four years before. Companies of boy players had a higher social status than the adult professionals, and, playing only in halls, they commanded a more affluent clientele. The boys performed only once a week, and the relative infrequency of their crowds, plus their skills as trained singers (they were choir-school children turned to making money for their choirmasters), proved less offensive to the local residents than a noisy adult company with its drums and trumpets. Leasing the Blackfriars to the boy company made a minor profit for the Burbages, who took the rent for eight years.

In the longer run, though, this arrangement provided a different means for the Burbage–Shakespeare company to advance its career. The boys' eight years of playing in their rented hall playhouse eventually made it possible for the company of adult players to renew Burbage's old plan of 1596. Shakespeare's company had been made the King's Men when James came to the throne in 1603, and their new patron gave them a status that made it impossible for the residents of Blackfriars to prevent them from implementing the original plan. During a lengthy closure of all the theaters because of a plague epidemic in 1608, the boys' manager surrendered his lease of the hall playhouse to the Burbages. They then took possession for their own company of the playhouse that their father had built for them twelve years before. They divided the new playhouse property among the leading players as they had done in 1599 with the Globe.

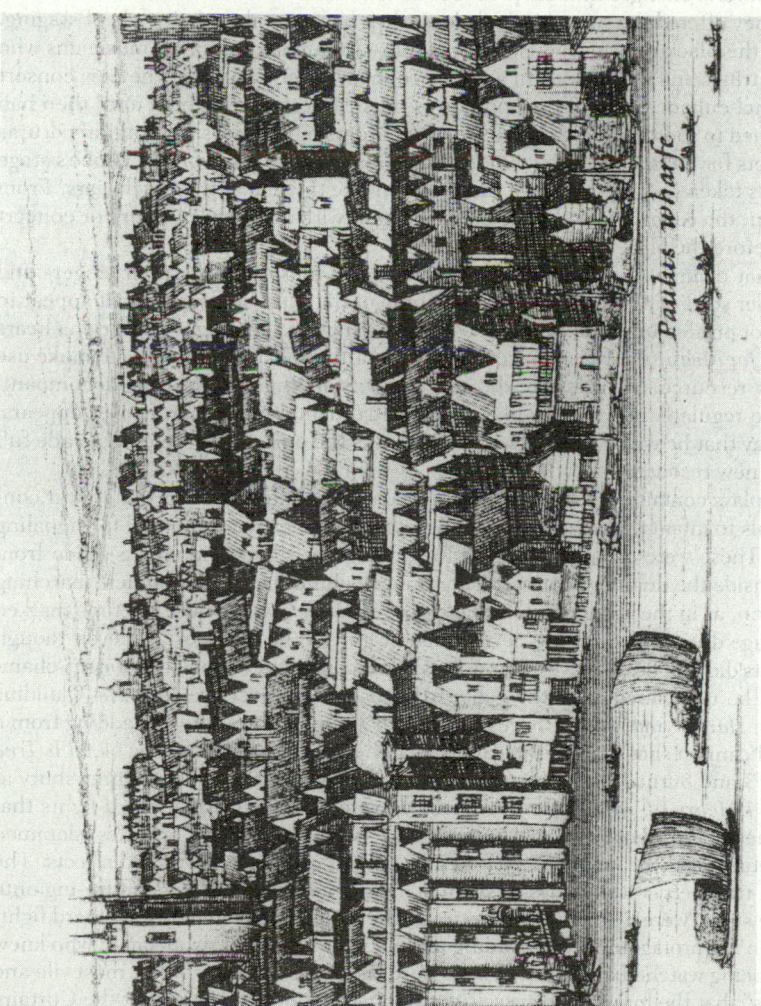

A section from Wenceslaus Hollar's "Long View" of London, printed in 1644. Drawn from a standpoint on the tower of the church that is now Southwark Cathedral, Hollar's view shows the roof of the great hall in which the Blackfriars playhouse was built. It can be seen as the long angled roof with two central chimneys, below and to the east of St. Bride's Church.

They were the King's Men, the leading company in the country, and their status after ten years of playing at the Globe was matched by their wealth. By the time theaters reopened late in 1609, the company had established a new system of playing.

The King's Men now had two playhouses, a large open amphitheater and a much smaller roofed hall. Instead of selling or renting one out and using the other for themselves, they decided to use both in turn, for half of each year. It was a reversion to the old system with the city inns, where through the summer they played in the large open yards and in the winter played at inns with big indoor rooms. This time, though, the company owned both playhouses. Their affluence and their high status are signaled by the fact that they chose to keep one of their playhouses idle while they used the other, despite there now being a shortage of playhouses in London. That affluence was needed in 1613, when the Globe burned down at a performance of *All Is True* (*Henry VIII*) and the company chose the much more expensive option of rebuilding it instead of reverting to the Blackfriars for both winter and summer. That decision, in its way, was the ultimate gesture of affection for their original playhouse. It was a costly gesture, but it meant that the Globe continued in use by the company until all the theaters were closed down by Parliament in 1642.

In 1609, when they reopened after the closure for plague, Shakespeare's company had made several changes in their procedures. The restart was at the Blackfriars, and although they offered the same kind of plays, they began to alter their style of staging. Along with the Blackfriars playhouse, they acquired a famous consort of musicians who played on strings and woodwinds in a music room set over the stage. The new consort was a distinct enhancement of the company's musical resources, which until then had been confined to song, the occasional use of recorders or hautboys, and military drums and trumpets for the scenes with soldiery. In 1608, a central room on the Globe's stage balcony was taken over to serve as a music room like the one at the Blackfriars. From this time on, the King's Men's performances began with a lengthy overture or concert of music before the play.

With that change, the plays themselves now had music to back their singers and provide other sorts of atmospheric effects. Some of the songs and music that appear in the plays not printed until the First Folio of 1623, such as the song that Mariana hears in *Measure for Measure* 4.1, may have been added after Shakespeare's time to make use of this new resource. Shakespeare did use songs, sometimes with string accompaniment, quite regularly in the early plays, but instrumental music hardly ever appears. The last play that he wrote alone, *The Tempest*, was the only one in which he made full use of this new resource.

All the plays containing soldiers and battles used the military drums that in war conveyed signals to infantry formations, as well as the trumpets that were used for signaling to cavalry. These were usually employed for offstage noises, sound effects made from "within" (inside the dressing room or tiring-house behind the stage). Soldiers marching in procession, as in the dead march at the close of *Hamlet*, would have the time marked by an onstage drum. Shakespeare never calls for guns to be fired onstage, even though other writers did, but he did have other noises at his command. A small cannon or "chamber" might be used, fired from the gable-fronted heavens over the stage, as Claudius demands in *Hamlet* and as the Chorus to Act 3 of *Henry V* notes. It was wadding from a ceremonial cannon shot that set the gallery thatch alight at a performance of *All Is True* in July 1613 and burned the Globe to the ground. Stage battles such as Shrewsbury at the end of *1 Henry IV*, written for the Theatre, were accompanied by sword fights that were not the duels of *Hamlet*'s finale but exchanges with broadswords or "foxes" slammed against metal shields or "targets." That action guaranteed emphatic sound effects. The drums and trumpets, with clashes of swords and a great deal of to-ing and fro-ing onto and off the stage, were highlighted in between the shouted dialogue by some hard fighting between the protagonists. The leading players were practiced swordsmen, who knew they were being watched by experts. These were the scenes of "four or five most vile and ragged foils" that the fourth Chorus self-consciously derided in *Henry V* at the Curtain.

The second great reason for noise in the amphitheaters was to mark storm and tempest. Stagehands used the kind of device that Jonson mocked in the Prologue to *Every Man in His Humour*, written for its 1616 publication. His play, wrote Jonson, was free from choruses that wafted you over the seas, "nor rolled bullet heard / To say, it thunders; nor tempestuous drum / Rumbles, to tell you when the storm doth come." For centuries, lead balls rolling down a tin trough were a standard way of making thunder noises in English theaters. The tempest in Act 3 of *King Lear* is heralded several times in the text before a stage direction, "Storm and tempest" (Folio 2.2.450), tells us that it has at last arrived. In 2.2, Cornwall notes its coming twice (Folio 2.2.452, 473). Kent comments on the "Foul weather" in his first line in Act 3, prefaced by the entry stage direction for Act 3, "Storm still," which is repeated for 3.2. Such stage directions appear in both texts (Q has "Storm" for the equivalent Scenes 8, 9, and also at 11, F's 3.4, where F omits any further reference to these noises). These explicit signals indicate that the stagehands provided offstage noises, for all that Lear himself outstorms them with his violent speeches in 3.2.

The main question about the storm scenes in *King Lear* is this: with such consistent emphasis on storm in the language, what was the design behind the stage directions? In the centuries that *Lear* has been restaged, the tempest has been made to roar offstage in a wide variety of ways, often with so much effect that, in the face of complaints that the storm noises made it difficult for the audience to hear the words, some modern productions reduced the storm to solely visual effects, or even left Lear's own raging language to express it unsupported. But the two stage directions indicate that in the original performances the "storm in nature" was not left to Lear himself to convey. The two "Storm still" directions in the Folio suggest a constant rumbling, not the intermittent crashes that might allow Lear to conduct a dialogue with the occasional outbursts of storm noises, as some modern productions have done.

Shakespeare left regrettably few stage directions to indicate the special tricks or properties that he wanted. Curtained beds are called for in *Othello* 5.2 and *Cymbeline* 2.2, and there is the specification "Stocks brought out" in *King Lear* 2.2.132. Small and portable things like papers were a much more common device, from the letters in *The Two Gentlemen of Verona* 1.2.46, 1.3.44, and 2.1.95 to Lear's map at 1.1.35. Across the whole thirty-eight plays, though, there are very few such directions. Shakespeare's economy in preparing his scripts is a major impediment to the modern reader. He hardly ever bothered to note the standard physical gestures, such as kneeling or doffing a hat, and did little more to specify any special effects. Nonetheless, it is important not to imagine elaborate devices or actions where the text does not call for them. On the whole, the demands Shakespeare made of his fellows for staging his plays appear to have been remarkably modest. Since he was a company shareholder, his parsimony may have had a simple commercial motive. Stage properties cost the company money, and one had to be confident of a new play's popularity before investing much in its staging.

There may have been other reasons for avoiding extravagant staging spectacles. Shakespeare made little use of the discovery space until the last plays, for instance, for reasons that we can only guess at. The few definite discoveries in the plays include Portia's caskets in *The Merchant of Venice*, Falstaff sleeping off his sack in *1 Henry IV* 2.5.482, the body of Polonius in *Hamlet*, Hermione's statue in *The Winter's Tale* 5.3.20, and the lovers in *The Tempest* 5.1.173, who are found when discovered to be playing chess. The audience's shock when Hermione moves and comes out of the discovery space onto the main stage is rare in Shakespeare: in every other play, whether comedy or tragedy, the audience knows far more than the characters onstage about what is going on. Shakespeare matched this late innovation in *The Winter's Tale* with his last play, *The Tempest*. After the preliminary and soothing concert by the resident Blackfriars musicians, it opens with a storm at sea so realistic that it includes that peculiarly distinctive stage direction "Enter Mariners, wet" (1.1.46). That startling piece of stage realism turns out straightaway to be not real at all but a piece of stage magic.

LATER PLAYS

Hamlet

"Who's there?" Shakespeare's most famous play begins. The question, turned back on the tragedy itself, has haunted actors, audiences and readers for centuries. *Hamlet* is an enigma. Mountains of feverish speculation have only deepened the interlocking mysteries: Why does Hamlet delay avenging the murder of his father by Claudius, his father's brother? How much guilt does Hamlet's mother, Gertrude, who has since married Claudius, bear in this crime? How trustworthy is the ghost of Hamlet's father, who has returned from the grave to demand that Hamlet avenge his murder? Is vengeance morally justifiable in this play, or is it to be condemned? What exactly *is* the ghost, and where has it come from? Why is the ghost, visible to everyone in the first act, visible only to Hamlet in Act 3? Is Hamlet's madness feigned or true, a strategy masquerading as a reality or a reality masquerading as a strategy? Does Hamlet, who once loved Ophelia, continue to love her in spite of his apparent cruelty? Does Ophelia, crushed by that cruelty and driven mad by Hamlet's murder of her father, Polonius, actually intend to drown herself, or does she die accidentally? What enables Hamlet to pass from thoughts of suicide to faith in God's providence, from "To be, or not to be" to "Let be"? What was Hamlet trying to say before death stopped his speech at the close?

Shakespeare probably wrote *Hamlet* in 1600 (shortly after *Julius Caesar,* to which Polonius seems to allude at 3.2.93), but the precise date of composition is uncertain, and this uncertainty is compounded by the exceptionally complex state of the text. *The Tragedie of Hamlet, Prince of Denmarke* is included in the First Folio of 1623, but most editions of the play since the eighteenth century have incorporated passages that appear only in an earlier text, the Second Quarto, dated 1604 and entitled *The Tragicall Historie of Hamlet, Prince of Denmarke.* In the present edition of the play, based on the Folio text, lines that appear only in the Second Quarto are indented and numbered separately, so that readers will be able to assess the difference between the two versions. (Further information on these texts and on the First or so-called Bad Quarto is given in the Textual Note.) *Hamlet* is a monument of world literature, but it is a monument built on shifting sands.

With a text so fraught with uncertainty, it is tempting to think that our unresolved questions are largely the result of the perplexities that must inevitably come with the passage of time and the vagaries of editors. Yet the play in all its versions seems designed to provoke such perplexities. "What art thou?" Horatio asks the Ghost, and the question, unanswered, is echoed again and again until it seems to touch on everything: "Is it not like the King?" (1.1.57); "Why seems it so particular with thee?" (1.2.75); "What does this mean, my lord?" (1.4.8); "Whither wilt thou lead me?" (1.5.1); "What's Hecuba to him, or he to Hecuba, / That he should weep for her?" (2.2.536–37); "Why wouldst thou be a breeder of sinners?" (3.1.122–23); "What should such fellows as I do crawling between heaven and earth?" (3.1.127–28); "Do you see nothing there?" (3.4.122); "What is it ye would see?" (5.2.306). The dream of getting answers to such questions tantalizes many of the play's characters and drives them to scrutinize one another. But the task is maddeningly difficult. When Hamlet repeatedly asks Guildenstern, one of the school friends whom his uncle has set to spy on him, to play the recorder, Guildenstern protests that he does not know how. "You would play upon me," Hamlet returns, "you would seem to know my stops, you would pluck out the heart of my mystery. . . . do you think I am easier to be played on than a pipe?" (3.2.335–40).

Hamlet at once invites and resists interrogation. He is, more than any theatrical

A man may not marrie his

- Mother. / Stepmother. / Wiues mother. — The right afcending line, and firft degree.

- Sonnes daughter. / Daughters daughter. / Wiues fonnes daughter. / Wiues daughters daughter. — The right defcēding line and fecond degree.

- Daughter. / Wiues daughter. / Sonnes wife. — The right defcending line and firft degree.

- Sifter. / Wiues fifter. / Brothers wife. — The equall collateral line, and firft degree.

- Fathers fifter. / Mothers fifter. / Fathers brothers wife. — The vnequall collaterall line, and fecond degree.

30 Therfore fhall ye keepe mine ordinances, that ye doe not any of the abhominable cuftomes, which haue been done before you.

Table of prohibited marriages. From William Clerke, *The Triall of Bastardie* (London, 1594).

character before and perhaps since, a figure constructed around an unseen or secret core. Such a figure in the theater is something of a paradox, since all that exists of any character onstage is what is seen and heard there. But from his place onstage at the center of a courtly world in which he is "the observed of all observers" and hence a person allowed virtually no privacy, Hamlet insists that he has "that within which passeth show" (1.2.85). What is it that he has "within"? In the nineteenth century, following a suggestion by the German poet Johann Wolfgang von Goethe, critics frequently argued that Hamlet has within him the soul of a poet, too sensitive, delicate, and complex to endure the cruel pressures of a coarse world. In the twentieth century, following a suggestion by the founder of psychoanalysis, Sigmund Freud, many critics have speculated that Hamlet has within him an unresolved Oedipus complex, a sexual desire for his mother that prevents him from taking decisive action against the man who has done in reality the thing that Hamlet unconsciously desires to do: kill his father and marry his mother. On occasion, this psychological speculation has been challenged by a political one: Hamlet hides within himself a spirit of political resistance, a subversive challenge to a corrupt, illegitimate regime shored up by lies, spies, and treachery.

These recurrent attempts to pluck out the heart of Hamlet's mystery are a modern continuation of an interpretive activity that goes on throughout the play itself. Attempting to solve the riddle of Hamlet's strange behavior, Polonius speculates that the Prince is desperately lovesick for his daughter, but Claudius concludes, after spying on Hamlet's conversation with Ophelia, that "his affections do not that way tend" (3.1.161). Rosencrantz and Guildenstern propose that Hamlet is suffering from ambition—after all, though Denmark is an elective monarchy, the Prince could have hoped to succeed his father on the throne—but Hamlet vehemently refutes the charge: "O God, I could be bounded in a nutshell and count myself a king of infinite space, were it not that I have bad dreams" (2.2.248–50). Claudius doubts that Hamlet is mad and, even though he never directly articulates this suspicion, seems to fear that the Prince somehow knows of his secret crime. But Hamlet's painful interiority, his melancholy insistence that he has something "within," is already clear from his first appearance, before the Ghost's revelation. Gertrude therefore seems wiser to argue that her son's distemper at least originates in "his father's death and our o'er-hasty marriage" (2.2.57).

As we first encounter him, Hamlet is a young man in deep mourning, which his mother and uncle both urge him to cease. The death of fathers is natural and inevitable, they point out, and while it is customary to grieve, it is unreasonable to persist obstinately in sorrow. Hamlet responds that his grief is not a theatrical performance, a mere costume to be put on and then discarded. When he is alone onstage a few moments later, he discloses, in the first of his famous soliloquies, a near-suicidal despair and a corrosive bitterness centered on the haste with which his mother has remarried. This bitterness is intensified by Hamlet's idealized image of his father and by painful memories of what had seemed to him his parents' perfect mutual love. As he broods on the brief time between his father's death and his mother's remarriage, Hamlet's mind convulsively shortens the interval: "two months," "nay, not so much, not two," "within a month."

At such moments—and there are many in the play—the audience seems to have direct access to the protagonist's tormented inner life. That life appears startlingly raw and unscripted, but the impression is actually the consequence of Shakespeare's sophisticated poetic skills. Hamlet's soliloquies are carefully crafted rhetorical performances. Thus, for example, the celebrated lines that begin "To be, or not to be; that is the question" (3.1.58ff.) have the structure of a formal academic debate on the subject of suicide: prudently considering both sides of the question and rehearsing venerable commonplaces, Hamlet does not once use the words "I" or "me." Yet here and elsewhere his words manage with astonishing vividness to convey the spontaneous rhythms of a mind in motion. Shakespeare had anticipated this achievement in such plays as *Richard II, 1 Henry IV,* and *Julius Caesar:* King Richard, Prince Hal, and Brutus all have intimate moments in which they seem to disclose the troubled faces that are normally hidden behind expressionless social masks. But in its moral complexity, psychological depth, and philosophical power, *Hamlet* seems to mark an epochal shift not only in Shakespeare's own career but in Western drama; it is as if the play were giving birth to a whole new kind of literary subjectivity. This subjectivity—the sense of being inside a character's psyche and following its twists and turns—is to a large degree an effect of language, the product of dramatic poetry and prose of unprecedented intensity. In order to convey a traumatized mind struggling to articulate perceptions of a shattered world, Shakespeare developed a complex syntax and a remarkably expanded diction. Take the moment, for example, in which Hamlet broods about the spectacle of Fortinbras's army marching off to fight to the death for a worthless piece of ground. Hamlet is struck by the absurd waste of lives and wealth, but then his agonized consciousness of his failure to act more quickly to avenge his father's death begins to transform his thinking. The strain in the syntax reflects the strain of a mind queasily in motion:

> Rightly to be great
> Is not to stir without great argument,
> But greatly to find quarrel in a straw
> When honour's at the stake.
> (4.4.9.43–9.46)

So, too, by one scholar's count, Shakespeare introduced over six hundred words in *Hamlet* that he had not used before. Many of these words—"self-slaughter," "unweeded," "fanged," "malefaction," "unpolluted," "compulsive," and so on—do not appear, at least in the form or with the meaning they have here, in any previous English text. The innovative inwardness is not restricted to scenes in which Hamlet is alone onstage, nor is it restricted to the Prince himself; indeed, many of the deepest psychic revelations in the play are conveyed not in moments of isolation but in disturbing exchanges, intimate encounters in which love and poison are intertwined.

These innovations are not called for by the story itself. In *Hamlet,* as in so many of his plays, Shakespeare was recycling narratives long in circulation. The legendary tale of Hamlet (Amleth) was already recounted at length in the late twelfth-century *Danish History* compiled in Latin by Saxo the Grammarian. (The tale was retold in French in François de Belleforest's 1570 collection *Histoires Tragiques*.) In Saxo's version, the unscrupulous Feng ambushes and kills his brother Horwendil and marries Horwendil's wife, Gerutha. Horwendil and Gerutha had a son, Amleth, who undertakes to avenge his father. In doing so, the son suffers no pangs of conscience, since in pre-Christian Denmark revenge was not a violation of the moral or religious law but a filial obligation. And he needs no ghost to inform him of what happened and

experiences no sickening uncertainty about his uncle's guilt, since the murder is public knowledge. Amleth's problem is survival: young and surrounded by Feng's hench-
men, his every move is carefully watched. In order to avert suspicion and buy time, the
cunning avenger pretends to be feebleminded. His strategy works: with the active
assistance of his mother, Amleth eventually succeeds in killing his uncle, along with
the uncle's followers, and is enthusiastically proclaimed King of Denmark.

This is the rough outline of the story that Shakespeare inherited, along, it seems,
with at least one other version about which we know tantalizingly little: by 1589, English audiences had evidently seen a play, now lost, on the theme of Hamlet. Apparently,
this play—which scholars call the Ur (original)-*Hamlet*—featured a ghost who cried,
"Hamlet, revenge!" On the basis of the barest shreds of contemporary evidence, scholars have constructed elaborate theories about this supposed source play, but there is
little agreement among them. Assuming that there was an Elizabethan staging of the
story that preceded Shakespeare's, its author remains unknown. Many scholars have
assigned it to Thomas Kyd, who wrote *The Spanish Tragedy* (c. 1587), one of the most
successful and enduring Elizabethan plays. *The Spanish Tragedy* itself has features that
strikingly anticipate Shakespeare's tragedy, including a ghost impatient for revenge, a
secret crime, a hero tormented by uncertainty and self-reproach, the strategic feigning
of a madness that seems disturbingly close to the real thing, a woman who goes mad
from grief and commits suicide, a play within the play, and a final slaughter that wipes
out much of the royal family and court, along with the avenger himself. Kyd's play is
entirely structured around the problem of revenge—"wild justice," in Francis Bacon's
haunting phrase—and gave rise to a whole genre of revenge plays in which *Hamlet* participates.

These plays generally share certain conventional assumptions. First, revenge is an
individual response to an intolerable wrong or a public insult. It is an unauthorized, violent action in a world whose institutions seem unable or unwilling to satisfy a craving
for justice. Second, since institutional channels are closed and since the criminal is
usually either hidden or well protected, revenge almost always follows a devious path
toward its violent end. Third, the revenger is in the grip of an inner compulsion: his
course of action may be motivated by institutional failure—for example, the mechanisms of justice are in the hands of the criminals themselves—but even if these mechanisms were operating perfectly, they would not allow the psychic satisfactions of
revenge. Fourth, revengers generally need their victims to know what is happening and
why: satisfaction depends on a moment of declaration and vindication. And fifth,
revenge is a universal imperative more powerful than the pious injunctions of any particular belief system, including Christianity itself.

Shakespeare had already produced a sensationally violent version of these conventions in *Titus Andronicus*. In *Hamlet*, he at once reproduces them and calls them into
question. The audience knows for certain—from Claudius's tortured attempt to pray
in Act 3—that there has been a "foul murder," a fratricide successfully covered over by
the story that a serpent stung the sleeping King. But Hamlet does not overhear
Claudius's confession and has only the questionable testimony of the Ghost. That testimony is open to question because the nature of the Ghost is open to question. The
Ghost speaks as if he were condemned to a term of suffering in the realm Catholics
called purgatory:

> Doomed for a certain term to walk the night,
> And for the day confined to fast in fires
> Till the foul crimes done in my days of nature
> Are burnt and purged away.
>
> (1.5.10–13)

But Protestant theologians vehemently denied that purgatory existed and argued that
spirits thought to be ghosts were in fact devils sent to lure humans into sinful actions.
Hamlet responds at first as if he believes the Ghost to be the authentic spirit of his

The man in prayer. By Mair von Landshut (1499).

father returned from the dead, but he subsequently expresses serious doubts—"The spirit that I have seen / May be the devil" (2.2.575–76)—and in the play's most famous soliloquy he speaks of death as "the undiscovered country from whose bourn / No traveller returns" (3.1.81–82).

The theatrical test Hamlet devises to authenticate the Ghost's accusation—carefully watching the reaction of his uncle to *The Mousetrap*—appears to resolve any doubts: "I'll take the Ghost's word," Hamlet exults, after the King has stormed out in a rage, "for a thousand pound" (3.2.263–64). Yet even here Shakespeare introduces an occasion for uncertainty: after all, the murderer in the play within the play is "one Lucianus, nephew to the King" (3.2.223). Claudius's anger could have arisen from the spectacle of the player-nephew killing his player-uncle and not from the spectacle of his own hidden crime. The effect on the audience is not so much to cast doubt on the Ghost's word as to uncouple Hamlet's inner life once again from the external world, even at the moment that he himself thinks they are at last securely linked.

This uncoupling, this sense of inward thoughts and feelings painfully cut off from the world around him, haunts virtually all of Hamlet's relationships. When he speaks with his old school friends Rosencrantz and Guildenstern, with the courtier Osric, or with Polonius, he is deliberately evasive, but his exchanges with Ophelia are equally oblique and baffling. Even with his intimate friend Horatio, there is some gap across which Hamlet struggles to speak: "There are more things in heaven and earth, Horatio," Hamlet says after his first encounter with the Ghost, "than are dreamt of in our philosophy" (1.5.168–69). (The quarto variant—"in your philosophy"—marks the gap between them still more sharply.) When Hamlet directly confronts his mother with the charge of murder, she reacts with astonishment. The painful words that follow, Hamlet's weird, tormented admonition to his mother to shun her husband's bed, do indeed seem to strike home: "These words like daggers," Gertrude exclaims, "enter in mine ears" (3.4.85). But the Ghost's sudden reappearance, visible this time only to Hamlet (and, of course, to the audience), convinces his mother that her son is mad. "Do you see nothing there?" asks Hamlet, to which his mother, certain that her son is hallucinating, replies steadfastly, "Nothing at all, yet all that is I see" (3.4.122–23).

Ironically, the distance between what Hamlet sees and what those around him see is smallest in the case of Claudius, since both share a knowledge of the secret crime that has poisoned the kingdom, and each maneuvers against the other throughout the play. But their fatal opposition never rises to full, open view until the final violent seconds, nor does Hamlet ever establish unequivocal, unambiguous public confirmation of his uncle's guilt. It would have been easy for Shakespeare to provide such confirmation—for example, in a last speech by the mortally wounded usurper—but he chooses instead to leave what Horatio calls "th' yet unknowing world" (5.2.323) in the dark. Until the explosion of treason and murder, the horrified bystanders know only a court in which the loving Claudius appeals to Hamlet as his "son" and wagers on his skill in fencing. Hamlet begins an explanation—"O I could tell you"—but he is cut short by death. The effect is to extend Hamlet's tragic isolation, his gnawing inward pain, all the way to his final silence.

What would it take to get rid of this pain? The possibility of cleansing, definitive action at once continually tantalizes and eludes the Prince. Such action is embodied in the soldier Fortinbras, but if Hamlet finds some way of easing his mental anguish, it is not through any comparable martial exploit, nor is it through the secret plotting undertaken by Laertes. The fact that both Fortinbras and Laertes are also attempting

Swordsmen. From *Vincentio Saviolo his Practise* (London, 1595).

to avenge the deaths of fathers underscores the shared crisis of dynastic succession but only intensifies the contrast with Hamlet's spiritual journey. The calm to which he gives voice near the play's close—"There's a special providence in the fall of a sparrow. If it be now, 'tis not to come. If it be not to come, it will be now. If it be not now, yet it will come. The readiness is all" (5.2.157–60)—descends upon him *before,* not as a result of, his revenge. The act of revenge itself happens in a flash of rage, without planning, without any self-vindicating declaration by Hamlet to Claudius, and without any public confession of guilt by the usurper. Revenge leaves the Prince not with inner satisfaction but with intense anxiety over his "wounded name."

Standing on a stage littered with corpses, Horatio promises to fulfill Hamlet's dying request to tell his story, but his account of "carnal, bloody, and unnatural acts," though it may be accurate, must be inadequate to the play we have just witnessed. For *Hamlet* situates the need for revenge in a context that goes beyond any crime, however heinous, and that seems resistant to violent solutions. Before the Ghost disclosed his uncle's villainy, Hamlet was suffering from the traumas of mortality: the searing pain of his father's death, a troubled recognition of his mother's sexuality, a sickening awareness of the vulnerability and corruptibility of the flesh. There was a time, the play implies, when Hamlet embodied all the hopes and aspirations of his age and his own vision of human possibility was unbounded—"What a piece of work is a man!"—but that vision has given way to bitter disillusionment: "And yet to me what is this quintessence of dust?" (2.2.293–94, 297–98).

Renaissance psychologists had a word for Hamlet's condition: melancholy, a state of spiritual desolation akin to madness but also to the literary and artistic genius. In Hamlet's melancholy consciousness, human existence has been reduced to dust at its dustiest. Although Claudius's secret crime is a political act that has poisoned the public sphere, the roots of Hamlet's despair seem to lie in a more intractably inward place, a place perhaps less consonant with revenge than with suicide. If there were only the evil usurper to depose, Hamlet might compass a straightforward course of action, but his soul-sickness has receding layers: beyond political corruption, there is the time-serving shallowness of his friends Rosencrantz and Guildenstern, and beyond this there is Ophelia's dismayingly compliant obedience to her father, and beyond this there is his mother's disturbing carnality, and beyond this there is the ongoing, endlessly transformative, morally indifferent cycle of life itself. For Hamlet, the quintessence of dust is not only the cold, inert matter produced by the nauseating triumph of death—the flesh of Alexander the Great metamorphosed into a plug of dirt stopping up a beer barrel—but also living matter pullulating with tenacious, meaningless vitality, produced by the equally nauseating triumph of life. "We fat all creatures else to fat us," Hamlet tells Claudius, "and we fat ourselves for maggots" (4.3.22–23).

In a world pervaded by decay, the process of natural renewal has come to seem grotesque and disgusting:

> 'Tis an unweeded garden
> That grows to seed; things rank and gross in nature
> Possess it merely.
>
> (1.2.135–37)

These lines immediately give way to bitter reflections on his mother's sexual appetite: in Hamlet's diseased consciousness, the spectacle of nature run riot, of uncontrolled breeding and feeding, centers on the body of woman. His bitterness at his mother's remarriage spreads like a stain to include all women, including the woman he had once ardently courted. "Get thee to a nunnery," Hamlet urges Ophelia, as if the only virtuous course of action were renunciation of the flesh. "Why wouldst thou be a breeder of sinners?" (3.1.122–23) Even this desperate advice seems to be undermined by Hamlet's obsessive sense of rampant female sexuality and of his own corruption, since in Elizabethan slang "nunnery" could also be a term for "brothel."

The fragile Ophelia begins to crack under the strain of Hamlet's misogynistic revulsion. Gertrude, who takes the full force of this revulsion, does not lose her wits, but when confronted alone by her son, she fears for her life. Both women sense the violence and despair seething in Hamlet beneath what he calls his "antic disposition" (1.5.173). That disposition, manifested in his disordered dress and in the "wild and whirling words" (1.5.137) that he begins to speak after encountering the Ghost, casts Hamlet in the strange role of jester in the court in which he is the mourning son and the heir apparent. Of all Shakespeare's tragic heroes, he is at once the saddest and the funniest. His blend of sarcasm, riddling, and sly wordplay initially strikes those around him as folly, but this first impression continually gives way to an uneasy awareness of hidden meanings: Claudius, alert to danger, notes that "there's something in his soul / O'er which his melancholy sits on brood" (3.1.163–64). The "something" Claudius senses is in part the murderous design of the revenger, but it is also the philosophical meditation on life and death that haunts Hamlet throughout the play. This meditation reaches a climax in the graveyard, where Hamlet, trading zany quibbles with one of the gravediggers, directly confronts the corruption and decay that had obsessed him ever since his father's death. If there is any release for Hamlet from this obsession—and it is not clear that there is—it comes from an unflinching gaze at a skull, the skull of the jester Yorick, but also, by extension, his father's skull and his own.

STEPHEN GREENBLATT

TEXTUAL NOTE

Hamlet exists in three distinct early texts. The relationship among these texts, along with a mountain of speculation about an earlier theatrical version of the story, now lost, have occupied scholars for decades. These are some of the bare facts. A printer named James Roberts placed an entry in the Stationers' Register on July 26, 1602, for "A booke called the Revenge of Hamlett Prince Denmarke as yt was latelie Acted by the Lord Chamberleyne his servantes." The first known edition (Q1) is a Quarto dated 1603, printed not by Roberts but by Nicholas Ling and John Trundell. This edition, "*The Tragicall Historie of HAMLET Prince of Denmarke By William Shake-speare,*" is a text markedly inferior, except for a few details, to the others and, at 2,200 type lines long, markedly shorter. Generally regarded as a highly suspect version of the play, it is often referred to as the "bad Quarto"—often differing markedly even when it overlaps with the other versions. (The Prince's most famous soliloquy, for example, begins "To be or not to be, ay there's the point.") Only two copies of this Quarto, first identified in 1823, are known to exist; one is in the British Library in London, the other in the Huntington Library in San Marino, California.

A second edition (Q2), dated 1604, was printed by James Roberts. The title page advertises itself as "Newly imprinted and enlarged to almost as much againe as it was, according to the true and perfect Coppie." At 3,800 type lines, Q2 makes good on its claim to substantial enlargement, and scholars tend to agree that the printer's shop set the text from the playwright's own handwritten draft, or "foul papers," occasionally supplemented by consultation with Q1. Q2 was reprinted once, without significant alteration, during Shakespeare's lifetime.

If Shakespeare's manuscript is behind Q2, what is the source of the substantially different Q1? The most widely accepted theory, first proposed in 1941 by G. I. Duthie (*The 'Bad' Quarto of Hamlet*), is that Q1 is the product of memorial reconstruction. That is, one or more actors in the play reported what they remembered to a scribe, who prepared copy for the printer. Scholars have conjectured that the principal reporter was the actor who played Marcellus and probably doubled as Valtemand and Lucianus, since the accuracy of the text, as measured by the subsequent editions, greatly improves whenever those characters are onstage. Along with virtually every other aspect of the textual history of *Hamlet,* this appeal to memorial reconstruction is a subject of continuing scholarly debate.

The third major version of the play appeared in 1623 in the First Folio (F), where it is entitled *The Tragedie of Hamlet, Prince of Denmarke.* This edition differs in important ways from Q2: there are a great many small changes, along with some substantial cuts and additions. Most recent editors believe that F was set not from the author's own draft but from a scribal transcript, possibly from a promptbook prepared while Shakespeare was still active in the company. Such a promptbook would normally have been made by annotating a fair copy of the author's foul papers. In other words, the text of *Hamlet* in F is probably closer than Q2 to the play as it was performed in the theater when Shakespeare was alive.

Traditionally, many editors regarded any changes introduced in the passage from the author's own draft to the transcript prepared for the prompter (and thus in the case of *Hamlet* from Q2 to F) as corruptions of the text. Their goal, then, was to remove the corruptions and restore the play to its original state, the text as the author had conceived it. But most if not all of the passages that appear in F and not in Q2 seem unmistakably by Shakespeare himself, while the passages that appear in Q2 and not in F seem equally authentic. Consequently, editors were forced to conjecture that the compositors of Q2 had in 1604 unaccountably omitted the passages that appear in F, while the compositors of the Folio had similarly omitted those passages that only appear in Q2. As early as the eighteenth century, *Hamlet's* editors routinely conflated Q2 and F, incorporating in a single text as much as possible of both versions of the play.

The Oxford editors broke with this tradition. They observed that since Shakespeare was an active member of his company, the passage from foul papers to promptbook was not necessarily a corruption of his text. Rather, it could as easily have been the occasion for deliberate authorial revision, drawing upon his own second thoughts as well as the suggestions of his trusted professional colleagues. Close study of the differences between Q2 and F suggests the strong possibility of such revision, reflecting a coherent strategy. The Oxford editors hypothesized that Shakespeare himself prepared a fair copy of the foul papers from which Q2 was set, that in making that fair copy he revised the text in a number of ways, and that F derives, at one or possibly more removes, from that fair copy. Therefore, since the Oxford editors concluded that Shakespeare's own revisions are reflected in F, they adopted F as the control text.

In keeping with this decision, the *Oxford Shakespeare* relegated passages from Q2 that do not appear in F to an appendix. This format enables readers to imagine more readily the version of *Hamlet* thought to have been revised for performance during Shakespeare's own lifetime, but it has certain disadvantages, the principal of which is that only a reader extremely familiar with the play can easily imagine exactly how the Q2 passages functioned in what everyone agrees was a version of the play also written by Shakespeare. Moreover, since several of these passages have long been regarded as integral parts of the play, their relegation to an appendix makes it difficult for readers to participate fully in the great cultural conversation about *Hamlet* that has occupied artists, critics, and scholars for generations. Accordingly, the *Norton Shakespeare,* while following the Oxford text, has moved the Q2 passages from the appendix to the body of the play. But in order not to once again produce a conflated text, the Q2 passages are indented, printed in a different typeface, and numbered in such a way as to make clear their provenance. Also, at the points where the Folio and the Q2 passages directly overlap (3.4.70, 3.4.151, and 5.2.154), the overlapping lines are repeated. Those who wish to read the Folio version of *Hamlet* can thus simply skip over the offset Q2 passages, while at the same time it is possible for readers to see clearly the place that the Q2 passages occupy.

The First Quarto (Q1) of *Hamlet,* published in 1603, was evidently cobbled together from the memory of one or more of the actors in a production of Shakespeare's play. The text is notoriously defective, as its version of Hamlet's most famous soliloquy suggests:*

Q1 [cf. 3.1.58ff.]

To be, or not to be; ay, there's the point.
To die, to sleep: is that all? Ay all.
No, to sleep, to dream; ay marry, there it goes.
For in that dream of death, when we awake
And borne before an everlasting judge
From whence no passenger ever returned,
The undiscovered country at whose sight
The happy smile and the accursed damned—
But for this, the joyful hope of this,
Who'd bear the scorns and flattery of the world,
Scorned by the right rich, the rich cursed of the poor,
The widow being oppressed, the orphan wronged,
The taste of hunger or a tyrant's reign,
And thousand more calamities besides,
To grunt and sweat under this weary life,
When that he may his full quietus make
With a bare bodkin? Who would this endure,
But for a hope of something after death,
Which puzzles the brain and doth confound the sense,
Which makes us rather bear those evils we have
Than fly to others that we know not of?
Ay that. O, this conscience makes cowards of us all.—
Lady, in thy orisons be all my sins remembered.

Between the two authoritative versions of the play, the Second Quarto (Q2: 1604) and the Folio (F: 1623), there are many substantial differences, most notably the Q2-only passages that this edition indents and prints in a different typeface. In addition to these major alterations, apparently the consequence of Shakespeare's own revision of his play, there are many other small but suggestive differences between Q2 and F that also seem to reflect shifting authorial intentions. A sampling of these follows:

2.2.212ff.

Q2:	F:
HAMLET You cannot take from me anything that I will not more willingly part withal: except my life, except my life, except my life.	HAMLET You cannot, sir, take from me anything that I will more willingly part withal: except my life, my life.

5.1.166ff.

Q2:	F:
FIRST CLOWN This same skull, sir, was sir Yorick's skull, the King's jester.	FIRST CLOWN This same skull, sir, this same skull, sir, was Yorick's skull, the King's jester.

*Modernization from Kathleen O. Irace, ed., *The First Quarto of Hamlet* (New York: Cambridge University Press, 1998).

HAMLET This?

FIRST CLOWN E'en that.

HAMLET Alas, poor Yorick. I knew him, Horatio—a fellow of infinite jest, of most excellent fancy. He hath bore me on his back a thousand times; and now how abhorred in my imagination it is! My gorge rises at it. Here hung those lips that I have kissed I know not how oft. Where be your gibes now, your gambols, your songs, your flashes of merriment that were wont to set the table on a roar? Not one now to mock your own grinning?

HAMLET This?

FIRST CLOWN E'en that.

HAMLET Let me see. Alas, poor Yorick. I knew him, Horatio—a fellow of infinite jest, of most excellent fancy. He hath borne me on his back a thousand times; and how abhorred my imagination is! My gorge rises at it. Here hung those lips that I have kissed I know not how oft. Where be your gibes now, your gambols, your songs, your flashes of merriment that were wont to set the table on a roar? No one now to mock your own jeering?

5.1.196ff.

Q2:

HAMLET Imperious Caesar, dead and
turned to clay,
Might stop a hole to keep the wind
away.
O, that the earth which kept the world
in awe
Should patch a wall t'expel the water's
flaw.
But soft, but soft, awhile. Here
comes the King.

F:

HAMLET Imperial Caesar, dead and
turned to clay,
Might stop a hole to keep the wind away.
O, that the earth which kept the world
in awe
Should patch a wall t'expel the winter's
flaw.
But soft, but soft; aside. Here comes
the King.

5.2.297ff.

Q2:

HAMLET But I do prophecy th'election
lights
On Fortinbras. He has my dying voice.
So tell him, with th'occurrants, more
and less,
Which have solicited. The rest is
silence.

HORATIO Now cracks a noble heart.

F:

HAMLET But I do prophecy th'election
lights
On Fortinbras. He has mydying voice.
So tell him, with th'occurrants, more
and less,
Which have solicited. The rest is
silence.
O, O, O, O!

HORATIO Now crack a noble heart.

SELECTED BIBLIOGRAPHY

Adelman, Janet. "Man and His Wife Is One Flesh: *Hamlet* and the Confrontation with the Maternal Body." *Suffocating Mothers: Fantasies of Maternal Origin in Shakespeare's Plays, "Hamlet" to "The Tempest."* New York: Routledge, 1992. 11–37. For Shakespeare, fully realized female sexuality (in the form of Gertrude) gives birth not only to fallen and contaminated man, but also to tragedy itself.

Bradley, A. C. *Shakespearean Tragedy: Lectures on "Hamlet," "Othello," "King Lear," "Macbeth."* 1904. 3rd ed. Basingstoke, Eng.: Macmillan, 1992. Hamlet's character—at the center of the tragedy that bears his name—is dominated by a morbid melancholy that weakens his ability to love and impedes his ability to act.

De Grazia, Margreta. *"Hamlet" Without Hamlet.* Cambridge, Mass.: Cambridge University Press, 2007. The elusiveness of Hamlet's inner life is a largely modern critical invention, obscuring the dispossession that Renaissance audiences would have seen as the tragedy's central crisis.

Eliot, T. S. "Hamlet and His Problems." *The Sacred Wood: Essays on Poetry and Criticism.* London: Methuen, 1920. *Hamlet* proves deficient as a work of art: the prince's disproportionate confusion about his condition reflects Shakespeare's own confusion concerning the proper assembly of his diverse literary materials.

Garber, Marjorie. "*Hamlet*: Giving Up the Ghost." *Shakespeare's Ghost Writers: Literature as Uncanny Causality.* New York: Methuen, 1987. 124–76. Simultaneously constituting and dissolving the self, the Ghost haunts the unstable relationship between action and memory; Shakespeare himself has a similarly haunting purchase on the modern imagination.

Greenblatt, Stephen. *Hamlet in Purgatory.* Princeton: Princeton University Press, 2001. *Hamlet* exploits and transforms into theatrical ritual the fears and desires generated by the Catholic cult of purgatory, a cult banned by Tudor Protestantism.

Maguire, Laurie. "'Actions that a man might play': Mourning, Memory, Editing." *Performance Research* 7 (2002): 66–76. Editors of Shakespeare searching for one "true" text of the play should take a hint from Hamlet himself: single viewpoints (whether ontological or editorial) ultimately bow to the daunting yet rich reality of multiplicity.

McGee, Arthur. *The Elizabethan Hamlet.* New Haven: Yale University Press, 1987. Hamlet emerges as a sophisticated manifestation of Vice from the medieval morality-play tradition.

Showalter, Elaine. "Representing Ophelia: Women, Madness, and the Responsibilities of Feminist Criticism." *Shakespeare and the Question of Theory.* Ed. Patricia Parker and Geoffrey Hartman. New York: Methuen, 1985. 77–94. A survey of shifting cultural attitudes toward the representation of Ophelia serves as a barometer of ideological conflict and as a contribution to the evolving discourse of feminist criticism.

Targoff, Ramie. "The Performance of Prayer: Sincerity and Theatricality in Early Modern England." *Representations* 60 (1997): 49–69. Hamlet's misreading of Claudius's prayer is neither accidental nor further evidence of his inability to act; rather, it is symptomatic of early modern Protestant anxieties over how to determine sincerity and hypocrisy.

Wilson, J. Dover. *What Happens in "Hamlet."* 3rd ed. Cambridge, Mass.: Cambridge University Press, 1951. In grappling with the play's dramatic difficulties, especially the problematic "Mouse-trap" scene, we more nearly approach "the secret of Hamlet's character."

See also the creative uses of *Hamlet* in Johann Wolfgang von Goethe's *Wilhelm Meister's Apprenticeship* (1796); James Joyce's *Ulysses* (1922); Tom Stoppard's *Rosencrantz and Guildenstern Are Dead* (1967); Heiner Müller's *Die Hamletmaschine* (1978); and John Updike's *Gertrude and Claudius* (2000).

Films

Hamlet. 1948. Dir. Laurence Olivier. UK. 155 min. In this black-and-white film, Olivier's Hamlet is an oedipal prince, tormented by a desire to kill his father and sleep with his mother (played in the film by an actress only two years older than Olivier).

Gamlet. 1964. Dir. Grigori Kozintsev and Iosif Shapiro. Soviet Union. 148 min. A black-and-white Cold-war *Hamlet,* in Russian, set in a prisonlike Elsinore.

Hamlet. 1990. Dir. Franco Zeffirelli. UK. 130 min. Naturalistic medieval scenes, with Glenn Close's strong Gertrude in an oedipally charged relationship with Mel Gibson's Hamlet.

Hamlet. 1996. Dir. Kenneth Branagh. UK. 242 min. (cut version 150 min.). Opulent, full-text epic rendered in the mirrored halls of a palatial nineteenth-century Austrian court.

Hamlet. 2000. Dir. Michael Almereyda. USA. 112 min. Inspired by director Akira Kurosawa, Almereyda updates the play to modern New York and draws on communications technologies such as videocameras, fax machines, and computers.

The Tragedy of Hamlet, Prince of Denmark

THE PERSONS OF THE PLAY

GHOST of Hamlet, the late King of Denmark
KING CLAUDIUS, his brother
QUEEN GERTRUDE of Denmark, widow of King Hamlet, now
   wife of Claudius
Prince HAMLET, son of King Hamlet and Queen Gertrude
POLONIUS, a lord
LAERTES, son of Polonius
OPHELIA, daughter of Polonius
REYNALDO, servant of Polonius
HORATIO
ROSENCRANTZ } friends of Prince Hamlet
GUILDENSTERN
FRANCISCO
BARNARDO } soldiers
MARCELLUS
VALTEMAND
CORNELIUS
OSRIC } courtiers
GENTLEMEN
A SAILOR
Two CLOWNS, a gravedigger and his companion
A PRIEST
FORTINBRAS, Prince of Norway
A CAPTAIN in his army
AMBASSADORS from England
PLAYERS, who play the parts of the PROLOGUE, PLAYER KING,
   PLAYER QUEEN, and LUCIANUS, in *The Mousetrap*
Lords, messengers, attendants, guards, soldiers, followers of
   Laertes, sailors

1.1

Enter BARNARDO *and* FRANCISCO, *two sentinels* [*at several° doors*]   *separate*

BARNARDO   Who's there?
FRANCISCO   Nay, answer me.[1] Stand and unfold° yourself.   *identify*
BARNARDO   Long live the King!
FRANCISCO   Barnardo?
BARNARDO   He.
FRANCISCO   You come most carefully° upon your hour.   *dutifully; cautiously*
5 BARNARDO   'Tis now struck twelve. Get thee to bed, Francisco.
FRANCISCO   For this relief much thanks. 'Tis bitter cold,
  And I am sick at heart.

BARNARDO   Have you had quiet guard?

FRANCISCO   Not a mouse stirring.

BARNARDO   Well, good night.
　　　If you do meet Horatio and Marcellus,
10　　The rivals° of my watch, bid them make haste.　　　　　　　　　*partners*
　　　　　　　Enter HORATIO *and* MARCELLUS

FRANCISCO   I think I hear them—Stand! Who's there?

HORATIO   Friends to this ground.°　　　　*country*

MARCELLUS   And liegemen° to the Dane.[2]　　　　　　*sworn servants*

FRANCISCO   Give° you good night.　　　　*God give*

MARCELLUS   O farewell, honest soldier. Who hath relieved you?

FRANCISCO   Barnardo has my place. Give you good night.　　*Exit*

15　MARCELLUS   Holla, Barnardo!

BARNARDO   Say—what, is Horatio there?

HORATIO   A piece of him.

BARNARDO   Welcome, Horatio. Welcome, good Marcellus.

MARCELLUS[3]   What, has this thing appeared again tonight?

20　BARNARDO   I have seen nothing.

MARCELLUS   Horatio says 'tis but our fantasy,
　　　And will not let belief take hold of him
　　　Touching this dreaded sight twice seen of us.
　　　Therefore I have entreated him along
25　With us to watch the minutes of this night,
　　　That if again this apparition come
　　　He may approve° our eyes and speak to it.[4]　　*verify the evidence of*

HORATIO   Tush, tush, 'twill not appear.

BARNARDO   Sit down a while,
　　　And let us once again assail your ears,
30　That are so fortified against our story,
　　　What we two nights have seen.

HORATIO   Well, sit we down,
　　　And let us hear Barnardo speak of this.

BARNARDO   Last night of all,°　　　　　　　　　*Just last night*
　　　When yon same star that's westward from the pole°　　*polestar*
35　Had made his° course t'illume that part of heaven　　　　*its*
　　　Where now it burns, Marcellus and myself,
　　　The bell then beating one—
　　　　　Enter the GHOST [*in complete armour, holding a trun-*
　　　　　cheon, with his beaver up][5]

MARCELLUS   Peace, break thee off. Look where it comes again.

BARNARDO   In the same figure like the King that's dead.

40　MARCELLUS [*to* HORATIO]   Thou art a scholar—speak to it, Horatio.

BARNARDO   Looks it not like the King?—Mark it, Horatio.

HORATIO   Most like. It harrows me with fear and wonder.

BARNARDO   It would° be spoke to.　　　　　　　　*wishes to*

MARCELLUS   Question it, Horatio.

HORATIO   [*to the* GHOST]   What art thou that usurp'st[6] this time of night,
45　Together with that fair and warlike form
　　　In which the majesty of buried Denmark°　　　　*the buried King*

---

2. King of Denmark.

3. Q2 gives this line to Horatio.

4. A ghost was believed to speak only when spoken to. As a precaution, the experiment will be conducted by an educated man (Horatio) who knows Latin (the language effective for exorcising demonic spirits).

5. Holding a baton (military commander's sign of office), with his visor ("beaver") raised.

6. Wrongfully seize (both the night and the shape of the King). The familiar "thou" would be an inappropriate form of address for a real King.

Did sometimes° march? By heaven, I charge thee speak.   *formerly*

MARCELLUS   It is offended.

BARNARDO   See, it stalks away.

HORATIO [*to the* GHOST]   Stay, speak, speak, I charge thee speak.

Exit GHOST

50   MARCELLUS   'Tis gone, and will not answer.

BARNARDO   How now, Horatio? You tremble and look pale.

Is not this something more than fantasy?

What think you on't?°   *of it*

HORATIO   Before my God, I might not this believe

55   Without the sensible° and true avouch°   *sensory / testimony*

Of mine own eyes.

MARCELLUS   Is it not like the King?

HORATIO   As thou art to thyself.

Such was the very armour he had on

60   When he th'ambitious Norway° combated.   *King of Norway*

So frowned he once when in an angry parley°   *debate*

He smote the sledded Polacks[7] on the ice.

'Tis strange.

MARCELLUS   Thus twice before, and just at this dead hour,

65   With martial stalk hath he gone by our watch.

HORATIO   In what particular thought to work[8] I know not,

But in the gross and scope of my opinion[9]

This bodes some strange eruption° to our state.   *calamity*

MARCELLUS   Good now,° sit down, and tell me, he that knows,   *(an entreaty: Good sir, now)*

70   Why this same strict and most observant watch

So nightly toils the subject of the land,[1]

And why such daily cast° of brazen cannon,   *production*

And foreign mart° for implements of war,   *trade*

Why such impress° of shipwrights, whose sore task   *drafting*

75   Does not divide the Sunday from the week:

What might be toward° that this sweaty haste   *impending*

Doth make the night joint-labourer with the day,

Who is't that can inform me?

HORATIO   That can I—

At least the whisper goes so: our last king,

80   Whose image even but now appeared to us,

Was as you know by Fortinbras of Norway,

Thereto pricked° on by a most emulate° pride,   *spurred / rivalrous*

Dared to the combat; in which our valiant Hamlet—

For so this side of our known world esteemed him—

85   Did slay this Fortinbras, who by a sealed compact[2]

Well ratified by law and heraldry[3]

Did forfeit with his life all those his lands

Which he stood seized on° to the conqueror;   *held possession of*

Against the which a moiety competent°   *an equal portion*

90   Was gagèd° by our King, which had returned[4]   *staked*

To the inheritance° of Fortinbras   *ownership*

Had he been vanquisher, as by the same cov'nant

And carriage of the article designed[5]

7. Poles who traveled by sled.
8. *In . . . work*: What precise theory to follow.
9. But in my general opinion.
1. *So . . . land*: Requires the country's subjects to toil every night.
2. A mutually agreed-upon contract ("compact") to which each set his seal.
3. Properly ratified in accordance with civil law and the law of arms.
4. Which would have gone.
5. And execution of the contract's provision.

His fell to Hamlet. Now sir, young Fortinbras,
95 Of unimprovèd° mettle hot and full,   *untested; untrained*
Hath in the skirts° of Norway here and there   *outlying parts*
Sharked up a list[6] of landless[7] resolutes
For food and diet to some enterprise
That hath a stomach in't,[8] which is no other—
100 And it doth well° appear unto our state—   *obviously*
But to recover of us by strong hand[9]
And terms compulsative° those foresaid lands   *forcible*
So by his father lost. And this, I take it,
Is the main motive of our preparations,
105 The source of this our watch, and the chief head°   *source*
Of this post-haste and rummage[1] in the land.[2]
106.1 BARNARDO *I think it be no other but e'en so.*
Well may it sort° that this portentous figure   *be fitting*
Comes armèd through our watch so like the king
That was and is the question° of these wars.   *cause*
106.5 HORATIO *A mote° it is to trouble the mind's eye.*   *speck of dust*
In the most high and palmy° state of Rome,   *flourishing*
A little ere the mightiest Julius fell,
The graves stood tenantless, and the sheeted° dead   *shrouded*
Did squeak and gibber in the Roman streets
106.10 *At stars with trains of fire,[3] and dews of blood,*
Disasters[4] in the sun; and the moist star,[5]
Upon whose influence Neptune's empire stands,°   *depends*
Was sick almost to doomsday with eclipse.[6]
And even the like precurse° of feared events,   *forerunner*
106.15 *As harbingers preceding still° the fates,*   *always*
And prologue to the omen°coming on,   *disastrous event*
Have heaven and earth together demonstrated
Unto our climature° and countrymen.   *region*
Enter the GHOST [*as before*]
But soft,° behold—lo where it comes again!   *hush*
I'll cross[7] it though it blast° me.—Stay, illusion.   *wither*
[*The* GHOST] *spreads his arms*
If thou hast any sound or use of voice,
110 Speak to me.
If there be any good thing to be done
That may to thee do ease and grace to me,
Speak to me.
If thou art privy to thy country's fate
115 Which happily° foreknowing may avoid,   *perhaps; fortunately*
O speak!
Or if thou hast uphoarded in thy life
Extorted treasure in the womb of earth—

---

6. Gathered together indiscriminately (as a shark takes prey) a band ("list").
7. Q1, Q2 print "lawless," which accurately conveys Horatio's view of these men; F's "landless," however, provides a more specific motive for their enlistment.
8. *For . . . in't:* The men will "feed" his enterprise; they are fed in return for their service. *stomach:* courageous action; challenge to the pride (of both the Prince and his men).
9. By main force (punning on the name "Fortinbras," literally "strong arm").
1. Of this feverish activity and commotion.

2. After this line, Q2 contains the following passage, 106.1–106.18, omitted in F.
3. "At" is emended from Q2's "As," which would require another verb.
4. Malevolent influences (astrological term).
5. The moon, thought to control tides by drawing water out of the sea ("Neptune's empire," line 106.12).
6. Eclipses of sun and moon would accompany Christ's return to earth on Judgment Day (see Revelation 6:12).
7. Confront, cross its path; also, make the sign of the cross (to counter its evil influence).

For which, they say, you spirits oft walk in death—

The cock crows

120   Speak of it, stay and speak.—Stop it, Marcellus.

MARCELLUS   Shall I strike at it with my partisan?°   *spear-handled blade*

HORATIO   Do, if it will not stand.

BARNARDO   'Tis here.

HORATIO   'Tis here.

                                        Exit GHOST

MARCELLUS   'Tis gone.

  We do it wrong, being so majestical,

125   To offer it the show of violence,

  For it is as the air invulnerable,

  And our vain blows malicious mockery.

BARNARDO   It was about to speak when the cock crew.

HORATIO   And then it started like a guilty thing

130   Upon a fearful summons. I have heard

  The cock, that is the trumpet to the morn,

  Doth with his lofty and shrill-sounding throat

  Awake the god of day,[8] and at his warning,

  Whether in sea or fire, in earth or air,

135   Th'extravagant and erring[9] spirit hies°   *hurries*

  To his confine;° and of the truth herein   *enclosure*

  This present object° made probation.°   *example / proof*

MARCELLUS   It faded on the crowing of the cock.

  Some say that ever 'gainst° that season comes   *always when*

140   Wherein our saviour's birth is celebrated

  The bird of dawning singeth all night long;

  And then, they say, no spirit can walk abroad,

  The nights are wholesome; then no planets strike,[1]

  No fairy takes,° nor witch hath power to charm,   *bewitches*

145   So hallowed and so gracious° is the time.   *full of God's grace*

HORATIO   So have I heard, and do in part believe it.

  But look, the morn in russet mantle clad

  Walks o'er the dew of yon high eastern hill.

  Break we our watch up, and by my advice

150   Let us impart what we have seen tonight

  Unto young Hamlet; for upon my life,

  This spirit, dumb to us, will speak to him.

  Do you consent we shall acquaint him with it,

  As needful in our loves,[2] fitting our duty?

155 MARCELLUS   Let's do't, I pray; and I this morning know

  Where we shall find him most conveniently.   *Exeunt*

1.2

Flourish. Enter CLAUDIUS, *King of Denmark,* GERTRUDE
the Queen, [*members of the*] *Council,* [*such*] *as* POLON-
IUS, *his son* LAERTES *and* [*daughter*] OPHELIA, [*Prince*]
    HAMLET [*dressed in black*], *cum aliis*°   *with others*

KING CLAUDIUS   Though yet of Hamlet our[1] dear brother's death

  The memory be green, and that it us befitted

---

8. The sun god, Phoebus Apollo.
9. Wandering out of its boundaries.
1. When they were in certain unfavorable astrological positions, heavenly bodies were thought to exercise a negative influence on earthly events.

2. As necessary because of the love we have for him.
1.2 Location: The castle.
1. My. (Kings often referred to themselves in the plural, the royal "we," although in the lines that follow, Claudius may also be talking about Danes in general.)

To bear our hearts in grief and our whole kingdom
To be contracted in one brow of woe,[2]
5   Yet so far hath discretion fought with nature°   *natural love*
That we with wisest sorrow think on him
Together with remembrance of ourselves.[3]
Therefore our sometime° sister, now our queen,[4]   *former*
Th'imperial jointress° of this warlike state,   *joint possessor*
10   Have we as 'twere with a defeated joy,
With one auspicious and one dropping eye,[5]
With mirth in funeral and with dirge in marriage,
In equal scale weighing delight and dole,°   *sorrow*
Taken to wife. Nor have we herein barred°   *excluded; contradicted*
15   Your better wisdoms, which have freely gone
With this affair along. For all, our thanks.
Now follows that you know° young Fortinbras,   *should be informed that*
Holding a weak supposal° of our worth,   *a poor opinion*
Or thinking by our late dear brother's death
20   Our state to be disjoint° and out of frame,°   *fractured / order*
Co-leaguèd with the dream of his advantage,[6]
He hath not failed to pester us with message
Importing° the surrender of those lands   *Concerning*
Lost by his father, with all bonds° of law,   *legal procedures*
25   To our most valiant brother. So much for him.
       Enter VALTEMAND *and* CORNELIUS
Now for ourself, and for this time of meeting,
Thus much the business is: we have here writ
To Norway, uncle of young Fortinbras—
Who, impotent and bed-rid, scarcely hears
30   Of this his nephew's purpose—to suppress
His further gait° herein, in that the levies,   *progress*
The lists, and full proportions are all made
Out of his subject;[7] and we here dispatch
You, good Cornelius, and you, Valtemand,
35   For bearers of this greeting to old Norway,
Giving to you no further personal power
To business with the King more than the scope
Of these dilated° articles allow.   *lengthy*
Farewell, and let your haste commend your duty.[8]
40 VALTEMAND   In that and all things will we show our duty.
KING CLAUDIUS   We doubt it nothing,° heartily farewell.   *not at all*
       Exeunt VALTEMAND *and* CORNELIUS
And now, Laertes, what's the news with you?
You told us of some suit. What is't, Laertes?
You cannot speak of reason to the Dane°   *the Danish King*
45   And lose your voice. What wouldst thou beg, Laertes,

---

2. To be drawn together into a collective expression of mourning (playing on "the frowning brow of a mourner").

3. *we . . . ourselves*: "He is not wise that is not wise for himself" was proverbial.

4. English canon law forbade marriage between former brother- and sister-in-law (Leviticus 18:16; Book of Common Prayer); it was on this ground that Henry VIII annulled his marriage to his brother's widow and married Anne Boleyn, Queen Elizabeth's mother. The relationship between Claudius and Gertrude could thus be regarded as incestuous. In some early Germanic soci-

eties, however, a new King customarily married the late King's widow.

5. One eye looking hopefully, the other downcast, or "dropping" tears.

6. Reinforced by the illusion of his own advantageous position.

7. *in that . . . subject*: since the moneys, enlistments, and forces are made up of his (the King of Norway's) subjects.

8. Let your swift departure (rather than elaborate speeches) show your loyalty.

That shall not be my offer, not thy asking?⁹
The head is not more native¹ to the heart,
The hand more instrumental to the mouth,
Than is the throne of Denmark to thy father.
What wouldst thou have, Laertes?

50 LAERTES   Dread my° lord,   *My revered*
Your leave° and favour° to return to France,   *permission / approval*
From whence though willingly I came to Denmark
To show my duty in your coronation,
Yet now I must confess, that duty done,
55 My thoughts and wishes bend again towards France
And bow them to your gracious leave and pardon.²

KING CLAUDIUS   Have you your father's leave? What says Polonius?
POLONIUS   He hath, my lord, wrung from me my slow leave
By laboursome petition, and at last
60 Upon his will° I sealed my hard° consent.   *desire / reluctant*
I do beseech you give him leave to go.

KING CLAUDIUS   Take thy fair hour,³ Laertes. Time be thine,
And thy best graces spend it at thy will.⁴
But now, my cousin⁵ Hamlet, and my son—
65 HAMLET   A little more than kin and less than kind⁶

KING CLAUDIUS   How is it that the clouds still hang on you?
HAMLET   Not so, my lord, I am too much i'th' sun.⁷
QUEEN GERTRUDE   Good Hamlet, cast thy nightly colour⁸ off,
And let thine eye look like a friend on Denmark.⁹
70 Do not for ever with thy vailèd lids°   *downcast eyes*
Seek for thy noble father in the dust.
Thou know'st 'tis common—all that lives must die,
Passing through nature to eternity.
HAMLET   Ay, madam, it is common.¹

QUEEN GERTRUDE   If it be,
75 Why seems it so particular° with thee?   *personal*
HAMLET   Seems, madam? Nay, it *is*. I know not 'seems'.
'Tis not alone my inky cloak, good-mother,²
Nor customary suits of solemn black,
Nor windy suspiration° of forced breath,   *sighs*
80 No, nor the fruitful° river in the eye,   *copious*
Nor the dejected haviour° of the visage,   *expression*
Together with all forms, moods, shows of grief
That can denote me truly. These indeed 'seem',
For they are actions that a man might play;
85 But I have that within which passeth show—
These but the trappings and the suits of woe.

---

9. *What wouldst . . . asking:* What could you ask of me that I would not offer before you asked?
1. Naturally connected; an allusion to the "body politic," headed by the King and having as its heart the King's council.
2. And humbly ask you to grant permission to depart.
3. Opportunity (while you are young).
4. *Time . . . will:* Your time is your own; use it in accordance with your best qualities.
5. Kinsman (outside one's immediate family).
6. "The nearer in kin the less in kindness" was proverbial. Hamlet's riddling comment indicates first that there is little warmth in their new, only nominally closer

relationship. Playing on "kind" in the sense of natural type or offspring, however, he also refers to the incestuousness of the marriage that has produced their unnatural kinship.
7. In the sunshine of Claudius's favor; also, punning on "son."
8. Black mourning garments and melancholic behavior.
9. Both the King of Denmark and the country.
1. Commonplace (?); crude (?).
2. Stepmother. The hyphen, an editorial addition to F's "good Mother," calls attention to the ironic implication of Hamlet's words.

KING CLAUDIUS   'Tis sweet and commendable in your nature, Hamlet,
To give these mourning duties to your father;
But you must know your father lost a father;
90   That father lost, lost his; and the survivor bound
In filial obligation for some term
To do obsequious sorrow.[3] But to persever
In obstinate condolement° is a course   *lamenting*
Of impious stubbornness, 'tis unmanly grief,
95   It shows a will most incorrect° to heaven,   *unsubmissive*
A heart unfortified, a mind impatient,[4]
An understanding simple° and unschooled;   *childish*
For what we know must be, and is as common
As any the most vulgar thing to sense,[5]
100   Why should we in our peevish opposition
Take it to heart? Fie, 'tis a fault to heaven,
A fault against the dead, a fault to nature,
To reason most absurd, whose common theme
Is death of fathers, and who still° hath cried   *always*
105   From the first corpse[6] till he that died today,
'This must be so'. We pray you throw to earth
This unprevailing° woe, and think of us   *unavailing*
As of a father; for let the world take note
You are the most immediate° to our throne,   *next in succession*
110   And with no less nobility° of love   *purity; generosity*
Than that which dearest father bears his son
Do I impart towards you. For your intent
In going back to school in Wittenberg,[7]
It is most retrograde° to our desire,   *contrary*
115   And we beseech you bend you° to remain   *yield; agree*
Here in the cheer and comfort of our eye,
Our chiefest courtier, cousin, and our son.
QUEEN GERTRUDE   Let not thy mother lose her prayers, Hamlet.
I pray thee stay with us, go not to Wittenberg.
120   HAMLET   I shall in all my best obey you, madam.
KING CLAUDIUS   Why, 'tis a loving and a fair reply.
Be as ourself in Denmark. [*To* GERTRUDE] Madam, come.
This gentle and unforced accord of Hamlet
Sits smiling to° my heart; in grace° whereof,   *Pleases / honor*
125   No jocund health that Denmark° drinks today   *the King*
But the great cannon to the clouds shall tell,°   *sound*
And the King's rouse[8] the heavens shall bruit again,°   *loudly echo*
Re-speaking earthly thunder. Come, away.
                    Flourish. Exeunt all but HAMLET
HAMLET   O that this too too solid[9] flesh would melt,
130   Thaw, and resolve° itself into a dew,   *dissolve*
Or that the Everlasting had not fixed
His canon° 'gainst self-slaughter! O God, O God,   *law*
How weary, stale, flat, and unprofitable

3. To mourn as befits obsequies, or funeral ceremonies.
4. A heart not strengthened (against emotion or misfortune), a mind unprepared to suffer.
5. As the most obvious and ordinary thing we perceive
using our senses.
6. That of Abel, the first human to die, murdered by his
brother, Cain.

7. The birthplace of Protestantism, the university of
Luther and Faustus; many Danes studied there.
8. Bout of drinking.
9. F's reading; Q2 has "sallied," a possible spelling of
"sullied." Editors have seen wordplay on "sallied,"
assailed, or, alternatively, salty, tear-soaked (salting
was a method of preserving meat), and "sullied," or contaminated, ill used. "Solid" accords best with "melt."

Seem to me all the uses° of this world!   *customs; business*
135 Fie on't, ah fie, fie! 'Tis an unweeded garden
That grows to seed; things rank and gross in nature
Possess it merely.° That it should come to this—   *entirely*
But two months dead—nay, not so much, not two—
So excellent a king, that was to this
140 Hyperion to a satyr,[1] so loving to my mother
That he might not beteem° the winds of heaven   *permit*
Visit her face too roughly! Heaven and earth,
Must I remember? Why, she would hang on him
As if increase of appetite had grown
145 By what it fed on, and yet within a month—
Let me not think on't; frailty, thy name is woman—
A little month, or ere° those shoes were old   *before*
With which she followed my poor father's body,
Like Niobe, all tears,[2] why she, even she—
150 O God, a beast that wants discourse of reason[3]
Would have mourned longer!—married with mine uncle,
My father's brother, but no more like my father
Than I to Hercules; within a month,
Ere yet the salt of most unrighteous tears
155 Had left the flushing of her gallèd° eyes,   *inflamed*
She married. O most wicked speed, to post°   *hurry*
With such dexterity to incestuous sheets!
It is not, nor it cannot come to good.
But break, my heart, for I must hold my tongue.

    Enter HORATIO, MARCELLUS, *and* BARNARDO

  HORATIO Hail to your lordship.
160 HAMLET   I am glad to see you well.
Horatio—or I do forget myself.
  HORATIO The same, my lord, and your poor servant ever.
  HAMLET Sir, my good friend; I'll change° that name with you.   *exchange*
And what make you from[4] Wittenberg, Horatio?—
Marcellus.
165 MARCELLUS My good lord.
  HAMLET I am very glad to see you. [*To* BARNARDO] Good even, sir.—
But what in faith make you from Wittenberg?
  HORATIO A truant disposition, good my lord.
  HAMLET I would not have your enemy say so,
170 Nor shall you do mine ear that violence
To make it truster° of your own report   *believer*
Against yourself. I know you are no truant.
But what is your affair in Elsinore?
We'll teach you to drink deep ere you depart.
175 HORATIO My lord, I came to see your father's funeral.
  HAMLET I prithee do not mock me, fellow-student;
I think it was to see my mother's wedding.
  HORATIO Indeed, my lord, it followed hard upon.
  HAMLET Thrift, thrift, Horatio. The funeral baked meats°   *meat pies and pastries*
180 Did coldly° furnish forth the marriage tables.   *when cold*
Would I had met my dearest° foe in heaven   *most hated*

---

1. *So . . . satyr:* That King was to this as the sun god (Hyperion, a Titan) is to a lustful half goat (mythological companion of the wine god, Bacchus).
2. Niobe's fourteen children were killed by Apollo and Artemis to punish her for boasting about them. She continued to weep bitterly even after she was turned to stone.
3. That lacks the faculty of rational thought.
4. What are you doing away from.

Ere I had ever seen that day, Horatio.
My father—methinks I see my father.

HORATIO   O where, my lord?

HAMLET   In my mind's eye, Horatio.

185 HORATIO   I saw him once. A° was a goodly king.   *He*

HAMLET   A was a man. Take him for all in all,
I shall not look upon his like again.

HORATIO   My lord, I think I saw him yesternight.

HAMLET   Saw? Who?

190 HORATIO   My lord, the King your father.

HAMLET   The King my father?

HORATIO   Season° your admiration° for a while   *Moderate / amazement*
With an attent° ear till I may deliver,   *attentive*
Upon the witness of these gentlemen,
This marvel to you.

195 HAMLET   For God's love let me hear!

HORATIO   Two nights together had these gentlemen,
Marcellus and Barnardo, on their watch,
In the dead waste° and middle of the night,   *stillness*
Been thus encountered. A figure like your father,

200 Armed at all points° exactly, cap-à-pie,°   *details / head to foot*
Appears before them, and with solemn march
Goes slow and stately by them. Thrice he walked
By their oppressed and fear-surprisèd eyes
Within his truncheon's[5] length, whilst they distilled°   *dissolved*

205 Almost to jelly with the act° of fear   *effect*
Stand dumb and speak not to him. This to me
In dreadful secrecy impart they did,
And I with them the third night kept the watch,
Where, as they had delivered, both in time,

210 Form of the thing, each word made true and good,
The apparition comes. I knew your father;
These hands are not more like.[6]

HAMLET   But where was this?

MARCELLUS   My lord, upon the platform where we watched.

HAMLET   Did you not speak to it?

HORATIO   My lord, I did,

215 But answer made it none; yet once methought
It lifted up it° head and did address   *its*
Itself to motion like as it would speak,[7]
But even° then the morning cock crew loud,   *just*
And at the sound it shrunk in haste away
And vanished from our sight.

220 HAMLET   'Tis very strange.

HORATIO   As I do live, my honoured lord, 'tis true,
And we did think it writ down° in our duty   *prescribed*
To let you know of it.

HAMLET   Indeed, indeed, sirs; but this troubles me.—
Hold you the watch tonight?

225 BARNARDO *and* MARCELLUS   We do, my lord.

HAMLET   Armed, say you?

BARNARDO *and* MARCELLUS   Armed, my lord.

---

5. Officer's baton (see stage direction at 1.1.37).
6. These hands are not more like each other than the apparition was like King Hamlet.

7. *address . . . speak:* start to move as though it wished to speak.

HAMLET   From top to toe?

BARNARDO *and* MARCELLUS   My lord, from head to foot.

HAMLET   Then saw you not his
  face.

HORATIO   O yes, my lord, he wore his beaver up.

HAMLET   What° looked he? Frowningly?   *How*

HORATIO   A countenance more
  In sorrow than in anger.

230 HAMLET   Pale or red?

HORATIO   Nay, very pale.

HAMLET   And fixed his eyes upon you?

HORATIO   Most constantly.

HAMLET   I would I had been there.

HORATIO   It would have much amazed you.

235 HAMLET   Very like, very like. Stayed it long?

HORATIO   While one with moderate haste might tell° a hundred.   *count*

BARNARDO *and* MARCELLUS   Longer, longer.

HORATIO   Not when I saw't.

HAMLET   His beard was grizzly,° no?   *gray*

240 HORATIO   It was as I have seen it in his life,
  A sable silvered.[8]

HAMLET   I'll watch tonight. Perchance
  'Twill walk[9] again.

HORATIO   I warrant° you it will.   *guarantee*

HAMLET   If it assume my noble father's person
  I'll speak to it though hell itself should gape
245 And bid me hold my peace. I pray you all,
  If you have hitherto concealed this sight,
  Let it be treble[1] in your silence still,
  And whatsoever else shall hap° tonight,   *occur*
  Give it an understanding but no tongue.
250 I will requite your loves. So fare ye well.
  Upon the platform 'twixt eleven and twelve
  I'll visit you.

ALL THREE   Our duty to your honour.

HAMLET   Your love, as mine to you. Farewell.

                                 Exeunt [all but HAMLET]

  My father's spirit in arms! All is not well.
255 I doubt° some foul play. Would the night were come.   *suspect*
  Till then, sit still, my soul. Foul deeds will rise,
  Though all the earth o'erwhelm them, to men's eyes.   *Exit*

1.3

Enter LAERTES *and* OPHELIA, *his sister*

LAERTES   My necessaries are inbarqued.°   Farewell.   *aboard ship*
  And, sister, as the winds give benefit
  And convoy is assistant,[1] do not sleep
  But let me hear from you.

OPHELIA   Do you doubt that?

5 LAERTES   For Hamlet and the trifling of his favour,

---

8. Black sprinkled with white.
9. "Wake," F's reading, suggests a return to consciousness.
1. Triply (F's reading); most editors follow Q2's "ten-

able" (that is, able to be held).
1.3 Location: Polonius's apartments in the castle.
1. And means of transport is available.

Hold it a fashion and a toy in blood,
A violet in the youth of primy nature,
Forward[2] not permanent, sweet not lasting,
The perfume and suppliance° of a minute,   *diversion*
No more.

OPHELIA   No more but so?

10 LAERTES   Think it no more.
For nature crescent° does not grow alone   *growing*
In thews° and bulk, but as his temple° waxes   *muscles / body*
The inward service° of the mind and soul   *responsibility*
Grows wide withal.° Perhaps he loves you now,   *along with it*
15 And now no soil° nor cautel° doth besmirch   *stain / deception*
The virtue of his will;° but you must fear,   *intentions; desires*
His greatness weighed,[3] his will is not his own,
For he himself is subject to his birth.
He may not, as unvalued° persons do,   *common*
20 Carve for himself,[4] for on his choice depends
The sanity[5] and health of the whole state;
And therefore must his choice be circumscribed
Unto the voice° and yielding° of that body[6]   *vote / consent*
Whereof he is the head. Then if he says he loves you,
25 It fits° your wisdom so far to believe it   *befits*
As he in his peculiar sect and force[7]
May give his saying deed,[8] which is no further
Than the main° voice of Denmark goes withal.   *collective*
Then weigh what loss your honour may sustain
30 If with too credent° ear you list° his songs,   *trusting / listen to*
Or lose your heart, or your chaste treasure open
To his unmastered° importunity.   *uncontrolled*
Fear it, Ophelia, fear it, my dear sister,
And keep within the rear of your affection,[9]
35 Out of the shot and danger of desire.
The chariest° maid is prodigal enough   *most careful; modest*
If she unmask her beauty to the moon.[1]
Virtue itself scapes not calumnious strokes.
The canker galls the infants[2] of the spring
40 Too oft before their buttons be disclosed,°   *buds are open*
And in the morn and liquid dew of youth
Contagious blastments° are most imminent.   *blights*
Be wary then; best safety lies in fear;
Youth to itself rebels, though none else near.[3]
45 OPHELIA   I shall th'effect of this good lesson keep
As watchman to my heart; but, good my brother,
Do not, as some ungracious° pastors do,   *ungodly*
Show me the steep and thorny way to heaven
Whilst like a puffed° and reckless libertine   *proud*

---

2. *a toy . . . / Forward:* a passing sexual fancy, a flower of his natural impulses in their prime, early blooming ("forward").
3. When his high rank is considered.
4. Help himself to his own choice of the roast (proverbially, to choose for himself).
5. Well-being, emended from F's "sanctity"; Q2 prints "safety."
6. Body politic; nation.
7. His special rank and power (F). Q2 (and most editors) give "particular act and place," which has been interpreted as "power of action and social position."

8. May act on his promise.
9. And be restrained, despite the forward march of your feelings.
1. *prodigal . . . moon:* risk-taking enough if she exposes herself to the chaste moon. (Upper-class women wore masks to screen their complexions from the sun.) Q2 introduces lines 36, 38, and 39 with quotation marks, identifying these sentences as proverbial or noteworthy.
2. The cankerworm injures the shoots.
3. Young people are naturally rebellious, even without provocation.

50   Himself the primrose path of dalliance treads
         And recks° not his own rede.°   *heeds / advice*

LAERTES   O fear me not.°   *fear not for me*

        Enter POLONIUS

         I stay too long—but here my father comes.
         A double blessing is a double grace;
         Occasion smiles upon a second leave.[4]

55 POLONIUS   Yet here, Laertes? Aboard, aboard, for shame!
         The wind sits in the shoulder° of your sail,   *at the back*
         And you are stayed° for. There—my blessing with thee,   *waited*
         And these few precepts in thy memory
         See thou character.° Give thy thoughts no tongue,   *inscribe*
60   Nor any unproportioned° thought his act.   *unruly*
         Be thou familiar° but by no means vulgar.[5]   *friendly*
         The friends thou hast, and their adoption tried,°   *their friendship tested*
         Grapple them to thy soul with hoops of steel,
         But do not dull° thy palm with entertainment[6]   *callous*
65   Of each new-hatched unfledged comrade. Beware
         Of entrance to a quarrel, but being in,
         Bear't° that th'opposèd may beware of thee.   *Manage it so*
         Give every man thine ear but few thy voice.
         Take each man's censure,° but reserve thy judgement.   *opinion*
70   Costly thy habit° as thy purse can buy,   *dress*
         But not expressed in fancy;° rich not gaudy;   *bizarre excess*
         For the apparel oft proclaims the man,
         And they in France of the best rank and station
         Are of all most select and generous chief in that.[7]
75   Neither a borrower nor a lender be,
         For loan oft loses both itself and friend,
         And borrowing dulls the edge of husbandry.°   *economy*
         This above all—to thine own self be true,
         And it must follow, as the night the day,
80   Thou canst not then be false to any man.
         Farewell—my blessing season° this in thee.   *mature*

LAERTES   Most humbly do I take my leave, my lord.

POLONIUS   The time invites you. Go; your servants tend.°   *wait*

LAERTES   Farewell, Ophelia, and remember well
         What I have said to you.

85 OPHELIA   'Tis in my memory locked,
         And you yourself shall keep the key of it.

LAERTES   Farewell.   *Exit*

POLONIUS   What is't, Ophelia, he hath said to you?

OPHELIA   So please you, something touching the Lord Hamlet.

90 POLONIUS   Marry,[8] well bethought.
         'Tis told me he hath very oft of late
         Given private time to you, and you yourself
         Have of your audience° been most free and bounteous.   *attention*
         If it be so—as so 'tis put on° me,   *suggested to*
95   And that in way of caution—I must tell you
         You do not understand yourself so clearly

---

4. Favorable circumstances provide us with a second farewell.
5. Indiscriminately social.
6. Greeting (handshaking).

7. Are of all people the most adept at displaying rank in fine appearance.
8. By the Virgin Mary, a mild oath.

As it behoves my daughter and your honour.
What is between you? Give me up the truth.

OPHELIA He hath, my lord, of late made many tenders°   *offers*
100 Of his affection to me.

POLONIUS Affection, pooh! You speak like a green girl
Unsifted° in such perilous circumstance.   *Inexperienced*
Do you believe his 'tenders' as you call them?

OPHELIA I do not know, my lord, what I should think.

105 POLONIUS Marry, I'll teach you: think yourself a baby
That you have ta'en his tenders for true pay,
Which are not sterling.⁹ Tender° yourself more dearly,   *Value; protect*
Or—not to crack the wind of the poor phrase,
Running it thus¹—you'll tender me a fool.²

110 OPHELIA My lord, he hath importuned me with love
In honourable fashion—

POLONIUS Ay, fashion° you may call it. Go to,³ go to.   *conventional flattery*

OPHELIA And hath given countenance° to his speech, my lord,   *authority*
With all the vows of heaven.

115 POLONIUS Ay, springes to catch woodcocks.⁴ I do know
When the blood burns how prodigal° the soul   *lavishly*
Lends the tongue vows. These blazes, daughter,
Giving more light than heat, extinct° in both   *extinguished*
Even in their promise as it is a-making,
120 You must not take for fire. From this time, daughter,
Be somewhat scanter of your maiden presence.
Set your entreatments at a higher rate
Than a command to parley.⁵ For Lord Hamlet,
Believe so much in° him, that he is young,   *concerning*
125 And with a larger tether may he walk
Than may be given you. In few,° Ophelia,   *brief*
Do not believe his vows, for they are brokers,°   *go-betweens*
Not of the dye which their investments° show,   *clerical vestments*
But mere imploratators° of unholy suits,   *solicitors*
130 Breathing° like sanctified and pious bawds   *Speaking*
The better to beguile. This is for all—
I would not, in plain terms, from this time forth
Have you so slander° any moment leisure   *disgrace*
As to give words or talk with the Lord Hamlet.
135 Look to't, I charge you. Come your ways.°   *Come along*

OPHELIA I shall obey, my lord.   *Exeunt*

1.4

Enter [Prince] HAMLET, HORATIO, *and* MARCELLUS

HAMLET The air bites shrewdly,° it is very cold.   *sharply*

HORATIO It is a nipping and an eager° air.   *a bitter*

HAMLET What hour now?

HORATIO I think it lacks of twelve.

5 MARCELLUS No, it is struck.

HORATIO Indeed? I heard it not. Then it draws near the season°   *time*
Wherein the spirit held his wont° to walk.   *was accustomed*

---

9. Genuine currency.
1. *crack . . . thus:* ruin the phrase with overworking (like a "broken-winded" horse).
2. A multiple pun: make me look foolish; seem yourself a fool; show me a baby (idiomatically, a "fool").

3. That's enough; come, come.
4. (Obvious) traps for proverbially gullible birds.
5. *Set . . . parley:* Do not negotiate a surrender (of your chastity) just because he asks to speak with you.
1.4 Location: The castle's battlements.

A flourish of trumpets, and two pieces [of ordnance]°   *cannons*
goes off

What does this mean, my lord?

HAMLET   The King doth wake tonight and takes his rouse,
10   Keeps wassail, and the swagg'ring upspring reels,[1]
And as he drains his draughts of Rhenish° down   *Rhine wine*
The kettle-drum and trumpet thus bray out
The triumph of his pledge.[2]

HORATIO   Is it a custom?

15   HAMLET   Ay, marry is't,
And to my mind, though I am native here
And to the manner° born, it is a custom   *custom*
More honoured in the breach than the observance.[3]
18.1   *This heavy-headed revel east and west*
Makes us traduced and taxed of other nations.
They clepe° us drunkards, and with swinish phrase   *call*
Soil our addition;° and indeed it takes   *reputation*
18.5   *From our achievements, though performed at height,°*   *excellently*
The pith° and marrow of our attribute.°   *heart / attributed glory*
So, oft itchances in particular men
That, for some vicious mole of nature[4] in them—
As in their birth,° wherein they are not guilty,   *parentage*
18.10   *Since nature cannot choose his° origin,*   *its*
By the o'ergrowth of some complexion,[5]
Oft breaking down the pales° and forts of reason,   *fences; boundaries*
Or by some habit that too much o'erleavens
The form of plausive manners[6]—that these men,
18.15   *Carrying, I say, the stamp of one defect,*
Being nature's livery or fortune's star,[7]
His virtues else be they as pure as grace,
As infinite as man may undergo,°   *sustain*
Shall in the general censure° take corruption   *the public opinion*
18.20   *From that particular fault. The dram of evil[8]*
Doth all the noble substance over-daub[9]
To his own scandal.°   *shame*

Enter GHOST *[as before]*

HORATIO   Look, my lord, it comes.

20   HAMLET   Angels and ministers of grace defend us!
Be thou a spirit of health or goblin° damned,   *demon*
Bring with thee airs° from heaven or blasts[1] from hell,   *gentle breezes*
Be thy intents wicked or charitable,
Thou com'st in such a questionable shape
25   That I will speak to thee. I'll call thee Hamlet,
King, father, royal Dane. O answer me!

---

1. *The King . . . reels*: The King revels and carouses rather than sleeping, has a drinking party ("wassail"), and staggers ("reels") through a wild German dance.
2. His success in draining his cup upon making a toast.
3. Which is more honored in being broken than in being observed. After this line, Q2 has the following passage, 18.1–18.22, omitted in F (possibly in deference to the English Queen, Anne of Denmark).
4. Natural blemish that tends to vice.
5. By the disproportionate amount of one humor (see note to 2.2.310–11), and thus an unbalanced personality.
6. *o'erleavens . . . manners*: changes the whole effect of otherwise pleasing ("plausive") manners for the worse (as

too much yeast ruins a batch of bread).
7. Being a congenital defect (the "livery," or clothing, given by nature) or a blemish caused by fortune (the influence of chance astrological events).
8. Tiny amount (eighth of an ounce) of bad qualities. This is a conjectural emendation of Q2's "eale," although there is no consensus on the correct reading.
9. *Doth . . . over-daub*: Obscures the virtuous essence with adhering dirt. Emended from Q2's "of a doubt," an incomplete thought; "often dout" (extinguish) is another plausible correction.
1. Pestilent gusts.

Let me not burst in ignorance, but tell
Why thy canonized° bones, hearsèd° in death,   *consecrated / coffined*
Have burst their cerements,° why the sepulchre   *grave clothes*
30   Wherein we saw thee quietly enurned°   *entombed*
Hath oped his ponderous and marble jaws
To cast thee up again. What may this mean,
That thou, dead corpse, again in complete steel,°   *armor*
Revisitst thus the glimpses of the moon,[2]
35   Making night hideous, and we fools of nature[3]
So horridly to shake our disposition°   *mental foundations*
With thoughts beyond the reaches of our souls?
Say, why is this? Wherefore? What should we do?
              GHOST *beckons* HAMLET
HORATIO   It beckons you to go away with it
40   As if it some impartment° did desire   *communication*
To you alone.
MARCELLUS [*to* HAMLET]   Look with what courteous action
It wafts° you to a more removèd ground.   *beckons*
But do not go with it.
HORATIO [*to* HAMLET]   No, by no means.
HAMLET   It will not speak. Then will I follow it.
HORATIO   Do not, my lord.
45   HAMLET   Why, what should be the fear?
I do not set my life at a pin's fee,°   *value*
And for my soul, what can it do to that,
Being a thing immortal as itself?
       [GHOST *beckons* HAMLET]
It waves me forth again. I'll follow it.
50   HORATIO   What if it tempt you toward the flood,° my lord,   *sea*
Or to the dreadful summit of the cliff
That beetles o'er° his base into the sea,   *overhangs*
And there assume some other horrible form
Which might deprive your sovereignty of reason
55   And draw you into madness? Think of it.[4]
55.1   *The very place puts toys of desperation,[5]*
        Without more motive,° into every brain   *cause*
        That looks so many fathoms to the sea
        And hears it roar beneath.
       [GHOST *beckons* HAMLET]
HAMLET   It wafts me still. [*To* GHOST] Go on, I'll follow thee.
MARCELLUS   You shall not go, my lord.
HAMLET   Hold off your hand.
HORATIO   Be ruled. You shall not go.
HAMLET   My fate cries out,
And makes each petty artere° in this body   *artery*
60   As hardy as the Nemean lion's[6] nerve.
       [GHOST *beckons* HAMLET]
Still am I called. Unhand me, gentlemen.
By heav'n, I'll make a ghost of him that lets° me.   *hinders*
I say, away! [*To* GHOST] Go on, I'll follow thee.
                Exeunt GHOST *and* HAMLET

---

2. *glimpses of the moon:* (earth lit by) flickering moonlight.
3. Mere mortals (terrified by encounters with the supernatural).
4. After this line, Q2 has the following passage, 55.1–55.4, omitted in F.
5. Imaginings of despair and suicide.
6. A ferocious beast killed by Hercules.

HORATIO   He waxes desperate with imagination.
65   MARCELLUS   Let's follow. 'Tis not fit thus to obey him.
HORATIO   Have after.° To what issue° will this come?   *Go on / end*
MARCELLUS   Something is rotten in the state of Denmark.
HORATIO   Heaven will direct it.
MARCELLUS   Nay, let's follow him.   *Exeunt*

1.5

Enter GHOST, *and* [*Prince*] HAMLET [*following*]

HAMLET   Whither wilt thou lead me? Speak. I'll go no further.
GHOST   Mark me.
HAMLET   I will.
GHOST   My hour is almost come
   When I to sulph'rous and tormenting flames
   Must render up myself.
HAMLET   Alas, poor ghost!
5   GHOST   Pity me not, but lend thy serious hearing
   To what I shall unfold.
HAMLET   Speak, I am bound to hear.
GHOST   So art thou to revenge when thou shalt hear.
HAMLET   What?
GHOST   I am thy father's spirit,
10   Doomed for a certain term to walk the night,
   And for the day confined to fast° in fires   *do penance*
   Till the foul crimes done in my days of nature°   *my natural life*
   Are burnt and purged away. But that I am forbid
   To tell the secrets of my prison-house
15   I could a tale unfold whose lightest word
   Would harrow up thy soul, freeze thy young blood,
   Make thy two eyes like stars start from their spheres,
   Thy knotty and combinèd locks to part,
   And each particular hair to stand on end
20   Like quills upon the fretful porcupine.
   But this eternal blazon[1] must not be
   To ears of flesh and blood. List,° Hamlet, list, O list!   *Listen*
   If thou didst ever thy dear father love—
HAMLET   O God!
25   GHOST   Revenge his foul and most unnatural murder.
HAMLET   Murder?
GHOST   Murder most foul, as in the best it is,
   But this most foul, strange, and unnatural.
HAMLET   Haste, haste me to know it, that with wings as swift
30   As meditation or the thoughts of love
   May sweep to my revenge.
GHOST   I find thee apt,
   And duller shouldst thou be than the fat° weed   *gross*
   That rots itself[2] in ease on Lethe wharf[3]
   Wouldst thou not stir in this. Now, Hamlet, hear.
35   'Tis given out that, sleeping in mine orchard,
   A serpent stung me. So the whole ear of Denmark
   Is by a forgèd process° of my death   *a fabricated account*

1.5 Location: Scene continues.
1. Catalogue or display of the afterlife's mysteries.
2. Decays under its own excessive growth (F). Q1, Q2

print "roots itself," another possible reading.
3. In classical mythology, Lethe was the river of forget-fulness in Hades.

Rankly abused.° But know, thou noble youth,   *deceived*
The serpent that did sting thy father's life
40 Now wears his crown.

HAMLET   O my prophetic soul! Mine uncle?

GHOST   Ay, that incestuous, that adulterate° beast,   *adulterous*
With witchcraft of his wit, with traitorous gifts°—   *abilities; presents*
O wicked wit and gifts, that have the power
45 So to seduce!—won to his shameful lust
The will of my most seeming-virtuous queen.
O Hamlet, what a falling off was there!—
From me, whose love was of that dignity
That it went hand-in-hand even with the vow
50 I made to her in marriage, and to decline
Upon a wretch whose natural gifts were poor
To° those of mine.   *Compared to*
But virtue, as it never will be moved,
Though lewdness court it in a shape of heaven,
55 So lust, though to a radiant angel linked,
Will sate itself[4] in a celestial bed,
And prey on garbage.
But soft, methinks I scent the morning's air.
Brief let me be. Sleeping within mine orchard,
60 My custom always in the afternoon,
Upon my secure hour thy uncle stole
With juice of cursèd hebenon[5] in a vial,
And in the porches° of mine ears did pour   *entranceways*
The leperous distilment,[6] whose effect
65 Holds such an enmity with blood of man
That swift as quicksilver it courses through
The natural gates and alleys of the body,
And with a sudden vigour it doth posset°   *curdle*
And curd, like eager° droppings into milk,   *acid (like wine)*
70 The thin and wholesome blood. So did it mine;
And a most instant tetter° barked about,[7]   *scaly rash*
Most lazar-like,° with vile and loathsome crust,   *leperlike*
All my smooth body.
Thus was I, sleeping, by a brother's hand
75 Of life, of crown, of queen at once dispatched,°   *deprived*
Cut off even in the blossoms of my sin,[8]
Unhouseled, dis-appointed, unaneled,[9]
No reck'ning made, but sent to my account
With all my imperfections on my head.[1]
80 O horrible, O horrible, most horrible!
If thou hast nature° in thee, bear it not.   *natural feeling*
Let not the royal bed of Denmark be
A couch for luxury° and damnèd incest.   *lechery*
But howsoever thou pursuest this act,
85 Taint not thy mind,[2] nor let thy soul contrive
Against thy mother aught.° Leave her to heaven,   *any punishment*

---

4. Will become satiated (and unable to find further pleasure).
5. A poison, possibly henbane.
6. Distillation causing skin to become scaly (as in leprosy, a disease familiar in Elizabethan England).
7. Covered the body like bark.
8. Cut off when my sins were full-blown, flourishing.

9. Without the sacrament of the Eucharist, without death-bed confession and absolution, and without extreme unction, the ritual anointing of those who are close to death.
1. *No . . . head:* Without having made restitution for my sins, but sent to the Last Judgment liable for all my faults.
2. Do not let yourself be corrupted.

And to those thorns that in her bosom lodge
To prick and sting her. Fare thee well at once.
The glow-worm shows the matin° to be near,   *morning*
90   And gins° to pale his uneffectual fire.   *begins*
Adieu, adieu, Hamlet. Remember me.   *Exit*
HAMLET   O all you host of heaven! O earth! What else?
And shall I couple° hell? O fie! Hold, hold, my heart,   *add*
And you, my sinews, grow not instant old,
95   But bear me stiffly up. Remember thee?
Ay, thou poor ghost, while memory holds a seat
In this distracted globe.³ Remember thee?
Yea, from the table° of my memory   *tablet; book*
I'll wipe away all trivial fond° records,   *foolish*
100   All saws of books, all forms, all pressures past,⁴
That youth and observation copied there,
And thy commandment all alone shall live
Within the book and volume of my brain
Unmixed with baser matter. Yes, yes, by heaven.
105   O most pernicious woman!
O villain, villain, smiling, damnèd villain!
My tables,⁵
My tables—meet it is I set it down
That one may smile and smile and be a villain.
110   At least I'm sure it may be so in Denmark.
        [*He writes*]
So, uncle, there you are. Now to my word:°   *watchword; motto*
It is 'Adieu, adieu, remember me'.
I have sworn't.
HORATIO *and* MARCELLUS [*within*]   My lord, my lord.
        Enter HORATIO *and* MARCELLUS
115   MARCELLUS [*calling*]   Lord Hamlet!
HORATIO   Heaven secure him.
HAMLET   So be it.
HORATIO [*calling*]   Illo, ho, ho, my lord.
HAMLET   Hillo, ho, ho, boy; come, bird, come.⁶
120   MARCELLUS   How is't, my noble lord?
HORATIO [*to* HAMLET]   What news, my lord?
HAMLET   O wonderful!
HORATIO   Good my lord, tell it.
HAMLET   No, you'll reveal it.
HORATIO   Not I, my lord, by heaven.
MARCELLUS   Nor I, my lord.
125   HAMLET   How say you then, would heart of man once think it?
But you'll be secret?
HORATIO *and* MARCELLUS   Ay, by heav'n, my lord.
HAMLET   There's ne'er a villain dwelling in all Denmark
But he's an arrant° knave.   *a downright*
HORATIO   There needs no ghost, my lord, come from the grave
To tell us this.
130   HAMLET   Why, right, you are i'th' right,
And so without more circumstance° at all   *elaborate speech*

3. Confused head; disordered world; often also taken as a reference to the Globe Theatre and the audience.
4. All adages from books, all images or customs, all past impressions.
5. Scholars and others might carry two writing tables hinged together, as a notebook.
6. Hamlet parodies a falconer's call.

I hold it fit that we shake hands and part,
You as your business and desires shall point you—
For every man has business and desire,

135   Such as it is—and for mine own poor part,
Look you, I'll go pray.

HORATIO   These are but wild and whirling words, my lord.

HAMLET   I'm sorry they offend you, heartily,
Yes, faith, heartily.

HORATIO   There's no offence, my lord.

140 HAMLET   Yes, by Saint Patrick,[7] but there is, Horatio,
And much offence, too. Touching this vision here,
It is an honest° ghost, that let me tell you.   *a reliable; a genuine*
For your desire to know what is between us,
O'ermaster't as you may. And now, good friends,

145   As you are friends, scholars, and soldiers,
Give me one poor request.

HORATIO   What is't, my lord? We will.

HAMLET   Never make known what you have seen tonight.

HORATIO *and* MARCELLUS   My lord, we will not.

HAMLET   Nay, but swear't.

HORATIO   In faith, my lord, not I.[8]

MARCELLUS   Nor I, my lord, in faith.

HAMLET   Upon my sword.[9]

150 MARCELLUS   We have sworn, my lord, already.

HAMLET   Indeed, upon my sword, indeed.
            GHOST *cries under the stage*

GHOST   Swear.

HAMLET   Ah ha, boy, sayst thou so? Art thou there, truepenny?°—   *trusty fellow*
Come on. You hear this fellow in the cellarage.
Consent to swear.

HORATIO   Propose the oath, my lord.

155 HAMLET   Never to speak of this that you have seen,
Swear by my sword.

GHOST [*under the stage*]   Swear.
           [*They swear*]

HAMLET   *Hic et ubique?*[1] Then we'll shift our ground.—
Come hither, gentlemen,

160   And lay your hands again upon my sword.
Never to speak of this that you have heard,
Swear by my sword.

GHOST [*under the stage*]   Swear.
           [*They swear*]

HAMLET   Well said, old mole. Canst work i'th' earth so fast?

165   A worthy pioneer.[2]—Once more remove,° good friends.   *move*

HORATIO   O day and night, but this is wondrous strange!

HAMLET   And therefore as a stranger give it welcome.[3]
There are more things in heaven and earth, Horatio,
Than are dreamt of in our philosophy.[4] But come,

---

7. Perhaps because Patrick was thought to be keeper of purgatory.
8. I will indeed not reveal it.
9. Swearing on a sword was a fairly common practice because the hilt and blade form a cross.
1. Here and everywhere (Latin).

2. Army trench digger.
3. As if it had a guest's right to courteous hospitality.
4. Human speculative knowledge. Q2 and most editors print "your philosophy"; F's "our" shows Hamlet himself still trying to reconcile his own understanding with the supernatural revelations.

170 Here as before, never, so help you mercy,
How strange or odd soe'er I bear myself—
As I perchance hereafter shall think meet
To put an antic disposition on⁵—
That you at such time seeing me never shall,
175 With arms encumbered° thus, or this headshake,   *folded*
Or by pronouncing of some doubtful° phrase   *ambiguous*
As 'Well, we know' or 'We could an if° we would',   *an if=if*
Or 'If we list° to speak', or 'There be, an if they might',⁶   *liked*
Or such ambiguous giving out, to note
180 That you know aught° of me—this not to do,   *anything*
So grace and mercy at your most need help you, swear.
GHOST [*under the stage*]   Swear.
        [*They swear*]
HAMLET   Rest, rest, perturbèd spirit.—So, gentlemen,
With all my love I do commend me to you,
185 And what so poor a man as Hamlet is
May do t'express his love and friending° to you,   *friendship*
God willing, shall not lack.° Let us go in together,   *be left undone*
And still° your fingers on your lips, I pray.   *always*
The time is out of joint.° O cursèd spite   *dislocated; disordered*
190 That ever I was born to set it right!
Nay, come,⁷ let's go together.   *Exeunt*

2.1

Enter old POLONIUS *with his man* REYNALDO

POLONIUS   Give him this money and these notes, Reynaldo.
REYNALDO   I will, my lord.
POLONIUS   You shall do marv'lous wisely, good Reynaldo,
Before you visit him to make enquire
Of his behaviour.
5 REYNALDO   My lord, I did intend it.
POLONIUS   Marry, well said, very well said. Look you, sir,
Enquire me° first what Danskers° are in Paris,   *for me / Danes*
And how, and who, what means,° and where they keep,°   *wealth; income / lodge*
What company, at what expense; and finding
10 By this encompassment and drift of question¹
That they do know my son, come you more nearer
Than your particular demands will touch it.²
Take you,° as 'twere, some distant knowledge of him,   *Pretend*
As thus: 'I know his father and his friends,
15 And in part him'—do you mark this, Reynaldo?
REYNALDO   Ay, very well, my lord.
POLONIUS   'And in part him, but', you may say, 'not well,
But if't be he I mean, he's very wild,
Addicted so and so'; and there put on him°   *attribute to him*
20 What forgeries° you please—marry, none so rank³   *made-up tales*
As may dishonour him, take heed of that—
But, sir, such wanton,° wild, and usual slips   *unrestrained*

---

5. To assume the behavior of a madman.
6. There are those who would speak if they were allowed.
7. The others are politely waiting for Hamlet, the Prince, to lead the way; he insists on informality.
2.1 Location: Polonius's apartments in the castle.

1. By this roundabout and indirect way of inquiry.
2. *come . . . it:* you will come closer to the truth than by direct questions.
3. Excessive; foul.

As are companions noted and most known
To youth and liberty.

25 REYNALDO   As gaming, my lord?

POLONIUS   Ay, or drinking, fencing, swearing,
Quarrelling, drabbing°—you may go so far.   *whoring*

REYNALDO   My lord, that would dishonour him.

POLONIUS   Faith, no, as you may season° it in the charge.   *mitigate*

30 You must not put another scandal on him,
That he is open° to incontinency.°   *inclined / sexual excess*
That's not my meaning—but breathe his faults so quaintly
That they may seem the taints of liberty,[4]
The flash and outbreak of a fiery mind,

35 A savageness in unreclaimèd° blood,   *unchecked*
Of general assault.[5]

REYNALDO   But, my good lord—

POLONIUS   Wherefore should you do this?

REYNALDO   Ay, my lord.
I would know that.

POLONIUS   Marry, sir, here's my drift,
And I believe it is a fetch of warrant:[6]

40 You laying these slight sullies on my son,
As 'twere a thing a little soiled i'th' working,[7]
Mark you, your party° in converse, him you would sound,°   *partner / sound out*
Having° ever seen in the prenominate crimes[8]   *If he has*
The youth you breathe of guilty, be assured

45 He closes° with you in this consequence:[9]   *confides*
'Good sir', or so, or 'friend', or 'gentleman',
According to the phrase° and the addition[1]   *expression*
Of man and country.

REYNALDO   Very good, my lord.

POLONIUS   And then, sir, does a° this—a does—   *he*
50 what was I about to say? By the mass, I was about to say something. Where did I leave?

REYNALDO   At 'closes in the consequence', at 'friend',
Or so', and 'gentleman'.

POLONIUS   At 'closes in the consequence'—ay, marry,
55 He closes with you thus: 'I know the gentleman,
I saw him yesterday'—or t'other day,
Or then, or then—'with such and such, and, as you say,
There was a° gaming, there o'ertook in 's rouse,   *he*
There falling out° at tennis', or perchance   *quarreling*

60 'I saw him enter such a house of sale',
Videlicet,° a brothel, or so forth. See you now,   *That is to say*
Your bait of falsehood takes this carp of truth;
And thus do we of wisdom and of reach°   *wide understanding*
With windlasses and with assays of bias[2]

65 By indirections find directions° out.   *real tendencies*
So, by my former° lecture and advice,   *preceding*
Shall you my son. You have me,° have you not?   *my meaning*

---

4. Faults resulting from freedom of action.
5. Which afflicts all young men.
6. *fetch of warrant*: justifiable trick (F). Q2 has "fetch of wit" (clever scheme).
7. Stained by education in the ways of the world, "shop soiled."

8. Aforesaid faults.
9. To the following effect.
1. Title of address.
2. And with indirect tests, like the curved line, or "bias," that a weighted bowling ball describes. *windlasses*: round-about paths (a hunter's circuit to intercept game).

REYNALDO	My lord, I have.	
POLONIUS	God b'wi' ye. Fare ye well.	
70 REYNALDO	Good my lord.	
POLONIUS	Observe his inclination in° yourself.	*for*
REYNALDO	I shall, my lord.	
POLONIUS	And let him ply° his music.	*work at*
REYNALDO	Well, my lord.	

Enter OPHELIA

POLONIUS   Farewell.   *Exit* REYNALDO
75   How now, Ophelia, what's the matter?
OPHELIA   Alas, my lord, I have been so affrighted.
POLONIUS   With what, i'th' name of God?
OPHELIA   My lord, as I was sewing in my chamber,
   Lord Hamlet, with his doublet all unbraced,°   *jacket all unfastened*
80   No hat upon his head, his stockings fouled,
   Ungartered, and down-gyvèd to his ankle,³
   Pale as his shirt, his knees knocking each other,
   And with a look so piteous in purport
   As if he had been loosèd out of hell
85   To speak of horrors, he comes before me.
POLONIUS   Mad for thy love?
OPHELIA   My lord, I do not know,
   But truly I do fear it.
POLONIUS   What said he?
OPHELIA   He took me by the wrist and held me hard,
   Then goes he to the length of all his arm,
90   And with his other hand thus o'er his brow
   He falls to such perusal of my face
   As a° would draw it. Long stayed he so.   *As if he*
   At last, a little shaking of mine arm,
   And thrice his head thus waving up and down,
95   He raised a sigh so piteous and profound
   That it did seem to shatter all his bulk
   And end his being. That done, he lets me go,
   And, with his head over his shoulder turned,
   He seemed to find his way without his eyes,
100   For out o' doors he went without their help,
   And to the last bended their light⁴ on me.
POLONIUS   Come, go with me. I will go seek the King.
   This is the very ecstasy° of love,   *insanity*
   Whose violent property fordoes° itself   *nature destroys*
105   And leads the will to desperate undertakings
   As oft as any passion under heaven
   That does afflict our natures. I am sorry—
   What, have you given him any hard words of late?
OPHELIA   No, my good lord, but as you did command
110   I did repel his letters and denied
   His access to me.
POLONIUS   That hath made him mad.
   I am sorry that with better speed and judgement
   I had not quoted° him. I feared he did but trifle   *observed*

---

3. Fallen round his ankles, like a prisoner's fetters, or
"gyves."

4. Sight was thought to result from both sending light
out and taking it in through the eyes.

And meant to wreck thee.[5] But beshrew my jealousy!°   *curse my suspicion*
115 By heaven, it is as proper to our age
To cast beyond ourselves[6] in our opinions
As it is common for the younger sort
To lack discretion. Come, go we to the King.
This must be known, which, being kept close, might move
120 More grief to hide than hate to utter love.[7]   *Exeunt*

2.2

Flourish. Enter KING [CLAUDIUS] *and* QUEEN [GER-
TRUDE], ROSENCRANTZ *and* GUILDENSTERN,[1] *cum aliis*

KING CLAUDIUS   Welcome, dear Rosencrantz and Guildenstern.
Moreover° that we much did long to see you,   *Beyond the fact*
The need we have to use you did provoke
Our hasty sending.° Something have you heard   *summons*
5 Of Hamlet's transformation—so I call it,
Since not th'exterior nor the inward man
Resembles that° it was. What it should be,   *what*
More than his father's death, that thus hath put him
So much from th'understanding of himself,
10 I cannot deem of.[2] I entreat you both
That, being of so young days[3] brought up with him,
And since so neighboured° to his youth and humour,°   *familiar / temperament*
That you vouchsafe your rest[4] here in our court
Some little time, so by your companies
15 To draw him on to pleasures, and to gather,
So much as from occasions° you may glean,   *opportunities*
Whether aught to us unknown afflicts him thus
That, opened,° lies within our remedy.   *if disclosed*
QUEEN GERTRUDE   Good gentlemen, he hath much talked of you,
20 And sure I am two men there is not living
To whom he more adheres.[5] If it will please you
To show us so much gentry° and good will   *courtesy*
As to expend your time with us a while
For the supply and profit of our hope,[6]
25 Your visitation shall receive such thanks
As fits a king's remembrance.
ROSENCRANTZ   Both your majesties
Might, by the sovereign power you have of° us,   *over*
Put your dread° pleasures more into command   *reverend*
Than to entreaty.
GUILDENSTERN   But we both obey,
30 And here give up ourselves in the full bent[7]
To lay our service freely at your feet
To be commanded.
KING CLAUDIUS   Thanks, Rosencrantz and gentle Guildenstern.

---

5. To ruin you through seduction.
6. *as proper . . . ourselves:* as natural to us old men to go too far and (like hunting dogs) lose the scent, thus erring out of caution.
7. *which . . . love:* we may incur hatred by revealing (Hamlet's) love, but to conceal it may cause greater suffering. *close:* secret.
2.2 Location: A stateroom in the castle.
1. Historical figures with these names are mentioned in an ambassador's report to Queen Elizabeth sent from Elsinore in 1588.
2. Judge (F). Q2 prints "dream."
3. From such an early age.
4. That you agree to stay.
5. To whom he is more attached.
6. *For . . . hope:* To provide support for and furtherance of our hope.
7. To the fullest extent (like an archer's bow, fully drawn).

QUEEN GERTRUDE   Thanks, Guildenstern and gentle Rosencrantz.
35   And I beseech you instantly to visit
      My too-much changèd son.—Go, some of ye,
      And bring the gentlemen where Hamlet is.
GUILDENSTERN   Heavens make our presence and our practices
      Pleasant and helpful to him.
QUEEN GERTRUDE   Ay, amen!
            Exeunt ROSENCRANTZ *and* GUILDENSTERN [*with others*]
            Enter POLONIUS
40   POLONIUS   Th'ambassadors from Norway, my good lord,
      Are joyfully returned.
KING CLAUDIUS   Thou still° hast been the father of good news.   *always*
POLONIUS   Have I, my lord? Assure you, my good liege,
      I hold my duty, as I hold my soul,
45   Both to my God and to my gracious King.
      And I do think—or else this brain of mine
      Hunts not the trail of policy° so sure   *cleverness*
      As it hath used to do—that I have found
      The very cause of Hamlet's lunacy.
50   KING CLAUDIUS   O speak of that, that I do long to hear!
POLONIUS   Give first admittance to th'ambassadors.
      My news shall be the fruit° to that great feast.   *dessert*
KING CLAUDIUS   Thyself do grace to them, and bring them in.
            [*Exit* POLONIUS]
      He tells me, my sweet queen, that he hath found
55   The head° and source of all your son's distemper.   *origin; chief part*
QUEEN GERTRUDE   I doubt⁸ it is no other but the main°—   *main matter*
      His father's death and our o'er-hasty marriage.
KING CLAUDIUS   Well, we shall sift him.°   *interrogate (Polonius)*
            Enter POLONIUS, VALTEMAND, *and* CORNELIUS
                        Welcome, my good friends.
      Say, Valtemand, what from our brother° Norway?   *fellow monarch*
60   VALTEMAND   Most fair return of greetings and desires.°   *good wishes*
      Upon our first⁹ he sent out to suppress
      His nephew's levies, which to him appeared
      To be a preparation 'gainst the Polack;°   *King of Poland*
      But better looked into, he truly found
65   It was against your highness; whereat grieved
      That so his sickness, age, and impotence
      Was falsely borne in hand,¹ sends out arrests
      On Fortinbras,² which he, in brief, obeys,
      Receives rebuke from Norway, and, in fine,°   *conclusion*
70   Makes vow before his uncle never more
      To give th'essay of arms³ against your majesty;
      Whereon old Norway, overcome with joy,
      Gives him three thousand crowns in annual fee°   *income*
      And his commission to employ those soldiers
75   So levied as before, against the Polack,
      With an entreaty herein further shown,
            [*He gives a letter to* CLAUDIUS]
      That it might please you to give quiet pass

8. Fear, suspect. *distemper:* unbalanced mind.
9. When we first raised the matter.
1. Disloyally taken advantage of, tricked.
2. *arrests / On Fortinbras:* orders commanding Fortin-

bras to stop his preparations and (presumably) present
himself to explain them.
3. To mount a military challenge.

Through your dominions for his enterprise
On such regards of safety and allowance[4]
As therein are set down.

80 KING CLAUDIUS   It likes° us well,   *pleases*
And at our more considered° time we'll read,   *suitable for thought*
Answer, and think upon this business.
Meantime we thank you for your well-took labour.
Go to your rest; at night we'll feast together.
85 Most welcome home.

Exeunt [VALTEMAND *and* CORNELIUS]

POLONIUS   This business is very well ended.
My liege, and madam, to expostulate°   *debate*
What majesty should be, what duty is,
Why day is day, night night, and time is time,
90 Were nothing but to waste night, day, and time.
Therefore, since brevity is the soul of wit,
And tediousness the limbs and outward flourishes,°   *rhetorical devices*
I will be brief. Your noble son is mad—
'Mad' call I it, for to define true madness,
95 What is't but to be nothing else but mad?
But let that go.

QUEEN GERTRUDE   More matter with less art.

POLONIUS   Madam, I swear I use no art at all.
That he is mad, 'tis true; 'tis true 'tis pity,
And pity 'tis 'tis true—a foolish figure,°   *figure of speech*
100 But farewell it, for I will use no art.
Mad let us grant him, then; and now remains
That we find out the cause of this effect—
Or rather say 'the cause of this *defect*',
For this effect defective[5] comes by cause.
105 Thus it remains, and the remainder thus.
Perpend.°   *Consider*
I have a daughter—have whilst she is mine°—   *until she marries*
Who in her duty and obedience, mark,
Hath given me this. Now gather and surmise.

[He reads a] letter

110 'To the celestial and my soul's idol, the most beautified Ophelia'—that's an ill phrase, a vile phrase, 'beautified' is a vile
phrase. But you shall hear—'these in° her excellent white   *these words unto*
bosom, these'.

QUEEN GERTRUDE   Came this from Hamlet to her?

115 POLONIUS   Good madam, stay° a while. I will be faithful.[6]   *wait*
'Doubt thou the stars are fire,
   Doubt that the sun doth move,
Doubt° truth to be a liar,   *Suspect*
   But never doubt I love.
120 O dear Ophelia, I am ill at these numbers.[7] I have not art to
reckon my groans.[8] But that I love thee best, O most best,
believe it. Adieu.
   Thine evermore, most dear lady, whilst this
   machine is° to him,   *this body belongs*

---

4. *On . . . allowance:* Conditions regarding your realm's
safety, subject to your approval.
5. This consequence showing a lack of something (Hamlet's reason).

6. I will accurately read out the letter's contents.
7. Hamlet is both bad at writing verse and lovesick while
he is writing.
8. Count my groans; also, number my groans metrically.

Hamlet.'

125 This in obedience hath my daughter showed me,
And more above° hath his solicitings,   *in addition*
As they fell out° by time, by means, and place,   *occurred*
All given to mine ear.
KING CLAUDIUS   But how hath she
Received his love?
POLONIUS   What do you think of me?
130 KING CLAUDIUS   As of a man faithful and honourable.
POLONIUS   I would fain° prove so. But what might you think,   *be glad to*
When I had seen this hot love on the wing,
As I perceived it—I must tell you that—
Before my daughter told me, what might you,
135 Or my dear majesty your queen here, think,
If I had played the desk or table-book,⁹
Or given my heart a winking mute and dumb,¹
Or looked upon this love with idle sight—
What might you think? No, I went round° to work,   *directly*
140 And my young mistress thus I did bespeak:°   *address*
'Lord Hamlet is a prince out of thy star.°   *above your sphere*
This must not be'. And then I precepts gave her,
That she should lock herself from his resort,°   *visits*
Admit no messengers, receive no tokens;
145 Which done, she took the fruits of my advice,
And he, repulsèd—a short tale to make—
Fell into a sadness, then into a fast,
Thence to a watch,° thence into a weakness,   *an insomnia*
Thence to a lightness,° and, by this declension,°   *dizziness / decline*
150 Into the madness wherein now he raves,
And all we° wail for.   *of us*
KING CLAUDIUS [*to* GERTRUDE]   Do you think 'tis this?
QUEEN GERTRUDE   It may be; very likely.
POLONIUS   Hath there been such a time—I'd fain know that—
155 That I have positively said ' 'Tis so'
When it proved otherwise?
KING CLAUDIUS   Not that I know.
POLONIUS [*touching his head, then his shoulder*]
Take this from this if this be otherwise.
If circumstances lead me I will find
Where truth is hid, though it were hid indeed
Within the centre.°   *middle of the earth*
160 KING CLAUDIUS   How may we try° it further?   *test*
POLONIUS   You know sometimes he walks four hours together
Here in the lobby.
QUEEN GERTRUDE   So he does indeed.
POLONIUS   At such a time I'll loose my daughter to him.
[*To* CLAUDIUS] Be you and I behind an arras° then.   *a tapestry*
165 Mark the encounter. If he love her not,
And be not from his reason fall'n thereon,°   *on that account*

9. If I had recorded the perception (in my memory) but   1. Or made my heart close its eyes and remain silent.
kept it hidden.

Let me be no assistant for a state,
But keep a farm and carters.°   *wagon drivers*

KING CLAUDIUS   We will try it.

Enter [Prince] HAMLET, *[madly attired,] reading on a*
book[2]

QUEEN GERTRUDE   But look where sadly° the poor wretch comes   *gravely*
reading.

170   POLONIUS   Away, I do beseech you both, away.
I'll board him presently.° O give me leave.[3]   *accost him immediately*

Exit KING *and* QUEEN

How does my good Lord Hamlet?

HAMLET   Well, God-'a'-mercy.[4]

POLONIUS   Do you know me, my lord?

175   HAMLET   Excellent, excellent well. You're a fishmonger.

POLONIUS   Not I, my lord.

HAMLET   Then I would you were so honest a man.

POLONIUS   Honest, my lord?

HAMLET   Ay, sir. To be honest, as this world goes, is to be one
180   man picked out of ten thousand.

POLONIUS   That's very true, my lord.

HAMLET   For if the sun breed maggots in a dead dog, being a
good kissing carrion[5]—have you a daughter?

POLONIUS   I have, my lord.

185   HAMLET   Let her not walk i'th' sun.[6] Conception[7] is a blessing,
but not as your daughter may conceive. Friend, look to't.°   *take care*

POLONIUS   [*aside*]   How say you by that? Still harping on my
daughter. Yet he knew me not at first—a° said I was a fish-   *he*
monger. A is far gone, far gone, and truly, in my youth I suf-
190   fered much extremity for love, very near this. I'll speak to him
again.—What do you read, my lord?

HAMLET   Words, words, words.

POLONIUS   What is the matter,[8] my lord?

HAMLET   Between who?

195   POLONIUS   I mean the matter you read, my lord.

HAMLET   Slanders, sir; for the satirical slave° says here that old   *scoundrel*
men have grey beards, that their faces are wrinkled, their eyes
purging° thick amber° or plum-tree gum, and that they have a   *discharging / resin*
plentiful lack of wit,° together with most weak hams.° All which,   *intellect / thighs*
200   sir, though I most powerfully and potently believe, yet I hold
it not honesty° to have it thus set down; for you yourself, sir,   *honorable*
should be old as I am—if, like a crab, you could go backward.

POLONIUS   [*aside*]   Though this be madness, yet there is method
in't.—Will you walk out of the air,[9] my lord?

205   HAMLET   Into my grave.

POLONIUS   Indeed, that is out o'th' air. [*Aside*] How pregnant°   *meaningful*
sometimes his replies are! A happiness° that often madness hits   *An appropriateness*

2. Hamlet possibly has two entrances here, the first at
the inner stage ("lobby," line 162) and the second at the
outer stage representing the audience chamber, where
Claudius, Gertrude, and Polonius are talking. Hamlet
would thus have overheard Polonius's plan before they
notice him reading (line 169). (See 2.1.79–82 for
Ophelia's description of Hamlet's attire.)
3. Excuse me (politely asking the King and Queen to
leave).
4. Thank you (used with inferiors).

5. Piece of flesh good for kissing. Dead matter was
thought to breed maggots, especially in sunlight.
6. Walk out in public or (as in 1.2.67) expose herself too
much to a Prince's (or son's) love.
7. The ability to form ideas; pregnancy.
8. Content, although Hamlet deliberately takes it as
"subject of a quarrel."
9. Outdoor air was regarded as a hazard for the sick;
Polonius may mean "out of the draughts," since the
scene seems to be set indoors.

on, which reason and sanity could not so prosperously° be   *successfully*
delivered of. I will leave him, and suddenly° contrive the means   *immediately*
210 of meeting between him and my daughter.—My lord, I will
take my leave of you.

HAMLET   You cannot, sir, take from me anything that I will more
willingly part withal°—except my life, my life, my life.   *with*

POLONIUS [*going*]   Fare you well, my lord.

215 HAMLET   These tedious old fools!

               Enter GUILDENSTERN *and* ROSENCRANTZ[1]

POLONIUS   You go to seek the Lord Hamlet. There he is.

ROSENCRANTZ   God save you, sir.

GUILDENSTERN [*to* POLONIUS]   Mine honoured lord.

                                               [*Exit* POLONIUS]

ROSENCRANTZ [*to* HAMLET]   My most dear lord.

220 HAMLET   My ex'llent good friends. How dost thou, Guildenstern? Ah, Rosencrantz—good lads, how do ye both?

ROSENCRANTZ   As the indifferent° children of the earth.   *ordinary*

GUILDENSTERN   Happy° in that we are not over-happy,   *Fortunate*
On Fortune's cap we are not the very button.°   *highest point*

225 HAMLET   Nor the soles of her shoe?

ROSENCRANTZ   Neither, my lord.

HAMLET   Then you live about her waist, or in the middle of her
favour?

GUILDENSTERN   Faith, her privates[2] we.

230 HAMLET   In the secret parts of Fortune? O, most true, she is a
strumpet.° What's the news?   *whore*

ROSENCRANTZ   None, my lord, but that the world's grown
honest.

HAMLET   Then is doomsday near. But your news is not true. Let
235 me question more in particular. What have you, my good
friends, deserved at the hands of Fortune that she sends you to
prison hither?

GUILDENSTERN   Prison, my lord?

HAMLET   Denmark's a prison.

240 ROSENCRANTZ   Then is the world one.

HAMLET   A goodly[3] one, in which there are many confines,°   *enclosures*
wards,° and dungeons, Denmark being one o'th' worst.   *cells*

ROSENCRANTZ   We think not so, my lord.

HAMLET   Why, then 'tis none to you, for there is nothing either
245 good or bad but thinking makes it so. To me it is a prison.

ROSENCRANTZ   Why, then your ambition makes it one; 'tis too
narrow for your mind.

HAMLET   O God, I could be bounded in a nutshell and count
myself a king of infinite space, were it not that I have bad
250 dreams.

GUILDENSTERN   Which dreams indeed are ambition; for the very
substance of the ambitious is merely the shadow of a dream.

HAMLET   A dream itself is but a shadow.

ROSENCRANTZ   Truly, and I hold ambition of so airy and light a
255 quality that it is but a shadow's shadow.

---

1. In F, Rosencrantz and Guildenstern enter after line
215; in Q1, after line 211; in Q2, after line 213. Because
Polonius addresses them at line 216, this seems the best
place for their entry.

2. A triple pun: private persons holding no office; intimate friends; private parts, genitalia.
3. Spacious; fine.

HAMLET   Then are our beggars bodies, and our monarchs and outstretched heroes the beggars' shadows.[4] Shall we to th' court? For, by my fay,° I cannot reason.   *faith*

ROSENCRANTZ *and* GUILDENSTERN   We'll wait upon° you.   *accompany*

260   HAMLET   No such matter.° I will not sort° you with the rest of my   *Certainly not / class*
servants, for, to speak to you like an honest man, I am most
dreadfully attended.° But in the beaten way[5] of friendship, what   *waited upon*
make you° at Elsinore?   *are you doing*

ROSENCRANTZ   To visit you, my lord, no other occasion.

265   HAMLET   Beggar that I am, I am even poor in thanks, but I thank
you; and sure, dear friends, my thanks are too dear a halfpenny.[6] Were you not sent for? Is it your own inclining? Is it
a free° visitation? Come, deal justly with me. Come, come. Nay,   *voluntary*
speak.

270   GUILDENSTERN   What should we say, my lord?

HAMLET   Why, anything—but to th' purpose. You were sent for,
and there is a kind of confession in your looks which your mod-
esties[7] have not craft enough to colour.° I know the good King   *disguise*
and Queen have sent for you.

275   ROSENCRANTZ   To what end, my lord?

HAMLET   That you must teach me. But let me conjure° you by   *solemnly request*
the rights of our fellowship, by the consonancy° of our youth,   *harmonious friendship*
by the obligation of our ever-preserved love, and by what more
dear a better proposer could charge you withal, be even° and   *level*
280   direct with me whether you were sent for or no.

ROSENCRANTZ [*to* GUILDENSTERN]   What say you?

HAMLET   Nay then, I have an eye of° you—if you love me, hold   *on*
not off.

GUILDENSTERN   My lord, we were sent for.

285   HAMLET   I will tell you why. So shall my anticipation prevent°   *forestall*
your discovery, and your secrecy to the King and Queen moult
no feather.[8] I have of late—but wherefore I know not—lost all
my mirth, forgone all custom of exercise; and indeed it goes so
heavily with my disposition[9] that this goodly frame,° the earth,   *structure*
290   seems to me a sterile promontory. This most excellent canopy
the air, look you, this brave o'erhanging,[1] this majestical roof
fretted° with golden fire—why, it appears no other thing to me   *adorned*
than a foul and pestilent congregation° of vapours. What a   *mass*
piece of work is a man! How noble in reason, how infinite in
295   faculty,° in form and moving how express[2] and admirable, in   *natural powers*
action how like an angel, in apprehension how like a god—the
beauty of the world, the paragon of animals! And yet to me
what is this quintessence of dust?[3] Man delights not me—no,

4. *Then . . . shadows:* Then beggars, being without ambition, are not shadows but have substance; if monarchs and heroes (who ambitiously "stretch" too far) are shadows and only substantial bodies can cast shadows, they must be the beggars' shadows.
5. Well-worn track (plain words).
6. Too expensive at a halfpenny (not worth a halfpenny); perhaps also, too expensive by a halfpenny for me to give in return for such worthless information.
7. Senses of decency.
8. Remain unimpaired. To pull the feathers off a reputation meant to detract from it.
9. *it goes . . . disposition:* I am so heavy with melancholy.

F, however, prints "heavenly" for Q2's "heavily," which, if accepted, gives a startling image of Hamlet's impatient world-weariness.
1. This splendid overhang (F). Most editions give Q2's "o'erhanging firmament" (heavens). In either case, the image may refer to the "heavens," the roof overhanging the Elizabethan stage, which was decorated with stars.
2. Precise; expressive.
3. It was thought that the heavenly bodies were composed of a fifth element ("quintessence"), superior to the other four (earth, air, fire, and water) and also the purest distillation of earthly objects. Hamlet thinks of humanity as dust at its dustiest.

nor woman neither, though by your smiling you seem to say
300 so.

ROSENCRANTZ   My lord, there was no such stuff in my thoughts.

HAMLET   Why did you laugh, then, when I said 'Man delights
not me'?

ROSENCRANTZ   To think, my lord, if you delight not in man what
305 lenten entertainment[4] the players shall receive from you. We
coted° them on the way, and hither are they coming to offer   passed
you service.

HAMLET   He that plays the King shall be welcome; his majesty
shall have tribute of me. The adventurous Knight shall use his
310 foil° and target,° the Lover shall not sigh gratis,° the Humorous   sword / shield / for free
Man shall end his part in peace,[5] the Clown shall make those
laugh whose lungs are tickled o'th' sear,[6] and the Lady shall say
her mind freely, or the blank verse shall halt for't.[7] What players are they?

315 ROSENCRANTZ   Even those you were wont to take delight in, the
tragedians° of the city.   actors

HAMLET   How chances it they travel? Their residence° both in   (in the city)
reputation and profit was better both ways.

ROSENCRANTZ   I think their inhibition comes by the means of
320 the late innovation.[8]

HAMLET   Do they hold the same estimation° they did when I was   esteem
in the city? Are they so followed?

ROSENCRANTZ   No, indeed, they are not.

HAMLET   How comes it? Do they grow rusty?

325 ROSENCRANTZ   Nay, their endeavour keeps° in the wonted° pace.   continues / accustomed
But there is, sir, an eyrie of children, little eyases,[9] that cry out
on the top of question[1] and are most tyrannically° clapped for't.   outrageously
These are now the fashion, and so berattle° the common   noisily abuse
stages[2]—so they call them—that many wearing rapiers are
330 afraid of goose-quills,[3] and dare scarce come thither.

HAMLET   What, are they children? Who maintains 'em? How are
they escoted?° Will they pursue the quality° no longer than   provided for / profession
they can sing?[4] Will they not say afterwards, if they should grow
themselves to common players—as it is like° most will, if their   likely
335 means° are not better—their writers do them wrong to make   financial options
them exclaim against their own succession?°   later employment

ROSENCRANTZ   Faith, there has been much to-do on both sides,
and the nation° holds it no sin to tarre° them to controversy.   populace / goad
There was for a while no money bid for argument unless the
340 poet and the player went to cuffs in the question.[5]

HAMLET   Is't possible?

---

4. Welcome. Lent was a period of penitence and fasting (when London theaters were closed).
5. *the Humorous . . . peace:* the eccentric (governed by
excess of one humor, or mood-influencing bodily fluid)
should be allowed to rant on without disturbance.
6. Whose lungs are primed to laugh. (The "sear" is the
part of a gun holding back the hammer until the trigger
releases it.)
7. *and the Lady . . . for't:* if the lady is not allowed to
speak all her part, the poetry will "halt," or limp (fail to
scan).
8. Comes from recent fashion (probably the rage for boy-
acting companies). An "inhibition" could be either a hin-
drance or an official prohibition. (Elizabethan theaters

were commonly closed at signs of political instability.)
9. Young hawks. A company of boy actors flourished at
the private Blackfriars Theatre, leased from the
Burbages, from 1600 to 1608. *eyrie:* nest for a bird of
prey.
1. That yell over their critics' voices.
2. Public theaters (such as the Globe).
3. That gentlemen are afraid of the poet's satirical pen.
4. Only until their voices break.
5. *no money . . . question:* nothing offered for the plot (or
draft) of a play unless it added to the dispute between the
children's dramatists and the public theater companies.
went to cuffs: came to blows.

GUILDENSTERN   O, there has been much throwing about of
brains.[6]

HAMLET   Do the boys carry it° away?   *(the victory)*

345   ROSENCRANTZ   Ay, that they do, my lord, Hercules and his load
too.[7]

HAMLET   It is not strange; for mine uncle is King of Denmark,
and those that would make mows° at him while my father lived   *grimaces*
give twenty, forty, an hundred ducats apiece for his picture in

350   little.° 'Sblood,[8] there is something in this more than natural,   *miniature*
if philosophy could find it out.

         A *flourish*[9] *for the* PLAYERS

GUILDENSTERN   There are the players.

HAMLET   Gentlemen, you are welcome to Elsinore. Your hands,
come. Th'appurtenance° of welcome is fashion and ceremony.   *fitting accompaniment*

355   Let me comply with you in the garb,[1] lest my extent° to the   *offering (of welcome)*
players—which, I tell you, must show fairly° outward—should   *courteously*
more appear like entertainment° than yours.   *(warm) welcome*

         [*He shakes hands with them*]

You are welcome. But my uncle-father and aunt-mother are
deceived.

360   GUILDENSTERN   In what, my dear lord?

HAMLET   I am but mad north-north-west;[2] when the wind is
southerly, I know a hawk from a handsaw.[3]

         Enter POLONIUS

POLONIUS   Well be with you, gentlemen.

HAMLET [*aside*]   Hark you, Guildenstern, and you too—at each

365   ear a hearer—that great baby you see there is not yet out of
his swathing-clouts.°   *swaddling clothes*

ROSENCRANTZ [*aside*]   Haply° he's the second time come to   *Perhaps*
them, for they say an old man is twice a child.

HAMLET [*aside*]   I will prophesy he comes to tell me of the play-

370   ers. Mark it.—You say right, sir, for o' Monday morning, 'twas
so indeed.

POLONIUS   My lord, I have news to tell you.

HAMLET   My lord, I have news to tell you. When Roscius[4] was
an actor in Rome—

375   POLONIUS   The actors are come hither, my lord.

HAMLET   Buzz, buzz.[5]

POLONIUS   Upon mine honour—

HAMLET   Then came each actor on his ass.

POLONIUS   The best actors in the world, either for tragedy, com-

380   edy, history, pastoral, pastorical-comical, historical-pastoral,
tragical-historical, tragical-comical-historical-pastoral, scene
individable[6] or poem unlimited.[7] Seneca cannot be too heavy,

6. A great battle of wits.

7. In the course of one of his labors, Hercules held up
the world on his shoulders while Atlas (its usual support)
ran an errand; Hercules bearing the world was the sign of
the Globe.

8. By God's blood.

9. Trumpet flourishes often heralded dramatic performances.

1. Let me follow accepted forms in the recognized
manner (by shaking hands).

2. The smallest compass point away from true north,
and thus not far from sane; or possibly, only mad on

occasions when the wind blows from the north-
northwest.

3. A small saw, and possibly a variant of "heronshaw"
(heron).

4. The most famous ancient Roman actor, a rather dated
news item.

5. A response to stale news.

6. Probably, play with no breaks in performance, or play
observing the unity of place (and presumably the other
classical unities). Shakespeare parodies the classifica-
tions of contemporary dramatic theorists.

7. (Dramatic) poem unrestricted by classical rules.

nor Plautus too light.[8] For the law of writ and the liberty,[9] these
are the only men.

385 HAMLET O Jephthah, judge of Israel, what a treasure hadst
thou![1]

POLONIUS What a treasure had he, my lord?

HAMLET Why,
        'One fair daughter and no more,
390   The which he lovèd passing° well'.   *surpassingly*

POLONIUS [*aside*] Still on my daughter.

HAMLET Am I not i'th' right, old Jephthah?

POLONIUS If you call me Jephthah, my lord, I have a daughter
that I love passing well.

395 HAMLET Nay, that follows not.[2]

POLONIUS What follows then, my lord?

HAMLET Why

                'As by lot°   *chance*
                God wot',°   *knows*
400 and then you know

                'It came to pass
                As most like° it was'—   *probable*
the first row° of the pious chanson° will show you more, for   *stanza / ballad*
look where my abridgements[3] come.

        Enter four or five PLAYERS

405 You're welcome, masters, welcome all.—I am glad to see thee
well.—Welcome, good friends.—O, my old friend! Thy face is
valanced° since I saw thee last. Com'st thou to beard° me in   *fringed (with beard) / defy*
Denmark?—What, my young lady and mistress.[4] By'r Lady,
your ladyship is nearer heaven than when I saw you last by the
410 altitude of a chopine.° Pray God your voice, like a piece of   *high platform shoe*
uncurrent gold, be not cracked within the ring.[5]—Masters, you
are all welcome. We'll e'en to't like French falc'ners,[6] fly at
anything we see. We'll have a speech straight.° Come, give us   *right away*
a taste of your quality.° Come, a passionate speech.   *professional skill*

415 FIRST PLAYER What speech, my good lord?

HAMLET I heard thee speak me a speech once, but it was never
acted, or, if it was, not above once; for the play, I remember,
pleased not the million. 'Twas caviare to the general.° But it   *populace*
was—as I received it, and others whose judgements in such
420 matters cried in the top of[7] mine—an excellent play, well
digested° in the scenes, set down with as much modesty° as   *organized / restraint*
cunning. I remember one said there was no sallets[8] in the lines
to make the matter savoury, nor no matter in the phrase that
might indict the author of affectation, but called it an honest
425 method, as wholesome as sweet, and by very much more handsome than fine.[9] One speech in it I chiefly loved, 'twas Aeneas'
tale to Dido, and thereabout of it especially where he speaks of

8. The best-known Roman playwrights, masters of
tragedy and comedy, respectively.
9. For plays where classical rules are either observed or
abandoned.
1. Jephthah vowed that if he defeated the Ammonites,
he would sacrifice the first living thing he saw on his
return. He won, and his daughter became the sacrificial
victim (Judges 11). "Jephthah, Judge of Israel" was the
title of a popular ballad, the "pious chanson" from
which Hamlet subsequently quotes or sings.
2. Polonius's having a daughter is not a logical consequence of Hamlet's calling him Jephthah.

3. Those who cut me short; also, entertainments.
4. The boy who played female roles.
5. A coin was no longer legal tender if the circle or ring
enclosing the monarch's head was broken (by "clip-
ping," or trimming off small amounts of gold).
6. We'll go to work at once. (French falconers seem to
have been regarded as experts, willing to try any potential
prey.)
7. *cried . . . of*: outweighed.
8. Literally, salads (seasoned dishes); highly flavored, or
"salty" (lecherous).
9. Beautifully crafted rather than showy.

Priam's slaughter.[1] If it live in your memory, begin at this
line—let me see, let me see:
430 'The rugged° Pyrrhus,[2] like th'Hyrcanian beast'°—   *savage / tiger*
'tis not so. It begins with Pyrrhus—
'The rugged Pyrrhus, he whose sable° arms,   *black*
Black as his purpose, did the night resemble
When he lay couchèd° in the ominous horse,[3]   *hidden*
435 Hath now this dread and black complexion° smeared   *appearance*
With heraldry° more dismal. Head to foot   *heraldic colors*
Now is he total gules,° horridly tricked°   *all red / inked over*
With blood of fathers, mothers, daughters, sons,
Baked and impasted with° the parching° streets,   *encrusted by / fiery*
440 That lend a tyrranous and damnèd light
To their vile murders. Roasted in wrath and fire,
And thus o'er-sizèd[4] with coagulate gore,
With eyes like carbuncles[5] the hellish Pyrrhus
Old grandsire Priam seeks.'
445 So, proceed you.

POLONIUS Fore God, my lord, well spoken, with good accent
and good discretion.

FIRST PLAYER   'Anon° he finds him,   *Soon*
Striking too short at Greeks. His antique sword,
450 Rebellious to his arm, lies where it falls,
Repugnant° to command. Unequal match,   *Resistant*
Pyrrhus at Priam drives, in rage strikes wide;
But with the whiff and wind of his fell° sword   *fierce*
Th'unnervèd° father falls. Then senseless Ilium,[6]   *strengthless*
455 Seeming to feel his blow, with flaming top
Stoops to his° base, and with a hideous crash   *its*
Takes prisoner Pyrrhus' ear. For lo, his sword,
Which was declining° on the milky° head   *descending / white*
Of reverend Priam, seemed i'th' air to stick.
460 So, as a painted tyrant,[7] Pyrrhus stood,
And, like a neutral to his will and matter,[8]
Did nothing.
But as we often see against° some storm   *before*
A silence in the heavens, the rack° stand still,   *cloud banks*
465 The bold winds speechless, and the orb° below   *earth*
As hush as death, anon the dreadful thunder
Doth rend the region:° so, after Pyrrhus' pause,   *sky*
A rousèd vengeance sets him new a-work;
And never did the Cyclops'[9] hammers fall
470 On Mars his° armour, forged for proof eterne,[1]   *(Mars's)*
With less remorse° than Pyrrhus' bleeding sword   *pity; hesitation*
Now falls on Priam.
Out, out, thou strumpet Fortune! All you gods,
In general synod, take away her power,

1. The murder of the Trojan King Priam, at the end of the Trojan War; adapted from Virgil's *Aeneid*, possibly via Christopher Marlowe's *Dido, Queen of Carthage*. Aeneas recounts the story of Priam's slaughter to his beloved, Dido.
2. Also known as Neoptolemus, he came to Troy to avenge the death of his father, the Greek hero Achilles.
3. The Trojan horse, full of Greek warriors.
4. As though coated with sizing, the thick liquid used to prepare a canvas for painting.
5. Gems supposed to glow with their own light.
6. The citadel of Troy.
7. Tyrant depicted in a painting and so incapable of moving.
8. And as one indifferent toward his intention and the action at hand.
9. The three one-eyed giants who served as armorers to the classical gods and heroes.
1. To remain impenetrable forever.

475 Break all the spokes and fellies from her wheel,[2]
And bowl the round nave° down the hill of heaven,°   *wheel hub / Mt. Olympus*
As low as to the fiends!'

POLONIUS   This is too long.

HAMLET   It shall to the barber's, with your beard.°   [*To* FIRST   *It shall be cut short*
480 PLAYER] Prithee, say on. He's for a jig[3] or a tale of bawdry, or
he sleeps. Say on, come to Hecuba.

FIRST PLAYER   'But who, O who had seen the mobbled°   *veiled; muffled*
queen'—

HAMLET   'The mobbled queen'?

POLONIUS   That's good; 'mobbled queen' is good.

485 FIRST PLAYER   'Run barefoot up and down, threat'ning the flames
With bisson rheum;° a clout° upon that head   *blinding tears / cloth*
Where late the diadem stood, and for a robe,
About her lank and all o'er-teemèd[4] loins,
A blanket in th'alarm of fear caught up—
490 Who this had seen, with tongue in venom steeped,
'Gainst Fortune's state° would treason have pronounced.   *rule*
But if the gods themselves did see her then,
When she saw Pyrrhus make malicious sport
In mincing with his sword her husband's limbs,
495 The instant burst of clamour that she made—
Unless things mortal move them not at all—
Would have made milch° the burning eyes of heaven,   *milky; moist*
And passion° in the gods.'   *suffering; pity*

POLONIUS   Look whe'er° he has not turned his colour, and has   *whether*
500 tears in 's eyes. [*To* FIRST PLAYER] Prithee, no more.

HAMLET [*to* FIRST PLAYER]   'Tis well. I'll have thee speak out the
rest soon. [*To* POLONIUS] Good my lord, will you see the play-
ers well bestowed?° Do ye hear?—let them be well used,° for   *lodged / treated*
they are the abstracts° and brief chronicles of the time. After   *summaries*
505 your death you were better have a bad epitaph than their ill
report while you live.

POLONIUS   My lord, I will use them according to their desert.

HAMLET   God's bodykins,° man, much better. Use every man   *By God's dear body*
after° his desert, and who should scape whipping? Use them   *according to*
510 after your own honour and dignity—the less they deserve, the
more merit is in your bounty. Take them in.

POLONIUS [*to* PLAYERS]   Come, sirs.   *Exit*

HAMLET [*to* PLAYERS]   Follow him, friends. We'll hear a play
tomorrow. Dost thou hear me, old friend? Can you play the
515 murder of Gonzago?

PLAYERS   Ay, my lord.

HAMLET   We'll ha't° tomorrow night. You could for a need° study   *have it / if necessary*
a speech of some dozen or sixteen lines which I would set down
and insert in't, could ye not?

520 PLAYERS   Ay, my lord.

HAMLET   Very well. Follow that lord, and look you mock him
not.

Exeunt PLAYERS[5]

2. The power of Fortune's ever-turning wheel, raising
and lowering men in succession, was proverbial. *fellies:*
curved sections of a wooden wheel rim.
3. A ridiculous piece of poetry, or the dance that followed
many plays (unrelated to the drama).
4. Completely worn out with childbearing. (Hecuba was

supposed to have borne seventeen or more children.)
5. In F and Q1, the players leave after line 524. In Q2,
they leave with Polonius after line 512. Their exit has
been relocated here to coincide with Hamlet's command
that they follow Polonius.

My good friends, I'll leave you till night. You are welcome to
Elsinore.
525 ROSENCRANTZ   Good my lord.
HAMLET   Ay, so. God b'wi'° ye.   *Exeunt [all but]* HAMLET   *be with*
                                  Now I am alone.
O, what a rogue and peasant slave am I!
Is it not monstrous that this player here,
But° in a fiction, in a dream of passion,   *Merely*
530   Could force his soul so to his whole conceit[6]
That from her° working all his visage wanned,°   *(the soul's) / grew pale*
Tears in his eyes, distraction in 's aspect,
A broken voice, and his whole function suiting
With forms to his conceit?[7] And all for nothing.
535   For Hecuba!
What's Hecuba to him, or he to Hecuba,
That he should weep for her? What would he do
Had he the motive and the cue for passion
That I have? He would drown the stage with tears,
540   And cleave the general ear[8] with horrid speech,
Make mad the guilty and appal the free,°   *innocent*
Confound the ignorant, and amaze° indeed   *bewilder*
The very faculty of eyes and ears. Yet I,
A dull and muddy-mettled° rascal, peak°   *dull-spirited / mope*
545   Like John-a-dreams,° unpregnant of[9] my cause,   *a sleepy idler*
And can say nothing—no, not for a king
Upon whose property° and most dear life   *rightful sovereignty*
A damned defeat[1] was made. Am I a coward?
Who calls me villain, breaks my pate° across,   *head*
550   Plucks off my beard and blows it in my face,
Tweaks me by th' nose, gives me the lie i'th' throat
As deep as to the lungs?[2] Who does me this?
Ha? 'Swounds,° I should take it; for it cannot be   *By God's wounds*
But I am pigeon-livered and lack gall[3]
555   To make oppression bitter, or ere this
I should 'a' fatted all the region kites[4]
With this slave's offal. Bloody, bawdy villain!
Remorseless, treacherous, lecherous, kindless villain!
O, vengeance!—
560   Why, what an ass am I? Ay, sure, this is most brave,°   *fine*
That I, the son of the dear murderèd,°   *the dear murdered man*
Prompted to my revenge by heaven and hell,
Must, like a whore, unpack my heart with words
And fall a-cursing like a very drab,°   *whore*
565   A scullion![5] Fie upon't, foh!—About,° my brain.   *Into action*
I have heard that guilty creatures sitting at a play
Have by the very cunning° of the scene   *artfulness*
Been struck so to the soul that presently°   *immediately*
They have proclaimed their malefactions;
570   For murder, though it have no tongue, will speak

---

6. Could make his innermost being conform so well with
his imagined situation.
7. *his whole . . . conceit:* the action of his whole body in
outward accord with his imagination.
8. The ears of people generally.
9. Not quickened into action by.

1. An act of overthrow worthy of damnation.
2. *gives . . . lungs:* calls me a thoroughgoing liar.
3. Pigeons were thought not to secrete gall, a bitter fluid
produced by the liver and the supposed source of anger.
4. All the kites (birds of prey) in the sky ("region").
5. Kitchen servant.

With most miraculous organ. I'll have these players
Play something like the murder of my father
Before mine uncle. I'll observe his looks,
I'll tent° him to the quick. If a° but blench,   probe (a wound) / he
575 I know my course. The spirit that I have seen
May be the devil, and the devil hath power
T'assume a pleasing shape; yea, and perhaps,
Out of my weakness and my melancholy—
As he is very potent with such spirits⁶—
580 Abuses° me to damn me. I'll have grounds   Deceives
More relative° than this. The play's the thing   relevant
Wherein I'll catch the conscience of the King.   *Exit*

3.1

Enter KING [CLAUDIUS], QUEEN [GERTRUDE], POLONIUS,
OPHELIA, ROSENCRANTZ, GUILDENSTERN, *and lords*

KING CLAUDIUS   [*to* ROSENCRANTZ *and* GUILDENSTERN]
And can you by no drift of circumstance¹
Get from him why he puts on this confusion,
Grating so harshly all his days of quiet
With turbulent and dangerous lunacy?
5 ROSENCRANTZ   He does confess he feels himself distracted,°   confused; agitated
But from what cause a will by no means speak.
GUILDENSTERN   Nor do we find him forward° to be sounded,°   eager / probed
But with a crafty madness keeps aloof
When we would bring him on to some confession
10 Of his true state.
QUEEN GERTRUDE   Did he receive you well?
ROSENCRANTZ   Most like a gentleman.
GUILDENSTERN   But with much forcing of his disposition.°   mood
ROSENCRANTZ   Niggard of question,² but of° our demands   to
Most free in his reply.
15 QUEEN GERTRUDE   Did you assay° him   try to persuade
To any pastime?
ROSENCRANTZ   Madam, it so fell out that certain players
We o'er-raught° on the way. Of these we told him,   passed
And there did seem in him a kind of joy
20 To hear of it. They are about the court,
And, as I think, they have already order
This night to play before him.
POLONIUS   'Tis most true,
And he beseeched me to entreat your majesties
To hear and see the matter.
25 KING CLAUDIUS   With all my heart; and it doth much content me
To hear him so inclined.—Good gentlemen,
Give him a further edge,° and drive his purpose on   stimulus; appetite
To these delights.
ROSENCRANTZ   We shall, my lord.
Exeunt ROSENCRANTZ *and* GUILDENSTERN
30 KING CLAUDIUS   Sweet Gertrude, leave us too,
For we have closely° sent for Hamlet hither,   privately

6. *Out of . . . spirits:* It was thought that those afflicted
with too much black bile, a humor (fluid), or "spirit"
(distillation) became melancholy and subject to halluci-
nations, which in turn made them easily tricked by the

devil. *potent with:* powerful over.
3.1 Location: The castle.
1. By no carefully directed conversation.
2. Reluctant to offer conversation.

That he, as 'twere by accident, may here
Affront° Ophelia.   *Confront*
Her father and myself, lawful espials,°   *spies*
35 Will so bestow ourselves that, seeing unseen,
We may of their encounter frankly judge,
And gather by him, as he is behaved,
If 't be th'affliction of his love or no
That thus he suffers for.
QUEEN GERTRUDE   I shall obey you.
40 And for your part, Ophelia, I do wish
That your good beauties be the happy cause
Of Hamlet's wildness; so shall I hope your virtues
Will bring him to his wonted° way again,   *customary*
To both your honours.
OPHELIA   Madam, I wish it may.
                              [*Exit* GERTRUDE]
45 POLONIUS Ophelia, walk you here.—Gracious,° so please you, *Your Grace*
We will bestow ourselves.—Read on this book,
That show of such an exercise may colour
Your loneliness.[3] We are oft to blame in this:
'Tis too much proved° that with devotion's visage   *true in experience*
50 And pious action we do sugar o'er
The devil himself.
KING CLAUDIUS   O, 'tis too true.
[*Aside*] How smart° a lash that speech doth give my conscience. *sharp*
The harlot's cheek, beautied with plast'ring° art,   *cosmetic; healing*
Is not more ugly to the thing that helps it[4]
55 Than is my deed to my most painted word.
O heavy burden!
POLONIUS I hear him coming. Let's withdraw, my lord.
                    Exeunt [CLAUDIUS *and* POLONIUS]
            Enter [*Prince*] HAMLET
HAMLET To be, or not to be; that is the question:
Whether 'tis nobler in the mind to suffer
60 The slings and arrows of outrageous fortune,
Or to take arms against a sea of troubles,
And, by opposing, end them. To die, to sleep—
No more, and by a sleep to say we end
The heartache and the thousand natural shocks
65 That flesh is heir to—'tis a consummation
Devoutly to be wished. To die, to sleep.
To sleep, perchance to dream. Ay, there's the rub,[5]
For in that sleep of death what dreams may come
When we have shuffled° off this mortal coil°   *cast / turmoil; flesh*
70 Must give us pause. There's the respect°   *consideration*
That makes calamity of so long life,[6]
For who would bear the whips and scorns of time,
Th'oppressor's wrong, the proud man's contumely,°   *scornful abuse*
The pangs of disprized° love, the law's delay,   *unvalued*
75 The insolence of office,° and the spurns[7]   *bureaucrats*

---

3. *may . . . loneliness:* may explain your solitude, and also
give it a virtuous or pious look. The "book" is a prayer
book or devotional text.
4. *to . . . it:* compared to the artificially beautiful surface
that covers it.

5. Obstacle in the game of bowls, an impediment to the
ball's intended path.
6. Makes adversity so long-lived (as opposed to quickly
ended in suicide).
7. Kicks, insults.

That patient merit of th'unworthy takes,[8]
When he himself might his quietus make[9]
With a bare bodkin?° Who would these fardels° bear,   *mere dagger / burdens*
To grunt and sweat under a weary life,
80 But that the dread of something after death,
The undiscovered country from whose bourn°   *border*
No traveller returns, puzzles the will,
And makes us rather bear those ills we have
Than fly to others that we know not of?
85 Thus conscience[1] does make cowards of us all,
And thus the native hue° of resolution   *ruddy complexion*
Is sicklied o'er with the pale cast° of thought,   *tint*
And enterprises of great pith and moment[2]
With this regard° their currents turn awry,   *consideration*
90 And lose the name of action. Soft you, now,[3]
The fair Ophelia!—Nymph, in thy orisons°   *prayers*
Be all my sins remembered.
OPHELIA   Good my lord,
How does your honour for this many a day?
HAMLET   I humbly thank you, well, well, well.
95 OPHELIA   My lord, I have remembrances of yours
That I have longèd long to redeliver.
I pray you now receive them.
HAMLET   No, no, I never gave you aught.
OPHELIA   My honoured lord, you know right well you did,
100 And with them words of so sweet breath composed
As made the things more rich. Their perfume lost,
Take these again; for to the noble mind
Rich gifts wax° poor when givers prove unkind.   *grow*
There, my lord.
105 HAMLET   Ha, ha? Are you honest?°   *chaste; truthful*
OPHELIA   My lord.
HAMLET   Are you fair?
OPHELIA   What means your lordship?
HAMLET   That if you be honest and fair, your honesty should
110 admit no discourse to[4] your beauty.
OPHELIA   Could beauty, my lord, have better commerce° than   *dealings*
with honesty?
HAMLET   Ay, truly, for the power of beauty will sooner transform
honesty from what it is to a bawd than the force of honesty can
115 translate beauty into his° likeness. This was sometime a par-   *its (honesty's)*
adox, but now the time[5] gives it proof. I did love you once.
OPHELIA   Indeed, my lord, you made me believe so.
HAMLET   You should not have believed me, for virtue cannot so
inoculate our old stock but we shall relish of it.[6] I loved you
120 not.
OPHELIA   I was the more deceived.
HAMLET   Get thee to a nunnery.[7] Why wouldst thou be a breeder

---

8. That the deserving has to accept patiently from the unworthy.
9. A paid-off account was marked "Quietus est" ("laid to rest").
1. Both consciousness (introspective knowledge) and moral conscience.
2. Of profundity and importance (F). Q2 gives "pitch," meaning "height" (in the context of a falcon's flight).
3. Wait a moment (an expression of surprise).

4. No familiar conversation with.
5. This was formerly an uncredited opinion, but now the present age.
6. *You . . . it:* Virtue grafted onto fallen human nature cannot eradicate completely the taste ("relish") of original sin.
7. By entering a nunnery, Ophelia will take a vow of life-long chastity. But in Elizabethan slang, "nunnery" could also mean "brothel."

of sinners? I am myself indifferent honest,° but yet I could | *moderately virtuous*
accuse me of such things that it were better my mother had not
125 borne me. I am very proud, revengeful, ambitious, with more
offences at my beck° than I have thoughts to put them in, imag- | *command*
ination to give them shape, or time to act them in. What should
such fellows as I do crawling between heaven and earth? We
are arrant° knaves, all. Believe none of us. Go thy ways to a | *downright*
130 nunnery. Where's your father?

OPHELIA   At home, my lord.

HAMLET   Let the doors be shut upon him, that he may play the
fool nowhere but in 's own house. Farewell.

OPHELIA   O help him, you sweet heavens!

135 HAMLET   If thou dost marry, I'll give thee this plague for thy
dowry: be thou as chaste as ice, as pure as snow, thou shalt not
escape calumny. Get thee to a nunnery, go, farewell. Or if thou
wilt needs marry, marry a fool; for wise men know well enough
what monsters[8] you° make of them. To a nunnery, go, and | *you women*
140 quickly, too. Farewell.

OPHELIA   O heavenly powers, restore him!

HAMLET   I have heard of your paintings,° too, well enough. God | *cosmetics*
hath given you one face, and you make yourselves another. You
jig, you amble, and you lisp,[9] and nickname God's creatures,[1]
145 and make your wantonness your ignorance.[2] Go to, I'll no
more on't.° It hath made me mad. I say we will have no more | *of it*
marriages. Those that are married already—all but one—shall
live. The rest shall keep as they are. To a nunnery, go.   *Exit*

OPHELIA   O what a noble mind is here o'erthrown!
150 The courtier's, soldier's, scholar's eye, tongue, sword,
Th'expectancy and rose of the fair state,
The glass° of fashion and the mould of form,[3] | *mirror image*
Th'observed of all observers, quite, quite, down!
And I, of ladies most deject and wretched,
155 That sucked the honey of his music vows,
Now see that noble and most sovereign reason
Like sweet bells jangled out of tune and harsh;
That unmatched form and feature of blown° youth | *fully blossoming*
Blasted° with ecstasy.° O woe is me, | *Withered / madness*
160 T'have seen what I have seen, see what I see!

Enter KING [CLAUDIUS] *and* POLONIUS

KING CLAUDIUS   Love? His affections° do not that way tend, | *emotions*
Nor what he spake, though it lacked form a little,
Was not like madness. There's something in his soul
O'er which his melancholy sits on brood,
165 And I do doubt° the hatch and the disclose[4] | *fear*
Will be some danger; which to prevent
I have in quick determination
Thus set it down:° he shall with speed to England | *resolved it*
For the demand of our neglected tribute.[5]

8. Alluding to the belief that cuckolds grew horns, but Hamlet may mean a more spiritual or psychological transformation as well.
9. *You jig . . . lisp:* You dance (or sing), walk with an affectedly easy gait, and speak artificially.
1. Use new and fashionable names instead of the God-given ones.
2. *make . . . ignorance:* "play dumb" to excuse your (seductive) affectations.
3. Pattern of decorum.
4. Public disclosure.
5. Although the play is set in a Renaissance world, Claudius's words invoke a distant medieval past, when England paid tribute to Denmark.

170   Haply° the seas and countries different,   *Perhaps; with luck*
    With variable objects,[6] shall expel
    This something-settled° matter in his heart,   *somewhat rooted*
    Whereon his brains still° beating puts him thus   *constantly*
    From fashion of himself.[7] What think you on't?
175 POLONIUS   It shall do well. But yet do I believe
    The origin and commencement of this grief
    Sprung from neglected° love.—How now, Ophelia?   *unrequited*
    You need not tell us what Lord Hamlet said;
    We heard it all.—My lord, do as you please,
180   But, if you hold it fit, after the play
    Let his queen mother all alone entreat him
    To show his griefs. Let her be round° with him,   *blunt*
    And I'll be placed, so please you, in the ear°   *within earshot*
    Of all their conference. If she find him not,[8]
185   To England send him, or confine him where
    Your wisdom best shall think.
KING CLAUDIUS   It shall be so.
    Madness in great ones must not unwatched go.   *Exeunt*

3.2

Enter [Prince] HAMLET *and two or three of the* PLAYERS

HAMLET   Speak the speech, I pray you, as I pronounced it to
    you—trippingly on the tongue; but if you mouth it,[1] as many
    of your players do, I had as lief° the town-crier had spoke my   *willingly*
    lines. Nor do not saw the air too much with your hand, thus,
5   but use all gently; for in the very torrent, tempest, and as I may
    say the whirlwind of your passion, you must acquire and beget
    a temperance that may give it smoothness. O, it offends me to
    the soul to hear a robustious,° periwig-pated° fellow tear a pas-   *bombastic / wig-wearing*
    sion to tatters, to very rags, to split the ears of the groundlings,[2]
10   who for the most part are capable of nothing but inexplicable
    dumb shows[3] and noise. I would have such a fellow whipped
    for o'erdoing Termagant. It out-Herods Herod.[4] Pray you avoid
    it.
A PLAYER   I warrant your honour.[5]
15 HAMLET   Be not too tame, neither; but let your own discretion
    be your tutor. Suit the action to the word, the word to the
    action, with this special observance: that you o'erstep not the
    modesty° of nature. For anything so overdone is from° the pur-   *moderation / opposed to*
    pose of playing, whose end, both at the first and now, was and
20   is to hold as 'twere the mirror up to nature, to show virtue her
    own feature, scorn her own image, and the very age and body
    of the time his form and pressure.[6] Now this overdone, or come
    tardy° off, though it make the unskilful[7] laugh, cannot but   *faultily*
    make the judicious grieve; the censure of the which one[8] must

6. With different sights or interests.
7. *puts . . . himself*: makes him unlike his normal self.
8. If she fails to discover his secret.
3.2 Location: A stateroom of the castle.
1. If you speak exaggeratedly.
2. Spectators standing on the ground before the stage (the cheapest area).
3. Brief mimed scenes giving the plot of the scene to follow (see 3.2.122ff.). By Shakespeare's time, this once-common device was out of fashion.
4. It surpasses the excesses of Herod, who, as a char-

acter in medieval cycle plays, was famous for his ranting. Termagant, an imaginary deity supposedly worshipped by Muslims, takes the form of a violent speaking idol in medieval drama.
5. I assure your Honor (that we will avoid it).
6. *the very . . . pressure*: the true state of things at present, in shape ("form") and likeness (as a stamp pressed in wax).
7. Undiscriminating.
8. The judgment of one of whom (judicious persons).

25   in your allowance o'erweigh a whole theatre of others. O, there
    be players that I have seen play, and heard others praise, and
    that highly, not to speak it profanely,[9] that neither having the
    accent of Christians nor the gait of Christian, pagan, nor no
    man, have so strutted and bellowed that I have thought some
30   of nature's journeymen[1] had made men, and not made them
    well, they imitated humanity so abominably.

A PLAYER   I hope we have reformed that indifferently° with us,   *moderately well*
    sir.

HAMLET   O, reform it altogether. And let those that play your
35   clowns speak no more than is set down for them; for there be
    of° them that will themselves laugh to set° on some quantity of   *some of / urge*
    barren° spectators to laugh too, though in the mean time some   *unthinking*
    necessary question of the play be then to be considered. That's
    villainous, and shows a most pitiful ambition in the fool that
40   uses it. Go make you ready.   *Exeunt* PLAYERS
          Enter POLONIUS, GUILDENSTERN, *and* ROSENCRANTZ
    [*To* POLONIUS] How now, my lord? Will the King hear this
    piece of work?

POLONIUS   And the Queen too, and that presently.°   *immediately*

HAMLET   Bid the players make haste.   *Exit* POLONIUS
    Will you two help to hasten them?

45 ROSENCRANTZ *and* GUILDENSTERN   We will, my lord.   *Exeunt*

HAMLET   What ho, Horatio!
          Enter HORATIO

HORATIO   Here, sweet lord, at your service.

HAMLET   Horatio, thou art e'en as just° a man   *honest; balanced*
    As e'er my conversation coped withal.[2]

HORATIO   O my dear lord—

HAMLET   Nay, do not think I flatter;
50   For what advancement° may I hope from thee,   *political favors*
    That no revenue hast but thy good spirits
    To feed and clothe thee? Why should the poor be flattered?
    No, let the candied° tongue lick absurd pomp,   *flattering*
    And crook the pregnant° hinges of the knee   *ready (to bow)*
55   Where thrift may follow feigning.[3] Dost thou hear?—
    Since my dear soul was mistress of her choice
    And could of° men distinguish, her election   *between*
    Hath sealed thee for herself;[4] for thou hast been
    As one in suff'ring all that suffers nothing,
60   A man that Fortune's buffets and rewards
    Hath ta'en with equal thanks; and blest are those
    Whose blood° and judgement are so well commingled   *passion*
    That they are not a pipe for Fortune's finger
    To sound what stop° she please. Give me that man   *finger holes; notes*
65   That is not passion's slave, and I will wear him
    In my heart's core, ay, in my heart of heart,
    As I do thee. Something too much of this.
    There is a play tonight before the King.
    One scene of it comes near the circumstance

---

9. Meaning no blasphemy (by implying as he goes on
to do that some humans were not created by God).
1. Hired assistants to the master craftsmen, still learning their trade.
2. As I ever encountered in my dealings with men.

3. Where prosperity may result from (flattering) lies.
Most editions follow Q2's "fawning."
4. Has marked you as her own (on a document, a legal
sign of possession).

70 Which I have told thee of my father's death.
I prithee, when thou seest that act afoot,
Even with the very comment of thy soul⁵
Observe mine uncle. If his occulted° guilt   *hidden*
Do not itself unkennel in one speech,
75 It is a damnèd ghost that we have seen,
And my imaginations are as foul
As Vulcan's stithy.⁶ Give him heedful note,
For I mine eyes will rivet to his face,
And after, we will both our judgements join
To censure of his seeming.⁷

80 HORATIO   Well, my lord.
If a° steal aught the whilst this play is playing   *he*
And scape detecting, I will pay the theft.
            Enter trumpets and kettle drums. Sound a flourish
HAMLET   They are coming to the play. I must be idle.°   *mad; unoccupied*
Get you a place.
            Danish march. Enter KING [CLAUDIUS], QUEEN [GER-
            TRUDE], POLONIUS, OPHELIA, ROSENCRANTZ, GUILDEN-
            STERN, *and other lords attendant, with* [*the King's*]
            guard carrying torches
KING CLAUDIUS   How fares⁸ our cousin° Hamlet?   *kinsman*
85 HAMLET   Excellent, i'faith, of the chameleon's dish. I eat the air,
promise-crammed.⁹ You cannot feed capons¹ so.
KING CLAUDIUS   I have nothing with this answer, Hamlet. These
words are not mine.
HAMLET   No, nor mine now. [*To* POLONIUS] My lord, you played
90 once i'th' university, you say.
POLONIUS   That I did, my lord, and was accounted a good actor.
HAMLET   And what did you enact?
POLONIUS   I did enact Julius Caesar. I was killed i'th' Capitol.²
Brutus killed me.
95 HAMLET   It was a brute part of him to kill so capital a calf°   *such a prize fool*
there.—Be the players ready?
ROSENCRANTZ   Ay, my lord, they stay° upon your patience.   *wait*
QUEEN GERTRUDE   Come hither, my good Hamlet. Sit by me.
HAMLET   No, good-mother,° here's mettle³ more attractive.   *stepmother*
            [*He sits by* OPHELIA]
100 POLONIUS [*aside*]   O ho, do you mark that?
HAMLET [*to* OPHELIA]   Lady, shall I lie in your lap?
OPHELIA   No, my lord.
HAMLET   I mean my head upon your lap?
OPHELIA   Ay, my lord.
105 HAMLET   Do you think I meant country matters?⁴
OPHELIA   I think nothing, my lord.
HAMLET   That's a fair thought to lie between maids' legs.

---

5. With your utmost critical faculty.
6. Smithy, or forge, of Vulcan, the Roman blacksmith
god.
7. To judge by his outward reaction.
8. How does; Hamlet's response puns on "fare" as food
and drink.
9. The chameleon was supposed to live on air. Hamlet
puns on "heir," referring to Claudius's insubstantial
promise of the succession.
1. Castrated cocks, crammed or fattened for the table

(and a term for a fool).
2. Perhaps an allusion to Shakespeare's own *Julius Caesar*; the actor who first played Polonius may also have
played the part of Caesar.
3. A disposition (punning on magnetically attractive
"metal").
4. Rustic doings (with an obscene pun on "cunt"). The
punning continues in the following lines, where "nothing" suggests the female genitals (often linked to the
shape of a zero), and "thing" the male genitals.

OPHELIA What is, my lord?

HAMLET No thing.

110 OPHELIA You are merry, my lord.

HAMLET Who, I?

OPHELIA Ay, my lord.

HAMLET O God, your only jig-maker![5] What should a man do
but be merry? For look you how cheerfully my mother looks,
115 and my father died within 's° two hours.   *these*

OPHELIA Nay, 'tis twice two months, my lord.

HAMLET So long? Nay then, let the devil wear black, for I'll have
a suit of sables.[6] O heavens, die two months ago and not forgotten yet! Then there's hope a great man's memory may outlive
120 his life half a year. But, by'r Lady, a must build churches then,
or else shall a suffer not thinking on,[7] with the hobby-horse,
whose epitaph is 'For O, for O, the hobby-horse is forgot.'[8]

Hautboys° play. The dumb show enters. Enter a KING   *Oboes*
and a QUEEN very lovingly, the QUEEN embracing him.
She kneels and makes show of protestation unto him. He
takes her up and declines° his head upon her neck. He   *leans*
lays him down upon a bank of flowers. She, seeing him
asleep, leaves him. Anon comes in a fellow, takes off his
crown, kisses it, and pours poison in the King's ears, and
exits. The QUEEN returns, finds the KING dead, and
makes passionate action. The poisoner, with some two or
three mutes,° comes in again, seeming to lament with   *nonspeaking actors*
her. The dead body is carried away. The poisoner woos
the QUEEN with gifts. She seems loath and unwilling a
while, but in the end accepts his love. Exeunt [the
PLAYERS]

OPHELIA What means this, my lord?

HAMLET Marry, this is miching *malhecho*.° That means mis-   *sneaking wrongdoing*
125 chief.

OPHELIA Belike this show imports the argument° of the play.   *plot*

Enter PROLOGUE

HAMLET We shall know by this fellow. The players cannot keep
counsel,° they'll tell all.   *a secret*

OPHELIA Will a tell us what this show meant?

130 HAMLET Ay, or any show that you'll show him. Be not you
ashamed to show, he'll not shame to tell you what it means.

OPHELIA You are naught,° you are naught. I'll mark the play.   *indecent*

PROLOGUE For us and for our tragedy
Here stooping to your clemency,
135 We beg your hearing patiently.   *[Exit]*

HAMLET Is this a prologue, or the posy of a ring?[9]

OPHELIA 'Tis brief, my lord.

HAMLET As woman's love.

Enter the [PLAYER] KING and his QUEEN

PLAYER KING Full thirty times hath Phoebus' cart[1] gone round

---

5. The leading comic actor often devised and performed
the farcical song and dance concluding a play. *only:* unri-
valed.

6. Sable is both an expensive fur for cloaks and trim and
the heraldic term for "black"; Hamlet simultaneously for-
swears his ascetic mourning and vows to continue it.

7. He shall have to endure being forgotten.

8. The hobbyhorse, a man with a mock horse's body
strapped round his waist, was a figure in May Day morris dances (under attack in Shakespeare's time by religious reformers). "The hobby horse is forgot" seems to
have been a ballad refrain.

9. The motto engraved in a ring.

1. Apollo's chariot (the sun).

140 Neptune's salt wash and Tellus' orbèd ground,[2]
And thirty dozen moons with borrowed sheen°   *reflected light*
About the world have times twelve thirties been
Since love our hearts and Hymen° did our hands   *goddess of marriage*
Unite commutual in most sacred bands.

145 PLAYER QUEEN   So many journeys may the sun and moon
Make us again count o'er ere love be done.
But woe is me, you are so sick of late,
So far from cheer and from your former state,
That I distrust° you. Yet, though I distrust,   *am worried about*

150 Discomfort° you my lord it nothing must.   *Sadden*
For women's fear and love holds quantity,[3]
In neither aught, or in extremity.[4]
Now what my love is, proof° hath made you know,   *experience*
And as my love is sized,° my fear is so.[5]   *in quantity*

154.1 *Where love is great, the littlest doubts are fear:*
Where little fears grow great, great love grows there.

155 PLAYER KING   Faith, I must leave thee, love, and shortly too.
My operant° powers their functions leave° to do,   *vital / cease*
And thou shalt live in this fair world behind,
Honoured, beloved; and haply° one as kind   *perhaps*
For husband shalt thou—

PLAYER QUEEN   O, confound the rest!

160 Such love must needs be treason in my breast.
In second husband let me be accurst;
None wed the second but who killed the first.

HAMLET   Wormwood,[6] wormwood.

PLAYER QUEEN   The instances° that second marriage move°   *motives / prompt*
165 Are base respects of thrift,° but none of love.   *considerations of profit*
A second time I kill my husband dead
When second husband kisses me in bed.

PLAYER KING   I do believe you think what now you speak;
But what we do determine oft we break.
170 Purpose is but the slave to[7] memory,
Of violent birth but poor validity,°   *enduring strength*
Which now like fruit unripe sticks on the tree,
But fall unshaken when they mellow be.
Most necessary 'tis that we forget
175 To pay ourselves what to ourselves is debt.[8]
What to ourselves in passion we propose,
The passion ending, doth the purpose lose.
The violence of either grief or joy
Their own enactures with themselves destroy.[9]
180 Where joy most revels, grief doth most lament;
Grief joys, joy grieves, on slender accident.[1]
This world is not for aye,° nor 'tis not strange   *eternity*
That even our loves should with our fortunes change;

---

2. *Neptune's . . . ground:* The salty flood of the sea god and the round foundation of Tellus (the earth).
3. Are in equal proportions. Q2 includes one other line before this one: "For women fear too much, even as they love / And women's fear . . ."
4. *In . . . extremity:* Either love and fear are both absent, or both are extremely strong.
5. After this line, Q2 has a couplet, 154.1–154.2, omitted in F.
6. A bitter herb taken medicinally (hence, "a bitter pill to swallow").
7. Our intentions serve and depend on.
8. *Most . . . debt:* It is inevitable (or necessary for our well-being) that we neglect to fulfill those promises made to ourselves.
9. *The violence . . . destroy:* Extreme grief and joy destroy themselves, and the motive for action vanishes with them.
1. On account of a small, unforeseen event.

	For 'tis a question left us yet to prove	
185	Whether love lead fortune or else fortune love.	
	The great man down, you mark his favourite flies;	
	The poor advanced° makes friends of enemies.	*promoted*
	And hitherto° doth love on fortune tend,°	*to this extent / attend*
	For who not needs shall never lack a friend,	
190	And who in want a hollow friend doth try°	*test*
	Directly seasons him[2] his enemy.	
	But orderly to end where I begun,	
	Our wills and fates do so contrary run[3]	
	That our devices still° are overthrown;	*our plans always*
195	Our thoughts are ours, their ends° none of our own.	*results*
	So think thou wilt no second husband wed;	
	But die thy thoughts when thy first lord is dead.	

PLAYER QUEEN   Nor earth to me give food, nor heaven light,
Sport and repose lock from me day and night,[4]

199.1	*To desperation turn my trust and hope;*	
	An anchor's cheer[5] in prison be my scope.°	*extent (of good)*
200	Each opposite[6] that blanks° the face of joy	*makes pale*
	Meet what I would have well and it destroy,	
	Both here and hence pursue me lasting strife	
	If, once a widow, ever I be wife.	

HAMLET   If she should break it now!

PLAYER KING [*to* PLAYER QUEEN]

205	'Tis deeply sworn. Sweet, leave me here a while.	
	My spirits grow dull, and fain° I would beguile	*gladly*
	The tedious day with sleep.	

PLAYER QUEEN   Sleep rock thy brain,
And never come mischance between us twain.

                    [PLAYER KING] *sleeps. Exit* [PLAYER QUEEN]

HAMLET [*to* GERTRUDE]   Madam, how like you this play?

210   QUEEN GERTRUDE   The lady protests too much, methinks.

HAMLET   O, but she'll keep her word.

KING CLAUDIUS   Have you heard the argument?° Is there no   *plot*
offence in't?

HAMLET   No, no, they do but jest, poison in jest. No offence i'th'
215   world.

KING CLAUDIUS   What do you call the play?

HAMLET   *The Mousetrap.* Marry, how? Tropically.[7] This play is
the image of a murder done in Vienna. Gonzago is the Duke's
name, his wife Baptista.[8] You shall see anon. 'Tis a knavish
220   piece of work; but what o' that? Your majesty, and we that have
free° souls, it touches[9] us not. Let the galled jade wince, our   *guiltless*
withers are unwrung.[1]

                    Enter [PLAYER] LUCIANUS
This is one Lucianus, nephew to the King.

---

2. Immediately hardens him, as timber is seasoned for use.
3. What we desire and what is destined to happen are so opposed.
4. After this line, Q2 has a couplet omitted in F, 199.1–199.2.
5. Food for an anchorite (ascetic religious hermit).
6. Each adverse force.
7. As a trope, or rhetorical figure (perhaps punning on

"trap").
8. That is, the Player King and Queen (called "Duke" and "Duchess" throughout Q1). Shakespeare seems to base *The Mousetrap* on an extremely muddled version of the Duke of Urbino's alleged 1538 murder by Luigi Gonzaga.
9. Wounds; concerns.
1. Let the chafed horse wince, our shoulders are not rubbed sore.

OPHELIA   You are as good as a chorus,[2] my lord.

225 HAMLET   I could interpret between you and your love if I could see the puppets dallying.[3]

OPHELIA   You are keen,° my lord, you are keen.   *sharply satirical*

HAMLET   It would cost you a groaning to take off mine edge.[4]

OPHELIA   Still better, and worse.[5]

230 HAMLET   So you mis-take your husbands.[6] [*To* LUCIANUS] Begin, murderer. Pox, leave thy damnable° faces and begin. Come: *grimacing*
'the croaking raven doth bellow for revenge'.[7]

PLAYER LUCIANUS   Thoughts black, hands apt, drugs fit, and time
      agreeing,
Confederate° season, else no creature seeing;   *Complicit*

235 Thou mixture rank° of midnight weeds collected,   *foul*
With Hecate's ban[8] thrice blasted, thrice infected,
Thy natural magic and dire property°   *quality*
On wholesome life usurp immediately.

[*He*] *pours the poison in* [*the Player King's*] *ears*

HAMLET   A poisons him i'th' garden for 's estate.° His name's   *position; state*

240 Gonzago. The story is extant, and writ in choice Italian. You shall see anon how the murderer gets the love of Gonzago's wife.

OPHELIA   The King rises.

HAMLET   What, frighted with false fire?[9]

245 QUEEN GERTRUDE [*to* CLAUDIUS]   How fares my lord?

POLONIUS   Give o'er the play.

KING CLAUDIUS   Give me some light. Away.

COURTIERS   Lights, lights, lights![1]

Exeunt all but HAMLET *and* HORATIO

HAMLET   Why, let the stricken deer go weep,[2]

250   The hart ungallèd° play,   *unafflicted*
   For some must watch,° while some must sleep,   *stay awake*
   So runs the world away.[3]

Would not this,° sir, and a forest of feathers,[4] if the rest of my   (The Mousetrap)
fortunes turn Turk° with me, with two Provençal roses on my   *renegade*

255 razed[5] shoes, get me a fellowship in a cry of players,[6] sir?

HORATIO   Half a share.

HAMLET   A whole one, I.
   For thou dost know, O Damon[7] dear,
   This realm dismantled° was   *deprived*

260   Of Jove himself, and now reigns here
   A very, very—pajock.[8]

---

2. The Chorus explained the forthcoming action. In puppet shows, a choric narrator, or "interpreter," announced the characters' names and spoke the dialogue.
3. Flirting. Hamlet uses "interpret" here in the sense of acting as the go-between, or pander, for two lovers.
4. To satisfy my sexual appetite (leading to groaning in either sexual intercourse or childbirth).
5. Wittier, and more obscene.
6. With these false promises ("for better and for worse"), you take your husbands in marriage and cheat on them.
7. Misquoted from *The True Tragedy of Richard III* (c. 1591; not to be confused with Shakespeare's own *Richard III*).
8. Curse by the goddess of witchcraft.
9. Fireworks or blank cartridges.
1. This line is spoken by Polonius in Q2 and by "All"
in F.
2. A deer was thought to weep when mortally wounded. These four lines are probably from a lost ballad.
3. That's the way of the world.
4. Plumes, worn often onstage.
5. Decorated with slashes. *Provençal roses:* large rosettes concealing shoelaces.
6. *a fellowship . . . players:* a profit-sharing partnership in a pack ("cry") of actors (such as Shakespeare had in the Lord Chamberlain's Men).
7. Damon and Pythias were legendary ideals of friendship.
8. "Patchock" (rare, meaning something like "oaf"), or "peacock," emblem of the sin of pride. (The expected rhyme word would be "ass.")

HORATIO   You might have rhymed.

HAMLET   O good Horatio, I'll take the Ghost's word for a thousand pound. Didst perceive?

265   HORATIO   Very well, my lord.

HAMLET   Upon the talk of the pois'ning?

HORATIO   I did very well note him.

Enter ROSENCRANTZ *and* GUILDENSTERN

HAMLET   Ah ha! Come, some music, come, the recorders,
For if the King like not the comedy,

270   Why then, belike he likes it not, pardie.°   *indeed* (pardieu)
Come, some music.

GUILDENSTERN   Good my lord, vouchsafe me a word with you.

HAMLET   Sir, a whole history.

GUILDENSTERN   The King, sir—

275   HAMLET   Ay, sir, what of him?

GUILDENSTERN   Is in his retirement° marvellous distempered.   *withdrawal*

HAMLET   With drink, sir?

GUILDENSTERN   No, my lord, rather with choler.⁹

HAMLET   Your wisdom should show itself more richer° to signify   *resourceful*

280   this to his doctor, for for me to put him to his purgation¹ would
perhaps plunge him into far more choler.

GUILDENSTERN   Good my lord, put your discourse into some
frame,° and start° not so wildly from my affair.   *order / jump away*

HAMLET   I am tame, sir. Pronounce.

285   GUILDENSTERN   The Queen your mother, in most great affliction of spirit, hath sent me to you.

HAMLET   You are welcome.

GUILDENSTERN   Nay, good my lord, this courtesy is not of the
right breed.° If it shall please you to make me a wholesome°   *kind; nobility / sane*

290   answer, I will do your mother's commandment; if not, your
pardon° and my return shall be the end of my business.   *permission to go*

HAMLET   Sir, I cannot.

GUILDENSTERN   What, my lord?

HAMLET   Make you a wholesome answer. My wit's diseased. But,

295   sir, such answers as I can make, you shall command; or rather,
as you say, my mother. Therefore no more, but to the matter.
My mother, you say?

ROSENCRANTZ   Then thus she says: your behaviour hath struck
her into amazement and admiration.°   *bewilderment*

300   HAMLET   O wonderful son, that can so astonish a mother! But is
there no sequel at the heels of this mother's admiration?

ROSENCRANTZ   She desires to speak with you in her closet° ere   *private chamber*
you go to bed.

HAMLET   We shall obey, were she ten times our mother. Have

305   you any further trade with us?

ROSENCRANTZ   My lord, you once did love me.

HAMLET   So I do still, by these pickers and stealers.²

ROSENCRANTZ   Good my lord, what is your cause of distemper?

9. Both anger (Guildenstern's meaning) and indiges-
tion (Hamlet's). In Renaissance medical psychology,
each was a symptom of too much yellow bile—an
imbalance ("distemper") of the bodily fluids (humors).
1. A complicated pun: bloodletting; spiritual purging
(confession and absolution); legal purging (clearing oneself of a crime).
2. Hands. (The catechism in the Book of Common
Prayer includes a promise to "keep my hands from picking and stealing, and my tongue from evil speaking,
lying, and slandering.")

You do freely° bar the door of your own liberty if you deny your   *voluntarily*
310   griefs to your friend.

HAMLET   Sir, I lack advancement.

ROSENCRANTZ   How can that be when you have the voice of the
King himself for your succession in Denmark?

HAMLET   Ay, but 'while the grass grows . . .'³—the proverb is
315   something° musty.   *somewhat*

                 Enter one with a recorder⁴

O, the recorder. Let me see. [*To* ROSENCRANTZ *and* GUILDEN-
STERN, *taking them aside*] To withdraw° with you, why do you   *speak privately*
go about to recover the wind of me as if you would drive me
into a toil?⁵

320   GUILDENSTERN   O my lord, if my duty be too bold, my love is
too unmannerly.⁶

HAMLET   I do not well understand that. Will you play upon this
pipe?

GUILDENSTERN   My lord, I cannot.

325   HAMLET   I pray you.

GUILDENSTERN   Believe me, I cannot.

HAMLET   I do beseech you.

GUILDENSTERN   I know no touch of it, my lord.

HAMLET   'Tis as easy as lying. Govern these ventages° with your   *finger holes*
330   fingers and thumb, give it breath with your mouth, and it will
discourse most excellent music. Look you, these are the stops.°   *finger holes; notes*

GUILDENSTERN   But these cannot I command to any utterance
of harmony. I have not the skill.

HAMLET   Why, look you now, how unworthy a thing you make
335   of me! You would play upon me, you would seem to know my
stops, you would pluck out the heart of my mystery, you would
sound° me from my lowest note to the top of my compass;° and   *fathom; play on / range*
there is much music, excellent voice in this little organ,° yet   *musical instrument*
cannot you make it speak. 'Sblood, do you think I am easier to
340   be played on than a pipe? Call me what instrument you will,
though you can fret⁷ me, you cannot play upon me.

                 Enter POLONIUS

God bless you, sir.

POLONIUS   My lord, the Queen would speak with you, and presently.

345   HAMLET   Do you see yonder cloud that's almost in shape of a
camel?

POLONIUS   By th' mass, and 'tis: like a camel, indeed.

HAMLET   Methinks it is like a weasel.

POLONIUS   It is backed like a weasel.

350   HAMLET   Or like a whale.

POLONIUS   Very like a whale.

HAMLET   Then will I come to my mother by and by. [*Aside*]
They fool me to the top of my bent.⁸ [*To* POLONIUS] I will come
by and by.

355   POLONIUS   I will say so.

HAMLET   'By and by' is easily said.   *Exit* [POLONIUS]

---

3. "While the grass grows, the horse starves."
4. Q2 has "Enter the Players with Recorders."
5. *go . . . toil:* both conspire and take a roundabout
course in order to get to the windward (like a hunter
using his own smell to drive quarry to a waiting snare,
or "toil").

6. If I have been discourteous in pursuing what is my
duty, my love for you is to blame.
7. Irritate, punning on "frets of stringed instruments,"
which regulate fingering and pitch.
8. They go along with my foolishness to its limit, or to
the limit of my endurance.

Leave me, friends. [*Exeunt* ROSENCRANTZ *and* GUILDENSTERN]
'Tis now the very witching time of night,
When churchyards yawn, and hell itself breathes out
360 Contagion to this world. Now could I drink hot blood,
And do such bitter business as the day
Would quake to look on. Soft, now to my mother.
O heart, lose not thy nature!° Let not ever   *natural affection*
The soul of Nero[9] enter this firm° bosom.   *resolved*
365 Let me be cruel, not unnatural.
I will speak daggers to her, but use none.
My tongue and soul in this be hypocrites[1]—
How in my words somever[2] she be shent,°   *rebuked*
To give them seals[3] never my soul consent.   *Exit*

3.3

Enter KING [CLAUDIUS], ROSENCRANTZ, *and* GUILDEN-
STERN

KING CLAUDIUS   I like him not, nor stands it safe with us
To let his madness range. Therefore prepare you.
I your commission will forthwith dispatch,
And he to England shall along with you.
5 The terms of our estate[1] may not endure
Hazard so dangerous as doth hourly grow
Out of his lunacies.[2]

GUILDENSTERN   We will ourselves provide.
Most holy and religious fear° it is   *care*
To keep those many many bodies safe
10 That live and feed upon your majesty.

ROSENCRANTZ   The single° and peculiar° life is bound   *individual / private*
With all the strength and armour of the mind
To keep itself from noyance;° but much more   *harm*
That spirit upon whose weal° depends and rests   *well-being*
15 The lives of many. The cease° of majesty   *decease*
Dies not alone, but like a gulf° doth draw   *whirlpool*
What's near it with it. It is a massy° wheel   *massive*
Fixed on the summit of the highest mount,
To whose huge spokes ten thousand lesser things
20 Are mortised° and adjoined, which° when it falls   *affixed / so that*
Each small annexment, petty consequence,
Attends° the boist'rous ruin. Never alone   *Accompanies*
Did the King sigh, but with a general groan.

KING CLAUDIUS   Arm° you, I pray you, to this speedy voyage, *Prepare*
25 For we will fetters put upon this fear
Which now goes too free-footed.

ROSENCRANTZ *and* GUILDENSTERN   We will haste us.
                                        Exeunt [*both*]

Enter POLONIUS

POLONIUS   My lord, he's going to his mother's closet.
Behind the arras° I'll convey myself   *wall tapestry*
To hear the process.° I'll warrant she'll tax him home.[3]   *proceedings*

---

9. The Roman Emperor Nero reputedly murdered his
mother, in one account, by cutting open her womb.
1. Let me appear and speak as if I intended violence
(though I do not).
2. However much by my words.
3. To confirm them with visible deeds.

3.3 Location: The castle.
1. The responsibilities of our position.
2. Mad actions, apparently a revision in F of Q2's
"browes" (an ambiguous term suggesting "brain,"
"expressions," or "effrontery").
3. I'm sure she will rebuke him thoroughly.

30 And, as you said—and wisely was it said—
    'Tis meet° that some more audience than a mother,   *fitting*
    Since nature makes them partial, should o'erhear
    The speech of vantage.° Fare you well, my liege.   *in addition*
    I'll call upon you ere you go to bed,
    And tell you what I know.
35 KING CLAUDIUS   Thanks, dear my lord.

                                                      Exit [POLONIUS]

    O, my offence is rank! It smells to heaven.
    It hath the primal eldest curse⁴ upon't,
    A brother's murder. Pray can I not.
    Though inclination be as sharp as will,⁵
40 My stronger guilt defeats my strong intent,
    And like a man to double business bound⁶
    I stand in pause where I shall first begin,
    And both neglect. What if this cursèd hand
    Were thicker than itself with brother's blood,⁷
45 Is there not rain enough in the sweet heavens
    To wash it white as snow?⁸ Whereto serves mercy
    But to confront the visage of offence?⁹
    And what's in prayer but this twofold force,
    To be forestallèd° ere we come to fall,   *prevented*
50 Or pardoned being down? Then I'll look up.
    My fault is past—but O, what form of prayer
    Can serve my turn? 'Forgive me my foul murder'?
    That cannot be, since I am still possessed
    Of those effects for which I did the murder—
55 My crown, mine own ambition, and my queen.
    May one be pardoned and retain th'offence?¹
    In the corrupted currents of this world
    Offence's gilded° hand may shove by justice,   *bribing*
    And oft 'tis seen the wicked prize² itself
60 Buys out the law. But 'tis not so above.
    There is no shuffling,° there the action lies   *evasion*
    In his true nature,³ and we ourselves compelled
    Even to the teeth and forehead of⁴ our faults
    To give in evidence.⁵ What then? What rests?°   *remains to be done*
65 Try what repentance can. What can it not?
    Yet what can it when one cannot repent?
    O wretched state, O bosom black as death,
    O limèd⁶ soul that, struggling to be free,
    Art more engaged!° Help, angels! Make assay.°   *entangled / some attempt*
70 Bow, stubborn knees; and heart with strings of steel,

---

4. The first, oldest curse (God's curse on Cain for murdering his brother, Abel; see Genesis 4:10–12).
5. Though my desire (to pray) is as strong as my determination to do so.
6. Committed to two different goals.
7. Were covered with a layer of brother's blood deeper than the hand's thickness.
8. Compare Isaiah 1:15–18: "And though ye make many prayers, I will not hear: for your hands are full of blood. Wash you, make you clean; take away the evil of your works from before mine eyes. . . . though your sins were as crimson, they shall be made white as snow."

9. *Whereto . . . offence:* What purpose has mercy if not to oppose sin face to face?
1. And keep what was gained from the crime.
2. The profits from wickedness.
3. *the action . . . nature:* the deed appears in its true form; legal proceedings are properly conducted.
4. *Even . . . of:* Even face to face with. (English law provided for the confrontation of the accused and the witnesses.)
5. To testify. In English law, one cannot be forced to give evidence against oneself; heavenly justice is different.
6. Caught as if in birdlime, a sticky substance smeared on twigs to catch birds.

Be soft as sinews of the new-born babe.
All may be well.

     [He kneels.]
     Enter [Prince] HAMLET *[behind him]*

HAMLET   Now might I do it pat,° now a° is praying,   *neatly / he*
And now I'll do't,

     [He draws his sword]
             and so a goes to heaven,
75   And so am I revenged. That would be scanned.[7]
A villain kills my father, and for that
I, his sole son, do this same villain send
To heaven.
O, this is hire and salary, not revenge!
80   A took my father grossly, full of bread,[8]
With all his crimes broad blown,[9] as flush° as May;   *vigorously thriving*
And how his audit° stands, who knows save heaven?   *spiritual account*
But in our circumstance and course of thought[1]
'Tis heavy with him. And am I then revenged
85   To take him in the purging of his soul,
When he is fit and seasoned° for his passage?   *made ready*
No.

     [He sheathes his sword]
Up, sword, and know thou a more horrid hint.°   *occasion*
When he is drunk asleep, or in his rage,
90   Or in th'incestuous pleasure of his bed,
At gaming, swearing, or about some act
That has no relish° of salvation in't,   *trace*
Then trip him that his heels may kick at heaven,
And that his soul may be as damned and black
95   As hell whereto it goes. My mother stays.°   *waits*
This physic[2] but prolongs thy sickly days.   *Exit*
KING CLAUDIUS   My words fly up, my thoughts remain below.
Words without thoughts never to heaven go.   *Exit*

3.4

     Enter QUEEN GERTRUDE *and* POLONIUS

POLONIUS   A will come straight.° Look you lay home to him.[1]   *immediately*
Tell him his pranks have been too broad° to bear with,   *outrageous*
And that your grace hath screened and stood between
Much heat and him. I'll silence me e'en here.
5   Pray you be round° with him.   *blunt*
HAMLET *(within)*   Mother, mother, mother!
QUEEN GERTRUDE   I'll warr'nt you. Fear° me not. Withdraw; I   *Doubt*
   hear him coming.

     *[*POLONIUS *hides behind the arras.]*
     Enter [Prince] HAMLET

HAMLET   Now, mother, what's the matter?
QUEEN GERTRUDE   Hamlet, thou hast thy father much offended.
10 HAMLET   Mother, you have my father much offended.

---

7. That needs careful evaluation.
8. Not spiritually prepared. Compare Ezekiel 16:49:
"Behold, this was the iniquity of thy sister Sodom, pride,
fullness of bread, and abundance of idleness."
9. With all his sins in full bloom.
1. But in our indirect and limited way of knowing on

earth.
2. Medicine (both Claudius's prayer and Hamlet's
postponement of the revenge).
3.4 Location: The Queen's private chamber.
1. Be sure to rebuke him thoroughly.

QUEEN GERTRUDE   Come, come, you answer with an idle tongue.

HAMLET   Go, go, you question with a wicked tongue.

QUEEN GERTRUDE   Why, how now,° Hamlet?   *what's this*

HAMLET   What's the matter now?

QUEEN GERTRUDE   Have you forgot me?²

HAMLET   No, by the rood,° not so.   *Cross of Christ*

15   You are the Queen, your husband's brother's wife.
      But—would you were not so—you are my mother.

QUEEN GERTRUDE   Nay, then, I'll set those to you that can speak.³

HAMLET   Come, come, and sit you down. You shall not budge.
      You go not till I set you up a glass°   *mirror*

20   Where you may see the inmost part of you.

QUEEN GERTRUDE   What wilt thou do? Thou wilt not murder me?
      Help, help, ho!

POLONIUS [*behind the arras*]   What ho! Help, help, help!

HAMLET   How now, a rat? Dead for a ducat, dead.⁴
      [*He thrusts his sword through the arras.*] *Kills* POLONIUS

POLONIUS   O, I am slain!

QUEEN GERTRUDE [*to* HAMLET]   O me, what hast thou done?

25   HAMLET   Nay, I know not. Is it the King?

QUEEN GERTRUDE   O, what a rash and bloody deed is this!

HAMLET   A bloody deed—almost as bad, good-mother,°   *stepmother*
      As kill a king and marry with his brother.

QUEEN GERTRUDE   As kill a king?

HAMLET   Ay, lady, 'twas my word.

30   [*To* POLONIUS] Thou wretched, rash, intruding fool, farewell.
      I took thee for thy better. Take thy fortune.
      Thou find'st to be too busy° is some danger.—   *nosy*
      Leave wringing of your hands. Peace, sit you down,
      And let me wring your heart; for so I shall

35   If it be made of penetrable stuff,
      If damnèd custom° have not brassed it so   *sinful habit*
      That it is proof and bulwark against sense.⁵

QUEEN GERTRUDE   What have I done, that thou dar'st wag thy tongue
      In noise so rude against me?

HAMLET   Such an act

40   That blurs the grace and blush of modesty,
      Calls virtue hypocrite, takes off the rose
      From the fair forehead of an innocent love
      And sets a blister there,⁶ makes marriage vows
      As false as dicers' oaths—O, such a deed

45   As from the body of contraction° plucks   *marriage contract*
      The very soul, and sweet religion makes
      A rhapsody⁷ of words. Heaven's face doth glow,°   *blush*
      Yea, this solidity and compound mass⁸
      With tristful° visage, as against the doom,⁹   *sad*
      Is thought-sick at the act.

50   QUEEN GERTRUDE   Ay me, what act,

---

2. Forgotten the respect you owe to me as your mother.
3. *that can speak:* who can deal with someone as impossibly rude as you.
4. I bet a ducat I have killed it.
5. *brassed . . . sense:* made it so brasslike (or brazen) that it is impenetrably fortified against natural feeling ("sense").

6. Prostitutes, among other criminals, were branded on the forehead during the sixteenth and seventeenth centuries.
7. Meaningless jumble.
8. Solid earth (a compound of the four elements).
9. As if preparing for the Last Judgment.

That roars so loud and thunders in the index?[1]
HAMLET   Look here upon this picture, and on this,
    The counterfeit presentment° of two brothers.   *painted portrayal*
    See what a grace was seated on this brow—
55   Hyperion's° curls, the front° of Jove himself,   *The sun god's / forehead*
    An eye like Mars,° to threaten or command,   *the god of war*
    A station like the herald Mercury[2]
    New lighted° on a heaven-kissing hill;   *alighted*
    A combination and a form indeed
60   Where every god did seem to set his seal
    To give the world assurance of a man.
    This *was* your husband. Look you now what follows.
    Here *is* your husband, like a mildewed ear°   *ear of grain*
    Blasting° his wholesome brother. Have you eyes?   *Infesting*
65   Could you on this fair mountain leave° to feed,   *cease*
    And batten on this moor?[3] Ha, have you eyes?
    You cannot call it love, for at your age
    The heyday in the blood[4] is tame, it's humble,
    And waits° upon the judgement; and what judgement   *follows*
70   Would step from this to this?[5]
70.1   *Sense[6] sure you have,*
      Else could you not have motion; but sure that sense
      Is apoplexed,° for madness would not err,   *paralyzed*
      Nor sense to ecstasy was ne'er so thralled
70.5   *But it reserved some quantity of choice*
      To serve in such a difference.[7] What devil was't
      That thus hath cozened you at hoodman-blind?[8]
      Eyes without feeling, feeling without sight,
      Ears without hands or eyes, smelling sans all,[9]
70.10   *Or but a sickly part of one true sense*
      Could not so mope.[1]
                 What devil was't
    That thus hath cozened you at hood-man blind?[2]
    O shame, where is thy blush? Rebellious hell,
    If thou canst mutine° in a matron's bones,   *mutiny*
    To flaming youth let virtue be as wax
75   And melt in her° own fire. Proclaim no shame   *(youth's)*
    When the compulsive ardour gives the charge,°   *order to attack*
    Since frost itself as actively doth burn,
    And reason panders will.[3]
QUEEN GERTRUDE   O Hamlet, speak no more!
    Thou turn'st mine eyes into my very soul,
80   And there I see such black and grainèd° spots   *engrained*
    As will not leave their tinct.°   *lose their color*
HAMLET   Nay, but to live
    In the rank sweat of an enseamèd° bed,   *a greasy*

---

1. Table of contents; preface.
2. A stance like the winged herald of the gods.
3. And glut yourself on this poor pastureland (possibly punning on "blackamoor").
4. The excitement of sexual passion.
5. After "this?" Q2 has a longer version, 70.1–70.11, of Hamlet's subsequent one and a half lines.
6. Sensation; the five senses (sight, smell, hearing, taste, and touch).
7. *ne'er . . . difference:* never so enslaved by madness that it did not retain some ability to choose between such different men ("sense" connoting "reason").

8. See note to line 71.
9. *sans all:* without any other sense. Cf. Psalm 115:5–6 on idolaters: "Eyes have they, but they see not: They have ears but they hear not: noses have they, but they smell not."
1. Could not be so obtuse.
2. That in this way has cheated you in blindman's buff (as if her second husband had been put in her way while she was groping blindfolded).
3. And mature reason abets lust (rather than restraining it).

Stewed in corruption, honeying and making love
Over the nasty sty—

QUEEN GERTRUDE   O, speak to me no more!
85   These words like daggers enter in mine ears.
No more, sweet Hamlet.

HAMLET   A murderer and a villain,
A slave that is not twenti'th part the tithe°   *one-tenth*
Of your precedent° lord, a vice⁴ of kings,   *previous*
A cutpurse° of the empire and the rule,   *pickpocket*
90   That from a shelf the precious diadem stole
And put it in his pocket—

QUEEN GERTRUDE   No more.

HAMLET   A king of shreds and patches⁵—

Enter GHOST *in his nightgown*⁶

Save me and hover o'er me with your wings,
95   You heavenly guards! [*To* GHOST] What would you, gracious figure?

QUEEN GERTRUDE   Alas, he's mad.

HAMLET [*to* GHOST]   Do you not come your tardy son to chide,
That, lapsed in time and passion,⁷ lets go by
Th'important° acting of your dread command?   *urgent*
O, say!

100 GHOST   Do not forget. This visitation
Is but to whet thy almost blunted purpose.
But look, amazement on thy mother sits.
O, step between her and her fighting soul.
Conceit° in weakest bodies strongest works.   *Imagination*
105 Speak to her, Hamlet.

HAMLET   How is it with you, lady?

QUEEN GERTRUDE   Alas, how is't with you,
That you do bend your eye on vacancy,
And with th'incorporal° air do hold discourse?   *bodiless*
110 Forth at your eyes your spirits wildly peep,
And, as the sleeping soldiers in th'alarm,°   *call to arms*
Your bedded hair, like life in excrements,⁸
Start up and stand on end. O gentle son,
Upon the heat and flame of thy distemper°   *unbalanced mind*
115 Sprinkle cool patience! Whereon do you look?

HAMLET   On him, on him. Look you how pale he glares.
His form and cause conjoined,⁹ preaching to stones,
Would make them capable. [*To* GHOST] Do not look
                          upon me,
Lest with this piteous action you convert°   *change (to mercy)*
120 My stern effects.° Then what I have to do   *intended acts*
Will want true colour¹—tears perchance° for blood.   *perhaps*

QUEEN GERTRUDE   To whom do you speak this?

HAMLET   Do you see nothing there?

QUEEN GERTRUDE   Nothing at all, yet all that is I see.

HAMLET   Nor did you nothing hear?

QUEEN GERTRUDE   No, nothing but ourselves.

---

4. In morality plays, the buffoon who personified evil.
5. *shreds and patches:* motley, the costume of a jester.
6. The nightgown is specified only in Q1; Q2 and F
leave open the possibility that the Ghost is appearing
again in his armor.
7. *lapsed . . . passion:* having allowed time to pass and

passionate dedication (to revenge) to fade.
8. In insensate outgrowths (used of nails and hair).
bedded: (formerly) flat and inert.
9. His appearance joined with his reason for appearing.
1. Will not be as it should (since he cries colorless tears
instead of shedding red blood).

125 HAMLET   Why, look you there. Look how it steals away.
     My father, in his habit[2] as° he lived.   *when; as if*
     Look where he goes even now out at the portal.

                                                   Exit GHOST

     QUEEN GERTRUDE   This is the very coinage of your brain.
     This bodiless creation ecstasy
     Is very cunning in.[3]

130 HAMLET   Ecstasy?
     My pulse as yours doth temperately keep time,
     And makes as healthful music. It is not madness
     That I have uttered. Bring me to the test,
     And I the matter will reword,° which madness   *repeat exactly*
135   Would gambol° from. Mother, for love of grace   *skitter away*
     Lay not a flattering unction[4] to your soul
     That not your trespass but my madness speaks.
     It will but skin° and film the ulcerous place   *cover*
     Whilst rank corruption, mining° all within,   *undermining*
140   Infects unseen. Confess yourself to heaven;
     Repent what's past, avoid what is to come,
     And do not spread the compost o'er the weeds
     To make them ranker. Forgive me this my virtue,°   *virtuous exhortation*
     For in the fatness° of these pursy° times   *grossness / flatulent*
145   Virtue itself of vice must pardon beg,
     Yea, curb° and woo for leave° to do him good.   *bow / permission*

     QUEEN GERTRUDE   O Hamlet, thou hast cleft my heart in twain!

     HAMLET   O, throw away the worser part of it,
     And live the purer with the other half!
150   Good night—but go not to mine uncle's bed.
     Assume° a virtue if you have it not.[5]   *Put on (actions of)*
151.1   *That monster custom, who all sense doth eat,*
     Of habits devilish,[6] is angel yet in this:
     That to the use° of actions fair and good   *habitual practice*
     He likewise gives a frock or livery
151.5   *That aptly° is put on. Refrain tonight,*   *quickly*
     And that shall lend a kind of easiness
     To the next abstinence, the next more easy—
     For use almost can change the stamp of nature—
     And either in° the devil, or throw him out   *let in*
151.10   *With wondrous potency.*
     Refrain tonight,
     And that shall lend a kind of easiness
     To the next abstinence. Once more, good night;
155   And when you are desirous to be blest,
     I'll blessing beg of you. For this same lord,
     I do repent. But heaven hath pleased it so
     To punish me with this, and this with me,
     That I must be their scourge and minister.[7]
160   I will bestow° him, and will answer well[8]   *dispose of*
     The death I gave him. So, again, good night.

---

2. Dress and bearing.
3. *This bodiless . . . in*: This type of hallucination is a particular skill ("cunning") of madness.
4. Do not apply an ointment that relieves pain but does not heal (contrasted to a sacramental unction that blesses the soul).

5. Q2 has the following longer version (151.1–151.10) of lines 152–54 (*Refrain . . . abstinence*).
6. Emended from Q2's "devil," apparently in compressed opposition to "angel."
7. Heaven's agent of punishment.
8. Will take responsibility for.

I must be cruel only to be kind.
Thus bad begins, and worse remains behind.[9]

QUEEN GERTRUDE   What shall I do?

165 HAMLET   Not this, by no means, that I bid you do:
Let the bloat King tempt you again to bed,
Pinch wanton on your cheek, call you his mouse,
And let him for a pair of reechy° kisses,   *filthy*
Or paddling° in your neck with his damned fingers,   *fondly fingering*
170 Make you to ravel° all this matter out,   *disclose*
That I essentially am not in madness,
But mad in craft.° 'Twere good you let him know,   *cunning*
For who that's but° a queen, fair, sober, wise,   *only*
Would from a paddock,° from a bat, a gib,°   *toad / tomcat*
175 Such dear concernings° hide? Who would do so?   *Such vital affairs*
No, in despite of sense and secrecy,
Unpeg the basket on the house's top,
Let the birds fly, and, like the famous ape,
To try conclusions in the basket creep,
180 And break your own neck down.[1]

QUEEN GERTRUDE   Be thou assured, if words be made of breath,
And breath of life, I have no life to breathe
What thou hast said to me.

HAMLET   I must to England.
You know that?

QUEEN GERTRUDE   Alack, I had forgot.
185 'Tis so concluded on.[2]

185.1 HAMLET   *There's letters sealed, and my two schoolfellows—*
Whom I will trust as I will adders fanged—
They bear the mandate, they must sweep my way
And marshal me to knavery[3] Let it work,°   *proceed*
185.5 *For 'tis the sport to have the engineer[4]*
Hoised with his own petard;[5] and't shall go hard
But I will delve one yard below their mines°   *military tunnels*
And blow them at the moon. O, 'tis most sweet
When in one line two crafts directly meet.[6]

HAMLET   This man shall set me packing.
I'll lug the guts into the neighbour room.
Mother, good night indeed. This counsellor
Is now most still, most secret, and most grave,
Who was in life a foolish prating knave.—
190 Come, sir, to draw toward an end with you.[7]—
Good night, mother.   *Exit, tugging in* POLONIUS

---

9. To follow. Q2 here adds, "One word more good
Lady."
1. *like . . . down:* a tale presumably involving an ape who
opened a wicker cage full of birds and released them from
the rooftop; after climbing into the basket, he tried to imitate their flight to freedom but died in the fall. *try conclusions:* test the results.
2. Q2 contains the following additional passage.
3. *sweep . . . knavery:* prepare my path and escort me

into a trap (also, and provoke me to crime).
4. Designer and builder of "engines" (military devices).
5. Blown skyward by his own bomb (for breaching
enemy fortifications).
6. That is, when two devious plots ("crafts") meet along
the same path of tunneling (a standard technique in siege
warfare).
7. To conclude my dealings with you (punning on
"draw" as "drag").

4.1

Enter KING CLAUDIUS *to* QUEEN GERTRUDE[1]

KING CLAUDIUS   There's matter in these sighs, these profound heaves;
You must translate. 'Tis fit we understand them.
Where is your son?[2]

3.1   QUEEN GERTRUDE   *Bestow this place on us a little while*
Exeunt [ROSENCRANTZ *and* GUILDENSTERN]
Ah, my good lord, what have I seen tonight!

5   KING CLAUDIUS   What, Gertrude? How does Hamlet?

QUEEN GERTRUDE   Mad as the sea and wind when both contend
Which is the mightier. In his lawless fit,
Behind the arras hearing something stir,
He whips his rapier out and cries 'A rat, a rat!',
10   And in his brainish apprehension° kills   *brain-sick notion*
The unseen good old man.

KING CLAUDIUS   O heavy deed!
It had been so with us° had we been there.   *me (royal "we")*
His liberty is full of threats to all—
To you yourself, to us, to everyone.
15   Alas, how shall this bloody deed be answered?°   *accounted for*
It will be laid to° us, whose providence°   *blamed on / foresight*
Should have kept short,° restrained, and out of haunt[3]   *closely tethered*
This mad young man. But so much was our love,
We would not understand what was most fit,
20   But, like the owner° of a foul disease,   *victim*
To keep it from divulging,° let it feed   *being seen*
Even on the pith of life. Where is he gone?

QUEEN GERTRUDE   To draw apart the body he hath killed,
O'er whom—his very madness, like some ore°   *vein of gold*
25   Among a mineral° of metals base,   *mine*
Shows itself pure—a° weeps for what is done.   *he*

KING CLAUDIUS   O Gertrude, come away!
The sun no sooner shall the mountains touch
But we will ship him hence; and this vile deed
30   We must with all our majesty and skill
Both countenance° and excuse.—Ho, Guildenstern!   *condone*
Enter ROSENCRANTZ *and* GUILDENSTERN
Friends both, go join you with some further aid.
Hamlet in madness hath Polonius slain,
And from his mother's closet hath he dragged him.
35   Go seek him out, speak fair, and bring the body
Into the chapel. I pray you haste in this.
Exeunt [ROSENCRANTZ *and* GUILDENSTERN]
Come, Gertrude, we'll call up our wisest friends
To let them know both what we mean to do
And what's untimely done.[4]

39.1   *So envious slander,*[5]
Whose whisper o'er the world's diameter,°   *whole extent*

4.1 Location: The castle.
1. The action continues, Gertrude remaining onstage. (Act divisions in the play are not authorial.) In Q2, Rosencrantz and Guildenstern enter with Claudius.
2. In Q2, Rosencrantz and Guildenstern, having entered with Claudius and Gertrude, can exit here (see line 3.1).

3. Public gatherings.
4. After "done," Q2 has the following passage, 39.1–39.5, omitted in F.
5. The phrase is conjectural. Q2 is missing a half line that contains the subject of the sentence.

As level as the cannon to his blank,[6]
Transports his poisoned shot, may miss our name

39.5 And hit the woundless° air.   invulnerable
                                          O, come away!
40 My soul is full of discord and dismay.   *Exeunt*

4.2

Enter [Prince] HAMLET
HAMLET Safely stowed.
ROSENCRANTZ *and* GUILDENSTERN (*within*) Hamlet, Lord Hamlet!
HAMLET What noise? Who calls on Hamlet?
Enter ROSENCRANTZ and GUILDENSTERN
                                        O, here they come.
ROSENCRANTZ What have you done, my lord, with the dead body?
5 HAMLET Compounded° it with dust, whereto 'tis kin.   Mixed
ROSENCRANTZ Tell us where 'tis, that we may take it thence
  And bear it to the chapel.
HAMLET Do not believe it.
ROSENCRANTZ Believe what?
10 HAMLET That I can keep your counsel and not mine own.[1]
  Besides, to be demanded of° a sponge—what replication°   questioned by / reply
  should be made by the son of a king?
ROSENCRANTZ Take you me for a sponge, my lord?
HAMLET Ay, sir, that soaks up the King's countenance,° his   favor
15 rewards, his authorities. But such officers do the King best service in the end. He keeps them, like an ape an apple in the
  corner of his jaw, first mouthed to be last swallowed. When he
  needs what you have gleaned, it is but squeezing you, and,
  sponge, you shall be dry again.
20 ROSENCRANTZ I understand you not, my lord.
HAMLET I am glad of it. A knavish speech sleeps in a foolish
  ear.[2]
ROSENCRANTZ My lord, you must tell us where the body is, and
  go with us to the King.
25 HAMLET The body is with the King, but the King is not with the
  body.[3] The King is a thing—
GUILDENSTERN A thing, my lord?
HAMLET Of nothing. Bring me to him. Hide fox, and all after.[4]
                    [*Exit running, pursued by the others*]

4.3

Enter KING [CLAUDIUS][1]
KING CLAUDIUS I have sent to seek him, and to find the body.
  How dangerous is it that this man goes loose!
  Yet must not we put the strong law on him.
  He's loved of° the distracted° multitude,   by / unreasonable

---

6. As straight as the cannon at a target at point-blank range. (The cannon would be tilted to aim at a distant target.)
4.2 Location: Scene continues.
1. Hamlet plays on two senses of "counsel": That I can follow your advice and not keep my secret.
2. An insulting remark is not perceived by a fool.
3. A riddle. Hamlet may mean that Polonius is gone to the afterlife with King Hamlet but Claudius is still alive; or he may refer to the legal theory of the "king's two bod-

ies" (one the king's natural body, the other the immortal abstract body of the state).
4. From the children's game fox-and-hounds, similar to hide-and-seek.
4.3 Location: Scene continues.
1. Q2 reads, "Enter King and two or three," thus allowing the ensuing lines to be spoken to other characters rather than treating them as a soliloquy or directed to the audience.

5   Who like not in their judgement but their eyes,[2]
     And where 'tis so, th'offender's scourge° is weighed,   *punishment*
     But never the offence. To bear° all smooth and even,   *manage*
     This sudden sending him away must seem
     Deliberate pause.° Diseases desperate grown   *Careful planning*
10   By desperate appliance° are relieved,   *remedy*
     Or not at all.

         Enter ROSENCRANTZ

                How now, what hath befall'n?

ROSENCRANTZ   Where the dead body is bestowed, my lord,
     We cannot get from him.

KING CLAUDIUS   But where is he?

ROSENCRANTZ   Without, my lord, guarded to know your pleasure.

15 KING CLAUDIUS   Bring him before us.

ROSENCRANTZ   Ho, Guildenstern! Bring in my lord.

         Enter [*Prince*] HAMLET *and* GUILDENSTERN

KING CLAUDIUS   Now, Hamlet, where's Polonius?

HAMLET   At supper.

KING CLAUDIUS   At supper? Where?

20 HAMLET   Not where he eats, but where a is eaten.[3] A certain
     convocation of politic° worms are e'en° at him. Your worm is   *cunning / now*
     your only emperor for diet.[4] We fat all creatures else° to fat us,   *besides ourselves*
     and we fat ourselves for maggots. Your fat king and your lean
     beggar is but variable service°—two dishes, but to one table.   *different courses*
25 That's the end.

KING CLAUDIUS   Alas, alas!

HAMLET   A man may fish with the worm that hath eat of a king,
     and eat of the fish that hath fed of that worm.

KING CLAUDIUS   What dost thou mean by this?

30 HAMLET   Nothing but to show you how a king may go a progress°   *royal journey*
     through the guts of a beggar.

KING CLAUDIUS   Where is Polonius?

HAMLET   In heaven. Send thither to see. If your messenger find
     him not there, seek him i'th' other place yourself. But indeed,
35 if you find him not this month, you shall nose him as you go
     up the stairs into the lobby.

KING CLAUDIUS [*to* ROSENCRANTZ]   Go seek him there.

HAMLET [*to* ROSENCRANTZ]   A will stay till ye come.

                  [*Exit* ROSENCRANTZ]

KING CLAUDIUS   Hamlet, this deed of thine, for thine especial safety—
40 Which we do tender° as we dearly grieve   *value*
     For that which thou hast done—must send thee hence
     With fiery quickness. Therefore prepare thyself.
     The barque is ready, and the wind at help,
     Th'associates tend,° and everything is bent°   *companions wait / poised*
45 For England.

HAMLET   For England?

KING CLAUDIUS   Ay, Hamlet.

---

2. Who choose not by reason but by external appearance.
3. Possibly an allusion to the Eucharist (Lord's Supper), in which the body of Christ is consumed in the form of bread.
4. *Your worm . . . diet:* The average worm is the only creature with a diet superior to a King's. The Diet (Council) of Emperor Charles V at Worms in 1521 called on Luther to defend his new doctrine. A scholar at Hamlet's university at Wittenberg, Luther maintained that faith alone, rather than sacramental ritual, was the basis of salvation.

HAMLET   Good.

KING CLAUDIUS   So is it if thou knew'st our purposes.

50   HAMLET   I see a cherub[5] that sees them. But come, for England.
Farewell, dear mother.

KING CLAUDIUS   Thy loving father, Hamlet.

HAMLET   My mother. Father and mother is man and wife, man
and wife is one flesh,[6] and so my mother. Come, for England.

Exit

55   KING CLAUDIUS [to GUILDENSTERN]   Follow him at foot.° Tempt   his heel
him with speed aboard.
Delay it not. I'll have him hence tonight.
Away, for everything is sealed and done
That else leans° on th'affair. Pray you, make haste.   bears

[Exit GUILDENSTERN]

And, England,[7] if my love thou hold'st at aught°—   any value
60   As my great power thereof may give thee sense,[8]
Since yet thy cicatrice° looks raw and red   scar
After the Danish sword, and thy free awe[9]
Pays homage to us—thou mayst not coldly set°   indifferently view
Our sovereign process, which imports at full,[1]
65   By letters conjuring to that effect,
The present° death of Hamlet. Do it, England,   immediate
For like the hectic° in my blood he rages,   fever
And thou must cure me. Till I know 'tis done,
Howe'er my haps,° my joys were ne'er begun.   Exit   fortunes

4.4

Enter FORTINBRAS *with a drum and his army over the
stage*

FORTINBRAS   Go, captain, from me greet the Danish king.
Tell him that by his licence° Fortinbras   permission
Claims the conveyance of° a promised march   escort for
Over his kingdom. You know the rendezvous.
5   If that his majesty would aught with us,
We shall express our duty in his eye,°   presence
And let him know so.

CAPTAIN   I will do't, my lord.   [Exit]

FORTINBRAS   Go safely[1] on.   Exeunt [marching]

Enter [Prince] HAMLET, ROSENCRANTZ, [GUILDENSTERN,] *etc.*

9.1   HAMLET [to the CAPTAIN]   *Good sir, whose powers° are these?*   forces

CAPTAIN   *They are of Norway, sir.*

HAMLET   *How purposed, sir, I pray you?*

CAPTAIN   *Against some part of Poland.*

HAMLET   *Who commands them, sir?*

CAPTAIN   *The nephew to old Norway, Fortinbras.*

9.5   HAMLET   *Goes it against the main° of Poland, sir,*   heart
Or for some frontier?

CAPTAIN   *Truly to speak, and with no addition,°*   exaggeration

---

5. The keen-sighted second order of angels, cherubim
symbolized heavenly knowledge.
6. As stated in Genesis 2:23 and the marriage rite of
the Book of Common Prayer.
7. King of England.
8. May give you a reason to feel the value of that love.
9. Your respect unconstrained (by an army of occupa-

tion).
1. Our sovereign command, which signifies in detailed
instructions.
4.4 Location: The Danish coast.
1. In Q2, "softly" (that is, slowly, circumspectly). In Q2,
the captain remains onstage, and the scene continues
with the following passage, 9.1–9.56.

We go to gain a little patch of ground
That hath in it no profit but the name.
9.10 To pay five ducats, five, I would not farm° it,   *lease*
Nor will it yield to Norway or the Pole
A ranker rate, should it be sold in fee.²

HAMLET   Why then, the Polack never will defend it.

CAPTAIN   Yes, it is already garrisoned.

9.15 HAMLET   Two thousand souls and twenty thousand ducats
Will now³ debate the question of this straw.°   *trifle*
This is th'imposthume° of much wealth and peace,   *abscess*
That inward breaks and shows no cause without⁴
Why the man dies. I humbly thank you, sir.

CAPTAIN   God buy° you, sir.   [*Exit*]   *be with*

9.20 ROSENCRANTZ   Will't please you go, my lord?

HAMLET   I'll be with you straight. Go a little before
[*Exeunt all but* HAMLET]

How all occasions do inform against° me   *accuse*
And spur my dull revenge! What is a man
If his chief good and market° of his time   *profit*
9.25 Be but to sleep and feed?—a beast, no more.
Sure, he that made us with such large discourse,°   *reasoning faculty*
Looking before and after,⁵ gave us not
That capability° and god-like reason   *intelligence*
To fust° in us unused. Now whether it be   *grow moldy*
9.30 Bestial oblivion,⁶ or some craven scruple
Of thinking too precisely on th'event—
A thought which, quartered, hath but one part wisdom
And ever three parts coward—I do not know
Why yet I live to say 'This thing's to do',
9.35 Sith° I have cause, and will, and strength, and means,   *Since*
To do't. Examples gross as earth exhort me,
Witness this army of such mass and charge,°   *cost*
Led by a delicate and tender° prince,   *young*
Whose spirit with divine ambition puffed°   *inspired*
9.40 Makes mouths at the invisible event,⁷
Exposing what is mortal and unsure
To all that fortune, death, and danger dare,
Even for an eggshell. Rightly to be great
Is not to stir without great argument,
9.45 But greatly to find quarrel in a straw
When honour's at the stake.⁸ How stand I, then,
That have a father killed, a mother stained,
Excitements° of my reason and my blood,   *Urgings*
And let all sleep while, to my shame, I see
9.50 The imminent death of twenty thousand men
That, for a fantasy and trick° of fame,   *fragile trifle*
Go to their graves like beds, fight for a plot
Whereon the numbers cannot try the cause,⁹

---

2. Sold outright as a freehold. *ranker rate:* more generous
return.
3. Oxford's emendation of Q2's "Will not."
4. That ruptures internally without external symptom.
5. Able to see past and future.
6. Animal-like inability to remember.

7. Shows a scornful face to unforeseeable outcomes.
8. *Rightly . . . stake:* These lines, syntactically ambiguous, seem to mean that true greatness lies not in rational restraint but in noble action. *the stake:* post to which a bull or bear was fastened for baiting.
9. Which is not big enough for the armies to fight on.

Which is not tomb enough and continent°   *container*
9.55   To hide the slain. O, from this time forth
My thoughts be bloody or be nothing worth!   *Exit*

4.5

Enter QUEEN GERTRUDE *and* HORATIO

QUEEN GERTRUDE   I will not speak with her.

HORATIO[1]   She is importunate,
Indeed distraught. Her mood will needs be pitied.

QUEEN GERTRUDE   What would she have?

HORATIO   She speaks much of her father, says she hears
5   There's tricks i'th' world, and hems, and beats her heart,
Spurns enviously at straws,[2] speaks things in doubt°   *obscurely*
That carry but half sense. Her speech is nothing,
Yet the unshapèd use° of it doth move   *incoherent manner*
The hearers to collection.° They aim° at it,   *inference / guess*
10   And botch° the words up fit to° their own thoughts,   *patch / to match*
Which,° as her winks and nods and gestures yield them,   *(words)*
Indeed would make one think there might be thought,
Though nothing sure, yet much unhappily.[3]

QUEEN GERTRUDE   'Twere good she were spoken with, for she may strew
15   Dangerous conjectures in ill-breeding minds.
Let her come in.

[HORATIO *withdraws to admit* OPHELIA]

QUEEN GERTRUDE   To my sick soul, as sin's true nature is,
Each toy° seems prologue to some great amiss.°   *triviality / calamity*
So full of artless jealousy° is guilt,   *uncontrolled suspicion*
20   It spills itself in fearing to be spilt.

Enter OPHELIA *distracted, playing on a lute, and her
hair down, singing*[4]

OPHELIA   Where is the beauteous majesty of Denmark?

QUEEN GERTRUDE   How now,° Ophelia?   *What's this*

OPHELIA (*sings*) How should I your true love know
From another one?—
25   By his cockle hat and staff,
And his sandal shoon.[5]

QUEEN GERTRUDE   Alas, sweet lady, what imports° this song?   *means*

OPHELIA   Say you? Nay, pray you, mark.°   *listen*
(*Song*)   He is dead and gone, lady,
30   He is dead and gone.
At his head a grass-green turf,
At his heels a stone.

QUEEN GERTRUDE   Nay, but Ophelia—

OPHELIA   Pray you, mark.
35   (*Song*)   White his shroud as the mountain snow—

Enter KING [CLAUDIUS]

QUEEN GERTRUDE   Alas, look here, my lord.

4.5 Location: A public room of the castle.
1. As in F. In Q2, lines 1–2 and 4–13 are spoken by a
"Gent.," while Horatio comments on them in lines
14–15 (assigned in F to Gertrude).
2. Kicks bitterly (takes offense) at the slightest thing.
3. Though they reveal nothing for certain, her words

could lead to unfortunate impressions.
4. F simply notes that Ophelia enters distracted; the
additional details are taken from Q1.
5. Shoes. *cockle hat:* a cockle-shell badge worn in the
hat was a pilgrim's memento of St. James's shrine at
Compostela in Spain.

OPHELIA (*Song*)   Larded° with sweet flowers,   *Garnished*
   Which bewept to the grave did—not⁶—go
   With true-love showers.°   *tears*
40 KING CLAUDIUS   How do ye, pretty lady?

OPHELIA   Well, God'ield° you. They say the owl was a baker's   *God yield (reward)*
daughter.⁷ Lord, we know what we are, but know not what we
may be. God be at your table!

KING CLAUDIUS [*to* GERTRUDE]   Conceit° upon her father.   *Brooding imagination*

45 OPHELIA   Pray you, let's have no words of this, but when they ask
you what it means, say you this.
  (*Song*)   Tomorrow is Saint Valentine's day,
   All in the morning betime,°   *early*
   And I a maid at your window
50   To be your Valentine.
   Then up he rose, and donned his clothes,
   And dupped° the chamber door;   *unlatched*
   Let in the maid, that out a maid
   Never departed more.
55 KING CLAUDIUS   Pretty Ophelia—

OPHELIA   Indeed, la? Without an oath, I'll make an end on't.°   *of it*
  (*Song*)   By Gis,° and by Saint Charity,   *Jesus*
   Alack, and fie for shame!
   Young men will do't if they come to't,
60   By Cock,⁸ they are to blame.
   Quoth she 'Before you tumbled me,
   You promised me to wed.'
   So would I 'a' done, by yonder sun,
   An° thou hadst not come to my bed.   *If*
65 KING CLAUDIUS [*to* GERTRUDE]   How long hath she been thus?

OPHELIA   I hope all will be well. We must be patient. But I cannot choose but weep to think they should lay him i'th' cold
ground. My brother shall know of it. And so I thank you for
your good counsel. Come, my coach! Good night, ladies, good
70 night, sweet ladies, good night, good night.   *Exit*

KING CLAUDIUS [*to* HORATIO]   Follow her close. Give her good
   watch, I pray you.   [*Exit* HORATIO]
O, this is the poison of deep grief! It springs
All from her father's death. O Gertrude, Gertrude,
When sorrows come they come not single spies,°   *scouts*
75 But in battalions. First, her father slain;
Next, your son gone, and he most violent author
Of his own just remove; the people muddied,°   *confused*
Thick and unwholesome in their thoughts and whispers
For good Polonius' death; and we have done but greenly°   *naively*
80 In hugger-mugger° to inter him; poor Ophelia   *secrecy*
Divided from herself and her fair judgement,
Without the which we are pictures or mere beasts;
Last, and as much containing° as all these,   *and as important*
Her brother is in secret come from France,

6. By adding "not," Ophelia changes the song's words and meter to fit the circumstances of Polonius's burial (see lines 79–80).
7. A folktale: Christ turned a baker's daughter into an owl because when he asked for food, she would give him only a small loaf.
8. A corruption of "God" in very mild swearing (playing on "penis").

85 Feeds on this wonder, keeps himself in clouds,°   *unverified suspicion*
And wants° not buzzers° to infect his ear   *lacks / scandal mongers*
With pestilent speeches of his father's death;
Wherein necessity, of matter beggared,
Will nothing stick our persons to arraign
90 In ear and ear.⁹ O my dear Gertrude, this,
Like to a murd'ring-piece,¹ in many places
Gives me superfluous° death.   *redundant*
    A noise within
QUEEN GERTRUDE   Alack, what noise is this?
KING CLAUDIUS   Where is my Switzers?² Let them guard the door.
    Enter a MESSENGER
What is the matter?
MESSENGER   Save yourself, my lord.
95 The ocean, overpeering of his list,³
Eats not the flats with more impetuous⁴ haste
Than young Laertes, in a riotous head,°   *insurrection; tidal wave*
O'erbears your officers. The rabble call him lord,
And, as° the world were now but° to begin,   *as if / only now*
100 Antiquity forgot, custom not known,
The ratifiers and props of every word,⁵
They cry 'Choose we! Laertes shall be king.'
Caps, hands, and tongues applaud it to the clouds,
'Laertes shall be king, Laertes king.'
105 QUEEN GERTRUDE   How cheerfully on the false trail they cry!⁶
    A noise within
O, this is counter,⁷ you false Danish dogs!
KING CLAUDIUS   The doors are broke.
    Enter LAERTES *with [his* FOLLOWERS *at the door]*
LAERTES   Where is the King?—Sirs, stand you all without.
ALL HIS FOLLOWERS   No, let's come in.
110 LAERTES   I pray you, give me leave.
ALL HIS FOLLOWERS   We will, we will.
LAERTES   I thank you. Keep the door.   *[Exeunt* FOLLOWERS*]*
      O thou vile king,
Give me my father.
QUEEN GERTRUDE   Calmly, good Laertes.
LAERTES   That drop of blood that's calm proclaims me bastard,
115 Cries cuckold to my father, brands the harlot
Even here between the chaste unsmirchèd brow
Of my true mother.
KING CLAUDIUS   What is the cause, Laertes,
That thy rebellion looks so giant-like?—
Let him go, Gertrude. Do not fear° our person.   *fear for*
120 There's such divinity doth hedge a king

9. *Wherein . . . ear:* In which affair, because they have no real information and need to give some account, they will not hesitate to whisper accusations against us.
1. Small cannon that fired shrapnel.
2. Company of Swiss mercenaries (employed as royal bodyguards in many European countries).
3. Rising over its boundary at the shore.
4. Spelled "impittious" in F and "impitious" in Q2, probably meaning "merciless" as well as "rash." *flats:* low-

lying countryside.
5. *Antiquity . . . word:* Ignoring history and traditional precedents, which give meaning, order, and stability to society by fixing the agreed-upon meaning of political contracts (and of any truth expressed in language).
6. How enthusiastically they run after the wrong scent (like a pack of hounds hunting the murderer of Polonius).
7. This is following the quarry's trail, but in the wrong direction.

That treason can but peep to what it would,[8]
Acts little of his will.—Tell me, Laertes,
Why thou art thus incensed.—Let him go, Gertrude.—
Speak, man.

LAERTES   Where is my father?

KING CLAUDIUS   Dead.

QUEEN GERTRUDE [*to* LAERTES]   But not by him.

125 KING CLAUDIUS   Let him demand his fill.

LAERTES   How came he dead? I'll not be juggled with.°   deceived
To hell, allegiance! Vows to the blackest devil!
Conscience and grace to the profoundest pit!
I dare damnation. To this point° I stand,   resolve
130 That both the worlds I give to negligence,[9]
Let come what comes. Only I'll be revenged
Most throughly° for my father.   thoroughly

KING CLAUDIUS   Who shall stay° you?   prevent

LAERTES   My will, not all the world;
135 And for my means, I'll husband them so well
They shall go far with little.

KING CLAUDIUS   Good Laertes,
If you desire to know the certainty
Of your dear father's death, is't writ in your revenge
That, sweepstake,[1] you will draw° both friend and foe,   take from
140 Winner and loser?

LAERTES   None but his enemies.

KING CLAUDIUS   Will you know them then?

LAERTES   To his good friends thus wide I'll ope my arms,
And, like the kind life-rend'ring pelican,
Repast them with my blood.[2]

145 KING CLAUDIUS   Why, now you speak
Like a good child and a true gentleman.
That I am guiltless of your father's death,
And am most sensibly° in grief for it,   sympathetically
It shall as level° to your judgement pierce   directly
150 As day does to your eye.

        A noise within

VOICES [*within*]   Let her come in.[3]

LAERTES How now, what noise is that?

        Enter OPHELIA [*as before*]

O heat dry up my brains! Tears seven times salt
Burn out the sense and virtue° of mine eye!   natural power
155 By heaven, thy madness shall be paid by weight
Till our scale turns the beam.[4] O rose of May,
Dear maid, kind sister, sweet Ophelia!
O heavens, is't possible a young maid's wits
Should be as mortal as an old man's life?
160 Nature is fine in love, and where 'tis fine

---

8. That treason can only glance furtively at what it would like to do.
9. That both this world and the next do not matter to me.
1. Indiscriminately. (The winner of a sweepstake gained the stakes of all other players.)
2. The female pelican was supposed to feed, and even revive, its young with blood from a wound it pecked in its

own breast. *Repast:* Feed.
3. This line is assigned to no one in F but rather appears in italic following the stage direction "A noise within." Q2 gives the line to Laertes.
4. *shall . . . beam:* shall be atoned for until vengeance outweighs the injury of madness (thus tilting the "scale" of justice).

It sends some precious instance of itself
After the thing it loves.[5]
OPHELIA *(Song)*   They bore him barefaced on the bier,
                        Hey non nony, nony, hey nony,
165   And on his grave rained many a tear—
Fare you well, my dove.
LAERTES   Hadst thou thy wits and didst persuade° revenge,   *argue for*
It could not move thus.
OPHELIA   You must sing 'Down, a-down', and you, 'Call him a
170   down-a'. O, how the wheel[6] becomes it! It is the false steward
that stole his master's daughter.[7]
LAERTES   This nothing's more than matter.[8]
OPHELIA   There's rosemary, that's for remembrance. Pray, love,
remember. And there is pansies; that's for thoughts.[9]
175   LAERTES   A document in madness—thoughts and remembrance
fitted.
OPHELIA   There's fennel for you, and columbines.[1] There's rue
for you, and here's some for me. We may call it herb-grace o'
Sundays. O, you must wear your rue with a difference.[2] There's
180   a daisy. I would give you some violets,[3] but they withered all
when my father died. They say a made a good end.
(Song)   For bonny sweet Robin is all my joy.
LAERTES   Thought and affliction, passion, hell itself
She turns to favour° and to prettiness.   *beauty*
185   OPHELIA *(Song)*   And will a not come again,
                        And will a not come again?
                        No, no, he is dead,
                        Go to thy death-bed,
                        He never will come again.

190   His beard as white as snow,
                        All flaxen° was his poll.°   *white / head*
                        He is gone, he is gone,
                        And we cast away moan.
                        God 'a' mercy on his soul.
195   And of all Christian souls, I pray God. God b'wi' ye.
                        Exeunt OPHELIA [*and* GERTRUDE]
LAERTES   Do you see this, O God?
KING CLAUDIUS   Laertes, I must commune with your grief,
Or you deny me right. Go but apart,
Make choice of whom° your wisest friends you will,   *whichever of*
200   And they shall hear and judge 'twixt you and me.
If by direct or by collateral° hand   *an agent's*
They find us touched,° we will our kingdom give,   *involved in guilt*

---

5. *Nature . . . loves:* Human nature is made most ethere-ally pure by love and sends a precious token ("instance") of itself after the object of its love. Laertes struggles to say that because of Ophelia's great love for her father, her sanity departed with him.
6. Probably refrain, although possibly spinning wheel (at which women sang ballads) or Fortune's wheel. "Down, a-down" resembles the refrain of recorded ballads.
7. *false . . . daughter:* the tale is unknown; Laertes seems to recognize it.
8. This nonsense signifies more than coherent speech.
9. *There's . . . thoughts:* Ophelia, recalling the flowers'

symbolic significance, distributes them to Laertes, Gertrude, and Claudius.
1. Columbines were associated with ingratitude or marital infidelity, fennel with flattery.
2. In heraldry, minor branches of a family were distin-guished by a "difference," a variation or addition to the coat of arms. Ophelia probably means "for a different reason." Rue is associated with repentance, and Ophelia identifies it with the "herb of grace" (wormwood), since penitence depended on and enabled God's blessing.
3. Representing faithfulness; daisies could symbolize dissembling seduction.

Our crown, our life, and all that we call ours,
To you in satisfaction.° But if not, *recompense*
205 Be you content to lend your patience to us,
And we shall jointly labour with your soul
To give it due content.
LAERTES   Let this be so.
His means of death, his obscure burial—
No trophy, sword, nor hatchment[4] o'er his bones,
210 No noble rite nor formal ostentation°— *rite of grief*
Cry to be heard, as 'twere from heaven to earth,
That I must call't in question.[5]
KING CLAUDIUS   So you shall;
And where th'offence is, let the great axe fall.
I pray you go with me.   *Exeunt*

4.6

Enter HORATIO *with* [*a* SERVANT]

HORATIO   What are they that would speak with me?
SERVANT   Sailors, sir. They say they have letters for you.
HORATIO   Let them come in.   [*Exit* SERVANT]
I do not know from what part of the world
5 I should be greeted if not from Lord Hamlet.

Enter SAILOR[S]

A SAILOR   God bless you, sir.
HORATIO   Let him bless thee too.
A SAILOR   A shall, sir, an't° please him. There's a letter for you, *if it*
sir. It comes from th'ambassador that was bound for England—
10 if your name be Horatio, as I am let to know it is.
HORATIO (*reads*)   'Horatio, when thou shalt have overlooked° *read*
this, give these fellows some means° to the King. They have *access*
letters for him. Ere we were two days old at sea, a pirate of very
warlike appointment° gave us chase. Finding ourselves too slow *equipment*
15 of sail, we put on a compelled valour, and in the grapple I
boarded them. On the instant they got clear of our ship, so I
alone became their prisoner. They have dealt with me like
thieves of mercy; but they knew what they did:[1] I am to do a
good turn for them. Let the King have the letters I have sent,
20 and repair thou° to me with as much haste as thou wouldst fly *come*
death. I have words to speak in thine ear will make thee dumb,
yet are they much too light for the bore° of the matter. These *caliber; size*
good fellows will bring thee where I am. Rosencrantz and
Guildenstern hold their course for England. Of them I have
25 much to tell thee. Farewell.
He that thou knowest thine,
Hamlet.'
Come, I will give you way° for these your letters, *means of delivery*
And do't the speedier that you may direct me
30 To him from whom you brought them.   *Exeunt*

---

4. Lozenge-shaped tablet bearing a coat of arms, carried in funeral processions and deposited near the tomb. *trophy*: memorial (often consisting of real or symbolic weapons and armor).
5. I must demand an explanation of it.
4.6 Location: The castle.

1. *They have . . . did:* They have been merciful, but with the expectation of a return. Hamlet recalls the thieves crucified next to Christ (one of whom he blessed) and Christ's plea of forgiveness for those who "know not what they do" (Luke 23:34–43).

4.7

Enter KING [CLAUDIUS] *and* LAERTES

KING CLAUDIUS   Now must your conscience my acquittance seal,[1]
And you must put me in your heart for friend,
Sith° you have heard, and with a knowing ear,   *Since*
That he which hath your noble father slain
5   Pursued my life.

LAERTES   It well appears. But tell me
Why you proceeded not against these feats,°   *acts*
So crimeful and so capital° in nature,   *punishable by death*
As by your safety, wisdom, all things else,
You mainly° were stirred up.   *greatly*

KING CLAUDIUS   O, for two special reasons,
10   Which may to you perhaps seem much unsinewed,°   *uncompelling*
And yet to me they're strong. The Queen his mother
Lives almost by his looks; and for myself—
My virtue or my plague, be it either which—
She's so conjunctive to my life and soul
15   That, as the star moves not but in his sphere,[2]
I could not but by her. The other motive
Why to a public count° I might not go   *accounting*
Is the great love the general gender° bear him,   *the common people*
Who, dipping all his faults in their affection,
20   Would, like the spring that turneth wood to stone,[3]
Convert his guilts to graces; so that my arrows,
Too slightly timbered for so loud a wind,
Would have reverted to my bow again,
And not where I had aimed them.

25   LAERTES   And so have I a noble father lost,
A sister driven into desp'rate terms,
Who has, if praises may go back again,[4]
Stood challenger, on mount, of all the age
For her perfections.[5] But my revenge will come.

30   KING CLAUDIUS   Break not your sleeps for that. You must not think
That we are made of stuff so flat and dull
That we can let our beard be shook with danger,[6]
And think it pastime. You shortly shall hear more.
I loved your father, and we love ourself.
35   And that, I hope, will teach you to imagine—
                    Enter a MESSENGER *with letters*
How now? What news?

MESSENGER   Letters, my lord, from Hamlet.
This to your majesty; this to the Queen.

KING CLAUDIUS   From Hamlet? Who brought them?

MESSENGER   Sailors, my lord, they say. I saw them not.
40   They were given me by Claudio. He received them.

KING CLAUDIUS   Laertes, you shall hear them.—Leave us.
                                                                                    Exit MESSENGER

4.7 Location: Claudius's private apartments.
1. *my acquittance seal:* affirm my innocence (of Polonius's death).
2. According to Ptolemeic astronomy, heavenly bodies moved in hollow spheres. *conjunctive* (line 14): closely united (as two planets were said astronomically to be "in conjunction" when they appeared close).
3. In limestone-rich areas (such as south Warwickshire),

concentrations in spring water may be great enough to petrify absorbent objects.
4. May refer to what was (but is no longer).
5. *Stood . . . perfections:* Conspicuously challenged the world to match her perfections.
6. That I can allow anyone to endanger me with contemptuous behavior.

[*Reads*] 'High and mighty, you shall know I am set naked° on   destitute
your kingdom. Tomorrow shall I beg leave to see your kingly
eyes, when I shall, first asking your pardon,° thereunto recount   permission
45   th'occasions of my sudden and more strange return.
                                                   Hamlet.'
What should this mean? Are all the rest come back?
Or is it some abuse,° and no such thing?   deception
LAERTES   Know you the hand?
KING CLAUDIUS   'Tis Hamlet's character.°   handwriting
50   'Naked'—and in a postscript here he says
'Alone'. Can you advise me?
LAERTES   I'm lost in it, my lord. But let him come.
It warms the very sickness in my heart
That I shall live and tell him to his teeth,
55   'Thus diddest thou'.[7]
KING CLAUDIUS   If it be so, Laertes—
As how should it be so, how otherwise?[8]—
Will you be ruled by me?
LAERTES   If so° you'll not o'errule me to a peace.   Provided that
KING CLAUDIUS   To thine own peace. If he be now returned,
60   As checking at[9] his voyage, and that he means
No more to undertake it, I will work him
To an exploit, now ripe in my device,°   planning
Under the which he shall not choose but fall;
And for his death no wind of blame shall breathe;
65   But even his mother shall uncharge° the practice°   not accuse / connivance
And call it accident.[1]
66.1   LAERTES   My lord, I will be ruled,
           The rather if you could devise it so
           That I might be the organ.°   agent
           KING CLAUDIUS   *It falls right.*
           You have been talked of, since your travel, much,
66.5   *And that in Hamlet's hearing, for a quality*
           Wherein they say you shine. Your sum of parts°   abilities
           Did not together pluck such envy from him
           As did that one, and that, in my regard,
           Of the unworthiest siege.°   lowest rank
           LAERTES   *What part is that, my lord?*
66.10   KING CLAUDIUS   *A very ribbon in the cap of youth,*
           Yet needful too, for youth no less becomes°   is suited by
           The light and careless livery that it wears
           Than settled age his sables and his weeds
           Importing health and graveness.[2]
                                         Some two months since
Here was a gentleman of Normandy.
I've seen myself, and served against, the French,
And they can well° on horseback; but this gallant   are skilled
70   Had witchcraft in't. He grew into his seat,
And to such wondrous doing brought his horse

---

7. This which I do now to you, you did to my father.
8. *As . . . otherwise:* How could Hamlet be returning,
and yet how else could he have sent this letter?
9. As one who has been diverted from ("checking at" is
a term from falconry).

1. After "accident," Q2 has the following passage,
66.1–66.14, omitted in F.
2. *his . . . graveness:* its rich gowns trimmed with sable,
garments ("weeds") signifying concern for prosperity
and dignity.

As had he been incorpsed and demi-natured[3]
With the brave beast. So far he passed my thought
That I in forgery of shapes and tricks[4]
Come short of what he did.

75   LAERTES   A Norman was't?

KING CLAUDIUS   A Norman.

LAERTES   Upon my life, Lamord.

KING CLAUDIUS   The very same.

LAERTES   I know him well. He is the brooch° indeed,   *ornament*
And gem, of all the nation.

KING CLAUDIUS   He made confession° of you,   *testimonial*

80   And gave you such a masterly report
For art and exercise in your defence,
And for your rapier most especially,
That he cried out 'twould be a sight indeed
If one could match you.[5]

84.1   *Th'escrimers° of their nation*   *fencers*
He swore had neither motion, guard, nor eye
If you opposed them.

                           Sir, this report of his

85   Did Hamlet so envenom with his envy
That he could nothing do but wish and beg
Your sudden° coming o'er to play with him.   *immediate*
Now, out of this—

LAERTES   What out of this, my lord?

KING CLAUDIUS   Laertes, was your father dear to you?

90   Or are you like the painting of a sorrow,
A face without a heart?

LAERTES   Why ask you this?

KING CLAUDIUS   Not that I think you did not love your father,
But that I know love is begun by time,°   *circumstance*
And that I see, in passages of proof,[6]

95   Time qualifies° the spark and fire of it.[7]   *moderates*
95.1   *There lives within the very flame of love*
A kind of wick or snuff[8] that will abate it,
And nothing is at a like° goodness still,°   *an equal / always*
For goodness, growing to a plurisy,[9]
95.5   *Dies in his own too much.° That we would do*   *overabundance*
We should do when we would, for this 'would' changes,
And hath abatements and delays as many
As there are tongues, are hands, are accidents;
And then this 'should' is like a spendthrift's sigh,
95.10   *That hurts by easing.[1] But to the quick° of th'ulcer—*   *center*
Hamlet comes back. What would you undertake
To show yourself your father's son in deed
More than in words?

LAERTES   To cut his throat i'th' church.

---

3. As if he had been in the same body and had half the nature of (the image of a centaur).
4. That I in my very imagination ("forgery") of figures and skillful feats of horsemanship.
5. After "you," Q2 has the following passage, 84.1–84.3, omitted in F.
6. From experiences that have tested this.
7. After this line, Q2 has the following passage, 95.1–

95.10, omitted in F.
8. Burned part of the wick (which causes smoke and reduces light if not removed).
9. A chest inflammation, metaphorically like a fire in the heart; thought to take its name from the Latin for "more" (*plus*) and to be caused by an excess of humors (and so playing on "excess").
1. A sigh was thought to use up a drop of blood.

KING CLAUDIUS   No place indeed should murder sanctuarize.[2]
100   Revenge should have no bounds. But, good Laertes,
Will you do this?—keep close within your chamber.
Hamlet returned shall know you are come home.
We'll put on those shall[3] praise your excellence,
And set a double varnish on the fame
105   The Frenchman gave you; bring you, in fine,° together,   *conclusion*
And wager on your heads. He, being remiss,°   *unwary*
Most generous,° and free from all contriving,   *noble*
Will not peruse the foils; so that with ease,
Or with a little shuffling, you may choose
110   A sword unbated, and, in a pass of practice,[4]
Requite him for your father.
LAERTES   I will do't,
And for that purpose I'll anoint my sword.
I bought an unction° of a mountebank°   *ointment / quack*
So mortal that, but dip a knife in it,
115   Where it draws blood no cataplasm° so rare,   *poultice*
Collected from all simples° that have virtue°   *herbs / potency*
Under the moon, can save the thing from death
That is but scratched withal.° I'll touch my point   *with it*
With this contagion, that if I gall° him slightly,   *prick*
It may be death.
120   KING CLAUDIUS   Let's further think of this;
Weigh what convenience both of time and means
May fit us to our shape.[5] If this should fail,
And that our drift look° through our bad performance,   *our intention be seen*
'Twere better not essayed. Therefore this project
125   Should have a back or second[6] that might hold
If this should blast in proof.[7] Soft, let me see.
We'll make a solemn wager on your cunnings . . .°   *skills*
I ha't! When in your motion° you are hot and dry—   *exercise*
As make your bouts more violent to that end—
130   And that he calls for drink, I'll have prepared him
A chalice for the nonce,° whereon but sipping,   *occasion*
If he by chance escape your venomed stuck,°   *thrust*
Our purpose may hold there.—
          Enter QUEEN [GERTRUDE]
                              How now, sweet Queen?
QUEEN GERTRUDE   One woe doth tread upon another's heel,
135   So fast they follow. Your sister's drowned, Laertes.
LAERTES   Drowned? O, where?
QUEEN GERTRUDE   There is a willow grows aslant a brook
That shows his hoar leaves[8] in the glassy stream.
Therewith fantastic garlands did she make
140   Of crow-flowers, nettles, daisies, and long purples,[9]

2. Give sanctuary to a murderer. In English tradition, a criminal remained invulnerable to secular authority for most crimes (save sacrilege and treason) as long as he took refuge in a church.
3. *We'll . . . shall:* I shall incite some people to.
4. In a treacherous thrust. *unbated:* unblunted (as recreational or practice foils were).
5. May make us ready to put into effect our plot and to assume the roles we are to play.
6. Should have reserve soldiers (military metaphor for the plotting).
7. Should blow up in our faces when put to the test (like a cannon).
8. The willow leaf is gray-white ("hoar") on the undersides (reflected from below by the water). The willow was an emblem of mourning and of forsaken love.
9. Early purple orchises. *crow-flowers:* common name for several wildflowers, including Ragged Robin and bluebells (often appearing beside long purples in woodland and sharing their association with fertility).

That liberal shepherds give a grosser[1] name,
But our cold° maids do dead men's fingers call them.   *chaste*
There on the pendent boughs her crownet° weeds   *garlanded*
Clamb'ring to hang,[2] an envious sliver° broke,   *a malicious twig*
145   When down the weedy trophies and herself
Fell in the weeping brook. Her clothes spread wide,
And mermaid-like a while they bore her up;
Which time she chanted snatches of old tunes,
As one incapable° of her own distress,   *uncomprehending*
150   Or like a creature native and endued
Unto that element.[3] But long it could not be
Till that her garments, heavy with their drink,
Pulled the poor wretch from her melodious lay°   *song*
To muddy death.
155 LAERTES   Alas, then is she drowned.
QUEEN GERTRUDE   Drowned, drowned.
LAERTES   Too much of water hast thou, poor Ophelia,
And therefore I forbid my tears. But yet
It is our trick;° nature her custom holds,   *characteristic way*
Let shame say what it will.
                [*He weeps*]
160   When these are gone,
The woman will be out.[4] Adieu, my lord.
I have a speech of fire that fain° would blaze,   *gladly*
But that this folly douts° it.   *Exit*   *extinguishes*
KING CLAUDIUS   Let's follow, Gertrude.
How much I had to do to calm his rage!
165   Now fear I this will give it start again;
Therefore let's follow.   *Exeunt*

5.1

Enter two CLOWNS° *carrying a spade and a pickaxe*   *rustics; peasants*
FIRST CLOWN   Is she to be buried in Christian burial that wilfully
    seeks her own salvation?[1]
SECOND CLOWN   I tell thee she is, and therefore make her grave
    straight.° The coroner hath sat on her,[2] and finds it Christian   *right away*
5   burial.[3]
FIRST CLOWN   How can that be unless she drowned herself in
    her own defence?
SECOND CLOWN   Why, 'tis found so.
FIRST CLOWN   It must be *se offendendo*,[4] it cannot be else; for
10   here lies the point: if I drown myself wittingly, it argues an act;
    and an act hath three branches: it is to act, to do, and to per-
    form. Argal[5] she drowned herself wittingly.

1. More indecent. Among the recorded names for the purple orchis are "priest's-pintle" (penis), "dog's cullions" (testicles), "goat's cullions," and "fool's ballochs." *liberal:* free-spoken.
2. Deserted lovers proverbially hung garlands on willows.
3. *native . . . element:* naturally fit to live in water.
4. *When . . . out:* When I have cried my tears, the feminine side of my nature will be gone with them.
5.1 Location: A churchyard.
1. Probably a mistake for "damnation"; suicide was a mortal sin. Ordinarily, suicides would not receive a "Christian burial" (in consecrated ground with the church's blessing and ritual).
2. Conducted an inquest on the cause of her death.
3. And has given the verdict that she is eligible for a Christian burial (in effect, a decision that Ophelia did not drown herself).
4. A mangled version of *se defendendo*, the term for "killing in self-defense."
5. For "ergo," or "therefore." The argument parodies a famous law case of 1554 concerning suicide by drowning, in which the act was said to have three parts: imagination, resolution, and perfection (accomplishment).

SECOND CLOWN   Nay, but hear you, Goodman Delver.[6]

FIRST CLOWN   Give me leave. Here lies the water—good. Here

15 stands the man—good. If the man go to this water and drown
himself, it is, will he nill he,° he goes. Mark you that. But if the   *willy-nilly*
water come to him and drown him, he drowns not himself;
argal he that is not guilty of his own death shortens not his own
life.

20 SECOND CLOWN   But is this law?

FIRST CLOWN   Ay, marry, is't: coroner's quest° law.   *inquest*

SECOND CLOWN   Will you ha' the truth on't? If this had not been
a gentlewoman, she should have been buried out o' Christian
burial.

25 FIRST CLOWN   Why, there thou sayst,° and the more pity that   *how right you are*
great folk should have count'nance° in this world to drown or   *privilege*
hang themselves more than their even° Christian. Come, my   *fellow*
spade. There is no ancient gentlemen but gardeners, ditchers,
and gravemakers; they hold up° Adam's profession.   *carry on*
        [FIRST CLOWN *digs*]

30 SECOND CLOWN   Was he a gentleman?

FIRST CLOWN   A was the first that ever bore arms.[7]

SECOND CLOWN   Why, he had none.

FIRST CLOWN   What, art a heathen? How dost thou understand
the Scripture? The Scripture says Adam digged. Could he dig

35 without arms? I'll put another question to thee. If thou answer-
est me not to the purpose, confess thyself[8]—

SECOND CLOWN   Go to.[9]

FIRST CLOWN   What is he that builds stronger than either the
mason, the shipwright, or the carpenter?

40 SECOND CLOWN   The gallows-maker; for that frame° outlives a   *structure*
thousand tenants.

FIRST CLOWN   I like thy wit well, in good faith. The gallows does°   *serves*
well. But how does it well? It does well to those that do ill. Now
thou dost ill to say the gallows is built stronger than the church,

45 argal the gallows may do well to thee. To't again, come.

SECOND CLOWN   'Who builds stronger than a mason, a shipwright, or a carpenter?'

FIRST CLOWN   Ay, tell me that, and unyoke.[1]

SECOND CLOWN   Marry, now I can tell.

50 FIRST CLOWN   To't.

SECOND CLOWN   Mass,° I cannot tell.   *By the Mass*
        Enter [*Prince*] HAMLET *and* HORATIO *afar off*

FIRST CLOWN   Cudgel thy brains no more about it, for your dull
ass will not mend° his pace with beating; and when you are   *improve*
asked this question next, say 'a grave-maker'; the houses that he

55 makes lasts till doomsday. Go, get thee to Johan.[2] Fetch me a
stoup° of liquor.   [*Exit* SECOND CLOWN]   *flagon*
(*Sings*) In youth when I did love, did love,
        Methought it was very sweet

---

6. Master Digger ("Goodman" was the ordinary title in
addressing a man by his occupation).
7. Those bearing a family coat of arms were officially
recognized as gentlemen; playing on "limbs."
8. "Confess thyself and be hanged" was proverbial.

9. An expression of impatience.
1. Rest your wits from work (like draft animals).
2. *Johan:* unknown (presumably a neighborhood ale-
house keeper).

To contract°-O-the time for-a-my behove,°   *shorten / advantage*
60   O methought there-a-was nothing-a-meet.[3]

HAMLET   Has this fellow no feeling of his business that a sings at
grave-making?

HORATIO   Custom hath made it in him a property of easiness.[4]

HAMLET   'Tis e'en so; the hand of little employment hath the
65   daintier sense.[5]

FIRST CLOWN (*sings*) But age with his stealing steps
                    Hath caught me in his clutch,
                    And hath shipped me intil the land,°   *into the earth*
                    As if I had never been such.

        [*He throws up a skull*]

70   HAMLET   That skull had a tongue in it and could sing once. How
the knave jowls° it to th' ground as if 'twere Cain's jawbone,   *slams*
that did the first murder! This might be the pate of a politician
which this ass o'er-offices,[6] one that would circumvent God,
might it not?

75   HORATIO   It might, my lord.

HAMLET   Or of a courtier, which could say 'Good morrow, sweet
lord. How dost thou, good lord?' This might be my lord such a
one, that praised my lord such a one's horse when a meant to
beg it, might it not?

80   HORATIO   Ay, my lord.

HAMLET   Why, e'en so, and now my lady Worm's, chapless,° and   *lacking a lower jaw*
knocked about the mazard° with a sexton's spade. Here's fine   *head*
revolution,[7] an° we had the trick° to see't. Did these bones cost   *if / ability*
no more the breeding but to play at loggats with 'em?[8] Mine
85   ache to think on't.

FIRST CLOWN (*sings*) A pickaxe and a spade, a spade,
                    For and° a shrouding-sheet;   *And also*
                    O, a pit of clay for to be made
                    For such a guest is meet.

        [*He throws up another skull*]

90   HAMLET   There's another. Why might not that be the skull of a
lawyer? Where be his quiddits[9] now, his quillets,° his cases, his   *quibbles*
tenures,° and his tricks? Why does he suffer this rude knave   *property titles*
now to knock him about the sconce° with a dirty shovel, and   *head*
will not tell him of his action of battery?[1] H'm! This fellow
95   might be in 's time a great buyer of land, with his statutes, his
recognizances, his fines, his double vouchers, his recoveries.[2]
Is this the fine° of his fines and the recovery° of his recoveries,   *end / profit*
to have his fine° pate full of fine° dirt? Will his vouchers vouch[3]   *subtle / fine-grained*
him no more of his purchases, and double ones too, than the

3. *meet:* suitable. The Clown sings garbled snatches
of Thomas Lord Vaux's poem "The Aged Lover Re-
nounceth Love," printed in *Tottel's Miscellany* (1557).
The extrametrical "O"s and "A"s are probably grunts
while digging.
4. *a property of easiness:* something he can do without
distress.
5. Has more delicate feeling (because not hardened by
calluses).
6. *o'er-offices:* lords it over because of his position, pulls
rank on. A "politician" was a schemer for political advantage.
7. Reversal of fortune (literally, the turning of Fortune's

wheel).
8. Was it so inexpensive and easy to bring these bones to
maturity that they can be treated as loggats (small
wooden clubs thrown at a stake)?
9. Subtle distinctions.
1. Legal prosecution for assault.
2. Fines and recoveries were both kinds of lawsuits
brought to make legal an agreement to transfer land
ownership. The "double voucher" summoned two witnesses to attest to the land's ownership in these cases.
statutes: mortgages on land, often linked with "recognizances" (bonds acknowledging a particular debt).
3. Guarantee.

100 length and breadth of a pair of indentures?⁴ The very convey-
     ances° of his lands will hardly lie in this box;° and must th'in-   *deeds / deed box; coffin*
     heritor° himself have no more, ha?   *owner*

HORATIO   Not a jot more, my lord.

HAMLET   Is not parchment made of sheepskins?

105 HORATIO   Ay, my lord, and of calf-skins too.

HAMLET   They are sheep and calves° that seek out assurance⁵ in   *simpletons and fools*
     that. I will speak to this fellow. [*To the* FIRST CLOWN] Whose
     grave's this, sirrah?⁶

FIRST CLOWN   Mine, sir.

110 (*Sings*)   O, a pit of clay for to be made
                        For such a guest is meet.

HAMLET   I think it be thine indeed, for thou liest in't.

FIRST CLOWN   You lie out on't, sir, and therefore it is not yours.
     For my part, I do not lie in't, and yet it is mine.

115 HAMLET   Thou dost lie in't, to be in't and say 'tis thine. 'Tis for
     the dead, not for the quick;° therefore thou liest.   *living*

FIRST CLOWN   'Tis a quick° lie, sir, 'twill away again from me to   *nimble*
     you.

HAMLET   What man dost thou dig it for?

120 FIRST CLOWN   For no man, sir.

HAMLET   What woman, then?

FIRST CLOWN   For none, neither.

HAMLET   Who is to be buried in't?

FIRST CLOWN   One that was a woman, sir; but, rest her soul, she's
125 dead.

HAMLET   How absolute° the knave is! We must speak by the   *precise*
     card,⁷ or equivocation will undo us. By the Lord, Horatio, these
     three years I have taken note of it. The age is grown so picked°   *punctilious*
     that the toe of the peasant comes so near the heel of the court-
130 ier he galls his kibe.° [*To the* FIRST CLOWN] How long hast thou   *chafes his heel sore*
     been a grave-maker?

FIRST CLOWN   Of all the days i'th' year I came to't that day that
     our last King Hamlet o'ercame Fortinbras.

HAMLET   How long is that since?

135 FIRST CLOWN   Cannot you tell that? Every fool can tell that. It
     was the very day that young Hamlet was born—he that was
     mad and sent into England.

HAMLET   Ay, marry, why was he sent into England?

FIRST CLOWN   Why, because a was mad. A shall recover his wits
140 there; or if a do not, 'tis no great matter there.

HAMLET   Why?

FIRST CLOWN   'Twill not be seen in him there. There the men
     are as mad as he.

HAMLET   How came he mad?

145 FIRST CLOWN   Very strangely, they say.

HAMLET   How strangely?

FIRST CLOWN   Faith, e'en with losing his wits.

HAMLET   Upon what ground?⁸

---

4. The two copies of a document (written on one sheet
and separated by an irregular cut so that they could later
be proved to be part of one transaction). The dead man's
property (his grave) is hardly bigger than these elaborate
papers.
5. Security, playing on the legal conveyance of a property

title.
6. An address used with inferiors.
7. With precisely defined meanings (literally, by the
directions marked on a mariner's compass card).
8. From what cause? (The Clown takes him to mean "In
what country?")

FIRST CLOWN   Why, here in Denmark. I have been sexton here,
150   man and boy, thirty years.
HAMLET   How long will a man lie i'th' earth ere he rot?
FIRST CLOWN   I'faith, if a be not rotten before a die—as we have
    many pocky corpses nowadays, that will scarce hold the laying
    in⁹—a will last you some eight year or nine year. A tanner will
155   last you nine year.
HAMLET   Why he more than another?
FIRST CLOWN   Why, sir, his hide is so tanned with his trade that
    a will keep out water a great while, and your water is a sore
    decayer of your whoreson° dead body. Here's a skull, now. This   *vile*
160   skull has lain in the earth three-and-twenty years.
HAMLET   Whose was it?
FIRST CLOWN   A whoreson mad fellow's it was. Whose do you
    think it was?
HAMLET   Nay, I know not.
165   FIRST CLOWN   A pestilence on him for a mad rogue—a poured a
    flagon of Rhenish° on my head once! This same skull, sir, was   *Rhine wine*
    Yorick's skull, the King's jester.
HAMLET   This?
FIRST CLOWN   E'en that.
170   HAMLET   Let me see.
        [*He takes the skull*]
    Alas, poor Yorick. I knew him, Horatio—a fellow of infinite
    jest, of most excellent fancy. He hath borne me on his back a
    thousand times; and now, how abhorred my imagination is! My
    gorge rises at it. Here hung those lips that I have kissed I know
175   not how oft. Where be your gibes now, your gambols, your
    songs, your flashes of merriment that were wont to set the table
    on a roar? Not one now to mock your own grinning? Quite
    chop-fallen?¹ Now get you to my lady's chamber and tell her,
    let her paint an inch thick, to this favour° she must come. Make   *appearance*
180   her laugh at that. Prithee, Horatio, tell me one thing.
HORATIO   What's that, my lord?
HAMLET   Dost thou think Alexander looked o' this fashion i'th'
    earth?
HORATIO   E'en so.
185   HAMLET   And smelt so? Pah!
        [*He throws the skull down*]
HORATIO   E'en so, my lord.
HAMLET   To what base uses we may return, Horatio! Why may
    not imagination trace the noble dust of Alexander till a find it
    stopping a bung-hole?°   *opening of a cask*
190   HORATIO   'Twere to consider too curiously° to consider so.   *oversubtly*
HAMLET   No, faith, not a jot; but to follow him thither with mod-
    esty° enough, and likelihood to lead it, as thus: Alexander died,   *reasonable speculation*
    Alexander was buried, Alexander returneth into dust, the dust
    is earth, of earth we make loam,² and why of that loam whereto
195   he was converted might they not stop a beer-barrel?
    Imperial Caesar, dead and turned to clay,
    Might stop a hole to keep the wind away.
    O, that that earth which kept the world in awe

---

9. *pocky . . . in*: bodies riddled with venereal disease that   1. Dejected; also, with a dropped or lost lower jaw.
hardly keep from disintegrating during their burial rites.   2. A mix of clay and straw used as plaster.

Should patch a wall t'expel the winter's flaw!°   *violent wind*
But soft, but soft; aside.

> [HAMLET *and* HORATIO *stand aside*.] *Enter* KING [CLAU-
> DIUS], QUEEN [GERTRUDE], LAERTES, *and a coffin, with*
> [*a* PRIEST *and*] *lords attendant*

200   Here comes the King,
The Queen, the courtiers—who is that they follow,
And with such maimèd rites?³ This doth betoken
The corpse they follow did with desp'rate hand
Fordo it° own life. 'Twas of some estate.°   *Bring down its / rank*
Couch we° a while, and mark.   *Let's lie low*

205 LAERTES   What ceremony else?
HAMLET [*aside to* HORATIO]   That is Laertes, a very noble youth. Mark.
LAERTES   What ceremony else?
PRIEST   Her obsequies have been as far enlarged
As we have warrantise.° Her death was doubtful,⁴   *proper sanction*
210 And but that great command o'ersways the order⁵
She should in ground unsanctified have lodged
Till the last trumpet. For° charitable prayers,   *Rather than*
Shards, flints, and pebbles should be thrown on her,
Yet here she is allowed her virgin rites,
215 Her maiden strewments,⁶ and the bringing home
Of bell and burial.⁷
LAERTES   Must there no more be done?
PRIEST   No more be done.
We should profane the service of the dead
220 To sing sage° requiem and such rest to her   *solemn*
As to peace-parted° souls.   *peacefully deceased*
LAERTES   Lay her i'th' earth,
And from her fair and unpolluted flesh
May violets spring. I tell thee, churlish priest,
A minist'ring angel shall my sister be
225 When thou liest howling.°   *(in hell)*
HAMLET [*aside*]   What, the fair Ophelia!
QUEEN GERTRUDE [*scattering flowers*]   Sweets to the sweet. Farewell.
I hoped thou shouldst have been my Hamlet's wife.
I thought thy bride-bed to have decked, sweet maid,
And not t'have strewed thy grave.
230 LAERTES   O, treble woe
Fall ten times treble on that cursèd head
Whose wicked deed thy most ingenious sense⁸
Deprived thee of!—Hold off the earth a while,
Till I have caught her once more in mine arms.

> [LAERTES] *leaps into the grave*

235 Now pile your dust upon the quick and dead
Till of this flat a mountain you have made
To o'ertop old Pelion, or the skyish head
Of blue Olympus.⁹

---

3. Truncated ceremonies (ordinarily grand for a court funeral).
4. That is, possibly suicide.
5. And if royal authority had not prevailed over the usual ecclesiastical procedure.
6. Flowers strewed over the casket or grave. Throughout northern Europe, funerary flowers of an unmarried girl often included a special wreath that was sometimes afterward hung in the church. (Q2's "crants" [garlands] for F's "rites" specifically evokes this practice.)
7. *the bringing . . . burial*: the taking her to her resting place with the ritual passing bells and funeral service.
8. Quick, perceptive intelligence.
9. In Greek mythology, giants piled Pelion (a mountain in Thessaly) on top of Mount Ossa in an attempt to climb Mount Olympus.

HAMLET [*coming forward*]   What is he whose grief
    Bears such an emphasis,[1] whose phrase° of sorrow   *rhetoric*
240   Conjures the wand'ring stars° and makes them stand   *planets*
    Like wonder-wounded° hearers? This is I,   *awestruck*
    Hamlet the Dane.[2]
               HAMLET *leaps in after* LAERTES
LAERTES   The devil take thy soul.
HAMLET   Thou pray'st not well.
245   I prithee take thy fingers from my throat,
    For though I am not splenative° and rash,   *quick-tempered*
    Yet have I something in me dangerous,
    Which let thy wiseness fear. Away thy hand.
KING CLAUDIUS   [*to* LORDS]   Pluck them asunder.
QUEEN GERTRUDE   Hamlet, Hamlet!
ALL THE LORDS   Gentlemen!
250   HORATIO [*to* HAMLET]   Good my lord, be quiet.
HAMLET   Why, I will fight with him upon this theme
    Until my eyelids will no longer wag.°   *blink*
QUEEN GERTRUDE   O my son, what theme?
HAMLET   I loved Ophelia. Forty thousand brothers
255   Could not, with all their quantity of love,
    Make up my sum.—What wilt thou do for her?
KING CLAUDIUS   O, he is mad, Laertes.
QUEEN GERTRUDE [*to* LAERTES]   For love of God, forbear him.°   *let him alone*
HAMLET [*to* LAERTES]   'Swounds,° show me what thou'lt do.   *By Christ's wounds*
260   Woot° weep, woot fight, woot fast, woot tear thyself,   *Wilt thou*
    Woot drink up eisel,° eat a crocodile?   *vinegar*
    I'll do't. Dost thou come here to whine,
    To outface me with leaping in her grave?
    Be buried quick with her, and so will I.
265   And if thou prate of mountains, let them throw
    Millions of acres on us, till our ground,
    Singeing his pate° against the burning zone,°   *his head / sun's sphere*
    Make Ossa[3] like a wart. Nay, an° thou'lt mouth,°   *if / speak excessively*
    I'll rant as well as thou.
KING CLAUDIUS [*to* LAERTES] This is mere madness,
270   And thus a while the fit will work on him.
    Anon,° as patient as the female dove   *Soon*
    When that her golden couplets are disclosed,°   *chicks are hatched*
    His silence will sit drooping.
HAMLET [*to* LAERTES]   Hear you, sir,
    What is the reason that you use me thus?
275   I loved you ever. But it is no matter.
    Let Hercules himself do what he may,
    The cat will mew, and dog will have his day.[4]   *Exit*
KING CLAUDIUS   I pray you, good Horatio, wait upon him.
                          [*Exit*] HORATIO
    [*To* LAERTES] Strengthen your patience in° our last night's   *with*
       speech.
280   We'll put the matter to the present push.°—   *the immediate trial*
    Good Gertrude, set some watch over your son.—

---

1. A violent expression.
2. Normally the title of the King of Denmark.
3. Greek mountain (see note to line 238).

4. *Let . . . day:* Despite Laertes' Herculean ranting, my
   day will come.

This grave shall have a living monument.[5]
An hour of quiet shortly shall we see;
Till then, in patience our proceeding be.　　　　　*Exeunt*

5.2

Enter [Prince] HAMLET *and* HORATIO

HAMLET　So much for this, sir. Now, let me see, the other.°　　*other matter*
　　You do remember all the circumstance?°　　　*state of things then*
HORATIO　Remember it, my lord!
HAMLET　Sir, in my heart there was a kind of fighting
5　That would not let me sleep. Methought I lay
　　Worse than the mutines in the bilboes.[1] Rashly°—　　*Impulsively*
　　And praised be rashness for it: let us know°　　*acknowledge*
　　Our indiscretion° sometime serves us well　　*unreasoned action*
　　When our dear plots do pall,° and that should teach us　*grow weak*
10　There's a divinity that shapes our ends,
　　Rough-hew them° how we will—　　*Form them roughly*
HORATIO　That is most certain.
HAMLET　　　　　　　　　Up from my cabin,
　　My sea-gown scarfed about me in the dark,
15　Groped I to find out them, had my desire,
　　Fingered° their packet, and in fine° withdrew　　*Stole / finally*
　　To mine own room again, making so bold,
　　My fears forgetting manners, to unseal
　　Their grand commission; where I found, Horatio—
20　O royal knavery!—an exact command,
　　Larded° with many several° sorts of reasons　*Elaborated / different*
　　Importing° Denmark's health, and England's, too,　*Concerning*
　　With ho! such bugs and goblins in my life,[2]
　　That on the supervise,° no leisure bated,°　*reading / allowed*
25　No, not to stay° the grinding of the axe,　　*await*
　　My head should be struck off.
HORATIO　　　　　　　　　　Is't possible?
HAMLET　[*giving it to him*]　Here's the commission. Read it at more leisure.
　　But wilt thou hear me how I did proceed?
HORATIO　I beseech you.
30　HAMLET　Being thus benetted round with villainies—
　　Ere I could make a prologue to my brains,
　　They had begun the play[3]—I sat me down,
　　Devised a new commission, wrote it fair.[4]
　　I once did hold it, as our statists° do,　　*statesmen*
35　A baseness to write fair, and laboured much
　　How to forget that learning;[5] but, sir, now
　　It did me yeoman's service.[6] Wilt thou know
　　Th'effect of what I wrote?
HORATIO　　　　　　　　　Ay, good my lord.

5. A lasting memorial; hinting that Hamlet, now "living," will soon be sacrificed to Ophelia's memory.
5.2 Location: A stateroom of the castle.
1. Worse than the mutineers in the ankle fetters.
2. Such fanciful horrors that would result were I to remain alive. *bugs*: bugbears.
3. *Ere . . . play*: Hamlet's brains "acted" before he consciously thought out a plan.
4. In the professional handwriting of finished (published) documents.

5. *I once . . . learning*: In the sixteenth century, the upper echelons of government became increasingly professionalized; Hamlet implies that these newly elevated officials are prone to snobbish pretensions, covering up their education as common clerks, and he confesses that he once shared their snobbery.
6. It served me valiantly. English yeomen (free landholders) were famous for military strength, supposedly because they fought for their national interest rather than for base pay.

HAMLET   An earnest conjuration° from the King,   *appeal*
40   As England was his faithful tributary,
As love between them like the palm should flourish,
As peace should still her wheaten garland[7] wear
And stand a comma[8] 'tween their amities,
And many such like 'as'es of great charge,[9]
45   That on the view and know of these contents,
Without debatement further more or less,
He should the bearers put to sudden death,
Not shriving-time[1] allowed.
HORATIO   How was this sealed?
HAMLET   Why, even in that was heaven ordinant.°   *guiding*
50   I had my father's signet in my purse,
Which was the model of that Danish seal;
Folded the writ up in the form of th'other,
Subscribed° it, gave't th'impression,° placed it safely,   *Signed / seal (in wax)*
The changeling[2] never known. Now the next day
55   Was our sea-fight; and what to this was sequent°   *subsequent*
Thou know'st already.
HORATIO   So Guildenstern and Rosencrantz go to't.
HAMLET   Why, man, they did make love to this employment.
They are not near my conscience. Their defeat°   *destruction*
60   Doth by their own insinuation grow.
'Tis dangerous when the baser nature comes
Between the pass and fell incensèd points[3]
Of mighty opposites.°   *opponents*
HORATIO   Why, what a king is this!
HAMLET   Does it not, think'st thee, stand me now upon[4]—
65   He that hath killed my king and whored my mother,
Popped in between th'election and my hopes,
Thrown out his angle° for my proper° life,   *fishhook/own*
And with such coz'nage°—is't not perfect conscience   *trickery*
To quit° him with this arm? And is't not to be damned   *requite*
70   To let this canker° of our nature come   *cancerous sore*
In° further evil?   *Into*
HORATIO   It must be shortly known to him from England
What is the issue° of the business there.   *result*
HAMLET   It will be short. The interim's mine,
75   And a man's life's no more than to say 'one'.[5]
But I am very sorry, good Horatio,
That to Laertes I forgot myself;
For by the image° of my cause I see   *mirror's reflection*
The portraiture of his. I'll court his favours.
80   But sure, the bravery° of his grief did put me   *ostentation*
Into a tow'ring passion.
HORATIO   Peace, who comes here?
Enter young OSRIC, *a courtier* [*taking off his hat*]

---

7. Like the palm tree, an emblem of peace and prosperity.
8. And hold their interests separate but still connected (unlike a period, which would cut off "amity").
9. Weighty clauses beginning with "as"; asses bearing heavy loads.
1. Time for final confession and absolution, a part of the state ritual of legal executions.

2. A malicious elf child substituted for an infant, as Hamlet swaps his counterfeit letter for their authentic one.
3. *the pass . . . points*: fencing language; the thrust ("pass") and fiercely angry ("fell") rapiers.
4. Rest incumbent upon me.
5. And life lasts no longer than it takes to pronounce ("say") the monosyllable "one."

OSRIC   Your lordship is right welcome back to Denmark.

HAMLET   I humbly thank you, sir. [*To* HORATIO] Dost know this
water-fly?

85   HORATIO   No, my good lord.

HAMLET   Thy state is the more gracious,° for 'tis a vice to know   *blessed*
him. He hath much land, and fertile. Let a beast be lord of
beasts, and his crib shall stand at the king's mess.[6] 'Tis a chuff,°   *rich boor; jackdaw*
but, as I say, spacious in the possession of dirt.

90   OSRIC   Sweet lord, if your friendship were at leisure I should
impart a thing to you from his majesty.

HAMLET   I will receive it, sir, with all diligence of spirit. Put your
bonnet° to his right use; 'tis for the head.   *hat*

OSRIC   I thank your lordship, 'tis very hot.

95   HAMLET   No, believe me, 'tis very cold. The wind is northerly.

OSRIC   It is indifferent° cold, my lord, indeed.   *rather*

HAMLET   Methinks it is very sultry and hot for my complexion.°   *constitution*

OSRIC   Exceedingly, my lord. It is very sultry, as 'twere—I cannot
tell how. But, my lord, his majesty bade me signify to you that

100   a° has laid a great wager on your head. Sir, this is the matter.   *he*

HAMLET   I beseech you, remember.[7]

OSRIC   Nay, good my lord, for mine ease, in good faith.[8]

102.1   *Sir here is newly come to court Laertes, believe me, an*
absolute gentleman, full of most excellent differences,°   *superior qualities*
of very soft° society and great showing.° Indeed, to speak   *pleasing / appearance*
feelingly° of him, he is the card or calendar of gentry,[9]   *appreciatively*

102.5   *for you shall find in him the continent of what part[1] a*
gentleman would see.

HAMLET   *Sir, his definement suffers no perdition in you,[2]*
though I know to divide him inventorially would dizzy
th'arithmetic of memory, and yet but yaw neither in

102.10   *respect of his quick sail.[3] But in the verity of extolment,°*   *in truthful praise*
I take him to be a soul of great article,[4] and his infusion°   *inborn essence*
of such dearth° and rareness as, to make true diction[5] of   *preciousness*
him, his semblable° is his mirror, and who else would   *likeness*
trace him his umbrage, nothing more.[6]

102.15   OSRIC   *Your lordship speaks most infallibly of him.*

HAMLET   *The concernancy,° sir? Why do we wrap the gen-*   *relevance (to us)*
tleman in our more rawer breath?[7]

OSRIC   *Sir?*

HORATIO   *Is't not possible to understand in another*

102.20   *tongue? You will to't, sir, rarely.[8]*

HAMLET   *What imports the nomination° of this gentleman?*   *mention*

OSRIC   *Of Laertes?*

6. *Let . . . mess:* If an animal owned enough herds, even
it might find a place at the King's table. *crib:* manger.
7. "Remember your courtesy," the conventional expression inviting a subordinate to put his hat back on.
8. A conventional expression declining Hamlet's invitation. Q2 adds the following passage, lines 102.1–102.34,
in place of lines 103–4, placing a comma instead of a
period after "faith."
9. The model of gentlemanly behavior. *card:* chart or
map. *calendar:* account book, directory.
1. Attribute or quality, playing on "region" (to which
Laertes is the "card"). *continent:* embodiment, continuing the geographical pun.
2. Your picture of him ("definement") loses none of the
man's real excellence.

3. *to divide . . . sail:* to list his qualities individually would
confuse the memory's reckoning up (through recount-
ing vast numbers), and yet only steer erratically ("yaw")
around Laertes' skills—that is, the description would
only approximate his virtues.
4. Large scope (?); excellent qualities (?).
5. To speak truly.
6. And whoever imitates him is like his shadow
("umbrage"), not the real thing at all.
7. Our less refined words (since we are so much inferior to Laertes).
8. *Is't . . . rarely:* Can't he understand his words in
another man's mouth? You will have your joke, sir, splendidly.

HORATIO [*aside to* HAMLET]   *His purse is empty already; all*
      's golden words are spent.

102.25   HAMLET [*to* OSRIC]   *Of him, sir.*

OSRIC   *I know you are not ignorant—*

HAMLET   *I would you did, sir; yet, in faith, if you did it*
      would not much approve° me. Well, sir?   commend

OSRIC   *You are not ignorant of what excellence Laertes is.*

102.30   HAMLET   *I dare not confess that, lest I should compare*
      with him in excellence.[9] *But to know a man well were*
      to know himself.[1]

OSRIC   *I mean, sir, for his weapon. But in the imputation*
      laid on him by them, in his meed° he's unfellowed.°   merit / unmatched
      Sir, you are not ignorant of what excellence Laertes is at his
      weapon.

105   HAMLET   What's his weapon?

OSRIC   Rapier and dagger.

HAMLET   That's two of his weapons. But well.

OSRIC   The King, sir, hath wagered with him six Barbary horses,
      against the which he imponed,° as I take it, six French rapiers   staked

110   and poniards, with their assigns° as girdle,° hanger,[2] or so.   accessories / sword belt
      Three of the carriages, in faith, are very dear to fancy, very
      responsive to the hilts, most delicate carriages, and of very lib-
      eral conceit.[3]

HAMLET   What call you the carriages?[4]

114.1   HORATIO   [*aside to* HAMLET]   *I know you must be edified*
      by the margin[5] *ere you had done.*

115   OSRIC   The carriages, sir, are the hangers.

HAMLET   The phrase would be more germane to the matter if we
      could carry cannon by our sides. I would it might be hangers
      till then. But on: six Barbary horses against six French swords,
      their assigns, and three liberal-conceited carriages—that's the

120   French bet against the Danish. Why is this 'imponed', as you
      call it?

OSRIC   The King, sir, hath laid,° sir, that in a dozen passes   placed his bet
      between you and him he shall not exceed you three hits.[6] He
      hath on't twelve for nine,[7] and it would come to immediate

125   trial if your lordship would vouchsafe the answer.[8]

HAMLET   How if I answer no?

OSRIC   I mean, my lord, the opposition of your person in trial.

HAMLET   Sir, I will walk here in the hall. If it please his majesty,
      'tis the breathing° time of day with me. Let the foils be brought;   exercising

130   the gentleman willing, an° the King hold his purpose, I will   if
      win for him an I can. If not, I'll gain nothing but my shame
      and the odd hits.

OSRIC   Shall I re-deliver you e'en so?

HAMLET   To this effect, sir; after what flourish your nature will.

---

9. Claim to match him (since, proverbially, only excellence recognizes excellence).
1. For in order to know another man truly, one must
know oneself.
2. Attaching straps.
3. *are . . . conceit:* capture the imagination ("fancy")
and match or echo ("respond to") the ornamentation on
the rapiers' hilts; further, they are finely wrought ("delicate") and of an elaborate ("liberal") design.
4. Osric's inflated term for "hangers," or straps. Here Q2
adds the following aside by Horatio, lines 114.1–114.2.

5. Must be informed by an explanatory note (from the
margin of a book).
6. Laertes must score three more "hits" than Hamlet
out of twelve bouts of swordplay to win the wager.
7. If "he" is Laertes, Osric may mean "He has bet twelve
passes for nine hits" (a greater challenge than the King's
terms, by which he would only need eight hits to win).
8. Would accept the challenge (Osric's meaning, and
the only honorable response). In the next line, Hamlet
deliberately misunderstands "answer" as "(any) reply."

135 OSRIC   I commend my duty° to your lordship.   dedicate my service
HAMLET   Yours, yours.   [*Exit* OSRIC]
He does well to commend° it himself; there are no tongues   recommend
else for 's turn.°   purpose
HORATIO   This lapwing runs away with the shell on his head.[9]
140 HAMLET   A did comply with his dug[1] before a sucked it. Thus
has he—and many more of the same bevy that I know the
drossy° age dotes on—only got the tune of the time and out-   worthless
ward habit of encounter,[2] a kind of yeasty collection which
carries them through and through the most fanned and win-
145 nowed opinions;[3] and do but blow them to their trial, the
bubbles are out.[4]

Enter a LORD

146.1 LORD [*to* HAMLET]   *My lord, his majesty commended him
to you by young Osric, who brings back to him that you
attend him in the hall. He sends to know if your pleasure
hold to play with Laertes, or that you will take longer*
146.5 *time.*
HAMLET   *I am constant to my purposes; they follow the
King's pleasure. If his fitness speaks, mine is ready, now
or whensoever, provided I be so able as now.*
LORD   *The King and Queen and all are coming down.*
146.10 HAMLET   *In happy time.*
LORD   *The Queen desires you to use some gentle entertainment[5] to Laertes before you fall to play.*
HAMLET   *She well instructs me.*   [*Exit* LORD]
HORATIO   *You will lose, my lord.*
HORATIO   You will lose this wager, my lord.
HAMLET   I do not think so. Since he went into France, I have
been in continual practice. I shall win at the odds. But thou
150 wouldst not think how all here about my heart—but it is no
matter.
HORATIO   Nay, good my lord—
HAMLET   It is but foolery, but it is such a kind of gain-giving° as   misgiving
would perhaps trouble a woman.
155 HORATIO   If your mind dislike anything, obey it. I will forestall
their repair° hither, and say you are not fit.   coming
HAMLET   Not a whit. We defy augury. There's a special provi-
dence[6] in the fall of a sparrow. If it be now, 'tis not to come.
If it be not to come, it will be now. If it be not now, yet it will
160 come. The readiness is all. Since no man has aught of what he
leaves, what is't to leave betimes?[7]

9. The newly hatched chicks of the plover ("lapwing") were supposed to scurry about still wearing their eggshells, a reference to the bonnet that Osric has finally put back on as well as to the courtier's brainless chirping.
1. He bowed politely to his mother's breast.
2. *the tune . . . encounter:* the fashionable turns of speech ("tune of the time") and the formulas ('habit') of courteous conversation ("encounter").
3. *a kind of . . . opinions:* their empty clichés get them through or pass for the most carefully considered wisdom (which is "fanned and winnowed" like wheat separated from chaff during threshing). *yeasty collection:* a frothy and inflated repertoire of speech and behavior.
4. And if you test them by blowing on them—as Hamlet does by speaking to Osric—they pop and dissolve. In Q2, the following passage, lines 146.1–146.14, replaces Horatio's line in F, "You will lose this wager, my lord."

5. To behave with conciliatory courtesy. Shakespeare seems to have considered two alternative explanations for Hamlet's final graciousness toward Laertes; here, in Q2, the Queen's maternal guidance nudges him to it, while F instead supplies Hamlet's own regret for his graveside brawling in 5.2.76–81.
6. God's direction for a specific event (over and above "general providence," the whole shape of God's design). Compare Matthew 10:29. The specifically Protestant theology of God's predestinating power is more explicit in Q1's version of this line: "There's a predestinate providence / In the fall of a sparrow."
7. Since man does not truly possess what he must leave behind him (worldly things and earthly flesh), why does it matter to leave them sooner ("betimes")? Q2 reads "Since no man of ought he leaves, knows what is't to leave betimes, let be."

Enter KING [CLAUDIUS], QUEEN [GERTRUDE], LAERTES,
and lords, with [OSRIC *and*] *other attendants with trum-*
pets, drums, cushions, foils, and gauntlets; a table, and
flagons of wine on it

KING CLAUDIUS   Come, Hamlet, come, and take this hand from me.
HAMLET [*to* LAERTES]   Give me your pardon, sir. I've done you wrong;
   But pardon't as you are a gentleman.
165   This presence° knows,   *royal company*
   And you must needs have heard, how I am punished
   With sore distraction.° What I have done   *agitation; insanity*
   That might your nature, honour, and exception°   *disapproval*
   Roughly awake, I here proclaim was madness.
170   Was't Hamlet wronged Laertes? Never Hamlet.
   If Hamlet from himself be ta'en away,
   And when he's not himself does wrong Laertes,
   Then Hamlet does it not, Hamlet denies it.
   Who does it then? His madness. If't be so,
175   Hamlet is of the faction that is wronged.
   His madness is poor Hamlet's enemy.
   Sir, in this audience
   Let my disclaiming from a purposed evil[8]
   Free me so far in your most generous thoughts
180   That I have shot mine arrow o'er the house
   And hurt my brother.[9]
LAERTES   I am satisfied in nature,
   Whose motive in this case should stir me most
   To my revenge. But in my terms of honour[1]
   I stand aloof, and will no reconcilement
185   Till by some elder masters of known honour
   I have a voice and precedent of peace[2]
   To keep my name ungored;° but till that time   *my reputation intact*
   I do receive your offered love like love,
   And will not wrong it.
HAMLET   I do embrace it freely,
190   And will this brothers' wager frankly° play.—   *freely*
   [*To attendants*]   Give us the foils. Come on.
LAERTES [*to attendants*]   Come, one for me.
HAMLET   I'll be your foil,[3] Laertes. In mine ignorance
   Your skill shall, like a star i'th' darkest night,
   Stick° fiery off indeed.   *Sparkle; jab*
195 LAERTES   You mock me, sir.
HAMLET   No, by this hand.
KING CLAUDIUS   Give them the foils, young Osric. Cousin Hamlet,
   You know the wager?
HAMLET   Very well, my lord.
   Your grace hath laid the odds o'th' weaker side.
200 KING CLAUDIUS   I do not fear it; I have seen you both.
   But since he is bettered,° we have therefore odds.°   *favored / handicapping*
LAERTES   [*taking a foil*]   This is too heavy; let me see another.

---

8. Let my disavowal of evil intention.
9. F's reading is "mother."
1. But where my social standing as a man of honor is
concerned.
2. *Till . . . peace:* Until the consensus of men of author-

itative standing, judging by the standards of tradition
(precedent), holds that I can make an honorable peace.
3. Flattering contrast. Jewels were often set with a
piece of metal foil under them to increase their glitter.

HAMLET [*taking a foil*]   This likes° me well. These foils have all   *pleases*
      a° length?   *the same*

OSRIC   Ay, my good lord.
      [HAMLET *and* LAERTES] *prepare to play*

KING CLAUDIUS [*to attendants*]   Set me the stoups° of wine upon   *flagons*
205   that table.
      If Hamlet give the first or second hit,
      Or quit in answer of the third exchange,[4]
      Let all the battlements their ordnance° fire.   *canons*
      The King shall drink to Hamlet's better breath,°   *energy*
210   And in the cup an union[5] shall he throw
      Richer than that which four successive kings
      In Denmark's crown have worn. Give me the cups,
      And let the kettle° to the trumpet speak,   *kettledrum*
      The trumpet to the cannoneer without,
215   The cannons to the heavens, the heaven to earth,
      'Now the King drinks to Hamlet'.
              Trumpets the while [*he drinks*]
                           Come, begin.
      And you, the judges, bear a wary eye.

HAMLET [*to* LAERTES]   Come on, sir.

LAERTES   Come, my lord.
      They play

220 HAMLET   One.

LAERTES   No.

HAMLET [*to* OSRIC]   Judgement.

OSRIC   A hit, a very palpable hit.

LAERTES   Well, again.

225 KING CLAUDIUS   Stay.° Give me drink. Hamlet, this pearl is thine.   *Stop*
      Here's to thy health.—
           Drum [*and*] *trumpets sound, and shot goes off*
                    Give him the cup.

HAMLET   I'll play this bout first. Set it by a while.—
      Come.
      They play again
      Another hit. What say you?

LAERTES   A touch, a touch, I do confess.

KING CLAUDIUS   Our son shall win.

230 QUEEN GERTRUDE   He's fat° and scant of breath.—   *sweaty*
      Here, Hamlet, take my napkin.° Rub thy brows.   *handkerchief*
      The Queen carouses to thy fortune, Hamlet.

HAMLET   Good madam.

KING CLAUDIUS   Gertrude, do not drink.

QUEEN GERTRUDE   I will, my lord, I pray you pardon me.
      She drinks [*then offers the cup to* HAMLET]

235 KING CLAUDIUS [*aside*]   It is the poisoned cup; it is too late.

HAMLET   I dare not drink yet, madam; by and by.

QUEEN GERTRUDE [*to* HAMLET]   Come, let me wipe thy face.

LAERTES [*aside to* CLAUDIUS]   My lord, I'll hit him now.

KING CLAUDIUS [*aside to* LAERTES]   I do not think't.

240 LAERTES [*aside*]   And yet 'tis almost 'gainst my conscience.

---

4. Or repay Laertes' victories by winning the third
bout.
5. A pearl, of exceptional quality. Claudius is perhaps

proposing to dissolve the gem, as Cleopatra did in a
much-repeated legend.

HAMLET   Come for the third, Laertes, you but dally.
I pray you pass° with your best violence.   thrust
I am afeard you make a wanton° of me.   spoiled child
LAERTES   Say you so? Come on.
                    [*They*] *play*
OSRIC   Nothing neither way.
LAERTES [*to* HAMLET]   Have at you now!
          [LAERTES *wounds* HAMLET.] *In scuffling, they change*
          rapiers[6] [*and* HAMLET *wounds* LAERTES]
245 KING CLAUDIUS [*to attendants*]   Part them, they are incensed.
HAMLET [*to* LAERTES]   Nay, come again.
          The QUEEN *falls down*[7]
OSRIC   Look to the Queen there, ho!
HORATIO   They bleed on both sides. [*To* HAMLET] How is't, my lord?
OSRIC   How is't, Laertes?
LAERTES   Why, as a woodcock to mine own springe,° Osric.   snare
250 I am justly killed with mine own treachery.
HAMLET   How does the Queen?
KING CLAUDIUS   She swoons to see them bleed.
QUEEN GERTRUDE   No, no, the drink, the drink! O my dear Hamlet,
The drink, the drink—I am poisoned.   [*She dies*]
HAMLET   O villainy! Ho! Let the door be locked!   [*Exit* OSRIC]
255 Treachery, seek it out.
LAERTES   It is here, Hamlet. Hamlet, thou art slain.
No med'cine in the world can do thee good.
In thee there is not half an hour of life.
The treacherous instrument is in thy hand,
260 Unbated° and envenomed. The foul practice   Not blunted
Hath turned itself on me. Lo, here I lie,
Never to rise again. Thy mother's poisoned.
I can no more. The King, the King's to blame.
HAMLET   The point envenomed too? Then, venom, to thy work.
          [*He*] *hurts* KING [CLAUDIUS]
265 ALL THE COURTIERS   Treason, treason!
KING CLAUDIUS   O yet defend me, friends! I am but hurt.
HAMLET   Here, thou incestuous, murd'rous, damnèd Dane,
Drink off this potion. Is thy union[8] here?
Follow my mother.   KING [CLAUDIUS] *dies*
LAERTES   He is justly served.
270 It is a poison tempered° by himself.   mixed
Exchange forgiveness with me, noble Hamlet.
Mine and my father's death come not upon thee,[9]
Nor thine on me.   LAERTES *dies*
HAMLET   Heaven make thee free of it! I follow thee.
275 I am dead, Horatio. Wretched Queen, adieu!
You that look pale and tremble at this chance,
That are but mutes° or audience to this act,   nonspeaking actors
Had I but time—as this fell sergeant[1] Death
Is strict in his arrest—O, I could tell you—

6. *In . . . rapiers*: from F. While Q2 lacks any stage direction here, Q1 has "They catch one another's Rapiers," suggesting that each combatant is trying to disarm the other with his free hand. Q1 also supplies daggers at line 161; these would presumably have been dropped so that each man would have a free hand.
7. This stage direction and the one at line 253 are taken from Q1, where they occur together.
8. Referring to both the pearl and his incestuous marriage to Gertrude.
9. May your soul not be judged accountable for our murders.
1. As this fierce sheriff's officer.

280 But let it be. Horatio, I am dead,
Thou liv'st. Report me and my cause aright
To the unsatisfied.

HORATIO   Never believe it.
I am more an antique Roman than a Dane.[2]
Here's yet some liquor left.

HAMLET   As thou'rt a man,

285 Give me the cup. Let go. By heaven, I'll ha't.
O God, Horatio, what a wounded name,
Things standing thus unknown, shall live behind me!
If thou didst ever hold me in thy heart,
Absent thee from felicity a while,

290 And in this harsh world draw thy breath in pain
To tell my story.

                    March afar off, and shout within
                              What warlike noise is this?

                    Enter OSRIC

OSRIC   Young Fortinbras, with conquest come from Poland,
To th'ambassadors of England gives
This warlike volley.°   *military salute*

HAMLET   O, I die, Horatio!

295 The potent poison quite o'ercrows[3] my spirit.
I cannot live to hear the news from England,
But I do prophesy th'election lights
On Fortinbras. He has my dying voice.[4]
So tell him, with th'occurrents,° more and less,   *events*

300 Which have solicited.[5] The rest is silence.
O, O, O, O![6]   HAMLET *dies*

HORATIO   Now cracks a noble heart. Good night, sweet prince,
And flights of angels sing thee to thy rest.—
Why does the drum come hither?

                    Enter FORTINBRAS *with the English* AMBASSADORS, *with*
                    drumme[r], colours, and attendants

305 FORTINBRAS   Where is this sight?

HORATIO   What is it ye would see?
If aught of woe or wonder, cease your search.

FORTINBRAS   This quarry cries on havoc.[7] O proud death,
What feast is toward° in thine eternal cell   *preparing*

310 That thou so many princes at a shot
So bloodily hast struck!

AMBASSADOR   The sight is dismal,
And our affairs from England come too late.
The ears are senseless that should give us hearing
To tell him° his commandment is fulfilled,   *(Claudius)*

315 That Rosencrantz and Guildenstern are dead.
Where should we have our thanks?

HORATIO   Not from his mouth,
Had it th'ability of life to thank you.

---

2. Ancient ("antique") Romans generally regarded suicide as preferable to dishonor; in particular, they believed
that servants or retainers should not outlive their master's overthrow.
3. Announces triumph over, like the victorious rooster in
a cockfight.
4. Vote. Because Denmark is an elective monarchy, Fortinbras can only become King by receiving the "voice,"
or vote, of electors like Hamlet.

5. Some editors assume that the sentence is grammat-
ically incomplete, broken off by death. Hamlet seems to
refer to the events that have moved ("solicited") him to
have his story told and to give his support to Fortinbras.
6. These exclamations, omitted from Q2, might be
suggestive stage directions for death throes, rather than
scripted cries.
7. All this slaughtered game ("quarry") proclaims a
massacre.

He never gave commandment for their death.
But since so jump° upon this bloody question°   *immediately / matter*
320 You from the Polack wars, and you from England,
Are here arrived, give order that these bodies
High on a stage be placèd to the view;
And let me speak to th' yet unknowing world
How these things came about. So shall you hear
325 Of carnal, bloody, and unnatural acts,
Of accidental judgements,° casual° slaughters,   *retributions / chance*
Of deaths put on° by cunning and forced cause;   *instigated*
And, in this upshot, purposes mistook
Fall'n on th'inventors' heads. All this can I
Truly deliver.
330 FORTINBRAS   Let us haste to hear it,
And call the noblest to the audience.
For me, with sorrow I embrace my fortune.
I have some rights of memory[8] in this kingdom,
Which now to claim my vantage° doth invite me.   *favorable opportunity*
335 HORATIO   Of that I shall have also cause to speak,
And from his mouth whose voice will draw on more.[9]
But let this same be presently performed,
Even whiles men's minds are wild, lest more mischance
On° plots and errors happen.   *On top of*
FORTINBRAS   Let four captains
340 Bear Hamlet like a soldier to the stage,
For he was likely, had he been put on,°   *put to the test*
To have proved° most royally; and for his passage,   *shown himself ; acted*
The soldiers' music and the rites of war
Speak loudly for him.
345 Take up the body. Such a sight as this
Becomes the field,[1] but here shows° much amiss.   *appears*
Go, bid the soldiers shoot.
                        Exeunt, marching [with the bodies]; after
                        the which, a peal of ordnance are shot off

---

8. *of memory:* unforgotten; traditional.   1. Is most appropriate to a battlefield.
9. Whose choice will induce more votes of support.

Troilus and Cressida

Audiences or readers who come to *Troilus and Cressida* (1601–02) from the *Iliad* are in for a shock. Where Homer sings of heroic conflict culminating in the epic battle between Hector and Achilles, Shakespeare gives center stage to a love story that, like the events of the Trojan War itself, he treats in skeptical, arguably cynical, fashion. Where Homer finds tragic grandeur in the events he portrays, Shakespeare finds only carnage, a carnage not relieved by a romantic plot that ends in disillusionment. This unfamiliar recasting of traditional material produces a darkly ironic view of sexuality and politics that feels radically modern.

Shakespeare knew Homer through George Chapman's *Seaven Bookes of the Iliades of Homere* (1598) and perhaps through earlier English and French translations. (The frontispiece from Chapman's *Homer* suggests the standard view of the Trojan War at the time.) More generally, the English monarchy had long traced its lineage back to Troy. For the titular figures—and, hence, for his core narrative—Shakespeare almost certainly drew on Geoffrey Chaucer's *Troilus and Criseyde* (1380s), which views the central relationship through the code of courtly love and produces an aristocratic medieval tragedy from the failure of that love. Shakespeare was also indebted to a range of other texts: classical (Virgil's *Aeneid,* Ovid's *Metamorphoses,* perhaps several plays of Euripides), medieval (John Lydgate's *Troy Book,* early fifteenth century), and Renaissance (probably including Robert Greene's *Euphues His Censure to Philautus,* 1587). In *Doctor Faustus* (1592), a tragedy that broadly influenced Shakespeare, Christopher Marlowe's titular figure lovingly apostrophizes Helen of Troy: "Was this the face that launched a thousand ships, / And burned the topless towers of Ilium?" And in 1599, a London theatrical company apparently performed Thomas Dekker and Henry Chettle's *Troyelles and Cresseda,* but only a fragmentary list of little more than stage entrances and exits survives today. The lost drama may have covered the same territory as *Troilus and Cressida* from an epic, didactic, and sentimental perspective to which Shakespeare and his company, perceiving the commercial opportunities of a rival work on the topic, stingingly replied.

Less speculative is the ironic effect *Troilus and Cressida* achieves by self-consciously retelling a familiar story. The lovers swear oaths of fidelity that, as the audience but not the characters realize, anticipate their quite different literary reputations. Cressida's uncle, the go-between Pandarus, provides a summary: "If ever you prove false one to another, . . . let all pitiful goers-between be called to the world's end after my name: call them all panders. Let all constant men be Troiluses, all false women Cressids, and all brokers-between panders" (3.2.185–90). Here Pandarus's initial neutrality ("If ever you prove false one to another") reverts to the traditional sexual double standard, a shift predictive of the outcome and already voiced in the lovers' immediately preceding speeches, where only Cressida's faithfulness is open to question. Similarly, the military plot calls attention to the very different Homeric version of its tale. Achilles is outfought by Hector and must avail himself of the Trojan's chivalric generosity: "Pause, if thou wilt" (5.6.14). Achilles then treacherously employs his soldiers, the Myrmidons, to ambush and kill Hector:

> HECTOR   I am unarmed. Forgo this vantage, Greek.
> ACHILLES   Strike, fellows, strike! This is the man I seek.
> . . . .
> On, Myrmidons, and cry you all amain,
> 'Achilles hath the mighty Hector slain!'
>
> (5.9.9–14)

In addition to deflating the epic account, the passage explains how that false account arose in the first place. Such literary self-consciousness reconciles conflicting interpretations while helping to produce a movement toward increasing bitterness.

The play breaks in equally startling fashion with the drama Shakespeare composed in the first half of his career. The romantic comedies from *Two Gentlemen of Verona* (1590–91) to *Twelfth Night* (1601) generally focus on romantic attachment and conclude in marriage. By contrast, *Troilus and Cressida* moves from extramarital sex to infidelity, recriminations, deception, self-deception, venereal disease, and despair. The English history plays from *The First Part of the Contention of the Two Famous Houses of York and Lancaster* (2 *Henry VI*; 1591) to *Henry V* (1599) usually turn on martial action

Title page of the *Iliad* of Homer in George Chapman's translation (1611?). Shakespeare probably used the less complete 1598 edition.

in defense of the state. Again in contrast, *Troilus and Cressida* casts doubt on the moral legitimacy of war, increasingly seen as an arena of mindless brutality.

Nonetheless, the play hardly emerges from nowhere. First, its negativity is partly anticipated in the sources, beginning with the *Iliad*. That poem's nostalgic admiration for warrior culture is tinged with an awareness of human suffering. Robert Henryson's *Testament of Cresseid* (late fifteenth century) moralistically punishes Cressida's infidelity by the infliction of leprosy, and William Caxton's *Recuyell of the Historyes of Troye* (the first English printed book, about 1474) has a jaundiced view of the Trojan War. Similarly, Shakespeare's earlier comedies and histories hint at the dyspeptic vision of *Troilus and Cressida*. More important, London stage practice of the period provides a suggestive context. The children's theaters that reopened in 1599 popularized misogynistic dramatic satire, to which *Troilus and Cressida* responds. The play arguably participates in the battle of rival playwrights at the turn of the century, known as the Poets' War. The ridiculous figure of Ajax may satirize Ben Jonson, whose own drama had criticized Shakespeare's works. And the railing Thersites perhaps points to John Marston, the most vituperative of the satiric playwrights. Within Shakespeare's own oeuvre, *Troilus and Cressida*'s tone anticipates the so-called problem plays, *Measure for Measure* and *All's Well That Ends Well*. Further, beginning in 1599 with *Julius Caesar*, Shakespeare initiated a decade-long appropriation of classical history in which—to oversimplify—Rome is the subject of tragedy and Greece of satire. But a satiric streak and especially a loathing of women, sexuality, and the diseased body are major strands within Shakespeare's tragic period as a whole (1599–1608), appearing at least as early as *Hamlet* (1600), with which *Troilus and Cressida* has much in common.

Finally, because the play is hardly homogeneous in tone, it sometimes connects with less bitter motifs in Shakespeare's earlier work. Troilus's initial state echoes the comically extravagant romantic excess in which Duke Orsino begins *Twelfth Night*. When asked by an attendant whether he will hunt the "hart" (deer, with a pun on "heart," line 16), the Duke explains that when he first saw Olivia, he was

> . . . turned into a hart,
> And my desires, like fell and cruel hounds,
> E'er since pursue me.
>
> (1.1.20–22)

Lovesick Troilus also renounces the hunt:

> Why should I war without the walls of Troy
> That find such cruel battle here within?
> Each Trojan that is master of his heart,
> Let him to field—Troilus, alas, hath none.
>
> (1.1.2–5)

This opening succeeds the military exposition of the Prologue and is followed by scenes of sexual comedy, cynical politics, satiric abuse, and perverse idealism. By the time any of these perspectives is repeated, one-third of the play is over. *Troilus and Cressida* thus entertains a dizzying multiplicity of views: one of its salient features is its generic hybridity.

Hence, even though ironic disillusionment becomes increasingly pervasive, it does not subsume all other perspectives. As a result, the nature of the work has always provoked disagreement. Early seventeenth-century references label it variously a history, a comedy, and a tragedy. By adding satire to the list, twentieth-century critics intensified the uncertainty of their predecessors. Although Shakespeare's entire career is marked by the mixing of genres and by the consequent violation of neoclassical norms that separated comedy sharply from tragedy, *Troilus and Cressida* represents an extreme. The play never adopts a consistent outlook in its dismantling of the leading aristocratic narrative forms—medieval chivalric romance and classical epic.

This disorientation is also produced within particular scenes. Even with the general darkening of tone, the play eschews a homogenized outlook. In Act 5, Scene 2, one of Shakespeare's most celebrated forays into eavesdropping, Diomedes and Cressida have an assignation, Troilus and Ulysses secretly watch them, Thersites covertly observes both pairs of figures, and the audience sees all five characters. Cressida's behavior elicits judgments from Diomedes and especially from Cressida herself; it also produces the following commentary.

> ULYSSES   . . . Cressid was here but now.
> TROILUS   Let it not be believed, for womanhood.

A neuer writer, to an euer
reader. Newes.

Eternall reader, you haue heere a new play, neuer stal'd with the Stage, neuer clapper-clawd with the palmes of the vulger, and yet passing full of the palme comicall; for it is a birth of your braine, that neuer vnder-tooke any thing commicall, vainely: And were but the vaine names of commedies changde for the titles of Commodities, or of Playes for Pleas; you should see all those grand censors, that now stile them such vanities, flock to them for the maine grace of their grauities: especially this authors Commedies, that are so fram'd to the life, that they serue for the most common Commentaries, of all the actions of our liues, shewing such a dexteritie, and power of witte, that the most displeased with Playes, are pleasd with his Commedies. And all such dull and heauy-witted worldlings, as were neuer capable of the witte of a Commedie, comming by report of them to his representations, haue found that witte there, that they neuer found in them-selues, and haue parted better wittied then they came: feeling an edge of witte set vpon them, more then euer they dreamd they had braine to grinde it on. So much and such sauored salt of witte is in his Commedies, that they seeme (for their height of pleasure) to be borne in that sea that brought forth Venus. Amongst all there is none more witty then this: And had I time I would comment vpon it, though I know it needs not, (for so

¶ 2   much

This prefatory epistle (continued on the facing page) was added to the second state of the 1609 Quarto of *Troilus and Cressida* (Qb). It is not found in the first state (Qa) or in the First Folio (F) and is not included in the present edition. See the Textual Note.

Think: we had mothers. Do not give advantage
To stubborn critics, apt without a theme
For depravation to square the general sex
By Cressid's rule. Rather, think this not Cressid.
ULYSSES What hath she done, Prince, that can soil our mothers?
TROILUS Nothing at all, unless that this were she.
THERSITES [aside] Will a swagger himself out on's own eyes?
(5.2.128–36)

Troilus oscillates between misogynistic generalization and idealistic denial of Cressida's infidelity, Ulysses rejects extrapolation from individual to gender, and Thersites ridicules Troilus's willful blindness. This pattern suggests that the play's view is broader than Thersites'. What that view is, however, is another matter. Although the audience apparently

THE EPISTLE.

much as will make you thinke your testerne well bestowd) but for so much worth, as euen poore I know to be stuft in it. It deserues such a labour, as well as the best Commedy in Terence or Plautus. And beleeue this, that when hee is gone, and his Commedies out of sale, you will scramble for them, and set vp a new English Inquisition. Take this for a warning, and at the perrill of your pleasures losse, and Iudgements, refuse not, nor like this the lesse, for not being sullied, with the smoaky breath of the multitude; but thinke fortune for the scape it hath made amongst you. Since by the grand possessors wills I beleeue you should haue prayd for them rather then beene prayd. And so I leaue all such to bee prayd for (for the states of their wits healths) that will not praise it.
Vale.

occupies a privileged position, it must synthesize incompatible perspectives and recognize that its privilege cannot guarantee comprehensive judgment. Rather, multiple eavesdropping onstage opens up an infinite regress that extends to the spectators, thereby undermining interpretive certainty. This uncertainty holds throughout *Troilus and Cressida*.

The play's urge to provide philosophical rationales for even the most trivial actions intensifies this effect. The characters disagree with each other and with themselves in the sense that their words bear little relation to their deeds. If this discrepancy had a casual feel to it, it might be easy to overlook. But the linkage of policy questions to foundational principles highlights the practical irrelevance of those principles. Further, since the military story remains almost devoid of combat until Act 5, the play sustains interest by relying on talk and on decisions about how—or even whether—to prosecute the war. In the meeting of the Greek leaders (1.3), Ulysses considers Achilles' defection from the war an illustration of the disruption of "degree" (1.3.82)—of a hierarchically ordered world—by mere power. His is the most famous speech in the play, and it is often read as Shakespeare's own orthodox credo. The dramatic context undermines this judgment, however. Ulysses' humanely conservative political vision sits oddly with the manipulative scheme that he immediately proposes in the same scene to return Achilles to the fray. Similarly, Ulysses complains that Patroclus amuses Achilles by satirically impersonating the other Greek leaders. To illustrate, he reproduces Patroclus's performances, in the process ridiculing Agamemnon and Nestor. And his own satiric voice is repeatedly heard, most often on the subject of Ajax.

A similar slippage from lofty precept to dubious behavior marks the corresponding Trojan council (2.2), hence establishing a parallel between the contending camps. In debating with Troilus the merits of fighting for Helen, Hector asserts, "Every tithe-soul, 'mongst many thousand dimes [souls], / Hath been as dear as Helen" (2.2.18–19). He continues:

> HECTOR   Brother, she [Helen] is not worth what she doth cost
> The holding.
> TROILUS   What's aught but as 'tis valued?
> HECTOR   But value dwells not in particular will.
> It holds his estimate and dignity
> As well wherein 'tis precious of itself
> As in the prizer.
>
> (2.2.50–55)

In response to Troilus's subjective view, then, Hector offers an objective standard that, he insists, must carry equal weight.

Undeterred, Troilus argues against returning Helen to end the war by appealing to constancy of purpose.

> I take today a wife, and my election
> Is led on in the conduct of my will;
>
> . . . .
> . . . How may I avoid—
> Although my will distaste what it elected—
> The wife I chose? There can be no evasion
> To blench from this and to stand firm by honour.
>
> (2.2.60–67)

Troilus's defense of marital commitment unwittingly militates against his own position, however. Helen is Menelaus's wife, not Paris's, and Troilus himself gives no thought to marrying Cressida. Even Hector, the noblest character in the play, cannot make good on his words. Claiming that to keep Helen is both self-destructive and immoral, he wins the debate with Troilus (and Paris). But partly inspired by the desire for chivalric glory, he collapses intellectually, agreeing to continue fighting for the Trojans' "dignities," the very aristocratic honor he had just seen through.

The friendly chivalric combat between two noble kinsmen, Hector and Ajax. From Geffrey Whitney, *A Choice of Emblemes* (1586).

The Trojan council of war is echoed at least twice. Hector's disabused view of Helen is more bitterly refracted when Paris asks who deserves her more, "myself or Menelaus" (4.1.56). Diomedes replies,

> He merits well to have her that doth seek her,
> Not making any scruple of her soilure,
> With such a hell of pain and world of charge;
> And you as well to keep her that defend her,
> Not palating the taste of her dishonour,
> With such a costly loss of wealth and friends.
>
> (4.1.57–62)

In addition, Helen is branded a "whore" by both Thersites and Diomedes (2.3.65, 4.1.68) before that term comes to be attached to Cressida. Misogyny thus informs anti-war sentiment—the play's dominant position. Second, however, when the Greek leaders earlier snub Achilles to get him to fight, Ulysses tells the shaken warrior that value consists not in merit but in reputation—almost the opposite of Hector's position. And the play provides no resolution to this argument.

The romantic plot also holds contradictory outlooks in tension. Reacting against earlier twentieth-century criticism that identified with Troilus, recent discussions have looked skeptically at the male lover and sympathetically at the woman who apparently betrays him. Troilus has a mundane goal: "Her bed is India; there she lies, a pearl" (1.1.96). This sensual motivation turns Cressida into an object of exchange. The idealized image of love he articulates elsewhere is not simply ironized by this jarring juxtaposition: the metaphor parallels the businesslike enterprise of seduction in which Pandarus is so instrumental. When Troilus calls himself as "skilless as unpractised infancy" and "simpler than the infancy of truth" (1.1.12, 3.2.157), he continues his self-regarding rhetoric in a different vein, distances himself from his own sexually aggressive behavior, and arguably imagines sexual intercourse between adults as the relationship between infant and mother. Troilus also fears a subsequent letdown: he worries "that the will is infinite and the execution confined; that the desire is boundless and the act a slave to limit" (3.2.76–77).

Disappointment is Cressida's anxiety as well, although her concern is male inconstancy: "Yet hold I off. Women are angels, wooing; / Things won are done. Joy's soul lies in the doing" (1.2.264–65). Cressida's ambivalence turns on the conviction, deeply embedded in gender inequality, that female sexual surrender cools male ardor. She seems to act out of multiple motives—love and sexual desire, vulnerability, fear of betrayal, the possibility of the self-betrayal of her feelings out of the need to protect herself, and the tendency to understand herself as others define her. The play validates this ambivalence. She has been abandoned by her father, and her remaining relative seeks only to send her to bed with Troilus. Following their first and only night together, the lovers' common fear is realized. Troilus cheerfully gets up to leave, over Cressida's objections. The news that she will be swapped for Antenor—will literally become an object of exchange—elicits passionate refusal from her but immediate resignation from him. Although her reference to "the merry Greeks" (4.5.55) arouses Troilus's jealousy, Cressida interprets his renewed passion as further devaluation of her. Upon her arrival in the enemy camp, she is kissed by the Greek leaders in a scene that has been taken to reveal everything from her wantonness to a near gang rape. Reunited with a father who delivers her to Diomedes, she acts with characteristic ambiguity, perhaps combining ambivalence, a sense of entrapment, desperation, weakness, desire, and manipulation.

But one should not simply reverse Troilus's self-understanding, seeing him as victimizer and Cressida as victim. The play provides the material for competing interpretations without privileging any of them. In a way, this uncertainty does not matter. Troilus and Cressida's relationship is a zero-sum game in that however one explains their behavior, the effect is to undermine ideals that prove to have been overrated all along. Ambiguity and degradation also mark the military climax, in which Hector compounds his failure in the Trojan council by disastrous chivalric generosity. Driven by honor, he insists on fighting, although he is warned not to, and the fate of Troy hangs on his health. Ulysses, Ajax, and Troilus all remark on his habit of sparing a defeated foe. This habit is accompanied by the assumption, despite clear evidence to the contrary, that others operate similarly. Thus, when Hector disarms before Achilles comes upon him, he becomes an easy target. With this implicit judgment of Hector, the play universalizes its critique. The result is a near moral vacuum. Although aristocratic norms retain a vestige of their former appeal, the struggle to live—and die—by them is scarcely worth the effort. The play may thus gesture toward the political crisis at the end of Elizabeth's reign, highlighted by the execution of the Earl of Essex, whose ambitious factionalism (perhaps echoed in Achilles) and chivalric competitiveness (perhaps exemplified by Hector) more generally marked the behavior of competing groups of courtiers who had long sought the queen's favor.

The systematic ambiguity of *Troilus and Cressida,* though perhaps not its movement toward disillusionment, is intensified by the early publishing history of the play. (See the Textual Note.) The First Quarto emphasizes Troilus, Cressida, and Pandarus on the title page and is prefaced by an anonymous prose epistle that defines the work as a comedy. (See the facsimile reproduction of the epistle on pages 208–209.) The version in the First Folio (1623) is called a tragedy and lacks the epistle, instead introducing the play by a verse Prologue that says nothing of the lovers while focusing on the Trojan War itself, which it treats in heroic terms. In other words, the two texts set up antithetical expectations for their readers. The Quarto closes much as it opens—with Pandarus's lewd and satiric identification with the audience. (See the indented text after 5.11.31.) Although the Folio provides the same conclusion, perhaps it was meant to end with Troilus's despairing, vengeful response to Hector's death. That hypothesis governs the present edition, which views the Folio as the revised and, hence, more authoritative text. Although beginnings and endings cannot determine the meaning of a play, they have disproportionate weight. The modified Folio printed here, like the Quarto, provides a consistent frame around the play, with the difference that the frame is heroic rather than satiric. But the present text does not convert satire into tragedy; in any version, there is satire as well as tragedy. The present text, then, slightly reduces the likelihood that tragic elements will be drowned in a sea of bitter irony.

The Quarto's satiric thrust and the claim in its epistle that the work was never performed in a public theater have given rise to the theory that it was composed for, or even limited to, elite private performance—possibly at one of the Inns of Court (law schools) or at Cambridge. This view, often supported by emphasis on the play's Latinate language, legal references, and penchant for philosophical argument, is contradicted by contemporary documents and is certainly at odds with Shakespeare's normal practice. Possibly, however, *Troilus and Cressida* was relatively unsuccessful at the Globe; probably, it was influenced by the Inns of Court; possibly it was performed there, at Cambridge, or in both locales. Whatever the truth, the debate about the nature and location of the early audience reproduces the ambivalence about the genre of *Troilus and Cressida*: coterie performance implies satire; the public stage, tragedy.

This uncertainty did not sit well with neoclassical writers. In 1679, John Dryden removed "that heap of rubbish" which prevented the play from being a proper tragedy. He has Cressida remain true to Troilus but commit suicide, and he uses Achilles to kill off Troilus. Dryden's radical adaptation was occasionally staged between 1679 and 1734. Thereafter, *Troilus and Cressida* went unperformed until 1898, perhaps because of its grim outlook. Especially in the last fifty years, however, its unsettling proliferation of incompatible meanings and bitter view of love and war have made it extremely popular. Just as Shakespeare's history plays were mobilized to support patriotic sentiment, *Troilus and Cressida* has given expression to antiwar views—on the eve of both world wars, repeatedly during the Vietnam War in the 1960s and 1970s, and recently with reference to the Balkans. Consequently, Thersites sometimes becomes the central spokesman of the play; Ulysses, advocate of traditional hierarchy, accordingly is ironized. Similarly, increased sympathy for Cressida inspired by feminism has led to a complementary depreciation of Troilus.

But does the play offer an alternative system of positive values, even if those values cannot be openly articulated? In this explicitly sexual work, the best place to look may be moments with only an implicitly sexual undertone. The ceremonial exchanges between the leaders of the rival armies suggest the lure of homosocial coupling, which simultaneously excludes women and drives the men back to battle. Performances since the 1960s have frequently been sensitive to this motif. Hector challenges "the fair'st of Greece," by which he means not a woman but a man, and indeed a man who will "dare avow her [his mistress's] beauty and her worth / In other arms than hers" (1.3.262, 268–69). Ulysses resorts to similar wordplay when trying to persuade Achilles to overcome the scruples of heterosexual love: "Better would it fit Achilles much / To throw down Hector than Polyxena" (3.3.200–01).

But one cannot consistently link either misogyny to antiwar views or same-sex bonding to a warrior ethos. Everything has a flip side. An ambivalent imagistic pattern connecting women, effeminacy, and sexual deviation comes closest to providing a countervision to the heroic ethos. Cassandra interrupts the Trojan council with prophecies of doom, a tactic she repeats with equal lack of success in seconding Andromache's efforts to prevent Hector from entering battle near the end of the play. Priam sums up the primarily female forces urging inaction when he tells Hector, "Go back. / Thy wife hath dreamt, thy mother hath had visions, / Cassandra doth foresee" (5.3.64–66). Paris reports, "I would fain have armed today, but my Nell [Helen] would not have it so" (3.1.127–28). And Achilles' not-so-secret love for Polyxena keeps him out of the war entirely: "Fall, Greeks; fail, fame; honour, or go or stay. / My major vow lies here; this I'll obey" (5.1.38–39). More strikingly, the warriors internalize the female perspective. Achilles has "a woman's longing, / . . . To see great Hector in his weeds of peace" (3.3.230–32). Troilus cannot fight because his love for Cressida makes him "weaker than a woman's tear, / . . . Less valiant than the virgin in the night" (1.1.9–11). Hector echoes the sentiment in opening his attack on the war: "There is no lady . . . / More ready to cry out, 'Who knows what follows?' / Than Hector is" (2.2.10–13). Ajax calls the play's leading satirist "Mistress Thersites" (2.1.34), and when faced with "a bastard son of Priam's" (5.8.7) on the battlefield, Thersites makes an illogical, if life-saving, argument: "I am a bastard, too. I love bastards. . . . Take heed: the quarrel's most ominous to us. If the son of a whore fight for a whore, he tempts judgement" (5.8.8–13). Here, Thersites' cowardice conjures up a brotherhood of sexual illegitimacy opposed to meaningless slaughter. Finally, Patroclus complains to Achilles that their enforced leisure makes him loathed as "an effeminate man" (3.3.211):

> . . . I stand condemned for this.
> They think my little stomach to the war
> And your great love to me restrains you thus.
> (3.3.212–14)

What "they think" may be true. Thersites calls Patroclus "Achilles' brach" (bitch hound, 2.1.109), later describing him as "Achilles' male varlet . . . his masculine whore" (5.1.14–16). The death of "my sweet Patroclus" (5.1.32) causes Achilles to break his vow and seek revenge, just as the loss of Cressida turns Troilus toward savagery. In a play about the most famous war in Western literature, opposition to battle brings disgrace. But in such moments—moments of sexual, romantic, or familial intimacy rooted in female or homoerotic experience—an alternative to both aristocratic values and their ironic deflation can be glimpsed.

WALTER COHEN

TEXTUAL NOTE

The textual history of *Troilus and Cressida* (1601–02) poses complex problems of potential interpretive significance. In early 1603, "The booke of Troilus and Cresseda as yt is acted by my lo: Chamberlens Men" was listed in the Stationers' Register—a necessary prelude to authorized publication. In fact, the play was not published; a second entry in the Stationers' Register, this one from 1609, now refers to "THE history of Troylus and Cressida," but with no mention of theatrical performance. The First Quarto (Q) appeared the same year in two distinct states. The earlier version, like the 1609 Stationers' Register, calls it "THE Historie of Troylus and Cresseida" but echoes the 1603 Stationers' Register in evoking stage history—"As it was acted by the Kings Maiesties seruants at the Globe." (Shakespeare's acting company, the Lord Chamberlain's Men, became the King's Men after James succeeded Elizabeth on the throne in 1603.) The second version's title page announces "THE Famous Historie of Troylus and Cresseid," goes on to emphasize their love and Pandarus's role, and omits any mention of performance. That omission is developed in a new prefatory epistle, which calls the play a comedy, appeals to elite literary taste by saying that it was never acted in the public theater, and implies—correctly, it seems—that publication is unauthorized.

Moreover, when the First Folio (F) was being prepared for publication in 1623, *Troilus and Cressida* was originally intended to follow *Romeo and Juliet* in the tragedy section. But after only three pages of it were set, printing was discontinued. The play was finally incorporated at the last minute, too late to be mentioned in the Catalogue (table of contents). It excluded the epistle but included a new Prologue, a reset version of its Folio first page, the remaining two pages of the original and incomplete Folio printing, and newly set type for the remainder of the play. It was placed between *All Is True (Henry VIII)*, the last of the histories, and *Coriolanus*, which was meant to be the first of the tragedies. In this intermediate zone, the work in effect became the initial tragedy of the volume, bearing the title "THE TRAGEDIE OF Troylus and Cressida."

Beyond revealing an uncertainty about genre that has continued to the present day, this twenty-year sequence leaves a number of issues obscure. Why was the play not published in 1603: lack of authorization, fear of political reprisals, or, most likely, no real intention to publish? Was it performed at the Globe (probably) or just for an elite audience at the law schools known as the Inns of Court or Cambridge (perhaps in addition to, less likely instead of, the Globe)? Why did the printer of Q change the title page and insert the prefatory epistle in midstream: access to new information, discovery of the epistle at the end of the play manuscript, desire to distance the work from the King's Men, or, most likely, hope of selling more copies? When was the epistle written: 1603 or, more likely, 1609? None of these questions admits of a definitive answer. The delay in printing the Folio version, however, is perhaps less mysterious: it may have been necessitated by copyright troubles that were subsequently resolved.

Equally contentious are the questions about Q and F—their nature, the texts that stand behind them, their relationship to each other. Both, scholars agree, are authoritative in the sense of ultimately deriving from authorial manuscripts. After that, there is less agreement. Q appears to derive from a copy of Shakespeare's draft that has been revised, probably—but not certainly—by Shakespeare. The three pages of the false start in printing the F version are based exclusively on Q, and presumably the initial intention was to follow this procedure throughout the play. But most of the actual F text relies on a substantively different manuscript of *Troilus and Cressida* that usually, but not always, seems to represent an earlier Shakespearean version than the one behind Q. This version has been annotated for performance and hence is a promptbook. In addition, after the first three pages F intermittently relies on Q. It is likely, then, that the F *Troilus* derives from both the manuscript and Q. (Alternatively, it may depend solely on the promptbook manuscript after the first three pages, but that manuscript then would have been influenced by Q.) Accordingly, neither Q nor F has clear priority. The Oxford editors, however, believe that only F incorporates Shakespeare's revisions. Thus, except in a few long passages (1.1.0–1.2.215, 2.2.103–209, 3.3.1–95, and 4.6.0–64), this edition tends to follow F.

For the most part, the consequences of this decision are modest. Both Q and F end with an epilogue spoken by Pandarus, introduced by a three-line exchange between him and Troilus in which Troilus angrily dismisses him. Only F, however, includes almost the identical three lines at the end of Act 5, Scene 3. Both locations cannot be correct. But since this earlier placement occurs only in F and hence is viewed by the Oxford editors as Shakespeare's final judgment on the matter, it is retained in the present edition while Pandarus's epilogue is cut and printed as an indented passage. This excision, the exclusion of the epistle as well as other (very brief) passages found in Q but not F, and the inclusion of the Prologue as well as other (somewhat longer) passages found in F but not Q all point in the same direction. They slightly reduce the satiric elements in the portrayal of Troilus, Cressida, and Pandarus and, more important, downplay the central love affair and shift the focus to the Trojan War itself. These thematic matters are treated in greater detail in the Introduction.

Neither Q nor F has act or scene divisions, with the exception of the first scene in F, which is labeled *"Actus Primus. Scœna Prima."* Editors have supplied these divisions since the early eighteenth century. This edition, unlike most of its predecessors, begins a new scene each time the stage is cleared. Accordingly, Act 4 includes a new Scene 3 after 4.2.75 and a new Scene 7 after 4.6.119, for a total of seven scenes rather than the conventional five. Similarly, Act 5 has a new Scene 8 after 5.7.8, for a total of eleven rather than ten scenes. These changes are discussed in the footnotes.

SELECTED BIBLIOGRAPHY

Bednarz, James P. *Shakespeare and the Poets' War.* New York: Columbia University Press, 2001. 32–52, 257–64. Links the play to the satirical Poets' War of about 1599–1602, with Ajax representing Ben Jonson and Thersites John Marston.

Bredbeck, Gregory W. *Sodomy and Interpretation: Marlowe to Milton.* Ithaca, N.Y.: Cornell University Press, 1991. 33–47. Satire and statecraft joined in the (unjustified) charge of sodomy against Patroclus, a strategy that serves Greek political ends in a chaotic world.

Charnes, Linda. " 'So Unsecret to Ourselves': Notorious Identity and the Material Subject in Shakespeare's *Troilus and Cressida*." *Shakespeare Quarterly* 40 (1989): 413–40. The characters' literary reputation as fixed identities against which they struggle in the effort to assert their own subjectivity.

Girard, René. "The Politics of Desire in *Troilus and Cressida*." *Shakespeare and the Question of Theory.* Ed. Patricia Parker and Geoffrey Hartman. New York: Methuen, 1985. 188–209. The love plot and the war plot as instances of mimetic desire (desire inspired by emulous rivalry); generally sympathetic to Cressida and unsympathetic to Troilus.

Grady, Hugh. *Shakespeare's Universal Wolf: Studies in Early Modern Reification.* Oxford: Clarendon, 1996. 58–94. Argues that, philosophically, the play negates all value, seeing a world, from which it dissents, dominated by desire, power, capital, and instrumental reason unlinked to ethics.

James, Heather. *Shakespeare's Troy: Drama, Politics, and the Translation of Empire.* New York: Cambridge University Press, 1997. 85–118. Shakespeare's refusal to choose among alternative versions of the Troy legend, some of which trace a direct lineage from the Trojan to the English monarchy, the result being a conflicted play rooted in the late Elizabethan crisis.

Mallin, Eric S. "Emulous Factions and the Collapse of Chivalry: *Troilus and Cressida*." *Representations* 29 (1990): 145–79. Links the play to the nostalgic chivalry of the Essex faction at court, in tension with the actual reality of self-interested greed.

Martin, Priscilla, ed. *Shakespeare, "Troilus and Cressida": A Casebook.* London: Macmillan, 1976. Three hundred years of criticism beginning in 1679, concentrating on 1945–1975.

Shirley, Frances A., ed. *Troilus and Cressida.* New York: Cambridge University Press, 2005. Performance history, followed by a text of the play with notes on staging from various productions.

Yachnin, Paul. "The Perfection of Ten": Populuxe Art and Artisanal Value in *Troilus and Cressida*." *Shakespeare Quarterly* 56 (2005): 306–28. *Troilus and Cressida* as an upscale, deluxe satire performed by a popular, artisan acting company whose need to win audience approval informs the play's debates about value and reputation.

FILM

Troilus & Cressida. 1981. Dir. Jonathan Miller. UK. 190 min. Relatively conservative BBC production that steers clear of homoeroticism but that offers a spirited, rather than a debased, Cressida and makes use of TV's resources by utilizing both broad background shots and intimate close-ups.

Troilus and Cressida

THE PERSONS OF THE PLAY

PROLOGUE

Trojans

PRIAM, King of Troy
HECTOR ⎫
DEIPHOBUS ⎪
HELENUS, a priest ⎬ his sons
PARIS ⎪
TROILUS ⎪
MARGARETON, a bastard ⎭
CASSANDRA, Priam's daughter, a prophetess
ANDROMACHE, wife of Hector
AENEAS ⎫
ANTENOR ⎬ commanders
PANDARUS, a lord
CRESSIDA, his niece
CALCHAS, her father, who has joined the Greeks
HELEN, wife of Menelaus, now living with Paris
ALEXANDER, servant of Cressida
Servants of Troilus, musicians, soldiers, attendants

Greeks

AGAMEMNON, Commander-in-Chief
MENELAUS, his brother
NESTOR
ULYSSES
ACHILLES
PATROCLUS, his companion
DIOMEDES
AJAX
THERSITES
MYRMIDONS, soldiers of Achilles
Servants of Diomedes, soldiers

Prologue

[*Enter the* PROLOGUE *armed*][1]

PROLOGUE   In Troy there lies the scene. From isles of Greece
The princes orgulous, their high blood chafed,[2]
Have to the port of Athens sent their ships,
Fraught° with the ministers and instruments   *Weighted down*
5   Of cruel war. Sixty-and-nine, that wore

Prologue
1. In armor (see line 23); perhaps referring to Ben Jonson's prologue to *Poetaster* (1601), in which an armed figure appears to defend Jonson's embattled reputation among playwrights. *Troilus and Cressida*'s Ajax is sometimes seen as a further jab at Jonson's warlike posturing. The Prologue first appeared in F. Modern editions tend

to include an epistle to the reader either before the opening list of characters, in the notes, or in an appendix. The epistle prefaced the second state of Q and was probably not written by Shakespeare. It is excluded here, but a photograph of it as it appeared in Q is provided. See the Textual Note and Introduction.
2. The princes proud, their noble blood heated.

Their crownets° regal, from th'Athenian bay   *coronets*
Put forth toward Phrygia,[3] and their vow is made
To ransack Troy, within whose strong immures°   *fortifications*
The ravishèd° Helen, Menelaus' queen,   *kidnapped (sexual)*
10 With wanton Paris sleeps—and that's the quarrel.
To Tenedos° they come,   *island near Troy*
And the deep-drawing barques[4] do there disgorge
Their warlike freightage; now on Dardan[5] plains
The fresh and yet unbruisèd Greeks do pitch
15 Their brave pavilions.° Priam's six-gated city—   *finely arrayed tents*
Dardan and Timbria, Helias, Chetas, Troien,
And Antenorides—with massy staples°   *bolt holes*
And corresponsive and full-filling bolts
Spar up the sons of Troy.[6]
20 Now expectation, tickling skittish° spirits   *excitable*
On one and other side, Trojan and Greek,
Sets all on hazard.° And hither am I come,   *at stake*
A Prologue armed—but not in confidence
Of author's pen or actor's voice,[7] but suited
25 In like conditions as our argument[8]—
To tell you, fair beholders, that our play
Leaps o'er the vaunt° and firstlings of those broils, *preliminaries*
Beginning in the middle,[9] starting thence away
To what may be digested in a play.
30 Like or find fault; do as your pleasures are;
Now, good or bad, 'tis but the chance of war.   [*Exit*]

1.1

Enter PANDARUS, *and* TROILUS [*armed*]

TROILUS Call here my varlet.° I'll unarm again.   *page (of genteel birth)*
Why should I war without° the walls of Troy   *outside*
That° find such cruel battle here within?°   *Who / in myself*
Each Trojan that is master of his heart,
5 Let him to field—Troilus, alas, hath none.[1]
PANDARUS Will this gear° ne'er be mended?   *affair*
TROILUS The Greeks are strong, and skilful to their strength,[2]
Fierce to their skill, and to their fierceness valiant.
But I am weaker than a woman's tear,
10 Tamer than sleep, fonder° than ignorance,   *sillier*
Less valiant than the virgin in the night,
And skilless as unpractised infancy.
PANDARUS Well, I have told you enough of this. For my part, I'll

---

3. The region around Troy (now northwestern Turkey).
4. Boats riding deeply in the water (because they are heavily laden).
5. Trojan. Dardanus was the mythical founder of the city.
6. The sons of Troy shut up the six-gated city. (But the inverted syntax also suggests that the city, whose six gates the Prologue has just named, shuts in "the sons of Troy.")
7. *not . . . voice*: not confident of success at writing or acting.
8. *suited . . . argument*: dressed appropriately for our subject (unlike Jonson's).
9. On the model of epic poetry in the Homeric tradition and as recommended by the ancient Latin poet Horace

in his *Art of Poetry*. Despite the play's classical subject matter, the double plot and generic hybridity deviate from what Renaissance critics understood to be classical dramatic norms. But the play comes close to observing two of the three supposedly Aristotelian unities (of time, place, and action) by compressing events after Act 1, Scene 2, into little more than forty-eight hours and by restricting the scene to Troy and its immediate surroundings.
1.1 Location: Troy.
1. Has no heart for battle (having lost his heart to Cressida).
2. And as skilled as they are strong.

not meddle nor make° no farther. He that will have a cake out   *be involved (proverbial)*
15   of the wheat must tarry° the grinding.   *wait for*
    TROILUS   Have I not tarried?
    PANDARUS   Ay, the grinding; but you must tarry the boulting.°   *sifting*
    TROILUS   Have I not tarried?
    PANDARUS   Ay, the boulting; but you must tarry the leavening.
20   TROILUS   Still have I tarried.
    PANDARUS   Ay, to the leavening; but here's yet in the word 'here-
    after' the kneading, the making of the cake, the heating the
    oven, and the baking—nay, you must stay the cooling too, or
    ye may chance burn your lips.
25   TROILUS   Patience herself, what goddess e'er she be,
    Doth lesser blench at suff'rance[3] than I do.
    At Priam's royal table do I sit
    And when fair Cressid comes into my thoughts—
    So, traitor![4] 'When she comes'? When is she thence?
30   PANDARUS   Well, she looked yesternight fairer than ever I saw
    her look, or any woman else.
    TROILUS   I was about to tell thee: when my heart,
    As wedged° with a sigh, would rive° in twain,   *divided / tear apart*
    Lest Hector or my father should perceive me
35   I have, as when the sun doth light askance,°   *obliquely*
    Buried this sigh in wrinkle of a smile.
    But sorrow that is couched° in seeming gladness   *concealed*
    Is like that mirth fate turns to sudden sadness.
    PANDARUS   An° her hair were not somewhat darker than Hel-   *If*
40   en's[5]—well, go to,° there were no more comparison between   *say no more*
    the women. But, for my part, she is my kinswoman; I would
    not, as they term it, 'praise'° her. But I would somebody had   *compliment; appraise*
    heard her talk yesterday, as I did. I will not dispraise your sister
    Cassandra's wit, but—
45   TROILUS   O Pandarus! I tell thee, Pandarus,
    When I do tell thee 'There my hopes lie drowned',
    Reply not in how many fathoms deep
    They lie endrenched. I tell thee I am mad
    In Cressid's love; thou answer'st 'She is fair',
50   Pourest in the open ulcer of my heart
    Her eyes, her hair, her cheek, her gait, her voice;
    Handlest in thy discourse, O, that her hand,[6]
    In whose comparison all whites are ink
    Writing their own reproach, to° whose soft seizure°   *compared to / grasp*
55   The cygnet's down is harsh, and spirit of sense[7]
    Hard as the palm of ploughman. This thou tell'st me—
    As true thou tell'st me—when I say I love her.
    But saying thus, instead of oil and balm
    Thou lay'st in every gash that love hath given me
60   The knife that made it.
    PANDARUS   I speak no more than truth.

---

3. Shies away less from suffering. (Shakespeare presumably means more, not "lesser.")
4. Troilus considers himself a "traitor" to Cressida for
ever forgetting her.
5. Pandarus shows the standard Elizabethan hostility to
dark hair or a dark complexion.

6. *Handlest . . . hand:* You treat in your discussion, O,
that hand of hers. (Troilus's use of "handlest" reminds
him of Cressida's hand.)
7. The quintessential medium of feeling or touch that
conveyed sense impressions from body to mind.

TROILUS   Thou dost not speak so much.

PANDARUS   Faith, I'll not meddle in it. Let her be as she is. If she
be fair, 'tis the better for her; an she be not, she has the mends°   *cure (cosmetics)*
65   in her own hands.

TROILUS   Good Pandarus, how now, Pandarus!

PANDARUS   I have had my labour for my travail.° Ill thought on   *my pains as payment*
of her and ill thought on of you. Gone between and between,
but small thanks for my labour.

70   TROILUS   What, art thou angry, Pandarus? What, with me?

PANDARUS   Because she's kin to me, therefore she's not so fair as
Helen. An she were not kin to me, she would be as fair o'
Friday as Helen is on Sunday.[8] But what care I? I care not an
she were a blackamoor. 'Tis all one to me.

75   TROILUS   Say I she is not fair?

PANDARUS   I do not care whether you do or no. She's a fool to
stay behind her father.[9] Let her to the Greeks—and so I'll tell
her the next time I see her. For my part, I'll meddle nor make
no more i'th' matter.

80   TROILUS   Pandarus—

PANDARUS   Not I.

TROILUS   Sweet Pandarus—

PANDARUS   Pray you, speak no more to me. I will leave all as I
found it. And there an end.   *Exit*

         Alarum°   *Trumpet call to arms*

85   TROILUS   Peace, you ungracious clamours! Peace, rude sounds!
Fools on both sides. Helen must needs be fair
When with your blood you daily paint° her thus.   *daub (as with rouge)*
I cannot fight upon this argument.°   *on these grounds*
It is too starved a subject° for my sword.   *too weak a reason*
90   But Pandarus—O gods, how do you plague me!
I cannot come to Cressid but by Pandar,
And he's as tetchy to be° wooed to woo   *touchy about being*
As she is stubborn-chaste against all suit.
Tell me, Apollo, for thy Daphne's love,[1]
95   What Cressid is, what Pandar, and what we?
Her bed is India;[2] there she lies, a pearl.
Between our Ilium° and where she resides   *Priam's palace*
Let it be called the wild and wand'ring flood,
Ourself the merchant, and this sailing Pandar
100   Our doubtful° hope, our convoy,° and our barque.   *uncertain / escort*

         Alarum. Enter AENEAS

AENEAS   How now, Prince Troilus? Wherefore not afield?

TROILUS   Because not there. This woman's answer sorts,°   *is fitting*
For womanish it is to be from thence.
What news, Aeneas, from the field today?

105   AENEAS   That Paris is returnèd home, and hurt.

TROILUS   By whom, Aeneas?

AENEAS   Troilus, by Menelaus.

---

8. *An . . . Sunday:* If she weren't my kinswoman (with the
result that my praise seems biased), she'd be as beautiful
in everyday dress as Helen is in her finest clothes.
9. She's a fool not to leave with her father, Calchas, a
prophet who deserted to the Greeks, having foreseen
their victory.

1. For your love of Daphne. Daphne was a nymph who
prayed (successfully) to be turned into a bay tree to escape
the advances of Apollo, god of poetry.
2. Source of jewels, precious metals, exotic spices, and
rich fabrics.

TROILUS   Let Paris bleed, 'tis but a scar to scorn:
　　　　　Paris is gored with Menelaus' horn.[3]

　　　　　　　　Alarum

AENEAS   Hark what good sport is out of town° today.　　　　　　*outside Troy*
110　TROILUS   Better at home, if 'would I might' were 'may'.
　　　　　But to the sport abroad—are you bound thither?
AENEAS   In all swift haste.
TROILUS　　　　　　　　　　　　Come, go we then together.　*Exeunt*

1.2

Enter [above] CRESSIDA *and her [servant* ALEXANDER]

CRESSIDA   Who were those went by?
ALEXANDER　　　　　　　　　　Queen Hecuba and Helen.
CRESSIDA   And whither go they?
ALEXANDER　　　　　　　　　Up to the eastern tower,
　　　　　Whose height commands as subject all the vale,°　　　　　　*valley*
　　　　　To see the battle. Hector, whose patience
5　　　　Is as a virtue fixed,° today was moved.°　　　　　*unwavering / angry*
　　　　　He chid Andromache and struck his armourer
　　　　　And, like as there were husbandry in war,
　　　　　Before the sun rose[1] he was harnessed light,°　　　*in lightweight armor*
　　　　　And to the field goes he, where every flower
10　　　Did as a prophet weep° what it foresaw　　　　*Was wet with dew at*
　　　　　In Hector's wrath.
CRESSIDA　　　　　　What was his cause of anger?
ALEXANDER   The noise° goes this: there is among the Greeks　　　*rumor*
　　　　　A lord of Trojan blood, nephew° to Hector;　　　　　*relation*
　　　　　They call him Ajax.
CRESSIDA　　　　　　　Good,° and what of him?　　　　　*Well*
15　ALEXANDER   They say he is a very man *per se*,°　　　　*unique man*
　　　　　And stands alone.°　　　　　　　　　　　　*is preeminent*
CRESSIDA　　　　　So do all men
　　　　　Unless they are drunk, sick, or have no legs.
ALEXANDER   This man, lady, hath robbed many beasts of their
　　　　　particular additions:° he is as valiant as the lion, churlish as the　　*characteristics*
20　　　bear, slow as the elephant—a man into whom nature hath so
　　　　　crowded humours[2] that his valour is crushed into folly, his folly
　　　　　farced° with discretion. There is no man hath a virtue that he　　*stuffed*
　　　　　hath not a glimpse° of, nor any man an attaint° but he carries　*hint / flaw*
　　　　　some stain of it. He is melancholy without cause and merry
25　　　against the hair;° he hath the joints of everything, but every-　*against the grain*
　　　　　thing so out of joint that he is a gouty Briareus, many hands
　　　　　and no use, or purblind Argus, all eyes and no sight.[3]
CRESSIDA   But how should this man that makes me smile make
　　　　　Hector angry?
30　ALEXANDER   They say he yesterday coped° Hector in the battle　　*engaged*
　　　　　and struck him down, the disdain° and shame whereof hath　*indignation*
　　　　　ever since kept Hector fasting and waking.

---

3. *'tis . . . horn:* it's just a trivial wound (or a wound given
in return for Paris's scorn of Menelaus): Paris is wounded
by the emblem of the cuckold (having seduced Helen,
Menelaus's wife).
1.2 Location: Troy.
1. *Like . . . rose:* as if there were prudent management in
war as in agriculture, where the conscientious laborer

gets up before dawn. The comparison continues with
"field" and "flower" (line 9).
2. Peculiarities. Humors were the four main bodily fluids
and were believed to determine a person's temperament.
3. He is a giant (Briareus), whose hundred hands are
ruined by gout, or totally blind Argus, whose hundred eyes
Juno deprived of sight because he fell asleep guarding Io.

	CRESSIDA Who comes here?	
	ALEXANDER Madam, your uncle Pandarus.	
	Enter PANDARUS [*above*]	
35	CRESSIDA Hector's a gallant man.	
	ALEXANDER As may be in the world, lady.	
	PANDARUS What's that? What's that?	
	CRESSIDA Good morrow, uncle Pandarus.	
	PANDARUS Good morrow, cousin° Cressid. What do you talk	*relation*
40	of?— Good morrow, Alexander.—How do you, cousin? When	
	were you at Ilium?	
	CRESSIDA This morning, uncle.	
	PANDARUS What were you talking of when I came? Was Hector	
	armed and gone ere ye came to Ilium? Helen was not up, was	
45	she?	
	CRESSIDA Hector was gone but Helen was not up?	
	PANDARUS E'en so. Hector was stirring early.	
	CRESSIDA That were we talking of, and of his anger.	
	PANDARUS Was he angry?	
50	CRESSIDA So he° says here.	*Alexander*
	PANDARUS True, he was so. I know the cause too. He'll lay about	
	him today, I can tell them that. And there's Troilus will not	
	come far behind him. Let them take heed of Troilus, I can tell	
	them that too.	
55	CRESSIDA What, is he angry too?	
	PANDARUS Who, Troilus? Troilus is the better man of the two.	
	CRESSIDA O Jupiter! There's no comparison.	
	PANDARUS What, not between Troilus and Hector? Do you	
	know a man if you see him?	
60	CRESSIDA Ay, if I ever saw him before and knew him.[4]	
	PANDARUS Well, I say Troilus is Troilus.°	*(that special man)*
	CRESSIDA Then you say as I say, for I am sure	
	He is not Hector.	
	PANDARUS No, nor Hector is not Troilus, in some degrees.°	*respects*
65	CRESSIDA 'Tis just to each of them: he is himself.	
	PANDARUS Himself? Alas, poor Troilus, I would he were.	
	CRESSIDA So he is.	
	PANDARUS Condition I had gone barefoot to India.[5]	
	CRESSIDA He is not Hector.	
70	PANDARUS Himself? No, he's not himself. Would a° were him-	*he*
	self! Well, the gods are above, time must friend or end.° Well,	*befriend or kill him*
	Troilus, well, I would my heart were in her body. No, Hector	
	is not a better man than Troilus.	
	CRESSIDA Excuse me.[6]	
75	PANDARUS He is elder.	
	CRESSIDA Pardon me, pardon me.	
	PANDARUS Th'other's not come to't.° You shall tell me another	*his prime; intercourse*
	tale when th'other's come to't. Hector shall not have his will[7]	
	this year.	
80	CRESSIDA He shall not need it if he have his own.	
	PANDARUS Nor his qualities.	

---

4. Here and in the following lines, Cressida obstinately takes Pandarus's figurative language literally. Recognized him; met an ideal man; saw him from the front ("before") and had sexual intercourse with ("knew") him.

5. If I'd gone barefoot (on pilgrimage) to India—an impossibility.

6. Cressida disagrees, as in line 76.

7. Troilus's resolve; Troilus's sexual desire.

CRESSIDA   No matter.

PANDARUS   Nor his beauty.

CRESSIDA   'Twould not become him; his own's better.

85 PANDARUS   You have no judgement, niece. Helen herself swore
     th'other day that Troilus for a brown favour,[8] for so 'tis, I must
     confess—not brown neither—

CRESSIDA   No, but brown.

PANDARUS   Faith, to say truth, brown and not brown.

90 CRESSIDA   To say the truth, true and not true.

PANDARUS   She praised his complexion above Paris'.

CRESSIDA   Why, Paris hath colour enough.

PANDARUS   So he has.

CRESSIDA   Then Troilus should° have too much. If she praised   *must therefore*

95 him above, his° complexion is higher than his;° he having col-   *Troilus's / Paris's*
     our enough, and the other higher, is too flaming a praise for
     a good complexion. I had as lief Helen's golden tongue had
     commended Troilus for a copper nose.[9]

PANDARUS   I swear to you, I think Helen loves him better than

100 Paris.

CRESSIDA   Then she's a merry Greek[1] indeed.

PANDARUS   Nay, I am sure she does. She came to him th'other
     day into the compassed° window, and you know he has not past   *bay*
     three or four hairs on his chin—

105 CRESSIDA   Indeed, a tapster's° arithmetic may soon bring his par-   *the simplest*
     ticulars therein to a total.

PANDARUS   Why, he is very young—and yet will he within three
     pound lift as much as his brother Hector.

CRESSIDA   Is he so young a man and so old a lifter?°   *so practiced a thief*

110 PANDARUS   But to prove to you that Helen loves him: she came
     and puts me° her white hand to his cloven chin.   *puts me = puts*

CRESSIDA   Juno have mercy! How came it cloven?

PANDARUS   Why, you know, 'tis dimpled. I think his smiling
     becomes him better than any man in all Phrygia.

115 CRESSIDA   O he smiles valiantly.

PANDARUS   Does he not?

CRESSIDA   O yes, an't were a cloud in autumn.[2]

PANDARUS   Why, go to then. But to prove to you that Helen loves
     Troilus—

120 CRESSIDA   Troilus will stand to the proof[3] if you'll prove it so.

PANDARUS   Troilus? Why, he esteems her no more than I esteem
     an addle° egg.   *rotten*

CRESSIDA   If you love an addle egg as well as you love an idle
     head you would eat chickens i'th' shell.[4]

125 PANDARUS   I cannot choose but laugh to think how she tickled
     his chin. Indeed, she has a marvellous white hand, I must
     needs confess—

CRESSIDA   Without the rack.°   *being tortured*

PANDARUS   And she takes upon her to spy a white hair on his

130 chin.

<hr/>

8. Notwithstanding his (unfashionably) dark or tanned
face.
9. Red nose, caused by drinking; perhaps also an artificial
nose, made necessary by syphilis.
1. Slang for a reveler or wanton, implying good
fellowship and superficiality; here, appropriately applied

to Helen and more generally to the Greeks, at least as
they treat Cressida.
2. As if he were a rain cloud.
3. Will uphold the proof; will have an erection.
4. An addled egg often resulted from the chick dying
during hatching.

CRESSIDA Alas, poor chin! Many a wart is richer.°   (*in hairs*)

PANDARUS But there was such laughing! Queen Hecuba laughed
that° her eyes ran o'er.   *so much that*

CRESSIDA With millstones.⁵

135 PANDARUS And Cassandra laughed.

CRESSIDA But there was a more temperate fire under the pot of
her eyes⁶—or did her eyes run o'er too?

PANDARUS And Hector laughed.

CRESSIDA At what was all this laughing?

140 PANDARUS Marry,⁷ at the white hair that Helen spied on Troilus'
chin.

CRESSIDA An't had been a green hair I should have laughed too.

PANDARUS They laughed not so much at the hair as at his pretty°   *witty*
answer.

145 CRESSIDA What was his answer?

PANDARUS Quoth she, 'Here's but two-and-fifty hairs on your
chin, and one of them is white.'

CRESSIDA This is her question.

PANDARUS That's true, make no question of that. 'Two-and-fifty

150 hairs,' quoth he, 'and one white? That white hair is my father,
and all the rest are his sons.'⁸ 'Jupiter!' quoth she, 'which of
these hairs° is Paris my husband?' 'The forked⁹ one,' quoth he,   *pun on "heirs"*
'pluck't out and give it him.' But there was such laughing, and
Helen so blushed and Paris so chafed° and all the rest so   *(was) so irritated*

155 laughed, that it passed.°   *surpassed description*

CRESSIDA So let it now, for it has been a great while going by.

PANDARUS Well, cousin, I told you a thing yesterday. Think on't.

CRESSIDA So I do.

PANDARUS I'll be sworn 'tis true. He will weep you an't° were a   *for you as if he*

160 man born in April.°   *month of showers*

CRESSIDA And I'll spring up in his tears an't° were a nettle   *as if I*
against° May.   *in anticipation of*

A retreat [is] sound[ed]

PANDARUS Hark, they are coming from the field. Shall we stand
up here and see them as they pass toward Ilium? Good niece,

165 do, sweet niece Cressida.

CRESSIDA At your pleasure.

PANDARUS Here, here, here's an excellent place, here we may
see most bravely.° I'll tell you them all by their names as they   *very finely*
pass by, but mark Troilus above the rest.

Enter AENEAS [*passing by below*]

170 CRESSIDA Speak not so loud.

PANDARUS That's Aeneas. Is not that a brave° man? He's one of   *splendid; courageous*
the flowers° of Troy, I can tell you. But mark Troilus; you shall   *finest men*
see anon.

Enter ANTENOR [*passing by below*]

CRESSIDA Who's that?

175 PANDARUS That's Antenor. He has a shrewd wit, I can tell you,

---

5. A hard-hearted person was proverbially said to weep
millstones rather than tears. Cressida doesn't think the
story is particularly funny.
6. Cassandra's tears are "more temperate" because she
was associated with mournful, doom-laden prophecy.
Cressida imagines tears of laughter as a pot boiling over.

7. An oath based on the name of the Virgin Mary, here
meaning "Why," elsewhere "Indeed."
8. Priam reputedly had fifty sons. The "forked" hair (line
152) apparently counts as two.
9. Like a cuckold's horns, thereby suggesting Helen's
unfaithfulness to Paris.

and he's a man good enough. He's° one o'th' soundest judge- *He has*
ments in Troy whosoever,° and a proper man of person.[1] When *of any man*
comes Troilus? I'll show you Troilus anon. If he see me you
shall see him nod at me.

180 CRESSIDA Will he give you the nod?

PANDARUS You shall see.

CRESSIDA If he do, the rich shall have more.[2]

    Enter HECTOR [*passing by below*]

PANDARUS That's Hector, that, that, look you, that. There's a
fellow!— Go thy way, Hector!—There's a brave man, niece. O

185 brave Hector! Look how he looks. There's a countenance. Is't
not a brave man?

CRESSIDA O a brave man.

PANDARUS Is a° not? It does a man's heart good. Look you what *he*
hacks are on his helmet. Look you yonder, do you see? Look

190 you there. There's no jesting. There's laying on, take't off who
will,[3] as they say. There be hacks.

CRESSIDA Be those with swords?

    Enter PARIS [*passing by below*]

PANDARUS Swords, anything, he cares not. An the devil come to
him it's all one.° By God's lid° it does one's heart good. Yonder *the same / eyelid*

195 comes Paris, yonder comes Paris. Look ye yonder, niece. Is't
not a gallant° man too? Is't not? Why, this is brave now. Who *fine*
said he came hurt home today? He's not hurt. Why, this will
do Helen's heart good now, ha! Would I could see Troilus now.
You shall see Troilus anon.

    Enter HELENUS [*passing by below*]

200 CRESSIDA Who's that?

PANDARUS That's Helenus. I marvel where Troilus is. That's
Helenus. I think he went not forth today. That's Helenus.

CRESSIDA Can Helenus fight, uncle?

PANDARUS Helenus? No—yes, he'll fight indifferent° well. I mar- *fairly*

205 vel where Troilus is.

    [*A Shout*]

Hark, do you not hear the people cry 'Troilus'? Helenus is a
priest.

    Enter TROILUS [*passing by below*]

CRESSIDA What sneaking fellow comes yonder?

PANDARUS Where? Yonder? That's Deiphobus.—'Tis Troilus!

210 There's a man, niece, h'm? Brave Troilus, the prince of chivalry!

CRESSIDA Peace, for shame, peace.

PANDARUS Mark him, note him. O brave Troilus! Look well
upon him, niece. Look you how his sword is bloodied and

215 his helm more hacked than Hector's, and how he looks and
how he goes.° O admirable youth! He ne'er saw three-and- *walks*
twenty. —Go thy way, Troilus, go thy way!—Had I a sister were
a grace,[4] or a daughter a goddess, he should take his choice. O
admirable man! Paris? Paris is dirt to him, and I warrant Helen

220 to change° would give an eye to boot. *exchange*

    Enter common soldiers [*passing by below*]

---

1. Good-looking man.
2. If Troilus acknowledges Pandarus with a nod, this will make Pandarus even more of a noddy, a fool.
3. There's hard fighting, denials notwithstanding (with wordplay: "laying on" versus "take't off").
4. The three Graces were goddesses of beauty and charm.

CRESSIDA   Here comes more.

PANDARUS   Asses, fools, dolts. Chaff and bran, chaff and bran.
Porridge° after meat. I could live and die i'th' eyes of Troilus.   *Soup*
Ne'er look, ne'er look, the eagles are gone. Crows and daws,°   *jackdaws; fools*
225   crows and daws. I had rather be such a man as Troilus than
Agamemnon and all Greece.

CRESSIDA   There is among the Greeks Achilles, a better man
than Troilus.

PANDARUS   Achilles? A drayman,° a porter, a very camel.   *cart driver*

230   CRESSIDA   Well, well.

PANDARUS   Well, well? Why, have you any discretion? Have you   ~~demonstrative~~
any eyes? Do you know what a man is? Is not birth,° beauty,   *lineage*
good shape, discourse,° manhood, learning, gentleness,° virtue,   *eloquence / gentility*
youth, liberality, and so forth, the spice and salt that season a
235   man?

CRESSIDA   Ay, a minced[5] man—and then to be baked with no
date in the pie, for then the man's date is out.[6]

PANDARUS   You are such another woman!° One knows not at   *like other women*
what ward you lie.[7]

240   CRESSIDA   Upon my back to defend my belly,[8] upon my wit to
defend my wiles, upon my secrecy° to defend mine honesty,[9]   *privacy; genitals*
my mask to defend my beauty,° and you to defend all these—   *(from sun)*
and at all these wards I lie at a thousand watches.[1]

PANDARUS   Say one of your watches.

245   CRESSIDA   'Nay, I'll watch you for that'—and that's one of the
chiefest of them too.[2] If I cannot ward what I would not have
hit,° I can watch you for° telling how I took the blow— unless   *(sexually) / from*
it swell past hiding,° and then it's past watching.   *(from pregnancy)*

PANDARUS   You are such another!

Enter BOY

250   BOY   Sir, my lord would instantly speak with you.

PANDARUS   Where?

BOY   At your own house.

PANDARUS   Good boy, tell him I come.   [*Exit* BOY]
I doubt° he be hurt. Fare ye well, good niece.   *fear*

255   CRESSIDA   Adieu, uncle.

PANDARUS   I'll be with you, niece, by and by.

CRESSIDA   To bring, uncle?

PANDARUS   Ay, a token from Troilus.

CRESSIDA   By the same token, you are a bawd.°   *pander; pimp*

Exeunt PANDARUS [*and* ALEXANDER]

260   Words, vows, gifts, tears, and love's full sacrifice
He offers in another's enterprise;
But more in Troilus thousandfold I see
Than in the glass° of Pandar's praise may be.   *mirror*
Yet hold I off. Women are angels, wooing;[3]

---

5. Affected (punning on "mincemeat" to suggest the
multiple ingredients of Troilus and thus beginning to
develop Pandarus's "spice and salt" metaphor).
6. The man is flavorless; out of date; not in female genitalia.
7. A man doesn't know what position of defense in fencing ("ward") you adopt. (A man doesn't know how to deal
with you.)
8. Vagina. Lying on one's back is not, of course, the obvious way to defend one's virginity.

9. Reputation.
1. Ways of guarding; hours of the night; the duties of a
watchman (playing on "watch" and "ward," line 243);
devotional exercises (line 244). "Watch" as a verb is also
implied: observe (line 245); prevent (line 246); worry
(line 247).
2. Presumably the immediately preceding phrase is one
of her chief devotional exercises.
3. Men call women angels only while wooing them.

265 Things won are done. Joy's soul lies in the doing.
That she beloved knows naught that knows not this:
Men price the thing ungained more than it is.°   *is worth*
That she was never yet that ever knew
Love got so sweet as when desire did sue.[4]
270 Therefore this maxim out of° love I teach: *taken from*
Achievement is command; ungained, beseech.[5]
Then though my heart's contents[6] firm love doth bear,
Nothing of that shall from mine eyes appear.   *Exit*

1.3

Sennet.° Enter AGAMEMNON, NESTOR, ULYSSES, DIO-   *Fanfare*
MEDES, [*and*] MENELAUS, *with others*

AGAMEMNON   Princes, what grief hath set the jaundice° on your cheeks?   *sickliness*
The ample proposition that hope makes
In all designs begun on earth below
Fails in the promised largeness. Checks° and disasters   *Obstacles*
5 Grow in the veins[1] of actions highest reared,
As knots, by the conflux° of meeting sap,   *confluence*
Infects the sound pine and diverts his° grain   *its*
Tortive° and errant° from his course of growth.   *Contorted / straying*
Nor, princes, is it matter new to us
10 That we come short of our suppose° so far   *intention*
That after seven years' siege yet Troy walls stand,
Sith° every action that hath gone before,   *Since*
Whereof we have record, trial did draw
Bias and thwart,[2] not answering° the aim   *living up to*
15 And that unbodied figure° of the thought   *theoretical design*
That gave't surmisèd shape. Why then, you princes,
Do you with cheeks abashed behold our works,
And think them shames, which are indeed naught else
But the protractive trials of great Jove
20 To find persistive constancy in men?
The fineness of which mettle° is not found   *temperament; metal*
In fortune's love—for then the bold and coward,
The wise and fool, the artist° and unread,   *learned*
The hard and soft, seem all affined° and kin.   *related*
25 But in the wind and tempest of her frown
Distinction with a loud and powerful fan,
Puffing at all, winnows the light away,[3]
And what hath mass or matter by itself
Lies rich in virtue and unminglèd.
30 NESTOR   With due observance of° thy godly seat,°   *respect to / throne*
Great Agamemnon, Nestor shall apply°   *gloss*
Thy latest words. In the reproof of° chance   *rebuff by; rebuttal of*
Lies the true proof of men. The sea being smooth,
How many shallow bauble°-boats dare sail   *toy*
35 Upon her patient breast, making their way

---

4. *That . . . sue:* No woman has ever known making love with a man to be as sweet as when it is still desired for the first time.
5. Once a woman yields, the man controls her; what the man doesn't have he must plead for.
6. *contents':* happiness; *con'tents:* substance.
1.3 Location: The Greek camp outside Troy.

1. It is assumed that trees have veins through which sap flows.
2. *trial . . . thwart:* attempting the deed ("action") called it into being crookedly and in a manner at odds with the purpose.
3. The comparison is to light, dry chaff blown away from grain.

With those of nobler bulk!
But let the ruffian Boreas° once enrage   *North wind*
The gentle Thetis,[4] and anon behold
The strong-ribbed barque through liquid mountains cut,
40 Bounding between the two moist elements°   *(water and air)*
Like Perseus' horse.° Where's then the saucy° boat   *(winged Pegasus) / bold*
Whose weak untimbered sides but even° now   *just*
Co-rivalled greatness? Either to harbour fled,
Or made a toast for Neptune.[5] Even so
45 Doth valour's show and valour's worth divide
In storms of fortune. For in her° ray and brightness   *(fortune's)*
The herd hath more annoyance by the breese°   *gadfly*
Than by the tiger; but when the splitting wind
Makes flexible the knees° of knotted° oaks   *tough timber / gnarled*
50 And flies flee under shade, why then the thing of courage,°   *brave person*
As roused with rage, with rage doth sympathize,[6]
And with an accent tuned in selfsame key
Retorts to chiding fortune.
ULYSSES   Agamemnon,
Thou great commander, nerve° and bone of Greece,   *sinew*
55 Heart of our numbers,° soul and only spirit   *troops*
In whom the tempers and the minds of all
Should be shut up,° hear what Ulysses speaks.   *encapsulated*
Besides th'applause° and approbation   *approval*
The which, [*to* AGAMEMNON] most mighty for thy place and
sway,°   *position and power*
60 And thou, [*to* NESTOR] most reverend for thy stretched-out life,
I give to both your speeches—which were such
As, Agamemnon, every hand of Greece
Should hold up high in brass,° and such again   *record permanently*
As, venerable Nestor, hatched[7] in silver,
65 Should with a bond of air, strong as the axle-tree[8]
On which the heavens ride, knit all Greeks' ears
To his experienced tongue—yet let it please both,
Thou [*to* AGAMEMNON] great, and [*to* NESTOR] wise, to hear Ulysses speak.
AGAMEMNON   Speak, Prince of Ithaca, and be't of less expect°   *likelihood*
70 That matter needless, of importless burden,°   *irrelevant meaning*
Divide thy lips, than we are confident
When rank° Thersites opes his mastic° jaws   *rancid / abusive*
We shall hear music, wit, and oracle.
ULYSSES   Troy, yet upon his basis,° had been down   *still standing*
75 And the great Hector's sword had lacked a master
But for these instances:°   *causes*
The specialty° of rule hath been neglected.   *rights and duties*
And look how many° Grecian tents do stand   *however many*
Hollow° upon this plain: so many hollow° factions.   *Empty / false*
80 When that the general is not like the <u>hive</u>
To whom the foragers° shall all repair,   *food collectors*
What honey is expected? Degree° being vizarded,°   *Rank / concealed*

4. Sea goddess (mother of Achilles), here standing for the sea.
5. Morsel of toasted bread, floated in wine, for the god of the sea.
6. Himself enraged, behaves like the raging storm.
7. Etched with parallel lines, as if inlaid with precious metal (alluding to Nestor's white hair and beard, or his wrinkled face).
8. *bond of air*: persuasive rhetoric. *axle-tree*: the axis on which the universe was imagined to revolve, earth being at the center.

Th'unworthiest shows as fairly in the masque
[   ].⁹

85   The heavens themselves, the planets, and this centre°   *(the earth)*
Observe degree, priority, and place,
Infixture,° course, proportion, season, form,   *Fixity*
Office° and custom, in all line of order.   *Function*
And therefore is the glorious planet Sol¹
90   In noble eminence enthroned and sphered°   *placed in orbit*
Amidst the other,° whose med'cinable² eye   *rest*
Corrects the ill aspects° of planets evil   *astrological influence*
And posts° like the commandment of a king,   *hastens*
Sans° check, to good and bad. But when the planets   *Without*
95   In evil mixture to disorder wander,³
What plagues and what portents, what mutiny?
What raging of the sea, shaking of earth?
Commotion in the winds, frights, changes,° horrors   *political strife*
Divert and crack, rend and deracinate°   *uproot*
100 The unity and married calm of states
Quite from their fixture. O when degree is shaked,
Which is the ladder to all high designs,
The enterprise is sick. How could communities,
Degrees in schools,° and brotherhoods° in cities,   *Academic rank / guilds*
105 Peaceful commerce from dividable° shores,   *isolated*
The primogenity° and due of birth,   *primogeniture*
Prerogative of age, crowns, sceptres, laurels,
But by degree stand in authentic place?
Take but degree away, untune that string,
110 And hark what discord follows. Each thing meets
In mere oppugnancy.° The bounded waters   *total antagonism*
Should lift their bosoms higher than the shores
And make a sop° of all this solid globe;   *lump of soaked bread*
Strength should be lord of imbecility,°   *weakness*
115 And the rude son should strike his father dead.
Force should be right—or rather, right and wrong,
Between whose endless jar justice resides,⁴
Should lose their names, and so should justice too.
Then everything includes itself in° power,   *comes down to*
120 Power into will,° will into appetite;   *egotism; lust*
And appetite, an universal wolf,
So doubly seconded with will and power,
Must make perforce an universal prey,°   *seizing*
And last eat up himself. Great Agamemnon,
125 This chaos, when degree is suffocate,
Follows the choking.
And this neglection of degree it is
That by a pace goes backward in a purpose
It hath to climb.⁵ The general's disdained
130 By him one step below; he, by the next;
That next, by him beneath. So every step,

---

9. A line providing the contrast to 'Th'unworthiest" may be lost.
1. In the Ptolemaic system, the sun was thought to be a planet revolving round the earth.
2. Curative. The eyes were thought to see by emitting rays—like the sun. Kings sometimes claimed a similar ability to cure.

3. The word "planets" means "wanderers," referring to their apparently erratic course, as seen from earth. *evil mixture*: wicked coupling.
4. Justice stands between the clashing ("jar") of the opposing contenders.
5. *That . . . climb*: That drops back step by step when it intends to climb.

Examped by the first pace that is sick
Of his superior, grows to an envious fever
Of pale and bloodless emulation.°   *sick rivalry*
135   And 'tis this fever that keeps Troy on foot,°   *standing*
Not her own sinews. To end a tale of length:
Troy in our weakness lives, not in her strength.
   NESTOR   Most wisely hath Ulysses here discovered°   *revealed*
The fever whereof all our power is sick.
140   AGAMEMNON   The nature of the sickness found, Ulysses,
What is the remedy?
   ULYSSES   The great Achilles, whom opinion° crowns   *consensus*
The sinew and the forehand° of our host,°   *strongest / army*
Having his ear full of his airy° fame   *lofty; insubstantial*
145   Grows dainty of° his worth, and in his tent   *too conscious of*
Lies mocking our designs. With him Patroclus
Upon a lazy bed the livelong day
Breaks scurrile° jests   *scurrilous*
And, with ridiculous and awkward action°   *gesture*
150   Which, slanderer, he 'imitation' calls,
He pageants° us. Sometime, great Agamemnon,   *mimics*
Thy topless deputation° he puts on,   *supreme rank*
And like a strutting player, whose conceit
Lies in his hamstring[6] and doth think it rich
155   To hear the wooden dialogue and sound
'Twixt his stretched footing and the scaffoldage,[7]
Such to-be-pitied and o'er-wrested seeming°   *pitiful imitation*
He acts thy greatness in. And when he speaks
'Tis like a chime a-mending, with terms unsquared[8]
160   Which from the tongue of roaring Typhon[9] dropped
Would seem hyperboles. At this fusty° stuff   *stale; bombastic*
The large Achilles on his pressed[1] bed lolling
From his deep chest laughs out a loud applause,
Cries 'Excellent! 'Tis Agamemnon just.°   *exactly*
165   Now play me Nestor, hem° and stroke thy beard,   *(as in "ahem")*
As he being dressed to° some oration.'   *preparing for*
That's done as near as the extremest ends
Of parallels, as like as Vulcan and his wife.[2]
Yet god° Achilles still cries, 'Excellent!   *semidivine (ironic)*
170   'Tis Nestor right. Now play him me, Patroclus,
Arming to answer in° a night alarm'.   *respond to*
And then forsooth the faint° defects of age   *weak*
Must be the scene of mirth: to cough and spit,
And with a palsy, fumbling on his gorget,°   *throat armor*
175   Shake in and out the rivet.° And at this sport   *fastening bolt*
Sir Valour dies,° cries, 'O enough, Patroclus!   *(laughing)*
Or give me ribs of steel. I shall split all
In pleasure of my spleen.'° And in this fashion   *(seat of mirth)*
All our abilities, gifts, natures, shapes,

---

6. *whose . . . hamstring*: whose brains are in his thighs.
7. *To hear . . . scaffoldage*: To hear the sound of his long, powerful strides (and dull speech?) on the platform stage.
8. Like bells being repaired (or tuned?), with ill-fitting expressions.
9. Monster with a hundred heads, each uttering the cry of a different beast; eventually buried by Jupiter under (and so associated with) a volcano.

1. Weighed down (by Achilles).
2. *as near . . . wife*: as closely as the ends of parallel lines (which, since they are equidistant, never meet), and as the ugly, limping god Vulcan, the smith, resembles his beautiful wife Venus. Ulysses is stressing how bad the acting is, while at the same time covertly belittling Agamemnon and Nestor.

180	Severals and generals of grace exact,[3]	
	Achievements, plots, orders, preventions,°	*precautions*
	Excitements° to the field or speech for truce,	*Urgings*
	Success or loss, what is or is not, serves	
	As stuff for these two to make paradoxes.°	*absurdities*
185	NESTOR And in the imitation of these twain	
	Who, as Ulysses says, opinion crowns	
	With an imperial voice, many are infect.°	*infected*
	Ajax is grown self-willed and bears his head	
	In such a rein,° in full as proud a place	*So high*
190	As broad Achilles, and keeps° his tent like him,	*stays within*
	Makes factious feasts, rails on° our state of war	*complains about*
	Bold as an oracle, and sets Thersites,	
	A slave whose gall° coins slanders like a mint,	*rancor*
	To match us in comparisons with dirt,	
195	To weaken and discredit our exposure,°	*exposed position*
	How rank° so ever rounded in with° danger.	*densely / hemmed in by*
	ULYSSES They tax° our policy and call it cowardice,	*criticize*
	Count wisdom as no member of the war,	
	Forestall prescience° and esteem no act	*advance planning*
200	But that of hand. The still and mental parts	
	That do contrive how many hands shall strike	
	When fitness° calls them on, and know by measure	*the right moment*
	Of their observant toil the enemy's weight,°	*power*
	Why, this hath not a finger's dignity.	
205	They call this 'bed-work', 'mapp'ry',° 'closet war'.	*mere mapping; planning*
	So that the ram that batters down the wall,	
	For the great swinge and rudeness of his poise[4]	
	They place before° his hand that made the engine,°	*exalt above / (the ram)*
	Or those that with the finesse° of their souls	*subtlety*
210	By reason guide his execution.°	*the ram's use*
	NESTOR Let this be granted, and Achilles' horse	
	Makes many Thetis' sons.[5]	
	Tucket°	*Trumpet call*
	AGAMEMNON What trumpet?	
	Look, Menelaus.	
	MENELAUS From Troy.	
	Enter AENEAS [*and a trumpeter*]	
	AGAMEMNON What would you fore° our tent?	*before*
215	AENEAS Is this great Agamemnon's tent I pray you?	
	AGAMEMNON Even this.	
	AENEAS May one that is a herald and a prince	
	Do a fair message to his kingly ears?	
	AGAMEMNON With surety° stronger than Achilles' arm,	*security*
220	Fore all the Greekish heads, which with one voice	
	Call Agamemnon heart and general.	
	AENEAS Fair leave and large° security. How may	*generous*
	A stranger to those most imperial looks	
	Know them from eyes of other mortals?	
	AGAMEMNON How?	
225	AENEAS Ay, I ask that I might waken reverence	

---

3. Supreme merits, possessed individually and in common.
4. Because of the impetus and violence of its impact.

5. *Let . . . sons*: If this is true, then Achilles' horse is worth many Achilleses. Thetis was the mother of Achilles.

And on the cheek be ready with a blush
Modest as morning when she coldly eyes
The youthful Phoebus.[6]
Which is that god in office, guiding men?
230   Which is the high and mighty Agamemnon?
AGAMEMNON [*to the Greeks*]   This Trojan scorns us, or the men of Troy
Are ceremonious courtiers.
AENEAS   Courtiers as free,° as debonair,° unarmed,   *generous / gracious*
As bending° angels—that's their fame in peace.   *ministering*
235   But when they would seem soldiers they have galls,[7]
Good arms, strong joints, true swords—and great Jove's acorn[8]
Nothing so full of heart.° But peace, Aeneas,   *courage; nutmeat*
Peace, Trojan; lay thy finger on thy lips.
The worthiness of praise distains° his worth,   *stains*
240   If that the praised himself bring the praise forth.
But what, repining,° the enemy commends,   *grudging(ly)*
That breath fame blows; that praise, sole pure, transcends.
AGAMEMNON   Sir, you of Troy, call you yourself Aeneas?
AENEAS   Ay, Greek,° that is my name.   *cheater (slang)*
AGAMEMNON   What's your affair, I pray you?
245   AENEAS   Sir, pardon, 'tis for Agamemnon's ears.
AGAMEMNON   He hears naught privately that comes from Troy.
AENEAS   Nor I from Troy come not to whisper him.
I bring a trumpet to awake his ear,
To set his sense on the attentive bent,
And then to speak.
250   AGAMEMNON   Speak frankly° as the wind.   *freely*
It is not Agamemnon's sleeping hour.
That thou shalt know, Trojan, he is awake,
He tells thee so himself.
AENEAS   Trumpet,° blow loud.   *Trumpeter*
Send thy brass voice through all these lazy tents,
255   And every Greek of mettle let him know
What Troy means fairly shall be spoke aloud.
        The trumpet sound[s]
We have, great Agamemnon, here in Troy
A prince called Hector—Priam is his father—
Who in this dull and long-continued truce
260   Is resty° grown. He bade me take a trumpet   *lazy*
And to this purpose speak: 'Kings, princes, lords,
If there be one among the fair'st of Greece
That holds his honour higher than his ease,
That seeks his praise more than he fears his peril,
265   That knows his valour and knows not his fear,
That loves his mistress more than in confession
With truant vows to her own lips he loves,[9]
And dare avow her beauty and her worth
In other arms than hers°—to him this challenge.   *armor; Hector's arms*
270   Hector in view of Trojans and of Greeks
Shall make it good, or do his best to do it:
He hath a lady wiser, fairer, truer,
Than ever Greek did compass° in his arms,   *hold*

6. *Modest . . . Phoebus:* Modest as Aurora, the blushing
dawn personified, when she coldly eyes Apollo, the sun
god ("youthful" because it is early morning).
7. But when it is time for them to be warriors, their courageous tempers do not tolerate mistreatment.
8. The oak was Jupiter's tree.
9. *That . . . loves:* Who will declare his love with stronger
proof (deeds) than unreliable, private promises.

And will tomorrow with his trumpet call
275   Midway between your tents and walls of Troy
To rouse a Grecian that is true in love.
If any come, Hector shall honour him.
If none, he'll say in Troy when he retires
The Grecian dames are sunburnt° and not worth   *not fair*
280   The splinter° of a lance.' Even so much.   *breaking; fragment*
AGAMEMNON   This shall be told our lovers, Lord Aeneas.
If none of them have soul in such a kind,
We left them all at home. But we are soldiers,
And may that soldier a mere recreant prove
285   That means not, hath not,[1] or is not in love.
If then one is, or hath, or means to be,
That one meets Hector. If none else, I'll be he.
NESTOR [*to* AENEAS]   Tell him of Nestor, one that was a man
When Hector's grandsire sucked. He is old now,
290   But if there be not in our Grecian mould°   *character; model*
One noble man that hath one spark of fire
To answer for his love, tell him from me
I'll hide my silver beard in a gold beaver°   *helmet's face guard*
And in my vambrace° put this withered brawn,°   *forearm armor / arm*
295   And meeting him will tell him that my lady
Was fairer than his grandam, and as chaste
As may be in the world. His youth in flood,°   *Despite his youth*
I'll prove this truth with my three drops of blood.
AENEAS   Now heavens forbid such scarcity of youth.
300   ULYSSES   Amen.
AGAMEMNON   Fair Lord Aeneas, let me touch° your hand.   *shake*
To our pavilion shall I lead you first.
Achilles shall have word of this intent;
So shall each lord of Greece, from tent to tent.
305   Yourself shall feast with us before you go,
And find the welcome of a noble foe.
            Exeunt. Manent° ULYSSES *and* NESTOR   *Remain*
ULYSSES   Nestor!
NESTOR   What says Ulysses?
ULYSSES   I have a young
Conception in my brain; be you my time[2]
To bring it to some shape.
NESTOR   What is't?
ULYSSES   This 'tis:
310   Blunt wedges rive° hard knots. The seeded pride   *split*
That hath to this maturity blown° up   *swelled*
In rank° Achilles must or° now be cropped   *overgrown / either*
Or, shedding,° breed a nursery of like evil   *dropping its seed*
To overbulk° us all.   *overrun*
NESTOR   Well, and how?
315   ULYSSES   This challenge that the gallant Hector sends,
However it is spread in general name,
Relates in purpose only to Achilles.
NESTOR   The purpose is perspicuous,° even as substance°   *easy to see / wealth*
Whose grossness little characters sum up.[3]

---

1. Who does not aim (to be), has never been.
2. *Conception . . . time*: The primary meaning (unfolding
of a plan) metaphorically extended to pregnancy's onset
and gestation period, the latter associated with the male

and aged Nestor, who is oddly associated with this female
and ordinarily youthful activity, presumably because he
embodies the passage of time.
3. Whose size is reckoned by small figures (on paper).

320 And, in the publication, make no strain[4]
But that Achilles, were his brain as barren
As banks of Libya°—though, Apollo knows,   *the Sahara desert*
'Tis dry° enough—will with great speed of judgement,   *infertile; empty*
Ay with celerity, find Hector's purpose
325 Pointing on him.°   *himself*

ULYSSES And wake him to the answer, think you?

NESTOR Yes, 'tis most meet.° Who may you else oppose,   *fitting*
That can from Hector bring his honour off,
If not Achilles? Though't be a sportful combat,
330 Yet in this trial much opinion° dwells,   *reputation*
For here the Trojans taste our dear'st repute
With their fin'st palate. And trust to me, Ulysses,
Our imputation° shall be oddly poised[5]   *reputation*
In this wild° action: for the success,   *uncontrollable*
335 Although particular, shall give a scantling
Of good or bad unto the general[6]—
And in such indices,° although small pricks   *tables of contents*
To° their subsequent volumes, there is seen   *Compared to*
The baby figure of the giant mass
340 Of things to come at large. It is supposed
He that meets Hector issues from our choice,
And choice, being mutual act of all our souls,
Makes merit her election,° and doth boil,   *grounds of choice*
As 'twere, from forth us all a man distilled
345 Out of our virtues—who miscarrying,°   *should he lose*
What heart from hence receives the conqu'ring part
To steel a strong opinion to themselves?[7]
Which entertained, limbs are e'en his instruments,
In no less working than are swords and bows
350 Directive by the limbs.[8]

ULYSSES   Give pardon to my speech:
Therefore 'tis meet° Achilles meet not Hector.   *appropriate*
Let us like merchants show our foulest wares
And think perchance they'll sell. If not,
The lustre of the better yet to show°   *not yet shown*
355 Shall show the better. Do not consent
That ever Hector and Achilles meet,
For both our honour and our shame in this
Are dogged with two strange followers.°   *surprising results*

NESTOR I see them not with my old eyes. What are they?

360 ULYSSES What glory our Achilles shares° from Hector,   *gains*
Were he not proud we all should wear° with him.   *share*
But he already is too insolent,
And we were better parch in Afric sun
Than in the pride and salt° scorn of his eyes,   *bitter*
365 Should he scape Hector fair. If he were foiled,
Why then we did our main opinion° crush   *common reputation*
In taint of° our best man. No, make a lott'ry,   *In the dishonor of*

---

4. And, with the announcement, do not doubt.
5. Disproportionately judged.
6. *the success . . . general*: the outcome, although relating only to one person, shall serve as an example of the whole army's abilities.
7. *What . . . themselves*: What (Greek) warriors could possibly get a sense of victory from this that would make them feel more confident?; what motivation will the Trojans get from this to make them feel more confident?
8. *Which . . . limbs*: Assuming that this confidence ("strong opinion") is received from the victory, the soldiers' limbs become the mechanisms ("instruments") of that confidence in the same way that swords and bows are subject to direction by the limbs themselves.

And by device let blockish° Ajax draw   *blockheaded*
The sort° to fight with Hector. Among ourselves   *lot*
370   Give him allowance° as the worthier man—   *acknowledgment*
For that will physic the great Myrmidon,[9]
Who broils in° loud applause, and make him fall°   *is excited by / lower*
His crest, that prouder than blue Iris[1] bends.
If the dull brainless Ajax come safe off,
375   We'll dress him up in voices;° if he fail,   *sing his praises*
Yet go we under our opinion still
That we have better men. But hit or miss,
Our project's life° this shape of sense° assumes: *success / rationale*
Ajax employed plucks down Achilles' plumes.
380   NESTOR   Now, Ulysses, I begin to relish thy advice,
And I will give a taste of it forthwith
To Agamemnon. Go we to him straight.°   *immediately*
Two curs shall tame each other; pride alone
Must tarre the mastiffs on,[2] as 'twere° their bone.   *Exeunt*   *if it were*

2.1

Enter AJAX *and* THERSITES

AJAX   Thersites.

THERSITES   Agamemnon—how if he had boils, full,° all over,   *(of pus)*
generally?

AJAX   Thersites.

5   THERSITES   And those boils did run? Say so, did not the General
run then? Were not that a botchy core?°   *ulcerous center*

AJAX   Dog.

THERSITES   Then there would come some matter° from him. I   *pus; sense*
see none now.

10   AJAX   Thou bitch-wolf's son, canst thou not hear? Feel then.
[*He*] *strikes* [THERSITES]

THERSITES   The plague of Greece upon thee, thou mongrel[1]
beef-witted° lord!   *dumb as an ox*

AJAX   Speak then, thou unsifted leaven,° speak! I will beat[2] thee   *dough*
into handsomeness.°   *decency; good looks*

15   THERSITES   I shall sooner rail thee into wit and holiness. But I
think thy horse will sooner con° an oration than thou learn a   *memorize*
prayer without book.°   *by heart*
[AJAX *strikes him*]
Thou canst strike, canst thou? A red murrain° o' thy jade's[3]   *bloody plague*
tricks.

20   AJAX   Toad's stool![4]
[*He strikes* THERSITES]
Learn me° the proclamation.   *Instruct me (about)*

THERSITES   Dost thou think I have no sense,° thou strikest me   *feeling*
thus?

AJAX   The proclamation.

25   THERSITES   Thou art proclaimed a fool, I think.

AJAX   Do not, porcupine,[5] do not. My fingers itch.°   *(to hit you)*

---

9. Will give medicine to (purge) Achilles, who led the
Myrmidons.
1. Goddess of the rainbow; blue flower.
2. Must incite these large, aggressive dogs.
2.1 Location: The Greek camp.
1. Ajax's mother was Trojan; hence, he was of mixed

breed, "mongrel."
2. Punning on the pounding of bread dough.
3. Temperamental horse's.
4. Toadstools were once thought to be a toad's poisonous
excrement (stool).

THERSITES   I would thou didst itch from head to foot. An° I had   *If*
the scratching of thee, I would make thee the loathsomest
scab in Greece.

30 AJAX   I say, the proclamation.

THERSITES   Thou grumblest and railest every hour on Achilles,
and thou art as full of envy at his greatness as Cerberus is at
Proserpina's[6] beauty, ay, that thou barkest at him.

AJAX   Mistress[7] Thersites.

35 THERSITES   Thou shouldst strike him.

AJAX   Cobloaf.°   *Small crusty loaf*

THERSITES   He would pun° thee into shivers° with his fist, as a   *pound / pieces*
sailor breaks a biscuit.

AJAX   You whoreson cur.
[*He strikes* THERSITES]

40 THERSITES   Do! Do!°   *Go on*

AJAX   Thou stool° for a witch.   *privy*
[*He strikes* THERSITES]

THERSITES   Ay, do, do! Thou sodden-witted° lord, thou hast in   *boiled-brained*
thy skull no more brain than I have in mine elbows. An *asnico*°   *little ass*
may tutor thee. Thou scurvy valiant ass, thou art here but to
45 thrash Trojans, and thou art bought and sold[8] among those of
any wit like a barbarian slave. If thou use° to beat me, I will   *continue*
begin at thy heel and tell what thou art by inches, thou thing
of no bowels,° thou.   *with no pity*

AJAX   You dog.

50 THERSITES   You scurvy lord.

AJAX   You cur.
[*He strikes* THERSITES]

THERSITES   Mars his idiot!° Do, rudeness! Do, camel, do, do!   *God of war's jester*

Enter ACHILLES *and* PATROCLUS

ACHILLES   Why, how now, Ajax? Wherefore do ye thus?
How now, Thersites? What's the matter, man?

55 THERSITES   You see him there? Do you?

ACHILLES   Ay. What's the matter?

THERSITES   Nay, look upon him.

ACHILLES   So I do. What's the matter?

THERSITES   Nay, but regard him well.

60 ACHILLES   'Well'? Why, I do so.

THERSITES   But yet you look not well upon him.[9] For whoso-
mever you take him to be, he is Ajax.°   *a jakes = toilet*

ACHILLES   I know that, fool.

THERSITES   Ay, but 'that fool' knows not himself.[1]

65 AJAX   Therefore I beat thee.[2]

THERSITES   Lo,° lo, lo, lo, what modicums of wit he utters. His   *Behold (sarcastic)*
evasions have ears thus long.[3] I have bobbed° his brain more   *thumped*

---

5. The porcupine's sharp quills were emblematic of the
satirist (here, Thersites).
6. Cerberus was the monstrous three-headed dog who
guarded the gate of Hades. Proserpina was Queen of
Hades and wife of Pluto, god of the underworld.
7. Because a woman's only weapon was thought to be her
tongue, because Thersites is a coward, or because he is
believed to be homosexual.
8. You are traded like goods—hence, treated as an object,
treated contemptuously.
9. Thersites is probably feigning amazement that Achil-

les can look at Ajax and yet not see what a fool he is; but
he may also mean that Achilles does not do well to favor
("look . . . upon") him.
1. Thersites deliberately understands Achilles' line without the intended comma: "I know that fool" (Ajax), rather
than "I know that [fact], fool."
2. Ajax thinks Thersites is calling himself (rather than
Ajax) a "fool" who does not know himself.
3. His efforts to dodge witty rejoinders are like an
ass's—hence asinine.

than he has beat my bones. I will° buy nine sparrows for a   *can*
penny, and his *pia mater*° is not worth the ninth part of a spar-   *brain*
70   row. This lord, Achilles—Ajax, who wears his wit in his belly
and his guts in his head—I'll tell you what I say of him.

ACHILLES   What?

THERSITES   I say, this Ajax—

         [AJAX *threatens to strike him*]

ACHILLES   Nay, good Ajax.

75   THERSITES   Has not so much wit—

         [AJAX *threatens to strike him*]

ACHILLES [*to* AJAX]   Nay, I must hold° you.   *restrain*

THERSITES   As will stop the eye of Helen's needle,[4] for whom he
comes to fight.

ACHILLES   Peace, fool.

80   THERSITES   I would have peace and quietness, but the fool° will   *Ajax*
not. He, there, that he, look you there.

AJAX   O thou damned cur I shall—

ACHILLES [*to* AJAX]   Will you set your wit to° a fool's?   *against*

THERSITES   No, I warrant you, for a fool's will shame it.

85   PATROCLUS   Good words,° Thersites.   *Speak with restraint*

ACHILLES [*to* AJAX]   What's the quarrel?

AJAX   I bade the vile owl[5] go learn me the tenor of the proclamation, and he rails upon me.

THERSITES   I serve thee not.

90   AJAX   Well, go to, go to.

THERSITES   I serve here voluntary.°   *as a volunteer*

ACHILLES   Your last service was sufferance. 'Twas not voluntary:
no man is beaten voluntary. Ajax was here the voluntary, and
you as under an impress.[6]

95   THERSITES   E'en so. A great deal of your wit, too, lies in your
sinews, or else there be liars. Hector shall have a great catch an
a° knock out either of your brains. A were as good° crack a   *if he / might as well*
fusty° nut with no kernel.   *rotten*

ACHILLES   What, with me too, Thersites?

100   THERSITES   There's Ulysses and old Nestor, whose wit was
mouldy ere your grandsires had nails on their toes, yoke you
like draught oxen and make you plough up the war.°   *(pun on ware = crops)*

ACHILLES   What? What?

THERSITES   Yes, good sooth. To° Achilles! To, Ajax, to—   *(urging on the oxen)*

105   AJAX   I shall cut out your tongue.

THERSITES   'Tis no matter. I shall speak as much wit as thou
afterwards.

PATROCLUS   No more words, Thersites, peace.

THERSITES   I will hold my peace when Achilles' brach° bids me,   *bitch*
110   shall I?

ACHILLES   There's for you, Patroclus.

THERSITES   I will see you hanged like clodpolls° ere I come any   *blockheads*
more to your tents. I will keep where there is wit stirring, and
leave the faction of fools.   *Exit*

115   PATROCLUS   A good riddance.

---

4. "Eye" perhaps alludes to "vagina"; "needle" is also   6. As a conscript; being hit as though with a stamp (by
obscene. *stop*: fill.   Ajax).
5. The owl is associated with evil portent.

ACHILLES [*to* AJAX]   Marry, this, sir, is proclaimed through all our host:
That Hector, by the fifth hour° of the sun,   *11 A.M.*
Will with a trumpet 'twixt our tents and Troy
Tomorrow morning call some knight to arms
120   That hath a stomach,° and such a one that dare   *appetite for combat*
Maintain—I know not what. 'Tis trash. Farewell.
AJAX   Farewell. Who shall answer him?
ACHILLES   I know not. 'Tis put to lott'ry. Otherwise,
He knew his man.   [*Exeunt* ACHILLES *and* PATROCLUS]
125   AJAX   O, meaning you? I will go learn more of it.   *Exit*

2.2

[*Sennet.*] *Enter* [*King*] PRIAM, HECTOR, TROILUS, PARIS,
and HELENUS

PRIAM   After so many hours, lives, speeches spent,
Thus once again says Nestor from the Greeks:
'Deliver Helen, and all damage else—
As honour, loss of time, travail,° expense,   *hard labor*
5   Wounds, friends, and what else dear° that is consumed   *beloved; costly*
In hot digestion of this cormorant° war—   *rapacious*
Shall be struck off.'° Hector, what say you to't?   *expunged*
HECTOR   Though no man lesser fears the Greeks than I,
As far as toucheth my particular,° yet, dread Priam,   *own concerns*
10   There is no lady of more softer bowels,°   *compassion*
More spongy to suck in° the sense of fear,   *able to absorb*
More ready to cry out, 'Who knows what follows?'
Than Hector is. The wound of peace is surety,[1]
Surety secure; but modest doubt is called
15   The beacon° of the wise, the tent[2] that searches   *lighthouse*
To th' bottom of the worst. Let Helen go.
Since the first sword was drawn about this question,
Every tithe-soul, 'mongst many thousand dimes,
Hath been as dear as Helen[3]—I mean, of ours.
20   If we have lost so many tenths of ours
To guard a thing not ours—nor worth to us,
Had it our name, the value of one ten[4]—
What merit's in that reason which denies
The yielding of her up?
TROILUS   Fie, fie, my brother!
25   Weigh you the worth and honour of a king
So great as our dread father in a scale
Of common ounces? Will you with counters° sum   *worthless chips*
The past-proportion of his infinite,[5]
And buckle in a waist most fathomless[6]
30   With spans° and inches so diminutive   *nine inches*
As fears and reasons?° Fie, for godly shame!   *(pun on "raisins")*
HELENUS   No marvel though you bite so sharp at reasons,

2.2 Location: The palace in Troy.
1. (Overconfident) sense of security.
2. Surgeon's probe.
3. *Every . . . Helen:* Every soul taken to pay the tithe (a tenth of one's goods, paid as a tax), among many thousand "dimes" (tenths; tithes paid, through soldiers' deaths), has been as valuable as Helen.
4. Even if Helen were Trojan, the value of one-tenth (one

of the men lost).
5. Add up the infinitude of his measurelessness.
6. Most immeasurable even in fathoms (6 foot lengths, used in calculating sea depths). "Waist" puns on "waste" as uninhabited expanse, especially the ocean, and as the squandering of resources (the second unintended by Troilus).

You are so empty of them. Should not our father
Bear the great sway of his affairs with reason
35 Because your speech hath none that tells him so?
TROILUS   You are for dreams and slumbers, brother priest.
You fur your gloves with 'reason'.[7] Here are your reasons:
You know an enemy intends you harm,
You know a sword employed is perilous,
40 And reason flies the object of all harm.°   *any sight of danger*
Who marvels then, when Helenus beholds
A Grecian and his sword, if he do set
The very wings of reason to his heels
And fly like chidden Mercury[8] from Jove,
45 Or like a star disorbed?° Nay, if we talk of reason,   *a shooting star*
Let's shut our gates and sleep. Manhood and honour
Should have hare° hearts, would they but fat their thoughts   *timid*
With this crammed° reason. Reason and respect°   *fattened / deliberation*
Make livers° pale and lustihood° deject.   *courage / energy*
50 HECTOR   Brother, she is not worth what she doth cost
The holding.°   *To keep*
TROILUS   What's aught but as 'tis valued?[9]
HECTOR   But value dwells not in particular will.°   *individual desire*
It holds his° estimate and dignity   *its*
As well wherein 'tis precious of itself
55 As in the prizer. 'Tis mad idolatry
To make the service° greater than the god;   *the devotion paid*
And the will dotes that is inclinable
To what infectiously itself affects
Without some image of th'affected merit.[1]
60 TROILUS   I take today a wife, and my election°   *choice*
Is led on in the conduct° of my will;   *under the guidance*
My will enkindled by mine eyes and ears,
Two traded° pilots 'twixt the dangerous shores   *experienced*
Of will and judgement. How may I avoid—
65 Although my will distaste what it elected—
The wife I chose? There can be no evasion
To blench° from this and to stand firm by honour.   *shy away*
We turn not back° the silks upon° the merchant   *don't return / to*
When we have spoiled them; nor the remainder viands°   *uneaten food*
70 We do not throw in unrespective° sewer   *undiscriminating*
Because we now are full. It was thought meet°   *appropriate that*
Paris should do some vengeance on the Greeks.
Your breath of full consent bellied° his sails;   *swelled*
The seas and winds, old wranglers,° took a truce   *opponents*
75 And did him service. He touched the ports desired,
And for an old aunt whom the Greeks held captive[2]
He brought a Grecian queen,° whose youth and freshness   *pun on quean = whore?*

7. You rationalize your desire for comfort.
8. Messenger of the gods, usually pictured with wings on his heels. Mercury was once arraigned before Jove for stealing cattle and was ordered to go and return them.
9. That is, no absolute measure of value exists; there is only the esteem granted to an object by particular individuals.
1. *the will . . . merit:* the will is foolishly obsessed that is committed to what it likes in a sick way (having caught

this desire like a disease), without some conception of that object's real value. The point is related to Jesus' attack on the scribes and Pharisees in Matthew 23, for instance verse 19: "whether is greater, the offering, or the altar which sanctifieth the offering?"
2. Hesione, Priam's sister, kidnapped by the Greeks; "aunt" is also slang for "whore." The "vengeance" (line 72) is for the kidnapping.

Wrinkles Apollo's and makes stale the morning.[3]
Why keep we her? The Grecians keep our aunt.
80 Is she worth keeping? Why, she is a pearl
Whose price hath launched above a thousand ships[4]
And turned crowned kings to merchants.
If you'll avouch 'twas wisdom Paris went—
As you must needs, for you all cried, 'Go, go!';
85 If you'll confess he brought home noble prize—
As you must needs, for you all clapped your hands
And cried, 'Inestimable!'—why do you now
The issue° of your proper° wisdoms rate,°   *result / own / berate*
And do a deed that never fortune did:[5]
90 Beggar the estimation[6] which you prized
Richer than sea and land? O theft most base,
That we have stol'n what we do fear to keep!
But thieves unworthy of a thing so stol'n,
That in their country did them that disgrace
95 We fear to warrant in our native place.[7]
CASSANDRA [*within*]
Cry, Trojans, cry!
PRIAM   What noise? What shriek is this?
TROILUS   'Tis our mad sister. I do know her voice.
CASSANDRA [*within*]   Cry, Trojans!
HECTOR   It is Cassandra.

Enter CASSANDRA[8] *raving, with her hair about her ears*

100 CASSANDRA   Cry, Trojans, cry! Lend me ten thousand eyes
And I will fill them with prophetic tears.
HECTOR   Peace, sister, peace.
CASSANDRA   Virgins and boys, mid-age, and wrinkled old,°   *old people*
Soft infancy that nothing canst° but cry,   *can do*
105 Add to my clamours. Let us pay betimes°   *in advance*
A moiety° of that mass° of moan to come.   *portion / sum*
Cry, Trojans, cry! Practise your eyes with tears.°   *Learn to weep*
Troy must not be, nor goodly Ilium stand.
Our firebrand[9] brother, Paris, burns us all.
110 Cry, Trojans, cry! Ah Helen, and ah woe!
Cry, cry 'Troy burns!'—or else let Helen go.   *Exit*
HECTOR   Now, youthful Troilus, do not these high strains
Of divination in our sister work
Some touches of remorse? Or is your blood
115 So madly hot that no discourse of reason,
Nor fear of bad success° in a bad cause,   *outcome*
Can qualify° the same?   *moderate*
TROILUS   Why, brother Hector,
We may not think the justness of each act
Such and no other than the event doth form it,[1]

3. Helen's "youth and freshness" by comparison make Apollo's (hence also the sun's) "youth and freshness" seem old and rosy dawn seem dried out (but also, unintentionally on Troilus's part, sluttish).
4. A well-worn phrase even when Marlowe used it in *Doctor Faustus*: "Was this the face that launched a thousand ships?" Here given a mercantile turn.
5. And act more erratically than fortune.
6. Deem worthless the valued object.
7. *That . . . place*: (We Trojans) who in Greece dishonored the Greeks but back home are afraid to stand up for what we did.
8. Apollo gave Cassandra the gift of prophecy to win her love, but because she rejected his wooing, he cursed her by causing her prophecies to be disregarded.
9. When pregnant with Paris, Hecuba dreamed of giving birth to a firebrand.
1. *We . . . it*: We must not judge the "justness" of our cause only by the results.

120 Nor once deject° the courage of our minds   *reduce*
Because Cassandra's mad. Her brainsick raptures
Cannot distaste° the goodness of a quarrel   *make distasteful*
Which hath our several honours all engaged
To make it gracious.° For my private part,   *righteous; successful*
125 I am no more touched° than all Priam's sons.   *implicated*
And Jove forbid there should be done amongst us
Such things as might offend the weakest spleen
To fight for and maintain.²

PARIS   Else might the world convince° of levity   *convict*
130 As well my undertakings as your counsels.
But I attest° the gods, your full consent   *call to witness*
Gave wings to my propension° and cut off   *leaning*
All fears attending on so dire a project.
For what, alas, can these my single arms?°   *can my arms do alone*
135 What propugnation° is in one man's valour   *defense*
To stand the push° and enmity of those   *thrust*
This quarrel would excite?° Yet I protest,   *incite to battle*
Were I alone to pass° the difficulties   *endure*
And had as ample power as I have will,
140 Paris should ne'er retract what he hath done
Nor faint in the pursuit.

PRIAM   Paris, you speak
Like one besotted° on your sweet delights.   *drunk*
You have the honey still, but these the gall.
So° to be valiant is no praise at all.   *In such circumstances*
145 PARIS   Sir, I propose not merely to myself°   *for my own benefit*
The pleasures such a beauty brings with it,
But I would have the soil of her fair rape³
Wiped off in honourable keeping her.
What treason were it to the ransacked° queen,   *carried off as plunder*
150 Disgrace to your great worths, and shame to me,
Now to deliver her possession up
On terms of base compulsion? Can it be
That so degenerate a strain° as this   *impulse*
Should once set footing in your generous° bosoms?   *noble*
155 There's not the meanest spirit on our party
Without a heart to dare or sword to draw
When Helen is defended; nor none so noble
Whose life were ill bestowed or death unfamed
Where Helen is the subject. Then I say:
160 Well may we fight for her whom we know well
The world's large spaces cannot parallel.

HECTOR   Paris and Troilus, you have both said well,
But on the cause and question now in hand
Have glossed° but superficially—not much   *commented*
165 Unlike young men, whom Aristotle thought
Unfit to hear moral philosophy.⁴
The reasons you allege do more conduce
To the hot passion of distempered blood
Than to make up a free determination

---

2. *And Jove . . . maintain:* We ("Priam's sons") shouldn't undertake something unless even the least courageous of us is willing to fight to defend it.
3. The defilement (of Helen or Paris, or both) resulting

from her proper (also, beautiful) abduction (also, sexual violation).
4. Political philosophy. This is an anachronistic reference to Aristotle's *Nicomachean Ethics* 1.3.

170 'Twixt right and wrong; for pleasure and revenge
Have ears more deaf than adders⁵ to the voice
Of any true decision. Nature craves
All dues be rendered to their owners. Now,
What nearer debt in all humanity
175 Than wife is to the husband? If this law
Of nature be corrupted through affection,°   *lust*
And that great minds, of partial° indulgence   *though prejudiced*
To their benumbèd° wills, resist the same,   *dulled*
There is a law in each well-ordered nation
180 To curb those raging appetites that are
Most disobedient and refractory.°   *stubborn*
If Helen then be wife to Sparta's king,
As it is known she is, these moral laws
Of nature and of nations speak aloud
185 To have her back returned. Thus to persist
In doing wrong extenuates not wrong,
But makes it much more heavy. Hector's opinion
Is this in way of° truth—yet ne'ertheless,   *with respect to*
My sprightly° brethren, I propend° to you   *spirited / incline*
190 In resolution to keep Helen still;
For 'tis a cause that hath no mean dependence
Upon our joint and several° dignities.   *separate*
TROILUS   Why, there you touched the life of our design.
Were it not glory that we more affected°   *desired*
195 Than the performance of our heaving spleens,°   *acting on our anger*
I would not wish a drop of Trojan blood
Spent more in her defence. But, worthy Hector,
She is a theme of honour and renown,
A spur to valiant and magnanimous° deeds,   *noble*
200 Whose present courage may beat down our foes,
And fame in time to come canonize° us—   *glorify*
For I presume brave Hector would not lose
So rich advantage of a promised glory
As smiles upon the forehead° of this action   *countenance*
For the wide world's revenue.
205 HECTOR   I am yours,
You valiant offspring of great Priamus.
I have a roisting° challenge sent amongst   *boisterous*
The dull and factious nobles of the Greeks
Will shriek amazement to their drowsy spirits.
210 I was advertised their great general⁶ slept
Whilst emulation° in the army crept;   *jealous rivalry*
This I presume will wake him.   [*Flourish.*] *Exeunt*

2.3

Enter THERSITES

THERSITES   How now, Thersites? What, lost in the labyrinth of
thy fury? Shall the elephant Ajax carry it° thus? He beats me   *get away with it*
and I rail at him. O worthy satisfaction! Would it were other-

---

5. Adders were proverbially deaf. See Psalms 58:4–5:
"like the deaf adder that stoppeth his ear. Which heareth
not the voice of the enchanter, though he be most expert
in charming."
6. I was told that Achilles (Agamemnon?) slept.
2.3 Location: The Greek camp, outside Achilles' tent.

wise: that I could beat him whilst he railed at me. 'Sfoot,° I'll   *God's foot*
5   learn to conjure and raise devils but I'll see some issue of my
spiteful execrations.[1] Then there's Achilles: a rare engineer.[2] If
Troy be not taken till these two undermine it, the walls will
stand till they fall of themselves. O thou great thunder-darter of
Olympus, forget that thou art Jove, the king of gods; and Mer-
10   cury, lose all the serpentine craft of thy caduceus,[3] if ye take
not that little, little, less than little wit from them that they
have—which short-armed ignorance[4] itself knows is so abun-
dant—scarce it will not in circumvention° deliver a fly from a   *craftiness*
spider without drawing their massy irons° and cutting the web.   *swords*
15   After this, the vengeance on the whole camp—or rather, the
Neapolitan bone-ache,° for that methinks is the curse depen-   *syphilis*
dent° on those that war for a placket.[5] I have said my prayers,   *impending*
and devil Envy say 'Amen'.—What ho! My lord Achilles!

Enter PATROCLUS [*at the door to the tent*]

PATROCLUS   Who's there? Thersites? Good Thersites, come in
20   and rail.   [*Exit*]

THERSITES   If I could ha' remembered a gilt counterfeit, thou
wouldst not have slipped out of my contemplation;[6] but it is no
matter. Thyself upon thyself![7] The common curse of mankind,
folly and ignorance, be thine in great revenue!° Heaven bless°   *amounts / save*
25   thee from a tutor, and discipline come not near thee! Let thy
blood° be thy direction° till thy death! Then if she that lays thee   *lust / guide*
out says thou art a fair corpse, I'll be sworn and sworn upon't
she never shrouded any but lazars.°   *lepers; sick bodies*

[*Enter* PATROCLUS]

Amen.—Where's Achilles?
30   PATROCLUS   What, art thou devout? Wast thou in prayer?

THERSITES   Ay. The heavens hear me!

PATROCLUS   Amen.

Enter ACHILLES

ACHILLES   Who's there?

PATROCLUS   Thersites, my lord.

35   ACHILLES   Where? Where? O where?—Art thou come? Why,
my cheese,° my digestion, why hast thou not served thyself   *digestive aid*
into my table so many meals? Come: what's Agamemnon?

THERSITES   Thy commander, Achilles.—Then tell me, Patroclus, what's Achilles?

40   PATROCLUS   Thy lord, Thersites. Then tell me, I pray thee,
what's Thersites?

THERSITES   Thy knower, Patroclus. Then tell me, Patroclus,
what art thou?

PATROCLUS   Thou mayst tell, that knowest.

45   ACHILLES   O tell, tell.

THERSITES   I'll decline the whole question.[8] Agamemnon com-

---

1. *but I'll . . . execrations:* if I must, in order to get tangible results from my contemptuous curses. "Spiteful"
keeps its unintended sense of "malicious."
2. Constructor of military earthworks and machines.
3. Mercury's emblem, a rod entwined by snakes.
Known for "craft," Mercury was the patron of thieves.
4. Ignorance is "short-armed" because most things are
beyond its grasp.
5. Petticoat; woman; woman's genitalia (obscene).

6. If I could have remembered a fake gold coin (worthless
Patroclus), you wouldn't have been forgotten (punning on
"slip," a counterfeit coin) in my devout meditation (which
focused on Ajax and Achilles, but only to curse them).
7. To be Patroclus is the worst possible fate—hence,
Thersites' curse on him is to be himself.
8. I'll recite in order the entire subject under investigation. "Decline," "Derive" (line 55), and "positive" (line
58) are all grammatical terms.

mands Achilles, Achilles is my lord, I am Patroclus' knower,
and Patroclus is a fool.

PATROCLUS You rascal.

50 THERSITES Peace, fool, I have not done.

ACHILLES [*to* PATROCLUS] He is a privileged man.[9]—Proceed,
Thersites.

THERSITES Agamemnon is a fool, Achilles is a fool, Thersites is
a fool, and as aforesaid Patroclus is a fool.

55 ACHILLES Derive this.° Come.   *Show your reasoning*

THERSITES Agamemnon is a fool to offer to command Achilles;
Achilles is a fool to be commanded of Agamemnon; Thersites
is a fool to serve such a fool; and Patroclus is a fool positive.°   *absolute*

PATROCLUS Why am I a fool?

60 THERSITES Make that demand to the Creator. It suffices me
thou art. Look you, who comes here?

> *Enter* AGAMEMNON, ULYSSES, NESTOR, DIOMEDES, AJAX,
> *and* CALCHAS

ACHILLES Patroclus, I'll speak with nobody.—Come in with me,
Thersites.   *Exit*

THERSITES Here is such patchery,° such juggling° and such   *foolery / deception*
65 knavery. All the argument is a whore and a cuckold. A good
quarrel to draw[1] emulous° factions and bleed to death upon.   *envious*
Now the dry serpigo° on the subject, and war and lechery con-   *skin disease*
found all.   [*Exit*]

AGAMEMNON [*to* PATROCLUS] Where is Achilles?

70 PATROCLUS Within his tent; but ill-disposed,° my lord.   *unwell; bad-tempered*

AGAMEMNON Let it be known to him that we are here.
He faced° our messengers, and we lay by   *bullied*
Our appertainments,° visiting of him.   *rights of rank*
Let him be told so, lest perchance he think
75 We dare not move the question of our place,°   *assert our authority*
Or know not what we are.

PATROCLUS   I shall so say to him.   [*Exit*]

ULYSSES We saw him at the opening of his tent.
He is not sick.

AJAX Yes, lion-sick:° sick of proud heart. You may call it 'melan-   *sick with pride*
80 choly'[2] if you will favour the man, but by my head 'tis pride.
But why? Why? Let him show us the cause. [*To* AGAMEMNON]
A word, my lord.

> [AJAX *and* AGAMEMNON *talk apart*]

NESTOR What moves Ajax thus to bay at him?

ULYSSES Achilles hath inveigled° his fool from him.   *enticed away*

85 NESTOR Who? Thersites?

ULYSSES He.

NESTOR Then will Ajax lack matter,[3] if he have lost his argument.°   *subject matter*

ULYSSES No, you see, he *is* his argument that *has* his argument:[4]
90 Achilles.

NESTOR All the better—their fraction° is more our wish than   *division*

9. An acknowledged fool could speak with impunity.
1. Attract to itself, like a magnet; extract, like a sword; tear to pieces; drag to execution.
2. A fashionable philosophical malady.
3. Something to say; sense; pus.

4. Achilles is the person who is Ajax's argument. Since Achilles has taken Thersites (who used to be Ajax's object of derision) as the object of his derision, Ajax has transferred his scorn from Thersites to Achilles.

their faction.° But it was a strong council that a fool could dis-   *union in rebellion*
unite.°   *(ironic)*
ULYSSES   The amity that wisdom knits not, folly may easily untie.
          Enter PATROCLUS
95   Here comes Patroclus.
NESTOR   No Achilles with him.
ULYSSES   The elephant hath joints, but none for courtesy:[5] his
legs are legs for necessity, not for flexure.°   *bending*
PATROCLUS [*to* AGAMEMNON]   Achilles bids me say he is much sorry
100 If anything more than your sport and pleasure
Did move your greatness and this noble state°   *company*
To call upon him. He hopes it is no other
But for your health and your digestion's sake:
An after-dinner's breath.°   *exercise*
AGAMEMNON   Hear you, Patroclus.
105 We are too well acquainted with these answers.
But his evasion, winged thus swift with scorn,
Cannot outfly° our apprehensions.°   *escape / understanding*
Much attribute° he hath, and much the reason   *reputation*
Why we ascribe it to him. Yet all his virtues,
110 Not virtuously on his own part beheld,
Do in our eyes begin to lose their gloss,
Yea, and like fair fruit in an unwholesome dish
Are like to rot untasted. Go and tell him
We come to speak with him—and you shall not sin
115 If you do say we think him over-proud
And under-honest, in self-assumption° greater   *his own opinion*
Than in the note of judgement. And worthier than himself
Here tend° the savage strangeness° he puts on,   *wait on / aloofness*
Disguise the holy strength of their command,
120 And underwrite in an observing kind°   *submit compliantly to*
His humorous predominance[6]—yea, watch
His pettish lunes,[7] his ebbs, his flows, as if
The passage and whole carriage° of this action   *means and ends*
Rode on his tide. Go tell him this, and add
125 That if he overhold° his price so much   *overestimate*
We'll none of him, but let him, like an engine
Not portable, lie under this report:
'Bring action hither, this cannot go to war.'
A stirring° dwarf we do allowance give   *bustling*
130 Before a sleeping giant. Tell him so.
PATROCLUS   I shall, and bring his answer presently.°   *immediately*
AGAMEMNON   In second voice° we'll not be satisfied;   *By proxy (Patroclus)*
We come to speak with him.—Ulysses, enter you.
          Exit ULYSSES [*with* PATROCLUS]
AJAX   What is he more than another?
135 AGAMEMNON   No more than what he thinks he is.[8]
AJAX   Is he so much? Do you not think he thinks himself a better
man than I am?
AGAMEMNON   No question.

5. The elephant's supposed lack of knee joints made it resemble a proud, unbowing man.
6. His idiosyncratic assumption of superiority; the domination of one particular "humor" (temperament)—pride.
7. His fits of madness (caused by the moon's changing phases; as the moon also produces sea tides, hence "ebbs," "flows," and "tide," lines 122, 124). "Lunes" is an editorial emendation of F's "lines."
8. He's the only one with a high opinion of him; he's worth as much as he thinks he is.

AJAX Will you subscribe his thought, and say he is?

140 AGAMEMNON No, noble Ajax. You are as strong, as valiant, as
 wise, no less noble, much more gentle, and altogether more
 tractable.

AJAX Why should a man be proud? How doth pride grow? I
 know not what it is.

145 AGAMEMNON Your mind is the clearer, Ajax, and your virtues
 the fairer. He that is proud eats up himself. Pride is his own
 glass,° his own trumpet, his own chronicle—and whatever   *its own mirror*
 praises itself but in the deed devours the deed in the praise.[9]

          Enter ULYSSES

AJAX I do hate a proud man as I hate the engendering° of toads.   *mating*

150 NESTOR [*aside*] Yet he loves himself. Is't not strange?

ULYSSES Achilles will not to the field tomorrow.

AGAMEMNON What's his excuse?

ULYSSES   He doth rely on none,
 But carries on the stream of his dispose°   *disposition*
 Without observance or respect of any,

155 In will peculiar and in self-admission.[1]

AGAMEMNON Why, will he not, upon our fair request,
 Untent his person and share the air with us?

ULYSSES Things small as nothing, for request's sake only,[2]
 He makes important. Possessed° he is with greatness,   *Bewitched*

160 And speaks not to himself but with a pride
 That quarrels at self-breath.[3] Imagined worth
 Holds in his blood such swoll'n and hot discourse
 That 'twixt his mental and his active parts
 Kingdomed Achilles[4] in commotion° rages   *insurrection*

165 And batters 'gainst himself. What should I say?
 He is so plaguy proud that the death tokens of it[5]
 Cry 'No recovery'.

AGAMEMNON   Let Ajax go to him.
 [*To* AJAX] Dear lord, go you and greet him in his tent.
 'Tis said he holds you well and will be led,

170 At your request, a little from himself.°   *from his self-conceit*

ULYSSES O Agamemnon, let it not be so.
 We'll consecrate the steps that Ajax makes
 When they go from Achilles. Shall the proud lord
 That bastes his arrogance with his own seam[6]

175 And never suffers matter° of the world   *the affairs*
 Enter his thoughts, save° such as do revolve   *except*
 And ruminate° himself—shall he be worshipped   *turn on*
 Of that° we hold an idol more than he?   *By one who*
 No, this thrice-worthy and right valiant lord

180 Must not so stale his palm,° nobly acquired,   *sully his honor*
 Nor by my will assubjugate° his merit,   *reduce to subjection*
 As amply titled as Achilles' is,
 By going to Achilles—
 That were to enlard his fat-already pride

---

9. Whatever self-praise arises except from silently performing the noble deed itself destroys the deed by the act
of praising it.
1. In self-will and in acknowledgment of only his own
authority.
2. Merely because they are asked for.
3. *And . . . self-breath:* Achilles is not even satisfied with

what he himself has to say in praise of his merits; he is too
proud to talk even to himself.
4. Achilles' body is imagined as a state at civil war.
5. He is so annoyingly (diseasedly) proud that the fatal
signs of plague.
6. Fat; appearance. Achilles is accused of feeding self-
flattery to his already inflated arrogance.

185 And add more coals to Cancer[7] when he burns
     With entertaining great Hyperion.°   *the sun*
     This lord go to him? Jupiter forbid,
     And say in thunder 'Achilles, go to him'.
     NESTOR [*aside to* DIOMEDES] O this is well. He rubs the vein of him.°   *stirs up Ajax*
190 DIOMEDES [*aside to* NESTOR] And how his silence drinks up this applause.
     AJAX If I go to him, with my armèd fist
     I'll pash° him o'er the face.   *smash*
     AGAMEMNON   O no, you shall not go.
     AJAX An a° be proud with me, I'll feeze° his pride.   *If he / take care of*
     Let me go to him.
195 ULYSSES Not for the worth that hangs upon our quarrel.°   *(with Troy)*
     AJAX A paltry insolent fellow.
     NESTOR [*aside*] How he describes himself!
     AJAX Can he not be sociable?
     ULYSSES [*aside*] The raven chides blackness.
200 AJAX I'll let his humour's blood.[8]
     AGAMEMNON [*aside*] He will be the physician that should be the
       patient.
     AJAX An all men were o' my mind—
     ULYSSES [*aside*] Wit would be out of fashion.
205 AJAX A should not bear it so. A should eat swords[9] first. Shall
       pride carry it?
     NESTOR [*aside*] An't would, you'd carry half.
     AJAX A would have ten shares.[1]
     ULYSSES [*aside*] I will knead him; I'll make him supple.° He's   *compliant*
210   not yet through warm.[2]
     NESTOR [*aside*] Farce° him with praises. Pour in, pour in! His   *Stuff; sauce*
       ambition is dry.°   *thirsty*
     ULYSSES [*to* AGAMEMNON] My lord, you feed too much on this dislike.
     NESTOR [*to* AGAMEMNON] Our noble general, do not do so.
215 DIOMEDES [*to* AGAMEMNON] You must prepare to fight without Achilles.
     ULYSSES Why, 'tis this naming of him° does him harm.   *(as our sole hope)*
     Here is a man°—but 'tis before his face.   *Ajax*
     I will be silent.
     NESTOR   Wherefore should you so?
     He is not emulous,° as Achilles is.   *hungry for praise*
220 ULYSSES Know the whole world he is as valiant—
     AJAX A whoreson dog, that shall palter° thus with us—would he   *deal evasively*
       were a Trojan!
     NESTOR What a vice were it in Ajax now—
     ULYSSES If he were proud—
     DIOMEDES   Or covetous of praise—
     ULYSSES Ay, or surly borne—
225 DIOMEDES   Or strange,° or self-affected.°   *aloof / egotistical*
     ULYSSES [*to* AJAX] Thank the heavens, lord, thou art of sweet
       composure.°   *temperament*

---

7. And add fuel to the fire. Cancer is the sign of the
Zodiac that begins on June 21—hence, a symbol of summer heat.
8. I'll cure his illness (pride) by bloodletting, as a doctor
would to get rid of surplus humors.
9. He wouldn't carry on so. He would be defeated in
combat (eat his words).
1. Probably alluding to the ten shares into which the
Lord Chamberlain's Men's assets were divided—hence,

everything.
2. Warm all through. In F, the speech prefixes for lines
208–09 are reversed. In the arrangement printed here,
Ajax's line refers to Achilles and Ulysses', to Ajax, whom
Ulysses says he plans to manipulate further. In F's version,
Ulysses gets the first line, which refers to Ajax, who in the
next two lines describes what he'll do to Achilles. Q has
still another approach, and additional variations are found
in modern editions.

Praise him that got thee, she that gave thee suck.
Famed be thy tutor, and thy parts of nature°   *natural attributes*
Thrice famed beyond, beyond all erudition.³
230 But he that disciplined thine arms to fight—
Let Mars divide eternity in twain,
And give him half. And for thy vigour,
Bull-bearing Milo⁴ his addition° yield   *reputation*
To sinewy Ajax. I will not praise thy wisdom,
235 Which like a bourn, a pale, a shore confines⁵
Thy spacious and dilated° parts. Here's Nestor,   *ample; famous*
Instructed by the antiquary° times: *ancient*
He must, he is, he cannot but be, wise.
But pardon, father Nestor: were your days
240 As green⁶ as Ajax', and your brain so tempered,°   *composed*
You should not have the eminence of° him,   *be superior to*
But be as° Ajax.   *equal to*
AJAX   Shall I call you father?°   *guide*
ULYSSES Ay, my good son.
DIOMEDES   Be ruled by him, Lord Ajax.
ULYSSES [*to* AGAMEMNON] There is no tarrying here: the hart Achilles
245 Keeps thicket.° Please it our great general°   *stays home / Agamemnon*
To call together all his state° of war.   *council*
Fresh kings° are come today to Troy; tomorrow   *Reinforcements*
We must with all our main of power° stand fast.   *utmost strength*
And here's a lord, come knights from east to west°   *the whole world*
250 And cull their flower,⁷ Ajax shall cope° the best.   *match*
AGAMEMNON Go we to counsel. Let Achilles sleep.
Light boats sail swift, though greater hulks draw deep.⁸ *Exeunt*

3.1

Music sounds within. Enter PANDARUS [*at one door*] *and*
a SERVANT [*at another door*]

PANDARUS Friend? You. Pray you, a word. Do not you follow the
young Lord Paris?
SERVANT Ay, sir, when he goes before me.
PANDARUS You depend upon him,° I mean.   *serve him*
5 SERVANT Sir, I do depend upon the Lord.°   *God; Paris*
PANDARUS You depend upon a notable gentleman; I must needs
praise him.
SERVANT The Lord be praised!
PANDARUS You know me—do you not?
10 SERVANT Faith, sir, superficially.
PANDARUS Friend, know me better. I am the Lord Pandarus.
SERVANT I hope I shall know your honour better.¹
PANDARUS I do desire it.

---

3. Ajax's glory exceeds anything scholars might say about it. Also ironic: learning constitutes no part of it.
4. Famous Greek athlete who bore a four-year-old bull on his shoulders.
5. Which like a boundary, a fence, a shore limits the uses of (probably ironic).
6. Young, fresh; immature; gullible.
7. And choose their best men.
8. We will progress more swiftly without Achilles (perhaps alluding to the famous success of "light" English ships against the "greater hulks" of the Spanish

Armada). This line is doubly ironic: on the one hand, Ajax can hardly be called a "light boat"; on the other, the Greeks as a whole have already been associated with "deep-drawing" boats in the Prologue (line 12).
3.1 Location: Troy's palace.
1. I hope to get to know you better. I hope to learn of an improvement in your spiritual health. The double meaning here is typical of the servant's playful mockery of Pandarus, which partly contrasts Pandarus' secular concerns with more important, albeit anachronistic, Christian ones.

SERVANT   You are in the state of grace?[2]

15 PANDARUS   Grace? Not so, friend. 'Honour' and 'lordship' are my
titles. What music is this?

SERVANT   I do but partly know, sir. It is music in parts.

PANDARUS   Know you the musicians?

SERVANT   Wholly, sir.

20 PANDARUS   Who play they to?

SERVANT   To the hearers, sir.

PANDARUS   At whose pleasure, friend?

SERVANT   At mine, sir, and theirs that love music.

PANDARUS   'Command' I mean, friend.

25 SERVANT   Who shall I command, sir?

PANDARUS   Friend, we understand not one another. I am too
courtly and thou too cunning. At whose request do these men
play?

SERVANT   That's to't° indeed, sir. Marry, sir, at the request of   *to the point*

30 Paris my lord, who's there in person; with him, the mortal°   *living; fatal*
Venus, the heart-blood of beauty, love's visible soul°—   *love incarnate*

PANDARUS   Who, my cousin Cressida?

SERVANT   No, sir, Helen. Could not you find out that by her
attributes?

35 PANDARUS   It should seem, fellow, that thou hast not seen the
Lady Cressid. I come to speak with Paris from the Prince Troilus. I will make a complimental° assault upon him, for my busi-   *courteous*
ness seethes.°   *boils; is pressing*

SERVANT   Sodden business! There's a stewed[3] phrase, indeed.

Enter PARIS *and* HELEN [*attended by musicians*]

40 PANDARUS   Fair be to you, my lord, and to all this fair company.
Fair desires in all fair measure fairly guide them—especially
to you, fair Queen. Fair thoughts be your fair pillow.

HELEN   Dear lord, you are full of fair words.

PANDARUS   You speak your fair pleasure, sweet Queen. [*To* PARIS]

45 Fair prince, here is good broken music.[4]

PARIS   You have broke° it, cousin,[5] and by my life you shall make   *interrupted*
it whole again. You shall piece it out° with a piece of your   *repair it*
performance.° —Nell, he is full of harmony.   *performed by you*

PANDARUS   Truly, lady, no.

50 HELEN   O sir.

[*She tickles him*]

PANDARUS   Rude,° in sooth, in good sooth very rude.   *Unskilled; unmusical*

PARIS   Well said, my lord. Will you say so in fits?[6]

PANDARUS   I have business to my lord, dear Queen.—My lord,
will you vouchsafe me a word?

55 HELEN   Nay, this shall not hedge° us out. We'll hear you sing,   *keep*
certainly.

PANDARUS   Well, sweet Queen, you are pleasant with° me.—But   *teasing*
marry, thus, my lord: my dear lord and most esteemed friend,
your brother Troilus—

2. Theologically (deliberately misunderstanding Pandarus's "desire" in line 13 as a wish for moral improvement rather than social acquaintance). Pandarus
proceeds to misunderstand "grace" as the status of
being called "your grace" (a Duke's title).
3. "Stewed" (overdone, literally and metaphorically;
associated with stews, or brothels) puns on "sodden,"
which means "boiled" (picking up on "seethes," line 38);

is stupid; is drunk; is being treated for venereal disease.
4. Music for instruments of different kinds—for
example, strings and woodwind.
5. Kinsman (used especially by sovereigns to noblemen, whether or not related).
6. Would you please say (do you insist on saying) so in
sections of songs or music (fits and starts; spasms of
laughter)?

60 HELEN My lord Pandarus, honey-sweet lord.

PANDARUS Go to, sweet Queen, go to!—commends himself
most affectionately to you.

HELEN You shall not bob° us out of our melody. If you do, our   *swindle*
melancholy[7] upon your head.

65 PANDARUS Sweet Queen, sweet Queen, that's a sweet Queen.
Ay, faith—

HELEN And to make a sweet lady sad is a sour offence.

PANDARUS Nay, that shall not serve your turn; that shall it not,
in truth, la. Nay, I care not for such words. No, no.—And, my

70 lord, he desires you that, if the King call for him at supper, you
will make his excuse.

HELEN My lord Pandarus.

PANDARUS What says my sweet Queen, my very very sweet
Queen?

75 PARIS What exploit's in hand? Where sups he tonight?

HELEN Nay, but my lord—

PANDARUS What says my sweet Queen? My cousin will fall out
with you.[8]

HELEN [to PARIS] You must not° know where he sups.   *are not supposed to*

80 PARIS I'll lay my life, with my dispenser[9] Cressida.

PANDARUS No, no! No such matter. You are wide.° Come, your   *way off target*
dispenser is sick.

PARIS Well, I'll make 's° excuse.   *his*

PANDARUS Ay, good my lord. Why should you say Cressida? No,

85 your poor dispenser's sick.

PARIS 'I spy.'[1]

PANDARUS You spy? What do you spy?—[To a musician] Come,
give me an instrument.—Now, sweet Queen.

HELEN Why, this is kindly done!

90 PANDARUS My niece is horrible° in love with a thing you have,   *horribly*
sweet Queen.

HELEN She shall have it, my lord—if it be not my lord Paris.

PANDARUS He? No, she'll none of him. They two are twain.°   *estranged*

HELEN Falling in,[2] after falling out,° may make them three.   *arguing*

95 PANDARUS Come, come, I'll hear no more of this. I'll sing you a
song now.

HELEN Ay, ay, prithee. Now by my troth, sweet lord, thou hast a
fine forehead.[3]

[She strokes his forehead]

PANDARUS Ay, you may, you may.°   *(go on)*

100 HELEN Let thy song be love. 'This love will undo us all.' O
Cupid, Cupid, Cupid!

PANDARUS Love? Ay, that it shall,° i'faith.   *(be); (undo us)*

PARIS Ay, good now,° 'Love, love, nothing but love'.   *please*

PANDARUS In good truth, it° begins so.   *the song; love*

---

7. May our "melancholy" mood (supposedly cured by
music) be.
8. *What . . . you:* If you (Helen) keep interrupting, my
"cousin" Paris (as in line 46) will be angry with you; if
you keep inquiring about private affairs, my "cousin"
Cressida will be angry with you.
9. Excuser (of Troilus's failure to attend dinner); pro-
visioner (again, of dinner); bestower of (sexual) favors;
dispenser of cures (with "sick," lines 82, 85, a remedy

for Troilus's lovesickness). Here and in lines 82 and 85,
"dispenser" is an editorial emendation for "disposer," of
uncertain meaning but perhaps suggesting that Cressida can do what she likes with Troilus and Paris.
1. I understand (alluding to a child's game).
2. "Falling in" sexually, so as to produce a child.
3. Impudence; modesty; sign of male beauty; hint of
cuckoldry.

105 [*Sings*] Love, love, nothing but love, still° love, still more!	*always*
For O love's bow	
Shoots buck and doe.°	*male and female*
The shaft° confounds	*arrow; penis*
Not that it wounds	
110 But tickles still the sore.⁴	
These lovers cry 'O! O!', they die.°	*perish; have an orgasm*
Yet that which seems the wound to kill°	*mortal wound*
Doth turn 'O! O!' to 'ha ha he!'⁵	
115 So dying love lives still.	
'O! O!' a while, but 'ha ha ha!'	
'O! O!' groans out for 'ha ha ha!'—	

Heigh-ho.

HELEN   In love—ay, faith, to the very tip of the nose.

PARIS   He eats nothing but doves,° love, and that breeds hot *emblem of true love*
120   blood, and hot blood begets hot thoughts, and hot thoughts
beget hot deeds, and hot deeds is love.

PANDARUS   Is this the generation° of love: hot blood, hot thoughts, *genealogy*
and hot deeds? Why, they are vipers. Is love a generation of
vipers?⁶

[*Alarum*]

125   Sweet lord, who's afield today?

PARIS   Hector, Deiphobus, Helenus, Antenor, and all the gal-
lantry of Troy. I would fain have° armed today, but my Nell *like to have*
would not have it so. How chance my brother Troilus went
not?

130 HELEN   He hangs the lip° at something. You know all, Lord Pan- *looks despondent*
darus.

PANDARUS   Not I, honey-sweet Queen. I long to hear how they
sped today.— You'll remember your brother's excuse?

PARIS   To a hair.°   *Exactly*

135 PANDARUS   Farewell, sweet Queen.

HELEN   Commend me to your niece.

PANDARUS   I will, sweet Queen.   [*Exit*]

Sound a retreat

PARIS   They're come from field. Let us to Priam's hall
To greet the warriors. Sweet Helen, I must woo you
140 To help unarm our Hector. His stubborn buckles,
With these your white enchanting fingers touched,
Shall more obey than to the edge of steel° *sword blade*
Or force of Greekish sinews. You shall do more
Than all the island kings:° disarm great Hector. *Greek lords*

145 HELEN   'Twill make us proud to be his servant, Paris;
Yea, what he shall receive of us in duty
Gives us more palm in° beauty than we have— *fame for*
Yea, overshines ourself.

PARIS   Sweet above thought, I love thee!

Exeunt

---

4. Wound; four-year-old buck.
5. Turns pain to joy; turns ecstasy to derision.
6. Anachronistic allusion, not intended by Pandarus,

to a biblical phrase—for instance, the "generation of
vipers" in Matthew 23:33, promising damnation.

3.2

Enter PANDARUS [*at one door*] *and Troilus'* MAN [*at another door*]

PANDARUS   How now, where's thy master? At my cousin
 Cressida's?

MAN   No, sir, he stays for you to conduct him thither.

 Enter TROILUS

PANDARUS   O here he comes.—How now, how now?

5 TROILUS   Sirrah, walk off.   [*Exit* MAN]

PANDARUS   Have you seen my cousin?

TROILUS   No, Pandarus, I stalk about her door
 Like a strange° soul upon the Stygian banks   *newly arrived*
 Staying for waftage.¹ O be thou my Charon,
10 And give me swift transportance to those fields²
 Where I may wallow° in the lily beds   *roll around*
 Proposed for° the deserver. O gentle Pandar,³   *Promised to*
 From Cupid's shoulder pluck his painted° wings   *brightly colored*
 And fly with me to Cressid.

15 PANDARUS   Walk here i'th' orchard.° I'll bring her straight. *Exit*   *garden*

TROILUS   I am giddy. Expectation whirls me round.
 Th'imaginary relish° is so sweet   *pleasant anticipation*
 That it enchants my sense. What will it be
 When that the wat'ry° palates taste indeed   *watering*
20 Love's thrice-repurèd nectar?⁴ Death, I fear me,
 Swooning destruction, or some joy too fine,°   *exquisite*
 Too subtle-potent, tuned too sharp in sweetness°   *(musically)*
 For the capacity of my ruder powers.
 I fear it much, and I do fear besides
25 That I shall lose distinction° in my joys,   *power to discriminate*
 As doth a battle° when they charge on heaps   *army*
 The enemy flying.

 Enter PANDARUS

PANDARUS   She's making her ready. She'll come straight.° You   *immediately*
 must be witty now. She does so blush, and fetches her wind° so   *breath*
30 short as if she were frayed with a spirit.⁵ I'll fetch her. It is the
 prettiest villain!° She fetches her breath as short as a new-ta'en⁶   *(affectionate)*
 sparrow.   *Exit*

TROILUS   Even such a passion doth embrace my bosom.
 My heart beats thicker° than a feverous pulse,   *faster*
35 And all my powers do their bestowing° lose,   *function*
 Like vassalage at unawares° encount'ring   *vassals unexpectedly*
 The eye of majesty.

 Enter PANDARUS, [*with*] CRESSIDA [*veiled*]

PANDARUS [*to* CRESSIDA]   Come, come, what need you blush?
 Shame's a baby. [*To* TROILUS] Here she is now. Swear the oaths
40 now to her that you have sworn to me. [*To* CRESSIDA] What,
 are you gone again? You must be watched ere you be made
 tame,⁷ must you? Come your ways, come your ways. An you
 draw backward, we'll put you i'th' thills.⁸ [*To* TROILUS] Why do

---

3.2 Location: Cressida's garden.
1. Waiting to be ferried across. The dead were carried across the river Styx into the underworld by the ferryman Charon.
2. The Elysian Fields, which were reserved for the blessed dead ("the deserver" line 12).
3. The shortened form of the name here helps define

Pandarus as a pander.
4. Thrice-purified drink of the gods (giving immortality).
5. Frightened by a ghost.
6. Just captured.
7. Hawks were kept awake at night to tame them.
8. If you back away, we'll back you, like a horse, into the shafts of a cart.

you not speak to her?   [*To* CRESSIDA] Come, draw this curtain,
45 and let's see your picture.⁹ [*He unveils her*] Alas the day! How
loath you are to offend daylight! An't were dark, you'd close°   *agree; unite*
sooner. So, so. [*To* TROILUS] Rub on, and kiss the mistress.¹
[*They kiss*] How now, a kiss in fee farm!° Build there, carpenter,   *perpetual land tenure*
the air° is sweet. Nay, you shall fight your hearts out ere I part   *her breath*
50 you. The falcon as the tercel,² for° all the ducks i'th' river. Go   *I'd bet*
to, go to.

TROILUS   You have bereft me of all words, lady.

PANDARUS   Words pay no debts; give her deeds. But she'll
bereave you o'th' deeds° too, if she call your activity° in ques-   *wear you out / virility*
55 tion. [*They kiss*] What, billing° again? Here's 'in witness   *kissing*
whereof the parties interchangeably'.³ Come in, come in. I'll
go get a fire.°   [*Exit*]   *(for the bedroom)*

CRESSIDA   Will you walk in, my lord?

TROILUS   O Cressida, how often have I wished me thus.

60 CRESSIDA   Wished, my lord? The gods grant—O, my lord!

TROILUS   What should they grant? What makes this pretty abrup-
tion?° What too-curious dreg° espies my sweet lady in the foun-   *pause / speck of dirt*
tain of our love?

CRESSIDA   More dregs than water, if my fears have eyes.

65 TROILUS   Fears make devils of cherubims;° they never see truly.   *predict the worst*

CRESSIDA   Blind fear, that seeing° reason leads, finds safer foot-   *clear-sighted*
ing than blind reason, stumbling without fear. To fear the worst
oft cures the worse.

TROILUS   O let my lady apprehend no fear. In all Cupid's pag-
70 eant there is presented no monster.

CRESSIDA   Nor nothing monstrous neither?

TROILUS   Nothing but our undertakings,° when we vow to weep   *promises*
seas, live in fire, eat rocks, tame tigers, thinking it harder for
our mistress to devise imposition enough° than for us to   *a big enough challenge*
75 undergo any difficulty imposed. This is the monstruosity in
love, lady—that the will is infinite and the execution confined;
that the desire is boundless and the act° a slave to limit.   *(sex) act*

CRESSIDA   They say all lovers swear more performance than they
are able, and yet reserve an ability that they never perform:
80 vowing more than the perfection of ten,° and discharging less   *(lovers)*
than the tenth part of one. They that have the voice of lions
and the act of hares, are they not monsters?

TROILUS   Are there such? Such are not we. Praise us as we are
tasted;° allow° us as we prove. Our head shall go bare till merit   *tested / praise*
85 crown it. No perfection in reversion⁴ shall have a praise in
present. We will not name desert° before his° birth, and being   *mention merit / its*
born his addition° shall be humble. Few words to fair faith.⁵   *title*
Troilus shall be such to Cressid as what envy can say worst
shall be a mock for his truth;⁶ and what truth can speak truest,
90 not truer⁷ than Troilus.

CRESSIDA   Will you walk in, my lord?

---

9. Cressida's face is veiled. Pictures were curtained for
protection against light and dust.
1. Metaphor from the game of bowls: keep on course,
and touch gently the master ball (a small ball at which
bowls were aimed).
2. The female hawk as (eagerly as) the male.
3. A garbled version of a betrothal; also a contractual
legal formula completed by the words "have set their

hands and seals."
4. No perfection by right of eventual succession (like
lands or title)—hence, in the future.
5. Brevity goes with honesty (proverbial).
6. *as . . . truth*: that envy's most malicious comment on
Troilus can only be to mock him for constancy.
7. *not truer*: could not be more reliable.

Enter PANDARUS

PANDARUS What, blushing still? Have you not done talking yet?

CRESSIDA Well, uncle, what folly° I commit I dedicate to you.   *whatever indiscretion*

PANDARUS I thank you for that. If my lord get a boy of you, you'll

95 give him me. Be true to my lord. If he flinch,° chide me for it.   *(sexually)*

TROILUS [*to* CRESSIDA] You know now your hostages:° your uncle's   *pledges*
    word and my firm faith.

PANDARUS Nay, I'll give my word for her too. Our kindred,
    though they be long ere they are wooed, they are constant

100 being won. They are burrs, I can tell you: they'll stick where
    they are thrown.°   *laid (sexual)*

CRESSIDA Boldness comes to me now, and brings me heart.
    Prince Troilus, I have loved you night and day
    For many weary months.

105 TROILUS Why was my Cressid then so hard to win?

CRESSIDA Hard to seem won; but I was won, my lord,
    With the first glance that ever—pardon me:
    If I confess much, you will play the tyrant.
    I love you now, but till now not so much

110 But I might master it. In faith, I lie:
    My thoughts were like unbridled children, grown
    Too headstrong for their mother. See, we fools!
    Why have I blabbed? Who shall be true to us,°   *women*
    When we are so unsecret to ourselves?°   *betray ourselves*

115 But though I loved you well, I wooed you not—
    And yet, good faith, I wished myself a man,
    Or that we women had men's privilege
    Of speaking first. Sweet, bid me hold my tongue,
    For in this rapture I shall surely speak

120 The thing I shall repent. See, see, your silence,
    Cunning in dumbness, in my weakness draws
    My soul of counsel° from me. Stop my mouth.   *most secret thoughts*

TROILUS And shall, albeit sweet music issues thence.
    [*He kisses her*]

PANDARUS Pretty, i' faith.

125 CRESSIDA [*to* TROILUS] My lord, I do beseech you pardon me.
    'Twas not my purpose thus to beg a kiss.
    I am ashamed. O heavens, what have I done?
    For this time will I take my leave, my lord.

TROILUS Your leave, sweet Cressid?

130 PANDARUS Leave? An you take leave till tomorrow morning—

CRESSIDA Pray you, content you.°   *be quiet*

TROILUS   What offends you, lady?

CRESSIDA Sir, mine own company.

TROILUS You cannot shun yourself.

CRESSIDA Let me go and try.

135 I have a kind of self resides with you—
    But an unkind° self, that itself will leave   *unnatural*
    To be another's fool. Where is my wit?
    I would be gone. I speak I know not what.

TROILUS Well know they what they speak that speak so wisely.

140 CRESSIDA Perchance, my lord, I show more craft° than love,   *cunning*
    And fell so roundly° to a large° confession   *openly / full*
    To angle for° your thoughts. But you are wise,   *fish for*

Or else you love not[8]—for to be wise and love
Exceeds man's might: that dwells with gods above.

145 TROILUS   O that I thought it could be in a woman—
As, if it can, I will presume in° you—   *it to be in*
To feed for aye° her lamp and flames of love,   *forever*
To keep her constancy in plight° and youth,   *health*
Outliving beauty's outward,° with a mind   *exterior*
150 That doth renew swifter than blood° decays;   *passion*
Or that persuasion could but thus convince me
That my integrity and truth to you
Might be affronted° with the match and weight°   *met / same amount*
Of such a winnowed[9] purity in love.
155 How were I then uplifted! But alas,
I am as true as truth's simplicity,°   *truth itself*
And simpler° than the infancy of truth.   *more naive*
CRESSIDA   In that I'll war° with you.   *compete*
TROILUS   O virtuous fight,
When right with right wars who shall be most right.
160 True swains in love shall in the world to come
Approve° their truth by Troilus. When their rhymes,   *Attest*
Full of protest,° of oath and big compare,[1]   *protestation*
Wants° similes, truth tired with iteration°—   *Lack / repetition*
'As true as steel, as plantage to the moon,[2]
165 As sun to day, as turtle° to her mate,   *turtledove*
As iron to adamant,° as earth to th' centre'[3]—   *a magnet*
Yet, after all comparisons of truth,
As truth's authentic author to be cited,
'As true as Troilus' shall crown up the verse
And sanctify the numbers.°   *verses*
170 CRESSIDA   Prophet may you be!
If I be false, or swerve a hair from truth,
When time is old and hath forgot itself,
When water drops have worn the stones of Troy
And blind oblivion swallowed cities up,
175 And mighty states characterless are grated[4]
To dusty nothing, yet let memory
From false° to false among false maids in love   *falsehood*
Upbraid my falsehood. When they've said, 'as false
As air, as water, wind or sandy earth,
180 As fox to lamb, or wolf to heifer's calf,
Pard° to the hind, or stepdame to her son',   *Panther; leopard*
Yea, let them say, to stick the heart° of falsehood,   *hit the bullseye*
'As false as Cressid'.
PANDARUS   Go to, a bargain made. Seal it, seal it. I'll be the wit-
185 ness. Here I hold your hand; here, my cousin's.[5] If ever you
prove false one to another, since I have taken such pain to
bring you together, let all pitiful goers-between be called to the
world's end after my name: call them all panders. Let all con-

8. Alternative explanations for why he has made no "large confession" (line 141).
9. Grain is "winnowed" (separated from worthless light chaff).
1. Exaggerated comparisons.
2. Plants were supposed to be affected in growth by the moon.
3. The earth's surface to the earth's center, or axis.
4. Are ground up unrecorded.
5. Taking hands before a witness could be regarded as a (civil) marriage.

stant men be Troiluses, all false women Cressids, and all
190 brokers-between° panders. Say 'Amen'.   *pimps*
TROILUS   Amen.
CRESSIDA   Amen.
PANDARUS   Amen. Whereupon I will show you a chamber with
a bed—which bed, because it shall not speak of your pretty
195 encounters, press it to death.[6] Away!

Exeunt [TROILUS *and* CRESSIDA]

And Cupid grant all tongue-tied maidens° here   *male or female virgins*
Bed, chamber, pander to provide this gear.°   *Exit*   *equipment*

3.3

Flourish. Enter ULYSSES, DIOMEDES, NESTOR, AGAMEM-
NON, MENELAUS, [AJAX,] *and* CALCHAS[1]

CALCHAS   Now, princes, for the service I have done you,
Th'advantage° of the time prompts me aloud   *opportunity*
To call for recompense. Appear° it to your mind   *Let it appear*
That through the sight I bear in things to come
5   I have abandoned Troy, left my profession,°   *priestly role*
Incurred a traitor's name, exposed myself
From certain and possessed conveniences
To doubtful fortunes, sequest'ring° from me all   *divorcing*
That time, acquaintance, custom, and condition°   *position*
10   Made tame° and most familiar to my nature,   *accustomed*
And here to do you service am become
As new into the world, strange, unacquainted.
I do beseech you, as in way of taste,°   *a foretaste*
To give me now a little benefit
15   Out of those many registered in promise°   *many promised things*
Which you say live to come° in my behalf.   *wait to be fulfilled*
AGAMEMNON   What wouldst thou of us, Trojan? Make demand.
CALCHAS   You have a Trojan prisoner called Antenor,
Yesterday took. Troy holds him very dear.
20   Oft have you—often have you thanks therefor°—   *for it*
Desired my Cressid in right great exchange,[2]
Whom Troy hath still denied. But this Antenor
I know is such a wrest[3] in their affairs
That their negotiations° all must slack,   *affairs of state*
25   Wanting his manage,° and they will almost   *guidance*
Give us a prince of blood,° a son of Priam,   *a royal prince*
In change of° him. Let him be sent, great princes,   *exchange for*
And he shall buy my daughter, and her presence
Shall quite strike off° all service I have done   *annul*
In most accepted° pain.   *willingly undertaken*
30   AGAMEMNON   Let Diomedes bear him,
And bring us Cressid hither; Calchas shall have
What he requests of us. Good Diomed,
Furnish you fairly° for this interchange;   *completely ready yourself*
Withal° bring word if Hector will tomorrow   *At the same time*
35   Be answered in his challenge. Ajax is ready.

6. Customary punishment for an accused person who
remained silent and would not plead.
3.3 Location: The Greek camp.
1. Calchas is Cressida's father, a Trojan priest siding
with the Greeks.

2. In return for someone important.
3. Tuning key for a stringed instrument (hence probably related to "slack," line 24); peg for tightening a sur-
gical ligature.

DIOMEDES This shall I undertake, and 'tis a burden
Which I am proud to bear.   *Exit* [*with* CALCHAS]
        Enter ACHILLES *and* PATROCLUS *in their tent*
ULYSSES Achilles stands i'th' entrance of his tent.
Please it our general pass strangely° by him,   *aloofly*
40 As if he were forgot; and, princes all,
Lay negligent and loose° regard upon him.   *casual*
I will come last. 'Tis like he'll question me
Why such unplausive° eyes are bent, why turned on him.   *unapproving*
If so, I have derision medicinable°   *health-giving scorn*
45 To use° between your strangeness and his pride,   *act as intermediary*
Which his own will shall have desire to drink.
It may do good. Pride hath no other glass
To show itself but pride;[4] for supple knees°   *bowing and scraping*
Feed arrogance and are the proud man's fees.°   *expected reward*
50 AGAMEMNON We'll execute your purpose and put on
A form° of strangeness as we pass along.   *appearance*
So do each lord, and either greet him not
Or else disdainfully, which shall shake him more
Than if not looked on. I will lead the way.
        [*They pass by the tent, in turn*]
55 ACHILLES What, comes the general to speak with me?
You know my mind: I'll fight no more 'gainst Troy.
AGAMEMNON [*to* NESTOR] What says Achilles? Would he aught with us?
NESTOR [*to* ACHILLES] Would you, my lord, aught with the general?
ACHILLES   No.
NESTOR [*to* AGAMEMNON] Nothing, my lord.
AGAMEMNON   The better.
        [*Exeunt* AGAMEMNON *and* NESTOR]
ACHILLES [*to* MENELAUS]   Good day, good day.
60 MENELAUS How do you? How do you?   [*Exit*]
ACHILLES [*to* PATROCLUS]
What, does the cuckold scorn me?
AJAX   How now, Patroclus?
ACHILLES Good morrow, Ajax.
AJAX   Ha?
ACHILLES   Good morrow.
AJAX Ay, and good next day too.   *Exit*
ACHILLES [*to* PATROCLUS] What mean these fellows? Know they
        not Achilles?
65 PATROCLUS They pass by strangely. They were used to bend,
To send their smiles before them to Achilles,
To come as humbly as they use° to creep   *are accustomed*
To holy altars.
ACHILLES   What, am I poor° of late?   *insignificant*
'Tis certain, greatness once fall'n out with fortune
70 Must fall out with men too. What the declined is
He shall as soon read in the eyes of others
As feel in his own fall; for men, like butterflies,
Show not their mealy° wings but to the summer,   *powdery*
And not a man, for being simply man,
75 Hath any honour, but° honour for those honours   *but instead has*
That are without° him—as place, riches, and favour: *external to*

---

4. *Pride . . . pride:* A proud person recognizes excessive pride only when shown it in others.

Prizes of accident° as oft as merit;   *that come by chance*
Which, when they fall, as being slippery standers° —   *on an uncertain base*
The love that leaned on them, as slippery too—
80   Doth one° pluck down another, and together   *The one doth*
Die in the fall. But 'tis not so with me.
Fortune and I are friends. I do enjoy
At ample point° all that I did possess,   *Fully*
Save° these men's looks—who do methinks find out   *Except*
85   Something not worth in me such rich beholding°   *attention*
As they have often given. Here is Ulysses;
I'll interrupt his reading. How now, Ulysses?
ULYSSES   Now, great Thetis' son.
ACHILLES   What are you reading?
90   ULYSSES   A strange fellow here
Writes me that man, how dearly ever parted,°   *however valuably endowed*
How much in having, or without or in,⁵
Cannot make boast to have that which he hath,
Nor feels not what he owes,° but by reflection—   *owns*
95   As when his virtues, shining upon others,
Heat them, and they retort° that heat again   *cast back*
To the first givers.
ACHILLES   This is not strange, Ulysses.
The beauty that is borne here in the face
The bearer knows not, but commends itself
100   To others' eyes. Nor doth the eye itself,
That most pure spirit of sense,° behold itself,   *of the five senses*
Not going from itself; but eye to eye opposed
Salutes each other with each other's form.⁶
For speculation° turns not to itself   *sight*
105   Till it hath travelled and is mirrored there
Where it may see itself. This is not strange at all.
ULYSSES   I do not strain at° the position° —   *question / thesis*
It is familiar—but at the author's drift;
Who in his circumstance expressly° proves   *in detail explicitly*
110   That no man is the lord of anything,
Though in and of him there be much consisting,°   *value*
Till he communicate his parts° to others.   *qualities*
Nor doth he of himself know them for aught°   *as valuable*
Till he behold them formèd in th'applause
115   Where they're extended—who,° like an arch,° reverb'rate   *(the applauders) / vault*
The voice again; or, like a gate of steel
Fronting° the sun, receives and renders back   *Facing*
His figure° and his heat. I was much rapt in this,   *Its appearance*
And apprehended here immediately
120   The unknown Ajax.
Heavens, what a man is there! A very horse,
That has he knows not what.° Nature, what things there are,   *doesn't know himself*
Most abject in regard and dear in use.°   *Despised but useful*
What things again, most dear in the esteem
125   And poor in worth. Now shall we see tomorrow
An act that very° chance doth throw upon him.   *pure*

---

5. However much he possesses, either externally or internally.
6. *Not going . . . form:* Being unable to leave itself; but two eyes (in two people), looking at each other, can show both people their images.

Ajax renowned? O heavens, what some men do,
While some men leave to do.°   *leave undone*
How some men creep in skittish Fortune's hall
130   Whiles others play the idiots in her eyes;[7]
How one man eats into another's pride
While pride is fasting in his wantonness.[8]
To see these Grecian lords! Why, even already
They clap the lubber° Ajax on the shoulder,   *lout*
135   As if his foot were on brave Hector's breast
And great Troy shrinking.°   *cowering; declining*
ACHILLES   I do believe it,
For they passed by me as misers do by beggars,
Neither gave to me good word nor look.
What, are my deeds forgot?
ULYSSES   Time hath, my lord,
140   A wallet° at his back, wherein he puts   *satchel*
Alms for oblivion, a great-sized monster[9]
Of ingratitudes. Those scraps are good deeds past,
Which are devoured as fast as they are made,
Forgot as soon as done. Perseverance, dear my lord,
145   Keeps honour bright. To have done° is to hang   *rely on past deeds*
Quite out of fashion, like a rusty mail°   *coat of armor*
In monumental mock'ry.° Take the instant way,   *a useless monument*
For honour travels in a strait so narrow,
Where one but goes abreast.° Keep then the path,   *must go single file*
150   For emulation hath a thousand sons
That one by one pursue: if you give way,
Or hedge aside from the direct forthright,°   *straightforward path*
Like to an entered tide they all rush by
And leave you hindmost;
155   Or, like a gallant horse fall'n in first rank,
Lie there for pavement to the abject rear,°   *worthless rearguard*
O'errun and trampled on. Then what they do in present,
Though less than yours in past, must o'ertop yours.
For Time is like a fashionable host,
160   That slightly shakes his parting guest by th' hand
And, with his arms outstretched as he would° fly,   *as if he wanted to*
Grasps in the comer. Welcome ever smiles,
And Farewell goes out sighing. O let not virtue seek
Remuneration for the thing it was;
165   For beauty, wit,
High birth, vigour of bone,° desert in service,°   *strength / worthiness*
Love, friendship, charity, are subjects all
To envious and calumniating time.
One touch of nature° makes the whole world kin°—   *natural fault / similar*
170   That all with one consent praise new-born gauds,°   *toys*
Though they are made and moulded of things past,
And give to dust that is a little gilt°   *gilded*
More laud than gilt o'er-dusted.°   *older treasures*
The present eye praises the present object.
175   Then marvel not, thou great and complete man,

---

7. While others act like fools to get Fortune's attention;
do nothing to get Fortune's attention.
8. While the second man in effect starves his pride,
and hence his reputation, through his odd behavior.

9. *Alms for oblivion*: Feats that won't be remembered.
Traditionally, if you wore your satchel behind you, it
contained your vices, which you in this way forgot.
monster: time or, more likely, oblivion.

That all the Greeks begin to worship Ajax,
Since things in motion sooner catch the eye
Than what not stirs. The cry° went once on thee,   approval
And still it might, and yet it may again,
180   If thou wouldst not entomb thyself alive
And case° thy reputation in thy tent,   shut up
Whose glorious deeds but in these fields of late
Made emulous missions 'mongst the gods themselves,[1]
And drove great Mars to faction.°   to take sides

ACHILLES   Of this my privacy
I have strong reasons.
185   ULYSSES   But 'gainst your privacy
The reasons are more potent and heroical.
'Tis known, Achilles, that you are in love
With one of Priam's daughters.°   Polyxena

ACHILLES   Ha? Known?
ULYSSES   Is that a wonder?
The providence that's in a watchful state[2]
190   Knows almost every grain of Pluto's[3] gold,
Finds bottom in th'uncomprehensive° deeps,   unimaginable
Keeps place with aught,[4] and almost like the gods
Do infant thoughts unveil in their dumb cradles.[5]
There is a mystery, with whom relation°   report
195   Durst never meddle, in the soul of state,
Which hath an operation more divine
Than breath or pen can give expressure° to.   expression
All the commerce° that you have had with Troy   dealings
As perfectly is ours as yours,[6] my lord;
200   And better would it fit Achilles much
To throw down° Hector than Polyxena.   (in war); (in love)
But it must grieve young Pyrrhus° now at home,   Achilles' son
When fame shall in his island sound her trump
And all the Greekish girls shall tripping sing,
205   'Great Hector's sister did Achilles win,
But our great Ajax bravely beat down *him*'.°   (Hector)
Farewell, my lord. I as your lover° speak.   good friend
The fool slides o'er the ice that you should break.[7]   [*Exit*]

PATROCLUS   To this effect, Achilles, have I moved you.
210   A woman impudent° and mannish grown   immodest
Is not more loathed than an effeminate° man   cowardly
In time of action. I stand condemned for this.
They think my little stomach to° the war   appetite for
And your great love to me restrains you thus.
215   Sweet, rouse yourself, and the weak wanton Cupid
Shall from your neck unloose his amorous fold°   embrace
And like a dew-drop from the lion's mane
Be shook to air.

ACHILLES   Shall Ajax fight with Hector?
PATROCLUS   Ay, and perhaps receive much honour by him.

---

1. Caused the gods to join the fight on both sides in an effort to match Achilles.
2. Government foresight is compared to divine "providence"—perhaps ironically.
3. God of the underworld (regularly identified with Plutus, god of wealth).
4. Stays abreast of everything.
5. *Do . . . cradles:* Discovers thoughts before they are spoken.
6. Is as well known to us (the other Greek leaders) as to you.
7. Perhaps: Ajax (the fool) is engaged in superficial action, whereas only you can initiate real combat.

220 ACHILLES   I see my reputation is at stake.
My fame is shrewdly gored.°   *severely wounded*
PATROCLUS   O then beware:
Those wounds heal ill that men do give themselves.
Omission to do what is necessary
Seals a commission to a blank of danger,[8]
225 And danger like an ague subtly taints
Even then when we sit idly in the sun.[9]
ACHILLES   Go call Thersites hither, sweet Patroclus.
I'll send the fool to Ajax, and desire him
T'invite the Trojan lords after the combat
230 To see us here unarmed. I have a woman's longing,
An appetite that I am sick withal,°   *with*
To see great Hector in his weeds° of peace,   *garments*

         Enter THERSITES

To talk with him and to behold his visage
Even to my full of view.°—A labour saved.   *in full view*
235 THERSITES   A wonder!
ACHILLES   What?
THERSITES   Ajax goes up and down the field, as° asking for him-   *as if*
self.[1]
ACHILLES   How so?
240 THERSITES   He must° fight singly tomorrow with Hector, and is   *is to*
so prophetically proud of an heroical cudgelling° that he raves   *(by Hector)*
in saying nothing.
ACHILLES   How can that be?
THERSITES   Why, a° stalks up and down like a peacock—a stride   *he*
245 and a stand; ruminates like an hostess that hath no arithmetic
but her brain to set down her reckoning;[2] bites his lip with a
politic regard,° as who should say 'There were wit in this head,   *judicious expression*
an't would out'°—and so there is; but it lies as coldly in him as   *if it would come out*
fire in a flint, which will not show without knocking.° The   *striking (into flame)*
250 man's undone for ever, for if Hector break not his neck i'th'
combat he'll break't himself in vainglory. He knows not me. I
said, 'Good morrow, Ajax', and he replies, 'Thanks, Agamemnon'. What think you of this man that takes me for the Gen-
eral? He's grown a very land-fish,° languageless, a monster. A   *unnatural creature*
255 plague of opinion! A man may wear it on both sides like a
leather jerkin.[3]
ACHILLES   Thou must be my ambassador to him, Thersites.
THERSITES   Who, I? Why, he'll answer nobody. He professes not
answering.° Speaking is for beggars. He wears his tongue in's   *refuses to respond*
260 arms. I will put on° his presence. Let Patroclus make demands   *imitate*
to me. You shall see the pageant of Ajax.
ACHILLES   To him, Patroclus. Tell him I humbly desire the valiant Ajax to invite the most valorous Hector to come unarmed
to my tent, and to procure safe-conduct for his person of the
265 magnanimous and most illustrious six-or-seven-times-honoured
captain-general of the Grecian army, Agamemnon; et cetera.
Do this.

8. Gives danger free rein (literally, provides danger
with a blank warrant to fill in as it pleases).
9. *danger . . . sun:* danger, like a fever, insidiously weakens (causes shivering) even when one is sitting in the sun.
1. Punning on "Ajax" and "a jakes" (a toilet), the point
presumably being that Ajax is so terrified by battle, he
cannot help relieving himself.
2. Like the hostess at an inn whose mathematical inep-
titude makes it hard for her to work out the bill.
3. A plague on conceit (or reputation)! One can wear it
either way (conceit or reputation) like a reversible
jacket (but it's still the same pride).

PATROCLUS [*to* THERSITES]   Jove bless great Ajax!

THERSITES   H'm.

270   PATROCLUS   I come from the worthy Achilles—

THERSITES   Ha?

PATROCLUS   Who most humbly desires you to invite Hector to
his tent—

THERSITES   H'm!

275   PATROCLUS   And to procure safe-conduct from Agamemnon.

THERSITES   Agamemnon?

PATROCLUS   Ay, my lord.

THERSITES   Ha!

PATROCLUS   What say you to't?

280   THERSITES   God b'wi' you,° with all my heart.   *(dismissive)*

PATROCLUS   Your answer, sir?

THERSITES   If tomorrow be a fair day, by eleven o'clock it will go
one way or other. Howsoever, he shall pay for me ere° he has   *pay dearly before*
me.

285   PATROCLUS   Your answer, sir?

THERSITES   Fare ye well, with all my heart.

ACHILLES   Why, but he is not in this tune,° is he?   *mood*

THERSITES   No, but he's out o' tune thus. What music will be in
him when Hector has knocked out his brains, I know not. But
290   I am feared° none, unless the fiddler Apollo get his sinews to   *afraid*
make catlings⁴ on.

ACHILLES   Come, thou shalt bear a letter to him straight.

THERSITES   Let me carry another to his horse, for that's the more
capable° creature.   *intelligent*

295   ACHILLES   My mind is troubled like a fountain stirred,
And I myself see not the bottom of it.   [*Exit with* PATROCLUS]

THERSITES   Would the fountain of your mind were clear again,
that I might water an ass at it. I had rather be a tick in a sheep
than such a valiant ignorance.°   *Exit*   *puffed-up fool*

4.1

Enter at one door AENEAS *with a torch; at another* PARIS,
DEIPHOBUS, ANTENOR, [*and*] DIOMEDES *the Grecian,
with torch*[*-bearers*]

PARIS   See, ho! Who is that there?

DEIPHOBUS   It is the Lord Aeneas.

AENEAS   Is the Prince there in person?
Had I so good occasion to lie long
5   As you, Prince Paris, nothing but heavenly business
Should rob my bed-mate of my company.

DIOMEDES   That's my mind too. Good morrow, Lord Aeneas.

PARIS   A valiant Greek, Aeneas, take his hand.
Witness the process of your speech,¹ wherein
10   You told how Diomed e'en a whole week by days°   *every day*
Did haunt you in the field.

AENEAS [*to* DIOMEDES]   Health to you, valiant sir,
During all question of° the gentle truce.   *conversations during*
But when I meet you armed, as black defiance

---

4. Instrument strings made of catgut.

4.1 Location: A street in Troy.

1. *Witness . . . speech:* As the thrust of your narrative
made clear (that he is valiant).

As heart can think or courage execute.

15 DIOMEDES The one and other Diomed embraces.
Our bloods are now in calm; and so long, health.
But when contention and occasion meet,°   *it's time to fight*
By Jove I'll play the hunter for thy life
With all my force, pursuit, and policy.°   *cunning*
20 AENEAS And thou shalt hunt a lion that will fly
With his face backward.[2] In humane gentleness,
Welcome to Troy. Now by Anchises' life,
Welcome indeed! By Venus'[3] hand I swear
No man alive can love in such a sort°   *to such an extent*
25 The thing he means to kill more excellently.
DIOMEDES We sympathize.° Jove, let Aeneas live—   *feel the same*
If to my sword his fate be not the glory—
A thousand complete courses of the sun;
But, in mine emulous honour,[4] let him die
30 With every joint a wound—and that, tomorrow.
AENEAS We know each other well.
DIOMEDES We do, and long to know each other worse.
PARIS This is the most despitefull'st gentle greeting,
The noblest hateful love, that e'er I heard of.
35 What business, lord, so early?
AENEAS I was sent for to the King; but why, I know not.
PARIS His purpose meets you:° 'twas to bring this Greek   *I'll tell you why*
To Calchas' house, and there to render him,
For the enfreed Antenor, the fair Cressid.
40 Let's have your company, or if you please
Haste there before us. [*Aside*] I constantly° do think—   *firmly*
Or rather, call my thought a certain knowledge—
My brother Troilus lodges there tonight.
Rouse him and give him note of our approach,
45 With the whole quality° wherefore. I fear   *cause*
We shall be much unwelcome.
AENEAS [*aside*]   That I assure you.
Troilus had rather Troy were borne to Greece
Than Cressid borne from Troy.
PARIS [*aside*]   There is no help.
The bitter disposition of the time
50 Will have it so.
[*Aloud*] On, lord, we'll follow you.
AENEAS Good morrow all.   *Exit*
PARIS And tell me, noble Diomed—faith, tell me true,
Even in the soul of sound good-fellowship—
55 Who in your thoughts merits fair Helen most,
Myself or Menelaus?
DIOMEDES   Both alike.
He merits well to have her that doth seek her,
Not making any scruple of her soilure,°   *issue of her dishonor*
With such a hell of pain and world of charge;°   *expense*
60 And you as well to keep her that defend her,
Not palating the taste of° her dishonour,   *Not even tasting*

---

2. In the imagery of heraldry for chivalric combat, a lion walking and looking back over his shoulder; also, Aeneas will still fight even as he retreats.

3. Anchises and Venus, the goddess of love, were Aeneas's parents.
4. If his death will increase my honor.

With such a costly loss of wealth and friends.
He like a puling° cuckold would drink up   *whining*
The lees and dregs of a flat 'tamèd piece;⁵
65   You like a lecher out of whorish loins
Are pleased to breed out your inheritors.
Both merits poised,° each weighs nor less nor more,   *weighed in the scales*
But he as he: which heavier for a whore?⁶
PARIS   You are too bitter to your countrywoman.
70   DIOMEDES   She's bitter to her country. Hear me, Paris.
For every false drop in her bawdy veins
A Grecian's life hath sunk; for every scruple°   *tiny unit of weight*
Of her contaminated carrion° weight   *putrid*
A Trojan hath been slain. Since she could speak
75   She hath not given so many good words breath
As, for her, Greeks and Trojans suffered death.
PARIS   Fair Diomed, you do as chapmen° do: *merchants*
Dispraise the thing that you desire to buy.
But we in silence hold this virtue well:°   *act similarly*
80   We'll but commend what we intend to sell.⁷—
Here lies our way.   *Exeunt*

4.2

Enter TROILUS *and* CRESSIDA

TROILUS   Dear, trouble not yourself. The morn is cold.
CRESSIDA   Then, sweet my lord, I'll call mine uncle down.
He shall unbolt the gates.
TROILUS   Trouble him not.
To bed, to bed! Sleep lull those pretty eyes
5   And give as soft attachment° to thy senses   *imprisonment*
As to infants empty of all thought.
CRESSIDA   Good morrow, then.
TROILUS   I prithee now, to bed.
CRESSIDA   Are you aweary of me?
10   TROILUS   O Cressida! But that the busy day,
Waked by the lark, hath roused the ribald° crows,   *offensively noisy*
And dreaming night will hide our joys no longer,
I would not from thee.
CRESSIDA   Night hath been too brief.
TROILUS   Beshrew the witch! With venomous wights¹ she stays
15   As hideously as hell, but flies° the grasps of love   *flees*
With wings more momentary-swift than thought.
You will catch cold and curse me.
CRESSIDA   Prithee, tarry. You men will never tarry.
O foolish Cressid! I might have still held off,
20   And then you would have tarried.—Hark, there's one up.
[*She veils herself*]
PANDARUS [*within*]   What's° all the doors open here?   *Why are*
TROILUS   It is your uncle.
CRESSIDA   A pestilence on him! Now will he be mocking.
I shall have such a life.

---

5. Of a stale insipid (penetrated) cask of wine (woman).
6. But one the same as the other: which more deserves
(is made sadder by) the whore?
7. We'll praise only what we're trying to sell. (But we

don't intend to bargain for Helen and so won't praise her.)
4.2 Location: Cressida's house.
1. Curse the night! With evil people (who are hateful to
each other).

Enter PANDARUS

25 PANDARUS How now, how now, how go° maidenheads?   *what's the price of*
    [*To* CRESSIDA] Here, you, maid! Where's my cousin Cressid?²
  CRESSIDA [*unveiling*] Go hang yourself. You naughty, mocking uncle!
    You bring me to do°—and then you flout me too.   *have sex*
  PANDARUS To do what? To do what?—Let her say what.—What
30 have I brought you to do?
  CRESSIDA Come, come, beshrew° your heart. You'll ne'er be good,   *curses on*
    Nor suffer others.°   *let others be good*
  PANDARUS Ha ha! Alas, poor wretch. Ah, poor *capocchia*,° hast   *simpleton; foreskin*
    not slept tonight? Would he not—a naughty man—let it sleep?
35 A bugbear° take him.   *goblin*
  CRESSIDA [*to* TROILUS] Did not I tell you? Would he were
    knocked i'th' head.°   *killed*

One knocks [*within*]

    Who's that at door?—Good uncle, go and see.—
    My lord, come you again into my chamber.
    You smile and mock me, as if I meant naughtily.
40 TROILUS Ha ha!
  CRESSIDA Come, you are deceived, I think of no such thing.

[*One*] knock[*s within*]

    How earnestly they knock! Pray you come in.
    I would not for half Troy have you seen here.

Exeunt [TROILUS *and* CRESSIDA]

  PANDARUS Who's there? What's the matter? Will you beat down
45 the door?

[*He opens the door. Enter* AENEAS]

    How now, what's the matter?
  AENEAS Good morrow, lord, good morrow.
  PANDARUS Who's there? My Lord Aeneas? By my troth,
    I knew you not. What news with you so early?
  AENEAS Is not Prince Troilus here?
50 PANDARUS   Here? What should he do here?
  AENEAS Come, he is here, my lord. Do not deny him.
    It doth import° him much to speak with me.   *concern*
  PANDARUS Is he here, say you? It's more than I know, I'll be
    sworn. For my own part, I came in late. What should he do
55 here?
  AENEAS Whoa! Nay, then. Come, come, you'll do him wrong
    Ere you are ware.° You'll be so true to him   *aware*
    To be false to him.° Do not you know of him,   *As to harm him*
    But yet go fetch him hither. Go.

[*Exit* PANDARUS]³

Enter TROILUS

60 TROILUS How now, what's the matter?
  AENEAS My lord, I scarce have leisure to salute you,
    My matter is so rash.° There is at hand   *urgent*
    Paris your brother and Deiphobus,
    The Grecian Diomed, and our Antenor

---

2. Pandarus pretends not to recognize Cressida, now that she is no longer a virgin. It is possible that he addresses her as "maid" (line 26) because she is wearing a veil, which suggests a modesty appropriate to virgins. 3. Editors usually keep him on and have Cressida enter alone at what is the beginning of 4.3 in this edition.

65   Delivered to us—and for him° forthwith,   *(Antenor)*
        Ere the first sacrifice, within this hour,
        We must give up to Diomedes' hand
        The Lady Cressida.

TROILUS   Is it so concluded?

AENEAS   By Priam and the general state° of Troy.   *council*

70   They are at hand, and ready to effect it.

TROILUS   How my achievements mock me.
        I will go meet them—and, my Lord Aeneas,
        We° met by chance: you did not find me here.   *(Pretend that) we*

AENEAS   Good, good, my lord: the untold secrecies° of nature   *untold secrets*

75   Have not more gift in taciturnity.   *Exeunt*

4.3

Enter PANDARUS *and* CRESSIDA[1]

PANDARUS   Is't possible? No sooner got but lost. The devil take
        Antenor! The young prince will go mad. A plague upon Ante-
        nor! I would they had broke 's neck.

CRESSIDA   How now? What's the matter? Who was here?

5   PANDARUS   Ah, ah!

CRESSIDA   Why sigh you so profoundly? Where's my lord?
        Gone? Tell me, sweet uncle, what's the matter?

PANDARUS   Would I were as deep under the earth as I am above.

CRESSIDA   O the gods! What's the matter?

10 PANDARUS   Pray thee, get thee in. Would thou hadst ne'er been
        born. I knew thou wouldst be his death. O poor gentleman! A
        plague upon Antenor!

CRESSIDA   Good uncle, I beseech you on my knees; I beseech
        you, what's the matter?

15 PANDARUS   Thou must be gone, wench, thou must be gone.
        Thou art changed° for Antenor. Thou must to thy father, and   *exchanged*
        be gone from Troilus. 'Twill be his death. 'Twill be his bane.
        He cannot bear it.

CRESSIDA   O you immortal gods! I will not go.

20 PANDARUS   Thou must.

CRESSIDA   I will not, uncle. I have forgot my father.
        I know no touch of consanguinity,
        No kin, no love, no blood, no soul, so near me
        As the sweet Troilus. O you gods divine,

25   Make Cressid's name the very crown° of falsehood   *height*
        If ever she leave Troilus. Time, force, and death
        Do to this body what extremity you can,
        But the strong base and building of my love
        Is as the very centre of the earth,

30   Drawing all things to it. I'll go in and weep—

PANDARUS   Do, do.

CRESSIDA   Tear my bright hair, and scratch my praisèd cheeks,
        Crack my clear voice with sobs, and break my heart
        With sounding 'Troilus'. I will not go from Troy.   *Exeunt*

4.3 Location: Scene continues.
 1. Most modern editions do not mark a scene break here;   this affects the numbering of the following lines and
                                     scenes. See note to 4.2.59 and Textual Note.

4.4

Enter PARIS, TROILUS, AENEAS, DEIPHOBUS, ANTENOR,
and DIOMEDES

PARIS   It is great morning,° and the hour prefixed°   *daylight / arranged*
    Of her delivery to this valiant Greek
    Comes fast upon us. Good my brother Troilus,
    Tell you the lady what she is to do,
    And haste her to the purpose.
5 TROILUS   Walk into her house.
    I'll bring her to the Grecian presently°—   *immediately*
    And to his hand when I deliver her,
    Think it an altar, and thy brother Troilus
    A priest, there off'ring to it his own heart.
10 PARIS   I know what 'tis to love,
    And would,° as I shall pity, I could help.—   *wish*
    Please you walk in, my lords?   *Exeunt*

4.5

Enter PANDARUS *and* CRESSIDA

PANDARUS   Be moderate, be moderate.
CRESSIDA   Why tell you me of moderation?
    The grief is fine,° full, perfect that I taste,   *undiluted*
    And violenteth° in a sense° as strong   *rages / manner*
5 As that which causeth it.° How can I moderate it?   *(her love)*
    If I could temporize with° my affection   *adjust to*
    Or brew° it to a weak and colder palate,°   *dilute / taste*
    The like allayment° could I give my grief.   *dilution*
    My love admits no qualifying dross;°   *modifying impurity*
10 No more° my grief, in such a precious loss.   *Any more than does*

Enter TROILUS

PANDARUS   Here, here, here he comes. Ah, sweet ducks!
CRESSIDA [*embracing him*]   O Troilus, Troilus!
PANDARUS   What a pair of spectacles° is here! Let me embrace   *sights*
    you too. 'O heart', as the goodly saying is,
15   'O heart, heavy heart,
          Why sigh'st thou without breaking?'
    where he answers again
         'Because thou canst not ease thy smart
           By friendship nor by speaking.'
20 There was never a truer rhyme. Let us cast away nothing, for
    we may live to have need of such a verse. We see it, we see it.
    How now, lambs?
TROILUS   Cressid, I love thee in so strained° a purity   *refined*
    That the blest gods, as° angry with my fancy°—   *as if / love*
25 More bright in zeal than the devotion which
    Cold lips blow to their deities—take thee from me.
CRESSIDA   Have the gods envy?
PANDARUS   Ay, ay, ay, ay, 'tis too plain a case.
CRESSIDA   And is it true that I must go from Troy?
TROILUS   A hateful truth.
30 CRESSIDA   What, and from Troilus too?
TROILUS   From Troy and Troilus.

4.4 Location: Outside Cressida's house.   4.5 Location: Inside Cressida's house.

CRESSIDA   Is't possible?

TROILUS   And suddenly°—where injury of° chance   *immediately / injurious*
Puts back° leave-taking, jostles roughly by   *Prevents*
All time of pause, rudely beguiles° our lips   *deprives*
35   Of all rejoindure,° forcibly prevents   *joining again*
Our locked embrasures, strangles our dear vows
Even in the birth of our own labouring breath.°   *(as in childbirth)*
We two, that with so many thousand sighs
Did buy each other, must poorly sell ourselves
40   With the rude brevity and discharge of one.°   *(sigh)*
Injurious Time now with a robber's haste
Crams his rich thiev'ry up, he knows not how.[1]
As many farewells as be stars in heaven,
With distinct breath and consigned° kisses to them,   *ratifying*
45   He fumbles up° into a loose adieu   *clumsily combines*
And scants us with a single famished kiss,
Distasted[2] with the salt of broken° tears.   *interrupted*

        Enter AENEAS

AENEAS   My lord, is the lady ready?

TROILUS [*to* CRESSIDA]   Hark, you are called. Some say the *genius*° so   *guardian spirit*
50   Cries 'Come!' to him that instantly must die.
[*To* PANDARUS] Bid them have patience. She shall come anon.

PANDARUS   Where are my tears? Rain, to lay this wind,° or my   *allay my sighs*
heart will be blown up by the root.   [*Exit with* AENEAS]

CRESSIDA   I must then to the Grecians.

TROILUS   No remedy.

55   CRESSIDA   A woeful Cressid 'mongst the merry Greeks![3]
When shall we see again?

TROILUS   Hear me, my love: be thou but true of heart—

CRESSIDA   I true? How now! What wicked deem° is this?   *thought*

TROILUS   Nay, we must use expostulation° kindly,   *conversation*
60   For it° is parting from us.   *the opportunity*
I speak not 'Be thou true' as fearing thee—
For I will throw my glove to° Death himself   *challenge*
That there's no maculation° in thy heart—   *stain of infidelity*
But 'Be thou true' say I, to fashion in°   *introduce*
65   My sequent° protestation: 'Be thou true,   *following*
And I will see thee'.

CRESSIDA   O you shall be exposed, my lord, to dangers
As infinite as imminent. But I'll be true.

TROILUS   And I'll grow friend with danger. Wear this sleeve.[4]

70   CRESSIDA   And you this glove. When shall I see you?

TROILUS   I will corrupt the Grecian sentinels
To° give thee nightly visitation.   *In order that I may*
But yet, be true.

CRESSIDA   O heavens! 'Be true' again!

75   TROILUS   Hear why I speak it, love.
The Grecian youths are full of quality,
Their loving well composed, with gifts of nature flowing,
And swelling o'er with arts° and exercise.°   *education / practice*
How novelty may move, and parts with person,°   *talent and good looks*
80   Alas, a kind of godly° jealousy—   *divinely sanctioned*

1. Compresses his stolen goods (farewell kisses) into a
short period, distractedly.
2. Made distasteful.

3. Common phrase for licentious revelers, here also
meant literally.
4. Often detachable in Elizabethan dress.

Which I beseech you call a virtuous sin—
Makes me afeard.

CRESSIDA   O heavens, you love me not!

TROILUS   Die I a villain then!

85   In this I do not call your faith° in question   *fidelity*
So mainly° as my merit.[5] I cannot sing,   *much*
Nor heel the high lavolt, nor sweeten talk,[6]
Nor play at subtle games—fair virtues all,
To which the Grecians are most prompt and pregnant.°   *ready*
90   But I can tell that in each grace of these
There lurks a still and dumb-discoursive° devil   *silently communicating*
That tempts most cunningly. But be not tempted.

CRESSIDA   Do you think I will?

TROILUS   No, but something may be done that we will not,°   *do not will*
95   And sometimes we are devils to ourselves,
When we will tempt the frailty of our powers,
Presuming on their changeful potency.°   *unreliable strength*

AENEAS (*within*)   Nay, good my lord!

TROILUS   Come, kiss, and let us part.

PARIS [*at the door*]   Brother Troilus?

TROILUS   Good brother, come you hither,
100   And bring Aeneas and the Grecian with you. *Exit* [PARIS]

CRESSIDA   My lord, will you be true?

TROILUS   Who, I? Alas, it is my vice, my fault.
Whiles others fish with craft° for great opinion,°   *guile / reputation*
I with great truth catch mere simplicity;[7]
105   Whilst some with cunning gild their copper crowns,°   *coins; heads*
With truth and plainness I do wear° mine bare.   *dress; erode*

       Enter [PARIS, AENEAS, ANTENOR, DEIPHOBUS, *and* DIO-
       MEDES]

Fear not my truth. The moral° of my wit   *maxim*
Is 'plain and true!'; there's all the reach of it.—
Welcome, Sir Diomed. Here is the lady
110   Which for Antenor we deliver you.
At the port,° lord, I'll give her to thy hand,   *gate of the city*
And by the way possess° thee what she is.   *instruct*
Entreat° her fair, and by my soul, fair Greek,   *Treat*
If e'er thou stand at mercy of my sword,
115   Name Cressid, and thy life shall be as safe
As Priam is in Ilium.

DIOMEDES   Fair Lady Cressid,
So please you, save the thanks this prince expects.[8]
The lustre in your eye, heaven in your cheek,
Pleads your fair usage;° and to Diomed   *treatment*
120   You shall be mistress, and command him wholly.

TROILUS   Grecian, thou dost not use me courteously,
To shame the zeal of my petition towards thee
In praising her. I tell thee, lord of Greece,
She is as far high-soaring o'er thy praises

---

5. Deserts; good works, deserving of salvation (picking up the religious language of the preceding lines, especially "faith," line 85).
6. Nor dance the "lavolt" (which involved spectacular jumps), nor flatter.
7. Absolute rusticity (sincerity).
8. *save . . . expects:* you won't need to thank Troilus for the good treatment I will give you.

125   As thou unworthy to be called her servant.[9]
        I charge thee use her well, even for my charge;°   *simply at my command*
        For, by the dreadful Pluto, if thou dost not,
        Though the great bulk Achilles be thy guard
        I'll cut thy throat.
    DIOMEDES   O be not moved,° Prince Troilus.   *angry*
130   Let me be privileged by my place and message
        To be a speaker free. When I am hence
        I'll answer to my lust.° And know you, lord,   *do as I please*
        I'll nothing do on charge.° To her own worth   *command*
        She shall be prized; but that° you say 'Be't so',   *simply because*
135   I'll speak it in my spirit and honour 'No!'
    TROILUS   Come, to the port.—I'll tell thee, Diomed,
        This brave° shall oft make thee to hide thy head.—   *boast*
        Lady, give me your hand, and as we walk
        To our own selves bend we our needful talk.
                [Exeunt TROILUS, CRESSIDA, *and* DIOMEDES*]*
          [A] trumpet sound[s]
    PARIS   Hark, Hector's trumpet.
140   AENEAS   How have we spent this morning?
        The Prince must think me tardy and remiss,
        That swore to ride before him in the field.
    PARIS   'Tis Troilus' fault. Come, come to field with him.
    DEIPHOBUS   Let us make ready straight.
145   AENEAS   Yea, with a bridegroom's fresh alacrity
        Let us address° to tend on Hector's heels.   *prepare*
        The glory of our Troy doth this day lie
        On his fair worth and single chivalry.   *Exeunt*

4.6

Enter AJAX *armed*, ACHILLES, PATROCLUS, AGAMEMNON,
  MENELAUS, ULYSSES, NESTOR[, *a trumpeter, and others*]
    AGAMEMNON   Here art thou in appointment° fresh and fair,   *equipment*
        Anticipating time[1] with starting° courage.   *bounding*
        Give with thy trumpet a loud note to Troy,
        Thou dreadful° Ajax, that the appallèd air   *causing fear*
5   May pierce the head of the great combatant
        And hale° him hither.   *draw*
    AJAX   Thou trumpet,° there's my purse.   *trumpeter*
          [He gives him money]
        Now crack thy lungs and split thy brazen pipe.°   *trumpet; windpipe*
        Blow, villain,° till thy spherèd bias° cheek   *servant / puffed-out*
        Outswell the colic of puffed Aquilon.[2]
10   Come, stretch thy chest and let thy eyes spout blood;
        Thou blow'st for Hector.
          [The trumpet sounds]
    ULYSSES   No trumpet answers.
    ACHILLES   'Tis but early days.
    AGAMEMNON   Is not yond Diomed with Calchas' daughter?
15   ULYSSES   'Tis he. I ken° the manner of his gait.   *recognize*

---

9. Like "mistress" (line 120), a cliché of courtly love.
4.6 Location: Between the Greek camp and Troy.
1. Ajax has not waited for Hector to appear with his
challenge.

2. Outswells the intestinal pain (from bloating) of the
north wind (Aquilon). (Winds on contemporary maps
were represented as human heads blowing.)

He rises on the toe: that spirit of his
In aspiration lifts him from the earth.
     [*Enter* DIOMEDES *and* CRESSIDA]
AGAMEMNON [*to* DIOMEDES]   Is this the Lady Cressid?
DIOMEDES   Even she.
AGAMEMNON   Most dearly welcome to the Greeks, sweet lady.
     [*He kisses her*]
20 NESTOR [*to* CRESSIDA]   Our General doth salute you with a kiss.
ULYSSES   Yet is the kindness but particular;°   *from only one of us*
'Twere better she were kissed in general.
NESTOR   And very courtly counsel. I'll begin.
     [*He kisses her*]
So much for Nestor.
25 ACHILLES   I'll take that winter° from your lips, fair lady.   *Nestor's old age*
     [*He kisses her*]
Achilles bids you welcome.
MENELAUS [*to* CRESSIDA]   I had good argument° for kissing once.   *Helen*
PATROCLUS   But that's no argument for kissing now;
For thus [*stepping between them*] popped° Paris in his   *thrust in*
   hardiment,°   *boldness; hardness*
30 And parted thus you and your argument.
     [*He kisses her*]
ULYSSES [*aside*]   O deadly gall, and theme of all our scorns!
For which we lose our heads to gild his horns.°   *cuckold's horns*
PATROCLUS [*to* CRESSIDA]   The first was Menelaus' kiss; this, mine.
Patroclus kisses you.
     [*He kisses her again*]
MENELAUS   O this is trim.°   *excellent*
35 PATROCLUS [*to* CRESSIDA]   Paris and I kiss evermore° for him.   *always*
MENELAUS   I'll have my kiss, sir.—Lady, by your leave.
CRESSIDA   In kissing do you render or receive?
MENELAUS   Both take and give.
CRESSIDA   I'll make my match to live,°   *bet my life*
The kiss you take is better than you give.
40 Therefore no kiss.
MENELAUS   I'll give you boot:° I'll give you three for one.   *profit*
CRESSIDA   You are an odd[3] man: give even or give none.
MENELAUS   An odd man, lady? Every man is odd.
CRESSIDA   No, Paris is not—for you know 'tis true
45 That you are odd, and he is even° with you.   *has gotten even*
MENELAUS   You fillip me o'th' head.[4]
CRESSIDA   No, I'll be sworn.
ULYSSES   It were no match, your nail against his horn.[5]
May I, sweet lady, beg a kiss of you?
CRESSIDA   You may.
ULYSSES   I do desire it.
CRESSIDA   Why, beg too.
50 ULYSSES   Why then, for Venus' sake, give me a kiss,
When Helen is a maid again, and his°—   *Menelaus's*
CRESSIDA   I am your debtor; claim it when 'tis due.

ULYSSES Never's my day,° and then a kiss of you. *the due date*

DIOMEDES Lady, a word. I'll bring you to your father.

   [*They talk apart*]

NESTOR A woman of quick sense.° *intelligence; sexuality*

55 ULYSSES   Fie, fie upon her!

There's language in her eye, her cheek, her lip;

Nay, her foot speaks. Her wanton spirits look out° *are exposed*

At every joint and motive° of her body. *moving limb*

O these encounterers so glib of tongue,

60 That give accosting° welcome ere it comes, *an approach*

And wide unclasp the tables° of their thoughts *tablets*

To every ticklish° reader, set them down° *lustful / mark them*

For sluttish spoils of opportunity° *As easy sexual prey*

And daughters of the game.° *prostitutes*

                    Exeunt [DIOMEDES *and* CRESSIDA]

         Flourish

65 ALL   The Trojans' trumpet.° *(Trojan strumpet)*

   Enter all of Troy: HECTOR [*armed*], PARIS, AENEAS, HELE-

   NUS, *and attendants* [*among them* TROILUS]

AGAMEMNON Yonder comes the troop.

AENEAS [*coming forward*] Hail, all you state° of Greece! What *noblemen*

   shall be done° *rewarded*

To him that victory commands? Or do you purpose

A victor shall be known? Will you° the knights *Do you wish that*

70 Shall to the edge of all extremity° *the death*

Pursue each other, or shall they be divided

By any voice or order of the field?[6]

Hector bade ask.

AGAMEMNON   Which way would Hector have it?

AENEAS He cares not; he'll obey conditions.° *your choice*

75 ACHILLES 'Tis done like Hector—but securely° done, *too boldly*

A little proudly, and great deal disprising° *underestimating*

The knight opposed.

AENEAS   If not Achilles, sir,

What is your name?

ACHILLES   If not Achilles, nothing.

AENEAS Therefore Achilles. But whate'er, know this:

80 In the extremity of great and little,

Valour and pride excel themselves in Hector,

The one° almost as infinite as all, *(valor)*

The other° blank as nothing. Weigh him well, *(pride)*

And that which looks like pride is courtesy.

85 This Ajax is half made of Hector's blood,[7]

In love whereof half Hector stays at home.

Half heart, half hand, half Hector comes to seek

This blended knight, half Trojan and half Greek.

ACHILLES A maiden° battle, then? O I perceive you. *bloodless*

   [*Enter* DIOMEDES]

90 AGAMEMNON Here is Sir Diomed.—Go, gentle knight,

Stand by our Ajax. As you and Lord Aeneas

Consent° upon the order° of their fight, *Decide / terms*

---

6. By any umpire or rules of combat?   7. Ajax was Priam's nephew.

So be it: either to the uttermost
Or else a breath.°   *bout of exercise*

[*Exeunt* AJAX, DIOMEDES, HECTOR, *and* AENEAS][8]
The combatants being kin

95 Half stints their strife before their strokes begin.

ULYSSES   They are opposed already.

AGAMEMNON   What Trojan is that same that looks so heavy?°   *sorrowful*

ULYSSES   The youngest son of Priam, a true knight:
     They call him Troilus.

100 Not yet mature, yet matchless-firm of word,
     Speaking in deeds and deedless in his tongue;°   *not boastful*
     Not soon provoked, nor being provoked soon calmed;
     His heart and hand both open and both free.°   *generous*
     For what he has he gives; what thinks, he shows;

105 Yet gives he not till judgement guide his bounty,°   *generosity*
     Nor dignifies an impare° thought with breath.   *unworthy*
     Manly as Hector but more dangerous,
     For Hector in his blaze of wrath subscribes°   *relents*
     To tender objects, but he in heat of action

110 Is more vindicative° than jealous love.   *vindictive*
     They call him Troilus, and on him erect
     A second hope as fairly built as Hector.
     Thus says Aeneas, one that knows the youth
     Even to his inches, and with private soul[9]

115 Did in great Ilium thus translate° him to me.   *describe*

          Alarum

AGAMEMNON   They are in action.

NESTOR   Now, Ajax, hold thine own!

TROILUS   Hector, thou sleep'st! Awake thee!

AGAMEMNON   His blows are well disposed. There, Ajax!   [*Exeunt*]

4.7

[*Enter* HECTOR *and* AJAX *fighting, and* AENEAS *and* DIO-
MEDES *interposing.*] *Trumpets cease*[1]

DIOMEDES   You must no more.

AENEAS   Princes, enough, so please you.

AJAX   I am not warm yet. Let us fight again.

DIOMEDES   As Hector pleases.

HECTOR   Why then will I no more.—
     Thou art, great lord, my father's sister's son,

5   A cousin-german° to great Priam's seed.   *first cousin*
     The obligation of our blood forbids
     A gory emulation° 'twixt us twain.   *competition*
     Were thy commixtion° Greek and Trojan so°   *blending / such*
     That thou couldst say 'This hand is Grecian all,

10   And this is Trojan; the sinews of this leg
     All Greek, and this all Troy; my mother's blood
     Runs on the dexter° cheek, and this sinister°   *right / left*
     Bounds in my father's,' by Jove multipotent°   *most powerful*
     Thou shouldst not bear from me a Greekish member°   *part of the body*

---

8. The combat might take place onstage.
9. *Even . . . soul:* In utmost detail, and in confidence.
4.7 Location: Scene continues.

1. Most modern editions do not mark a scene break
here; this affects the numbering of the following lines
as well as the following scenes. See Textual Note.

15   Wherein my sword had not impressure made
    Of our rank° feud. But the just gods gainsay°   *heated / prohibit*
    That any drop thou borrowed'st from thy mother,
    My sacred aunt, should by my mortal sword
    Be drained. Let me embrace thee, Ajax.
20   By him that thunders,° thou hast lusty arms.   *Jupiter*
    Hector would have them fall upon him thus.°   *in an embrace*
    Cousin, all honour to thee.
AJAX   I thank thee, Hector.
    Thou art too gentle and too free a man.
    I came to kill thee, cousin, and bear hence
25   A great addition° earnèd in thy death.   *title*
HECTOR   Not Neoptolemus² so mirable,°   *wonderful*
    On whose bright crest° Fame with her loud'st oyez°   *helmet / hear ye*
    Cries 'This is he!', could promise to himself
    A thought of added honour torn from Hector.
30 AENEAS   There is expectance here from both the sides
    What further you will do.
HECTOR   We'll answer it:
    The issue° is embracement.—Ajax, farewell.   *conclusion*
AJAX   If I might in entreaties find success,
    As seld° I have the chance, I would desire   *seldom*
35   My famous cousin to our Grecian tents.
DIOMEDES   'Tis Agamemnon's wish—and great Achilles
    Doth long to see unarmed the valiant Hector.
HECTOR   Aeneas, call my brother Troilus to me,
    And signify this loving interview
40   To the expecters of our Trojan part.°   *awaiting Trojans*
    Desire them home.°   [*Exit* AENEAS]   *to go home*
                Give me thy hand, my cousin.
    I will go eat with thee, and see your knights.
          Enter AGAMEMNON *and the rest* [AENEAS, ULYSSES,
          MENELAUS, NESTOR, ACHILLES, PATROCLUS, TROILUS,
          and others]
AJAX   Great Agamemnon comes to meet us here.
HECTOR [*to* AENEAS]   The worthiest of them,° tell me name by name.   *the Greeks*
45   But for Achilles, mine own searching eyes
    Shall find him by his large and portly size.
AGAMEMNON [*embracing him*]   Worthy of arms, as welcome as to° one   *as you can be to*
    That would be rid of such an enemy.
    But that's no welcome. Understand more clear:
50   What's past and what's to come is strewed with husks
    And formless ruin of oblivion,
    But in this extant° moment faith and troth,   *present*
    Strained purely from all hollow bias-drawing,³
    Bids thee with most divine integrity
55   From heart of very heart, 'Great Hector, welcome!'
HECTOR   I thank thee, most imperious° Agamemnon.   *imperial*
AGAMEMNON [*to* TROILUS]   My well-famed lord of Troy, no less to you.
MENELAUS   Let me confirm my princely brother's greeting.
    You brace° of warlike brothers, welcome hither.   *pair*
          [*He embraces* HECTOR *and* TROILUS]

---

2. Achilles' son Pyrrhus (but Shakespeare may have   3. Freed from all insincerity and indirectness.
thought Neoptolemus was Achilles' surname).

HECTOR [*to* AENEAS] Who must we answer?

60 AENEAS   The noble Menelaus.

HECTOR O, you, my lord! By Mars his° gauntlet, thanks.   *Mars's*

   Mock not that I affect° th'untraded° oath.   *choose / unfamiliar*

   Your quondam° wife swears still by Venus' glove.[4]   *former*

   She's well, but bade me not commend her to you.

65 MENELAUS Name her not now, sir. She's a deadly theme.

HECTOR O, pardon. I offend.

NESTOR I have, thou gallant Trojan, seen thee oft,

   Labouring for destiny,[5] make cruel way

   Through ranks of Greekish youth, and I have seen thee

70 As hot as Perseus° spur thy Phrygian steed,   *(on winged Pegasus)*

   And seen thee scorning forfeits and subduements,[6]

   When thou hast hung° th'advancèd sword i'th' air,   *kept high*

   Not letting it decline° on the declined,°   *fall / fallen*

   That I have said unto my standers-by,

75 'Lo, Jupiter is yonder, dealing life'.[7]

   And I have seen thee pause and take thy breath,

   When that a ring of Greeks have hemmed thee in,

   Like an Olympian,° wrestling. This have I seen;   *a god*

   But this thy countenance, still° locked in steel,   *always*

80 I never saw till now. I knew thy grandsire[8]

   And once fought with him. He was a soldier good,

   But—by great Mars, the captain of us all—

   Never like thee. Let an old man embrace thee;

   And, worthy warrior, welcome to our tents.

          [*He embraces* HECTOR]

85 AENEAS [*to* HECTOR] 'Tis the old Nestor.

HECTOR Let me embrace thee, good old chronicle,°   *record of history*

   That hast so long walked hand in hand with time.

   Most reverend Nestor, I am glad to clasp thee.

NESTOR I would my arms could match thee in contention°   *in battle*

90 As they contend with thee in courtesy.

HECTOR I would they could.

NESTOR Ha! By this white beard I'd fight with thee tomorrow.

   Well, welcome, welcome! I have seen the time.[9]

ULYSSES I wonder now how yonder city stands

95 When we have here her base and pillar by us?

HECTOR I know your favour,° Lord Ulysses, well.   *face*

   Ah, sir, there's many a Greek and Trojan dead

   Since first I saw yourself and Diomed

   In Ilium on your Greekish embassy.

100 ULYSSES Sir, I foretold you then what would ensue.

   My prophecy is but half his journey yet;

   For yonder walls that pertly front your town,

   Yon towers whose wanton° tops do buss° the clouds,   *reckless / kiss*

   Must kiss their own feet.

HECTOR   I must not believe you.

105 There they stand yet, and modestly I think

   The fall of every Phrygian stone will cost

---

4. *Venus' glove*: contrasting with Mars's gauntlet and alluding to Venus's adultery with Mars; possibly with an obscene innuendo.
5. Doing the Fates' work for them.
6. Scorning those whose lives might have been forfeit and (possible) conquests.
7. Giving life being the gods' prerogative.
8. Laomedon, builder of Troy's walls.
9. That is, the time when I could have met you in combat.

A drop of Grecian blood. The end crowns all,
And that old common arbitrator Time
Will one day end it.

ULYSSES   So to him we leave it.
110   Most gentle and most valiant Hector, welcome.
          [*He embraces him*]
          After the General, I beseech you next
          To feast with me and see me at my tent.
ACHILLES   I shall forestall thee, Lord Ulysses. [*To* HECTOR] Thou!°   (*insulting*)
          Now, Hector, I have fed mine eyes on thee.
115   I have with exact view perused° thee, Hector,   *minutely looked over*
          And quoted° joint by joint.   *taken note*
HECTOR   Is this Achilles?
ACHILLES   I am Achilles.
HECTOR   Stand fair,° I pray thee, let me look on thee.   *open to view*
ACHILLES   Behold thy fill.
120   HECTOR   Nay, I have done already.
ACHILLES   Thou art too brief. I will the second time,
          As° I would buy thee, view thee limb by limb.   *As though*
HECTOR   O, like a book of sport° thou'lt read me o'er.   *hunting manual*
          But there's more in me than thou understand'st.
125   Why dost thou so oppress[1] me with thine eye?
ACHILLES   Tell me, you heavens, in which part of his body
          Shall I destroy him—whether there, or there, or there—
          That I may give the local wound a name,
          And make distinct the very breach whereout
130   Hector's great spirit flew? Answer me, heavens.
HECTOR   It would discredit the blest gods, proud man,
          To answer such a question. Stand again.°   *Let me look again*
          Think'st thou to catch my life so pleasantly°   *easily*
          As to prenominate° in nice° conjecture   *name in advance / exact*
          Where thou wilt hit me dead?
135   ACHILLES   I tell thee, yea.
HECTOR   Wert thou the oracle to tell me so,
          I'd not believe thee. Henceforth guard thee well.
          For I'll not kill thee there, nor there, nor there,
          But, by the forge that stithied° Mars his helm,   *forged*
140   I'll kill thee everywhere, yea, o'er and o'er.—
          You wisest Grecians, pardon me this brag:
          His insolence draws folly from my lips.
          But I'll endeavour deeds to match these words,
          Or may I never—
AJAX   Do not chafe thee,° cousin.—   *get angry*
145   And you, Achilles, let these threats alone,
          Till accident or purpose bring you to't.
          You may have every day enough of Hector,
          If you have stomach.° The general state,° I fear,   *appetite / Greek lords*
          Can scarce entreat you to be odd° with him.   *at odds*
150   HECTOR [*to* ACHILLES]   I pray you, let us see you in the field.
          We have had pelting° wars since you refused   *paltry*
          The Grecians' cause.
ACHILLES   Dost thou entreat me, Hector?

---

1. Molest; in heraldry, place a perpendicular or diagonal stripe across an animal (continuing the metaphor of Hector as a hunted animal from "book of sport," line 123).

Tomorrow do I meet thee, fell as death;
Tonight, all friends.

HECTOR   Thy hand upon that match.

155 AGAMEMNON   First, all you peers of Greece, go to my tent.
There in the full convive you.° Afterwards,   *feast together*
As Hector's leisure and your bounties shall
Concur together, severally entreat° him.   *individually invite*
Beat loud the taborins,° let the trumpets blow,   *small drums*
160 That this great soldier may his welcome know.
    [Flourish.] Exeunt [all but TROILUS *and* ULYSSES]
TROILUS   My Lord Ulysses, tell me, I beseech you,
In what place of the field doth Calchas keep?°   *reside*
ULYSSES   At Menelaus' tent, most princely Troilus.
There Diomed doth feast with him tonight—
165 Who neither looks on heaven nor on earth,
But gives all gaze and bent° of amorous view   *inclination*
On the fair Cressid.
TROILUS   Shall I, sweet lord, be bound to you so much,
After we part from Agamemnon's tent,
To bring me thither?
170 ULYSSES   You shall command me, sir.
As gentle° tell me, of what honour was   *courteously*
This Cressida in Troy? Had she no lover there
That wails her absence?
TROILUS   O sir, to such as boasting show their scars°   *brag of past wounds*
175 A mock is due. Will you walk on, my lord?
She was beloved, she loved; she is, and doth.
But still sweet love is food for fortune's tooth.   *Exeunt*

5.1

Enter ACHILLES *and* PATROCLUS

ACHILLES   I'll heat his blood with Greekish wine tonight,
Which with my scimitar I'll cool° tomorrow.   *expose to air*
Patroclus, let us feast him to the height.
PATROCLUS   Here comes Thersites.

Enter THERSITES

ACHILLES   How now, thou core° of envy,   *(of an ulcer)*
5 Thou crusty botch[1] of nature, what's the news?
THERSITES   Why, thou picture° of what thou seemest, and idol   *mere image*
of idiot-worshippers, here's a letter for thee.
ACHILLES   From whence, fragment?°   *scrap of leftovers*
THERSITES   Why, thou full dish of fool,[2] from Troy.
    [ACHILLES *reads the letter*]
10 PATROCLUS   Who keeps the tent now?[3]
THERSITES   The surgeon's box or the patient's wound.
PATROCLUS   Well said, adversity.° And what need these tricks?   *perversity*
THERSITES   Prithee be silent, boy. I profit not by thy talk. Thou
art thought to be Achilles' male varlet.°   *servant; concubine?*
15 PATROCLUS   'Male varlet', you rogue? What's that?
THERSITES   Why, his masculine whore. Now the rotten diseases

---

5.1. Location: The Greek camp, near Achilles' tent.
1. You scab-encrusted (bad-tempered) boil.
2. Punning on the name of a dessert, probably clotted
cream or egg custard.

3. Who stays in the tent now? Thersites can no longer
taunt Achilles for remaining indoors. But Thersites
deliberately mistakes Patroclus to mean the surgeon's
probe or lint used to clean a wound.

of the south, guts-griping, ruptures, catarrhs, loads o' gravel
i'th' back, lethargies, cold palsies, and the like,[4] take and take
again such preposterous discoveries!°   *revealed perversion*

19.1   THERSITES   *Why, his masculine whore. Now the rotten*
           diseases of the south, the guts-griping, ruptures, loads
           o' gravel in the back, lethargies, cold palsies, raw eyes,
           dirt-rotten livers, wheezing lungs, bladders full of
19.5   *impostume,° sciaticas, lime-kilns° i'th' palm, incur-*   *abscess / burning*
           able bone-ache, and the rivelled fee-simple of the
           tetter,[5] take and take again such preposterous dis-
           coveries.

20   PATROCLUS   Why, thou damnable box of envy thou, what
    mean'st thou to curse thus?
    THERSITES   Do I curse thee?
    PATROCLUS   Why, no, you ruinous butt,° you whoreson indistin-   *leaky tub*
    guishable cur,° no.   *formless beast*
25   THERSITES   No? Why art thou then exasperate?° Thou idle   *irritated*
    immaterial skein of sleave-silk, thou green sarsenet flap[6] for a
    sore eye,[7] thou tassel of a prodigal's purse, thou! Ah, how the
    poor world is pestered with such waterflies!° Diminutives of   *tiny, flashy insects*
    nature.
30   PATROCLUS   Out, gall!
    THERSITES   Finch egg!°   *(small, gaudy egg)*
    ACHILLES   My sweet Patroclus, I am thwarted quite
    From my great purpose in tomorrow's battle.
    Here is a letter from Queen Hecuba,
35   A token from her daughter, my fair love,
    Both taxing° me, and gaging° me to keep   *reproving / binding*
    An oath that I have sworn. I will not break it.
    Fall, Greeks; fail, fame; honour, or° go or stay.   *either*
    My major vow lies here; this I'll obey.—
40   Come, come, Thersites, help to trim° my tent.   *decorate*
    This night in banqueting must all be spent.—
    Away, Patroclus.   *Exeunt* [ACHILLES *and* PATROCLUS]
    THERSITES   With too much blood° and too little brain these two   *passion*
    may run mad, but if with too much brain and too little blood
45   they do, I'll be a curer of madmen.[8] Here's° Agamemnon: an   *Take*
    honest fellow enough, and one that loves quails,° but he has   *(as food); prostitutes*
    not so much brain as ear-wax. And the goodly transformation
    of Jupiter there, his brother the bull,[9] the primitive° statue and   *archetypal*
    oblique° memorial of cuckolds, a thrifty shoeing-horn in a   *perverse*
50   chain, hanging at his brother's leg:[1] to what form but that he is
    should wit larded with malice and malice farced° with wit turn   *stuffed*
    him to? To an ass were nothing: he is both ass and ox. To an
    ox were nothing: he is both ox and ass. To be a dog, a mule, a
    cat, a fitchew,[2] a toad, a lizard, an owl, a puttock,° or a herring   *kite*

---

4. These may be separate diseases, but they can nearly
all be symptoms of venereal disease. *south:* referring to
the arrival of venereal disease in Europe after the Cru-
sades and its association with Italy, particularly Naples.
loads . . . back: kidney stones. *lethargies:* inertia. *palsies:*
paralysis. *and the like:* for the additional diseases listed
in Q's more elaborate version of this speech, see the
indented passage following (lines 19.1–19.8).
5. Incurable syphilis, and the shriveled absolute possession (as of property) of skin disease.
6. *Thou idle . . . flaps:* You insubstantial fine silk

thread, you immature patch of silk fabric.
7. Possible symptom of venereal disease.
8. A paradox and distinct improbability: a fool curing a
madman.
9. Jupiter made himself into a bull to rape Europa; but
Menelaus is bull-like for almost the opposite reason—
he has the horns of a cuckold.
1. A convenient tool (the shoehorn, suggested by the
cuckold's horn, was sometimes worn on "a chain")
available to serve Agamemnon; also, always underfoot.
2. Polecat (proverbially lecherous and stinking).

55 without a roe,° I would not care; but to be Menelaus!—I would   *(of no value)*
conspire against destiny. Ask me not what I would be if I were
not Thersites, for I care not to be° the louse of a lazar, so[3] I   *wouldn't mind being*
were not Menelaus.—Hey-day, sprites and fires.[4]

Enter HECTOR, AJAX, AGAMEMNON, ULYSSES, NESTOR,
[MENELAUS, TROILUS,] *and* DIOMEDES, *with lights*

AGAMEMNON   We go wrong, we go wrong.

AJAX   No, yonder 'tis:
There, where we see the light.

60 HECTOR   I trouble you.

AJAX   No, not a whit.

Enter ACHILLES

ULYSSES   Here comes himself° to guide you.   *the man himself*

ACHILLES   Welcome, brave Hector. Welcome, princes all.

AGAMEMNON [*to* HECTOR]   So now, fair prince of Troy, I bid good night.
Ajax commands the guard to tend on you.

65 HECTOR   Thanks and good night to the Greeks' general.

MENELAUS   Good night, my lord.

HECTOR   Good night, sweet Lord Menelaus.

THERSITES [*aside*]   Sweet draught![5] 'Sweet', quoth a?° Sweet   ~~sweet~~   *he*
sink,° sweet sewer.   *cesspool*

ACHILLES   Good night and welcome both at once, to those

70 That go or tarry.

AGAMEMNON   Good night.

Exeunt AGAMEMNON [*and*] MENELAUS

ACHILLES   Old Nestor tarries, and you too, Diomed.
Keep Hector company an hour or two.

DIOMEDES   I cannot, lord. I have important business

75 The tide° whereof is now.—Good night, great Hector.   *time*

HECTOR   Give me your hand.

ULYSSES [*aside to* TROILUS]   Follow his torch, he goes to Calchas' tent.
I'll keep you company.

TROILUS [*aside*]   Sweet sir, you honour me.

HECTOR [*to* DIOMEDES]   And so good night.

ACHILLES   Come, come, enter my tent.

Exeunt [DIOMEDES, *followed by* ULYSSES *and* TROILUS,
at one door; and ACHILLES, HECTOR, AJAX, *and* NESTOR
at another door]

80 THERSITES   That same Diomed's a false-hearted rogue, a most
unjust knave. I will no more trust him when he leers° than I   *smiles*
will a serpent when he hisses. He will spend his mouth and
promise like Brabbler the hound, but when he performs astronomers foretell it: that is prodigious, there will come some

85 change.[6] The sun borrows of the moon[7] when Diomed keeps
his word. I will rather leave to see Hector than not to dog him.[8]
They say he keeps a Trojan drab,° and uses the traitor Calchas   *whore*
his tent. I'll after.—Nothing but lechery! All incontinent varlets!   *Exit*

---

3. The louse of a leper, as long as.
4. The Greeks approach with torches, suggesting night; Thersites imagines them to be light-bearing spirits.
5. Drink; team of beasts used for pulling wagons; cesspool, toilet.
6. *He will . . . change:* He will bark and "promise" (that there is prey) like a hound that is noisy (quarrelsome), even when off the scent, but when he actually "per-

forms" (acts in good faith, keeps his word), astronomers make predictions on that basis: it is such a rare event that they consider it an ominous warning of a cosmic happening (often indicative of massive political upheaval).
7. It was well known that the moon's light was merely a reflection of the sun's.
8. I'll stop seeing Hector rather than give up tailing Diomedes.

5.2

Enter DIOMEDES

DIOMEDES   What, are you up here? Ho! Speak!

CALCHAS [*at the door*]   Who calls?

DIOMEDES   Diomed. Calchas, I think. Where's your daughter?

CALCHAS [*at the door*]   She comes to you.

Enter TROILUS *and* ULYSSES [*unseen*]

5   ULYSSES [*aside*]   Stand where the torch may not discover° us.   disclose

TROILUS [*aside*]   Cressid comes forth to him.

Enter CRESSIDA

DIOMEDES   How now, my charge?

CRESSIDA   Now, my sweet guardian. Hark, a word with you.

[*She whispers to him.*]

[*Enter* THERSITES, *unseen*]

TROILUS [*aside*]   Yea, so familiar?

ULYSSES [*aside*]   She will sing any man at first sight.[1]

10   THERSITES [*aside*]   And any man may sing her, if he can take her
clef. She's noted.[2]

DIOMEDES   Will you remember?

CRESSIDA   Remember? Yes.

DIOMEDES   Nay, but do then,

15   And let your mind be coupled with your words.

TROILUS [*aside*]   What should she remember?

ULYSSES [*aside*]   List!°   Listen

CRESSIDA   Sweet honey Greek, tempt me no more to folly.°   promiscuity

THERSITES [*aside*]   Roguery.

20   DIOMEDES   Nay, then!

CRESSIDA   I'll tell you what—

DIOMEDES   Fo, fo! Come, tell a pin.° You are forsworn.   tell me nothing

CRESSIDA   In faith, I cannot.° What would you have me do?   do as I promised

THERSITES [*aside*]   A juggling trick: to be secretly open.[3]

25   DIOMEDES   What did you swear you would bestow on me?

CRESSIDA   I prithee, do not hold me to mine oath.
Bid me do anything but that, sweet Greek.

DIOMEDES   Good night.

TROILUS [*aside*]   Hold, patience!

ULYSSES [*aside*]   How now, Trojan?

CRESSIDA   Diomed.

30   DIOMEDES   No, no, good night. I'll be your fool no more.

TROILUS [*aside*]   Thy better must.°   (be Cressida's fool)

CRESSIDA   Hark, one word in your ear.

[*She whispers to him*]

TROILUS [*aside*]   O plague and madness!

ULYSSES [*aside*]   You are movèd, Prince. Let us depart, I pray you,

35   Lest your displeasure should enlarge itself
To wrathful terms. This place is dangerous,
The time right deadly. I beseech you go.

TROILUS [*aside*]   Behold, I pray you.

ULYSSES [*aside*]   Nay, good my lord, go off.
You flow° to great distraction. Come, my lord.   rise; flood

TROILUS [*aside*]   I prithee, stay.

5.2 Location: Outside Calchas's tent.
1. As in sight reading of music; Cressida does not need
to know the man beforehand to play (upon) him.
2. *if . . . noted*: if he can take her musical key (also, her

cleft, or pudenda). She's like music written down; she's
notorious.
3. *juggling*: often meant sexual dexterity. *open*: public;
available for sexual intercourse.

40   ULYSSES [*aside*]   You have not patience. Come.

     TROILUS [*aside*]   I pray you, stay. By hell and all hell's torments,

       I will not speak a word.

     DIOMEDES   And so good night.

     CRESSIDA   Nay, but you part in anger.

     TROILUS [*aside*]   Doth that grieve thee?

       O withered truth!

     ULYSSES [*aside*]   Why, how now, lord?

     TROILUS [*aside*]   By Jove,

45   I will be patient.

            [DIOMEDES *starts to go*]

     CRESSIDA   Guardian! Why, Greek!

     DIOMEDES   Fo, fo! Adieu. You palter.°   *equivocate*

     CRESSIDA   In faith, I do not. Come hither once again.

     ULYSSES [*aside*]   You shake, my lord, at something. Will you go?

       You will break out.

     TROILUS [*aside*]   She strokes his cheek.

50   ULYSSES [*aside*]   Come, come.

     TROILUS [*aside*]   Nay, stay. By Jove, I will not speak a word.

       There is between my will and all offences°   *any bad deeds*

       A guard° of patience. Stay a little while.   *barrier*

     THERSITES [*aside*]   How the devil Luxury° with his fat rump and   *lust*

55   potato⁴ finger tickles these together! Fry, lechery, fry.⁵

     DIOMEDES   But will you then?

     CRESSIDA   In faith, I will, la. Never trust me else.

     DIOMEDES   Give me some token for the surety of it.

     CRESSIDA   I'll fetch you one.   *Exit*

60   ULYSSES [*aside*]   You have sworn patience.

     TROILUS [*aside*]   Fear me not, sweet lord.

       I will not be myself, nor have cognition°   *awareness*

       Of what I feel. I am all patience.

            Enter CRESSIDA [*with Troilus' sleeve*]

     THERSITES [*aside*]   Now the pledge! Now, now, now.

65   CRESSIDA   Here Diomed, keep this sleeve.

     TROILUS [*aside*]   O beauty, where is thy faith?

     ULYSSES [*aside*]   My lord.

     TROILUS [*aside*]   I will be patient; outwardly I will.

     CRESSIDA   You look upon that sleeve. Behold it well.

70   He loved me—O false wench!—give't me again.

           [*She takes it back*]

     DIOMEDES   Whose was't?

     CRESSIDA   It is no matter, now I ha't again.

       I will not meet with you tomorrow night.

       I prithee, Diomed, visit me no more.

75   THERSITES [*aside*]   Now she sharpens.⁶ Well said, whetstone.

     DIOMEDES   I shall have it.

     CRESSIDA   What, this?

     DIOMEDES   Ay, that.

     CRESSIDA   O all you gods! O pretty pretty pledge!

80   Thy master now lies thinking on his bed

       Of thee and me, and sighs, and takes my glove

       And gives memorial° dainty kisses to it—   *in remembrance*

---

4. The Spanish, or sweet, potato was thought to be an aphrodisiac.

5. In the fires of lust and of hell.

6. Becomes harsh; whets his desire.

DIOMEDES   As I kiss thee.
[*He snatches the sleeve*]
CRESSIDA   Nay, do not snatch it from me.
He that takes that doth take my heart withal.
85 DIOMEDES   I had your heart before; this follows it.
TROILUS [*aside*]   I did swear patience.
CRESSIDA   You shall not have it, Diomed. Faith, you shall not.
I'll give you something else.
DIOMEDES   I will have this. Whose was it?
CRESSIDA   It is no matter.
DIOMEDES   Come, tell me whose it was?
90 CRESSIDA   'Twas one's that loved me better than you will.
But now you have it, take it.
DIOMEDES   Whose was it?
CRESSIDA   By all Diana's waiting-women[7] yond,
And by herself, I will not tell you whose.
DIOMEDES   Tomorrow will I wear it on my helm,
95 And grieve° his spirit that dares not challenge it.   afflict
TROILUS [*aside*]   Wert thou the devil and wor'st it on thy horn,
It should be challenged.
CRESSIDA   Well, well, 'tis done, 'tis past—and yet it is not.
I will not keep my word.
DIOMEDES   Why then, farewell.
100 Thou never shalt mock Diomed again.
CRESSIDA   You shall not go. One cannot speak a word
But it straight starts you.°   makes you run off
DIOMEDES   I do not like this fooling.
TROILUS [*aside*]   Nor I, by Pluto—but that that likes° not you   pleases
Pleases me best.
DIOMEDES   What, shall I come? The hour—
105 CRESSIDA   Ay, come. O Jove, do come. I shall be plagued.[8]
DIOMEDES   Farewell till then.
CRESSIDA   Good night. I prithee, come.
Exit [DIOMEDES]
Troilus, farewell. One eye yet looks on thee,
But with my heart the other eye doth see.
Ah, poor our° sex! This fault in us I find: our poor
110 The error of our eye directs our mind.
What error° leads must err. O then conclude: wandering
Minds swayed by eyes are full of turpitude.   *Exit*
THERSITES [*aside*]   A proof of strength she could not publish more[9]
Unless she said, 'My mind is now turned whore'.
ULYSSES   All's done, my lord.
TROILUS   It is.
115 ULYSSES   Why stay we then?
TROILUS   To make a recordation to my soul
Of every syllable that here was spoke.
But if I tell how these two did co-act,
Shall I not lie in publishing a truth?
120 Sith yet there is a credence in my heart,
An esperance° so obstinately strong,   hope

7. The stars (Diana being the goddess of the moon and, ironically, of chastity).
8. Vexed; teased (but also alluding to her eventual fate in late medieval narrative, as a leper). See the Introduction.
9. She could not make a strong proof known more clearly.

That doth invert th'attest° of eyes and ears,   *reverse the testimony*
As if those organs had deceptious° functions   *deceptive*
Created only to calumniate.
Was Cressid here?

125 ULYSSES   I cannot conjure,° Trojan.   *produce a ghost*

TROILUS   She was not, sure.

ULYSSES   Most sure, she was.

TROILUS   Why, my negation hath no taste of madness.

ULYSSES   Nor mine, my lord. Cressid was here but now.

TROILUS   Let it not be believed, for° womanhood.   *for the sake of*

130   Think: we had mothers. Do not give advantage
    To stubborn critics, apt without a theme
    For depravation° to square the general sex   *denigration*
    By Cressid's rule.[1] Rather, think this not Cressid.

ULYSSES   What hath she done, Prince, that can soil our mothers?

135 TROILUS   Nothing at all, unless that this were she.

THERSITES [*aside*]   Will a swagger himself out on's own eyes?[2]

TROILUS   This, she? No, this is Diomed's Cressida.
    If beauty have a soul, this is not she.
    If souls guide vows, if vows be sanctimonies,°   *sacred things*
140   If sanctimony° be the gods' delight,   *sanctity*
    If there be rule in unity itself,°   *unity is indivisible*
    This is not she. O madness of discourse,°   *reason*
    That cause[3] sets up with and against thyself!
    Bifold authority, where reason can revolt
145   Without perdition, and loss assume all reason
    Without revolt![4] This is and is not Cressid.
    Within my soul there doth conduce° a fight   *come together*
    Of this strange nature, that a thing inseparate°   *indivisible*
    Divides more wider than the sky and earth,
150   And yet the spacious breadth of this division
    Admits no orifex° for a point as subtle°   *orifice / fine*
    As Ariachne's[5] broken woof° to enter.   *weaving thread*
    Instance,° O instance, strong as Pluto's gates: *Evidence*
    Cressid is mine, tied with the bonds of heaven.
155   Instance, O instance, strong as heaven itself:
    The bonds of heaven are slipped, dissolved, and loosed,   Gordian knot
    And with another knot, five-finger-tied,[6]
    The fractions° of her faith, orts° of her love,   *pieces / leftover scraps*
    The fragments, scraps, the bits and greasy relics
160   Of her o'er-eaten° faith, are bound to Diomed.   *eaten-away; surfeited*

ULYSSES   May worthy Troilus e'en be half attached
    With that which here his passion doth express?[7]

TROILUS   Ay, Greek, and that shall be divulgèd well

---

1. *to square . . . rule:* to measure all women by the standard of Cressida.
2. Will he bluster himself out of (the evidence of) his own eyes?
3. Case; plea (where, here, defendant and plaintiff are one).
4. *Bifold . . . revolt:* The meaning is obscure. Perhaps: Divided authority, where reason (belief in the testimony of the senses) can revolt against itself (by claiming that this is not in fact Cressida) without being accused of loss of reason ("perdition"); and where loss of reason (inability to trust the senses), without rebelling against reason, can lay claim to being the highest form of reason precisely

because the sensual evidence, which ought to be the highest form of reason, lies (because this cannot be Cressida).
5. A conflation of Arachne the weaver, turned into a spider by Athena for overweening pride in her work, and Ariadne, who gave Theseus a ball of thread to mark his way out of the Labyrinth of her father.
6. United by human hands (Cressida's and Diomedes'), as opposed to "the bonds of heaven" (line 156); evilly consummated (alluding to the devil's five fingers, symbolizing the steps to lechery).
7. *May . . . express:* Can worthy Troilus be even half as affected as he seems to be?

In characters as red as Mars his° heart   *Mars's*
165 Inflamed with Venus. Never did young man fancy°   *love*
With so eternal and so fixed a soul.
Hark, Greek: as much as I do Cressid love,
So much by weight hate I her Diomed.
That sleeve is mine that he'll bear in his helm.
170 Were it a casque° composed by Vulcan's[8] skill,   *helmet*
My sword should bite it. Not the dreadful spout
Which shipmen do the hurricano° call,   *waterspout*
Constringed° in mass by the almighty sun,   *Drawn together*
Shall dizzy° with more clamour Neptune's ear   *stun*
175 In his descent, than shall my prompted° sword   *eager*
Falling on Diomed.
THERSITES [*aside*]   He'll tickle it for his concupy.[9]
TROILUS   O Cressid, O false Cressid! False, false, false.
Let all untruths stand by° thy stainèd name,   *be compared with*
And they'll seem glorious.
180 ULYSSES   O contain yourself.
Your passion draws ears hither.
        Enter AENEAS
AENEAS [*to* TROILUS]   I have been seeking you this hour, my lord.
Hector by this° is arming him in Troy.   *by this time*
Ajax your guard stays to conduct you home.
185 TROILUS   Have° with you, Prince.—My courteous lord, adieu.—   *I shall come*
Farewell, revolted fair; and Diomed,
Stand fast and wear a castle° on thy head.   *strong defense*
ULYSSES   I'll bring you to the gates.
TROILUS   Accept distracted thanks.
        Exeunt TROILUS, AENEAS, *and* ULYSSES
THERSITES   Would I could meet that rogue Diomed! I would
190 croak like a raven.[1] I would bode,° I would bode. Patroclus will   *foretell evil*
give me anything for the intelligence° of this whore. The parrot   *secret information*
will not do more for an almond[2] than he for a commodious
drab.° Lechery, lechery, still wars and lechery! Nothing else   *willing whore*
holds fashion. A burning devil° take them!   *Exit*   *venereal disease*

5.3

        Enter HECTOR [*armed*] *and* ANDROMACHE
ANDROMACHE   When was my lord so much ungently tempered
To stop his ears against admonishment?
Unarm, unarm, and do not fight today.
HECTOR   You train° me to offend you. Get you in.   *teach*
5 By all the everlasting gods, I'll go.
ANDROMACHE   My dreams will sure prove ominous to the day.°   *true omens of the day*
HECTOR   No more, I say.
        Enter CASSANDRA
CASSANDRA   Where is my brother Hector?
ANDROMACHE   Here, sister, armed and bloody in intent.
Consort° with me in loud and dear° petition,   *Join / earnest*

---

8. Smith of the gods, Vulcan made armor for various classical heroes, most notably Achilles.
9. (Probably) Troilus will "tickle" (beat [ironic]) Diomedes' helmet for his lust (his concubine).

1. Proverbially birds of ill omen.
2. *The parrot . . . almond:* Proverbial for a brainless passion for a trivial delicacy.
5.3 Location: Priam's palace.

10 Pursue we him on knees—for I have dreamed
Of bloody turbulence, and this whole night
Hath nothing been but shapes and forms of slaughter.

CASSANDRA   O 'tis true.

HECTOR   Ho! Bid my trumpet sound.

CASSANDRA   No notes of sally, for the heavens, sweet brother.

15 HECTOR   Begone, I say. The gods have heard me swear.

CASSANDRA   The gods are deaf to hot and peevish° vows.   *headstrong*
They° are polluted off'rings, more abhorred   *Rash vows*
Than spotted livers° in the sacrifice.   *ruined offerings*

ANDROMACHE [*to* HECTOR]   O, be persuaded. Do not count it holy
20 To hurt by being just.° It is as lawful,   *true to your vow*
For we would° give much, to use violent thefts,   *Because we want to*
And rob in the behalf of charity.

CASSANDRA   It is the purpose that makes strong the vow,
But vows to every purpose must not° hold.   *do not have to*
Unarm, sweet Hector.

25 HECTOR   Hold you still,° I say.   *Stop it*
Mine honour keeps the weather[1] of my fate.
Life every man holds dear, but the dear° man   *worthy*
Holds honour far more precious-dear than life.

Enter TROILUS [*armed*]

How now, young man, mean'st thou to fight today?

30 ANDROMACHE [*aside*]   Cassandra, call my father° to persuade.   *father-in-law*

Exit CASSANDRA

HECTOR   No, faith, young Troilus. Doff thy harness,° youth.   *Disarm*
I am today i'th' vein of° chivalry.   *mood for*
Let grow thy sinews till their knots be strong,
And tempt not yet the brushes° of the war.   *encounters*
35 Unarm thee, go—and doubt thou not, brave boy,
I'll stand today for thee and me and Troy.

TROILUS   Brother, you have a vice of mercy in you,
Which better fits a lion[2] than a man.

HECTOR   What vice is that? Good Troilus, chide me for it.

40 TROILUS   When many times the captive° Grecian falls   *miserable*
Even in the fan and wind of your fair sword,[3]
You bid them rise and live.

HECTOR   O 'tis fair play.

TROILUS   Fool's play, by heaven, Hector.

45 HECTOR   How now! How now!

TROILUS   For th' love of all the gods,
Let's leave the hermit pity with our mother
And, when we have our armours buckled on,
The venomed vengeance ride upon our swords,
50 Spur them to ruthful° work, rein them from ruth.°   *woeful / pity*

HECTOR   Fie, savage, fie!

TROILUS   Hector, then 'tis wars.°   *then it's a true war*

HECTOR   Troilus, I would not have you fight today.

TROILUS   Who should withhold me?
Not fate, obedience, nor the hand of Mars

---

1. My honor stays to windward (in sailing, a ship windward of another takes its wind, and so gets the better of it).
2. Lions were said not to attack any animal that sub-

mitted to them.
3. The rapidly moving sword is like a fan, blowing his enemies down before he reaches them.

55   Beck'ning with fiery truncheon⁴ my retire,
       Not Priamus and Hecuba on knees,
       Their eyes o'er-gallèd° with recourse° of tears,   *sore / repeated flow*
       Nor you, my brother, with your true sword drawn
       Opposed to hinder me, should stop my way
60   But by my ruin.
              Enter PRIAM *and* CASSANDRA
    CASSANDRA   Lay hold upon him, Priam, hold him fast.
       He is thy crutch: now if thou loose thy stay,°   *prop*
       Thou on him leaning and all Troy on thee,
       Fall all together.
    PRIAM   Come, Hector, come. Go back.
65   Thy wife hath dreamt, thy mother hath had visions,
       Cassandra doth foresee, and I myself
       Am like a prophet suddenly enrapt°   *inspired*
       To tell thee that this day is ominous.
       Therefore come back.
    HECTOR   Aeneas is afield,
70   And I do stand engaged to many Greeks,
       Even in the faith of valour,° to appear   *warrior's honor*
       This morning to them.
    PRIAM   Ay, but thou shalt not go.
    HECTOR [*kneeling*]   I must not break my faith.
75   You know me dutiful; therefore, dear sire,
       Let me not shame respect,° but give me leave   *duty to a parent*
       To take that course, by your consent and voice,
       Which you do here forbid me, royal Priam.
    CASSANDRA   O Priam, yield not to him.
    ANDROMACHE   Do not, dear father.
80   HECTOR   Andromache, I am offended with you.
       Upon the love you bear me, get you in.   *Exit* ANDROMACHE
    TROILUS   This foolish, dreaming, superstitious girl
       Makes all these bodements.°   *warnings*
    CASSANDRA   O farewell, dear Hector.
       Look how thou diest; look how thy eye turns pale;
85   Look how thy wounds do bleed at many vents.
       Hark how Troy roars, how Hecuba cries out,
       How poor Andromache shrills her dolours forth.
       Behold: distraction, frenzy, and amazement
       Like witless antics° one another meet,   *buffoons*
90   And all cry 'Hector, Hector's dead, O Hector!'
    TROILUS   Away, away!
    CASSANDRA   Farewell. Yet soft:° Hector, I take my leave.   *wait a moment*
       Thou dost thyself and all our Troy deceive.   *Exit*
    HECTOR [*to* PRIAM]   You are amazed, my liege, at her exclaim.°   *outcry*
95   Go in and cheer the town. We'll forth and fight,
       Do deeds of praise, and tell you them at night.
    PRIAM   Farewell. The gods with safety stand about thee.
            [*Exeunt* PRIAM *and* HECTOR *severally.°*] *Alarum*   *separately*
    TROILUS   They are at it, hark! Proud Diomed, believe
       I come to lose my arm or win my sleeve.
               Enter PANDARUS
100   PANDARUS   Do you hear, my lord, do you hear?

---

4. Staff of office (carried by the marshal of a formal combat).

TROILUS What now?

PANDARUS Here's a letter come from yon poor girl.

TROILUS Let me read.

[TROILUS *reads the letter*]

105 PANDARUS A whoreson phthisic,° a whoreson rascally phthisic so   *consumptive cough*
troubles me, and the foolish fortune of this girl, and what one
thing, what another, that I shall leave you one o' these days.
And I have a rheum° in mine eyes too, and such an ache in my   *watery discharge*
bones° that unless a man were cursed I cannot tell what to   *(suggesting syphilis)*
think on't.—What says she there?

TROILUS [*tearing the letter*] Words, words, mere words, no mat-
110 ter from the heart.

Th'effect° doth operate another way.   *Her action*

Go, wind, to wind: there turn and change together.[5]

My love with words and errors° still she feeds,   *lies*

But edifies another with her deeds.

115 PANDARUS Why, but hear you—

TROILUS Hence, broker-lackey!° Ignomy° and shame   *pimp / Ignominy*
Pursue thy life, and live aye with thy name. *Exeunt* [*severally*][6]

5.4

Alarum. Enter THERSITES [*in*] *excursions*°   *advancing troops*

THERSITES Now they are clapper-clawing° one another. I'll go   *thrashing*
look on. That dissembling abominable varlet Diomed has got
that same scurvy doting foolish young knave's sleeve of Troy°   *Trojan knave's sleeve*
there in his helm. I would fain see them meet, that that same
5 young Trojan ass that loves the whore there might send that
Greekish whoremasterly villain with the sleeve back to the dissembling luxurious drab of a sleeveless errand.[1] O'th' t'other
side, the policy° of those crafty swearing rascals—that stale old   *statecraft; scheming*
mouse-eaten dry cheese Nestor and that same dog-fox° Ulys-   *crafty one*
10 ses—is proved not worth a blackberry.° They set me up° in *proved worthless / set up*
policy that mongrel cur Ajax against that dog of as bad a kind
Achilles. And now is the cur Ajax prouder than the cur Achilles, and will not arm today—whereupon the Grecians began
to proclaim barbarism,[2] and policy grows into an ill opinion.° *gets a bad reputation*

Enter DIOMEDES, [*followed by*] TROILUS

15 Soft, here comes sleeve and t'other.

TROILUS [*to* DIOMEDES] Fly not, for shouldst thou take the river Styx[3]
I would swim after.

DIOMEDES   Thou dost miscall retire.°   *mistake my retreat*
I do not fly, but advantageous care°   *tactical caution*
Withdrew me from the odds of multitude. Have at thee!

[*They fight*]

20 THERSITES Hold thy whore, Grecian! Now for thy whore, Trojan! Now the sleeve, now the sleeve!

[*Exit* DIOMEDES, *driving in* TROILUS]

Enter HECTOR [*behind*]

---

5. Go, empty words, into the breeze: there, along with the air, toss about ("turn" was often used of sexual infidelity).
6. The last three lines of this scene are not in Q. A similar exchange occurs at the end of the play in both Q and F. See indented passage after 5.11.31 and Textual Note.
5.4 Location: The rest of the play takes place on the battlefield.
1. To the lying, lecherous slut on a pointless errand (punning on the actual sleeve).
2. Began to set up whim and ignorance in authority ("barbarism" being normally contrasted with "Greek").
3. Even if you should enter the river of the underworld (as prey hoping to make the hunter lose the scent).

HECTOR   What art thou, Greek? Art thou for Hector's match?
     Art thou of blood° and honour?   *nobility*
THERSITES   No, no, I am a rascal, a scurvy railing knave, a very
25   filthy rogue.
HECTOR   I do believe thee: live.⁴
THERSITES   God-a-mercy,° that thou wilt believe me—   *Thank God*
                                                                          [*Exit* HECTOR]
     but a plague break thy neck for frighting me. What's become
     of the wenching rogues? I think they have swallowed one
30   another. I would laugh at that miracle—yet in a sort lechery
     eats itself. I'll seek them.   *Exit*

                                   5.5
                    Enter DIOMEDES *and* SERVANTS
DIOMEDES   Go, go, my servant, take thou Troilus' horse.
     Present the fair steed to my Lady Cressid.
     Fellow, commend my service to her beauty.
     Tell her I have chastised the amorous Trojan,
     And am her knight by proof.°   *(of deeds)*
5 SERVANT   I go, my lord.   [*Exit*]
                    Enter AGAMEMNON
AGAMEMNON   Renew, renew! The fierce Polydamas
     Hath beat down Menon; bastard Margareton
     Hath Doreus prisoner,
     And stands colossus-wise waving his beam°   *spearshaft*
10   Upon the pashèd° corpses of the kings   *smashed*
     Epistropus and Cedius; Polixenes is slain,
     Amphimacus and Thoas deadly hurt,
     Patroclus ta'en or slain, and Palamedes
     Sore hurt and bruised; the dreadful sagittary¹
15   Appals our numbers.° Haste we, Diomed,   *soldiers*
     To reinforcement, or we perish all.
                    Enter NESTOR [*with Patroclus' body*]
NESTOR   Go, bear Patroclus' body to Achilles,
     And bid the snail-paced Ajax arm for shame.
                              [*Exit one or more with the body*]
     There is a thousand Hectors in the field.
20   Now here he fights on Galathe his horse,
     And there lacks work; anon he's there afoot,
     And there they fly or die, like scalèd schools²
     Before the belching° whale. Then is he yonder,   *spouting*
     And there the strawy Greeks, ripe for his edge,°   *sword blade*
25   Fall down before him like the mower's swath.
     Here, there, and everywhere he leaves and takes,³
     Dexterity so obeying appetite
     That what he will he does, and does so much
     That proof° is called impossibility.   *his achievement*
                    Enter ULYSSES
30 ULYSSES   O courage, courage, princes! Great Achilles
     Is arming, weeping, cursing, vowing vengeance.

---

4. Here Hector is at once contemptuous and merciful.   2. Scaly (armor-clad) schools of fish.
5.5   3. He spares and kills; possibly, he "leaves" the dead
1. A legendary centaurlike beast, armed with bow and   and "takes" on the living.
arrows.

Patroclus' wounds have roused his drowsy blood,
Together with his mangled Myrmidons,
That noseless, handless, hacked and chipped come to him

35   Crying on° Hector. Ajax hath lost a friend   *Complaining of*
And foams at mouth, and he is armed and at it,
Roaring for Troilus—who hath done today
Mad and fantastic execution,
Engaging and redeeming of° himself   *Risking and saving*

40   With such a careless force and forceless care°   *effortless diligence*
As if that luck, in very spite of cunning,°   *his foes' skill*
Bade him win all.

        Enter AJAX

AJAX   Troilus, thou coward Troilus!   *Exit*

DIOMEDES   Ay, there, there!   *Exit*

45   NESTOR   So, so, we draw together.°   *join forces*

        Enter ACHILLES

ACHILLES   Where is this Hector?
Come, come, thou brave boy-queller, show thy face.
Know what it is to meet Achilles angry.
Hector! Where's Hector? I will none but Hector.   *Exeunt*

5.6

        Enter AJAX

AJAX   Troilus, thou coward Troilus! Show thy head!

        Enter DIOMEDES

DIOMEDES   Troilus, I say! Where's Troilus?

AJAX   What wouldst thou?

DIOMEDES   I would correct° him.   *chastise*

AJAX   Were I the general, thou shouldst have my office

5   Ere° that correction.—Troilus, I say! What, Troilus!   *Before you should have*

        Enter TROILUS

TROILUS   O traitor Diomed! Turn thy false face, thou traitor,
And pay the life thou ow'st me for my horse.

DIOMEDES   Ha, art thou there?

AJAX   I'll fight with him alone. Stand, Diomed.

10   DIOMEDES   He is my prize; I will not look upon.°   *be a spectator*

TROILUS   Come, both you cogging° Greeks, have at you both!   *cheating*
       [*They fight.*]

        Enter HECTOR

HECTOR   Yea, Troilus? O well fought, my youngest brother!

       Exit TROILUS [*driving* DIOMEDES *and* AJAX *in*]

        Enter ACHILLES [*behind*]

ACHILLES   Now do I see thee.—Ha! Have at thee, Hector.
       [*They fight.* ACHILLES *is bested*]

HECTOR   Pause, if thou wilt.

15   ACHILLES   I do disdain thy courtesy, proud Trojan.
Be happy that my arms are out of use.°   *practice*
My rest and negligence befriends thee now;
But thou anon shalt hear of me again.
Till when, go seek thy fortune.   *Exit*

HECTOR   Fare thee well.

20   I would have been much more a fresher man
Had I expected thee.

        Enter TROILUS [*in haste*]

How now, my brother?

TROILUS   Ajax hath ta'en° Aeneas. Shall it be?   *taken captive*
No, by the flame of yonder glorious heaven,
He shall not carry him. I'll be ta'en too,
25   Or bring him off.° Fate, hear me what I say: *rescue Aeneas*
I reck° not though thou end my life today.   *Exit*   *care*

Enter one in [sumptuous] armour

HECTOR   Stand, stand, thou Greek! Thou art a goodly mark.°   *target*
No? Wilt thou not? I like thy armour well.
I'll frush° it and unlock the rivets all,   *smash*
But I'll be master of it.   [*Exit one in armour*]
30   Wilt thou not, beast, abide?
Why then, fly on; I'll hunt thee for thy hide.   *Exit*

5.7

Enter ACHILLES *with Myrmidons*

ACHILLES   Come here about me, you my Myrmidons.
Mark what I say. Attend me where I wheel;°   *range*
Strike not a stroke, but keep yourselves in breath,
And when I have the bloody Hector found,
5   Empale° him with your weapons round about.   *Fence in*
In fellest° manner execute your arms.   *fiercest*
Follow me, sirs, and my proceedings eye.
It is decreed Hector the great must die.   *Exeunt*

5.8

Enter MENELAUS *and* PARIS, [*fighting, then*] THERSITES[1]

THERSITES   The cuckold and the cuckold-maker are at it.—
Now, bull! Now, dog! 'Loo,[2] Paris, 'loo! Now, my double-
horned[3] Spartan! 'Loo, Paris, 'loo! The bull has the game.°   *is winning*
Ware° horns, ho!   *Exit* MENELAUS, [*driving in*] PARIS   *Beware*

Enter BASTARD [*behind*]

5   BASTARD   Turn, slave, and fight.
THERSITES   What art thou?
BASTARD   A bastard son of Priam's.
THERSITES   I am a bastard, too. I love bastards. I am bastard
begot, bastard instructed, bastard in mind, bastard in valour,
10   in everything illegitimate. One bear will not bite another, and
wherefore should one bastard? Take heed: the quarrel's most
ominous to us. If the son of a whore fight for a whore, he tempts
judgement. Farewell, bastard.   [*Exit*]
BASTARD   The devil take thee, coward.   *Exit*

5.9

Enter HECTOR [*dragging the one in sumptuous armour*]

HECTOR [*taking off the helmet*]   Most putrefièd core, so fair without,
Thy goodly armour thus hath cost thy life.
Now is my day's work done. I'll take good breath.
Rest, sword: thou hast thy fill of blood and death.

5.8
1. Most modern editions do not mark a scene break
here; this affects the numbering of the following lines
and scenes. See Textual Note.

2. Halloo (shout to encourage dogs chasing game or in
bullbaiting).
3 Two-horned, like a bull; horned because a cuckold.
5.9

[*He disarms.*]
Enter ACHILLES *and his Myrmidons* [*surrounding*
HECTOR]

5 ACHILLES   Look, Hector, how the sun begins to set,
How ugly night comes breathing at his heels.
Even with the veil[1] and dark'ning of the sun
To close the day up, Hector's life is done.
HECTOR   I am unarmed. Forgo this vantage, Greek.
10 ACHILLES   Strike, fellows, strike! This is the man I seek.
[*The Myrmidons kill* HECTOR]
So, Ilium, fall thou. Now, Troy, sink down.
Here lies thy heart, thy sinews, and thy bone.—
On, Myrmidons, and cry you all amain,°   *with full force*
'Achilles hath the mighty Hector slain!'
[*A*] *retreat* [*is sounded*]
15 Hark, a retire upon our Grecian part.
[*Another retreat is sounded*]
A MYRMIDON   The Trojan trumpets sound the like, my lord.
ACHILLES   The dragon wing of night o'erspreads the earth
And, stickler°-like, the armies separates.   *referee (in combat)*
My half-supped° sword, that frankly° would have fed,   *half-satisfied / freely*
20 Pleased with this dainty bait,° thus goes to bed.   *snack*
[*He sheathes his sword*]
Come, tie his body to my horse's tail.
Along the field I will the Trojan trail.   *Exeunt* [*dragging the bodies*]

5.10

[*A*] *retreat* [*is*] *sound*[*ed*]. *Enter* AGAMEMNON, AJAX,
MENELAUS, NESTOR, DIOMEDES, *and the rest, marching.*
[*A*] *shout* [*within*]

AGAMEMNON   Hark, hark! What shout is that?
NESTOR   Peace, drums.
MYRMIDONS (*within*)   Achilles!
Achilles! Hector's slain! Achilles!
DIOMEDES   The bruit° is: Hector's slain, and by Achilles.   *report*
AJAX   If it be so, yet bragless let it be.
5 Great Hector was a man as good as he.
AGAMEMNON   March patiently along. Let one be sent
To pray Achilles see us at our tent.
If in his death the gods have us befriended,
Great Troy is ours, and our sharp° wars are ended.   *fierce*
Exeunt [*marching*]

5.11

Enter AENEAS, PARIS, ANTENOR, *and* DEIPHOBUS
AENEAS   Stand, ho! Yet are we masters of the field.
Never go home; here starve[1] we out the night.
Enter TROILUS
TROILUS   Hector is slain.
ALL THE OTHERS   Hector? The gods forbid.

---

1. At the same time as the setting.
5.11

1. Wait in discomfort; outlast, kill by starvation (the
night being imagined as a city under siege).

TROILUS He's dead, and at the murderer's horse's tail

5   In beastly sort° dragged through the shameful field.   *manner*
      Frown on, you heavens; effect your rage with speed;
      Sit, gods, upon your thrones, and smite at Troy.
      I say, at once: let your brief plagues be mercy,[2]
      And linger not our sure destructions on.

10 AENEAS My lord, you do discomfort all the host.°   *army*
    TROILUS You understand me not that tell me so.
      I do not speak of flight, of fear of death,
      But dare all imminence that gods and men
      Address their dangers in.[3] Hector is gone.

15   Who shall tell Priam so, or Hecuba?
      Let him that will a screech-owl aye° be called   *voice of doom always*
      Go into Troy and say their Hector's dead.
      There is a word° will Priam turn to stone,   *sentence*
      Make wells and Niobes[4] of the maids and wives,

20   Cold statues of the youth, and in a word
      Scare Troy out of itself. But march away.
      Hector is dead; there is no more to say.
      Stay yet.—You vile abominable tents
      Thus proudly pitched upon our Phrygian plains,

25   Let Titan° rise as early as he dare,   *sun god Hyperion*
      I'll through and through you! And thou great-sized coward,°   *Achilles*
      No space of earth shall sunder our two hates.
      I'll haunt thee like a wicked conscience still,
      That mouldeth goblins swift as frenzy's thoughts.

30   Strike a free march! To Troy with comfort° go: *this one comfort*
      Hope of revenge shall hide our inward woe. *[Exeunt marching]*[5]
      [Enter PANDARUS]

31.1 PANDARUS *But hear you, hear you.*
    TROILUS *Hence, broker-lackey. [Strikes him] Ignomy and shame*
      Pursue thy like, and live aye with thy name. Exeunt [all but PANDARUS]
    PANDARUS *A goodly medicine for my aching bones. O*
31.5   *world, world, world!—thus is the poor agent despised.*
      O traitors and bawds, how earnestly are you set a° work,   *to*
      and how ill requited! Why should our endeavour be so
      desired and the performance so loathed? What verse
      for it? What instance° for it? Let me see,   *traditional saying*
31.10   *Full merrily the humble-bee doth sing*
      Till he hath lost his honey and his sting,
      And being once subdued in armèd tail,[6]
      Sweet honey and sweet notes together fail.
      Good traders in the flesh, set this in your painted cloths:[7]
31.15   *As many as be here of Pandar's hall,°*   *guild hall*
      Your eyes, half out,[8] *weep out at Pandar's fall.*
      Or if you cannot weep, yet give some groans,
      Though not for me, yet for your aching bones.°   *(from syphilis)*
      Brethren and sisters of the hold-door trade,°   *Pimps and bawds*

---

2. Be mercifully quick in destruction.
3. *But . . . in:* But dare all impending danger that gods and men prepare for me.
4. Mythical Queen of Thebes, who wept so much at the murder of her children by the gods that the gods turned her into a statue that flowed with water.
5. For the extended conclusion with Pandarus's epilogue, see indented passage below (lines 31.1–31.24).

The exit marked here is deferred until line 31.3. For discussion, see the Textual Note and Introduction.
6. And having lost his sting: alluding to impotence caused by venereal disease.
7. Inexpensive substitutes for tapestries, often including moralistic inscriptions.
8. Half-blinded by venereal disease.

31.20 *Some two months hence my will shall here be made.*[9]
It should be now, but that my fear is this:
Some gallèd goose of Winchester would hiss.[1]
Till then I'll sweat[2] and seek about for eases,
And at that time bequeath you my diseases.   *Exit*

---

9. "Here" is possibly a reference to the stage of the Globe and hence the promise of a sequel that never materialized; it has also been taken to refer to an Inn of Court, where young men studied law, a plausible place to make a "will" and thus hypothesized by some scholars to be the location of the first performance. See the Introduction.

1. A prostitute or customer afflicted with venereal disease, from the diocese of Winchester (which had jurisdiction over Southwark, home of both the brothels and the Globe), would disapprove—of the will and/or the play.
2. Usual treatment for venereal disease.

Sir Thomas More: *Passages Attributed to Shakespeare*

The play *Sir Thomas More* was originally composed between late 1592 and mid-1595, probably in 1592–93, by Anthony Munday, Henry Chettle, and perhaps a third writer (Thomas Dekker?). Sometime later, perhaps in 1593–94 or 1603–04, Shakespeare seems to have participated in its revision. The original version was designed for Lord Strange's Men, who presumably intended to stage it at their regular theater, the Rose. Drawing on Raphael Holinshed's *Chronicles of England, Scotland, and Ireland* (1587), Nicholas Harpsfield's *Life and Death of Sir Thomas Moore,* and Thomas Stapleton's Latin biography *Vita Thomae Mori,* the play conforms to the popular tragic model known in Latin as *de casibus virorum illustrium* (on the fall of illustrious men). It follows the career of More—leading English Renaissance humanist and author of *Utopia,* Lord Chancellor of England and persecutor of Protestants, and, finally, Catholic martyr when the religious tide turned. The work focuses on his success as sheriff in peacefully quelling the anti-alien London riots of May Day 1517; his elevation to the post of Lord Chancellor; and his eventual execution for refusing to subscribe to certain of the King's articles. Throughout and especially at the end, the witty and wise protagonist is treated with almost uncritical admiration.

Strange's Men specialized in plays on English subjects with a loosely nationalist appeal; they also liked to live dangerously. *Sir Thomas More* was doubly dangerous. First, even though it carefully converts the issue that led to More's death (papal versus royal supremacy of the church) into a less concrete conflict between worldly authority and individual conscience that would appeal to a Puritan-leaning audience, it sympathetically dramatizes the life of a Catholic martyr killed by Henry VIII, the father of the ruling Protestant monarch, Queen Elizabeth. Second, although it shows More successfully preventing popular protest that historically he was unable to control, the play exploits contemporary antiforeign resentment, which was noticeable by late 1592 and led to rioting and harsh government reprisals between 1593 and 1595. On neither issue does the absolute monarch end up looking particularly good. Before the first performance, however, the censor, Sir Edmund Tilney, Master of the Revels, demanded substantial rewriting, in particular a toning down of the attack on foreigners and the elimination of the scene dramatizing the 1517 rebellion against them. Apparently before the manuscript could be revised, an outbreak of plague closed the theaters for most of the period from mid-1592 to mid-1594, and the actors abandoned the play.

Early in the seventeenth century, the text was revised for performance—possibly at the Fortune, the regular theater of Lord Admiral's Men/Prince Henry's Men, conceivably at the Globe by Shakespeare's company, the Lord Chamberlain's Men/King's Men. (On James I's accession in 1603, Prince Henry and his father, the King, assumed the patronage of the Lord Admiral's and Lord Chamberlain's companies.) The play fit the strategy of the Lord Admiral's Men in the years immediately after 1600, when they specialized in revivals from the Strange's repertory of the early 1590s and the Admiral's own of 1594–97. Also, during the same period, both the Lord Admiral's and the Lord Chamberlain's Men mounted a number of plays set during the reign of Henry VIII. A new monarch and the absence of the dangerous political context of the 1590s allowed the revisers to imagine how they might take account of the censor's earlier concerns. But they could not disregard the fact that the play as originally written required more actors than were in either company, and they adapted the text accordingly. No record of performance exists.

For the original version, Anthony Munday (manuscript Hand S) had copied out the entire text, modifying the work of his collaborator(s). The revision, which also significantly improved the quality of the play, was undertaken by Henry Chettle (Hand A), Thomas Dekker (Hand E), probably Thomas Heywood (Hand B), a playhouse scribe (Hand C), and very probably Shakespeare (Hand D). The result, "The Booke of Sir Thomas Moore" (British Library, MS Harleian 7368)—where "Booke" means theatrical promptbook—is arguably the messiest and most extensively revised dramatic manuscript

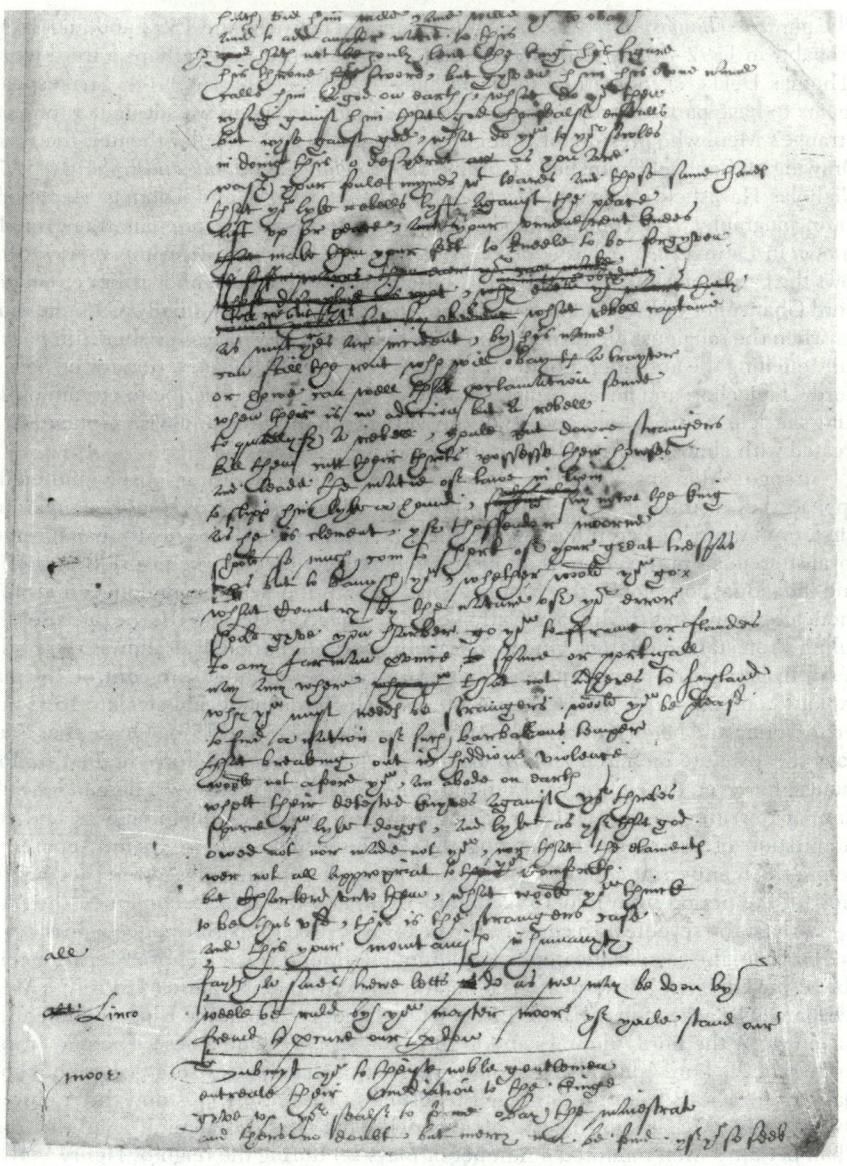

From Anthony Munday and others, "The Booke of Sir Thomas Moore" (British Library MS Harleian 7368), fol. 9a. This is the most legible of the pages believed to be in Shakespeare's hand.

of the age. It was not printed until the nineteenth century. It is worth emphasizing the existence of other possible explanations—three in particular—of the text besides the one offered here. The revisions may have occurred immediately following the initial composition of the play, either before or after Tilney's censorship. Second, a small minority denies that Shakespeare is Hand D. Third and most striking, it has been argued that Hand D, whatever his identity, was one of the original playwrights rather than a reviser.

Hand D is present in the first of the two passages printed here, Add.II.D (Addition II, Hand D; 8ʳ, 8ᵛ, 9ʳ), which was subsequently edited by Hand C, partly to make it conform to the other revisions. If Add.II.D is Shakespearean, it is by far the longest extant specimen of Shakespeare's handwriting and as such is of considerable scholarly, as well as theatrical and literary, value. It shows what a Shakespearean first draft looks like and, hence, some of the challenges a scribe or printer had to contend with. The attribution to Shakespeare is based on resemblances to his other extant handwriting (almost exclusively signatures), spelling similarities to printed texts that probably are directly based on manuscripts in Shakespeare's hand, and stylistic affinities. The text printed here excludes the emendations that Hand C made to Add.II.D. Normally, this edition opts for the theatrical, rather than the authorial, version of a play on the grounds that Shakespeare was aware of and accepted the revisions introduced by his acting company when preparing his manuscript for the stage. In this instance, however, his involvement in rehearsal and performance is less likely than usual. The second passage included here, Add.III (folio 11*ᵇ), is in Hand C and is attributed to Shakespeare, with somewhat less confidence, on stylistic grounds. Normally, as well, this edition prints an entire play rather than a fragment. Here, however, Shakespeare's contribution is small and his involvement probably late—long after the play had been conceptualized and, indeed, written. The entire play is available, however, online at the *Norton Shakespeare* Web site.

Add.II.D constitutes almost the first two-thirds of what one modern edition calls Scene 6 and another Act 2, Scene 3. Earlier in the play, the citizens of London, angered by the high-handed, legally protected behavior of foreigners, prepare to take bloody revenge. Here, More, acting on behalf of a state otherwise prepared to meet force with force, talks the assembled crowd out of violence and into submission to the King. Shakespeare's revision belittles the protesters, depriving them of an individuality they possessed earlier in the play and reducing them to the idiotic fear of disease-causing foreign vegetables (the parsnip and the pumpkin, lines 10–19). Although the rhetoric of More's arguments for obedience is clever and even arresting in its evocation of "the wretched strangers" leaving England (line 81), the claims are orthodox and traditional. They may represent changes from the original manuscript and, like the imagery, certainly have parallels in Shakespeare's other plays, most tellingly in Ulysses' speech on degree in 1.3 of *Troilus and Cressida* (probably from 1602). Even though the lines seem at least partly designed to reassure the censor, their political implications also point in a different direction. Once the crowd has listened to More, whom they already trust and respect, they willingly submit to royal authority. The text demonstrates the fundamental decency of the common folk. And More's brilliant success provides a plausible, if historically inaccurate, explanation of his appointment as Lord Chancellor.

Like Ulysses' speech, however, More's is undermined by the rest of the play. The passage also engages in powerfully ironic foreshadowing at the expense of the monarchy. More promises,

> Submit you to these noble gentlemen,
> Entreat their mediation to the King,
> Give up yourself to form, obey the magistrate,
> And there's no doubt but mercy may be found,
> If you so seek it.

(lines 157–61)

There is, however, a "doubt": Lincoln goes to the scaffold, his noble death anticipating More's own fate. More also insists that

> . . . to the King God hath his office lent
> . . . .
>   . . . What do you then,
> Rising 'gainst him that God himself installs,
> But rise 'gainst God?
>   (lines 107, 113–15)

The equation of God and King, the divine sanction for royal authority—these are the principles that More repudiates at the cost of his life. A similar effect is achieved in Add.III, which opens Scene 8 of one modern edition and Act 3, Scene 1, of another. Newly named Lord Chancellor, More soliloquizes on the suddenness of his ascent, in which he sees evidence of a providential force at odds with explanations based on "our fortunes" (line 2; Fortune is usually represented in *de casibus* tragedy by the image of the turning wheel). This view leads him to predict, accurately, that "to be great / Is" to be "greatly undone" (lines 19–21)—where the greatness of the undoing can refer both to the height from which he falls and to the stature of the cause for which he goes to his death.

WALTER COHEN

SELECTED BIBLIOGRAPHY

Fox, Alistair. "The Paradoxical Design of *The Book of Sir Thomas More.*" *Renaissance and Reformation/Renaissance et Réforme* n.s. 5 (1981): 162–73. Includes discussion of the symbolic resonance of the dramatic interlude that More puts on for the Lord Mayor (Scene 9).

Gabrieli, Vittorio. "*Sir Thomas More*: Sources, Characters, Ideas." *Moreana* 23 (June 1986): 17–43. The central study of the play's sources.

Howard-Hill, T. H., ed. *Shakespeare and "Sir Thomas More": Essays on the Play and Its Shakespearian Interest*. Cambridge, Eng.: Cambridge University Press, 1989. A collection of articles dealing with both authorship issues and critical interpretation.

Levine, Nina S. "Citizens' Games: Differentiating Collaboration and *Sir Thomas More.*" *Shakespeare Quarterly* 58 (2007): 31–64. Investigates the analogy between collaborative authorship and the subject of that collaboration, rebellious citizen solidarity.

Masten, Jeffrey. "More or Less: Editing the Collaborative." *Shakespeare Studies* 29 (2001): 109–31. Argues for including the full play, rather than just the Shakespearean portions, in editions of Shakespeare, thus avoiding a practice that underemphasizes the unity of the work.

McMillin, Scott. *The Elizabethan Theatre and "The Book of Sir Thomas More."* Ithaca, N.Y.: Cornell University Press, 1987. Interprets the play in the context of theatrical practice at the time, arguing that Shakespeare was part of the collaboration that originally composed the play rather than one of its revisers.

Munday, Anthony, and others. Revised by Henry Chettle, Thomas Dekker, Thomas Heywood, and William Shakespeare. *Sir Thomas More: A Play*. Ed. Vittorio Gabrieli and Giorgio Melchiori. The Revels Plays series. Manchester: Manchester University Press, 1990. Annotated modern edition of the play.

Wentersdorf, Karl P. "On 'Momtanish Inhumanyty' in *Sir Thomas More.*" *Studies in Philology* 103 (2006): 178–85. Argues that More criticizes the citizens' hostility to foreigners as Muslim inhumanity.

Sir Thomas More: *Passages Attributed to Shakespeare*

Add.II.D

[*John*] LINCOLN [*a broker*],° DOLL, BETTS, [SHERWIN (*a*   *buying and selling agent*
goldsmith), *and prentices*° *armed; Thomas* MORE (*sheriff*   *apprentices*
of the City of London), *the other sheriff, Sir Thomas*
PALMER, *Sir Roger* CHOLMELEY,] *and a* SERJEANT-*at-*
arms [*stand aloof*]

LINCOLN [*to the prentices*]   Peace, hear me! He that will not see°   *tolerate*
   a red herring at a Harry groat,° butter at eleven pence a pound,   *cost of fourpence*
   meal at nine shillings a bushel, and beef at four nobles a stone,
   list[1] to me.

5 OTHER   It will come to that pass if strangers be suffered.[2] Mark
   him.

LINCOLN   Our country is a great eating country; argo,[3] they eat
   more in our country than they do in their own.

OTHER   By a halfpenny loaf a day, troy weight.°   *standard measure*

10 LINCOLN   They bring in strange roots,[4] which is merely° to the   *entirely*
   undoing of poor prentices, for what's a sorry parsnip[5] to a good
   heart?

OTHER   Trash, trash. They breed sore eyes, and 'tis enough to
   infect the city with the palsy.

15 LINCOLN   Nay, it has infected it with the palsy, for these bastards
   of dung[6]—as you know, they grow in dung—have infected us,
   and it is our infection will make the city shake, which partly
   comes through the eating of parsnips.

OTHER   True, and pumpions° together.   *pumpkins*

SERJEANT [*coming forward*]   What say you to the mercy of the
20   King?
   Do you refuse it?

LINCOLN   You would have us upon th'hip,° would you? No,   *at a disadvantage*
   marry, do we not. We accept of the King's mercy; but we will
   show no mercy upon the strangers.

25 SERJEANT   You are the simplest things
   That ever stood in such a question.[7]

LINCOLN   How say you now? Prentices 'simple'? [*To the pren-*
   tices] Down with him!

ALL   Prentices simple! Prentices simple!

Add.II.D Location: St. Martin's Lane, London; May Day
1517.
1. *noble:* gold coin worth 6 shillings 8 pence. *stone:* 14
pounds. *list:* listen. These prices would have seemed high
to a contemporary audience.
2. If foreigners ("strangers" means "foreigners" throughout the scene) are allowed (to remain in London).
3. As Lincoln says, England had a reputation for gluttony. *argo:* for Latin *ergo* (therefore).

4. Foreign vegetables.
5. Lincoln confuses parsnips with potatoes, which were
introduced to England from the Americas in the 1580s
and were rumored to cause disease.
6. Illegitimate growths made still more repugnant by
their association with excrement; perhaps merely abusive.
7. Stood their ground in such circumstances (against
the King's wishes).

Enter the Lord MAYOR, [*the Earl of*] SURREY, [*and the Earl of*] SHREWSBURY

30　SHERIFF [*to the prentices*]　Hold in the King's name! Hold!

　　SURREY [*to the prentices*]　Friends, masters, countrymen—

　　MAYOR [*to the prentices*]　Peace ho, peace! I charge you, keep
　　　　the peace!

　　SHREWSBURY [*to the prentices*]　My masters, countrymen—

　　SHERWIN　The noble Earl of Shrewsbury, let's hear him.

35　BETTS　We'll hear the Earl of Surrey.

　　LINCOLN　The Earl of Shrewsbury.

　　BETTS　We'll hear both.

　　ALL　Both, both, both, both!

　　LINCOLN　Peace, I say peace! Are you men of wisdom, or what
40　　are you?

　　SURREY　What you will have them,° but not men of wisdom.　　*Whatever you call them*

　　SOME　We'll not hear my Lord of Surrey.

　　OTHERS　No, no, no, no, no! Shrewsbury, Shrewsbury!

　　MORE [*to the nobles and officers*]　Whiles they are o'er the bank
　　　　of their obedience,
45　　Thus will they bear down all things.[8]

　　LINCOLN [*to the prentices*]　Sheriff More speaks. Shall we hear
　　　　Sheriff More speak?

　　DOLL　Let's hear him. A keeps a plentiful shrievaltry,[9] and a
　　　　made my brother Arthur Watchins Sergeant Safe's yeoman.°　　*assistant*
50　　Let's hear Sheriff More.

　　ALL　Sheriff More, More, More, Sheriff More!

　　MORE　Even by the rule you have among yourselves,
　　　　Command still audience.°　　*quiet hearing*

　　SOME　Surrey, Surrey!

55　OTHERS　More, More!

　　LINCOLN *and* BETTS　Peace, peace, silence, peace!

　　MORE　You that have voice and credit with the number,°　　*the crowd*
　　　　Command them to a stillness.

　　LINCOLN　A plague on them! They will not hold their peace.
60　　The devil cannot rule them.

　　MORE　Then what a rough and riotous charge° have you,　　*people in your care; duty*
　　　　To lead those that the devil cannot rule.
　　　　[*To the prentices*] Good masters, hear me speak.

　　DOLL　Ay, by th' mass, will we. More, thou'rt a good house-
65　　keeper,[1] and I thank thy good worship for my brother Arthur
　　　　Watchins.

　　ALL　Peace, peace!

　　MORE　Look, what you do offend you cry upon,[2]
　　　　That is the peace. Not one of you here present,
70　　Had there such fellows lived when you were babes
　　　　That could have topped the peace as now you would,
　　　　The peace wherein you have till now grown up
　　　　Had been ta'en from you, and the bloody times
　　　　Could not have brought you to the state of men.[3]

8. The image is of water flooding over the banks (of obedience), destroying everything in its path.
9. He ("A") is a generous sheriff.
1. Patron; head of a well-to-do household.
2. By yelling "peace" (though you call for peace), you break the peace. More's speeches to the crowd, especially lines 79–94, echo Ulysses' speech on degree in *Troilus and Cressida* 1.3.74–137, in particular lines 110–24. Both of these sincere expositions of orthodoxy are ironized by the ensuing events.
3. *Not one . . . men:* If such peace breakers as you had been around when you were children, you wouldn't have had peaceful times to grow up in, and you wouldn't have lived to become men.

75 Alas, poor things, what is it you have got,
Although we grant you get the thing you seek?

BETTS Marry, the removing of the strangers, which cannot
choose but much advantage the poor handicrafts° of the city.   *craftspeople*

MORE Grant them removed, and grant that this your noise

80 Hath chid down all the majesty of England.[4]
Imagine that you see the wretched strangers,
Their babies at their backs, with their poor luggage
Plodding to th' ports and coasts for transportation,
And that you sit as kings in your desires,[5]

85 Authority quite silenced by your brawl
And you in ruff of your opinions clothed:[6]
What had you got? I'll tell you. You had taught
How insolence and strong hand° should prevail,   *force*
How order should be quelled—and by this pattern

90 Not one of you should live an agèd man,
For other ruffians as their fancies wrought
With selfsame hand, self reasons, and self right
Would shark° on you, and men like ravenous fishes   *prey*
Would feed on one another.

95 DOLL Before God, that's as true as the gospel.

BETTS Nay, this'° a sound fellow, I tell you. Let's mark° him.   *this is / listen to*

MORE Let me set up before your thoughts, good friends,
One supposition,° which if you will mark   *proposition*
You shall perceive how horrible a shape

100 Your innovation° bears. First, 'tis a sin   *rebellion*
Which oft th'apostle° did forewarn us of,   *Paul (Romans 13:1–5)*
Urging obedience to authority;
And 'twere no error if I told you all
You were in arms 'gainst God.

105 ALL Marry, God forbid that!

MORE Nay, certainly you are.
For to the King God hath his office lent
Of dread,° of justice, power and command,   *fearful respect*
Hath bid him rule and willed you to obey;

110 And to add ampler majesty to this,
He hath not only lent the King his figure,
His throne and sword, but given him his own name,
Calls him a god on earth. What do you then,
Rising 'gainst him that God himself installs,

115 But rise 'gainst God?[7] What do you to your souls
In doing this? O desperate as you are,
Wash your foul minds with tears, and those same hands
That you like rebels lift against the peace
Lift up for peace; and your unreverent knees,

120 Make them your feet. To kneel to be forgiven
Is safer wars than ever you can make,
Whose discipline is riot.[8]

---

4. *grant that . . . England*: suppose your action overthrew the state.
5. You get what you want; your wishes are obeyed.
6. And you wearing the clothes ("ruff" was a fancy starched collar; also, the highest pride) befitting the rank and authority you think you deserve (alluding to Elizabethan sumptuary laws, which determined, according to rank and income, the clothes one was permitted to wear).
7. More argues in this speech that the monarch's authority has divine sanction—ironically, a position that, as the end of the play reveals, he later repudiated at the cost of his life.
8. *Is . . . riot*: Is a safer means of fighting (for your goals) than your rebellion.

In, in, to your obedience!⁹ Why, even your hurly°   *riot*
Cannot proceed but by obedience.

125   What rebel captain,
As mut'nies are incident,° by his name   *about to happen*
Can still the rout?° Who will obey a traitor?   *quiet the rabble*
Or how can well that proclamation sound,
When there is no addition° but 'a rebel'   *title of rank*

130   To qualify° a rebel? You'll put down strangers,   *signify*
Kill them, cut their throats, possess their houses,
And lead the majesty of law in lyam°   *on a leash*
To slip° him like a hound—alas, alas!   *release*
Say now the King,

135   As he is clement° if th'offender mourn,°   *merciful / repent*
Should so much come too short of your great trespass¹
As but to banish you: whither would you go?
What country, by° the nature of your error,   *in light of*
Should give you harbour? Go you to France or Flanders,

140   To any German province, Spain or Portugal,
Nay, anywhere that not adheres² to England—
Why, you must needs° be strangers. Would you be pleased   *necessarily*
To find a nation of such barbarous temper
That breaking out in hideous violence

145   Would not afford you an abode on earth,
Whet° their detested knives against your throats,   *But would whet*
Spurn you like dogs, and like as if that God
Owed° not nor made not you, nor that the elements   *Owned*
Were not all appropriate° to your comforts   *suitable*

150   But chartered unto° them, what would you think   *reserved only for*
To be thus used? This is the strangers' case,
And this your mountainish³ inhumanity.

ONE [*to the others*]   Faith, a° says true. Let's do as we may be   *he*
     done by.⁴

155 ANOTHER [*to* MORE]   We'll be ruled by you, Master More, if
     you'll stand our friend to procure our pardon.

MORE   Submit you to these noble gentlemen,
     Entreat their mediation to the King,
     Give up yourself to form,° obey the magistrate,   *correct behavior*

160   And there's no doubt but mercy may be found,
     If you so seek it.⁵

Add.III

Enter [*Sir Thomas*] MORE

MORE   It is in heaven that I am thus and thus,¹
     And that which we profanely term our fortunes
     Is the provision of the power above,
     Fitted and shaped just to that strength of nature

5   Which we are born withal.° Good God, good God,   *with*
     That I from such an humble bench² of birth

---

9. Get back within the boundaries of your obedience.
1. Should reduce by so much the punishment for your great offense.
2. Anywhere whose customs don't conform.
3. Gross, coarse. Possibly a contraction of Mahometan-ish, or Muslim.
4. Proverbial. From the Sermon on the Mount (Matthew 7:12 and Luke 6:31).

5. In the event, More's intercession is unable to save Lincoln, whose noble death on the scaffold foreshadows More's own and, like his, reflects badly on the King—the dying men's loyal words notwithstanding.
Add.III Location: The chancery staterooms in Westminster.
1. It is up to heaven that I am one thing and then another.
2. Legal position; foot of the table: hence, origin.

Should step as 'twere up to my country's head
And give the law out there; ay, in my father's life
To take prerogative and tithe of knees[3]
10   From elder kinsmen, and him bind by my place
To give the smooth and dexter way to me[4]
That owe it him by nature!° Sure these things,   *by birth*
Not physicked° by respect, might turn our blood   *regulated*
To much corruption. But More, the more thou hast
15   Either of honour, office, wealth and calling,
Which might accite° thee to embrace and hug them,   *entice*
The more do thou e'en° serpents' natures think them: *even*
Fear their gay skins, with thought of their sharp stings,
And let this be thy maxim: to be great
20   Is, when the thread of hazard is once spun,
A bottom great wound up, greatly undone.[5]

3. *To . . . knees:* To have preeminence and the deference of having others curtsy.
4. *and him . . . me:* and for my rank to force ("bind") someone ("him") to yield the right-hand side and the smooth part of the road.
5. *to be great . . . undone:* worldly power, when the thread that Fortune ("hazard") allots has been all wound up onto a big spool ("bottom"; or, when the hazards of reaching a high position have been surmounted), simply means a greater fall (or, falling only for something important). In Greek mythology, the end of a life occurred when the Fates cut a person's thread. Regardless of the exact interpretation of the passage, it accurately predicts More's fate.

Measure for Measure

A young man is in grave trouble with the law, and his beautiful sister goes to the magistrate to plead for mercy. The magistrate offers to remit the penalty if the sister will sleep with him. It is an old story in more ways than one. Shakespeare knew several sixteenth-century versions: the Italian Giovanbattista Giraldi Cinthio produced both prose and dramatic renderings, and in 1578 the English playwright George Whetstone published *Promos and Cassandra,* the most important source for *Measure for Measure.* Shakespeare took the title of his play from Jesus' Sermon on the Mount: "Judge not, that ye be not judged. For with what judgment ye judge, ye shall be judged: and with what measure ye mete, it shall be measured to you again" (Matthew 7:1–2). Jesus' advice combines threat with promise: a prudent fear of heavenly retaliation persuades believers not to pass judgment themselves, while at the same time, an apparent abdication of equity is folded into an overall scheme of just compensation. As we shall see, the passage in all its complexity complements the intricacies of Shakespeare's treatment of the ancient tale.

Measure for Measure was performed in 1604 at a pivotal moment in Shakespeare's career. The play is the last in a long series of comedies that explore complex issues of sex, marriage, and personal identity. Its tone, themes, and methods of characterization, however, veer close to tragedy, the genre that largely, though not exclusively, preoccupied Shakespeare in the years immediately following. Many critics, therefore, classify *Measure for Measure* as a "problem" comedy. The designation attests both to the difficult moral issues that the play confronts and to the boldness with which it stretches— some would say shatters—the normal limits of comic form.

The play's distinctiveness becomes evident almost immediately. In Act 1, Scene 2, Claudio and his pregnant lover, Juliet, appear in the custody of the Provost, being led away to prison. Their crime is premarital sex; the penalty, for Claudio at least, is death. The seriousness of their situation is not in itself unusual: "The course of true love never did run smooth," Lysander remarks in *A Midsummer Night's Dream,* and if it did, it would hardly make an engrossing dramatic subject. Nonetheless, Claudio's initial description of his plight is quite remarkable:

> LUCIO   Why, how now, Claudio? Whence comes this restraint?
> CLAUDIO   From too much liberty, my Lucio, liberty.
> As surfeit is the father of much fast,
> So every scope, by the immoderate use,
> Turns to restraint. Our natures do pursue,
> Like rats that raven down their proper bane,
> A thirsty evil; and when we drink, we die.
>
> (1.2.104–10)

Claudio likens his passion for his beloved to a rat's craving for poison: compulsive, irrational, and self-destructive. Excessive indulgence, or "surfeit," inevitably brings regret and punishment in its train. Claudio sounds as if he is describing the most arrant kind of lust, although, as he will subsequently explain, he is actually "precontracted" to Juliet, bound by a promise of marriage that many in Renaissance England saw as providing conjugal privileges. (Shakespeare himself may have subscribed to this view, since his wife gave birth to their daughter five months after their wedding. More pertinently, the Duke, in his guise as a friar, affirms that the precontract sanctions Mariana's intimacy with Angelo later in the play.) Interestingly, however, neither Claudio nor Juliet is inclined to argue that their devotion to one another mitigates their guilt. Instead, they admit that they have committed "fornication," a severely condemnatory term that conflates all kinds of sex outside of marriage under the same rubric, recognizing no difference between long-term relationships and sheerest promiscuity.

As the play continues, it becomes clear that Claudio's imagery of suicidal animalism, havoc, and pollution is not merely the consequence of his immediate agitation, but expresses a profound assumption of the society in which he lives. For his sister, Isabella, sexual intercourse is "what I abhor to name" (3.1.100); the Duke deplores Pompey's "filthy vice" and Juliet's "most offenseful act"; the wise Escalus acknowledges Claudio's "error" even as he attempts to alleviate his punishment. Few doubt that human sexuality is an essentially sordid matter, a sign of degradation rather than a means of creativity or love. Occasional glimpses of an alternative vision—Lucio's brief, radiant analogy between Juliet's pregnancy and agricultural fertility, for instance—by their very rarity reinforce the prevailing pessimism.

Such austere views of human sexuality have ancient roots. When the Duke calls Vienna's sex laws "needful bits and curbs to headstrong weeds" (1.3.20), he recalls an image from Plato, who compared the desiring part of the soul to a useful but refractory horse, which the rational part of the soul needs to keep strictly bridled and under firm control. When Isabella refers to erotic desire as a "natural guiltiness" (2.2.142), she draws upon a traditional Christian connection between sexuality and original sin, the disobedience committed by Adam and Eve in the Garden of Eden and passed on to all their offspring as a kind of intrinsic pollution.

To say that a view is traditional, however, is not to say that it is inevitable. What makes sexuality so troublesome in this particular play? In Shakespeare's earlier, more optimistic comedies, the prospect of heterosexual consummation usually seems automatically to entail marriage, so that the weddings with which the plays conclude seem to follow spontaneously from the eroticism that fuels the plot. By marrying and establishing a family, the young couples simultaneously satisfy their mutual yearning for one another, and their community's demand for clear kinship structures and for orderly means of transferring property to "legitimate" members of a new generation. In *Measure for Measure*, however, the link between heterosexual desire and marriage seems to have snapped. Claudio and Juliet defer their wedding day; Angelo abandons Mariana; Lucio refuses to support his child or marry its mother. Prostitution flourishes. Rampant promiscuity makes syphilis a familiar ailment and a standard topic for nervous jokes.

Charioteer with two galloping horses. From Geffrey Whitney, *A Choice of Emblemes* (1586).

Once carnal desire comes unhinged from the institution of marriage, it begins to seem subversive of personal and civic order. And if one believes, rightly or wrongly, that one's sexuality is intrinsically antisocial and depraved, then complete sexual renunciation might seem the wisest course. In *Measure for Measure*, the morally ambitious characters—the Duke, Angelo, and Isabella—initially assume that their virtue is tied up with, perhaps even identical with, their chastity. "Believe not that the dribbling dart of love / Can pierce a complete bosom," the Duke boasts to the Friar (1.3.2–3). Angelo attempts to protect his reputation for austerity even as he hopelessly compromises his scruples in secret. Isabella believes that sleeping with Angelo will defile her forever, even if she does so in order to save her brother's life.

The value of celibacy is endorsed by characters who do not themselves aspire to such high standards of conduct. Lucio is a libertine, but he believes that Isabella's intention to enter a nunnery renders her "a thing enskied and sainted" (1.4.33). Likewise, Pompey admits that his life as a pimp "does stink in some sort, sir" (3.1.283). A few of those who cannot be chaste themselves are, like Claudio, capable of moments of shame or self-loathing; others, like Lucio, shruggingly accept their lack of saintliness. The Vienna of *Measure for Measure* is full of people unlikely to be enlisted for projects of social or spiritual improvement: the moronic Elbow, the impenitent Pompey, the unregenerate Mistress Overdone, the "gravel-hearted" Barnardine, the heedless First and Second Gentlemen, the gullible Froth. These people are part of the commonwealth, subject to the law, and willy-nilly part, too, of a Catholic church that aspires—unlike some of the Protestant sects of Shakespeare's time—to include the entire community. Should the laws of this community reflect its stringent ideals or the actual behavior of most of its members? Throughout the play, those who aspire to belong to a principled moral elite deplore the weaknesses of the reprobate. At the same time, because the rascals in *Measure for Measure* are so vividly memorable, the play also suggests that moral "failure" is often at least as humanly compelling as moral excellence is—at least moral excellence defined in the narrow, self-denying terms that prevail in Vienna.

For the intransigent majority unable or unwilling to control the horses of lust, the "needful bits and curbs" of which the Duke speaks impose an external system of repression. Such a system would not have been unfamiliar to Shakespeare's original audience. Courts administered by the Church of England prosecuted many sexual infractions: among them fathering or giving birth to a bastard, committing adultery or bigamy, deserting a spouse, reneging on a wedding engagement, or groundlessly accusing others of such transgressions. Convicted individuals could be fined, whipped, displayed in the marketplace, or made to announce their sins in church. (Thus Claudio and Juliet are paraded about the streets of Vienna before being taken to prison, to humiliate them and to serve as an example for others.) Repeat offenders were excommunicated, or cast out of the church.

Underlying such proceedings was the assumption, as in *Measure for Measure,* that morality could and should be legislated; that the sexual conduct of individuals was the business of the entire community. Indeed, in the early seventeenth century, when Shakespeare was writing *Measure for Measure,* an increasingly powerful group of Puritans, or "precisians," argued that the church courts' punishments were far too mild. Threats of disgrace and excommunication failed to deter the most egregious offenders, who had no reputation to lose and were unlikely to fret at their exclusion from church. Moreover, shaming punishments worked less well in the increasingly busy, heterogeneous neighborhoods of Jacobean London than they had in the smaller rural communities for which they had originally been designed.

In *Measure for Measure,* the repeated characterization of Angelo as "precise" associates him with the rigorists of Shakespeare's time; and since Viennese justice treats Claudio more strictly than it does professionals in the sex trade, the question of what constitutes adequate severity is certainly at issue. Perhaps, then, the play comprises Shakespeare's reflection on an issue of contemporary concern: what would happen if, as some argued, sexual misconduct could be punished with death? At the same time, Shakespeare carefully distinguishes the world of his play from seventeenth-century England, most obviously by making Vienna a Catholic city peopled with the nuns and friars who had been eliminated from Protestant England over half a century earlier. For despite obvious connections between *Measure for Measure* and some of the issues of its own day, Shakespeare's play hardly constitutes a clear policy recommendation. He is more deeply attentive to general issues about the often-vexed relationship between civic life and human passion, and between religious commitment and the conduct of secular affairs. What happens to individuals and a community when sexuality is viewed as transgressive, when it becomes the subject of public discipline? Is it possible or advisable to regulate sexual behavior through the courts? How do religious convictions affect the experience of sexual desire? These concerns resonate in an era like our own, characterized by a lack of consensus in religion and in sexual mores, by widespread transformations in the institution of marriage, and by debates over the extent to which the state ought to monitor the sexual behavior of citizens.

In *Measure for Measure*, Angelo's disastrous career suggests one possible effect of strict sexual self-denial: that the habits of restraint can themselves provoke sexual excitement. Rigid and self-righteous, Angelo seems not to have experienced the violence of desire until Isabella's first visit on behalf of her brother awakens his appetite:

> What's this? What's this? Is this her fault or mine?
> The tempter or the tempted, who sins most, ha?
> Not she; nor doth she tempt; but it is I
> That, lying by the violet in the sun,
> Do, as the carrion does, not as the flower,
> Corrupt with virtuous season.
>
> (2.2.167–72)

Like Claudio, Angelo thinks of passion in terms of death and decay, but the resemblance between the two men ends there. Angelo imagines himself as tainted meat rotting all the

Jost Amman, Poor Clare nun, from *Cleri totius Romanae ecclesiae subjecti* (1585).

faster under the very sun that gives life to innocent, lovely things. What ought to improve Angelo—his keen appreciation for the presence of virtue—makes him worse.

Angelo is sexually aroused by prohibition. Mariana loves him, and his relationship with her breaches no social norms; he discards her. Isabella is ostentatiously pristine, and her nun's habit marks her as taboo; he finds her irresistible. In order to extract pleasure from the encounter, however, Angelo must force himself to remain aware of the principles he attempts so flagrantly to violate. If he rationalized his behavior or blamed it on Isabella, he would lose the nearly sensual luxury of self-hatred. Therefore, the lucidity with which Angelo analyzes his own motives leads not to penitence but to an increasing moral recklessness. His inclination to categorize all sexual conduct as transgressive actually makes his offense easier to commit. Propositioning Isabella in their second meeting together, he tells her: "I have begun, / And now I give my sensual race the rein" (2.4.159–60). Angelo explains why he cannot govern himself with the same image the Duke used to underscore the necessity of control. Once embarked on the "sensual race," he imagines, there is no alternative to utter abandon.

For Isabella, however, sleeping with Angelo is out of the question. Some modern critics have found her defiance heroic, others chilling or selfish. Doubtless in Shakespeare's time, she elicited a similarly mixed response. Shakespeare alters his source story considerably to expand Isabella's role and specify its implications more exactly. In Whetstone's *Promos and Cassandra,* the sister has no plans to enter a convent, and she eventually goes to bed with the deputy in order to save her brother's life. For Isabella, by contrast, virginity is a principled choice, not an accident of youth. The vow of lifelong, religiously dedicated chastity she plans to take is a matter about which Shakespeare's contemporaries had conflicting feelings. One effect of England's break with the Catholic Church had been a spectacular change in official attitudes toward celibacy. While Catholics honored sexual renunciation and demanded that their clergy remain chaste, Protestants discouraged veneration of the Virgin Mary, abolished convents and monasteries, and urged clergy to marry. Despite these alterations, however, a powerful appreciation for virginity and belief in its semimagical powers persisted in Reformation England, cut loose from its explicitly religious moorings. The effect of Shakespeare's innovations on Whetstone, then, is both to heighten the ambivalence of the story and to focus the moral spotlight on Isabella's convictions and the choices that follow from them.

Isabella believes that she would damn herself by sleeping with Angelo.

> Better it were a brother died at once
> Than that a sister, by redeeming him,
> Should die for ever.
>
> (2.4.107–9)

Is she right? St. Augustine, the most influential Christian writer on sexual morality, insists that since sin is a property of the will, not a physical state, persons who are forced to perform sexual acts are blameless. If chastity is a state of mind, then the fate of Isabella's body is possibly independent of, and irrelevant to, the fate of her soul. Perhaps, in fact, by acquiescing to Angelo, Isabella would perform an act of charity, generously sacrificing her own preferences for Claudio's benefit. On the other hand, female "virtue" has traditionally been defined in physical as well as mental terms, so that chastity, the spiritual attitude, is hard to separate from virginity, the bodily condition. Moreover, Isabella is not exactly a rape victim; she must, as Angelo says, "fit her consent" to his proposal. Does that consent, however reluctant, contaminate her with his sin? Quite possibly. Would it permanently unsuit her for her religious vocation? Quite possibly. Clearly it is reasonable, then, for Isabella to be cautious; and no one, says Augustine, is obliged to put him- or herself in eternal peril merely in order to save the life of another person.

Since, however, Shakespeare characteristically translates sweeping moral questions into scrupulously personal terms, apparently reasonable general maxims do not entirely suffice to explain Isabella's motives. On one hand, her obstinacy seems justified after the fact, when Angelo decides to execute Claudio, because clearly her capitulation would not have saved her brother's life. On the other hand, Isabella's obsession with her own purity seems excessive, especially in 3.1, when it manifests itself in gross insensitivity to her plaintive, terrified brother. Moreover, her fervent yearning for constraint, like Angelo's, seems luridly imbued with sadomasochism.

> were I under the terms of death,
> Th'impression of keen whips I'd wear as rubies,
> And strip myself to death as to a bed
> That longing have been sick for, ere I'd yield
> My body up to shame.

$$(2.4.100–04)$$

At such moments, Isabella seems not to be exterminating or transcending her own sexuality, but redirecting it in ways of which she is not entirely conscious. She not only shares Angelo's assumption that the sexual act is a defilement, but like him she finds discipline exciting. With all our disapproval of Angelo's abuse of power and our sympathy with Isabella's indignation, we can still see how their conflict arises as much from their similarities as from their differences.

Isabella's difficulty is hard to resolve because it is unclear how much her chastity is worth. Is it more valuable than her brother's life? Is it more valuable than her own life, which she would throw down for Claudio, she claims, "as frankly as a pin" (3.1.105)? Is it only fair, as Angelo claims, to yield him her body as compensation for overlooking Claudio's offense, or is "lawful mercy . . . nothing kin to foul redemption" (2.4.113–14)? Shakespeare provides no answer to these questions, but the conflict they produce yields the play's most vividly realized interactions. As the title suggests, *Measure for Measure* is obsessed with problems of substitution and commensurability—from the opening scene in which Angelo takes over as the Duke's deputy to Angelo's proposal that Isabella vindicate Claudio by committing his sin herself, to the bed trick that replaces Isabella with Mariana, to the Provost's exchange of Ragusine's head for Claudio's. Even the most apparently trivial comic interchanges persistently echo the concern with equivalence, proportionality, and relative priority: the Gentlemen argue about whether they are cut from lists or velvet; Pompey and Abhorson debate the relative standing of bawd and hangman.

Questions of equivalence seem to underlie the very possibility of justice, even the possibility of any ethical thinking. When a person commits a misdeed, restoring the status quo ante is usually impossible. Thus the wrongdoer ought, we feel, either to make adequate restitution or to suffer in rough proportion to the anguish he or she has caused, rendering, in the biblical phrase, measure for measure. In sexual matters, however, such problems of equivalence are murky, because there is no consensus regarding how apparently straightforward bodily acts ought to be interpreted. Angelo compares Claudio's offense to murder and counterfeiting; Lucio thinks it is trivial, "a game of tick-tack" (1.2.167). What seem to be the same actions can be evaluated in wildly different ways, depending on one's frame of reference: to the abstemious Angelo, Claudio's behavior looks like gross debauchery, while to Mistress Overdone's dissolute patrons, it looks positively restrained. Motives alter what seem to be the same actions, so that we are inclined to regard Claudio more leniently than Lucio, who abandoned his mistress after making her pregnant. So do outcomes: the bed trick means that Angelo, intending to commit an impermissible act, in fact performs a licit one, unknowingly laying the groundwork for his pardon in the final scene.

The commitment of several characters to a Christian religious vocation further complicates the possibility of establishing some kind of commensurability. Isabella, especially, assumes that spiritual goods like honor and purity are infinitely more important than secular, visible possessions. In her system of values, a promise of ardent prayer constitutes the most potent bribe she can offer Angelo, beside which gold is barren and trivial. The counterintuitive otherworldliness of Isabella's concept of commensurability is central to Christianity, a religion founded on the spectacularly lopsided substitution of the blameless Christ for sinful humanity in the system of God's justice. But since such religious convictions are not subject to the verification of the senses, they are open to challenge by those more firmly attached to the things of this world. For Claudio, any fate seems better than death. His hierarchy of priorities is different from Isabella's, and so, therefore, are his conceptions of commensurability.

How are such drastic discrepancies between the various characters' moral and social outlooks to be reconciled? The agent for bringing order and justice is Duke Vincentio, a concealed authority who learns everybody's secrets in the course of the play. Far from providing an authoritative solution to the play's ethical impasse, however, the Duke has elicited almost as much controversy as Isabella. Some critics see him as a version of God, "like power divine," as Angelo declares in the final scene. Some have suggested that the Duke was meant to compliment the diffident King James I, who at the time of the play's first performance had just ascended the English throne, after the death of his extroverted predecessor, Elizabeth I. More skeptical critics see the Duke as a schemer who foists his dirty work onto political subordinates and meddles impudently, even sacrilegiously, with the lives of his subjects.

The Duke's function as clergyman reflects the fact that the problems of *Measure for Measure* can only be solved by someone who can obtain access to the concealed realm of motives and intentions, a privilege usually reserved for a confessor. But merely knowing such information will not bring practical redress of injustice. So at the same time, unlike a clergyman, he must retain the secular ruler's ability to mandate changes in the world in order to bring matters to a satisfactory conclusion. A prince disguised as a friar, the Duke bridges, however unsteadily, the gap between knowledge and power. An actual sovereign with such prerogatives would approach tyranny—for that reason, the functions of priest and lay magistrate were ordinarily separated even in Shakespeare's time, when church and state were far more closely allied than they are today. In the play's fictional Vienna, however, the Duke's sweeping authority conveniently allows him to impose a resolution.

There are limits to Vincentio's power. Not even a Duke can sequester erotic fervor from the cruelty and disorder with which it has proven to be so intimately and insidiously allied. Not even a Duke can make passion tractable. The best he can manage is to introduce his subjects to some socially sanctioned medium between celibacy and abandon. Marriage in *Measure for Measure* is thus patently not a happy aspiration but a stopgap measure imposed on reluctant or noncommittal individuals, for whom the alternative in several cases is death. Indeed, Lucio, forthright as usual, complains that marriage is a worse fate than hanging; the others are distinctly muted in their response to the Duke's nuptial stratagems. Claudio and Juliet are given no lines in which to celebrate their reunion; nor do we hear that Angelo, who claims to "crave death more willingly than mercy" (5.1.470), is grateful to be preserved as Mariana's husband. Isabella remains silent in the face of the Duke's unexpected proposal of marriage, leaving it an open question whether she is overwhelmed with joy or gripped with horror, whether the Duke provides her with a socially and personally satisfying alternative to the cloister or merely recapitulates Angelo's harassment.

The pro forma quality of the coupling with which *Measure for Measure* concludes suggests that marital union is not, finally, the resolution toward which the play most convincingly moves. Most of the last scene is devoted to finding a way out of the difficulties posed by the radical moral incommensurabilities described above. In quick succession, the Duke's trial rehearses the normal outcome of Isabella's complaint—her condemnation and Angelo's exoneration—and then demonstrates that in this instance, almost miraculously, Angelo's secret vice will be made manifest after all. But this disclosure does not end the play, for the Duke's plan demands that Isabella plead for Angelo's life "against all sense," as the Sermon on the Mount commands her to do. The simple asceticism of the flesh with which *Measure for Measure* begins is displaced at last by a more subtle and exacting asceticism of the spirit, as Isabella renounces the hunger for vengeance in favor of a forgiveness that goes very much against the grain. Only this principled willingness to overlook injury and tolerate difference, the play seems to imply, can still the jostling among heterogeneous moral perspectives that endlessly complicate life in Vienna.

KATHARINE EISAMAN MAUS

TEXTUAL NOTE

The First Folio (1623, F) is the only authoritative text for most of *Measure for Measure,* and the *Norton Shakespeare* in general follows F closely. This text has some puzzling features. In F's 1.2, Claudio's imprisonment is first announced by Mistress Overdone, then shortly thereafter described by Pompey to Mistress Overdone, who seems unaware of the situation she has just related. The Oxford editors believe that *Measure for Measure* was adapted by Thomas Middleton for a performance after Shakespeare's death. In this scene, they argue, F reproduces in succession both the adapted text and the passage it was designed to replace. The same theory would explain some curious features of the action at the end of Act 3 and the beginning of Act 4: Mariana's song seems to have been taken from *The Bloody Brother,* a play first performed around 1617, and the Duke's soliloquy during the absence of Mariana and Isabella is irrelevant to its context. The adapter, in the course of rewriting the beginning of Act 4, probably switched this soliloquy with the one at the end of Act 3.

Because the line between adapted and original material is impossible to recover with any certainty, this edition does not attempt to restore a supposedly "Shakespearean" version of the play, but instead reconstructs the version presumably performed by the King's Men a few years before the printing of the Folio. This reconstruction departs from F only in omitting the short, redundant Shakespearean passage. The omitted passage is reproduced as an appendix, as is the soliloquy at the end of Act 3 as the Oxford editors believe Shakespeare originally wrote it (see Additional Passages). Mariana's song at the beginning of Act 4 has been collated with the authoritative manuscript originally belonging to John Wilson, the composer who set the lyric to music; as a result, F's "but" in line 6 has been emended to "though."

SELECTED BIBLIOGRAPHY

Adelman, Janet. "Bed Tricks: On Marriage as the End of Comedy in *All's Well That Ends Well* and *Measure for Measure.*" *Shakespeare's Personality.* Ed. Norman H. Holland, Sidney Homan, and Bernard J. Paris. Berkeley: University of California Press, 1989. 151–74. Sexuality as defilement and marriage as punishment in *Measure for Measure.*

Baines, Barbara. "Assaying the Power of Chastity in *Measure for Measure.*" *Studies in English Literature* 30 (1990): 248–98. Isabella's chastity as an active virtue in the Vienna of *Measure for Measure.*

Bennett, Josephine Waters. *"Measure for Measure" as Royal Entertainment.* New York: Columbia University Press, 1966. The play as it reflects James I's court, political philosophy, and royal persona.

Bloom, Harold, ed. *William Shakespeare's "Measure for Measure."* New York: Chelsea House, 1987. Anthology of critical essays.

Dollimore, Jonathan. "Transgression and Surveillance in *Measure for Measure.*" *Political Shakespeare: New Essays in Cultural Materialism.* Ed. Jonathan Dollimore and Alan Sinfield. Ithaca, N.Y.: Cornell University Press, 1985. 72–87.

Engle, Lars. "*Measure for Measure* and Modernity: The Problem of the Skeptic's Authority." *Shakespeare and Modernity: Early Modern to Millennium.* Ed. Hugh Grady. New York: Routledge, 2000. 85–104. Ethical relativism and difficulties of judgment.

Hawkins, Harriett. *Measure for Measure*. Boston: Twayne, 1987. Chapters on stage history, critical reception, and the play's major interpretive cruxes.

Knight, G. Wilson. "*Measure for Measure* and the Gospels." *The Wheel of Fire: Essays in Interpretation of Shakespeare's Sombre Tragedies*. London: Oxford University Press, 1930. 80–106. Duke Vincentio as godlike: *Measure for Measure* as a Christian play.

Maus, Katharine Eisaman. "Sexual Secrecy in *Measure for Measure*." *Inwardness and Theater in the English Renaissance*. Chicago: University of Chicago Press, 1995. 157–81. Sexual privacy as a challenge for legal supervision and as the grounds for character in *Measure for Measure*.

Shell, Marc. *The End of Kinship: "Measure for Measure," Incest, and the Ideal of Universal Siblinghood*. Stanford: Stanford University Press, 1988. Proper and improper exchanges in the Christian world of *Measure for Measure*, in which everyone is a brother or sister to everyone else.

Shuger, Debora Kuller. *Political Theologies in Shakespeare's England: The Sacred and the State in "Measure for Measure."* New York: Palgrave, 2001. *Measure for Measure* shows the intimate connection between problems of governance and religion in early modern Europe.

Wheeler, Richard P. *Shakespeare's Development* and *the Problem Comedies: Turn and Counter-Turn*. Berkeley: University of California Press, 1981. 1–33, 92–153. Detailed psychoanalytic interpretation.

FILM

Measure for Measure. 1979. Dir. Desmond Davis. UK. BBC-TV production. Nuanced performances from the entire ensemble, particularly Tim Pigott-Smith (Angelo), Kenneth Colley (Duke), Kate Nelligan (Isabella), and Frank Middlemass (Pompey).

Measure for Measure

THE PERSONS OF THE PLAY

Vincentio, the DUKE of Vienna
ANGELO, appointed his deputy
ESCALUS, an old lord, appointed Angelo's secondary
CLAUDIO, a young gentleman
JULIET, betrothed to Claudio
ISABELLA, Claudio's sister, novice to a sisterhood of nuns
LUCIO, a 'fantastic'
Two other such GENTLEMEN
FROTH, a foolish gentleman
MISTRESS OVERDONE, a bawd
POMPEY, her clownish servant
A PROVOST
ELBOW, a simple constable
A JUSTICE
ABHORSON, an executioner
BARNARDINE, a dissolute condemned prisoner
MARIANA, betrothed to Angelo
A BOY, attendant on Mariana
FRIAR PETER
FRANCESCA, a nun
VARRIUS, a lord, friend to the Duke
Lords, officers, citizens, servants

1.1

Enter DUKE, ESCALUS, [*and other*] *lords*

DUKE   Escalus.

ESCALUS   My lord.

DUKE   Of government the properties to unfold°   explain
    Would seem in me t'affect° speech and discourse,   love; show off
5   Since I am put° to know that your own science°   obliged / knowledge
    Exceeds in that the lists° of all advice   limits
    My strength can give you. Then no more remains
    But this: to° your sufficiency,° as your worth is able,   rely on / ability
    And let them¹ work. The nature of our people,
10 Our city's institutions and the terms°   procedures
    For common justice, you're as pregnant° in   expert
    As art° and practice hath enrichèd any   learning
    That we remember.
        [*He gives* ESCALUS *papers*]
                              There is our commission,
    From which we would not have you warp.°   deviate
    [*To a lord*]   Call hither,
15 I say bid come before us, Angelo.   [*Exit lord*]

1.1 Location: The play takes place in Vienna. Some
scene locations can merely be inferred. This scene may
be set in the Duke's palace.

1. The referent of "them" is unclear. Perhaps a line is
missing.

[*To* ESCALUS] What figure of us think you he will bear?[2]—
For you must know we have with special soul°   *deliberation*
Elected° him our absence to supply,°   *Chosen / make up for*
Lent him our terror, dressed him with our love,
20   And given his deputation° all the organs°   *deputyship / instruments*
Of our own power. What think you of it?

ESCALUS   If any in Vienna be of worth
To undergo° such ample grace° and honour,   *sustain / favor*
It is Lord Angelo.

                    Enter ANGELO

DUKE   Look where he comes.
25   ANGELO   Always obedient to your grace's will,
I come to know your pleasure.

DUKE   Angelo,
There is a kind of character[3] in thy life
That to th'observer doth thy history°   *life story*
Fully unfold. Thyself and thy belongings°   *endowments*
30   Are not thine own so proper° as to waste   *exclusively*
Thyself upon thy virtues, they on thee.
Heaven doth with us as we with torches do,
Not light them for themselves; for if our virtues
Did not go forth of° us, 'twere all alike   *from*
35   As if we had them not.[4] Spirits are not finely touched
But to fine issues;[5] nor nature never lends
The smallest scruple° of her excellence   *bit*
But, like a thrifty goddess, she determines°   *ordains*
Herself the glory of a creditor,
40   Both thanks and use.° But I do bend° my speech   *interest / direct*
To one that can my part in him advertise.°   *make known*
Hold[6] therefore, Angelo.
In our remove be thou at full ourself.
Mortality° and mercy in Vienna   *Power to kill*
45   Live in thy tongue and heart. Old Escalus,
Though first in question, is thy secondary.[7]
Take thy commission.

ANGELO   Now good my lord,
Let there be some more test made of my metal°   *(variant of "mettle")*
Before so noble and so great a figure
Be stamped upon it.

50   DUKE   No more evasion.
We have with leavened° and preparèd choice   *fermented (mature)*
Proceeded to you; therefore take your honours.
        [ANGELO *takes his commission*]
Our haste from hence is of so quick condition
That it prefers itself, and leaves unquestioned[8]
55   Matters of needful value. We shall write to you
As time and our concernings° shall importune,°   *affairs / demand*
How it goes with us; and do look° to know   *expect*
What doth befall you here. So fare you well.

---

2. How do you think he will represent me (with the royal
plural)? Angelo is imagined bearing his ruler's image like
a coin; compare "metal" in line 48.
3. Handwriting; engraved pattern.
4. *Heaven . . . not*: similarly, Jesus, in Matthew 5:14–16,
tells his followers not to hide their light under a bushel.

5. *Spirits . . . issues*: Spirits are not made fine except to
do fine deeds.
6. Silence; take (this commission).
7. Though first to be addressed, is your subordinate.
8. That it takes precedence, and leaves unconsidered.

To th' hopeful execution do I leave you
Of your commissions.

60   ANGELO   Yet give leave, my lord,
That we may bring you something° on the way.   °some distance
DUKE   My haste may not admit° it;   °permit
Nor need you, on mine honour, have to do
With⁹ any scruple. Your scope is as mine own,
65   So to enforce or qualify° the laws   °mitigate
As to your soul seems good. Give me your hand.
I'll privily away. I love the people,
But do not like to stage me° to their eyes.   °display myself
Though it do well,° I do not relish well   °is politically useful
70   Their loud applause and *aves*° vehement;   °salutations
Nor do I think the man of safe discretion°   °sound judgment
That does affect° it. Once more, fare you well.   °desire
ANGELO   The heavens give safety to your purposes!
ESCALUS   Lead forth and bring you back in happiness!
75   DUKE   I thank you. Fare you well.   *Exit*
ESCALUS   I shall desire you, sir, to give me leave
To have free° speech with you; and it concerns me   °frank
To look into the bottom of my place.¹
A power I have, but of what strength and nature
80   I am not yet instructed.°   °informed
ANGELO   'Tis so with me. Let us withdraw together,
And we may soon our satisfaction have
Touching that point.
ESCALUS   I'll wait upon° your honour.   *Exeunt*   °accompany

1.2

Enter LUCIO, *and two other* GENTLEMEN

LUCIO   If the Duke with the other dukes come not to composi-
tion° with the King of Hungary, why then, all the dukes fall   °agreement
upon° the King.   °attack
FIRST GENTLEMAN   Heaven grant us its peace, but not the King
5   of Hungary's!
SECOND GENTLEMAN   Amen.
LUCIO   Thou concludest like the sanctimonious pirate, that went
to sea with the Ten Commandments, but scraped° one out of   °erased
the table.°   °tablet
10   SECOND GENTLEMAN   'Thou shalt not steal'?
LUCIO   Ay, that he razed.
FIRST GENTLEMAN   Why, 'twas a commandment to command
the captain and all the rest from their functions: they put forth
to steal. There's not a soldier of us all that in the thanksgiving
15   before meat° do relish the petition well that prays for peace.   °food
SECOND GENTLEMAN   I never heard any soldier dislike° it.   °express aversion to
LUCIO   I believe thee, for I think thou never wast where grace
was said.
SECOND GENTLEMAN   No? A dozen times at least.
20   FIRST GENTLEMAN   What, in metre?
LUCIO   In any proportion,° or in any language.   °meter

---

9. *have to do / With:* worry about.
1. To examine my duties thoroughly.
1.2. Location: A street or public place. In F, as here, the
scene begins with what is evidently an interpolation

introduced after Shakespeare's death. A reconstruction
of the original opening appears at the end of the play as
Additional Passage A.

FIRST GENTLEMAN   I think, or in any religion.

LUCIO   Ay, why not? Grace is grace despite of all controversy;[1] as
      for example, thou thyself art a wicked villain despite of all
25   grace.

FIRST GENTLEMAN   Well, there went but a pair of shears between us.[2]

LUCIO   I grant—as there may between the lists° and the velvet.   selvages
      Thou art the list.

FIRST GENTLEMAN   And thou the velvet. Thou art good velvet,
30   thou'rt a three-piled[3] piece, I warrant thee. I had as lief° be a   had rather
      list of an English kersey° as be piled as thou art pilled,[4] for a   wool cloth
      French velvet. Do I speak feelingly° now?   to the point; painfully

LUCIO   I think thou dost, and indeed with most painful feeling°   conviction
      of thy speech. I will out of thine own confession learn to begin°   drink to
35   thy health, but whilst I live forget to drink after thee.°   (to avoid infection)

FIRST GENTLEMAN   I think I have done myself wrong,° have I   laid myself open to that
      not?

SECOND GENTLEMAN   Yes, that thou hast, whether thou art
      tainted or free.°   sick or well

        Enter [MISTRESS OVERDONE]

40   LUCIO   Behold, behold, where Madam Mitigation° comes! I   (of sexual desire)
      have purchased as many diseases under her roof as come to—

SECOND GENTLEMAN   To what, I pray?

LUCIO   Judge.°   Guess

SECOND GENTLEMAN   To three thousand dolours° a year?   pains; dollars

45   FIRST GENTLEMAN   Ay, and more.

LUCIO   A French crown° more.   coin; syphilitic sore

FIRST GENTLEMAN   Thou art always figuring° diseases in me, but   imagining
      thou art full of error—I am sound.°   healthy

LUCIO   Nay not, as one would say, healthy, but so sound° as   resounding
50   things that are hollow—thy bones are hollow,[5] impiety° has   wickedness
      made a feast of thee.

FIRST GENTLEMAN [*to* MISTRESS OVERDONE]   How now, which of
      your hips has the most profound sciatica?[6]

MISTRESS OVERDONE   Well, well! There's one yonder arrested
55   and carried to prison was worth five thousand of you all.

SECOND GENTLEMAN   Who's that, I pray thee?

MISTRESS OVERDONE   Marry° sir, that's Claudio, Signor Claudio.   By the Virgin Mary

FIRST GENTLEMAN   Claudio to prison? 'Tis not so.

MISTRESS OVERDONE   Nay, but I know 'tis so. I saw him arrested,
60   saw him carried away; and, which is more, within these three
      days his head to be chopped off.

LUCIO   But after° all this fooling, I would not have it so. Art thou   despite
      sure of this?

MISTRESS OVERDONE   I am too sure of it, and it is for getting
65   Madame Julietta with child.

LUCIO   Believe me, this may be. He promised to meet me two
      hours since and he was ever precise in promise-keeping.

---

1. Referring to the religious controversy over whether human beings are saved by divine grace or by good works. *grace:* divine favor; prayer before a meal.
2. We are cut from the same cloth.
3. Very plush; full of rectal sores (a symptom of syphilis). Lucio accuses the First Gentleman of being a "list," a selvage or edging of inferior cloth; the Gentleman retorts that he'd rather be a plain selvage than an expensively "piled" velvet like Lucio. Lucio then uses the Gentleman's knowledge of "piles" to score a point against him.
4. Ruined; made bald (a sign of syphilis, the "French pox"). Syphilitic sores were covered with velvet patches.
5. Syphilis causes bones to become brittle.
6. Ache in the sciatic vein of the hip, associated with venereal disease.

SECOND GENTLEMAN   Besides, you know, it draws° something   *approaches*
near to the speech we had to such a purpose.

70   FIRST GENTLEMAN   But most of all agreeing with the proclamation.

LUCIO   Away; let's go learn the truth of it.

Exeunt [LUCIO *and* GENTLEMEN]

MISTRESS OVERDONE   Thus, what with the war, what with the
sweat,° what with the gallows, and what with poverty, I am cus-   *plague*
tom-shrunk.°   *short on customers*

Enter [POMPEY *the*] *Clown*

75   How now, what's the news with you?

POMPEY   You have not heard of the proclamation, have you?

MISTRESS OVERDONE   What proclamation, man?

POMPEY   All houses in the suburbs[7] of Vienna must be plucked° down.   *torn*

MISTRESS OVERDONE   And what shall become of those in the city?

80   POMPEY   They shall stand for seed.[8] They had gone down too,
but that a wise burgher put in° for them.   *citizen interceded*

MISTRESS OVERDONE   But shall all our houses of resort in the
suburbs be pulled down?

POMPEY   To the ground, mistress.

85   MISTRESS OVERDONE   Why, here's a change indeed in the commonwealth. What shall become of me?

POMPEY   Come, fear not you. Good counsellors° lack no clients.   *attorneys*
Though you change your place, you need not change your
trade. I'll be your tapster still. Courage, there will be pity taken
90   on you. You that have worn your eyes almost out in the service,[9] you will be considered.°   *recompensed*

[*A noise within*]

MISTRESS OVERDONE   What's to do° here, Thomas Tapster?[1]   *the matter*
Let's withdraw!

Enter PROVOST,° CLAUDIO, JULIET,[2] [*and*] *officers;* LUCIO   *jailer*
and [*the*] *two* GENTLEMEN

POMPEY   Here comes Signor Claudio, led by the Provost to
95   prison; and there's Madame Juliet.

Exeunt [MISTRESS OVERDONE *and* POMPEY]

CLAUDIO [*to the* PROVOST]   Fellow, why dost thou show me thus
to th' world?
Bear me to prison, where I am committed.

PROVOST   I do it not in evil disposition,
But from Lord Angelo by special charge.

100   CLAUDIO   Thus can the demigod Authority
Make us pay down for our offence, by weight,°   *fully*
The bonds of ° heaven. On whom it will, it will;[3]   *obligations to*
On whom it will not, so; yet still 'tis just.

LUCIO   Why, how now, Claudio? Whence comes this restraint?

105   CLAUDIO   From too much liberty,° my Lucio, liberty.   *looseness*
As surfeit is the father of much fast,°   *gluttony precedes fasting*
So every scope,° by the immoderate use,   *freedom*
Turns to restraint. Our natures do pursue,

---

7. London brothels ("houses") were located outside the
city walls, where civic authorities had difficulty controlling them.
8. Grain for the next crop; semen.
9. "Eye" was slang for "female genital"; blindness is
another symptom of syphilis.
1. Stock name for a tapster (bartender).

2. Claudio and Juliet are perhaps wearing white sheets of
penance; such public humiliations were common punishments for sexual transgressions.
3. Paul has God say in Romans 9:15: "I will have mercy
on him, to whom I will show mercy: and will have compassion on him, on whom I will have compassion."

	Like rats that raven° down their proper bane,°	*devour / poison*
110	A thirsty evil; and when we drink, we die.	
	LUCIO If I could speak so wisely under an arrest, I would send	
	for certain of my creditors.[4] And yet, to say the truth, I had as	
	lief have the foppery° of freedom as the morality of imprison-	*folly*
	ment. What's thy offence, Claudio?	
115	CLAUDIO What but to speak of would offend again.	
	LUCIO What, is't murder?	
	CLAUDIO No.	
	LUCIO Lechery?	
	CLAUDIO Call it so.	
	PROVOST Away, sir; you must go.	
	CLAUDIO One word, good friend.	
	[*The* PROVOST *shows assent*]	
	Lucio, a word with you.	
120	LUCIO A hundred, if they'll do you any good.	
	[CLAUDIO *and* LUCIO *speak apart*]	
	Is lechery so looked after?	
	CLAUDIO Thus stands it with me. Upon a true contract,[5]	
	I got possession of Julietta's bed.	
	You know the lady; she is fast° my wife,	*nearly; entirely*
125	Save that we do the denunciation° lack	*declaration*
	Of outward order.° This we came not to	*public ceremony*
	Only for propagation° of a dower	*enlargement*
	Remaining in the coffer of her friends,°	*relatives*
	From whom we thought it meet° to hide our love	*appropriate*
130	Till time had made them for° us. But it chances	*favorably disposed to*
	The stealth of our most mutual° entertainment	*reciprocal; intimate*
	With character too gross° is writ on Juliet.	*writing too large*
	LUCIO With child, perhaps?	
	CLAUDIO Unhapp'ly even so.	
	And the new deputy now for the Duke—	
135	Whether it be the fault and glimpse° of newness,	*glitter*
	Or whether that the body public be	
	A horse whereon the governor doth ride,	
	Who, newly in the seat, that it may know	
	He can command, lets it straight° feel the spur—	*immediately*
140	Whether the tyranny be in his place,°	*office*
	Or in his eminence that fills it up—	
	I stagger in.° But this new governor	*hesitate to say*
	Awakes me all the enrollèd° penalties	*recorded*
	Which have, like unscoured armour, hung by th' wall	
145	So long that fourteen zodiacs° have gone round,	*years*
	And none of them been worn; and, for a name,°	*reputation*
	Now puts the drowsy and neglected act	
	Freshly on me. 'Tis surely for a name.	
	LUCIO I warrant° it is; and thy head stands so tickle° on thy	*I'm sure / insecurely*
150	shoulders that a milkmaid, if she be in love, may sigh it off.[6]	
	Send after the Duke, and appeal to him.	

---

4. Who, Lucio implies, would have him arrested for nonpayment of debts.
5. A secret plighting of troth, as opposed to public nuptials; in seventeenth-century England, such a contract could constitute legal marriage if made in the present tense ("I marry you" rather than "I will marry you") and followed by sexual consummation. The nature of the contract between Claudio and Juliet is unclear.
6. That a milkmaid's lovesick sigh may blow it off (with wordplay on "maidenhead").

CLAUDIO   I have done so, but he's not to be found.
I prithee, Lucio, do me this kind service.
This day my sister should the cloister enter,
155   And there receive her approbation.°   *become a novice*
Acquaint her with the danger of my state.
Implore her in my voice that she make friends
To the strict deputy. Bid herself assay° him.   *try*
I have great hope in that, for in her youth
160   There is a prone° and speechless dialect   *eager; submissive*
Such as move men; beside, she hath prosperous art°   *skill*
When she will play with reason and discourse,
And well she can persuade.
LUCIO   I pray she may—as well for the encouragement of thy
165   like,° which else would stand under grievous imposition,° as for   *those like you / burden*
the enjoying of thy life, who I would be sorry should be thus
foolishly lost at a game of tick-tack.[7] I'll to her.
CLAUDIO   I thank you, good friend Lucio.
LUCIO   Within two hours.
170   CLAUDIO   Come, officer; away.
                Exeunt [LUCIO *and* GENTLEMEN *at one door;*
                     CLAUDIO, JULIET, PROVOST, *and officers at another*]

1.3

Enter DUKE *and* [a] FRIAR
DUKE   No, holy father, throw away that thought.
Believe not that the dribbling[1] dart of love
Can pierce a complete° bosom. Why I desire thee   *an invulnerable*
To give me secret harbour hath a purpose
5   More grave and wrinkled° than the aims and ends   *(suggesting aged wisdom)*
Of burning youth.
FRIAR   May your grace speak of it?
DUKE   My holy sir, none better knows than you
How I have ever loved the life removed,°   *retired*
And held in idle price° to haunt assemblies   *thought it frivolous*
10   Where youth and cost a witless bravery° keeps.   *pointless ostentation*
I have delivered to Lord Angelo—
A man of stricture° and firm abstinence—   *self-restraint*
My absolute power and place here in Vienna;
And he supposes me travelled to Poland—
15   For so I have strewed it in the common ear,°   *ears of common people*
And so it is received.° Now, pious sir,   *believed*
You will demand of me why I do this.
FRIAR   Gladly, my lord.
DUKE   We have strict statutes and most biting laws,
20   The needful bits and curbs to headstrong weeds,[2]
Which for this fourteen years we have let slip;°   *slide*
Even like an o'ergrown lion in a cave
That goes not out to prey. Now, as fond° fathers,   *doting*
Having bound up the threat'ning twigs of birch
25   Only to stick it in their children's sight
For terror, not to use, in time the rod

7. A kind of backgammon scored by placing pegs into holes; with sexual innuendo.
1.3 Location: A Friar's cell.
1. Inadequate, like an arrow shot without sufficient force.

2. Since "bits and curbs" are parts of bridles, many editors emend "weeds" to "jades" or "steeds," but the Oxford English Dictionary records several instances of "weed" as a slang term for a worthless horse.

More mocked becomes than feared: so our decrees,
Dead to infliction,° to themselves are dead;   *Never inflicted*
And Liberty plucks Justice by the nose,[3]
30 The baby beats the nurse, and quite athwart
Goes all decorum.

FRIAR   It rested in° your grace   *remained possible for*
To unloose this tied-up Justice when you pleased,
And it in you more dreadful would have seemed
Than in Lord Angelo.

DUKE   I do fear, too dreadful.
35 Sith° 'twas my fault to give the people scope,   *Since*
'Twould be my tyranny to strike and gall° them   *chafe*
For what I bid them do—for we bid this be done
When evil deeds have their permissive pass,°   *unhindered passage*
And not the punishment. Therefore indeed, my father,
40 I have on Angelo imposed the office,
Who may in th'ambush° of my name strike home,   *under cover*
And yet my nature never in the fight
T'allow in slander.° And to behold his sway,°   *To permit slander / rule*
I will as 'twere a brother of your order
45 Visit both prince° and people. Therefore, I prithee,   *ruler*
Supply me with the habit, and instruct me
How I may formally in person bear°   *behave in character*
Like a true friar. More reasons for this action
At our more leisure shall I render you.
50 Only this one: Lord Angelo is precise,°   *puritanical*
Stands at a guard with envy,° scarce confesses   *on guard against desire*
That his blood flows, or that his appetite
Is more to bread than stone. Hence shall we see
If power change purpose, what our seemers be.   *Exeunt*

1.4

Enter ISABELLA, *and* FRANCESCA, *a nun*

ISABELLA   And have you nuns no farther privileges?
FRANCESCA   Are not these large° enough?   *generous*
ISABELLA   Yes, truly. I speak not as desiring more,
But rather wishing a more strict restraint
5 Upon the sisterhood, the votarists of Saint Clare.
LUCIO (*within*)   Ho, peace be in this place!
ISABELLA [*to* FRANCESCA]   Who's that which calls?
FRANCESCA   It is a man's voice. Gentle Isabella.
Turn you the key, and know° his business of° him.   *find out / from*
You may, I may not; you are yet unsworn.
10 When you have vowed, you must not speak with men
But in the presence of the prioress.
Then if you speak, you must not show your face;
Or if you show your face, you must not speak.
     [LUCIO *calls within*]
He calls again. I pray you answer him.
     [*She stands aside*][1]
15 ISABELLA   Peace and prosperity! Who is't that calls?
     [*She opens the door*]

---

3. Licentiousness insults the administration of law.

1.4 Location: A convent of St. Clare, an order known for austere discipline.

1. Or Francesca may exit here.

[*Enter* LUCIO]

LUCIO   Hail, virgin, if you be—as those cheek-roses°   *glowing cheeks*
     Proclaim you are no less. Can you so stead° me   *help*
     As bring me to the sight of Isabella,
     A novice of this place, and the fair sister
20   To her unhappy° brother Claudio?   *unfortunate*
ISABELLA   Why her unhappy brother? Let me ask,
     The rather for I now must make you know
     I am that Isabella, and his sister.
LUCIO   Gentle and fair, your brother kindly greets you.
25   Not to be weary° with you, he's in prison.   *tedious*
ISABELLA   Woe me! For what?
LUCIO   For that which, if myself might be his judge,
     He should receive his punishment in thanks.
     He hath got his friend° with child.   *lover*
ISABELLA   Sir, make me not your story.°   *don't tell me tales*
30   LUCIO   'Tis true. I would not—though 'tis my familiar° sin   *habitual*
     With maids to seem the lapwing,[2] and to jest
     Tongue far from heart—play with all virgins so.
     I hold you as a thing enskied° and sainted   *placed in heaven*
     By your renouncement, an immortal spirit,
35   And to be talked with in sincerity
     As with a saint.
ISABELLA   You do blaspheme the good in mocking me.
LUCIO   Do not believe it. Fewness° and truth, 'tis thus: *In few words*
     Your brother and his lover have embraced.
40   As those that feed grow full, as blossoming time
     That from the seedness° the bare fallow° brings   *sowing / plowland*
     To teeming foison,° even so her plenteous womb   *abundance*
     Expresseth his full tilth° and husbandry.[3]   *tillage*
ISABELLA   Someone with child by him? My cousin Juliet?
45   LUCIO   Is she your cousin?
ISABELLA   Adoptedly,° as schoolmaids change° their names   *By choice / exchange*
     By vain° though apt affection.   *foolish*
LUCIO   She it is.
ISABELLA   O, let him marry her!
LUCIO   This is the point.
     The Duke is very strangely gone from hence;
50   Bore many gentlemen—myself being one—
     In hand and hope of action;[4] but we do learn,
     By those that know the very nerves° of state,   *sinews (inward secrets)*
     His giving out° were of an infinite distance   *What he proclaimed*
     From his true-meant design. Upon° his place,   *In*
55   And with full line° of his authority,   *extent*
     Governs Lord Angelo—a man whose blood
     Is very snow-broth;° one who never feels   *melted snow*
     The wanton stings and motions° of the sense,   *stimulants and impulses*
     But doth rebate° and blunt his natural edge   *dull*
60   With profits of the mind, study, and fast.
     He, to give fear to use° and liberty,   *custom*
     Which have for long run by the hideous law

---

2. Bird that cries alarm when far from its nest, a common figure for deception.
3. Cultivation (punning on "husband").
4. *Bore . . . action:* Deceived us into hoping for some military action.

As mice by lions, hath picked out an act°   *a statute*
Under whose heavy° sense your brother's life   *oppressive*
65 Falls into forfeit. He arrests him on it,
And follows close the rigour of the statute
To make him an example. All hope is gone,
Unless you have the grace by your fair prayer
To soften Angelo. And that's my pith°   *essence*
70 Of business 'twixt you and your poor brother.

ISABELLA   Doth he so seek his life?

LUCIO   Has censured° him already,   *sentenced*
And, as I hear, the Provost hath a warrant
For's execution.

ISABELLA   Alas, what poor
Ability's in me to do him good?

75 LUCIO   Assay the power you have.

ISABELLA   My power? Alas, I doubt.

LUCIO   Our doubts are traitors,
And makes us lose the good we oft might win,
By fearing to attempt. Go to Lord Angelo;
80 And let him learn to know, when maidens sue,
Men give like gods, but when they weep and kneel,
All their petitions are as freely theirs
As° they themselves would owe° them.   *As if / were to own*

ISABELLA   I'll see what I can do.

LUCIO   But speedily.

ISABELLA   I will about it straight,°   *immediately*
85 No longer staying but to give the Mother°   *Mother Superior*
Notice of my affair.° I humbly thank you.   *business*
Commend me to my brother. Soon at night
I'll send him certain word of my success.°   *fortune (good or bad)*

LUCIO   I take my leave of you.

ISABELLA   Good sir, adieu.

> *Exeunt* [ISABELLA *and* FRANCESCA *at one door,*
> LUCIO *at another door*]

2.1

Enter ANGELO, ESCALUS, *and servants;* [a] JUSTICE

ANGELO   We must not make a scarecrow of the law,
Setting it up to fear° the birds of prey,   *frighten*
And let it keep one shape till custom make it
Their perch, and not their terror.

ESCALUS   Ay, but yet
5 Let us be keen, and rather cut a little
Than fall and bruise to death. Alas, this gentleman
Whom I would save had a most noble father.
Let but your honour know—
Whom I believe to be most strait° in virtue—   *rigorous*
10 That in the working of your own affections,°   *passions*
Had time cohered with place, or place with wishing,
Or that the resolute acting of your blood°   *desire*
Could have attained th'effect° of your own purpose—   *fulfillment*
Whether you had not sometime in your life

_____
2.1 Location: The court of justice.

15   Erred in this point which now you censure° him,   *condemn in*
     And pulled the law upon you.
     ANGELO   'Tis one thing to be tempted, Escalus,
     Another thing to fall. I not° deny   *do not*
     The jury passing on the prisoner's life
20   May in the sworn twelve have a thief or two
     Guiltier than him they try. What knows the law¹
     That thieves do pass on thieves? What's open° made to justice,   *evident*
     That justice seizes. 'Tis very pregnant:°   *clear*
     The jewel that we find, we stoop and take't
25   Because we see it, but what we do not see
     We tread upon and never think of it.
     You may not so extenuate his offence
     For° I have had such faults; but rather tell me,   *Because*
     When I that censure him do so offend,
30   Let mine own judgement pattern out° my death,   *give precedent for*
     And nothing come in partial.° Sir, he must die.   *no allowances be made*
     ESCALUS   Be it as your wisdom will.
     ANGELO   Where is the Provost?
          Enter PROVOST
     PROVOST   Here, if it like your honour.
     ANGELO   See that Claudio
     Be execute by nine tomorrow morning.
35   Bring him his confessor, let him be prepared,
     For that's the utmost of his pilgrimage.°   [*Exit* PROVOST]   *life's journey*
     ESCALUS   Well, heaven forgive him, and forgive us all!
     Some rise by sin, and some by virtue fall.
     Some run from brakes of vice,² and answer none;°   *not at all*
40   And some condemnèd for a fault alone.°   *single imperfection*
          Enter ELBOW, FROTH, POMPEY, *and officers*
     ELBOW   Come, bring them away. If these be good people in a
     commonweal, that do nothing but use their abuses° in com-   *do their bad deeds*
     mon houses,° I know no law. Bring them away.   *brothels*
     ANGELO   How now, sir? What's your name? And what's the matter?
45   ELBOW   If it please your honour, I am the poor Duke's constable,
     and my name is Elbow. I do lean° upon justice, sir; and do   *depend*
     bring in here before your good honour two notorious benefactors.³
     ANGELO   Benefactors? Well! What benefactors are they?
     Are they not malefactors?
50   ELBOW   If it please your honour, I know not well what they are;
     but precise⁴ villains they are, that I am sure of, and void of all
     profanation° in the world that good Christians ought to have.   *(for "reverence")*
     ESCALUS [*to* ANGELO]   This comes off° well; here's a wise officer!   *turns out*
     ANGELO   Go to, what quality° are they of? Elbow is your name?   *rank*
55   Why dost thou not speak, Elbow?
     POMPEY   He cannot, sir; he's out at elbow.⁵
     ANGELO   What are you, sir?
     ELBOW   He, sir? A tapster, sir, parcel bawd;° one that serves a bad   *part-time pimp*

---

1. What does the law know; who knows what law.
2. F has "brakes of ice," a famous crux; often amended
as here. *brakes:* thickets.
3. Elbow comically misuses words; here he means
"malefactors," criminals.

4. Elbow means "precious"; "precise" (morally scrupulous) is elsewhere applied to Angelo.
5. Ragged; perplexed at the sound of his name. Pompey
loves to play on the double meanings of words.

woman whose house, sir, was, as they say, plucked down in the
60   suburbs; and now she professes a hot-house,° which I think is   *pretends to run a sauna*
  a very ill house too.

ESCALUS   How know you that?

ELBOW   My wife, sir, whom I detest° before heaven and your   *(for "protest")*
  honour—

65 ESCALUS   How, thy wife?

ELBOW   Ay, sir, whom I thank heaven is an honest woman—

ESCALUS   Dost thou detest her therefor?

ELBOW   I say, sir, I will detest myself also, as well as she, that this
  house, if it be not a bawd's house, it is pity of her life,° for it is   *a great pity*
70   a naughty° house.   *wicked*

ESCALUS   How dost thou know that, constable?

ELBOW   Marry, sir, by my wife, who, if she had been a woman
  cardinally° given, might have been accused in fornication,   *(for "carnally")*
  adultery, and all uncleanliness there.

75 ESCALUS   By the woman's means?

ELBOW   Ay, sir, by Mistress Overdone's means. But as she° spit   *(Elbow's wife)*
  in his° face, so she defied him.   *(Pompey's)*

POMPEY [*to* ESCALUS]   Sir, if it please your honour, this is not so.

ELBOW   Prove it before these varlets° here, thou honourable   *villains*
80   man, prove it.

ESCALUS [*to* ANGELO]   Do you hear how he misplaces?°   *confuses his words*

POMPEY   Sir, she came in great with child, and longing—saving
  your honour's reverence°—for stewed prunes.[6] Sir, we had but   *excuse the expression*
  two in the house, which at that very distant° time stood, as it   *(for "instant")*
85   were, in a fruit dish[7]—a dish of some threepence; your honours
  have seen such dishes; they are not china dishes, but very good
  dishes.

ESCALUS   Go to, go to, no matter for the dish, sir.

POMPEY   No, indeed, sir, not of° a pin; you are therein in the   *worth*
90   right. But to the point. As I say, this Mistress Elbow, being, as I
  say, with child, and being great-bellied, and longing, as I said,
  for prunes; and having but two in the dish, as I said, Master
  Froth here, this very man, having eaten the rest, as I said, and,
  as I say, paying for them very honestly; for, as you know, Master
95   Froth, I could not give you threepence again.°   *in change*

FROTH   No, indeed.

POMPEY   Very well. You being, then, if you be remembered,
  cracking the stones of the foresaid prunes—

FROTH   Ay, so I did indeed.

100 POMPEY   Why, very well.—I telling you then, if you be remembered, that such a one and such a one were past cure of the
  thing you wot of,[8] unless they kept very good diet, as I told
  you—

FROTH   All this is true.

105 POMPEY   Why, very well then—

ESCALUS   Come, you are a tedious fool. To the purpose. What
  was done to Elbow's wife that he hath cause to complain of?
  Come me° to what was done to her.   *Get*

POMPEY   Sir, your honour cannot come to that yet.[9]

---

6. Commonly served in brothels; also suggesting "testicles" in the series of double entendres that follows.
7. Slang term for "female genital."

8. Euphemism for syphilis. *wot:* know.
9. Taking "done" in the sexual sense, Pompey pretends
shock at Escalus's salaciousness.

110   ESCALUS   No, sir, nor I mean it not.°   *I don't mean that*

        POMPEY   Sir, but you shall come to it, by your honour's leave.
        And I beseech you, look into° Master Froth here, sir, a man of   *consider*
        fourscore pound a year,[1] whose father died at Hallowmas°—   *Nov. 1, All Saint's Day*
        was't not at Hallowmas, Master Froth?

115   FROTH   All Hallow Eve.°   *Halloween*

        POMPEY   Why, very well. I hope here be truths. He, sir, sitting,
        as I say, in a lower° chair, sir—'twas in the Bunch of Grapes,[2]   *reclining?*
        where indeed you have a delight to sit, have you not?

        FROTH   I have so, because it is an open room,[3] and good for
120   winter.

        POMPEY   Why, very well then. I hope here be truths.

        ANGELO   This will last out a night in Russia,
        When nights are longest there. [*To* ESCALUS] I'll take my leave,
        And leave you to the hearing of the cause,°   *case*
125   Hoping you'll find good cause to whip them all.

        ESCALUS   I think no less. Good morrow to your lordship.

                                              Exit [ANGELO]

        Now, sir, come on, what was done to Elbow's wife, once more?

        POMPEY   Once, sir? There was nothing done to her once.

        ELBOW   I beseech you, sir, ask him what this man did to my wife.

130   POMPEY   I beseech your honour, ask me.

        ESCALUS   Well, sir, what did this gentleman to her?

        POMPEY   I beseech you, sir, look in this gentleman's face. Good
        Master Froth, look upon his honour. 'Tis for a good purpose.
        Doth your honour mark° his face?   *note*

135   ESCALUS   Ay, sir, very well.

        POMPEY   Nay, I beseech you, mark it well.

        ESCALUS   Well, I do so.

        POMPEY   Doth your honour see any harm in his face?

        ESCALUS   Why, no.

140   POMPEY   I'll be supposed° upon a book° his face is the worst   *(for "deposed") / Bible*
        thing about him. Good, then—if his face be the worst thing
        about him, how could Master Froth do the constable's wife any
        harm? I would know that of your honour.

        ESCALUS   He's in the right, constable; what say you to it?

145   ELBOW   First, an it like° you, the house is a respected[4] house;   *if it please*
        next, this is a respected fellow; and his mistress is a respected
        woman.

        POMPEY [*to* ESCALUS]   By this hand, sir, his wife is a more
        respected person than any of us all.

150   ELBOW   Varlet, thou liest; thou liest, wicked varlet. The time is
        yet to come that she was ever respected with man, woman, or
        child.

        POMPEY   Sir, she was respected with him before he married with her.

        ESCALUS   Which is the wiser here, justice or iniquity? [*To*
155   ELBOW] Is this true?

        ELBOW [*to* POMPEY]   O thou caitiff, O thou varlet, O thou wicked
        Hannibal![5] I respected with her before I was married to her?
        [*To* ESCALUS] If ever I was respected with her, or she with

---

1. Eighty pounds was a low income for a gentleman. The father's recent death means that Froth has just come into his inheritance.
2. A room in a tavern.

3. A public room (where fires were kept burning).
4. For "suspected."
5. Blunder for "cannibal"; also, both Hannibal and Pompey were famous generals of ancient times.

me, let not your worship think me the poor Duke's officer. [*To*
160 POMPEY] Prove this, thou wicked Hannibal,[6] or I'll have mine
action of battery° on thee.   *(for "slander")*

ESCALUS   If he took° you a box o'th' ear you might have your   *struck*
action of slander too.

ELBOW   Marry, I thank your good worship for it. What is't your
165 worship's pleasure I shall do with this wicked caitiff?°   *knave*

ESCALUS   Truly, officer, because he hath some offences in him
that thou wouldst discover° if thou couldst, let him continue in   *expose*
his courses° till thou knowest what they are.   *conduct*

ELBOW   Marry, I thank your worship for it.—Thou seest, thou
170 wicked varlet now, what's come upon thee. Thou art to continue now, thou varlet, thou art to continue.

ESCALUS [*to* FROTH]   Where were you born, friend?

FROTH   Here in Vienna, sir.

ESCALUS   Are you of fourscore pounds a year?

175 FROTH   Yes, an't please you, sir.

ESCALUS   So. [*To* POMPEY] What trade are you of, sir?

POMPEY   A tapster, a poor widow's tapster.

ESCALUS   Your mistress's name?

POMPEY   Mistress Overdone.

180 ESCALUS   Hath she had any more than one husband?

POMPEY   Nine, sir—Overdone by the last.[7]

ESCALUS   Nine?—Come hither to me, Master Froth. Master
Froth, I would not have you acquainted with tapsters. They will
draw you,[8] Master Froth, and you will hang them.° Get you   *get them hanged*
185 gone, and let me hear no more of you.

FROTH   I thank your worship. For mine own part, I never come
into any room in a tap-house but I am drawn in.

ESCALUS   Well, no more of it, Master Froth. Farewell.

[*Exit* FROTH]

Come you hither to me, Master Tapster. What's your name,
190 Master Tapster?

POMPEY   Pompey.

ESCALUS   What else?

POMPEY   Bum, sir.

ESCALUS   Troth, and your bum is the greatest thing about you;
195 so that, in the beastliest sense, you are Pompey the Great.[9]
Pompey, you are partly a bawd, Pompey, howsoever you colour
it in being a tapster, are you not? Come, tell me true; it shall
be the better for you.

POMPEY   Truly, sir, I am a poor fellow that would live.

200 ESCALUS   How would you live, Pompey? By being a bawd? What
do you think of the trade, Pompey? Is it a lawful trade?

POMPEY   If the law would allow it, sir.

ESCALUS   But the law will not allow it, Pompey; nor it shall not°   *nor shall it*
be allowed in Vienna.

205 POMPEY   Does your worship mean to geld and spay all the youth
of the city?

ESCALUS   No, Pompey.

---

6. Ancient Carthaginian general who waged war
against Rome; possibly Escalus means "cannibal."
7. She takes her name from Overdone, her last husband; her last husband wore her out.

8. Get you beer; steal your substance; convey you to execution.
9. The Roman general Pompey was surnamed "the
Great."

POMPEY   Truly, sir, in my poor opinion they will to't then. If your
worship will take order° for the drabs° and the knaves, you need   *measures / whores*
210   not to fear the bawds.
ESCALUS   There is pretty orders beginning, I can tell you. It is
but heading° and hanging.   *beheading*
POMPEY   If you head and hang all that offend that way but for
ten year together, you'll be glad to give out a commission° for   *an order*
215   more heads. If this law hold° in Vienna ten year, I'll rent the   *remain*
fairest house in it after threepence a bay.[1] If you live to see this
come to pass, say Pompey told you so.
ESCALUS   Thank you, good Pompey; and in requital of° your   *return for*
prophecy, hark you. I advise you, let me not find you before
220   me again upon any complaint whatsoever; no, not for° dwelling   *even for*
where you do. If I do, Pompey, I shall beat you to your tent,
and prove a shrewd Caesar to you;[2] in plain dealing, Pompey,
I shall have you whipped. So for this time, Pompey, fare you well.
POMPEY   I thank your worship for your good counsel; [*aside*] but
225   I shall follow it as the flesh and fortune shall better determine.
Whip me? No, no; let carman° whip his jade.°   *cart driver / horse*
The valiant heart's not whipped out of his trade.   *Exit*
ESCALUS   Come hither to me, Master Elbow; come hither, Master Constable. How long have you been in this place of con-
230   stable?
ELBOW   Seven year and a half, sir.
ESCALUS   I thought, by the readiness in the office, you had continued in it some time. You say seven years together?
ELBOW   And a half, sir.
235   ESCALUS   Alas, it hath been great pains to you. They do you
wrong to put you so oft upon't. Are there not men in your ward
sufficient° to serve it?   *fit*
ELBOW   Faith, sir, few of any wit in such matters. As they are
chosen, they are glad to choose me for them. I do it for some
240   piece of money, and go through with all.
ESCALUS   Look° you bring me in the names of some six or seven,   *See that*
the most sufficient of your parish.
ELBOW   To your worship's house, sir?
ESCALUS   To my house. Fare you well.
      [*Exit* ELBOW *with officers*]
245   What's o'clock, think you?
JUSTICE   Eleven, sir.
ESCALUS   I pray you home to dinner with me.[3]
JUSTICE   I humbly thank you.
ESCALUS   It grieves me for the death of Claudio,
250   But there's no remedy.
JUSTICE   Lord Angelo is severe.
ESCALUS   It is but needful.
Mercy is not itself that oft looks so.
Pardon is still° the nurse of second woe.   *always*
255   But yet, poor Claudio! There is no remedy.
Come, sir.   *Exeunt*

1. Townhouse rental was based on the number of front
windows ("bays").
2. Julius Caesar defeated Pompey in 48 B.C.E. *shrewd:*
harsh.
3. Dinner was served at midday. *pray:* ask.

2.2

Enter PROVOST [*and a*] SERVANT

SERVANT   He's hearing of a cause;° he will come straight.°   *case / right away*
I'll tell him of you.

PROVOST   Pray you do.   [*Exit* SERVANT]
                                    I'll know
His pleasure; maybe he will relent. Alas,
He° hath but as offended in a dream.   *(Claudio)*
5   All sects,° all ages, smack° of this vice; and he   *kinds of people / partake*
To die for't!

Enter ANGELO

ANGELO   Now, what's the matter, Provost?

PROVOST   Is it your will Claudio shall die tomorrow?

ANGELO   Did not I tell thee yea? Hadst thou not order?
Why dost thou ask again?

PROVOST   Lest I might be too rash.
10   Under your good correction, I have seen
When after execution judgement hath
Repented o'er his doom.°   *sentence*

ANGELO   Go to; let that be mine.°   *my concern*
Do you your office, or give up your place,
And you shall well be spared.°   *easily be done without*

PROVOST   I crave your honour's pardon.
15   What shall be done, sir, with the groaning Juliet?
She's very near her hour.°   *(of childbirth)*

ANGELO   Dispose of her
To some more fitter place, and that with speed.

[*Enter* SERVANT]

SERVANT   Here is the sister of the man condemned
Desires access to you.

ANGELO   Hath he a sister?
20   PROVOST   Ay, my good lord; a very virtuous maid,
And to be shortly of a sisterhood,
If not already.

ANGELO   Well, let her be admitted.   [*Exit* SERVANT]
See you the fornicatress be removed.
Let her have needful but not lavish means.
There shall be order° for't.   *written direction*

Enter LUCIO *and* ISABELLA

25   PROVOST   God save your honour.

ANGELO   Stay a little while. [*To* ISABELLA] You're welcome.
What's your will?

ISABELLA   I am a woeful suitor to your honour.
Please° but your honour hear me.   *If it please*

ANGELO   Well, what's your suit?

ISABELLA   There is a vice that most I do abhor,
30   And most desire should meet the blow of justice,
For which I would not plead, but that I must;
For which I must not plead, but that I am
At war 'twixt will and will not.

ANGELO   Well, the matter?

ISABELLA   I have a brother is condemned to die.

2.2 Location: A room in the court of justice.

35 I do beseech you, let it be his fault,°   *his fault be condemned*
    And not my brother.
  PROVOST [*aside*]   Heaven give thee moving graces!°   *the gift of persuasion*
  ANGELO   Condemn the fault, and not the actor° of it?   *doer*
    Why, every fault's condemned ere it be done.
    Mine were the very cipher of a function,
40   To fine° the faults whose fine° stands in record,   *condemn / penalty*
    And let go by° the actor.   *leave unpunished*
  ISABELLA   O just but severe law!
    I had a brother, then. Heaven keep your honour.
  LUCIO [*aside to* ISABELLA]   Give't not o'er° so. To him again;   *Don't give up*
    entreat him.
    Kneel down before him; hang upon° his gown.   *cling to*
45   You are too cold. If you should need a pin,
    You could not with more tame a tongue desire it.
    To him, I say!
  ISABELLA [*to* ANGELO]   Must he needs° die?   *necessarily*
  ANGELO   Maiden, no remedy.
50   ISABELLA   Yes, I do think that you might pardon him,
    And neither heaven nor man grieve at the mercy.
  ANGELO   I will not do't.
  ISABELLA   But can you if you would?
  ANGELO   Look what° I will not, that I cannot do.   *Whatever*
  ISABELLA   But might you do't, and do the world no wrong,
55   If so your heart were touched with that remorse°   *pity*
    As mine is to him?
  ANGELO   He's sentenced; 'tis too late.
  LUCIO [*aside to* ISABELLA]   You are too cold.
  ISABELLA   Too late? Why, no; I that do speak a word
60   May call° it again. Well, believe this,   *retract*
    No ceremony° that to great ones 'longs,   *symbolic accessory*
    Not the king's crown, nor the deputed sword,
    The marshal's truncheon, nor the judge's robe,
    Become them with one half so good a grace
65   As mercy does.
    If he had been as you and you as he,
    You would have slipped like him, but he, like you,
    Would not have been so stern.
  ANGELO   Pray you be gone.
  ISABELLA   I would to heaven I had your potency,°   *power*
70   And you were Isabel! Should it then be thus?
    No; I would tell what 'twere to be a judge,
    And what a prisoner.
  LUCIO [*aside to* ISABELLA]   Ay, touch him;[1] there's the vein.°   *that's the style*
  ANGELO   Your brother is a forfeit of the law,
    And you but waste your words.
  ISABELLA   Alas, alas!
75   Why, all the souls that were were forfeit[2] once,
    And He that might the vantage° best have took   *advantage*
    Found out° the remedy.[3] How would you be   *Procured*
    If He which is the top° of judgement should   *highest pattern or source*
    But judge you as you are? O, think on that,

1. Influence him; but perhaps Isabella touches Angelo's arm or garment here.
2. Lost (as a result of Adam and Eve's disobedience).
3. By saving all mankind in the person of Christ.

80	And mercy then will breathe within your lips,
	Like man new made.° *renewed by faith*
	ANGELO Be you content, fair maid.° *(with play on "new made")*
	It is the law, not I, condemn your brother.
	Were he my kinsman, brother, or my son,
	It should be thus with him. He must die tomorrow.
85	ISABELLA Tomorrow? O, that's sudden! Spare him, spare him!
	He's not prepared for death. Even for our kitchens
	We kill the fowl of season.° Shall we serve heaven *at the proper time*
	With less respect than we do minister
	To our gross selves? Good good my lord, bethink you:
90	Who is it that hath died for this offence?
	There's many have committed it.
	LUCIO [*aside*] Ay, well said.
	ANGELO The law hath not been dead, though it hath slept.
	Those many had not dared to do that evil
	If the first that did th'edict infringe
95	Had answered for his deed. Now 'tis awake,
	Takes note of what is done, and, like a prophet,
	Looks in a glass° that shows what future evils, *mirror*
	Either raw,° or by remissness new conceived *unripe*
	And so in progress to be hatched and born,
100	Are now to have no successive degrees,[4]
	But ere they live, to end.
	ISABELLA Yet show some pity.
	ANGELO I show it most of all when I show justice,
	For then I pity those I do not know
	Which a dismissed° offence would after gall,° *Whom a pardoned / hurt*
105	And do him right that, answering° one foul wrong, *paying for*
	Lives not to act another. Be satisfied.
	Your brother dies tomorrow. Be content.
	ISABELLA So you must be the first that gives this sentence,
	And he that suffers. O, it is excellent
110	To have a giant's strength, but it is tyrannous
	To use it like a giant.
	LUCIO [*aside to* ISABELLA] That's well said.
	ISABELLA Could great men thunder
	As Jove[5] himself does, Jove would never be quiet,
115	For every pelting° petty officer *paltry*
	Would use his heaven for thunder, nothing but thunder.
	Merciful heaven,
	Thou rather with thy sharp and sulphurous° bolt *fiery*
	Split'st the unwedgeable and gnarlèd oak
120	Than the soft myrtle. But man, proud man,
	Dressed in a little brief authority,
	Most ignorant of what he's most assured,
	His glassy° essence, like an angry ape[6] *fragile; illusory*
	Plays such fantastic tricks before high heaven
125	As makes the angels weep, who, with our spleens,[7]
	Would all themselves laugh mortal.

4. Future stages of development.
5. King of the Roman gods, whose weapon was the thunderbolt.
6. A figure of grotesque mimicry.
7. Thought to be the seat of laughter.

LUCIO [*aside to* ISABELLA]　O, to him, to him, wench!° He will　　　　*girl*
　　　relent.

　　　He's coming;° I perceive't.　　　　　　　　　　　　　　　　　　*yielding*

PROVOST [*aside*]　　　　　　　Pray heaven she win him!

ISABELLA　We cannot weigh our brother with ourself.[8]

130　　Great men may jest with saints; 'tis wit in them,
　　　But in the less,° foul profanation.　　　　　　　　　　　　*ordinary people*

LUCIO [*aside to* ISABELLA]　Thou'rt i'th' right, girl. More o' that.

ISABELLA　That in the captain's but a choleric word,
　　　Which in the soldier is flat blasphemy.

135　LUCIO [*aside to* ISABELLA]　Art advised o' that?° More on't.　　*So you know about that*

ANGELO　Why do you put° these sayings upon me?　　　　　　　*impose*

ISABELLA　Because authority, though it err like others,
　　　Hath yet a kind of medicine in itself
　　　That skins the vice o'th' top.[9] Go to your bosom;

140　　Knock there, and ask your heart what it doth know
　　　That's like my brother's fault. If it confess
　　　A natural guiltiness, such as is his,
　　　Let it not sound a thought upon your tongue
　　　Against my brother's life.

ANGELO [*aside*]　　　　　　She speaks, and 'tis such sense°　　*sound advice*

145　　That my sense breeds° with it. [*To* ISABELLA] Fare you well.　*desire increases*

ISABELLA　Gentle my° lord, turn back.　　　　　　　　　　　　*My gracious*

ANGELO　I will bethink me.° Come again tomorrow.　　　　　　*consider*

ISABELLA　Hark how I'll bribe you; good my lord, turn back.

ANGELO　How, bribe me?

150　ISABELLA　Ay, with such gifts that° heaven shall share with° you.　*as / apportion to*

LUCIO [*aside to* ISABELLA]　You had marred all else.

ISABELLA　Not with fond° shekels of the tested° gold,　　　　*foolish / refined*
　　　Or stones,° whose rate° are either rich or poor　　　　　*jewels / value*
　　　As fancy values them; but with true prayers,

155　　That shall be up at heaven and enter there
　　　Ere sunrise, prayers from preservèd° souls,　　　　　　　*protected*
　　　From fasting maids whose minds are dedicate
　　　To nothing temporal.

ANGELO　Well, come to me tomorrow.

160　LUCIO [*aside to* ISABELLA]　Go to;° 'tis well; away.　　　　*Come on*

ISABELLA　Heaven keep your honour[1] safe.

ANGELO [*aside*]　Amen;
　　　For I am that way going to temptation,
　　　Where prayer is crossed.°　　　　　　　　　　　*corrupted; frustrated*

ISABELLA　　　　　　　At what hour tomorrow
　　　Shall I attend your lordship?

165　ANGELO　　　　　　　At any time fore noon.

ISABELLA　God save your honour.

ANGELO [*aside*]　　　　　From thee; even from thy virtue.

　　　　　　[*Exeunt* ISABELLA, LUCIO, *and* PROVOST]

　　　What's this? What's this? Is this her fault or mine?
　　　The tempter or the tempted, who sins most, ha?
　　　Not she; nor doth she tempt; but it is I

170　　That, lying by the violet in the sun,
　　　Do, as the carrion does, not as the flower,

8. We cannot judge others as we judge ourselves.
9. That causes a skin to grow over the sore.

1. Isabella calls Angelo "your honor" as a term of respect;
Angelo understands the phrase as referring to his virtue.

Corrupt with virtuous season.° Can it be   *Rot in fine weather*
That modesty may more betray our sense°   *seduce our appetite*
Than woman's lightness?° Having waste ground enough,   *licentiousness*
175 Shall we desire to raze the sanctuary,
And pitch° our evils there? O, fie, fie, fie!   *hurl; set up*
What dost thou, or what art thou, Angelo?
Dost thou desire her foully for those things
That make her good? O, let her brother live!
180 Thieves for their robbery have authority,
When judges steal themselves. What, do I love her,
That I desire to hear her speak again,
And feast upon her eyes? What is't I dream on?
O cunning enemy,° that, to catch a saint,°   *(Satan) / holy person*
185 With saints dost bait thy hook! Most dangerous
Is that temptation that doth goad us on
To sin in loving virtue. Never could the strumpet,
With all her double vigour°—art and nature—   *twofold power*
Once stir my temper;° but this virtuous maid   *excite me*
190 Subdues me quite. Ever till now
When men were fond,° I smiled, and wondered how.   *Exit*   *infatuated*

2.3

Enter [at one door] the DUKE, *[disguised as a friar,] and*
[at another door, the] PROVOST

DUKE   Hail to you, Provost!—so I think you are.

PROVOST   I am the Provost. What's your will, good friar?

DUKE   Bound by my charity and my blest order,
I come to visit the afflicted spirits
5 Here in the prison.¹ Do me the common right°   *right of all clerics*
To let me see them, and to make me know
The nature of their crimes, that I may minister
To them accordingly.

PROVOST   I would do more than that, if more were needful.

    Enter JULIET

10 Look, here comes one, a gentlewoman of mine,°   *in my care*
Who, falling in the flaws° of her own youth,   *faults; gusts of passion*
Hath blistered her report.° She is with child,   *reputation*
And he that got° it, sentenced—a young man   *begot*
More fit to do another such offence
15 Than die for this.

DUKE   When must he die?

PROVOST   As I do think, tomorrow.
[*To* JULIET] I have provided for you. Stay a while,
And you shall be conducted.

20 DUKE   Repent you, fair one, of the sin you carry?

JULIET   I do, and bear the shame most patiently.

DUKE   I'll teach you how you shall arraign° your conscience,   *accuse*
And try your penitence if it be sound
Or hollowly put on.

25 JULIET   I'll gladly learn.

DUKE   Love you the man that wronged you?

JULIET   Yes, as I love the woman that wronged him.

2.3 Location: The prison.
1. Echoing 1 Peter 3:19: "He . . . went, and preached unto the spirits that were in prison."

DUKE So then it seems your most offenceful act	
Was mutually committed?	
JULIET Mutually.	
30 DUKE Then was your sin of heavier° kind than his.	graver
JULIET I do confess it and repent it, father.	
DUKE 'Tis meet° so, daughter. But lest you do repent	appropriate
As that° the sin hath brought you to this shame—	Because
Which sorrow is always toward ourselves, not heaven,	
35 Showing we would not spare heaven[2] as we love it,	
But as we stand in fear—	
JULIET I do repent me as it is an evil,	
And take the shame with joy.	
DUKE There rest.°	remain
Your partner, as I hear, must die tomorrow,	
40 And I am going with instruction to him.	
Grace go with you. *Benedicite!*° *Exit*	Bless you
JULIET Must die tomorrow? O injurious law,	
That respites me a life[3] whose very comfort	
Is still a dying horror!	
PROVOST 'Tis pity of° him. *Exeunt*	for

2.4

Enter ANGELO

ANGELO   When I would pray and think, I think and pray
To several° subjects: heaven hath my empty words, — different
Whilst my invention,° hearing not my tongue, — imagination
Anchors on Isabel; God in my mouth,
5 As if I did but only chew his name,
And in my heart the strong and swelling evil
Of my conception.[1] The state° whereon I studied — statecraft; dignity
Is like a good thing, being often read,
Grown seared° and tedious. Yea, my gravity, — arid
10 Wherein—let no man hear me—I take pride,
Could I with boot° change for an idle plume[2] — advantage
Which the air beats in vain. O place,° O form,° — rank / formality
How often dost thou with thy case,° thy habit,° — appearance / dress
Wrench awe from fools, and tie the wiser souls
15 To thy false seeming! Blood, thou art blood.[3]
Let's write 'good angel'[4] on the devil's horn—
'Tis now the devil's crest.° — heraldic device

Enter SERVANT

                    How now? Who's there?
SERVANT   One Isabel, a sister, desires access to you.
ANGELO   Teach her the way.   [*Exit* SERVANT]
                    O heavens,
20 Why does my blood thus muster° to my heart, — crowd
Making both it unable° for itself, — weak
And dispossessing all my other parts
Of necessary fitness?
So play° the foolish throngs with one that swoons— — act

2. Relieve heaven from distress.
3. Pregnant women were spared the death penalty, at least until after childbirth.
2.4 Location: A room in the court of justice.
1. *the strong . . . conception:* the wickedness of my idea; original sin, inherited through the parents.

2. A frivolous feather, as worn in the hats of rakish youths.
3. That is, basic passions cannot be eradicated (contrasts with 1.4.56–58).
4. With pun on Angelo's name.

25   Come all to help him, and so stop the air
    By which he should revive—and even so
    The general subject° to a well-wished king   *common people*
    Quit their own part° and, in obsequious fondness,°   *place / foolish love*
    Crowd to his presence, where their untaught° love   *ignorant*
    Must needs appear offence.

             Enter ISABELLA

30   How now, fair maid?
  ISABELLA   I am come to know your pleasure.
  ANGELO [*aside*]   That you might know[5] it would much better please me
    Than to demand° what 'tis. [*To* ISABELLA] Your brother cannot live.   *ask*
  ISABELLA   Even so.° Heaven keep your honour.[6]   *So be it*
35 ANGELO   Yet may he live a while, and it may be
    As long as you or I. Yet he must die.
  ISABELLA   Under your sentence?
  ANGELO   Yea.
  ISABELLA   When, I beseech you?—that in his reprieve,
40   Longer or shorter, he may be so fitted°   *prepared*
    That his soul sicken not.
  ANGELO   Ha, fie, these filthy vices! It were as good
    To pardon him that hath from nature stolen
    A man already made,[7] as to remit°   *excuse*
45   Their saucy sweetness that do coin God's image
    In stamps that are forbid.[8] 'Tis all as easy
    Falsely° to take away a life true° made   *Wrongly / legitimately*
    As to put metal[9] in restrainèd° moulds,   *forbidden*
    To make a false one.
50 ISABELLA   'Tis set down so in heaven, but not in earth.
  ANGELO   Say you so? Then I shall pose° you quickly.   *ask*
    Which had you rather: that the most just law
    Now took your brother's life, or, to redeem him,
    Give up your body to such sweet uncleanness
    As she that he hath stained?
55 ISABELLA   Sir, believe this.
    I had rather give my body than my soul.
  ANGELO   I talk not of your soul. Our compelled sins
    Stand more for number than for account.[1]
  ISABELLA   How say you?
  ANGELO   Nay, I'll not warrant that,[2] for I can speak
60   Against the thing I say. Answer to this.
    I now, the voice of the recorded law,
    Pronounce a sentence on your brother's life.
    Might there not be a charity in sin
    To save this brother's life?
  ISABELLA   Please° you to do't,   *If it please*
65   I'll take it as a peril to my soul
    It is no sin at all, but charity.
  ANGELO   Pleased you to do't at peril of your soul
    Were equal poise° of sin and charity.   *balance*

---

5. With pun on "carnal knowledge."
6. A form of farewell.
7. *hath . . . made*: has committed murder.
8. *coin . . . forbid*: counterfeit God's image (by begetting illegitimate children).

9. Variant spelling of "mettle" (spirit). Some thought the child's spirit was conveyed in its father's semen.
1. *Our . . . account*: Sins we are forced to commit fill out the list but are not held against us.
2. I'll not guarantee that to be true.

ISABELLA That I do beg his life, if it be sin,
70   Heaven let me bear it. You granting° of my suit,   *Supposing you grant*
        If that be sin, I'll make it my morn prayer
        To have it added to the faults of mine,
        And nothing of your answer.
ANGELO   Nay, but hear me.
        Your sense pursues not mine.[3] Either you are ignorant,
75   Or seem so craftily, and that's not good.
ISABELLA Let me be ignorant, and in nothing good
        But graciously° to know I am no better.   *by God's grace*
ANGELO Thus wisdom wishes to appear most bright
        When it doth tax° itself: as these black masks[4]   *reprove*
80   Proclaim an enshield° beauty ten times louder   *a shielded*
        Than beauty could, displayed. But mark me.
        To be received° plain, I'll speak more gross.°   *understood / clearly*
        Your brother is to die.
ISABELLA So.°   *Yes*
85 ANGELO And his offence is so, as it appears,
        Accountant° to the law upon that pain.°   *Accountable / penalty*
ISABELLA True.
ANGELO Admit° no other way to save his life—   *Suppose*
        As I subscribe not° that nor any other—   *agree to neither*
90   But, in the loss of question,[5] that you his sister,
        Finding yourself desired of such a person
        Whose credit with the judge, or own great place,°   *rank*
        Could fetch your brother from the manacles
        Of the all-binding law, and that there were
95   No earthly mean to save him, but that either
        You must lay down the treasures of your body
        To this supposed,° or else to let him suffer—   *supposed man*
        What would you do?
ISABELLA As much for my poor brother as myself.
100   That is, were I under the terms° of death,   *sentence*
        Th'impression of keen whips I'd wear as rubies,
        And strip myself to death as to a bed
        That longing have been sick for, ere I'd yield
        My body up to shame.
105 ANGELO Then must your brother die.
ISABELLA And 'twere the cheaper way.
        Better it were a brother died at once
        Than that a sister, by redeeming him,
        Should die for ever.°   *be eternally damned*
110 ANGELO Were not you then as cruel as the sentence
        That you have slandered so?
ISABELLA Ignominy in ransom and free pardon
        Are of two houses;° lawful mercy   *different families*
        Is nothing kin to foul redemption.
115 ANGELO You seemed of late to make the law a tyrant,
        And rather proved° the sliding of your brother   *argued*
        A merriment than a vice.
ISABELLA O pardon me, my lord. It oft falls out
        To have what we would° have, we speak not what we mean.   *wish to*

---

3. You don't follow my meaning; your desire is not   4. Worn at court entertainments.
aroused by mine.   5. For the sake of discussion.

120   I something° do excuse the thing I hate   *to some extent*
        For his advantage that I dearly love.
        ANGELO   We are all frail.[6]
        ISABELLA   Else° let my brother die—   *Otherwise*
        If not a federy,° but only he,   *confederate*
        Owe and succeed thy weakness.[7]
        ANGELO   Nay, women are frail too.
125   ISABELLA   Ay, as the glasses° where they view themselves,   *mirrors*
        Which are as easy broke as they make forms.
        Women? Help, heaven! Men their creation° mar   *origin*
        In profiting by them. Nay, call us ten times frail,
        For we are soft as our complexions are,
        And credulous to false prints.[8]
130   ANGELO   I think it well,°   *agree completely*
        And from this testimony of your own sex,
        Since I suppose we are made to be no stronger
        Than faults may shake our frames, let me be bold.°   *presumptuous*
        I do arrest° your words. Be that you are;   *seize upon*
135   That is, a woman. If you be more,° you're none.   *(that is, better)*
        If you be one, as you are well expressed°   *shown to be*
        By all external warrants,° show it now,   *evidence*
        By putting on the destined livery.[9]
        ISABELLA   I have no tongue° but one. Gentle my lord,   *speech*
140   Let me entreat you speak the former language.
        ANGELO   Plainly conceive, I love you.
        ISABELLA   My brother did love Juliet,
        And you tell me that he shall die for it.
        ANGELO   He shall not, Isabel, if you give me love.
145   ISABELLA   I know your virtue hath a licence[1] in't,
        Which seems a little fouler than it is,
        To pluck on° others.   *test; mislead*
        ANGELO   Believe me, on mine honour,
        My words express my purpose.
        ISABELLA   Ha, little honour to be much believed,
150   And most pernicious purpose! Seeming, seeming!
        I will proclaim° thee, Angelo; look for't.   *denounce*
        Sign me a present° pardon for my brother,   *an immediate*
        Or with an outstretched throat I'll tell the world aloud
        What man thou art.
        ANGELO   Who will believe thee, Isabel?
155   My unsoiled name, th'austereness of my life,
        My vouch° against you, and my place i'th' state,   *attestation*
        Will so your accusation overweigh
        That you shall stifle in your own report,°   *story; reputation*
        And smell of calumny. I have begun,
160   And now I give my sensual race the rein.
        Fit thy consent to my sharp appetite.
        Lay by all nicety and prolixious° blushes   *coyness and excessive*
        That banish what they sue for. Redeem thy brother
        By yielding up thy body to my will,

---

6. Echoing Ecclesiasticus 8:5: "We are all worthy blame."
7. Own and inherit the weakness under discussion, or the weakness that you possess.
8. And receptive to false impressions; referring to Angelo's counterfeiting imagery, lines 45ff.
9. That is, by accepting women's sexual destiny and subjection to men. *livery*: servant's uniform.
1. Liberty to seem licentious.

165 Or else he must not only die the death,
     But thy unkindness° shall his death draw out   *unnaturalness*
     To ling'ring sufferance.° Answer me tomorrow,   *torment*
     Or by the affection° that now guides me most,   *passion*
     I'll prove a tyrant to him. As for you,
170 Say what you can, my false o'erweighs your true.   *Exit*

ISABELLA To whom should I complain? Did I tell this,
     Who would believe me? O perilous mouths,
     That bear in them one and the selfsame tongue
     Either of condemnation or approof,°   *approval*
175 Bidding the law make curtsy° to their will,   *submit*
     Hooking both right and wrong to th'appetite,
     To follow as it draws! I'll to my brother.
     Though he hath fall'n by prompture° of the blood,   *instigation*
     Yet hath he in him such a mind of honour
180 That had he twenty heads to tender° down   *pay*
     On twenty bloody blocks, he'd yield them up
     Before his sister should her body stoop
     To such abhorred pollution.
     Then Isabel live chaste, and brother die:
185 More than our brother is our chastity.
     I'll tell him yet of Angelo's request,
     And fit his mind to death, for his soul's rest.   *Exit*

3.1

Enter DUKE *[disguised as a friar]*, CLAUDIO, *and* PROVOST

DUKE So then you hope of pardon from Lord Angelo?
CLAUDIO The miserable have no other medicine
     But only hope.
     I've hope to live, and am prepared to die.
5 DUKE Be absolute° for death. Either death or life   *resolved*
     Shall thereby be the sweeter. Reason thus with life.
     If I do lose thee, I do lose a thing
     That none but fools would keep. A breath thou art,
     Servile to all the skyey influences[1]
10   That dost this habitation where thou keep'st°   *live*
     Hourly afflict. Merely° thou art death's fool,°   *Utterly / dupe*
     For him thou labour'st by thy flight to shun,
     And yet runn'st toward him still.° Thou art not noble,   *always*
     For all th'accommodations° that thou bear'st   *material comforts*
15   Are nursed by baseness.[2] Thou'rt by no means valiant,
     For thou dost fear the soft and tender fork°   *forked tongue*
     Of a poor worm.° Thy best of rest is sleep,   *snake*
     And that thou oft provok'st,° yet grossly fear'st   *summon*
     Thy death, which is no more. Thou art not thyself,°   *self-contained*
20   For thou exist'st on many a thousand grains
     That issue out of dust.° Happy thou art not,   *grow from the ground*
     For what thou hast not, still thou striv'st to get,
     And what thou hast, forget'st. Thou art not certain,°   *stable*
     For thy complexion° shifts to strange effects   *temperament*
25   After° the moon. If thou art rich, thou'rt poor,[3]   *Following*

3.1 Location: The prison.
1. Subject to all the influences of the heavenly bodies.
2. Are grown from plants and animals; made by lower-class people.

3. From Revelation 3:17: "For thou sayest, I am rich and increased with goods, and have need of nothing, and knowest not how thou art wretched and miserable, and poor, and blind, and naked."

For like an ass whose back with ingots bows,
Thou bear'st thy heavy riches but a journey,
And death unloads thee. Friend hast thou none,
For thine own bowels,° which do call thee sire,   *offspring*
30   The mere effusion° of thy proper° loins,   *very emission / own*
Do curse the gout, serpigo,° and the rheum,°   *skin disease / congestion*
For ending thee no sooner. Thou hast nor youth nor age,
But as it were an after-dinner's sleep
Dreaming on both; for all thy blessèd youth
35   Becomes as agèd,° and doth beg the alms°   *as if old / for money*
Of palsied eld;° and when thou art old and rich,   *old people*
Thou hast neither heat,° affection, limb,° nor beauty,   *desire / strength*
To make thy riches pleasant. What's in this
That bears the name of life? Yet in this life
40   Lie hid more thousand° deaths; yet death we fear   *a thousand more*
That makes these odds° all even.   *irregularities*
CLAUDIO   I humbly thank you.
To sue° to live, I find I seek to die,   *ask*
And seeking death, find life.[4] Let it come on.
ISABELLA [*within*]   What ho! Peace here, grace, and good company!
45   PROVOST   Who's there? Come in; the wish deserves a welcome.
DUKE [*to* CLAUDIO]   Dear sir, ere long I'll visit you again.
CLAUDIO   Most holy sir, I thank you.
          Enter ISABELLA
ISABELLA   My business is a word or two with Claudio.
PROVOST   And very welcome. Look, signor, here's your sister.
DUKE   Provost, a word with you.
50   PROVOST   As many as you please.
          [*The* DUKE *and* PROVOST *draw aside*]
DUKE   Bring me to hear them speak where I may be concealed.
          [*They conceal themselves*]
CLAUDIO   Now sister, what's the comfort?
ISABELLA   Why, as all comforts are: most good, most good indeed.
Lord Angelo, having affairs to heaven,
55   Intends you for his swift ambassador,
Where you shall be an everlasting leiger.°   *resident ambassador*
Therefore your best appointment° make with speed.   *preparation*
Tomorrow you set on.°   *forward*
CLAUDIO   Is there no remedy?
ISABELLA   None but such remedy as, to save a head,
60   To cleave a heart in twain.
CLAUDIO   But is there any?
ISABELLA   Yes, brother, you may live.
There is a devilish mercy in the judge,
If you'll implore it, that will free your life,
But fetter you till death.
65   CLAUDIO   Perpetual durance?°   *imprisonment*
ISABELLA   Ay, just,° perpetual durance; a restraint,   *exactly so*
Though all the world's vastidity° you had,   *vastness*
To a determined scope.[5]
CLAUDIO   But in what nature?

---

4. Echoing Matthew 16:25: "For whosoever will save his life, shall lose it: and whosoever shall lose his life for my sake, shall find it."

5. Constricted space (by the awareness of the means by which he had been saved).

ISABELLA   In such a one as you consenting to't
70   Would bark[6] your honour from that trunk° you bear,   *body; tree trunk*
        And leave you naked.
CLAUDIO   Let me know the point.
ISABELLA   O, I do fear thee, Claudio, and I quake
        Lest thou a feverous° life shouldst entertain,°   *feverish / cherish*
        And six or seven winters more respect°   *esteem*
75   Than a perpetual honour. Dar'st thou die?
        The sense° of death is most in apprehension,°   *awareness / anticipation*
        And the poor beetle that we tread upon
        In corporal sufferance° finds a pang as great   *bodily suffering*
        As when a giant dies.
CLAUDIO   Why give you me this shame?
80   Think you I can a resolution fetch°   *derive*
        From flow'ry° tenderness? If I must die,   *florid*
        I will encounter darkness as a bride,
        And hug it in mine arms.
ISABELLA   There spake my brother; there my father's grave
85   Did utter forth a voice. Yes, thou must die.
        Thou art too noble to conserve a life
        In base appliances.° This outward-sainted deputy,   *ignoble means*
        Whose settled° visage and deliberate word   *composed*
        Nips youth i'th' head[7] and follies doth enew°   *drive into hiding*
90   As falcon doth the fowl, is yet a devil.
        His filth within being cast,[8] he would appear
        A pond as deep as hell.
CLAUDIO   The precise[9] Angelo?
ISABELLA   O, 'tis the cunning livery of hell
        The damnedest body to invest° and cover   *dress*
95   In precise guards!° Dost thou think, Claudio: *trimmings*
        If I would yield him my virginity,
        Thou might'st be freed!
CLAUDIO   O heavens, it cannot be!
ISABELLA   Yes, he would give't thee, from this rank offence,
        So to offend him still.[1] This night's the time
100   That I should do what I abhor to name,
        Or else thou diest tomorrow.
CLAUDIO   Thou shalt not do't.
ISABELLA   O, were it but my life,
        I'd throw it down for your deliverance
        As frankly° as a pin.   *freely*
105 CLAUDIO   Thanks, dear Isabel.
ISABELLA   Be ready, Claudio, for your death tomorrow.
CLAUDIO   Yes. Has he affections in him
        That thus can make him bite the law by th' nose°   *flout the law*
        When he would force it? Sure it is no sin,
110   Or of the deadly seven[2] it is the least.
ISABELLA   Which is the least?
CLAUDIO   If it were damnable, he being so wise,
        Why would he for the momentary trick°   *trifle*

6. Strip off, like bark from a tree.
7. As a hawk kills a bird.
8. Cleaned out; measured; vomited.
9. F has "prenzie" here and in line 95; some editors
emend (as here) to "precise," others to "princely."

1. *give't thee . . . still*: grant you freedom in return for his
foul sin, so that you might continue offending him.
2. Seven deadly sins (pride, lechery, envy, anger, covet-
ousness, gluttony, and sloth).

Be perdurably fined?° O Isabel!   *eternally punished*
115 ISABELLA   What says my brother?
CLAUDIO   Death is a fearful thing.
ISABELLA   And shamèd life a hateful.
CLAUDIO   Ay, but to die, and go we know not where;
To lie in cold obstruction,° and to rot;   *congealment*
120 This sensible warm motion° to become   *conscious warm body*
A kneaded clod, and the dilated° spirit   *expansive; released*
To bath in fiery floods, or to reside
In thrilling° region of thick-ribbèd ice;   *bitterly cold*
To be imprisoned in the viewless° winds,   *unseeing; invisible*
125 And blown with restless violence round about
The pendent° world; or to be worse than worst   *hanging in space*
Of those that lawless and incertain thought[3]
Imagine howling—'tis too horrible!
The weariest and most loathèd worldly life
130 That age, ache, penury, and imprisonment
Can lay on nature is a paradise
To what we fear of death.
ISABELLA   Alas, alas!
CLAUDIO   Sweet sister, let me live.
135 What sin you do to save a brother's life,
Nature dispenses with° the deed so far   *excuses*
That it becomes a virtue.
ISABELLA   O, you beast!
O faithless coward, O dishonest wretch,
Wilt thou be made a man° out of my vice?   *given life*
140 Is't not a kind of incest to take life
From thine own sister's shame? What should I think?
Heaven shield° my mother played my father fair,   *forbid*
For such a warpèd slip of wilderness°   *shoot of wild stock*
Ne'er issued from his blood. Take my defiance,°   *rejection*
145 Die, perish! Might but my bending down
Reprieve thee from thy fate, it should proceed.
I'll pray a thousand prayers for thy death,
No word to save thee.
CLAUDIO   Nay, hear me, Isabel.
150 ISABELLA   O fie, fie, fie!
Thy sin's not accidental,° but a trade.°   *casual / habit*
Mercy to thee would prove itself a bawd.[4]
'Tis best that thou diest quickly.
          [*She parts from* CLAUDIO]
CLAUDIO   O hear me, Isabella.
DUKE [*coming forward to* ISABELLA]   Vouchsafe a word, young
155 sister, but one word.
ISABELLA   What is your will?
DUKE   Might you dispense with your leisure,° I would by and by   *spare the time*
have some speech with you. The satisfaction I would require
is likewise your own benefit.
160 ISABELLA   I have no superfluous leisure; my stay must be stolen
out of other affairs; but I will attend° you a while.   *await*
DUKE [*standing aside with* CLAUDIO]   Son, I have overheard what
hath passed between you and your sister. Angelo had never the

3. Of those whom unbridled and dubious conjecture.   4. By facilitating sinful behavior.

purpose to corrupt her; only he hath made an assay°   *a trial*
165 of her virtue, to practise his judgement with the disposition of
natures. She, having the truth of honour° in her, hath made   *chastity*
him that gracious° denial which he is most glad to receive. I   *virtuous*
am confessor to Angelo, and I know this to be true. Therefore
prepare yourself to death. Do not falsify° your resolution with   *corrupt*
170 hopes that are fallible. Tomorrow you must die. Go to your
knees and make ready.

CLAUDIO   Let me ask my sister pardon. I am so out of love with
life that I will sue to be rid of it.

DUKE   Hold you there.° Farewell.   *Remain so resolved*

[CLAUDIO *joins* ISABELLA][5]

175 Provost, a word with you.

PROVOST [*coming forward*]   What's your will, father?

DUKE   That now you are come, you will be gone. Leave me a
while with the maid. My mind° promises with my habit° no   *intention / friar's gown*
loss shall touch her by my company.

180 PROVOST   In good time.°   *Exit* [*with* CLAUDIO]   *Very well*

DUKE   The hand that hath made you fair hath made you good.
The goodness that is cheap in beauty makes beauty brief in
goodness;[6] but grace,° being the soul of your complexion,° shall   *virtue / constitution*
keep the body of it ever fair. The assault that Angelo hath made
185 to you fortune hath conveyed to my understanding; and but
that frailty hath examples° for his falling, I should wonder at   *precedents*
Angelo. How will you do to content this substitute,° and to save   *deputy*
your brother?

ISABELLA   I am now going to resolve him. I had rather my
190 brother die by the law than my son should be unlawfully born.
But O, how much is the good Duke deceived in Angelo! If ever
he return and I can speak to him, I will open my lips in vain,
or discover° his government.[7]   *expose*

DUKE   That shall not be much amiss. Yet as the matter now
195 stands, he will avoid° your accusation: he made trial of you   *quash*
only. Therefore fasten your ear on my advisings. To the love I
have in doing good, a remedy presents itself. I do make myself
believe that you may most uprighteously do a poor wronged
lady a merited benefit, redeem your brother from the angry
200 law, do no stain to your own gracious person, and much please
the absent Duke, if peradventure he shall ever return to have
hearing of this business.

ISABELLA   Let me hear you speak farther. I have spirit to do anything that appears not foul in the truth of my spirit.

205 DUKE   Virtue is bold, and goodness never fearful. Have you not
heard speak of Mariana, the sister of Frederick, the great soldier
who miscarried° at sea?   *perished*

ISABELLA   I have heard of the lady, and good words went with
her name.

210 DUKE   She should this Angelo have married, was affianced to her
oath, and the nuptial appointed;° between which time of the   *wedding day set*
contract and limit° of the solemnity, her brother Frederick was   *date*
wrecked at sea, having in that perished vessel the dowry of his

---

5. The Duke's conversation with the Provost provides an
opportunity for a silent reconciliation.
6. The goodness that is little valued by the beautiful

makes beauty short-lived.
7. Conduct; mode of governing.

sister. But mark how heavily this befell to the poor gentle-
215 woman. There she lost a noble and renowned brother, in his
love toward her ever most kind and natural; with him, the portion and sinew° of her fortune, her marriage dowry; with both,   *mainstay*
her combinate° husband, this well-seeming Angelo.   *betrothed*
ISABELLA   Can this be so? Did Angelo so leave her?
220 DUKE   Left her in her tears, and dried not one of them with his
comfort; swallowed° his vows whole, pretending° in his discov-   *retracted / alleging*
eries of dishonour;° in few, bestowed her on her own lamenta-   *unchastity*
tion, which she yet wears for his sake; and he, a marble° to her   *impervious*
tears, is washed with them, but relents not.
225 ISABELLA   What a merit were it in death to take this poor maid
from the world! What corruption in this life, that it will let this
man live! But how out of this can she avail?°   *profit*
DUKE   It is a rupture that you may easily heal, and the cure of it
not only saves your brother, but keeps you from dishonour in
230 doing it.
ISABELLA   Show me how, good father.
DUKE   This forenamed maid hath yet in her the continuance of
her first affection.° His unjust unkindness, that in all reason   *passion*
should have quenched her love, hath, like an impediment in
235 the current, made it more violent and unruly. Go you to
Angelo, answer his requiring with a plausible obedience, agree
with his demands to the point;° only refer yourself to this advan-   *exactly*
tage: first, that your stay with him may not be long; that the
time may have all shadow° and silence in it; and the place   *darkness*
240 answer to convenience. This being granted in course, and now
follows all. We shall advise this wronged maid to stead up° your   *fulfill*
appointment, go in your place. If the encounter acknowledge
itself° hereafter, it may compel him to her recompense; and   *becomes known*
hear, by this is your brother saved, your honour untainted, the
245 poor Mariana advantaged, and the corrupt deputy scaled.[8] The
maid will I frame° and make fit for his attempt. If you think   *prepare*
well to carry this, as you may, the doubleness of the benefit
defends the deceit from reproof. What think you of it?
ISABELLA   The image of it gives me content already, and I trust
250 it will grow to a most prosperous perfection.°   *completion*
DUKE   It lies much in your holding up. Haste you speedily to
Angelo. If for this night he entreat you to his bed, give him
promise of satisfaction. I will presently to Saint Luke's; there
at the moated grange° resides this dejected[9] Mariana. At that   *country house*
255 place call upon me; and dispatch° with Angelo, that it may be   *settle*
quickly.
ISABELLA   I thank you for this comfort. Fare you well, good
father.   *Exit*
        Enter ELBOW, [POMPEY *the*] *Clown, and officers*[1]
ELBOW   Nay, if there be no remedy for it but that you will needs°   *you must*
260 buy and sell men and women like beasts, we shall have all the
world drink brown and white bastard.°   *sweet wine (with pun)*
DUKE   O heavens, what stuff is here?
POMPEY   'Twas never merry world since, of two usuries,[2] the

---

8. Overreached; weighed (and found wanting).
9. Depressed; rejected.
1. The rest of the scene takes place on the street. Some

editors begin a new scene here, though the Duke remains
onstage.
2. Lending of money at interest; prostitution.

merriest was put down, and the worser allowed by order of law,[3]
265 a furred gown° to keep him warm—and furred with fox on   *(worn by usurers)*
lambskins too, to signify that craft,° being richer than inno-   *cunning*
cency, stands for the facing.[4]

ELBOW   Come your way, sir.—Bless you, good father friar.[5]

DUKE   And you, good brother father. What offence hath this man
270 made you, sir?

ELBOW   Marry, sir, he hath offended the law; and, sir, we take
him to be a thief, too, sir, for we have found upon him, sir, a
strange picklock,° which we have sent to the deputy.   *skeleton key*

DUKE [*to* POMPEY]   Fie, sirrah, a bawd,° a wicked bawd!   *pimp*
275 The evil that thou causest to be done,
That is thy means to live. Do thou but think
What 'tis to cram a maw or clothe a back
From such a filthy vice. Say to thyself,
'From their abominable and beastly touches
280 I drink, I eat, array° myself, and live'.   *dress*
Canst thou believe thy living is a life,
So stinkingly depending?° Go mend, go mend.   *dependent*

POMPEY   Indeed it does stink in some sort, sir. But yet, sir, I
would prove—

285 DUKE   Nay, if the devil have given thee proofs for sin,
Thou wilt prove° his.—Take him to prison, officer.   *prove to be*
Correction° and instruction must both work   *Punishment*
Ere this rude° beast will profit.°   *barbarous / improve*

ELBOW   He must before the deputy, sir; he has given him warn-
290 ing. The deputy cannot abide a whoremaster. If he be a whore-
monger and comes before him, he were as good go a mile on
his errand.[6]

DUKE   That° we were all as some would seem to be—   *Would that*
Free from our faults, or faults from seeming free.°   *free from seeming*

295 ELBOW   His neck will come to° your waist: a cord,[7] sir.   *end up like*

    Enter LUCIO

POMPEY   I spy comfort, I cry bail. Here's a gentleman, and a
friend of mine.

LUCIO   How now, noble Pompey? What, at the wheels of Caesar? Art thou led in triumph?[8] What, is there none of Pygmali-
300 on's images[9] newly made woman to be had now, for putting
the hand in the pocket and extracting clutched?[1] What reply,
ha? What sayst thou to this tune, matter, and method?[2] Is't not
drowned i'th' last rain,[3] ha? What sayst thou, trot?° Is the world   *bawd*
as it was, man? Which is the way? Is it sad and few words? Or
305 how? The trick° of it?   *style*

DUKE   Still° thus and thus; still worse!   *Always*

LUCIO   How doth my dear morsel thy mistress? Procures she still, ha?

---

3. A statute of 1570 allowed interest of 10 percent or less.
4. Is used to trim the garment; displays itself to the world.
5. Absurd, since "friar" means "brother"; hence the Duke's reply.
6. *he were . . . errand:* he would be better doing anything rather than that.
7. Encircled by a rope, as the friar's cord encircles his waist.

8. After Roman victories, vanquished generals were paraded behind the chariot wheels of their conquerors.
9. In classical legend, the sculptor Pygmalion fell in love with one of his statues, who was given life by Venus, the goddess of love; with a play on "become a woman" (lose one's virginity).
1. Clenched, with money for bail.
2. This style, topic, and sequence of thought.
3. Overwhelmed with recent misfortune.

POMPEY   Troth, sir, she hath eaten up° all her beef,° and she is   *worn out / prostitutes*
   herself in the tub.[4]

310 LUCIO   Why, 'tis good, it is the right of it, it must be so. Ever
   your fresh whore and your powdered[5] bawd; an unshunned°   *unavoidable*
   consequence, it must be so. Art going to prison, Pompey?

POMPEY   Yes, faith, sir.

LUCIO   Why 'tis not amiss, Pompey. Farewell. Go; say I sent thee
315   thither. For debt, Pompey, or how?

ELBOW   For being a bawd, for being a bawd.

LUCIO   Well then, imprison him. If imprisonment be the due of
   a bawd, why, 'tis his right. Bawd is he doubtless, and of antiq-
   uity° too—bawd born.° Farewell, good Pompey. Commend me   *long standing / at birth*
320   to the prison, Pompey. You will turn good husband° now, Pom-   *householder*
   pey; you will keep the house.

POMPEY   I hope, sir, your good worship will be my bail?

LUCIO   No, indeed, will I not, Pompey; it is not the wear.° I will   *fashion*
   pray, Pompey, to increase your bondage. If you take it not
325   patiently, why, your mettle° is the more. Adieu, trusty Pom-   *spirit; shackles*
   pey.— Bless you, friar.

DUKE   And you.

LUCIO   Does Bridget paint° still, Pompey, ha?   *use cosmetics*

ELBOW [*to* POMPEY]   Come your ways, sir, come.

330 POMPEY [*to* LUCIO]   You will not bail me then, sir?

LUCIO   Then, Pompey, nor now.—What news abroad,° friar,   *in the world*
   what news?

ELBOW [*to* POMPEY]   Come your ways, sir, come.

LUCIO   Go to kennel, Pompey,[6] go.

                    [*Exeunt* ELBOW, POMPEY, *and officers*]

335   What news, friar, of the Duke?

DUKE   I know none. Can you tell me of any?

LUCIO   Some say he is with the Emperor of Russia; other some,°   *some others*
   he is in Rome. But where is he, think you?

DUKE   I know not where; but wheresoever, I wish him well.

340 LUCIO   It was a mad, fantastical trick° of him to steal from the   *eccentric caprice*
   state, and usurp the beggary he was never born to. Lord Angelo
   dukes it° well in his absence; he puts transgression to't.[7]   *plays the Duke*

DUKE   He does well in't.

LUCIO   A little more lenity to lechery would do no harm in him.
345   Something too crabbed° that way, friar.   *Somewhat too harsh*

DUKE   It is too general a vice, and severity must cure it.

LUCIO   Yes, in good sooth, the vice is of a great° kindred, it is   *an extensive; powerful*
   well allied.° But it is impossible to extirp° it quite, friar, till   *connected / extirpate*
   eating and drinking be put down. They say this Angelo was not
350   made by man and woman, after this downright[8] way of creation. Is it true, think you?

DUKE   How should he be made, then?

LUCIO   Some report a sea-maid° spawned him, some that he was   *mermaid*
   begot between two stockfishes.° But it is certain that when he   *dried fish*
355   makes water his urine is congealed ice; that I know to be true.
   And he is a motion ungenerative;[9] that's infallible.°   *certain*

DUKE   You are pleasant,° sir, and speak apace.°   *merry / unrestrainedly*

---

4. Pickling tub for preserving ("powdering") beef; sweating tub for curing venereal disease.
5. Pickled; covered with cosmetic powder.
6. "Pompey" was a common dog's name.

7. He prosecutes lawbreaking vigorously.
8. In accordance with this straightforward.
9. An impotent puppet.

LUCIO Why, what a ruthless thing is this in him, for the rebellion of a codpiece[1] to take away the life of a man! Would the
360 Duke that is absent have done this? Ere he would have hanged
a man for the getting° a hundred bastards, he would have paid   *begetting*
for the nursing a thousand. He had some feeling of the sport,
he knew the service,° and that instructed him to mercy.   *(of prostitution)*
DUKE I never heard the absent Duke much detected° for   *accused*
365 women; he was not inclined that way.
LUCIO O sir, you are deceived.
DUKE 'Tis not possible.
LUCIO Who, not the Duke? Yes, your beggar of fifty; and his
use° was to put a ducat in her clack-dish.[2] The Duke had cro-   *custom*
370 chets° in him. He would be drunk too, that let me inform you.   *odd notions*
DUKE You do him wrong, surely.
LUCIO Sir, I was an inward° of his. A shy fellow was the Duke,   *intimate*
and I believe I know the cause of his withdrawing.
DUKE What, I prithee, might be the cause?
375 LUCIO No, pardon, 'tis a secret must be locked within the teeth
and the lips. But this I can let you understand. The greater file
of the subject° held the Duke to be wise.   *majority of the people*
DUKE Wise? Why, no question but he was.
LUCIO A very superficial, ignorant, unweighing° fellow.   *injudicious*
380 DUKE Either this is envy° in you, folly, or mistaking. The very   *malice*
stream° of his life, and the business he hath helmed,° must,   *course / steered*
upon a warranted need,° give him a better proclamation.° Let   *necessarily / reputation*
him be but testimonied° in his own bringings-forth,° and he   *proven / public actions*
shall appear to the envious a scholar, a statesman, and a soldier.
385 Therefore you speak unskilfully,° or, if your knowledge be   *ignorantly*
more, it is much darkened in your malice.
LUCIO Sir, I know him and I love him.
DUKE Love talks with better knowledge, and knowledge with
dearer love.
390 LUCIO Come, sir, I know what I know.
DUKE I can hardly believe that, since you know not what you
speak. But if ever the Duke return, as our prayers are he may,
let me desire you to make your answer before him. If it be
honest you have spoke, you have courage to maintain it. I am
395 bound to call upon° you; and I pray you, your name?   *accuse*
LUCIO Sir, my name is Lucio, well known to the Duke.
DUKE He shall know you better, sir, if I may live to report you.
LUCIO I fear you not.
DUKE O, you hope the Duke will return no more, or you imag-
400 ine me too unhurtful an opposite.° But indeed I can do you   *adversary*
little harm; you'll forswear this again.°   *at another time*
LUCIO I'll be hanged first. Thou art deceived in me, friar. But
no more of this. Canst thou tell if Claudio die tomorrow or no?
DUKE Why should he die, sir?
405 LUCIO Why? For filling a bottle with a tundish.° I would the   *funnel (with innuendo)*
Duke we talk of were returned again; this ungenitured agent°   *sexless deputy*
will unpeople the province with continency. Sparrows° must   *(proverbially lustful)*
not build in his house-eaves, because they are lecherous. The
Duke yet would have dark deeds darkly answered:° he would   *secretly requited*
410 never bring them to light. Would he were returned. Marry, this

---

1. Padded pouch worn over a man's breeches.   2. Begging bowl (with sexual innuendo).

Claudio is condemned for untrussing.° Farewell, good friar. I   *undoing his leggings*
prithee pray for me. The Duke, I say to thee again, would eat
mutton on Fridays.[3] He's not past it yet, and, I say to thee, he
would mouth° with a beggar, though she smelt° brown bread   *kiss / smelled of*
415   and garlic.[4] Say that I said so. Farewell.   *Exit*

DUKE   No might nor greatness in mortality°   *mortal existence*
Can censure scape;° back-wounding calumny[5]   *escape censure*
The whitest virtue strikes. What king so strong
Can tie the gall° up in the slanderous tongue?   *rancor*
      Enter ESCALUS, PROVOST, *and* [MISTRESS OVERDONE]
But who comes here?

420 ESCALUS [*to the* PROVOST]   Go, away with her to prison.

MISTRESS OVERDONE   Good my lord, be good to me. Your honour is accounted a merciful man, good my lord.

ESCALUS   Double and treble admonition,[6] and still forfeit in the
same kind!° This would make mercy swear[7] and play the tyrant.   *way*

425 PROVOST   A bawd of eleven years' continuance, may it please
your honour.

MISTRESS OVERDONE   My lord, this is one Lucio's information°   *accusation*
against me. Mistress Kate Keepdown was with child by him in
the Duke's time; he promised her marriage. His child is a year
430   and a quarter old come Philip and Jacob.[8] I have kept it myself;
and see how he goes about° to abuse° me.   *out of his way / injure*

ESCALUS   That fellow is a fellow of much licence. Let him be
called before us. Away with her to prison. Go to, no more
words. Provost, my brother° Angelo will not be altered; Claudio   *colleague*
435   must die tomorrow. Let him be furnished with divines, and
have all charitable preparation.[9] If my brother wrought by° my   *acted according to*
pity, it should not be so with him.

PROVOST   So please you, this friar hath been with him and
advised him for th'entertainment° of death.   *acceptance*
      [*Exeunt* PROVOST *and* MISTRESS OVERDONE]

440 ESCALUS   Good even, good father.

DUKE   Bliss and goodness on you.

ESCALUS   Of whence are you?

DUKE   Not of this country, though my chance° is now   *fortune*
To use it for my time.° I am a brother   *dwell here at present*
445   Of gracious order, late come from the See°   *Vatican*
In special business from his Holiness.

ESCALUS   What news abroad i'th' world?

DUKE   None, but that there is so great a fever on goodness that
the dissolution of it must cure it.[1] Novelty is only in request,°   *alone in demand*
450   and it is as dangerous to be aged in° any kind of course as it is   *habituated to*
virtuous to be inconstant in any undertaking. There is scarce
truth° enough alive to make societies secure, but security[2]   *honesty; loyalty*
enough to make fellowships° accursed. Much upon° this riddle *partnerships/According to*
runs the wisdom of the world. This news is old enough, yet it

---

3. *mutton:* prostitute (slang); it was forbidden to eat meat
on Fridays.
4. The food of the poor.
5. *back-wounding calumny:* slander ("calumny") is cowardly because it is not done to the victim's face.
6. Exceeding that recommended by Paul in Titus 3:10:
"Reject him that is an heretic, after once or twice admonition."
7. Varying the proverbial "make a saint swear."

8. May 1 was the Feast of St. Philip and St. James
(Jacob), but also the time of sexually licentious May Day
festivities, when the child was presumably conceived.
9. Spiritual preparation enjoined by Christian charity.
1. *there is . . . it:* that is, goodness is so sick that only
death will "cure" it.
2. Financial bonds liable to forfeit; blind trustfulness.
societies: association with others.

455   is every day's news. I pray you, sir, of what disposition was the Duke?

    ESCALUS   One that, above all other strifes, contended especially
    to know himself.[3]

    DUKE   What pleasure was he given to?

    ESCALUS   Rather rejoicing to see another merry than merry at

460   anything which professed° to make him rejoice; a gentleman   *attempted*
    of all temperance. But leave we him to his events,° with a   *affairs*
    prayer they may prove prosperous, and let me desire to know°   *ask*
    how you find Claudio prepared. I am made to understand that
    you have lent him visitation.°   *visited him*

465   DUKE   He professes to have received no sinister measure° from   *unjust treatment*
    his judge, but most willingly humbles himself to the determi-
    nation° of justice. Yet had he framed° to himself, by the instruc-   *sentence / imagined*
    tion of his frailty, many deceiving promises of life, which I, by
    my good leisure,° have discredited to him; and now is he   *gradually*

470   resolved to die.

    ESCALUS   You have paid the heavens your function, and the pris-
    oner the very debt of your calling.[4] I have laboured for the
    poor gentleman to the extremest shore° of my modesty, but my   *utmost limit*
    brother-justice have I found so severe that he hath forced me

475   to tell him he is indeed Justice.[5]

    DUKE   If his own life answer° the straitness° of his proceeding, it   *correspond to / strictness*
    shall become him well; wherein if he chance to fail, he hath
    sentenced° himself.   *condemned*

    ESCALUS   I am going to visit the prisoner. Fare you well.

480   DUKE   Peace be with you.   *[Exit* ESCALUS*]*[6]
    He who the sword of heaven[7] will bear
    Should be as holy as severe,
    Pattern in himself to know,
    Grace to stand, and virtue go,[8]

485   More nor less to others paying
    Than by self-offences° weighing.   *his own offenses*
    Shame to him whose cruel striking
    Kills for faults of his own liking!
    Twice treble shame on Angelo,

490   To weed my vice,[9] and let his grow!
    O, what may man within him hide,
    Though angel on the outward side!
    How may likeness made in crimes[1]
    Make my practice on the times

495   To draw with idle spiders' strings
    Most ponderous and substantial things?[2]
    Craft against vice I must apply.
    With Angelo tonight shall lie
    His old betrothèd but despisèd.

500   So disguise shall, by th' disguisèd,[3]
    Pay with falsehood false exacting,
    And perform an old contracting.   *Exit*

---

3. "Know thyself" was proverbial advice.
4. You have repaid the heavens for giving you your vocation, and given the prisoner all he can expect of a friar.
5. Absolute justice personified.
6. For a reconstruction of the following episodes as they
were originally written, see Additional Passage B.
7. The authority of a ruler, conferred by God.
8. When to stand firm, and when to take action (?).

9. The Duke speaks as a representative sinner.
1. How can the similarity between Claudio's and
Angelo's offenses.
2. *To draw . . . things:* the law was proverbially compared
to a spider's web, which caught small insects but which
large insects could break through. *idle:* ineffectual.
3. Mariana, "disguised" as Isabella.

4.1

MARIANA [*discovered with a*] BOY *singing*

BOY   Take, O take those lips away

    That so sweetly were forsworn,°   *perjured*

  And those eyes, the break of day

    Lights° that do mislead° the morn;   *Suns / guide falsely*

5   But my kisses bring again, bring again,°   *return*

    Seals of love, though sealed in vain, sealed in vain.

Enter DUKE [*disguised as a friar*]

MARIANA   Break off thy song, and haste thee quick away.

  Here comes a man of comfort, whose advice

  Hath often stilled my brawling° discontent.   [*Exit* BOY]   *clamorous*

10   I cry you mercy,° sir, and well could wish   *beg your pardon*

  You had not found me here so musical.

  Let me excuse me, and believe me so:°   *in this*

  My mirth it much displeased, but pleased my woe.[1]

DUKE   'Tis good; though music oft hath such a charm°   *magic spell*

15   To make bad good,° and good provoke to harm. I pray you tell   *bad appear good*

  me, hath anybody enquired for me here today? Much upon°   *at about*

  this time have I promised here to meet.

MARIANA   You have not been enquired after; I have sat here all day.

Enter ISABELLA

DUKE   I do constantly° believe you; the time is come even now.   *assuredly*

20   I shall crave your forbearance° a little. Maybe I will call upon   *departure; patience*

  you anon, for some advantage to yourself.

MARIANA   I am always bound to you.   *Exit*

DUKE   Very well met, and welcome.

  What is the news from this good deputy?

25 ISABELLA   He hath a garden circummured° with brick,   *walled about*

  Whose western side is with a vineyard backed;

  And to that vineyard is a planckèd° gate,   *made of planks*

  That makes his opening with this bigger key.

  This other doth command a little door

30   Which from the vineyard to the garden leads.

  There have I made my promise

  Upon the heavy° middle of the night   *In the gloomy*

  To call upon him.

DUKE   But shall you on your knowledge° find this way?   *with this information*

35 ISABELLA   I have ta'en a due and wary note upon't.

  With whispering and most guilty diligence,

  In action all of precept,° he did show me   *With explanatory gestures*

  The way twice o'er.

DUKE   Are there no other tokens°   *signs*

  Between you 'greed concerning her observance?[2]

40 ISABELLA   No, none, but only a repair° i'th' dark,   *journey to the place*

  And that I have possessed° him my most° stay   *informed / longest*

  Can be but brief, for I have made him know

  I have a servant comes with me along

  That stays upon° me, whose persuasion is   *waits for*

  I come about my brother.

45 DUKE   'Tis well borne up.°   *maintained*

4.1 Location: Mariana's house. Probably Mariana and the Boy are "discovered" by drawing back a curtain to reveal the characters within an alcove at the back of the stage.

1. The music drove away mirth but nurtured melancholy.
2. That she (Mariana) must observe.

I have not yet made known to Mariana
A word of this.—What ho, within! Come forth!
       Enter MARIANA
[*To* MARIANA] I pray you be acquainted with this maid.
She comes to do you good.

ISABELLA   I do desire the like.

50 DUKE [*to* MARIANA]   Do you persuade yourself° that I respect you?   *believe*
MARIANA   Good friar, I know you do, and so have found it.
DUKE   Take then this your companion° by the hand,   *partner*
Who hath a story ready for your ear.
I shall attend your leisure;° but make haste,   *wait until you are ready*
The vaporous night approaches.
55 MARIANA [*to* ISABELLA]   Will't please you walk aside?
       Exeunt [MARIANA *and* ISABELLA]
DUKE[3]   O place° and greatness, millions of false° eyes   *rank / misjudging*
Are stuck° upon thee; volumes of report°   *fixed / rumors*
Run with their false and most contrarious quest°   *misguided inquiry*
Upon thy doings; thousand escapes° of wit   *sallies*
60 Make thee the father° of their idle dream,°   *subject / fantasy*
And rack[4] thee in their fancies.
       Enter MARIANA *and* ISABELLA
              Welcome. How agreed?
ISABELLA   She'll take the enterprise upon her, father,
If you advise it.
DUKE   It is not my consent,
But my entreaty too.
ISABELLA [*to* MARIANA]   Little have you to say
65 When you depart from him but, soft and low,
'Remember now my brother'.
MARIANA   Fear me not.[5]
DUKE   Nor, gentle daughter, fear you not at all.
He is your husband on a pre-contract.°   *formal betrothal*
To bring you thus together 'tis no sin,
70 Sith that° the justice of your title to him   *Since*
Doth flourish° the deceit. Come, let us go.   *give propriety to*
Our corn's to reap, for yet our tilth's° to sow.   *Exeunt*   *tilled land*

4.2
       Enter PROVOST *and* [POMPEY]
PROVOST   Come hither, sirrah. Can you cut off a man's head?
POMPEY   If the man be a bachelor, sir, I can; but if he be a married man, he's his wife's head,[1] and I can never cut off a woman's head.[2]
5 PROVOST   Come, sir, leave me° your snatches,° and yield me a   *stop / quips*
direct answer. Tomorrow morning are to die Claudio and Bar-
nardine. Here is in our prison a common executioner, who in
his office lacks a helper. If you will take it on you to assist him,
it shall redeem you from your gyves;° if not, you shall have   *fetters*

---

3. The following lines, which seem out of context, may
have originally been part of the Duke's soliloquy at the
end of Act 3.
4. Misrepresent (literally, "torture by stretching").
5. Rely upon me; but the Duke takes "fear" in its modern
sense.

4.2 Location: The prison.
1. Alluding to Paul's doctrine "the husband is the wife's
head," Ephesians 5:23.
2. Playing on "married woman's maidenhead," an
improbability.

10   your full time of imprisonment, and your deliverance with an
       unpitied° whipping; for you have been a notorious bawd.   *unmerciful*

POMPEY   Sir, I have been an unlawful bawd time out of mind,
       but yet I will be content to be a lawful hangman. I would be
       glad to receive some instruction from my fellow partner.

15 PROVOST   What ho, Abhorson! Where's Abhorson there?

           Enter ABHORSON

ABHORSON   Do you call, sir?

PROVOST   Sirrah, here's a fellow will help you tomorrow in your
       execution. If you think it meet, compound with him by the
       year,[3] and let him abide here with you; if not, use him for the
20   present, and dismiss him. He cannot plead his estimation° with   *reputation*
       you; he hath been a bawd.

ABHORSON   A bawd, sir? Fie upon him, he will discredit our mystery.[4]

PROVOST   Go to, sir, you weigh equally; a feather will turn the scale.

                                          Exit

POMPEY   Pray, sir, by your good favour°—for surely, sir, a good   *permission*
25   favour° you have, but that you have a hanging look[5]—do you   *face*
       call, sir, your occupation a mystery?

ABHORSON   Ay, sir, a mystery.

POMPEY   Painting,[6] sir, I have heard say is a mystery; and your
       whores, sir, being members of my occupation, using painting,
30   do prove my occupation a mystery. But what mystery there
       should be in hanging, if I should be hanged I cannot imagine.

ABHORSON   Sir, it is a mystery.

POMPEY   Proof.

ABHORSON   Every true man's apparel fits your thief[7]—

35 POMPEY   If it be too little for your thief, your true man thinks it
       big enough.° If it be too big for your thief, your thief thinks it   *a big enough loss*
       little enough.° So every true man's apparel fits your thief.   *a small enough gain*

           Enter PROVOST

PROVOST   Are you agreed?

POMPEY   Sir, I will serve him, for I do find your hangman is
40   a more penitent trade than your bawd—he doth oftener ask
       forgiveness.[8]

PROVOST [*to* ABHORSON]   You, sirrah, provide your block and
       your axe tomorrow, four o'clock.

ABHORSON [*to* POMPEY]   Come on, bawd, I will instruct thee in
45   my trade. Follow.

POMPEY   I do desire to learn, sir, and I hope, if you have occasion
       to use me for your own turn, you shall find me yare.° For truly,   *skillful; eager*
       sir, for your kindness I owe you a good turn.[9]

PROVOST   Call hither Barnardine and Claudio.

                   Exeunt [ABHORSON *and* POMPEY]

50   Th'one has my pity; not a jot the other,
       Being a murderer, though he were my brother.

           Enter CLAUDIO

       Look, here's the warrant, Claudio, for thy death.
       'Tis now dead midnight, and by eight tomorrow
       Thou must be made immortal. Where's Barnardine?

---

3. Settle regular terms of employment with him.
4. Profession, requiring specialized skills and training.
5. Downcast expression; hangman's face.
6. Artist's occupation; use of cosmetics.
7. Abhorson implies that the thief assumes the character of an honest man by stealing his clothing; he also suggests an analogy between the thief and the hangman, who was awarded the clothes of his victims.
8. Executioners customarily asked forgiveness of their victims before killing them.
9. Favor; turning off the scaffold.

55 CLAUDIO   As fast locked up in sleep as guiltless labour
When it lies starkly° in the travailer's° bones.   *stiffly / worker's*
He will not wake.
PROVOST   Who can do good on him?
Well, go prepare yourself.
[*Knocking within*]
                              But hark, what noise?
Heaven give your spirits comfort!   [*Exit* CLAUDIO]
[*Knocking again*]
                              By and by!
60 I hope it is some pardon or reprieve
For the most gentle Claudio.
        Enter DUKE [*disguised as a friar*]
                              Welcome, father.
DUKE   The best and wholesom'st spirits of the night
Envelop you, good Provost! Who called here of late?
PROVOST   None since the curfew[1] rung.
65 DUKE   Not Isabel?
PROVOST   No.
DUKE   They will then, ere't be long.
PROVOST   What comfort is for Claudio?
DUKE   There's some in hope.
70 PROVOST   It is a bitter° deputy.   *cruel*
DUKE   Not so, not so; his life is paralleled
Even with the stroke and line[2] of his great justice.
He doth with holy abstinence subdue
That in himself which he spurs on his power
75 To qualify° in others. Were he mealed° with that   *moderate / stained*
Which he corrects, then were he tyrannous;
But this being so, he's just.
        [*Knocking within*]
                              Now are they come.
        [*The* PROVOST *goes to a door*]
This is a gentle Provost. Seldom when°   *Rarely*
The steelèd° jailer is the friend of men.   *hard-hearted*
        [*Knocking within*]
        [*To* PROVOST] How now, what noise? That spirit's possessed
80   with haste
That wounds th'unlisting postern° with these strokes.   *unyielding door*
PROVOST   There he° must stay until the officer   (*the messenger*)
Arise to let him in. He° is called up.   (*the officer*)
DUKE   Have you no countermand for Claudio yet,
But he must die tomorrow?
85 PROVOST   None, sir, none.
DUKE   As near the dawning, Provost, as it is,
You shall hear more ere morning.
PROVOST   Happily°   *Perhaps*
You something know, yet I believe there comes
No countermand. No such example° have we;   *precedent*
90 Besides, upon the very siege° of justice   *seat*
Lord Angelo hath to the public ear
Professed the contrary.

---

1. Evening bell, rung at 9:00 P.M.
2. Exact course; also suggesting ax blows and hanging ropes.

Enter a MESSENGER
    This is his lordship's man.
  DUKE   And here comes Claudio's pardon.
95 MESSENGER [*giving a paper to* PROVOST] My lord hath sent you
    this note, and by me this further charge: that you swerve not
    from the smallest article of it, neither in time, matter, or other
    circumstance. Good morrow; for, as I take it, it is almost day.
  PROVOST   I shall obey him.   [*Exit* MESSENGER]
100 DUKE [*aside*] This is his pardon, purchased by such sin
    For which the pardoner himself is in.
    Hence hath offence his° quick celerity,   *its*
    When it is borne in high authority.
    When vice makes mercy, mercy's so extended
105   That for the fault's love[3] is th'offender friended.°—   *befriended*
    Now sir, what news?
  PROVOST   I told you: Lord Angelo, belike thinking me remiss in
    mine office, awakens me with this unwonted putting-on;°   *urging*
    methinks strangely, for he hath not used° it before.   *practiced*
110 DUKE   Pray you let's hear.
  PROVOST [*reading the letter*] 'Whatsoever you may hear to the
    contrary, let Claudio be executed by four of the clock, and in
    the afternoon Barnardine. For my better satisfaction, let me
    have Claudio's head sent me by five. Let this be duly per-
115   formed, with a thought that more depends on it than we must
    yet deliver.° Thus fail not to do your office, as you will answer   *make known*
    it at your peril.'
    What say you to this, sir?
  DUKE   What is that Barnardine, who is to be executed in th'afternoon?
120 PROVOST   A Bohemian born, but here nursed up and bred; one
    that is a prisoner nine years old.°   *nine years a prisoner*
  DUKE   How came it that the absent Duke had not either deliv-
    ered him to his liberty or executed him? I have heard it was
    ever his manner to do so.
125 PROVOST   His friends still° wrought reprieves for him; and indeed   *continually*
    his fact,° till now in the government of Lord Angelo, came not   *crime*
    to an undoubtful° proof.   *a certain*
  DUKE   It is now apparent?
  PROVOST   Most manifest, and not denied by himself.
130 DUKE   Hath he borne himself penitently in prison? How seems
    he to be touched?°   *affected*
  PROVOST   A man that apprehends death no more dreadfully but as
    a drunken sleep; careless, reckless, and fearless of what's past,
    present, or to come; insensible of mortality, and desperately
135   mortal.[4]
  DUKE   He wants° advice.   *needs*
  PROVOST   He will hear none. He hath evermore had the liberty
    of the prison. Give him leave to escape hence, he would not.
    Drunk many times a day, if not many days entirely° drunk. We   *continuously*
140   have very oft awaked him as if to carry him to execution, and
    showed him a seeming warrant for it; it hath not moved him at all.
  DUKE   More of him anon. There is written in your brow, Provost,
    honesty and constancy. If I read it not truly, my ancient skill

---

3. For love of the fault.   4. Reckless of death, and in a state of mortal sin.

beguiles me. But in the boldness° of my cunning,° I will lay   *confidence / skill*
145 myself in hazard.[5] Claudio, whom here you have warrant to
execute, is no greater forfeit to the law than Angelo who hath
sentenced him. To make you understand this in a manifested
effect,° I crave but four days' respite, for the which you are to   *clear demonstration*
do me both a present° and a dangerous courtesy.°   *an immediate / favor*
150 PROVOST   Pray sir, in what?
DUKE   In the delaying death.
PROVOST   Alack, how may I do it, having the hour limited, and
an express command under penalty to deliver his head in the
view of Angelo? I may make my case as Claudio's to cross° this   *oppose*
155 in the smallest.
DUKE   By the vow of mine order, I warrant you, if my instructions
may be your guide, let this Barnardine be this morning executed, and his head borne to Angelo.
PROVOST   Angelo hath seen them both, and will discover° the   *discern*
160 favour.
DUKE   O, death's a great disguiser, and you may add to it. Shave
the head and tie the beard, and say it was the desire of the
penitent to be so bared before his death; you know the course
is common. If anything fall to you upon° this more than thanks   *as a result of*
165 and good fortune, by the saint whom I profess,[6] I will plead
against it with my life.
PROVOST   Pardon me, good father, it is against my oath.
DUKE   Were you sworn to the Duke or to the deputy?
PROVOST   To him and to his substitutes.
170 DUKE   You will think you have made no offence if the Duke
avouch° the justice of your dealing?   *vouch for*
PROVOST   But what likelihood is in that?
DUKE   Not a resemblance,° but a certainty. Yet since I see you   *likelihood*
fearful, that neither my coat,° integrity, nor persuasion can with   *religious garb*
175 ease attempt you,° I will go further than I meant, to pluck all   *win you over*
fears out of you. [*Showing a letter*] Look you, sir, here is the
hand and seal of the Duke. You know the character,° I doubt   *handwriting*
not, and the signet is not strange to you?
PROVOST   I know them both.
180 DUKE   The contents of this is the return of the Duke. You shall
anon° over-read it at your pleasure, where you shall find within   *right away*
these two days he will be here. This is a thing that Angelo
knows not, for he this very day receives letters of strange tenor,
perchance of the Duke's death, perchance entering into some
185 monastery; but by chance nothing of what is writ.° Look, th'un-   *written here*
folding star[7] calls up the shepherd. Put not yourself into amaze-
ment° how these things should be. All difficulties are but easy   *perplexity*
when they are known. Call your executioner, and off with Bar-
nardine's head. I will give him a present shrift,° and advise him   *an immediate confession*
190 for a better place. Yet° you are amazed; but this° shall abso-   *Still / (the letter)*
lutely resolve you.° Come away, it is almost clear dawn.   *free you from doubt*

Exeunt

5. I will bet on it; I will put myself in peril.   7. Morning star (which tells the shepherd he may
6. The patron saint of my order.   safely release the sheep from the fold).

4.3

Enter [POMPEY]

POMPEY   I am as well acquainted here as I was in our house of
profession.[1] One would think it were Mistress Overdone's own
house, for here be many of her old customers. First, here's
young Master Rash; he's in for a commodity[2] of brown paper
5   and old ginger, nine score and seventeen pounds, of which he
made five marks ready money.[3] Marry, then ginger[4] was not
much in request, for the old women were all dead.[5] Then is
there here one Master Caper,° at the suit of Master Threepile[6]   *fashionable dance*
the mercer,° for some four suits of peach-coloured satin, which   *cloth dealer*
10   now peaches° him a beggar. Then have we here young Dizzy,   *impeaches; declares*
and young Master Deepvow, and Master Copperspur and Mas-
ter Starve-lackey[7] the rapier and dagger man,[8] and young Drop-
hair[9] that killed lusty Pudding,° and Master Forthright the   *stuffed guts*
tilter,° and brave Master Shoe-tie the great traveller,[1] and wild   *fencer*
15   Half-can that stabbed Pots,[2] and I think forty more, all great
doers in our trade, and are now 'for the Lord's sake'.[3]

Enter ABHORSON

ABHORSON   Sirrah, bring Barnardine hither.
POMPEY   Master Barnardine! You must rise[4] and be hanged,
Master Barnardine!
20   ABHORSON   What ho, Barnardine!
BARNARDINE [*within*]   A pox o' your throats! Who makes that
noise there? What are you?
POMPEY   Your friends, sir; the hangman. You must be so good,
sir, to rise and be put to death.
25   BARNARDINE   Away, you rogue, away! I am sleepy.
ABHORSON   Tell him he must awake, and that quickly too.
POMPEY   Pray, Master Barnardine, awake till you are executed,
and sleep afterwards.
ABHORSON   Go in to him and fetch him out.
30   POMPEY   He is coming, sir, he is coming. I hear his straw rustle.
ABHORSON   Is the axe upon the block, sirrah?
POMPEY   Very ready, sir.

Enter BARNARDINE

BARNARDINE   How now, Abhorson, what's the news with you?
ABHORSON   Truly, sir, I would desire you to clap into[5] your pray-
35   ers, for, look you, the warrant's come.
BARNARDINE   You rogue, I have been drinking all night. I am not
fitted for't.
POMPEY   O, the better, sir; for he that drinks all night, and is
hanged betimes° in the morning, may sleep the sounder all the   *early*
40   next day.

Enter DUKE [*disguised as a friar*]

4.3 Location: Scene continues.
1. Religious house ("nunnery" was slang for "brothel").
2. To evade the statutory limit on interest, usurers would
give borrowers part of their loan in practically worthless
"commodities," which they were supposed to sell for
ready money. *he's in for*: he's in for falling into debt over.
3. Rash paid 197 pounds for the "commodity," a very
large sum, and sold it for about 3.3 pounds.
4. Used to make warming tonics.
5. Presumably victims of the 1603 plague, mentioned
earlier by Mistress Overdone.

6. Richest sort of velvet.
7. One who fails to feed his servants.
8. Suggesting a reputation for brawling.
9. Premature baldness was a sign of syphilis.
1. Observer of foreign fashions (probably ironic).
2. Suggesting drinking cups.
3. The cry of prisoners begging from the prison grate.
Prisoners had to pay for their own food and lodging.
4. Get out of bed; mount the scaffold.
5. Immediately begin; join your hands for.

ABHORSON [*to* BARNARDINE]   Look you, sir, here comes your
   ghostly° father. Do we jest now, think you?   *spiritual*
DUKE [*to* BARNARDINE]   Sir, induced by my charity, and hearing
   how hastily you are to depart, I am come to advise you, comfort
45   you, and pray with you.
BARNARDINE   Friar, not I. I have been drinking hard all night,
   and I will have more time to prepare me, or they shall beat out
   my brains with billets.° I will not consent to die this day, that's   *thick sticks*
   certain.
50 DUKE   O sir, you must; and therefore, I beseech you,
   Look forward on the journey you shall go.
BARNARDINE   I swear I will not die today, for any man's persuasion.
DUKE   But hear you—
BARNARDINE   Not a word. If you have anything to say to me,
55   come to my ward,° for thence will not I today.   *Exit*   *cell*
DUKE   Unfit to live or die. O gravel° heart!   *(i.e., hard)*
   After him, fellows; bring him to the block.
                        [*Exeunt* ABHORSON *and* POMPEY]

      Enter PROVOST

PROVOST   Now, sir, how do you find the prisoner?
DUKE   A creature unprepared, unmeet° for death;   *unfit*
60   And to transport° him in the mind he is   *execute (euphemistic)*
   Were damnable.
PROVOST   Here in the prison, father,
   There died this morning of a cruel fever
   One Ragusine, a most notorious pirate,
   A man of Claudio's years, his beard and head
65   Just of his colour. What if we do omit°   *disregard*
   This reprobate till he were well inclined,
   And satisfy the deputy with the visage
   Of Ragusine, more like to Claudio?
DUKE   O, 'tis an accident that heaven provides.
70   Dispatch it presently; the hour draws on
   Prefixed° by Angelo. See this be done,   *Fixed in advance*
   And sent according to command, whiles I
   Persuade this rude° wretch willingly to die.   *uncivilized*
PROVOST   This shall be done, good father, presently.
75   But Barnardine must die this afternoon;
   And how shall we continue° Claudio,   *maintain*
   To save me from the danger that might come
   If he were known alive?
DUKE   Let this be done:
   Put them in secret holds,° both Barnardine and Claudio.   *cells*
80   Ere twice the sun hath made his journal° greeting   *daily*
   To yonder generation,[6] you shall find
   Your safety manifested.
PROVOST   I am your free dependant.°   *willing servant*
DUKE   Quick, dispatch, and send the head to Angelo.
                         Exit [PROVOST]
   Now will I write letters to Angelo[7]—
85   The Provost, he shall bear them—whose contents
   Shall witness to him I am near at home,

6. That is, the people outside the prison.
7. "Angelo" may be an error for "Varrius," whom the Duke meets outside the city in 4.5.

And that by great injunctions° I am bound   *for compelling reasons*
To enter publicly. Him I'll desire
To meet me at the consecrated fount

90 A league below the city, and from thence,
By cold gradation° and well-balanced form,   *deliberate degrees*
We shall proceed with Angelo.

    Enter PROVOST [*with Ragusine's head*]

PROVOST   Here is the head; I'll carry it myself.
DUKE   Convenient° is it. Make a swift return,   *Suitable*

95 For I would commune° with you of such things   *confer*
That want no ear but yours.
PROVOST   I'll make all speed.   *Exit*
ISABELLA [*within*]   Peace, ho, be here!
DUKE   The tongue of Isabel. She's come to know

100 If yet her brother's pardon be come hither;
But I will keep her ignorant of her good,
To make her heavenly comforts of° despair   *out of*
When it is least expected.
ISABELLA [*within*]   Ho, by your leave!

    Enter ISABELLA

DUKE   Good morning to you, fair and gracious daughter.
105 ISABELLA   The better, given me° by so holy a man.   *so greeted*
Hath yet the deputy sent my brother's pardon?
DUKE   He hath released him, Isabel, from the world.
His head is off and sent to Angelo.
ISABELLA   Nay, but it is not so.
DUKE   It is no other.

110 Show your wisdom, daughter, in your close° patience.   *silent*
ISABELLA   O, I will to° him and pluck out his eyes!   *will go to*
DUKE   You shall not be admitted to his sight.
ISABELLA [*weeping*]   Unhappy Claudio! Wretched Isabel!
Injurious world! Most damnèd Angelo!

115 DUKE   This nor° hurts him, nor profits you a jot.   *neither*
Forbear it, therefore; give your cause° to heaven.   *grievance*
Mark what I say, which you shall find
By every syllable a faithful verity.
The Duke comes home tomorrow—nay, dry your eyes—

120 One of our convent, and his confessor,
Gives me this instance.° Already he hath carried   *indication*
Notice to Escalus and Angelo,
Who do prepare to meet him at the gates,
There to give up their power. If you can pace° your wisdom   *train to walk*

125 In that good path that I would wish it go,
And you shall have your bosom° on this wretch,   *desire*
Grace° of the Duke, revenges to your heart,   *Favor*
And general honour.
ISABELLA   I am directed by you.
DUKE   This letter, then, to Friar Peter give.

130 'Tis that he sent me of the Duke's return.
Say by this token I desire his company
At Mariana's house tonight. Her cause and yours
I'll perfect° him withal, and he shall bring you   *fully instruct*
Before the Duke, and to the head of° Angelo   *and directly to*

135 Accuse him home and home.° For my poor self,   *to the utmost*
I am combinèd° by a sacred vow,   *bound*

And shall be absent. [*Giving the letter*] Wend you° with this letter.   *Depart*
Command these fretting° waters from your eyes   *agitated; corrosive*
With a light heart. Trust not my holy order
If I pervert° your course.   *lead astray*
    Enter LUCIO
                        Who's here?
140 LUCIO   Good even.°   *evening*
Friar, where's the Provost?
DUKE   Not within, sir.
LUCIO   O pretty Isabella, I am pale at mine heart to see thine
eyes so red. Thou must be patient. I am fain to dine and sup
with water and bran;[8] I dare not for my head fill my belly; one
145 fruitful° meal would set me to't.[9] But they say the Duke will be   *plentiful*
here tomorrow. By my troth, Isabel, I loved thy brother. If the
old fantastical° Duke of dark corners° had been at home, he   *capricious/secret places*
had lived.   [*Exit* ISABELLA]
DUKE   Sir, the Duke is marvellous° little beholden to your   *remarkably*
150 reports; but the best is, he lives not° in them.   *is not to be found*
LUCIO   Friar, thou knowest not the Duke so well as I do. He's a
better woodman[1] than thou tak'st him for.
DUKE   Well, you'll answer° this one day. Fare ye well.   *account for*
LUCIO   Nay, tarry, I'll go along with thee. I can tell thee pretty
155 tales of the Duke.
DUKE   You have told me too many of him already, sir, if they be
true; if not true, none were enough.
LUCIO   I was once before him for getting a wench with child.
DUKE   Did you such a thing?
160 LUCIO   Yes, marry, did I; but I was fain to forswear it. They would
else° have married me to the rotten medlar.[2]   *otherwise*
DUKE   Sir, your company is fairer° than honest. Rest you well.   *more speciously pleasant*
LUCIO   By my troth, I'll go with thee to the lane's end. If bawdy
talk offend you, we'll have very little of it. Nay, friar, I am a
165 kind of burr; I shall stick.   *Exeunt*

4.4

    Enter ANGELO *and* ESCALUS
ESCALUS   Every letter he hath writ hath disvouched other.°   *repudiated the others*
ANGELO   In most uneven and distracted manner. His actions
show much like to madness. Pray heaven his wisdom be not
tainted.° And why meet him at the gates, and redeliver our   *impaired*
5 authorities there?
ESCALUS   I guess not.
ANGELO   And why should we proclaim it in an hour before his
entering, that if any crave redress of injustice, they should
exhibit° their petitions in the street?   *present*
10 ESCALUS   He shows his reason for that—to have a dispatch° of   *prompt settlement*
complaints, and to deliver us from devices° hereafter, which   *contrivances*
shall then have no power to stand against us.
ANGELO   Well, I beseech you let it be proclaimed.
Betimes° i'th' morn I'll call you at your house.   *Early*

---

8. Diet thought to suppress lust.
9. Would incite me to lechery.
1. Hunter (literally, of game; here, of women).

2. Kind of pear eaten when rotten; slang for "prostitute."
4.4 Location: Vienna.

15   Give notice to such men of sort and suit°   *rank and retinue*
     As are to meet him.
     ESCALUS   I shall, sir. Fare you well.
     ANGELO   Good night.   *Exit* [ESCALUS]
     This deed unshapes° me quite, makes me unpregnant°   *destroys/unready*
20   And dull to all proceedings. A deflowered maid,
     And by an eminent body[1] that enforced°   *exerted; raped*
     The law against it! But that her tender shame
     Will not proclaim against her maiden loss,°   *loss of virginity*
     How might she tongue° me! Yet reason dares her no,[2]   *reproach*
25   For my authority bears off a credent bulk,[3]
     That no particular° scandal once can touch   *private; single*
     But it confounds° the breather. He should have lived,   *confutes; overthrows*
     Save that his riotous youth, with dangerous sense,°   *sensibility; sensuality*
     Might in the times to come have ta'en revenge
30   By° so receiving a dishonoured life   *Because of*
     With ransom of such shame. Would yet he had lived.
     Alack, when once our grace we have forgot,
     Nothing goes right; we would, and we would not.   *Exit*

                              4.5
     Enter DUKE, [*in his own habit*] *and* FRIAR PETER
     DUKE   These letters at fit time deliver me.
     The Provost knows our purpose and our plot.
     The matter being afoot, keep° your instruction,   *observe*
     And hold you ever to our special drift,°   *purpose*
5   Though sometimes you do blench° from this to that   *swerve*
     As cause doth minister.° Go call at Flavio's house,   *serve*
     And tell him where I stay. Give the like notice
     To Valentinus, Rowland, and to Crassus,
     And bid them bring the trumpets° to the gate.   *trumpeters*
     But send me Flavius first.
10   FRIAR PETER   It shall be speeded well.°   [*Exit*]   *quickly done*
                    Enter VARRIUS
     DUKE   I thank thee, Varrius; thou hast made good haste.
     Come, we will walk.° There's other of our friends   *withdraw*
     Will greet us here anon. My gentle° Varrius!   *Exeunt*   *noble*

                              4.6
     Enter ISABELLA *and* MARIANA
     ISABELLA   To speak so indirectly° I am loath—   *evasively*
     I would say the truth, but to accuse him so,
     That is your part—yet I am advised to do it,
     He says, to veil full purpose.
     MARIANA   Be ruled by him.
5   ISABELLA   Besides, he tells me that if peradventure
     He speak against me on the adverse side,
     I should not think it strange, for 'tis a physic°   *medicine*
     That's bitter to sweet end.
                    Enter [FRIAR] PETER
     MARIANA   I would Friar Peter—

---

1. Person (also suggesting the physical body).
2. Makes her dare not.
3. Sustains such massive credibility.

4.5 Location: Outside the city.
4.6 Location: A street near the city gates.

10   ISABELLA   O, peace; the friar is come.

FRIAR PETER   Come, I have found you out a stand° most fit,   *place*
Where you may have such vantage° on the Duke   *advantageous position*
He shall not pass you. Twice have the trumpets sounded.[1]
The generous° and gravest citizens   *noble*
15   Have hent° the gates, and very near upon   *reached*
The Duke is ent'ring; therefore hence, away.   *Exeunt*

5.1

Enter [at one door] DUKE, VARRIUS, *[and] lords; [at
another door]* ANGELO, ESCALUS, LUCIO, *citizens [and
officers]*

DUKE   *[to* ANGELO*]*   My very worthy cousin,° fairly met.   *fellow nobleman*
[To ESCALUS*]* Our old and faithful friend, we are glad to see you.

ANGELO *and* ESCALUS   Happy return be to your royal grace.

DUKE   Many and hearty thankings to you both.
5   We have made enquiry of you, and we hear
Such goodness of your justice that our soul
Cannot but yield you forth to public thanks,
Forerunning more requital.°   *greater reward*

ANGELO   You make my bonds° still greater.   *obligations*

DUKE   O, your desert speaks loud, and I should wrong it
10   To lock it in the wards° of covert bosom,   *prison cells*
When it deserves with characters° of brass   *letters*
A forted° residence 'gainst the tooth of time   *fortified*
And razure° of oblivion. Give me your hand,   *erasure*
And let the subject° see, to make them know   *people*
15   That outward courtesies would fain proclaim
Favours that keep° within. Come, Escalus,   *dwell*
You must walk by us on our other hand,
And good supporters[1] are you.

        [They walk forward]
        *Enter [*FRIAR*]* PETER *and* ISABELLA

FRIAR PETER   Now is your time. Speak loud, and kneel before him.
20   ISABELLA *[kneeling]*   Justice, O royal Duke! Vail your regard°   *Look down*
Upon a wronged—I would fain° have said, a maid.   *like to*
O worthy prince, dishonour not your eye
By throwing it on any other object,
Till you have heard me in my true complaint,
25   And given me justice, justice, justice, justice!

DUKE   Relate your wrongs. In what? By whom? Be brief.
Here is Lord Angelo shall give you justice.
Reveal yourself° to him.   *(your complaint)*

ISABELLA   O worthy Duke,
You bid me seek redemption of the devil.
30   Hear me yourself, for that which I must speak
Must either punish me, not being believed,
Or wring redress from you. Hear me, O hear me, hear!

ANGELO   My lord, her wits, I fear me, are not firm.
She hath been a suitor to me for her brother,
Cut off° by course of justice.   *Executed*
35   ISABELLA *[standing]*   By course of justice!

---

1. The third flourish will signal the Duke's arrival.
5.1 Location: The city gates.

1. Attendants; in heraldry, "supporters" are figures
depicted beside a shield, holding it up.

ANGELO   And she will speak most bitterly and strange.

ISABELLA   Most strange, but yet most truly, will I speak.
    That Angelo's forsworn, is it not strange?
    That Angelo's a murderer, is't not strange?
40   That Angelo is an adulterous thief,
    An hypocrite, a virgin-violator,
    Is it not strange, and strange?

DUKE   Nay, it is ten times strange!

ISABELLA   It is not truer he is Angelo
    Than this is all as true as it is strange.
45   Nay, it is ten times true, for truth is truth
    To th'end of reck'ning.[2]

DUKE   Away with her. Poor soul,
    She speaks this in th'infirmity of sense.

ISABELLA   O prince, I conjure° thee, as thou believ'st   *appeal to*
    There is another comfort than this world,
50   That thou neglect me not with that opinion
    That I am touched with madness. Make not impossible
    That which but seems unlike.° 'Tis not impossible   *unlikely*
    But° one, the wicked'st caitiff° on the ground,   *That/villain*
    May seem as shy,° as grave, as just, as absolute,°   *reserved/perfect*
55   As Angelo; even so may Angelo,
    In all his dressings, characts,[3] titles, forms,°   *formalities*
    Be an arch-villain. Believe it, royal prince,
    If he be less, he's nothing; but he's more,
    Had I more name for badness.

DUKE   By mine honesty,
60   If she be mad, as I believe no other,
    Her madness hath the oddest frame° of sense,   *shape*
    Such a dependency° of thing on thing   *connected sequence*
    As e'er I heard in madness.

ISABELLA   O gracious Duke,
    Harp not on that, nor do not banish reason
65   For inequality;[4] but let your reason serve
    To make the truth appear where it seems hid,
    And hide the false seems° true.   *that seems*

DUKE   Many that are not mad
    Have sure more lack of reason. What would you say?

ISABELLA   I am the sister of one Claudio,
70   Condemned upon the act of° fornication   *decree against*
    To lose his head, condemned by Angelo.
    I, in probation of a sisterhood,
    Was sent to by my brother, one Lucio
    As° then the messenger.   *Being*

LUCIO   That's I, an't like your grace.
75   I came to her from Claudio, and desired her
    To try her gracious fortune with Lord Angelo
    For her poor brother's pardon.

ISABELLA   That's he indeed.

DUKE [*to* LUCIO]   You were not bid to speak.

---

2. *for truth . . . reck'ning*: echoing 1 Esdras 4:38: "But truth doth abide, and is strong forever, and liveth and reigneth for ever and ever." *reck'ning*: day of reckoning.

3. Signs (of office).
4. Difference in rank (between Isabella and Angelo); discrepancy (between my report and what seems true).

LUCIO   No, my good lord,
  Nor wished to hold my peace.
80 DUKE   I wish you now, then. Pray you take note of it;
  And when you have a business for yourself,
  Pray heaven you then be perfect.
LUCIO   I warrant° your honour.   *assure*
DUKE   The warrant's[5] for yourself; take heed to't.
ISABELLA   This gentleman told somewhat of my tale—
85 LUCIO   Right.
DUKE   It may be right, but you are i'the wrong
  To speak before your time. [*To* ISABELLA] Proceed.
ISABELLA   I went
  To this pernicious caitiff deputy—
DUKE   That's somewhat madly spoken.
ISABELLA   Pardon it;
  The phrase is to the matter.°   *appropriate*
90 DUKE   Mended again.
  The matter; proceed.
ISABELLA   In brief, to set the needless process by,[6]
  How I persuaded, how I prayed and kneeled,
  How he refelled° me, and how I replied—   *repelled*
95 For this was of much length—the vile conclusion
  I now begin with grief and shame to utter.
  He would not, but by gift of my chaste body
  To his concupiscible° intemperate lust,   *desirous*
  Release my brother; and after much debatement,
100 My sisterly remorse confutes° mine honour,   *overcomes*
  And I did yield to him. But the next morn betimes,
  His purpose surfeiting,° he sends a warrant   *satisfied*
  For my poor brother's head.
DUKE   This is most likely!
ISABELLA   O, that it were as like° as it is true!   *probable*
105 DUKE   By heaven, fond° wretch, thou knows't not what thou speak'st,   *foolish*
  Or else thou art suborned against his honour
  In hateful practice.° First, his integrity   *conspiracy*
  Stands without blemish. Next, it imports no reason°   *makes no sense*
  That with such vehemency he should pursue
110 Faults proper° to himself. If he had so offended,   *belonging*
  He would have weighed thy brother by himself,
  And not have cut him off. Someone hath set you on.°   *incited you*
  Confess the truth, and say by whose advice
  Thou cam'st here to complain.
ISABELLA   And is this all?
115 Then, O you blessèd ministers° above,   *angels*
  Keep me in patience, and with ripened time
  Unfold the evil which is here wrapped up
  In countenance![7] Heaven shield your grace from woe,
  As I, thus wronged, hence unbelievèd go.
120 DUKE   I know you'd fain be gone. An officer!
  To prison with her.
            [*An officer guards* ISABELLA]
                    Shall we thus permit

---

5. That is, for arrest, punning on the verb in line 83.   7. In false appearance; in royal favor.
6. To skip unnecessary parts of the story.

A blasting° and a scandalous breath to fall   *blighting*
On him so near us? This needs must be a practice.°   *conspiracy*
Who knew of your intent and coming hither?

125 ISABELLA   One that I would were here, Friar Lodowick.[8]

[*Exit, guarded*]

DUKE   A ghostly father, belike. Who knows that Lodowick?

LUCIO   My lord, I know him. 'Tis a meddling friar;
I do not like the man. Had he been lay, my lord,
For certain words he spake against your grace

130 In your retirement, I had swinged° him soundly.   *beat*

DUKE   Words against me? This'° a good friar, belike!   *This is*
And to set on this wretched woman here
Against our substitute! Let this friar be found.

[*Exit one or more*]

LUCIO   But yesternight, my lord, she and that friar,

135 I saw them at the prison. A saucy friar,
A very scurvy fellow.

FRIAR PETER   Blessed be your royal grace!
I have stood by, my lord, and I have heard
Your royal ear abused. First hath this woman
Most wrongfully accused your substitute,

140 Who is as free from touch or soil with her
As she from one ungot.°   *not yet begotten*

DUKE   We did believe no less.
Know you that Friar Lodowick that she speaks of?

FRIAR PETER   I know him for a man divine and holy,
Not scurvy, nor a temporary meddler,[9]

145 As he's reported by this gentleman;
And, on my trust, a man that never yet
Did, as he vouches,° misreport your grace.   *asserts*

LUCIO   My lord, most villainously; believe it.

FRIAR PETER   Well, he in time may come to clear himself;

150 But at this instant he is sick, my lord,
Of a strange fever. Upon his mere° request,   *Solely at his*
Being come to knowledge that there was complaint
Intended 'gainst Lord Angelo, came I hither
To speak, as from his mouth, what he doth know

155 Is true and false, and what he with his oath
And all probation° will make up full clear   *proof*
Whensoever he's convented.° First, for this woman: *summoned*
To justify° this worthy nobleman,   *vindicate*
So vulgarly and personally accused,

160 Her shall you hear disprovèd to her eyes,
Till she herself confess it.

DUKE   Good friar, let's hear it.

[*Exit* FRIAR PETER]

Do you not smile at this, Lord Angelo?
O heaven, the vanity of wretched fools!
Give us some seats.

[*Seats are brought in*]
          Come, cousin Angelo,

---

8. Evidently the Duke's name when in disguise.   9. Meddler in temporal matters.

165   In this I'll be impartial; be you judge
       Of your own cause.[1]
                    [*The* DUKE *and* ANGELO *sit*]
                Enter [FRIAR PETER *and*] MARIANA [*veiled*]
                    Is this the witness, friar?
       First let her show her face, and after speak.
MARIANA   Pardon, my lord, I will not show my face
       Until my husband bid me.
170 DUKE   What, are you married?
MARIANA   No, my lord.
DUKE   Are you a maid?°   *unmarried woman; virgin*
MARIANA   No, my lord.
DUKE   A widow then?
175 MARIANA   Neither, my lord.
DUKE   Why, you are nothing then; neither maid, widow, nor wife!
LUCIO   My lord, she may be a punk,° for many of them are nei-   *prostitute*
       ther maid, widow, nor wife.
DUKE   Silence that fellow. I would° he had some cause to prattle   *wish*
180   for himself.°   *(in his own defense)*
LUCIO   Well, my lord.
MARIANA   My lord, I do confess I ne'er was married,
       And I confess besides, I am no maid.
       I have known[2] my husband, yet my husband
185   Knows not that ever he knew me.
LUCIO   He was drunk then, my lord, it can be no better.
DUKE   For the benefit of silence, would thou wert so too.
LUCIO   Well, my lord.
DUKE   This is no witness for Lord Angelo.
190 MARIANA   Now I come to't, my lord.
       She that accuses him of fornication
       In self-same manner doth accuse my husband,
       And charges him, my lord, with such a time
       When I'll depose° I had him in mine arms   *testify*
195   With all th'effect° of love.   *manifestations*
ANGELO   Charges she more than me?
MARIANA   Not that I know.
DUKE   No? You say your husband.
MARIANA   Why just,° my lord, and that is Angelo,   *just so*
       Who thinks he knows that he ne'er knew my body,
       But knows, he thinks, that he knows Isabel's.
200 ANGELO   This is a strange abuse.° Let's see thy face.   *imposture*
MARIANA [*unveiling*]   My husband bids me; now I will unmask.
       This is that face, thou cruel Angelo,
       Which once thou swor'st was worth the looking on.
       This is the hand which, with a vowed contract,
205   Was fast belocked in thine. This is the body
       That took away the match° from Isabel,   *assignation*
       And did supply° thee at thy garden-house   *satisfy*
       In her imagined person.
DUKE [*to* ANGELO]   Know you this woman?
210 LUCIO   Carnally, she says.
DUKE   Sirrah, no more!

---

1. Ironically recalling the principle that no one ought   2. Had sexual intercourse with.
to judge his or her own cause.

LUCIO   Enough, my lord.

ANGELO   My lord, I must confess I know this woman;

And five years since there was some speech of marriage

215 Betwixt myself and her, which was broke off,

Partly for that her promisèd proportions°   *dowry*

Came short of composition,° but in chief   *the agreed sum*

For that her reputation was disvalued°   *discredited*

In levity;° since which time of five years   *For wantonness*

220 I never spake with her, saw her, nor heard from her,

Upon my faith and honour.

MARIANA [*kneeling before the* DUKE]   Noble prince,

As there comes light from heaven, and words from breath,

As there is sense° in truth, and truth in virtue,   *significance*

I am affianced this man's wife, as strongly

225 As words could make up vows. And, my good lord,

But Tuesday night last gone, in's garden-house,

He knew me as a wife. As this is true,

Let me in safety raise me from my knees,

Or else forever be confixèd° here,   *fixed firmly*

A marble monument.

230 ANGELO   I did but smile till now.

Now, good my lord, give me the scope° of justice.   *extent*

My patience here is touched.° I do perceive   *irritated*

These poor informal° women are no more   *disorderly*

But instruments° of some more mightier member°   *agents/power*

235 That sets them on. Let me have way, my lord,

To find this practice out.

DUKE [*standing*]   Ay, with my heart,

And punish them even to your height of pleasure.—

Thou foolish friar, and thou pernicious woman

Compact with° her that's gone, think'st thou thy oaths,   *In league with*

240 Though they would swear down each particular saint,

Were testimonies against his worth and credit

That's sealed in approbation?° You, Lord Escalus,   *ratified by proof*

Sit with my cousin; lend him your kind pains

To find out this abuse, whence 'tis derived.

245 There is another friar that set them on.

Let him be sent for.

[ESCALUS *sits*]

FRIAR PETER   Would he were here, my lord, for he indeed

Hath set the women on to this complaint.

Your Provost knows the place where he abides,

And he may fetch him.

250 DUKE [*to one or more*]   Go, do it instantly.   [*Exit one or more*]

[*To* ANGELO] And you, my noble and well-warranted cousin,

Whom it concerns to hear this matter forth,°   *out*

Do with your injuries as seems you best

In any chastisement. I for a while will leave you,

255 But stir not you till you have well determined°   *passed judgment*

Upon these slanderers.

ESCALUS   My lord, we'll do it throughly.°   *thoroughly*

Exit [DUKE]

Signor Lucio, did not you say you knew that Friar Lodowick to

be a dishonest person?

LUCIO   *Cucullus non facit monachum:*[3] honest in nothing but in
260   his clothes; and one that hath spoke most villainous speeches
         of the Duke.

ESCALUS   We shall entreat you to abide here till he come, and
         enforce° them against him. We shall find this friar a notable   urge
         fellow.

265 LUCIO   As any in Vienna, on my word.

ESCALUS   Call that same Isabel here once again; I would speak
         with her.   [*Exit one or more*]
         [*To* ANGELO] Pray you, my lord, give me leave to question. You
         shall see how I'll handle her.

270 LUCIO   Not better than he, by her own report.

ESCALUS   Say you?

LUCIO   Marry, sir, I think if you handled her privately, she would
         sooner confess; perchance publicly she'll be ashamed.

ESCALUS   I will go darkly° to work with her.   privately; soberly

275 LUCIO   That's the way, for women are light[4] at midnight.
                        Enter ISABELLA [*guarded*]

ESCALUS [*to* ISABELLA]   Come on, mistress, here's a gentle-
         woman denies all that you have said.
                Enter DUKE [*disguised as a friar, hooded, and*] PROVOST

LUCIO   My lord, here comes the rascal I spoke of, here with the
         Provost.

280 ESCALUS   In very good time. Speak not you to him till we call
         upon you.

LUCIO   Mum.

ESCALUS [*to the* DUKE]   Come, sir, did you set these women on
         to slander Lord Angelo? They have confessed you did.

285 DUKE   'Tis false.

ESCALUS   How! Know you where you are?

DUKE   Respect to your great place, and let the devil
         Be sometime honoured fore his burning throne.[5]
         Where is the Duke? 'Tis he should hear me speak.

290 ESCALUS   The Duke's in° us, and we will hear you speak.   power is vested in
         Look you speak justly.°   accurately

DUKE   Boldly at least.
         [*To* ISABELLA *and* MARIANA]   But O, poor souls,
         Come you to seek the lamb here of the fox,
         Good night to your redress! Is the Duke gone?
         Then is your cause gone too. The Duke's unjust
295   Thus to retort° your manifest appeal,°   cast back / accusation
         And put your trial in the villain's mouth
         Which here you come to accuse.

LUCIO   This is the rascal, this is he I spoke of.

ESCALUS   Why, thou unreverend and unhallowed° friar,   impious
300   Is't not enough thou hast suborned these women
         To accuse this worthy man but, in foul mouth,
         And in the witness of his proper° ear,   own
         To call him villain, and then to glance° from him   ricochet
         To th' Duke himself, to tax° him with injustice?   reproach

---

3. The hood does not make the monk (proverbial).
4. Licentious; exploiting the unintentional sexual suggestion of Escalus's "go darkly to work."

5. *let . . . throne:* that is, the devil, too, seated on his
throne in hell, seems a figure of honor. *fore:* before.

305   Take him hence; to th' rack with him. We'll touse° you   *tear*
      Joint by joint—but we will know his[6] purpose.
      What, 'unjust'?

DUKE   Be not so hot. The Duke
      Dare no more stretch this finger of mine than he
      Dare rack his own. His subject am I not,
310   Nor here provincial.[7] My business in this state
      Made me a looker-on here in Vienna,
      Where I have seen corruption boil and bubble
      Till it o'errun the stew;° laws for all faults,   *cauldron; brothel*
      But faults so countenanced that the strong statutes
315   Stand like the forfeits[8] in a barber's shop,
      As much in mock as mark.

ESCALUS   Slander to th' state!
      Away with him to prison.

ANGELO   What can you vouch against him, Signor Lucio?
320   Is this the man that you did tell us of?

LUCIO   'Tis he, my lord.—Come hither, goodman Bald-pate.[9]
      Do you know me?

DUKE   I remember you, sir, by the sound of your voice.[1] I met
      you at the prison, in the absence of the Duke.

325   LUCIO   O, did you so? And do you remember what you said of
      the Duke?

DUKE   Most notedly, sir.

LUCIO   Do you so, sir? And was the Duke a fleshmonger,° a fool,   *whoremaster*
      and a coward, as you then reported him to be?

330   DUKE   You must, sir, change persons with me ere you make that
      my report. You indeed spoke so of him, and much more, much
      worse.

LUCIO   O, thou damnable fellow! Did not I pluck thee by the
      nose° for thy speeches?   *(gesture of contempt)*

335   DUKE   I protest I love the Duke as I love myself.

ANGELO   Hark how the villain would close[2] now, after his trea-
      sonable abuses.

ESCALUS   Such a fellow is not to be talked withal. Away with him
      to prison. Where is the Provost? Away with him to prison. Lay
340   bolts° enough upon him. Let him speak no more. Away with   *fetters*
      those giglets° too, and with the other confederate companion.[3]   *strumpets*
            [MARIANA *is raised to her feet, and is guarded.*
            The PROVOST *makes to seize the* DUKE]

DUKE   Stay, sir, stay a while.

ANGELO   What, resists he? Help him, Lucio.

LUCIO [*to the* DUKE]   Come, sir; come, sir; come, sir! Foh,° sir!   *(expression of disgust)*
345   Why, you bald-pated lying rascal, you must be hooded, must
      you? Show your knave's visage, with a pox to you! Show your
      sheep-biting face,[4] and be hanged an hour![5] Will't not off?
            [*He pulls off the friar's hood, and discovers the* DUKE.
            ANGELO *and* ESCALUS *rise*]

---

6. The friar's; the confusion of pronouns suggests Escalus's fury.
7. Subject to local ecclesiastical authorities.
8. Jocular list of penalties for minor infractions.
9. Mr. Bald-head: "goodman" was a form of address for
a man below the rank of gentleman; friars shaved their
heads.
1. The friar's hood presumably covers his face so that he

cannot see Lucio.
2. Conclude; hide himself; come to a settlement.
3. Fellow (contemptuous).
4. Like the wolf in sheep's clothing.
5. Jocular way of saying "be hanged." Animals were
sometimes executed like human beings for destroying life
or property.

DUKE   Thou art the first knave that e'er madest a duke.
    First, Provost, let me bail these gentle three.
350   [*To* LUCIO] Sneak not away, sir, for the friar and you
    Must have a word anon. [*To one or more*] Lay hold on him.
LUCIO   This may prove worse than hanging.
DUKE [*to* ESCALUS] What you have spoke, I pardon. Sit you down.
    We'll borrow place° of him.   *seat; office*
    [ESCALUS *sits*]
    [*To* ANGELO]   Sir, by your leave.
    [*He takes Angelo's seat*]
355 Hast thou or° word or wit or impudence   *either*
    That yet can do thee office?° If thou hast,   *service*
    Rely upon it till my tale be heard,
    And hold no longer out.
ANGELO   O my dread lord,
    I should be guiltier than my guiltiness
360 To think I can be undiscernible,
    When I perceive your grace, like power divine,
    Hath looked upon my passes.[6] Then, good prince,
    No longer session° hold upon my shame,   *inquiry*
    But let my trial be mine own confession.
365 Immediate sentence then, and sequent° death, *thereafter*
    Is all the grace I beg.
DUKE   Come hither, Mariana.
    [*To* ANGELO] Say, wast thou e'er contracted to this woman?
ANGELO   I was, my lord.
DUKE   Go, take her hence and marry her instantly.
370 Do you the office, friar; which consummate,°   *finished*
    Return him here again. Go with him, Provost.
        Exeunt [ANGELO, MARIANA, FRIAR PETER, *and the* PROVOST]
ESCALUS   My lord, I am more amazed at his dishonour
    Than at the strangeness of it.°   *(the situation)*
DUKE   Come hither, Isabel.
    Your friar is now your prince. As I was then
375 Advertising° and holy to your business,   *Attentive*
    Not changing heart with habit I am still
    Attorneyed° at your service.   *Engaged as advocate*
ISABELLA   O, give me pardon,
    That I, your vassal, have employed and pained° *troubled*
    Your unknown sovereignty.
DUKE   You are pardoned, Isabel.
380 And now, dear maid, be you as free° to us.   *generous*
    Your brother's death I know sits at your heart,
    And you may marvel why I obscured myself,
    Labouring to save his life, and would not rather
    Make rash remonstrance° of my hidden power *demonstration*
385 Than let him so be lost. O most kind maid,
    It was the swift celerity of his death,
    Which I did think with slower foot came on,
    That brained° my purpose. But peace be with him! *killed*
    That life is better life, past fearing death,
390 Than that which lives to fear. Make it your comfort,
    So happy is your brother.

---

6. Actions, trespasses; recalling Job 34:21: "For his eyes are upon the ways of man, and he seeth all his goings."

ISABELLA   I do, my lord.

          Enter ANGELO, MARIANA, [FRIAR] PETER, [*and*] PROVOST

DUKE   For this new-married man approaching here,

    Whose salt° imagination yet hath wronged   *salacious*

    Your well-defended honour, you must pardon

395   For Mariana's sake; but as he adjudged° your brother—   *condemned*

    Being criminal in double violation

    Of sacred chastity and of promise-breach,

    Thereon dependent, for your brother's life—

    The very mercy° of the law cries out   *Even the merciful aspect*

400   Most audible, even from his proper° tongue,   *its own*

    'An Angelo for Claudio, death for death'.

    Haste still° pays haste, and leisure° answers leisure;   *always / deliberation*

    Like doth quit° like, and measure still for measure.   *requite*

    Then, Angelo, thy fault's thus manifested,

405   Which, though° thou wouldst deny, denies thee vantage.°   *even if / (i.e., clemency)*

    We do condemn thee to the very block

    Where Claudio stooped to death, and with like haste.

    Away with him.

MARIANA   O my most gracious lord,

    I hope you will not mock me with a husband!

410 DUKE   It is your husband mocked you with a husband.

    Consenting to the safeguard of your honour,

    I thought your marriage fit; else imputation,°   *censure*

    For that he knew you, might reproach your life,

    And choke your good to come.° For his possessions,   *ruin your prospects*

415 Although by confiscation they are ours,[7]

    We do enstate and widow you° with all,   *give you widow's rights*

    To buy you a better husband.

MARIANA   O my dear lord,

    I crave no other, nor no better man.

DUKE   Never crave him; we are definitive.°   *resolute*

MARIANA   Gentle my liege—

420 DUKE   You do but lose your labour.—

    Away with him to death. [*To* LUCIO] Now, sir, to you.

MARIANA [*kneeling*]   O my good lord!—Sweet Isabel, take my part;

    Lend me your knees, and all my life to come

    I'll lend you all my life to do you service.

425 DUKE   Against all sense you do importune her.

    Should she kneel down in mercy of this fact,°   *crime*

    Her brother's ghost his pavèd bed° would break,   *stone-covered grave*

    And take her hence in horror.

MARIANA   Isabel,

    Sweet Isabel, do yet but kneel by me.

430 Hold up your hands; say nothing; I'll speak all.

    They say best men are moulded out of faults,

    And, for the most,° become much more the better   *most part*

    For being a little bad. So may my husband.

    O Isabel, will you not lend a knee?

DUKE   He dies for Claudio's death.

435 ISABELLA [*kneeling*]   Most bounteous sir,

    Look, if it please you, on this man condemned

    As if my brother lived. I partly think

---

7. Because a felon's property was forfeit to the crown.

A due sincerity governed his deeds,
Till he did look on me. Since it is so,
440 Let him not die. My brother had but justice,
In that he did the thing for which he died.
For Angelo,
His act did not o'ertake his bad intent,
And must be buried° but as an intent   (*i.e., forgotten*)
445 That perished by the way. Thoughts are no subjects,[8]
Intents but merely thoughts.
MARIANA   Merely, my lord.
DUKE   Your suit's unprofitable. Stand up, I say.
          [MARIANA *and* ISABELLA *stand*]
I have bethought me of another fault.
Provost, how came it Claudio was beheaded
At an unusual hour?
450 PROVOST   It was commanded so.
DUKE   Had you a special warrant for the deed?
PROVOST   No, my good lord, it was by private message.
DUKE   For which I do discharge you of your office.
Give up your keys.
PROVOST   Pardon me, noble lord.
455 I thought it was a fault, but knew it not,
Yet did repent me after more advice;°   *deliberation*
For° testimony whereof one in the prison   *As*
That should by private order else° have died   *otherwise*
I have reserved alive.
460 DUKE   What's he?
PROVOST   His name is Barnardine.
DUKE   I would thou hadst done so by Claudio.
Go fetch him hither. Let me look upon him.   [*Exit* PROVOST]
ESCALUS   I am sorry one so learned and so wise
465 As you, Lord Angelo, have still° appeared,   *always*
Should slip so grossly, both in the heat of blood
And lack of tempered judgement afterward.
ANGELO   I am sorry that such sorrow I procure,°   *cause*
And so deep sticks it in my penitent heart
470 That I crave death more willingly than mercy.
'Tis my deserving, and I do entreat it.
          Enter BARNARDINE *and* PROVOST; CLAUDIO, [*muffled,*°   *with his face wrapped*
          and] JULIET
DUKE   Which is that Barnardine?
PROVOST   This, my lord.
DUKE   There was a friar told me of this man.
[*To* BARNARDINE] Sirrah, thou art said to have a stubborn soul
475 That apprehends no further than this world,
And squar'st° thy life according. Thou'rt condemned;   *frames*
But, for those earthly faults,[9] I quit° them all,   *pardon*
And pray thee take this mercy to provide
For better times to come.—Friar, advise him.
480 I leave him to your hand. [*To* PROVOST] What muffled fellow's that?
PROVOST   This is another prisoner that I saved,
Who should have died when Claudio lost his head,
As like almost to Claudio as himself.

---

8. Thoughts are not subject to prosecution.   9. Offenses subject to earthly punishment.

[*He unmuffles* CLAUDIO]

DUKE [*to* ISABELLA]   If he be like your brother, for his sake

485 Is he pardoned; and for your lovely sake

Give me your hand, and say you will be mine.¹

He is my brother° too. But fitter time for that.   *(as a brother-in-law)*

By this Lord Angelo perceives he's safe.

Methinks I see a quick'ning in his eye.

490 Well, Angelo, your evil quits° you well.   *recompenses*

Look that you love your wife, her worth worth° yours.   *being equal to*

I find an apt remission° in myself;   *inclination to mercy*

And yet here's one in place° I cannot pardon.   *present*

[*To* LUCIO] You, sirrah, that knew me for a fool, a coward,

495 One all of luxury,° an ass, a madman,   *lasciviousness*

Wherein have I so deserved of you

That you extol me thus?

LUCIO   Faith, my lord, I spoke it but according to the trick.° If   *fashion*

you will hang me for it, you may; but I had rather it would

500 please you I might be whipped.

DUKE   Whipped first, sir, and hanged after.

Proclaim it, Provost, round about the city,

If any woman wronged by this lewd fellow,

As I have heard him swear himself there's one

505 Whom he begot with child, let her appear,

And he shall marry her. The nuptial finished,

Let him be whipped and hanged.

LUCIO   I beseech your highness, do not marry me to a whore.

Your highness said even now I made you a duke; good my lord,

510 do not recompense me in making me a cuckold.

DUKE   Upon mine honour, thou shalt marry her.

Thy slanders I forgive, and therewithal

Remit thy other forfeits.°—Take him to prison,   *punishments*

And see our pleasure herein executed.

515 LUCIO   Marrying a punk, my lord, is pressing to death,² whip-

ping, and hanging.

DUKE   Slandering a prince deserves it.   [*Exit* LUCIO *guarded*]

She, Claudio, that you wronged, look you restore.³

Joy to you, Mariana. Love her, Angelo.

520 I have confessed her,° and I know her virtue.   *been her confessor*

Thanks, good friend Escalus, for thy much goodness.

There's more behind° that is more gratulate.°   *to come / gratifying*

Thanks, Provost, for thy care and secrecy.

We shall employ thee in a worthier place.

525 Forgive him, Angelo, that brought you home

The head of Ragusine for Claudio's.

Th'offence pardons itself. Dear Isabel,

I have a motion° much imports your good,   *proposal*

Whereto, if you'll a willing ear incline,

530 What's mine is yours, and what is yours is mine.

[*To all*] So bring° us to our palace, where we'll show   *accompany*

What's yet behind that's meet you all should know.   [*Exeunt*]

---

1. It is not clear how Isabella responds to the Duke's pro-   2. Executing by crushing under heavy weights.
posal of marriage.   3. To her good name, by marrying her.

Additional Passages

The text of *Measure for Measure* given in this edition is probably that of an adapted version made for Shakespeare's company after his death. Adaptation seems to have affected two passages, printed below as the Oxford editors believe Shakespeare to have written them.

A. 1.2.0.1–104

The passage begins with seven lines that the adapter (believed to be Thomas Middleton) intended to be replaced by 1.2.52–71 of the play as printed here. The adapter must have contributed all of 1.2.0.1–74, which in the earliest and subsequent printed texts precede the discussion between the clown (Pompey) and the bawd (Mistress Overdone) about Claudio's arrest. Lucio's entry alone at line 36 below, some eleven lines after his reentry with the two Gentlemen and the Provost's party in the adapted text, probably represents Shakespeare's original intention. In his version, Juliet, present but silent in the adapted text both in 1.2 and 5.1, probably did not appear in either scene; accordingly, the words "and there's Madam Juliet" (1.2.95) must also be the reviser's work, and do not appear below.

Enter POMPEY *and* MISTRESS OVERDONE, *meeting*
MISTRESS OVERDONE   How now, what's the news with you?
POMPEY   Yonder man is carried to prison.
MISTRESS OVERDONE   Well! What has he done?
POMPEY   A woman.
5   MISTRESS OVERDONE   But what's his offence?
POMPEY   Groping for trouts[1] in a peculiar° river.   *private*
MISTRESS OVERDONE   What, is there a maid[2] with child by him?
POMPEY   No, but there's a woman with maid[3] by him: you have
    not heard of the proclamation, have you?
10   MISTRESS OVERDONE   What proclamation, man?
POMPEY   All houses in the suburbs of Vienna must be plucked down.
MISTRESS OVERDONE   And what shall become of those in the city?
POMPEY   They shall stand for seed. They had gone down too, but
    that a wise burgher put in for them.
15   MISTRESS OVERDONE   But shall all our houses of resort in the
    suburbs be pulled down?
POMPEY   To the ground, mistress.
MISTRESS OVERDONE   Why, here's a change indeed in the com-
    monwealth. What shall become of me?
20   POMPEY   Come, fear not you. Good counsellors lack no clients.
    Though you change your place, you need not change your
    trade. I'll be your tapster still. Courage, there will be pity taken
    on you. You that have worn your eyes almost out in the service,
    you will be considered.
      A noise within
25   MISTRESS OVERDONE   What's to do here, Thomas Tapster?
    Let's withdraw!
      Enter the PROVOST *and* CLAUDIO
POMPEY   Here comes Signor Claudio, led by the Provost to
    prison.   *Exeunt* MISTRESS OVERDONE *and* POMPEY
CLAUDIO   Fellow, why dost thou show me thus to th' world?
30   Bear me to prison, where I am committed.
PROVOST   I do it not in evil disposition,

---

1. Literally, a way of catching trout by tickling their bellies.
2. Young woman (but Pompey understands "virgin").
3. Pregnant with a baby girl.

But from Lord Angelo by special charge.

CLAUDIO   Thus can the demigod Authority
Make us pay down for our offence, by weight,
35   The bonds of heaven. On whom it will, it will;
On whom it will not, so; yet still 'tis just.

       Enter LUCIO

LUCIO   Why, how now, Claudio? Whence comes this restraint?

B. 3.1.479–4.1.65

Before revision, there would have been no act break and no song; the lines immediately
following the song would also have been absent. The Duke's soliloquies "He who the
sword of heaven will bear" and "O place and greatness" have evidently been transposed
in revision; in the original, the end of "O place and greatness" would have led straight
on to the Duke's meeting with Isabella and then Mariana.

ESCALUS   I am going to visit the prisoner. Fare you well.
DUKE   Peace be with you.   *Exit* ESCALUS
O place and greatness, millions of false eyes
Are stuck upon thee; volumes of report
5   Run with their false and most contrarious quest
Upon thy doings; thousand escapes of wit
Make thee the father of their idle dream,
And rack thee in their fancies.

       Enter ISABELLA

DUKE   Very well met.
What is the news from this good deputy?
10   ISABELLA   He hath a garden circummured with brick,
Whose western side is with a vineyard backed;
And to that vineyard is a planchèd gate,
That makes his opening with this bigger key.
This other doth command a little door
15   Which from the vineyard to the garden leads.
There have I made my promise
Upon the heavy middle of the night
To call upon him.
DUKE   But shall you on your knowledge find this way?
20   ISABELLA   I have ta'en a due and wary note upon't.
With whispering and most guilty diligence,
In action all of precept, he did show me
The way twice o'er.
DUKE   Are there no other tokens
Between you 'greed concerning her observance?
25   ISABELLA   No, none, but only a repair i'th' dark,
And that I have possessed him my most stay
Can be but brief, for I have made him know
I have a servant comes with me along
That stays upon me, whose persuasion is
I come about my brother.
30   DUKE   'Tis well borne up.
I have not yet made known to Mariana
A word of this.—What ho, within! Come forth!

       Enter MARIANA

[*To* MARIANA] I pray you be acquainted with this maid.
She comes to do you good.

ISABELLA   I do desire the like.

35   DUKE [to MARIANA]   Do you persuade yourself that I respect you?

MARIANA   Good friar, I know you do, and so have found it.

DUKE   Take then this your companion by the hand,
    Who hath a story ready for your ear.
    I shall attend your leisure; but make haste,
    The vaporous night approaches.

40   MARIANA   Will't please you walk aside.

    Exeunt MARIANA *and* ISABELLA

DUKE   He who the sword of heaven will bear
    Should be as holy as severe,
    Pattern in himself to know,
    Grace to stand, and virtue go,
45   More nor less to others paying
    Than by self-offences weighing.
    Shame to him whose cruel striking
    Kills for faults of his own liking!
    Twice treble shame on Angelo,
50   To weed my vice, and let his grow!
    O, what may man within him hide,
    Though angel on the outward side!
    How may likeness made in crimes
    Make my practice on the times
55   To draw with idle spiders' strings
    Most ponderous and substantial things?
    Craft against vice I must apply.
    With Angelo tonight shall lie
    His old betrothed but despisèd.
60   So disguise shall, by th' disguisèd,
    Pay with falsehood false exacting,
    And perform an old contracting.

    Enter MARIANA *and* ISABELLA

    Welcome. How agreed?

ISABELLA   She'll take the enterprise upon her, father,
65   If you advise it.

Othello

"The problem of the twentieth century is the problem of the color-line." So prophesied the African American intellectual and activist W. E. B. Du Bois in his classic study *The Souls of Black Folk* (1903) just as the century began. Du Bois's prediction may have been premature with respect to Shakespearean tragedy, where *Hamlet, King Lear,* and *Macbeth* continued to dominate critical attention throughout most of the twentieth century. But today, *Othello* (1602–03) speaks to readers and audiences alike with unusual power, largely because it explores race and racism in unsettling fashion. Does this emphasis, centered on the dark skin of the title character, belatedly recognize a crucial issue previously neglected or misconstrued? Alternatively, does the recent preoccupation with race impose contemporary concerns on material with a different orientation?

Yes, to both questions. Interpretation is always influenced by both past and present—here by the play itself, together with its theatrical and critical heritage, and by the current preoccupations of contemporary audiences and readers. A complex work elicits different responses in different times or places: in *Othello*, to oversimplify, one issue (jealousy) was formerly more prominent, while another (race) has emerged—or reemerged—only recently. Neither race nor jealousy is the play's sole concern. *Othello* provocatively investigates gender and sexuality. It is preoccupied with class conflict, morality, and metaphysics. And it sets its central domestic disaster against the international conflict between Venetians and Turks over the island of Cyprus—a religious, political, and military antagonism that subtly informs the characters' catastrophic personal relationships.

This thematic range can be investigated by looking at Shakespeare's handling of his sources, at his unusual manipulation of dramatic genres and, hence, of audience expectations, at the psychology of Iago and Othello as well as their interaction, and, finally, at race itself. Much of *Othello*'s plot—but little of its outlook, characterization, or language—derives from Giovanbattista Giraldi Cinthio's *De gli hecatommithi* ("Hundred Tales," third decade, seventh story, 1565). In Shakespeare's version, racial issues are more persistent. The play here draws primarily on the 1600 translation of *A Geographical Historie of Africa* by Leo Africanus, a Moroccan Muslim who had been captured by Christian pirates and brought to Rome, where he converted to Catholicism. The public world of Venetian-Turkish affairs, absent from Cinthio, probably derives from Richard Knolles's *Generall Historie of the Turkes* (1603). Minor characters are given interesting twists. For instance, Emilia, the wife of Iago, the story's villain, is passive in Cinthio but in Shakespeare speaks for the rights of women, stands by Desdemona, Othello's wife, and ultimately brings her own husband down—at the cost of her life. The changes to Iago and Othello are even more consequential. Unlike *De gli hecatommithi*'s malefactor, who is motivated by unrequited lust for Desdemona and anger that she has refused his advances, Shakespeare's Iago loathes Othello and is determined to destroy him. His manipulative mastery is given greater scope, thereby enhancing a sense of his power as well as his fathomless viciousness. Similarly, by making Othello Desdemona's killer (Iago's job in Cinthio) and by having him publicly acknowledge his responsibility for the act, Shakespeare increases the character's guilt as well as his grandeur—the latter further enhanced by an elevation in social status from his position in the source. Thus *Othello*, unlike *De gli hecatommithi*, ties everything to the central murder.

The manipulation of generic expectations in *Othello* produces multiple perspectives on the plot. Though familiar with the classical dramatic genres of comedy and tragedy, Shakespeare was also influenced by late medieval–early Renaissance morality plays and

Two views of "the Moor" (one Arab or Berber, the other sub-Saharan), suggesting the range of images Shakespeare may have had in mind. Left: the Moroccan ambassador to Queen Elizabeth I (1600); right: "a Moor," from Cesare Vecellio, *De gli habiti antichi et moderni* (1590).

by Renaissance experimentation with hybrid forms. Hence, all of his plays are mixtures. The distinctiveness of *Othello,* however, lies not in the copresence of comic and tragic elements—a common feature in Shakespearean drama—but in the work's daring experiments with shifting generic frameworks. Its opening act, probably Shakespeare's invention, employs a strategy of studied indirection. It is night in a city—Venice, we are later told (1.1.107). Plot and character are presented in nonspecific terms: Roderigo is irritated that Iago "shouldst know of this," "of such a matter"—a matter concerning a "him" (1.1.3, 5, 6), an unnamed personage invoked only by pronouns until the snide reference to "his Moorship" (1.1.32). The play's first audiences might have connected this character with the titular figure, even though Othello himself does not appear on stage until scene 2 and is not named until scene 3. Iago tells Roderigo to "call up her father" (1.1.67), again without identifying "her" or "her father." The two men provoke Brabanzio, "her father," in similarly oblique fashion, only gradually revealing that Roderigo's "this" is a sexual relationship and, still later, that it is a marriage. Their imprecision about "this" encourages the audience to wonder what kind of play they are watching. It turns out to be a romantic comedy. Iago and Roderigo's strategy is aimed at persuading Brabanzio to nullify the union. They do get Brabanzio's aid, but they do not get what they want. Against the cultural norms of Shakespeare's time and subsequent centuries, the play celebrates Othello's grandeur, Desdemona's assertive autonomy (she wooed him), and the result—marriage between Moor and Venetian, old and young, black and white. The initial suppression of the names of the lovers renders them as character types to which stylized attributes, however misleading, can be attached before their individuality emerges. The darkness and the urban setting point to romantic concerns. The villain's machinations fail; the opposition of the old father, a standard blocking figure in stage comedy, proves ineffectual; the Duke, the play's highest ranking character, ratifies the marriage. It has all been so easy. Midway through the third scene, the story is over.

Except, of course, that it isn't. A new obstacle to marital bliss has arisen—the Turk-ish fleet's threat to Cyprus. The Venetian Senate dispatches Othello there to defend the interests of the state. To these vicissitudes of war the play adds the trial of separation. Although Desdemona will join Othello, she travels separately—with Iago. Before Venetian ships reach Cyprus, however, a storm destroys the Turkish armada. But by removing one danger, the storm creates two others. Will Desdemona be safe at sea? Will Othello? Romantic comedy has modulated into romance in the manner of late antique Greek and Roman prose fiction: faithful lovers, separated by storms, must undergo pro-longed suffering before their final reunion. But Desdemona soon arrives unharmed; Othello promptly follows. By early in the second act, the play has apparently resolved issues of race and ethnicity, love and sexuality, religious and military hostilities. But less than halfway through the play, romantic comedy and romance both give way to domes-tic tragedy, a popular dramatic form of the time, usually set in England, in which female marital infidelity leads to disaster. Since there is no adultery, however, this third generic movement does not automatically occur. Iago must fabricate pretexts for Othello's sex-ual jealousy, a sensibility often associated on the Renaissance English stage with mod-ern Italy and the Mediterranean. Accordingly, as we'll later see, neither comedy nor romance is ever definitively rejected.

These multiple formal perspectives—comedy, romance, domestic tragedy—help generate a correspondingly complex treatment of the characters and their interaction. The play begins with Iago. We quickly learn that "his Moorship," presumably a for-eigner to Venice, has chosen as his lieutenant Cassio, an unproven gentleman from Florence and, hence, also a foreigner of sorts. Iago, the battle-tested, homegrown common soldier, deeply resents the slight. Out for himself and passed over for promo-tion, Iago is a young man on the make driven by class, regional, and ethnic resentment and willing to use others as means to his ends. Moreover, he has no illusions about those means. For instance, he anticipates that Brabanzio's opposition to his daughter's marriage will fail because of Othello's military importance to Venice (1.1.145–160). But Iago is more than a cool calculator; he is also tortured by a superheated sexual jeal-ousy. Although he lacks any evidence, he believes that Othello has become Emilia's lover. He invents the sexual liaison between Cassio and Desdemona in order to sup-plant Cassio as lieutenant and make Othello jealous, arguing to himself that the charge of adultery he knows he has simply made up is actually real. Here, perhaps, we glimpse Iago's own sexual anxieties. Thus, he acknowledges his lust for Desdemona, explaining, however, that it is motivated by a desire to do to Othello what he assumes Othello has already done to him. And he converts his careerist resentment of Cassio into a fear that Cassio, too, will become Emilia's lover (2.1.273–299).

Furthermore, Iago enjoys the sport of ruining Othello's life. In this respect, he descends from a key figure of the earlier English morality plays—the Vice, a semisec-ularized devil who employs his comic verve to try to destroy his virtuous antagonists and whose colloquial intimacy with the audience often half-succeeds in winning that audi-ence over. His diabolism is emphasized throughout the play. As he explains,

> When devils will the blackest sins put on,
> They do suggest at first with heavenly shows,
> As I do now.
>
> (2.3.325–27)

Similarly, Othello concludes:

> OTHELLO I look down towards his feet, but that's a fable.
> [*To* IAGO] If that thou beest a devil I cannot kill thee.
> [*He wounds* IAGO]
> . . . .
> IAGO   I bleed, sir, but not killed.
>
> (5.2.292–94)

The "fable" is that the devil's feet are cloven hooves. If Iago is the devil, he cannot die, a point he mockingly makes by insisting he is "not killed."

For more than a century, *Othello* in performance has often been Iago's show, partly because he wittily speaks to—not just before—the audience. Iago is also extremely talkative, uttering two hundred more lines than Othello himself—indeed, more than any other Shakespearean character except Hamlet. Thus, he potentially dominates a play that deploys the smallest cast in Shakespearean tragedy and that, after the first act, conforms to the Aristotelian unities of time, place, and action that Shakespeare normally ignores. As a matter of fact, his prominence has proven a recurrent problem, since it runs the risk of belittling Othello.

On the other hand, Iago's various motives help the play offer multiple accounts of Othello as well. Why does Othello move from nobly loving husband to insanely jealous murderer? If Iago is driven by resentment and jealousy, Othello is a savage fool. But if Iago is devilish, the play acquires a religious cast. Othello's soul hangs in the balance; in repudiating his good "angel" (5.2.140) and succumbing to temptation, he reenacts the fall. Faced with a supernatural adversary, Othello is less culpable. Hence, the longstanding debate about the protagonist's character cannot be resolved: Othello is noble victim and barbaric dupe.

Indeed, the disastrous outcome partly results from Iago's ability to turn Desdemona's and Othello's very nobility against them. Desdemona's bold, generous spirit becomes evidence of her affair with Cassio. Othello's "free and open nature" enables him to "be led by th' nose" (1.3.381, 383). Iago can also count on Othello's military resoluteness. Before Othello becomes jealous, he has staked everything on Desdemona: "My life upon her faith" (1.3.293). His grief at Desdemona's supposed betrayal, combining the martial and the marital, is at first moving in its stately repetitions:

> Farewell the tranquil mind, farewell content,
> Farewell the plumèd troops and the big wars
> That makes ambition virtue! O, farewell,
> Farewell the neighing steed and the shrill trump.
> (3.3.353–56)

But as Othello's psyche breaks down, incoherent prose supplants measured verse: "Handkerchief—confessions—handkerchief. . . . Pish! Noses, ears, and lips! Is't possible? Confess? Handkerchief? O devil! *He falls down in a trance*" (4.1.36–41, s.d.).

Put another way, Othello is out of his element. A soldier since childhood, he knows little of peacetime urban existence. He should feel at home on Cyprus, a military prize. But when the Turkish threat dissipates, the island becomes the typical other world of Shakespearean drama, where all characters are displaced and fundamental change occurs. In particular, Cyprus's ancient association with sexual license emerges. Although this seems antithetical to republican Venice's sobriety, we come to suspect that Venice is no better. As a result, Othello is more vulnerable to Iago's influence than he would be on the battlefield. He accepts narratives about himself and Desdemona composed from the repugnant sexual—and especially misogynist—stereotypes of European society that also torment Iago. Brabanzio warns Othello: "She has deceived her father, and may thee" (1.3.292). Iago retrieves the thought:

> IAGO She did deceive her father, marrying you.
> . . . .
> OTHELLO   And so she did.
> (3.3.210–12)

As Iago's thinking has revealed, sexual guilt need be merely plausible. "'Tis probable, and palpable to thinking," Brabanzio argues, that Othello used magic on Desdemona (1.2.77). The Duke rejects mere assertion and "poor likelihoods" (1.3.108). But Iago gets away with "imputation, and strong circumstances" (3.3.411) rather than "ocular proof" (3.3.365), because Othello cannot challenge Iago's cynical view of sexuality:

"In Venice they do let God see the pranks / They dare not show their husbands" (3.3.206–07). Hence, Iago's description of Cassio and Desdemona in the play's recurrent animal imagery—"as prime as goats, as hot as monkeys" (3.3.408)—returns in Othello's "Goats and monkeys!" (4.1.260). This outcome seems to depend, however, on Iago's ability to elicit Othello's own sexual anxieties.

The sexual loathing Othello reveals here may also be inspired by Desdemona's directness:

> That I did love the Moor to live with him,
> My downright violence and storm of fortunes
> May trumpet to the world.
>
> (1.3.247–49)

Othello registers the allure and the threat of such erotic boldness when he and Desdemona are reunited on Cyprus: "If it were now to die / 'Twere now to be most happy," where "to die" also means to have an orgasm (2.1.186–87). Christian doctrine sometimes considered excessive marital sexual pleasure a form of adultery. Earlier, Iago plots "after some time to abuse Othello's ears / That he is too familiar with his wife" (1.3.377–78). "He" is presumably Cassio, to whom Iago has recently referred. But the nearer mention of Othello and the pronoun confusion—since "his" must refer to Othello—suggest that Othello experiences his own sexual desire as adulterous, that following sexual consummation of his marriage (if that actually occurs) he projects this desire onto Cassio, and that he punishes his sexual feelings by killing Desdemona.

Not surprisingly, the conclusion also encourages an ambivalent view of Othello. Shakespeare emphasizes Desdemona's innocent victimization by dramatizing her obedience to her husband.

> DESDEMONA O, falsely, falsely murdered!
> . . . .
> A guiltless death I die.
> EMILIA   O, who hath done this deed?
> DESDEMONA Nobody, I myself. Farewell.
> Commend me to my kind lord. O, farewell!
>
> (5.2.126–34)

A loyally subordinate Desdemona is more conventionally reassuring than the Desdemona who flouted convention to marry Othello. This diminution of female autonomy retreats from Desdemona's bolder position early in the play, which is itself echoed by Emilia's brave, principled defiance at the end. Yet Desdemona's final words may indicate a masochistic submissiveness as unsettling as her previous behavior or perhaps, taken from a Christian perspective, a paradox—the simultaneous assertion of suicide (a mortal sin) and guiltlessness. Her words also increase Othello's guilt and underscore the mistreatment of women that we see as well in both Iago's relationship with Emilia and Cassio's with Bianca, the courtesan who loves him.

Othello himself believes he is administering secular justice or performing a religious ritual in killing Desdemona. But his rage forces him to "call what I intend to do / A murder, which I thought a sacrifice" (5.2.69–70). Confronted with Desdemona's innocence, he assumes the same role—this time, however, executing himself. But suicide evokes Christian despair and certainty of damnation as well as disinterested justice and ancient Stoic heroism. Similarly, one may disagree with Othello's conviction that he is "an honourable murderer," "one not easily jealous" (5.2.300, 354).

The persistence of a comic outlook further complicates our judgment. As in Shakespeare's earlier romantic comedy *Much Ado About Nothing* (1598), information sufficient to unmask the villain's slandering of female sexual propriety has always been available. Further, Othello speculates that Desdemona's infidelity arises because "I am declined / Into the vale of years" (3.3.269–70), thereby invoking farce's standard cuckolding of old man by young woman, of January by May. Similarly, Emilia oxymoronically calls Othello a "murderous coxcomb" (fool) and asks a familiar comic question: "What should such a fool / Do with so good a wife?" (5.2.240–41). The play then concludes by literalizing the metaphorical destination of romantic comedy—the marriage bed, here present in grimly parodic form.

A pervasive association between sex and death also promotes ambivalence. The fatal "napkin," or handkerchief, indicative of aristocratic privilege but important because of its very triviality, symbolically captures these feelings. Presented, according to Othello, to his mother by "an Egyptian . . . charmer," the handkerchief combines the magic and ethnic exoticism Othello earlier repudiates in defending his marriage to Desdemona. It enabled his mother to "subdue my father / Entirely to her love" (3.4.57–58). Or perhaps not. Othello ultimately offers a more prosaic account: "It was a handkerchief, an antique token / My father gave my mother" (5.2.223–24). "Spotted with strawberries" (3.3.440), it may evoke the blood Desdemona loses with her virginity on the marriage bed. Desdemona has Emilia "lay on my bed my wedding sheets" (4.2.108); Othello anticipates that "thy bed, lust-stained, shall with lust's blood be spotted" (5.1.37). This association between sexual pleasure and death is then enacted. Attracted by his sleeping wife, Othello cannot resist kissing her: "Be thus when thou art dead, and I will kill thee / And love thee after" (5.2.18–19). He recalls this necrophilic perversity at his own death: "I kissed thee ere I killed thee. No way but this: / Killing myself, to die upon a kiss" (5.2.368–69), where "die" once again carries a secondary sexual sense. Romance's movement toward reuniting long-separated lovers takes the form of a postmortem embrace. Furthermore, this concluding tableau includes not only Othello and Desdemona but perhaps Emilia as well, whose dying wish is to "lay me by my mistress' side!" (5.2.244). If so, we witness the very ménage à trois or intimate bedroom relationship between Emilia and Othello that Iago invoked to motivate his revenge.

What, then, of race? It is there from the start. Iago warns Brabanzio that "an old black ram / Is tupping your white ewe" (1.1.88–89). The arousal of Brabanzio's fear of miscegenation works. The old man cannot believe that his daughter would ever "run . . . to the sooty bosom / Of such a thing as thou" (1.2.71–72). He is wrong, however, not just about Desdemona but also about the sympathies of the Venetian Senate. As the Duke explains, "Your son-in-law is far more fair than black" (1.3.289). Yet this victory is uncomfortable: the praise arises from the negative connotations of blackness. Hence, when Othello seeks to understand his wife's betrayal, he adopts these connotations literally—"Haply for I am black" (3.3.267)—and metaphorically—"My name . . . is now begrimed and black / As mine own face" (3.3.391–93).

The manner of Turkish tyrannie over Christian slaves.

Compare Othello's last speech before killing himself (5.2.361–65). Woodcut, from F. Knight, *A Relation of Seavan Yeares Slaverie Under the Turkes of Argeire . . .* (1640).

The language of color in the play draws on the biblical association of blackness and evil, Elizabethan prejudice toward black Africans resident in England, ethnographic accounts of passionately jealous Africans, and the early stages of the slave trade. Yet it lacks the full racist import it subsequently acquired. Renaissance thought was innocent of the biological view of ethnic difference that triumphed in the nineteenth century. Othello's mention of being "sold to slavery" (1.3.137), given its Mediterranean context, has more to do with social hierarchy and religious difference than skin color. Until the late seventeenth century, *Othello*'s commentators make little of Othello's appearance, although they assume, in line with most of the play's language, that he is black—a position rejected in the nineteenth century and still sometimes challenged today. (See the two renderings of Moors on page 376.) Shakespeare also followed less prominent, more sympathetic accounts of Moors, deriving from subordinate strains in both travel literature and the religious tradition. The racial issues of *Othello* are, therefore, both like and unlike those of the present, with which they are connected partly by the unbroken influence of the play itself.

These issues have produced powerful contradictory reactions on the stage, where *Othello* has always been one of Shakespeare's most popular works. Well into the twentieth century, audiences and critics often agreed with Brabanzio, seeing in the conclusion the triumph of Othello's barbaric African essence over his civilized European surface. When they defended his nobility, they denied he was black. "Othello *was a white* man," Mary Preston of Baltimore wrote in 1869. A compromise resolution offered by the actor Herbert Beerbohm Tree in 1912 suggests the underlying racist agreement between antithetical conclusions about Othello's skin color: "Othello was an Oriental, not a Negro: a stately Arab of the best caste."

But especially when Othello is played by an actor of sub-Saharan descent, performances have seemed to strike a blow for freedom—on the Continent following the revolutions of 1848, in czarist Russia on the eve of the liberation of the serfs, after 1863 and the emancipation of American slaves, in World War II America, and in the final years of South African apartheid. The 1943 American *Othello*, featuring what may have been the American theater's first kiss between a black actor (Paul Robeson) and a white actress, was at the time the longest-running production of any Shakespearean play in the United States. Yet commentators of African descent have sometimes taken the opposite view—that a black actor as Othello runs the risk of reinforcing racial stereotypes. The problem for a white actor is even graver. With the recent return on the stage to the pre-1800 conviction that Othello is black, productions have steered away from white performers in the part, fearing that they would produce minstrel-show figures in blackface reminiscent of nineteenth-century burlesques of the play—precisely the charge sometimes made against Laurence Olivier's 1965 portrayal.

This history inevitably affects contemporary understanding of the conclusion of the play, when race seems to return literally with a vengeance. The alien connotations of the handkerchief are echoed by the ethnic rhetoric of Othello's last long speech, in which the conflict of civilizations reemerges in the Moor's identification with the exotic non-European, non-Christian world. In the quarto version (see the Textual Note), Othello is "like the base Indian" who "threw a pearl away / Richer than all his tribe" (5.2.356–57). But the Folio reads "base Iudean" (Judean) and hence may allude to Judas, betrayer of Christ, or to Herod the Great, murderer of his wife, Mariamne, out of jealousy. Othello "drops tears as fast as the Arabian trees / Their medicinable gum" (5.2.359–60). He asks his listeners to remind the Venetian state

> that in Aleppo once,
> Where a malignant and a turbaned Turk
> Beat a Venetian and traduced the state,
> I took by th' throat the circumcisèd dog
> And smote him thus.
> *He stabs himself*
> (5.2.361–65, s.d.)

In Act 1, Othello, an orthodox Christian and loyal servant of the state, agrees to defend Venice from the Turks—to protect Christianity from a Muslim people with whom Moors were linked on religious, political, and military grounds. By having Venice send Othello to that island to protect Christian interests from the forces of Islam, Shakespeare inserts his protagonist into a defining struggle of the age. In Act 5, Othello remembers that he defended Venice from the Turks once before. This recollection is the occasion for his suicide, a deed that splits him in two. Othello is agent and object of justice, servant and enemy of the Christian state. As a "base Iudean" and "circumcisèd dog," he is a Jew. Circumcision also makes him a Turk. The external military conflict returns as internal division within Othello's soul. Othello half assumes an ethnic and religious otherness to exorcise his guilt. The development of the plot both undermines and validates ethnocentric and racist stereotypes. But is this conclusion really about race, or does it turn instead on religious—and, hence, cultural—antagonism? The question resonates in today's world, where the "problem of the color-line" seems both related to and distinct from the persistence, in the eastern Mediterranean and beyond, of the very religious and military conflicts evoked by *Othello*. Hence, the uneasiness of the ending, where the unwarranted projection of guilt entirely beyond the confines of Europe is the precondition of that noble acceptance of responsibility with which Othello so memorably leaves the world and the play.

WALTER COHEN

TEXTUAL NOTE

The Tragedy of Othello, the Moore of Venice survives in two early authoritative versions—the First Quarto of 1622 (Q) and the First Folio of the following year (F). Extensive study of the background and relationship of the two texts has yet to produce anything close to a consensus. The Oxford editors hypothesize that F uses a scribal copy of Shakespeare's own revision of his earlier manuscript preserved in Q. On the other hand, Q more accurately preserves Shakespeare's characteristic spelling and punctuation, its stage directions are fuller and more authorial (although some were probably added later), and it contains more than fifty oaths excluded from F presumably in response to the Profanity Act of 1606. It is also the only Shakespearean Quarto with act divisions. In order to capture these features, the version printed here uses Q for these details. But it includes the roughly 160 lines from F not found in Q, and it usually prefers F to Q in the over one thousand places where their wording differs. In general, then, F is the primary source for the language, whereas Q provides the spelling, punctuation, oaths, and to some extent stage directions. Act divisions are the same in the two versions. Other modern editions of the play, although differing in their assumptions and in many details, produce broadly similar texts.

The passages unique to F fall into three main categories. In Act 1, Roderigo's and Brabanzio's accusations against Othello are longer. Second, beginning in Act 3, F provides Othello with greater opportunity to express his anguish. Finally and most important, the last two acts of F provide fuller parts for Desdemona (mainly by giving her the willow song in 4.3) and Emilia. These passages tend to place F further away from cynicism and disillusionment than is Q. Some of the more extensive or striking differences from Q are mentioned in the notes. By contrast, differences in Iago's role between Q and F are minor and incidental. The excision of oaths places the scribal transcript for F after 1606. Perhaps the Profanity Act necessitated certain limited revisions for a revival in 1606 or later. Perhaps then or at another time, the Oxford editors hypothesize, Shakespeare introduced more substantive changes—occasionally in the oaths, more often in the characters themselves.

Various alternatives to this approach appear in the scholarly literature on the play. One recent explanation is worthy of particular note, however. According to this argument, the 160 lines found only in F are part of the original text. Q represents an abridgment designed for performance and, for the most part, dictated to a scribe by the actors who initially played the parts. If this is so (and it currently seems the most persuasive hypothesis), the thematic differences between Q and F suggested above would represent not two distinct stages in Shakespeare's career but two different versions of the same play—the *Othello* performed for some or all audiences in the early seventeenth century and the version available to readers and potentially to spectators at least from 1623 on, though perhaps earlier as well.

SELECTED BIBLIOGRAPHY

Barthelemy, Anthony Gerard, ed. *Critical Essays on Shakespeare's "Othello."* New York: Hall, 1994. A collection of important essays (including Boose, Fineman, Loomba, Neely, Neill, Newman), mainly from the 1970s and 1980s, focusing on race and gender.

Danson, Lawrence. "England, Islam, and the Mediterranean Drama: *Othello* and Others." *Journal for Early Modern Cultural Studies* 2.2 (2002): 1–25. Contextual study of East and West, showing the instability of standard distinctions among Moor, Turk, Jew, and Christian.

Greenblatt, Stephen. *Renaissance Self-Fashioning: From More to Shakespeare*. Chicago: University of Chicago Press, 1980. 222–54. Othello's narrative self-fashioning and its subversion by Desdemona's submission and Iago's malice; a central essay for modern *Othello* scholarship and for New Historicist criticism generally.

Hankey, Julie, ed. *Othello*. 2nd ed. New York: Cambridge University Press, 2005. History of performance (stage, film, and television), with an extensive list of productions over 400 years and a text of the play with theatrical annotations.

Neill, Michael, ed. *Othello, the Moor of Venice*. Oxford: Clarendon, 2006. Outstanding scholarly edition with a book-length critical introduction.

Nostbakken, Faith, ed. *Understanding "Othello": A Student Casebook to Issues, Sources, and Historical Documents*. Westport, Conn.: Greenwood Press, 2000. Extensive excerpts from Renaissance sources, including Cinthio and Knowles; briefer selections from literary and performance criticism; suggestions of contemporary relevance (O.J. Simpson, Bill Clinton, etc.).

Orlin, Lena Cowen, ed. *Othello*. New York: Palgrave Macmillan, 2004. Leading essays since 1990, mostly on gender and marriage (Berger, Bristol, Sinfield) or race and reception (Bartels, Singh, Hodgdon, Albanese).

Pechter, Edward. *"Othello" and Interpretive Traditions*. Iowa City: University of Iowa Press, 1999. Relatively traditional account of the play's power that recognizes the inextricable link between text and interpretation while arguing for the continuing influence of earlier critical debates on current scholarship.

Potter, Lois. *Othello*. Shakespeare in Performance series. Manchester: Manchester University Press, 2002. Manchester: Manchester University Press, 2002. Focus on recent stagings, live or electronic, seeing Paul Robeson's performances from the 1930s to the 1950s as the defining events in modern productions of the play.

Wain, John, ed. *Shakespeare, "Othello": A Casebook*. London: Macmillan, 1971. Classic essays by Rymer, Johnson, Coleridge, Bradley, Eliot, Knight, Empson, Leavis, Gardner, Bayley, Auden, Coghill.

FILMS

Othello. 1952. Dir. Orson Welles. USA. 93 min. This black-and-white film stars Welles as Othello. Famous for its innovative and disorienting camera work more than for its acting.

Othello. 1965. Dir. Stuart Burge and John Dexter. UK. 165 min. Film of a stage performance, with Laurence Olivier as Othello and Maggie Smith as Desdemona. Notable not only for the white actor's effort fully to impersonate a black African—seen at the time as both troubling and moving—but also for Smith's spirited Desdemona, a break with the prior stage tradition of representing the character as a passive victim.

Othello. 1988. Dir. Janet Suzman. South Africa/UK. 187 min. Film of the controversial South African stage performance (the first with a black African actor and a white actress) that became a form of antiapartheid protest.

Othello. 1995. Dir. Oliver Parker. USA/UK. 123 min. First version made for film with an African American, Laurence Fishburne, as Othello. Kenneth Branagh as Iago dominates the play (as often happens with Iago). Ironically, racial issues are muted.

O. 2001. Dir. Tim Blake Nelson. USA. 95 min. Set in a contemporary high school, centered on a basketball player, Odin (Mekhi Phifer), in love with Desi (Julia Stiles), undone by Hugo (Josh Hartnett); also with Martin Sheen.

The Tragedy of Othello
the Moor of Venice

THE PERSONS OF THE PLAY

OTHELLO, the Moor of Venice
DESDEMONA, his wife
Michael CASSIO, his lieutenant
BIANCA, a courtesan, in love with Cassio
IAGO, the Moor's ensign
EMILIA, Iago's wife
A CLOWN, a servant of Othello
The DUKE of Venice
BRABANZIO, Desdemona's father, a senator of Venice
GRAZIANO, Brabanzio's brother
LODOVICO, kinsman of Brabanzio
SENATORS of Venice
RODERIGO, a Venetian gentleman, in love with Desdemona
MONTANO, Governor of Cyprus
A HERALD
A MESSENGER
Attendants, officers, sailors, gentlemen of Cyprus, musicians

1.1

Enter IAGO[1] *and* RODERIGO

RODERIGO   Tush, never tell me!° I take it much unkindly   (*Annoyance; disbelief*)
    That thou, Iago, who hast had my purse
    As if the strings were thine, shouldst know of this.
IAGO   'Sblood,° but you'll not hear me!   *By Christ's blood*
5   If ever I did dream of such a matter, abhor me.
RODERIGO   Thou told'st me thou didst hold him in thy hate.
IAGO   Despise me
    If I do not. Three great ones of the city,
    In personal suit to make me his lieutenant,
10   Off-capped° to him; and by the faith of man   *Took off their caps*
    I know my price, I am worth no worse a place.
    But he, as loving his own pride and purposes,
    Evades them with a bombast circumstance[2]
    Horribly stuffed with epithets of war,°   *military jargon*
15   Nonsuits° my mediators; for 'Certes,'° says he,   *Denies / Certainly*
    'I have already chose my officer.'
    And what was he?
    Forsooth, a great arithmetician,[3]
    One Michael Cassio, a Florentine,

1.1 Location: A street in Venice.
1. Iago's name may be related to Santiago Matamoros, St. James the Moor Slayer, the patron saint of Spain.
2. With an inflated circumlocution. *bombast:* cotton pad-

ding in clothes, a metaphor picked up by "stuffed" (line 14) and possibly "suit" (line 9) and "Nonsuits" (line 15).
3. Implying that Cassio's knowledge of war is purely theoretical.

20 A fellow almost damned in a fair wife,[4]
    That° never set a squadron in the field   *Who*
    Nor the division° of a battle° knows   *ordering / battalion*
    More than a spinster°—unless the bookish theoric,°   *housewife / learning*
    Wherein the togaed consuls can propose[5]
25 As masterly as he. Mere prattle without practice
    Is all his soldiership; but he, sir, had th'election,
    And I—of whom his eyes had seen the proof
    At Rhodes, at Cyprus, and on other grounds
    Christened and heathen—must be beleed° and calmed°   *without wind / becalmed*
30 By debitor and creditor. This counter-caster,[6]
    He in good time° must his lieutenant be,   *indeed (scornful)*
    And I—God bless the mark!°—his Moorship's ensign.[7]   *God help us*
RODERIGO   By heaven, I rather would have been his hangman.
IAGO   Why, there's no remedy. 'Tis the curse of service.
35 Preferment goes by letter and affection,[8]
    And not by old gradation,° where each second   *traditional seniority*
    Stood heir to th' first. Now, sir, be judge yourself
    Whether I in any just term am affined°   *am bound in any just way*
    To love the Moor.[9]
40 RODERIGO   I would not follow him then.
IAGO   O sir, content you.°   *be content*
    I follow him to serve my turn upon him.
    We cannot all be masters, nor all masters
    Cannot be truly followed. You shall mark
45 Many a duteous and knee-crooking knave
    That, doting on his own obsequious bondage,
    Wears out his time much like his master's ass
    For naught but provender,° and when he's old, cashiered.°   *animal feed / fired*
    Whip me° such honest knaves. Others there are   *The hell with*
50 Who, trimmed° in forms and visages of duty,   *outwardly decorated*
    Keep yet their hearts attending on themselves,
    And, throwing but shows of service on their lords,
    Do well thrive by 'em, and when they have lined their coats,
    Do themselves homage. These fellows have some soul,
55 And such a one do I profess myself—for, sir,
    It is as sure as you are Roderigo,
    Were I the Moor I would not be Iago.
    In following him I follow but myself.
    Heaven is my judge, not I for° love and duty,   *I am not driven by*
60 But seeming so for my peculiar° end.   *personal*
    For when my outward action doth demonstrate
    The native act and figure[1] of my heart

---

4. Obscure. Cassio has not yet met Bianca and is unmarried, although in Shakespeare's source he is. Perhaps Shakespeare's error, a reference to Cassio as a ladies' man, or an oblique, debatable anticipation of the main plot.
5. In which the toga-wearing senators can debate.
6. *debitor and creditor, counter-caster:* pejorative terms for an accountant (Cassio).
7. As "ensign," Iago is something like a standard-bearer or third-in-command. He clearly ranks below "lieutenant" Cassio, the second-in-command. This reference to "his Moorship" is also the first indication about whom Iago has been complaining.

8. Promotion comes through connections and favoritism.
9. A Moor was a Muslim of the mixed Berber and Arab people inhabiting northwest Africa. This term, like the comparison of Othello to a "Barbary horse" (an Arab, line 113), formerly led to the denial of Othello's blackness. But the passages describing Othello's appearance—"thick-lips," "black ram," "sooty bosom," "black Othello," "I am black," "black / As mine own face" (1.1.66, 1.1.88, 1.2.71, 2.3.27–28, 3.3.267, 3.3.392–93)—seem to have greater weight. "Moor" often meant sub-Saharan African in the Renaissance.
1. The innate operation (or motivation) and shape (or nature).

In compliment extern,° 'tis not long after   *outward appearance*
But I will wear my heart upon my sleeve
65 For daws° to peck at. I am not what I am.   *crowlike birds*
RODERIGO   What a full fortune does the thick-lips owe°   *own*
If he can carry't thus!
IAGO   Call up her father,
Rouse him, make after him, poison his delight,
Proclaim him in the streets; incense her kinsmen,
70 And, though he in a fertile climate dwell,
Plague him with flies. Though that his joy be joy,
Yet throw such chances of vexation on't
As it may lose some colour.
RODERIGO   Here is her father's house. I'll call aloud.
75 IAGO   Do, with like timorous accent° and dire yell   *frightening tone*
As when, by night and negligence, the fire
Is spied in populous cities.
RODERIGO [*calling*]   What ho, Brabanzio, Signor Brabanzio, ho!
IAGO [*calling*]   Awake, what ho, Brabanzio, thieves, thieves, thieves!
80 Look to your house, your daughter, and your bags.
Thieves, thieves!
     [*Enter* BRABANZIO [*in his nightgown*] *at a window
     above*
BRABANZIO   What is the reason of this terrible summons?
What is the matter there?
RODERIGO   Signor, is all your family within?
IAGO   Are your doors locked?
85 BRABANZIO   Why, wherefore ask you this?
IAGO   'Swounds,° sir, you're robbed. For shame, put on your   *By Christ's wounds*
   gown.
Your heart is burst, you have lost half your soul.
Even now, now, very now, an old black ram
Is tupping° your white ewe. Arise, arise!   *copulating with*
90 Awake the snorting° citizens with the bell,   *snoring*
Or else the devil will make a grandsire of you.
Arise, I say.
BRABANZIO   What, have you lost your wits?
RODERIGO   Most reverend signor, do you know my voice?
BRABANZIO   Not I. What are you?
95 RODERIGO   My name is Roderigo.
BRABANZIO   The worser welcome.
I have charged thee not to haunt about my doors.
In honest plainness thou hast heard me say
My daughter is not for thee, and now in madness,
100 Being full of supper and distempering° draughts,   *destabilizing*
Upon malicious bravery° dost thou come   *defiance*
To start° my quiet.   *upset*
RODERIGO   Sir, sir, sir.
BRABANZIO   But thou must needs be sure
105 My spirits and my place° have in their power   *rank*
To make this bitter to thee.
RODERIGO   Patience, good sir.
BRABANZIO   What tell'st thou me of robbing? This is Venice.
My house is not a grange.°   *country house*
RODERIGO   Most grave Brabanzio,

In simple and pure soul I come to you.

110 IAGO [*to* BRABANZIO]   'Swounds, sir, you are one of those that will
not serve God if the devil bid you. Because we come to do you
service and you think we are ruffians, you'll have your daughter
covered with a Barbary horse,² you'll have your nephews° neigh   grandsons
to you, you'll have coursers for cousins and jennets for ger-
115   mans.³

BRABANZIO   What profane wretch art thou?

IAGO   I am one, sir, that comes to tell you your daughter and the
Moor are now making the beast with two backs.°   copulating

BRABANZIO   Thou art a villain.

IAGO   You are a senator.

120 BRABANZIO   This thou shalt answer.° I know thee, Roderigo.   account for

RODERIGO   Sir, I will answer anything. But I beseech you,
If't be your pleasure and most wise consent⁴—
As partly I find it is—that your fair daughter,
At this odd-even° and dull watch o'th' night,   late (around midnight)
125   Transported with no worse nor better guard
But with a knave of common° hire, a gondolier,   public
To the gross clasps of a lascivious Moor—
If this be known to you, and your allowance,°   allowed by you
We then have done you bold and saucy wrongs.
130   But if you know not this, my manners tell me
We have your wrong rebuke. Do not believe
That, from° the sense of all civility,   in opposition to
I thus would play and trifle with your reverence.
Your daughter, if you have not given her leave,
135   I say again hath made a gross revolt,
Tying her duty, beauty, wit, and fortunes
In an extravagant and wheeling stranger⁵
Of here and everywhere. Straight° satisfy yourself.   Immediately
If she be in her chamber or your house,
140   Let loose on me the justice of the state
For thus deluding you.

BRABANZIO [*calling*]   Strike on the tinder,° ho!   A light
Give me a taper,° call up all my people.   candle
This accident° is not unlike my dream;   event
Belief of it oppresses me already.
Light, I say, light!   *Exit*

145 IAGO   Farewell, for I must leave you.
It seems not meet° nor wholesome to my place   proper
To be produced°—as, if I stay, I shall—   presented as witness
Against the Moor, for I do know the state,
However this may gall him with some check,°   reprimand
150   Cannot with safety cast° him, for he's embarked°   dismiss / committed
With such loud reason° to the Cyprus wars,   vociferous, just support
Which even now stands in act,° that, for their souls,   are taking place
Another of his fathom° they have none   caliber
To lead their business, in which regard—

---

2. Horse from northwest coastal Africa; an Arab; sug-   4. Lines 122–138 do not appear in Q.
gesting barbarism.   5. In a vagrant and vagabond foreigner (perhaps sug-
3. *coursers:* strong horses. *cousins:* kinsmen. *jennets:*   gesting a planet wandering off course).
small Spanish horses. *germans:* close relatives.

155 Though I do hate him as I do hell pains—
     Yet for necessity of present life
     I must show out a flag and sign of love,
     Which is indeed but sign. That you shall surely find him,
     Lead to the Sagittary[6] the raisèd search,°   *awakened searchers*
160 And there will I be with him. So farewell.   *Exit*
     Enter [below] BRABANZIO *in his nightgown, and servants*
         with torches

     BRABANZIO   It is too true an evil. Gone she is,
     And what's to come of my despisèd time°   *lifetime*
     Is naught but bitterness. Now, Roderigo,
     Where didst thou see her?—O unhappy girl!—
165 With the Moor, sayst thou?—Who would be a father?—
     How didst thou know 'twas she?—O, she deceives me
     Past thought!—What said she to you? [*To servants*] Get more tapers,
     Raise all my kindred.   [*Exit one or more*]
     [*To* RODERIGO]   Are they married, think you?
     RODERIGO   Truly, I think they are.
170 BRABANZIO   O heaven, how got she out? O, treason of the blood!
     Fathers, from hence trust not your daughters' minds
     By what you see them act. Is there not charms°   *magic*
     By which the property° of youth and maidhood°   *attribute / virginity*
     May be abused? Have you not read, Roderigo,
     Of some such thing?
175 RODERIGO   Yes, sir, I have indeed.
     BRABANZIO [*to servants*]   Call up my brother. [*To* RODERIGO] O,
         would you had had her.
     [*To servants*] Some one way, some another.   [*Exit one or more*]
     [*To* RODERIGO]   Do you know
     Where we may apprehend her and the Moor?
     RODERIGO   I think I can discover him, if you please
180 To get good guard and go along with me.
     BRABANZIO   Pray you lead on. At every house I'll call;
     I may command° at most. [*Calling*] Get weapons, ho,   *demand help*
     And raise some special officers of night.
     On, good Roderigo. I will deserve° your pains.   *Exeunt*   *reward*

1.2

     Enter OTHELLO, IAGO, *and attendants with torches*
     IAGO   Though in the trade of war I have slain men,
     Yet do I hold it very stuff ° o'th' conscience   *essence*
     To do no contrived° murder. I lack iniquity,   *premeditated*
     Sometime, to do me service. Nine or ten times
5   I had thought to've yerked him° here, under the ribs.   *stabbed (Roderigo)*
     OTHELLO   'Tis better as it is.
     IAGO   Nay, but he prated,
     And spoke such scurvy and provoking terms
     Against your honour
     That, with the little godliness I have,

---

6. Perhaps indicating an inn named for the astrological sign Sagitarius, where Othello and Desdemona are staying. It may also suggest Othello himself, since Sagitarius is depicted as a centaur (a mythological being part man, part horse), and Iago has already likened Othello to a "Barbary horse."
1.2 Location: Another street in Venice, before Othello's lodgings.

10   I did full hard forbear him.[1] But I pray you, sir,
    Are you fast° married? Be assured of this: *legitimately*
    That the magnifico° is much beloved,   *(Brabanzio)*
    And hath in his effect a voice potential°   *powerful*
    As double as the Duke's. He will divorce you,
15   Or put upon you what restraint or grievance
    The law, with all his might to enforce it on,
    Will give him cable.°   *scope*
OTHELLO   Let him do his spite.
    My services which I have done the signory°   *Venetian government*
    Shall out-tongue his complaints. 'Tis yet to know°—   *not publicly known*
20   Which, when I know that boasting is an honour,
    I shall promulgate—I fetch my life and being
    From men of royal siege,° and my demerits°   *rank / deserts*
    May speak unbonneted[2] to as proud a fortune
    As this that I have reached. For know, Iago,
25   But that I love the gentle Desdemona
    I would not my unhousèd° free condition   *unconfined*
    Put into circumscription and confine
    For the seas' worth.
                Enter CASSIO *and officers, with torches*
                      But look, what lights come yond?
IAGO   Those are the raisèd father and his friends.
    You were best go in.
30 OTHELLO   Not I. I must be found.
    My parts,° my title, and my perfect soul[3]   *qualities*
    Shall manifest me rightly. Is it they?
IAGO   By Janus,° I think no.   *two-faced Roman god*
OTHELLO   The servants of the Duke, and my lieutenant!
35   The goodness of the night upon you, friends.
    What is the news?
CASSIO   The Duke does greet you, general,
    And he requires your haste-post-haste appearance
    Even on the instant.
OTHELLO   What is the matter, think you?
CASSIO   Something from Cyprus, as I may divine;
40   It is a business of some heat.° The galleys   *urgency*
    Have sent a dozen sequent° messengers   *successive*
    This very night at one another's heels,
    And many of the consuls, raised and met,
    Are at the Duke's already. You have been hotly called for,
45   When, being not at your lodging to be found,
    The senate sent about three several quests
    To search you out.
OTHELLO   'Tis well I am found by you.
    I will but spend a word here in the house
    And go with you.   *[Exit]*
CASSIO   Ensign, what makes he here?
50 IAGO   Faith, he tonight hath boarded a land-carrack.°   *large merchant ship*
    If it prove lawful prize, he's made for ever.
CASSIO   I do not understand.

---

1. I barely restrained myself from attacking him.   3. My clear conscience.
2. Without deference; modestly.

IAGO	He's married.	
CASSIO	To who?	

Enter BRABANZIO, RODERIGO, *and* OFFICERS, *with lights and weapons*

IAGO   Marry,° to—   *By Mary (mild oath)*
   [*Enter* OTHELLO]
   [*To* OTHELLO] Come, captain, will you go?
OTHELLO   Have with you.°   *Let's go*
55 CASSIO   Here comes another troop to seek for you.
   IAGO   It is Brabanzio. General, be advised.
   He comes to bad intent.
OTHELLO   Holla, stand, there!
RODERIGO [*to* BRABANZIO]   Signor, it is the Moor.
BRABANZIO   Down with him, thief!
   IAGO [*drawing his sword*]   You, Roderigo? Come, sir, I am for you.
60 OTHELLO   Keep up° your bright swords, for the dew will rust 'em.   *Put away*
   [*To* BRABANZIO] Good signor, you shall more command with years
   Than with your weapons.
BRABANZIO   O thou foul thief, where hast thou stowed my daughter?
   Damned as thou art, thou hast enchanted her,
65 For I'll refer me to all things of sense,[4]
   If she in chains of magic were not bound,
   Whether a maid so tender, fair, and happy,
   So opposite to marriage that she shunned
   The wealthy curlèd darlings of our nation,
70 Would ever have, t'incur a general mock,
   Run from her guardage to the sooty bosom
   Of such a thing as thou—to fear, not to delight.
   Judge me the world if 'tis not gross in sense[5]
   That thou hast practised on her with foul charms,
75 Abused her delicate youth with drugs or minerals
   That weakens motion. I'll have't disputed on.°   *argued by experts*
   'Tis probable, and palpable to thinking.
   I therefore apprehend and do attach° thee   *arrest*
   For an abuser of the world, a practiser
80 Of arts inhibited and out of warrant.°   *prohibited and illegal*
   [*To* OFFICERS] Lay hold upon him. If he do resist,
   Subdue him at his peril.
OTHELLO   Hold your hands,
   Both you of my inclining° and the rest.   *following*
   Were it my cue to fight, I should have known it
85 Without a prompter. Whither will you that I go
   To answer this your charge?
BRABANZIO   To prison, till fit time
   Of law and course of direct session
   Call thee to answer.
OTHELLO   What if I do obey?
   How may the Duke be therewith satisfied,
90 Whose messengers are here about my side
   Upon some present business of the state
   To bring me to him?
OFFICER [*to* BRABANZIO]   'Tis true, most worthy signor.

4. For I'll ask, relying on common sense.
5. If it is not patently obvious. Lines 73–78 do not appear in Q.

The Duke's in council, and your noble self,
I am sure, is sent for.

BRABANZIO   How, the Duke in council?

95   In this time of the night? Bring him away.°   *along*
Mine's not an idle cause. The Duke himself,
Or any of my brothers of the state,
Cannot but feel this wrong as 'twere their own;
For if such actions may have passage free,

100   Bondslaves and pagans shall our statesmen be.   *Exeunt*

1.3

Enter [the] DUKE *and* SENATORS *set at a table, with*
lights and OFFICERS

DUKE   There is no composition in these news
That gives them credit.[1]

FIRST SENATOR   Indeed, they are disproportioned.°   *inconsistent*
My letters say a hundred and seven galleys.

DUKE   And mine a hundred-forty.

SECOND SENATOR   And mine two hundred.

5   But though they jump not on a just account°—   *don't exactly agree*
As, in these cases, where the aim reports
'Tis oft with difference[2]—yet do they all confirm
A Turkish fleet, and bearing up to Cyprus.

DUKE   Nay, it is possible enough to judgement.

10   I do not so secure me in the error,
But the main article I do approve
In fearful sense.[3]

SAILOR *(within)*   What ho, what ho, what ho!

Enter [a] SAILOR

OFFICER   A messenger from the galleys.

DUKE   Now, what's the business?

SAILOR   The Turkish preparation° makes for Rhodes.   *battle-ready fleet*

15   So was I bid report here to the state
By Signor Angelo.[4]

DUKE *[to* SENATORS*]*   How say you by this change?

FIRST SENATOR   This cannot be,
By no assay° of reason—'tis a pageant   *test*

20   To keep us in false gaze. When we consider
The importancy of Cyprus to the Turk,
And let ourselves again but understand
That, as it more concerns the Turk than Rhodes,
So may he with more facile question bear it,[5]

25   For that it stands not in such warlike brace,
But altogether lacks th'abilities
That Rhodes is dressed in—if we make thought of this,
We must not think the Turk is so unskilful
To leave that latest° which concerns him first,   *last*

30   Neglecting an attempt of ease and gain
To wake and wage° a danger profitless.   *risk*

1.3 Location: A Venetian council room.
1. *There . . . credit:* The reports lack the consistency
that would make them believable.
2. *where . . . difference:* where the reports are esti-
mates, there are often discrepancies among them.
3. *I do not . . . sense:* I am not so reassured by the discrepancies as to dismiss the main concern—the

approach of the Turkish fleet.
4. Not mentioned elsewhere in the play, Angelus Sori-
anus was a Venetian sea captain who received the Venetian ambassador bearing from Constantinople the
Turkish ultimatum to surrender Cyprus shortly before
its capture by the Turks in 1571.
5. So also can the Turkish fleet more easily win it.

DUKE   Nay, in all confidence, he's not for Rhodes.

OFFICER   Here is more news.

Enter a MESSENGER

MESSENGER   The Ottomites,° reverend and gracious,   *Ottoman Turks*

35   Steering with due course toward the Isle of Rhodes,

Have there injointed them with an after° fleet.   *joined with another*

FIRST SENATOR   Ay, so I thought. How many, as you guess?

MESSENGER   Of thirty sail, and now they do restem°   *retrace*

Their backward course, bearing with frank appearance

40   Their purposes toward Cyprus. Signor Montano,

Your trusty and most valiant servitor,

With his free duty recommends you thus,[6]

And prays you to believe him.

DUKE   'Tis certain then for Cyprus.

Marcus Luccicos,[7] is not he in town?

45   FIRST SENATOR   He's now in Florence.

DUKE   Write from us to him post-post-haste. Dispatch.

Enter BRABANZIO, OTHELLO, RODERIGO, IAGO, CASSIO,

and officers

FIRST SENATOR   Here comes Brabanzio and the valiant Moor.

DUKE   Valiant Othello, we must straight° employ you   *immediately*

Against the general enemy° Ottoman.   *(of all Christendom)*

50   [*To* BRABANZIO] I did not see you. Welcome, gentle° signor.   *noble*

We lacked your counsel and your help tonight.

BRABANZIO   So did I yours. Good your grace, pardon me.

Neither my place,° nor aught I heard of business,   *official duty*

Hath raised me from my bed, nor doth the general care

55   Take hold on me; for my particular grief

Is of so floodgate and o'erbearing nature

That it engluts and swallows other sorrows,

And it is still itself.[8]

DUKE   Why, what's the matter?

BRABANZIO   My daughter, O, my daughter!

SENATORS   Dead?

BRABANZIO   Ay, to me.

60   She is abused,° stol'n from me, and corrupted   *deluded*

By spells and medicines bought of mountebanks.°   *quacks*

For nature so preposterously to err,

Being not deficient, blind, or lame of sense,

Sans° witchcraft could not.   *Without*

65   DUKE   Whoe'er he be that in this foul proceeding

Hath thus beguiled your daughter of herself

And you of her, the bloody book of law

You shall yourself read in the bitter letter

After your own sense, yea, though our proper son

70   Stood in your action.[9]

BRABANZIO   Humbly I thank your grace.

Here is the man, this Moor, whom now it seems

Your special mandate for the state affairs

Hath hither brought.

SENATORS   We are very sorry for't.

---

6. With his freely given loyalty reports to you thus.
7. Not mentioned elsewhere in the play.
8. *That . . . itself:* That my "grief" can incorporate other "sorrows" without being affected.

9. *You shall . . . action:* You yourself shall interpret the law as you see fit even if my own son is the one you accuse.

DUKE [*to* OTHELLO]   What in your own part can you say to this?

75 BRABANZIO   Nothing but this is so.

OTHELLO   Most potent, grave, and reverend signors,
My very noble and approved good masters,
That I have ta'en away this old man's daughter,
It is most true, true I have married her.

80 The very head and front° of my offending   *height and breadth*
Hath this extent, no more. Rude° am I in my speech,   *Unpolished*
And little blessed with the soft phrase of peace,
For since these arms of mine had seven years' pith°   *strength*
Till now some nine moons wasted,° they have used   *Nine months ago*

85 Their dearest° action in the tented field,   *most valued*
And little of this great world can I speak
More than pertains to feats of broils° and battle.   *combats*
And therefore little shall I grace my cause
In speaking for myself. Yet, by your gracious patience,

90 I will a round° unvarnished tale deliver   *plain*
Of my whole course of love, what drugs, what charms,
What conjuration and what mighty magic—
For such proceeding I am charged withal°—   *with*
I won his daughter.

BRABANZIO   A maiden never bold,

95 Of spirit so still and quiet that her motion
Blushed at herself¹—and she in spite of nature,
Of years, of country, credit,° everything,   *reputation*
To fall in love with what she feared to look on!
It is a judgement maimed and most imperfect

100 That will confess perfection so could err
Against all rules of nature, and must° be driven   *(we therefore) must*
To find out practices of cunning hell
Why this should be. I therefore vouch again
That with some mixtures powerful o'er the blood,°   *passions*

105 Or with some dram conjured° to this effect,   *enchanted dose*
He wrought upon her.

DUKE   To vouch this is no proof
Without more wider and more overt test
Than these thin habits and poor likelihoods
Of modern seeming do prefer against him.²

110 A SENATOR   But Othello, speak.
Did you by indirect and forcèd courses°   *means*
Subdue and poison this young maid's affections,
Or came it by request and such fair question°   *conversation*
As soul to soul affordeth?

OTHELLO   I do beseech you,

115 Send for the lady to the Sagittary,
And let her speak of me before her father.
If you do find me foul in her report,
The trust, the office I do hold of you
Not only take away, but let your sentence
Even fall upon my life.

120 DUKE [*to* OFFICERS]   Fetch Desdemona hither.

---

1. *her . . . herself*: she blushed at herself at the slightest provocation.
2. *Without . . . him*: Without fuller and more direct
testimony than mere appearances and conjecture based
on currently popular beliefs against him.

OTHELLO   Ensign, conduct them. You best know the place.

Exit [IAGO *with*] *two or three* [*officers*]

    And till she come, as truly as to heaven

    I do confess the vices of my blood,°   *sins of passion*

    So justly to your grave ears I'll present

125   How I did thrive in this fair lady's love,

    And she in mine.

DUKE   Say it, Othello.

OTHELLO   Her father loved me, oft invited me,

    Still° questioned me the story of my life   *Constantly*

    From year to year, the battles, sieges, fortunes

130   That I have passed.

    I ran it through even from my boyish days

    To th' very moment that he bade me tell it,

    Wherein I spoke of most disastrous chances,°   *events*

    Of moving accidents° by flood and field,   *events*

135   Of hair-breadth scapes i'th' imminent deadly breach,[3]

    Of being taken by the insolent foe

    And sold to slavery, of my redemption thence,

    And portance° in my traveller's history,   *conduct*

    Wherein of antres° vast and deserts idle,   *caves*

140   Rough quarries, rocks, and hills whose heads touch heaven,

    It was my hint° to speak. Such was my process,°   *occasion / story*

    And of the cannibals that each other eat,

    The Anthropophagi,[4] and men whose heads

    Do grow beneath their shoulders. These things to hear

145   Would Desdemona seriously incline,

    But still the house affairs would draw her thence,

    Which ever as° she could with haste dispatch   *Whenever*

    She'd come again, and with a greedy ear

    Devour up my discourse; which I observing,

150   Took once a pliant° hour, and found good means   *convenient*

    To draw from her a prayer of earnest heart

    That I would all my pilgrimage dilate,°   *relate*

    Whereof by parcels she had something heard,

    But not intentively.° I did consent,   *continuously*

155   And often did beguile her of her tears

    When I did speak of some distressful stroke

    That my youth suffered. My story being done,

    She gave me for my pains a world of kisses.[5]

    She swore in faith 'twas strange, 'twas passing° strange,   *exceptionally*

160   'Twas pitiful, 'twas wondrous pitiful.

    She wished she had not heard it, yet she wished

    That heaven had made her such a man.[6] She thankèd me,

    And bade me, if I had a friend that loved her,

    I should but teach him how to tell my story,

165   And that would woo her. Upon this hint I spake.

    She loved me for the dangers I had passed,

    And I loved her that she did pity them.

    This only is the witchcraft I have used.

---

3. In the deadly gaps in a fortification.
4. Man-eaters. The term is from the ancient Roman writer Pliny the Elder. Shakespeare was also indebted to the travel literature of the Middle Ages (*Mandeville's Travels*) and the Renaissance (Hakluyt's *Principal*

Navigations, among others).
5. F reads "kisses," Q "sighs." It is hard to explain "kisses" as a textual error.
6. Made such a man for her; made her into such a man.

Enter DESDEMONA, IAGO, *and attendants*
    Here comes the lady. Let her witness it.

170 DUKE   I think this tale would win my daughter, too.—
    Good Brabanzio,
    Take up this mangled matter at the best.°   *Make the best of this*
    Men do their broken weapons rather use
    Than their bare hands.

BRABANZIO   I pray you hear her speak.

175 If she confess that she was half the wooer,
    Destruction on my head if my bad blame
    Light on the man! Come hither, gentle mistress.
    Do you perceive in all this noble company
    Where most you owe obedience?

DESDEMONA   My noble father,

180 I do perceive here a divided duty.
    To you I am bound for life and education.
    My life and education both do learn° me   *teach*
    How to respect you. You are the lord of duty,
    I am hitherto your daughter. But here's my husband,
185 And so much duty as my mother showed
    To you, preferring you before her father,
    So much I challenge° that I may profess   *assert*
    Due to the Moor my lord.

BRABANZIO   God b'wi'you, I ha' done.
    Please it your grace, on to the state affairs.
190 I had rather to adopt a child than get° it.   *beget*
    Come hither, Moor.
    I here do give thee that° with all my heart   *that which*
    Which, but° thou hast already, with all my heart   *except that*
    I would keep from thee. [*To* DESDEMONA] For your sake, jewel,
195 I am glad at soul I have no other child,
    For thy escape would teach me tyranny,
    To hang clogs⁷ on 'em. I have done, my lord.

DUKE   Let me speak like yourself, and lay a sentence°   *draw a moral*
    Which, as a grece° or step, may help these lovers   *step*
200 Into your favour.
    When remedies are past, the griefs are ended
    By seeing the worst which late on hopes depended.⁸
    To mourn a mischief that is past and gone
    Is the next way to draw new mischief on.
205 What cannot be preserved when fortune takes,
    Patience her injury a mockery makes.⁹
    The robbed that smiles steals something from the thief;
    He robs himself that spends a bootless° grief.   *pointless*

BRABANZIO   So let the Turk of Cyprus us beguile,
210 We lose it not so long as we can smile.
    He bears the sentence° well that nothing bears   *saying; judgment*
    But the free comfort which from thence he hears,
    But he bears both the sentence and the sorrow
    That, to pay grief, must of poor patience borrow.
215 These sentences, to sugar or to gall,°   *both sweet and bitter*

---

7. Blocks of wood tied to criminals' legs to keep them from escaping.
8. By seeing those things come to pass that caused grief in anticipation. The Duke paints the moral in rhyming couplets, to which Brabanzio replies in kind.
9. Patience laughs at what cannot be helped (and thus reduces the "injury").

Being strong on both sides, are equivocal.
But words are words. I never yet did hear
That the bruised heart was piercèd[1] through the ear. I humbly
beseech you proceed to th'affairs of state.

220 DUKE   The Turk with a most mighty preparation makes for
Cyprus. Othello, the fortitude of the place is best known to
you, and though we have there a substitute of most allowed
sufficiency,° yet opinion, a more sovereign mistress of effects,   *known ability*
throws a more safer voice on you.[2] You must therefore be con-
225 tent to slubber° the gloss of your new fortunes with this more   *soil*
stubborn° and boisterous expedition.   *rougher*

OTHELLO   The tyrant custom, most grave senators,
Hath made the flinty and steel couch of war
My thrice-driven° bed of down. I do agnize°   *sifted / acknowledge*
230 A natural and prompt alacrity
I find in hardness,° and do undertake   *hardship*
This present wars against the Ottomites.
Most humbly therefore bending to your state,°   *authority*
I crave fit disposition for my wife,
235 Due reference of place and exhibition,[3]
With such accommodation and besort°   *suitable attendance*
As levels with her breeding.

DUKE   Why, at her father's!

BRABANZIO   I will not have it so.

240 OTHELLO   Nor I.

DESDEMONA   Nor would I there reside,
To put my father in impatient thoughts
By being in his eye. Most gracious Duke,
To my unfolding° lend your prosperous° ear,   *proposal / receptive*
245 And let me find a charter° in your voice   *an authorization*
T'assist my simpleness.

DUKE   What would you, Desdemona?

DESDEMONA   That I did love the Moor to live with him,
My downright violence and storm of fortunes[4]
May trumpet to the world. My heart's subdued
250 Even to the very quality of my lord.[5]
I saw Othello's visage in his mind,
And to his honours and his valiant parts°   *qualities*
Did I my soul and fortunes consecrate;
So that, dear lords, if I be left behind,
255 A moth of peace, and he go to the war,
The rites° for why I love him are bereft me,   *(of love); (of war?)*
And I a heavy interim shall support
By his dear absence. Let me go with him.

OTHELLO [*to the* DUKE]   Let her have your voice.
260 Vouch with me heaven, I therefor beg it not
To please the palate of my appetite,
Nor to comply with heat°—the young affects[6]   *sexual passion*
In me defunct—and proper° satisfaction,   *personal; fitting*

---

1. Surgically lanced (and presumably cured).
2. *opinion . . . you*: public opinion, which determines
what gets done, finds greater security with you.
3. Proper accommodation and maintenance.
4. My outright defiance of custom.
5. *My heart's . . . lord*: I love him for what he is (military,

adventurous). Q reads "utmost pleasure" for "very
quality"—an openly sexual formulation that makes
Desdemona's response one of subordination rather
than of identification, sexual and otherwise.
6. The youthful desires.

But to be free° and bounteous to her mind;   *liberal*
265 And heaven defend your good souls that you think
I will your serious and great business scant
When she is with me. No, when light-winged toys°   *diversions*
Of feathered Cupid seel° with wanton dullness   *blind*
My speculative and officed instruments,[7]
270 That my disports° corrupt and taint my business,   *sexual pleasures*
Let housewives make a skillet of my helm,
And all indign° and base adversities   *undignified*
Make head against my estimation.[8]
DUKE Be it as you shall privately determine,
275 Either for her stay or going. Th'affair cries haste,
And speed must answer it.
A SENATOR [*to* OTHELLO]   You must away tonight.
DESDEMONA Tonight, my lord?
DUKE   This night.
OTHELLO   With all my heart.
DUKE At nine i'th' morning here we'll meet again.
Othello, leave some officer behind,
280 And he shall our commission bring to you,
And such things else of quality and respect°   *weight and importance*
As doth import° you.   *concern*
OTHELLO   So please your grace, my ensign.
A man he is of honesty[9] and trust.
To his conveyance I assign my wife,
285 With what else needful your good grace shall think
To be sent after me.
DUKE   Let it be so.
Good night to everyone. [*To* BRABANZIO] And, noble signor,
If virtue no delighted° beauty lack,   *delightful*
Your son-in-law is far more fair than black.
290 A SENATOR Adieu, brave Moor. Use Desdemona well.
BRABANZIO Look to her,° Moor, if thou hast eyes to see.   *Watch her carefully*
She has deceived her father, and may thee.
        Exeunt [DUKE, BRABANZIO, CASSIO, SENATORS,
                    and officers]
OTHELLO My life upon her faith. Honest Iago,
My Desdemona must I leave to thee.
295 I prithee let thy wife attend on her,
And bring them after in the best advantage.[1]
Come, Desdemona. I have but an hour
Of love, of worldly matter and direction
To spend with thee. We must obey the time.
        Exeunt [OTHELLO *the*] *Moor and* DESDEMONA
300 RODERIGO Iago.
IAGO What sayst thou, noble heart?
RODERIGO What will I do, think'st thou?
IAGO Why, go to bed and sleep.
RODERIGO I will incontinently° drown myself.   *immediately*
305 IAGO If thou dost, I shall never love thee after. Why, thou silly
gentleman!

---

7. My duty-bound faculties of sense.   of them deeply ironic, some unwittingly so.
8. Raise an army against my good reputation.   1. And bring them along at the most favorable moment.
9. The first of many references to Iago's "honesty," all

RODERIGO   It is silliness to live when to live is torment; and then
have we a prescription° to die when death is our physician.   *right; doctor's order*

IAGO   O, villainous!° I ha' looked upon the world for four times   *absurd; immoral?*
310   seven years, and since I could distinguish betwixt a benefit and
an injury I never found man that knew how to love himself.
Ere I would say I would drown myself for the love of a guinea-
hen,° I would change my humanity with a baboon.   *woman*

RODERIGO   What should I do? I confess it is my shame to be so
315   fond, but it is not in my virtue° to amend it.   *native ability*

IAGO   Virtue? A fig!° 'Tis in ourselves that we are thus or thus.   *(an obscenity)*
Our bodies are our gardens, to the which our wills are garden-
ers; so that if we will plant nettles or sow lettuce, set hyssop° and   *mint herb*
weed up thyme, supply it with one gender of herbs or distract it
320   with many, either to have it sterile with idleness° or manured   *noncultivation*
with industry, why, the power and corrigible authority° of this   *ability to decide*
lies in our wills. If the beam° of our lives had not one scale of   *(as on a scale)*
reason to peise° another of sensuality, the blood and baseness   *counterweigh*
of our natures would conduct us to most preposterous conclu-
325   sions. But we have reason to cool our raging motions,° our car-   *appetites*
nal stings, our unbitted° lusts; whereof I take this that you call   *unrestrained*
love to be a sect or scion.°   *offshoot*

RODERIGO   It cannot be.

IAGO   It is merely a lust of the blood and a permission of the will.
330   Come, be a man. Drown thyself? Drown cats and blind pup-
pies. I have professed me thy friend, and I confess me knit to
thy deserving with cables of perdurable° toughness. I could   *durable*
never better stead° thee than now. Put money in thy purse.   *help*
Follow thou the wars, defeat thy favour with an usurped beard.[2]
335   I say, put money in thy purse. It cannot be long that Desdemona should continue her love to the Moor—put money in
thy purse—nor he his to her. It was a violent commencement°   *an abruptly begun affair*
in her, and thou shalt see an answerable sequestration[3]—put
but money in thy purse. These Moors are changeable in their
340   wills—fill thy purse with money. The food that to him now
is as luscious as locusts[4] shall be to him shortly as bitter as
coloquintida.[5] She must change for youth. When she is sated
with his body, she will find the error of her choice. Therefore
put money in thy purse. If thou wilt needs° damn thyself, do it   *If you must*
345   a more delicate way than drowning. Make all the money thou
canst. If sanctimony° and a frail vow betwixt an erring° barbar-   *holy rite / a wandering*
ian and a super-subtle° Venetian be not too hard for my wits   *highly sensitive*
and all the tribe of hell, thou shalt enjoy her; therefore make
money. A pox o' drowning thyself—it is clean out of the way.°   *of no use*
350   Seek thou rather to be hanged in compassing° thy joy than to   *encompassing*
be drowned and go without her.

RODERIGO   Wilt thou be fast° to my hopes if I depend on the   *duty bound*
issue?°   *outcome*

IAGO   Thou art sure of me. Go, make money. I have told thee
355   often, and I re-tell thee again and again, I hate the Moor. My
cause is hearted,° thine hath no less reason. Let us be conjunc-   *heartfelt*
tive° in our revenge against him. If thou canst cuckold him,   *joined*

---

2. Disguise your appearance with a fake beard.   5. Colocynth, a purgative—one of Iago's many refer-
3. A correspondingly abrupt separation.   ences to the digestive tract.
4. A sweet, exotic fruit, perhaps carob or honeysuckle.

thou dost thyself a pleasure, me a sport. There are many events
in the womb of time, which will be delivered. Traverse,° go,　　　*Go (to arms)*
360　provide thy money. We will have more of this tomorrow.
Adieu.

RODERIGO　Where shall we meet i'th' morning?

IAGO　　　　　　　　　　　　　　　　At my lodging.

RODERIGO　I'll be with thee betimes.°　　　　　　　　　　*early*

IAGO　　　　　　　　　　Go to, farewell—
Do you hear, Roderigo?

RODERIGO　　　　　　　I'll sell all my land.　　　*Exit*

365　IAGO　Thus do I ever make my fool my purse—
For I mine own gained knowledge should profane
If I would time expend with such a snipe°　　　　　　　*fool*
But for my sport and profit. I hate the Moor,
And it is thought abroad° that 'twixt my sheets　　　　*rumored*
370　He has done my office. I know not if't be true,
But I, for mere suspicion in that kind,
Will do° as if for surety. He holds° me well:　　　*act / esteems*
The better shall my purpose work on him.
Cassio's a proper° man. Let me see now,　　　　　　*handsome*
375　To get his place, and to plume up° my will　　　　　*gratify*
In double knavery—how, how? Let's see.
After some time to abuse Othello's ears
That he is too familiar with his wife;⁶
He hath a person and a smooth dispose°　　　　　　　*manner*
380　To be suspected, framed to make women false.
The Moor is of a free° and open nature,　　　　　　　*liberal*
That thinks men honest that but seem to be so,
And will as tenderly° be led by th' nose　　　　　　　*easily*
As asses are.
385　I ha't. It is ingendered. Hell and night
Must bring this monstrous birth to the world's light.　　*Exit*

2.1

Enter [below] MONTANO, *Governor of Cyprus; two other*
GENTLEMEN *[above]*

MONTANO　What from the cape can you discern at sea?

FIRST GENTLEMEN　Nothing at all. It is a high-wrought flood.°　　*very rough sea*
I cannot 'twixt the heaven and the main°　　　　　　　*sea*
Descry° a sail.　　　　　　　　　　　　　　　　　　　*Discern*

5　MONTANO　Methinks the wind hath spoke aloud at land.
A fuller blast ne'er shook our battlements.
If it ha' ruffianed° so upon the sea,　　　　　　　　　*raged*
What ribs of oak, when mountains melt on them,
Can hold the mortise?¹ What shall we hear of this?

10　SECOND GENTLEMEN　A segregation° of the Turkish fleet;　　*separation*
For do but stand upon the foaming shore,
The chidden billow² seems to pelt the clouds,
The wind-shaked surge with high and monstrous mane

---

6. "He" is Cassio (as in line 379), but "his" refers to
Othello—a potential confusion of pronouns.
2.1 Location: A seaport in Cyprus; outdoors near the
harbor.
1. *What . . . mortise:* What ship (with "ribs of oak")

can hold its joints ("mortise") together when "mountains" of water pour on it?
2. The surging ocean, rebuked ("chidden") by the wind
(or repulsed by the land).

Seems to cast water on the burning Bear
15 And quench the guards of th'ever-fixèd Pole.[3]
I never did like molestation view°   *see such a tumult*
On the enchafèd flood.

MONTANO   If that the Turkish fleet
Be not ensheltered and embayed, they are drowned.
It is impossible to bear it out.

Enter a THIRD GENTLEMEN

20 THIRD GENTLEMEN   News, lads! Our wars are done.
The desperate tempest hath so banged the Turks
That their designment° halts. A noble ship of Venice   *plan*
Hath seen a grievous wrack and sufferance
On most part of their fleet.

25 MONTANO   How, is this true?

THIRD GENTLEMEN   The ship is here put in,
A Veronessa.[4] Michael Cassio,
Lieutenant to the warlike Moor Othello,
Is come on shore; the Moor himself at sea,
30 And is in full commission here for Cyprus.

MONTANO   I am glad on't; 'tis a worthy governor.

THIRD GENTLEMEN   But this same Cassio, though he speak of comfort
Touching the Turkish loss, yet he looks sadly,°   *seriously*
And prays the Moor be safe, for they were parted
With foul and violent tempest.

35 MONTANO   Pray heavens he be,
For I have served him, and the man commands
Like a full soldier. Let's to the sea-side, ho!—
As well to see the vessel that's come in
As to throw out our eyes for brave Othello,
40 Even till we make the main and th'aerial blue
An indistinct regard.[5]

THIRD GENTLEMEN   Come, let's do so,
For every minute is expectancy
Of more arrivance.

Enter CASSIO

CASSIO   Thanks, you the valiant of this warlike isle
45 That so approve the Moor! O, let the heavens
Give him defence against the elements,
For I have lost him on a dangerous sea.

MONTANO   Is he well shipped?

CASSIO   His barque is stoutly timbered, and his pilot
50 Of very expert and approved allowance.°   *known ability*
Therefore my hopes, not surfeited to death,°   *not excessive*
Stand in bold cure.°   *likely to be rewarded*

VOICES (*within*)   A sail, a sail, a sail!

CASSIO   What noise?

A GENTLEMAN   The town is empty. On the brow° o'th' sea   *cliff at the edge*
55 Stand ranks of people, and they cry 'A sail!'

CASSIO   My hopes do shape him° for the governor.   *make it out to be*
A shot

---

3. *burning Bear*: the constellation Ursa Minor. *guards*:
probably two stars in the constellation that point in a
line to the polestar, also in Ursa Minor.
4. Meaning unclear: originally from Verona, though now

used by the Venetians; a cutter; possibly meant to modify
not "ship" but Cassio, although he is Florentine (1.1.19).
5. *Even . . . regard*: Until we can't distinguish sea from
sky.

A GENTLEMAN   They do discharge their shot of courtesy—
Our friends, at least.
CASSIO   I pray you, sir, go forth,
And give us truth who 'tis that is arrived.
60 A GENTLEMAN   I shall.   *Exit*
MONTANO   But, good lieutenant, is your general wived?
CASSIO   Most fortunately. He hath achieved a maid
That paragons° description and wild fame,   *stands above*
One that excels the quirks of blazoning° pens,   *praise-giving*
65 And in th'essential vesture of creation
Does tire the engineer.[6]
             Enter GENTLEMAN
                    How now, who has put in?
GENTLEMAN   'Tis one Iago, ensign to the general.
CASSIO   He's had most favourable and happy speed.
Tempests themselves, high seas, and howling winds,
70 The guttered° rocks and congregated° sands,   *jagged / accumulated*
Traitors ensteeped° to enclog the guiltless keel,   *underwater*
As having sense of beauty do omit°   *forgo*
Their mortal° natures, letting go safely by   *deadly*
The divine Desdemona.
MONTANO   What is she?
75 CASSIO   She that I spake of, our great captain's captain,
Left in the conduct of the bold Iago,
Whose footing here anticipates our thoughts
A sennight's speed.[7] Great Jove, Othello guard,
And swell his sail with thine own powerful breath,
80 That he may bless this bay with his tall ship,
Make love's quick pants in Desdemona's arms,
Give renewed fire to our extincted spirits,
And bring all Cyprus comfort.
             Enter DESDEMONA, IAGO, EMILIA, *and* RODERIGO
                    O, behold,
The riches of the ship is come on shore!
85 You men of Cyprus, let her have your knees.
             [MONTANO *and the* GENTLEMEN *make curtsy to*
             DESDEMONA]
Hail to thee, lady, and the grace of heaven
Before, behind thee, and on every hand
Enwheel thee round!
DESDEMONA   I thank you, valiant Cassio.
What tidings can you tell me of my lord?
90 CASSIO   He is not yet arrived, nor know I aught
But that he's well and will be shortly here.
DESDEMONA   O, but I fear—how lost you company?
CASSIO   The great contention of the sea and skies
Parted our fellowship.
95 VOICES (*within*)   A sail, a sail!
CASSIO   But hark, a sail.
             [*A shot*]
A GENTLEMAN   They give their greeting to the citadel.
This likewise is a friend.

6. *in . . . engineer*: whose natural beauty exhausts the poet's capacity to invent praise.   7. *Whose . . . speed*: Whose arrival predates our expectations by a week.

CASSIO   See for the news. [*Exit* GENTLEMAN]
Good ensign, you are welcome. [*Kissing* EMILIA] Welcome, mistress.

100 Let it not gall your patience, good Iago,
That I extend my manners. 'Tis my breeding
That gives me this bold show of courtesy.

IAGO   Sir, would she give you so much of her lips
As of her tongue she oft bestows on me,
105 You would have enough.

DESDEMONA   Alas, she has no speech![8]

IAGO   In faith, too much.
I find it still when I ha' leave to sleep.
Marry, before your ladyship, I grant,
110 She puts her tongue a little in her heart,[9]
And chides with thinking.

EMILIA   You ha' little cause to say so.

IAGO   Come on, come on. You are pictures out of door,
Bells in your parlours; wildcats in your kitchens,
Saints in your injuries; devils being offended,
115 Players in your housewifery, and hussies in your beds.[1]

DESDEMONA   O, fie upon thee, slanderer!

IAGO   Nay, it is true, or else I am a Turk.
You rise to play and go to bed to work.

EMILIA   You shall not write my praise.

IAGO   No, let me not.

120 DESDEMONA   What wouldst write of me, if thou shouldst praise me?

IAGO   O, gentle lady, do not put me to't,
For I am nothing if not critical.

DESDEMONA   Come on, essay°—there's one gone to the harbour?   *try*

IAGO   Ay, madam.

125 DESDEMONA   I am not merry, but I do beguile°   *disguise*
The thing I am° by seeming otherwise.   *(worried for Othello)*
Come, how wouldst thou praise me?

IAGO   I am about it, but indeed my invention
Comes from my pate as birdlime[2] does from frieze°—   *coarse wool cloth*
130 It plucks out brains and all. But my muse labours,°   *(in childbirth)*
And thus she is delivered:
If she be fair and wise, fairness and wit,
The one's for use, the other useth it.[3]

DESDEMONA   Well praised! How if she be black and witty?

135 IAGO   If she be black and thereto have a wit,
She'll find a white that shall her blackness fit.[4]

DESDEMONA   Worse and worse.

EMILIA   How if fair and foolish?

IAGO   She never yet was foolish that was fair,
For even her folly° helped her to an heir.   *foolishness; lechery*

140 DESDEMONA   These are old fond° paradoxes, to make fools laugh   *foolish*
i'th' alehouse.

---

8. Perhaps: Alas, the accused scolding chatterbox is not even rising to her own defense (both a defense of Emilia and a prod for her to speak).
9. She keeps her (critical) thoughts to herself.
1. *You are . . . beds:* Iago shifts from Emilia to women generally in this speech. *pictures:* models of silent propriety. *Bells:* Noisy. *kitchens:* perhaps domestic affairs generally, rather than a specific room. *Saints:* Martyrs.

Players in your housewifery: Deceptive in managing household expenses. *hussies:* wanton (perhaps businesslike, or sparing of sexual favors).
2. Sticky substance used to trap small birds.
3. *The one's . . . it:* Intelligence makes use of beauty.
4. *black:* dark-haired or dark-complexioned. *white:* fair-skinned person ("wight" means "person"). *fit:* (sexual).

What miserable praise hast thou for her
That's foul° and foolish?   ugly

IAGO   There's none so foul and foolish thereunto,°   to boot
145   But does foul° pranks which fair and wise ones do.   lascivious

DESDEMONA   O heavy ignorance! Thou praisest the worst best.
But what praise couldst thou bestow on a deserving woman
indeed—one that, in the authority of her merit, did justly put
on the vouch° of very malice itself?   compel the approval

150   IAGO   She that was ever fair and never proud,
Had tongue at will and yet was never loud,
Never lacked gold and yet went never gay,°   lavishly clothed
Fled from her wish, and yet said 'Now I may';[5]
She that, being angered, her revenge being nigh,
155   Bade her wrong stay° and her displeasure fly;   sense of injury end
She that in wisdom never was so frail
To change the cod's head for the salmon's tail;[6]
She that could think and ne'er disclose her mind,
See suitors following, and not look behind—
160   She was a wight, if ever such wights were—

DESDEMONA   To do what?

IAGO   To suckle fools, and chronicle small beer.[7]

DESDEMONA   O most lame and impotent conclusion! Do not
learn of him, Emilia, though he be thy husband. How say you,
165   Cassio, is he not a most profane and liberal° counsellor?   outspoken

CASSIO   He speaks home, madam. You may relish him more in°   as
the soldier than in the scholar.

                [CASSIO and DESDEMONA talk apart]

IAGO [aside]   He takes her by the palm. Ay, well said°—whisper.   well done
With as little a web as this will I ensnare as great a fly as Cassio.
170   Ay, smile upon her, do. I will gyve° thee in thine own court-   shackle
ship.° You say true, 'tis so indeed. If such tricks as these strip   courtliness
you out of your lieutenantry, it had been better you had not
kissed your three fingers[8] so oft, which now again you are most
apt to play the sir° in. Very good, well kissed, an excellent   gentleman
175   curtsy, 'tis so indeed; yet again your fingers to your lips? Would
they were clyster-pipes° for your sake.   enema tubes

                Trumpets within

[Aloud] The Moor—I know his trumpet.

CASSIO   'Tis truly so.

DESDEMONA   Let's meet him and receive him.

CASSIO   Lo where he comes!

                Enter OTHELLO and attendants

OTHELLO [to DESDEMONA]   O my fair warrior!

DESDEMONA   My dear Othello.

180   OTHELLO   It gives me wonder great as my content
To see you here before me. O my soul's joy,
If after every tempest come such calms,
May the winds blow till they have wakened death,
And let the labouring barque° climb hills of seas   small ship

---

5. Voluntarily withstood temptation even when given the choice.
6. To make an unworthy exchange. Probably also suggesting sexual infidelity: "cod" means "penis," and "tail" equals "vulva."

7. To breast-feed babies and keep track of trivial domestic goods. That is, such perfect virtue suits only a dull, complacent, decidedly ungenteel housewife.
8. Kissing one's own hand was a common courtly gesture from a gentleman to a lady.

185   Olympus-high,[9] and duck again as low
        As hell's from heaven. If it were now to die[1]
        'Twere now to be most happy, for I fear
        My soul hath her content so absolute
        That not another comfort like to this
        Succeeds° in unknown fate.°   *will follow / future*

190 DESDEMONA   The heavens forbid
        But that our loves and comforts should increase
        Even as our days do grow.

OTHELLO   Amen to that, sweet powers!
        I cannot speak enough of this content.
        It stops me here, it is too much of joy.
195   And this, *(they kiss)* and this, the greatest discords be
        That e'er our hearts shall make.

IAGO *[aside]*   O, you are well tuned now,
        But I'll set down the pegs that make this music,[2]
        As honest as I am.

OTHELLO   Come, let us to the castle.
        News, friends: our wars are done, the Turks are drowned.
200   How does my old acquaintance of this isle?—
        Honey, you shall be well desired° in Cyprus,   *welcomed*
        I have found great love amongst them. O my sweet,
        I prattle out of fashion, and I dote
        In mine own comforts. I prithee, good Iago,
205   Go to the bay and disembark my coffers.
        Bring thou the master° to the citadel.   *captain*
        He is a good one, and his worthiness
        Does challenge° much respect. Come, Desdemona.—   *deserve*
        Once more, well met at Cyprus!

                      Exeunt OTHELLO *and* DESDEMONA
                      [with all but IAGO *and* RODERIGO*]*

210 IAGO *[to an attendant as he goes out]*   Do thou meet me pres-
        ently at the harbour.   *[To* RODERIGO*]* Come hither. If thou beest
        valiant—as they say base° men being in love have then a nobil-   *lowly born*
        ity in their natures more than is native to them—list° me. The   *listen to*
        lieutenant tonight watches on the court of guard.[3] First, I
215   must tell thee this: Desdemona is directly in love with him.

RODERIGO   With him? Why, 'tis not possible!

IAGO   Lay thy finger thus,° and let thy soul be instructed. Mark   *Be silent*
        me with what violence she first loved the Moor, but for brag-
        ging and telling her fantastical lies. To love him still for prat-
220   ing?—let not thy discreet heart think it. Her eye must be fed,
        and what delight shall she have to look on the devil? When the
        blood is made dull with the act of sport, there should be again
        to inflame it, and to give satiety a fresh appetite, loveliness in
        favour,° sympathy in years, manners, and beauties, all which   *looks*
225   the Moor is defective in. Now, for want of these required con-
        veniences,° her delicate tenderness will find itself abused,°   *compatibilities / revolted*
        begin to heave the gorge,° disrelish and abhor the Moor. Very   *feel nausea*
        nature will instruct her in it and compel her to some second
        choice. Now, sir, this granted—as it is a most pregnant° and   *obvious; (sexual)*

---

9. Mt. Olympus, home of the Greek gods and hence too high for mortals.
1. To perish; to have an orgasm.

2. I'll untune (by loosening) the "pegs" that hold the strings of a musical instrument taut.
3. Cassio is in charge of the watch at the guardhouse.

230 unforced position—who stands so eminent in the degree of⁴
this fortune as Cassio does?—a knave very voluble,° no further   *facile*
conscionable° than in putting on the mere form of civil and   *no more ethical*
humane seeming for the better compass° of his salt° and most   *achievement* /*lewd*
hidden loose affection. Why, none; why, none—a slipper° and   *slippery*
235 subtle knave, a finder of occasion, that has an eye can stamp
and counterfeit advantages,⁵ though true advantage never present itself, a devilish knave! Besides, the knave is handsome,
young, and hath all those requisites in him that folly° and green   *wantonness*
minds look after. A pestilent° complete knave, and the woman   *damnably*
240 hath found him already.

RODERIGO I cannot believe that in her. She's full of most blessed
condition.

IAGO Blessed fig's end!° The wine she drinks is made of grapes.   *(obscene)*
If she had been blessed, she would never have loved the Moor.
245 Blessed pudding!° Didst thou not see her paddle with the palm   *sausage*
of his hand? Didst not mark that?

RODERIGO Yes, that I did, but that was but courtesy.

IAGO Lechery, by this hand; an index and obscure prologue to
the history of lust and foul thoughts.⁶ They met so near with
250 their lips that their breaths embraced together. Villainous
thoughts, Roderigo! When these mutualities so marshal the
way, hard at hand comes the master and main exercise,⁷ th'in-
corporate° conclusion. Pish! But, sir, be you ruled by me. I have   *in the flesh*
brought you from Venice. Watch you tonight. For the com-
255 mand, I'll lay't upon you.⁸ Cassio knows you not; I'll not be far
from you. Do you find some occasion to anger Cassio, either
by speaking too loud, or tainting° his discipline, or from what   *insulting*
other course you please, which the time shall more favourably
minister.°   *provide*
260 RODERIGO Well.

IAGO Sir, he's rash and very sudden in choler, and haply° may   *perhaps*
strike at you. Provoke him that he may, for even out of that will
I cause these of Cyprus to mutiny, whose qualification shall
come into no true taste again⁹ but by the displanting of Cassio.
265 So shall you have a shorter journey to your desires by the means
I shall then have to prefer° them, and the impediment most   *promote*
profitably removed, without the which there were no expectation of our prosperity.

RODERIGO I will do this, if you can bring it to any opportunity.
270 IAGO I warrant thee. Meet me by and by at the citadel. I must
fetch his necessaries° ashore. Farewell.   *Othello's possessions*

RODERIGO Adieu.   *Exit*

IAGO That Cassio loves her, I do well believe it.
That she loves him, 'tis apt and of great credit.°   *likely and believable*
275 The Moor—howbe't that I endure him not—
Is of a constant, loving, noble nature,
And I dare think he'll prove to Desdemona
A most dear° husband. Now I do love her too,   *affectionate; costly*
Not out of absolute lust—though peradventure

---

4. *in the degree of:* as next in line for.
5. Who can (like a counterfeiter) create his own opportunities.
6. *an . . . thoughts:* the analogy is to a dirty book. *index:*
table of contents. *obscure:* encoded. *history:* story.

7. When these intimacies have cleared the way, the
main event follows close behind. Here, the analogy is to
an official procession.
8. Stand watch tonight. I'll see that you receive orders.
9. *whose . . . again:* who will not be adequately appeased.

280	I stand accountant° for as great a sin—	*accountable*
	But partly led to diet° my revenge	*feed*
	For that I do suspect the lusty Moor	
	Hath leapt into my seat,° the thought whereof	*slept with my wife*
	Doth, like a poisonous mineral, gnaw my inwards;°	*innards*
285	And nothing can or shall content my soul	
	Till I am evened with him, wife for wife—	
	Or failing so, yet that I put the Moor	
	At least into a jealousy so strong	
	That judgement cannot cure, which thing to do,	
290	If this poor trash of Venice whom I trace	
	For his quick hunting stand the putting on,[1]	
	I'll have our Michael Cassio on the hip,°	*at my mercy*
	Abuse° him to the Moor in the rank garb°—	*Slander / "hot" manner*
	For I fear Cassio with my nightcap,° too—	*(as sexual rival)*
295	Make the Moor thank me, love me, and reward me	
	For making him egregiously an ass,	
	And practising upon° his peace and quiet	*undermining*
	Even to madness. 'Tis here,° but yet confused.	*My plan is here*
	Knavery's plain face is never seen till used. *Exit*	

2.2

Enter Othello's HERALD *reading a proclamation*

HERALD   It is Othello's pleasure—our noble and valiant general—that, upon certain tidings now arrived importing the
mere perdition° of the Turkish fleet, every man put himself   *entire loss*
into triumph: some to dance, some to make bonfires, each man
5   to what sport and revels his addiction° leads him; for besides   *inclination*
these beneficial news, it is the celebration of his nuptial. So
much was his pleasure should be proclaimed. All offices° are   *storehouses*
open, and there is full liberty of feasting from this present hour
of five till the bell have told eleven. Heaven bless the isle of
10 Cyprus and our noble general, Othello!   *Exit*

2.3

Enter OTHELLO, DESDEMONA, CASSIO, *and attendants*

OTHELLO Good Michael, look you to the guard tonight.		
Let's teach ourselves that honourable stop°		*self-restraint*
Not to outsport° discretion.		*pass the limits of*
CASSIO Iago hath direction what to do,		
5 But notwithstanding, with my personal eye		
Will I look to't.		
OTHELLO Iago is most honest.		
Michael, good night. Tomorrow with your earliest		
Let me have speech with you. [*To* DESDEMONA] Come, my dear love,		
The purchase made, the fruits are to ensue.		
10 That profit's yet to come 'tween me and you.[1]		
[*To* CASSIO] Good night.		

Exeunt OTHELLO, DESDEMONA [*and attendants*]

Enter IAGO

---

1. *If . . . on:* If Roderigo, whom I follow (?), train (?),
put weights on to slow him down (?), is successfully set
on the hunt when incited.

2.2 Location: A street in Cyprus.
2.3 Location: The citadel at Cyprus.
1. We haven't yet consummated our marriage.

CASSIO   Welcome, Iago. We must to the watch.

IAGO   Not this hour, lieutenant; 'tis not yet ten o'th' clock. Our
general cast° us thus early for the love of his Desdemona, who   dismissed
15 let us not therefore blame. He hath not yet made wanton the
night with her, and she is sport for Jove.

CASSIO   She's a most exquisite lady.

IAGO   And I'll warrant her full of game.

CASSIO   Indeed, she's a most fresh and delicate creature.

20 IAGO   What an eye she has! Methinks it sounds a parley° to prov-   (military) call
ocation.

CASSIO   An inviting eye, and yet, methinks, right modest.

IAGO   And when she speaks, is it not an alarum° to love?   a call (to arms)

CASSIO   She is indeed perfection.

25 IAGO   Well, happiness to their sheets. Come, lieutenant. I have
a stoup° of wine, and here without are a brace° of Cyprus gal-   two quarts / pair
lants that would fain have a measure° to the health of black   would like to drink
Othello.

CASSIO   Not tonight, good Iago. I have very poor and unhappy
30 brains for drinking. I could well wish courtesy would invent
some other custom of entertainment.

IAGO   O, they are our friends! But one cup. I'll drink for you.

CASSIO   I ha' drunk but one cup tonight, and that was craftily
qualified,° too, and behold what innovation° it makes here! I   well diluted / disorder
35 am infortunate in the infirmity, and dare not task my weakness
with any more.

IAGO   What, man, 'tis a night of revels, the gallants desire it!

CASSIO   Where are they?

IAGO   Here at the door. I pray you call them in.

40 CASSIO   I'll do't, but it dislikes me.°   *Exit*   I don't like doing it

IAGO   If I can fasten but one cup upon him,
With that which he hath drunk tonight already
He'll be as full of quarrel and offence
As my young mistress' dog. Now my sick fool Roderigo,
45 Whom love hath turned almost the wrong side out,
To Desdemona hath tonight caroused
Potations pottle-deep, and he's to watch.[2]
Three else of Cyprus—noble swelling° spirits   proud
That hold their honours in a wary distance,[3]
50 The very elements° of this warlike isle—   typical residents
Have I tonight flustered with flowing cups,
And they watch too. Now 'mongst this flock of drunkards
Am I to put our Cassio in some action
That may offend the isle.
          Enter MONTANO, CASSIO, GENTLEMEN, *and* [*servants
          with wine*]
                              But here they come.
55 If consequence do but approve my dream,[4]
My boat sails freely both with wind and stream.°   current

CASSIO   Fore God, they have given me a rouse° already.   full draft

MONTANO   Good faith, a little one; not past a pint,
As I am a soldier.

IAGO   Some wine, ho!

---

2. *caroused . . . watch:* consumed drink to the bottom   3. Who are touchy about their honor.
of the tankard, and he's assigned guard duty.   4. If events turn out as I hope.

60 [*Sings*]   And let me the cannikin° clink, clink,   *drinking vessel*
           And let me the cannikin clink.
               A soldier's a man,
               O, man's life's but a span,
           Why then, let a soldier drink.
65   Some wine, boys!
CASSIO   Fore God, an excellent song.
IAGO   I learned it in England, where indeed they are most potent
     in potting.[5] Your Dane, your German, and your swag°-bellied   *hanging*
     Hollander—drink, ho!—are nothing to your English.
70 CASSIO   Is your Englishman so exquisite in his drinking?
IAGO   Why, he drinks you with facility your Dane dead drunk.
     He sweats not to overthrow your Almain.° He gives your Hol-   *German*
     lander a vomit ere the next pottle° can be filled.   *tankard*
CASSIO   To the health of our general!
75 MONTANO   I am for it, lieutenant, and I'll do you justice.°   *match your drinking*
IAGO   O sweet England!
     [*Sings*]   King Stephen was and a worthy peer,
               His breeches cost him but a crown;
               He held them sixpence all too dear,
80   With that he called the tailor lown.°   *lout*
           He was a wight of high renown,
               And thou art but of low degree.
           'Tis pride° that pulls the country down,   *ostentatious clothing*
               Then take thy auld cloak about thee.
85   Some wine, ho!
CASSIO   Fore God, this is a more exquisite song than the other.
IAGO   Will you hear't again?
CASSIO   No, for I hold him to be unworthy of his place that does
     those things. Well, God's above all, and there be souls must be
90   saved, and there be souls must not be saved.[6]
IAGO   It's true, good lieutenant.
CASSIO   For mine own part—no offence to the general, nor any
     man of quality°—I hope to be saved.   *rank*
IAGO   And so do I too, lieutenant.
95 CASSIO   Ay, but, by your leave, not before me. The lieutenant is
     to be saved before the ensign. Let's ha' no more of this. Let's to
     our affairs. God forgive us our sins. Gentlemen, let's look to
     our business. Do not think, gentlemen, I am drunk. This is my
     ensign, this is my right hand, and this is my left. I am not drunk
100   now. I can stand well enough, and I speak well enough.
GENTLEMEN   Excellent well.
CASSIO   Why, very well then. You must not think then that I am
     drunk.   *Exit*
MONTANO   To th' platform, masters. Come, let's set the watch.
               [*Exeunt* GENTLEMEN]
105 IAGO   You see this fellow that is gone before—
     He's a soldier fit to stand by Caesar
     And give direction; and do but see his vice.
     'Tis to his virtue a just equinox,°   *of equal size*
     The one as long as th'other. 'Tis pity of him.
110   I fear the trust Othello puts him in,

---

5. Most adept at drinking.
6. Referring to the idea of predestination, the belief
held by Calvinist Protestants that some souls are destined from the outset to be saved and others damned.

On some odd time of his infirmity,
Will shake this island.

MONTANO   But is he often thus?

IAGO   'Tis evermore his prologue to his sleep.
He'll watch the horologe a double set[7]
If drink rock not his cradle.

115   MONTANO   It were well
The general were put in mind of it.
Perhaps he sees it not, or his good nature
Prizes the virtue that appears in Cassio,
And looks not on his evils. Is not this true?

                    Enter RODERIGO

120   IAGO   [*aside*]   How now, Roderigo!
I pray you after the lieutenant, go.   *Exit* RODERIGO

MONTANO   And 'tis great pity that the noble Moor
Should hazard such a place as his own second
With one of an engraffed° infirmity.   ingrained

125   It were an honest action to say so
To the Moor.

IAGO   Not I, for this fair island!
I do love Cassio well, and would do much
To cure him of this evil.

VOICES   (*within*)   Help, help!

IAGO   But hark, what noise?

                    Enter CASSIO, *driving in* RODERIGO

130   CASSIO   'Swounds, you rogue, you rascal!

MONTANO   What's the matter, lieutenant?

CASSIO   A knave teach me my duty?—I'll beat the knave into a
twiggen° bottle.   wicker-cased

RODERIGO   Beat me?

135   CASSIO   Dost thou prate, rogue?

MONTANO   Nay, good lieutenant, I pray you, sir, hold your hand.

CASSIO   Let me go, sir, or I'll knock you o'er the mazard.°   head

MONTANO   Come, come, you're drunk.

CASSIO   Drunk?

                    They fight

140   IAGO   [*to* RODERIGO]   Away, I say. Go out and cry a mutiny.
                                        [*Exit* RODERIGO]
Nay, good lieutenant. God's will, gentlemen!
Help, ho! Lieutenant! Sir! Montano! Sir!
Help, masters. Here's a goodly watch indeed.

                    A bell rung

Who's that which rings the bell? Diablo,° ho!   The devil

145   The town will rise. God's will, lieutenant, hold.
You'll be ashamed for ever.

                    Enter OTHELLO *and attendants, with weapons*

OTHELLO   What is the matter here?

MONTANO   'Swounds, I bleed still. I am hurt to th' death.
                    [*Attacking* CASSIO] He dies.

OTHELLO   Hold, for your lives!

IAGO   Hold, ho, lieutenant, sir, Montano, gentlemen!

150   Have you forgot all place of sense and duty?
Hold, the general speaks to you. Hold, hold, for shame.

---

7. He'll stay up twice around the clock.

OTHELLO Why, how now, ho? From whence ariseth this?
Are we turned Turks, and to ourselves do that
Which heaven hath forbid the Ottomites?°   *(by raising a storm)*
155 For Christian shame, put by this barbarous brawl.
He that stirs next to carve for his own rage°   *draw a sword in anger*
Holds his soul light. He dies upon his motion.
Silence that dreadful bell—it frights the isle
From her propriety.
        [*Bell stops*]
                    What is the matter, masters?
160 Honest Iago, that looks dead with grieving,
Speak. Who began this? On thy love I charge thee.
IAGO I do not know. Friends all but now, even now,
In quarter° and in terms like bride and groom   *Under control*
Devesting them° for bed; and then but now—   *Getting undressed*
165 As if some planet° had unwitted men—   *astrological influence*
Swords out, and tilting one at others' breasts
In opposition bloody. I cannot speak
Any beginning to this peevish odds,°   *silly quarrel*
And would in action glorious I had lost
170 Those legs that brought me to a part of it.
OTHELLO How comes it, Michael, you are thus forgot?
CASSIO I pray you pardon me. I cannot speak.
OTHELLO Worthy Montano, you were wont be° civil.   *you used to be*
The gravity and stillness of your youth
175 The world hath noted, and your name is great
In mouths of wisest censure.° What's the matter,   *judgment*
That you unlace your reputation thus,
And spend your rich opinion° for the name   *reputation*
Of a night-brawler? Give me answer to it.
180 MONTANO Worthy Othello, I am hurt to danger.
Your officer Iago can inform you,
While I spare speech—which something now offends me°—   *somewhat now pains me*
Of all that I do know; nor know I aught
By me that's said or done amiss this night,
185 Unless self-charity° be sometimes a vice,   *care of oneself*
And to defend ourselves it be a sin
When violence assails us.
OTHELLO   Now, by heaven,
My blood begins my safer guides to rule,
And passion, having my best judgement collied,°   *darkened*
190 Essays to lead the way. 'Swounds, if I stir,
Or do but lift this arm, the best of you
Shall sink in my rebuke. Give me to know
How this foul rout began, who set it on,
And he that is approved in this offence,
195 Though he had twinned with me, both at a birth,
Shall lose me. What, in a town of war
Yet° wild, the people's hearts brimful of fear,   *Still*
To manage° private and domestic quarrel   *carry on*
In night, and on the court and guard of safety!8
200 'Tis monstrous. Iago, who began't?
MONTANO [*to* IAGO] If partially affined° or leagued in office   *biased (for Cassio)*

8. And at the place where safety and security are at stake (on the night watch).

Thou dost deliver more or less than truth,
Thou art no soldier.
IAGO   Touch me not so near.
I had rather ha' this tongue cut from my mouth
205   Than it should do offence to Michael Cassio.
Yet I persuade myself to speak the truth
Shall nothing wrong him. This it is, general.
Montano and myself being in speech,
There comes a fellow crying out for help,
210   And Cassio following him with determined sword
To execute upon° him. Sir, this gentleman   To attack
Steps in to Cassio, and entreats his pause.
Myself the crying fellow did pursue,
Lest by his clamour, as it so fell out,
215   The town might fall in fright. He, swift of foot,
Outran my purpose, and I returned, the rather
For that I heard the clink and fall of swords
And Cassio high in oath, which till tonight
I ne'er might say before. When I came back—
220   For this was brief—I found them close together
At blow and thrust, even as again they were
When you yourself did part them.
More of this matter cannot I report,
But men are men. The best sometimes forget.
225   Though Cassio did some little wrong to him,
As men in rage strike those that wish them best,
Yet surely Cassio, I believe, received
From him that fled some strange indignity
Which patience could not pass.°   let pass
OTHELLO   I know, Iago,
230   Thy honesty and love doth mince° this matter,   minimize
Making it light to Cassio. Cassio, I love thee,
But never more be officer of mine.
          Enter DESDEMONA, *attended*
Look if my gentle love be not raised up.
I'll make thee an example.
235   DESDEMONA   What is the matter, dear?
OTHELLO   All's well now, sweeting.
Come away to bed. [*To* MONTANO] Sir, for your hurts
Myself will be your surgeon. [*To attendants*] Lead him off.
          [*Exeunt attendants with* MONTANO]
Iago, look with care about the town,
240   And silence those whom this vile brawl distracted.
Come, Desdemona. 'Tis the soldier's life
To have their balmy slumbers waked with strife.
          Exeunt [OTHELLO *the*] *Moor*, DESDEMONA,
                                    and attendants
IAGO   What, are you hurt, lieutenant?
CASSIO   Ay, past all surgery.
245   IAGO   Marry, God forbid.
CASSIO   Reputation, reputation, reputation—O, I ha' lost my rep-
utation, I ha' lost the immortal part of myself, and what remains
is bestial! My reputation, Iago, my reputation.
IAGO   As I am an honest man, I thought you had received some
250   bodily wound. There is more sense in that than in reputation.

Reputation is an idle and most false imposition,° oft got without   *artificial notion*
merit and lost without deserving. You have lost no reputation
at all unless you repute yourself such a loser. What, man, there
are more ways to recover the general again. You are but now
255   cast in his mood—a punishment more in policy⁹ than in malice, even so as one would beat his offenceless dog to affright an
imperious lion. Sue to° him again, and he's yours.   *Petition*

CASSIO   I will rather sue to be despised than to deceive so good
a commander with so slight, so drunken, and so indiscreet an
260   officer. Drunk, and speak parrot,° and squabble? Swagger,   *rant on*
swear, and discourse fustian° with one's own shadow? O thou   *nonsense*
invisible spirit of wine, if thou hast no name to be known by,
let us call thee devil.

IAGO   What was he that you followed with your sword? What had
265   he done to you?

CASSIO   I know not.

IAGO   Is't possible?

CASSIO   I remember a mass of things, but nothing distinctly; a
quarrel, but nothing wherefore.° O God, that men should put   *but not why*
270   an enemy in their mouths° to steal away their brains! That we   *should drink*
should with joy, pleasance, revel, and applause transform our-
selves into beasts!

IAGO   Why, but you are now well enough. How came you thus
recovered?

275   CASSIO   It hath pleased the devil drunkenness to give place to
the devil wrath. One unperfectness shows me another, to make
me frankly despise myself.

IAGO   Come, you are too severe a moraller. As the time, the
place, and the condition of this country stands, I could heartily
280   wish this had not befallen; but since it is as it is, mend it for
your own good.

CASSIO   I will ask him for my place again. He shall tell me I am
a drunkard. Had I as many mouths as Hydra,¹ such an answer
would stop them all. To be now a sensible man, by and by a
285   fool, and presently a beast! O, strange! Every inordinate cup is
unblessed, and the ingredient is a devil.

IAGO   Come, come. Good wine is a good familiar creature, if it
be well used. Exclaim no more against it. And, good lieutenant,
I think you think I love you.

290   CASSIO   I have well approved° it, sir—I drunk?   *tested*

IAGO   You or any man living may be drunk at a time, man. I'll
tell you what you shall do. Our general's wife is now the general. I may say so in this respect, for that he hath devoted and
given up himself to the contemplation, mark, and denotement°   *observation*
295   of her parts° and graces. Confess yourself freely to her. Impor-   *qualities*
tune her help to put you in your place again. She is of so free,°   *generous*
so kind, so apt, so blessed a disposition, she holds it a vice in
her goodness not to do more than she is requested. This broken
joint between you and her husband entreat her to splinter,°   *heal with a splint*
300   and, my fortunes against any lay° worth naming, this crack of   *wager*
your love shall grow stronger than it was before.

CASSIO   You advise me well.

---

9. *cast . . . policy:* dismissed in anger—a matter of   1. A mythical serpent with many heads who grew two
policy (of public example).   more when one was cut off.

IAGO   I protest,° in the sincerity of love and honest kindness.   *insist*

CASSIO   I think it freely, and betimes° in the morning I will   *early*
305   beseech the virtuous Desdemona to undertake for me. I am
       desperate of my fortunes if they check° me here.   *stop*

IAGO   You are in the right. Good night, lieutenant. I must to the
       watch.

CASSIO   Good night, honest Iago.   *Exit*

310 IAGO   And what's he then that says I play the villain,
       When this advice is free I give, and honest,
       Probal° to thinking, and indeed the course   *Wise*
       To win the Moor again? For 'tis most easy
       Th'inclining° Desdemona to subdue   *The well-disposed*
315   In any honest suit. She's framed as fruitful°   *generous*
       As the free elements; and then for her
       To win the Moor, were't to renounce his baptism,
       All seals and symbols of redeemèd sin,
       His soul is so enfettered to her love
320   That she may make, unmake, do what she list,
       Even as her appetite° shall play the god   *wishes*
       With his weak function.° How am I then a villain,   *faculties*
       To counsel Cassio to this parallel° course   *suitable*
       Directly to his good? Divinity° of hell: *Theology*
325   When devils will the blackest sins put on,
       They do suggest at first with heavenly shows,
       As I do now; for whiles this honest fool
       Plies Desdemona to repair his fortune,
       And she for him pleads strongly to the Moor,
330   I'll pour this pestilence into his ear:
       That she repeals him° for her body's lust,   *appeals for him*
       And by how much she strives to do him good
       She shall undo her credit with the Moor.
       So will I turn her virtue into pitch,²
335   And out of her own goodness make the net
       That shall enmesh them all.
                   Enter RODERIGO
                             How now, Roderigo?

RODERIGO   I do follow here in the chase, not like a hound that
       hunts, but one that fills up the cry.° My money is almost spent,   *a pack follower*
       I ha' been tonight exceedingly well cudgelled, and I think the
340   issue will be I shall have so much° experience for my pains: *only so much*
       and so, with no money at all and a little more wit, return again
       to Venice.

IAGO   How poor are they that ha' not patience!
       What wound did ever heal but by degrees?
345   Thou know'st we work by wit and not by witchcraft,
       And wit depends on dilatory° time.   *drawn-out*
       Does't not go well? Cassio hath beaten thee,
       And thou by that small hurt hast cashiered° Cassio.   *dismissed*
       Though other things grow fair against the sun,
350   Yet fruits that blossom first will first be ripe.³
       Content thyself a while. By the mass,° 'tis morning.   *(a mild oath)*

---

2. Black, sticky substance used as a snare. The more the thing caught in it tries to escape, the more stuck it becomes.

3. *Though . . . ripe:* Although others may appear to be prospering, your plan will be successful soonest because started first.

Pleasure and action make the hours seem short.
Retire thee. Go where thou art billeted.
Away, I say. Thou shalt know more hereafter.
Nay, get thee gone.   *Exit* RODERIGO
355   Two things are to be done.
My wife must move for Cassio to her mistress.
I'll set her on.
Myself a while to draw the Moor apart,
And bring him jump° when he may Cassio find   exactly
360   Soliciting his wife. Ay, that's the way.
Dull not device by coldness and delay.⁴   *Exit*

3.1

Enter CASSIO *with* MUSICIANS

CASSIO   Masters, play here—I will content° your pains—   reward
Something that's brief, and bid 'Good morrow, general'.
[*Music*.] *Enter* CLOWN
CLOWN   Why, masters, ha' your instruments been in Naples,
that they speak i'th' nose thus?¹
5   MUSICIAN   How, sir, how?
CLOWN   Are these, I pray you, wind instruments?²
MUSICIAN   Ay, marry are they, sir.
CLOWN   O, thereby hangs a tail.
MUSICIAN   Whereby hangs a tale, sir?
10 CLOWN   Marry, sir, by many a wind instrument that I know. But
masters, here's money for you, and the general so likes your
music that he desires you, for love's sake, to make no more
noise with it.
MUSICIAN   Well, sir, we will not.
15 CLOWN   If you have any music that may not° be heard, to't again;   cannot
but, as they say, to hear music the general does not greatly care.
MUSICIAN   We ha' none such, sir.
CLOWN   Then put up your pipes in your bag, for I'll away. Go,
vanish into air, away.   *Exeunt* MUSICIANS
20 CASSIO   Dost thou hear, my honest friend?
CLOWN   No, I hear not your honest friend, I hear you.
CASSIO   Prithee, keep up thy quillets.° There's a poor piece of   pack up your puns
gold for thee. If the gentlewoman that attends the general's wife
be stirring, tell her there's one Cassio entreats her a little favour
25   of speech. Wilt thou do this?
CLOWN   She is stirring, sir. If she will stir hither, I shall seem° to   arrange
notify unto her.
CASSIO   Do, good my friend.   *Exit* CLOWN
Enter IAGO
In happy time,° Iago.   Well met
IAGO   You ha' not been abed, then.
CASSIO   Why, no. The day had broke
30   Before we parted. I ha' made bold, Iago,
To send in to your wife. My suit to her

---

4. Don't let sluggishness and slowness to act weaken
the plot.
3.1 Location: Outside Othello and Desdemona's room.
1. That they sound so nasal; perhaps a reference to
venereal disease, often associated with Naples, or a

phallic or anal joke.
2. The exchange that follows depends on the connections between wind instruments, flatulence, and
"tale/tail."

Is that she will to virtuous Desdemona
Procure me some access.

IAGO   I'll send her to you presently,°   *immediately*
35 And I'll devise a mean to draw the Moor
Out of the way, that your converse and business
May be more free.

CASSIO   I humbly thank you for't.   *Exit* IAGO
I never knew a Florentine more kind and honest.
            Enter EMILIA

EMILIA   Good morrow, good lieutenant. I am sorry
40 For your displeasure, but all will sure be well.
The general and his wife are talking of it,
And she speaks for you stoutly. The Moor replies
That he you hurt is of great fame in Cyprus,
And great affinity,° and that in wholesome wisdom   *well connected*
45 He might not but refuse you. But he protests he loves you,
And needs no other suitor but his likings
To take the saf'st occasion by the front°   *forelock*
To bring you in again.

CASSIO   Yet I beseech you,
If you think fit, or that it may be done,
50 Give me advantage of some brief discourse
With Desdemon alone.

EMILIA   Pray you come in.
I will bestow you where you shall have time
To speak your bosom° freely.   *heart*

CASSIO   I am much bound to you.
                                                          Exeunt

3.2
            Enter OTHELLO, IAGO, *and* GENTLEMEN

OTHELLO   These letters give, Iago, to the pilot,
And by him do my duties° to the senate.   *send my respects*
That done, I will be walking on the works.°   *fortifications*
Repair there to me.

IAGO   Well, my good lord, I'll do't.   *[Exit]*
5 OTHELLO   This fortification, gentlemen—shall we see't?
A GENTLEMAN   We'll wait upon your lordship.   *Exeunt*

3.3
            Enter DESDEMONA, CASSIO, *and* EMILIA

DESDEMONA   Be thou assured, good Cassio, I will do
All my abilities in thy behalf.

EMILIA   Good madam, do. I warrant it grieves my husband
As if the cause were his.

5 DESDEMONA   O, that's an honest fellow. Do not doubt, Cassio,
But I will have my lord and you again
As friendly as you were.

CASSIO   Bounteous madam,
Whatever shall become of Michael Cassio
He's never anything but your true servant.

10 DESDEMONA   I know't. I thank you. You do love my lord.
You have known him long, and be you well assured

3.2 Location: The citadel.   3.3 Location: The citadel's garden.

He shall in strangeness stand no farther off
Than in a politic distance.[1]
CASSIO   Ay, but, lady,
That policy may either last so long,
15   Or feed upon such nice and wat'rish diet,
Or breed itself so out of circumstance,[2]
That, I being absent and my place supplied,°   *filled*
My general will forget my love and service.
DESDEMONA   Do not doubt° that. Before Emilia here   *fear*
20   I give thee warrant° of thy place. Assure thee,   *assurance*
If I do vow a friendship I'll perform it
To the last article. My lord shall never rest.
I'll watch him tame, and talk him out of patience.[3]
His bed shall seem a school, his board a shrift.°   *confessional*
25   I'll intermingle everything he does
With Cassio's suit. Therefore be merry, Cassio,
For thy solicitor° shall rather die   *advocate*
Than give thy cause away.°   *up*

                Enter OTHELLO *and* IAGO

EMILIA   Madam, here comes my lord.
CASSIO   Madam, I'll take my leave.
DESDEMONA   Why, stay, and hear me speak.
30   CASSIO   Madam, not now. I am very ill at ease,
Unfit for mine own purposes.
DESDEMONA   Well, do your discretion.   *Exit* CASSIO
IAGO   Ha! I like not that.
OTHELLO   What dost thou say?
35   IAGO   Nothing, my lord. Or if, I know not what.
OTHELLO   Was not that Cassio parted from my wife?
IAGO   Cassio, my lord? No, sure, I cannot think it,
That he would steal away so guilty-like
Seeing your coming.
40   OTHELLO   I do believe 'twas he.
DESDEMONA   How now, my lord?
I have been talking with a suitor here,
A man that languishes in your displeasure.
OTHELLO   Who is't you mean?
45   DESDEMONA   Why, your lieutenant, Cassio; good my lord,
If I have any grace or power to move you,
His present reconciliation take;°   *Accept him now*
For if he be not one that truly loves you,
That errs in ignorance and not in cunning,°   *not knowingly*
50   I have no judgement in an honest face.
I prithee call him back.
OTHELLO   Went he hence now?
DESDEMONA   Yes, faith, so humbled
That he hath left part of his grief with me
55   To suffer with him. Good love, call him back.
OTHELLO   Not now, sweet Desdemon. Some other time.
DESDEMONA   But shall't be shortly?
OTHELLO   The sooner, sweet, for you.

---

1. *He . . . distance:* He will distance himself from you
only as much as good diplomacy requires.
2. *Or feed . . . circumstance:* Or persist based on such
unimportant and poor justifications, or continue by
chance.
3. I'll keep him awake until he obeys me, and talk to
him beyond his endurance.

DESDEMONA Shall't be tonight at supper?
OTHELLO   No, not tonight.
DESDEMONA Tomorrow dinner,° then?   *midday meal*
OTHELLO   I shall not dine at home.
60   I meet the captains at the citadel.
DESDEMONA Why then, tomorrow night, or Tuesday morn,
        On Tuesday noon, or night, on Wednesday morn—
        I prithee name the time, but let it not
        Exceed three days. In faith, he's penitent,
65   And yet his trespass, in our common reason°—   *normal judgment*
        Save that, they say, the wars must make example
        Out of her° best—is not almost a fault   *(war's)*
        T'incur a private check.⁴ When shall he come?
        Tell me, Othello. I wonder in my soul
70   What you would ask me that I should deny,
        Or stand so mamm'ring° on? What, Michael Cassio,   *hesitating*
        That came a-wooing with you, and so many a time
        When I have spoke of you dispraisingly
        Hath ta'en your part—to have so much to-do
75   To bring him in?° By'r Lady, I could do much.⁵   *into favor*
OTHELLO   Prithee, no more. Let him come when he will.
        I will deny thee nothing.
DESDEMONA   Why, this is not a boon.
        'Tis as I should entreat you wear your gloves,
        Or feed on nourishing dishes, or keep you warm,
80   Or sue to you to do a peculiar° profit   *particular*
        To your own person. Nay, when I have a suit
        Wherein I mean to touch your love indeed,
        It shall be full of poise° and difficult weight,   *balanced judgment*
        And fearful to be granted.
OTHELLO   I will deny thee nothing,
85   Whereon I do beseech thee grant me this:
        To leave me but a little to myself.
DESDEMONA Shall I deny you? No. Farewell, my lord.
OTHELLO Farewell, my Desdemona. I'll come to thee straight.°   *immediately*
DESDEMONA Emilia, come. [*To* OTHELLO] Be as your fancies
            teach° you.   *as your whims lead*
90   Whate'er you be, I am obedient.
                    Exeunt DESDEMONA *and* EMILIA
OTHELLO Excellent wretch!° Perdition catch my soul   *(affectionate)*
        But I do love thee, and when I love thee not,
        Chaos is come again.
IAGO   My noble lord.
95 OTHELLO What dost thou say, Iago?
IAGO   Did Michael Cassio, when you wooed my lady,
        Know of your love?
OTHELLO He did, from first to last. Why dost thou ask?
IAGO   But for a satisfaction of my thought,
        No further harm.
100 OTHELLO   Why of thy thought, Iago?
IAGO   I did not think he had been acquainted with her.
OTHELLO O yes, and went between us very oft.
IAGO   Indeed?

---

4. *is . . . check:* is barely worth even private criticism.   5. Do much to make you regret your reluctance (?).

OTHELLO   Indeed? Ay, indeed. Discern'st thou aught in that?
105   Is he not honest?

IAGO   Honest, my lord?

OTHELLO   Honest? Ay, honest.

IAGO   My lord, for aught I know.

OTHELLO   What dost thou think?

IAGO   Think, my lord?

110   OTHELLO   'Think, my lord?' By heaven, thou echo'st me
As if there were some monster in thy thought
Too hideous to be shown! Thou dost mean something.
I heard thee say even now thou liked'st not that,
When Cassio left my wife. What didst not like?
115   And when I told thee he was of my counsel°   *in my confidence*
In my whole course of wooing, thou cried'st 'Indeed?'
And didst contract and purse thy brow together
As if thou then hadst shut up in thy brain
Some horrible conceit.° If thou dost love me,   *thought*
120   Show me thy thought.

IAGO   My lord, you know I love you.

OTHELLO   I think thou dost,
And for° I know thou'rt full of love and honesty,   *since*
And weigh'st thy words before thou giv'st them breath,
125   Therefore these stops° of thine fright me the more;   *reluctances*
For such things in a false disloyal knave
Are tricks of custom,° but in a man that's just,   *habitual*
They're close dilations,[6] working from the heart
That passion cannot rule.°   *control*

IAGO   For Michael Cassio,
130   I dare be sworn I think that he is honest.

OTHELLO   I think so too.

IAGO   Men should be what they seem,
Or those that be not, would they might seem none.[7]

OTHELLO   Certain, men should be what they seem.

IAGO   Why then, I think Cassio's an honest man.

135   OTHELLO   Nay, yet there's more in this.
I prithee speak to me as to thy thinkings,
As thou dost ruminate, and give thy worst of thoughts
The worst of words.

IAGO   Good my lord, pardon me.
Though I am bound to every act of duty,
140   I am not bound to that all slaves are free to.[8]
Utter my thoughts? Why, say they are vile and false,
As where's that palace whereinto foul things
Sometimes intrude not? Who has that breast so pure
But some uncleanly apprehensions
145   Keep leets and law-days, and in sessions sit
With meditations lawful?[9]

OTHELLO   Thou dost conspire against thy friend,° Iago,   *(Othello)*
If thou but think'st him wronged and mak'st his ear
A stranger to thy thoughts.

IAGO   I do beseech you,

6. Involuntary revelations of interior, close-kept secrets.
7. *Or . . . none:* If only those who are not what they seem didn't seem to be what they are not.
8. I am not obligated to reveal my inner thoughts,
something about which even slaves have a choice.
9. *uncleanly . . . lawful:* illegitimate thoughts meet in court ("leets") from time to time (on "law-days") and debate (in court "sessions") with legitimate ones.

<table>
<tr><td>150</td><td>Though I perchance am vicious° in my guess—</td><td>mistaken</td></tr>
</table>

150 Though I perchance am vicious° in my guess—   mistaken
   As I confess it is my nature's plague
   To spy into abuses, and oft my jealousy
   Shapes faults that are not—that your wisdom then,
   From one that so imperfectly conceits,°   imagines
155 Would take no notice, nor build yourself a trouble
   Out of his scattering° and unsure observance.   incoherent
   It were not for your quiet nor your good,
   Nor for my manhood, honesty, and wisdom,
   To let you know my thoughts.
OTHELLO   What dost thou mean?
160 IAGO   Good name in man and woman, dear my lord,
   Is the immediate jewel of their souls.
   Who steals my purse steals trash; 'tis something, nothing;
   'Twas mine, 'tis his, and has been slave to thousands.
   But he that filches from me my good name
165 Robs me of that which not enriches him
   And makes me poor indeed.
OTHELLO   By heaven, I'll know thy thoughts.
IAGO   You cannot, if my heart were in your hand;
   Nor shall not whilst 'tis in my custody.
OTHELLO   Ha!
IAGO   O, beware, my lord, of jealousy.
170 It is the green-eyed monster which doth mock
   The meat it feeds on.[1] That cuckold lives in bliss
   Who, certain of his fate, loves not his wronger.[2]
   But O, what damnèd minutes tells he o'er
   Who dotes yet doubts, suspects yet fondly loves!
175 OTHELLO   O misery!
IAGO   Poor and content is rich, and rich enough,
   But riches fineless° is as poor as winter   boundless
   To him that ever fears he shall be poor.
   Good God the souls of all my tribe defend
   From jealousy!
180 OTHELLO   Why, why is this?
   Think'st thou I'd make a life of jealousy,
   To follow still the changes of the moon°   To renew endlessly
   With fresh suspicions? No, to be once in doubt
   Is once to be resolved.° Exchange me for a goat   to be finally settled
185 When I shall turn the business of my soul
   To such exsufflicate and blowed° surmises   inflated and blown-up
   Matching thy inference. 'Tis not to make me jealous
   To say my wife is fair, feeds well, loves company,
   Is free of speech, sings, plays, and dances well.
190 Where virtue is, these are more virtuous,
   Nor from mine own weak merits will I draw
   The smallest fear or doubt of her revolt,°   or fear of her betrayal
   For she had eyes and chose me. No, Iago,
   I'll see before I doubt; when I doubt, prove;
195 And on the proof, there is no more but this:
   Away at once with love or jealousy.

---

1. *which . . . on:* that tortures, as it consumes, the heart of the jealous person.   2. Who, knowing it is his fate to be cuckolded, doesn't love his wife.

IAGO   I am glad of this, for now I shall have reason
      To show the love and duty that I bear you
      With franker spirit. Therefore, as I am bound,
200   Receive it from me. I speak not yet of proof.
      Look to your wife. Observe her well with Cassio.
      Wear your eyes thus: not jealous, nor secure.
      I would not have your free and noble nature
      Out of self-bounty be abused.[3] Look to't.
205   I know our country disposition well.
      In Venice they do let God see the pranks
      They dare not show their husbands; their best conscience
      Is not to leave't undone, but keep't unknown.
OTHELLO   Dost thou say so?
210 IAGO   She did deceive her father, marrying you,
      And when she seemed to shake and fear your looks
      She loved them most.
OTHELLO   And so she did.
IAGO   Why, go to,° then.   *that's it*
      She that so young could give out such a seeming,
      To seel her father's eyes up close as oak,[4]
215   He thought 'twas witchcraft! But I am much to blame.
      I humbly do beseech you of your pardon
      For too much loving you.
OTHELLO   I am bound to thee for ever.
IAGO   I see this hath a little dashed your spirits.
OTHELLO   Not a jot, not a jot.
IAGO   I'faith, I fear it has.
220   I hope you will consider what is spoke
      Comes from my love. But I do see you're moved.
      I am to pray you not to strain my speech
      To grosser issues,° nor to larger reach   *greater conclusions*
      Than to suspicion.
225 OTHELLO   I will not.
IAGO   Should you do so, my lord,
      My speech should fall into such vile success
      Which my thoughts aimed not. Cassio's my worthy friend.
      My lord, I see you're moved.
OTHELLO   No, not much moved.
230   I do not think but Desdemona's honest.
IAGO   Long live she so, and long live you to think so!
OTHELLO   And yet how nature, erring from itself—
IAGO   Ay, there's the point; as, to be bold with you,
      Not to affect° many proposèd matches   *desire*
235   Of her own clime, complexion, and degree,
      Whereto we see in all things nature tends.
      Foh, one may smell in such a will most rank,
      Foul disproportions, thoughts unnatural!
      But pardon me. I do not in position°   *argument*
240   Distinctly speak of her, though I may fear
      Her will,° recoiling° to her better judgement,   *desire / submitting*
      May fall to match you with her country forms[5]
      And happily° repent.   *perhaps*

---

3. Be deceived on account of your own goodness.   father's eyes as tightly as oak (a fine-grained wood).
4. Perhaps: To cover ("seel" means "to blind") her   5. May happen to compare you with Venetian standards.

OTHELLO   Farewell, farewell.
  If more thou dost perceive, let me know more.
245 Set on thy wife to observe. Leave me, Iago.
IAGO [*going*]   My lord, I take my leave.
OTHELLO   Why did I marry? This honest creature doubtless
  Sees and knows more, much more, than he unfolds.
IAGO [*returning*]   My lord, I would I might entreat your honour
250 To scan this thing no farther. Leave it to time.
  Although 'tis fit that Cassio have his place—
  For sure he fills it up with great ability—
  Yet, if you please to hold him off a while,
  You shall by that perceive him and his means.[6]
255 Note if your lady strain his entertainment°   *urge his reception*
  With any strong or vehement importunity.
  Much will be seen in that. In the mean time,
  Let me be thought too busy° in my fears—   *meddlesome*
  As worthy cause I have to fear I am—
260 And hold her free,° I do beseech your honour.   *believe her innocent*
OTHELLO   Fear not my government.°   *self-conduct*
IAGO   I once more take my leave.
                                                    Exit
OTHELLO   This fellow's of exceeding honesty,
  And knows all qualities° with a learned spirit   *(human) types*
  Of human dealings. If I do prove her haggard,°   *wild (falconry)*
265 Though that her jesses were my dear heart-strings
  I'd whistle her off and let her down the wind
  To prey at fortune.[7] Haply for° I am black,   *Perhaps because*
  And have not those soft parts of conversation°   *easy manners*
  That chamberers° have; or for I am declined   *gallants*
270 Into the vale of years—yet that's not much—
  She's gone. I am abused,° and my relief   *deceived*
  Must be to loathe her. O curse of marriage,
  That we can call these delicate creatures ours
  And not their appetites! I had rather be a toad
275 And live upon the vapour of a dungeon
  Than keep a corner in the thing I love
  For others' uses. Yet 'tis the plague of great ones;
  Prerogatived° are they less than the base.°   *Privileged / lowborn*
  'Tis destiny unshunnable, like death.
280 Even then this forkèd plague is fated to us
  When we do quicken.[8]
            Enter DESDEMONA *and* EMILIA
                        Look where she comes.
  If she be false, O then heaven mocks itself!
  I'll not believe't.
DESDEMONA   How now, my dear Othello?
  Your dinner, and the generous° islanders   *noble*
285 By you invited, do attend° your presence.   *wait for*
OTHELLO   I am to blame.
DESDEMONA   Why do you speak so faintly? Are you not well?
OTHELLO   I have a pain upon my forehead here.°   *(from cuckold's horns)*

6. Method (for restoring himself to favor).
7. *Though . . . fortune:* Even if what tied her ("jesses" were leg straps put on a hawk) were my own heartstrings, I'd set her loose downwind forever to hunt on her own.
8. *Even . . . quicken:* The "plague" of horns (imagined to grow from the forehead of a cuckold) is our fate as soon as we live.

DESDEMONA   Faith, that's with watching.° 'Twill away again.   *from lack of sleep*
290   Let me but bind it hard, within this hour
      It will be well.
OTHELLO   Your napkin° is too little.   *handkerchief*
         [*He puts the napkin from him. It drops*]
      Let it alone. Come, I'll go in with you.
DESDEMONA   I am very sorry that you are not well.
                        Exeunt OTHELLO *and* DESDEMONA
EMILIA [*taking up the napkin*]   I am glad I have found this napkin.
295   This was her first remembrance from the Moor.
      My wayward husband hath a hundred times
      Wooed me to steal it, but she so loves the token—
      For he conjured her⁹ she should ever keep it—
      That she reserves it evermore about her
300   To kiss and talk to. I'll ha' the work ta'en out,°   *embroidery copied*
      And give't Iago. What he will do with it,
      Heaven knows, not I.
      I nothing,° but to please his fantasy.   *intend nothing*
            Enter IAGO
IAGO   How now, what do you here alone?
305   EMILIA   Do not you chide. I have a thing for you.
IAGO   You have a thing for me? It is a common thing.¹
EMILIA   Ha?
IAGO   To have a foolish wife.
EMILIA   O, is that all? What will you give me now
310   For that same handkerchief?
IAGO   What handkerchief?
EMILIA   What handkerchief?
      Why, that the Moor first gave to Desdemona,
      That which so often you did bid me steal.
315   IAGO   Hast stol'n it from her?
EMILIA   No, faith, she let it drop by negligence,
      And to th'advantage° I, being here, took't up.   *taking the occasion*
      Look, here 'tis.
IAGO   A good wench! Give it me.
EMILIA   What will you do with it, that you have been so earnest
      To have me filch it?
320   IAGO   Why, what is that to you?
         [*He takes the napkin*]
EMILIA   If it be not for some purpose of import,
      Give't me again. Poor lady, she'll run mad
      When she shall lack it.
IAGO   Be not acknown on't.° I have use for it. Go, leave me.   *Don't let it be known*
                        Exit EMILIA
325   I will in Cassio's lodging lose this napkin,
      And let him find it. Trifles light as air
      Are to the jealous confirmations strong
      As proofs of holy writ. This may do something.
      The Moor already changes with my poison.
330   Dangerous conceits° are in their natures poisons,   *ideas*
      Which at the first are scarce found to distaste,
      But, with a little act° upon the blood,   *effect*

---

9. Made her swear; perhaps also an unwitting backward glance at Brabanzio's charge in 1.3 that Othello
employed witchcraft to win Desdemona.
1. It is a vagina ("thing") available to all.

Burn like the mines of sulphur.[2]

Enter OTHELLO

                                                         I did say so.

Look where he comes. Not poppy nor mandragora[3]

335   Nor all the drowsy syrups of the world

Shall ever medicine thee to that sweet sleep

Which thou owedst° yesterday.   *owned*

OTHELLO   Ha, ha, false to me?

IAGO   Why, how now, general? No more of that.

340   OTHELLO   Avaunt, be gone. Thou hast set me on the rack.

I swear 'tis better to be much abused°   *mistreated; deceived*

Than but to know't a little.

IAGO   How now, my lord?

OTHELLO   What sense had I of her stol'n hours of lust?

I saw't not, thought it not; it harmed not me.

345   I slept the next night well, fed well, was free and merry.

I found not Cassio's kisses on her lips.

He that is robbed, not wanting° what is stol'n,   *missing*

Let him not know't and he's not robbed at all.

IAGO   I am sorry to hear this.

350   OTHELLO   I had been happy if the general camp,

Pioneers° and all, had tasted her sweet body,   *Manual laborers*

So° I had nothing known. O, now for ever   *If*

Farewell the tranquil mind, farewell content,

Farewell the plumèd troops and the big wars

355   That makes ambition virtue! O, farewell,

Farewell the neighing steed and the shrill trump,

The spirit-stirring drum, th'ear-piercing fife,

The royal banner, and all quality,°   *aspects*

Pride,° pomp, and circumstance° of glorious war!   *Magnificence / ceremony*

360   And O, you mortal engines° whose rude throats   *deadly cannons*

Th'immortal Jove's dread clamours° counterfeit,   *thunderclaps*

Farewell! Othello's occupation's gone.

IAGO   Is't possible, my lord?

OTHELLO   [*taking* IAGO *by the throat*]   Villain, be sure thou prove

                 my love a whore.

365   Be sure of it. Give me the ocular proof,

Or, by the worth of mine eternal soul,

Thou hadst been better have been born a dog

Than answer my waked wrath.

IAGO   Is't come to this?

OTHELLO   Make me to see't, or at the least so prove it

370   That the probation° bear no hinge nor loop   *proof*

To hang a doubt on, or woe upon thy life.

IAGO   My noble lord.

OTHELLO   If thou dost slander her and torture me,

Never pray more; abandon all remorse,

375   On horror's head horrors accumulate,

Do deeds to make heaven weep, all earth amazed,

For nothing canst thou to damnation add

Greater than that.

---

2. Pliny the Elder describes two islands of sulfur between mainland Italy and Sicily that were rumored to be always on fire.

3. A sleep-inducing substance made from the mandrake root.

IAGO   O grace, O heaven forgive me!
     Are you a man? Have you a soul or sense?
380   God buy you, take mine office.[4] O wretched fool,°   *(to himself)*
     That lov'st to make thine honesty a vice!°   *fault*
     O monstrous world, take note, take note, O world,
     To be direct and honest is not safe!
     I thank you for this profit,° and from hence   *profitable lesson*
385   I'll love no friend, sith° love breeds such offence.   *since*
OTHELLO   Nay, stay. Thou shouldst be honest.
IAGO   I should be wise, for honesty's a fool,
     And loses that° it works for.   *what*
OTHELLO   By the world,[5]
     I think my wife be honest, and think she is not.
390   I think that thou art just, and think thou art not.
     I'll have some proof. My name, that was as fresh
     As Dian's[6] visage, is now begrimed and black
     As mine own face. If there be cords, or knives,
     Poison, or fire, or suffocating streams,
395   I'll not endure it. Would I were satisfied!
IAGO   I see, sir, you are eaten up with passion.
     I do repent me that I put it to you.
     You would be satisfied?
OTHELLO   Would? Nay, and I will.
IAGO   And may. But how, how satisfied, my lord?
400   Would you, the supervisor,° grossly gape on,   *observer*
     Behold her topped?
OTHELLO   Death and damnation! O!
IAGO   It were a tedious° difficulty, I think,   *painful*
     To bring them to that prospect. Damn them then
     If ever mortal eyes do see them bolster°   *share a pillow*
405   More° than their own!° What then, how then?   *Other / own eyes*
     What shall I say? Where's satisfaction?
     It is impossible you should see this,
     Were they as prime° as goats, as hot as monkeys,   *lustful*
     As salt as wolves in pride,[7] and fools as gross
410   As ignorance made drunk. But yet I say,
     If imputation, and strong circumstances[8]
     Which lead directly to the door of truth,
     Will give you satisfaction, you might ha't.
OTHELLO   Give me a living reason she's disloyal.
415 IAGO   I do not like the office,
     But sith I am entered in this cause so far,
     Pricked to't° by foolish honesty and love,   *Prodded on*
     I will go on. I lay with Cassio lately,
     And being troubled with a raging tooth,
420   I could not sleep. There are a kind of men
     So loose of soul that in their sleeps
     Will mutter their affairs. One of this kind is Cassio.
     In sleep I heard him say 'Sweet Desdemona,
     Let us be wary, let us hide our loves',
425   And then, sir, would he grip and wring my hand,

---

4. Good-bye, I resign my official position (ensign).
5. Othello's speech (lines 388–95) does not appear in Q.
6. Diana, goddess of chastity and of the (pale) moon.
The Second Quarto (1630) replaces "My" (line 391)

with "Her," a plausible but arguably less powerful reading that lacks textual authority.
7. As lecherous as wolves in heat.
8. If inference and strong circumstantial evidence.

Cry 'O, sweet creature!', then kiss me hard,
As if he plucked up kisses by the roots,
That grew upon my lips, lay his leg o'er my thigh,
And sigh, and kiss, and then cry 'Cursèd fate,
430   That gave thee to the Moor!'
OTHELLO   O, monstrous, monstrous!
IAGO   Nay, this was but his dream.
OTHELLO   But this denoted a foregone conclusion.°   *an earlier event*
IAGO   'Tis a shrewd doubt,° though it be but a dream,   *reasonable fear*
435   And this may help to thicken other proofs
That do demonstrate thinly.
OTHELLO   I'll tear her all to pieces.
IAGO   Nay, yet be wise; yet we see nothing done.
She may be honest yet. Tell me but this:
Have you not sometimes seen a handkerchief
440   Spotted with strawberries in your wife's hand?
OTHELLO   I gave her such a one. 'Twas my first gift.
IAGO   I know not that, but such a handkerchief—
I am sure it was your wife's—did I today
See Cassio wipe his beard with.
OTHELLO   If it be that—
445 IAGO   If it be that, or any that was hers,
It speaks against her with the other proofs.
OTHELLO   O that the slave° had forty thousand lives!   *(Cassio)*
One is too poor, too weak for my revenge.
Now do I see 'tis true. Look here, Iago.
450   All my fond love thus do I blow to heaven—'tis gone.
Arise, black vengeance, from the hollow hell.
Yield up, O love, thy crown and hearted throne°   *rule of the heart*
To tyrannous hate! Swell, bosom, with thy freight,°   *burden*
For 'tis of aspics'° tongues.   *poison snakes'*
IAGO   Yet be content.
OTHELLO   O, blood, blood, blood!
455 IAGO   Patience, I say. Your mind may change.
OTHELLO   Never, Iago. Like to the Pontic Sea,°   *Black Sea*
Whose icy current and compulsive course
Ne'er knows retiring ebb, but keeps due on
To the Propontic and the Hellespont,[9]
460   Even so my bloody thoughts with violent pace
Shall ne'er look back, ne'er ebb to humble love,
Till that a capable° and wide revenge   *capacious*
Swallow them up.
        [*He kneels*]
                  Now, by yon marble heaven,
In the due reverence of a sacred vow
I here engage my words.
465 IAGO   Do not rise yet.
        IAGO *kneels*[1]
Witness you ever-burning lights above,
You elements that clip° us round about,   *embrace (sexual?)*
Witness that here Iago doth give up

---

9. The Propontic was the body of water bounded by the straits of Bosphorus and the Dardanelles (Hellespont), the latter strait leading to the Aegean.
1. Parody of the marriage ceremony.

The execution° of his wit, hands, heart   *command*
470   To wronged Othello's service. Let him command,
And to obey shall be in me remorse,°   *pity (for Othello)*
What bloody business ever.°   *soever*
     [*They rise*]

OTHELLO   I greet thy love,
Not with vain thanks, but with acceptance bounteous,
And will upon the instant put thee to't.°   *immediately test it*
475   Within these three days let me hear thee say
That Cassio's not alive.

IAGO   My friend is dead.
'Tis done at your request; but let her live.

OTHELLO   Damn her, lewd minx!° O, damn her, damn her!   *wanton*
Come, go with me apart. I will withdraw
480   To furnish me with some swift means of death
For the fair devil. Now art thou my lieutenant.

IAGO   I am your own for ever.   *Exeunt*

3.4
Enter DESDEMONA, EMILIA, *and the* CLOWN

DESDEMONA   Do you know, sirrah,[1] where Lieutenant Cassio
lies?

CLOWN   I dare not say he lies anywhere.

DESDEMONA   Why, man?

5   CLOWN   He's a soldier, and for me to say a soldier lies, 'tis stabbing.

DESDEMONA   Go to. Where lodges he?

CLOWN   To tell you where he lodges is to tell you where I lie.

DESDEMONA   Can anything be made of this?

10   CLOWN   I know not where he lodges, and for me to devise a
lodging and say he lies here, or he lies there, were to lie in
mine own throat.°   *lie outrageously*

DESDEMONA   Can you enquire him out, and be edified by
report?

15   CLOWN   I will catechize the world for him; that is, make questions, and by them answer.

DESDEMONA   Seek him, bid him come hither, tell him I have
moved° my lord on his behalf, and hope all will be well.   *petitioned*

CLOWN   To do this is within the compass° of man's wit, and   *scope*
20   therefore I will attempt the doing it.   *Exit*

DESDEMONA   Where should° I lose the handkerchief, Emilia?   *did*

EMILIA   I know not, madam.

DESDEMONA   Believe me, I had rather have lost my purse
Full of crusadoes,° and but° my noble Moor   *gold coins / but that*
25   Is true of mind, and made of no such baseness
As jealous creatures are, it were enough
To put him to ill thinking.

EMILIA   Is he not jealous?

DESDEMONA   Who, he? I think the sun where he was born
Drew all such humours from him.
     Enter OTHELLO

EMILIA   Look where he comes.

30   DESDEMONA   I will not leave him now till Cassio

3.4 Location: Before the citadel.   1. A form of address to an inferior.

Be called to him. How is't with you, my lord?

OTHELLO   Well, my good lady. [*Aside*] O hardness to dissemble!—
How do you, Desdemona?

DESDEMONA   Well, my good lord.

OTHELLO   Give me your hand. This hand is moist, my lady.

35   DESDEMONA   It hath felt no age, nor known no sorrow.

OTHELLO   This argues fruitfulness and liberal heart.[2]
Hot, hot and moist—this hand of yours requires
A sequester from liberty; fasting, and prayer,
Much castigation, exercise devout,

40   For here's a young and sweating devil here
That commonly rebels. 'Tis a good hand,
A frank° one.   *(sexually) open*

DESDEMONA   You may indeed say so,
For 'twas that hand that gave away my heart.

OTHELLO   A liberal hand. The hearts of old gave hands,

45   But our new heraldry is hands, not hearts.[3]

DESDEMONA   I cannot speak of this. Come now, your promise.

OTHELLO   What promise, chuck?°   *woodchuck (affectionate)*

DESDEMONA   I have sent to bid Cassio come speak with you.

OTHELLO   I have a salt and sorry rheum° offends me.   *badly watering eyes*
Lend me thy handkerchief.

50   DESDEMONA [*offering a handkerchief*]   Here, my lord.

OTHELLO   That which I gave you.

DESDEMONA   I have it not about me.

OTHELLO   Not?

DESDEMONA   No, faith, my lord.

OTHELLO   That's a fault. That handkerchief
Did an Egyptian to my mother give.

55   She was a charmer,° and could almost read   *sorceress*
The thoughts of people. She told her, while she kept it
'Twould make her amiable,° and subdue my father   *desirable*
Entirely to her love; but if she lost it,
Or made a gift of it, my father's eye

60   Should hold her loathèd, and his spirits should hunt
After new fancies. She, dying, gave it me,
And bid me, when my fate would have me wived,
To give it her.° I did so, and take heed on't.   *to my wife*
Make it a darling, like your precious eye.

65   To lose't or give't away were such perdition°   *loss; damnation*
As nothing else could match.

DESDEMONA   Is't possible?

OTHELLO   'Tis true. There's magic in the web of it.
A sibyl° that had numbered in the world   *female prophet*
The sun to course two hundred compasses[4]

70   In her prophetic fury sewed the work.
The worms were hallowed that did breed the silk,
And it was dyed in mummy,[5] which the skilful
Conserved of° maidens' hearts.   *Preserved out of*

DESDEMONA   I'faith, is't true?

---

2. This demonstrates fertility (perhaps, by implication, lust) and a generous (loose) heart. A moist hand was thought to be a sign of active desire.
3. These days the joining of hands doesn't signify the joining of hearts.
4. *that . . . compasses*: who was two hundred years old.
5. Fluid drained from mummified bodies, supposedly magical.

	OTHELLO	Most veritable. Therefore look to't well.	
75	DESDEMONA	Then would to God that I had never seen it!	
	OTHELLO	Ha, wherefore?	
	DESDEMONA	Why do you speak so startingly and rash?	
	OTHELLO	Is't lost? Is't gone? Speak, is't out o'th' way?	
	DESDEMONA	Heaven bless us!	
80	OTHELLO	Say you?	
	DESDEMONA	It is not lost, but what an if° it were?	an if=if
	OTHELLO	How?	
	DESDEMONA	I say it is not lost.	
	OTHELLO	Fetch't, let me see't.	
	DESDEMONA	Why, so I can, sir, but I will not now.	

85   This is a trick to put me from my suit.
        Pray you let Cassio be received again.

	OTHELLO	Fetch me the handkerchief. My mind misgives.	
	DESDEMONA	Come, come, you'll never meet a more sufficient° man.	complete
	OTHELLO	The handkerchief.	
	DESDEMONA	I pray, talk me of Cassio.	
	OTHELLO	The handkerchief.	
90	DESDEMONA	A man that all his time	

        Hath founded his good fortunes on your love,
        Shared dangers with you—

	OTHELLO	The handkerchief.	
	DESDEMONA	I'faith, you are to blame.	
95	OTHELLO	'Swounds!	Exit
	EMILIA	Is not this man jealous?	
	DESDEMONA	I ne'er saw this before.	

        Sure there's some wonder in this handkerchief.
        I am most unhappy in the loss of it.

	EMILIA	'Tis not a year or two shows us a man.[6]	
100		They are all but° stomachs, and we all but food.	nothing but

        They eat us hungrily, and when they are full,
        They belch us.

        Enter IAGO *and* CASSIO
        Look you, Cassio and my husband.

	IAGO [*to* CASSIO]	There is no other way. 'Tis she must do't,	

        And lo, the happiness![7] Go and importune her.

105	DESDEMONA	How now, good Cassio? What's the news with you?	
	CASSIO	Madam, my former suit. I do beseech you	

        That by your virtuous means I may again
        Exist and be a member of his love
        Whom I, with all the office of my heart,
110   Entirely honour. I would not be delayed.

        If my offence be of such mortal° kind   *deadly*
        That nor° my service past, nor present sorrows,   *neither*
        Nor purposed merit in futurity
        Can ransom me into his love again,
115   But to know so° must be my benefit.   *Even to know this*
        So° shall I clothe me in a forced content,   *If so*
        And shut° myself up in some other course   *give*
        To fortune's alms.

	DESDEMONA	Alas, thrice-gentle Cassio!	

---

6. Probably: It doesn't take long to see what men are made of.   7. What a happy coincidence (seeing Desdemona).

My advocation is not now in tune.[8]

120 My lord is not my lord, nor should I know him
Were he in favour° as in humour altered.   *appearance*
So help me every spirit sanctified
As I have spoken for you all my best,
And stood within the blank of° his displeasure   *in the aim of*
125 For my free speech! You must a while be patient.
What I can do I will, and more I will
Than for myself I dare. Let that suffice you.

IAGO   Is my lord angry?

EMILIA   He went hence but now,
And certainly in strange unquietness.

130 IAGO   Can he be angry? I have seen the cannon
When it hath blown his ranks into the air,
And, like the devil, from his very arm
Puffed his own brother;[9] and is he angry?
Something of moment then. I will go meet him.
135 There's matter in't indeed, if he be angry.

DESDEMONA   I prithee do so.   *Exit* IAGO
                Something sure of state,[1]
Either from Venice or some unhatched practice°   *unfinished plot*
Made demonstrable here in Cyprus to him,
Hath puddled his clear spirit; and in such cases
140 Men's natures wrangle with inferior things,
Though great ones are their object. 'Tis even so;
For let our finger ache and it indues°   *induces*
Our other, healthful members even to a sense
Of pain. Nay, we must think men are not gods,
145 Nor of them look for such observancy°   *careful attention*
As fits the bridal.° Beshrew me° much, Emilia, *wedding / (mild curse)*
I was—unhandsome° warrior as I am—   *unskilled*
Arraigning his unkindness with my soul;
But now I find I had suborned the witness,
And he's indicted falsely.[2]

150 EMILIA   Pray heaven it be
State matters, as you think, and no conception
Nor no jealous toy° concerning you.   *whim*

DESDEMONA   Alas the day, I never gave him cause.

EMILIA   But jealous souls will not be answered so.
155 They are not ever jealous for the cause,
But jealous for they're jealous. It is a monster
Begot upon itself, born on itself.

DESDEMONA   Heaven keep the monster from Othello's mind.

EMILIA   Lady, amen.

160 DESDEMONA   I will go seek him. Cassio, walk here about.
If I do find him fit I'll move your suit,
And seek to effect it to my uttermost.

CASSIO   I humbly thank your ladyship.

               Exeunt DESDEMONA *and* EMILIA

Enter BIANCA[3]

BIANCA Save you,° friend Cassio.   *God save you*

CASSIO   What make° you from home?   *brings*

165 How is't with you, my most fair Bianca?
I'faith, sweet love, I was coming to your house.

BIANCA And I was going to your lodging, Cassio.
What, keep a week away? Seven days and nights,
Eightscore-eight hours, and lovers' absent hours

170 More tedious than the dial eightscore times![4]
O weary reckoning!°   *calculating*

CASSIO   Pardon me, Bianca,
I have this while with leaden thoughts been pressed,
But I shall in a more continuate° time   *opportune*
Strike off° this score of absence. Sweet Bianca,   *Make up*
Take me this work out.°   *Copy this embroidery*
[*He gives her Desdemona's napkin*]

175 BIANCA   O Cassio, whence came this?
This is some token from a newer friend.
To the felt absence now I feel a cause.
Is't come to this? Well, well.

CASSIO   Go to,° woman.   *Stop it*
Throw your vile guesses in the devil's teeth,

180 From whence you have them. You are jealous now
That this is from some mistress, some remembrance.
No, by my faith, Bianca.

BIANCA   Why, whose is it?

CASSIO I know not, neither. I found it in my chamber.
I like the work well. Ere it be demanded°—   *sought out*

185 As like° enough it will—I would have it copied.   *likely*
Take it, and do't, and leave me for this time.

BIANCA Leave you? Wherefore?

CASSIO I do attend here on the general,
And think it no addition,° nor my wish,   *(to my cause)*
To have him see me womaned.

190 BIANCA   Why, I pray you?

CASSIO Not that I love you not.

BIANCA   But that you do not love me.
I pray you bring me on the way a little,
And say if I shall see you soon at night.

CASSIO 'Tis but a little way that I can bring you,

195 For I attend here; but I'll see you soon.

BIANCA 'Tis very good. I must be circumstanced.[5]
                                                        Exeunt

4.1

Enter IAGO *and* OTHELLO

IAGO Will you think so?

OTHELLO   Think so, Iago?

IAGO What, to kiss in private?

OTHELLO   An unauthorized kiss.

---

3. "Bianca" means "white" in Italian—perhaps part of
the play's ironic reversal of conventional color imagery,
given that Bianca is a "customer" (courtesan, 4.1.117).
4. *lovers'* . . . *times:* each hour lovers are parted is eight

score (160) times more tedious than normal clock time.
5. Content with what circumstances offer.
4.1 Location: Before the citadel.

IAGO   Or to be naked with her friend in bed
An hour or more, not meaning any harm?
5   OTHELLO   Naked in bed, Iago, and not mean harm?
It is hypocrisy against the devil.[1]
They that mean virtuously and yet do so,
The devil their virtue tempts, and they tempt heaven.[2]
IAGO   If they do nothing, 'tis a venial slip.°   *an excusable sin*
10   But if I give my wife a handkerchief—
OTHELLO   What then?
IAGO   Why then, 'tis hers, my lord, and being hers,
She may, I think, bestow't on any man.
OTHELLO   She is protectress of her honour, too.
15   May she give that?
IAGO   Her honour is an essence that's not seen.
They° have it very oft that have it not.   *They are reputed to*
But for the handkerchief—
OTHELLO   By heaven, I would most gladly have forgot it.
20   Thou said'st—O, it comes o'er my memory
As doth the raven o'er the infectious house,[3]
Boding to all!—he had my handkerchief.
IAGO   Ay, what of that?
OTHELLO   That's not so good now.
IAGO   What if I had said I had seen him do you wrong,
25   Or heard him say—as knaves be such abroad,[4]
Who having by their own importunate suit
Or voluntary dotage of some mistress
Convincèd or supplied° them, cannot choose   *Seduced or satisfied*
But they must blab—
OTHELLO   Hath he said anything?
30   IAGO   He hath, my lord. But, be you well assured,
No more than he'll unswear.
OTHELLO   What hath he said?
IAGO   Faith, that he did—I know not what he did.
OTHELLO   What, what?
IAGO   Lie—
OTHELLO   With her?
IAGO   With her, on her, what
you will.
OTHELLO   Lie with her? Lie on her? We say 'lie on her' when
35   they belie° her. Lie with her? 'Swounds, that's fulsome!°   *slander / nauseating*
Handkerchief—confessions—handkerchief. To[5] confess and be
hanged for his labour. First to be hanged and then to confess!
I tremble at it. Nature would not invest herself in such shadowing passion without some instruction.[6] It is not words that
40   shakes me thus. Pish! Noses, ears, and lips! Is't possible? Confess? Handkerchief? O devil!
    He falls down in a trance

---

1. *Naked . . . devil*: By showing every sign of committing adultery but then stopping just in time, they deliberately mislead the devil, who wrongly takes their
apparent intention to sin at face value (just as an ordinary hypocrite deceives by professing virtue).
2. *They . . . heaven*: Those who mean well ("virtuously")
but act in this lascivious fashion ("so") make it easy for the
devil successfully to tempt them, and they push heaven to
the point where it may not be able to forgive them (?).

3. The raven was thought to be an ill omen and a carrier of plague. *infectious*: plague-infested.
4. As such knaves do exist in the world.
5. Lines 36–41 do not appear in Q. Arguably, these
lines provide more time for Othello to drive himself to
distraction and hence make his collapse more plausible.
6. *Nature . . . instruction*: It isn't natural that I would
feel such overwhelming ("shadowing") emotion (jealousy) unless there were some cause for it.

IAGO   Work on; my medicine works. Thus credulous fools are caught,
　　And many worthy and chaste dames even thus,
　　All guiltless, meet reproach. What ho, my lord!
　　My lord, I say. Othello!

Enter CASSIO

45　　　　　　　　　　　　How now, Cassio?
CASSIO   What's the matter?
IAGO   My lord is fall'n into an epilepsy.
　　This is his second fit. He had one yesterday.
CASSIO   Rub him about the temples.
IAGO   　　　　　　　　　　No, forbear.
50　The lethargy° must have his° quiet course. 　　　　　　　　*trance / its*
　　If not, he foams at mouth, and by and by
　　Breaks out to savage madness. Look, he stirs.
　　Do you withdraw yourself a little while,
　　He will recover straight.° When he is gone 　　　　　　　*immediately*
55　I would on great occasion° speak with you. 　[*Exit* CASSIO] 　*important matters*
　　How is it, general? Have you not hurt your head?[7]
OTHELLO   Dost thou mock me?
IAGO   　　　　　　　　I mock you not, by heaven.
　　Would you would bear your fortune like a man.
OTHELLO   A hornèd man's a monster and a beast.
60　IAGO   There's many a beast then in a populous city,
　　And many a civil° monster. 　　　　　　　　　　　*city-dwelling*
OTHELLO   Did he confess it?
IAGO   Good sir, be a man.
　　Think every bearded fellow that's but yoked
65　May draw with you.[8] There's millions now alive
　　That nightly lie in those unproper beds
　　Which they dare swear peculiar.[9] Your case is better.
　　O, 'tis the spite of hell, the fiend's arch-mock,° 　　*devil's greatest mock*
　　To lip° a wanton in a secure° couch 　　　　　*kiss / an unsuspected*
70　And to suppose her chaste! No, let me know,
　　And knowing what I am,° I know what she shall be. 　　*(a cuckold)*
OTHELLO   O, thou art wise, 'tis certain.
IAGO   　　　　　　　　　　Stand you a while apart.
　　Confine yourself but in a patient list.° 　　　　　　　　*boundary*
　　Whilst you were here, o'erwhelmèd with your grief—
75　A passion most unsuiting such a man—
　　Cassio came hither. I shifted him away,
　　And laid good 'scuse upon your ecstasy,° 　　　　　　　*for your fit*
　　Bade him anon return and here speak with me,
　　The which he promised. Do but encave° yourself, 　　　　　*hide*
80　And mark the fleers,° the gibes and notable scorns 　　　　*sneers*
　　That dwell in every region of his face.
　　For I will make him tell the tale anew,
　　Where, how, how oft, how long ago, and when
　　He hath and is again to cope° your wife. 　　　　　　*copulate with*
85　I say, but mark his gesture. Marry, patience,
　　Or I shall say you're all-in-all in spleen,° 　　　*completely impulsive*
　　And nothing of a man.

---

7. Othello takes this as suggesting that he has grown cuckold's horns.
8. *every . . . you:* every married man ("yoked," like an ox, to his wife and hence to cuckoldry) labors ("draws")
under the same fate.
9. *That . . . peculiar:* Who lie in beds that don't belong entirely to them but that they would swear are exclusively their own.

OTHELLO   Dost thou hear, Iago?
   I will be found most cunning in my patience,
   But—dost thou hear?—most bloody.
IAGO   That's not amiss,
90   But yet keep time° in all. Will you withdraw?   *maintain control*
     [OTHELLO *stands apart*]
   Now will I question Cassio of Bianca,
   A hussy that by selling her desires
   Buys herself bread and cloth. It is a creature
   That dotes on Cassio—as 'tis the strumpet's plague
95   To beguile many and be beguiled by one.
   He, when he hears of her, cannot restrain
   From the excess of laughter.
     Enter CASSIO
                   Here he comes.
   As he shall smile, Othello shall go mad;
   And his unbookish° jealousy must conster°   *ignorant / construe*
100   Poor Cassio's smiles, gestures, and light behaviours
   Quite in the wrong. How do you now, lieutenant?
CASSIO   The worser that you give me the addition
   Whose want even kills me.
IAGO   Ply Desdemona well and you are sure on't.
105   Now, if this suit lay in Bianca's power,
   How quickly should you speed!
CASSIO [*laughing*]   Alas, poor caitiff!°   *wretch*
OTHELLO [*aside*]   Look how he laughs already.
IAGO   I never knew a woman love man so.
110 CASSIO   Alas, poor rogue! I think i'faith she loves me.
OTHELLO [*aside*]   Now he denies it faintly, and laughs it out.
IAGO   Do you hear, Cassio?
OTHELLO [*aside*]   Now he importunes him
   To tell it o'er. Go to, well said, well said.
IAGO   She gives it out that you shall marry her.
   Do you intend it?
115 CASSIO   Ha, ha, ha!
OTHELLO [*aside*]   Do ye triumph, Roman,[1] do you triumph?
CASSIO   I marry! What, a customer?° Prithee, bear some charity   *courtesan*
   to my wit°—do not think it so unwholesome. Ha, ha, ha!   *sense*
OTHELLO [*aside*]   So, so, so, so. They laugh that wins.
120 IAGO   Faith, the cry goes that you marry her.
CASSIO   Prithee, say true.
IAGO   I am a very villain else.°   *if it's not true*
OTHELLO [*aside*]   Ha' you scored° me? Well.   *scored off*
CASSIO   This is the monkey's own giving out.° She is persuaded *Bianca's own story*
125   I will marry her out of her own love and flattery, not out of my
   promise.
OTHELLO [*aside*]   Iago beckons me. Now he begins the story.
     [OTHELLO *draws closer*]
CASSIO   She was here even now. She haunts me in every place.
   I was the other day talking on the sea-bank with certain Vene-
130   tians, and thither comes the bauble,° and falls me thus about   *toy*
   my neck.

---

1. Perhaps Othello draws on associations either with Rome's imperial successes (and subsequent collapse) or with the Roman practice of holding celebratory processions.

OTHELLO [*aside*]   Crying 'O dear Cassio!' as it were. His gesture
    imports° it.   *indicates*
CASSIO   So hangs and lolls and weeps upon me, so shakes and
135   pulls me—ha, ha, ha!
OTHELLO [*aside*]   Now he tells how she plucked him to my
    chamber. O, I see that nose of yours, but not that dog I shall
    throw it to!²
CASSIO   Well, I must leave her company.
    Enter BIANCA
140   IAGO   Before me, look where she comes.
CASSIO   'Tis such another fitchew!³ Marry, a perfumed one. [*To*
    BIANCA] What do you mean by this haunting of me?
BIANCA   Let the devil and his dam° haunt you. What did you   *mother*
    mean by that same handkerchief you gave me even now? I was
145   a fine fool to take it. I must take out° the whole work—a likely   *copy*
    piece of work,° that you should find it in your chamber and   *an implausible story*
    know not who left it there. This is some minx's token, and I
    must take out the work. There, give it your hobby-horse.° [*Giv-*   *loose woman*
    ing CASSIO *the napkin*] Wheresoever you had it, I'll take out
150   no work on't.
CASSIO   How now, my sweet Bianca, how now, how now?
OTHELLO [*aside*]   By heaven, that should° be my handkerchief.   *must*
BIANCA   An° you'll come to supper tonight, you may. An you will   *If*
    not, come when you are next prepared for.⁴   *Exit*
155   IAGO   After her, after her.
CASSIO   Faith, I must, she'll rail in the streets else.
IAGO   Will you sup there?
CASSIO   Faith, I intend so.
IAGO   Well, I may chance to see you, for I would very fain speak
160   with you.
CASSIO   Prithee, come, will you?
IAGO   Go to, say no more.   *Exit* CASSIO
OTHELLO   How shall I murder him, Iago?
IAGO   Did you perceive how he laughed at his vice?
165   OTHELLO   O Iago!
IAGO   And did you see the handkerchief?
OTHELLO   Was that mine?
IAGO   Yours, by this hand. And to see how he prizes the foolish
    woman your wife. She gave it him, and he hath given it his
170   whore.
OTHELLO   I would have him nine years a-killing.⁵ A fine woman,
    a fair woman, a sweet woman.
IAGO   Nay, you must forget that.
OTHELLO   Ay, let her rot and perish, and be damned tonight, for
175   she shall not live. No, my heart is turned to stone; I strike it,
    and it hurts my hand. O, the world hath not a sweeter creature!
    She might lie by an emperor's side, and command him tasks.
IAGO   Nay, that's not your way.°   *(the way to think)*
OTHELLO   Hang her, I do but say what she is—so delicate with
180   her needle, an admirable musician. O, she will sing the savage-
    ness out of a bear! Of so high and plenteous wit and invention.°   *imagination*

---

2. *I see . . . to:* I'm envisioning my revenge, but the time
is not yet quite right. Cutting off the enemy's nose was
understood as a form of retribution.
3. Polecat, associated with prostitutes because of its

bad smell and presumed lecherousness.
4. Come next time I prepare for you (never).
5. I would spend nine years killing him.

IAGO   She's the worse for all this.

OTHELLO   O, a thousand, a thousand times! And then of so gen-
tle° a condition.   *highly born*

185 IAGO   Ay, too gentle.°   *generous (sexually)*

OTHELLO   Nay, that's certain. But yet the pity of it, Iago. O, Iago,
the pity of it, Iago!

IAGO   If you are so fond° over her iniquity, give her patent° to   *foolish / license*
offend; for if it touch not you, it comes near nobody.

190 OTHELLO   I will chop her into messes.° Cuckold me!   *pieces of food*

IAGO   O, 'tis foul in her.

OTHELLO   With mine officer.

IAGO   That's fouler.

OTHELLO   Get me some poison, Iago, this night. I'll not expostu-
195 late with her, lest her body and beauty unprovide my mind°   *weaken my resolve*
again. This night, Iago.

IAGO   Do it not with poison. Strangle her in her bed, even the
bed she hath contaminated.

OTHELLO   Good, good, the justice of it pleases, very good.

200 IAGO   And for Cassio, let me be his undertaker.° You shall hear   *murderer*
more by midnight.

OTHELLO   Excellent good.
        A trumpet
What trumpet is that same?

IAGO   I warrant, something from Venice.
        Enter LODOVICO, DESDEMONA, *and attendants*

205 'Tis Lodovico. This comes from the Duke. See, your wife's with
him.

LODOVICO   God save the worthy general.

OTHELLO   With all my heart,° sir.   *Thank you*

LODOVICO [*giving* OTHELLO *a letter*]   The Duke and the senators
210 of Venice greet you.

OTHELLO   I kiss the instrument° of their pleasures.°   *bearer / commands*
        [*He reads the letter*]

DESDEMONA   And what's the news, good cousin Lodovico?

IAGO [*to* LODOVICO]   I am very glad to see you, signor. Welcome
to Cyprus.

215 LODOVICO   I thank you. How does Lieutenant Cassio?

IAGO   Lives, sir.

DESDEMONA   Cousin, there's fall'n between him and my lord
An unkind° breach. But you shall make all well.   *unnatural*

OTHELLO   Are you sure of that?

220 DESDEMONA   My lord.

OTHELLO [*reads*]   'This fail you not to do as you will'—

LODOVICO   He did not call, he's busy in the paper.
Is there division 'twixt my lord and Cassio?

DESDEMONA   A most unhappy one. I would do much

225 T'atone° them, for the love I bear to Cassio.   *To reconcile*

OTHELLO   Fire and brimstone!

DESDEMONA   My lord?

OTHELLO   Are you wise?

DESDEMONA   What, is he angry?

LODOVICO   Maybe the letter moved him,
For, as I think, they do command him home,
Deputing Cassio in his government.°   *official position*

230 DESDEMONA   By my troth, I am glad on't.

OTHELLO   Indeed!

DESDEMONA   My lord?

OTHELLO [to DESDEMONA]   I am glad to see you mad.[6]

DESDEMONA   Why, sweet Othello!

235   OTHELLO   Devil!
       [He strikes her]

DESDEMONA   I have not deserved this.

LODOVICO   My lord, this would not be believed in Venice,
Though I should swear I saw't. 'Tis very much.°   *going too far*
Make her amends, she weeps.

OTHELLO   O, devil, devil!

240   If that the earth could teem with° woman's tears,   *become pregnant by*
Each drop she falls would prove a crocodile.[7]
Out of my sight!

DESDEMONA [going]   I will not stay to offend you.

LODOVICO   Truly, an obedient lady.
I do beseech your lordship call her back.

245   OTHELLO   Mistress!

DESDEMONA [returning]   My lord?

OTHELLO [to LODOVICO]   What would you° with her, sir?   *do you wish*

LODOVICO   Who, I, my lord?

OTHELLO   Ay, you did wish that I would make her turn.°   *return*

250   Sir, she can turn and turn,° and yet go on   *(sexually)*
And turn again, and she can weep, sir, weep,
And she's obedient, as you say, obedient,
Very obedient. [To DESDEMONA] Proceed you in your tears.
[To LODOVICO] Concerning this, sir—[To DESDEMONA] O well
      painted passion!
[To LODOVICO] I am commanded home. [To DESDEMONA] Get

255   you away.
I'll send for you anon. [To LODOVICO] Sir, I obey the mandate,
And will return to Venice. [To DESDEMONA] Hence, avaunt!°   *begone*
                       [Exit DESDEMONA]
[To LODOVICO] Cassio shall have my place, and, sir, tonight
I do entreat that we may sup together.

260   You are welcome, sir, to Cyprus. Goats and monkeys![8]   *Exit*

LODOVICO   Is this the noble Moor whom our full senate
Call all-in-all sufficient? Is this the nature
Whom passion could not shake, whose solid virtue
The shot of accident nor dart of chance
Could neither graze nor pierce?

265   IAGO   He is much changed.

LODOVICO   Are his wits safe? Is he not light of brain?

IAGO   He's that he is. I may not breathe my censure
What he might be. If what he might he is not,
I would to heaven he were.[9]

LODOVICO   What, strike his wife!

270   IAGO   Faith, that was not so well. Yet would I knew

---

6. Perhaps Othello is pleased that she's rejoicing in Cassio's promotion and hence revealing their adulterous affair, which she would be "mad" to do in public and in front of him.

7. Each drop would cause the earth to conceive a crocodile (crocodiles proverbially wept false tears for their victims).

8. Symbols of lust.

9. *I may . . . were:* I won't express my judgment on whether he is sane. If he is sane, I wish he were insane (because only that would excuse his bad behavior); if he is not sane, I wish he were.

That stroke would prove the worst.

LODOVICO   Is it his use,°   *custom*
    Or did the letters work upon his blood°   *passions*
    And new-create his fault?

IAGO   Alas, alas.
    It is not honesty in me to speak
275   What I have seen and known. You shall observe him,
    And his own courses° will denote him so   *actions*
    That I may save my speech. Do but go after,
    And mark how he continues.

LODOVICO   I am sorry that I am deceived in him.   *Exeunt*

4.2

Enter OTHELLO *and* EMILIA

OTHELLO   You have seen nothing then?
EMILIA   Nor ever heard, nor ever did suspect.
OTHELLO   Yes, you have seen Cassio and she together.
EMILIA   But then I saw no harm, and then I heard
5   Each syllable that breath made up between 'em.
OTHELLO   What, did they never whisper?
EMILIA   Never, my lord.
OTHELLO   Nor send you out o'th' way?
EMILIA   Never.
10   OTHELLO   To fetch her fan, her gloves, her mask, nor nothing?
EMILIA   Never, my lord.
OTHELLO   That's strange.
EMILIA   I durst, my lord, to wager she is honest,
    Lay down my soul at stake. If you think other,
15   Remove your thought; it doth abuse your bosom.
    If any wretch ha' put this in your head,
    Let heaven requite it with the serpent's curse,[1]
    For if she be not honest, chaste, and true,
    There's no man happy; the purest of their wives
    Is foul as slander.
20   OTHELLO   Bid her come hither. Go.   *Exit* EMILIA
    She says enough, yet she's a simple bawd
    That cannot say as much.[2] This is a subtle whore,
    A closet lock and key° of villainous secrets,   *A hider*
    And yet she'll kneel and pray—I ha' seen her do't.

Enter DESDEMONA *and* EMILIA

DESDEMONA   My lord, what is your will?
25   OTHELLO   Pray you, chuck, come hither.
DESDEMONA   What is your pleasure?
OTHELLO   Let me see your eyes.
    Look in my face.
DESDEMONA   What horrible fancy's this?
OTHELLO [*to* EMILIA]   Some of your function,[3] mistress.
30   Leave procreants° alone, and shut the door,   *copulators*
    Cough or cry 'Hem' if anybody come.
    Your mystery, your mystery°—nay, dispatch.   *Exit* EMILIA   *profession*
DESDEMONA   Upon my knees, what doth your speech import?

4.2 Location: The citadel.   2. *yet . . . much:* yet it would be a simpleminded go-
1. In Genesis, the curse that God laid on the serpent   between who can't say as much as she did.
who deceived Eve.   3. Fulfill your bawd's function by guarding the door.

I understand a fury in your words,
But not the words.

35 OTHELLO   Why, what art thou?

DESDEMONA   Your wife, my lord, your true and loyal wife.

OTHELLO   Come, swear it, damn thyself,
Lest, being° like one of heaven, the devils themselves   *appearing*
Should fear to seize thee. Therefore be double-damned:
Swear thou art honest.

40 DESDEMONA   Heaven doth truly know it.

OTHELLO   Heaven truly knows that thou art false as hell.

DESDEMONA   To whom, my lord? With whom? How am I false?

OTHELLO [*weeping*]   Ah, Desdemon, away, away, away!

DESDEMONA   Alas, the heavy day! Why do you weep?

45 Am I the motive of these tears, my lord?
If haply° you my father do suspect   *perhaps*
An instrument of this your calling back,
Lay not your blame on me. If you have lost him,
I have lost him too.

OTHELLO   Had it pleased God

50 To try me with affliction; had He rained
All kind of sores and shames on my bare head,
Steeped me in poverty to the very lips,
Given to captivity me and my utmost hopes,
I should have found in some place of my soul

55 A drop of patience. But, alas, to make me
The fixèd figure for the time of scorn
To point his slow and moving finger at[4]—
Yet could I bear that too, well, very well.
But there where I have garnered° up my heart,   *stored*

60 Where either I must live or bear no life,
The fountain[5] from the which my current runs
Or else dries up—to be discarded thence,
Or keep it as a cistern for foul toads
To knot and gender° in! Turn thy complexion there,   *To couple and engender*

65 Patience,[6] thou young and rose-lipped cherubin,
Ay, here look grim as hell.

DESDEMONA   I hope my noble lord esteems me honest.

OTHELLO   O, ay—as summer flies are in the shambles,°   *slaughterhouse*
That quicken even with blowing.[7] O thou weed,

70 Who art so lovely fair, and smell'st so sweet,
That the sense aches at thee—would thou hadst ne'er been born!

DESDEMONA   Alas, what ignorant sin have I committed?

OTHELLO   Was this fair paper, this most goodly book,
Made to write 'whore' upon? What committed?

75 Committed?[8] O thou public commoner,°   *prostitute*
I should make very forges of my cheeks,
That would to cinders burn up modesty,
Did I but speak thy deeds. What committed?

---

4. *The fixed . . . at:* The designated object of scorn for this scornful time to point (as on a clock face) its slowly moving hand at.
5. Spring. The language here imagines Desdemona as the source of Othello's potential offspring.
6. *Turn . . . / Patience:* Change color at the thought of that, Patience. Or perhaps Patience and the "cherubin"

(end of line) are Desdemona, whom Othello directs to gaze at his own face or a mirror.
7. Who come to life (or bring their offspring to life and hence make the meat foul) as soon as the eggs are deposited. The point seems to be the speed of breeding, inferred from Desdemona's supposed infidelity.
8. Lines 75–78 do not appear in Q.

Heaven stops the nose at it, and the moon winks;°   *closes its eyes*
80   The bawdy° wind, that kisses all it meets,   *promiscuous*
       Is hushed within the hollow mine of earth°   *within a cave*
       And will not hear't. What committed?
DESDEMONA   By heaven, you do me wrong.
OTHELLO   Are not you a strumpet?
85 **DESDEMONA**   No, as I am a Christian.
       If to preserve this vessel for my lord
       From any other foul unlawful touch
       Be not to be a strumpet, I am none.
OTHELLO   What, not a whore?
DESDEMONA   No, as I shall be saved.
90 **OTHELLO**   Is't possible?
DESDEMONA   O heaven forgive us!
OTHELLO   I cry you mercy° then.   *I beg your pardon*
       I took you for that cunning whore of Venice
       That married with Othello. [*Calling*] You, mistress,
95   That have the office opposite to Saint Peter
       And keeps the gate of hell,
                    Enter EMILIA
                              you, you, ay, you.
       We ha' done our course.° [*Giving money*] There's money for your pains.   *business*
       I pray you, turn the key and keep our counsel.   *Exit*
EMILIA   Alas, what does this gentleman conceive?°   *believe*
100   How do you, madam? How do you, my good lady?
DESDEMONA   Faith, half asleep.
EMILIA   Good madam, what's the matter with my lord?
DESDEMONA   With who?
EMILIA   Why, with my lord, madam.
DESDEMONA   Who is thy lord?
EMILIA   He that is yours, sweet lady.
105 **DESDEMONA**   I ha' none. Do not talk to me, Emilia.
       I cannot weep, nor answers have I none
       But what should go by water.° Prithee tonight   *appear in tears*
       Lay on my bed my wedding sheets, remember.
       And call thy husband hither.
EMILIA   Here's a change indeed.   *Exit*
110 **DESDEMONA**   'Tis meet° I should be used so, very meet.   *fitting*
       How have I been behaved, that he might stick
       The small'st opinion on my least misuse?⁹
                    Enter IAGO *and* EMILIA
IAGO   What is your pleasure, madam? How is't with you?
DESDEMONA   I cannot tell. Those that do teach young babes
115   Do it with gentle means and easy tasks.
       He might ha' chid me so, for, in good faith,
       I am a child to chiding.
IAGO   What is the matter, lady?
EMILIA   Alas, Iago, my lord hath so bewhored her,°   *called her whore*
       Thrown such despite° and heavy terms upon her,   *spite*
120   That true hearts cannot bear it.
DESDEMONA   Am I that name, Iago?
IAGO   What name, fair lady?
DESDEMONA   Such as she said my lord did say I was.

9. *that . . . misuse:* perhaps, which would cause him to suspect even slightly the least fault.

EMILIA   He called her whore. A beggar in his drink

125   Could not have laid such terms upon his callet.°   *whore*

IAGO   Why did he so?

DESDEMONA   I do not know. I am sure I am none such.

IAGO   Do not weep, do not weep. Alas the day!

EMILIA   Hath she forsook so many noble matches,

130   Her father and her country and her friends,

To be called whore? Would it not make one weep?

DESDEMONA   It is my wretched fortune.

IAGO   Beshrew° him for't.   *Curse*

How comes this trick° upon him?   *behavior*

DESDEMONA   Nay, heaven doth know.

EMILIA   I will be hanged if some eternal villain,

135   Some busy° and insinuating rogue,   *meddling*

Some cogging,° cozening° slave, to get some office,   *deceiving / cheating*

Have not devised this slander. I will be hanged else.

IAGO   Fie, there is no such man. It is impossible.

DESDEMONA   If any such there be, heaven pardon him.

140   EMILIA   A halter° pardon him, and hell gnaw his bones!   *hangman's noose*

Why should he call her whore? Who keeps her company?

What place, what time, what form, what likelihood?

The Moor's abused by some most villainous knave,

Some base, notorious knave, some scurvy fellow.

145   O heaven, that such companions thou'dst unfold,°   *reveal*

And put in every honest hand a whip

To lash the rascals naked through the world,

Even from the east to th' west!

IAGO   Speak within door.°   *more softly*

EMILIA   O, fie upon them. Some such squire° he was   *fellow*

150   That turned your wit the seamy side without,°   *wrong side out*

And made you to suspect me with the Moor.

IAGO   You are a fool. Go to.

DESDEMONA   O God, Iago,

What shall I do to win my lord again?

Good friend, go to him; for by this light of heaven,

I know not how I lost him.

              [*She kneels*]

155   Here I kneel.[1]

If e'er my will did trespass 'gainst his love,

Either in discourse of thought or actual deed,

Or that mine eyes, mine ears, or any sense

Delighted them in any other form,[2]

160   Or that I do not yet,° and ever did,   *still*

And ever will—though he do shake me off

To beggarly divorcement—love him dearly,

Comfort forswear me.° Unkindness may do much,   *Deny me divine solace*

And his unkindness may defeat my life,

But never taint my love.

              [*She rises*]

165   I cannot say 'whore'.

It does abhor me[3] now I speak the word.

1. Lines 155–68 (beginning with "Here") do not   3. Fill me with abhorrence; make me abhorrent, with a
appear in Q.   pun on "ab-whore."
2. Took pleasure in anyone but him.

To do the act that might the addition° earn,   *label*
Not the world's mass of vanity° could make me.   *all worldly splendor*

IAGO   I pray you, be content. 'Tis but his humour.°   *mood*

170   The business of the state does him offence,
And he does chide with you.

DESDEMONA   If 'twere no other!

IAGO   It is but so, I warrant.

         [*Flourish within*]

Hark how these instruments summon you to supper.

175   The messengers of Venice stays the meat.°   *are waiting to eat*
Go in, and weep not. All things shall be well.

         Exeunt DESDEMONA *and* EMILIA

       Enter RODERIGO

How now, Roderigo?

RODERIGO   I do not find that thou deal'st justly with me.

IAGO   What in the contrary?

180   RODERIGO   Every day thou daff'st me with some device,[4] Iago,
and rather, as it seems to me now, keep'st from me all conve-
niency° than suppliest me with the least advantage of hope. I   *opportunity*
will indeed no longer endure it, nor am I yet persuaded to put
up in peace what already I have foolishly suffered.

185   IAGO   Will you hear me, Roderigo?

RODERIGO   Faith, I have heard too much, for your words and
performances are no kin together.

IAGO   You charge me most unjustly.

RODERIGO   With naught but truth. I have wasted myself out of

190   my means. The jewels you have had from me to deliver Desdemona would half have corrupted a votarist.° You have told me   *nun*
she hath received 'em, and returned me expectations and comforts of sudden respect and acquaintance, but I find none.

IAGO   Well, go to,° very well.   *(expresses remonstrance)*

195   RODERIGO   'Very well', 'go to'! I cannot go to,° man, nor 'tis not   *succeed sexually*
very well. Nay, I think it is scurvy, and begin to find myself
fopped° in it.   *made a fool*

IAGO   Very well.

RODERIGO   I tell you 'tis not very well. I will make myself known

200   to Desdemona. If she will return me my jewels, I will give
over my suit and repent my unlawful solicitation. If not, assure
yourself I will seek satisfaction of you.

IAGO   You have said° now.   *finished*

RODERIGO   Ay, and said nothing but what I protest intendment

205   of doing.

IAGO   Why, now I see there's mettle in thee, and even from this
instant do build on thee a better opinion than ever before. Give
me thy hand, Roderigo. Thou hast taken against me a most just
exception, but yet I protest I have dealt most directly in thy

210   affair.

RODERIGO   It hath not appeared.

IAGO   I grant, indeed, it hath not appeared, and your suspicion
is not without wit and judgement. But, Roderigo, if thou hast
that in thee indeed which I have greater reason to believe now

215   than ever—I mean purpose, courage, and valour—this night
show it. If thou the next night following enjoy not Desdemona,

---

4. You put me off with some trick.

take me from this world with treachery, and devise engines plots against
for° my life. possibility

RODERIGO   Well, what is it? Is it within reason and compass?°

220 IAGO   Sir, there is especial commission come from Venice to
depute Cassio in Othello's place.

RODERIGO   Is that true? Why then, Othello and Desdemona
return again to Venice.

IAGO   O no, he goes into Mauritania,[5] and takes away with him

225 the fair Desdemona, unless his abode be lingered here by some
accident, wherein none can be so determinate° as the remov- effectual
ing of Cassio.

RODERIGO   How do you mean 'removing' of him?

IAGO   Why, by making him uncapable of Othello's place—

230 knocking out his brains.

RODERIGO   And that you would have me to do.

IAGO   Ay, if you dare do yourself a profit and a right. He sups
tonight with a harlotry, and thither will I go to him. He knows
not yet of his honourable fortune.° If you will watch his going his promotion

235 thence, which I will fashion° to fall out between twelve and arrange
one, you may take him at your pleasure. I will be near, to second your attempt, and he shall fall between us. Come, stand
not amazed at it, but go along with me. I will show you such a
necessity in his death that you shall think yourself bound to put

240 it on him. It is now high supper-time, and the night grows to
waste. About it.

RODERIGO   I will hear further reason for this.

IAGO   And you shall be satisfied. *Exeunt*

4.3

Enter OTHELLO, DESDEMONA, LODOVICO, EMILIA, *and
attendants*

LODOVICO   I do beseech you, sir, trouble yourself no further.

OTHELLO   O, pardon me, 'twill do me good to walk.

LODOVICO [*to* DESDEMONA]   Madam, good night. I humbly thank
your ladyship.

DESDEMONA   Your honour is most welcome.

OTHELLO Will you walk, sir?

5 O, Desdemona!

DESDEMONA   My lord?

OTHELLO   Get you to bed on th'instant. I will be returned forthwith. Dismiss your attendant there. Look't be done.

DESDEMONA   I will, my lord.

Exeunt [OTHELLO, LODOVICO, *and attendants*]

10 EMILIA   How goes it now? He looks gentler than he did.

DESDEMONA   He says he will return incontinent.° *immediately*
He hath commanded me to go to bed,
And bid me to dismiss you.

EMILIA Dismiss me?

DESDEMONA   It was his bidding. Therefore, good Emilia,

15 Give me my nightly wearing, and adieu.
We must not now displease him.

EMILIA   I would you had never seen him.

DESDEMONA   So would not I. My love doth so approve him

---

5. Country in the western Sahara. 4.3 Location: Scene continues.

That even his stubbornness, his checks, his frowns—
20 Prithee unpin me—have grace and favour in them.
        [EMILIA *helps* DESDEMONA *to undress*]
EMILIA   I have laid those sheets you bade me on the bed.
DESDEMONA   All's one.° Good faith, how foolish are our minds!   *It doesn't matter*
    If I do die before thee, prithee shroud me
    In one of these same sheets.
EMILIA   Come, come, you talk.
25 DESDEMONA   My mother had a maid called Barbary.[1]
    She was in love, and he she loved proved mad
    And did forsake her. She had a song of willow.
    An old thing 'twas, but it expressed her fortune,
    And she died singing it. That song tonight
30 Will not go from my mind. I[2] have much to do
    But to[3] go hang my head all at one side
    And sing it, like poor Barbary. Prithee, dispatch.
EMILIA   Shall I go fetch your nightgown?
DESDEMONA   No. Unpin me here.
    This Lodovico is a proper man.
EMILIA   A very handsome man.
35 DESDEMONA   He speaks well.
EMILIA   I know a lady in Venice would have walked barefoot to
    Palestine for a touch of his nether lip.
DESDEMONA [*sings*] 'The poor soul sat sighing by a sycamore tree,
        Sing all a green willow.[4]
40 Her hand on her bosom, her head on her knee,
        Sing willow, willow, willow.
    The fresh streams ran by her and murmured her moans,
        Sing willow, willow, willow.
    Her salt tears fell from her and softened the stones,
45   Sing willow'—
    Lay by these.—
                        'willow, willow.'
    Prithee, hie thee.° He'll come anon.   *hurry*
    'Sing all a green willow must be my garland.
50 Let nobody blame him, his scorn I approve'—
    Nay, that's not next. Hark, who is't that knocks?
EMILIA   It's the wind.
DESDEMONA [*sings*] 'I called my love false love, but what said he then?[5]
        Sing willow, willow, willow.
55 If I court more women, you'll couch with more men.'
    So, get thee gone. Good night. Mine eyes do itch.
    Doth that bode weeping?
EMILIA   'Tis neither here nor there.
DESDEMONA   I have heard it said so. O, these men, these men![6]
    Dost thou in conscience think—tell me, Emilia—
60 That there be women do abuse their husbands
    In such gross kind?°   *fashion*
EMILIA   There be some such, no question.
DESDEMONA   Wouldst thou do such a deed for all the world?
EMILIA   Why, would not you?

---

1. Iago compares Othello to a "Barbary horse" in 1.1.113.
2. Lines 30–51 ("I . . . next") do not appear in Q.
3. I can barely bring myself not to.
4. A conventional symbol of disappointed love.
5. Lines 53–55 do not appear in Q.
6. Lines 58–61 do not appear in Q.

DESDEMONA   No, by this heavenly light.

EMILIA   Nor I neither, by this heavenly light. I might do't as well
65   i'th' dark.

DESDEMONA   Wouldst thou do such a deed for all the world?

EMILIA   The world's a huge thing. It is a great price for a small
vice.

DESDEMONA   In truth, I think thou wouldst not.

70   **EMILIA**   In truth, I think I should, and undo't when I had done.
Marry, I would not do such a thing for a joint ring,[7] nor for
measures of lawn,° nor for gowns, petticoats, nor caps, nor any   *linen*
petty exhibition;° but for all the whole world? Ud's° pity, who   *gift / God's*
would not make her husband a cuckold to make him a mon-
75   arch? I should venture purgatory for't.

DESDEMONA   Beshrew me if I would do such a wrong
For the whole world.

EMILIA   Why, the wrong is but a wrong i'th' world, and having
the world for your labour, 'tis a wrong in your own world, and
80   you might quickly make it right.

DESDEMONA   I do not think there is any such woman.

EMILIA   Yes, a dozen, and as many
To th' vantage as would store the world they played for.[8]
But I do think it is their husbands' faults[9]
85   If wives do fall. Say that they slack their duties,°   *marital duties*
And pour our treasures into foreign laps,[1]
Or else break out in peevish jealousies,
Throwing restraint upon us; or say they strike us,
Or scant our former having in despite:[2]
90   Why, we have galls;° and though we have some grace,   *tempers*
Yet have we some revenge. Let husbands know
Their wives have sense like them. They see, and smell,
And have their palates both for sweet and sour,
As husbands have. What is it that they do
95   When they change us for others? Is it sport?
I think it is. And doth affection° breed it?   *lust*
I think it doth. Is't frailty that thus errs?
It is so, too. And have not we affections,
Desires for sport, and frailty, as men have?
100   Then let them use us well, else let them know
The ills we do, their ills instruct us so.

DESDEMONA   Good night, good night. God me such uses° send   *habits*
Not to pick bad from bad, but by bad mend![3]   *Exeunt*

5.1

Enter IAGO *and* RODERIGO

IAGO   Here, stand behind this bulk.° Straight° will he come.   *shop stall / Right away*
Wear thy good rapier bare, and put it home.°   *drive it into him*
Quick, quick, fear nothing. I'll be at thy elbow.
It makes us or it mars us. Think on that,
5   And fix most firm thy resolution.

RODERIGO   Be near at hand. I may miscarry in't.

---

7. A cheap ring in separable halves.
8. *and . . . for:* and as many more as it would take to
populate the world they gained by doing it.
9. Lines 84–101 do not appear in Q.
1. And give the semen that belongs to us to other women.

2. Or reduce our allowances out of spite.
3. Not to take bad behavior as an example, but to know
what to avoid.
5.1 Location: A street in Cyprus.

IAGO   Here at thy hand. Be bold, and take thy stand.
RODERIGO [*aside*]   I have no great devotion to the deed,
    And yet he hath given me satisfying reasons.
10   'Tis but a man gone. Forth my sword—he dies!
IAGO [*aside*]   I have rubbed this young quat° almost to the sense,°   *pimple / to the quick*
    And he grows angry. Now, whether he kill Cassio
    Or Cassio him, or each do kill the other,
    Every way makes my gain. Live Roderigo,°   *If Roderigo lives*
15   He calls me to a restitution large
    Of gold and jewels that I bobbed from him°   *defrauded him of*
    As gifts to Desdemona.
    It must not be. If Cassio do remain,
    He hath a daily beauty in his life
20   That makes me ugly; and besides, the Moor
    May unfold° me to him—there stand I in much peril.   *reveal*
    No, he must die. But so, I hear him coming.
    Enter CASSIO
RODERIGO   I know his gait, 'tis he. [*Attacking* CASSIO] Villain, thou diest.
CASSIO   That thrust had been mine enemy indeed,
25   But that my coat is better° than thou know'st.   *thicker; more armored*
    I will make proof of° thine.   *test*
    [*He stabs* RODERIGO, *who falls*]
RODERIGO   O, I am slain!
    [IAGO *wounds* CASSIO *in the leg from behind. Exit* IAGO]
CASSIO [*falling*]   I am maimed for ever. Help, ho, murder, murder!
    Enter OTHELLO [*above*]
OTHELLO   The voice of Cassio. Iago keeps his word.
RODERIGO   O, villain that I am!
30 OTHELLO   It is even so.
CASSIO   O, help, ho! Light, a surgeon!
OTHELLO   'Tis he. O brave Iago, honest and just,
    That hast such noble sense of thy friend's wrong—
    Thou teachest me. Minion,° your dear lies dead,   *Hussy*
35   And your unblessed fate hies.° Strumpet, I come.   *damnation hurries on*
    Forth of° my heart those charms, thine eyes, are blotted.   *Out of*
    Thy bed, lust-stained, shall with lust's blood be spotted.   *Exit*
    Enter LODOVICO *and* GRAZIANO
CASSIO   What ho, no watch, no passage?° Murder, murder!   *passersby*
GRAZIANO   'Tis some mischance. The voice is very direful.
40 CASSIO   O, help!
LODOVICO   Hark.
RODERIGO   O wretched villain!
LODOVICO   Two or three groan. 'Tis heavy° night.   *dark*
    These may be counterfeits. Let's think't unsafe
45   To come into° the cry without more help.   *go near*
RODERIGO   Nobody come? Then shall I bleed to death.
    Enter IAGO *with a light*
LODOVICO   Hark.
GRAZIANO   Here's one comes in his shirt, with light and weapons.
IAGO   Who's there? Whose noise is this that cries on murder?
LODOVICO   We do not know.
50 IAGO   Do not you hear a cry?
CASSIO   Here, here. For heaven's sake, help me.
IAGO   What's the matter?
GRAZIANO [*to* LODOVICO]   This is Othello's ensign, as I take it.

LODOVICO   The same indeed, a very valiant fellow.

IAGO [*to* CASSIO]   What are you here that cry so grievously?

55 CASSIO   Iago—O, I am spoiled, undone by villains.
Give me some help.

IAGO   O me, lieutenant, what villains have done this?

CASSIO   I think that one of them is hereabout
And cannot make away.

IAGO   O treacherous villains!
[*To* LODOVICO *and* GRAZIANO] What are you there? Come in
60   and give some help.

RODERIGO   O, help me there!

CASSIO   That's one of 'em.

IAGO [*stabbing* RODERIGO]   O murderous slave! O villain!

RODERIGO   O damned Iago! O inhuman dog!

65 IAGO   Kill men i'th' dark? Where be these bloody thieves?
How silent is this town! Ho, murder, murder!
[*To* LODOVICO *and* GRAZIANO] What may you be? Are you of
good or evil?

LODOVICO   As you shall prove us, praise us.

IAGO   Signor Lodovico.

LODOVICO   He, sir.

70 IAGO   I cry you mercy. Here's Cassio hurt by villains.

GRAZIANO   Cassio?

IAGO   How is't, brother?

CASSIO   My leg is cut in two.

IAGO   Marry, heaven forbid!

75   Light, gentlemen. I'll bind it with my shirt.
                  Enter BIANCA

BIANCA   What is the matter, ho? Who is't that cried?

IAGO   Who is't that cried?

BIANCA   O my dear Cassio,
My sweet Cassio, O, Cassio, Cassio!

IAGO   O notable strumpet! Cassio, may you suspect

80   Who they should be that have thus mangled you?

CASSIO   No.

GRAZIANO   I am sorry to find you thus. I have been to seek you.

IAGO   Lend me a garter. So. O for a chair,°   *litter*
To bear him easily hence!

85 BIANCA   Alas, he faints. O, Cassio, Cassio, Cassio!

IAGO   Gentlemen all, I do suspect this trash
To be a party in this injury.
Patience a while, good Cassio. Come, come,
Lend me a light. [*Going to* RODERIGO] Know we this face or no?

90   Alas, my friend, and my dear countryman.
Roderigo? No—yes, sure—O heaven, Roderigo!

GRAZIANO   What, of Venice?

IAGO   Even he, sir. Did you know him?

GRAZIANO   Know him? Ay.

95 IAGO   Signor Graziano, I cry your gentle pardon.
These bloody accidents must excuse my manners
That so neglected you.

GRAZIANO   I am glad to see you.

IAGO   How do you, Cassio? O, a chair, a chair!

GRAZIANO   Roderigo.

IAGO   He, he, 'tis he.

[*Enter attendants with a chair*]

100   O, that's well said, the chair!
Some good man bear him carefully from hence.
I'll fetch the general's surgeon. [*To* BIANCA] For you, mistress,
Save you your labour. He that lies slain here, Cassio,
Was my dear friend. What malice was between you?

105 CASSIO   None in the world, nor do I know the man.
     IAGO [*to* BIANCA]   What, look you pale? [*To attendants*] O, bear
            him out o'th' air.[1]
     [*To* LODOVICO *and* GRAZIANO] Stay you, good gentlemen.
                           [*Exeunt attendants with* CASSIO *in the chair*
                                and with Roderigo's body]
     [*To* BIANCA]   Look you pale, mistress?
     [*To* LODOVICO *and* GRAZIANO] Do you perceive the ghastness° of her eye?   *terror*
     [*To* BIANCA] Nay, an° you stare we shall hear more anon.   *if*

110   [*To* LODOVICO *and* GRAZIANO] Behold her well; I pray you look upon her.
Do you see, gentlemen? Nay, guiltiness
Will speak, though tongues were out of use.
          Enter EMILIA

     EMILIA   Alas, what is the matter? What is the matter, husband?
     IAGO   Cassio hath here been set on in the dark
115 By Roderigo and fellows that are scaped.
He's almost slain, and Roderigo dead.
     EMILIA   Alas, good gentleman! Alas, good Cassio!
     IAGO   This is the fruits of whoring. Prithee, Emilia,
Go know of Cassio where he supped tonight.
120 [*To* BIANCA] What, do you shake at that?
     BIANCA   He supped at my house, but I therefore shake not.
     IAGO   O, did he so? I charge you go with me.
     EMILIA [*to* BIANCA]   O, fie upon thee, strumpet!
     BIANCA   I am no strumpet, but of life as honest
As you that thus abuse me.
125 EMILIA   As I? Fough, fie upon thee!
     IAGO   Kind gentlemen, let's go see poor Cassio dressed.
     [*To* BIANCA] Come, mistress, you must tell's another tale.
Emilia, run you to the citadel
And tell my lord and lady what hath happed.
Will you go on afore?   [*Exit* EMILIA]
130 [*Aside*]   This is the night
That either makes me or fordoes° me quite.   *Exeunt*   *undoes*

5.2

Enter OTHELLO *with a light.* [*He draws back a curtain,
revealing*] DESDEMONA [*asleep*] *in her bed*

     OTHELLO   It is the cause,[1] it is the cause, my soul.
Let me not name it to you, you chaste stars.
It is the cause. Yet I'll not shed her blood,
Nor scar that whiter skin of hers than snow,
5 And smooth as monumental alabaster.°   *stone used in tombs*
Yet she must die, else she'll betray more men.
Put out the light, and then put out the light.[2]

---

1. Out of the open air (thought to be bad for wounds).
5.2 Location: Desdemona and Othello's bedroom.
1. What matters is Desdemona's infidelity; the "cause" of justice, which Othello sees himself defending, as in the subsequent lines.
2. This and the following lines compare the light of Othello's lamp or torch to Desdemona's "light" of life.

If I quench thee, thou flaming minister,°   *light that serves me*
I can again thy former light restore
10   Should I repent me; but once put out thy light,
Thou cunning'st pattern of excelling nature,[3]
I know not where is that Promethean heat[4]
That can thy light relume.° When I have plucked thy rose   *relight*
I cannot give it vital growth again.
15   It needs must wither. I'll smell thee on the tree.
      [*He kisses her*]
O balmy breath, that dost almost persuade
Justice to break her sword! One more, one more.
Be thus when thou art dead, and I will kill thee
And love thee after. One more, and that's the last.
      He kisses her
20   So sweet was ne'er so fatal. I must weep,
But they are cruel tears. This sorrow's heavenly,
It strikes where it doth love.[5] She wakes.

DESDEMONA   Who's there? Othello?

OTHELLO   Ay, Desdemona.

25 DESDEMONA   Will you come to bed, my lord?

OTHELLO   Have you prayed tonight, Desdemon?

DESDEMONA   Ay, my lord.

OTHELLO   If you bethink yourself of any crime
Unreconciled as yet to heaven and grace,
30   Solicit° for it straight.   *Ask forgiveness*

DESDEMONA   Alack, my lord, what may you mean by that?

OTHELLO   Well, do it, and be brief. I will walk by.
I would not kill thy unpreparèd spirit.
No, heavens forfend! I would not kill thy soul.

DESDEMONA   Talk you of killing?

OTHELLO   Ay, I do.

35 DESDEMONA   Then heaven
Have mercy on me.

OTHELLO   Amen, with all my heart.

DESDEMONA   If you say so, I hope you will not kill me.

OTHELLO   Hum!

DESDEMONA   And yet I fear you, for you're fatal then
40   When your eyes roll so. Why I should fear I know not,
Since guiltiness I know not, but yet I feel I fear.

OTHELLO   Think on thy sins.

DESDEMONA   They are loves I bear to you.

OTHELLO   Ay, and for that thou diest.

45 DESDEMONA   That death's unnatural that kills for loving.
Alas, why gnaw you so your nether lip?
Some bloody passion shakes your very frame.
These are portents, but yet I hope, I hope
They do not point on me.

OTHELLO   Peace, and be still.

DESDEMONA   I will so. What's the matter?

50 OTHELLO   That handkerchief
Which I so loved and gave thee, thou gav'st to Cassio.

---

3. You most cleverly wrought example of nature's work.
4. Life-giving fire. In Greek mythology, Prometheus stole fire from heaven to give it to humankind; in a different tradition, he is credited with animating humankind from clay.
5. See Hebrews 12:6: "For whom the Lord loveth, he chasteneth."

DESDEMONA   No, by my life and soul. Send for the man
    And ask him.
OTHELLO   Sweet soul, take heed, take heed of perjury.
55   Thou art on thy deathbed.
DESDEMONA   Ay, but not yet to die.
OTHELLO   Presently.°   *Immediately*
    Therefore confess thee freely of thy sin,
    For to deny each article with oath
60   Cannot remove nor choke the strong conception
    That I do groan withal.⁶ Thou art to die.
DESDEMONA   Then Lord have mercy on me.
OTHELLO   I say amen.
DESDEMONA   And have you mercy, too. I never did
    Offend you in my life, never loved Cassio
65   But with such general warranty of heaven
    As I might love. I never gave him token.
OTHELLO   By heaven, I saw my handkerchief in's hand.
    O perjured woman! Thou dost stone° my heart,   *harden*
    And makes me call what I intend to do
70   A murder, which I thought a sacrifice.
    I saw the handkerchief.
DESDEMONA   He found it, then.
    I never gave it him. Send for him hither.
    Let him confess a truth.
OTHELLO   He hath confessed.
DESDEMONA   What, my lord?
OTHELLO   That he hath usèd thee.
75   DESDEMONA   How, unlawfully?
OTHELLO   Ay.
DESDEMONA   He will not say so.
OTHELLO   No, his mouth is stopped.
    Honest Iago hath ta'en order for't.
80   DESDEMONA   O, my fear interprets! What, is he dead?
OTHELLO   Had all his hairs been lives, my great revenge
    Had stomach for 'em all.
DESDEMONA [*weeping*]   Alas, he is betrayed, and I undone.
OTHELLO   Out, strumpet! Weep'st thou for him to my face?
85   DESDEMONA   O, banish me, my lord, but kill me not.
OTHELLO [*attacking her*]   Down, strumpet.
DESDEMONA   Kill me tomorrow; let me live tonight.
OTHELLO   Nay, an you strive—
DESDEMONA   But half an hour.
90   OTHELLO   Being done, there is no pause.⁷
DESDEMONA   But while I say one prayer.
OTHELLO   It is too late.
        He smothers her
DESDEMONA   O Lord, Lord, Lord!
        EMILIA *at the door*
EMILIA (*within*)   My lord, my lord, what ho, my lord, my lord!
95   OTHELLO   What noise is this? Not dead? Not yet quite dead?
    I that am cruel am yet merciful.

---

6. *Cannot . . . withal:* Cannot stop the strong conviction   makes me groan so. The metaphor is from childbirth.
I have in your guilt (or the firm plan to kill you), which   7. Now that I've started, there's no stopping.

I would not have thee linger in thy pain.
So, so.
EMILIA [*within*]   What ho, my lord, my lord!
OTHELLO   Who's there?
EMILIA [*within*]   O, good my lord, I would speak a word with you.
OTHELLO [*calling*]   Yes.—'Tis Emilia. [*Calling*] By
100   and by!—She's dead.
'Tis like she comes to speak of Cassio's death.
The noise was high.° Ha! No more moving.   *commotion was loud*
Still as the grave. Shall she come in? Were't good?
I think she stirs again. No. What's best to do?
105   If she come in, she'll sure speak to my wife.
My wife, my wife! What wife? I ha' no wife.
O insupportable, O heavy hour!
Methinks it should be now a huge eclipse
Of sun and moon, and that th'affrighted globe
110   Should yawn at alteration.[8]
EMILIA [*within*]   I do beseech you
That I may speak with you. O, good my lord!
OTHELLO   I had forgot thee.—O, come in, Emilia.—
Soft,° by and by. Let me the curtains draw.   *Quiet*
[*He closes the bed-curtains*]
Where art thou?
[*He opens the door.*] *Enter* EMILIA
What's the matter with thee now?
115   EMILIA   O my good lord, yonder's foul murder's done.
OTHELLO   What, now?
EMILIA   But° now, my lord.   *Just*
OTHELLO   It is the very error° of the moon,   *deviation*
She comes more nearer earth than she was wont,
120   And makes men mad.
EMILIA   Cassio, my lord, hath killed a young Venetian
Called Roderigo.
OTHELLO   Roderigo killed
And Cassio killed?
EMILIA   No, Cassio is not killed.
OTHELLO   Not Cassio killed? Then murder's out of tune,
125   And sweet revenge grows harsh.
DESDEMONA   O, falsely, falsely murdered!
EMILIA   O Lord, what cry is that?
OTHELLO   That? What?
EMILIA   Out and alas, that was my lady's voice!
[*She opens the bed-curtains*]
130   Help, help, ho, help! O lady, speak again!
Sweet Desdemona, O sweet mistress, speak!
DESDEMONA   A guiltless death I die.
EMILIA   O, who hath done this deed?
DESDEMONA   Nobody, I myself. Farewell.
Commend me to my kind lord. O, farewell!   *She dies*
OTHELLO   Why, how should she be murdered?
135   EMILIA   Alas, who knows?
OTHELLO   You heard her say herself it was not I.
EMILIA   She said so, I must needs report the truth.

8. Should gape at the change. Earthquakes were associated with eclipses.

OTHELLO She's like a liar gone to burning hell.
'Twas I that killed her.

140 EMILIA O, the more angel she, and you the blacker devil!

OTHELLO She turned to folly,° and she was a whore.   *wantonness*

EMILIA Thou dost belie her, and thou art a devil.

OTHELLO She was false as water.

EMILIA   Thou art rash as fire
To say that she was false. O, she was heavenly true!

145 OTHELLO Cassio did top her. Ask thy husband else.°   *if you doubt it*
O, I were damned beneath all depth in hell
But that I did proceed upon just grounds
To this extremity! Thy husband knew it all.

EMILIA My husband?

OTHELLO   Thy husband.

EMILIA   That she was false to wedlock?

150 OTHELLO Ay, with Cassio. Had she been true,
If heaven would make me such another world
Of one entire and perfect chrysolite°   *topaz*
I'd not have sold her for it.

EMILIA   My husband?

OTHELLO Ay, 'twas he that told me on her first.

155 An honest man he is, and hates the slime
That sticks on filthy deeds.

EMILIA   My husband?

OTHELLO What needs this iterance?° Woman, I say thy husband.   *repetition*

EMILIA O mistress, villainy hath made mocks with° love.⁹   *at*
My husband say she was false?

OTHELLO   He, woman.

160 I say thy husband. Dost understand the word?
My friend, thy husband, honest, honest Iago.

EMILIA If he say so, may his pernicious soul
Rot half a grain a day. He lies to th' heart.
She was too fond of her most filthy bargain.

165 OTHELLO Ha?

EMILIA Do thy worst.
This deed of thine is no more worthy heaven
Than thou wast worthy her.

OTHELLO   Peace, you were best.°   *it would be best for you*

EMILIA Thou hast not half that power to do me harm

170 As I have to be hurt. O gull,° O dolt,   *fool*
As ignorant as dirt! Thou hast done a deed—
I care not for thy sword, I'll make thee known
Though I lost twenty lives. Help, help, ho! Help!
The Moor hath killed my mistress. Murder, murder!

Enter MONTANO, GRAZIANO, *and* IAGO

175 MONTANO What is the matter? How now, general?

EMILIA O, are you come, Iago? You have done well,
That men must lay their murders on your neck.

GRAZIANO What is the matter?

EMILIA [*to* IAGO] Disprove this villain if thou beest a man.

180 He says thou told'st him that his wife was false.
I know thou didst not. Thou'rt not such a villain.
Speak, for my heart is full.

---

9. Lines 158–61 do not appear in Q.

IAGO   I told him what I thought, and told no more
Than what he found himself was apt and true.

185   EMILIA   But did you ever tell him she was false?

IAGO   I did.

EMILIA   You told a lie, an odious, damnèd lie,
Upon my soul a lie, a wicked lie.
She false with Cassio? Did you say with Cassio?

190   IAGO   With Cassio, mistress. Go to, charm° your tongue.   silence

EMILIA   I will not charm my tongue. I am bound to speak.
My mistress here lies murdered in her bed.[1]

MONTANO *and* GRAZIANO   O heavens forfend!

EMILIA [*to* IAGO]   And your reports have set the murder on.

195   OTHELLO   Nay, stare not, masters. It is true indeed.

GRAZIANO   'Tis a strange truth.

MONTANO   O monstrous act!

EMILIA   Villainy, villainy, villainy!
I think upon't, I think. I smell't. O villainy!
I thought so then. I'll kill myself for grief.

200   O villainy, villainy!

IAGO   What, are you mad? I charge you get you home.

EMILIA   Good gentlemen, let me have leave to speak.
'Tis proper I obey him, but not now.
Perchance, Iago, I will ne'er go home.

OTHELLO   O, O, O!

          OTHELLO *falls on the bed*

205   EMILIA   Nay, lay thee down and roar,
For thou hast killed the sweetest innocent
That e'er did lift up eye.°   (to heaven)

OTHELLO [*rising*]   O, she was foul!
[*To* GRAZIANO] I scarce did know you, uncle. There lies your niece,
Whose breath indeed these hands have newly stopped.

210   I know this act shows° horrible and grim.   appears

GRAZIANO   Poor Desdemon, I am glad thy father's dead.
Thy match was mortal to him, and pure grief
Shore his old thread in twain.[2] Did he live now
This sight would make him do a desperate turn,°   act

215   Yea, curse his better angel from his side,
And fall to reprobance.[3]

OTHELLO   'Tis pitiful. But yet Iago knows
That she with Cassio hath the act of shame
A thousand times committed. Cassio confessed it,

220   And she did gratify his amorous works
With that recognizance° and pledge of love   token
Which I first gave her. I saw it in his hand.
It was a handkerchief, an antique token
My father gave my mother.

EMILIA   O God! O heavenly God!

IAGO   'Swounds, hold your peace!

225   EMILIA   'Twill out, 'twill out. I peace?
No, I will speak as liberal as the north.[4]
Let heaven, and men, and devils, let 'em all,
All, all cry shame against me, yet I'll speak.

---

1. Lines 192–200 do not appear in Q.
2. Cut the thread of his life.
3. Suicide, the unforgivably sinful act of despair.
4. As freely as the north wind.

IAGO Be wise and get you home.

230 EMILIA I will not.
              [IAGO *draws his sword*]

GRAZIANO [*to* IAGO] Fie, your sword upon a woman?

EMILIA O thou dull Moor, that handkerchief thou speak'st of
  I found by fortune and did give my husband,
  For often, with a solemn earnestness—
235 More than indeed belonged to such a trifle—
  He begged of me to steal't.

IAGO   Villainous whore!

EMILIA She give it Cassio? No, alas, I found it,
  And I did give't my husband.

IAGO   Filth, thou liest.

EMILIA By heaven I do not, I do not, gentlemen.
240 O murderous coxcomb!° What should such a fool   *fool*
  Do with so good a wife?

OTHELLO   Are there no stones° in heaven   *thunderbolts*
  But what serves for the thunder? Precious° villain!   *Absolute*
      The Moor runs at IAGO. [MONTANO *disarms* OTHELLO.]
      IAGO [*wounds*] *his wife*

GRAZIANO The woman falls. Sure he hath killed his wife.

EMILIA Ay, ay. O, lay me by my mistress' side!   *Exit* IAGO

245 GRAZIANO He's gone, but his wife's killed.

MONTANO 'Tis a notorious villain. Take you this weapon
  Which I have here recovered from the Moor.
  Come, guard the door without. Let him not pass,
  But kill him rather. I'll after that same villain,
  For 'tis a damnèd slave.   *Exeunt* MONTANO *and* GRAZIANO

250 OTHELLO   I am not valiant neither,
  But every puny whipster° gets my sword.   *insignificant person*
  But why should honour outlive honesty?[5]
  Let it go all.

EMILIA   What did thy song bode, lady?[6]
  Hark, canst thou hear me? I will play the swan,
255 And die in music. [*Sings*] 'Willow, willow, willow.'—
  Moor, she was chaste. She loved thee, cruel Moor.
  So come my soul to bliss as I speak true.
  So, speaking as I think, alas, I die.   *She dies*

OTHELLO I have another weapon in this chamber.
260 It was a sword of Spain, the ice-brook's temper.°   *tempered in icy water*
  O, here it is. [*Calling*] Uncle, I must come forth.

GRAZIANO (*within*) If thou attempt it, it will cost thee dear.
  Thou hast no weapon, and perforce must suffer.

OTHELLO Look in upon me then, and speak with me,
265 Or, naked° as I am, I will assault thee.   *unarmed*
      [*Enter* GRAZIANO]

GRAZIANO What is the matter?

OTHELLO   Behold, I have a weapon;
  A better never did itself sustain
  Upon a soldier's thigh. I have seen the day
  That, with this little arm and this good sword,
270 I have made my way through more impediments

---

5. Why should military reputation outlive integrity?
6. Lines 253–55 ("What . . . willow.'—") do not appear in Q.

	Than twenty times your stop.° But O, vain boast!	*power to stop*
	Who can control his fate? 'Tis not so now.	
	Be not afraid, though you do see me weaponed.	
	Here is my journey's end, here is my butt[7]	
275	And very sea-mark° of my utmost sail.	*beacon*
	Do you go back dismayed? 'Tis a lost° fear.	*an unnecessary*
	Man but a rush° against Othello's breast	*Aim even a reed*
	And he retires. Where should Othello go?	
	[*To* DESDEMONA] Now, how dost thou look now? O ill-starred wench,	
280	Pale as thy smock! When we shall meet at count°	*Judgment Day*
	This look of thine will hurl my soul from heaven,	
	And fiends will snatch at it.	
	[*He touches her*]	
	Cold, cold, my girl,	
	Even like thy chastity. O cursèd, cursèd slave!	
	Whip me, ye devils,	
285	From the possession of this heavenly sight.	
	Blow me about in winds, roast me in sulphur,	
	Wash me in steep-down gulfs of liquid fire!	
	O Desdemon! Dead Desdemon! Dead! O! O!	
	Enter LODOVICO, MONTANO, IAGO [*guarded by*] *officers,*	
	with CASSIO *in a chair*	
	LODOVICO Where is this rash and most unfortunate man?	
290	OTHELLO That's he that was Othello. Here I am.	
	LODOVICO Where is that viper? Bring the villain forth.	
	OTHELLO I look down towards his feet,[8] but that's a fable.	
	[*To* IAGO] If that thou beest a devil I cannot kill thee.	
	[*He wounds* IAGO]	
	LODOVICO Wrench his sword from him.	
	[*Officers disarm* OTHELLO]	
	IAGO I bleed, sir, but not killed.	
295	OTHELLO I am not sorry, neither. I'd have thee live,	
	For in my sense° 'tis happiness to die.	*state of feeling*
	LODOVICO O thou Othello, that was once so good,	
	Fall'n in the practice° of a cursèd slave,	*plot*
	What shall be said to thee?	
	OTHELLO Why, anything;	
300	An honourable murderer, if you will,	
	For naught I did in hate, but all in honour.	
	LODOVICO This wretch hath part confessed his villainy.	
	Did you and he consent in Cassio's death?	
	OTHELLO Ay.	
305	CASSIO Dear general, I never gave you cause.	
	OTHELLO I do believe it, and I ask your pardon.	
	Will you, I pray, demand that demi-devil	
	Why he hath thus ensnared my soul and body?	
	IAGO Demand me nothing. What you know, you know.	
310	From this time forth I never will speak word.	
	LODOVICO [*to* IAGO] What, not to pray?	
	GRAZIANO [*to* IAGO] Torments° will ope your lips.	*Tortures*
	OTHELLO Well, thou dost best.	
	LODOVICO Sir, you shall understand what hath befall'n,	
315	Which as, I think, you know not. Here is a letter,	

---

7. Goal. Lines 273–79 do not appear in Q.   8. To look for the devil's cloven feet.

Found in the pocket of the slain Roderigo,
And here another. The one of them imports
The death of Cassio, to be undertook
By Roderigo.

320 OTHELLO   O villain!

CASSIO   Most heathenish and most gross.°   *monstrous*

LODOVICO   Now here's another discontented paper
Found in his pocket too, and this it seems
Roderigo meant to've sent this damnèd villain,

325 But that, belike,° Iago in the interim   *most likely*
Came in and satisfied him.

OTHELLO [*to* IAGO]   O thou pernicious caitiff!°   *wretch*
How came you, Cassio, by that handkerchief
That was my wife's?

CASSIO   I found it in my chamber,

330 And he himself confessed it, but even now,
That there he dropped it for a special purpose
Which wrought to his desire.

OTHELLO   O fool, fool, fool!

CASSIO   There is besides in Roderigo's letter
How he upbraids Iago, that he made him

335 Brave° me upon the watch, whereon it came   *Defy*
That I was cast;° and even but now he spake   *dismissed*
After long seeming dead, Iago hurt him,
Iago set him on.

LODOVICO [*to* OTHELLO]   You must forsake this room and go with us.

340 Your power and your command is taken off,
And Cassio rules in Cyprus. For this slave,
If there be any cunning cruelty
That can torment him much and hold him° long,   *(alive)*
It shall be his. You shall close° prisoner rest   *tightly confined*

345 Till that the nature of your fault be known
To the Venetian state. [*To officers*] Come, bring away.

OTHELLO   Soft you,° a word or two before you go.   *Wait*
I have done the state some service, and they know't.
No more of that. I pray you, in your letters,

350 When you shall these unlucky deeds relate,
Speak of me as I am. Nothing extenuate,
Nor set down aught in malice. Then must you speak
Of one that loved not wisely but too well,
Of one not easily jealous but, being wrought,

355 Perplexed in the extreme; of one whose hand,
Like the base Indian, threw a pearl away
Richer than all his tribe;⁹ of one whose subdued° eyes,   *(by grief)*
Albeit unusèd to the melting mood,
Drops tears as fast as the Arabian trees

360 Their medicinable gum.° Set you down this,   *myrrh*
And say besides that in Aleppo once,
Where a malignant and a turbaned Turk
Beat a Venetian and traduced the state,
I took by th' throat the circumcisèd dog

9. Othello supposes an uncivilized "Indian" unaware of the value of a pearl. Compare this reading from Q with F's "Judean," which may suggest malice rather than ignorance by alluding to Judas (betrayer of Christ) or perhaps Herod (who killed his wife Mariamne out of jealousy). "Judean" also anticipates "circumcisèd" (line 364) and hence an identification of Othello with Jews.

365 And smote him thus.
       He stabs himself
LODOVICO   O bloody period!°   *conclusion; sentence*
GRAZIANO   All that is spoke is marred.
OTHELLO [*to* DESDEMONA]   I kissed thee ere I killed thee. No way but this:
   Killing myself, to die upon a kiss.[1]   *He* [*kisses* DESDEMONA *and*] *dies*
370 CASSIO   This did I fear, but thought he had no weapon,
   For he was great of heart.
LODOVICO [*to* IAGO]   O Spartan dog,°   *notoriously savage*
   More fell° than anguish, hunger, or the sea,   *cruel*
   Look on the tragic loading of this bed.
   This is thy work. The object poisons sight.
   Let it be hid.
         [*They close the bed-curtains*]
375   Graziano, keep the house,
   And seize upon the fortunes of the Moor,
   For they succeed on you. [*To* CASSIO] To you, Lord Governor,
   Remains the censure° of this hellish villain.   *sentence*
   The time, the place, the torture, O, enforce it!
380   Myself will straight aboard, and to the state
   This heavy act with heavy heart relate.   *Exeunt* [*with Emilia's body*]

---

1. At 5.2.244, the dying Emilia says, "O, lay me by my mistress' side!" She then addresses Desdemona in a way that suggests that her wish has been granted. If it has, however, the presence of her body intrudes upon the concluding tableau of the dead Desdemona being kissed by the dying Othello, where "die" in line 369, as earlier, has the secondary sense of "orgasm."

All's Well That Ends Well

In innumerable old folktales, an unknown or lowborn young man of great courage, intelligence, or expertise addresses himself to a serious peril: a dragon no one can slay, a riddle no one can solve, a wound no one can cure. The grateful recipient of his aid— a king or mighty duke—rewards the youth with marriage to a princess who would ordinarily be far above his station. *All's Well That Ends Well* retells this popular tale of fantastic upward mobility but with the genders reversed: the resourceful young quester is female, the marital prize male. Shakespeare did not invent the reversal; he adapted his plot from a story in Boccaccio's *Decameron* that is itself a retelling of a traditional tale. But *All's Well That Ends Well* considerably heightens the heroine's risk-taking initiative, making Helen's adventures in the first two acts correspond more precisely, in sexually transposed form, to the masculine quest-romance pattern.

Even today, this reversal makes the story seem problematic. In the customary masculine version, no one inquires into the feelings of the noblewoman who is the champion's prize. But in *All's Well,* when a man becomes a reward, he reacts with astonished anger:

> BERTRAM   My wife, my liege? I shall beseech your highness,
> In such a business give me leave to use
> The help of mine own eyes.
> KING   Know'st thou not, Bertram,
> What she has done for me?
> BERTRAM   Yes, my good lord,
> But never hope to know why I should marry her.
>   (2.3.102–6)

After the wedding ceremony, Bertram flees without consummating the union. He leaves behind a letter detailing for Helen two apparently impossible conditions she must satisfy before he will consider her his wife: "When thou canst get the ring upon my finger, which never shall come off, and show me a child begotten of thy body that I am father to, then call me husband" (3.2.55–57).

Folklorists have traced the second part of the play, in which Helen ingeniously fulfills Bertram's stipulations, to yet another old tale, that of the "clever wench" who ultimately wins a reluctant husband's affection by turning his recalcitrance to her own benefit. In Helen's case, however, her "unfeminine" audacity both before and after her wedding has repelled some commentators. Others have expressed doubts about Helen's bed trick, wherein she secretly substitutes herself for another woman and becomes pregnant by the spouse who thinks he loathes her. How, they wonder, could such a maneuver possibly convert anyone, much less Bertram, into a loving husband?

By rewriting the comic plot, then, Shakespeare makes the difference in conventional expectations for men and women vividly clear. His revisions implicitly challenge those conventions, making them seem artificial and restrictive. At the same time, the deviations from comic norms in *All's Well* also might be taken as reflecting badly on the hero and heroine. The generic uneasiness of the play has led some critics to classify it as a "problem comedy," a category that also includes *Measure for Measure* and sometimes *Troilus and Cressida.* Editors conjecture that all three plays were written between 1602 and 1606, a period in which Shakespeare was largely preoccupied with tragedy: *Hamlet, Othello, King Lear, Timon of Athens, Macbeth,* and *Antony and Cleopatra* are roughly contemporaneous compositions. The "problem comedies" often seem closer in theme and tone to these tragedies than to the sunnier romantic comedies Shakespeare wrote in the 1590s.

Nonetheless, *All's Well* has obvious connections to Shakespeare's earlier achievements. In *The Merchant of Venice, As You Like It,* and *Much Ado About Nothing,* Shakespeare had gradually developed the dramatic possibilities of an articulate, assertive, and sympathetic heroine—a kind of character virtually without precedent in the Western tradition. Helen is recognizably one of this company: generally beloved by those around her, premaritally chaste but intensely sexual, tenacious in pursuit of the man she desires. Bertram is likewise a version of a standard Shakespearean type: the immature youth who finds aggressively "masculine" enterprises like hunting or war emotionally easier to negotiate than the complications of heterosexual intimacy. Bertram's predecessors include the unwilling Adonis in *Venus and Adonis,* the naive Claudio in *Much Ado About Nothing,* the edgily unself-conscious Hotspur of *1 Henry IV,* and the narcissistic young man of the sonnets. Both Helen and Bertram, however, "push the envelop" of their generic type. No previous comic heroine finds herself, as Helen does, publicly repudiated by the man she loves, and thus none need show herself as relentless as Helen in seeking a remedy. And Bertram is surely the most perfidious, and the most thoroughly disgraced, of Shakespeare's callow males.

In its portrayal of older characters, too, *All's Well* seems to develop out of Shakespeare's previous romantic plays. In much Greek and Roman comedy, parents or parent surrogates attempt to hinder their children's sexual happiness, and as a young playwright Shakespeare adhered to this ancient convention. In *A Midsummer Night's Dream* and *Romeo and Juliet,* written in the mid-1590s, parents are killjoys who block the glorious passions of youth out of mere peevishness. But in *The Merchant of Venice,* written a year or two later, Shylock's paternal possessiveness contrasts with the wise policy of Portia's father, whose strict constraints upon his daughter's marital options in fact ensure her happiness. In *Much Ado About Nothing* (1598), the sexually anxious young couples seem incapable of forming heterosexual pairs without the intervention of elders and friends. In *All's Well That Ends Well,* the marriage between Helen and Bertram is unthinkable without the support of the Countess and the King; the match is also roundly endorsed by the elderly courtier Lafeu. If the oldsters are culpable, it is for pushing the young people together prematurely, not for keeping them apart.

Arguably this change in perspective is a consequence of Shakespeare's own aging. By the time he wrote *All's Well,* he was the father of two marriageable daughters, and surviving records indicate that he had strong opinions about the men they wed. At any rate, the role of family members in Shakespeare's romantic plays becomes more benign, even essential for the pairing-off with which the comedies conclude; by the time of the late romances, in fact, the primary dramatic emphasis tends to be less on the young couple than on their parents. Seen in such a light, *All's Well* marks an important transition in the generational dynamics of Shakespearean comedy.

At the same time, the expanded role of family and friends in "making a match" seems to reflect an increasing pessimism about sex. In both *All's Well* and *Measure for Measure,* mutual desire fails to flower spontaneously between eligible bachelors and maidens. Moreover, even when desire is somehow kindled, its relationship to the institution of lifelong monogamy seems difficult. In *All's Well,* erotic passion burns hottest not when it is gratified but when its goal is still unattained. Bertram wants Diana only so long as she rebuffs him:

> Madding my eagerness with her restraint,
> As all impediments in fancy's course
> Are motives of more fancy.
>
> (5.3.215–17)

Once he imagines he has deflowered her, he deserts her without compunction. Bertram behaves reprehensibly, and yet Helen's more steadfast love, too, seems at least in part an effect of distance and difficulty. In Act 1, she declares Bertram to be a "bright particular star," fascinating although inaccessible, and perhaps *because* inaccessible. The obstacles Bertram places in the way of their union seem to make him all the more precious in Helen's eyes and to stimulate her extraordinary efforts to win his affections. But the more resolutely she strives to catch him, the more difficult it becomes to imagine her content with him once he is caught.

In sexual matters, apparently, as soon as one gets what one thinks one wants, it no longer seems so intensely appealing. "Success" brings disillusion in its train. In *All's Well,* this unfortunate arrangement is reflected in passages and episodes that oscillate painfully between imagined extremes of distance and intimacy. In Act 2, Helen frets about the social gap that separates her from Bertram: he seems too alien for her. But when the Countess pleads that Helen consider her a "mother," Helen suffers a paroxysm of anxiety on the opposite count: that she and Bertram may be all too closely allied. "God's mercy, maiden!" exclaims the Countess. "Does it curd thy blood / To say I am thy mother?" (1.3.133–34). Helen's hysterical overreaction suggests that she fears being "too close" at the same time she fears being "too remote." Later in *All's Well,* the bed trick rehearses, in another key, a similar paradox of intimacy and distance. Fleeing his home and a spouse closely associated with his upbringing, Bertram lusts after a foreign woman. But this foreigner turns out, unbeknownst to him, to be his own wife.

Thus the fundamental structure of sexual desire seems inimical to a durably happy marriage, but marriage nonetheless remains the only socially approved arena for sexual expression. Caught in this dilemma, lovers simply cannot be trusted to make proper arrangements among themselves. The community therefore assumes a new prominence in initiating and regulating marriages. In *All's Well,* two means of such regulation are central to the plot. The first is the institution of wardship, a remnant of the feudal system. Minors who inherited estates automatically fell into the care of their feudal superiors: the King in Bertram's case, the Countess in Helen's. Once the guardian chose a marriage partner of suitable social rank for the "ward," the ward could not refuse the match except by forfeiting much of his property; thus the tense exchange in 2.3 between Bertram and the King about Helen's qualifications in this respect.

Another form of external pressure is brought to bear upon Bertram at the end of the play, when Helen once again appeals to the King to enforce her claim. The hearing that ensues resembles those of the ecclesiastical courts, judicial bodies that settled complaints of sexual misconduct in early modern England. The conflicting testimony of Diana and Bertram painfully recalls the proceedings of the "bawdy courts," as they were popularly known: interminable prosecutions and counterprosecutions for premarital fornication, breach of promise, adultery, child support, and sexual slander—cases in which, as here, evidence was often hard to come by and truth difficult to unearth.

In the early seventeenth century, both wardship and the judicial regulation of sexual conduct were topics of considerable controversy. Some people fiercely resented any meddling in their domestic and sexual affairs, but others wanted the courts to monitor such behavior even more aggressively. Likewise, some attacked wardship on the grounds that guardians often trampled on the

Drummers before an encampment. From Geffrey Whitney, *A Choice of Emblemes* (1586).

personal inclinations of the ward, while others argued that young heirs and heiresses required supervision to prevent their seduction by unscrupulous gold diggers. In both cases, the point at issue is whether sexual conduct is an essentially personal matter or a matter for public concern. By making both the custom of wardship and the procedures of the bawdy courts crucial to the plot of *All's Well,* Shakespeare seems to endorse the assumption upon which both institutions are premised: that individuals are not competent to manage their own sexual lives, and that stern legal measures are required to coerce the likes of Bertram into matrimony.

A comedy normally depicts the progress of young lovers toward marriage, and in *All's Well,* Bertram's stubborn resistance to his generically mandated fate has important consequences. The protagonists of almost all comedies undergo some kind of suffering in the middle acts of the play, but that suffering is overcome. The happy ending retrospectively makes the hardships that preceded it seem worthwhile; conversely, pain validates and gives an appropriate significance to the concluding felicities. Despite its cheerful once-and-for-all title, *All's Well That Ends Well* does not conform to this time-worn pattern. Instead, the play constantly derails narrative expectations and promises endings that turn out to be mirages. Helen cures the King and weds Bertram, but the story is not yet over. She must then encounter Bertram somehow (whether by accident or design is unclear) and arrange to bed him. Then she must make sure she is pregnant; then she must return to France to beg justice of the King. The action continues past the point where one would expect it to terminate, again and again requiring the expenditure of additional effort and ingenuity on Helen's part: early in Act 5, even the King's court turns out to be surprisingly difficult to locate.

Helen's stamina is not demanded of the other characters, but they, too, persist willy-nilly after one might have expected them to subside, and they resurface after one might have expected them to vanish. The King is preparing for his own death when Helen's arrival returns him to the life he had resigned himself to losing. Later, Bertram believes that by fleeing Italy for France he has left Helen behind; similarly, he forsakes Diana. But the two women decline to evaporate. They reappear together in a scene that begins with the King announcing that "the nature of [Bertram's] great offence is dead" (5.3.23), then revives and exacerbates his offense, then declares it buried once more.

Occasion with her forelock. From Geffrey Whitney, *A Choice of Emblemes* (1586). She must be "taken by the forelock"—that is, at the moment when she presents herself; the back of her head is bald to signify that once she is past, she can no longer be grasped. See *All's Well That Ends Well* 5.3.40.

These aborted endings, continual deferrals, unanticipated reemergences, and surprising persistences inevitably make the actual end of the play seem rather arbitrary. Eventually it becomes hard to credit the permanence of any resolution, any happy ending. When, in the play's final lines, the King blithely promises Diana her choice of husbands from among his stable of remaining wards, *All's Well* may seem not to be drawing to a close, but merely to be forecasting its own reiteration. The play's open-endedness has generated both dismay and appreciation, depending on the temperament of the critic and, often, on his or her convictions about literary form. Those who prefer celebratory and romantic modes often find the play's lack of convincing closure a disturbing flaw. Those who find the happy endings of most comedies wishful and unrealistic tend to applaud Shakespeare's eschewal of easy answers.

Once again, *All's Well*'s apparent noncompliance with "normal" comic practice implicitly suggests limitations inherent in the comic forms it forsakes. In 2.4, when Helen asks Lavatch whether the Countess is well, Lavatch replies that "she is not well," despite the fact that "she's very well and wants nothing i'th' world." To the baffled Helen, Lavatch goes on to explain that he does not consider the Countess well because "she's not in heaven, whither God send her quickly" (lines 2ff.). In Lavatch's mind, only the dead are happy, a notion that gives a distinctly uncomical twist to the concept of ending well. Consciously or not, Lavatch echoes a long tradition of classical and Christian thought that emphasizes the misery of this world and defers true happiness until after death. In 4.3, the first Lord Dumaine relates this apparently inevitable misery to the intransigence of human passions, an intransigence imagined in the Christian tradition in terms of original sin. "As we are ourselves, what things are we" (lines 19–20). Only divine grace can remedy the defects of human nature in general and of human sexuality in particular. Only another world can offer the prospect of true, lasting felicity. But comedy is a secular mode, lacking the means to represent heaven or divine intervention, and to that extent its happy endings must be illusory or partial. *All's Well* is not unique among Shakespearean comedies in gesturing beyond the mundane, imperfect world with which plays are necessarily concerned, to an ideal world that cannot be directly represented in the theater. Lorenzo's discussion of the music of the spheres in *The Merchant of Venice* and Isabella's acute conviction of divine mentorship in *Measure for Measure* likewise have the effect of implicitly contrasting the limited bliss of comic endings with an unlimited, indescribable counterpart.

But although absolute fulfillment may be impossible in this world, relative improvements are surely feasible. In *All's Well,* it seems that a community can constructively intervene to correct, at least provisionally, some of the grosser imperfections of individuals. In Act 4, Bertram acknowledges that he has misjudged Paroles and at the end of the play begs pardon for his behavior, finally promising to love his wife "ever ever dearly." These apparent changes of heart are not motivated by an instinctive sense of regret for his past actions or by a spontaneous upwelling of love for Helen. Rather, the vigorous efforts of his mother, his king, his friends, and his wife force him onto the path that seems best for him whether he likes it or not. Those critics who find his apparent reformation at the end of the play unconvincing are often those skeptical of whether this kind of social pressure will suffice to rescue Bertram from himself. If, however, we are to believe that Bertram is salvageable, as the play implies, then we must acknowledge the effectiveness of the community's efforts to rectify him.

Obviously a society can have these beneficial effects on its more wayward members only if its moral intuitions are fundamentally sound, and only if its coercive resources have the potential to induce heartfelt, lasting change. The King can force Bertram to marry Helen and to acknowledge the legitimacy of the child in her womb. But such decrees will ensure Bertram's *love* of Helen only if his inner convictions somehow follow from, or develop out of, his external submission to the King's commands. How actual—not merely apparent—compliance might be achieved is suggested in a speech in which the King warmly remembers Bertram's father, the late Count of Roussillon. The old Count, according to the King, adhered to a traditional aristocratic code: he was careful to speak no more than he was willing to defend with his sword. Thought, word, and deed were thus inextricable. The King characterizes this inextricability as "honor," for honor and its corollary, shame, bridge the gap between external behavior and private states of mind, internalizing social scruples so that the aristocrat behaves well even in the absence of obvious incentives or punishments. At best, honor is thus a "clock to itself," a self-regulating mechanism. Only when that clock fails to function properly— as it fails in Bertram's case—must the same results be compelled by clumsier, more obviously extrinsic means.

In his comments on the old Count, the King claims that the up-and-coming generation has an insufficiently vivid conception of honor and its importance:

> Such a man
> Might be a copy to these younger times,
> Which followed well would demonstrate them now
> But goers-backward.
>
> (1.2.45–48)

The danger of such a regression is embodied in Paroles, whose name means "words." Paroles exhibits all the superficial signs of courtiership—wit, lavish dress, a familiarity with military and courtly jargons—without any of the real skills or virtues those signs are supposed to indicate. Paroles endangers the social processes by which the world of *All's Well* is imagined to operate, estranging externals from inner substance and subversively demonstrating limitations in the courtly code of honor. He is tightly connected to Bertram, not merely through their friendship but by similarities in their circumstances. The staged drum trick on Paroles coincides temporally with the unstageable bed trick on Bertram, and there are clear thematic parallels as well: both victims are blind, morally as well as literally, to plots perpetrated by close acquaintances masquerading as strangers.

Still, Paroles's menace should not be overestimated. Everyone except Bertram sees through him instantly, and Bertram's inability to discern Paroles's pretenses is a telling mark of his immaturity. Once Bertram finally recognizes that Paroles is a "counterfeit module," moreover, he recoils violently from his former friend and adviser. Bertram may be gauche and inattentive, but he recognizes gross cowardice when he sees it, and in that rudimentary recognition of the difference between honorable and dishonorable conduct will lie the possibility of his reform.

Paroles, then, both incarnates Bertram's flaws and diminishes Bertram's culpability. "Your son was misled with a snipped-taffeta fellow there," opines Lafeu indignantly to the Countess, "whose villainous saffron would have made all the unbaked and doughy youth of a nation in his colour" (4.5.1–3). If, in the world of *All's Well*, good associates and benign forms of institutional duress can maneuver Bertram in the right direction, then bad associates and bad customs likewise have the power to exacerbate his worst impulses. On the other hand, unlike a sterner and more principled character, the "unbaked" Bertram retains the capacity to be reformed, like a lump of dough, despite his unpromising shape.

In less obvious ways, Paroles's presence in *All's Well* also deflects criticism from Helen. Helen's marital plans involve, as she herself admits, quite startling social ambi-

Foppish camp follower. Peter Flötner (mid-sixteenth century).

tions. Marrying Bertram will elevate her from the relatively large gentry class to a tiny elite at the pinnacle of the social pyramid. In a hierarchically stratified society where people are supposed to "know their places," such aspirations might well seem disruptive. But Paroles, a cruder and less principled social climber, helps clarify the actually *conservative* nature of Helen's desires. In marked contrast to the craven Paroles, Helen is willing to certify her words with her body as honorable aristocrats are supposed to do, proposing to sacrifice life and reputation if her promises to cure the King prove empty. Helen's conviction that words must suit actions, that her tongue must obey her hand, marks her as "noble" despite her lack of material resources, and gain her the respect of the older members of the nobility, such as the King, the Countess, and Lafeu. Thus marriage to Bertram seems to remedy an unaccountable lapse in the proper social order, rather than to create a breach in that order.

Left deliberately vague is what relationship, if any, merit really has with birth. On the one hand, Helen's excellence seems to belie her humble origins; on the other hand, although both Helen and Diana are poor, it is carefully specified that they are not "base" persons of artisan or peasant stock. Their gentility, however modest, seems to lend their upward mobility a respectability that Paroles's attempts at self-promotion can never possess. Paroles thus draws off criticism that Helen might otherwise attract for violating class boundaries. Similarly, his presence in the play serves partially to allay criticism of Helen's sexual transgressiveness: his boastful inaction is so obviously worse than Helen's vigorous but possibly "unfeminine" enterprise that once again he seems an instructive example that tells in Helen's favor.

Although Paroles functions as a scapegoat of sorts, at the end of the play he does not suffer the scapegoat's usual cruel fate. After his disgrace, his dramatic function as corrupter of Bertram and foil to Helen is evidently complete, and we might imagine that we have seen the last of him. But like so many other characters in *All's Well*, good and bad, Paroles has a surprising durability. "Simply the thing I am," he declares, "shall make me live" (4.3.310–11). Like Helen and Diana, he reappears in the final scenes, reinserting himself, in a reduced capacity, into a world that had scorned him. The partial, incremental improvement promised by the conclusion of *All's Well That Ends Well* may from some points of view seem disappointing. But its pessimism inspires a certain tolerance, a forbearance that allows even the ridiculous or debased to find a home.

KATHARINE EISAMAN MAUS

TEXTUAL NOTE

All's Well That Ends Well was first printed in the Folio of 1623 (F), and all subsequent editions have relied on that text. The presence in F of some stage directions that explain rather than merely indicate the action, as well as variant speech prefixes in different scenes (for instance, "Countess," "Mother," "Old Countess"), suggests that the printed text was prepared directly from Shakespeare's "foul papers," or manuscript draft. Some textual scholars believe that before printing, this manuscript must have been further annotated by the King's Men's bookkeeper, the person who prepared play texts for performance. Unfortunately, perhaps because of difficulties reading the foul papers, the compositors did a poor job of setting up the text, forcing later editors to make an unusual number of conjectural emendations.

The Oxford edition preserves the Folio act divisions and the traditional editorial (that is, non-Shakespearean) scene divisions. For those familiar with other editions of the play, the primary novelty of the Oxford text will be its decision to use "Helen" instead of "Hellena" to designate the heroine. In fact, the latter form occurs only four times in the play and only once in dialogue, so the Oxford editors argue that Shakespeare's preference was clearly for the two-syllable name.

SELECTED BIBLIOGRAPHY

Bradbrook, Muriel. "Virtue Is the True Nobility: A Study of the Structure of *All's Well That Ends Well*." *Review of English Studies* n.s. 1 (1950): 289–301. True nobility of virtue, as exemplified by Helen, versus the false nobility of birth, as exemplified by Bertram.

Calderwood, James L. "Styles of Knowing in *All's Well*." *Modern Language Quarterly* 25 (1964): 272–94. Sexuality and honor for Helen and Bertram.

Donaldson, Ian. "*All's Well That Ends Well*: Shakespeare's Play of Endings." *Essays in Criticism* 27 (1977): 34–55. Discusses the play's preoccupation with endings and its problematic final scene.

Engle, Lars. "Shakespeare Normativity in *All's Well That Ends Well*." *Shakespeare Studies Today*. Ed. Graham Bradshaw, Tom Bishop, and Mark Turner. Shakespeare International Yearbook 4. Burlington, Vt.: Ashgate, 2004. 264–79. The establishment and violation of norms in *All's Well That Ends Well*.

Frye, Northrop. *The Myth of Deliverance: Reflections on Shakespeare's Problem Comedies*. Toronto: University of Toronto Press, 1983. General discussion of patterns of reversal in the problem comedies.

Hodgdon, Barbara. "The Making of Virgins and Mothers: Sexual Signs, Substitute Scenes, and Doubled Presences in *All's Well That Ends Well*." *Philological Quarterly* 66 (1987): 47–72. The character of Helen, as Shakespeare develops it from the source story in Boccaccio's *Decameron*.

Huston, J. Dennis, "'Some Stain of Soldier': The Functions of Paroles in *All's Well That Ends Well*." *Shakespeare Quarterly* 21 (1970): 431–38. Paroles compared with Helen.

Muir, Kenneth, and Stanley Wells, eds. *Aspects of Shakespeare's "Problem Plays": Articles Reprinted from Shakespeare Survey*. New York: Cambridge University Press, 1982. Essays on *Measure for Measure, All's Well That Ends Well*, and *Troilus and Cressida*, with selected reviews of theater productions from 1953 to 1976.

Parker, Patricia. "*All's Well That Ends Well*: Increase and Multiply." *Creative Imitation: New Essays on Renaissance Literature in Honor of Thomas M. Greene*. Ed. David Quint, Margaret Ferguson, G. W. Pigman, and Wayne Rebhorn. Binghamton, N.Y.: Medieval & Renaissance Texts & Studies, 1992. 355–90. Linguistic and sexual deferral and displacement as the key to abundance in *All's Well That Ends Well*.

Traister, Barbara Howard. "'Doctor She': Healing and Sex in *All's Well That Ends Well*." *A Companion to Shakespeare Works*, IV: *Poems, Problem Comedies, Late Plays*. Blackwell Companions to Literature and Culture 20. Ed. Richard Dutton and Jean E. Howard. Malden, Mass.: Blackwell, 2003. 333–47. Helen as lovesick physician.

Wheeler, Richard P. "Imperial Love and the Dark House: *All's Well That Ends Well*." *Shakespeare's Development and the Problem Comedies: Turn and Counter-Turn*. Berkeley: University of California Press, 1981. 35–91. Detailed psychoanalytic reading.

Zitner, Sheldon P. *All's Well That Ends Well*. Boston: Twayne, 1989. Stage and reception histories as well as critical commentary on the play.

FILM

All's Well That Ends Well. 1981. Dir. Elijah Moshinsky. UK. 142 min. From BBC-TV. An elegant production, with sets and lighting that recall the paintings of Vermeer and Caravaggio. Compelling performances from Angela Down (Helen), Celia Johnson (Countess), Donald Sinden (King), and Ian Charleson (Bertram).

All's Well That Ends Well

The Persons of the Play

The Dowager COUNTESS of Roussillon
BERTRAM, Count of Roussillon, her son
HELEN, an orphan, attending on the Countess
LAVATCH, a Clown, the Countess's servant
REYNALDO, the Countess's steward
PAROLES, Bertram's companion
The KING of France
LAFEU, an old lord
FIRST LORD DUMAINE
SECOND LORD DUMAINE } brothers
INTERPRETER, a French soldier
A GENTLEMAN Austringer
The DUKE of Florence
WIDOW Capilet
DIANA, her daughter
MARIANA, a friend of the Widow
Lords, attendants, soldiers, citizens

1.1

Enter young BERTRAM *Count of Roussillon, his mother*
[*the* COUNTESS], HELEN, [*and*] *Lord* LAFEU, *all in black*

COUNTESS   In delivering my son from me I bury a second husband.[1]

BERTRAM   And I in going, madam, weep o'er my father's death
anew; but I must attend° his majesty's command, to whom I   heed
5 am now in ward,[2] evermore in subjection.

LAFEU   You shall find of the King a husband,° madam; you, sir,   patron
a father. He that so generally° is at all times good must of neces-   universally
sity hold° his virtue to you, whose worthiness would stir it up   uphold
where it wanted° rather than lack it where there is such abun-   was lacking
10 dance.

COUNTESS   What hope is there of his majesty's amendment?°   improvement

LAFEU   He hath abandoned his physicians,[3] madam, under
whose practices he hath persecuted time with hope,[4] and finds
no other advantage in the process but only the losing of hope
15 by time.

COUNTESS   This young gentlewoman had a father—O that 'had':
how sad a passage° 'tis!—whose skill was almost as great as his   expression; passing away
honesty;° had it° stretched so far, would have made nature   integrity / (his skill)
immortal, and death should have play for lack of work. Would
20 for the King's sake he were living. I think it would be the death
of the King's disease.

1.1 Location: Bertram's palace in Roussillon, in south-
west France.
1. Giving up my son grieves me as much as my husband's death (playing on "deliver" as "give birth").
2. Upon the old Count's death, the King becomes guardian of Bertram's estate until he comes of age. A guardian

could arrange his ward's marriage, provided the match
was with a social equal.
3. Playing on the usual "His physicians have abandoned
him" (given up hope of his cure).
4. Afflicted his days by hoping for a cure.

LAFEU   How called you the man you speak of, madam?

COUNTESS   He was famous, sir, in his profession, and it was his
   great right to be so: Gérard de Narbonne.[5]

25   LAFEU   He was excellent indeed, madam. The King very lately
   spoke of him, admiringly and mourningly. He was skilful
   enough to have lived still, if knowledge could be set up against
   mortality.

BERTRAM   What is it, my good lord, the King languishes of?

30   LAFEU   A fistula,° my lord.   °abscess (often anal)

BERTRAM   I heard not of it before.

LAFEU   I would it were not notorious.°—Was this gentlewoman   °known to everyone
   the daughter of Gérard de Narbonne?

COUNTESS   His sole child, my lord, and bequeathed to my over-
35   looking.[6] I have those hopes of her good that her education°   °upbringing
   promises; her dispositions she inherits, which makes fair gifts°   °abilities
   fairer—for where an unclean mind carries virtuous qualities,°   °acquired skills
   there commendations go with pity:° they are virtues and traitors   °mingle with regret
   too.[7] In her they are the better for their simpleness.° She   °purity
40   derives° her honesty and achieves her goodness.   °inherits

LAFEU   Your commendations, madam, get from her tears.

COUNTESS   'Tis the best brine a maiden can season° her praise   °preserve (as with salt)
   in. The remembrance of her father never approaches her heart
   but the tyranny of her sorrows takes all livelihood° from her   °liveliness
45   cheek.—No more of this, Helen. Go to, no more, lest it be
   rather thought you affect° a sorrow than to have—   °make a show of

HELEN   I do affect a sorrow indeed, but I have it too.

LAFEU   Moderate lamentation is the right of the dead, excessive
   grief the enemy to the living.

50   COUNTESS   If the living be not enemy to the grief, the excess
   makes it soon mortal.°   °fatal

BERTRAM [kneeling]   Madam, I desire your holy wishes.°   °blessing

LAFEU   How understand we that?[8]

COUNTESS   Be thou blessed, Bertram, and succeed thy father
55   In manners° as in shape. Thy blood and virtue[9]   °behavior
   Contend for empire in thee, and thy goodness
   Share with thy birthright. Love all, trust a few,
   Do wrong to none. Be able° for thine enemy   °a match for
   Rather in power than use,[1] and keep thy friend
60   Under thy own life's key.[2] Be checked° for silence   °criticized
   But never taxed for speech.° What heaven more will   °rebuked for chatter
   That thee may furnish° and my prayers pluck down,   °embellish
   Fall on thy head. Farewell. [To LAFEU] My lord,
   'Tis an unseasoned° courtier. Good my lord,   °immature
   Advise him.

65   LAFEU   He cannot want the best
   That shall attend his love.[3]

COUNTESS   Heaven bless him!—Farewell, Bertram.

BERTRAM [rising]   The best wishes that can be forged° in your   °fashioned
   thoughts be servants to you.°   [Exit COUNTESS]   °assist you

---

5. Town just north of Roussillon.
6. Guardianship (Helen is the Countess's ward, as
Bertram is the King's).
7. Because the skills are used for evil purposes.
8. Possibly a misplaced line; possibly Lafeu thinks
Bertram's interruption discourteous.

9. (May) your noble birth and acquired goodness.
1. By having power, rather than using it.
2. keep . . . key: safeguard your friend's life as you do
your own.
3. He . . . love: He will not lack the best advice my
affection for him can supply.

70 [*To* HELEN] Be comfortable° to my mother, your mistress, and   *comforting*
make much of her.

LAFEU   Farewell, pretty lady. You must hold the credit° of your   *uphold the reputation*
father.   *Exeunt* BERTRAM *and* LAFEU

HELEN   O were that all! I think not on my father,
75 And these great tears grace his remembrance more
Than those I shed for him.[4] What was he like?
I have forgot him. My imagination
Carries no favour° in't but Bertram's.   *face; liking; love token*
I am undone. There is no living, none,
80 If Bertram be away. 'Twere all one
That° I should love a bright particular star   *It is just as if*
And think to wed it, he is so above me.
In his bright radiance and collateral[5] light
Must I be comforted, not in his sphere.
85 Th'ambition in my love thus plagues itself.
The hind° that would be mated by the lion   *doe*
Must die for love. 'Twas pretty, though a plague,
To see him every hour, to sit and draw
His archèd brows, his hawking° eye, his curls,   *sharp*
90 In our heart's table°—heart too capable°   *drawing table / receptive*
Of every line and trick° of his sweet favour.°   *trait / face*
But now he's gone, and my idolatrous fancy°   *love*
Must sanctify his relics.[6] Who comes here?
         Enter PAROLES
One that goes with him. I love him for his sake—
95 And yet I know him a notorious liar,
Think him a great way° fool, solely° a coward.   *mostly a / completely*
Yet these fixed evils sit so fit in him°   *fit him so well*
That they take place[7] when virtue's steely bones°   *rigid severity*
Looks bleak i'th' cold wind. Withal, full oft we see
100 Cold wisdom waiting on superfluous folly.

PAROLES   Save° you, fair queen.   *God save*

HELEN   And you, monarch.

PAROLES   No.

HELEN   And no.

105 PAROLES   Are you meditating on virginity?

HELEN   Ay. You have some stain° of soldier in you, let me ask   *tinge*
you a question. Man is enemy to virginity: how may we barri-
cado° it against him?   *barricade*

PAROLES   Keep him out.

110 HELEN   But he assails, and our virginity, though valiant in the
defence, yet is weak. Unfold to us some warlike resistance.

PAROLES   There is none. Man, setting down before° you, will   *laying siege to*
undermine you and blow you up.[8]

HELEN   Bless our poor virginity from underminers and blowers-
115 up. Is there no military policy° how virgins might blow up   *strategy*
men?

PAROLES   Virginity being blown down, man will quicklier be
blown up.° Marry,[9] in blowing him down again, with the   *have an erection*

---

4. *grace . . . him:* are a better tribute to my father than those (few) tears I actually shed for him.
5. Rotating in a separate orbit (in Ptolomaic astronomy).
6. Must worship what reminds me of him.
7. Take precedence.

8. *undermine you:* dig tunnels under you (to plant explosives). *blow you up:* punning on "inflate," "make you pregnant."
9. By Mary (a mild oath).

breach yourselves made you lose your city. It is not politic° in *expedient*
120 the commonwealth of nature to preserve virginity. Loss of virginity is rational increase,[1] and there was never virgin got° till *begotten*
virginity was first lost. That° you were made of is mettle° to *What / substance*
make virgins. Virginity by being once lost may be ten times
found;° by being ever kept it is ever lost. 'Tis too cold a com- *reproduced tenfold*
125 panion, away with't.

HELEN   I will stand for't° a little, though therefore I die a virgin. *defend it*

PAROLES   There's little can be said in't.° 'Tis against the rule of *for it*
nature. To speak on the part of virginity is to accuse your mothers, which is most infallible disobedience. He that hangs him-
130 self is a virgin:[2] virginity murders itself, and should be buried
in highways, out of all sanctified limit,[3] as a desperate
offendress against nature. Virginity breeds mites, much like a
cheese;[4] consumes itself to the very paring, and so dies with
feeding his own stomach.° Besides, virginity is peevish, proud, *pride*
135 idle, made of self-love—which is the most inhibited° sin in the *prohibited*
canon.° Keep it not, you cannot choose but lose by't. Out *scriptures*
with't![5] Within t'one year it will make itself two, which is a
goodly increase, and the principal[6] itself not much the worse.
Away with't.

140 HELEN   How might one do, sir, to lose it to her own liking?

PAROLES   Let me see. Marry, ill, to like him that ne'er it likes.[7]
'Tis a commodity will lose the gloss with lying:° the longer kept, *remaining idle*
the less worth. Off with't while 'tis vendible.° Answer the time *salable*
of request.[8] Virginity like an old courtier wears her cap out of
145 fashion, richly suited° but unsuitable,° just like the brooch and *dressed / inappropriate*
the toothpick, which wear not now.[9] Your date° is better in *fruit; age*
your pie and your porridge than in your cheek, and your virginity, your old virginity, is like one of our French withered pears:[1]
it looks ill, it eats drily, marry, 'tis a withered pear—it was for-
150 merly better, marry, yet 'tis a withered pear. Will you anything
with it?

HELEN   Not my virginity, yet . . .[2]
There° shall your master have a thousand loves, *(At court)*
A mother and a mistress and a friend,
155 A phoenix,[3] captain, and an enemy,
A guide, a goddess, and a sovereign,
A counsellor, a traitress, and a dear:
His humble ambition, proud humility,
His jarring concord and his discord dulcet,[4]
160 His faith, his sweet disaster, with a world
Of pretty fond adoptious christendoms
That blinking Cupid gossips.[5] Now shall he—
I know not what he shall. God send him well.
The court's a learning place, and he is one—

---

1. *rational increase*: judicious growth in the human ("rational") population.
2. A suicide, like a virgin, is a self-destroyer.
3. Consecrated ground (in which suicides were denied burial).
4. Cheese was thought to generate spontaneously the mites that fed on it.
5. Get rid of it; put it out at interest.
6. Original investment (the woman's body).
7. To please him who doesn't appreciate virginity.

8. Respond to demand (greatest in youth).
9. Which are no longer in fashion.
1. Dried pears (suggesting aged female genitals).
2. Not with *my* virginity: not my virginity *yet* (but soon).
3. The mythical phoenix was a one-of-a-kind bird; hence, marvelous, unique being.
4. Harmonious (all these oxymorons were typical of courtly love poetry).
5. *pretty . . . gossips:* foolish nicknames given when blind Cupid is godfather at a christening.

165	PAROLES What one, i'faith?	
	HELEN That I wish well. 'Tis pity.	
	PAROLES What's pity?	
	HELEN That wishing well had not a body in't	
	Which might be felt,° that we, the poorer born,	*perceived*
170	Whose baser stars do shut us up in wishes,⁶	
	Might with effects of them follow our friends	
	And show what we alone must° think, which never	*must only*
	Returns us thanks.°	*wins us gratitude*

Enter [*a*] PAGE

	PAGE Monsieur Paroles, my lord calls for you. [*Exit*]	
175	PAROLES Little Helen, farewell. If I can remember thee I will	
	think of thee at court.	
	HELEN Monsieur Paroles, you were born under a charitable star.	
	PAROLES Under Mars,⁷ I.	
	HELEN I especially think *under* Mars.	
180	PAROLES Why '*under* Mars'?	
	HELEN The wars hath so kept you under that you must needs be	
	born under Mars.	
	PAROLES When he was predominant.°	*in the ascendant*
	HELEN When he was retrograde,⁸ I think rather.	
185	PAROLES Why think you so?	
	HELEN You go so much backward when you fight.	
	PAROLES That's for advantage.°	*tactical gain*
	HELEN So is running away, when fear proposes the safety. But	
	the composition° that your valour and fear makes in you is a	*truce; mixture*
190	virtue of a good wing,⁹ and I like the wear° well.	*habit; fashion*
	PAROLES I am so full of businesses I cannot answer thee acutely.	
	I will return perfect courtier, in the which my instruction shall	
	serve to naturalize° thee, so thou wilt be capable of a courtier's	*familiarize*
	counsel and understand what advice shall thrust upon thee;	
195	else thou diest in thine unthankfulness, and thine ignorance	
	makes thee away.° Farewell. When thou hast leisure say thy	*puts an end to you*
	prayers; when thou hast none remember thy friends.¹ Get thee	
	a good husband and use° him as he uses thee. So farewell.	*treat*
	[*Exit*]	
	HELEN Our remedies oft in ourselves do lie	
200	Which we ascribe to heaven. The fated° sky	*destiny-ordaining*
	Gives us free scope, only doth backward pull	
	Our slow designs when we ourselves are dull.°	*sluggish*
	What power is it which mounts my love so high,²	
	That makes me see and cannot feed mine eye?	
205	The mightiest space in fortune nature brings	
	To join like likes and kiss like native things.³	
	Impossible be strange° attempts to those	*unusual*
	That weigh their pains in sense⁴ and do suppose	
	What hath been cannot be. Who ever strove	
210	To show her merit that did miss° her love?	*fail to achieve*

6. Whose less elevated destinies confine us merely to wishing.
7. The planet was identified with the god of war.
8. Retreating (said of a planet's apparent movement relative to the zodiac).
9. *of a good wing*: that is, rapid in flight; also, with large shoulder flaps. Paroles is foppishly dressed.
1. Unclear: perhaps, Say your prayers when you have the chance, and when you're too busy, rely on your friends instead.
2. Which elevates my love to so lofty an object.
3. *The mightiest . . . things*: Natural affect brings persons greatly distant in rank together as if they were similar and conjoins them as if they had a common origin.
4. Who vividly imagine the difficulties.

The King's disease—my project may deceive me,
But my intents are fixed and will not leave me.   *Exit*

1.2

A flourish of cornetts.° Enter the KING *of France with let-*   horn fanfare
ters, [the two LORDS DUMAINE,*] and divers attendants*

KING   The Florentines and Sienese are by th'ears,°   quarreling
Have fought with equal fortune, and continue
A braving° war.   defiant; gallant

FIRST LORD DUMAINE   So 'tis reported, sir.

KING   Nay, 'tis most credible: we here receive it

5   A certainty vouched from our cousin° Austria,   fellow sovereign
With caution that the Florentine will move° us   entreat
For speedy aid—wherein our dearest friend°   (the Duke of Austria)
Prejudicates° the business, and would seem   Prejudges
To have us make denial.

FIRST LORD DUMAINE   His love and wisdom

10   Approved° so to your majesty may plead   Proven
For amplest credence.

KING   He hath armed° our answer,   hardened
And Florence is denied before he comes.
Yet for our gentlemen that mean to see
The Tuscan service, freely have they leave
To stand on either part.°   fight on either side

15   SECOND LORD DUMAINE   It well may serve
A nursery to[1] our gentry, who are sick°   pining
For breathing° and exploit.   exercise

KING   What's he comes here?

Enter BERTRAM, LAFEU, *and* PAROLES

FIRST LORD DUMAINE   It is the Count Roussillon, my good lord,
Young Bertram.

KING *[to* BERTRAM*]*   Youth, thou bear'st thy father's face.

20   Frank° nature, rather curious° than in haste,   generous / meticulous
Hath well composed thee. Thy father's moral parts°   qualities
Mayst thou inherit, too. Welcome to Paris.

BERTRAM   My thanks and duty are your majesty's.

KING   I would I had that corporal soundness now

25   As when thy father and myself in friendship
First tried our soldiership. He did look far°   see deeply
Into the service° of the time, and was   military service
Discipled of° the bravest. He lasted long,   Followed by; taught by
But on us both did haggish° age steal on,   witchlike; malevolent

30   And wore us out of act.° It much repairs me   action
To talk of your good father. In his youth
He had the wit which I can well observe
Today in our young lords, but they may jest
Till their own scorn return to them unnoted[2]

35   Ere they can hide their levity in honour.[3]
So like a courtier,° contempt nor bitterness   paradigm of courtesy
Were in his pride° or sharpness;[4] if they were   self-esteem

---

1.2 Location: The King's court at Paris.
1. As a training school for.
2. *they may . . . unnoted:* their ridicule merely rebounds
upon them, ignored by others.

3. Before they can compensate for their frivolity with
noble acts.
4. Keenness of wit.

His equal had awaked them,[5] and his honour—
Clock to itself°—knew the true minute when   *Self-regulating*
40 Exception° bid him speak, and at this time   *Disapproval*
His tongue obeyed his hand.[6] Who were below him
He used as creatures of another place,[7]
And bowed his eminent top° to their low ranks,   *head*
Making them proud of his humility,
45 In their poor praise he humbled.[8] Such a man
Might be a copy° to these younger times,   *model*
Which followed well would demonstrate them now
But goers-backward.°   *backsliders*

BERTRAM   His good remembrance, sir,
Lies richer in your thoughts than on his tomb.
50 So in approof° lives not his epitaph   *confirmation*
As in your royal speech.

KING   Would I were with him! He would always say—
Methinks I hear him now; his plausive° words   *praiseworthy*
He scattered not in ears, but grafted them[9]
55 To grow there and to bear. 'Let me not live'—
This his good melancholy oft began
On the catastrophe° and heel of pastime,   *end*
When it was out°—'Let me not live', quoth he,   *finished*
'After my flame lacks oil, to be the snuff[1]
60 Of younger spirits, whose apprehensive° senses   *quick*
All but new things disdain, whose judgements are
Mere fathers of their garments,[2] whose constancies°   *loyalties*
Expire before their fashions.' This he wished.
I after him do after° him wish too,   *in harmony with*
65 Since I nor wax nor honey can bring home,
I quickly were dissolvèd° from my hive   *removed*
To give some labourers room.

SECOND LORD DUMAINE   You're lovèd, sir.
They that least lend it you° shall lack° you first.   *grant you love / miss*

KING   I fill a place, I know't.—How long is't, Count,
70 Since the physician at your father's died?
He was much famed.

BERTRAM   Some six months since, my lord.

KING   If he were living I would try him yet.—
Lend me an arm.—The rest have worn me out
With several applications.° Nature and sickness   *various treatments*
75 Debate it at their leisure.[3] Welcome, Count.
My son's no dearer.

BERTRAM   Thank your majesty.   [*Flourish.*] *Exeunt*

1.3

Enter the COUNTESS, [REYNALDO *her*] *steward, and*
[*behind,* LAVATCH *her*] *clown*

COUNTESS   I will now hear. What say you of this gentlewoman?

---

5. *if they were . . . them:* if ever he spoke bitterly or contemptuously, it was to a social equal.
6. He said no more than he would back up with action.
7. He treated as people of a higher station.
8. He willingly humbled himself to praise their poor selves.
9. He did not strew (words) superficially among his hearers (like seed), but planted them permanently (as twigs

of fruit trees are grafted to a tree trunk).
1. Burned upper wick, which if not trimmed keeps the lower part from burning properly.
2. *whose judgements . . . garments:* whose mental prowess creates only new clothes.
3. Argue over my condition at length.
1.3 Location: Roussillon.

REYNALDO Madam, the care I have had to even your content[1] I
wish might be found in the calendar° of my past endeavours,   record
for then we wound our modesty and make foul the clearness of
5   our deservings, when of ourselves we publish° them.   advertise
COUNTESS What does this knave here? [*To* LAVATCH] Get you
gone, sirrah. The complaints I have heard of you I do not all
believe. 'Tis my slowness that I do not, for I know you lack not
folly to commit them and have ability enough to make such
10   knaveries yours.
LAVATCH 'Tis not unknown to you, madam, I am a poor fellow.
COUNTESS Well, sir?
LAVATCH No, madam, 'tis not so well that I am poor, though
many of the rich are damned. But if I may have your ladyship's
15   good will to go to the world,° Isbel the woman° and I will do as   marry / maidservant
we may.[2]
COUNTESS Wilt thou needs be a beggar?
LAVATCH I do beg your good will in this case.
COUNTESS In what case?
20   LAVATCH In Isbel's case and mine own. Service is no heritage,[3]
and I think I shall never have the blessing of God till I have
issue o' my body, for they say bairns° are blessings.   children
COUNTESS Tell me thy reason why thou wilt marry.
LAVATCH My poor body, madam, requires it. I am driven on by
25   the flesh, and he must needs go that the devil drives.
COUNTESS Is this all your worship's reason?
LAVATCH Faith, madam, I have other holy reasons,[4] such as they
are.
COUNTESS May the world know them?
30   LAVATCH I have been, madam, a wicked creature, as you—and
all flesh and blood—are, and indeed I do marry that I may
repent.[5]
COUNTESS Thy marriage sooner than thy wickedness.
LAVATCH I am out o' friends, madam, and I hope to have friends
35   for my wife's sake.
COUNTESS Such friends are thine enemies, knave.
LAVATCH You're shallow,° madam—in great friends, for the   a superficial judge
knaves come to do that for me which I am aweary of. He that
ears° my land spares my team, and gives me leave to in° the   plows / harvest
40   crop. If I be his cuckold, he's my drudge. He that comforts my
wife is the cherisher of my flesh and blood; he that cherishes
my flesh and blood loves my flesh and blood; he that loves my
flesh and blood is my friend; *ergo,* he that kisses my wife is my
friend. If men could be contented to be what they are,° there   (cuckolds)
45   were no fear in marriage. For young Chairbonne the puritan
and old Poisson the papist,[6] howsome'er their hearts are sev-
ered in religion, their heads are both one:° they may jowl°   identical / bump
horns together like any deer i'th' herd.[7]
COUNTESS Wilt thou ever be a foul-mouthed and calumnious
50   knave?

1. To meet your desires.
2. Will do our best (with sexual pun on "do").
3. A servant has little to leave his children (proverbial; with sexual pun on "service").
4. Other motives sanctified by the marriage ceremony; with puns on "holy" ("hole-y") and "reasons" ("raisings").
5. That I may make my illicit sexual activity lawful (but alluding to the proverb "Marry in haste and repent at leisure").
6. *chair bonne:* good meat (French). *poisson:* fish. Catholics ate fish on fast days, but Puritans rejected the custom.
7. Cuckolds were supposed to have horns in their foreheads.

LAVATCH   A prophet? Ay, madam, and I speak the truth the next°   most direct
   way.
   [*He sings*]   For I the ballad will repeat,
            Which men full true shall find:
55   Your marriage comes by destiny,
            Your cuckoo sings by kind.[8]
COUNTESS   Get you gone, sir. I'll talk with you more anon.
REYNALDO   May it please you, madam, that he bid Helen come
   to you? Of her I am to speak.
60 COUNTESS [*to* LAVATCH]   Sirrah, tell my gentlewoman I would
   speak with her. Helen, I mean.
LAVATCH [*sings*]
      'Was this fair face the cause', quoth she,[9]
      'Why the Grecians sackèd Troy?
      Fond° done, done fond. Was this[1] King Priam's joy?'   Foolishly; lovingly
65   With that she sighèd as she stood,
      With that she sighèd as she stood,
         And gave this sentence° then: maxim
      'Among nine bad if one be good,
      Among nine bad if one be good,
70   There's yet one good in ten.'
COUNTESS   What, 'one good in ten'? You corrupt[2] the song,
   sirrah.
LAVATCH   One good *woman* in ten, madam, which is a purifying
   o'th' song. Would God would serve the world so all the year!
75 We'd find no fault with the tithe-woman[3] if I were the parson.
   One in ten, quoth a?° An° we might have a good woman born   did he say / If
   but ere every blazing star,° or at an earthquake, 'twould mend   comet
   the lottery° well. A man may draw his heart out ere a pluck[4]   improve the odds
   one.
80 COUNTESS   You'll be gone, sir knave, and do as I command you.
LAVATCH   That man should be at woman's command, and yet
   no hurt done! Though honesty be no puritan,[5] yet it will do no
   hurt;° it will wear the surplice of humility over the black gown   harm
   of a big heart.[6] I am going, forsooth. The business is for Helen
85 to come hither.   *Exit*
COUNTESS   Well now.
REYNALDO   I know, madam, you love your gentlewoman
   entirely.
COUNTESS   Faith, I do. Her father bequeathed her to me, and
90 she herself without other advantage[7] may lawfully make title
   to° as much love as she finds. There is more owing her than is   claim
   paid, and more shall be paid her than she'll demand.
REYNALDO   Madam, I was very late° more near her than I think   recently
   she wished me. Alone she was, and did communicate to her
95 self, her own words to her own ears; she thought, I dare vow for

---

8. *by kind:* according to its nature (the cuckoo's song was supposed to mock cuckolds).
9. Lavatch is reminded of the "fair face" of Helen of Troy, the most famous cuckold maker. *she:* probably Hecuba, wife of Priam and mother of Paris, Helen's lover.
1. *this:* probably refers to Paris.
2. Debase (the original presumably had "one bad in ten," referring to Paris, Priam's only bad son).
3. One-tenth of the parish produce was tithed to the church.

4. Before he draw (as from a lottery).
5. Though my honest self is not morally strict.
6. *it will wear . . . heart:* that is, Lavatch will conceal his pride under apparent meekness. Some Puritan ministers obeyed English ecclesiastical law by wearing the surplice, or priestly garment, but with a black Calvinist gown underneath.
7. Even without any interest accrued (Helen being regarded as the "principal" bequeathed by her father).

her, they touched not any stranger sense.[8] Her matter° was, she   subject
loved your son. Fortune, she said, was no goddess, that had put
such difference betwixt their two estates;° Love no god, that   social stations
would not extend his might only where qualities were level;[9]
100   Dian° no queen of virgins, that would suffer her poor knight   goddess of chastity
surprised[1] without rescue in the first assault or ransom after-
ward. This she delivered in the most bitter touch° of sorrow that   strain
e'er I heard virgin exclaim in; which I held my duty speedily to
acquaint you withal, sithence° in the loss that may happen it   since
105   concerns you something to know it.
COUNTESS   You have discharged this honestly. Keep it to yourself. Many likelihoods informed me of this before, which hung
so tott'ring in the balance that I could neither believe nor misdoubt.° Pray you, leave me. Stall° this in your bosom, and I   doubt / Enclose
110   thank you for your honest care. I will speak with you further
anon.   *Exit steward*
        Enter HELEN
COUNTESS [*aside*]   Even so it was with me when I was young.
        If ever we are nature's, these° are ours: this thorn   (love pangs)
        Doth to our rose of youth rightly belong.
115   Our blood° to us, this to our blood is born;   passions
        It is the show° and seal of nature's truth,   sign
        Where love's strong passion is impressed in youth.
        By our remembrances of days foregone,
        Such were our faults—or° then we thought them none.   although
120   Her eye is sick on't.° I observe her now.   with it
HELEN   What is your pleasure, madam?
COUNTESS   You know, Helen,
        I am a mother to you.
HELEN   Mine honourable mistress.
COUNTESS   Nay, a mother.
        Why not a mother? When I said 'a mother',
125   Methought you saw a serpent. What's in 'mother'
        That you start at it? I say I am your mother,
        And put you in the catalogue of those
        That were enwombèd mine. 'Tis often seen
        Adoption strives with nature, and choice breeds
130   A native slip to us from foreign seeds.[2]
        You ne'er oppressed me with a mother's groan,°   (in childbirth)
        Yet I express to you a mother's care.
        God's mercy, maiden! Does it curd thy blood
        To say I am thy mother? What's the matter,
135   That this distempered° messenger of wet,°   disturbed / rain; tears
        The many-coloured Iris,[3] rounds thine eye?
        Why, that you are my daughter?
HELEN   That I am not.
COUNTESS   I say I am your mother.
HELEN   Pardon, madam.
        The Count Roussillon cannot be my brother.
140   I am from humble, he from honoured name;
        No note° upon my parents, his all noble.   distinction

8. Any other persons' hearing.   2. *choice . . . seeds*: a twig chosen from foreign seed
9. Would not exercise his power except where rank was   becomes, once engrafted, part of our plant.
equal.   3. Goddess of rainbows (Helen's tear-filled eyes are iri-
1. Would allow her poor devotee to be captured.   descent).

My master, my dear lord he is, and I
His servant live and will his vassal die.
He must not be my brother.

COUNTESS   Nor I your mother?

145 HELEN   You are my mother, madam. Would you were—
So° that my lord your son were not my brother—   *Provided*
Indeed my mother! Or were you both our mothers°   *mother of us both*
I care no more for than I do for heaven,
So I were not his sister. Can 't no other
150 But, I your daughter, he must be my brother?

COUNTESS   Yes, Helen, you might be my daughter-in-law.
God shield you mean it not! 'Daughter' and 'mother'
So strive upon your pulse. What, pale again?
My fear hath catched your fondness.° Now I see   *love; folly*
155 The myst'ry of your loneliness, and find
Your salt tears' head.° Now to all sense 'tis gross:°   *source / obvious*
You love my son. Invention[4] is ashamed
Against° the proclamation of thy passion   *In the face of*
To say thou dost not. Therefore tell me true,
160 But tell me then 'tis so—for look, thy cheeks
Confess it t'one to th'other, and thine eyes
See it so grossly shown in thy behaviours
That in their kind° they speak it. Only sin   *after their fashion*
And hellish obstinacy tie thy tongue,
165 That truth should be suspected.° Speak, is't so?   *doubted*
If it be so you have wound a goodly clew;[5]
If it be not, forswear't.° Howe'er,° I charge thee,   *deny it / In any case*
As heaven shall work in me for thine avail,°   *benefit*
To tell me truly.

HELEN   Good madam, pardon me.

COUNTESS   Do you love my son?

170 HELEN   Your pardon, noble mistress.

COUNTESS   Love you my son?

HELEN   Do not you love him, madam?

COUNTESS   Go not about.[6] My love hath in't a bond
Whereof the world takes note.° Come, come, disclose   *society recognizes*
The state of your affection, for your passions
Have to the full appeached.°   *informed against you*

175 HELEN   Then I confess,
Here on my knee, before high heaven and you,
That before you° and next unto high heaven   *even more than I love you*
I love your son.
My friends° were poor but honest; so's my love.   *relatives*
180 Be not offended, for it hurts not him
That he is loved of me. I follow him not
By any token° of presumptuous suit,°   *manifestations / wooing*
Nor would I have him till I do deserve him,
Yet never know how that desert should be.
185 I know I love in vain, strive against hope;
Yet in this captious° and intenable° sieve   *receptive / unretentive*
I still° pour in the waters of my love   *continually*
And lack not to lose still.° Thus, Indian-like,   *And keep losing it*

4. (Your) capacity to invent excuses.   6. Don't beat around the bush.
5. You have made a fine tangle of thread (mess).

Religious in mine error, I adore
190 The sun that looks upon his worshipper
But knows of him no more. My dearest madam,
Let not your hate encounter with° my love   oppose
For loving where you do; but if yourself,
Whose agèd honour cites° a virtuous youth,   testifies to
195 Did ever in so true a flame of liking
Wish chastely and love dearly, that your Dian
Was both herself and Love,[7] then give pity
To her whose state is such that cannot choose
But lend and give where she is sure to lose,
200 That seeks to find not that° her search implies,   what
But riddle-like[8] lives sweetly where she dies.

COUNTESS   Had you not lately an intent—speak truly—
To go to Paris?

HELEN   Madam, I had.

205 COUNTESS   Wherefore? Tell true.

HELEN   I will tell truth, by grace itself I swear.
You know my father left me some prescriptions
Of rare and proved effects, such as his reading
And manifest° experience had collected   obvious
210 For general sovereignty,° and that he willed me   effectiveness
In heedfull'st reservation° to bestow them,   With most sparing care
As notes whose faculties inclusive were
More than they were in note.[9] Amongst the rest
There is a remedy, approved,° set down,   tested
215 To cure the desperate languishings whereof
The King is rendered lost.°   held to be dying

COUNTESS   This was your motive
For Paris, was it? Speak.

HELEN   My lord your son made me to think of this,
Else Paris and the medicine and the King
220 Had from the conversation of my thoughts
Haply° been absent then.   Perhaps

COUNTESS   But think you, Helen,
If you should tender° your supposèd aid,   offer
He would receive it? He and his physicians
Are of a° mind: he, that they cannot help him;   one
225 They, that they cannot help. How shall they credit
A poor unlearnèd virgin, when the schools,
Embowelled° of their doctrine, have left off   Emptied
The danger to itself?

HELEN   There's something in't
More than my father's skill, which was the great'st
230 Of his profession, that his good receipt°   prescription
Shall for my legacy be sanctified
By th' luckiest stars in heaven, and would your honour
But give me leave to try success,° I'd venture   test the outcome
The well-lost life of mine on his grace's cure
235 By such a day, an hour.

COUNTESS   Dost thou believe't?

---

7. Venus, goddess of erotic love, is usually the antagonist
of Diana, goddess of chastity; Helen's love reconciles
them.

8. Paradoxically; retaining her secret.
9. *As . . . note:* As prescriptions of greater powers than
were recognized.

HELEN   Ay, madam, knowingly.[1]

COUNTESS   Why, Helen, thou shalt have my leave and love,
Means and attendants, and my loving greetings
240 To those of mine in court. I'll stay at home
And pray God's blessing into thy attempt.
Be gone tomorrow, and be sure of this:
What I can help thee to, thou shalt not miss.°   *Exeunt*   lack

2.1

Flourish cornetts. Enter the KING [*carried in a chair*],
with [*the two* LORDS DUMAINE,] *divers young lords tak-*
ing leave for the Florentine war, [*and* BERTRAM] *and*
PAROLES

KING   Farewell, young lords. These warlike principles°   military precepts
Do not throw from you. And you, my lords,[1] farewell.
Share the advice betwixt you; if both gain all,
The gift doth stretch itself as 'tis received,
And is enough for both.

5 FIRST LORD DUMAINE   'Tis our hope, sir,
After well-entered soldiers,[2] to return
And find your grace in health.

KING   No, no, it cannot be—and yet my heart
Will not confess he owes° the malady   it owns
10 That doth my life besiege. Farewell, young lords.
Whether I live or die, be you the sons
Of worthy Frenchmen; let higher° Italy—   northern
Those bated° that inherit but the fall   dwindled peoples
Of the last monarchy[3]—see that you come
15 Not to woo honour but to wed it. When
The bravest questant° shrinks, find what you seek,   seeker
That fame may cry you loud.° I say farewell.   acclaim you loudly

FIRST LORD DUMAINE   Health at your bidding serve your majesty.

KING   Those girls of Italy, take heed of them.
20 They say our French lack language to deny
If they demand.° Beware of being captives[4]   request
Before you serve.°   (militarily)

BOTH LORDS DUMAINE   Our hearts receive your warnings.

KING   Farewell.—Come hither to me.
        [*Some lords stand aside with the* KING]

FIRST LORD DUMAINE [*to* BERTRAM]   O my sweet lord, that you
        will stay behind us.

PAROLES   'Tis not his fault, the spark.°   spirited person

25 SECOND LORD DUMAINE   O 'tis brave° wars.   splendid

PAROLES   Most admirable! I have seen those wars.

BERTRAM   I am commanded° here, and kept a coil° with   (to stay) / fussed over
'Too young' and 'the next year' and ''tis too early'.

PAROLES   An° thy mind stand to't, boy, steal away bravely.   If

30 BERTRAM   I shall stay here the forehorse to a smock,[5]
Creaking my shoes on the plain masonry,[6]

---

1. Fully aware of what I am doing.
2.1 Location: The King's palace.
1. Presumably leaving to take the opposite side in the war.
2. After we are well initiated as soldiers.
3. Perhaps the Holy Roman Empire, the Medici, or the

papacy.
4. Of your mistresses.
5. Lead horse of a team driven by a woman (figuratively, part of a dancing couple).
6. Level stonework (of the palace floors, in contrast to the rough battlefield).

Till honour be bought up,° and no sword worn   *all acquired (by others)*
But one to dance with. By heaven, I'll steal away.

FIRST LORD DUMAINE   There's honour in the theft.

PAROLES   Commit it, Count.

35   SECOND LORD DUMAINE   I am your accessary.° And so, farewell.   *accomplice*

BERTRAM   I grow° to you,   *am deeply attached*
And our parting is a tortured body.

FIRST LORD DUMAINE   Farewell, captain.

SECOND LORD DUMAINE   Sweet Monsieur Paroles.

PAROLES   Noble heroes, my sword and yours are kin. Good
40   sparks and lustrous, a word, good mettles.° You shall find in the   *spirits; sword blades*
regiment of the Spinii one Captain Spurio, with his cicatrice,°   *scar*
an emblem of war, here on his sinister° cheek. It was this very   *left*
sword entrenched it. Say to him I live, and observe his reports°   *note his reply*
for me.

45   FIRST LORD DUMAINE   We shall, noble captain.

PAROLES   Mars dote on you for his novices.

                        [Exeunt both LORDS DUMAINE*]*

  [To BERTRAM*]* What will ye do?

BERTRAM   Stay° the King.   *Await*

PAROLES   Use a more spacious ceremony° to the noble lords.   *expansive courtesy*
50   You have restrained yourself within the list° of too cold an   *limit*
adieu. Be more expressive to them, for they wear themselves
in the cap of the time,[7] there do muster true gait;[8] eat, speak,
and move under the influence of the most received° star—and   *fashionable*
though the devil lead the measure,° such are to be followed.   *dance*
55   After them, and take a more dilated° farewell.   *extended*

BERTRAM   And I will do so.

PAROLES   Worthy fellows, and like to prove most sinewy sword-
men.   *Exeunt [*BERTRAM *and* PAROLES*]*

       Enter LAFEU *[to the* KING*]*

LAFEU *[kneeling]*   Pardon, my lord, for me and for my tidings.

60   KING   I'll fee[9] thee to stand up.

LAFEU *[rising]*   Then here's a man stands that has bought his pardon.
I would you had kneeled, my lord, to ask me mercy,
And that at my bidding you could so stand up.

KING   I would I had, so I had broke thy pate°   *head*
And asked thee mercy for't.

65   LAFEU   Good faith, across![1]
But my good lord, 'tis thus: will you be cured
Of your infirmity?

KING   No.

LAFEU   O will you eat
No grapes, my royal fox?[2] Yes, but you will,
My noble grapes, an if° my royal fox   *an if=if*
70   Could reach them. I have seen a medicine°   *physician; remedy*
That's able to breathe life into a stone,
Quicken° a rock, and make you dance canary°   *Animate / a lively dance*
With sprightly fire and motion; whose simple° touch   *mere; medicinal herb*
Is powerful to araise King Pépin,[3] nay,

---

7. Are ornaments of fashion.
8. Display grace of movement.
9. Pay (not merely "pardon").
1. A weak jest: in tilting, a blow "across" is a bad hit.

2. In Aesop, a fox pretends not to want a bunch of grapes he cannot reach.
3. Eighth-century French King.

75   To give great Charlemagne[4] a pen in's hand,
    And write to her a love-line.
    KING   What 'her' is this?
    LAFEU   Why, Doctor She. My lord, there's one arrived,
    If you will see her. Now by my faith and honour,
    If seriously I may convey my thoughts
80   In this my light deliverance,° I have spoke   *mode of speaking*
    With one that in her sex, her years, profession,°   *claims of skill*
    Wisdom and constancy, hath amazed me more
    Than I dare blame my weakness.° Will you see her—   *(as an old man)*
    For that is her demand—and know her business?
    That done, laugh well at me.
85   KING   Now, good Lafeu,
    Bring in the admiration,° that we with thee   *marvel*
    May spend our wonder too, or take off thine
    By wond'ring how thou took'st° it.   *came by*
    LAFEU   Nay, I'll fit° you,   *satisfy*
    And not be all day neither.
                 [He goes to the door]
90   KING   Thus he his special nothing° ever prologues.   *trifles*
    LAFEU *[to* HELEN, *within]*   Nay, come your ways.°   *come along*
            Enter HELEN
    KING   This haste hath wings indeed.
    LAFEU *[to* HELEN*]*   Nay, come your ways.
    This is his majesty. Say your mind to him.
95   A traitor[5] you do look like, but such traitors
    His majesty seldom fears. I am Cressid's uncle,[6]
    That dare leave two together. Fare you well.
            Exeunt [all but the KING *and* HELEN*]*
    KING   Now, fair one, does your business follow us?
    HELEN   Ay, my good lord. Gérard de Narbonne was my father;
    In what he did profess, well found.°   *found to be good*
100   KING   I knew him.
    HELEN   The rather will I spare my praises towards him;
    Knowing him is enough. On's° bed of death   *On his*
    Many receipts he gave me, chiefly one
    Which, as the dearest issue[7] of his practice,
105   And of his old experience th'only darling,
    He bade me store up as a triple° eye   *third*
    Safer than mine own two, more dear. I have so,
    And hearing your high majesty is touched
    With that malignant cause wherein the honour
110   Of my dear father's gift stands chief in power,[8]
    I come to tender it and my appliance°   *treatment*
    With all bound° humbleness.   *dutiful*
    KING   We thank you, maiden,
    But may not be so credulous of cure,
    When our most learnèd doctors leave us, and
115   The congregated College[9] have concluded
    That labouring art° can never ransom nature   *medical skill*
    From her inaidable estate.° I say we must not   *condition*

---

4. Pépin's son, founder of the Holy Roman Empire.
5. Because she avoids the King's gaze.
6. Pandarus, the go-between for Troilus and Cressida and archetypal pimp.
7. Best product; favorite child.
8. *malignant . . . power:* disease for which my father's honored gift is most effective.
9. Assembled College of Physicians.

So stain our judgement or corrupt our hope,
To prostitute° our past-cure malady   submit
120   To empirics,[1] or to dissever so
Our great self and our credit,[2] to esteem
A senseless help,° when help past sense we deem.   An unbelievable cure

HELEN   My duty then shall pay me for my pains.
I will no more enforce mine office° on you,   service
125   Humbly entreating from your royal thoughts
A modest one[3] to bear me back again.

KING   I cannot give thee less, to be called grateful.
Thou thought'st to help me, and such thanks I give
As one near death to those that wish him live.
130   But what at full I know, thou know'st no part;°   not at all
I knowing all my peril, thou no art.

HELEN   What I can do can do no hurt to try,
Since you set up your rest° 'gainst remedy.   stake everything
He that of greatest works is finisher
135   Oft does them by the weakest minister.
So holy writ in babes hath judgement shown
When judges have been babes;[4] great floods have flow'n
From simple sources, and great seas have dried.
When miracles have by th' great'st been denied.
140   [   ][5]
Oft expectation fails, and most oft there
Where most it promises, and oft it hits°   succeeds
Where hope is coldest and despair most fits.

KING   I must not hear thee. Fare thee well, kind maid.
145   Thy pains, not used, must by thyself be paid:
Proffers not took reap thanks° for their reward.   only thanks

HELEN   Inspirèd merit so by breath is barred.[6]
It is not so with him that all things knows
As 'tis with us that square our guess by shows;[7]
150   But most it is presumption in us when
The help of heaven we count the act of men.
Dear sir, to my endeavours give consent.
Of heaven, not me, make an experiment.
I am not an impostor, that proclaim
155   Myself against the level of mine aim,[8]
But know I think, and think I know most sure,
My art is not past° power, nor you past cure.   without

KING   Art thou so confident? Within what space
Hop'st thou my cure?

HELEN   The great'st grace lending grace,
160   Ere twice the horses of the sun shall bring
Their fiery coacher his diurnal ring,°   daily round
Ere twice in murk and occidental damp

1. Physicians whose methods were based on experience rather than on medical theory. In early modern Europe, "theoretical" practitioners, like the members of the French College of Physicians, often considered their "empirical" colleagues mere quacks; the "empirics" usually hailed from lower social classes and had less formal education.
2. *to dissever . . . credit*: to open such a gap between my royal station and my gullibility.
3. A favorable thought appropriate to a woman and a subject.
4. *So . . . babes*: "Thou hast hid these things from the wise and men of understanding, and hast opened them unto babes" (Matthew 11:25).
5. The Oxford editors conjecture a lost line here.
6. Divinely inspired virtue is thus denied by human speech.
7. Who base our conjectures on appearances.
8. *proclaim . . . aim*: boast in advance of the accuracy of my aim; declare myself to be different from what I am.

Moist Hesperus° hath quenched her sleepy lamp,   *the evening star*
Or four-and-twenty times the pilot's glass°   *hourglass*
165 Hath told the thievish minutes how they pass,
What is infirm from your sound parts shall fly,
Health shall live free, and sickness freely die.

KING Upon thy certainty and confidence
What dar'st thou venture?°   *risk*

HELEN   Tax° of impudence,   *Accusation*
170 A strumpet's boldness, a divulgèd shame;
Traduced by odious ballads, my maiden's name
Seared[9] otherwise, nay—worse of worst—extended[1]
With vilest torture, let my life be ended.

KING Methinks in thee some blessèd spirit doth speak,
175 His powerful sound within an organ weak;
And what impossibility would slay
In common sense, sense saves another way.[2]
Thy life is dear, for all that life can rate
Worth name of life in thee hath estimate:°   *is present*
180 Youth, beauty, wisdom, courage, all
That happiness and prime[3] can happy call.
Thou this to hazard needs must intimate[4]
Skill infinite, or monstrous desperate.
Sweet practiser,° thy physic I will try,   *practitioner; schemer*
185 That ministers thine own death if I die.

HELEN If I break time, or flinch in property[5]
Of what I spoke, unpitied let me die,
And well deserved. Not helping, death's my fee.
But if I help, what do you promise me?

KING Make thy demand.

190 HELEN   But will you make it even?°   *satisfy it*

KING Ay, by my sceptre and my hopes of heaven.

HELEN Then shalt thou give me with thy kingly hand
What husband in thy power I will command.
Exempted be from me the arrogance
195 To choose from forth the royal blood of France,
My low and humble name to propagate
With any branch or image of thy state;°   *royal place*
But such a one, thy vassal, whom I know
Is free for me to ask, thee to bestow.

200 KING Here is my hand. The premises observed,°   *conditions fulfilled*
Thy will by my performance shall be served.
So make the choice of thy own time, for I,
Thy resolved patient, on thee still° rely.   *always*
More should I question thee, and more I must,
205 Though more to know could not be more to trust:
From whence thou cam'st, how tended on°—but rest   *attended*
Unquestioned[6] welcome, and undoubted blessed.—
Give me some help here, ho! If thou proceed
As high as word, my deed shall match thy deed.

Flourish. Exeunt [the KING, carried, and HELEN]

---

9. Branded (like a criminal).
1. Prolonged; stretched on the rack.
2. *sense . . . way:* makes sense in another, uncommon way.
3. That good fortune and the springtime of life.

4. For you to risk this must suggest.
5. If I fail to meet the deadline or fall short in the particulars.
6. Not having been asked; unquestionably.

2.2

Enter the COUNTESS *and* [LAVATCH] *the clown*

COUNTESS   Come on, sir. I shall now put you to the height[1] of
your breeding.

LAVATCH   I will show myself highly fed and lowly taught.[2] I know
my business is but to the court.

5   COUNTESS   'To the court'? Why, what place make you special,
when you put off° that with such contempt? 'But to the court'! ························ *dismiss*

LAVATCH   Truly, madam, if God have lent a man any manners
he may easily put it off° at court. He that cannot make a leg,° ········ *lose it; take it off / bow*
put off's cap, kiss his hand, and say nothing, has neither leg,

10   hands, lip, nor cap, and indeed such a fellow, to say precisely,
were not for the court. But for me, I have an answer will serve
all men.

COUNTESS   Marry, that's a bountiful answer that fits all questions.

LAVATCH   It is like a barber's chair that fits all buttocks: the pin°- ················ *pointed*

15   buttock, the quatch°-buttock, the brawn-buttock, or any but- ·················· *fat*
tock.

COUNTESS   Will your answer serve fit to all questions?

LAVATCH   As fit as ten groats is for the hand of an attorney, as
your French crown[3] for your taffeta punk,° as Tib's rush[4] for ·············· *prostitute*

20   Tom's forefinger, as a pancake[5] for Shrove Tuesday, a morris° ·············· *morris dance*
for May Day, as the nail to his hole, the cuckold to his horn, as
a scolding quean° to a wrangling knave, as the nun's lip to the ·············· *whore*
friar's mouth, nay as the pudding° to his skin. ······························· *sausage*

COUNTESS   Have you, I say, an answer of such fitness for all ques-

25   tions?

LAVATCH   From beyond your duke to beneath your constable, it
will fit any question.

COUNTESS   It must be an answer of most monstrous size that
must fit all demands.

30   LAVATCH   But a trifle neither,° in good faith, if the learned ·············· *No, just a trifle*
should speak truth of it. Here it is, and all that belongs to't. Ask
me if I am a courtier. It shall do you no harm to learn.

COUNTESS   To be young again, if we could! I will be a fool in
question, hoping to be the wiser by your answer. I pray you, sir,

35   are you a courtier?

LAVATCH   O Lord, sir![6]—There's a simple putting off. More,
more, a hundred of them.

COUNTESS   Sir, I am a poor friend of yours that loves you.

LAVATCH   O Lord, sir!—Thick,° thick, spare not me. ······················ *Quick*

40   COUNTESS   I think, sir, you can eat none of this homely° meat. ·············· *plain*

LAVATCH   O Lord, sir!—Nay, put me to't, I warrant you.

COUNTESS   You were lately whipped, sir, as I think.

LAVATCH   O Lord, sir!—Spare not me.

COUNTESS   Do you cry 'O Lord, sir!' at your whipping, and 'spare

45   not me'? Indeed, your 'O Lord, sir!' is very sequent[7] to your
whipping. You would answer very well[8] to a whipping, if you
were but bound to't.[9]

2.2 Location: Bertram's palace.
1. Make you display your best manners.
2. Spoiled children were called "better fed than taught."
3. Coin; bald head (from syphilis, the "French disease").
4. Reed twisted into a ring for use in folk marriage, with
sexual innuendo.
5. Traditionally eaten on Shrove Tuesday, the day before

the beginning of Lent.
6. A voguish catchphrase that evades an answer by
appearing to wonder at the question. *putting off*: evasion.
7. Follows naturally upon (as a plea for mercy).
8. Reply cleverly to; be a fitting recipient of.
9. Required to answer; tied to a whipping post.

LAVATCH   I ne'er had worse luck in my life in my 'O Lord, sir!' I
see things may serve long, but not serve ever.

50   COUNTESS   I play the noble housewife° with the time, to enter-   *good steward (ironic)*
tain it so merrily with a fool.

LAVATCH   O Lord, sir!—Why, there't serves well again.

COUNTESS   An end, sir! To your business: give Helen this,
   [*She gives him a letter*]
And urge her to a present° answer back.   *immediate*

55   Commend me to my kinsmen and my son.
This is not much.

LAVATCH   Not much commendation to them?

COUNTESS   Not much employment for you. You understand me.

LAVATCH   Most fruitfully. I am there before my legs.

60   COUNTESS   Haste you again.°   *Exeunt* [*severally*]   *back again*

2.3

Enter [BERTRAM,] LAFEU [*with a ballad*], *and* PAROLES

LAFEU   They say miracles are past, and we have our philosophical persons to make modern and familiar things supernatural
and causeless.[1] Hence is it that we make trifles of terrors,
ensconcing ourselves into° seeming knowledge when we   *sheltering ourselves with*
5   should submit ourselves to an unknown fear.°   *awe of the unknown*

PAROLES   Why, 'tis the rarest argument° of wonder that hath   *best instance*
shot out in our latter° times.   *recent*

BERTRAM   And so 'tis.

LAFEU   To be relinquished of the artists[2]—

10   PAROLES   So I say—both of Galen and Paracelsus.[3]

LAFEU   Of all the learned and authentic Fellows[4]—

PAROLES   Right, so I say.

LAFEU   That gave him out incurable—

PAROLES   Why, there 'tis, so say I too.

15   LAFEU   Not to be helped.

PAROLES   Right, as 'twere a man assured of a—

LAFEU   Uncertain life and sure death.

PAROLES   Just,° you say well, so would I have said.   *Exactly*

LAFEU   I may truly say it is a novelty to the world.

20   PAROLES   It is indeed. If you will have it in showing,° you shall   *demonstrated*
read it in [*pointing to the ballad*] what-do-ye-call there.

LAFEU [*reads*]   'A showing of a heavenly effect in an earthly
actor.'

PAROLES   That's it, I would have said the very same.

25   LAFEU   Why, your dolphin[5] is not lustier.° Fore me, I speak in   *more sportive*
respect°—   *respectfully*

PAROLES   Nay, 'tis strange, 'tis very strange, that is the brief° and   *short*
the tedious° of it, and he's of a most facinorous° spirit that will   *long / wicked*
not acknowledge it to be the—

30   LAFEU   Very hand of heaven.

PAROLES   Ay, so I say.

LAFEU   In a most weak—

PAROLES   And debile minister° great power, great transcendence,   *feeble agent*

2.3 Location: The King's palace.
1. To make supernatural things, without apparent cause,
seem commonplace and easily explained.
2. Abandoned by the scholars.
3. Galen was a second-century Greek physician, the tra-

ditional medical authority; Paracelsus was a sixteenth-
century Swiss physician who tried to reform Galen's
teachings.
4. Accredited members of the College of Physicians.
5. Punning on "dauphin," heir to the French throne.

which should indeed give us a further use to be made than
35   alone the recov'ry of the king, as to be—
LAFEU   Generally° thankful.   *Universally*
      Enter the KING, HELEN, *and attendants*
PAROLES   I would have said it, you say well. Here comes the King.
LAFEU   *Lustig,*° as the Dutchman says. I'll like a maid the better   *Frolicsome*
    whilst I have a tooth in my head.[6]
      [*The* KING *and* HELEN *dance*]
40   Why, he's able to lead her a coranto.°   *running dance*
PAROLES   *Mort du vinaigre,*[7] is not this Helen?
LAFEU   Fore God, I think so.
KING   Go call before me all the lords in court.
                         [*Exit one or more*]
    Sit, my preserver, by thy patient's side,
      [*The* KING *and* HELEN *sit*]
45   And with this healthful hand whose banished sense°   *sense of feeling*
    Thou hast repealed,° a second time receive   *restored*
    The confirmation of my promised gift,
    Which but attends° thy naming.   *awaits*
      Enter four LORDS
    Fair maid, send forth thine eye. This youthful parcel°   *group*
50   Of noble bachelors stand at my bestowing,[8]
    O'er whom both sovereign power and father's voice
    I have to use. Thy frank election° make.   *free choice*
    Thou hast power to choose, and they none to forsake.
HELEN   To each of you one fair and virtuous mistress
55   Fall[9] when love please. Marry, to each but one.
LAFEU [*aside*]   I'd give bay Curtal and his furniture[1]
    My mouth no more were broken[2] than these boys',
    And writ° as little beard.   *laid claim to*
KING [*to* HELEN]   Peruse them well.
    Not one of these but had a noble father.
60 HELEN   Gentlemen,
    Heaven hath through me restored the King to health.
ALL [*but* HELEN]   We understand it, and thank heaven for you.
HELEN   I am a simple maid, and therein wealthiest
    That I protest I simply am a maid.—
65   Please it your majesty, I have done already.
    The blushes in my cheeks thus whisper me:
    'We blush that thou shouldst choose; but, be° refused,   *if you are*
    Let the white death sit on thy cheek for ever,
    We'll ne'er come there again.'
KING   Make choice and see.
70   Who shuns thy love shuns all his love in me.
HELEN [*rising*]   Now, Dian, from thy altar do I fly,
    And to imperial Love, that god most high,
    Do my sighs stream.
      [*She addresses her to a* LORD]
              Sir, will you hear my suit?
FIRST LORD   And grant it.

---

6. *whilst . . . head:* so long as I have a taste for pleasure ("sweet tooth"); until I've degenerated into complete senility.
7. Death of the vinegar—a pseudo-French oath.
8. Are in my power to bestow (because they are his wards).
9. Befall, with the suggestion of a sexual "fall."
1. I'd give my dock-tailed bay horse and his trappings.
2. Contained broken teeth; of a boy's voice, "broken" at puberty; of a horse, "broken" to the bit.

HELEN   Thanks, sir. All the rest is mute.°   *I will say no more*

75 LAFEU [*aside*]   I had rather be in this choice than throw
        ambs-ace[3] for my life.

HELEN [*to another* LORD]   The honour, sir, that flames in your fair eyes,[4]
    Before I speak, too threat'ningly replies.
    Love make your fortunes twenty times above
    Her that so wishes,° and her humble love.   *makes this wish*

SECOND LORD   No better, if you please.

80 HELEN   My wish receive,
    Which great Love grant. And so I take my leave.

LAFEU [*aside*]   Do all they deny her?[5] An they were sons of mine
    I'd have them whipped, or I would send them to th' Turk to
    make eunuchs of.

85 HELEN [*to another* LORD]   Be not afraid that I your hand should take;
    I'll never do you wrong for your own sake.
    Blessing upon your vows,° and in your bed   *marriage vows*
    Find fairer fortune, if you ever wed.

LAFEU [*aside*]   These boys are boys of ice, they'll none have her.

90 Sure they are bastards to the English, the French ne'er got°   *begot*
    'em.

HELEN [*to another* LORD]   You are too young, too happy, and too good
    To make yourself a son out of my blood.

FOURTH LORD   Fair one, I think not so.

95 LAFEU [*aside*]   There's one grape° yet. I am sure thy father drunk   *fruit of a noble stock*
    wine,[6] but if thou beest not an ass I am a youth of fourteen. I
    have known° thee already.   *found out*

HELEN [*to* BERTRAM]   I dare not say I take you, but I give
    Me and my service ever whilst I live

100 Into your guiding power.—This is the man.

KING   Why then, young Bertram, take her, she's thy wife.

BERTRAM   My wife, my liege? I shall beseech your highness,
    In such a business give me leave to use
    The help of mine own eyes.

KING   Know'st thou not, Bertram,
    What she has done for me?

105 BERTRAM   Yes, my good lord,
    But never hope° to know why I should marry her.   *expect*

KING   Thou know'st she has raised me from my sickly bed.

BERTRAM   But follows it, my lord, to bring me down
    Must answer for your raising? I know her well:

110 She had her breeding° at my father's charge.   *upbringing*
    A poor physician's daughter, my wife? Disdain
    Rather corrupt° me ever.   *ruin*

KING   'Tis only title° thou disdain'st in her, the which   *rank*
    I can build up. Strange is it that our bloods,

115 Of colour, weight, and heat, poured all together,
    Would quite confound distinction,[7] yet stands off °   *separated*
    In differences so mighty. If she be
    All that is virtuous, save what thou dislik'st—
    'A poor physician's daughter'—thou dislik'st

3. Two aces (the lowest throw in dice); a joking under-
statement.
4. The pride of rank that shows in your look.
5. Either Lafeu, standing apart, misunderstands what is
happening, or (less probably) the lords' polite replies are
belied by their evident relief when Helen rejects them.
6. Was red-blooded (wine was supposed to turn directly
into blood).
7. Confuse the effort to distinguish.

120   Of virtue for the name.° But do not so.   *(lack of) a title*
        From lowest place when virtuous things proceed,
        The place is dignified by th' doer's deed.
        Where great additions° swell's, and virtue none,   *titles*
        It is a dropsied[8] honour. Good alone°   *in itself*
125   Is good without a name, vileness is so:
        The property° by what it is should go,   *quality*
        Not by the title. She is young, wise, fair.
        In these to nature she's immediate heir,
        And these breed honour. That is honour's scorn
130   Which challenges° itself as honour's born   *makes claims for*
        And is not like the sire; honours thrive
        When rather from our acts we them derive
        Than our foregoers. The mere word's a slave,
        Debauched° on every tomb, on every grave   *Debased*
135   A lying trophy,° and as oft is dumb   *memorial*
        Where dust and dammed° oblivion is the tomb   *stopped-up*
        Of honoured bones indeed. What should be said?
        If thou canst like this creature as a maid,
        I can create the rest. Virtue and she
140   Is her own dower;[9] honour and wealth from me.
    BERTRAM   I cannot love her, nor will strive° to do't.   *attempt*
    KING   Thou wrong'st thyself. If thou shouldst strive to choose—
    HELEN   That you are well restored, my lord, I'm glad.
        Let the rest go.
145   KING   My honour's at the stake, which to defeat
        I must produce my power. Here, take her hand,
        Proud, scornful boy, unworthy this good gift,
        That dost in vile misprision° shackle up   *wrongful disdain*
        My love and her desert; that canst not dream
150   We, poising us in her defective scale,
        Shall weigh thee to the beam;[1] that wilt not know
        It is in us° to plant thine honour where   *in our power*
        We please to have it grow. Check° thy contempt;   *Restrain*
        Obey our will, which travails in° thy good;   *labors for*
155   Believe not thy disdain, but presently
        Do thine own fortunes that obedient right
        Which both thy duty owes and our power claims,
        Or I will throw thee from my care for ever
        Into the staggers[2] and the careless lapse°   *fall; ruin*
160   Of youth and ignorance, both my revenge and hate
        Loosing upon thee in the name of justice
        Without all terms of° pity. Speak. Thine answer. *any concessions to*
    BERTRAM [*kneeling*]   Pardon, my gracious lord, for I submit
        My fancy° to your eyes. When I consider   *perceptions; affection*
165   What great creation[3] and what dole° of honour   *portion*
        Flies where you bid it, I find that she, which late
        Was in my nobler thoughts most base, is now
        The praisèd of the King; who, so ennobled,
        Is as 'twere born so.

---

8. Unhealthily swollen.   of the balance shall raise your (lighter) side. (The King
9. *Virtue . . . dower*: Her own marriage gift is virtue and   uses the royal plural.)
herself.   2. Confusion (literally, a horse disease).
1. *We . . . beam*: Adding my weight to her deficient side   3. Creating of greatness.

KING   Take her by the hand
170 And tell her she is thine; to whom I promise
A counterpoise, if not to thy estate
A balance more replete.[4]
BERTRAM [*rising*]   I take her hand.
KING   Good fortune and the favour of the King
Smile upon this contract, whose ceremony
175 Shall seem expedient on the now-born brief,[5]
And be performed tonight. The solemn feast
Shall more attend upon the coming space,
Expecting absent friends.[6] As thou lov'st her
Thy love's to me religious;° else, does err.   properly devoted
[*Flourish.*] *Exeunt* [*all but*] PAROLES *and* LAFEU,
[*who*] *stay behind, commenting on this wedding*

180 LAFEU   Do you hear, monsieur? A word with you.
PAROLES   Your pleasure, sir.
LAFEU   Your lord and master did well to make his recantation.
PAROLES   Recantation? My lord? My master?
LAFEU   Ay. Is it not a language I speak?
185 PAROLES   A most harsh one, and not to be understood without
bloody succeeding.° My master?   consequences
LAFEU   Are you companion to the Count Roussillon?
PAROLES   To any count, to all counts, to what is man.°   whatever is manly
LAFEU   To what is count's man;° count's master is of another   servant
190 style.
PAROLES   You are too old, sir. Let it satisfy you,[7] you are too old.
LAFEU   I must tell thee, sirrah, I write 'Man',[8] to which title age
cannot bring thee.
PAROLES   What I dare too well do I dare not do.[9]
195 LAFEU   I did think thee for two ordinaries° to be a pretty wise   meals
fellow. Thou didst make tolerable vent° of thy travel; it might   talk passibly
pass. Yet the scarves and the bannerets[1] about thee did mani-
foldly dissuade me from believing thee a vessel of too great a
burden.° I have now found thee;[2] when I lose thee again I care   tonnage
200 not. Yet art thou good for nothing but taking up,[3] and that
thou'rt scarce worth.
PAROLES   Hadst thou not the privilege of antiquity[4] upon thee—
LAFEU   Do not plunge thyself too far in anger, lest thou hasten
thy trial, which if—Lord have mercy on thee for a hen! So, my
205 good window of lattice,[5] fare thee well. Thy casement I need
not open, for I look through thee. Give me thy hand.
PAROLES   My lord, you give me most egregious indignity.
LAFEU   Ay, with all my heart, and thou art worthy of it.
PAROLES   I have not, my lord, deserved it.
210 LAFEU   Yes, good faith, every dram° of it, and I will not bate°   one-eighth ounce / remit
thee a scruple.°   one-third dram
PAROLES   Well, I shall be wiser.
LAFEU   E'en as soon as thou canst, for thou hast to pull at a

4. *A counterpoise . . . replete*: A dowry equal to, if not greater than, your own estate.
5. Shall expedite this newly made decree.
6. *The solemn . . . friends*: The wedding reception will be postponed until relatives and friends can arrive.
7. Don't force me to avenge your insult.
8. I claim myself to be a man.
9. What I have the courage for (fighting), your age prevents me from doing.
1. Streamers (which remind Lafeu of a ship's pennants).
2. Discovered what you are.
3. Rebuking; arresting; drafting as a soldier.
4. Exemption (from combat) because of age.
5. Paroles is easily seen through despite his affectation; his fancy "latticework" of scarves suggests a lattice window.

smack o'th' contrary.[6] If ever thou beest bound in thy scarf and
215 beaten thou shall find what it is to be proud of thy bondage. I
have a desire to hold° my acquaintance with thee, or rather my   *maintain*
knowledge, that I may say in the default,° 'He is a man I know'.   *in the event*

PAROLES   My lord, you do me most insupportable vexation.

LAFEU   I would it were hell-pains for thy sake, and my poor
220 doing[7] eternal; for doing[8] I am past, as I will by thee, in what
motion age will give me leave.   *Exit*

PAROLES   Well, thou hast a son shall take this disgrace off me.
Scurvy, old, filthy, scurvy lord. Well, I must be patient. There
is no fettering of authority. I'll beat him, by my life, if I can
225 meet him with any convenience, an° he were double and dou-   *if*
ble a lord. I'll have no more pity of his age than I would have
of—I'll beat him, an if I could but meet him again.

                Enter LAFEU

LAFEU   Sirrah, your lord and master's married. There's news for
you: you have a new mistress.

230 PAROLES   I most unfeignedly beseech your lordship to make
some reservation of your wrongs.° He is my good lord; whom I   *restrain your abuse*
serve above is my master.

LAFEU   Who? God?

PAROLES   Ay, sir.

235 LAFEU   The devil it is that's thy master. Why dost thou garter up[9]
thy arms o' this fashion? Dost make hose of thy sleeves? Do
other servants so? Thou wert best set thy lower part where thy
nose stands. By mine honour, if I were but two hours younger
I'd beat thee. Methink'st thou art a general offence° and every   *public nuisance*
240 man should beat thee. I think thou wast created for men to
breathe° themselves upon thee.   *exercise*

PAROLES   This is hard and undeserved measure, my lord.

LAFEU   Go to, sir. You were beaten in Italy for picking a kernel
out of a pomegranate,[1] you are a vagabond and no true travel-
245 ler, you are more saucy with lords and honourable personages
than the commission° of your birth and virtue gives you her-   *warrant*
aldry.° You are not worth another word, else I'd call you knave.   *entitles you*
I leave you.   *Exit*

PAROLES   Good, very good, it is so then. Good, very good, let it
250 be concealed awhile.

                [*Enter* BERTRAM]

BERTRAM   Undone and forfeited to cares for ever.

PAROLES   What's the matter, sweetheart?

BERTRAM   Although before the solemn priest I have sworn,
I will not bed her.

255 PAROLES   What, what, sweetheart?

BERTRAM   O my Paroles, they have married me.
I'll to the Tuscan wars and never bed her.

PAROLES   France is a dog-hole, and it no more merits
The tread of a man's foot. To th' wars!

260 BERTRAM   There's letters from my mother. What th'import is
I know not yet.

PAROLES   Ay, that would be known. To th' wars, my boy, to th' wars!

---

6. *pull . . . contrary*: drink a quantity of the opposite   8. Activity (with sexual suggestion).
quality.   9. Tie up (commenting again on Paroles's outfit).
7. My poor attempt to vex you.   1. *for picking . . . pomegranate*: on the slightest pretext.

He wears his honour in a box unseen°   *(with sexual innuendo)*
That hugs his kicky-wicky° here at home,   *darling*
265 Spending his manly marrow in her arms,
Which should sustain the bound and high curvet°   *leap*
Of Mars's fiery steed. To other regions!
France is a stable, we that dwell in't jades.[2]
Therefore to th' war.

270 BERTRAM   It shall be so. I'll send her to my house,
Acquaint my mother with my hate to her,
And wherefore I am fled, write to the King
That which I durst not speak. His present gift[3]
Shall furnish me to° those Italian fields   *equip me for*
275 Where noble fellows strike. Wars is no strife
To° the dark house and the detested wife.   *Compared to*

PAROLES   Will this *capriccio*° hold in thee? Art sure?   *caprice*
BERTRAM   Go with me to my chamber and advise me.
I'll send her straight away. Tomorrow
280 I'll to the wars, she to her single sorrow.

PAROLES   Why, these balls bound,[4] there's noise in it. 'Tis hard:
A young man married is a man that's marred.
Therefore away, and leave her bravely. Go.
The King has done you wrong, but hush 'tis so.°   *Exeunt*   *but don't say so*

2.4

Enter HELEN *reading a letter, and* [LAVATCH *the*] *clown*

HELEN   My mother greets me kindly. Is she well?
LAVATCH   She is not well,[1] but yet she has her health. She's very
merry, but yet she is not well. But thanks be given she's very
well and wants° nothing i'th' world. But yet she is not well.   *lacks*
5 HELEN   If she be very well, what does she ail
That she's not very well?
LAVATCH   Truly, she's very well indeed, but for two things.
HELEN   What two things?
LAVATCH   One, that she's not in heaven, whither God send her
10 quickly. The other, that she's in earth, from whence God send
her quickly.

Enter PAROLES

PAROLES   Bless you, my fortunate lady.
HELEN   I hope, sir, I have your good will to have
Mine own good fortunes.
15 PAROLES   You had my prayers to lead them° on, and to keep   *(your good fortunes)*
them on have them still.—O my knave, how does my old lady?
LAVATCH   So that you had her wrinkles and I her money, I
would she did[2] as you say.
PAROLES   Why, I say nothing.
20 LAVATCH   Marry, you are the wiser man, for many a man's°   *servant's*
tongue shakes out[3] his master's undoing. To say nothing, to do
nothing, to know nothing, and to have nothing, is to be a great
part of your title,[4] which is within a very little of nothing.
PAROLES   Away, thou'rt a knave.

---

2. Worthless horses; sluts. Paroles considers staying in
France effeminating.
3. Wedding present just bestowed.
4. Are bouncing now (from tennis); that is, that's how it
should be done.

2.4 Location: The King's palace.
1. The dead were said to be well, because in heaven.
2. Perhaps playing on "died."
3. Inadvertently tumbles out.
4. Status; playing on "tittle," "tiny amount."

25   LAVATCH   You should have said, sir, 'Before⁵ a knave, thou'rt a
         knave'—that's 'Before me,⁶ thou'rt a knave'. This had been
         truth, sir.
     PAROLES   Go to, thou art a witty fool. I have found° thee.   *seen through*
     LAVATCH   Did you find me in yourself, sir, or were you taught to
30   find me?
     PAROLES   In⁷ myself, knave.
     LAVATCH   The search, sir, was profitable, and much fool may you
         find in you, even to the world's pleasure and the increase of
         laughter.
35   PAROLES   [*to* HELEN]   A good knave, i'faith, and well fed.°   *"better fed than taught"*
         Madam, my lord will go away tonight.
         A very serious business calls on him.
         The great prerogative and rite of love,
         Which as your due time claims, he does acknowledge,
40   But puts it off to a compelled restraint:
         Whose want and whose delay is strewed with sweets,
         Which they distil now in the curbèd time,⁸
         To make the coming hour o'erflow with joy,
         And pleasure drown the brim.
     HELEN   What's his will else?
45   PAROLES   That you will take your instant leave o'th' King,
         And make° this haste as your own good proceeding,   *represent*
         Strengthened with what apology you think
         May make it probable need.⁹
     HELEN   What more commands he?
     PAROLES   That having this obtained, you presently
         Attend° his further pleasure.°   *Await / command*
50   HELEN   In everything
         I wait upon his will.
     PAROLES   I shall report it so.
     HELEN   I pray you.   *Exit* PAROLES [*at one door*]
         Come, sirrah.
                                          Exeunt [*at another door*]

                              2.5
                   Enter LAFEU *and* BERTRAM
     LAFEU   But I hope your lordship thinks not him a soldier.
     BERTRAM   Yes, my lord, and of very valiant approof.°   *proven valor*
     LAFEU   You have it from his own deliverance.°   *report*
     BERTRAM   And by other warranted testimony.
5   LAFEU   Then my dial° goes not true. I took this lark for a   *clock*
         bunting.¹
     BERTRAM   I do assure you, my lord, he is very great in knowledge,
         and accordingly° valiant.   *correspondingly*
     LAFEU   I have then sinned against his experience and trans-
10   gressed against his valour—and my state that way is dangerous,²
         since I cannot yet find in my heart to repent. Here he comes. I
         pray you make us friends. I will pursue the amity.

5. Even in comparison with; in the presence of.
6. An expression like "Upon my soul"; Lavatch insinuates that Paroles is another knave.
7. By (reinterpreted in lines 31–33 by Lavatch). This
speech is not in F, but clearly some such reply should go
here.
8. *whose delay . . . time:* the delay of which multiplies its

sweetness, as distillation intensifies perfumes.
9. May make the need for haste probable.
2.5 Location: The King's palace.
1. I underestimated him (since the bunting looks like a
lark but does not sing).
2. In that respect risks damnation.

Enter PAROLES

PAROLES [*to* BERTRAM]   These things shall be done, sir.

LAFEU [*to* BERTRAM]   Pray you, sir, who's his tailor?[3]

15 PAROLES   Sir!

LAFEU   O, I know him well.[4] Ay, 'Sir', he; 'Sir''s a good workman,
a very good tailor.

BERTRAM [*aside to* PAROLES]   Is she gone to the King?

PAROLES   She is.

20 BERTRAM   Will she away tonight?

PAROLES   As you'll have her.

BERTRAM   I have writ my letters, casketed my treasure,
Given order for our horses, and tonight,
When I should take possession of the bride,

25 End ere I do begin.

LAFEU [*aside*]   A good traveller is something° at the latter end of   an asset
a dinner,[5] but one that lies three-thirds and uses a known truth
to pass a thousand nothings with, should be once heard and
thrice beaten. [*To* PAROLES]   God save you, captain.

30 BERTRAM [*to* PAROLES]   Is there any unkindness between my
lord and you, monsieur?

PAROLES   I know not how I have deserved to run into my lord's
displeasure.

LAFEU   You have made shift° to run into't, boots and spurs and   arranged

35 all, like him that leaped into the custard,[6] and out of it you'll
run again, rather than suffer question for your residence.[7]

BERTRAM   It may be you have mistaken him, my lord.

LAFEU   And shall do so ever, though I took him at's prayers. Fare
you well, my lord, and believe this of me: there can be no

40 kernel in this light nut. The soul of this man is his clothes.
Trust him not in matter of heavy° consequence. I have kept of   serious
them tame,[8] and know their natures.—Farewell, monsieur. I
have spoken better of you than you have wit or will[9] to deserve
at my hand, but we must do good against evil.   *Exit*

45 PAROLES   An idle lord, I swear.

BERTRAM   I think not so.

PAROLES   Why, do you not know him?

BERTRAM   Yes, I do know him well, and common speech
Gives him a worthy pass.° Here comes my clog.[1]   report

Enter HELEN[*, attended*]

50 HELEN   I have, sir, as I was commanded from you,
Spoke with the King, and have procured his leave
For present parting; only he desires
Some private speech with you.

BERTRAM   I shall obey his will.
You must not marvel, Helen, at my course,

55 Which holds not colour° with the time, nor does   is not in keeping
The ministration and requirèd office
On my particular.[2] Prepared I was not
For such a business, therefore am I found

---

3. Mocking Paroles's clothes.
4. Lafeu pretends "Sir" is the tailor's name.
5. When stories are welcome.
6. At the annual Lord Mayor's feast in London, a jester leaped into an enormous custard pie.
7. Rather than explain how you got there.

8. These kinds of tame animals.
9. The intelligence or intention.
1. Weighty fetter, "ball and chain."
2. *The ministration . . . particular*: The particular duty incumbent on me (as a husband).

So much unsettled. This drives me to entreat you
60   That presently you take your way for home,
      And rather muse° than ask why I entreat you,   *wonder*
      For my respects° are better than they seem,   *reasons*
      And my appointments° have in them a need   *purposes*
      Greater than shows itself at the first view
65   To you that know them not. This to my mother.
                 [*He gives her a letter*]
      'Twill be two days ere I shall see you, so
      I leave you to your wisdom.
HELEN   Sir, I can nothing say
      But that I am your most obedient servant.
BERTRAM   Come, come, no more of that.
HELEN   And ever shall
70   With true observance° seek to eke out that   *dutiful service*
      Wherein toward me my homely stars° have failed   *humble birth*
      To equal my great fortune.
BERTRAM   Let that go.
      My haste is very great. Farewell. Hie° home.   *Hurry*
HELEN   Pray sir, your pardon.
BERTRAM   Well, what would you say?
75   HELEN   I am not worthy of the wealth I owe,°   *own*
      Nor dare I say 'tis mine—and yet it is—
      But like a timorous thief most fain° would steal   *gladly*
      What law does vouch mine own.
BERTRAM   What would you have?
HELEN   Something, and scarce so much: nothing indeed.
80   I would not tell you what I would, my lord. Faith, yes:
      Strangers and foes do sunder° and not kiss.   *separate*
BERTRAM   I pray you, stay° not, but in haste to horse.   *delay*
HELEN   I shall not break your bidding, good my lord.—
      Where are my other men?—Monsieur, farewell.
                 Exeunt HELEN [*and attendants at one door*]
85   BERTRAM   Go thou toward home, where I will never come
      Whilst I can shake my sword or hear the drum.—
      Away, and for our flight.
PAROLES   Bravely. *Coraggio!*°   *Courage*
                 Exeunt [*at another door*]

3.1

Flourish of trumpets. Enter the DUKE *of Florence* [*and
the*] *two* [LORDS DUMAINE], *with a troop of soldiers*
DUKE   So that from point to point now have you heard
      The fundamental reasons of this war,
      Whose great decision° hath much blood let forth,   *process of resolution*
      And more thirsts after.
FIRST LORD DUMAINE   Holy seems the quarrel
5   Upon your grace's part; black and fearful
      On the opposer.
DUKE   Therefore we marvel much our cousin France
      Would in so just a business shut his bosom
      Against our borrowing prayers.°   *entreaties for aid*
SECOND LORD DUMAINE   Good my lord,
10   The reasons of our state I cannot yield

3.1 Location: Florence.

But° like a common and an outward man°   *Except / an outsider*
That the great figure° of a council frames   *image*
By self-unable motion;° therefore dare not   *inadequate guess*
Say what I think of it, since I have found
15   Myself in my incertain grounds° to fail   *conjectures*
As often as I guessed.
DUKE   Be it his pleasure.
FIRST LORD DUMAINE   But I am sure the younger of our nation,
That surfeit on° their ease, will day by day   *have had too much of*
Come here for physic.[1]
DUKE   Welcome shall they be,
20   And all the honours that can fly° from us   *proceed*
Shall on them settle. You know your places well;
When better fall,[2] for your avails they fell.
Tomorrow to the field.   *Flourish.* [*Exeunt*]

3.2

Enter the COUNTESS [*with a letter,*] *and* [LAVATCH *the*]
clown

COUNTESS   It hath happened all as I would have had it, save that
he comes not along with her.
LAVATCH   By my troth, I take my young lord to be a very melancholy man.
5   COUNTESS   By what observance, I pray you?
LAVATCH   Why, he will look upon his boot and sing, mend° the   *adjust*
ruff° and sing, ask questions and sing, pick his teeth and sing.   *boot's cuff*
I know a man that had this trick of melancholy sold a goodly
manor for a song.
10   COUNTESS   Let me see what he writes, and when he means to
come.
      [*She opens the letter and reads*]
LAVATCH [*aside*]   I have no mind to Isbel since I was at court.
Our old lings[1] and our Isbels o'th' country are nothing like your
old ling and your Isbels o'th' court. The brains of my Cupid's
15   knocked out, and I begin to love as an old man loves money:
with no stomach.°   *appetite*
COUNTESS   What have we here?
LAVATCH   E'en that you have there.   *Exit*
COUNTESS [*reads the letter aloud*]   'I have sent you a daughter-in-
20   law. She hath recovered° the King and undone me. I have wed-   *cured*
ded her, not bedded her, and sworn to make the "not"° eternal.   *punning on "knot"*
You shall hear I am run away; know it before the report come.
If there be breadth enough in the world I will hold a long
distance. My duty to you.
25   Your unfortunate son,
                          Bertram.'
This is not well, rash and unbridled boy,
To fly the favours of so good a King,
To pluck° his indignation on thy head   *pull down*
30   By the misprizing° of a maid too virtuous   *undervaluing*
For the contempt of empire.°   *an emperor*

---

1. Cure (through bloodletting).   3.2 Location: Roussillon, Bertram's palace.
2. When better places fall vacant.   1. Salt cod (slang for "penis").

Enter [LAVATCH *the*] *clown*

LAVATCH O madam, yonder is heavy° news within, between two   *sad*
    soldiers and my young lady.

COUNTESS What is the matter?

35 LAVATCH Nay, there is some comfort in the news, some comfort.
    Your son will not be killed so soon as I thought he would.

COUNTESS Why should he be killed?

LAVATCH So say I, madam—if he run away, as I hear he does.
    The danger is in standing to't;[2] that's the loss of men, though it

40   be the getting° of children. Here they come will tell you more.   *begetting*
    For my part, I only heard your son was run away.   [*Exit*]

    Enter HELEN [*with a letter,*] *and* [*the*] *two* [LORDS
    DUMAINE]

SECOND LORD DUMAINE [*to the* COUNTESS] Save you, good
    madam.

HELEN Madam, my lord is gone, for ever gone.

45 FIRST LORD DUMAINE Do not say so.

COUNTESS [*to* HELEN] Think upon patience.—Pray you, gentlemen,
    I have felt so many quirks of joy and grief
    That the first face° of neither on the start°   *appearance / suddenly*
    Can woman me unto't.[3] Where is my son, I pray you?

FIRST LORD DUMAINE Madam, he's gone to serve the Duke of
50   Florence.
    We met him thitherward,° for thence we came,   *going there*
    And, after some dispatch° in hand at court,   *business*
    Thither we bend again.

HELEN Look on his letter, madam: here's my passport.°   *vagabond's license*
    [*She reads aloud*]

55   'When thou canst get the ring upon my finger, which never
    shall come off, and show me a child begotten of thy body that
    I am father to, then call me husband; but in such a "then" I
    write a "never".'
    This is a dreadful sentence.

COUNTESS Brought you this letter, gentlemen?

60 FIRST LORD DUMAINE   Ay, madam,
    And for the contents' sake are sorry for our pains.

COUNTESS I prithee, lady, have a better cheer.
    If thou engrossest° all the griefs are thine   *monopolize*
    Thou robb'st me of a moiety.° He was my son,   *share*
65   But I do wash his name out of my blood,
    And thou art all my° child.—Towards Florence is he?   *my only*

FIRST LORD DUMAINE Ay, madam.

COUNTESS   And to be a soldier?

FIRST LORD DUMAINE Such is his noble purpose, and—believe't—
    The Duke will lay upon him all the honour
    That good convenience claims.°   *That is suitable*

70 COUNTESS   Return you thither?

SECOND LORD DUMAINE Ay, madam, with the swiftest wing of speed.

HELEN 'Till I have no wife, I have nothing in France.'
    'Tis bitter.

COUNTESS Find you that there?

75 HELEN Ay, madam.

---

2. In standing one's ground (in love and war).   3. Can make me weep like a woman.

SECOND LORD DUMAINE   'Tis but the boldness of his hand,
    Haply,° which his heart was not consenting to.   *Perhaps*
COUNTESS   Nothing in France until he have no wife?
    There's nothing here that is too good for him
80   But only she, and she deserves a lord
    That twenty such rude boys might tend upon
    And call her, hourly, mistress. Who was with him?
SECOND LORD DUMAINE   A servant only, and a gentleman
    Which I have sometime known.
85 COUNTESS   Paroles, was it not?
SECOND LORD DUMAINE   Ay, my good lady, he.
COUNTESS   A very tainted fellow, and full of wickedness.
    My son corrupts a well-derivèd° nature   *nobly born*
    With his inducement.
SECOND LORD DUMAINE   Indeed, good lady,
90   The fellow has a deal of that too much,
    Which holds him much to have.[4]
COUNTESS   You're welcome, gentlemen.
    I will entreat you when you see my son
    To tell him that his sword can never win
    The honour that he loses. More I'll entreat you
    Written to bear along.
95 FIRST LORD DUMAINE   We serve you, madam,
    In that and all your worthiest affairs.
COUNTESS   Not so, but° as we change° our courtesies.   *except / exchange*
    Will you draw near?   *Exeunt* [*all but* HELEN]
HELEN   'Till I have no wife I have nothing in France.'
100 Nothing in France until he has no wife.
    Thou shalt have none, Roussillon, none in France;
    Then hast thou all again. Poor lord, is't I
    That chase thee from thy country and expose
    Those tender limbs of thine to the event°   *outcome*
105 Of the none-sparing war? And is it I
    That drive thee from the sportive court, where thou
    Wast shot at with fair eyes, to be the mark
    Of smoky muskets? O you leaden messengers°   *(bullets)*
    That ride upon the violent speed of fire,
110 Fly with false aim, cleave the still-piecing air[5]
    That sings with piercing, do not touch my lord.
    Whoever shoots at him, I set him there.
    Whoever charges on his forward° breast,   *brave; proud; advancing*
    I am the caitiff° that do hold him to't,   *wretch*
115 And though I kill him not, I am the cause
    His death was so effected. Better 'twere
    I met the ravin° lion when he roared   *ravenous*
    With sharp constraint of hunger; better 'twere
    That all the miseries which nature owes°   *human nature possesses*
120 Were mine at once. No, come thou home, Roussillon,
    Whence honour but of danger wins a scar,[6]
    As oft it loses all. I will be gone;
    My being here it is that holds thee hence.

---

4. Has all too much persuasive power, which greatly profits him.
5. Air that is constantly repairing itself.
6. *Whence . . . scar:* From where honor at best can win a scar.

Shall I stay here to do't? No, no, although
125   The air of paradise did fan the house
And angels officed all.⁷ I will be gone,
That pitiful° rumour may report my flight   *pitying*
To consolate° thine ear. Come night, end day;   *console*
For with the dark, poor thief, I'll steal away.   *Exit*

3.3

Flourish. Enter the DUKE *of Florence,* [BERTRAM,] *a
drum[mer] and trumpet[ers], soldiers, and* PAROLES

DUKE [*to* BERTRAM]   The general of our horse° thou art, and we,   *cavalry*
Great in our hope, lay° our best love and credence°   *wager / trust*
Upon thy promising fortune.
BERTRAM   Sir, it is
A charge° too heavy for my strength, but yet   *load*
5   We'll strive to bear it for your worthy sake
To th'extreme edge of hazard.°   *limit of danger*
DUKE   Then go thou forth,
And Fortune play upon thy prosperous helm
As thy auspicious mistress.
BERTRAM   This very day,
Great Mars, I put myself into thy file.°   *line of soldiers*
10   Make me but like my thoughts, and I shall prove
A lover of thy drum, hater of love.   *Exeunt*

3.4

Enter the COUNTESS *and* [REYNALDO *her*] *steward* [*with
a letter*]

COUNTESS   Alas! And would you take the letter of her?
Might you not know she would do as she has done,
By sending me a letter? Read it again.
REYNALDO [*reads the*] *letter*¹   'I am Saint Jaques' pilgrim,² thither gone.
5   Ambitious love hath so in me offended
That barefoot plod I the cold ground upon
With sainted vow my faults to have amended.
Write, write, that from the bloody course of war
My dearest master, your dear son, may hie.°   *hurry*
10   Bless him at home in peace, whilst I from far
His name with zealous fervour sanctify.°   *(in prayer)*
His taken° labours bid him me forgive;   *undertaken*
I, his despiteful Juno,³ sent him forth
From courtly friends, with camping foes to live,
15   Where death and danger dogs the heels of worth.
He is too good and fair for death and me;
Whom⁴ I myself embrace to set him free.'
COUNTESS   Ah, what sharp stings are in her mildest words!
Reynaldo, you did never lack advice° so much   *discretion*
20   As letting her pass so. Had I spoke with her,
I could have well diverted her intents,
Which thus she hath prevented.

---

7. Performed all household tasks.
3.3 Location: Florence.
3.4 Location: Roussillon, Bertram's palace.
1. The letter forms a sonnet.
2. A pilgrim to the shrine of St. James (presumably in

Compostella in Spain).
3. Cruel goddess of marriage (who oppressed Hercules
by assigning him twelve supposedly impossible tasks).
4. Death (but the suggestion "Bertram" may be deliberate).

REYNALDO   Pardon me, madam.
  If I had given you this at over-night°   *last night*
  She might have been o'erta'en—and yet she writes
  Pursuit would be but vain.
25 COUNTESS   What angel shall
  Bless this unworthy husband? He cannot thrive
  Unless her prayers, whom heaven delights to hear
  And loves to grant, reprieve him from the wrath
  Of greatest justice. Write, write, Reynaldo,
30 To this unworthy husband of his wife.
  Let every word weigh heavy of° her worth,   *emphasize*
  That he does weigh too light; my greatest grief,
  Though little he do feel it, set down sharply.
  Dispatch the most convenient messenger.
35 When haply° he shall hear that she is gone,   *Perhaps when*
  He will return, and hope I may that she,
  Hearing so much, will speed her foot again,
  Led hither by pure love. Which of them both
  Is dearest to me I have no skill in sense
40 To make distinction. Provide° this messenger.   *Make ready*
  My heart is heavy and mine age is weak;
  Grief would have tears, and sorrow bids me speak.   *Exeunt*

3.5

  A tucket° afar off. Enter [an] old WIDOW *of Florence, her*   *trumpet call*
  daughter [DIANA], *and* MARIANA, *with other citizens*
WIDOW   Nay, come, for if they do approach the city we shall
  lose° all the sight.   *miss*
DIANA   They say the French Count has done most honourable
  service.
5 WIDOW   It is reported that he has taken their° greatest com-   *(the Sienese)*
  mander, and that with his own hand he slew the Duke's
  brother. [*Tucket*] We have lost our labour; they are gone a contrary way. Hark. You may know by their trumpets.
MARIANA   Come, let's return° again, and suffice ourselves with   *go home*
10 the report of it.—Well, Diana, take heed of this French earl.
  The honour of a maid is her name,° and no legacy is so rich as   *reputation*
  honesty.°   *chastity*
WIDOW [*to* DIANA]   I have told my neighbour how you have been
  solicited by a gentleman, his companion.
15 MARIANA   I know that knave, hang him! One Paroles. A filthy
  officer° he is in those suggestions° for the young earl. Beware   *agent / solicitings*
  of them, Diana; their promises, enticements, oaths, tokens, and
  all their engines° of lust, are not the things they go¹ under.   *devices*
  Many a maid hath been seduced by them; and the misery is,
20 example, that so terrible shows in the wreck of maidenhood,
  cannot for all that dissuade succession,° but that they are limed *prevent it recurring*
  with the twigs² that threatens them. I hope I need not to advise
  you further, but I hope your own grace° will keep you where   *virtue*
  you are, though there were no further danger° known but the   *(pregnancy)*
25 modesty which is so lost.
DIANA   You shall not need to fear° me.   *fear for*

3.5 Location: Florence.   2. *they . . . twigs*: other virgins are entrapped (sticky
1. Concealed themselves.   lime was applied to twigs to catch birds).

Enter HELEN [*dressed as a pilgrim*]

WIDOW   I hope so. Look, here comes a pilgrim. I know she will
   lie at my house; thither they send one another. I'll question
   her.

30   God save you, pilgrim. Whither are you bound?

HELEN   To Saint Jaques le Grand.
   Where do the palmers° lodge, I do beseech you?   *pilgrims*

WIDOW   At the 'Saint Francis' here beside the port.°   *city gate*

HELEN   Is this the way?

WIDOW   Ay, marry, is't.
          [*Sound of*] *a march, far off*

35   Hark you, they come this way. If you will tarry,
   Holy pilgrim, but till the troops come by,
   I will conduct you where you shall be lodged,
   The rather for I think I know your hostess
   As ample° as myself.   *well*

40   HELEN   Is it yourself?

WIDOW   If you shall please so, pilgrim.

HELEN   I thank you, and will stay upon° your leisure.   *await*

WIDOW   You came, I think, from France?

HELEN   I did so.

WIDOW   Here you shall see a countryman of yours
   That has done worthy service.

45   HELEN   His name, I pray you?

DIANA   The Count Roussillon. Know you such a one?

HELEN   But by the ear, that hears most nobly of him;
   His face I know not.

DIANA   Whatsome'er° he is,   *Whatever kind of man*
   He's bravely taken° here. He stole from France,   *highly regarded*

50   As 'tis reported; for the King had married him
   Against his liking. Think you it is so?

HELEN   Ay, surely, mere° the truth. I know his lady.   *simply*

DIANA   There is a gentleman that serves the Count
   Reports but coarsely of her.

HELEN   What's his name?

DIANA   Monsieur Paroles.

55   HELEN   O, I believe with him:
   In argument of praise,³ or to° the worth   *compared to*
   Of the great Count himself, she is too mean°   *lowly*
   To have her name repeated. All her deserving°   *Her only merit*
   Is a reservèd honesty,° and that   *preserved chastity*
   I have not heard examined.°   *questioned*

60   DIANA   Alas, poor lady.
   'Tis a hard bondage to become the wife
   Of a detesting lord.

WIDOW   I warr'nt, good creature, wheresoe'er she is
   Her heart weighs sadly. This young maid might do her
   A shrewd turn° if she pleased.   *nasty trick*

65   HELEN   How do you mean?
   Maybe the amorous Count solicits her
   In the unlawful purpose.

WIDOW   He does indeed,
   And brokes° with all that can in such a suit   *bargains*

---

3. As a topic of praise.

Corrupt the tender honour of a maid,
70   But she is armed for him, and keeps her guard
     In honestest defence.
MARIANA   The gods forbid else.

     *Enter, [with] drum and colours, [BERTRAM,] PAROLES,
     and the whole army*

WIDOW   So, now they come.
     That is Antonio, the Duke's eldest son;
     That, Escalus.
HELEN   Which is the Frenchman?
75 DIANA   He—
     That with the plume. 'Tis a most gallant fellow.
     I would he loved his wife. If he were honester⁴
     He were much goodlier. Is't not
     A handsome gentleman?
80 HELEN   I like him well.
DIANA   'Tis pity he is not honest.
     Yond's that same knave that leads him to those places.
     Were I his lady, I would poison
     That vile rascal.
HELEN   Which is he?
DIANA   That jackanapes°   monkey
85   With scarves. Why is he melancholy?
HELEN   Perchance he's hurt i'th' battle.
PAROLES [*aside*]   Lose our drum?⁵ Well.
MARIANA   He's shrewdly° vexed at something.   badly
     Look, he has spied us.
WIDOW [*to* PAROLES]   Marry, hang you!
90 MARIANA [*to* PAROLES]   And your courtesy,° for a ring-carrier.°   bow / go-between

     Exeunt [BERTRAM, PAROLES, and the army]

WIDOW   The troop is past. Come, pilgrim, I will bring you
     Where you shall host.° Of enjoined penitents⁶   lodge
     There's four or five to great Saint Jaques bound
     Already at my house.
HELEN   I humbly thank you.
95   Please it° this matron and this gentle maid   If it please
     To eat with us tonight, the charge and thanking
     Shall be for me. And to requite you further,
     I will bestow some precepts of° this virgin   advice on
     Worthy the note.
WIDOW *and* MARIANA   We'll take your offer kindly.°   gratefully

                              Exeunt

                    3.6
     Enter [BERTRAM] and the [two Captains DUMAINE]
SECOND LORD DUMAINE [*to* BERTRAM]   Nay, good my lord, put
     him to't.° Let him have his way.   (to the test)
FIRST LORD DUMAINE [*to* BERTRAM]   If your lordship find him not
     a hilding,° hold me no more in your respect.   worthless wretch
5 SECOND LORD DUMAINE [*to* BERTRAM]   On my life, my lord, a
     bubble.
BERTRAM   Do you think I am so far deceived in him?
SECOND LORD DUMAINE   Believe it, my lord. In mine own direct

---

4. More honorable (and chaste).
5. A military disgrace.
6. Those sworn to a penitential pilgrimage.
3.6 Location: The Florentine camp.

knowledge—without any malice, but to speak of him as° my   *as if he were*
10   kinsman—he's a most notable coward, an infinite and endless
liar, an hourly promise-breaker, the owner of no one good
quality worthy your lordship's entertainment.°   *patronage*

FIRST LORD DUMAINE [*to* BERTRAM]   It were fit you knew him,
lest reposing° too far in his virtue, which he hath not, he might   *trusting*
15   at some great and trusty business, in a main danger, fail you.

BERTRAM   I would I knew in what particular action to try him.

FIRST LORD DUMAINE   None better than to let him fetch off° his   *back*
drum, which you hear him so confidently undertake to do.

SECOND LORD DUMAINE [*to* BERTRAM]   I, with a troop of Floren-
20   tines, will suddenly surprise° him. Such I will have whom I am   *ambush*
sure he knows not from the enemy; we will bind and hood-
wink° him so, that he shall suppose no other but that he is   *blindfold*
carried into the laager° of the adversary's when we bring him   *camp*
to our own tents. Be but your lordship present at his examina-
25   tion: if he do not, for the promise of his life and in the highest
compulsion of base fear, offer to betray you, and deliver all the
intelligence° in his power against you, and that with the divine   *information*
forfeit of his soul upon oath, never trust my judgement in anything.

30 FIRST LORD DUMAINE [*to* BERTRAM]   O, for the love of laughter,
let him fetch his drum. He says he has a stratagem for't. When
your lordship sees the bottom° of his success in't, and to what   *entirety*
metal this counterfeit lump of ore will be melted, if you give
him not John Drum's entertainment,[1] your inclining° cannot   *partiality*
35   be removed. Here he comes.

       Enter PAROLES

SECOND LORD DUMAINE   O [*aside*] for the love of laughter
[*aloud*] hinder not the honour of his design; let him fetch off
his drum in any hand.°   *case*

BERTRAM [*to* PAROLES]   How now, monsieur? This drum sticks
40   sorely in your disposition.°   *troubles you sorely*

FIRST LORD DUMAINE   A pox on't, let it go. 'Tis but a drum.

PAROLES   But a drum? Is't but a drum? A drum so lost! There
was excellent command: to charge in with our horse° upon our   *cavalry*
own wings° and to rend our own soldiers!   *flank units*

45 FIRST LORD DUMAINE   That was not to be blamed in the command
of the service. It was a disaster° of war that Caesar himself   *an accident*
could not have prevented, if he had been there to command.

BERTRAM   Well, we cannot greatly condemn our success.[2] Some
dishonour we had in the loss of that drum, but it is not to be
50   recovered.

PAROLES   It might have been recovered.

BERTRAM   It might, but it is not now.

PAROLES   It *is* to be recovered. But that the merit of service is
seldom attributed to the true and exact performer, I would have
55   that drum or another, or '*hic iacet*'.[3]

BERTRAM   Why, if you have a stomach,° to't, monsieur. If you   *an inclination*
think your mystery in stratagem° can bring this instrument of   *tactical skill*
honour again into his native quarter,° be magnanimous° in the   *back home / valiant*

---

1. *John Drum's entertainment*: ignominious dismissal   3. Here lies (Latin): Paroles imagines himself dying in an
(proverbial).   attempt to recover the drum.
2. The general success of the battle.

enterprise and go on. I will grace° the attempt for a worthy   *honor*
60   exploit. If you speed° well in it, the Duke shall both speak of it   *succeed*
and extend to you what further becomes his greatness, even to
the utmost syllable of your worthiness.

PAROLES   By the hand of a soldier, I will undertake it.

BERTRAM   But you must not now slumber in it.

65 PAROLES   I'll about it this evening, and I will presently pen down
my dilemmas,[4] encourage myself in my certainty, put myself
into my mortal preparation;[5] and by midnight look to hear further from me.

BERTRAM   May I be bold to acquaint his grace you are gone
70   about it?

PAROLES   I know not what the success will be, my lord, but the
attempt I vow.

BERTRAM   I know thou'rt valiant, and to the possibility° of thy   *utmost capacity*
soldiership will subscribe° for thee. Farewell.   *vouch*

75 PAROLES   I love not many words.   *Exit*

SECOND LORD DUMAINE   No more than a fish loves water. [*To*
BERTRAM] Is not this a strange fellow, my lord, that so confidently seems to undertake this business, which he knows is not
to be done? Damns himself to do, and dares better be damned
80   than to do't.

FIRST LORD DUMAINE [*to* BERTRAM]   You do not know him, my
lord, as we do. Certain it is that he will steal himself into a
man's favour, and for a week escape a great deal of discoveries,[6]
but when you find him out, you have° him ever after.   *understand*

85 BERTRAM   Why, do you think he will make no deed° at all of this   *endeavor*
that so seriously he does address himself unto?

SECOND LORD DUMAINE   None in the world, but return with an
invention,° and clap upon you two or three probable° lies. But   *tall tale / plausible*
we have almost emboskéd[7] him. You shall see his fall tonight;
90   for indeed he is not for your lordship's respect.

FIRST LORD DUMAINE [*to* BERTRAM]   We'll make you some sport
with the fox ere we case° him. He was first smoked[8] by the old   *skin*
Lord Lafeu. When his disguise and he is parted, tell me what
a sprat° you shall find him, which you shall see this very night.   *tiny fish*

95 SECOND LORD DUMAINE   I must go look my twigs.° He shall be   *see to my bird trap*
caught.

BERTRAM   Your brother, he shall go along with me.

SECOND LORD DUMAINE   As't please your lordship. I'll leave you.
                                                            [*Exit*]

BERTRAM   Now will I lead you to the house, and show you
100   The lass I spoke of.

FIRST LORD DUMAINE   But you say she's honest.°   *chaste*

BERTRAM   That's all the fault. I spoke with her but once
And found her wondrous cold, but I sent to her
By this same coxcomb that we have i'th' wind°   *are stalking*
105   Tokens and letters, which she did re-send,°   *return*
And this is all I have done. She's a fair creature.
Will you go see her?

FIRST LORD DUMAINE   With all my heart, my lord.   *Exeunt*

---

4. I will immediately reflect on my difficulties.
5. Spiritual preparation for death; readying of fatal
weapons.

6. *escape . . . discoveries:* largely get away with it.
7. Cornered; run to exhaustion (hunting term).
8. Forced into the open, like a fox smoked from its hole.

3.7

Enter HELEN *and the* WIDOW

HELEN   If you misdoubt° me that I am not she,   doubt
I know not how I shall assure you further
But I shall lose the grounds I work upon.[1]

WIDOW   Though my estate° be fall'n, I was well born,   fortune
5   Nothing acquainted with these businesses,
And would not put my reputation now
In any staining act.

HELEN   Nor would I wish you.
First give me trust° the Count he is my husband,   trust me that
And what to your sworn counsel° I have spoken   secrecy
10   Is so° from word to word, and then you cannot,   true
By° the good aid that I of you shall borrow,   With respect to
Err in bestowing it.

WIDOW   I should believe you,
For you have showed me that which well approves°   confirms
You're great in fortune.

HELEN   Take this purse of gold,
15   And let me buy your friendly help thus far,
Which I will over-pay, and pay again
When I have found it.° The Count he woos your daughter,   succeeded
Lays down his wanton siege before her beauty,
Resolved to carry° her. Let her in fine° consent,   conquer / the end
20   As we'll direct her how 'tis best to bear° it.   manage
Now his important blood° will naught deny   importunate passion
That she'll demand. A ring the County° wears,   Count
That downward hath succeeded in his house
From son to son some four or five descents°   generations
25   Since the first father wore it. This ring he holds
In most rich choice;° yet in his idle° fire   estimation / crazy
To buy his will° it would not seem too dear,   lust
Howe'er repented after.

WIDOW   Now I see the bottom of your purpose.

30   HELEN   You see it lawful then. It is no more
But that your daughter ere she seems as won
Desires this ring; appoints him an encounter;
In fine, delivers me to fill the time,°   keep the appointment
Herself most chastely absent. After,
35   To marry her° I'll add three thousand crowns   As her dowry
To what is passed already.

WIDOW   I have yielded.
Instruct my daughter how she shall persever,
That time and place with this deceit so lawful
May prove coherent.° Every night he comes   fitting
40   With musics of all sorts, and songs composed
To her unworthiness.[2] It nothing steads° us   avails
To chide him from our eaves, for he persists
As if his life lay on't.

HELEN   Why then tonight
Let us essay° our plot, which if it speed°   attempt / succeed

---

3.7 Location: The widow's house, Florence.   2. To my humble daughter; to persuade my daughter to
1. *But . . . upon:* Unless I give up what my plot depends   unworthy deeds.
upon (and reveal my identity to Bertram).

45   Is wicked meaning° in a lawful deed   *intention (Bertram's)*
     And lawful meaning° in a wicked act,   *intention (Helen's)*
     Where both not sin, and yet a sinful fact.³
     But let's about it.   *[Exeunt]*

4.1

Enter [SECOND LORD DUMAINE], *with five or six other
soldiers, in ambush*

SECOND LORD DUMAINE   He can come no other way but by this
    hedge corner. When you sally° upon him, speak what terrible°   *rush / ferocious*
    language you will. Though you understand it not yourselves,
    no matter, for we must not seem to understand him, unless°   *except*
5   some one among us, whom we must produce for an interpreter.
INTERPRETER   Good captain, let me be th'interpreter.
SECOND LORD DUMAINE   Art not acquainted with him? Knows he
    not thy voice?
INTERPRETER   No, sir, I warrant you.
10 SECOND LORD DUMAINE   But what linsey-woolsey¹ hast thou to
    speak to us again?
INTERPRETER   E'en such as you speak to me.
SECOND LORD DUMAINE   He must think us some band of strang-
    ers° i'th' adversary's entertainment.° Now he hath a smack² of   *foreigners / service*
15   all neighbouring languages, therefore we must every one be a
    man of his own fancy. Not to know what we speak one to
    another, so° we seem to know, is to know straight° our purpose: *provided / suffices for*
    choughs'° language, gabble enough and good enough. As for   *crows*
    you, interpreter, you must seem very politic.° But couch,° ho!   *cunning / hide*
20   Here he comes, to beguile° two hours in a sleep, and then to   *while away*
    return and swear the lies he forges.
        [They hide.] Enter PAROLES. *[Clock strikes]*
PAROLES   Ten o'clock. Within these three hours 'twill be time
    enough to go home. What shall I say I have done? It must be a
    very plausive° invention that carries it. They begin to smoke°   *plausible / suspect*
25   me, and disgraces have of late knocked too often at my door. I
    find my tongue is too foolhardy, but my heart hath the fear of
    Mars before it, and of his creatures, not daring the reports of
    my tongue.³
SECOND LORD DUMAINE *[aside]*   This is the first truth that e'er
30   thine own tongue was guilty of.
PAROLES   What the devil should move me to undertake the
    recovery of this drum, being not ignorant of the impossibility,
    and knowing I had no such purpose? I must give myself some
    hurts, and say I got them in exploit. Yet slight ones will not
35   carry it. They will say, 'Came you off with so little?' And great
    ones I dare not give. Wherefore, what's the instance?° Tongue,   *evidence*
    I must put you into a butter-woman's⁴ mouth, and buy myself
    another of Bajazet's mute,⁵ if you prattle me into these perils.
SECOND LORD DUMAINE *[aside]*   Is it possible he should know
40   what he is, and be that he is?

---

3. Deed (as Bertram intends it).
4.1 Location: Outside the Florentine camp.
1. Hodgepodge (literally, cloth of mixed linen and wool
fibers).
2. Smattering.

3. *my heart . . . tongue:* I am frightened by the god of war
and his followers, not daring to do what I have boasted.
4. Proverbially talkative.
5. *of . . . mute:* from the Turkish sultan's servant (whose
tongue was cut off to ensure his discretion).

PAROLES   I would the cutting of my garments would serve the
turn, or the breaking of my Spanish sword.

SECOND LORD DUMAINE [*aside*]   We cannot afford° you so.   accommodate

PAROLES   Or the baring° of my beard, and to say it was in strat-   shaving
45   agem.

SECOND LORD DUMAINE [*aside*]   'Twould not do.

PAROLES   Or to drown my clothes, and say I was stripped.

SECOND LORD DUMAINE [*aside*]   Hardly serve.

PAROLES   Though I swore I leapt from the window of the citadel?

50   SECOND LORD DUMAINE [*aside*]   How deep?

PAROLES   Thirty fathom.°   fathom = 6 feet

SECOND LORD DUMAINE [*aside*]   Three great oaths would scarce
make that be believed.

PAROLES   I would I had any drum of the enemy's. I would swear
55   I recovered it.

SECOND LORD DUMAINE [*aside*]   You shall hear one anon.°   immediately

PAROLES   A drum now of the enemy's—
              Alarum° within. [*The ambush rushes forth*]   Call to arms

SECOND LORD DUMAINE   *Throca movousus, cargo, cargo, cargo.*

SOLDIERS [*severally*]   *Cargo, cargo, cargo, villianda par corbo,*
60   *cargo.*
              [*They seize and blindfold him*]

PAROLES   O ransom, ransom, do not hide mine eyes.

INTERPRETER   *Boskos thromuldo boskos.*

PAROLES   I know you are the Moscows° regiment,   Russian
And I shall lose my life for want of language.
65   If there be here German or Dane, Low Dutch,
Italian, or French, let him speak to me,
I'll discover° that which shall undo the Florentine.   reveal

INTERPRETER   *Boskos vauvado.*—
I understand thee, and can speak thy tongue.—
70   *Kerelybonto.*—Sir,
Betake thee to thy faith,° for seventeen poniards   Say your prayers
Are at thy bosom.

PAROLES   O!

INTERPRETER   O pray, pray, pray!—
Manka revania dulche?

SECOND LORD DUMAINE   *Oscorbidulchos volivorco.*

75   INTERPRETER   The general is content to spare thee yet,
And, hoodwinked⁶ as thou art, will lead thee on⁷
To gather from thee. Haply° thou mayst inform   Perhaps
Something to save thy life.

PAROLES   O let me live,
And all the secrets of our camp I'll show,
80   Their force, their purposes; nay, I'll speak that
Which you will wonder at.

INTERPRETER   But wilt thou faithfully?⁸

PAROLES   If I do not, damn me.

INTERPRETER   *Acordo linta.*—
Come on, thou art granted space.°   breathing space
              Exeunt [*all but* SECOND LORD DUMAINE *and a* SOLDIER]
              A short alarum within

---

6. Blindfolded; punning on "deceived."   8. Truthfully; loyally (ironic).
7. Will take you elsewhere; will deceive you further.

SECOND LORD DUMAINE   Go tell the Count Roussillon and my brother
85   We have caught the woodcock,[9] and will keep him muffled°   *blindfolded*
    Till we do hear from them.
SOLDIER   Captain, I will.
SECOND LORD DUMAINE   A° will betray us all unto ourselves.   *He*
    Inform on° that.   *Report*
SOLDIER   So I will, sir.
SECOND LORD DUMAINE   Till then I'll keep him dark and safely
90   locked.

Exeunt [severally]

4.2

Enter BERTRAM *and the maid called* DIANA

BERTRAM   They told me that your name was Fontibel.
DIANA   No, my good lord, Diana.
BERTRAM   Titled° goddess,   *Called*
    And worth it, with addition.[1] But, fair soul,
    In your fine frame hath love no quality?
5   If the quick° fire of youth light not your mind,   *vital*
    You are no maiden but a monument.°   *statue*
    When you are dead you should be such a one
    As you are now, for you are cold and stern,
    And now you should be as your mother was
10   When your sweet self was got.°   *begotten*
DIANA   She then was honest.
BERTRAM   So should you be.
DIANA   No.
    My mother did but duty; such, my lord,
    As you owe to your wife.
BERTRAM   No more o' that.
15   I prithee do not strive against my vows.[2]
    I was compelled to her, but I love thee
    By love's own sweet constraint, and will for ever
    Do thee all rights of service.
DIANA   Ay, so you serve us
    Till we serve you.° But when you have our roses,   *(sexually)*
20   You barely° leave our thorns to prick ourselves,   *only; exposed*
    And mock us with our bareness.
BERTRAM   How have I sworn!
DIANA   'Tis not the many oaths that makes the truth,
    But the plain single vow that is vowed true.
    What is not holy, that we swear not by,
25   But take the high'st to witness; then pray you, tell me,
    If I should swear by Jove's great attributes
    I loved you dearly, would you believe my oaths
    When I did love you ill?° This has no holding,[3]   *poorly; irreligiously*
    To swear by him whom I protest to love
30   That I will work against him. Therefore your oaths
    Are words and poor conditions but unsealed,[4]
    At least in my opinion.

---

9. Proverbially stupid bird.
4.2 Location: The widow's house, Florence.
1. *worth it, with addition:* you more than deserve to be called a goddess; with wordplay on "addition" as an honorific title. The goddess Diana was the patroness of chas-

tity, an "addition" that hardly bodes well for Bertram.
2. Do not quarrel with me about my wedding vows.
3. Consistency; binding power.
4. *words . . . unsealed:* contracts without the validating seal.

BERTRAM   Change it, change it.
　　Be not so holy-cruel. Love is holy,
　　And my integrity ne'er knew the crafts°   *deceptive plays*
35　　That you do charge men with. Stand no more off,
　　But give thyself unto my sick desires,
　　Who then recovers. Say thou art mine, and ever
　　My love as it begins shall so persever.
DIANA　　I see that men make toys e'en such a surance⁵
40　　That we'll forsake ourselves. Give me that ring.
BERTRAM　　I'll lend it thee, my dear, but have no power
　　To give it from me.
DIANA　　　　　　　　Will you not, my lord?
BERTRAM　　It is an honour 'longing to our house,°   *family line*
　　Bequeathèd down from many ancestors,
45　　Which were the greatest obloquy° i'th' world   *disgrace*
　　In me to lose.
DIANA　　　　　　　Mine honour's such a ring.
　　My chastity's the jewel of our house,
　　Bequeathèd down from many ancestors,
　　Which were the greatest obloquy i'th' world
50　　In me to lose. Thus your own proper wisdom⁶
　　Brings in the champion Honour on my part°   *side*
　　Against your vain assault.
BERTRAM　　　　　　　　　Here, take my ring.
　　My house, mine honour, yea my life be thine,
　　And I'll be bid° by thee.   *commanded*
55　DIANA　　When midnight comes, knock at my chamber window.
　　I'll order take my mother shall not hear.
　　Now will I charge you in the bond of truth,
　　When you have conquered my yet maiden bed,
　　Remain there but an hour, nor speak to me—
60　　My reasons are most strong, and you shall know them
　　When back again this ring shall be delivered—
　　And on your finger in the night I'll put
　　Another ring that, what° in time proceeds,   *whatever*
　　May token° to the future our past deeds.   *betoken*
65　　Adieu till then; then, fail not. You have won
　　A wife of° me, though there my hope be done.⁷   *in; through*
BERTRAM　　A heaven on earth I have won by wooing thee.
DIANA　　For which live long to thank both heaven and me.
　　You may so in the end.   [*Exit* BERTRAM]
70　　My mother told me just how he would woo,
　　As if she sat in's heart. She says all men
　　Have the like oaths. He had sworn to marry me
　　When his wife's dead; therefore I'll lie with him
　　When I am buried. Since Frenchmen are so braid,°   *deceitful*
75　　Marry° that will; I live and die a maid.   *Let those marry*
　　Only, in this disguise I think't no sin
　　To cozen° him that would unjustly win.   *Exit*   *cheat*

---

5. Men treat trifles as if they were such guarantees of
good faith.
6. Wisdom in your own affairs.

7. My marriage hopes are ruined; my hope of aiding
Helen is accomplished.

4.3

Enter the two Captains [DUMAINE] *and some two or*
three soldiers

FIRST LORD DUMAINE You have not given him his mother's
letter?

SECOND LORD DUMAINE I have delivered it an hour since. There
is something in't that stings his nature, for on the reading it
5 he changed almost into another man.

FIRST LORD DUMAINE He has much worthy° blame laid upon   deserved
him for shaking off so good a wife and so sweet a lady.

SECOND LORD DUMAINE Especially he hath incurred the everlasting displeasure of the King, who had even tuned his bounty
10 to sing happiness to him.¹ I will tell you a thing, but you shall
let it dwell darkly° with you.   secretly

FIRST LORD DUMAINE When you have spoken it 'tis dead, and I
am the grave of it.

SECOND LORD DUMAINE He hath perverted a young gentle-
15 woman here in Florence of a most chaste renown,° and this   reputation
night he fleshes his will² in the spoil of her honour. He hath
given her his monumental° ring, and thinks himself made in   memorial
the unchaste composition.°   bargain

FIRST LORD DUMAINE Now God delay our rebellion!° As we are   stifle our unruliness
20 ourselves,° what things are we.   without divine aid

SECOND LORD DUMAINE Merely° our own traitors. And as in the   Absolutely
common course of all treasons we still° see them reveal them-   always
selves° till they attain to their abhorred ends, so he that in this (their true nature)
action contrives° against his own nobility, in his proper stream   plots
25 o'erflows himself.³

FIRST LORD DUMAINE Is it not meant damnable° in us to be   meant to be mortal sin
trumpeters of our unlawful intents? We shall not then have his
company tonight?

SECOND LORD DUMAINE Not till after midnight, for he is dieted°   restricted
30 to his hour.

FIRST LORD DUMAINE That approaches apace. I would gladly
have him see his company anatomized,° that he might take a   companion exposed
measure of his own judgements, wherein so curiously° he had   carefully
set this counterfeit.⁴

35 SECOND LORD DUMAINE We will not meddle with him° till he°   (Paroles) / (Bertram)
come, for his presence must be the whip of the other.

FIRST LORD DUMAINE In the mean time, what hear you of these
wars?

SECOND LORD DUMAINE I hear there is an overture of peace.

40 FIRST LORD DUMAINE Nay, I assure you, a peace concluded.

SECOND LORD DUMAINE What will Count Roussillon do then?
Will he travel higher,° or return again into France?   further

FIRST LORD DUMAINE I perceive by this demand you are not altogether of his council.°   in his confidence

45 SECOND LORD DUMAINE Let it be forbid, sir; so should I be a
great deal of his act.⁵

FIRST LORD DUMAINE Sir, his wife some two months since fled

4.3 Location: The Florentine camp.
1. Who had previously readied his generosity to make
him happy (with musical metaphor).
2. He feeds his lust (hounds were "fleshed," or rewarded,
with a piece of meat from their prey, or "spoil").

3. *in his . . . himself*: dissipates himself outside his appropriate channel.
4. False jewel (Paroles).
5. An accessory to his deeds.

from his house. Her pretence° is a pilgrimage to Saint Jaques   *purpose*
le Grand, which holy undertaking with most austere sancti-
50   mony° she accomplished, and there residing, the tenderness of   *piety*
her nature became as a prey to her grief : in fine,° made a groan   *conclusion*
of her last breath, and now she sings in heaven.

SECOND LORD DUMAINE   How is this justified?°   *verified*

FIRST LORD DUMAINE   The stronger part of it by her own letters,
55   which makes her story true even to the point of her death. Her
death itself, which could not be her office to say is come, was
faithfully confirmed by the rector of the place.

SECOND LORD DUMAINE   Hath the Count all this intelligence?

FIRST LORD DUMAINE   Ay, and the particular confirmations,
60   point from point, to the full arming° of the verity.°   *corroboration / truth*

SECOND LORD DUMAINE   I am heartily sorry that he'll be glad of
this.

FIRST LORD DUMAINE   How mightily sometimes we make us
comforts of our losses.

65   SECOND LORD DUMAINE   And how mightily some other times we
drown our gain in tears. The great dignity that his valour hath
here acquired for him shall at home be encountered° with a   *opposed*
shame as ample.

FIRST LORD DUMAINE   The web° of our life is of a mingled yarn,   *fabric*
70   good and ill together. Our virtues would be proud if our faults
whipped them not, and our crimes would despair if they were
not cherished by our virtues.

         Enter a [SERVANT]

How now? Where's your master?

SERVANT   He met the Duke in the street, sir, of whom he hath
75   taken a solemn leave. His lordship will° next morning for   *intends to leave*
France. The Duke hath offered him letters of commendations
to the King.

SECOND LORD DUMAINE   They shall be no more than needful
there, if they were more than they can commend.[6]

         Enter [BERTRAM]

80   FIRST LORD DUMAINE   They cannot be too sweet for the King's
tartness. Here's his lordship now. How now, my lord, is't not
after midnight?

BERTRAM   I have tonight dispatched sixteen businesses, a
month's length apiece. By an abstract of success:° I have *con-*   *list of items*
géd with° the Duke, done my adieu with his nearest, buried a   *taken leave of*
85   wife, mourned for her, writ to my lady mother I am returning,
entertained my convoy,° and between these main parcels of dis-   *arranged my transport*
patch° affected many nicer° needs. The last was the greatest,   *business / more delicate*
but that I have not ended yet.

90   SECOND LORD DUMAINE   If the business be of any difficulty, and
this morning your departure hence, it requires haste of your
lordship.

BERTRAM   I mean the business is not ended, as fearing to hear of
it hereafter. But shall we have this dialogue between the Fool
95   and the Soldier? Come, bring forth this counterfeit model,° has   *image (of soldiership)*
deceived me like a double-meaning° prophesier.   *ambiguous*

SECOND LORD DUMAINE   Bring him forth.   [*Exit one or more*]
He's sat i'th' stocks all night, poor gallant knave.

---

6. Even if they were more commendatory than they possibly could be.

BERTRAM   No matter, his heels have deserved it in usurping his
100   spurs[7] so long. How does he carry himself?
SECOND LORD DUMAINE   I have told your lordship already, the
        stocks carry him. But to answer you as you would be under-
        stood, he weeps like a wench that had shed° her milk. He hath   *spilled*
        confessed himself to Morgan, whom he supposes to be a friar,
105   from the time of his remembrance[8] to this very instant° disaster   *present*
        of his setting i'th' stocks. And what think you he hath con-
        fessed?
BERTRAM   Nothing of me, has a?°   *he*
SECOND LORD DUMAINE   His confession is taken, and it shall be
110   read to his face. If your lordship be in't, as I believe you are,
        you must have the patience to hear it.
            Enter PAROLES [*guarded and*] *blindfolded, with* [*his*]
            Interpreter
BERTRAM   A plague upon him! Muffled!° He can say nothing of   *Blindfolded*
        me.
FIRST LORD DUMAINE [*aside to* BERTRAM]   Hush, hush.
115   SECOND LORD DUMAINE [*aside to* BERTRAM]   Hoodman[9] comes.
        [*Aloud*] *Porto tartarossa.*
INTERPRETER [*to* PAROLES]   He calls for the tortures. What will
        you say without 'em?
PAROLES   I will confess what I know without constraint. If ye
120   pinch me like a pasty° I can say no more.   *piecrust*
INTERPRETER   *Bosko chimurcho.*
SECOND LORD DUMAINE   *Boblibindo chicurmurco.*
INTERPRETER   You are a merciful general.—Our general bids
        you answer to what I shall ask you out of a note.
125   PAROLES   And truly, as I hope to live.
INTERPRETER [*reads*]   'First demand of him how many horse° the   *horsemen*
        Duke is strong.'—What say you to that?
PAROLES   Five or six thousand, but very weak and unserviceable.
        The troops are all scattered and the commanders very poor
130   rogues, upon my reputation and credit, and as I hope to live.
INTERPRETER   Shall I set down your answer so?
PAROLES   Do. I'll take the sacrament on't, how and which way
        you will.[1]
FIRST LORD DUMAINE[2] [*aside*]   All's one to him.
135   BERTRAM [*aside*]   What a past-saving slave is this!
FIRST LORD DUMAINE [*aside*]   You're deceived, my lord. This is
        Monsieur Paroles, the 'gallant militarist'—that was his own
        phrase—that had the whole theoric° of war in the knot of his   *theory*
        scarf, and the practice in the chape° of his dagger.   *scabbard tip*
140   SECOND LORD DUMAINE [*aside*]   I will never trust a man again for
        keeping his sword clean, nor believe he can have everything in
        him by wearing his apparel neatly.
INTERPRETER [*to* PAROLES]   Well, that's set down.
PAROLES   'Five or six thousand horse,' I said—I will say true—'or
145   thereabouts' set down, for I'll speak truth.
FIRST LORD DUMAINE [*aside*]   He's very near the truth in this.

7. Symbolic of knightly valor.
8. As far back as he can recall.
9. The blindfold player in blindman's buff.

1. According to whatever rite you prefer.
2. F attributes this remark to Bertram.

BERTRAM [*aside*]   But I con him no thanks° for't in the   °*feel no gratitude*
nature° he delivers it.   °*manner*

PAROLES   'Poor rogues', I pray you say.

150   INTERPRETER   Well, that's set down.

PAROLES   I humbly thank you, sir. A truth's a truth. The rogues
are marvellous poor.

INTERPRETER [*reads*]   'Demand of him of what strength they are
a-foot.'—What say you to that?

155   PAROLES   By my troth, sir, if I were to die this present hour, I will
tell true. Let me see, Spurio a hundred and fifty; Sebastian so
many;° Corambus so many; Jaques so many; Guillaume,   °*the same number*
Cosmo, Lodowick, and Gratii, two hundred fifty each; mine
own company, Chitopher, Vaumond, Bentii, two hundred fifty
160   each. So that the muster file, rotten and sound,³ upon my life
amounts not to fifteen thousand poll,° half of the which dare   °*heads*
not shake the snow from off their cassocks° lest they shake   °*cloaks*
themselves to pieces.

BERTRAM [*aside*]   What shall be done to him?

165   FIRST LORD DUMAINE [*aside*]   Nothing, but let him have thanks.
[*To* INTERPRETER] Demand of him my condition, and what
credit I have with the Duke.

INTERPRETER [*to* PAROLES]   Well, that's set down. [*Reads*] 'You
shall demand of him, whether one Captain Dumaine be i'th'
170   camp, a Frenchman; what his reputation is with the Duke;
what his valour, honesty, and expertness in wars; or whether he
thinks it were not possible with well-weighing° sums of gold to   °*heavy; persuasive*
corrupt him to a revolt.'—What say you to this? What do you
know of it?

175   PAROLES   I beseech you let me answer to the particular of the
inter'gatories.° Demand them singly.   °*judicial questions*

INTERPRETER   Do you know this Captain Dumaine?

PAROLES   I know him. A was a botcher's° prentice in Paris, from   °*clothes mender*
whence he was whipped for getting the sheriff's fool⁴ with
180   child—a dumb innocent° that could not say him nay.   °*idiot*

BERTRAM [*aside to* FIRST LORD DUMAINE]   Nay, by your leave,
hold your hands, though I know his brains are forfeit to the
next tile that falls.⁵

INTERPRETER   Well, is this captain in the Duke of Florence's
185   camp?

PAROLES   Upon my knowledge he is, and lousy.

FIRST LORD DUMAINE [*aside*]   Nay, look not so upon me: we shall
hear of your lordship anon.

INTERPRETER   What is his reputation with the Duke?

190   PAROLES   The Duke knows him for no other but a poor officer
of mine, and writ to me this other day to turn him out o'th'
band. I think I have his letter in my pocket.

INTERPRETER   Marry, we'll search.

PAROLES   In good sadness,° I do not know. Either it is there, or it   °*all seriousness*
195   is upon a file with the Duke's other letters in my tent.

INTERPRETER   Here 'tis, here's a paper. Shall I read it to you?

PAROLES   I do not know if it be it or no.

BERTRAM [*aside*]   Our interpreter does it well.

---

3. The total roll, sick and able-bodied.   5. I know he's close to sudden death.
4. Mentally retarded girl.

FIRST LORD DUMAINE [*aside*] Excellently.

200 INTERPRETER [*reads the letter*] 'Dian, the Count's a fool, and full of gold.'

PAROLES That is not the Duke's letter, sir. That is an advertise-
ment° to a proper maid in Florence, one Diana, to take heed   admonition
of the allurement of one Count Roussillon, a foolish idle boy,
but for all that very ruttish.° I pray you, sir, put it up again.   lecherous

205 INTERPRETER Nay, I'll read it first, by your favour.

PAROLES My meaning in't, I protest, was very honest in the
behalf of the maid, for I knew the young Count to be a dangerous and lascivious boy, who is a whale to virginity, and devours
up all the fry° it finds.   tiny fish

210 BERTRAM [*aside*] Damnable both-sides rogue.

INTERPRETER [*reads*] 'When he swears oaths, bid him drop gold,
   and take it.
   After he scores he never pays the score.°   bill
   Half-won is match well made; match, and well make it.[6]
   He ne'er pays after-debts,[7] take it before.

215 And say a soldier, Dian, told thee this:
   Men are to mell° with, boys are not to kiss.   meddle (sexually)
   For count° of this, the Count's a fool, I know it,   on account
   Who pays before,° but not when he does owe it.   in advance
          Thine, as he vowed to thee in thine ear,

220   Paroles.'

BERTRAM [*aside*] He shall be whipped through the army with
this rhyme in's[8] forehead.

SECOND LORD DUMAINE [*aside*] This is your devoted friend, sir,
the manifold linguist and the armipotent° soldier.   mighty-in-arms

225 BERTRAM [*aside*] I could endure anything before but a cat,[9] and
now he's a cat to me.

INTERPRETER I perceive, sir, by the general's looks, we shall be
fain° to hang you.   obliged

PAROLES My life, sir, in any case! Not that I am afraid to die,
230 but that, my offences being many, I would repent out the
remainder of nature.° Let me live, sir, in a dungeon, i'th' stocks,   my natural life
or anywhere, so I may live.

INTERPRETER We'll see what may be done, so you confess freely.
Therefore once more to this Captain Dumaine. You have
235 answered to his reputation with the Duke, and to his valour.
What is his honesty?

PAROLES He will steal, sir, an egg out of a cloister. For rapes and
ravishments he parallels Nessus.[1] He professes° not keeping of   makes a practice of
oaths; in breaking 'em he is stronger than Hercules. He will lie,
240 sir, with such volubility that you would think truth were a fool.
Drunkenness is his best virtue, for he will be swine-drunk, and
in his sleep he does little harm, save to his bedclothes; but they
about him know his conditions,° and lay him in straw. I have   habits
but little more to say, sir, of his honesty. He has everything that
245 an honest man should not have; what an honest man should
have, he has nothing.

FIRST LORD DUMAINE [*aside*] I begin to love him for this.

---

6. Negotiating a good bargain is half the battle, so be
sure to bargain well.
7. Debts payable after receipt of goods.
8. On his (whores and their customers, when punished
by public whipping, were often made to wear signs indicating their transgressions).
9. A common phobia, but "cat" is also a term of contempt, usually referring to a spiteful or sluttish woman.
1. Centaur who attempted to rape Hercules' wife.

BERTRAM [*aside*]   For this description of thine honesty? A pox
upon him! For me, he's more and more a cat.

250   INTERPRETER   What say you to his expertness in war?

PAROLES   Faith, sir, he's led the drum before the English tragedi-
ans.[2] To belie him I will not, and more of his soldiership I
know not, except in that country he had the honour to be the
officer at a place there called Mile End,[3] to instruct for the
255   doubling of files.[4] I would do the man what honour I can, but
of this I am not certain.

FIRST LORD DUMAINE [*aside*]   He hath out-villained villainy so far
that the rarity° redeems him.   *uniqueness*

BERTRAM [*aside*]   A pox on him! He's a cat still.

260   INTERPRETER   His qualities being at this poor price, I need not
to ask you if gold will corrupt him to revolt.

PAROLES   Sir, for a *quart d'écu*[5] he will sell the fee-simple° of   *absolute ownership*
his salvation, the inheritance of it, and cut th'entail from all
remainders,[6] and a perpetual succession for it perpetually.

265   INTERPRETER   What's his brother, the other Captain Dumaine?

SECOND LORD DUMAINE [*aside*]   Why does he ask him of me?

INTERPRETER   What's he?

PAROLES   E'en a crow o'th' same nest. Not altogether so great as
the first in goodness, but greater a great deal in evil. He excels
270   his brother for a coward, yet his brother is reputed one of the
best that is. In a retreat he outruns any lackey;[7] marry, in coming on° he has the cramp.   *advancing*

INTERPRETER   If your life be saved will you undertake to betray
the Florentine?

275   PAROLES   Ay, and the captain of his horse, Count Roussillon.

INTERPRETER   I'll whisper with the general and know his pleasure.

PAROLES   I'll no more drumming. A plague of all drums! Only
to seem to deserve well, and to beguile the supposition° of that   *judgment*
280   lascivious young boy, the Count, have I run into this danger.
Yet who would have suspected an ambush where I was taken?

INTERPRETER   There is no remedy, sir, but you must die. The
general says you that have so traitorously discovered° the secrets   *revealed*
of your army, and made such pestiferous reports of men very
285   nobly held,° can serve the world for no honest use; therefore   *regarded*
you must die.—Come, headsman, off with his head.

PAROLES   O Lord, sir!—Let me live, or let me see my death!

INTERPRETER   That shall you, and take your leave of all your
friends.
                    [*He unmuffles* PAROLES]
290   So, look about you. Know you any here?

BERTRAM   Good morrow, noble captain.

SECOND LORD DUMAINE   God bless you, Captain Paroles.

FIRST LORD DUMAINE   God save you, noble captain.

SECOND LORD DUMAINE   Captain, what greeting will you° to my   *do you desire*
295   Lord Lafeu? I am for° France.   *off to*

FIRST LORD DUMAINE   Good captain, will you give me a copy of
the sonnet you writ to Diana in behalf of the Count Roussillon?

2. He's banged the drum to help advertise plays.
3. Where the London citizen militia drilled.
4. Simple drill exercise, in which the men stand in two
rows.

5. Quarter-crown, French coin of small value.
6. Prevent its succession to any future heirs.
7. Footman who runs before his master's coach.

An° I were not a very coward I'd compel it of you. But fare you   *If*
well.   *Exeunt [all but* PAROLES *and the* INTERPRETER]

300   INTERPRETER   You are undone, captain—all but your scarf ; that
has a knot on't yet.

PAROLES   Who cannot be crushed with a plot?

INTERPRETER   If you could find out a country where but women
were that had received so much shame, you might begin an

305   impudent° nation. Fare ye well, sir. I am for France too. We   *a shameless*
shall speak of you there.   *Exit*

PAROLES   Yet am I thankful. If my heart were great
'Twould burst at this. Captain I'll be no more,
But I will eat and drink and sleep as soft

310   As captain shall. Simply the thing I am
Shall make me live.° Who knows himself a braggart,   *sustain me*
Let him fear this, for it will come to pass
That every braggart shall be found an ass.
Rust, sword; cool, blushes; and Paroles live

315   Safest in shame; being fooled, by fool'ry thrive.
There's place and means for every man alive.
I'll after them.   *Exit*

4.4

Enter HELEN, WIDOW, *and* DIANA

HELEN   That you may well perceive I have not wronged you,
One of the greatest in the Christian world
Shall be my surety;° fore whose throne 'tis needful,   *guarantee*
Ere I can perfect mine intents, to kneel.

5   Time was, I did him a desirèd office
Dear almost as his life; which gratitude
Through flinty Tartar's bosom¹ would peep forth
And answer 'Thanks'. I duly am informed
His grace is at Marseilles, to which place

10   We have convenient convoy.° You must know   *suitable transport*
I am supposèd dead. The army breaking,°   *disbanding*
My husband hies him home, where, heaven aiding,
And by the leave of my good lord the King,
We'll be before our welcome.°   *before we're expected*

WIDOW   Gentle madam,
15   You never had a servant to whose trust
Your business was more welcome.

HELEN   Nor you, mistress,
Ever a friend whose thoughts more truly labour
To recompense your love. Doubt not but heaven
Hath brought me up to be your daughter's dower,

20   As it hath fated her to be my motive°   *means*
And helper to a husband. But O, strange men,
That can such sweet use make of what they hate,
When saucy trusting of the cozened° thoughts   *deceived*
Defiles the pitchy night;² so lust doth play

25   With what it loathes, for° that which is away.   *in the place of*
But more of this hereafter. You, Diana,

4.4 Location: The widow's house, Florence.
1. Even from a savage's stony heart (Tartars, residents of
central Asia, were considered barbaric by western Europeans).
2. *When . . . night:* When lascivious yielding to deceit
defiles even the black night.

Under my poor instructions yet must suffer
Something in my behalf.

DIANA   Let death and honesty°   *chastity*
Go with your impositions, I am yours,
Upon° your will to suffer.   *At*

30   HELEN   Yet,° I pray you.—   *A little longer*
But with that word° the time will bring on summer,   *("Yet")*
When briers shall have leaves as well as thorns
And be as sweet° as sharp. We must away,   *fragrant*
Our wagon is prepared, and time revives us.

35   All's well that ends well; still the fine's° the crown.   *end*
Whate'er the course, the end is the renown.°   *Exeunt*   *what is remembered*

4.5

Enter [LAVATCH *the*] *clown, old* [COUNTESS], *and* LAFEU

LAFEU   No, no, no, your son was misled with a snipped-taffeta[1]
fellow there, whose villainous saffron[2] would have made all the
unbaked and doughy youth of a nation in his colour. Else, your
daughter-in-law had been alive at this hour, and your son here
5   at home, more advanced by the King than by that red-tailed
humble-bee[3] I speak of.

COUNTESS   I would a° had not known him. It was the death of   *he*
the most virtuous gentlewoman that ever nature had praise for
creating. If she had partaken of my flesh and cost me the
10   dearest groans of a mother I could not have owed her a more
rooted love.

LAFEU   'Twas a good lady, 'twas a good lady. We may pick a
thousand salads ere we light on such another herb.

LAVATCH   Indeed, sir, she was the sweet marjoram of the salad,
15   or rather the herb of grace.°   *rue*

LAFEU   They are not grass,[4] you knave, they are nose-herbs.°   *fragrant plants*

LAVATCH   I am no great Nebuchadnezzar,[5] sir, I have not much
skill in grace.

LAFEU   Whether° dost thou profess thyself, a knave or a fool?   *Which*

20   LAVATCH   A fool, sir, at a woman's service, and a knave at a
man's.

LAFEU   Your distinction?

LAVATCH   I would cozen° the man of his wife and do his service.   *cheat*

LAFEU   So you were a knave at his service indeed.

25   LAVATCH   And I would give his wife my bauble,[6] sir, to do her
service.

LAFEU   I will subscribe° for thee, thou art both knave and fool.   *vouch*

LAVATCH   At your service.

LAFEU   No, no, no.

30   LAVATCH   Why, sir, if I cannot serve you I can serve as great a
prince as you are.

LAFEU   Who's that? A Frenchman?

LAVATCH   Faith, sir, a has an English name, but his phys'namy[7]
is more hotter in France than there.

35   LAFEU   What prince is that?

4.5 Location: Bertram's palace.
1. Silk slashed to show a contrasting lining.
2. Yellow dye, used for pastry; the coward's color.
3. Bumblebee (noisy, colorful, and useless).
4. Misconstruing "grace."

5. In Daniel 4:28–34, the King of Babylon who, lacking
spiritual "grace," went mad and ate "grass."
6. Fool's rod (suggesting "penis").
7. Physiognomy, face (in Elizabethan pronunciation,
punning on "name").

LAVATCH   The Black Prince,[8] sir, alias the prince of darkness,
alias the devil.

LAFEU   Hold thee, there's my purse. I give thee not this to sug-
gest° thee from thy master thou talk'st of; serve him still.   *lure*

40 LAVATCH   I am a woodland fellow, sir, that always loved a great
fire, and the master I speak of ever keeps a good fire. But since
he is the prince of the world, let the nobility remain in's court;
I am for the house with the narrow gate,[9] which I take to be
too little for pomp to enter. Some that humble themselves may,
45 but the many will be too chill and tender,[1] and they'll be for
the flow'ry way that leads to the broad gate and the great fire.

LAFEU   Go thy ways. I begin to be aweary of thee, and I tell thee
so before,° because I would not fall out with thee. Go thy ways.   *in advance*
Let my horses be well looked to, without any tricks.

50 LAVATCH   If I put any tricks upon 'em, sir, they shall be jades'
tricks,[2] which are their own right by the law of nature.   *Exit*

LAFEU   A shrewd° knave and an unhappy.   *bitter*

COUNTESS   So a is. My lord that's gone made himself much sport
out of him; by his authority he remains here, which he thinks
55 is a patent° for his sauciness, and indeed he has no pace,° but   *license / restraint*
runs where he will.

LAFEU   I like him well, 'tis not amiss. And I was about to tell you,
since I heard of the good lady's death and that my lord your
son was upon his return home, I moved the King my master to
60 speak in the behalf of my daughter; which, in the minority of
them both, his majesty out of a self-gracious remembrance[3] did
first propose. His highness hath promised me to do it; and to
stop up the displeasure he hath conceived against your son,
there is no fitter matter. How does your ladyship like it?

65 COUNTESS   With very much content, my lord, and I wish it happily effected.

LAFEU   His highness comes post° from Marseilles, of as able   *speedily*
body as when he numbered thirty. A will be here tomorrow, or
I am deceived by him° that in such intelligence° hath seldom   *someone / information*
70 failed.

COUNTESS   It rejoices me that I hope I shall see him ere I die. I
have letters that my son will be here tonight. I shall beseech
your lordship to remain with me till they meet together.

LAFEU   Madam, I was thinking with what manners I might safely
75 be admitted.°   *invited to be present*

COUNTESS   You need but plead your honourable privilege.[4]

LAFEU   Lady, of that I have made a bold charter,[5] but, I thank
my God, it holds yet.

Enter [LAVATCH *the*] *clown*

LAVATCH   O madam, yonder's my lord your son with a patch of
80 velvet[6] on's face. Whether there be a scar under't or no, the
velvet knows; but 'tis a goodly patch of velvet. His left cheek is

---

8. Punning on the nickname of Edward III's eldest son,
who conquered the French.
9. "Enter in at the strait gate; for it is the wide gate, and
broad way that leadeth to destruction, and many there be
which go in thereat. Because the gate is strait and the way
narrow that leadeth unto life, and few there be that find
it" (Matthew 7:13–14; see also Luke 13:24). The devil is
called the "prince of this world" in John 12:31 and elsewhere.

1. Fainthearted and self-indulgent.
2. Contemptible tricks; playing on the sense "tricks
played on horses."
3. Recollection prompted by his own graciousness.
4. Privilege due your honor.
5. Made as bold a claim as I dare.
6. Used to cover a battle wound or a facial sore from
syphilis.

a cheek of two pile and a half,[7] but his right cheek is worn bare.

LAFEU A scar nobly got, or a noble scar, is a good liv'ry° of hon- *uniform*
our. So belike° is that. *probably*

85 LAVATCH But it is your carbonadoed[8] face.

LAFEU [*to the* COUNTESS] Let us go see your son, I pray you. I
long to talk with the young noble soldier.

LAVATCH Faith, there's a dozen of 'em, with delicate fine hats,
and most courteous feathers, which bow the head and nod at
90 every man. *Exeunt*

5.1

Enter HELEN, WIDOW, *and* DIANA, *with two attendants*

HELEN But this exceeding posting° day and night *this hasty riding*
Must wear your spirits low. We cannot help it.
But since you have made the days and nights as one
To wear° your gentle limbs in my affairs, *tire*
5 Be bold° you do so grow in my requital° *confident / repayment*
As nothing can unroot you.

Enter a GENTLE[MAN] *Austringer*° *keeper of hawks*
In happy time!° *Just at the right time*
This man may help me to his majesty's ear,
If he would spend his power.—God save you, sir.

GENTLEMAN And you.

10 HELEN Sir, I have seen you in the court of France.

GENTLEMAN I have been sometimes there.

HELEN I do presume, sir, that you are not fall'n
From the report that goes upon your goodness,
And therefore, goaded with most sharp occasions° *urgent circumstances*
15 Which lay nice° manners by, I put° you to *scrupulous / urge*
The use of your own virtues, for the which
I shall continue thankful.

GENTLEMAN What's your will?

HELEN That it will please you
To give this poor petition to the King,
20 And aid me with that store of power you have
To come into his presence.

GENTLEMAN The King's not here.

HELEN Not here, sir?

GENTLEMAN Not indeed.
He hence removed° last night, and with more haste *departed*
25 Than is his use.° *custom*

WIDOW Lord, how we lose our pains.

HELEN All's well that ends well yet,
Though time seem so adverse, and means unfit.—
I do beseech you, whither is he gone?

30 GENTLEMAN Marry, as I take it, to Roussillon,
Whither I am going.

HELEN I do beseech you, sir,
Since you are like to see the King before me,
Commend° the paper to his gracious hand, *Present*
Which I presume shall render you no blame,

7. The thickest velvet was three-piled; Lavatch invents
an imaginary next best.
8. Slashed (like meat for broiling) in battle or by a sur-

geon, to treat a syphilitic eruption.
5.1 Location: Marseilles.

35 But rather make you thank your pains for it.
    I will come after you with what good speed
    Our means will make us means.°   resources will permit
    GENTLEMAN [*taking the paper*]   This I'll do for you.
    HELEN   And you shall find yourself to be well thanked,
    Whate'er falls more. We must to horse again.—
40 Go, go, provide.   [*Exeunt severally*]

5.2
Enter [LAVATCH] *and* PAROLES[, *with a letter*]

PAROLES   Good Master Lavatch, give my Lord Lafeu this letter.
    I have ere now, sir, been better known to you, when I have held
    familiarity with fresher clothes. But I am now, sir, muddied in
    Fortune's mood, and smell somewhat strong of her strong
5   displeasure.
LAVATCH   Truly, Fortune's displeasure is but sluttish if it smell
    so strongly as thou speakest of. I will henceforth eat no fish of
    Fortune's butt'ring.° Prithee allow the wind.[1]   prepared by Fortune
PAROLES   Nay, you need not to stop your nose, sir, I spake but by
10 a metaphor.
LAVATCH   Indeed, sir, if your metaphor stink I will stop my nose,
    or against any man's metaphor. Prithee get thee further.
PAROLES   Pray you, sir, deliver me this paper.
LAVATCH   Foh, prithee stand away. A paper from Fortune's close-
15 stool° to give to a nobleman! Look, here he comes himself.   toilet
        Enter LAFEU
    Here is a pur[2] of Fortune's, sir, or of Fortune's cat—but not a
    musk-cat[3]—that has fallen into the unclean fish-pond of her
    displeasure and, as he says, is muddied withal. Pray you, sir,
    use the carp[4] as you may, for he looks like a poor, decayed,
20 ingenious, foolish, rascally knave. I do pity his distress in my
    similes of comfort, and leave him to your lordship.   *Exit*
PAROLES   My lord, I am a man whom Fortune hath cruelly
    scratched.
LAFEU   And what would you have me to do? 'Tis too late to pare
25 her nails now. Wherein have you played the knave with For-
    tune that she should scratch you, who of herself is a good lady
    and would not have knaves thrive long under her? There's a
    quart d'écu for you. Let the justices[5] make you and Fortune
    friends; I am for other business.
30 PAROLES   I beseech your honour to hear me one single word—
LAFEU   You beg a single penny more. Come, you shall ha't. Save
    your word.°   breath
PAROLES   My name, my good lord, is Paroles.
LAFEU   You beg more than one word[6] then. Cox my passion!°   By God's passion
35 Give me your hand. How does your drum?
PAROLES   O my good lord, you were the first that found me.
LAFEU   Was I, in sooth? And I was the first that lost thee.
PAROLES   It lies in you, my lord, to bring me in some grace,[7] for
    you did bring me out.°   out of favor

5.2 Location: Roussillon.
1. Stand downwind of me.
2. Piece of dung; cat's purr; knave (in the card game post and pair).
3. Civet cat, a source of perfume.

4. Fish often bred in mud ponds; chatterbox.
5. Of the peace, responsible for beggars.
6. Playing on "Paroles," "words."
7. Into some favor (but Lafeu takes "grace" in its religious sense).

40   LAFEU   Out upon thee, knave! Dost thou put upon me at once
            both the office of God and the devil? One brings thee in grace,
            and the other brings thee out.

                    [*Trumpets sound*]

            The King's coming; I know by his trumpets. Sirrah, enquire
            further after me. I had talk of you last night. Though you are a
45   fool and a knave, you shall eat. Go to, follow.
      PAROLES   I praise God for you.   [*Exeunt*]

5.3

Flourish. Enter KING, *old* [COUNTESS], LAFEU, *and attendants*

      KING   We lost a jewel of° her, and our esteem°   *in /* (*own*) *worth*
            Was made much poorer by it. But your son,
            As mad in folly, lacked the sense to know
            Her estimation home.°   *value to the full*
      COUNTESS   'Tis past, my liege,
5   And I beseech your majesty to make° it   *consider*
            Natural rebellion done i'th' blade° of youth,   *greenness*
            When oil and fire, too strong for reason's force,
            O'erbears it and burns on.
      KING   My honoured lady,
            I have forgiven and forgotten all,
10   Though my revenges were high[1] bent upon him
            And watched° the time to shoot.   *vigilantly waited*
      LAFEU   This I must say—
            But first I beg my pardon—the young lord
            Did to his majesty, his mother, and his lady
            Offence of mighty note, but to himself
15   The greatest wrong of all. He lost a wife
            Whose beauty did astonish the survey°   *observation*
            Of richest° eyes, whose words all ears took captive, *most experienced*
            Whose dear perfection hearts that scorned to serve
            Humbly called mistress.
      KING   Praising what is lost
20   Makes the remembrance dear. Well, call him hither.
            We are reconciled, and the first view shall kill
            All repetition.[2] Let him not ask our pardon.
            The nature of his great offence is dead,
            And deeper than oblivion we do bury
25   Th'incensing relics° of it. Let him approach   *infuriating reminders*
            A stranger, no offender; and inform him
            So 'tis our will he should.
      ATTENDANT   I shall, my liege.   [*Exit*]
      KING [*to* LAFEU]   What says he to your daughter? Have you spoke?
      LAFEU   All that he is hath reference° to your highness.   *is submitted*
30   KING   Then shall we have a match. I have letters sent me
            That sets him high in fame.

                    Enter BERTRAM [*with a patch of velvet on his left cheek,
                    and kneels*]

      LAFEU   He looks well on't.
      KING [*to* BERTRAM]   I am not a day of season,°   *constant weather*
            For thou mayst see a sunshine and a hail

5.3 Location: Roussillon.   2. Rehearsal of past grievances.
1. To the utmost (like a taut bow).

35   In me at once. But to the brightest beams
     Distracted° clouds give way; so stand thou forth.   *Agitated; broken*
     The time is fair again.

BERTRAM   My high-repented blames,°   *much-repented faults*
     Dear sovereign, pardon to me.

KING   All is whole.°   *healed*
     Not one word more of the consumèd time.
40   Let's take the instant by the forward top,³
     For we are old, and on our quick'st decrees
     Th'inaudible and noiseless foot of time
     Steals ere we can effect them. You remember
     The daughter of this lord?

45   BERTRAM   Admiringly, my liege. At first
     I stuck° my choice upon her, ere my heart   *fixed*
     Durst make too bold a herald of my tongue;
     Where, the impression of mine eye enfixing,⁴
     Contempt his scornful perspective⁵ did lend me,
50   Which warped the line of every other favour,°   *face*
     Stained a fair colour° or expressed it stolen,⁶   *complexion*
     Extended or contracted all proportions
     To a most hideous object. Thence it came
     That she° whom all men praised and whom myself,   *(Helen)*
55   Since I have lost, have loved, was in mine eye
     The dust that did offend it.

KING   Well excused.
     That thou didst love her strikes some scores° away   *debits*
     From the great count.° But love that comes too late,   *reckoning*
     Like a remorseful° pardon slowly carried,   *compassionate; regretful*
60   To the grace-sender turns a sour offence,
     Crying, 'That's good that's gone.' Our rash faults
     Make trivial price of° serious things we have,   *Underestimate*
     Not knowing them until we know their grave.°   *lose them forever*
     Oft our displeasures, to ourselves unjust,
65   Destroy our friends and after weep° their dust.   *mourn over*
     Our own love waking° cries to see what's done,   *coming to its senses*
     While shameful hate sleeps out the afternoon.
     Be this sweet Helen's knell, and now forget her.
     Send forth your amorous token for fair Maudlin.°   *Lafeu's daughter*
70   The main consents are had, and here we'll stay
     To see our widower's second marriage day.

COUNTESS⁷   Which better than the first, O dear heaven, bless!
     Or ere they meet, in me, O nature, cease.⁸

LAFEU [*to* BERTRAM]   Come on, my son, in whom my house's name
75   Must be digested,⁹ give a favour from you
     To sparkle in the spirits of my daughter,
     That she may quickly come.
           [BERTRAM *gives* LAFEU *a ring*]
                               By my old beard
     And ev'ry hair that's on't, Helen that's dead
     Was a sweet creature. Such a ring as this,

3. Let's seize time by the forelock; proverbial for "taking a present opportunity."
4. Once the impression of Lafeu's daughter was implanted in my heart.
5. Distorting optical glass.

6. Declared it artificial.
7. In F, the King speaks these lines.
8. Before they come to resemble one another, let me die.
9. Absorbed (because Maudlin is his only child and will take Bertram's name).

80   The last° that ere I took her leave at court,   *last time*
    I saw upon her finger.[1]

BERTRAM   Hers it was not.

KING   Now pray you let me see it; for mine eye,
    While I was speaking, oft was fastened to't.

        [LAFEU *gives him the ring*]

    This ring was mine, and when I gave it Helen
85   I bade her, if her fortunes ever stood
    Necessitied to° help, that by this token   *In need of*
    I would relieve her. Had you that craft to reave° her   *deprive*
    Of what should stead° her most?   *aid*

BERTRAM   My gracious sovereign,
    Howe'er it pleases you to take it so,
    The ring was never hers.

90 **COUNTESS**   Son, on my life
    I have seen her wear it, and she reckoned it
    At her life's rate.°   *value*

LAFEU   I am sure I saw her wear it.

BERTRAM   You are deceived, my lord, she never saw it.
    In Florence was it from a casement thrown me,
95   Wrapped in a paper which contained the name
    Of her that threw it. Noble she was, and thought
    I stood ingaged.[2] But when I had subscribed
    To mine own fortune,° and informed her fully   *admitted my situation*
    I could not answer in that course of honour
100   As she had made the overture, she ceased
    In heavy satisfaction,° and would never   *sad acceptance*
    Receive the ring again.

KING   Plutus° himself,   *god of riches*
    That knows the tinct and multiplying med'cine,[3]
    Hath not in nature's mystery more science°   *expertise*
105   Than I have in this ring. 'Twas mine, 'twas Helen's,
    Whoever gave it you. Then if you know
    That you are well acquainted with yourself,[4]
    Confess 'twas hers, and by what rough enforcement
    You got it from her. She called the saints to surety°   *guarantee*
110   That she would never put it from her finger
    Unless she gave it to yourself in bed,
    Where you have never come, or sent it us
    Upon° her great disaster.   *On the occasion of*

BERTRAM   She never saw it.

KING   Thou speak'st it falsely, as I love mine honour,
115   And mak'st conjectural fears to come into me
    Which I would fain° shut out. If it should prove   *gladly*
    That thou art so inhuman—'twill not prove so.
    And yet I know not. Thou didst hate her deadly,
    And she is dead, which nothing but to close
120   Her eyes myself could win me to believe,
    More than to see this ring.—Take him away.
    My fore-past proofs,[5] howe'er the matter fall,°   *befalls*

---

1. See 4.2.60–64.
2. Pledged to her (alternatively, "ungaged," not promised to anyone else).
3. Alchemical elixir for turning other metals into gold.
4. That you know who you are; that you are willing to admit your actions.
5. My evidence already in hand.

Shall tax° my fears of little vanity,°   *accuse / foolishness*
Having vainly feared too little. Away with him.
We'll sift this matter further.

125 BERTRAM   If you shall prove
This ring was ever hers, you shall as easy
Prove that I husbanded her bed in Florence,
Where yet she never was.   [*Exit guarded*]
     Enter the GENTLEMAN [*Austringer with a paper*]
KING   I am wrapped in dismal thinkings.

130 GENTLEMAN   Gracious sovereign,
Whether I have been to blame or no, I know not.
Here's a petition from a Florentine
Who hath for four or five removes come short
To tender it herself.[6] I undertook it,

135 Vanquished thereto by the fair grace and speech
Of the poor suppliant, who by this° I know   *now*
Is here attending. Her business looks° in her   *shows itself*
With an importing° visage, and she told me   *urgent*
In a sweet verbal brief° it did concern   *summary*

140 Your highness with herself.
KING [*reads*] *a letter*   'Upon his many protestations to marry me
when his wife was dead, I blush to say it, he won me. Now is
the Count Roussillon a widower, his vows are forfeited to me,[7]
and my honour's paid to him. He stole from Florence, taking

145 no leave, and I follow him to his country for justice. Grant it
me, O King! In you it best lies; otherwise a seducer flourishes
and a poor maid is undone.

                         Diana Capilet.'
LAFEU   I will buy me a son-in-law in a fair,[8] and toll or this.[9] I'll

150 none of him.
KING   The heavens have thought well on thee, Lafeu,
To bring forth this discov'ry.—Seek these suitors.
Go speedily and bring again the Count.   *Exit one or more*
I am afeard the life of Helen, lady,
Was foully snatched.
         Enter BERTRAM [*guarded*]

155 COUNTESS   Now justice on the doers!
KING [*to* BERTRAM]   I wonder, sir, since wives are monsters to you,
And that° you fly them as you swear them lordship,[1]   *since*
Yet you desire to marry.
         Enter WIDOW *and* DIANA
               What woman's that?
DIANA   I am, my lord, a wretched Florentine,

160 Derivèd° from the ancient Capilet.   *Descended*
My suit, as I do understand, you know,
And therefore know how far I may be pitied.
WIDOW [*to the* KING]   I am her mother, sir, whose age and
     honour
Both suffer under this complaint we bring,

165 And both° shall cease without your remedy.   *(life and honor)*
KING   Come hither, Count. Do you know these women?

---

6. *Who . . . herself*: Who has for four or five changes of royal residence failed to arrive in time to deliver it herself.
7. His promises have fallen due.
8. Notorious for unreliable merchandise.
9. Pay a tax for the privilege of selling this one (Bertram).
1. As soon as you vow to wed them.

BERTRAM My lord, I neither can nor will deny
But that I know them. Do they charge me further?

DIANA Why do you look so strange upon your wife?

BERTRAM [to the KING] She's none of mine, my lord.

170 DIANA   If you shall marry
You give away this° hand, and that is mine;   (Bertram's)
You give away heaven's vows, and those are mine;
You give away myself, which is known mine,
For I by vow am so embodied yours
175 That she which marries you must marry me,
Either both or none.

LAFEU [to BERTRAM] Your reputation comes too short for my
daughter, you are no husband for her.

BERTRAM [to the KING] My lord, this is a fond° and desp'rate   foolish
creature
180 Whom sometime I have laughed with. Let your highness
Lay a more noble thought upon mine honour
Than for to think that I would sink it here.

KING Sir, for my thoughts, you have them ill to friend²
Till your deeds gain them. Fairer prove your honour
Than in my thought it lies.

185 DIANA   Good my lord,
Ask him upon his oath if he does think
He had not my virginity.

KING What sayst thou to her?

BERTRAM She's impudent, my lord,
190 And was a common gamester° to the camp.   prostitute

DIANA [to the KING] He does me wrong, my lord. If I were so
He might have bought me at a common price.
Do not believe him. O behold this ring,
Whose high respect° and rich validity°   worth / value
195 Did lack a parallel; yet for all that
He gave it to a commoner o'th' camp,
If I be one.

COUNTESS   He blushes and 'tis hit.°   that hit the mark
Of six preceding ancestors, that gem;
Conferred by testament to th' sequent issue°   following generation
200 Hath it been owed° and worn. This is his wife.   owned
That ring's a thousand proofs.

KING [to DIANA]   Methought you said°   (perhaps in the letter)
You saw one here in court could witness it.

DIANA I did, my lord, but loath am to produce
So bad an instrument. His name's Paroles.

205 LAFEU I saw the man today, if man he be.

KING Find him and bring him hither.   [Exit one]

BERTRAM   What of him?
He's quoted° for a most perfidious slave   noted
With all the spots o'th' world taxed and debauched,
Whose nature sickens but to speak a truth.
210 Am I or° that or this for what he'll utter,   either
That will speak anything?

KING   She hath that ring of yours.

BERTRAM I think she has. Certain it is I liked her

---

2. you . . . friend: they are no friends of yours.

And boarded° her i'th' wanton way of youth.   *made advances to*
She knew her distance and did angle for me,
215   Madding° my eagerness with her restraint,   *Maddening*
As all impediments in fancy's° course   *love's*
Are motives° of more fancy; and in fine°   *causes / the end*
Her inf'nite cunning with her modern° grace   *commonplace*
Subdued me to her rate.° She got the ring,   *price*
220   And I had that which my inferior might
At market price have bought.
        DIANA   I must be patient.
You that have turned off a first so noble wife
May justly diet° me. I pray you yet—   *starve (of favor)*
Since you lack virtue I will lose a husband—
225   Send for your ring, I will return it home,
And give me mine again.
        BERTRAM   I have it not.
        KING [*to* DIANA]   What ring was yours, I pray you?
        DIANA   Sir, much like the same upon your finger.
230   KING   Know you this ring? This ring was his of late.
        DIANA   And this was it I gave him being abed.
        KING   The story then goes false you threw it him
Out of a casement?
        DIANA   I have spoke the truth.
                Enter PAROLES
        BERTRAM [*to the* KING]   My lord, I do confess the ring was hers.
235   KING   You boggle shrewdly;[3] every feather starts° you.—   *startles*
Is this the man you speak of?
        DIANA   Ay, my lord.
        KING [*to* PAROLES]   Tell me, sirrah—but tell me true, I charge you,
Not fearing the displeasure of your master,
Which on your just proceeding I'll keep off—
240   By° him and by this woman here what know you?   *About*
        PAROLES   So please your majesty, my master hath been an hon-
ourable gentleman. Tricks he hath had in him which gentlemen have.
        KING   Come, come, to th' purpose. Did he love this woman?
245   PAROLES   Faith, sir, he did love her, but how?
        KING   How, I pray you?
        PAROLES   He did love her, sir, as a gentleman loves a woman.
        KING   How is that?
        PAROLES   He loved her, sir, and loved her not.
250   KING   As thou art a knave and no knave. What an equivocal companion is this!
        PAROLES   I am a poor man, and at your majesty's command.
        LAFEU [*to the* KING]   He's a good drum,[4] my lord, but a
naughty° orator.   *bad*
        DIANA [*to* PAROLES]   Do you know he promised me marriage?
255   PAROLES   Faith, I know more than I'll speak.
        KING   But wilt thou not speak all thou know'st?
        PAROLES   Yes, so please your majesty. I did go between them, as
I said; but more than that, he loved her, for indeed he was mad
for her and talked of Satan and of limbo and of Furies and I

3. You take fright violently; you attempt to evade the   4. Capable only of noise; Lafeu probably also refers to
point wickedly (or incompetently).   Paroles's earlier adventures.

260   know not what. Yet I was in that° credit with them at that time   *so much*
       that I knew of their going to bed and of other motions,° as   *proposals*
       promising her marriage and things which would derive me ill
       will to speak of. Therefore I will not speak what I know.

    KING   Thou hast spoken all already, unless thou canst say they
265   are married. But thou art too fine° in thy evidence, therefore   *hairsplitting*
      stand aside.—
      This ring you say was yours.

    DIANA   Ay, my good lord.

    KING   Where did you buy it? Or who gave it you?

    DIANA   It was not given me, nor I did not buy it.

    KING   Who lent it you?

270   DIANA   It was not lent me neither.

    KING   Where did you find it then?

    DIANA   I found it not.

    KING   If it were yours by none of all these ways,
      How could you give it him?

    DIANA   I never gave it him.

    LAFEU [*to the* KING]   This woman's an easy glove, my lord, she
275   goes off and on at pleasure.

    KING [*to* DIANA]   This ring was mine. I gave it his first wife.

    DIANA   It might be yours or hers for aught I know.

    KING [*to attendants*]   Take her away, I do not like her now.
      To prison with her. And away with him.—
280   Unless thou tell'st me where thou hadst this ring
      Thou diest within this hour.

    DIANA   I'll never tell you.

    KING [*to attendants*]   Take her away.

    DIANA   I'll put in bail, my liege.

    KING   I think thee now some common customer.°   *prostitute*

    DIANA   By Jove, if ever I knew° man 'twas you.   *(carnally)*

285   KING   Wherefore hast thou accused him all this while?

    DIANA   Because he's guilty, and he is not guilty.
      He knows I am no maid, and he'll swear to't;
      I'll swear I am a maid, and he knows not.
      Great King, I am no strumpet; by my life,
290   I am either maid or else this old man's° wife.   *(Lafeu's)*

    KING [*to attendants*]   She does abuse our ears. To prison with her.

    DIANA   Good mother, fetch my bail.   [*Exit* WIDOW]
                            Stay, royal sir.
    The jeweller that owes° the ring is sent for,   *owns*
    And he shall surety me.° But for this lord,   *be my security*
295   Who hath abused me as he knows himself,
    Though yet he never harmed me, here I quit° him.   *acquit; repay; leave*
    He knows himself my bed he hath defiled,
    And at that time he got his wife with child.
    Dead though she be she feels her young one kick.
300   So there's my riddle; one that's dead is quick.°   *alive; pregnant*
    And now behold the meaning.
             Enter HELEN *and* WIDOW

    KING   Is there no exorcist°   *conjurer*
    Beguiles the truer office° of mine eyes?   *function*
    Is't real that I see?

    HELEN   No, my good lord,

'Tis but the shadow° of a wife you see,   ghost; imitation
The name and not the thing.
305 BERTRAM   Both, both. O, pardon!
HELEN   O, my good lord, when I was like° this maid   in the place of
    I found you wondrous kind. There is your ring.
    And, look you, here's your letter. This it says:
    'When from my finger you can get this ring,
310 And are by me with child,' et cetera. This is done.
    Will you be mine now you are doubly won?
BERTRAM [to the KING]   If she, my liege, can make me know this clearly
    I'll love her dearly, ever ever dearly.
HELEN   If it appear not plain and prove untrue,
315 Deadly divorce step between me and you.—
    O my dear mother, do I see you living?
LAFEU   Mine eyes smell onions, I shall weep anon.
    [To PAROLES] Good Tom Drum, lend me a handkerchief. So,
    I thank thee. Wait on me home, I'll make sport with thee. Let
320 thy curtsies alone, they are scurvy ones.
KING [to HELEN]   Let us from point to point this story know
    To make the even° truth in pleasure flow.   plain
    [To DIANA] If thou be'st yet a fresh uncroppèd flower,
    Choose thou thy husband and I'll pay thy dower.
325 For I can guess that by thy honest aid
    Thou kept'st a wife herself, thyself a maid.
    Of that and all the progress more and less[5]
    Resolvèdly° more leisure shall express.   So questions are resolved
    All yet seems well; and if it end so meet,°   properly
330 The bitter past, more welcome is the sweet.
        Flourish

Epilogue

The King's a beggar now the play is done.
All is well ended if this suit be won:
That you express content,° which we will pay   (by applause)
With strife° to please you, day exceeding° day.   trying / after
5 Ours be your patience then, and yours our parts:[1]
Your gentle hands lend us, and take our hearts.   Exeunt

---

5. The course of events, great and small.

Epilogue
1. *Ours . . . parts:* We will wait patiently, like an audience, while you take the active part.

The Life of Timon of Athens

In a jewelry advertisement, a handsome man and a beautiful woman share a rapturous embrace. A large diamond sparkles on the woman's finger; apparently, the impressive ring symbolizes a love equally magnificent. Although the deliberate confusion of emotional and financial investments seems crass once it is explicitly recognized, the ad can only be effective at selling jewelry if it captures something people know, or wish, to be true. What does love have to do with money? How closely entwined are friendship and material self-interest? Are persons esteemed for intrinsic personal characteristics or for the glamour of their possessions? Are affluent communities or prosperous individuals especially likely to confuse sheer wealth with other forms of value?

Timon of Athens asks such questions with a relentlessness unusual for Shakespeare. To many readers and audiences, the play has seemed uncharacteristic in other respects as well: its schematic plot and vivid but static characters evoke the morality drama of Shakespeare's predecessors or the satiric drama of his contemporaries more closely than the other tragedies that Shakespeare was writing around this time. Some argue that *Timon of Athens* was never finished; others suggest that the play is a collaborative work, about a third of which was written by Shakespeare's fellow dramatist Thomas Middleton. Nonetheless, some connections between *Timon* and Shakespeare's other plays are clear enough. The plot derives from that Shakespearean favorite, Plutarch's *Lives*, which also provided the sources for *Julius Caesar*, *Antony and Cleopatra*, and *Coriolanus*. *Timon* has strong affinities to *The Merchant of Venice* in its concern with the connections between affectional and monetary bonds, and between material and intangible goods. The play's jaundiced view of ancient Greece recalls *Troilus and Cressida,* as does its evasion of ordinary generic categories: although its protagonist dies at the end, its title does not promise a tragedy but merely a "life." The hero's sensational degradation from preeminence to utter penury, and his ferociously misanthropic reaction to that humiliation, has often prompted comparison with *King Lear.*

Timon opens on a panorama of glittering abundance. Purveyors of luxury goods— art, poems, jewels, textiles—flock to Timon's palace in hope of reward. Like advertisers today, they claim that their goods have a symbolic significance that goes beyond their obvious beauty or utility: these items give concrete expression to the ineffable virtues of their possessor. "Things of like value differing in the owners/Are prizèd by their masters," fawns the Jeweller. "You mend the jewel by the wearing it" (1.1.174–75, 176). The guests at Timon's sumptuous banquet are likewise loud in their admiration for their host. Their conversation turns almost obsessively upon Timon's apparently inexhaustible fortune.

And no wonder—for Timon seems not merely rich but unique. His generosity is characterized by what the Poet calls "magic of bounty," an outflow uncannily unbalanced by any apparent countereffort at acquisition. While ordinary owners have the power merely to transfer, not actually to generate, new goods, Timon seems freed from such basic material laws. He dispenses his "bounty" as if he were a god empowered to create wealth from nothing. But Timon's "magic" relies on a trick that he himself resolutely ignores. Using his lands as collateral, he borrows the money he needs to buy rich presents and keep a lavish table. The recipients of his hospitality are often the same men to whom he is indebted.

To Timon's surprise but hardly to the audience's, his elaborate charade collapses in the play's second act. Why has he behaved so self-destructively? We are given clues to his motives when, in the course of his banquet, he and his guests explicitly and implicitly offer several theories about the relationship of his "bounty" both to the social weal and to his own self-conception. Timon desires love and admiration, and in Athenian society, as in many others, money proves a potent way of getting both. The adjectives "good," "worthy," "free," "kind," "gentle," and "noble" echo through the first act—their simultaneously economic and moral significance tending to break down any difference between the two domains. When Ventidius offers to return the large sum that Timon has spent releasing him from prison, Timon refuses:

> You mistake my love.
> I gave it freely ever, and there's none
> Can truly say he gives if he receives.
> (1.2.8–10)

Typically, love and money are here almost inextricable. Is the "it" that Timon freely gives the love to which he refers in the previous line or the money he has bestowed upon Ventidius? Moreover, Timon's generosity is entangled with pride and with a desire for mastery. By always giving, never receiving, Timon attempts to force his beneficiaries into an endlessly grateful and therefore subordinate role. His conduct recalls that of the chiefs of the native American tribes of the Pacific Northwest, who consolidated their status by "potlatches," great parties at which they would give away virtually all their possessions, thus compelling their guests to serve them in the future. In such a system, divesting oneself of wealth, not accumulating it, is the primary mode of acquiring status.

In the socioeconomic world of the potlatch, in which the recipient of a gift is profoundly obliged to the donor, Timon might well escape serious financial danger. His "courtiers" would attempt to repay him, in kind or in service. Timon briefly imagines such a system when he rhapsodizes at his dinner party: "We are born to do benefits; and what better or properer can we call our own than the riches of our friends? O, what a precious comfort 'tis to have so many like brothers commanding one another's fortunes!" (1.2.95–98). Unfortunately, not only is this communitarian vision at odds with Timon's insistence on entirely unilateral gift-giving, but it is grossly out of kilter with the covetous society in which he actually lives. When Timon pays Ventidius's debt, Ventidius's messenger declares that "your lordship ever binds him" (1.1.106); likewise the First Lord claims to be "virtuously bound" by Timon's generosity (1.2.221). Yet by the middle of Act 2, they have already lost any sense of commitment to their erstwhile benefactor. Timon's "bonds," the legal instruments that enable his lenders to seize his lands when he forfeits cash repayment, turn out to be more "binding" than the unwritten ties of gratitude. In Athens, tangible goods are considered more real than intangible ones, legal commitments more real than obligations informally imposed.

Apemantus, the Cynic philosopher, hovering on the margins of Timon's dinner party, introduces an alternative economic language early in the play: the audience's perception of the entire banquet extravaganza is filtered through his commentary. For Timon, magnanimity apparently comes naturally, and gifts express sociability. For Apemantus, by contrast, people are naturally greedy and antisocial: protestations of friendship and gratitude hypocritically conceal an impulse to accumulate wealth at the expense of another, just as lavishness hypocritically conceals a desire for adulation. In such circumstances, the Cynic philosopher preserves his safety and integrity by repudiating his need both for property and for other people:

> Immortal gods, I crave no pelf.
> I pray for no man but myself.
> Grant I may never prove so fond
> To trust a man on his oath or bond,

> Or a harlot for her weeping,
> Or a dog that seems a-sleeping,
> Or a keeper with my freedom,
> Or my friends if I should need 'em.
> (1.2.61–68)

To Timon's generous trustfulness, Apemantus counterpoises a self-protective suspicion. The difference in the way the two men conceive of human nature correlates with a difference in the way they imagine the material world. Timon believes that wealth is endlessly renewable and thus endlessly sharable without decrease. Apemantus believes that resources are strictly limited and that one person's gain must entail another person's loss. Thus what Timon sees as banquet pleasantries amount, in Apemantus's view, to a form of cannibalism. "O you gods, what a number of men eats Timon, and he sees 'em not! It grieves me to see so many dip their meat in one man's blood" (1.2.38–40). Both of these apparently opposite attitudes, however—Timon's romanticism and Apemantus's reductiveness—are actually rooted in a conviction that one's possessions, or the lack of them, centrally determine the way one thinks of oneself and interacts with other people. Arguably, Apemantus's cannibal imagery makes the shared materialism of the two men's attitudes especially obvious to a Christian audience; for that vision of Timon's banquet parodies, in grotesquely literal terms, the dispersal of Christ's spiritual body in the communion ceremony.

Most scholars believe that *Timon of Athens* was written between 1605 and 1608, several years after the accession of James I to the English throne. There are good reasons why Timon's particular economic dilemma would interest dramatists observing the contemporary scene in these years. If the play was, as many argue, left unfinished and unproduced, perhaps it was too incendiary to be safely performed in Jacobean England: although most of Shakespeare's plays reflect to some extent the time in which they were written, *Timon* is unusual in its brutally direct topical relevance. In the first decade of the seventeenth century, the traditional aristocratic virtues of openhanded generosity and carelessness of expense were coming into increasingly acute conflict with the limited means upon which the great nobles could actually draw. As England became an international trading power, luxuries once unheard of became available to people with the money to buy them. As tastes grew more sophisticated, noblemen who wished to impress peers and subordinates with the splendor of their

Penthesilea, Queen of the Amazons. Drawing by Inigo Jones. From *The Masque of Queenes,* by Beu Jonson.

"bounty" were forced into ever greater expenditures. The result was an extraordinary expansion in the credit markets. The worst offender in this respect was King James, who—like Timon—showered his favorites with expensive gifts, a habit that created staggering deficits in the Royal Exchequer. By 1608, royal indebtedness had reached crisis proportions, and other members of the upper aristocracy were likewise floating on a sea of debt and credit.

Shakespeare, or Shakespeare and Middleton, thus bear witness to a society in the process of a crucial economic transition—a transition that affects more than financial matters narrowly defined. In the first act, Timon assumes that his money transactions are accompanied by affection on the part of the giver and gratitude on the part of the recipient. In an informal, small-scale credit system, the difference between love and money, and between loans and gifts, may indeed become blurred, for friends may help one another financially on occasion. In Jacobean England, however, the inability of the upper classes to live within their means overstrained the limits of "friendly understanding": for few people then or now lend really substantial sums of money out of sheer amiability. Borrowing and lending thus increasingly became business matters transacted between relative strangers, divorced from rather than continuous with friendship and patronage relationships. Usury, a practice traditionally deplored and even illegal, was nonetheless widespread and increasingly accepted as a necessary fact of life.

A fiscally prudent, hardworking businessman, Shakespeare may well have been shocked on occasion at the profligacy of the patrons upon whose expansiveness he and his theater company partly depended. Certainly he recognized acutely that the motives of the Poet and the Painter do not differ from the motives of the other courtiers: "artists" in Athens are as venal as everybody else. What seems to have intrigued him most, however, is the way in which an apparently rather limited social phenomenon—aristocratic reliance on credit—necessarily affects social and even biological relations that seem far removed from money lending. Uniquely among Shakespeare's plays, Timon is nearly bereft of women. The few who do briefly appear—the Amazons of Act 1, Alcibiades' whores in Act 4—are pointedly excluded from the "normal" marital relationships in which most socially useful reproductive activity traditionally takes place. In this nearly all-male world, the language of erotic intimacy is reserved for interactions among men. Exchanges of money and commodities take over some of the functions of procreative sexual intimacy, an appropriation that can easily be construed as perverse or depraved. Lending money at interest seems especially corrupt: Timon of Athens draws upon an ancient tradition of imagining usury to be a form of unnatural "breeding." After his disillusionment, Timon continually and deliberately conflates lust with greed, the venereal with the venal. Syphilis and its symptoms are not merely analogies for, but are perhaps even the consequences of, economic iniquity.

Despite the virtual absence of actual women, allegorical representations of female power play an important rhetorical role in Timon of Athens. The first half of the play is dominated by the allegorical figure of Dame Fortune. The Poet describes her as a "sovereign lady . . . upon a high and pleasant hill" (1.1.69, 64), huge, omnipotent, and whimsical, raising and crushing her struggling male subjects for no apparent reason. In the second half of the play, "Mother Earth" has some of the same threatening demeanor. The ruined Timon forsakes Athens for the wilderness outside it, rather as Shakespeare's lovers had done in that drastically different play A Midsummer Night's Dream. In Dream, the woods outside Athens are a lushly sexual place, but in Timon, roughly the same geographical locale is unusually harsh and minimalist. Like the whores to whom Timon compares her, Mother Earth is barren, refusing to surrender the roots for which Timon digs and instead yielding only the gold he had hoped to flee. Thus, for all the energy spent exposing the "unnaturalness" of Athenians' economic relations, a potentially restorative "natural" alternative is wholly lacking.

In many respects, Timon's disillusioned ferocity simply inverts, recoils from, the generous courtesy he had manifested throughout Act 1. Yet not everything changes: there is a clear continuity to Timon's personality in the first and second half of the play. Initially, as a wealthy patron and benefactor, Timon isolates himself from others by making himself a god of generosity. Later, as an indigent, he similarly sets himself apart, cursing mankind with all the immoderation with which he once blessed it. Shakespeare was fascinated throughout his career by self-absorbed, almost solipsistic characters: Adonis in *Venus and Adonis*, the young man of the sonnets, Malvolio in *Twelfth Night* "sick of self love." Timon exemplifies an extreme version of this egocentrism, his sense of his own separateness untouched even after his conception of human nature has been poisoned at its source. He not only dies alone, but mysteriously manages to bury himself and engrave his own epitaph: an epitaph that typically, and perversely, both demands that passersby remember him and orders them to "seek not my name" (5.5.73).

The necessarily social medium of the drama finds true hermits impossible to accommodate. For most of Acts 4 and 5, various acquaintances crowd to Timon's cave as they once crowded to his palace, some to commiserate or to offer advice, some to investigate rumors that Timon had discovered gold while digging for roots to eat. The disillusioned Timon no longer wants gold, because it has value only insofar as it can be exchanged, and thus requires that its users form relationships with other human beings. So, ironically, the man who once blessed his "friends" with treasure once again gives it away to them, this time with his curses. The sense of separateness Timon has always possessed makes satiric alienation congenial to him; but, like many satirists, he is an ambiguous figure. The satirist can tell truths about society because his disengagement gives him the standing to criticize practices he regards as corrupt. At the same time, his observational acuteness—his refusal to accept the complacencies of the majority—bespeaks a certain imbalance. The satirist's misanthropy coexists curiously with an inability to mind his own business. The tone of the play's latter acts thus becomes profoundly equivocal. Are we supposed to agree with Timon that virtually all human values and activities can be plausibly reduced to money and the greed for it? Certainly, the action of the play gives us ample reason to share his disgust at his erstwhile friends. Or is his rage disproportionate to the adversities he endures? Just as the Timon of the early acts can be variously characterized as noble and foolish, the later Timon has seemed to some critics a sublimely disappointed idealist, to others a petulant whiner.

A few characters suggest that Timon's unmitigated misanthropy is too simple and incomplete. The steward Flavius's loyalty to his former master defies the terms of Timon's blanket condemnation of all humankind, as Timon reluctantly acknowledges. Throughout *Timon*, low-ranking characters—having less to gain from greed—display an acute sense of gratitude and obligation sadly lacking in their "betters." All Timon's servants, not merely Flavius, seem dismayed by their master's ruin; and in 3.4, the usurers' servants, talking among themselves, freely condemn the commands they are forced to carry out. But Timon prefers to believe that rapacity is a universal human trait, not a more limited, class-linked phenomenon. Reduced to rags and roots though he is, Timon cannot help being a snob. And to some extent, his status consciousness seems justified: for if the servants are kindhearted, they are also ineffectual, disqualified by low rank from remedying the social problems they witness.

Alcibiades provides a more formidable alternative to the Athenian usurers, although the connection between this subplot and the main action is sketchy. Certainly he does not escape, or seek to disentangle, the interconnections between love and money that eventually seem so poisonous to Timon: when he visits Timon in the cave, he comes with a prostitute on each arm. Nonetheless, in his brief appearances, Alcibiades testifies to the existence of a less restricted, more complex sociopolitical world than the one we witness for most of the play. Whereas, for instance, Timon's function in Athens seems mainly to give expensive dinner parties, Alcibiades insists that Timon has performed important military services for the state: that his "bounty" has had a political and executive, as well as a sheerly economic, aspect. Unfortunately, the relationship between Timon and Alcibiades, as well as the relationship between the city's politics and its social organization, is left largely undeveloped in the text of the play as it has

Dame Fortune, blind, standing on a ball with wings (to show how quickly her favors may fly away). From George Wither, *A Collection of Emblemes* (1635).

come down to us. The soldier, pursuing his vocation in the bleak world beyond the city walls, is imagined as partly outside the economic system in which other characters are enmeshed. Like the hermit-satirist, he has the special credibility that comes with distance. But whereas Timon's detachment is the product of a merely negative disgust, Alcibiades' involves allegiance to a different set of positive values. In 3.6, not only does he risk himself to defend a friend, but the terms of his defense hint at a code of behavior divorced from cash rewards and penalties.

At the end of the play, after Timon's death, the Athenian senators invite Alcibiades and his army back into the city. He will, they hope, "approach the fold and cull th'infected forth" (5.5.43), as a shepherd kills the sick animals of his flock in order to keep disease from spreading to the remainder. The senators argue that greed is merely the failing of a degenerate few, not the universal human trait Timon had believed it to be. Alcibiades seems to accept this claim, agreeing to renounce the indiscriminate violence of a war against all Athens in favor of the more targeted punishment of particular offenders. But the play entertains this alternative view of Timon's plight too late and too hastily to carry much conviction, and the apparent optimism of the conclusion thus seems unearned. How Alcibiades' invasion will reform Athens is hard to imagine.

KATHARINE EISAMAN MAUS

TEXTUAL NOTE

The only source for *Timon* is the First Folio of 1623 (F), and the circumstances of its publication seem to have been unusual. Evidently the decision to include *Timon* in

Shakespeare's collected works was made quite late; it was inserted into a space early in F that had been originally designated for the longer *Troilus and Cressida,* a play for which the printer initially had trouble obtaining copyright. This peculiarity, especially when viewed in light of the play's many rough edges and inconsistencies, has led scholars to speculate that *Timon* seemed, to the Folio compilers, to be marginal to Shakespeare's oeuvre. Some scholars believe, on the basis of analyzing vocabulary, stage directions, spelling, and style, that *Timon* is a collaborative text jointly authored by Shakespeare and Thomas Middleton. Others suggest that whatever its authorship, the play was abandoned before it reached the final stages of revision. There is no evidence that the play was ever performed, but such firm evidence is often lacking in the scanty surviving documents: the record is similarly silent on such plays as *As You Like It, Troilus and Cressida, All's Well That Ends Well,* and *Antony and Cleopatra.*

SELECTED BIBLIOGRAPHY

Chorost, Michael. "Biological Finance in Shakespeare's *Timon of Athens.*" *English Literary Renaissance* 21 (1991): 349–70. Gift and money economies in *Timon,* and the language of biological reproduction in which they are described.

Empson, William. "Timon's Dog." *The Structure of Complex Words.* London: Chatto & Windus, 1951. The dog as an icon of both flattery and cynicism in *Timon.*

Jowett, John. "Middleton and Debt in *Timon of Athens.*" *Money and the Age of Shakespeare: Essays in New Economic Criticism.* Ed. Linda Woodbridge. New York: Palgrave Macmillan, 2003. The play reflects the economic attitudes of Thomas Middleton, Shakespeare's probable collaborator.

Kahn, Coppélia. "'Magic of Bounty': *Timon of Athens,* Jacobean Patronage, and Maternal Power." *Shakespeare Quarterly* 38 (1987): 34–57. *Timon's* links to the contradictory practices of Jacobean court patronage.

Nuttall, A. D. *Timon of Athens.* Harvester New Critical Introductions to Shakespeare. Hemel Hempstead, Eng.: Harvester Wheatsheaf, 1989. Chapters on stage history and critical reception, followed by a detailed commentary on the play.

Paster, Gail Kern. *The Idea of the City in the Age of Shakespeare.* Athens: University of Georgia Press, 1985. 99–108. *Timon's* bleak vision of urban life, as enacted in the hero's transformation from philanthropist to misanthrope.

Scott, Alison V. *Selfish Gifts: The Politics of Exchange and English Courtly Literature, 1580–1628.* Madison, N.J.: Fairleigh Dickinson University Press, 2005. Describes the culture of patronage and self-seeking upon which *Timon* comments.

FILM

Timon of Athens. 1981. Dir. Jonathan Miller. UK. 128 min. Sepia-toned BBC-TV production featuring Athenians in Jacobean dress. Jonathan Pryce stars as an initially clueless and eventually very battered Timon. Effectively slimy performances in the subsidiary roles.

The Life of Timon of Athens

THE PERSONS OF THE PLAY

TIMON of Athens
A POET
A PAINTER
A JEWELLER
A MERCHANT
A mercer
LUCILIUS, one of Timon's servants
An OLD ATHENIAN
LORDS and SENATORS of Athens
VENTIDIUS, one of Timon's false friends
ALCIBIADES, an Athenian captain
APEMANTUS, a churlish philosopher
One dressed as CUPID in the masque
LADIES dressed as Amazons in the masque
FLAVIUS, Timon's steward
FLAMINIUS } Timon's servants
SERVILIUS }
Other SERVANTS of Timon
A FOOL
A PAGE
CAPHIS
ISIDORE'S SERVANT } servants to Timon's creditors
Two of VARRO'S SERVANTS }
LUCULLUS }
LUCIUS } flattering lords
SEMPRONIUS }
LUCULLUS' SERVANT
LUCIUS' SERVANT
Three STRANGERS, one called Hostillius
TITUS' SERVANT }
HORTENSIUS' SERVANT } other servants to Timon's creditors
PHILOTUS' SERVANT }
PHRYNIA } whores with Alcibiades
TIMANDRA }
The banditti, THIEVES
SOLDIER of Alcibiades' army
Messengers, attendants, soldiers

1.1

Enter POET [*at one door*], PAINTER [*carrying a picture at another door, followed by*] JEWELLER, MERCHANT, *and Mercer, at several doors*

POET   Good day, sir.
PAINTER   I am glad you're well.
POET   I have not seen you long. How goes the world?

1.1 Location: Timon's house, Athens.

PAINTER   It wears,° sir, as it grows.°   *wears out / ages*

POET   Ay, that's well known.

But what particular rarity, what strange,

5   Which manifold record° not matches?—See,   *all recorded history*

Magic of bounty,° all these spirits thy power   *generosity*

Hath conjured to attend.

[MERCHANT *and* JEWELLER *meet. Mercer passes over the*
stage, and exits]

                                              I know the merchant.

PAINTER   I know them both. Th'other's a jeweller.

MERCHANT [*to* JEWELLER]   O, 'tis a worthy lord!°   *(Timon)*

JEWELLER   Nay, that's most fixed.°   *definite*

10   MERCHANT   A most incomparable man, breathed,° as it were,   *trained; inspired*

To an untirable and continuate° goodness.   *habitual*

He passes.°   *excels*

JEWELLER [*showing a jewel*]   I have a jewel here.

MERCHANT   O, pray, let's see't. For the Lord Timon, sir?

JEWELLER   If he will touch the estimate.° But for that—   *meet the price*

15   POET [*to himself*]   'When we for recompense have praised the vile,

It stains the glory in that happy° verse   *appropriate*

Which aptly sings the good.'

MERCHANT [*to* JEWELLER]   'Tis a good form.°   *shape*

JEWELLER   And rich. Here is a water,° look ye.   *luster*

PAINTER [*to* POET]   You are rapt, sir, in some work, some dedication

To the great lord.[1]

20   POET   A thing slipped idly from me.

Our poesy is as a gum° which oozes   *sap*

From whence 'tis nourished. The fire i'th' flint

Shows not till it be struck; our gentle flame

Provokes° itself, and like the current flies   *Generates*

25   Each bound it chafes.[2] What have you there?

PAINTER   A picture, sir. When comes your book forth?

POET   Upon the heels of my presentment,[3] sir.

Let's see your piece.

PAINTER [*showing the picture*]   'Tis a good piece.

POET   So 'tis. This comes off well and excellent.

PAINTER   Indifferent.°   *So-so*

30   POET   Admirable. How this grace

Speaks his own standing![4] What a mental power

This eye shoots forth! How big imagination

Moves in this lip! To th' dumbness° of the gesture   *muteness*

One might interpret.°   *supply words*

35   PAINTER   It is a pretty mocking° of the life.   *imitation*

Here is a touch; is't good?

POET   I will say of it,

It tutors nature. Artificial strife°   *The striving of art*

Lives in these touches livelier than life.

                Enter certain Senators

PAINTER   How this lord is followed!

40   POET   The senators of Athens. Happy man!

PAINTER   Look, more.

---

1. Poets dedicated their volumes to wealthy patrons in
hopes of financial reward.
2. *like . . . chafes:* like the river overflows restricting

banks.
3. As soon as I have presented it formally (to Timon).
4. Imparts the dignity of his estate.

[The Senators pass over the stage, and exeunt]

POET   You see this confluence, this great flood of visitors.
    I have in this rough work shaped out a man
    Whom this beneath[5] world doth embrace and hug
45   With amplest entertainment.° My free drift°   *hospitality / meaning*
    Halts not particularly,[6] but moves itself
    In a wide sea of tax.[7] No levelled malice
    Infects one comma in the course I hold,
    But flies an eagle flight, bold and forth° on,   *straight*
50   Leaving no tract° behind.   *trace*

PAINTER   How shall I understand you?

POET   I will unbolt° to you.   *disclose*
    You see how all conditions, how all minds,
    As well of glib and slipp'ry creatures as
55   Of grave and austere quality, tender° down   *give*
    Their service to Lord Timon. His large fortune,
    Upon his good and gracious nature hanging,
    Subdues and properties° to his love and tendance°   *appropriates / attendance*
    All sorts of hearts; yea, from the glass-faced[8] flatterer
60   To Apemantus, that few things loves better
    Than to abhor himself; even he drops down
    The knee before him, and returns° in peace,   *leaves*
    Most rich in Timon's nod.

PAINTER   I saw them speak together.

POET   Sir, I have upon a high and pleasant hill
65   Feigned° Fortune to be throned. The base o'th' mount   *Imagined*
    Is ranked with all deserts,[9] all kind of natures
    That labour on the bosom of this sphere
    To propagate their states.° Amongst them all   *improve their fortunes*
    Whose eyes are on this sovereign lady fixed
70   One do I personate of Lord Timon's frame,
    Whom Fortune with her ivory hand wafts° to her,   *beckons*
    Whose present grace° to present slaves and servants   *graciousness*
    Translates his rivals.[1]

PAINTER   'Tis conceived to scope.°   *correctly*
    This throne, this Fortune, and this hill, methinks,
75   With one man beckoned from the rest below,
    Bowing his head against the steepy mount
    To climb his happiness,° would be well expressed   *good fortune*
    In our condition.[2]

POET   Nay, sir, but hear me on.
    All those which were his fellows° but of late,   *equals*
80   Some better than his value, on the moment
    Follow his strides, his lobbies fill with tendance,[3]
    Rain sacrificial° whisperings in his ear,   *respectful*
    Make sacred even his stirrup,[4] and through him
    Drink the free air.

---

5. Sublunar (in Ptolomaic astronomy, the earth was the center of the universe and the moon its closest satellite; things beyond the moon were eternally fixed, but things in the sublunar "sphere" died or changed).
6. Does not criticize individuals.
7. In general satire (the Oxford editors substitute "tax" [criticism] for F's "wax"). *levelled*: aimed (at a particular person).
8. Reflecting his patron's moods.

9. Is lined with people of all degrees of virtue.
1. *to present . . . rivals*: instantly converts Timon's rivals to his slaves and servants.
2. *would . . . condition*: would be a good expression of the human condition; would make a good design for a painter.
3. *his . . . tendance*: crowd his rooms to visit him.
4. By holding it reverently as he mounts.

PAINTER   Ay, marry, what of these?

85 POET   When Fortune in her shift and change of mood

Spurns° down her late belovèd, all his dependants,   *Kicks*

Which laboured after him to the mountain's top

Even on their knees and hands, let him fall down,

Not one accompanying his declining foot.

90 PAINTER   'Tis common.

A thousand moral paintings I can show

That shall demonstrate these quick blows of Fortune's

More pregnantly° than words. Yet you do well   *forcibly*

To show Lord Timon that mean° eyes have seen   *base people's*

95 The foot above the head.

Trumpets sound. Enter TIMON [*wearing a rich jewel*],
with a MESSENGER *from Ventidius;* LUCILIUS *and other*
Servants attending. TIMON *address*[*es*] *himself courte-*
ously to every suitor [*then speaks to the* MESSENGER]

TIMON   Imprisoned is he, say you?

MESSENGER   Ay, my good lord. Five talents[5] is his debt,

His means most short, his creditors most strait.°   *severe*

Your honourable letter he desires

100 To those° have shut him up, which failing,   *those who*

Periods° his comfort.   *Ends*

TIMON   Noble Ventidius! Well,

I am not of that feather° to shake off   *sort*

My friend when he must need me. I do know him

A gentleman that well deserves a help,

105 Which he shall have. I'll pay the debt and free him.

MESSENGER   Your lordship ever binds° him.   *obligates*

TIMON   Commend me to him. I will send his ransom;

And, being enfranchised,° bid him come to me.   *set free*

'Tis not enough to help the feeble up,

110 But to support him after. Fare you well.

MESSENGER   All happiness to your honour.   *Exit*

Enter an OLD ATHENIAN

OLD ATHENIAN   Lord Timon, hear me speak.

TIMON   Freely, good father.

OLD ATHENIAN   Thou hast a servant named Lucilius.

TIMON   I have so. What of him?

115 OLD ATHENIAN   Most noble Timon, call the man before thee.

TIMON   Attends he here or no? Lucilius!

LUCILIUS [*coming forward*]   Here at your lordship's service.

OLD ATHENIAN   This fellow here, Lord Timon, this thy creature,

By night frequents my house. I am a man

120 That from my first have been inclined to thrift,

And my estate deserves an heir more raised°   *exalted*

Than one which holds a trencher.[6]

TIMON   Well, what further?

OLD ATHENIAN   One only daughter have I, no kin else

On whom I may confer what I have got.

125 The maid is fair, o'th' youngest for a bride,

And I have bred her° at my dearest cost   *brought her up*

---

5. A large unit of money, usually taken as equivalent to several thousand dollars. Shakespeare seems undecided about how much a "talent" is worth in *Timon,* and his inconsistencies are often cited as evidence for incomplete revision of the text.

6. Platter (one who waits on table).

In qualities of the best. This man of thine
Attempts her love. I prithee, noble lord,
Join with me to forbid him her resort.°   company
130 Myself have spoke in vain.
TIMON   The man is honest.
OLD ATHENIAN   Therefore he will be,[7] Timon.
His honesty rewards him in itself;
It must not bear° my daughter.   carry off
135 TIMON   Does she love him?
OLD ATHENIAN   She is young and apt.°   impressionable
Our own precedent° passions do instruct us   former
What levity's in youth.
TIMON [to LUCILIUS]   Love you the maid?
LUCILIUS   Ay, my good lord, and she accepts of it.
140 OLD ATHENIAN   If in her marriage my consent be missing,
I call the gods to witness, I will choose
Mine heir from forth the beggars of the world,
And dispossess her all.
TIMON   How shall she be endowed°   What dowry will she have
If she be mated with an equal husband?
145 OLD ATHENIAN   Three talents on the present; in future, all.
TIMON   This gentleman of mine hath served me long.
To build his fortune I will strain a little,
For 'tis a bond° in men. Give him thy daughter.   duty of friendship
What you bestow in him I'll counterpoise,
And make him weigh with her.
150 OLD ATHENIAN   Most noble lord,
Pawn me to this your honour,[8] she is his.
TIMON   My hand to thee; mine honour on my promise.
LUCILIUS   Humbly I thank your lordship. Never may
That state or fortune fall into my keeping
155 Which is not owed to you.
                          Exeunt [LUCILIUS *and* OLD ATHENIAN]
POET [*presenting a poem to* TIMON]   Vouchsafe° my labour, and   Accept
      long live your lordship!
TIMON   I thank you. You shall hear from me anon.°   soon
      Go not away. [*To* PAINTER] What have you there, my friend?
PAINTER   A piece of painting, which I do beseech
      Your lordship to accept.
160 TIMON   Painting is welcome.
The painting is almost the natural° man;   actual
For since dishonour traffics° with man's nature,   has dealings
He is but outside;° these pencilled figures are   only superficial
Even such as they give out.[9] I like your work,
165 And you shall find I like it. Wait attendance
Till you hear further from me.
PAINTER   The gods preserve ye!
TIMON   Well fare you, gentleman. Give me your hand.
We must needs dine together. [*To* JEWELLER] Sir, your jewel
Hath suffered under[1] praise.
JEWELLER   What, my lord, dispraise?

7. He will behave honorably (and chastely).   1. Has been inundated by (but the Jeweller misunder-
8. If you pledge your honor to do this.   stands).
9. Just what they profess to be.

170   TIMON   A mere° satiety of commendations.   *An utter*
        If I should pay you for't as 'tis extolled
        It would unclew° me quite.   *ruin*
      JEWELLER   My lord, 'tis rated
        As those which sell would give;[2] but you well know
        Things of like value differing in the owners
175   Are prizèd by their masters.[3] Believe't, dear lord,
        You mend° the jewel by the wearing it.   *improve*
      TIMON   Well mocked.°   *You're kidding*
      MERCHANT   No, my good lord, he speaks the common tongue°   *general opinion*
        Which all men speak with him.

           Enter APEMANTUS

      TIMON   Look who comes here.
180   Will you be chid?
      JEWELLER   We will bear,° with your lordship.   *suffer*
      MERCHANT   He'll spare none.
      TIMON   Good morrow to thee, gentle Apemantus.
      APEMANTUS   Till I be gentle, stay thou for thy good morrow—
185   When thou art Timon's dog, and these knaves honest.[4]
      TIMON   Why dost thou call them knaves? Thou know'st them not.
      APEMANTUS   Are they not Athenians?
      TIMON   Yes.
      APEMANTUS   Then I repent not.
190   JEWELLER   You know me, Apemantus?
      APEMANTUS   Thou know'st I do. I called thee by thy name.
      TIMON   Thou art proud, Apemantus!
      APEMANTUS   Of nothing so much as that I am not like Timon.
      TIMON   Whither art going?
195   APEMANTUS   To knock out an honest Athenian's brains.
      TIMON   That's a deed thou'lt die for.
      APEMANTUS   Right, if doing nothing[5] be death by th' law.
      TIMON   How likest thou this picture, Apemantus?
      APEMANTUS   The best for the innocence.[6]
200   TIMON   Wrought he not well that painted it?
      APEMANTUS   He wrought better that made the painter, and yet
        he's but a filthy piece of work.
      PAINTER   You're a dog.[7]
      APEMANTUS   Thy mother's of my generation. What's she, if I be a dog?
205   TIMON   Wilt dine with me, Apemantus?
      APEMANTUS   No, I eat not[8] lords.
      TIMON   An° thou shouldst, thou'dst anger ladies.   *If*
      APEMANTUS   O, they eat lords. So they come by great bellies.
      TIMON   That's a lascivious apprehension.[9]
210   APEMANTUS   So thou apprehend'st it; take it for thy labour.
      TIMON   How dost thou like this jewel, Apemantus?
      APEMANTUS   Not so well as plain dealing, which will not cost a
        man a doit.°   *tiny coin*
      TIMON   What dost thou think 'tis worth?

---

2. At what a merchant would pay (the wholesale price).
3. Are valued as their owners are valued.
4. *stay . . . honest:* wait for a polite greeting until you are changed into your own dog or (an equally likely prospect) these crooks become honest.
5. Since there are no honest Athenians.

6. For its inability to harm anyone.
7. "Dog" is not merely a term of contempt; Apemantus was a Cynic philosopher, a school whose name derived from the Greek *kynē*, "dog."
8. I do not devour the substance of.
9. Interpretation; grasping.

APEMANTUS   Not worth my thinking.

215   POET   How now, poet?

POET   How now, philosopher?

APEMANTUS   Thou liest.

POET   Art not one?

APEMANTUS   Yes.

220   POET   Then I lie not.

APEMANTUS   Art not a poet?

POET   Yes.

APEMANTUS   Then thou liest. Look in thy last work, where thou
hast feigned him° a worthy fellow.   *(Timon)*

225   POET   That's not feigned, he is so.

APEMANTUS   Yes, he is worthy of thee, and to pay thee for thy
labour. He that loves to be flattered is worthy o'th' flatterer.
Heavens, that I were a lord!

TIMON   What wouldst do then, Apemantus?

230   APEMANTUS   E'en as Apemantus does now: hate a lord with my heart.

TIMON   What, thyself?

APEMANTUS   Ay.

TIMON   Wherefore?

APEMANTUS   That I had no augury[1] but to be a lord.—Art not
235   thou a merchant?

MERCHANT   Ay, Apemantus.

APEMANTUS   Traffic confound° thee, if the gods will not!   *May business ruin*

MERCHANT   If traffic do it, the gods do it.

APEMANTUS   Traffic's thy god, and thy god confound thee!

Trumpet sounds. Enter a MESSENGER

240   TIMON   What trumpet's that?

MESSENGER   'Tis Alcibiades, and some twenty horse°   *horsemen*
All of companionship.°   *in one group*

TIMON [*to Servants*]   Pray entertain them. Give them guide to us.

[*Exit one or more Servants*]

[*To* JEWELLER] You must needs dine with me.
[*To* POET]   Go not you hence

245   Till I have thanked you. [*To* PAINTER] When dinner's done
Show me this piece. [*To all*] I am joyful of your sights.°   *to see you*

Enter ALCIBIADES *with* [*his horsemen*]

Most welcome, sir!

APEMANTUS [*aside*]   So, so, there.
Aches contract and starve° your supple joints!   *ruin*

250   That there should be small love 'mongst these sweet knaves,
And all this courtesy! The strain of man's bred out°   *degenerated*
Into baboon and monkey.

ALCIBIADES [*to* TIMON]   Sir, you have saved my longing,° and I   *anticipated my desire*
feed
Most hungrily on your sight.

TIMON   Right welcome, sir!

255   Ere we depart, we'll share a bounteous time
In different pleasures. Pray you, let us in.

Exeunt [*all but* APEMANTUS]

Enter two LORDS

FIRST LORD   What time o' day is't, Apemantus?

APEMANTUS   Time to be honest.

---

1. Foresight (so I could avoid it).

	FIRST LORD	That time serves still.°	*always*
	APEMANTUS	The most accursèd thou, that still omitt'st° it.	*do not take advantage of*
260	SECOND LORD	Thou art going to Lord Timon's feast?	
	APEMANTUS	Ay, to see meat fill knaves, and wine heat fools.	
	SECOND LORD	Fare thee well, fare thee well.	
	APEMANTUS	Thou art a fool to bid me farewell twice.	
	SECOND LORD	Why, Apemantus?	

APEMANTUS   Shouldst have kept one to thyself, for I mean to give
265   thee none.

FIRST LORD   Hang thyself!

APEMANTUS   No, I will do nothing at thy bidding. Make thy
    requests to thy friend.

SECOND LORD   Away, unpeaceable dog, or I'll spurn° thee hence.   *kick*   270

APEMANTUS   I will fly, like a dog, the heels o'th' ass.   *Exit*

FIRST LORD   He's opposite° to humanity. Come, shall we in,   *antagonistic*
    And taste Lord Timon's bounty? He outgoes°   *surpasses*
    The very heart° of kindness.   *essence*

275 SECOND LORD   He pours it out. Plutus the god of gold
    Is but his steward; no meed° but he repays   *gift*
    Sevenfold above itself; no gift to him
    But breeds the giver a return exceeding
    All use of quittance.°   *customary interest rates*

FIRST LORD   The noblest mind he carries
280   That ever governed man.

SECOND LORD   Long may he live in fortunes! Shall we in?

FIRST LORD   I'll keep you company.   *Exeunt*

1.2

Hautboys° playing loud music. A great banquet served in   *Oboes*
[FLAVIUS *and Servants attending*]; *and then enter*
TIMON, [ALCIBIADES,] *the* [SENATORS], *the Athenian*
LORDS, [*and*] VENTIDIUS *which* TIMON *redeemed from*
prison. Then comes, dropping° after all, APEMANTUS, *dis-*   *entering casually*
contentedly, like himself°   *in everyday clothes*

VENTIDIUS   Most honoured Timon, it hath pleased the gods to
    remember
    My father's age and call him to long peace.°   *eternal rest*
    He is gone happy, and has left me rich.
    Then, as in grateful virtue I am bound
5   To your free° heart, I do return those talents,   *generous*
    Doubled with thanks and service, from whose help
    I derived liberty.

TIMON   O, by no means,
    Honest Ventidius. You mistake my love.
    I gave it freely ever, and there's none
10   Can truly say he gives if he receives.
    If our betters play at that game,° we must not dare   *pretend generosity*
    To imitate them. Faults that are rich° are fair.   *of rich people*

VENTIDIUS   A noble spirit!
    [*The* LORDS *stand with ceremony*]

TIMON   Nay, my lords,
    Ceremony was but devised at first
15   To set a gloss on¹ faint deeds, hollow welcomes,

1.2 Location: Timon's banqueting room.   1. To give a fine appearance to.

Recanting goodness,[2] sorry ere 'tis shown;
But where there is true friendship, there needs none.°   no ceremony
Pray sit. More welcome are ye to my fortunes
Than my fortunes to me.
      [*They sit*]

20 FIRST LORD   My lord, we always have confessed it.

APEMANTUS   Ho, ho, confessed it? Hanged it, have you not?

TIMON   O, Apemantus! You are welcome.

APEMANTUS   No,
You shall not make me welcome.
I come to have thee° thrust me out of doors.   provoke you to

25 TIMON   Fie, thou'rt a churl.° Ye've got a humour there   rude one
Does not become a man; 'tis much to blame.
They say, my lords, *Ira furor brevis est*,[3]
But yon man is ever angry.
Go, let him have a table by himself,
30 For he does neither affect° company   like
Nor is he fit for't, indeed.

APEMANTUS   Let me stay at thine apperil,° Timon.   risk
I come to observe, I give thee warning on't.

TIMON   I take no heed of thee; thou'rt an Athenian,
35 Therefore welcome. I myself would have no power:[4]
Prithee, let my meat make thee silent.

APEMANTUS   I scorn thy meat. 'Twould choke me, for I should
ne'er flatter thee. O you gods, what a number of men eats
Timon, and he sees 'em not! It grieves me to see so many dip
40 their meat in one man's blood; and all° the madness is, he   the height of
cheers them up,° too.   encourages them
I wonder men dare trust themselves with men.
Methinks they should invite them without knives:[5]
Good for their meat, and safer for their lives.
45 There's much example for't. The fellow that sits next him, now
parts° bread with him, pledges the breath of him in a divided   shares
draught,[6] is the readiest man to kill him. 'T'as been proved. If
I were a huge° man, I should fear to drink at meals,   great
Lest they should spy my windpipe's dangerous notes.[7]
50 Great men should drink with harness° on their throats.   armor

TIMON [*drinking to a* LORD]   My lord, in heart; and let the
health° go round.   shared cup

SECOND LORD   Let it flow° this way, my good lord.   circulate

APEMANTUS   'Flow this way'? A brave° fellow; he keeps his tides[8]   fine (ironic)
55 well. Those healths will make thee and thy state look ill,
Timon.
Here's that which is too weak to be a sinner:
Honest water, which ne'er left man i'th' mire.
This and my food are equals; there's no odds.
60 Feasts are too proud to give thanks to the gods.
          Apemantus' grace
Immortal gods, I crave no pelf.°   property (contemptuous)

---

2. Generosity that demands repayment or that is immediately revoked.
3. Anger is brief insanity (Latin).
4. Wish no power to silence you.
5. Renaissance dinner guests brought their own silver-
ware.

6. *pledges . . . draught:* toasts his health in a shared cup.
7. *my . . . notes:* the indications, when I drink, of where
my windpipe is (so they can cut my throat).
8. He observes his opportunity (joking, with wordplay on
"flow," that the Second Lord is ensuring that he gets
plenty to drink).

I pray for no man but myself.
Grant I may never prove so fond°   *foolish*
To trust man on his oath or bond,
65   Or a harlot for her weeping,
Or a dog that seems a-sleeping,
Or a keeper° with my freedom,   *jailer*
Or my friends if I should need 'em.
Amen. So fall to't.
70   Rich men sin, and I eat root.
          [*He eats*]
Much good dich° thy good heart, Apemantus.   *may it do*

TIMON   Captain Alcibiades, your heart's in the field° now.   *battlefield*

ALCIBIADES   My heart is ever at your service, my lord.

TIMON   You had rather be at a breakfast of enemies° than a din-   *(at a battle)*
75   ner of friends.

ALCIBIADES   So they were bleeding new, my lord; there's no
meat like 'em. I could wish my best friend at such a feast.

APEMANTUS   Would all those flatterers were thine enemies then,
That thou mightst kill 'em and bid me to 'em.

80   FIRST LORD [*to* TIMON]   Might we but have that happiness, my
lord, that you would once use our hearts,⁹ whereby we might
express some part of our zeals,° we should think ourselves for   *love*
ever perfect.°   *happy*

TIMON   O, no doubt, my good friends, but the gods themselves
85   have provided that I shall have much help from you. How had
you been my friends else? Why have you that charitable title°   *loving name*
from thousands, did not you chiefly belong to my heart? I have
told more of you to myself than you can with modesty speak in
your own behalf; and thus far I confirm you.¹ 'O you gods,'
90   think I, 'what need we have any friends if we should ne'er have
need of 'em? They were the most needless creatures living,
should we ne'er have use for 'em, and would most resemble
sweet instruments hung up in cases, that keeps their sounds to
themselves.' Why, I have often wished myself poorer, that I
95   might come nearer to you. We are born to do benefits; and
what better or properer° can we call our own than the riches of   *more suitably*
our friends? O, what a precious comfort 'tis to have so many
like brothers commanding° one another's fortunes! O, joy's   *having at their command*
e'en made away° ere't can be born: mine eyes cannot hold out   *destroyed (by tears)*
100   water, methinks. To forget their° faults, I drink to you.   *(my eyes')*

APEMANTUS   Thou weep'st to make them drink, Timon.

SECOND LORD [*to* TIMON]   Joy had the like° conception in our eyes,   *some kind of*
And at that instant like a babe sprung up.

APEMANTUS   Ho, ho, I laugh to think that babe a bastard.²

105   THIRD LORD [*to* TIMON]   I promise you, my lord, you moved me much.

APEMANTUS   Much!
          [*A*] tucket° sound[*s within*]   *trumpet flourish*

TIMON   What means that trump?
          Enter SERVANT
How now?

SERVANT   Please you, my lord, there are certain ladies most desir-
110   ous of admittance.

---

9. Would make trial of our affection.   2. That is, the guests' tears are illegitimate.
1. In your claim to be my friends.

TIMON   Ladies? What are their wills?

SERVANT   There comes with them a forerunner, my lord, which
    bears that office° to signify their pleasures.°   *function / desires*

TIMON   I pray let them be admitted.

    Enter [one as] CUPID

115   CUPID   Hail to thee, worthy Timon, and to all
    That of his bounties taste! The five best senses
    Acknowledge thee their patron, and come freely
    To gratulate° thy plenteous bosom.° Th'ear,   *greet / generous heart*
    Taste, touch, smell, all, pleased from thy table rise.

120   They° only now come but to feast thine eyes.   *(the masques)*

TIMON   They're welcome all. Let 'em have kind admittance.
    Music make their welcome!   *[Exit* CUPID*]*

FIRST LORD   You see, my lord, how ample you're beloved.

    [Music.] Enter a masque of LADIES *[as] Amazons, with*
    lutes in their hands, dancing and playing

APEMANTUS   Hey-day, what a sweep of vanity comes this way!

125   They dance? They are madwomen.
    Like madness is the glory° of this life   *vainglory*
    As this pomp shows to a little oil and root.³
    We make ourselves fools to disport° ourselves,   *amuse*
    And spend our flatteries to drink° those men   *toast; drink up*

130   Upon whose age we void° it up again   *old age we spit*
    With poisonous spite and envy.
    Who lives that's not depravèd or depraves?
    Who dies that bears not one spurn° to their graves   *insult*
    Of their friends' gift?°   *giving*

135   I should fear those that dance before me now
    Would one day stamp upon me. 'T'as been done.
    Men shut their doors against a setting sun.

    The LORDS *rise from table with much adoring of* TIMON;
    and to show their loves each singles out an Amazon, and
    all dance, men with women, a lofty strain or two to the
    hautboys, and cease

TIMON   You have done our pleasures much grace, fair ladies,
    Set a fair fashion on° our entertainment,   *Made elegant*

140   Which was not half so beautiful and kind.
    You have added worth unto't and lustre,
    And entertained me with mine own device.⁴
    I am to thank you for't.

FIRST LADY   My lord, you take us even at the best.⁵

145   APEMANTUS   Faith; for the worst is filthy, and would not hold
    taking,⁶ I doubt me.

TIMON   Ladies, there is an idle° banquet 'tends you.   *a trifling*
    Please you to dispose° yourselves.   *seat*

ALL LADIES   Most thankfully, my lord.   *Exeunt [*LADIES*]*

150   TIMON   Flavius.

FLAVIUS   My lord.

TIMON   The little casket bring me hither.

FLAVIUS   Yes, my lord. *[Aside]* More jewels yet?
    There is no crossing him in's humour,°   *whim*

---

3. As this feast compares to a meager meal.
4. Plan. Timon may be implying that he himself
arranged the entertainment or merely that it was
designed for him by his admirers.

5. You consider our efforts in the best possible light.
6. Would not be worth noting; would not endure sexual
penetration (because of venereal disease).

155   Else I should tell him well, i'faith I should.
           When all's spent, he'd be crossed[7] then, an° he could.   *if*
           'Tis pity bounty had not eyes behind,[8]
           That man might ne'er be wretched for his mind.[9]   *Exit*

     FIRST LORD   Where be our men?

160   SERVANT   Here, my lord, in readiness.

     SECOND LORD   Our horses.   [*Exit* SERVANT]
              [*Enter* FLAVIUS *with the casket. He gives it to* TIMON *and
              exits*]

     TIMON   O my friends, I have one word to say to you.
           Look you, my good lord,
           I must entreat you honour me so much

165   As to advance° this jewel. Accept and wear it,   *improve (by your worth)*
           Kind my lord.

     FIRST LORD   I am so far already in your gifts.

     ALL LORDS   So are we all.
              [TIMON *gives them jewels.*]
              Enter a SERVANT

     FIRST SERVANT   My lord, there are certain nobles of the senate

170   newly alighted and come to visit you.

     TIMON   They are fairly° welcome.   [*Exit* SERVANT]   *graciously*
              Enter FLAVIUS

     FLAVIUS   I beseech your honour, vouchsafe me a word; it does
     concern you near.

     TIMON   Near? Why then, another time I'll hear thee. I prithee,

175   let's be provided to show them entertainment.

     FLAVIUS   I scarce know how.
              Enter a [SECOND SERVANT]

     SECOND SERVANT   May it please your honour, Lord Lucius
           Out of his free love hath presented to you
           Four milk-white horses trapped° in silver.   *bedecked*

180   TIMON   I shall accept them fairly. Let the presents
           Be worthily entertained.°   [*Exit* SERVANT]   *accepted*
              Enter a [THIRD SERVANT]
               How now, what news?

     THIRD SERVANT   Please you, my lord, that honourable gentleman
           Lord Lucullus entreats your company tomorrow to hunt with
           him, and has sent your honour two brace° of greyhounds.   *pairs*

185   TIMON   I'll hunt with him, and let them be received
           Not without fair reward.   [*Exit* SERVANT]

     FLAVIUS [*aside*]   What will this come to?
           He commands us to provide and give great gifts,
           And all out of an empty coffer;
           Nor will he know his purse, or yield° me this: *allow*

190   To show him what a beggar his heart is,
           Being of no power to make his wishes good.
           His promises fly so beyond his state°   *estate*
           That what he speaks is all in debt, he owes
           For every word. He is so kind that he now

195   Pays interest for't. His land's put to their books.°   *mortgaged*
           Well, would I were gently put out of office
           Before I were forced out.

---

7. He'd want to have his debts canceled.
8. 'Tis a pity generosity is not more careful.

9. *for his mind:* because of his (generous) intentions.

Happier is he that has no friend to feed
Than such that do e'en enemies exceed.[1]
I bleed inwardly for my lord.   *Exit*

200 TIMON [*to the* LORDS]   You do yourselves
Much wrong, you bate° too much of your own merits.   *undervalue*
[*To* SECOND LORD] Here, my lord, a trifle of our love.

SECOND LORD   With more than common thanks I will receive it.

THIRD LORD   O, he's the very soul of bounty!

205 TIMON [*to* FIRST LORD]   And now I remember, my lord, you gave
good words the other day of a bay courser I rode on. 'Tis yours,
because you liked it.

FIRST LORD   O I beseech you pardon me, my lord, in that.[2]

TIMON   You may take my word, my lord, I know no man
210 Can justly praise but what he does affect.°   *desire*
I weigh my friends' affection with mine own.
I'll tell you true, I'll call to° you.   *on*

ALL LORDS   O, none so welcome.

TIMON   I take all and your several visitations
So kind to heart, 'tis not enough to give.
215 Methinks I could deal kingdoms to my friends,
And ne'er be weary. Alcibiades,
Thou art a soldier, therefore seldom rich.
[*Giving a present*] It comes in charity to thee, for all thy living
Is 'mongst the dead, and all the lands thou hast
Lie in a pitched field.

220 ALCIBIADES   Ay, defiled[3] land, my lord.

FIRST LORD   We are so virtuously bound—

TIMON   And so am I to you.

SECOND LORD   So infinitely endeared°—   *obliged*

TIMON   All to you. Lights, more lights!

225 FIRST LORD   The best of happiness, honour, and fortunes
Keep with you, Lord Timon.

TIMON   Ready for his friends.

                    Exeunt [*all but* TIMON *and* APEMANTUS]

APEMANTUS   What a coil's° here,   *commotion is*
Serving of becks° and jutting-out of bums!   *bowing*
230 I doubt whether their legs° be worth the sums   *curtsies*
That are given for 'em. Friendship's full of dregs.
Methinks false hearts should never have sound legs.
Thus honest fools lay out their wealth on curtseys.

TIMON   Now, Apemantus, if thou wert not sullen
235 I would be good to thee.

APEMANTUS   No, I'll nothing; for if I should be bribed too, there
would be none left to rail upon thee, and then thou wouldst
sin the faster. Thou giv'st so long, Timon, I fear me thou wilt
give away thyself in paper° shortly. What needs these feasts,   *promissory notes*
240 pomps, and vainglories?

TIMON   Nay, an you begin to rail on society once, I am sworn
not to give regard° to you.   *pay attention*
Farewell, and come with better music.   *Exit*

---

1. Who ruin themselves faster than enemies could.
2. That is, I wasn't hinting for the horse.
3. Lined with ranks of soldiers; punning on Ecclesias-

ticus 13:1, "He that toucheth pitch, shall be defiled with
it."

APEMANTUS   So.
Thou wilt not hear me now, thou shalt not then.
245 I'll lock thy heaven° from thee. O, that men's ears should be *(my redemptive guidance)*
To counsel deaf, but not to flattery!   *Exit*

2.1
Enter a SENATOR *[with bonds]*

SENATOR   And late five thousand. To Varro and to Isidore
He owes nine thousand, besides my former sum,
Which makes it five-and-twenty. Still in motion
Of raging waste![1] It cannot hold,° it will not.   *last*
5 If I want gold, steal but a beggar's dog
And give it Timon, why, the dog coins gold.
If I would sell my horse and buy twenty more
Better than he, why, give my horse to Timon—
Ask nothing, give it him—it foals me straight,[2]
10 And able horses. No porter[3] at his gate,
But rather one that smiles and still invites
All that pass by. It cannot hold. No reason
Can sound his state in safety.[4] Caphis ho!
Caphis, I say!
          Enter CAPHIS
CAPHIS   Here, sir. What is your pleasure?
15 SENATOR   Get on your cloak and haste you to Lord Timon.
Importune him for my moneys. Be not ceased°   *put off*
With slight denial, nor then silenced when
'Commend me to your master', and the cap
Plays in the right hand,[5] thus; but tell him
20 My uses cry to me, I must serve my turn
Out of mine own,[6] his days and times are past,
And my reliances on his fracted° dates   *broken*
Have smit° my credit. I love and honour him,   *hurt*
But must not break my back to heal his finger.
25 Immediate are my needs, and my relief
Must not be tossed and turned[7] to me in words,
But find supply immediate. Get you gone.
Put on a most importunate aspect,
A visage of demand, for I do fear
30 When every feather sticks in his own wing[8]
Lord Timon will be left a naked gull,°   *an unfledged bird; dupe*
Which flashes now a phoenix. Get you gone.
CAPHIS   I go, sir.
SENATOR *[giving him bonds]*   Take the bonds along with you,
And have the dates in count.°   *reckoned up*
CAPHIS   I will, sir.
SENATOR   Go.
          Exeunt [severally]°   *separately*

2.1 Location: A Senator's house.
1. *Still . . . waste:* Still keeping up unending extrava-gance.
2. It immediately gives birth.
3. Gatekeeper (who restricts entrance). *able horses:* full-grown horses (not "foals," baby horses).
4. *No reason . . . safety:* No rational person can investi-gate his financial situation and believe it safe.
5. *when . . . hand:* that is, with friendly speech and ges-tures.
6. *serve . . . own:* pay for my needs with my own money.
7. Returned (like a tennis ball).
8. When everything is returned to its proper owner.

2.2

Enter [FLAVIUS *the*] *Steward, with many bills in his hand*

FLAVIUS   No care, no stop; so senseless of expense
That he will neither know how to maintain it
Nor cease his flow of riot,° takes no account   *his wastefulness*
How things go from him, nor resumes° no care   *takes*
5   Of what is to continue. Never mind
Was to be so unwise to be so kind.¹
What shall be done? He will not hear till feel.°   *he suffers*
    [*A sound of horns within*]
I must be round° with him, now he comes from hunting. *frank*
Fie, fie, fie, fie!

    Enter CAPHIS [*at one door*] *and* [SERVANTS *of*] *Isidore
    and Varro* [*at another door*]

10   CAPHIS   Good even, Varro. What, you come for money?
VARRO'S SERVANT   Is't not your business too?
CAPHIS   It is; and yours too, Isidore?
ISIDORE'S SERVANT   It is so.
CAPHIS   Would we were all discharged.
VARRO'S SERVANT   I fear it.
CAPHIS   Here comes the lord.

    Enter TIMON *and his train* [*amongst them* ALCIBIADES,
    as from hunting]

TIMON   So soon as dinner's done we'll forth again,
    My Alcibiades.
    [CAPHIS *meets* TIMON]
15   With me? What is your will?
CAPHIS   My lord, here is a note of certain dues.°   *debts*
TIMON   Dues? Whence are you?
CAPHIS   Of Athens here, my lord.
TIMON   Go to my steward.
20   CAPHIS   Please it your lordship, he hath put me off,
    To the succession of new days, this month.°   *every day for a month*
    My master is awaked° by great occasion°   *driven / need*
    To call upon his own,° and humbly prays you   *own money*
    That with your other noble parts you'll suit²
    In giving him his right.
25   TIMON   Mine honest friend,
    I prithee but repair° to me next morning.   *come back*
CAPHIS   Nay, good my lord.
TIMON   Contain thyself, good friend.
VARRO'S SERVANT   One Varro's servant, my good lord.
ISIDORE'S SERVANT [*to* TIMON]   From Isidore. He humbly prays
    your speedy payment.
30   CAPHIS [*to* TIMON]   If you did know, my lord, my master's wants—
VARRO'S SERVANT [*to* TIMON]   'Twas due on forfeiture,³ my lord,
    six weeks and past.
ISIDORE'S SERVANT [*to* TIMON]   Your steward puts me off, my
    lord, and I
    Am sent expressly to your lordship.

2.2 Location: Before Timon's house.
1. *Never . . . kind*: Never was anyone so idiotically generous.
2. That you'll act in accordance with your noble qualities.
3. On penalty of forfeiting the security.

TIMON   Give me breath.—
   I do beseech you, good my lords, keep on.°   *go ahead*
   I'll wait upon you instantly.
         [*Exeunt* ALCIBIADES *and Timon's train*]
35   [*To* FLAVIUS]   Come hither. Pray you,
   How goes the world, that I am thus encountered
   With clamorous demands of broken bonds
   And the detention of° long-since-due debts,   *failure to pay*
   Against my honour?
FLAVIUS [*to* SERVANTS]   Please you, gentlemen,
40   The time is unagreeable to this business;
   Your importunacy cease till after dinner,
   That I may make his lordship understand
   Wherefore you are not paid.
TIMON [*to* SERVANTS]   Do so, my friends.
   [*To* FLAVIUS] See them well entertained.   *Exit*
FLAVIUS   Pray draw near. *Exit*
       Enter APEMANTUS *and* FOOL
45 CAPHIS   Stay, stay, here comes the fool with Apemantus.
   Let's ha' some sport with 'em.
VARRO'S SERVANT   Hang him, he'll abuse us.
ISIDORE'S SERVANT   A plague upon him, dog!
VARRO'S SERVANT   How dost, fool?
50 APEMANTUS   Dost dialogue with thy shadow?[4]
VARRO'S SERVANT   I speak not to thee.
APEMANTUS   No, 'tis to thyself. [*To* FOOL] Come away.
ISIDORE'S SERVANT [*to* VARRO'S SERVANT]   There's the fool[5] hangs
   on your back already.
55 APEMANTUS   No, thou stand'st single:° thou'rt not on him yet.   *alone (in being a fool)*
CAPHIS [*to* ISIDORE'S SERVANT]   Where's the fool now?
APEMANTUS   He last asked the question. Poor rogues' and usu-
   rers' men, bawds between gold and want.[6]
ALL SERVANTS   What are we, Apemantus?
60 APEMANTUS   Asses.
ALL SERVANTS   Why?
APEMANTUS   That you ask me what you are, and do not know
   yourselves. Speak to 'em, fool.
FOOL   How do you, gentlemen?
65 ALL SERVANTS   Gramercies,° good fool. How does your mistress?   *Many thanks*
FOOL   She's e'en° setting on water to scald such chickens[7] as you   *just now*
   are. Would we could see you at Corinth.[8]
APEMANTUS   Good; gramercy.
       Enter PAGE [*with two letters*]
FOOL   Look you, here comes my mistress' page.
70 PAGE   Why, how now, captain? What do you in this wise company? How dost thou, Apemantus?
APEMANTUS   Would I had a rod[9] in my mouth, that I might
   answer thee profitably.

---

4. With your reflection (implying that Varro's servant is also a fool).
5. The name "fool." In Renaissance England, wrong-doers were punished by being made to wear signs declaring their offenses.
6. *bawds . . . want:* go-betweens making deals between moneylenders and those who need loans.
7. In order to remove the feathers (a "plucked bird" was a hoodwinked fool; compare 2.1.31); also, syphilitics were "sweated" in tubs of very hot water.
8. Greek city famous for prostitution.
9. From Proverbs 26:3–4: "Unto the horse belongeth a whip, to the ass a bridle, and a rod to the fool's back. Answer not a fool according to his foolishness, lest thou also be like him."

PAGE Prithee, Apemantus, read me the superscription° of these   *address*
75   letters. I know not which is which.

APEMANTUS Canst not read?

PAGE No.

APEMANTUS There will little learning die then that day thou art
     hanged. This is to Lord Timon, this to Alcibiades. Go, thou
80   wast born a bastard, and thou'lt die a bawd.

PAGE Thou wast whelped a dog, and thou shalt famish° a dog's   *die*
     death. Answer not; I am gone.   *Exit*

APEMANTUS E'en so thou outrunn'st grace.[1] Fool, I will go with
     you to Lord Timon's.

85 FOOL Will you leave me there?

APEMANTUS If Timon stay at home.[2] [*To* SERVANTS] You three
     serve three usurers?

ALL SERVANTS Ay. Would they served us.°   *treated us well*

APEMANTUS So would I: as good a trick as ever hangman served
90   thief.

FOOL Are you three usurers' men?

ALL SERVANTS Ay, fool.

FOOL I think no usurer but has a fool to his servant. My mistress
     is one,[3] and I am her fool. When men come to borrow of your
95   masters they approach sadly and go away merry, but they enter
     my mistress's house merrily and go away sadly.[4] The reason of
     this?

VARRO'S SERVANT I could render one.

APEMANTUS Do it then, that we may account thee a whore-
100 master and a knave, which notwithstanding thou shalt be no
     less esteemed.

VARRO'S SERVANT What is a whoremaster, fool?

FOOL A fool in good clothes, and something like thee. 'Tis a
     spirit; sometime 't appears like a lord, sometime like a lawyer,
105 sometime like a philosopher with two stones[5] more than's° arti- *than his*
     ficial one. He is very often like a knight; and generally in all
     shapes that man goes up and down in from fourscore to thir-
     teen, this spirit walks in.

VARRO'S SERVANT Thou art not altogether a fool.

110 FOOL Nor thou altogether a wise man. As much foolery as I
     have, so much wit thou lack'st.

APEMANTUS That answer might have become° Apemantus.   *suited*
     Enter TIMON *and* [FLAVIUS *the*] Steward

ALL SERVANTS Aside, aside, here comes Lord Timon.

APEMANTUS Come with me, fool, come.

115 FOOL I do not always follow lover, elder brother, and woman:[6]
     sometime the philosopher   [*Exeunt* APEMANTUS *and* FOOL]

FLAVIUS [*to* SERVANTS] Pray you, walk near. I'll speak with you
     anon.   *Exeunt* [SERVANTS]

TIMON You make me marvel wherefore ere this time
120 Had you not fully laid my state before me,[7]
     That I might so have rated° my expense   *regulated*
     As I had leave of means.°   *As means permitted*

---

1. You run away from profitable instruction.
2. There will be a fool at Timon's house as long as he is
at home.
3. She is a "usurer" in the sense that she lends her body
for financial gain; the connection between usury and
prostitution was traditional.

4. According to Aristotle, all creatures are sad after sexual intercourse.
5. Testicles. In alchemy, the "philosopher's stone" was
thought to turn base metals into gold.
6. All figures associated with folly.
7. Described my financial status.

FLAVIUS   You would not hear me.
  At many leisures I proposed—
TIMON   Go to.°   *(impatient exclamation)*
  Perchance some single vantages° you took,   *isolated opportunities*
125   When my indisposition° put you back,   *disinclination*
  And that unaptness made your minister°   *allowed you*
  Thus to excuse yourself.
FLAVIUS   O my good lord,
  At many times I brought in my accounts,
  Laid them before you; you would throw them off
130   And say you summed them in mine honesty.[8]
  When for some trifling present you have bid me
  Return so much,° I have shook my head and wept,   *a large sum*
  Yea, 'gainst th'authority of manners° prayed you   *with rude bluntness*
  To hold your hand more close. I did endure
135   Not seldom nor no slight checks° when I have   *rebukes*
  Prompted you in° the ebb of your estate   *Urged you to note*
  And your great flow of debts. My lovèd lord—
  Though you hear now too late, yet now's a time°—   *better late than never*
  The greatest of your having[9] lacks a half
  To pay your present debts.
140   TIMON   Let all my land be sold.
FLAVIUS   'Tis all engaged,° some forfeited and gone,   *mortgaged*
  And what remains will hardly stop the mouth
  Of present dues.° The future comes apace.   *debts*
  What shall defend the interim, and at length°   *in the long term*
145   How goes our reck'ning?
TIMON   To Lacedaemon° did my land extend.   *Sparta*
FLAVIUS   O my good lord, the world is but a word.
  Were it all yours to give it in a breath,
  How quickly were it gone.
TIMON   You tell me true.
150   FLAVIUS   If you suspect my husbandry° or falsehood,   *household management*
  Call me before th'exactest auditors
  And set me on the proof. So the gods bless me,
  When all our offices° have been oppressed   *kitchens and workrooms*
  With riotous feeders, when our vaults have wept
155   With drunken spilth° of wine, when every room   *spilling*
  Hath blazed with lights and brayed with minstrelsy,
  I have retired me to a wasteful cock,[1]
  And set mine eyes at flow.
TIMON   Prithee, no more.
FLAVIUS   'Heavens,' have I said, 'the bounty of this lord!
160   How many prodigal bits° have slaves and peasants   *extravagant morsels*
  This night englutted! Who is not Timon's?°   *devoted to Timon*
  What heart, head, sword, force, means, but is Lord Timon's?
  Great Timon, noble, worthy, royal Timon!
  Ah, when the means are gone that buy this praise,
165   The breath is gone whereof this praise is made.
  Feast won, fast° lost; one cloud of winter show'rs,   *quickly; while fasting*
  These flies are couched.'°   *lying unseen*
TIMON   Come, sermon me no further.

8. You gauged their accuracy by my honesty.
9. The most generous estimate of your wealth.

1. I have sat down beside a wine spout, left wastefully flowing.

No villainous° bounty yet hath passed my heart.   *shameful*
Unwisely, not ignobly, have I given.

170   Why dost thou weep? Canst thou the conscience° lack   *conviction*
To think I shall lack friends? Secure thy heart.
If I would broach° the vessels of my love   *tap (like a wine barrel)*
And try the argument° of hearts by borrowing,   *test the contents*
Men and men's fortunes could I frankly° use   *as freely*
As I can bid thee speak.

175   FLAVIUS   Assurance bless your thoughts!²
TIMON   And in some sort° these wants of mine are crowned°   *respect / exalted*
That I account them blessings, for by these
Shall I try friends. You shall perceive how you
Mistake my fortunes. I am wealthy in my friends.—

180   Within there, Flaminius, Servilius!
Enter [FLAMINIUS, SERVILIUS, *and a* THIRD] SERVANT
ALL SERVANTS   My lord, my lord.
TIMON   I will dispatch you severally,°   *separately*
[*To* SERVILIUS] You to Lord Lucius,
[*To* FLAMINIUS]   to Lord Lucullus you—
I hunted with his honour today—
[*To* THIRD SERVANT] You to Sempronius. Commend me to
     their loves,

185   And I am proud, say, that my occasions° have   *needs*
Found time° to use 'em toward a supply of money.   *occasion*
Let the request be fifty talents.°   *(a huge sum)*
FLAMINIUS   As you have said, my lord.   [*Exeunt* SERVANTS]
FLAVIUS   Lord Lucius and Lucullus? Hmh!

190   TIMON   Go you, sir, to the senators,
Of whom, even to the state's best health,³ I have
Deserved this hearing. Bid 'em send o'th' instant
A thousand talents to me.
FLAVIUS   I have been bold,
For that I knew it the most general° way,   *usual*

195   To them, to use your signet⁴ and your name;
But they do shake their heads, and I am here
No richer in return.
TIMON   Is't true? Can't be?
FLAVIUS   They answer in a joint and corporate voice
That now they are at fall,° want° treasure, cannot   *low ebb / lack*

200   Do what they would, are sorry, you are honourable,
But yet they could have wished—they know not—
Something hath been amiss—a noble nature
May catch a wrench°—would all were well—'tis pity;   *suffer a misfortune*
And so, intending° other serious matters,   *pretending; attending to*

205   After distasteful looks and these hard fractions,°   *phrases*
With certain half-caps° and cold moving nods   *reluctant salutations*
They froze me into silence.
TIMON   You gods reward them!
Prithee, man, look cheerly.° These old fellows   *cheerful*
Have their ingratitude in them hereditary.

210   Their blood is caked, 'tis cold, it seldom flows.
'Tis lack of kindly⁵ warmth they are not kind;

---

2. May your hopes be well founded.
3. Greatest welfare (see 4.3.92–95).
4. Signet ring (token of authorization).
5. Natural (punning on "caring").

And nature as it grows again toward earth°   the grave
Is fashioned for the journey dull and heavy.
Go to Ventidius. Prithee, be not sad.
215   Thou art true and honest—ingenuously° I speak—   candidly
No blame belongs to thee. Ventidius lately
Buried his father, by whose death he's stepped
Into a great estate. When he was poor,
Imprisoned, and in scarcity of friends,
220   I cleared him with five talents. Greet him from me.
Bid him suppose some good° necessity   urgent
Touches his friend, which craves to be remembered
With° those five talents. That had, give't these fellows   By return of
To whom 'tis instant due. Ne'er speak or think
225   That Timon's fortunes 'mong his friends can sink.
FLAVIUS   I would I could not think it. That thought is bounty's foe:
Being free° itself, it thinks all others so.   *Exeunt [severally]*   generous

<h2 style="text-align:center">3.1</h2>

[*Enter*] FLAMINIUS, [*with a box under his cloak,*] *waiting
to speak with* [LUCULLUS]. *From his master, enters a* SER-
VANT *to him*

LUCULLUS' SERVANT   I have told my lord of you. He is coming
down to you.
FLAMINIUS   I thank you, sir.
          Enter LUCULLUS
LUCULLUS' SERVANT   Here's my lord.
5   LUCULLUS [*aside*]   One of Lord Timon's men? A gift, I warrant.
Why, this hits right; I dreamt of a silver basin and ewer°   pitcher
tonight.—Flaminius, honest Flaminius, you are very respec-
tively° welcome, sir. [*To his* SERVANT] Fill me some wine.   respectfully
                    [*Exit* SERVANT]
And how does that honourable, complete, free-hearted gentle-
10   man of Athens, thy very bountiful good lord and master?
FLAMINIUS   His health is well, sir.
LUCULLUS   I am right glad that his health is well, sir. And what
hast thou there under thy cloak, pretty Flaminius?
FLAMINIUS   Faith, nothing but an empty box, sir, which in my
15   lord's behalf I come to entreat your honour to supply, who,
having great and instant° occasion to use fifty talents, hath sent   urgent
to your lordship to furnish him, nothing doubting your present°   immediate
assistance therein.
LUCULLUS   La, la, la, la, 'nothing doubting' says he? Alas, good
20   lord! A noble gentleman 'tis, if he would not keep so good a
house.° Many a time and often I ha' dined with him and told   such lavish hospitality
him on't, and come again to supper to him of purpose to have
him¹ spend less; and yet he would embrace no counsel, take
no warning by my coming. Every man has his fault, and hon-
25   esty° is his. I ha' told him on't, but I could ne'er get him from't.   generosity
          Enter SERVANT, *with wine*
SERVANT   Please your lordship, here is the wine.
LUCULLUS   Flaminius, I have noted thee always wise.
    [*Drinking*]   Here's to thee!
FLAMINIUS   Your lordship speaks your pleasure.°   It pleases you to say so

---

3.1 Location: Lucullus's house.   1. *of . . . him*: in order to persuade him to.

30 LUCULLUS   I have observed thee always for a towardly° prompt   *promising*
spirit, give thee thy due, and one that knows what belongs to
reason;° and canst use the time well if the time use thee well.[2]   *is reasonable*
[*Drinking*] Good parts in thee![3]
[*To his* SERVANT] Get you gone, sirrah.   [*Exit* SERVANT]

35 Draw nearer, honest Flaminius. Thy lord's a bountiful gentleman; but thou art wise, and thou know'st well enough,
although thou com'st to me, that this is no time to lend money,
especially upon bare° friendship without security. [*Giving*   *mere*
coins] Here's three solidares° for thee. Good boy, wink at me,[4]   *shillings*

40 and say thou saw'st me not. Fare thee well.

FLAMINIUS   Is't possible the world should so much differ,°   *alter*
And we alive that lived?
          [*He throws the coins at* LUCULLUS]
                    Fly, damnèd baseness,
To him that worships thee.

LUCULLUS   Ha! Now I see thou art a fool, and fit for thy master.
                                                                    Exit

45 FLAMINIUS   May these add to the number that may scald thee.°   *(in hell)*
Let molten coin be thy damnation,
Thou disease of a friend, and not himself.°   *not a true friend*
Has friendship such a faint and milky heart
It turns° in less than two nights? O you gods,   *curdles*

50 I feel my master's passion!° This slave   *suffering*
Unto this hour has my lord's meat in him.
Why should it thrive and turn to nutriment,
When he is turned to poison?
O, may diseases only work upon't;

55 And when he's sick to death, let not that part of nature
Which my lord paid for be of any power
To expel sickness, but prolong his hour.°   *Exit*   *(of suffering)*

3.2
Enter LUCIUS, *with three* STRANGERS

LUCIUS   Who, the Lord Timon? He is my very good friend, and
an honourable gentleman.

FIRST STRANGER   We know him for no less, though we are but
strangers to him. But I can tell you one thing, my lord, and

5 which I hear from common rumours: now Lord Timon's happy
hours are done and past, and his estate shrinks from him.

LUCIUS   Fie, no, do not believe it. He cannot want for money.

SECOND STRANGER   But believe you this, my lord, that not long
ago one of his men was with the Lord Lucullus to borrow so

10 many talents—nay, urged extremely for't, and showed what
necessity belonged to't, and yet was denied.

LUCIUS   How?

SECOND STRANGER   I tell you, denied, my lord.

LUCIUS   What a strange case was that! Now before the gods, I am

15 ashamed on't. Denied that honourable man? There was very
little honour showed in't. For my own part, I must needs confess I have received some small kindnesses from him, as money,
plate, jewels, and suchlike trifles—nothing comparing to his;

---

2. *canst . . . thee well*: know how to use an opportunity.   4. Close your eyes to me.
3. To your good qualities (a toast).   3.2 Location: A public place.

yet had he not mistook him[1] and sent to me, I should ne'er
20 have denied his occasion so many talents.

Enter SERVILIUS

SERVILIUS [*aside*] See, by good hap yonder's my lord. I have
sweat° to see his honour. [*To* LUCIUS] My honoured lord! *hurried*

LUCIUS Servilius! You are kindly met, sir. Fare thee well. Commend me to thy honourable virtuous lord, my very exquisite° *extraordinary*
25 friend.

SERVILIUS May it please your honour, my lord hath sent—

LUCIUS Ha! What has he sent? I am so much endeared° to that *obliged*
lord, he's ever sending. How shall I thank him, think'st thou?
And what has he sent now?

30 SERVILIUS He's only sent his present occasion now, my lord,
requesting your lordship to supply his instant use with so many
talents.

LUCIUS I know his lordship is but merry with me.
He cannot want fifty-five hundred[2] talents.

35 SERVILIUS But in the mean time he wants less, my lord.
If his occasion were not virtuous
I should not urge it half so faithfully.

LUCIUS Dost thou speak seriously, Servilius?

SERVILIUS Upon my soul, 'tis true, sir.

40 LUCIUS What a wicked beast was I to disfurnish myself against
such a good time[3] when I might ha' shown myself honourable!
How unluckily it happened that I should purchase the day
before a little part,° and undo a great deal of honour! Servilius, *small investment*
now before the gods I am not able to do, the more beast I, I
45 say. I was sending to use° Lord Timon myself—these gentle- *make use of*
men can witness—but I would not for the wealth of Athens I
had done't now. Commend me bountifully to his good lord-
ship; and I hope his honour will conceive the fairest° of me *think the best*
because I have no power to be kind. And tell him this from me:
50 I count it one of my greatest afflictions, say, that I cannot plea-
sure° such an honourable gentleman. Good Servilius, will you *gratify*
befriend me so far as to use mine own words to him?

SERVILIUS Yes, sir, I shall.

LUCIUS I'll look you out° a good turn, Servilius. *Exit* SERVILIUS *seek to do you*
55 True as you said: Timon is shrunk indeed;
And he that's once denied will hardly speed.° *Exit* *prosper*

FIRST STRANGER Do you observe this, Hostilius?

SECOND STRANGER Ay, too well.

FIRST STRANGER Why, this is the world's soul,° and just of the *essence*
same piece° *(of cloth)*
Is every flatterer's spirit. Who can call him his friend
60 That dips in the same dish?[4] For, in my knowing,
Timon has been this lord's father° *patron*
And kept his° credit with his purse, *sustained (Lucius's)*
Supported his estate; nay, Timon's money
Has paid his men their wages. He ne'er drinks,
65 But Timon's silver treads upon his lip;
And yet—O see the monstrousness of man

1. Not overestimated Lucullus's generosity.
2. This number possibly retains Shakespeare's revision
from "five hundred" to "fifty" or vice versa.
3. *disfurnish . . . time:* be unprepared for such a fine

occasion.
4. Alluding to Judas's betrayal of Christ after the Last
Supper.

When he looks out° in an ungrateful shape!—   *shows himself*
He does deny him, in respect of his,[5]
What charitable men afford to beggars.
THIRD STRANGER   Religion groans at it.
70 FIRST STRANGER   For mine own part,
I never tasted° Timon in my life,   *had experience of*
Nor came any of his bounties over me
To mark me for his friend; yet I protest,
For his right noble mind, illustrious virtue,
75 And honourable carriage,°   *conduct*
Had his necessity made use of me
I would have put my wealth into donation°   *given my wealth*
And the best half should have returned to him,
So much I love his heart. But I perceive
80 Men must learn now with pity to dispense,
For policy° sits above conscience.   *Exeunt*   *calculation*

3.3

Enter [Timon's] THIRD SERVANT, with SEMPRONIUS,
another of Timon's friends

SEMPRONIUS   Must he needs trouble me in't? Hmh! 'Bove all others?
He might have tried Lord Lucius or Lucullus;
And now Ventidius is wealthy too,
Whom he redeemed from prison. All these
Owes their estates unto him.
5 SERVANT   My lord,
They have all been touched° and found base metal,   *tested for purity*
For they have all denied him.
SEMPRONIUS   How, have they denied him?
Has Ventidius and Lucullus denied him,
And does he send to me? Three? Hmh!
10 It shows but little love or judgement in him.
Must I be his last refuge? His friends, like physicians,
Thrive, give him over;[1] must I take th' cure upon me?
He's much disgraced me in't. I'm angry at him,
That might have known my place.[2] I see no sense for't
15 But his occasions might have wooed me first,
For, in my conscience,° I was the first man   *on my word*
That e'er receivèd gift from him.
And does he think so backwardly of me now
That I'll requite it last? No.
20 So it may prove an argument° of laughter   *a subject*
To th' rest, and I 'mongst lords be thought a fool.
I'd rather than the worth of thrice the sum
He'd sent to me first, but for my mind's sake.[3]
I'd such a courage to do him good. But now return,
25 And with their faint reply this answer join:
Who bates° mine honour shall not know my coin.   *Exit*   *undervalues*
SERVANT   Excellent. Your lordship's a goodly villain. The devil
knew not what he did when he made man politic°— he   *calculating*
crossed[4] himself by't, and I cannot think but in the end the

---

5. In proportion to what he owns.
3.3 Location: Sempronius's house.
1. Thrive, while abandoning him to death.
2. That is, his place in Timon's list of friends.

3. If only on account of my disposition to him.
4. Thwarted (by making men his equal); canceled from
the list of debtors.

30 villainies of man will set him clear.⁵ How fairly° this lord strives   *fully; speciously*
to appear foul! Takes virtuous copies° to be wicked, like those⁶   *precepts*
that under hot ardent zeal would set whole realms on fire; of
such a nature is his politic love.
This was my lord's best hope. Now all are fled
35 Save only the gods. Now his friends are dead.
Doors that were ne'er acquainted with their wards°   *locks*
Many a bounteous year must be employed
Now to guard sure° their master;   *safely*
And this is all a liberal° course allows: *generous*
40 Who cannot keep his wealth must keep his house.⁷   *Exit*

3.4

Enter Varro's [two SERVANTS], *meeting others, all [* SER-
VANTS *of]* Timon's *creditors, to wait for his coming out.*
*Then enter [*SERVANTS *of]* Lucius, [Titus,] *and Horten-*
sius

VARRO'S FIRST SERVANT   Well met; good morrow, Titus and
    Hortensius.
TITUS' SERVANT   The like to you, kind Varro.
HORTENSIUS' SERVANT   Lucius, what, do we meet together?
LUCIUS' SERVANT   Ay, and I think one business does command
    us all,
For mine is money.
5 TITUS' SERVANT   So is theirs and ours.
            Enter [a SERVANT *of]* Philotus
LUCIUS' SERVANT   And Sir Philotus too!
PHILOTUS' SERVANT   Good day at once.
LUCIUS' SERVANT   Welcome, good brother. What do you think
    the hour?
PHILOTUS' SERVANT   Labouring for° nine.   *Approaching*
LUCIUS' SERVANT   So much?
10 PHILOTUS' SERVANT   Is not my lord seen yet?
LUCIUS' SERVANT   Not yet.
PHILOTUS' SERVANT   I wonder on't; he was wont to shine° at   *used to rise*
    seven.
LUCIUS' SERVANT   Ay, but the days are waxed shorter with him.
    You must consider that a prodigal course
15 Is like the sun's,¹
    But not, like his,° recoverable. I fear   *(the sun's)*
    'Tis deepest winter in Lord Timon's purse; that is,
    One may reach deep enough, and yet find little.
PHILOTUS' SERVANT   I am of° your fear for that.   *I share*
20 TITUS' SERVANT   I'll show you how t'observe a strange event.
    Your lord sends now for money?
HORTENSIUS' SERVANT   Most true, he does.
TITUS' SERVANT   And he wears jewels now of Timon's gift,
    For° which I wait for money.   *For the purchase of*
HORTENSIUS' SERVANT   It is against my heart.°   *desire*
25 LUCIUS' SERVANT   Mark how strange it shows.
    Timon in this should pay more than he owes,

---

5. Will make him look innocent; will free him from debt.
6. Religious fanatics; perhaps alludes to the Catholic
Gunpowder Plot to blow up King and Parliament.

7. Must stay indoors (for fear of arrest).
3.4 Location: Timon's house.
1. That is, waning after the summer solstice.

And e'en° as if your lord should wear rich jewels   *just*
And send for money for 'em.[2]

HORTENSIUS' SERVANT   I'm weary of this charge,° the gods can   *task*
    witness.

30   I know my lord hath spent of Timon's wealth,
    And now ingratitude makes it worse than stealth.°   *stealing*

VARRO'S FIRST SERVANT
    Yes; mine's three thousand crowns. What's yours?

LUCIUS' SERVANT   Five thousand, mine.

VARRO'S FIRST SERVANT   'Tis much° deep, and it should seem by th' sum   *very*
    Your master's confidence was above mine,°   *(my master's)*
    Else surely his° had equalled.   *(my master's loan)*

        Enter FLAMINIUS

35 TITUS' SERVANT   One of Lord Timon's men.

LUCIUS' SERVANT   Flaminius! Sir, a word. Pray, is my lord
    Ready to come forth?

FLAMINIUS   No, indeed he is not.

TITUS' SERVANT   We attend his lordship.
    Pray signify so much.

40 FLAMINIUS   I need not tell
    Him that; he knows you are too diligent.

        Enter [FLAVIUS *the*] *Steward, muffled in a cloak*

LUCIUS' SERVANT   Ha, is not that his steward muffled so?
    He goes away in a cloud.° Call him, call him.   *concealed; in trouble*

TITUS' SERVANT [*to* FLAVIUS]   Do you hear, sir?

45 VARRO'S SECOND SERVANT [*to* FLAVIUS]   By your leave, sir.

FLAVIUS   What do ye ask of me, my friend?

TITUS' SERVANT   We wait for certain money here, sir.

FLAVIUS   Ay,
    If money were as certain as your waiting,
    'Twere sure enough.

50   Why then preferred° you not your sums and bills   *brought forward*
    When your false masters ate of my lord's meat?
    Then they could smile and fawn upon his debts,
    And take down th'int'rest into their glutt'nous maws.
    You do yourselves but wrong to stir me up.

55   Let me pass quietly.
    Believe't, my lord and I have made an end.°   *finished with each other*
    I have no more to reckon, he to spend.

LUCIUS' SERVANT   Ay, but this answer will not serve.

FLAVIUS   If 'twill not serve[3] 'tis not so base as you,
60   For you serve knaves.   *Exit*

VARRO'S FIRST SERVANT   How? What does his cashiered° worship   *dismissed*
    mutter?

VARRO'S SECOND SERVANT   No matter what; he's poor, and that's
    revenge enough. Who can speak broader[4] than he that has no
65   house to put his head in? Such may rail against great buildings.

        Enter SERVILIUS

TITUS' SERVANT   O, here's Servilius. Now we shall know some
    answer.

SERVILIUS   If I might beseech you, gentlemen, to repair° some   *return*

---

2. And demand payment from Timon for supplying them.   4. More freely; more out of doors.
3. Suffice (but in line 60, "wait on").

70 other hour, I should derive° much from't; for, take't of my soul,   *gain*
my lord leans wondrously to discontent. His comfortable° tem-   *cheerful*
per has forsook him. He's much out of health, and keeps his
chamber.

LUCIUS' SERVANT   Many do keep their chambers are not sick,⁵
And if it be so far beyond his health
75 Methinks he should the sooner pay his debts
And make a clear way to the gods.

SERVILIUS   Good gods!

TITUS' SERVANT   We cannot take this for an answer, sir.

FLAMINIUS [*within*]   Servilius, help! My lord, my lord!

Enter TIMON *in a rage*

TIMON   What, are my doors opposed against my passage?
80 Have I been ever free,° and must my house   *at liberty; generous*
Be my retentive° enemy, my jail?   *confining; niggardly*
The place which I have feasted, does it now,
Like all mankind, show me an iron heart?

LUCIUS' SERVANT   Put in° now, Titus.   *Make your claim*

TITUS' SERVANT   My lord, here is my bill.

LUCIUS' SERVANT   Here's mine.

85 HORTENSIUS' SERVANT   And mine, my lord.

VARRO'S FIRST *and* SECOND SERVANTS   And ours, my lord.

PHILOTUS' SERVANT   All our bills.

TIMON   Knock me down with 'em, cleave me to the girdle.⁶

LUCIUS' SERVANT   Alas, my lord.

90 TIMON   Cut my heart in° sums.   *into*

TITUS' SERVANT   Mine fifty talents.

TIMON   Tell° out my blood.   *Count*

LUCIUS' SERVANT   Five thousand crowns, my lord.

TIMON   Five thousand drops pays that. What yours? And yours?

VARRO'S FIRST SERVANT   My lord—

95 VARRO'S SECOND SERVANT   My lord—

TIMON   Tear me, take me, and the gods fall upon you.   *Exit*

HORTENSIUS' SERVANT   Faith, I perceive our masters may throw
their caps at° their money. These debts may well be called des-   *cease pursuing*
perate° ones, for a madman owes 'em.   *Exeunt*   *hopeless; insane*

3.5

Enter TIMON [*and* FLAVIUS]

TIMON   They have e'en put¹ my breath from me, the slaves.
Creditors? Devils!

FLAVIUS   My dear lord—

TIMON   What if it should be so?²

5 FLAVIUS   My lord—

TIMON   I'll have it so. My steward!

FLAVIUS   Here, my lord.

TIMON   So fitly?° Go bid all my friends again: *conveniently*
Lucius, Lucullus, and Sempronius—all luxors,° all.   *lechers*
I'll once more feast the rascals.

FLAVIUS   O my lord,
10 You only speak from your distracted soul.

---

5. That is, they are avoiding arrest for debt.
6. Timon puns on "bills" (line 87) as weapons (halberds).
3.5 Location: Scene continues.

1. Have taken (referring to Timon's breathlessness and to the proverb "Air is free").
2. Timon is referring to a plan he has just thought of.

There is not so much left to furnish out
A moderate table.

TIMON   Be it not in thy care.°   *your responsibility*
Go, I charge thee, invite them all. Let in the tide
Of knaves once more. My cook and I'll provide.

Exeunt [*severally*]

3.6

Enter three SENATORS *at one door*

FIRST SENATOR   My lords, you have my voice to't.° The fault's°   *vote for it / crime is*
      bloody.
      'Tis necessary he should die.
      Nothing emboldens sin so much as mercy.

SECOND SENATOR   Most true; the law shall bruise 'im.

[*Enter*] ALCIBIADES [*at another door*], *with attendants*

5 ALCIBIADES   Honour, health, and compassion to the senate!

FIRST SENATOR   Now, captain.

ALCIBIADES   I am an humble suitor to your virtues;
      For pity is the virtue° of the law,   *essence*
      And none but tyrants use it cruelly.
10   It pleases time and fortune to lie heavy
      Upon a friend of mine, who in hot blood
      Hath stepped into° the law, which is past depth   *(as into quicksand)*
      To those that without heed do plunge into't.
      He is a man, setting his feat° aside,   *deed*
15   Of comely virtues;
      Nor did he soil the fact with cowardice—
      An honour in him which buys out his fault°—   *redeems his crime*
      But with a noble fury and fair spirit,
      Seeing his reputation touched to death,°   *fatally besmirched*
20   He did oppose his foe;
      And with such sober and unnoted[1] passion
      He did behave° his anger, ere 'twas spent,   *control*
      As if he had but proved an argument.

FIRST SENATOR   You undergo° too strict a paradox,   *undertake*
25   Striving to make an ugly deed look fair.
      Your words have took such pains as if they laboured
      To bring manslaughter into form,[2] and set quarrelling
      Upon the head° of valour—which indeed   *In the category of*
      Is valour misbegot, and came into the world
30   When sects and factions were newly born.
      He's truly valiant that can wisely suffer
      The worst that man can breathe,° and make his wrongs his   *utter*
            outsides°   *merely external things*
      To wear them like his raiment carelessly,
      And ne'er prefer° his injuries to his heart   *promote*
35   To bring it into danger.
      If wrongs be evils and enforce us kill,
      What folly 'tis to hazard life for ill!

ALCIBIADES   My lord—

FIRST SENATOR   You cannot make gross sins look clear.
      To revenge is no valour, but to bear.°   *endure (is valor)*

3.6 Location: The Senate house.   2. To make manslaughter legal.
1. Unnoticed (because moderate).

40 ALCIBIADES   My lords, then, under favour,° pardon me   *by your leave*
       If I speak like a captain.
       Why do fond° men expose themselves to battle,   *foolish*
       And not endure all threats, sleep upon't,
       And let the foes quietly cut their throats
45   Without repugnancy?° If there be   *resistance*
       Such valour in the bearing,° what make we   *enduring*
       Abroad?[3] Why then, women are more valiant
       That stay at home if bearing carry it,°   *wins the day*
       And the ass more captain than the lion, the felon
50   Loaden with irons° wiser than the judge,   *shackles*
       If wisdom be in suffering. O my lords,
       As you are great, be pitifully good.°   *good in showing pity*
       Who cannot condemn rashness in cold blood?
       To kill, I grant, is sin's extremest gust,°   *outburst*
55   But in defence, by mercy,[4] 'tis most just.
       To be in anger is impiety,
       But who is man that is not angry?
       Weigh but the crime with this.
  SECOND SENATOR   You breathe in vain.
  ALCIBIADES   In vain?
       His service done at Lacedaemon and Byzantium
60   Were a sufficient briber for his life.
  FIRST SENATOR   What's that?
  ALCIBIADES   Why, I say, my lords, he's done fair° service,   *fine*
       And slain in fight many of your enemies.
       How full of valour did he bear himself
       In the last conflict, and made plenteous wounds!
65 SECOND SENATOR   He has made too much plenty with 'em.
       He's a sworn rioter;° he has a sin   *committed reveler*
       That often drowns him and takes his valour prisoner.[5]
       If there were no foes, that were enough
       To overcome him. In that beastly fury
70   He has been known to commit outrages
       And cherish factions.° 'Tis inferred° to us   *foster dissension / alleged*
       His days are foul and his drink dangerous.
  FIRST SENATOR   He dies.
  ALCIBIADES   Hard fate! He might have died in war.
       My lords, if not for any parts° in him—   *good qualities*
75   Though his right arm might purchase his own time[6]
       And be in debt to none—yet more to move you,
       Take° my deserts to his and join 'em both.   *Combine*
       And for I know
       Your reverend ages love security,[7]
80   I'll pawn my victories, all my honour to you
       Upon his good returns.°   *repayment (of your trust)*
       If by this crime he owes the law his life,
       Why, let the war receive't in valiant gore,
       For law is strict, and war is nothing more.
85 FIRST SENATOR   We are for law; he dies. Urge it no more,
       On height of our° displeasure. Friend or brother,   *At risk of our highest*

3. *what make we / Abroad*: why do we (men) go outdoors?   6. Though performance in battle might redeem him for
4. But self-defense, considered mercifully.   the duration of his life.
5. *sin . . . prisoner*: that is, drunkenness.   7. Collateral (as on a loan); safety.

He forfeits his own blood that spills another.

ALCIBIADES   Must it be so? It must not be.
My lords, I do beseech you know me.

SECOND SENATOR   How?

ALCIBIADES   Call me to your remembrances.

90 THIRD SENATOR   What?

ALCIBIADES   I cannot think but your age has forgot me.
It could not else° be I should prove so base   *otherwise*
To sue and be denied such common grace.
My wounds ache at you.

FIRST SENATOR   Do you dare our anger?

95 'Tis in few words, but spacious° in effect: *great*
We banish thee for ever.

ALCIBIADES   Banish me?
Banish your dotage, banish usury
That makes the senate ugly.

FIRST SENATOR   If after two days' shine
Athens contain thee, attend our weightier judgement;

100 And, not to swell your spirit,° he shall be   *anger*
Executed presently.°   *Exeunt* [SENATORS *and attendants*]   *immediately*

ALCIBIADES   Now the gods keep you old enough that you may live
Only in bone,° that none may look on you!   *as skeletons*
I'm worse than mad. I have kept back their foes

105 While they have told° their money and let out   *counted*
Their coin upon large interest—I myself,
Rich only in large hurts. All those for this?
Is this the balsam° that the usuring senate   *ointment*
Pours into captains' wounds? Banishment!

110 It comes not ill; I hate not to be banished.
It is a cause worthy my spleen and fury,
That I may strike at Athens. I'll cheer up
My discontented troops, and lay for hearts.°   *win their support*
'Tis honour with most lands° to be at odds.   *the richest*

115 Soldiers should brook° as little wrongs as gods.   *Exit*   *endure*

3.7

Enter divers [of Timon's] friends, [amongst them LUCUL-
LUS, LUCIUS, SEMPRONIUS, *and other* LORDS *and Senators,] at several doors*

FIRST LORD   The good time of day to you, sir.

SECOND LORD   I also wish it to you. I think this honourable lord
did but try° us this other day.   *test*

FIRST LORD   Upon that were my thoughts tiring[1] when we
5   encountered.° I hope it is not so low with him as he made it   *met*
seem in the trial of his several friends.

SECOND LORD   It should not be, by the persuasion° of his new   *evidence*
feasting.

FIRST LORD   I should think so. He hath sent me an earnest invit-
10   ing, which many my near occasions° did urge me to put off, but   *my many urgent affairs*
he hath conjured me beyond them, and I must needs appear.

SECOND LORD   In like manner was I in debt° to my importunate   *I needed to attend*
business, but he would not hear my excuse. I am sorry when
he sent to borrow of me that my provision was out.

3.7 Location: Timon's house.   1. Feeding (as a hawk tears flesh).

15 FIRST LORD   I am sick of that grief too, as I understand how all
    things go.[2]
    SECOND LORD   Every man hears so. What would he have bor-
    rowed of you?
    FIRST LORD   A thousand pieces.
20 SECOND LORD   A thousand pieces?
    FIRST LORD   What of you?
    SECOND LORD   He sent to me, sir—
        [*Loud music.*] *Enter* TIMON *and attendants*
    Here he comes.
    TIMON   With all my heart, gentlemen both; and how fare you?
25 FIRST LORD   Ever at the best, hearing well of your lordship.
    SECOND LORD   The swallow follows not summer more willing
    than we your lordship.
    TIMON [*aside*]   Nor more willingly leaves winter, such summer
    birds are men.—Gentlemen, our dinner will not recompense
30 this long stay. Feast your ears with the music a while, if they
    will fare° so harshly o'th' trumpets' sound; we shall to't   *sustain themselves*
    presently.
    FIRST LORD   I hope it remains not unkindly with your lordship
    that I returned you an empty messenger.
35 TIMON   O sir, let it not trouble you.
    SECOND LORD   My noble lord—
    TIMON   Ah, my good friend, what cheer?
        [*A table and stools are*] *brought in*
    SECOND LORD   My most honourable lord, I am e'en° sick of   *utterly*
    shame that when your lordship this other day sent to me I was
40 so unfortunate a beggar.
    TIMON   Think not on't, sir.
    SECOND LORD   If you had sent but two hours before—
    TIMON   Let it not cumber° your better remembrance.—Come,   *burden*
    bring in all together.
        [*Enter Servants with covered dishes*]
45 SECOND LORD   All covered dishes.
    FIRST LORD   Royal cheer,° I warrant you.   *dining*
    THIRD LORD   Doubt not that, if money and the season can yield it.
    FIRST LORD   How do you? What's the news?
    THIRD LORD   Alcibiades is banished. Hear you of it?
50 FIRST and SECOND LORDS   Alcibiades banished?
    THIRD LORD   'Tis so, be sure of it.
    FIRST LORD   How, how?
    SECOND LORD   I pray you, upon what?°   *what grounds*
    TIMON   My worthy friends, will you draw near?
55 THIRD LORD   I'll tell you more anon. Here's a noble feast
    toward.°   *coming up*
    SECOND LORD   This is the old[3] man still.
    THIRD LORD   Will't hold, will't hold?°   *last*
    SECOND LORD   It does; but time will°—and so—   *"time will tell"*
60 THIRD LORD   I do conceive.°   *understand*
    TIMON   Each man to his stool with that spur° as he would to the   *speed*
    lip of his mistress. Your diet shall be in all places alike. Make

---

2. *as . . . go:* now that I understand the real situation.   3. Familiar (in his generosity).

not a city feast[4] of it, to let the meat cool ere we can agree
upon the first place.° Sit, sit. The gods require our thanks.   *place of honor*
            They sit
65   You great benefactors, sprinkle our society with thankfulness.
      For your own gifts make yourselves praised; but reserve still[5] to
      give, lest your deities be despised. Lend to each man enough
      that one need not lend to another; for were your godheads to
      borrow of men, men would forsake the gods. Make the meat
70   be beloved more than the man that gives it. Let no assembly of
      twenty be without a score of villains. If there sit twelve women
      at the table, let a dozen of them be as they are. The rest of your
      foes, O gods—the senators of Athens, together with the
      common tag° of people—what is amiss in them, you gods,   *mob*
75   make suitable for destruction. For these my present friends, as
      they are to me nothing, so in nothing bless them; and to noth-
      ing are they welcome.—Uncover, dogs, and lap.
            [*The dishes are uncovered, and seen to be full of
            steaming water and stones*]
      SOME LORDS   What does his lordship mean?
      OTHER LORDS   I know not.
80   TIMON   May you a better feast never behold,
      You knot of mouth-friends.[6] Smoke and lukewarm water
      Is your perfection. This is Timon's last,
      Who, stuck and spangled with your flattery,
      Washes it off, and sprinkles in your faces
      Your reeking° villainy.   *steaming; stinking*
            [*He throws water in their faces*]
85   Live loathed and long,
      Most smiling, smooth, detested parasites,
      Courteous destroyers, affable wolves, meek bears,
      You fools of fortune, trencher-friends,° time's flies,[7]   *mealtime friends*
      Cap-and-knee° slaves, vapours, and minute-jacks![8]   *Sycophantic*
90   Of man and beast the infinite malady[9]
      Crust you quite o'er.
            [*A LORD is going*]
                              What, dost thou go?
      Soft,° take thy physic° first. Thou too, and thou.   *Wait / medicine*
            [*He beats them*]
      Stay, I will lend thee money, borrow none.
            [*Exeunt LORDS, leaving caps and gowns*]
      What, all in motion? Henceforth be no feast
95   Whereat a villain's not a welcome guest.
      Burn house! Sink Athens! Henceforth hated be
      Of Timon man and all humanity!   *Exit*
            Enter the Senators [and] other LORDS
      FIRST LORD   How now, my lords?
      SECOND LORD   Know you the quality° of Lord Timon's fury?   *nature*
      THIRD LORD   Push!° Did you see my cap?   *(impatient expression)*
100   FOURTH LORD   I have lost my gown.
      FIRST LORD   He's but a mad lord, and naught but humours°   *unstable moods*

---

4. Feast as given by London dignitaries, in which seating
arrangements were thought socially significant.
5. But always hold back something.
6. You group of insincere (or gluttonous) friends.

7. That is, vanishing in cold weather.
8. Mannekins that strike bells on medieval clocks; hence,
timeservers.
9. May every disease of man and beast.

sways him. He gave me a jewel th'other day, and now he has
beat it out of my hat.

Did you see my jewel?

THIRD LORD   Did you see my cap?

SECOND LORD   Here 'tis.

FOURTH LORD   Here lies my gown.

105 FIRST LORD   Let's make no stay.

SECOND LORD   Lord Timon's mad.

THIRD LORD   I feel't upon my bones.

FOURTH LORD   One day he gives us diamonds, next day stones.

                                              Exeunt

4.1

Enter TIMON

TIMON   Let me look back upon thee. O thou wall
    That girdles in those wolves, dive in the earth,
    And fence not Athens! Matrons, turn incontinent!°   *unchaste*
    Obedience fail in children! Slaves and fools,
5   Pluck the grave wrinkled senate from the bench
    And minister in their steads! To general filths°   *common whores*
    Convert o'th' instant, green[1] virginity!
    Do't in your parents' eyes. Bankrupts, hold fast!°   *refuse to pay*
    Rather than render back, out with your knives,
10 And cut your trusters'° throats. Bound° servants, steal! *creditors'/Indentured*
    Large-handed robbers your grave masters are,
    And pill° by law. Maid, to thy master's bed!   *plunder*
    Thy mistress is o'th' brothel. Son of sixteen,
    Pluck the lined° crutch from thy old limping sire;   *padded*
15 With it beat out his brains! Piety and fear,
    Religion to the gods, peace, justice, truth,
    Domestic awe,[2] night rest, and neighbourhood,°   *neighborliness*
    Instruction, manners, mysteries,° and trades,   *crafts*
    Degrees,° observances,[3] customs, and laws,   *Social ranks*
20 Decline to your confounding° contraries,   *destroying*
    And let confusion live! Plagues incident to men,
    Your potent and infectious fevers heap
    On Athens, ripe for stroke!° Thou cold sciatica,° *to be struck/nerve pain*
    Cripple our senators, that their limbs may halt°   *limp*
25 As lamely as their manners! Lust and liberty,°   *licentiousness*
    Creep in the minds and marrows[4] of our youth,
    That 'gainst the stream of virtue they may strive
    And drown themselves in riot!° Itches, blains,°   *debauchery/sores*
    Sow all th'Athenian bosoms, and their crop
30 Be general leprosy! Breath infect breath,
    That their society,° as their friendship, may   *company*
    Be merely° poison!   *wholly*
        He tears off his clothing
                          Nothing I'll bear from thee
    But nakedness, thou detestable town;
    Take thou that too, with multiplying bans.°   *curses*
35 Timon will to the woods, where he shall find

4.1 Location: Outside the walls of Athens.
1. Young, newly menstruating girls often suffered anemia, then called "greensickness" and thought to be cur-
able by sexual satisfaction.

2. Household government.
3. Respectful customs.
4. Thought to be the site of vigor; proverbially melted by
lust.

Th'unkindest beast more kinder[5] than mankind.
The gods confound—hear me you good gods all—
Th'Athenians, both within and out that wall;
And grant, as Timon grows, his hate may grow
40   To the whole race of mankind, high and low.
Amen.   *Exit*

4.2

Enter [FLAVIUS *the*] *Steward, with two or three* SERVANTS

FIRST SERVANT   Hear you, master steward, where's our master?
Are we undone, cast off, nothing remaining?
FLAVIUS   Alack, my fellows, what should I say to you?
Let me be recorded: by the righteous gods,
I am as poor as you.
5   FIRST SERVANT   Such a house broke,
So noble a master fall'n? All gone, and not
One friend to take his° fortune by the arm   *(Timon's)*
And go along with him?
SECOND SERVANT   As we do turn our backs
From our companion thrown into his grave,
10   So his familiars to[1] his buried fortunes
Slink all away, leave their false vows with him
Like empty purses picked; and his poor self,
A dedicated° beggar to the air,   *Abandoned as a*
With his disease of all-shunned poverty,
Walks like contempt alone.
               Enter other SERVANTS
15   More of our fellows.
FLAVIUS   All broken implements of a ruined house.
THIRD SERVANT   Yet do our hearts wear Timon's livery.°   *servants' uniforms*
That see I by our faces. We are fellows still,
Serving alike in sorrow. Leaked is our barque,°   *sailboat*
20   And we, poor mates, stand on the dying° deck   *sinking*
Hearing the surges'° threat. We must all part   *waves'*
Into this sea of air.
FLAVIUS   Good fellows all,
The latest° of my wealth I'll share amongst you.   *last bit*
Wherever we shall meet, for Timon's sake
25   Let's yet be fellows. Let's shake our heads and say,
As 'twere a knell unto our master's fortunes,
'We have seen better days.'
          [*He gives them money*]
                 Let each take some.
Nay, put out all your hands. Not one word more.
Thus part we rich in sorrow, parting poor.
          [*They*] *embrace, and* [*the* SERVANTS] *part several ways*
30   O, the fierce° wretchedness that glory brings us!   *excessive*
Who would not wish to be from wealth exempt,
Since riches point to misery and contempt?
Who would be so mocked with glory, or to live
But in a dream of friendship,

---

5. Gentler; more nearly akin.
4.2 Location: Timon's house.

1. So his intimate friends from (a "familiar" could also be a flattering devil).

35 To have his pomp and all what state compounds[2]
But only painted like his varnished friends?
Poor honest lord, brought low by his own heart,
Undone by goodness! Strange, unusual blood°   *disposition*
When man's worst sin is he does too much good!
40 Who then dares to be half so kind again?
For bounty, that makes° gods, does still mar men.   *characterizes*
My dearest lord, blessed to be most accursed,
Rich only to be wretched, thy great fortunes
Are made thy chief afflictions. Alas, kind lord!
45 He's flung in rage from this ingrateful seat°   *residence*
Of monstrous friends;
Nor has he with him to supply° his life,   *resources to maintain*
Or that° which can command it.   *(money)*
I'll follow and enquire him out.
50 I'll ever serve his mind with my best will.
Whilst I have gold I'll be his steward still.   *Exit*

4.3

Enter TIMON [*from his cave*] *in the woods* [*half naked,*
and with a spade]

TIMON O blessèd breeding sun,[1] draw from the earth
Rotten° humidity; below thy sister's[2] orb   *Putrid*
Infect the air. Twinned brothers of one womb,
Whose procreation, residence,° and birth   *time in the womb*
5 Scarce is dividant,° touch them with several° fortunes,   *separable / different*
The greater scorns the lesser. Not nature,
To whom all sores° lay siege, can bear great fortune   *afflictions*
But by contempt of nature.[3]
It is the pasture lards[4] the brother's sides,
10 The want that makes him lean.
Raise me[5] this beggar and demit that lord,
The senator shall bear contempt hereditary,°   *as if he had inherited it*
The beggar native° honour. Who dares, who dares   *inborn*
In purity of manhood stand upright
15 And say 'This man's a flatterer'? If one be,
So are they all, for every grece° of fortune   *step on the staircase*
Is smoothed by that below.[6] The learnèd pate°   *head*
Ducks° to the golden fool. All's obliquy;°   *Bows / deviousness*
There's nothing level° in our cursèd natures   *straight; consistent*
20 But direct villainy. Therefore be abhorred
All feasts, societies, and throngs of men.
His semblable,° yea, himself, Timon disdains.   *His own image*
Destruction fang° mankind. Earth, yield me roots.   *seize*
  [*He digs*]
Who seeks for better of thee, sauce his palate
With thy most operant° poison.   *potent*
  [*He finds gold*]
25   What is here?

---

2. And all that splendor is made of.
4.3 Location: Outside Athens.
1. The sun was supposed to be able to generate vermin spontaneously and to foment infection.
2. The moon's; see note to 1.1.44.
3. Without scorning those of like nature.

4. Fattens ("pasture" suggests both owning and eating from the land).
5. This "me" is an example of the so-called ethic dative (literally, "for me"), used to emphasize the verb. See also line 112.
6. By the people standing on the step below.

Gold? Yellow, glittering, precious gold?
No, gods, I am no idle° votarist: *frivolous*
Roots, you clear heavens. Thus much of this will make
Black white, foul fair, wrong right,
30   Base noble, old young, coward valiant.
Ha, you gods! Why this, what, this, you gods? Why, this
Will lug your priests and servants from your sides,
Pluck stout men's pillows from below their heads.°   *(to kill them)*
This yellow slave
35   Will knit and break religions, bless th'accursed,
Make the hoar° leprosy adored, place° thieves,   *gray/appoint to office*
And give them title, knee,° and approbation   *kneeling*
With senators on the bench. This is it
That makes the wappered° widow wed again.   *worn out*
40   She whom the spittle house° and ulcerous sores   *hospital*
Would cast the gorge° at, this embalms and spices   *vomit*
To th'April day[7] again. Come, damnèd earth,°   *gold*
Thou common whore of mankind, that puts odds°   *quarrels*
Among the rout° of nations; I will make thee   *rabble*
Do[8] thy right nature.
      March afar off
45   Ha, a drum! Thou'rt quick;[9]
But yet I'll bury thee.
      [He buries gold]
                       Thou'lt go, strong thief,
When gouty keepers of thee cannot stand.
      [He keeps some gold]
Nay, stay thou out for earnest.°   *as a pledge*
      Enter ALCIBIADES, *with* [*soldiers playing*] *drum and fife,*
      in warlike manner; and PHRYNIA *and* TIMANDRA
ALCIBIADES   What art thou there? Speak.
TIMON   A beast, as thou art. The canker[1] gnaw thy heart
50   For showing me again the eyes of man.
ALCIBIADES   What is thy name? Is man so hateful to thee
That art thyself a man?
TIMON   I am Misanthropos,° and hate mankind.   *man-hater (Greek)*
For thy part, I do wish thou wert a dog,
That I might love thee something.°   *somewhat*
55 ALCIBIADES   I know thee well,
But in thy fortunes am unlearned and strange.[2]
TIMON   I know thee too, and more than that I know thee
I not desire° to know. Follow thy drum.   *do not desire*
With man's blood paint the ground gules,° gules.   *red (heraldic term)*
60   Religious canons, civil laws, are cruel;
Then what should war be? This fell° whore of thine   *dreadful*
Hath in her more destruction than thy sword,
For all her cherubin look.
PHRYNIA   Thy lips rot off!°   *(as in syphilis)*
TIMON   I will not kiss thee; then the rot returns
65   To thine own lips again.
ALCIBIADES   How came the noble Timon to this change?

7. To youthful freshness.   9. Swift to bring strife; alive.
8. Act according to (by concealing gold and yielding   1. Spreading ulcer; cankerworm.
roots).   2. Am ignorant and unacquainted.

TIMON   As the moon does, by wanting° light to give.   *lacking*
    But then renew I could not like the moon;
    There were no suns to borrow of.

70 ALCIBIADES   Noble Timon, what friendship may I do thee?

TIMON   None but to maintain my opinion.

ALCIBIADES   What is it, Timon?

TIMON   Promise me friendship, but perform none. If thou wilt
    promise, the gods plague thee, for thou art a man. If thou dost

75   not perform, confound° thee, for thou art a man.   *damn*

ALCIBIADES   I have heard in some sort° of thy miseries.   *to some extent*

TIMON   Thou saw'st them when I had prosperity.

ALCIBIADES   I see them now; then was a blessèd time.

TIMON   As thine is now, held with a brace° of harlots.   *pair*

80 TIMANDRA   Is this th'Athenian minion,° whom the world   *favorite*
    Voiced° so regardfully?   *Spoke of*

TIMON   Art thou Timandra?

TIMANDRA   Yes.

TIMON   Be a whore still. They love thee not that use thee.
    Give them diseases, leaving with thee their lust.

85   Make use of thy salt° hours: season° the slaves   *lecherous / prepare*
    For tubs and baths,[3] bring down rose-cheeked youth
    To the tub-fast and the diet.

TIMANDRA   Hang thee, monster!

ALCIBIADES   Pardon him, sweet Timandra, for his wits
    Are drowned and lost in his calamities.

90   I have but little gold of late, brave Timon,
    The want whereof doth daily make° revolt   *cause*
    In my penurious band. I have heard and grieved
    How cursèd Athens, mindless of thy worth,
    Forgetting thy great deeds, when neighbour states

95   But for thy sword and fortune trod upon them[4]—

TIMON   I prithee, beat thy drum and get thee gone.

ALCIBIADES   I am thy friend, and pity thee, dear Timon.

TIMON   How dost thou pity him whom thou dost trouble?
    I had rather be alone.

ALCIBIADES   Why, fare thee well.
    Here is some gold for thee.

100 TIMON   Keep it. I cannot eat it.

ALCIBIADES   When I have laid proud Athens on a heap—

TIMON   Warr'st thou 'gainst Athens?

ALCIBIADES   Ay, Timon, and have cause.

TIMON   The gods confound them all in thy conquest,
    And thee after, when thou hast conquerèd.

ALCIBIADES   Why me, Timon?

105 TIMON   That by killing of villains
    Thou wast born to conquer my country.
    Put up thy gold.
        [*He gives* ALCIBIADES *gold*]
        Go on; here's gold; go on.
    Be as a planetary plague[5] when Jove
    Will o'er some high-viced city hang his poison

---

3. Used, with "diet" (line 87), to treat venereal disease.
4. Alcibiades suggests that Timon's money and military expertise saved Athens in the past.

5. Plagues were thought to be caused by the influence of the other planets.

110 In the sick air. Let not thy sword skip one.
Pity not honoured age for his white beard;
He is an usurer. Strike me° the counterfeit matron;   *Strike for me*
It is her habit° only that is honest,   *attire*
Herself's a bawd. Let not the virgin's cheek
115 Make soft thy trenchant° sword; for those milk paps°   *cutting / breasts*
That through the window-bars° bore at men's eyes   *openwork bodice*
Are not within the leaf° of pity writ;   *page*
But set them down horrible traitors. Spare not the babe
Whose dimpled smiles from fools exhaust° their mercy.   *draw out*
120 Think it a bastard whom the oracle
Hath doubtfully° pronounced thy throat shall cut,   *ambiguously*
And mince it sans° remorse. Swear against objects.⁶   *without*
Put armour on thine ears and on thine eyes
Whose proof° nor yells of mothers, maids, nor babes,   *strength*
125 Nor sight of priests in holy vestments bleeding,
Shall pierce a jot. There's gold to pay thy soldiers.
Make large confusion, and, thy fury spent,
Confounded be thyself. Speak not. Be gone.
ALCIBIADES   Hast thou gold yet? I'll take the gold thou giv'st me,
130 Not all thy counsel.
TIMON   Dost thou or dost thou not, heaven's curse upon thee!
PHRYNIA *and* TIMANDRA   Give us some gold, good Timon. Hast
          thou more?
TIMON   Enough to make a whore forswear her trade,
And to make wholesomeness a bawd. Hold up, you sluts,
Your aprons mountant.⁷
          [*He throws gold into their aprons*]
135   You are not oathable,⁸
Although I know you'll swear, terribly swear,
Into strong shudders and to heavenly agues°   *fevers*
Th'immortal gods that hear you. Spare your oaths;
I'll trust to your conditions.° Be whores still,   *occupations; characters*
140 And he whose pious breath seeks to convert you,
Be strong in whore, allure him, burn him up.°   *inflame him; infect him*
Let your close° fire predominate his smoke;⁹   *secret*
And be no turncoats. Yet may your pain-sick months
Be quite contrary,° and thatch your poor thin roofs   *Make you suffer intensely*
145 With burdens of the dead¹—some that were hanged,
No matter. Wear them, betray with them; whore still;
Paint° till a horse may mire° upon your face.   *Use cosmetics / get stuck*
A pox of wrinkles!
PHRYNIA *and* TIMANDRA   Well, more gold; what then?
Believe't that we'll do anything for gold.
150 TIMON   Consumptions° sow   *Diseases*
In hollow bones of man, strike their sharp shins,²
And mar men's spurring.³ Crack the lawyer's voice,
That he may never more false title plead
Nor sound his quillets° shrilly. Hoar the flamen⁴   *quibbles (wordplay)*

---

6. Vow not to listen to protests.
7. Your skirts lifted ("mountant," a heraldic term, puns
on "sexual mounting").
8. Capable of being bound on oath.
9. Overcome his "pious breath" (line 140).
1. *thatch . . . dead:* wear wigs made of corpses' hair to

cover your syphilitic baldness.
2. Syphilis causes bone degeneration.
3. Horseback riding; sexual intercourse. *Crack:* Ruin (an
ulcerous larynx is an effect of syphilis).
4. Whiten the priest (with syphilis or leprosy).

155 That scolds against the quality° of flesh   *nature*
And not believes himself. Down with the nose,
Down with it flat;⁵ take the bridge quite away
Of him that his particular° to foresee   *self-interest*
Smells from the general weal.⁶ Make curled-pate ruffians bald,
160 And let the unscarred braggarts of the war
Derive some pain from you. Plague all,
That your activity may defeat and quell
The source of all erection.⁷ There's more gold.
Do you damn others, and let this damn you;
165 And ditches grave you all!⁸

PHRYNIA *and* TIMANDRA   More counsel with more money, boun-
    teous Timon.

TIMON   More whore, more mischief first; I have given you earnest.°   *a down payment*
ALCIBIADES   Strike up the drum towards Athens. Farewell, Timon.
    If I thrive well, I'll visit thee again.
170 TIMON   If I hope well, I'll never see thee more.
ALCIBIADES   I never did thee harm.
TIMON   Yes, thou spok'st well of me.
ALCIBIADES   Call'st thou that harm?
TIMON   Men daily find it.° Get thee away,   *discover it to be so*
And take thy beagles° with thee.   *fawning curs (the whores)*
175 ALCIBIADES   We but offend him. Strike!
                    Exeunt [to drum and fife, all but TIMON]
TIMON   That nature, being sick of° man's unkindness,   *through excess of*
    Should yet be hungry!
        [*He digs the earth*]
                    Common° mother—thou   *Universal*
Whose womb unmeasurable and infinite breast
Teems° and feeds all, whose selfsame mettle°   *Breeds / substance*
180 Whereof thy proud child, arrogant man, is puffed
Engenders the black toad and adder blue,
The gilded newt and eyeless venomed worm,
With all th'abhorrèd births below crisp° heaven   *clear*
Whereon Hyperion's quick'ning° fire doth shine—   *the sun's life-giving*
185 Yield him who all thy human sons do hate
From forth thy plenteous bosom, one poor root.
Ensear° thy fertile and conceptious womb;   *Dry up*
Let it no more bring out ingrateful man.
Go great° with tigers, dragons, wolves, and bears;   *pregnant*
190 Teem with new monsters whom thy upward° face   *upturned*
Hath to the marbled mansion° all above   *heavens*
Never presented.
        [*He finds a root*]
                    O, a root! Dear thanks.
Dry up thy marrows,° vines, and plough-torn leas,°   *pulpy fruits / fields*
Whereof ingrateful man with liquorish draughts⁹
195 And morsels unctuous° greases his pure mind,   *oily*
That from it all consideration° slips!—   *rationality*

---

5. Syphilis sometimes caused the bridge of the nose to collapse.
6. The image suggests a dog leaving the pack to pursue its own quarry.
7. Sexual erection; social advancement.
8. May you all suffer squalid deaths.
9. Sweet, lust-inducing drinks.

Enter APEMANTUS

More man? Plague, plague!

APEMANTUS I was directed hither. Men report

Thou dost affect° my manners, and dost use them. *like; imitate*

200 TIMON 'Tis then because thou dost not keep a dog

Whom I would imitate. Consumption catch thee!

APEMANTUS This is in thee a nature but infected,[1]

A poor unmanly melancholy, sprung

From change of fortune. Why this spade, this place,

205 This slave-like habit,° and these looks of care? *costume*

Thy flatterers yet wear silk, drink wine, lie soft,

Hug their diseased perfumes,° and have forgot *perfumed women*

That ever Timon was. Shame not these woods

By putting on the cunning of a carper.[2]

210 Be thou a flatterer now, and seek to thrive

By that which has undone thee. Hinge thy knee,

And let his very breath whom thou'lt observe° *pay court to*

Blow off thy cap. Praise his most vicious strain,° *trait*

And call it excellent. Thou wast told thus.

215 Thou gav'st thine ears like tapsters° that bade welcome *bartenders*

To knaves and all approachers. 'Tis most just

That thou turn rascal.° Hadst thou wealth again, *knave; solitary deer*

Rascals should have't. Do not assume my likeness.

TIMON Were I like thee, I'd throw away myself.

220 APEMANTUS Thou hast cast away thyself being like thyself—

A madman so long, now a fool. What, think'st

That the bleak air, thy boisterous chamberlain,° *personal servant*

Will put thy shirt on warm? Will these mossed trees

That have outlived the eagle page° thy heels *follow at*

225 And skip when thou point'st out?[3] Will the cold brook,

Candied° with ice, caudle thy morning taste[4] *Encrusted*

To cure thy o'ernight's surfeit? Call the creatures

Whose naked natures live in° all the spite *exposed to*

Of wreakful° heaven, whose bare unhousèd trunks° *vengeful / bodies*

230 To the conflicting elements exposed

Answer° mere nature; bid them flatter thee. *Obey*

O, thou shalt find—

TIMON A fool of thee! Depart.

APEMANTUS I love thee better now than e'er I did.

TIMON I hate thee worse.

APEMANTUS Why?

TIMON Thou flatter'st misery.

235 APEMANTUS I flatter not, but say thou art a caitiff.° *wretch*

TIMON Why dost thou seek me out?

APEMANTUS To vex thee.

TIMON Always a villain's office, or a fool's.

Dost please thyself in't?

APEMANTUS Ay.

TIMON What, a knave too?

APEMANTUS If thou didst put this sour cold habit° on *dress; disposition*

240 To castigate thy pride, 'twere well; but thou

---

1. That is, not innately misanthropic or converted by philosophical argument.
2. The knowledge of a faultfinder.
3. And jump to get whatever you indicate.
4. Give you a hot drink in the morning.

Dost it enforcèdly.° Thou'dst courtier be again   °by compulsion
Wert thou not beggar. Willing misery
Outlives incertain° pomp, is crowned[5] before.   °insecure
The one° is filling still,° never complete;   °("incertain pomp")/°always
245   The other at high wish.[6] Best state, contentless,[7]
Hath a distracted and most wretched being,
Worse than the worst, content.[8]
Thou shouldst desire to die, being miserable.
TIMON   Not by his breath that is more miserable.[9]
250   Thou art a slave whom fortune's tender arm
With favour never clasped, but bred a dog.
Hadst thou like us from our first swathe proceeded[1]
The sweet degrees[2] that this brief world affords
To such as° may the passive drudges of it   °To those who
255   Freely command, thou wouldst have plunged thyself
In general riot,° melted down thy youth   °debauchery
In different beds of lust, and never learned
The icy precepts of respect,° but followed   °restraint; judgment
The sugared game° before thee. But myself,   °sweet quarry
260   Who had the world as my confectionary,
The mouths, the tongues, the eyes and hearts of men
At duty,° more than I could frame° employment,   °my service/°provide
That numberless upon me stuck, as leaves
Do on the oak, have with one winter's brush
265   Fell from their boughs, and left me open, bare
For every storm that blows—I to bear this,
That never knew but better,° is some burden.   °anything but good fortune
Thy nature did commence in sufferance,° time   °suffering
Hath made thee hard° in't. Why shouldst thou hate men?   °hardened
270   They never flattered thee. What hast thou given?
If thou wilt curse, thy father, that poor rag,°   °wretch
Must be thy subject, who in spite put stuff
To[3] some she-beggar and compounded° thee   °constituted
Poor rogue hereditary.° Hence, be gone.   °by birth
275   If thou hadst not been born the worst of men
Thou hadst been a knave and flatterer.
APEMANTUS   Art thou proud yet?
TIMON   Ay, that I am not thee.
APEMANTUS   I that I was
No prodigal.
280   TIMON   I that I am one now.
Were all the wealth I have shut up° in thee   °contained
I'd give thee leave to hang it. Get thee gone.
That° the whole life of Athens were in this!   °Would that
Thus would I eat it.
        [*He bites the root*]
APEMANTUS [*offering food*]   Here, I will mend° thy feast.   °improve
285   TIMON   First mend my company: take away thyself.
APEMANTUS   So I shall mend mine own by th' lack of thine.

---

5. Finds fulfillment.
6. (Misery) at the height of its wish.
7. The greatest prosperity, if not contented.
8. The least prosperity, living contented.
9. Not at the command of someone even unhappier

than I.
1. From our swaddling clothes mounted.
2. Social ranks; steps on Fortune's ladder.
3. *put stuff/To*: ejaculated into.

TIMON 'Tis not well mended so, it is but botched;[4]
　　　　If not, I would it were.

APEMANTUS　　　　　　　What wouldst thou have to[5] Athens?

TIMON　Thee thither in a whirlwind. If thou wilt,
290　　Tell them there I have gold. Look, so I have.

APEMANTUS　Here is no use for gold.

TIMON　　　　　　　　　　　　The best and truest,
　　　　For here it sleeps and does no hirèd harm.

APEMANTUS　Where liest a-nights, Timon?

TIMON　Under that's above me.° Where feed'st thou a-days,　　*(the sky)*
295　　Apemantus?

APEMANTUS　Where my stomach finds meat;° or rather, where I eat it.　　*food*

TIMON　Would poison were obedient, and knew my mind!

APEMANTUS　Where wouldst thou send it?

TIMON　To sauce thy dishes.

300　APEMANTUS　The middle of humanity thou never knewest, but
　　　　the extremity of both ends. When thou wast in thy gilt and thy
　　　　perfume, they mocked thee for too much curiosity;° in thy rags　　*delicacy*
　　　　thou know'st none, but art despised for the contrary. There's a
　　　　medlar[6] for thee; eat it.

305　TIMON　On what I hate I feed not.

APEMANTUS　Dost hate a medlar?

TIMON　Ay, though it look like thee.

APEMANTUS　An° thou'dst hated meddlers sooner, thou shouldst　　*If*
　　　　have loved thyself better now. What man didst thou ever know
310　　unthrift° that was beloved after[7] his means?　　*prodigal*

TIMON　Who, without those means thou talk'st of, didst thou ever
　　　　know beloved?

APEMANTUS　Myself.

TIMON　I understand thee: thou hadst some means to keep a dog.[8]

315　APEMANTUS　What things in the world canst thou nearest com-
　　　　pare to thy flatterers?

TIMON　Women nearest; but men, men are the things them
　　　　selves. What wouldst thou do with the world, Apemantus, if it
　　　　lay in thy power?

320　APEMANTUS　Give it the beasts, to be rid of the men.

TIMON　Wouldst thou have thyself fall in the confusion° of men,　　*overthrow*
　　　　and remain a beast with the beasts?

APEMANTUS　Ay, Timon.

TIMON　A beastly ambition, which the gods grant thee t'attain to.
325　　If thou wert the lion, the fox would beguile thee. If thou wert
　　　　the lamb, the fox would eat thee. If thou wert the fox, the lion
　　　　would suspect thee when peradventure° thou wert accused by　　*perchance*
　　　　the ass. If thou wert the ass, thy dullness would torment thee,
　　　　and still° thou lived'st but as a breakfast to the wolf. If thou wert　　*always*
330　　the wolf, thy greediness would afflict thee, and oft thou
　　　　shouldst hazard thy life for thy dinner. Wert thou the unicorn,
　　　　pride and wrath would confound thee, and make thine own
　　　　self the conquest of thy fury.[9] Wert thou a bear, thou wouldst

4. It is fixed badly (because Apemantus will still have to
endure himself).
5. Have conveyed to (but Timon changes the meaning).
6. A pear eaten when rotten; with puns in the following
lines on "lecher," "whore," and "interfering person."
7. In proportion to; after losing. *means:* money.

8. Which flattered its master for meager reward (or perhaps "dog" refers to Apemantus himself).
9. The legendary unicorn could be trapped by a hunter
who stood in front of a tree; when the unicorn charged,
the hunter stepped aside, and the unicorn's horn stuck
fast in the tree.

be killed by the horse.[1] Wert thou a horse, thou wouldst be
335 seized by the leopard. Wert thou a leopard, thou wert german°   related
to the lion, and the spots of thy kindred[2] were jurors on thy life;
all thy safety were remotion,° and thy defence absence. What   remaining away
beast couldst thou be that were not subject to a beast? And
what a beast art thou already, that seest not thy loss in transfor-
340 mation![3]

APEMANTUS   If thou couldst please me with speaking to me, thou
mightst have hit upon it here.[4] The commonwealth of Athens
is become a forest of beasts.

TIMON   How, has the ass broke the wall, that thou art out of the city?

345 APEMANTUS   Yonder comes a poet and a painter.[5] The plague of
company light upon thee! I will fear to catch it, and give way.°   go away
When I know not what else to do, I'll see thee again.

TIMON   When there is nothing living but thee, thou shalt be
welcome. I had rather be a beggar's dog than Apemantus.

350 APEMANTUS   Thou art the cap[6] of all the fools alive.

TIMON   Would thou wert clean enough to spit upon.

APEMANTUS   A plague on thee! Thou art too bad to curse.

TIMON   All villains that do stand by thee are pure.°   (by comparison)

APEMANTUS   There is no leprosy but what thou speak'st.

355 TIMON   If I name thee.
I'd beat thee, but I should infect my hands.

APEMANTUS   I would my tongue could rot them off.

TIMON   Away, thou issue° of a mangy dog!   offspring; discharge
Choler does kill me that thou art alive.
360 I swoon to see thee.

APEMANTUS   Would thou wouldst burst!

TIMON   Away, thou tedious rogue!
   [He throws a stone at APEMANTUS]
I am sorry I shall lose a stone by thee.

APEMANTUS   Beast!

365 TIMON   Slave!

APEMANTUS   Toad!

TIMON   Rogue, rogue, rogue!
I am sick of this false world, and will love naught
But even° the mere necessities upon't.   Except
370 Then, Timon, presently° prepare thy grave.   at once
Lie where the light foam of the sea may beat
Thy gravestone daily. Make thine epitaph,
That death in° me at others' lives may laugh.   through
   [He looks on the gold]
O, thou sweet king-killer, and dear divorce
375 'Twixt natural son and sire; thou bright defiler
Of Hymen's° purest bed; thou valiant Mars;[7]   god of marriage
Thou ever young, fresh, loved, and delicate wooer,
Whose blush° doth thaw the consecrated snow[8]   glow
That lies on Dian's lap; thou visible god,
380 That sold'rest close impossibilities[9]

---

1. Bears were supposedly hated by horses.
2. Lion's crimes; leopard's spots.
3. Being transformed to a beast.
4. thou . . . here: what you've just said would please me.
5. They do not appear until 5.1 (perhaps a sign of revision).
6. Supreme instance (with wordplay on "fool's cap").
7. Adulterous lover of Venus and the god of war.
8. The snow of chastity, of which the goddess Diana was patroness.
9. That tightly solders together incompatible things.

And mak'st them kiss, that speak'st with every tongue
To every purpose; O thou touch° of hearts: *touchstone*
Think thy slave man rebels, and by thy virtue°   *power*
Set them into confounding odds,° that beasts   *men at ruinous strife*
May have the world in empire.
385   APEMANTUS   Would 'twere so,
But not till I am dead. I'll say thou'st gold.
Thou wilt be thronged to shortly.
        TIMON   Thronged to?
        APEMANTUS   Ay.
        TIMON   Thy back,[1] I prithee.
        APEMANTUS   Live, and love thy misery.
        TIMON   Long live so, and so die. I am quit.°   *rid of you*
                *Enter the Banditti [*THIEVES]
390   APEMANTUS   More things like men. Eat, Timon, and abhor
        them.   *Exit*
        FIRST THIEF   Where should he have° this gold? It is some poor   *have obtained; have put*
        fragment, some slender ort° of his remainder. The mere want   *scrap*
        of gold and the falling-from of his friends drove him into this
395   melancholy.
        SECOND THIEF   It is noised° he hath a mass of treasure.   *rumored*
        THIRD THIEF   Let us make the assay° upon him. If he care not   *test; assault*
        for't, he will supply us easily. If he covetously reserve it, how
        shall 's get it?
400   SECOND THIEF   True, for he bears it not about him; 'tis hid.
        FIRST THIEF   Is not this he?
        OTHER THIEVES   Where?
        SECOND THIEF   'Tis his description.
        THIRD THIEF   He, I know him.
405   ALL THIEVES [*coming forward*]   Save° thee, Timon.   *God save*
        TIMON   Now, thieves.
        ALL THIEVES   Soldiers, not thieves.
        TIMON   Both, too, and women's sons.
        ALL THIEVES   We are not thieves, but men that much do want.°   *are very needy*
        TIMON   Your greatest want is, you want much of meat.°   *food*
410   Why should you want? Behold, the earth hath roots.
        Within this mile break forth a hundred springs.
        The oaks bear mast,° the briars scarlet hips.[2]   *acorns (fed to swine)*
        The bounteous housewife nature on each bush
        Lays her full mess° before you. Want? Why want?   *serving*
415   FIRST THIEF   We cannot live on grass, on berries, water,
        As beasts and birds and fishes.
        TIMON   Nor on the beasts themselves, the birds and fishes;
        You must eat men. Yet thanks I must you con°   *render*
        That you are thieves professed, that you work not
420   In holier shapes; for there is boundless theft
        In limited° professions. [*Giving gold*] Rascal thieves,   *legitimate*
        Here's gold. Go suck the subtle° blood o'th' grape   *delicate; deceptive*
        Till the high fever seethe° your blood to froth,   *boil (by drunkenness)*
        And so scape hanging.° Trust not the physician;   *(by dying of a fever)*
425   His antidotes are poison, and he slays
        More than you rob. Take wealth and lives together.
        Do villainy; do, since you protest° to do't,   *openly profess*

---

1. Show me your back (go away).   2. Rose hips (sour fruit).

Like workmen.° I'll example you with³ thievery.   *skilled artisans*
The sun's a thief, and with his great attraction°   *power to draw up*
430 Robs the vast sea. The moon's an arrant⁴ thief,
And her pale fire she snatches from the sun.
The sea's a thief, whose liquid surge resolves°   *melts*
The moon into salt tears.⁵ The earth's a thief,
That feeds and breeds by a composture° stol'n   *manure*
435 From gen'ral° excrement. Each thing's a thief.   *universal*
The laws, your curb and whip,° in their rough power   *restraint and punishment*
Has unchecked theft.⁶ Love not yourselves. Away,
Rob one another. There's more gold. Cut throats;
All that you meet are thieves. To Athens go,
440 Break open shops; nothing can you steal
But thieves do lose it. Steal no less for° this I give you,   *because of*
And gold confound you howsoe'er.° Amen.   *whatever you do*

THIRD THIEF   He's almost charmed me from my profession by
persuading me to it.

445 FIRST THIEF   'Tis in the malice° of mankind that he thus advises   *out of hatred*
us, not to have us thrive in our mystery.°   *profession*

SECOND THIEF   I'll believe him as⁷ an enemy, and give over my
trade.

FIRST THIEF   Let us first see peace in Athens.° There is no time   *(an unlikely prospect)*
450 so miserable but a man may be true.°   *Exeunt* THIEVES   *may repent*

    Enter [FLAVIUS *the*] *Steward to* TIMON

FLAVIUS   O you gods!
Is yon despised and ruinous° man my lord,   *ruined*
Full of decay and failing? O monument
And wonder of good deeds evilly bestowed!⁸
455 What an alteration of honour has desp'rate want made!
What viler thing upon the earth than friends,
Who can bring noblest minds to basest ends!
How rarely does it meet with this time's guise,
When man was wished to love his enemies!⁹
460 Grant I may ever love and rather woo
Those that would mischief me than those that do!¹
    [TIMON *sees him*]
He's caught me in his eye. I will present
My honest grief unto him, and as my lord
Still serve him with my life.—My dearest master.

TIMON   Away! What art thou?

465 FLAVIUS   Have you forgot me, sir?

TIMON   Why dost ask that? I have forgot all men;
Then if thou grant'st thou'rt man, I have forgot thee.

FLAVIUS   An honest poor servant of yours.

TIMON   Then I know thee not. I never had
470 Honest man about me; ay, all I kept were knaves,
To serve in meat° to villains.   *serve food*

FLAVIUS   The gods are witness,
Ne'er did poor steward wear a truer grief

---

3. I'll give you precedents for.
4. Unmitigated; a wandering. The moon was considered auspicious to thieves.
5. Tides supposedly resulted from the sea drawing moisture from the moon.
6. Have unlimited power to steal.
7. As I would an enemy (that is, not at all).

8. Bestowed on ungrateful people.
9. *How . . . enemies:* How perfectly it accords with the customary exhortation to love one's enemies (since friends are one's undoing).
1. Those who would like to injure me, rather than those who really do so.

For his undone lord than mine eyes for you.

TIMON   What, dost thou weep? Come nearer then; I love thee

475 Because thou art a woman,° and disclaim'st   (*in weeping*)
Flinty mankind whose eyes do never give°   *succumb*
But thorough° lust and laughter. Pity's sleeping.   *through*
Strange times, that weep with laughing, not with weeping!

FLAVIUS   I beg of you to know me, good my lord,
T'accept my grief,

[*He offers his money*]

480   and whilst this poor wealth lasts
To entertain° me as your steward still.   *employ*

TIMON   Had I a steward
So true, so just, and now so comfortable?°   *comforting*
It almost turns my dangerous° nature mild.   *savage*

485 Let me behold thy face. Surely this man
Was born of woman.
Forgive my general and exceptless° rashness,   *indiscriminate*
You perpetual sober gods! I do proclaim
One honest man—mistake me not, but one,

490 No more, I pray—and he's a steward.
How fain° would I have hated all mankind,   *willingly*
And thou redeem'st thyself! But all save thee
I fell° with curses.   *cut down*
Methinks thou art more honest now than wise,

495 For by oppressing and betraying me
Thou mightst have sooner got another service;
For many so arrive at second masters
Upon° their first lord's neck. But tell me true—   *By stepping on*
For I must ever doubt, though ne'er so sure—

500 Is not thy kindness subtle,° covetous,   *treacherous*
A usuring kindness, and, as rich men deal gifts,
Expecting in return twenty for one?

FLAVIUS   No, my most worthy master, in whose breast
Doubt and suspect,° alas, are placed too late.   *suspicion*

505 You should have feared false times when you did feast.
Suspect still° comes where an estate is least.   *always*
That which I show, heaven knows, is merely love,
Duty and zeal to your unmatchèd mind,
Care of your food and living; and, believe it,

510 My most honoured lord,
For° any benefit that points to me,   *As for*
Either in hope° or present, I'd exchange   *the future*
For this one wish: that you had power and wealth
To requite° me by making rich yourself.   *repay*

515 TIMON   Look thee, 'tis so. Thou singly honest man,
[*He gives* FLAVIUS *gold*]
Here, take. The gods, out of my misery,
Has sent thee treasure. Go, live rich and happy,
But thus conditioned:[2] thou shalt build from° men,   *away from*
Hate all, curse all, show charity to none,

520 But let the famished flesh slide from the bone
Ere thou relieve the beggar. Give to dogs
What thou deniest to men. Let prisons swallow 'em,

2. But on this condition.

Debts wither 'em to nothing; be men° like blasted woods,   *let men be*
And may diseases lick up their false bloods.
And so farewell, and thrive.

525 FLAVIUS   O, let me stay
And comfort you, my master.

TIMON   If thou hat'st curses,
Stay not. Fly whilst thou art blest and free.
Ne'er see thou man, and let me ne'er see thee.

        Exeunt [TIMON *into his cave,* FLAVIUS *another way*]

5.1

       Enter POET *and* PAINTER

PAINTER   As I took note of the place, it cannot be far where he
abides.

POET   What's to be thought of him? Does the rumour hold for
true that he's so full of gold?

5 PAINTER   Certain. Alcibiades reports it. Phrynia and Timandra
had gold of him. He likewise enriched poor straggling soldiers
with great quantity. 'Tis said he gave unto his steward a mighty
sum.

POET   Then this breaking° of his has been but a try° for his   *bankruptcy / test*
10   friends?

PAINTER   Nothing else. You shall see him a palm[1] in Athens
again, and flourish with the highest. Therefore 'tis not amiss
we tender our loves to him in this supposed distress of his. It
will show honestly in us, and is very likely to load our purposes°   *to reward our efforts*
15 with what they travail° for, if it be a just and true report that   *labor; travel*
goes° of his having.°   *circulates / property*

POET   What have you now to present unto him?

PAINTER   Nothing at this time, but my visitation; only I will
promise him an excellent piece.

20 POET   I must serve him so too, tell him of an intent that's coming
toward him.

PAINTER   Good as the best.°   *That's excellent*

       Enter TIMON *from his cave* [*unobserved*]

Promising is the very air° o'th' time; it opens the eyes of expec-   *fashion*
tation. Performance is ever the duller for his° act, and but in   *its*
25 the plainer and simpler kind of people the deed of saying° is   *doing what one says*
quite out of use. To promise is most courtly and fashionable.
Performance is a kind of will or testament which argues a great
sickness in his judgement that makes it.[2]

TIMON [*aside*]   Excellent workman, thou canst not paint a man
30 so bad as is thyself.

POET [*to* PAINTER]   I am thinking what I shall say I have provided
for him. It must be a personating° of himself, a satire against   *representation*
the softness of prosperity, with a discovery° of the infinite flat-   *revelation*
teries that follow youth and opulency.

35 TIMON [*aside*]   Must thou needs stand° for a villain in thine own   *model*
work? Wilt thou whip thine own faults in other men? Do so; I
have gold for thee.

POET [*to* PAINTER]   Nay, let's seek him.

5.1 Location: Outside Athens.
1. The highest tree: alluding to Psalm 92:12, "The righteous shall flourish like a palm tree."

2. That is, only those close to death worry about fulfilling their vows.

	Then do we sin against our own estate°	condition in life
40	When we may profit meet° and come too late.	make a profit
	PAINTER True.	
	When the day serves,° before black-cornered night,	allows
	Find what thou want'st by free and offered light.	
	Come.	
45	TIMON [aside] I'll meet you at the turn.³ What a god's gold,	
	That he is worshipped in a baser temple	
	Than where swine feed!	
	'Tis thou that rigg'st the barque° and plough'st the foam,	puts sails on the boat
	Settlest admirèd reverence in a slave.⁴	
50	To thee be worship, and thy saints for aye°	ever
	Be crowned with plagues, that thee alone obey.	
	Fit° I meet them.	It is fit

[He comes forward to them]

	POET Hail, worthy Timon!	
	PAINTER Our late noble master!	
	TIMON Have I once° lived to see two honest men?	really
55	POET Sir, having often of your open bounty tasted,	
	Hearing you were retired,° your friends fall'n off,	had gone away
	Whose thankless natures, O abhorrèd spirits,	
	Not all the whips of heaven are large enough—	
	What, to you,	
60	Whose star-like nobleness gave life and influence⁵	
	To their whole being! I am rapt,° and cannot cover	overwhelmed
	The monstrous bulk of this ingratitude	
	With any size⁶ of words.	
	TIMON Let it go naked; men may see't the better.	
65	You that are honest, by being what you are	
	Make them° best seen and known.	(the "abhorrèd spirits")
	PAINTER He and myself	
	Have travelled° in the great show'r of your gifts,	walked
	And sweetly felt it.	
	TIMON Ay, you are honest men.	
	PAINTER We are hither come to offer you our service.	
70	TIMON Most honest men. Why, how shall I requite you?	
	Can you eat roots and drink cold water? No.	
	POET and PAINTER What we can do we'll do to do you service.	
	TIMON You're honest men. You've heard that I have gold,	
	I am sure you have. Speak truth; you're honest men.	
75	PAINTER So it is said, my noble lord, but therefor	
	Came not my friend nor I.	
	TIMON Good honest men. [To PAINTER] Thou draw'st a counterfeit°	picture; fake
	Best in all Athens; thou'rt indeed the best;	
	Thou counterfeit'st most lively.	
	PAINTER So so, my lord.	
80	TIMON E'en so, sir, as I say. [To POET] And for thy fiction,°	poetry; lying
	Why, thy verse swells with stuff so fine and smooth	
	That thou art even natural° in thine art.	lifelike; idiotic
	But for all this, my honest-natured friends,	
	I must needs say you have a little fault.	

3. I'll meet you when you come around the corner; I'll trick you in return.
4. Makes an unworthy person be revered.
5. Explained astrologically, "influence" was a substance thought to stream forth from stars and affect events on earth.
6. Amount; sizing, a layer applied to walls prior to painting.

85 Marry, 'tis not monstrous in you, neither wish I
    You take much pains to mend.
POET *and* PAINTER   Beseech your honour
    To make it known to us.
TIMON   You'll take it ill.
POET *and* PAINTER   Most thankfully, my lord.
TIMON   Will you indeed?
90 POET *and* PAINTER   Doubt it not, worthy lord.
TIMON   There's never a one of you but trusts a knave
    That mightily deceives you.
POET *and* PAINTER   Do we, my lord?
TIMON   Ay, and you hear him cog,° see him dissemble,   *cheat*
    Know his gross patchery,° love him, feed him,   *roguery*
95 Keep° in your bosom; yet remain assured   *Keep him*
    That he's a made-up° villain.   *complete*
PAINTER   I know none such, my lord.
POET   Nor I.
TIMON   Look you, I love you well. I'll give you gold,
100 Rid me these villains from your companies.
    Hang them or stab them, drown them in a draught,°   *stream; cesspool*
    Confound° them by some course, and come to me,   *Destroy*
    I'll give you gold enough.
POET *and* PAINTER   Name them, my lord, let's know them.
TIMON   You that way and you this—but two in company—
105 Each man apart, all single and alone,
    Yet an arch-villain keeps him company.[7]
    [*To* PAINTER] If where thou art two villains shall not be,
    Come not near him. [*To* POET] If thou wouldst not reside
    But where one villain is, then him abandon.
110 Hence; pack!° [*Striking him*] There's gold. You came for gold,   *go away*
        ye slaves.
    [*Striking* PAINTER] You have work for me; there's payment.
        Hence!
    [*Striking* POET]   You are an alchemist;[8] make gold of that.
    Out, rascal dogs!   *Exeunt* [POET *and* PAINTER *one way,*
                                        TIMON *into his cave*]

5.2

Enter [FLAVIUS *the*] *Steward and two* SENATORS
FLAVIUS   It is in vain that you would speak with Timon,
    For he is set so only to himself°   *so self-isolated*
    That nothing but himself which looks like man
    Is friendly with° him.   *congenial to*
FIRST SENATOR   Bring us to his cave.
5   It is our part and promise to th'Athenians
    To speak with Timon.
SECOND SENATOR   At all times alike
    Men are not still° the same. 'Twas time and griefs   *always*
    That framed him thus. Time with his fairer hand
    Offering the fortunes of his former days,
10 The former man may make him. Bring us to him,
    And chance it as it may.

---

7. That is, both of you are archvillains.
8. That is, one who can translate base metal (the beating)

into gold.
5.2 Location: Scene continues.

FLAVIUS   Here is his cave.
     [*Calling*] Peace and content be here! Lord Timon, Timon,
     Look out and speak to friends. Th'Athenians
     By two of their most reverend senate greet thee.
15   Speak to them, noble Timon.

               Enter TIMON *out of his cave*

TIMON   Thou sun that comforts, burn! Speak and be hanged.
     For each true word a blister, and each false°   *let each false word*
     Be as a cantherizing° to the root o'th' tongue,   *cauterizing*
     Consuming it with speaking.
FIRST SENATOR   Worthy Timon—
20 TIMON   Of none but such as you, and you of Timon.[1]
FIRST SENATOR   The senators of Athens greet thee, Timon.
TIMON   I thank them, and would send them back the plague
     Could I but catch it for them.
FIRST SENATOR   O, forget
     What we are sorry for, ourselves in thee.[2]
25   The senators with one consent of° love   *unanimous*
     Entreat thee back to Athens, who have thought
     On special dignities° which vacant lie   *titles; offices*
     For thy best use and wearing.
SECOND SENATOR   They confess
     Toward thee forgetfulness too general-gross,°   *obvious and extreme*
30   Which now the public body,° which doth seldom   *republic*
     Play the recanter,° feeling in itself   *Change its mind*
     A lack of Timon's aid, hath sense withal
     Of it own fail,° restraining° aid to Timon;   *failure / withholding*
     And send forth us to make their sorrowed render,°   *to apologize sadly*
35   Together with a recompense more fruitful
     Than their offence can weigh down by the dram;[3]
     Ay, even such heaps and sums of love and wealth
     As shall to thee blot out what wrongs were theirs,
     And write in thee the figures[4] of their love,
     Ever to read them thine.
40 TIMON   You witch° me in it,   *bewitch*
     Surprise me to the very brink of tears.
     Lend me a fool's heart and a woman's eyes,
     And I'll beweep these comforts, worthy senators.
FIRST SENATOR   Therefore so please thee to return with us,
45   And of our Athens, thine and ours, to take
     The captainship, thou shalt be met with thanks,
     Allowed° with absolute power, and thy good name   *Vested*
     Live with authority. So soon we shall drive back
     Of Alcibiades th'approaches wild,
50   Who, like a boar too savage, doth root up
     His country's peace.
SECOND SENATOR   And shakes his threat'ning sword
     Against the walls of Athens.
FIRST SENATOR   Therefore, Timon—
TIMON   Well, sir, I will; therefore I will, sir, thus.
     If Alcibiades kill my countrymen,
55   Let Alcibiades know this of Timon:

---

1. That is, we deserve each other.   3. Can outweigh even by painstaking calculation.
2. In the injuries we did you.   4. Distinctive marks; numbers in an account book.

That Timon cares not. But if he sack fair Athens,
And take our goodly agèd men by th' beards,
Giving our holy virgins to the stain°   (by rape)
Of contumelious,° beastly, mad-brained war,   insolent
60 Then let him know, and tell him Timon speaks it
In pity of our agèd and our youth,
I cannot choose but tell him that I care not;
And—let him take't at worst[5]—for their knives care not
While you have throats to answer.° For myself,   suitable for cutting
65 There's not a whittle° in th' unruly camp   pocket knife
But I do prize it at my love before
The reverend'st throat in Athens. So I leave you
To the protection of the prosperous gods,
As thieves to keepers.
FLAVIUS [to SENATORS]   Stay not; all's in vain.
70 TIMON   Why, I was writing of my epitaph.
It will be seen tomorrow. My long sickness
Of health and living now begins to mend,
And nothing° brings me all things. Go; live still.   oblivion
Be Alcibiades your plague, you his,
And last so long enough.
75 FIRST SENATOR   We speak in vain.
TIMON   But yet I love my country, and am not
One that rejoices in the common wrack°   ruin
As common bruit° doth put it.   rumor
FIRST SENATOR   That's well spoke.
TIMON   Commend me to my loving countrymen—
80 FIRST SENATOR   These words become your lips as they pass
through them.
SECOND SENATOR   And enter in our ears like great triumphers[6]
In their applauding gates.[7]
TIMON   Commend me to them,
And tell them that to ease them of their griefs,
Their fears of hostile strokes, their aches, losses,
85 Their pangs of love, with other incident throes°   natural torments
That nature's fragile vessel doth sustain
In life's uncertain voyage, I will some kindness do them.
I'll teach them to prevent° wild Alcibiades' wrath.   forestall
FIRST SENATOR [aside]   I like this well; he will return again.
90 TIMON   I have a tree which grows here in my close°   enclosure
That mine own use° invites me to cut down,   purpose
And shortly must I fell it. Tell my friends,
Tell Athens, in the sequence of degree°   in order of rank
From high to low throughout, that whoso please
95 To stop affliction, let him take his haste,
Come hither ere my tree hath felt the axe,
And hang himself. I pray you do my greeting.
FLAVIUS [to SENATORS]   Trouble him no further. Thus you still
shall find him.
TIMON   Come not to me again, but say to Athens,
100 Timon hath made his everlasting mansion°   (his grave)
Upon the beachèd verge° of the salt flood,°   edge / sea

5. Interpret what I say in the worst possible way.   7. Gates full of applauding fellow citizens.
6. Like conquerors returning home.

Who once a day with his embossèd° froth   *foaming*
The turbulent surge shall cover. Thither come,
And let my gravestone be your oracle.°   *source of revelation*
105 Lips, let four° words go by, and language end.   *(that is, few)*
What is amiss, plague and infection mend.
Graves only be men's works, and death their gain.
Sun, hide thy beams. Timon hath done his reign.

Exit [into his cave]

FIRST SENATOR   His discontents are unremovably
110 Coupled to nature.°   *Intrinsic to his nature*
SECOND SENATOR   Our hope in him is dead. Let us return,
And strain what other means is left unto us
In our dear peril.
FIRST SENATOR   It requires swift foot.   *Exeunt*

5.3

Enter two other SENATORS, *with a* MESSENGER

THIRD SENATOR   Thou hast painfully discovered.[1] Are his files°   *troops*
As full as thy report?
MESSENGER   I have spoke the least.°   *estimated low*
Besides, his expedition° promises   *speed*
Present° approach.   *Immediate*
5 FOURTH SENATOR   We stand much hazard if they bring not Timon.
MESSENGER   I met a courier, one mine ancient friend,
Whom, though in general part° we were opposed,   *public matters*
Yet our old love made° a particular force   *exerted*
And made us speak like friends. This man was riding
10 From Alcibiades to Timon's cave
With letters of entreaty which imported°   *urged*
His fellowship i'th' cause against your city,
In part for his sake moved.

Enter the other SENATORS

THIRD SENATOR   Here come our brothers.
FIRST SENATOR   No talk of Timon; nothing of him expect.
15 The enemy's drum is heard, and fearful scouring°   *hostile action*
Doth choke the air with dust. In, and prepare.
Ours is the fall, I fear, our foe's the snare.   *Exeunt*

5.4

Enter a SOLDIER, *in the woods, seeking* TIMON

SOLDIER   By all description, this should be the place.
Who's here? Speak, ho! No answer?
[He discovers a gravestone]
                                  What is this?
Dead, sure, and this his grave. What's on this tomb
I cannot read. The character I'll take with wax.[1]
5 Our captain hath in every figure° skill,   *kind of writing*
An aged° interpreter, though young in days.   *experienced*
Before proud Athens he's set down by this,°   *laid siege by this time*
Whose fall the mark° of his ambition is.   *Exit*   *goal*

5.3 Location: Outside the walls of Athens.   5.4 Location: Outside Athens.
1. Carefully reconnoitered; told us painful news.   1. By making an impression of the letters.

5.5

Trumpets sound. Enter ALCIBIADES *with his powers,°*   army
before Athens

ALCIBIADES   Sound° to this coward and lascivious town   Proclaim
Our terrible approach.
              A parley[1] sound[s]. The SENATORS *appear upon the*
              walls[2]
Till now you have gone on and filled the time
With all licentious measure,[3] making your wills
5   The scope of justice.[4] Till now myself and such
As slept° within the shadow of your power   dwelled
Have wandered with our traversed[5] arms, and breathed
Our sufferance[6] vainly. Now the time is flush
When crouching marrow,° in the bearer strong,   latent vigor
10   Cries of itself 'No more'; now breathless° wrong   exhausted
Shall sit and pant in your great chairs of ease,
And pursy° insolence shall break his wind°   short-winded / pant; fart
With fear and horrid° flight.   terrified
FIRST SENATOR   Noble and young,
When thy first griefs were but a mere conceit,°   only merely imagined
15   Ere thou hadst power or we had cause of fear,
We sent to thee to give thy rages balm,
To wipe out our ingratitude with loves
Above their quantity.[7]
SECOND SENATOR   So did we woo
Transformèd Timon to our city's love
20   By humble message and by promised means.°   wealth
We were not all unkind, nor all deserve
The common° stroke of war.   indiscriminate
FIRST SENATOR   These walls of ours
Were not erected by their hands from whom
You have received your grief; nor are they such
25   That these great tow'rs, trophies,° and schools[8] should fall   monuments
For private faults in them.°   (the offenders)
SECOND SENATOR   Nor are they living
Who were the motives that you first went out.[9]
Shame that they wanted° cunning, in excess,   lacked
Hath broke their hearts. March, noble lord,
30   Into our city with thy banners spread.
By decimation and a tithèd death,[1]
If thy revenges hunger for that food
Which nature loathes, take thou the destined tenth,
And by the hazard of the spotted die
Let die the spotted.[2]
35   FIRST SENATOR   All have not offended.
For those that were,° it is not square° to take,   (living) / fair
On those that are, revenges. Crimes like lands
Are not inherited. Then, dear countryman,
Bring in thy ranks, but leave without° thy rage.   outside

5.5 Location: Outside the walls of Athens.
1. Trumpet call to negotiate.
2. Probably on the upper gallery at stage rear.
3. All kinds of licentious conduct.
4. *making . . . justice:* making justice conform to your whims.
5. Crossed (as part of military training).

6. *breathed / Our sufferance:* voiced our grievances.
7. *loves . . . quantity:* friendly gestures greater than your grievances.
8. Public buildings.
9. Who were those who prompted your banishment.
1. Killing one of every ten person, chosen by lot.
2. Corrupt (punning on the spots of dice).

40 Spare thy Athenian cradle° and those kin   *birthplace*
 Which, in the bluster of thy wrath, must fall
 With those that have offended. Like a shepherd
 Approach the fold and cull th'infected forth,°   *pick out the corrupt*
 But kill not all together.

SECOND SENATOR   What thou wilt,
45 Thou rather shalt enforce it with thy smile
 Than hew to't with thy sword.

FIRST SENATOR   Set but thy foot
 Against our rampired° gates and they shall ope,   *barricaded*
 So° thou wilt send thy gentle heart before   *If*
 To say thou'lt enter friendly.

SECOND SENATOR   Throw thy glove,
50 Or any token° of thine honour else,   *pledge*
 That thou wilt use the wars as thy redress,
 And not as our confusion.° All thy powers°   *ruin / army*
 Shall make their harbour° in our town till we   *lodging*
 Have sealed° thy full desire.   *satisfied*

ALCIBIADES [*throwing up a glove*] Then there's my glove.
55 Descend, and open your uncharged ports.°   *unattacked gates*
 Those enemies of Timon's and mine own
 Whom you yourselves shall set out for reproof°   *select for punishment*
 Fall, and no more; and to atone° your fears   *appease*
 With my more noble meaning, not a man°   *soldier*
60 Shall pass his quarter° or offend the stream   *leave his assigned place*
 Of regular justice[3] in your city's bounds
 But shall be remedied to° your public laws   *punished according to*
 At heaviest answer.°   *penalty*

BOTH SENATORS 'Tis most nobly spoken.
65 ALCIBIADES Descend, and keep your words.
    [*Trumpets sound. Exeunt* SENATORS *from the walls.*]
    Enter [SOLDIER, *with a tablet of wax*]

SOLDIER My noble general, Timon is dead,
 Entombed upon the very hem° o'th' sea;   *edge*
 And on his gravestone this insculpture,° which   *inscription*
 With wax I brought away, whose soft impression
70 Interprets for my poor ignorance.

      ALCIBIADES *reads the Epitaph*

ALCIBIADES 'Here lies a wretched corpse,
  Of wretched soul bereft.
  Seek not my name. A plague consume
  You wicked caitiffs° left!   *wretches*
75 Here lie I, Timon, who alive
  All living men did hate.
  Pass by and curse thy fill, but pass
  And stay not here thy gait.'
 These well express in thee thy latter spirits.°   *sentiments*
80 Though thou abhorred'st in us our human griefs,
 Scorned'st our brains' flow[4] and those our droplets which
 From niggard[5] nature fall, yet rich conceit°   *imagination*
 Taught thee to make vast Neptune weep for aye°   *ever*
 On thy low grave, on faults forgiven. Dead

---

3. *offend . . . justice:* violate the ordinary laws.
4. Tears were thought to exude from the brain.

5. "Niggard" because teardrops are tiny compared with the sea, Neptune (line 83).

85   Is noble Timon, of whose memory
         Hereafter more.
                 [*Enter* SENATORS *through the gates*]
                         Bring me into your city,
         And I will use the olive° with my sword,   (*symbol of peace*)
         Make war breed peace, make peace stint° war, make each   *stop*
         Prescribe to other as each other's leech.[6]
90   Let our drums strike.   [*Drums.*] *Exeunt* [*through the gates*]

---

6. Physician (because war purges peace of its decadence, and peace purges war of its violence).

King Lear

You have, King James told his eldest son a few years before Shakespeare wrote *King Lear,* a double obligation to love God: first because He made you a man, and second because He made you "a little God to sit on his Throne, and rule over other men." Whatever the realities of Renaissance kingship—realities that included the stern necessity of compromise, reciprocity, and restraint—the idea of sovereignty was closely linked to fantasies of divine omnipotence. From his exalted height, the sovereign looked down upon the tiny figures of the ordinary mortals below him. Their hopes, the material conditions of their miserable existence, their names, were of little interest, and yet the King knew that they too were looking back up at him. "For kings being public persons," James uneasily acknowledged, are set "upon a public stage, in the sight of all the people; where all the beholders' eyes are attentively bent to look and pry in the least circumstance of their secretist drifts." Under such circumstances, the sovereign's dream was to command, like God, not only unquestioning obedience but unqualified love.

In *King Lear,* Shakespeare explores the dark consequences of this dream not only in the state but also in the family, where the Renaissance father increasingly styled himself "a little God." If, as the play opens, the aged Lear, exercising his imperious will and demanding professions of devotion, is "every inch a king," he is also by the same token every inch a father, the absolute ruler of a family that conspicuously lacks the alternative authority of a mother. Shakespeare's play invokes this royal and paternal sovereignty only to chronicle its destruction in scenes of astonishing cruelty and power. The very words "every inch a king" are spoken not by the confident figure of supreme authority whom we glimpse in the first moments but by the ruined old man who perceives in his feverish rage and madness that the fantasy of omnipotence is a fraud: "When the rain came to wet me once, and the wind to make me chatter; when the thunder would not peace at my bidding, there I found 'em, there I smelt 'em out. Go to, they are not men o' their words. They told me I was everything; 'tis a lie, I am not ague-proof" (4.5.98–102; all quotations, except where noted, are from *The Tragedy of King Lear*).

"They told me I was everything": Shakespeare's culture continually staged public rituals of deference to authority. These rituals—kneeling, bowing, uncovering the head, and so forth—enacted respect for wealth, caste, power, and, at virtually every level of society, age. Jacobean England had a strong official regard for the rights and privileges of age. It told itself that, by the will of God and the natural order of things, authority gravitated to the old, particularly to old men, and it contrived to ensure that this proper, sanctified arrangement of society be everywhere respected.

"'Tis a lie": Shakespeare's culture continually told itself at the same time that without the control of property and the threat of punishment, any claim to authority was chillingly vulnerable to the ruthless ambitions of the young, the restless, and the discontented. The incessant, ritualized spectacles of sovereignty have a nervous air, as if no one quite believed all the grand claims to divine sanction for the rule of Kings and fathers, as if those who ruled both states and families secretly feared that the elaborate hierarchical structure could vanish like a mirage, exposing their shivering, defenseless bodies. *King Lear* relentlessly stages this horrifying descent toward what the ruined King, contemplating the filthy, naked body of a mad beggar, calls "the thing itself": "Unaccommodated man is no more but such a poor, bare, forked animal as thou art" (3.4.95–97). Lear and the Earl of Gloucester, another old man whose terrible fate closely parallels Lear's, repeatedly look up at the heavens and call upon the gods for help, but the gods are silent. The despairing Gloucester concludes that the universe is actively malevolent—"As flies to wanton boys are we to th' gods; / They kill us for their sport" (4.1.37–38)—but the awful silence of the gods may equally be a sign of their indifference or their nonexistence.

The story of King Lear and his three daughters had been often told when Shakespeare undertook to make it the subject of a tragedy. The play, performed at court in December 1605, was probably written and first performed somewhat earlier, though not before 1603, since it contains allusions to a florid piece of anti-Catholic propaganda published in that year: Samuel Harsnett's *Declaration of Egregious Popish Imposture* (the source of the colorful names of the "foul fiends" by whom Shakespeare's mad beggar claims to be possessed). Thus scholars generally assign Shakespeare's composition of *King Lear* to 1604–05, shortly after *Othello* (c. 1603–04) and before *Macbeth* (c. 1606): an astounding succession of tragic masterpieces.

King Lear first appeared in print in a Quarto published in 1608 entitled *M. William Shak-speare: His True Chronicle Historie of the life and death of King Lear;* a substantially different text, entitled *The Tragedie of King Lear* and grouped with the other tragedies, was printed in the 1623 First Folio. From the eighteenth century, when the difference between the two texts was first noted, editors, assuming that they were imperfect versions of the identical play, customarily conflated them, blending together the approximately one hundred Folio lines not printed in the Quarto with the approximately three hundred quarto lines not printed in the Folio and selecting as best they could among the hundreds of particular alternative readings. But there is a growing scholarly consensus that the 1608 text of *Lear* represents the play as Shakespeare first wrote it and that the 1623 text represents a substantial revision. (See the Textual Note for further discussion.) Since this revision includes significant structural changes as well as many local details, the two texts provide a precious opportunity to glimpse Shakespeare's creative process as an artist and the collaborative work of his theater company. Accordingly, the *Norton Shakespeare* prints *The History of King Lear* and *The Tragedy of King Lear* on facing pages; in addition, a modern conflated version of the play follows, so that readers will be able to judge for themselves the effects of the familiar editorial practice of stitching together the two texts.

When *King Lear* was first performed, it may have struck contemporaries as strangely timely in the wake of a lawsuit that had occurred in late 1603. The two elder daughters of a doddering gentleman named Sir Brian Annesley attempted to get their father legally certified as insane, thereby enabling themselves to take over his estate, while his youngest daughter vehemently protested on her father's behalf. The youngest daughter's name happened to be Cordell, a name uncannily close to that of Lear's youngest daughter, Cordelia, who tries to save her father from the malevolent designs of her older sisters.

Cordeilla Queene. From Raphael Holinshed, *The Firste Volume of the Chronicles of England, Scotlande, and Irelande* (1577).

The Annesley case is worth invoking not only because it may have caught Shakespeare's attention but also because it directs our own attention to the ordinary family tensions and fears around which *King Lear*, for all of its wildness, violence, and strangeness, is constructed. Though the Lear story has the mythic quality of a folktale (specifically, it resembles both the tale of Cinderella and the tale told in many cultures of a daughter who falls into disfavor for telling her father she loves him as much as salt), it was rehearsed in Shakespeare's time as a piece of authentic British history from the very ancient past (c. 800

B.C.E.) and as an admonition to contemporary fathers not to put too much trust in the flattery of their children: "Remember what happened to old King Lear . . ." In some versions of the story, including Shakespeare's, the warning centers on a decision to retire.

Retirement has come to seem a routine event, but in the patriarchal, gerontocratic culture of Tudor and Stuart England, it was generally shunned. When through illness or extreme old age it became unavoidable, retirement put a severe strain on the politics and psychology of deference by driving a wedge between status—what Lear at society's pinnacle calls "the name and all th'addition to a king" (1.1.134)—and power. In both the state and the family, the strain could be somewhat eased by transferring power to the eldest legitimate male successor, but as the families of both the legendary Lear and the real Brian Annesley showed, such a successor did not always exist. In the absence of a male heir, the aged Lear, determined to "shake all cares and business" from himself and confer them on "younger strengths," attempts to divide his kingdom equally among his daughters so that, as he puts it, "future strife / May be prevented now" (1.1.37–38, 42–43). But this attempt is a disastrous failure. Critics have often argued that the roots of the failure lie in the division of the kingdom, that any parceling out of the land on a map would itself have provoked in the audience an ominous shudder, as it is clearly meant to do when the rebels spread out a map in anticipation of a comparable division in 1 Henry IV. But the principal focus of Shakespeare's tragedy seems to lie elsewhere: Lear's folly is not (or not only) that he retires or even that he divides his kingdom—the play opens with the Earl of Gloucester and the Earl of Kent commenting without apparent disapproval on the scrupulous equality of the shares—but rather that he rashly disinherits the only child who truly loves him, his youngest daughter.

Shakespeare contrives moreover to show that the problem with which his characters are grappling does not simply result from the absence of a son and heir. In his most brilliant and complex use of a double plot, he intertwines the story of Lear and his three daughters with the story of Gloucester and his two sons, a tale he adapted from an episode in Philip Sidney's prose romance Arcadia. Gloucester has a legitimate heir, his elder son, Edgar, as well as an illegitimate son, Edmond, and in this family the tragic conflict originates not in an unusual manner of transferring property from one generation to another but rather in the reverse: Edmond seethes with murderous resentment at the disadvantage entirely customary for someone in his position, both as a younger son and as what was called a "base" or "natural" child. "Thou, nature, art my goddess," he declares:

Wherefore should I
Stand in the plague of custom and permit
The curiosity of nations to deprive me
For that I am some twelve or fourteen moonshines
Lag of a brother? Why 'bastard'? Wherefore 'base'?
(1.2.1–6)

For the seductive and ruthlessly ambitious Edmond, the social order and the language used to articulate it are merely arbitrary constraints, obstacles to the triumph of his will. He schemes to tear down the obstacles by playing on his father's fears, cleverly planting a forged letter in which his older brother appears to be plotting against his father's life. The letter's chilling sentences express Edmond's own impatience, his hatred of the confining power of custom, his disgusted observation of "the oppression of aged tyranny, who sways not as it hath power but as it is suffered" (1.2.48–49). Gloucester is predictably horrified and incensed; these are, as Edmond cunningly knows, the cold sentiments that the aged fear lie just beneath the surface of deference and flattery. The forged letter reflects back as well on the scene in which Gloucester himself has just participated: a scene in which everyone, with the exception of the Earl of Kent, has tamely suffered a tyrannical old man to banish his youngest daughter for her failure to flatter him.

Why does Lear, who has already drawn up the map dividing the kingdom, stage the love test? In Shakespeare's principal source, an anonymous play called The True

Stargazing. From John Cypriano, *A Most Strange and Wonderfull Prophesie* (1595). "I should have been that I am had the maidenliest star in the firmament twinkled on my bastardizing" (1.2.119–21).

Chronicle History of King Leir (published in 1605 but dating from 1594 or earlier), there is a gratifyingly clear answer. Leir's strong-willed daughter Cordella has vowed that she will only marry a man whom she herself loves; Leir wishes her to marry the man he chooses for his own dynastic purposes. He stages the love test, anticipating that in competing with her sisters Cordella will declare that she loves her father best, at which point Leir will demand that she prove her love by marrying the suitor of his choice. The stratagem backfires, but its purpose is clear.

By stripping his character of a comparable motive, Shakespeare makes Lear's act seem stranger, at once more arbitrary and more rooted in deep psychological needs. His Lear is a man who has determined to retire from power but who cannot endure dependence. Unwilling to lose his identity as an absolute authority both in the state and in the family, he arranges a public ritual—"Which of you shall we say doth love us most?" (1.1.49)—whose aim seems to be to allay his own anxiety by arousing it in his children. Since the shares have already been apportioned, Lear evidently wants his daughters to engage in a competition for his bounty without having to endure any of the actual consequences of such a competition; he wants, that is, to produce in them something like the effect of theater, where emotions run high and their practical effects are negligible. But in this absolutist theater Cordelia refuses to perform: "What shall Cordelia speak? Love and be silent" (1.1.60). When she says "Nothing," a word that echoes darkly throughout the play, Lear hears what he most dreads: emptiness, loss of respect, the extinction of identity. And when, under further interrogation, she declares that she loves her father "according to my bond" (1.1.91), Lear understands these words too to be the equivalent of "nothing."

As Cordelia's subsequent actions demonstrate, his youngest daughter's bond is in reality a sustaining, generous love, but it is a love that ultimately leads to her death. Here Shakespeare makes an even more startling departure not only from *The True Chronicle History of King Leir* but from all his known sources. The earliest of these, the account in Geoffrey of Monmouth's twelfth-century *Historia Regum Britanniae*, sets the pattern repeated in John Higgins's *Mirour for Magistrates* (1574 edition), William Warner's *Albions England* (1586), Raphael Holinshed's *Chronicles of England, Scotlande, and Irelande* (2nd ed., 1587), and Edmund Spenser's *Faerie Queene* (1590, 2.10.27–32): the aged Lear is overthrown by his wicked daughters and their husbands, but he is restored to the throne by the army of his good daughter's husband, the King of France. The story then is one of loss and restoration: Lear resumes his reign, and when, "made ripe for death" by old age, as Spenser puts it, he dies, he is succeeded by Cordelia. The conclusion is not unequivocally happy; in all of the known chronicles, Cordelia rules worthily for several years and then, after being deposed and imprisoned by her nephews, in despair commits suicide. But Shakespeare's ending is unprecedented in its tragic devastation. When in Act 5 Lear suddenly enters with the lifeless body of Cordelia in his arms, the original audience, secure in the expectation of a very different resolution, must have been doubly shocked, a shock cruelly reinforced when the signs that she might be reviving—"This feather stirs. She lives" (5.3.239)—all prove false. Lear apparently dies in the grip of the illusion that he detects some breath on his daughter's lips, but we know that Cordelia will, as he says a moment earlier, "come no more. / Never, never, never, never, never" (5.3.282–83).

Those five reiterated words, the bleakest pentameter line Shakespeare ever wrote, are the climax of an extraordinary poetics of despair that is set in motion when Lear disinherits Cordelia and when Gloucester credits Edmond's lies about Edgar. *King Lear* has seemed to many modern readers and audiences the greatest of Shakespeare's tragedies precisely because of its anguished look into the heart of darkness, but its vision of suffering and evil has not always commanded unequivocal admiration. In the eighteenth century, Samuel Johnson wrote, "I was many years ago so shocked by Cordelia's death that I know not whether I ever endured to read again the last scenes of the play till I undertook to revise them as an editor." Johnson's contemporaries preferred a revision of Shakespeare's tragedy undertaken in 1681 by Nahum Tate. Finding the play "a Heap of Jewels, unstrung, and unpolish't," Tate proceeded to restring them in order to save Cordelia's life and to produce the unambiguous and happy triumph of the forces of good.

Only in the nineteenth century was Shakespeare's deeply pessimistic ending—the old generation dead or dying, the survivors shaken to the core, the ruling families all broken with no impending marriage to promise renewal—generally restored to theatrical performance and the tragedy's immense power fully acknowledged. Even passionate admirers of *King Lear,* however, continued to express deep uneasiness, repeatedly noting not only its unbearably painful close but also what Johnson first called the "improbability of Lear's conduct" and Samuel Taylor Coleridge termed the plot's "glaring absurdity." Above all, critics questioned whether the tragedy was suitable for the stage. Coleridge compared the suffering Lear to one of Michelangelo's titanic figures, but the grandeur invoked by the comparison led his contemporary Charles Lamb to conclude flatly that "Lear is essentially impossible to be represented on stage." "To see Lear acted," Lamb wrote, "to see an old man tottering about the stage with a walking stick, turned out of doors by his daughters in a rainy night, has nothing in it but what is painful and disgusting." In such a view, *King Lear* could only be staged successfully in the imagination; there alone would Lear's passion be perceived not like ordinary human suffering but rather, in the marvelous characterization of another Romantic critic, William Hazlitt, "like a sea, swelling, chafing, raging, without bound, without hope, without beacon, or anchor." In the theater of the mind, Shakespeare's play could assume its true, stupendous proportions, enabling the reader to grasp its ultimate meaning. That meaning, the great early twentieth-century critic A. C. Bradley wrote, is that we must "renounce the world, hate it, and lose it gladly. The only real thing in it is the soul, with its courage, patience, devotion. And nothing outward can touch that." These are stirring words, but what about the body?

Brilliant modern stage performances and, more recently, films belying the view that *King Lear* is unactable have underscored not only the play's acute theatrical sophistication and self-awareness but also its emphasis on the body's inescapable centrality. If Shakespeare explores the extremes of the mind's anguish and the soul's devotion, he never forgets that his characters have bodies as well, bodies that have needs, cravings, and terrible vulnerabilities. When in this tragedy characters fall from high station, they plunge unprotected into a world of violent storms, murderous cruelty, and physical horror. The old King wanders raging on the heath, through a wild night of thunder and rain. Disguised as Poor Tom, a mad beggar possessed by demons, Gloucester's son Edgar enacts a life of utmost degradation: "Poor Tom, that eats the swimming frog, the toad, the tadpole, the wall-newt and the water; that in the fury of his heart, when the foul fiend rages, eats cowdung for salads, swallows the old rat and the ditch-dog, drinks the green mantle of the standing pool" (3.4.115–19). Gloucester's fate is even more terrible: betrayed by his son Edmond, he is seized in his own house by Lear's sadistic daughter Regan and her husband, Cornwall, tied to a chair, brutally interrogated, blinded, and then thrust bleeding out of doors.

Mental anguish in *King Lear,* then, is closely intertwined with physical anguish; the terrifying forces that are released by Lear's folly crash down upon both body and soul, just as the storm that rages on the heath seems at once an objective event and a symbolic representation of Lear's innermost being. The greatest expression of this intertwining in the play is Lear's madness, which brings together a devastating loss of identity, a relentless, radical assault on the hypocrisies of authority, and a demented, nauseated loathing of female sexuality. The loathing culminates in a fit of retching—"Fie, fie, fie; pah, pah!"—followed by Lear's delusional attempt to find a physical remedy for his psychic pain: "Give me an ounce of civet, good apothecary, sweeten my imagination" (4.5.123–24). In fact, relief from the chaotic rage of madness comes in the wake of a deep, restorative sleep and a change of garments.

The body in *King Lear* is a site not only of abject misery, nausea, and pain but of care and a nascent moral awareness. In the midst of his mad ravings, Lear turns to the shivering Fool and asks, "Art cold?" (3.2.67). The simple question anticipates his recognition a few moments later that there is more suffering in the world than his own:

> Poor naked wretches, wheresoe'er you are,
> That bide the pelting of this pitiless storm,
> How shall your houseless heads and unfed sides,
> Your looped and windowed raggedness, defend you
> From seasons such as these? O, I have ta'en
> Too little care of this.
>
> (3.4.28–33)

And if the world seems largely unjust and indifferent to human suffering, there are nonetheless throughout the play constant manifestations of generosity of body as well

Tom Durie (1614). By Marcus Gheeraerts the Younger. Durie was the jester of Anne of Denmark, who was married to James I.

as soul. "Help me, help me!" cries the frightened Fool, to which Kent (disguised in order to serve the King who has banished him) says simply, "Give me thy hand" (3.4.39–40). "What are you?" says the blind Gloucester to the son he has unjustly disinherited, to which the son, also in disguise, replies similarly, "Give me your hand" (4.5.213, 216). (In a moving moment from the History of . . . King Lear, absent from the Folio version, two of Gloucester's servants not only react with horror to their master's blinding but also resolve to assist him: "Go thou. I'll fetch some flax and whites of eggs / To apply to his bleeding face. Now heaven help him!" [14.103–04].) Such signs of goodness and empathy do not outweigh the harshness of the physical world of the play, let alone cancel out the vicious cruelty of certain of its inhabitants, but they do qualify its moral bleakness.

It is possible to detect in King Lear one of the great structural rhythms of Christianity: a passage through suffering, humiliation, and pain to a transcendent wisdom and love. Lear's initial actions were blind and selfish, but he comes to acknowledge his folly and, in an immensely poignant scene, to kneel down before the daughter he has wronged. Gloucester too learns that he was blind, even when his eyes could see, and he passes, by means of Edgar's strange deception at the imaginary cliff, from suicidal despair to patient resignation. "Men must endure / Their going hence even as their coming hither," Edgar wisely counsels his father. "Ripeness is all" (5.2.9–11). For a time, evil seems to flourish in the world, but the wicked do not ultimately triumph. The sadistic Duke of Cornwall is fatally wounded by his own morally upright servant, Edmond is killed by the brother he had tried to destroy, the loathsome Oswald is clubbed to death trying to murder Gloucester, one wicked sister poisons the other and then kills herself. Against self-interest and in the face of intolerable pressure, goodness shines forth. The Earl of Kent, banished by the rash Lear, dons a disguise in order to serve his King and master, and there are comparable acts of devoted service and self-sacrificing love from Edgar, Cordelia, and that remarkable figure the Fool. In one of the comic masterpieces of the sixteenth century, The Praise of Folly, the great Dutch humanist Erasmus used the fool as an emblem of the deepest Christian wisdom, revealed only when the pride, cruelty, and ambition of the world are shattered by a cleansing laughter. The shattering in King Lear is tragically violent and deadly, but the presence of the truth-telling Fool seems to point toward a comparable revelation.

Yet King Lear, set in a pagan world, resists the redemptive optimism that underlies the Christian vision (an optimism that led Dante to call his poem of damnation and salvation The Divine Comedy). The Fool's unnervingly perceptive observations sound far more corrosive than loving—he is, in Lear's words, "a bitter fool" (1.4.121)—and he disappears altogether in the third act. His moments of insight and those of all the other characters in the play are radically unstable, like brilliant flashes of lightning in a vast, dark landscape. Hence, for example, Lear's recognition of his folly in banishing Cordelia for her "most small fault" (1.4.228) is immediately followed by his hideous cursing of Goneril. His moving acknowledgment of the suffering of the poor, naked wretches is immediately followed by his inability to see the poor naked wretch before him in any terms but his own: "Didst thou give all to thy two daughters, / And art thou come to this?" (3.4.47–48). And his appeal to patient resignation—"When we are born, we cry that we are come / To this great stage of fools" (4.5.172–73)—is immediately followed by a mad fantasy of revenge: "Then kill, kill, kill, kill, kill, kill!" (4.5.177). Every time we seem to have reached firm moral ground, the ground shifts, and we are kept, as Johnson observed, in "a perpetual tumult of indignation, pity, and hope." There are moments of apparent resolution: "Let's away to prison," says Lear to the weeping Cordelia, when they are captured by the enemy. "We two alone will sing like birds i'th' cage" (5.3.8–9). But a more terrible fate lies before them. "Some good I mean to do," says the dying Edmond, "despite of mine own nature" (5.3.217–18). But his attempt to send a reprieve and therefore in some measure to redeem himself comes too late. The play's nightmarish events continually lurch ahead of intentions, and even efforts to say "I have seen the worst" are frustrated.

The tragedy is not only that the intervals of moral resolution, mental lucidity, and spiritual calm are so brief, continually giving way to feverish grief and rage, but also that the modest human understandings, moving in their simplicity, cost such an enormous amount of pain. Edgar saves his father from despair but also in some sense breaks his father's heart. Cordelia's steadfast honesty, her refusal to flatter the father she loves, may be admirable but has disastrous consequences, and her attempt to save Lear only leads to her own death. For a sublime moment, Lear actually *sees* his daughter, understands her separateness, acknowledges her existence—

> Do not laugh at me,
> For as I am a man, I think this lady
> To be my child, Cordelia—

but it has taken the destruction of virtually his whole world for him to reach this recognition (4.6.61–63).

An apocalyptic dream of last judgment and redemption hovers over the entire tragedy, but it is a dream forever deferred. At the sight of the howling Lear with the dead Cordelia in his arms, the bystanders can only ask a succession of stunned questions:

> KENT   Is this the promised end?
> EDGAR   Or image of that horror?
>
> (5.3.237–38)

Lear's own question a moment later seems the most terrible and the most important: "Why should a dog, a horse, a rat have life, / And thou no breath at all?" (5.3.281–82). It is a sign of *King Lear*'s astonishing freedom from orthodoxy that it refuses to offer any of the conventional answers to this question, answers that largely serve to conceal or deflect the mourner's anguish. Shakespeare's tragedy asks us not to turn away from evil, folly, and unbearable human pain but, seeing them face-to-face, to strengthen our capacity to speak the truth, to endure, and to love.

STEPHEN GREENBLATT

TEXTUAL NOTE

The textual traces of *King Lear* have probably given scholars more cause for debate than any of Shakespeare's other works. The debate centers on the relative authority of the two early texts of the tragedy, the First Quarto (Q1) and the First Folio (F), and the relationship between them. Q1 contains approximately three hundred lines that do not appear in F; F prints approximately one hundred lines that are not in Q1. There are also hundreds of individual variants, some apparently negligible but others highly significant. To take a single instance, the closing lines of the play—by convention assigned to the person who will now govern the state—are in Q1 spoken by Albany, in F spoken by Edgar.

Q1 was first printed in December and January of 1607–08 in the shop of Nicholas Okes, a London printer, under the following title:

> M. William Shak-speare: His True Chronicle Historie of the life and death of King Lear and his three Daughters. With the vnfortunate life of Edgar, sonne and heire to the Earle of Gloster, and his sullen and assumed humor of Tom of Bedlam: As it was played before the Kings Maiestie at Whitehall vpon S. Stephans night in Christmas Hollidayes. By his Maiesties seruants playing vsually at the Gloabe on the Banckeside. London, Printed for Nathaniel Butter, and are to be sold at his shop in Pauls Church-yard at the signe of the Pide Bull neere St. Austins Gate. 1608.

Of the print run, only twelve copies have been found. Q1 was set, most scholars agree, from Shakespeare's own draft, his "foul papers." That Q1 was printed from such a draft and not from a scribe's copy or a promptbook promises strong authority. However, there are difficulties.

Peculiarities within the text and variations among the twelve copies suggest that

Okes's printing shop was not quite up to the task set by this long, complex play. *King Lear* appears indeed to have been the first play Okes attempted. There was clearly a shortage of typeface, particularly of full stops and colons: this may help to explain anomalous aspects of lineation and punctuation. Evidently, two compositors worked together on the play, one perhaps reading aloud while the other set the type; this may have caused what often appear to be aural errors in the text. And these errors, which may have been compounded by difficulties in reading the copy, might have been avoided had the printer's copy come from an experienced scribe rather than from Shakespeare's own handwriting, which appears at some points to have been illegible. The result is a text of great importance but tantalizing uncertainty. While no critics doubt that Q1 represents a legitimate early version of *King Lear*, it is a version whose authority is compromised by a succession of readings that are often confusing and sometimes nonsensical.

At a time when it was generally accepted that Q1 and F were, for all their differences, derived from one original text, now lost, these textual difficulties were relatively easily handled: the editor, positing a single ideal form of the play "behind" or "before" the versions that were printed, would conflate the two texts, weaving together the lines that appear in only one or the other version and correcting Q1 with reference to F or (in a much smaller number of instances) F with reference to Q1. The Oxford editors, upon whose work this edition is based, broke decisively with this tradition of conflation. Instead, they edited and printed Q1 and F as separate and distinct texts. In so doing, they gave up the luxury of editorial cross-referencing. As the principal Oxford editor of *King Lear*, Gary Taylor, points out, "The entire purpose of editing Q and F separately is to preserve the integrity of each, and such a purpose is not well served by importing revised readings into an unrevised fabric." Oxford therefore sought, insofar as possible, to emend Q1, where necessary, as if F did not exist.

Such emendation is almost unnecessary in the altogether more straightforward text of the First Folio, which appeared in 1623 as *The Tragedie of King Lear*. In contrast to Q1, F differentiates carefully between prose and verse, shows consistency in spelling, and offers detailed stage directions. The Folio also characteristically divides the play into acts and scenes. These differences, along with the cuts and the additional passages, are all the more striking if F is basically derived, as Oxford contends, from the text known as Q2. For this Second Quarto, printed in 1619 (three years after Shakespeare's death) although falsely dated 1608, is only a slightly improved copy of Q1. While spelling and punctuation were somewhat corrected and some attempts were made to emend difficult words and phrases, no independent manuscript was used to prepare Q2. Therefore, when the compositors sat down to print F, their copy of Q2, Oxford maintains, must have been annotated using an independent manuscript. What was the source of this manuscript? The Oxford editors think it likely that the manuscript was a scribal copy, perhaps a promptbook, that derived ultimately from Q1.

Though F is thus linked, if indirectly, to Q1, the fact remains that two quite different texts of the play exist. Efforts over the years to conflate them in the search for a hypothetical master text have been partly responsible for the neglect that Q1 has generally suffered and for the failure to explore fully the extraordinary opportunity that the survival of these distinct versions of the play presents. Each version has its own integrity; each contains passages intrinsically its own. In addition, the Quarto may give us a precious glimpse, as the Oxford editor notes, of the play "as Shakespeare first conceived it, probably before it was performed," while the Folio represents a revision made probably two or three years after the play had been first written and performed. The Folio, then, with its substantial cuts and its small additions, its streamlining and its subtle shifts in emphasis, is the more theatrical text.

The *Norton Shakespeare* presents Q1 and F on facing pages so that readers can compare them easily. In order to make it possible to read them independently of one another, both texts are glossed and footnoted. In addition, we offer a conflated version of *King Lear*, prepared by Barbara K. Lewalski, so that readers can encounter the tragedy in the form that it assumed in most editions from the eighteenth century until very recently.

SELECTED BIBLIOGRAPHY

Booth, Stephen. "On the Greatness of *King Lear*." *"King Lear," "Macbeth," Indefinition and Tragedy*. New Haven: Yale University Press, 1983. 1–57. Shakespeare's tragedy compels readers and audience through its power of indefiniteness: the play's characters, categories, and boundaries melt and blur, disclosing the instability of all attempts to impose order on the world.

Cavell, Stanley. "The Avoidance of Love: A Reading of *King Lear*." *Disowning Knowledge in Six Plays of Shakespeare*. Cambridge: Cambridge University Press, 1987. 39–124. To face the frightening isolation of all humans, to grasp the difference between the knowledge of love and the acknowledgment of love, to understand that in order to see one must also allow oneself to be seen, to endure the shame of exposure—these are among *King Lear*'s radical insights.

de Grazia, Margreta. "The Ideology of Superfluous Things: *King Lear* as Period Piece." *Subject and Object in Renaissance Culture*. Ed. Margreta de Grazia, Maureen Quilligan, and Peter Stallybrass. Cambridge: Cambridge University Press, 1996. 17–42. Far from being protomodern, the play depicts a world where persons and things cannot be separated and superfluity is a sign of apocalypse.

Greenblatt, Stephen. "Shakespeare and the Exorcists." *Shakespearean Negotiations: The Circulation of Social Energy in Renaissance England*. Berkeley: University of California Press, 1988. 94–128. Shakespeare draws theatrical energy from the contemporary practice of exorcism, a ritualized encounter with evil attacked by Protestant officials as a vicious, histrionic fraud.

Holland, Peter, ed. *King Lear and Its Afterlife: Shakespeare Survey* 55 (2002): 1–180. Treating four centuries of adaptations, appropriations, performances, and interpretations, this essay collection focuses on plays, songs, and novels that draw on *King Lear*.

Jones, John. *Shakespeare at Work*. Oxford: Oxford University Press, 1995. Close attention to the Folio revisions of the quarto text of the play discloses a cunning symbolic design that links Lear's craziness with an obsession with quantity.

Kronenfeld, Judy. *"King Lear" and the Naked Truth: Rethinking the Language of Religion and Resistance*. Durham, N.C.: Duke University Press, 1998. The play should be understood not through deconstruction or new historicism but through the common Christian culture that gave its terms meaning outside a polemical context.

Leggatt, Alexander. *King Lear*. 2nd ed. Manchester: Manchester University Press, 2004. Interpretive problems are explored through the history of twentieth-century stage and film productions.

Nuttall, A. D. "King Lear." *Why Does Tragedy Give Pleasure?* Oxford: Clarendon, 1996. 81–105. The play gives pleasure not by sealing off suffering in poetic form but by destroying the expected recognition and closure of tragedy.

Taylor, Gary, and Michael Warren, eds. *The Division of the Kingdoms: Shakespeare's Two Versions of "King Lear."* Oxford: Clarendon, 1983. This essay collection presents the case for the quarto and Folio texts as distinct works and explores the consequences for interpreting *King Lear*.

FILMS

Korol Lir. 1969. Dir. Grigori Kozintsev and Iosif Shapiro. Soviet Union. 139 min. This black-and-white film presents a wizened but childlike Lear in a peasant-filled wasteland; a romantic fable in the Christian Middle Ages.

King Lear. 1971. Dir. Peter Brook. UK. 137 min. Men in pelts wander in a primitive tundra. Breaks in cinematic realism signal Lear's decline. With Paul Scofield and Jack MacGowran.

King Lear. 1983. Dir. Michael Elliott. UK. 158 min. Laurence Olivier, nearly eighty, in his final *Lear*. A television production that opens at Stonehenge.

Ran. 1985. Dir. Akira Kurosawa. Japan. 160 min. Set in sixteenth-century feudal Japan, the story, loosely adapted from Shakespeare, is noted for its elegaic battle sequences and orgies of red. In Japanese. With Tatsuya Nakadai and Akira Terao.

King Lear. 1998. Dir. Richard Eyre. UK. 150 min. Garish hues and torch-lit interiors for an especially cruel Lear, with equally vicious Regan and Goneril. With Ian Holm and Victoria Hamilton.

The History of King Lear

THE PERSONS OF THE PLAY

LEAR, King of Britain
GONORIL, Lear's eldest daughter
Duke of ALBANY, her husband
REGAN, Lear's second daughter
Duke of CORNWALL, her husband
CORDELIA, Lear's youngest daughter
King of FRANCE   } suitors of Cordelia
Duke of BURGUNDY
Earl of KENT, later disguised as Caius
Earl of GLOUCESTER
EDGAR, elder son of Gloucester, later disguised as Tom o' Bedlam
EDMUND, bastard son of Gloucester
OLD MAN, a tenant of Gloucester
CURAN, Gloucester's retainer
Lear's FOOL
OSWALD, Gonoril's steward
Three SERVANTS of Cornwall
DOCTOR, attendant on Cordelia
Three CAPTAINS
A HERALD
A KNIGHT
A MESSENGER
Gentlemen, servants, soldiers, followers, trumpeters, others

Scene 1

*Enter [the Earl of] KENT, [the Earl of] GLOUCESTER,[1]
and Bastard [EDMUND]*

KENT I thought the King had more affected° the Duke of   favored
Albany° than Cornwall.   Scotland
GLOUCESTER   It did always seem so to us, but now in the division
of the kingdoms it appears not° which of the Dukes he values   is not clear
5   most; for equalities° are so weighed° that curiosity in neither   shares / equal
can make choice of either's moiety.[2]
KENT   Is not this your son, my lord?
GLOUCESTER   His breeding,° sir, hath been at my charge.[3] I have   upbringing
so often blushed to acknowledge him that now I am brazed° to   hardened
10   it.
KENT   I cannot conceive° you.   comprehend
GLOUCESTER   Sir, this young fellow's mother could,[4] whereupon
she grew round-wombed and had indeed, sir, a son for her cradle ere she had a husband for her bed. Do you smell a fault?[5]

Scene 1 Location: King Lear's court.
1. Pronounced "Gloster."
2. *that . . . moiety:* that careful scrutiny ("curiosity") of
both parts cannot determine which portion ("moiety")
is preferable.

3. My responsibility; at my cost.
4. Could conceive; punning on biological conception.
5. Sin, wrongdoing; female genitals.

The Tragedy of King Lear

THE PERSONS OF THE PLAY

LEAR, King of Britain
GONERIL, Lear's eldest daughter
Duke of ALBANY, her husband
REGAN, Lear's second daughter
Duke of CORNWALL, her husband
CORDELIA, Lear's youngest daughter
King of FRANCE } suitors of Cordelia
Duke of BURGUNDY
Earl of KENT, later disguised as Caius
Earl of GLOUCESTER
EDGAR, elder son of Gloucester, later disguised as Tom o' Bedlam
EDMOND, bastard son of Gloucester
OLD MAN, Gloucester's tenant
CURAN, Gloucester's retainer
Lear's FOOL
OSWALD, Goneril's steward
A SERVANT of Cornwall
A KNIGHT
A HERALD
A CAPTAIN
Gentlemen, servants, soldiers, attendants, messengers

1.1

Enter [the Earl of] KENT, *[the Earl of]* GLOUCESTER,[1]
and EDMOND

KENT I thought the King had more affected° the Duke of   *favored*
Albany° than Cornwall.   *Scotland*

GLOUCESTER It did always seem so to us, but now in the division of
the kingdom it appears not° which of the Dukes he values   *is not clear*
5   most; for qualities are so weighed that curiosity in neither can
make choice of either's moiety.[2]

KENT Is not this your son, my lord?

GLOUCESTER His breeding,° sir, hath been at my charge.[3] I have   *upbringing*
so often blushed to acknowledge him that now I am brazed°   *hardened*
10 to't.

KENT I cannot conceive° you.   *comprehend*

GLOUCESTER Sir, this young fellow's mother could,[4] whereupon
she grew round-wombed and had indeed, sir, a son for her
cradle ere she had a husband for her bed. Do you smell a fault?[5]

1.1 Location: King Lear's court.
1. Pronounced "Gloster."
2. *for . . . moiety:* because their qualities are so evenly
weighted that careful scrutiny ("curiosity") of both parts

cannot determine which portion ("moiety") is preferable.
3. My responsibility; at my cost.
4. Could conceive; punning on biological conception.
5. Sin, wrongdoing; female genitals.

15   KENT   I cannot wish the fault undone, the issue° of it being so   *offspring; result*
        proper.°   *handsome; right*
      GLOUCESTER   But I have, sir, a son by order of law,° some year   *legitimate son*
        elder than this, who yet is no dearer in my account.° Though   *estimation*
        this knave° came something saucily⁶ into the world before he   *scamp; fellow*
20   was sent for, yet was his mother fair, there was good sport at his
        making, and the whoreson° must be acknowledged. [*To*   *rogue; bastard*
        EDMUND] Do you know this noble gentleman, Edmund?
      EDMUND   No, my lord.
      GLOUCESTER [*to* EDMUND]   My lord of Kent. Remember him
25   hereafter as my honourable friend.
      EDMUND [*to* KENT]   My services to your lordship.
      KENT   I must love you, and sue° to know you better.   *seek*
      EDMUND   Sir, I shall study deserving.°   *shall learn to deserve*
      GLOUCESTER [*to* KENT]   He hath been out° nine years, and away   *away; abroad*
30   he shall again.
                Sound a sennet°   *fanfare of trumpets*
        The King is coming.
                Enter one bearing a coronet, then [King] LEAR, *then the*
                Dukes of ALBANY *and* CORNWALL; *next* GONORIL, REGAN,
                CORDELIA, *with followers*
      LEAR   Attend° my lords of France and Burgundy, Gloucester.   *Attend upon; escort*
      GLOUCESTER   I shall, my liege.°   [*Exit*]   *feudal superior*
      LEAR   Meantime we° will express our darker° purposes.   *(royal "we") / more secret*
35   The map there. Know we have divided
        In three our kingdom, and 'tis our first intent
        To shake all cares and business off our state,°   *position (as King)*
        Confirming them on younger years.
        The two great princes, France and Burgundy—
40   Great rivals in our youngest daughter's love—
        Long in our court have made their amorous sojourn,
        And here are to be answered. Tell me, my daughters,
        Which of you shall we say doth love us most,
        That° we our largest bounty° may extend   *So that / generosity*
45   Where merit doth most challenge it?°   *best claims it*
        Gonoril, our eldest born, speak first.
      GONORIL   Sir, I do love you more than words can wield° the matter;   *convey*
        Dearer than eyesight, space,° or liberty;   *freedom of movement*
        Beyond what can be valued, rich or rare;
50   No less than life; with grace, health, beauty, honour;
        As much as child e'er loved, or father, friend;°   *or friend*
        A love that makes breath° poor and speech unable.   *language*
        Beyond all manner of so much° I love you.   *Beyond all comparison*
      CORDELIA [*aside*]   What shall Cordelia do? Love and be silent.
55   LEAR [*to* GONORIL]   Of all these bounds° even from this line to this,   *regions*
        With shady forests and wide skirted meads,°   *broad meadows*

---

6. Somewhat rudely; somewhat shamefully.

15 KENT   I cannot wish the fault undone, the issue° of it being so   *offspring; result*
proper.°   *handsome; right*
GLOUCESTER   But I have a son, sir, by order of law,° some year   *legitimate son*
older than this, who yet is no dearer in my account.° Though   *estimation*
this knave° came something saucily⁶ to the world before he was   *scamp; fellow*
20 sent for, yet was his mother fair, there was good sport at his
making, and the whoreson° must be acknowledged. [*To*   *rogue; bastard*
EDMOND] Do you know this noble gentleman, Edmond?
EDMOND   No, my lord.
GLOUCESTER [*to* EDMOND]   My lord of Kent. Remember him
25 hereafter as my honourable friend.
EDMOND [*to* KENT]   My services to your lordship.
KENT   I must love you, and sue° to know you better.   *seek*
EDMOND   Sir, I shall study deserving.°   *shall learn to deserve*
GLOUCESTER [*to* KENT]   He hath been out° nine years, and away   *away; abroad*
30 he shall again.
               Sennet°   *Fanfare of trumpets*
The King is coming.
      Enter King LEAR, [*the Dukes of*] CORNWALL [*and*]
      ALBANY, GONERIL, REGAN, CORDELIA, *and attendants*
LEAR   Attend° the lords of France and Burgundy, Gloucester.   *Attend upon; escort*
GLOUCESTER   I shall, my lord.   *Exit*
LEAR   Meantime we° shall express our darker° purpose.   *(royal "we") / more secret*
35 Give me the map there. Know that we have divided
In three our kingdom, and 'tis our fast° intent   *fixed*
To shake all cares and business from our age,
Conferring them on younger strengths while we
Unburdened crawl toward death. Our son° of Cornwall,   *son-in-law*
40 And you, our no less loving son of Albany,
We have this hour a constant will to publish⁷
Our daughters' several dowers,° that future strife   *individual dowries*
May be prevented now. The princes France and Burgundy—
Great rivals in our youngest daughter's love—
45 Long in our court have made their amorous sojourn,
And here are to be answered. Tell me, my daughters—
Since now we will divest us both of rule,
Interest° of territory, cares of state—   *Legal title*
Which of you shall we say doth love us most,
50 That° we our largest bounty° may extend   *So that / generosity*
Where nature doth with merit challenge?⁸ Goneril,
Our eldest born, speak first.
GONERIL   Sir, I love you more than words can wield° the matter;   *convey*
Dearer than eyesight, space,° and liberty;   *freedom of movement*
55 Beyond what can be valued, rich or rare,
No less than life; with grace, health, beauty, honour;
As much as child e'er loved or father found;
A love that makes breath° poor and speech unable.   *language*
Beyond all manner of so much° I love you.   *Beyond all comparison*
CORDELIA [*aside*]   What shall Cordelia speak? Love and be
60   silent.
LEAR [*to* GONERIL]   Of all these bounds° even from this line to this,   *regions*
With shadowy forests and with champaigns riched,°   *enriched plains*
With plenteous rivers and wide-skirted meads,°   *broad meadows*

---

6. Somewhat rudely; somewhat shamefully.
7. A fixed determination to announce publicly.

8. *Where . . . challenge*: To the one whose natural love
and deserving lay claim (to our generosity).

We make thee lady. To thine and Albany's issue°   *children; heirs*
Be this perpetual.—What says our second daughter?
Our dearest Regan, wife to Cornwall, speak.
60 REGAN   Sir, I am made
Of the self-same mettle° that my sister is,   *spirit; substance*
And prize me at her worth.° In my true heart   *believe myself her equal*
I find she names my very deed of love—
Only she came short, that° I profess   *in that*
65 Myself an enemy to all other joys
Which the most precious square of sense possesses,[7]
And find I am alone felicitate°   *am only made happy*
In your dear highness' love.
CORDELIA [*aside*]   Then poor Cordelia—
And yet not so, since I am sure my love's
70 More richer than my tongue.
LEAR [*to* REGAN]   To thee and thine hereditary ever
Remain this ample third of our fair kingdom,
No less in space, validity,° and pleasure   *value*
Than that confirmed° on Gonoril. [*To* CORDELIA] But now our joy,   *fixed*
75 Although the last, not least in our dear love:
What can you say to win a third more opulent
Than your sisters?
CORDELIA   Nothing, my lord.
LEAR   How? Nothing can come of nothing.[8] Speak again.
80 CORDELIA   Unhappy that I am, I cannot heave
My heart into my mouth. I love your majesty
According to my bond,° nor more nor less.   *filial duty*
LEAR   Go to, go to, mend your speech a little
Lest it may mar your fortunes.
CORDELIA   Good my lord,
85 You have begot me, bred me, loved me.
I return those duties back as are right fit—
Obey you, love you, and most honour you.
Why have my sisters husbands if they say
They love you all°? Haply° when I shall wed   *completely / Perhaps; if lucky*
90 That lord whose hand must take my plight° shall carry   *marriage vow; condition*
Half my love with him, half my care and duty.
Sure, I shall never marry like my sisters,
To love my father all.
LEAR   But goes this with thy heart?
95 CORDELIA   Ay, good my lord.
LEAR   So young and so untender?
CORDELIA   So young, my lord, and true.°   *honest; faithful*
LEAR   Well, let it be so. Thy truth then be thy dower;
For by the sacred radiance of the sun,
100 The mysteries of Hecate[9] and the night,
By all the operation of the orbs
From whom we do exist and cease to be,[1]

---

7. *Which . . . possesses:* That the body can enjoy. *precious square of sense:* measure of sensibility; or, perhaps, balanced and sensitive perception. The square may represent the even mixture of the body's four fluids, or humors.
8. *Ex nihilo nihil fit,* a maxim derived from Aristotle, was accepted by the Christian Middle Ages with the single exception of God having created the world out of nothing.

9. A classical goddess of the moon and the patron of witchcraft, she was associated with the underworld, Hades.
1. *By all . . . be:* Referring to the belief that the movements of stars and planets ("orbs") corresponded to physical and spiritual motions in a person and thus controlled his or her fate.

We make thee lady. To thine and Albany's issues°   *children; heirs*
65   Be this perpetual.—What says our second daughter?
Our dearest Regan, wife of Cornwall?
REGAN   I am made of that self° mettle° as my sister,   *same / spirit; substance*
And prize me at her worth.° In my true heart   *believe myself her equal*
I find she names my very deed of love—
70   Only she comes too short, that° I profess   *in that*
Myself an enemy to all other joys
Which the most precious square of sense possesses,[9]
And find I am alone felicitate°   *am only made happy*
In your dear highness' love.
CORDELIA [*aside*]   Then poor Cordelia—
75   And yet not so, since I am sure my love's
More ponderous° than my tongue.   *weighty*
LEAR [*to* REGAN]   To thee and thine hereditary ever
Remain this ample third of our fair kingdom,
No less in space, validity,° and pleasure   *value*
80   Than that conferred on Goneril. [*To* CORDELIA] Now our joy,
Although our last and least,° to whose young love   *youngest; smallest*
The vines of France and milk of Burgundy
Strive to be interested:° what can you say to draw   *admitted*
A third more opulent than your sisters? Speak.
85 CORDELIA   Nothing, my lord.
LEAR   Nothing?
CORDELIA   Nothing.
LEAR   Nothing will come of nothing.[1] Speak again.
CORDELIA   Unhappy that I am, I cannot heave
90   My heart into my mouth. I love your majesty
According to my bond,° no more nor less.   *filial duty*
LEAR   How, how, Cordelia? Mend your speech a little
Lest you may mar your fortunes.
CORDELIA   Good my lord,
You have begot me, bred me, loved me.
95   I return those duties back as are right fit—
Obey you, love you, and most honour you.
Why have my sisters husbands if they say
They love you all°? Haply° when I shall wed   *completely / Perhaps; if lucky*
That lord whose hand must take my plight° shall carry   *marriage vow; condition*
100   Half my love with him, half my care and duty.
Sure, I shall never marry like my sisters.
LEAR   But goes thy heart with this?
CORDELIA   Ay, my good lord.
LEAR   So young and so untender?
105 CORDELIA   So young, my lord, and true.°   *honest; faithful*
LEAR   Let it be so. Thy truth then be thy dower;
For by the sacred radiance of the sun,
The mysteries of Hecate[2] and the night,
By all the operation of the orbs
110   From whom we do exist and cease to be,[3]

9. *Which . . . possesses:* That the body can enjoy. *precious square of sense:* measure of sensibility; or, perhaps, balanced and sensitive perception. The square may represent the even mixture of the body's four fluids, or humors.
1. *Ex nihilo nihil fit,* a maxim derived from Aristotle, was accepted by the Christian Middle Ages with the single exception of God having created the world out of nothing.

2. A classical goddess of the moon and the patron of witchcraft, she was associated with the underworld, Hades.
3. *By all . . . be:* Referring to the belief that the movements of stars and planets ("orbs") corresponded to physical and spiritual motions in a person and thus controlled his or her fate.

Here I disclaim all my paternal care,
Propinquity,° and property of blood,°   *Closeness / kinship*
105 And as a stranger to my heart and me
Hold thee from this° for ever. The barbarous Scythian,[2]   *this time*
Or he that makes his generation
Messes[3] to gorge his appetite,
Shall be as well neighboured, pitied, and relieved
As thou, my sometime° daughter.   *former*
110 KENT   Good my liege—
LEAR   Peace, Kent. Come not between the dragon and his wrath.
I loved her most, and thought to set my rest[4]
On her kind nursery.° [*To* CORDELIA] Hence, and avoid my sight!—   *care*
So be my grave my peace[5] as here I give
115 Her father's heart from her. Call France. Who stirs?[6]
Call Burgundy.   [*Exit one or more*]
            Cornwall and Albany,
With my two daughters' dowers digest° this third.   *incorporate*
Let pride, which she calls plainness,° marry her.   *directness*
I do invest you jointly in my power,
120 Pre-eminence, and all the large effects°   *outward shows; trappings*
That troop with° majesty. Ourself by monthly course,   *accompany*
With reservation of° an hundred knights   *legal right to retain*
By you to be sustained, shall our abode
Make with you by due turns. Only we still retain
125 The name and all the additions° to a king.   *prerogatives*
The sway,° revenue, execution of the rest,   *power*
Belovèd sons, be yours; which to confirm,
This crownet[7] part betwixt you.
KENT   Royal Lear,
Whom I have ever honoured as my king,
130 Loved as my father, as my master followed,
As my great patron thought on in my prayers—
LEAR   The bow is bent and drawn; make from° the shaft.   *get clear of*
KENT   Let it fall° rather, though the fork° invade   *strike here / arrowhead*
The region of my heart. Be Kent unmannerly
135 When Lear is mad. What wilt thou do, old man?
Think'st thou that duty shall have dread to speak
When power to flattery bows? To plainness° honour's bound   *plain speaking*
When majesty stoops to folly. Reverse thy doom,°   *Revoke your sentence*
And in thy best consideration check°   *halt*
140 This hideous rashness. Answer my life my judgement,[8]
Thy youngest daughter does not love thee least,
Nor are those empty-hearted whose low sound
Reverbs no hollowness.°   *Echoes no insincerity*
LEAR   Kent, on thy life, no more!
KENT   My life I never held but as a pawn°   *chess piece; stake*
145 To wage° against thy enemies, nor fear to lose it,   *wager*
Thy safety being the motive.

---

2. Notoriously savage Crimean nomads of classical
antiquity.
3. *he . . . / Messes*: he who makes meals of his parents
or his children.
4. To secure my repose; to stake my all, as in the card
game known as primero.

5. So may I rest in peace (probably an oath).
6. Does nobody stir? An order, with the force of "Get
moving."
7. Cordelia's crown, symbol of the endowment she has
forsworn.
8. *Answer . . . judgement*: I'll stake my life on my opinion.

Here I disclaim all my paternal care,
Propinquity,° and property of blood,°   Closeness / kinship
And as a stranger to my heart and me
Hold thee from this° for ever. The barbarous Scythian,[4]   this time
115 Or he that makes his generation messes[5]
To gorge his appetite, shall to my bosom
Be as well neighboured, pitied, and relieved
As thou, my sometime° daughter.   former
KENT   Good my liege—
LEAR   Peace, Kent.
120 Come not between the dragon and his wrath.
I loved her most, and thought to set my rest[6]
On her kind nursery.° [*To* CORDELIA] Hence, and avoid my sight!—   care
So be my grave my peace[7] as here I give
Her father's heart from her. Call France. Who stirs?[8]
Call Burgundy.   [*Exit one or more*]
125   Cornwall and Albany,
With my two daughters' dowers digest° the third.   incorporate
Let pride, which she calls plainness,° marry her.   directness
I do invest you jointly with my power,
Pre-eminence, and all the large effects°   outward shows; trappings
130 That troop with° majesty. Ourself by monthly course,   accompany
With reservation of° an hundred knights   legal right to retain
By you to be sustained, shall our abode
Make with you by due turn. Only we shall retain
The name and all th'addition° to a king. The sway,°   prerogatives / power
135 Revenue, execution of the rest,
Belovèd sons, be yours; which to confirm,
This crownet[9] part between you.
KENT   Royal Lear,
Whom I have ever honoured as my king,
Loved as my father, as my master followed,
140 As my great patron thought on in my prayers—
LEAR   The bow is bent and drawn; make from° the shaft.   get clear of
KENT   Let it fall° rather, though the fork° invade   strike here / arrowhead
The region of my heart. Be Kent unmannerly
When Lear is mad. What wouldst thou do, old man?
145 Think'st thou that duty shall have dread to speak
When power to flattery bows? To plainness° honour's bound   plain speaking
When majesty falls to folly. Reserve° thy state,°   Retain / rule; position
And in thy best consideration check°   halt
This hideous rashness. Answer my life my judgement,[1]
150 Thy youngest daughter does not love thee least,
Nor are those empty-hearted whose low sounds
Reverb no hollowness.°   Echo no insincerity
LEAR   Kent, on thy life, no more!
KENT   My life I never held but as a pawn°   chess piece; stake
To wage° against thine enemies, ne'er feared to lose it,   wager
Thy safety being motive.°   (my) motivation

4. Notoriously savage Crimean nomads of classical antiquity.
5. *he . . . messes:* he who makes meals of his parents or his children.
6. To secure my repose; to stake my all, as in the card game known as primero.
7. So may I rest in peace (probably an oath).
8. Does nobody stir? An order, with the force of "Get moving."
9. Cordelia's crown, symbol of the endowment she has forsworn.
1. *Answer . . . judgement:* I'll stake my life on my opinion.

LEAR   Out of my sight!

KENT   See better, Lear, and let me still° remain   *always*
        The true blank° of thine eye.   *precise bull's-eye*

LEAR   Now, by Apollo—

KENT   Now, by Apollo, King, thou swear'st thy gods in vain.[9]

LEAR [*making to strike him*]   Vassal, recreant!°   *villain; unbeliever*

150 KENT   Do, kill thy physician,
        And the fee bestow upon the foul disease.[1]
        Revoke thy doom, or whilst I can vent clamour
        From my throat I'll tell thee thou dost evil.

LEAR   Hear me; on thy allegiance hear me!

155   Since thou hast sought to make us break our vow,
        Which we durst never yet, and with strayed° pride   *wayward; erring*
        To come between our sentence and our power,
        Which nor our nature nor our place[2] can bear,
        Our potency made good° take thy reward: *demonstrated*

160   Four days we do allot thee for provision
        To shield thee from dis-eases° of the world,   *discomforts*
        And on the fifth to turn thy hated back
        Upon our kingdom. If on the next day following
        Thy banished trunk° be found in our dominions,   *body*

165   The moment is thy death. Away! By Jupiter,
        This shall not be revoked.

KENT   Why, fare thee well, King; since thus thou wilt appear,
        Friendship lives hence, and banishment is here.
        [*To* CORDELIA] The gods to their protection take thee, maid,

170   That rightly thinks, and hast most justly said.
        [*To* GONORIL *and* REGAN] And your large speeches may your deeds approve,[3]
        That good effects may spring from words of love.
        Thus Kent, O princes, bids you all adieu;
        He'll shape his old course in a country new.   [*Exit*]
            Enter [*the King of*] FRANCE *and* [*the Duke of*] BUR-
            GUNDY, *with* GLOUCESTER

175 GLOUCESTER   Here's France and Burgundy, my noble lord.

LEAR   My lord of Burgundy,
        We first address towards you, who with a king
        Hath rivalled for our daughter: what in the least
        Will you require in present dower with her
        Or cease your quest of love?

180 BURGUNDY   Royal majesty,
        I crave no more than what your highness offered;
        Nor will you tender° less.   *offer*

LEAR   Right noble Burgundy,
        When she was dear to us we did hold her so;
        But now her price is fallen. Sir, there she stands.

185   If aught within that little seeming substance,[4]
        Or all of it, with our displeasure pieced,°   *joined*
        And nothing else, may fitly like° your grace,   *please*
        She's there, and she is yours.

---

9. You invoke your gods falsely and without effect.   3. And let your actions live up to your fine words.
1. *kill . . . disease:* you would not only kill the doctor   4. *little seeming substance:* one who appears insub-
but hand his fee over to the disease.   stantial; one who will not pretend.
2. Which neither my temperament nor my royal position.

155   LEAR   Out of my sight!

        KENT   See better, Lear, and let me still° remain   *always*

        The true blank° of thine eye.   *precise bull's-eye*

        LEAR   Now, by Apollo—

        KENT   Now, by Apollo, King, thou swear'st thy gods in vain.[2]

        LEAR *[making to strike him]*   O vassal! Miscreant!°   *Villain; unbeliever*

        ALBANY *and* CORDELIA   Dear sir, forbear.

160   KENT *[to* LEAR*]*   Kill thy physician, and thy fee bestow

        Upon the foul disease.[3] Revoke thy gift,

        Or whilst I can vent clamour from my throat

        I'll tell thee thou dost evil.

        LEAR   Hear me, recreant;° on thine allegiance hear me!   *traitor*

165   That thou hast sought to make us break our vows,

        Which we durst never yet, and with strained° pride   *overblown*

        To come betwixt our sentence and our power,

        Which nor our nature nor our place[4] can bear,

        Our potency made good° take thy reward: *demonstrated*

170   Five days we do allot thee for provision

        To shield thee from disasters of the world,

        And on the sixth to turn thy hated back

        Upon our kingdom. If on the seventh day following

        Thy banished trunk° be found in our dominions,   *body*

175   The moment is thy death. Away! By Jupiter,

        This shall not be revoked.

        KENT   Fare thee well, King; sith° thus thou wilt appear,   *since*

        Freedom lives hence, and banishment is here.

        [To CORDELIA*]* The gods to their dear shelter take thee, maid,

180   That justly think'st, and hast most rightly said.

        [To GONERIL *and* REGAN*]* And your large speeches may your deeds approve,[5]

        That good effects may spring from words of love.

        Thus Kent, O princes, bids you all adieu;

        He'll shape his old course in a country new.   *Exit*

              Flourish.° Enter GLOUCESTER *with [the King of]*   *Fanfare of trumpets*

              FRANCE, *[the Duke of]* BURGUNDY, *attendants*

185   CORDELIA   Here's France and Burgundy, my noble lord.

        LEAR   My lord of Burgundy,

        We first address toward you, who with this King

        Hath rivalled for our daughter: what in the least

        Will you require in present dower with her

        Or cease your quest of love?

190   BURGUNDY   Most royal majesty,

        I crave no more than hath your highness offered;

        Nor will you tender° less.   *offer*

        LEAR   Right noble Burgundy,

        When she was dear to us we did hold her so;

        But now her price is fallen. Sir, there she stands.

195   If aught within that little seeming substance,[6]

        Or all of it, with our displeasure pieced,°   *joined*

        And nothing more, may fitly like° your grace,   *please*

        She's there, and she is yours.

---

2. You invoke your gods falsely and without effect.
3. *Kill . . . disease:* You would not only kill the doctor but hand his fee over to the disease.
4. Which neither my temperament nor my royal position.

5. And let your actions live up to your fine words.
6. *little seeming substance:* one who appears insubstantial; one who will not pretend.

BURGUNDY   I know no answer.

LEAR   Sir, will you with those infirmities she owes,°   owns
190   Unfriended, new-adopted to our hate,
       Covered with our curse and strangered° with our oath,   estranged
       Take her or leave her?

BURGUNDY   Pardon me, royal sir.
       Election makes not up on such conditions.⁵

LEAR   Then leave her, sir; for by the power that made me,
195   I tell you° all her wealth. [To FRANCE] For° you, great King,   inform you of / As for
       I would not from your love make such a stray°   stray so far
       To° match you where I hate, therefore beseech you   As to
       To avert your liking° a more worthier way   To turn your affections
       Than on a wretch whom nature is ashamed
200   Almost to acknowledge hers.

FRANCE   This is most strange, that she that even but now
       Was your best object, the argument° of your praise,   theme
       Balm of your age, most best, most dearest,
       Should in this trice° of time commit a thing   moment
205   So monstrous to dismantle°   as to strip off; disrobe
       So many folds of favour. Sure, her offence
       Must be of such unnatural degree
       That monsters it,° or your fore-vouched affections   makes it monstrous
       Fall'n into taint;⁶ which to believe of her
210   Must be a faith that reason without miracle
       Could never plant in me.

CORDELIA [to LEAR]   I yet beseech your majesty,
       If for I want° that glib and oily art   because I lack
       To speak and purpose not°—since what I well intend,   and not intend
215   I'll do't before I speak—that you acknow°   acknowledge
       It is no vicious blot, murder, or foulness,
       No unclean action or dishonoured step
       That hath deprived me of your grace and favour,
       But even the want of that for which I am rich—
220   A still-soliciting° eye, and such a tongue   An always-begging
       As I am glad I have not, though not to have it
       Hath lost me in your liking.

LEAR   Go to, go to.
       Better thou hadst not been born than not to have pleased me better.

FRANCE   Is it no more but this—a tardiness in nature,
225   That often leaves the history unspoke
       That it intends to do?⁷—My lord of Burgundy,
       What say you to the lady? Love is not love
       When it is mingled with respects° that stands   considerations
       Aloof from the entire point. Will you have her?
230   She is herself a dower.

BURGUNDY   Royal Lear,
       Give but that portion which yourself proposed,
       And here I take Cordelia by the hand,
       Duchess of Burgundy—

LEAR   Nothing. I have sworn.

---

5. A choice cannot be made under those terms.
6. or . . . taint: or else the love you earlier swore for
Cordelia must be regarded with suspicion. "Or" may
also mean "before," in which case the phrase would

mean "before the love you once proclaimed could have
decayed."
7. a tardiness . . . do: a natural reserve that inhibits
voicing one's intentions.

BURGUNDY   I know no answer.

LEAR   Will you with those infirmities she owes,°   owns
200   Unfriended, new adopted to our hate,
       Dowered with our curse and strangered° with our oath,   estranged
       Take her or leave her?

BURGUNDY   Pardon me, royal sir.
       Election makes not up in such conditions.[7]

LEAR   Then leave her, sir; for by the power that made me,
205   I tell you° all her wealth. [*To* FRANCE] For° you, great King,   inform you of / As for
       I would not from your love make such a stray°   stray so far
       To° match you where I hate, therefore beseech you   As to
       T'avert your liking° a more worthier way   To turn your affections
       Than on a wretch whom nature is ashamed
       Almost t'acknowledge hers.

210 FRANCE   This is most strange,
       That she whom even but now was your best object,
       The argument° of your praise, balm of your age,   theme
       The best, the dear'st, should in this trice° of time   moment
       Commit a thing so monstrous to dismantle°   as to strip off; disrobe
215   So many folds of favour. Sure, her offence
       Must be of such unnatural degree
       That monsters it,° or your fore-vouched affection   makes it monstrous
       Fall into taint;[8] which to believe of her
       Must be a faith that reason without miracle
220   Should never plant in me.

CORDELIA [*to* LEAR]   I yet beseech your majesty,
       If for I want° that glib and oily art   because I lack
       To speak and purpose not°—since what I well intend,   and not intend
       I'll do't before I speak—that you make known
225   It is no vicious blot, murder, or foulness,
       No unchaste action or dishonoured step
       That hath deprived me of your grace and favour,
       But even the want of that for which I am richer—
       A still-soliciting° eye, and such a tongue   An always-begging
230   That I am glad I have not, though not to have it
       Hath lost me in your liking.

LEAR   Better thou
       Hadst not been born than not t'have pleased me better.

FRANCE   Is it but this—a tardiness in nature,
       Which often leaves the history unspoke
235   That it intends to do?[9]—My lord of Burgundy,
       What say you to the lady? Love's not love
       When it is mingled with regards° that stands   considerations
       Aloof from th'entire point. Will you have her?
       She is herself a dowry.

BURGUNDY [*to* LEAR]   Royal King,
240   Give but that portion which yourself proposed,
       And here I take Cordelia by the hand,
       Duchess of Burgundy.

LEAR   Nothing. I have sworn. I am firm.

---

7. A choice cannot be made under those terms.
8. *or . . . taint:* or else the love you earlier swore for
Cordelia must be regarded with suspicion. "Or" may
also mean "before," in which case the phrase would

mean "before the love you once proclaimed could have
decayed."
9. *a tardiness . . . do:* a natural reserve that inhibits
voicing one's intentions.

BURGUNDY [*to* CORDELIA]   I am sorry, then, you have so lost a father

235　That you must lose a husband.

CORDELIA   Peace be with Burgundy; since that respects

Of fortune are his love, I shall not be his wife.

FRANCE   Fairest Cordelia, that art most rich, being poor;

Most choice, forsaken; and most loved, despised:

240　Thee and thy virtues here I seize upon.

Be it lawful, I take up what's cast away.

Gods, gods! 'Tis strange that from their cold'st neglect

My love should kindle to inflamed respect.°—　　　　　*ardent regard*

Thy dowerless daughter, King, thrown to my chance,

245　Is queen of us, of ours, and our fair France.

Not all the dukes in wat'rish° Burgundy　　　　　*irrigated; watery; weak*

Shall buy this unprized° precious maid of me.—　　　　*unappreciated*

Bid them farewell, Cordelia, though unkind.°　　　　*though they are unkind*

Thou losest here,° a better where° to find.　　　　*this place / place*

250　LEAR   Thou hast her, France. Let her be thine, for we

Have no such daughter, nor shall ever see

That face of hers again. Therefore be gone,

Without our grace, our love, our benison.°—　　　　　*blessing*

Come, noble Burgundy.

　　　　　　　[*Flourish.*] *Exeunt* LEAR *and* BURGUNDY [*then*

　　　　　　　ALBANY, CORNWALL, GLOUCESTER, EDMUND,

　　　　　　　　　　　　　　and followers]

FRANCE [*to* CORDELIA]　　　Bid farewell to your sisters.

255　CORDELIA   Ye jewels of our father, with washed eyes

Cordelia leaves you. I know you what you are,

And like a sister am most loath to call

Your faults as they are named.° Use well our father.　　*are properly called*

To your professèd bosoms° I commit him.　　　　*publicly proclaimed love*

260　But yet, alas, stood I within his grace

I would prefer° him to a better place.　　　　　*promote; recommend*

So farewell to you both.

GONORIL   Prescribe not us our duties.

REGAN   Let your study

265　Be to content your lord, who hath received you

At fortune's alms.[8] You have obedience scanted,°　　　*neglected*

And well are worth the worst that you have wanted.[9]

CORDELIA   Time shall unfold what pleated cunning hides.

Who covers faults, at last shame them derides.[1]

Well may you prosper.

270　FRANCE　　　　　　　Come, fair Cordelia.

　　　　　　　　　Exeunt FRANCE *and* CORDELIA

GONORIL   Sister, it is not a little I have to say of what most nearly

appertains to us both. I think our father will hence tonight.

REGAN   That's most certain, and with you. Next month with us.

GONORIL   You see how full of changes° his age is. The observa-　　*fickleness*

275　tion we have made of it hath not been little.[2] He always loved

our sister most, and with what poor judgement he hath now

cast her off appears too gross.°　　　　　　　*blatant*

---

8. As a charitable gift from Dame Fortune.
9. And you deserve to get no more love (from your husband) than you have given (to your father). "Want"
plays on its alternative meanings of "lack" and "desire."

1. *Who . . . derides:* Those who hide their faults will in
the end be put to shame.
2. We have observed it more than a little.

BURGUNDY [*to* CORDELIA]   I am sorry, then, you have so lost a father
That you must lose a husband.

245 CORDELIA   Peace be with Burgundy;
Since that respect and fortunes are his love,
I shall not be his wife.

FRANCE   Fairest Cordelia, that art most rich, being poor;
Most choice, forsaken; and most loved, despised:
250 Thee and thy virtues here I seize upon.
Be it lawful, I take up what's cast away.
Gods, gods! 'Tis strange that from their cold'st neglect
My love should kindle to inflamed respect.°—   *ardent regard*
Thy dowerless daughter, King, thrown to my chance,
255 Is queen of us, of ours, and our fair France.
Not all the dukes of wat'rish° Burgundy   *irrigated; watery; weak*
Can buy this unprized° precious maid of me.—   *unappreciated*
Bid them farewell, Cordelia, though unkind.°   *though they are unkind*
Thou losest here,° a better where° to find.   *this place / place*

260 LEAR   Thou hast her, France. Let her be thine, for we
Have no such daughter, nor shall ever see
That face of hers again. Therefore be gone,
Without our grace, our love, our benison.°—   *blessing*
Come, noble Burgundy.

Flourish. Exeunt [all but FRANCE
and the sisters]

FRANCE   Bid farewell to your sisters.
265 CORDELIA   Ye jewels of our father, with washed eyes
Cordelia leaves you. I know you what you are,
And like a sister am most loath to call
Your faults as they are named.° Love well our father.   *are properly called*
To your professèd bosoms° I commit him.   *publicly proclaimed love*
270 But yet, alas, stood I within his grace
I would prefer° him to a better place.   *promote; recommend*
So farewell to you both.

REGAN   Prescribe not us our duty.

GONERIL   Let your study
275 Be to content your lord, who hath received you
At fortune's alms.[1] You have obedience scanted,°   *neglected*
And well are worth the want that you have wanted.[2]

CORDELIA   Time shall unfold what pleated cunning hides,
Who covert faults at last with shame derides.[3]
Well may you prosper.

280 FRANCE   Come, my fair Cordelia.

Exeunt FRANCE *and* CORDELIA

GONERIL   Sister, it is not little I have to say of what most nearly
appertains to us both. I think our father will hence tonight.

REGAN   That's most certain, and with you. Next month with us.

GONERIL   You see how full of changes° his age is. The observa-   *fickleness*
285 tion we have made of it hath been little.° He always loved our   *meticulous*
sister most, and with what poor judgement he hath now cast
her off appears too grossly.°   *blatantly*

1. As a charitable gift from Dame Fortune.
2. And you deserve to get no more love (from your husband) than you have given (to your father). "Want"
plays on its alternative meanings of "lack" and "desire."
3. *Time . . . derides:* Time eventually exposes and
shames all hidden faults.

REGAN   'Tis the infirmity of his age; yet he hath ever but slen-
derly known himself.

280 GONORIL   The best and soundest of his time hath been but rash;[3]
then° must we look to receive from his age not alone the imper-   *therefore*
fection of long-engrafted condition,° but therewithal unruly   *deep-rooted habit*
waywardness that infirm and choleric years bring with them.

REGAN   Such unconstant starts[4] are we like° to have from him as   *likely*
285 this of Kent's banishment.

GONORIL   There is further compliment° of leave-taking between   *ceremony*
France and him. Pray, let's hit° together. If our father carry   *join; strike*
authority with such dispositions[5] as he bears, this last surrender°   *abdication*
of his will but offend° us.   *harm*

290 REGAN   We shall further think on't.

GONORIL   We must do something, and i'th' heat.°   *Exeunt*   *quickly*

Scene 2

Enter Bastard [EDMUND]

EDMUND   Thou, nature, art my goddess. To thy law
My services are bound.[1] Wherefore° should I   *Why*
Stand in the plague of custom[2] and permit
The curiosity° of nations to deprive me   *legal niceties*
5 For that° I am some twelve or fourteen moonshines°   *Because / months*
Lag of° a brother? Why 'bastard'? Wherefore 'base',   *Younger than*
When my dimensions are as well compact,°   *composed*
My mind as generous,° and my shape as true   *noble*
As honest° madam's issue?   *married; chaste*
10 Why brand they us with 'base, base bastardy',
Who in the lusty stealth of nature take
More composition and fierce quality[3]
Than doth within a stale, dull-eyed bed go
To the creating a whole tribe of fops°   *fools*
15 Got° 'tween a sleep and wake? Well then,   *Begotten*
Legitimate Edgar, I must have your land.
Our father's love is to° the bastard Edmund   *as much to*
As to the legitimate. Well, my legitimate, if
This letter speed° and my invention° thrive,   *succeed / plot*
20 Edmund the base shall to° th' legitimate.   *match up to; usurp*
I grow, I prosper. Now gods, stand up for bastards!
Enter GLOUCESTER. [EDMUND *reads a letter*]

GLOUCESTER   Kent banished thus, and France in choler parted,°   *in anger departed*
And the King gone tonight,° subscribed° his power,   *last night / limited*
Confined to exhibition[4]—all this done
25 Upon the gad?°—Edmund, how now? What news?   *spur of the moment*

EDMUND   So please your lordship, none.

---

3. *The . . . rash:* Even in the prime of his life he was impetuous.
4. Such impulsive outbursts.
5. Frame of mine.
Scene 2 Location: The Earl of Gloucester's house.
1. Edmund declares the raw force of unsocialized and unregulated existence, as opposed to human law, to be his ruler; ironically, "nature" also means "natural filial affection." A "natural" was another word for "bastard" (illegitimate child).
2. Submit to the imposition of inheritance law.

3. *Who . . . quality:* Whose begetting, by reason of its furtiveness and heightened excitement, requires better execution and more vigor. Alternatively (with "take" meaning "give"), whose begetting produces (a person of) more mixture and vigor. "Composition," or mixture, may refer to the belief that the perfect offspring was conceived from an equal quantity of male and female essence and that physical and mental abnormalities were caused by a predominance of one or the other.
4. Pension; mere show without force.

REGAN 'Tis the infirmity of his age; yet he hath ever but slen-
derly known himself.

290 GONERIL The best and soundest of his time hath been but rash;[4]
then° must we look from his age to receive not alone the imper- *therefore*
fections of long-engrafted condition,° but therewithal the *deep-rooted habit*
unruly waywardness that infirm and choleric years bring with
them.

295 REGAN Such unconstant starts[5] are we like° to have from him as *likely*
this of Kent's banishment.

GONERIL There is further compliment° of leave-taking between *ceremony*
France and him. Pray you, let us sit together. If our father carry
authority with such disposition[6] as he bears, this last surrender° *abdication*
300 of his will but offend° us. *harm*

REGAN We shall further think of it.

GONERIL We must do something, and i'th' heat.° *Exeunt* *quickly*

1.2

Enter Bastard [EDMOND]

EDMOND Thou, nature, art my goddess. To thy law
My services are bound.[1] Wherefore° should I *Why*
Stand in the plague of custom[2] and permit
The curiosity° of nations to deprive me *legal niceties*
5 For that° I am some twelve or fourteen moonshines° *Because / months*
Lag of° a brother? Why 'bastard'? Wherefore 'base', *Younger than*
When my dimensions are as well compact,° *composed*
My mind as generous,° and my shape as true *noble*
As honest° madam's issue? Why brand they us *married; chaste*
10 With 'base', with 'baseness, bastardy—base, base'—
Who in the lusty stealth of nature take
More composition and fierce quality[3]
Than doth within a dull, stale, tirèd bed
Go to th' creating a whole tribe of fops° *fools*
15 Got° 'tween a sleep and wake? Well then, *Begotten*
Legitimate Edgar, I must have your land.
Our father's love is to° the bastard Edmond *as much to*
As to th' legitimate. Fine word, 'legitimate'.
Well, my legitimate, if this letter speed° *succeed*
20 And my invention° thrive, Edmond the base *plot*
Shall to° th' legitimate. I grow, I prosper. *match up to; usurp*
Now gods, stand up for bastards!

Enter GLOUCESTER. [EDMOND *reads a letter*]

GLOUCESTER Kent banished thus, and France in choler parted,° *in anger departed*
And the King gone tonight,° prescribed° his power, *last night / limited*
25 Confined to exhibition[4]—all this done
Upon the gad?°—Edmond, how now? What news? *spur of the moment*

EDMOND So please your lordship, none.

---

4. *The . . . rash:* Even in the prime of his life he was
impetuous.
5. Such impulsive outbursts.
6. Frame of mind.
1.2 Location: The Earl of Gloucester's house.
1. Edmond declares the raw force of unsocialized and
unregulated existence, as opposed to human law, to be
his ruler; ironically, "nature" also means "natural filial
affection." A "natural" was another word for "bastard"
(illegitimate child).
2. Submit to the imposition of inheritance law.

3. *Who . . . quality:* Whose begetting, by reason of its
furtiveness and heightened excitement, requires better
execution and more vigor. Alternatively (with "take"
meaning "give"), whose begetting produces (a person
of) more mixture and vigor. "Composition," or mixture,
may refer to the belief that the perfect offspring was
conceived from an equal quantity of male and female
essence and that physical and mental abnormalities
were caused by a predominance of one or the other.
4. Pension; mere show without force.

GLOUCESTER   Why so earnestly seek you to put up that letter?

EDMUND   I know no news, my lord.

GLOUCESTER   What paper were you reading?

30 EDMUND   Nothing, my lord.

GLOUCESTER   No? What needs then that terrible dispatch° of it   *frightened haste*
into your pocket? The quality of nothing hath not such need
to hide itself. Let's see. Come, if it be nothing I shall not need
spectacles.

35 EDMUND   I beseech you, sir, pardon me. It is a letter from my
brother that I have not all o'er-read; for so much as I have
perused, I find it not fit for your liking.°   *pleasure*

GLOUCESTER   Give me the letter, sir.

EDMUND   I shall offend either to detain or give it. The contents,
40 as in part I understand them, are to blame.

GLOUCESTER   Let's see, let's see.

EDMUND   I hope for my brother's justification he wrote this but
as an assay or taste[5] of my virtue.

[*He gives* GLOUCESTER] *a letter*

GLOUCESTER (*reads*)   'This policy of age makes the world bitter
45 to the best of our times,[6] keeps our fortunes from us till our
oldness cannot relish them. I begin to find an idle and fond°   *a useless and foolish*
bondage in the oppression of aged tyranny, who sways not as
it hath power but as it is suffered.[7] Come to me, that of this I
may speak more. If our father would sleep till I waked him, you
50 should enjoy half his revenue for ever and live the beloved of
your brother,

                                           Edgar.'

Hum, conspiracy! 'Slept till I waked him, you should enjoy half
his revenue'—my son Edgar! Had he a hand to write this, a
55 heart and brain to breed it in? When came this to you? Who
brought it?

EDMUND   It was not brought me, my lord, there's the cunning
of it. I found it thrown in at the casement° of my closet.°   *window / private room*

60 GLOUCESTER   You know the character° to be your brother's?   *handwriting*

EDMUND   If the matter° were good, my lord, I durst swear it were   *content*
his; but in respect of that, I would fain° think it were not.   *gladly*

GLOUCESTER   It is his.

EDMUND   It is his hand, my lord, but I hope his heart is not in
the contents.

65 GLOUCESTER   Hath he never heretofore sounded you° in this   *sounded you out*
business?

EDMUND   Never, my lord; but I have often heard him maintain
it to be fit that, sons at perfect age° and fathers declining, his   *at maturity*
father should be as ward[8] to the son, and the son manage the
70 revenue.

GLOUCESTER   O villain, villain—his very opinion in the letter!
Abhorred villain, unnatural, detested, brutish villain—worse
than brutish! Go, sir, seek him, ay, apprehend him. Abominable villain! Where is he?

---

5. *but . . . taste:* simply as a proof or test. Both terms
derive from metallurgy.
6. The established primacy of the elderly embitters us
at the prime of our lives. *policy:* statecraft; craftiness;
established order.

7. *who . . . suffered:* which rules not because it is powerful but because it is permitted to ("suffered").
8. A child under eighteen years who was legally dependent, often orphaned.

GLOUCESTER   Why so earnestly seek you to put up that letter?

EDMOND   I know no news, my lord.

30   GLOUCESTER   What paper were you reading?

EDMOND   Nothing, my lord.

GLOUCESTER   No? What needed then that terrible dispatch° of it   *frightened haste*
into your pocket? The quality of nothing hath not such need
to hide itself. Let's see. Come, if it be nothing I shall not need
35   spectacles.

EDMOND   I beseech you, sir, pardon me. It is a letter from my
brother that I have not all o'er-read; and for so much as I have
perused, I find it not fit for your o'erlooking.

GLOUCESTER   Give me the letter, sir.

40   EDMOND   I shall offend either to detain or give it. The contents,
as in part I understand them, are to blame.

GLOUCESTER   Let's see, let's see.

EDMOND   I hope for my brother's justification he wrote this but
as an assay or taste[5] of my virtue.

[*He gives* GLOUCESTER *a letter*]

45   GLOUCESTER (*reads*)   'This policy and reverence of age makes
the world bitter to the best of our times,[6] keeps our fortunes
from us till our oldness cannot relish them. I begin to find an
idle and fond° bondage in the oppression of aged tyranny, who   *a useless and foolish*
sways not as it hath power but as it is suffered.[7] Come to me,
50   that of this I may speak more. If our father would sleep till I
waked him, you should enjoy half his revenue for ever and live
the beloved of your brother,

Edgar.'

Hum, conspiracy! 'Sleep till I wake him, you should enjoy half
55   his revenue'—my son Edgar! Had he a hand to write this, a
heart and brain to breed it in? When came you to this? Who
brought it?

EDMOND   It was not brought me, my lord, there's the cunning
of it. I found it thrown in at the casement° of my closet.°   *window / private room*

60   GLOUCESTER   You know the character° to be your brother's?   *handwriting*

EDMOND   If the matter° were good, my lord, I durst swear it were   *content*
his; but in respect of that, I would fain° think it were not.   *gladly*

GLOUCESTER   It is his.

EDMOND   It is his hand, my lord, but I hope his heart is not in
65   the contents.

GLOUCESTER   Has he never before sounded° you in this   *sounded you out*
business?

EDMOND   Never, my lord; but I have heard him oft maintain it
to be fit that, sons at perfect age° and fathers declined, the   *at maturity*
70   father should be as ward[8] to the son, and the son manage his
revenue.

GLOUCESTER   O villain, villain—his very opinion in the letter!
Abhorred villain, unnatural, detested, brutish villain—worse
than brutish! Go, sirrah,[9] seek him. I'll apprehend him. Abom-
75   inable villain! Where is he?

---

5. *but . . . taste:* simply as a proof or test. Both terms
derive from metallurgy.
6. The established primacy of the elderly embitters us
at the prime of our lives. *policy:* statecraft; craftiness;
established order.
7. *who . . . suffered:* which rules not because it is pow-

erful but because it is permitted to ("suffered").
8. A child under eighteen years who was legally dependent, often orphaned.
9. A form of address used with children or social inferiors.

75 EDMUND   I do not well know, my lord. If it shall please you to suspend your indignation against my brother till you can derive
from him better testimony of this intent, you should run a cer-
tain° course; where° if you violently proceed against him, mis-   *safe; reliable / whereas*
taking his purpose, it would make a great gap in your own
80 honour and shake in pieces the heart of his obedience. I dare
pawn down° my life for him he hath wrote this to feel° my   *I dare stake / feel out*
affection to your honour, and to no further pretence of danger.[9]
GLOUCESTER   Think you so?
EDMUND   If your honour judge it meet,° I will place you where   *appropriate*
85 you shall hear us confer of this, and by an auricular° assurance   *audible*
have your satisfaction, and that without any further delay
than this very evening.
GLOUCESTER   He cannot be such a monster.
EDMUND   Nor is not, sure.
90 GLOUCESTER   To his father, that so tenderly and entirely loves
him—heaven and earth! Edmund seek him out, wind me into
him.[1] I pray you, frame° your business after your own wisdom.   *arrange*
I would unstate myself to be in a due resolution.[2]
EDMUND   I shall seek him, sir, presently,° convey° the business   *immediately / carry out*
95 as I shall see means, and acquaint you withal.°   *therewith*
GLOUCESTER   These late° eclipses in the sun and moon portend   *recent*
no good to us.[3] Though the wisdom of nature can reason thus
and thus, yet nature finds itself scourged by the sequent
effects.[4] Love cools, friendship falls off, brothers divide; in cities
100 mutinies, in countries discords, palaces treason, the bond
cracked between son and father. Find out this villain,
Edmund; it shall lose thee nothing. Do it carefully. And the
noble and true-hearted Kent banished, his offence honesty!
Strange, strange!   [*Exit*]
105 EDMUND   This is the excellent foppery° of the world: that when   *foolishness*
we are sick in fortune—often the surfeit° of our own behav-   *excesses*
iour—we make guilty of° our disasters the sun, the moon, and   *we hold responsible for*
the stars, as if we were villains by necessity, fools by heavenly
compulsion, knaves, thieves, and treacherers° by spherical pre-   *traitors*
110 dominance,[5] drunkards, liars, and adulterers by an enforced
obedience of planetary influence, and all that we are evil in by
a divine thrusting on.° An admirable° evasion of whoremaster   *imposition / amazing*
man, to lay his goatish disposition to the charge of stars![6] My
father compounded° with my mother under the Dragon's tail   *coupled*
115 and my nativity was under Ursa Major,[7] so that it follows I am
rough and lecherous. Fut!° I should have been that° I am had   *By Christ's foot / what*
the maidenliest star of the firmament twinkled on my bastardy.
Edgar . . .

9. No further intention to do harm.
1. Worm your way into his confidence (with "me" as an
intensifier); worm your way into his confidence for me
("me" as a dative of respect).
2. I would give up everything to have my doubts resolved.
3. Lunar and solar eclipses that were seen in London
about a year before the play's first recorded performance would have added spice to this superstitious
belief in the role of heavenly bodies as augurs of misfortune.
4. *Though . . . effects:* Though natural science may

explain the eclipses this way or that, nature (and family bonds) suffers in the effects that follow.
5. By the ascendancy of a particular planet. In the universe as conceived by Ptolemy, the planets revolved
about the earth on crystalline spheres.
6. *to lay . . . stars:* to hold the stars responsible for his
lustful desires. In Greek mythology, the satyr, a creature
with goatlike characteristics, was notoriously lecherous.
7. Constellations: *Dragon's tail* = Draco and *Ursa
Major* = Great Bear.

EDMOND I do not well know, my lord. If it shall please you to
suspend your indignation against my brother till you can derive
from him better testimony of his intent, you should run a cer-
tain° course; where° if you violently proceed against him, mis- *safe; reliable / whereas*
80 taking his purpose, it would make a great gap in your own
honour and shake in pieces the heart of his obedience. I dare
pawn down° my life for him that he hath writ this to feel° my *I dare stake / feel out*
affection to your honour, and to no other pretence of danger.[1]
GLOUCESTER Think you so?
85 EDMOND If your honour judge it meet,° I will place you where *appropriate*
you shall hear us confer of this, and by an auricular° assurance *audible*
have your satisfaction, and that without any further delay
than this very evening.
GLOUCESTER He cannot be such a monster. Edmond, seek him
90 out, wind me into him,[2] I pray you. Frame° the business after *Arrange*
your own wisdom. I would unstate myself to be in a due
resolution.[3]
EDMOND I will seek him, sir, presently,° convey° the business as *immediately / carry out*
I shall find means, and acquaint you withal.° *therewith*
95 GLOUCESTER These late° eclipses in the sun and moon portend *recent*
no good to us.[4] Though the wisdom of nature can reason it
thus and thus, yet nature finds itself scourged by the sequent
effects.[5] Love cools, friendship falls off, brothers divide; in
cities, mutinies; in countries, discord; in palaces, treason; and
100 the bond cracked 'twixt son and father. This villain of mine
comes under the prediction: there's son against father. The
King falls from bias of nature:[6] there's father against child. We
have seen the best of our time. Machinations, hollowness,° *insincerity*
treachery, and all ruinous disorders follow us disquietly to our
105 graves. Find out this villain, Edmond; it shall lose thee nothing.
Do it carefully. And the noble and true-hearted Kent banished,
his offence honesty! 'Tis strange. *Exit*
EDMOND This is the excellent foppery° of the world: that when *foolishness*
we are sick in fortune—often the surfeits° of our own behav- *excesses*
110 iour—we make guilty of° our disasters the sun, the moon, and *we hold responsible for*
stars, as if we were villains on necessity, fools by heavenly
compulsion, knaves, thieves, and treachers by spherical predominance,[7] drunkards, liars, and adulterers by an enforced
obedience of planetary influence, and all that we are evil in by
115 a divine thrusting on.° An admirable° evasion of whoremaster *imposition / amazing*
man, to lay his goatish disposition on the charge of a star![8] My
father compounded° with my mother under the Dragon's tail *coupled*
and my nativity was under Ursa Major,[9] so that it follows I
am rough and lecherous. Fut!° I should have been that° I am *By Christ's foot / what*
120 had the maidenliest star in the firmament twinkled on my
bastardizing.

1. No other intention to do harm.
2. Worm your way into his confidence (with "me" as an intensifier); worm your way into his confidence for me ("me" as a dative of respect).
3. I would give up everything to have my doubts resolved.
4. Lunar and solar eclipses that were seen in London about a year before the play's first recorded performance would have added spice to this superstitious belief in the role of heavenly bodies as augurs of misfortune.
5. *Though . . . effects:* Though natural science may explain the eclipses this way or that, nature (and family bonds) suffers in the effects that follow.

6. The King deviates from his natural inclination. In the game of bowls, the "bias" ("course") is the eccentric path taken by the weighted ball when thrown.
7. By the ascendancy of a particular planet. In the universe as conceived by Ptolemy, the planets revolved about the earth on crystalline spheres.
8. *to lay . . . star:* to hold a star responsible for his lustful desires. In Greek mythology, the satyr, a creature with goatlike characteristics, was notoriously lecherous.
9. Constellations: *Dragon's tail* = Draco and *Ursa Major* = Great Bear.

Enter EDGAR

   and on's cue out he comes, like the catastrophe° of the old   *resolution*
120 comedy; mine° is villainous melancholy, with a sigh like them   *my cue; my role*
   of Bedlam.[8]—O, these eclipses do portend these divisions.

EDGAR How now, brother Edmund, what serious contemplation
   are you in?

EDMUND I am thinking, brother, of a prediction I read this
125 other day, what should follow these eclipses.

EDGAR Do you busy yourself about that?

EDMUND I promise you, the effects he writ of succeed° unhap-   *follow*
   pily, as of unnaturalness between the child and the parent,
   death, dearth, dissolutions of ancient amities, divisions in state,
130 menaces and maledictions against king and nobles, needless
   diffidences,° banishment of friends, dissipation of cohorts,[9]   *baseless suspicions*
   nuptial breaches, and I know not what.

EDGAR How long have you been a sectary astronomical?°   *a devotee of astrology*

EDMUND Come, come, when saw you my father last?

135 EDGAR Why, the night gone by.

EDMUND Spake you with him?

EDGAR Two hours together.

EDMUND Parted you in good terms? Found you no displeasure
   in him by word or countenance?°   *appearance; demeanor*

140 EDGAR None at all.

EDMUND Bethink yourself wherein you may have offended him,
   and at my entreaty forbear° his presence till some little time   *avoid*
   hath qualified° the heat of his displeasure, which at this instant   *moderated*
   so rageth in him that with the mischief of your person it would
145 scarce allay.[1]

EDGAR Some villain hath done me wrong.

EDMUND That's my fear, brother. I advise you to the best. Go
   armed. I am no honest man if there be any good meaning
   towards you. I have told you what I have seen and heard but
150 faintly, nothing like the image and horror of it. Pray you, away.

EDGAR Shall I hear from you anon?

EDMUND I do serve you in this business.   *Exit* EDGAR
   A credulous father, and a brother noble,
   Whose nature is so far from doing harms
155 That he suspects none; on whose foolish honesty
   My practices° ride easy. I see the business.[2]   *plots*
   Let me, if not by birth, have lands by wit.°   *intelligence*
   All with me's meet that I can fashion fit.[3]   *Exit*

---

8. Like the inmates of Bedlam. "Bethlehem," shortened to "Bedlam," was the name of the oldest and best-
known London madhouse.
9. Scattering of forces.
1. *with . . . allay:* even harming you bodily would
hardly relieve his anger; alternatively, with the irritant

of your presence, it (Gloucester's anger) would not be
abated.
2. It is now clear to me what needs to be done.
3. Anything is fine by me as long as I can make it serve
my purpose. *meet:* justifiable; appropriate.

Enter EDGAR

Pat° he comes, like the catastrophe° of the old comedy. My cue   *On cue / resolution*
is villainous melancholy, with a sigh like Tom o' Bedlam.[1]
[*He reads a book*]
—O, these eclipses do portend these divisions. Fa, so, la, mi.[2]

125   EDGAR   How now, brother Edmond, what serious contemplation
are you in?

EDMOND   I am thinking, brother, of a prediction I read this
other day, what should follow these eclipses.

EDGAR   Do you busy yourself with that?

130   EDMOND   I promise you, the effects he writes of succeed° unhap-   *follow*
pily. When saw you my father last?

EDGAR   The night gone by.

EDMOND   Spake you with him?

EDGAR   Ay, two hours together.

135   EDMOND   Parted you in good terms? Found you no displeasure
in him by word nor countenance?°   *appearance; demeanor*

EDGAR   None at all.

EDMOND   Bethink yourself wherein you may have offended him,
and at my entreaty forbear° his presence until some little time   *avoid*

140   hath qualified° the heat of his displeasure, which at this instant   *moderated*
so rageth in him that with the mischief of your person it
would scarcely allay.[3]

EDGAR   Some villain hath done me wrong.

EDMOND   That's my fear. I pray you have a continent forbear-

145   ance° till the speed of his rage goes slower; and, as I say, retire   *restrained absence*
with me to my lodging, from whence I will fitly° bring you to   *when suitable*
hear my lord speak. Pray ye, go. There's my key. If you do stir
abroad, go armed.

EDGAR   Armed, brother?

150   EDMOND   Brother, I advise you to the best. I am no honest man
if there be any good meaning toward you. I have told you what
I have seen and heard but faintly, nothing like the image and
horror of it. Pray you, away.

EDGAR   Shall I hear from you anon?

155   EDMOND   I do serve you in this business.   *Exit* [EDGAR]
A credulous father, and a brother noble,
Whose nature is so far from doing harms
That he suspects none; on whose foolish honesty
My practices° ride easy. I see the business.[4]   *plots*

160   Let me, if not by birth, have lands by wit.°   *intelligence*
All with me's meet that I can fashion fit.[5]   *Exit*

---

1. The usual name for lunatic beggars; "Bethlehem," shortened to "Bedlam," was the name of the oldest and best-known London madhouse.
2. The portion of the scale Edmund sings is an augmented fourth, an interval considered at this time very discordant; it was sometimes referred to as "the devil in music." *divisions*: social fractures; melodic embellishments.
3. *with . . . allay*: even harming you bodily ("mischief") would hardly relieve his anger; alternatively, with the irritant of your presence, it (Gloucester's anger) would not be abated.
4. It is now clear to me what needs to be done.
5. Anything is fine by me as long as I can make it serve my purpose. *meet*: justifiable; appropriate.

Scene 3

Enter GONORIL *and Gentleman* [OSWALD]

GONORIL   Did my father strike my gentleman
For chiding of his fool?

OSWALD   Yes, madam.

GONORIL   By day and night he wrongs me. Every hour
He flashes into one gross crime° or other   *offense*
5   That sets us all at odds. I'll not endure it.
His knights grow riotous, and himself upbraids us
On every trifle. When he returns from hunting
I will not speak with him. Say I am sick.
If you come slack of former services[1]
10   You shall do well; the fault of it I'll answer.°   *answer for*

[*Hunting horns within*]

OSWALD   He's coming, madam. I hear him.

GONORIL   Put on what weary negligence you please,
You and your fellow servants. I'd have it come in° question.   *into*
If he dislike it, let him to our sister,
15   Whose mind and mine I know in that are one,
Not to be overruled. Idle° old man,   *Foolish*
That still would manage those authorities
That he hath given away! Now, by my life,
Old fools are babes again, and must be used
20   With checks as flatteries, when they are seen abused.[2]
Remember what I tell you.

OSWALD   Very well, madam.

GONORIL   And let his knights have colder looks among you.
What grows of it, no matter. Advise your fellows so.
I would breed from hence occasions, and I shall,
25   That I may speak.[3] I'll write straight° to my sister   *straightaway*
To hold my very° course. Go prepare for dinner.   *exact*

Exeunt [*severally*]°   *separately*

Scene 4

Enter KENT [*disguised*]

KENT   If but as well[1] I other accents borrow
That can my speech diffuse,° my good intent   *disguise*
May carry through itself to that full issue°   *result*
For which I razed my likeness.[2] Now, banished Kent,
5   If thou canst serve where thou dost stand condemned,
Thy master, whom thou lov'st, shall find thee full of labour.°   *ready for work*

Enter LEAR [*and servants from hunting*]

LEAR   Let me not stay° a jot for dinner. Go get it ready.   *wait*

[*Exit one*]

[*To* KENT] How now, what° art thou?   *who*

KENT   A man, sir.

10   LEAR   What dost thou profess?[3] What wouldst thou with us?

KENT   I do profess to be no less than I seem, to serve him truly

---

Scene 3 Location: The Duke of Albany's castle.
1. If you offer him less service (and respect) than before.
2. *Old . . . abused*: When foolish old men act like children, rebukes are the kindest treatment when kind treatment is abused.
3. *I would . . . speak*: I wish to foster situations, and I shall, in which to speak my mind.

Scene 4 Location: As before.
1. As well as disguising my appearance.
2. Disguised my appearance; shaved off my beard (with a pun on "razor").
3. What is your job (profession)? Kent, in reply, uses "profess" punningly to mean "claim."

1.3

Enter GONERIL *and Steward* [OSWALD]

GONERIL Did my father strike my gentleman
For chiding of his fool?

OSWALD   Ay, madam.

GONERIL By day and night he wrongs me. Every hour
He flashes into one gross crime° or other   *offense*
5 That sets us all at odds. I'll not endure it.
His knights grow riotous, and himself upbraids us
On every trifle. When he returns from hunting
I will not speak with him. Say I am sick.
If you come slack of former services[1]
10 You shall do well; the fault of it I'll answer.°   *answer for*

     [*Horns within*]

OSWALD He's coming, madam. I hear him.

GONERIL Put on what weary negligence you please,
You and your fellows.° I'd have it come to question. *servants*
If he distaste° it, let him to my sister,   *dislike*
15 Whose mind and mine I know in that are one.
Remember what I have said.

OSWALD   Well, madam.

GONERIL And let his knights have colder looks among you.
What grows of it, no matter. Advise your fellows so.
I'll write straight° to my sister to hold my course. *straightaway*
20 Prepare for dinner.   *Exeunt* [*severally*]° *separately*

1.4

Enter KENT [*disguised*]

KENT If but as well[1] I other accents borrow
That can my speech diffuse,° my good intent   *disguise*
May carry through itself to that full issue°   *result*
For which I razed my likeness.[2] Now, banished Kent,
5 If thou canst serve where thou dost stand condemned,
So may it come° thy master, whom thou lov'st,   *come to pass*
Shall find thee full of labours.°   *helpful; keen*

   Horns within.° Enter LEAR *and attendants* [*from* *Hunting horns offstage*
   hunting][3]

LEAR Let me not stay° a jot for dinner. Go get it ready. *wait*

          [*Exit one*]

 [*To* KENT] How now, what° art thou?   *who*
10 KENT A man, sir.

LEAR What dost thou profess?[4] What wouldst thou with us?

KENT I do profess to be no less than I seem, to serve him truly

---

1.3 Location: The Duke of Albany's castle.
1. If you offer him less service (and respect) than before.
1.4 Location: As before.
1. As well as disguising my appearance.
2. Disguised my appearance; shaved off my beard (with a pun on "razor").

3. The attendants include at least one knight. Critics of James I complained that he devalued honors by granting too many knighthoods and that he squandered too much time in hunting.
4. What is your job (profession)? Kent, in reply, uses "profess" punningly to mean "claim."

that will put me in trust, to love him that is honest, to converse°   *associate*
with him that is wise and says little, to fear judgement, to fight
when I cannot choose,° and to eat no fish.⁴   *when I must*

15 LEAR What art thou?

KENT A very honest-hearted fellow, and as poor as the King.

LEAR If thou be as poor for a subject as he is for a king, thou'rt
poor enough. What wouldst thou?

KENT Service.

20 LEAR Who wouldst thou serve?

KENT You.

LEAR Dost thou know me, fellow?

KENT No, sir, but you have that in your countenance which I
would fain° call master.   *gladly*

25 LEAR What's that?

KENT Authority.

LEAR What services canst do?

KENT I can keep honest counsel,° ride, run, mar a curious tale   *keep secrets*
in telling it,⁵ and deliver a plain message bluntly. That which
30 ordinary men are fit for I am qualified in; and the best of me
is diligence.

LEAR How old art thou?

KENT Not so young to love a woman for singing, nor so old to
dote on her for anything. I have years on my back forty-eight.

35 LEAR Follow me. Thou shalt serve me, if I like thee no worse
after dinner. I will not part from thee yet.—Dinner, ho, dinner!
Where's my knave, my fool? Go you and call my fool hither.
                                                    [*Exit one*]

        Enter steward [OSWALD]
You, sirrah, where's my daughter?

OSWALD So please you—   [*Exit*]

40 LEAR What says the fellow there? Call the clotpoll° back.   *blockhead*
                        [*Exeunt* SERVANT *and* KENT]
Where's my fool? Ho, I think the world's asleep.
        [*Enter* KENT *and a* SERVANT]
How now, where's that mongrel?

KENT He says, my lord, your daughter is not well.

LEAR Why came not the slave back to me when I called him?

45 SERVANT Sir, he answered me in the roundest° manner he   *bluntest; rudest*
would not.

LEAR A° would not?   *He*

SERVANT My lord, I know not what the matter is, but to my
judgement your highness is not entertained with that ceremo-
50 nious affection as you were wont.° There's a great abatement   *accustomed to*
appears as well in the general dependants° as in the Duke him-   *servants*
self also, and your daughter.

LEAR Ha, sayst thou so?

SERVANT I beseech you pardon me, my lord, if I be mistaken, for
55 my duty cannot be silent when I think your highness wronged.

---

4. And not to be a Catholic or penitent (Catholics were   5. That is, Kent's plain, blunt speech would make him
obliged to eat fish on specified occasions and as   ill suited to tell a convoluted ("curious") tale.
penance); alternatively, to be a manly man, meat eater.

that will put me in trust, to love him that is honest, to converse°   *associate*
with him that is wise and says little, to fear judgement, to fight
15   when I cannot choose,° and to eat no fish.[5]   *when I must*
    LEAR   What art thou?
    KENT   A very honest-hearted fellow, and as poor as the King.
    LEAR   If thou be'st as poor for a subject as he's for a king, thou'rt
    poor enough. What wouldst thou?
20   KENT   Service.
    LEAR   Who wouldst thou serve?
    KENT   You.
    LEAR   Dost thou know me, fellow?
    KENT   No, sir, but you have that in your countenance which I
25   would fain° call master.   *gladly*
    LEAR   What's that?
    KENT   Authority.
    LEAR   What services canst do?
    KENT   I can keep honest counsel,° ride, run, mar a curious tale   *keep secrets*
30   in telling it,[6] and deliver a plain message bluntly. That which
    ordinary men are fit for I am qualified in; and the best of me
    is diligence.
    LEAR   How old art thou?
    KENT   Not so young, sir, to love a woman for singing, nor so old
35   to dote on her for anything. I have years on my back forty-eight.
    LEAR   Follow me. Thou shalt serve me, if I like thee no worse
    after dinner. I will not part from thee yet. Dinner, ho, dinner!
    Where's my knave, my fool? Go you and call my fool hither.
            [*Exit one*]
        Enter Steward [OSWALD]
    You, you, sirrah, where's my daughter?
40   OSWALD   So please you—   *Exit*
    LEAR   What says the fellow there? Call the clotpoll° back.   *blockhead*
            [*Exit a knight*]
    Where's my fool? Ho, I think the world's asleep.
        [*Enter a* KNIGHT]
    How now? Where's that mongrel?
  KNIGHT   He says, my lord, your daughter is not well.
45   LEAR   Why came not the slave back to me when I called him?
  KNIGHT   Sir, he answered me in the roundest° manner he would   *bluntest; rudest*
    not.
    LEAR   A° would not?   *He*
  KNIGHT   My lord, I know not what the matter is, but to my judge-
50   ment your highness is not entertained with that ceremonious
    affection as you were wont.° There's a great abatement of kind-   *accustomed to*
    ness appears as well in the general dependants° as in the   *servants*
    Duke himself also, and your daughter.
    LEAR   Ha, sayst thou so?
55   KNIGHT   I beseech you pardon me, my lord, if I be mistaken, for
    my duty cannot be silent when I think your highness wronged.

---

5. And not to be a Catholic or penitent (Catholics were obliged to eat fish on specified occasions and as penance); alternatively, to be a manly man, meat eater.

6. That is, Kent's plain, blunt speech would make him ill suited to tell a convoluted ("curious") tale.

LEAR   Thou but rememberest° me of mine own conception.° I   *remind/perception*
have perceived a most faint neglect of late, which I have rather
blamed as mine own jealous curiosity[6] than as a very pretence°   *a true intention*
and purport of unkindness. I will look further into't. But
60   where's this fool? I have not seen him these two days.
SERVANT   Since my young lady's going into France, sir, the fool
hath much pined away.
LEAR   No more of that, I have noted it. Go you and tell my
daughter I would speak with her.   [*Exit one*]
65   Go you, call hither my fool.   [*Exit one*]
          [*Enter* OSWALD *crossing the stage*]
O you, sir, you, sir, come you hither. Who am I, sir?
OSWALD   My lady's father.
LEAR   My lady's father? My lord's knave, you whoreson dog, you
slave, you cur!
70   OSWALD   I am none of this, my lord, I beseech you pardon me.
LEAR   Do you bandy looks with me, you rascal?
          [LEAR *strikes him*]
OSWALD   I'll not be struck, my lord—
KENT [*tripping him*]   Nor tripped neither, you base football-
player.[7]
75   LEAR [*to* KENT]   I thank thee, fellow. Thou serv'st me, and I'll
love thee.
KENT [*to* OSWALD]   Come, sir, I'll teach you differences.° Away,   *(of rank)*
away. If you will measure your lubber's length again,[8] tarry;
but away if you have wisdom.   [*Exit* OSWALD]
80   LEAR   Now, friendly knave, I thank thee.
          Enter [*Lear's*] FOOL
There's earnest of° thy service.   *downpayment for*
          [*He gives* KENT *money*]
FOOL   Let me hire him, too. [*To* KENT] Here's my coxcomb.°   *fool's cap*
LEAR   How now, my pretty knave, how dost thou?
FOOL [*to* KENT]   Sirrah, you were best take my coxcomb.
85   KENT   Why, fool?
FOOL   Why, for taking one's part that's out of favour. Nay, an
thou canst not smile as the wind sits, thou'lt catch cold shortly.[9]
There, take my coxcomb. Why, this fellow hath banished two
on's daughters[1] and done the third a blessing against his will. If
90   thou follow him, thou must needs wear my coxcomb. [*To*
LEAR] How now, nuncle?° Would I had two coxcombs and two   *(mine) uncle*
daughters.
LEAR   Why, my boy?
FOOL   If I gave them my living° I'd keep my coxcombs myself.[2]   *goods*
95   There's mine; beg another off thy daughters.
LEAR   Take heed, sirrah—the whip.

---

6. *jealous curiosity:* paranoid concern with niceties.
7. Football was a rough street game played by the poor.
8. If you will be stretched out by me again. *lubber:*
clumsy oaf.
9. *an . . . shortly:* if you can't keep in favor with those in

power, you will soon find yourself left out in the cold.
1. By abdicating, Lear has in effect prevented his eldest daughters from any longer being his subjects, just
as if he had "banished" them.
2. I'd be twice as much a fool.

LEAR   Thou but rememberest° me of mine own conception.° I   *remind / perception*
have perceived a most faint neglect of late, which I have rather
blamed as mine own jealous curiosity[7] than as a very pretence°   *a true intention*
60   and purpose of unkindness. I will look further into't. But
where's my fool? I have not seen him these two days.

KNIGHT   Since my young lady's going into France, sir, the fool
hath much pined away.

LEAR   No more of that, I have noted it well. Go you and tell my
65   daughter I would speak with her.   [*Exit one*]
Go you, call hither my fool.   [*Exit one*]
        Enter Steward [OSWALD *crossing the stage*]
O you, sir, you, come you hither, sir, who am I, sir?

OSWALD   My lady's father.

LEAR   My lady's father? My lord's knave, you whoreson dog, you
70   slave, you cur!

OSWALD   I am none of these, my lord, I beseech your pardon.

LEAR   Do you bandy looks with me, you rascal?
        [LEAR *strikes him*]

OSWALD   I'll not be strucken, my lord.

KENT [*tripping him*]   Nor tripped neither, you base football
75   player.[8]

LEAR   [*to* KENT]   I thank thee, fellow. Thou serv'st me, and I'll
love thee.

KENT [*to* OSWALD]   Come, sir, arise, away. I'll teach you differences.° Away, away. If you will measure your lubber's length   *(of rank)*
80   again,[9] tarry; but away, go to. Have you wisdom? So.
                    [*Exit* OSWALD]

LEAR   Now, my friendly knave, I thank thee.
        Enter [*Lear's*] FOOL
There's earnest of° thy service.   *downpayment for*
        [*He gives* KENT *money*]

FOOL   Let me hire him, too. [*To* KENT] Here's my coxcomb.°   *fool's cap*

LEAR   How now, my pretty knave, how dost thou?

85   FOOL [*to* KENT]   Sirrah, you were best take my coxcomb.

LEAR   Why, my boy?

FOOL   Why? For taking one's part that's out of favour. [*To* KENT]
Nay, an thou canst not smile as the wind sits, thou'lt catch cold
shortly.[1] There, take my coxcomb. Why, this fellow has
90   banished two on's daughters[2] and did the third a blessing
against his will. If thou follow him, thou must needs wear my
coxcomb. [*To* LEAR] How now, nuncle?°   Would I had two cox-   *(mine) uncle*
combs and two daughters.

LEAR   Why, my boy?

95   FOOL   If I gave them all my living° I'd keep my coxcombs   *goods*
myself.[3] There's mine; beg another off thy daughters.

LEAR   Take heed, sirrah—the whip.

---

7. *jealous curiosity:* paranoid concern with niceties.
8. Football was a rough street game played by the poor.
9. If you will be stretched out by me again. *lubber:*
clumsy oaf.
1. *an . . . shortly:* if you can't keep in favor with those in

power, you will soon find yourself left out in the cold.
2. By abdicating, Lear has in effect prevented his eldest daughters from any longer being his subjects, just
as if he had "banished" them.
3. I'd be twice as much a fool.

FOOL   Truth is a dog that must to° kennel. He must be whipped   go to
out when Lady the brach[3] may stand by the fire and stink.

LEAR   A pestilent gall° to me!   annoyance; bitterness

100 FOOL [to KENT]   Sirrah, I'll teach thee a speech.

LEAR   Do.

FOOL   Mark it, uncle.

          Have more than thou showest,
          Speak less than thou knowest,
105   Lend less than thou owest,°   own
          Ride more than thou goest,°   walk
          Learn° more than thou trowest,°   Hear / believe
          Set less than thou throwest,[4]
          Leave thy drink and thy whore,
110   And keep in-a-door,
          And thou shalt have more
          Than two tens to a score.[5]

LEAR   This is nothing, fool.

FOOL   Then, like the breath° of an unfee'd° lawyer, you gave me   speech / unpaid
115 nothing for't. Can you make no use of nothing, uncle?

LEAR   Why no, boy. Nothing can be made out of nothing.

FOOL [to KENT]   Prithee, tell him so much the rent of his land
comes to.[6] He will not believe a fool.

LEAR   A bitter fool.

120 FOOL   Dost know the difference, my boy, between a bitter fool
and a sweet fool?

LEAR   No, lad. Teach me.

FOOL [sings]   That lord that counselled thee
                  To give away thy land,
125   Come, place him here by me;
                  Do thou for him stand.°   represent him
                  The sweet and bitter fool
                  Will presently appear,
                  The one in motley[7] here,
130   The other found out there.

LEAR   Dost thou call me fool, boy?

FOOL   All thy other titles thou hast given away. That thou wast
born with.

KENT [to LEAR]   This is not altogether fool,[8] my lord.

135 FOOL   No, faith; lords and great men will not let me. If I had a
monopoly out, they would have part on't, and ladies too, they
will not let me have all the fool to myself—they'll be snatching. Give me an egg, nuncle, and I'll give thee two crowns.

LEAR   What two crowns shall they be?

140 FOOL   Why, after I have cut the egg in the middle and eat up
the meat,° the two crowns of the egg. When thou clovest° thy   edible part / cleaved
crown i'th' middle and gavest away both parts, thou borest° thy   you carried
ass o'th'° back o'er the dirt. Thou hadst little wit° in thy bald   on your / sense
crown when thou gavest thy golden one away. If I speak like
145 myself° in this, let him be whipped that first finds it so.[9]   (like a fool)

3. Lady the bitch. Pet dogs were often called "Lady"   on "rent" meaning "torn," "divided."
such and such. The allusion is to Regan and Gonoril,   7. Multicolored dress of a court jester.
who are now being preferred to truthful Cordelia.   8. Foolish, folly. In the next line, the Fool takes "alto-
4. Don't gamble everything on a single cast of the dice. gether fool" to mean "one who has cornered the market
5. And thou . . . score: And there will be more than two on folly."
tens in your twenty—that is, you will become richer.   9. that . . . so: who first discovers for himself that this
6. Remind him that no land means no rent; with a pun   is true; who first considers this to be foolish.

FOOL   Truth's a dog must to° kennel. He must be whipped out   go to
     when the Lady Brach⁴ may stand by th' fire and stink.

100 LEAR   A pestilent gall° to me!   annoyance; bitterness

FOOL [*to* KENT]   Sirrah, I'll teach thee a speech.

LEAR   Do.

FOOL   Mark it, nuncle:
           Have more than thou showest,
105   Speak less than thou knowest,
           Lend less than thou owest,°   own
           Ride more than thou goest,°   walk
           Learn° more than thou trowest,°   Hear / believe
           Set less than thou throwest,⁵
110   Leave thy drink and thy whore,
           And keep in-a-door,
           And thou shalt have more
           Than two tens to a score.⁶

KENT   This is nothing, fool.

115 FOOL   Then 'tis like the breath° of an unfee'd° lawyer: you gave   speech / unpaid
     me nothing for't. [*To* LEAR] Can you make no use of nothing,
     nuncle?

LEAR   Why no, boy. Nothing can be made out of nothing.

FOOL [*to* KENT]   Prithee, tell him so much the rent of his land
120   comes to.⁷ He will not believe a fool.

LEAR   A bitter fool.

FOOL   Dost know the difference, my boy, between a bitter fool
     and a sweet one?

LEAR   No, lad. Teach me.

125 FOOL   Nuncle, give me an egg, and I'll give thee two crowns.

LEAR   What two crowns shall they be?

FOOL   Why, after I have cut the egg i'th' middle and eat up the
     meat,° the two crowns of the egg. When thou clovest° thy   edible part / cleaved
     crown i'th' middle and gavest away both parts, thou borest°   you carried
130   thine ass o'th'° back o'er the dirt. Thou hadst little wit° in thy   on your / sense
     bald crown when thou gavest thy golden one away. If I speak
     like myself° in this, let him be whipped that first finds it so.⁸   (like a fool)

---

4. Lady Bitch. Pet dogs were often called "Lady" such and such. The allusion is to Regan and Goneril, who are now being preferred to truthful Cordelia.
5. Don't gamble everything on a single cast of the dice.
6. *And thou . . . score:* And there will be more than two

tens in your twenty—that is, you will become richer.
7. Remind him that no land means no rent; with a pun on "rent" meaning "torn," "divided."
8. *that . . . so:* who first discovers for himself that this is true; who first considers this to be foolish.

[*Sings*]   Fools had ne'er less wit in a year,
            For wise men are grown foppish.[1]
            They know not how their wits do wear,
            Their manners are so apish.°   *stupid; imitative*

150 LEAR   When were you wont° to be so full of songs, sirrah?   *accustomed*

FOOL   I have used° it, nuncle, ever since thou madest thy daugh-   *practiced*
ters thy mother; for when thou gavest them the rod and puttest
down thine own breeches,
   [*Sings*]   Then they for sudden joy did weep,
155   And I for sorrow sung,
             That such a king should play bo-peep°   *a child's game*
             And go the fools among.
Prithee, nuncle, keep a schoolmaster that can teach thy fool
to lie. I would fain learn to lie.

160 LEAR   An° you lie, we'll have you whipped.   *If*

FOOL   I marvel what kin° thou and thy daughters are. They'll   *how alike*
have me whipped for speaking true, thou wilt have me
whipped for lying, and sometime I am whipped for holding my
peace. I had rather be any kind of thing than a fool; and yet I
165 would not be thee, nuncle. Thou hast pared thy wit o' both
sides and left nothing in the middle.
        Enter GONORIL
Here comes one of the parings.

LEAR   How now, daughter, what makes that frontlet[2] on?
Methinks you are too much o' late i'th' frown.

170 FOOL   Thou wast a pretty fellow when thou hadst no need to
care for her frown. Now thou art an O without a figure.[3] I am
better than thou art, now. I am a fool; thou art nothing. [*To*
GONORIL] Yes, forsooth, I will hold my tongue; so your face
bids me, though you say nothing.
175   [*Sings*]   Mum, mum.
            He that keeps neither crust nor crumb,
            Weary of all, shall want° some.   *lack; be in need of*
That's a shelled peascod.°   *empty pea pod; nothing*

GONORIL [*to* LEAR]   Not only, sir, this your all-licensed° fool,   *unrestrained*
180 But other of your insolent retinue
Do hourly carp and quarrel, breaking forth
In rank° and not-to-be-endurèd riots.   *foul; spreading*
Sir, I had thought by making this well known unto you
To have found a safe° redress, but now grow fearful,   *sure*
185 By what yourself too late° have spoke and done,   *recently*
That you protect this course, and put it on°   *encourage it*
By your allowance; which if you should, the fault
Would not scape censure, nor the redress sleep
Which in the tender of a wholesome weal
190 Might in their working do you that offence,
That else were shame, that then necessity
Must call discreet proceedings.[4]

---

1. *Fools . . . foppish:* Professional fools have never been as witless since wise men have lately outdone them in idiocy.
2. Band worn on the forehead; here, a metaphor for "frown."
3. A zero without a preceding digit; nothing.
4. *which if you . . . proceedings:* if you do approve (of your attendants' behavior), you will not escape criticism, nor will it be without retribution, which for the common good will cause you pain. While this would otherwise be improper, it will be seen as a prudent ("discreet") action under the circumstances. *tender of:* concern for. *weal:* state, commonwealth. *then necessity:* the demands of the time.

[*Sings*] Fools had ne'er less grace in a year,
            For wise men are grown foppish,[9]
135   And know not how their wits to wear,
            Their manners are so apish.°   *stupid; imitative*
LEAR When were you wont° to be so full of songs, sirrah?   *accustomed*
FOOL I have used° it, nuncle, e'er since thou madest thy daugh-   *practiced*
      ters thy mothers; for when thou gavest them the rod and
140   puttest down thine own breeches,
[*Sings*] Then they for sudden joy did weep,
            And I for sorrow sung,
            That such a king should play bo-peep°   *a child's game*
            And go the fools among.
145   Prithee, nuncle, keep a schoolmaster that can teach thy fool
      to lie. I would fain learn to lie.
LEAR An° you lie, sirrah, we'll have you whipped.   *If*
FOOL I marvel what kin° thou and thy daughters are. They'll   *how alike*
      have me whipped for speaking true, thou'lt have me whipped
150   for lying, and sometimes I am whipped for holding my peace.
      I had rather be any kind o' thing than a fool; and yet I would
      not be thee, nuncle. Thou hast pared thy wit o' both sides and
      left nothing i'th' middle.
            Enter GONERIL
      Here comes one o' the parings.
155 LEAR How now, daughter? What makes that frontlet[1] on?
      You are too much of late i'th' frown.
FOOL Thou wast a pretty fellow when thou hadst no need to
      care for her frowning. Now thou art an O without a figure.[2] I
      am better than thou art, now. I am a fool; thou art nothing.
160   [*To* GONERIL] Yes, forsooth, I will hold my tongue; so your face
      bids me, though you say nothing.
      [*Sings*] Mum, mum.
                He that keeps nor crust nor crumb,
                Weary of all, shall want° some.   *lack; be in need of*
165   That's a shelled peascod.°   *empty pea pod; nothing*
GONERIL [*to* LEAR] Not only, sir, this your all-licensed° fool,   *unrestrained*
      But other of your insolent retinue
      Do hourly carp and quarrel, breaking forth
      In rank° and not-to-be-endurèd riots. Sir,   *foul; spreading*
170   I had thought by making this well known unto you
      To have found a safe° redress, but now grow fearful,   *sure*
      By what yourself too late° have spoke and done,   *recently*
      That you protect this course, and put it on°   *encourage it*
      By your allowance; which if you should, the fault
175   Would not scape censure, nor the redresses sleep
      Which in the tender of a wholesome weal
      Might in their working do you that offence,
      Which else were shame, that then necessity
      Will call discreet proceeding.[3]

---

9. *Fools . . . foppish:* Professional fools have never been as witless since wise men have lately outdone them in idiocy.
1. Band worn on the forehead; here, a metaphor for "frown."
2. A zero without a preceding digit; nothing.
3. *which if you . . . proceeding:* if you do approve (of your attendants' behavior), you will not escape criticism, nor will it be without retribution, which for the common good will cause you pain. While this would otherwise be improper, it will be seen as a prudent ("discreet") action under the circumstances. *tender of:* concern for. *weal:* state, commonwealth. *then necessity:* the demands of the time.

FOOL [*to* LEAR]   For, you trow, nuncle,
   [*Sings*]   The hedge-sparrow fed the cuckoo⁵ so long

195   That it had it° head bit off by it young;°   *its / (the young cuckoo)*
   so out went the candle, and we were left darkling.°   *in the dark*

LEAR [*to* GONORIL]   Are you our daughter?

GONORIL   Come, sir, I would° you would make use of that good wisdom   *wish*
   Whereof I know you are fraught,° and put away   *full*

200   These dispositions° that of late transform you   *moods; attitudes*
   From what you rightly are.

FOOL   May not an ass know when the cart draws the horse?
   [*Sings*] 'Whoop, jug,⁶ I love thee!'

LEAR   Doth any here know me? Why, this is not Lear.

205   Doth Lear walk thus, speak thus? Where are his eyes?
   Either his notion° weakens, or his discernings   *intellect*
   Are lethargied. Sleeping or waking, ha?
   Sure, 'tis not so.
   Who is it that can tell me who I am?

210   Lear's shadow? I would° learn that, for by the marks°   *wish to / evidence*
   Of sovereignty, knowledge, and reason
   I should be false persuaded I had daughters.

FOOL   Which° they will make an obedient father.   *Whom*

LEAR [*to* GONORIL]   Your name, fair gentlewoman?

GONORIL   Come, sir,

215   This admiration° is much of the savour   *excessive amazement*
   Of other your new pranks. I do beseech you
   Understand my purposes aright,
   As you are old and reverend, should° be wise.   *you should*
   Here do you keep a hundred knights and squires,

220   Men so disordered,° so debauched and bold   *disorderly*
   That this our court, infected with their manners,
   Shows° like a riotous inn, epicurism°   *Appears / gluttony*
   And lust make more like to a tavern, or brothel,
   Than a great palace. The shame itself doth speak

225   For instant remedy. Be thou desired,
   By her that else will take the thing she begs,
   A little to disquantity your train,°   *to reduce your retinue*
   And the remainder that shall still depend°   *be retained*
   To be such men as may besort° your age,   *befit*
   That know themselves° and you.   *Who know their place*

230 LEAR   Darkness and devils!
   Saddle my horses, call my train together!—   [*Exit one or more*]
   Degenerate bastard, I'll not trouble thee.
   Yet° have I left a daughter.   *Still*

GONORIL   You strike my people, and your disordered rabble
235   Make servants of their betters.
        Enter Duke [*of* ALBANY]

---

5. The cuckoo lays its eggs in other birds' nests.   6. Nickname for "Joan"; sobriquet for a whore.

180   FOOL [*to* LEAR]   For, you know, nuncle,

         [*Sings*]   The hedge-sparrow fed the cuckoo[4] so long

              That it's had it° head bit off by it young;°   *its* / *(the young cuckoo)*

         so out went the candle, and we were left darkling.°   *in the dark*

      LEAR [*to* GONERIL]   Are you our daughter?

185   GONERIL   I would° you would make use of your good wisdom,   *wish*

         Whereof I know you are fraught,° and put away   *full*

         These dispositions° which of late transport you   *moods; attitudes*

         From what you rightly are.

      FOOL   May not an ass know when the cart draws the horse?

190   [*Sings*] 'Whoop, jug,[5] I love thee!'

      LEAR   Does any here know me? This is not Lear.

         Does Lear walk thus, speak thus? Where are his eyes?

         Either his notion° weakens, his discernings   *intellect*

         Are lethargied—ha, waking?° 'Tis not so.   *am I awake*

195   Who is it that can tell me who I am?

      FOOL   Lear's shadow.

      LEAR [*to* GONERIL]   Your name, fair gentlewoman?

      GONERIL   This admiration,° sir, is much o'th' savour   *excessive amazement*

         Of other your new pranks. I do beseech you

200   To understand my purposes aright,

         As you are old and reverend, should° be wise.   *you should*

         Here do you keep a hundred knights and squires,

         Men so disordered,° so debauched and bold   *disorderly*

         That this our court, infected with their manners,

205   Shows° like a riotous inn. Epicurism° and lust   *Appears* / *Gluttony*

         Makes it more like a tavern or a brothel

         Than a graced° palace. The shame itself doth speak   *an honored*

         For instant remedy. Be then desired,

         By her that else will take the thing she begs,

210   A little to disquantity your train,°   *to reduce your retinue*

         And the remainders that shall still depend°   *be retained*

         To be such men as may besort° your age,   *befit*

         Which know themselves° and you.   *Who know their place*

      LEAR   Darkness and devils!

         Saddle my horses, call my train together!—   [*Exit one or more*]

215   Degenerate bastard, I'll not trouble thee.

         Yet° have I left a daughter.   *Still*

      GONERIL   You strike my people, and your disordered rabble

         Make servants of their betters.

          Enter ALBANY

---

4. The cuckoo lays its eggs in other birds' nests.   5. Nickname for "Joan"; sobriquet for a whore.

LEAR   We that too late repent's—O sir, are you come?
        Is it your will that we—prepare my horses.   [*Exit one or more*]
        Ingratitude, thou marble-hearted fiend,
        More hideous when thou show'st thee in a child
240   Than the sea-monster—[*to* GONORIL] detested kite,° thou liest.   *carrion-eating hawk*
        My train are men of choice and rarest parts,°   *qualities*
        That all particulars of duty know,
        And in the most exact regard support
        The worships of° their name. O most small fault,   *honor accorded*
245   How ugly didst thou in Cordelia show,
        That, like an engine, wrenched my frame of nature
        From the fixed place,[7] drew from my heart all love,
        And added to the gall! O Lear, Lear!
        Beat at this gate° that let thy folly in   *(his head)*
250   And thy dear° judgement out.—Go, go, my people!   *precious*
ALBANY   My lord, I am guiltless as I am ignorant.
LEAR   It may be so, my lord. Hark, nature, hear:
        Dear goddess, suspend thy purpose if
        Thou didst intend to make this creature fruitful.
255   Into her womb convey sterility.
        Dry up in her the organs of increase,
        And from her derogate° body never spring   *debased*
        A babe to honour her. If she must teem,°   *breed*
        Create her child of spleen,° that it may live   *malice*
260   And be a thwart disnatured° torment to her.   *a perverse unnatural*
        Let it stamp wrinkles in her brow of youth,
        With cadent° tears fret° channels in her cheeks,   *flowing / carve*
        Turn all her mother's pains and benefits°   *cares and kind actions*
        To laughter and contempt, that she may feel—
265   That she may feel
        How sharper than a serpent's tooth it is
        To have a thankless child.—Go, go, my people!
                    [*Exeunt* LEAR, KENT, FOOL, *and servants*]
ALBANY   Now, gods that we adore, whereof comes this?
GONORIL   Never afflict yourself to know the cause,
270   But let his disposition have that scope
        That dotage gives it.
                    [*Enter* LEAR *and* FOOL]
LEAR   What, fifty of my followers at a clap?
        Within a fortnight?
ALBANY   What is the matter, sir?
LEAR   I'll tell thee. [*To* GONORIL] Life and death! I am ashamed
275   That thou hast power to shake my manhood thus,
        That these hot tears, that break from me perforce°   *against my will*
        And should make thee—worst blasts and fogs upon thee!
        Untented woundings° of a father's curse   *Undressed wounds*
        Pierce every sense about thee! Old fond° eyes,   *foolish*

---

7. *like . . . place*: as a machine (or lever) dislocated my natural affections from their proper foundations.

LEAR   Woe that° too late repents!   *Woe to him who*
       Is it your will? Speak, sir.—Prepare my horses.
                                         [*Exit one or more*]
220   Ingratitude, thou marble-hearted fiend,
       More hideous when thou show'st thee in a child
       Than the sea-monster—
ALBANY   Pray sir, be patient.
LEAR [*to* GONERIL]   Detested kite,° thou liest.   *carrion-eating hawk*
225   My train are men of choice and rarest parts,°   *qualities*
       That all particulars of duty know,
       And in the most exact regard support
       The worships of° their name. O most small fault,   *honors accorded*
       How ugly didst thou in Cordelia show,
230   Which, like an engine, wrenched my frame of nature
       From the fixed place,[6] drew from my heart all love,
       And added to the gall! O Lear, Lear, Lear!
       Beat at this gate° that let thy folly in   *(his head)*
       And thy dear° judgement out.—Go, go, my people!   *precious*
235 ALBANY   My lord, I am guiltless, as I am ignorant
       Of what hath moved you.
LEAR   It may be so, my lord.
       Hear, nature; hear, dear goddess, hear:
       Suspend thy purpose if thou didst intend
       To make this creature fruitful.
240   Into her womb convey sterility.
       Dry up in her the organs of increase,
       And from her derogate° body never spring   *debased*
       A babe to honour her. If she must teem,°   *breed*
       Create her child of spleen,° that it may live   *malice*
245   And be a thwart disnatured° torment to her.   *a perverse unnatural*
       Let it stamp wrinkles in her brow of youth,
       With cadent° tears fret° channels in her cheeks,   *flowing / carve*
       Turn all her mother's pains and benefits°   *cares and kind actions*
       To laughter and contempt, that she may feel—
250   That she may feel
       How sharper than a serpent's tooth it is
       To have a thankless child. Away, away!
                              Exeunt [LEAR, KENT, *and attendants*]
ALBANY   Now, gods that we adore, whereof comes this?
GONERIL   Never afflict yourself to know more of it,
255   But let his disposition have that scope
       As° dotage gives it.   *Which*
                   Enter LEAR
LEAR   What, fifty of my followers at a clap?
       Within a fortnight?
ALBANY   What's the matter, sir?
LEAR   I'll tell thee. [*To* GONERIL] Life and death! I am ashamed
260   That thou hast power to shake my manhood thus,
       That these hot tears, which break from me perforce,°   *against my will*
       Should make thee worth them. Blasts and fogs upon thee!
       Th'untented woundings° of a father's curse   *The undressed wounds*
       Pierce every sense about thee! Old fond° eyes,   *foolish*

---

6. *like . . . place:* as a machine (or lever) dislocated my natural affections from their proper foundations.

280   Beweep° this cause again I'll pluck you out   *If you weep over*
         And cast you, with the waters that you make,
         To temper° clay. Yea,   *soften*
         Is't come to this? Yet have I left a daughter
         Whom, I am sure, is kind and comfortable.°   *comforting*
285   When she shall hear this of thee, with her nails
         She'll flay thy wolvish visage. Thou shalt find
         That I'll resume the shape which thou dost think
         I have cast off for ever; thou shalt, I warrant thee.   [*Exit*]
        GONORIL   Do you mark that, my lord?
290   ALBANY   I cannot be so partial,° Gonoril,   *biased*
         To° the great love I bear you—   *Because of*
        GONORIL   Come, sir, no more.—
         You, more knave than fool, after your master!
        FOOL   Nuncle Lear, nuncle Lear, tarry, and take the fool with
         thee.
295   A fox when one has caught her,
                     And such a daughter,
                     Should sure° to the slaughter,   *surely be sent*
                     If my cap would buy a halter.°   *collar; noose*
                     So, the fool follows after.   [*Exit*]

300   GONORIL   What, Oswald, ho!
               [*Enter* OSWALD]
        OSWALD   Here, madam.
        GONORIL   What, have you writ this letter to my sister?
        OSWALD   Yes, madam.
        GONORIL   Take you some company, and away to horse.
305   Inform her full of my particular fears,
         And thereto add such reasons of your own
         As may compact° it more. Get you gone,   *compound*
          And after, your retinue.   [*Exit* OSWALD]
                   Now, my lord,
         This milky gentleness and course of yours,
310   Though I dislike not, yet under pardon°   *begging your pardon*
         You're much more ataxed° for want of wisdom   *taken to task; censured*
         Than praised for harmful mildness.
        ALBANY   How far your eyes may pierce° I cannot tell.   *foresee*
         Striving to better aught,° we mar what's well.   *anything*
315   GONORIL   Nay, then—
        ALBANY   Well, well, the event.°   *Exeunt*   *let's see the outcome*

265   Beweep° this cause again I'll pluck ye out   *If you weep over*
        And cast you, with the waters that you loose,°   *let loose*
        To temper° clay. Ha! Let it be so.   *soften*
        I have another daughter
        Who, I am sure, is kind and comfortable.°   *comforting*
270   When she shall hear this of thee, with her nails
        She'll flay thy wolvish visage. Thou shalt find
        That I'll resume the shape which thou dost think
        I have cast off for ever.   *Exit*

GONERIL   Do you mark that?

ALBANY   I cannot be so partial,° Goneril,   *biased*
275   To° the great love I bear you—   *Because of*

GONERIL   Pray you, content.° What, Oswald, ho!—   *be quiet*
        You, sir, more knave than fool, after your master.

FOOL   Nuncle Lear, nuncle Lear,
        Tarry, take the fool with thee.
280   A fox when one has caught her,
        And such a daughter,
        Should sure° to the slaughter,   *surely be sent*
        If my cap would buy a halter.°   *collar; noose*
        So, the fool follows after.   *Exit*

285 GONERIL   This man hath had good counsel—a hundred knights?
        'Tis politic° and safe to let him keep   *prudent*
        At point° a hundred knights, yes, that on every dream,   *Armed*
        Each buzz,° each fancy, each complaint, dislike,   *rumor*
        He may enguard° his dotage with their powers   *protect*
290   And hold our lives in mercy.—Oswald, I say!

ALBANY   Well, you may fear too far.

GONERIL   Safer than trust too far.
        Let me still° take away the harms I fear,   *always*
        Not° fear still to be taken. I know his heart.   *Rather than*
        What he hath uttered I have writ my sister.
295   If she sustain him and his hundred knights
        When I have showed th'unfitness—

            Enter Steward [OSWALD]

                         How now, Oswald?
        What, have you writ that letter to my sister?

OSWALD   Ay, madam.

GONERIL   Take you some company, and away to horse.
300   Inform her full of my particular fear,
        And thereto add such reasons of your own
        As may compact° it more. Get you gone,   *compound*
        And hasten your return.   [*Exit* OSWALD]
                   No, no, my lord,
        This milky gentleness and course of yours,
305   Though I condemn not, yet under pardon°   *begging your pardon*
        You are much more attasked° for want of wisdom   *taken to task; censured*
        Than praised for harmful mildness.

ALBANY   How far your eyes may pierce° I cannot tell.   *foresee*
        Striving to better, oft we mar what's well.
310 GONERIL   Nay, then—

ALBANY   Well, well, th'event.°   *Exeunt*   *let's see the outcome*

Scene 5

Enter LEAR, KENT [*disguised, and*] FOOL

LEAR [*to* KENT]   Go you before° to Gloucester¹ with these letters.   *on ahead*
Acquaint my daughter no further with anything you know than
comes from her demand out of the letter.² If your diligence be
not speedy, I shall be there before you.

5   KENT   I will not sleep, my lord, till I have delivered your letter.

                                                  Exit

FOOL   If a man's brains were in his heels, were't not in danger of
kibes?°   *chilblains*

LEAR   Ay, boy.

FOOL   Then, I prithee, be merry: thy wit shall ne'er go slipshod.³

10   LEAR   Ha, ha, ha!

FOOL   Shalt° see thy other daughter will use thee kindly, for   *Thou shalt*
though she's as like this as a crab° is like an apple, yet I   *crab apple; sour apple*
con° what I can tell.   *know*

LEAR   Why, what canst thou tell, my boy?

15   FOOL   She'll taste as like this as a crab doth to a crab. Thou canst
not tell why one's nose stands in the middle of his face?

LEAR   No.

FOOL   Why, to keep his eyes on either side 's nose, that what a
man cannot smell out, a° may spy into.   *he*

20   LEAR   I did her wrong.

FOOL   Canst tell how an oyster makes his shell?

LEAR   No.

FOOL   Nor I neither; but I can tell why a snail has a house.

LEAR   Why?

25   FOOL   Why, to put his head in, not to give it away to his daughter
and leave his horns without a case.⁴

LEAR   I will forget my nature.⁵ So kind a father!
Be my horses ready?

FOOL   Thy asses° are gone about them. The reason why the   *(servants)*
30   seven stars° are no more than seven is a pretty reason.   *the Pleiades*

LEAR   Because they are not eight.

FOOL   Yes. Thou wouldst make a good fool.

LEAR   To take't again perforce⁶—monster ingratitude!

FOOL   If thou wert my fool, nuncle, I'd have thee beaten for
35   being old before thy time.

LEAR   How's that?

FOOL   Thou shouldst not have been old before thou hadst been
wise.

LEAR   O, let me not be mad, sweet heaven!
40   I would not be mad.
Keep me in temper.° I would not be mad.   *sane*

Scene 5 Location: Before Albany's castle.
1. To Gloucestershire, where Cornwall and Regan
reside.
2. *than . . . letter:* other than such questions as are
prompted by the letter.
3. Literally, your brains will not wear slippers (to warm
feet that are afflicted with chilblains); feet of any intelligence would not walk toward Regan.

4. Protective covering for his head, or concealment for
his horns (horns were the conventional sign of a cuckold). The Fool reflects the cynical view, common in the
period, that all married men are inevitably cuckolded.
5. Lose my fatherly feelings. *nature:* character.
6. To take it back by force. Lear may refer to Gonoril's
treachery, or he may be contemplating resuming his
authority.

1.5

Enter LEAR, KENT [*disguised, the First*] GENTLEMAN, *and*
FOOL

LEAR [*to the* GENTLEMAN,[1] *giving him a letter*] Go you before° to   °*on ahead*
Gloucester[2] with these letters.   [*Exit* GENTLEMAN]
[*To* KENT, *giving him a letter*] Acquaint my daughter no further with anything you know than comes from her demand
5   out of the letter.[3] If your diligence be not speedy, I shall be
there afore you.

KENT   I will not sleep, my lord, till I have delivered your letter.

Exit

FOOL   If a man's brains were in's heels, were't not in danger of
kibes?°   °*chilblains*
10 LEAR   Ay, boy.

FOOL   Then, I prithee, be merry: thy wit shall not go slipshod.[4]

LEAR   Ha, ha, ha!

FOOL   Shalt° see thy other daughter will use thee kindly, for   °*Thou shalt*
though she's as like this as a crab's° like an apple, yet I can tell   *crab apple; sour apple*
15 what I can tell.

LEAR   What canst tell, boy?

FOOL   She will taste as like this as a crab does to a crab. Thou
canst tell why one's nose stands i'th' middle on 's° face?   °*of one's*

LEAR   No.

20 FOOL   Why, to keep one's eyes of either side 's nose, that what a
man cannot smell out, a° may spy into.   °*he*

LEAR   I did her wrong.

FOOL   Canst tell how an oyster makes his shell?

LEAR   No.

25 FOOL   Nor I neither; but I can tell why a snail has a house.

LEAR   Why?

FOOL   Why, to put 's head in, not to give it away to his daughters
and leave his horns without a case.[5]

LEAR   I will forget my nature.[6] So kind a father!
30 Be my horses ready?

FOOL   Thy asses° are gone about 'em. The reason why the seven   °(*servants*)
stars° are no more than seven is a pretty reason.   *the Pleiades*

LEAR   Because they are not eight.

FOOL   Yes, indeed, thou wouldst make a good fool.

35 LEAR   To take't again perforce[7]—monster ingratitude!

FOOL   If thou wert my fool, nuncle, I'd have thee beaten for
being old before thy time.

LEAR   How's that?

FOOL   Thou shouldst not have been old till thou hadst been
40 wise.

LEAR   O, let me not be mad, not mad, sweet heaven!
Keep me in temper.° I would not be mad.   °*sane*

1.5 Location: Before Albany's castle.
1. Most editors address this entire speech to Kent,
since in Q the first gentleman does not appear here.
2. To Gloucestershire, where Cornwall and Regan
reside.
3. *than . . . letter:* other than such questions as are
prompted by the letter.
4. Literally, your brains will not wear slippers (to warm
feet that are afflicted with chilblains); feet of any intelligence would not walk toward Regan.
5. Protective covering for his head, or concealment for
his horns (horns were the conventional sign of a cuckold). The Fool reflects the cynical view, common in the
period, that all married men are inevitably cuckolded.
6. Lose my fatherly feelings. *nature:* character.
7. To take it back by force. Lear may refer to Goneril's
treachery, or he may be contemplating resuming his
authority.

[*Enter a* SERVANT]

Are the horses ready?

SERVANT   Ready, my lord.

LEAR [*to* FOOL]   Come, boy.   *Exeunt* [LEAR *and* SERVANT]

FOOL   She that is maid now, and laughs at my departure,

45   Shall not be a maid long, except things be cut shorter.[7] *Exit*

Scene 6

Enter Bastard [EDMUND] *and* CURAN, *meeting*

EDMUND   Save° thee, Curan.   *God save*

CURAN   And you, sir. I have been with your father, and given

          him notice that the Duke of Cornwall and his duchess will be

          here with him tonight.

5   EDMUND   How comes that?

CURAN   Nay, I know not. You have heard of the news abroad?—

          I mean the whispered ones, for there are yet but ear-bussing

          arguments.[1]

EDMUND   Not. I pray you, what are they?

10   CURAN   Have you heard of no likely wars towards° twixt the two   *impending*

          Dukes of Cornwall and Albany?

EDMUND   Not a word.

CURAN   You may then in time. Fare you well, sir.   [*Exit*]

EDMUND   The Duke be here tonight! The better, best.

15   This weaves itself perforce° into my business.   *necessarily*

          Enter EDGAR [*at a window above*]

          My father hath set guard to take my brother,

          And I have one thing of a queasy question[2]

          Which must ask briefness. Wit and fortune help!—

          Brother, a word. Descend, brother, I say.

          [EDGAR *climbs down*]

20   My father watches. O, fly this place.

          Intelligence is given where you are hid.

          You have now the good advantage of the night.

          Have you not spoken 'gainst the Duke of Cornwall aught?°   *anything*

          He's coming hither now, in the night, i'th' haste,

25   And Regan with him. Have you nothing said

          Upon his party° against the Duke of Albany?   *On his (Cornwall's) side*

          Advise you°—   *Consider carefully*

EDGAR   I am sure on't,° not a word.   *of it*

EDMUND   I hear my father coming. Pardon me.

          In cunning I must draw my sword upon you.

30   Seem to defend yourself. Now, quit you° well.   *acquit yourself*

          [*Calling*]   Yield, come before my father. Light here, here!

          [*To* EDGAR] Fly, brother, fly! [*Calling*] Torches, torches! [*To*

             EDGAR] So, farewell.   [*Exit* EDGAR]

          Some blood drawn on me would beget opinion°   *produce the impression*

          Of my more fierce endeavour.

             He wounds his arm

---

7. *She . . . shorter:* A girl who would laugh at my leaving
would be so foolish that she could not remain a virgin for
long; "things" refers both to the unfolding event and to
penises.

Scene 6 Location: Gloucester's castle.
1. Barely whispered affairs. *bussing:* buzzing.
2. And I have a hazardous and delicate problem.

[*Enter the* FIRST GENTLEMAN]

How now, are the horses ready?

FIRST GENTLEMAN   Ready, my lord.

LEAR [*to* FOOL]   Come, boy.

45   FOOL   She that's a maid now, and laughs at my departure,
        Shall not be a maid long, unless things be cut shorter.[8]

                                                        Exeunt

2.1

Enter Bastard [EDMOND] *and* CURAN, *severally*

EDMOND   Save° thee, Curan.   God save

CURAN   And you, sir. I have been with your father, and given
    him notice that the Duke of Cornwall and Regan his duchess
    will be here with him this night.

5   EDMOND   How comes that?

CURAN   Nay, I know not. You have heard of the news abroad?—
    I mean the whispered ones, for they are yet but ear-kissing
    arguments.[1]

EDMOND   Not I. Pray you, what are they?

10   CURAN   Have you heard of no likely wars toward° twixt the Dukes   impending
    of Cornwall and Albany?

EDMOND   Not a word.

CURAN   You may do then in time. Fare you well, sir.   *Exit*

EDMOND   The Duke be here tonight! The better, best.

15   This weaves itself perforce° into my business.   necessarily

Enter EDGAR [*at a window above*]

My father hath set guard to take my brother,
And I have one thing of a queasy question[2]
Which I must act. Briefness and fortune work!°—   be with me
Brother, a word, descend. Brother, I say.

[EDGAR *climbs down*]

20   My father watches. O sir, fly this place.
Intelligence is given where you are hid.
You have now the good advantage of the night.
Have you not spoken 'gainst the Duke of Cornwall?
He's coming hither, now, i'th' night, i'th' haste,

25   And Regan with him. Have you nothing said
Upon his party° 'gainst the Duke of Albany?   On his (Cornwall's) side
Advise yourself.°   Consider carefully

EDGAR   I am sure on't,° not a word.   of it

EDMOND   I hear my father coming. Pardon me.
In cunning I must draw my sword upon you.

30   Draw. Seem to defend yourself. Now, quit you° well.   acquit yourself
[*Calling*] Yield, come before my father. Light ho, here!
[*To* EDGAR] Fly, brother! [*Calling*] Torches, torches!
[*To* EDGAR]   So, farewell.

                                          Exit EDGAR

Some blood drawn on me would beget opinion°   produce the impression
Of my more fierce endeavour.

        [*He wounds his arm*]

---

8. *She . . . shorter:* A girl who would laugh at my leaving would be so foolish that she could not remain a virgin for long; "things" refers both to the unfolding event
and to penises.

2.1 Location: Gloucester's castle.
1. Barely whispered affairs.
2. And I have a hazardous and delicate problem.

                                    I have seen
35 Drunkards do more than this in sport. [*Calling*] Father, father!
    Stop, stop! Ho, help!
                Enter GLOUCESTER [*and others*]
    GLOUCESTER   Now, Edmund, where is the villain?
    EDMUND   Here stood he in the dark, his sharp sword out,
    Warbling of wicked charms, conjuring the moon
    To stand 's° auspicious mistress.   *To act as his*
    GLOUCESTER   But where is he?
    EDMUND   Look, sir, I bleed.
40 GLOUCESTER   Where is the villain, Edmund?
    EDMUND   Fled this way, sir, when by no means he could—
    GLOUCESTER   Pursue him, go after.   [*Exeunt others*]
                By no means what?
    EDMUND   Persuade me to the murder of your lordship,
    But that° I told him the revengive gods   *In response to that*
45 'Gainst parricides did all their thunders bend,
    Spoke with how manifold and strong a bond
    The child was bound to the father. Sir, in fine,°   *finally*
    Seeing how loathly opposite° I stood   *opposed*
    To his unnatural purpose, with fell° motion,   *deadly*
50 With his preparèd sword he charges home°   *strikes to the heart of*
    My unprovided° body, lanced° mine arm;   *unprotected / struck*
    But when he saw my best alarumed spirits
    Bold in the quarrel's rights,[3] roused to the encounter,
    Or° whether ghasted° by the noise I made   *Either / frightened*
55 Or [   ] I know not,[4]
    But suddenly he fled.
    GLOUCESTER   Let him fly far,
    Not in this land shall he remain uncaught,
    And found, dispatch.° The noble Duke my master,   *And once found, killed*
    My worthy arch° and patron, comes tonight.   *lord*
60 By his authority I will proclaim it
    That he which finds him shall deserve our thanks,
    Bringing the murderous caitiff° to the stake;[5]   *wretch*
    He that conceals him, death.
    EDMUND   When I dissuaded him from his intent
65 And found him pitched° to do it, with curst° speech   *resolved / bitter*
    I threatened to discover° him. He replied,   *expose*
    'Thou unpossessing bastard, dost thou think
    If I would stand against thee, could the reposure°   *placing*
    Of any trust, virtue, or worth in thee
70 Make thy words faithed?° No, what I should deny—   *credible*
    As this I would, ay, though thou didst produce
    My very character[6]—I'd turn it all
    To[7] thy suggestion, plot, and damned pretence,°   *intent*
    And thou must make a dullard of the world
75 If they not thought the profits of my death

---

3. *my best . . . rights:* that I was fully roused to action, made brave by righteousness.
4. From the jumbled syntax, it appears likely that Q has accidentally omitted a verse line that, in the Oxford editors' conjecture, would have begun with "Or" and ended with "I know not."

5. Treachery and rebellion were crimes for which one could be burned.
6. Handwriting; but also, a true summary of my character.
7. *I'd . . . / To:* I'd blame it all on.

I have seen drunkards
35   Do more than this in sport. [*Calling*] Father, father!
Stop, stop! Ho, help!
        Enter GLOUCESTER, *and servants with torches*
GLOUCESTER   Now, Edmond, where's the villain?
EDMOND   Here stood he in the dark, his sharp sword out,
Mumbling of wicked charms, conjuring the moon
To stand 's° auspicious mistress.   *To act as his*
GLOUCESTER   But where is he?
EDMOND   Look, sir, I bleed.
40   GLOUCESTER   Where is the villain, Edmond?
EDMOND   Fled this way, sir, when by no means he could—
GLOUCESTER   Pursue him, ho! Go after.   [*Exeunt servants*]
                        By no means what?
EDMOND   Persuade me to the murder of your lordship,
But that° I told him the revenging gods   *In response to that*
45   'Gainst parricides did all the thunder bend,
Spoke with how manifold and strong a bond
The child was bound to th'father. Sir, in fine,°   *finally*
Seeing how loathly opposite° I stood   *opposed*
To his unnatural purpose, in fell° motion   *deadly*
50   With his preparèd sword he charges home°   *strikes to the heart of*
My unprovided° body, latched° mine arm;   *unprotected / struck*
And when he saw my best alarumed spirits
Bold in the quarrel's right,[3] roused to th'encounter,
Or whether ghasted° by the noise I made,   *frightened*
Full suddenly he fled.
55   GLOUCESTER   Let him fly far,
Not in this land shall he remain uncaught,
And found, dispatch.° The noble Duke my master,   *And once found, killed*
My worthy arch° and patron, comes tonight.   *lord*
By his authority I will proclaim it
60   That he which finds him shall deserve our thanks,
Bringing the murderous coward to the stake;[4]
He that conceals him, death.
EDMOND   When I dissuaded him from his intent
And found him pitched° to do it, with curst° speech   *resolved / bitter*
65   I threatened to discover° him. He replied,   *expose*
'Thou unpossessing bastard, dost thou think
If I would stand against thee, would the reposal°   *placing*
Of any trust, virtue, or worth in thee
Make thy words faithed?° No, what I should deny—   *credible*
70   As this I would, ay, though thou didst produce
My very character[5]—I'd turn it all
To[6] thy suggestion, plot, and damnèd practice,°   *scheming*
And thou must make a dullard of the world
If they not thought the profits of my death

---

3. *my best . . . right*: that I was fully roused to action, made brave by righteousness.
4. Treachery and rebellion were crimes for which one could be burned.

5. Handwriting; but also, a true summary of my character.
6. *I'd . . . / To*: I'd blame it all on.

Were very pregnant and potential spurs
To make thee seek it.'[8]

GLOUCESTER   Strong° and fastened° villain!   *Flagrant / incorrigible*
  Would he deny his letter? I never got° him.   *begot*
  [*Trumpets within*]
  Hark, the Duke's trumpets. I know not why he comes.
80 All ports° I'll bar. The villain shall not scape.   *seaports; exits*
  The Duke must grant me that; besides, his picture
  I will send far and near, that all the kingdom
  May have note of him[9]—and of my land,
  Loyal and natural° boy, I'll work the means   *loving; illegitimate*
85 To make thee capable.°   *legally able to inherit*

      Enter the Duke of CORNWALL [*and* REGAN]

CORNWALL   How now, my noble friend? Since I came hither,
  Which I can call but now, I have heard strange news.

REGAN   If it be true, all vengeance comes too short
  Which can pursue the offender. How dost, my lord?

90 GLOUCESTER   Madam, my old heart is cracked, is cracked.

REGAN   What, did my father's godson seek your life?
  He whom my father named, your Edgar?

GLOUCESTER   Ay, lady, lady; shame would have it hid.

REGAN   Was he not companion with the riotous knights
95 That tend° upon my father?   *attend*

GLOUCESTER   I know not, madam. 'Tis too bad, too bad.

EDMUND   Yes, madam, he was.

REGAN   No marvel, then, though° he were ill affected.°   *that / ill disposed*
  'Tis they have put him on° the old man's death,   *have urged him to seek*
100 To have the spoil and waste of his revenues.
  I have this present evening from my sister
  Been well informed of them, and with such cautions
  That if they come to sojourn at my house
  I'll not be there.

CORNWALL   Nor I, assure thee, Regan.
105 Edmund, I heard that you have shown your father
  A childlike office.°   *filial service*

EDMUND   'Twas my duty, sir.

GLOUCESTER [*to* CORNWALL]   He did betray his practice,°   *uncover his (Edgar's) plot*
      and received
  This hurt you see striving to apprehend him.

CORNWALL   Is he pursued?

GLOUCESTER   Ay, my good lord.
110 CORNWALL   If he be taken, he shall never more
  Be feared of doing harm. Make your own purpose
  How in my strength you please.[1] For you, Edmund,
  Whose virtue and obedience doth this instant
  So much commend itself, you shall be ours.
115 Natures of such deep trust we shall much need.
  You we first seize on.

EDMUND   I shall serve you truly,
  However else.°   *If nothing else*

GLOUCESTER [*to* CORNWALL]   For him I thank your grace.

8. *And thou . . . it:* And do you think the world so stupid that it could not see the benefit you would get from my death (and thus a motive for plotting to kill me)? *pregnant:* full. *potential spurs:* powerful temptations.
9. Likenesses of outlaws were drawn up, printed, and publicly displayed, sometimes with an offer of reward as in "Wanted" posters.
1. *Make . . . please:* Devise your plots making use of my forces and authority as you see fit.

75 Were very pregnant and potential spirits
To make thee seek it.'[7]

GLOUCESTER   O strange° and fastened° villain!   *unnatural / incorrigible*
Would he deny his letter, said he?

Tucket° within   *Flourish of trumpets*

Hark, the Duke's trumpets. I know not why he comes.
All ports° I'll bar. The villain shall not scape.   *seaports; exits*
80 The Duke must grant me that; besides, his picture
I will send far and near, that all the kingdom
May have due note of him[8]—and of my land,
Loyal and natural° boy, I'll work the means   *loving; illegitimate*
To make thee capable.°   *legally able to inherit*

Enter CORNWALL, REGAN, *and attendants*

85 CORNWALL How now, my noble friend? Since I came hither,
Which I can call but now, I have heard strange news.

REGAN If it be true, all vengeance comes too short
Which can pursue th'offender. How dost, my lord?

GLOUCESTER O madam, my old heart is cracked, it's cracked.

90 REGAN What, did my father's godson seek your life?
He whom my father named, your Edgar?

GLOUCESTER O lady, lady, shame would have it hid!

REGAN Was he not companion with the riotous knights
That tend° upon my father?   *attend*

95 GLOUCESTER I know not, madam. 'Tis too bad, too bad.

EDMOND Yes, madam, he was of that consort.°   *company*

REGAN No marvel, then, though° he were ill affected.°   *that / ill disposed*
'Tis they have put him on° the old man's death,   *have urged him to seek*
To have th'expense° and spoil of his revenues.   *use*
100 I have this present evening from my sister
Been well informed of them, and with such cautions
That if they come to sojourn at my house
I'll not be there.

CORNWALL   Nor I, assure thee, Regan.
Edmond, I hear that you have shown your father
A childlike office.°   *filial service*

105 EDMOND   It was my duty, sir.

GLOUCESTER [*to* CORNWALL] He did bewray his practice,°   *uncover his (Edgar's) plot*
and received
This hurt you see striving to apprehend him.

CORNWALL Is he pursued?

GLOUCESTER   Ay, my good lord.

CORNWALL If he be taken, he shall never more
110 Be feared of doing harm. Make your own purpose
How in my strength you please.[9] For you, Edmond,
Whose virtue and obedience doth this instant
So much commend itself, you shall be ours.
Natures of such deep trust we shall much need.
You we first seize on.

115 EDMOND   I shall serve you, sir,
Truly, however else.°   *if nothing else*

GLOUCESTER [*to* CORNWALL] For him I thank your grace.

7. *And thou . . . it:* And do you think the world so stupid that it could not see the benefit you would get from my death (and thus a motive for plotting to kill me)? *pregnant:* full. *potential spirits:* powerful temptations.
8. Likenesses of outlaws were drawn up, printed, and publicly displayed, sometimes with an offer of reward as in "Wanted" posters.
9. *Make . . . please:* Devise your plots making use of my forces and authority as you see fit.

CORNWALL You know not why we came to visit you—

REGAN This out-of-season threat'ning dark-eyed night—

120 Occasions, noble Gloucester, of some poise,° *weight*
Wherein we must have use of your advice.
Our father he hath writ, so hath our sister,
Of differences° which I least thought it fit *quarrels*
To answer from our home. The several° messengers *various*
125 From hence attend° dispatch. Our good old friend, *await*
Lay comforts to your bosom, and bestow
Your needful° counsel to our business, *badly needed*
Which craves the instant use.[2]

GLOUCESTER I serve you, madam.
130 Your graces are right welcome. *Exeunt*

Scene 7

Enter KENT, [*disguised, at one door,*] *and Steward*
[OSWALD *at another door*]

OSWALD Good even° to thee, friend. Art° of the house? *evening / Are you a servant*

KENT Ay.

OSWALD Where may we set our horses?

KENT I'th' mire.

5 OSWALD Prithee, if thou love me,° tell me. *if you will be so kind*

KENT I love thee not.

OSWALD Why then, I care not for thee.

KENT If I had thee in Lipsbury pinfold[1] I would make thee care
for me.

10 OSWALD Why dost thou use° me thus? I know thee not. *treat*

KENT Fellow, I know thee.

OSWALD What dost thou know me for?

KENT A knave, a rascal, an eater of broken meats,° a base, proud, *scraps*
shallow, beggarly, three-suited, hundred-pound, filthy worsted-
15 stocking knave;[2] a lily-livered, action-taking knave; a whoreson,
glass-gazing, superfinical rogue; one-trunk-inheriting slave;[3]
one that wouldst be a bawd in way of good service,[4] and art
nothing but the composition° of a knave, beggar, coward, pan- *combination*
der, and the son and heir of a mongrel bitch, whom I will beat
20 into clamorous whining if thou deny the least syllable of the
addition.[5]

OSWALD What a monstrous fellow art thou, thus to rail on one
that's neither known of° thee nor knows thee! *by*

KENT What a brazen-faced varlet° art thou, to deny thou *rascal*
25 knowest me! Is it two days ago since I beat thee and tripped
up thy heels before the King? Draw, you rogue; for though it
be night, the moon shines.

[*He draws his sword*]

---

2. Which requires immediate attention.
Scene 7 Location: Before Gloucester's house.
1. If I had you in the enclosure of my mouth (gripped
in my teeth). Lipsbury is probably an invented place-
name. *pinfold:* pen, animal enclosure.
2. *three-suited . . . knave:* Oswald is being called a poor
imitation of a gentleman. Servants were permitted
three suits a year; one hundred pounds was the minimum qualification for the purchase of one of King
James's knighthoods; a gentleman would wear silk, not

"worsted" (of thick woolen material), stockings.
3. *lily-livered:* cowardly. *action-taking:* litigious, one
who would rather use the law than his fists. *glass-
gazing:* mirror-gazing. *superfinical:* overly finicky, fastidious. *one-trunk-inheriting:* owning only what would
fill one trunk.
4. *one that . . . service:* one who would even be a pimp
if called upon.
5. Of the descriptions Kent has just applied to him.
addition: title (used ironically).

CORNWALL   You know not why we came to visit you—
REGAN   Thus out of season, threading dark-eyed night—
120   Occasions, noble Gloucester, of some poise,°   weight
Wherein we must have use of your advice.
Our father he hath writ, so hath our sister,
Of differences° which I least thought it fit   quarrels
To answer from our home. The several° messengers   various
125   From hence attend° dispatch. Our good old friend,   await
Lay comforts to your bosom, and bestow
Your needful° counsel to our businesses,   badly needed
Which craves the instant use.[1]
GLOUCESTER   I serve you, madam.
130   Your graces are right welcome.   *Flourish. Exeunt*

2.2

Enter KENT, *[disguised,] and Steward* [OSWALD], *severally*

OSWALD   Good dawning to thee, friend. Art° of this house?   *Are you a servant*
KENT   Ay.
OSWALD   Where may we set our horses?
KENT   I'th' mire.
5   OSWALD   Prithee, if thou lov'st me,° tell me.   *if you will be so kind*
KENT   I love thee not.
OSWALD   Why then, I care not for thee.
KENT   If I had thee in Lipsbury pinfold[1] I would make thee care
for me.
10   OSWALD   Why dost thou use° me thus? I know thee not.   treat
KENT   Fellow, I know thee.
OSWALD   What dost thou know me for?
KENT   A knave, a rascal, an eater of broken meats,° a base, proud,   scraps
shallow, beggarly, three-suited, hundred-pound, filthy worsted-
15   stocking knave;[2] a lily-livered, action-taking, whoreson, glass-
gazing, super-serviceable, finical rogue; one-trunk-inheriting
slave;[3] one that wouldst be a bawd in way of good service,[4] and
art nothing but the composition° of a knave, beggar, coward,   combination
pander, and the son and heir of a mongrel bitch, one whom I
20   will beat into clamorous whining if thou deniest the least syllable of thy addition.[5]
OSWALD   Why, what a monstrous fellow art thou, thus to rail on
one that is neither known of° thee nor knows thee!   by
KENT   What a brazen-faced varlet° art thou, to deny thou   rascal
25   knowest me! Is it two days since I tripped up thy heels and
beat thee before the King? Draw, you rogue; for though it be
night, yet the moon shines.
[He draws his sword]

---

1. Which require immediate attention.
2.2 Location: Before Gloucester's house.
1. If I had you in the enclosure of my mouth (gripped in my teeth). Lipsbury is probably an invented place-name. *pinfold*: pen, animal enclosure.
2. *three-suited . . . knave*: Oswald is being called a poor imitation of a gentleman. Servants were permitted three suits a year; one hundred pounds was the minimum qualification for the purchase of one of King James's knighthoods; a gentleman would wear silk, not

"worsted" (of thick woolen material), stockings.
3. *lily-livered*: cowardly. *action-taking*: litigious, one who would rather use the law than his fists. *glass-gazing*: mirror-gazing. *super-serviceable*: overly officious, or too ready to serve. *finical*: finicky, fastidious. *one-trunk-inheriting*: owning only what would fill one trunk.
4. *one that . . . service*: one who would even be a pimp if called upon.
5. Of the descriptions Kent has just applied to him. *addition*: title (used ironically).

I'll make a sop of the moonshine[6] o' you. Draw, you whoreson,
cullionly barber-monger,[7] draw!

30 OSWALD   Away. I have nothing to do with thee.

KENT   Draw, you rascal. You bring letters against the King, and
take Vanity the puppet's part against the royalty of her father.[8]
Draw, you rogue, or I'll so carbonado[9] your shanks—draw, you
rascal, come your ways!°   *come forward*

35 OSWALD   Help, ho, murder, help!

KENT   Strike, you slave! Stand, rogue! Stand, you neat° slave,   *elegant; foppish*
strike!

OSWALD   Help, ho, murder, help!

Enter EDMUND *with his rapier drawn,* [*then*] GLOUCES-
TER, [*then*] *the Duke* [CORNWALL] *and Duchess*
[REGAN]

EDMUND [*parting them*]   How now, what's the matter?

40 KENT   With you, goodman boy. An° you please come, I'll flesh   *If*
you.[1] Come on, young master.

GLOUCESTER   Weapons? Arms? What's the matter here?

CORNWALL   Keep peace, upon your lives. He dies that strikes
again. What's the matter?

45 REGAN   The messengers from our sister and the King.

CORNWALL [*to* KENT *and* OSWALD]   What's your difference?°   *quarrel*
Speak.

OSWALD   I am scarce in breath, my lord.

KENT   No marvel, you have so bestirred your valour, you cow-
50 ardly rascal. Nature disclaims° in thee; a tailor[2] made thee.   *disowns her part*

CORNWALL   Thou art a strange fellow—a tailor make a man?

KENT   Ay, a tailor, sir. A stone-cutter or a painter could not have
made him so ill° though he had been but two hours at the   *so badly*
trade.

55 GLOUCESTER   Speak yet; how grew your quarrel?

OSWALD   This ancient ruffian, sir, whose life I have spared at
suit of° his grey beard—   *on account of*

KENT   Thou whoreson Z,[3] thou unnecessary letter—[*to* CORN-
WALL] my lord, if you'll give me leave I will tread this unboulted°   *unsifted; coarse*
60 villain into mortar and daub the walls of a jakes° with him. [*To*   *privy; toilet*
OSWALD] Spare my grey beard, you wagtail?[4]

CORNWALL   Peace, sir. You beastly knave, have you no
reverence?°   *respect*

KENT   Yes, sir, but anger has a privilege.

65 CORNWALL   Why art thou angry?

KENT   That such a slave as this should wear a sword,
That° wears no honesty. Such smiling rogues   *Who*
As these, like rats, oft bite those cords[5] in twain
Which are too entrenched° to unloose, smooth° every passion   *intricate / flatter*
70 That in the natures of their lords rebel,

6. Kent proposes so to skewer and pierce Oswald that
his body might soak up moonlight. *sop:* piece of bread
to be steeped or dunked in soup.
7. *cullionly barber-monger:* despicable frequenter of
hairdressers. *cullion:* testicle.
8. *and take . . . father:* and support Gonoril, here depicted as a dressed-up doll whose pride is contrasted
with Lear's kingliness.
9. Slash or score as one would the surface of meat in
preparation for broiling.

1. I'll initiate you into fighting, as a hunting dog is
given the taste of blood to rouse it for the chase.
2. Tailors, considered effeminate, were stock objects of
mockery.
3. The letter Z (zed) was considered superfluous and
omitted from many dictionaries.
4. A common English bird that takes its name from the
up-and-down flicking of its tail; this, and its characteristic hopping from foot to foot, causes it to appear nervous.
5. Bonds of kinship, affection, marriage, or rank.

I'll make a sop o'th' moonshine of you,[6] you whoreson, cullionly barber-monger,[7] draw!

30 OSWALD Away. I have nothing to do with thee.

KENT Draw, you rascal. You come with letters against the King, and
take Vanity the puppet's part against the royalty of her father.[8]
Draw, you rogue, or I'll so carbonado[9] your shanks—draw, you
rascal, come your ways!°   *come forward*

35 OSWALD Help, ho, murder, help!

KENT Strike, you slave! Stand, rogue! Stand, you neat° slave,   *elegant; foppish*
strike!

OSWALD Help, ho, murder, murder!

    Enter Bastard [EDMOND], [*then*] CORNWALL, REGAN,
    GLOUCESTER, [*and*] *servants*

EDMOND How now, what's the matter? Part.

40 KENT With you, goodman boy. If you please, come, I'll flesh
ye.[1] Come on, young master.

GLOUCESTER Weapons? Arms? What's the matter here?

CORNWALL Keep peace, upon your lives. He dies that strikes
again. What is the matter?

45 REGAN The messengers from our sister and the King.

CORNWALL [*to* KENT *and* OSWALD] What is your difference?°   *quarrel*
Speak.

OSWALD I am scarce in breath, my lord.

KENT No marvel, you have so bestirred your valour, you cow-
50 ardly rascal. Nature disclaims° in thee; a tailor[2] made thee.   *disowns her part*

CORNWALL Thou art a strange fellow—a tailor make a man?

KENT A tailor, sir. A stone-cutter or a painter could not have
made him so ill° though they had been but two years o'th'°   *so badly / at the*
trade.

55 CORNWALL Speak yet; how grew your quarrel?

OSWALD This ancient ruffian, sir, whose life I have spared at suit
of° his grey beard—   *on account of*

KENT Thou whoreson Z,[3] thou unnecessary letter—[*to* CORN-
WALL] my lord, if you'll give me leave I will tread this unbolted°   *unsifted; coarse*
60 villain into mortar and daub the wall of a jakes° with him. [*To*   *privy; toilet*
OSWALD] Spare my grey beard, you wagtail?[4]

CORNWALL Peace, sirrah.
You beastly knave, know you no reverence?°   *respect*

KENT Yes, sir, but anger hath a privilege.

65 CORNWALL Why art thou angry?

KENT That such a slave as this should wear a sword,
Who wears no honesty. Such smiling rogues as these,
Like rats, oft bite the holy cords[5] a-twain
Which are too intrince° t'unloose, smooth° every passion   *intricate / flatter*
70 That in the natures of their lords rebel;

---

6. Kent proposes so to skewer and pierce Oswald that
his body might soak up moonlight. *sop*: piece of bread
to be steeped or dunked in soup.
7. *cullionly barber-monger*: despicable frequenter of
hairdressers. *cullion*: testicle.
8. *and take . . . father*: and support Goneril, here
depicted as a dressed-up doll whose pride is contrasted
with Lear's kingliness.
9. Slash or score as one would the surface of meat in
preparation for broiling.

1. I'll initiate you into fighting, as a hunting dog is
given the taste of blood to rouse it for the chase.
2. Tailors, considered effeminate, were stock objects of
mockery.
3. The letter Z (zed) was considered superfluous and
omitted from many dictionaries.
4. A common English bird that takes its name from the
up-and-down flicking of its tail; this, and its characteristic hopping from foot to foot, causes it to appear nervous.
5. Bonds of kinship, affection, marriage, or rank.

Bring oil to fire, snow to their colder moods,
Renege,° affirm, and turn their halcyon beaks[6]   *Deny*
With every gale and vary° of their masters,   *mood*
Knowing naught, like dogs, but following.
75   [*To* OSWALD] A plague upon your epileptic° visage!   *distorted; grimacing*
Smile you° my speeches as° I were a fool?   *Do you smile at / as if*
Goose, an I had you upon Sarum Plain
I'd send you cackling home to Camelot.[7]
CORNWALL   What, art thou mad, old fellow?
GLOUCESTER [*to* KENT]   How fell you out?
80   Say that.
KENT   No contraries° hold more antipathy   *opposites*
Than I and such a knave.
CORNWALL   Why dost thou call him knave?
What's his offence?
KENT   His countenance likes° me not.   *pleases*
CORNWALL   No more perchance does mine, or his, or hers.
85   KENT   Sir, 'tis my occupation to be plain:
I have seen better faces in my time
Than stands on any shoulder that I see
Before me at this instant.
CORNWALL   This is a fellow
Who, having been praised for bluntness, doth affect
90   A saucy roughness, and constrains the garb
Quite from his nature.[8] He cannot flatter, he.
He must be plain, he must speak truth.
An they will take't, so; if not, he's plain.[9]
These kind of knaves I know, which in this plainness
95   Harbour more craft and more corrupter ends
Than twenty silly-ducking observants
That stretch their duties nicely.[1]
KENT   Sir, in good sooth, or in sincere verity,
Under the allowance of your grand aspect,[2]
100   Whose influence, like the wreath of radiant fire
In flickering Phoebus' front°—   *the sun god's forehead*
CORNWALL   What mean'st thou by this?
KENT   To go out of my dialect,° which you discommend so   *normal mode of speech*
much. I know, sir, I am no flatterer. He that beguiled you in a
plain accent was a plain knave, which for my part I will not
105   be, though I should win your displeasure to entreat me to't.[3]
CORNWALL [*to* OSWALD]   What's the offence you gave him?

6. It was believed that the kingfisher (in Greek, *hal-cyon*) could be used as a weather vane when dead: suspended by a fine thread, its beak would turn whatever way the wind blew.
7. *Goose . . . Camelot*: Comparing him to a cackling goose, Kent tells Oswald that if he had him on Salisbury Plain, he would drive him all the way to Camelot, legendary home of King Arthur.
8. *and constrains . . . nature*: and assumes the appearance though it is untrue to his real self. Alternatively (with "his" meaning "its"), and distorts the true shape of plainness from what it naturally is (by turning it into disrespect).
9. If they will accept (Kent's attitude), well and good;

if not, he is a plainspoken man (and does not care).
1. *Than . . . nicely*: Than twenty obsequious attendants who constantly bow idiotically, and who perform their functions with excessive diligence ("nicely").
2. With the permission of your great countenance. "Aspect" also refers to the astrological position of a planet; Kent's bombastic language here raises Cornwall to the mock-heroic proportions of a heavenly body.
3. *He that . . . to't*: The person who tried to hoodwink you with plain speaking was, indeed, a pure knave—something I won't be, even if you were to beg me to be one (a plain knave, or flatterer).

Being oil to fire, snow to the colder moods,
Renege,° affirm, and turn their halcyon beaks⁶   *Deny*
With every gall and vary° of their masters,   *irritation and mood*
Knowing naught, like dogs, but following.
75 [*To* OSWALD] A plague upon your epileptic° visage!   *distorted; grimacing*
Smile you° my speeches as° I were a fool?   *Do you smile at / as if*
Goose, an I had you upon Sarum Plain
I'd drive ye cackling home to Camelot.⁷

CORNWALL What, art thou mad, old fellow?
GLOUCESTER [*to* KENT]   How fell you out?
80 Say that.
KENT No contraries° hold more antipathy   *opposites*
Than I and such a knave.
CORNWALL   Why dost thou call him knave?
What is his fault?°   *offense*
KENT   His countenance likes° me not.   *pleases*
CORNWALL No more perchance does mine, nor his, nor hers.
85 KENT Sir, 'tis my occupation to be plain:
I have seen better faces in my time
Than stands on any shoulder that I see
Before me at this instant.
CORNWALL   This is some fellow
Who, having been praised for bluntness, doth affect
90 A saucy roughness, and constrains the garb
Quite from his nature.⁸ He cannot flatter, he;
An honest mind and plain, he must speak truth.
An they will take't, so; if not, he's plain.⁹
These kind of knaves I know, which in this plainness
95 Harbour more craft and more corrupter ends
Than twenty silly-ducking observants
That stretch their duties nicely.¹
KENT Sir, in good faith, in sincere verity,
Under th'allowance of your great aspect,²
100 Whose influence, like the wreath of radiant fire
On flick'ring Phoebus' front°—   *the sun god's forehead*
CORNWALL   What mean'st by this?
KENT To go out of my dialect,° which you discommend so   *normal mode of speech*
much. I know, sir, I am no flatterer. He that beguiled you in
a plain accent was a plain knave, which for my part I will not be,
105 though I should win your displeasure to entreat me to't.³
CORNWALL [*to* OSWALD] What was th'offence you gave him?

---

6. It was believed that the kingfisher (in Greek, *halcyon*) could be used as a weather vane when dead: suspended by a fine thread, its beak would turn whatever way the wind blew.
7. *Goose . . . Camelot:* Comparing him to a cackling goose, Kent tells Oswald that if he had him on Salisbury Plain, he would drive him all the way to Camelot, legendary home of King Arthur.
8. *and constrains . . . nature:* and assumes the appearance though it is untrue to his real self. Alternatively (with "his" meaning "its"), and distorts the true shape of plainness from what it naturally is (by turning it into disrespect).
9. If they will accept (Kent's attitude), well and good; if

not, he is a plainspoken man (and does not care).
1. *Than . . . nicely:* Than twenty obsequious attendants who constantly bow idiotically, and who perform their functions with excessive diligence ("nicely").
2. With the permission of your great countenance. "Aspect" also refers to the astrological position of a planet; Kent's bombastic language here raises Cornwall to the mock-heroic proportions of a heavenly body.
3. *He that . . . to't:* The person who tried to hoodwink you with plain speaking was, indeed, a pure knave—something I won't be, even if you were to beg me to be one (a plain knave, or flatterer).

OSWALD   I never gave him any.
It pleased the King his master very late°   lately
To strike at me upon his misconstruction,°   misunderstanding (me)
When he, conjunct,° and flattering his displeasure,   in league with
110   Tripped me behind; being down, insulted,° railed,   I being down, he insulted
And put upon him such a deal of man
That worthied him,⁴ got praises of the King
For him attempting who was self-subdued,⁵
And in the fleshment° of this dread exploit   excitement; flush
Drew on me here again.

115   KENT   None of these rogues and cowards
But Ajax is their fool.⁶
CORNWALL [calling]   Bring forth the stocks, ho!—
You stubborn, ancient knave, you reverend° braggart,   old; revered
We'll teach you.
KENT   I am too old to learn.
Call not your stocks for me. I serve the King,
120   On whose employments I was sent to you.
You should do small respect, show too bold malice
Against the grace° and person° of my master,   majesty / personal honor
Stocking° his messenger.   By stocking
CORNWALL [calling]   Fetch forth the stocks!—
As I have life and honour, there shall he sit till noon.
125   REGAN   Till noon?—till night, my lord, and all night too.
KENT   Why, madam, if I were your father's dog
You could not use me so.
REGAN   Sir, being° his knave, I will.   since you are
          [Stocks brought out]
CORNWALL   This is a fellow of the selfsame nature
Our sister° speaks of.—Come, bring away the stocks.   sister-in-law
130   GLOUCESTER   Let me beseech your grace not to do so.
His fault is much, and the good King his master
Will check° him for't. Your purposed° low correction   reprimand / intended
Is such as basest and contemnèd wretches
For pilf'rings and most common trespasses
135   Are punished with. The King must take it ill
That he's so slightly valued in his messenger,
Should have him thus restrained.
CORNWALL   I'll answer° that.   be responsible for
REGAN   My sister may receive it much more worse
To have her gentlemen abused, assaulted,
140   For following° her affairs. Put in his legs.   carrying out
          [They put KENT in the stocks]
Come, my good lord, away!
                    [Exeunt all but GLOUCESTER and KENT]
GLOUCESTER   I am sorry for thee, friend. 'Tis the Duke's pleasure,
Whose disposition, all the world well knows,
Will not be rubbed° nor stopped. I'll entreat for thee.   obstructed

---

4. And put . . . him: And put on such a show of manliness that he was thought a worthy fellow.
5. For attacking a man who had already surrendered
(Kent attacking Oswald).

6. None . . . fool: Such rogues and cowards as these
talk as if they were greater warriors (and blusterers)
than Ajax; such rogues always make even mighty Ajax
out to be a fool.

OSWALD   I never gave him any.
It pleased the King his master very late°   *lately*
To strike at me upon his misconstruction,°   *misunderstanding (me)*
When he, compact,° and flattering his displeasure,   *in league with*
110 Tripped me behind; being down, insulted,° railed,   *I being down, he insulted*
And put upon him such a deal of man
That worthied him,⁴ got praises of the King
For him attempting who was self-subdued,⁵
And in the fleshment° of this dread exploit   *excitement; flush*
Drew on me here again.
115 KENT   None of these rogues and cowards
But Ajax is their fool.⁶
CORNWALL   Fetch forth the stocks!
                          [*Exeunt some servants*]
You stubborn, ancient knave, you reverend° braggart,   *old; revered*
We'll teach you.
KENT   Sir, I am too old to learn.
Call not your stocks for me. I serve the King,
120 On whose employment I was sent to you.
You shall do small respect, show too bold malice
Against the grace° and person° of my master,   *majesty / personal honor*
Stocking° his messenger.   *By stocking*
CORNWALL [*calling*]   Fetch forth the stocks!—
As I have life and honour, there shall he sit till noon.
125 REGAN   Till noon?—till night, my lord, and all night too.
KENT   Why, madam, if I were your father's dog
You should not use me so.
REGAN   Sir, being° his knave, I will.   *since you are*
          [*Stocks brought out*]
CORNWALL   This is a fellow of the selfsame colour°   *character*
Our sister° speaks of.—Come, bring away the stocks.   *sister-in-law*
130 GLOUCESTER   Let me beseech your grace not to do so.
The King his master needs must take it ill
That he, so slightly valued in his messenger,
Should have him thus restrained.
CORNWALL   I'll answer° that.   *be responsible for*
          [*They put* KENT *in the stocks*]
REGAN   My sister may receive it much more worse
135 To have her gentlemen abused, assaulted.
CORNWALL   Come, my good lord, away!
                  Exeunt [*all but* GLOUCESTER *and* KENT]
GLOUCESTER   I am sorry for thee, friend. 'Tis the Duke's pleasure,
Whose disposition, all the world well knows,
Will not be rubbed° nor stopped. I'll entreat for thee.   *obstructed*

---

4. *And put . . . him:* And put on such a show of manliness that he was thought a worthy fellow.
5. For attacking a man who had already surrendered
(Kent attacking Oswald).

6. *None . . . fool:* Such rogues and cowards as these
talk as if they were greater warriors (and blusterers)
than Ajax; such rogues always make even mighty Ajax
out to be a fool.

145   KENT   Pray you, do not, sir. I have watched° and travelled hard.   *gone without sleep*
      Some time I shall sleep out; the rest I'll whistle.
      A good man's fortune may grow out at heels.[7]
      Give° you good morrow.   *God give*
  GLOUCESTER   The Duke's to blame in this; 'twill be ill took.
                                        [*Exit*]

150   KENT   Good King, that must approve° the common say:°   *prove / saying*
      Thou out of heaven's benediction com'st
      To the warm sun.[8]
        [*He takes out a letter*]
      Approach, thou beacon[9] to this under globe,
      That by thy comfortable beams I may
155   Peruse this letter. Nothing almost sees miracles
      But misery.[1] I know 'tis from Cordelia,
      Who hath now fortunately been informed
      Of my obscurèd° course, and shall find time   *hidden; disguised*
      For this enormous state,° seeking to give   *awful state of affairs*
160   Losses their remedies. All weary and overwatched,°   *too long awake*
      Take vantage,° heavy eyes, not to behold   *the opportunity*
      This shameful lodging. Fortune, good night;
      Smile; once more turn thy wheel.[2]   *Sleeps*
        Enter EDGAR
  EDGAR   I heard myself proclaimed,°   *declared an outlaw*
      And by the happy° hollow of a tree   *opportune*
165   Escaped the hunt. No port° is free, no place   *seaport; exit*
      That guard and most unusual vigilance
      Does not attend my taking.° While° I may scape   *await my capture / Until*
      I will preserve myself, and am bethought°   *resolved*
      To take the basest and most poorest shape
170   That ever penury in contempt of° man   *for*
      Brought near to beast. My face I'll grime with filth,
      Blanket my loins, elf all my hair with knots,[3]
      And with presented° nakedness outface   *exposed*
      The wind and persecution of the sky.
175   The country gives me proof and precedent
      Of Bedlam beggars who with roaring voices
      Strike° in their numbed and mortified° bare arms   *Stick / deadened*
      Pins, wooden pricks, nails, sprigs of rosemary,
      And with this horrible object° from low farms,   *spectacle*
180   Poor pelting° villages, sheep-cotes and mills   *paltry; contemptible*
      Sometime with lunatic bans,° sometime with prayers   *curses*
      Enforce their charity. 'Poor Tuelygod,[4] Poor Tom!'
      That's something yet. Edgar I nothing am.[5]   *Exit*
        Enter King [LEAR, FOOL, *and a* KNIGHT]
  LEAR   'Tis strange that they should so depart from home
      And not send back my messenger.

7. The fortunes of even good men sometimes wear thin.
8. *Thou . . . sun*: You come from the blessing of heaven into the heat of the sun (go from good to bad).
9. It is arguable whether Kent here refers to the sun or the moon.
1. *Nothing . . . misery*: Only those suffering misery are granted miracles; any comfort seems miraculous to those who are miserable.

2. The goddess Fortune was traditionally depicted with a wheel to signify her mutability and caprice. She was believed to take pleasure in arbitrarily lowering those at the top of her wheel and raising those at the bottom.
3. Tangle the hair into "elf locks," supposed to be a favorite trick of malicious elves.
4. A word of unknown origin.
5. Edgar, I am nothing; I am no longer Edgar.

140 KENT   Pray do not, sir. I have watched° and travelled hard.   *gone without sleep*
Some time I shall sleep out; the rest I'll whistle.
A good man's fortune may grow out at heels.[7]
Give° you good morrow.   *God give*
GLOUCESTER   The Duke's to blame in this; 'twill be ill taken.
                                                           Exit
145 KENT   Good King, that must approve° the common say:°   *prove / saying*
Thou out of heaven's benediction com'st
To the warm sun.[8]
[*He takes out a letter*]
Approach, thou beacon[9] to this under globe,
That by thy comfortable beams I may
150 Peruse this letter. Nothing almost sees miracles
But misery.[1] I know 'tis from Cordelia,
Who hath now fortunately been informed
Of my obscurèd° course, and shall find time   *hidden; disguised*
For this enormous state,° seeking to give   *awful state of affairs*
155 Losses their remedies. All weary and o'erwatched,°   *too long awake*
Take vantage,° heavy eyes, not to behold   *the opportunity*
This shameful lodging. Fortune, good night;
Smile once more; turn thy wheel.[2]   [*He sleeps*]
Enter EDGAR
EDGAR   I heard myself proclaimed,°   *declared an outlaw*
And by the happy° hollow of a tree   *opportune*
160 Escaped the hunt. No port° is free, no place   *seaport; exit*
That guard and most unusual vigilance
Does not attend my taking.° Whiles° I may scape   *await my capture / Until*
I will preserve myself, and am bethought°   *resolved*
To take the basest and most poorest shape
165 That ever penury in contempt of° man   *for*
Brought near to beast. My face I'll grime with filth,
Blanket my loins, elf all my hairs in knots,[3]
And with presented° nakedness outface   *exposed*
The winds and persecutions of the sky.
170 The country gives me proof and precedent
Of Bedlam beggars who with roaring voices
Strike° in their numbed and mortified° arms   *Stick / deadened*
Pins, wooden pricks, nails, sprigs of rosemary,
And with this horrible object° from low farms,   *spectacle*
175 Poor pelting° villages, sheep-cotes and mills   *paltry; contemptible*
Sometime with lunatic bans,° sometime with prayers   *curses*
Enforce their charity. 'Poor Tuelygod,[4] Poor Tom.'
That's something yet. Edgar I nothing am.[5]   *Exit*
Enter LEAR, FOOL, *and* [*the* FIRST] GENTLEMAN[6]
LEAR   'Tis strange that they should so depart from home
And not send back my messenger.

---

7. The fortunes of even good men sometimes wear thin.
8. *Thou . . . sun:* You come from the blessing of heaven into the heat of the sun (go from good to bad).
9. It is arguable whether Kent here refers to the sun or the moon.
1. *Nothing . . . misery:* Only those suffering misery are granted miracles; any comfort seems miraculous to those who are miserable.
2. The goddess Fortune was traditionally depicted with a wheel to signify her mutability and caprice. She was

believed to take pleasure in arbitrarily lowering those at the top of her wheel and raising those at the bottom.
3. Tangle the hair into "elf locks," supposed to be a favorite trick of malicious elves.
4. A word of unknown origin.
5. Edgar, I am nothing; I am no longer Edgar.
6. F seems to reserve "a Gentleman" (referred to as "First Gentleman" in this edition) for this particular character, who returns in 5.3.

185 KNIGHT　　　　　　　　　　As I learned,
　　　The night before there was no purpose°　　　　　　　　　*intention*
　　　Of his remove.°　　　　　　　　　　　　　　　　*change of residence*
　　KENT [*waking*]　　Hail to thee, noble master.
　　LEAR　How! Mak'st thou this shame thy pastime?
　　FOOL　Ha, ha, look, he wears cruel garters![6] Horses are tied by
190　　the heads, dogs and bears by th' neck, monkeys by th' loins,
　　　and men by th' legs. When a man's over-lusty at legs,[7] then he
　　　wears wooden nether-stocks.°　　　　　　　　　　　*knee socks*
　　LEAR [*to* KENT]　What's° he that hath so much thy place° mistook　　*Who's / position*
　　　To set thee here?
　　KENT　　　　　　　　　It is both he and she:
　　　Your son° and daughter.　　　　　　　　　　　　　*son-in-law*
　　LEAR　　　　　　　　No.
　　KENT　　　　　　　　　Yes.
195　LEAR　　　　　　　　　No, I say.
　　KENT　I say yea.
　　LEAR　　　　　　No, no, they would not.
　　KENT　　　　　　　　　　　Yes, they have.
　　LEAR　By Jupiter, I swear no. They durst not do't,
　　　They would not, could not do't. 'Tis worse than murder,
　　　To do upon respect[8] such violent outrage.
200　Resolve° me with all modest° haste which way　　　　　*Inform / reasonable*
　　　Thou mayst deserve or they propose this usage,
　　　Coming from us.
　　KENT　　　　　　　My lord, when at their home
　　　I did commend° your highness' letters to them,　　　　*deliver*
　　　Ere I was risen from the place that showed
205　My duty kneeling, came there a reeking° post°　　　*steaming / messenger*
　　　Stewed in his haste, half breathless, panting forth
　　　From Gonoril, his mistress, salutations,
　　　Delivered letters spite of intermission,[9]
　　　Which presently° they read, on whose contents　　　　*immediately*
210　They summoned up their meiny,° straight° took horse,　　*retinue / straightaway*
　　　Commanded me to follow and attend
　　　The leisure of their answer, gave me cold looks;
　　　And meeting here the other messenger,
　　　Whose welcome I perceived had poisoned mine—
215　Being the very° fellow that of late　　　　　　　　　*same*
　　　Displayed so saucily° against your highness—　　　*Acted so insolently*
　　　Having more man° than wit° about me, drew.　　　*courage / sense*
　　　He raised the house with loud and coward cries.
　　　Your son and daughter found this trespass worth°　　　*deserving of*
220　This shame which here it suffers.

---

6. Worsted garters, punning on "crewel," a thin yarn.
The Fool is actually referring to the stocks in which
Kent's feet are held.
7. When a man's liable to run away.

8. To do to one who deserves respect.
9. Regardless of interrupting me; despite the interrup-
tions in his account (as he gasped for breath).

180 FIRST GENTLEMAN As I learned,
The night before there was no purpose in them°   *they had no intention*
Of this remove.°   *change of residence*
KENT [*waking*]   Hail to thee, noble master.
LEAR   Ha! Mak'st thou this shame thy pastime?
KENT   No, my lord.
FOOL   Ha, ha, he wears cruel garters![7] Horses are tied by the
185 heads, dogs and bears by th' neck, monkeys by th' loins, and
men by th' legs. When a man's overlusty at legs,[8] then he wears
wooden nether-stocks.°   *knee socks*
LEAR [*to* KENT]   What's° he that hath so much thy place° mistook   *Who's / position*
To set thee here?
KENT   It is both he and she:
Your son° and daughter.   *son-in-law*
LEAR   No.
KENT   Yes.
190 LEAR   No, I say.
KENT   I say yea.
LEAR   By Jupiter, I swear no.
KENT   By Juno,[9] I swear ay.
LEAR   They durst not do't,
They could not, would not do't. 'Tis worse than murder,
To do upon respect[1] such violent outrage.
195 Resolve° me with all modest° haste which way   *Inform / reasonable*
Thou mightst deserve or they impose this usage,
Coming from us.
KENT   My lord, when at their home
I did commend° your highness' letters to them,   *deliver*
Ere I was risen from the place that showed
200 My duty kneeling, came there a reeking° post°   *steaming / messenger*
Stewed in his haste, half breathless, painting° forth   *panting*
From Goneril, his mistress, salutations,
Delivered letters spite of intermission,[2]
Which presently° they read, on whose contents   *immediately*
205 They summoned up their meiny,° straight° took horse,   *retinue / straightaway*
Commanded me to follow and attend
The leisure of their answer, gave me cold looks;
And meeting here the other messenger,
Whose welcome I perceived had poisoned mine—
210 Being the very° fellow which of late   *same*
Displayed so saucily° against your highness—   *Acted so insolently*
Having more man° than wit° about me, drew.   *courage / sense*
He raised the house with loud and coward cries.
Your son and daughter found this trespass worth°   *deserving of*
215 The shame which here it suffers.

---

7. Worsted garters, punning on "crewel," a thin yarn.   whom she constantly quarreled.
The Fool is actually referring to the stocks in which   1. To do to one who deserves respect.
Kent's feet are held.   2. Regardless of interrupting me; despite the interrup-
8. When a man's liable to run away.   tions in his account (as he gasped for breath).
9. Queen of the Roman gods and wife of Jupiter, with

LEAR   O, how this mother° swells up toward my heart!   *hysteria*
    Histerica passio, down, thou climbing sorrow;[1]
    Thy element's° below.—Where is this daughter?   *natural place is*

KENT   With the Earl, sir, within.

LEAR   Follow me not; stay there.
                                              [*Exit*]

KNIGHT [*to* KENT]   Made you no more offence than what you
225   speak of?

KENT   No. How chance the King comes with so small a train?

FOOL   An° thou hadst been set in the stocks for that question,   *If*
  thou hadst well deserved it.

KENT   Why, fool?

230 FOOL   We'll set thee to school to an ant, to teach thee there's no
  labouring in the winter.[2] All that follow their noses are led by
  their eyes but blind men, and there's not a nose among a hun-
  dred but can smell him that's stinking.° Let go thy hold when   *(as his fortunes decay)*
  a great wheel runs down a hill, lest it break thy neck with fol-
235   lowing it; but the great one that goes up the hill,[3] let him draw
  thee after. When a wise man gives thee better counsel, give me
  mine again. I would have none but knaves follow it, since a
  fool gives it.
  [*Sings*]   That sir that serves for gain
240   And follows but for form,
           Will pack° when it begin to rain,   *pack up and go*
           And leave thee in the storm.

           But I will tarry, the fool will stay,
           And let the wise man fly.
245   The knave turns fool that runs away,[4]
           The fool no knave, pardie.°   *by God* (pardieu)

KENT   Where learnt you this, fool?

FOOL   Not in the stocks.
        Enter LEAR *and* GLOUCESTER

LEAR   Deny to speak with me? They're sick, they're weary?
250   They travelled hard tonight?—mere insolence,
  Ay, the images of revolt and flying off.[5]
  Fetch me a better answer.

---

1. Histerica . . . *sorrow: Hysterica passio* (a Latin
expression originating in the Greek *steiros,* "suffering in
the womb") was an inflammation of the senses. In Renaissance medicine, vapors from the abdomen were
thought to rise up through the body, and in women, the
uterus itself to wander around.
2. Ants, proverbially prudent, do not work in winter.

Implicitly, a wise person should know better than to
look for sustenance to an old man who has fallen on
wintry times.
3. A great wheel is a figure for Lear and of Fortune's
wheel itself, which has swung downward.
4. The scoundrel who runs away is the real fool.
5. *images of:* signs of. *flying off:* desertion; insurrection.

FOOL   Winter's not gone yet if the wild geese fly that way.[3]

[*Sings*]   Fathers that wear rags
                           Do make their children blind,[4]
                       But fathers that bear bags
220   Shall see their children kind.
                       Fortune, that arrant whore,
                           Ne'er turns the key° to th' poor.   *opens the door*
        But for all this thou shalt have as many dolours[5] for thy daugh-
        ters as thou canst tell° in a year.   *count*
225 LEAR   O, how this mother° swells up toward my heart!   *hysteria*
        Histerica passio down, thou climbing sorrow;[6]
        Thy element's° below.—Where is this daughter?   *natural place is*
     KENT   With the Earl, sir, here within.
     LEAR   Follow me not; stay here.
                                                                          Exit
     FIRST GENTLEMAN [*to* KENT]   Made you no more offence but
        what you speak of?
230 KENT   None.
        How chance the King comes with so small a number?
     FOOL   An° thou hadst been set i'th' stocks for that question,   *If*
        thou'dst well deserved it.
     KENT   Why, Fool?
235 FOOL   We'll set thee to school to an ant, to teach thee there's no
        labouring i'th' winter.[7] All that follow their noses are led by
        their eyes but blind men, and there's not a nose among twenty
        but can smell him that's stinking.° Let go thy hold when a great   *(as his fortunes decay)*
        wheel runs down a hill,[8] lest it break thy neck with follow-
240 ing; but the great one that goes upward, let him draw thee
        after. When a wise man gives thee better counsel, give me
        mine again. I would have none but knaves follow it, since a
        fool gives it.
        [*Sings*]   That sir which serves and seeks for gain
245   And follows but for form,
                         Will pack° when it begin to rain,   *pack up and go*
                           And leave thee in the storm.

                       But I will tarry, the fool will stay,
                           And let the wise man fly.
250   The knave turns fool that runs away,[9]
                           The fool no knave, pardie.°   *by God* (*pardieu*)
     KENT   Where learned you this, Fool?
     FOOL   Not i'th' stocks, fool.
             Enter LEAR *and* GLOUCESTER
     LEAR   Deny to speak with me? They are sick, they are weary,
255 They have travelled all the night?—mere fetches,°   *ruses; pretexts*
        The images of revolt and flying off.[1]
        Fetch me a better answer.

---

3. That is, things will get worse before they get better.
4. Blind to their father's needs.
5. Pain, sorrow; punning on "dollar," the English term for the German "thaler," a large silver coin.
6. Histerica . . . *sorrow: Hysterica passio* (a Latin expression originating in the Greek *steiros,* "suffering in the womb") was an inflammation of the senses. In Renaissance medicine, vapors from the abdomen were thought to rise up through the body, and in women, the uterus itself to wander around.
7. Ants, proverbially prudent, do not work in winter. Implicitly, a wise person should know better than to look for sustenance to an old man who has fallen on wintry times.
8. A great wheel is a figure for Lear and of Fortune's wheel itself, which has swung downward.
9. The scoundrel who runs away is the real fool.
1. *images of:* signs of. *flying off:* desertion; insurrection.

GLOUCESTER   My dear lord,
      You know the fiery quality° of the Duke,   *disposition*
      How unremovable and fixed he is
      In his own course.
255 LEAR   Vengeance, death, plague, confusion!°   *destruction*
      What 'fiery quality'? Why, Gloucester, Gloucester, I'd
      Speak with the Duke of Cornwall and his wife.
      GLOUCESTER   Ay, my good lord.
      LEAR   The King would speak with Cornwall; the dear father
260 Would with his daughter speak, commands, tends° service.   *awaits*
      'Fiery'? The Duke?—tell the hot Duke that Lear—
      No, but not yet. Maybe he is not well.
      Infirmity doth still° neglect all office°   *always / obligation*
      Whereto our health is bound. We are not ourselves
265 When nature, being oppressed, commands the mind
      To suffer with the body. I'll forbear,
      And am fallen out with my more headier will,[6]
      To take° the indisposed and sickly fit   *mistake*
      For the sound man.—Death on my state,[7]
270 Wherefore° should he sit here? This act persuades me   *Why*
      That this remotion° of the Duke and her   *remoteness; aloofness*
      Is practice° only. Give me my servant forth.   *trickery*
      Tell the Duke and 's wife I'll speak with them,
      Now, presently.° Bid them come forth and hear me,   *at once*
275 Or at their chamber door I'll beat the drum
      Till it cry sleep to death.[8]
      GLOUCESTER   I would have all well
      Betwixt you.   [*Exit*]
      LEAR   O, my heart, my heart!
      FOOL   Cry to it, nuncle, as the cockney° did to the eels when she *Londoner (city woman)*
      put 'em i'th' paste° alive. She rapped 'em o'th' coxcombs° with   *pie; pastry / heads*
280 a stick, and cried 'Down, wantons,° down!' 'Twas her brother   *rogues*
      that, in pure kindness to his horse, buttered his hay.[9]

            Enter Duke [of CORNWALL] *and* REGAN [GLOUCESTER,
            and others]

      LEAR   Good morrow to you both.
      CORNWALL   Hail to your grace.
            [KENT *here set at liberty*]
      REGAN   I am glad to see your highness.
285 LEAR   Regan, I think you are. I know what reason
      I have to think so. If thou shouldst not be glad
      I would divorce me from thy mother's shrine,
      Sepulchring° an adultress. [*To* KENT] Yea, are you free?   *Because it entombed*
      Some other time for that.—Belovèd Regan,
290 Thy sister is naught.° O, Regan, she hath tied   *wicked; nothing*
      Sharp-toothed unkindness like a vulture here.[1]
      I can scarce speak to thee. Thou'lt not believe
      Of how deplored a quality—O, Regan!

6. And disagree with my (earlier) more rash intention.
7. May my royal authority end (an oath). Ironically, this
has already happened.
8. Till the noise kills sleep.

9. Like that of his sister (who wanted to make eel pie
without killing the eels), his kindness was misplaced:
horses will not eat buttered hay.
1. Lear probably gestures to his heart.

GLOUCESTER   My dear lord,
  You know the fiery quality° of the Duke,   *disposition*
  How unremovable and fixed he is
  In his own course.
260 LEAR   Vengeance, plague, death, confusion!°   *destruction*
  'Fiery'? What 'quality'? Why, Gloucester, Gloucester,
  I'd speak with the Duke of Cornwall and his wife.
GLOUCESTER   Well, my good lord, I have informed them so.
LEAR   'Informed them'? Dost thou understand me, man?
265 GLOUCESTER   Ay, my good lord.
LEAR   The King would speak with Cornwall; the dear father
  Would with his daughter speak, commands, tends° service.   *awaits*
  Are they 'informed' of this? My breath and blood—
  'Fiery'? The 'fiery' Duke—tell the hot Duke that—
270   No, but not yet. Maybe he is not well.
  Infirmity doth still° neglect all office°   *always / obligation*
  Whereto our health is bound. We are not ourselves
  When nature, being oppressed, commands the mind
  To suffer with the body. I'll forbear,
275   And am fallen out with my more headier will,[2]
  To take° the indisposed and sickly fit   *mistake*
  For the sound man.—Death on my state,[3] wherefore°   *why*
  Should he sit here? This act persuades me
  That this remotion° of the Duke and her   *remoteness; aloofness*
280   Is practice° only. Give me my servant forth.   *trickery*
  Go tell the Duke and 's wife I'd speak with them,
  Now, presently.° Bid them come forth and hear me,   *at once*
  Or at their chamber door I'll beat the drum
  Till it cry sleep to death.[4]
GLOUCESTER   I would have all well betwixt you.
                                 Exit
285 LEAR   O me, my heart! My rising heart! But down.
FOOL   Cry to it, nuncle, as the cockney° did to the eels when she   *Londoner (city woman)*
  put 'em i'th' paste° alive. She knapped 'em o'th' coxcombs°   *pie; pastry / heads*
  with a stick, and cried 'Down, wantons,° down!' 'Twas her   *rogues*
  brother that, in pure kindness to his horse, buttered his hay.[5]
        Enter CORNWALL, REGAN, GLOUCESTER, [*and*] *servants*
290 LEAR   Good morrow to you both.
CORNWALL   Hail to your grace.
          KENT *here set at liberty*
REGAN   I am glad to see your highness.
LEAR   Regan, I think you are. I know what reason
  I have to think so. If thou shouldst not be glad
295   I would divorce me from thy mother's shrine,
  Sepulchring° an adultress. [*To* KENT] O, are you free?   *Because it entombed*
  Some other time for that.
                        [*Exit* KENT]
              Belovèd Regan,
  Thy sister's naught.° O, Regan, she hath tied   *wicked; nothing*
  Sharp-toothed unkindness like a vulture here.[6]
300   I can scarce speak to thee. Thou'lt not believe
  With how depraved a quality—O, Regan!

---

2. And disagree with my (earlier) more rash intention.
3. May my royal authority end (an oath). Ironically, this has already happened.
4. Till the noise kills sleep.

5. Like that of his sister (who wanted to make eel pie without killing the eels), his kindness was misplaced: horses will not eat buttered hay.
6. Lear probably gestures to his heart.

REGAN   I pray you, sir, take patience. I have hope
295   You less know how to value her desert
        Than she to slack her duty.²

LEAR   My curses on her.
REGAN   O sir, you are old.
        Nature° in you stands on the very verge   *Life*
300   Of her confine.° You should be ruled and led   *Of its limit*
        By some discretion° that discerns your state   *discreet person*
        Better than you yourself. Therefore I pray
        That to our sister you do make return;
        Say you have wronged her, sir.
LEAR   Ask her forgiveness?
305   Do you mark how this becomes the house?³
        [*Kneeling*] 'Dear daughter, I confess that I am old.
        Age° is unnecessary. On my knees I beg   *An old man*
        That you'll vouchsafe me raiment,° bed, and food.'   *promise me clothing*
REGAN   Good sir, no more. These are unsightly tricks.
        Return you to my sister.
310 LEAR [*rising*]   No, Regan.
        She hath abated° me of half my train,   *deprived*
        Looked black upon me, struck me with her tongue
        Most serpent-like upon the very heart.
        All° the stored vengeances of heaven fall   *Let all*
315   On her ungrateful top!° Strike her young bones,   *head*
        You taking° airs, with lameness!   *infectious; malignant*
CORNWALL   Fie, fie, sir.
LEAR   You nimble lightnings, dart your blinding flames
        Into her scornful eyes. Infect her beauty,
        You fen-sucked fogs drawn by the pow'rful sun⁴
        To fall and blast her pride.
320 REGAN   O, the blest gods!
        So will you wish on me when the rash mood—
LEAR   No, Regan. Thou shalt never have my curse.
        Thy tender-hested° nature shall not give   *pledged to tenderness*
        Thee o'er to harshness. Her eyes are fierce, but thine
325   Do comfort and not burn. 'Tis not in thee
        To grudge my pleasures, to cut off my train,
        To bandy hasty words, to scant my sizes,°   *reduce my allowances*
        And, in conclusion, to oppose the bolt°   *to lock the door*
        Against my coming in. Thou better know'st
330   The offices° of nature, bond of childhood,   *duties*
        Effects° of courtesy, dues of gratitude.   *Actions*
        Thy half of the kingdom hast thou not forgot,
        Wherein I thee endowed.

---

2. *I have . . . duty:* I expect that you are worse at valu-
ing her deservings than she is at neglecting her duty.
The double negative here ("less," "scant") is acceptable
Jacobean usage.

3. Do you see how appropriate this is among members
of a family (spoken ironically)?
4. The sun was thought to suck poisonous vapors from
marshy ground.

REGAN   I pray you, sir, take patience. I have hope
    You less know how to value her desert
    Than she to scant her duty.[7]
LEAR   Say, how is that?
305 REGAN   I cannot think my sister in the least
    Would fail her obligation. If, sir, perchance
    She have restrained the riots of your followers,
    'Tis on such ground and to such wholesome end
    As clears her from all blame.
310 LEAR   My curses on her.
REGAN   O sir, you are old.
    Nature° in you stands on the very verge   *Life*
    Of his confine.° You should be ruled and led   *Of its limit*
    By some discretion° that discerns your state   *discreet person*
315   Better than you yourself. Therefore I pray you
    That to our sister you do make return;
    Say you have wronged her.
LEAR   Ask her forgiveness?
    Do you but mark how this becomes the house?[8]
    [*Kneeling*] 'Dear daughter, I confess that I am old.
320   Age° is unnecessary. On my knees I beg   *An old man*
    That you'll vouchsafe me raiment,° bed, and food.' *promise me clothing*
REGAN   Good sir, no more. These are unsightly tricks.
    Return you to my sister.
LEAR [*rising*]   Never, Regan.
    She hath abated° me of half my train,   *deprived*
325   Looked black upon me, struck me with her tongue
    Most serpent-like upon the very heart.
    All° the stored vengeances of heaven fall   *Let all*
    On her ingrateful top!° Strike her young bones,   *head*
    You taking° airs, with lameness!   *infectious; malignant*
CORNWALL   Fie, sir, fie.
330 LEAR   You nimble lightnings, dart your blinding flames
    Into her scornful eyes. Infect her beauty,
    You fen-sucked fogs drawn by the pow'rful sun[9]
    To fall and blister.
REGAN   O, the blest gods!
    So will you wish on me when the rash mood is on.
335 LEAR   No, Regan. Thou shalt never have my curse.
    Thy tender-hafted[1] nature shall not give
    Thee o'er to harshness. Her eyes are fierce, but thine
    Do comfort and not burn. 'Tis not in thee
    To grudge my pleasures, to cut off my train,
340   To bandy hasty words, to scant my sizes,°   *reduce my allowances*
    And, in conclusion, to oppose the bolt°   *to lock the door*
    Against my coming in. Thou better know'st
    The offices° of nature, bond of childhood,   *duties*
    Effects° of courtesy, dues of gratitude.   *Actions*
345   Thy half o'th' kingdom hast thou not forgot,
    Wherein I thee endowed.

7. *I have . . . duty:* I expect that you are worse at valuing her deservings than she is at neglecting her duty. The double negative here ("less," "scant") is acceptable Jacobean usage.
8. Do you see how appropriate this is among members of a family (spoken ironically)?
9. The sun was thought to suck poisonous vapors from marshy ground.
1. Tender-handled; firmly set in a tender disposition (as a knife blade into its haft).

REGAN   Good sir, to th' purpose.°   *get to the point*
LEAR   Who put my man i'th' stocks?
          [*Trumpets within*]
CORNWALL   What trumpet's that?
          Enter Steward [OSWALD]
335   REGAN   I know't, my sister's. This approves° her letters   *confirms*
          That she would soon be here. [*To* OSWALD] Is your lady come?
      LEAR   This is a slave whose easy-borrowed pride[5]
          Dwells in the fickle grace of her a° follows.   *he*
          [*He strikes* OSWALD]
          Out, varlet,° from my sight!   *wretch*
CORNWALL   What means your grace?
          Enter GONORIL
340   GONORIL   Who struck my servant? Regan, I have good hope
          Thou didst not know on't.°   *of it*
      LEAR   Who comes here? O heavens,
          If you do love old men, if your sweet sway
          Allow obedience, if yourselves are old,
          Make it your cause! Send down and take my part.
345   [*To* GONORIL] Art not ashamed to look upon this beard?
          O Regan, wilt thou take her by the hand?
      GONORIL   Why not by the hand, sir? How have I offended?
          All's not offence that indiscretion finds
          And dotage terms so.
      LEAR   O sides,[6] you are too tough!
350   Will you yet hold?—How came my man i'th' stocks?
      CORNWALL   I set him there, sir; but his own disorders°   *disorderly behavior*
          Deserved much less advancement.[7]
      LEAR   You? Did you?
      REGAN   I pray you, father, being weak, seem so.°   *behave so*
          If till the expiration of your month
355   You will return and sojourn with my sister,
          Dismissing half your train, come then to me.
          I am now from home, and out of that provision
          Which shall be needful for your entertainment.
      LEAR   Return to her, and fifty men dismissed?
360   No, rather I abjure all roofs, and choose
          To be a comrade with the wolf and owl,
          To wage against the enmity of the air
          Necessity's sharp pinch.[8] Return with her?
          Why, the hot-blood in France that dowerless took
365   Our youngest born—I could as well be brought
          To knee° his throne and, squire-like, pension beg   *kneel to*
          To keep base life afoot. Return with her?
          Persuade me rather to be slave and sumpter°   *packhorse*
          To this detested groom.°   *(Oswald)*
      GONORIL   At your choice, sir.
370   LEAR   Now I prithee, daughter, do not make me mad.
          I will not trouble thee, my child. Farewell.
          We'll no more meet, no more see one another.
          But yet thou art my flesh, my blood, my daughter—

---

5. Unmerited and unpaid-for arrogance; "pride" may also refer to Oswald's fine clothing received for his services to Gonoril.
6. Chest, where Lear's heart is swelling with emotion.
7. Deserved far worse treatment.

8. *To wage . . . pinch*: To counter the harshness of the elements with the hardness brought on by necessity. *pinch*: stress, pressure. Oxford has transposed lines 361 and 362.

REGAN   Good sir, to th' purpose.°   *get to the point*
LEAR   Who put my man i'th' stocks?
       Tucket within
CORNWALL   What trumpet's that?
       Enter Steward [OSWALD]
REGAN   I know't, my sister's. This approves° her letter   *confirms*
      That she would soon be here. [*To* OSWALD] Is your lady come?
350   LEAR   This is a slave whose easy-borrowed pride[2]
      Dwells in the sickly grace of her a° follows.   *he*
      [*To* OSWALD] Out, varlet,° from my sight!   *wretch*
CORNWALL   What means your grace?
      Enter GONERIL
LEAR   Who stocked my servant? Regan, I have good hope
      Thou didst not know on't.° Who comes here? O heavens,   *of it*
355   If you do love old men, if your sweet sway
      Allow obedience, if you yourselves are old,
      Make it your cause! Send down and take my part.
      [*To* GONERIL] Art not ashamed to look upon this beard?
      O Regan, will you take her by the hand?
360   GONERIL   Why not by th' hand, sir? How have I offended?
      All's not offence that indiscretion finds
      And dotage terms so.
LEAR   O sides,[3] you are too tough!
      Will you yet hold?—How came my man i'th' stocks?
CORNWALL   I set him there, sir; but his own disorders°   *disorderly behavior*
      Deserved much less advancement.[4]
365   LEAR   You? Did you?
REGAN   I pray you, father, being weak, seem so.°   *behave so*
      If till the expiration of your month
      You will return and sojourn with my sister,
      Dismissing half your train, come then to me.
370   I am now from home, and out of that provision
      Which shall be needful for your entertainment.
LEAR   Return to her, and fifty men dismissed?
      No, rather I abjure all roofs, and choose
      To be a comrade with the wolf and owl,
375   To wage against the enmity o'th' air
      Necessity's sharp pinch.[5] Return with her?
      Why, the hot-blooded France, that dowerless took
      Our youngest born—I could as well be brought
      To knee° his throne and, squire-like, pension beg   *kneel to*
380   To keep base life afoot. Return with her?
      Persuade me rather to be slave and sumpter°   *packhorse*
      To this detested groom.°   *(Oswald)*
GONERIL   At your choice, sir.
LEAR   I prithee, daughter, do not make me mad.
      I will not trouble thee, my child. Farewell.
385   We'll no more meet, no more see one another.
      But yet thou art my flesh, my blood, my daughter—

---

2. Unmerited and unpaid-for arrogance; "pride" may also refer to Oswald's fine clothing received for his services to Goneril.
3. Chest, where Lear's heart is swelled with emotion.
4. Deserved far worse treatment.

5. *To wage . . . pinch:* To counter the harshness of the elements with the hardness brought on by necessity. *pinch:* stress, pressure. Oxford has transposed lines 374 and 375.

Or rather a disease that lies within my flesh,
375 Which I must needs call mine. Thou art a boil,
A plague-sore, an embossèd° carbuncle   *a swollen*
In my corrupted blood. But I'll not chide thee.
Let shame come when it will, I do not call° it.   *call upon*
I do not bid the thunder-bearer° shoot,   *(Jove)*
380 Nor tell tales of thee to high-judging Jove.
Mend° when thou canst; be better at thy leisure.   *Make amends*
I can be patient, I can stay with Regan,
I and my hundred knights.

REGAN   Not altogether so, sir.
I look not for° you yet, nor am provided   *I did not expect*
385 For your fit welcome. Give ear, sir, to my sister;
For those that mingle reason with your passion[9]
Must be content to think you are old, and so—
But she knows what she does.

LEAR   Is this well° spoken now?   *earnestly*

REGAN   I dare avouch° it, sir. What, fifty followers?   *vouch for*
390 Is it not well? What should you need of more,
Yea, or so many, sith° that both charge° and danger   *since / expense*
Speaks 'gainst so great a number? How in a house
Should many people under two commands
Hold amity? 'Tis hard, almost impossible.

395 GONORIL   Why might not you, my lord, receive attendance
From those that she calls servants, or from mine?

REGAN   Why not, my lord? If then they chanced to slack° you,   *neglect*
We could control them. If you will come to me—
For now I spy a danger—I entreat you
400 To bring but five-and-twenty; to no more
Will I give place or notice.°   *acknowledgment*

LEAR   I gave you all.

REGAN   And in good time° you gave it.   *it was about time*

LEAR   Made you my guardians, my depositaries,°   *trustees*
405 But kept a reservation° to be followed   *reserved a right*
With such a number. What, must I come to you
With five-and-twenty, Regan? Said you so?

REGAN   And speak't again, my lord. No more with me.

LEAR   Those wicked creatures yet do seem well favoured°   *attractive*
410 When others are more wicked. Not being the worst
Stands in some rank of praise.[1] [*To* GONORIL] I'll go with thee.
Thy fifty yet doth double five-and-twenty,
And thou art twice her love.

GONORIL   Hear me, my lord.
What need you five-and-twenty, ten, or five,
415 To follow in a house where twice so many
Have a command to tend you?

REGAN   What needs one?

LEAR   O, reason not the need! Our basest beggars
Are in the poorest thing superfluous.[2]
Allow not° nature more than nature needs,   *If you don't allow*
420 Man's life is cheap as beast's. Thou art a lady.

9. For those who temper your passionate argument
with their own calm reasoning.
1. Deserves some degree ("rank") of praise.

2. *Our . . . superfluous*: Even the lowliest beggars have
something more than the barest minimum.

Or rather a disease that's in my flesh,
Which I must needs call mine. Thou art a boil,
A plague-sore or embossèd° carbuncle   swollen
390   In my corrupted blood. But I'll not chide thee.
Let shame come when it will, I do not call° it.   call upon
I do not bid the thunder-bearer° shoot,   (Jove)
Nor tell tales of thee to high-judging Jove.
Mend° when thou canst; be better at thy leisure.   Make amends
395   I can be patient, I can stay with Regan,
I and my hundred knights.
REGAN   Not altogether so.
I looked not for° you yet, nor am provided   I did not expect
For your fit welcome. Give ear, sir, to my sister;
For those that mingle reason with your passion⁶
400   Must be content to think you old, and so—
But she knows what she does.
LEAR   Is this well° spoken?   earnestly
REGAN   I dare avouch° it, sir. What, fifty followers?   vouch for
Is it not well? What should you need of more,
Yea, or so many, sith° that both charge° and danger   since / expense
405   Speak 'gainst so great a number? How in one house
Should many people under two commands
Hold amity? 'Tis hard, almost impossible.
GONERIL   Why might not you, my lord, receive attendance
From those that she calls servants, or from mine?
410   REGAN   Why not, my lord? If then they chanced to slack° ye,   neglect
We could control them. If you will come to me—
For now I spy a danger—I entreat you
To bring but five and twenty; to no more
Will I give place or notice.°   acknowledgment
415   LEAR   I gave you all.
REGAN   And in good time° you gave it.   it was about time
LEAR   Made you my guardians, my depositaries,°   trustees
But kept a reservation° to be followed   reserved a right
With such a number. What, must I come to you
420   With five and twenty? Regan, said you so?
REGAN   And speak't again, my lord. No more with me.
LEAR   Those wicked creatures yet do look well favoured°   attractive
When others are more wicked. Not being the worst
Stands in some rank of praise.⁷ [To GONERIL] I'll go with thee.
425   Thy fifty yet doth double five and twenty,
And thou art twice her love.
GONERIL   Hear me, my lord.
What need you five and twenty, ten, or five,
To follow in a house where twice so many
Have a command to tend you?
REGAN   What need one?
430   LEAR   O, reason not the need! Our basest beggars
Are in the poorest thing superfluous.⁸
Allow not° nature more than nature needs,   If you don't allow
Man's life is cheap as beast's. Thou art a lady.

6. For those who temper your passionate argument   8. *Our . . . superfluous:* Even the lowliest beggars have
with their own calm reasoning.   something more than the barest minimum.
7. Deserves some degree ("rank") of praise.

If only to go warm were gorgeous,
Why, nature needs not what thou, gorgeous, wearest,
Which scarcely keeps thee warm.[3] But for true need—
You heavens, give me that patience,° patience I need.   endurance
425   You see me here, you gods, a poor old fellow,
As full of grief as age, wretchèd in both.
If it be you that stirs these daughters' hearts
Against their father, fool me not so much
To bear it tamely.[4] Touch me with noble anger.
430   O, let not women's weapons, water-drops,
Stain my man's cheeks! No, you unnatural hags,
I will have such revenges on you both
That all the world shall—I will do such things—
What they are, yet I know not; but they shall be
435   The terrors of the earth. You think I'll weep.
No, I'll not weep.
              [Storm within]
I have full cause of weeping, but this heart
Shall break into a hundred thousand flaws°   fragments
Or ere° I'll weep.—O fool, I shall go mad!   Before
              Exeunt LEAR, [GLOUCESTER,] KENT, [KNIGHT,] and FOOL
440   CORNWALL   Let us withdraw. 'Twill be a storm.
REGAN   This house is little. The old man and his people
Cannot be well bestowed.°   lodged
GONORIL   'Tis his own blame;
Hath put himself from° rest, and must needs taste his folly.   deprived himself of
REGAN   For his particular° I'll receive him gladly,   single self
445   But not one follower.
CORNWALL   So am I purposed. Where is my lord of Gloucester?
REGAN   Followed the old man forth.
              Enter GLOUCESTER
                                        He is returned.
GLOUCESTER   The King is in high rage, and will° I know not whither.   will go
REGAN   'Tis good to give him way. He leads himself.
450   GONORIL [to GLOUCESTER]   My lord, entreat him by no means to stay.
GLOUCESTER   Alack, the night comes on, and the bleak winds
Do sorely rustle. For many miles about
There's not a bush.
REGAN   O sir, to wilful men
The injuries that they themselves procure
455   Must be their schoolmasters. Shut up your doors.
He is attended with a desperate° train,   violent
And what they may incense° him to, being apt   incite
To have his ear abused,° wisdom bids fear.   deceived
CORNWALL   Shut up your doors, my lord. 'Tis a wild night.
460   My Regan counsels well. Come out o'th' storm.   Exeunt

---

3. If . . . thee warm: If gorgeousness in clothes is measured by the warmth they provide, your elaborate
clothes are superfluous, for they barely cover your body.

4. fool . . . tamely: do not make me so foolish as to
accept it meekly.

If only to go warm were gorgeous,
435 Why, nature needs not what thou, gorgeous, wear'st,
Which scarcely keeps thee warm.⁹ But for true need—
You heavens, give me that patience,° patience I need.   *endurance*
You see me here, you gods, a poor old man,
As full of grief as age, wretchèd in both.
440 If it be you that stirs these daughters' hearts
Against their father, fool me not so much
To bear it tamely.¹ Touch me with noble anger,
And let not women's weapons, water-drops,
Stain my man's cheeks. No, you unnatural hags,
445 I will have such revenges on you both
That all the world shall—I will do such things—
What they are, yet I know not; but they shall be
The terrors of the earth. You think I'll weep.
No, I'll not weep. I have full cause of weeping,
     Storm and tempest
450 But this heart shall break into a hundred thousand flaws°   *fragments*
Or ere° I'll weep.—O Fool, I shall go mad!   *Before*
    Exeunt [LEAR, FOOL, GENTLEMAN, *and* GLOUCESTER]
CORNWALL   Let us withdraw. 'Twill be a storm.
REGAN   This house is little. The old man and 's people
  Cannot be well bestowed.°   *lodged*
GONERIL   'Tis his own blame;
455 Hath put himself from° rest, and must needs taste his folly.   *deprived himself of*
REGAN   For his particular° I'll receive him gladly,   *single self*
  But not one follower.
GONERIL   So am I purposed.
  Where is my lord of Gloucester?
CORNWALL   Followed the old man forth.
    Enter GLOUCESTER
                        He is returned.
GLOUCESTER   The King is in high rage.
460 CORNWALL   Whither is he going?
GLOUCESTER   He calls to horse, but will° I know not whither.   *will go*
CORNWALL   'Tis best to give him way. He leads himself.
GONERIL [*to* GLOUCESTER]   My lord, entreat him by no means to stay.
GLOUCESTER   Alack, the night comes on, and the high winds
465 Do sorely ruffle.° For many miles about   *bluster*
  There's scarce a bush.
REGAN   O sir, to wilful men
  The injuries that they themselves procure
  Must be their schoolmasters. Shut up your doors.
  He is attended with a desperate° train,   *violent*
470 And what they may incense° him to, being apt   *incite*
  To have his ear abused,° wisdom bids fear.   *deceived*
CORNWALL   Shut up your doors, my lord. 'Tis a wild night.
  My Regan counsels well. Come out o'th' storm.   *Exeunt*

---

9. *If . . . thee warm:* If gorgeousness in clothes is measured by the warmth they provide, your elaborate clothes are superfluous, for they barely cover your body.

1. *fool . . . tamely:* do not make me so foolish as to accept it meekly.

Scene 8

[*Storm.*] *Enter* KENT [*disguised,*] *and* [FIRST] GENTLE-
MAN, *at several°* doors   separate

KENT   What's here, beside foul weather?

FIRST GENTLEMAN   One minded like the weather,
Most unquietly.

KENT   I know you. Where's the King?

FIRST GENTLEMAN   Contending with the fretful element;
Bids the wind blow the earth into the sea

5   Or swell the curlèd waters 'bove the main,°   mainland
That things might change or cease; tears his white hair,
Which the impetuous blasts, with eyeless rage,
Catch in their fury and make nothing of;
Strives in his little world of man to outstorm

10 The to-and-fro-conflicting wind and rain.
This night, wherein the cub-drawn bear would couch,[1]
The lion and the belly-pinchèd wolf
Keep their fur dry, unbonneted° he runs,   hatless; uncrowned
And bids what will take all.

KENT   But who is with him?

15 FIRST GENTLEMAN   None but the fool, who labours to outjest
His heart-struck injuries.[2]

KENT   Sir, I do know you,
And dare upon the warrant of my art[3]
Commend a dear° thing to you. There is division,   Entrust a crucial
Although as yet the face of it be covered

20 With mutual cunning, 'twixt Albany and Cornwall;
But true it is. From France there comes a power
Into this scattered kingdom, who already,
Wise in° our negligence, have secret feet   Aware of
In some of our best ports, and are at point°   ready

25 To show their open banner. Now to you:
If on my credit you dare build° so far   If you trust me
To make your speed to Dover, you shall find
Some that will thank you, making just° report   accurate
Of how unnatural and bemadding° sorrow   maddening

30 The King hath cause to plain.°   complain
I am a gentleman of blood and breeding,
And from some knowledge and assurance offer
This office° to you.   role; duty

FIRST GENTLEMAN   I will talk farther with you.

35 KENT   No, do not.
For confirmation that I am much more
Than my out-wall,° open this purse, and take   outward appearance
What it contains. If you shall see Cordelia—
As fear not but you shall—show her this ring

40 And she will tell you who your fellow° is,   (Kent himself)

Scene 8 Location: Bare, open country.
1. In which even the bear, though starving, having been sucked dry ("drawn") by its cub, would not go out to forage.

2. *to outjest:* to relieve with laughter; to exorcise through ridicule. *heart-struck injuries:* injuries (from the betrayal of his paternal love) that penetrated to the heart.
3. On the basis of my skill (at judging people).

3.1

Storm still. Enter KENT *[disguised] and [the* FIRST*] GEN-*
TLEMAN, severally°   separately

KENT   Who's there, besides foul weather?

FIRST GENTLEMAN   One minded like the weather,
Most unquietly.

KENT   I know you. Where's the King?

FIRST GENTLEMAN   Contending with the fretful elements;
Bids the wind blow the earth into the sea

5   Or swell the curlèd waters 'bove the main,°   mainland
That things might change or cease.

KENT   But who is with him?

FIRST GENTLEMAN   None but the Fool, who labours to outjest
His heart-struck injuries.[1]

KENT   Sir, I do know you,
And dare upon the warrant of my note[2]

10   Commend a dear° thing to you. There is division,   Entrust a crucial
Although as yet the face of it is covered
With mutual cunning, 'twixt Albany and Cornwall,
Who have—as who have not that their great stars
Throned and set high[3]—servants, who seem no less,°   who appear as such

15   Which are to France the spies and speculations°   observers
Intelligent of[4] our state. What hath been seen,
Either in snuffs and packings° of the Dukes,   quarrels and plots
Or the hard rein° which both of them hath borne   treatment
Against the old kind King; or something deeper,

20   Whereof perchance these are but furnishings°—   pretexts

FIRST GENTLEMAN   I will talk further with you.

KENT   No, do not.
For confirmation that I am much more
Than my out-wall,° open this purse, and take   outward appearance
What it contains. If you shall see Cordelia—

25   As fear not but you shall—show her this ring
And she will tell you who that fellow° is   (Kent himself)

3.1 Location: Bare, open country.
1. *to outjest:* to relieve with laughter; to exorcise through
ridicule. *heart-struck injuries:* injuries (from the betrayal
of his paternal love) that penetrated to the heart.

2. On the basis of my skill (at judging people).
3. *as . . . high:* as has everybody who has been favored
by destiny.
4. Supplying intelligence about; too well informed of.

That yet you do not know. Fie on this storm!
I will go seek the King.

FIRST GENTLEMAN　　　　　　Give me your hand.
Have you no more to say?

KENT　　　　　　　　　　Few words, but to effect°　　　　　*but in importance*
More than all yet: that when we have found the King—
45　　In which endeavour I'll° this way, you that—　　　　　*I'll go*
He that first lights on him holla the other.　　*Exeunt severally*

Scene 9

[*Storm.*] *Enter* LEAR *and* FOOL

LEAR　Blow, wind, and crack your cheeks! Rage, blow,
You cataracts and hurricanoes,[1] spout
Till you have drenched the steeples, drowned the cocks!°　　*weather vanes*
You sulphurous and thought-executing fires,[2]
5　　Vaunt-couriers° to oak-cleaving thunderbolts,　　　　　*Forerunners*
Singe my white head; and thou all-shaking thunder,
Smite flat the thick rotundity of the world,
Crack nature's mould, all germens° spill at once　　　　*seeds*
That make ingrateful man.

10　FOOL　O nuncle, court holy water[3] in a dry house is better than
this rain-water out o' door. Good nuncle, in, and ask thy daughters blessing. Here's a night pities neither wise man nor fool.

LEAR　Rumble thy bellyful; spit, fire; spout, rain.
Nor rain, wind, thunder, fire are my daughters.
15　　I tax° not you, you elements, with unkindness.　　　　*blame*
I never gave you kingdom, called you children.
You owe me no subscription.° Why then, let fall　　*obedience; allegiance*
Your horrible pleasure. Here I stand your slave,
A poor, infirm, weak and despised old man,
20　　But yet I call you servile ministers,°　　　　　　　*agents*
That have with two pernicious daughters joined
Your high engendered battle° 'gainst a head　　　*heaven-bred forces*
So old and white as this. O, 'tis foul!

FOOL　He that has a house to put his head in has a good
25　　headpiece.°　　　　　　　　　　　　　　　　　*hat; brain*
[*Sings*]　　The codpiece that will house
　　　　　　Before the head has any,
　　　　　　The head and he shall louse,
　　　　　　So beggars marry many.[4]
30　　　　　The man that makes his toe
　　　　　　What he his heart should make
　　　　　　Shall have a corn cry woe,
　　　　　　And turn his sleep to wake[5]—
for there was never yet fair woman but she made mouths in a
35　　glass.[6]

Scene 9 Location: As before.
1. *cataracts*: floodgates of the heavens. *hurricanoes*:
waterspouts (water from both sky and sea).
2. *thought-executing fires*: lightning that strikes as
swiftly as thought.
3. Sprinkled blessings of a courtier, flattery.
4. *The codpiece . . . many*: Whoever finds his penis a
lodging before providing shelter for his head will end up
in lice-infested poverty and live in married beggary. *cod-*

piece: a pouchlike covering for the male genitals, often
conspicuous, particularly in the costume of a fool.
5. *The man . . . wake*: The man who values an inferior
part of his body over the part that is truly valuable will
suffer from and lose sleep over that inferior part.
6. She practiced making pretty faces in a mirror. The
Fool probably refers to Regan's and Gonoril's vanity, or
the line may be thrown in to soften the harshness of his
satire.

That yet you do not know. Fie on this storm!
I will go seek the King.

FIRST GENTLEMAN   Give me your hand. Have you no more to say?

30   KENT   Few words, but to effect° more than all yet: *but in importance*
That when we have found the King—in which your pain
That way, I'll this⁵—he that first lights on him
Holla the other.   *Exeunt [severally]*

3.2

Storm still. Enter LEAR *and* FOOL

LEAR   Blow, winds, and crack your cheeks! Rage, blow,
You cataracts and hurricanoes,¹ spout
Till you have drenched our steeples, drowned the cocks!°   *weather vanes*
You sulph'rous and thought-executing fires,²

5   Vaunt-couriers° of oak-cleaving thunderbolts,   *Forerunners*
Singe my white head; and thou all-shaking thunder,
Strike flat the thick rotundity o'th' world,
Crack nature's moulds, all germens° spill at once   *seeds*
That makes ingrateful man.

10   FOOL   O nuncle, court holy water³ in a dry house is better than
this rain-water out o' door. Good nuncle, in, ask thy daughters
blessing. Here's a night pities neither wise men nor fools.

LEAR   Rumble thy bellyful; spit, fire; spout, rain.
Nor rain, wind, thunder, fire are my daughters.

15   I tax° not you, you elements, with unkindness.   *blame*
I never gave you kingdom, called you children.
You owe me no subscription.° Then let fall   *obedience; allegiance*
Your horrible pleasure. Here I stand your slave,
A poor, infirm, weak and despised old man,

20   But yet I call you servile ministers,°   *agents*
That will with two pernicious daughters join
Your high-engendered battles° 'gainst a head   *heaven-bred forces*
So old and white as this. O, ho, 'tis foul!

FOOL   He that has a house to put 's head in has a good

25   headpiece.°   *hat; brain*
[*Sings*]   The codpiece that will house
                    Before the head has any,
                The head and he shall louse,
                    So beggars marry many.⁴

30   The man that makes his toe
                    What he his heart should make
                Shall of a corn cry woe,
                    And turn his sleep to wake⁵—
for there was never yet fair woman but she made mouths in a

35   glass.⁶

---

5. *in which . . . this:* in which effort you will go that
way and I this way.
3.2 Location: As before.
1. *cataracts:* floodgates of the heavens. *hurricanoes:*
waterspouts (water from both sky and sea).
2. *thought-executing fires:* lightning that strikes as
swiftly as thought.
3. Sprinkled blessings of a courtier; flattery.
4. *The codpiece . . . many:* Whoever finds his penis a
lodging before providing shelter for his head will end up
in lice-infested poverty and live in married beggary.

codpiece: a pouchlike covering for the male genitals,
often conspicuous, particularly in the costume of a
fool.
5. *The man . . . wake:* The man who values an inferior
part of his body over the part that is truly valuable will
suffer from and lose sleep over that inferior part.
6. She practiced making pretty faces in a mirror. The
Fool probably refers to Regan's and Goneril's vanity, or
the line may be thrown in to soften the harshness of his
satire.

LEAR   No, I will be the pattern of all patience.
    [He sits.] Enter KENT *[disguised]*
  I will say nothing.
KENT   Who's there?
FOOL   Marry, here's grace and a codpiece—that's a wise man
40 and a fool.[7]
KENT *[to* LEAR*]*   Alas, sir, sit you here? Things that love night
  Love not such nights as these. The wrathful skies
  Gallow° the very wanderers of the dark   *Frighten*
  And makes them keep° their caves. Since I was man   *keep inside*
45 Such sheets of fire, such bursts of horrid thunder,
  Such groans of roaring wind and rain I ne'er
  Remember to have heard. Man's nature cannot carry°   *bear*
  The affliction nor the force.
LEAR   Let the great gods,
  That keep this dreadful pother° o'er our heads,   *commotion*
50 Find out their enemies now. Tremble, thou wretch
  That hast within thee undivulgèd crimes
  Unwhipped of° justice; hide thee, thou bloody hand,   *Unpunished by*
  Thou perjured and thou simular° man of virtue   *simulating; pretending*
  That art incestuous; caitiff,° in pieces shake,   *wretch*
55 That under covert and convenient seeming°   *fitting hypocrisy*
  Hast practised on° man's life;   *against*
  Close° pent-up guilts, rive° your concealèd centres   *Secret / split open*
  And cry these dreadful summoners grace.[8]
  I am a man more sinned against than sinning.
60 KENT   Alack, bare-headed?
  Gracious my lord, hard by here is a hovel.
  Some friendship will it lend you 'gainst the tempest.
  Repose you there whilst I to this hard house°—   *household*
  More hard than is the stone whereof 'tis raised,
65 Which° even but now, demanding° after you,   *Who / I demanding*
  Denied me to come in—return and force
  Their scanted° courtesy.   *niggardly*
LEAR   My wit begins to turn.
  [To FOOL*]* Come on, my boy. How dost, my boy? Art cold?
  I am cold myself.—Where is this straw, my fellow?
70 The art° of our necessities is strange,   *skill; alchemy*
  That can make vile things precious. Come, your hovel.—
  Poor fool and knave, I have one part of my heart
  That sorrows yet for thee.
FOOL *[sings]*[9]   He that has a little tiny wit,°   *sense*
75   With heigh-ho, the wind and the rain,
        Must make content with his fortunes fit,
        For the rain it raineth every day.
LEAR   True, my good boy. *[To* KENT*]* Come, bring us to this hovel.
                     [Exeunt]

---

7. The supposedly wise King is symbolized by royal
grace, the Fool by his codpiece (here, slang for "penis").
The Fool speaks ironically: the King, as he has pointed
out, is now the foolish one. *Marry:* By the Virgin Mary
(a mild oath).

8. And pray for mercy from these elements that bring
you to justice.
9. The following song is an adaptation of one sung by
Feste at the end of *Twelfth Night.*

Enter KENT [*disguised*]

LEAR   No, I will be the pattern of all patience.
        I will say nothing.

KENT   Who's there?

FOOL   Marry, here's grace and a codpiece—that's a wise man
40   and a fool.[7]

KENT [*to* LEAR]   Alas, sir, are you here? Things that love night
        Love not such nights as these. The wrathful skies
        Gallow° the very wanderers of the dark   *Frighten*
        And make them keep° their caves. Since I was man   *keep inside*
45   Such sheets of fire, such bursts of horrid thunder,
        Such groans of roaring wind and rain I never
        Remember to have heard. Man's nature cannot carry°   *bear*
        Th'affliction nor the fear.

LEAR   Let the great gods,
        That keep this dreadful pother° o'er our heads,   *commotion*
50   Find out their enemies now. Tremble, thou wretch
        That hast within thee undivulgèd crimes
        Unwhipped of° justice; hide thee, thou bloody hand,   *Unpunished by*
        Thou perjured and thou simular° of virtue   *simulator; pretender*
        That art incestuous; caitiff,° to pieces shake,   *wretch*
55   That under covert and convenient seeming°   *fitting hypocrisy*
        Has practised on° man's life; close° pent-up guilts,   *against / secret*
        Rive° your concealing continents° and cry   *Split open / coverings*
        These dreadful summoners grace.[8] I am a man
        More sinned against than sinning.

KENT   Alack, bare-headed?
60   Gracious my lord, hard by here is a hovel.
        Some friendship will it lend you 'gainst the tempest.
        Repose you there while I to this hard house°—   *household*
        More harder than the stones whereof 'tis raised,
        Which° even but now, demanding° after you,   *Who / I demanding*
65   Denied me to come in—return and force
        Their scanted° courtesy.   *niggardly*

LEAR   My wits begin to turn.
        [*To* FOOL] Come on, my boy. How dost, my boy? Art cold?
        I am cold myself.—Where is this straw, my fellow?
        The art° of our necessities is strange,   *skill; alchemy*
70   And can make vile things precious. Come, your hovel.—
        Poor fool and knave, I have one part in my heart
        That's sorry yet for thee.

FOOL [*Sings*][9]   He that has and° a little tiny wit,°   *even / sense*
                With heigh-ho, the wind and the rain,
75   Must make content with his fortunes fit,
                Though the rain it raineth every day.

LEAR   True, boy. [*To* KENT] Come, bring us to this hovel.

                        Exeunt [LEAR *and* KENT]

---

7. The supposedly wise King is symbolized by royal
grace, the Fool by his codpiece (here, slang for "penis").
The Fool speaks ironically: the King, as he has pointed
out, is now the foolish one. *Marry*: By the Virgin Mary
(a mild oath).

8. *and cry . . . grace:* and pray for mercy from these elements that bring you to justice.
9. The following song is an adaptation of one sung by
Feste at the end of *Twelfth Night.*

Scene 10

Enter GLOUCESTER *and the Bastard* [EDMUND], *with lights*

GLOUCESTER   Alack, alack, Edmund, I like not this
Unnatural dealing. When I desired their leave
That I might pity° him, they took from me   *relieve*
The use of mine own house, charged me on pain
5   Of their displeasure neither to speak of him,
Entreat for him, nor any way sustain him.

EDMUND   Most savage and unnatural!

GLOUCESTER   Go to,° say you nothing. There's a division betwixt   *(an expletive)*
the Dukes, and a worse matter than that. I have received a
10   letter this night—'tis dangerous to be spoken—I have locked
the letter in my closet.° These injuries the King now bears will   *private chamber*
be revenged home.° There's part of a power° already landed.   *to the hilt / an army*
We must incline to¹ the King. I will seek him and privily°   *secretly; privately*
relieve him. Go you and maintain talk with the Duke, that my
15   charity be not of him perceived. If he ask for me, I am ill and
gone to bed. Though I die for't—as no less is threatened me—
the King my old master must be relieved. There is some
strange thing toward.° Edmund, pray you be careful.   *Exit*   *coming*

EDMUND   This courtesy,° forbid° thee, shall the Duke   *act of kindness / forbidden*
20   Instantly know, and of that letter too.
This seems a fair deserving,² and must draw me
That which my father loses: no less than all.
The younger rises when the old do fall.   *Exit*

Scene 10 Location: At Gloucester's castle.
1. We must take the side of.

2. This seems an action that deserves to be rewarded.

FOOL   This is a brave night to cool a courtesan.[1] I'll speak a
        prophecy ere I go:[2]

80   When priests are more in word than matter;°   *real virtue*
        When brewers mar their malt with water;
        When nobles are their tailors' tutors,[3]
        No heretics burned, but wenches' suitors,[4]
        Then shall the realm of Albion°   *Britain*
85   Come to great confusion.°   *decay*

        When every case in law is right;°   *just*
        No squire in debt nor no poor knight;
        When slanders do not live in tongues,
        Nor cutpurses° come not to throngs;   *pickpockets*
90   When usurers tell their gold i'th' field,[5]
        And bawds and whores do churches build,
        Then comes the time, who lives to see't,
        That going° shall be used° with feet.   *walking / practiced*
        This prophecy Merlin shall make; for I live before his time.[6]

                                                            Exit

3.3

Enter GLOUCESTER *and* EDMOND

GLOUCESTER   Alack, alack, Edmond, I like not this unnatural
    dealing. When I desired their leave that I might pity° him, they   *relieve*
    took from me the use of mine own house, charged me on pain
    of perpetual displeasure neither to speak of him, entreat for
5   him, or any way sustain him.

EDMOND   Most savage and unnatural!

GLOUCESTER   Go to,° say you nothing. There is division between   *(an expletive)*
    the Dukes, and a worse matter than that. I have received a let-
    ter this night—'tis dangerous to be spoken—I have locked
10 the letter in my closet.° These injuries the King now bears will   *private chamber*
    be revenged home.° There is part of a power already footed.[1]   *to the hilt*
    We must incline to[2] the King. I will look° him and privily°   *seek / secretly; privately*
    relieve him. Go you and maintain talk with the Duke, that my
    charity be not of him perceived. If he ask for me, I am ill and
15 gone to bed. If I die for't—as no less is threatened me—the
    King my old master must be relieved. There is strange things
    toward,° Edmond; pray you be careful.   *Exit*   *coming*

EDMOND   This courtesy,° forbid° thee, shall the Duke   *act of kindness / forbidden*
    Instantly know, and of that letter too.
20 This seems a fair deserving,[3] and must draw me
    That which my father loses: no less than all.
    The younger rises when the old doth fall.   *Exit*

---

1. To cool even the hot lusts of a prostitute.
2. What follows is a parody of the pseudo-Chaucerian
"Merlin's Prophecy" from *The Arte of English Poesie*. In
F, lines 84–85 follow line 91.
3. When noblemen follow fashion more closely than
their tailors do.
4. When the only heretics burned are faithless lovers,
who burn from venereal disease.
5. When usurers can count their profits openly (because

they have no shady dealings to hide).
6. Merlin was the great wizard at the legendary court
of King Arthur. Lear's Britain is set in an even more distant past.
3.3 Location: At Gloucester's castle.
1. Part of an army already landed.
2. We must take the side of.
3. This seems an action that deserves to be rewarded.

Scene 11

[*Storm.*] *Enter* LEAR, KENT [*disguised*], *and* FOOL

KENT   Here is the place, my lord. Good my lord, enter.
    The tyranny of the open night's too rough
    For nature° to endure.   *human weakness*
LEAR   Let me alone.
KENT   Good my lord, enter here.
LEAR   Wilt break my heart?
5 KENT   I had rather break mine own. Good my lord, enter.
LEAR   Thou think'st 'tis much that this contentious storm
    Invades us to the skin. So 'tis to thee;
    But where the greater malady is fixed,°   *rooted*
    The lesser is scarce felt. Thou'dst shun a bear,
10   But if thy flight lay toward the roaring sea
    Thou'dst meet the bear i'th' mouth. When the mind's free,°   *unburdened*
    The body's delicate.° This tempest in my mind   *sensitive*
    Doth from my senses take all feeling else
    Save° what beats there: filial ingratitude.   *Except*
15   Is it not as° this mouth should tear this hand   *as if*
    For lifting food to't? But I will punish sure.
    No, I will weep no more.—
    In such a night as this! O Regan, Gonoril,
    Your old kind father, whose frank heart gave you all—
20   O, that way madness lies. Let me shun that.
    No more of that.
KENT   Good my lord, enter.
LEAR   Prithee, go in thyself. Seek thy own ease.
    This tempest will not give me leave to° ponder   *allow me to*
    On things would hurt me more; but I'll go in.   [*Exit* FOOL]
25   Poor naked wretches, wheresoe'er you are,
    That bide° the pelting of this pitiless night,   *endure; dwell in*
    How shall your houseless heads and unfed sides,°   *starved ribs*
    Your looped and windowed[1] raggedness, defend you
    From seasons such as these? O, I have ta'en
30   Too little care of this. Take physic, pomp,[2]
    Expose thyself to feel what wretches feel,
    That thou mayst shake the superflux[3] to them
    And show the heavens more just.
               [*Enter* FOOL]
FOOL   Come not in here, nuncle; here's a spirit. Help me, help
35 me!
KENT   Give me thy hand. Who's there?
FOOL   A spirit. He says his name's Poor Tom.
KENT   What art thou that dost grumble there in the straw?
    Come forth.

Scene 11 Location: Open country, before a cattle shed.
1. *looped and windowed*: full of holes and vents; "windowed" could also refer to cloth worn through to semi-
transparency, like the oilcloth window "panes" of the
poor.

2. Cure yourself, pompous person.
3. Superfluity; bodily discharge, suggested by "physic"
(which also has the meaning of "purgative") in line 30.
Excess here is also excess of wealth.

3.4

Enter LEAR, KENT [*disguised*], *and* FOOL

KENT   Here is the place, my lord. Good my lord, enter.
The tyranny of the open night's too rough
For nature° to endure.   *human weakness*

Storm still

LEAR   Let me alone.

KENT   Good my lord, enter here.

LEAR   Wilt break my heart?

5   KENT   I had rather break mine own. Good my lord, enter.

LEAR   Thou think'st 'tis much that this contentious storm
Invades us to the skin. So 'tis to thee;
But where the greater malady is fixed,°   *rooted*
The lesser is scarce felt. Thou'dst shun a bear,
10 But if thy flight lay toward the roaring sea
Thou'dst meet the bear i'th' mouth. When the mind's free,°   *unburdened*
The body's delicate.° This tempest in my mind   *sensitive*
Doth from my senses take all feeling else
Save° what beats there: filial ingratitude.   *Except*
15 Is it not as° this mouth should tear this hand   *as if*
For lifting food to't? But I will punish home.°   *thoroughly*
No, I will weep no more.—In such a night
To shut me out? Pour on, I will endure.
In such a night as this! O Regan, Goneril,
20 Your old kind father, whose frank heart gave all—
O, that way madness lies. Let me shun that.
No more of that.

KENT   Good my lord, enter here.

LEAR   Prithee, go in thyself. Seek thine own ease.
This tempest will not give me leave to° ponder   *allow me to*
25 On things would hurt me more; but I'll go in.
[*To* FOOL] In, boy; go first. [*Kneeling*] You houseless poverty°—   *poor*
Nay, get thee in. I'll pray, and then I'll sleep.   *Exit* [FOOL]
Poor naked wretches, wheresoe'er you are,
That bide° the pelting of this pitiless storm,   *endure; dwell in*
30 How shall your houseless heads and unfed sides,°   *starved ribs*
Your looped and windowed[1] raggedness, defend you
From seasons such as these? O, I have ta'en
Too little care of this. Take physic, pomp,[2]
Expose thyself to feel what wretches feel,
35 That thou mayst shake the superflux[3] to them
And show the heavens more just.

Enter FOOL, *and* EDGAR [*as a Bedlam beggar in the hovel*]

EDGAR   Fathom and half![4] Fathom and half! Poor Tom!

FOOL   Come not in here, nuncle. Here's a spirit. Help me, help me!

40 KENT   Give me thy hand. Who's there?

FOOL   A spirit, a spirit. He says his name's Poor Tom.

KENT   What art thou that dost grumble there i'th' straw?
Come forth.

3.4 Location: Open country, before a cattle shed.
1. *looped and windowed*: full of holes and vents; "windowed" could also refer to cloth worn through to semitransparency, like the oilcloth window "panes" of the poor.
2. Cure yourself, pompous person.

3. Superfluity; bodily discharge, suggested by "physic" (which also has the meaning of "purgative") in line 33. Excess here is also excess of wealth.
4. "Nine feet," a sailor's cry when taking soundings to gauge the depth of water.

[Enter EDGAR *as a bedlam beggar]*

40 EDGAR   Away, the foul fiend follows me. Through the sharp
hawthorn blows the cold wind.[4] Go to thy cold bed and warm
thee.[5]

LEAR   Hast thou given all to thy two daughters,
And art thou come to this?

45 EDGAR   Who gives anything to Poor Tom, whom the foul fiend
hath led through fire and through ford and whirlypool, o'er bog
and quagmire; that has laid knives under his pillow and halters
in his pew, set ratsbane by his potage,[6] made him proud of
heart to ride on a bay trotting-horse over four-inched bridges,[7]
50 to course° his own shadow for° a traitor. Bless thy five wits,[8]   hunt / as
Tom's a-cold! Bless thee from whirlwinds, star-blasting, and tak-
ing.[9] Do Poor Tom some charity, whom the foul fiend vexes.
There could I have him, now, and there, and there again.[1]

LEAR   What, has his daughters brought him to this pass?

55 *[To* EDGAR] Couldst thou save nothing? Didst thou give them all?

FOOL   Nay, he reserved a blanket, else we had been all shamed.

LEAR *[to* EDGAR]   Now all the plagues that in the pendulous° air   overhanging; portentous
Hang fated o'er men's faults fall on thy daughters!

KENT   He hath no daughters, sir.

60 LEAR   Death, traitor! Nothing could have subdued nature
To such a lowness but his unkind daughters.
[To EDGAR] Is it the fashion that discarded fathers
Should have thus little mercy on their flesh?
Judicious punishment: 'twas this flesh begot
65 Those pelican[2] daughters.

EDGAR   Pillicock sat on pillicock's hill; a lo, lo, lo.[3]

FOOL   This cold night will turn us all to fools and madmen.

EDGAR   Take heed o'th' foul fiend; obey thy parents; keep thy
word justly; swear not; commit not with man's sworn spouse:
70 set not thy sweet heart on proud array.[4] Tom's a-cold.

LEAR   What hast thou been?

EDGAR   A servingman, proud in heart and mind, that curled my
hair, wore gloves in my cap,[5] served the lust of my mistress'
heart, and did the act of darkness with her; swore as many oaths
75 as I spake words, and broke them in the sweet face of heaven;
one that slept in the contriving of lust, and waked to do it. Wine
loved I deeply, dice dearly, and in woman out-paramoured the
Turk.[6] False of heart, light of ear,° bloody of hand; hog in sloth,   rumor-hungry
fox in stealth, wolf in greediness, dog in madness, lion in prey.
80 Let not the creaking of shoes[7] nor the rustlings of silks betray

4. *Through . . . wind:* Perhaps a fragment from a ballad.
5. *Go . . . thee:* This expression is also used by the drunken beggar Christopher Sly in *The Taming of the Shrew,* Induction 1.
6. *laid knives . . . potage:* these are all means by which the foul fiend tempts Tom to commit suicide. *halters:* nooses. *ratsbane:* rat poison. *potage:* soup.
7. Impossibly narrow, and probably suicidal to attempt without diabolical help.
8. The five wits were common wit, imagination, fantasy, estimation, and memory (from medieval and Renaissance cognitive theory).
9. *whirlwinds, star-blasting:* malign astrological influences capable of causing sickness or death. *taking:* infection; bewitchment.

1. As Edgar speaks this sentence, he might kill vermin on his body as if they were devils.
2. Greedy. Young pelicans were reputed to feed on blood from the wounds they made in their mother's breast; in some versions, they first killed their father.
3. A fragment of an old rhyme, followed by hunting cries or a ballad refrain; "Pillicock" was both a term of endearment and a euphemism for "penis."
4. *obey . . . array:* these are fragments from the Ten Commandments.
5. Favors from his mistress. In Petrarchan poetry, wooers are "servants" to their ladies.
6. And had more women than the sultan had in his royal harem.
7. Creaking shoes were a fashionable affectation.

[EDGAR *comes forth*]

EDGAR   Away, the foul fiend follows me. Thorough the sharp
45   hawthorn blow the winds.[5] Hm! Go to thy cold bed and warm
thee.[6]

LEAR   Didst thou give all to thy two daughters,
And art thou come to this?

EDGAR   Who gives anything to Poor Tom, whom the foul fiend
50   hath led through fire and through flame, through ford and
whirlpool, o'er bog and quagmire; that hath laid knives under
his pillow and halters in his pew, set ratsbane by his porridge,[7]
made him proud of heart to ride on a bay trotting-horse over
four-inched[8] bridges, to course° his own shadow for° a traitor.   *hunt / as*
55   Bless thy five wits,[9] Tom's a-cold! O, do, de, do, de, do de. Bless
thee from whirlwinds, star-blasting, and taking.[1] Do Poor Tom
some charity, whom the foul fiend vexes. There could I have
him now, and there, and there again, and there.[2]

Storm still

LEAR   Has his daughters brought him to this pass?
60   [*To* EDGAR] Couldst thou save nothing? Wouldst thou give 'em all?

FOOL   Nay, he reserved a blanket, else we had been all shamed.

LEAR [*to* EDGAR]   Now all the plagues that in the pendulous° air   *overhanging; portentous*
Hang fated o'er men's faults light on thy daughters!

KENT   He hath no daughters, sir.

65   LEAR   Death, traitor! Nothing could have subdued nature
To such a lowness but his unkind daughters.
[*To* EDGAR] Is it the fashion that discarded fathers
Should have thus little mercy on their flesh?
Judicious punishment: 'twas this flesh begot
70   Those pelican[3] daughters.

EDGAR   Pillicock sat on Pillicock Hill; alow, alow, loo, loo.[4]

FOOL   This cold night will turn us all to fools and madmen.

EDGAR   Take heed o'th' foul fiend; obey thy parents; keep thy
words' justice; swear not; commit not with man's sworn spouse;
75   set not thy sweet heart on proud array.[5] Tom's a-cold.

LEAR   What hast thou been?

EDGAR   A servingman, proud in heart and mind, that curled my
hair, wore gloves[6] in my cap, served the lust of my mistress'
heart, and did the act of darkness with her; swore as many oaths
80   as I spake words, and broke them in the sweet face of heaven;
one that slept in the contriving of lust, and waked to do it. Wine
loved I deeply, dice dearly, and in woman out-paramoured the
Turk.[7] False of heart, light of ear,° bloody of hand; hog in sloth,   *rumor-hungry*
fox in stealth, wolf in greediness, dog in madness, lion in prey.
85   Let not the creaking of shoes[8] nor the rustling of silks betray

5. *Thorough . . . winds:* Perhaps a fragment from a ballad.
6. *Go . . . thee:* This expression is also used by the
drunken beggar Christopher Sly in *The Taming of the
Shrew*, Induction 1.
7. *laid knives . . . porridge:* these are all means by
which the foul fiend tempts Tom to commit suicide.
halters: nooses. *ratsbane:* rat poison.
8. Impossibly narrow, and probably suicidal to attempt
without diabolical help.
9. The five wits were common wit, imagination, fantasy, estimation, and memory (from medieval and Renaissance cognitive theory).
1. *whirlwinds, star-blasting:* malign astrological influences capable of causing sickness or death. *taking:*
infection; bewitchment.

2. As Edgar speaks this sentence, he might kill vermin
on his body as if they were devils.
3. Greedy. Young pelicans were reputed to feed on
blood from the wounds they made in their mother's
breast; in some versions, they first killed their father.
4. A fragment of an old rhyme, followed by hunting
cries or a ballad refrain; "Pillicock" was both a term of
endearment and a euphemism for "penis."
5. *obey . . . array:* these are fragments from the Ten
Commandments.
6. Favors from his mistress. In Petrarchan poetry, wooers are "servants" to their ladies.
7. And had more women than the sultan had in his
royal harem.
8. Creaking shoes were a fashionable affectation

thy poor heart to women. Keep thy foot[8] out of brothel, thy
hand out of placket,[9] thy pen from lender's book, and defy
the foul fiend. Still through the hawthorn blows the cold
wind. Heigh no nonny. Dolphin, my boy, my boy! Cease, let
85 him trot by.[1]

LEAR Why, thou wert better in thy grave than to answer° with   *encounter*
thy uncovered body this extremity of the skies.° Is man no more   *violent weather*
but this? Consider him well. Thou owest the worm no silk, the
beast no hide, the sheep no wool, the cat[2] no perfume. Here's
90 three on 's° are sophisticated; thou art the thing itself. Unac-   *of us*
commodated[3] man is no more but such a poor, bare, forked°   *two-legged*
animal as thou art. Off, off, you lendings!° Come on, be true.   *borrowed clothes*

FOOL Prithee, nuncle, be content. This is a naughty° night to   *foul*
swim in. Now a little fire in a wild° field were like an old lech-   *barren; lustful*
95 er's heart—a small spark, all the rest on 's° body cold. Look,   *of his*
here comes a walking fire.

        Enter GLOUCESTER [*with a torch*]

EDGAR This is the foul fiend Flibbertigibbet.[4] He begins at cur-
few° and walks till the first cock.° He gives the web and the   *9:00 P.M. / midnight*
pin,[5] squinies° the eye, and makes the harelip; mildews the   *causes squints in*
100 white° wheat, and hurts the poor creature of earth.   *near-ripe*
[*Sings*] Swithin footed thrice the wold,[6]
         A met the night mare and her nine foal;[7]
             Bid her alight
             And her troth plight,°   *And gave her word*
105   And aroint thee,° witch, aroint thee!   *begone*

KENT [*to* LEAR] How fares your grace?

LEAR   What's° he?   *Who's*

KENT [*to* GLOUCESTER] Who's there? What is't you seek?

GLOUCESTER What are you there? Your names?

EDGAR Poor Tom, that eats the swimming frog, the toad, the
110 tadpole, the wall-newt and the water;° that in the fury of his   *water newt*
heart, when the foul fiend rages, eats cowdung for salads,° swal-   *savories*
lows the old rat and the ditch-dog,[8] drinks the green mantle° of   *scum*
the standing pool; who is whipped from tithing° to tithing, and   *parish*
stock-punished,° and imprisoned; who hath had three suits to   *put in stocks*
115 his back, six shirts to his body,
             Horse to ride, and weapon to wear.
             But mice and rats and such small deer[9]
             Hath been Tom's food for seven long year—
         Beware my follower. Peace, Smolking;° peace, thou fiend!   *a Harsnett devil*
120 GLOUCESTER [*to* LEAR] What, hath your grace no better company?
EDGAR The Prince of Darkness is a gentleman;
         Modo he's called, and Mahu[1]—

---

8. Punning on the French *foutre* ("fuck").
9. Slits in skirts or petticoats.
1. These phrases are probably snatches from songs
and proverbs. "Dolphin" is an imagined animal or devil
or the heir to the French throne ("dauphin," which
Shakespeare usually Anglicizes), or all three.
2. Civet cat, in Shakespeare's time the major source of
musk for perfume.
3. Naked; without the trappings of civilization.
4. A devil drawn from folk beliefs but famous for his
prominent place in Samuel Harsnett's *Declaration
of Egregious Popish Impostures* (1603); the frequent
borrowings from Harsnett in *King Lear* set the earliest

possible composition date for the play.
5. *web and the pin*: cataract.
6. Swithin, an early English saint famous for healing,
traversed the hilly countryside three times.
7. *night mare*: a demon that is not necessarily in the
shape of a horse; "foal" can also signify the folds, or
coils, of a snake. A: He.
8. A dog found dead in a ditch.
9. *deer*: animals. These verses are adapted from a
romance popular in Shakespeare's time, *Bevis of Hampton*.
1. Modo and Mahu, more Harsnett devils, were commanding generals of the hellish troops.

thy poor heart to woman. Keep thy foot[9] out of brothels, thy
hand out of plackets,[1] thy pen from lenders' books, and defy
the foul fiend. Still through the hawthorn blows the cold wind,
says suum, mun, nonny. Dauphin, my boy! Boy, *cessez*;° let   *stop*
90   him trot by.[2]

    Storm still

LEAR   Thou wert better in a grave than to answer° with thy uncov-   *encounter*
ered body this extremity of the skies.° Is man no more than this?   *violent weather*
Consider him well. Thou owest the worm no silk, the beast
no hide, the sheep no wool, the cat[3] no perfume. Ha, here's
95   three on 's° are sophisticated; thou art the thing itself. Unac-   *of us*
commodated[4] man is no more but such a poor, bare, forked°   *two-legged*
animal as thou art. Off, off, you lendings!° Come, unbutton   *borrowed clothes*
here.

    Enter GLOUCESTER *with a torch*

FOOL   Prithee, nuncle, be contented. 'Tis a naughty° night to   *foul*
100   swim in. Now a little fire in a wild° field were like an old lech-   *barren; lustful*
er's heart—a small spark, all the rest on 's° body cold. Look,   *of his*
here comes a walking fire.

EDGAR   This is the foul fiend Flibbertigibbet.[5] He begins at cur-
few° and walks till the first cock.° He gives the web and the   *9:00 P.M. / midnight*
105   pin,[6] squints the eye, and makes the harelip; mildews the
white° wheat, and hurts the poor creature of earth.   *near-ripe*
[*Sings*]   Swithin footed thrice the wold,[7]
     A met the night mare and her nine foal,[8]
       Bid her alight
110   And her troth plight,°   *And gave her word*
     And aroint thee,° witch, aroint thee!   *begone*

KENT [*to* LEAR]   How fares your grace?

LEAR   What's° he?   *Who's*

KENT [*to* GLOUCESTER]   Who's there? What is't you seek?

GLOUCESTER   What are you there? Your names?

115   EDGAR   Poor Tom, that eats the swimming frog, the toad, the
tadpole, the wall-newt and the water;° that in the fury of his   *water newt*
heart, when the foul fiend rages, eats cowdung for salads,° swal-   *savories*
lows the old rat and the ditch-dog,[9] drinks the green mantle° of   *scum*
the standing pool; who is whipped from tithing° to tithing, and   *parish*
120   stocked,° punished, and imprisoned; who hath had three suits   *put in stocks*
to his back, six shirts to his body,
       Horse to ride, and weapon to wear;
       But mice and rats and such small deer[1]
       Have been Tom's food for seven long year.
125   Beware my follower. Peace, Smulkin;° peace, thou fiend!   *a Harsnett devil*

GLOUCESTER [*to* LEAR]   What, hath your grace no better company?

EDGAR   The Prince of Darkness is a gentleman.
Modo he's called, and Mahu.[2]

---

9. Punning on the French *foutre* ("fuck").
1. Slits in skirts or petticoats.
2. These phrases are probably snatches from songs
and proverbs. *Dauphin*: the heir to the French throne,
sometimes identified with the devil by the English.
3. Civet cat, in Shakespeare's time the major source of
musk for perfume.
4. Naked; without the trappings of civilization.
5. A devil drawn from folk beliefs but famous for his
prominent place in Samuel Harsnett's *Declaration of
Egregious Popish Impostures* (1603); the frequent borrowings from Harsnett in *King Lear* set the earliest
possible composition date for the play.

6. *web and the pin*: cataract.
7. Swithin, an early English saint famous for healing,
traversed the hilly countryside three times.
8. *night mare*: a demon that is not necessarily in the
shape of a horse; "foal" can also signify the folds, or
coils, of a snake. *A*: He.
9. A dog found dead in a ditch.
1. *deer*: animals. These verses are adapted from a
romance popular in Shakespeare's time, *Bevis of Hampton*.
2. Modo and Mahu, more Harsnett devils, were commanding generals of the hellish troops.

GLOUCESTER [*to* LEAR]   Our flesh and blood is grown so vile, my lord,
    That it doth hate what gets° it.   *begets*
EDGAR   Poor Tom's a-cold.
125 GLOUCESTER [*to* LEAR]   Go in with me. My duty cannot suffer°   *permit me*
    To obey in all your daughters' hard commands.
    Though their injunction be to bar my doors
    And let this tyrannous night take hold upon you,
    Yet have I ventured to come seek you out
130 And bring you where both food and fire is ready.
LEAR   First let me talk with this philosopher.
    [*To* EDGAR] What is the cause of thunder?
KENT   My good lord,
    Take his offer; go into the house.
LEAR   I'll talk a word with this most learnèd Theban.°   *Greek sage*
135 [*To* EDGAR] What is your study?°   *field of expertise*
EDGAR   How to prevent the fiend, and to kill vermin.
LEAR   Let me ask you one word in private.
            [*They converse apart*]
KENT [*to* GLOUCESTER]   Importune him to go, my lord.
    His wits begin to unsettle.
GLOUCESTER   Canst thou blame him?
140 His daughters seek his death. O, that good Kent,
    He said it would be thus, poor banished man!
    Thou sayst the King grows mad; I'll tell thee, friend,
    I am almost mad myself. I had a son,
    Now outlawed° from my blood; a° sought my life   *disowned / he*
145 But lately, very late.° I loved him, friend;   *recently*
    No father his son dearer. True to tell thee,
    The grief hath crazed my wits. What a night's this!
    [*To* LEAR] I do beseech your grace—
LEAR   O, cry you mercy.°   *beg your pardon*
    [*To* EDGAR] Noble philosopher, your company.
EDGAR   Tom's a-cold.
150 GLOUCESTER   In, fellow, there in t'hovel; keep thee warm.
LEAR   Come, let's in all.
KENT   This way, my lord.
LEAR   With him!
    I will keep still with my philosopher.
KENT [*to* GLOUCESTER]   Good my lord, soothe° him; let him take   *humor*
    the fellow.
155 GLOUCESTER   Take him you on.°   *on ahead*
KENT [*to* EDGAR]   Sirrah, come on. Go along with us.
LEAR [*to* EDGAR]   Come, good Athenian.°   *Greek philosopher*
GLOUCESTER   No words, no words. Hush.
EDGAR   Child Roland² to the dark tower come,
        His word° was still 'Fie, fo, and fum;   *motto / always*
160   I smell the blood of a British³ man.'
                        [*Exeunt*]

---

2. *Child:* an aspirant to knighthood. Roland is the
famous hero of the Charlemagne legends.
3. "An Englishman" usually appears in this rhyme from

the cycle of tales of which "Jack and the Beanstalk" is
the best known. The alteration befits Lear's ancient
Britain.

GLOUCESTER [*to* LEAR]   Our flesh and blood, my lord, is grown so vile

    That it doth hate what gets° it.   *begets*

130   EDGAR   Poor Tom's a-cold.

GLOUCESTER [*to* LEAR]   Go in with me. My duty cannot suffer°   *permit me*

    T'obey in all your daughters' hard commands.

    Though their injunction be to bar my doors

    And let this tyrannous night take hold upon you,

135   Yet have I ventured to come seek you out

    And bring you where both fire and food is ready.

LEAR   First let me talk with this philosopher.

    [*To* EDGAR] What is the cause of thunder?

KENT   Good my lord, take his offer; go into th' house.

140   LEAR   I'll talk a word with this same learnèd Theban.°   *Greek sage*

    [*To* EDGAR] What is your study?°   *field of expertise*

EDGAR   How to prevent the fiend, and to kill vermin.

LEAR   Let me ask you one word in private.

    [*They converse apart*]

KENT [*to* GLOUCESTER]   Importune him once more to go, my lord.

    His wits begin t'unsettle.

145   GLOUCESTER   Canst thou blame him?

    Storm still

    His daughters seek his death. Ah, that good Kent,

    He said it would be thus, poor banished man!

    Thou sayst the King grows mad; I'll tell thee, friend,

    I am almost mad myself. I had a son,

150   Now outlawed° from my blood; a° sought my life   *disowned / he*

    But lately, very late.° I loved him, friend;   *recently*

    No father his son dearer. True to tell thee,

    The grief hath crazed my wits. What a night's this!

    [*To* LEAR] I do beseech your grace—

LEAR   O, cry you mercy,° sir!   *beg your pardon*

    [*To* EDGAR] Noble philosopher, your company.

155   EDGAR   Tom's a-cold.

GLOUCESTER   In, fellow, there in t'hovel; keep thee warm.

LEAR   Come, let's in all.

KENT   This way, my lord.

LEAR   With him!

    I will keep still with my philosopher.

KENT [*to* GLOUCESTER]   Good my lord, soothe° him; let him take   *humor*

    the fellow.

160   GLOUCESTER   Take him you on.°   *on ahead*

KENT [*to* EDGAR]   Sirrah, come on. Go along with us.

LEAR [*to* EDGAR]   Come, good Athenian.°   *Greek philosopher*

GLOUCESTER   No words, no words. Hush.

EDGAR   Child Roland³ to the dark tower came,

    His word° was still° 'Fie, fo, and fum;   *motto / always*

165   I smell the blood of a British⁴ man.'   *Exeunt*

---

3. *Child*: an aspirant to knighthood. Roland is the famous hero of the Charlemagne legends.

4. "An Englishman" usually appears in this rhyme from the cycle of tales of which "Jack and the Beanstalk" is the best known. The alteration befits Lear's ancient Britain.

Scene 12

Enter CORNWALL *and Bastard* [EDMUND]

CORNWALL　I will have my revenge ere I depart the house.

EDMUND　How, my lord, I may be censured,° that nature° thus　　*judged / kinship*
gives way to loyalty, something fears me° to think of.　　*I am somewhat afraid*

CORNWALL　I now perceive it was not altogether your brother's
5　evil disposition made him seek his° death, but a provoking　　*(Gloucester's)*
merit set a-work by a reprovable badness in himself.[1]

EDMUND　How malicious is my fortune, that I must repent to be
just! This is the letter he spoke of, which approves him an
intelligent party to the advantages of France.[2] O heavens, that
10　his treason were not, or not I the detector!

CORNWALL　Go with me to the Duchess.

EDMUND　If the matter of this paper be certain, you have mighty
business in hand.

CORNWALL　True or false, it hath made thee Earl of Gloucester.
15　Seek out where thy father is, that he may be ready for our
apprehension.°　　*arrest*

EDMUND [*aside*]　If I find him comforting the King, it will stuff
his° suspicion more fully.　[*To* CORNWALL] I will persever in my　　*(Cornwall's)*
course of loyalty, though the conflict be sore between that and
20　my blood.°　　*filial duty*

CORNWALL　I will lay trust upon thee, and thou shalt find a
dearer father in my love.　　*Exeunt*

Scene 13

Enter GLOUCESTER *and* LEAR, KENT [*disguised*], FOOL,
and EDGAR [*as a Bedlam beggar*]

GLOUCESTER　Here is better than the open air; take it thankfully.
I will piece out° the comfort with what addition I can. I will　　*augment*
not be long from you.

KENT　All the power of his wits have given way to impatience;[1]
5　the gods° discern your kindness!　　[*Exit* GLOUCESTER]　　*may the gods*

EDGAR　Fraretto° calls me, and tells me Nero is an angler in　　*a Harsnett devil*
the lake of darkness.[2] Pray, innocent; beware the foul fiend.

FOOL [*to* LEAR]　Prithee, nuncle, tell me whether a madman be
a gentleman or a yeoman.[3]

10　LEAR　A king, a king! To have a thousand
With red burning spits come hissing in upon them!

EDGAR　The foul fiend bites my back.

FOOL [*to* LEAR]　He's mad that trusts in the tameness of a wolf, a
horse's health, a boy's love, or a whore's oath.

15　LEAR　It shall be done. I will arraign° them straight.°　　*prosecute / immediately*
[*To* EDGAR] Come, sit thou here, most learnèd justicer.
[*To* FOOL] Thou sapient sir, sit here.—No, you she-foxes—

EDGAR　Look where he stands and glares. Want'st thou eyes at
troll-madam?[4]

Scene 12　Location: At Gloucester's castle.
1. *a provoking . . . himself*: Gloucester's own wickedness
deservedly triggered the blameworthy evil in Edgar.
2. *which . . . France*: which proves him a spy and
informer to him in the aid of France; "party," or faction, was
usually a term of opprobrium in the Renaissance.
Scene 13　Location: Within an outbuilding of Gloucester's.
1. Rage; inability to bear more suffering.

2. In Chaucer's *Monk's Tale*, the infamously cruel
Roman Emperor Nero is found fishing in hell (lines
485–86).
3. A free landowner but not a member of the gentry,
lacking official family arms and the distinctions they
confer. Shakespeare seems to have procured a coat of
arms for his father in 1596.
4. *troll*: a board game using small balls. *eyes*: eyeballs (?).
to troll: to fish; to sing.

3.5

Enter CORNWALL *and* EDMOND

CORNWALL   I will have my revenge ere I depart his house.

EDMOND   How, my lord, I may be censured,° that nature° thus   *judged / kinship*
gives way to loyalty, something fears me° to think of.   *I am somewhat afraid*

CORNWALL   I now perceive it was not altogether your brother's
5   evil disposition made him seek his° death, but a provoking   *(Gloucester's)*
merit set a-work by a reprovable badness in himself.[1]

EDMOND   How malicious is my fortune, that I must repent to be
just! This is the letter which he spoke of, which approves him
an intelligent party to the advantages of France.[2] O heavens,
10   that this treason were not, or not I the detector!

CORNWALL   Go with me to the Duchess.

EDMOND   If the matter of this paper be certain, you have mighty
business in hand.

CORNWALL   True or false, it hath made thee Earl of Gloucester.
15   Seek out where thy father is, that he may be ready for our
apprehension.°   *arrest*

EDMOND [*aside*]   If I find him comforting the King, it will stuff
his° suspicion more fully. [*To* CORNWALL] I will persever in my   *(Cornwall's)*
course of loyalty, though the conflict be sore between that and
20   my blood.°   *filial duty*

CORNWALL   I will lay trust upon thee, and thou shalt find a
dearer father in my love.   *Exeunt*

3.6

Enter KENT [*disguised*], *and* GLOUCESTER

GLOUCESTER   Here is better than the open air; take it thankfully.
I will piece out° the comfort with what addition I can. I will   *augment*
not be long from you.

KENT   All the power of his wits have given way to his impa-
5   tience;[1] the gods° reward your kindness!   Exit GLOUCESTER   *may the gods*
Enter LEAR, EDGAR [*as a Bedlam beggar*], *and* FOOL

EDGAR   Frateretto° calls me, and tells me Nero is an angler in the   *a Harsnett devil*
lake of darkness.[2] Pray, innocent, and beware the foul fiend.

FOOL   Prithee, nuncle, tell me whether a madman be a gentleman or a yeoman.[3]

10   LEAR   A king, a king!

FOOL   No, he's a yeoman that has a gentleman to° his son; for   *for*
he's a mad yeoman that sees his son a gentleman before him.

LEAR   To have a thousand with red burning spits
Come hissing in upon 'em!

3.5 Location: At Gloucester's castle.
1. *a provoking . . . himself*: Gloucester's own wickedness deservedly triggered the blameworthy evil in Edgar.
2. *which . . . France*: which proves him a spy and informer in the aid of France; "party," or faction, was usually a term of opprobrium in the Renaissance.
3.6 Location: Within an outbuilding of Gloucester's.
1. Rage; inability to bear more suffering.

2. In Chaucer's *Monk's Tale,* the infamously cruel Roman Emperor Nero is found fishing in hell (lines 485–86).
3. A free landowner but not a member of the gentry, lacking official family arms and the distinctions they confer. Shakespeare seems to have procured a coat of arms for his father in 1596.

20   [*Sings*]   Come o'er the burn, Bessy, to me.⁵

FOOL [*sings*]   Her boat hath a leak,⁶
          And she must not speak
          Why she dares not come over to thee.

EDGAR   The foul fiend haunts Poor Tom in the voice of a night-
25 ingale. Hoppedance° cries in Tom's belly for two white° her-   *a demon / fresh*
ring. Croak° not, black angel: I have no food for thee.   *Growl*

KENT [*to* LEAR]   How do you, sir? Stand you not so amazed.
Will you lie down and rest upon the cushions?

LEAR   I'll see their trial first. Bring in the evidence.
30   [*To* EDGAR] Thou robèd man of justice, take thy place;
    [*to* FOOL] And thou, his yokefellow of equity,°   *partner of law*
    Bench° by his side. [*To* KENT] You are o'th' commission,°   *Sit / judiciary*
    Sit you, too.

EDGAR   Let us deal justly.
35   [*Sings*]   Sleepest or wakest thou, jolly shepherd?
          Thy sheep be in the corn,°   *grain*
          And for one blast of thy minikin° mouth   *dainty*
          Thy sheep shall take no harm.
    Purr, the cat⁷ is grey.
40 LEAR   Arraign her first. 'Tis Gonoril. I here take my oath before
this honourable assembly she kicked the poor King her father.

FOOL   Come hither, mistress. Is your name Gonoril?

LEAR   She cannot deny it.

FOOL   Cry you mercy, I took you for a join-stool.⁸

45 LEAR   And here's another, whose warped looks proclaim
What store° her heart is made on.° Stop her there.   *material / of*
Arms, arms, sword, fire, corruption in the place!
False justicer, why hast thou let her scape?

EDGAR   Bless thy five wits.

50 KENT [*to* LEAR]   O pity! Sir, where is the patience now
That you so oft have boasted to retain?

EDGAR [*aside*]   My tears begin to take his part so much
They'll mar my counterfeiting.

LEAR   The little dogs and all,°   *Even the little dogs*
Tray, Blanch, and Sweetheart—see, they bark at me.

55 EDGAR   Tom will throw his head at° them.—Avaunt,° you curs!   *will threaten? / Begone*
        Be thy mouth or° black or white,   *either*
        Tooth that poisons° if it bite,   *gives rabies*
        Mastiff, greyhound, mongrel grim,
        Hound or spaniel, brach° or him,   *bitch*
60   Bobtail tyke or trundle-tail,⁹
        Tom will make them weep and wail;
        For with throwing thus my head,
        Dogs leap the hatch,¹ and all are fled.
    Loudla, doodla! Come, march to wakes° and fairs   *parish festivals*
65 And market towns. Poor Tom, thy horn is dry.²

---

5. From an old song. *burn:* a small stream.
6. She has venereal disease; punning on "boat" as body and "burn" as genital discomfort.
7. Purr the cat is another devil; such devils in the shape of cats were the familiars of witches.
8. I beg your pardon, I mistook you for a stool. An idiom of the day expressing annoyance at being

slighted. Here the part of Gonoril is actually being played by a stool.
9. Short-tailed mongrel or long-tailed.
1. Dogs leap over the lower half of a divided door.
2. A begging formula that refers to the horn vessel that vagabonds carried for drink; the covert sense is that Edgar has run out of Bedlamite inspiration.

EDGAR   **Bless thy five wits.**

15   KENT [*to* LEAR]   O, pity! Sir, where is the patience now
      That you so oft have boasted to retain?

EDGAR [*aside*]   My tears begin to take his part so much
      They mar my counterfeiting.

LEAR   The little dogs and all,°   *Even the little dogs*
      Tray, Blanch, and Sweetheart—see, they bark at me.

20   EDGAR   Tom will throw his head at° them.—Avaunt,° you curs!   *will threaten? / Begone*
      Be thy mouth or° black or white,   *either*
      Tooth that poisons° if it bite,   *gives rabies*
      Mastiff, greyhound, mongrel grim,
      Hound or spaniel, brach° or him,   *bitch*
25   Bobtail tyke or trundle-tail,[4]
      Tom will make him weep and wail;
      For with throwing thus my head,
      Dogs leapt the hatch,[5] and all are fled.
      Do, de, de, de. Sese![6] Come, march to wakes° and fairs   *parish festivals*
30   And market towns. Poor Tom, thy horn is dry.[7]

---

4. Short-tailed mongrel or long-tailed.
5. Dogs leaped over the lower half of a divided door.
6. Apparently nonsense, although "Sese" may be a version of the French *cessez* ("stop" or "hush").

7. A begging formula that refers to the horn vessel that vagabonds carried for drink; the covert sense is that Edgar has run out of Bedlamite inspiration.

LEAR   Then let them anatomize° Regan; see what breeds about   dissect
    her heart. Is there any cause in nature that makes this hardness?
    [*To* EDGAR] You, sir, I entertain° you for one of my hundred,   retain
    only I do not like the fashion of your garments. You'll say they
70   are Persian° attire; but let them be changed.   oriental; splendid
KENT   Now, good my lord, lie here a while.
LEAR   Make no noise, make no noise. Draw the curtains.° So, so,   bed curtains
    so. We'll go to supper i'th' morning. So, so, so.
         [*He sleeps.*] *Enter* GLOUCESTER
GLOUCESTER [*to* KENT]   Come hither, friend. Where is the King
75   my master?
KENT   Here, sir, but trouble him not; his wits are gone.
GLOUCESTER   Good friend, I prithee take him in thy arms.
    I have o'erheard a plot of death upon° him.   against
    There is a litter ready. Lay him in't
80   And drive towards Dover, friend, where thou shalt meet
    Both welcome and protection. Take up thy master.
    If thou shouldst dally half an hour, his life,
    With thine and all that offer to defend him,
    Stand in assurèd loss.° Take up, take up,   Are certainly doomed
85   And follow me, that will to some provision
    Give thee quick conduct.[3]
KENT [*to* LEAR]   Oppressèd nature sleeps.
    This rest might yet have balmed° thy broken sinews°   soothed / nerves
    Which, if convenience° will not allow,   circumstances
    Stand in hard cure.° [*To* FOOL] Come, help to bear thy   Will be hard to cure
    master.
    Thou must not stay behind.
90 GLOUCESTER   Come, come away.
                   Exeunt [*all but* EDGAR]
EDGAR   When we our betters see bearing our° woes,   our same
    We scarcely think our miseries our foes.
    Who alone suffers, suffers most i'th' mind,
    Leaving free° things and happy shows° behind.   carefree / scenes
95   But then the mind much sufferance doth o'erskip
    When grief hath mates, and bearing° fellowship.   pain; suffering
    How light and portable my pain seems now,
    When that which makes me bend, makes the King bow.
    He° childed as I fathered. Tom, away.   He is
100   Mark the high noises,° and thyself bewray°   important rumors / reveal
    When false opinion, whose wrong thoughts defile thee,
    In thy just proof repeals and reconciles thee.[4]
    What° will hap° more tonight, safe scape the King!   Whatever / chance
    Lurk, lurk.   [*Exit*]

---

3. *that . . . conduct:* who will quickly guide you to some
supplies.

4. *In . . . thee:* When true evidence pardons you and
reconciles you (with your father).

LEAR   Then let them anatomize° Regan; see what breeds about   dissect
    her heart. Is there any cause in nature that makes these hard-
    hearts? [*To* EDGAR] You, sir, I entertain° for one of my hundred,   retain
    only I do not like the fashion of your garments. You will say
35   they are Persian;° but let them be changed.   oriental; splendid
KENT   Now, good my lord, lie here and rest a while.
LEAR   Make no noise, make no noise. Draw the curtains.° So, so.   bed curtains
    We'll go to supper i'th' morning.
        [*He sleeps*]
FOOL   And I'll go to bed at noon.
        Enter GLOUCESTER
GLOUCESTER [*to* KENT]   Come hither, friend. Where is the King
40   my master?
KENT   Here, sir, but trouble him not; his wits are gone.
GLOUCESTER   Good friend, I prithee take him in thy arms.
    I have o'erheard a plot of death upon° him.   against
    There is a litter ready. Lay him in't
45   And drive toward Dover, friend, where thou shalt meet
    Both welcome and protection. Take up thy master.
    If thou shouldst dally half an hour, his life,
    With thine and all that offer to defend him,
    Stand in assurèd loss.° Take up, take up,   *Are certainly doomed*
50   And follow me, that will to some provision
    Give thee quick conduct.[8] Come, come away.
        Exeunt [KENT *carrying* LEAR *in his arms*]

8. *that . . . conduct:* who will quickly guide you to some supplies.

Scene 14

Enter CORNWALL *and* REGAN, *and* GONORIL *and Bastard*
[EDMUND, *and* SERVANTS]

CORNWALL [*to* GONORIL]   Post° speedily to my lord your husband.   Ride
Show him this letter. The army of France is landed.
[*To* SERVANTS] Seek out the villain Gloucester. [*Exeunt some*]

REGAN   Hang him instantly.

GONORIL   Pluck out his eyes.

CORNWALL   Leave him to my displeasure.—

5   Edmund, keep you our sister° company. The revenges we are   *sister-in-law*
bound[1] to take upon your traitorous father are not fit for your
beholding. Advise the Duke where you are going, to a most
festinate preparation;[2] we are bound° to the like. Our posts°   *committed / messengers*
shall be swift, and intelligence° betwixt us.—   *convey information*
10   Farewell, dear sister. Farewell, my lord of Gloucester.

            Enter Steward [OSWALD]
How now, where's the King?

OSWALD   My lord of Gloucester hath conveyed him hence.
Some five- or six-and-thirty of his° knights,   *(Lear's)*
Hot questants° after him, met him at gate,   *searchers*
15   Who, with some other of the lord's° dependants,   *(Gloucester's)*
Are gone with him towards Dover, where they boast
To have well-armèd friends.

CORNWALL   Get horses for your mistress.   [*Exit* OSWALD]

GONORIL   Farewell, sweet lord, and sister.

CORNWALL   Edmund, farewell.

            Exeunt GONORIL *and Bastard* [EDMUND]
20   [*To* SERVANTS]   Go seek the traitor Gloucester.
Pinion him° like a thief; bring him before us.   *Tie his arms*
            [*Exeunt other* SERVANTS]
Though we may not pass° upon his life   *pass sentence*
Without the form° of justice, yet our power   *official proceedings*
Shall do a curtsy[3] to our wrath, which men
25   May blame but not control. Who's there—the traitor?

            Enter GLOUCESTER *brought in by two or three*
REGAN   Ingrateful fox, 'tis he.

CORNWALL [*to* SERVANTS]   Bind fast his corky° arms.   *withered*

GLOUCESTER   What means your graces? Good my friends, consider
You are my guests. Do me no foul play, friends.

CORNWALL [*to* SERVANTS]   Bind him, I say—

REGAN   Hard, hard! O filthy traitor!

30   GLOUCESTER   Unmerciful lady as you are, I am true.

CORNWALL [*to* SERVANTS]   To this chair bind him. [*To* GLOUCES-
TER] Villain, thou shalt find—
            [REGAN *plucks Gloucester's beard*]°   *(an extreme insult)*

GLOUCESTER   By the kind gods, 'tis most ignobly done,
To pluck me by the beard.

REGAN   So white,° and such a traitor!   *white-haired; venerable*

Scene 14 Location: At Gloucester's castle.
1. Bound by duty; expected by destiny.
2. *Advise . . . preparation:* When you reach Albany, tell

the Duke to prepare quickly.
3. Shall allow a courtesy or indulgence; shall bow to.

3.7

Enter CORNWALL, REGAN, GONERIL, *Bastard* [EDMOND], *and* SERVANTS

CORNWALL [*to* GONERIL]   Post° speedily to my lord your husband.   *Ride*
show him this letter. the army of France is landed.
[*To* SERVANTS] Seek out the traitor Gloucester. [*Exeunt some*]

REGAN   Hang him instantly.

GONERIL   Pluck out his eyes.

CORNWALL   Leave him to my displeasure.

5   Edmond, keep you our sister° company.   *sister-in-law*
The revenges we are bound¹ to take upon your traitorous father
are not fit for your beholding. Advise the Duke where you are
going, to a most festinate preparation;² we are bound° to the   *committed*
like. Our posts° shall be swift and intelligent° betwixt us. [*To messengers / well informed*

10   GONERIL] Farewell, dear sister. [*To* EDMOND] Farewell, my lord
of Gloucester.

Enter Steward [OSWALD]

How now, where's the King?

OSWALD   My lord of Gloucester hath conveyed him hence.
Some five or six and thirty of his° knights,   *(Lear's)*
15   Hot questrists° after him, met him at gate,   *searchers*
Who, with some other of the lord's° dependants,   *(Gloucester's)*
Are gone with him toward Dover, where they boast
To have well-armèd friends.

CORNWALL   Get horses for your mistress.   *Exit* [OSWALD]

20   GONERIL   Farewell, sweet lord, and sister.

CORNWALL   Edmond, farewell. [*Exeunt* GONERIL *and* EDMOND]
[*To* SERVANTS]   Go seek the traitor Gloucester.
Pinion him° like a thief; bring him before us.   *Tie his arms*
[*Exeunt other* SERVANTS]
Though well we may not pass° upon his life   *pass sentence*
Without the form° of justice, yet our power   *official proceedings*
25   Shall do a curtsy³ to our wrath, which men
May blame but not control.

Enter GLOUCESTER *and* SERVANTS
Who's there—the traitor?

REGAN   Ingrateful fox, 'tis he.

CORNWALL [*to* SERVANTS]   Bind fast his corky° arms.   *withered*

GLOUCESTER   What means your graces? Good my friends, consider
You are my guests. Do me no foul play, friends.

CORNWALL [*to* SERVANTS]   Bind him, I say.

30   REGAN   Hard, hard! O filthy traitor!

GLOUCESTER   Unmerciful lady as you are, I'm none.

CORNWALL [*to* SERVANTS]   To this chair bind him. [*To* GLOUCES-
TER] Villain, thou shalt find—
[REGAN *plucks Gloucester's beard*]°   *(an extreme insult)*

GLOUCESTER   By the kind gods, 'tis most ignobly done,
To pluck me by the beard.

35   REGAN   So white,° and such a traitor?   *white-haired; venerable*

3.7 Location: At Gloucester's castle.
1. Bound by duty; expected by destiny.
2. *Advise . . . preparation:* When you reach Albany, tell

the Duke to prepare quickly.
3. Shall allow a courtesy or indulgence; shall bow to.

35 GLOUCESTER   Naughty° lady,   *Wicked*
These hairs which thou dost ravish from my chin
Will quicken° and accuse thee. I am your host.   *come alive*
With robbers' hands my hospitable favours°   *features*
You should not ruffle° thus. What will you do?   *snatch at*
40 CORNWALL   Come, sir, what letters had you late° from France?   *lately*
REGAN   Be simple,° answerer, for we know the truth.   *direct*
CORNWALL   And what confederacy have you with the traitors
Late footed° in the kingdom?   *landed*
REGAN   To whose hands
You have sent the lunatic King. Speak.
45 GLOUCESTER   I have a letter guessingly set down,[4]
Which came from one that's of a neutral heart,
And not from one opposed.
CORNWALL   Cunning.
REGAN   And false.
CORNWALL   Where hast thou sent the King?
GLOUCESTER   To Dover.
REGAN   Wherefore° to Dover? Wast thou not charged° at peril—   *Why / commanded*
50 CORNWALL   Wherefore to Dover? Let him first answer that.
GLOUCESTER   I am tied to th' stake, and I must stand the course.[5]
REGAN   Wherefore to Dover, sir?
GLOUCESTER   Because I would not see thy cruel nails
Pluck out his poor old eyes, nor thy fierce sister
55 In his anointed[6] flesh rash° boarish fangs.   *slash; cut*
The sea, with such a storm as his bowed head
In hell-black night endured, would have buoyed° up   *risen*
And quenched the stellèd° fires. Yet, poor old heart,   *stars'*
He holped° the heavens to rage.   *helped*
60 If wolves had at thy gate howled that dern° time,   *dreary; dreadful*
Thou shouldst have said 'Good porter, turn the key;°   *(to open the door)*
All cruels I'll subscribe.'[7] But I shall see
The wingèd vengeance[8] overtake such children.
CORNWALL   See't shalt thou never.—Fellows,° hold the chair.—   *Servants*
65 Upon those eyes of thine I'll set my foot.
GLOUCESTER   He that will think° to live till he be old   *Whoever hopes*
Give me some help!—O cruel! O ye gods!
        [CORNWALL *pulls out one of* GLOUCESTER's *eyes and*
        stamps on it]
REGAN [*to* CORNWALL]   One side will mock another; t'other, too.
CORNWALL [*to* GLOUCESTER]   If you see vengeance—
SERVANT   Hold your hand, my lord.
70 I have served you ever since I was a child,
But better service have I never done you
Than now to bid you hold.
REGAN   How now, you dog!

---

4. Written without confirmation; speculative.
5. An image from bearbaiting, in which a bear on a short tether had to fight off the assault of dogs.
6. Consecrated with holy oils (as part of a King's coronation).
7. The cruelty of all creatures (but not yours) I can

accept ("subscribe"). Oxford emends F ("else subscribe") and Q ("else subscrib'd"); the line is usually paraphrased "All other cruel beasts would have pity, but not you."
8. Swift or heaven-sent revenge; either an angel of God or the Furies, who were flying executors of divine vengeance in classical mythology.

GLOUCESTER   Naughty° lady,   *Wicked*
    These hairs which thou dost ravish from my chin
    Will quicken° and accuse thee. I am your host.   *come alive*
    With robbers' hands my hospitable favours°   *features*
40 You should not ruffle° thus. What will you do?   *snatch at*
CORNWALL   Come, sir, what letters had you late° from France?   *lately*
REGAN   Be simple-answered,° for we know the truth.   *straightforward*
CORNWALL   And what confederacy have you with the traitors
    Late footed° in the kingdom?   *landed*
REGAN   To whose hands
45 You have sent the lunatic King. Speak.
GLOUCESTER   I have a letter guessingly set down,[4]
    Which came from one that's of a neutral heart,
    And not from one opposed.
CORNWALL   Cunning.
REGAN   And false.
CORNWALL   Where hast thou sent the King?
GLOUCESTER   To Dover.
50 REGAN   Wherefore° to Dover? Wast thou not charged° at peril—   *Why / commanded*
CORNWALL   Wherefore to Dover?—Let him answer that.
GLOUCESTER   I am tied to th' stake, and I must stand the course.[5]
REGAN   Wherefore to Dover?
GLOUCESTER   Because I would not see thy cruel nails
55   Pluck out his poor old eyes, nor thy fierce sister
    In his anointed[6] flesh stick boarish fangs.
    The sea, with such a storm as his bare head
    In hell-black night endured, would have buoyed° up   *risen*
    And quenched the stellèd° fires.   *stars'*
60 Yet, poor old heart, he holp° the heavens to rain.   *helped*
    If wolves had at thy gate howled that stern time,
    Thou shouldst have said 'Good porter, turn the key;°   *(to open the door)*
    All cruels I'll subscribe.'[7] But I shall see
    The wingèd vengeance[8] overtake such children.
65 CORNWALL   See't shalt thou never.—Fellows,° hold the chair.—   *Servants*
    Upon these eyes of thine I'll set my foot.
GLOUCESTER   He that will think° to live till he be old   *Whoever hopes*
    Give me some help!—O cruel! O you gods!
        [CORNWALL *pulls out one of* GLOUCESTER's *eyes and*
        stamps on it]
REGAN [*to* CORNWALL]   One side will mock another; th'other, too.
CORNWALL [*to* GLOUCESTER]   If you see vengeance—
70 SERVANT   Hold your hand, my lord.
    I have served you ever since I was a child,
    But better service have I never done you
    Than now to bid you hold.
REGAN   How now, you dog!

---

4. Written without confirmation; speculative.
5. An image from bearbaiting, in which a bear on a short tether had to fight off the assault of dogs.
6. Consecrated with holy oils (as part of a King's coronation).
7. The cruelty of all creatures (but not yours) I can accept ("subscribe"). Oxford emends F ("else subscribe") and Q ("else subscrib'd"); the line is usually paraphrased "All other cruel beasts would have pity, but not you."
8. Swift or heaven-sent revenge; either an angel of God or the Furies, who were flying executors of divine vengeance in classical mythology.

SERVANT   If you did wear a beard upon your chin
I'd shake it on this quarrel.[9] [*To* CORNWALL] What do you mean?°   *intend*
75 CORNWALL   My villein!°   *servant; villain*
SERVANT   Why then, come on, and take the chance of anger.[1]
[*They*] *draw and fight*
REGAN [*to another* SERVANT]   Give me thy sword. A peasant stand up thus!
She takes a sword and runs at him behind
SERVANT [*to* GLOUCESTER]   O, I am slain, my lord! Yet have you one eye left
To see some mischief° on him.   *injury*
[REGAN *stabs him again*]
O!   [*He dies*]
80 CORNWALL   Lest it see more, prevent it. Out, vile jelly!
[*He pulls out* GLOUCESTER's *other eye*]
Where is thy lustre now?
GLOUCESTER   All dark and comfortless. Where's my son Edmund?
Edmund, enkindle all the sparks of nature[2]
To quite° this horrid act.   *requite; avenge*
REGAN   Out, villain!
85 Thou call'st on him that hates thee. It was he
That made the overture° of thy treasons to us,   *revelation*
Who is too good to pity thee.
GLOUCESTER   O, my follies! Then Edgar was abused.°   *slandered*
Kind gods, forgive me that, and prosper him!
90 REGAN [*to* SERVANTS]   Go thrust him out at gates, and let him smell
His way to Dover. [*To* CORNWALL] How is't, my lord? How
look you?°   *How do you feel*
CORNWALL   I have received a hurt. Follow me, lady.
[*To* SERVANTS] Turn out that eyeless villain. Throw this slave
Upon the dunghill.
[*Exit one or more with* GLOUCESTER *and the body*]
Regan, I bleed apace.
95 Untimely comes this hurt. Give me your arm.
Exeunt [CORNWALL *and* REGAN]
SECOND SERVANT   I'll never care what wickedness I do
If this man come to good.[3]
THIRD SERVANT   If she live long
And in the end meet the old° course of death,   *usual*
Women will all turn monsters.
100 SECOND SERVANT   Let's follow the old Earl and get the bedlam°   *madman*
To lead him where he would. His roguish madness
Allows itself to anything.
THIRD SERVANT   Go thou. I'll fetch some flax and whites of eggs
To apply to his bleeding face. Now heaven help him!
Exeunt [*severally*]

---

9. I'd pluck it over this point; I'd issue a challenge.
1. Take the risk of fighting when angry; take the fortune of one who is governed by his anger.
2. All the warmth of filial love; all the anger that your

father has received such treatment.
3. *I'll . . . good:* Because this may be a sign that evil goes unpunished. *this man:* Cornwall.

SERVANT   If you did wear a beard upon your chin

75   I'd shake it on this quarrel.⁹ [*To* CORNWALL] What do you mean?°   *intend*

CORNWALL   My villein!°   *servant; villain*

SERVANT   Nay then, come on, and take the chance of anger.¹

    [*They draw and fight*]

REGAN [*to another* SERVANT]   Give me thy sword. A peasant stand up thus!

    [*She*] *kills him*

SERVANT [*to* GLOUCESTER]   O, I am slain. My lord, you have one eye left

    To see some mischief° on him.   *injury*

    [REGAN *stabs him again*]

80   O!   [*He dies*]

CORNWALL   Lest it see more, prevent it. Out, vile jelly!

    [*He pulls out* GLOUCESTER'*s other eye*]

    Where is thy lustre now?

GLOUCESTER   All dark and comfortless. Where's my son Edmond?

    Edmond, enkindle all the sparks of nature²

    To quite° this horrid act.   *requite; avenge*

85   REGAN   Out, treacherous villain!

    Thou call'st on him that hates thee. It was he

    That made the overture° of thy treasons to us,   *revelation*

    Who is too good to pity thee.

GLOUCESTER   O, my follies! Then Edgar was abused.°   *slandered*

90   Kind gods, forgive me that, and prosper him!

REGAN [*to* SERVANTS]   Go thrust him out at gates, and let him smell

    His way to Dover.   *Exit* [*one or more*] *with* GLOUCESTER

             How is't, my lord? How look you?°   *How do you feel*

CORNWALL   I have received a hurt. Follow me, lady.

    [*To* SERVANTS] Turn out that eyeless villain. Throw this slave

95   Upon the dunghill. Regan, I bleed apace.

    Untimely comes this hurt. Give me your arm.

                           Exeunt [*with the body*]

---

9. I'd pluck it over this point; I'd issue a challenge.
1. Take the risk of fighting when angry; take the fortune of one who is governed by his anger.

2. All the warmth of filial love; all the anger that your father has received such treatment.

Scene 15

Enter EDGAR [*as a Bedlam beggar*]

EDGAR   Yet better thus and known to be contemned°   *despised*
Than still° contemned and flattered. To be worst,   *always*
The low'st and most dejected thing of fortune,
Stands still in esperance, lives not in fear.[1]
5   The lamentable change is from the best;
The worst returns to laughter.[2]

Enter GLOUCESTER *led by an* OLD MAN

Who's here? My father, parti-eyed?[3] World, world, O world!
But that thy strange mutations make us hate thee,
Life would not yield to age.[4]

[EDGAR *stands aside*]

OLD MAN [*to* GLOUCESTER]   O my good lord,
10   I have been your tenant and your father's tenant
This fourscore—

GLOUCESTER   Away, get thee away, good friend, be gone.
Thy comforts° can do me no good at all;   *assistance*
Thee they may hurt.

15   OLD MAN   Alack, sir, you cannot see your way.

GLOUCESTER   I have no way, and therefore want no eyes.
I stumbled when I saw. Full oft 'tis seen
Our means secure us, and our mere defects
Prove our commodities.[5] Ah dear son Edgar,
20   The food° of thy abusèd° father's wrath—   *fuel; prey / deceived*
Might I but live to see thee in° my touch   *through*
I'd say I had eyes again.

OLD MAN   How now? Who's there?

EDGAR [*aside*]   O gods! Who is't can say 'I am at the worst'?
I am worse than e'er I was.

OLD MAN   'Tis poor mad Tom.

25   EDGAR [*aside*]   And worse I may be yet. The worst is not
As long as we can say 'This is the worst.'

OLD MAN [*to* EDGAR]   Fellow, where goest?

GLOUCESTER   Is it a beggarman?

OLD MAN   Madman and beggar too.

30   GLOUCESTER   A° has some reason, else he could not beg.   *He*
In the last night's storm I such a fellow saw,
Which made me think a man a worm. My son
Came then into my mind, and yet my mind
Was then scarce friends with him. I have heard more since.
35   As flies to wanton° boys are we to th' gods;   *playful; careless*
They kill us for their sport.

Scene 15   Location: Open country.
1. *Stands . . . fear:* Remains in hope ("esperance") because there is no fear of falling further.
2. *The lamentable . . . laughter:* The change to be lamented is one that alters the best of circumstances; the worst luck can only improve.
3. Multicolored like a fool's costume (red with blood under white dressings).
4. *But . . . age:* If there were no strange reversals of fortune to make the world hateful, we would not consent to aging and death.
5. *Our means . . . commodities:* Our wealth makes us overconfident, and our utter deprivation proves to be beneficial.

4.1

Enter EDGAR [*as a Bedlam beggar*]

EDGAR Yet better thus and known to be contemned°   *despised*
Than still° contemned and flattered. To be worst,   *always*
The low'st and most dejected thing of fortune,
Stands still in esperance, lives not in fear.[1]
5   The lamentable change is from the best;
The worst returns to laughter.[2] Welcome, then,
Thou unsubstantial air that I embrace.
The wretch that thou hast blown unto the worst
Owes nothing° to thy blasts.   *(because he can't pay)*

Enter GLOUCESTER [*led by*] *an* OLD MAN

But who comes here?
10   My father, parti-eyed?[3] World, world, O world!
But that thy strange mutations make us hate thee,
Life would not yield to age.[4]

[EDGAR *stands aside*]

OLD MAN [*to* GLOUCESTER]   O my good lord,
I have been your tenant and your father's tenant
These fourscore years.

15   GLOUCESTER   Away, get thee away, good friend, be gone.
Thy comforts° can do me no good at all;   *assistance*
Thee they may hurt.

OLD MAN   You cannot see your way.

GLOUCESTER   I have no way, and therefore want no eyes.
I stumbled when I saw. Full oft 'tis seen
20   Our means secure us, and our mere defects
Prove our commodities.[5] O dear son Edgar,
The food° of thy abusèd° father's wrath—   *fuel; prey / deceived*
Might I but live to see thee in° my touch   *through*
I'd say I had eyes again.

OLD MAN   How now? Who's there?

25   EDGAR [*aside*]   O gods! Who is't can say 'I am at the worst'?
I am worse than e'er I was.

OLD MAN [*to* GLOUCESTER]   'Tis poor mad Tom.

EDGAR [*aside*]   And worse I may be yet. The worst is not
So long as we can say 'This is the worst.'

OLD MAN [*to* EDGAR]   Fellow, where goest?

30   GLOUCESTER   Is it a beggarman?

OLD MAN   Madman and beggar too.

GLOUCESTER   A° has some reason, else he could not beg.   *He*
I'th' last night's storm I such a fellow saw,
Which made me think a man a worm. My son
35   Came then into my mind, and yet my mind
Was then scarce friends with him. I have heard more since.
As flies to wanton° boys are we to th' gods;   *playful; careless*
They kill us for their sport.

4.1 Location: Open country.
1. *Stands . . . fear:* Remains in hope ("esperance") because there is no fear of falling further.
2. *The lamentable . . . laughter:* The change to be lamented is one that alters the best of circumstances; the worst luck can only improve.
3. Multicolored like a fool's costume (red with blood under white dressings).
4. *But . . . age:* If there were no strange reversals of fortune to make the world hateful, we would not consent to aging and death.
5. *Our means . . . commodities:* Our wealth makes us overconfident, and our utter deprivation proves to be beneficial.

EDGAR [*aside*]   How should this be?
Bad is the trade that must play fool to sorrow,[6]
Ang'ring itself and others.
          [*He comes forward*]
                         Bless thee, master.

GLOUCESTER   Is that the naked fellow?

OLD MAN   Ay, my lord.

40 GLOUCESTER   Then prithee, get thee gone. If for my sake
Thou wilt o'ertake us hence a mile or twain
I'th' way toward Dover, do it for ancient love,[7]
And bring some covering for this naked soul,
Who I'll entreat to lead me.

OLD MAN   Alack, sir, he is mad.

45 GLOUCESTER   'Tis the time's plague when[8] madmen lead the blind.
Do as I bid thee; or rather do thy pleasure.
Above the rest, be gone.

OLD MAN   I'll bring him the best 'parel° that I have,   apparel; clothing
Come on't what will.   [*Exit*]

GLOUCESTER   Sirrah, naked fellow!

50 EDGAR   Poor Tom's a-cold. I cannot dance it farther.[9]

GLOUCESTER   Come hither, fellow.

EDGAR   Bless thy sweet eyes, they bleed.

GLOUCESTER   Know'st thou the way to Dover?

EDGAR   Both stile and gate, horseway and footpath. Poor Tom
55 hath been scared out of his good wits. Bless thee, goodman,°   commoner
from the foul fiend. Five fiends have been in Poor Tom at
once, as Obidicut of lust, Hobbididence prince of dumbness,
Mahu of stealing, Modo of murder, Flibbertigibbet of mocking
and mowing,° who since possesses chambermaids and waiting-   making faces
60 women. So bless thee, master.

GLOUCESTER   Here, take this purse, thou whom the heavens' plagues
Have humbled to all strokes.° That I am wretched   to accept all blows
Makes thee the happier. Heavens deal so still.°   always
Let the superfluous and lust-dieted man[1]
65 That stands° your ordinance,° that will not see   resists / authority
Because he does not feel, feel your power quickly.
So distribution should undo excess,
And each man have enough. Dost thou know Dover?

EDGAR   Ay, master.

70 GLOUCESTER   There is a cliff whose high and bendìng° head   overhanging
Looks saucily in the confinèd deep.[2]
Bring me but to the very brim of it
And I'll repair the misery thou dost bear
With something rich about me. From that place
75 I shall no leading need.

EDGAR   Give me thy arm.
Poor Tom shall lead thee.   [*Exit* EDGAR *guiding* GLOUCESTER]

---

6. It is a bad business to have to play the fool in the face of sorrow.
7. For the sake of our long and loyal relationship (as master and servant).
8. The time is truly sick when.
9. I cannot continue the charade.
1. Let the overprosperous man who indulges his appetite.
2. Looks fearsomely into the straits below.

EDGAR [*aside*]   How should this be?
Bad is the trade that must play fool to sorrow,[6]
Ang'ring itself and others.
        [*He comes forward*]
40   Bless thee, master.
GLOUCESTER   Is that the naked fellow?
OLD MAN   Ay, my lord.
GLOUCESTER   Get thee away. If for my sake
   Thou wilt o'ertake us hence a mile or twain
   I'th' way toward Dover, do it for ancient love,[7]
45   And bring some covering for this naked soul,
   Which I'll entreat to lead me.
OLD MAN   Alack, sir, he is mad.
GLOUCESTER   'Tis the time's plague when[8] madmen lead the blind.
   Do as I bid thee; or rather do thy pleasure.
   Above the rest, be gone.
50 OLD MAN   I'll bring him the best 'parel° that I have,   *apparel; clothing*
   Come on't what will.   *Exit*
GLOUCESTER   Sirrah, naked fellow!
EDGAR   Poor Tom's a-cold. [*Aside*] I cannot daub it further.[9]
GLOUCESTER   Come hither, fellow.
EDGAR   [*aside*]   And yet I must.
   [*To* GLOUCESTER] Bless thy sweet eyes, they bleed.
GLOUCESTER   Know'st thou the way to Dover?
55 EDGAR   Both stile and gate, horseway and footpath. Poor Tom
   hath been scared out of his good wits. Bless thee, goodman's°   *commoner's*
   son, from the foul fiend.
GLOUCESTER   Here, take this purse, thou whom the heavens' plagues
   Have humbled to all strokes.° That I am wretched   *to accept all blows*
60   Makes thee the happier. Heavens deal so still.°   *always*
   Let the superfluous and lust-dieted man[1]
   That slaves° your ordinance,° that will not see   *defers to / authority*
   Because he does not feel, feel your power quickly.
   So distribution should undo excess,
65   And each man have enough. Dost thou know Dover?
EDGAR   Ay, master.
GLOUCESTER   There is a cliff whose high and bending° head   *overhanging*
   Looks fearfully in the confinèd deep.[2]
   Bring me but to the very brim of it
70   And I'll repair the misery thou dost bear
   With something rich about me. From that place
   I shall no leading need.
EDGAR   Give me thy arm.
   Poor Tom shall lead thee.   *Exit* [EDGAR *guiding* GLOUCESTER]

---

6. It is a bad business to have to play the fool in the face of sorrow.
7. For the sake of our long and loyal relationship (as master and servant).
8. The time is truly sick when.
9. I cannot continue the charade. *daub:* mask, plaster.
1. Let the overprosperous man who indulges his appetite.
2. Looks fearsomely into the straits below.

Scene 16

Enter [at one door] GONORIL *and Bastard [*EDMUND*]*

GONORIL   Welcome, my lord. I marvel our mild husband
Not° met us on the way.   *Has not*

*Enter [at another door] Steward [*OSWALD*]*

Now, where's your master?

OSWALD   Madam, within; but never man so changed.
I told him of the army that was landed;
5   He smiled at it. I told him you were coming;
His answer was 'The worse.' Of Gloucester's treachery
And of the loyal service of his son
When I informed him, then he called me sot,°   *fool*
And told me I had turned the wrong side out.[1]
10   What he should most defy seems pleasant to him;
What like, offensive.

GONORIL *[to* EDMUND*]*   Then shall you go no further.
It is the cowish° terror of his spirit   *cowardly*
That dares not undertake. He'll not feel wrongs
Which tie him to an answer.[2] Our wishes on the way
15   May prove effects.[3] Back, Edmund, to my brother.°   *brother-in-law*
Hasten his musters° and conduct his powers.°   *call-up of troops / armies*
I must change arms at home, and give the distaff[4]
Into my husband's hands. This trusty servant
Shall pass between us. Ere long you are like° to hear,   *likely*
20   If you dare venture in your own behalf,
A mistress's° command. Wear this. Spare speech.   *(playing on "lover's")*
Decline your head. This kiss, if it durst speak,
Would stretch thy spirits up into the air.
[She kisses him]
Conceive,° and fare you well.   *Understand (my meaning)*
25   EDMUND   Yours in° the ranks of death.   *even in*
GONORIL   My most dear Gloucester.   *[Exit* EDMUND*]*
To thee a woman's services are due;
My foot usurps my body.[5]
OSWALD   Madam, here comes my lord. *Exit*
[Enter ALBANY*]*
GONORIL   I have been worth the whistling.[6]
ALBANY   O Gonoril,
30   You are not worth the dust which the rude wind
Blows in your face. I fear your disposition.
That nature which contemns it° origin   *despises its*
Cannot be bordered certain° in itself.   *be defended securely*
She that herself will sliver and disbranch°   *split*
35   From her material sap perforce must wither,
And come to deadly use.[7]

Scene 16 Location: Before Albany's castle.
1. I had reversed things (by mistaking loyalty for
treachery).
2. *He'll . . . answer:* He'll ignore insults that would provoke him to retaliate.
3. May be put into action.
4. A device used in spinning and so emblematic of the
female role. To "change arms," therefore, is to swap the
insignia of male and female identity.
5. Continuing the inversion of roles, Albany, who should

be the head of the family, is seen by Gonoril as a sub-
servient member with no right to control her.
6. At one time, you would have come to welcome me
home; referring to the proverb "It is a poor dog that is
not worth the whistling."
7. *She . . . use:* The allusion is probably biblical: "But
that which beareth thorns and briers is reproved, and is
near unto cursing; whose end is to be burned" (Hebrews
6:8). *come to deadly use:* be destroyed; be used for
burning.

4.2

Enter GONERIL [*and*] *Bastard* [EDMOND *at one door*]
and Steward [OSWALD *at another*]

GONERIL   Welcome, my lord. I marvel our mild husband
Not° met us on the way. [*To* OSWALD] Now, where's your master?   *Has not*

OSWALD   Madam, within; but never man so changed.
I told him of the army that was landed;

5   He smiled at it. I told him you were coming;
His answer was 'The worse'. Of Gloucester's treachery
And of the loyal service of his son
When I informed him, then he called me sot,°   *fool*
And told me I had turned the wrong side out.[1]

10   What most he should dislike seems pleasant to him;
What like, offensive.

GONERIL [*to* EDMOND]   Then shall you go no further.
It is the cowish° terror of his spirit   *cowardly*
That dares not undertake. He'll not feel wrongs
Which tie him to an answer.[2] Our wishes on the way

15   May prove effects.[3] Back, Edmond, to my brother.°   *brother-in-law*
Hasten his musters° and conduct his powers.°   *call-up of troops / armies*
I must change names° at home, and give the distaff[4]   *exchange roles*
Into my husband's hands. This trusty servant
Shall pass between us. Ere long you are like° to hear,   *likely*

20   If you dare venture in your own behalf,
A mistress's° command. Wear this. Spare speech.   *(playing on "lover's")*
Decline your head. This kiss, if it durst speak,
Would stretch thy spirits up into the air.
[*She kisses him*]
Conceive,° and fare thee well.   *Understand (my meaning)*

25   EDMOND   Yours in° the ranks of death.   *even in*

GONERIL   My most dear Gloucester.   *Exit* [EDMOND]
O, the difference of man and man!
To thee a woman's services are due;
My fool usurps my body.[5]

OSWALD   Madam, here comes my lord.
Enter ALBANY

GONERIL   I have been worth the whistling.[6]

30   ALBANY   O Goneril,
You are not worth the dust which the rude wind
Blows in your face.

4.2 Location: Before Albany's castle.
1. I had reversed things (by mistaking loyalty for treachery).
2. *He'll . . . answer:* He'll ignore insults that would provoke him to retaliate.
3. May be put into action.

4. Spinning staff, the female insignia that she wishes to exchange for Albany's manly sword.
5. My idiot husband presumes to possess me.
6. At one time, you would have come to welcome me home; referring to the proverb "It is a poor dog that is not worth the whistling."

GONORIL   No more. The text is foolish.

ALBANY Wisdom and goodness to the vile seem vile;
    Filths savour but themselves. What have you done?
    Tigers, not daughters, what have you performed?
40   A father, and a gracious, agèd man,
    Whose reverence even the head-lugged° bear would lick,   *dragged by the head*
    Most barbarous, most degenerate, have you madded.°   *driven mad*
    Could my good-brother° suffer you to do it—   *brother-in-law*
    A man, a prince by him so benefacted?
45   If that the heavens do not their visible spirits
    Send quickly down to tame these vile offences,
    It will come,
    Humanity must perforce° prey on itself,   *inevitably*
    Like monsters of the deep.

GONORIL   Milk-livered° man,   *Cowardly*
50   That bear'st a cheek for blows, a head for wrongs;[8]
    Who hast not in thy brows an eye discerning
    Thine honour from thy suffering;[9] that not know'st
    Fools do those villains pity who are punished
    Ere they have done their mischief: where's thy drum?°   *(to muster troops)*
55   France spreads his banners in our noiseless° land,   *peaceful*
    With plumèd helm thy flaxen biggin° threats,   *nightcap; child's cap*
    Whiles thou, a moral° fool, sits still and cries   *moralizing*
    'Alack, why does he so?'

ALBANY   See thyself, devil.
    Proper deformity shows not in the fiend
    So horrid as in woman.[1]
60 GONORIL   O vain° fool!   *useless*

ALBANY Thou changèd and self-covered[2] thing, for shame
    Bemonster not thy feature. Were't my fitness°   *If it were appropriate*
    To let these hands obey my blood,
    They are apt enough to dislocate and tear
65   Thy flesh and bones. Howe'er° thou art a fiend,   *Although*
    A woman's shape doth shield thee.

GONORIL Marry your manhood, mew[3]—

      Enter [SECOND] GENTLEMAN

ALBANY What news?

SECOND GENTLEMAN O my good lord, the Duke of Cornwall's dead,
    Slain by his servant going to put out
    The other eye of Gloucester.
70 ALBANY   Gloucester's eyes?

SECOND GENTLEMAN A servant that he bred, thralled with
      remorse,°   *shaken with pity*
    Opposed against the act, bending° his sword   *directing*
    To° his great master, who thereat enraged   *Against*

---

8. *for wrongs*: fit for abuse; ready for cuckold's horns.
9. *discerning . . . suffering*: that can distinguish between an insult to your honor and something you should patiently endure.
1. *Proper . . . woman*: Deformity (of morals) is appropriate in the devil and so less horrid than in woman, from whom virtue is expected. Albany may hold a mirror in front of Gonoril, since Jacobean women sometimes wore small mirrors attached to their dresses.
2. Altered and with your true (womanly) self concealed.
3. Get control of your manhood—restrain ("mew") it. Alternatively, assert your feeble masculinity (with a derisive catcall, "mew").

GONERIL   Milk-livered° man,   *Cowardly*
That bear'st a cheek for blows, a head for wrongs;[7]
Who hast not in thy brows an eye discerning
Thine honour from thy suffering[8]—

35 ALBANY   See thyself, devil.
Proper deformity shows not in the fiend
So horrid as in woman.[9]
GONERIL   O vain° fool!   *useless*

Enter a MESSENGER
MESSENGER   O my good lord, the Duke of Cornwall's dead,
Slain by his servant going to put out
The other eye of Gloucester.
40 ALBANY   Gloucester's eyes?
MESSENGER   A servant that he bred, thrilled with remorse,°   *shaken with pity*
Opposed against the act, bending° his sword   *directing*
To° his great master, who thereat enraged   *Against*

---

7. *for wrongs:* fit for abuse; ready for cuckold's horns.
8. *discerning . . . suffering:* that can distinguish
between an insult to your honor and something you
should patiently endure.
9. *Proper . . . woman:* Deformity (of morals) is appropriate in the devil and so less horrid than in woman,
from whom virtue is expected. Albany may hold a mirror in front of Goneril, since Jacobean women sometimes wore small mirrors attached to their dresses.

Flew on him, and amongst them felled him dead,
75 But not without that harmful stroke which since
Hath plucked him after.[4]
ALBANY   This shows you are above,
You justicers,° that these our nether crimes[5]   *judges*
So speedily can venge. But O, poor Gloucester!
Lost he his other eye?
SECOND GENTLEMAN   Both, both, my lord.
80 [*To* GONORIL] This letter, madam, craves a speedy answer.
'Tis from your sister.
GONORIL [*aside*]   One way I like this well;[6]
But being° widow, and my Gloucester with her,   *her being*
May all the building on my fancy pluck
Upon my hateful life.[7] Another way
85 The news is not so took.[8]—I'll read and answer.   *Exit*
ALBANY   Where was his son when they did take his eyes?
SECOND GENTLEMAN   Come with my lady hither.
ALBANY   He is not here.
SECOND GENTLEMAN   No, my good lord; I met him back° again.   *returning*
ALBANY   Knows he the wickedness?
90 SECOND GENTLEMAN   Ay, my good lord; 'twas he informed against him,
And quit the house on purpose that their punishment
Might have the freer course.
ALBANY   Gloucester, I live
To thank thee for the love thou showed'st the King,
And to revenge thy eyes.—Come hither, friend.
95 Tell me what more thou knowest.   *Exeunt*

Scene 17

Enter KENT [*disguised,*] *and* [FIRST] GENTLEMAN

KENT   Why the King of France is so suddenly gone back know
you no reason?
FIRST GENTLEMAN   Something he left imperfect° in the state   *unsettled*
Which, since his coming forth, is thought of;° which   *remembered*
5 Imports° to the kingdom so much fear and danger   *Portends*
That his personal return was most required
And necessary.
KENT   Who hath he left behind him general?
FIRST GENTLEMAN   The Maréchal° of France, Monsieur la Far.   *Marshall*
10 KENT   Did your letters pierce the Queen to any demonstration
of grief?
FIRST GENTLEMAN   Ay, sir. She took them, read them in my presence,
And now and then an ample tear trilled down
Her delicate cheek. It seemed she was a queen
15 Over her passion who,° most rebel-like,   *which*
Sought to be king o'er her.

---

4. Has sent him to follow his servant into death.
5. Lower crimes, and so committed on earth, but also suggesting that the deeds smack of the netherworld of hell.
6. Because a political rival has been eliminated.

7. *May . . . life:* May pull down all of my built-up fantasies and thus make my life hateful.
8. The news may be taken otherwise.
Scene 17 Location: Near the French camp at Dover.

Flew on him, and amongst them felled him dead,
45   But not without that harmful stroke which since
Hath plucked him after.[1]

ALBANY   This shows you are above,
You justicers,° that these our nether crimes[2]   judges
So speedily can venge. But O, poor Gloucester!
Lost he his other eye?

MESSENGER   Both, both, my lord.—
50   This letter, madam, craves a speedy answer.
'Tis from your sister.

GONERIL [aside]   One way I like this well;[3]
But being° widow, and my Gloucester with her,   her being
May all the building in my fancy pluck
Upon my hateful life.[4] Another way
55   The news is not so tart.°—I'll read and answer.   bitter
                                        [Exit with OSWALD]

ALBANY   Where was his son when they did take his eyes?

MESSENGER   Come with my lady hither.

ALBANY   He is not here.

MESSENGER   No, my good lord; I met him back° again.   returning

ALBANY   Knows he the wickedness?

60   MESSENGER   Ay, my good lord; 'twas he informed against him,
And quit the house on purpose that their punishment
Might have the freer course.

ALBANY   Gloucester, I live
To thank thee for the love thou showed'st the King,
And to revenge thine eyes.—Come hither, friend.
65   Tell me what more thou know'st.   Exeunt

---

1. Has sent him to follow his servant into death.
2. Lower crimes, and so committed on earth, but also suggesting that the deeds smack of the netherworld of hell.

3. Because a political rival has been eliminated.
4. May . . . life: May pull down all of my built-up fantasies and thus make my life hateful.

KENT   O, then it moved her.

FIRST GENTLEMAN   Not to a rage. Patience and sorrow strove
      Who should express her goodliest.¹ You have seen
      Sunshine and rain at once; her smiles and tears
20   Were like, a better way. Those happy smilets
      That played on her ripe lip seemed not to know
      What guests were in her eyes, which parted thence
      As pearls from diamonds dropped. In brief,
      Sorrow would be a rarity° most beloved   gem
      If all could so become it.²

25 KENT   Made she no verbal question?

FIRST GENTLEMAN   Faith, once or twice she heaved the name of 'father'
      Pantingly forth as if it pressed her heart,
      Cried 'Sisters, sisters, shame of ladies, sisters,
      Kent, father, sisters, what, i'th' storm, i'th' night,
30   Let piety not be believed!'³ There she shook
      The holy water from her heavenly eyes
      And clamour° mastered, then away she started°   crying / sprang
      To deal with grief alone.

KENT   It is the stars,
      The stars above us govern our conditions,
35   Else one self mate and make⁴ could not beget
      Such different issues.° You spoke not with her since?   offspring

FIRST GENTLEMAN   No.

KENT   Was this before the King returned?

FIRST GENTLEMAN   No, since.

KENT   Well, sir, the poor distressèd Lear's i'th' town,
40   Who sometime in his better tune° remembers   state of mind
      What we are come about, and by no means
      Will yield° to see his daughter.   consent

FIRST GENTLEMAN   Why, good sir?

KENT   A sovereign shame so elbows° him: his own unkindness,   prods; nudges
      That stripped her from his benediction, turned her
45   To foreign casualties,° gave her dear rights   risks
      To his dog-hearted daughters—these things sting
      His mind so venomously that burning shame
      Detains him from Cordelia.

FIRST GENTLEMAN   Alack, poor gentleman!

KENT   Of Albany's and Cornwall's powers you heard not?

50 FIRST GENTLEMAN   'Tis so; they are afoot.

KENT   Well, sir, I'll bring you to our master Lear,
      And leave you to attend him. Some dear cause°   Some important reason
      Will in concealment wrap me up a while.
      When I am known aright you shall not grieve°   repent
55   Lending me this acquaintance.° I pray you go   news
      Along with me.   Exeunt

---

1. Which should best express her feelings.
2. If everyone wore it so beautifully.
3. Never believe in piety (pity, or filial respect); piety can-
4. Or else the same pair of spouses; "mate" and "make"
not exist.
may describe either partner.

Scene 18

Enter [Queen] CORDELIA, DOCTOR, *and others*

CORDELIA   Alack, 'tis he! Why, he was met even now,
As mad as the racked sea, singing aloud,
Crowned with rank fumitor and furrow-weeds,[1]
With burdocks, hemlock, nettles, cuckoo-flowers,
5   Darnel, and all the idle° weeds that grow   useless
In our sustaining corn. The centuries° send forth.   battalions
Search every acre in the high-grown field,
And bring him to our eye.   [*Exit one or more*]
                              What can man's wisdom
In the restoring° his bereavèd sense,   Do to restore
10   He that can help him
Take all my outward° worth.   material
DOCTOR   There is means, madam.
Our foster-nurse of nature[2] is repose,
The which he lacks. That to provoke in him
15   Are many simples operative,[3] whose power
Will close the eye of anguish.
CORDELIA   All blest secrets,
All you unpublished virtues° of the earth,   obscure healing plants
Spring with my tears, be aidant and remediate°   healing and remedial
In the good man's distress!—Seek, seek for him,
20   Lest his ungoverned rage dissolve the life
That wants° the means to lead it.   lacks
              Enter MESSENGER
MESSENGER   News, madam.
The British powers° are marching hitherward.   armies
CORDELIA   'Tis known before; our preparation stands
In expectation of them.—O dear father,
25   It is thy business that I go about;[4]
Therefore great France
My mourning and important° tears hath pitied.   urgent; solicitous
No blown° ambition doth our arms incite,   inflated
But love, dear love, and our aged father's right.[5]
30   Soon may I hear and see him!   *Exeunt*

Scene 18 Location: The French camp at Dover.
1. Fumitor was used against brain sickness. Furrow-weeds, like the other weeds in the following lines, grow in the furrows of plowed fields.
2. *Our . . . nature:* That which comforts and nourishes human nature.
3. *That . . . operative:* To induce that ("repose") in him,
there are many effective medicinal herbs.
4. The line echoes Christ's explanation of his mission in Luke 2:49, "I must go about my father's business."
5. *No . . . right:* 1 Corinthians 13:4–5 in the Bishops' Bible (1568) says that love "swelleth not, dealeth not dishonestly, seeketh not her own."

4.3

Enter with drum and colours, [Queen] CORDELIA, GEN-
TLEMEN, *and soldiers*

CORDELIA   Alack, 'tis he! Why, he was met even now,
   As mad as the vexèd sea, singing aloud,
   Crowned with rank fumitor and furrow-weeds,[1]
   With burdocks, hemlock, nettles, cuckoo-flowers,
5   Darnel, and all the idle° weeds that grow   *useless*
   In our sustaining corn. A century° send forth.   *battalion (100 men)*
   Search every acre in the high-grown field,
   And bring him to our eye.   [*Exit one or more*]
                   What can man's wisdom
   In the restoring° his bereavèd sense,   *Do to restore*
10 He that helps him take all my outward° worth.   *material*
FIRST GENTLEMAN   There is means, madam.
   Our foster-nurse of nature[2] is repose,
   The which he lacks. That to provoke in him
   Are many simples operative,[3] whose power
   Will close the eye of anguish.
15 CORDELIA   All blest secrets,
   All you unpublished virtues° of the earth,   *obscure healing plants*
   Spring with my tears, be aidant and remediate°   *healing and remedial*
   In the good man's distress!—Seek, seek for him,
   Lest his ungoverned rage dissolve the life
   That wants° the means to lead it.   *lacks*
        Enter [a] MESSENGER
20 MESSENGER   News, madam.
   The British powers° are marching hitherward.   *armies*
CORDELIA   'Tis known before; our preparation stands
   In expectation of them.—O dear father,
   It is thy business that I go about;[4]
25 Therefore great France
   My mourning and importuned° tears hath pitied.   *importunate; solicitous*
   No blown° ambition doth our arms incite,   *inflated*
   But love, dear love, and our aged father's right.[5]
   Soon may I hear and see him!   *Exeunt*

4.3 Location: The French camp at Dover.
1. Fumitor was used against brain sickness. Furrow-weeds, like the other weeds in the following lines, grow in the furrows of plowed fields.
2. *Our . . . nature:* That which comforts and nourishes human nature.
3. *That . . . operative:* To induce that ("repose") in him,

there are many effective medicinal herbs.
4. The line echoes Christ's explanation of his mission in Luke 2:49, "I must go about my father's business."
5. *No . . . right:* 1 Corinthians 13:4–5 in the Bishops' Bible (1568) says that love "swelleth not, dealeth not dishonestly, seeketh not her own."

Scene 19

Enter REGAN *and Steward* [OSWALD]

REGAN But are my brother's powers° set forth?   *(Albany's forces)*

OSWALD   Ay, madam.

REGAN Himself in person?

OSWALD   Madam, with much ado.°   *trouble*
Your sister is the better soldier.

REGAN Lord Edmund spake not with your lord at home?

5 OSWALD No, madam.

REGAN What might import° my sister's letters to him?   *mean*

OSWALD I know not, lady.

REGAN Faith, he is posted° hence on serious matter.   *hurried*
It was great ignorance, Gloucester's eyes being out,

10 To let him live. Where he arrives he moves
All hearts against us. Edmund, I think, is gone,
In pity of his misery,° to dispatch   *(ironic)*
His 'nighted° life, moreover to descry°   *darkened / investigate*
The strength o'th' army.

15 OSWALD I must needs after° with my letters, madam.   *go after*

REGAN Our troop sets forth tomorrow. Stay with us.
The ways are dangerous.

OSWALD   I may not, madam.
My lady charged° my duty in this business.   *commanded*

REGAN Why should she write to Edmund? Might not you

20 Transport her purposes by word? Belike°—   *Perhaps*
Something, I know not what. I'll love° thee much: *reward*
Let me unseal the letter.

OSWALD   Madam, I'd rather—

REGAN I know your lady does not love her husband.
I am sure of that, and at her late° being here   *recently*

25 She gave strange oeillades° and most speaking looks   *amorous glances*
To noble Edmund. I know you are of her bosom.°   *in her confidence*

OSWALD I, madam?

REGAN I speak in understanding,° for I know't.   *with certainty*
Therefore I do advise you take this note.°   *take note of this*

30 My lord is dead. Edmund and I have talked,
And more convenient° is he for my hand   *appropriate*
Than for your lady's. You may gather° more.   *infer*
If you do find him, pray you give him this,[1]
And when your mistress hears thus much from you,

35 I pray desire her call her wisdom to her.[2]
So, farewell.
If you do chance to hear of that blind traitor,
Preferment falls on him that cuts him off.°   *cuts his life short*

OSWALD Would I could meet him, madam. I would show
What lady I do follow.

40 REGAN   Fare thee well.   *Exeunt* [*severally*]

Scene 19 Location: At Gloucester's castle.   2. *desire . . . to her:* tell her to come to her senses.
1. This information, but possibly another letter or token.

4.4

Enter REGAN *and Steward* [OSWALD]

REGAN But are my brother's powers° set forth? *(Albany's forces)*

OSWALD Ay, madam.

REGAN Himself in person there?

OSWALD Madam, with much ado.° *trouble*
Your sister is the better soldier.

REGAN Lord Edmond spake not with your lord at home?

5 OSWALD No, madam.

REGAN What might import° my sister's letters to him? *mean*

OSWALD I know not, lady.

REGAN Faith, he is posted° hence on serious matter. *hurried*
It was great ignorance, Gloucester's eyes being out,

10 To let him live. Where he arrives he moves
All hearts against us. Edmond, I think, is gone,
In pity of his misery,° to dispatch *(ironic)*
His 'nighted° life, moreover to descry° *darkened / investigate*
The strength o'th' enemy.

15 OSWALD I must needs after,° madam, with my letter. *go after*

REGAN Our troops set forth tomorrow. Stay with us.
The ways are dangerous.

OSWALD I may not, madam.
My lady charged° my duty in this business. *commanded*

REGAN Why should she write to Edmond? Might not you

20 Transport her purposes by word? Belike°— *Perhaps*
Some things—I know not what. I'll love° thee much: *reward*
Let me unseal the letter.

OSWALD Madam, I had rather—

REGAN I know your lady does not love her husband.
I am sure of that, and at her late° being here *recently*

25 She gave strange oeillades° and most speaking looks *amorous glances*
To noble Edmond. I know you are of her bosom.° *in her confidence*

OSWALD I, madam?

REGAN I speak in understanding.° Y'are, I know't. *with certainty*
Therefore I do advise you take this note.° *take note of this*

30 My lord is dead. Edmond and I have talked,
And more convenient° is he for my hand *appropriate*
Than for your lady's. You may gather° more. *infer*
If you do find him, pray you give him this,[1]
And when your mistress hears thus much from you,

35 I pray desire her call her wisdom to her.[2]
So, fare you well.
If you do chance to hear of that blind traitor,
Preferment falls on him that cuts him off.° *cuts his life short*

OSWALD Would I could meet him, madam. I should show
What party I do follow.

40 REGAN Fare thee well. *Exeunt* [*severally*]

4.4 Location: At Gloucester's castle.
1. This information, but possibly another letter or token.

2. *desire . . . to her*: tell her to come to her senses.

Scene 20

Enter EDGAR [*disguised as a peasant, with a staff, guiding the blind*] GLOUCESTER

GLOUCESTER When shall we come to th' top of that same° hill? agreed-upon
EDGAR You do climb up it now. Look how we labour.
GLOUCESTER Methinks the ground is even.
EDGAR   Horrible steep.
  Hark, do you hear the sea?
GLOUCESTER   No, truly.
5 EDGAR Why, then your other senses grow imperfect
  By your eyes' anguish.
GLOUCESTER   So may it be indeed.
  Methinks thy voice is altered, and thou speak'st
  With better phrase and matter° than thou didst. sense
EDGAR You're much deceived. In nothing am I changed
  But in my garments.
10 GLOUCESTER   Methinks you're better spoken.
EDGAR Come on, sir, here's the place. Stand still. How fearful
  And dizzy 'tis to cast one's eyes so low!
  The crows and choughs° that wing the midway air[1] jackdaws
  Show° scarce so gross° as beetles. Halfway down Appear / big
15 Hangs one that gathers samphire,° dreadful trade! seaweed
  Methinks he seems no bigger than his head.
  The fishermen that walk upon the beach
  Appear like mice, and yon tall anchoring barque° ship
  Diminished to her cock,° her cock a buoy dinghy
20 Almost too small for sight. The murmuring surge
  That on the unnumbered° idle pebble chafes innumerable
  Cannot be heard, it's so high. I'll look no more,
  Lest my brain turn and the° deficient sight my
  Topple° down headlong. Topple me
GLOUCESTER   Set me where you stand.
25 EDGAR Give me your hand. You are now within a foot
  Of th'extreme verge. For all beneath the moon
  Would I not leap upright.[2]
GLOUCESTER   Let go my hand.
  Here, friend, 's another purse; in it a jewel
  Well worth a poor man's taking. Fairies and gods
30 Prosper it[3] with thee! Go thou farther off.
  Bid me farewell, and let me hear thee going.
EDGAR Now fare you well, good sir.
  [*He stands aside*]
GLOUCESTER   With all my heart.
EDGAR [*aside*] Why I do trifle thus with his despair
  Is done to cure it.
GLOUCESTER   O you mighty gods,
  He kneels
35 This world I do renounce, and in your sights
  Shake patiently my great affliction off!

Scene 20 Location: Near Dover.
1. The air between cliff and sea.
2. I would not jump up and down (for fear of losing my

balance).
3. Make it increase. Fairies were sometimes held to
hoard and multiply treasure.

4.5

Enter EDGAR *[disguised as a peasant, with a staff, guid-*
ing the blind] GLOUCESTER

GLOUCESTER   When shall I come to th' top of that same° hill?   *agreed-upon*
EDGAR   You do climb up it now. Look how we labour.
GLOUCESTER   Methinks the ground is even.
EDGAR   Horrible steep.
     Hark, do you hear the sea?
GLOUCESTER   No, truly.
5   EDGAR   Why, then your other senses grow imperfect
     By your eyes' anguish.
GLOUCESTER   So may it be indeed.
     Methinks thy voice is altered, and thou speak'st
     In better phrase and matter° than thou didst.   *sense*
EDGAR   You're much deceived. In nothing am I changed
     But in my garments.
10   GLOUCESTER   Methinks you're better spoken.
EDGAR   Come on, sir, here's the place. Stand still. How fearful
     And dizzy 'tis to cast one's eyes so low!
     The crows and choughs° that wing the midway air[1]   *jackdaws*
     Show° scarce so gross° as beetles. Halfway down   *Appear / big*
15   Hangs one that gathers samphire,° dreadful trade!   *seaweed*
     Methinks he seems no bigger than his head.
     The fishermen that walk upon the beach
     Appear like mice, and yon tall anchoring barque°   *ship*
     Diminished to her cock,° her cock a buoy   *dinghy*
20   Almost too small for sight. The murmuring surge
     That on th'unnumbered° idle pebble chafes   *innumerable*
     Cannot be heard so high. I'll look no more,
     Lest my brain turn and the° deficient sight   *my*
     Topple° down headlong.   *Topple me*
GLOUCESTER   Set me where you stand.
25   EDGAR   Give me your hand. You are now within a foot
     Of th'extreme verge. For all beneath the moon
     Would I not leap upright.[2]
GLOUCESTER   Let go my hand.
     Here, friend, 's another purse; in it a jewel
     Well worth a poor man's taking. Fairies and gods
30   Prosper it[3] with thee! Go thou further off.
     Bid me farewell, and let me hear thee going.
EDGAR   Now fare ye well, good sir.
     [He stands aside]
GLOUCESTER   With all my heart.
EDGAR *[aside]*   Why I do trifle thus with his despair
     Is done to cure it.
GLOUCESTER *[kneeling]* O you mighty gods,
35   This world I do renounce, and in your sights
     Shake patiently my great affliction off!

4.5 Location: Near Dover.
1. The air between cliff and sea.
2. I would not jump up and down (for fear of losing my
balance).
3. Make it increase. Fairies were sometimes held to
hoard and multiply treasure.

If I could bear it longer, and not fall
To quarrel° with your great opposeless wills,   *Into conflict*
My snuff and loathèd part of nature⁴ should
40   Burn itself out. If Edgar live, O bless him!—
Now, fellow, fare thee well.

EDGAR   Gone, sir. Farewell.
       [GLOUCESTER] *falls* [*forward*]
[*Aside*] And yet I know not how conceit may rob
The treasury of life, when life itself
Yields to the theft.⁵ Had he been where he thought,
45   By this° had thought been past.—Alive or dead?   *now*
[*To* GLOUCESTER] Ho you, sir; hear you, sir? Speak.
[*Aside*] Thus might he pass° indeed. Yet he revives.   *pass away*
[*To* GLOUCESTER] What are you, sir?

GLOUCESTER   Away, and let me die.

EDGAR   Hadst thou been aught° but goss'mer, feathers, air,   *anything*
50   So many fathom down precipitating°   *plunging*
Thou hadst shivered° like an egg. But thou dost breathe,   *shattered*
Hast heavy substance, bleed'st not, speak'st, art sound.
Ten masts a-length° make not the altitude   *end to end*
Which thou hast perpendicularly fell.
55   Thy life's a miracle. Speak yet again.

GLOUCESTER   But have I fallen, or no?

EDGAR   From the dread summit of this chalky bourn.⁶
Look up a-height. The shrill-gorged° lark so far   *shrill-throated*
Cannot be seen or heard. Do but look up.

60   GLOUCESTER   Alack, I have no eyes.
Is wretchedness deprived° that benefit   *deprived of*
To end itself by death? 'Twas yet some comfort
When misery could beguile° the tyrant's rage   *cheat*
And frustrate his proud will.

EDGAR   Give me your arm.
65   Up. So, how now? Feel you your legs? You stand.

GLOUCESTER   Too well, too well.

EDGAR   This is above all strangeness.
Upon the crown of the cliff what thing was that
Which parted from you?

GLOUCESTER   A poor unfortunate beggar.

EDGAR   As I stood here below, methoughts his eyes
70   Were two full moons. A had a thousand noses,
Horns whelked° and waved like the enridgèd sea.   *twisted*
It was some fiend. Therefore, thou happy father,°   *lucky old man*
Think that the clearest° gods, who made their honours   *purest; most illustrious*
Of men's impossibilities,⁷ have preserved thee.

75   GLOUCESTER   I do remember now. Henceforth I'll bear
Affliction till it do cry out itself
'Enough, enough,' and die. That thing you speak of,
I took it for a man. Often would it say

---

4. The scorched and hateful remnant of my lifetime.
snuff: end of a candlewick.
5. *And yet . . . theft*: Edgar worries that the imagined scenario ("conceit") he has invented may be enough to kill
his father, particularly as Gloucester wishes for ("yields

to") his own death.
6. The white chalk cliffs of Dover, which make a boundary ("bourn") between land and sea.
7. *who . . . impossibilities*: who attained honor for themselves by performing deeds impossible to men.

If I could bear it longer, and not fall
To quarrel° with your great opposeless wills,   *Into conflict*
My snuff and loathèd part of nature⁴ should
40   Burn itself out. If Edgar live, O bless him!—
Now, fellow, fare thee well.

EDGAR   Gone, sir. Farewell.
       [GLOUCESTER *falls forward*]
[*Aside*] And yet I know not how conceit may rob
The treasury of life, when life itself
Yields to the theft.⁵ Had he been where he thought,
45   By this° had thought been past.—Alive or dead?   *now*
[*To* GLOUCESTER] Ho, you, sir, friend; hear you, sir? Speak.
[*Aside*] Thus might he pass° indeed. Yet he revives.   *pass away*
[*To* GLOUCESTER] What are you, sir?

GLOUCESTER   Away, and let me die.

EDGAR   Hadst thou been aught° but gossamer, feathers, air,   *anything*
50   So many fathom down precipitating°   *plunging*
Thou'dst shivered° like an egg. But thou dost breathe,   *shattered*
Hast heavy substance, bleed'st not, speak'st, art sound.
Ten masts a-length° make not the altitude   *end to end*
Which thou hast perpendicularly fell.
55   Thy life's a miracle. Speak yet again.

GLOUCESTER   But have I fall'n, or no?

EDGAR   From the dread summit of this chalky bourn.⁶
Look up a-height. The shrill-gorged° lark so far   *shrill-throated*
Cannot be seen or heard. Do but look up.

60   GLOUCESTER   Alack, I have no eyes.
Is wretchedness deprived° that benefit   *deprived of*
To end itself by death? 'Twas yet some comfort
When misery could beguile° the tyrant's rage   *cheat*
And frustrate his proud will.

EDGAR   Give me your arm.
65   Up, so. How is't? Feel you your legs? You stand.

GLOUCESTER   Too well, too well.

EDGAR   This is above all strangeness.
Upon the crown o'th' cliff what thing was that
Which parted from you?

GLOUCESTER   A poor unfortunate beggar.

EDGAR   As I stood here below, methoughts his eyes
70   Were two full moons. He had a thousand noses,
Horns whelked° and wavèd like the enragèd sea.   *twisted*
It was some fiend. Therefore, thou happy father,°   *lucky old man*
Think that the clearest° gods, who make them honours   *purest; most illustrious*
Of men's impossibilities,⁷ have preserved thee.

75   GLOUCESTER   I do remember now. Henceforth I'll bear
Affliction till it do cry out itself
'Enough, enough,' and die. That thing you speak of,
I took it for a man. Often 'twould say

---

4. The scorched and hateful remnant of my lifetime.
snuff: end of a candlewick.
5. *And yet . . . theft*: Edgar worries that the imagined scenario ("conceit") he has invented may be enough to kill
his father, particularly as Gloucester wishes for ("yields

to") his own death.
6. The white chalk cliffs of Dover, which make a boundary ("bourn") between land and sea.
7. *who . . . impossibilities*: who attain honor for themselves by performing deeds impossible to men.

'The fiend, the fiend!' He led me to that place.

EDGAR   Bear free and patient thoughts.

Enter LEAR *mad* [*crowned with weeds and flowers*]

80   But who comes here?
The safer sense will ne'er accommodate
His master thus.[8]

LEAR   No, they cannot touch me for coining.[9] I am the King
himself.

85   EDGAR   O thou side-piercing sight!

LEAR   Nature is above art in that respect.[1] There's your press-
money.[2] That fellow handles his bow like a crow-keeper.[3] Draw
me a clothier's yard.[4] Look, look, a mouse! Peace, peace, this
toasted cheese will do it.°   There's my gauntlet. I'll prove it on   (*lure the mouse*)
90   a giant.[5] Bring up the brown bills.[6] O, well flown, bird,° in the   arrow
air. Ha! Give the word.°   password

EDGAR   Sweet marjoram.[7]

LEAR   Pass.

GLOUCESTER   I know that voice.

95   LEAR   Ha, Gonoril! Ha, Regan! They flattered me like a dog,°   *fawningly*
and told me I had white hairs in my beard ere the black ones
were there.[8] To say 'ay' and 'no' to everything I said 'ay' and
'no' to was no good divinity.[9] When the rain came to wet me
once, and the wind to make me chatter, when the thunder
100   would not peace at my bidding, there I found° them, there I   *understood*
smelt them out. Go to, they are not men of their words. They
told me I was everything; 'tis a lie, I am not ague-proof.°   *immune to illness*

GLOUCESTER   The trick° of that voice I do well remember.   *peculiarity*
Is't not the King?

LEAR   Ay, every inch a king.

[GLOUCESTER *kneels*]

105   When I do stare, see how the subject quakes!
I pardon that man's life. What was thy cause?°   *crime*
Adultery? Thou shalt not die for adultery.
No, the wren goes to't, and the small gilded fly
Does lecher in my sight.

110   Let copulation thrive, for Gloucester's bastard son
Was kinder to his father than my daughters
Got 'tween the lawful sheets. To't, luxury,° pell-mell,   *lechery*
For I lack soldiers. Behold yon simp'ring dame,
Whose face between her forks presageth snow,[1]
115   That minces° virtue, and does shake the head   *affects*
To hear of° pleasure's name: *even of*
The fitchew nor the soilèd horse[2] goes to't
With a more riotous appetite. Down from the waist

---

8. *The . . . thus:* A sane mind would never allow its possessor to dress up this way.
9. Because minting money was the prerogative of the
King, nobody could overtake or equal ("touch") him.
1. My true feelings will always outvalue others' hypocrisy;
my natural supremacy surpasses any attempt to create a
false new reign. This image may also be based on coining
(see note 9, above).
2. Fee paid to a soldier impressed, or forced, into the
army.
3. A person hired as a scarecrow, and thus unfit for anything else.
4. Draw the bowstring the full length of the arrow (a
standard English arrow was a cloth yard [37 inches]

long).
5. I'll defend my stand even against a giant. To throw
down an armored glove ("gauntlet") was to issue a challenge.
6. Brown painted pikes; the soldiers carrying them.
7. Used medicinally against madness.
8. Told me I had wisdom before age.
9. *no good divinity:* poor theology (because insincere);
from James 5:12, "Let your yea be yea; nay, nay."
1. Whose expression implies cold chastity. "Face" refers
to the area between her legs ("forks"), as well as to her
literal facial expression as framed by the aristocratic lady's
starched headpiece, also called a "fork."
2. Neither the polecat nor a horse full of fresh grass.

'The fiend, the fiend!' He led me to that place.

EDGAR Bear free and patient thoughts.

Enter LEAR [*mad, crowned with weeds and flowers*]

80   But who comes here?
The safer sense will ne'er accommodate
His master thus.[8]

LEAR No, they cannot touch me° for crying. I am the King   *lay hands on me*
himself.

85 EDGAR O thou side-piercing sight!

LEAR Nature's above art in that respect.[9] There's your press-
money.[1] That fellow handles his bow like a crow-keeper.[2] Draw
me a clothier's yard.[3] Look, look, a mouse! Peace, peace, this
piece of toasted cheese will do't.° There's my gauntlet. I'll   *(lure the mouse)*
90 prove it on a giant.[4] Bring up the brown bills.[5] O, well flown,
bird,° i'th' clout,° i'th' clout! Whew! Give the word.°   *arrow / bull's-eye / password*

EDGAR Sweet marjoram.[6]

LEAR Pass.

GLOUCESTER I know that voice.

95 LEAR Ha! Goneril with a white beard? They flattered me like a
dog,° and told me I had the white hairs in my beard ere the   *fawningly*
black ones were there.[7] To say 'ay' and 'no' to everything that I
said 'ay' and 'no' to was no good divinity.[8] When the rain came
to wet me once, and the wind to make me chatter; when the
100 thunder would not peace at my bidding, there I found° 'em,   *understood*
there I smelt 'em out. Go to, they are not men o' their words.
They told me I was everything; 'tis a lie, I am not ague-proof.°   *immune to illness*

GLOUCESTER The trick° of that voice I do well remember.   *peculiarity*
Is't not the King?

LEAR   Ay, every inch a king.

[GLOUCESTER *kneels*]

105 When I do stare, see how the subject quakes!
I pardon that man's life. What was thy cause?°   *crime*
Adultery? Thou shalt not die. Die for adultery!
No, the wren goes to't, and the small gilded fly
Does lecher in my sight. Let copulation thrive,
110 For Gloucester's bastard son
Was kinder to his father than my daughters
Got 'tween the lawful sheets. To't, luxury,° pell-mell,   *lechery*
For I lack soldiers. Behold yon simp'ring dame,
Whose face between her forks presages snow,[9]
115 That minces° virtue, and does shake the head   *affects*
To hear of° pleasure's name.   *even of*
The fitchew nor the soilèd horse[1] goes to't
With a more riotous appetite. Down from the waist

---

8. *The . . . thus:* A sane mind would never allow its possessor to dress up this way.
9. My true feelings will always outvalue others' hypocrisy;
my natural supremacy surpasses any attempt to create a
false new reign. This image may also be based on coining.
1. Fee paid to a soldier impressed, or forced, into the
army.
2. A person hired as a scarecrow, and thus unfit for anything else.
3. Draw the bowstring the full length of the arrow (a
standard English arrow was a cloth yard [37 inches]
long).
4. I'll defend my stand even against a giant. To throw

down an armored glove ("gauntlet") was to issue a challenge.
5. Brown painted pikes; the soldiers carrying them.
6. Used medicinally against madness.
7. Told me I had wisdom before age.
8. *no good divinity:* poor theology (because insincere);
from James 5:12, "Let your yea be yea; nay, nay."
9. Whose expression implies cold chastity. "Face"
refers to the area between her legs ("forks") as well as
to her literal facial expression as framed by the aristocratic lady's starched headpiece, also called a "fork."
1. Neither the polecat nor a horse full of fresh grass.

They're centaurs,[3] though women all above.

120   But° to the girdle° do the gods inherit;°   *Only / waist / own*
       Beneath is all the fiend's. There's hell,[4] there's darkness,
       There's the sulphury pit, burning, scalding,
       Stench, consummation. Fie, fie, fie; pah, pah!
       Give me an ounce of civet,[5] good apothecary,

125   To sweeten my imagination.
       There's money for thee.

GLOUCESTER   O, let me kiss that hand!

LEAR   Here, wipe it first; it smells of mortality.

GLOUCESTER   O ruined piece° of nature! This great world   *masterpiece*
       Shall so wear out to naught.[6] Do you know me?

130   LEAR   I remember thy eyes well enough. Dost thou squiny°   *squint*
       on me?
       No, do thy worst, blind Cupid, I'll not love.
       Read thou that challenge. Mark the penning of 't.

GLOUCESTER   Were all the letters suns, I could not see one.

135   EDGAR [*aside*]   I would not take° this from report; it is,   *believe*
       And my heart breaks at it.

LEAR [*to* GLOUCESTER]   Read.

GLOUCESTER   What—with the case° of eyes?   *sockets*

LEAR   O ho, are you there with me?[7] No eyes in your head, nor

140   no money in your purse? Your eyes are in a heavy case,[8] your
       purse in a light; yet you see how this world goes.

GLOUCESTER   I see it feelingly.°   *by touch; painfully*

LEAR   What, art mad? A man may see how the world goes with
       no eyes; look with thy ears. See how yon justice rails upon yon

145   simple° thief. Hark in thy ear: handy-dandy,[9] which is the thief,   *lowly; innocent*
       which is the justice? Thou hast seen a farmer's dog bark at a
       beggar?

GLOUCESTER   Ay, sir.

LEAR   An the creature° run from the cur, there thou mightst   *If the wretch*

150   behold the great image of authority. A dog's obeyed in office.
       Thou rascal beadle,[1] hold° thy bloody hand.   *restrain*
       Why dost thou lash that whore? Strip thine own back.
       Thy blood as hotly lusts to use her in that kind°   *way*
       For which thou whip'st her. The usurer hangs the cozener.[2]

155   Through tattered rags small vices do appear;
       Robes and furred gowns hides all. Get thee glass eyes,
       And, like a scurvy politician,[3] seem
       To see the things thou dost not. No tears, now.
       Pull off my boots. Harder, harder! So.

160   EDGAR [*aside*]   O, matter and impertinency° mixed—   *sense and nonsense*
       Reason in madness!

---

3. Lecherous mythological creatures that have a human body to the waist and the legs and torso of a horse below.
4. Shakespeare's frequent term for female genitals.
5. Exotic perfume derived from the sex glands of the civet cat.
6. Shall decay to nothing in the same way. In Renaissance philosophy, humans were analogous to the cosmos, standing for the whole in miniature and as its masterpiece.

7. Is that what you are telling me?
8. In a sad condition; playing on "case" as "sockets."
9. Pick a hand, as in a child's game.
1. The parish officer responsible for whippings.
2. The ruinous moneylender, prosperous enough to be made a judge, convicts the ordinary cheat.
3. A vile schemer. In early modern England, "politician" meant an ambitious, even Machiavellian, upstart.

They're centaurs,[2] though women all above.
But° to the girdle° do the gods inherit;°   *Only / waist / own*
Beneath is all the fiend's. There's hell,[3] there's darkness, there
is the sulphurous pit, burning, scalding, stench, consumption.
Fie, fie, fie; pah, pah! Give me an ounce of civet,[4] good apothe-
cary, sweeten my imagination.
There's money for thee.

GLOUCESTER   O, let me kiss that hand!

LEAR   Let me wipe it first; it smells of mortality.

GLOUCESTER   O ruined piece° of nature! This great world   *masterpiece*
Shall so wear out to naught.[5] Dost thou know me?

LEAR   I remember thine eyes well enough. Dost thou squiny°   *squint*
at me?
No, do thy worst, blind Cupid, I'll not love.
Read thou this challenge. Mark but the penning of it.

GLOUCESTER   Were all thy letters suns, I could not see.

EDGAR [*aside*]   I would not take° this from report; it is,   *believe*
And my heart breaks at it.

LEAR [*to* GLOUCESTER]   Read.

GLOUCESTER   What—with the case° of eyes?   *socket*

LEAR   O ho, are you there with me?[6] No eyes in your head, nor
no money in your purse? Your eyes are in a heavy case,[7] your
purse in a light; yet you see how this world goes.

GLOUCESTER   I see it feelingly.°   *by touch; painfully*

LEAR   What, art mad? A man may see how this world goes with
no eyes; look with thine ears. See how yon justice rails upon
yon simple° thief. Hark in thine ear: change places, and handy-   *lowly; innocent*
dandy,[8] which is the justice, which is the thief? Thou hast seen
a farmer's dog bark at a beggar?

GLOUCESTER   Ay, sir.

LEAR   An the creature° run from the cur, there thou mightst   *If the wretch*
behold the great image of authority. A dog's obeyed in office.
Thou rascal beadle,[9] hold° thy bloody hand.   *restrain*
Why dost thou lash that whore? Strip thy own back.
Thou hotly lusts to use her in that kind°   *way*
For which thou whip'st her. The usurer hangs the cozener.[1]
Through tattered clothes great vices do appear;
Robes and furred gowns hide all. Plate° sin with gold,   *Armor; gild*
And the strong lance of justice hurtless° breaks;   *harmlessly*
Arm it in rags, a pygmy's straw does pierce it.
None does offend, none, I say none. I'll able° 'em.   *authorize*
Take that of me, my friend, who have the power
To seal th'accuser's lips. Get thee glass eyes,
And, like a scurvy politician,[2] seem
To see the things thou dost not. Now, now, now, now!
Pull off my boots. Harder, harder! So.

EDGAR [*aside*]   O, matter and impertinency° mixed—   *sense and nonsense*
Reason in madness!

---

2. Lecherous mythological creatures that have a human body to the waist and the legs and torso of a horse below.
3. Shakespeare's frequent term for female genitals.
4. Exotic perfume derived from the sex glands of the civet cat.
5. Shall decay to nothing in the same way. In Renaissance philosophy, humans were analogous to the cosmos, standing for the whole in miniature and as its masterpiece.

6. Is that what you are telling me?
7. In a sad condition; playing on "case" as "sockets."
8. Pick a hand, as in a child's game.
9. The parish officer responsible for whippings.
1. The ruinous moneylender, prosperous enough to be made a judge, convicts the ordinary cheat.
2. A vile schemer. In early modern England, "politician" meant an ambitious, even Machiavellian, upstart.

LEAR   If thou wilt weep my fortune, take my eyes.
I know thee well enough: thy name is Gloucester.
Thou must be patient. We came crying hither.
165   Thou know'st the first time that we smell the air
We wail and cry. I will preach to thee. Mark me.
GLOUCESTER   Alack, alack, the day!
LEAR *[removing his crown of weeds]*[4]   When we are born, we cry
        that we are come
To this great stage of fools. This'° a good block.[5]   *This is*
170   It were a delicate° stratagem to shoe   *subtle*
A troop of horse with felt;[6] and when I have stole upon
These son-in-laws, then kill, kill, kill, kill, kill, kill!
            Enter three GENTLEMEN
FIRST GENTLEMAN   O, here he is. Lay hands upon him, sirs.
[*To* LEAR] Your most dear—
175   LEAR   No rescue? What, a prisoner? I am e'en
The natural fool[7] of fortune. Use° me well.   *Treat*
You shall have ransom. Let me have a surgeon;
I am cut to the brains.
FIRST GENTLEMAN   You shall have anything.
180   LEAR   No seconds?° All myself?   *supporters*
Why, this would make a man a man of salt,[8]
To use his eyes for garden water-pots,
Ay, and laying° autumn's dust.   *settling*
FIRST GENTLEMAN   Good sir—
LEAR   I will die bravely,[9] like a bridegroom.
185   What, I will be jovial. Come, come,
I am a king, my masters, know you that?
FIRST GENTLEMAN   You are a royal one, and we obey you.
LEAR   Then there's life° in't. Nay, an° you get it, you shall get it   *hope / if*
with running.   *Exit running [pursued by two* GENTLEMEN]
190   FIRST GENTLEMAN   A sight most pitiful in the meanest wretch,
Past speaking in a king. Thou hast one daughter
Who redeems nature from the general curse
Which twain hath brought her to.[1]
EDGAR   Hail, gentle° sir.   *noble*
195   FIRST GENTLEMAN   Sir, speed you.° What's your will?   *God speed you*
EDGAR   Do you hear aught of a battle toward?°   *coming*
FIRST GENTLEMAN   Most sure and vulgar,° everyone hears that   *commonly known*
That can distinguish sense.°   *Who can understand*
EDGAR   But, by your favour,
200   How near's the other army?
FIRST GENTLEMAN   Near and on speedy foot, the main;°   *main army*
        descriers°   *scouts*
Stands on the hourly thoughts.°   *Are expected forthwith*
EDGAR   I thank you, sir. That's all.

---

4. Like a preacher, removing his hat in the pulpit.
5. Stage (often called "scaffold" and hence linked to executioner's block); block used to shape a felt hat (such as
the hat removed by a preacher before a sermon); mounting block (such as the stump or stock Lear may have sat
on to remove his boots).
6. Hat material, to muffle the sound of the approaching
cavalry.
7. Born plaything; playing on "natural" as "mentally
deficient."

8. A man reduced to nothing but the salt his tears
deposit.
9. With courage; showily. "Die" plays on the Renaissance sense of "have an orgasm."
1. Who . . . to: Who restores proper meaning and order
to a universe plagued by the crimes of the other two
daughters; alluding to the fall of humankind and the natural world caused by the sin of Adam and Eve and to the
universal redemption brought about by Christ's sacrifice.

LEAR   If thou wilt weep my fortunes, take my eyes.
I know thee well enough: thy name is Gloucester.
Thou must be patient. We came crying hither.
Thou know'st the first time that we smell the air
170   We waul and cry. I will preach to thee. Mark.

GLOUCESTER   Alack, alack the day!

LEAR [*removing his crown of weeds*][3]   When we are born, we cry
    That we are come
To this great stage of fools. This'° a good block.[4]   *This is*
It were a delicate° stratagem to shoe   *subtle*
175   A troop of horse with felt.[5] I'll put't in proof,°   *to the test*
And when I have stol'n upon these son-in-laws,
Then kill, kill, kill, kill, kill, kill!

                        Enter a GENTLEMAN

FIRST GENTLEMAN   O, here he is. Lay hand upon him. [*To* LEAR] Sir,
Your most dear daughter—
180 LEAR   No rescue? What, a prisoner? I am even
The natural fool[6] of fortune. Use° me well.   *Treat*
You shall have ransom. Let me have surgeons;
I am cut to th' brains.

FIRST GENTLEMAN   You shall have anything.

185 LEAR   No seconds?° All myself?   *supporters*
Why, this would make a man a man of salt,[7]
To use his eyes for garden water-pots.
I will die bravely,[8] like a smug° bridegroom. What,   *an elegant*
I will be jovial. Come, come, I am a king.
190   Masters, know you that?

FIRST GENTLEMAN   You are a royal one, and we obey you.

LEAR   Then there's life° in't. Come, an° you get it, you shall get   *hope / if*
it by running. Sa, sa, sa, sa![9]

                        Exit [*running*]

FIRST GENTLEMAN   A sight most pitiful in the meanest wretch,
195   Past speaking in a king. Thou hast a daughter
Who redeems nature from the general curse
Which twain have brought her to.[1]

EDGAR   Hail, gentle° sir.   *noble*

FIRST GENTLEMAN   Sir, speed you.° What's your will?   *God speed you*

200 EDGAR   Do you hear aught, sir, of a battle toward?°   *coming*

FIRST GENTLEMAN   Most sure and vulgar,° everyone hears that   *commonly known*
That can distinguish sound.

EDGAR   But, by your favour,
How near's the other army?

205 FIRST GENTLEMAN   Near and on speedy foot. The main descry°   *appearance*
Stands in the hourly thought.°   *Is expected forthwith*

EDGAR   I thank you, sir. That's all.

---

3. Like a preacher removing his hat in the pulpit.
4. Stage (often called "scaffold" and hence linked to executioner's block); block used to shape a felt hat (such as
the hat removed by a preacher before a sermon); mounting block (such as the stump or stock Lear may have sat
on to remove his boots).
5. Hat material, to muffle the sound of the approaching
cavalry.
6. Born plaything; playing on "natural" as "mentally
deficient."

7. A man reduced to nothing but the salt his tears
deposit.
8. With courage; showily. "Die" plays on the Renaissance sense of "have an orgasm."
9. A cry to encourage dogs in the hunt.
1. *Who . . . to:* Who restores proper meaning and order
to a universe plagued by the crimes of the other two
daughters; alluding to the fall of humankind and the natural world caused by the sin of Adam and Eve and to the
universal redemption brought about by Christ's sacrifice.

FIRST GENTLEMAN   Though that the Queen on° special cause°   *for / reason*
    is here,
    Her army is moved on.

EDGAR   I thank you, sir.   *Exit* GENTLEMAN

205   GLOUCESTER   You ever gentle gods, take my breath from me.
    Let not my worser spirit² tempt me again
    To die before you please.

EDGAR   Well pray you, father.³

GLOUCESTER   Now, good sir, what are you?

210   EDGAR   A most poor man, made lame by fortune's blows,
    Who by the art of known and feeling° sorrows   *profound*
    Am pregnant to° good pity. Give me your hand,   *disposed to feel*
    I'll lead you to some biding.°   *resting place*

GLOUCESTER [*rising*]   Hearty thanks.
    The bounty and the benison of heaven
    To send thee boot to boot.⁴

        Enter Steward [OSWALD]

215   OSWALD   A proclaimed prize!⁵ Most happy!°   *lucky*
    That eyeless head of thine was first framed° flesh   *made of*
    To raise my fortunes. Thou most unhappy traitor,
    Briefly thyself remember.⁶ The sword is out
    That must destroy thee.

GLOUCESTER   Now let thy friendly hand
    Put strength enough to't.

220   OSWALD [*to* EDGAR]   Wherefore, bold peasant,
    Durst thou support a published° traitor? Hence,   *proclaimed*
    Lest the infection° of his fortune take   *(deathly) sickness*
    Like° hold on thee. Let go his arm.   *The same*

EDGAR   'Chill⁷ not let go, sir, without 'cagion.°   *occasion*

225   OSWALD   Let go, slave, or thou diest.

EDGAR   Good gentleman, go your gate.° Let poor volk pass. An   *be on your way*
    'chud° have been swaggered out of my life, it would not have   *If I could*
    been so long by a vortnight. Nay, come not near the old man.
    Keep out, 'che vor' ye, or I'll try whether your costard or my
230   baton be the harder;⁸ I'll be plain with you.

OSWALD   Out, dunghill!

        They fight

EDGAR   'Chill pick your teeth, sir. Come, no matter for your
    foins.°   *sword thrusts*

    [EDGAR *knocks him down*]

OSWALD   Slave, thou hast slain me. Villain, take my purse.
235   If ever thou wilt thrive, bury my body,
    And give the letters which thou find'st about me
    To Edmund, Earl of Gloucester. Seek him out
    Upon° the British party. O untimely death! Death!   *He dies*   *Within*

---

2. Wicked inclination; bad angel.
3. A term of respect for an elderly man.
4. To send you reward in addition (to my thanks).
5. A wanted man, with a bounty on his life.
6. Recollect and pray forgiveness for your sins.

7. I will; dialect from Somerset was a stage convention for peasant dialogue.
8. *'che vor' ye . . . harder:* I warrant you, or I'll test whether your head or my cudgel is harder. *costard:* a kind of apple.

FIRST GENTLEMAN   Though that the Queen on° special cause° is   *for / reason*
    here,
    Her army is moved on.
EDGAR   I thank you, sir.   *Exit* [GENTLEMAN]
GLOUCESTER   You ever gentle gods, take my breath from me.
210   Let not my worser spirit² tempt me again
    To die before you please.
EDGAR   Well pray you, father.³
GLOUCESTER   Now, good sir, what are you?
EDGAR   A most poor man, made tame to fortune's blows,
215   Who by the art of known and feeling° sorrows   *profound*
    Am pregnant to° good pity. Give me your hand,   *disposed to feel*
    I'll lead you to some biding.°   *resting place*
GLOUCESTER [*rising*]   Hearty thanks.
    The bounty and the benison of heaven
    To boot and boot.⁴
        Enter Steward [OSWALD]
OSWALD   A proclaimed prize!⁵ Most happy!°   *lucky*
220   That eyeless head of thine was first framed° flesh   *made of*
    To raise my fortunes. Thou old unhappy traitor,
    Briefly thyself remember.⁶ The sword is out
    That must destroy thee.
GLOUCESTER   Now let thy friendly hand
    Put strength enough to't.
OSWALD [*to* EDGAR]   Wherefore, bold peasant,
225   Durst thou support a published° traitor? Hence,   *proclaimed*
    Lest that th'infection° of his fortune take   *(deathly) sickness*
    Like° hold on thee. Let go his arm.   *The same*
EDGAR   'Chill⁷ not let go, sir, without vurther 'cagion.°   *further occasion*
OSWALD   Let go, slave, or thou diest.
230 EDGAR   Good gentleman, go your gate,° and let poor volk pass.   *be on your way*
    An 'chud ha'° been swaggered out of my life, 'twould not ha'   *If I could have*
    been so long as 'tis by a vortnight. Nay, come not near th'old
    man. Keep out, 'che vor' ye, or I's' try whether your costard or
    my baton be the harder;⁸ I'll be plain with you.
235 OSWALD   Out, dunghill!
EDGAR   'Chill pick your teeth, sir. Come, no matter vor your
    foins.°   *sword thrusts*
        [EDGAR *knocks him down*]
OSWALD   Slave, thou hast slain me. Villain, take my purse.
    If ever thou wilt thrive, bury my body,
240   And give the letters which thou find'st about me
    To Edmond, Earl of Gloucester. Seek him out
    Upon° the English party. O untimely death! Death!   [*He dies*]   *Within*

---

2. Wicked inclination; bad angel.
3. A term of respect for an elderly man.
4. In addition to my thanks, and may it bring you some
worldly reward.
5. A wanted man, with a bounty on his life.
6. Recollect and pray forgiveness for your sins.

7. I will; dialect from Somerset was a stage convention
for peasant dialogue.
8. *'che vor' ye . . . harder:* I warrant you, or I shall test
whether your head or my cudgel is harder. *costard:* a kind
of apple.

EDGAR I know thee well—a serviceable° villain, *an officious*
240 As duteous to the vices of thy mistress
As badness would desire.
GLOUCESTER What, is he dead?
EDGAR Sit you down, father. Rest you.
    [GLOUCESTER *sits*]
Let's see his pockets. These letters that he speaks of
245 May be my friends. He's dead; I am only sorrow° *sorry*
He had no other deathsman.° Let us see. *executioner*
Leave,° gentle wax;⁹ and manners, blame us not. *By your leave*
To know our enemies' minds we'd rip their hearts;
Their° papers is more lawful. *To rip their*
    [*He reads*] *a letter*
250 'Let your reciprocal vows be remembered. You have many
opportunities to cut him off. If your will want° not, time and *lacks*
place will be fruitfully offered. There is nothing done° if he *accomplished*
return the conqueror; then am I the prisoner, and his bed my
jail, from the loathed warmth whereof, deliver me, and supply° *fill*
255 the place for your labour.¹
    Your—wife, so I would say—your affectionate
        servant, and for you her own for venture,²
                                            Gonoril.'
O indistinguished space of woman's wit³—
260 A plot upon her virtuous husband's life,
And the exchange° my brother!—Here in the sands *substitute*
Thee I'll rake up,° the post unsanctified° *cover up / unholy messenger*
Of murderous lechers, and in the mature time° *when the time is ripe*
With this ungracious° paper strike the sight *ungodly*
265 Of the death-practisèd Duke.⁴ For him 'tis well
That of thy death and business I can tell. [*Exit with the body*]
GLOUCESTER The King is mad. How stiff is my vile sense,⁵
That I stand up and have ingenious feeling⁶
Of my huge sorrows! Better I were distraught;° *mad*
270 So should my thoughts be fencèd from my griefs,
And woes by wrong° imaginations lose *false*
The knowledge of themselves.
    A drum afar off. [*Enter* EDGAR]
EDGAR   Give me your hand.
Far off methinks I hear the beaten drum.
Come, father, I'll bestow° you with a friend. *lodge*
        Exit [EDGAR *guiding* GLOUCESTER]

9. The wax seal on the letter.
1. *for your labour:* as a reward for your endeavors, and
for further sexual exertion.
2. *for you . . . venture:* one willing to risk all for you; all
yours, if you dare be so bold.
3. Limitless extent of woman's cunning.

4. Of the Duke whose death is plotted.
5. How obstinate is my unwanted power of reason.
6. That I remain upright and firm in my sanity and
have rational perceptions.

EDGAR I know thee well—a serviceable° villain,   *an officious*
As duteous to the vices of thy mistress
245 As badness would desire.
GLOUCESTER What, is he dead?
EDGAR Sit you down, father. Rest you.
　　　　　[GLOUCESTER *sits*]
Let's see these pockets. The letters that he speaks of
May be my friends. He's dead; I am only sorrow°   *sorry*
250 He had no other deathsman.° Let us see.   *executioner*
Leave,° gentle wax,⁹ and manners; blame us not.   *By your leave*
To know our enemies' minds we rip their hearts;
Their° papers is more lawful.   *To rip their*
　　　　　Reads the letter
'Let our reciprocal vows be remembered. You have many
255 opportunities to cut him off. If your will want° not, time and   *lacks*
place will be fruitfully offered. There is nothing done° if he   *accomplished*
return the conqueror; then am I the prisoner, and his bed my
jail, from the loathed warmth whereof, deliver me, and supply°   *fill*
the place for your labour.¹
260 　　　　Your—wife, so I would say,—affectionate
　　　　servant, and for you her own for venture,²
　　　　　　　　　　　　　　　Goneril.'
O indistinguished space of woman's will³—
A plot upon her virtuous husband's life,
265 And the exchange° my brother!—Here in the sands   *substitute*
Thee I'll rake up,° the post unsanctified°   *cover up / unholy messenger*
Of murderous lechers, and in the mature time°   *when the time is ripe*
With this ungracious° paper strike the sight   *ungodly*
Of the death-practised Duke.⁴ For him 'tis well
270 That of thy death and business I can tell. [*Exit with the body*]
GLOUCESTER The King is mad. How stiff is my vile sense,⁵
That I stand up and have ingenious feeling⁶
Of my huge sorrows! Better I were distraught,°   *mad*
So should my thoughts be severed from my griefs,
　　　　　Drum afar off
275 And woes by wrong° imaginations lose   *false*
The knowledge of themselves.
　　　　　[*Enter* EDGAR]
EDGAR　　　　　　　　　　　Give me your hand.
Far off methinks I hear the beaten drum.
Come, father, I'll bestow° you with a friend.   *lodge*
　　　　　Exit [EDGAR *guiding* GLOUCESTER]

9. The wax seal on the letter.
1. *for your labour:* as a reward for your endeavors, and for further sexual exertion.
2. *for you . . . venture:* one willing to risk all for you; all yours, if you dare be so bold.
3. Limitless extent of woman's willfulness. As with "hell" in line 121, "will" might also refer to a woman's genitals.
4. Of the Duke whose death is plotted.
5. How obstinate is my unwanted power of reason.
6. That I remain upright and firm in my sanity and have rational perceptions.

Scene 21

[*Soft music.*] *Enter* CORDELIA, *and* KENT [*disguised*]

CORDELIA   O thou good Kent,
How shall I live and work to match thy goodness?
My life will be too short, and every measure° fail me.   attempt
KENT   To be acknowledged, madam, is o'erpaid.°   is more than enough
5   All my reports go[1] with the modest truth,
Nor more, nor clipped, but so.[2]
CORDELIA   Be better suited.°   attired
These weeds° are memories of those worser hours.   clothes
I prithee put them off.
KENT   Pardon me, dear madam.
Yet to be known shortens my made intent.[3]
10   My boon I make it[4] that you know° me not   acknowledge
Till time and I think meet.°   suitable
CORDELIA   Then be't so, my good lord.

[*Enter* DOCTOR *and* FIRST GENTLEMAN]

How does the King?
DOCTOR   Madam, sleeps still.
CORDELIA   O you kind gods,
Cure this great breach in his abusèd nature;
The untuned and hurrying senses O wind up[5]
Of this child-changèd[6] father!
15   DOCTOR   So please your majesty
That we may wake the King? He hath slept long.
CORDELIA   Be governed by your knowledge, and proceed
I'th' sway° of your own will. Is he arrayed?°   By the authority / clothed
FIRST GENTLEMAN   Ay, madam. In the heaviness of his sleep
20   We put fresh garments on him.
DOCTOR   Good madam, be by when we do awake him.
I doubt not of his temperance.°   calmness
CORDELIA   Very well.
DOCTOR   Please you draw near. Louder the music there!

[LEAR *is discovered*° *asleep*]   revealed

CORDELIA   O my dear father, restoration hang
25   Thy medicine on my lips, and let this kiss
Repair those violent harms that my two sisters
Have in thy reverence° made!   aged dignity
KENT   Kind and dear princess!
CORDELIA   Had you not[7] been their father, these white flakes°   locks of hair
Had challenged° pity of them. Was this a face   Would have provoked
30   To be exposed against the warring winds,
To stand against the deep dread-bolted thunder
In the most terrible and nimble stroke
Of quick cross-lightning, to watch°—poor *perdu*[8]—   to stand guard

---

Scene 21 Location: The French camp at Dover.
1. May all accounts of me agree.
2. Not greater or less, but exactly the modest amount I deserve.
3. Revealing myself now would abort my designs.
4. The reward I beg is.
5. *The . . . up:* Reorder his confused and delirious mind.

The image is of tightening the strings of a lute.
6. Changed by his children; changed into a child; playing on a musical key change.
7. Even if you had not.
8. Lost one; in military terms, a dangerously exposed sentry.

4.6

Enter CORDELIA, KENT [*disguised*], *and* [*the* FIRST] GEN-
TLEMAN

CORDELIA   O thou good Kent, how shall I live and work
To match thy goodness? My life will be too short,
And every measure° fail me.   *attempt*

KENT   To be acknowledged, madam, is o'erpaid.°   *is more than enough*

5   All my reports go[1] with the modest truth,
Nor more, nor clipped, but so.[2]

CORDELIA   Be better suited.°   *attired*
These weeds° are memories of those worser hours.   *clothes*
I prithee put them off.

KENT   Pardon, dear madam.
Yet to be known shortens my made intent.[3]

10   My boon I make it[4] that you know° me not   *acknowledge*
Till time and I think meet.°   *suitable*

CORDELIA   Then be't so, my good lord.—
How does the King?

FIRST GENTLEMAN   Madam, sleeps still.

CORDELIA   O you kind gods,
Cure this great breach in his abusèd nature;
Th'untuned and jarring senses O wind up[5]
Of this child-changèd[6] father!

15   FIRST GENTLEMAN   So please your majesty
That we may wake the King? He hath slept long.

CORDELIA   Be governed by your knowledge, and proceed
I'th' sway° of your own will. Is he arrayed?°   *By the authority / clothed*

FIRST GENTLEMAN   Ay, madam. In the heaviness of sleep
20   We put fresh garments on him.

Enter LEAR [*asleep*,] *in a chair carried by servants*
Be by, good madam, when we do awake him.
I doubt not of his temperance.°   *calmness*

CORDELIA   O my dear father, restoration hang
Thy medicine on my lips, and let this kiss
25   Repair those violent harms that my two sisters
Have in thy reverence° made!   *aged dignity*

KENT   Kind and dear princess!

CORDELIA   Had you not[7] been their father, these white flakes°   *locks of hair*
Did challenge° pity of them. Was this a face   *Would have provoked*
To be opposed against the warring winds?

4.6 Location: The French camp at Dover.
1. May all accounts of me agree.
2. Not greater or less, but exactly the modest amount I deserve.
3. Revealing myself now would abort my designs.
4. The reward I beg is.
5. *Th'untuned . . . up:* Reorder his confused and delirious mind. The image is of tightening the strings of a lute.
6. Changed by his children; changed into a child; playing on a musical key change.
7. Even if you had not.

With this thin helm?° Mine injurer's mean'st dog,   *helmet (of hair)*
35   Though he had bit me, should have stood that night
      Against my fire. And wast thou fain,° poor father,   *glad*
      To hovel thee with swine and rogues forlorn
      In short° and musty straw? Alack, alack,   *scant; broken*
      'Tis wonder that thy life and wits at once
40   Had not concluded all!° [*To* DOCTOR] He wakes. Speak to him.   *altogether*
DOCTOR   Madam, do you; 'tis fittest.
CORDELIA [*to* LEAR]   How does my royal lord? How fares your majesty?
LEAR   You do me wrong to take me out o'th' grave.
      Thou art a soul in bliss, but I am bound
45   Upon a wheel of fire, that mine own tears
      Do scald like molten lead.[9]
CORDELIA   Sir, know me.
LEAR   You're a spirit, I know. Where did you die?
CORDELIA [*to the* DOCTOR]   Still, still far wide!°   *unbalanced*
DOCTOR   He's scarce awake. Let him alone a while.
50   LEAR   Where have I been? Where am I? Fair daylight?
      I am mightily abused.° I should e'en die with pity   *wronged; deceived*
      To see another thus. I know not what to say.
      I will not swear these are my hands. Let's see:
      I feel this pin prick. Would I were assured
      Of my condition.
55   CORDELIA [*kneeling*]   O look upon me, sir,
      And hold your hands in benediction o'er me.
      No, sir, you must not kneel.
LEAR   Pray do not mock.
      I am a very foolish, fond° old man,   *silly*
      Fourscore and upward, and to deal plainly,
60   I fear I am not in my perfect mind.
      Methinks I should know you, and know this man;
      Yet I am doubtful, for I am mainly° ignorant   *entirely*
      What place this is; and all the skill I have
      Remembers not these garments; nor I know not
65   Where I did lodge last night. Do not laugh at me,
      For as I am a man, I think this lady
      To be my child, Cordelia.
CORDELIA   And so I am.
LEAR   Be your tears wet?[1] Yes, faith. I pray, weep not.
      If you have poison for me, I will drink it.
70   I know you do not love me; for your sisters
      Have, as I do remember, done me wrong.
      You have some cause; they have not.
CORDELIA   No cause, no cause.

---

9. *but I . . . lead*: Lear puts himself in either hell or pur-   accounts.
gatory, both places of such punishment in medieval   1. Are your tears real?; is this really happening?

30	Mine enemy's dog, though he had bit me, should have stood	
	That night against my fire. And wast thou fain,° poor father,	glad
	To hovel thee with swine and rogues forlorn	
	In short° and musty straw? Alack, alack,	scant; broken
	'Tis wonder that thy life and wits at once	
35	Had not concluded all!° [*To the* GENTLEMAN] He wakes. Speak	altogether
	to him.	

FIRST GENTLEMAN   Madam, do you; 'tis fittest.

CORDELIA [*to* LEAR]   How does my royal lord? How fares your majesty?

LEAR   You do me wrong to take me out o'th' grave.

    Thou art a soul in bliss, but I am bound

40   Upon a wheel of fire, that mine own tears

    Do scald like molten lead.[8]

CORDELIA   Sir, do you know me?

LEAR   You are a spirit, I know. Where did you die?

CORDELIA [*to the* GENTLEMAN]   Still, still far wide!°   *unbalanced*

FIRST GENTLEMAN   He's scarce awake. Let him alone a while.

45	LEAR Where have I been? Where am I? Fair daylight?	
	I am mightily abused.° I should ev'n die with pity	wronged; deceived
	To see another thus. I know not what to say.	
	I will not swear these are my hands. Let's see:	
	I feel this pin prick. Would I were assured	
50	Of my condition.	

CORDELIA [*kneeling*]   O look upon me, sir,

    And hold your hands in benediction o'er me.

    You must not kneel.

LEAR   Pray do not mock.

	I am a very foolish, fond° old man,	silly
	Fourscore and upward,	
55	Not an hour more nor less; and to deal plainly,	
	I fear I am not in my perfect mind.	
	Methinks I should know you, and know this man;	
	Yet I am doubtful, for I am mainly° ignorant	entirely
	What place this is; and all the skill I have	
60	Remembers not these garments; nor I know not	
	Where I did lodge last night. Do not laugh at me,	
	For as I am a man, I think this lady	
	To be my child, Cordelia.	

CORDELIA   And so I am, I am.

LEAR   Be your tears wet?[9] Yes, faith. I pray, weep not.

65   If you have poison for me, I will drink it.

    I know you do not love me; for your sisters

    Have, as I do remember, done me wrong.

    You have some cause; they have not.

CORDELIA   No cause, no cause.

---

8. *but I . . . lead:* Lear puts himself in either hell or purgatory, both places of such punishment in medieval accounts.

9. Are your tears real?; is this really happening?

LEAR   Am I in France?
KENT   In your own kingdom, sir.
75   LEAR   Do not abuse° me.   *deceive; mock*
DOCTOR   Be comforted, good madam. The great rage
    You see is cured in him, and yet it is danger
    To make him even o'er° the time he has lost.   *go over*
    Desire him to go in; trouble him no more
80   Till further settling.°   *Until his mind eases*
CORDELIA [*to* LEAR]   Will't please your highness walk?
LEAR   You must bear with me.
    Pray now, forget and forgive. I am old
    And foolish.   *Exeunt. Manent°* KENT *and* [FIRST] GENTLEMAN   *Remain*
FIRST GENTLEMAN   Holds it true, sir, that the Duke
    Of Cornwall was so slain?
85   KENT   Most certain, sir.
FIRST GENTLEMAN   Who is conductor° of his people?   *commander*
KENT   As 'tis said,
    The bastard son of Gloucester.
FIRST GENTLEMAN   They say Edgar,
    His banished son, is with the Earl of Kent
    In Germany.
KENT   Report° is changeable.   *Rumor*
90   'Tis time to look about.° The powers of the kingdom   *prepare defenses*
    Approach apace.
FIRST GENTLEMAN   The arbitrement° is   *encounter*
    Like to be bloody. Fare you well, sir.   [*Exit*]
KENT   My point and period[2] will be throughly wrought,
    Or° well or ill, as this day's battle's fought.   *Exit*   *For*

Scene 22

Enter EDMUND, REGAN, *and their powers*

EDMUND   Know° of the Duke if his last purpose hold,[1]   *Inquire*
    Or whether since he is advised by aught[2]
    To change the course. He's full of abdication[3]
    And self-reproving. Bring his constant pleasure.°   *his settled intent*
                  [*Exit one or more*]
5   REGAN   Our sister's man is certainly miscarried.[4]
EDMUND   'Tis to be doubted,° madam.   *feared*
REGAN   Now, sweet lord,
    You know the goodness I intend upon you.
    Tell me but truly—but then speak the truth—
    Do you not love my sister?
EDMUND   Ay: honoured° love.   *honorable*
10   REGAN   But have you never found my brother's way
    To the forfended[5] place?

---

2. The purpose and end of my life; literally, the full stop.
Scene 22 Location: The British camp near Dover.
1. If his previous intention (to wage war) remains firm.
2. Since then anything has persuaded him.

3. A tendency to give up his intentions or put aside his responsibilities.
4. Has surely come to grief by some accident.
5. Forbidden (to Edmund, because it is adulterous).

LEAR   Am I in France?
70 KENT   In your own kingdom, sir.
LEAR   Do not abuse° me.   *deceive; mock*
FIRST GENTLEMAN   Be comforted, good madam. The great rage
You see is killed in him. Desire him to go in.
Trouble him no more till further settling.°   *until his mind eases*
75 CORDELIA [*to* LEAR]   Will't please your highness walk?
LEAR   You must bear with me. Pray you now, forget
And forgive. I am old and foolish.   *Exeunt*

5.1

Enter with drum and colours° EDMOND, REGAN, GENTLE-   *regimental flags*
MEN, *and soldiers*
EDMOND   Know° of the Duke if his last purpose hold,[1]   *Inquire*
Or whether since he is advised by aught[2]
To change the course. He's full of abdication[3]
And self-reproving. Bring his constant pleasure.°   *his settled intent*
[*Exit one or more*]
5 REGAN   Our sister's man is certainly miscarried.[4]
EDMOND   'Tis to be doubted,° madam.   *feared*
REGAN   Now, sweet lord,
You know the goodness I intend upon you.
Tell me but truly—but then speak the truth—
Do you not love my sister?
EDMOND   In honoured° love.   *honorable*
10 REGAN   But have you never found my brother's way
To the forfended[5] place?

5.1 Location: The British camp near Dover.
1. If his previous intention (to wage war) remains firm.
2. Since then anything has persuaded him.
3. A tendency to give up his intentions or put aside his

responsibilities.
4. Has surely come to grief by some accident.
5. Forbidden (to Edmond, because it is adulterous).

EDMUND   That thought abuses° you.   *deceives*

REGAN   I am doubtful°   *suspicious*
That you have been conjunct° and bosomed with° her,   *complicit/enamored of*
As far as we call hers.[6]

15   EDMUND   No, by mine honour, madam.

REGAN   I never shall endure her. Dear my lord,
Be not familiar° with her.   *intimate*

EDMUND   Fear° me not.   *Doubt*
She and the Duke her husband—

            Enter ALBANY *and* GONORIL *with troops*

20   GONORIL [*aside*]   I had rather lose the battle than that sister
Should loosen° him and me.   *disunite*

ALBANY [*to* REGAN]   Our very loving sister, well bemet,°   *met*
For this I hear: the King is come to his daughter,
With others whom the rigour° of our state°   *harshness / government*

25   Forced to cry out. Where I could not be honest°   *honorable*
I never yet was valiant. For this business,
It touches° us as France invades our land;   *concerns*
Yet bold's the King, with others whom I fear.[7]
Most just and heavy causes make oppose.[8]

EDMUND   Sir, you speak nobly.

30   REGAN   Why is this reasoned?[9]

GONORIL   Combine together 'gainst the enemy;
For these domestic poor particulars°   *minor details*
Are not to° question here.   *the*

ALBANY   Let us then determine with the ensign° of war   *experienced officer(s)*
On our proceedings.

35   EDMUND   I shall attend you
Presently° at your tent.   [*Exit with his powers*]   *In a moment*

REGAN   Sister, you'll go with us?

GONORIL   No.

REGAN   'Tis most convenient.° Pray you go with us.[1]   *suitable*

GONORIL [*aside*]   O ho, I know the riddle!° [*To* REGAN] I will go. *disguised meaning*

            Enter EDGAR [*disguised as a peasant*]

40   EDGAR [*to* ALBANY]   If e'er your grace had speech with man so poor,
Hear me one word.

ALBANY [*to the others*]   I'll overtake you.

                        Exeunt [*all but* ALBANY *and* EDGAR]
                            Speak.

EDGAR   Before you fight the battle, ope this letter.
If you have victory, let the trumpet sound
For him that brought it. Wretched though I seem,

45   I can produce a champion that will prove°   *defend*
What is avouchèd° there. If you miscarry,°   *asserted / perish*
Your business of the world hath so an end.
Fortune love you—

ALBANY   Stay till I have read the letter.

---

6. In total intimacy; all the way.
7. Albany expresses his ambivalence. The invasion concerns us insofar as we are facing a French army in our lands. On the other hand, King Lear, along with other powerful forces, is boldly claiming his own land.
8. Fair and serious causes are driven into opposition.
9. What is the point of this kind of speech?
1. Regan wants Gonoril to go with Albany and her, rather than with Edmund.

EDMOND   No, by mine honour, madam.

REGAN   I never shall endure her. Dear my lord,
   Be not familiar° with her.   *intimate*

EDMOND   Fear° me not.   *Doubt*

15   She and the Duke her husband—
            Enter with drum and colours ALBANY, GONERIL, [*and*]
            soldiers

ALBANY [*to* REGAN]   Our very loving sister, well bemet.°   *met*
   [*To* EDMOND] Sir, this I heard: the King is come to his daughter,
   With others whom the rigour° of our state°   *harshness / government*
   Forced to cry out.

REGAN   Why is this reasoned?⁶

20   GONERIL   Combine together 'gainst the enemy;
   For these domestic and particular broils°   *minor details*
   Are not the question here.

ALBANY   Let's then determine with th'ensign° of war   *experienced officer(s)*
   On our proceeding.

REGAN   Sister, you'll go with us?⁷

25   GONERIL   No.

REGAN   'Tis most convenient.° Pray go with us.   *suitable*

GONERIL [*aside*]   O ho, I know the riddle!° [*To* REGAN] I will go.   *disguised meaning*
            Enter EDGAR [*disguised as a peasant*]

EDGAR [*to* ALBANY]   If e'er your grace had speech with man so poor,
   Hear me one word.

ALBANY [*to the others*]   I'll overtake you.   *Exeunt both the armies*
                          Speak.

30   EDGAR   Before you fight the battle, ope this letter.
   If you have victory, let the trumpet sound
   For him that brought it. Wretched though I seem,
   I can produce a champion that will prove°   *defend*
   What is avouchèd° there. If you miscarry,°   *asserted / perish*
35   Your business of the world hath so an end,
   And machination° ceases. Fortune love you.   *plotting*

ALBANY   Stay till I have read the letter.

---

6. What is the point of this kind of speech?
7. Regan wants Goneril to go with Albany and her, rather than with Edmond.

50 EDGAR   I was forbid it.
　　When time shall serve, let but the herald cry,
　　And I'll appear again.
　ALBANY   Why, fare thee well.
　　I will o'erlook the paper.　　　　　　　　　*Exit* [EDGAR]
　　　　　Enter EDMUND
55 EDMUND   The enemy's in view; draw up your powers.°　　　*troops*
　　　[*He offers* ALBANY *a paper*]
　　Here is the guess° of their great strength and forces　*estimate*
　　By diligent discovery;° but your haste　　　　　　*spying*
　　Is now urged on you.
　ALBANY　　　　　　　We will greet the time.²　　　*Exit*
　EDMUND   To both these sisters have I sworn my love,
60　Each jealous° of the other as the stung　　　　*suspicious*
　　Are of the adder. Which of them shall I take?—
　　Both?—one?—or neither? Neither can be enjoyed
　　If both remain alive. To take the widow
　　Exasperates, makes mad, her sister Gonoril,
65　And hardly° shall I carry out my side,°　*with difficulty / plan*
　　Her husband being alive. Now then, we'll use
　　His countenance³ for the battle, which being done,
　　Let her that would be rid of him devise
　　His speedy taking off. As for his mercy
70　Which he intends to Lear and to Cordelia,
　　The battle done, and they within our power,
　　Shall° never see his pardon; for my state°　*They shall / condition*
　　Stands on° me to defend, not to debate.　*Exit*　*Obliges*

Scene 23

*Alarum.*¹ *Enter the powers of France over the stage* [*led
by*] CORDELIA *with her father in her hand.* [*Then*] *enter*
EDGAR [*disguised as a peasant, guiding*] GLOUCESTER

　EDGAR   Here, father,² take the shadow of this bush
　　For your good host;° pray that the right may thrive　*shelter*
　　If ever I return to you again
　　I'll bring you comfort.　　　　　　　　　*Exit*
　GLOUCESTER　　　　　Grace go with you, sir.
　　Alarum and retreat.° [*Enter* EDGAR]　　*trumpet signal*
5 EDGAR   Away, old man. Give me thy hand. Away.
　　King Lear hath lost, he and his daughter ta'en.
　　Give me thy hand. Come on.
　GLOUCESTER   No farther, sir. A man may rot even° here.　*right*
　EDGAR   What, in ill thoughts again? Men must endure
10　Their going hence even as their coming hither.
　　Ripeness is all.³ Come on.　[*Exit* EDGAR *guiding* GLOUCESTER]

2. We will be ready to meet the occasion.
3. Authority or backing; also suggesting "face," to be used like a mask for Edmund's ambition.
Scene 23 Location: The rest of the play takes place near the battlefield.
1. Trumpet call to battle.

2. See note to 20.208.
3. To await the destined time is the most important thing, as fruit falls only when ripe (playing on Gloucester's "rot," line 8); readiness for death is our only duty (compare *Hamlet* 5.2.160, "The readiness is all").

EDGAR   I was forbid it.
When time shall serve, let but the herald cry,
And I'll appear again.

40   ALBANY   Why, fare thee well.
I will o'erlook thy paper.   *Exit* [EDGAR]
         Enter EDMOND

EDMOND   The enemy's in view; draw up your powers.°   *troops*
         [*He offers* ALBANY *a paper*]
Here is the guess° of their true strength and forces   *estimate*
By diligent discovery;° but your haste   *spying*
Is now urged on you.

45   ALBANY   We will greet the time.[8]   *Exit*

EDMOND   To both these sisters have I sworn my love,
Each jealous° of the other as the stung   *suspicious*
Are of the adder. Which of them shall I take?—
Both?—one?—or neither? Neither can be enjoyed

50   If both remain alive. To take the widow
Exasperates, makes mad, her sister Goneril,
And hardly° shall I carry out my side,°   *with difficulty / plan*
Her husband being alive. Now then, we'll use
His countenance[9] for the battle, which being done,

55   Let her who would be rid of him devise
His speedy taking off. As for the mercy
Which he intends to Lear and to Cordelia,
The battle done, and they within our power,
Shall° never see his pardon; for my state°   *They shall / condition*

60   Stands on° me to defend, not to debate.   *Exit*   *Obliges*

5.2

Alarum within.[1] *Enter with drum and colours* LEAR, COR-
DELIA, *and soldiers over the stage; and exeunt. Enter*
EDGAR [*disguised as a peasant, guiding*] GLOUCESTER

EDGAR   Here, father,[2] take the shadow of this tree
For your good host;° pray that the right may thrive.   *shelter*
If ever I return to you again
I'll bring you comfort.

GLOUCESTER   Grace go with you, sir.   *Exit* [EDGAR]
         Alarum and retreat° within. Enter EDGAR   *trumpet signal*

5   EDGAR   Away, old man. Give me thy hand. Away.
King Lear hath lost, he and his daughter ta'en.
Give me thy hand. Come on.

GLOUCESTER   No further, sir. A man may rot even° here.   *right*

EDGAR   What, in ill thoughts again? Men must endure

10   Their going hence even as their coming hither.
Ripeness is all.[3] Come on.

GLOUCESTER   And that's true, too.
         [*Exit* EDGAR *guiding* GLOUCESTER]

---

8. We will be ready to meet the occasion.
9. Authority or backing; also suggesting "face," to be used like a mask for Edmond's ambition.
5.2 Location: The rest of the play takes place near the battlefield.
1. Trumpet call to battle (backstage).

2. See note to 4.5.212.
3 To await the destined time is the most important thing, as fruit falls only when ripe (playing on Gloucester's "rot," line 8); readiness for death is our only duty (compare *Hamlet* 5.2.160, "The readiness is all").

Scene 24

Enter EDMUND *with* LEAR *and* CORDELIA *prisoners*[*, a*
CAPTAIN, *and soldiers*]

EDMUND   Some officers take them away. Good guard
　　Until their greater pleasures[1] best be known
　　That are to censure° them.　　　　　　　　　　　　　　　　　*judge*
CORDELIA [*to* LEAR]　　　　　We are not the first
　　Who with best meaning° have incurred the worst.　　　　*intention*
5　For thee, oppressèd King, am I cast down,°　　　　(*into unhappiness*)
　　Myself could else outfrown false fortune's frown.[2]
　　Shall we not see these daughters and these sisters?
LEAR   No, no. Come, let's away to prison.
　　We two alone will sing like birds i'th' cage.
10　When thou dost ask me blessing, I'll kneel down
　　And ask of thee forgiveness; so we'll live,
　　And pray, and sing, and tell old tales, and laugh
　　At gilded butterflies,[3] and hear poor rogues
　　Talk of court news, and we'll talk with them too—
15　Who loses and who wins, who's in, who's out,
　　And take upon 's the mystery of things
　　As if we were God's spies; and we'll wear out°　　　　　*outlast*
　　In a walled prison packs and sects of great ones
　　That ebb and flow by th' moon.[4]
EDMUND [*to soldiers*]　　　　　Take them away.
20　LEAR [*to* CORDELIA]   Upon such sacrifices,[5] my Cordelia,
　　The gods themselves throw incense. Have I caught thee?
　　He that parts us shall bring a brand from heaven
　　And fire us hence like foxes.[6] Wipe thine eyes.
　　The goodyear shall devour 'em, flesh and fell,[7]
25　Ere they shall make us weep. We'll see 'em starve first. Come.
　　　　　　　　　　　[*Exeunt all but* EDMUND *and* CAPTAIN]
EDMUND   Come hither, captain. Hark.
　　Take thou this note. Go follow them to prison.
　　One step I have advanced° thee; if thou dost　　　　　*promoted*
　　As this instructs thee, thou dost make thy way
30　To noble fortunes. Know thou this: that men
　　Are as the time is. To be tender-minded
　　Does not become a sword.° Thy great employment　　*befit a swordsman*
　　Will not bear question.° Either say thou'lt do't,　　　*discussion*
　　Or thrive by other means.
CAPTAIN　　　　　　I'll do't, my lord.
35　EDMUND   About it, and write 'happy' when thou hast done.[8]
　　Mark, I say, instantly, and carry it° so　　　　　　　*carry it out*
　　As I have set it down.
CAPTAIN　　　　　　I cannot draw a cart,
　　Nor eat dried oats.° If it be man's work, I'll do't.　　[*Exit*]　　(*like a horse*)

Scene 24
1. *Good . . . pleasures:* Guard them well until the desires
of those greater persons.
2. Otherwise, I could be defiant in the face of bad fortune.
3. Gaudy courtiers.
4. *packs . . . moon:* followers and factions of important
people whose position at court varies as the tide.
5. Upon such sacrifices as we are or as you have made.

6. *shall . . . foxes:* must have divine aid to do so. The
image is of using a torch to smoke foxes out of their holes,
or, in the case of Lear and Cordelia, prison cells.
7. *flesh and fell:* meat and skin; entirely. The precise
meaning of "goodyear" has not been explained; it may
signify simply the passage of time or may suggest some
ominous, destructive power.
8. Go to it, and call yourself happy when you are done.

5.3

Enter in conquest with drum and colours EDMOND; LEAR
and CORDELIA *as prisoners; soldiers; a* CAPTAIN

EDMOND   Some officers take them away. Good guard
    Until their greater pleasures[1] first be known
    That are to censure° them.   *judge*
CORDELIA [*to* LEAR]   We are not the first
    Who with best meaning° have incurred the worst.   *intention*
5 For thee, oppressèd King, I am cast down,°   *(into unhappiness)*
    Myself could else outfrown false fortune's frown.[2]
    Shall we not see these daughters and these sisters?
LEAR   No, no, no, no. Come, let's away to prison.
    We two alone will sing like birds i'th' cage.
10 When thou dost ask me blessing, I'll kneel down
    And ask of thee forgiveness; so we'll live,
    And pray, and sing, and tell old tales, and laugh
    At gilded butterflies,[3] and hear poor rogues
    Talk of court news, and we'll talk with them too—
15 Who loses and who wins, who's in, who's out,
    And take upon 's the mystery of things
    As if we were God's spies; and we'll wear out°   *outlast*
    In a walled prison packs and sects of great ones
    That ebb and flow by th' moon.[4]
EDMOND [*to soldiers*]   Take them away.
20 LEAR   Upon such sacrifices,[5] my Cordelia,
    The gods themselves throw incense. Have I caught thee?
    He that parts us shall bring a brand from heaven
    And fire us hence like foxes.[6] Wipe thine eyes.
    The goodyear shall devour them, flesh and fell,[7]
25 Ere they shall make us weep. We'll see 'em starved first. Come.
            Exeunt [all but EDMOND *and* CAPTAIN]
EDMOND   Come hither, captain. Hark.
    Take thou this note. Go follow them to prison.
    One step I have advanced° thee; if thou dost   *promoted*
    As this instructs thee, thou dost make thy way
30 To noble fortunes. Know thou this: that men
    Are as the time is. To be tender-minded
    Does not become a sword.° Thy great employment   *befit a swordsman*
    Will not bear question.° Either say thou'lt do't,   *discussion*
    Or thrive by other means.
CAPTAIN   I'll do't, my lord.
35 EDMOND   About it, and write 'happy' when thou'st done.[8]
    Mark, I say, instantly, and carry it° so   *carry it out*
    As I have set it down.   *Exit* CAPTAIN

5.3
1. *Good . . . pleasures:* Guard them well until the desires
of those greater persons.
2. Otherwise, I could be defiant in the face of bad fortune.
3. Gaudy courtiers.
4. *packs . . . moon:* followers and factions of important
people whose position at court varies as the tide.
5. Upon such sacrifices as we are or as you have made.

6. *shall . . . foxes:* must have divine aid to do so. The
image is of using a torch to smoke foxes out of their holes,
or, in the case of Lear and Cordelia, prison cells.
7. *flesh and fell:* meat and skin; entirely. The precise
meaning of "goodyear" has not been explained; it may
signify simply the passage of time or may suggest some
ominous, destructive power.
8. Go to it, and call yourself happy when you are done.

Enter Duke [of ALBANY], *the two ladies* [GONORIL *and*
REGAN, *another* CAPTAIN], *and others*

ALBANY [*to* EDMUND]   Sir, you have showed today your valiant
   strain,°   *qualities; birth*
40 And fortune led you well. You have the captives
 That were the opposites° of this day's strife.   *opponents*
 We do require then of you, so to use° them   *treat*
 As we shall find their merits and our safety
 May equally determine.

EDMUND   Sir, I thought it fit
45 To send the old and miserable King
 To some retention° and appointed guard,   *confinement*
 Whose° age has charms in it, whose title more,   *(Lear's)*
 To pluck the common bosom[9] on his side
 And turn our impressed lances° in our eyes   *conscripted lancers*
50 Which[1] do command them. With him I sent the Queen,
 My reason all the same, and they are ready
 Tomorrow, or at further space,° to appear   *at a future point*
 Where you shall hold your session.° At this time   *court of judgment*
 We sweat and bleed. The friend hath lost his friend,
55 And the best quarrels in the heat are cursed
 By those that feel their sharpness.[2]
 The question of Cordelia and her father
 Requires a fitter place.

ALBANY   Sir, by your patience,
 I hold you but a subject of° this war,   *in waging*
 Not as a brother.

60 REGAN   That's as we list° to grace him.   *choose*
 Methinks our pleasure should have been demanded[3]
 Ere you had spoke so far. He led our powers,°   *armies*
 Bore the commission of my place and person,
 The which immediate° may well stand up   *close connection*
 And call itself your brother.

65 GONORIL   Not so hot.°   *Not so fast*
 In his own grace° he doth exalt himself   *merit*
 More than in your advancement.[4]

REGAN   In my right
 By me invested, he compeers° the best.   *equals*

GONORIL   That were the most[5] if he should husband you.

REGAN   Jesters do oft prove prophets.

70 GONORIL   Holla, holla—
 That eye that told you so looked but asquint.[6]

REGAN   Lady, I am not well, else I should answer
 From a full-flowing stomach.° [*To* EDMUND] General,   *anger*
 Take thou my soldiers, prisoners, patrimony.
75 Witness the world that I create thee here
 My lord and master.

---

9. To garner the affection of the populace.
1. *in our eyes / Which:* in the eyes of us who.
2. *And . . . sharpness:* And in the heat of battle, even the
most just wars are cursed by those who must suffer the
fighting.

3. I think you should have inquired into my wishes.
4. In the honors you confer upon him.
5. That investiture would be complete.
6. Squinting was a proverbial effect of jealousy, because
of the tendency to look suspiciously at potential rivals.

Flourish. Enter ALBANY, GONERIL, REGAN, [*drummer,*
trumpeter and] *soldiers*

ALBANY   Sir, you have showed today your valiant strain,°   qualities; birth
And fortune led you well. You have the captives
Who were the opposites° of this day's strife.   opponents
I do require them of you, so to use° them   treat
As we shall find their merits and our safety
May equally determine.

EDMOND   Sir, I thought it fit
To send the old and miserable King
To some retention° and appointed guard,   confinement
Whose° age had charms in it, whose title more,   (Lear's)
To pluck the common bosom⁹ on his side
And turn our impressed lances° in our eyes   conscripted lancers
Which¹ do command them. With him I sent the Queen,
My reason all the same, and they are ready
Tomorrow, or at further space,° t'appear   at a future point
Where you shall hold your session.°   court of judgment

ALBANY   Sir, by your patience,
I hold you but a subject of° this war,   in waging
Not as a brother.

REGAN   That's as we list° to grace him.   choose
Methinks our pleasure might have been demanded²
Ere you had spoke so far. He led our powers,°   armies
Bore the commission of my place and person,
The which immediacy° may well stand up   close connection
And call itself your brother.

GONERIL   Not so hot.°   Not so fast
In his own grace° he doth exalt himself   merit
More than in your addition.³

REGAN   In my rights
By me invested, he compeers° the best.   equals

ALBANY   That were the most⁴ if he should husband you.

REGAN   Jesters do oft prove prophets.

GONERIL   Holla, holla—
That eye that told you so looked but asquint.⁵

REGAN   Lady, I am not well, else I should answer
From a full-flowing stomach.° [*To* EDMOND] General,   anger
Take thou my soldiers, prisoners, patrimony.
Dispose of them, of me. The walls° is thine.   fortress of my heart
Witness the world that I create thee here
My lord and master.

---

9. To garner the affection of the populace.
1. *in our eyes / Which*: in the eyes of us who.
2. I think you should have inquired into my wishes.
3. In the honors you confer upon him.

4. That investiture would be complete.
5. Squinting was a proverbial effect of jealousy, because
of the tendency to look suspiciously at potential rivals.

GONORIL   Mean you to enjoy him, then?

ALBANY   The let-alone° lies not in your good will.   veto

EDMUND   Nor in thine, lord.

ALBANY   Half-blooded° fellow, yes.   Bastard

EDMUND   Let the drum strike[7] and prove my title good.

80 ALBANY   Stay yet, hear reason. Edmund, I arrest thee
     On capital treason, and in thine attaint[8]
     This gilded serpent.   [To REGAN] For your claim, fair sister,°   sister-in-law
     I bar it in the interest of my wife.
     'Tis she is subcontracted to this lord,
85   And I, her husband, contradict the banns.°   announcement of marriage
     If you will marry, make your love to me.
     My lady is bespoke.—Thou art armed, Gloucester.
     If none appear to prove upon thy head
     Thy heinous, manifest, and many treasons,
          [He throws down a glove]
90   There is my pledge. I'll prove it on thy heart,
     Ere I taste bread, thou art in nothing less°   in no way less guilty
     Than I have here proclaimed thee.

REGAN   Sick, O sick!

GONORIL [aside]   If not, I'll ne'er trust poison.

EDMUND [to ALBANY, throwing down a glove]
95   There's my exchange. What° in the world he is   Whoever
     That names me traitor, villain-like he lies.
     Call by thy trumpet. He that dares, approach;
     On him, on you—who not?—I will maintain
     My truth and honour firmly.

100 ALBANY   A herald, ho!

EDMUND   A herald, ho, a herald!

ALBANY   Trust to thy single virtue,° for thy soldiers,   your unassisted power
     All levied in my name, have in my name
     Took their discharge.

REGAN   This sickness grows upon me.

105 ALBANY   She is not well. Convey her to my tent.
          [Exit one or more with REGAN]
     [Enter a HERALD and a trumpeter]
     Come hither, herald. Let the trumpet sound,
     And read out this.

---

7. Perhaps to announce the betrothal, or a challenge.
8. And in order to accuse you; and as one who shares your corruption or crime.

GONERIL   Mean you to enjoy him?

ALBANY   The let-alone° lies not in your good will.   *veto*

EDMOND   Nor in thine, lord.

ALBANY   Half-blooded° fellow, yes.   *Bastard*

REGAN [*to* EDMOND]   Let the drum strike⁶ and prove my title thine.

75   ALBANY   Stay yet, hear reason. Edmond, I arrest thee
      On capital treason, and in thy attaint⁷
      This gilded serpent. [*To* REGAN] For your claim, fair sister,°   *sister-in-law*
      I bar it in the interest of my wife.
      'Tis she is subcontracted to this lord,
80   And I, her husband, contradict your banns.°   *announcement of marriage*
      If you will marry, make your loves to me.
      My lady is bespoke.

GONERIL   An interlude!°   *A farce*

ALBANY   Thou art armed, Gloucester. Let the trumpet sound.
      If none appear to prove upon thy person
85   Thy heinous, manifest, and many treasons,
      There is my pledge.
            [*He throws down a glove*]
                I'll make° it on thy heart,   *prove*
      Ere I taste bread, thou art in nothing less°   *in no way less guilty*
      Than I have here proclaimed thee.

REGAN   Sick, O sick!

90   GONERIL [*aside*]   If not, I'll ne'er trust medicine.°   *poison (euphemistic)*

EDMOND [*to* ALBANY, *throwing down a glove*]   There's my
           exchange. What° in the world he is   *whoever*
      That names me traitor, villain-like he lies.
      Call by the trumpet. He that dares, approach;
      On him, on you,—who not?—I will maintain
      My truth and honour firmly.

95   ALBANY   A herald, ho!
          Enter a HERALD
      [*To* EDMOND] Trust to thy single virtue,° for thy soldiers,   *your unassisted power*
      All levied in my name, have in my name
      Took their discharge.

REGAN   My sickness grows upon me.

ALBANY   She is not well. Convey her to my tent.
               [*Exit one or more with* REGAN]
100   Come hither, herald. Let the trumpet sound,
      And read out this.

---

6. Perhaps to announce the betrothal, or a challenge.
7. And in order to accuse you; and as one who shares your corruption or crime.

SECOND CAPTAIN Sound, trumpet!
    [*Trumpeter sounds*]
HERALD [*reads*] 'If any man of quality or degree in the host of
110 the army will maintain upon Edmund, supposed Earl of
  Gloucester, that he's a manifold traitor, let him appear at the
  third sound of the trumpet. He is bold in his defence.'
EDMUND Sound! [*Trumpeter sounds*] Again!
    Enter EDGAR, [*armed,*] *at the third sound, a trumpet*
    before him
ALBANY [*to the* HERALD] Ask him his purposes, why he appears
  Upon this call o'th' trumpet.
115 HERALD [*to* EDGAR]   What° are you?   *Who*
  Your name and quality,° and why you answer   *degree; rank*
  This present summons?
EDGAR   O, know my name is lost,
  By treason's tooth bare-gnawn and canker-bit.°   *worm-eaten*
  Yet ere I move't,° where is the adversary   *make my declaration*
  I come to cope withal?°   *to encounter with*
120 ALBANY   Which is that adversary?
EDGAR What's he that speaks for Edmund, Earl of Gloucester?
EDMUND Himself. What sayst thou to him?
EDGAR   Draw thy sword,
  That° if my speech offend a noble heart   *So that*
  Thy arm may do thee justice. Here is mine.
    [*He draws his sword*]
125 Behold, it is the privilege of my tongue,
  My oath, and my profession. I protest,
  Maugre° thy strength, youth, place, and eminence,   *Despite*
  Despite thy victor-sword and fire-new° fortune,   *newly minted*
  Thy valour and thy heart,° thou art a traitor,   *courage*
130 False to thy gods, thy brother, and thy father,
  Conspirant 'gainst this high illustrious prince,
  And from th'extremest upward° of thy head   *top*
  To the descent° and dust beneath thy feet   *lowest part; sole*
  A most toad-spotted⁹ traitor. Say thou no,
135 This sword, this arm, and my best spirits are bent°   *ready*
  To prove upon thy heart, whereto I speak,
  Thou liest.
EDMUND   In wisdom I should ask thy name,
  But since thy outside looks so fair and warlike,
  And that° thy tongue some say¹ of breeding breathes,   *since*
140 My right of knighthood° I disdain and spurn.   *(to ask your name)*
  Here do I toss those treasons to thy head,
  With the hell-hated° lie o'erturn thy heart,   *hated as much as hell*

---

9. Venomous, like a toad; spotted with disgrace.   1. Taste (from "assay"); utterance.

A trumpet sounds

HERALD [*reads*]   'If any man of quality or degree within the lists
of the army will maintain upon Edmond, supposed Earl of
Gloucester, that he is a manifold traitor, let him appear by the
105 third sound of the trumpet. He is bold in his defence.'

First trumpet

Again.

Second trumpet

Again.

Third trumpet

Trumpet answers within. Enter EDGAR, *armed*

ALBANY [*to the* HERALD]   Ask him his purposes, why he appears
Upon this call o'th' trumpet.

HERALD [*to* EDGAR]   What° are you?   *Who*
110 Your name, your quality,° and why you answer   *degree; rank*
This present summons?

EDGAR   Know, my name is lost,
By treason's tooth bare-gnawn and canker-bit.°   *worm-eaten*
Yet am I noble as the adversary
I come to cope.°   *to encounter*

ALBANY   Which is that adversary?

115 EDGAR   What's he that speaks for Edmond, Earl of Gloucester?

EDMOND   Himself. What sayst thou to him?

EDGAR   Draw thy sword,
That° if my speech offend a noble heart   *So that*
Thy arm may do thee justice. Here is mine.
[*He draws his sword*]
Behold, it is the privilege of mine honour,
120 My oath, and my profession. I protest,
Maugre° thy strength, place, youth, and eminence,   *Despite*
Despite thy victor-sword and fire-new° fortune,   *newly minted*
Thy valour and thy heart,° thou art a traitor,   *courage*
False to thy gods, thy brother, and thy father,
125 Conspirant 'gainst this high illustrious prince,
And from th'extremest upward° of thy head   *top*
To the descent° and dust below thy foot   *lowest part; sole*
A most toad-spotted[8] traitor. Say thou no,
This sword, this arm, and my best spirits are bent°   *ready*
130 To prove upon thy heart, whereto I speak,
Thou liest.

EDMOND   In wisdom I should ask thy name,
But since thy outside looks so fair and warlike,
And that° thy tongue some say[9] of breeding breathes,   *since*
What safe and nicely I might well demand
135 By rule of knighthood I disdain and spurn.[1]
Back do I toss those treasons to thy head,
With the hell-hated° lie o'erwhelm thy heart,   *hated as much as hell*

8. Venomous, like a toad; spotted with disgrace.
9. Taste (from "assay"); utterance.
1. *What . . . spurn:* What I have a right to know and what
would be prudent and technically correct to ask, I disdain to inquire about.

Which, for° they yet glance by and scarcely bruise,   *since*
This sword of mine shall give them instant way°   *access*
145 Where they shall rest for ever. Trumpets, speak!
      [*Flourish. They fight.* EDMUND *is vanquished*]
ALL[2]   Save° him, save him!   *Spare*
GONORIL   This is mere practice,° Gloucester.   *trickery*
By the law of arms thou art not bound to answer
An unknown opposite.° Thou art not vanquished,   *opponent*
But cozened and beguiled.°   *cheated and deceived*
ALBANY   Stop your mouth, dame,
150 Or with this paper shall I stopple° it.   *plug*
Thou worse than anything, read thine own evil.
Nay, no tearing, lady. I perceive you know't.
GONORIL   Say if I do, the laws are mine, not thine.
Who shall arraign° me for't?   *prosecute*
ALBANY   Most monstrous!
Know'st thou this paper?
155 GONORIL   Ask me not what I know.   *Exit*
ALBANY   Go after her. She's desperate. Govern° her.   *Restrain*
      [*Exit one or more*]
EDMUND   What you have charged me with, that have I done,
And more, much more. The time will bring it out.
'Tis past, and so am I.   [*To* EDGAR] But what art thou,
160 That hast this fortune on me?[3] If thou beest noble,
I do forgive thee.
EDGAR   Let's exchange charity.°   *forgiveness*
I am no less in blood than thou art, Edmund.
If more, the more ignobly thou hast wronged me.
      [*He takes off his helmet*]
My name is Edgar, and thy father's son.
165 The gods are just, and of our pleasant vices
Make instruments to scourge us.
The dark and vicious place where thee he got[4]
Cost him his eyes.
EDMUND   Thou hast spoken truth.
The wheel° is come full circled. I am here.[5]   *Fortune's wheel*
170 ALBANY [*to* EDGAR]   Methought thy very gait did prophesy
A royal nobleness. I must embrace thee.
Let sorrow split my heart if I did ever hate
Thee or thy father.
EDGAR   Worthy prince, I know't.
175 ALBANY   Where have you hid yourself?
How have you known the miseries of your father?
EDGAR   By nursing them, my lord. List° a brief tale,   *Listen to*
And when 'tis told, O that my heart would burst!
The bloody proclamation to escape[6]
180 That followed me so near—O, our lives' sweetness,

---

2. Both Q and F give this speech to "Alb." (for "Albany"), which may be a compositor's mistake for "All."
3. Who have this good fortune at my expense.
4. The adulterous bed in which you were born; or, possibly, the vagina. *got:* begot.
5. Back at the lowest point.
6. In order to escape the sentence of death.

	Which, for° they yet glance by and scarcely bruise,	*since*
	This sword of mine shall give them instant way°	*access*
140	Where they shall rest for ever. Trumpets, speak!	
	Alarums. [They] fight. [EDMOND is vanquished]	
	ALL[2] Save° him, save him!	*Spare*
	GONERIL This is practice,° Gloucester.	*trickery*
	By th' law of arms thou wast not bound to answer	
	An unknown opposite.° Thou art not vanquished,	*opponent*
	But cozened and beguiled.°	*cheated and deceived*
	ALBANY Shut your mouth, dame,	
145	Or with this paper shall I stopple° it.	*plug*
	[*To* EDMOND] Hold,° sir, thou worse than any name: read	*Behold*
	thine own evil.	
	[*To* GONERIL] No tearing, lady. I perceive you know it.	
	GONERIL Say if I do, the laws are mine, not thine.	
	Who can arraign° me for't? *Exit*	*prosecute*
	ALBANY Most monstrous!—	
	O, know'st thou this paper?	
150	EDMOND Ask me not what I know.	
	ALBANY Go after her. She's desperate. Govern° her.	*Restrain*
	[*Exit one or more*]	
	EDMOND What you have charged me with, that have I done,	
	And more, much more. The time will bring it out.	
	'Tis past, and so am I. [*To* EDGAR] But what art thou,	
155	That hast this fortune on me?[3] If thou'rt noble,	
	I do forgive thee.	
	EDGAR Let's exchange charity.°	*forgiveness*
	I am no less in blood than thou art, Edmond.	
	If more, the more thou'st wronged me.	
	[*He takes off his helmet*]	
	My name is Edgar, and thy father's son.	
160	The gods are just, and of our pleasant vices	
	Make instruments to plague us.	
	The dark and vicious place where thee he got[4]	
	Cost him his eyes.	
	EDMOND Thou'st spoken right. 'Tis true.	
	The wheel° is come full circle. I am here.[5]	*Fortune's wheel*
165	ALBANY [*to* EDGAR] Methought thy very gait did prophesy	
	A royal nobleness. I must embrace thee.	
	Let sorrow split my heart if ever I	
	Did hate thee or thy father.	
	EDGAR Worthy prince, I know't.	
170	ALBANY Where have you hid yourself?	
	How have you known the miseries of your father?	
	EDGAR By nursing them, my lord. List° a brief tale,	*Listen to*
	And when 'tis told, O that my heart would burst!	
	The bloody proclamation to escape[6]	
175	That followed me so near—O, our lives' sweetness,	

2. Both Q and F give this speech to "Alb." (for "Albany"), which may be a compositor's mistake for "All."
3. Who have this good fortune at my expense.
4. The adulterous bed in which you were born; or, possibly, the vagina. *got:* begot.
5. Back at the lowest point.
6. In order to escape the sentence of death.

That with the pain of death would hourly die
Rather than die at once!⁷—taught me to shift
Into a madman's rags, to assume a semblance
That very° dogs disdained; and in this habit   even
185   Met I my father with his bleeding rings,°   sockets
The precious stones° new-lost; became his guide,   eyes
Led him, begged for him, saved him from despair;
Never—O father!—revealed myself unto him
Until some half hour past, when I was armed.
190   Not sure, though hoping, of this good success,°   conclusion
I asked his blessing, and from first to last
Told him my pilgrimage; but his flawed° heart—   cracked
Alack, too weak the conflict to support—
'Twixt two extremes of passion, joy and grief,
Burst smilingly.
195   EDMUND   This speech of yours hath moved me,
And shall perchance do good. But speak you on—
You look as you had something more to say.
ALBANY   If there be more, more woeful, hold it in,
For I am almost ready to dissolve,°   melt into tears
Hearing of this.
200   EDGAR   This would have seemed a period°   conclusion
To such as love not sorrow; but another
To amplify,° too much would make much more,   enlarge; extend
And top extremity.
Whilst I was big in clamour° came there in a man   lamenting loudly
205   Who, having seen me in my worst estate,
Shunned my abhorred society; but then, finding
Who 'twas that so endured, with his strong arms
He fastened on my neck and bellowed out
As he'd burst heaven; threw him on my father,
210   Told the most piteous tale of Lear and him°   himself
That ever ear received, which in recounting
His grief grew puissant° and the strings of life   powerful
Began to crack. Twice then the trumpets sounded,
And there I left him tranced.
ALBANY   But who was this?
215   EDGAR   Kent, sir, the banished Kent, who in disguise
Followed his enemy king,⁸ and did him service
Improper° for a slave.   Unfit even
        Enter [SECOND GENTLEMAN] with a bloody knife
SECOND GENTLEMAN   Help, help!
ALBANY   What kind of help?
What means that bloody knife?
SECOND GENTLEMAN   It's hot, it smokes.
It came even from the heart of—
ALBANY   Who, man? Speak.
220   SECOND GENTLEMAN   Your lady, sir, your lady; and her sister
By her is poisonèd—she hath confessed it.

7. our . . . once: how sweet must life be that we prefer   8. Because Lear had previously banished him. enemy:
the constant pain of dying to death itself.   hostile.

That we the pain of death would hourly die
Rather than die at once![7]—taught me to shift
Into a madman's rags, t'assume a semblance
That very° dogs disdained; and in this habit   *even*
180   Met I my father with his bleeding rings,°   *sockets*
Their precious stones° new-lost; became his guide,   *eyes*
Led him, begged for him, saved him from despair;
Never—O fault!—revealed myself unto him
Until some half hour past, when I was armed.
185   Not sure, though hoping, of this good success,°   *conclusion*
I asked his blessing, and from first to last
Told him our pilgrimage; but his flawed° heart—   *cracked*
Alack, too weak the conflict to support—
'Twixt two extremes of passion, joy and grief,
Burst smilingly.
190   EDMOND   This speech of yours hath moved me,
And shall perchance do good. But speak you on—
You look as you had something more to say.
     ALBANY   If there be more, more woeful, hold it in,
For I am almost ready to dissolve,°   *melt into tears*
195   Hearing of this.

         Enter a GENTLEMAN [*with a bloody knife*]
     GENTLEMAN   Help, help, O help!
     EDGAR   What kind of help?
     ALBANY   Speak, man.
     EDGAR   What means this bloody knife?
     GENTLEMAN   'Tis hot, it smokes.
It came even from the heart of—O, she's dead!
     ALBANY   Who dead? Speak, man.
200   GENTLEMAN   Your lady, sir, your lady; and her sister
By her is poisoned. She confesses it.

---

7. *our . . . once:* how sweet must life be that we prefer the constant pain of dying to death itself.

EDMUND   I was contracted to them both; all three
      Now marry° in an instant.   unite (in death)
ALBANY   Produce their bodies, be they alive or dead.
225   This justice of the heavens, that makes us tremble,
      Touches us not with pity.
                      Enter KENT [*as himself*]
EDGAR   Here comes Kent, sir.
ALBANY   O, 'tis he; the time will not allow
      The compliment that very manners urges.⁹
KENT   I am come
230   To bid my king and master aye° good night.   forever
      Is he not here?
ALBANY   Great thing of° us forgot!—   by
      Speak, Edmund; where's the King, and where's Cordelia?
                The bodies of GONORIL *and* REGAN *are brought in*
      Seest thou this object,° Kent?   spectacle
KENT   Alack, why thus?
235   EDMUND   Yet° Edmund was beloved.   Despite all
      The one the other poisoned for my sake,
      And after slew herself.
ALBANY   Even so.—Cover their faces.
EDMUND   I pant for life. Some good I mean to do,
      Despite of my own nature. Quickly send,
240   Be brief° in't, to th' castle; for my writ¹   speedy
      Is on the life of Lear and on Cordelia.
      Nay, send in time.
ALBANY   Run, run, O run!
EDGAR   To who, my lord? Who hath the office?° Send   commission
      Thy token of reprieve.
245   EDMUND   Well thought on! Take my sword. The captain,
      Give it the° captain.   to the
ALBANY   Haste thee for thy life.
                                          [*Exit* SECOND CAPTAIN]
EDMUND   He hath commission from thy wife and me
      To hang Cordelia in the prison, and
      To lay the blame upon her own despair,
250   That she fordid herself.²
ALBANY   The gods defend her!—Bear him hence a while.
                                     [*Exeunt some with* EDMUND]
          Enter LEAR *with* CORDELIA *in his arms* [*followed by the*
          SECOND CAPTAIN]
LEAR   Howl, howl, howl, howl! O, you are men of stones.
      Had I your tongues and eyes, I would use them so
      That heaven's vault should crack. She's gone for ever.
255   I know when one is dead and when one lives.
      She's dead as earth.

---

9. The ceremony that barest custom demands.   texts for the play, Cordelia does in fact kill herself after
1. Order of execution.   reigning for some years.
2. Destroyed herself. In most of Shakespeare's source

EDMOND I was contracted to them both; all three
  Now marry° in an instant.   *unite (in death)*

EDGAR   Here comes Kent.
  Enter KENT [*as himself*]

ALBANY Produce the bodies, be they alive or dead.
  Goneril's and Regan's bodies brought out
205   This judgement of the heavens, that makes us tremble,
  Touches us not with pity.—O, is this he?
  [*To* KENT] The time will not allow the compliment
  Which very manners urges.[8]

KENT   I am come
  To bid my king and master aye° good night.   *forever*
  Is he not here?

210 ALBANY   Great thing of° us forgot!—   *by*
  Speak, Edmond; where's the King, and where's Cordelia?—
  Seest thou this object,° Kent?   *spectacle*

KENT Alack, why thus?

EDMOND Yet° Edmond was beloved.   *Despite all*
215   The one the other poisoned for my sake,
  And after slew herself.

ALBANY   Even so.—Cover their faces.

EDMOND I pant for life. Some good I mean to do,
  Despite of mine own nature. Quickly send,
  Be brief° in it, to th' castle; for my writ[9]   *speedy*
220   Is on the life of Lear and on Cordelia.
  Nay, send in time.

ALBANY   Run, run, O run!

EDGAR To who, my lord?—Who has the office?° Send   *commission*
  Thy token of reprieve.

EDMOND Well thought on! Take my sword. The captain,
  Give it the° captain.   *to the*

225 EDGAR   Haste thee for thy life.
             [*Exit the* GENTLEMAN]

EDMOND [*to* ALBANY] He hath commission from thy wife and me
  To hang Cordelia in the prison, and
  To lay the blame upon her own despair,
  That she fordid herself.[1]

230 ALBANY The gods defend her!—Bear him hence a while.
          [*Exeunt some with* EDMOND]
  Enter LEAR *with* CORDELIA *in his arms [followed by the*
  GENTLEMAN]

LEAR Howl, howl, howl, howl! O, you are men of stones.
  Had I your tongues and eyes, I'd use them so
  That heaven's vault should crack. She's gone for ever.
  I know when one is dead and when one lives.
  She's dead as earth.

---

8. *the compliment . . . urges:* the ceremony that barest custom demands.
9. Order of execution.

1. Destroyed herself. In most of Shakespeare's source texts for the play, Cordelia does in fact kill herself after reigning for some years.

[*He lays her down*]
                                 Lend me a looking-glass.
If that her breath will mist or stain the stone,[3]
Why, then she lives.
KENT   Is this the promised end?[4]
EDGAR   Or image of that horror?
ALBANY   Fall and cease.[5]
260   LEAR   This feather stirs. She lives. If it be so,
It is a chance which does redeem all sorrows
That ever I have felt.
KENT [*kneeling*]   Ah, my good master!
LEAR   Prithee, away.
EDGAR   'Tis noble Kent, your friend.
LEAR   A plague upon you, murderous traitors all.
265   I might have saved her; now she's gone for ever.—
Cordelia, Cordelia: stay a little. Ha?
What is't thou sayst?—Her voice was ever soft,
Gentle, and low, an excellent thing in women.—
I killed the slave that was a-hanging thee.
SECOND CAPTAIN   'Tis true, my lords, he did.
270   LEAR   Did I not, fellow?
I have seen the day with my good biting falchion°   *light sword*
I would have made them skip. I am old now,
And these same crosses spoil me.[6] [*To* KENT] Who are you?
Mine eyes are not o' the best, I'll tell you straight.°   *recognize you soon*
275   KENT   If fortune bragged of two she loved or hated,[7]
One of them we behold.
LEAR   Are not you Kent?
KENT   The same, your servant Kent. Where is your servant
Caius?°   *(Kent's pseudonym)*
LEAR   He's a good fellow, I can tell you that.
He'll strike, and quickly too. He's dead and rotten.
280   KENT   No, my good lord, I am the very man—
LEAR   I'll see that straight.[8]
KENT   That from your first of difference and decay[9]
Have followed your sad steps.
LEAR   You're welcome hither.
KENT   Nor no man else.[1] All's cheerless, dark, and deadly.°   *deathly*
285   Your eldest daughters have fordone° themselves,   *destroyed*
And desperately° are dead.   *in despair*
LEAR   So think I, too.

3. Mica, or stone polished to a mirror finish.
4. Doomsday; expected end of the play. In no version of
the story previous to Shakespeare's does Cordelia die at
this point.
5. Let the world collapse and end.
6. And these recent adversities have weakened me;
and these parries I could once match would now
destroy me.
7. If Fortune bragged of two she treated only with good

or terrible extremes; "or" may be a variant of "ere," giving the meaning "loved before she hated."
8. I'll attend to that shortly; I'll comprehend that in a
moment.
9. Who from the beginning of your alteration and deterioration.
1. No, neither I nor anyone else is welcome. Alternatively, I am that man, not disguised as anyone else.

[*He lays her down*]

235　　　　　　　　　　　　Lend me a looking-glass.
　　　If that her breath will mist or stain the stone,[2]
　　　Why, then she lives.

KENT　　　　　　　　　Is this the promised end?[3]

EDGAR　Or image of that horror?

ALBANY　　　　　　　　　　Fall and cease.[4]

LEAR　This feather stirs. She lives. If it be so,
240　　　It is a chance which does redeem all sorrows
　　　That ever I have felt.

KENT [*kneeling*]　　　　O, my good master!

LEAR　Prithee, away.

EDGAR　　　　　　　　'Tis noble Kent, your friend.

LEAR　A plague upon you, murderers, traitors all.
　　　I might have saved her; now she's gone for ever.—
245　　　Cordelia, Cordelia: stay a little. Ha?
　　　What is't thou sayst?—Her voice was ever soft,
　　　Gentle, and low, an excellent thing in woman.—
　　　I killed the slave that was a-hanging thee.

GENTLEMAN　'Tis true, my lords, he did.

LEAR　　　　　　　　　　Did I not, fellow?
250　　　I have seen the day with my good biting falchion°　　　*light sword*
　　　I would have made them skip. I am old now,
　　　And these same crosses spoil me.[5]　[*To* KENT] Who are you?
　　　Mine eyes are not o'th' best, I'll tell you straight.°　　　*recognize you soon*

KENT　If fortune brag of two she loved and hated,
　　　One of them we behold.[6]

255　LEAR　　　　　　　　　This' a dull sight.[7]
　　　Are you not Kent?

KENT　The same, your servant Kent.
　　　Where is your servant Caius?°　　　　　　(*Kent's pseudonym*)

LEAR　He's a good fellow, I can tell you that.
260　　　He'll strike, and quickly too. He's dead and rotten.

KENT　No, my good lord, I am the very man—

LEAR　I'll see that straight.[8]

KENT　That from your first of difference and decay[9]
　　　Have followed your sad steps.

LEAR　　　　　　　　　You're welcome hither.

265　KENT　Nor no man else.[1] All's cheerless, dark, and deadly.°　　　*deathly*
　　　Your eldest daughters have fordone° themselves,　　　*destroyed*
　　　And desperately° are dead.　　　　　　　　　*in despair*

LEAR　　　　　　　　　Ay, so think I.

2. Mica, or stone polished to a mirror finish.
3. Doomsday; expected end of the play. In no version of the story previous to Shakespeare's does Cordelia die at this point.
4. Let the world collapse and end.
5. And these recent adversities have weakened me; and these parries I could once match would now destroy me.
6. *If . . . behold:* If there were only two supreme examples in the world of Fortune's ability to raise up and cast down, Lear would be one; alternatively, we are each of us one (Lear and Kent are here looking at each other).
7. This is a sad sight; my vision is failing.
8. I'll attend to that shortly; I'll comprehend that in a moment.
9. Who from the beginning of your alteration and deterioration.
1. No, neither I nor anyone else is welcome. Alternatively, I am that man, not disguised as anyone else.

ALBANY He knows not what he sees; and vain° it is   *in vain*
That we present us to him.
EDGAR   Very bootless.°   *futile*
    Enter [another] CAPTAIN
THIRD CAPTAIN [*to* ALBANY] Edmund is dead, my lord.
ALBANY   That's but a trifle here.—
290 You lords and noble friends, know our intent.
What comfort to this great decay° may come   *ruin; destruction*
Shall be applied; for us, we will resign
During the life of this old majesty
To him our absolute power; [*to* EDGAR *and* KENT] you to your rights,
295 With boot° and such addition° as your honours   *reward / distinction*
Have more than merited. All friends shall taste
The wages of their virtue, and all foes
The cup of their deservings.—O see, see!
LEAR And my poor fool² is hanged. No, no life.
300 Why should a dog, a horse, a rat have life,
And thou no breath at all? O, thou wilt come no more.
Never, never, never.—Pray you, undo
This button. Thank you, sir. O, O, O, O!
EDGAR He faints. [*To* LEAR] My lord, my lord!
305 LEAR Break, heart, I prithee break.
EDGAR Look up, my lord.
KENT Vex not his ghost.³ O, let him pass. He hates him
That would upon the rack⁴ of this tough world
Stretch him out longer.
    [LEAR *dies*]
EDGAR   O, he is gone indeed.
310 KENT The wonder is he hath endured so long.
He but usurped his life.⁵
ALBANY [*to attendants*] Bear them from hence. Our present business
Is to general woe. [*To* KENT *and* EDGAR] Friends of my soul, you twain
Rule in this kingdom, and the gored° state sustain.   *wounded; bloody*
315 KENT I have a journey, sir, shortly to go:
My master calls, and I must not say no.
ALBANY The weight of this sad time we must obey,
Speak what we feel, not what we ought to say.
The oldest have borne most. We that are young
320 Shall never see so much, nor live so long.
                    [*Exeunt carrying the bodies*]

---

2. A term of endearment, here used for Cordelia, though it also recalls the disappearance of Lear's Fool after Scene 13.

3. Do not disturb his departing soul.
4. Instrument of torture, used to stretch its victims.
5. From death, which already had a claim on it.

ALBANY   He knows not what he says; and vain° is it   *in vain*
     That we present us to him.
               Enter a MESSENGER
EDGAR   Very bootless.°   *futile*
MESSENGER [*to* ALBANY]   Edmond is dead, my lord.
270 ALBANY   That's but a trifle here.—
     You lords and noble friends, know our intent.
     What comfort to this great decay° may come   *ruin; destruction*
     Shall be applied; for us, we will resign
     During the life of this old majesty
     To him our absolute power;
275 [*To* EDGAR *and* KENT]   you to your rights,
     With boot° and such addition° as your honours   *reward / distinction*
     Have more than merited. All friends shall taste
     The wages of their virtue, and all foes
     The cup of their deservings.—O see, see!
280 LEAR   And my poor fool[2] is hanged. No, no, no life?
     Why should a dog, a horse, a rat have life,
     And thou no breath at all? Thou'lt come no more.
     Never, never, never, never, never.
     [*To* KENT] Pray you, undo this button. Thank you, sir.
285 Do you see this? Look on her. Look, her lips.
     Look there, look there.   *He dies*
EDGAR   He faints.   [*To* LEAR] My lord, my lord!
KENT [*to* LEAR]   Break, heart, I prithee break.
EDGAR [*to* LEAR]   Look up, my lord.
KENT   Vex not his ghost.[3] O, let him pass. He hates him
     That would upon the rack[4] of this tough world
     Stretch him out longer.
290 EDGAR   He is gone indeed.
KENT   The wonder is he hath endured so long.
     He but usurped his life.[5]
ALBANY   Bear them from hence. Our present business
     Is general woe. [*To* EDGAR *and* KENT] Friends of my soul, you twain
295 Rule in this realm, and the gored° state sustain.   *wounded; bloody*
KENT   I have a journey, sir, shortly to go:
     My master calls me; I must not say no.
EDGAR   The weight of this sad time we must obey,
     Speak what we feel, not what we ought to say.
300 The oldest hath borne most. We that are young
     Shall never see so much, nor live so long.
               Exeunt with a dead march [carrying the bodies]

---

2. A term of endearment, here used for Cordelia, though it also recalls the disappearance of Lear's Fool after 3.6.

3. Do not disturb his departing soul.
4. Instrument of torture, used to stretch its victims.
5. From death, which already had a claim on it.

King Lear

A CONFLATED TEXT

The Persons of the Play

LEAR, King of Britain
GONERIL, Lear's eldest daughter
Duke of ALBANY, her husband
REGAN, Lear's second daughter
Duke of CORNWALL, her husband
CORDELIA, Lear's youngest daughter
King of FRANCE }
Duke of BURGUNDY } suitors of Cordelia
Earl of KENT, later disguised as Caius
Earl of GLOUCESTER
EDGAR, elder son of Gloucester, later disguised as Tom o' Bedlam
EDMUND, bastard son of Gloucester
OLD MAN, Gloucester's tenant
CURAN, Gloucester's retainer
Lear's FOOL
OSWALD, Goneril's steward
A DOCTOR
A CAPTAIN
A GENTLEMAN
A HERALD
SERVANTS to Cornwall
Knights, officers, messengers, soldiers, attendants

1.1

Enter KENT, GLOUCESTER,[1] *and* EDMUND

KENT I thought the king had more affected° the Duke of   *favored*
Albany° than Cornwall.   *Scotland*

GLOUCESTER It did always seem so to us; but now, in the division of the kingdom, it appears not° which of the dukes he   *is not clear*
5 values most; for equalities° are so weighed,° that curiosity in *shares / equal*
neither can make choice of either's moiety.[2]

KENT Is not this your son, my lord?

GLOUCESTER His breeding,° sir, hath been at my charge.[3] I have   *upbringing*
so often blushed to acknowledge him, that now I am brazed°   *hardened*
10 to it.

KENT I cannot conceive° you.   *comprehend*

GLOUCESTER Sir, this young fellow's mother could;[4] whereupon
she grew round-wombed, and had, indeed, sir, a son for her
cradle ere she had a husband for her bed. Do you smell a
15 fault?[5]

1.1 Location: King Lear's court.
1. Pronounced "Gloster."
2. *that . . . moiety*: that careful scrutiny ("curiosity") of both parts cannot determine which portion ("moiety") is preferable.
3. My responsibility; at my cost.
4. Could conceive; punning on biological conception.
5. Sin, wrongdoing; female genitals.

KENT   I cannot wish the fault undone, the issue° of it being so   *offspring; result*
         proper.°   *handsome; right*
GLOUCESTER   But I have, sir, a son by order of law,° some year   *legitimate son*
         elder than this, who yet is no dearer in my account.° Though   *estimation*
20   this knave° came something saucily⁶ into the world before he   *scamp; fellow*
         was sent for, yet was his mother fair; there was good sport at his
         making, and the whoreson° must be acknowledged. Do you   *rogue; bastard*
         know this noble gentleman, Edmund?
EDMUND   No, my lord.
25   GLOUCESTER   My lord of Kent. Remember him hereafter as my
         honorable friend.
EDMUND   My services to your lordship.
KENT   I must love you, and sue° to know you better.   *seek*
EDMUND   Sir, I shall study deserving.°   *shall learn to deserve*
30   GLOUCESTER   He hath been out° nine years, and away he shall   *away; abroad*
         again. (*Sound a sennet*)° The king is coming.   *fanfare of trumpets*

> *Enter one bearing a coronet, then King* LEAR, CORN-
> WALL, ALBANY, GONERIL, REGAN, CORDELIA, *and atten-*
> *dants*

LEAR   Attend the lords of France and Burgundy, Gloucester.
GLOUCESTER   I shall, my liege.°   *feudal superior*

> *Exeunt* GLOUCESTER *and* EDMUND

LEAR   Meantime we° shall express our darker° purpose.   *(royal "we") / more secret*
35   Give me the map there. Know that we have divided
         In three our kingdom; and 'tis our fast° intent   *fixed*
         To shake all cares and business from our age,
         Conferring them on younger strengths, while we
         Unburthened crawl toward death. Our son° of Cornwall,   *son-in-law*
40   And you, our no less loving son of Albany,
         We have this hour a constant will to publish⁷
         Our daughters' several dowers,° that future strife   *individual dowries*
         May be prevented now. The princes, France and Burgundy,
         Great rivals in our youngest daughter's love,
45   Long in our court have made their amorous sojourn,
         And here are to be answered. Tell me, my daughters—
         Since now we will divest us, both of rule,
         Interest° of territory, cares of state—   *Legal title*
         Which of you shall we say doth love us most?
50   That° we our largest bounty° may extend   *So that / generosity*
         Where nature doth with merit challenge.⁸ Goneril,
         Our eldest-born, speak first.
GONERIL   Sir, I love you more than words can wield° the matter;   *convey*
         Dearer than eye-sight, space,° and liberty;   *freedom of movement*
55   Beyond what can be valued, rich or rare;
         No less than life, with grace, health, beauty, honor;
         As much as child e'er loved, or father found;
         A love that makes breath° poor, and speech unable;   *language*
         Beyond all manner of so much° I love you.   *Beyond all comparison*
60   CORDELIA (*aside*)   What shall Cordelia speak? Love, and be silent.
LEAR   Of all these bounds,° even from this line to this,   *regions*
         With shadowy forests and with champains riched,°   *enriched plains*
         With plenteous rivers and wide-skirted meads,°   *broad meadows*

---

6. Somewhat rudely; somewhat shamefully.   8. *Where . . . challenge:* To the one whose natural love
7. A fixed determination to announce publicly.   and deserving lay claim (to our generosity).

We make thee lady: to thine and Albany's issue°   *children; heirs*
65   Be this perpetual. What says our second daughter,
    Our dearest Regan, wife to Cornwall? Speak.
REGAN   Sir, I am made
    Of the self-same metal° that my sister is,   *spirit; substance*
    And prize me at her worth.° In my true heart   *believe myself her equal*
70   I find she names my very deed of love;
    Only she comes too short, that° I profess   *in that*
    Myself an enemy to all other joys,
    Which the most precious square of sense possesses,[9]
    And find I am alone felicitate°   *am only made happy*
    In your dear highness' love.
75 CORDELIA (*aside*)   Then poor Cordelia!
    And yet not so; since, I am sure, my love's
    More ponderous° than my tongue.   *weighty*
LEAR   To thee and thine hereditary ever
    Remain this ample third of our fair kingdom;
80   No less in space, validity,° and pleasure,   *value*
    Than that conferred on Goneril. Now, our joy,
    Although our last and least;° to whose young love   *youngest; smallest*
    The vines of France and milk of Burgundy
    Strive to be interessed,° what can you say to draw   *admitted*
85   A third more opulent than your sisters? Speak.
CORDELIA   Nothing, my lord.
LEAR   Nothing?
CORDELIA   Nothing.
LEAR   Nothing will come of nothing,[1] speak again.
90 CORDELIA   Unhappy that I am, I cannot heave
    My heart into my mouth. I love your majesty
    According to my bond;° nor more nor less.   *filial duty*
LEAR   How, how, Cordelia! mend your speech a little,
    Lest it may mar your fortunes.
CORDELIA   Good my lord,
95   You have begot me, bred me, loved me; I
    Return those duties back as are right fit,
    Obey you, love you, and most honor you.
    Why have my sisters husbands, if they say
    They love you all°? Haply,° when I shall wed,   *completely / Perhaps; if lucky*
100   That lord whose hand must take my plight° shall carry   *marriage vow; condition*
    Half my love with him, half my care and duty.
    Sure, I shall never marry like my sisters,
    To love my father all.
LEAR   But goes thy heart with this?
105 CORDELIA   Ay, good my lord.
LEAR   So young, and so untender?
CORDELIA   So young, my lord, and true.°   *honest; faithful*
LEAR   Let it be so! Thy truth, then, be thy dower!
    For, by the sacred radiance of the sun,
110   The mysteries of Hecate,[2] and the night;

9. **Which . . . *possesses*:** That the body can enjoy. *precious square of sense:* measure of sensibility; or, perhaps, balanced and sensitive perception. The square may represent the even mixture of the body's four fluids, or humors. 1. *Ex nihilo nihil fit,* a maxim derived from Aristotle, was accepted by the Christian Middle Ages with the single exception of God having created the world out of nothing. 2. A classical goddess of the moon and the patron of witchcraft, she was associated with the underworld, Hades.

By all the operation of the orbs *legal & astronomical*
From whom we do exist and cease to be;[3]
Here I disclaim all my paternal care,
Propinquity° and property of blood,°   *Closeness / kinship*
115 And as a stranger to my heart and me
Hold thee, from this,° for ever. The barbarous Scythian,[4]   *this time*
Or he that makes his generation messes[5]
To gorge his appetite, shall to my bosom
Be as well neighbored, pitied, and relieved,
As thou my sometime° daughter.   *former*
120 KENT   Good my liege—
    LEAR   Peace, Kent!
Come not between the dragon and his wrath.
I loved her most, and thought to set my rest[6]
On her kind nursery.° Hence, and avoid my sight!   *care*
125 So be my grave my peace,[7] as here I give
Her father's heart from her! Call France; who stirs?[8]
Call Burgundy. Cornwall and Albany,
With my two daughters' dowers digest° this third: *incorporate*
Let pride, which she calls plainness,° marry her.   *directness*
130 I do invest you jointly with my power,
Pre-eminence, and all the large effects°   *outward shows; trappings*
That troop with° majesty. Ourself, by monthly course,   *accompany*
With reservation of° an hundred knights,   *legal right to retain*
By you to be sustained, shall our abode
135 Make with you by due turns. Only we still retain
The name, and all the additions° to a king;   *prerogatives*
The sway,° revenue, execution of the rest,   *power*
Beloved sons, be yours; which to confirm,
This coronet[9] part betwixt you.
    KENT   Royal Lear,
140 Whom I have ever honored as my king,
Loved as my father, as my master followed,
As my great patron thought on in my prayers—
    LEAR   The bow is bent and drawn, make from° the shaft.   *get clear of*
    KENT   Let it fall° rather, though the fork° invade   *strike home / arrowhead*
145 The region of my heart: be Kent unmannerly,
When Lear is mad. What wilt thou do, old man?
Think'st thou that duty shall have dread to speak,
When power to flattery bows? To plainness° honor's bound,   *plain speaking*
When majesty stoops to folly. Reverse thy doom,°   *Revoke your sentence*
150 And, in thy best consideration, check°   *halt*
This hideous rashness. Answer my life my judgment,[1]
Thy youngest daughter does not love thee least;
Nor are those empty-hearted whose low sounds
Reverb no hollowness.°   *Echo no insincerity*
    LEAR   Kent, on thy life, no more.
155 KENT   My life I never held but as a pawn°   *chess piece; stake*

---

3. *By all . . . be*: Referring to the belief that the movements of stars and planets ("orbs") corresponded to physical and spiritual motions in a person and thus controlled his or her fate.
4. Notoriously savage Crimean nomads of classical antiquity.
5. *he . . . messes*: he who makes meals of his parents or his children.

6. To secure my repose; to stake my all, as in the card game known as primero.
7. So may I rest in peace (probably an oath).
8. Does nobody stir? An order, with the force of "Get moving."
9. Cordelia's crown, symbol of the endowment she has forsworn.
1. *Answer . . . judgment*: I'll stake my life on my opinion.

	To wage° against thy enemies; nor fear to lose it,	*wager*
	Thy safety being the motive.
LEAR	Out of my sight!
KENT	See better, Lear; and let me still° remain	*always*
	The true blank° of thine eye.	*precise bull's-eye*
LEAR	Now, by Apollo—
160 KENT	Now, by Apollo, king,
	Thou swear'st thy gods in vain.²
LEAR	O, vassal! miscreant!°	*villain; unbeliever*

Laying his hand on his sword

ALBANY
CORNWALL } Dear sir, forbear.

KENT   Do;
165   Kill thy physician, and the fee bestow
Upon thy foul disease.³ Revoke thy doom;
Or, whilst I can vent clamor from my throat,
I'll tell thee thou dost evil.

LEAR   Hear me, recreant!°   *traitor*
On thine allegiance, hear me!
Since thou hast sought to make us break our vow,
170   Which we durst never yet, and with strained° pride   *overblown*
To come between our sentence and our power,
Which nor our nature nor our place⁴ can bear,
Our potency made good,° take thy reward.   *demonstrated*
Five days we do allot thee, for provision
175   To shield thee from diseases of the world;
And on the sixth to turn thy hated back
Upon our kingdom: if, on the tenth day following,
Thy banished trunk° be found in our dominions,   *body*
The moment is thy death. Away! by Jupiter,
180   This shall not be revoked.

KENT   Fare thee well, king. Sith° thus thou wilt appear,   *Since*
Freedom lives hence, and banishment is here.
(*To* CORDELIA) The gods to their dear shelter take thee, maid,
That justly think'st, and hast most rightly said!
185   (*To* REGAN *and* GONERIL) And your large speeches may your deeds approve,⁵
That good effects may spring from words of love.
Thus Kent, O princes, bids you all adieu;
He'll shape his old course in a country new.   *Exit*
    Flourish.° *Re-enter* GLOUCESTER, *with* FRANCE, BUR-   *Fanfare of trumpets*
    GUNDY, *and attendants*

GLOUCESTER   Here's France and Burgundy, my noble lord.
190 LEAR   My lord of Burgundy,
We first address towards you, who with this king
Hath rivaled for our daughter. What, in the least,
Will you require in present dower with her,
Or cease your quest of love?

BURGUNDY   Most royal majesty,
195   I crave no more than what your highness offered,
Nor will you tender° less.   *offer*

LEAR   Right noble Burgundy,

---

2. You invoke your gods falsely and without effect.
3. *Kill . . . disease:* You would not only kill the doctor but hand his fee over to the disease.

4. Which neither my temperament nor my royal position.
5. And let your actions live up to your fine words.

When she was dear to us, we did hold her so;
But now her price is fallen. Sir, there she stands;
If aught within that little seeming substance,[6]
200 Or all of it, with our displeasure pieced,°   *joined*
And nothing more, may fitly like° your grace,   *please*
She's there, and she is yours.
BURGUNDY   I know no answer.
LEAR   Will you, with those infirmities she owes,°   *owns*
Unfriended, new-adopted to our hate,
205 Dowered with our curse, and strangered° with our oath,   *estranged*
Take her, or leave her?
BURGUNDY   Pardon me, royal sir;
Election makes not up on such conditions.[7]
LEAR   Then leave her, sir; for, by the power that made me,
I tell you° all her wealth. (*To* FRANCE) For° you, great king,   *inform you of / As for*
210 I would not from your love make such a stray°   *stray so far*
To° match you where I hate; therefore beseech you   *As to*
To avert your liking° a more worthier way   *To turn your affections*
Than on a wretch whom nature is ashamed
Almost to acknowledge hers.
FRANCE   This is most strange,
215 That she, whom even but now was your best object,
The argument° of your praise, balm of your age,   *theme*
Most best, most dearest, should in this trice° of time *moment*
Commit a thing so monstrous, to dismantle°   *as to strip off; disrobe*
So many folds of favor. Sure, her offense
220 Must be of such unnatural degree,
That monsters it,° or your fore-vouched affection   *makes it monstrous*
Fall'n into taint;[8] which to believe of her,
Must be a faith that reason without miracle
Could never plant in me.
CORDELIA   I yet beseech your majesty—
225 If for I want° that glib and oily art,   *because I lack*
To speak and purpose not°—since what I well intend,   *and not intend*
I'll do't before I speak—that you make known
It is no vicious blot, murder, or foulness,
No unchaste action, or dishonored step,
230 That hath deprived me of your grace and favor;
But even for want of that for which I am richer,
A still-soliciting° eye, and such a tongue   *An always-begging*
As I am glad I have not, though not to have it
Hath lost me in your liking.
LEAR   Better thou
235 Hadst not been born than not to have pleased me better.
FRANCE   Is it but this—a tardiness in nature
Which often leaves the history unspoke
That it intends to do?[9] My lord of Burgundy,
What say you to the lady? Love's not love
240 When it is mingled with regards° that stands   *considerations*

---

6. *little seeming substance:* one who appears insubstantial; one who will not pretend.
7. A choice cannot be made under those terms.
8. *or . . . taint:* or else the love you earlier swore for Cordelia must be regarded with suspicion. "Or" may also

mean "before," in which case the phrase would mean "before the love you once proclaimed could have decayed."
9. *a tardiness . . . do:* a natural reserve that inhibits voicing one's intentions.

Aloof from th' entire point. Will you have her?
She is herself a dowry.

BURGUNDY   Royal Lear,
Give but that portion which yourself proposed,
And here I take Cordelia by the hand,
245 Duchess of Burgundy.

LEAR Nothing! I have sworn; I am firm.

BURGUNDY I am sorry, then, you have so lost a father
That you must lose a husband.

CORDELIA   Peace be with Burgundy!
Since that respects of fortune are his love,
250 I shall not be his wife.

FRANCE Fairest Cordelia, that art most rich, being poor;
Most choice, forsaken; and most loved, despised!
Thee and thy virtues here I seize upon:
Be it lawful I take up what's cast away.
255 Gods, gods! 't is strange that from their cold'st neglect
My love should kindle to inflamed respect.°   ardent regard
Thy dowerless daughter, king, thrown to my chance,
Is queen of us, of ours, and our fair France.
Not all the dukes of waterish° Burgundy   irrigated; watery; weak
260 Can buy this unprized° precious maid of me.   unappreciated
Bid them farewell, Cordelia, though unkind;°   though they are unkind
Thou losest here,° a better where° to find.   this place / place

LEAR Thou hast her, France; let her be thine; for we
Have no such daughter, nor shall ever see
265 That face of hers again. Therefore be gone
Without our grace, our love, our benison.°   blessing
Come, noble Burgundy.
        Flourish. Exeunt all but FRANCE, GONERIL, REGAN, *and*
                CORDELIA

FRANCE Bid farewell to your sisters.

CORDELIA The jewels of our father, with washed eyes
270 Cordelia leaves you. I know you what you are,
And like a sister am most loath to call
Your faults as they are named.° Love well our father.   are properly called
To your professed bosoms° I commit him;   publicly proclaimed love
But yet, alas, stood I within his grace,
275 I would prefer° him to a better place.   promote; recommend
So, farewell to you both.

REGAN Prescribe not us our duties.

GONERIL   Let your study
Be to content your lord, who hath received you
At fortune's alms.[1] You have obedience scanted,°   neglected
280 And well are worth the want that you have wanted.[2]

CORDELIA Time shall unfold what pleated cunning hides:
Who cover faults, at last shame them derides.[3]
Well may you prosper!

FRANCE   Come, my fair Cordelia.
                Exeunt FRANCE *and* CORDELIA

---

1. As a charitable gift from Dame Fortune.
2. And you deserve to get no more love (from your husband) than you have given (to your father). "Want" plays

on its alternative meanings of "lack" and "desire."
3. Those who hide their faults will in the end be put to
shame.

GONERIL   Sister, it is not a little I have to say of what most nearly
285   appertains to us both. I think our father will hence to-night.
REGAN   That's most certain, and with you; next month with us.
GONERIL   You see how full of changes° his age is; the observation   *fickleness*
we have made of it hath not been little:[4] he always loved our
sister most; and with what poor judgment he hath now cast her
290   off appears too grossly.°   *blatantly*
REGAN   'Tis the infirmity of his age; yet he hath ever but slen-
derly known himself.
GONERIL   The best and soundest of his time hath been but rash;[5]
then° must we look to receive from his age, not alone the   *therefore*
295   imperfections of long-engraffed condition,° but therewithal the   *deep-rooted habit*
unruly waywardness that infirm and choleric years bring with
them.
REGAN   Such unconstant starts[6] are we like° to have from him as   *likely*
this of Kent's banishment.
300   GONERIL   There is further compliment° of leave-taking between   *ceremony*
France and him. Pray you, let's hit° together: if our father carry   *join; strike*
authority with such dispositions[7] as he bears, this last surren-
der° of his will but offend° us.   *abdication / harm*
REGAN   We shall further think on 't.
305   GONERIL   We must do something, and i' the heat.°   *Exeunt*   *quickly*

1.2

Enter EDMUND, *with a letter*

EDMUND   Thou, nature, art my goddess; to thy law
My services are bound.[1] Wherefore° should I   *Why*
Stand in the plague of custom,[2] and permit
The curiosity° of nations to deprive me,   *legal niceties*
5   For that° I am some twelve or fourteen moonshines°   *Because / months*
Lag of° a brother? Why bastard? wherefore base?   *Younger than*
When my dimensions are as well compact,°   *composed*
My mind as generous° and my shape as true,   *noble*
As honest° madam's issue? Why brand they us   *married; chaste*
10   With base? with baseness? bastardy? base, base?
Who, in the lusty stealth of nature, take
More composition and fierce quality[3]
Than doth, within a dull, stale, tired bed,
Go to creating a whole tribe of fops,°   *fools*
15   Got° 'tween asleep and wake? Well, then,   *Begotten*
Legitimate Edgar, I must have your land.
Our father's love is to° the bastard Edmund   *as much to*
As to the legitimate. Fine word—'legitimate'!
Well, my legitimate, if this letter speed,°   *succeed*
20   And my invention° thrive, Edmund the base   *plot*

---

4. We have observed it more than a little.
5. *The . . . rash:* Even in the prime of his life he was impetuous.
6. Such impulsive outbursts.
7. Frame of mind.
1.2 Location: The Earl of Gloucester's house.
1. Edmund declares the raw force of unsocialized and unregulated existence, as opposed to human law, to be his ruler; ironically, "nature" also means "natural filial affection." A "natural" was another word for "bastard" (illegitimate child).

2. Submit to the imposition of inheritance law.
3. *Who . . . quality:* Whose begetting, by reason of its furtiveness and heightened excitement, requires better execution and more vigor. Alternatively (with "take" meaning "give"), whose begetting produces (a person of) more mixture and vigor. "Composition," or mixture, may refer to the belief that the perfect offspring was conceived from an equal quantity of male and female essence and that physical and mental abnormalities were caused by a predominance of one or the other.

Shall top° the legitimate. I grow; I prosper.   *overcome; usurp*
Now, gods, stand up for bastards!
      Enter GLOUCESTER

GLOUCESTER   Kent banished thus? and France in choler
      parted?°   *in anger departed*
      And the king gone tonight?° subscribed° his power?   *last night / limited*
25   Confirmed to exhibition?[4] All this done
      Upon the gad?° Edmund, how now! what news?   *spur of the moment*

EDMUND   So please your lordship, none. *Putting up the letter*

GLOUCESTER   Why so earnestly seek you to put up that letter?

EDMUND   I know no news, my lord.

30 GLOUCESTER   What paper were you reading?

EDMUND   Nothing, my lord.

GLOUCESTER   No? What needed, then, that terrible dispatch° of   *frightened haste*
      it into your pocket? The quality of nothing hath not such need
      to hide itself. Let's see. Come, if it be nothing, I shall not need
35   spectacles.

EDMUND   I beseech you, sir, pardon me. It is a letter from my
      brother, that I have not all o'er-read; and for so much as I have
      perused, I find it not fit for your o'er-looking.

GLOUCESTER   Give me the letter, sir.

40 EDMUND   I shall offend, either to detain or give it. The contents,
      as in part I understand them, are to blame.

GLOUCESTER   Let's see, let's see.

EDMUND   I hope, for my brother's justification, he wrote this but
      as an essay or taste[5] of my virtue.

45 GLOUCESTER (*reads*) "This policy and reverence of age makes
      the world bitter to the best of our times;[6] keeps our fortunes
      from us till our oldness cannot relish them. I begin to find an
      idle and fond° bondage in the oppression of aged tyranny; who   *a useless and foolish*
      sways, not as it hath power, but as it is suffered.[7] Come to me,
50   that of this I may speak more. If our father would sleep till I
      waked him, you should enjoy half his revenue for ever, and live
      the beloved of your brother, Edgar."
      Hum—conspiracy!—"Sleep till I waked him—you should
      enjoy half his revenue"—My son Edgar! Had he a hand to
55   write this? a heart and brain to breed it in?—When came this
      to you? who brought it?

EDMUND   It was not brought me, my lord; there's the cunning of
      it; I found it thrown in at the casement° of my closet.°   *window / private room*

GLOUCESTER   You know the character° to be your brother's?   *handwriting*

60 EDMUND   If the matter° were good, my lord, I durst swear it were   *content*
      his; but, in respect of that, I would fain° think it were not.   *gladly*

GLOUCESTER   It is his.

EDMUND   It is his hand, my lord; but I hope his heart is not in
      the contents.

65 GLOUCESTER   Hath he never heretofore sounded you° in this   *sounded you out*
      business?

EDMUND   Never, my lord. But I have heard him oft maintain it
      to be fit, that, sons at perfect age,° and fathers declining, the   *at maturity*

---

4. Established as mere show; relegated to pension.
5. *but . . . taste:* simply as a proof or test. Both terms derive from metallurgy.
6. The established primacy of the elderly embitters us at the prime of our lives. *policy:* statecraft; craftiness; established order.
7. *who . . . suffered:* which rules not because it is powerful but because it is permitted to ("suffered").

father should be as ward[8] to the son, and the son manage his
70 revenue.

GLOUCESTER   O villain, villain! His very opinion in the letter!
Abhorred villain! Unnatural, detested, brutish villain! worse
than brutish! Go, sirrah,[9] seek him. I'll apprehend him. Abominable villain! Where is he?

75 EDMUND   I do not well know, my lord. If it shall please you to
suspend your indignation against my brother till you can derive
from him better testimony of his intent, you shall run a certain°   safe; reliable
course; where,° if you violently proceed against him, mistaking   whereas
his purpose, it would make a great gap in your own honor and
80 shake in pieces the heart of his obedience. I dare pawn down°   I dare stake
my life for him that he hath wrote this to feel° my affection to   feel out
your honor, and to no further pretense of danger.[1]

GLOUCESTER   Think you so?

EDMUND   If your honor judge it meet,° I will place you where   appropriate
85 you shall hear us confer of this, and by an auricular° assurance   audible
have your satisfaction; and that without any further delay than
this very evening.

GLOUCESTER   He cannot be such a monster—

EDMUND   Nor is not, sure.

90 GLOUCESTER   To his father, that so tenderly and entirely loves
him. Heaven and earth! Edmund, seek him out; wind me into
him,[2] I pray you; frame° the business after your own wisdom. I   arrange
would unstate myself, to be in a due resolution.[3]

EDMUND   I will seek him, sir, presently;° convey° the business as   immediately / carry out
95 I shall find means, and acquaint you withal.°   therewith

GLOUCESTER   These late° eclipses in the sun and moon portend   recent
no good to us.[4] Though the wisdom of nature can reason it
thus and thus, yet nature finds itself scourged by the sequent
effects.[5] Love cools, friendship falls off, brothers divide; in
100 cities, mutinies; in countries, discord; in palaces, treason; and
the bond cracked 'twixt son and father. This villain of mine
comes under the prediction; there's son against father. The
king falls from bias of nature;[6] there's father against child. We
have seen the best of our time. Machinations, hollowness,°   insincerity
105 treachery, and all ruinous disorders, follow us disquietly to our
graves. Find out this villain, Edmund; it shall lose thee nothing; do it carefully. And the noble and true-hearted Kent banished! his offence, honesty! 'Tis strange.   *Exit*

EDMUND   This is the excellent foppery° of the world, that, when   foolishness
110 we are sick in fortune, often the surfeit° of our own behavior,   excesses
we make guilty of° our disasters the sun, the moon, and the   we hold responsible for
stars; as if we were villains by necessity; fools by heavenly com-
pulsion; knaves, thieves, and treachers,° by spherical predomi-   traitors

8. A child under eighteen years who was legally dependent, often orphaned.
9. A form of address used with children or social inferiors.
1. No further intention to do harm.
2. Worm your way into his confidence (with "me" as an
intensifier); worm your way into his confidence for me
("me" as a term of respect).
3. I would give up everything to have my doubts resolved.
4. Lunar and solar eclipses that were seen in London

about a year before the play's first recorded performance
would have added spice to this superstitious belief in
the role of heavenly bodies as augurs of misfortune.
5. *Though . . . effects:* Though natural science may
explain the eclipses this way or that, nature (and family
bonds) suffers in the effects that follow.
6. The King deviates from his natural inclination. In the
game of bowls, the "bias" ("course") is the eccentric
path taken by the weighted ball when thrown.

nance;[7] drunkards, liars, and adulterers, by an enforced obedience of planetary influence; and all that we are evil in, by a
divine thrusting on.° An admirable° evasion of whore-master   *imposition / amazing*
man, to lay his goatish disposition to the charge of a star![8] My
father compounded° with my mother under the dragon's tail,   *coupled*
and my nativity was under Ursa Major,[9] so that it follows, I am
rough and lecherous. Fut!° I should have been that° I am, had   *By Christ's foot / what*
the maidenliest star in the firmament twinkled on my bas-
tardizing. Edgar—

    Enter EDGAR

and pat° he comes like the catastrophe° of the old comedy. My   *on cue / resolution*
cue is villainous melancholy, with a sigh like Tom o' Bedlam.[1]
O, these eclipses do portend these divisions! Fa, sol, la, mi.[2]

EDGAR   How now, brother Edmund? What serious contemplation are you in?

EDMUND   I am thinking, brother, of a prediction I read this
other day, what should follow these eclipses.

EDGAR   Do you busy yourself about that?

EDMUND   I promise you, the effects he writes of succeed° unhap-   *follow*
pily; as of unnaturalness between the child and the parent;
death, dearth, dissolutions of ancient amities; divisions in state,
menaces and maledictions against king and nobles; needless
diffidences,° banishment of friends, dissipation of cohorts,[3]   *baseless suspicions*
nuptial breaches, and I know not what.

EDGAR   How long have you been a sectary astronomical?°   *a devotee of astrology*

EDMUND   Come, come! When saw you my father last?

EDGAR   Why, the night gone by.

EDMUND   Spake you with him?

EDGAR   Ay, two hours together.

EDMUND   Parted you in good terms? Found you no displeasure
in him by word or countenance?°   *appearance; demeanor*

EDGAR   None at all.

EDMUND   Bethink yourself wherein you may have offended him;
and at my entreaty forbear° his presence till some little time   *avoid*
hath qualified° the heat of his displeasure; which at this instant *moderated*
so rageth in him, that with the mischief of your person it would
scarcely allay.[4]

EDGAR   Some villain hath done me wrong.

EDMUND   That's my fear. I pray you, have a continent forbear-
ance° till the speed of his rage goes slower; and, as I say, retire   *restrained absence*
with me to my lodging, from whence I will fitly° bring you to   *when suitable*
hear my lord speak. Pray ye, go! There's my key. If you do stir
abroad, go armed.

EDGAR   Armed, brother?

EDMUND   Brother, I advise you to the best. Go armed. I am no
honest man if there be any good meaning towards you. I have

---

7. By the ascendancy of a particular planet. In the universe as conceived by Ptolemy, the planets revolved about
the earth on crystalline spheres.
8. *to lay . . . star:* to hold a star responsible for his lustful
desires. In Greek mythology, the satyr, a creature with
goatlike characteristics, was notoriously lecherous.
9. Constellations: *Dragon's tail* = Draco and *Ursa
Major* = Great Bear.
1. The usual name for lunatic beggars; "Bethlehem,"
shortened to "Bedlam," was the name of the oldest and

best-known London madhouse.
2. The portion of the scale Edmund sings is an augmented fourth, an interval considered at this time very
discordant; it was sometimes referred to as "the devil in
music." *divisions:* social fractures; melodic embellishments.
3. Scattering of forces.
4. *with . . . allay:* even harming you bodily would hardly
relieve his anger; alternatively, with the irritant of your
presence, it (Gloucester's anger) would not be abated.

told you what I have seen and heard; but faintly, nothing like
160   the image and horror of it. Pray you, away!
EDGAR   Shall I hear from you anon?
EDMUND   I do serve you in this business.   *Exit* EDGAR
   A credulous father, and a brother noble,
   Whose nature is so far from doing harms,
165   That he suspects none; on whose foolish honesty
   My practices° ride easy! I see the business.[5]   *plots*
   Let me, if not by birth, have lands by wit:°   *intelligence*
   All with me's meet that I can fashion fit.[6]   *Exit*

1.3

Enter GONERIL, *and* OSWALD, *her steward*

GONERIL   Did my father strike my gentleman for chiding of his fool?
OSWALD   Yes, madam.
GONERIL   By day and night he wrongs me; every hour
   He flashes into one gross crime° or other,   *offense*
5   That sets us all at odds. I'll not endure it.
   His knights grow riotous, and himself upbraids us
   On every trifle. When he returns from hunting,
   I will not speak with him. Say I am sick.
   If you come slack of former services,[1]
10   You shall do well; the fault of it I'll answer.°   *answer for*
OSWALD   He's coming, madam; I hear him.
     Horns within°   *Hunting horns offstage*
GONERIL   Put on what weary negligence you please,
   You and your fellows.° I'd have it come to question.   *servants*
   If he dislike it, let him to our sister,
15   Whose mind and mine, I know, in that are one,
   Not to be overruled. Idle° old man,   *Foolish*
   That still would manage those authorities
   That he hath given away! Now, by my life,
   Old fools are babes again, and must be used
20   With checks as flatteries, when they are seen abused.[2]
   Remember what I tell you.
OSWALD   Well, madam.
GONERIL   And let his knights have colder looks among you.
   What grows of it, no matter; advise your fellows so.
   I would breed from hence occasions, and I shall,
25   That I may speak.[3] I'll write straight° to my sister,   *straightaway*
   To hold my very° course. Prepare for dinner.   *Exeunt*   *exact*

1.4

Enter KENT, *disguised*

KENT   If but as well[1] I other accents borrow,
   That can my speech defuse,° my good intent   *disguise*
   May carry through itself to that full issue°   *result*
   For which I razed my likeness.[2] Now, banished Kent,

---

5. It is now clear to me what needs to be done.
6. Anything is fine by me as long as I can make it serve my purpose. *meet:* justifiable; appropriate.
1.3 Location: The Duke of Albany's castle.
1. If you offer him less service (and respect) than before.
2. *Old . . . abused:* When foolish old men act like children, rebukes are the kindest treatment when kind treat-

ment is abused.
3. *I would . . . speak:* I wish to foster situations, and I shall, in which to speak my mind.
1.4 Location: As before.
1. As well as disguising my appearance.
2. Disguised my appearance; shaved off my beard (with a pun on "razor").

5   If thou canst serve where thou dost stand condemned,

So may it come,° thy master, whom thou lovest,   *come to pass*

Shall find thee full of labors.°   *helpful; keen*

        Horns within. Enter LEAR, KNIGHTS, *and attendants*[3]

LEAR   Let me not stay° a jot for dinner; go get it ready.   *wait*

                               Exit an attendant

How now! What° art thou?   *Who*

10 KENT   A man, sir.

LEAR   What dost thou profess?[4] What wouldst thou with us?

KENT   I do profess to be no less than I seem; to serve him truly

that will put me in trust; to love him that is honest; to converse°   *associate*

with him that is wise and says little; to fear judgment; to fight

15   when I cannot choose;° and to eat no fish.[5]   *when I must*

LEAR   What art thou?

KENT   A very honest-hearted fellow, and as poor as the king.

LEAR   If thou be as poor for a subject as he is for a king, thou art

poor enough. What wouldst thou?

20 KENT   Service.

LEAR   Who wouldst thou serve?

KENT   You.

LEAR   Dost thou know me, fellow?

KENT   No, sir; but you have that in your countenance which I

25   would fain° call master.   *gladly*

LEAR   What's that?

KENT   Authority.

LEAR   What services canst thou do?

KENT   I can keep honest counsel,° ride, run, mar a curious tale   *keep secrets*

30   in telling it,[6] and deliver a plain message bluntly. That which

ordinary men are fit for, I am qualified in; and the best of me

is diligence.

LEAR   How old art thou?

KENT   Not so young, sir, to love a woman for singing, nor so old

35   to dote on her for anything. I have years on my back forty-eight.

LEAR   Follow me; thou shalt serve me. If I like thee no worse

after dinner, I will not part from thee yet. Dinner, ho dinner!

Where's my knave? my fool? Go you, and call my fool hither.

                               Exit an attendant

        Enter OSWALD

You, you, sirrah, where's my daughter?

40 OSWALD   So please you—   *Exit*

LEAR   What says the fellow there? Call the clotpoll° back.   (*Exit*   *blockhead*

a KNIGHT) Where's my fool, ho? I think the world's asleep.

        Re-enter KNIGHT

How now! where's that mongrel?

KNIGHT   He says, my lord, your daughter is not well.

45 LEAR   Why came not the slave back to me when I called him?

KNIGHT   Sir, he answered me in the roundest° manner, he would   *bluntest; rudest*

not.

LEAR   He would not!

KNIGHT   My lord, I know not what the matter is; but, to my judg-

---

3. Critics of James I complained that he devalued honors by granting too many knighthoods and that he squandered too much time in hunting.

4. What is your job (profession)? Kent, in reply, uses "profess" punningly to mean "claim."

5. And not to be a Catholic or penitent (Catholics were obliged to eat fish on specified occasions and as penance); alternatively, to be a manly man, a meat eater.

6. That is, Kent's plain, blunt speech would make him ill suited to tell a convoluted ("curious") tale.

50   ment, your highness is not entertained with that ceremonious
affection as you were wont,° there's a great abatement of kind-   *accustomed to*
ness appears as well in the general dependants° as in the duke   *servants*
himself also and your daughter.

LEAR   Ha! sayest thou so?

55 KNIGHT   I beseech you pardon me, my lord, if I be mistaken; for
my duty cannot be silent when I think your highness wronged.

LEAR   Thou but rememberest° me of mine own conception.° I   *remind / perception*
have perceived a most faint neglect of late; which I have
rather blamed as mine own jealous curiosity[7] than as a very

60 pretense° and purpose of unkindness. I will look further into 't.   *a true intention*
But where's my fool? I have not seen him this two days.

KNIGHT   Since my young lady's going into France, sir, the fool
hath much pined away.

LEAR   No more of that; I have noted it well. Go you and tell my

65 daughter I would speak with her.   *Exit* KNIGHT
Go you, call hither my fool. ·   *Exit an attendant*
      Re-enter OSWALD
O, you sir, you! Come you hither, sir. Who am I, sir?

OSWALD   My lady's father.

LEAR   "My lady's father"! My lord's knave! You whoreson dog!

70 you slave! you cur!

OSWALD   I am none of these, my lord; I beseech your pardon.

LEAR   Do you bandy looks with me, you rascal? (*Striking him*)

OSWALD   I'll not be struck, my lord.

KENT   Nor tripped neither, you base foot-ball player.[8]
      Tripping up his heels

75 LEAR   I thank thee, fellow; thou servest me, and I'll love thee.

KENT   Come, sir, arise, away! I'll teach you differences.° Away,   *(of rank)*
away! If you will measure your lubber's length again,[9] tarry; but
away! Go to! Have you wisdom? so.   *Pushes* OSWALD *out*

LEAR   Now, my friendly knave, I thank thee: there's earnest of°   *downpayment for*

80 thy service. (*Giving* KENT *money*)
      Enter FOOL

FOOL   Let me hire him too. Here's my coxcomb.°   *fool's cap*
      Offering KENT *his cap*

LEAR   How now, my pretty knave! How dost thou?

FOOL   Sirrah, you were best take my coxcomb.

KENT   Why, fool?

85 FOOL   Why, for taking one's part that's out of favor. Nay, an thou
canst not smile as the wind sits, thou'lt catch cold shortly.[1]
There, take my coxcomb! Why, this fellow has banished two
on's daughters,[2] and did the third a blessing against his will. If
thou follow him, thou must needs wear my coxcomb. How

90 now, nuncle!° Would I had two coxcombs and two daughters!   *(mine) uncle*

LEAR   Why, my boy?

FOOL   If I gave them all my living,° I'd keep my coxcombs   *goods*
myself.[3] There's mine; beg another of thy daughters.

LEAR   Take heed, sirrah; the whip.

95 FOOL   Truth's a dog must to° kennel; he must be whipped out,   *go to*

---

7. *jealous curiosity:* paranoid concern with niceties.
8. Football was a rough street game played by the poor.
9. If you will be stretched out by me again. *lubber:*
clumsy oaf.
1. *an . . . shortly:* if you can't keep in favor with those
in power, you will soon find yourself left out in the cold.
2. By abdicating, Lear has in effect prevented his eldest daughters from any longer being his subjects, just
as if he had "banished" them.
3. I'd be twice as much a fool.

when Lady the brach[4] may stand by the fire and stink.

LEAR   A pestilent gall° to me!   *annoyance; bitterness*

FOOL   Sirrah, I'll teach thee a speech.

LEAR   Do.

100   FOOL   Mark it, nuncle:

Have more than thou showest,
Speak less than thou knowest,
Lend less than thou owest,°   *own*
Ride more than thou goest,°   *walk*

105   Learn° more than thou trowest,°   *Hear / believe*
Set less than thou throwest,[5]
Leave thy drink and thy whore,
And keep in-a-door,
And thou shalt have more

110   Than two tens to a score.[6]

KENT   This is nothing, fool.

FOOL   Then 'tis like the breath° of an unfeed° lawyer; you gave   *speech / unpaid*
me nothing for 't. Can you make no use of nothing, nuncle?

LEAR   Why, no, boy; nothing can be made out of nothing.

115   FOOL   (*to* KENT)   Prithee, tell him, so much the rent of his land
comes to.[7] He will not believe a fool.

LEAR   A bitter fool!

FOOL   Dost thou know the difference, my boy, between a bitter
fool and a sweet fool?

120   LEAR   No, lad; teach me.

FOOL   That lord that counseled thee
To give away thy land,
Come place him here by me,
Do thou for him stand:°   *represent him*

125   The sweet and bitter fool
Will presently appear;
The one in motley[8] here,
The other found out there.

LEAR   Dost thou call me fool, boy?

130   FOOL   All thy other titles thou hast given away; that thou wast
born with.

KENT   This is not altogether fool,[9] my lord.

FOOL   No, faith, lords and great men will not let me; if I had a
monopoly out, they would have part on 't: and ladies too, they

135   will not let me have all fool to myself; they'll be snatching.
Give me an egg, nuncle, and I'll give thee two crowns.

LEAR   What two crowns shall they be?

FOOL   Why, after I have cut the egg i' the middle, and eat up the
meat,° the two crowns of the egg. When thou clovest° thy   *edible part / cleaved*

140   crown i' the middle, and gavest away both parts, thou borest°   *you carried*
thy ass on thy back o'er the dirt. Thou hadst little wit° in thy   *sense*
bald crown, when thou gavest thy golden one away. If I speak
like myself° in this, let him be whipped that first finds it so.[1]   *(like a fool)*

---

4. Lady the bitch. Pet dogs were often called "Lady"
such and such. The allusion is to Regan and Goneril,
who are now being preferred to truthful Cordelia.
5. Don't gamble everything on a single cast of the
dice.
6. *And thou . . . score:* And there will be more than two
tens in your twenty—that is, you will become richer.

7. Remind him that no land means no rent; with a pun
on "rent" meaning "torn," "divided."
8. Multicolored dress of a court jester.
9. Foolish, folly. In the next line, the Fool takes "altogether
fool" to mean "one who has cornered the market on folly."
1. *that . . . so:* who first discovers for himself that this
is true; who first considers this to be foolish.

Singing

    Fools had ne'er less wit in a year;

145   For wise men are grown foppish,[2]

    They know not how their wits to wear,

    Their manners are so apish.°   *stupid; imitative*

LEAR When were you wont° to be so full of songs, sirrah?   *accustomed*

FOOL I have used° it, nuncle, ever since thou madest thy daugh-   *practiced*

150   ters thy mother; for when thou gavest them the rod, and put'st

down thine own breeches,

Singing

    Then they for sudden joy did weep,

      And I for sorrow sung,

    That such a king should play bo-peep,°   *a child's game*

155   And go the fools among.

Prithee, nuncle, keep a schoolmaster that can teach thy fool

to lie. I would fain learn to lie.

LEAR An° you lie, sirrah, we'll have you whipped.   *If*

FOOL I marvel what kin° thou and thy daughters are. They'll   *how alike*

160   have me whipped for speaking true, thou'lt have me whipped

for lying; and sometimes I am whipped for holding my peace.

I had rather be any kind o' thing than a fool; and yet I would

not be thee, nuncle; thou hast pared thy wit o' both sides, and

left nothing i' the middle. Here comes one o' the parings.

Enter GONERIL

165 LEAR How now, daughter! What makes that frontlet[3] on?

Methinks you are too much of late i' the frown.

FOOL Thou wast a pretty fellow when thou hadst no need to

care for her frowning; now thou art an O without a figure.[4] I

am better than thou art now; I am a fool, thou art nothing. [*To*

170 GONERIL] Yes, forsooth, I will hold my tongue; so your face bids

me, though you say nothing. Mum, mum,

    He that keeps nor crust nor crum,

    Weary of all, shall want° some.   *lack; be in need of*

(*Pointing to* LEAR) That's a shealed peascod.°   *empty pea pod; nothing*

175 GONERIL Not only, sir, this your all-licensed° fool,   *unrestrained*

But other of your insolent retinue

Do hourly carp and quarrel, breaking forth

In rank° and not-to-be-endured riots. Sir,   *foul; spreading*

I had thought, by making this well known unto you,

180 To have found a safe° redress; but now grow fearful,   *sure*

By what yourself too late° have spoke and done,   *recently*

That you protect this course, and put it on°   *encourage it*

By your allowance; which if you should, the fault

Would not 'scape censure, nor the redresses sleep,

185 Which, in the tender of a wholesome weal,

Might in their working do you that offense,

Which else were shame, that then necessity

Will call discreet proceeding.[5]

---

2. *Fools . . . foppish:* Professional fools have never been as witless since wise men have lately outdone them in idiocy.

3. Band worn on the forehead; here, a metaphor for "frown."

4. A zero without a preceding digit; nothing.

5. *which if you . . . proceeding:* if you do approve (of your attendants' behavior), you will not escape criticism, nor will it be without retribution, which for the common good will cause you pain. While this would otherwise be improper, it will be seen as a prudent ("discreet") action under the circumstances. *tender of:* concern for. *weal:* state, commonwealth. *then necessity:* the demands of the time.

FOOL   For, you know, nuncle,

190   The hedge-sparrow fed the cuckoo[6] so long,

                That it had it° head bit off by it young.°   *its / (the young cuckoo)*

        So, out went the candle, and we were left darkling.°   *in the dark*

LEAR   Are you our daughter?

GONERIL   Come, sir.

195   I would° you would make use of that good wisdom,   *wish*

        Whereof I know you are fraught,° and put away   *full*

        These dispositions,° that of late transform you   *moods; attitudes*

        From what you rightly are.

FOOL   May not an ass know when the cart draws the horse?

200   Whoop, Jug![7] I love thee.

LEAR   Doth any here know me? This is not Lear.

        Doth Lear walk thus? speak thus? Where are his eyes?

        Either his notion° weakens, his discernings   *intellect*

        Are lethargied—Ha! waking?° 'Tis not so.   *am I awake*

205   Who is it that can tell me who I am?

FOOL   Lear's shadow.

LEAR   I would° learn that; for, by the marks° of sovereignty,   *wish to / evidence*

        knowledge, and reason, I should be false persuaded I had

        daughters.

210   FOOL   Which° they will make an obedient father.   *Whom*

LEAR   Your name, fair gentlewoman?

GONERIL   This admiration,° sir, is much o' the savor   *excessive amazement*

        Of other your new pranks. I do beseech you

        To understand my purposes aright.

215   As you are old and reverend, you should be wise.

        Here do you keep a hundred knights and squires;

        Men so disordered,° so deboshed° and bold,   *disorderly / debauched*

        That this our court, infected with their manners,

        Shows° like a riotous inn. Epicurism° and lust   *Appears / Gluttony*

220   Make it more like a tavern or a brothel

        Than a graced° palace. The shame itself doth speak   *an honored*

        For instant remedy; be then desired

        By her, that else will take the thing she begs,

        A little to disquantity your train;°   *to reduce your retinue*

225   And the remainder that shall still depend,°   *be retained*

        To be such men as may besort° your age,   *befit*

        And know themselves° and you.   *know their place*

LEAR   Darkness and devils!

        Saddle my horses! call my train together!

        Degenerate bastard! I'll not trouble thee.

230   Yet° have I left a daughter.   *Still*

GONERIL   You strike my people, and your disordered rabble

        Make servants of their betters.

                Enter ALBANY

LEAR   Woe that° too late repents!—(*To* ALBANY)   *Woe to him who*

        O, sir, are you come?

235   Is it your will? Speak, sir. Prepare my horses!

        Ingratitude, thou marble-hearted fiend,

        More hideous when thou show'st thee in a child

        Than the sea-monster!

---

6. The cuckoo lays its eggs in other birds' nests.   7. Nickname for "Joan"; sobriquet for a whore.

ALBANY   Pray, sir, be patient.

LEAR (*to* GONERIL)   Detested kite!° thou liest: *carrion-eating hawk*

240 My train are men of choice and rarest parts,°   *qualities*
       That all particulars of duty know,
       And in the most exact regard support
       The worships of° their name. O most small fault,   *honors accorded*
       How ugly didst thou in Cordelia show!
245 That, like an engine, wrench'd my frame of nature
       From the fixed place;⁸ drew from my heart all love,
       And added to the gall. O Lear, Lear, Lear!
       Beat at this gate, that let thy folly in, (*striking his head*)
       And thy dear° judgment out! Go, go, my people.   *precious*
250 ALBANY   My lord, I am guiltless, as I am ignorant
       Of what hath moved you.

LEAR   It may be so, my lord.
       Hear, Nature, hear! dear goddess, hear!
       Suspend thy purpose, if thou didst intend
       To make this creature fruitful!
255 Into her womb convey sterility!
       Dry up in her the organs of increase;
       And from her derogate° body never spring   *debased*
       A babe to honor her! If she must teem,°   *breed*
       Create her child of spleen,° that it may live   *malice*
260 And be a thwart, disnatured° torment to her!   *a perverse, unnatural*
       Let it stamp wrinkles in her brow of youth;
       With cadent° tears fret° channels in her cheeks;   *flowing / carve*
       Turn all her mother's pains and benefits°   *cares and kind actions*
       To laughter and contempt, that she may feel
265 How sharper than a serpent's tooth it is
       To have a thankless child! Away, away!   *Exit*

ALBANY   Now, gods that we adore, whereof comes this?

GONERIL   Never afflict yourself to know the cause;
       But let his disposition have that scope
270 That dotage gives it.
                    Re-enter LEAR

LEAR   What, fifty of my followers at a clap?
       Within a fortnight?

ALBANY   What's the matter, sir?

LEAR   I'll tell thee. (*To* GONERIL) Life and death! I am ashamed
       That thou hast power to shake my manhood thus;
275 That these hot tears, which break from me perforce,°   *against my will*
       Should make thee worth them. Blasts and fogs upon thee!
       The untented woundings° of a father's curse   *The undressed wounds*
       Pierce every sense about thee! Old fond° eyes,   *foolish*
       Beweep° this cause again, I'll pluck ye out,   *If you weep over*
280 And cast you, with the waters that you lose,
       To temper° clay. Yea, is it come to this?   *soften*
       Let it be so. Yet have I left a daughter,
       Who, I am sure, is kind and comfortable.°   *comforting*
       When she shall hear this of thee, with her nails
285 She'll flay thy wolvish visage. Thou shalt find
       That I'll resume the shape which thou dost think
       I have cast off for ever; thou shalt, I warrant thee.

---

8. *like . . . place:* as a machine (or lever) dislocated my natural affections from their proper foundations.

Exeunt LEAR, KENT, *and attendants*

GONERIL. Do you mark that, my lord?

ALBANY   I cannot be so partial,° Goneril,   *biased*

290   To° the great love I bear you—   *Because of*

GONERIL   Pray you, content.° What, Oswald, ho! (*To the* FOOL)   *be quiet*
      You sir, more knave than fool, after your master!

FOOL   Nuncle Lear, nuncle Lear, tarry and take the fool with
      thee.

295   A fox, when one has caught her,
                               And such a daughter,
                               Should sure° to the slaughter,   *surely be sent*
                               If my cap would buy a halter:°   *collar; noose*
                               So the fool follows after.   *Exit*

GONERIL   This man hath had good counsel!—a hundred
300   knights?
         'Tis politic° and safe to let him keep   *prudent*
         At point° a hundred knights? Yes, that on every dream,   *Armed*
         Each buzz,° each fancy, each complaint, dislike,   *rumor*
         He may enguard° his dotage with their powers,   *protect*
305   And hold our lives in mercy. Oswald, I say!

ALBANY   Well, you may fear too far.

GONERIL   Safer than trust too far:
         Let me still° take away the harms I fear,   *always*
         Not° fear still to be taken. I know his heart.   *Rather than*
         What he hath uttered I have writ my sister.
310   If she sustain him and his hundred knights,
         When I have showed the unfitness—
                Re-enter OSWALD

                                                  How now, Oswald!
         What, have you writ that letter to my sister?

OSWALD   Yes, madam.

GONERIL   Take you some company, and away to horse!
315   Inform her full of my particular fear,
         And thereto add such reasons of your own
         As may compact° it more. Get you gone,   *compound*
         And hasten your return.   *Exit* OSWALD
         No, no, my lord,
320   This milky gentleness and course of yours
         Though I condemn not, yet, under pardon,°   *begging your pardon*
         You are much more attaxed° for want of wisdom   *taken to task; censured*
         Than praised for harmful mildness.

ALBANY   How far your eyes may pierce° I cannot tell: *foresee*
325   Striving to better, oft we mar what's well.

GONERIL   Nay, then—

ALBANY   Well, well; the event.°   *Exeunt*   *let's see the outcome*

1.5

Enter LEAR, KENT, *and* FOOL

LEAR   Go you before° to Gloucester[1] with these letters. Acquaint   *on ahead*
my daughter no further with any thing you know than comes
from her demand out of the letter.[2] If your diligence be not
speedy, I shall be there afore you.

5   KENT   I will not sleep, my lord, till I have delivered your letter.

Exit

FOOL   If a man's brains were in 's heels, were't not in danger of
kibes?°   *chilblains*

LEAR   Ay, boy.

FOOL   Then, I prithee, be merry; thy wit shall ne'er go slip-shod.[3]

10   LEAR   Ha, ha, ha!

FOOL   Shalt° see thy other daughter will use thee kindly; for   *Thou shalt*
though she's as like this as a crab's° like an apple, yet I can tell   *crab apple; sour apple*
what I can tell.

LEAR   Why, what canst thou tell, my boy?

15   FOOL   She will taste as like this as a crab does to a crab. Thou
canst tell why one's nose stands i' the middle on's° face?   *of one's*

LEAR   No.

FOOL   Why, to keep one's eyes of either side's nose, that what a
man cannot smell out, 'a° may spy into.   *he*

20   LEAR   I did her wrong—

FOOL   Canst tell how an oyster makes his shell?

LEAR   No.

FOOL   Nor I neither; but I can tell why a snail has a house.

LEAR   Why?

25   FOOL   Why, to put his head in; not to give it away to his daughters, and leave his horns without a case.[4]

LEAR   I will forget my nature.[5] So kind a father! Be my horses
ready?

FOOL   Thy asses° are gone about 'em. The reason why the seven   *(servants)*

30   stars° are no more than seven is a pretty reason.   *the Pleiades*

LEAR   Because they are not eight?

FOOL   Yes, indeed. Thou wouldst make a good fool.

LEAR   To take 't again perforce![6] Monster ingratitude!

FOOL   If thou wert my fool, nuncle, I'd have thee beaten for

35   being old before thy time.

LEAR   How's that?

FOOL   Thou shouldst not have been old till thou hadst been wise.

LEAR   O, let me not be mad, not mad, sweet heaven!
Keep me in temper;° I would not be mad!   *sane*

Enter GENTLEMEN

40   How now! Are the horses ready?

GENTLEMEN   Ready, my lord.

LEAR   Come, boy.

FOOL   She that's a maid now, and laughs at my departure,

1.5 Location: Before Albany's castle.
1. To Gloucestershire, where Cornwall and Regan
reside.
2. *than . . . letter:* other than such questions as are
prompted by the letter.
3. Literally, your brains will not wear slippers (to warm
feet that are afflicted with chilblains); feet of any intelligence would not walk toward Regan.

4. Protective covering for his head or concealment for his
horns (horns were the conventional sign of a cuckold).
The Fool reflects the cynical view, common in the
period, that all married men are inevitably cuckolded.
5. Lose my fatherly feelings. *nature:* character.
6. To take it back by force. Lear may refer to Goneril's
treachery, or he may be contemplating resuming his
authority.

Shall not be a maid long, unless things be cut shorter.[7]

Exeunt

2.1

Enter EDMUND *and* CURAN *meeting*

EDMUND Save° thee, Curan.   *God save*

CURAN And you, sir. I have been with your father, and given
    him notice that the Duke of Cornwall and Regan his duchess
    will be here with him this night.

5 EDMUND How comes that?

CURAN Nay, I know not. You have heard of the news abroad—
    I mean the whispered ones, for they are yet but ear-bussing
    arguments?[1]

EDMUND Not I. Pray you, what are they?

10 CURAN Have you heard of no likely wars toward,° 'twixt the   *impending*
    Dukes of Cornwall and Albany?

EDMUND Not a word.

CURAN You may do, then, in time. Fare you well, sir.   *Exit*

EDMUND The duke be here tonight? The better! best!

15 This weaves itself perforce° into my business.   *necessarily*
    My father hath set guard to take my brother;
    And I have one thing, of a queasy question,[2]
    Which I must act. Briefness and fortune, work!°   *be with me*
    Brother, a word! Descend! Brother, I say!

Enter EDGAR

20 My father watches. O sir, fly this place!
    Intelligence is given where you are hid.
    You have now the good advantage of the night.
    Have you not spoken 'gainst the Duke of Cornwall?
    He's coming hither; now, i' the night, i' the haste,

25 And Regan with him: have you nothing said
    Upon his party° 'gainst the Duke of Albany?   *On his (Cornwall's) side*
    Advise yourself.°   *Consider carefully*

EDGAR   I am sure on't,° not a word.   *of it*

EDMUND I hear my father coming. Pardon me!
    In cunning I must draw my sword upon you:

30 Draw; seem to defend yourself; now quit you° well.   *acquit yourself*
    Yield! Come before my father. Light, ho, here!
    Fly, brother. Torches, torches! So farewell.   *Exit* EDGAR
    Some blood drawn on me would beget opinion°   *produce the impression*
      (*wounds his arm*)
    Of my more fierce endeavor. I have seen drunkards

35 Do more than this in sport. Father, father!
    Stop, stop! No help?

Enter GLOUCESTER, *and servants with torches*

GLOUCESTER Now, Edmund, where's the villain?

EDMUND Here stood he in the dark, his sharp sword out,
    Mumbling of wicked charms, conjuring the moon
    To stand° auspicious mistress,—   *To act as his*

40 GLOUCESTER   But where is he?

EDMUND Look, sir, I bleed.

---

7. *She . . . shorter:* A girl who would laugh at my leaving would be so foolish that she could not remain a virgin for long; "things" refers both to the unfolding event
and to penises.

2.1 Location: Gloucester's castle.
1. Barely whispered affairs. *bussing:* buzzing.
2. And I have a hazardous and delicate problem.

GLOUCESTER   Where is the villain, Edmund?
EDMUND   Fled this way, sir. When by no means he could—
GLOUCESTER   Pursue him, ho! Go after.   *Exeunt some servants*
    By no means what?
45 EDMUND   Persuade me to the murder of your lordship;
    But that° I told him, the revenging gods   *In response to that*
    'Gainst parricides did all their thunders bend;
    Spoke, with how manifold and strong a bond
    The child was bound to the father; sir, in fine,°   *finally*
50   Seeing how loathly opposite° I stood   *opposed*
    To his unnatural purpose, in fell° motion,   *deadly*
    With his prepared sword, he charges home°   *strikes to the heart of*
    My unprovided° body, lanched° mine arm: *unprotected / struck*
    But when he saw my best alarumed spirits,
55   Bold in the quarrel's right,[3] roused to the encounter,
    Or whether gasted° by the noise I made,   *frightened*
    Full suddenly he fled.
GLOUCESTER   Let him fly far.
    Not in this land shall he remain uncaught;
    And found—dispatch.° The noble duke my master,   *And once found—killed*
60   My worthy arch° and patron, comes to-night: *lord*
    By his authority I will proclaim it,
    That he which finds him shall deserve our thanks,
    Bringing the murderous caitiff° to the stake;[4]   *wretch*
    He that conceals him, death.
65 EDMUND   When I dissuaded him from his intent,
    And found him pight° to do it, with curst° speech   *resolved / bitter*
    I threatened to discover° him. He replied,   *expose*
    "Thou unpossessing bastard! dost thou think
    If I would stand against thee, would the reposal°   *placing*
70   Of any trust, virtue, or worth in thee
    Make thy words faithed?° No. What I should deny—   *credible*
    As this I would; ay, though thou didst produce
    My very character[5]—I'd turn it all
    To[6] thy suggestion, plot, and damned practice:°   *scheming*
75   And thou must make a dullard of the world,
    If they not thought the profits of my death
    Were very pregnant and potential spurs
    To make thee seek it."[7]
GLOUCESTER   Strong° and fast'ned° villain!   *Flagrant / incorrigible*
    Would he deny his letter? I never got° him.   *begot*
    Tucket° within   *Flourish of trumpets*
80   Hark, the Duke's trumpets! I know not why he comes.
    All ports° I'll bar; the villain shall not 'scape;   *seaports; exits*
    The duke must grant me that. Besides, his picture[8]
    I will send far and near, that all the kingdom
    May have due note of him; and of my land,
85   Loyal and natural° boy, I'll work the means   *loving; illegitimate*
    To make thee capable.°   *legally able to inherit*

3. *my best . . . right*: that I was fully roused to action, made brave by righteousness.
4. Treachery and rebellion were crimes for which one could be burned.
5. Handwriting; but also, a true summary of my character.
6. *I'd . . . / To*: I'd blame it all on.

7. *And thou . . . it*: And do you think the world so stupid that it could not see the benefit you would get from my death (and thus a motive for plotting to kill me)? *pregnant*: full. *potential spurs*: powerful temptations.
8. Likenesses of outlaws were drawn up, printed, and publicly displayed, sometimes with an offer of reward as in "Wanted" posters.

Enter CORNWALL, REGAN, *and attendants*

CORNWALL   How now, my noble friend! Since I came hither,
    (Which I can call but now) I have heard strange news.
REGAN   If it be true, all vengeance comes too short

90   Which can pursue the offender. How dost, my lord?
GLOUCESTER   O, madam, my old heart is cracked, is cracked!
REGAN   What, did my father's godson seek your life?
    He whom my father named? Your Edgar?
GLOUCESTER   O, lady, lady, shame would have it hid!

95 REGAN   Was he not companion with the riotous knights
    That tend° upon my father?   *attend*
GLOUCESTER   I know not, madam. 'Tis too bad, too bad!
EDMUND   Yes, madam, he was of that consòrt.°   *company*
REGAN   No marvel, then, though° he were ill affected.° *that / ill disposed*

100 'Tis they have put him on° the old man's death, *have urged him to seek*
    To have th' expense° and waste of his revènues.   *use*
    I have this present evening from my sister
    Been well informed of them; and with such cautions
    That if they come to sojourn at my house,
    I'll not be there.

105 CORNWALL   Nor I, assure thee, Regan.
    Edmund, I hear that you have shown your father
    A child-like office.°   *filial service*
EDMUND   'Twas my duty, sir.
GLOUCESTER   He did bewray his practice,° and received *uncover his (Edgar's) plot*
    This hurt you see, striving to apprehend him.
CORNWALL   Is he pursued?

110 GLOUCESTER   Ay, my good lord.
CORNWALL   If he be taken, he shall never more
    Be feared of doing harm. Make your own purpose,
    How in my strength you please.⁹ For you, Edmund,
    Whose virtue and obedience doth this instant

115 So much commend itself, you shall be ours.
    Natures of such deep trust we shall much need;
    You we first seize on.
EDMUND   I shall serve you, sir,
    Truly, however else.°   *if nothing else*
GLOUCESTER   For him I thank your grace.
CORNWALL   You know not why we came to visit you—

120 REGAN   Thus out of season, threading dark-eyed night.
    Occasions, noble Gloucester, of some poise,°   *weight*
    Wherein we must have use of your advice:
    Our father he hath writ, so hath our sister,
    Of differences,° which I least thought of fit   *quarrels*

125 To answer from our home. The several° messengers *various*
    From hence attend° dispatch. Our good old friend, *await*
    Lay comforts to your bosom, and bestow
    Your needful° counsel to our business,   *badly needed*
    Which craves the instant use.¹
GLOUCESTER   I serve you, madam.

130 Your graces are right welcome.   *Exeunt*

---

9. *Make . . . please:* Devise your plots making use of my   1. Which requires immediate attention.
forces and authority as you see fit.

2.2

Enter KENT *and* OSWALD, *severally*°   *separately*

OSWALD   Good dawning to thee, friend. Art° of this house?   *Are you a servant*
KENT   Ay.
OSWALD   Where may we set our horses?
KENT   I' the mire.
5   OSWALD   Prithee, if thou lovest me,° tell me.   *if you will be so kind*
KENT   I love thee not.
OSWALD   Why, then, I care not for thee.
KENT   If I had thee in Lipsbury pinfold,[1] I would make thee care
    for me.
10   OSWALD   Why dost thou use° me thus? I know thee not.   *treat*
KENT   Fellow, I know thee.
OSWALD   What dost thou know me for?
KENT   A knave; a rascal; an eater of broken meats;° a base, proud,   *scraps*
    shallow, beggarly, three-suited, hundred-pound, filthy, worsted-
15   stocking knave;[2] a lily-livered, action-taking knave; a whoreson,
    glass-gazing, superserviceable, finical rogue; one-trunk-inher-
    iting slave;[3] one that wouldst be a bawd in way of good service,[4]
    and art nothing but the composition° of a knave, beggar, cow-   *combination*
    ard, pandar, and the son and heir of a mongrel bitch; one
20   whom I will beat into clamorous whining, if thou deniest the
    least syllable of thy addition.[5]
OSWALD   Why, what a monstrous fellow art thou, thus to rail on
    one that is neither known of° thee nor knows thee!   *by*
KENT   What a brazen-faced varlet° art thou, to deny thou   *rascal*
25   knowest me! Is it two days ago since I tripped up thy heels, and
    beat thee before the king? Draw, you rogue! For, though it be
    night, yet the moon shines. I'll make a sop of the moonshine[6]
    of you. Draw, you whoreson cullionly barber-monger,[7] draw!
    Drawing his sword
OSWALD   Away! I have nothing to do with thee.
30   KENT   Draw, you rascal! You come with letters against the king,
    and take Vanity the puppet's part against the royalty of her
    father.[8] Draw, you rogue, or I'll so carbonado[9] your shanks!
    Draw, you rascal! Come your ways!°   *Come forward*
OSWALD   Help, ho! murther! help!
35   KENT   Strike, you slave! Stand, rogue! Stand, you neat° slave!   *elegant; foppish*
    Strike! [*Beating him*]
OSWALD   Help, ho! muther! murther!
    Enter EDMUND *with his rapier drawn,* CORNWALL,
    REGAN, GLOUCESTER, *and servants*

2.2 Location: Before Gloucester's house.
1. If I had you in the enclosure of my mouth (gripped in my teeth). Lipsbury is probably an invented place-name. *pinfold:* pen, animal enclosure.
2. *three-suited . . . knave:* Oswald is being called a poor imitation of a gentleman. Servants were permitted three suits a year; one hundred pounds was the minimum qualification for the purchase of one of King James's knighthoods; a gentleman would wear silk, not "worsted" (of thick woolen material), stockings.
3. *lily-livered:* cowardly. *action-taking:* litigious, one who would rather use the law than his fists. *glass-gazing:* mirror-gazing. *superserviceable:* overly officious, or too ready to serve. *finical:* finicky, fastidious. *one-trunk-inheriting:* owning only what would fill one trunk.

4. *one that . . . service:* one who would even be a pimp if called upon.
5. Of the descriptions Kent has just applied to him. *addition:* title (used ironically).
6. Kent proposes so to skewer and pierce Oswald that his body might soak up moonlight. *sop:* piece of bread to be steeped or dunked in soup.
7. *cullionly barber-monger:* despicable frequenter of hairdressers. *cullion:* testicle.
8. *and take . . . father:* and support Goneril, here depicted as a dressed-up doll whose pride is contrasted with Lear's kingliness.
9. Slash or score as one would the surface of meat in preparation for broiling.

EDMUND How now! What's the matter?
    Parts them

KENT With you, goodman boy, an° you please! Come, I'll flesh   *if*
40   ye!¹ Come, on, young master!

GLOUCESTER Weapons! arms! What's the matter here?

CORNWALL Keep peace, upon your lives!
    He dies that strikes again. What is the matter?

REGAN The messengers from our sister and the king.

45 CORNWALL What is your difference?° Speak.   *quarrel*

OSWALD I am scarce in breath, my lord.

KENT No marvel, you have so bestirred your valor. You cowardly
    rascal, nature disclaims° in thee; a tailor made thee.   *disowns her part*

CORNWALL Thou art a strange fellow. A tailor² make a man?

50 KENT Ay, a tailor, sir. A stone-cutter or a painter could not have
    made him so ill,° though he had been but two hours at the   *so badly*
    trade.

CORNWALL Speak yet, how grew your quarrel?

OSWALD This ancient ruffian, sir, whose life I have spared at suit
55   of° his gray beard—   *on account of*

KENT Thou whoreson zed!³ thou unnecessary letter! My lord, if
    you will give me leave, I will tread this unbolted° villain into   *unsifted; coarse*
    mortar, and daub the walls of a jakes° with him. Spare my gray   *privy; toilet*
    beard, you wagtail?⁴

60 CORNWALL Peace, sirrah!
    You beastly knave, know you no reverence?°   *respect*

KENT Yes, sir, but anger hath a privilege.

CORNWALL Why art thou angry?

KENT That such a slave as this should wear a sword,
65   Who wears no honesty. Such smiling rogues as these,
    Like rats, oft bite the holy cords⁵ a-twain
    Which are too intrinse° t' unloose; smooth° every passion   *intricate / flatter*
    That in natures of their lords rebel;
    Bring oil to fire, snow to their colder moods;
70   Renege,° affirm, and turn their halcyon beaks⁶   *Deny*
    With every gale and vary° of their masters,   *mood*
    Knowing nought, like dogs, but following.
    A plague upon your epileptic° visage!   *distorted; grimacing*
    Smile you° my speeches, as° I were a fool?   *Do you smile at / as if*
75   Goose, if I had you upon Sarum plain
    I'd drive ye cackling home to Camelot.⁷

CORNWALL What, art thou mad, old fellow?

GLOUCESTER How fell you out? say that.

KENT No contraries° hold more antipathy   *opposites*
80   Than I and such a knave.

CORNWALL Why dost thou call him knave? What's his offense?

KENT His countenance likes° me not.   *pleases*

CORNWALL No more, perchance, does mine, nor his, nor hers.

---

1. I'll initiate you into fighting, as a hunting dog is given the taste of blood to rouse it for the chase.
2. Tailors, considered effeminate, were stock objects of mockery.
3. The letter Z (zed) was considered superfluous and omitted from many dictionaries.
4. A common English bird that takes its name from the up-and-down flicking of its tail; this, and its characteristic hopping from foot to foot, causes it to appear nervous.

5. Bonds of kinship, affection, marriage, or rank.
6. It was believed that the kingfisher (in Greek, *halcyon*) could be used as a weather vane when dead: suspended by a fine thread, its beak would turn whatever way the wind blew.
7. *Goose . . . Camelot:* Comparing him to a cackling goose, Kent tells Oswald that if he had him on Salisbury Plain, he would drive him all the way to Camelot, legendary home of King Arthur.

KENT   Sir, 'tis my occupation to be plain.
85   I have seen better faces in my time
Than stands on any shoulder that I see
Before me at this instant.
CORNWALL   This is some fellow,
Who, having been praised for bluntness, doth affect
A saucy roughness, and constrains the garb
90   Quite from his nature.[8] He cannot flatter, he,
An honest mind and plain, he must speak truth!
An they will take it, so; if not, he's plain.[9]
These kind of knaves I know, which in this plainness
Harbor more craft and more corrupter ends
95   Than twenty silly ducking observants
That stretch their duties nicely.[1]
KENT   Sir, in good sooth, in sincere verity,
Under the allowance of your great aspect,[2]
Whose influence, like the wreath of radiant fire
On flickering Phoebus' front,°   *the sun god's forehead*
100 CORNWALL   What mean'st by this?
KENT   To go out of my dialect,° which you discommend so   *normal mode of speech*
much. I know, sir, I am no flatterer. He that beguiled you in a
plain accent was a plain knave; which for my part I will not be,
though I should win your displeasure to entreat me to 't.[3]
105 CORNWALL   What was the offense you gave him?
OSWALD   I never gave him any:
It pleased the king his master very late°   *lately*
To strike at me, upon his misconstruction,°   *misunderstanding (me)*
When he, conjunct,° and flattering his displeasure,   *in league with*
110   Tripped me behind; being down, insulted,° railed,   *I being down, he insulted*
And put upon him such a deal of man,
That worthied him,[4] got praises of the king
For him attempting who was self-subdued;[5]
And, in the fleshment° of this dread exploit,   *excitement; flush*
Drew on me here again.
115 KENT   None of these rogues and cowards
But Ajax is their fool.[6]
CORNWALL   Fetch forth the stocks!
You stubborn miscreant knave, you reverent° braggart,   *old; revered*
We'll teach you—
KENT   Sir, I am too old to learn.
120   Call not your stocks for me. I serve the king;
On whose employment I was sent to you:
You shall do small respect, show too bold malice
Against the grace° and person° of my master,   *majesty / personal honor*

---

8. *and constrains . . . nature*: and assumes the appearance though it is untrue to his real self. Alternatively (with "his" meaning "its"), and distorts the true shape of plainness from what it naturally is (by turning it into disrespect).
9. If they will accept (Kent's attitude), well and good; if not, he is a plainspoken man (and does not care).
1. *Than . . . nicely*: Than twenty obsequious attendants who constantly bow idiotically, and who perform their functions with excessive diligence ("nicely").
2. With the permission of your great countenance. "Aspect" also refers to the astrological position of a planet; Kent's bombastic language here raises Cornwall

to the mock-heroic proportions of a heavenly body.
3. *He that . . . to 't*: The person who tried to hoodwink you with plain speaking was, indeed, a pure knave—something I won't be, even if you were to beg me to be one (a plain knave, or flatterer).
4. *And put . . . him*: And put on such a show of manliness that he was thought a worthy fellow.
5. For attacking a man who had already surrendered (Kent attacking Oswald).
6. *None . . . fool*: Such rogues and cowards as these talk as if they were greater warriors (and blusterers) than Ajax; such rogues always make even mighty Ajax out to be a fool.

Stocking° his messenger.   *By stocking*

125   CORNWALL   Fetch forth the stocks! As I have life and honor.
There shall he sit till noon.

REGAN   Till noon? Till night, my lord, and all night too!

KENT   Why, madam, if I were your father's dog,
You should not use me so.

REGAN   Sir, being° his knave, I will.   *since you are*

130   CORNWALL   This is a fellow of the self-same color°   *character*
Our sister° speaks of. Come, bring away the stocks!   *sister-in-law*

        Stocks brought out

GLOUCESTER   Let me beseech your grace not to do so.
His fault is much, and the good king his master
Will check° him for't. Your purposed° low correction   *reprimand / intended*

135   Is such as basest and contemned'st wretches
For pilferings and most common trespasses
Are punished with: the king must take it ill,
That he, so slightly valued in his messenger,
Should have him thus restrained.

CORNWALL   I'll answer° that.   *be responsible for*

140   REGAN   My sister may receive it much more worse,
To have her gentleman abused, assaulted,
For following° her affairs. Put in his legs.   *carrying out*

        KENT *is put in the stocks*

Come, my good lord, away.

        Exeunt all but GLOUCESTER *and* KENT

GLOUCESTER   I am sorry for thee, friend: 'tis the duke's pleasure,

145   Whose disposition, all the world well knows,
Will not be rubbed° nor stopped: I'll entreat for thee.   *obstructed*

KENT   Pray, do not sir. I have watched° and traveled hard;   *gone without sleep*
Some time I shall sleep out, the rest I'll whistle.
A good man's fortune may grow out at heels:[7]

150   Give° you good morrow!   *God give*

GLOUCESTER   The duke's to blame in this; 't will be ill-taken.

                      Exit

KENT   Good king, that must approve° the common saw,°   *prove / saying*
Thou out of heaven's benediction comest
To the warm sun![8]

155   Approach, thou beacon[9] to this under globe,
That by thy comfortable beams I may
Peruse this letter! Nothing almost sees miracles
But misery.[1] I know 'tis from Cordelia,
Who hath most fortunately been informed

160   Of my obscurèd° course; (*reads*) "and shall find time   *hidden; disguised*
From this enormous state,° seeking to give   *awful state of affairs*
Losses their remedies." All weary and o'er-watched,°   *too long awake*
Take vantage,° heavy eyes, not to behold   *the opportunity*
This shameful lodging.

165   Fortune, good night; smile once more; turn thy wheel![2]

                      Sleeps

---

7. The fortunes of even good men sometimes wear thin.
8. *Thou . . . sun:* You come from the blessing of heaven into the heat of the sun (go from good to bad).
9. It is arguable whether Kent here refers to the sun or the moon.
1. *Nothing . . . misery:* Only those suffering misery are granted miracles; any comfort seems miraculous to those who are miserable.
2. The goddess Fortune was traditionally depicted with a wheel to signify her mutability and caprice. She was believed to take pleasure in arbitrarily lowering those at the top of her wheel and raising those at the bottom.

2.3

Enter EDGAR

EDGAR I heard myself proclaimed;°   *declared an outlaw*
    And by the happy° hollow of a tree   *opportune*
    Escaped the hunt. No port° is free; no place,   *seaport; exit*
    That guard, and most unusual vigilance,
5 Does not attend my taking.° Whiles° I may 'scape,   *await my capture / Until*
    I will preserve myself; and am bethought°   *resolved*
    To take the basest and most poorest shape
    That ever penury, in contempt of° man,   *for*
    Brought near to beast. My face I'll grime with filth,
10 Blanket my loins, elf[1] all my hair in knots,
    And with presented° nakedness out-face   *exposed*
    The winds and persecutions of the sky.
    The country gives me proof and precedent
    Of Bedlam beggars, who, with roaring voices,
15 Strike° in their numbed and mortified° bare arms   *Stick / deadened*
    Pins, wooden pricks, nails, sprigs of rosemary;
    And with this horrible object,° from low farms,   *spectacle*
    Poor pelting° villages, sheep-cotes, and mills,   *paltry; contemptible*
    Sometime with lunatic bans,° sometime with prayers,   *curses*
20 Enforce their charity. Poor Turlygod![2] poor Tom!
    That's something yet! Edgar I nothing am.[3]   *Exit*

2.4

Enter LEAR, FOOL, *and* GENTLEMAN

LEAR 'Tis strange that they should so depart from home,
    And not send back my messenger.

GENTLEMAN   As I learned,
    The night before there was no purpose in them°   *they had no intention*
    Of this remove.°   *change of residence*

KENT   Hail to thee, noble master!

5 LEAR Ha!
    Makest thou this shame thy pastime?

KENT   No, my lord.

FOOL Ha, ha! he wears cruel garters.[1] Horses are tied by the
    heads, dogs and bears by the neck, monkeys by the loins, and
    men by the legs. When a man's over-lusty at legs,[2] then he
10 wears wooden nether-stocks.°   *knee socks*

LEAR What's° he that hath so much thy place° mistook   *Who's / position*
    To set thee here?

KENT   It is both he and she;
    Your son° and daughter.   *son-in-law*

LEAR No.

15 KENT Yes.

LEAR No, I say.

KENT I say, yea.

LEAR No, no, they would not!

KENT Yes, yes, they have!

2.3 Location: As before.
1. Tangle the hair into "elf locks," supposed to be a
favorite trick of malicious elves.
2. A word of unknown origin.
3. Edgar, I am nothing; I am no longer Edgar.

2.4 Location: As before.
1. Worsted garters, punning on "crewel," a thin yarn.
The Fool is actually referring to the stocks in which
Kent's feet are held.
2. When a man's liable to run away.

20	LEAR	By Jupiter, I swear, no!	
	KENT	By Juno,[3] I swear, aye!	

LEAR   They durst not do 't;
They would not, could not do 't. 'Tis worse than murder,
To do upon respect[4] such violent outrage.
Resolve° me, with all modest° haste, which way   *Inform / reasonable*
25   Thou mightst deserve, or they impose, this usage,
Coming from us.

KENT   My lord, when at their home
I did commend° your highness' letters to them,   *deliver*
Ere I was risen from the place that showed
My duty kneeling, came there a reeking° post,°   *steaming / messenger*
30   Stewed in his haste, half breathless, panting forth
From Goneril his mistress, salutations;
Delivered letters, spite of intermission,[5]
Which presently° they read; on whose contènts,   *immediately*
They summoned up their meiny,° straight° took horse;   *retinue / straightaway*
35   Commanded me to follow, and attend
The leisure of their answer, gave me cold looks,
And meeting here the other messenger,
Whose welcome, I perceived, had poisoned mine—
Being the very° fellow that of late   *same*
40   Displayed so saucily° against your highness—   *Acted so insolently*
Having more man° than wit° about me, drew.   *courage / sense*
He raised the house with loud and coward cries.
Your son and daughter found this trespass worth°   *deserving of*
The shame which here it suffers.

45   FOOL   Winter's not gone yet, if the wild-geese fly that way.[6]
             Fathers that wear rags
                 Do make their children blind;[7]
             But fathers that bear bags
                 Shall see their children kind.
50   Fortune, that arrant whore,
                 Ne'er turns the key° to the poor.   *opens the door*
But, for all this, thou shalt have as many dolors[8] for thy daugh-
ters as thou canst tell° in a year.   *count*

LEAR   O, how this mother° swells up toward my heart!   *hysteria*
55   *Hysterica passio*, down, thou climbing sorrow,[9]
Thy element's° below! Where is this daughter?   *natural place is*

KENT   With the earl, sir, here within.

LEAR   Follow me not; stay here.
                                                              Exit

GENTLEMAN   Made you no more offenses but what you speak of?

KENT   None. How chance the king comes with so small a train?

60   FOOL   An° thou hadst been set i' the stocks for that question,   *If*
thou hadst well deserved it.

KENT   Why, fool?

FOOL   We'll set thee to school to an ant, to teach thee there's no

---

3. Queen of the Roman gods and wife of Jupiter, with
whom she constantly quarreled.
4. To do to one who deserves respect.
5. Regardless of interrupting me; despite the interrup-
tions in his account (as he gasped for breath).
6. That is, things will get worse before they get better.
7. Blind to their father's needs.
8. Pains, sorrows; punning on "dollar," the English term

for the German "thaler," a large silver coin.
9. Hysterica . . . *sorrow*: *Hysterica passio* (a Latin expression originating in the Greek *steiros*, "suffering in the
womb") was an inflammation of the senses. In Renaissance medicine, vapors from the abdomen were thought
to rise up through the body, and in women, the uterus
itself to wander around.

laboring i' the winter.[1] All that follow their noses are led by
their eyes but blind men, and there's not a nose among twenty
but can smell him that's stinking.° Let go thy hold when a great   *(as his fortunes decay)*
wheel runs down a hill,[2] lest it break thy neck with following
it; but the great one that goes up the hill, let him draw thee
after. When a wise man gives thee better counsel, give me
mine again. I would have none but knaves follow it, since a
fool gives it.

    That sir which serves and seeks for gain,
     And follows but for form,
    Will pack° when it begins to rain,   *pack up and go*
     And leave thee in the storm.
    But I will tarry; the fool will stay,
     And let the wise man fly.
    The knave turns fool that runs away;[3]
     The fool no knave, perdy.°   *by God (pardieu)*

KENT Where learned you this, fool?

FOOL Not i' the stocks, fool.

   Re-enter LEAR, *with* GLOUCESTER

LEAR Deny to speak with me? They are sick? they are weary?
They have traveled all the night? Mere fetches;°   *ruses; pretexts*
The images of revolt and flying off.[4]
Fetch me a better answer.

GLOUCESTER   My dear lord,
You know the fiery quality° of the duke;   *disposition*
How unremoveable and fixed he is
In his own course.

LEAR Vengeance! plague! death! confusion!°   *destruction*
Fiery? what quality? Why, Gloucester, Gloucester,
I'd speak with the Duke of Cornwall and his wife.

GLOUCESTER Well, my good lord, I have informed them so.

LEAR Informed them! Dost thou understand me, man?

GLOUCESTER Ay, my good lord.

LEAR The king would speak with Cornwall; the dear father
Would with his daughter speak, commands her service.
Are they informed of this? My breath and blood!
Fiery? the fiery duke? Tell the hot duke that—
No, but not yet. May be he is not well.
Infirmity doth still° neglect all office°   *always / obligation*
Whereto our health is bound; we are not ourselves
When nature, being oppressed, commands the mind
To suffer with the body. I'll forbear;
And am fallen out with my more headier will,[5]
To take° the indisposed and sickly fit   *mistake*
For the sound man. Death on my state![6] Wherefore°   *Why*
   looking on KENT
Should he sit here? This act persuades me
That this remotion° of the duke and her   *remoteness, aloofness*
Is practice° only. Give me my servant forth.   *trickery*

---

1. Ants, proverbially prudent, do not work in winter.
Implicitly, a wise person should know better than to look
for sustenance to an old man who has fallen on wintry
times.
2. A great wheel is a figure for Lear and of Fortune's
wheel itself, which has swung downward.

3. The scoundrel who runs away is the real fool.
4. *images of*: signs of. *flying off*: desertion; insurrection.
5. And disagree with my (earlier) more rash intention.
6. May my royal authority end (an oath). Ironically, this
has already happened.

110   Go tell the duke and 's wife I'd speak with them,
            Now, presently!° Bid them come forth and hear me,   *at once*
            Or at their chamber-door I'll beat the drum
            Till it cry sleep to death.[7]

     GLOUCESTER   I would have all well betwixt you.   *Exit*

115   LEAR   O me, my heart, my rising heart! but, down!

     FOOL   Cry to it, nuncle, as the cockney° did to the eels when she   *Londoner (city woman)*
            put 'em i' the paste° alive; she knapped 'em o' the coxcombs°   *pie; pastry / heads*
            with a stick, and cried "Down, wantons,° down!" 'Twas her   *rogues*
            brother that, in pure kindness to his horse, buttered his hay.[8]

                 Enter CORNWALL, REGAN, GLOUCESTER, *and servants*

     LEAR   Good morrow to you both.

120   CORNWALL   Hail to your grace!

         KENT *is set at liberty*

     REGAN   I am glad to see your highness.

     LEAR   Regan, I think you are; I know what reason
            I have to think so. If thou shouldst not be glad,
            I would divorce me from thy mother's tomb,

125   Sepulchring° an adultress. (*To* KENT) O, are you free?   *Because it entombed*
            Some other time for that. Belovèd Regan,
            Thy sister's naught.° O Regan, she hath tied   *wicked; nothing*
            Sharp-toothed unkindness, like a vulture, here!

         Points to his heart

            I can scarce speak to thee; thou'lt not believe

130   With how depraved a quality—O Regan!

     REGAN   I pray you, sir, take patience. I have hope
            You less know how to value her desert
            Than she to scant her duty.[9]

     LEAR   Say, how is that?

     REGAN   I cannot think my sister in the least

135   Would fail her obligation. If, sir, perchance
            She have restrained the riots of your followers,
            'Tis on such ground, and to such wholesome end,
            As clears her from all blame.

     LEAR   My curses on her!

     REGAN   O, sir, you are old;

140   Nature° in you stands on the very verge   *Life*
            Of her confine.° You should be ruled and led   *Of its limit*
            By some discretion,° that discerns your state   *discreet person*
            Better than you yourself. Therefore, I pray you,
            That to our sister you do make return;
            Say you have wronged her, sir.

145   LEAR   Ask her forgiveness?
            Do you but mark how this becomes the house:[1]
            "Dear daughter, I confess that I am old; (*kneeling*)
            Age° is unnecessary. On my knees I beg   *An old man*
            That you'll vouchsafe me raiment,° bed, and food."   *promise me clothing*

150   REGAN   Good sir, no more! These are unsightly tricks.
            Return you to my sister.

---

7. Till the noise kills sleep.
8. Like that of his sister (who wanted to make eel pie without killing the eels), his kindness was misplaced: horses will not eat buttered hay.
9. *I have . . . duty:* I expect that you are worse at valuing her deservings than she is at neglecting her duty. The double negative here ("less," "scant") is acceptable Jacobean usage.
1. Do you see how appropriate this is among members of a family (spoken ironically)?

LEAR (*rising*)   Never, Regan!
  She hath abated° me of half my train;   *deprived*
  Looked black upon me; struck me with her tongue
  Most serpent-like, upon the very heart.
155 All° the stored vengeances of heaven fall   *Let all*
  On her ingrateful top!° Strike her young bones,   *head*
  You taking° airs, with lameness!   *infectious; malignant*
CORNWALL   Fie, sir, fie!
LEAR You nimble lightnings, dart your blinding flames
  Into her scornful eyes! Infect her beauty,
160 You fen-sucked fogs, drawn by the powerful sun,[2]
  To fall and blast her pride!
REGAN O the blest gods! so will you wish on me,
  When the rash mood is on.
LEAR No, Regan, thou shalt never have my curse.
165 Thy tender-hefted[3] nature shall not give
  Thee o'er to harshness. Her eyes are fierce; but thine
  Do comfort and not burn. 'Tis not in thee
  To grudge my pleasures, to cut off my train,
  To bandy hasty words, to scant my sizes,°   *reduce my allowances*
170 And in conclusion to oppose the bolt°   *to lock the door*
  Against my coming in. Thou better know'st
  The offices° of nature, bond of childhood,   *duties*
  Effects° of courtesy, dues of gratitude;   *Actions*
  Thy half o' the kingdom hast thou not forgot,
  Wherein I thee endowed.
175 REGAN   Good sir, to the purpose.°   *get to the point*
LEAR Who put my man i' the stocks?
     Tucket within
CORNWALL   What trumpet's that?
REGAN I know't, my sister's. This approves° her letter,   *confirms*
  That she would soon be here.
     Enter OSWALD
               Is your lady come?
LEAR This is a slave, whose easy-borrowed pride[4]
180 Dwells in the fickle grace of her he follows.
  Out varlet,° from my sight!   *wretch*
CORNWALL   What means your grace?
LEAR Who stocked my servant? Regan, I have good hope
  Thou didst not know on 't.°   *of it*
     Enter GONERIL
  Who comes here? O heavens,
185 If you do love old men, if your sweet sway
  Allow obedience, if yourselves are old,
  Make it your cause! Send down, and take my part!
  (*To* GONERIL) Art not ashamed to look upon this beard?
  O Regan, wilt thou take her by the hand?
190 GONERIL Why not by the hand, sir? How have I offended?
  All's not offense that indiscretion finds
  And dotage terms so.
LEAR   O sides,[5] you are too tough!

2. The sun was thought to suck poisonous vapors from marshy ground.
3. Tenderly placed; firmly set in a tender disposition (as a knife blade into its haft).
4. Unmerited and unpaid-for arrogance; "pride" may also refer to Oswald's fine clothing received for his services to Goneril.
5. Chest, where Lear's heart is swelling with emotion.

Will you yet hold? How came my man i' the stocks?

CORNWALL   I set him there, sir; but his own disorders°   *disorderly behavior*
Deserved much less advancement.[6]

195   LEAR   You! did you?

REGAN   I pray you, father, being weak, seem so.°   *behave so*
If, till the expiration of your month,
You will return and sojourn with my sister,
Dismissing half your train, come then to me.
200   I am now from home, and out of that provision
Which shall be needful for your entertainment.

LEAR   Return to her, and fifty men dismissed?
No, rather I abjure all roofs, and choose
To wage against the enmity o' the air;
205   To be a comrade with the wolf and owl—
Necessity's sharp pinch![7] Return with her?
Why, the hot-blooded France, that dowerless took
Our youngest born, I could as well be brought
To knee° his throne, and, squire-like, pension beg   *kneel to*
210   To keep base life afoot. Return with her?
Persuade me rather to be slave and sumpter°   *packhorse*
To this detested groom. (*Pointing at* OSWALD)

GONERIL   At your choice, sir.

LEAR   I prithee, daughter, do not make me mad.
I will not trouble thee, my child; farewell.
215   We'll no more meet, no more see one another.
But yet thou art my flesh, my blood, my daughter;
Or rather a disease that's in my flesh,
Which I must needs call mine. Thou art a boil,
A plague-sore, an embossed° carbuncle,   *a swollen*
220   In my corrupted blood. But I'll not chide thee;
Let shame come when it will, I do not call° it.   *call upon*
I do not bid the Thunder-bearer° shoot,   *(Jove)*
Nor tell tales of thee to high-judging Jove.
Mend° when thou canst; be better at thy leisure.   *Make amends*
225   I can be patient, I can stay with Regan,
I and my hundred knights.

REGAN   Not altogether so.
I looked not for° you yet, nor am provided   *I did not expect*
For your fit welcome. Give ear, sir, to my sister;
For those that mingle reason with your passion[8]
230   Must be content to think you old, and so—
But she knows what she does.

LEAR   Is this well° spoken?   *earnestly*

REGAN   I dare avouch° it, sir. What, fifty followers?   *vouch for*
Is it not well? What should you need of more?
Yea, or so many, sith° that both charge° and danger   *since / expense*
235   Speak 'gainst so great a number? How, in one house,
Should many people, under two commands,
Hold amity? 'T is hard; almost impossible.

GONERIL   Why might not you, my lord, receive attendance
From those that she calls servants, or from mine?

---

6. Deserved far worse treatment.
7. *To wage . . . pinch:* To counter, like predators, the harshness of the elements with the hardness brought on by necessity. *pinch:* stress, pressure.
8. For those who temper your passionate argument with their own calm reasoning.

240	REGAN Why not, my lord? If then they chanced to slack° you,
	We could control them. If you will come to me—
	For now I spy a danger—I entreat you
	To bring but five-and-twenty. To no more
	Will I give place or notice.°
	LEAR I gave you all—
245	REGAN And in good time° you gave it.
	LEAR Made you my guardians, my depositaries;°
	But kept a reservation° to be followed
	With such a number. What, must I come to you
	With five-and-twenty, Regan? Said you so?
250	REGAN And speak't again, my lord; no more with me.
	LEAR Those wicked creatures yet do look well-favored,°
	When others are more wicked; not being the worst
	Stands in some rank of praise.[9] (To GONERIL) I'll go with thee:
	Thy fifty yet doth double five-and-twenty,
	And thou art twice her love.
255	GONERIL Hear me, my lord.
	What need you five-and-twenty, ten, or five,
	To follow in a house where twice so many
	Have a command to tend you?
	REGAN What need one?
	LEAR O, reason not the need! Our basest beggars
260	Are in the poorest thing superfluous.[1]
	Allow not° nature more than nature needs,
	Man's life's as cheap as beast's. Thou art a lady;
	If only to go warm were gorgeous,
	Why, nature needs not what thou gorgeous wear'st,
265	Which scarcely keeps thee warm.[2] But, for true need—
	You heavens, give me that patience,° patience I need!
	You see me here, you gods, a poor old man,
	As full of grief as age; wretched in both!
	If it be you that stirs these daughters' hearts
270	Against their father, fool me not so much
	To bear it tamely;[3] touch me with noble anger,
	And let not women's weapons, water-drops,
	Stain my man's cheeks! No, you unnatural hags,
	I will have such revenges on you both,
275	That all the world shall—I will do such things—
	What they are, yet I know not; but they shall be
	The terrors of the earth! You think I'll weep;
	No, I'll not weep.
	I have full cause of weeping, but this heart
280	Shall break into a hundred thousand flaws°
	Or ere° I'll weep. O fool, I shall go mad!

Exeunt LEAR, GLOUCESTER, KENT, *and* FOOL.
Storm and tempest

	CORNWALL Let us withdraw; 't will be a storm.
	REGAN This house is little; the old man and his people
	Cannot be well bestowed.°

Right-margin glosses:
- *neglect* (240)
- *acknowledgment* (244)
- *it was about time* (245)
- *trustees* (246)
- *reserved a right* (247)
- *attractive* (251)
- *If you don't allow* (261)
- *endurance* (266)
- *fragments* (280)
- *Before* (281)
- *lodged*

---

9. Deserves some degree ("rank") of praise.
1. *Our . . . superfluous:* Even the lowliest beggars have something more than the barest minimum.
2. *If . . . thee warm:* If gorgeousness in clothes is mea-sured by the warmth they provide, your elaborate clothes are superfluous, for they barely cover your body.
3. *fool . . . tamely:* do not make me so foolish as to accept it meekly.

285 GONERIL   'Tis his own blame; hath put himself from° rest,   *deprived himself of*
And must needs taste his folly.

REGAN   For his particular,° I'll receive him gladly,   *single self*
But not one follower.

GONERIL   So am I purposed.
Where is my lord of Gloucester?

290 CORNWALL   Followed the old man forth. He is returned.

            Re-enter GLOUCESTER

GLOUCESTER   The king is in high rage.

CORNWALL   Whither is he going?

GLOUCESTER   He calls to horse, but will° I know not whither.   *will go*

CORNWALL   'Tis best to give him way; he leads himself.

GONERIL   My lord, entreat him by no means to stay.

295 GLOUCESTER   Alack, the night comes on, and the bleak winds
Do sorely ruffle.° For many miles about   *bluster*
There's scarce a bush.

REGAN   O, sir, to willful men,
The injuries that they themselves procure
Must be their schoolmasters. Shut up your doors.

300 He is attended with a desperate° train;   *violent*
And what they may incense° him to, being apt   *incite*
To have his ear abused,° wisdom bids fear.   *deceived*

CORNWALL   Shut up your doors, my lord; 'tis a wild night.
My Regan counsels well. Come out o' the storm.   *Exeunt*

3.1

            Storm still. Enter KENT *and a* GENTLEMAN, *at several°*   *separate*
            doors

KENT   Who's there, besides foul weather?

GENTLEMAN   One minded like the weather, most unquietly.

KENT   I know you. Where's the king?

GENTLEMAN   Contending with the fretful elements;

5 Bids the wind blow the earth into the sea,
Or swell the curlèd waters 'bove the main,°   *mainland*
That things might change or cease; tears his white hair,
Which the impetuous blasts, with eyeless rage,
Catch in their fury, and make nothing of;

10 Strives in his little world of man to out-scorn
The to-and-fro-conflicting wind and rain.
This night, wherein the cub-drawn bear would couch,[1]
The lion and the belly-pinchèd wolf
Keep their fur dry, unbonneted° he runs,   *hatless; uncrowned*
And bids what will take all.

15 KENT   But who is with him?

GENTLEMAN   None but the fool, who labors to out-jest
His heart-struck injuries.[2]

KENT   Sir, I do know you;
And dare, upon the warrant of my note,[3]
Commend a dear° thing to you. There is division,   *Entrust a crucial*

20 Although as yet the face of it be covered

3.1 Location: Bare, open country.
1. In which even the bear, though starving, having been sucked dry ("drawn") by its cub, would not go out to forage.

2. *to out-jest*: to relieve with laughter; to exorcise through ridicule. *heart-struck injuries*: injuries (from the betrayal of his paternal love) that penetrated to the heart.
3. On the basis of my skill (at judging people).

With mutual cunning, 'twixt Albany and Cornwall;
Who have—as who have not, that their great stars
Throned and set high?[4]—servants, who seem no less,°   *who appear as such*
Which are to France the spies and speculations°   *observers*
25   Intelligent of[5] our state. What hath been seen,
Either in snuffs and packings° of the dukes,   *quarrels and plots*
Or the hard rein° which both of them have borne   *treatment*
Against the old kind king; or something deeper,
Whereof perchance these are but furnishings;°   *pretexts*
30   But, true it is, from France there comes a power
Into this scattered kingdom; who already,
Wise in° our negligence, have secret feet   *Aware of*
In some of our best ports, and are at point°   *ready*
To show their open banner. Now to you:
35   If on my credit you dare build° so far   *If you trust me*
To make your speed to Dover, you shall find
Some that will thank you, making just° report   *accurate*
Of how unnatural and bemadding° sorrow   *maddening*
The king hath cause to plain.°   *complain*
40   I am a gentleman of blood and breeding;
And, from some knowledge and assurance, offer
This office° to you.   *role; duty*
GENTLEMAN   I will talk further with you.
KENT   No, do not.
For confirmation that I am much more
45   Than my out-wall,° open this purse, and take   *outward appearance*
What it contains. If you shall see Cordelia—
As fear not but you shall—show her this ring,
And she will tell you who your fellow° is   *(Kent himself)*
That yet you do not know. Fie on this storm!
50   I will go seek the king.
GENTLEMAN   Give me your hand. Have you no more to say?
KENT   Few words, but, to effect,° more than all yet;   *in importance*
That, when we have found the king—in which your pain
That way, I'll this[6]—he that first lights on him
55   Holla the other.   *Exeunt severally*

3.2

Enter LEAR *and* FOOL. *Storm still*
LEAR   Blow, winds, and crack your cheeks! rage! blow!
You cataracts and hurricanoes,[1] spout
Till you have drenched our steeples, drowned the cocks!°   *weather vanes*
You sulphurous and thought-executing fires,[2]
5   Vaunt-couriers° to oak-cleaving thunderbolts,   *Forerunners*
Singe my white head! And thou, all-shaking thunder,
Smite flat the thick rotundity o' the world!
Crack Nature's molds, all germens° spill at once,   *seeds*
That make ingrateful man!

---

4. *as . . . high:* as has everybody who has been favored by
destiny.
5. Supplying intelligence about; too well informed of.
6. *in which . . . this:* in which effort you will go that way
and I this way.

3.2 Location: As before.
1. *cataracts:* floodgates of the heavens. *hurricanoes:*
waterspouts (water from both sky and sea).
2. *thought-executing fires:* lightning that strikes as swiftly
as thought.

10 FOOL   O nuncle, court holy-water[3] in a dry house is better than
        this rain-water out o' door. Good nuncle, in, and ask thy daugh-
        ters' blessing! Here's a night pities neither wise man nor fool.

LEAR   Rumble thy bellyful! Spit, fire! spout, rain!
        Nor rain, wind, thunder, fire, are my daughters:
15   I tax° not you, you elements, with unkindness;   *blame*
        I never gave you kingdom, called you children,
        You owe me no subscription.° Then let fall   *obedience; allegiance*
        Your horrible pleasure. Here I stand, your slave,
        A poor, infirm, weak, and despised old man.
20   But yet I call you servile ministers,°   *agents*
        That have with two pernicious daughters joined
        Your high engendered battles° 'gainst a head   *heaven-bred forces*
        So old and white as this. O! O! 't is foul!

FOOL   He that has a house to put 's head in has a good head-
25   piece.°   *hat; brain*
                 The cod-piece that will house
                    Before the head has any,
                 The head and he shall louse;
                    So beggars marry many.[4]
30   The man that makes his toe
                    What he his heart should make
                 Shall of a corn cry woe,
                    And turn his sleep to wake.[5]
        For there was never yet fair woman but she made mouths in a
35   glass.[6]

LEAR   No, I will be the pattern of all patience; I will say nothing.
                    Enter KENT

KENT   Who's there?

FOOL   Marry, here's grace and a cod-piece; that's a wise man and
        a fool.[7]

40 KENT   Alas, sir, are you here? things that love night
        Love not such nights as these; the wrathful skies
        Gallow° the very wanderers of the dark,   *Frighten*
        And make them keep° their caves. Since I was man,   *keep inside*
        Such sheets of fire, such bursts of horrid thunder,
45   Such groans of roaring wind and rain, I never
        Remember to have heard. Man's nature cannot carry°   *bear*
        The affliction nor the fear.

LEAR   Let the great gods,
        That keep this dreadful pother° o'er our heads,   ~~forensic~~   *commotion*
        Find out their enemies now. Tremble, thou wretch,
50   That hast within thee undivulgèd crimes,
        Unwhipped of° justice. Hide thee, thou bloody hand;   *Unpunished by*
        Thou perjured, and thou simular° of virtue   *simulator; pretender*

---

3. Sprinkled blessings of a courtier; flattery.
4. *The cod-piece . . . many:* Whoever finds his penis a
lodging before providing shelter for his head will end up
in lice-infested poverty and live in married beggary. *codpiece:* a pouchlike covering for the male genitals, often
conspicuous, particularly in the costume of a fool.
5. *The man . . . wake:* The man who values an inferior
part of his body over the part that is truly valuable will
suffer from and lose sleep over that inferior part.

6. She practiced making pretty faces in a mirror. The
Fool probably refers to Regan's and Goneril's vanity, or
the line may be thrown in to soften the harshness of his
satire.
7. The supposedly wise King is symbolized by royal
grace, the Fool by his codpiece (here, slang for "penis").
The Fool speaks ironically: the King, as he has pointed
out, is now the foolish one. *Marry:* By the Virgin Mary (a
mild oath).

That are incestuous. Caitiff,° to pieces shake,   *Wretch*
That under covert and convenient seeming°   *fitting hypocrisy*
55   Hast practiced on° man's life. Close° pent-up guilts   *against / Secret*
Rive° your concealing continents,° and cry   *Split open / coverings*
These dreadful summoners grace.[8] I am a man
More sinned against than sinning.

KENT   Alack, bare-headed?
Gracious my lord, hard by here is a hovel;
60   Some friendship will it lend you 'gainst the tempest.
Repose you there, while I to this hard house°—   *household*
More harder than the stones whereof 'tis raised,
Which° even but now, demanding° after you,   *Who / I demanding*
Denied me to come in—return, and force
Their scanted° courtesy.   *niggardly*

65 LEAR   My wits begin to turn.
Come on, my boy. How dost, my boy? Art cold?
I am cold myself. Where is this straw, my fellow?
The art° of our necessities is strange,   *skill; alchemy*
That can make vile things precious. Come, your hovel.
70   Poor fool and knave, I have one part in my heart
That's sorry yet for thee.

FOOL (*singing*)[9]
           He that has and° a little tiny wit°—   *even / sense*
           With hey, ho, the wind and the rain—
           Must make content with his fortunes fit,
75   Though the rain it raineth every day.

LEAR   True, boy. Come, bring us to this hovel.
                        Exeunt LEAR *and* KENT

FOOL   This is a brave night to cool a courtesan.[1]
I'll speak a prophecy ere I go:[2]
           When priests are more in word than matter;°   *real virtue*
80   When brewers mar their malt with water;
           When nobles are their tailors' tutors;[3]
           No heretics burned, but wenches' suitors;[4]
           When every case in law is right;°   *just*
           No squire in debt, nor no poor knight;
85   When slanders do not live in tongues,
           Nor cutpurses° come not to throngs;   *pickpockets*
           When usurers tell their gold i' the field,[5]
           And bawds and whores do churches build;
           Then shall the realm of Albion°   *Britain*
90   Come to great confusion.°   *decay*
Then comes the time, who lives to see 't,
That going° shall be used° with feet.   *walking / practiced*
This prophecy Merlin shall make; for I live before his time.[6]
                            Exit

---

8. *and cry . . . grace:* and pray for mercy from these elements that bring you to justice.
9. The following song is an adaptation of one sung by Feste at the end of *Twelfth Night.*
1. To cool even the hot lusts of a prostitute.
2. What follows is a parody of the pseudo-Chaucerian "Merlin's Prophecy" from *The Arte of English Poesie.*
3. When noblemen follow fashion more closely than their tailors do.
4. When the only heretics burned are faithless lovers, who burn from venereal disease.
5. When usurers can count their profits openly (because they have no shady dealings to hide).
6. Merlin was the great wizard at the legendary court of King Arthur. Lear's Britain is set in an even more distant past.

3.3

Enter GLOUCESTER *and* EDMUND

GLOUCESTER Alack, alack, Edmund, I like not this unnatural
dealing. When I desired their leave that I might pity° him, they   *relieve*
took from me the use of mine own house; charged me, on pain
of their perpetual displeasure, neither to speak of him, entreat
5 for him, nor any way sustain him.

EDMUND Most savage and unnatural!

GLOUCESTER Go to;° say you nothing. There's a division betwixt   *(an expletive)*
the dukes, and a worse matter than that. I have received a letter
this night; 'tis dangerous to be spoken; I have locked the letter
10 in my closet.° These injuries the king now bears will be   *private chamber*
revenged home;° there's part of a power already footed;[1] we   *to the hilt*
must incline to[2] the king. I will seek him, and privily° relieve   *secretly; privately*
him. Go you and maintain talk with the duke, that my charity
be not of him perceived if he ask for me, I am ill, and gone to
15 bed. Though I die for it, as no less is threatened me, the king
my old master must be relieved. There is some strange thing
toward,° Edmund; pray you, be careful.   *Exit*   *coming*

EDMUND This courtesy,° forbid° thee, shall the duke   *act of kindness / forbidden*
Instantly know, and of that letter too.
20 This seems a fair deserving,[3] and must draw me
That which my father loses—no less than all.
The younger rises when the old doth fall.   *Exit*

3.4

Enter LEAR, KENT, *and* FOOL

KENT Here is the place, my lord; good my lord, enter:
The tyranny of the open night's too rough
For nature° to endure.   *human weakness*

Storm still

LEAR Let me alone.

KENT Good my lord, enter here.
5 LEAR   Wilt break my heart?

KENT I had rather break mine own. Good my lord, enter.

LEAR Thou think'st 'tis much that this contentious storm
Invades us to the skin. So 'tis to thee;
But where the greater malady is fixed,°   *rooted*
10 The lesser is scarce felt. Thou'dst shun a bear;
But if thy flight lay toward the raging sea,
Thou'dst meet the bear i' the mouth. When the mind's free,°   *unburdened*
The body's delicate.° The tempest in my mind   *sensitive*
Doth from my senses take all feeling else
15 Save° what beats there. Filial ingratitude!   *Except*
Is it not as° this mouth should tear this hand   *as if*
For lifting food to 't? But I will punish home.°   *thoroughly*
No, I will weep no more. In such a night
To shut me out! Pour on; I will endure.
20 In such a night as this! O Regan, Goneril!
Your old kind father, whose frank heart gave all—
O, that way madness lies; let me shun that;
No more of that.

3.3 Location: At Gloucester's castle.   3. This seems an action that deserves to be rewarded.
1. Part of an army already landed.   3.4 Location: Open country, before a cattle shed.
2. We must take the side of.

KENT   Good my lord, enter here.
LEAR   Prithee, go in thyself; seek thine own ease:
25   This tempest will not give me leave to° ponder   *allow me to*
        On things would hurt me more. But I'll go in.
        (*To the* FOOL) In, boy; go first. You houseless poverty°—   *poor*
        Nay, get thee in. I'll pray, and then I'll sleep.
                        FOOL *goes in*
        Poor naked wretches, whereso'er you are,
30   That bide° the pelting of this pitiless storm,   *endure; dwell in*
        How shall your houseless heads and unfed sides,°   *starved ribs*
        Your looped and windowed[1] raggedness, defend you
        From seasons such as these? O, I have ta'en
        Too little care of this! Take physic, pomp;[2]
35   Expose thyself to feel what wretches feel,
        That thou mayst shake the superflux[3] to them,
        And show the heavens more just.
EDGAR   (*within*)   Fathom and half,[4] fathom and half!
        Poor Tom!
                The FOOL *runs out from the hovel*
40 FOOL   Come not in here, nuncle, here's a spirit.
        Help me, help me!
KENT   Give me thy hand. Who's there?
FOOL   A spirit, a spirit! He says his name's poor Tom.
KENT   What art thou that dost grumble there i' the straw? Come
45   forth.
                Enter EDGAR *disguised as a madman*
EDGAR   Away! the foul fiend follows me!
        Through the sharp hawthorn blows the cold wind.[5]
        Humh! go to thy cold bed, and warm thee.[6]
LEAR   Hast thou given all to thy two daughters? And art thou
50   come to this?
EDGAR   Who gives any thing to poor Tom? whom the foul fiend
        hath led through fire and through flame, through ford and
        whirlpool, o'er bog and quagmire; that hath laid knives under
        his pillow and halters in his pew; set ratsbane by his porridge;[7]
55   made him proud of heart, to ride on a bay trotting-horse over
        four-inched bridges,[8] to course° his own shadow for° a traitor.   *hunt / as*
        Bless thy five wits![9] Tom's a-cold—O, do, de, do de, do de.
        Bless thee from whirlwinds, star-blasting, and taking![1] Do poor
        Tom some charity, whom the foul fiend vexes: there could I
60   have him now—and there—and there again, and there.[2]
                Storm still
LEAR   What, has his daughters brought him to this pass?
        Couldst thou save nothing? Didst thou give them all?

---

1. *looped and windowed:* full of holes and vents; "windowed" could also refer to cloth worn through to semi-transparency, like the oilcloth window "panes" of the poor.
2. Cure yourself, pompous person.
3. Superfluity; bodily discharge, suggested by "physic" (which also has the meaning of "purgative") in line 34. Excess here is also excess of wealth.
4. "Nine feet," a sailor's cry when taking soundings to gauge the depth of water.
5. *Through . . . wind:* Perhaps a fragment from a ballad.
6. *go . . . thee:* this expression is also used by the drunken beggar Christopher Sly in *The Taming of the Shrew,* Induction 1.

7. *laid knives . . . porridge:* these are all means by which the foul fiend tempts Tom to commit suicide. *halters:* nooses. *ratsbane:* rat poison.
8. Impossibly narrow, and probably suicidal to attempt without diabolical help.
9. The five wits were common wit, imagination, fantasy, estimation, and memory (from medieval and Renaissance cognitive theory).
1. *whirlwinds, star-blasting:* malign astrological influences capable of causing sickness or death. *taking:* infection; bewitchment.
2. As Edgar speaks this sentence, he might kill vermin on his body as if they were devils.

FOOL   Nay, he reserved a blanket, else we had been all shamed.

LEAR   Now, all the plagues that in the pendulous° air   *overhanging; portentous*

65   Hang fated o'er men's faults light on thy daughters!

KENT   He hath no daughters, sir.

LEAR   Death, traitor! nothing could have subdued nature
        To such a lowness but his unkind daughters.
        Is it the fashion that discarded fathers

70   Should have thus little mercy on their flesh?
        Judicious punishment! 't was this flesh begot
        Those pelican³ daughters.

EDGAR   Pillicock sat on Pillicock-hill.
        Halloo, halloo, loo, loo!⁴

75 FOOL   This cold night will turn us all to fools and madmen.

EDGAR   Take heed o' the foul fiend; obey thy parents; keep thy
        word justly; swear not; commit not with man's sworn spouse;
        set not thy sweet heart on proud array.⁵ Tom's a-cold.

LEAR   What hast thou been?

80 EDGAR   A serving-man, proud in heart and mind; that curled my
        hair; wore gloves in my cap;⁶ served the lust of my mistress'
        heart, and did the act of darkness with her; swore as many oaths
        as I spake words, and broke them in the sweet face of heaven:
        one that slept in the contriving of lust, and waked to do it. Wine

85   loved I deeply, dice dearly; and in woman out-paramoured the
        Turk.⁷ False of heart, light of ear,° bloody of hand; hog in sloth,   *rumor-hungry*
        fox in stealth, wolf in greediness, dog in madness, lion in prey.
        Let not the creaking of shoes⁸ nor the rustling of silks betray
        thy poor heart to woman. Keep thy foot⁹ out of brothels, thy

90   hand out of plackets,¹ thy pen from lenders' books, and defy
        the foul fiend. Still through the hawthorn blows the cold wind:
        Says suum, mun, ha, no, nonny. Dolphin my boy, my boy,
        sessa! let him trot by.²

        Storm still

LEAR   Why, thou wert better in thy grave than to answer° with thy   *encounter*

95   uncovered body this extremity of the skies.° Is man no more than   *violent weather*
        this? Consider him well. Thou owest the worm no silk, the beast
        no hide, the sheep no wool, that cat³ no perfume. Ha! here's
        three on's° are sophisticated! Thou art the thing itself; unac-   *of us*
        commodated⁴ man is no more but such a poor, bare, forked°   *two-legged*

100   animal as thou art. Off, off, you lendings!° come unbutton   *borrowed clothes*
        here.

        Tearing off his clothes

FOOL   Prithee, nuncle, be contented; 'tis a naughty° night to   *foul*
        swim in. Now a little fire in a wild° field were like an old lech-   *barren; lustful*
        er's heart; a small spark, all the rest on's° body cold. Look, here   *of his*

105   comes a walking fire.

        Enter GLOUCESTER, *with a torch*

---

3. Greedy. Young pelicans were reputed to feed on blood from the wounds they made in their mother's breast; in some versions, they first killed their father.

4. A fragment of an old rhyme, followed by hunting cries or a ballad refrain; "Pillicock" was both a term of endearment and a euphemism for "penis."

5. *obey . . . array:* these are fragments from the Ten Commandments.

6. Favors from his mistress. In Petrarchan poetry, wooers are "servants" to their ladies.

7. And had more women than the sultan had in his royal harem.

8. Creaking shoes were a fashionable affectation.

9. Punning on the French *foutre* ("fuck").

1. Slits in skirts or petticoats.

2. These phrases are probably snatches from songs and proverbs. "Dolphin" is an imagined animal or devil or the heir to the French throne ("dauphin," which Shakespeare usually Anglicized), or all three.

3. Civet cat, in Shakespeare's time the major source of musk for perfume.

4. Naked; without the trappings of civilization.

EDGAR   This is the foul fiend Flibbertigibbet.[5] He begins at cur-
few,° and walks till the first cock.° He gives the web and the   9:00 P.M. / midnight
pin,[6] squinies[7] the eye, and makes the hare-lip; mildews the
white° wheat, and hurts the poor creature of earth.   near-ripe

110   St. Withold footed thrice the old;[8]
He met the night-mare and her nine-fold;[9]
Bid her alight,
And her troth plight,°   And gave her word
And, aroint thee,° witch, aroint thee!   begone

115   KENT   How fares your grace?

LEAR   What's° he?   Who's

KENT   Who's there? What is't you seek?

GLOUCESTER   What are you there? Your names?

EDGAR   Poor Tom, that eats the swimming frog, the toad, the
120   tadpole, the wall-newt and the water;° that in the fury of his   water newt
heart, when the foul fiend rages, eats cow-dung for sallets;°   savories
swallows the old rat and the ditch-dog;[1] drinks the green man-
tle° of the standing-pool; who is whipped from tithing to tith-   scum
ing,° and stock-punished,° and imprisoned; who hath had three   parish / put in stocks
125   suits to his back, six shirts to his body, horse to ride, and weapon
to wear;
But mice and rats, and such small deer,[2]
Have been Tom's food for seven long year.
Beware my follower. Peace, Smulkin;° peace, thou fiend!   a Harsnett devil

130   GLOUCESTER   What, hath your grace no better company?

EDGAR   The prince of darkness is a gentleman. Modo he's call'd,
and Mahu.[3]

GLOUCESTER   Our flesh and blood is grown so vile, my lord,
That it doth hate what gets° it.   begets

135   EDGAR   Poor Tom's a-cold.

GLOUCESTER   Go in with me. My duty cannot suffer°   permit me
To obey in all your daughters' hard commands:
Though their injunction be to bar my doors,
And let this tyrannous night take hold upon you
140   Yet have I ventured to come seek you out.
And bring you where both fire and food is ready.

LEAR   First let me talk with this philosopher.
What is the cause of thunder?

KENT   Good my lord, take his offer; go into the house.

145   LEAR   I'll take a word with this same learned Theban.°   Greek sage
What is your study?°   field of expertise

EDGAR   How to prevent the fiend, and to kill vermin.

LEAR   Let me ask you one word in private.

KENT   Importune him once more to go, my lord;
His wits begin to unsettle.

150   GLOUCESTER   Canst thou blame him?
   Storm still

---

5. A devil drawn from folk beliefs but famous for his prominent place in Samuel Harsnett's *Declaration of Egregious Popish Impostures* (1603); the frequent borrowings from Harsnett in *King Lear* set the earliest possible composition date for the play.
6. *web and the pin:* cataract.
7. Causes squints in.
8. St. Withold traversed the hilly countryside three times. *old:* wold, uplands.

9. *night-mare:* a demon that is not necessarily in the shape of a horse. *fold:* familiar, demon.
1. A dog found dead in a ditch.
2. *deer:* animals. These verses are adapted from a romance popular in Shakespeare's time, *Bevis of Hampton.*
3. Modo and Mahu, more Harsnett devils, were commanding generals of the hellish troops.

His daughters seek his death; ah, that good Kent!
He said it would be thus, poor banished man!
Thou say'st the king grows mad; I'll tell thee, friend,
I am almost mad myself. I had a son,
155   Now outlawed° from my blood. He sought my life.   *disowned*
But lately, very late.° I loved him, friend;   *recently*
No father his son dearer. True to tell thee,
The grief hath crazed my wits. What a night's this!
I do beseech your grace—
LEAR   O, cry you mercy,° sir.   *beg your pardon*
160   Noble philosopher, your company.
EDGAR   Tom's a-cold.
GLOUCESTER   In, fellow, there, into the hovel; keep thee warm.
LEAR   Come, let's in all.
               This way, my lord.
KENT   With him!
LEAR   I will keep still with my philosopher.
165   KENT   Good my lord, soothe° him; let him take the fellow.   *humor*
GLOUCESTER   Take him you on.°   *on ahead*
KENT   Sirrah, come on; go along with us.
LEAR   Come, good Athenian.°   *Greek philosopher*
GLOUCESTER   No words, no words: hush.
170   EDGAR   Child Rowland[4] to the dark tower came,
His word° was still°—Fie, foh, and fum,   *motto / always*
I smell the blood of a British[5] man.   *Exeunt*

3.5

Enter CORNWALL *and* EDMUND
CORNWALL   I will have my revenge ere I depart his house.
EDMUND   How, my lord, I may be censured,° that nature° thus   *judged / kinship*
gives way to loyalty, something fears me° to think of.   *I am somewhat afraid*
CORNWALL   I now perceive, it was not altogether your brother's
5   evil disposition made him seek his° death; but a provoking   *(Gloucester's)*
merit, set a-work by a reproveable badness in himself.[1]
EDMUND   How malicious is my fortune, that I must repent to
be just! This is the letter he spoke of, which approves him an
intelligent party to the advantages of France.[2] O heavens! that
10   this treason were not, or not I the detector!
CORNWALL   Go with me to the duchess.
EDMUND   If the matter of this paper be certain, you have mighty
business in hand.
CORNWALL   True or false, it hath made thee Earl of Gloucester.
15   Seek out where thy father is, that he may be ready for our
apprehension.°   *arrest*
EDMUND (*aside*)   If I find him comforting the king, it will stuff
his° suspicion more fully.—I will persèver in my course of loy-   *(Cornwall's)*
alty, though the conflict be sore between that and my blood.°   *filial duty*
20   CORNWALL   I will lay trust upon thee, and thou shalt find a
dearer father in my love.   *Exeunt*

---

4. *Child*: an aspirant to knighthood. Roland is the famous hero of the Charlemagne legends.
5. "An Englishman" usually appears in this rhyme from the cycle of tales of which "Jack and the Beanstalk" is the best known. The alteration befits Lear's ancient Britain.
3.5 Location: At Gloucester's castle.

1. *a provoking . . . himself*: Gloucester's own wickedness deservedly triggered the blameworthy evil in Edgar.
2. *which . . . France*: which proves him a spy and informer in the aid of France; "party," or faction, was usually a term of opprobrium in the Renaissance.

3.6

Enter GLOUCESTER, LEAR, KENT, FOOL, *and* EDGAR

GLOUCESTER   Here is better than the open air; take it thankfully.
    I will piece out° the comfort with what addition I can; I will   *augment*
    not be long from you.

KENT   All the power of his wits have given sway to his impa-
5   tience:[1] the gods° reward your kindness!   *Exit* GLOUCESTER   *may the gods*

EDGAR   Frateretto° calls me; and tells me Nero is an angler in the   *a Harsnett devil*
    lake of darkness.[2] Pray, innocent, and beware the foul fiend.

FOOL   Prithee, nuncle, tell me whether a madman be a gentle-
    man or a yeoman?[3]

10 LEAR   A king, a king!

FOOL   No, he's a yeoman that has a gentleman to° his son; for   *for*
    he's a mad yeoman that sees his son a gentleman before him.

LEAR   To have a thousand with red burning spits
    Come hissing in upon 'em—

15 EDGAR   The foul fiend bites my back.

FOOL   He's mad that trusts in the tameness of a wolf, a horse's
    health, a boy's love, or a whore's oath.

LEAR   It shall be done; I will arraign° them straight.°   *prosecute / immediately*
    (*To* EDGAR) Come, sit thou here, most learned justicer;
20   (*to the* FOOL) Thou, sapient sir, sit here. Now, you she foxes!

EDGAR   Look, where he stands and glares! Wantest thou eyes° at   *observers*
    trial, madam?

FOOL   Come o'er the bourn, Bessy, to me[4]—
             Her boat hath a leak,[5]
25   And she must not speak
           Why she dares not come over to thee.

EDGAR   The foul fiend haunts poor Tom in the voice of a night-
    ingale. Hopdance° cries in Tom's belly for two white° herring.   *a demon / fresh*
    Croak° not, black angel; I have no food for thee.   *Growl*

30 KENT   How do you, sir? Stand you not so amazed:
    Will you lie down and rest upon the cushions?

LEAR   I'll see their trial first. Bring in the evidence.
    (*To* EDGAR) Thou robed man of justice, take thy place;
    (*to the* FOOL) And thou, his yoke-fellow of equity,°   *partner of law*
35   Bench° by his side. (*To* KENT) You are o' the commission,°   *Sit / judiciary*
    Sit you too.

EDGAR   Let us deal justly.
           Sleepest or wakest thou, jolly shepherd?
           Thy sheep be in the corn;°   *grain*
40   And for one blast of thy minikin° mouth,   *dainty*
           Thy sheep shall take no harm.
    Pur! the cat[6] is gray.

LEAR   Arraign her first; 'tis Goneril. I here take my oath before
    this honorable assembly, she kicked the poor king her father.

45 FOOL   Come hither, mistress. Is your name Goneril?

LEAR   She cannot deny it.

3.6 Location: Within an outbuilding of Gloucester's.
1. Rage; inability to bear more suffering.
2. In Chaucer's *Monk's Tale*, the infamously cruel Roman Emperor Nero is found fishing in hell (lines 485–86).
3. A free landowner but not a member of the gentry, lacking official family arms and the distinctions they confer.

Shakespeare seems to have procured a coat of arms for his father in 1596.
4. From an old song. *bourn*: a small stream.
5. She has venereal disease; punning on "boat" as body and "burn" as genital discomfort.
6. Pur the cat is another devil; such devils in the shape of cats were the familiars of witches.

FOOL   Cry you mercy, I took you for a joint-stool.[7]

LEAR   And here's another, whose warped looks proclaim
What store° her heart is made on.° Stop her there!   *material / of*
50   Arms, arms, sword, fire! Corruption in the place!
False justicer, why hast thou let her 'scape?

EDGAR   Bless thy five wits!

KENT   O pity! Sir, where is the patience now,
That you so oft have boasted to retain?

55   EDGAR (*aside*)   My tears begin to take his part so much,
They'll mar my counterfeiting.

LEAR   The little dogs and all,°   *Even the little dogs*
Tray, Blanch, and Sweet-heart, see, they bark at me.

EDGAR   Tom will throw his head at° them. Avaunt,° you curs!   *will threaten? / Begone*
60   Be thy mouth or° black or white,   *either*
Tooth that poisons° if it bite;   *gives rabies*
Mastiff, greyhound, mongrel grim,
Hound or spaniel, brach° or him,   *bitch*
Or bobtail tike or trundle-tail.[8]
65   Tom will make them weep and wail:
For, with throwing thus my head,
Dogs leap the hatch,[9] and all are fled.
Do de, de, de. Sessa![1] Come, march to wakes° and fairs and   *parish festivals*
market-towns. Poor Tom, thy horn is dry.[2]

70   LEAR   Then let them anatomize° Regan; see what breeds about   *dissect*
her heart. Is there any cause in nature that makes these hard
hearts? (*To* EDGAR) You, sir, I entertain° for one of my hundred;   *retain*
I do not like the fashion of your garments. You will say they are
Persian;° but let them be changed.   *oriental; splendid*

75   KENT   Now, good my lord, lie there and rest awhile.

LEAR   Make no noise, make no noise; draw the curtains.° So, so,   *bed curtains*
so. We'll go to supper i' the morning.

FOOL   And I'll go to bed at noon.

[*Re-enter* GLOUCESTER]

GLOUCESTER   Come hither, friend. Where is the king my master?

80   KENT   Here, sir; but trouble him not; his wits are gone.

GLOUCESTER   Good friend, I prithee, take him in thy arms;
I have o'erheard a plot of death upon° him: *against*
There is a litter ready; lay him in 't
And drive towards Dover, friend, where thou shalt meet
85   Both welcome and protection. Take up thy master.
If thou shouldst dally half an hour, his life,
With thine, and all that offer to defend him,
Stand in assured loss.° Take up, take up!   *Are certainly doomed*
And follow me, that will to some provision
Give thee quick conduct.[3]

90   KENT   Oppressèd nature sleeps:
This rest might yet have balmed° thy broken sinews,°   *soothed / nerves*
Which, if convenience will not allow,

---

7. I beg your pardon, I mistook you for a stool. An idiom
of the day expressing annoyance at being slighted. Here
the part of Goneril is actually being played by a stool.
8. Short-tailed mongrel or long-tailed.
9. Dogs leap over the lower half of a divided door.
1. Apparently nonsense, although "Sessa" may be a ver-

sion of the French *cessez* ("stop" or "hush").
2. A begging formula that refers to the horn vessel that
vagabonds carried for drink; the covert sense is that Edgar
has run out of Bedlamite inspiration.
3. *that . . . conduct:* who will quickly guide you to some
supplies.

Stand in hard cure.° (*To the* FOOL) Come, help to bear thy   *Will be hard to cure*
   master:
  Thou must not stay behind.
GLOUCESTER   Come come, away.
                       Exeunt all but EDGAR

95 EDGAR   When we our betters see bearing our° woes,   *our same*
  We scarcely think our miseries our foes.
  Who alone suffers suffers most i' the mind,
  Leaving free° things and happy shows° behind: *carefree / scenes*
  But then the mind much sufferance doth o'erskip
100 When grief hath mates, and bearing° fellowship.   *pain; suffering*
  How light and portable my pain seems now,
  When that which makes me bend makes the king bow;
  He° childed as I fathered! Tom, away!   *He is*
  Mark the high noises,° and thyself bewray°   *important rumors / reveal*
105 When false opinion, whose wrong thought defiles thee,
  In thy just proof repeals and reconciles thee.[4]
  What° will hap° more tonight, safe 'scape the king!   *Whatever / chance*
  Lurk, lurk.   *Exit*

3.7

Enter CORNWALL, REGAN, GONERIL, EDMUND, *and ser-*
vants

CORNWALL (*to* GONERIL)   Post° speedily to my lord your hus-   *Ride*
  band; show him this letter. The army of France is landed. Seek
  out the villain Gloucester.   *Exeunt some of the servants*
REGAN   Hang him instantly.
5 GONERIL   Pluck out his eyes.
CORNWALL   Leave him to my displeasure. Edmund, keep you
  our sister° company. The revenges we are bound[1] to take   *sister-in-law*
  upon your traitorous father are not fit for your beholding.
  Advise the duke, where you are going, to a most festinate prep-
10 aration.[2] We are bound° to the like. Our posts° shall be swift and   *committed / messengers*
  intelligent° betwixt us. Farewell, dear sister: farewell, my lord of   *well informed*
  Gloucester.
          Enter OSWALD
  How now! Where's the king?
OSWALD   My lord of Gloucester hath conveyed him hence.
15 Some five or six and thirty of his° knights,   *(Lear's)*
  Hot questrists° after him, met him at gate;   *searchers*
  Who, with some other of the lords° dependants,   *(Gloucester's)*
  Are gone with him towards Dover; where they boast
  To have well-armed friends.
CORNWALL   Get horses for your mistress.
20 GONERIL   Farewell, sweet lord, and sister.
CORNWALL   Edmund, farewell.
          Exeunt GONERIL, EDMUND, *and* OSWALD
  Go seek the traitor Gloucester,
  Pinion him° like a thief, bring him before us.   *Tie his arms*
          Exeunt other servants
  Though well we may not pass° upon his life   *pass sentence*

---

4. *In . . . thee:* When true evidence pardons you and
reconciles you (with your father).
3.7 Location: At Gloucester's castle.

1. Bound by duty; expected by destiny.
2. *Advise . . . preparation:* When you reach Albany, tell
the Duke to prepare quickly.

25   Without the form° of justice, yet our power   *official proceedings*
        Shall do a courtesy[3] to our wrath, which men
        May blame, but not control. Who's there? the traitor?
        Enter GLOUCESTER, *brought in by two or three*
    REGAN   Ingrateful fox! 'tis he.
    CORNWALL   Bind fast his corky° arms.   *withered*
30   GLOUCESTER   What mean your graces? Good my friends, consider
        You are my guests. Do me no foul play, friends.
    CORNWALL   Bind him, I say.
        Servants bind him
    REGAN   Hard, hard. O filthy traitor!
    GLOUCESTER   Unmerciful lady as you are, I'm none.
    CORNWALL   To this chair bind him. Villain, thou shalt find—
                 REGAN *plucks his beard*°   *(an extreme insult)*
35   GLOUCESTER   By the kind gods, 'tis most ignobly done
        To pluck me by the beard.
    REGAN   So white,° and such a traitor!   *white-haired; venerable*
    GLOUCESTER   Naughty° lady,   *Wicked*
        These hairs, which thou dost ravish from my chin,
        Will quicken,° and accuse thee. I am your host.   *come alive*
40   With robbers' hands my hospitable favors°   *features*
        You should not ruffle° thus. What will you do?   *snatch at*
    CORNWALL   Come, sir, what letters had you late° from France?   *lately*
    REGAN   Be simple° answered, for we know the truth.   *straightforwardly*
    CORNWALL   And what confederacy have you with the traitors
45   Late footed° in the kingdom?   *landed*
    REGAN   To whose hands have you sent the lunatic king? Speak.
    GLOUCESTER   I have a letter guessingly set down,[4]
        Which came from one that's of a neutral heart,
        And not from one opposed.
    CORNWALL   Cunning.
    REGAN   And false.
50   CORNWALL   Where hast thou sent the king?
    GLOUCESTER   To Dover.
    REGAN   Wherefore° to Dover? Wast thou not charged° at peril—   *Why / commanded*
    CORNWALL   Wherefore to Dover? Let him first answer that.
    GLOUCESTER   I am tied to the stake, and I must stand the
55   course.[5]
    REGAN   Wherefore to Dover?
    GLOUCESTER   Because I would not see thy cruel nails
        Pluck out his poor old eyes; nor thy fierce sister
        In his anointed[6] flesh stick boarish fangs.
60   The sea, with such a storm as his bare head
        In hell-black night endured, would have buoyed° up,   *risen*
        And quenched the stellèd° fires.   *stars'*
        Yet, poor old heart, he holp° the heavens to rage.   *helped*
        If wolves had at thy gate howled that dern° time,   *dreary; dreadful*
65   Thou shouldst have said "Good porter, turn the key."°   *(to open the door)*
        All cruels else subscribed.[7] But I shall see
        The wingèd vengeance[8] overtake such children.

---

3. Shall allow a courtesy or indulgence; shall bow to.
4. Written without confirmation; speculative.
5. An image from bearbaiting, in which a bear on a short tether had to fight off the assault of dogs.
6. Consecrated with holy oils (as part of a King's corona-

tion).
7. All other cruel creatures yielded to compassion.
8. Swift or heaven-sent revenge; either an angel of God or the Furies, who were flying executors of divine vengeance in classical mythology.

CORNWALL   See 't shalt thou never. Fellows,° hold the chair.   *Servants*
    Upon these eyes of thine I'll set my foot.
70 GLOUCESTER   He that will think° to live till he be old,   *Whoever hopes*
    Give me some help! O cruel! O ye gods! [CORNWALL *pulls out*
    one of GLOUCESTER'*s eyes and stamps on it*]
REGAN   One side will mock another. The other too!
CORNWALL   If you see vengeance—
FIRST SERVANT   Hold your hand, my lord:
    I have served you ever since I was a child;
75 But better service have I never done you
    Than now to bid you hold.
REGAN   How now, you dog!
FIRST SERVANT   If you did wear a beard upon your chin,
    I'd shake it on this quarrel.⁹
80 REGAN   What do you mean?°   *intend*
CORNWALL   My villain!°   *servant; villain*
FIRST SERVANT   Why, then, come on, and take the chance of anger.¹
REGAN   Give me thy sword. A peasant stand up thus!
    CORNWALL *is wounded.*
    Takes a sword, and runs at him behind
FIRST SERVANT   O, I am slain! My lord, you have one eye left
85 To see some mischief° on him. O!   *Dies*   *injury*
CORNWALL   Lest it see more, prevent it. Out, vile jelly! [*He pulls*
    out GLOUCESTER'*s other eye*]
    Where is thy luster now?
GLOUCESTER   All dark and comfortless. Where's my son Edmund?
    Edmund, enkindle all the sparks of nature,²
    To quit° this horrid act.   *requite; avenge*
90 REGAN   Out, treacherous villain!
    Thou call'st on him that hates thee. It was he
    That made the overture° of thy treasons to us;   *revelation*
    Who is too good to pity thee.
GLOUCESTER   O my follies! Then Edgar was abused.°   *slandered*
95 Kind gods, forgive me that, and prosper him!
REGAN   Go thrust him out at gates, and let him smell
    His way to Dover.   *Exit one with* GLOUCESTER
    How is't, my lord? how look you?°   *how do you feel*
CORNWALL   I have received a hurt. Follow me, lady;
100 Turn out that eyeless villain. Throw this slave
    Upon the dunghill. Regan, I bleed apace.
    Untimely comes this hurt. Give me your arm.
                        Exit CORNWALL *led by* REGAN
SECOND SERVANT   I'll never care what wickedness I do,
    If this man come to good.³
THIRD SERVANT   If she live long,
105 And in the end meet the old° course of death,   *usual*
    Woman will all turn monsters.
SECOND SERVANT   Let's follow the old earl, and get the Bedlam°   *madman*
    To lead him where he would. His roguish madness
    Allows itself to any thing.
110 THIRD SERVANT   Go thou; I'll fetch some flax and whites of eggs

---

9. I'd pluck it over this point; I'd issue a challenge.
1. Take the risk of fighting when angry; take the fortune of one who is governed by his anger.
2. All the warmth of filial love; all the anger that your

father has received such treatment.
3. *I'll . . . good:* because this may be a sign that evil goes unpunished. *this man:* Cornwall.

To apply to his bleeding face. Now, heaven help him!

Exeunt severally

4.1

Enter EDGAR

EDGAR Yet better thus, and known to be contemned°   *despised*
Than still° contemned and flattered. To be worst,   *always*
The lowest and most dejected thing of fortune,
Stands still in esperance, lives not in fear.[1]
5 The lamentable change is from the best;
The worst returns to laughter.[2] Welcome, then,
Thou unsubstantial air that I embrace!
The wretch that thou hast blown unto the worst
Owes nothing° to thy blasts. But who comes here?   *(because he can't pay)*

Enter GLOUCESTER, *led by an* OLD MAN

10 My father, parti-eyed?[3] World, world, O world!
But that thy strange mutrations make us hate thee,
Life would not yield to age.[4]

OLD MAN O, my good lord, I have been your tenant, and your
father's tenant, these fourscore years.

15 GLOUCESTER Away, get thee away! Good friend, be gone.
Thy comforts° can do me no good at all;   *assistance*
Thee they may hurt.

OLD MAN Alack, sir, you cannot see your way.

GLOUCESTER I have no way, and therefore want no eyes;
20 I stumbled when I saw. Full oft 'tis seen,
Our means secure us, and our mere defects
Prove our commodities.[5] O dear son Edgar,
The food° of thy abusèd° father's wrath!   *fuel; prey / despised*
Might I but live to see thee in° my touch,   *through*
I'd say I had eyes again!

25 OLD MAN   How now! Who's there?

EDGAR (*aside*) O gods! Who is't can say "I am at the worst"?
I am worse than e'er I was.

OLD MAN   'Tis poor mad Tom.

EDGAR (*aside*) And worse I may be yet: the worst is not
So long as we can say "This is the worst."

OLD MAN Fellow, where goest?

30 GLOUCESTER   Is it a beggar-man?

OLD MAN Madman and beggar too.

GLOUCESTER He has some reason, else he could not beg.
I' the last night's storm I such a fellow saw;
Which made me think a man a worm. My son
35 Came then into my mind, and yet my mind
Was then scarce friends with him. I have heard more since.
As flies to wanton° boys are we to the gods;   *playful; careless*
They kill us for their sport.

EDGAR (*aside*)   How should this be?
Bad is the trade that must play fool to sorrow,[6]

4.1 Location: Open country.
1. *Stands . . . fear:* Remains in hope ("esperance")
because there is no fear of falling further.
2. *The lamentable . . . laughter:* The change to be
lamented is one that alters the best of circumstances; the
worst luck can only improve.
3. Multicolored like a fool's costume (red with blood
under white dressings).

4. *But . . . age:* If there were no strange reversals of fortune to make the world hateful, we would not consent
to aging and death.
5. *Our means . . . commodities:* Our wealth makes us
overconfident, and our utter deprivation proves to be
beneficial.
6. It is a bad business to have to play the fool in the face
of sorrow.

40 Angering itself and others.—Bless thee, master!
GLOUCESTER   Is that the naked fellow?
OLD MAN   Ay, my lord.
GLOUCESTER   Then, prithee, get thee gone. If, for my sake,
Thou wilt o'ertake us, hence a mile or twain,
I' the way toward Dover, do it for ancient love;[7]
45 And bring some covering for this naked soul,
Who I'll entreat to lead me.
OLD MAN   Alack, sir, he is mad.
GLOUCESTER   'Tis the times' plague, when[8] madmen lead the blind.
Do as I bid thee, or rather do thy pleasure;
Above the rest, be gone.
50 OLD MAN   I'll bring him the best 'parel° that I have,   *apparel; clothing*
Come on 't what will.   *Exit*
GLOUCESTER   Sirrah, naked fellow—
EDGAR   Poor Tom's a-cold. (*Aside*) I cannot daub it further.[9]
GLOUCESTER   Come hither, fellow.
55 EDGAR (*aside*)   And yet I must.—Bless thy sweet eyes, they bleed.
GLOUCESTER   Know'st thou the way to Dover?
EDGAR   Both stile and gate, horse-way and foot-path. Poor Tom
hath been scared out of his good wits. Bless thee, good man's
son, from the foul fiend! Five fiends have been in Poor Tom at
60 once; of lust, as Obidicut; Hobbididance, prince of dumbness;
Mahu, of stealing; Modo, of murder; Flibbertigibbet, of mop-
ping and mowing,° who since possesses chambermaids and   *making faces*
waiting-women. So, bless thee, master!
GLOUCESTER   Here, take this purse, thou whom the heavens' plagues
65 Have humbled to all strokes.° That I am wretched   *to accept all blows*
Makes thee the happier. Heavens, deal so still!°   *always*
Let the superfluous and lust-dieted man,[1]
That slaves° your ordinance,° that will not see   *defers to / authority*
Because he doth not feel, feel your power quickly;
70 So distribution should undo excess,
And each man have enough. Dost thou know Dover?
EDGAR   Ay, master.
GLOUCESTER   There is a cliff, whose high and bending° head   *overhanging*
Looks fearfully in the confinèd deep.[2]
75 Bring me but to the very brim of it,
And I'll repair the misery thou dost bear
With something rich about me. From that place
I shall no leading need.
EDGAR   Give me thy arm.
Poor Tom shall lead thee.   *Exeunt*

4.2

Enter GONERIL *and* EDMUND
GONERIL   Welcome, my lord. I marvel our mild husband
Not° met us on the way.   *Has not*
Enter OSWALD
                 Now where's your master?
OSWALD   Madam, within, but never man so changed.
I told him of the army that was landed;

---

7. For the sake of our long and loyal relationship (as master and servant).
8. The time is truly sick when.
9. I cannot continue the charade. *daub*: mask, plaster.

1. Let the overprosperous man who indulges his appetite.
2. Looks fearsomely into the straits below.
4.2 Location: Before Albany's castle.

5   He smiled at it. I told him you were coming;
       His answer was "The worse." Of Gloucester's treachery,
       And of the loyal service of his son,
       When I informed him, then he called me sot,°   fool
       And told me I had turned the wrong side out.[1]
10   What most he should dislike seems pleasant to him;
       What like, offensive.
GONERIL (*to* EDMUND)   Then shall you go no further.
       It is the cowish° terror of his spirit,   cowardly
       That dares not undertake. He'll not feel wrongs
       Which tie him to an answer.[2] Our wishes on the way
15   May prove effects.[3] Back, Edmund, to my brother;°   brother-in-law
       Hasten his musters° and conduct his powers.°   call-up of troops / armies
       I must change arms at home, and give the distaff[4]
       Into my husband's hands. This trusty servant
       Shall pass between us. Ere long you are like° to hear,   likely
20   If you dare venture in your own behalf,
       A mistress's° command. Wear this; spare speech;   (*playing on "lover's"*)
          (*giving a favor*)
       Decline your head. This kiss, if it durst speak,
       Would stretch thy spirits up into the air.
       Conceive,° and fare thee well.   Understand my meaning
EDMUND   Yours in° the ranks of death.   even in
25 GONERIL   My most dear Gloucester!
                                   Exit EDMUND
       O, the difference of man and man!
       To thee a woman's services are due:
       My fool usurps my body.[5]
OSWALD   Madam, here comes my lord.   *Exit*
          Enter ALBANY
GONERIL   I have been worth the whistling.[6]
30 ALBANY   O Goneril!
       You are not worth the dust which the rude wind
       Blows in your face. I fear your disposition.
       That nature, which contemns it° origin,   despises its
       Cannot be bordered certain° in itself.   be defended securely
35   She that herself will sliver and disbranch°   split
       From her material sap, perforce must wither
       And come to deadly use.[7]
GONERIL   No more; the text is foolish.
ALBANY   Wisdom and goodness to the vile seem vile;
40   Filths savor but themselves. What have you done?
       Tigers, not daughters, what have you performed?
       A father, and a gracious aged man,
       Whose reverence even the head-lugged° bear would lick,   dragged by the head
       Most barbarous, most degenerate, have you madded°   driven mad
45   Could my good brother° suffer you to do it?   brother-in-law
       A man, a prince, by him so benefited!

---

1. I had reversed things (by mistaking loyalty for treachery).
2. *He'll . . . answer:* He'll ignore insults that would provoke him to retaliate.
3. May be put into action.
4. A device used in spinning and so emblematic of the female role. To "change arms," therefore, is to swap the insignia of male and female identity.
5. My idiot husband presumes to possess me.

6. At one time, you would have come to welcome me home; referring to the proverb "It is a poor dog that is not worth the whistling."
7. *She . . . use:* The allusion is probably biblical: "But that which beareth thorns and briers is reproved, and is near unto cursing; whose end is to be burned" (Hebrews 6:8). *come to deadly use:* be destroyed; be used for burning.

If that the heavens do not their visible spirits
Send quickly down to tame these vild° offenses,   *wild; vile*
It will come,
50 Humanity must perforce° prey on itself,   *inevitably*
Like monsters of the deep.
GONERIL   Milk-livered° man!   *Cowardly*
That bear'st a cheek for blows, a head for wrongs:[8]
Who hast not in thy brows an eye discerning
Thine honor from thy suffering;[9] that not know'st
55 Fools do those villains pity who are punished
Ere they have done their mischief. Where's thy drum?°   *(to muster troops)*
France spreads his banners in our noiseless° land,   *peaceful*
With plumèd helm thy state begins to threat;
Whiles thou, a moral° fool, sit'st still, and criest   *moralizing*
"Alack, why does he so?"
60 ALBANY   See thyself, devil!
Proper deformity shows not in the fiend
So horrid as in woman.[1]
GONERIL   O vain° fool!   *useless*
ALBANY   Thou changèd and self-covered[2] thing, for shame,
Be-monster not thy feature. Were't my fitness°   *If it were appropriate*
65 To let these hands obey my blood,
They are apt enough to dislocate and tear
Thy flesh and bones. Howe'er° thou art a fiend,   *Although*
A woman's shape doth shield thee.
GONERIL   Marry, your manhood! mew![3]
    Enter a MESSENGER
70 ALBANY   What news?
MESSENGER   O, my good lord, the Duke of Cornwall's dead;
Slain by his servant, going to put out
The other eye of Gloucester.
ALBANY   Gloucester's eyes?
MESSENGER   A servant that he bred, thrilled with remorse,°   *shaken with pity*
75 Opposed against the act, bending° his sword   *directing*
To° his great master; who, thereat enraged,   *Against*
Flew on him, and amongst them felled him dead;
But not without that harmful stroke, which since
Hath plucked him after.[4]
ALBANY   This shows you are above,
80 You justicers,° that these our nether crimes[5]   *judges*
So speedily can venge! But, O poor Gloucester!
Lost he his other eye?
MESSENGER   Both, both, my lord.
This letter, madam, craves a speedy answer;
'T is from your sister.
85 GONERIL *(aside)*   One way I like this well;[6]
But being° a widow, and my Gloucester with her,   *her being*

8. *for wrongs:* fit for abuse; ready for cuckold's horns.
9. *discerning . . . suffering:* that can distinguish between an insult to your honor and something you should patiently endure.
1. *Proper . . . woman:* Deformity (of morals) is appropriate in the devil and so less horrid than in woman, from whom virtue is expected. Albany may hold a mirror in front of Goneril, since Jacobean women sometimes wore small mirrors attached to their dresses.

2. Altered and with your true (womanly) self concealed.
3. Some manhood! (spoken derisively). *Marry:* By the Virgin Mary. *mew:* a derisive catcall.
4. Has sent him to follow his servant into death.
5. Lower crimes, and so committed on earth, but also suggesting that the deeds smack of the netherworld of hell.
6. Because a political rival has been eliminated.

May all the building in my fancy pluck
Upon my hateful life.[7] Another way,
The news is not so tart.°—I'll read, and answer.   *Exit*   bitter
90 ALBANY   Where was his son when they did take his eyes?
MESSENGER   Come with my lady hither.
ALBANY   He is not here.
MESSENGER   No, my good lord; I met him back° again.   returning
ALBANY   Knows he the wickedness?
MESSENGER   Ay, my good lord; 'twas he informed against him;
95 And quit the house on purpose, that their punishment
Might have the freer course.
ALBANY   Gloucester, I live
To thank thee for the love thou show'dst the king,
And to revenge thine eyes. Come hither, friend.
Tell me what more thou know'st.   *Exeunt*

4.3

Enter KENT *and a* GENTLEMAN

KENT   Why the King of France is so suddenly gone back know
you the reason?
GENTLEMAN   Something he left imperfect° in the state, which   unsettled
since his coming forth is thought of;° which imports° to the   remembered / portends
5 kingdom so much fear and danger, that his personal return was
most required and necessary.
KENT   Who hath he left behind him general?
GENTLEMAN   The Marshall of France, Monsieur LaFar.
KENT   Did your letters pierce the queen to any demonstration of grief?
10 GENTLEMAN   Ay, sir. She took them, in my presence;
And now and then an ample tear trilled down
Her delicate cheek. It seemed she was a queen
Over her passion, who,° most rebel-like,   which
Sought to be king o'er her.
KENT   O, then it moved her.
15 GENTLEMAN   Not to a rage. Patience and sorrow strove
Who should express her goodliest.[1] You have seen
Sunshine and rain at once: her smiles and tears
Were like a° better way. Those happy smilets,   Were similar in a
That played on her ripe lip, seemed not to know
20 What guests were in her eyes, which parted thence,
As pearls from diamonds dropped. In brief,
Sorrow would be a rarity° most beloved,   gem
If all could so become it.[2]
KENT   Made she no verbal question?
GENTLEMAN   'Faith, once or twice she heaved the name of "father"
25 Pantingly forth, as if it pressed her heart;
Cried "Sisters! sisters! Shame of ladies! sisters!
Kent! father! sisters! What, i' the storm? i' the night?
Let pity not be believed!"[3] There she shook
The holy water from her heavenly eyes,
30 And clamor moistened.[4] Then away she started°   sprang
To deal with grief alone.

7. *May . . . life*: May pull down all of my built-up fantasies and thus make my life hateful.
4.3 Location: Near the French camp at Dover.
1. Which should best express her feelings.

2. If everyone wore it so beautifully.
3. Never believe in pity; compassion cannot exist.
4. And moistened her anguish (with tears).

KENT   It is the stars,
       The stars above us, govern our conditions;
       Else one self mate and make⁵ could not beget
       Such different issues.° You spoke not with her since?   *offspring*
35 GENTLEMAN   No.
    KENT   Was this before the king returned?
    GENTLEMAN   No, since.
    KENT   Well, sir, the poor distressed Lear's i' the town;
       Who sometime, in his better tune,° remembers   *state of mind*
       What we are come about, and by no means
       Will yield° to see his daughter.   *consent*
40 GENTLEMAN   Why, good sir?
    KENT   A sovereign shame so elbows° him; his own unkindness,   *prods; nudges*
       That stripped her from his benediction, turned her
       To foreign casualties,° gave her dear rights   *risks*
       To his dog-hearted daughters, these things sting
45   His mind so venomously, that burning shame
       Detains him from Cordelia.
    GENTLEMAN   Alack, poor gentleman!
    KENT   Of Albany's and Cornwall's powers you heard not?
    GENTLEMAN   'Tis so, they are afoot.
    KENT   Well, sir, I'll bring you to our master Lear,
50   And leave you to attend him. Some dear cause°   *Some important reason*
       Will in concealment wrap me up awhile;
       When I am known aright, you shall not grieve°   *repent*
       Lending me this acquaintance.° I pray you, go   *news*
       Along with me.   *Exeunt*

                          4.4
       Enter, with drum and colors, CORDELIA, DOCTOR, *and*
       soldiers
    CORDELIA   Alack, 'tis he! Why, he was met even now
       As mad as the vexed sea; singing aloud;
       Crowned with rank fumiter and furrow-weeds,¹
       With hor-docks, hemlock, nettles, cuckoo-flowers,
5   Darnel, and all the idle° weeds that grow   *useless*
       In our sustaining corn. A century° send forth;   *battalion (100 men)*
       Search every acre in the high-grown field,
       And bring him to our eye.   *Exit an officer*
       What can man's wisdom
10   In the restoring° his bereaved sense?   *Do to restore*
       He that helps him take all my outward° worth.   *material*
    DOCTOR   There is means, madam.
       Our foster-nurse of nature² is repose,
       The which he lacks. That to provoke in him,
15   Are many simples operative,³ whose power
       Will close the eye of anguish.
    CORDELIA   All blest secrets,
       All you unpublished virtues° of the earth,   *obscure healing plants*
       Spring with my tears! be aidant and remediate°   *healing and remedial*

---

5. Or else the same pair of spouses; "mate" and "make"
may describe either partner.
4.4 Location: The French camp at Dover.
1. Fumiter was used against brain sickness. Furrow-
weeds, like the other weeds in the following lines, grow
in the furrows of plowed fields.
2. *Our . . . nature:* That which comforts and nourishes
human nature.
3. *That . . . operative:* To induce that ("repose") in him,
there are many effective medicinal herbs.

In the good man's distress! Seek, seek for him;
20   Lest his ungoverned rage dissolve the life
That wants° the means to lead it.   *lacks*

Enter a MESSENGER

MESSENGER   News, madam;
The British powers° are marching hitherward.   *armies*
CORDELIA   'Tis known before; our preparation stands
In expectation of them. O dear father,
25   It is thy business that I go about;[4]
Therefore great France
My mourning and importuned° tears hath pitied.   *importunate; solicitous*
No blown° ambition doth our arms incite,   *inflated*
But love, dear love, and our aged father's right.[5]
30   Soon may I hear and see him!   *Exeunt*

4.5

Enter REGAN *and* OSWALD

REGAN   But are my brother's powers° set forth?   *(Albany's forces)*
OSWALD   Ay, madam.
REGAN   Himself in person there?
OSWALD   Madam, with much ado.°   *trouble*
Your sister is the better soldier.
5   REGAN   Lord Edmund spake not with your lord at home?
OSWALD   No, madam.
REGAN   What might import° my sister's letter to him?   *mean*
OSWALD   I know not, lady.
REGAN   Faith, he is posted° hence on serious matter.   *hurried*
10   It was great ignorance, Gloucester's eyes being out,
To let him live. Where he arrives he moves
All hearts against us. Edmund, I think, is gone,
In pity of his misery,° to dispatch   *(ironic)*
His nighted° life; moreover, to descry°   *darkened / investigate*
15   The strength o' the enemy.
OSWALD   I must needs after° him, madam, with my letter.   *go after*
REGAN   Our troops set forth tomorrow. Stay with us;
The ways are dangerous.
OSWALD   I may not, madam:
My lady charged° my duty in this business.   *commanded*
20   REGAN   Why should she write to Edmund? Might not you
Transport her purposes by word? Belike,°   *Perhaps*
Something—I know not what. I'll love° thee much,   *reward*
Let me unseal the letter.
OSWALD   Madam, I had rather—
REGAN   I know your lady does not love her husband;
25   I am sure of that; and at her late° being here   *recently*
She gave strange oeillades° and most speaking looks   *amorous glances*
To noble Edmund. I know you are of her bosom.°   *in her confidence*
OSWALD   I, madam?
REGAN   I speak in understanding;° y'are, I know't.   *with certainty*
30   Therefore I do advise you, take this note:°   *take note of this*
My lord is dead; Edmund and I have talked;

---

4. The line echoes Christ's explanation of his mission in Luke 2:49: "I must go about my father's business."
5. *No . . . right:* 1 Corinthians 13:4–5 in the Bishops' Bible (1568) says that love "swelleth not, dealeth not dishonestly, seeketh not her own."
4.5 Location: At Gloucester's castle.

And more convenient° is he for my hand   *appropriate*
Than for your lady's. You may gather° more.   *infer*
If you do find him, pray you, give him this;[1]
35   And when your mistress hears thus much from you,
I pray, desire her call her wisdom to her.[2]
So, fare you well.
If you do chance to hear of that blind traitor,
Preferment falls on him that cuts him off.°   *cuts his life short*
40 OSWALD   Would I could meet him, madam! I should show
What party I do follow.
REGAN   Fare thee well.   *Exeunt*

4.6

Enter GLOUCESTER, *and* EDGAR *dressed like a peasant*

GLOUCESTER   When shall we come to the top of that same° hill?   *agreed-upon*
EDGAR   You do climb up it now. Look how we labor.
GLOUCESTER   Methinks the ground is even.
EDGAR   Horrible steep.
Hark, do you hear the sea?
GLOUCESTER   No, truly.
5 EDGAR   Why, then, your other senses grow imperfect
By your eyes' anguish.
GLOUCESTER   So may it be, indeed.
Methinks thy voice is altered, and thou speakest
In better phrase and matter° than thou didst.   *sense*
EDGAR   Y'are much deceived. In nothing am I changed
But in my garments.
10 GLOUCESTER   Methinks y'are better spoken.
EDGAR   Come on, sir; here's the place. Stand still. How fearful
And dizzy 'tis, to cast one's eyes so low!
The crows and choughs° that wing the midway air[1]   *jackdaws*
Show° scarce so gross° as beetles. Halfway down   *Appear / big*
15 Hangs one that gathers sampire,° dreadful trade!   *seaweed*
Methinks he seems no bigger than his head.
The fishermen, that walk upon the beach,
Appear like mice; and yond tall anchoring bark,°   *ship*
Diminished to her cock;° her cock, a buoy   *dinghy*
20 Almost too small for sight. The murmuring surge,
That on the unnumbered° idle pebble chafes,   *innumerable*
Cannot be heard so high. I'll look no more,
Lest my brain turn, and the° deficient sight   *my*
Topple° down headlong.   *Topple me*
GLOUCESTER   Set me where you stand.
25 EDGAR   Give me your hand. You are now within a foot
Of th' extreme verge. For all beneath the moon
Would I not leap upright.[2]
GLOUCESTER   Let go my hand.
Here, friend, 's another purse; in it a jewel
Well worth a poor man's taking. Fairies and gods
30 Prosper it[3] with thee! Go thou farther off;
Bid me farewell, and let me hear thee going.

---

1. This information, but possibly another letter or token.
2. *desire . . . to her:* tell her to come to her senses.
4.6 Location: Near Dover.
1. The air between cliff and sea.

2. I would not jump up and down (for fear of losing my balance).
3. Make it increase. Fairies were sometimes held to hoard and multiply treasure.

EDGAR   Now fare you well, good sir.

GLOUCESTER   With all my heart.

EDGAR (*aside*)   Why I do trifle thus with his despair
    Is done to cure it.

GLOUCESTER (*kneeling*)   O you mighty gods!
35   This world I do renounce, and, in your sights,
    Shake patiently my great affliction off.
    If I could bear it longer, and not fall
    To quarrel° with your great opposeless wills,   Into conflict
    My snuff and loathèd part of nature⁴ should
40   Burn itself out. If Edgar live, O, bless him!
    Now, fellow, fare thee well.
                He falls forward and swoons

EDGAR   Gone, sir; farewell.—
    And yet I know not how conceit may rob
    The treasury of life, when life itself
    Yields to the theft.⁵ Had he been where he thought,
45   By this° had thought been past. Alive or dead?   now
    Ho, you sir! friend! Hear you, sir? speak!
    Thus might he pass° indeed. Yet he revives.   pass away
    What are you, sir?

GLOUCESTER   Away, and let me die.

EDGAR   Hadst thou been aught° but gossamer, feathers, air,   anything
50   So many fathom down precipitating,°   plunging
    Thou'dst shivered° like an egg; but thou dost breathe;   shattered
    Hast heavy substance; bleed'st not; speak'st; art sound.
    Ten masts at each° make not the altitude   end to end
    Which thou hast perpendicularly fell.
55   Thy life's a miracle. Speak yet again.

GLOUCESTER   But have I fallen, or no?

EDGAR   From the dread summit of this chalky bourn.⁶
    Look up a-height; the shrill-gorged° lark so far   shrill-throated
    Cannot be seen or heard. Do but look up.

60 GLOUCESTER   Alack, I have no eyes.
    Is wretchedness deprived° that benefit,   deprived of
    To end itself by death? 'Twas yet some comfort,
    When misery could beguile° the tyrant's rage,   cheat
    And frustrate his proud will.

EDGAR   Give me your arm.
65   Up—so. How is 't? Feel you your legs? You stand.

GLOUCESTER   Too well, too well.

EDGAR   This is above all strangeness.
    Upon the crown o' the cliff, what thing was that
    Which parted from you?

GLOUCESTER   A poor unfortunate beggar.

EDGAR   As I stood here below, methought his eyes
70   Were two full moons; he had a thousand noses,
    Horns whelked° and waved like the enridgèd sea: twisted
    It was some fiend. Therefore, thou happy father,°   lucky old man
    Think that the clearest° gods, who make them honors   purest; most illustrious
    Of men's impossibilities,⁷ have preserved thee.

4. The scorched and hateful remnant of my lifetime. *snuff*: end of a candlewick.
5. *And yet . . . theft*: Edgar worries that the imagined scenario ("conceit") he has invented may be enough to kill his father, particularly as Gloucester wishes for ("yields to") his own death.
6. The white chalk cliffs of Dover, which make a boundary ("bourn") between land and sea.
7. *who . . . impossibilities*: who attain honor for themselves by performing deeds impossible to men.

75 GLOUCESTER I do remember now. Henceforth I'll bear
      Affliction till it do cry out itself
      "Enough, enough," and die. That thing you speak of,
      I took it for a man; often 't would say
      "The fiend, the fiend"—he led me to that place.
80 EDGAR Bear free and patient thoughts. But who comes here?
      Enter LEAR, *fantastically dressed with wild flowers*
      The safer sense will ne'er accommodate
      His master thus.[8]
      LEAR No, they cannot touch me for coining;[9] I am the king
      himself.
85 EDGAR O thou side-piercing sight!
      LEAR Nature's above art in that respect.[1] There's your press-
      money.[2] That fellow handles his bow like a crow-keeper.[3] Draw
      me a clothier's yard.[4] Look, look, a mouse! Peace, peace; this
      piece of toasted cheese will do 't.° There's my gauntlet; I'll   (lure the mouse)
90 prove it on a giant.[5] Bring up the brown bills.[6] O, well flown,
      bird!° i' the clout,° i' the clout. Hewgh! Give the word.°   arrow / bull's-eye / password
      EDGAR Sweet marjoram.[7]
      LEAR Pass.
      GLOUCESTER I know that voice.
95 LEAR Ha! Goneril, with a white beard! They flattered me like a
      dog;° and told me I had white hairs in my beard ere the black   fawningly
      ones were there.[8] To say "aye" and "no" to everything that I
      said!—"Aye" and "no" too was no good divinity.[9] When the
      rain came to wet me once, and the wind to make me chatter;
100 when the thunder would not peace at my bidding; there I
      found° 'em, there I smelt 'em out. Go to, they are not men o'   understood
      their words! They told me I was everything. 'Tis a lie, I am not
      ague-proof.°   immune to illness
      GLOUCESTER The trick° of that voice I do well remember.   peculiarity
      Is 't not the king?
105 LEAR   Aye, every inch a king!
      When I do stare, see how the subject quakes.
      I pardon that man's life. What was thy cause?°   crime
      Adultery?
      Thou shalt not die. Die for adultery? No.
110 The wren goes to 't, and the small gilded fly
      Does lecher in my sight.
      Let copulation thrive; for Gloucester's bastard son
      Was kinder to his father than my daughters
      Got 'tween the lawful sheets. To 't luxury,° pell-mell!   lechery
115 For I lack soldiers. Behold yond simpering dame,
      Whose face between her forks presages snow;[1]

8. *The . . . thus:* A sane mind would never allow its possessor to dress up this way.
9. Because minting money was the prerogative of the
King, nobody could overtake or equal ("touch") him.
1. My true feelings will always outvalue others' hypocrisy;
my natural supremacy surpasses any attempt to create a
false new reign. This image may also be based on coining
(see note 9, above).
2. Fee paid to a soldier impressed, or forced, into the
army.
3. A person hired as a scarecrow, and thus unfit for anything else.
4. Draw the bowstring the full length of the arrow (a
standard English arrow was a cloth yard [37 inches]

long).
5. I'll defend my stand even against a giant. To throw
down an armored glove ("gauntlet") was to issue a challenge.
6. Brown painted pikes; the soldiers carrying them.
7. Used medicinally against madness.
8. Told me I had wisdom before age.
9. *no good divinity:* poor theology (because insincere);
from James 5:12, "Let your yea be yea; nay, nay."
1. Whose expression implies cold chastity. "Face" refers
to the area between her legs ("forks"), as well as to her
literal facial expression as framed by the aristocratic
lady's starched headpiece, also called a "fork."

	That minces° virtue, and does shake the head	*affects*
	To hear of° pleasure's name;	*even of*
	The fitchew, nor the soilèd horse,[2] goes to 't	
120	With a more riotous appetite.	
	Down from the waist they are Centaurs,[3]	
	Though women all above.	
	But° to the girdle° do the gods inherit.°	*Only / waist / own*
	Beneath is all the fiends'; there's hell,[4] there's darkness,	
125	There's the sulphurous pit, burning, scalding,	
	Stench, consumption! Fie, fie, fie! pah! pah!	
	Give me an ounce of civet,[5] good apothecary,	
	To sweeten my imagination.	
	There's money for thee.	

GLOUCESTER   O, let me kiss that hand!

LEAR   Let me wipe it first; it smells of mortality.

GLOUCESTER   O ruined piece° of nature! This great world *masterpiece*
Shall so wear out to nought.[6] Dost thou know me?

LEAR   I remember thine eyes well enough. Dost thou squiny° at *squint*
me? No, do thy worst, blind Cupid; I'll not love. Read thou this
challenge; mark but the penning of it.

GLOUCESTER   Were all the letters suns, I could not see one.

EDGAR (*aside*)   I would not take° this from report. It is, *believe*
And my heart breaks at it.

LEAR   Read.

GLOUCESTER   What, with the case° of eyes? *socket*

LEAR   O, ho, are you there with me?[7] No eyes in your head, nor
no money in your purse? Your eyes are in a heavy case,[8] your
purse in a light. Yet you see how this world goes.

GLOUCESTER   I see it feelingly.° *by touch; painfully*

LEAR   What, art mad? A man may see how this world goes with
no eyes. Look with thine ears. See how yond justice rails upon
yond simple° thief. Hark, in thine ear. Change places and, *lowly; innocent*
handy-dandy,[9] which is the justice, which is the thief? Thou
hast seen a farmer's dog bark at a beggar?

GLOUCESTER   Aye, sir.

LEAR   And the creature° run from the cur? There thou mightst *wretch*
behold the great image of authority: a dog's obeyed in office.
Thou rascal beadle,[1] hold° thy bloody hand! *restrain*
Why dost thou lash that whore? Strip thine own back;
Thou hotly lusts to use her in that kind° *way*
For which thou whipp'st her. The usurer hangs the cozener.[2]
Through tattered clothes small vices do appear;
Robes and furred gowns hide all. Plate° sin with gold, *Armor; gild*
And the strong lance of justice hurtless° breaks; *harmlessly*
Arm it in rags, a pigmy's straw does pierce it.
None does offend, none, I say, none; I'll able° 'em; *authorize*
Take that of me, my friend, who have the power
To seal the accuser's lips. Get thee glass eyes;

2. Neither the polecat nor a horse full of fresh grass.
3. Lecherous mythological creatures that have a human body to the waist and the torso of a horse below.
4. Shakespeare's frequent term for female genitals.
5. Exotic perfume derived from the sex glands of the civet cat.
6. Shall decay to nothing in the same way. In Renaissance philosophy, humans were perfectly analogous to the cosmos, standing for the whole in miniature and as its masterpiece.
7. Is that what you are telling me?
8. In a sad condition; playing on "case" as "sockets."
9. Pick a hand, as in a child's game.
1. The parish officer responsible for whippings.
2. The ruinous moneylender, prosperous enough to be made a judge, convicts the ordinary cheat.

165　And, like a scurvy politician,[3] seem
　　　To see the things thou dost not. Now, now, now, now!
　　　Pull off my boots. Harder, harder! So.
　EDGAR　O, matter and impertinency° mixed!　　　　　　　*sense and nonsense*
　　　Reason in madness!
170　LEAR　If thou wilt weep my fortunes, take my eyes.
　　　I know thee well enough; thy name is Gloucester:
　　　Thou must be patient. We came crying hither;
　　　Thou knows't, the first time that we smell the air,
　　　We wail and cry. I will preach to thee. Mark.
　　　　　　LEAR *takes off his crown of weeds and flowers*[4]
175　GLOUCESTER　Alack, alack the day!
　LEAR　When we are born, we cry that we are come
　　　To this great stage of fools. This'° a good block;[5]　　　　*This is*
　　　It were a delicate° stratagem, to shoe　　　　　　　　　　*subtle*
　　　A troop of horse with felt.[6] I'll put 't in proof;°　　　　*to the test*
180　And when I have stol'n upon these sons-in-law,
　　　Then, kill, kill, kill, kill, kill, kill!
　　　　　　Enter a GENTLEMAN, *with attendants*
　GENTLEMAN　O, here he is; lay hand upon him. Sir,
　　　Your most dear daughter—
　LEAR　No rescue? What, a prisoner? I am even
185　The natural fool[7] of fortune. Use° me well;　　　　　　　*Treat*
　　　You shall have ransom. Let me have surgeons;
　　　I am cut to the brains.
　GENTLEMAN　　　　　　　You shall have any thing.
　LEAR　No seconds?° all myself?　　　　　　　　　　　　*supporters*
　　　Why, this would make a man a man of salt,[8]
190　To use his eyes for garden water-pots,
　　　Aye, and laying° autumn's dust.　　　　　　　　　　　*settling*
　GENTLEMAN　　　　　　　Good sir—
　LEAR　I will die bravely,[9] like a smug° bridegroom. What!　　*an elegant*
　　　I will be jovial. Come, come; I am a king,
　　　My masters, know you that?
195　GENTLEMAN　You are a royal one, and we obey you.
　LEAR　Then there's life° in't. Nay, if you get it, you shall get it　*hope*
　　　with running. Sa, sa, sa, sa.[1]　(*Exit running; attendants follow*)
　GENTLEMAN　A sight most pitiful in the meanest wretch,
　　　Past speaking of in a king! Thou hast one daughter,
200　Who redeems nature from the general curse
　　　Which twain have brought her to.[2]
　EDGAR　Hail, gentle° sir.　　　　　　　　　　　　　　　*noble*
　GENTLEMAN　　　　　　　Sir, speed you.° What's your will?　*God speed you*
　EDGAR　Do you hear aught, sir, of a battle toward?°　　　　*coming*
　GENTLEMAN　Most sure and vulgar.° Everyone hears that,　　*commonly known*
　　　Which° can distinguish sound.　　　　　　　　　　　*Who*

3. A vile schemer. In early modern England, "politician" meant an ambitious, even Machiavellian, upstart.
4. Like a preacher, removing his hat in the pulpit.
5. Stage (often called "scaffold" and hence linked to executioner's block); block used to shape a felt hat (such as the hat removed by a preacher before a sermon); mounting block (such as the stump or stock Lear may have sat on to remove his boots).
6. Hat material, to muffle the sound of the approaching cavalry.
7. Born plaything; playing on "natural" as "mentally

deficient."
8. A man reduced to nothing but the salt his tears deposit.
9. With courage; showily. "Die" plays on the Renaissance sense of "have an orgasm."
1. A cry to encourage dogs in the hunt.
2. *Who . . . to:* Who restores proper meaning and order to a universe plagued by the crimes of the other two daughters; alluding to the fall of humankind and the natural world caused by the sin of Adam and Eve and to the universal redemption brought about by Christ's sacrifice.

205 EDGAR   But, by your favor,
How near's the other army?

GENTLEMAN   Near and on speedy foot. The main descry°   *appearance*
Stands on the hourly thought.°   *Is expected forthwith*

EDGAR   I thank you, sir. That's all.

210 GENTLEMAN   Though that the queen on° special cause° is here,   *for / reason*
Her army is moved on.

EDGAR   I thank you, sir.   *Exit* GENTLEMAN

GLOUCESTER   You ever-gentle gods, take my breath from me;
Let not my worser spirit[3] tempt me again
To die before you please!

EDGAR   Well pray you, father.[4]

215 GLOUCESTER   Now, good sir, what are you?

EDGAR   A most poor man, made tame to fortune's blows;
Who, by the art of known and feeling° sorrows,   *profound*
Am pregnant to° good pity. Give me your hand,   *disposed to feel*
I'll lead you to some biding.°   *resting place*

GLOUCESTER   Hearty thanks.

220 The bounty and the benison of heaven
To boot, and boot![5]

           Enter OSWALD

OSWALD   A proclaimed prize![6] Most happy!°   *lucky*
That eyeless head of thine was first framed° flesh   *made of*
To raise my fortunes. Thou old unhappy traitor,

225 Briefly thyself remember.[7] The sword is out
That must destroy thee.

GLOUCESTER   Now let thy friendly hand
Put strength enough to 't.

           EDGAR *interposes*

OSWALD   Wherefore, bold peasant.
Darest thou support a published° traitor? Hence,   *proclaimed*
Lest that the infection° of his fortune take   *(deadly) sickness*

230 Like° hold on thee. Let go his arm.   *The same*

EDGAR   Chill[8] not let go, zir, without vurther 'casion.°   *further occasion*

OSWALD   Let go, slave, or thou diest!

EDGAR   Good gentleman, go your gait,° and let poor volk pass.   *walk on*
An chud ha'° bin zwaggered out of my life, 't would not ha' bin   *If I could have*

235 zo long as 'tis by a vortnight. Nay, come not near th' old man;
keep out, che vor ye, or ise try whether your costard or my
ballow be the harder.[9] Chill be plain with you.

OSWALD   Out, dunghill!

EDGAR   Chill pick your teeth, zir. Come! No matter vor your

240 foins.°   *sword thrusts*

      They fight, and EDGAR *knocks him down*

OSWALD   Slave, thou hast slain me. Villain, take my purse.
If ever thou wilt thrive, bury my body;
And give the letters which thou find'st about me
To Edmund earl of Gloucester. Seek him out

245 Upon° the British party. O, untimely death!   *Within*
Death!   *He dies*

---

3. Wicked inclination; bad angel.
4. A term of respect for an elderly man.
5. In addition to my thanks, and may it bring you some worldly reward.
6. A wanted man, with a bounty on his life.
7. Recollect and pray forgiveness for your sins.

8. I will; dialect from Somerset was a stage convention for peasant dialogue.
9. *che vor ye . . . harder:* I warrant you, or I shall test whether your head or my cudgel is harder. *costard:* a kind of apple.

EDGAR   I know thee well: a serviceable° villain;   *an officious*
    As duteous to the vices of thy mistress
    As badness would desire.
GLOUCESTER   What, is he dead?
250 EDGAR   Sit you down, father; rest you.
    Let's see his pockets; the letters that he speaks of
    May be my friends. He's dead; I am only sorry
    He had no other death'sman.° Let us see.   *executioner*
    Leave,° gentle wax;[1] and, manners blame us not.   *By your leave*
255 To know our enemies' minds, we'd rip their hearts;
    Their° papers, is more lawful.   *To rip their*
    (*Reads*) "Let our reciprocal vows be remembered. You have
    many opportunities to cut him off. If your will want° not, time *lacks*
    and place will be fruitfully offered. There is nothing done,° if *accomplished*
260 he return the conqueror. Then am I the prisoner, and his bed my
    jail; from the loathed warmth whereof deliver me, and supply°   *fill*
    the place for your labor.[2]
                        Your—wife, so I would say—
                        Affectionate servant,
265   Goneril."
    O undistinguished space of woman's will![3]
    A plot upon her virtuous husband's life;
    And the exchange° my brother! Here, in the sands,   *substitute*
    Thee I'll rake up,° the post unsanctified°   *cover up / unholy messenger*
270 Of murderous lechers; and in the mature time°   *when the time is ripe*
    With this ungracious° paper strike the sight   *ungodly*
    Of the death-practiced duke.[4] For him 'tis well
    That of thy death and business I can tell.
GLOUCESTER   The king is mad. How stiff is my vile sense,[5]
275 That I stand up, and have ingenious feeling[6]
    Of my huge sorrows! Better I were distract;°   *mad*
    So should my thoughts be severed from my griefs,
    And woes by wrong° imaginations lose   *false*
    The knowledge of themselves.
         Drum afar off
    EDGAR   Give me your hand.
280 Far off, methinks, I hear the beaten drum.
    Come, father, I'll bestow° you with a friend.   *Exeunt*   *lodge*

4.7
Enter CORDELIA, KENT, DOCTOR, *and a* GENTLEMAN
CORDELIA   O thou good Kent, how shall I live and work,
    To match thy goodness? My life will be too short,
    And every measure° fail me.   *attempt*
KENT   To be acknowledged, madam, is o'erpaid.°   *is more than enough*
5 All my reports go[1] with the modest truth;
    Nor more nor clipped, but so.[2]
CORDELIA   Be better suited.°   *attired*
    These weeds° are memories of those worser hours.   *clothes*
    I prithee, put them off.

1. The wax seal on the letter.
2. *for your labor:* as a reward for your endeavors, and
for further sexual exertion.
3. Limitless extent of woman's willfulness. As with "hell"
in line 124, "will" might also refer to a woman's genitals.
4. Of the Duke whose death is plotted.
5. How obstinate is my unwanted power of reason.

6. That I remain upright and firm in my sanity and
have rational perceptions.
4.7 Location: The French camp at Dover.
1. May all accounts of me agree.
2. Not greater or less, but exactly the modest amount I
deserve.

KENT   Pardon me, dear madam;
     Yet to be known shortens my made intent.[3]
10   My boon I make it,[4] that you know° me not   *acknowledge*
     Till time and I think meet.°   *suitable*
CORDELIA   Then be 't so, my good lord. (*To the* DOCTOR) How
          does the king?
DOCTOR   Madam, sleeps still.
CORDELIA   O you kind gods,
15   Cure this great breach in his abusèd nature!
     The untuned and jarring senses, O, wind up[5]
     Of this child-changèd[6] father!
DOCTOR   So please your majesty
     That we may wake the king? He hath slept long.
CORDELIA   Be governed by your knowledge, and proceed
20   I' the sway° of your own will. Is he arrayed?°   *By the authority / clothed*
          Enter LEAR *in a chair carried by servants*
GENTLEMAN   Aye, madam. In the heaviness of his sleep
     We put fresh garments on him.
DOCTOR   Be by, good madam, when we do awake him;
     I doubt not of his temperance.°   *calmness*
CORDELIA   Very well.
          Music
25   DOCTOR   Please you, draw near. Louder the music there!
CORDELIA   O my dear father! Restoration hang
          Thy medicine on my lips; and let this kiss
          Repair those violent harms that my two sisters
          Have in thy reverence° made!   *aged dignity*
KENT   Kind and dear princess!
30   CORDELIA   Had you not[7] been their father, these white flakes°   *locks of hair*
     Had challenged° pity of them. Was this a face   *Would have provoked*
     To be opposed against the warring winds?
     To stand against the deep dread-bolted thunder?
     In the most terrible and nimble stroke
35   Of quick, cross lightning? to watch°—poor perdu![8]—   *to stand guard*
     With this thin helm?° Mine enemy's dog,   *helmet (of hair)*
     Though he had bit me, should have stood that night
     Against my fire; and wast thou fain,° poor father,   *glad*
     To hovel thee with swine, and rogues forlorn,
40   In short° and musty straw? Alack, alack!   *scant; broken*
     'Tis wonder that thy life and wits at once
     Had not concluded all.° He wakes; speak to him.   *altogether*
DOCTOR   Madam, do you; 'tis fittest.
CORDELIA   How does my royal lord? How fares your majesty?
45   LEAR   You do me wrong to take me out o' the grave.
     Thou art a soul in bliss; but I am bound
     Upon a wheel of fire, that mine own tears
     Do scald like molten lead.[9]
CORDELIA   Sir, do you know me?
LEAR   You are a spirit, I know. When did you die?
50   CORDELIA   Still, still, far wide!°   *unbalanced*

---

3. Revealing myself now would abort my designs.
4. The reward I beg is.
5. *The . . . up:* Reorder his confused and delirious mind. The image is of tightening the strings of a lute.
6. Changed by his children; changed into a child; playing on a musical key change.

7. Even if you had not.
8. Lost one; in military terms, a dangerously exposed sentry.
9. *but I . . . lead:* Lear puts himself in either hell or purgatory, both places of such punishment in medieval accounts.

DOCTOR   He's scarce awake. Let him alone awhile.

LEAR   Where have I been? Where am I? Fair daylight?
  I am mightily abused.° I should e'en die with pity,   *wronged; deceived*
  To see another thus. I know not what to say.
55 I will not swear these are my hands. Let's see.
  I feel this pin prick. Would I were assured
  Of my condition!

CORDELIA   O, look upon me, sir,
  And hold your hands in benediction o'er me:
  No, sir, you must not kneel.

60 LEAR   Pray, do not mock me.
  I am a very foolish fond° old man,   *silly*
  Fourscore and upward, not an hour more nor less;
  And, to deal plainly,
  I fear I am not in my perfect mind.
65 Methinks I should know you, and know this man;
  Yet I am doubtful; for I am mainly° ignorant   *entirely*
  What place this is; and all the skill I have
  Remembers not these garments; nor I know not
  Where I did lodge last night. Do not laugh at me;
70 For, as I am a man, I think this lady
  To be my child Cordelia.

CORDELIA   And so I am, I am.

LEAR   Be your tears wet?[1] Yes, faith. I pray, weep not.
  If you have poison for me, I will drink it.
  I know you do not love me; for your sisters
75 Have, as I do remember, done me wrong.
  You have some cause, they have not.

CORDELIA   No cause, no, cause.

LEAR   Am I in France?

KENT   In your own kingdom, sir.

LEAR   Do not abuse° me.   *deceive; mock*

DOCTOR   Be comforted, good madam. The great rage,
80 You see, is killed in him; and yet it is danger
  To make him even o'er° the time he has lost.   *go over*
  Desire him to go in. Trouble him no more
  Till further settling.°   *Until his mind eases*

CORDELIA   Will't please your highness walk?

LEAR   You must bear with me:
85 Pray you now, forget and forgive. I am old and foolish.

          Exeunt all but KENT *and* GENTLEMAN

GENTLEMAN   Holds it true, sir, that the Duke of Cornwall was so
  slain?

KENT   Most certain, sir.

GENTLEMAN   Who is conductor° of his people?   *commander*

90 KENT   As 'tis said, the bastard son of Gloucester.

GENTLEMAN   They say Edgar, his banished son, is with the Earl
  of Kent in Germany.

KENT   Report° is changeable. 'Tis time to look about.° The pow-   *Rumor/prepare defenses*
  ers of the kingdom approach apace.

95 GENTLEMAN   The arbitrement° is like to be bloody. Fare you   *encounter*
  well, sir.   *Exit*

KENT   My point and period[2] will be throughly wrought,
  Or° well or ill, as this day's battle's fought.   *Exit*   *For*

---

1. Are your tears real?; is this really happening?   2. The purpose and end of my life; literally, the full stop.

5.1

Enter, with drum and colors,° EDMUND, REGAN, GENTLE-   °*regimental flags*
MAN, *and soldiers*

EDMUND   Know° of the duke if his last purpose hold,[1]   °*Inquire*
Or whether since he is advised by aught[2]
To change the course. He's full of alteration°   °*indecision*
And self-reproving. Bring his constant pleasure.°   °*his settled intent*

To a GENTLEMAN, *who goes out*

5   REGAN   Our sister's man is certainly miscarried.[3]
EDMUND   'Tis to be doubted,° madam.   °*feared*
REGAN   Now, sweet lord,
You know the goodness I intend upon you.
Tell me—but truly—but then speak the truth,
Do you not love my sister?
EDMUND   In honored° love.   °*honorable*
10   REGAN   But have you never found my brother's way
To the forfended[4] place?
EDMUND   That thought abuses° you.   °*deceives*
REGAN   I am doubtful° that you have been conjunct°   °*suspicious / complicit*
And bosomed with° her, as far as we call hers.[5]   °*enamored of*
EDMUND   No, by mine honor, madam.
15   REGAN   I never shall endure her. Dear my lord,
Be not familiar° with her.   °*intimate*
EDMUND   Fear° me not.   °*Doubt*
She and the duke her husband!

Enter, with drum and colors, ALBANY, GONERIL, *and
soldiers*

GONERIL (*aside*)   I had rather lose the battle than that sister
Should loosen° him and me.   °*disunite*
20   ALBANY   Our very loving sister, well be-met.
Sir, this I hear: the king is come to his daughter,
With others whom the rigor° of our state°   °*harshness / government*
Forced to cry out. Where I could not be honest,°   °*honorable*
I never yet was valiant. For this business,
25   It toucheth° us, as France invades our land,   °*concerns*
Not bolds the king, with others, whom, I fear,
Most just and heavy causes make oppose.[6]
EDMUND   Sir, you speak nobly.
REGAN   Why is this reasoned?[7]
GONERIL   Combine together 'gainst the enemy;
30   For these domestic and particular broils°   °*minor details*
Are not the question here.
ALBANY   Let's then determine
With the ancient° of war on our proceeding.   °*experienced officer*
EDMUND   I shall attend you presently° at your tent.   °*in a moment*
REGAN   Sister, you'll go with us?[8]
35   GONERIL   No.
REGAN   'Tis most convenient;° pray you, go with us.   °*suitable*
GONERIL (*aside*)   O, ho, I know the riddle.°—I will go.   °*disguised meaning*
As they are going out, enter EDGAR *disguised*

5.1   Location: The British camp near Dover.
1. If his previous intention (to wage war) remains firm.
2. Since then anything has persuaded him.
3. Has surely come to grief by some accident.
4. Forbidden (to Edmund, because it is adulterous).
5. In total intimacy; all the way.
6. *It . . . oppose:* This is of concern to us because France

lands on our soil, not because it emboldens the King and
others, who, I am afraid, have been provoked for good
and solid reasons.
7. What is the point of this kind of speech?
8. Regan wants Goneril to go with Albany and her,
rather than with Edmund.

EDGAR   If e'er your grace had speech with man so poor,
Hear me one word.

ALBANY   I'll overtake you. Speak.

Exeunt all but ALBANY *and* EDGAR

40 EDGAR   Before you fight the battle, ope this letter.
If you have victory, let the trumpet sound
For him that brought it. Wretched though I seem,
I can produce a champion that will prove°   *defend*
What is avouched° there. If you miscarry,°   *asserted / perish*
45 Your business of the world hath so an end,
And machination° ceases. Fortune love you!   *plotting*

ALBANY   Stay till I have read the letter.

EDGAR   I was forbid it.
When time shall serve, let but the herald cry,
And I'll appear again.

50 ALBANY   Why, fare thee well. I will o'erlook thy paper.

Exit EDGAR

Re-enter EDMUND

EDMUND   The enemy 's in view; draw up your powers.°   *troops*
Here is the guess° of their true strength and forces   *estimate*
By diligent discovery;° but your haste   *spying*
Is now urged on you.

ALBANY   We will greet the time.[9]   *Exit*

55 EDMUND   To both these sisters have I sworn my love;
Each jealous° of the other, as the stung   *suspicious*
Are of the adder. Which of them shall I take?
Both? one? or neither? Neither can be enjoyed,
If both remain alive. To take the widow
60 Exasperates, makes mad her sister Goneril;
And hardly° shall I carry out my side,°   *with difficulty / plan*
Her husband being alive. Now then we'll use
His countenance[1] for the battle; which being done,
Let her who would be rid of him devise
65 His speedy taking off. As for the mercy
Which he intends to Lear and to Cordelia,
The battle done, and they within our power,
Shall° never see his pardon; for my state°   *They shall / condition*
Stands on° me to defend, not to debate.   '   *Exit*   *Obliges*

5.2

Alarum within.[1] *Enter, with drum and colors,* LEAR, COR-
DELIA, *and soldiers, over the stage; and exeunt.*
Enter EDGAR *and* GLOUCESTER

EDGAR   Here, father,[2] take the shadow of this tree
For your good host;° pray that the right may thrive: *shelter*
If ever I return to you again,
I'll bring you comfort.

GLOUCESTER   Grace go with you, sir!   *Exit* EDGAR

Alarum and retreat° within. Re-enter EDGAR   *trumpet signal*

5 EDGAR   Away, old man! give me thy hand! away!

---

9. We will be ready to meet the occasion.
1. Authority or backing; also suggesting "face," to be
used like a mask for Edmund's ambition.
5.2 Location: The rest of the play takes place near the
battlefield.
1. Trumpet call to battle (backstage).
2. See note to 4.6.214.

King Lear hath lost, he and his daughter ta'en.
Give me thy hand! come on!

GLOUCESTER   No farther, sir; a man may rot even° here.   *right*

EDGAR   What, in ill thoughts again? Men must endure
10   Their going hence, even as their coming hither;
Ripeness is all.³ Come on!

GLOUCESTER   And that's true, too.   *Exeunt*

5.3

Enter, in conquest, with drum and colors, EDMUND;
LEAR *and* CORDELIA, *prisoners;* CAPTAIN, SOLDIERS, *etc.*

EDMUND   Some officers take them away. Good guard,
Until their greater pleasures¹ first be known
That are to censure° them.   *judge*

CORDELIA   We are not the first
Who, with best meaning,° have incurred the worst.   *intention*
5   For thee, oppressèd king, am I cast down;°   *(into unhappiness)*
Myself could else out-frown false Fortune's frown.²
Shall we not see these daughters and these sisters?

LEAR   No, no, no, no! Come, let's away to prison.
We two alone will sing like birds i' the cage.
10   When thou dost ask me blessing, I'll kneel down,
And ask of thee forgiveness. So we'll live,
And pray, and sing, and tell old tales, and laugh
At gilded butterflies,³ and hear poor rogues
Talk of court news; and we'll talk with them too,
15   Who loses and who wins; who 's in, and who 's out;
And take upon 's the mystery of things,
As if we were Gods' spies; and we'll wear out,°   *outlast*
In a walled prison, packs and sects of great ones,
That ebb and flow by the moon.⁴

EDMUND   Take them away.

20   LEAR   Upon such sacrifices,⁵ my Cordelia,
The gods themselves throw incense. Have I caught thee?
He that parts us shall bring a brand from heavens,
And fire us hence like foxes.⁶ Wipe thine eyes;
The good-years shall devour them, flesh and fell,⁷
25   Ere they shall make us weep! We'll see 'em starved first.
Come.   *Exeunt* LEAR *and* CORDELIA, *guarded*

EDMUND   Come hither, captain; hark.
Take thou this note (*giving a paper*). Go follow them to prison:
One step I have advanced° thee. If thou dost   *promoted*
30   As this instructs thee, thou dost make thy way
To noble fortunes. Know thou this, that men
Are as the time is. To be tender-minded
Does not become a sword.° Thy great employment   *befit a swordsman*

---

3. To await the destined time is the most important thing, as fruit falls only when ripe (playing on Gloucester's "rot," line 8); readiness for death is our only duty (compare *Hamlet* 5.2.160, "The readiness is all").
5.3
1. *Good . . . pleasures:* Guard them well until the desires of those greater persons.
2. Otherwise, I could be defiant in the face of bad fortune.
3. Gaudy courtiers.

4. *packs . . . moon:* followers and factions of important people whose positions at court vary as the tide.
5. Upon such sacrifices as we are or as you have made.
6. *shall . . . foxes:* must have divine aid to do so. The image is of using a torch to smoke foxes out of their holes, or, in the case of Lear and Cordelia, prison cells.
7. *flesh and fell:* meat and skin; entirely. The precise meaning of "good-years" has not been explained; it may signify simply the passage of time or may suggest some ominous, destructive power.

Will not bear question.° Either say thou'lt do 't,   *discussion*
Or thrive by other means.
35 CAPTAIN   I'll do 't, my lord.
EDMUND   About it; and write happy when thou hast done.[8]
Mark, I say, instantly; and carry it° so   *carry it out*
As I have set it down.
CAPTAIN   I cannot draw a cart, nor eat dried oats;°   *(like a horse)*
40 If it be a man's work, I'll do it.   *Exit*
          Flourish. Enter ALBANY, GONERIL, REGAN, *another* CAP-
          TAIN, *and soldiers*
ALBANY   Sir, you have showed today your valiant strain,°   *qualities; birth*
And fortune led you well. You have the captives
That were the opposites° of this day's strife.   *opponents*
I do require them of you, so to use° them   *treat*
45 As we shall find their merits and our safety
May equally determine.
EDMUND   Sir, I thought it fit
To send the old and miserable king
To some retention° and appointed guard;   *confinement*
Whose° age has charms in it, whose title more,   *(Lear's)*
50 To pluck the common bosom[9] on his side,
And turn our impressed lances° in our eyes   *conscripted lancers*
Which[1] do command them. With him I sent the queen;
My reason all the same; and they are ready
Tomorrow, or at further space,° t' appear   *at a future point*
55 Where you shall hold your session.° At this time   *court of judgment*
We sweat and bleed; the friend hath lost his friend;
And the best quarrels, in the heat, are cursed
By those that feel their sharpness.[2]
The question of Cordelia and her father
Requires a fitter place.
60 ALBANY   Sir, by your patience,
I hold you but a subject of° this war,   *in waging*
Not as a brother.
REGAN   That's as we list° to grace him.   *choose*
Methinks our pleasure might have been demanded,[3]
Ere you had spoken so far. He led our powers;°   *armies*
65 Bore the commission of my place and person;
The which immediacy° may well stand up,   *close connection*
And call itself your brother.
GONERIL   Not so hot!°   *Not so fast*
In his own grace° he doth exalt himself,   *merit*
More than in your addition.[4]
REGAN   In my rights,
70 By me invested, he compeers° the best.   *equals*
GONERIL   That were the most,[5] if he should husband you.
REGAN   Jesters do oft prove prophets.
GONERIL   Holla, holla!
That eye that told you so looked but a-squint.[6]

8. Go to it, and call yourself happy when you are done.
9. To garner the affection of the populace.
1. *in our eyes / Which:* in the eyes of us who.
2. *And . . . sharpness:* And in the heat of battle, even the most just wars are cursed by those who must suffer the fighting.
3. I think you should have inquired into my wishes.
4. In the honors you confer upon him.
5. That investiture would be complete.
6. Squinting was a proverbial effect of jealousy, because of the tendency to look suspiciously at potential rivals.

REGAN   Lady, I am not well; else I should answer
75   From a full-flowing stomach.° General,   *anger*
   Take thou my soldiers, prisoners, patrimony:
   Dispose of them, of me; the walls° are thine.   *fortress of my heart*
   Witness the world, that I create thee here
   My lord and master.
GONERIL   Mean you to enjoy him?
80 ALBANY   The let-alone° lies not in your good will.   *veto*
EDMUND   Nor in thine, lord.
ALBANY   Half-blooded° fellow, yes.   *Bastard*
REGAN (*to* EDMUND)   Let the drum strike,[7] and prove my title thine.
ALBANY   Stay yet; hear reason. Edmund, I arrest thee
   On capital treason; and, in thine attaint,[8]
   This gilded serpent (*pointing to* GONERIL). For your claim, fair
85   sister,°   *sister-in-law*
   I bar it in the interest of my wife;
   'Tis she is sub-contracted to this lord,
   And I, her husband, contradict your banes.°   *announcement of marriage*
   If you will marry, make your loves to me,
   My lady is bespoke.
90 GONERIL   An interlude!°   *A farce*
ALBANY   Thou art armed, Gloucester. Let the trumpet sound.
   If none appear to prove upon thy head
   Thy heinous, manifest, and many treasons,
   There is my pledge (*throwing down a glove*); I'll prove it on thy heart,
95   Ere I taste bread, thou art in nothing less°   *in no way less guilty*
   Than I have proclaimed thee.
REGAN   Sick, O, sick!
GONERIL (*aside*)   If not, I'll ne'er trust medicine.°   *poison (euphemistic)*
EDMUND   There's my exchange (*throwing down a glove*). What°   *Whoever*
     in the world he is
   That names me traitor, villain-like he lies.
100   Call by thy trumpet. He that dares approach,
   On him, on you, who not? I will maintain
   My truth and honor firmly.
ALBANY   A herald, ho!
EDMUND   A herald, ho, a herald!
ALBANY   Trust to thy single virtue;° for thy soldiers,   *your unassisted power*
105   All levied in my name, have in my name
   Took their discharge.
REGAN   My sickness grows upon me.
ALBANY   She is not well; convey her to my tent.   *Exit* REGAN, *led*
      Enter a HERALD
   Come hither, herald—Let the trumpet sound—
   And read out this.
CAPTAIN   Sound, trumpet! (*A trumpet sounds*)
110 HERALD [*reads*]   "If any man of quality or degree within the
   lists of the army will maintain upon Edmund, supposed Earl of
   Gloucester, that he is a manifold traitor, let him appear by the
   third sound of the trumpet. He is bold in his defense."
EDMUND   Sound! (*First trumpet*)
115 HERALD   Again! (*Second trumpet*)

---

7. Perhaps to announce the betrothal, or a challenge.
8. And in order to accuse you; and as one who shares your corruption or crime.

HERALD Again! (*Third trumpet*)
    Trumpet answers within
    Enter EDGAR, *at the third sound, armed, with a trumpet*
    before him

ALBANY Ask him his purposes, why he appears
    Upon this call o' the trumpet.

HERALD   What° are you?   *Who*
    Your name, your quality?° and why you answer   *degree; rank*
    This present summons?

120 EDGAR   Know, my name is lost;
    By treason's tooth bare-gnawn and canker-bit.°   *worm-eaten*
    Yet am I noble as the adversary
    I come to cope.°   *to encounter*

ALBANY   Which is that adversary?

EDGAR What's he that speaks for Edmund Earl of Gloucester?

EDMUND Himself. What say'st thou to him?

125 EDGAR   Draw thy sword,
    That,° if my speech offend a noble heart,   *So that*
    Thy arm may do thee justice. Here is mine.
    Behold, it is the privilege of mine honors,
    My oath, and my profession. I protest,

130   Maugre° thy strength, youth, place, and eminence, *Despite*
    Despite thy victor sword and fire-new° fortune, *newly minted*
    Thy valor and thy heart,° thou art a traitor;   *courage*
    False to thy gods, thy brother, and thy father;
    Conspirant 'gainst this high-illustrious prince;

135   And, from the extremest upward° of thy head   *top*
    To the descent° and dust below thy foot,   *lowest part; sole*
    A most toad-spotted[9] traitor. Say thou "No,"
    This sword, this arm, and my best spirits, are bent° *ready*
    To prove upon thy heart, whereto I speak,
    Thou liest.

140 EDMUND   In wisdom I should ask thy name;
    But, since thy outside looks so fair and warlike
    And that thy tongue some say of breeding breathes,
    What safe and nicely I might well delay
    By rule of knighthood, I disdain and spurn.[1]

145   Back do I toss these treasons to thy head;
    With the hell-hated° lie o'erwhelm thy heart; *hated as much as hell*
    Which, for° they yet glance by and scarcely bruise, *since*
    This sword of mine shall give them instant way,° *access*
    Where they shall rest for ever. Trumpets, speak!
    Alarums. They fight. EDMUND *falls*

ALBANY Save° him, save him!   *Spare*

150 GONERIL   This is practice,° Gloucester: *trickery*
    By the law of arms thou wast not bound to answer
    An unknown opposite.° Thou art not vanquished, *opponent*
    But cozened and beguiled.°   *cheated and deceived*

ALBANY   Shut your mouth, dame,
    Or with this paper shall I stople° it.   *plug*

155   Thou worse than any name, read thine own evil.
    No tearing, lady! I perceive you know it.

---

9. Venomous, like a toad; spotted with disgrace.
1. *And . . . spurn:* And since your speech may suggest high birth, I will not stick safely and meticulously to the rules of knighthood (which do not require a knight to fight an unknown opponent) and refuse to fight you.

Gives the letter to EDMUND

GONERIL   Say, if I do, the laws are mine, not thine.
Who can arraign° me for 't?   *prosecute*

ALBANY   Most monstrous! oh!
Know'st thou this paper?

GONERIL   Ask me not what I know.   *Exit*

160   ALBANY   Go after her: she's desperate; govern° her.   *restrain*

EDMUND   What you have charged me with, that have I done;
And more, much more; the time will bring it out.
'Tis past, and so am I. But what art thou
That hast this fortune on me?[2] If thou 'rt noble,
I do forgive thee.

165   EDGAR   Let's exchange charity.°   *forgiveness*
I am no less in blood than thou art, Edmund;
If more, the more thou hast wronged me.
My name is Edgar, and thy father's son.
The gods are just, and of our pleasant vices
170   Make instruments to plague us.
The dark and vicious place where thee he got[3]
Cost him his eyes.

EDMUND   Thou hast spoken right, 'tis true;
The wheel° is come full circle! I am here.[4]   *Fortune's wheel*

ALBANY   Methought thy very gait did prophesy
175   A royal nobleness. I must embrace thee.
Let sorrow split my heart, if ever I
Did hate thee or thy father!

EDGAR   Worthy prince. I know 't.

ALBANY   Where have you hid yourself?
How have you known the miseries of your father?

180   EDGAR   By nursing them, my lord. List° a brief tale;   *Listen to*
And when 'tis told, O, that my heart would burst!
The bloody proclamation to escape,[5]
That followed me so near—O, our lives' sweetness!
That we the pain of death would hourly die
185   Rather than die at once![6]—taught me to shift
Into a madman's rags; to assume a semblance
That very° dogs disdained; and in this habit   *even*
Met I my father with his bleeding rings,°   *sockets*
Their precious stones° new lost; became his guide,   *eyes*
190   Led him, begged for him, saved him from despair;
Never—O fault!—revealed myself unto him,
Until some half-hour past, when I was armed:
Not sure, though hoping, of this good success,°   *conclusion*
I asked his blessing, and from first to last
195   Told him my pilgrimage. But his flawed° heart—   *cracked*
Alack, too weak the conflict to support!—
'Twixt two extremes of passion, joy and grief,
Burst smilingly.

EDMUND   This speech of yours hath moved me,
And shall perchance do good; but speak you on;
200   You look as you had something more to say.

---

2. Who have this good fortune at my expense.
3. The adulterous bed in which you were born; or, possibly, the vagina. *got:* begot.
4. Back at the lowest point.

5. In order to escape the sentence of death.
6. *our . . . once:* how sweet must life be that we prefer
the constant pain of dying to death itself.

ALBANY   If there be more, more woeful, hold it in;
  For I am almost ready to dissolve,°   *melt into tears*
  Hearing of this.
EDGAR   This would have seemed a period° *conclusion*
  To such as love not sorrow; but another,
205 To amplify° too much would make much more, *enlarge; extend*
  And top extremity.
  Whilst I was big in clamor° came there in a man, *lamenting loudly*
  Who, having seen me in my worst estate,
  Shunned my abhorred society; but then, finding
210 Who 'twas that so endured, with his strong arms
  He fastened on my neck, and bellowed out
  As he'd burst heaven; threw him on my father;
  Told the most piteous tale of Lear and him° *himself*
  That ever ear received; which in recounting
215 His grief grew puissant,° and the strings of life *powerful*
  Began to crack. Twice then the trumpets sounded,
  And there I left him tranced.
ALBANY   But who was this?
EDGAR Kent, sir, the banished Kent; who in disguise
  Followed his enemy king,[7] and did him service
220 Improper° for a slave.   *Unfit even*
    Enter a GENTLEMAN, *with a bloody knife*
GENTLEMAN Help, help, O, help!
EDGAR   What kind of help?
ALBANY   Speak, man.
EDGAR What means that bloody knife?
GENTLEMAN   'Tis hot, it smokes,
  It came even from the heart of—O, she's dead!
ALBANY Who dead? speak, man.
225 GENTLEMAN Your lady, sir, your lady! and her sister
  By her is poisoned; she hath confessed it.
EDMUND I was contracted to them both. All three
  Now marry° in an instant.   *unite (in death)*
    Enter KENT
EDGAR   Here comes Kent.
ALBANY Produce their bodies, be they alive or dead:
230 This judgment of the heavens, that makes us tremble,
  Touches us not with pity.   *Exit* GENTLEMAN
      O, is this he?
  The time will not allow the compliment
  Which very manners urges.[8]
KENT   I am come
  To bid my king and master aye° good night. *forever*
  Is he not here?
235 ALBANY   Great thing of° us forgot!   *by*
  Speak, Edmund, where's the king? and where's Cordelia?
  See'st thou this object,° Kent?   *spectacle*
    The bodies of GONERIL *and* REGAN *are brought in*
KENT Alack, why thus?
EDMUND   Yet° Edmund was beloved. *Despite all*

---

7. Because Lear had previously banished him. *enemy:* 8. *the compliment . . . urges:* the ceremony that barest
hostile.   custom demands.

The one the other poisoned for my sake,
240 And after slew herself.

ALBANY Even so. Cover their faces.

EDMUND I pant for life. Some good I mean to do,
Despite of mine own nature. Quickly send,
Be brief° in it, to the castle; for my writ⁹   *speedy*
245 Is on the life of Lear and on Cordelia:
Nay, send in time.

ALBANY   Run, run, O, run!

EDGAR To who, my lord? Who hath the office?° send   *commission*
Thy token of reprieve.

EDMUND   Well thought on. Take my sword,
Give it the° captain.   *to the*

250 ALBANY   Haste thee for thy life.   *Exit* EDGAR

EDMUND He hath commission from thy wife and me
To hang Cordelia in the prison, and
To lay the blame upon her own despair,
That she fordid herself.¹

255 ALBANY The gods defend her! Bear him hence awhile.

                                        EDMUND *is borne off*

          Re-enter LEAR, *with* CORDELIA *dead in his arms;* EDGAR,
          CAPTAIN, *and others following*

LEAR Howl, howl, howl, howl! O, you are men of stones:
Had I your tongues and eyes, I'd use them so
That heaven's vault should crack. She's gone forever!
I know when one is dead, and when one lives;
260 She's dead as earth. Lend me a looking-glass;
If that her breath will mist or stain the stone,²
Why, then she lives.

KENT   Is this the promised end?³

EDGAR Or image of that horror?

ALBANY   Fall, and cease!⁴

LEAR This feather stirs; she lives! If it be so,
265 It is a chance which does redeem all sorrows
That ever I have felt.

KENT (*kneeling*)   O my good master!

LEAR Prithee, away.

EDGAR   'Tis noble Kent, your friend.

LEAR A plague upon you, murderers, traitors all!
I might have saved her; now she's gone for ever!
270 Cordelia, Cordelia! stay a little. Ha!
What is 't thou say'st? Her voice was ever soft,
Gentle, and low, an excellent thing in woman.
I killed the slave that was a-hanging thee.

GENTLEMAN 'Tis true, my lords, he did.

LEAR   Did I not, fellow?
275 I have seen the day, with my good biting falchion°   *light sword*
I would have made them skip: I am old now,

---

9. Order of execution.
1. Destroyed herself. In most of Shakespeare's source texts for the play, Cordelia does in fact kill herself after reigning for some years.
2. Mica, or stone polished to a mirror finish.

3. Doomsday; expected end of the play. In no version of the story previous to Shakespeare's does Cordelia die at this point.
4. Let the world collapse and end.

And these same crosses spoil me.[5] Who are you?
Mine eyes are not o' the best. I'll tell you straight.°   *recognize you soon*
KENT   If fortune brag of two she loved and hated,
280   One of them we behold.[6]
LEAR   This is a dull sight.[7] Are you not Kent?
KENT   The same,
Your servant Kent. Where is your servant Caius?°   *(Kent's pseudonym)*
LEAR   He's a good fellow, I can tell you that;
He'll strike, and quickly too. He's dead and rotten.
285   KENT   No, my good lord; I am the very man—
LEAR   I'll see that straight.[8]
KENT   That, from your first of difference and decay,[9]
Have followed your sad steps.
LEAR   You are welcome hither.
KENT   Nor no man else.[1] All's cheerless, dark, and deadly.°   *deathly*
290   Your eldest daughters have fordone° themselves,   *destroyed*
And desperately° are dead.   *in despair*
LEAR   Aye, so I think.
ALBANY   He knows not what he says; and vain° it is   *in vain*
That we present us to him.
EDGAR   Very bootless.°   *futile*

        Enter a CAPTAIN

CAPTAIN   Edmund is dead, my lord.
ALBANY   That's but a trifle here.
295   You lords and noble friends, know our intent.
What comfort to this great decay° may come   *ruin; destruction*
Shall be applied. For us, we will resign,
During the life of this old majesty,
To him our absolute power; (*to* EDGAR *and* KENT) you, to your
    rights;
300   With boot,° and such addition° as your honors   *reward / distinction*
Have more than merited. All friends shall taste
The wages of their virtue, and all foes
The cup of their deserving. O, see, see!
LEAR   And my poor fool[2] is hanged! No, no, no life!
305   Why should a dog, a horse, a rat, have life,
And thou no breath at all? Thou'lt come no more,
Never, never, never, never, never!
Pray you, undo this button. Thank you, sir.
Do you see this? Look on her, look, her lips,
Look there, look there!   *Dies*
310   EDGAR   He faints! My lord, my lord!
KENT   Break, heart; I prithee, break!
EDGAR   Look up, my lord.
KENT   Vex not his ghost.[3] O, let him pass! He hates him much
That would upon the rack[4] of this tough world
Stretch him out longer.
EDGAR   He is gone, indeed.

5. And these recent adversities have weakened me; and
these parries I could once match would now destroy me.
6. *If . . . behold:* If there were only two supreme examples
in the world of Fortune's ability to raise up and cast down,
Lear would be one; alternatively, we are each of us one
(Lear and Kent are here looking at each other).
7. This is a sad sight; my vision is failing.
8. I'll attend to that shortly; I'll comprehend that in a
moment.

9. Who from the beginning of your alteration and deterioration.
1. No, neither I nor anyone else is welcome. Alternatively, I am that man, not disguised as anyone else.
2. A term of endearment, here used for Cordelia, though
it also recalls the disappearance of Lear's Fool after 3.6.
3. Do not disturb his departing soul.
4. Instrument of torture, used to stretch its victims.

315 KENT   The wonder is, he hath endured so long.
      He but usurped his life.[5]
    ALBANY   Bear them from hence. Our present business
      Is general woe. (*To* KENT *and* EDGAR) Friends of my soul, you twain
      Rule in this realm, and the gored° state sustain.   *wounded; bloody*
320 KENT   I have a journey, sir, shortly to go;
      My master calls me, I must not say no.
    EDGAR   The weight of this sad time we must obey;
      Speak what we feel, not what we ought to say.
      The oldest hath borne most; we that are young
325   Shall never see so much, nor live so long.
                          Exeunt, with dead march

---

5. From death, which already had a claim on it.

Macbeth

On May 19, 1603, a scant two months after the death of Queen Elizabeth and the accession to the English throne of the Scottish King James, Shakespeare's company, the Lord Chamberlain's Men, was formally declared to be the King's Men. The players had every reason to be grateful to their new royal master for this lucrative distinction and attentive to his pleasure and interest. It has long been argued that one of the most striking signs of their gratitude is *Macbeth*, based on a story from Scottish history particularly apt for a monarch who traced his line back to Banquo, the noble thane whose murder Macbeth orders after he has killed King Duncan.

In Shakespeare's principal historical source, Raphael Holinshed's *Chronicles of England, Scotland, and Ireland* (1587), Banquo aids Macbeth in the murder of the King. Shakespeare suppresses this complicity. The witches (or "weird sisters") who tell Macbeth that he will be king tell Banquo that he will be the father of kings, but Banquo seems determined not to be drawn into any conspiratorial attempt to realize these prophecies. When, just before Duncan's assassination, Macbeth indirectly asks for his support, Banquo speaks of keeping his "allegiance clear" (2.1.27). Macbeth's only co-conspirator, then, is his wife. Innocent of the crime against Duncan, Banquo is killed because Macbeth fears and envies him and because he wishes to keep the crown he has seized from passing, as the witches had prophesied, to Banquo's heirs. Other significant changes Shakespeare made in his source materials further intensify Macbeth's isolation and his evil: in Holinshed's *Chronicles,* Duncan is a relatively young and feeble ruler, and Macbeth, having dispatched him, goes on to reign brilliantly for ten years. As Shakespeare staged the story, Duncan is a mature and virtuous king, and Scotland under the tyrant Macbeth is in the grip of a nightmare from which it will eventually awaken into the happy rule of Banquo's descendants.

As is so often the case with Shakespeare, we do not have a secure date for either the composition or the first performance of *Macbeth*. The first printed text is in the 1623 First Folio, but the play, usually dated 1606, has always seemed the most topical of Shakespeare's great tragedies, cannily alert at once to King James's personal obsessions and to contemporary events. The most unnerving of those events was the Gunpowder Plot, an attempt by a small group of conspirators, embittered by what they perceived as James's unwillingness to extend toleration to Roman Catholics, to set off a massive explosion that would blow up the King and his family along with most of the government. On the night before the intended attempt, the plot was foiled by the arrest of one of the principal conspirators, Guy Fawkes, who revealed under torture the names of his collaborators.

Among those hunted down, brought to trial, and executed for the Gunpowder Plot was Father Henry Garnet, head of the clandestine Jesuit mission in England. Garnet pleaded innocent, but the government prosecutors made much of the fact that he was the author of *A Treatise of Equivocation,* a book showing how to give misleading or ambiguous answers under oath. At a harrowing moment in *Macbeth,* in the immediate wake of the murder of the sleeping King Duncan, an insistent knocking is heard at the castle gate. (The knocking is a simple device, but in performance it almost always has a thrilling effect, famously characterized by the Romantic critic Thomas De Quincey as the reflux of the human upon the fiendish.) A porter, roused by the hammering on the door but still half drunk from the evening's revelry, appears. As he grumblingly goes to unlock the gate, he imagines that he is the gatekeeper in hell, opening the door to new arrivals. "Here's an equivocator," he says of one of these imaginary sinners, "that could swear in both the scales against either scale, who committed treason enough for God's sake, yet could not equivocate to heaven. O, come in, equivocator" (2.3.8–11). This treasonous equivocator knocking on hell's gate is almost certainly an allusion to the recently executed Henry Garnet.

The Gunpowder Plot was only one of the King's sources of anxiety. Not surprising for someone whose mother and father had both been killed, James had a horror of assassination and was convinced that there were many plots against his life. He also held a powerful conviction that a king was a sacred figure, God's own representative on earth. Regicide, in this view, was close to the ultimate crime, a demonic assault not simply on an individual and a community but on the fundamental order of the universe. James, who had written a learned book on witchcraft, suspected the hand of the devil in any plot against an anointed king, believed that witches had at various points in his own life conspired to harm him or render him impotent, and feared the existence of occult, invisible forces bent on bringing all things to ruin.

In several of his earlier plays, most notably in *Richard II*, Shakespeare's characters give voice to the theory that the King is God's deputy on earth and, consequently, that attacks upon him are evil, but kingship's claim to sacred authority is voiced exceptionally powerfully in *Macbeth* (not in Scotland alone, but also in neighboring England, where, as Malcolm tells Macduff, the touch of the pious King Edward cures disease). Exceptionally powerful, too, in this play is the metaphysical horror of regicide. The murder of Duncan is marked in the natural world with dreadful signs and portents and in the human world with an overpowering sense of devastation ironically given its most eloquent expression by the murderer Macbeth:

Henry IV of France (1553–1610) administers the royal touch, thought to cure scrofula. An etching by Pierre Firens, in André Du Laurens's *De mirabilii strumas sanandi vi solis Galliae regibus . . .* (Paris, 1609). See *Macbeth* 4.3.142–60.

Renown and grace is dead.
The wine of life is drawn, and the mere lees
Is left this vault to brag of.

(2.3.90–92)

Macbeth is speaking hypocritically—"look like the innocent flower," his wife had earlier counseled him, "but be the serpent under't" (1.5.63–64)—and yet, at least in one
interpretation of the part, he is saying what he himself knows to be the grim truth. Far
more than any other of Shakespeare's villains, more than the homicidal Richard III, the
treacherous Claudius in *Hamlet*, and the cold-hearted Iago in *Othello*, Macbeth is fully
aware of the wickedness of his deeds and is tormented by this awareness. Endowed with
a clear-eyed grasp of the difference between good and evil, he chooses evil, even though
the choice horrifies and sickens him.

Before he has taken the irrevocable step, Macbeth tries to recover his moral bear-
ings. The deed he is contemplating, he begins by telling himself, would work only if he
could control all consequences, so that his blow "might be the be-all and the end-all"
(1.7.5). But he grasps that there is no possibility of such complete control and therefore no hope of practical success. His thoughts then turn to the overwhelming ethical
arguments against the murder: he is not only the King's kinsman and subject but also
his host, "who should against his murderer shut the door, / Not bear the knife myself"
(1.7.15–16). And from these considerations, practical and ethical, Macbeth's restless,
brooding mind rises higher, imagining that the murdered Duncan's virtues will plead
like angels against the "deep damnation of his taking-off,"

And pity, like a naked new-born babe,
Striding the blast, or heaven's cherubin, horsed
Upon the sightless couriers of the air,
Shall blow the horrid deed in every eye
That tears shall drown the wind.

(1.7.21–25)

No one else in the play has a moral sensibility so intense or so visionary, no one else
imagines so vividly the forces that lie beyond the ordinary and familiar horizon of
human experience. Macbeth understands exactly what is at stake and what he must
do: "We will," he tells his wife decisively, "proceed no further in this business"
(1.7.31).

Why, then, does he change his mind and commit a crime he cannot even contem-
plate without horror? A significant part of the answer lies in the instigation of his formidable wife. When we first glimpse Lady Macbeth, she is reading a letter. (Reading
was by no means a universal achievement for women of the early seventeenth century,
let alone the eleventh, when the play's events are set, but Shakespeare frequently represents it in his plays in a variety of contexts.) The letter makes her burn with visions
of the "golden round" that "fate and metaphysical aid" (1.5.26–27) seem to have conferred upon her husband. But even though she speaks of the crown as if it were already
on Macbeth's head, she fears that he is too full of the "milk of human kindness"
(1.5.15) to seize what has been promised him. She resolves then to "chastise" her husband, to urge him, in a phrase taken from archery that has a strong sexual undercurrent, to screw his courage to the sticking place. Lady Macbeth manipulates him in two
principal ways. The first is through sexual taunting:

Art thou afeard
To be the same in thine own act and valour
As thou art in desire?
. . . .
When you durst do it, then you were a man

(1.7.39–41, 49)

And the second is through the terrible force of her determination:

> I have given suck, and know
> How tender 'tis to love the babe that milks me.
> I would, while it was smiling in my face,
> Have plucked my nipple from his boneless gums
> And dashed the brains out, had I so sworn
> As you have done to this.
>
> (1.7.54–59)

These words, and the gestures that viscerally intensify them onstage, cannot by themselves account for Macbeth's decision. He counters his wife's sexual taunting with a clear sense of the proper boundaries of his identity as a male and as a human being: "I dare do all that may become a man; / Who dares do more is none" (1.7.46–47). As for Lady Macbeth's fantasy of murdering her infant, its horror might have served rather to deter Macbeth from his unnatural crime than to spur him toward it. Virtually everyone is subject to terrible dreams and lawless fantasies—"Merciful powers," Banquo prays, "restrain in me the cursèd thoughts that nature / Gives way to in repose" (2.1.7–9)— but not everyone crosses the fatal line from criminal desire to criminal act.

That in crossing this line Macbeth murders a man toward whom he should be grateful, loyal, and protective, deepens the mystery of his crime, linking it to a long current of theological and philosophical brooding on the nature of evil. For St. Augustine, the great fourth-century church father, evil in its most radical form is gratuitous—that is, without an explicable rationale or motivation—and this notion of gratuitousness haunts subsequent thinkers, including those far from Christian orthodoxy. Thus the Florentine Niccolò Machiavelli, notorious in the sixteenth century for freethinking, writes in Chapter 37 of his *Discourses* that "when men are no longer obliged to fight from necessity, they fight from ambition, which passion is so powerful in the hearts of men that it never leaves them, no matter to what height they may rise." The reason for this, Machiavelli proposes, is that "nature has created men so that they desire everything, but are unable to attain it; desire being thus always greater than the faculty of acquiring, discontent with what they have and dissatisfaction with themselves result from it."

Macbeth and Lady Macbeth act on ambition, restless desire, and a will to power normally kept in check by the pragmatic, ethical, and religious considerations to which the wavering Macbeth initially gives voice. Lady Macbeth in effect works to liberate that will to power in her husband, freeing him from his "sickly" fears of damnation so that he can act with a ruthless blend of murderous violence and cunning. In her radically disenchanted, coolly skeptical view, the murder of the King can be undertaken without fear of guilty conscience, vengeful ghosts, or divine judgment: "The sleeping and the dead," she tells her shaken husband, "are but as pictures. 'Tis the eye of childhood / That fears a painted devil" (2.2.51–53).

This reassurance, Shakespeare's tragedy shows, is hopelessly shallow. As the spectral dagger, the ghost sitting in Macbeth's chair, and the indelible bloodstains on Lady Macbeth's hands all chillingly demonstrate, the secure distinction between representation and reality, the dead and the living, repeatedly breaks down, not simply for the characters but for the spectators as well. In most productions, the dagger and the blood are visible only to the diseased minds of the murderers, but Banquo's ghost is almost always palpably present onstage, visible to the audience as well as to the unhinged Macbeth, though invisible to everyone around him. Moreover, the dream of a "clean" regicide proves psychologically untenable: the seizure of the crown leads to feverish sleeplessness, brooding anxiety about security, and an overwhelming sense of defilement. Macbeth and Lady Macbeth are equally devastated, but the psychological trajectory in the wake of the crime is not the same for the two conspirators. Initially frozen in moral numbness, Lady Macbeth experiences a gradual decomposition, a growing horror that breaks forth unforgettably in the sleepwalking scene with her compulsive attempts to free herself of the smell and stain of blood: "All the perfumes of Arabia will not sweeten this little hand" (5.1.42–43). Initially gripped by a heightened sensitivity to fear, a dread that threatens inward decomposition, Macbeth experiences a gradual hardening and deadening of the self until he reaches a state of absolute numbness:

> Tomorrow, and tomorrow, and tomorrow
> Creeps in this petty pace from day to day
> To the last syllable of recorded time.
>
> (5.5.18–20)

The assassination also proves, as Macbeth had foreseen, politically untenable. There is always someone who escapes the murderer's net, someone who poses a threat or seeks to redress an injury or simply remembers what it felt like to be free and unafraid. It is impossible to tie up all the loose ends, to break the chain of action and reaction, to reach a stable resting place. There are no clean murders. One crime leads to another and then to another without bringing the criminal any closer to the security or contentment that each desperate act is meant to achieve. Macbeth cannot stop the bloody acts; instead he must multiply and extend them. Where Lady Macbeth had only fantasized the murder of children, Macbeth actually undertakes that and other crimes until he dreams, in his half-crazed words to the "secret, black, and midnight hags" (4.1.64), of universal destruction.

It is Macbeth's first encounter with these hags—the weird (or, in the original spelling, "weyward" or "weyard") sisters—that seems to initiate his descent toward murder and tyranny. But what kind of power do these malevolent bearded women have over Macbeth? Are they responsible, by magical influence or by planting the idea in his mind, for his decision to kill Duncan? Are they somehow privy to a predestined fate, as if they have seen the script of the tragedy before it is performed? Or, alternatively, are they uncanny emblems of Macbeth's psychological condition, a kind of screen onto which he projects his "horrible imaginings" (1.3.137)? The word "weird," in one of its etymologies, derives from the Old English word for "fate," but do the women Shakespeare depicts, trafficking in ambiguous prophecies, fretting over village squabbles, mumbling charms, actually control destiny (or, what amounts to the same thing, the

Macbeth and Banquo encounter the weird sisters (1.3). From Raphael Holinshed, *The Firste Volume of the Chronicles of England, Scotlande, and Irelande* (1577).

tragedy's plot)? What is the nature of these strange creatures that "look not like th'inhabitants o'th' earth," as Banquo observes, "and yet are on't" (1.3.39–40)?

Actors' responses to these questions have ranged wildly, though virtually all productions have recognized that the witches' scenes are among the most theatrically powerful and compelling in the play and that it matters a great deal whether they are made up to look grotesque or stately, perversely comical or terrifying. Scholarly responses have been complicated by the high probability that not all of the witchcraft scenes are by Shakespeare himself: it appears that 3.5 and part of 4.1, the scenes featuring the goddess Hecate, were added to the play some time after its first performance and incorporate songs derived from Thomas Middleton's play *The Witch*. (The Folio text of *Macbeth* cites only the first words of these songs, which are given in full in this edition.) But even if we set aside the problems raised by these interpolated scenes, the status of the witches in Shakespeare's play remains uncertain and seems to be so by design. "What are you?" asks Macbeth when he first encounters the eerie, sexually ambiguous figures, and he receives in reply his own name: "All hail, Macbeth" (1.3.45–46). Banquo urgently renews the inquiry, asking the creatures before his eyes if they truly exist or are only figments of his imagination; but his question, too, remains unanswered. When Macbeth and Banquo demand to know more, the witches vanish: "what seemed corporal / Melted as breath into the wind" (1.3.79–80). "As breath into the wind"—*Macbeth* is a tragedy of meltings, vanishing boundaries, and liminal states.

Much of the play transpires on the border between fantasy and reality, a sickening betwixt and between where a "horrid image" in the mind has the uncanny power to produce bodily effects "against the use of nature" (1.3.134, 136), where one mind is present to the innermost fantasies of another, where manhood threatens to vanish and murdered men walk and blood cannot be washed off. If these effects could be unequivocally attributed to the agency of the witches, the audience would at least have the security of a defined and focused fear. Alternatively, if the witches could be definitively dismissed as fantasy or fraud, the audience would at least have the clear-eyed certainty of witnessing human causes in an altogether secular world. But instead, Shakespeare achieves the remarkable effect of a nebulous infection, a bleeding of the demonic into the secular and the secular into the demonic.

The most famous instance of this effect is Lady Macbeth's great invocation of the "spirits / That tend on mortal thoughts" (1.5.38–39) to unsex her, fill her with cruelty, make thick her blood, and exchange her milk for gall. The speech appears to be a conjuration of demonic powers, an act of witchcraft in which the "murd'ring ministers" (1.5.46) are directed to bring about a set of changes in her body. She calls these ministers "sightless substances" (1.5.47): though invisible, they are—as she conceives them—not figures of speech or projections of her mind, but objective, substantial beings or forces. (Macbeth similarly seems to imagine invisible but objective forces when he speaks of "the sightless couriers of the air," 1.7.23.) But the fact that the spirits she invokes are "sightless" already moves this passage away from the literal existence of the weird sisters and toward the metaphorical use of "spirits" in her speech of a few moments earlier: "Hie thee hither, / That I may pour my spirits in thine ear" (1.5.23–24). The spirits she speaks of here are manifestly figurative—they refer to the bold words, the undaunted mettle, and the sexual taunts with which she intends to incite Macbeth to murder Duncan—but, like all of her expressions of will and passion, they strain toward bodily realization, even as they convey a psychic and hence invisible inwardness. That is, there is something uncannily literal about Lady Macbeth's influence on her husband, as if marital intimacy were akin to demonic possession, as if she had contrived to inhabit his mind, as if, in other words, she had literally poured her spirits in his ear. Conversely, there is something uncannily figurative about the "sightless substances" she invokes, as if the spirit world, the realm of "fate and metaphysical aid," were only a metaphor for her blind and murderous desires, as if the weird sisters were condensations of her own breath.

Witchcraft in Scotland. From *Newes from Scotland* (1591).

In Shakespeare's plays, as in those of his contemporaries, evildoers may wreak havoc for a time, but in the final restoration of order and justice, they and their principal accomplices are almost inevitably punished. Thus, at the close of *Macbeth*, not only are Macbeth and Lady Macbeth dead, but the victorious Malcolm also speaks of settling scores with "the cruel ministers / Of this dead butcher and his fiend-like queen" (5.11.34–35). Yet though the play has deeply implicated the witches in Macbeth's monstrous assault on the fabric of civilized life, there is no gesture toward punishing them, no sign that the victors are even aware of their existence. This omission is the more striking if we recall that at the time Shakespeare wrote his play, the authorities in England and Scotland were bringing women to trial on charges of witchcraft and executing them. The theatrical power of *Macbeth* seems bound up with its refusal to resolve the questions raised by the witches. At once marginal and central to the play, they are only briefly and intermittently onstage, but they are still suggestively present when we cannot see them, when the threats they embody are absorbed in the ordinary relations of everyday life.

"There's no art / To find the mind's construction in the face" (1.4.11–12), says the baffled Duncan about a man who had betrayed his trust, but Macbeth confronts a deeper perplexity, an appalling mystery within himself:

> My thought, whose murder yet is but fantastical,
> Shakes so my single state of man that function
> Is smothered in surmise, and nothing is
> But what is not.
>
> (1.3.138–41)

The witches have something to do with this inner torment, but what that something is remains as elusive as the dagger that Macbeth sees before him, handle toward his hand. Scotland is sick, "almost afraid to know itself" (4.3.166). But the sickness cannot be isolated in a conspiracy of witches. If violence stirs in the hinterlands, where marauding armies struggle, it breeds more murderously still in the inmost circles of the realm, where the ruler feels most secure: "This castle hath a pleasant seat," says Duncan, going unwittingly to his death:

> The air
> Nimbly and sweetly recommends itself
> Unto our gentle senses.
>
> (1.6.1–3)

If the mind is subject to "supernatural soliciting" (1.3.129) from some bizarre place, it is gripped still more terribly and irresistibly by "horrible imaginings" (1.3.137) from within. If there is sexual disturbance out on the heath, where the bearded hags stir the ingredients of their hideous caldron, there is deeper sexual disturbance at home, in the murderous intimacy of the marriage bond: "When you durst do it, then you were a man" (1.7.49). If you are worried about losing your manhood, it is not enough to hunt for witches; look to your wife. If you are anxious about your future, scrutinize your best friends: "He was a gentleman on whom I built / An absolute trust" (1.4.13–14). If you are worried about interior temptation, fear your own dreams:

> Merciful powers,
> Restrain in me the cursèd thoughts that nature
> Gives way to in repose.
>
> (2.1.7–9)

And if you fear spiritual desolation, turn your eyes on the contents not only of the hideous caldron but of your skull: "O, full of scorpions is my mind, dear wife!" (3.2.37).

The men who persecuted witches in Shakespeare's age were determined to compel full confessions, to pass judgment, and to escape from the terror of the inexplicable, the unforeseen, the aimlessly malignant. In *Macbeth*, the audience is given something better than confession, for it has visible proof of the demonic in action, but this visibility turns out to be as maddeningly equivocal or frustrating as the witches' riddling words. The "wayward" witches appear and disappear, their promises and prophecies all tricks, like practical jokes with appalling consequences. The language of the play subverts the illusory certainties of sight, and the forces of renewed order, Malcolm and Macduff, are themselves strangely unstable. Malcolm, who spins an elaborate fantasy of his own viciousness, and Macduff, who abandons his wife and children to their slaughter, are peculiar emblems of a renewed, divinely sanctioned order. Shakespeare may have set out to flatter the King, but it is difficult to see how the King, if he paid any attention to the tragedy that the King's Men offered him, could be reassured. The ambiguities of demonic agency are never resolved, and its horror spreads like a mist through a murky landscape. "What is't you do?" Macbeth asks the weird sisters. "A deed without a name" (4.1.65).

By the play's close, Macbeth has begun "to doubt th'equivocation of the fiend, / That lies like truth" (5.5.41–42). Equivocations are lies with mental reservations, words with double meanings, puns, twists of emphasis, and plays on false interpretations (such as the meaning of the phrase "not of woman born"). Like the witches—and, for that matter, like concepts of gender and authority and social order—language in *Macbeth* is a boundary stalker, neither a trustworthy guide nor a manifest illusion. Words sit dangerously in a middle ground; they must be brought under control, but they always threaten to slide into lies or magic charms or riddles or sheer emptiness. It is this emptiness with which Macbeth seems haunted at the end, with his vision of life as

> a tale
> Told by an idiot, full of sound and fury,
> Signifying nothing.
>
> (5.5.25–27)

If the closing moments of the play invite us to recoil from this black hole—after all, the tyrant is killed—they invite us to recoil from too confident and simple a celebration of the triumph of grace. For somewhere beyond the immediate circle of order restored, the witches are dancing around the caldron, and, the play seems to imply, the caldron is in every one of us.

STEPHEN GREENBLATT

TEXTUAL NOTE

The only authoritative text of *Macbeth* is the First Folio (1623), which consequently serves as the control text in this edition. Scholars generally agree that the Folio version (F) was based on a promptbook, a transcript derived, in all likelihood, from Shakespeare's rough draft of the play. F appears to be a fairly reliable record of its manuscript source, the promptbook.

There are, however, signs that this source was itself an abbreviated version of the play as first written and performed, for the text in F is considerably shorter than that of any of the other major tragedies. Moreover, the Folio's *Macbeth* appears to be a version of the play revised, sometime after Shakespeare had ceased to be active with the King's Men, for a court performance in the presence of King James. Scholars have long suspected that it contains material not by Shakespeare. In particular, the two songs referred to in 3.5 and 4.1 of F only by their opening phrases ("Come away, come away, &c.," "Blacke Spirits, &c.") are very likely by the playwright Thomas Middleton. Songs with the same opening phrases appear in a manuscript of Middleton's unsuccessful play *The Witch* (c. 1613) and are restored in full in this edition of *Macbeth*.

Middleton may have been personally responsible for the revision of *Macbeth* reflected in the Folio text. He could, in addition to the songs, have added all of 3.5 (which seems to diverge stylistically from the rest of the play) as well as parts of 4.1, particularly Hecate's speeches.

SELECTED BIBLIOGRAPHY

Adelman, Janet. "'Born of Woman': Fantasies of Maternal Power in *Macbeth*." *Cannibals, Witches, and Divorce: Estranging the Renaissance*. Ed. Marjorie Garber. Baltimore: Johns Hopkins University Press, 1987. 90–121. *Macbeth* represents dueling fantasies of absolute, destructive female power and of escape from that power; masculine authority is consolidated in the end by eliminating the feminine.

Bradley, A. C. *Shakespearean Tragedy: Lectures on "Hamlet," "Othello," "King Lear," "Macbeth."* London: Macmillan, 1905. The most concentrated, classical, and fast-paced of Shakespeare's great tragedies, *Macbeth* produces unequaled dread with its dark atmosphere and sublime central characters.

Calderwood, James L. *If It Were Done: "Macbeth" and Tragic Action*. Amherst: University of Massachusetts Press, 1986. *Macbeth* subverts the models of *Hamlet* and Aristotelian poetics, interrogating the nature of tragedy and the role of violence as both a threat to and a source of social order.

Greenblatt, Stephen. "Shakespeare Bewitched." *New Historical Literary Study: Essays on Reproducing Texts, Representing History*. Ed. Jeffrey N. Cox and Larry J. Reynolds. Princeton: Princeton University Press, 1993. 108–35. In writing *Macbeth,* Shakespeare drew both upon the King's belief in witchcraft and upon a skeptical critique of such belief by Reginald Scot.

Howard, Jean E. "Shakespeare, Geography, and the Work of Genre on the Early Modern Stage." *Modern Language Quarterly* 64.3 (2003): 299–322. Scotland's mingled contemporary reputation for nobility and savagery allowed Shakespeare to desacralize kingship.

Kastan, David Scott. "Macbeth and the 'Name of the King.'" *Shakespeare After Theory*. New York: Routledge, 1999. 165–82. Insistent doubling, blending the figures of the king and tyrant, undermines the attempt in *Macbeth* to contain violence by restoring moral order.

Mullaney, Steven. "Lying Like Truth: Riddle, Representation, and Treason." *The Place of the Stage: License, Play, and Power in Renaissance England*. Chicago: University of Chicago Press, 1988. 116–34. Like the Jacobean spectacle of a traitor on the scaffold, *Macbeth* reveals the generative power of equivocation, challenging the absolutes of royal authority.

Norbrook, David. "Macbeth and the Politics of Historiography." *Politics of Discourse: The Literature and History of Seventeenth-Century England*. Ed. Kevin Sharpe and Steven N. Zwicker. Berkeley: University of California Press, 1987. 78–116. Embroiled in seventeenth-century debates over writing Scottish history, Shakespeare raised the specter of justified regicide even as he drew on King James's monarchist views.

Orgel, Stephen. "*Macbeth* and the Antic Round." *The Authentic Shakespeare, and Other Problems of the Early Modern Stage*. New York: Routledge, 2002. 159–72. Revisions to the witches' scenes link theatrical spectacle to psychological inwardness and heighten the paradoxical role of women.

Wells, Robin Headlam. "'Arms and the Man': *Macbeth*." *Shakespeare on Masculinity*. New York: Cambridge University Press, 2000. 117–43. *Macbeth* blurs Gospel and classical epic conceptions of manhood, questioning the terms of King James's rule.

FILMS

Macbeth. 1948. Dir. Orson Welles. USA. 107 min. Expressionist, low-budget production, starring Welles and Jeanette Nolan.

Throne of Blood. 1957. Dir. Akira Kurosawa. Japan. 105 min. Kabuki-influenced production set in feudal Japan stars Toshirô Mifune and Isuzu Yamada.

Macbeth. 1971. Dir. Roman Polanski. UK/USA. 140 min. Bleak, misty, bloody vision, with strikingly young leads Jon Finch and Francesca Annis.

Macbeth. 1979. Dir. Philip Casson. UK. 146 min. Minimalist production for television with doubling actors and simple sets. Ian McKellen and Judi Dench star.

Scotland, PA. 2001. Dir. Billy Morrissette. USA. 104 min. Comic recasting in a 1970s American fast-food joint.

The Tragedy of Macbeth

THE PERSONS OF THE PLAY

KING DUNCAN of Scotland

MALCOLM
DONALBAIN } his sons

A CAPTAIN in Duncan's army

MACBETH, Thane of Glamis, later Thane of Cawdor, then King
    of Scotland

A PORTER at Macbeth's castle

Three MURDERERS attending on Macbeth

SEYTON, servant of Macbeth

LADY MACBETH, Macbeth's wife

A DOCTOR of Physic
A Waiting-GENTLEWOMAN } attending on Lady Macbeth

BANQUO, a Scottish thane

FLEANCE, his son

MACDUFF, Thane of Fife

LADY MACDUFF, his wife

MACDUFF'S SON

LENNOX
ROSS
ANGUS } Scottish Thanes
CAITHNESS
MENTEITH

SIWARD, Earl of Northumberland

YOUNG SIWARD, his son

An English DOCTOR

HECATE, Queen of the Witches

Six WITCHES

Three APPARITIONS, one an armed head, one a bloody child,
    one a child crowned

A SPIRIT LIKE A CAT

Other SPIRITS

An OLD MAN

A MESSENGER

MURDERERS

SERVANTS

A show of eight kings; Lords and Thanes, attendants, soldiers,
    drummers

1.1

Thunder and lightning. Enter three WITCHES

FIRST WITCH   When shall we three meet again?
  In thunder, lightning, or in rain?[1]

SECOND WITCH   When the hurly-burly's° done,   *tumult is*
  When the battle's lost and won.

5   THIRD WITCH   That will be ere the set of sun.

1.1 Location: An open place.   1. Witches were thought to be able to cause bad weather.

FIRST WITCH   Where the place?
SECOND WITCH   Upon the heath.
THIRD WITCH   There to meet with Macbeth.
FIRST WITCH   I come, Grimalkin.
SECOND WITCH   Paddock² calls.
THIRD WITCH   Anon.°   *At once*
10   ALL   Fair is foul, and foul is fair,
      Hover through the fog and filthy air.   *Exeunt*

1.2

Alarum within. Enter KING [DUNCAN], MALCOLM, DON-
ALBAIN, LENNOX, *with attendants, meeting a bleeding*
CAPTAIN°   *staff officer*

KING DUNCAN   What bloody man is that? He can report,
      As seemeth by his plight, of the revolt
      The newest state.
MALCOLM   This is the sergeant
      Who like a good and hardy soldier fought
5   'Gainst my captivity. Hail, brave friend.
      Say to the King the knowledge of the broil°   *battle*
      As thou didst leave it.
CAPTAIN   Doubtful it stood,
      As two spent° swimmers that do cling together   *exhausted*
      And choke their art.¹ The merciless Macdonald—
10   Worthy to be a rebel, for to that°   *that end*
      The multiplying villainies of nature²
      Do swarm upon him—from the Western Isles°   *Hebrides and Ireland*
      Of kerns and galloglasses³ is supplied,
      And fortune on his damnèd quarry⁴ smiling
15   Showed° like a rebel's whore. But all's too weak,   *Appeared*
      For brave Macbeth—well he deserves that name!°—   *epithet*
      Disdaining fortune, with his brandished steel
      Which smoked with bloody execution,
      Like valour's minion°   *favorite*
20   Carved out his passage till he faced the slave,°   *(Macdonald)*
      Which° ne'er shook hands nor bade farewell to him   *Who*
      Till he unseamed him from the nave to th' chops·⁵
      And fixed his head upon our battlements.
KING DUNCAN   O valiant cousin,° worthy gentleman!   *kinsman*
25   CAPTAIN   As whence the sun 'gins his reflection⁶
      Shipwrecking storms and direful thunders break,
      So from that spring° whence comfort seemed to come   *source; (season)*
      Discomfort swells.° Mark, King of Scotland, mark.   *wells up*
      No sooner justice had, with valour armed,
30   Compelled these skipping° kerns to trust their heels   *mobile; fleeing*
      But the Norwegian lord, surveying vantage,°   *seeing his chance*
      With furbished° arms and new supplies of men   *polished*
      Began a fresh assault.
KING DUNCAN   Dismayed not this our captains, Macbeth and Banquo?

---

2. Paddock, a toad, and Grimalkin, a gray cat, are the witches' familiars, or attendant evil spirits.
1.2 Location: A camp near the battlefield.
1. And confound their skill in swimming.
2. The evil aspects of his own nature; the villainous progeny of nature (the mercenaries).
3. *kerns:* lightly armed Irish foot soldiers. *galloglasses:* ax-wielding horsemen.

4. Its condemned victim. Fortune smiled temporarily on Macdonald, although it had already marked him for destruction. Many editions emend "quarry" to "quarrel."
5. Ripped him open from the navel to the jaw, as one would rip open the seam of a garment.
6. Begins its return after the spring equinox, thought to cause turbulent weather.

35 CAPTAIN Yes, as sparrows eagles, or the hare the lion!
    If I say sooth I must report they were
    As cannons overcharged with double cracks,[7]
    So they doubly redoubled strokes upon the foe.
    Except° they meant to bathe in reeking wounds   *Unless*
40 Or memorize another Golgotha,[8]
    I cannot tell—
    But I am faint. My gashes cry for help.
KING DUNCAN So well thy words become thee as thy wounds:
    They smack of honour both.—Go get him surgeons.
                                    [*Exit* CAPTAIN *with attendants*]
        Enter ROSS *and* ANGUS
    Who comes here?
45 MALCOLM   The worthy Thane[9] of Ross.
LENNOX What haste looks through his eyes! So should he look
    That seems to° speak things strange.   *seems about to*
ROSS   God save the King.
KING DUNCAN Whence cam'st thou, worthy thane?
ROSS   From Fife, great King,
    Where the Norwegian banners flout° the sky   *mock*
50 And fan our people cold.°   *cold with fear*
    Norway° himself, with terrible numbers,   *The King of Norway*
    Assisted by that most disloyal traitor
    The Thane of Cawdor, began a dismal° conflict,   *an ominous*
    Till that° Bellona's bridegroom,[1] lapped in proof,[2]   *Until*
55 Confronted him with self-comparisons,°   *comparable deeds*
    Point° against point, rebellious arm 'gainst arm,   *Swordpoint*
    Curbing his lavish° spirit; and to conclude,   *wild*
    The victory fell on us—
KING DUNCAN   Great happiness.
ROSS   That now
    Sweno, the Norways'° king, craves composition;°   *Norwegians' / a truce*
60 Nor would we deign him burial of his men
    Till he disbursèd at Saint Colum's inch[3]
    Ten thousand dollars[4] to our general use.
KING DUNCAN No more that Thane of Cawdor shall deceive
    Our bosom interest.[5] Go pronounce his present° death,   *immediate*
65 And with his former title greet Macbeth.
ROSS I'll see it done.
KING DUNCAN What he hath lost, noble Macbeth hath won.
                            Exeunt severally°   *separately*

1.3

Thunder. Enter the three WITCHES
FIRST WITCH Where hast thou been, sister?
SECOND WITCH Killing swine.
THIRD WITCH   Sister, where thou?
FIRST WITCH A sailor's wife had chestnuts in her lap,
    And munched, and munched, and munched. 'Give me,' quoth I.

7. Overloaded with double charges of gunpowder.
8. Or make the battlefield as memorable as Golgotha, the "place of skulls" where Jesus was crucified.
9. Title of Scottish nobility.
1. Macbeth, imagined as husband to Bellona, the Roman goddess of war.
2. Clad in tested armor.

3. Incholm, the island of St. Columba in the Firth of Forth.
4. German and Spanish coins (first minted in the sixteenth century, five hundred years after the events of the play).
5. Our closest concerns.
1.3 Location: An open place.

5   'Aroint thee,° witch,' the rump-fed runnion¹ cries.   *Begone*
       Her husband's to Aleppo gone, master o'th' *Tiger*.
       But in a sieve I'll thither sail,
       And like a rat without a tail
       I'll do, I'll do, and I'll do.
10   SECOND WITCH   I'll give thee a wind.
       FIRST WITCH   Thou'rt kind.
       THIRD WITCH   And I another.
       FIRST WITCH   I myself have all the other,°   *others*
       And the very ports they blow,°   *blow from*
15   All the quarters° that they know   *directions*
       I'th' shipman's card.°   *compass card*
       I'll drain him dry as hay.
       Sleep shall neither night nor day
       Hang upon his penthouse lid.²
20   He shall live a man forbid.°   *cursed*
       Weary sennights° nine times nine   *weeks*
       Shall he dwindle, peak,° and pine.   *waste away*
       Though his barque cannot be lost,
       Yet it shall be tempest-tossed.
       Look what I have.
25   SECOND WITCH   Show me, show me.
       FIRST WITCH   Here I have a pilot's thumb,
       Wrecked as homeward he did come.
                       Drum within
       THIRD WITCH   A drum, a drum—
       Macbeth doth come.
30   ALL [*dancing in a ring*]   The weird³ sisters hand in hand,
       Posters° of the sea and land,   *Swift travelers*
       Thus do go about, about,
       Thrice to thine, and thrice to mine,
       And thrice again to make up nine.
35   Peace! The charm's wound up.
                       Enter MACBETH *and* BANQUO
       MACBETH   So foul and fair a day I have not seen.
       BANQUO   How far is't called° to Forres?—What are these,   *said to be*
       So withered, and so wild in their attire,
       That look not like th'inhabitants o'th' earth
40   And yet are on't?—Live you, or are you aught
       That man may question?° You seem to understand me   *converse with*
       By each at once her choppy° finger laying   *chapped*
       Upon her skinny lips. You should be women,
       And yet your beards forbid me to interpret
       That you are so.
45   MACBETH [*to the* WITCHES]   Speak, if you can. What are you?
       FIRST WITCH   All hail, Macbeth! Hail to thee, Thane of Glamis.
       SECOND WITCH   All hail, Macbeth! Hail to thee, Thane of Cawdor.
       THIRD WITCH   All hail, Macbeth, that shalt be king hereafter!
       BANQUO   Good sir, why do you start and seem to fear
50   Things that do sound so fair? [*To the* WITCHES] I'th' name of truth,
       Are ye fantastical° or that indeed   *imaginary*

1. The fat-rumped, mangy slut.   3. F: "weyward," from the Old English "wyrd," meaning
2. Eyelid, which projects out over the eye like the slop-   "fate."
ing roof of a penthouse.

Which outwardly ye show? My noble partner
You greet with present grace° and great prediction   *title*
Of noble having° and of royal hope,   *estate*
55   That he seems rapt withal.[4] To me you speak not.
If you can look into the seeds of time
And say which grain will grow and which will not,
Speak then to me, who neither beg nor fear
Your favours nor your hate.
60   FIRST WITCH   Hail!
SECOND WITCH   Hail!
THIRD WITCH   Hail!
FIRST WITCH   Lesser than Macbeth, and greater.
SECOND WITCH   Not so happy,° yet much happier.   *fortunate*
65   THIRD WITCH   Thou shalt get° kings, though thou be none.   *beget*
So all hail, Macbeth and Banquo!
FIRST WITCH   Banquo and Macbeth, all hail!
MACBETH   Stay, you imperfect° speakers, tell me more.   *incomplete*
By Sinel's° death I know I am Thane of Glamis,   *Macbeth's father*
70   But how of Cawdor? The Thane of Cawdor lives,
A prosperous gentleman, and to be king
Stands not within the prospect of belief,
No more than to be Cawdor. Say from whence
You owe° this strange intelligence,° or why   *possess / information*
75   Upon this blasted° heath you stop our way   *blighted*
With such prophetic greeting. Speak, I charge you.
          [*The*] WITCHES *vanish*
BANQUO   The earth hath bubbles, as the water has,
And these are of them. Whither are they vanished?
MACBETH   Into the air, and what seemed corporal°   *corporeal*
80   Melted as breath into the wind. Would they had stayed.
BANQUO   Were such things here as we do speak about,
Or have we eaten on the insane root[5]
That takes the reason prisoner?
MACBETH   Your children shall be kings.
BANQUO   You shall be king.
85   MACBETH   And Thane of Cawdor too. Went it not so?
BANQUO   To th' self-same tune and words. Who's here?
          Enter ROSS *and* ANGUS
ROSS   The King hath happily received, Macbeth,
The news of thy success, and when he reads°   *considers*
Thy personal venture° in the rebels' sight   *exploits*
90   His wonders and his praises do contend
Which should be thine or his; silenced with that,[6]
In viewing o'er the rest o'th' self-same day
He finds thee in the stout Norwegian ranks,
Nothing° afeard of what thyself didst make,   *Not at all*
95   Strange images° of death. As thick as hail   *forms*
Came post° with post, and every one did bear   *messenger*
Thy praises in his kingdom's great defence,
And poured them down before him.
ANGUS [*to* MACBETH]   We are sent

---

4. He seems entranced by these predictions.
5. Of the root causing insanity, possibly hemlock.
6. *His wonders . . . that:* Duncan does not know whether

to speak of his astonishment or his admiration, and so
is silent.

To give thee from our royal master thanks;
100 Only to herald thee into his sight,
Not pay thee.

ROSS   And, for an earnest° of a greater honour,   *a pledge*
He bade me from him call thee Thane of Cawdor,
In which addition,° hail, most worthy thane,   *title*
For it is thine.

105 BANQUO   What, can the devil speak true?

MACBETH   The Thane of Cawdor lives. Why do you dress me
In borrowed robes?

ANGUS   Who was the thane lives yet,
But under heavy judgement bears that life
Which he deserves to lose. Whether he was combined°   *allied*
110 With those of Norway, or did line the rebel°   *support Macdonald*
With hidden help and vantage,° or that with both   *benefit*
He laboured in his country's wrack,[7] I know not;
But treasons capital, confessed, and proved
Have overthrown him.

MACBETH [*aside*]   Glamis, and Thane of Cawdor.
115 The greatest is behind.° [*To* ROSS *and* ANGUS] Thanks for your pains.   *to come*
[*To* BANQUO] Do you not hope your children shall be kings
When those that gave the thane of Cawdor to me
Promised no less to them?

BANQUO   That, trusted home,°   *completely*
Might yet enkindle° you unto the crown,   *encourage*
120 Besides the thane of Cawdor. But 'tis strange,
And oftentimes to win us to our harm
The instruments of darkness tell us truths,
Win us with honest trifles to betray's°   *betray us*
In deepest consequence.
125 [*To* ROSS *and* ANGUS] Cousins, a word, I pray you.

MACBETH [*aside*]   Two truths are told
As happy prologues to the swelling act[8]
Of the imperial theme [*To* ROSS *and* ANGUS] I thank you, gentlemen.
[*Aside*] This supernatural soliciting°   *temptation*
130 Cannot be ill, cannot be good. If ill,
Why hath it given me earnest of success
Commencing in a truth? I am Thane of Cawdor.
If good, why do I yield to that suggestion
Whose horrid image doth unfix my hair
135 And make my seated heart knock at my ribs
Against the use° of nature? Present fears   *custom*
Are less than horrible imaginings.
My thought, whose murder yet is but fantastical,[9]
Shakes so my single state of man[1] that function°   *capacity to act*
140 Is smothered in surmise,° and nothing is   *speculation*
But what is not.

BANQUO [*to* ROSS *and* ANGUS]
                    Look how our partner's rapt.

MACBETH [*aside*]   If chance will have me king, why, chance may crown me
Without my stir.°   *effort*

---

7. He worked to bring about his country's ruin.
8. To the developing action, or climactic dramatic
action.
9. In which murder is so far only a fantasy.

1. My undivided self. Macbeth feels that his wholeness
is coming apart under the pressure of his criminal
thought.

BANQUO [*to* ROSS *and* ANGUS]
           New honours come upon him,
Like our strange° garments, cleave not to their mould°   *new / wearer's form*
But with the aid of use.

145 MACBETH [*aside*]   Come what come may,
Time and the hour runs through the roughest day.[2]

BANQUO   Worthy Macbeth, we stay° upon your leisure.   *wait; attend*

MACBETH   Give me your favour.° My dull brain was wrought°   *pardon / agitated*
With things forgotten. [*To* ROSS *and* ANGUS] Kind gentlemen,
    your pains
150 Are registered° where every day I turn   *recorded (in my memory)*
The leaf to read them. Let us toward the King.
[*Aside to* BANQUO] Think upon what hath chanced, and at
    more time,
The interim having weighed it, let us speak
Our free hearts° each to other.   *unconcealed thoughts*

155 BANQUO   Very gladly.

MACBETH   Till then, enough. [*To* ROSS *and* ANGUS] Come, friends.
                            Exeunt

1.4

Flourish. Enter KING [DUNCAN], LENNOX, MALCOLM,
DONALBAIN, *and attendants*

KING DUNCAN   Is execution done on Cawdor? Are not
Those in commission[1] yet returned?

MALCOLM   My liege,
They are not yet come back. But I have spoke
With one that saw him die, who did report
5 That very frankly he confessed his treasons,
Implored your highness' pardon, and set forth
A deep repentance. Nothing in his life
Became him like the leaving it. He died
As one that had been studied° in his death   *practiced*
10 To throw away the dearest thing he owed°   *owned*
As 'twere a careless° trifle.   *an uncared-for*

KING DUNCAN   There's no art
To find the mind's construction in the face.
He was a gentleman on whom I built
An absolute trust.
      Enter MACBETH, BANQUO, ROSS, *and* ANGUS
[*To* MACBETH] O worthiest cousin,
15 The sin of my ingratitude even now
Was heavy on me! Thou art so far before°   *ahead*
That swiftest wing of recompense is slow
To overtake thee. Would thou hadst less deserved,
That the proportion both of thanks and payment
20 Might have been mine.[2] Only I have left to say,
'More is thy due than more than all can pay'.

MACBETH   The service and the loyalty I owe,
In doing it, pays itself. Your highness' part
Is to receive our duties, and our duties

---

2. *Come . . . day:* What must happen will happen one way or another.
1.4 Location: A camp near the battlefield.

1. Those charged to execute Cawdor.
2. *That . . . mine:* That the King's rewards would be generously proportional to Macbeth's dessert.

25   Are to your throne and state children and servants
      Which do but what they should by doing everything
      Safe toward° your love and honour.   °To safeguard

KING DUNCAN   Welcome hither.
      I have begun to plant thee, and will labour
      To make thee full of growing.—Noble Banquo,
30   That hast no less deserved, nor must be known
      No less to have done so, let me enfold thee
      And hold thee to my heart.

BANQUO   There if I grow
      The harvest is your own.

KING DUNCAN   My plenteous joys,
      Wanton° in fullness, seek to hide themselves   °Unrestrained
35   In drops of sorrow. Sons, kinsmen, thanes,
      And you whose places are the nearest,° know   °nearest to the throne
      We will establish our estate³ upon
      Our eldest, Malcolm, whom we name hereafter
      The Prince of Cumberland;⁴ which honour must
40   Not unaccompanied invest him only,⁵
      But signs of nobleness, like stars, shall shine
      On all deservers. [To MACBETH] From hence to Inverness,°   °Macbeth's estate
      And bind us further to you.⁶

MACBETH   The rest is labour which is not used for you.⁷
45   I'll be myself the harbinger,⁸ and make joyful
      The hearing of my wife with your approach;
      So humbly take my leave.

KING DUNCAN   My worthy Cawdor.

MACBETH [aside]   The Prince of Cumberland—that is a step
      On which I must fall down or else o'erleap,
50   For in my way it lies. Stars, hide your fires,
      Let not light see my black and deep desires;
      The eye wink at the hand;⁹ yet let that be°   °be done
      Which the eye fears, when it is done, to see.   Exit

KING DUNCAN   True, worthy Banquo, he is full so valiant,¹
55   And in his commendations I am fed.
      It is a banquet to me. Let's after him,
      Whose care is gone before to bid us welcome.
      It is a peerless kinsman.   Flourish. Exeunt

1.5

Enter [LADY MACBETH,] with a letter

LADY MACBETH [reading]   'They met me in the day of success,
      and I have learned by the perfect'st° report they have more in   °most accurate
      them than mortal knowledge. When I burned in desire to ques-
      tion them further, they made themselves air, into which they
5   vanished. Whiles I stood rapt in the wonder of it came missives°   °messengers
      from the King, who all-hailed me "Thane of Cawdor", by
      which title before these weird sisters saluted me, and referred
      me to the coming on of time with "Hail, King that shalt be!"

3. We will settle the succession of the kingdom. At the
time, the Scottish crown was not hereditary.
4. Title of the Scottish heir apparent.
5. which . . . only: honors will not be bestowed on
Malcolm alone.
6. And make me further indebted to you by your hospitality.

7. Even repose seems wearisome when it is not dedicated to your purposes.
8. Forerunner; messenger sent ahead to arrange royal
lodgings.
9. Let the eye deliberately ignore what the hand does.
1. As valiant as you say.
1.5 Location: Inverness, Macbeth's castle.

This have I thought good to deliver° thee, my dearest partner   *inform*
10 of greatness, that thou mightst not lose the dues of rejoicing
by being ignorant of what greatness is promised thee. Lay it
to thy heart, and farewell.'
Glamis thou art, and Cawdor, and shalt be
What thou art promised. Yet do I fear° thy nature.   *doubt*
15 It is too full o'th' milk of human kindness
To catch the nearest° way. Thou wouldst be great,   *most expedient*
Art not without ambition, but without
The illness° should attend it. What thou wouldst highly,   *wickedness (that)*
That wouldst thou holily; wouldst not play false,
20 And yet wouldst wrongly win. Thou'dst have, great Glamis,
That which cries 'Thus thou must do' if thou have it,
And that which rather thou dost fear to do
Than wishest should be undone. Hie° thee hither,   *Hasten*
That I may pour my spirits in thine ear
25 And chastise with the valour of my tongue
All that impedes thee from the golden round°   *crown*
Which fate and metaphysical° aid doth seem   *supernatural*
To have thee crowned withal.°   *with*
        Enter [a SERVANT]
                                   What is your tidings?
SERVANT   The King comes here tonight.
LADY MACBETH   Thou'rt mad to say it.
30 Is not thy master with him, who, were't so,
Would have informed for preparation?
SERVANT   So please you, it is true. Our thane is coming,
One of my fellows had the speed of° him,   *outdistanced*
Who, almost dead for breath, had scarcely more
Than would make up his message.
35 LADY MACBETH   Give him tending;
He brings great news.   *Exit [*SERVANT]
                        The raven[1] himself is hoarse
That croaks the fatal entrance of Duncan
Under my battlements. Come, you spirits
That tend on mortal° thoughts, unsex me here,   *attend deadly*
40 And fill me from the crown to the toe top-full
Of direst cruelty. Make thick my blood,
Stop up th'access and passage to remorse,°   *pity*
That no compunctious visitings of nature
Shake my fell° purpose, nor keep peace° between   *cruel / intervene*
45 Th'effect and it.[2] Come to my woman's breasts,
And take my milk for° gall, you murd'ring ministers,°   *in exchange for / agents*
Wherever in your sightless° substances   *invisible*
You wait on° nature's mischief. Come, thick night,   *assist*
And pall° thee in the dunnest° smoke of hell,   *envelop / darkest*
50 That my keen knife see not the wound it makes,
Nor heaven peep through the blanket of the dark
To cry 'Hold, hold!'
        Enter MACBETH
                        Great Glamis, worthy Cawdor,
Greater than both by the all-hail hereafter,

---

1. The raven was considered a bird of ill omen.   2. My purpose and its accomplishment.

Thy letters have transported me beyond
55 This ignorant present, and I feel now
The future in the instant.

MACBETH   My dearest love,
Duncan comes here tonight.

LADY MACBETH   And when goes hence?

MACBETH Tomorrow, as he purposes.

LADY MACBETH   O never
Shall sun that morrow see.
60 Your face, my thane, is as a book where men
May read strange matters. To beguile the time,
Look like the time;³ bear welcome in your eye,
Your hand, your tongue; look like the innocent flower,
But be the serpent under't. He that's coming
65 Must be provided for; and you shall put
This night's great business into my dispatch,°   management
Which shall to all our nights and days to come
Give solely sovereign sway and masterdom.

MACBETH We will speak further.

LADY MACBETH   Only look up clear.°   appear innocent
70 To alter favour⁴ ever is to fear.
Leave all the rest to me.   *Exeunt*

1.6

Hautboys° and torches. Enter KING [DUNCAN], MAL-   Oboes
COLM, DONALBAIN, BANQUO, LENNOX, MACDUFF, ROSS,
ANGUS, *and attendants*

KING DUNCAN This castle hath a pleasant seat.° The air   location
Nimbly and sweetly recommends itself
Unto our gentle senses.

BANQUO   This guest of summer,
The temple-haunting martlet,¹ does approve°   prove
5 By his loved mansionry° that the heavens' breath   nest building
Smells wooingly here. No jutty,° frieze,   projection
Buttress, nor coign of vantage° but this bird   convenient corner
Hath made his pendant bed and procreant° cradle;   for breeding
Where they most breed and haunt I have observed
The air is delicate.

Enter LADY [MACBETH]

10 KING DUNCAN   See, see, our honoured hostess!
The love that follows us sometime is our trouble,
Which still we thank as love.² Herein I teach you
How you shall bid God 'ield us for your pains,
And thank us for your trouble.³

LADY MACBETH   All our service
15 In every point twice done, and then done double,
Were° poor and single° business to contend   Would be / small
Against those honours deep and broad wherewith
Your majesty loads our house. For those of old,
And the late dignities heaped up to them,

3. *To . . . like the time:* To deceive the world, match your
expression to the occasion.
4. To alter your facial expression and thereby arouse
suspicion.
1.6 Location: Outside Macbeth's castle.

1. A bird, the martin, that often built its nest in churches.
2. *The . . . love:* Love bestowed upon us sometimes
causes us inconvenience, but we are still grateful for it.
3. *How . . . trouble:* Ask God to reward ("yield") me for
the trouble I cause you.

We rest your hermits.[4]

20 KING DUNCAN   Where's the Thane of Cawdor?
We coursed him at the heels,° and had a purpose   *followed him closely*
To be his purveyor;[5] but he rides well,
And his great love, sharp as his spur, hath holp° him   *helped*
To his home before us. Fair and noble hostess,
We are your guest tonight.

25 LADY MACBETH   Your servants ever
Have theirs, themselves, and what is theirs in count°   *in trust*
To make their audit at your highness' pleasure,
Still to return your own.[6]

KING DUNCAN   Give me your hand.
Conduct me to mine host. We love him highly,
30 And shall continue our graces towards him.
By your leave,[7] hostess.   *Exeunt*

1.7

Hautboys. Torches. Enter a sewer° and divers servants   *butler*
with dishes and service over the stage. Then enter MACBETH

MACBETH   If it were done when 'tis done, then 'twere well
It were done quickly. If th'assassination
Could trammel up the consequence, and catch
With his surcease success:[1] that but this blow
5 Might be the be-all and the end-all, here,°   *in this world*
But here upon this bank and shoal[2] of time,
We'd jump° the life to come. But in these cases   *risk*
We still have judgement[3] here, that° we but teach   *in that*
Bloody instructions which, being taught, return
10 To plague th'inventor. This even-handed° justice   *impartial*
Commends th'ingredience° of our poisoned chalice   *contents*
To our own lips. He's here in double trust:
First, as I am his kinsman and his subject,
Strong both against the deed; then, as his host,
15 Who should against his murderer shut the door,
Not bear the knife myself. Besides, this Duncan
Hath borne his faculties° so meek, hath been   *authority*
So clear° in his great office, that his virtues   *blameless*
Will plead like angels, trumpet-tongued against
20 The deep damnation of his taking-off,°   *murder*
And pity, like a naked new-born babe,
Striding the blast,[4] or heaven's cherubin, horsed
Upon the sightless couriers[5] of the air,
Shall blow the horrid deed in every eye

4. We remain your beadsmen (monks hired to pray for
their employers).
5. Attendant who preceded the King when he traveled
and procured foodstuffs for the royal party.
6. *Your servants . . . own:* Your servants hold all that they
have in trust from you, and they are always ready to settle accounts and return to you what is yours.
7. By your permission. A request for permission to leave
or perhaps for a formal kiss.
1.7 Location: A courtyard or an anteroom in Macbeth's
castle.
1. *If th'assassination . . . success:* If only I could gain

success with Duncan's death (his "surcease"); if only
the assassination were the end of the matter. *trammel up
the consequence:* restrain the subsequent sequence of
events, as in a trammel, or net.
2. Sandbar. The mortal span is seen as a narrow piece of
land in the river of time. F has "Schoole," and "bank"
may also mean "bench," suggesting that life is a time of
instruction and probation.
3. We are invariably punished.
4. Astride the storm provoked by Duncan's death.
5. The invisible runners, the winds.

25   That tears shall drown the wind.[6] I have no spur
          To prick the sides of my intent, but only
          Vaulting ambition which o'erleaps itself
          And falls on th'other.[7]

Enter LADY [MACBETH]

                          How now? What news?

LADY MACBETH   He has almost supped. Why have you left the chamber?

MACBETH   Hath he asked for me?

30 LADY MACBETH   Know you not he has?

      MACBETH   We will proceed no further in this business.
          He hath honoured me of late, and I have bought°   *won*
          Golden opinions from all sorts of people,
          Which would be worn now in their newest gloss,
          Not cast aside so soon.

35 LADY MACBETH   Was the hope drunk
          Wherein you dressed yourself? Hath it slept since?
          And wakes it now to look so green° and pale   *sickly*
          At what it did so freely? From this time
          Such I account thy love. Art thou afeard
40   To be the same in thine own act and valour
          As thou art in desire? Wouldst thou have that°   *(the crown)*
          Which thou esteem'st the ornament of life,
          And live a coward in thine own esteem,
          Letting 'I dare not' wait upon 'I would',
          Like the poor cat i'th' adage?[8]

45 MACBETH   Prithee, peace.
          I dare do all that may become a man;
          Who dares do more is none.

      LADY MACBETH   What beast was't then
          That made you break° this enterprise to me?   *broach*
          When you durst do it, then you were a man;
50   And to be more than what you were, you would
          Be so much more the man. Nor time nor place
          Did then adhere,° and yet you would make both.   *agree*
          They have made themselves, and that their fitness now
          Does unmake you. I have given suck, and know
55   How tender 'tis to love the babe that milks me.
          I would, while it was smiling in my face,
          Have plucked my nipple from his boneless gums
          And dashed the brains out, had I so sworn
          As you have done to this.

      MACBETH   If we should fail?

      LADY MACBETH   We fail![9]
60   But screw your courage to the sticking-place[1]
          And we'll not fail. When Duncan is asleep—
          Whereto the rather shall his day's hard journey
          Soundly invite him—his two chamberlains°   *bedroom attendants*
          Will I with wine and wassail° so convince°   *carousing / overpower*
65   That memory, the warder° of the brain,   *guard*
          Shall be a fume, and the receipt° of reason   *receptacle*

---

6. Tears will fall like heavy rain, which was believed to still the wind.

7. The other side. The image is of a rider vaulting over his horse instead of into his saddle, or of a horseman who clears a high obstacle but falls on the other side.

8. Proverbial: "The cat would eat fish but does not dare to wet her feet."

9. F: "faile?"

1. The notch on a crossbow that holds the string, which is cranked or screwed taut.

A limbeck[2] only. When in swinish sleep
Their drenchèd natures lies as in a death,
What cannot you and I perform upon
70 Th'unguarded Duncan? What not put upon
His spongy officers, who shall bear the guilt
Of our great quell?°   *murder*
MACBETH   Bring forth men-children only,
For thy undaunted mettle° should compose   *substance*
Nothing but males. Will it not be received,°   *believed*
75 When we have marked with blood those sleepy two
Of his own chamber and used their very daggers,
That they have done't?
LADY MACBETH   Who dares receive it other,
As we shall make our griefs and clamour roar
Upon his death?
MACBETH   I am settled, and bend up
80 Each corporal° agent to this terrible feat.   *bodily*
Away, and mock° the time with fairest show.   *deceive*
False face must hide what the false heart doth know.

                                        Exeunt

                    2.1
          Enter BANQUO *and* FLEANCE, *with a torch*
          before him
BANQUO   How goes the night, boy?[1]
FLEANCE   The moon is down. I have not heard the clock.
BANQUO   And she goes down at twelve.
FLEANCE   I take't 'tis later, sir.
BANQUO [*giving* FLEANCE *his sword*]   Hold, take my sword.
          There's husbandry° in heaven,   *thrift*
5 Their candles are all out. Take thee that,[2] too.
A heavy summons° lies like lead upon me,   *summons to sleep*
And yet I would not sleep. Merciful powers,[3]
Restrain in me the cursèd thoughts that nature
Gives way to in repose.
          Enter MACBETH, *and a servant with a torch*
                              Give me my sword. Who's there?
10 MACBETH   A friend.
BANQUO   What, sir, not yet at rest? The King's a-bed.
He hath been in unusual pleasure, and
Sent forth great largesse° to your offices.[4]   *gifts*
This diamond he greets your wife withal
15 By the name of most kind hostess, and shut up°   *concluded*
In measureless content.
MACBETH   Being unprepared
Our will became the servant to defect,
Which else should free have wrought.[5]
BANQUO   All's well.
I dreamt last night of the three weird sisters.
To you they have showed some truth.

2. Alembic, the upper part of a still to which fumes rise.
The wine will make the memory a fume that will fill and
cloud the brain, the "receptacle of reason."
2.1 Location: The courtyard of Macbeth's castle.
1. How much of the night has passed?
2. Some article of clothing or armor.

3. Angels invoked as protection against demons.
4. Household departments.
5. *Being . . . wrought*: Our desire to entertain the King
liberally was constrained by the fact that we were unprepared. *defect*: deficiency. *free*: freely.

20 MACBETH   I think not of them;
    Yet, when we can entreat an hour to serve,
    We would spend it in some words upon that business
    If you would grant the time.
    BANQUO   At your kind'st leisure.
    MACBETH   If you shall cleave to my consent when 'tis,⁶
    It shall make honour for you.
25 BANQUO   So° I lose none   Provided
    In seeking to augment it, but still keep
    My bosom franchised° and allegiance clear,°   guiltless / unstained
    I shall be counselled.°   receptive
    MACBETH   Good repose the while.
30 BANQUO   Thanks, sir. The like to you.
                                   Exeunt BANQUO [and FLEANCE]
    MACBETH [to the Servant]   Go bid thy mistress, when my drink is ready,
    She strike upon the bell. Get thee to bed.   Exit [Servant]
    Is this a dagger which I see before me,
    The handle toward my hand? Come, let me clutch thee.
35 I have thee not, and yet I see thee still.
    Art thou not, fatal vision, sensible°   perceptible
    To feeling as to sight? Or art thou but
    A dagger of the mind, a false creation
    Proceeding from the heat-oppressèd° brain?   fevered
40 I see thee yet, in form as palpable
    As this which now I draw.
    Thou marshall'st° me the way that I was going,   guide
    And such an instrument I was to use.
    Mine eyes are made the fools o'th' other senses,
45 Or else worth all the rest. I see thee still,
    And on thy blade and dudgeon gouts° of blood,   and handle drops
    Which was not so before. There's no such thing.
    It is the bloody business which informs°   creates shapes
    Thus to mine eyes. Now o'er the one half-world
50 Nature seems dead, and wicked dreams abuse°   deceive
    The curtained sleep. Witchcraft celebrates
    Pale Hecate's offerings,⁷ and withered murder,
    Alarumed° by his sentinel the wolf,   Roused
    Whose howl's his watch,° thus with his stealthy pace, watchword
55 With Tarquin's⁸ ravishing strides, towards his design°   prey
    Moves like a ghost. Thou sure and firm-set earth,
    Hear not my steps which way they walk, for fear
    Thy very stones prate of my whereabout,
    And take the present horror° from the time,   terrible stillness
60 Which now suits with it. Whiles I threat, he lives.
    Words to the heat of deeds too cold breath gives.
          A bell rings
    I go, and it is done. The bell invites me.
    Hear it not, Duncan; for it is a knell
    That summons thee to heaven or to hell.   Exit

6. If you will support my opinion or my cause when the   8. A Roman prince who ravished the chaste matron
time comes.   Lucrece. Shakespeare tells the story in *The Rape of*
7. Sacrificial rites offered to Hecate, Greek goddess of *Lucrece.*
witchcraft and of the moon.

2.2

Enter LADY [MACBETH]

LADY MACBETH   That which hath made them drunk hath made me bold.
What hath quenched them hath given me fire. Hark, peace!—
It was the owl that shrieked, the fatal bellman°   *night watchman*
Which gives the stern'st good-night.[1] He is about it.
5   The doors are open, and the surfeited grooms°   *attendants*
Do mock their charge° with snores. I have drugged their   *duty*
possets°   *mulled milk and wine*
That death and nature do contend about them
Whether they live or die.

Enter MACBETH [*above*]

MACBETH   Who's there? What ho?   [*Exit*]

LADY MACBETH   Alack, I am afraid they have awaked,
10   And 'tis not done. Th'attempt and not the deed
Confounds° us. Hark!—I laid their daggers ready;   *Ruins*
He could not miss 'em. Had he not resembled
My father as he slept, I had done't.

      [*Enter* MACBETH *below*]

                                My husband!

MACBETH   I have done the deed. Didst thou not hear a noise?
15   LADY MACBETH   I heard the owl scream and the crickets cry.
Did not you speak?

MACBETH   When?

LADY MACBETH   Now.

MACBETH   As I descended?

LADY MACBETH   Ay.

MACBETH   Hark!—Who lies i'th' second chamber?

LADY MACBETH   Donalbain.

MACBETH [*looking at his hands*]   This is a sorry sight.

LADY MACBETH   A foolish thought, to say a sorry sight.

20   MACBETH   There's one did laugh in's sleep, and one cried 'Murder!'
That they did wake each other. I stood and heard them.
But they did say their prayers and addressed them°   *settled themselves*
Again to sleep.

LADY MACBETH   There are two lodged together.

MACBETH   One cried 'God bless us' and 'Amen' the other,
25   As° they had seen me with these hangman's[2] hands.   *As if*
List'ning their fear I could not say 'Amen'
When they did say 'God bless us.'

LADY MACBETH   Consider it not so deeply.

MACBETH   But wherefore could not I pronounce 'Amen'?
30   I had most need of blessing, and 'Amen'
Stuck in my throat.

LADY MACBETH   These deeds must not be thought°   *thought on*
After these ways. So, it will make us mad.

MACBETH   Methought I heard a voice cry 'Sleep no more,
Macbeth does murder sleep'—the innocent sleep,
35   Sleep that knits up the ravelled sleave° of care,   *tangled skein*
The death of each day's life, sore labour's bath,

2.2 **Location:** Scene continues with only a brief pause.   2. Bloodstained. The hangman had to disembowel and
1. A bell was rung outside the cells of condemned pris-   quarter his victims.
oners the night before they were to be executed.

Balm of hurt minds, great nature's second course,[3]
Chief nourisher in life's feast—
LADY MACBETH   What do you mean?
MACBETH   Still it cried 'Sleep no more' to all the house,
40   'Glamis hath murdered sleep, and therefore Cawdor
Shall sleep no more, Macbeth shall sleep no more.'
LADY MACBETH   Who was it that thus cried? Why, worthy thane,
You do unbend° your noble strength to think   slacken
So brain-sickly of things. Go get some water
45   And wash this filthy witness° from your hand.   evidence
Why did you bring these daggers from the place?
They must lie there. Go, carry them, and smear
The sleepy grooms with blood.
MACBETH   I'll go no more.
I am afraid to think what I have done,
Look on't again I dare not.
50   LADY MACBETH   Infirm of purpose!
Give me the daggers. The sleeping and the dead
Are but as pictures. 'Tis the eye of childhood
That fears a painted devil. If he do bleed
I'll gild[4] the faces of the grooms withal,
For it must seem their guilt.   *Exit*
                    Knock within
55   MACBETH   Whence is that knocking?—
How is't with me when every noise appals me?
What hands are here! Ha, they pluck out mine eyes.
Will all great Neptune's ocean wash this blood
Clean from my hand? No, this my hand will rather
60   The multitudinous seas incarnadine,°   turn red
Making the green one red.[5]
                    Enter LADY [MACBETH]
LADY MACBETH   My hands are of your colour, but I shame
To wear a heart so white.
                    Knock [*within*]
                    I hear a knocking
At the south entry. Retire we to our chamber.
65   A little water clears us of this deed.
How easy is it then! Your constancy
Hath left you unattended.[6]
                    Knock [*within*]
                    Hark, more knocking.
Get on your nightgown, lest occasion call us
And show us to be watchers.[7] Be not lost
70   So poorly in your thoughts.
MACBETH   To know my deed 'twere best not know myself.[8]
                    Knock [*within*]
Wake Duncan with thy knocking. I would thou couldst.
                    Exeunt

---

3. Second, and most nourishing, course of a meal; second, or alternative, habit or practice.
4. Coat as if with gold leaf. Gold was often called red;
compare 2.3.109.
5. *one red:* entirely red.

6. *Your . . . unattended:* Your resolve has deserted you.
7. Those who have stayed awake.
8. It is better that I lose consciousness altogether than
face my deed.

2.3

Enter a PORTER. *Knocking within*

PORTER   Here's a knocking indeed! If a man were porter of hell-
gate he should have old° turning the key.   *plenty of*

Knock [within]

Knock, knock, knock. Who's there, i'th' name of Beelzebub?°   *name of a devil*
Here's a farmer that hanged himself on th'expectation of
5   plenty.[1] Come in time![2] Have napkins° enough about you; here   *handkerchiefs*
you'll sweat for't.

Knock [within]

Knock, knock. Who's there, in th'other devil's name? Faith,
here's an equivocator[3] that could swear in both the scales
against either scale, who committed treason enough for God's
10   sake, yet could not equivocate to heaven. O, come in, equivocator.

Knock [within]

Knock, knock, knock. Who's there? 'Faith, here's an English
tailor come hither for stealing out of a French hose.[4] Come in,
tailor. Here you may roast your goose.[5]

Knock [within]

15   Knock, knock. Never at quiet. What are you?—But this place
is too cold for hell. I'll devil-porter it no further. I had thought
to have let in some of all professions that go the primrose way
to th'everlasting bonfire.

Knock [within]

Anon, anon!

[He opens the gate]

20   I pray you remember the porter.

Enter MACDUFF *and* LENNOX

MACDUFF   Was it so late, friend, ere you went to bed
That you do lie so late?

PORTER   Faith, sir, we were carousing till the second cock,° and   *3:00 A.M.*
drink, sir, is a great provoker of three things.

25   MACDUFF   What three things does drink especially provoke?

PORTER   Marry,° sir, nose-painting,[6] sleep, and urine. Lechery,   *Indeed*
sir, it provokes and unprovokes: it provokes the desire but it
takes away the performance. Therefore much drink may be
said to be an equivocator with lechery: it makes him and it
30   mars him; it sets him on and it takes him off; it persuades him
and disheartens him, makes him stand to° and not stand to; in   *maintain an erection*
conclusion, equivocates him in a sleep,[7] and, giving him the
lie,[8] leaves him.

MACDUFF   I believe drink gave thee the lie last night.

35   PORTER   That it did, sir, i'the very throat on me;[9] but I requited

---

2.3 Location: Scene continues, perhaps after a short pause.
1. *Here's . . . plenty:* A farmer had hoarded grain to sell at high prices but was ruined by a crop surplus that forced prices down.
2. Good timing.
3. One who speaks ambiguously. An allusion to the Jesuit doctrine that a seemingly false statement was not a lie (and therefore not repugnant to God) if the speaker had in mind a different meaning in which the utterance was true. Possibly an allusion to the 1606 trial of the Jesuit Henry Garnet for involvement in the Gunpowder Plot to blow up the Houses of Parliament; Father Garnet had

written a treatise defending equivocation for Catholics being persecuted for their beliefs.
4. Tight-fitting breeches, which would easily reveal the tailor's attempt to skimp on the cloth supplied him for their manufacture. He had apparently been able to do so undetected when loose-fitting breeches were in fashion.
5. Heat your smoothing iron.
6. Reddening of the nose through drink.
7. Gives him an erotic experience in dreams only.
8. An elaborate pun: calling him a liar; laying him out flat; making him urinate ("lye," or urine).
9. *i'the . . . me:* provoking a duel by insulting me with a deliberate lie.

him for his lie, and, I think, being too strong for him, though
he took up my legs sometime, yet I made a shift to cast him.[1]

MACDUFF   Is thy master stirring?

Enter MACBETH

Our knocking has awaked him: here he comes.   [*Exit* PORTER]

LENNOX [*to* MACBETH]   Good morrow, noble sir.

40   MACBETH   Good morrow, both.

MACDUFF   Is the King stirring, worthy thane?

MACBETH   Not yet.

MACDUFF   He did command me to call timely° on him.   early
I have almost slipped the hour.

MACBETH   I'll bring you to him.

MACDUFF   I know this is a joyful trouble to you,
45   But yet 'tis one.

MACBETH   The labour we delight in physics pain.[2]
This is the door.

MACDUFF   I'll make so bold to call,
For 'tis my limited° service.   *Exit* MACDUFF   appointed

LENNOX   Goes the King hence today?

MACBETH   He does; he did appoint so.

50   LENNOX   The night has been unruly. Where we lay
Our chimneys were blown down, and, as they say,
Lamentings heard i'th' air, strange screams of death,
And prophesying with accents terrible
Of dire combustion° and confused events   tumult
55   New-hatched to th' woeful time. The obscure bird[3]
Clamoured the livelong night. Some say the earth
Was feverous and did shake.

MACBETH   'Twas a rough night.

LENNOX   My young remembrance cannot parallel
A fellow to it.

Enter MACDUFF

MACDUFF   O horror, horror, horror!
60   Tongue nor heart cannot conceive nor name thee.

MACBETH *and* LENNOX   What's the matter?

MACDUFF   Confusion° now hath made his masterpiece.   Ruin
Most sacrilegious murder hath broke ope
The Lord's anointed temple° and stole thence   (the King's body)
65   The life o'th' building.

MACBETH   What is't you say—the life?

LENNOX   Mean you his majesty?

MACDUFF   Approach the chamber and destroy your sight
With a new Gorgon.[4] Do not bid me speak.
See, and then speak yourselves. *Exeunt* MACBETH *and* LENNOX
70   Awake, awake!
Ring the alarum bell. Murder and treason!
Banquo and Donalbain, Malcolm, awake!
Shake off this downy sleep, death's counterfeit,
And look on death itself. Up, up, and see
75   The great doom's image.° Malcolm, Banquo,   replica of Doomsday
As from your graves rise up, and walk like sprites

1. *being . . . cast him:* the effects of drunkenness are   3. The owl, bird of darkness.
described in the language of a wrestling match. *cast:*   4. A mythical monster with a woman's figure and snakes
throw off; vomit.   for hair, the sight of whose face turned beholders to
2. Pleasure in labor mitigates its laboriousness.   stone. Medusa was one of the three Gorgons.

To countenance° this horror.   *suit; behold*
        Bell rings. Enter LADY [MACBETH]

LADY MACBETH   What's the business,
  That such a hideous trumpet calls to parley
  The sleepers of the house? Speak, speak.

MACDUFF   O gentle lady,
80   'Tis not for you to hear what I can speak.
  The repetition° in a woman's ear   *report*
  Would murder as it fell.
        Enter BANQUO
                  O Banquo, Banquo,
  Our royal master's murdered!

LADY MACBETH   Woe, alas—
  What, in our house?

BANQUO   Too cruel anywhere.
85   Dear Duff, I prithee contradict thyself,
  And say it is not so.
        Enter MACBETH, LENNOX, *and* ROSS

MACBETH   Had I but died an hour before this chance°   *occurrence*
  I had lived a blessèd time, for from this instant
  There's nothing serious in mortality.°   *worth living for*
90   All is but toys.° Renown and grace is dead.   *trifles*
  The wine of life is drawn, and the mere lees
  Is left this vault° to brag of.   *wine vault; world*
        Enter MALCOLM *and* DONALBAIN

DONALBAIN   What is amiss?

MACBETH   You are, and do not know't.
95   The spring, the head, the fountain of your blood
  Is stopped, the very source of it is stopped.

MACDUFF   Your royal father's murdered.

MALCOLM   O, by whom?

LENNOX   Those of his chamber, as it seemed, had done't.
  Their hands and faces were all badged° with blood,   *marked*
100 So were their daggers, which, unwiped, we found
  Upon their pillows. They stared and were distracted.
  No man's life was to be trusted with them.

MACBETH   O, yet I do repent me of my fury
  That I did kill them.

MACDUFF   Wherefore did you so?
105 MACBETH   Who can be wise, amazed, temp'rate and furious,
  Loyal and neutral in a moment? No man.
  Th'expedition° of my violent love   *haste*
  Outran the pauser,° reason. Here lay Duncan,   *delayer*
  His silver skin laced with his golden blood,
110 And his gashed stabs looked like a breach in nature
  For ruin's wasteful° entrance; there the murderers,   *destructive*
  Steeped in the colours of their trade, their daggers
  Unmannerly breeched[5] with gore. Who could refrain,
  That had a heart to love, and in that heart
  Courage to make 's love known?
115 LADY MACBETH   Help me hence, ho!

MACDUFF   Look to the lady.

MALCOLM [*aside to* DONALBAIN] Why do we hold our tongues,

---

5. Covered—as if with breeches—with blood.

That most may claim this argument° for ours?   subject
DONALBAIN [aside to MALCOLM]   What should be spoken here,
    where our fate,
Hid in an auger-hole,° may rush and seize us?   in a cranny; in ambush
Let's away. Our tears are not yet brewed.
120 MALCOLM [aside to DONALBAIN]   Nor our strong sorrow
Upon the foot of motion.[6]
  BANQUO   Look to the lady;
            [Exit LADY MACBETH, attended]
And when we have our naked frailties hid,°   clothed
That suffer in exposure, let us meet
And question° this most bloody piece of work,   discuss
125 To know it further. Fears and scruples° shake us.   doubts
In the great hand of God I stand, and thence
Against the undivulged pretence I fight
Of treasonous malice.[7]
MACDUFF   And so do I.
ALL   So all.
MACBETH   Let's briefly° put on manly readiness,°   quickly / clothes; resolve
And meet i'th' hall together.
130 ALL   Well contented.
      Exeunt [all but MALCOLM and DONALBAIN]
MALCOLM   What will you do? Let's not consort with them.
To show an unfelt sorrow is an office
Which the false man does easy. I'll to England.
DONALBAIN   To Ireland, I. Our separated fortune
135 Shall keep us both the safer. Where we are
There's daggers in men's smiles. The nea'er in blood,
The nearer bloody.[8]
MALCOLM   This murderous shaft that's shot
Hath not yet lighted,° and our safest way   fallen
Is to avoid the aim. Therefore to horse,
140 And let us not be dainty of° leave-taking,   polite about
But shift° away. There's warrant° in that theft   slip / justification
Which steals itself[9] when there's no mercy left.   Exeunt

2.4

    Enter ROSS with an OLD MAN
OLD MAN   Threescore and ten I can remember well,
Within the volume of which time I have seen
Hours dreadful and things strange, but this sore night
Hath trifled former knowings.[1]
  ROSS   Ha, good father,
5   Thou seest the heavens, as troubled with man's act,
Threatens his bloody stage. By th' clock 'tis day,
And yet dark night strangles the travelling lamp.°   sun
Is't night's predominance° or the day's shame   ascendancy
That darkness does the face of earth entomb
When living light should kiss it?
10 OLD MAN   'Tis unnatural,

---

6. Nor . . . motion: Nor has our strong sorrow yet begun   nearer the danger of murder.
to express itself.   9. Which steals itself: Malcolm alludes to the fact that he
7. Against . . . malice: I will fight against the hidden pur-   and Donalbain intend to "steal" away from the castle.
pose behind this treasonous act.   2.4 Location: Not far from Macbeth's castle.
8. The nea'er . . . bloody: The closer the kinship, the   1. Has made previous experiences seem trifling.

Even like the deed that's done. On Tuesday last
A falcon, tow'ring in her pride of place,[2]
Was by a mousing owl[3] hawked at and killed.

ROSS   And Duncan's horses— a thing most strange and certain—
15   Beauteous and swift, the minions° of their race,   *darlings*
Turned wild in nature, broke their stalls, flung out,
Contending 'gainst obedience, as° they would   *as if*
Make war with mankind.

OLD MAN   'Tis said they ate each other.

ROSS   They did so, to th'amazement of mine eyes
That looked upon't.

                    Enter MACDUFF

20   Here comes the good Macduff.
How goes the world, sir, now?

MACDUFF   Why, see you not?

ROSS   Is't known who did this more than bloody deed?

MACDUFF   Those that Macbeth hath slain.

ROSS   Alas the day,
What good could they pretend?[4]

MACDUFF   They were suborned.°   *bribed*
25   Malcolm and Donalbain, the King's two sons,
Are stol'n away and fled, which puts upon them
Suspicion of the deed.

ROSS   'Gainst nature still.
Thriftless ambition, that will raven up°   *devour*
Thine own life's means! Then 'tis most like
30   The sovereignty will fall upon Macbeth.

MACDUFF   He is already named and gone to Scone[5]
To be invested.

ROSS   Where is Duncan's body?

MACDUFF   Carried to Colmekill,[6]
35   The sacred storehouse of his predecessors,
And guardian of their bones.

ROSS   Will you to Scone?

MACDUFF   No, cousin, I'll to Fife.[7]

ROSS   Well, I will thither.

MACDUFF   Well, may you see things well done there. Adieu,
Lest our old robes sit easier than our new.

40   ROSS   Farewell, father.

OLD MAN   God's benison° go with you, and with those   *blessing*
That would make good of bad, and friends of foes.

                                        Exeunt severally

3.1

        Enter BANQUO

BANQUO   Thou hast it now: King, Cawdor, Glamis, all
As the weird women promised; and I fear
Thou played'st most foully for't. Yet it was said
It should not stand in thy posterity,[1]
5   But that myself should be the root and father

---

2. Mounting to her highest point in the sky before swooping down.
3. An owl that usually feeds on mice.
4. What good could they expect to gain from the murder?
5. Ancient royal city where Scottish Kings were invested

with the ceremonial symbols of authority.
6. Iona, the burial place of Scottish Kings.
7. Macduff is the Thane of Fife.
3.1 Location: The royal palace at Forres.
1. It should not pass to your descendants.

Of many kings. If there come truth from them—

As upon thee, Macbeth, their speeches shine°—   *smile favorably*

Why by the verities on thee made good

May they not be my oracles as well,

10   And set me up in hope? But hush, no more.

       Sennet° sounded. Enter MACBETH *as King*, LADY MAC-   *Trumpet call*

       BETH *as Queen*, LENNOX, ROSS, *lords, and attendants*

MACBETH   Here's our chief guest.

LADY MACBETH   If he had been forgotten

It had been as a gap in our great feast,

And all-thing° unbecoming.   *entirely*

MACBETH [*to* BANQUO]   Tonight we hold a solemn° supper, sir,   *formal*

And I'll request your presence.

15   BANQUO   Let your highness

Command upon me, to the which my duties

Are with a most indissoluble tie

For ever knit.

MACBETH   Ride you this afternoon?

20   BANQUO   Ay, my good lord.

MACBETH   We should have else desired your good advice,

Which still° hath been both grave° and prosperous,   *always / weighty*

In this day's council; but we'll talk tomorrow.

Is't far you ride?

25   BANQUO   As far, my lord, as will fill up the time

'Twixt this and supper. Go not my horse the better,[2]

I must become a borrower of the night

For a dark hour or twain.

MACBETH   Fail not our feast.

30   BANQUO   My lord, I will not.

MACBETH   We hear our bloody cousins are bestowed°   *lodged*

In England and in Ireland, not confessing

Their cruel parricide, filling their hearers

With strange invention.° But of that tomorrow,   *falsehood*

35   When therewithal we shall have cause of state

Craving us jointly.[3] Hie you to horse. Adieu,

Till you return at night. Goes Fleance with you?

BANQUO   Ay, my good lord. Our time does call upon 's.

MACBETH   I wish your horses swift and sure of foot,

40   And so I do commend° you to their backs.   *entrust*

Farewell.   *Exit* BANQUO

Let every man be master of his time

Till seven at night. To make society

The sweeter welcome, we will keep ourself

45   Till supper-time alone. While° then, God be with you.   *Till*

         Exeunt [all but MACBETH *and a* SERVANT]

Sirrah, a word with you. Attend those men

Our pleasure?

SERVANT   They are, my lord, without° the palace gate.   *outside*

MACBETH   Bring them before us.   *Exit* SERVANT

                     To be thus is nothing

50   But to be safely thus.[4] Our fears in° Banquo   *of*

2. If my horse does not go faster than I expect.
3. *cause . . . jointly:* state business demanding our joint attention.

4. *To be thus . . . thus:* To be a King is no good unless one can reign in safety ("thus" refers to "King").

Stick° deep, and in his royalty of nature°   *Prick / natural nobility*
Reigns that which would be feared. 'Tis much he dares,
And to° that dauntless temper of his mind   *added to*
He hath a wisdom that doth guide his valour
55 To act in safety. There is none but he
Whose being I do fear, and under him
My genius° is rebuked as, it is said,[5]   *tutelary spirit*
Mark Antony's was by Caesar.° He chid the sisters   *Octavius Caesar*
When first they put the name of king upon me,
60 And bade them speak to him. Then, prophet-like,
They hailed him father to a line of kings.
Upon my head they placed a fruitless crown,
And put a barren sceptre in my grip,
Thence to be wrenched with° an unlineal hand,   *by*
65 No son of mine succeeding. If't be so,
For Banquo's issue have I filed° my mind,   *defiled*
For them the gracious° Duncan have I murdered,   *full of grace*
Put rancours° in the vessel of my peace   *bitterness*
Only for them, and mine eternal jewel°   *soul*
70 Given to the common enemy of man°   *(the devil)*
To make them kings, the seeds of Banquo kings.
Rather than so, come fate into the list°   *arena*
And champion me to th'utterance.[6] Who's there?
     Enter Servant and two MURDERERS
[*To the Servant*] Now go to the door, and stay there till we call.
                         Exit Servant
75 Was it not yesterday we spoke together?
MURDERERS   It was, so please your highness.
MACBETH   Well then, now
Have you considered of my speeches? Know
That it was he in the times past which held you
So under° fortune, which you thought had been   *out of favor with*
80 Our innocent self. This I made good to you
In our last conference, passed in probation° with you   *reviewed the proof*
How you were borne in hand,° how crossed,° the instruments,[7] *deceived / thwarted*
Who wrought with them, and all things else that might
To half a soul, and to a notion crazed,[8]
Say 'Thus did Banquo'.
85 FIRST MURDERER   You made it known to us.
MACBETH   I did so, and went further, which is now
Our point of second meeting. Do you find
Your patience so predominant in your nature
That you can let this go? Are you so gospelled[9]
90 To pray for this good man and for his issue,
Whose heavy hand hath bowed you to the grave
And beggared yours° for ever?   *your family*
FIRST MURDERER   We are men, my liege.
MACBETH   Ay, in the catalogue ye go for men,
As hounds and greyhounds, mongrels, spaniels, curs,
95 Shoughs, water-rugs, and demi-wolves[1] are clept°   *called*

---

5. Said by Plutarch. Shakespeare paraphrases him in
Antony and Cleopatra (2.3).
6. And fight with me in single combat to the death.
7. Agents.

8. Even to a half-wit or to a crazed mind.
9. Imbued with the gospel spirit.
1. Shaggy lapdogs, water dogs (for fowling), and cross-breeds between wolf and dog.

All by the name of dogs. The valued file²
Distinguishes the swift, the slow, the subtle,
The housekeeper,° the hunter, every one   watchdog
According to the gift which bounteous nature
100   Hath in him closed;° whereby he does receive   enclosed
Particular addition from the bill
That writes them all alike.³ And so of men.
Now, if you have a station° in the file,   position
Not i'th' worst rank of manhood, say't,
105   And I will put that business in your bosoms
Whose execution takes your enemy off,
Grapples you to the heart and love of us,
Who wear our health but sickly in his life,
Which in his death were perfect.
SECOND MURDERER   I am one, my liege,
110   Whom the vile blows and buffets of the world
Hath so incensed that I am reckless what
I do to spite the world.
FIRST MURDERER   And I another,
So weary with disasters, tugged with° fortune,   mauled by
That I would set° my life on any chance   risk
To mend it or be rid on't.
115   MACBETH   Both of you
Know Banquo was your enemy.
MURDERERS   True, my lord.
MACBETH   So is he mine, and in such bloody distance°   enmity
That every minute of his being thrusts
Against my near'st of life;⁴ and though I could
120   With barefaced power sweep him from my sight
And bid my will avouch° it, yet I must not,   warrant
For° certain friends that are both his and mine,   Because of
Whose loves I may not drop, but wail° his fall   must bewail
Who I myself struck down. And thence it is
125   That I to your assistance do make love,°   I crave your aid
Masking the business from the common eye
For sundry weighty reasons.
SECOND MURDERER   We shall, my lord,
Perform what you command us.
FIRST MURDERER   Though our lives—
MACBETH   Your spirits shine through you. Within this hour at most
130   I will advise you where to plant yourselves,
Acquaint you with the perfect spy o'th' time,
The moment on't;⁵ for't must be done tonight,
And something° from the palace; always thought°   at some distance / remember
That I require a clearness;⁶ and with him,
135   To leave no rubs° nor botches in the work,   flaws
Fleance, his son, that keeps him company—
Whose absence is no less material to me
Than is his father's—must embrace the fate
Of that dark hour. Resolve yourselves apart.⁷
I'll come to you anon.

---

2. List specifying the value of the cataloged items.
3. *Particular . . . alike:* Distinction apart from a catalog
that lists them indiscriminately.
4. My most vital part, the heart.

5. *Acquaint . . . on't:* I will give you full and precise
instructions as to when it is to be done.
6. A clearance (from suspicion).
7. Make up your minds privately.

140 MURDERERS   We are resolved, my lord.
    MACBETH   I'll call upon you straight. Abide within.

                              [*Exeunt* MURDERERS]

    It is concluded. Banquo, thy soul's flight,
    If it find heaven, must find it out tonight.   *Exit*

3.2

                  Enter LADY [MACBETH] *and a* SERVANT

    LADY MACBETH   Is Banquo gone from court?
    SERVANT   Ay, madam, but returns again tonight.
    LADY MACBETH   Say to the King I would attend his leisure
       For a few words.
5   SERVANT   Madam, I will.   *Exit*
    LADY MACBETH   Naught's had, all's spent,
       Where our desire is got without content.°   *happiness*
       'Tis safer to be that which we destroy
       Than by destruction dwell in doubtful joy.

                  Enter MACBETH

10   How now, my lord, why do you keep alone,
       Of sorriest° fancies your companions making,   *most wretched*
       Using° those thoughts which should indeed have died   *Entertaining*
       With them they think on? Things without all remedy
       Should be without regard.° What's done is done.   *not considered*
15 MACBETH   We have scorched° the snake, not killed it.   *slashed*
       She'll close° and be herself, whilst our poor malice   *heal*
       Remains in danger of her former tooth.[1]
       But let the frame of things disjoint, both the worlds suffer,[2]
       Ere we will eat our meal in fear, and sleep
20   In the affliction of these terrible dreams
       That shake us nightly. Better be with the dead,
       Whom we to gain our peace have sent to peace,
       Than on the torture° of the mind to lie   *rack*
       In restless ecstasy.° Duncan is in his grave.   *frenzy*
25   After life's fitful fever he sleeps well.
       Treason has done his worst. Nor steel nor poison,
       Malice domestic, foreign levy,[3] nothing
       Can touch him further.
    LADY MACBETH   Come on, gentle my lord,
       Sleek o'er your rugged looks, be bright and jovial
       Among your guests tonight.
30 MACBETH   So shall I, love,
       And so I pray be you. Let your remembrance
       Apply° to Banquo. Present him eminence°   *Be given / favor*
       Both with eye and tongue; unsafe the while that we
       Must lave our honours in these flattering streams[4]
35   And make our faces visors° to our hearts,   *masks*
       Disguising what they are.
    LADY MACBETH   You must leave this.
    MACBETH   O, full of scorpions is my mind, dear wife!
       Thou know'st that Banquo and his Fleance lives.

3.2 Location: The palace.
1. *our . . . tooth:* we remain in danger of her fangs, which
are as dangerous as they were before she was slashed.
poor malice: weak enmity.
2. Let the universe fall apart, and heaven and earth

suffer destruction.
3. An army levied abroad against Scotland.
4. *unsafe . . . streams:* we are unsafe at present, so we
must make our reputations look clean by flattering others; we are unsafe as long as we must flatter.

LADY MACBETH   But in them nature's copy's[5] not eterne.°   *everlasting*

40 MACBETH   There's comfort yet, they are assailable.
Then be thou jocund. Ere the bat hath flown
His cloistered° flight, ere to black Hecate's summons   *restricted*
The shard-borne[6] beetle with his drowsy hums
Hath rung night's yawning peal,[7] there shall be done
A deed of dreadful note.
45 LADY MACBETH   What's to be done?
MACBETH   Be innocent of the knowledge, dearest chuck,[8]
Till thou applaud the deed.—Come, seeling[9] night,
Scarf up° the tender eye of pitiful day,   *Blindfold*
And with thy bloody and invisible hand
50 Cancel and tear to pieces that great bond°   *(Banquo's lease on life)*
Which keeps me pale. Light thickens, and the crow
Makes wing to th' rooky° wood.   *full of rooks*
Good things of day begin to droop and drowse,
Whiles night's black agents to their preys do rouse.
55 Thou marvell'st at my words; but hold thee still.
Things bad begun make strong themselves by ill.
So prithee go with me.   *Exeunt*

3.3

Enter three MURDERERS
FIRST MURDERER [*to* THIRD MURDERER]   But who did bid thee
      join with us?
THIRD MURDERER   Macbeth.
SECOND MURDERER [*to* FIRST MURDERER]   He needs not our mis-
      trust, since he delivers
Our offices and what we have to do
To the direction just.[1]
FIRST MURDERER [*to* THIRD MURDERER]   Then stand with us.
5   The west yet glimmers with some streaks of day.
Now spurs the lated° traveller apace   *belated*
To gain the timely inn, and near approaches
The subject of our watch.
THIRD MURDERER   Hark, I hear horses.
BANQUO [*within*]   Give us a light there, ho!
SECOND MURDERER   Then 'tis he. The rest
10   That are within the note of expectation°   *list of expected guests*
Already are i'th' court.
FIRST MURDERER   His horses go about.[2]
THIRD MURDERER   Almost a mile; but he does usually,
So all men do, from hence to th' palace gate
Make it their walk.
          Enter BANQUO *and* FLEANCE *with a torch*
SECOND MURDERER [*aside*]   A light, a light.
THIRD MURDERER [*aside*]   'Tis he.
15   FIRST MURDERER [*aside*]   Stand to't.

---

5. Lease on life (a copyhold lease was subject to cancellation and therefore "not eterne"); the individual human cast from nature's mold.
6. Carried on scaly wings; born in dung ("shards").
7. Macbeth likens the beetle's humming to a bell, signaling the time for sleep.
8. Chick (term of endearment).

9. Eye-closing. Falcons' eyelids were sewn shut ("seeled") as part of their training.
3.3 Location: Near the palace.
1. *He . . . just:* We need not mistrust this man, since he knows perfectly Macbeth's instructions to us.
2. Are led (by servants) to the stables.

BANQUO   It will be rain tonight.

FIRST MURDERER   Let it come down.

     [FIRST MURDERER *strikes out the torch. The others attack*
     BANQUO]

BANQUO   O, treachery! Fly, good Fleance, fly, fly, fly!
     Thou mayst revenge.—O slave!   [*He dies. Exit* FLEANCE]

THIRD MURDERER   Who did strike out the light?

20 FIRST MURDERER   Was't not the way?°   *proper thing*

THIRD MURDERER   There's but one down. The son is fled.

SECOND MURDERER   We have lost best half of our affair.

FIRST MURDERER   Well, let's away and say how much is done.

                              Exeunt [*with Banquo's body*]

3.4

     Banquet prepared. Enter MACBETH [*as King*], LADY [MAC-
     BETH *as Queen*], ROSS, LENNOX, *Lords, and attendants.*
     [LADY MACBETH *sits*]

MACBETH   You know your own degrees;° sit down. At first and last[1]   *ranks; places*
     The hearty welcome.

LORDS   Thanks to your majesty.

     [*They sit*]

MACBETH   Ourself will mingle with society
     And play the humble host. Our hostess keeps her state,°   *chair of state*

5 But in best time we will require° her welcome.   *request*

LADY MACBETH   Pronounce it for me, sir, to all our friends,
     For my heart speaks they are welcome.

     Enter FIRST MURDERER [*to the door*]

MACBETH   See, they encounter° thee with their hearts' thanks.   *answer*
     Both sides are even. Here I'll sit, i'th' midst.

10 Be large° in mirth. Anon we'll drink a measure   *unrestrained*
     The table round. [*To* FIRST MURDERER]   There's blood upon thy face.

FIRST MURDERER [*aside to* MACBETH]   'Tis Banquo's, then.

MACBETH   'Tis better thee without than he within.[2]
     Is he dispatched?

15 FIRST MURDERER   My lord, his throat is cut. That I did for him.

MACBETH   Thou art the best o'th' cut-throats. Yet he's good
     That did the like for Fleance. If thou didst it,
     Thou art the nonpareil.°   *paragon (without equal)*

FIRST MURDERER   Most royal sir,
     Fleance is scaped.

20 MACBETH   Then comes my fit again; I had else been perfect,
     Whole as the marble, founded° as the rock,   *immovable*
     As broad and general° as the casing° air,   *unconstrained / surrounding*
     But now I am cabined, cribbed,° confined, bound in   *penned up*
     To saucy° doubts and fears. But Banquo's safe?   *importunate*

25 FIRST MURDERER   Ay, my good lord. Safe in a ditch he bides,
     With twenty trenchèd gashes on his head,
     The least a death to nature.

MACBETH   Thanks for that.
     There the grown serpent lies. The worm° that's fled   *young serpent*
     Hath nature that in time will venom breed,

3.4 Location: The palace.   2. Better on you than inside him.
1. To one and all.

30 No teeth for th' present. Get thee gone. Tomorrow
We'll hear ourselves° again.   *Exit* [FIRST] MURDERER   *confer*
LADY MACBETH   My royal lord,
You do not give the cheer.° The feast is sold   *entertain*
That is not often vouched, while 'tis a-making,
'Tis given with welcome.³ To feed° were best at home.   *Mere eating*
35 From thence° the sauce to meat is ceremony,   *Away from home*
Meeting were° bare without it.   *Company would be*
          Enter the Ghost of Banquo, and sits in Macbeth's place
MACBETH   Sweet remembrancer.°   *reminder*
Now good digestion wait on appetite,
And health on both.
LENNOX   May't please your highness sit?
MACBETH   Here had we now our country's honour roofed⁴
40 Were the graced person of our Banquo present,
Who may I rather challenge for° unkindness   *accuse of*
Than pity for mischance.
ROSS   His absence, sir,
Lays blame upon his promise. Please't your highness
To grace us with your royal company?
MACBETH   The table's full.
45 LENNOX   Here is a place reserved, sir.
MACBETH   Where?
LENNOX   Here, my good lord. What is't that moves your highness?
MACBETH   Which of you have done this?
LORDS   What, my good lord?
MACBETH [*to the Ghost*]   Thou canst not say I did it. Never shake
50 Thy gory locks at me.
ROSS [*rising*]   Gentlemen, rise. His highness is not well.
LADY MACBETH [*rising*]   Sit, worthy friends. My lord is often thus,
And hath been from his youth. Pray you, keep seat.
The fit is momentary. Upon a thought°   *In a moment*
55 He will again be well. If much you note him
You shall offend him, and extend his passion.°   *prolong his suffering*
Feed, and regard him not.
          [*She speaks apart with* MACBETH]
          Are you a man?
MACBETH   Ay, and a bold one, that dare look on that
Which might appal the devil.
LADY MACBETH   O proper stuff!°   *mere nonsense*
60 This is the very painting of your fear;
This is the air-drawn dagger⁵ which you said
Led you to Duncan. O, these flaws° and starts,   *outbursts*
Impostors to° true fear, would well become   *compared with*
A woman's story at a winter's fire
65 Authorized by her grandam. Shame itself,
Why do you make such faces? When all's done
You look but on a stool.
MACBETH   Prithee see there. Behold, look, lo—how say you?
Why, what care I? If thou canst nod, speak, too!
70 If charnel-houses and our graves must send

---

3. *The . . . welcome:* A feast is like a purchased meal if
the guests are not assured often that they are welcome.

4. All the Scottish nobility under one roof.
5. The dagger made of, or carried on, the air.

Those that we bury back, our monuments
Shall be the maws of kites.[6]   *[Exit Ghost]*
LADY MACBETH   What, quite unmanned in folly?
MACBETH   If I stand here, I saw him.
LADY MACBETH   Fie, for shame!
MACBETH   Blood hath been shed ere now, i'th' olden time,
75   Ere human statute purged the gentle weal;[7]
Ay, and since, too, murders have been performed
Too terrible for the ear. The time has been
That, when the brains were out, the man would die,
And there an end. But now they rise again
80   With twenty mortal murders° on their crowns,°   *deadly wounds / heads*
And push us from our stools. This is more strange
Than such a murder is.
LADY MACBETH *[aloud]*   My worthy lord,
Your noble friends do lack you.
MACBETH   I do forget.
Do not muse° at me, my most worthy friends.   *wonder*
85   I have a strange infirmity which is nothing
To those that know me. Come, love and health to all,
Then I'll sit down.
To an [attendant]   Give me some wine. Fill full.
      Enter Ghost
I drink to th' general joy of th'whole table,
And to our dear friend Banquo, whom we miss.
90   Would he were here. To all and him we thirst,°   *drink*
And all to all.[8]
LORDS   Our duties, and the pledge.°   *toast*
      [They drink]
MACBETH *[seeing the Ghost]*   Avaunt, and quit my sight! Let the
    earth hide thee.
Thy bones are marrowless, thy blood is cold.
Thou hast no speculation° in those eyes   *sight*
Which thou dost glare with.
95 LADY MACBETH   Think of this, good peers,
But as a thing of custom. 'Tis no other;
Only it spoils the pleasure of the time.
MACBETH   What man dare, I dare.
Approach thou like the ruggèd Russian bear,
100   The armed° rhinoceros, or th'Hyrcan[9] tiger;   *armored*
Take any shape but that,° and my firm nerves°   *(Banquo's) / sinews*
Shall never tremble. Or be alive again,
And dare me to the desert° with thy sword.   *deserted place*
If trembling I inhabit then,[1] protest me
105   The baby of a girl.[2] Hence, horrible shadow,
Unreal mock'ry, hence!   *[Exit Ghost]*
           Why so, being gone,
I am a man again. Pray you sit still.
LADY MACBETH   You have displaced the mirth, broke the good meeting
With most admired° disorder.   *wondered at*

---

6. *If . . . kites:* If the dead return from their graves, nothing will prevent them from being consumed by birds of prey.
7. Before human or humane (Elizabethans did not spell the two words differently) law cleansed the commonwealth and made it peaceable.
8. All good wishes to everyone.
9. From Hyrcania, a region near the Caspian Sea.
1. If then I tremble; if, trembling, I stay indoors.
2. A baby girl; a girl's doll.

MACBETH   Can such things be
110 And overcome° us like a summer's cloud,   *pass over*
Without our special wonder? You make me strange
Even to the disposition that I owe,[3]
When now I think you can behold such sights
And keep the natural ruby of your cheeks
When mine is blanched with fear.
115 ROSS   What sights, my lord?
LADY MACBETH   I pray you, speak not. He grows worse and worse.
Question enrages° him. At once, good night.   *Talk aggravates*
Stand not upon the order of your going,
But go at once.[4]
LENNOX   Good night, and better health
Attend his majesty.
120 LADY MACBETH   A kind good-night to all.   *Exeunt Lords*
MACBETH   It will have blood, they say. Blood will have blood.
Stones have been known to move, and trees to speak,
Augurs° and understood relations[5] have   *Auguries*
By maggot-pies and choughs and rooks[6] brought forth°   *revealed*
125 The secret'st man of blood.° What is the night?[7]   *murderer*
LADY MACBETH   Almost at odds with morning, which is which.
MACBETH   How sayst thou[8] that Macduff denies his person
At our great bidding?
LADY MACBETH   Did you send to him, sir?
MACBETH   I hear it by the way,° but I will send.   *indirectly*
130 There's not a one of them but in his house
I keep a servant fee'd.° I will° tomorrow,   *paid to spy / will go*
And betimes° I will, to the weird sisters.   *early*
More shall they speak, for now I am bent° to know   *determined*
By the worst means the worst. For mine own good
135 All causes° shall give way. I am in blood   *other concerns*
Stepped in so far that, should I° wade no more,°   *were I to / no farther*
Returning were° as tedious as go° o'er.   *would be / going*
Strange things I have in head that will to hand,
Which must be acted ere they may be scanned.[9]
140 LADY MACBETH   You lack the season° of all natures, sleep.   *preservative*
MACBETH   Come, we'll to sleep. My strange and self-abuse°   *self-delusion*
Is the initiate fear that wants hard use.[1]
We are yet but young in deed.°   *Exeunt*   *crime*

3.5

Thunder. Enter the three WITCHES *meeting* HECATE

FIRST WITCH   Why, how now, Hecate? You look angerly.
HECATE   Have I not reason, beldams° as you are?   *hags*
Saucy and over-bold, how did you dare
To trade and traffic with Macbeth
5   In riddles and affairs of death,
And I, the mistress of your charms,
The close° contriver of all harms,   *secret*

---

3. *You . . . owe:* You make me a stranger to my own
nature, which I had supposed brave.
4. *Stand . . . once:* Do not follow the order of precedence
in departing, but all go at once.
5. Formerly hidden, now revealed relationships between
causes and effects.
6. Magpies, traditionally sacrificed by augurers, and
birds (choughs and rooks) of the crow family.

7. What time of night is it?
8. What do you think of the fact that.
9. *ere . . . scanned:* at once, before they can be considered.
1. Is the fear of a novice who lacks toughening experience.
3.5 Location: An open place.

	Was never called to bear my part	
	Or show the glory of our art?—	
10	And, which is worse, all you have done	
	Hath been but for a wayward son,	
	Spiteful and wrathful, who, as others do,	
	Loves for his own ends, not for you.	
	But make amends now. Get you gone,	
15	And at the pit of Acheron°	river in hell
	Meet me i'th' morning. Thither he	
	Will come to know his destiny.	
	Your vessels and your spells provide,	
	Your charms and everything beside.	
20	I am for th'air. This night I'll spend	
	Unto a dismal and a fatal end.[1]	
	Great business must be wrought ere noon.	
	Upon the corner of the moon	
	There hangs a vap'rous drop profound.[2]	
25	I'll catch it ere it come to ground,	
	And that, distilled by magic sleights,	
	Shall raise such artificial sprites[3]	
	As by the strength of their illusion	
	Shall draw him on to his confusion.	
30	He shall spurn fate, scorn death, and bear	
	His hopes 'bove wisdom, grace, and fear;	
	And you all know security°	overconfidence
	Is mortals' chiefest enemy.	
	SPIRITS [*singing dispersedly within*]° Come away, come away.	offstage
35	Hecate, Hecate, come away.	
	HECATE Hark, I am called! My little spirit, see,	
	Sits in a foggy cloud and stays for me.	

[The Song]

	SPIRITS [*within*] Come away, come away,[4]	
	Hecate, Hecate, come away.	
40	HECATE I come, I come, I come, I come,	
	With all the speed I may,	
	With all the speed I may.	
	Where's Stadlin?	
	SPIRIT [*within*] Here.	
	HECATE Where's Puckle?	
	ANOTHER SPIRIT [*within*] Here.	
	OTHER SPIRITS [*within*] And Hoppo, too, and Hellwain, too,	
45	We lack but you, we lack but you.	
	Come away, make up the count.	
	HECATE I will but 'noint,[5] and then I mount.	
	[*Spirits appear above.* A SPIRIT LIKE A CAT *descends*]	
	SPIRITS [*above*] There's one comes down to fetch his dues,	
	A kiss, a coll,° a sip of blood,	an embrace
50	And why thou stay'st so long I muse,° I muse,	wonder
	Since the air's so sweet and good.	
	HECATE O, art thou come? What news, what news?	

1. Working toward a disastrous and fateful end.
2. Of deep or hidden significance; ready to fall.
3. Spirits produced by magic art.
4. The Folio only includes the first line of this song: the remaining lines, supplied here, come from a song with the same opening words from Thomas Middleton's play *The Witch* (c. 1613). See Textual Note.
5. Anoint myself, perhaps with an ointment to enable flying.

SPIRIT LIKE A CAT   All goes still to our delight.
    Either come, or else refuse, refuse.
55 HECATE   Now I am furnished° for the flight.   *provided*
    [*She ascends with the* SPIRIT *and sings*]
    Now I go, now I fly,
    Malkin my sweet spirit and I.
SPIRITS *and* HECATE   O what a dainty pleasure 'tis
        To ride in the air
60   When the moon shines fair,
    And sing, and dance, and toy,° and kiss.   *play amorously*
    Over woods, high rocks and mountains,
    Over seas and misty fountains,
    Over steeples, towers and turrets,
65   We fly by night 'mongst troops of spirits.
    No ring of bells to our ears sounds,
    No howls of wolves, no yelps of hounds.
    No, not the noise of waters-breach°   *breaking waves*
    Or cannons' throat our height can reach.
70 SPIRITS [*above*]   No ring of bells to our ears sounds,
    No howls of wolves, no yelps of hounds.
    No, not the noise of waters-breach
    Or cannons' throat our height can reach.
    [*Exeunt into the heavens the*
    SPIRIT LIKE A CAT *and* HECATE]
FIRST WITCH   Come, let's make haste. She'll soon be back again.
        Exeunt

3.6

Enter LENNOX *and another* LORD

LENNOX   My former speeches have but hit your thoughts,
    Which can interpret farther.[1] Only I say
    Things have been strangely borne.° The gracious Duncan   *carried on*
    Was pitied of Macbeth: marry, he was dead;[2]
5   And the right valiant Banquo walked too late,
    Whom you may say, if't please you, Fleance killed,
    For Fleance fled: men must not walk too late.
    Who cannot want the thought° how monstrous   *can help thinking*
    It was for Malcolm and for Donalbain
10   To kill their gracious father? Damnèd fact,°   *deed*
    How it did grieve Macbeth! Did he not straight
    In pious° rage the two delinquents tear,   *loyal*
    That were the slaves of drink, and thralls° of sleep?   *slaves*
    Was not that nobly done? Ay, and wisely too,
15   For 'twould have angered any heart alive
    To hear the men deny't. So that I say
    He has borne all things well, and I do think
    That had he Duncan's sons under his key—
    As, an't° please heaven, he shall not—they should find   *if it*
20   What 'twere to kill a father. So should Fleance.
    But peace, for from broad words,[3] and 'cause he failed
    His presence at the tyrant's feast, I hear

3.6 Location: Somewhere in Scotland.
1. *My . . . farther:* What I have said has coincided with your thoughts. I need not say more; you can draw your own further conclusions.

2. *The . . . dead:* Macbeth pitied Duncan after he was dead, but not before. *of:* by.
3. As a result of his plain speaking.

Macduff lives in disgrace. Sir, can you tell
Where he bestows himself?°   *lodges*

LORD   The son of Duncan

25 From whom this tyrant holds° the due of birth°   *withholds / birthright*
Lives in the English court, and is received
Of the most pious Edward[4] with such grace
That the malevolence of fortune nothing
Takes from his high respect.[5] Thither Macduff

30 Is gone to pray the holy King upon his aid°   *in aid of Malcolm*
To wake Northumberland and warlike Siward,
That by the help of these—with Him above
To ratify the work—we may again
Give to our tables meat,° sleep to our nights,   *food*

35 Free from our feasts and banquets bloody knives,[6]
Do faithful homage, and receive free[7] honours,
All which we pine for now. And this report
Hath so exasperate their king° that he   *exasperated (Macbeth)*
Prepares for some attempt of war.

40 LENNOX   Sent he to Macduff?

LORD   He did, and with° an absolute 'Sir, not I,'   *on receiving*
The cloudy messenger turns me his back
And hums, as who should say 'You'll rue the time
That clogs me with this answer.'[8]

LENNOX   And that well might

45 Advise him to a caution t'hold what distance
His wisdom can provide.[9] Some holy angel
Fly to the court of England and unfold
His message ere he come, that a swift blessing
May soon return to this our suffering country
Under a hand accursed.[1]

50 LORD   I'll send my prayers with him.

                                                             Exeunt

4.1

[*A Cauldron.*] *Thunder. Enter the three* WITCHES

FIRST WITCH   Thrice the brinded° cat hath mewed.   *brindled; streaked*

SECOND WITCH   Thrice, and once the hedge-pig° whined.   *hedgehog*

THIRD WITCH   Harpier° cries ''Tis time, 'tis time.'   *(her familiar)*

FIRST WITCH   Round about the cauldron go,

5 In the poisoned entrails throw.
Toad that under cold stone
Days and nights has thirty-one
Sweltered venom sleeping got,[1]
Boil thou first i'th' charmèd pot.

10 ALL   Double, double, toil and trouble,
Fire burn, and cauldron bubble.

4. *received . . . Edward*: received by the saintly King Edward (Edward the Confessor, reigned 1042–1066).
5. Does not deprive Malcolm of respect.
6. Free our feasts from bloody knives.
7. Freely given; enjoyed in freedom.
8. *He did . . . answer*: Macduff says, "Sir, not I." The scowling ("cloudy") messenger from Macbeth turns his back and hums. His rudeness seems to say ominously, "You'll rue the time that burdens ('clogs') me with this

answer."
9. *And . . . provide*: Warn Macduff to keep as far from Macbeth as he can.
1. *country . . . accursed*: country suffering under an accursed hand.
4.1 Location: A cave with a boiling caldron.
1. *has . . . got*: has for thirty-one days and nights exuded poison formed during sleep.

SECOND WITCH   Fillet° of a fenny° snake,   *Slice / from the swamps*
In the cauldron boil and bake.
Eye of newt and toe of frog,
15   Wool of bat and tongue of dog,
Adder's fork° and blind-worm's sting,   *forked tongue*
Lizard's leg and owlet's wing,
For a charm of powerful trouble,
Like a hell-broth boil and bubble.
20 ALL   Double, double, toil and trouble,
Fire burn, and cauldron bubble.
THIRD WITCH   Scale of dragon, tooth of wolf,
Witches' mummy,° maw and gulf²   *mummified flesh*
Of the ravined° salt-sea shark,   *ravenous; glutted*
25   Root of hemlock digged i'th' dark,
Liver of blaspheming Jew,
Gall of goat, and slips of yew
Slivered° in the moon's eclipse,   *Cut off*
Nose of Turk, and Tartar's³ lips,
30   Finger of birth-strangled babe
Ditch-delivered by a drab,°   *whore*
Make the gruel thick and slab.°   *viscous*
Add thereto a tiger's chaudron°   *entrails*
For th'ingredience of our cauldron.
35 ALL   Double, double, toil and trouble,
Fire burn, and cauldron bubble.
SECOND WITCH   Cool it with a baboon's blood,
Then the charm is firm and good.
        Enter HECATE *and the other three* WITCHES
HECATE   O, well done! I commend your pains,
40   And everyone shall share i'th' gains.
And now about the cauldron sing
Like elves and fairies in a ring,
Enchanting all that you put in.
        Music and a song
HECATE   Black spirits and white, red spirits and grey,⁴
45   Mingle, mingle, mingle, you that mingle may.
FOURTH WITCH   Titty,⁵ Tiffin, keep it stiff in;
        Firedrake, Puckey, make it lucky;
            Liard, Robin, you must bob in.
ALL   Round, around, around, about, about,
50   All ill come running in, all good keep out.
FOURTH WITCH   Here's the blood of a bat.
HECATE   Put in that, O put in that!
FIFTH WITCH   Here's leopard's bane.
HECATE   Put in a grain.
55 FOURTH WITCH   The juice of toad, the oil of adder.
FIFTH WITCH   Those will make the younker° madder.   *fashionable young man*
HECATE   Put in, there's all, and rid the stench.
A WITCH   Nay, here's three ounces of a red-haired wench.
ALL   Round, around, around, about, about,
60   All ill come running in, all good keep out.

---

2. Stomach and gullet.   song; see Textual Note.
3. Both thought of as cruel pagans.   5. The proper names are the names of spirits.
4. As in 3.5, the Folio only includes the first line of this

SECOND WITCH   By the pricking of my thumbs,
      Something wicked this way comes.
      [*Knock within*]
      Open, locks, whoever knocks.
      Enter MACBETH

MACBETH   How now, you secret, black, and midnight hags,
    What is't you do?

65   ALL THE WITCHES   A deed without a name.

MACBETH   I conjure you by that which you profess,°   *the black arts*
    Howe'er you come to know it, answer me.
    Though you untie the winds and let them fight
    Against the churches, though the yeasty° waves   *foamy*
70   Confound° and swallow navigation up,   *Defeat*
    Though bladed corn° be lodged° and trees blown down, *ripe wheat / beaten down*
    Though castles topple on their warders' heads,
    Though palaces and pyramids do slope°   *bend*
    Their heads to their foundations, though the treasure
75   Of nature's germens[6] tumble all together
    Even till destruction sicken,° answer me   *be surfeited*
    To what I ask you.

FIRST WITCH   Speak.

SECOND WITCH   Demand.

THIRD WITCH   We'll answer.

FIRST WITCH   Say if thou'dst rather hear it from our mouths
    Or from our masters.

MACBETH   Call 'em, let me see 'em.

80   FIRST WITCH   Pour in sow's blood that hath eaten
    Her nine farrow;° grease that's sweaten°   *litter of nine / sweated*
    From the murderer's gibbet° throw   *gallows*
    Into the flame.

ALL THE WITCHES   Come high or low,
    Thyself and office° deftly show.   *function*
    Thunder. FIRST APPARITION: *an armed*° *head*   *armored*

MACBETH   Tell me, thou unknown power—

85   FIRST WITCH   He knows thy thought.
    Hear his speech, but say thou naught.

FIRST APPARITION   Macbeth, Macbeth, Macbeth, beware Macduff,
    Beware the Thane of Fife. Dismiss me. Enough.
    [APPARITION] *descends*

MACBETH   Whate'er thou art, for thy good caution thanks.
90   Thou hast harped° my fear aright. But one word more— *guessed*

FIRST WITCH   He will not be commanded. Here's another,
    More potent than the first.
    Thunder. SECOND APPARITION: *a bloody child*

SECOND APPARITION   Macbeth, Macbeth, Macbeth.

MACBETH   Had I three ears I'd hear thee.

95   SECOND APPARITION   Be bloody, bold, and resolute. Laugh to scorn
    The power of man, for none of woman born
    Shall harm Macbeth.
    [APPARITION] *descends*

MACBETH   Then live, Macduff—what need I fear of thee?
    But yet I'll make assurance double sure,

6. Seeds from which all nature grows. According to Renaissance theories of biology, if they were tumbled together, they would become barren or produce only monsters.

100 And take a bond of fate thou shalt not live,[7]
That I may tell pale-hearted fear it lies,
And sleep in spite of thunder.
          Thunder. THIRD APPARITION: *a child crowned, with a*
          tree in his hand[8]
                              What is this
That rises like the issue of a king,
And wears upon his baby-brow the round
And top° of sovereignty?   crown
105 ALL THE WITCHES   Listen, but speak not to't.
THIRD APPARITION Be lion-mettled, proud, and take no care
Who chafes, who frets, or where conspirers are.
Macbeth shall never vanquished be until
Great Birnam Wood to high Dunsinane Hill
Shall come against him.
          [APPARITION] *descends*
110 MACBETH   That will never be.
Who can impress° the forest, bid the tree   *force into service*
Unfix his earth-bound root? Sweet bodements,° good!   *omens*
Rebellious dead,[9] rise never till the wood
Of Birnam rise, and on's high place Macbeth
115 Shall live the lease of nature,° pay his breath   *natural life span*
To time and mortal custom.[1] Yet my heart
Throbs to know one thing. Tell me, if your art
Can tell so much, shall Banquo's issue ever
Reign in this kingdom?
ALL THE WITCHES   Seek to know no more.
120 MACBETH I will be satisfied. Deny me this,
And an eternal curse fall on you! Let me know.
          [*The cauldron sinks.*] *Hautboys*
Why sinks that cauldron? And what noise° is this?   *music*
FIRST WITCH Show.
SECOND WITCH Show.
125 THIRD WITCH Show.
ALL THE WITCHES Show his eyes and grieve his heart,
Come like shadows, so depart.
          A show of eight kings, [*the*] *last with a glass*° *in his*   *mirror*
          hand; and BANQUO
MACBETH Thou art too like the spirit of Banquo. Down!
Thy crown does sear mine eyeballs. And thy hair,
130 Thou other gold-bound brow, is like the first.
A third is like the former. Filthy hags,
Why do you show me this?—A fourth? Start,° eyes!   *Bulge out*
What, will the line stretch out to th' crack of doom?
Another yet? A seventh? I'll see no more—
135 And yet the eighth appears, who bears a glass
Which shows me many more; and some I see
That twofold balls and treble sceptres[2] carry.

---

7. By killing Macduff, Macbeth hopes to bind fate to its promise that no man of woman born shall harm Macbeth.
8. Signifying Malcolm. The tree anticipates 5.5.31ff.
9. Perhaps Banquo. Some editors emend to "Rebellious head" or "Rebellion's head," where "head" means "army."

1. The custom of mortality; natural death.
2. James I was crowned twice, once as King of Scotland and later as King of England. He carried one orb at each coronation. "Treble sceptres" refers to the fact that he held two scepters in the English coronation and one in the Scottish, or perhaps to his claim to be King of Britain, France, and Ireland.

Horrible sight! Now I see 'tis true,
For the blood-baltered[3] Banquo smiles upon me,
And points at them for his.[4]

[*Exeunt kings and* BANQUO]

140   What, is this so?

HECATE   Ay, sir, all this is so. But why
Stands Macbeth thus amazedly?°   *entranced*
Come, sisters, cheer we up his sprites,°   *spirits*
And show the best of our delights.
145   I'll charm the air to give a sound
While you perform your antic round,°   *fantastic dance*
That this great king may kindly say
Our duties did his welcome pay.[5]

Music. The WITCHES *dance, and vanish*

MACBETH   Where are they? Gone? Let this pernicious hour
150   Stand aye° accursèd in the calendar.   *ever*
Come in, without there.

Enter LENNOX

LENNOX   What's your grace's will?
MACBETH   Saw you the weird sisters?
LENNOX   No, my lord.
MACBETH   Came they not by you?
LENNOX   No, indeed, my lord.
MACBETH   Infected be the air whereon they ride,
155   And damned all those that trust them. I did hear
The galloping of horse. Who was't came by?
LENNOX   'Tis two or three, my lord, that bring you word
Macduff is fled to England.
MACBETH   Fled to England?
LENNOX   Ay, my good lord.
160 MACBETH [*aside*]   Time, thou anticipat'st° my dread exploits.   *forestall*
The flighty purpose never is o'ertook
Unless the deed go with it.[6] From this moment
The very firstlings° of my heart shall be   *first notions*
The firstlings° of my hand. And even now,   *first acts*
165   To crown my thoughts with acts, be it thought and done:
The castle of Macduff I will surprise,
Seize upon Fife, give to th'edge o'th' sword
His wife, his babes, and all unfortunate souls
That trace him in his line. No boasting like a fool;
170   This deed I'll do before this purpose cool.
But no more sights! [*To* LENNOX] where are these gentlemen?
come bring me where they are.   *Exeunt*

4.2

Enter MACDUFF'S WIFE, *her son, and* ROSS

LADY MACDUFF   What had he done to make him fly the land?
ROSS   You must have patience, madam.
LADY MACDUFF   He had none.

---

3. Having hair matted with blood.
4. Banquo was the legendary founder of the Stuart dynasty.
5. Our service repaid the welcome he gave us.

6. *The flighty . . . it:* The fleeting intention is never realized unless the deed is done immediately.
4.2 Location: Macduff's castle in Fife.

His flight was madness. When our actions do not,
Our fears do make us traitors.[1]

ROSS   You know not
5   Whether it was his wisdom or his fear.

LADY MACDUFF   Wisdom—to leave his wife, to leave his babes,
His mansion, and his titles° in a place   *estates*
From whence himself does fly? He loves us not,
He wants° the natural touch,° for the poor wren,   *lacks / affection*
10   The most diminutive of birds, will fight,
Her young ones in her nest, against the owl.
All is the fear and nothing is the love;
As little is the wisdom, where the flight
So runs against all reason.

ROSS   My dearest coz,°   *kinswoman*
15   I pray you school° yourself. But for your husband,   *control*
He is noble, wise, judicious, and best knows
The fits o'th' season.[2] I dare not speak much further,
But cruel are the times when we are traitors
And do not know ourselves;[3] when we hold rumour
20   From what we fear, yet know not what we fear,[4]
But float upon a wild and violent sea
Each way and none.[5] I take my leave of you;
Shall° not be long but° I'll be here again.   *It shall / before*
Things at the worst will cease, or else climb upward
25   To what they were before. My pretty cousin,°   *(Macduff's son)*
Blessing upon you!

LADY MACDUFF   Fathered he is, and yet he's fatherless.

ROSS   I am so much a fool, should I stay longer
It would be my disgrace and your discomfort.[6]
I take my leave at once.   *Exit*

30 LADY MACDUFF   Sirrah, your father's dead,
And what will you do now? How will you live?

MACDUFF'S SON   As birds do, mother.

LADY MACDUFF   What, with worms and flies?

MACDUFF'S SON   With what I get, I mean, and so do they.

LADY MACDUFF   Poor° bird, thou'dst never fear the net nor lime,[7]   *Pitiful*
35   The pitfall nor the gin.°   *snare*

MACDUFF'S SON   Why should I, mother? Poor° birds they are not   *Worthless*
set for.
My father is not dead, for all your saying.

LADY MACDUFF   Yes, he is dead. How wilt thou do for a father?

MACDUFF'S SON   Nay, how will you do for a husband?

40 LADY MACDUFF   Why, I can buy me twenty at any market.

MACDUFF'S SON   Then you'll buy 'em to sell again.

LADY MACDUFF   Thou speak'st with all thy wit, and yet, i'faith,
with wit enough for thee.

MACDUFF'S SON   Was my father a traitor, mother?

45 LADY MACDUFF   Ay, that he was.

---

1. *When . . . traitors:* Even when we have committed no
treason, our fear of suspicion makes us behave as though
we are guilty.
2. The violent convulsions of the present time; what
befits the time.
3. *we . . . ourselves:* we are denounced as traitors but do
not know why; we have no self-knowledge.

4. *when . . . fear:* when we believe rumors inspired by our
fears, but those fears are themselves vague.
5. In every direction, and so finally in none.
6. I would disgrace myself and embarrass you by
weeping (or perhaps by lingering).
7. Birdlime, a sticky substance smeared on twigs to catch
small birds.

MACDUFF'S SON What is a traitor?

LADY MACDUFF Why, one that swears and lies.[8]

MACDUFF'S SON And be all traitors that do so?

LADY MACDUFF Everyone that does so is a traitor, and must be

50 hanged.

MACDUFF'S SON And must they all be hanged that swear° and   *speak profanely*
lie?

LADY MACDUFF Every one.

MACDUFF'S SON Who must hang them?

55 LADY MACDUFF Why, the honest men.

MACDUFF'S SON Then the liars and swearers are fools, for there
are liars and swearers enough to beat the honest men and hang
up them.

LADY MACDUFF Now God help thee, poor monkey! But how wilt

60 thou do for a father?

MACDUFF'S SON If he were dead you'd weep for him. If you
would not, it were a good sign that I should quickly have a
new father.

LADY MACDUFF Poor prattler, how thou talk'st!

Enter a MESSENGER

65 MESSENGER Bless you, fair dame. I am not to you known,
Though in your state of honour I am perfect.[9]
I doubt° some danger does approach you nearly.   *fear*
If you will take a homely° man's advice,   *plain*
Be not found here. Hence with your little ones!

70 To fright you thus methinks I am too savage,
To do worse to you were fell cruelty,[1]
Which is too nigh your person.[2] Heaven preserve you.
I dare abide no longer.   *Exit* MESSENGER

LADY MACDUFF   Whither should I fly?
I have done no harm. But I remember now

75 I am in this earthly world, where to do harm
Is often laudable, to do good sometime
Accounted dangerous folly. Why then, alas,
Do I put up that womanly defence
To say I have done no harm?

Enter MURDERERS

     What are these faces?

80 A MURDERER Where is your husband?

LADY MACDUFF I hope in no place so unsanctified
Where such as thou mayst find him.

A MURDERER   He's a traitor.

MACDUFF'S SON Thou liest, thou shag-haired villain.

A MURDERER [*stabbing him*]   What, you egg!
Young fry° of treachery!   *spawn*

MACDUFF'S SON   He has killed me, mother.

85 Run away, I pray you.

[*He dies.*] *Exit* [MACDUFF'S WIFE] *crying 'Murder!'*

[*followed by* MURDERERS *with the Son's body*]

---

8. Takes an oath and breaks it.
9. Though I know perfectly well your high rank (an
apology for bursting in).
1. *To fright . . . cruelty:* Even to frighten you by speaking

of such danger is savage; actually to harm you would be
brutal ("fell") cruelty.
2. Such cruelty is already too near you.

4.3

Enter MALCOLM *and* MACDUFF

MALCOLM   Let us seek out some desolate shade, and there
Weep our sad bosoms empty.

MACDUFF   Let us rather
Hold fast the mortal° sword, and like good men   deadly
Bestride our downfall birthdom.[1] Each new morn
5   New widows howl, new orphans cry, new sorrows
Strike heaven on the face that° it resounds   so that
As if it felt with Scotland and yelled out
Like syllable of dolour.°   A similar cry of pain

MALCOLM   What I believe I'll wail,
What know believe; and what I can redress,
10   As I shall find the time to friend,° I will.   favorable
What you have spoke it may be so, perchance.
This tyrant, whose sole° name blisters our tongues,   mere
Was once thought honest. You have loved him well.
He hath not touched° you yet. I am young, but something   injured
15   You may discern of him through me:[2] and wisdom°   it's prudent
To offer up a weak poor innocent lamb
T'appease an angry god.

MACDUFF   I am not treacherous.

MALCOLM   But Macbeth is.
20   A good and virtuous nature may recoil
In an imperial charge.[3] But I shall crave your pardon.
That which you are my thoughts cannot transpose.°   transform
Angels are bright still, though the brightest° fell.   (Lucifer)
Though all things foul would wear the brows of grace,
Yet grace must still look so.[4]

MACDUFF   I have lost my hopes.[5]

25   MALCOLM   Perchance even there where I did find my doubts.[6]
Why in that rawness° left you wife and child,   unprotected condition
Those precious motives,° those strong knots of love,   inducements to devotion
Without leave-taking? I pray you,
30   Let not my jealousies° be your dishonours,   suspicions
But mine own safeties.° You may be rightly just,   safeguards
Whatever I shall think.

MACDUFF   Bleed, bleed, poor country!
Great tyranny, lay thou thy basis° sure,   foundation
For goodness dare not check thee. Wear thou thy wrongs;°   wrongful gains
35   The title is affeered.° Fare thee well, lord.   confirmed
I would not be the villain that thou think'st
For the whole space that's in the tyrant's grasp,
And the rich east to boot.°   as well

MALCOLM   Be not offended.
I speak not as in absolute fear° of you.   complete distrust
40   I think our country sinks beneath the yoke.
It weeps, it bleeds, and each new day a gash
Is added to her wounds. I think withal°   nonetheless

4.3 Location: England, before King Edward's palace.
1. Stand in defense over our downtrodden native land.
2. *I . . . me*: I am inexperienced, but you might gain favor
with Macbeth by betraying me. Many editions emend
"discern" to "deserve."
3. *recoil . . . charge*: give way to a royal command.

4. *Though . . . so*: Though everything evil disguises itself
as virtue, virtue still looks like itself.
5. Hopes of Malcolm's help in a campaign against Macbeth.
6. Doubts of Macduff's loyalty, because he has left his
wife and children.

There would be hands uplifted in my right,
And here from gracious England° have I offer   *the King of England*
45 Of goodly thousands. But for all this,
When I shall tread upon the tyrant's head,
Or wear it on my sword, yet my poor country
Shall have more vices than it had before,
More suffer, and more sundry° ways, than ever,   *in more various*
By him that shall succeed.
50 MACDUFF   What° should he be?   *Who*
MALCOLM   It is myself I mean, in whom I know
All the particulars° of vice so grafted   *varieties*
That when they shall be opened° black Macbeth   *disclosed*
Will seem as pure as snow, and the poor state
55 Esteem him as a lamb, being compared
With my confineless° harms.   *infinite*
MACDUFF   Not in the legions
Of horrid hell can come a devil more damned
In evils to top Macbeth.
MALCOLM   I grant him bloody,
Luxurious,° avaricious, false, deceitful,   *Lecherous*
60 Sudden,° malicious, smacking of every sin   *Violent*
That has a name. But there's no bottom, none,
In my voluptuousness. Your wives, your daughters,
Your matrons, and your maids could not fill up
The cistern of my lust, and my desire
65 All continent° impediments would o'erbear   *restraining; chaste*
That did oppose my will. Better Macbeth
Than such an one to reign.
MACDUFF   Boundless intemperance
In nature° is a tyranny. It hath been   *human nature*
Th'untimely emptying of the happy throne,
70 And fall of many kings. But fear not yet°   *nevertheless*
To take upon you what is yours. You may
Convey° your pleasures in a spacious plenty   *Manage secretly*
And yet seem cold.° The time° you may so hoodwink.° *indifferent / age / deceive*
We have willing dames enough. There cannot be
75 That vulture in you to devour so many
As will to greatness dedicate themselves,
Finding it so inclined.
MALCOLM   With this there grows
In my most ill-composed affection° such   *character*
A staunchless° avarice that were I king   *An insatiable*
80 I should cut off the nobles for their lands,
Desire his jewels and this other's house,
And my more having would be as a sauce
To make me hunger more, that I should forge
Quarrels unjust against the good and loyal,
Destroying them for wealth.
85 MACDUFF   This avarice
Sticks deeper, grows with more pernicious root
Than summer-seeming[7] lust, and it hath been
The sword° of our slain kings. Yet do not fear.   *undoing*
Scotland hath foisons° to fill up your will   *plenty*

---

7. Appropriate to youth ("summer") but passing with age, unlike avarice; summerlike.

90 Of your mere own.⁸ All these are portable,°   *bearable*
    With other graces weighed.
    MALCOLM   But I have none. The king-becoming graces,
    As justice, verity, temp'rance, stableness,
    Bounty, perseverance, mercy, lowliness,°   *humility*
95 Devotion, patience, courage, fortitude,
    I have no relish° of them, but abound   *trace*
    In the division° of each several° crime,   *variations / separate*
    Acting it many ways. Nay, had I power I should
    Pour the sweet milk of concord into hell,
100 Uproar the universal peace, confound
    All unity on earth.
    MACDUFF   O Scotland, Scotland!
    MALCOLM   If such a one be fit to govern, speak.
    I am as I have spoken.
    MACDUFF   Fit to govern?
    No, not to live. O nation miserable,
105 With an untitled° tyrant bloody-sceptered,   *a usurping*
    When shalt thou see thy wholesome days again,
    Since that the truest issue of thy throne
    By his own interdiction° stands accursed   *declaration of unfitness*
    And does blaspheme his breed?° Thy royal father   *disgrace his heritage*
110 Was a most sainted king. The Queen that bore thee,
    Oft'ner upon her knees than on her feet,
    Died⁹ every day she lived. Fare thee well.
    These evils thou repeat'st upon thyself
    Hath banished me from Scotland. O, my breast—
    Thy hope ends here!
115 MALCOLM   Macduff, this noble passion,
    Child of integrity, hath from my soul
    Wiped the black scruples,° reconciled my thoughts   *dark suspicions*
    To thy good truth and honour. Devilish Macbeth
    By many of these trains° hath sought to win me   *stratagems*
120 Into his power, and modest wisdom° plucks me   *prudent moderation*
    From over-credulous haste; but God above
    Deal between thee and me, for even now
    I put myself to thy direction and
    Unspeak° mine own detraction, here abjure   *Retract*
125 The taints and blames I laid upon myself
    For° strangers to my nature. I am yet   *As*
    Unknown to woman, never was forsworn,
    Scarcely have coveted what was mine own,
    At no time broke my faith, would not betray
130 The devil to his fellow, and delight
    No less in truth than life. My first false-speaking
    Was this upon myself. What I am truly
    Is thine and my poor country's to command,
    Whither indeed, before thy here-approach,
135 Old Siward with ten thousand warlike men,
    Already at a point,° was setting forth.   *prepared*
    Now we'll together; and the chance of goodness

---

8. *Scotland . . . own:* Scotland is bountiful enough to   9. Dead to the world. ("By your rejoicing which I have in
satisfy your greed with your own royal property alone.   Christ Jesus our Lord, I die daily," 1 Corinthians 15:31).

Be like our warranted quarrel!¹—Why are you silent?

MACDUFF   Such welcome and unwelcome things at once
140   'Tis hard to reconcile.

                    Enter a DOCTOR

MALCOLM   Well, more anon. [*To the* DOCTOR] Comes the King
      forth, I pray you?

DOCTOR   Ay, sir. There are a crew of wretched souls
      That stay° his cure. Their malady convinces   *await*
      The great essay of art,² but at his touch,
145   Such sanctity hath Heaven given his hand,
      They presently amend.°   *heal*

MALCOLM   I thank you, doctor.   *Exit* [DOCTOR]

MACDUFF   What's the disease he means?

MALCOLM   'Tis called the evil³—
      A most miraculous work in this good King,
      Which often since my here-remain in England
150   I have seen him do. How he solicits° heaven   *moves by entreaty*
      Himself best knows, but strangely visited° people,   *afflicted*
      All swoll'n and ulcerous, pitiful to the eye,
      The mere° despair of surgery, he cures,   *utter*
      Hanging a golden stamp° about their necks,   *coin*
155   Put on with holy prayers; and 'tis spoken,
      To the succeeding royalty he leaves
      The healing benediction. With this strange virtue°   *power*
      He hath a heavenly gift of prophecy,
      And sundry blessings hang about his throne
      That speak him full of grace.°   *divine grace*

                    Enter ROSS

160 MACDUFF   See who comes here.

MALCOLM   My countryman, but yet I know° him not.   *recognize*

MACDUFF   My ever gentle cousin, welcome hither.

MALCOLM   I know him now. Good God betimes° remove   *quickly*
      The means that makes us strangers!

ROSS   Sir, amen.

MACDUFF   Stands Scotland where it did?

165 ROSS   Alas, poor country,
      Almost afraid to know itself. It cannot
      Be called our mother, but our grave, where nothing
      But who knows nothing is once seen to smile;⁴
      Where sighs and groans and shrieks that rend the air
170   Are made, not marked;° where violent sorrow seems   *noticed*
      A modern ecstasy.° The dead man's knell   *commonplace emotion*
      Is there scarce asked for who,⁵ and good men's lives
      Expire before the flowers in their caps,
      Dying or ere° they sicken.   *before*

MACDUFF   O relation°   *report*
      Too nice° and yet too true!   *detailed*

175 MALCOLM   What's the newest grief?

ROSS   That of an hour's age doth hiss the speaker;⁶
      Each minute teems° a new one.   *yields*

1. *the . . . quarrel:* may the chance of success be equal to
the justice of our cause.
2. *convinces . . . art:* defeats the best efforts of medical
skill.
3. "The king's evil," scrofula, thought to be cured by the
royal touch.
4. No one smiles except he who knows nothing.
5. Scarcely anyone asks for whom it is rung.
6. Cause the speaker to be hissed for telling old news.

MACDUFF How does my wife?
ROSS Why, well.
MACDUFF And all my children?
ROSS Well, too.
MACDUFF The tyrant has not battered at their peace?
180 ROSS No, they were well at peace when I did leave 'em.
MACDUFF Be not a niggard of your speech. How goes't?
ROSS When I came hither to transport the tidings
Which I have heavily° borne, there ran a rumour   *gravely*
Of many worthy fellows that were out,°   *in arms*
185 Which was to my belief witnessed the rather°   *made more credible*
For that I saw the tyrant's power° afoot.   *army*
Now is the time of° help. [*To* MALCOLM] Your eye in scotland   *moment for*
Would create soldiers, make our women fight
To doff° their dire distresses.   *remove*
MALCOLM Be't their comfort
190 We are coming thither. Gracious England hath
Lent us good Siward and ten thousand men;
An older and a better soldier none°   *there is none*
That Christendom gives out.°   *proclaims; provides*
ROSS Would I could answer
This comfort with the like. But I have words
195 That would be howled out in the desert air
Where hearing should not latch° them.   *catch*
MACDUFF What concern they—
The general cause, or is it a fee-grief°   *private woe*
Due to° some single breast?   *Owned by*
ROSS No mind that's honest
But in it shares some woe, though the main part
Pertains to you alone.
200 MACDUFF If it be mine,
Keep it not from me; quickly let me have it.
ROSS Let not your ears despise my tongue for ever,
Which shall possess them with the heaviest sound
That ever yet they heard.
MACDUFF H'm, I guess at it.
205 ROSS Your castle is surprised, your wife and babes
Savagely slaughtered. To relate the manner
Were on the quarry of these murdered deer
To add the death of you.[7]
MALCOLM Merciful heaven!
[*To* MACDUFF] What, man, ne'er pull your hat upon your
   brows.°   *conceal your grief*
210 Give sorrow words. The grief that does not speak
Whispers the o'erfraught° heart and bids it break.   *overburdened*
MACDUFF My children too?
ROSS Wife, children, servants, all
That could be found.
MACDUFF And I must be° from thence!   *had to be*
My wife killed too?
ROSS I have said.
MALCOLM Be comforted.

7. To tell how they were murdered would be to add your death to the heap of slaughtered game ("quarry").

215   Let's make us medicines of our great revenge
     To cure this deadly grief.
   MACDUFF   He has no children. All my pretty ones?
     Did you say all? O hell-kite! All?
     What, all my pretty chickens and their dam
220   At one fell swoop?
   MALCOLM   Dispute° it like a man.   *Fight*
   MACDUFF   I shall do so,
     But I must also feel it as a man.
     I cannot but remember such things were
225   That were most precious to me. Did heaven look on
     And would not take their part? Sinful Macduff,
     They were all struck for° thee. Naught° that I am,   *on account of / Wicked*
     Not for their own demerits but for mine
     Fell slaughter on their souls. Heaven rest them now.
230   MALCOLM   Be this the whetstone of your sword. Let grief
     Convert° to anger: blunt not the heart, enrage it.   *Be changed*
   MACDUFF   O, I could play the woman with mine eyes
     And braggart with my tongue! But gentle heavens
     Cut short all intermission.° Front to front°   *delay / Face-to-face*
235   Bring thou this fiend of Scotland and myself.
     Within my sword's length set him. If he scape,
     Heaven forgive him too.
   MALCOLM   This tune goes manly.
     Come, go we to the King. Our power° is ready;   *army*
     Our lack is nothing but our leave.[8] Macbeth
240   Is ripe for shaking, and the powers above
     Put on their instruments.[9] Receive what cheer you may:
     The night is long that never finds the day.   *Exeunt*

5.1

Enter a DOCTOR *of Physic° and a Waiting-*   *Physician*
   GENTLEWOMAN

   DOCTOR   I have two nights watched with you, but can perceive
     no truth in your report. When was it she last walked?
   GENTLEWOMAN   Since his majesty went into the field° I have   *battlefield*
     seen her rise from her bed, throw her nightgown upon her,
5   unlock her closet,° take forth paper, fold it, write upon't, read   *chest*
     it, afterwards seal it, and again return to bed, yet all this while
     in a most fast sleep.
   DOCTOR   A great perturbation in nature, to receive at once the
     benefit of sleep and do the effects of watching°. In this slum-   *act as if awake*
10   bery agitation° besides her walking and other actual° perfor-   *movement / active*
     mances, what at any time have you heard her say?
   GENTLEWOMAN   That, sir, which I will not report after her.
   DOCTOR   You may to me; and 'tis most meet° you should.   *proper*
   GENTLEWOMAN   Neither to you nor anyone, having no witness to
15   confirm my speech.
         Enter LADY [MACBETH] *with a taper*
     Lo you, here she comes. This is her very guise,° and, upon my   *exact habit*
     life, fast asleep. Observe her. Stand close.°   *concealed*

---

8. We have only to take leave of the King.   5.1 Location: Macbeth's castle in Dunsinane.
9. Arm themselves; set us to work as their agents.

DOCTOR   How came she by that light?

GENTLEWOMAN   Why, it stood by her. She has light by her con-
20   tinually. 'Tis her command.

DOCTOR   You see her eyes are open.

GENTLEWOMAN   Ay, but their sense are shut.

DOCTOR   What is it she does now? Look how she rubs her hands.

GENTLEWOMAN   It is an accustomed action with her, to seem
25   thus washing her hands. I have known her continue in this a
      quarter of an hour.

LADY MACBETH   Yet here's a spot.

DOCTOR   Hark, she speaks. I will set down what comes from her
      to satisfy° my remembrance the more strongly.   *support*

30   LADY MACBETH   Out, damned spot; out, I say. One, two,—why,
      then 'tis time to do't. Hell is murky. Fie, my lord, fie, a soldier
      and afeard? What need we fear who knows it when none can
      call our power to account? Yet who would have thought the
      old man to have had so much blood in him?

35   DOCTOR   Do you mark that?

LADY MACBETH   The Thane of Fife had a wife. Where is she
      now? What, will these hands ne'er be clean? No more o' that,
      my lord, no more o' that. You mar all with this starting.°   *startled movement*

DOCTOR   Go to, go to.°   You have known what you should not.   *(expression of reproof)*

40   GENTLEWOMAN   She has spoke what she should not, I am sure of
      that. Heaven knows what she has known.

LADY MACBETH   Here's the smell of the blood still. All the per-
      fumes of Arabia will not sweeten this little hand. O, O, O!

DOCTOR   What a sigh is there! The heart is sorely charged.°   *burdened*

45   GENTLEWOMAN   I would not have such a heart in my bosom for
      the dignity° of the whole body.   *worth*

DOCTOR   Well, well, well.

GENTLEWOMAN   Pray God it be, sir.

DOCTOR   This disease is beyond my practice.° Yet I have known   *skill*
50   those which have walked in their sleep who have died holily in
      their beds.

LADY MACBETH   Wash your hands, put on your nightgown, look
      not so pale. I tell you yet again, Banquo's buried. He cannot
      come out on's° grave.   *of his*

55   DOCTOR   Even so?

LADY MACBETH   To bed, to bed. There's knocking at the gate.
      Come, come, come, come, give me your hand. What's done
      cannot be undone. To bed, to bed, to bed.   *Exit*

DOCTOR   Will she go now to bed?

60   GENTLEWOMAN   Directly.

DOCTOR   Foul whisp'rings are abroad. Unnatural deeds
      Do breed unnatural troubles; infected minds
      To their deaf pillows will discharge their secrets.
      More needs she the divine° than the physician.   *priest*
65   God, God forgive us all! Look after her.
      Remove from her the means of all annoyance,°   *self-injury*
      And still keep eyes upon her. So, good night.
      My mind she has mated,° and amazed my sight.   *bewildered*
      I think, but dare not speak.

GENTLEWOMAN   Good night, good doctor.   *Exeunt*

5.2

Enter MENTEITH, CAITHNESS, ANGUS, LENNOX, *soldiers,*
[*with a drummer*] *and colours*

MENTEITH   The English power is near, led on by Malcolm,
    His uncle Siward, and the good Macduff.
    Revenges burn in them, for their dear causes
    Would to the bleeding° and the grim alarm°   *bloody / call to battle*
    Excite° the mortified° man.   *Rouse / insensible; dead*

5 ANGUS   Near Birnam Wood
    Shall we well° meet them. That way are they coming.   *doubtless*
CAITHNESS   Who knows if Donalbain be with his brother?
LENNOX   For certain, sir, he is not. I have a file°   *roster*
    Of all the gentry. There is Siward's son,
10   And many unrough° youths that even now   *beardless*
    Protest their first of manhood.[1]
MENTEITH   What does the tyrant?
CAITHNESS   Great Dunsinane he strongly fortifies.
    Some say he's mad, others that lesser hate him
    Do call it valiant fury; but for certain
15 He cannot buckle his distempered° cause   *disease-swollen*
    Within the belt of rule.°   *restraint*
ANGUS   Now does he feel
    His secret murders sticking on his hands.
    Now minutely° revolts upbraid his faith-breach.   *every minute*
    Those he commands move only in command,°   *under constraint*
20 Nothing in love. Now does he feel his title
    Hang loose about him, like a giant's robe
    Upon a dwarfish thief.
MENTEITH   Who then shall blame
    His pestered° senses to recoil and start   *tormented*
    When all that is within him does condemn
    Itself for being there?
25 CAITHNESS   Well, march we on
    To give obedience where 'tis truly owed.
    Meet we the medicine° of the sickly weal,°   *(Malcolm) / state*
    And with him pour we in our country's purge,
    Each drop of us.
LENNOX   Or so much as it needs
30 To dew° the sovereign° flower and drown the weeds.   *bedew / royal; curative*
    Make we our march towards Birnam.   *Exeunt, marching*

5.3

Enter MACBETH, [*the*] DOCTOR [*of Physic*], *and attendants*

MACBETH   Bring me no more reports. Let them fly all.°   *Let all thanes desert*
    Till Birnam Wood remove to Dunsinane
    I cannot taint° with fear. What's the boy Malcolm?   *be infected*
    Was he not born of woman? The spirits that know
5 All mortal consequences° have pronounced me thus: *human destinies*
    'Fear not, Macbeth. No man that's born of woman
    Shall e'er have power upon thee.' Then fly, false thanes,
    And mingle with the English epicures.[1]
    The mind I sway° by and the heart I bear   *rule myself*

5.2 Location: The country near Dunsinane.   5.3 Location: Macbeth's castle in Dunsinane.
1. Declare for the first time that they are men.   1. Lovers of easy, luxurious living.

10   Shall never sag with doubt nor shake with fear.
                    Enter SERVANT
            The devil damn thee black, thou cream-faced loon!°   rogue
            Where gott'st thou that goose look?
    SERVANT   There is ten thousand—
    MACBETH   Geese, villain?
    SERVANT   Soldiers, sir.
15 MACBETH   Go prick thy face and over-red thy fear,[2]
            Thou lily-livered[3] boy. What soldiers, patch?°   fool
            Death of° thy soul, those linen cheeks of thine   on
            Are counsellors to fear.° What soldiers, whey-face?   Teach others to fear
    SERVANT   The English force, so please you.
    MACBETH   Take thy face hence.   [*Exit* SERVANT]
20   Seyton!—I am sick at heart
            When I behold—Seyton, I say!—This push°   crisis
            Will cheer[4] me ever or disseat° me now.   dethrone
            I have lived long enough. My way of life
            Is fall'n into the sere,° the yellow leaf,   withered state
25   And that which should accompany old age,
            As° honour, love, obedience, troops of friends,   Such as
            I must not look to have, but in their stead
            Curses, not loud but deep, mouth-honour,° breath   lip service
            Which the poor heart would fain deny and dare not.
30   Seyton!
                    Enter SEYTON
    SEYTON   What's your gracious pleasure?
    MACBETH   What news more?
    SEYTON   All is confirmed, my lord, which was reported.
    MACBETH   I'll fight till from my bones my flesh be hacked.
            Give me my armour.
35 SEYTON   'Tis not needed yet.
    MACBETH   I'll put it on.
            Send out more horses. Skirr° the country round.   Scour
            Hang those that talk of fear. Give me mine armour.
            How does your patient, doctor?
    DOCTOR   Not so sick, my lord,
40   As she is troubled with thick-coming fancies
            That keep her from her rest.
    MACBETH   Cure her of that.
            Canst thou not minister to a mind diseased,
            Pluck from the memory a rooted sorrow,
            Raze out the written troubles of[5] the brain,
45   And with some sweet oblivious° antidote   causing forgetfulness
            Cleanse the fraught bosom of that perilous stuff
            Which weighs upon the heart?
    DOCTOR   Therein the patient
            Must minister to himself.
    MACBETH   Throw physic° to the dogs; I'll none of it.   medicine
50   [*To an attendant*] Come, put mine armour on. Give me my staff.°   lance
            Seyton, send out. Doctor, the thanes fly from me.

---

2. Redden your fearful pallor.
3. Lacking blood in your liver (thought to be the seat of
courage); cowardly.

4. Comfort; enthrone or establish (punning on "cheer/
chair").
5. Erase the troubles engraved in.

[*To an attendant*] Come, sir, dispatch.°—If thou couldst, doctor, cast   *hurry*
The water[6] of my land, find her disease,
And purge it to a sound and pristine health,
55   I would applaud thee to the very echo,
That should applaud again.   [*To an attendant*] Pull't off, I say.[7]
[*To the* DOCTOR] what rhubarb, cyme,° or what purgative drug   *senna (medicinal plant)*
Would scour° these English hence? Hear'st thou of them?   *purge*

DOCTOR   Ay, my good lord. Your royal preparation
Makes us hear something.

60   MACBETH [*to an attendant*]   Bring it[8] after me.
I will not be afraid of death and bane°   *destruction*
Till Birnam Forest come to Dunsinane.

DOCTOR [*aside*]   Were I from Dunsinane away and clear,
Profit again should hardly draw me here.[9]   *Exeunt*

5.4

Enter MALCOLM, SIWARD, MACDUFF, SIWARD'S SON, MEN-
TEITH, CAITHNESS, ANGUS, *and* SOLDIERS, *marching,*
[*with a drummer*] *and colours*

MALCOLM   Cousins, I hope the days are near at hand
That chambers° will be safe.   *bedrooms*

MENTEITH   We doubt it nothing.°   *not at all*

SIWARD   What wood is this before us?

MENTEITH   The wood of Birnam.

MALCOLM   Let every soldier hew him down a bough
5   And bear't before him. Thereby shall we shadow°   *conceal*
The numbers of our host, and make discovery°   *reconnaissance*
Err in report of us.

A SOLDIER   It shall be done.

SIWARD   We learn no other but the confident tyrant
Keeps still in Dunsinane, and will endure
Our setting down before°'t.   *laying siege to*

10   MALCOLM   'Tis his main hope,
For where there is advantage° to be gone,   *opportunity*
Both more and less° have given him the revolt,   *great and lowly*
And none serve with him but constrainèd things,
Whose hearts are absent too.

MACDUFF   Let our just censures
15   Attend the true event,[1] and put we on
Industrious soldiership.

SIWARD   The time approaches
That will with due decision make us know
What we shall say we have, and what we owe.
Thoughts speculative their unsure hopes relate,
20   But certain issue strokes must arbitrate;[2]
Towards which, advance the war.   *Exeunt, marching*

---

6. *cast / The water*: analyze the urine as a method of diagnosis.
7. A piece of armor is not properly fitted; Macbeth orders the attendant to take it off.
8. The armor not yet on Macbeth.
9. No large fees could lure me back.

5.4 Location: The country near Birnam Wood.
1. *Let . . . event*: Let our judgments await the actual outcome.
2. *Thoughts . . . arbitrate*: Speculation produces hopes and unconfirmed optimism, but the issue will only be decided by action.

5.5

Enter MACBETH, SEYTON, *and soldiers, with [a drummer]*
and colours

MACBETH   Hang out our banners on the outward walls.
  The cry is still 'They come.' Our castle's strength
  Will laugh a siege to scorn. Here let them lie
  Till famine and the ague eat them up.
5 Were they not forced° with those that should be ours   *reinforced*
  We might have met them dareful,° beard to beard,   *boldly*
  And beat them backward home.
      A cry within of women
                              What is that noise?
SEYTON   It is the cry of women, my good lord.   *[Exit]*
MACBETH   I have almost forgot the taste of fears.
10 The time has been my senses would have cooled°   *been chilled with terror*
  To hear a night-shriek, and my fell of hair°   *hair on my skin*
  Would at a dismal treatise° rouse and stir   *story*
  As life were in't. I have supped full with horrors.
  Direness, familiar to my slaughterous thoughts,
  Cannot once start° me.   *startle*
      [Enter SEYTON*]*
15   Wherefore was that cry?
SEYTON   The Queen, my lord, is dead.
MACBETH   She should have died hereafter.[1]
  There would have been a time for such a word.
  Tomorrow, and tomorrow, and tomorrow
  Creeps in this petty pace from day to day
20 To the last syllable of recorded time,
  And all our yesterdays have lighted fools
  The way to dusty death. Out, out, brief candle.
  Life's but a walking shadow, a poor player
  That struts and frets his hour upon the stage,
25 And then is heard no more. It is a tale
  Told by an idiot, full of sound and fury,
  Signifying nothing.
      Enter a MESSENGER
                          Thou com'st to use
  Thy tongue: thy story quickly.
MESSENGER   Gracious my lord,
  I should report that which I say I saw,
  But know not how to do't.
30 MACBETH   Well, say, sir.
MESSENGER   As I did stand my watch upon the hill
  I looked toward Birnam, and anon methought
  The wood began to move.
MACBETH   Liar and slave!
MESSENGER   Let me endure your wrath if't be not so.
35 Within this three mile may you see it coming.
  I say, a moving grove.
MACBETH   If thou speak'st false
  Upon the next tree shalt thou hang alive
  Till famine cling° thee. If thy speech be sooth,°   *wither / truth*

5.5 Location: Macbeth's castle.
1. She would certainly have died someday; she should have died at another, more peaceful time.

I care not if thou dost for me as much.
40 I pall° in resolution, and begin   *fail*
To doubt th'equivocation of the fiend,
That lies like truth. 'Fear not till Birnam Wood
Do come to Dunsinane'—and now a wood
Comes toward Dunsinane. Arm, arm, and out.
45 If this which he avouches does appear
There is nor flying hence nor tarrying here.
I 'gin to be aweary of the sun,
And wish th'estate° o'th' world were now undone.   *ordered structure*
Ring the alarum bell. [*Alarums*] Blow wind, come wrack,°   *ruin*
50 At least we'll die with harness° on our back.   *Exeunt*   *armor*

5.6

Enter MALCOLM, SIWARD, MACDUFF, *and their army with*
boughs, [with a drummer] and colours

MALCOLM   Now near enough. Your leafy screens throw down,
And show° like those you are.   *appear*
                    [*They throw down the boughs*]
                                                                You, worthy uncle,
Shall with my cousin, your right noble son,
Lead our first battle.° Worthy Macduff and we   *battalion*
5 Shall take upon's what else remains to do
According to our order.°   *battle plan*
SIWARD   Fare you well.
Do we but find the tyrant's power° tonight,   *army*
Let us be beaten if we cannot fight.
MACDUFF   Make all our trumpets speak, give them all breath,
10 Those clamorous harbingers of blood and death.
                                        Exeunt. Alarums continued

5.7

Enter MACBETH

MACBETH   They have tied me to a stake. I cannot fly,
But bear-like I must fight the course.[1] What's he
That was not born of woman? Such a one
Am I to fear, or none.
                    Enter YOUNG SIWARD
5 YOUNG SIWARD   What is thy name?
MACBETH   Thou'lt be afraid to hear it.
YOUNG SIWARD   No, though thou call'st thyself a hotter name
Than any is in hell.
MACBETH   My name's Macbeth.
YOUNG SIWARD   The devil himself could not pronounce a title
More hateful to mine ear.
10 MACBETH   No, nor more fearful.
YOUNG SIWARD   Thou liest, abhorrèd tyrant. With my sword
I'll prove the lie thou speak'st.
                    [*They*] *fight, and* YOUNG SIWARD [*is*] *slain*
MACBETH   Thou wast born of woman,

5.6 Location: As before.
5.7 Location: As before.
1. Referring to the practice of bearbaiting, in which a
bear was tied to a stake and set upon by dogs. *course:*
round of bearbaiting.

But swords I smile at, weapons laugh to scorn,
Brandished by man that's of a woman born.

Exit [with the body]

5.8

Alarums. Enter MACDUFF

MACDUFF   That way the noise is. Tyrant, show thy face!
If thou beest slain and with° no stroke of mine,   by
My wife and children's ghosts will haunt me still.°   always
I cannot strike at wretched kerns,° whose arms   Irish foot soldiers
5   Are hired to bear their staves.° Either thou, Macbeth,   spears
Or else my sword with an unbattered edge
I sheathe again undeeded.¹ There thou shouldst be;
By this great clatter one of greatest note
Seems bruited.° Let me find him, fortune,   announced
10 And more I beg not.   *Exit. Alarums*

5.9

Enter MALCOLM *and* SIWARD

SIWARD   This way, my lord. The castle's gently rendered.°   surrendered
The tyrant's people on both sides do fight.
The noble thanes do bravely in the war.
The day almost itself professes yours,
And little is to do.
5 MALCOLM   We have met with foes
That strike beside us.¹
SIWARD   Enter, sir, the castle.   *Exeunt. Alarum*

5.10

Enter MACBETH

MACBETH   Why should I play the Roman fool,° and die   the suicide
On mine own sword? Whiles I see lives, the gashes
Do better upon them.

Enter MACDUFF

MACDUFF   Turn, hell-hound, turn.
MACBETH   Of all men else I have avoided thee.
5   But get thee back. My soul is too much charged
With blood of thine already.
MACDUFF   I have no words;
My voice is in my sword, thou bloodier villain
Than terms can give thee out.°   words can describe
[*They*] *fight; alarum*
MACBETH   Thou losest labour.°   waste effort
As easy mayst thou the intrenchant° air   incapable of being cut
10 With thy keen sword impress° as make me bleed.   mark
Let fall thy blade on vulnerable crests;
I bear a charmèd life, which must not yield
To one of woman born.
MACDUFF   Despair° thy charm,   Despair of
And let the angel° whom thou still hast served   (evil) spirit

---

5.8 Location: Before Macbeth's castle; the battle continues.
1. Having accomplished no deeds.
5.9 Location: Before Macbeth's castle.
1. Fight on our side; deliberately miss us.
5.10 Location: Scene continues.

<table>
<tr><td>15</td><td>Tell thee Macduff was from his mother's womb</td><td></td></tr>
</table>

15   Tell thee Macduff was from his mother's womb
     Untimely° ripped.   *Prematurely*
MACBETH   Accursèd be that tongue that tells me so,
     For it hath cowed° my better part of man;   *intimidated*
     And be these juggling fiends no more believed,
20   That palter° with us in a double sense,   *equivocate*
     That keep the word of promise to our ear
     And break it to our hope. I'll not fight with thee.
MACDUFF   Then yield thee, coward,
     And live to be the show and gaze° o'th' time.   *spectacle*
25   We'll have thee as our rarer monsters° are,   *prodigies*
     Painted upon a pole,[1] and underwrit
     'Here may you see the tyrant.'
MACBETH   I will not yield
     To kiss the ground before young Malcolm's feet,
     And to be baited° with the rabble's curse.   *harassed*
30   Though Birnam Wood be come to Dunsinane,
     And thou opposed being of no woman born,
     Yet I will try the last.° Before my body   *the last resort*
     I throw my warlike shield. Lay on, Macduff,
     And damned be him that first cries 'Hold, enough!'
                            Exeunt fighting. Alarums
     [*They*] *enter fighting, and* MACBETH [*is*] *slain.* [*Exit* MAC-
     DUFF *with Macbeth's body*]

5.11

Retreat[1] *and flourish. Enter with* [*a drummer*] *and col-
ours* MALCOLM, SIWARD, ROSS, *thanes, and soldiers*
MALCOLM   I would° the friends we miss were safe arrived.   *wish*
SIWARD   Some must go off;° and yet by these[2] I see   *die*
     So great a day as this is cheaply bought.
MALCOLM   Macduff is missing, and your noble son.
5   ROSS [*to* SIWARD]   Your son, my lord, has paid a soldier's debt.
     He only lived but till he was a man,
     The which no sooner had his prowess confirmed
     In the unshrinking station[3] where he fought,
     But like a man he died.
SIWARD   Then he is dead?
10   ROSS   Ay, and brought off the field. Your cause of sorrow
     Must not be measured by his worth, for then
     It hath no end.
SIWARD   Had he his hurts before?°   *on his front*
ROSS   Ay, on the front.
SIWARD   Why then, God's soldier be he.
     Had I as many sons as I have hairs
15   I would not wish them to a fairer death;
     And so his knell is knolled.
MALCOLM   He's worth more sorrow,
     And that I'll spend for him.
SIWARD   He's worth no more.

---

1. Painted on a cloth or board supported by a pole as a
form of advertisement.
5.11 Location: Within the castle.

1. A trumpet call signaling the end of the battle.
2. To judge from those who are present.
3. Post from which he did not shrink.

	They say he parted° well and paid his score,	*departed*
	And so God be with him. Here comes newer comfort.	

Enter MACDUFF *with Macbeth's head*

20	MACDUFF [*to* MALCOLM] Hail, King, for so thou art. Behold where stands[4]	
	Th'usurper's cursèd head. The time is free.°	*free from tyranny*
	I see thee compassed with thy kingdom's pearl,[5]	
	That speak my salutation in their minds,	
	Whose voices I desire aloud with mine:	
	Hail, King of Scotland!	
25	ALL BUT MALCOLM Hail, King of Scotland!	

Flourish

	MALCOLM We shall not spend a large expense of time	
	Before we reckon with° your several loves	*make an accounting of*
	And make us even with you.° My thanes and kinsmen,	*reward your loyalty*
	Henceforth be earls, the first that ever Scotland	
30	In such an honour named. What's more to do	
	Which would be planted newly with the time,[6]	
	As calling home our exiled friends abroad,	
	That fled the snares of watchful tyranny,	
	Producing forth[7] the cruel ministers°	*agents*
35	Of this dead butcher and his fiend-like queen—	
	Who, as 'tis thought, by self and violent hands°	*her own violent hands*
	Took off her life—this and what needful else	
	That calls upon us, by the grace of grace	
	We will perform in measure, time, and place.[8]	
40	So thanks to all at once, and to each one,	
	Whom we invite to see us crowned at Scone.	

Flourish. Exeunt Omnes°   *all*

---

4. Presumably upon a pole or lance.
5. I see you surrounded by your nobles, here called the "pearl" of the kingdom.
6. Which should be performed at the beginning of this

new era.
7. Bringing forward for trial.
8. In due order, at the proper time and place.

Antony and Cleopatra

What if Shakespeare had had second thoughts about *Romeo and Juliet*? He might have tried something a little different. In this version, the lovers, neither youthful nor married to each other, are involved in a long-standing, adulterous relationship. Romeo, thinking Juliet dead because she has sent a messenger with that lie, kills himself—though with a sword rather than poison. He partly bungles the job, however, and hence takes a while to die. Juliet resolves to follow him, but she delays for the entire fifth act before killing herself—though with poison rather than a sword. And when they are both finally dead, the audience may be less likely to lament the loss of "star-crossed lovers" than celebrate the fulfillment of a heroic passion.

In the event Shakespeare did have second thoughts about *Romeo and Juliet*; he called these second thoughts *Antony and Cleopatra* (late 1606–early 1607). The last of Shakespeare's three love tragedies, the play also rewrites *Othello*, the middle work of this group, converting its threat from the East, there represented by the Turks, into both a threat and an opportunity from the East, here represented by the Egyptians. All three tragedies set their domestic concerns thematically against the backdrop of bloody political conflict, but formally against the expectations of romantic comedy. All three seem like comedies that somehow get derailed. But *Antony and Cleopatra* replaces the emphasis on youth of romantic comedy, of *Romeo and Juliet*, and even of Desdemona in *Othello* with the most sustained, complex portrayal of mature love in Shakespeare's dramatic career.

In Shakespeare's romantic comedies, problem plays, and romances, the female protagonist often dominates the scene. But in the tragedies that Shakespeare composed from roughly 1599 to 1608, *Antony and Cleopatra* is the only such candidate. Moreover, following a series of tragedies—*Hamlet, Othello, King Lear,* and *Macbeth*—in which the protagonist's psychology is consistently probed, *Antony and Cleopatra* almost completely avoids soliloquy. Antony's and Cleopatra's motives often remain opaque—arguably, even to themselves. We never definitively learn why Antony thinks marriage to Octavia will solve his political problems, why Cleopatra flees at Actium, why she negotiates with Caesar in the last act. Instead of self-revelation, the play offers contradictory framing commentary by minor figures. These external perspectives help impart an epic feel, as do the geographical and scenic shifts, which also produce a loose, fragmentary, and capacious structure alien to classically inspired notions of proper dramatic form. *Antony and Cleopatra* is thus a new, transitional kind of tragedy. Its restlessness is of a piece with that of *Pericles*, perhaps the next play Shakespeare wrote and the first of his late romances. And the intimations of transcendence with which *Antony and Cleopatra* ends point toward the magical or supernatural resolutions of the romances more generally.

The play may also be compared to Shakespeare's other Roman tragedies, *Julius Caesar* and *Coriolanus*. All are based on Thomas North's translation of *Plutarch's Lives of the Noble Grecians and Romanes* (1579)—Shakespeare's favorite source, with the exception of Raphael Holinshed's *Chronicles of England, Scotland, and Ireland,* and one that he follows closely here. All three plays rely heavily on blank verse while almost entirely avoiding rhyme. Here Shakespeare may have followed the Earl of Surrey's sixteenth-century blank-verse translation of part of the *Aeneid* (19 B.C.E.), Virgil's epic of the legendary founding of Rome, itself understood as an allegory of the city-state's bloody transition from republic (rule by senatorial aristocracy) to empire (monarchical power) in the poet's own day.

Octavius Caesar, later known as Augustus, as on this medal. From Guillaume Du Choul, *Discours de la Religion des Anciens Romains* (1567 ed.).

It is this transition that Shakespeare dramatizes in *Julius Caesar* and *Antony and Cleopatra*. Chronologically, *Antony* picks up where *Julius Caesar* leaves off. That earlier play focuses on Caesar's assassination by republicans, led by Brutus and Cassius, and the assassins' subsequent defeat at the hands of Mark Antony (Caesar's lieutenant) and Octavius Caesar (Caesar's young grandnephew and adoptive son). *Antony and Cleopatra*, which covers the period from 40 to 30 b.c.e., completes the narrative of Roman civil war and the final destruction of the Republic. The dominant military power throughout the Mediterranean and beyond, Rome is ruled by the triumvirate of Lepidus, Octavius Caesar, and Mark Antony, who govern, respectively, the Mediterranean portions of Africa, Europe, and Asia. Accordingly, *Antony and Cleopatra* partly turns away from *Julius Caesar*'s emphasis on the struggle over Rome's internal political system, looking instead to Rome's external imperial domains. Correspondingly, the stylistic restraint fitted to Brutus's republican restraint gives way to an extravagant, hyperbolic verse in accord with the empire's expansive grandeur. This would thus seem the theater for heroic, legendary, even mythic performance: Antony is associated with Hercules, and Antony and Cleopatra are repeatedly compared to Mars and Venus.

Yet *Antony and Cleopatra* actually investigates the possibility of such performance in a postheroic world. It offers an epic view of the political arena but deprives that arena of heroic significance. Mark Antony and Octavius Caesar contend for political supremacy, but the love between Antony and Cleopatra increasingly occupies center stage. The work then asks whether heroic meaning can be transplanted to the ostensibly private terrain of love. Much of the play's fascination arises from this intertwining of empire and sexuality. Plutarch and other classical writers were preoccupied with what for them was the opposition between the political and moral virtue of the conquering West, and the luxurious, feminized sexuality of the older civilizations of the subjugated East. This understanding of empire reemerged in the Renaissance during a new era of Western expansion, marked by an increasingly racialized and still sexualized view of non-European peoples. Just months before the probable first performance of the play, King James authorized the establishment of an English colony in North America—an undertaking that resulted in the founding of Jamestown the following year. As in other western European countries at the time, Rome was the central model of imperial greatness. The view of Egypt was more mixed, however: it was both the preeminent source of ancient wisdom and a land that, even though Rome had defeated it, threatened to transmit its decadence to the victors.

Accordingly, *Antony and Cleopatra* itself seems designed to elicit complicated judgments. This has often proven difficult in performance. Long supplanted on the stage by John Dryden's *All for Love* (1678), which recasts Shakespeare's story as a tragedy of private life, the play came into its own only after 1800 in the heyday of the British Empire, with Cleopatra routinely embodying Oriental sexual vice. The text initially seems to justify this interpretation: Rome is contrasted to Egypt, West to East, the conquerors to the conquered. Rapid shifts of scene across enormous distances accentuate this division. A sober, masculine military ethos opposes a frivolous, feminized, and sexualized court. Political opportunism drives Antony's marriage to Octavia, love and sexual desire his relationship with Cleopatra; he chooses between fidelity to a chaste, white wife and adultery with a promiscuous, "tawny," "black" seductress (1.1.6, 1.5.28). That seductress has a smaller political role than in Plutarch—a change which accentuates the basic conflict. Where Caesar employs rational self-interest (he is the "universal landlord," 3.13.72), Antony revels in extravagant generosity and challenges Caesar to one-on-one combat. Young Caesar is a bureaucrat of the future, old Antony a warrior of the past. Caesar's concerns are public, Antony's private. Antony is guilty by association with his brother and his previous wife, Fulvia, who attack Caesar. By contrast, Caesar promises that "the time of universal peace is near" (4.6.4), an assertion that anticipates the *Pax Romana* (Roman peace) he instituted throughout the Empire and the birth of Christ in a Roman province during his long rule.

Yet the play seems to create such dichotomies only to undermine them. Antony boasts of his valor at Philippi, while Caesar "alone / Dealt on lieutenantry" (battled exclusively through his officers; 3.11.38–39). Earlier, however, Antony's "officer" Ventidius remarks, "Caesar and Antony have ever won / More in their officer than person" (3.1.16–17). Caesar's promise of "universal peace" is anticipated in a version of Christ's Last Supper that Antony shares with his followers.

> Tend me tonight.
> Maybe it is the period of your duty.
> Haply you shall not see me more; or if,
> A mangled shadow. Perchance tomorrow
> You'll serve another master.
>
> (4.2.24–28)

Enobarbus, who functions like a skeptical chorus, criticizes Antony for moving his friends to tears. But that skepticism is itself challenged. It leads Enobarbus to become a Judas figure who betrays his master by defecting to Caesar and who dies shortly thereafter, his heart broken by Antony's generosity.

Even the geographical contrast of the play partly dissolves into parallelisms: Roman war is eroticized, Egyptian love is militarized. The external representation of the lovers' relationship, the absence of scenes of them alone, and their pride in exhibiting their affair intensify the feeling that love and war influence each other, that there is no distinction between public and private. Furthermore, love is on both sides of the divide. Late in the play, Antony, focused exclusively on Cleopatra, is heroically preceded in suicide by his aptly named servant Eros (love), a figure from Plutarch. But when the work opens, Antony's neglect of military command is criticized as "this dotage of our General's" by Philo (again, "love"; 1.1.1), a figure invented by Shakespeare.

The eroticization of Rome also takes the form of powerful feelings directed toward Antony. Octavius Caesar at times acts almost as if he were the son—rather than grandnephew and adopted son—of Cleopatra's former lover, Julius Caesar, whose paternal role Antony has usurped. Octavius Caesar is disgusted by Antony and Cleopatra's theatrical coronation:

> At the feet sat
> Caesarion, whom they call my father's son,
> And all the unlawful issue that their lust
> Since then hath made between them.
>
> (3.6.5–8)

Here, there is a possible confusion between Antony and the older Caesar and a definite one between Caesarion and the younger Caesar, both of whom are "my father's son." At Antony's death, Caesar movingly recalls his foe:

> . . . thou, my brother, my competitor
> In top of all design, my mate in empire,
> Friend and companion in the front of war,

> The arm of mine own body, and the heart
> Where mine his thoughts did kindle.
>   (5.1.42–46)

This outpouring of emotion leads in contradictory directions. By calling Antony his "brother" and "mate," and by invoking a meeting of "heart" and mind, Caesar on the one hand suggests an intimacy between the two men that recalls Renaissance celebrations of close male friendship but that also borders on the erotic. On the other hand, he neutralizes any filial anxiety he may feel by describing Antony first as "my brother" and then as a subordinate, "the arm of mine own body."

Most important, this strategy of undermining apparent distinctions has the effect of draining the political world of meaning. *Julius Caesar*'s struggle between republic and empire arises only peripherally in *Antony and Cleopatra,* where it is voiced by Pompey (2.6.15–19), who is bought off, attacked, and finally murdered by the triumvirs. The Republic is thus all but dead when *Antony and Cleopatra* opens. Egypt's independence is at stake, although this occurs only to Cleopatra—belatedly and perhaps duplicitously. That leaves only the conflict between Antony and Caesar, a conflict, however, that simply concerns the desires of two ambitious men. The end of the Roman civil war is also important, but it is hard either to celebrate the victory of Caesar or lament the defeat of Antony. The disabused view of political power that emerges could be construed as an implicit critique of the centralizing monarchs of Shakespeare's own time.

On the other hand, the political symbolism of the two men is certainly antithetical. Caesar astutely adopts republican style, whereas Antony offends Roman sensibilities by taking on monarchical trappings (3.6.1–19). Antony's antagonist does not emulate the older Caesar, whose sexual and military conquests were intertwined (3.13.82–85). Hence the younger Caesar represents not the preservation but the diminution of traditional Roman values, a constriction of a heroic culture of which Antony is the last survivor. The play insists that politics and sex (or any kind of grandeur) are irrevocably sundered, that one can no longer have it both ways.

Certainly, Antony and Cleopatra cannot. The play characterizes Antony and Cleopatra through a language of greatness, shared by the protagonists and minor figures alike, only to subvert that rhetoric through still other commentary and, even more, through the behavior of Antony and Cleopatra themselves. Although Shakespeare makes them more sympathetic than they are in Plutarch, they remain maddeningly self-absorbed and self-destructive—lying, ignoring urgent business, acting impulsively, bullying underlings, reveling in vulgarity, apparently betraying each other. They are also militarily peripheral, as the fighting scenes, except for the first Battle of Alexandria, testify. Shakespeare's uncharacteristic decision to follow the practice of classical theater and keep all combat offstage leaves only a feeling of being let down, as helpless observers report on the debacle. Thus, Enobarbus laments at Actium:

> Naught, naught, all naught! I can behold no longer.
> Th'*Antoniad,* the Egyptian admiral,
> With all their sixty, fly and turn the rudder.
>   (3.10.1–3)

At the last battle of the play, it is Antony's turn:

> All is lost.
> This foul Egyptian hath betrayèd me.
> My fleet hath yielded to the foe, and yonder
> They cast their caps up, and carouse together
> Like friends long lost.
>   (4.13.9–13)

But this is not the whole story or even, in the end, most of it. Antony and Cleopatra are great not despite their failings but because of them. Inability to fit into Caesar's narrowed world of self-discipline sets them apart. Their outsized grandeur can be described only through paradoxical hyperbole. Antony's heart "is become the bellows and the fan / To cool a gipsy's lust": his heart is a fan that cools Cleopatra's lust by satisfying it, but in so doing he rekindles her passion, as if his heart were also a bellows (1.1.9–10). Similarly, when Cleopatra meets Antony, "pretty dimpled boys" (2.2.208) attend her

> With divers-coloured fans whose wind did seem
> To glow the delicate cheeks which they did cool,
> And what they undid did.
>
> (2.2.209–11)

And when told that marriage to Octavia will force Antony to abandon Cleopatra, Enobarbus demurs in the play's most famous lines:

> Never. He will not.
> Age cannot wither her, nor custom stale
> Her infinite variety. Other women cloy
> The appetites they feed, but she makes hungry
> Where most she satisfies.
>
> (2.2.239–43)

These passages might be considered accounts of insatiable middle-aged lust. The trick of the play is to convince the audience that they are really about love. Antony's feelings may seem easier to believe than Cleopatra's: he is the one who gives up an empire. By contrast, Cleopatra's combination of teasing frivolity, comic jealousy, and cold calculation have rendered her motives suspect. Yet Shakespeare gives her passages of extraordinary dignity early in the play, when Antony decides to leave her upon hearing of his wife Fulvia's death.

> Courteous lord, one word.
> Sir, you and I must part; but that's not it.
> Sir, you and I have loved; but there's not it;
> That you know well. Something it is I would—
> O, my oblivion is a very Antony,
> And I am all forgotten.
>
> (1.3.87–92)

Cleopatra experiences something more than she can express. Its articulation, therefore, initially takes the form of a failure to articulate. There is an echo of this later, when Enobarbus attempts to describe her to his fellow Romans: "her own person . . . beggared all description" (2.2.203–04). Here, however, Cleopatra tries to convey her meaning through a witticism: her forgetfulness makes her like Antony, who is forgetful of her. She forgets and is forgotten. But when Antony misses the point, thinking he has merely witnessed idle wordplay, she corrects him.

> 'Tis sweating labour
> To bear such idleness so near the heart
> As Cleopatra this. But sir, forgive me,
> . . . .
> . . . be deaf to my unpitied folly,
> And all the gods go with you.
>
> (1.3.94–100)

In short, Cleopatra's playfulness is the mere surface of her essential depth, a depth that involves a "sweating labour" like that of childbirth.

The last two acts put that depth to the test, ultimately making Cleopatra the play's central character. *Antony and Cleopatra*'s geographical restlessness diminishes as the protagonists' sphere of activity is reduced to Alexandria. Cleopatra sends Antony a fabricated, manipulative report of her death, he botches his suicide in response, and she then refuses to leave her monument to attend him as he lies dying. Instead, she hoists him up to her with the comment, "Here's sport indeed. How heavy weighs my lord!" (4.16.33), where "sport" is both playful and bitter, where "weighs" carries both physical and psychological meaning, and, hence, where the scene as a whole combines grotesque comedy with genuine pathos. Structurally, Antony's presumably climactic death becomes a mere false ending that shifts the burden of significance to the final act. Egypt and Cleopatra are what matter. Egypt has been associated throughout with the over-flowing that Antony is faulted for at the outset. Antony declares his love for Cleopatra by rejecting the state he rules: "Let Rome in Tiber melt, and the wide arch / Of the ranged empire fall" (1.1.35–36). Upon hearing of Antony's marriage to Octavia, Cleopatra prays, "Melt Egypt into Nile, and kindly creatures / Turn all to serpents!" (2.5.78–79). This apocalyptic imagery, which dissolves all distinction, anticipates Antony's loss of self when he thinks Cleopatra has betrayed him. His body seems to him as "indistinct / As water is in water" (4.15.10–11). The language of liquefaction is also connected to the confusion of gender identity. Antony

> is not more manlike
> Than Cleopatra, nor the queen of Ptolemy
> More womanly than he.
>
> (1.4.5–7)

And Cleopatra reports, "I . . . put my tires and mantles on him whilst / I wore his sword Philippan" (2.5.21–23). Depending on one's perspective, this behavior either danger-ously confuses gender roles, thereby leading to Antony's ignominious flight at Actium, or overcomes a destructive opposition.

Cleopatra herself, who metaphorically overflows boundaries, is literally linked to Egypt throughout the play. In particular, she is specifically identified with the Egyptian goddess Isis (3.6.17), who is invoked several times in the play, probably on the basis of Plutarch's *On Isis and Osiris*. Isis is the sister-wife of Osiris, whom she restores after he is pursued to his death by his brother-rival, Typhon. The conclusion thus seeks the regenerative powers of the Nile in Cleopatra. It asks whether she really is the equiva-lent of Isis, whether she really is the wife of Antony (Osiris), whether she really does restore him after he is pursued to his death by his brother (Caesar).

This is the work of Cleopatra's suicide, which makes good on these imagistic pat-terns, retrospectively justifying Antony's decision to die for her. We may desire the pro-tagonists' deaths in Shakespeare's earlier tragedies, perhaps because life no longer has any meaning for these characters. But *Antony and Cleopatra* goes further: it convinces us that the suicides of the two lovers is a heroic achievement, that anything less would constitute abject failure. The ending also evokes the synthesis precluded by the play's dichotomies but implied by its more subtle patterns. Cleopatra dies the death of a Roman man:

> My resolution's placed, and I have nothing
> Of woman in me. Now from head to foot
> I am marble-constant. Now the fleeting moon
> No planet is of mine.
>
> (5.2.234–37)

She also dies the death of a faithful Roman wife:

> . . . methinks I hear
> Antony call. I see him rouse himself
> To praise my noble act. . . .
> . . . Husband, I come.
> Now to that name my courage prove my title.
>
> (5.2.274–79)

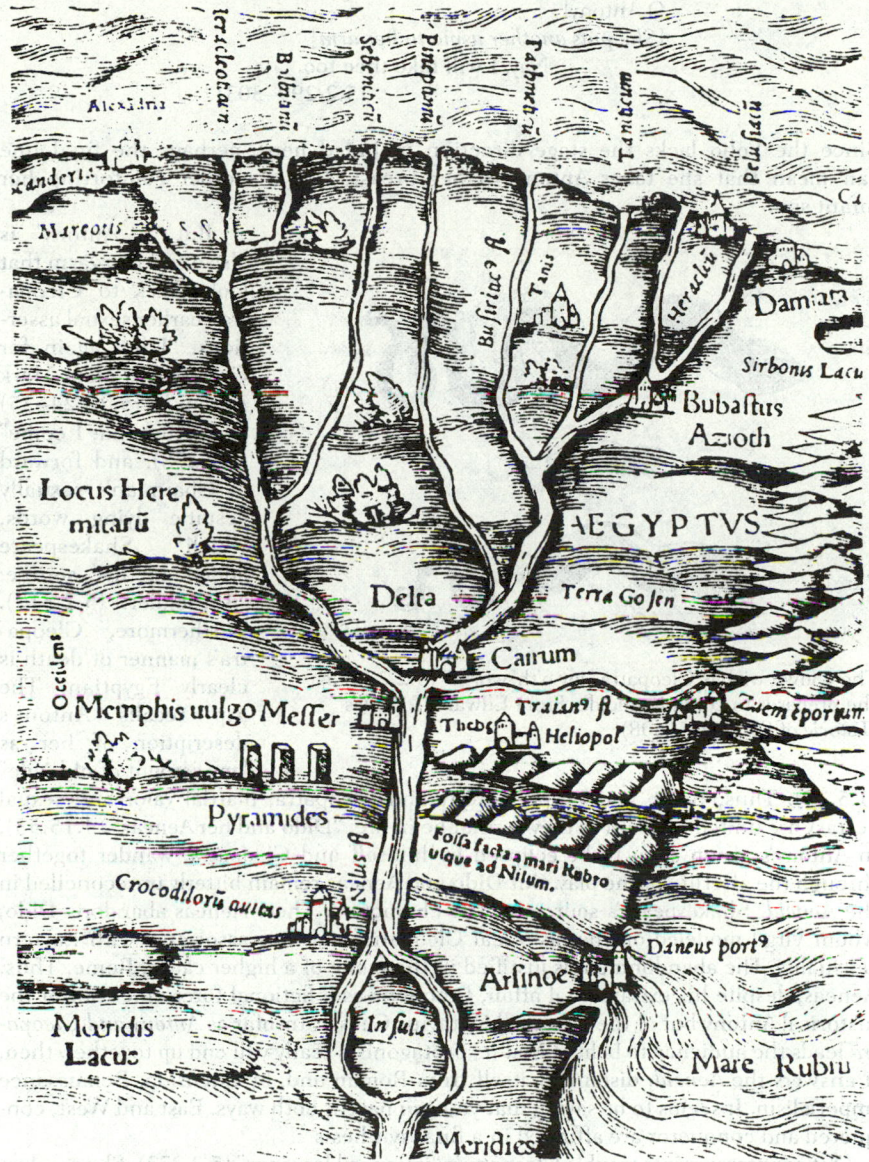

The Nile delta, showing the northern end of the river as it flows into the Mediterranean Sea. Alexandria is visible near the upper left-hand corner. From a map in Sebastian Münster's *Cosmographiae universalis* (1550).

And in taking the poisonous asp to her breast, she may become a Roman mother as well, in a passage that recalls her earlier representation of intense feeling in the language of childbirth:

> Peace, peace.
> Dost thou not see my baby at my breast,
> That sucks the nurse asleep?
> . . . .
> As sweet as balm, as soft as air, as gentle.

O Antony!
[*She puts another aspic to her arm*]
Nay, I will take thee too.
(5.2.299–303)

Since the Folio lacks the stage direction included here, perhaps the final line can mean that she takes Antony to her breast, like a mother comforting her infant son.

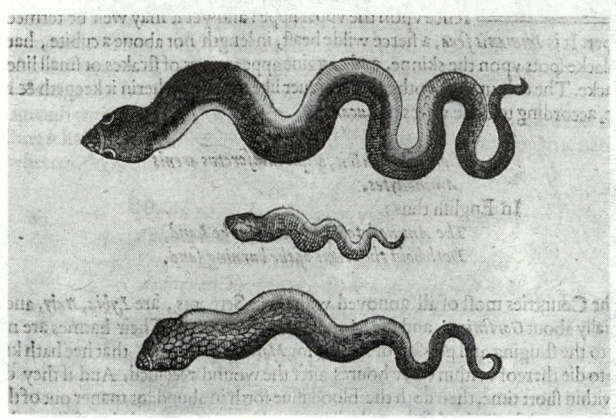

The Clown wishes Cleopatra "joy o'th' worm" (5.2.270) as she prepares to commit suicide. From Edward Topsell's *Historie of Serpents* (1608).

But "O Antony" is also a cry of orgasm that looks back to Cleopatra's earlier sexual assertions, "I am again for Cydnus / To meet Mark Antony" (5.2.224–25) and "Husband, I come" (5.2.278), and forward to Charmian's sexually ecstatic dying words, which Shakespeare added to his source: "Ah, soldier!" (5.2.319). Furthermore, Cleopatra's manner of death is clearly Egyptian. The asp recalls Antony's description of her as "my serpent of old Nile" (1.5.25). Thus, Rome and Egypt, Antony and Cleopatra, martial valor and sexual ecstasy are united in death as they cannot be in life. "Dido and her Aeneas" (4.15.53), in Antony's vision soon to be eclipsed by himself and Cleopatra, wander together through the afterlife of the play. But Dido and Aeneas remain bitterly unreconciled in the *Aeneid,* Shakespeare's source for the characters. There Aeneas abandons Dido, whom Virgil modeled on the historical Cleopatra and thus associated with Eastern sensuality. The abandonment is justified in the name of a higher cause, Rome. Thus, Aeneas, despite his extramarital affair, functions as a fictional forerunner not of the historical Antony but of the historical Octavius Caesar. Insofar as *Antony and Cleopatra* leads the audience to believe that its protagonists really will end up together, then, it answers the *Aeneid,* distancing itself from Roman and, by extension, Renaissance imperialism. It seems to be saying that you *can* have it both ways. East and West, conquered and conqueror are affirmed in a final synthesis.

Yet countercurrents trouble Cleopatra's "immortal longings" (5.2.272). She resolves on suicide not when she learns that Antony killed himself for her but when she becomes certain that Caesar plans to lead her in a humiliating triumph in Rome. Recognizing that her suicide will ruin Caesar's plans, she takes pleasure in imagining that Antony will "mock / The luck of Caesar," that the asp will "call great Caesar ass / Unpolicied" (5.2.276–77, 298–99). The concluding triumphant rhetoric thus cleans up earlier dubious behavior and puts the best face on defeat. Heroic aristocratic individualism can act in the world only by leaving it. Moreover, the domestic Cleopatra of the conclusion might seem the reduction to a conventional gender role of a woman who challenged sexual hierarchy. At her death, Cleopatra "lies / A lass unparalleled" (5.2.305–06). This alliterative eulogy juxtaposes the Latinate "unparalleled," typical of the extravagant rhetoric of the play, with the homespun "lass." Both stylistically and semantically, that humble word also matches Cleopatra's own rhetoric—"Husband," "baby," and "nurse." Moreover, in echoing her contempt for "Caesar [the] ass / Unpolicied," the phrase praises her at his expense. Alternatively, however, has *Antony and Cleopatra* instead presented "lies alas unparalleled?"

The answer depends on the relationship between the ending and the partly incompatible material that has preceded it. Most, though not all, critics have found the conclusion affirmative. But the work registers ambivalence to the last. This duality is captured in Cleopatra's account of the response she expects in Rome:

> The quick comedians
> Extemporally will stage us, and present
> Our Alexandrian revels. Antony
> Shall be brought drunken forth, and I shall see
> Some squeaking Cleopatra boy my greatness
> I'th' posture of a whore.
>
> (5.2.212–17)

Cleopatra shudders at the absurdity of a boy actor badly impersonating her, yet the part of Cleopatra in *Antony and Cleopatra* was originally performed by a boy. This reminder punctures the dramatic illusion just when it seems most essential. It looks back to Cleopatra's deliberate blurring of gender division. And it emphasizes the artifice of Cleopatra herself, a veteran actress in her final performance. Shakespeare here flaunts the power of his medium. But if it is impossible to "boy" Cleopatra's "greatness," to represent her adequately, perhaps that is an invitation, as she has earlier suggested, to look beyond what can be shown, to take seriously her "immortal longings."

WALTER COHEN

TEXTUAL NOTE

The Tragedie of Anthonie, and Cleopatra was published in the First Folio of 1623 (F), which also gives the forms *Anthony and Cleopater* in other references to the title of the play. "Anthony & Cleopatra" was entered on May 20, 1608, in the Stationers' Register, a listing of books intended for legal publication. As it happened, the play went unpublished; this entry may have been designed to prevent someone else from printing it. Both stylistic tests and probable verbal echoes in other plays suggest a date of late 1606 or possibly early 1607. The Folio version is ultimately based on an authorial manuscript but perhaps by way of a transcript. There is no evidence of the revisions necessary for theatrical performance. Thus, the stage directions list characters who have no role in the scene or even the entire play (characters excluded from the present edition); are insufficient at various points, especially in the closing scenes at Cleopatra's monument; and (like the speech prefixes) contain some authorial errors.

The play presents problems in modernizing proper names and in verse lineation. In addition, but less problematically, it has no act or scene divisions after an initial "Actus Primus. Scoena Prima." The ones supplied here follow editorial practice standard since the eighteenth century, except in starting a new scene after 4.7.3 (because the stage is cleared). This decision, of course, changes the scene numbering for the remainder of the act.

SELECTED BIBLIOGRAPHY

Archer, John Michael. "Antiquity and Degeneration in *Antony and Cleopatra*." *Race, Ethnicity, and Power in the Renaissance.* Ed. Joyce Green MacDonald. Madison, N.J.: Fairleigh Dickinson University Press, 1997. 145–64. The ambivalent image of

Egypt in the Renaissance, combining reverence for its antique wisdom with anxiety about contagious decadence.

Bloom, Harold, ed. *William Shakespeare's "Antony and Cleopatra."* New York: Chelsea House, 1988. Eight heterogeneous essays by important critics from the 1970s and 1980s.

Deats, Sara Munson, ed. *Antony and Cleopatra: New Critical Essays.* New York: Routledge, 2005. Fourteen new essays, including a long opening survey of criticism and performance by the editor.

Drakakis, John, ed. *"Antony and Cleopatra," William Shakespeare.* New York: St. Martin's, 1994. Twelve heterogeneous essays by leading critics, mainly from the 1970s and 1980s.

Holderness, Graham, Bryan Loughrey, and Andrew Murphy, eds. *Shakespeare: The Roman Plays.* London: Longman, 1996. Three essays on *Antony and Cleopatra* from the 1980s and 1990s, focusing on psychoanalytical and political issues.

Loomba, Ania. *Shakespeare, Race, and Colonialism.* Oxford: Oxford University Press, 2002. 112–34. Links of empire, gender ambiguity, skin color, gypsies, and role playing.

Madeleine, Richard, ed. *Antony and Cleopatra.* Cambridge: Cambridge University Press, 1998. Book-length history of productions of *Antony and Cleopatra*, combined with an edition of the play annotated with accounts of various performance decisions.

Rose, Mark, ed. *Twentieth Century Interpretations of "Antony and Cleopatra": A Collection of Critical Essays.* Englewood Cliffs, N.J.: Prentice-Hall, 1977. A dozen statements and essays from major critics, from 1945 to 1975, mostly formalist in character, with some attention to historical background.

Wofford, Susanne L. *Shakespeare's Late Tragedies: A Collection of Critical Essays.* Upper Saddle River, N.J.: Prentice Hall, 1996. Five essays on *Antony and Cleopatra* from the 1980s and 1990s, plus substantial discussion of the play in three other more general pieces; primarily issues of subjectivity, race, gender, empire, and performance.

Wood, Nigel, ed. *Antony and Cleopatra.* Buckingham, Eng.: Open University Press, 1996. Four essays connecting theory to interpretation, from the perspectives of mimetic rivalry, postcolonialism, polysemous gynocentrism, and genre.

FILM

Antony and Cleopatra. 1974. Dir. Jon Scoffield. UK. 161 min. Based on the 1972 Royal Shakespeare Company performance, starring Janet Suzman as an intelligent, tawny, feminist Cleopatra. Focuses on love at the expense of politics.

The Tragedy of
Antony and Cleopatra

THE PERSONS OF THE PLAY

MARK ANTONY (Marcus Antonius), triumvir of Rome

DEMETRIUS
PHILO
Domitius ENOBARBUS
VENTIDIUS
SILIUS
EROS
CAMIDIUS
SCARUS
DECRETAS
} friends and followers of Antony

Octavius CAESAR, triumvir of Rome
OCTAVIA, his sister

MAECENAS
AGRIPPA
TAURUS
DOLABELLA
THIDIAS
GALLUS
PROCULEIUS
} friends and followers of Caesar

LEPIDUS, triumvir of Rome
Sextus POMPEY (Pompeius)

MENECRATES
MENAS
VARRIUS
} friends of Pompey

CLEOPATRA, Queen of Egypt

CHARMIAN
IRAS
ALEXAS
MARDIAN, a eunuch
DIOMED
SELEUCUS
} attending on Cleopatra

A SOOTHSAYER
An AMBASSADOR
MESSENGERS
A BOY who sings
A SENTRY and men of his WATCH
Men of the GUARD
An EGYPTIAN
A CLOWN
SERVANTS
SOLDIERS
Eunuchs, attendants, captains, soldiers, servants

1.1

Enter DEMETRIUS *and* PHILO

PHILO   Nay, but this dotage° of our General's   *absurd infatuation*
    O'erflows the measure.[1] Those his goodly eyes,
    That o'er the files and musters°of the war   *lines of troops*
    Have glowed like plated° Mars, now bend, now turn   *armored*
5   The office° and devotion of their view   *duty*
    Upon a tawny front.[2] His captain's heart,
    Which in the scuffles of great fights hath burst
    The buckles on his breast, reneges all temper,[3]
    And is become the bellows and the fan
    To cool a gipsy's° lust.   *Egyptian's; hussy's*

      Flourish.° Enter ANTONY, CLEOPATRA, *her ladies, the*   *Trumpet fanfare*
      train,° with eunuchs fanning her   *retinue*
10   Look where they come.
    Take but good note, and you shall see in him
    The triple pillar of the world[4] transformed
    Into a strumpet's fool. Behold and see.

CLEOPATRA [*to* ANTONY]   If it be love indeed, tell me how much.
15 ANTONY   There's beggary° in the love that can be reckoned.   *little value*
CLEOPATRA   I'll set a bourn° how far to be beloved.   *boundary*
ANTONY   Then must thou needs find out new heaven, new earth.[5]

      Enter a MESSENGER

MESSENGER   News, my good lord, from Rome.
ANTONY   Grates° me: the sum.°   *Irks / summary*
20 CLEOPATRA   Nay, hear them, Antony.
    Fulvia° perchance is angry; or who knows   *Antony's wife*
    If the scarce-bearded Caesar[6] have not sent
    His powerful mandate to you: 'Do this, or this,
    Take in° that kingdom and enfranchise° that.   *Annex / liberate*
25   Perform't, or else we damn thee.'
ANTONY   How,° my love?   *What*
CLEOPATRA   Perchance? Nay, and most like.[7]
    You must not stay here longer. Your dismission°   *marching orders*
    Is come from Caesar, therefore hear it, Antony.
30   Where's Fulvia's process°—Caesar's, I would say—both? *summons*
    Call in the messengers. As I am Egypt's queen,
    Thou blushest, Antony, and that blood of thine
    Is Caesar's homager;° else so thy cheek pays shame *Pays Caesar homage*
    When shrill-tongued Fulvia scolds. The messengers!
35 ANTONY   Let Rome in Tiber melt, and the wide arch
    Of the ranged° empire fall. Here is my space.   *orderly; extensive*
    Kingdoms are clay. Our dungy° earth alike   *made of manure*
    Feeds beast as man. The nobleness of life
    Is to do thus;° when such a mutual pair   *act as we do; embrace*
40   And such a twain can do't—in which I bind

1.1 Location: Cleopatra's palace, Alexandria.
1. Goes beyond suitable bounds.
2. A face or forehead of dark complexion (referring to Cleopatra; see the Introduction); military "front," or battle line.
3. Abandons all temperance ("temper" is also the hardness of tempered steel).
4. Antony, Octavius Caesar, and Lepidus were the three triumvirs ruling the Roman Empire (most of the known world, for Romans).

5. Alluding anachronistically to Revelation 21:1 ("I saw a new heaven, and a new earth") and to the discovery of the New World. This second meaning may connect to the imperial theme of the play—its sense of geographical expansiveness and European geographical expansion.
6. The opening of the play is set in 40 B.C.E., when Octavius Caesar was twenty-three; Antony was almost twenty years his senior.
7. It is most likely, rather than merely possible, that Fulvia is angry.

On pain of punishment the world to weet°—   *recognize*
We stand up peerless.
CLEOPATRA [*aside*]   Excellent falsehood!
Why did he marry Fulvia and not love her?
I'll seem the fool I am not. [*To* ANTONY] Antony
Will be himself.[8]
45   ANTONY   But stirred[9] by Cleopatra.
Now, for the love of Love and her soft hours
Let's not confound° the time with conference° harsh.   *ruin / conversation*
There's not a minute of our lives should stretch
Without some pleasure now. What sport° tonight?   *entertainment*
CLEOPATRA   Hear the ambassadors.
50   ANTONY   Fie, wrangling queen,
Whom everything becomes—to chide, to laugh,
To weep; how every passion fully strives
To make itself, in thee, fair and admired!
No messenger but thine;[1] and all alone
55   Tonight we'll wander through the streets and note
The qualities of people. Come, my queen.
Last night you did desire it. [*To the* MESSENGER] Speak not to us.
                     Exeunt [ANTONY *and* CLEOPATRA] *with the train*
                       [*and by another door the* MESSENGER]
DEMETRIUS   Is Caesar with° Antonius prized° so slight?   *by / esteemed*
PHILO   Sir, sometimes when he is not Antony
60   He comes too short of that great property°   *unique characteristic*
Which still° should go with Antony.   *always*
DEMETRIUS   I am full sorry
That he approves° the common liar who   *proves correct*
Thus speaks of him at Rome; but I will hope
Of better deeds tomorrow. Rest you happy.   *Exeunt*

1.2

Enter ENOBARBUS, *a* SOOTHSAYER, CHARMIAN, IRAS, MAR-
DIAN *the eunuch,* ALEXAS [*and attendants*]
CHARMIAN   Lord Alexas, sweet Alexas, most anything Alexas,
almost most absolute° Alexas, where's the soothsayer that you   *perfect*
praised so to th' Queen?
O that I knew this husband, which you say
Must charge his horns[1] with garlands!
5   ALEXAS   Soothsayer!
SOOTHSAYER   Your will?
CHARMIAN   Is this the man? Is't you, sir, that know things?
SOOTHSAYER   In nature's infinite book of secrecy
A little I can read.
10   ALEXAS [*to* CHARMIAN]   Show him your hand.
ENOBARBUS [*calling*]   Bring in the banquet° quickly,   *light meal; dessert*
Wine enough Cleopatra's health to drink.
        [*Enter servants with food and wine, and exeunt*]
CHARMIAN [*to* SOOTHSAYER]   Good sir, give me good fortune.
SOOTHSAYER   I make not, but foresee.

---

8. *I'll . . . himself*: I'll appear to believe Antony's falsehood, although I am really not so credulous; he will continue in his folly. (But Antony construes the words he
hears as a compliment. It is also possible that Antony
hears Cleopatra's entire speech.)

9. Aroused; motivated; disturbed.
1. I will hear only what you have to say.
1.2 Location: Scene continues.
1. Must adorn his (proverbial) cuckold's horns.

CHARMIAN   Pray then, foresee me one.

15 SOOTHSAYER   You shall be yet
   Far fairer than you are.

CHARMIAN   He means in flesh.°   *(by getting fatter)*

IRAS   No, you shall paint° when you are old.   *use cosmetics*

CHARMIAN   Wrinkles forbid!

ALEXAS   Vex not his prescience. Be attentive.

CHARMIAN   Hush!

SOOTHSAYER   You shall be more beloving than beloved.

20 CHARMIAN   I had rather heat my liver with drinking.[2]

ALEXAS   Nay, hear him.

CHARMIAN   Good now,° some excellent fortune! Let me be mar-   *Please; fine; begin*
   ried to three kings in a forenoon and widow them all. Let me
   have a child at fifty to whom Herod of Jewry[3] may do homage.

25 Find° me to marry me with Octavius Caesar, and companion   *Find in my palm*
   me° with my mistress.   *make me equal*

SOOTHSAYER   You shall outlive the lady whom you serve.

CHARMIAN   O, excellent! I love long life better than figs.[4]

SOOTHSAYER   You have seen and proved° a fairer former fortune   *undergone*
30 Than that which is to approach.

CHARMIAN   Then belike° my children shall have no names.°   *likely / be bastards*
   Prithee, how many boys and wenches must I have?

SOOTHSAYER   If every of your wishes had a womb,
   And fertile every wish, a million.

35 CHARMIAN   Out, fool—I forgive thee for a witch.[5]

ALEXAS   You think none but your sheets are privy to your wishes.

CHARMIAN [to the SOOTHSAYER]   Nay, come, tell Iras hers.

ALEXAS   We'll know all our fortunes.

ENOBARBUS   Mine, and most of our fortunes, tonight shall be
40 drunk to bed.

IRAS [showing her hand to the SOOTHSAYER]   There's a palm
   presages chastity,° if nothing else.   *(a dry palm)*

CHARMIAN   E'en as the o'erflowing Nilus presageth famine.[6]

IRAS   Go, you wild° bedfellow, you cannot soothsay.   *licentious*

45 CHARMIAN   Nay, if an oily palm° be not a fruitful prognostica-   *(sign of sensuality)*
   tion,° I cannot scratch mine ear. [To the SOOTHSAYER] Prithee,   *sign of fertility*
   tell her but a workaday° fortune.   *an everyday*

SOOTHSAYER   Your fortunes are alike.

IRAS   But how, but how? Give me particulars.

50 SOOTHSAYER   I have said.

IRAS   Am I not an inch of fortune better than she?

CHARMIAN   Well, if you were but an inch of fortune better than
   I, where would you choose it?

IRAS   Not in my husband's nose.°   *(sexual innuendo)*

55 CHARMIAN   Our worser° thoughts heavens mend! Alexas—come,   *lascivious*
   his fortune, his fortune. O, let him marry a woman that cannot
   go, sweet Isis,[7] I beseech thee, and let her die too, and give him

2. Both falling in love and excessive drinking were thought to inflame the liver, the seat of the passions.
3. Anachronistic: Charmian wants homage to her child even from Herod, Cleopatra's enemy, who was to become proverbial for his brutality to children when he slaughtered the Holy Innocents in an effort to kill the infant Jesus.
4. Genitalia (possibly proverbial); lines 27–28 also foreshadow 5.2.229–319.

5. Since you are a soothsayer, I will let you speak freely and will not persecute you as a witch; I will forgive your outlandish prognostications because they are unlikely to come true.
6. Ironic: the silt brought down by the flooding Nile each year gave Egypt its fertile soil.
7. Egyptian goddess of fertility, as well as of the earth and moon. For the comparison of Cleopatra to Isis, see the Introduction. go: come (sexual); bear children.

a worse, and let worse follow worse till the worst of all follow
him laughing to his grave, fiftyfold a cuckold. Good Isis, hear
60   me this prayer, though thou deny me a matter of more weight;
good Isis, I beseech thee.

IRAS   Amen, dear goddess, hear that prayer of the people. For as
it is a heart-breaking to see a handsome man loose-wived,° so it   *wedded to an adulteress*
is a deadly sorrow to behold a foul knave uncuckolded. There-
65   fore, dear Isis, keep decorum,° and fortune him accordingly.   *do the right thing*

CHARMIAN   Amen.

ALEXAS   Lo now, if it lay in their hands to make me a cuckold,
they would make themselves whores but they'd do't.[8]

        Enter CLEOPATRA

ENOBARBUS   Hush, here comes Antony.

CHARMIAN   Not he, the Queen.

CLEOPATRA   Saw you my lord?

ENOBARBUS   No, lady.

70   CLEOPATRA   Was he not here?

CHARMIAN   No, madam.

CLEOPATRA   He was disposed to mirth, but on the sudden
A Roman° thought hath struck him. Enobarbus!   *of Rome; serious*

ENOBARBUS   Madam?

75   CLEOPATRA   Seek him, and bring him hither. Where's Alexas?

ALEXAS   Here at your service. My lord approaches.

        Enter ANTONY *with a* MESSENGER

CLEOPATRA   We will not look upon him. Go with us.

        Exeunt [all but ANTONY *and the* MESSENGER]

MESSENGER   Fulvia thy wife first came into the field.°   *battlefield*

ANTONY   Against my brother Lucius?[9]

80   MESSENGER   Ay, but soon that war had end, and the time's state°   *situation at the time*
Made friends of them, jointing their force 'gainst Caesar,
Whose better issue° in the war from Italy   *greater success*
Upon the first encounter drave them.°   *drove them out*

ANTONY   Well, what worst?

MESSENGER   The nature of bad news infects the teller.[1]

85   ANTONY   When it concerns the fool or coward. On.
Things that are past are done. With me 'tis thus:
Who tells me true, though in his tale lie death,
I hear him as° he flattered.   *as if*

MESSENGER   Labienus[2]—
This is stiff news—hath with his Parthian force

90   Extended° Asia; from Euphrates   *Seized*
His conquering banner shook, from Syria
To Lydia and to Ionia,
Whilst—

ANTONY   Antony, thou wouldst say—

MESSENGER   O, my lord!

ANTONY   Speak to me home.° Mince not the general tongue.[3]   *plainly*

95   Name Cleopatra as she is called in Rome.

8. *but they'd do't:* in order to do so.
9. Lucius Antonius, Roman consul.
1. Makes the teller hated by the hearer. For examples,
see 2.5 and 3.1.
2. Quintus Labienus, who was sent by Brutus and Cassius following their killing of Julius Caesar (see *Julius
Caesar*) to garner support from the Parthians, an Asian
people whose empire came to include much of Meso-

potamia (Iraq) and Persia (Iran) and who regularly warred
with Rome. After Brutus's and Cassius's defeat at Philippi
by Antony, Octavius Caesar, and Lepidus, Labienus
defected to take command of the Parthian army and
began a war against the Romans, conquering some of
their provinces in the Middle East (lines 90–92)—provinces Antony was supposed to protect.
3. Do not play down common opinion.

Rail thou in Fulvia's phrase,° and taunt my faults   *words*
With such full licence as both truth and malice
Have power to utter. O, then we bring forth weeds
When our quick° winds lie still, and our ills told us   *living; fertile*
100   Is as our earing.[4] Fare thee well a while.
MESSENGER   At your noble pleasure.   *Exit* MESSENGER
       Enter another MESSENGER
ANTONY   From Sicyon,[5] ho, the news? Speak there.
SECOND MESSENGER   The man from Sicyon—
ANTONY   Is there such a one?
SECOND MESSENGER   He stays upon° your will.   *He attends*
ANTONY   Let him appear.
           [*Exit* SECOND MESSENGER]
105   These strong Egyptian fetters I must break,
Or lose myself in dotage.
       Enter another MESSENGER *with a letter*
                  What are you?
THIRD MESSENGER   Fulvia thy wife is dead.
ANTONY   Where died she?
THIRD MESSENGER   In Sicyon.
Her length of sickness, with what else more serious
Importeth thee° to know, this bears.   *Is important for you*
       [*He gives* ANTONY *the letter*]
110   ANTONY   Forbear° me.   *Leave*
           [*Exit* THIRD MESSENGER]
There's a great spirit gone. Thus did I desire it.
What our contempts doth often hurl from us
We wish it ours again. The present pleasure,
By revolution low'ring,[6] does become
115   The opposite of itself. She's° good being gone;   *Fulvia is*
The hand could° pluck her back that shoved her on.   *would wish to*
I must from this enchanting° queen break off.   *spellbinding*
Ten thousand harms more than the ills I know
My idleness doth hatch. How now, Enobarbus!
       Enter ENOBARBUS
ENOBARBUS   What's your pleasure, sir?
120   ANTONY   I must with haste from hence.
ENOBARBUS   Why, then we kill[7] all our women. We see how
mortal an unkindness is to them; if they suffer our departure,
death's the word.
ANTONY   I must be gone.
125   ENOBARBUS   Under a compelling occasion let women die. It
were pity to cast them away for nothing, though between them
and a great cause they should be esteemed nothing. Cleopatra
catching but the least noise of this dies instantly. I have seen
her die twenty times upon far poorer moment.° I do think there   *for far less reason*
130   is mettle° in death, which commits some loving act upon her,   *(sexual) potency; courage*
she hath such a celerity° in dying.   *speed*
ANTONY   She is cunning past man's thought.

---

4. *O . . . earing:* Antony compares his recent behavior to an unplowed field: just as the field sprouts weeds when it remains untilled (by hand or) by a "quick" (fertile) wind, he falls into "ill" habits when he is not forced to face criticism (to undergo "earing," plowing).
5. City in Greece where Antony left Fulvia.

6. Growing lower by turning (as of a wheel, such as Fortune's).
7. Alluding to achieving an orgasm. Throughout the scene "kill," "death," and "dying" all carry this bawdy resonance. "Nothing," which Enobarbus repeats, may refer to the female genitals.

ENOBARBUS Alack, sir, no. Her passions are made of nothing but
the finest part of pure love. We cannot call her winds and
135 waters sighs and tears; they are greater storms and tempests than
almanacs can report. This cannot be cunning in her; if it be,
she makes a shower of rain as well as Jove.[8]

ANTONY Would I had never seen her!

ENOBARBUS O, sir, you had then left unseen a wonderful piece
140 of work,° which not to have been blessed withal° would have   *masterpiece / with*
discredited your travel.[9]

ANTONY Fulvia is dead.

ENOBARBUS Sir.

ANTONY Fulvia is dead.

145 ENOBARBUS Fulvia?

ANTONY Dead.

ENOBARBUS Why, sir, give the gods a thankful sacrifice. When it
pleaseth their deities to take the wife of a man from him, it
shows to man the tailors of the earth; comforting therein that
150 when old robes° are worn out there are members[1] to make new.   *clothes; women*
If there were no more women but Fulvia, then had you indeed
a cut, and the case to be lamented. This grief is crowned with
consolation; your old smock brings forth a new petticoat, and
indeed the tears live in an onion that should water this sorrow.[2]

155 ANTONY The business she hath broachèd in the state
Cannot endure my absence.

ENOBARBUS And the business you have broached here cannot
be without you, especially that of Cleopatra's, which wholly
depends on your abode.°   *staying on here*

160 ANTONY No more light answers. Let our officers
Have notice what we purpose. I shall break
The cause of our expedience° to the Queen,   *haste*
And get her leave to part; for not alone
The death of Fulvia, with more urgent touches,°   *concerns*
165 Do strongly speak to us, but the letters too
Of many our contriving friends[3] in Rome
Petition us at home.° Sextus Pompeius   *to go home*
Hath given the dare to Caesar and commands
The empire of the sea.[4] Our slippery° people,   *inconstant*
170 Whose love is never linked to the deserver
Till his deserts are past, begin to throw°   *ascribe (the title of)*
Pompey the Great and all his dignities
Upon his son, who—high in name and power,
Higher than both in blood and life°—stands up   *vitality and energy*
175 For the main soldier;[5] whose quality, going on,
The sides o'th' world may danger.[6] Much is breeding
Which, like the courser's hair, hath yet but life,
And not a serpent's poison.[7] Say our pleasure,

---

8. Jupiter; ruler of the gods: one of his duties was governing rain.
9. Would have cast doubt on your success as a traveler.
Travel also suggests travail, or work, as in "piece of work"
(lines 139–40).
1. Limbs; sexual organs. The sexual innuendo is continued in "cut" (line 152: severe blow; slash in a garment;
vagina, "case" (line 152: situation; set of clothes; vagina),
and "broachèd" (line 155, 157: opened or pricked).
2. *the tears . . . sorrow:* real tears are not called for.
3. Of many friends acting on our behalf.

4. Sextus Pompey was the younger son of Pompey the
Great, who was a foe of Julius Caesar (see *Julius Caesar*
1.1). Previously an outlaw, the Pompey of the play had
gained control of the shipping routes around Sicily.
5. *stands . . . soldier:* acts like the leading soldier.
6. *whose . . . danger:* whose accomplishments and character, should they continue to succeed, might endanger the
entire arrangement of the world.
7. A horse's ("courser's," line 177) hair was believed to
become a live snake if put in water.

To such whose place° is under us, requires   °rank
Our quick remove from hence.

180   ENOBARBUS   I shall do't. [*Exeunt severally*]

1.3

Enter CLEOPATRA, CHARMIAN, ALEXAS, *and* IRAS

CLEOPATRA   Where is he?

CHARMIAN   I did not see him since.°   °recently

CLEOPATRA [*to* ALEXAS]   See where he is, who's with him, what he does.
I did not send you.[1] If you find him sad,°   °serious
Say I am dancing; if in mirth, report

5   That I am sudden sick. Quick, and return.   [*Exit* ALEXAS]

CHARMIAN   Madam, methinks, if you did love him dearly,
You do not hold the method° to enforce   °act appropriately
The like from him.

CLEOPATRA   What should I do I do not?°   °What else should I do

CHARMIAN   In each thing give him way; cross him in nothing.

10   CLEOPATRA   Thou teachest like a fool, the way to lose him.

CHARMIAN   Tempt° him not so too far. Iwis,° forbear.   °Test / °Indeed
In time we hate that which we often fear.

          Enter ANTONY

But here comes Antony.

CLEOPATRA   I am sick and sullen.°   °dispirited

ANTONY   I am sorry to give breathing° to my purpose.   °voice

15   CLEOPATRA   Help me away, dear Charmian, I shall fall.
It cannot be thus long—the sides of nature[2]
Will not sustain it.

ANTONY   Now, my dearest queen.

CLEOPATRA   Pray you, stand farther from me.

ANTONY   What's the matter?

CLEOPATRA   I know by that same eye there's some good news.

20   What says the married woman°—you may go?   °(Fulvia)
Would she had never given you leave to come.
Let her not say 'tis I that keep you here.
I have no power upon you; hers you are.

ANTONY   The gods best know—

CLEOPATRA   O, never was there queen

25   So mightily betrayed! Yet at the first
I saw the treasons planted.

ANTONY   Cleopatra—

CLEOPATRA   Why should I think you can be mine and true—
Though you in swearing shake the thronèd gods[3]—
Who have been false to Fulvia? Riotous madness,

30   To be entangled with those mouth-made° vows   °hypocritical
Which break themselves in swearing.°   °as they are made

ANTONY   Most sweet queen—

CLEOPATRA   Nay, pray you, seek no colour° for your going,   °excuse
But bid farewell and go. When you sued staying,°   °entreated to remain
Then was the time for words; no going then.

35   Eternity was in our[4] lips and eyes,
Bliss in our brow's bent;° none our parts so poor   °curve
to shake.

1.3 Location: Scene continues.
1. Do not say I sent you.
2. This cannot go on much longer—the bodily frame.
3. When Jupiter swore an oath, Olympus was supposed

to shake.
4. My (royal plural); possibly also the conventional first
person plural.

But was a race of heaven.[5] They are so still,
Or thou, the greatest soldier of the world,
Art turned the greatest liar.

ANTONY   How now, lady!

40   CLEOPATRA   I would I had thy inches.° Thou shouldst know   size (phallic)
There were a heart in Egypt.[6]

ANTONY   Hear me, Queen.
The strong necessity of time commands
Our services a while, but my full heart
Remains in use° with you. Our Italy   in trust

45   Shines o'er with civil swords.° Sextus Pompeius   swords of civil war
Makes his approaches to the port of Rome.[7]
Equality of two domestic powers
Breed scrupulous faction.° The hated, grown to strength,   distrustful dissent
Are newly grown to love.° The condemned° Pompey,   popularity / banished

50   Rich in his father's honour, creeps° apace   insinuates himself
Into the hearts of such as have not thrived
Upon the present state,° whose numbers threaten;   government
And quietness, grown sick of rest, would purge
By any desperate change.[8] My more particular,°   personal motivation

55   And that which most with you should safe° my going,   sanction
Is Fulvia's death.

CLEOPATRA   Though age from folly could not give me freedom,
It does from childishness. Can Fulvia die?

ANTONY   She's dead, my queen.

[He offers letters]

60   Look here, and at thy sovereign leisure read
The garboils° she awaked. At the last, best,[9]   upheavals
See when and where she died.

CLEOPATRA   O most false love!
Where be the sacred vials[1] thou shouldst fill
With sorrowful water? Now I see, I see,

65   In Fulvia's death how mine received shall be.

ANTONY   Quarrel no more, but be prepared to know
The purposes I bear, which are° or cease   continue
As you shall give th'advice. By the fire°   sun
That quickens Nilus' slime,[2] I go from hence

70   Thy soldier-servant, making peace or war
As thou affects.°   choose

CLEOPATRA   Cut my lace,[3] Charmian, come.
But let it be. I am quickly ill and well;
So[4] Antony loves.

ANTONY   My precious queen, forbear,
And give true evidence° to his love, which stands   be an honest witness
An honourable trial.

75   CLEOPATRA   So Fulvia told me.

---

5. *none . . . heaven*: Even my poorest attributes were
heavenly.
6. There were courage (to respond to such insults) in the
country (Queen) of Egypt.
7. Ostia (16 miles from Rome).
8. *And . . . change*: And peace, made ill by inactivity,
wishes to purge itself of impurities by a violently acting
remedy.
9. The best news last; Fulvia was at her best at the end of
her life.

1. Renaissance writers thought that the Romans filled
small bottles with tears to place in graves; also, where are
your sad and watery eyes ("vials")?
2. That causes plants to grow in the silt that the Nile
deposits.
3. Cutting the strings would be quicker than untying the
lace on her bodice to relieve her from her feigned fainting spell.
4. Thus (falsely); as long as.

I prithee turn aside and weep for her,
Then bid adieu to me, and say the tears
Belong to Egypt.° Good now, play one scene   *Cleopatra*
Of excellent dissembling, and let it look
Like perfect honour.

80   ANTONY   You'll heat my blood.° No more.   *make me angry*

    CLEOPATRA   You can do better yet; but this is meetly.°   *fairly good (acting)*

    ANTONY   Now by my sword—

    CLEOPATRA   And target.[5] Still he mends.°   *improves*
But this is not the best. Look, prithee, Charmian,
How this Herculean Roman does become

85   The carriage of his chafe.[6]

    ANTONY   I'll leave you, lady.

    CLEOPATRA   Courteous lord, one word.
Sir, you and I must part; but that's not it.
Sir, you and I have loved; but there's not it;

90   That you know well. Something it is I would—
O, my oblivion is a very Antony,
And I am all forgotten.[7]

    ANTONY   But that your royalty
Holds idleness your subject, I should take you
For idleness itself.[8]

    CLEOPATRA   'Tis sweating labour°   *work; birth pains*

95   To bear such idleness° so near the heart   *flippancy; laziness*
As Cleopatra this. But sir, forgive me,
Since my becomings° kill me when they do not   *transformations; graces*
Eye° well to you. Your honour calls you hence,   *Look*
Therefore be deaf to my unpitied folly,

100   And all the gods go with you. Upon your sword
Sit laurel victory,[9] and smooth success
Be strewed before your feet.

    ANTONY   Let us go.
Come. Our separation so abides and flies[1]
That thou residing here goes yet with me,

105   And I hence fleeting, here remain with thee.
Away.   *Exeunt* [*severally*]

1.4

Enter Octavius CAESAR *reading a letter,* LEPIDUS, *and
their train*

    CAESAR   You may see, Lepidus, and henceforth know,
It is not Caesar's natural vice to hate
Our great competitor.° From Alexandria   *ally; rival*
This is the news: he fishes, drinks, and wastes

5   The lamps of night in revel; is not more manlike
Than Cleopatra, nor the queen of Ptolemy[1]

---

5. Shield. Cleopatra parodies the blustering oaths of
heroic drama.
6. *does . . . chafe:* emulates Hercules, his heroic ancestor,
with his posture of rage.
7. *my . . . forgotten:* my memory has deserted me as you
are doing, and I have forgotten everything (am totally forgotten—by Antony).
8. *But . . . itself:* If you were not queen over your flippancy and hence in full control of it, I would think that
you were flippancy itself.

9. *Upon . . . victory:* May your military exploits receive
the laurel wreath as the reward for victory.
1. Consists so much of both remaining together and
being separated (in that we are united by the shared experience of it).
1.4 Location: Rome.
1. Julius Caesar had commanded Cleopatra to marry her
half brother Ptolemy XIV (acceptable within the Egyptian royal family); she was said to have had Ptolemy poisoned.

More womanly than he; hardly gave audience[2]
Or vouchsafed to think he had partners. You shall find there°   (the letter); (Egypt)
A man who is the abstract° of all faults   paradigm
That all men follow.

10 LEPIDUS   I must not think there are
Evils enough to darken all his goodness.
His faults in him seem as the spots of heaven,°   stars
More fiery by night's blackness; hereditary
Rather than purchased;° what he cannot change   acquired
15 Than° what he chooses.   Rather than

CAESAR   You are too indulgent. Let's grant it is not
Amiss to tumble on the bed of Ptolemy,
To give a kingdom for a mirth,° to sit   joke
And keep the turn of° tippling with a slave,   take turns at
20 To reel the streets at noon, and stand the buffet°   come to blows
With knaves that smells of sweat. Say° this becomes him—   Even if
As his composure° must be rare indeed   And his character
Whom these things cannot blemish—yet must Antony
No way excuse his foils° when we do bear   faults
25 So great weight in° his lightness. If he filled   as a result of
His vacancy° with his voluptuousness,   leisure
Full surfeits and the dryness of his bones[3]
Call on° him for't. But to confound° such time   Afflict / waste
That drums° him from his sport, and speaks as loud   summons
30 As his own state° and ours— 'tis to be chid   public responsibility
As we rate° boys who, being mature in knowledge,   upbraid
Pawn their experience to their present pleasure,
And so rebel to judgement.[4]
    Enter a MESSENGER

LEPIDUS   Here's more news.
MESSENGER   Thy biddings have been done, and every hour,
35 Most noble Caesar, shalt thou have report
How 'tis abroad. Pompey is strong at sea,
And it appears he is beloved of those
That only have feared Caesar.[5] To the ports
The discontents° repair, and men's reports   discontented people
Give him° much wronged.   [Exit]   Say he is
40 CAESAR   I should have known no less.
It hath been taught us from the primal state[6]
That he which is was wished until he were,[7]
And the ebbed° man, ne'er loved till ne'er worth love,   fallen
Comes deared° by being lacked. This common body,°   Is loved / The people
45 Like to a vagabond flag° upon the stream,   drifting reed
Goes to, and back, lackeying° the varying tide,   following slavishly
To rot itself with motion.
    [Enter a SECOND MESSENGER]

SECOND MESSENGER   Caesar, I bring thee word
Menecrates and Menas, famous pirates,°   (allied with Pompey)
Makes the sea serve them, which they ear° and wound   plow
50 With keels of every kind. Many hot inroads

---

2. Hardly listened (to Octavius's messengers, in 1.1).
3. *Full . . . bones:* Ill health caused by overeating and venereal disease.
4. *being . . . judgement:* old enough to know better, abandon their wisdom in favor of momentary pleasure, and

thus act against their better judgment.
5. That obeyed Caesar only out of fear.
6. Since the first society was organized.
7. That man who rules was supported until he began to rule.

They make in Italy. The borders maritime°   *coastal territories*
Lack blood° to think on't, and flush° youth revolt.   *Go pallid / spirited*
No vessel can peep forth but 'tis as soon
Taken as seen; for Pompey's name strikes more
Than could his war resisted.[8]   [*Exit*]

55 CAESAR   Antony,
Leave thy lascivious wassails.° When thou once   *drunken revels*
Was beaten from Modena,[9] where thou slew'st
Hirtius and Pansa, consuls, at thy heel
Did famine follow, whom thou fought'st against—
60 Though daintily brought up—with patience more
Than savages could suffer. Thou didst drink
The stale° of horses, and the gilded° puddle   *urine / slime-covered*
Which beasts would cough at.° Thy palate then did deign°   *refuse (to drink) / accept*
The roughest berry on the rudest hedge.
65 Yea, like the stag when snow the pasture sheets,°   *covers*
The barks of trees thou browsed.° On the Alps   *fed upon*
It is reported thou didst eat strange flesh,
Which some did die to look on; and all this—
It wounds thine honour that I speak it now—
70 Was borne so like a soldier that thy cheek
So much as lanked° not.   *grew thin*
LEPIDUS   'Tis pity of him.
CAESAR   Let his shames quickly
Drive him to Rome. 'Tis time we twain
75 Did show ourselves i'th' field; and to that end
Assemble we immediate council. Pompey
Thrives in our idleness.
LEPIDUS   Tomorrow, Caesar,
I shall be furnished to inform you rightly
Both what° by sea and land I can be able°   *what forces / assemble*
To front° this present time.   *To confront the enemy at*
80 CAESAR   Till which encounter
It is my business, too. Farewell.
LEPIDUS   Farewell, my lord. What you shall know meantime
Of stirs° abroad I shall beseech you, sir,   *incidents*
To let me be partaker.
85 CAESAR   Doubt not, sir. I knew it for my bond.°   *Exeunt*   *responsibility*

1.5

Enter CLEOPATRA, CHARMIAN, IRAS, *and* MARDIAN

CLEOPATRA   Charmian!
CHARMIAN   Madam?
CLEOPATRA [*yawning*]   Ha, ha. Give me to drink mandragora.[1]
CHARMIAN   Why, madam?
5 CLEOPATRA   That I might sleep out this great gap of time
My Antony is away.
CHARMIAN   You think of him too much.
CLEOPATRA   O, 'tis treason!
CHARMIAN   Madam, I trust not so.
CLEOPATRA   Thou, eunuch Mardian!

8. *Pompey's . . . resisted:* Pompey's name alone is more powerful than his forces would be if confronted in battle.
9. Site of a battle in which Antony was defeated by the combined armies of Octavius Caesar and the Roman Sen-ate, at the instigation of Cicero.
1.5 Location: Alexandria.
1. A narcotic, made from the mandrake plant.

MARDIAN   What's your highness' pleasure?

CLEOPATRA   Not now to hear thee sing.[2] I take no pleasure

10   In aught[3] an eunuch has. 'Tis well for thee

That, being unseminared,° thy freer thoughts   *castrated*

May not fly forth of Egypt. Hast thou affections?°   *desires*

MARDIAN   Yes, gracious madam.

CLEOPATRA   Indeed?

15 MARDIAN   Not in deed, madam, for I can do° nothing   *(sexually)*

But what indeed is honest° to be done.   *chaste; moral*

Yet have I fierce affections, and think

What Venus did with Mars.[4]

CLEOPATRA   O, Charmian,

Where think'st thou he is now? Stands he or sits he?

20   Or does he walk? Or is he on his horse?

O happy horse, to bear the weight of Antony!

Do bravely, horse, for wot'st° thou whom thou mov'st?—   *know*

The demi-Atlas[5] of this earth, the arm°   *champion*

And burgonet° of men. He's speaking now,   *helmet; guardian*

25   Or murmuring 'Where's my serpent of old Nile?'[6]—

For so he calls me. Now I feed myself

With most delicious poison. Think on me,

That am with Phoebus'° amorous pinches black,   *the sun god*

And wrinkled deep in time. Broad-fronted° Caesar,°   *Broad-browed / (Julius)*

30   When thou wast here above the ground I was

A morsel for a monarch, and great Pompey[7]

Would stand and make his eyes grow in my brow.

There would he anchor his aspect,° and die°   *gaze / (sexual)*

With looking on his life.

        Enter ALEXAS

ALEXAS   Sovereign of Egypt, hail!

35 CLEOPATRA   How much unlike art thou Mark Antony!

Yet, coming from him, that great medicine[8] hath

With his tinct° gilded thee. How goes it   *power; color*

With my brave° Mark Antony?   *magnificent*

ALEXAS   Last thing he did, dear Queen,

He kissed—the last of many doubled kisses—

40   This orient[9] pearl. His speech sticks in my heart.

CLEOPATRA   Mine ear must pluck it thence.

ALEXAS   'Good friend,' quoth he,

'Say the firm° Roman to great Egypt° sends   *loyal; resolute / Cleopatra*

This treasure of an oyster; at whose foot,

To mend° the petty present, I will piece°   *improve / add to*

45   Her opulent throne with kingdoms. All the East,

Say thou, shall call her mistress.' So he nodded,

And soberly did mount an arm-jaunced steed,[1]

---

2. Castrati were used in Italian music from the end of the sixteenth century, and Shakespeare associates singing eunuchs with the eastern Mediterranean in *Twelfth Night* and *A Midsummer Night's Dream;* they are not thought to have been used as singers in ancient Rome.

3. In anything; in the nothing. The eunuch has nothing instead of testicles.

4. Venus, goddess of love (married to Vulcan), and Mars, god of war, were lovers.

5. Octavius and Antony between them rule the world—Lepidus having conveniently been forgotten—as Atlas bore it on his shoulders.

6. See 2.7.25–26 for the superstition that snakes formed spontaneously in the Nile mud; the asp in particular was associated with Isis, with whom Cleopatra identifies herself.

7. Gnaeus Pompey, older brother of Sextus Pompey (the character in this play) and son of Pompey the Great. But Cleopatra's phrasing makes him sound like the father.

8. Elixir of life: sought by alchemists, it was thought to be able to turn base metals to gold and cure all disease.

9. From India (more lustrous than European pearls).

1. Steed jolted by one in armor (or by its own armor).

Who neighed so high that what I would have spoke
Was beastly dumbed° by him.   *drowned out*
CLEOPATRA   What, was he sad or merry?
50   ALEXAS   Like to the time o'th' year between the extremes
Of hot and cold, he was nor° sad nor merry.   *neither*
CLEOPATRA   O well divided° disposition! Note him,   *balanced*
Note him, good Charmian, 'tis the man; but note him.
He was not sad, for he would shine on those
55   That make their looks by his;[2] he was not merry,
Which seemed to tell them his remembrance lay
In Egypt with his joy; but between both.
O heavenly mingle! Be'st thou sad or merry,
The violence of either thee becomes;
60   So does it no man else. Met'st thou my posts?°   *messengers*
ALEXAS   Ay, madam, twenty several° messengers.   *separate*
Why do you send so thick?
CLEOPATRA   Who's° born that day   *Whoever is*
When I forget to send to Antony
Shall die a beggar. Ink and paper, Charmian!
65   Welcome, my good Alexas. Did I, Charmian,
Ever love Caesar so?
CHARMIAN   O, that brave Caesar!
CLEOPATRA   Be choked with such another emphasis!
Say 'the brave Antony'.
CHARMIAN   The valiant Caesar.
CLEOPATRA   By Isis, I will give thee bloody teeth
70   If thou with Caesar paragon° again   *compare*
My man of men.
CHARMIAN   By your most gracious pardon,
I sing but after you.
CLEOPATRA   My salad days,
When I was green° in judgement, cold in blood,°   *immature / feeling*
To say as I said then. But come, away,
75   Get me ink and paper.
He shall have every day a several greeting,
Or I'll unpeople Egypt.[3]   *Exeunt*

2.1

Enter POMPEY, MENECRATES, *and* MENAS, *in warlike*
manner
POMPEY   If the great gods be just, they shall assist
The deeds of justest men.
MENECRATES   Know, worthy Pompey,
That what they do delay they not deny.
POMPEY   Whiles we are suitors to their throne, decays
The thing we sue for.[1]
5   MENECRATES   We, ignorant of ourselves,
Beg often our own harms, which the wise powers
Deny us for our° good; so find we profit   *our own*
By losing of our prayers.
POMPEY   I shall do well.

2. Who are dependent on his mood; who reflect his
appearance in their own.
3. If not, it will be only because I have run out of Egyptians to act as messengers (or, because I have killed all

Egyptians).
2.1 Location: Pompey's headquarters (in Sicily).
1. *Whiles . . . for:* While we are beseeching the gods, what
we request is losing its value.

The people love me, and the sea is mine.
10 My powers are crescent,° and my auguring° hope   *growing / prophesying*
Says it° will come to th' full.[2] Mark Antony   *(my military power)*
In Egypt sits at dinner, and will make
No wars without doors.[3] Caesar gets money where
He loses hearts. Lepidus flatters both,
15 Of° both is flattered; but he neither loves,°   *By / loves neither*
Nor either cares for him.

MENAS   Caesar and Lepidus
Are in the field; a mighty strength they carry.

POMPEY   Where have you this? 'Tis false.

MENAS   From Silvius, sir.

POMPEY   He dreams. I know they are in Rome together,
20 Looking° for Antony. But all the charms° of love,   *Waiting / incantations*
Salt° Cleopatra, soften thy waned[4] lip.   *Lecherous*
Let witchcraft join with beauty, lust with both
Tie up the libertine, in a field of feasts
Keep his brain fuming;° Epicurean[5] cooks   *drunk*
25 Sharpen with cloyless sauce[6] his appetite,
That sleep and feeding may prorogue° his honour   *postpone*
Even till a Lethe'd dullness[7]—

Enter VARRIUS

                    How now, Varrius?

VARRIUS   This is most certain that I shall deliver:
Mark Antony is every hour in Rome
30 Expected. Since he went from Egypt, 'tis
A space for farther travel.[8]

POMPEY   I could have given less° matter   *less crucial*
A better ear. Menas, I did not think
This amorous surfeiter would have donned his helm°   *helmet*
For such a petty war. His soldiership
35 Is twice the other twain. But let us rear°   *elevate*
The higher our opinion,° that our stirring   *(of ourselves)*
Can from the lap of Egypt's widow[9] pluck
The ne'er lust-wearied Antony.

MENAS   I cannot hope°   *suppose*
Caesar and Antony shall well greet together.
40 His wife that's dead did trespasses to° Caesar,   *offended against*
His brother warred upon him, although, I think,
Not moved° by Antony.   *prompted*

POMPEY   I know not, Menas,
How lesser enmities may give way to greater.
Were't not that we stand up against them all,
45 'Twere pregnant° they should square° between themselves,   *evident / argue*
For they have entertainèd° cause enough   *sustained*
To draw their swords. But how the fear of us
May cement their divisions,° and bind up   *unite them*

---

2. Like the "crescent" moon.
3. Outside doors. Antony is concerned only with the wars of love, conducted indoors.
4. Withered; decreased, like the moon, perhaps in implicit contrast to the "crescent" and potentially "full" moon of Pompey's "powers" (lines 10–11).
5. The philosopher Epicurus and his followers believed that the gods took no interest in men's actions and that the only aim of life was to seek pleasure.

6. Sauce that never wearies or disgusts.
7. Drinking the water of Lethe, one of the rivers bounding Hades, caused total loss of memory.
8. Sufficient time to have traveled even farther (than between Egypt and Rome).
9. Cleopatra had married one of her brothers, Ptolemy XIV, whom she later seems to have had murdered. See note to 1.4.6.

The petty difference, we yet not know.
50 Be't as our gods will have't; it only stands
Our lives upon to use¹ our strongest hands.
Come, Menas.   *Exeunt*

2.2

Enter ENOBARBUS *and* LEPIDUS

LEPIDUS   Good Enobarbus, 'tis a worthy deed,
And shall become you well, to entreat your captain
To soft and gentle speech.
ENOBARBUS   I shall entreat him
To answer like himself.¹ If Caesar move° him,   *angers*
5 Let Antony look over Caesar's head
And speak as loud as Mars. By Jupiter,
Were I the wearer of Antonio's beard
I would not shave't today.²
LEPIDUS   'Tis not a time
For private stomaching.°   *quarrels*
ENOBARBUS   Every time
10 Serves for the matter that is then born in't.
LEPIDUS   But small to greater matters must give way.
ENOBARBUS   Not if the small come first.
LEPIDUS   Your speech is passion.°   *not reasoned*
But pray you, stir no embers° up. Here comes   *old resentments*
The noble Antony.

Enter [at one door] ANTONY *and* VENTIDIUS

ENOBARBUS   And yonder Caesar.

Enter [at another door] CAESAR, MAECENAS, *and* AGRIPPA

15 ANTONY [*to* VENTIDIUS]   If we compose° well here, to Parthia.   *reach agreement*
Hark, Ventidius.
CAESAR   I do not know,
Maecenas; ask Agrippa.
LEPIDUS[*to* CAESAR *and* ANTONY]   Noble friends,
That which combined us was most great; and let not
A leaner° action rend us. What's amiss,   *less important*
20 May it be gently heard. When we debate
Our trivial difference loud,° we do commit   *loudly; violently*
Murder in° healing wounds. Then, noble partners,   *in the process of*
The rather for° I earnestly beseech,   *Especially because*
Touch you the sourest points with sweetest terms,
Nor curstness grow° to th' matter.   *Do not let ill temper add*
25 ANTONY   'Tis spoken well.
Were we° before our armies, and to° fight,   *If we were / about to*
I should do thus.³

[ANTONY *and* CAESAR *embrace.*] *Flourish*

CAESAR   Welcome to Rome.
ANTONY   Thank you.
30 CAESAR   Sit.
ANTONY   Sit, sir.
CAESAR   Nay then.

---

1. *it . . . use:* our lives depend entirely on the use of.
2.2 Location: Rome.
1. To answer in a manner appropriate to his character
(greatness?; dissipation?).
2. Plucking a man's beard was an insult; Enobarbus

wants Antony to give Octavius the chance to insult him.
Possibly, Enobarbus is suggesting not that Antony act
heroically but that he merely look the part.
3. Formally embrace you, as I do now; possibly, speak as
you request.

[*They sit*]

ANTONY   I learn you take things ill which are not so,
Or being,° concern you not.   *being ill*

CAESAR   I must be laughed at
35   If or° for nothing or a little I   *either*
Should say myself offended, and with you
Chiefly i'th'° world; more laughed at that I should   *Of all the*
Once name you derogately,° when to sound your name   *censoriously*
It not concernèd me.

40   ANTONY   My being in Egypt, Caesar, what was't to you?

CAESAR   No more than my residing here at Rome
Might be to you in Egypt. Yet if you there
Did practise on° my state, your being in Egypt   *scheme against*
Might be my question.°   *concern*

ANTONY   How intend you 'practised'?

45   CAESAR   You may be pleased to catch at° mine intent   *grasp*
By what did here befall me. Your wife and brother
Made wars upon me, and their contestation
Was theme for you. You were the word of war.[4]

ANTONY   You do mistake the business. My brother never
50   Did urge me in his act.[5] I did enquire° it,   *inquire into*
And have my learning from some true reports°   *reliable sources*
That drew their swords with you. Did he not rather
Discredit my authority with yours,
And make the wars alike against my stomach,°   *wish*
55   Having alike° your cause? Of this, my letters   *Since I shared*
Before did satisfy you. If you'll patch a quarrel,
As matter whole you have to make it with,[6]
It must not be with this.

CAESAR   You praise yourself
By laying defects of judgement to me, but
You patched up your excuses.

60   ANTONY   Not so, not so.
I know you could not lack, I am certain on't,
Very necessity of this thought,[7] that I,
Your partner in the cause 'gainst which he fought,
Could not with graceful eyes attend[8] those wars
65   Which fronted° mine own peace. As for my wife,   *opposed*
I would you had her spirit in such another.
The third o'th' world is yours, which with a snaffle[9]
You may pace° easy, but not such a wife.   *train to walk*

ENOBARBUS   Would we had all such wives, that the men might
70   go to wars with the women.

ANTONY   So much uncurbable,° her garboils,° Caesar,   *uncontrollable / tumults*
Made out of her impatience—which not wanted°   *did not lack*
Shrewdness of policy too—I grieving grant
Did you too much disquiet, for that you must
But° say I could not help it.   *Only*

75   CAESAR   I wrote to you

---

4. *contestation . . . war*: war was meant as an example for
you to follow (had you as its theme); Your name was the
war cry (war was waged in your name).
5. Claimed to be acting as my proxy.
6. *If . . . with*: If you'll patch together an old quarrel with
trivia, when you have enough material to make a new one

(or, possibly, as if you had enough material to make one).
7. *I know . . . thought*: I'm confident that you must have
been aware.
8. Could not look with approval on.
9. Bridle (one without a curb, for good-tempered horses).

When, rioting in Alexandria, you
Did pocket up my letters, and with taunts
Did gibe my missive out of audience.¹

ANTONY   Sir, he fell upon° me ere admitted, then.   broke in on
80   Three kings I had newly feasted, and did want
Of what I was² i'th' morning; but next day
I told him of myself,° which was as much   my situation
As to have asked him pardon. Let this fellow
Be nothing° of our strife. If we contend,   Be no part
Out of our question° wipe him.   dispute
85   CAESAR   You have broken
The article° of your oath, which you shall never   terms
Have tongue to charge me with.

LEPIDUS   Soft, Caesar.

ANTONY   No, Lepidus, let him speak.
90   The honour is sacred which he talks on now,
Supposing that I lacked it.³ But on, Caesar:
The article of my oath—

CAESAR   To lend me arms and aid when I required them,
The which you both denied.

ANTONY   Neglected, rather,
95   And then when poisoned hours had bound me up
From mine own knowledge.⁴ As nearly as I may
I'll play the penitent to you, but mine honesty
Shall not make poor my greatness, nor my power
Work without it.⁵ Truth is that Fulvia,
100   To have me out of Egypt, made wars here,
For which myself, the ignorant motive, do
So far ask pardon as befits mine honour°   dignity
To stoop in such a case.

LEPIDUS   'Tis noble spoken.

MAECENAS   If it might please you to enforce no further
105   The griefs° between ye; to forget them quite   grievances
Were to remember that the present need
Speaks to atone you.°   Is to reconcile you

LEPIDUS   Worthily spoken, Maecenas.

ENOBARBUS   Or if you borrow one another's love for the instant,
you may, when you hear no more words of Pompey, return it
110   again. You shall have time to wrangle in when you have nothing else to do.

ANTONY   Thou art a soldier only. Speak no more.

ENOBARBUS   That truth should be silent I had almost forgot.

ANTONY   You wrong this presence,° therefore speak no more.   (noble) company
115   ENOBARBUS   Go to, then; your considerate stone.⁶

CAESAR   I do not much dislike the matter,° but   content
The manner of his speech, for't cannot be
We shall remain in friendship, our conditions°   dispositions
So diff'ring in their acts. Yet if I knew
120   What hoop should hold us staunch,° from edge to edge   watertight; bound

---

1. Scoffed my messenger out of your (public) hearing (referring to 1.1).
2. *did . . . was*: was not myself.
3. *The honour . . . it*: What Caesar speaks of now is my sacred honor, which he assumes I lack (even assuming I lack it).
4. *bound . . . knowledge*: prevented me from realizing what I was doing.
5. *mine . . . it*: my honorable behavior (in admitting a fault) will not diminish my power, nor shall my power operate without honor.
6. Very well, then; still and silent, but capable of thought.

O'th' world I would pursue it.

AGRIPPA   Give me leave, Caesar.

CAESAR   Speak, Agrippa.

AGRIPPA   Thou hast a sister by the mother's side,
125   Admired Octavia. Great Mark Antony
Is now a widower.

CAESAR   Say not so, Agrippa.
If Cleopatra heard you, your reproof
Were well deserved of rashness.[7]

ANTONY   I am not married, Caesar. Let me hear
130   Agrippa further speak.

AGRIPPA   To hold you in perpetual amity,
To make you brothers, and to knit your hearts
With an unslipping knot, take Antony°   *let Antony take*
Octavia to° his wife; whose beauty claims   *for*
135   No worse a husband than the best of men;
Whose virtue and whose general graces speak
That which none else can utter.[8] By this marriage
All little jealousies° which now seem great,   *mistrusts*
And all great fears which now import° their dangers,   *bring along*
140   Would then be nothing. Truths would be tales
Where now half-tales be truths.[9] Her love to both
Would each to other and all loves to both
Draw after her. Pardon what I have spoke,
For 'tis a studied, not a present° thought,   *sudden*
By duty ruminated.

145   ANTONY   Will Caesar speak?

CAESAR   Not till he hears how Antony is touched°   *reacts*
With° what is spoke already.   *To*

ANTONY   What power is in Agrippa,
If I would say 'Agrippa, be it so',
To make this good?

150   CAESAR   The power of Caesar,
And his power unto Octavia.

ANTONY   May I never
To this good purpose, that so fairly shows,
Dream of impediment![1] Let me have thy hand.
Further this act of grace, and from this hour
155   The heart of brothers govern in our loves
And sway our great designs.

CAESAR   There's my hand.
[ANTONY *and* CAESAR *clasp hands*]
A sister I bequeath° you whom no brother   *hand over to*
Did ever love so dearly. Let her live
To join our kingdoms and our hearts; and never
Fly off our loves again.[2]

160   LEPIDUS   Happily, amen.

ANTONY   I did not think to draw my sword 'gainst Pompey,
For he hath laid strange° courtesies and great   *uncommon*

---

7. *your . . . rashness:* the reproof you would receive would
befit your rashness.
8. *speak . . . utter:* speak for themselves; speak more
powerfully than in any other woman.
9. *Truths . . . truths:* True reports, even if they were disturbing, could be passed over, regarded as hearsay, where
now incomplete rumors are accepted as truth.

1. *May . . . impediment:* alluding to the Anglican marriage service, as does sonnet 116: "Let me not to the marriage of true minds / Admit impediments." *so fairly shows:*
appears so attractive.
2. *never . . . again:* may our love for each other never
again desert us.

Of late upon me. I must thank him only,°   *at least*
Lest my remembrance° suffer ill report;   *gratitude*
At heel of° that, defy him.   *Right after*

165   LEPIDUS   Time calls upon's.
Of° us must Pompey presently° be sought,   *By / immediately*
Or else he seeks out us.

ANTONY   Where lies he?

CAESAR   About the Mount Misena.³

ANTONY   What is his strength
By land?

CAESAR   Great and increasing, but by sea
He is an absolute master.

170   ANTONY   So is the fame.°   *report*
Would we had spoke together.° Haste we for it;   *(earlier)*
Yet ere we put ourselves in arms, dispatch we
The business we have talked of.

CAESAR   With most gladness,
And do° invite you to my sister's view,   *I do*
Whither straight I'll lead you.

175   ANTONY   Let us, Lepidus,
Not lack your company.

LEPIDUS   Noble Antony,
Not sickness should detain me.

Flourish. Exeunt. Manent ENOBARBUS, AGRIPPA,
and MAECENAS

MAECENAS [*to* ENOBARBUS]   Welcome from Egypt, sir.

ENOBARBUS   Half the heart° of Caesar, worthy Maecenas! My   *Beloved friend*
180   honourable friend, Agrippa!

AGRIPPA   Good Enobarbus!

MAECENAS   We have cause to be glad that matters are so well
digested.° You stayed well by't⁴ in Egypt.   *settled*

ENOBARBUS   Ay, sir, we did sleep day out of countenance,⁵ and
185   made the night light° with drinking.   *bright; merry*

MAECENAS   Eight wild boars roasted whole at a breakfast and but
twelve persons there—is this true?

ENOBARBUS   This was but as a fly by° an eagle. We had much   *compared with*
more monstrous matter of feast, which worthily deserved noting.

190   MAECENAS   She's a most triumphant° lady, if report be square° to   *magnificent / fair*
her.

ENOBARBUS   When she first met Mark Antony, she pursed up
his heart upon the river of Cydnus.⁶

AGRIPPA   There she appeared indeed, or my reporter devised° well   *imagined*
195   for her.

ENOBARBUS   I will tell you.
The barge° she sat in, like a burnished throne   *oar-driven ship*
Burned on the water. The poop° was beaten gold;   *upper deck*
Purple° the sails, and so perfumèd that   *(royal dye)*
200   The winds were love-sick with them. The oars were silver,
Which to the tune of flutes kept stroke, and made
The water which they beat to follow faster,
As° amorous of their strokes. For° her own person,   *As if / As for*

---

3. Misenum, a hilly outcropping at the north end of the   not see what it looked like.
Bay of Naples.   6. She took possession of his heart on the Cydnus River
4. You hung in there; you had a high old time.   in Cilicia, Asia Minor (Turkey), on which the city of Tar-
5. We disconcerted day by sleeping through it, and did   sus stood.

It beggared all description. She did lie
205 In her pavilion—cloth of gold, of tissue[7]—
O'er-picturing that Venus where we see
The fancy outwork nature.[8] On each side her
Stood pretty dimpled boys, like smiling Cupids,
With divers-coloured fans whose wind did seem
210 To glow° the delicate cheeks which they did cool, *make glow*
And what they undid did.

AGRIPPA   O, rare for Antony!

ENOBARBUS   Her gentlewomen, like the Nereides,° *sea nymphs*
So many mermaids, tended her i'th' eyes,° *under her watchful eyes*
And made their bends adornings.[9] At the helm
215 A seeming mermaid steers. The silken tackle° *sails and ropes*
Swell with the touches of those flower-soft hands
That yarely frame° the office. From the barge *artfully carry out*
A strange invisible perfume hits the sense
Of the adjacent wharfs.° The city cast *banks*
220 Her people out upon° her, and Antony, *toward*
Enthroned i'th' market-place, did sit alone,
Whistling to th'air, which but for vacancy[1]
Had° gone to gaze on Cleopatra too, *Would have*
And made a gap in nature.

AGRIPPA   Rare Egyptian!

225 ENOBARBUS   Upon her landing Antony sent to her,
Invited her to supper. She replied
It should be better he became her guest,
Which she entreated. Our courteous Antony,
Whom ne'er the word of 'No' woman heard speak,
230 Being barbered ten times o'er, goes to the feast,
And for his ordinary° pays his heart *public meal at an inn*
For what his eyes eat only.

AGRIPPA   Royal wench!
She made great Caesar° lay his sword to bed. *(Julius)*
He ploughed her, and she cropped.[2]

ENOBARBUS   I saw her once
235 Hop forty paces through the public street,
And having lost her breath, she spoke and panted,
That° she did make defect° perfection, *So that / her panting*
And breathless, pour breath forth.

MAECENAS   Now Antony
Must leave her utterly.

ENOBARBUS   Never. He will not.
240 Age cannot wither her, nor custom stale° *familiarity diminish*
Her infinite variety. Other women cloy
The appetites they feed, but she makes hungry
Where most she satisfies. For vilest things
Become themselves° in her, that° the holy priests *Are becoming / so that*
245 Bless her when she is riggish.° *acts like a slut*

---

7. Fabric interwoven with gold thread.
8. *O'er-picturing . . . nature:* Outdoing even the picture of Venus in which the artist outdid nature.
9. Made their curtsies additions to the decoration.
1. Which if not for the fact that its absence would have left a vacuum (already in Shakespeare's time proverbially impossible in nature).
2. She bore Caesarion. After the assassination of Julius

Caesar in 44 B.C.E., Cleopatra returned from Rome, where she had accompanied him, to Egypt. There she reigned with their son, who became Ptolemy XV, after she ordered the death of her half brother and previous co-ruler Ptolemy XIV. On Ptolemy XIV, see 1.4.6 with note and 2.1.37 with note. On Antony and Cleopatra's plans for Ptolemy XV, see 3.6.1–16. On Ptolemy XV's fate, see note to 5.2.352.

MAECENAS If beauty, wisdom, modesty can settle
 The heart of Antony, Octavia is
 A blessèd lottery° to him.   *prize*

AGRIPPA   Let us go.
 Good Enobarbus, make yourself my guest
 Whilst you abide here.

250 ENOBARBUS   Humbly, sir, I thank you.   *Exeunt*

2.3

Enter ANTONY [*and*] CAESAR; OCTAVIA *between them*

ANTONY The world and my great office will sometimes
 Divide me from your bosom.

OCTAVIA   All which time,
 Before the gods my knee shall bow my prayers
 To them for you.

ANTONY   Good night, sir. My Octavia,
5 Read not my blemishes in the world's report.
 I have not kept my square,° but that° to come *stayed in line / what's*
 Shall all be done by th' rule.¹ Good night, dear lady.
 Good night, sir.

CAESAR Good night.   *Exeunt* [CAESAR *and* OCTAVIA]
 Enter SOOTHSAYER

10 ANTONY Now, sirrah.² You do wish yourself in Egypt?

SOOTHSAYER Would I had never come from thence, nor you
 Gone thither.

ANTONY   If you can, your reason?

SOOTHSAYER I see it in my motion,° have it not in my tongue. *intuition*
 But yet hie° you to Egypt again.   *hurry*

ANTONY   Say to me
15 Whose fortunes shall rise higher: Caesar's or mine?

SOOTHSAYER Caesar's. Therefore, O Antony, stay not by his side.
 Thy daemon, that thy spirit³ which keeps thee, is
 Noble, courageous, high, unmatchable,
 Where Caesar's is not. But near him thy angel
20 Becomes afeard, as° being o'erpowered. Therefore *as if*
 Make space enough between you.

ANTONY   Speak this no more.

SOOTHSAYER To none but thee; no more but when⁴ to thee.
 If thou dost play with him at any game
 Thou art sure to lose; and of° that natural luck   *by*
25 He beats thee 'gainst the odds. Thy lustre thickens° *Your brightness dims*
 When he shines by. I say again, thy spirit
 Is all afraid to govern thee near him;
 But he away, 'tis noble.

ANTONY   Get thee gone.
 Say to Ventidius I would speak with him. *Exit* [SOOTHSAYER]
30 He shall to Parthia; be it art or hap,°   *talent or luck*
 He° hath spoken true. The very dice obey him,° *(the soothsayer) / (Caesar)*
 And in our sports my better cunning° faints   *capability*
 Under his chance.° If we draw lots, he speeds.° *luck / succeeds*

2.3 Location: Rome.
1. Regulation; ruler, as unit of measure (picking up "square," line 6, a measuring tool).
2. Term by which a subordinate or social inferior is

addressed.
3. *Thy daemon . . . spirit:* Your guardian angel, which is the spirit.
4. *no more but when:* only.

His cocks do win the battle still of° mine   *always against*
35 When it is all to nought, and his quails ever
 Beat mine, inhooped, at odds.[5] I will to Egypt;
 And though I make this marriage for my peace,
 I'th' East my pleasure lies.
    Enter VENTIDIUS
         O, come, Ventidius.
 You must to Parthia, your commission's ready.
40 Follow me, and receive't.   *Exeunt*

2.4

Enter LEPIDUS, MAECENAS, *and* AGRIPPA

LEPIDUS Trouble yourselves no further. Pray you, hasten
 Your generals after.[1]
AGRIPPA   Sir, Mark Antony
 Will e'en but° kiss Octavia, and we'll follow.   *merely*
LEPIDUS Till I shall see you in your soldier's dress,
 Which will become you both, farewell.
5 MAECENAS   We shall,
 As I conceive the journey, be at the Mount° *Mount Misenum*
 Before you, Lepidus.
LEPIDUS   Your way is shorter.
 My purposes do draw me° much about.   *force me to go*
 You'll win two days upon me.
MAECENAS *and* AGRIPPA   Sir, good success.
10 LEPIDUS Farewell.   *Exeunt* [MAECENAS *and* AGRIPPA *at one*
          door, LEPIDUS *at another*]

2.5

Enter CLEOPATRA, CHARMIAN, IRAS, *and* ALEXAS

CLEOPATRA Give me some music—music, moody° food *melancholy*
 Of us that trade in love.
CHARMIAN, IRAS, *and* ALEXAS The music, ho!
    Enter MARDIAN, *the eunuch*
CLEOPATRA Let it alone. Let's to billiards. Come, Charmian.
CHARMIAN My arm is sore. Best play with Mardian.
5 CLEOPATRA As well a woman with an eunuch played
 As with a woman. Come, you'll play with me, sir?
MARDIAN As well as I can, madam.
CLEOPATRA And when good will is showed, though't come too short[1]
 The actor may plead pardon. I'll none now.° *I won't play now*
10 Give me mine angle.° We'll to th' river. There, *fishing rod*
 My music playing far off, I will betray°   *catch*
 Tawny-finned fishes. My bended hook shall pierce
 Their slimy jaws, and as I draw them up
 I'll think them every one an Antony,
 And say 'Ah ha, you're caught!'
15 CHARMIAN   'Twas merry when
 You wagered on your angling, when your diver

---

5. *When . . . odds:* When the odds completely favor me,
and when our quails are placed in a round enclosure to
make them fight, his always beat mine, against all odds.
2.4 Location: Rome.

1. *hasten . . . after:* follow your leaders.
2.5 Location: Alexandria.
1. Referring to Mardian's sexual incapacity.

Did hang a salt° fish on his hook, which he   *preserved*
With fervency drew up.
CLEOPATRA   That time—O times!—
I laughed him out of patience, and that night
20   I laughed him into patience, and next morn,
Ere the ninth hour, I drunk him to his bed,
Then put my tires and mantles° on him whilst   *headdresses and robes*
I wore his sword Philippan.[2]
       Enter a MESSENGER
                 O, from Italy.
Ram thou thy fruitful tidings in mine ears,
That long time have been barren.
25   MESSENGER   Madam, madam!
CLEOPATRA   Antonio's dead. If thou say so, villain,
Thou kill'st thy mistress; but well and free,
If thou so yield° him, there is gold, and here   *report*
My bluest veins to kiss—a hand that kings
Have lipped, and trembled kissing.
30   MESSENGER   First, madam, he is well.
CLEOPATRA   Why, there's more gold. But, sirrah, mark: we use
To say the dead are well. Bring it to that,
The gold I give thee will I melt and pour
Down thy ill-uttering throat.
35   MESSENGER   Good madam, hear me.
CLEOPATRA   Well, go to, I will.
But there's no goodness in thy face. If Antony
Be free and healthful, so tart a favour°   *so sour an expression*
To trumpet such good tidings! If not well,
40   Thou shouldst come like a Fury[3] crowned with snakes,
Not like a formal° man.   *Not in the shape of a*
MESSENGER   Will't please you hear me?
CLEOPATRA   I have a mind to strike thee ere thou speak'st.
Yet if thou say Antony lives, is well,
Or friends with Caesar, or not captive to him,
45   I'll set thee in a shower of gold, and hail
Rich pearls upon thee.
MESSENGER   Madam, he's well.
CLEOPATRA   Well said.
MESSENGER   And friends with Caesar.
CLEOPATRA   Thou'rt an honest man.
MESSENGER   Caesar and he are greater friends than ever.
CLEOPATRA   Make thee a fortune from me.
MESSENGER   But yet, madam—
50   CLEOPATRA   I do not like 'But yet'; it does allay°   *dissipate*
The good precedence.° Fie upon 'But yet'.   *preceding good news*
'But yet' is as a jailer to bring forth
Some monstrous malefactor. Prithee, friend,
Pour out the pack of matter to mine ear,°   *Give me all the news*
55   The good and bad together. He's friends with Caesar,
In state of health, thou sayst; and, thou sayst, free.
MESSENGER   Free, madam? No, I made no such report.
He's bound unto Octavia.

2. The sword with which Antony had beaten Brutus   3. In Greek mythology, a female avenging spirit.
and Cassius at Philippi.

CLEOPATRA	For what good turn?°	*good deed*
MESSENGER	For the best turn i'th' bed.	
CLEOPATRA	I am pale, Charmian.	
60 MESSENGER	Madam, he's married to Octavia.	
CLEOPATRA	The most infectious pestilence upon thee!	

       [*She*] *strikes him down*

MESSENGER	Good madam, patience!	
CLEOPATRA	What say you?	

       [*She*] *strikes him*

Hence, horrible villain, or I'll spurn° thine eyes   *kick*
Like balls before me. I'll unhair thy head,
       She hales° *him up and down*   *drags*
65 Thou shalt be whipped with wire and stewed in brine,
Smarting in ling'ring pickle.°   *salt water*

MESSENGER	Gracious madam,	

I that do bring the news made not the match.

CLEOPATRA	Say 'tis not so, a province I will give thee,	

And make thy fortunes proud. The blow thou hadst
70 Shall make thy peace for moving me to rage,
And I will boot° thee with what° gift beside   *compensate / whatever*
Thy modesty can beg.

MESSENGER	He's married, madam.	
CLEOPATRA	Rogue, thou hast lived too long.	

       [*She*] *draw*[*s*] *a knife*

MESSENGER	Nay then, I'll run.	

What mean you, madam? I have made no fault.   *Exit*
75 CHARMIAN   Good madam, keep yourself within yourself.°   *restrain yourself*
The man is innocent.

CLEOPATRA	Some innocents 'scape not the thunderbolt.	

Melt Egypt into Nile, and kindly° creatures   *harmless*
Turn all to serpents! Call the slave again.
80 Though I am mad I will not bite him. Call!

CHARMIAN	He is afeard to come.	
CLEOPATRA	I will not hurt him.	

       [*Exit* CHARMIAN]

These hands do lack nobility that they strike
A meaner° than myself, since I myself   *One of lower rank*
Have given myself the cause.°   *(by loving Antony)*
       Enter the MESSENGER *again* [*with* CHARMIAN]
                 Come hither, sir.
85 Though it be honest, it is never good
To bring bad news. Give to a gracious message
An host° of tongues, but let ill tidings tell   *A multitude*
Themselves when they be felt.[4]

MESSENGER	I have done my duty.	
90 CLEOPATRA	Is he married?	

I cannot hate thee worser than I do
If thou again say 'Yes'.

MESSENGER	He's married, madam.	
CLEOPATRA	The gods confound° thee! Dost thou hold there still?	*destroy*
MESSENGER	Should I lie, madam?	
CLEOPATRA	O, I would thou didst,	

95 So° half my Egypt were submerged and made   *Even if*
A cistern° for scaled snakes. Go, get thee hence.   *reservoir; chamber pot*

---

4. *let . . . felt*: bad news is best revealed by letting the victim feel the effects.

Hadst thou Narcissus[5] in thy face, to me
Thou wouldst appear most ugly. He is married?

MESSENGER I crave your highness' pardon.

CLEOPATRA   He is married?

100 MESSENGER Take no offence that I would not° offend you.   do not want to
To punish me for what you make me do
Seems much unequal.° He's married to Octavia.   most unfair

CLEOPATRA O that his fault should make a knave° of thee,   villain
That act not what thou'rt sure of!6 Get thee hence.

105 The merchandise which thou hast brought from Rome
Are all too dear for me. Lie they upon thy hand,7
And be undone° by 'em.   [*Exit* MESSENGER]   ruined (financially)

CHARMIAN   Good your highness, patience.

CLEOPATRA In praising Antony I have dispraised Caesar.

CHARMIAN Many times, madam.

110 CLEOPATRA I am paid for't now. Lead me from hence.
I faint. O Iras, Charmian—'tis no matter.
Go to the fellow, good Alexas, bid him
Report the feature° of Octavia: her years,   appearance
Her inclination;° let him not leave out   disposition

115 The colour of her hair. Bring me word quickly.   [*Exit* ALEXAS]
Let him for ever go—let him not, Charmian;
Though he be painted one way like a Gorgon,
The other way's a Mars.8 [*To* MARDIAN] Bid you Alexas
Bring me word how tall she is. Pity me, Charmian,

120 But do not speak to me. Lead me to my chamber.   *Exeunt*

2.6

Flourish. Enter POMPEY [*and*] MENAS *at one door, with*
[*a*] *drum*[*mer*] *and* [*a*] *trumpet*[*er*]; *at another,* CAESAR,
LEPIDUS, ANTONY, ENOBARBUS, MAECENAS, AGRIPPA, *with*
soldiers marching

POMPEY Your hostages I have, so have you mine,
And we shall talk before we fight.

CAESAR   Most meet°   fitting
That first we come to words, and therefore have we
Our written purposes° before us sent,   offers
5 Which if thou hast considered, let us know
If 'twill tie up° thy discontented sword   lead you to put aside
And carry back to Sicily much tall° youth   courageous
That else must perish here.

POMPEY   To you all three,
The senators alone° of this great world,   sole governors
10 Chief factors° for the gods: I do not know   agents
Wherefore° my father[1] should revengers want,°   why / lack

5. In Greek mythology, a surprisingly beautiful young
man.
6. Who do not commit the offense you know about;
who do not report the information you know.
7. Leave with your goods unsold.
8. Cleopatra imagines Antony as a figure in a perspective
painting: popular in Shakespeare's time, they showed different images according to the angle from which they
were viewed. In classical mythology, a Gorgon was one of
three female monsters with snakes for hair whose horrific
appearance could turn others to stone.
2.6 Location: Near Misenum, Italy.
1. Pompey the Great. The allusion in the following lines
is primarily to the events dramatized by Shakespeare in
Julius Caesar. After being defeated by Julius Caesar at
Pharsalia, Pompey the Great fled to Egypt and was there
assassinated by agents of Ptolemy, Cleopatra's half brother
(prior to the events in *Julius Caesar*). Julius Caesar was
then himself assassinated by the Roman republican conspirators, who included Cassius and Brutus. The triumvirs Antony, Octavius, and Lepidus defeated and killed
Brutus and Cassius at Philippi in revenge (see note to
1.2.88). The younger Pompey thus believes that by making war on the triumvirate, he avenges his father's death
and the deaths of Brutus and Cassius (and, therefore, he
fights for the Republic).

Having a son and friends, since Julius Caesar,
Who at Philippi the good Brutus ghosted,[2]
There saw you labouring for him.° What was't — *on his behalf*
15 That moved pale Cassius to conspire? And what
Made the all-honoured, honest° Roman Brutus, — *honorable*
With the armèd rest, courtiers° of beauteous freedom, — *seekers*
To drench° the Capitol but that they would — *(in blood)*
Have one man but a man?° And that is it — *(and not a king)*
20 Hath made me rig° my navy, at whose burden — *equip*
The angered ocean foams; with which I meant
To scourge th'ingratitude that despiteful Rome
Cast on my noble father.

CAESAR   Take your time.

ANTONY   Thou canst not fear° us, Pompey, with thy sails. — *intimidate*
25 We'll speak with° thee at sea. At land thou know'st — *engage*
How much we do o'ercount° thee. — *outnumber*

POMPEY   At land indeed
Thou dost o'ercount me of my father's house,[3]
But since the cuckoo builds not for himself,[4]
Remain in't as thou mayst.° — *as long as you can*

LEPIDUS   Be pleased to tell us—
30 For this is from the present°—how you take — *beside the point*
The offers we have sent you.

CAESAR   There's the point.

ANTONY   Which do not be entreated to,° but weigh — *convinced unfairly of*
What it is worth, embraced.° — *if you consent*

CAESAR   And what may follow,
To try a larger fortune?[5]

POMPEY   You have made me offer
35 Of Sicily, Sardinia; and I must
Rid all the sea of pirates; then to send
Measures of wheat to Rome; this 'greed upon,
To part with unhacked edges,° and bear back — *unused swords*
Our targes undinted.° — *shields untouched*

CAESAR, ANTONY, *and* LEPIDUS   That's our offer.

POMPEY   Know, then,
40 I came before you here a man prepared
To take this offer. But Mark Antony
Put me to some impatience. Though I lose
The praise of it by telling, you must know,
When Caesar and your brother were at blows,
45 Your mother came to Sicily, and did find
Her welcome friendly.

ANTONY   I have heard it, Pompey,
And am well studied for° a liberal thanks — *intend to offer*
Which I do owe you.

POMPEY   Let me have your hand.
       [POMPEY *and* ANTONY *shake hands*]
I did not think, sir, to have met you here.

---

2. Caesar appeared as a ghost to Brutus at the Battle of Philippi.
3. Plutarch records that Antony agreed to buy the elder Pompey's house but ultimately refused to pay for it.
4. The cuckoo lays eggs in the nests of other birds, rather than building a nest of its own.
5. If you try (by fighting us) for a still larger fortune than we have offered.

50 ANTONY The beds i'th' East are soft; and thanks to you,
That called me timelier° than my purpose° hither; *earlier / intention*
For I have gained by't.
CAESAR [*to* POMPEY]   Since I saw you last
There is a change upon you.
POMPEY   Well, I know not
What counts harsh fortune casts upon my face,[6]
55 But in my bosom shall she never come
To make my heart her vassal.
LEPIDUS   Well met here.
POMPEY I hope so, Lepidus. Thus we are agreed.
I crave our composition° may be written *pact*
And sealed between us.
CAESAR   That's the next to do.
60 POMPEY We'll feast each other ere we part, and let's
Draw lots who shall begin.° *act as host*
ANTONY That will I, Pompey.
POMPEY No, Antony, take the lot.
But, first or last, your fine Egyptian cookery
65 Shall have the fame. I have heard that Julius Caesar
Grew fat with feasting there.
ANTONY   You have heard much.
POMPEY I have fair° meanings, sir. *amicable*
ANTONY And fair° words to them. *(ironic)*
POMPEY Then so much have I heard,
70 And I have heard Apollodorus carried[7]—
ENOBARBUS No more o' that, he did so.
POMPEY   What, I pray you?
ENOBARBUS A certain queen to Caesar in a mattress.
POMPEY I know thee now. How far'st thou, soldier?
ENOBARBUS Well, and well am like to do, for I perceive
Four feasts are toward.° *to come*
75 POMPEY   Let me shake thy hand.
[POMPEY *and* ENOBARBUS *shake hands*]
I never hated thee. I have seen thee fight
When I have envied thy behaviour.
ENOBARBUS Sir, I never loved you much, but I ha' praised ye
When you have well deserved ten times as much
80 As I have said you did.
POMPEY Enjoy thy plainness.° It nothing ill becomes thee. *matter-of-fact speech*
Aboard my galley I invite you all.
Will you lead, lords?
CAESAR, ANTONY, *and* LEPIDUS Show's the way, sir.
POMPEY   Come.
Exeunt. Manent ENOBARBUS *and* MENAS
MENAS [*aside*] Thy father, Pompey, would ne'er have made this treaty.
85 [*To* ENOBARBUS] You and I have known,° sir. *met each other*
ENOBARBUS At sea, I think.
MENAS We have, sir.
ENOBARBUS You have done well by water.

---

6. What accounts cruel fortune calculates (by marking
notches, like wrinkles).
7. Alluding to the story that Cleopatra gained access to

her lover, Julius Caesar, by having herself rolled up in a
sleeping mat (told in Plutarch).

MENAS   And you by land.

90   ENOBARBUS   I will praise any man that will praise me, though it cannot be denied what I have done by land.

MENAS   Nor what I have done by water.

ENOBARBUS   Yes, something you can deny for your own safety. You have been a great thief by sea.

95   MENAS   And you by land.

ENOBARBUS   There I deny my land service; but give me your hand, Menas. If our eyes had authority,° here they might take   (*to make an arrest*)
two thieves kissing.[8]

    [*They shake hands*]

MENAS   All men's faces are true,° whatsome'er their hands are.   *honest*

100   ENOBARBUS   But there is never a fair woman has a true° face.   (*without makeup*)

MENAS   No slander;° they steal hearts.   *That's true*

ENOBARBUS   We came hither to fight with you.

MENAS   For my part, I am sorry it is turned to a drinking. Pompey doth this day laugh away his fortune.

105   ENOBARBUS   If he do, sure he cannot weep't back again.

MENAS   You've said,° sir. We looked not for Mark Antony here.   *spoken truly*
Pray you, is he married to Cleopatra?

ENOBARBUS   Caesar's sister is called Octavia.

MENAS   True, sir. She was the wife of Caius Marcellus.

110   ENOBARBUS   But she is now the wife of Marcus Antonius.

MENAS   Pray ye, sir?

ENOBARBUS   'Tis true.

MENAS   Then is Caesar and he for ever knit together.

ENOBARBUS   If I were bound to divine° of this unity I would not   *make predictions*
115   prophesy so.

MENAS   I think the policy of that purpose made more[9] in the marriage than the love of the parties.

ENOBARBUS   I think so, too. But you shall find the band that seems to tie their friendship together will be the very strangler
120   of their amity. Octavia is of a holy, cold, and still conversation.°   *disposition*

MENAS   Who would not have his wife so?

ENOBARBUS   Not he that himself is not so, which is Mark Antony. He will to his Egyptian dish again; then shall the sighs of Octavia blow the fire up in Caesar, and, as I said before, that
125   which is the strength of their amity shall prove the immediate author° of their variance.° Antony will use his affection where   *cause / enmity*
it is. He married but his occasion here.[1]

MENAS   And thus it may be. Come, sir, will you aboard? I have a health for you.

130   ENOBARBUS   I shall take it, sir. We have used our throats in Egypt.

MENAS   Come, let's away.   *Exeunt*

---

8. Arrest two thieves embracing; catch two thieving hands in a handshake, plotting together.
9. I think the politics of that "unity" weighed more heavily.

1. *Antony . . . here:* Antony will act on his desire where it really is located (Egypt). He married out of self-interest here.

2.7

Music plays. Enter two or three SERVANTS *with a banquet*[1]

FIRST SERVANT   Here they'll be, man. Some o' their plants are ill
rooted[2] already; the least wind i'th' world will blow them down.
SECOND SERVANT   Lepidus is high-coloured.
FIRST SERVANT   They have made him drink alms-drink.[3]
5   SECOND SERVANT   As they pinch one another by the disposition,[4]
he cries out 'No more!'—reconciles them to his entreaty° and   (to stop arguing)
himself to th' drink.
FIRST SERVANT   But it raises the greater war between him and his
discretion.
10   SECOND SERVANT   Why, this it is to have a name° in great men's   only a nominal place
fellowship. I had as lief° have a reed that will do me no service   just as soon
as a partisan I could not heave.[5]
FIRST SERVANT   To be called into a huge sphere and not to be
seen to move in't, are the holes where eyes should be which
15   pitifully disaster the cheeks.[6]

A sennet° sounded. Enter CAESAR, ANTONY, POMPEY,   flourish of trumpets
LEPIDUS, AGRIPPA, MAECENAS, ENOBARBUS, [*and*]
MENAS, *with other captains* [*and a boy*]

ANTONY [*to* CAESAR]   Thus do they, sir: they take the flow° o'th'   measure the depth
Nile
By certain scales i'th'° pyramid. They know   marks on the
By th' height, the lowness, or the mean,° if dearth   middle position
Or foison° follow. The higher Nilus swells   abundance
20   The more it promises; as it ebbs, the seedsman
Upon the slime and ooze scatters his grain,
And shortly comes to harvest.
LEPIDUS   You've strange serpents there?
ANTONY   Ay, Lepidus.
25   LEPIDUS   Your serpent of Egypt is bred now of your mud by the
operation of your sun; so is your crocodile.
ANTONY   They are so.
POMPEY   Sit, and some wine. A health to Lepidus!
[ANTONY, POMPEY, *and* LEPIDUS *sit*]
LEPIDUS   I am not so well as I should be, but I'll ne'er out.°   leave; miss a round
30   ENOBARBUS   Not till you have slept—I fear me you'll be in° till   remain; be drunk
then.
LEPIDUS   Nay, certainly, I have heard the Ptolemies' pyramises[7]
are very goodly things: without contradiction I have heard that.
MENAS [*aside to* POMPEY]   Pompey, a word.
POMPEY [*aside to* MENAS]   Say in mine ear; what is't?
35   MENAS [*aside to* POMPEY]   Forsake thy seat, I do beseech thee, captain,
And hear me speak a word.
POMPEY [*aside to* MENAS]   Forbear° me till anon.   Wait for
[*Aloud*] This wine for Lepidus!

2.7 Location: Pompey's galley, off Misenum.
1. One of the courses of the feast, possibly dessert.
2. *their . . . rooted:* the soles of the feet of the (drunken)
leaders are unsteady; the alliance between Antony and
Caesar is shaky.
3. Drink given out of charity; in this case, extra rounds
given to reconcile the parties each time they quarrel; one
too many.
4. As they irritate one another according to their natures.

5. As a spear I could not lift (position without power).
6. *To be . . . cheeks:* To be placed in high circles in which
one is incapable of moving is like having, instead of eyes,
empty eye sockets that disfigure one's face. (In Ptolemaic
astronomy, a planet "moves" within its "sphere," one of a
series of concentric circles of which the universe is
formed, with the earth at the center. A planet's ill influence causes "disaster," which literally means "bad star.")
7. Pyramids (drunken speech).

[MENAS] *whispers in* [*Pompey's*] *ear*

LEPIDUS   What manner o' thing is your crocodile?

ANTONY   It is shaped, sir, like itself, and it is as broad as it hath
40   breadth. It is just so high as it is, and moves with it° own organs.   its
It lives by that which nourisheth it, and the elements once out
of it, it transmigrates.[8]

LEPIDUS   What colour is it of?

ANTONY   Of it own colour, too.

45   LEPIDUS   'Tis a strange serpent.

ANTONY   'Tis so, and the tears of it are wet.[9]

CAESAR [*to* ANTONY]   Will this description satisfy him?

ANTONY   With the health that Pompey gives him; else he is a
very epicure.°   *an insatiable glutton*

50   POMPEY [*aside to* MENAS]   Go hang, sir, hang! Tell me of that? Away,
Do as I bid you. [*Aloud*] Where's this cup I called for?

MENAS [*aside to* POMPEY]   If for the sake of merit° thou wilt hear me,   *past deeds*
Rise from thy stool.

POMPEY [*rising*]   I think thou'rt mad. The matter?
[MENAS *and* POMPEY *stand apart*]

MENAS   I have ever held my cap off to° thy fortunes.   *ever served*

55   POMPEY   Thou hast served me with much faith. What's else to say?
Be jolly, lords.

ANTONY   These quicksands, Lepidus,
Keep off them, for you sink.

MENAS   Wilt thou be lord of all the world?

POMPEY   What sayst thou?

MENAS   Wilt thou be lord of the whole world? That's twice.

POMPEY   How should that be?

60   MENAS   But entertain° it   *consider*
And, though thou think me poor, I am the man
Will give thee all the world.

POMPEY   Hast thou drunk well?

MENAS   No, Pompey, I have kept me from the cup.
Thou art, if thou dar'st be, the earthly Jove.
65   Whate'er the ocean pales° or sky inclips°   *encloses / embraces*
Is thine, if thou wilt ha't.

POMPEY   Show me which way!

MENAS   These three world-sharers, these competitors,°   *allies*
Are in thy vessel. Let me cut the cable;
And when we are put off,° fall to their throats.   *(from shore)*
All there is thine.

70   POMPEY   Ah, this thou shouldst have done
And not have spoke on't. In me 'tis villainy,
In thee 't had been good service. Thou must know
'Tis not my profit that does lead mine honour;
Mine honour, it.[1] Repent that e'er thy tongue
75   Hath so betrayed thine act.[2] Being done unknown,
I should have found it afterwards well done,
But must condemn it now. Desist, and drink.

8. Passes into other forms of life: referring to Pythagoras's
theory, apparently of Egyptian origin, that at death the
soul moves into another newborn living thing.
9. Continuing the pattern of comically uninformative
self-identity, this line may also refer to hypocritical crocodile tears and hence to Pompey, as his ensuing exchange

with Menas suggests. See also 3.2.54–60 and 5.1.26–49.
1. *'Tis . . . it*: It is my honor that precedes or is the basis
of my profit.
2. Treacherously disclosed your intentions and so made
it impossible to carry them out.

[*He returns to the others*]

MENAS [*aside*]   For this, I'll never follow thy palled° fortunes more.   *diminished*
Who seeks and will not take when once 'tis offered,
Shall never find it more.

80   POMPEY   This health to Lepidus!
ANTONY   Bear him ashore.—I'll pledge it° for him, Pompey.   *drink the toast*
ENOBARBUS   Here's to thee, Menas!
MENAS   Enobarbus, welcome.
POMPEY   Fill till the cup be hid.
                [*One lifts* LEPIDUS, *drunk, and carries him off*]
ENOBARBUS   There's a strong fellow, Menas.
MENAS   Why?
85   ENOBARBUS   A° bears the third part of the world, man; seest not?   *He*
MENAS   The third part then is drunk. Would it were all,
That it might go on wheels.°   *easily; out of control*
ENOBARBUS   Drink thou, increase the reels.°   *revels; spinning*
MENAS   Come.
POMPEY   This is not yet an Alexandrian feast.
90   ANTONY   It ripens towards it. Strike the vessels,° ho!   *Open more casks*
Here's to Caesar!
CAESAR   I could well forbear't.
It's monstrous° labour when I wash my brain,   *unnatural*
An° it grow fouler.   *If as a result*
ANTONY   Be a child o'th' time.
95   CAESAR   Possess it, I'll make answer.³
But I had rather fast from all, four days,
Than drink so much in one.
ENOBARBUS [*to* ANTONY]   Ha, my brave Emperor,
Shall we dance now the Egyptian bacchanals,⁴
And celebrate our drink?
100   POMPEY   Let's ha't, good soldier.
ANTONY   Come, let's all take hands
Till that the conquering wine hath steeped our sense
In soft and delicate Lethe.°   *oblivion*
ENOBARBUS   All take hands.
Make battery to° our ears with the loud music.   *Besiege*
105   The while I'll place you, then the boy shall sing.
The holding° every man shall beat° as loud   *refrain / beat out*
As his strong sides can volley.°   *fire off*
        Music plays. ENOBARBUS *places them hand in hand*
BOY [*sings*]   Come, thou monarch of the vine,
              Plumpy Bacchus, with pink⁵ eyne!
110   In thy vats our cares be drowned,
              With thy grapes our hairs be crowned!
              Cup us till the world go round,
              Cup us till the world go round!
CAESAR   What would you more? Pompey, good night.
        [*To* ANTONY]   Good-brother,°   *Brother-in-law*
115   Let me request you off.° Our graver business   *to come ashore*
Frowns at this levity. Gentle lords, let's part.
You see we have burnt° our cheeks. Strong Enobarb   *flushed*

───────────────

3. Take it, and I'll drink, too; be in command of the time,   and revelry.
I say.   5. Half-closed and red from drinking.
4. Wild, drunken revels in honor of Bacchus, god of wine

Is weaker than the wine, and mine own tongue
Splits° what it speaks. The wild disguise° hath almost   *Deforms / drunkenness*
120   Anticked us° all. What needs more words? Good night.   *Made us clowns*
Good Antony, your hand.

POMPEY   I'll try you° on the shore.   *test your drinking*

ANTONY   And shall, sir. Give's your hand.

POMPEY   O Antony,
You have my father's house. But what, we are friends!
Come down into the boat.

                [Exeunt all but ENOBARBUS *and* MENAS*]*

ENOBARBUS   Take heed you fall not, Menas.

125 **MENAS**   I'll not° on shore.   *not go*
No, to my cabin. These drums, these trumpets, flutes, what!
Let Neptune hear we bid a loud farewell
To these great fellows. Sound and be hanged, sound out!

              Sound a flourish, with drums

ENOBARBUS *[throwing his cap in the air]*   Hoo, says a!° There's   *he*
my cap.

MENAS   Ho, noble captain, come!   *Exeunt*

3.1

Enter VENTIDIUS *[with* SILIUS *and other Roman soldiers]*
as it were in triumph; the dead body of Pacorus borne
before him

VENTIDIUS   Now, darting Parthia,[1] art thou struck; and now
Pleased fortune does of Marcus Crassus'[2] death
Make me revenger. Bear the King's son's body
Before our army. Thy° Pacorus, Orodes,   *Your son*
Pays this for Marcus Crassus.

5 **SILIUS**   Noble Ventidius,
Whilst yet with Parthian blood thy sword is warm,
The fugitive Parthians follow.[3] Spur through Media,[4]
Mesopotamia, and the shelters whither
The routed fly. So thy grand captain, Antony,
10 Shall set thee on triumphant° chariots and   *triumphal*
Put garlands on thy head.

VENTIDIUS   O Silius, Silius,
I have done enough. A lower place,° note well,   *man of low rank*
May make too great an act. For learn this, Silius:
Better to leave undone than by our deed
15 Acquire too high a fame when him we serve's away.
Caesar and Antony have ever won
More in their officer than person.[5] Sossius,
One of my place in Syria, his° lieutenant,   *(Antony's)*
For quick accumulation of renown,
20 Which he achieved by th' minute,° lost his favour.   *more every minute*
Who does i'th' wars more than his captain can
Becomes his captain's captain; and ambition,

3.1 Location: Syria.
1. Parthian cavalry advanced flinging darts, then retreated shooting arrows. "Parthia" here refers to both the nation and its King, Orodes.
2. A member, with Pompey the Great and Julius Caesar, of the first triumvirate, treacherously and cruelly killed in

defeat by Orodes in 53 B.C.E.
3. Chase the fleeing Parthians.
4. The land between Persia and Armenia, east of Mesopotamia—part of the Parthian Empire.
5. Owing more to the skill of their officers than to their own skill.

The soldier's virtue, rather makes choice of loss
Than gain which darkens him.°   eclipses his renown
25 I could do more to do Antonius good,
But 'twould offend him, and in his offence
Should my performance perish.°   lose its value
SILIUS   Thou hast, Ventidius, that°   (discretion)
Without the which a soldier and his sword
Grants scarce° distinction. Thou wilt write to Antony?   Scarcely admits of
30 VENTIDIUS   I'll humbly signify what in his name,
That magical word of war, we have effected;
How, with his banners and his well-paid ranks,
The ne'er-yet-beaten horse° of Parthia   cavalry
We have jaded° out o'th' field.   chased like tired nags
SILIUS   Where is he now?
35 VENTIDIUS   He purposeth to Athens; whither, with what haste
The weight we must convey with's will permit,
We shall appear before him.—On there; pass along.   *Exeunt*

3.2
Enter AGRIPPA *at one door,* ENOBARBUS *at another*

AGRIPPA   What, are the brothers parted?°   brothers-in-law gone
ENOBARBUS   They have dispatched° with Pompey; he is gone.   finished the business
The other three are sealing.° Octavia weeps   signing their pact
To part from Rome, Caesar is sad, and Lepidus
5   Since Pompey's feast, as Menas says, is troubled
With the green-sickness.[1]
AGRIPPA   'Tis a noble Lepidus.
ENOBARBUS   A very fine one. O, how he loves Caesar!
AGRIPPA   Nay, but how dearly he adores Mark Antony!
ENOBARBUS   Caesar? Why, he's the Jupiter of men.
10 AGRIPPA   What's Antony—the god of Jupiter?
ENOBARBUS   Spake you of Caesar? How, the nonpareil?°   incomparable
AGRIPPA   O Antony, O thou Arabian bird![2]
ENOBARBUS   Would you praise Caesar, say 'Caesar'; go no further.
AGRIPPA   Indeed, he plied them both with excellent praises.
15 ENOBARBUS   But he loves Caesar best; yet he loves Antony—
Hoo! Hearts, tongues, figures,° scribes, bards, poets, cannot   (of speech); numbers
Think, speak, cast,° write, sing, number°—hoo!—   calculate / make verses
His love to Antony. But as for Caesar—
Kneel down, kneel down, and wonder.
AGRIPPA   Both he loves.
ENOBARBUS   They are his shards,[3] and he their beetle.
         [*Trumpet within*]
20   So,
This is° to horse. Adieu, noble Agrippa.   calls us
AGRIPPA   Good fortune, worthy soldier, and farewell.
         Enter CAESAR, ANTONY, LEPIDUS, *and* OCTAVIA
ANTONY [to CAESAR]   No further, sir.

3.2 Location: Rome.
1. Anemia in adolescent, lovesick girls (hence, a feminizing attribute): here, used humorously for Lepidus's hangover and its effect, as well as ironically for his overblown affection for Caesar and Antony.
2. The phoenix, a legendary, self-resurrecting bird, only

one of which existed at a time. It was believed to live for several centuries, to die in flames, and to be reborn from its own ashes.
3. Dung patches (between which the beetle crawls to feed and breed); perhaps, wing cases (with which the beetle flies).

CAESAR   You take from me a great part of myself.
25 Use me well in't. Sister, prove such a wife
As my thoughts make thee, and as my farthest bond
Shall pass on thy approof.⁴ Most noble Antony,
Let not the piece° of virtue which is set   *paragon*
Betwixt us as the cement of our love
30 To keep it builded, be the ram to batter
The fortress of it; for better might we
Have loved without this mean° if on both parts   *intermediary*
This be not cherished.
ANTONY   Make me not offended
In° your distrust.   *By*
CAESAR   I have said.
ANTONY   You shall not find,
35 Though you be therein curious,° the least cause   *overly probing*
For what you seem to fear. So, the gods keep you,
And make the hearts of Romans serve your ends.
We will here part.
CAESAR   Farewell, my dearest sister, fare thee well.
40 The elements be kind to thee, and make
Thy spirits all of comfort. Fare thee well.
OCTAVIA [*weeping*]   My noble brother!
ANTONY   The April's in her eyes;° it is love's spring,   *She weeps*
And these the showers to bring it on. Be cheerful.
45 OCTAVIA   Sir, look well to my husband's° house, and—   *(Antony's)*
CAESAR   What, Octavia?
OCTAVIA   I'll tell you in your ear.
          [*She whispers to* CAESAR]
ANTONY   Her tongue will not obey her heart, nor can
Her heart inform her tongue—the swan's-down feather,
That stands upon the swell at full of tide,
50 And neither way inclines.⁵
ENOBARBUS [*aside to* AGRIPPA]   Will Caesar weep?
AGRIPPA [*aside to* ENOBARBUS]   He has a cloud in's face.
ENOBARBUS [*aside to* AGRIPPA]   He were the worse for that were he a horse;⁶
So is he, being a man.
AGRIPPA [*aside to* ENOBARBUS]   Why, Enobarbus,
55 When Antony found Julius Caesar dead
He cried almost to roaring, and he wept
When at Philippi he found Brutus slain.
ENOBARBUS [*aside to* AGRIPPA]   That year indeed he was trou-
          bled with a rheum.°   *flu; watery eyes*
What willingly he did confound° he wailed,°   *destroy / mourned*
Believe't, till I wept too.
60 CAESAR   No, sweet Octavia,
You shall hear from me still.° The time shall not   *constantly*
Outgo⁷ my thinking on° you.   *of*
ANTONY   Come, sir, come,
I'll wrestle with you in my strength of love.

---

4. *and as . . . approof:* and (such a wife) as to make my
largest contractual commitment (also, my closest tie of
affection: here, Caesar's to Octavia) approved on the basis
of what you will prove to be.
5. *the swan's-down . . . inclines:* (she is like) the feather of
a swan's down that floats in still water, unmoving (just as

she can't speak) when the tide is about to turn. Octavia's
emotions, balanced between brother and husband, are
too strong to allow speech.
6. A horse with a cloud—a dark rather than a white star
on its face—was supposedly ill tempered.
7. *The . . . / Outgo:* Even time will not endure beyond.

Look, here I have you [*embracing* CAESAR]; thus I let you go,
And give you to the gods.

65 CAESAR   Adieu, be happy.

LEPIDUS   Let all the number of the stars give light
To thy fair way.

CAESAR   Farewell, farewell.

      [*He*] *kisses* OCTAVIA

ANTONY   Farewell.

       Trumpets sound. Exeunt [ANTONY, OCTAVIA, *and*
         ENOBARBUS *at one door*, CAESAR, LEPIDUS, *and*
                       AGRIPPA *at another*]

3.3

     Enter CLEOPATRA, CHARMIAN, IRAS, *and* ALEXAS

CLEOPATRA   Where is the fellow?

ALEXAS   Half afeard to come.

CLEOPATRA   Go to, go to.

      Enter the MESSENGER *as before*
                 Come hither, sir.

ALEXAS   Good majesty,
Herod of Jewry[1] dare not look upon you
But when you are well pleased.

CLEOPATRA   That Herod's head

5 I'll have; but how, when Antony is gone,
Through whom I might command it?

      [*To the* MESSENGER]   Come thou near.

MESSENGER   Most gracious majesty!

CLEOPATRA   Didst thou behold
Octavia?

MESSENGER   Ay, dread Queen.

CLEOPATRA   Where?

MESSENGER   Madam, in Rome.
I looked her in the face, and saw her led

10 Between her brother and Mark Antony.

CLEOPATRA   Is she as tall as me?

MESSENGER   She is not, madam.

CLEOPATRA   Didst hear her speak? Is she shrill-tongued or low?

MESSENGER   Madam, I heard her speak. She is low-voiced.

CLEOPATRA   That's not so good.° He cannot like her long.   *favorable to Octavia*

15 CHARMIAN   Like her? O Isis, 'tis impossible!

CLEOPATRA   I think so, Charmian. Dull of tongue, and dwarfish.
What majesty is in her gait? Remember
If e'er thou looked'st on majesty.

MESSENGER   She creeps.
Her motion and her station° are as one.   *standing still*

20 She shows° a body rather than a life,   *seems to be*
A statue than° a breather.   *rather than*

CLEOPATRA   Is this certain?

MESSENGER   Or I have no observance.°   *powers of observation*

CHARMIAN   Three in Egypt
Cannot make better note.[2]

CLEOPATRA   He's very knowing,

3.3 Location: Alexandria.
1. Renowned for his irrational cruelty. See note to 1.2.24.

2. *Three . . . note:* There are not three better witnesses in all Egypt.

I do perceive't. There's nothing in her yet.
The fellow has good judgement.

25 CHARMIAN   Excellent.

CLEOPATRA [*to the* MESSENGER]   Guess at her years, I prithee.

MESSENGER   Madam,
She was a widow—

CLEOPATRA   Widow? Charmian, hark.

MESSENGER   And I do think she's thirty.°   *(Cleopatra was 38)*

CLEOPATRA   Bear'st thou her face in mind? Is't long or round?

30 MESSENGER   Round, even to faultiness.

CLEOPATRA   For the most part, too, they are foolish that are so.
Her hair—what colour?

MESSENGER   Brown, madam; and her forehead
As low as she would wish it.³

CLEOPATRA [*giving money*]   There's gold for thee.
Thou must not take my former sharpness ill.

35 I will employ thee back° again. I find thee   *to go back to Rome*
Most fit for business. Go, make thee ready.
Our letters are prepared.   [*Exit* MESSENGER]

CHARMIAN   A proper° man.   *An admirable*

CLEOPATRA   Indeed he is so. I repent me much
That so I harried him. Why, methinks, by him,°   *by his account*
This creature's no such thing.°   *nothing special*

40 CHARMIAN   Nothing, madam.

CLEOPATRA   The man hath seen some majesty, and should know.

CHARMIAN   Hath he seen majesty? Isis else defend,
And serving you so long!⁴

CLEOPATRA   I have one thing more to ask him yet, good Charmian.

45 But 'tis no matter. Thou shalt bring him to me
Where I will write. All may be well enough.

CHARMIAN   I warrant you, madam.   *Exeunt*

3.4

Enter ANTONY *and* OCTAVIA

ANTONY   Nay, nay, Octavia, not only that,
That were excusable, that and thousands more
Of semblable° import; but he hath waged   *like*
New wars 'gainst Pompey, made his will and read it

5 To public ear,¹ spoke scantly° of me;   *meanly*
When perforce he could not
But pay me terms of honour, cold and sickly
He vented them, most narrow measure° lent me.   *little credit*
When the best hint° was given him, he not took't,   *opportunity*
Or did it from his teeth.°   *insincerely*

10 OCTAVIA   O my good lord,
Believe not all, or if you must believe,
Stomach° not all. A more unhappy lady,   *Resent*
If this division chance, ne'er stood between,
Praying for both parts.

15 The good gods will mock me presently,°   *at once*

---

3. So that she would wish it no lower: high foreheads were admired.
4. *Isis . . . long*: He surely has, considering how long he's served you. *else defend*: prohibit that it not be so. There may be a double irony in the lines, with Charmian appar-

ently denying that anyone who has long served Cleopatra could recognize true majesty but not really meaning it.
3.4 Location: Athens.
1. Caesar's act implies promises to the public.

When I shall pray 'O, bless my lord and husband!',
Undo that prayer by crying out as loud
'O, bless my brother!' Husband win, win brother
Prays and destroys the prayer; no midway
'Twixt these extremes at all.

20 ANTONY   Gentle Octavia,
Let your best love draw to that point which seeks
Best to preserve it.[2] If I lose mine honour,
I lose myself. Better I were not yours
Than yours so branchless.° But, as you requested,   *amputated*
25 Yourself shall go between's. The meantime, lady,
I'll raise the preparation of a war
Shall stain your brother.° Make your soonest haste;   *hurt his reputation*
So° your desires are yours.   *In this way*
OCTAVIA   Thanks to my lord.
The Jove of power make me most weak, most weak,
30 Your reconciler! Wars 'twixt you twain would be
As if the world should cleave, and that slain men
Should solder° up the rift.   *close*
ANTONY   When it appears to you where this begins,°   *who started this*
Turn your displeasure that way, for our faults
35 Can never be so equal that your love
Can equally move with° them. Provide° your going,   *judge / Prepare for*
Choose your own company, and command what cost
Your heart has mind to.   *Exeunt*

3.5

Enter ENOBARBUS *and* EROS [*meeting*]

ENOBARBUS   How now, friend Eros?
EROS   There's strange news come, sir.
ENOBARBUS   What, man?
EROS   Caesar and Lepidus have made wars upon Pompey.
5 ENOBARBUS   This is old. What is the success?°   *outcome*
EROS   Caesar, having made use of him° in the wars 'gainst Pom-   *(Lepidus)*
  pey, presently denied him rivality,° would not let him partake   *equal partnership*
  in the glory of the action, and, not resting° here, accuses him   *stopping*
  of letters he had formerly wrote to Pompey; upon his° own   *(Caesar's)*
10 appeal° seizes him; so the poor third is up,° till death enlarge *accusation / imprisoned*
  his confine.
ENOBARBUS   Then, world, thou hast a pair of chops,° no more,°   *jaws / (than two)*
And throw° between them all the food thou hast,   *if you should throw*
They'll grind the one the other. Where's Antony?
15 EROS   He's walking in the garden, thus, and spurns°   *kicks*
The rush° that lies before him, cries 'Fool Lepidus!'   *rushes*
And threats the throat of that his officer°   *that officer of his*
That murdered Pompey.[1]
ENOBARBUS   Our great navy's rigged.°   *prepared*
EROS   For Italy and Caesar. More,° Domitius: *There's more (to say)*
20 My lord desires you presently. My news
I might have told hereafter.

---

2. *Let . . . it:* Choose the one of us (Antony or Caesar)
who best strives to preserve your love.
3.5 Location: Athens.
1. Historically, though Shakespeare leaves Antony's re-

sponsibility for the killing unclear, Pompey was said to
have been murdered at the command of Antony, who
here regrets the death because Pompey might have been
a useful ally against Caesar.

ENOBARBUS 'Twill be naught.[2]
    But let it be; bring me to Antony.
EROS   Come, sir.   *Exeunt*

3.6

Enter AGRIPPA, MAECENAS, *and* CAESAR

CAESAR   Contemning° Rome, he has done all this and more   *Despising*
    In Alexandria. Here's the manner of 't:
    I'th' market place on a tribunal° silvered,   *platform*
    Cleopatra and himself in chairs of gold
5   Were publicly enthroned. At the feet sat
    Caesarion, whom they call my father's[1] son,
    And all the unlawful issue that their lust
    Since then hath made between them. Unto her
    He gave the stablishment° of Egypt; made her   *full possession*
10 Of lower Syria, Cyprus, Lydia,[2]
    Absolute queen.
MAECENAS   This in the public eye?
CAESAR   I'th' common showplace, where they exercise.[3]
    His sons he there proclaimed the kings of kings;
    Great Media, Parthia, and Armenia
15 He gave to Alexander. To Ptolemy he assigned
    Syria, Cilicia, and Phoenicia. She
    In th'habiliments° of the goddess Isis   *costume*
    That day appeared, and oft before gave audience,
    As 'tis reported, so.°   *in this costume*
MAECENAS   Let Rome be thus informed.
20 AGRIPPA   Who, queasy with° his insolence already,   *sick of*
    Will their good thoughts call° from him.   *remove*
CAESAR   The people knows it,
    And have now received his accusations.
AGRIPPA   Who does he accuse?
CAESAR   Caesar, and that having in Sicily
25 Sextus Pompeius spoiled,° we had not rated° him *ransacked / allotted*
    His part o'th' isle.° Then does he say he lent me   *Sicily*
    Some shipping, unrestored.° Lastly, he frets   *not returned (by me)*
    That Lepidus of the triumvirate
    Should be deposed; and being,° that we detain   *being deposed*
    All his revenue.
30 AGRIPPA   Sir, this should be answered.
CAESAR   'Tis done already, and the messenger gone.
    I have told him Lepidus was grown too cruel,
    That he his high authority abused
    And did deserve his change. For° what I have conquered,   *As for*
35 I grant him part; but then in his Armenia,
    And other of his conquered kingdoms,
    I demand the like.
MAECENAS   He'll never yield to that.
CAESAR   Nor must not then be yielded to in this.

Enter OCTAVIA *with her train*

---

2. Of no consequence; extremely harmful.
3.6 Location: Rome.
1. Julius Caesar (who adopted his grandnephew Octavius as his son). See 2.2.233–34 with note and note to 5.2.352.

2. District on the west coast of Asia Minor. Shakespeare took the name from North's translation of Plutarch, but the original has Libya.
3. In the arena (theater), where they engage in sports (perform).

OCTAVIA   Hail, Caesar, and my lord; hail, most dear Caesar!
40 CAESAR   That ever I should call thee castaway!
OCTAVIA   You have not called me so, nor have you cause.
CAESAR   Why have you stol'n upon us thus? You come not
    Like Caesar's sister. The wife of Antony
    Should have an army for an usher, and
45   The neighs of horse to tell of her approach
    Long ere she did appear. The trees by th' way
    Should have borne men, and expectation fainted,
    Longing for what it had not. Nay, the dust
    Should have ascended to the roof of heaven,
50   Raised by your populous troops. But you are come
    A market maid to Rome, and have prevented°   *(by coming too early)*
    The ostentation° of our love; which, left unshown,   *public display*
    Is often left unloved.[4] We should have met you
    By sea and land, supplying every stage°   *(of the voyage)*
    With an augmented greeting.
55 OCTAVIA   Good my lord,
    To come thus was I not constrained, but did it
    On my free will. My lord, Mark Antony,
    Hearing that you prepared for war, acquainted
    My grievèd ear withal, whereon I begged
    His pardon for° return.   *permission to*
60 CAESAR   Which soon he granted,
    Being an obstruct 'tween his lust and him.
OCTAVIA   Do not say so, my lord.
CAESAR   I have eyes upon him,
    And his affairs come to me on the wind.
    Where is he now?
OCTAVIA   My lord, in Athens.
65 CAESAR   No, my most wrongèd sister. Cleopatra
    Hath nodded him to her. He hath given his empire
    Up to a whore; who° now are levying   *both of them*
    The kings o'th' earth for war. He hath assembled
    Bocchus, the King of Libya; Archelaus
70   Of Cappadocia; Philadelphos, King
    Of Paphlagonia; the Thracian King Adallas;
    King Malchus of Arabia; King of Pont;
    Herod of Jewry; Mithridates, King
    Of Comagene; Polemon and Amyntas,
75   The Kings of Mede and Lycaonia;[5]
    With a more larger° list of sceptres.   *yet longer*
OCTAVIA   Ay me most wretched,
    That have my heart parted betwixt two friends
    That does afflict each other!
CAESAR   Welcome hither.
    Your letters did withhold our° breaking forth   *restrain me from*
80   Till we perceived both how you were wrong° led   *wrongly*
    And we in negligent danger.° Cheer your heart.   *danger from negligence*
    Be you not troubled with the time,° which drives   *present business*
    O'er your content° these strong necessities;   *contentment*

---

4. Is often thought not to be love at all. Or, *which . . .*   leads to its actual decline.
unloved: lack of opportunity to demonstrate love often   5. All kings from the East.

But let determined things to destiny
85 Hold unbewailed their way.⁶ Welcome to Rome;
Nothing more dear to me. You are abused
Beyond the mark° of thought, and the high gods,　　　　　°limits
To do you justice, makes their ministers°　　　　　　　°agents
Of us and those that love you. Best of comfort,
And ever welcome to us.
90 AGRIPPA　　　　　　　　Welcome, lady.
MAECENAS　Welcome, dear madam.
　　　Each heart in Rome does love and pity you.
　　　Only th'adulterous Antony, most large°　　　　　　°unlimited
　　　In his abominations, turns you off,
95 And gives his potent regiment° to a trull°　　°powerful rule / whore
　　　That noises it° against us.　　　　　　　　　　　°cries out
OCTAVIA　　　　　　　　　　Is it so, sir?
CAESAR　Most certain. Sister, welcome. Pray you
　　　Be ever known to patience. My dear'st sister!　　*Exeunt*

3.7

Enter CLEOPATRA *and* ENOBARBUS

CLEOPATRA　I will be even with thee, doubt it not.
ENOBARBUS　But why, why, why?
CLEOPATRA　Thou hast forspoke° my being in these wars,　　°opposed
　　　And sayst it is not fit.
ENOBARBUS　　　　　　Well, is it, is it?
5 CLEOPATRA　Is't not denounced° against us? Why should not we　°Isn't war declared
　　　Be there in person?
ENOBARBUS [*aside*]　　Well, I could reply
　　　If we should serve with horse and mares together,
　　　The horse were merely lost;¹ the mares would bear°　°seduce; carry
　　　A soldier and his horse.
CLEOPATRA　　　　　　What is't you say?
10 ENOBARBUS　Your presence needs must puzzle° Antony,　　°distract
　　　Take from his heart, take from his brain, from's time
　　　What should not then be spared. He is already
　　　Traduced° for levity; and 'tis said in Rome　　　°Slandered
　　　That Photinus, an eunuch, and your maids
　　　Manage this war.
15 CLEOPATRA　　　　　Sink Rome,° and their tongues rot　°To hell with Rome
　　　That speak against us! A charge° we bear i'th' war,　°An expense; duty
　　　And as the president of my kingdom will
　　　Appear there for° a man. Speak not against it.　　°as if I were
　　　I will not stay behind.

Enter ANTONY *and* CAMIDIUS

ENOBARBUS　　　　　　Nay, I have done.
　　　Here comes the Emperor.
20 ANTONY　　　　　　Is it not strange, Camidius,
　　　That from Tarentum and Brundisium²
　　　He could so quickly cut° the Ionian° Sea　　°Cut across / Adriatic
　　　And take in° Toryne?°—You have heard on't, sweet?　°overrun / (near Actium)

---

6. *let . . . way:* let predetermined events go to their destined conclusions without complaint.
3.7 Location: Antony's camp, near Actium, Greece.
1. *If . . . lost:* If we take both male and female horses

(whores) to the wars, the males would have no hope of triumphing, because of the females ("merely" equals "mare-ly").
2. Ports in southeast Italy.

CLEOPATRA   Celerity is never more admired°   *wondered at*
　　Than by the negligent.

25　ANTONY　　　　　　　　　A good rebuke,
　　Which might have well becomed the best of men
　　To taunt at slackness. Camidius, we
　　Will fight with him by sea.

CLEOPATRA　　　　　　　　By sea—what else?

CAMIDIUS   Why will my lord do so?

ANTONY　　　　　　　　　　For that he dares us to't.

30　ENOBARBUS   So hath my lord dared him to single fight.

CAMIDIUS   Ay, and to wage this battle at Pharsalia,°   *(near Actium)*
　　Where Caesar fought with Pompey. But these offers
　　Which serve not for his vantage, he shakes off,
　　And so should you.

ENOBARBUS　　　　　Your ships are not well manned,
35　Your mariners are muleters,° reapers, people   *mule drivers*
　　Engrossed° by swift impress.° In Caesar's fleet   *Amassed / conscription*
　　Are those that often have 'gainst Pompey fought.
　　Their ships are yare,° yours heavy. No disgrace   *smooth running*
　　Shall fall° you for refusing him at sea,   *befall*
　　Being prepared for land.

40　ANTONY　　　　　　　　By sea, by sea.

ENOBARBUS   Most worthy sir, you therein throw away
　　The absolute soldiership you have by land;
　　Distract° your army, which doth most consist   *Divert*
　　Of war-marked footmen; leave unexecuted°   *untapped*
45　Your own renownèd knowledge; quite forgo
　　The way which promises assurance,° and   *victory*
　　Give up yourself merely° to chance and hazard   *completely*
　　From firm security.

ANTONY　　　　　　　I'll fight at sea.

CLEOPATRA   I have sixty sails, Caesar none better.

50　ANTONY   Our overplus of shipping will we burn,[3]
　　And with the rest full-manned, from th'head° of Actium   *promontory*
　　Beat th'approaching Caesar. But if we fail,
　　We then can do't at land.

　　　　　　Enter a MESSENGER
　　　　　　　　　　Thy business?

MESSENGER   The news is true, my lord. He is descried.°   *He has been seen*
55　Caesar has taken Toryne.

ANTONY   Can he be there in person? 'Tis impossible;
　　Strange that his power° should be. Camidius,   *his entire army*
　　Our nineteen legions thou shalt hold by land,
　　And our twelve thousand horse. We'll to our ship.
　　Away, my Thetis![4]

　　　　　　Enter a SOLDIER
60　　　　　　　　　How now, worthy soldier?

SOLDIER   O noble Emperor, do not fight by sea.
　　Trust not to rotten planks. Do you misdoubt
　　This sword and these my wounds? Let th'Egyptians

---

3. Antony seems to have burned his excess ("overplus")
ships because he did not have enough sailors to man
them adequately and feared that they could easily be
taken by Octavius Caesar.
4. Sea goddess, mother of the Greek hero Achilles.

And the Phoenicians go a-ducking;° we   *to sea*
65 Have used to conquer standing on the earth,
And fighting foot to foot.

ANTONY   Well, well; away!

Exeunt ANTONY, CLEOPATRA, *and* ENOBARBUS

SOLDIER   By Hercules, I think I am i'th' right.

CAMIDIUS   Soldier, thou art; but his whole action grows
Not in the power on't.⁵ So our leader's led,
And we are women's men.

70 SOLDIER   You keep by land
The legions and the horse whole, do you not?

CAMIDIUS   Marcus Octavius, Marcus Justeius,
Publicola and Caelius are for sea,
But we keep whole° by land. This speed of Caesar's   *stay undivided*
Carries beyond° belief.   *Exceeds*

75 SOLDIER   While he was yet in Rome
His power went out in such distractions°   *separate detachments*
As beguiled all spies.

CAMIDIUS   Who's his lieutenant, hear you?

SOLDIER   They say, one Taurus.

CAMIDIUS   Well I know the man.

Enter a MESSENGER

MESSENGER   The Emperor calls Camidius.

80 CAMIDIUS   With news the time's in labour, and throws forth
Each minute some.⁶   *Exeunt*

3.8

Enter CAESAR *with his army, marching* [*and* TAURUS]

CAESAR   Taurus!

TAURUS   My lord?

CAESAR   Strike not by land. Keep whole.° Provoke not battle   *Stay in reserve*
Till we have done at sea. [*Giving a scroll*] Do not exceed
5 The prescript° of this scroll. Our fortune lies   *written orders*
Upon this jump.°   *ploy*

Exit [CAESAR *and his army at one door,* TAURUS *at another*]

3.9

Enter ANTONY *and* ENOBARBUS

ANTONY   Set we our squadrons on yon side o'th' hill
In eye° of Caesar's battle,° from which place   *view / battle line*
We may the number of the ships behold,
And so proceed accordingly.   *Exeunt*

3.10

CAMIDIUS *marcheth with his land army one way over the*
stage, and TAURUS, *the lieutenant of Caesar,* [*with his*
army] *the other way. After their going in is heard the*
noise of a sea-fight. Alarum. Enter ENOBARBUS

ENOBARBUS   Naught, naught, all naught!° I can behold no longer.   *lost; ruined*
Th'*Antoniad*, the Egyptian admiral,°   *flagship*
With all their sixty, fly and turn the rudder.

---

5. His entire plan is made without taking into account   **3.8** Location: Near Actium.
his resources.   **3.9** Location: Scene continues.
6. *throws . . . some*: each minute, more news is born.   **3.10** Location: Scene continues.

To see't mine eyes are blasted.°   *(as if by lightning)*
    Enter SCARUS

SCARUS   Gods and goddesses—
    All the whole synod° of them!   *assembly*

5 ENOBARBUS   What's° thy passion?   *What provokes*

SCARUS   The greater cantle° of the world is lost   *corner; portion*
    With° very ignorance;° we have kissed away   *Through / idiocy*
    Kingdoms and provinces.

ENOBARBUS   How appears the fight?

SCARUS   On our side like the tokened pestilence,[1]

10   Where death is sure. Yon riband-red[2] nag of Egypt—
    Whom leprosy o'ertake!—i'th' midst o'th' fight—
    When vantage like a pair of twins appeared,[3]
    Both as the same, or rather ours the elder°—   *ours likely the stronger*
    The breese upon her,[4] like a cow in June,
    Hoists sails and flies.

15 ENOBARBUS   That I beheld.
    Mine eyes did sicken at the sight, and could not
    Endure a further view.

SCARUS   She once being luffed,[5]
    The noble ruin° of her magic, Antony,   *casualty*
    Claps on his sea-wing° and, like a doting mallard,°   *sails / male duck*
20   Leaving the fight in° height, flies after her.   *at its*
    I never saw an action of such shame.
    Experience, manhood, honour, ne'er before
    Did violate so itself.

ENOBARBUS   Alack, alack!
    Enter CAMIDIUS

CAMIDIUS   Our fortune on the sea is out of breath,
25   And sinks most lamentably. Had our general
    Been what he knew himself,° it had gone well.   *(to be)*
    O, he has given example for our flight
    Most grossly by his own.

ENOBARBUS   Ay, are you thereabouts?° Why then, good night   *of the same mind*
    indeed!

30 CAMIDIUS   Toward Peloponnesus are they fled.

SCARUS   'Tis easy to't,° and there I will attend   *to reach that place*
    What further comes.

CAMIDIUS   To Caesar will I render
    My legions and my horse. Six kings already
    Show me the way of yielding.

ENOBARBUS   I'll yet follow
35   The wounded chance° of Antony, though my reason   *fortune*
    Sits in the wind against me.°   [*Exeunt severally*]   *Opposes*

3.11

Enter ANTONY *with Attendants*

ANTONY   Hark, the land bids me tread no more upon't,
    It is ashamed to bear me. Friends, come hither.

---

1. Plague manifested in tokens (red spots presaging death).
2. Decked in red ribbons. This emendation of F's "ribau-dred"—a word of unclear meaning, if any—juxtaposes the image of Cleopatra bedecked like a horse or a whore with the red tokens of the plague.
3. When the fight could have gone either way.
4. Bitten by a gadfly; driven by a breeze.
5. Having prepared the ship's head to sail close to the wind (ready to leave).
3.11 Location: Alexandria.

I am so lated° in the world that I   *lost in the dark*
Have lost my way for ever. I have a ship
5 Laden with gold. Take that; divide it, fly,
And make your peace with Caesar.

ATTENDANTS   Fly? Not we.

ANTONY   I have fled myself, and have instructed cowards
To run and show their shoulders.° Friends, be gone.   *backs*
I have myself resolved upon a course
10 Which has no need of you. Be gone.
My treasure's in the harbour. Take it. O,
I followed that° I blush to look upon.   *that which*
My very hairs do mutiny, for the white
Reprove the brown for rashness, and they them°   *they the others*
15 For fear and doting. Friends, be gone. You shall
Have letters from me to some friends that will
Sweep° your way for you. Pray you, look not sad,   *Clear*
Nor make replies of loathness.° Take the hint°   *reluctance / chance*
Which my despair proclaims. Let that be left
20 Which leaves° itself. To the seaside straightway!   *ceases to be*
I will possess you of that ship and treasure.
Leave me, I pray, a little.° Pray you now,   *for a brief time*
Nay, do so; for indeed I have lost command.°   *authority*
Therefore I pray you; I'll see you by and by.

                        [*Exeunt attendants*]

     [*He*] *sits down.*

     Enter CLEOPATRA *led by* CHARMIAN, [IRAS,] *and* EROS

25 EROS   Nay, gentle madam, to him. Comfort him.

IRAS   Do, most dear Queen.

CHARMIAN   Do. Why, what else?

CLEOPATRA   Let me sit down. O Juno!

     [*She sits down*]

ANTONY   No, no, no, no, no.

30 EROS [*to* ANTONY]   See you here, sir?

ANTONY   O fie, fie, fie!

CHARMIAN   Madam.

IRAS   Madam. O good Empress!

EROS   Sir, sir.

35 ANTONY   Yes, my lord, yes. He° at Philippi kept   *(Octavius)*
His sword e'en like a dancer,° while I struck   *(for decoration only)*
The lean and wrinkled Cassius; and 'twas I
That the mad Brutus ended.° He alone   *defeated*
Dealt on lieutenantry,° and no practice had   *Fought through others*
40 In the brave squares° of war. Yet now—no matter.   *fine formations*

CLEOPATRA [*rising, to* CHARMIAN *and* IRAS]   Ah, stand by.

EROS   The Queen, my lord, the Queen.

IRAS   Go to him, madam.
Speak to him. He's unqualitied°   *lost his sense of self*
With very shame.

45 CLEOPATRA   Well then, sustain me. O!

EROS   Most noble sir, arise. The Queen approaches.
Her head's declined, and death will seize her but°   *unless*
Your comfort makes the rescue.

ANTONY   I have offended reputation;
A most unnoble swerving.°   *slippage*

50 EROS   Sir, the Queen.

ANTONY [*rising*]   O, whither hast thou led me, Egypt? See
    How I convey° my shame out of thine eyes°   *steal back / sight*
    By looking back° what I have left behind   *back on*
    'Stroyed° in dishonour.   *Destroyed*
CLEOPATRA   O, my lord, my lord,
55   Forgive my fearful sails! I little thought
    You would have followed.
ANTONY   Egypt, thou knew'st too well
    My heart was to thy rudder tied by th' strings,
    And thou shouldst tow me after. O'er my spirit
    Thy full supremacy thou knew'st, and that
60   Thy beck° might from the bidding of the gods   *call*
    Command me.
CLEOPATRA   O, my pardon!
ANTONY   Now I must
    To the young man[1] send humble treaties,° dodge   *appeals*
    And palter in the shifts of lowness,[2] who
    With half the bulk o'th' world played as I pleased,
65   Making and marring fortunes. You did know
    How much you were my conqueror, and that
    My sword, made weak by my affection,° would   *desire*
    Obey it on all cause.°   *for any reason*
CLEOPATRA   Pardon, pardon!
ANTONY Fall° not a tear, I say. One of them rates°   *Weep / is worth*
70   All that is won and lost. Give me a kiss.
        [*He kisses her*]
    Even this repays me. [*To an Attendant*]   We sent our school-
    master;°   *tutor to our children*
    Is a° come back? [*To* CLEOPATRA] Love, I am full of lead.   *he*
    [*Calling*] Some wine
    Within there, and our viands!° Fortune knows   *food*
    We scorn her most when most she offers blows.   *Exeunt*

3.12

Enter CAESAR, AGRIPPA, THIDIAS, *and* DOLABELLA, *with*
    others
CAESAR   Let him appear that's come from Antony.
    Know you him?
DOLABELLA   Caesar, 'tis his schoolmaster;
    An argument° that he is plucked, when hither   *A proof*
    He sends so poor a pinion° of his wing,   *an outer feather*
5   Which° had superfluous kings for messengers   *He who*
    Not many moons gone by.
        Enter AMBASSADOR *from Antony*
CAESAR   Approach and speak.
AMBASSADOR   Such as I am, I come from Antony.
    I was of late as petty° to his ends   *inconsequential*
    As is the morn-dew on the myrtle leaf
    To his grand sea.[1]
10 CAESAR   Be't so. Declare thine office.°   *business*
AMBASSADOR   Lord of his fortunes he salutes thee, and

---

1. Octavius Caesar at this time (31 B.C.E.) was thirty-two,
Antony fifty-one.
2. *dodge . . . lowness:* shuffle and play fast and loose in
the shifty ways of a man brought low.

3.12 Location: Caesar's camp, Egypt.
1. In relation to the great sea, ultimate source of dew,
that is Antony.

Requires° to live in Egypt; which not granted,   *Asks*
He lessens his requests, and to thee sues
To let him breathe between the heavens and earth,
15 A private man in Athens. This for him.
Next, Cleopatra does confess thy greatness,
Submits her to thy might, and of thee craves
The circle° of the Ptolemies for her heirs,   *crown*
Now hazarded to thy grace.°   *placed at your mercy*

CAESAR   For Antony,
20 I have no ears to his request. The Queen
Of audience nor desire shall fail, so² she
From Egypt drive her all-disgracèd friend,
Or take his life there. This if she perform
She shall not sue unheard. So to them both.

AMBASSADOR   Fortune pursue thee!

25 CAESAR   Bring° him through the bands.°   *Escort / ranks*
               [*Exit* AMBASSADOR, *attended*]
[*To* THIDIAS] To try thy eloquence now 'tis time. Dispatch.
From Antony win Cleopatra. Promise,
And in our name, what she requires. Add more
As thine invention° offers. Women are not   *imagination*
30 In° their best fortunes strong, but want will perjure   *While in*
The ne'er-touched vestal.³ Try thy cunning, Thidias.
Make thine own edict° for thy pains, which we   *Command your reward*
Will answer as a law.

THIDIAS   Caesar, I go.

CAESAR   Observe how Antony becomes his flaw,°   *reacts to his fall*
35 And what thou think'st his very action speaks
In every power that moves.⁴

THIDIAS   Caesar, I shall.
       Exeunt [CAESAR *and his train at one door, and*
                  THIDIAS *at another*]

3.13

Enter CLEOPATRA, ENOBARBUS, CHARMIAN, AND IRAS

CLEOPATRA   What shall we do, Enobarbus?

ENOBARBUS   Think,° and die.   *(about our misery)*

CLEOPATRA   Is Antony or we in fault for this?

ENOBARBUS   Antony only, that would make his will°   *lust*
Lord of his reason. What though° you fled   *What if*
5 From that great face of war, whose several ranges°   *battle lines*
Frighted each other? Why should he follow?
The itch of his affection should not then
Have nicked° his captainship, at such a point,   *bettered (gambling term)*
When half to half the world opposed, he being
10 The mooted° question. 'Twas a shame no less   *disputed*
Than was his loss, to course° your flying flags   *chase*
And leave his navy gazing.

CLEOPATRA   Prithee, peace.
       Enter the AMBASSADOR *with* ANTONY

---

2. Shall not fail to receive either a hearing or fulfillment
of her wishes, as long as.
3. *want . . . vestal*: need will make the purest virgin break
her vows.

4. *his very . . . moves*: his actions themselves reveal in
every move he makes.
3.13 Location: Alexandria.

ANTONY   Is that his answer?
AMBASSADOR   Ay, my lord.
ANTONY   The Queen shall then have courtesy, so° she   *as long as*
     Will yield us up.
AMBASSADOR   He says so.
15   ANTONY   Let her know't.
     [*To* CLEOPATRA] To the boy Caesar send this grizzled head,
     And he will fill thy wishes to the brim
     With principalities.
CLEOPATRA   That head, my lord?
ANTONY [*to the* AMBASSADOR]   To him again. Tell him he wears the rose
20   Of youth upon him, from which the world should note
     Something particular.° His coin, ships, legions,   *A success of his own*
     May be a coward's, whose ministers° would prevail   *aides; underlings*
     Under the service of a child as soon°   *as well*
     As i'th' command of Caesar. I dare him therefore
25   To lay his gay caparisons° apart   *showy adornments*
     And answer me declined,[1] sword against sword,
     Ourselves alone. I'll write it. Follow me.
               [*Exeunt* ANTONY *and* AMBASSADOR]
ENOBARBUS [*aside*]   Yes, like enough, high-battled° Caesar will   *with many troops*
     Unstate° his happiness and be staged to th' show[2]   *Overthrow*
30   Against a sworder! I see men's judgements are
     A parcel of° their fortunes, and things outward   *Consistent with*
     Do draw the inward quality after them
     To suffer all alike.° That he should dream,   *To decay together*
     Knowing all measures,[3] the full Caesar will
35   Answer° his emptiness! Caesar, thou hast subdued   *Fight; reply to*
     His judgement, too.
         Enter a SERVANT
SERVANT   A messenger from Caesar.
CLEOPATRA   What, no more ceremony? See, my women:
     Against the blown° rose may they stop their nose,   *decaying*
     That° kneeled unto the buds. Admit him, sir.   [*Exit* SERVANT]   *Who once*
40   ENOBARBUS [*aside*]   Mine honesty° and I begin to square.°   *honor / square off; argue*
     The loyalty well held° to fools does make   *given*
     Our faith mere° folly; yet he that can endure   *complete*
     To follow with allegiance a fall'n lord
     Does conquer him that did his master conquer,
     And earns a place i'th' story.
         Enter THIDIAS
45   CLEOPATRA   Caesar's will?
THIDIAS   Hear it apart.
CLEOPATRA   None but friends; say boldly.
THIDIAS   So haply° are they friends to Antony.   *possibly*
ENOBARBUS   He needs as many, sir, as Caesar has,
     Or needs not us.[4] If Caesar please, our master
50   Will leap to be his friend. For us, you know,
     Whose he is, we are: and that is Caesar's.

---

1. And meet me past my prime, in my misfortune.
2. Be displayed to the public gaze (as in the London theater or Roman gladiatorial combat).
3. Having known the best and worst of times ("all mea-

sures" of fortune, both "full[ness]" and "emptiness," line 35).
4. *Or needs not us*: If the situation is truly hopeless, he doesn't even need our friendship.

THIDIAS   So. [*To* CLEOPATRA] Thus, then, thou most renowned:
 Caesar entreats
 Not to consider° in what case thou stand'st   *be concerned*
 Further than he is Caesar.[5]

CLEOPATRA   Go on; right royal.°   *most generous*

55 THIDIAS   He knows that you embraced not Antony
 As you did love, but as you fearèd him.

CLEOPATRA   O.

THIDIAS   The scars upon your honour therefore he
 Does pity as constrainèd° blemishes,   *involuntary*
 Not as deserved.

60 CLEOPATRA   He is a god, and knows
 What is most right. Mine honour was not yielded,
 But conquered merely.

ENOBARBUS [*aside*]   To be sure of that
 I will ask Antony. Sir, sir, thou art so leaky
 That we must leave thee to thy sinking, for
65 Thy dearest quit thee.   *Exit*

THIDIAS   Shall I say to Caesar
 What you require° of him?—For he partly begs   *request*
 To be desired to give. It much would please him
 That of his fortunes you should make a staff
 To lean upon. But it would warm his spirits
70 To hear from me you had left Antony,
 And put your self under his shroud,°   *protection; burial sheet*
 The universal landlord.

CLEOPATRA   What's your name?

THIDIAS   My name is Thidias.

CLEOPATRA   Most kind messenger,
 Say to great Caesar this in deputation:°   *as my representative*
75 I kiss his conqu'ring hand. Tell him I am prompt
 To lay my crown at's feet, and there to kneel
 Till from his all-obeying° breath I hear   *which all obey*
 The doom of Egypt.[6]

THIDIAS   'Tis your noblest course.
 Wisdom and fortune combating together,
80 If that the former dare but what it can,[7]
 No chance may shake it. Give me grace to lay
 My duty on your hand.
   [*He kisses Cleopatra's hand*]

CLEOPATRA   Your Caesar's father oft,
 When he hath mused of taking kingdoms in,° *subduing kingdoms*
 Bestowed his lips on that unworthy place,
 As° it rained kisses.   *As if*
   Enter ANTONY *and* ENOBARBUS

85 ANTONY   Favours, by Jove that thunders!
 What art thou, fellow?

THIDIAS   One that but performs
 The bidding of the fullest[8] man, and worthiest
 To have command obeyed.

ENOBARBUS   You will be whipped.

---

5. Beyond remembering that he is Caesar—and hence
nobly generous in forgiving insult and injury (but with a
more sinister undertone as well).

6. What he destines for Egypt and its Queen.
7. If the wise man confines his daring to what is possible.
8. Most complete; most successful.

ANTONY [*calling*]   Approach, there!—Ah, you kite!⁹ Now, gods and devils,
90   Authority melts from me of late. When I cried 'Ho!',
     Like boys unto a muss¹ kings would start forth,
     And cry 'Your will?'—Have you no ears? I am
     Antony yet.
                Enter servant[s]
                   Take hence this jack,° and whip him.   knave
ENOBARBUS [*aside to* THIDIAS]   'Tis better playing with a lion's whelp°   cub
     Than with an old one dying.
95   ANTONY   Moon and stars!
     Whip him! Were't twenty of the greatest tributaries
     That do acknowledge Caesar, should I find them
     So saucy with the hand of she here—what's her name
     Since she was Cleopatra?² Whip him, fellows,
100 Till like a boy you see him cringe° his face,   distort
     And whine aloud for mercy. Take him hence.
THIDIAS   Mark Antony—
ANTONY   Tug him away. Being whipped,
     Bring him again. This jack of Caesar's shall
     Bear us an errand to him.   *Exeunt [servants] with* THIDIAS
105 You were half blasted° ere I knew you. Ha,   decayed
     Have I my pillow left unpressed in Rome,
     Forborne the getting° of a lawful race,   begetting
     And by a gem of women, to be abused
     By one that looks on feeders?°   parasites; servants
110 CLEOPATRA   Good my lord—
ANTONY   You have been a boggler° ever.   fickle one
     But when we in our viciousness grow hard—
     O misery on't!—the wise gods seel³ our eyes,
     In our own filth drop our clear judgements, make us
115 Adore our errors, laugh at's while we strut
     To our confusion.
CLEOPATRA   O, is't come to this?
ANTONY   I found you as a morsel cold upon
     Dead Caesar's trencher;° nay, you were a fragment°   plate / leftover
     Of Gnaeus Pompey's,⁴ besides what hotter hours
120 Unregistered in vulgar fame° you have   base gossip
     Luxuriously° picked out. For I am sure,   Wantonly
     Though you can guess what temperance should be,
     You know not what it is.
CLEOPATRA   Wherefore is this?
ANTONY   To let a fellow that will take rewards
125 And say 'God quit° you' be familiar with   repay
     My playfellow your hand, this kingly seal
     And plighter° of high hearts! O that I were   pledger
     Upon the hill of Basan to outroar
     The hornèd herd!⁵ For I have savage cause,
130 And to proclaim it civilly were like
     A haltered° neck which does the hangman thank   in the noose

9. Predator or whore, addressed to either Cleopatra or   them.
Thidias.   4. Older brother of the Pompey of the play and son of
1. Game in which small items were tossed to the ground   Pompey the Great. See note to 1.5.31.
for children to snatch and grab.   5. Alluding to the bulls of the hill of Basan (Bashan) in
2. Antony's question suggests that since Cleopatra's be- Psalms 68:15 and 22:12; Antony sees himself as a cuck-
havior has changed, her name must have changed as well. old (a man whose wife has committed adultery), conven-
3. Blind: hawks' eyes were sealed (sewn up) to tame   tionally imagined with horns.

For being yare° about him.   swift
        Enter a SERVANT *with* THIDIAS
                            Is he whipped?
SERVANT   Soundly, my lord.
ANTONY   Cried he, and begged a° pardon?   he
135 SERVANT   He did ask favour.
ANTONY [*to* THIDIAS]   If that thy father live, let him repent
        Thou wast not made his daughter; and be thou sorry
        To follow Caesar in his triumph, since
        Thou hast been whipped for following him. Henceforth
140   The white hand of a lady fever thee,[6]
        Shake thou to look on't. Get thee back to Caesar;
        Tell him thy entertainment.° Look° thou say   treatment / See that
        He makes me angry with him, for he seems
        Proud and disdainful, harping on what I am,
145   Not what he knew I was. He makes me angry,
        And at this time most easy 'tis to do't,
        When my good stars that were my former guides
        Have empty left their orbs,° and shot their fires   spheres
        Into th'abyss of hell. If he mislike
150   My speech and what is done, tell him he has
        Hipparchus, my enfranchèd° bondman, whom   emancipated
        He may at pleasure whip, or hang, or torture,
        As he shall like, to quit° me. Urge it thou.   requite
        Hence, with thy stripes,° be gone!   *Exit* [SERVANT *with*] THIDIAS   wounds
155 CLEOPATRA   Have you done yet?
ANTONY   Alack, our terrene moon[7]
        Is now eclipsed, and it portends alone
        The fall of Antony.
CLEOPATRA [*aside*]   I must stay his time.[8]
ANTONY   To flatter Caesar would you mingle eyes
        With one that ties his points?[9]
160 CLEOPATRA   Not know me yet?
ANTONY   Cold-hearted toward me?
CLEOPATRA   Ah, dear, if I be so,
        From my cold heart let heaven engender hail,
        And poison it in the source, and the first stone
        Drop in my neck: as it determines,° so   turns to liquid
165   Dissolve my life! The next Caesarion smite,
        Till by degrees the memory of my womb,°   my children
        Together with my brave Egyptians all,
        By the discandying° of this pelleted storm   dissolving
        Lie graveless till the flies and gnats of Nile
        Have buried them for prey!
170 ANTONY   I am satisfied.
        Caesar sits down in° Alexandria, where   besieges
        I will oppose his fate.[1] Our force by land
        Hath nobly held; our severed navy too
        Have knit again, and fleet,° threat'ning most sea-like.   are afloat
175   Where hast thou been, my heart?° Dost thou hear, lady?   bravery
        If from the field I shall return once more

6. May the white hand of a lady make you feverish.   9. *would . . . points:* would you flirt with one of his ser-
7. Terrestrial moon goddess—Cleopatra.   vants? *points:* laces (attaching stockings to other clothing).
8. I must hold my tongue until he is over his rage.   1. I will resist his apparently destined victory.

To kiss these lips, I will appear in blood.°   *bloody; vigorous*
I and my sword will earn our chronicle.°   *historical reputation*
There's hope in't yet.

CLEOPATRA   That's my brave lord.

180 ANTONY   I will be treble-sinewed, hearted, breathed,
And fight maliciously;° for when mine hours   *furiously*
Were nice² and lucky, men did ransom° lives   *buy their*
Of° me for jests;° but now I'll set my teeth,   *From / trinkets*
And send to darkness all that stop me. Come,
185 Let's have one other gaudy° night. Call to me   *merry*
All my sad captains. Fill our bowls once more.
Let's mock the midnight bell.³

CLEOPATRA   It is my birthday.
I had thought to've held it poor,° but since my lord   *modestly commemorated it*
Is Antony again, I will be Cleopatra.

190 ANTONY   We will yet do well.

CLEOPATRA   Call all his noble captains to my lord!

ANTONY   Do so. We'll speak to them, and tonight I'll force
The wine peep through their scars. Come on, my queen,
There's sap in't° yet. The next time I do fight   *vigor in (our cause)*
195 I'll make death love me, for I will contend°   *do battle*
Even with his pestilent° scythe. *Exeunt [all but* ENOBARBUS]   *plague-dealing*

ENOBARBUS   Now he'll outstare° the lightning. To be furious   *stare down*
Is to be frighted out of fear, and in that mood
The dove will peck the estridge;° and I see still°   *a kind of hawk / always*
200 A diminution in our captain's brain
Restores his heart. When valour preys on reason,
It eats the sword it fights with. I will seek
Some way to leave him.   *Exit*

4.1

Enter CAESAR, *reading a letter, with* AGRIPPA, MAECENAS,
and his army

CAESAR   He calls me boy, and chides as° he had power   *as though*
To beat me out of Egypt. My messenger
He hath whipped with rods, dares me to personal combat,
Caesar to Antony. Let the old ruffian know
5 I have many other ways to die; meantime,
Laugh at° his challenge.   *Mock*

MAECENAS   Caesar must think,
When one so great begins to rage, he's hunted
Even to falling. Give him no breath,° but now   *time to catch breath*
Make boot° of his distraction.° Never anger   *Take advantage / fury*
Made good guard for itself.

10 CAESAR   Let our best heads°   *officers*
Know that tomorrow the last of many battles
We mean to fight. Within our files° there are,   *troops*
Of those that served Mark Antony but late,
Enough to fetch him in.° See it done,   *capture him*
15 And feast the army. We have store to do't,
And they have earned the waste.° Poor Antony!   *Exeunt*   *expense*

---

2. *Were nice:* Permitted me to pick and choose, to act   the death knell that fate seems to ring for us.
with noble generosity; were lascivious; were pampered.   4.1 Location: Caesar's camp, before Alexandria.
3. Let's make a mockery of the hour by revelry; let's mock

4.2

Enter ANTONY, CLEOPATRA, ENOBARBUS, CHARMIAN,
IRAS, ALEXAS, *with others*

ANTONY   He will not fight with me, Domitius?

ENOBARBUS   No.

ANTONY   Why should he not?

ENOBARBUS   He thinks, being twenty times of better fortune,
He is twenty men to one.

ANTONY   Tomorrow, soldier,

5   By sea and land I'll fight. Or° I will live   *Either*
Or bathe my dying honour in the blood
Shall make it live again. Woot thou° fight well?   *Will you*

ENOBARBUS   I'll strike, and cry 'Take all!'°   *Winner take all*

ANTONY   Well said. Come on!
Call forth my household servants. Let's tonight
Be bounteous at our meal.

Enter SERVITORS

10   Give me thy hand.
Thou hast been rightly honest; so hast thou,
Thou, and thou, and thou; you have served me well,
And kings have been your fellows.°   *companions*

CLEOPATRA [*to* ENOBARBUS]   What means this?

ENOBARBUS [*to* CLEOPATRA]   'Tis one of those odd tricks which
    sorrow shoots
Out of the mind.

15   ANTONY [*to a* SERVITOR]   And thou art honest too.
I wish I could be made° so many men,   *split up into*
And all of you clapped up together in
An Antony, that I might do you service
So good as you have done.

SERVITORS   The gods forbid!

20   ANTONY   Well, my good fellows, wait on me tonight.
Scant not my cups, and make as much of me
As when mine empire was your fellow° too,   *fellow servant*
And suffered° my command.   *obeyed*

CLEOPATRA [*aside to* ENOBARBUS]   What does he mean?

ENOBARBUS [*aside to* CLEOPATRA]
To make his followers weep.

ANTONY   Tend me tonight.

25   Maybe it is the period° of your duty.   *end*
Haply° you shall not see me more; or if,°   *Maybe / if you do*
A mangled shadow.° Perchance tomorrow   *phantom*
You'll serve another master. I look on you
As one that takes his leave. Mine honest friends,

30   I turn you not away, but, like a master
Married to your good service, stay till death.
Tend me tonight two hours. I ask no more;
And the gods yield° you for't!   *reward*

ENOBARBUS   What mean you, sir,
To give them this discomfort? Look, they weep,

35   And I, an ass, am onion-eyed.° For shame,   *weepy*
Transform us not to women.

4.2 Location: Alexandria.

ANTONY   Ho, ho, ho,
   Now the witch take° me if I meant it thus!   *bewitch*
   Grace grow where those drops fall. My hearty friends,
   You take me in too dolorous a sense;
40   For I spake to you for your comfort, did desire you
   To burn this night with torches. Know, my hearts,
   I hope well of tomorrow, and will lead you
   Where rather I'll expect victorious life
   Than death and honour. Let's to supper, come,
45   And drown consideration.°   *Exeunt*   *serious thoughts*

4.3

Enter a company of SOLDIERS
FIRST SOLDIER   Brother, good night. Tomorrow is the day.
SECOND SOLDIER   It will determine one way. Fare you well.°   *Good luck*
   Heard you of nothing strange about° the streets?   *in*
FIRST SOLDIER   Nothing. What news?
5   SECOND SOLDIER   Belike° 'tis but a rumour. Good night to you.   *Most likely*
FIRST SOLDIER   Well, sir, good night.
            [*Enter*] *other* SOLDIERS, *meet*[*ing them*]
SECOND SOLDIER   Soldiers, have careful watch.
THIRD SOLDIER   And you. Good night, good night.
     They place themselves in every corner of the stage
SECOND SOLDIER   Here we;[1] an if° tomorrow   *an if=if*
   Our navy thrive, I have an absolute hope
   Our landmen will stand up.°   *make a stand*
FIRST SOLDIER   'Tis a brave army,
   And full of purpose.
     Music of the hautboys° is under the stage   *oboes*
SECOND SOLDIER   Peace, what noise?
10   FIRST SOLDIER   List, list!
SECOND SOLDIER   Hark!
FIRST SOLDIER   Music i'th' air.
THIRD SOLDIER   Under the earth.
FOURTH SOLDIER   It signs° well, does it not?   *bodes*
THIRD SOLDIER   No.
FIRST SOLDIER   Peace, I say!
   What should this mean?
SECOND SOLDIER   'Tis the god Hercules, whom Antony loved,
   Now leaves him.
15   FIRST SOLDIER   Walk. Let's see if other watchmen
   Do hear what we do.
SECOND SOLDIER   How now, masters?°   *good sirs*
ALL (*speak*[*ing*] *together*)[2]   How now?
   How now? Do you hear this?
FIRST SOLDIER   Ay. Is't not strange?
THIRD SOLDIER   Do you hear, masters? Do you hear?
FIRST SOLDIER   Follow the noise so far as we have quarter.[3]
   Let's see how it will give off.°   *end*
20   ALL   Content. 'Tis strange.   *Exeunt*

4.3 Location: Outside Cleopatra's palace, Alexandria.
1. Here are our positions.
2. Individual soldiers probably address different questions
and comments to one another rather than speaking in
chorus.
3. As far as the limit of our watch.

4.4

Enter ANTONY *and* CLEOPATRA, *with* [CHARMIAN *and*]
others

ANTONY [*calling*]   Eros, mine armour, Eros!

CLEOPATRA   Sleep a little.

ANTONY   No, my chuck.° Eros, come, mine armour, Eros!   °*my dear*
    Enter EROS [*with armour*]
  Come, good fellow, put thine iron on.¹
  If fortune be not ours today, it is
  Because we brave° her. Come.   °*dare*

5 CLEOPATRA   Nay, I'll help, too.
  What's this for?

ANTONY   Ah, let be, let be! Thou art
  The armourer of my heart. False, false!° This, this!   °*wrong*

CLEOPATRA   Sooth, la, I'll help. Thus it must be.
    [*She helps* ANTONY *to arm*]

ANTONY   Well, well,
  We shall thrive now. Seest thou, my good fellow?
  Go put on thy defences.°   °*armor*

10 EROS   Briefly,° sir.   °*Soon*

CLEOPATRA   Is not this buckled well?

ANTONY   Rarely, rarely.
  He that unbuckles this, till we do please
  To doff't° for our repose, shall hear a storm.   °*remove it*
  Thou fumblest, Eros, and my queen's a squire°   °*an attendant to a knight*
15 More tight° at this than thou. Dispatch.° O love,   °*able* / *Finish*
  That thou couldst see my wars today, and knew'st
  The royal occupation! Thou shouldst see
  A workman° in't.   °*An expert*
    Enter an armed SOLDIER
        Good morrow to thee. Welcome.
  Thou look'st like him that knows a warlike charge.°   °*purpose*
20 To business that we love we rise betime,°   °*early*
  And go to't with delight.

SOLDIER   A thousand, sir,
  Early though't be, have on their riveted trim,°   °*armor*
  And at the port expect you.
    Shout [*within*]. *Trumpets flourish. Enter* CAPTAINS *and*
    SOLDIERS

CAPTAIN   The morn is fair. Good morrow, General.

SOLDIERS   Good morrow, General.

25 ANTONY   'Tis well blown,² lads.
  This morning, like the spirit of a youth
  That means to be of note, begins betimes.
  So, so. Come, give me that. This way. Well said.°   °*Well done*
  Fare thee well, dame. Whate'er becomes of me,
  This is a soldier's kiss.
    [*He kisses* CLEOPATRA]
30   Rebukable
  And worthy shameful check° it were to stand   °*reprimand*
  On more mechanic° compliment. I'll leave thee   °*coarse*
  Now like a man of steel. You that will fight,

4.4 Location: Cleopatra's palace.
1. Clad me in that piece of armor of mine that you have.

2. Well sounded (of the trumpet); well started (of the
morning).

Follow me close. I'll bring you to't. Adieu.

Exeunt [all but CLEOPATRA *and* CHARMIAN]

CHARMIAN Please you retire to your chamber?

35 CLEOPATRA   Lead me.

He goes forth gallantly. That he and Caesar might
Determine this great war in single fight!
Then, Antony—but now! Well, on.   *Exeunt*

4.5

Trumpets sound. Enter ANTONY *and* EROS [*meeting a*
SOLDIER]

SOLDIER The gods make this a happy° day to Antony!   *fortunate*

ANTONY Would thou and those thy scars had once° prevailed   *earlier*
To make me fight at land!

SOLDIER   Hadst thou done so,
The kings that have revolted,° and the soldier   *deserted*
5 That has this morning left thee, would have still
Followed thy heels.

ANTONY   Who's gone this morning?

SOLDIER Who? One ever near thee. Call for Enobarbus,
He shall not hear thee, or from Caesar's camp
Say 'I am none of thine'.

ANTONY   What sayest thou?

SOLDIER Sir, he is with Caesar.

10 EROS [*to* ANTONY]   Sir, his chests and treasure
He has not with him.

ANTONY   Is he gone?

SOLDIER   Most certain.

ANTONY Go, Eros, send his treasure after. Do it.
Detain no jot, I charge thee. Write to him—
I will subscribe°—gentle adieus and greetings.   *sign my name*
15 Say that I wish he never find more cause
To change a master. O, my fortunes have
Corrupted honest men! Dispatch. Enobarbus!   *Exeunt*

4.6

Flourish. Enter AGRIPPA, CAESAR, *with* ENOBARBUS *and*
DOLABELLA

CAESAR Go forth, Agrippa, and begin the fight.
Our will is Antony be took alive.
Make it so known.

AGRIPPA   Caesar, I shall.   [*Exit*]

CAESAR The time of universal peace is near.¹
5 Prove this° a prosp'rous day, the three-nooked world²   *If this proves*
Shall bear the olive° freely.   *sign of peace*
Enter a MESSENGER

MESSENGER   Antony
Is come into the field.

CAESAR   Go charge Agrippa

4.5 Location: Antony's camp, Alexandria.
4.6 Location: Caesar's camp, Alexandria.
1. Octavius Caesar, later the Emperor Augustus, was
known for the *Pax Romana*—Roman peace—of his reign;
the phrase also alludes to the birth of Christ, which
occurred while Augustus was emperor. See the Introduction.

2. Three-cornered world. Referring (in descending order
of probability) to Europe, Asia, Africa (the triumvirate's
holdings); the three races descended from Noah's sons
(Japhet, Shem, Ham); earth, sea, sky. The three races of
Noah can to an extent be superimposed on the three continents and may connect with the later religious connotations of the Roman Empire. See the previous note.

Plant those that have revolted in the van,°   *front lines*
That Antony may seem to spend his fury
10   Upon himself.°   *On his former troops*

Exeunt [MESSENGER *at one door,* CAESAR *and*
DOLABELLA *at another*]

ENOBARBUS   Alexas did revolt, and went to Jewry on
Affairs of Antony; there did dissuade°   *persuade*
Great Herod to incline himself to Caesar
And leave his master, Antony. For this pains,
15   Caesar hath hanged him. Camidius and the rest
That fell away have entertainment° but   *employment*
No honourable trust. I have done ill,
Of which I do accuse myself so sorely
That I will joy no more.

Enter a SOLDIER *of Caesar's*

SOLDIER   Enobarbus, Antony
20   Hath after thee sent all thy treasure, with
His bounty overplus. The messenger
Came on my guard,° and at thy tent is now   *on my watch*
Unloading of his mules.

ENOBARBUS   I give it you.

25 SOLDIER   Mock not, Enobarbus,
I tell you true. Best you safed the bringer
Out of the host.[3] I must attend mine office,°   *look after my duties*
Or would have done't myself. Your Emperor
Continues still a Jove.   *Exit*

30 ENOBARBUS   I am alone the° villain of the earth,   *the single greatest*
And feel I am so most.° O Antony,   *I feel it most*
Thou mine of bounty, how wouldst thou have paid
My better service, when my turpitude
Thou dost so crown with gold! This blows° my heart.   *swells; bursts*
35   If swift thought° break it not, a swifter mean°   *regret / means (suicide)*
Shall outstrike thought; but thought will do't, I feel.
I fight against thee? No, I will go seek
Some ditch wherein to die. The foul'st best fits
My latter part of life.   *Exit*

4.7

Alarum. Enter AGRIPPA [*with*] *drum*[*mer*]*s and trum-*
pet[*er*]*s*

AGRIPPA   Retire!° We have engaged our selves too far.   *Sound the retreat*
Caesar himself has work,° and our oppression   *is sorely challenged*
Exceeds what we expected.   *Exeunt*

4.8

Alarums. Enter ANTONY, *and* SCARUS *wounded*

SCARUS   O my brave Emperor, this is fought indeed!
Had we done so at first, we had droven them home
With clouts° about their heads.   *bandages; blows*

ANTONY   Thou bleed'st apace.

---

3. *Best . . . host:* It would be best if you ensured safe conduct through the lines for the messenger who brought
the treasure.

4.7 Location: The battlefield, Alexandria.
4.8 Location: Scene continues.

SCARUS I had a wound here that was like a T,
But now 'tis made an H.[1]
          [*Retreat sounded*] *far off*
5 ANTONY   They do retire.
SCARUS We'll beat 'em into bench-holes.° I have yet   *latrine holes*
Room for six scotches° more.   *gashes*
          Enter EROS
EROS They are beaten, sir, and our advantage serves
For a fair victory.
SCARUS   Let us score° their backs   *slash*
10 And snatch 'em up as° we take hares, behind.   *in the same way as*
'Tis sport to maul a runner.°   *coward*
ANTONY [*to* EROS]   I will reward thee
Once for thy sprightly° comfort, and tenfold   *cheerful*
For thy good valour. Come thee on.
SCARUS   I'll halt° after.   *Exeunt*   *limp*

4.9

          Alarum. Enter ANTONY *again in a march;* [*drummers
          and trumpeters;*] SCARUS, *with others*
ANTONY We have beat him to his camp. Run one before,
And let the Queen know of our gests.°   [*Exit a soldier*]   *deeds*
                              Tomorrow,
Before the sun shall see's, we'll spill the blood
That has today escaped. I thank you all,
5 For doughty-handed° are you, and have fought   *brave*
Not as° you served the cause, but as't had been   *as though*
Each man's like mine. You have shown all Hectors.[1]
Enter the city, clip° your wives, your friends,   *embrace*
Tell them your feats whilst they with joyful tears
10 Wash the congealment from your wounds, and kiss
The honoured gashes whole.
          Enter CLEOPATRA
[*To* SCARUS]   Give me thy hand.
To this great fairy° I'll commend thy acts,   *enchantress*
Make her thanks bless thee.
          [*To* CLEOPATRA, *embracing her*] O thou day° o'th' world, *light*
Chain mine armed neck; leap thou, attire and all,
15 Through proof of harness° to my heart, and there   *impenetrable armor*
Ride on the pants° triumphing.   *heartbeats*
CLEOPATRA   Lord of lords!
O infinite virtue,° com'st thou smiling from   *valor*
The world's great snare uncaught?
ANTONY   My nightingale,
We have beat them to their beds. What, girl, though grey
20 Do something° mingle with our younger brown, yet ha' we   *somewhat*
A brain that nourishes our nerves,° and can   *muscles*
Get goal for goal of youth.[2] Behold this man.
Commend unto his lips thy favouring hand;
Kiss it, my warrior.

---

1. *wound . . . H:* the wound was originally shaped like a
T, but another gash across its bottom has made it look like
an H turned sideways (punning on "ache," pronounced
"aitch").
4.9 Location: Scene continues.

1. You have all fought like Hector (the greatest of the
Trojan warriors).
2. Compete with any youth. Antony is clearly referring
here to the "boy" Caesar, but also, possibly, to his own
boyhood.

[SCARUS *kisses Cleopatra's hand*]
                                He hath fought today
25 As if a god, in hate of mankind, had
   Destroyed in such a shape.
CLEOPATRA   I'll give thee, friend,
   An armour all of gold. It was a king's.
ANTONY He has deserved it, were it carbuncled°   *bejeweled*
   Like holy Phoebus' car.° Give me thy hand.   *the sun god's chariot*
30 Through Alexandria make a jolly march.
   Bear our hacked targets like° the men that owe° them.   *shields as befits / own*
   Had our great palace the capacity
   To camp° this host, we all would sup together   *put up*
   And drink carouses to the next day's fate,
35 Which promises royal° peril. Trumpeters,   *great*
   With brazen din blast you the city's ear;
   Make mingle with our rattling taborins,°   *small drums*
   That heaven and earth may strike their sounds together,
   Applauding our approach.   [*Trumpets sound.*] *Exeunt*

4.10

Enter a SENTRY *and his company;* ENOBARBUS *follows*

SENTRY If we be not relieved within this hour
   We must return to th' court of guard.° The night   *guardroom*
   Is shiny,° and they say we shall embattle°   *bright / go to battle*
   By th' second hour i'th' morn.
FIRST WATCH   This last day was
   A shrewd° one to's.   *bad*
5 ENOBARBUS   O bear me witness, night—
SECOND WATCH   What man is this?
FIRST WATCH   Stand close,° and list° him.   *hidden / listen to*
ENOBARBUS   Be witness to me, O thou blessèd moon,
   When men revolted° shall upon record   *deserters*
   Bear hateful memory, poor Enobarbus did
   Before thy face repent.
SENTRY   Enobarbus?
10 SECOND WATCH   Peace; hark further.
ENOBARBUS   O sovereign mistress of true melancholy,°   *(the moon)*
   The poisonous damp of night disponge° upon me,   *pour down*
   That life, a very rebel to my will,
   May hang no longer on me. Throw my heart
15 Against the flint and hardness of my fault,
   Which,° being dried with grief, will break to powder,   *(his heart)*
   And finish all foul thoughts. O Antony,
   Nobler than my revolt is infamous,
   Forgive me in thine own particular,[1]
20 But let the world rank me in register°   *its records*
   A master-leaver and a fugitive.°   *deserter*
   O Antony! O Antony!   [*He dies*][2]
FIRST WATCH   Let's speak to him.

4.10 Location: Caesar's camp.
1. In whatever aspects of this business concern only you.
2. Depending on how this moment is played, Enobarbus's death may not be obvious either to those onstage
or to the audience.

SENTRY   Let's hear him, for the things he speaks
May concern Caesar.
25   SECOND WATCH   Let's do so. But he sleeps.
SENTRY   Swoons, rather; for so bad a prayer as his
Was never yet for° sleep.   *in preparation for*
FIRST WATCH   Go we to him.
SECOND WATCH   Awake, sir, awake; speak to us.
FIRST WATCH   Hear you, sir?
SENTRY   The hand of death hath raught° him.   *taken*
    Drums afar off
                                        Hark, the drums
30   Demurely° wake the sleepers. Let us bear him   *With subdued sound*
To th' court of guard; he is of note. Our hour
Is fully out.°   *expired*
SECOND WATCH   Come on, then. He may recover yet.
                        Exeunt [with the body]

4.11

Enter ANTONY and SCARUS with their army
ANTONY   Their preparation is today by sea;
We please them not by land.
SCARUS   For both, my lord.
ANTONY   I would they'd fight i'th' fire or i'th' air;
We'd fight there too.[1] But this it is: our foot°   *foot soldiers*
5   Upon the hills adjoining to the city
Shall stay with us. Order for sea is given.
They have put forth° the haven—   *departed from*
Where their appointment° we may best discover,   *purpose; battle plan*
And look on their endeavour.   *Exeunt*

4.12

Enter CAESAR and his army
CAESAR   But being° charged, we will be still° by land—   *unless we're / inactive*
Which, as I take't, we shall, for his best force
Is forth to man his galleys. To the vales,°   *valleys*
And hold our best advantage.°   *Exeunt*   *take the best position*

4.13

Alarum afar off, as at a sea fight.
Enter ANTONY and SCARUS
ANTONY   Yet they are not joined.° Where yon pine does stand   *(in battle)*
I shall discover all. I'll bring thee word
Straight° how 'tis like° to go.   *Exit*   *Promptly / likely*
SCARUS   Swallows have built
In Cleopatra's sails their nests. The augurs°   *soothsayers*
5   Say they know not, they cannot tell, look grimly,
And dare not speak their knowledge. Antony
Is valiant, and dejected, and by starts
His fretted° fortunes give him hope and fear   *diminished*
Of what he has and has not.
    Enter ANTONY

4.11 Location: This and the next two scenes take place   1. As well as in the other elements, earth and water.
on the battlefield.   4.12
                                                              4.13

ANTONY   All is lost.

10   This foul Egyptian hath betrayèd me.
      My fleet hath yielded to the foe, and yonder
      They cast their caps up, and carouse together
      Like friends long lost. Triple-turned whore![1] 'Tis thou
      Hast sold me to this novice, and my heart
15   Makes only wars on thee. Bid them all fly;
      For when I am revenged upon my charm,°   *sorceress*
      I have done all. Bid them all fly. Be gone.   [*Exit* SCARUS]
      O sun, thy uprise shall I see no more.
      Fortune and Antony part here; even here
20   Do we shake hands.° All come to this? The hearts   *(before parting)*
      That spanieled° me at heels, to whom I gave   *fawned upon*
      Their wishes, do discandy,° melt their sweets   *melt*
      On blossoming Caesar; and this pine° is barked[2]   *(Antony)*
      That overtopped them all. Betrayed I am.
25   O this false soul of Egypt! This grave° charm,   *deadly*
      Whose eye becked° forth my wars and called them home,   *beckoned*
      Whose bosom was my crownet,° my chief end,°   *coronet / reward*
      Like a right° gipsy hath at fast and loose[3]   *true*
      Beguiled° me to the very heart of loss.°   *cheated / ruin*
      What, Eros, Eros!
           Enter CLEOPATRA
30   Ah, thou spell! Avaunt.°   *Leave me*
CLEOPATRA   Why is my lord enraged against his love?
ANTONY   Vanish, or I shall give thee thy deserving
      And blemish Caesar's triumph.° Let him take thee   *triumphal procession*
      And hoist thee up to the shouting plebeians;
35   Follow his chariot, like the greatest spot°   *taint*
      Of all thy sex; most monster-like be shown
      For poor'st diminutives,[4] for dolts, and let
      Patient Octavia plough thy visage up
      With her preparèd° nails.   *Exit* CLEOPATRA   *specially sharpened*
                          'Tis well thou'rt gone,
40   If it be well to live. But better 'twere
      Thou fell'st into° my fury, for one death   *a victim to*
      Might have prevented many. Eros, ho!
      The shirt of Nessus[5] is upon me. Teach me,
      Alcides, thou mine ancestor, thy rage.
45   Let me lodge Lichas on the horns o'th' moon,
      And with those hands that grasped the heaviest club
      Subdue my worthiest self. The witch shall die.
      To the young Roman boy she hath sold me, and I fall
      Under this plot. She dies for't. Eros, ho!   *Exit*

---

1. Cleopatra is "triple-turned" because disloyal to three (Julius Caesar, Pompey, and Antony); alluding to her changing political allegiances.
2. Stripped of its bark (and so killed).
3. *fast and loose*: a cheating game played by gypsies.
4. For the benefit of (in place of) the lowest people (dwarfs).
5. Hercules, also known as Alcides (line 44), with whom Antony is repeatedly compared, fatally wounded the centaur Nessus for trying to rape his wife, Deianira. Nessus gave her some of his blood, falsely claiming that it would act as a love potion. Years later, she smeared some of the deadly blood on a shirt and sent it to Hercules. Blaming Lichas (line 45), who had brought the shirt, Hercules cast him into the sea. When she realized what she had done, Deianira killed herself.

4.14

Enter CLEOPATRA, CHARMIAN, IRAS, MARDIAN

CLEOPATRA Help me, my women! O, he's more mad
　　Than Telamon for his shield;[1] the boar of Thessaly[2]
　　Was never so embossed.[3]

CHARMIAN　　　　　　　　To th' monument![4]
　　There lock yourself, and send him word you are dead.
5　　The soul and body rive° not more in parting　　　　　　*separate*
　　Than greatness going off.°　　　　　　　　　　　*leaving someone*

CLEOPATRA　　　　　　　　To th' monument!
　　Mardian, go tell him I have slain myself.
　　Say that the last I spoke was 'Antony',
　　And word it, prithee, piteously. Hence, Mardian,
10　　And bring me° how he takes my death. To th' monument!　　*bring me word*

Exeunt

4.15

Enter ANTONY *and* EROS

ANTONY　Eros, thou yet behold'st me?

EROS　　　　　　　　　　Ay, noble lord.

ANTONY　Sometime we see a cloud that's dragonish,°　　*in a dragon's shape*
　　A vapour sometime like a bear or lion,
　　A towered citadel, a pendent° rock,　　　　　　　　　*hanging*
5　　A forkèd mountain, or blue promontory
　　With trees upon't that nod unto the world
　　And mock our eyes with air. Thou hast seen these signs;
　　They are black vesper's pageants.[1]

EROS　　　　　　　　　　　Ay, my lord.

ANTONY　That which is now a horse even with a thought
10　　The rack distains,° and makes it indistinct　　　　　*cloud dims*
　　As water is in water.

EROS　　　　　　　　It does, my lord.

ANTONY　My good knave° Eros, now thy captain is　　　　*boy*
　　Even such a body. Here I am Antony,
　　Yet cannot hold this visible shape, my knave.
15　　I made these wars for Egypt, and the Queen—
　　Whose heart I thought I had, for she had mine,
　　Which whilst it was mine had annexed unto't
　　A million more, now lost—she, Eros, has
　　Packed cards° with Caesar, and false-played my glory　　*Stacked the deck*
20　　Unto an enemy's triumph.°　　　　　　　　　*victory; trump card*
　　Nay, weep not, gentle Eros. There is left us
　　Ourselves to end ourselves.

Enter MARDIAN
　　　　　　　　　　O thy vile lady,
　　She has robbed me of my sword!°　　　　　　　*valor; manhood*

MARDIAN　　　　　　　　　No, Antony,

4.14 Location: Alexandria.
1. Ajax, also known as Telemon, went mad and killed
himself after the capture of Troy when he was not
awarded Achilles' shield.
2. Sent by Diana to lay waste Calydon (killed by Meleager).
3. Was never so exhaustedly foaming at the mouth—that
is, was never driven to such extremity (a hunting term).

4. The tomb that Cleopatra, forseeing her death, had
built.
4.15 Location: Alexandria.
1. Illusory spectacles heralding the approach of night—
with a probable allusion to funerals and death. (Pageants
were originally moving stages on which miracle plays
were presented.)

My mistress loved thee, and her fortunes mingled
With thine entirely.

25 ANTONY   Hence, saucy° eunuch, peace!   disrespectful
She hath betrayed me, and shall die the death.

MARDIAN   Death of one person can be paid but once,
And that she has discharged. What thou wouldst do
Is done unto thy hand.° The last she spake   for you
30 Was 'Antony, most noble Antony!'
Then in the midst a tearing groan did break
The name of Antony. It was divided
Between her heart and lips.² She rendered° life,   gave up
Thy name so buried in her.

ANTONY   Dead, then?

MARDIAN   Dead.

35 ANTONY   Unarm, Eros.³ The long day's task is done,
And we must sleep. [*To* MARDIAN] That thou depart'st hence safe
Does pay thy labour richly. Go.   *Exit* MARDIAN
                           Off, pluck off.
          [EROS *helps* ANTONY *to unarm*]
The seven-fold shield⁴ of Ajax cannot keep
The battery° from my heart. O, cleave, my sides!   onslaught
40 Heart, once be stronger than thy continent;°   container
Crack thy frail case. Apace,° Eros, apace.   Quickly
No more a soldier. Bruisèd pieces,° do;   of armor
You have been nobly borne.—From me a while.   *Exit* EROS
I will o'ertake thee, Cleopatra, and
45 Weep for my pardon. So it must be, for now
All length° is torture. Since the torch° is out,   longer life / (Cleopatra)
Lie down, and stray no farther. Now all labour
Mars what it does; yea, very force entangles
Itself with strength.⁵ Seal,° then, and all is done.   Finish the deed
50 Eros!—I come, my queen.—Eros!—Stay for me.
Where souls do couch on flowers⁶ we'll hand in hand,
And with our sprightly port° make the ghosts gaze.   cheerful stance
Dido and her Aeneas shall want troops,⁷
And all the haunt° be ours. Come, Eros, Eros!   place; ghosts
          Enter EROS

EROS   What would my lord?

55 ANTONY   Since Cleopatra died
I have lived in such dishonour that the gods
Detest my baseness. I, that with my sword
Quartered the world, and o'er green Neptune's back°   on the sea
With ships made cities,⁸ condemn myself to lack°   for lacking
60 The courage of a woman; less noble mind
Than she which by her death our Caesar tells
'I am conqueror of myself.' Thou art sworn, Eros,

---

2. *It . . . lips:* It was half-uttered.
3. Here and in the following lines, the symbolic appropriateness of this historical figure's name ("Eros" means
"love") is stressed.
4. A shield made of brass lined with six thicknesses of
oxhide.
5. *very . . . strength:* strength defeats itself by its own exertions.
6. Lie ("couch") in the Elysian Fields of the blessed dead
in the mythological underworld.

7. Shall lack followers. Dido, Queen of Carthage, commits suicide after being abandoned by her lover Aeneas,
legendary Trojan founder of Rome, in Virgil's *Aeneid*;
they are not reconciled in the underworld. Dido, who
originally hailed from Phoenicia, is meant to recall Cleopatra. In leaving her, Aeneas places public responsibility
above personal desire—unlike Antony but very much like
Octavius Caesar, whom Virgil intended him to resemble.
8. Put so many ships to sea that the fleet resembled a city.

That when the exigent° should come, which now   *urgent need*
Is come indeed—when I should see behind me
65   Th'inevitable prosecution° of   *pursuit*
Disgrace and horror—that on my command
Thou then wouldst kill me. Do't. The time is come.
Thou strik'st not me; 'tis Caesar thou defeat'st.
Put colour in thy cheek.

EROS   The gods withhold me!°   *God forbid*
70   Shall I do that which all the Parthian darts,
Though enemy, lost aim and could not?

ANTONY   Eros,
Wouldst thou be windowed° in great Rome and see   *looking from a window*
Thy master thus with pleached° arms, bending down   *tied*
His corrigible° neck, his face subdued   *submissive*
75   To penetrative° shame, whilst the wheeled seat°   *piercing / chariot*
Of fortunate Caesar, drawn before him, branded
His baseness that ensued?[9]

EROS   I would not see't.

ANTONY   Come then; for with a wound I must be cured.
Draw that thy honest° sword, which thou hast worn   *honorable*
Most useful for thy country.

80   EROS   O sir, pardon me!

ANTONY   When I did make thee free, swor'st thou not then
To do this when I bade thee? Do it at once,
Or thy precedent° services are all   *earlier*
But accidents unpurposed.° Draw, and come.   *But pointless events*

85   EROS   Turn from me then that noble countenance
Wherein the worship° of the whole world lies.   *esteem; worth*

ANTONY [*turning away*]   Lo thee!

EROS   My sword is drawn.

ANTONY   Then let it do at once
The thing why thou hast drawn it.

EROS   My dear master,
90   My captain, and my Emperor: let me say,
Before I strike this bloody stroke, farewell.

ANTONY   'Tis said, man; and farewell.

EROS   Farewell, great chief. Shall I strike now?

ANTONY   Now, Eros.

[EROS *stabs himself*]

EROS   Why, there then, thus I do escape the sorrow
Of Antony's death.   [*He dies*]

95   ANTONY   Thrice nobler than myself,
Thou teachest me, O valiant Eros, what
I should and thou couldst not. My queen and Eros
Have by their brave instruction got upon° me   *gained ahead of*
A nobleness in record.° But I will be   *history*
100 A bridegroom in my death, and run into't
As to a lover's bed.[1] Come then, and, Eros,
Thy master dies thy scholar. To do thus
I learned of thee.

9. *branded . . . ensued:* indicated, as if by a criminal's brand, the humiliation of the man who followed.
1. *But . . . bed:* Death is here treated as a form of erotic union or climax, with Antony as the bridegroom and death (and Cleopatra) the bride.

[*He stabs*] *himself*
                              How, not dead? Not dead?
The guard, ho! O, dispatch° me!   *finish*
                    Enter a GUARD [*and* DECRETAS]
FIRST GUARD   What's the noise?

105 ANTONY   I have done my work ill, friends. O, make an end
Of what I have begun!
SECOND GUARD   The star is fall'n.
FIRST GUARD   And time is at his period.°   *its end*
ALL THE GUARDS   Alas
   And woe!
ANTONY   Let him that loves me strike me dead.
FIRST GUARD   Not I.
SECOND GUARD   Nor I.
THIRD GUARD   Nor anyone.   *Exeunt* [*the* GUARD]
110 DECRETAS   Thy death and fortunes bid thy followers fly.
                    [*He takes Antony's sword*]
   This sword but shown to Caesar, with this tidings,
   Shall enter me° with him.   *gain me favor*
                    Enter DIOMEDES
DIOMEDES   Where's Antony?
DECRETAS   There, Diomed, there.
DIOMEDES   Lives he? Wilt thou not answer, man?
                                             [*Exit* DECRETAS]
ANTONY   Art thou there, Diomed? Draw thy sword, and give me
Sufficing° strokes for death.   *Enough*
115 DIOMEDES   Most absolute lord,
   My mistress Cleopatra sent me to thee.
ANTONY   When did she send thee?
DIOMEDES   Now, my lord.
ANTONY   Where is she?
DIOMEDES   Locked in her monument. She had a prophesying fear
   Of what hath come to pass; for when she saw—
120 Which never shall be found°—you did suspect   *(to be true)*
   She had disposed° with Caesar, and that your rage   *made an alliance*
   Would not be purged, she sent word she was dead;
   But fearing since how it might work, hath sent
   Me to proclaim the truth; and I am come,
125 I dread, too late.
ANTONY   Too late, good Diomed. Call my guard, I prithee.
DIOMEDES   What ho, the Emperor's guard! The guard, what ho!
   Come, your lord calls.
                    Enter four or five of the GUARD *of Antony*
ANTONY   Bear me, good friends, where Cleopatra bides.°   *waits; dwells*
130 'Tis the last service that I shall command you.
FIRST GUARD   Woe, woe are we, sir, you may not live to wear
   All your true followers out.°   *outlive them*
ALL THE GUARDS   Most heavy day!
ANTONY   Nay, good my fellows, do not please sharp fate
   To grace° it with your sorrows. Bid that welcome   *By gracing*
135 Which comes to punish us, and we punish it,
   Seeming to bear it lightly. Take me up.
   I have led you oft; carry me now, good friends,
   And have my thanks for all.   *Exeunt bearing* ANTONY [*and* EROS]

4.16

Enter CLEOPATRA *and her maids aloft, with*
CHARMIAN *and* IRAS

CLEOPATRA   O Charmian, I will never go from hence.

CHARMIAN   Be comforted, dear madam.

CLEOPATRA   No, I will not.
All strange and terrible events are welcome,
But comforts we despise. Our size of sorrow,
5   Proportioned to our cause, must be as great
As that which makes it.

Enter DIOMEDES [*below*]

                                      How now? Is he dead?

DIOMEDES   His death's upon him, but not dead.
Look out o'th' other side your monument.
His guard have brought him thither.

Enter [*below*] ANTONY, [*borne by*] *the guard*

CLEOPATRA   O sun,
10   Burn the great sphere thou mov'st in; darkling¹ stand
The varying shore o'th' world! O Antony,
Antony, Antony! Help, Charmian,
Help, Iras, help, help, friends below!
Let's draw him hither.

ANTONY   Peace. Not Caesar's valour
15   Hath o'erthrown Antony, but Antony's
Hath triumphed on itself.

CLEOPATRA   So it should be,
That none but Antony should conquer Antony.
But woe 'tis so!

ANTONY   I am dying, Egypt, dying. Only
20   I here importune death° awhile until   *ask death to wait*
Of many thousand kisses the poor last
I lay upon thy lips.

CLEOPATRA   I dare not,° dear,   *dare not come down*
Dear, my lord, pardon. I dare not,
Lest I be taken. Nor th'imperious show°   *triumphal procession*
25   Of the full-fortuned Caesar ever shall
Be brooched° with me, if knife, drugs, serpents, have   *decorated*
Edge, sting, or operation.° I am safe.   *power*
Your wife, Octavia, with her modest eyes
And still conclusion,° shall acquire no honour   *silent judgment*
30   Demuring° upon me. But come, come, Antony.—   *Gazing solemnly*
Help me, my women.—We must draw thee up.
Assist, good friends.

ANTONY   O quick, or I am gone!

CLEOPATRA   Here's sport indeed. How heavy weighs my lord!
Our strength is all gone into heaviness,°   *sadness; weight*
35   That makes the weight. Had I great Juno's power
The strong-winged Mercury should fetch thee up
And set thee by Jove's side. Yet come a little.
Wishers were ever fools. O come, come, come!

4.16 Location: Cleopatra's monument, Alexandria.
1. *O . . . darkling:* For the spheres in which the sun, like
the planets and stars, was thought to move around the
earth, see note to 2.7.15. If the sun burned its sphere,
presumably it would move out of orbit, thus leaving the
earth in darkness ("darkling").

They heave ANTONY *aloft to* CLEOPATRA

And welcome, welcome! Die when thou hast lived,°   *lived again*
40   Quicken° with kissing. Had my lips that power,   *Revive*
    Thus would I wear them out.

        [*They kiss*]

ALL THE LOOKERS-ON   A heavy sight.

ANTONY   I am dying, Egypt, dying.
    Give me some wine, and let me speak a little.

45 CLEOPATRA   No, let me speak, and let me rail so high
    That the false hussy Fortune break her wheel,
    Provoked by my offence.°   *insults*

ANTONY   One word, sweet queen.
    Of Caesar seek your honour, with your safety. O!

CLEOPATRA   They do not go together.

ANTONY   Gentle, hear me.
50   None about Caesar trust but Proculeius.

CLEOPATRA   My resolution and my hands I'll trust,
    None about Caesar.

ANTONY   The miserable change now at my end
    Lament° nor sorrow at, but please your thoughts   *Neither lament*
55   In feeding them with those my former fortunes,
    Wherein I lived the greatest prince o'th' world,
    The noblest; and do now not basely die,
    Not cowardly put off my helmet to
    My countryman; a Roman by a Roman
60   Valiantly vanquished. Now my spirit is going;
    I can no more.

CLEOPATRA   Noblest of men, woot die?°   *will you*
    Hast thou no care of me? Shall I abide
    In this dull world, which in thy absence is
    No better than a sty?

        [ANTONY *dies*]

              O see, my women,
65   The crown o'th' earth doth melt. My lord!
    O, withered is the garland° of the war.   *crowning glory*
    The soldier's pole² is fall'n. Young boys and girls
    Are level now with men. The odds° is gone,   *distinction among humans*
    And there is nothing left remarkable
70   Beneath the visiting moon.

        [*She falls*]

CHARMIAN   O, quietness, lady!

IRAS   She's dead, too, our sovereign.

CHARMIAN   Lady!

IRAS   Madam!

CHARMIAN   O, madam, madam, madam!

IRAS   Royal Egypt, Empress!

CHARMIAN   Peace, peace, Iras!

CLEOPATRA [*recovering*]   No more but e'en° a woman, and   *just (no longer Queen)*
75   commanded
    By such poor passion as the maid that milks
    And does the meanest chores. It were for° me   *would befit*
    To throw my sceptre at the injurious gods,

2. Polestar; military standard; phallus.

To tell them that this world did equal theirs
80   Till they had stol'n our jewel. All's but naught.
Patience is sottish,° and impatience does   foolish
Become a dog that's mad. Then is it sin
To rush into the secret house of death
Ere death dare come to us? How do you, women?
85   What, what, good cheer! Why, how now, Charmian?
My noble girls! Ah, women, women! Look,
Our lamp is spent, it's out. Good sirs,° take heart;   (to the women)
We'll bury him, and then what's brave,° what's noble,   fine
Let's do it after the high Roman fashion,
90   And make death proud to take us. Come, away.
This case of that huge spirit now is cold.
Ah, women, women! Come. We have no friend
But resolution, and the briefest° end.   fastest

Exeunt [those above] bearing off Antony's body

5.1

Enter CAESAR *with his council of war:* AGRIPPA, DOLA-
    BELLA, [MAECENAS, GALLUS, PROCULEIUS]
CAESAR   Go to him, Dolabella, bid him yield.
Being so frustrate, tell him, he but mocks
The pauses that he makes.[1]
DOLABELLA   Caesar, I shall.   [*Exit*]

Enter DECRETAS *with the sword of Antony*
CAESAR   Wherefore is that? And what art thou that dar'st
Appear thus° to us?   with a drawn weapon
5   DECRETAS   I am called Decretas.
Mark Antony I served, who best was worthy
Best to be served. Whilst he stood up and spoke
He was my master, and I wore my life
To spend° upon his haters. If thou please   expend
10   To take me to thee, as I was to him
I'll be to Caesar; if thou pleasest not,
I yield thee up my life.
CAESAR   What is't thou sayst?
DECRETAS   I say, O Caesar, Antony is dead.
CAESAR   The breaking° of so great a thing should make   end; telling
15   A greater crack.° The rivèd° world   noise; fracture / split
Should have shook lions into civil° streets,   city
And citizens to their° dens. The death of Antony   (the lions')
Is not a single doom; in that name lay
A moiety° of the world.   half
DECRETAS   He is dead, Caesar,
20   Not by a public minister of justice,
Nor by a hirèd knife; but that self° hand   same
Which writ his honour in the acts it did
Hath, with the courage which the heart did lend it,
Splitted the heart. This is his sword;
25   I robbed his wound of it. Behold it stained
With his most noble blood.
CAESAR [*weeping*]   Look you, sad friends,

5.1 Location: Caesar's camp.   1. *he but . . . makes:* his delays are a mere mockery.

The gods rebuke me;° but it is a tidings   *(for his tears)*
To wash the eyes of kings.

AGRIPPA   And strange it is
That nature must compel us to lament
Our most persisted deeds.°   *What we persevered in*

30 MAECENAS   His taints and honours
Waged° equal with° him.   *Fought as if / in*

AGRIPPA   A rarer spirit never
Did steer humanity;° but you gods will give us   *govern (any) man*
Some faults to make us men. Caesar is touched.

MAECENAS   When such a spacious mirror's set before him
He needs must see himself.

35 CAESAR   O Antony,
I have followed° thee to this. But we do lance°   *pursued / wound to cure*
Diseases in our bodies. I must perforce
Have shown to thee such a declining day,[2]
Or look on thine. We could not stall° together   *live in peace*
40 In the whole world. But yet let me lament,
With tears as sovereign[3] as the blood of hearts,
That thou, my brother, my competitor°   *comrade; foe*
In top of all design,° my mate in empire,   *In the greatest ventures*
Friend and companion in the front of war,
45 The arm of mine own body, and the heart
Where mine his° thoughts did kindle—that our stars,   *its*
Unreconciliable, should divide
Our equalness° to this. Hear me, good friends—   *partnership*

Enter an EGYPTIAN

But I will tell you at some meeter season.°   *fitter time*
50 The business of this man looks out of him;
We'll hear him what he says.—Whence are you?

EGYPTIAN   A poor Egyptian, yet the Queen my mistress,
Confined in all she has, her monument,
Of thy intents desires instruction,
55 That she preparèdly may frame herself
To th' way she's forced to.

CAESAR   Bid her have good heart.
She soon shall know of us, by some of ours,
How honourable and how kindly we
Determine for her. For Caesar cannot live
To be ungentle.

60 EGYPTIAN   So; the gods preserve thee!   *Exit*

CAESAR   Come hither, Proculeius. Go, and say
We purpose her no shame. Give her what comforts
The quality° of her passion° shall require,   *strength / grief*
Lest in her greatness, by some mortal stroke,
65 She do defeat us; for her life in Rome
Would be eternal in our triumph.[4] Go,
And with your speediest bring us what she says
And how you find of her.

PROCULEIUS   Caesar, I shall.   *Exit*

---

2. *I must . . . day:* I would have had to exhibit my demise
to you. *perforce:* necessarily.
3. As efficacious (weeping seems to be paralleled with
bloodletting).
4. *her life . . . triumph:* her presence alive in Rome would
bring eternal renown to my triumphal procession.

CAESAR   Gallus, go you along.   [*Exit* GALLUS]
                                        Where's Dolabella,
        To second Proculeius?
70 ALL BUT CAESAR   Dolabella!
    CAESAR   Let him alone; for I remember now
        How he's employed. He shall in time be ready.
        Go with me to my tent, where you shall see
        How hardly° I was drawn into this war,   *unwillingly*
75   How calm and gentle I proceeded still
        In all my writings.° Go with me, and see   *letters to Antony*
        What I can show in this.   *Exeunt*

                            5.2

        Enter CLEOPATRA, CHARMIAN, IRAS, *and* MARDIAN
    CLEOPATRA   My desolation does begin to make
        A better life. 'Tis paltry to be Caesar.
        Not being Fortune, he's but Fortune's knave,°   *servant*
        A minister of her will. And it is great
5   To do that thing° that ends all other deeds,   *(suicide)*
        Which shackles accidents and bolts up change,
        Which sleeps and never palates more the dung,
        The beggar's nurse, and Caesar's.¹
                    Enter PROCULEIUS²
    PROCULEIUS   Caesar sends greeting to the Queen of Egypt,
10   And bids thee study on° what fair demands   *give thought to*
        Thou mean'st to have him grant thee.
    CLEOPATRA   What's thy name?
    PROCULEIUS   My name is Proculeius.
    CLEOPATRA   Antony
        Did tell me of you, bade me trust you; but
        I do not greatly care to be deceived,
15   That° have no use for trusting.³ If your master   *Because I*
        Would have a queen his beggar, you must tell him
        That majesty, to keep decorum, must
        No less beg than a kingdom. If he please
        To give me conquered Egypt for my son,
20   He gives me so much of mine own as° I   *that*
        Will kneel to him with thanks.
    PROCULEIUS   Be of good cheer.
        You're fall'n into a princely hand; fear nothing.
        Make your full reference° freely to my lord,   *case*
        Who is so full of grace that it flows over
25   On all that need. Let me report to him
        Your sweet dependency,° and you shall find   *meek obeisance*
        A conqueror that will pray in aid for kindness,⁴
        Where he for grace is kneeled to.
    CLEOPATRA   Pray you, tell him
        I am his fortune's vassal, and I send him
30   The greatness he has got.⁵ I hourly learn

5.2 Location: Cleopatra's monument.
1. *Which sleeps . . . Caesar's:* Which brings a sleep in which we no longer taste the produce of the earth (dung), nourisher of all from beggar to emperor.
2. Cleopatra and her women are inside the monument, the others outside it.
3. Cleopatra claims not to care whether she is deceived, in the hope that Proculeius will relax his guard and reveal

Caesar's intentions. But she may also mean that she doesn't like being deceived, knowing as she does the perils of misplaced trust.
4. Who will beg help in finding new ways to be kind.
5. *I am . . . got:* I do homage to his good fortune, and acknowledge the great position he has won. "Send him" may suggest Cleopatra's sense of superiority in conferring greatness upon Caesar.

A doctrine of obedience, and would gladly
Look him i'th' face.
PROCULEIUS   This I'll report, dear lady;
Have comfort, for I know your plight is pitied
Of° him that caused it.   By

[Enter Roman soldiers from behind]

35 PROCULEIUS *[to the soldiers]*   You see how easily she may be surprised.
Guard her till Caesar come.
IRAS   Royal Queen—
CHARMIAN   O Cleopatra, thou art taken, Queen!
CLEOPATRA *[drawing a dagger]*   Quick, quick, good hands!
PROCULEIUS *[disarming CLEOPATRA]*   Hold,
     worthy lady, hold!
Do not yourself such wrong, who are in this
Relieved° but not betrayed.   *Rescued*
40 CLEOPATRA   What, of° death too,   *deprived of*
That rids our dogs of languish?[6]
PROCULEIUS   Cleopatra,
Do not abuse my master's bounty by
Th'undoing of yourself. Let the world see
His nobleness well acted, which your death
Will never let come forth.°   *allow to be displayed*
45 CLEOPATRA   Where art thou, death?
Come hither, come. Come, come, and take a queen
Worth many babes and beggars.[7]
PROCULEIUS   O temperance, lady!
CLEOPATRA   Sir, I will eat no meat.° I'll not drink, sir.   *food*
If idle talk will once be necessary,[8]
50 I'll not sleep, neither. This mortal house° I'll ruin,   *My body*
Do Caesar what he can. Know, sir, that I
Will not wait pinioned[9] at your master's court,
Nor once be chastised with the sober eye
Of dull Octavia. Shall they hoist me up
55 And show me to the shouting varletry°   *rabble*
Of censuring Rome? Rather a ditch in Egypt
Be gentle grave unto me; rather on Nilus' mud
Lay me stark naked, and let the waterflies
Blow me into abhorring;[1] rather make
60 My country's high pyramides my gibbet,°   *gallows*
And hang me up in chains.
PROCULEIUS   You do extend
These thoughts of horror further than you shall
Find cause in Caesar.

Enter DOLABELLA

DOLABELLA   Proculeius,
What thou hast done thy master Caesar knows,
65 And he hath sent for thee. For the Queen,
I'll take her to my guard.
PROCULEIUS   So, Dolabella,
It shall content me best. Be gentle to her.

---

6. Which rids even our dogs of protracted demise.
7. *babes and beggars*: death's cheapest victims; those most often "relieved" (line 39) by the great.
8. (Even) if useless words are at times needed (to keep me awake); if I am forced to engage in pointless chatter.
9. Will not serve shackled (or, will not wait like a bird with clipped wings).
1. Lay their eggs on me (thereby breeding maggots) so that I become disgusting, abhorrent.

[*To* CLEOPATRA] To Caesar I will speak what° you shall please,   *whatever*
If you'll employ me to him.

CLEOPATRA   Say I would die. *Exit* PROCULEIUS

70   DOLABELLA   Most noble Empress, you have heard of me.

CLEOPATRA   I cannot tell.

DOLABELLA   Assuredly you know me.

CLEOPATRA   No matter, sir, what I have heard or known.
You laugh when boys or women tell their dreams;
Is't not your trick?°   *custom*

DOLABELLA   I understand not, madam.

75   CLEOPATRA   I dreamt there was an Emperor Antony.
O, such another sleep, that I might see
But such another man!

DOLABELLA   If it might please ye—

CLEOPATRA   His face was as the heav'ns, and therein stuck°   *were stuck*
A sun and moon, which kept their course and lighted
The little O o'th' earth.

80   DOLABELLA   Most sovereign creature—

CLEOPATRA   His legs bestrid° the ocean; his reared arm   *straddled*
Crested[2] the world. His voice was propertied
As all the tunèd spheres,[3] and that to friends;
But when he meant to quail° and shake the orb,°   *awe / globe*
85   He was as rattling thunder. For his bounty,
There was no winter in't; an autumn 'twas,
That grew the more by reaping. His delights
Were dolphin-like; they showed his back above°   *they rose above*
The element they lived in. In his livery°   *service*
90   Walked crowns and crownets.° Realms and islands were   *kings and princes*
As plates° dropped from his pocket.   *silver coins*

DOLABELLA   Cleopatra—

CLEOPATRA   Think you there was, or might be, such a man
As this I dreamt of?

DOLABELLA   Gentle madam, no.

CLEOPATRA   You lie, up to the hearing of the gods.
95   But if there be, or ever were one such,
It's past the size of dreaming.[4] Nature wants stuff
To vie strange forms with fancy; yet t'imagine
An Antony were nature's piece 'gainst fancy,
Condemning shadows quite.[5]

DOLABELLA   Hear me, good madam:
100   Your loss is as yourself, great, and you bear it
As answering to[6] the weight. Would I might never
O'ertake° pursued success but° I do feel,   *Achieve / unless*
By the rebound° of yours, a grief that smites   *reflection*
My very heart at root.

CLEOPATRA   I thank you, sir.
105   Know you what Caesar means to do with me?

DOLABELLA   I am loath to tell you what I would you knew.

CLEOPATRA   Nay, pray you, sir.

---

2. Formed a crest over (as in heraldry).
3. *was . . . spheres:* sounded like the music of the spheres, supposedly produced by the harmonious structure of the universe. See note to 2.7.15.
4. My vision of him surpasses what can be dreamed.
5. *Nature . . . quite:* Nature lacks material to compete

with the remarkable visions of the imagination in creating fantastic forms; but by imaging and creating Antony, nature has produced a masterpiece that outstrips even fancy and thus discredits imaginary conceptions.
6. *you . . . to:* you do justice to.

DOLABELLA	Though he be honourable—	
CLEOPATRA	He'll lead me then in triumph.	
DOLABELLA	Madam, he will, I know't.	

Flourish. Enter CAESAR, [*with*] PROCULEIUS, GALLUS,
MAECENAS, *and others of his train*

ALL°   Make way, there! Caesar!   *(Caesar's train)*

CAESAR   Which is the Queen of Egypt?

DOLABELLA [*to* CLEOPATRA]
     It is the Emperor, madam.

               CLEOPATRA *kneels*

110   CAESAR   Arise! You shall not kneel.
     I pray you rise, rise, Egypt.

CLEOPATRA [*rising*]   Sir, the gods

     Will have it thus.° My master and my lord   *that I obey you*
     I must obey.

CAESAR   Take to you no hard thoughts.
     The record of what injuries you did us,
115   Though written in our flesh, we shall remember
     As things but done by chance.

CLEOPATRA   Sole sir° o'th' world,   *lord*
     I cannot project° mine own cause so well   *lay out*
     To make it clear,° but do confess I have   *innocent seeming*
     Been laden with like frailties which before
     Have often shamed our sex.

120   CAESAR   Cleopatra, know
     We will extenuate rather than enforce.°   *emphasize (faults)*
     If you apply yourself° to our intents,   *conform*
     Which towards you are most gentle, you shall find
     A benefit in this change; but if you seek
125   To lay on me a cruelty° by taking   *charge of cruelty*
     Antony's course, you shall bereave yourself
     Of my good purposes and put your children
     To that destruction which I'll guard them from,
     If thereon you rely. I'll take my leave.

130   CLEOPATRA   And may through all the world![7] 'Tis yours, and we,
     Your scutcheons° and your signs of conquest, shall   *captured shields*
     Hang in what place you please. [*Giving a paper*] Here, my good lord.

CAESAR   You shall advise me in all for° Cleopatra.   *concerning*

CLEOPATRA   This is the brief° of money, plate, and jewels   *summary*
135   I am possessed of. 'Tis exactly valued,
     Not petty things admitted.° Where's Seleucus?   *Except trivial things*

         [*Enter* SELEUCUS]

SELEUCUS   Here, madam.

CLEOPATRA [*to* CAESAR]   This is my treasurer. Let him speak, my lord,
     Upon his peril, that I have reserved
140   To myself nothing. Speak the truth, Seleucus.

SELEUCUS   Madam, I had rather seal° my lips   *sew up*
     Than to my peril speak that which is not.

CLEOPATRA   What have I kept back?

SELEUCUS   Enough to purchase what you have made known.

145   CAESAR   Nay, blush not, Cleopatra. I approve
     Your wisdom in the deed.

CLEOPATRA   See, Caesar! O, behold

---

7. As you may (take your leave and go) anywhere (as ruler of the world).

	How pomp is followed!⁸ Mine° will now be yours,	*My followers*
	And should we shift estates,° yours would be mine.	*change positions*
	The ingratitude of this Seleucus does	
150	Even make me wild.—O slave, of no more trust	
	Than love that's hired! What, goest thou back? Thou shalt	
	Go back, I warrant thee; but I'll catch thine eyes	
	Though° they had wings. Slave, soulless villain, dog!	*Even if*
	O rarely° base!	*exceptionally*
	CAESAR Good Queen, let us entreat you.	
155	CLEOPATRA O Caesar, what a wounding shame is this,	
	That thou vouchsafing° here to visit me,	*stooping to come*
	Doing the honour of thy lordliness	
	To one so meek—that mine own servant should	
	Parcel° the sum of my disgraces by	*Particularize; add to*
160	Addition of his envy.° Say, good Caesar,	*spite*
	That I some lady° trifles have reserved,	*ladylike*
	Immoment toys,° things of such dignity	*Worthless trinkets*
	As we greet modern° friends withal;° and say	*everday / with*
	Some nobler token I have kept apart	
165	For Livia° and Octavia, to induce	*Caesar's wife*
	Their mediation—must I be unfolded	
	With° one that I have bred? The gods! It smites me	*Turned in by*
	Beneath the fall I have. [*To* SELEUCUS] Prithee, go hence,	
	Or I shall show the cinders° of my spirits	*smoldering coals*
170	Through th'ashes of my chance.° Wert thou a man°	*fortune / (not a eunuch)*
	Thou wouldst have mercy on me.	
	CAESAR Forbear, Seleucus.	
	[*Exit* SELEUCUS]	
	CLEOPATRA Be it known that we, the greatest, are misthought°	*misjudged*
	For things that others do; and when we fall	
	We answer others' merits in our name,⁹	
	Are therefore to be pitied.	
175	CAESAR Cleopatra,	
	Not what you have reserved nor what acknowledged	
	Put we i'th' roll of conquest. Still be't yours.	
	Bestow° it at your pleasure, and believe	*Dispense*
	Caesar's no merchant, to make prize° with you	*haggle*
180	Of things that merchants sold. Therefore be cheered.	
	Make not your thoughts your prisons.¹ No, dear Queen;	
	For we intend so to dispose you as	
	Yourself shall give us counsel. Feed and sleep.	
	Our care and pity is so much upon you	
185	That we remain your friend; and so adieu.	
	CLEOPATRA My master and my lord!	
	CAESAR Not so. Adieu.	
	Flourish. Exeunt CAESAR *and his train*	
	CLEOPATRA He words me, girls, he words me, that I should not	
	Be noble to myself.² But hark thee, Charmian.	
	[*She whispers to* CHARMIAN]	

8. How the great are served.
9. We are responsible for the deeds committed by others in our names (an effort to shift the blame to Seleucus).
1. Don't think yourself a prisoner; don't be imprisoned by (or in) your thoughts.
2. *He words . . . myself*: He puts me off from committing suicide with mere words.

IRAS   Finish, good lady. The bright day is done,
          And we are for the dark.
190 CLEOPATRA [*to* CHARMIAN]   Hie thee again.°   *Hurry back*
          I have spoke already, and it is provided.
          Go put it to the haste.°   *Do it quickly*
   CHARMIAN   Madam, I will.
                  Enter DOLABELLA
   DOLABELLA   Where's the Queen?
   CHARMIAN   Behold, sir.   [*Exit*]
   CLEOPATRA   Dolabella!
   DOLABELLA   Madam, as thereto sworn by your command—
195   Which my love makes religion° to obey—   *compels me*
          I tell you this: Caesar through Syria
          Intends his journey, and within three days
          You with your children will he send before.
          Make your best use of this. I have performed
200   Your pleasure, and my promise.
   CLEOPATRA   Dolabella,
          I shall remain your debtor.
   DOLABELLA   I your servant.
          Adieu, good Queen. I must attend on Caesar.
   CLEOPATRA   Farewell, and thanks.   *Exit* [DOLABELLA]
                                    Now, Iras, what think'st thou?
          Thou, an Egyptian puppet shall be shown
205   In Rome, as well as I. Mechanic slaves°   *Laborers*
          With greasy aprons, rules,° and hammers shall   *measuring sticks*
          Uplift us to the view. In their thick° breaths,   *foul*
          Rank° of gross diet,° shall we be enclouded,   *Stinking / coarse food*
          And forced to drink° their vapour.   *inhale*
   IRAS   The gods forbid!
210 CLEOPATRA   Nay, 'tis most certain, Iras. Saucy lictors°   *Insolent law officers*
          Will catch at us like strumpets, and scald° rhymers   *scurvy*
          Ballad us out o' tune. The quick comedians
          Extemporally° will stage us, and present   *In improvised manner*
          Our Alexandrian revels. Antony
215   Shall be brought drunken forth, and I shall see
          Some squeaking Cleopatra boy³ my greatness
          I'th' posture of a whore.
   IRAS   O, the good gods!
   CLEOPATRA   Nay, that's certain.
   IRAS   I'll never see't! For I am sure my nails
          Are stronger than mine eyes.
220 CLEOPATRA   Why, that's the way
          To fool their preparation and to conquer
          Their most absurd intents.
                  Enter CHARMIAN
                                    Now, Charmian!
          Show° me, my women, like a queen. Go fetch   *Dress*
          My best attires. I am again for Cydnus
225   To meet Mark Antony.⁴ Sirrah Iras, go.
          Now, noble Charmian, we'll dispatch° indeed,   *hurry; finish*

3. Cleopatra's part will be played by a boy (as it was in   4. See 2.2.192–232.
Shakespeare's day).

And when thou hast done this chore I'll give thee leave
To play till doomsday.—Bring our crown and all.   [*Exit* IRAS]
    A noise within
Wherefore's this noise?
    Enter a GUARDSMAN

GUARDSMAN   Here is a rural fellow
230   That will not be denied your highness' presence.
He brings you figs.
CLEOPATRA   Let him come in.   *Exit* GUARDSMAN
                    What° poor an instrument   *How*
May do a noble deed! He brings me liberty.
My resolution's placed,° and I have nothing   *unwavering*
235   Of woman in me. Now from head to foot
I am marble-constant. Now the fleeting° moon   *changeable*
No planet is of mine.
           Enter GUARDSMAN, *and* CLOWN° [*with a basket*]   *rustic*
GUARDSMAN   This is the man.
CLEOPATRA   Avoid,° and leave him.   *Exit* GUARDSMAN   *Withdraw*
                  Hast thou the pretty worm[5]
Of Nilus there, that kills and pains not?
240   CLOWN   Truly, I have him; but I would not be the party that
    should desire you to touch him, for his biting is immortal;[6]
    those that do die of it do seldom or never recover.
CLEOPATRA   Remember'st thou any that have died on't?
CLOWN   Very many, men, and women too. I heard of one of
245   them no longer than yesterday, a very honest° woman, but   *truthful; chaste*
    something given to lie,° as a woman should not do but in the   *fib; lie with men*
    way of honesty, how she died° of the biting of it, what pain she *perished; had an orgasm*
    felt. Truly, she makes a very good report o'th' worm; but he
    that will believe all that they say shall never be saved by half
250   that they do;[7] but this is most falliable:° the worm's an odd   *(error for "infallible")*
    worm.
CLEOPATRA   Get thee hence, farewell.
CLOWN   I wish you all joy of the worm.
CLEOPATRA   Farewell.
255   CLOWN   You must think this, look you, that the worm will do his
    kind.°   *what's in its nature*
CLEOPATRA   Ay, ay; farewell.
CLOWN   Look you, the worm is not to be trusted but in the keep-
    ing of wise people; for indeed there is no goodness in the worm.
260   CLEOPATRA   Take thou no care; it shall be heeded.
CLOWN   Very good. Give it nothing, I pray you, for it is not worth
    the feeding.
CLEOPATRA   Will it eat me?
CLOWN   You must not think I am so simple but I know the devil
265   himself will not eat a woman; I know that a woman is a dish
    for the gods, if the devil dress° her not. But truly, these same *prepare (food); clothe*
    whoreson° devils do the gods great harm in their women; for in   *accursed*
    every ten that they make, the devils mar five.

---

5. Snake or serpent. In the Clown's description (lines
244–51), the "worm" also suggests the penis.
6. Comic error: the Clown means the opposite, but as so
often with such malapropisms in Shakespeare, the mistake reveals an unintended truth. See Cleopatra's "Immortal longings" (line 272).

7. Perhaps the point is that a woman "given to lie" (line
246) is not to be believed. If Cleopatra acts on this "good
report o'th' worm," she will "never be saved" (lines 248–
49): she will die and, in Christian terms, will lose hope of
salvation by committing suicide.

CLEOPATRA Well, get thee gone, farewell.

270 CLOWN Yes, forsooth. I wish you joy o'th' worm.

Exit [leaving the basket]

[Enter IRAS *with a robe, crown, and other jewels]*

CLEOPATRA Give me my robe. Put on my crown. I have
Immortal longings in me. Now no more
The juice of Egypt's grape shall moist this lip.

*[*CHARMIAN *and* IRAS *help her to dress]*

Yare,° yare, good Iras, quick—methinks I hear   · Briskly
275 Antony call. I see him rouse himself
To praise my noble act. I hear him mock
The luck of Caesar, which the gods give men
To excuse their° after wrath. Husband, I come.   *(the gods')*
Now to that name my courage prove my title.
280 I am fire and air; my other elements
I give to baser life.[8] So, have you done?
Come then, and take the last warmth of my lips.

[She kisses them]

Farewell, kind Charmian. Iras, long farewell.

*[*IRAS *falls and dies]*

Have I the aspic° in my lips? Dost fall?   *asp*
285 If thou and nature can so gently part,
The stroke of death is as a lover's pinch,
Which hurts and is desired. Dost thou lie still?
If thus thou vanishest, thou tell'st the world
It is not worth leave-taking.

290 CHARMIAN Dissolve, thick cloud, and rain, that I may say
The gods themselves do weep.

CLEOPATRA   This proves me base.°   *ignoble*
If she first meet the curlèd° Antony   *curly-haired*
He'll make demand of° her, and spend that kiss *question; (sexual)*
Which is my heaven to have.

[She takes an aspic from the basket and puts it to her breast]

        Come, thou mortal wretch,° *deadly creature*
295 With thy sharp teeth this knot intrinsicate°   *intricate*
Of life at once untie. Poor venomous fool,
Be angry, and dispatch. O, couldst thou speak,
That I might hear thee call great Caesar ass
Unpolicied!°   *Outsmarted*

CHARMIAN O eastern star!°   *Venus; Cleopatra*

CLEOPATRA   Peace, peace.
300 Dost thou not see my baby at my breast,
That sucks the nurse asleep?

CHARMIAN   O, break! O, break!

CLEOPATRA As sweet as balm, as soft as air, as gentle.
O Antony!

[She puts another aspic to her arm]

   Nay, I will take thee too.
What° should I stay—   *[She] dies*   *Why*

---

8. *I am . . . life:* The "other elements" (line 280) are earth and water, the lower and heavier elements traditionally linked to women and thought to explain their fickleness. Cleopatra is particularly associated with these elements through her equation with (the mud of) Egypt. By asserting that she is only "fire and air," she is claiming to be manly (as in lines 234–35) and is also referring to the separation of the soul from the body at death.

CHARMIAN   In this vile world? So, fare thee well.
305   Now boast thee, death, in thy possession lies
      A lass unparalleled. Downy windows,° close,   *eyelids*
      And golden Phoebus never be beheld
      Of eyes again so royal. Your crown's awry.
      I'll mend it,° and then play—   *set it right*
            Enter the GUARD, *rustling° in*   *clattering*
310   FIRST GUARD   Where's the Queen?
      CHARMIAN   Speak softly. Wake her not.
      FIRST GUARD   Caesar hath sent—
      CHARMIAN   Too slow a messenger.
            [*She applies an aspic*]
      O come apace, dispatch! I partly feel thee.
      FIRST GUARD   Approach, ho! All's not well. Caesar's beguiled.°   *deceived*
315   SECOND GUARD   There's Dolabella sent from Caesar. Call him.
                                          [*Exit a* GUARDSMAN]
      FIRST GUARD   What work is here, Charmian? Is this well done?
      CHARMIAN   It is well done, and fitting for a princess
      Descended of so many royal kings.
      Ah, soldier!   CHARMIAN *dies*
            Enter DOLABELLA
      DOLABELLA   How goes it here?
      SECOND GUARD   All dead.
320   DOLABELLA   Caesar, thy thoughts
      Touch their effects° in this. Thyself art coming   *Are realized*
      To see performed the dreaded act which thou
      So sought'st to hinder.
      ALL   A way there, a way for Caesar!
            Enter CAESAR *and all his train, marching*
      DOLABELLA [*to* CAESAR]   O sir, you are too sure an augurer.
      That° you did fear is done.   *What*
325   CAESAR   Bravest at the last,
      She levelled at° our purposes, and, being royal,   *discerned rightly*
      Took her own way. The manner of their deaths?
      I do not see them bleed.
      DOLABELLA [*to a* GUARDSMAN]   Who was last with them?
      FIRST GUARD   A simple countryman that brought her figs.
      This was his basket.
      CAESAR   Poisoned, then.
330   FIRST GUARD   O Caesar,
      This Charmian lived but now; she stood and spake.
      I found her trimming up the diadem
      On her dead mistress; tremblingly she stood,
      And on the sudden dropped.
      CAESAR   O, noble weakness!
335   If they had swallowed poison, 'twould appear
      By external swelling; but she looks like sleep,
      As° she would catch another Antony   *As if*
      In her strong toil° of grace.   *snare*
      DOLABELLA   Here on her breast
      There is a vent of blood, and something blown.°   *emitted; swollen*
      The like is on her arm.
340   FIRST GUARD   This is an aspic's trail,
      And these fig-leaves have slime upon them such
      As th'aspic leaves upon the caves of Nile.

CAESAR   Most probable
That so she died; for her physician tells me
345   She hath pursued conclusions° infinite   *trial outcomes*
Of easy ways to die. Take up her bed,
And bear her women from the monument.
She shall be buried by her Antony.
No grave upon the earth shall clip° in it   *embrace*
350   A pair so famous. High events as these
Strike° those that make° them, and their story is   *Afflict / cause*
No less in pity than his glory⁹ which
Brought them to be lamented. Our army shall
In solemn show attend this funeral,
355   And then to Rome. Come, Dolabella, see
High order in this great solemnity.
                    Exeunt all [*soldiers bearing* CLEOPATRA *on her*
                              bed, CHARMIAN, *and* IRAS]

9. *their . . . glory:* there is no less pity in their story than there is glory in the exploits of Caesar. The immodesty of these lines, in the guise of praise, recalls Caesar's ambiguous grief, his combination of calculation and sentiment, at the news of Antony's death in 5.1. The historical Octavius Caesar went on to order the murder of Ptolemy XV (Caesarion), Cleopatra's son with Julius Caesar. Since Julius Caesar was Octavius's great-uncle and adoptive father, this act, which ended the Ptolemaic dynasty, might be seen as fraticide. See 2.1.37 with note, 2.2.233–34 with note, and 3.6.1–16 with note to line 6. By contrast, after Antony and Cleopatra's deaths, the historical Octavia, over her brother Octavius's objections, raised Anthony's children by Fulvia and Cleopatra, as well as her own five children with Antony and a previous husband.

Pericles, Prince of Tyre:
A Reconstructed Text

Pericles, Prince of Tyre (1607–08) was one of the most popular plays of its time and has proven effective in modern productions as well. Coherent and innovative, it brought a new dramatic genre—romance—into Shakespeare's work and, arguably, onto the English stage in general. As a text to be read, however, *Pericles* has sometimes proven more problematic. It is not clear whether the difficulty is intrinsic to the play or results from an almost irresistible but partly mistaken tendency to interpret it in light of Shakespeare's earlier works and thus to make unwarranted assumptions about plot, characterization, morality, dramaturgy, and style. Does the romance pattern fully succeed in mastering the messiness of the play's materials? Does the play raise but not resolve a series of social, political, and sexual anxieties, despite its considerable structural and thematic unity? Are these even the right questions to ask?

Shakespeare's younger contemporary Ben Jonson spoke for many subsequent critics in disparaging *Pericles* as "a mouldy tale . . . and stale," and in attributing its success on the stage to its use of "scraps out of every dish." It is easy to see what Jonson is talking about. In *Pericles,* a King adorns his palace walls with the skulls of his victims. A princess commits incest with her father. Another princess is kidnapped by pirates and sold to a brothel. Famine brings a city to its knees. An entire crew is lost in a tumultuous storm. Two royal families are sent to fiery destruction. And Pericles is almost deposed by his restless nobility.

From the perspective of genre, *Pericles* seems to enact a transition from one kind of romance to another. Pericles first looks like a knight-errant willing to risk death in his quest to win the beautiful maiden. But this standard mode of medieval romance quickly gives way to the manner of late antique Greek romance, in which the faithful and virtuous lovers must suffer separation and all manner of misfortune before their ultimate, triumphant reunion. Characteristically, then, Pericles does not act; he is acted upon. Bad things (as well as good) just keep happening to him. Every member of his family narrowly escapes death: two evade assassins sent by murderous monarchs, and the third survives burial at sea. Each is reported dead, only to experience apparently miraculous rebirth. The play seems consciously to eschew the complex probing of the protagonist's psyche that marks Shakespeare's immediately preceding tragic period in favor of clear-cut moral oppositions and an emphatic poetic justice. By the end of *Pericles,* the good have been rewarded and the bad annihilated, but, for the most part, not as a result of the protagonist's own efforts.

Indeed, Pericles does not even get to act out significant portions of his own destiny before the audience. Much of the story is told by Gower, the onstage presence of the fourteenth-century writer John Gower, whose major work, *Confessio Amantis,* is the most important direct source of *Pericles.* The eighth book of this verse narrative is devoted primarily to the tale of Apollonius of Tyre, which, via medieval intermediaries dating back to a fifth- or sixth-century Latin text, derives from a now-lost late classical Latin or, more probably, Greek romance influenced by *The Odyssey.* A different route through the medieval sources, this time incorporating the lives of early Christian saints who suffered persecution in brothels, leads to the other proximate source of the play, Laurence Twine's *Patterne of Painefull Adventures* (written by 1576; published 1594?). *Pericles* is the first dramatization of these lengthy traditions. The shift in the protagonist's name from "Apollonius" to "Pericles" may derive from still other strains in the Apollonius tradition; from

The true History of the Play of *Pericles*, as it was lately presented by the worthy and ancient Poet *John Gower*.

John Gower

Woodcut of John Gower, from the title page of *The Painfull Adventures of Pericles Prince of Tyre*, by George Wilkins (1608).

Sir Philip Sidney's *Arcadia* (1590), one of whose protagonists is named Pyrocles; or from one of Shakespeare's favorite sources, Plutarch's *Lives,* which perhaps provides still other characters' names. In addition to praising the renowned fifth-century-B.C.E. Athenian statesman Pericles, it harshly judges his rival and successor Cleon as well as the fourth-century general Lysimachus—all names of characters in the play.

Pericles follows its sources more faithfully than do many of Shakespeare's works. One sign of this fidelity is the retention of an episodic plot. More striking still is the appearance of Gower himself as a character. His role as chorus finds its predecessor in *Henry V* (1599), but Gower has the more specific function of giving a (pseudo-) medieval feel to the action. Although he eventually reverts to standard pentameter lines, he starts out primarily in the rhymed tetrameter couplets in which *Confessio Amantis* is written: "To sing a song that old was sung / From ashes ancient Gower is come" (1.1–2). In addition, the theatrical Gower's diction often echoes the medieval poet's, extending even to the use of deliberately antiquated language ("iwis" for "certainly," for example, at 5.2). His moralizing speeches are frequently graced by an unrealistic theatrical device—the dumb show. Further, Gower recounts much of the action in his eight monologues, as if to emphasize that poet's authorship of what sometimes feels like narrative, as opposed to dramatic, material. These strategies are all metatheatrical: they undermine the naturalistic illusion of the play, encouraging the audience to view events from a certain distance, to attend to the larger pattern that unfolds rather than becoming emotionally engaged. Part of the genius of *Pericles*, however, is ultimately to elicit that emotional engagement as well.

Gower's monologues also structure the play more effectively than does the division into five acts introduced by later editors (but not followed here). The scene often shifts within each of the seven main groupings, but there is always a central focus. Gower introduces Antioch and incest (Scene 1), Pentapolis and Pericles' wooing of Thaisa (5), Ephesus and the saving of Thaisa (10), Tarsus and the attempted murder of Marina (15), Mytilene and Marina's virtuous life in the brothel (18), Mytilene again and Marina's reunion with Pericles (20), and Ephesus and the reunion with Thaisa (22), before providing the brief epilogue with which the play concludes.

The actual authorship of *Pericles* is beset by unresolved questions, which are treated at length in the Textual Note. Here it is worth mentioning only that George Wilkins probably wrote most of the first nine scenes and Shakespeare most of the remaining thirteen. Acknowledgment of dual authorship is tied to the long-standing recognition of stylistic differences between the two parts of the play. Wilkins's section of the dialogue is closer to Gower's language than is Shakespeare's. Although both playwrights regularly compose verse in iambic pentameter, Wilkins uses far more end-stopped rhyming couplets than does Shakespeare. By contrast, Shakespeare's predilection for blank-verse enjambment, in which the phrase or idea does not conclude at the end of the line, produces a tension between syntax and verse form.

Thus Wilkins's Pericles decorously repudiates the incestuous Daughter of Antiochus:

> Fair glass of light, I loved you, and could still,
> Were not this glorious casket stored with ill.
> . . . .
> For he's no man on whom perfections wait
> That, knowing sin within, will touch the gate.
> . . . .
> But, being played upon before your time,
> Hell only danceth at so harsh a chime.
> (1.119–28)

Shakespeare's Pericles reacts to a storm in imagistically more complex but also more colloquial verse:

> . . . O still
> Thy deaf'ning dreadful thunders, gently quench
> Thy nimble sulph'rous flashes. . . .
> . . . .
> . . . The seaman's whistle
> Is as a whisper in the ears of death,
> Unheard.—Lychorida!—Lucina, O!
> Divinest patroness, and midwife gentle
> To those that cry by night, convey thy deity
> Aboard our dancing boat, make swift the pangs
> Of my queen's travails!—Now, Lychorida.
> (11.4–14)

As a result, Shakespeare's section of the play is theatrically livelier, the contrast with the increasingly frequent monologues by Gower correspondingly sharper. Pericles' meeting with the fishermen is the only episode by Wilkins that seems of a piece with such later parts of the play as the second tempest (quoted from above); the revival of Pericles' wife, Thaisa; the two brothel scenes; and the first recognition scene. And structurally, Pericles breaks neatly in two: in the first nine scenes, Pericles moves from felicity to misfortune and back to felicity; in the remaining thirteen, he simply repeats this pattern but with greater intensity.

Yet such distinctions are misleading. Many Renaissance plays were written by more than one dramatist; Shakespeare collaborated on about a quarter of his plays, mostly near the beginning and end of his career. Especially in performance, such works do not necessarily seem any less unified than single-author pieces. Even though its "feel" shifts, Pericles remains consistent throughout in motif—Pericles as a noble tree, his jewel-like family, destructive eating, providential storms, divine music.

Its episodes also echo one another, within and across the two parts of the play. The deadly skulls at Antiochus's palace are answered by the harmless jousting at Simonides' court, and the bad potential marriage to Antiochus's Daughter is echoed by the good real one to Simonides'. The incestuous relationship between Antiochus and his Daughter is contrasted with the lovingly innocent one between Pericles and Marina. Thaliart's foiled attempt to assassinate Pericles at Antiochus's behest anticipates Leonine's failed effort to murder Marina at Dionyza's. Cleon calls down the "curse of heav'n and men" (4.103) should his family ever prove ungrateful to Pericles, and when his family does so prove, "him and his they [his subjects] in his palace burn" (22.121). The storm that costs Pericles his men but leads him to Thaisa is paralleled by the later tempest that apparently disposes of Thaisa. The vigorous popular culture of the fishermen is set against the degraded popular culture of the brothel. The vow of chastity Simonides attributes to Thaisa to get rid of all her suitors except Pericles is fulfilled both in her genuine vow of chastity when she thinks Pericles gone forever and in Marina's successful defense of her chastity in the brothel. The apparent burial of Thaisa is duplicated in the apparent interment of her daughter. And, more broadly, the excessive love of Antiochus for his daughter and, in a different way, of Dionyza for hers are contrasted with the defective love of Cleon for his daughter and, arguably, of Pericles for Marina—until the end of the play, when Pericles demonstrates the appropriate love of father for daughter: neither too much nor too little.

Throughout, the play insists that the concatenation of miseries inflicted on Pericles and his family ultimately leads to a higher felicity. As noted earlier, this is the structure of tragicomic romance, the genre of nearly all of Shakespeare's final plays. Typically, *Pericles* recapitulates Shakespeare's previous work while reversing its chronology: the tragic mood of the early seventeenth century precedes the comic tone of the 1590s. The play echoes *King Lear* both in its storm scenes and in its reunion of ravaged father and redemptive daughter, who gives "another life / To Pericles thy father" (21.194–95); it then duplicates *The Comedy of Errors*, which draws on the same sources as *Pericles* in its concluding retrieval of the missing wife-turned-priestess from the temple of Diana at Ephesus.

Gower reassuringly emphasizes this larger pattern—"I'll show you those in trouble's reign, / Losing a mite, a mountain gain" (5.7–8)—which becomes especially prominent in Shakespeare's scenes due to the presiding benevolence of Diana. She is first mentioned when, according to Simonides, Thaisa opts for continued virginity (9.9). Then Thaisa invokes her upon awakening in an opened coffin, as does Pericles when he vows not to cut his hair until his baby, Marina, is married (12.102, 13.28). Thaisa becomes her priestess, and Marina places her virginity in the goddess's protection (14.12, 15.4, 16.131). Finally, after Pericles is reunited with Marina, Diana appears to him in a dream, promising him happiness only if he goes to her temple in Ephesus and publicly recounts his loss of Thaisa (21.224–34). This supernatural moment recalls Thaisa's quasi-magical preservation by Cerimon (of whom Pericles says, "The gods can have no mortal officer / More like a god than you," 22.85–86), anticipates Pericles' actual meeting with Thaisa in the final scene (where Diana is repeatedly mentioned), and follows hard upon Pericles' perhaps unique ability to hear "the music of the spheres" (21.214)—the sound of a heavenly harmony that extends to human affairs below. A

Scenic view of the temple of Diana, designed by Inigo Jones for the pastoral *Florentine* (1635).

special sensitivity to music has marked Pericles' family throughout. Pericles is "music's master," Thaisa awakens to "still and woeful music," and, most tellingly, Marina "sings like one immortal" (9.28, 12.86, 20.3).

Although these visual and auditory signs of a divine providence guiding the destiny of Pericles' family are pagan in form, they are Christian in content. Tragicomedy's movement from tribulation to triumph is modeled on the *felix culpa*, the fortunate fall of Adam and Eve that led to the redemptive coming of Christ. Antioch recalls the sinister side of Eden: Pericles will "taste the fruit of yon celestial tree / Or die in the adventure"; Antiochus praises the "golden fruit, but dang'rous to be touched" and later warns, "Touch not, upon thy life" (1.64–65, 71, 130). The eastern Mediterranean of late Greek antiquity in which *Pericles* is set also carries connotations of Judaism and early Christianity. Tyre is connected with the reigns of David and Solomon, and was captured by the Christian forces in the First Crusade. Antioch recalls the rebellion of the Maccabees; in addition, Peter and Paul preached there. Paul was born in Tarsus and had a lengthy ministry in Ephesus. The fishermen on the shore of Pentapolis are literally, like St. Peter, fishers of men. Amid talk of devouring whales (5.63–80), they fish out Pericles, whom "the sea hath cast upon [their] coast" (5.92) in a manner that recalls the biblical Jonah, understood in Christian allegory to prefigure Christ's resurrection. Thaisa later undergoes a similar resurrection; and at Mytilene, the Pander laments, "Neither is our profession any mystery, it's no calling" (16.32–33)—where both "mystery" and "calling" have religious reverberations.

In a final, typically moralistic speech, Gower tells the audience,

> In Pericles, his queen, and daughter seen,
> Although assailed with fortune fierce and keen,
> Virtue preserved from fell destruction's blast,
> Led on by heav'n, and crowned with joy at last.
> (22.110–13)

Although there is no ambiguity here, the play as a whole leaves room for doubts on structural, social and political, and sexual grounds. First, despite the overarching pattern of the triumph over a pagan "fortune" by an implicitly Christian "heav'n," Pericles' sufferings feel arbitrary. It is hard to understand, except according to fairy-tale logic, why his predecessors cannot solve Antiochus's obvious riddle or why the King advertises the very secret he wants to preserve. Similarly, the play does not explain why Pericles leaves his daughter at Tarsus or why Dionyza, eager to be rid of Marina, does not consider sending her home instead of murdering her. More important, the misfortunes in *Pericles* seem unrelenting, unconnected, and unrelated to the character or behavior of their victims. Yet this disjunction fails to inspire any Job-like reflections on injustice. In short, the triumph of divine providence is not fully integrated with the secular saga of misfortune. Perhaps, then, the play reveals a contingent relationship between human vicissitude and redemptive transcendence, thereby raising questions about its own ostensible program.

Second, *Pericles* bears a complicated relationship to its own social and political material. The representation of popular culture provides some of the play's most engaging scenes without, however, always linking up to the larger movement of the plot. The initial storm leaves Pericles "bereft / Unfortunately both of ships and men" (7.79–80). The fishermen who then help him repeatedly receive his praise:

> MASTER ... I can compare our rich misers to nothing so fitly as to a whale: a plays and tumbles, driving the poor fry before him, and at last devours them all at a mouthful. ...
> PERICLES [*aside*] A pretty moral.
> (5.68–73)

This disabused account, which may echo the language of the 1607 Midlands Uprising against landlord enclosures of the common lands, leads to a rebuke of the monarch: "If the good King Simonides were of my mind . . . we would purge the land of these drones that rob the bee of her honey" (5.80–84). But the complaint quickly disappears, leaving only the positive image of Pericles' future father-in-law. Similarly, although Pericles promises the fishermen "if that ever my low fortune's better, / I'll pay your bounties, till then rest your debtor" (5.177–78), the debt, which is usually honored in previous tales of Apollonius (including Twine's), is not recalled when Pericles' fortunes quickly improve.

The anticommercial outlook implicit in the Master's denunciation of "rich misers" also informs the brothel scenes, which, like Pericles' encounter with the fishermen, replaces the predominantly Greek Mediterranean setting of the plot with recognizably English characters. Prostitution is the only market-driven activity depicted in the play, although Gower later reports that Marina graduates to an honest livelihood. Earlier, the Bawd advises her in economic terms: "You have fortunes coming upon you. Mark me, you must seem to do that fearfully which you commit willingly, to despise profit where you have most gain. To weep that you live as ye do makes pity in your lovers. Seldom but that pity begets you a good opinion, and that opinion a mere profit" (16.101–06). Marina is thus urged to perform like an actor at one of London's professional theaters. With commerce almost reduced to the oldest profession, a profession widely practiced in the neighborhoods around the theaters, the play implicitly links itself to the very activity that it simultaneously depicts Marina nobly resisting.

Thus, despite successfully exploiting popular culture for theatrical effect, *Pericles* fails to incorporate that culture into the final reconciliation: the play concludes with a purely aristocratic and royal circle. This ending is tacitly anticipated by the linguistic class divisions of the popular scenes: the fishermen and the brothelkeepers speak prose, whereas Pericles and Marina favor blank verse. Nevertheless, *Pericles* is the only one of Shakespeare's romances written before the King's Men began performing during the winter at Blackfriars, a "private," elite, commercial theater. It was acted at the Globe, the preeminent "public" theater, and its success in the early seventeenth century attests to the enduring, at least partly popular appeal of its traditional romance plot.

Furthermore, *Pericles* seems to take its distance from absolute monarchy—in the fishermen's insistence on their rights and in popular political assertiveness at Tarsus. This is important because the political value of aristocratic leadership is questionable. Antioch has been ruled by an incestuous murderer, and there is no indication of his successor. The Governor of Tarsus lets his city slip into famine; his wife is an attempted murderer. Although the inhabitants eventually kill the couple, their own earlier behavior does not inspire confidence: "All poverty was scorned, and pride so great / The name of help grew odious to repeat" (4.30–31). Under duress they are even worse:

> Those mothers who to nuzzle up their babes
> Thought naught too curious are ready now
> To eat those little darlings whom they loved.
> (4.42–44)

The passage echoes in reverse the riddle's equation of cannibalism with incest—"I feed / On mother's flesh" (1.107–08)—while also recalling numerous other moments where "to eat" is to devour. Ephesus's future remains unspecified: Lord Cerimon acts as a private figure. The Governor of Mytilene frequents a brothel until Marina converts him; at the end of the play, the brothel remains, while the Governor, betrothed to Marina, leaves Mytilene in uncertain hands and goes off to rule Tyre.

Earlier, Pericles' departure from Tyre inspires aristocratic "mutiny" (10.29) and begins the practice of absentee landlordism that reaches its climax near the end of the play when his deputy, Helicanus, appoints Aeschines as *his* deputy and sets out with Pericles. Shortly thereafter, Pericles and Thaisa accede to the throne of Pentapolis, a society whose virtues and defects the fishermen have earlier dissected. The death of Thaisa's father, "the good Simonides," is treated not as an occasion for grief but as an opportunity to dole out kingdoms and break up a family that has only just been reunited.

This outcome may parallel the isolation of the various members of James I's family, an isolation emblematized by James's failure to come to the deathbeds of two of his children. Pericles' absenteeism may also reflect on James's style of governing. Alternatively, it may simply recognize the necessity of intergenerational separation for dynastic continuity, just as the redemptive role of Marina may reflect upon Shakespeare's relationship to his own daughter.

Yet *Pericles* also raises sexual doubts. Although the play subjects its protagonists to debased sexuality only to demonstrate their Diana-like purity, they perhaps do not escape unpolluted. In Gower's *Confessio Amantis*, Pericles' daughter is not Marina but Thaisa. From an extradramatic and extratextual perspective, then, sexual relations with Thaisa, which in Gower would have been incest, are here converted into perfectly appropriate marital intimacy. It is almost as if the name change allows Pericles to have the very experience castigated in Antioch under the protection of the marriage bond. When the nearly catatonic Pericles arrives in Mytilene, Lysimachus agrees that Marina might be the cure:

> She questionless, with her sweet harmony
> And other choice attractions, would alarum [Quarto has "allure"]
> And make a batt'ry through his deafened ports.
>
> (21.34–36)

"Alarum" in the second line works better with the last line, but the Quarto's reading goes well with "choice attractions"; thus, "allure" may be correct. If so, Lysimachus, ignorant of Marina's parentage, is suggesting a potentially unfamilial relationship between father and daughter. So, too, does Pericles. He addresses Marina as "thou that begett'st him that did thee beget" (21.182), a line that may simply express gratitude for bringing him back to life. These words recall the generational reversals of Antiochus's incestuous riddle: "He's father, son, and husband mild; / I mother, wife, and yet his child" (1.111–12).

Tragicomic romance often provides a nontragic resolution to the tale of Oedipus, Pericles' predecessor in solving murderous riddles. Do Pericles' words to Marina reverse or repeat Antiochus's riddle? Ambiguities such as this one trouble the providential pattern. By name Pericles recalls an Athenian virtue at odds with the quasi-allegorical landscape through which he travels, a landscape of Asiatic luxury and decadence, of an incest associated with tyranny whose primary alternative seems to be anarchy. In other words, the various social, political, and sexual ambiguities of *Pericles* bear less on the psychology or morality of the protagonist than on the overall import of the play.

Modern performances of *Pericles* have increasingly embraced the challenge posed by this pattern. Although some productions attempt to create naturalistic settings and complex characters, most respect *Pericles*'s relative indifference to such matters by exploiting what's unrealistic about the play and about Renaissance theater generally. First, the doubling of parts has led to the same actress playing Antiochus's Daughter and Marina, Marina and Thaisa, or Thaisa and Dionyza. This procedure can accentuate the differences between the paired characters; more often, however, it has generated an overtone of incest. Relatedly, when one actor plays all the Mediterranean kings, the stage is able to capture the underlying similarity, the repetitiousness, of Pericles' adventures and, hence, the formal, ritualistic quality of the work. Second, although the figure of Gower can establish intimacy between audience and action, the tendency has been to follow the German dramatist Bertolt Brecht in resisting empathy and identification. Gower's role is thus made to underscore the play's theatricality: it has at various times been sung, treated as a voice-over, and played by a street performer. The dramatized action itself has been represented as street theater, as the work of a traveling troupe, as Chinese opera, as an African-American boatswain's sea chantey to his fellow sailors aboard ship, as a child's picture book, as events in an asylum, as the floor show in a gay brothel. One consequence of these techniques has sometimes been an ironic, farcical approach to the absurdities of the plot. The price, however, is the failure of the climactic recognition scenes, which thrive on psychological nuance. Similar problems may arise with overtly political interpretations, though a feminist or multi-ethnic perspective can be a highly suggestive response to the text. Perhaps the solution, in reading as well as performance, is to refuse to level the unevenness of the play, remaining faithful to its various and complex registers.

WALTER COHEN

TEXTUAL NOTE

Pericles, Prince of Tyre poses insuperable textual problems. At some point between 1606 and 1608, most likely in late 1607 or early 1608, Shakespeare probably collaborated on a draft of *Pericles* with George Wilkins, a freelance playwright whose *Miseries of Inforst Mariage* had been successfully staged around 1606 by Shakespeare's company, the King's Men. The exact mechanism of the collaboration is unknown, but Wilkins seems to have composed most of Scenes 1–9 (Acts 1–2 in other modern editions) and Shakespeare most of Scenes 10–22 (Acts 3–5). Each dramatist may also have had a small share in the other's part: for instance, Wilkins seems to have been involved with Gower throughout, writing all of his fifth monologue (Scene 18) and his epilogue (end of Scene 22).

The central evidence for dual authorship and for the attribution to Wilkins is the stylistic disparity between the two sections of the play. The style of the first nine scenes shares a prosaic manner, end-stopped versification, and rhyming couplets with Wilkins's other works during these years. It does not resemble Shakespeare's style at any time (or that of anyone else besides Wilkins proposed so far). By contrast, the final thirteen scenes are in Shakespeare's characteristically idiosyncratic late style, marked by complex imagery and, even more notably, by a radical use of enjambment. At various times, scholars have offered alternative explanations—that Shakespeare wrote the first part of *Pericles* early in his career and came back to it years later; that he wrote it all at once but that the two parts were differently mangled on the path from his manuscript to the printed page; that he deliberately shifted styles midway through the play for aesthetic effect; or that he did collaborate, but with someone other than Wilkins. None of these claims is nearly as plausible as the assumption of joint authorship by Wilkins and Shakespeare.

The play was probably first performed between December 1607 and May 1608, and was apparently a commercial success at the Globe. The King's Men seem to have submitted the company's official promptbook of *Pericles* to the Stationers' Register May 20, 1608, ostensibly with intent to print. Since ownership of the play rested not with the playwright but with the company, however, their real purpose may have been to block Wilkins from illegally exploiting *Pericles*'s popularity by selling it to a publisher himself—something he seems to have done the previous year with *The Miseries of Inforst Mariage*. In the event, the play was not printed in 1608; nonetheless, if the King's Men were trying to stop publication, their strategy failed in at least two respects.

First, Wilkins published a prose rendering of the story entitled *The Painfull Adventures of Pericles Prince of Tyre* sometime in 1608. Its title page advertises its indebtedness to the theatrical version, which for the most part, primarily in Scenes 1–9, it resembles. Yet even in these early scenes, Wilkins's narrative is not as close to the play as might be expected. One purely speculative theory is that he was following not Shakespeare's *Pericles* but an earlier play. It is far more likely, however, that as a collaborating dramatist unattached to an acting company, he would not necessarily have retained a manuscript of the part he wrote and might never have had a personal copy of the entire, jointly authored piece. Indeed, given Wilkins's previous behavior, the King's Men may have made a point of keeping the text out of his hands. *The Painfull Adventures* thus seems to record Wilkins's memory of the play that he recently had helped to write. That memory is less accurate, of course, in the parts he did not compose.

Perhaps the King's Men were unable to prevent publication in another way as well. In 1609, one or more actors who had performed in *Pericles* may have sold it for publication. If so, he or they had to reassemble the text from memory, since an actor routinely possessed a written version of little more than his own part. Since the unauthorized publication of the manuscript would have hurt the interests of the company's actor-shareholders such as Shakespeare, the actors most likely to have gone to press are thus to be found elsewhere. Arguably (although this is disputed), the text was the work of the boy actor who played Lychorida and Marina, as well as some minor other parts, and of a hired man who may have been one of the fishermen and the Pander, again among other small roles. For this claim to hold, these two actors would also had to have acquired a copy of Gower's speeches: perhaps the boy was apprenticed to the actor-shareholder who played Gower.

Almost inevitably, an actor's report significantly differs not only from what Shakespeare wrote but also from what was actually performed. Evidence for this divergence in *Pericles* is to be found especially in the large number of errors in meter, but perhaps also in the repeated confusion of verse and prose (although this may be a product of printing) and in the high degree of verbal repetition. The conjectural identification of the actors who reconstructed the text is based on the relative absence of these defects from the speeches of the characters they presumably played and from the scenes in which they appear. Certainly, the process of reporting cannot account for the stylistic differences between the two parts of the play. The First Quarto (Q1) of *Pericles* was typeset in two printing houses: probably one compositor worked in the first shop, two in the second. But here, again, the division between shops and among compositors does not correspond to the stylistic shift beginning in Scene 10. Neither can compositorial error explain most of the defects in the text. And although the title page names Shakespeare as the author, four other plays published in Quarto before 1623 and attributed to William Shakespeare as well as three more assigned to "W.S." were clearly written by others.

As noted in the Introduction, *Pericles* remained extremely popular in the early seventeenth century. It was revived several times through 1631—at the Globe, on tour in the countryside, and before a more elite audience. The print record is similarly extensive: the Second Quarto (Q2) appeared in the same year as the first, 1609, with subsequent quartos in 1611, 1619, 1630, and 1635. Each was based on the previous Quarto, although Q6 also drew on Q4. But *Pericles* was excluded from the First Folio (F) in 1623, perhaps because the editors thought of it as a collaborative piece. It was published in the second issue of the Third Folio (1664), which relied on Q6; again in the Fourth Folio (1685), which used the Third Folio; and in some major early eighteenth-century editions. But the play then largely dropped out of Shakespeare's works until 1780, when Edmund Malone successfully reintroduced it and provided it with the act and scene divisions—both lacking in Q1—subsequent editors have usually accepted. The play has been routinely included in Shakespeare's canon since then.

Because all editions ultimately derive from Q1, *Pericles* occupies a unique status. For every other Shakespearean play with the ambiguous exception of *Richard III*, at least one early printed version apparently draws directly on either an authorial manuscript or a scribal transcript of it, such as a promptbook. (*Sir Thomas More* remained unpublished during the Renaissance and survives in an authorial manuscript.) Since no reasonably authoritative text of *Pericles* exists, even the claim that Q1 is a report of a performance cannot depend on comparison with a presumably more accurate version but must rely on internal evidence alone. Various unsatisfactory alternatives thus confront an editor. The most commonly adopted strategy in the last fifty years has been to emend the text only conservatively to increase its intelligibility. This approach has the obvious advantage of avoiding the introduction of many new deviations from the original play. On the other hand, it is unlikely to preserve the early printed version, the early performed version, or the authors' original version.

The Oxford editors have taken a different tack. In their original-spelling edition, they reprint Q1. In their modern-spelling edition, followed here, they take advantage of the probable dual authorship of the play and the survival of Wilkins's *Painfull Adventures,* which they treat as a reported text, like Q1. Primarily in Wilkins's share of the play (Scenes 1–9) and in the brothel scenes, this edition draws on *The Painfull Adventures (PA)* when the reporting in Q1 seems to be poor and when Wilkins's prose version seems superior in logic, language, or meter and is not invalidated as a report of the play by dependence on another printed source (Laurence Twine's *The Patterne of Painefull Adventures,* 1594?). Although the rationale for this procedure is clearly strengthened by the assumption that Wilkins wrote the first nine scenes, it is not completely dependent on it.

Wilkins's prose is often metrical, as if he were remembering verse drama. Emendation based on *PA* regularly involves the conversion of prose into verse, as well as a wide variety of discretionary decisions. This policy improves the sense in many places (especially Scene 2). Further, Q1 lacks but apparently refers to a short passage displaying Pericles' musical talent that is reconstructed here (Scene 8a). In addition, by following Wilkins's prose, the rationale for Pericles' marriage to Thaisa is shifted from the nobility of his birth to the nobility of his soul (Scene 9). The same strategy of borrowing, in this instance inspired by the suspicion—disputed by other editors—that Q1 reports a politically censored version of the dialogue between Marina and Lysimachus, initially places Lysimachus in a harsher light (Scene 19). Finally, because this edition's scene divisions often differ from those in other modern editions, the play is divided into scenes but not acts.

Although previous scholars and editors have drawn on *PA* and even engaged in conjectural reconstruction of long passages, this version of *Pericles* pursues such an approach more radically and is bound to remain controversial. It can be criticized not only if some of its underlying assumptions are faulty but even if all of them prove correct. The chance is nil that so many emendations, many of them major, will accurately reproduce what was originally written or performed. Yet this is to say no more than that the Oxford edition takes bigger risks than do its predecessors, but on a play where risk taking makes sense. As already noted, if Q1 is a reported text, other modern editions cannot possibly reproduce the original play at all accurately. This edition may deviate more widely than they do from the original version of *Pericles;* then, again, it may well approximate that version more closely.

So that readers can form their own judgments on this question, for each scene the notes provide the act and scene equivalents in most modern texts of *Pericles.* Where scene division departs from the editorial norm, the deviation is explained. More important, the notes also record every emendation drawn from *PA* that significantly alters the meaning, and every emendation that is one line or longer. Rationales for most of these changes are supplied as well. To avoid overloading the notes to the point of unreadability, less substantial changes appear only in the Textual Variants, which provide selected examples of the conversion in this edition of Q1's prose into verse and a complete record of the verbal borrowings from *PA,* with full quotation except where Wilkins's prose is exactly followed.

SELECTED BIBLIOGRAPHY

Archibald, Elizabeth. *Apollonius of Tyre: Medieval and Renaissance Themes and Variations, Including the Text of the "Historia Apollonii Regis Tyri" with an English Translation.* Cambridge, Eng.: Brewer, 1991. A study of the literary tradition that provided the source material for *Pericles.*

Frye, Susan. "Incest and Authority in *Pericles, Prince of Tyre.*" *Incest and the Literary Imagination.* Ed. Elizabeth Barnes. Gainesville: University Press of Florida, 2002. 39–58. Focuses on three key scenes (incest, tournament, reunion) to argue that incest—understood physically, politically, and psychologically—is tied to questions of the royal family's legitimacy.

Gossett, Suzanne. "'You not your child well loving': Text and Family Structure in *Pericles.*" *A Companion to Shakespeare's Works.* IV: *Poems, Problem Comedies, Late*

Plays. Ed. Richard Dutton and Jean E. Howard. Malden, Mass.: Blackwell, 2003. 348–64. The play as exploration of the proper love between parent and daughter (neither excessive nor deficient), perhaps rooted in Shakespeare's own family experience.

Halpern, Richard. *Shakespeare Among the Moderns*. Ithaca, N.Y.: Cornell University Press, 1997. 140–58. Weak internal causal logic of the plot combined with transcendent romance plan as symptomatic response to decaying older social order.

Jordan, Constance. *Shakespeare's Monarchies: Ruler and Subject in the Romances*. Ithaca, N.Y.: Cornell University Press, 1997. 35–67. A political reading of the play in light of humanist theory; the work espouses mixed or limited monarchy against divine right of kings.

Nevo, Ruth. *Shakespeare's Other Language*. New York: Methuen, 1987. 33–61. Antiochus as Pericles' double, revealing the incest fear the protagonist must flee in a journey through other doubles to an ambiguous resolution.

Orkin, Martin. *Local Shakespeares: Proximations and Power*. London: Routledge, 2005. 63–81. *Pericles* as meditation on male unruliness, in this way providing a partial critique of its own patriarchal romance resolution.

Palfrey, Simon. *Late Shakespeare: A New World of Words*. Oxford: Clarendon, 1997. 57–78. *Pericles* as a skeptical reworking of romance; Pericles as post-heroic protagonist, dependent on popular support.

Skeele, David. *Thwarting the Wayward Seas: A Critical and Theatrical History of Shakespeare's "Pericles" in the Nineteenth and Twentieth Centuries*. Newark: University of Delaware Press, 1998. Charts the shifts from nineteenth-century negative critical views combined with occasional spectacle-based productions, through modernist emphasis on the play's unity, to contemporary celebrations of its disunity.

———, ed. *"Pericles": Critical Essays*. New York: Garland, 2000. A collection of criticism beginning with Ben Jonson in the early seventeenth century and of theatrical reviews beginning in the mid-nineteenth. Modern critics include Knight, Felperin, Barber and Wheeler, Kahn, Mullaney, Adelman, and Novy, among others.

FILM

Pericles, Prince of Tyre. 1984. Dir. David Hugh Jones. UK. 177 min. Generally praised BBC production, naturalistic by TV-studio standards but not by those of big-budget movies.

Pericles, Prince of Tyre:
A Reconstructed Text

THE PERSONS OF THE PLAY

John GOWER, the Presenter
ANTIOCHUS, King of Antioch
His DAUGHTER
THALIART, a villain
PERICLES, Prince of Tyre
HELICANUS }
AESCHINES } two grave counsellors of Tyre
MARINA, Pericles' daughter
CLEON, Governor of Tarsus
DIONYZA, his wife
LEONINE, a murderer
KING SIMONIDES, of Pentapolis
THAISA, his daughter
Three FISHERMEN, his subjects
Five PRINCES, suitors of Thaisa
A MARSHAL
LYCHORIDA, Thaisa's nurse
A ship MASTER
CERIMON, a physician of Ephesus
PHILEMON, his servant
LYSIMACHUS, Governor of Mytilene
A BAWD
A PANDER
BOULT, servant to Bawd and Pander
DIANA, goddess of chastity
Lords, ladies, pages, messengers, sailors, pirates, knights,
gentlemen

Scene 1

Enter GOWER[1] [as Prologue]

GOWER To sing a song that old° was sung[2]   *of old*
From ashes ancient Gower is come,
Assuming man's infirmities°   *Donning mortal flesh*
To glad your ear and please your eyes.
5   It hath been sung at festivals,
On ember-eves and holy-ales,[3]
And lords and ladies in their lives
Have read it for restoratives.°   *as a medicine*

Scene 1 (Q1 lacks act and scene divisions; the present edition numbers scenes consecutively throughout, omitting act divisions [see the Textual Note]. Other modern versions treat Gower's monologue as a prologue and start Act 1, Scene 1, at line 43. This edition, however, assumes that the row of heads referred to by Gower and Antiochus ["yon," lines 40, 77] is seen from roughly the same position both times and is first revealed after line 39. But the heads could be visible from the start.)

Location: The palace at Antioch.
1. Fourteenth-century English poet, whose story of Apollonius of Tyre in the eighth book of his *Confessio Amantis* is an important source of the play. See the Introduction.
2. Like most of Gower's choruses in the play, this one is mainly in rhyming tetrameter couplets.
3. *ember-eves:* evenings before periods of religious fasting. *holy-ales:* country festivals.

	The purchase° is to make men glorious,	*benefit*
10	*Et bonum quo antiquius eo melius.*⁴	
	If you, born in these latter times	
	When wit's more ripe,° accept my rhymes,	*poetry's more advanced*
	And that° to hear an old man sing	*And if*
	May to your wishes pleasure bring,	
15	I life would wish, and that I might	
	Waste° it for you like taper°-light.	*Use it up / candle*
	This'° Antioch, then; Antiochus the Great⁵	*This is*
	Built up this city for his chiefest seat,°	*capital*
	The fairest in all Syria.	
20	I tell you what mine authors° say.	*sources*
	This king unto him took a fere°	*mate*
	Who died, and left a female heir	
	So buxom,° blithe, and full of face°	*lively / attractive?*
	As° heav'n had lent her all his° grace,	*As if / its*
25	With whom the father liking took,	
	And her to incest did provoke.	
	Bad child, worse father, to entice his own	
	To evil should° be done by none.	*that should*
	By custom what they did begin	
30	Was with long use account' no sin.⁶	
	The beauty of this sinful dame	
	Made many princes thither frame°	*go*
	To seek her as a bedfellow,	
	In marriage pleasures playfellow,	
35	Which to prevent he made a law	
	To keep her still,° and men in awe,	*always*
	That whoso asked her for his wife,	
	His riddle told not,⁷ lost his life.	
	So for her many a wight° did die,	*fellow*
	[*A row of heads is revealed*]	
40	As yon grim looks do testify.	
	What now ensues, to th' judgement of your eye	
	I give, my cause who best can justify.⁸ *Exit*	
	[*Sennet.*]° *Enter* [*King*] ANTIOCHUS, *Prince* PERICLES,⁹	*Trumpet*
	and [*lords and peers in their richest ornaments*]	
	ANTIOCHUS Young Prince of Tyre,¹ you have at large received°	*fully understood*
	The danger of the task you undertake.	
45	PERICLES I have, Antiochus, and with a soul	
	Emboldened with the glory of her praise	
	Think death no hazard in this enterprise.	
	ANTIOCHUS Music!	
	[*Music sounds*]	
	Bring in our daughter, clothèd like a bride	
50	Fit for th'embracements ev'n of Jove himself,	
	At whose conception, till Lucina reigned,	
	Nature this dowry gave to glad her presence:²	

4. And the older something good is, the better (Latin).
5. *Antioch . . . Antiochus:* Recalling the Maccabee rebellion and the missions of Peter and Paul.
6. *By . . . sin:* When what they started (incest) became a habit, they no longer experienced it as a sin.
7. If he failed to explain Antiochus's riddle.
8. *my . . . justify:* which (your eye's "judgement") will best perceive the truth of my story.
9. *Pericles:* Named after Pericles, the fifth-century

B.C.E. Athenian leader, from Plutarch's *Lives*, or Pyrocles, a protagonist in Sidney's *Arcadia* (1590).
1. *Tyre:* Associated with David and Solomon; captured by a Christian army in the First Crusade.
2. *At . . . presence:* During pregnancy, until my daughter was born (Lucina was the Roman goddess of childbirth, often equated with Diana), nature gave her this dowry to make her presence welcome (or to make her happy).

The senate-house of planets all did sit,
In her their best perfections to knit.[3]

Enter Antiochus' DAUGHTER

55　PERICLES　See where she comes, apparelled like the spring,
Graces her subjects,[4] and her thoughts the king
Of ev'ry virtue gives° renown to men;　　　　　　　　　　*that gives*
Her face the book of praises,[5] where is read
Nothing but curious° pleasures, as° from thence　　　*delicate / as if*
60　Sorrow were ever razed and testy wrath
Could never be her mild° companion.　　　　　　　*(modifies "her")*
You gods that made me man, and sway° in love,　　　　*hold sway*
That have inflamed desire in my breast
To taste the fruit of yon celestial tree
65　Or die in the adventure, be my helps,
As I am son and servant to your will,
To compass° such a boundless happiness.　　　　　　　*attain*
ANTIOCHUS　Prince Pericles—
PERICLES　That would be son to great Antiochus.
70　ANTIOCHUS　Before thee stands this fair Hesperides,
With golden fruit, but dang'rous to be touched,
　　[*He gestures towards the heads*]
For death-like dragons here affright thee hard.[6]
　　[*He gestures towards his* DAUGHTER]
Her heav'n-like face enticeth thee to view
Her countless° glory, which desert must gain;　　　　*(like the stars)*
75　And which without desert, because thine eye
Presumes to reach, all the whole heap° must die.　　*your whole body*
Yon sometimes° famous princes, like thyself　　　　　*at one time*
Drawn by report, advent'rous by° desire,　　　*taking a risk out of*
Tell thee with speechless tongues and semblants° bloodless　*appearances*
80　That without covering save yon field of stars
Here they stand, martyrs slain in Cupid's wars,
And with dead cheeks advise thee to desist
From going on° death's net, whom none resist.　　　　　*into*
PERICLES　Antiochus, I thank thee, who hath taught
85　My frail mortality to know itself,
And by those fearful objects to prepare
This body, like to them, to what I must;[7]
For death remembered should be like a mirror
Who tells us life's but breath, to trust it error.
90　I'll make my will then, and, as sick men do,
Who know the world, see heav'n, but feeling woe
Grip not at earthly joys as erst° they did,　　　　　　*previously*
So I bequeath a happy peace to you
And all good men, as ev'ry prince should do;
95　My riches to the earth from whence they came,
[*To the* DAUGHTER] But my unspotted fire of love to you.
[*To* ANTIOCHUS] Thus ready for the way of life or death,
I wait the sharpest blow, Antiochus.

3. *The . . . knit*: Astrological forces arranged to give her
every perfection.
4. With mastery of all human graces.
5. The anthology of all that is commendable.
6. *Before . . . hard*: The Hesperides (here representing
Antiochus's Daughter) were daughters of Hesperus inhabiting a garden where golden apples grew, whose entrance
was patrolled by a dragon. The "golden fruit, but dan-
g'rous to be touched," like "the fruit of yon celestial tree"
(line 64), also evokes Eden.
7. *to what I must*: for death.

ANTIOCHUS   Scorning advice, read the conclusion° then,   *riddle*
    [*He angrily throws down the riddle*]
100   Which read and not expounded, 'tis decreed,
    As these before thee, thou thyself shalt bleed.
DAUGHTER [*to* PERICLES]   Of all 'sayed° yet, mayst thou prove   *who have tried (assayed)*
        prosperous;
    Of all 'sayed yet, I wish thee happiness.
PERICLES   Like a bold champion I assume the lists,°   *enter combat*
105   Nor ask advice of any other thought
    But faithfulness and courage.
        [*He takes up and reads aloud*] *the riddle*
    I am no viper, yet I feed
    On mother's flesh which did me breed.[8]
    I sought a husband, in which labour
110   I found that kindness° in a father.   *kinship; affection*
    He's father, son, and husband mild;
    I mother, wife, and yet his child.
    How this may be and yet in two,°   *only two people*
    As you will live resolve it you.
115   Sharp physic is the last.[9] [*Aside*] But O, you powers
    That gives heav'n countless eyes° to view men's acts,   *(the stars)*
    Why cloud they not their sights perpetually
    If this be true which makes me pale to read it?
        [*He gazes on the* DAUGHTER]
    Fair glass° of light, I loved you, and could still,   *image*
120   Were not this glorious casket stored with ill.[1]
    But I must tell you now my thoughts revolt,
    For he's no man on whom perfections wait°   *(as servants)*
    That, knowing sin within, will touch the gate.
    You're a fair viol,[2] and your sense° the strings   *senses*
125   Who, fingered to make man his lawful music,
    Would draw heav'n down and all the gods to hearken,
    But, being played upon before your time,
    Hell only danceth at so harsh a chime.
    Good sooth,° I care not for you.   *Truly*
130 ANTIOCHUS   Prince Pericles, touch not,[3] upon thy life,
    For that's an article within our law
    As dang'rous as the rest. Your time's expired.
    Either expound now, or receive your sentence.
PERICLES   Great King,
135   Few love to hear the sins they love to act.
    'Twould braid° yourself too near° for me to tell it.   *upbraid / plainly*
    Who° has a book of all that monarchs do,   *Whoever*
    He's more secure to keep it shut than shown,
    For vice repeated, like the wand'ring wind,
140   Blows dust in others' eyes to spread itself;
    And yet the end of all is bought thus dear,
    The breath is gone, and the sore eyes see clear
    To stop the air would hurt them.[4] The blind mole casts

---

8. Vipers were thought to eat their way out of their mother's body at birth.
9. This final threat is harsh medicine.
1. If your body weren't so sinful.
2. Stringed instrument; vial.
3. Perhaps Pericles makes some movement that Anti-

ochus misinterprets (further Edenic overtones).
4. *For vice . . . them:* For with the breath used to speak word of others' sins, one blows irritating dust in the eyes of the offenders. But the consequence is merely the speaker's death, since the offenders nevertheless see well enough to stop the news-spreading breath.

Copped° hills towards heav'n to tell° the earth is thronged   *Peaked / tell that*
145 By man's oppression, and the poor worm doth die for't.[5]
Kings are earth's gods; in vice their law's their will,
And if Jove stray, who dares say Jove doth ill?
It is enough you know,° and it is fit,   *(that I know)*
What being more known grows worse,[6] to smother° it.   *conceal*
150 All love the womb that their first being bred;[7]
Then give my tongue like leave to love my head.
ANTIOCHUS *[aside]*   Heav'n, that I had thy head! He's found the
    meaning.
But I will gloze° with him. —Young Prince of Tyre,   *dissemble*
Though by the tenor of our strict edict,
155 Your exposition misinterpreting,
We might proceed to cancel° of your days,   *to the termination*
Yet hope, succeeding from so fair a tree[8]
As your fair self, doth tune° us otherwise.   *move*
Forty days longer we do respite you,
160 If by which time our secret be undone,
This mercy shows we'll joy in such a son.
And until then your entertain° shall be   *entertainment*
As doth befit your worth and our degree.
      [Flourish. Exeunt.] Manet PERICLES *solus°*   *Pericles remains alone*
PERICLES   How courtesy would seem° to cover sin   *lie*
165 When what is done is like an hypocrite,
The which is good in nothing but in sight.°   *appearance*
If it be true that I interpret false,
Then were it certain you were not so bad
As with foul incest to abuse your soul,
170 Where now you're both a father and a son
By your uncomely claspings with your child—
Which pleasures fits a husband, not a father—
And she, an eater of her mother's flesh,
By the defiling of her parents' bed,
175 And both like serpents are, who though they feed
On sweetest flowers, yet they poison breed.
Antioch, farewell, for wisdom sees those men°   *men who*
Blush not in actions blacker than the night
Will 'schew no course° to keep them from the light.   *eschew no means*
180 One sin, I know, another doth provoke.
Murder's as near to lust as flame to smoke.
Poison and treason are the hands of sin,
Ay, and the targets° to put off the shame.   *shields*
Then, lest my life be cropped to keep you clear,°   *(of blame)*
185 By flight I'll shun the danger which I fear.   *Exit*
     Enter ANTIOCHUS
ANTIOCHUS   He hath found the meaning, for the which we mean
To have his head. He must not live
To trumpet forth my infamy, nor tell the world
Antiochus doth sin in such a loathèd manner,

5. *The blind . . . for't:* When we blindly protest against the injustice of our superiors, we die (with "mole" meaning "worm"), or, less likely, innocent creatures suffer (here, the "mole" is different from the "worm" and may even destroy it).
6. Since bad deeds become worse for being known.
7. All love the daughter they raised when young (hence,

hinting at incest). The obvious meaning—all love their mother's womb—either is nonincestuous or gets the incest backward.
8. Hope of a correct answer (an heir), with the successful answer (succession) coming from such a fine specimen (Pericles' regal lineage).

190   And therefore instantly this prince must die,
     For by his fall my honour must keep high.
     Who attends us there?
          Enter THALIART
  THALIART   Doth your highness call?
  ANTIOCHUS   Thaliart, you are of our chamber,° Thaliart,   *my chamberlain*
     And to your secrecy our mind partakes°   *imparts*
195   Her° private actions. For your faithfulness   *Its*
     We will advance you, Thaliart. Behold,
     Here's poison, and here's gold.
     We hate the Prince of Tyre, and thou must kill him.
     It fits° thee not to ask the reason. Why?   *befits*
200   Because we bid it. Say, is it done?
  THALIART   My lord, 'tis done.
  ANTIOCHUS   Enough.
          Enter a MESSENGER [*hastily*]
     Let your breath cool yourself, telling your haste.[9]
  MESSENGER   Your majesty, Prince Pericles is fled.   [*Exit*]
  ANTIOCHUS [*to* THALIART]   As thou wilt live, fly after; like an
205   arrow
     Shot from a well-experienced archer hits
     The mark his eye doth level° at, so thou   *aim*
     Never return unless it be to say
     'Your majesty, Prince Pericles is dead.'
210   THALIART   If I can get him in my pistol's° length°   *(anachronism) / range*
     I'll make him sure° enough. Farewell, your highness.   *unthreatening (dead)*
  ANTIOCHUS   Thaliart, adieu.   [*Exit* THALIART]
          Till Pericles be dead
     My heart can lend no succour to my head.
          [*Exit. The heads are concealed*]

Scene 2

Enter PERICLES [*distempered*] *with his lords*
  PERICLES   Let none disturb us.   [*Exeunt lords*]
          Why should this change of thoughts,°   *changed state of mind*
     The sad companion, dull-eyed melancholy,
     Be my so used° a guest as not an hour   *accustomed*
     In the day's glorious walk or peaceful night,
5   The tomb where grief should sleep, can breed me quiet?
     Here pleasures court mine eyes, and mine eyes shun them,
     And danger, which I feared, 's° at Antioch,   *is*
     Whose arm seems far too short to hit me here.
     Yet neither pleasure's art can joy my spirits,
10   Nor yet care's author's distance comfort me.
     Then it is thus: the passions of the mind,°   *obsessions*
     That have their first conception by misdread,°   *fear*
     Have after-nourishment and life by care,°   *worry*
     And what was first but fear what might be done
15   Grows elder now, and cares it be not done.[1]
     And so with me. The great Antiochus,

---

9. Use your rapid breathing to cool yourself by explaining
the reason for your haste.
Scene 2 (Act 1, Scene 2, in other modern editions)
Location: The palace at Tyre.

1. *And what . . . done*: And what starts out as simple fear
matures into a more rational concern for safety.

'Gainst whom I am too little to contend,
Since he's so great can° make his will his act,   *that he can*
Will think me speaking though I swear to silence,
20   Nor boots it° me to say I honour him   *does it help*
If he suspect I may dishonour him.
And what may make him blush in being known,
He'll stop the course by which it might be known.
With hostile forces he'll o'erspread the land,
25   And with th'ostent° of war will look so huge   *display*
Amazement° shall drive courage from the state,   *Terror*
Our men be vanquished ere they do resist,
And subjects punished that ne'er thought offence,
Which care of them, not pity of myself,
30   Who am no more but as the tops of trees
Which fence° the roots they grow by and defend them,   *shield*
Makes both my body pine and soul to languish,
And punish that° before that he would punish.[2]   *(myself)*

    Enter all the LORDS, *[among them old* HELICANUS,*] to*
    PERICLES

FIRST LORD   Joy and all comfort in your sacred breast!
35 SECOND LORD   And keep your mind peaceful[3] and comfortable.
HELICANUS   Peace, peace, and give experience tongue.
    [*To* PERICLES] You[4] do not well so to abuse yourself,
    To waste your body here with pining sorrow,
    Upon whose safety doth depend the lives
40   And the prosperity of a whole kingdom.
    'Tis ill in you to do it, and no less
    Ill in your council not to contradict it.
    They do abuse the King that flatter him,
    For flatt'ry is the bellows blows° up sin;   *that blows*
45   The thing the which is flattered, but a spark,
    To which that wind gives heat and stronger glowing;
    Whereas reproof, obedient and in order,
    Fits kings as they are men, for they may err.
    When Signor Sooth[5] here does proclaim a peace
50   He flatters you, makes war upon your life.
        [*He kneels*]
    Prince, pardon me, or strike me if you please.
    I cannot be much lower than my knees.
PERICLES   All leave us else;° but let your cares o'erlook   *except Helicanus*
    What shipping and what lading's[6] in our haven,
    And then return to us.   [*Exeunt* LORDS]
55   Helicane, thou
    Hast movèd us. What seest thou in our looks?
HELICANUS   An angry brow, dread lord.
PERICLES   If there be such a dart° in princes' frowns,   *danger*
    How durst thy tongue move anger to our brows?
HELICANUS   How dares the plants look up to heav'n from
60   whence

---

2. *before . . . punish*: before he punishes me ("that").
3. Q1 has "And keep your mind till you return to us peaceful," a phrase that anticipates Pericles' "return to us" (line 55). The omission here eliminates the speaker's clairvoyance about a trip that no one else contemplates until line 111.
4. Lines 37–42 are not in Q1 but are adapted from Wilkins's *Painfull Adventures* (PA). They explain why Helicanus thinks Pericles has been, but should not be, flattered.
5. Mock name for a flatterer, a soother of egos.
6. *let . . . lading's*: look carefully to find out what vessels are coming and going and what cargo is.

They have their nourishment?

PERICLES   Thou knowest I have pow'r to take thy life from thee.

HELICANUS   I have ground the axe myself; do you but strike the
    blow.

PERICLES [*lifting him up*]   Rise, prithee, rise. Sit down. Thou art
    no flatterer,

65   I thank thee for it, and the heav'ns forbid
    That kings should let their ears hear their faults hid.
    Fit counsellor and servant for a prince,
    Who by thy wisdom mak'st a prince thy servant,
    What wouldst thou have me do?

HELICANUS   To bear with patience

70   Such griefs as you do lay upon yourself.

PERICLES   Thou speak'st like a physician, Helicanus,
    That ministers a potion unto me
    That thou wouldst tremble to receive thyself.
    Attend me,° then. I went to Antioch,   *Listen to me*

75   Where, as thou know'st, against the face of death
    I sought the purchase° of a glorious beauty   *acquisition*
    From whence an issue I might propagate,
    As children are heav'n's blessings: to parents, objects;[7]
    Are arms° to princes, and bring joys to subjects.   *weapons*

80   Her face was to mine eye beyond all wonder,
    The rest—hark in thine ear—as black as incest,
    Which by my knowledge found, the sinful father
    Seemed not to strike, but smooth.° But thou know'st this,   *smooth over*
    'Tis time to fear when tyrants seems to kiss;

85   Which fear so grew in me I hither fled
    Under the covering of careful night,
    Who seemed my good protector, and being here
    Bethought me what was past, what might succeed.°   *happen next*
    I knew him tyrannous, and tyrants' fears

90   Decrease not, but grow faster than the years.
    And should he doubt°—as doubt no° doubt he doth—   *suspect / as no*
    That I should open° to the list'ning air   *declare*
    How many worthy princes' bloods were shed
    To keep his bed of blackness unlaid ope,

95   To lop that doubt he'll fill this land with arms,
    And make pretence of wrong that I have done him,
    When all for mine—if I may call—offence
    Must feel war's blow, who° spares not innocence;   *which*
    Which love to all, of which thyself art one,
    Who now reproved'st me for't—

100 HELICANUS   Alas, sir.

PERICLES   Drew sleep out of mine eyes, blood from my cheeks,
    Musings into my mind, with thousand doubts,
    How I might stop this tempest ere it came,
    And, finding little comfort to relieve them,°   *(his subjects)*

105   I thought it princely charity to grieve them.°   *(by my sorrow)*

HELICANUS   Well, my lord, since you have giv'n me leave to
    speak,
    Freely will I speak. Antiochus you fear,

---

7. Objects of affection. This line, composed by the Oxford editors, fills a long-recognized gap in Q1 between lines 77 and 79.

And justly too, I think, you fear the tyrant,
Who either by public war or private treason
110 Will take away your life.
Therefore, my lord, go travel for a while,
Till that his rage and anger be forgot,
Or destinies do cut his thread of life.[8]
Your rule direct° to any; if to me,   assign
115 Day serves not light more faithful than I'll be.
PERICLES   I do not doubt thy faith,
But should he in my absence wrong thy liberties?°   jurisdictions
HELICANUS   We'll mingle our bloods together in the earth
From whence we had our being and our birth.
120 PERICLES   Tyre, I now look from thee then, and to Tarsus°   (St. Paul's birthplace)
Intend° my travel, where I'll hear from thee,   Direct
And by whose letters I'll dispose myself.
The care I had and have of subjects' good
On thee I lay, whose wisdom's strength can bear it.
125 I'll take thy word for faith, not ask thine oath;
Who° shuns not to break one will sure crack both.   He who
But in our orbs° we'll live so round° and safe   places / prudently
That time of both this truth shall ne'er convince:°   refute
Thou showed'st a subject's shine, I a true prince.°   Exeunt   prince's

Scene 3

Enter THALIART

THALIART   So this is Tyre, and this the court. Here must I kill
King Pericles, and if I do it and am caught I am like to be
hanged abroad, but[1] if I do it not, I am sure to be hanged at
home. 'Tis dangerous. Well, I perceive he was a wise fellow
5 and had good discretion that, being bid to ask what he would
of the King, desired he might know none of his secrets.[2] Now
do I see he had some reason for't, for if a king bid a man be a
villain, he's bound by the indenture° of his oath to be one.   servant's contract
Hush, here comes the lords of Tyre.

Enter HELICANUS [*and*] AESCHINES, *with
other lords*

10 HELICANUS   You shall not need, my fellow peers of Tyre,
Further to question of your King's departure.
His sealed° commission left in trust with me   (with royal wax)
Does speak sufficiently he's gone to travel.
THALIART [*aside*]   How? The King gone?
15 HELICANUS   If further yet you will be satisfied
Why, as it were unlicensed of your loves,°   without your approval
He would depart, I'll give some light unto you.
Being at Antioch—
THALIART [*aside*]   What from Antioch?
HELICANUS   Royal Antiochus, on what cause I know not,
20 Took some displeasure at him—at least he judged so—
And doubting lest° that he had erred or sinned,   And fearing
To show his sorrow he'd correct° himself;   he wished to punish

8. In Greek mythology, a person died when the three
Fates "cut his thread of life."
Scene 3 (Act 1, Scene 3)
Location: The palace at Tyre.
1. *if . . . but*: this is a conjectural editorial addition that

semantically balances Thaliart's reflection on the consequences of failure. *like*: likely. *abroad*: in Tyre.
2. According to Plutarch's *Lives* and Barnabe Riche in
Souldiers Wishe to Britons Welfare (1604), the poet Philip-
pides made this request of King Lysimachus of Thrace.

So puts himself unto the ship-man's toil,
With whom each minute threatens life or death.

25 THALIART [*aside*] Well, I perceive I shall not be hanged now,
Although I would.[3]
But since he's gone, the King's ears it must please
He scaped° the land to perish on the seas. *escaped*
I'll present myself.—Peace to the lords of Tyre.

30 Lord Thaliart am I, of Antioch.[4]

HELICANUS Lord Thaliart of Antioch is welcome.

THALIART From King Antiochus I come
With message unto princely Pericles,
But since my landing I have understood

35 Your lord's betook himself to unknown travels.
Now my message must return from whence it came.

HELICANUS We have no reason to enquire it,
Commended° to our master, not to us. *Directed*
Yet ere you shall depart, this we desire:

40 As friends to Antioch, we may feast° in Tyre. *Exeunt* *prepare a feast for you*

Scene 4

Enter CLEON, *the Governor of Tarsus, with* [DIONYZA]
his wife, and others

CLEON My Dionyza, shall we rest us here
And, by relating tales of others' griefs,
See if 'twill teach us to forget our own?

DIONYZA That were to blow at fire in hope to quench it,

5 For who digs° hills because they do aspire *whoever digs up*
Throws down one mountain to cast up a higher.
O my distressèd lord, e'en such our griefs are;
Here they're but felt and seen with midges' eyes,° *as small matters*
But like to groves, being topped° they higher rise. *pruned*

10 CLEON O Dionyza,
Who wanteth food and will not say he wants it,
Or can conceal his hunger till he famish?
Our tongues our sorrows dictate to sound° deep *proclaim; plumb*
Our woes into the air, our eyes to weep

15 Till lungs fetch breath that may proclaim them louder,
That, if heav'n slumber while their° creatures want, *(heaven's)*
They° may awake their° helps to comfort them. *(creatures) / (heaven's)*
I'll then discourse our woes, felt sev'ral years,
And, wanting° breath to speak, help me with tears. *when I'm out of*

20 DIONYZA As you think best, sir.

CLEON This Tarsus o'er which I have the government,
A city o'er whom plenty held full hand,° *generously presided*
For riches strewed herself ev'n in the streets,
Whose tow'rs bore heads so high they kissed the clouds,

25 And strangers ne'er beheld but wondered at,° *without admiring*
Whose men and dames so jetted° and adorned° *strutted / (themselves)*
Like one another's glass to trim them[1] by;
Their tables were stored full to glad the sight,
And not so much to feed on as delight.

---

3. Even if I return home (?); even if that's what I wanted.
4. This line is added by the Oxford editors to explain how Helicanus knows who Thaliart is. Alternatively, Helicanus might simply recognize a leading lord of the dominant regional power.

Scene 4 (Act 1, Scene 4)
Location: Tarsus.
1. Mirror to dress themselves. (Everyone was a model of fashion.)

30 All poverty was scorned, and pride so great
    The name of help grew odious to repeat.
DIONYZA O, 'tis too true.
CLEON But see what heav'n can do by this our change.
    Those mouths who but of late° earth, sea, and air   *just recently*
35 Were all too little to content and please,
    Although they gave their creatures in abundance,
    As houses are defiled for want° of use,   *by lack*
    They are now starved for want of exercise.
    Those palates who, not yet two summers younger,
40 Must have inventions° to delight the taste   *Demanded novel foods*
    Would now be glad of bread and beg for it.
    Those mothers who to nuzzle up° their babes   *raise*
    Thought naught too curious° are ready now   *exquisite*
    To eat those little darlings whom they loved.
45 So sharp are hunger's teeth that man and wife
    Draw lots who first shall die to lengthen life.°   *(of the other)*
    Here weeping stands a lord, there lies a lady dying,
    Here many sink, yet those which see them fall
    Have scarce strength left to give them burial.
50 Is not this true?
DIONYZA Our cheeks and hollow eyes do witness it.
CLEON O, let those cities that of plenty's cup
    And her prosperities so largely taste
    With their superfluous riots,° heed these tears!   *excessive indulgence*
55 The misery of Tarsus may be theirs.
                Enter a [fainting] LORD *[of Tarsus slowly]*
LORD Where's the Lord Governor?
CLEON Here. Speak out thy sorrows which thou bring'st in
                haste,
    For comfort is too far for us t'expect.
LORD We have descried upon our neighbouring shore
60 A portly sail° of ships make hitherward.   *stately fleet*
CLEON I thought as much.
    One sorrow never comes but brings an heir
    That may succeed as his inheritor,
    And so in ours. Some neighbour nation,
65 Taking advantage of our misery,
    Hath stuffed these hollow vessels with their power°   *soldiers*
    To beat us down, the which are down already,
    And make a conquest of unhappy men,°   *(me: Q1)*
    Whereas no glory's got to overcome.[2]
70 LORD That's the least fear,° for by the semblance   *not to be feared*
    Of their white flags displayed they bring us peace,
    And come to us as favourers, not foes.
CLEON Thou speak'st like him's untutored to repeat;[3]
    Who makes the fairest show means most deceit.
75 But bring they° what they will and what they can,   *let them bring*
    What need we fear?
    Our grave's the low'st,° and we are half-way there.   *lowest we can go*
    Go tell their gen'ral we attend° him here   *await*
    To know for what he comes, and whence he comes.

2. Where there's no glory in winning.
3. Like him who hasn't learned (the following lesson) by heart.

80   LORD   I go, my lord.   [*Exit*]

      CLEON   Welcome is peace, if he on peace consist;°   *resolve*

        If wars, we are unable to resist.

                Enter [*the* LORD *again conducting*] PERICLES *with atten-*
                dants

      PERICLES [*to* CLEON]   Lord Governor, for so we hear you are,

        Let not our ships and number of our men

85   Be like a beacon fixed t'amaze° your eyes.   *to terrify*

        We have heard your miseries as far as Tyre,

        Since entering your unshut gates have witnessed

        The widowed[4] desolation of your streets;

        Nor come we to add sorrow to your hearts,

90   But to relieve them of their heavy load;

        And these our ships, you happily° may think   *perhaps*

        Are like the Trojan horse was fraught within

        With bloody veins importing overthrow,[5]

        Are stored with corn to make your needy bread,

95   And give them life whom hunger starved half dead.

      ALL OF TARSUS [*falling on their knees and weeping*]   The gods of

          Greece protect you, and we'll pray for you!

      PERICLES   Arise, I pray you, rise.

        We do not look for reverence but for love,

        And harbourage for me, my ships and men.

100   CLEON   The which when any shall not gratify,

        Or pay you with unthankfulness in thought,

        Be it our wives, our children, or ourselves,

        The curse of heav'n and men succeed° their evils!   *follow from*

        Till when—the which I hope shall ne'er be seen—

105   Your grace is welcome to our town and us.

      PERICLES   Which welcome we'll accept, feast here a while,

        Until our stars that frown lend us a smile.   *Exeunt*

Scene 5

        Enter GOWER

      GOWER   Here have you seen a mighty king

        His child, iwis,° to incest bring;   *certainly*

        A better prince° and benign lord   *(Pericles)*

        Prove awe-full° both in deed and word.   *worthy of respect*

5   Be quiet then, as men should be,

        Till he hath passed necessity.[1]

        I'll show you those° in trouble's reign,   *those who*

        Losing a mite, a mountain gain.

        The good in conversation,[2]

10   To whom I give my benison,°   *blessing*

        Is still at Tarsus where each man

        Thinks all is writ he speken can,[3]

        And to remember what he does

---

4. *Since . . . widowed*: This line, adapted from *PA*, replaces Q1's "And seene the"; the substitution prevents the inference that Pericles has "seen" Tarsus's "desolation" "as far as Tyre."
5. *was . . . overthrow*: was laden ("fraught") with Greek soldiers ("bloody veins") who sacked the city.
Scene 5 (Other editions treat Gower's monologue as a prologue to Act 2 and start Act 2, Scene 1, at line 41. The present edition, however, interprets "here he comes" [line

39] as evidence that the scene does not change.) Location: The seashore at Pentapolis, which was the coastal area of Cyrenaica, in the northeast corner of what is now Libya. This scene locates it in Greece, however (line 100).
1. *necessity*: the suffering that is his lot.
2. The good man (Pericles) in conduct.
3. Archaic (as is often the case in Gower's speeches): Thinks all Pericles says is holy scripture ("writ").

His statue build to make him glorious.
15 But tidings to the contrary
Are brought your eyes. What need speak I?
                    Dumb show.[4]
        Enter at one door PERICLES *talking with* CLEON, *all the*
        train with them. Enter at another door a gentleman with
        a letter to PERICLES. PERICLES *shows the letter to* CLEON.
        PERICLES *gives the messenger a reward, and knights him.*
        Exeunt [with their trains] PERICLES *at one door and*
        CLEON *at another*
Good Helicane that stayed at home,
Not to eat honey like a drone
From others' labours, for that he strive
20 To killen bad, keep good alive,
And to fulfil his prince' desire
Sent word of all that haps in Tyre;
How Thaliart came full bent with° sin   intent on
And hid intent to murdren him,
25 And that in Tarsus was not best
Longer for him to make his rest.
He deeming so put forth to seas,
Where when men been° there's seldom ease,   are
For now the wind begins to blow;
30 Thunder above and deeps below
Makes such unquiet that the ship
Should° house him safe is wrecked and split,   Which should
And he, good prince, having all lost,
By waves from coast to coast is tossed.
35 All perishen of man, of pelf,°   goods
Ne aught escapend° but himself,   Nothing escaping
Till fortune, tired with doing bad,
Threw him ashore to give him glad.°   joy
        Enter PERICLES *wet [and half-naked]*
And here he comes. What shall be next
40 Pardon old Gower; this 'longs[5] the text.   [*Exit*]
        [*Thunder and lightning*]
PERICLES   Yet cease your ire, you angry stars of heaven!
Wind, rain, and thunder, remember earthly man
Is but a substance that must yield to you,
And I, as fits my nature, do obey you.
45 Alas, the seas hath cast me on the rocks,
Washed me from shore to shore, and left my breath
Nothing to think on but ensuing death.
Let it suffice the greatness of your powers
To have bereft a prince of all his fortunes,
50 And, having thrown him from your wat'ry grave,
Here to have death in peace is all he'll crave.
        [*He sits.*]
        Enter [two poor] FISHERMEN [*one the* MASTER, *the other*
        his man]
MASTER [*calling*]   What ho, Pilch![6]

---

4. In Renaissance drama, a brief pantomime performance used to advance the plot.
5. Continuing would lengthen Gower's speech too
much; or, 'longs: belongs to.

6. Nickname derived from a rustic leather garment. The
nicknames, homely references, and social critiques in this
scene have a distinctively English feel.

SECOND FISHERMAN [*calling*]   Ha, come and bring away the nets.

MASTER [*calling*]   What, Patchbreech,° I say! (*another nickname*)

[*Enter a* THIRD FISHERMAN *with a hood upon his head
and a filthy leathern pelt upon his back, unseemly clad,
and homely to behold. He brings nets to dry and repair*]

55 THIRD FISHERMAN   What say you, master?

MASTER   Look how thou stirrest now. Come away, or I'll fetch
th' with a wanion.[7]

THIRD FISHERMAN   Faith, master, I am thinking of the poor men
that were cast away before us° even now. *in our sight*

60 MASTER   Alas, poor souls, it grieved my heart to hear what pitiful
cries they made to us to help them when, well-a-day,° we could *alas*
scarce help ourselves.

THIRD FISHERMAN   Nay, master, said not I as much when I saw
the porpoise how he bounced and tumbled?° They say they're (*predictive of storms*)

65 half fish, half flesh. A plague on them, they ne'er come but I look
to be washed.° Master, I marvel how the fishes live in the sea. (*by a storm*)

MASTER   Why, as men do a-land°—the great ones eat up the *on land*
little ones. I can compare our rich misers to nothing so fitly as
to a whale: a° plays and tumbles, driving the poor fry before *he*

70 him, and at last devours them all at a mouthful. Such whales
have I heard on° o'th' land, who never leave gaping° till they *of / close their mouths*
swallowed the whole parish: church, steeple, bells, and all.

PERICLES [*aside*]   A pretty moral.

THIRD FISHERMAN   But, master, if I had been the sexton, I would

75 have been that day in the belfry.

SECOND FISHERMAN   Why, man?

THIRD FISHERMAN   Because he should have swallowed me, too,
and when I had been in his belly I would have kept such a
jangling of the bells that he should never have left till he cast° *vomited*

80 bells, steeple, church, and parish up again. But if the good
King Simonides were of my mind—

PERICLES [*aside*]   Simonides?

THIRD FISHERMAN   We would purge the land of these drones that
rob the bee of her honey.

85 PERICLES [*aside*]   How from the finny subject° of the sea[8] *citizens*
These fishers tell th'infirmities of men,
And from their wat'ry empire recollect° *gather*
All that may men approve or men detect!° *expose*
[*Coming forward*] Peace be at your labour, honest fishermen.

90 SECOND FISHERMAN   Honest, good fellow? What's that? If it be a day
fits you, scratch't out of the calendar, and nobody look after it.[9]

PERICLES   May° see the sea hath cast upon your coast— *You may*

SECOND FISHERMAN   What a drunken knave was the sea to cast
thee in our way![1]

95 PERICLES   A man, whom both the waters and the wind
In that vast tennis-court hath made the ball
For them to play upon,° entreats you pity him. *with*
He asks of you that never used to beg.

---

7. *Look . . . wanion:* Look how quick you are (ironic). Hurry along, or I'll beat you with a vengeance.
8. Although the Fishermen speak in prose, Pericles uses verse.
9. *Honest . . . after it:* If "honest" were a day in the calendar that suited someone in your sorry state, you could remove it without anyone noticing; honesty is so rare

already, no one would notice its departure. (Perhaps a line is missing before line 89, in which Pericles wishes the Fishermen good day.)
1. Like St. Peter, the Fishermen are literally fishers of men, who help save Pericles from the sea. Their discussion of whales also evokes the tale of Jonah. The scene is full of biblical echoes.

MASTER   No, friend, cannot you beg? Here's them° in our coun-   *There are those*
100   try of Greece gets° more with begging than we can do with   *who get*
      working.
SECOND FISHERMAN   Canst thou catch any fishes, then?
PERICLES   I never practised it.
SECOND FISHERMAN   Nay, then thou wilt starve, sure; for here's
105   nothing to be got nowadays unless thou canst fish for't.°   *get it by deception*
PERICLES   What I have been, I have forgot to know,
     But what I am, want teaches me to think on:
     A man thronged up° with cold; my veins are chill,   *overwhelmed*
     And have no more of life than may suffice
110   To give my tongue that heat to crave your help,
     Which if you shall refuse, when I am dead,
     For that° I am a man, pray see me burièd.   *Because*
             [*He falls down*]
MASTER   Die, quotha?° Now, gods forbid't an° I have a gown   *says he / if*
     here! [*To* PERICLES, *lifting him up from the ground*] Come, put
115   it on, keep thee warm. Now, afore me,° a handsome fellow!   *on my word*
     Come, thou shalt go home, and we'll have flesh for holidays,
     fish for fasting-days, and moreo'er puddings° and flapjacks, and   *sausages*
     thou shalt be welcome.
PERICLES   I thank you, sir.
120   SECOND FISHERMAN   Hark you, my friend, you said you could
     not beg?
PERICLES   I did but crave.
SECOND FISHERMAN   But crave? Then I'll turn craver too, an so I
     shall scape whipping.°   *(for begging)*
125   PERICLES   Why, are all your beggars whipped, then?
SECOND FISHERMAN   O, not all, my friend, not all; for if all your°   *the*
     beggars were whipped I would wish no better office than to be
     beadle.²
MASTER³   Thine office, knave—
130   SECOND FISHERMAN   Is to draw up the other nets. I'll go.
             [*Exit with* THIRD FISHERMAN]
PERICLES [*aside*]   How well this honest mirth becomes their
     labour!
MASTER [*seating himself by* PERICLES]   Hark you, sir, do you
     know where ye are?
135   PERICLES   Not well.
MASTER   Why, I'll tell you. This is called Pentapolis, and our
     king the good Simonides.
PERICLES   'The good Simonides' do you call him?
MASTER   Ay, sir, and he deserves so to be called for his peaceable
140   reign and good government.
PERICLES   He is a happy king, since from his subjects
     He gains the name of good by his government.
     How far is his court distant from this shore?
MASTER   Marry,° sir, some half a day's journey. And I'll tell you,   *To be sure*
145   he hath a fair daughter, and tomorrow is her birthday, and
     there are princes and knights come from all parts of the world
     to joust and tourney for her love.

---

2. Minor parish official who administered corporal punishment.
3. To improve the motivation of the Second Fisherman's

exit, this edition substitutes "MASTER . . . I'll go" for Q1's
continuation of the Second Fisherman's speech: "But
Master, I'll go draw up the net."

PERICLES   Were but my fortunes answerable
　　To my desires I could wish to make one° there.　　　　　　　　　*be one of the princes*
150　MASTER   O, sir, things must be as they may, and what a man
　　cannot get himself, he may lawfully deal for with his wife's soul.⁴
　　　　　　Enter the [other] two FISHERMEN *drawing up a net*
SECOND FISHERMAN   Help, master, help! Here's a fish hangs in
　　the net like a poor man's right in the law; 'twill hardly come out.
　　　　　　[Before help comes, up comes their prize]
　　Ha, bots on't,° 'tis come at last, and 'tis turned to a rusty armour.　　*a pox (plague) on it*
155　PERICLES   An armour, friends? I pray you let me see it.
　　[Aside] Thanks, fortune, yet that after all thy crosses°　　　　　*hardships*
　　Thou giv'st me somewhat to repair my losses,
　　And though° it was mine own, part of my heritage　　　　　　　　*Even though*
　　Which my dead father did bequeath to me
160　With this strict charge ev'n as he left his life:
　　'Keep it, my Pericles; it hath been a shield
　　'Twixt me and death,' and pointed to this brace,°　　　　　　　　*arm armor*
　　'For that° it saved me, keep it. In like necessity,　　　　　　　　*Because*
　　The which the Gods forfend,° the same may defend thee.'　　　　*forbid*
165　It kept° where I kept, I so dearly loved it,　　　　　　　　　　　*remained*
　　Till the rough seas that spares not any man
　　Took it in rage, though calmed have giv'n't again.
　　I thank thee for't. My shipwreck now's no ill,
　　Since I have here my° father gave in 's° will.　　　　　　　　　*what my / his*
170　MASTER   What mean you, sir?
PERICLES   To beg of you, kind friends, this coat of worth,
　　For it was sometime target° to a king.　　　　　　　　　　　　*once a shield*
　　I know it by this mark. He loved me dearly,
　　And for his sake I wish the having of it,
175　And that you'd guide me to your sov'reign's court,
　　Where with't I may appear a gentleman.
　　And if that ever my low fortune's better,
　　I'll pay your bounties,° till then rest your debtor.　　　　　　　*repay your generosity*
MASTER   Why, wilt thou tourney for the lady?
180　PERICLES   I'll show the virtue I have learned in arms.
MASTER   Why, d'ye take it, and the gods give thee good on't!
SECOND FISHERMAN   Ay, but hark you, my friend, 'twas we that
　　made° up this garment through the rough seams of the waters.　　*raised*
　　There are certain condolements,⁵ certain vails.° I hope, sir, if　　*tips*
185　you thrive, you'll remember from whence you had this.
PERICLES   Believe't, I will.
　　By your furtherance I'm clothed in steel,
　　And spite of all the rapture° of the sea　　　　　　　　　　　　*plundering*
　　This jewel holds his building° on my arm.　　　　　　　　　　　*its place*
190　Unto thy° value I will mount myself　　　　　　　　　　　　　　*(the jewel's)*
　　Upon a courser° whose delightsome steps　　　　　　　　　　　*a horse*
　　Shall make the gazer joy to see him tread.
　　Only, my friends, I yet am unprovided
　　Of a pair of bases.⁶
195　SECOND FISHERMAN   We'll sure provide. Thou shalt have my

best gown to make thee a pair, and I'll bring thee to the court
myself.

PERICLES   Then honour be but equal to my will,
This day I'll rise, or else add ill to ill.

[*Exeunt with nets and armour*]

Scene 6

[*Sennet.*] *Enter* KING SIMONIDES *and* THAISA *with*
[LORDS *in*] *attendance* [*and sit on two thrones*]

KING SIMONIDES   Are the knights ready to begin the triumph?°   *tournament*
FIRST LORD   They are, my liege,
And stay° your coming to present themselves.   *await*
KING SIMONIDES   Return° them we are ready; and our daughter,   *Answer*
5   In honour of whose birth these triumphs are,
Sits here like beauty's child, whom nature gat°   *conceived*
For men to see and, seeing, wonder at.

[*Exit one*]

THAISA   It pleaseth you, my father, to express
My commendations great, whose merit's less.
10   KING SIMONIDES   It's fit it should be so, for princes° are   *rulers*
A model which heav'n makes like to itself.
As jewels lose their glory if neglected,
So princes their renown, if not respected.
'Tis now your office, daughter, to entertain°   *review*
15   The labour of each knight in his device.[1]
THAISA   Which, to preserve mine honour, I'll perform.
    [*Flourish.*] *The first knight passes by* [*richly armed, and*
    his page before him, bearing his device on his shield,
    delivers it to the Lady THAISA]
KING SIMONIDES   Who is the first that doth prefer° himself?   *present*
THAISA   A knight of Sparta, my renownèd father,
And the device he bears upon his shield
20   Is a black Ethiop reaching at the sun.
The word, *Lux tua vita mihi.*[2]
    [*She presents it to the* KING]
KING SIMONIDES   He loves you well that holds his life of° you.   *receives his life from*
    [*He returns it to the page, who exits with the first*
    knight.]
    [*Flourish.*] *The second knight* [*passes by richly armed,*
    and his page before him, bearing his device on his
    shield, delivers it to the Lady THAISA]
Who is the second that presents himself?
THAISA   A prince of Macedon, my royal father,
25   And the device he bears upon his shield
An armèd knight that's conquered by a lady.
The motto thus: *Piùe per dolcezza che per forza.*[3]
    [*She presents it to the* KING]
KING SIMONIDES   You win him more by lenity than force.[4]

Scene 6 (Act 2, Scene 2)
Location: Pentapolis, area near the tournament arena,
including a reviewing stand.
1. The ingenuity of each knight's emblem on his shield.
2. Your light is my life (Latin).

3. More by gentleness than by force (Italian). Q1 precedes this phrase with the words "in Spanish"—probably
an error by the reporter. (See the Textual Note.)
4. Not in Q1; adapted from *PA.* Simonides comments
on three of the other five mottoes.

[*He returns it to the page, who exits with the second
knight.*]
[*Flourish. The*] *third knight* [*passes by richly armed, and
his page before him, bearing his device on his shield,
delivers it to the Lady* THAISA]
And what's the third?

THAISA   The third of Antioch,
30   And his device a wreath of chivalry.[5]
     The word, *Me pompae provexit apex.*[6]
     [*She presents it to the* KING]

KING SIMONIDES   Desire of renown he doth devise,
     The which hath drawn him to this enterprise.[7]
          [*He returns it to the page, who exits with the third
          knight.*]
          [*Flourish. The*] *fourth knight* [*passes by richly armed,
          and his page before him, bearing his device on his
          shield, delivers it to the Lady* THAISA]
     What is the fourth?

THAISA   A knight of Athens bearing[8]
35   A burning torch that's turnèd upside down.
     The word, *Qui me alit me extinguit.*[9]
          [*She presents it to the* KING]

KING SIMONIDES   Which shows that beauty hath this power and will,
     Which can as well inflame as it can kill.
          [*He returns it to the page, who exits with the fourth
          knight.*]
          [*Flourish. The*] *fifth knight* [*passes by richly armed, and
          his page before him, bearing his device on his shield,
          delivers it to the Lady* THAISA]
     And who the fifth?

THAISA   The fifth, a prince of Corinth,
40   Presents[1] an hand environèd with clouds,
     Holding out gold that's by the touchstone[2] tried.
     The motto thus: *Sic spectanda fides.*[3]
          [*She presents it to the* KING]

KING SIMONIDES   So faith is to be looked into.[4]
          [*He returns it to the page, who exits with the fifth
          knight.*]
          [*Flourish. The*] *sixth knight* [PERICLES, *in a rusty ar-
          mour, who, having neither page to deliver his shield
          nor shield to deliver, presents his device unto the Lady*
          THAISA]
     And what's the sixth and last, the which the knight himself
45   With such a graceful courtesy° delivereth?   *bow*

THAISA   He seems to be a stranger, but his present° is   *presented object*
     A withered branch that's only green at top.
     The motto, *In hac spe vivo.*°   *I live in this hope*

KING SIMONIDES   From the dejected state wherein he is
50   He hopes by you his fortunes yet may flourish.

5. (Heraldic term): twisted band that joins the crest and
the knight's helmet.
6. The summit of glory has led me on (Latin).
7. Lines 32–33 are not in Q1; adapted from *PA*.
8. Not in Q1; adapted from *PA*.
9. Who nourishes me extinguishes me.
1. Lines 39–40, adapted from *PA*, replace Q1's "The fift";

the substitution produces symmetry with the other
knights' introductions.
2. Black stone used to check the purity of gold and silver;
symbol of fidelity.
3. Thus is faith to be examined.
4. Not in Q1; adapted from *PA*.

FIRST LORD   He had need mean° better than his outward show   *must intend something*
Can any way speak in his just commend,°   *on his behalf*
For by his rusty outside he appears
T'have practised more the whipstock than the lance.[5]

55 SECOND LORD   He well may be a stranger,° for he comes   *foreigner*
Unto an honoured triumph strangely furnished.°   *bizarrely equipped*

THIRD LORD   And on set purpose let his armour rust
Until this day, to scour it in the dust.[6]

KING SIMONIDES   Opinion's but a fool, that makes us scan
60 The outward habit° for the inward man.   *costume*
        [Cornetts]°   *Ceremonial trumpets*
But stay, the knights are coming. We will withdraw
Into the gallery.   [Exeunt]
    [Cornetts and] great shouts [within], and all cry 'The
    mean° knight!'   *impoverished*

Scene 7

[A stately banquet is brought in.] Enter KING [SIMON-
IDES, THAISA and their train at one door, and at another
door a MARSHAL conducting PERICLES] and [the other]
KNIGHTS from tilting

KING SIMONIDES [to the KNIGHTS]   To say you're welcome were
    superfluous.
To place upon the volume of your deeds
As in a title page[1] your worth in arms
Were more than you expect, or more than's fit,
5 Since every worth in show° commends itself.   *in practice*
Prepare for mirth, for mirth becomes a feast.
You're princes, and my guests.

THAISA [to PERICLES]   But you, my knight and guest;
To whom this wreath of victory I give,
And crown you king of this day's happiness.

10 PERICLES   'Tis more by fortune, lady, than my merit.

KING SIMONIDES   Call it by what you will, the day is yours,
And here I hope is none that envies it.
In framing° artists art hath thus decreed,   *making*
To make some good, but others to exceed.
You are her laboured scholar.[2] [To THAISA] Come, queen
15   o'th' feast—
For, daughter, so you are—here take your place.
[To MARSHAL]   Marshal the rest as they deserve their grace.[3]

KNIGHTS   We are honoured much by good Simonides.

KING SIMONIDES   Your presence glads our days; honour we love,
20 For who hates honour hates the gods above.

MARSHAL [to PERICLES]   Sir, yonder is your place.

PERICLES   Some other is more fit.

FIRST KNIGHT   Contend not, sir, for we are gentlemen
Have° neither in our hearts nor outward eyes   *Who've*
Envied the great, nor shall the low despise.

---

5. *he appears . . . lance*: he looks more like a manual laborer (a "whipstock" was the handle of a whip used to drive workhorses) than a knight.
6. To polish it in the dust (when he loses).
Scene 7 (Act 2, Scene 3)
Location: The palace at Pentapolis.

1. Renaissance publishers often advertised the contents on the title page of a book ("volume").
2. Art (creative power) worked hard to make you.
3. Arrange the others according to the honor they deserve.

    PERICLES   You are right courteous knights.

25   KING SIMONIDES   Sit, sir, sit.

        [PERICLES *sits directly over against*° *the* KING *and*   *across from*
        THAISA. *The guests feed apace.* PERICLES *sits still and*
        eats nothing]

    [*Aside*] By Jove I wonder, that is king of thoughts,
    These cates distaste me, he but thought upon.[4]

    THAISA [*aside*]   By Juno, that is queen of marriage,
    I am amazed all viands that I eat

30   Do seem unsavoury, wishing him my meat.
    [*To the* KING] Sure he's a gallant gentleman.

    KING SIMONIDES   He's but a country gentleman.
    He's done no more than other knights have done.
    He's broke a staff° or so, so let it pass.   *an opponent's lance*

35   THAISA [*aside*]   To me he seems like diamond to glass.

    PERICLES [*aside*]   Yon king's to me like to my father's picture,
    Which tells me in what glory once he was—
    Had princes sit like stars about his throne,
    And he the sun for them to reverence.

40   None that beheld him but like lesser lights
    Did vail° their crowns to his supremacy;   *lower*
    Where now his son's a glow-worm in the night,
    The which hath fire in darkness, none in light;
    Whereby I see that time's the king of men;

45   He's both their parent and he is their grave,
    And gives them what he will, not what they crave.

    KING SIMONIDES   What, are you merry, knights?

    THE OTHER KNIGHTS   Who can be other in this royal presence?

    KING SIMONIDES   Here with a cup that's stored unto the brim,

50   As you do love, full[5] to your mistress' lips,
    We drink this health to you.

    THE OTHER KNIGHTS   We thank your grace.

    KING SIMONIDES   Yet pause a while. Yon knight doth sit too melancholy,
    As if the entertainment in our court
    Had not a show might countervail° his worth.   *that might equal*
    Note it not you, Thaisa?

55   THAISA   What is't to me, my father?

    KING SIMONIDES   O, attend, my daughter. Princes in this
    Should live like gods above, who freely give
    To everyone that come to honour them.
    And princes not so doing are like gnats

60   Which make a sound but, killed, are wondered at.[6]
    Therefore to make his entertain° more sweet,   *entertainment*
    Here bear this standing-bowl° of wine to him.   *bowl on a pedestal*

    THAISA   Alas, my father, it befits not me
    Unto a stranger knight to be so bold.

65   He may my proffer take for an offence,
    Since men take women's gifts for impudence.

    KING SIMONIDES   How? Do as I bid you, or you'll move° me else.   *anger*

    THAISA [*aside*]   Now, by the gods, he could not please me better.

---

4. *These . . . upon:* (I'm so taken with him that, merely)
thinking of him, I lose my appetite for delicacies.
5. Just as you love, fully (all the way).

6. Which, when dead, appear surprisingly small for all
the noise they made alive.

KING SIMONIDES   Furthermore, tell him we desire to know
70   Of whence he is, his name and parentage.
         [THAISA *bears the cup to* PERICLES]
THAISA   The King my father, sir, has drunk to you,
      Wishing it so much blood unto your life.
PERICLES   I thank both him and you, and pledge° him freely.   *drink to*
         [*He pledges the* KING]
THAISA   And further he desires to know of you
75   Of whence you are, your name and parentage.
PERICLES   A gentleman of Tyre, my name Pericles,
      My education been in arts° and arms,   *liberal arts*
      Who, looking for adventures in the world,
      Was by the rough unconstant seas bereft
80   Unfortunately both of ships and men,
      And after shipwreck driven upon this shore.
         [THAISA *returns to the* KING]
THAISA   He thanks your grace, names himself Pericles,
      A gentleman of Tyre, who, seeking adventures,
      Was solely by misfortune of the seas
85   Bereft of ships and men, cast on this shore.
KING SIMONIDES   Now by the gods I pity his mishaps,
      And will awake him from his melancholy.
         [SIMONIDES, *rising from his state, goes forthwith and*
            embraces PERICLES]
      Be[7] cheered, for what misfortune hath impaired° you of,   *deprived*
      Fortune by my help can repair° to you.   *restore*
90   My self and country both shall be your friends,
      And presently° a goodly milk-white steed   *directly*
      And golden spurs I first bestow upon you,
      The prizes due your merit, and ordained
      For this day's enterprise.
95 PERICLES   Your kingly courtesy I thankfully accept.
KING SIMONIDES   Come, gentlemen, we sit° too long on trifles,   *dwell*
      And waste the time which looks for other revels.
      Ev'n in your armours, as you are addressed,°   *dressed*
      Your limbs will well become a soldier's dance.
100   I will not have excuse with saying this,
      'Loud music° is too harsh for ladies' heads',   *The sound of armor*
      Since they love men in arms as well as beds.
         [*The* KNIGHTS] *dance*
      So° this was well asked, 'twas so well performed.   *Just as*
      Come, here's a lady that wants breathing° too.   *exercise*
105   [*To* PERICLES] And I have heard, sir, that the knights of Tyre
      Are excellent in making ladies trip,°   *dance; go astray*
      And that their measures° are as excellent.   *dances; means*
PERICLES   In those that practise them they are, my lord.
KING SIMONIDES   O, that's as much as you would be denied
110   Of your fair courtesy.[8] Unclasp, unclasp.[9]
         They dance
      Thanks, gentlemen, to all. All have done well,
      [*To* PERICLES] But you the best.—Lights, pages, to conduct

---

7. Lines 88–95 are not in Q1; they are adapted from *PA*
to improve the transition between lines 87 and 96.
8. *that's . . . courtesy:* that's just what your modesty dic-
tates you should say.

9. Remove (your armor); if the stage direction "*They
dance*" is misplaced in Q and really should follow
"unclasp," Simonides is presumably ordering Pericles and
Thaisa not to dance so intimately.

These knights unto their sev'ral° lodgings.—Yours, sir,   *separate*
We have giv'n order should be next our own.

115 PERICLES   I am at your grace's pleasure.

KING SIMONIDES   Princes, it is too late to talk of love,
      And that's the mark I know you level° at.   *aim*
      Therefore each one betake him to his rest;
      Tomorrow all for speeding do their best.[1]   [*Exeunt severally*]°   *separately*

Scene 8

Enter HELICANUS *and* AESCHINES

HELICANUS   No, Aeschines, know this of me:
      Antiochus from incest lived not free,
      For which the most high gods, not minding° longer   *wishing*
      To hold the vengeance that they had in store
5   Due to this heinous capital offence,
      Even in the height and pride of all his glory,
      When he was seated in a chariot
      Of an inestimable value, and
      His daughter with him, both apparelled all in jewels,[1]
10   A fire from heaven came and shrivelled up
      Their bodies e'en to loathing, for they so stunk
      That all those eyes adored° them ere their fall   *that adored*
      Scorn now their° hands should give them burial.   *that their*

AESCHINES   'Twas very strange.

HELICANUS   And yet but justice, for though
15   This king were great, his greatness was no guard
      To bar heav'n's shaft, but sin had his° reward.   *its*

AESCHINES   'Tis very true.

Enter three LORDS [*and stand aside*]

FIRST LORD   See, not a man in private conference
      Or council has respect° with him but he.°   *influence / (Aeschines)*

20 SECOND LORD   It shall no longer grieve° without reproof.   *cause us grief*

THIRD LORD   And cursed be he that will not second it.

FIRST LORD   Follow me, then.—Lord Helicane, a word.

HELICANUS   With me? And welcome. Happy day, my lords.

FIRST LORD   Know that our griefs° are risen to the top,   *grievances*
25   And now at length they overflow their banks.

HELICANUS   Your griefs? For what? Wrong not your prince you love.

FIRST LORD   Wrong not yourself, then, noble Helicane,
      But if the prince do live, let us salute him
      Or know what ground's made happy by his step,
30   And be resolved° he lives to govern us,   *reassured*
      Or dead, give 's° cause to mourn his funeral   *us*
      And leave us to our free election.

SECOND LORD   Whose death indeed's the strongest° in our   *(likelihood)*
            censure,°   *judgment*
      And knowing this—kingdoms without a head,
35   Like goodly buildings left without a roof,
      Soon fall to utter ruin—your noble self,
      That best know how to rule and how to reign,
      We thus submit unto as sovereign.

---

1. Each one do his best to succeed (in wooing the   **Scene 8** (Act 2, Scene 4)
Princess).   Location: Tyre, the Governor's house.
                                                     1. *both . . . jewels:* not in Q1; taken from *PA.*

ALL [*kneeling*]   Live, noble Helicane!

40 HELICANUS   By honour's cause, forbear your suffrages.°   *voting (for me)*

If that you love Prince Pericles, forbear.

[*The* LORDS *rise*]

Take I° your wish I leap into the seas   *If I accept*

Where's° hourly trouble for a minute's ease,   *Where there is*

But if I cannot win you to this love,[2]

45 A twelvemonth longer then let me entreat you

Further to bear the absence of your king;

If in which time expired he not return,

I shall with agèd patience bear your yoke.

Go, seek your noble prince like noble subjects,

50 And in your search spend your adventurous worth,

Whom if you find and win unto° return,   *persuade to*

You shall like diamonds sit about his crown.

FIRST LORD   To wisdom he's a fool that will not yield,

And since Lord Helicane enjoineth us,

55 We with our travels will endeavour us.

If in the world he live we'll seek him out;

If in his grave he rest, we'll find him there.[3]

HELICANUS   Then you love us, we you, and we'll clasp hands.

When peers thus knit, a kingdom ever stands.   *Exeunt*

Scene 8a

[*Enter* PERICLES *with* GENTLEMEN *with lights*]

FIRST GENTLEMAN   Here is your lodging, sir.

PERICLES   Pray leave me private.

Only for instant solace pleasure me

With[1] some delightful instrument, with which,

And with my former practice,° I intend   *(of music)*

5 To pass away the tediousness of night,

Though slumbers were more fitting.

FIRST GENTLEMAN   Presently.°   *At once*

[*Exit* FIRST GENTLEMAN]

SECOND GENTLEMAN   Your will's obeyed in all things, for our

master

Commanded you be disobeyed in nothing.

[*Enter* FIRST GENTLEMAN *with a stringed instrument*]

PERICLES   I thank you. Now betake you to your pillows,

10 And to the nourishment of quiet sleep.   [*Exeunt* GENTLEMEN]

[PERICLES *plays and sings*]

Day—that hath still that sovereignty to draw back

The empire of the night, though for a while

In darkness she usurp—brings morning on.

I will go give his grace that salutation

15 Morning requires of me.   [*Exit with instrument*]

---

2. Love of Pericles (line 41). This line appears in Q1 after line 48, thereby rendering incomprehensible the First Lord's willingness to "yield" (line 53) to the suggestion of searching for Pericles.

3. Lines 56–57 appear after line 29 in Q1. There, they make lines 30–32 problematic and, as in note 2, undermine the First Lord's agreement to travel.

Scene 8a (This scene is not in Q1 or other modern editions. It was adapted from *PA* and provides a reference point for Simonides' compliments in Scene 9, lines 23–28. See the Textual Note.)

Location: The palace at Pentapolis.

1. *pleasure me / With:* grant me.

Scene 9

Enter KING [SIMONIDES] *at one door reading of a letter,*
the KNIGHTS [*enter at another door and*] *meet him*

FIRST KNIGHT   Good morrow to the good Simonides.

KING SIMONIDES   Knights, from my daughter this I let you know:
  That for this twelvemonth she'll not undertake
  A married life. Her reason to herself
5 Is only known, which from her none can get.

SECOND KNIGHT   May we not have access to her, my lord?

KING SIMONIDES   Faith, by no means. It is impossible,
  She hath so strictly tied her to her chamber.
  One twelve moons more she'll wear Diana's liv'ry.[1]
10 This by the eye of Cynthia[2] hath she vowed,
  And on her virgin honour will not break it.

THIRD KNIGHT   Loath to bid farewell, we take our leaves.

[*Exeunt* KNIGHTS]

KING SIMONIDES   So, they are well dispatched. Now to my
      daughter's letter.
  She tells me here she'll wed the stranger knight,
15 Or never more to view nor° day nor light.[3]   neither
  I like that well. Nay, how absolute she's in't,
  Not minding whether I dislike or no!
  Mistress, t'is well, I do commend your choice,
  And will no longer have it be delayed.

Enter PERICLES

20 Soft, here he comes. I must dissemble that
  In show, I have determined on in heart.[4]

PERICLES   All fortune to the good Simonides.

KING SIMONIDES   To you as much, sir. I am beholden to you
  For your sweet music this last night. My ears,
25 I do protest, were never better fed
  With such delightful pleasing harmony.

PERICLES   It is your grace's pleasure to commend,
  Not my desert.

KING SIMONIDES   Sir, you are music's master.

PERICLES   The worst of all her scholars, my good lord.

KING SIMONIDES   Let me ask you one thing. What think you of
30   my daughter?

PERICLES   A most virtuous princess.

KING SIMONIDES   And fair, too, is she not?

PERICLES   As a fair day in summer; wondrous fair.

KING SIMONIDES   My daughter, sir, thinks very well of you;
  So well indeed that you must be her master
35 And she will be your scholar;° therefore look to it.°   student be prepared

PERICLES   I am unworthy for her schoolmaster.

KING SIMONIDES   She thinks not so. Peruse this writing else.°   if you doubt me

[*He gives the letter to* PERICLES, *who reads*]

PERICLES [*aside*]   What's here?—a letter that she loves the knight
      of Tyre?
  'Tis the King's subtlety to have my life.

Scene 9 (Act 2, Scene 5)
Location: The palace at Pentapolis.
1. She'll serve Diana, goddess of chastity.
2. Diana, also goddess of the moon.
3. After this line, Q1 has "Tis well Mistress, your choice

agrees with mine," which is omitted in this edition
because the same thoughts are expressed in lines 16 and
18.
4. *that . . . heart:* replace Q1's "it" (adapted from *PA*).
that / In show: outwardly what.

[*He prostrates himself at the King's feet*]

40 O, seek not to entrap me, gracious lord,
A stranger and distressèd gentleman
That never aimed so high to° love your daughter,   *as to*
But bent all offices to honour her.[5]
Never did thought of mine levy° offence,   *give*
45 Nor never did my actions yet commence
A deed might° gain her love or your displeasure.   *that might*

KING SIMONIDES Thou liest like a traitor.

PERICLES   Traitor?

KING SIMONIDES   Ay, traitor,
That thus disguised art stol'n into my court
With witchcraft of thy actions to bewitch
50 The yielding spirit of my tender child.

PERICLES [*rising*] Who calls me traitor, unless it be the King,
Ev'n in his bosom I will write the lie.°   *(with my sword)*

KING SIMONIDES [*aside*] Now, by the gods, I do applaud his
          courage.

PERICLES My actions are as noble as my blood,
55 That never relished of° a base descent.   *gave a hint of*
I came unto your court in search of honour,
And not to be a rebel to your state;
And he that otherwise accounts of me,
This sword shall prove he's honour's enemy.

60 KING SIMONIDES I shall prove otherwise, since both your practice°   *actions*
And her consent therein is evident
There, by my daughter's hand, as she can witness.[6]

          Enter THAISA

PERICLES [*to* THAISA] Then as you are as virtuous as fair,
By what you hope of heaven or desire
65 By your best wishes here i'th' world fulfilled,[7]
Resolve° your angry father if my tongue   *Inform*
Did e'er solicit, or my hand subscribe
To any syllable made° love to you.   *that made*

THAISA Why, sir, say if you had,
70 Who takes offence at that° would make me glad?   *what*

KING SIMONIDES How, minion, are you so peremptory?°   *determined*
[*Aside*] I am glad on't.—Is[8] this a fit match for you?
A straggling Theseus, born we know not where,[9]
One that hath neither blood nor merit
75 For thee to hope for, or himself to challenge°   *claim for himself*
Of thy perfections e'en the least allowance.°   *share*

THAISA [*kneeling*] Suppose his birth were base, when that° his life   *even though*
Shows that he is not so, yet he hath virtue,
The very ground of all nobility,
80 Enough to make him noble. I entreat you
To remember that I am in love,

---

5. After this line, Q1 has

    KING Thou hast bewitched my daughter,
        And thou art a villain.
    PERICLES By the Gods I have not.

This passage breaks up what is a single speech in *PA*. It is
omitted here and replaced by Simonides' speech at lines
47–50, which is adapted from *PA* and is more powerful.
bent all offices: performed all services.
6. Except for "she can witness," lines 60–62 are adapted

from *PA*; they replace Q1's "No? here comes my daughter, she can witness it," which echoes *Othello* 1.3.169.
The reporter of this passage may have played Desdemona.
7. *By what . . . fulfilled*: not in Q1; adapted from *PA*.
8. Lines 72–96, adapted from *PA*, replace Q1's "with all
my heart"; inclusion of this passage shifts the emphasis
from nobility of birth to nobility of soul.
9. Theseus was an Athenian hero of ambiguous parentage who sometimes mistreated women.

The power of which love cannot be confined
By th' power of your will. Most royal father,
What with my pen I have in secret written
85 With my tongue now I openly confirm,
Which is I have no life but in his love,
Nor any being but in joying of his worth.
KING SIMONIDES   Equals to equals, good to good is joined.
This not being so, the bavin° of your mind   *firewood*
90 In rashness kindled must again be quenched,
Or purchase° our displeasure.—And for you, sir,   *provoke*
First learn to know I banish you my court,
And yet I scorn our rage should stoop so low.
For your ambition, sir, I'll have your life.
95 THAISA [*to* PERICLES]   For every drop of blood he sheds of yours
He'll draw another from his only child.
KING SIMONIDES   I'll tame you, yea, I'll bring you in subjection.
Will you not having my consent
Bestow your love and your affections
100 Upon a stranger?—[*aside*] who for aught I know
May be, nor can I think the contrary,
As great in blood as I myself.
    [*He catches* THAISA *rashly by the hand*]
Therefore hear you, mistress: either frame° your will to mine—   *mold*
    [*He catches* PERICLES *rashly by the hand*]
And you, sir, hear you: either be ruled by me—
Or I shall make you
    [*He claps their hands together*]
105   man and wife.
Nay, come, your hands and lips must seal it too,
    [PERICLES *and* THAISA *kiss*]
And being joined, I'll thus your hopes destroy,
    [*He parts them*]
And for your further grief, God give you joy.
What, are you pleased?
THAISA   Yes, [*to* PERICLES] if you love me, sir.
110 PERICLES   Ev'n as my life° my blood that fosters it.   *as my life loves*
KING SIMONIDES   What, are you both agreed?
PERICLES *and* THAISA   Yes, if't please your majesty.
KING SIMONIDES   It pleaseth me so well that I will see you wed,
Then with what haste you can, get you to bed.   *Exeunt*

Scene 10

Enter GOWER
GOWER   Now sleep y-slackèd hath the rout,[1]
No din but snores the house about,
Made louder by the o'erfed breast
Of this most pompous° marriage feast.   *lavish*
5 The cat with eyne° of burning coal   *eyes*
Now couches fore the mouse's hole,
And crickets sing at th'oven's mouth
As the blither for their drouth.[2]
Hymen° hath brought the bride to bed,   *god of marriage*

Scene 10 (Act 3, Chorus)   2. As if happier for being dry.
1. Sleep has rendered everyone inactive.

10 Where by the loss of maidenhead
    A babe is moulded. Be attent,°   attentive
    And time that is so briefly spent°   spent onstage
    With your fine fancies quaintly eche.°   skillfully fill out
    What's dumb in show, I'll plain° with speech.   clarify

                    [Dumb show.]
        Enter PERICLES and SIMONIDES at one door with atten-
        dants. A messenger [comes hastily in to] them, kneels,
        and gives PERICLES a letter. PERICLES shows it SIMON-
        IDES; the lords kneel to him. Then enter THAISA with
        child, with LYCHORIDA, a nurse. The KING shows her the
        letter. She rejoices. She and PERICLES take leave of her
        father and depart [with LYCHORIDA at one door; SIMON-
        IDES and attendants depart at another]

15 By many a dern° and painful perch°   wild / patch of land
    Of Pericles the care-full search,
    By the four opposing coigns°   corners
    Which the world together joins,
    Is made with all due diligence
20 That horse and sail and high expense
    Can stead° the quest. At last from Tyre   sustain in
    Fame° answering the most strange enquire,°   Rumor / distant queries
    To th' court of King Simonides
    Are letters brought, the tenor these:
25 Antiochus and his daughter dead,
    The men of Tyrus on the head
    Of Helicanus would set on
    The crown of Tyre, but he will° none.   desires
    The mutiny there he hastes t'appease,
30 Says to 'em if King Pericles
    Come not home in twice six moons
    He, obedient to their dooms,°   judgments
    Will take the crown. The sum of this
    Brought hither to Pentapolis
35 Y-ravishèd° the regions round,   Enraptured
    And everyone with claps can° sound   started to
    'Our heir-apparent is a king!
    Who dreamt, who thought of such a thing?'
    Brief° he must hence depart to Tyre;   In short; quickly
40 His queen with child makes her desire—
    Which who shall cross?—along to go.
    Omit we all their dole and woe.
    Lychorida her nurse she takes,
    And so to sea. Their vessel shakes
45 On Neptune's billow. Half the flood°   sea
    Hath their keel cut, but fortune's mood
    Varies again. The grizzled° north   grisly
    Disgorges such a tempest forth
    That as a duck for life that dives,
50 So up and down the poor ship drives.
    The lady shrieks, and well-a-near°   alas
    Does fall in travail° with her fear,   Goes into labor
    And what ensues in this fell° storm   cruel
    Shall for itself itself perform;
55 I nill° relate; action may   will not

Conveniently the rest convey,
Which might not what by me is told.[3]
In your imagination hold°   think
This stage the ship, upon whose deck
60   The sea-tossed Pericles appears to speke.   [*Exit*]

Scene 11

[*Thunder and lightning.*] *Enter* PERICLES *a-shipboard*

PERICLES   The god of this great vast° rebuke these surges   vast sea
Which wash both heav'n and hell; and thou that hast
Upon the winds command, bind them in brass,
Having called them from the deep. O still°   quiet
5   Thy deaf'ning dreadful thunders, gently quench
Thy nimble sulph'rous flashes.—O, ho, Lychorida!
How does my queen?—Thou stormest venomously.
Wilt thou spit all thyself? The seaman's whistle
Is as a whisper in the ears of death,°   of a dead person
10   Unheard.—Lychorida!—Lucina,° O!   goddess of childbirth
Divinest patroness, and midwife gentle
To those that cry by night, convey thy deity
Aboard our dancing boat, make swift the pangs
Of my queen's travails!—Now, Lychorida.
Enter LYCHORIDA [*with an infant*]
15   LYCHORIDA   Here is a thing too young for such a place,
Who, if it had conceit,° would die, as I   understanding
Am like° to do. Take in your arms this piece   likely
Of your dead queen.
PERICLES   How, how, Lychorida?
LYCHORIDA   Patience, good sir, do not assist the storm.°   (*by ranting and tears*)
20   Here's all that is left living of your queen,
A little daughter. For the sake of it
Be manly, and take comfort.
PERICLES   O you gods!
Why do you make us love your goodly gifts,
And snatch them straight away? We here below
25   Recall° not what we give, and therein may   Demand back
Use honour with you.[1]
LYCHORIDA   Patience, good sir,
E'en for this charge.[2]
        [*She gives him the infant.* PERICLES, *looking mournfully
        upon it, shakes his head, and weeps*]
PERICLES   Now mild may be thy life,
For a more blust'rous birth had never babe;
Quiet and gentle thy conditions,° for   circumstances
30   Thou art the rudeliest welcome to this world
That e'er was prince's child; happy° what follows.   let be happy
Thou hast as chiding° a nativity   upsetting
As fire, air, water, earth, and heav'n can make
To herald thee from th' womb. Poor inch of nature,
35   Ev'n at the first thy loss is more than can

---

3. Which could not easily "convey" what I've related so
far.
Scene 11 (Act 3, Scene 1)
Location: At sea.

1. *therein . . . you:* so we can criticize you by this standard
of honor.
2. For the sake of this child.

Thy partage quit with all thou canst find here.[3]
Now the good gods throw their best eyes° upon't.   *look favorably*
        Enter [the MASTER *and a]* SAILOR
MASTER   What, courage, sir! God save you.
PERICLES   Courage enough, I do not fear the flaw;°   *squall*
40   It hath done to me its worst. Yet for the love
    Of this poor infant, this fresh new seafarer,
    I would it would be quiet.
MASTER *[calling]*   Slack the bow-lines, there.—Thou° wilt not,   *(the storm)*
    wilt thou? Blow, and split thyself.
45   SAILOR   But searoom,[4] an° the brine and cloudy billow kiss the   *if*
    moon, I care not.
MASTER *[to* PERICLES*]*   Sir, your queen must overboard. The sea
    works° high, the wind is loud, and will not lie° till the ship be   *surges / lie still*
    cleared of the dead.
50   PERICLES   That's but your superstition.
MASTER   Pardon us, sir; with us at sea it hath been still° observed,   *always*
    and we are strong in custom. Therefore briefly° yield 'er, for   *quickly*
    she must overboard straight.
PERICLES   As you think meet. Most wretched queen!
LYCHORIDA   Here she lies, sir.
        [She draws the curtains and discovers the body of Thaisa
        in a bed. PERICLES *gives* LYCHORIDA *the infant]*
55   PERICLES *[to* THAISA*]*   A terrible childbed hast thou had, my dear,
    No light, no fire. Th'unfriendly elements
    Forgot thee utterly, nor have I time
    To give thee hallowed to thy grave, but straight
    Must cast thee, scarcely coffined, in the ooze,°   *seabed*
60   Where, for° a monument upon thy bones   *in place of*
    And aye-remaining° lamps, the belching whale   *ever-burning*
    And humming water must o'erwhelm thy corpse,
    Lying with simple shells.—O Lychorida,
    Bid Nestor bring me spices, ink, and paper,
65   My casket and my jewels, and bid Nicander
    Bring me the satin coffer. Lay the babe
    Upon the pillow. Hie° thee whiles I say   *Hurry*
    A priestly farewell to her. Suddenly,° woman.   *Immediately*
                                    [Exit LYCHORIDA*]*
    SAILOR   Sir, we have a chest beneath the hatches caulked and
70   bitumed[5] ready.
PERICLES   I thank thee. *[To the* MASTER*]* Mariner, say, what coast is this?
MASTER   We are near Tarsus.
PERICLES   Thither, gentle mariner,
    Alter thy course from Tyre. When canst thou reach it?
MASTER   By break of day, if the wind cease.
PERICLES   Make for Tarsus.
75   There will I visit Cleon, for the babe
    Cannot hold out to Tyrus. There I'll leave it
    At careful nursing. Go thy ways,° good mariner.   *Get to it*
    I'll bring the body presently.
            *Exit [*MASTER *at one door and* SAILOR *beneath*
                the hatches. Exit PERICLES *to* THAISA,
                        closing the curtains]

3. *than . . . here:* than your share of anything you find   4. As long as we're at sea (safe from the rocks).
in this life can make up for.   5. *bitumed:* caulked with pitch.

Scene 12

Enter Lord CERIMON *with a [poor man and a] servant*

CERIMON   Philemon, ho!

Enter PHILEMON

PHILEMON   Doth my lord call?

CERIMON   Get fire and meat for those poor men.[1]

                                    [*Exit* PHILEMON]

'T'as been a turbulent and stormy night.

SERVANT   I have seen many, but such a night as this

5   Till now I ne'er endured.

CERIMON   Your master will be dead ere you return.

    There's nothing can be ministered in nature

    That can recover him. [*To poor man*] Give this to th' pothecary°   *druggist*

    And tell me how it works.

                        [*Exeunt poor man and servant*]

Enter two GENTLEMEN

FIRST GENTLEMAN   Good morrow.

SECOND GENTLEMAN   Good morrow to your lordship.

10   CERIMON   Gentlemen,

    Why do you stir so early?

FIRST GENTLEMAN   Sir,

    Our lodgings, standing bleak upon° the sea,   *exposed to*

    Shook as° the earth did quake.   *as if*

    The very principals° did seem to rend   *principal rafters*

15   And all to topple. Pure surprise and fear

    Made me to quit the house.

SECOND GENTLEMAN   That is the cause we trouble you so early;

    'Tis not our husbandry.°   *good work habits*

CERIMON   O, you say well.

FIRST GENTLEMAN   But I much marvel that your lordship should,

20   Having rich tire° about you, at this hour   *bed furniture*

    Shake off the golden slumber of repose. 'Tis most strange,

    Nature to be so conversant with pain,[2]

    Being thereto not compelled.

CERIMON   I held it ever;°   *always believed*

    Virtue and cunning° were endowments greater   *knowledge*

25   Than nobleness and riches. Careless heirs

    May the two latter darken and dispend,°   *expend*

    But immortality attends the former,

    Making a man a god. 'Tis known I ever°   *always*

    Have studied physic,° through which secret art,   *medicine*

30   By turning o'er authorities,° I have,   *reading learned texts*

    Together with my practice, made familiar

    To me and to my aid° the blest infusions   *assistant*

    That dwells in vegetives,[3] in metals, stones,

    And so can speak of the disturbances

35   That nature works, and of her cures, which doth give me

    A more content° and cause of true delight   *greater happiness*

    Than to be thirsty after tott'ring° honour,   *unstable*

    Or tie my pleasure up in silken bags°   *(of money)*

    To glad the fool and death.[4]

Scene 12 (Act 3, Scene 2)
Location: Cerimon's house in Ephesus.
1. Offstage supplicants. Qls "these poor men" might refer to characters onstage.

2. That your nature should be so accustomed to labor.
3. Beneficial substances in plants.
4. To gladden the fool who trusts in wealth, which death inherits.

SECOND GENTLEMAN   Your honour has
40 Through Ephesus poured forth your charity,
    And hundreds call themselves your creatures⁵ who by you
    Have been restored. And not alone your knowledge,
    Your personal pain,° but e'en your purse still° open   labor / always
    Hath built Lord Cerimon such strong renown
45 As time shall never—
            *Enter [*PHILEMON *and one] or* two⁶ *with a chest*
PHILEMON   So, lift there.
CERIMON   What's that?
PHILEMON   Sir, even now
    The sea tossed up upon our shore this chest.
    'Tis off some wreck.
50 CERIMON   Set't down. Let's look upon't.
SECOND GENTLEMAN   'Tis like a coffin, sir.
CERIMON   Whate'er it be,
    'Tis wondrous heavy.—Did the sea cast it up?
PHILEMON   I never saw so huge a billow, sir,
    Or a more eager.⁷
CERIMON   Wrench it open straight.
        [*The others start to work*]
55 If the sea's stomach be o'ercharged with gold
    'Tis by a good constraint of queasy fortune⁸
    It belches upon us.
SECOND GENTLEMAN   'Tis so, my lord.
CERIMON   How close° 'tis caulked and bitumed!   tightly
        [*They force the lid*]
                                    Soft,° it smells   But wait
    Most sweetly in my sense.
SECOND GENTLEMAN   A delicate odour.
60 CERIMON   As ever hit my nostril. So, up with it.
        [*They take the lid off*]
    O you most potent gods! What's here—a corpse?
SECOND GENTLEMAN
    Most strange.
CERIMON   Shrouded in cloth of state,° and crowned,   royal fabric
    Balmed and entreasured with full bags of spices.
    A passport,° too!   An identification paper
        [*He takes a paper from the chest*]
65 Apollo perfect me i'th' characters.⁹
    'Here I give to understand,
    If e'er this coffin drives a-land,
    I, King Pericles, have lost
    This queen worth all our mundane cost.°   earthly wealth
70 Who° finds her, give her burying;   Whoever
    She was the daughter of a king.
    Besides this treasure for a fee,
    The° gods requite his charity.'   May the

---

5. *call . . . creatures:* owe their lives to you.
6. "Philemon" replaces Q1's "two or three" here, "Servant" in the speech prefixes to lines 46–53, and "one" in the stage direction to line 84, in accord with the emphasis on one of Cerimon's assistants in Twine's *Patterne of Painefull Adventures* and in order to make sense of Philemon's appearance at the beginning of the scene.
7. *Did . . . eager:* In Q1, these lines appear after "bitumed" (line 58), where the question seems inappro-

priate. The passage is then followed by "Wrench it open," which repeats line 54. Here, "Or a more eager," adapted from *PA*, replaces Q1's "as tossed it upon shore" (which repeats Q1's "toss up upon our shore," line 49). These changes seek to remedy the possibly faulty memory of the reporters.
8. By the force of uncertain fortune that.
9. Apollo (patron of both scholars and physicians) help me read the writing correctly.

If thou liv'st, Pericles, thou hast a heart
75 That even cracks for woe. This chanced tonight.°   *occurred last night*
SECOND GENTLEMAN   Most likely, sir.
CERIMON   Nay, certainly tonight,
For look how fresh she looks. They were too rash
That threw her in the sea. Make a fire within.
Fetch hither all my boxes in my closet.   [*Exit* PHILEMON]
80 Death may usurp on nature many hours,
And yet the fire of life kindle again
The o'erpressed° spirits. I have heard   *overcome*
Of an Egyptian nine hours dead
Who was by good appliances° recovered.   *medical treatments*
          Enter [PHILEMON] *with napkins and fire*
85 Well said, well said, the fire and cloths.
The still° and woeful music that we have,   *soft*
Cause it to sound, beseech you.
          [*Music*]
                                        The vial° once more.   *(of medicine)*
How thou stirr'st,¹ thou block! The music there!
I pray you give her air.° Gentlemen,   *(pun on "heir")*
90 This queen will live. Nature awakes, a warmth
Breathes out of her. She hath not been entranced°   *unconscious*
Above five hours. See how she 'gins to blow°   *bloom*
Into life's flow'r again.
FIRST GENTLEMAN   The heavens
Through you increase our wonder, and set up
Your fame for ever.
95 CERIMON   She is alive. Behold,
Her eyelids, cases to those heav'nly jewels
Which Pericles hath lost,
Begin to part their fringes of bright gold.
The diamonds of a most praisèd water²   *luster*
100 Doth appear to make the world twice rich.²—Live,
And make us weep to hear your fate, fair creature,
Rare° as you seem to be.   *Exquisite*
          She moves
THAISA   O dear Diana,
Where am I? Where's my lord? What world is this?
SECOND GENTLEMAN
Is not this strange?
FIRST GENTLEMAN   Most rare.
CERIMON   Hush, gentle neighbours.
105 Lend me your hands. To the next chamber bear her.
Get linen. Now this matter must be looked to,
For her relapse is mortal.° Come, come,   *would be fatal*
And Aesculapius° guide us.   *They carry her away. Exeunt*   *god of healing*

Scene 13
Enter PERICLES *at Tarsus, with* CLEON *and* DIONYZA
          [*and* LYCHORIDA *with a babe*]
PERICLES   Most honoured Cleon, I must needs be gone.
My twelve months are expired, and Tyrus stands

---

1. How lively you are (ironic).
2. Once by the precious gold of her eyelids and again
by the jewels they conceal.

Scene 13 (Act 3, Scene 3)
Location: The Governor's house in Tarsus.

In a litigious° peace. You and your lady   *conflict-ridden*
Take from my heart all thankfulness. The gods
Make up the rest upon you!¹

5 CLEON   Your strokes of fortune,
   Though they hurt you mortally, yet glance
   Full woundingly on us.

DIONYZA   O your sweet queen!
   That the strict fates had pleased you'd brought her hither
   T'have blessed mine eyes with her!

PERICLES   We cannot but obey

10 The pow'rs above us. Should° I rage and roar   *Even if*
   As doth the sea she lies in, yet the end
   Must be as 'tis. My gentle babe Marina,
   Whom for° she was born at sea I have named so,   *because*
   Here I charge° your charity withal,° and leave her   *saddle / with*

15 The infant of your care, beseeching you
   To give her princely training, that she may be
   Mannered° as she is born.   *Instructed in manners*

CLEON   Fear not, my lord, but think
   Your grace, that fed my country with your corn—°
   For which the people's pray'rs still fall upon you—

20 Must in your child be thought on. If neglection
   Should therein make me vile, the common body°   *the people*
   By you relieved would force me to my duty.
   But if to that° my nature need a spur,   *that duty*
   The gods revenge it upon me and mine
   To th' end of generation.

25 PERICLES   I believe you.
   Your honour and your goodness teach me to't°   *to do so*
   Without your vows.—Till she be married, madam,
   By bright Diana, whom we honour all,
   Unscissored shall this hair of mine remain,

30 Though I show ill° in't. So I take my leave.   *look bad*
   Good madam, make me blessèd in your care
   In bringing up my child.

DIONYZA   I have one myself,
   Who shall not be more dear to my respect°   *attention*
   Than yours, my lord.

PERICLES   Madam, my thanks and prayers.

35 CLEON   We'll bring your grace e'en to the edge o'th' shore,
     Then give you up to th' masted Neptune° and   *ship-conveying sea*
     The gentlest winds of heaven.

PERICLES   I will embrace your offer.—Come, dear'st madam.—
   O, no tears, Lychorida, no tears.

40 Look to your little mistress, on whose grace°   *favor*
   You may depend hereafter.—Come, my lord.   [*Exeunt*]

Scene 14

Enter CERIMON *and* THAISA

CERIMON   Madam, this letter and some certain jewels
   Lay with you in your coffer, which are all
   At your command. Know you the character?°   *handwriting*

---

1. Give you the rest of what you deserve.   Scene 14 (Act 3, Scene 4)
                                      Location: Cerimon's house in Ephesus.

THAISA   It is my lord's. That I was shipped° at sea   *on a ship*
5   I well remember, ev'n on my eaning° time,   *birthing*
       But whether there delivered, by th' holy gods
       I cannot rightly say. But since King Pericles,
       My wedded lord, I ne'er shall see again,
       A vestal liv'ry[1] will I take me to,
10   And never more have joy.

CERIMON   Madam, if this you purpose° as ye speak,   *intend*
       Diana's temple is not distant far,
       Where till your date° expire you may abide.   *time of life*
       Moreover, if you please a niece of mine
15   Shall there attend you.

THAISA   My recompense is thanks, that's all,
       Yet my good will is great, though the gift small.   *Exeunt*

Scene 15

Enter GOWER

GOWER   Imagine Pericles arrived at Tyre,
       Welcomed and settled to his own desire.
       His woeful queen we leave at Ephesus,
       Unto Diana there 's a votaress.°   *as a devotee*
5   Now to Marina bend your mind,
       Whom our fast-growing scene must find
       At Tarsus, and by Cleon trained
       In music, letters; who hath gained
       Of education all the grace,
10   Which makes her both the heart and place°   *focal point*
       Of gen'ral wonder. But, alack,
       That monster envy, oft the wrack°   *ruin*
       Of earnèd praise, Marina's life
       Seeks to take off by treason's knife,
15   And in this kind° our Cleon has   *connection*
       One daughter, and a full-grown lass
       E'en ripe for marriage-rite. This maid
       Hight° Philoten, and it is said   *Is called*
       For certain in our story she
20   Would ever° with Marina be,   *always*
       Be't when they weaved the sleided° silk   *divided into filaments*
       With fingers long, small, white as milk;
       Or when she would with sharp nee'le° wound   *needle*
       The cambric° which she made more sound   *fine linen*
25   By hurting it, or when to th' lute
       She sung, and made the night bird° mute,   *nightingale*
       That still records° with moan; or when   *always sings*
       She would with rich and constant pen
       Vail° to her mistress Dian. Still   *Inscribe praises*
30   This Philoten contends in skill
       With absolute° Marina; so   *perfect*
       With dove of Paphos might the crow

---

1. Vestal virgin's uniform of religious chastity.
Scene 15 (Other modern editions treat Gower's monologue as a prologue to Act 4 and start Act 4, Scene 1, at
line 53. This edition assumes that the grave Marina goes
"to strew" [line 66] "is revealed" during Gower's speech
[stage direction after line 42], that Dionyza and Leonine
enter here, rather than [as in Q1] at the end of that
speech, and hence that the scene does not change.)
Location: Tarsus, near the seashore.

Vie feathers white.[1] Marina gets
All praises which are paid as debts,
35   And not as given.[2] This so darks°   *(by comparison)*
In Philoten all graceful marks
That Cleon's wife with envy rare°   *extreme*
A present murder does prepare
For good Marina, that her daughter
40   Might stand peerless by° this slaughter.   *by means of*
The sooner her vile thoughts to stead°   *help*
Lychorida, our nurse, is dead,

[A tomb is revealed]

And cursèd Dionyza hath
The pregnant instrument of wrath
45   Pressed for this blow.[3] Th'unborn event°   *outcome*
I do commend to your content,°   *(viewing) pleasure*
Only I carry wingèd Time
Post° on the lame feet of my rhyme,   *Quickly*
Which never could I so convey
50   Unless your thoughts went on my way.

Enter DIONYZA *with* LEONINE

Dionyza does appear,
With Leonine, a murderer.   *Exit*

DIONYZA   Thy oath remember. Thou hast sworn to do't.
'Tis but a blow, which never shall be known.
55   Thou canst not do a thing i'th' world so soon°   *quickly*
To yield thee so much profit. Let not conscience,
Which is but cold, or fanning love thy bosom
Unflame[4] too nicely,° nor let pity, which   *scrupulously*
E'en women have cast off, melt thee; but be
A soldier to thy purpose.
60   LEONINE   I will do't;
But yet she is a goodly creature.
DIONYZA   The fitter then the gods should have her.

Enter MARINA *[to the tomb] with a basket of flowers*

Here she comes, weeping her only nurse's death.
Thou art resolved.
LEONINE   I am resolved.
65   MARINA   No, I will rob Tellus of her weed°   *earth of its garment*
To strew thy grave with flow'rs. The yellows, blues,
The purple violets and marigolds
Shall as a carpet hang upon thy tomb
While summer days doth last. Ay me, poor maid,
70   Born in a tempest when my mother died,
This world to me is but a ceaseless storm
Whirring° me from my friends.   *Hurrying*
DIONYZA   How now, Marina, why do you keep alone?
How chance° my daughter is not with you?   *Why is it*
75   Do not consume your blood with sorrowing.[5]
Have you a nurse of me.[6] Lord, how your favour°   *appearance*
Is changed with this unprofitable woe!

---

1. *so . . . white:* so might the crow try to be whiter than
the dove. Paphos was a city sacred to Venus.
2. *Marina . . . given:* Marina's virtues compel praise,
whether or not one wants to.
3. Has prepared a ready means for the murder.

4. *or . . . / Unflame:* or cooling love blow out the murderous flame in your bosom. Editors variously emend Q1's
"in flaming, thy love bosom, enslave."
5. Sighs were thought to consume one's blood.
6. Let me be your nurse.

Give me your flowers. Come, o'er the sea margin°   *seashore*
Walk with Leonine. The air is piercing there,
80   And quick;° it sharps the stomach.° Come, Leonine,   *refreshing / appetite*
Take her by th' arm. Walk with her.

MARINA   No, I pray you,
I'll not bereave you of your servant.

DIONYZA   Come, come,
I love the King your father and yourself
With more than foreign heart.° We ev'ry day   *As if we were kin*
85   Expect him here. When he shall come and find
Our paragon to all reports thus blasted,[7]
He will repent the breadth of his great voyage,
Blame both my lord and me, that we have taken
No care to your best courses.° Go, I pray you,   *courses of action*
90   Walk and be cheerful once again; resume
That excellent complexion which did steal
The eyes of young and old. Care not for me.
I can go home alone.

MARINA   Well, I will go,
But truly I have no desire to it.

95   DIONYZA   Nay, I know 'tis good for you. Walk half an hour,
Leonine, at the least; remember
What I have said.

LEONINE   I warr'nt° you, madam.   *guarantee*

DIONYZA [to MARINA]   I'll leave you, my sweet lady, for a while.
Pray you walk softly, do not heat your blood.
What, I must have care of you!

100   MARINA   My thanks, sweet madam.

[*Exit* DIONYZA]

Is this wind westerly that blows?

LEONINE   South-west.

MARINA   When I was born the wind was north.

LEONINE   Was't so?

MARINA   My father, as nurse says, did never fear,
But cried 'Good seamen' to the mariners,
105   Galling° his kingly hands with haling° ropes,   *Irritating / pulling*
And, clasping to the mast, endured a sea
That almost burst the deck.

LEONINE   When was this?

MARINA   When I was born.
110   Never was waves nor wind more violent.
Once from the ladder tackle washes off
A canvas-climber.° 'Ha!' says one, 'wolt out?'[8]   *sailor in the rigging*
And with a dropping° industry they skip   *dripping-wet*
From stem to stern. The boatswain whistles, and
115   The master calls and trebles their confusion.

LEONINE   Come, say your prayers.

MARINA   What mean you?

LEONINE   If you require a little space for prayer
I grant it. Pray, but be not tedious.°   *drawn out*
120   The gods are quick of ear, and I am sworn
To do my work with haste.

7. Our universally admired paragon of beauty so   8. So you want to get off ship? (a cruel joke).
blighted.

MARINA   Why would you kill me?

LEONINE   To satisfy my lady.

MARINA   Why would she have me killed?

Now, as I can remember, by my troth°   faith
I never did her hurt in all my life.
125   I never spake bad word, nor did ill turn
To any living creature. Believe me, la.°   (exclamation)
I never killed a mouse nor hurt a fly.
I trod once on a worm against my will,
But I wept for it. How have I offended
130   Wherein my death might yield her any profit
Or my life imply her danger?

LEONINE   My commission
Is not to reason of the deed, but do't.

MARINA   You will not do't for all the world, I hope.
You are well favoured, and your looks foreshow
135   You have a gentle heart. I saw you lately
When you caught° hurt in parting two that fought.   got
Good sooth,° it showed well in you. Do so now.   Truly
Your lady seeks my life. Come you between,
And save poor me, the weaker.

LEONINE   [drawing out his sword] I am sworn,
140   And will dispatch.

                   Enter PIRATES [running]

FIRST PIRATE   Hold, villain.

            [LEONINE runs away and hides behind the tomb]

SECOND PIRATE   A prize,° a prize.   Booty (Marina)

THIRD PIRATE   Half-part,° mates, half-part. Come, let's have her   To be shared
aboard suddenly.°   quickly

                   Exeunt [PIRATES carrying MARINA]

         LEONINE [steals back]

145   LEONINE   These roguing° thieves serve the great pirate Valdes.⁹   law-breaking
An° they have seized Marina, let her go.   If
There's no hope she'll return. I'll swear she's dead
And thrown into the sea; but I'll see further.
Perhaps they will but please themselves upon her,°   will only rape her
150   Not carry her aboard. If she remain,
Whom they have ravished must by me be slain.

                   Exit. [The tomb is concealed]

Scene 16

[A brothel sign.] Enter [the PANDER, his wife] the BAWD
[and their man BOULT]¹

PANDER   Boult.

BOULT   Sir.

PANDER   Search the market narrowly.° Mytilene is full of gal-   carefully
lants. We lose too much money this mart° by being wenchless.   market time
5   BAWD   We were never so much out of creatures.° We have but   prostitutes
poor three, and they can do no more than they can do, and
they with continual action are even as good as rotten.°   have venereal disease

PANDER   Therefore let's have fresh ones, whate'er we pay for

9. Probably named after an admiral in the Spanish   brothel.
Armada.   1. Pander: sexual go-between, after Pandarus in Troilus
Scene 16 (Act 4, Scene 2)   and Cressida. Bawd: supplier of prostitutes. The name
Location: Mytilene, on the island of Lesbos; before a   "Boult" may have phallic connotations.

them. If there be not a conscience to be used[2] in every trade,
10 we shall never prosper.

BAWD Thou sayst true. 'Tis not our bringing up of poor bas-
tards°—as I think I have brought up some eleven—   *(that enriches us)*

BOULT Ay, to eleven, and brought them down again.[3] But shall
I search the market?

15 BAWD What else, man? The stuff we have, a strong wind will
blow it to pieces, they are so pitifully sodden.[4]

PANDER Thou sayst true. They're too unwholesome, o' con-
science.° The poor Transylvanian is dead that lay with the little   *on my conscience*
baggage.°   *prostitute*

20 BOULT Ay, she quickly pooped° him, she made him roast meat   *overcame (by disease)*
for worms. But I'll go search the market.   *Exit*

PANDER Three or four thousand chequins° were as pretty a pro-   *gold coins*
portion° to live quietly, and so give over.°   *sum / retire*

BAWD Why to give over, I pray you? Is it a shame to get° when   *earn*
25 we are old?

PANDER O, our credit comes not in like the commodity, nor the
commodity wages not with the danger.[5] Therefore if in our
youths we could pick up some pretty estate, 'twere not amiss to
keep our door hatched.° Besides, the sore terms we stand upon   *closed for business*
30 with the gods[6] will be strong° with us for giving o'er.   *a strong argument*

BAWD Come, other sorts offend as well as we.

PANDER As well as we? Ay, and better too; we offend worse. Nei-
ther is our profession any mystery,[7] it's no calling.° But here   *(religious) vocation*
comes Boult.

Enter BOULT *with the* PIRATES *and* MARINA

35 BOULT [*to the* PIRATES] Come your ways,° my masters,° you say   *Come along / gentlemen*
she's a virgin?

A PIRATE O sir, we doubt it not.

BOULT [*to* PANDER] Master, I have gone through° for this piece°   *bargained / (of flesh)*
you see. If you like her, so;° if not, I have lost my earnest.°   *fine / deposit*

40 BAWD Boult, has she any qualities?°   *accomplishments*

BOULT She has a good face, speaks well, and has excellent good
clothes. There's no farther necessity of qualities can° make her   *whose absence can*
be refused.

BAWD What's her price, Boult?

45 BOULT I cannot be bated one doit of[8] a hundred sesterces.

PANDER [*to* PIRATES] Well, follow me, my masters. You shall
have your money presently.° [*To* BAWD] Wife, take her in,   *immediately*
instruct her what she has to do, that she may not be raw in her
entertainment.[9]   [*Exeunt* PANDER *and* PIRATES]

50 BAWD Boult, take you the marks of her, the colour of her hair,
complexion, height, her age, with warrant of her virginity, and
cry 'He that will give most shall have her first.' Such a maidenhead were no cheap thing if men were as they have been. Get
this done as I command you.

---

2. If we don't proceed diligently; if conscience can't be
economically exploited; perhaps a comic blunder for "if
conscience is involved."
3. And brought them to prostitution when they turned
eleven.
4. Overboiled in the sweating tub as treatment for venereal disease.
5. Our reputation doesn't accumulate like our profit, nor

does the profit justify the danger (with extended economic wordplay: "credit," "commodity," "wages").
6. This out-of-character admission is part of the religious
undercurrent of the scene.
7. Any secret; any (holy) trade.
8. I cannot get the price reduced a penny (*doit*: small
coin) from.
9. May not be unprepared to entertain customers.

55 BOULT Performance shall follow.   *Exit*

MARINA Alack that Leonine was so slack, so slow.
He should have struck, not spoke; or that° these pirates,   *if only*
Not enough barbarous, had but o'erboard thrown me
To seek my mother.

60 BAWD Why lament you, pretty one?

MARINA That I am pretty.

BAWD Come, the gods have done their part in you.

MARINA I accuse them not.

BAWD You are light° into my hands, where you are like° to live.   *arrived / likely*

65 MARINA The more my fault°   *misfortune*
To scape his hands where I was like to die.

BAWD Ay, and you shall live in pleasure.

MARINA No.

BAWD Yes, indeed shall you, and taste gentlemen of all fashions.
70 You shall fare well. You shall have the difference of all complexions.[1] What, do you stop your ears?

MARINA Are you a woman?

BAWD What would you have me be an I be not a woman?

MARINA An honest° woman, or not a woman.   *A chaste*

75 BAWD Marry, whip the gosling! I think I shall have something to
do° with you. Come, you're a young foolish sapling, and must   *some trouble*
be bowed as I would have you.

MARINA The gods defend me!

80 BAWD If it please the gods to defend you by men, then men
must comfort you, men must feed you, men must stir you up.
        Enter BOULT
Now, sir, hast thou cried° her through the market?   *advertised*

BOULT I have cried her almost to° the number of her hairs. I   *down to*
have drawn her picture with my voice.

BAWD And I prithee tell me, how dost thou find the inclination
85 of the people, especially of the younger sort?

BOULT Faith, they listened to me as they would have hearkened
to their fathers' testament.° There was a Spaniard's mouth   *will*
watered as he went to bed to her very description.

BAWD We shall have him here tomorrow with his best ruff° on.   *collar*

90 BOULT Tonight, tonight. But mistress, do you know the French
knight that cowers i' the hams?[2]

BAWD Who, Monsieur Veroles?

BOULT Ay, he. He offered to cut a caper[3] at the proclamation,
but he made a groan at it, and swore he would see her
95 tomorrow.

BAWD Well, well, as for him, he brought his disease hither.[4]
Here he does but repair° it. I know he will come in our shadow   *renew*
to scatter his crowns of the sun.[5]

BOULT Well, if we had of every nation a traveller, we should
100 lodge them all with this sign.[6]

BAWD [*to* MARINA] Pray you, come hither a while. You have fortunes coming upon you.[7] Mark me, you must seem to do that

---

1. The variety of appearances (temperaments; ethnici-
ties).
2. Who crouches (from venereal disease).
3. He prepared to leap up and clap his heels together.
4. Englishmen called syphilis "the French disease." This
allusion is one indication of the distinctively English feel
of the scene; see also Scene 5.
5. He will come inside our house to spend his French

crowns; to lose hair from syphilis; to spend his money on
Marina ("sun," if Q1's "in the sun" is retained). With a
play on "shadow" and "sun."
6. We would draw them all here by my pictorial description of Marina.
7. You have prosperity (wealthy men) about to come to
(have an orgasm on top of) you.

fearfully which you commit willingly, to despise profit where
you have most gain. To weep that you live as ye do° makes pity　　*(by prostitution)*
105　in your lovers. Seldom but that pity begets you a good opinion,
and that opinion a mere° profit.　　　　　　　　　　　　　　*clear*

MARINA　I understand you not.

BOULT *[to* BAWD*]*　O, take her home,° mistress, take her home.　*inside; to task*
These blushes of hers must be quenched with some present
110　practice.

BAWD　Thou sayst true, i'faith, so they must, for your bride goes
to that with shame which is her way to go with warrant.°　　*legitimately*

BOULT　Faith, some do and some do not. But mistress, if I have
bargained for the joint°—　　　　　　　　　　　　　　　　*cut of meat*

115　BAWD　Thou mayst cut a morsel off the spit.°　　　　　　*deflower her*

BOULT　I may so.

BAWD　Who should deny it? *[To* MARINA*]* Come, young one, I
like the manner of your garments well.

BOULT　Ay, by my faith, they shall not be changed yet.[8]

120　BAWD *[giving him money]*　Boult, spend thou that in the town.
Report what a sojourner we have. You'll lose nothing by cus-
tom.[9] When nature framed this piece° she meant thee a good　*(of work); (of flesh)*
turn. Therefore say what a paragon she is, and thou reapest the
harvest out of thine own setting forth.

125　BOULT　I warrant you, mistress, thunder shall not so awake the
beds of eels[1] as my giving out her beauty stirs up the lewdly
inclined. I'll bring home some tonight.　　　　　　　*[Exit]*

BAWD　Come your ways, follow me.

MARINA　If fires be hot, knives sharp, or waters deep,
130　Untied I still my virgin knot will keep.[2]
Diana° aid my purpose.　　　　　　　　　　　　　　*goddess of chastity*

BAWD　What have we to do with Diana? Pray you, will you go
with me?　　　　　　　　　　　*Exeunt. [The sign is removed]*

Scene 17

Enter [in mourning garments] CLEON *and* DIONYZA

DIONYZA　Why, are you foolish? Can it be undone?

CLEON　O Dionyza, such a piece of slaughter
The sun and moon ne'er looked upon.

DIONYZA　I think you'll turn a child again.

5　CLEON　Were I chief lord of all this spacious world
I'd give it to undo the deed. A lady°　　　　　　　　　　　　*(Marina)*
Much less in blood than virtue, yet a princess
To equal any single crown o'th' earth
I'th' justice of compare.° O villain Leonine,　　　　*In a fair comparison*
10　Whom thou hast poisoned too,
If thou hadst drunk to him 't'ad been a kindness
Becoming well thy fact.[1] What canst thou say
When noble Pericles demands his child?

DIONYZA　That she is dead. Nurses are not the fates.

---

8. Exchanged or sold (for a prostitute's wardrobe), since
they proclaim her virginity and social status.
9. You'll profit from the resulting increase in our customers; (perhaps) you'll get your turn with Marina.
1. Eels were supposedly roused by thunder.
2. An "Untied . . . virgin knot" presumably means loss of
virginity—not what Marina wants. Perhaps her intent is

suggested by the pun of "knot" and "not"—hence, not
untied.
Scene 17 (Act 4, Scene 3)
Location: The Governor's house in Tarsus.
1. *If . . . fact*: If you had drunk his health (from the same
poison), the self-punishment would have fit the crime.

15   To foster is not ever° to preserve.   *always*
        She died at night. I'll say so. Who can cross° it,   *deny*
        Unless you play the pious innocent
        And, for an honest attribute,° cry out   *reputation*
        'She died by foul play.'
    CLEON   O, go to.° Well, well,   *(contemptuous)*
20   Of all the faults beneath the heav'ns the gods
        Do like this worst.
    DIONYZA   Be one of those that thinks
        The petty wrens of Tarsus will fly hence
        And open° this to Pericles. I do shame   *disclose*
        To think of what a noble strain° you are,   *bloodline*
        And of how cowed a spirit.
25   CLEON   To such proceeding
        Whoever but his approbation added,
        Though not his prime° consent, he did not flow   *prior*
        From honourable sources.
    DIONYZA   Be it so, then.
        Yet none does know but you how she came dead,
30   Nor none can know, Leonine being gone.
        She did distain° my child, and stood between   *stain (by comparison)*
        Her and her fortunes. None would look on her,
        But cast their gazes on Marina's face
        Whilst ours was blurted at,° and held a malkin°   *scorned / dirty peasant*
35   Not worth the time of day. It pierced me through,
        And though you call my course unnatural,
        You not your child well loving, yet I find
        It greets° me as an enterprise of kindness   *strikes*
        Performed to your sole daughter.
40   CLEON   Heavens forgive it.
    DIONYZA   And as for Pericles,
        What should he say? We wept after her hearse,
        And yet° we mourn. Her monument   *still*
        Is almost finished, and her epitaphs
45   In glitt'ring golden characters express
        A gen'ral praise to her and care in us,
        At whose expense 'tis done.
    CLEON   Thou art like the harpy,[2]
        Which, to betray, dost, with thine angel face,
         Seize in thine eagle talons.
50   DIONYZA   Ye're like one that superstitiously
        Do swear to th' gods that winter kills the flies,[3]
        But yet I know you'll do as I advise.   *Exeunt*

Scene 18

Enter GOWER

    GOWER   Thus time we waste,° and long leagues make we short,[1]   *pass quickly*
        Sail seas in cockles,° have and wish but for't,[2]   *seashells*
        Making to take° imagination   *Proceeding by*
        From bourn° to bourn, region to region.   *border*

---

2. Monstrous creature with a woman's face and an eagle's talons.
3. *Ye're . . . flies*: perhaps, You're so afraid of the gods that you'd feel it necessary to tell them insignificant and unalterable things they already know (that winter killed the flies).

Scene 18 Scene 18 (Act, Scene 4)
Location: Before Marina's tomb in Tarsus.
1. Here Gower speaks in pentameter couplets.
2. Get something merely by wishing for it.

5   By you being pardoned, we commit no crime
To use one language in each sev'ral clime°   *separate region*
Where our scene seems to live. I do beseech you
To learn of me, who stand i'th' gaps° to teach you   *(between scenes)*
The stages of our story: Pericles

10   Is now again thwarting° the wayward seas,   *crossing*
Attended on by many a lord and knight,
To see his daughter, all his life's delight.
Old Helicanus goes along. Behind
Is left to govern, if you bear in mind,

15   Old Aeschines, whom Helicanus late°   *recently*
Advanced in Tyre to great and high estate.°   *rank*
Well sailing ships and bounteous winds have brought
This king to Tarsus—think his pilot thought;[3]
So with his steerage shall your thoughts go on—

20   To fetch his daughter home, who first° is gone.   *already*
Like motes and shadows[4] see them move a while;
Your ears unto your eyes I'll reconcile.

                                [*Dumb show.*]

> *Enter* PERICLES *at one door with all his train,* CLEON
> *and* DIONYZA [*in mourning garments*] *at the other.*
> CLEON [*draws the curtain and*] *shows* PERICLES *the*
> *tomb, whereat* PERICLES *makes lamentation, puts on*
> *sack-cloth, and in a mighty passion° departs* [*followed by*   *sorrow*
> *his train.* CLEON *and* DIONYZA *depart at the other door*]

See how belief may suffer by foul show.°   *false appearances*
This borrowed passion stands for true-owed woe,[5]

25   And Pericles, in sorrow all devoured,
With sighs shot through, and biggest tears o'ershow'red,
Leaves Tarsus, and again embarks. He swears
Never to wash his face nor cut his hairs.
He puts on sack-cloth, and to sea. He bears

30   A tempest which his mortal vessel tears,[6]
And yet he rides it out. Now please you wit°   *know*
The epitaph is° for Marina writ   *that is*
By wicked Dionyza.

         [*He reads Marina's epitaph[7] on the tomb*]

'The fairest, sweetest, best lies here,

35   Who withered in her spring of year.°   *early in life*
In nature's garden, though by growth a bud,
She was the chiefest flower: she was good.'
No visor does become black villainy
So well as soft and tender flattery.

40   Let Pericles believe his daughter's dead
And bear his courses to be orderèd[8]
By Lady Fortune, while our scene must play
His daughter's woe and heavy well-a-day°   *lamentation*
In her unholy service. Patience then,

45   And think you now are all in Mytilene.

                                      Exit

---

3. Think that his pilot is swiftly traveling thought.
4. Like specks of dust in a sunbeam and like (theatrical) illusions.
5. Cleon and Dionyza's "woe" is "borrowed," not "true-owed" (owned); perhaps also a self-referential comment on the sorrow simulated by the actor playing Pericles.
6. *He bears . . . tears:* His suffering assaults his body.

(Note the internalization of the earlier storms.)
7. The four-line epitaph is from *PA*, which may preserve the author's revised version of this passage. Q1's ten-line version (see the Additional Passage at the end of the play) includes the first two lines here.
8. And allow his fate to be arranged.

Scene 19

[*A brothel sign.*] *Enter two* GENTLEMEN

FIRST GENTLEMAN   Did you ever hear the like?

SECOND GENTLEMAN   No, nor never shall do in such a place as
this, she being once gone.

FIRST GENTLEMAN   But to have divinity preached there—did you
5   ever dream of such a thing?

SECOND GENTLEMAN   No, no. Come, I am for no more bawdy
houses. Shall 's go hear the vestals sing?[1]

FIRST GENTLEMAN   I'll do anything now that is virtuous, but I am
out of the road of rutting° for ever.   *Exeunt*   *fornication*

Enter [PANDER,] BAWD [*and* BOULT]

10   PANDER   Well, I had rather than twice the worth of her she had
ne'er come here.

BAWD   Fie, fie upon her, she's able to freeze the god Priapus and
undo the whole of generation.[2] We must either get her ravished
or be rid of her. When she should do for clients her fitment°   *duty*
15   and do me the kindness of our profession,[3] she has° me her   *gives*
quirks, her reasons, her master reasons, her prayers, her knees,°   *(kneeling to plead)*
that she would make a puritan of the devil if he should
cheapen° a kiss of her.   *bargain for*

BOULT   Faith, I must ravish her, or she'll disfurnish us of all our
20   cavalleria° and make our swearers[4] priests.   *gentlemen customers*

PANDER   Now, the pox upon her green-sickness[5] for me.

BAWD   Faith, there's no way to be rid on't but by the way to the pox.°   *venereal disease*

Enter LYSIMACHUS [*disguised*]

Here comes the Lord Lysimachus, disguised.

BOULT   We should have both lord and loon° if the peevish bag-   *lowborn*
25   gage° would but give way to custom.[6]   *worthless woman*

LYSIMACHUS   How now, how° a dozen of virginities?   *how much for*

BAWD   Now, the gods to-bless your honour!

BOULT   I am glad to see your honour in good health.

LYSIMACHUS   You may so. 'Tis the better for you that your resort-
30   ers stand upon sound legs.[7] How now, wholesome iniquity°   *healthy whore*
have you, that a man may deal withal° and defy the surgeon?°   *with / avoid the doctor*

BAWD   We have here one, sir, if she would—but there never
came her like in Mytilene.

LYSIMACHUS   If she'd do the deed of darkness, thou wouldst say.

35   BAWD   Your honour knows what 'tis to say° well enough.   *what I mean*

LYSIMACHUS   Well, call forth, call forth.   [*Exit* PANDER]

BOULT   For flesh and blood, sir, white and red, you shall see a
rose. And she were a rose indeed, if she had but—[8]

LYSIMACHUS   What, prithee?

40   BOULT   O sir, I can be modest.

Scene 19 (Other modern editions divide this scene in
two: Act 4, Scene 5 [lines 1–9] and Scene 6 [lines 10–
211]. But the location remains in or around the brothel
throughout. This edition assumes both that there is no
gap in time between the two parts and that the modest
shifts in locale within the scene do not violate the relatively unspecific notion of place on the early seventeenth-
century stage.)
Location: The brothel in Mytilene.
1. Shall we go hear the vestal virgins (religious devotees)
sing?
2. Able to stop the "whole" (hole) work of breeding.

Priapus was the god of procreation, especially of male
virility and lechery. "The whole of" emends Q1's "a
whole."
3. Enable me to profit from her profession of prostitution;
perhaps also homoerotic: have sex with me.
4. Loyal (blasphemous) customers.
5. Moody stubbornness, supposedly caused by anemia in
young women; queasiness from lack of experience.
6. Customers; customary behavior. Q1 has "customers."
7. Rather than upon legs bent from venereal disease.
8. If she had but a thorn; if she were sexually experienced.

LYSIMACHUS   That dignifies the renown of a bawd no less than
    it gives a good report to a noble to be chaste.[9]
               Enter [PANDER *with*] MARINA

BAWD   Here comes that which grows to° the stalk, never plucked   *affixed to*
    yet, I can assure you. Is she not a fair creature?

45 LYSIMACHUS   Faith, she would serve after a long voyage at sea.
    Well, there's for you. Leave us.
           [*He pays the* BAWD]

BAWD   I beseech your honour give me leave: a word, and I'll
    have done presently.°   *be done soon*

LYSIMACHUS   I beseech you, do.

50 BAWD [*aside to* MARINA]   First, I would have you note this is an
    honourable man.

MARINA   I desire to find him so, that I may honourably know him.

BAWD   Next, he's the governor of this country, and a man whom
    I am bound to.

55 MARINA   If he govern the country you are bound to him indeed,
    but how honourable he is in that, I know not.

BAWD   Pray you, without any more virginal fencing, will you use
    him kindly? He will line your apron with gold.

MARINA   What he will do graciously I will thankfully receive.

60 LYSIMACHUS [*to* BAWD]   Ha' you done?

BAWD   My lord, she's not paced° yet. You must take some pains   *trained (like a horse)*
    to work her to your manège.[1] [*To* BOULT *and* PANDER] Come,
    we will leave his honour and hers together. Go thy ways.°   *Come along*
                Exeunt [PANDER,] BAWD [*and* BOULT]

LYSIMACHUS   Fair one, how long have you been at this trade?

65 MARINA   What trade, sir?

LYSIMACHUS   I cannot name it but I shall offend.

MARINA   I cannot be offended with my trade.
    Please you to name it.

LYSIMACHUS   How long have you been
Of this profession?

MARINA   E'er since I can remember.

70 LYSIMACHUS   Did you go to't° so young? Were you a gamester°   *copulate / loose woman*
    At five, or seven?

MARINA   Earlier too, sir,
If now I be one.

LYSIMACHUS   Why, the house you dwell in
Proclaimeth you a creature of sale.

MARINA   And do you know this house to be a place
75 Of such resort° and will come into it?   *purpose*
I hear say you're of honourable blood,
And are the governor of this whole province.

LYSIMACHUS   What, hath your principal° informed you who I am?   *employer*

MARINA   Who is my principal?

LYSIMACHUS   Why, your herb-woman;
80 She that sets seeds of shame, roots of iniquity.
        [MARINA *weeps*]
O, you've heard something of my pow'r, and so
Stand off aloof for a more serious wooing.

---

9. Than it gives a noble(wo)man a (falsely) good reputation for being chaste. Q1 has "number" for "noble."

1. To bring her under your control (from horsemanship).

But I protest to thee,
Pretty one, my authority can wink
85 At blemishes,² or can on faults look friendly;
Or my displeasure punish at my pleasure,
From which displeasure, not thy beauty shall
Privilege thee, nor my affection,° which   lust
Hath drawn me here, abate with further ling'ring.
90 Come bring me to some private place. Come, come.
    MARINA Let not authority, which teaches you
To govern others, be the means to make you
Misgovern much yourself.³
If you were born to honour,° show it now;   high status; virtue
95 If put upon you,⁴ make the judgement good
That thought you worthy of it. What⁵ reason's in
Your justice, who hath power over all,
To undo any? If you take from me
Mine honour, you're like him that makes a gap
100 Into forbidden ground, whom after
Too many enter, and of all their evils
Yourself are guilty. My life is yet unspotted;°   still free of sin
My chastity unstainèd ev'n in thought.
Then if your violence deface this building,°   body
105 The workmanship of heav'n, you do kill your honour,
Abuse your justice, and impoverish me.
My yet good lord, if there be fire before me,
Must I straight fly° and burn myself? Suppose this house—   go immediately
Which too too many feel such houses are—
110 Should be the doctor's patrimony, and
The surgeon's feeding;° follows it, that I   livelihood
Must needs infect myself to give them maint'nance?
    LYSIMACHUS How's this, how's this? Some more. Be sage.
    MARINA [kneeling]   For me
That am a maid, though most ungentle fortune
115 Have franked° me in this sty, where since I came   shut
Diseases have been sold dearer than physic—⁶
That the gods would set me free from this unhallowed place,
Though they did change me to the meanest° bird   humblest
That flies i'th' purer air!
    LYSIMACHUS [moved]   I did not think
120 Thou couldst have spoke so well, ne'er dreamt thou couldst.
    [He lifts her up with his hands]
Though I brought hither a corrupted mind,
Thy speech hath altered it,
    [He wipes the wet from her eyes]
                    and my foul thoughts
Thy tears so well hath laved° that they're now white.   cleansed
I came here meaning but to pay the price,

2. *can wink /At blemishes*: can refuse to see moral short-comings. Lines 84–89 are adapted from *PA* and replace Q1's "my authority shall not see thee, or else look friendly upon thee," which doesn't reflect as badly on Lysimachus. Here and in subsequent passages in this scene, *PA* may preserve Shakespeare's original words.
3. *Let . . . yourself*: not in Q1 adapted from *PA*.

4. If you were granted rank not by birth but by merit.
5. Lines 96–112 are not in Q1 but were adapted from *PA*. Q1's lines 94–96 ("If . . . it") and 113–19 ("For . . . air") seem inadequate to produce Lysimachus's response at line 113 and dramatic conversion at lines 119–20.
6. Sold at a higher price than medical treatment.

125 A piece of gold for thy virginity;
     Here's twenty to relieve thine honesty.[7]
     Persever still° in that clear way thou goest,   *always*
     And the gods strengthen thee.
MARINA   The good gods preserve you!
LYSIMACHUS The[8] very doors and windows savour vilely.
130 Fare thee well. Thou art a piece of virtue,
     The best wrought up° that ever nature made,[9]   *created*
     And I doubt not thy training hath been noble.
     A curse upon him, die he° like a thief,   *may he die*
     That robs thee of thy honour. Hold, here's more gold.
135 If thou dost hear from me, it shall be for thy good.
             [*Enter* BOULT *standing ready at the door, making his*
              obeisance unto him as LYSIMACHUS *should go out*]
BOULT   I beseech your honour, one piece for me.
LYSIMACHUS Avaunt,° thou damnèd door-keeper!   *Begone*
     Your house, but for this virgin that doth prop it,
     Would sink and overwhelm you. Away.   [*Exit*]
140 BOULT   How's this? We must take another course with you. If
     your peevish chastity, which is not worth a breakfast in the
     cheapest country under the cope,° shall undo a whole house-   *sky*
     hold, let me be gelded like a spaniel. Come your ways.
MARINA   Whither would you have me?
145 BOULT   I must have your maidenhead taken off, or the common
     executioner shall do it.[1] We'll have no more gentlemen driven
     away. Come your ways, I say.
             Enter BAWD [*and* PANDER]
BAWD   How now, what's the matter?
BOULT   Worse and worse, mistress, she has here spoken holy
150 words to the Lord Lysimachus.
BAWD   O, abominable!
BOULT   She makes our profession as it were to stink afore the
     face of the gods.
BAWD   Marry° hang her up for ever!   *(expresses irritation)*
155 BOULT   The nobleman would have dealt with her like a noble-
     man,[2] and she sent him away as cold as a snowball, saying his
     prayers, too.
PANDER   Boult, take her away. Use her at thy pleasure. Crack the
     ice of her virginity, and make the rest malleable.
160 BOULT   An if° she were a thornier piece of ground than she is,   *Even if*
     she shall be ploughed.
MARINA   Hark, hark, you gods!
BAWD   She conjures.° Away with her! Would she had never   *calls on the gods*
     come within my doors.—Marry, hang you!—She's born to
165 undo us.—Will you not go the way of womenkind? Marry,
     come up, my dish of chastity with rosemary and bays.[3]
             Exeunt [BAWD *and* PANDER]
BOULT [*catching her rashly by the hand*]   Come, mistress, come
     your way with me.

---

7. To assist your chastity. Lines 124–26, adapted from *PA*, replace Q1's "Hold here's gold for thee."
8. Q1 precedes these lines with "For me be you thoughten [understand], that I came with no ill intent, for to me."
9. Line 131 not in Q1; adapted from *PA*.

1. "Executioner shall do" replaces Q1's "hāg-man shall execute," producing wordplay on "maidenhead" and "executioner" (one who chops off heads).
2. Would have used her and rewarded her well.
3. The Bawd chides Marina for thinking herself too exquisite a dish (for making too much of her chastity).

MARINA   Whither wilt thou have me?

170   BOULT   To take from you the jewel you hold so dear.

MARINA   Prithee, tell me one thing first.

BOULT   Come, now, your one thing.

MARINA   What canst thou wish thine enemy to be?[4]

BOULT   Why, I could wish him to be° my master, or rather my   *(as bad as)*

175   mistress.

MARINA   Neither of these can be so bad as thou art,
　　Since they do better thee in their command.[5]
　　Thou hold'st a place the painèd'st° fiend of hell   *most tortured*
　　Would not in reputation change with thee,

180　　Thou damnèd doorkeeper to ev'ry coistrel°   *base fellow*
　　That comes enquiring for his Tib.°   *loose woman*
　　To th' choleric fisting of ev'ry rogue
　　Thy ear is liable.[6] Thy food is such
　　As hath been belched on by infected lungs.

185   BOULT   What would you have me do? Go to the wars, would
　　you, where a man may serve seven years for the loss of° a leg,   *only to lose*
　　and have not money enough in the end to buy him a wooden one?

MARINA   Do anything but this thou dost. Empty
　　Old receptacles or common sew'rs of filth,

190　　Serve by indenture° to the public hangman—   *as apprentice*
　　Any of these are yet better than this.
　　For what thou professest a baboon, could he speak,
　　Would own a name too dear.[7] Here's gold for thee.
　　If that thy master would make gain by me,

195　　Proclaim that I can sing, weave, sew, and dance,
　　With other virtues° which I'll keep from boast,   *accomplishments*
　　And I will undertake all these to teach.
　　I doubt not but this populous city will
　　Yield many scholars.°   *pupils*

200   BOULT   But can you teach all this you speak of?

MARINA   Prove° that I cannot, take me home again   *If you prove*
　　And prostitute me to the basest groom°   *lowest servant*
　　That doth frequent your house.

BOULT   Well, I will see what I can do for thee. If I can place

205   thee, I will.

MARINA   But amongst honest women.

BOULT   Faith, my acquaintance lies little amongst them; but
　　since my master and mistress hath bought you, there's no going
　　but by their consent. Therefore I will make them acquainted

210　　with your purpose, and I doubt not but I shall find them tracta-
　　ble enough. Come, I'll do for thee what I can. Come your ways.

Exeunt. [The sign is removed]

Scene 20

Enter GOWER

GOWER   Marina thus the brothel scapes, and chances[1]
　　Into an honest house, our story says.

---

4. What is the worst thing you could wish on your
enemy?
5. Since they can command you to do what even they
wouldn't do themselves.
6. *To . . . liable:* Even the lowest rogue would box your
ear if angry.
7. Would consider beneath him. Q1 follows this sen-

tence with "That the gods would safely deliver me from
this place: here"—a repetition of line 117 that is out of
place here.
Scene 20 (Act 5, Chorus)
1. Unlike Gower's other prologues, which are in tetrameter or, less often, pentameter rhyming couplets, this one
rhymes alternate pentameter lines.

She sings like one immortal, and she dances

As goddess-like to her admirèd lays.°   *songs*

5   Deep clerks she dumbs,[2] and with her nee'le° composes   *needle*

Nature's own shape, of bud, bird, branch, or berry,

That e'en her art sisters° the natural roses.   *equals*

Her inkle,° silk, twin with the rubied cherry;   *linen thread*

That° pupils lacks she none of noble race,   *So that*

10   Who pour their bounty on her, and her gain

She gives the cursèd Bawd. Here we her place,

And to her father turn our thoughts again.

We left him on the sea. Waves there him tossed,

Whence, driven tofore° the winds, he is arrived   *before*

15 Here where his daughter dwells, and on this coast

Suppose him now at anchor. The city strived°   *surpassed itself*

God Neptune's annual feast to keep, from whence

Lysimachus our Tyrian ship espies,

His° banners sable,° trimmed with rich expense;   *Its / black*

20   And to him° in his barge with fervour hies.   *it*

In your supposing° once more put your sight;   *imagination*

Of heavy° Pericles think this the barque,°   *sad / ship*

Where what is done in action, more if might,

Shall be discovered.[3] Please you sit and hark.   *Exit*

Scene 21

Enter HELICANUS [*above; below, enter*] *to him* [*at the first door*] *two* SAILORS [*one* OF TYRE, *the other* OF MYTI-LENE]

SAILOR OF TYRE [*to* SAILOR OF MYTILENE]   Lord Helicanus can

resolve[1] you, sir.

[*To* HELICANUS] There is a barge put off from Mytilene.

In it, Lysimachus, the governor,

Who craves to come aboard. What is your will?

HELICANUS   That he have his.

                 [*Exit* SAILOR OF MYTILENE *at first door*]

5   Call up some gentlemen.

                    [*Exit* HELICANUS *above*]

SAILOR OF TYRE   Ho, my lord calls!

Enter [*from below the stage*] *two or three*

GENTLEMEN[; *to them, enter* HELICANUS]

FIRST GENTLEMAN   What is your lordship's pleasure?

HELICANUS   Gentlemen, some of worth° would come aboard.   *some noble visitor*

I pray you, greet him fairly.

Enter LYSIMACHUS [*at first door, with the* SAILOR *and*

LORDS OF MYTILENE]

SAILOR OF MYTILENE [*to* LYSIMACHUS]   This is the man that can

in aught resolve° you.   *answer anything for*

10 LYSIMACHUS [*to* HELICANUS]   Hail, reverend sir; the gods preserve you!

HELICANUS   And you, sir, to outlive the age I am,

And die as I would do.

---

2. Her wisdom reduces learned men to silence.
3. *Where . . . discovered:* Where the stage action, which would show more if it could, will reveal what happens.

Scene 21 (Act 5, Scene 1)
Location: Pericles' ship, off Mytilene.
1. Answer. This line replaces Q1's "Where is Lord Heli-canus? He can resolve you, / O here he is sir."

LYSIMACHUS   You wish me well.
I am the governor of Mytilene;[2]
Being on shore, honouring of Neptune's triumphs,[3]
15   Seeing this goodly vessel ride before us,
I made to it to know of whence you are.
HELICANUS   Our vessel is of Tyre, in it our king,
A man who for this three months hath not spoken
To anyone, nor taken sustenance
20   But to prorogue° his grief.   extend
LYSIMACHUS   Upon what ground grew his distemp'rature?°   emotional disturbance
HELICANUS   'Twould be too tedious to tell it over,
But the main grief springs from the precious loss
Of a belovèd daughter and a wife.
LYSIMACHUS   May we not see him?
25   HELICANUS   See him, sir, you may,
But bootless° is your sight. He will not speak   pointless
To any.
LYSIMACHUS   Let me yet obtain my wish.
HELICANUS   Behold him.
            [HELICANUS draws a curtain, revealing PERICLES lying
            upon a couch with a long overgrown beard, diffused°   disorderly
            hair, undecent nails on his fingers, and attired in sack-
            cloth]
                        This was a goodly person
Till the disaster of one mortal° night   fatal
Drove him to this.
30   LYSIMACHUS [to PERICLES]   Sir, King, all hail. Hail, royal sir.
            [PERICLES shrinks himself down upon his pillow]
HELICANUS   It is in vain. He will not speak to you.
LORD OF MYTILENE   Sir, we have a maid in Mytilene I durst wager
Would win some words of him.
LYSIMACHUS   'Tis well bethought.
She questionless, with her sweet harmony
35   And other choice attractions, would alarum[4]
And make a batt'ry through his deafened ports,
Which now are midway stopped.° She in all happy,°   half closed / skillful
As the fair'st of all, among her fellow maids
Dwells now i'th' leafy shelter that abuts
40   Against the island's side. Go fetch her hither.   [Exit LORD]
HELICANUS   Sure, all effectless; yet nothing we'll omit
That bears recov'ry's name.° But since your kindness   That might cure him
We have stretched thus far, let us beseech you
That for our gold we may provision have,
45   Wherein we are not destitute for want,
But weary for the staleness.
LYSIMACHUS   O sir, a courtesy
Which if we should deny, the most just gods
For every graft° would send a caterpillar,   cultivated plant
And so inflict° our province. Yet once more   afflict (with famine)

2. This line replaces Q1's
    HELICANUS   First what is your place?
    LYSIMACHUS   I am the Governor of this place you lie
        before,
which appears after line 16, where it interrupts the dialogue and attributes to Helicanus a rudeness that seems
gratuitous, since he already knows who Lysimachus is
(see line 3).
3. Observing Neptune's festival.
4. Awaken (as a trumpet). Q1 has "allure," which
introduces a sexual innuendo (see the Introduction).

50   Let me entreat to know at large° the cause   *in detail*
       Of your king's sorrow.
HELICANUS   Sit, sir. I will recount it.
       [*Enter* LORD *with* MARINA *and another* MAID]
       But see, I am prevented.
LYSIMACHUS   O, here's the lady that I sent for.—
       Welcome, fair one.—Is't not a goodly presence?°   *Isn't she attractive*
55 HELICANUS   She's a gallant° lady.   *fine*
LYSIMACHUS   She's such a one that, were I well assured
       Came of gentle kind° or noble stock, I'd wish   *a gentry family*
       No better choice to think me rarely° wed.—   *superbly*
       Fair one, all goodness that consists in bounty
60   Expect e'en here, where is a kingly patient;
       If that thy prosperous and artificial feat°   *artful skill*
       Can draw him but to answer thee in aught,
       Thy sacred physic° shall receive such pay   *treatment*
       As thy desires can wish.
MARINA   Sir, I will use
65   My utmost skill in his recure,° provided   *cure*
       That none but I and my companion maid
       Be suffered° to come near him.   *permitted*
LYSIMACHUS [*to the others*]   Let us leave her,
       And the gods prosper her.   [*The men stand aside*]
       The Song⁵
LYSIMACHUS [*coming forward*]   Marked° he your music?   *Noticed*
MAID   No, nor looked on us.
LYSIMACHUS [*to the others*]   See, she will speak to him.
70 MARINA [*to* PERICLES]   Hail, sir; my lord, lend ear.
PERICLES   Hmh, ha!
       [*He roughly repulses her*]
MARINA   I am a maid,
       My lord, that ne'er before invited eyes,
       But have been gazed on like a comet.° She speaks,
75   My lord, that maybe hath endured a grief   *in awe*
       Might° equal yours, if both were justly weighed.   *That might*
       Though wayward fortune did malign my state,°   *reduce my status*
       My derivation was from ancestors
       Who stood equivalent with mighty kings,
80   But time hath rooted out⁶ my parentage,
       And to the world and awkward casualties°   *adverse events*
       Bound me in servitude. [*Aside*] I will desist.
       But there is something glows upon my cheek,
       And whispers in mine ear 'Stay till he speak.'
85 PERICLES   My fortunes, parentage, good parentage,
       To equal mine? Was it not thus? What say you?
MARINA   I said if you did know my parentage,
       My lord, you would not do me violence.
PERICLES   I do think so. Pray you, turn your eyes upon me.
90   You're like something that—what countrywoman?°   *what nationality*
       Here of these shores?
MARINA   No, nor of any shores,

---

5. The song is given in *PA*, which takes it from Twine's   one in particular.
Patterne of Painefull Adventures. The early texts of   6. Uprooted me from; obscured; killed.
Shakespeare often call for a song without specifying any

Yet I was mortally[7] brought forth, and am
No other than I seem.

PERICLES [*aside*]   I am great° with woe, and shall deliver   *pregnant*
    weeping.
95   My dearest wife was like this maid, and such
My daughter might have been. My queen's square brows,
Her stature to an inch, as wand-like straight,
As silver-voiced, her eyes as jewel-like,
And cased as richly, in pace° another Juno,   *stride*
100   Who starves the ears she feeds, and makes them hungry
The more she gives them speech.—Where do you live?

MARINA   Where I am but a stranger.° From the deck   *foreigner*
You may discern the place.

PERICLES   Where were you bred,
And how achieved you these endowments which
You make more rich to owe?°   *by your owning them*

105   MARINA   If I should tell
My history, it would seem like lies
Disdained in the reporting.°   *as soon as told*

PERICLES   Prithee speak.
Falseness cannot come from thee, for thou look'st
Modest as justice, and thou seem'st a palace
110   For the crowned truth to dwell in. I will believe thee,
And make my senses credit thy relation°   *trust your story*
To° points that seem impossible. Thou show'st   *Even to*
Like one I loved indeed. What were thy friends?°   *kin*
Didst thou not say, when I did push thee back—
115   Which was when I perceived thee—that thou cam'st
From good descending?

MARINA   So indeed I did.

PERICLES   Report thy parentage. I think thou said'st
Thou hadst been tossed from wrong to injury,
And that thou thought'st thy griefs might equal mine,
If both were opened.°   *revealed*

120   MARINA   Some such thing I said,
And said no more but what my circumstance
Did warrant° me was likely.   *assure*

PERICLES   Tell thy story.
If thine considered prove the thousandth part
Of my endurance,° thou art a man, and I   *suffering*
125   Have suffered like a girl. Yet thou dost look
Like patience gazing on kings' graves, and smiling
Extremity out of act.[8] What were thy friends?
How lost thou them? Thy name, my most kind[9] virgin?
Recount, I do beseech thee. Come, sit by me.
    [*She sits*]

MARINA   My name, sir, is Marina.

130   PERICLES   O, I am mocked,
And thou by some incensèd god sent hither
To make the world to laugh at me.

---

7. "Normally," not supernaturally, despite not being born
on "any shores"; perhaps also "fatally"—to her mother.
8. *Yet . . . act:* Yet you seem able to bear even the deaths
of Kings (like statues of Patience personified, perhaps

on royal tombs) and to face down the worst extremities
(especially suicidal despair) with a smile.
9. Sympathetic; related by blood ("kind" also meant
"kin").

MARINA   Patience, good sir,
Or here I'll cease.
PERICLES   Nay, I'll be patient.
Thou little know'st how thou dost startle me
To call thyself Marina.
135 MARINA   The name
Was given me by one that had some power:
My father, and a king.
PERICLES   How, a king's daughter,
And called Marina?
MARINA   You said you would believe me,
But not to be a troubler of your peace
I will end here.
140 PERICLES   But are you flesh and blood?
Have you a working pulse and are no fairy?
Motion° as well? Speak on. Where were you born,   *(of life)*
And wherefore called Marina?
MARINA   Called Marina
For I was born at sea.
PERICLES   At sea? What mother?
145 MARINA   My mother was the daughter of a king,
Who died when I was born, as my good nurse
Lychorida hath oft recounted weeping.
PERICLES   O, stop there a little! [*Aside*] This is the rarest dream
That e'er dulled sleep did mock sad fools withal.°   *with*
150 This cannot be my daughter, buried. Well.
[*To* MARINA] Where were you bred? I'll hear you more to th'
    bottom°   *the end*
Of your story, and never interrupt you.
MARINA   You will scarce believe me. 'Twere best I did give o'er.°   *stop*
PERICLES   I will believe you by the syllable
155 Of what you shall deliver. Yet give me leave.°   *(to ask)*
How came you in these parts? Where were you bred?
MARINA   The King my father did in Tarsus leave me,
Till cruel Cleon, with his wicked wife,
Did seek to murder me, and wooed a villain
160 To attempt the deed; who having drawn to do't,
A crew of pirates came and rescued me.
To Mytilene they brought me. But, good sir,
What will you° of me? Why do you weep? It may be   *What do you want*
You think me an impostor. No, good faith,
165 I am the daughter to King Pericles,
If good King Pericles be.°   *live*
PERICLES [*rising*]   Ho, Helicanus!
HELICANUS [*coming forward*]   Calls my lord?
PERICLES   Thou art a grave and noble counsellor,
170 Most wise in gen'ral. Tell me if thou canst
What this maid is, or what is like° to be,   *likely*
That thus hath made me weep.
HELICANUS   I know not.
But here's the regent, sir, of Mytilene
Speaks° nobly of her.   *Who speaks*
LYSIMACHUS   She would never tell
175 Her parentage. Being demanded that,
She would sit still and weep.

PERICLES   O Helicanus, strike me, honoured sir,
Give me a gash, put me to present° pain,   *immediate*
Lest this great sea of joys rushing upon me
180   O'erbear° the shores of my mortality   *Overflow*
And drown me with their sweetness! [*To* MARINA] O, come hither,
      [MARINA *stands*]
Thou that begett'st him that did thee beget,[1]
Thou that wast born at sea, buried at Tarsus,
And found at sea again!—O Helicanus,
185   Down on thy knees, thank the holy gods as loud
As thunder threatens us, this is Marina!
[*To* MARINA] What was thy mother's name? Tell me but that,
For truth can never be confirmed enough,
Though doubts did ever sleep.[2]
MARINA   First, sir, I pray,
What is your title?
190   PERICLES   I am Pericles
Of Tyre. But tell me now my drowned queen's name.
As in the rest thou hast been godlike perfect,°   *have been omniscient*
So prove but true in that, thou art my daughter,[3]
The heir of kingdoms, and another life
To Pericles thy father.
195   MARINA [*kneeling*]   Is it no more
To be your daughter than to say my mother's name?
Thaisa was my mother, who did end
The minute I began.
PERICLES   Now blessing on thee! Rise. Thou art my child.
      [MARINA *stands. He kisses her*]
200   [*To attendants*] Give me fresh garments.—Mine own, Helicanus!
Not dead at Tarsus, as she should have been[4]
By savage Cleon. She shall tell thee all,
When thou shalt kneel and justify in knowledge°   *satisfy yourself that*
She is thy very princess. Who is this?
205   HELICANUS   Sir, 'tis the governor of Mytilene,
Who, hearing of your melancholy state,
Did come to see you.
PERICLES [*to* LYSIMACHUS] I embrace you, sir.—
Give me my robes.
      [*He is attired in fresh robes*]
                  I am wild in my beholding.[5]
O heavens, bless my girl!
      [*Celestial music*]
                        But hark, what music?
210   Tell Helicanus, my Marina, tell him
O'er point by point, for yet he seems to doubt,
How sure you are my daughter. But what music?
HELICANUS   My lord, I hear none.
PERICLES   None? The music of the spheres![6] List,° my Marina.   *Listen*
LYSIMACHUS [*aside to the others*]   It is not good to cross him. Give

1. The possible sexual complications here, including incest, can be highlighted in performance by doubling the part of Marina with that of Thaisa or Antiochus's Daughter. (For the possible relevance of doubling the part of Marina to the transmission of the text, see the Textual Note.)
2. Even in the absence of doubts.
3. Line is not in Q1; it was added to fill a suspected gap.
4. As she was believed (intended) to be.
5. Unkempt in my appearance, ecstatic at what I see.
6. A sign of celestial harmony, brought about by the proper movement of the heavenly bodies around earth (hence a sign of divine order).

215   him way.

PERICLES   Rar'st sounds. Do ye not hear?

LYSIMACHUS   Music, my lord?

PERICLES   I hear most heav'nly music.

It raps° me unto list'ning, and thick slumber   compels

220   Hangs upon mine eyelids. Let me rest.

          [*He sleeps*]

LYSIMACHUS   A pillow for his head.

          [*To* MARINA *and others*]   Companion friends,

If this but answer to my just belief

I'll well remember° you. So leave him all.   reward; recall

          [*Exeunt all but* PERICLES]

DIANA [*descends from the heavens*]

DIANA   My temple stands in Ephesus. Hie thee thither,

225   And do upon mine altar sacrifice.

There when my maiden priests are met together,

At large discourse thy fortunes in this wise:

With a full voice[7] before the people all,

Reveal how thou at sea didst lose thy wife.

230   To mourn thy crosses,° with thy daughter's, call   losses

And give them repetition to the life.[8]

Perform my bidding, or thou liv'st in woe;

Do't, and rest happy, by my silver bow.[9]

Awake, and tell thy dream.   [DIANA *ascends into the heavens*]

235   PERICLES   Celestial Dian, goddess argentine,°   silver (like the moon)

I will obey thee. [*Calling*] Helicanus!

          [*Enter* HELICANUS, LYSIMACHUS, *and* MARINA]

HELICANUS   Sir?

PERICLES   My purpose was for Tarsus, there to strike

Th'inhospitable Cleon, but I am

For other service first. Toward Ephesus

240   Turn our blown° sails. Eftsoons° I'll tell thee why.   inflated / Later

          [*Exit* HELICANUS]

Shall we refresh us, sir, upon your shore,

And give you gold for such provision

As our intents will need?

LYSIMACHUS   With all my heart, sir,

And when you come ashore I have a suit.

245   PERICLES   You shall prevail, were it to woo my daughter,

For it seems you have been noble towards her.

LYSIMACHUS   Sir, lend me your arm.

PERICLES   Come, my Marina.

          Exit [PERICLES *with* LYSIMACHUS *at one arm,*

                    MARINA *at the other*]

Scene 22

          Enter GOWER

GOWER   Now our sands are almost run;

          More a little, and then dumb.°   silent

          This my last boon give me,

7. *At . . . voice:* Not in Q1; added to fill a suspected gap.
At large discourse: Tell in detail (in public). *wise:* way.
8. *call . . . life:* speak loudly and repeat exactly what
happened.
9. A crescent moon. Diana was goddess of the moon
and a renowned hunter.

Scene 22 Scene 22 (Other modern editions divide this
scene in two: Act 5, Scene 2 [Gower's monologue, lines
1–20] and Scene 3 [lines 21–125]. But they anom-
alously keep Thaisa and the temple of Diana onstage
across the scene break. Even Gower may remain.)
Location: The temple of Diana in Ephesus.

For such kindness must relieve me,

5 That you aptly will suppose°   *readily will imagine*
What pageantry, what feats, what shows,
What minstrelsy and pretty din
The regent° made in Mytilene   *Lysimachus*
To greet the King. So well he° thrived   *(Lysimachus)*

10 That he is promised to be wived
To fair Marina, but in no wise°   *way*
Till he° had done his sacrifice   *(Pericles)*
As Dian bade, whereto being bound
The int'rim, pray you, all confound.°   *skip*

15 In feathered° briefness sails are filled,   *winged*
And wishes fall out as they're willed.
At Ephesus the temple see:
    [*An altar,* THAISA *and other vestals are revealed*]
Our king, and all his company.
    Enter PERICLES, MARINA, LYSIMACHUS, HELICANUS[, CER-
    IMON, *with attendants*]
That he can hither come so soon

20 Is by your fancies' thankful doom.[1]
    [GOWER *stands aside*]
PERICLES   Hail, Dian. To perform thy just° command   *precise*
I here confess myself the King of Tyre,
Who, frighted from my country, did espouse
The fair Thaisa
    [THAISA *starts*]
           at Pentapolis.

25 At sea in childbed died she, but brought forth
A maid° child called Marina, who, O goddess,   *girl*
Wears yet thy silver liv'ry.[2] She at Tarsus
Was nursed with° Cleon, whom at fourteen years   *by*
He sought to murder, but her better stars

30 Bore her to Mytilene, 'gainst whose shore riding[3]
Her fortunes brought the maid aboard our barque,
Where, by her own most clear remembrance, she
Made known herself my daughter.
THAISA   Voice and favour°—   *appearance*
You are, you are—O royal Pericles!
    [*She falls*]

35 PERICLES   What means the nun? She dies. Help, gentlemen!
CERIMON   Noble sir,
If you have told Diana's altar true,
This is your wife.
PERICLES   Reverend appearer,° no.   *reverend-looking man*
I threw her overboard with these same arms.
CERIMON   Upon this coast, I warr'nt you.

40 PERICLES   'Tis most certain.
CERIMON   Look to the lady. O, she's but o'erjoyed.
Early one blustering morn this lady
Was thrown upon this shore. I oped the coffin,
Found there rich jewels, recovered° her, and placed her   *revived*

1. Thanks to your imaginations' agreement.
2. Still wears your uniform (remains a virgin).
3. *'gainst . . . riding:* where, as we rode at anchor.

Here in Diana's temple.

45 PERICLES   May we see them?

CERIMON Great sir, they shall be brought you to° my house,   *at*
 Whither I invite you. Look, Thaisa is
 Recoverèd.

THAISA   O, let me look upon him!
 If he be none of mine, my sanctity
50 Will to my sense bend no licentious ear,
 But curb it, spite of seeing.⁴ O, my lord,
 Are you not Pericles? Like him you spake,
 Like him you are. Did you not name a tempest,
 A birth and death?

55 PERICLES The voice of dead Thaisa!

THAISA That Thaisa
 Am I, supposèd dead and drowned.

PERICLES [*taking Thaisa's hand*] Immortal Dian!

THAISA Now I know you better.
60 When we with tears parted° Pentapolis,   *departed*
 The King my father gave you such a ring.

PERICLES This, this! No more, you gods. Your present kindness
 Makes my past miseries sports;° you shall do well   *trifles*
 That° on the touching of her lips I may   *If*
65 Melt, and no more be seen.—O come, be buried
 A second time within these arms.

     [*They embrace and kiss*]

MARINA [*kneeling to* THAISA] My heart
 Leaps to be gone into my mother's bosom.

PERICLES Look who kneels here: flesh of thy flesh, Thaisa,
 Thy burden at the sea, and called Marina
 For she was yielded° there.   *Because she was born*

70 THAISA [*embracing* MARINA] Blessed, and mine own!

HELICANUS [*kneeling to* THAISA]
 Hail, madam, and my queen.

THAISA   I know you not.

PERICLES You have heard me say, when I did fly from Tyre,
 I left behind an ancient substitute.
 Can you remember what I called the man?
75 I have named him oft.

THAISA 'Twas Helicanus then.

PERICLES Still confirmation.
 Embrace him, dear Thaisa; this is he.
 Now do I long to hear how you were found,
80 How possibly preserved, and who to thank—
 Besides the gods—for this great miracle.

THAISA Lord Cerimon, my lord. This is the man
 Through whom the gods have shown their pow'r, that can
 From first to last resolve° you.   *answer everything for*

PERICLES [*to* CERIMON] Reverend sir,
85 The gods can have no mortal officer
 More like a god than you. Will you deliver°   *explain*
 How this dead queen re-lives?

CERIMON   I will, my lord.
 Beseech you, first go with me to my house,

---

4. *my sanctity . . . seeing*: my religious vows will forbid my sense to feel desire, in spite of what I see.

Where shall be shown you all was° found with her,   *that was*
90 And told how in this temple she came° placed,   *came to be*
No needful thing omitted.

PERICLES   Pure Diana,
I bless thee for thy vision,° and will offer   *(in Scene 21)*
Nightly oblations° to thee.—Beloved Thaisa,   *offerings*
This prince, the fair betrothèd of your daughter,
95 At Pentapolis shall marry her.
[*To* MARINA] And now this ornament°   *this hair that*
Makes me look dismal will I clip to form,
And what this fourteen years no razor touched,
To grace thy marriage day I'll beautify.

100 THAISA   Lord Cerimon hath letters of good credit,°   *trustworthiness*
Sir, from Pentapolis: my father's dead.

PERICLES   Heav'n make a star of him! Yet there, my queen,
We'll celebrate their nuptials, and ourselves
Will in that kingdom spend our following days.
105 Our son and daughter shall in Tyrus reign.—
Lord Cerimon, we do our longing stay°   *delay our desire*
To hear the rest untold. Sir, lead's the way.

                  Exeunt [all but] GOWER

GOWER   In Antiochus and his daughter you have heard[5]
Of monstrous lust the due and just reward;
110 In Pericles, his queen, and daughter seen,°   *you have seen*
Although assailed with fortune fierce and keen,
Virtue preserved from fell° destruction's blast,   *cruel*
Led on by heav'n, and crowned with joy at last.
In Helicanus may you well descry
115 A figure of truth, of faith, of loyalty.
In reverend Cerimon there well appears
The worth that learnèd charity aye° wears.   *always*
For wicked Cleon and his wife, when fame°   *rumor*
Had spread their cursèd deed to° th' honoured name   *against*
120 Of Pericles, to rage the city turn,°   *turned*
That° him and his they in his palace burn.   *So that*
The gods for murder seemèd so content
To punish that, although not done, but meant.
So on your patience evermore attending,
125 New joy wait on you. Here our play has ending.   [*Exit*]

Additional Passage

Q gives this more expansive version of Marina's Epitaph (18.34–37):

'The fairest, sweetest, best lies here,
Who withered in her spring of year.
She was of Tyrus the King's° daughter,   *the King of Tyre's*
On whom foul death hath made this slaughter.
5 Marina was she called, and at her birth
Thetis,[1] being proud, swallowed° some part o'th' earth;   *flooded*

---

5. The second of Gower's speeches in pentameter couplets.
Additional Passage
1. A sea nymph here confused with Tethys, wife of Oceanus (in Greek mythology, the ruler of a river that

encircled the earth). The image in this passage is of the ocean (because of Thetis/Tethys) surging happily in response to Marina's birth and angrily in response to her death.

Therefore the earth, fearing to be o'erflowed,
Hath Thetis' birth-child on the heav'ns bestowed,
Wherefore she° does, and swears she'll never stint,   *(Thetis)*
10 Make raging batt'ry upon shores of flint.'°   *rocky shores*

Coriolanus

Hērōs, the Greek word for "hero," originally meant "warrior." By Homer's time, eight centuries before the birth of Christ, the term was already beginning to be applied by extension to other kinds of praiseworthy people, but even today the military connotations of the word remain strong. The Latin word for "virtue" has a similar history, as the ancient historian Plutarch remarks in his biography of Coriolanus, Shakespeare's principal source for his play. "Now in those days valiantness was honored in Rome above all other virtues: which they call *virtūs*, by the name of virtue itself, as including in that general name, all other special virtues besides. So that *virtūs* in the Latin, was as much as valiantness."

Writing *Coriolanus* in 1608, Shakespeare considers the extent to which excellence in battle translates into other forms of meritoriousness. He works in an ageless tradition, still vital in the twenty-first century, of exalting great warriors: the mythically dauntless Hercules and Theseus, the fierce battle chieftains of classical epic, the indomitable knights of medieval chivalric romance, the superheroes of modern films and comic books. Yet Shakespeare also deviates from that tradition. Caius Martius Coriolanus performs astonishing, almost superhuman, acts of strength and bravery in battle, fighting on behalf of a society that seems to venerate war. His aggressiveness ought to mesh perfectly, one would think, with the needs of the community. If successful belligerence is the highest, or only, form of excellence, then Coriolanus, the pre-eminent soldier, is a natural candidate for Rome's top leadership positions.

In fact, however, Coriolanus's career is disastrous. Despite his phenomenal military successes and despite Rome's esteem for warriors, Coriolanus not only fails to win election as consul (leader) of Rome but barely escapes the death penalty. He is banished from the city and eventually killed while in the employ of Rome's enemies. The relationship between the supposedly exemplary individual and the culture from which he springs seems anything but straightforward; so does the connection between "valiantness" and other forms of virtue.

What goes wrong in *Coriolanus*? Shakespeare suggests that his hero brings many of his problems upon his own head. Coriolanus succeeds as a warrior by channeling overpowering anger into feats of extraordinary strength, by refusing to calculate possible harm to himself or to others, and by preferring action to words. In the political domain, by contrast, relative goods are often more important than absolutes, negotiated compromises preferable to flat conquest. The ability to control oneself in the interests of manipulating others is crucial; so, too, is the capacity to predict the effects of one's own and other people's words and actions. Coriolanus's phenomenal forcefulness, such a superb advantage on the battlefield, cripples his effectiveness for other enterprises. His initial lack of political ambitions together with his hopeless awkwardness as a candidate suggest that his military prowess is not merely irrelevant to peacetime employment but indeed renders him politically incompetent or even dangerous.

Like most of Shakespeare's tragic heroes after Richard II, then, Coriolanus is betrayed not so much by his vices or shortcomings as by what, in different circumstances, would be his best traits. Shakespeare alters his source material in order to make this pattern more distinct. For instance, Shakespeare entirely omits Plutarch's account of the historical Coriolanus's considerable political savvy. Plutarch's Coriolanus had already played several influential political roles before he made his bid for the consulship. He underwent without apparent compunction the traditional rituals required of all seekers after office; the plebeians later repudiated him on the grounds of a long political record that, in Shakespeare, does not exist. After his exile, Plutarch's Coriolanus cleverly exacerbated class strife in Rome by selectively refraining from burning patrician estates as he approached the city with his Volscian army. Shakespeare's relentless but hotheaded character would hardly be capable of such a calculated act.

The effect of Shakespeare's changes is to open up a chasm that does not exist in his sources between military and civic values. The general Cominius, praising Coriolanus in the senate house, seems superficially to be echoing Plutarch's comment that "*virtūs* in the Latin, was as much as valiantness":

> It is held
> That valour is the chiefest virtue, and
> Most dignifies the haver. If it be,
> The man I speak of cannot in the world
> Be singly counterpoised.
>
> (2.2.79–83)

But even in the process of making his argument, Cominius appears, in his evasive passive constructions and his conditional "if," to be partly disowning it.

Coriolanus's tragedy is not, however, merely a matter of personal idiosyncrasy and self-destructiveness. His career is inseparable from the society that both exalts and repudiates him. During Coriolanus's lifetime in the late fifth century B.C.E., Rome had already embarked on the expansionist course that would culminate in its domination of Europe, North Africa, and the Middle East four hundred years later, in the time of Julius Caesar, Marcus Brutus, and Mark Antony. But in these early years, dreams of world rule were far in the future: Coriolanus's Rome was still battling the nearby Volscians. Roman bellicosity was a cultural tendency, not yet a clear pathway to empire. At home, Rome struggled to devise a new form of government. In Coriolanus's youth, Lucius Junius Brutus and his allies had driven out King Tarquin and his family on the grounds that they had been abusing their power (an episode upon which Shakespeare based his narrative poem *The Rape of Lucrece*). In place of the monarchy, Brutus instituted a republic: government not by a King but by a senate composed of patricians (aristocrats). For military and civic matters requiring executive authority, the senate elected consuls for short terms. Soon, however, this system proved inadequate, as the large plebeian, or working, class clamored for a say in the city's rule. In the aftermath of the uprising depicted in *Coriolanus* 1.1, the plebeians were granted the right to elect their own representatives, called tribunes.

In its eventual form, therefore, the Roman Republic was a "mixed" form of government that attempted to distribute rather than to concentrate power, as well as to balance the rights and privileges of various constituencies. Inventing republican institutions entailed addressing important questions about the nature of the polity and of citizenship. Is the Roman state, as Menenius suggests, an impersonal force "whose course will on / The way it takes" (1.1.60–61) no matter what the majority of the city's residents desire? Or does the state merely express collective opinion, as the plebeians insist when they cry, "The people are the city" (3.1.200)? Ought the Roman state to concern itself mainly with managing affairs within the city walls, or should its military undertakings outside the city take political precedence? Who has a voice in the government of the city, and on what basis is suffrage granted: class status? personal merit? place of residence? Does citizenship, as Coriolanus argues, primarily entail duties such as military service? Or is citizenship, as the tribunes assume, an entitlement, giving everyone a voice in political and judicial affairs?

For Shakespeare and his contemporaries, these were not questions of merely antiquarian interest. Most premodern states, including classical republics and Shakespeare's England, consisted of a relatively small, property-owning, politically empowered class and a large subpolitical population that was supposed to submit to the laws but that had no voting rights. But how small ought to be the privileged group, how large the disempowered group, and how distinct the differences between the two?

These were matters of hot debate in Jacobean England. King James I and his son Charles, who liked to associate themselves with the imagery of imperial Rome, were attracted by absolutist models of government in which the monarch exercised virtually unlimited sway. By contrast, their opponents in Parliament often invoked the Roman Republic, which dispersed power over consuls, senate, and tribunes, as an analogue to the English commonwealth with its monarch, House of Lords, and House of Commons.

Given the contemporary resonances of his story, Shakespeare's extensive alterations of Plutarch's account are fascinating. *Coriolanus* opens, as already mentioned, with an uprising among Rome's common people. According to Plutarch, the plebeians revolted because the moneyed patricians had promised easier terms on loans if the plebeians would agree to fight the nearby Sabines. After the plebeians acquitted themselves bravely in battle, the patricians reneged on the agreement and sold into slavery those debtors—many of them war veterans—who were bankrupted by high interest rates. Shakespeare's plebeians, by contrast, make only fleeting references to usury. Their main complaint is simple hunger: a familiar grievance to an English audience in 1608. Barely a year before *Coriolanus*'s first performance, food shortages precipitated serious rioting by the rural poor in the Midland counties west of London, where Stratford-upon-Avon was located. The rioters accused the rich of hoarding foodstuffs in hopes of higher prices and of having created a dearth by replacing the traditional cultivation of cereal grains with lucrative sheep farming. The rich countered that bad weather was to blame.

In updating the motives of his lower-class characters, Shakespeare translates Roman class conflicts into terms more immediate for his contemporaries. But his revision has other consequences, too: it minimizes the plebeians' political sophistication, their military indispensability, and much of the justification for their outrage. The famine might well be a natural rather than a political calamity: there is no hint of any prior betrayed agreement and no suggestion of unrewarded plebeian military service. Unlike Plutarch's plebeians, Shakespeare's are mediocre soldiers or worse: in *Coriolanus,* Shakespeare's Rome fails to appreciate Coriolanus's *virtūs* simply because the society is not, as Plutarch had claimed it to be, fully a warrior culture at all.

In Shakespeare's rendering, valor in battle seems less a "Roman" than a distinctively aristocratic trait, exercised and uniquely cherished by the patrician class. The difficulties Coriolanus experiences in trying to translate that valor into a civilian context reflect a persistent problem in defining the male aristocrat's proper role. Just as the equation of "valiantness" and "virtue" could fail in early republican Rome, it could also be seen to be failing in early modern England. In medieval times, noblemen had been feudally obliged to serve as battle captains over troops of their own vassals; the aristocrat's military function was his raison d'être, although proficiency in war was supposed to carry over into the management of civic affairs. In Shakespeare's time, the aristocrat's function was theoretically unchanged, but altered social circumstances placed it under increasing pressure. Throughout the late sixteenth and early seventeenth centuries, bureaucrats and policy makers like William Cecil, Robert Cecil, and Francis Bacon were sharply at odds with swashbuckling militarists like Walter Ralegh, King James's son Prince Henry, and Shakespeare's erstwhile patron the Earl of Essex. In these conflicts, the bureaucrats almost always had the advantage. Their skill at such tasks as overhauling the taxation system was hardly glamorous but proved indispensable for the newly powerful nation-state. By the early seventeenth century, the notion that the aristocrat rendered his most important service to his King on the battlefield seemed a remnant of a simpler age.

Coriolanus then, like Hotspur in Shakespeare's *1 Henry IV*, seems to embody a conception of aristocratic excellence whose historical moment, for better or worse, has already passed. Interestingly, a sense of the archaic quality of mighty warriors seems almost universal. Homer's epic heroes were already beginning to specialize their functions during the siege of Troy. For Plutarch, writing in the time of the Roman Empire, the original identification of aristocrat and warrior seems to have shattered in the long-ago days of the Roman Republic. Medieval writers locate both the flowering of knightly service and the beginning of its breakdown in the legendary fourth-century Arthurian court. Many Hollywood Westerns look back to a time in the nineteenth century when the older, rougher codes of the Indian fighter or nomadic frontiersman were being displaced by the values of permanent white settlers, including women and professional-caste men. From time immemorial, glorifying warriors has been tied up with nostalgia—not merely for the mighty soldier himself, but for a simpler, "manly" alternative to civilized complexities, an alternative always already lost.

In the tense dramatic milieu of *Coriolanus,* compounded from Shakespeare's own experience and what his sources provided him, the nature of his protagonist's heroism thus seems more intelligible and its failure less surprising. Since the heterogeneous Roman population has difficulty coming to any consensus about what it values, no single individual could possibly exemplify its ideals. Rather, Coriolanus possesses a narrow subset of traits more appealing to some groups (the patricians) than others (the plebeians) and more useful in some situations (war) than in others (peace). Coriolanus's mother, Volumnia, describing her son's education, suggests how his "heroism" has been developed by rigorously selecting for desired traits and just as sternly suppressing others.

> When yet he was but tenderbodied and the only son of my womb, when youth with comeliness plucked all gaze his way, when for a day of kings' entreaties a mother should not sell him an hour from her beholding, I, considering how honour would become such a person . . . was pleased to let him seek danger where he was like to find fame. To a cruel war I sent him, from whence he returned his brows bound with oak. I tell thee, daughter, I sprang not more in joy at first hearing he was a man-child than now in first seeing he had proved himself a man. (1.3.5–15)

Volumnia's own shrewdness and ferocity seems to belie the "naturalness" of a system that excludes women from politics and combat. Unlike Coriolanus's wife, Virgilia, Volumnia hardly seems content to stay home and do the sewing. But the incongruity between her personality and her prescribed social role does not render her skeptical of that role. Instead, she embraces her gendered destiny with characteristic zeal. In maternity she finds an improbable outlet for her own aggressiveness.

> The breasts of Hecuba
> When she did suckle Hector looked not lovelier
> Than Hector's forehead when it spit forth blood
> At Grecian sword, contemning.
> (1.3.37–40)

Symbolically equating milk and blood, the lactating mother with her wounded son, Volumnia both identifies vicariously with her war hero and wishes suffering upon him, delighting not merely in his triumphs but in his pain. Virgilia's conventionally feminine recoil from Volumnia's gory fantasies makes their aberrancy clear for the audience. In Volumnia, the discipline required to submit to rules of Roman womanliness seems to have generated a complicated sadomasochistic adaptation. She displaces her own forbidden bellicosity onto a dream of exaggerated masculinity and then attempts to realize that dream in her son.

Volumnia's ruthless mothering produces a man whose characteristic gesture is violently to resist whatever he perceives to be outside himself. Battle is Coriolanus's model for identity formation, and his ideal self is like an impermeably walled city. Overstated *differences*—between patrician and plebeian, between Roman and Volsce, between male and female, between man and boy—are the principles upon which Coriolanus has established his own sense of identity. Contempt and anger, like aggression, reinforce and clarify the boundaries of the self, marking it vividly off from those whom one hates, despises, or conquers. Coriolanus does not merely happen to be inflexible and narrow-minded; too much tolerance, too much sensitivity, would endanger him to the core. So would introspection, which might reveal an unwelcome complexity within. Coriolanus is hardly a taciturn character, but he is perhaps Shakespeare's most opaque tragic protagonist, for he is not inclined to reflect upon his own motives either in conversation or alone (indeed, he has only a single short soliloquy in the entire play). The great moments of Coriolanus's life are moments of embattled solitude: fighting by himself inside Corioles, standing alone for consul or separated from the Roman people after his exile, reflecting in an unaccompanied moment in Aufidius's hall, isolated in Corioles again at the end of the play, shouting at his old (and new) enemy: "Alone I did it" (5.6.117). He is thrilled by fantasies of absolute independence: "As if a man were author of himself / And knew no other kin" (5.3.36–37). With some justice, the hostile tribunes accuse him of wanting to be the only man left in Rome and of considering himself a god superior to ordinary mortals.

In his defiant self-sufficiency, however, Coriolanus is far needier than he acknowledges. When he allies himself with Aufidius, his former enemy, Aufidius's elated speech of welcome clarifies their shared dilemma.

> I loved the maid I married; never man
> Sighed truer breath. But that I see thee here,
> Thou noble thing, more dances my rapt heart
> Than when I first my wedded mistress saw
> Bestride my threshold. . . .
> . . . .
>   Thou hast beat me out
> Twelve several times, and I have nightly since
> Dreamt of encounters 'twixt thyself and me—
> We have been down together in my sleep,
> Unbuckling helms, fisting each other's throat—
> And waked half dead with nothing.
>   (4.5.113–25)

Coriolanus and the attack on Corioli. Jost Amman, from *Icones Livianae* (1572).

The combination of pain and pleasure to which Aufidius bears witness is strikingly reminiscent of Volumnia's maternal feelings, in which aggressiveness toward the beloved seems to loom so large. It is impossible here to distinguish hostility from attraction, competition from dependency, combat from homosexual embrace. The warrior loves his adversary because he needs a manly competitor against whom to establish his own identity. The striving for autonomy depends on the existence of something set off against, beside, or below it.

To distinguish oneself from other people, then, one must rely on them. "Thy valiantness was mine, thou suck'dst it from me," Volumnia informs her son (3.2.129). Coriolanus wants to imagine his courage and honor as intrinsically his own, rather than conferred by others. But "our virtues," as Aufidius claims, "lie in th'interpretation of the time" (4.7.49–50). Roman merit, inextricable from social goals and needs, demands an admiring audience. Even while he professes to despise flattery, Coriolanus takes pride in such apparently trivial honorific gestures as the surname or the oaken garland conferred upon him by those who value his services. Insignificant in themselves, such symbols acquire meaning from the way in which they are regarded by the group. The exiled Coriolanus defiantly insists that "there is a world elsewhere" (3.3.139), but it is impossible for him to retire to a quiet corner of Italy and live out his life in obscurity. He needs to prove himself against an enemy, but now that enemy, Rome, is the place from which his life has drawn its meaning. Threatening to annihilate the community that bore him, he puts himself in a painfully contradictory position.

Thus the superior is always dependent on the inferior, the inside on the outside, the civilized on the barbarian, the patrician on the plebeian, the performer on the audience, the man on the woman and on the boy, even while the "upper" term prides itself on its difference from its subordinate. Moreover, just as important, the dependency works in both directions, as the action of *Coriolanus* shows. If Coriolanus depends on the Roman populace in ways he refuses to recognize, so does the populace depend on him. By imagining it can dispense with him and what he represents, it comes close to bringing destruction on its head.

Since we hear an unusual amount about Coriolanus's boyhood, it is easy to see his self-contradictory desire for autonomy in terms of his simultaneous flight from and dependence on Volumnia. But that is an oversimplification: Coriolanus is not merely the product of a uniquely bad upbringing. His anxieties about autonomy and dependence, competitiveness and cooperation, are shared, in some form, by almost everyone in the play: they are aspects of social and political dilemmas, not merely individual neuroses. Early in the first scene, the First Citizen notes—perhaps enviously but also accurately—that the patricians enjoy seeing the lower classes suffer, because that suffering enhances their sense of comparative privilege. Who depends on whom, how far ought that dependency to extend, what forms ought it to take?

These concerns are powerfully evoked in the imagery of *Coriolanus*. It was a cliché already old in Plutarch's time, and still current in Shakespeare's, that human communities were modeled on individual bodies. In the optimistic version of this analogy, the state is a collection of harmoniously interrelated organs, each selflessly performing its own distinctive function in the service of the whole. Interconnectedness is the apparent moral of Menenius's "pretty tale" (1.1.80) of the belly in the opening scene. But even in Menenius's version, the analogy veers toward grotesquerie, the body-state becoming an apparently headless entity equipped with an unnaturally smiling belly. Elsewhere in *Coriolanus*, the body is less a marvel of smooth interaction than a site of disintegration: Coriolanus imagines the plebeians as "fragments" and as "voices" (1.1.212, 2.3.115–20); Menenius rebukes a malcontent he calls "the great toe of this assembly" (1.1.144). The mutilations of the battlefield begin to seem corporeal equivalents for a profound crisis of the body politic. The shared needs of embodied, vulnerable human beings for food, shelter, and defense provide an obvious material basis for societies. But individual bodies tend to be selfish, unwilling to forgo their own urgent requirements in the interests of a collective good, reluctant to admit their reliance on one another lest that reliance be made a pretext for exploitation. Once again, dependence and autonomy seem simultaneously antithetical and inextricable.

Because the body in *Coriolanus* is so often imagined in negative terms—as starving, wounded, or cut to pieces—attempts to escape corporeal limitation seem understandable, even laudable. In fact, Coriolanus's battlefield heroism seems largely a matter of refusing to acknowledge physical constraints: he is inexhaustible, undaunted by wounds or by danger. Late in the play, Menenius describes him as a kind of robot: "When he walks, he moves like an engine, and the ground shrinks before his treading" (5.4.15–16). But within a few lines, Menenius is proven wrong: blood relationships, the ties of the body, prove impossible for Coriolanus to disown. Volumnia, Virgilia, and young Martius come to the Volscian camp to plead for their city and their people; and in a capitulation he knows to be virtually suicidal, Coriolanus grasps his mother's hand.

Coriolanus is not only the last of Shakespeare's tragedies but the last of a series of plays about ancient Rome. It seems to look back upon, and to anatomize, social and individual pathologies that in *Julius Caesar* and even *Antony and Cleopatra* were merely hinted at: the way "Roman" valor on the battlefield, for instance, becomes both a flight from and a replacement for heterosexuality; the way aggression and repression undergird the psyches of Roman men and women; the way both sexes deform their personalities in order to conform to highly restrictive patterns of masculinity or femininity. While in *Julius Caesar* class tensions serve mainly to exalt the patrician class, here the plebeians' grievances, and their different priorities, are understandable. Coriolanus's inability to comprehend the plebeians is a telling sign of both his personal rigidity and the alienation of rich from poor. *Coriolanus* has seemed to many audiences a relentlessly bleak play, and no wonder. Subjecting both its formidable but unpleasant hero and his society to intense critical scrutiny, *Coriolanus*

Volumnia entreating Coriolanus. Jost Amman, from *Icones Livianae* (1572).

implies that no political arrangement could possibly satisfy human needs, portrayed here as incorrigibly self-contradictory.

KATHARINE EISAMAN MAUS

TEXTUAL NOTE

The 1623 First Folio is the only authority for *Coriolanus*. Some believe that the compositors set the Folio text of this play directly from Shakespeare's manuscript, but the Oxford editors argue that the immediate source for F was more likely to have been a promptbook. Stage directions are unusually elaborate and give important performance clues: for instance, the act divisions were clearly marked (since intermissions were observed at "private" theaters like the Blackfriars), and the specifications for small musical instruments like cornets also suggest a more intimate performance space. The F compositors may have had trouble reading the handwriting in the manuscript (whether it was Shakespeare's or a member of the theater company's). There are some obvious errors requiring emendation and some confusion in setting verse lines. On the whole, however, *Coriolanus* is not one of the more textually vexing of Shakespeare's plays.

SELECTED BIBLIOGRAPHY

Adelman, Janet. "'Anger's My Meat': Feeding, Dependency, and Aggression in *Coriolanus*." *Representing Shakespeare: New Psychoanalytic Essays*. Ed. Murray M. Schwartz and Coppélia Kahn. Baltimore: Johns Hopkins University Press, 1980. 129–49. Argues that the play's political and psychological anxieties crystallize around the figure of the mother who does not feed her children.

Barton, Anne. "Livy, Machiavelli, and Shakespeare's *Coriolanus*." *Shakespeare Survey* 38 (1985): 115–29. The Roman historian Livy and Machiavelli's commentary upon Livy as sources of inspiration for *Coriolanus*.

Bloom, Harold, ed. *William Shakespeare's "Coriolanus."* New York: Chelsea House, 1988. Anthology of critical essays.

Calderwood, James. "*Coriolanus*: Wordless Meanings and Meaningless Words." *Studies in English Literature* 6 (1966): 211–24. Problems of language in the play as they corollate with its psychological and political dilemmas.

Cantor, Paul A. "Part One: *Coriolanus*." *Shakespeare's Rome: Republic and Empire*. Ithaca, N.Y.: Cornell University Press, 1976. 55–124. Strengths and weaknesses of the Roman Republic as Shakespeare contrasts them with the later imperial system.

Cavell, Stanley. "Who Does the Wolf Love?" *Disowning Knowledge in Six Plays by Shakespeare*. Cambridge, Mass.: Cambridge University Press, 1987. 143–78. *Coriolanus*'s affinity with sacrificial feasts, especially the Christian ritual of Communion.

Fish, Stanley. "How to Do Things with Austin and Searle: Speech-Act Theory and Literary Criticism." *Is There a Text in This Class?: The Authority of Interpretive Communities*. Cambridge, Mass.: Harvard University Press, 1980. 197–245. Coriolanus's problems with speech-acts.

Goldberg, Jonathan. "The Anus in *Coriolanus*." *Historicism, Psychoanalysis, and Early Modern Culture*. Ed. Carla Mazzio and Doug Trevor. New York: Routledge, 2000. 260–271. Anal imagery and homoeroticism in the play.

Jorgensen, Paul. "Shakespeare's Coriolanus: Elizabethan Soldier." *PMLA* 64 (1949): 221–35. *Coriolanus* reflects the military problems of Shakespeare's era.

Patterson, Annabel. "Speak, Speak! The Popular Voice and the Jacobean State." *Shakespeare and the Popular Voice*. Cambridge, Mass.: Blackwood, 1989. *Coriolanus* and disenfranchised groups in Shakespeare's England.

Wheeler, David, ed. *"Coriolanus": Critical Essays*. New York: Garland, 1995. An anthology of essays and reviews of theatrical productions.

FILMS

Coriolanus. 1951. Dir. Paul Nickell. USA. This Westinghouse Studio One black-and-white abridged television version, interspersed with occasional ads for refrigerators and laundry appliances, is performed in modern dress and strongly marked by the recent traumas of fascism and World War II. Richard Greene is handsome but inexpressive in the role of Coriolanus.

Coriolanus. 1984. Dir. Elijah Moshinsky. UK. BBC-TV's spare, gripping production featuring Alan Howard as a tightly-wound Coriolanus, Mike Gwilym as a canny Aufidius, and Irene Worth as a terrifying Volumnia.

The Tragedy of Coriolanus

THE PERSONS OF THE PLAY

CAIUS MARTIUS, later surnamed CORIOLANUS ⎫
MENENIUS Agrippa   ⎬ patricians of
Titus LARTIUS ⎫   ⎭ Rome
COMINIUS   ⎬ generals
VOLUMNIA, Coriolanus' mother
VIRGILIA, his wife
YOUNG MARTIUS, his son
VALERIA, a chaste lady of Rome
SICINIUS Velutus ⎫
Junius BRUTUS   ⎬ tribunes of the Roman people
CITIZENS of Rome
SOLDIERS in the Roman army
Tullus AUFIDIUS, general of the Volscian army
His LIEUTENANT
His SERVINGMEN
CONSPIRATORS with Aufidius
Volscian LORDS
Volscian CITIZENS
SOLDIERS in the Volscian army
ADRIAN, a Volscian
NICANOR, a Roman
A Roman HERALD
MESSENGERS
AEDILES
A gentlewoman, an usher, Roman and Volscian senators and
    nobles, captains in the Roman army, officers, lictors

1.1

Enter a Company of mutinous CITIZENS *with staves,*
clubs, and other weapons

FIRST CITIZEN   Before we proceed any further, hear me speak.
ALL   Speak, speak.
FIRST CITIZEN   You are all resolved rather to die than to famish?
ALL   Resolved, resolved.
5   FIRST CITIZEN   First, you know Caius Martius is chief enemy to
    the people.
ALL   We know't, we know't.
FIRST CITIZEN   Let us kill him, and we'll have corn° at our own   *grain*
    price. Is't a verdict?°   *Do we agree*
10   ALL   No more talking on't, let it be done. Away, away.
SECOND CITIZEN   One word, good citizens.
FIRST CITIZEN   We are accounted poor citizens, the patricians
    good.° What authority[1] surfeits on would relieve us. If they   *noble; well off*
    would yield us but the superfluity° while it were wholesome°   *excess / still edible*
15   we might guess they relieved us humanely, but they think we

---

1.1 Location: A street in Rome.   1. The nobility.

are too dear.[2] The leanness that afflicts us, the object° of our   *visible fact*
misery, is as an inventory to particularize their abundance;[3] our
sufferance° is a gain to them. Let us revenge this with our pikes°   *distress / spears; pitch-*
ere we become rakes;[4] for the gods know I speak this in hunger   *forks*
20 for bread, not in thirst for revenge.

SECOND CITIZEN   Would you proceed especially against Caius
Martius?

THIRD CITIZEN   Against him first.

FOURTH CITIZEN   He's a very dog to° the commonalty.[5]   *persecutor of*

25 SECOND CITIZEN   Consider you what services he has done for his
country?

FIRST CITIZEN   Very well, and could be content to give him good
report for't, but that he pays himself with being proud.

FIFTH CITIZEN   Nay, but speak not maliciously.

30 FIRST CITIZEN   I say unto you, what he hath done famously,° he   *that has won fame*
did it to that end°—though soft-conscienced men can be con-   *(to advance his pride)*
tent to say 'it was for his country', 'he did it to please his mother,
and to be partly proud'°—which he is even to the altitude of   *partly out of pride*
his virtue.[6]

35 SECOND CITIZEN   What he cannot help in his nature you account a vice in him. You must in no way say he is covetous.

FIRST CITIZEN   If I must not, I need not be barren of accusations.
He hath faults, with surplus, to tire in repetition.
        Shouts within
What shouts are these? The other side o'th' city is risen. Why
40 stay we prating° here? To th' Capitol!   *chattering*

ALL   Come, come.
        Enter MENENIUS

FIRST CITIZEN   Soft,° who comes here?   *Wait*

SECOND CITIZEN   Worthy Menenius Agrippa, one that hath
always loved the people.

45 FIRST CITIZEN   He's one honest enough. Would all the rest were
so!

MENENIUS   What work's, my countrymen, in hand? Where go you
With bats° and clubs? The matter. Speak, I pray you.   *cudgels*

FIRST CITIZEN   Our business is not unknown to th' senate. They
50 have had inkling this fortnight what we intend to do, which now
we'll show 'em in deeds. They say poor suitors° have strong[7]   *petitioners*
breaths; they shall know we have strong arms, too.

MENENIUS   Why, masters,° my good friends, mine honest neigh-   *(artisans' title)*
bours,
Will you undo° yourselves?   *destroy*

55 FIRST CITIZEN   We cannot, sir. We are undone already.

MENENIUS   I tell you, friends, most charitable care
Have the patricians of you. For° your wants,   *As for*
Your suffering in this dearth,° you may as well   *famine*
Strike at the heaven with your staves as lift them
60 Against the Roman state, whose course will on
The way it takes, cracking ten thousand curbs[8]
Of more strong link asunder than can ever

---

2. We cost too much to preserve; we are too rich.
3. To make their prosperity stand out by comparison.
4. Rakes are proverbially thin; playing on "pikes."
5. Common people.

6. That is, his pride is equal to his valor.
7. Strong-smelling, from eating onions, the food of the poor.
8. Chain bits used to restrain unruly horses.

Appear in your impediment.[9] For the dearth,
The gods, not the patricians, make it, and
65 Your knees to them, not arms, must help. Alack,
You are transported by calamity
Thither where more attends° you, and you slander   *awaits*
The helms° o'th' state, who care for you like fathers,   *helmsmen*
When you curse them as enemies.
70 FIRST CITIZEN Care for us? True, indeed! They ne'er cared for
us yet: suffer us to famish, and their storehouses crammed with
grain; make edicts for usury[1] to support usurers; repeal daily
any wholesome act established against the rich; and provide
more piercing° statutes daily to chain up and restrain the poor.   *severe*
75 If the wars eat us not up, they will; and there's all the love they
bear us.
MENENIUS Either you must
Confess yourselves wondrous malicious
Or be accused of folly. I shall tell you
80 A pretty tale. It may be you have heard it,
But since it serves my purpose, I will venture
To stale't a little more.°   *To make it more familiar*
FIRST CITIZEN Well, I'll hear it, sir. Yet you must not think to
fob off our disgrace[2] with a tale. But an't° please you, deliver.   *if it*
85 MENENIUS There was a time when all the body's members,
Rebelled against the belly, thus accused it:
That only like a gulf° it did remain   *abyss*
I'th' midst o'th' body, idle and unactive,
Still cupboarding the viand,[3] never bearing
90 Like° labour with the rest; where th'other instruments°   *Equal / organs*
Did see and hear, devise, instruct, walk, feel,
And, mutually participate,° did minister   *participating*
Unto the appetite and affection° common   *desire*
Of the whole body. The belly answered—
95 FIRST CITIZEN Well, sir, what answer made the belly?
MENENIUS Sir, I shall tell you. With a kind of smile,
Which ne'er came from the lungs,° but even thus—   *(organs of laughter)*
For look you, I may make the belly smile
As well as speak—it tauntingly replied
100 To th' discontented members, the mutinous parts
That envied his receipt;° even so most fitly[4]   *what it received*
As you malign our senators for that°   *because*
They are not such as you.
FIRST CITIZEN   Your belly's answer—what?
The kingly crownèd head, the vigilant eye,
105 The counsellor heart, the arm our soldier,
Our steed the leg, the tongue our trumpeter,
With other muniments° and petty helps   *supports*
In this our fabric,° if that they—   *body*
MENENIUS   What then?
Fore me,° this fellow speaks! What then? What then?   *(an oath)*
110 FIRST CITIZEN Should by the cormorant° belly be restrained,   *rapacious*
Who is the sink° o'th' body—   *cesspool*

---

9. *than . . . impediment*: than you can ever offer in opposition.
1. Permitting the lending of money at interest (widely considered immoral, because it enriched wealthy lenders at the expense of poor borrowers).
2. Dismiss our hardship.
3. Always hoarding the food.
4. In just the way.

MENENIUS   Well, what then?

FIRST CITIZEN The former agents, if they did complain,
 What could the belly answer?

MENENIUS   I will tell you,
 If you'll bestow a small° of what you have little—   *small amount*
115 Patience—a while, you'st hear the belly's answer.

FIRST CITIZEN You're long about it.

MENENIUS   Note me this, good friend:
 Your° most grave belly was deliberate,   *This*
 Not rash like his accusers, and thus answered:
 'True is it, my incorporate° friends,' quoth he,   *united in one body*
120 'That I receive the general food at first
 Which you do live upon, and fit it is,
 Because I am the storehouse and the shop
 Of the whole body. But, if you do remember,
 I send it through the rivers of your blood
125 Even to the court, the heart, to th' seat° o'th' brain;   *throne*
 And through the cranks and offices[5] of man
 The strongest nerves° and small inferior veins   *muscles*
 From me receive that natural competency°   *sustenance*
 Whereby they live. And though that all at once'—
130 You my good friends, this says the belly, mark me—

FIRST CITIZEN Ay, sir, well, well.

MENENIUS   'Though all at once cannot
 See what I do deliver out to each,
 Yet I can make my audit up[6] that all
 From me do back receive the flour[7] of all
135 And leave me but the bran.' What say you to't?

FIRST CITIZEN It was an answer. How apply you this?

MENENIUS The senators of Rome are this good belly,
 And you the mutinous members. For examine
 Their counsels and their cares, digest[8] things rightly
140 Touching the weal o'th' common,[9] you shall find
 No public benefit which you receive
 But it proceeds or comes from them to you,
 And no way from yourselves. What do you think,
 You, the great toe of this assembly?

145 FIRST CITIZEN I the great toe? Why the great toe?

MENENIUS For that, being one o'th' lowest, basest, poorest
 Of this most wise rebellion, thou goest foremost.
 Thou rascal, that art worst in blood[1] to run,
 Lead'st first to win some vantage.°   *benefit*
150 But make you ready your stiff bats and clubs.
 Rome and her rats are at the point of battle.
 The one side must have bale.°   *injury*
   Enter MARTIUS   Hail, noble Martius!

MARTIUS Thanks.—What's the matter, you dissentious° rogues, *rebelling*
 That, rubbing the poor itch of your opinion,
 Make yourselves scabs?

155 FIRST CITIZEN   We have ever your good word.

MARTIUS He that will give good words to thee will flatter

---

5. Through the winding passages and workrooms.
6. Show on my balance sheet.
7. Nourishment (punning on "flower," or choicest part).
8. Interpret (playing on the belly's function).

9. Concerning the public good.
1. Most desperate; lowest born. *rascal:* wretch; inferior deer or dog.

Beneath abhorring. What would you have, you curs
That like nor° peace nor war? The one affrights you,   *neither*
The other makes you proud.° He that trusts to you,   *rebellious*
160 Where he should find you lions finds you hares,
Where foxes, geese. You are no surer, no,
Than is the coal of fire upon the ice,
Or hailstone in the sun. Your virtue° is   *characteristic skill*
To make him worthy whose offence subdues him,[2]
165 And curse that justice did it. Who deserves greatness
Deserves° your hate, and your affections° are   *Incurs / propensities*
A sick man's appetite, who desires most that
Which would increase his evil.° He that depends   *illness*
Upon your favours swims with fins of lead,
170 And hews down oaks with rushes. Hang ye! Trust ye?
With every minute you do change a mind,
And call him noble that was now° your hate,   *just now*
Him vile that was your garland.[3] What's the matter,
That in these several° places of the city   *various*
175 You cry against the noble senate, who,
Under the gods, keep you in awe, which else°   *who otherwise*
Would feed on one another?
        [*To* MENENIUS]   What's their seeking?
MENENIUS   For corn at their own rates,° whereof they say   *prices*
The city is well stored.
MARTIUS   Hang 'em! They say?
180 They'll sit by th' fire and presume to know
What's done i'th' Capitol,[4] who's like to rise,
Who thrives and who declines; side° factions and give out°   *side with / announce*
Conjectural marriages, making parties strong
And feebling such as stand not in their liking
185 Below their cobbled° shoes. They say there's grain enough!   *patched*
Would the nobility lay aside their ruth°   *compassion*
And let me use my sword, I'd make a quarry[5]
With thousands of these quartered[6] slaves as high
As I could pitch my lance.
190 MENENIUS   Nay, these are all most thoroughly persuaded,°   *appeased*
For though abundantly they lack discretion,
Yet are they passing° cowardly. But I beseech you,   *exceedingly*
What says the other troop?
MARTIUS   They are dissolved. Hang 'em.
They said they were an-hungry,° sighed forth proverbs—   *very hungry*
195 That hunger broke stone walls, that dogs° must eat,   *(even dogs)*
That meat was made for mouths, that the gods sent not
Corn for the rich men only. With these shreds
They vented° their complainings, which being answered,   *spoke; excreted*
And a petition granted them—a strange one,
200 To break the heart of generosity°   *the nobility*
And make bold power look pale—they threw their caps
As they would hang them on the horns o'th' moon,
Shouting their emulation.[7]

2. To extol the man whose wrongdoing makes him
liable to punishment.
3. Hero (traditionally wreathed with laurel or oak leaves).
4. The temple of Jupiter and hub of the Roman state.

5. A pile of animals killed in hunting.
6. Hacked to pieces (a punishment for treason).
7. Rivalry (either to shout loudest, or to defy the nobility).

MENENIUS   What is granted them?

MARTIUS   Five tribunes° to defend their vulgar wisdoms,   *representatives*

205   Of their own choice. One's Junius Brutus,

        Sicinius Velutus, and I know not. 'Sdeath,°   *God's death (an oath)*

        The rabble should have first unroofed the city

        Ere so prevailed with me! It will in time

        Win upon power° and throw forth greater themes   *Prevail upon authority*

210   For insurrection's arguing.

MENENIUS   This is strange.

MARTIUS [*to the* CITIZENS]   Go get you home, you fragments.°   *scraps of uneaten food*

            Enter a MESSENGER *hastily*

MESSENGER   Where's Caius Martius?

MARTIUS   Here. What's the matter?

215   MESSENGER   The news is, sir, the Volsces are in arms.

MARTIUS   I am glad on't. Then we shall ha' means to vent

        Our musty superfluity.°   *moldy excess*

            Enter SICINIUS, BRUTUS, COMINIUS, LARTIUS, *with other*

            SENATORS

                   See, our best elders.

FIRST SENATOR   Martius, 'tis true that you have lately told us.

        The Volsces are in arms.

MARTIUS   They have a leader,

220   Tullus Aufidius, that will put you to't.°   *to the test*

        I sin in envying his nobility,

        And were I anything but what I am,

        I would wish me only he.

COMINIUS   You have fought together!

MARTIUS   Were half to half the world by th' ears[8] and he

225   Upon my party,° I'd revolt to make   *side*

        Only my wars with him. He is a lion

        That I am proud to hunt.

FIRST SENATOR   Then, worthy Martius,

        Attend upon° Cominius to these wars.   *Serve under*

COMINIUS [*to* MARTIUS]   It is your former promise.

MARTIUS   Sir, it is,

230   And I am constant. Titus Lartius, thou

        Shalt see me once more strike at Tullus' face.

        What, art thou stiff?[9] Stand'st out?

LARTIUS   No, Caius Martius.

        I'll lean upon one crutch and fight with th'other

        Ere stay behind this business.

MENENIUS   O true bred!

235   FIRST SENATOR   Your company to th' Capitol, where I know

        Our greatest friends attend us.

LARTIUS [*to* COMINIUS]   Lead you on.

        [*To* MARTIUS] Follow Cominius. We must follow you,

        Right worthy° your priority.   *Who well deserve*

COMINIUS   Noble Martius.

FIRST SENATOR [*to the* CITIZENS]   Hence to your homes, be

          gone.

MARTIUS   Nay, let them follow.

240   The Volsces have much corn. Take these rats thither

---

8. If one-half of the world were fighting the other.   9. Obstinate (but Lartius understands "stiff with age").

To gnaw their garners.°   CITIZENS *steal away*   *storehouses*
        Worshipful mutineers,
Your valour puts well forth.¹ [*To the* SENATORS] Pray follow.
        Exeunt. Manent° SICINIUS *and* BRUTUS *Remain onstage*

SICINIUS Was ever man so proud as is this Martius?
BRUTUS He has no equal.
245 SICINIUS When we were chosen tribunes for the people—
BRUTUS Marked you his lip and eyes?
SICINIUS   Nay, but his taunts.
BRUTUS Being moved,° he will not spare to gird² the gods. *angry*
SICINIUS Bemock the modest moon.
BRUTUS The present wars devour him! He is grown
 Too proud to be so valiant.
250 SICINIUS   Such a nature,
 Tickled° with good success, disdains the shadow *Excited; flattered*
 Which he treads on at noon. But I do wonder
 His insolence can brook° to be commanded   *endure*
 Under Cominius.
BRUTUS   Fame, at the which he aims—
255 In whom already he's well graced—cannot
 Better be held nor more attained than by
 A place below the first; for what miscarries
 Shall be the general's fault, though he perform
 To th' utmost of a man, and giddy censure° *rash opinion*
260 Will then cry out of Martius 'O, if he
 Had borne the business!'
SICINIUS   Besides, if things go well,
 Opinion, that so sticks on° Martius, shall   *clings to*
 Of his demerits° rob Cominius.   *Of Cominius's deserts*
BRUTUS   Come,
 Half all Cominius' honours are to Martius,
265 Though Martius earned them not; and all his faults
 To Martius shall be honours, though indeed
 In aught he merit not.
SICINIUS   Let's hence and hear
 How the dispatch is made,° and in what fashion, *business is executed*
 More than his singularity,³ he goes
 Upon this present action.
270 BRUTUS   Let's along.   *Exeunt*

1.2

Enter AUFIDIUS, *with* SENATORS *of Corioles*

FIRST SENATOR So, your opinion is, Aufidius,
 That they of Rome are entered° in our counsels *instructed*
 And know how we proceed.
AUFIDIUS   Is it not yours?
 What ever have been thought on in this state
5 That could be brought to bodily act ere Rome
 Had circumvention?° 'Tis not four days gone *means to circumvent it*
 Since I heard thence.° These are the words. I think *from there*
 I have the letter here—yes, here it is.
  [*He reads the letter*]

---

1. Promises well, like a budding plant (ironic). 3. Apart from his idiosyncrasies.
2. He will not refrain from sneering at. 1.2 Location: Corioles, chief city of the Volscians.

'They have pressed a power,° but it is not known   *conscripted an army*
10   Whether for east or west. The dearth is great,
The people mutinous, and it is rumoured
Cominius, Martius your old enemy,
Who is of Rome worse hated than of you,
And Titus Lartius, a most valiant Roman,
15   These three lead on this preparation
Whither 'tis bent.° Most likely 'tis for you.   *Wherever it is bound*
Consider of it.'

FIRST SENATOR   Our army's in the field.
We never yet made doubt but Rome was ready
To answer us.

AUFIDIUS   Nor did you think it folly
20   To keep your great pretences° veiled till when   *aims*
They needs must show themselves, which in the hatching,
It seemed, appeared° to Rome. By the discovery   *became known*
We shall be shortened in our aim,° which was   *have to lower our sights*
To take in° many towns ere, almost, Rome   *seize*
Should know we were afoot.
25 SECOND SENATOR   Noble Aufidius,
Take your commission, hie° you to your bands.°   *haste / troops*
Let us alone to guard Corioles.
If they set down° before's, for the remove°   *encamp / to raise the siege*
Bring up your army, but I think you'll find
They've not prepared for us.
30 AUFIDIUS   O, doubt not that.
I speak from certainties. Nay, more,
Some parcels° of their power are forth already,   *parts*
And only hitherward.° I leave your honours.   *marching toward us*
If we and Caius Martius chance to meet,
35 'Tis sworn between us we shall ever strike°   *keep fighting*
Till one can do no more.

ALL THE SENATORS   The gods assist you!

AUFIDIUS   And keep your honours safe.

FIRST SENATOR   Farewell.

SECOND SENATOR   Farewell.

ALL   Farewell.

        Exeunt [AUFIDIUS *at one door,*
        SENATORS *at another door*]

1.3

Enter VOLUMNIA *and* VIRGILIA, *mother and wife to Mar-*
tius. They set them down on two low stools and sew

VOLUMNIA   I pray you, daughter, sing, or express yourself in a
more comfortable sort.° If my son were my husband, I should   *cheerful manner*
freelier rejoice in that absence wherein he won honour than in
the embracements of his bed where he would show most love.
5   When yet he was but tenderbodied and the only son of my
womb, when youth with comeliness plucked all gaze his way,
when for a day of kings' entreaties a mother should not sell him
an hour from her beholding, I, considering how honour would
become such a person°—that it was no better than, picture-   *handsome figure*
10 like, to hang by th' wall if renown made it not stir[1]—was

---

1.3 Location: Caius Martius's house, in Rome.   1. If desire for fame did not move it to action.

pleased to let him seek danger where he was like to find fame.
To a cruel war I sent him, from whence he returned his brows
bound with oak.[2] I tell thee, daughter, I sprang not more in joy
at first hearing he was a man-child than now in first seeing he
15 had proved himself a man.

VIRGILIA   But had he died in the business, madam, how then?

VOLUMNIA   Then his good report should have been my son. I
therein would have found issue. Hear me profess sincerely: had
I a dozen sons, each in my love alike, and none less dear than
20 thine and my good Martius', I had rather had eleven die nobly
for their country than one voluptuously surfeit out of action.[3]

     Enter a GENTLEWOMAN

GENTLEWOMAN   Madam, the Lady Valeria is come to visit you.

VIRGILIA [*to* VOLUMNIA]   Beseech you give me leave to retire
myself.°   *to go in*
25 VOLUMNIA   Indeed you shall not.
    Methinks I hear hither your husband's drum,
    See him pluck Aufidius down by th' hair;
    As children from a bear, the Volsces shunning° him.   *fleeing*
    Methinks I see him stamp thus, and call thus:
30   'Come on, you cowards, you were got° in fear   *begotten*
    Though you were born in Rome!' His bloody brow
    With his mailed° hand then wiping, forth he goes,   *armored*
    Like to a harvest-man that's tasked° to mow   *ordered*
    Or° all or lose his hire.°   *Either / pay*
35 VIRGILIA   His bloody brow? O Jupiter, no blood!
VOLUMNIA   Away, you fool! It more becomes a man
    Than gilt° his trophy. The breasts of Hecuba[4]   *gold leaf*
    When she did suckle Hector[5] looked not lovelier
    Than Hector's forehead when it spit forth blood
    At Grecian sword, contemning.°   *expressing contempt*
40   [*To the* GENTLEWOMAN]   Tell Valeria
    We are fit° to bid her welcome.   *Exit* GENTLEWOMAN   *ready*
VIRGILIA   Heavens bless my lord from fell° Aufidius!   *fierce*
VOLUMNIA   He'll beat Aufidius' head below his knee
    And tread upon his neck.

     Enter VALERIA, *with an usher and the* GENTLEWOMAN

45 VALERIA   My ladies both, good day to you.
VOLUMNIA   Sweet madam.
VIRGILIA   I am glad to see your ladyship.
VALERIA   How do you both? You are manifest housekeepers.[6]
    What are you sewing here? A fine spot,° in good faith. How   *embroidered design*
50   does your little son?
VIRGILIA   I thank your ladyship; well, good madam.
VOLUMNIA   He had rather see the swords and hear a drum
    than look upon his schoolmaster.
VALERIA   O' my word, the father's son! I'll swear 'tis a very pretty
55   boy. O' my troth, I looked upon him o' Wednesday half an
    hour together. He's such a confirmed° countenance! I saw him   *determined*
    run after a gilded butterfly, and when he caught it he let it go
    again, and after it again, and over and over° he comes, and up   *head over heels*

---

2. A garland of oak leaves (awarded to one who saved
the life of a Roman citizen in battle).
3. Indulge himself to excess away from the battlefield.
4. Trojan queen, mother of many sons.

5. The greatest Trojan warrior, killed by the Greek
Achilles (*see* Troilus and Cressida).
6. You are clearly being stay-at-homes.

again, catched it again. Or whether his fall enraged him, or
60 how 'twas, he did so set° his teeth and tear it! O, I warrant, how   *clench*
he mammocked° it!   *shredded*
VOLUMNIA   One on's° father's moods.   *of his*
VALERIA   Indeed, la, 'tis a noble child.
VIRGILIA   A crack,° madam.   *lively lad*
65 VALERIA   Come, lay aside your stitchery. I must have you play
the idle housewife° with me this afternoon.   *hussy*
VIRGILIA   No, good madam, I will not out of doors.
VALERIA   Not out of doors?
VOLUMNIA   She shall, she shall.
70 VIRGILIA   Indeed, no, by your patience. I'll not over the thresh-
old till my lord return from the wars.
VALERIA   Fie, you confine yourself most unreasonably. Come,
you must go visit the good lady that lies in.°   *is confined with child*
VIRGILIA   I will wish her speedy strength, and visit her with my
75 prayers, but I cannot go thither.
VOLUMNIA   Why, I pray you?
VIRGILIA   'Tis not to save labour, nor that I want love.°   *lack affection for her*
VALERIA   You would be another Penelope.[7] Yet they say all the
yarn she spun in Ulysses' absence did but fill Ithaca full of
80 moths. Come, I would your cambric° were sensible° as your   *fine white linen / sensitive*
finger, that you might leave pricking it for pity. Come, you
shall go with us.
VIRGILIA   No, good madam, pardon me, indeed I will not forth.
VALERIA   In truth, la, go with me, and I'll tell you excellent news
85 of your husband.
VIRGILIA   O, good madam, there can be none yet.
VALERIA   Verily, I do not jest with you: there came news from
him last night.
VIRGILIA   Indeed, madam?
90 VALERIA   In earnest, it's true. I heard a senator speak it. Thus it
is: the Volsces have an army forth, against whom Cominius the
general is gone with one part of our Roman power. Your lord
and Titus Lartius are set down before their city Corioles. They
nothing doubt prevailing,[8] and to make it brief wars. This is
95 true, on mine honour; and so, I pray, go with us.
VIRGILIA   Give me excuse,° good madam, I will obey you in   *Pardon me*
everything hereafter.
VOLUMNIA [to VALERIA]   Let her alone, lady. As she is now she
will but disease° our better mirth.   *trouble*
100 VALERIA   In truth, I think she would. Fare you well, then. Come,
good sweet lady. Prithee, Virgilia, turn thy solemness out o'
door and go along with us.
VIRGILIA   No, at a word, madam. Indeed, I must not. I wish you
much mirth.
105 VALERIA   Well then, farewell.
    Exeunt [VALERIA, VOLUMNIA, *and usher at one door,*
    VIRGILIA *and* GENTLEWOMAN *at another door*]

---

7. In Homer's *Odyssey*, Ulysses' wife, Penelope, pre-   secretly unravels each night.
tends during his protracted absence that she cannot   8. They don't at all doubt that they will prevail.
remarry until she finishes her weaving, which she

1.4

Enter MARTIUS, LARTIUS *with [a trumpeter and] drum
and colors,° with captains and soldiers [carrying scaling
ladders], as before the city Corioles;¹ to them a* MES-
SENGER   drummer and flag bearer

MARTIUS   Yonder comes news. A wager they have met.
LARTIUS   My horse to yours, no.
MARTIUS   'Tis done.
LARTIUS   Agreed.
MARTIUS [*to the* MESSENGER]   Say, has our general met the enemy?
MESSENGER   They lie in view, but have not spoke° as yet.   encountered
LARTIUS   So, the good horse is mine.
5   MARTIUS   I'll buy him of you.
LARTIUS   No, I'll nor° sell nor give him. Lend you him I will,   neither
For half a hundred years.
[*To the trumpeter*]   Summon the town.
MARTIUS [*to the* MESSENGER]   How far off lie these armies?
MESSENGER   Within
         this mile and half.
MARTIUS   Then shall we hear their 'larum,° and they ours.   call to arms
10   Now Mars,° I prithee, make us quick in work,   Roman god of war
That we with smoking° swords may march from hence   steaming (with blood)
To help our fielded friends.²
[*To the trumpeter*]   Come, blow thy blast.
         They sound a parley.³ Enter two SENATORS, *with others,
         on the walls of Corioles*
[*To the* SENATORS] Tullus Aufidius, is he within your walls?
FIRST SENATOR   No, nor a man that fears you less than he:
That's lesser than a little.
         Drum afar off
15   [*To the Volscians*]   Hark, our drums
Are bringing forth our youth. We'll break our walls
Rather than they shall pound us up.° Our gates,   confine us
Which yet seem shut, we have but pinned with rushes.°   hollow reeds
They'll open of themselves.
         Alarum far off
[*To the Romans*]   Hark you, far off
20   There is Aufidius. List what work he makes
Amongst your cloven° army.   divided; cut to pieces
         [*Exeunt Volscians from the walls*]
MARTIUS   O, they are at it!
LARTIUS   Their noise be our instruction. Ladders, ho!
         [*They prepare to assault the walls.*]
         Enter the army of the Volsces [from the gates]
MARTIUS   They fear us not, but issue° forth their city.   rush from
Now put your shields before your hearts, and fight
25   With hearts more proof ° than shields. Advance, brave Titus.   impenetrable
They do disdain us much beyond our thoughts,⁴
Which makes me sweat with wrath. Come on, my fellows.

1.4 Location: Before the walls of Corioles.
1. The rear of the stage represented the city walls, the
tiring-house door the gate, and the balcony the ramparts.
2. Our comrades in the battlefield.
3. Trumpet call for conference with the enemy.
4. More than we had imagined.

He that retires, I'll take him for a Volsce,
And he shall feel mine edge.°   *(sword edge)*
> *Alarum. The Romans are beat back [and exeunt]*
> *to their trenches[, the Volsces following]*

1.5

> *Enter [Roman* SOLDIERS, *in retreat, followed by]* MAR-
> TIUS, *cursing*

MARTIUS   All the contagion of the south[1] light on you,
You shames of Rome! You herd of—boils and plagues
Plaster you o'er, that you may be abhorred°   *(by your smell)*
Farther than seen, and one infect another
5   Against the wind a mile!° You souls of geese   *Even a mile upwind*
That bear the shapes of men, how have you run
From slaves that apes would beat! Pluto° and hell: *god of the underworld*
All hurt behind![2] Backs red, and faces pale
With flight and agued° fear! Mend and charge home,[3]   *shivering*
10 Or by the fires of heaven° I'll leave the foe   *the stars*
And make my wars on you. Look to't. Come on.
If you'll stand fast, we'll beat them to their wives,
As they us to our trenches. Follow.
> *[The Romans come forward towards the walls.]*
> *Another alarum, and [enter the army of the Volsces.]*
> MARTIUS *[beats them back through] the gates*
So, now the gates are ope. Now prove good seconds.°   *supporters*
15 'Tis for the followers fortune widens° them,   *opens*
Not for the fliers. Mark me, and do the like.
> *[He] enters the gates*
FIRST SOLDIER   Foolhardiness! Not I.
SECOND SOLDIER   Nor I.
> *Alarum continues. [The gates close,] and [*MARTIUS*] is*
> *shut in*
FIRST SOLDIER   See, they have shut him in.
THIRD SOLDIER   To th' pot,° I warrant him.   *cooking pot*
> *Enter* LARTIUS
LARTIUS   What is become of Martius?
FOURTH SOLDIER   Slain, sir, doubtless.
20 FIRST SOLDIER   Following the fliers at the very heels,
With them he enters, who upon the sudden
Clapped-to° their gates. He is himself alone   *Shut*
To answer° all the city.   *confront*
LARTIUS   O noble fellow,
Who sensibly° outdares his senseless sword   *though having sensation*
25 And, when it bows, stand'st up! Thou art lost, Martius.
A carbuncle entire,° as big as thou art,   *flawless ruby*
Were not so rich a jewel. Thou wast a soldier
Even to Cato's[4] wish, not fierce and terrible
Only in strokes, but with thy grim looks and
30 The thunder-like percussion of thy sounds
Thou mad'st thine enemies shake as if the world
Were feverous and did tremble.

1.5 Scene continues.
1. South wind (thought to carry disease).
2. An injury taken in flight was a disgrace.
3. Charge to the heart of their defenses.
4. Cato the Censor, Roman general and moralist.

Enter MARTIUS, *bleeding, assaulted by the enemy*

FIRST SOLDIER   Look, sir.

LARTIUS   O, 'tis Martius!

Let's fetch him off, or make remain alike.[5]

They fight, and all [exeunt] into the city

1.6

Enter certain ROMANS *with spoils*

FIRST ROMAN   This will I carry to Rome.

SECOND ROMAN   And I this.

THIRD ROMAN   A murrain° on't, I took this for silver.   plague
[*He throws it away.*]

Alarum continues still afar off. Enter MARTIUS, [*bleeding,*] *and* [LARTIUS] *with a trumpet[er]. Exeunt* [ROMANS
with spoils]

MARTIUS   See here these movers[1] that do prize their honours
5   At a cracked drachma!° Cushions, leaden spoons,   Greek coin
Irons of a doit,[2] doublets that hangmen would
Bury with those that wore them,[3] these base slaves,
Ere yet the fight be done, pack up. Down with them!
And hark what noise the general makes. To him.
10   There is the man of my soul's hate, Aufidius,
Piercing our Romans. Then, valiant Titus, take
Convenient numbers to make good° the city,   secure
Whilst I, with those that have the spirit, will haste
To help Cominius.

LARTIUS   Worthy sir, thou bleed'st.
15   Thy exercise hath been too violent
For a second course° of fight.   bout

MARTIUS   Sir, praise me not.
My work hath yet not warmed me. Fare you well.
The blood I drop is rather physical[4]
Than dangerous to me. To Aufidius thus
I will appear and fight.

20   LARTIUS   Now the fair goddess fortune
Fall deep in love with thee, and her great charms
Misguide thy opposers' swords! Bold gentleman,
Prosperity be thy page.°   *Success attend you*
                                                                            (Prosperity)

MARTIUS   Thy friend° no less
Than those she placeth highest. So farewell.

25   LARTIUS   Thou worthiest Martius!   [*Exit* MARTIUS]
Go sound thy trumpet in the market-place.
Call thither all the officers o'th' town,
Where they shall know our mind. Away.   *Exeunt* [*severally*]

1.7

Enter COMINIUS, *as it were in retire, with soldiers*

COMINIUS   Breathe you,° my friends. Well fought. We are come   *Get your breath back*
off[1]
Like Romans, neither foolish in our stands

---

5. Let's rescue him, or share his fate.
1.6 Location: Corioles.
1. Active persons (ironic); plunderers.
2. Worthless swords (a "doit" was a very small coin).
doublets: close-fitting jackets (common male attire in
Jacobean England).

3. That is, even a hangman, whose wage is his victim's
clothing, would spurn these garments.
4. Curative (bloodletting was a common medical practice).
1.7 Location: The battlefield.
1. We have retreated.

Nor cowardly in retire. Believe me, sirs,
We shall be charged again. Whiles we have struck,°   *we were fighting*
5   By interims and conveying gusts² we have heard
The charges of our friends. The Roman gods
Lead their successes as we wish our own,
That both our powers, with smiling fronts° encount'ring,   *faces; front ranks*
May give you° thankful sacrifice!   *(the gods)*
      Enter a MESSENGER
                            Thy news?
10   MESSENGER   The citizens of Corioles have issued,°   *(from the gates)*
And given to Lartius and to Martius battle.
I saw our party to their trenches driven,
And then I came away.
COMINIUS   Though thou speak'st truth,
Methinks thou speak'st not well. How long is't since?
15   MESSENGER   Above an hour, my lord.
COMINIUS   'Tis not a mile; briefly° we heard their drums.   *a short time ago*
How couldst thou in a mile confound° an hour,   *waste*
And bring thy news so late?
MESSENGER   Spies of the Volsces
Held me in chase, that I was forced to wheel°   *detour*
20   Three or four miles about; else had I, sir,
Half an hour since brought my report.   [*Exit*]
      Enter MARTIUS [*bloody*]
COMINIUS   Who's yonder,
That does appear as he were flayed? O gods!
He has the stamp° of Martius, and I have   *form*
Before-time° seen him thus.   *Previously*
MARTIUS   Come I too late?
25   COMINIUS   The shepherd knows not thunder from a tabor°   *small drum*
More than I know the sound of Martius' tongue
From every meaner° man.   *lesser*
MARTIUS   Come I too late?
COMINIUS   Ay, if you come not in the blood of others,
But mantled in your own.
MARTIUS   O, let me clip° ye   *clasp*
30   In arms as sound as when I wooed, in heart
As merry as when our nuptial day was done,
And tapers burnt to bedward!
      [*They embrace*]
COMINIUS   Flower of warriors! How is't with Titus Lartius?
MARTIUS   As with a man busied about decrees,
35   Condemning some to death and some to exile,
Ransoming him or pitying, threat'ning th'other;
Holding Corioles in the name of Rome
Even like a fawning greyhound in the leash,
To let him slip° at will.   *off the leash*
COMINIUS   Where is that slave
40   Which told me they had beat you to your trenches?
Where is he? Call him hither.
MARTIUS   Let him alone.
He did inform° the truth. But for our gentlemen,°   *report / (sarcastic)*
The common file°—a plague—tribunes for them?—   *sort*

---

2. At intervals, conveyed by the wind.

The mouse ne'er shunned the cat as they did budge°   *flinch*
From rascals worse than they.

45 COMINIUS   But how prevailed you?

MARTIUS   Will the time serve to tell? I do not think.
Where is the enemy? Are you lords o'th' field?
If not, why cease you till you are so?

COMINIUS   Martius, we have at disadvantage fought,
50 And did retire to win our purpose.°   *for tactical reasons*

MARTIUS   How lies their battle?° Know you on which side   *army*
They have placed their men of trust?

COMINIUS   As I guess, Martius,
Their bands i'th' vanguard are the Antiates,
Of their best trust; o'er them Aufidius,
Their very heart of hope.

55 MARTIUS   I do beseech you
By all the battles wherein we have fought,
By th' blood we have shed together, by th' vows we have made
To endure° friends, that you directly set me   *remain*
Against Aufidius and his Antiates,
60 And that you not delay the present,° but,   *matter at hand*
Filling the air with swords advanced and darts,
We prove° this very hour.   *try*

COMINIUS   Though I could wish
You were conducted to a gentle bath
And balms applied to you, yet dare I never
65 Deny your asking. Take your choice of those
That best can aid your action.

MARTIUS   Those are they
That most are willing. If any such be here—
As it were sin to doubt—that love this painting°   *(blood)*
Wherein you see me smeared; if any fear
70 Lesser his person than an ill report[3]
If any think brave death outweighs bad life,
And that his country's dearer than himself,
Let him alone, or so many so minded,
        [*He waves his sword*]
Wave thus to express his disposition,
75 And follow Martius.

        They all shout and wave their swords, [then some] take
        him up in their arms and [they] cast up their caps

O' me alone, make you a sword of me?
If these shows be not outward,° which of you   *superficial*
But is four Volsces? None of you but is
Able to bear against the great Aufidius
80 A shield as hard as his. A certain number—
Though thanks to all—must I select from all.
The rest shall bear the business in some other fight
As cause will be obeyed.° Please you to march,   *the situation requires*
And I shall quickly draw out my command,[4]
Which men are best inclined.

85 COMINIUS   March on, my fellows.
Make good this ostentation,° and you shall   *show of enthusiasm*
Divide in all[5] with us.   *Exeunt [marching]*

3. Less for his body than for his reputation.   5. Share the honor and winnings.
4. Select those I will command.

1.8

Enter LARTIUS [*through the gates of*] *Corioles, with*
drum and trumpet, a LIEUTENANT, *other soldiers, and a*
scout

LARTIUS [*to the* LIEUTENANT]   So, let the ports° be guarded. Keep your duties   gates
　As I have set them down. If I do send, dispatch
　Those centuries[1] to our aid. The rest will serve
　For a short holding.° If we lose the field   *brief occupation*
5　We cannot keep the town.

LIEUTENANT   Fear not our care, sir.

LARTIUS   Hence, and shut your gates upon's.   [*Exit* LIEUTENANT]
　[*To the scout*] Our guider, come; to th' Roman camp conduct us.

Exeunt toward COMINIUS *and* MARTIUS

1.9

Alarum, as in battle. Enter MARTIUS, [*bloody,*] *and*
AUFIDIUS *at several*° *doors*   *separate*

MARTIUS   I'll fight with none but thee, for I do hate thee
　Worse than a promise-breaker.

AUFIDIUS   We hate alike.
　Not Afric owns° a serpent I abhor   *Africa doesn't contain*
　More than thy fame and envy.° Fix thy foot.   *enviable reputation*

5 MARTIUS   Let the first budger die the other's slave,
　And the gods doom him after.

AUFIDIUS   If I fly, Martius,
　Holla° me like a hare.   *Shout in pursuit of*

MARTIUS   Within these three hours, Tullus,
　Alone I fought in your Corioles' walls,
　And made what work I pleased. 'Tis not my blood
10　Wherein thou seest me masked. For thy revenge,
　Wrench up thy power to th' highest.

AUFIDIUS   Wert thou the Hector
　That was the whip of your bragged progeny,[1]
　Thou shouldst not scape me here.

Here they fight, and certain Volsces come in the aid of
AUFIDIUS. MARTIUS *fights till* [*the Volsces*] *be driven in*
breathless[, MARTIUS *following*]

　Officious° and not valiant, you have shamed me   *Meddling*
15　In your condemnèd seconds.[2]

                                                      Exit

1.10

Alarum. A retreat is sounded. Flourish.[1] *Enter at one*
door COMINIUS *with the Romans, at another door* MAR-
TIUS *with his arm in a scarf*°   *sling*

COMINIUS [*to* MARTIUS]   If I should tell thee o'er this thy day's work
　Thou'lt not believe thy deeds. But I'll report it
　Where senators shall mingle tears with smiles,
　Where great patricians shall attend and shrug,°   *(with incredulity)*
5　I'th' end admire;° where ladies shall be frighted   *marvel*

1.8 Location: The gates of Corioles.
1. Companies of a hundred men.
1.9 Location: The battlefield.
1. Romans claimed descent from the Trojans; Hector,
the finest Trojan soldier, was the scourge ("whip") of the

Greeks.
2. Contemptible assistance.
1.10 Location: The battlefield.
1. Trumpet call for the entry of the victorious Romans.
retreat: signal to cease pursuit.

And, gladly quaked,° hear more; where the dull° tribunes,   *made to tremble / sullen*
That with the fusty° plebeians hate thine honours,   *moldy; stinking*
Shall say against their hearts° 'We thank the gods   *despite themselves*
Our Rome hath such a soldier.'
10 Yet cam'st thou to a morsel of this feast,
Having fully dined before.[2]

        Enter [LARTIUS,] *with his power,° from the pursuit*   *troops*

LARTIUS   O general,
Here is the steed, we the caparison.[3]
Hadst thou beheld—
MARTIUS   Pray now, no more. My mother,
Who has a charter° to extol her blood,°   *right / offspring*
15 When she does praise me grieves me. I have done
As you have done, that's what I can; induced
As you have been, that's for my country.
He that has but effected his good will[4]
Hath overta'en mine act.
COMINIUS   You shall not be
20 The grave of your deserving. Rome must know
The value of her own. 'Twere a concealment
Worse than a theft, no less than a traducement,°   *slander*
To hide your doings and to silence that
Which, to the spire and top of praises vouched,°   *declared*
25 Would seem but modest.° Therefore, I beseech you—   *inadequate*
In sign° of what you are, not to reward   *As a token*
What you have done—before our army hear me.
MARTIUS I have some wounds upon me, and they smart
To hear themselves remembered.
COMINIUS   Should they not,
30 Well might they fester 'gainst ingratitude,
And tent[5] themselves with death. Of all the horses—
Whereof we have ta'en good, and good store[6]—of all
The treasure in this field achieved and city,
We render you the° tenth, to be ta'en forth   *one*
35 Before the common distribution
At your only° choice.   *sole*
MARTIUS   I thank you, general,
But cannot make my heart consent to take
A bribe to pay my sword. I do refuse it,
And stand° upon my common part with those   *insist*
40 That have upheld the doing.

    A long flourish. They all cry 'Martius, Martius!' [and]
    cast up their caps and lances. COMINIUS *and* LARTIUS
    stand bare

May these same instruments which you profane
Never sound more. When drums and trumpets shall
I'th' field prove flatterers, let courts and cities be
Made all of false-faced soothing.[7] When steel grows
45 Soft as the parasite's° silk, let him be made   *flatterer's*

2. *Yet . . . before:* either "The feast of description is a morsel compared with the full dinner of your deeds," or "Your final onslaught was a mere morsel in addition to your earlier fighting."
3. That is, here is he who really did the work (Coriolanus, the horse); we are only the horse's trappings ("caparison").
4. Carried out his resolution.
5. Heal (a "tent" was a probe that cleansed a wound).
6. We have captured good quality and quantity.
7. Hypocritical compliments.

An overture for th' wars.[8] No more, I say.
For that I have not washed my nose that bled,
Or foiled some debile° wretch, which without note   feeble
Here's many else° have done, you shout me forth   others
50   In acclamations hyperbolical,°   In exaggerated praise
As if I loved my little[9] should be dieted°   fattened
In praises sauced with lies.
COMINIUS   Too modest are you,
More cruel to your good report than grateful
To us that give° you truly. By your patience,   describe
55   If 'gainst yourself you be incensed we'll put you,
Like one that means his proper harm,° in manacles,   harm to himself
Then reason safely with you. Therefore be it known,
As to us, to all the world, that Caius Martius
Wears this war's garland, in token of the which
60   My noble steed, known to the camp, I give him,
With all his trim belonging;° and from this time,   fine trappings
For what he did before Corioles, call him,
With all th'applause and clamour of the host,
Martius Caius Coriolanus. Bear th'addition°   title
65   Nobly ever!
            Flourish. Trumpets sound, and drums
ALL   Martius Caius Coriolanus!
CORIOLANUS [*to* COMINIUS]   I will go wash,
And when my face is fair° you shall perceive   clean
Whether I blush or no. Howbeit, I thank you.
70   I mean to stride° your steed, and at all times   bestride; ride on
To undercrest° your good addition   uphold
To th' fairness° of my power.   best
COMINIUS   So, to our tent,
Where, ere we do repose us, we will write
To Rome of our success. You, Titus Lartius,
75   Must to Corioles back. Send us to Rome
The best,[1] with whom we may articulate°   make terms
For their own good and ours.
LARTIUS   I shall, my lord.
CORIOLANUS   The gods begin to mock me. I, that now
Refused most princely gifts, am bound to beg
Of my lord general.
80   COMINIUS   Take't, 'tis yours. What is't?
CORIOLANUS   I sometime lay here in Corioles,
And at a poor man's house. He used° me kindly.   treated
He cried° to me; I saw him prisoner;   appealed
But then Aufidius was within my view,
85   And wrath o'erwhelmed my pity. I request you
To give my poor host freedom.
COMINIUS   O, well begged!
Were he the butcher of my son he should
Be free as is the wind. Deliver° him, Titus.   Free
LARTIUS   Martius, his name?
CORIOLANUS   By Jupiter, forgot!
90   I am weary, yea, my memory is tired.
Have we no wine here?

---

8. *let . . . wars*: a debated and perhaps corrupt passage: 9. Small achievement.
perhaps "let the parasite call soldiers to war."   1. The most noble Volscians.

COMINIUS   Go we to our tent.
The blood upon your visage dries; 'tis time
It should be looked to. Come.   *Exeunt. A flourish [of] cornetts*

1.11

Enter AUFIDIUS, *bloody, with two or three* SOLDIERS

AUFIDIUS   The town is ta'en.

A SOLDIER   'Twill be delivered back on good condition.[1]

AUFIDIUS   Condition?
I would I were a Roman, for I cannot,

5   Being a Volsce, be that I am.° Condition?   *what I am (proud)*
What good condition can a treaty find
I'th' part that is at mercy?° Five times, Martius,   *For the conquered side*
I have fought with thee; so often hast thou beat me,
And wouldst do so, I think, should we encounter
10   As often as we eat. By th' elements,
If e'er again I meet him beard to beard,
He's mine, or I am his! Mine emulation°   *rivalry*
Hath not that honour in't it had, for where°   *whereas*
I thought to crush him in an equal force,
15   True sword to sword, I'll potch° at him some way   *thrust*
Or° wrath or craft may get him.   *Either*

A SOLDIER   He's the devil.

AUFIDIUS   Bolder, though not so subtle. My valour, poisoned
With only suff'ring stain° by him, for him   *disgrace*
Shall fly out of itself. Nor sleep nor sanctuary,[2]
20   Being naked, sick, nor fane° nor Capitol,   *temple*
The prayers of priests nor times of sacrifice—
Embargements° all of fury—shall lift up   *Impediments*
Their rotten° privilege and custom 'gainst   *worn-out*
My hate to Martius. Where I find him, were it
25   At home upon° my brother's guard,° even there,   *under / protection*
Against the hospitable canon,° would I   *rule of hospitality*
Wash my fierce hand in's heart. Go you to th' city.
Learn how 'tis held, and what they are that must
Be hostages for Rome.

A SOLDIER   Will not you go?

30   AUFIDIUS   I am attended° at the cypress grove. I pray you—   *expected*
'Tis south the city mills—bring me word thither
How the world goes, that to the pace of it[3]
I may spur on my journey.

A SOLDIER   I shall, sir.

                Exeunt [AUFIDIUS *at one door,* SOLDIERS
                          at another door]

2.1

Enter MENENIUS *with the two tribunes of the people,*
SICINIUS *and* BRUTUS

MENENIUS   The augurer[1] tells me we shall have news tonight.

BRUTUS   Good or bad?

MENENIUS   Not according to the prayer of the people, for they
love not Martius.

1.11 Location: Outside Corioles.
1. Terms (Aufidius takes the meaning "state of being").
2. In early modern England, those who sought sanctuary in a church were protected from attack or legal pros-

ecution. *fly out of itself*: deviate from its nature.
3. In accordance with the situation.
2.1 Location: Rome.
1. Religious official who interpreted omens.

5	SICINIUS Nature teaches beasts to know their friends.	
	MENENIUS Pray you, who does the wolf love?	
	SICINIUS The lamb.	
	MENENIUS Ay, to devour him, as the hungry plebeians would	
	the noble Martius.	
10	BRUTUS He's a lamb indeed that baas like a bear.	
	MENENIUS He's a bear indeed that lives like a lamb.[2] You two	
	are old men. Tell me one thing that I shall ask you.	
	SICINIUS *and* BRUTUS Well, sir?	
	MENENIUS In what enormity is Martius poor in that you two	
15	have not in abundance?	
	BRUTUS He's poor in no one fault, but stored° with all.	well stocked
	SICINIUS Especially in pride.	
	BRUTUS And topping all others in boasting.	
	MENENIUS This is strange now. Do you two know how you are	
20	censured° here in the city—I mean of us o'th' right-hand file.[3]	judged
	Do you?	
	SICINIUS *and* BRUTUS Why, how are we censured?	
	MENENIUS Because—you talk of pride now—will you not be	
	angry?	
25	SICINIUS *and* BRUTUS Well, well, sir, well?	
	MENENIUS Why, 'tis no great matter, for a very little thief of	
	occasion will rob you of a great deal of patience.[4] Give your	
	dispositions the reins, and be angry at your pleasures—at the	
	least, if you take it as a pleasure to you in being so. You blame	
30	Martius for being proud?	
	BRUTUS We do it not alone, sir.	
	MENENIUS I know you can do very little alone, for your helps	
	are many, or else your actions would grow wondrous single.°	solitary; trivial
	Your abilities are too infant-like for doing much alone. You talk	
35	of pride. O that you could turn your eyes toward the napes of	
	your necks, and make but an interior survey of your good	
	selves! O that you could!	
	SICINIUS *and* BRUTUS What then, sir?	
	MENENIUS Why, then you should discover a brace° of unmer-	pair
40	iting, proud, violent, testy magistrates, alias fools, as any in	
	Rome.	
	SICINIUS Menenius, you are known well enough too.	
	MENENIUS I am known to be a humorous° patrician, and one	whimsical
	that loves a cup of hot wine with not a drop of allaying Tiber°	water
45	in't; said to be something imperfect in favouring the first com-	
	plaint,[5] hasty and tinder-like upon too trivial motion;° one that	provocation
	converses more with the buttock of the night than with the	
	forehead of the morning.[6] What I think, I utter, and spend my	
	malice in my breath. Meeting two such wealsmen° as you	statesmen
50	are—I cannot call you Lycurguses[7]—if the drink you give me	
	touch my palate adversely, I make a crooked face at it. I cannot	
	say your worships have delivered the matter well, when I find	
	the ass in compound with the major part of your syllables.[8] And	

2. That is, how can you accuse him of being a bear when he lives an innocent life?

3. Patrician class (who made up the right-hand "file," or line, in battle).

4. The least pretext will make you lose your temper.

5. *favouring the first complaint*: accepting the first ver- sion of a dispute I hear before considering the other side.

6. That experiences more late nights than early mornings.

7. Lycurgus was a famous Spartan lawgiver of the ninth century B.C.E.

8. I find stupidity mixed in most of what you say.

though I must be content to bear with those that say you are
55 reverend grave men, yet they lie deadly° that tell you have good   *extremely*
faces. If you see this in the map of my microcosm,[9] follows it
that I am known well enough too? What harm can your bisson
conspectuities° glean out of this character,[1] if I be known well   *dim vision*
enough too?
60 BRUTUS Come, sir, come, we know you well enough.
MENENIUS You know neither me, yourselves, nor anything. You
are ambitious for poor knaves' caps and legs.[2] You wear out a
good wholesome forenoon in hearing a cause between an
orange-wife and a faucet-seller,[3] and then rejourn° the contro-   *adjourn*
65 versy of threepence to a second day of audience.° When you   *hearing*
are hearing a matter between party and party, if you chance to
be pinched with the colic,° you make faces like mummers,[4] set   *intestinal gas*
up the bloody flag° against all patience, and in roaring for a   *declare war*
chamber-pot, dismiss the controversy bleeding,° the more   *unhealed*
70 entangled by your hearing. All the peace you make in their
cause is calling both the parties knaves. You are a pair of
strange ones.
BRUTUS Come, come, you are well understood to be a perfecter
giber for the table than a necessary bencher in the Capitol.[5]
75 MENENIUS Our very priests must become mockers if they shall
encounter such ridiculous subjects° as you are. When you   *objects; citizens*
speak best unto the purpose it is not worth the wagging of your
beards, and your beards deserve not so honourable a grave as
to stuff a botcher's° cushion or to be entombed in an ass's pack-   *clothes mender*
80 saddle.[6] Yet you must be saying 'Martius is proud', who, in a
cheap estimation,° is worth all your predecessors since Deuca-   *low estimate*
lion,[7] though peradventure some of the best of 'em were hereditary hangmen.[8] Good e'en to your worships. More of your conversation would infect my brain, being° the herdsmen of   *you two being*
85 the beastly plebeians. I will be bold to take my leave of you.
    [*He leaves*] BRUTUS *and* SICINIUS, [*who stand*] *aside*.
    Enter [*in haste*] VOLUMNIA, VIRGILIA, *and* VALERIA
How now, my as fair as noble ladies—and the moon,[9] were she
earthly, no nobler—whither do you follow your eyes so fast?
VOLUMNIA Honourable Menenius, my boy Martius approaches.
For the love of Juno, let's go.
90 MENENIUS Ha, Martius coming home?
VOLUMNIA Ay, worthy Menenius, and with most prosperous
approbation.[1]
MENENIUS [*throwing up his cap*] Take my cap, Jupiter, and I
thank thee! Hoo, Martius coming home?
95 VIRGILIA *and* VALERIA Nay, 'tis true.
VOLUMNIA Look, here's a letter from him. The state hath another, his wife another, and I think there's one at home for
you.

---

9. My face (thought to map the "little world" of the human body).
1. Verbal description.
2. For deferentially doffed caps and bent legs.
3. Between a woman fruit vendor and someone who sells taps for liquor barrels.
4. Dumb-show actors (who use exaggerated facial expressions).

5. *perfecter giber . . . Capitol*: better at dinner jests than at serving in the senate.
6. Hair from cut beards was used as stuffing.
7. Deucalion and his wife were sole survivors of a great flood; their son was the ancestor of the Greeks.
8. A very base occupation.
9. Diana, goddess of chastity.
1. Rich praise; happy success.

MENENIUS   I will make my very house reel tonight. A letter for
100   me?

VIRGILIA   Yes, certain, there's a letter for you; I saw't.

MENENIUS   A letter for me? It gives me an estate° of seven years'   *endowment; condition*
health, in which time I will make a lip° at the physician. The   *sneer*
most sovereign° prescription in Galen² is but empiricutic° and,   *effective / quackish*
105   to° this preservative, of no better report than a horse-drench.³   *compared with*
Is he not wounded? He was wont° to come home wounded.   *accustomed*

VIRGILIA   O, no, no, no!

VOLUMNIA   O, he is wounded, I thank the gods for't!

MENENIUS   So do I, too, if it be not too much. Brings a° victory   *If he brings*
110   in his pocket, the wounds become him.

VOLUMNIA   On's brows, Menenius. He comes the third time
home with the oaken garland.

MENENIUS   Has he disciplined Aufidius soundly?

VOLUMNIA   Titus Lartius writes they fought together, but Aufid-
115   ius got off.

MENENIUS   And 'twas time for him too, I'll warrant him that. An°   *If*
he had stayed by him, I would not have been so fidiussed⁴ for
all the chests in Corioles and the gold that's in them. Is the
senate possessed° of this?   *informed*

120   VOLUMNIA   Good ladies, let's go. Yes, yes, yes. The senate has
letters from the general, wherein he gives my son the whole
name° of the war. He hath in this action outdone his former   *credit*
deeds doubly.

VALERIA   In truth, there's wondrous things spoke of him.

125   MENENIUS   Wondrous, ay, I warrant you; and not without his
true purchasing.°   *truly earning it*

VIRGILIA   The gods grant them true.

VOLUMNIA   True? Pooh-whoo!

MENENIUS   True? I'll be sworn they are true. Where is he
130   wounded? [*To the tribunes*] God save your good worships. Martius is coming home. He has more cause to be proud. [*To*
VOLUMNIA] Where is he wounded?

VOLUMNIA   I'th' shoulder and i'th' left arm. There will be large
cicatrices° to show the people when he shall stand for his   *scars*
135   place.⁵ He received in the repulse of Tarquin⁶ seven hurts
i'th' body.

MENENIUS   One i'th' neck and two i'th' thigh—there's nine that
I know.

VOLUMNIA   He had before this last expedition twenty-five wounds
140   upon him.

MENENIUS   Now it's twenty-seven. Every gash was an enemy's
grave.

A shout and flourish
Hark, the trumpets.

VOLUMNIA   These are the ushers of Martius. Before him he car-
145   ries noise, and behind him he leaves tears.
Death, that dark spirit, in's nervy° arm doth lie,   *muscular*
Which being advanced, declines;° and then men die.   *being raised, descends*

---

2. Ancient medical authority still standard in the Renaissance (Galen actually lived six centuries after Coriolanus).
3. Horse medicine.
4. "Aufidiussed." Menenius's coinage for "beaten."

5. Will offer himself as a candidate for consul, republican Rome's highest office.
6. Martius's first military experience was in the war
against the former King Tarquin.

Trumpets sound a sennet.° Enter [in state] COMINIUS *the*   ceremonial flourish
general and LARTIUS, *between them* CORIOLANUS,
*crowned with an oaken garland, with captains and sol-
diers and a* HERALD

HERALD   Know, Rome, that all alone Martius did fight
Within Corioles' gates, where he hath won

150   With fame a name to° 'Martius Caius'; these   *in addition to*
In honour follows 'Coriolanus'.
Welcome to Rome, renownèd Coriolanus!
    A flourish sound[s]

ALL   Welcome to Rome, renownèd Coriolanus!

CORIOLANUS   No more of this, it does offend my heart.
Pray now, no more.

COMINIUS   Look, sir, your mother.

155   CORIOLANUS *[to* VOLUMNIA*]*   O,
You have, I know, petitioned all the gods
For my prosperity!°   *success*
    [He] kneels

VOLUMNIA   Nay, my good soldier, up,
My gentle Martius, worthy Caius,
    [He rises]
And, by deed-achieving honour newly named—

160   What is it?—'Coriolanus' must I call thee?
But O, thy wife!

CORIOLANUS *[to* VIRGILIA*]*   My gracious silence, hail.
Wouldst thou have laughed had I come coffined home,
That weep'st to see me triumph? Ah, my dear,
Such eyes the widows in Corioles wear,
And mothers that lack sons.

165   MENENIUS   Now the gods crown thee!

CORIOLANUS *[to* VALERIA*]*   And live you yet? O my sweet lady, pardon.

VOLUMNIA   I know not where to turn. O, welcome home!
And welcome, general, and you're welcome all!

MENENIUS   A hundred thousand welcomes! I could weep

170   And I could laugh, I am light and heavy.° Welcome!   *(of heart)*
A curse begnaw at very root on's heart
That is not glad to see thee. You are three
That Rome should dote on. Yet, by the faith of men,
We have some old crab-trees° here at home that will not   *(gnarled, sour men)*

175   Be grafted to your relish.° Yet welcome, warriors!   *liking*
We call a nettle but a nettle, and
The faults of fools but folly.

COMINIUS   Ever right.

CORIOLANUS   Menenius, ever, ever.

HERALD   Give way there, and go on.

180   CORIOLANUS *[to* VOLUMNIA *and* VIRGILIA*]*   Your hand, and yours.
Ere in our own house I do shade my head
The good patricians must be visited,
From whom I have received not only greetings,
But with them change of honours.°   *a new set of honors*

VOLUMNIA   I have lived

185   To see inherited° my very wishes,   *realized*
And the buildings of my fancy. Only
There's one thing wanting, which I doubt not but
Our Rome will cast upon thee.

CORIOLANUS   Know, good mother,
I had rather be their servant in my way
Than sway⁷ with them in theirs.

190   COMINIUS   On, to the Capitol.
      Flourish [of] cornetts. Exeunt in state, as before, [all
      but] BRUTUS *and* SICINIUS[, *who come forward*]

BRUTUS   All tongues speak of him, and the bleared sights°   *dim-sighted people*
Are spectacled to see him. Your prattling nurse
Into a rapture° lets her baby cry   *fit*
While she chats him;⁸ the kitchen malkin° pins   *wench*
195   Her richest lockram° 'bout her reechy° neck,   *linen / filthy*
Clamb'ring the walls to eye him. Stalls, bulks,⁹ windows
Are smothered up, leads filled and ridges horsed
With variable complexions,¹ all agreeing
In earnestness to see him. Seld-shown flamens°   *Seldom-seen priests*
200   Do press among the popular° throngs, and puff°   *plebeian / pant*
To win a vulgar station.° Our veiled dames   *a place in the crowd*
Commit the war of white and damask² in
Their nicely³ guarded cheeks to th' wanton spoil
Of Phoebus'° burning kisses. Such a pother°   *the sun's / commotion*
205   As if that whatsoever god who leads him°   *(Coriolanus)*
Were slily crept into his human powers
And gave him graceful posture.

SICINIUS   On the sudden°   *At once*
I warrant him consul.

BRUTUS   Then our office may
During his power° go sleep.   *term of authority*

210   SICINIUS   He cannot temp'rately transport° his honours   *convey*
From where he should begin and end,° but will   *to where he should end*
Lose those he hath won.

BRUTUS   In that there's comfort.

SICINIUS   Doubt not
The commoners, for whom we stand, but they
Upon their ancient malice⁴ will forget
215   With the least cause these his new honours, which°   *(which cause)*
That he will give them make I as little question
As⁵ he is proud to do't.

BRUTUS   I heard him swear,
Were he to stand for consul, never would he
Appear i'th' market-place nor on him put
220   The napless vesture° of humility,   *threadbare garment*
Nor, showing, as the manner is, his wounds
To th' people, beg their stinking breaths.°   *votes*

SICINIUS   'Tis right.

BRUTUS   It was his word. O, he would miss it° rather   *forgo the consulship*
Than carry° it, but by the suit of the gentry to him,   *go through with it*
And the desire of the nobles.

225   SICINIUS   I wish no better
Than have him hold that purpose, and to put it
In execution.

---

7. Rule; prevail; deviate from a straight course.
8. Discusses Coriolanus.
9. Framework projecting from shopfronts ("stalls").
1. *leads . . . complexions:* lead roofs filled and rooftops bestridden by all types of people.

2. The conflict between white and pink in delicate skin ("damask" refers to the dark-pink damask rose).
3. Fastidiously (by the veils they usually wear).
4. Because of their long-standing hostility.
5. *I as . . . as:* I have as little doubt as that.

BRUTUS   'Tis most like he will.

SICINIUS   It shall be to him then, as our good wills,°   *as our benefit requires*
A sure destruction.

BRUTUS   So it must fall out

230   To him, or our authority's for an end.
We must suggest° the people in what hatred   *insinuate to*
He still° hath held them; that to's power he would   *always*
Have made them mules, silenced their pleaders,°   *representatives*
And dispropertied° their freedoms, holding them   *taken away*

235   In human action and capacity
Of no more soul nor fitness for the world
Than camels in their war, who have their provand°   *food*
Only for bearing burdens, and sore blows
For sinking under them.

SICINIUS   This, as you say, suggested

240   At some time when his soaring insolence
Shall touch° the people—which time shall not want°   *kindle / be lacking*
If he be put upon't, and that's as easy
As to set dogs on sheep—will be his fire
To kindle their dry stubble,[6] and their blaze
Shall darken him for ever.

Enter a MESSENGER

245   BRUTUS   What's the matter?

MESSENGER   You are sent for to the Capitol. 'Tis thought
That Martius shall be consul. I have seen
The dumb men throng to see him, and the blind
To hear him speak. Matrons flung gloves,

250   Ladies and maids their scarves and handkerchiefs,
Upon him as he passed. The nobles bended
As to Jove's statue, and the commons made
A shower and thunder with their caps and shouts.
I never saw the like.

BRUTUS   Let's to the Capitol,

255   And carry with us ears and eyes for th' time,°   *present occasion*
But hearts for the event.°   *outcome*

SICINIUS   Have with you.°   *Exeunt*   *Let's go; I'm with you.*

2.2

Enter two OFFICERS, *to lay cushions, as it were
in the Capitol*

FIRST OFFICER   Come, come, they are almost here. How many
stand for consulships?

SECOND OFFICER   Three, they say, but 'tis thought of everyone
Coriolanus will carry it.

5   FIRST OFFICER   That's a brave fellow, but he's vengeance° proud   *intensely*
and loves not the common people.

SECOND OFFICER   Faith, there hath been many great men that
have flattered the people who ne'er loved them; and there be
many that they° have loved they know not wherefore,° so that   *(the people) / why*

10   if they love they know not why, they hate upon no better a
ground. Therefore for Coriolanus neither to care whether they
love or hate him manifests the true knowledge he has in° their   *of*

6. That is, Coriolanus's fiery insolence will kindle the   2.2 Location: The Capitol, Rome.
dry fuel of the plebeians' resentment.

disposition, and out of his noble carelessness lets them plainly
see't.

15 FIRST OFFICER   If he did not care whether he had their love or
no he waved indifferently[1] 'twixt doing them neither good nor
harm; but he seeks their hate with greater devotion than they
can render it him, and leaves nothing undone that may fully
discover° him their opposite.° Now to seem to affect° the mal-   *reveal / adversary / desire*
20 ice and displeasure of the people is as bad as that which he
dislikes, to flatter them for their love.

SECOND OFFICER   He hath deserved worthily of his country, and
his ascent is not by such easy degrees as those who, having been
supple and courteous to the people, bonneted,[2] without any
25 further deed to have them at all into their estimation and
report.° But he hath so planted his honours in their eyes   *good opinion*
and his actions in their hearts that for their tongues to be silent
and not confess so much were a kind of ingrateful injury. To
report otherwise were a malice that, giving itself the lie,[3] would
30 pluck reproof and rebuke from every ear that heard it.

FIRST OFFICER   No more of him. He's a worthy man. Make way,
they are coming.

> *A sennet. Enter the Patricians, and* [SICINIUS *and* BRU-
> TUS], *the tribunes of the people, lictors[4] before them;*
> CORIOLANUS, MENENIUS, COMINIUS *the consul.* [*The
> Patricians take their places and sit.*] SICINIUS *and* BRU-
> TUS *take their places by themselves.* CORIOLANUS *stands*

MENENIUS   Having determined of° the Volsces, and   *made a decision about*
To send for Titus Lartius, it remains
35 As the main point of this our after-meeting
To gratify° his noble service that   *reward*
Hath thus stood for his country. Therefore please you,
Most reverend and grave elders, to desire
The present consul and last° general   *recent*
40 In our well-found° successes to report   *happily encountered*
A little of that worthy work performed
By Martius Caius Coriolanus, whom
We met here both to thank and to remember
With honours like° himself.   *befitting*
    [CORIOLANUS *sits*]

FIRST SENATOR   Speak, good Cominius.
45 Leave nothing out for° length, and make us think   *on account of*
Rather our state's defective for requital
Than we to stretch it out.[5]
    [*To the tribunes*]   Masters o'th' people,
We do request your kindest ears and, after,
Your loving motion toward° the common body   *persuasion of*
To yield° what passes here.   *agree to*
50 SICINIUS   We are convented°   *met together*
Upon a pleasing treaty,° and have hearts   *subject for discussion*
Inclinable to honour and advance
The theme of our assembly.
BRUTUS   Which the rather

---

1. He would waver without caring.
2. Put their bonnets back on (after doffing them as a
gesture of respect).
3. Showing itself to be false.

4. Officers who attended upon magistrates.
5. *Rather our . . . out:* We lack resources for adequate
reward, rather than the will to reward him to the utmost.

We shall be blessed° to do if he remember   *happy*
55 A kinder value of the people than
He hath hereto prized them at.

MENENIUS   That's off, that's off.°   *irrelevant*
I would you rather had been silent. Please you
To hear Cominius speak?

BRUTUS   Most willingly,
But yet my caution was more pertinent
Than the rebuke you give it.

60 MENENIUS   He loves your people,
But tie him not to be their bedfellow.
Worthy Cominius, speak.

          CORIOLANUS *rises and offers° to go away*   *begins*
[*To* CORIOLANUS]   Nay, keep your place.

FIRST SENATOR   Sit, Coriolanus. Never shame to hear
What you have nobly done.

CORIOLANUS   Your honours' pardon,
65 I had rather have my wounds to heal again
Than hear say how I got them.

BRUTUS   Sir, I hope
My words disbenched° you not?   *unseated*

CORIOLANUS   No, sir, yet oft
When blows have made me stay I fled from words.
You soothed° not, therefore hurt not; but your people,   *flattered*
I love them as they weigh°—   *deserve*

70 MENENIUS   Pray now, sit down.

CORIOLANUS   I had rather have one scratch my head i'th' sun
When the alarum° were struck than idly sit   *battle summons*
To hear my nothings monstered.[6]   *Exit*

MENENIUS   Masters of the people,
Your multiplying spawn° how can he flatter—   *fast-breeding plebeians*
75 That's thousand to one good one—when you now see
He had rather venture all his limbs for honour
Than one on's° ears to hear it? Proceed, Cominius.   *of his*

COMINIUS   I shall lack voice; the deeds of Coriolanus
Should not be uttered feebly. It is held
80 That valour is the chiefest virtue, and
Most dignifies the haver. If it be,
The man I speak of cannot in the world
Be singly counterpoised.° At sixteen years,   *equaled by anyone*
When Tarquin made a head for° Rome, he fought   *raised an army against*
85 Beyond the mark° of others. Our then dictator,[7]   *reach*
Whom with all praise I point at, saw him fight
When with his Amazonian[8] chin he drove
The bristled lips° before him. He bestrid   *bearded soldiers*
An o'erpressed° Roman, and, i'th' consul's view,   *overwhelmed*
90 Slew three opposers. Tarquin's self he met,
And struck him on his knee. In that day's feats,
When he might act the woman in the scene,[9]
He proved best man i'th' field, and for his meed°   *reward*
Was brow-bound with the oak. His pupil age

---

6. My trivial actions treated as marvels.
7. Roman magistrate with absolute authority, elected during emergencies.

8. Beardless (like a female Amazon warrior).
9. Might be expected to be cowardly (with an allusion to boys acting women's parts in the theater).

95   Man-entered thus, he waxèd like a sea,
And in the brunt° of seventeen battles since   *violence*
He lurched° all swords of the garland. For this last   *cheated*
Before and in Corioles, let me say
I cannot speak him home.° He stopped the fliers,   *praise him enough*
100   And by his rare example made the coward
Turn terror into sport. As weeds before
A vessel under sail, so men obeyed
And fell below his stem.° His sword, death's stamp,   *prow*
Where it did mark, it took.[1] From face to foot
105   He was a thing of blood, whose every motion
Was timed[2] with dying cries. Alone he entered
The mortal° gate of th' city, which he, painted   *fatal*
With shunless destiny,[3] aidless came off,
And with a sudden reinforcement struck
110   Corioles like a planet.[4] Now all's his.
When by and by the din of war gan° pierce   *began to*
His ready° sense, then straight his doubled spirit   *alert*
Requickened° what in flesh was fatigate,°   *Reanimated / exhausted*
And to the battle came he, where he did
115   Run reeking[5] o'er the lives of men as if
'Twere a perpetual spoil;° and till we called   *slaughter*
Both field and city ours he never stood
To ease his breast with panting.
MENENIUS   Worthy man.
FIRST SENATOR   He cannot but with measure° fit the honours   *exactly*
Which we devise him.
120   COMINIUS   Our spoils he kicked at,°   *spurned*
And looked upon things precious as° they were   *as if*
The common muck of the world. He covets less
Than misery° itself would give, rewards   *poverty*
His deeds with doing them, and is content
To spend the time to° end it.   *merely in order to*
125   MENENIUS   He's right noble.
Let him be called for.
FIRST SENATOR   Call Coriolanus.
OFFICER   He doth appear.
             Enter CORIOLANUS
MENENIUS   The senate, Coriolanus, are well pleased
To make thee consul.
130   CORIOLANUS   I do owe them still°   *always*
My life and services.
MENENIUS   It then remains
That you do speak to the people.
CORIOLANUS   I do beseech you,
Let me o'erleap that custom, for I cannot
Put on the gown, stand naked,° and entreat them   *exposed*
135   For my wounds' sake to give their suffrage.
Please you that I may pass this doing.
SICINIUS   Sir, the people
Must have their voices,° neither will they bate°   *votes / forgo*

---

1. It made a clear imprint (of death).
2. Rhythmically accompanied.
3. *painted . . . destiny*: covered with the blood of his victims, unable to avoid their fate.
4. Planets were believed to have the power to afflict, or blast, people and places.
5. Steaming (with blood and sweat).

One jot of ceremony.
MENENIUS [*to* CORIOLANUS]   Put them not to't.°   *Do not defy them*
Pray you, go fit you° to the custom and   *adapt yourself*
140   Take to you, as your predecessors have,
Your honour with your form.°   *the custom prescribed you*
CORIOLANUS   It is a part
That I shall blush in acting, and might well
Be taken from the people.
BRUTUS [*to* SICINIUS]   Mark you that?
CORIOLANUS   To brag unto them 'Thus I did, and thus',
145   Show them th'unaching scars, which I should hide,
As if I had received them for the hire
Of their breath° only!   *voice*
MENENIUS   Do not stand° upon't.—   *insist*
We recommend° to you, tribunes of the people,   *commit*
Our purpose° to them; and to our noble consul   *proposal*
150   Wish we all joy and honour.
SENATORS   To Coriolanus come all joy and honour!
                    Flourish [of] cornetts, then exeunt. Manent
                                SICINIUS *and* BRUTUS
BRUTUS   You see how he intends to use the people.
SICINIUS   May they perceive's intent! He will require° them   *ask from*
As if he did contemn° what he requested   *scorn that*
Should be in them to give.
155   BRUTUS   Come, we'll inform them
Of our proceedings here. On th' market-place
I know they do attend° us.   [*Exeunt*]   *await*

                            2.3
            Enter seven or eight CITIZENS
FIRST CITIZEN   Once,° if he do require our voices we ought not   *In short*
    to deny him.
SECOND CITIZEN   We may, sir, if we will.
THIRD CITIZEN   We have power in ourselves to do it, but it is a
5   power that we have no power to do.° For if he show us his   *no justification to use*
    wounds and tell us his deeds, we are to put our tongues into
    those wounds[1] and speak for them; so if he tell us his noble
    deeds we must also tell him our noble acceptance of them.
    Ingratitude is monstrous, and for the multitude to be ingrateful
10   were to make a monster of the multitude, of the which we,
    being members, should bring ourselves to be monstrous mem-
    bers.
FIRST CITIZEN   And to make us no better thought of, a little help
    will serve;° for once we stood up about the corn, he himself   *it won't take much*
15   stuck° not to call us the many-headed multitude.   *hesitated*
THIRD CITIZEN   We have been called so of many, not that our
    heads are some brown, some black, some abram,° some bald,   *auburn*
    but that our wits are so diversely coloured; and truly I think if
    all our wits were to issue out of one skull, they would fly east,
20   west, north, south, and their consent of° one direct way should   *agreement to go*
    be at once to all the points o'th' compass.
SECOND CITIZEN   Think you so? Which way do you judge my
    wit would fly?

2.3 Location: The marketplace in Rome.   1. That is, let those wounds inspire our voices.

THIRD CITIZEN Nay, your wit will not so soon out as another
25 man's will, 'tis strongly wedged up in a blockhead. But if it
were at liberty, 'twould sure southward.[2]
SECOND CITIZEN Why that way?
THIRD CITIZEN To lose itself in a fog where, being three parts
melted away with rotten° dews, the fourth would return for con- *unwholesome*
30 science' sake, to help to get thee a wife.
SECOND CITIZEN You are never without your tricks. You may,
you may.° *(have your joke)*
THIRD CITIZEN Are you all resolved to give your voices? But
that's no matter, the greater part carries it.° I say, if he would *majority decides*
35 incline to° the people there was never a worthier man. *support*

Enter CORIOLANUS *in a gown of humility, with* MENENIUS

Here he comes, and in the gown of humility. Mark his behaviour. We are not to stay all together, but to come by him where
he stands by ones, by twos, and by threes. He's to make his
requests by particulars,° wherein every one of us has a single *to individuals*
40 honour in giving him our own voices with our own tongues.
Therefore follow me, and I'll direct you how you shall go by
him.
ALL THE CITIZENS Content, content. [*Exeunt* CITIZENS]
MENENIUS O sir, you are not right. Have you not known
The worthiest men have done't?
45 CORIOLANUS   What must I say?
'I pray, sir'? Plague upon't, I cannot bring
My tongue to such a pace. 'Look, sir, my wounds.
I got them in my country's service, when
Some certain of your brethren roared and ran
From th' noise of our own drums'?
50 MENENIUS   O me, the gods!
You must not speak of that, you must desire them
To think upon you.
CORIOLANUS   Think upon me? Hang 'em.
I would they would forget me like the virtues
Which our divines lose by 'em.[3]
MENENIUS   You'll mar all.
55 I'll leave you. Pray you, speak to 'em, I pray you,
In wholesome[4] manner.
CORIOLANUS   Bid them wash their faces
And keep their teeth clean.   *Exit* [MENENIUS]

Enter three of the CITIZENS

                      So, here comes a brace.
You know the cause, sir, of my standing here.
THIRD CITIZEN We do, sir. Tell us what hath brought you to't.
60 CORIOLANUS Mine own desert.
SECOND CITIZEN Your own desert?
CORIOLANUS Ay, but not mine own desire.
THIRD CITIZEN How not your own desire?
CORIOLANUS No, sir, 'twas never my desire yet to trouble the
65 poor with begging.
THIRD CITIZEN You must think if we give you anything we hope
to gain by you.

2. The south is associated with plague.   4. Proper (but Coriolanus takes it as "healthy").
3. Our priests vainly try to instill in them.

CORIOLANUS   Well then, I pray, your price o'th' consulship?
FIRST CITIZEN   The price is to ask it kindly.
70   CORIOLANUS   Kindly, sir, I pray let me ha't. I have wounds to
show you which shall be yours° in private. [*To* SECOND CITIZEN]   *yours to see*
Your good voice, sir. What say you?
SECOND CITIZEN   You shall ha't, worthy sir.
CORIOLANUS   A match,° sir. There's in all two worthy voices   *agreement*
75   begged. I have your alms. Adieu.
THIRD CITIZEN [*to the other* CITIZENS]   But this is something odd.
SECOND CITIZEN   An° 'twere to give again—but 'tis no matter.   *If*
                                   Exeunt [CITIZENS]
        Enter two other CITIZENS
CORIOLANUS   Pray you now, if it may stand° with the tune of your   *accord*
voices that I may be consul, I have here the customary gown.
80   FOURTH CITIZEN   You have deserved nobly of your country, and
you have not deserved nobly.
CORIOLANUS   Your enigma?
FOURTH CITIZEN   You have been a scourge to her enemies, you
have been a rod to her friends. You have not, indeed, loved the
85   common people.
CORIOLANUS   You should account me the more virtuous that I
have not been common° in my love. I will, sir, flatter my sworn   *indiscriminate*
brother the people to earn a dearer estimation of them. 'Tis° a   *(Flattery) is*
condition they account gentle.° And since the wisdom of their   *noble*
90   choice is rather to have my hat than my heart, I will practise
the insinuating nod and be off° to them most counterfeitly; that   *bareheaded*
is, sir, I will counterfeit the bewitchment° of some popular   *charisma*
man,° and give it bountiful to the desirers. Therefore, beseech   *demagogue*
you I may be consul.
95   FIFTH CITIZEN   We hope to find you our friend, and therefore
give you our voices heartily.
FOURTH CITIZEN   You have received many wounds for your
country.
CORIOLANUS   I will not seal° your knowledge with showing them.   *confirm*
100   I will make much of your voices, and so trouble you no farther.
BOTH CITIZENS   The gods give you joy, sir, heartily.
CORIOLANUS   Most sweet voices.   [*Exeunt* CITIZENS]
Better it is to die, better to starve,
Than crave the hire which first we do deserve.[5]
105   Why in this womanish toge[6] should I stand here
To beg of Hob and Dick[7] that does appear
Their needless vouches?° Custom calls me to't.   *votes*
What custom wills, in all things should we do't,
The dust on antique time would lie unswept,
110   And mountainous error be too highly heaped
For truth to o'erpeer.[8] Rather than fool it° so,   *act the fool*
Let the high office and the honour go
To one that would do thus. I am half through.
The one part suffered, the other will I do.
        Enter three CITIZENS *more*
115   Here come more voices.

---

5. Than beg for the wages we have already earned.
6. F has "woolvish toge"; some editors read "wolvish" or
"wool-less." The "toge" is the toga (gown of humility).
7. Any Tom, Dick, or Harry.
8. To look over the top.

Your voices! For your voices I have fought,
Watched° for your voices, for your voices bear   *Gone sleepless*
Of wounds two dozen odd; battles thrice six
I have seen and heard of for your voices, have
120   Done many things, some less, some more. Your voices!
Indeed I would be consul.

SIXTH CITIZEN   He has done nobly, and cannot go without any
honest man's voice.

SEVENTH CITIZEN   Therefore let him be consul. The gods give
125   him joy and make him good friend to the people!

ALL THE CITIZENS   Amen, amen. God save thee, noble consul!

CORIOLANUS   Worthy voices.   [*Exeunt* CITIZENS]
       Enter MENENIUS *with* BRUTUS *and* SICINIUS

MENENIUS   You have stood your limitation,° and the tribunes   *allotted time*
Endue° you with the people's voice. Remains   *Invest*
130   That in th' official marks° invested, you   *insignia*
Anon° do meet the senate.   *Immediately*

CORIOLANUS   Is this done?

SICINIUS   The custom of request° you have discharged.   *requesting votes*
The people do admit you, and are summoned
To meet anon upon your approbation.[9]

CORIOLANUS   Where, at the senate-house?

135 SICINIUS   There, Coriolanus.

CORIOLANUS   May I change these garments?

SICINIUS   You may, sir.

CORIOLANUS   That I'll straight do, and, knowing myself again,
Repair to th' senate-house.

MENENIUS   I'll keep you company. [*To the tribunes*] Will you along?

BRUTUS   We stay here for the people.

140 SICINIUS   Fare you well.
       Exeunt CORIOLANUS *and* MENENIUS
He has it now, and by his looks methinks
'Tis warm at's heart.[1]

BRUTUS   With a proud heart he wore
His humble weeds.° Will you dismiss the people?   *garments*
       Enter the Plebeians

SICINIUS   How now, my masters, have you chose this man?

145 FIRST CITIZEN   He has our voices, sir.

BRUTUS   We pray the gods he may deserve your loves.

SECOND CITIZEN   Amen, sir. To my poor unworthy notice
He mocked us when he begged our voices.

THIRD CITIZEN   Certainly. He flouted us downright.

150 FIRST CITIZEN   No, 'tis his kind of speech. He did not mock us.

SECOND CITIZEN   Not one amongst us save yourself but says
He used us scornfully. He should have showed us
His marks of merit, wounds received for's country.

SICINIUS   Why, so he did, I am sure.

ALL THE CITIZENS   No, no; no man saw 'em.

155 THIRD CITIZEN   He said he had wounds which he could show in private,
And with his hat, thus waving it in scorn,
'I would be consul,' says he. 'Agèd custom
But by your voices will not so permit me.
Your voices therefore.' When we granted that,

---

9. For your ratification as consul.   1. That is, he's well pleased.

160   Here was 'I thank you for your voices, thank you.
       Your most sweet voices. Now you have left your voices
       I have no further° with you.' Was not this mockery?   *(to do)*
     SICINIUS   Why either were you ignorant° to see't,   *were you either unable*
       Or, seeing it, of such childish friendliness
       To yield your voices?
165   BRUTUS [*to the* CITIZENS]   Could you not have told him
       As you were lessoned: when he had no power
       But was a petty servant to the state,
       He was your enemy, ever spake against
       Your liberties and the charters that you bear
170   I'th' body of the weal;° and now arriving°   *state / reaching*
       A place of potency and sway o'th' state,
       If he should still malignantly remain
       Fast foe to th' plebeii, your voices might
       Be curses to yourselves. You should have said
175   That as his worthy deeds did claim no less
       Than what he stood for,° so his gracious nature   *the office he sought*
       Would think upon you for your voices and
       Translate° his malice towards you into love,   *Change*
       Standing your friendly lord.
     SICINIUS [*to the* CITIZENS]   Thus to have said
180   As you were fore-advised had touched° his spirit   *tested*
       And tried his inclination, from him plucked
       Either his gracious promise which you might,
       As cause had called you up, have held him to,
       Or else it would have galled his surly nature,
185   Which easily endures not article°   *stipulation*
       Tying him to aught. So putting him to rage,
       You should have ta'en th'advantage of his choler°   *wrath*
       And passed him unelected.
    BRUTUS [*to the* CITIZENS]   Did you perceive
       He did solicit you in free contempt
190   When he did need your loves, and do you think
       That his contempt shall not be bruising to you
       When he hath power to crush? Why, had your bodies
       No heart among you? Or had you tongues to cry
       Against the rectorship of judgement?°   *rule of common sense*
     SICINIUS [*to the* CITIZENS]   Have you
195   Ere now denied the asker, and now again,
       Of him that did not ask but mock, bestow
       Your sued-for tongues?
    THIRD CITIZEN   He's not confirmed, we may deny him yet.
    SECOND CITIZEN   And will deny him.
200   I'll have five hundred voices of that sound.
    FIRST CITIZEN   I twice five hundred, and their friends to piece° 'em.   *add to*
    BRUTUS   Get you hence instantly, and tell those friends
       They have chose a consul that will from them take
       Their liberties, make them of no more voice
205   Than dogs that are as often beat for barking,
       As therefor kept to do so.
    SICINIUS [*to the* CITIZENS]   Let them assemble,
       And on a safer° judgement all revoke   *sounder*
       Your ignorant election. Enforce° his pride   *Emphasize*
       And his old hate unto you. Besides, forget not

210 With what contempt he wore the humble weed,
    How in his suit° he scorned you; but your loves,   *petition; apparel*
    Thinking upon his services, took from you
    Th'apprehension° of his present portance,°   *perception / demeanor*
    Which most gibingly, ungravely he did fashion
    After the inveterate hate he bears you.
215 BRUTUS [*to the* CITIZENS]   Lay
    A fault on us your tribunes, that we laboured
    No impediment between,² but that you must
    Cast your election on him.
    SICINIUS [*to the* CITIZENS]   Say you chose him
    More after our commandment than as guided
220 By your own true affections, and that your minds,
    Preoccupied with what you rather must do
    Than what you should, made you against the grain
    To voice him consul. Lay the fault on us.
    BRUTUS [*to the* CITIZENS]   Ay, spare us not. Say we read lectures to you,
225 How youngly he began to serve his country,
    How long continued, and what stock he springs of,
    The noble house o'th' Martians, from whence came
    That Ancus Martius, Numa's daughter's son,
    Who after great Hostilius here was king;
230 Of the same house Publius and Quintus were,
    That our best water brought by conduits hither;
    And Censorinus that was so surnamed,³
    And nobly named so, twice being censor,⁴
    Was his great ancestor.
    SICINIUS [*to the* CITIZENS]   One thus descended,
235 That hath beside well in his person wrought
    To be set high in place, we did commend
    To your remembrances, but you have found,
    Scaling° his present bearing with his past,   *Weighing*
    That he's your fixèd enemy, and revoke
    Your sudden° approbation.   *hasty*
240 BRUTUS [*to the* CITIZENS]   Say you ne'er had done't—
    Harp on that still—but by our putting on;°   *instigation*
    And presently when you have drawn° your number,   *gathered*
    Repair to th' Capitol.
    A CITIZEN   We will so.
    ANOTHER CITIZEN   Almost all
    Repent in their election.   *Exeunt* [CITIZENS]
    BRUTUS   Let them go on.
245 This mutiny were better put in hazard°   *risked*
    Than stay,° past doubt, for greater.   *await*
    If, as his nature is, he fall in rage
    With their refusal, both observe and answer
    The vantage of ⁵ his anger.
    SICINIUS   To th' Capitol, come.
250 We will be there before the stream o'th' people,
    And this shall seem, as partly 'tis, their own,
    Which we have goaded onward.   *Exeunt*

2. *we . . . between:* we refused to allow anything to stand in the way.
3. Line missing in F; reconstructed from Plutarch.
4. Roman magistrate who supervised public morals and drew up the census.
5. *answer the vantage of:* seize the opportunity provided by.

3.1

Cornetts. Enter CORIOLANUS, MENENIUS, *all the gentry;*°   patricians
COMINIUS, LARTIUS, *and other* SENATORS

CORIOLANUS   Tullus Aufidius then had made new head?°   raised a new army

LARTIUS   He had, my lord, and that it was which caused
  Our swifter composition.[1]

CORIOLANUS   So then the Volsces stand but as at first,
5   Ready when time shall prompt them to make raid
  Upon's again.

COMINIUS   They are worn,° lord consul, so   exhausted
  That we shall hardly in our ages see
  Their banners wave again.

CORIOLANUS [*to* LARTIUS]   Saw you Aufidius?

LARTIUS   On safeguard° he came to me, and did curse   Under safe-conduct
10   Against the Volsces for they had so vilely
  Yielded the town. He is retired to Antium.

CORIOLANUS   Spoke he of me?

LARTIUS   He did, my lord.

CORIOLANUS   How? What?

LARTIUS   How often he had met you sword to sword;
  That of all things upon the earth he hated
15   Your person most; that he would pawn his fortunes
  To hopeless restitution,[2] so he might
  Be called your vanquisher.

CORIOLANUS   At Antium lives he?

LARTIUS   At Antium.

20 CORIOLANUS   I wish I had a cause to seek him there,
  To oppose his hatred fully. Welcome home.

         Enter SICINIUS *and* BRUTUS

  Behold, these are the tribunes of the people,
  The tongues o'th' common mouth. I do despise them,
  For they do prank them° in authority   adorn themselves
25   Against all noble sufferance.[3]

SICINIUS   Pass no further.

CORIOLANUS   Ha, what is that?

BRUTUS   It will be dangerous to go on. No further.

CORIOLANUS   What makes this change?

30 MENENIUS   The matter?

COMINIUS   Hath he not passed° the noble and the common?   been accepted by

BRUTUS   Cominius, no.

CORIOLANUS   Have I had children's voices?

FIRST SENATOR   Tribunes, give way. He shall to th' market-place.

BRUTUS   The people are incensed against him.

SICINIUS   Stop,
  Or all will fall in broil.°   turmoil

35 CORIOLANUS   Are these your herd?
  Must these have voices, that can yield them now
  And straight° disclaim their tongues? What are your offices?   immediately
  You being their mouths, why rule you not their teeth?
  Have you not set them on?

MENENIUS   Be calm, be calm.

40 CORIOLANUS   It is a purposed° thing, and grows by plot   deliberate

---

3.1 Location: A street in Rome.
1. Agreement (about returning Corioles to the Volscians).
2. Without hope of recovery.
3. Beyond what the nobility can endure.

To curb the will of the nobility.
Suffer't, and live with such as cannot rule
Nor ever will be ruled.

BRUTUS   Call't not a plot.
The people cry you mocked them, and of late
45   When corn was given them gratis, you repined,
Scandalled° the suppliants for the people, called them   *Defamed*
Time-pleasers, flatterers, foes to nobleness.

CORIOLANUS   Why, this was known before.

BRUTUS   Not to them all.

CORIOLANUS   Have you informed them sithence?°   *since*

BRUTUS   How, I inform them?

50   CORIOLANUS   You are like to do such business.

BRUTUS   Not unlike
Each way to better yours.[4]

CORIOLANUS   Why then should I be consul? By yon clouds,
Let me deserve so ill as you, and make me
Your fellow tribune.

55   SICINIUS   You show too much of that°   *(quality)*
For which the people stir.° If you will pass   *are aroused*
To where you are bound,[5] you must enquire your way,
Which you are out of,° with a gentler spirit,   *strayed from*
Or never be so noble as a consul,
Nor yoke with him° for tribune.   *(Brutus)*

60   MENENIUS   Let's be calm.

COMINIUS   The people are abused, set on. This palt'ring°   *trifling*
Becomes not Rome, nor has Coriolanus
Deserved this so dishonoured rub,° laid falsely   *shameful obstruction*
I'th' plain way of his merit.

CORIOLANUS   Tell me of corn?
65   This was my speech, and I will speak't again.

MENENIUS   Not now, not now.

FIRST SENATOR   Not in this heat, sir, now.

CORIOLANUS   Now as I live,
I will. My nobler friends, I crave their pardons.
70   For the mutable rank-scented meinie,°   *multitude*
Let them regard me, as I do not flatter,
And therein behold themselves. I say again,
In soothing them we nourish 'gainst our Senate
The cockle° of rebellion, insolence, sedition,   *weed*
75   Which we ourselves have ploughed for, sowed, and scattered
By mingling them with us, the honoured number
Who lack not virtue, no, nor power, but that
Which they have given to beggars.

MENENIUS   Well, no more.

FIRST SENATOR   No more words, we beseech you.

CORIOLANUS   How, no more?
80   As for my country I have shed my blood,
Not fearing outward force, so shall my lungs
Coin words till their decay against those measles°   *skin eruptions*
Which we disdain should tetter° us, yet sought   *infect*
The very way to catch them.

---

4. *Not unlike . . . yours:* Not unlikely in every respect to   5. That is, the marketplace; the consulship.
do better than you.

85   BRUTUS   You speak o'th' people as if you were a god
        To punish, not a man of their infirmity.°   *with the same frailty*
      SICINIUS   'Twere well we let the people know't.
      MENENIUS   What, what, his choler?
      CORIOLANUS   Choler? Were I as patient as the midnight sleep,
        By Jove, 'twould be my mind.°   *opinion*
      SICINIUS   It is a mind
90   That shall remain a poison where it is,
        Not poison any further.
      CORIOLANUS   'Shall remain'?
        Hear you this Triton[6] of the minnows? Mark you
        His absolute 'shall'?
      COMINIUS   'Twas from the canon.°   *out of order*
      CORIOLANUS   'Shall'?
        O good but most unwise patricians, why,
95   You grave but reckless senators, have you thus
        Given Hydra[7] here to choose an officer
        That, with his peremptory 'shall', being but
        The horn and noise° o'th' monster's, wants not spirit   *noisy horn*
        To say he'll turn your current° in a ditch   *stream of power*
100   And make your channel his? If he have power,
        Then vail° your impotence; if none, awake°   *bow down / awake from*
        Your dangerous lenity.° If you are learned,   *forbearance*
        Be not as common fools; if you are not,
        Let them have cushions by° you. You are plebeians   *senate seats beside*
105   If they be senators, and they are no less
        When, both your voices blended, the great'st taste
        Most palates theirs.[8] They choose their magistrate,
        And such a one as he, who puts his 'shall',
        His popular° 'shall', against a graver bench[9]   *plebeian*
110   Than ever frowned in Greece. By Jove himself,
        It makes the consuls base, and my soul aches
        To know, when two authorities are up,°   *established*
        Neither supreme, how soon confusion°   *chaos*
        May enter 'twixt the gap of both and take°   *overthrow*
        The one by th' other.
115   COMINIUS   Well, on to th' market-place.
      CORIOLANUS   Whoever gave that counsel to give forth
        The corn o'th' storehouse gratis, as 'twas used
        Sometime in Greece—
      MENENIUS   Well, well, no more of that.
      CORIOLANUS   Though there the people had more absolute power—
120   I say they nourished disobedience, fed
        The ruin of the state.
      BRUTUS   Why shall the people give
        One that speaks thus their voice?
      CORIOLANUS   I'll give my reasons,
        More worthier than their voices. They know the corn
        Was not our recompense,° resting well assured   *a payment from us*
125   They ne'er did service for't. Being pressed° to th' war,   *conscripted*
        Even when the navel° of the state was touched,°   *center / threatened*

6. Neptune's trumpeter, a minor sea god.   8. *the great'st . . . theirs:* the result tastes more like (or ap-
7. Mythical many-headed snake, a common figure for   peals more to) them than you.
the multitude.   9. A more respected body.

	They would not thread° the gates. This kind of service	*go through*
	Did not deserve corn gratis. Being i'th' war,	
	Their mutinies and revolts, wherein they showed	
130	Most valour, spoke not° for them. Th'accusation	*did not speak well*
	Which they have often made against the senate,	
	All cause unborn,° could never be the native°	*Without any cause / source*
	Of our so frank° donation. Well, what then?	*liberal*
	How shall this bosom multiplied¹ digest	
135	The senate's courtesy? Let deeds express	
	What's like to be their words: 'We did request it,	
	We are the greater poll,° and in true fear	*number*
	They gave us our demands.' Thus we debase	
	The nature of our seats,° and make the rabble	*senatorial positions*
140	Call our cares fears, which will in time	
	Break ope the locks o'th' senate and bring in	
	The crows to peck the eagles.²	

MENENIUS   Come, enough.

BRUTUS   Enough with over-measure.

CORIOLANUS   No, take more.

	What may be sworn by, both divine and human,	
145	Seal° what I end withal!° This double worship,³	*Authorize / with*
	Where one part does disdain with cause, the other	
	Insult° without all reason, where gentry, title, wisdom	*Behave insolently*
	Cannot conclude but by the yea and no	
	Of general ignorance, it must omit°	*neglect*
150	Real necessities, and give way the while	
	To unstable slightness.° Purpose° so barred, it follows	*trifling / Purposefulness*
	Nothing is done to purpose.° Therefore beseech you—	*any effect*
	You that will be less fearful than discreet,°	*judicious*
	That love the fundamental part of state	
155	More than you doubt the change on't,⁴ that prefer	
	A noble life before a long, and wish	
	To jump° a body with a dangerous physic°	*risk / medicine*
	That's sure of death without it—at once pluck out	
	The multitudinous tongue;⁵ let them not lick	
160	The sweet which is their poison. Your dishonour	
	Mangles true judgement, and bereaves the state	
	Of that integrity which should become't,	
	Not having the power to do the good it would	
	For° th'ill which doth control't.⁶	*Because of*

BRUTUS   He's said enough.

| 165 | SICINIUS   He's spoken like a traitor, and shall answer | |
| | As traitors do. | |

CORIOLANUS   Thou wretch, despite° o'erwhelm thee!   *contempt*

	What should the people do with these bald° tribunes,	*paltry*
	On whom depending, their obedience fails	
	To th' greater bench?° In a rebellion,	*(of the senate)*
170	When what's not meet but what must be was law,⁷	
	Then were they chosen. In a better hour	

1. Multifarious belly (of the many-headed multitude).
2. The eagle not only is associated with courage and no-bility but is the symbol of Roman power.
3. Divided magistracy.
4. You fear changing it (by repudiating the tribunes).

5. The tongue of the multitude, as represented by the tribunes.
6. Overpower it.
7. When . . . law: When necessity rather than propriety prevailed. *meet*: proper.

Let what is meet be said it must be meet,[8]
And throw their power i'th' dust.

BRUTUS   Manifest treason.

SICINIUS   This a consul? No.

BRUTUS   The aediles,° ho!   *tribune's officers*

Enter an AEDILE

175   Let him be apprehended.

SICINIUS   Go call the people,   [*Exit* AEDILE]
[*To* CORIOLANUS]   in whose name myself
Attach° thee as a traitorous innovator,°   *Arrest / revolutionary*
A foe to th' public weal. Obey, I charge thee,
And follow to thine answer.°   *trial*

CORIOLANUS   Hence, old goat!

ALL THE PATRICIANS   We'll surety him.°   *ensure his compliance*

180   COMINIUS [*to* SICINIUS]   Aged sir, hands off.

CORIOLANUS [*to* SICINIUS]   Hence, rotten thing, or I shall shake thy bones
Out of thy garments.

SICINIUS   Help, ye citizens!

Enter a rabble of Plebeians, with the AEDILES

MENENIUS   On both sides more respect.

SICINIUS   Here's he
That would take from you all your power.

BRUTUS   Seize him, aediles.

ALL THE CITIZENS   Down with him, down with him!

185   SECOND SENATOR   Weapons, weapons, weapons!

They all bustle about CORIOLANUS

CITIZENS *and* PATRICIANS [*in dispersed cries*]   Tribunes! Patricians!
Citizens! What ho!
Sicinius! Brutus! Coriolanus! Citizens!

SOME CITIZENS *and* PATRICIANS   Peace, peace, peace! Stay! Hold! Peace!

MENENIUS   What is about to be? I am out of breath.

190   Confusion's° near; I cannot speak. You tribunes   *Chaos is*
To th' people, Coriolanus, patience!
Speak, good Sicinius.

SICINIUS   Hear me, people, peace.

ALL THE CITIZENS   Let's hear our tribune! Peace! Speak, speak, speak!

SICINIUS   You are at point° to lose your liberties.   *about*

195   Martius would have all from you—Martius
Whom late you have named for consul.

MENENIUS   Fie, fie, fie,
This is the way to kindle, not to quench.

FIRST SENATOR   To unbuild the city, and to lay all flat.

SICINIUS   What is the city but the people?

ALL THE CITIZENS   True,
The people are the city.

200   BRUTUS   By the consent of all
We were established the people's magistrates.

ALL THE CITIZENS   You so remain.

MENENIUS   And so are like to do.

CORIOLANUS   That is the way to lay the city flat,
To bring the roof to the foundation,
205   And bury all which yet distinctly ranges[9]
In heaps and piles of ruin.

8. Let what is proper be declared necessary.   9. Extends in orderly ranks.

SICINIUS   This deserves death.

BRUTUS   Or° let us stand to our authority,   *Either*
    Or let us lose it. We do here pronounce,
    Upon the part o'th' people in whose power
210 We were elected theirs, Martius is worthy
    Of present° death.   *immediate*

SICINIUS   Therefore lay hold of him,
    Bear him to th' rock Tarpeian;[1] and from thence
    Into destruction cast him.

BRUTUS   Aediles, seize him.

ALL THE CITIZENS   Yield, Martius, yield.

MENENIUS   Hear me one word.
215 Beseech you, tribunes, hear me but a word.

AEDILES   Peace, peace!

MENENIUS [*to the tribunes*]   Be that you seem, truly your country's friend,
    And temp'rately proceed to what you would
    Thus violently redress.

BRUTUS   Sir, those cold ways
220 That seem like prudent helps are very poisons
    Where the disease is violent. Lay hands upon him,
    And bear him to the rock.

          CORIOLANUS *draws his sword*

CORIOLANUS   No, I'll die here.
    There's some among you have beheld me fighting.
    Come, try upon yourselves what you have seen me.

225 MENENIUS   Down with that sword. Tribunes, withdraw a while.

BRUTUS   Lay hands upon him.

MENENIUS   Help Martius, help!
    You that be noble, help him, young and old.

ALL THE CITIZENS   Down with him, down with him!

        In this mutiny the tribunes, the AEDILES, *and the*
        people are beat in

MENENIUS [*to* CORIOLANUS]   Go get you to your house. Be gone, away!
    All will be naught else.

230 SECOND SENATOR [*to* CORIOLANUS]   Get you gone.

CORIOLANUS   Stand fast; we have as many friends as enemies.

MENENIUS   Shall it be put to that?

FIRST SENATOR   The gods forbid!
    [*To* CORIOLANUS]   I prithee, noble friend, home to thy house.
    Leave us to cure this cause.°   *disease*

MENENIUS   For 'tis a sore upon us
235 You cannot tent° yourself. Be gone, beseech you.   *treat*

COMINIUS   Come, sir, along with us.

CORIOLANUS   I would they were barbarians, as they are,
    Though in Rome littered;° not Romans, as they are not,   *born (like animals)*
    Though calved i'th' porch o'th' Capitol.

MENENIUS   Be gone.
240 Put not your worthy° rage into your tongue.   *justifiable*
    One time will owe° another.   *occasion will compensate*

CORIOLANUS   On fair ground
    I could beat forty of them.

MENENIUS   I could myself
    Take up a brace o'th' best of them, yea, the two tribunes.

---

1. The cliff from which murderers and traitors were hurled to their deaths.

COMINIUS   But now 'tis odds beyond arithmetic,°   *calculation*
245   And manhood° is called foolery when it stands   *courage*
      Against a falling fabric.°   *building*
      [*To* CORIOLANUS]   Will you hence
      Before the tag° return, whose rage doth rend   *rabble*
      Like interrupted° waters, and o'erbear   *overflowing*
      What they are used to bear?[2]
MENENIUS [*to* CORIOLANUS]   Pray you be gone.
250   I'll try whether my old wit be in request
      With those that have but little. This must be patched
      With cloth of any colour.[3]
COMINIUS   Nay, come away. *Exeunt* CORIOLANUS *and* COMINIUS
A PATRICIAN   This man has marred his fortune.
255   MENENIUS   His nature is too noble for the world.
      He would not flatter Neptune for his trident
      Or Jove for's power to thunder. His heart's his mouth.
      What his breast forges, that his tongue must vent,
      And, being angry, does forget that ever
      He heard the name of death.
            A noise within
260   Here's goodly work.
A PATRICIAN   I would they were abed.
MENENIUS   I would they were in Tiber.
      What the vengeance, could he not speak 'em fair?°   *speak to them politely*
            Enter BRUTUS *and* SICINIUS, *with the rabble again*
SICINIUS   Where is this viper
      That would depopulate the city and
      Be every man himself?
265   MENENIUS   You worthy tribunes—
SICINIUS   He shall be thrown down the Tarpeian rock
      With rigorous hands. He hath resisted law,
      And therefore law shall scorn° him further trial   *deny*
      Than the severity of the public° power,   *commoners'*
      Which he so sets at naught.
270   FIRST CITIZEN   He shall well know
      The noble tribunes are the people's mouths,
      And we their hands.
ALL THE CITIZENS   He shall, sure on't.
MENENIUS   Sir, sir.
SICINIUS   Peace!
MENENIUS   Do not cry havoc[4] where you should but hunt
      With modest warrant.
275   SICINIUS   Sir, how comes't that you
      Have help to make this rescue?[5]
MENENIUS   Hear me speak.
      As I do know the consul's worthiness,
      So can I name his faults.
SICINIUS   Consul? What consul?
280   MENENIUS   The consul Coriolanus.
BRUTUS   He consul?
ALL THE CITIZENS   No, no, no, no, no!

2. *o'erbear . . . bear:* overpower that to which they ordinarily submit.
3. *patched . . . colour:* mended by whatever means possible.
4. "Havoc" was the signal to an army to pillage.
5. Have helped to remove this prisoner from custody
("make rescue" is a legal term).

MENENIUS   If, by the tribunes' leave and yours, good people,
    I may be heard, I would crave a word or two,
285 The which shall turn° you to no further harm   *bring*
    Than so much loss of time.
SICINIUS   Speak briefly, then,
    For we are peremptory to dispatch
    This viperous traitor. To eject him hence
    Were but our danger, and to keep him here
290 Our certain death. Therefore it is decreed
    He dies tonight.
MENENIUS   Now the good gods forbid
    That our renownèd Rome, whose gratitude
    Towards her deservèd° children is enrolled   *deserving*
    In Jove's own book, like an unnatural dam°   *mother*
295 Should now eat up her own!
SICINIUS   He's a disease that must be cut away.
MENENIUS   O, he's a limb that has but a disease—
    Mortal to cut it off, to cure it easy.
    What has he done to Rome that's worthy death?
300 Killing our enemies, the blood he hath lost—
    Which I dare vouch is more than that he hath
    By many an ounce—he dropped it for his country;
    And what is left, to lose it by his country
    Were to us all that do't and suffer° it   *allow*
    A brand° to th' end o'th' world.   *stigma*
305 SICINIUS   This is clean cam.°   *completely perverse*
BRUTUS   Merely° awry. When he did love his country   *Absolutely*
    It honoured him.
SICINIUS   The service of the foot,
    Being once gangrened, is not then respected
    For what before it was.
BRUTUS   We'll hear no more.
310 Pursue him to his house and pluck him thence,
    Lest his infection, being of catching nature,
    Spread further.
MENENIUS   One word more, one word!
    This tiger-footed rage, when it shall find
    The harm of unscanned° swiftness, will too late   *heedless*
315 Tie leaden pounds° to's heels. Proceed by process,° *weights / due process*
    Lest parties°—as he is beloved—break out   *factions*
    And sack great Rome with Romans.
BRUTUS   If it were so?
SICINIUS [*to* MENENIUS]   What do ye talk?
320 Have we not had a taste of his obedience:
    Our aediles smote, ourselves resisted? Come.
MENENIUS   Consider this: he has been bred i'th' wars
    Since a could draw a sword, and is ill-schooled
    In bolted[6] language. Meal and bran° together   *Flour and husks*
325 He throws without distinction. Give me leave,
    I'll go to him and undertake to bring him
    Where he shall answer by a lawful form,
    In peace, to his utmost peril.[7]
FIRST SENATOR   Noble tribunes,

---

6. Sifted; that is, carefully considered.   7. Even at peril of his life.

It is the humane way. The other course
330 Will prove too bloody, and the end of it
Unknown to the beginning.

SICINIUS   Noble Menenius,
Be you then as the people's officer.
[*To the* CITIZENS] Masters, lay down your weapons.

BRUTUS   Go not home.

SICINIUS   Meet on the market-place. [*To* MENENIUS] We'll attend° you there,   *await*
335 Where if you bring not Martius, we'll proceed
In our first way.

MENENIUS   I'll bring him to you.
[*To the* SENATORS] Let me desire your company. He must come,
Or what is worst will follow.

FIRST SENATOR   Pray you, let's to him.

Exeunt [*tribunes and* CITIZENS *at one door,*
PATRICIANS *at another door*]

3.2

Enter CORIOLANUS, *with Nobles*

CORIOLANUS   Let them pull all about mine ears, present me
Death on the wheel or at wild horses' heels,
Or pile ten hills on the Tarpeian rock,
That the precipitation° might down stretch   *steepness*
5   Below the beam of sight, yet will I still
Be thus to them.

Enter VOLUMNIA

A PATRICIAN   You do the nobler.

CORIOLANUS   I muse° my mother   *wonder that*
Does not approve me further, who was wont
To call them woollen° vassals, things created   *coarsely clad*
To buy and sell with groats,° to show bare heads   *fourpenny pieces*
10   In congregations, to yawn, be still, and wonder,
When one but of my ordinance° stood up   *rank*
To speak of peace or war. [*To* VOLUMNIA] I talk of you.
Why did you wish me milder? Would you have me
False to my nature? Rather say I play
The man I am.

15   VOLUMNIA   O, sir, sir, sir,
I would have had you put your power well on
Before you had worn it out.

CORIOLANUS   Let go.°   *Stop*

VOLUMNIA   You might have been enough the man you are
With striving less to be so. Lesser had been
20   The taxings° of your dispositions if   *challenging*
You had not showed them how ye were disposed
Ere they lacked° power to cross you.   *Before they lost*

CORIOLANUS   Let them hang.

VOLUMNIA   Ay, and burn too.

Enter MENENIUS *with the* SENATORS

MENENIUS [*to* CORIOLANUS]   Come, come, you have been too rough,
          something too rough.
You must return and mend it.

25   FIRST SENATOR   There's no remedy

3.2 Location: Coriolanus's house.

Unless, by not so doing, our good city
Cleave in the midst and perish.

VOLUMNIA [*to* CORIOLANUS]   Pray be counselled.
I have a heart as little apt as yours,
But yet a brain that leads my use of anger
To better vantage.

30 MENENIUS   Well said, noble woman.
Before he should thus stoop to th' herd, but that
The violent fit o'th' time craves it as physic°   *medicine*
For the whole state, I would put mine armour on,
Which I can scarcely bear.

35 CORIOLANUS   What must I do?

MENENIUS   Return to th' tribunes.

CORIOLANUS   Well, what then, what then?

MENENIUS   Repent what you have spoke.

CORIOLANUS   For them? I cannot do it to the gods.
Must I then do't to them?

40 VOLUMNIA   You are too absolute,°   *inflexible*
Though therein you can never be too noble,
But when extremities° speak. I have heard you say,   *extreme situations*
Honour and policy,° like unsevered friends,   *tactical shrewdness*
I'th' war do grow together. Grant that, and tell me
45 In peace what each of them by th' other lose
That they combine not there.

CORIOLANUS   Tush, tush!

MENENIUS   A good demand.

VOLUMNIA   If it be honour in your wars to seem
The same° you are not, which for your best ends   *That which*
You adopt your policy, how is it less or worse
50 That it° shall hold companionship in peace   *(dissimulation)*
With honour, as in war, since that to both
It stands in like request?°   *need*

CORIOLANUS   Why force° you this?   *urge*

VOLUMNIA   Because that now it lies you on to speak to th' people,
Not by your own instruction,° nor by th' matter   *conviction*
55 Which your heart prompts you, but with such words
That are but roted° in your tongue, though but   *memorized*
Bastards and syllables of no allowance
To[1] your bosom's truth. Now this no more
Dishonours you at all than to take in°   *capture*
60 A town with gentle words, which else would put you
To your fortune[2] and the hazard of much blood.
I would dissemble with my nature where
My fortunes and my friends at stake required
I should do so in honour. I am in this°   *I speak in this for*
65 Your wife, your son, these senators, the nobles;
And you will rather show our general° louts   *common*
How you can frown than spend a fawn° upon 'em   *cringing courtesy*
For the inheritance° of their loves and safeguard   *acquisition*
Of what that want° might ruin.   *lack (of their loves)*

MENENIUS   Noble lady!
70 [*To* CORIOLANUS] Come, go with us, speak fair. You may salve° so,   *smooth over*

---

1. *Bastards . . . / To:* Illegitimate words not acknowledged
by.
2. *put . . . fortune:* force you to take your chances (in
battle).

Not what is dangerous present, but the loss
Of what is past.[3]

VOLUMNIA   I prithee now, my son,
    [*She takes his bonnet*]
Go to them with this bonnet° in thy hand,   hat
And thus far having stretched it—here be with them—
75 Thy knee bussing° the stones—for in such business   kissing
Action is eloquence, and the eyes of th' ignorant
More learnèd than the ears—waving° thy head,   repeatedly bowing
With often, thus, correcting thy stout heart,
Now humble[4] as the ripest mulberry
80 That will not hold the handling; or say to them
Thou art their soldier and, being bred in broils,°   tumults
Hast not the soft way which, thou dost confess,
Were fit for thee to use as they to claim,°   for them to expect
In asking their good loves; but thou wilt frame
85 Thyself, forsooth, hereafter theirs so far
As thou hast power and person.°   ability and authority
MENENIUS [*to* CORIOLANUS]   This but done
Even as she speaks, why, their hearts were yours;
For they have pardons, being asked, as free
As words to little purpose.
VOLUMNIA [*to* CORIOLANUS]   Prithee now,
90 Go, and be ruled, although I know thou hadst rather
Follow thine enemy in a fiery gulf
Than flatter him in a bower.°   arbor
          Enter COMINIUS
                              Here is Cominius.
COMINIUS   I have been i'th' market-place; and, sir, 'tis fit
You make strong party,° or defend yourself   gather strong support
95 By calmness or by absence. All's in anger.
MENENIUS   Only fair speech.
COMINIUS   I think 'twill serve, if he
Can thereto frame his spirit.
VOLUMNIA   He must, and will.
Prithee now, say you will, and go about it.
CORIOLANUS   Must I go show them my unbarbèd sconce?°   unhelmeted head
100 Must I with my base tongue give to my noble heart
A lie that it must bear? Well, I will do't.
Yet were there but this single plot° to lose,   (*Coriolanus's body*)
This mould° of Martius they to dust should grind it   form; earth
And throw't against the wind. To th' market-place.
105 You have put me now to such a part which never
I shall discharge to th' life.°   perform convincingly
COMINIUS   Come, come, we'll prompt you.
VOLUMNIA   I prithee now, sweet son, as thou hast said
My praises made thee first a soldier, so,
To have my praise for this, perform a part
Thou hast not done before.
110 CORIOLANUS   Well, I must do't.
Away, my disposition; and possess me
Some harlot's[5] spirit! My throat of war be turned,

---

3. *Not . . . past:* Not only the present danger, but what was   4. Malleable (or possibly a verb, "let droop").
lost before.   5. Vagabond; buffoon; prostitute.

Which choired° with my drum, into a pipe   *harmonized*
Small as an eunuch or the virgin voice
115   That babies lull asleep! The smiles of knaves
Tent° in my cheeks, and schoolboys' tears take up   *Encamp*
The glasses° of my sight! A beggar's tongue   *windows*
Make motion through my lips, and my armed knees,
Who bowed but in my stirrup, bend like his
120   That hath received an alms! I will not do't,
Lest I surcease° to honour mine own truth,   *cease*
And by my body's action teach my mind
A most inherent° baseness.   *fixed*

VOLUMNIA   At thy choice, then.
To beg of thee it is my more dishonour
125   Than thou of them. Come all to ruin. Let
Thy mother rather feel° thy pride than fear   *suffer*
Thy dangerous stoutness,° for I mock at death   *stubbornness*
With as big heart as thou. Do as thou list.°   *wish*
Thy valiantness was mine, thou sucked'st it from me,
But owe° thy pride thyself.   *own*
130   **CORIOLANUS**   Pray be content.
Mother, I am going to the market-place.
Chide me no more. I'll mountebank[6] their loves,
Cog° their hearts from them, and come home beloved   *Wheedle*
Of all the trades in Rome. Look, I am going.
135   Commend me to my wife. I'll return consul,
Or never trust to what my tongue can do
I'th' way of flattery further.

VOLUMNIA   Do your will.   *Exit* VOLUMNIA

COMINIUS   Away! The tribunes do attend you. Arm yourself
To answer mildly, for they are prepared
140   With accusations, as I hear, more strong
Than are upon you yet.

CORIOLANUS   The word is 'mildly'. Pray you let us go.
Let them accuse me by invention,° I   *with invented charges*
Will answer in mine honour.
145   **MENENIUS**   Ay, but mildly.

CORIOLANUS   Well, mildly be it, then—mildly.   *Exeunt*

3.3

Enter SICINIUS *and* BRUTUS

BRUTUS   In this point charge him home:[1] that he affects°   *desires*
Tyrannical power. If he evade us there,
Enforce° him with his envy° to the people,   *Urge against / malice*
And that the spoil got on° the Antiats   *booty taken from*
Was ne'er distributed.

Enter an AEDILE

               What, will he come?
5   **AEDILE**   He's coming.

BRUTUS   How accompanied?

AEDILE   With old Menenius, and those senators
That always favoured him.

SICINIUS   Have you a catalogue

---

6. Cajole (a mountebank was an itinerant quack who   3.3 Location: The marketplace.
sold his cures from an improvised platform).   1. Press charges against him forcefully.

	Of all the voices° that we have procured,	*votes*
	Set down by th' poll?°	*individually*
10	AEDILE I have, 'tis ready.	
	SICINIUS Have you collected them by tribes?²	
	AEDILE I have.	
	SICINIUS Assemble presently the people hither,	
	And when they hear me say 'It shall be so	
	I'th' right and strength o'th' commons', be it either	
15	For death, for fine, or banishment, then let them,	
	If I say 'Fine', cry 'Fine!', if 'Death', cry 'Death!',	
	Insisting on the old prerogative	
	And power i'th' truth o'th' cause.³	
	AEDILE I shall inform them.	
	BRUTUS And when such time they have begun to cry,	
20	Let them not cease, but with a din confused	
	Enforce the present execution⁴	
	Of what we chance to sentence.	
	AEDILE Very well.	
	SICINIUS Make them be strong, and ready for this hint	
	When we shall hap° to give't them.	*chance*
	BRUTUS [*to the* AEDILE] Go about it. [*Exit* AEDILE]	
25	Put him to choler° straight. He hath been used	*anger at once*
	Ever to conquer and to have his worth⁵	
	Of contradiction. Being once chafed,° he cannot	*excited*
	Be reined again to temperance. Then he speaks	
	What's in his heart, and that is there which looks	
30	With us⁶ to break his neck.	

        Enter CORIOLANUS, MENENIUS, *and* COMINIUS, *with*
        other [SENATORS *and* PATRICIANS]

	SICINIUS Well, here he comes.	
	MENENIUS [*to* CORIOLANUS] Calmly, I do beseech you.	
	CORIOLANUS Ay, as an hostler° that for th' poorest piece°	*stable keeper / coin*
	Will bear the knave by th' volume.⁷—Th'honoured gods	
35	Keep Rome in safety and the chairs of justice	
	Supplied with worthy men, plant love among's,	
	Throng our large temples with the shows° of peace,	*ceremonies*
	And not our streets with war!	
	FIRST SENATOR Amen, amen.	
40	MENENIUS A noble wish.	

        Enter the AEDILE *with the* CITIZENS

	SICINIUS Draw near, ye people.	
	AEDILE List to your tribunes. Audience!	
	Peace, I say.	
	CORIOLANUS First, hear me speak.	
	SICINIUS and BRUTUS Well, say.—Peace ho!	
	CORIOLANUS Shall I be charged no further than this present?°	*at this present time*
	Must all determine° here?	*be determined*
	SICINIUS I do demand	
45	If you submit you to the people's voices,	
	Allow° their officers, and are content	*Acknowledge*

---

2. Romans voted by tribes (districts) or by social class; the former method favored the plebeians.
3. *old prerogative . . . cause*: traditional right to determine the truth of the case.

4. Insist upon the immediate performance.
5. Enjoy his fill; establish his reputation from.
6. *looks / With us*: promises with our help.
7. Will endure being called knave any number of times.

To suffer lawful censure for such faults
As shall be proved upon you.

CORIOLANUS   I am content.

MENENIUS   Lo, citizens, he says he is content.
50   The warlike service he has done, consider. Think
Upon the wounds his body bears, which show
Like graves i'th' holy churchyard.

CORIOLANUS   Scratches with briers,
Scars to move laughter only.

MENENIUS   Consider further
That when he speaks not like a citizen,
55   You find him like a soldier. Do not take
His rougher accents for malicious sounds,
But, as I say, such as become a soldier
Rather than envy° you.   show hatred to

COMINIUS   Well, well, no more.

60   CORIOLANUS   What is the matter
That, being passed for consul with full voice,
I am so dishonoured that the very hour
You take it off again?

SICINIUS   Answer to us.

65   CORIOLANUS   Say, then. 'Tis true I ought so.

SICINIUS   We charge you that you have contrived to take
From Rome all seasoned° office, and to wind°   time-honored / insinuate
Yourself into a power tyrannical,
For which you are a traitor to the people.

CORIOLANUS   How, traitor?

70   MENENIUS   Nay, temperately—your promise.

CORIOLANUS   The fires i'th' lowest hell fold in° the people!   enfold
Call me their traitor, thou injurious° tribune?   insulting
Within thine eyes sat twenty thousand deaths,
In thy hands clutched as many millions, in
75   Thy lying tongue both numbers, I would say
'Thou liest' unto thee with a voice as free
As I do pray the gods.

SICINIUS   Mark you this, people?

ALL THE CITIZENS   To th' rock, to th' rock with him!

80   SICINIUS   Peace!
We need not put new matter to his charge.
What you have seen him do and heard him speak,
Beating your officers, cursing yourselves,
Opposing laws with strokes, and here defying
85   Those whose great power must try him—
Even this, so criminal and in such capital kind,[8]
Deserves th'extremest death.

BRUTUS   But since he hath
Served well for Rome—

CORIOLANUS   What do you prate° of service?   babble

BRUTUS   I talk of that that know it.

CORIOLANUS   You?

90   MENENIUS   Is this the promise that you made your mother?

COMINIUS   Know, I pray you—

8. Important; deserving death.

CORIOLANUS   I'll know no further.
    Let them pronounce the steep Tarpeian death,
    Vagabond exile, flaying, pent° to linger   *imprisoned*
    But with a grain a day, I would not buy
95   Their mercy at the price of one fair word,
    Nor check my courage° for what they can give   *restrain my spirit*
    To have't with saying 'Good morrow'.
SICINIUS   For that he has,
    As much as in him lies, from time to time
    Inveighed against the people, seeking means
100   To pluck away their power, as now at last
    Given hostile strokes, and that not in the presence
    Of dreaded justice, but on the ministers
    That doth distribute it, in the name o'th' people,
    And in the power of us the tribunes, we
105   E'en from this instant banish him our city
    In peril of precipitation
    From off the rock Tarpeian, never more
    To enter our Rome gates. I'th' people's name
    I say it shall be so.
ALL THE CITIZENS   It shall be so,
110   It shall be so. Let him away. He's banished,
    And it shall be so.
COMINIUS   Hear me, my masters and my common friends.
SICINIUS   He's sentenced. No more hearing.
COMINIUS   Let me speak.
    I have been consul, and can show for Rome
115   Her enemies' marks upon me. I do love
    My country's good with a respect more tender,
    More holy and profound, than mine own life,
    My dear wife's estimate,° her womb's increase,   *reputation*
    And treasure of my loins.° Then if I would   *(that is, children)*
    Speak that—
120 SICINIUS   We know your drift. Speak what?
BRUTUS   There's no more to be said, but he is banished,
    As enemy to the people and his country.
    It shall be so.
ALL THE CITIZENS   It shall be so, it shall be so.
CORIOLANUS   You common cry° of curs, whose breath I hate   *yelping pack*
125   As reek° o'th' rotten fens,° whose loves I prize   *vapor / swamps*
    As the dead carcasses of unburied men
    That do corrupt my air: I banish you.
    And here remain with your uncertainty.
    Let every feeble rumour shake your hearts;
130   Your enemies, with nodding of their plumes,°   *(helmet plumes)*
    Fan you into despair! Have the power still
    To banish your defenders, till at length
    Your ignorance—which finds not till it feels⁹—   *Seeking only to preserve*
    Making but reservation of° yourselves,
135   Still your own foes, deliver you
    As most abated° captives to some nation   *debased*
    That won you without blows! Despising

---

9. Which does not learn until it undergoes.

For° you the city, thus I turn my back.   *On account of*
There is a world elsewhere.
      Exeunt CORIOLANUS, COMINIUS, *and* [MENENIUS],
      with [*the rest of the Patricians. The* CITIZENS] *all shout,*
      and throw up their caps

140 AEDILE   The people's enemy is gone, is gone.
ALL THE CITIZENS   Our enemy is banished, he is gone. Hoo-oo!
SICINIUS   Go see him out at gates, and follow him
   As he hath followed you, with all despite.°   *contempt*
   Give him deserved vexation. Let a guard
145   Attend us through the city.
ALL THE CITIZENS   Come, come, let's see him out at gates. Come.
   The gods preserve our noble tribunes! Come.   *Exeunt*

4.1

   Enter CORIOLANUS, VOLUMNIA, VIRGILIA, MENENIUS,
   [*and*] COMINIUS, *with the young nobility of Rome*
CORIOLANUS   Come, leave your tears. A brief farewell. The beast
   With many heads butts me away. Nay, mother,
   Where is your ancient° courage? You were used   *former*
   To say extremities was the trier of spirits,
5   That common chances common men could bear,
   That when the sea was calm all boats alike
   Showed mastership in floating; fortune's blows
   When most struck home, being gentle wounded craves
   A noble cunning.[1] You were used to load me
10   With precepts that would make invincible
   The heart that conned° them.   *learned*
VIRGILIA   O heavens, O heavens!
CORIOLANUS   Nay, I prithee, woman—
VOLUMNIA   Now the red pestilence[2] strike all trades in Rome,
   And occupations° perish!   *handicrafts*
15 CORIOLANUS   What, what, what?
   I shall be loved when I am lacked. Nay, mother,
   Resume that spirit when you were wont to say,
   If you had been the wife of Hercules[3]
   Six of his labours you'd have done, and saved
20   Your husband so much sweat. Cominius,
   Droop not. Adieu. Farewell, my wife, my mother.
   I'll do well yet. Thou old and true Menenius,
   Thy tears are salter than a younger man's,
   And venomous to thine eyes. My sometime[4] general,
25   I have seen thee stern, and thou hast oft beheld
   Heart-hard'ning spectacles. Tell these sad women
   'Tis fond° to wail inevitable strokes   *as foolish*
   As 'tis to laugh at 'em. My mother, you wot° well   *know*
   My hazards still° have been your solace, and—   *always*
30   Believe't not lightly—though I go alone,
   Like to a lonely dragon that his fen
   Makes feared° and talked of more than seen, your son   *fearful*

4.1 Location: Near the city gates of Rome.
1. *being . . . cunning*: to suffer nobly requires a gentleman's skill.
2. Bubonic plague or typhoid.
3. Mythical hero of great strength who was assigned twelve near-impossible labors.
4. Former (addressing Cominius).

Will or° exceed the common° or be caught   *either/usual standard*
With cautelous° baits and practice.   *deceitful*

VOLUMNIA   My first son,

35   Whither will thou go? Take good Cominius
With thee a while. Determine on some course
More than a wild exposure to each chance
That starts° i'th' way before thee.   *leaps up*

VIRGILIA   O the gods!

COMINIUS   I'll follow thee a month, devise with thee

40   Where thou shalt rest, that thou mayst hear of us
And we of thee. So, if the time thrust forth
A cause for thy repeal,° we shall not send   *recall from banishment*
O'er the vast world to seek a single man,
And lose advantage,° which doth ever cool   *favorable occasion*
I'th' absence of the needer.

45   CORIOLANUS   Fare ye well.
Thou hast years upon thee, and thou art too full
Of the wars' surfeits to go rove with one
That's yet unbruised. Bring me but out at gate.
Come, my sweet wife, my dearest mother, and

50   My friends of noble touch.° When I am forth,   *proven nobility*
Bid me farewell, and smile. I pray you come.
While I remain above the ground you shall
Hear from me still, and never of me aught
But what is like me formerly.

MENENIUS   That's worthily

55   As any ear can hear. Come, let's not weep.
If I could shake off but one seven years
From these old arms and legs, by the good gods,
I'd with thee every foot.

CORIOLANUS   Give me thy hand. Come.   *Exeunt*

4.2

Enter the two tribunes, SICINIUS *and* BRUTUS, *with the*
AEDILE

SICINIUS [*to the* AEDILE]   Bid them all home. He's gone, and we'll no further.
The nobility are vexed, whom we see have sided
In his behalf.

BRUTUS   Now we have shown our power,
Let us seem humbler after it is done
Than when it was a-doing.

5   SICINIUS [*to the* AEDILE]   Bid them home.
Say their great enemy is gone, and they
Stand in their ancient strength.

BRUTUS   Dismiss them home.   *Exit* AEDILE

Enter VOLUMNIA, VIRGILIA [*weeping*], *and* MENENIUS
Here comes his mother.

SICINIUS   Let's not meet her.

10   BRUTUS   Why?

SICINIUS   They say she's mad.

BRUTUS   They have ta'en note of us. Keep on your way.

4.2 Location: Near the city gates of Rome.

VOLUMNIA O, you're well met! Th'hoarded plague o'th' gods
   Requite° your love!   *Repay*
MENENIUS   Peace, peace, be not so loud.
15 VOLUMNIA [*to the tribunes*] If that I could for weeping, you should hear—
   Nay, and you shall hear some. Will you be gone?
VIRGILIA [*to the tribunes*] You shall stay, too. I would I had the power
   To say so to my husband.
SICINIUS [*to* VOLUMNIA]   Are you mankind?[1]
VOLUMNIA Ay, fool. Is that a shame? Note but this, fool:
20   Was not a man my father? Hadst thou foxship°   *slyness*
   To banish him that struck more blows for Rome
   Than thou hast spoken words?
SICINIUS   O blessèd heavens!
VOLUMNIA More noble blows than ever thou wise words,
   And for Rome's good. I'll tell thee what—yet go.
25   Nay, but thou shalt stay too. I would my son
   Were in Arabia,[2] and thy tribe before him,
   His good sword in his hand.
SICINIUS   What then?
VIRGILIA   What then?
   He'd make an end of thy posterity.
VOLUMNIA Bastards and all.
30   Good man, the wounds that he does bear for Rome!
MENENIUS Come, come, peace.
SICINIUS I would he had continued to his country
   As he began, and not unknit° himself   *untied*
   The noble knot he made.
BRUTUS   I would he had.
35 VOLUMNIA 'I would he had'! 'Twas you incensed the rabble—
   Cats that can judge as fitly of his worth
   As I can of those mysteries which heaven
   Will not have earth to know.
BRUTUS [*to* SICINIUS] Pray, let's go.
40 VOLUMNIA Now pray, sir, get you gone.
   You have done a brave deed. Ere you go, hear this:
   As far as doth the Capitol exceed
   The meanest house in Rome, so far my son—
   This lady's husband here, this, do you see?—
45   Whom you have banished does exceed you all.
BRUTUS Well, well, we'll leave you.
SICINIUS   Why stay we to be baited
   With one that wants° her wits?   *Exeunt tribunes*   *lacks*
VOLUMNIA   Take my prayers with you.
   I would the gods had nothing else to do
   But to confirm my curses. Could I meet 'em
50   But once a day, it would unclog° my heart   *unburden*
   Of what lies heavy to't.
MENENIUS   You have told them home[3]
   And, by my troth, you have cause. You'll sup° with me?   *dine*
VOLUMNIA Anger's my meat, I sup upon myself,
   And so shall starve with feeding.

1. Male (thus to speak in public); Volumnia takes the   places to hide.
word to mean "human."   3. Scolded them thoroughly.
2. That is, in a desert without political institutions or

[*To* VIRGILIA]   Come, let's go.
55 Leave this faint puling and lament as I do,
In anger, Juno-like.⁴ Come, come, come.

Exeunt VOLUMNIA *and* VIRGILIA

MENENIUS   Fie, fie, fie.   *Exit*

4.3

Enter [NICANOR,] *a Roman, and* [ADRIAN,] *a Volsce*

NICANOR   I know you well, sir, and you know me. Your name, I
think, is Adrian.

ADRIAN   It is so, sir. Truly, I have forgot you.

NICANOR   I am a Roman, and my services are, as you are, against
5 'em.° Know you me yet?   (the Romans)

ADRIAN   Nicanor, no?

NICANOR   The same, sir.

ADRIAN   You had more beard when I last saw you, but your
favour° is well approved° by your tongue. What's the news in   face / attested
10 Rome? I have a note° from the Volscian state to find you out   instruction
there. You have well saved me a day's journey.

NICANOR   There hath been in Rome strange insurrections, the
people against the senators, patricians, and nobles.

ADRIAN   Hath been?—is it ended then? Our state thinks not so.
15 They are in a most warlike preparation, and hope to come
upon them in the heat of their division.

NICANOR   The main blaze of it is past, but a small thing would
make it flame again, for the nobles receive so to heart the banishment of that worthy Coriolanus that they are in a ripe apt-
20 ness to take all power from the people, and to pluck from them
their tribunes for ever. This lies glowing,° I can tell you, and is   smoldering
almost mature for the violent breaking out.

ADRIAN   Coriolanus banished?

NICANOR   Banished, sir.

25 ADRIAN   You will be welcome with this intelligence, Nicanor.

NICANOR   The day° serves well for them° now. I have heard it   moment / (the Volscians)
said the fittest time to corrupt a man's wife is when she's fallen
out with her husband. Your noble Tullus Aufidius will appear
well in these wars, his great opposer Coriolanus being now in
30 no request of° his country.   unvalued by

ADRIAN   He cannot choose.° I am most fortunate thus acciden-   He is bound to
tally to encounter you. You have ended my business, and I will
merrily accompany you home.

NICANOR   I shall between this and supper tell you most strange
35 things from Rome, all tending to the good of their adversaries.
Have you an army ready, say you?

ADRIAN   A most royal one—the centurions and their charges distinctly billeted already in th'entertainment,¹ and to be on foot
at an hour's warning.

40 NICANOR   I am joyful to hear of their readiness, and am the man,
I think, that shall set them in present° action. So, sir, heartily   immediate
well met, and most glad of your company.

---

4. Goddess of marriage and childbirth (and frequently
infuriated by the infidelities of her husband, Jupiter, king
of the gods).

4.3 Location: A road between Rome and Antium.
1. *their . . . entertainment:* the men under their command
already listed unit by unit on the payroll.

ADRIAN   You take my part° from me, sir. I have the most cause to   lines
    be glad of yours.

45 NICANOR   Well, let us go together.   *Exeunt*

4.4

Enter CORIOLANUS *in mean apparel, disguised*
and muffled

CORIOLANUS   A goodly city is this Antium. City,
  'Tis I that made thy widows. Many an heir
  Of these fair edifices fore my wars°   *before my onslaught*
  Have I heard groan and drop. Then know me not,
5 Lest that thy wives with spits and boys with stones
  In puny battle slay me.

Enter a CITIZEN

                Save° you, sir.   *God save*

CITIZEN   And you.
CORIOLANUS   Direct me, if it be your will,
  Where great Aufidius lies. Is he in Antium?

CITIZEN   He is, and feasts the nobles of the state
  At his house this night.
10 CORIOLANUS   Which is his house, beseech you?

CITIZEN   This here before you.

CORIOLANUS   Thank you, sir. Farewell.

                      Exit CITIZEN

  O world, thy slippery turns! Friends now fast sworn,
  Whose double bosoms seem to wear one heart,
  Whose hours, whose bed, whose meal and exercise
15 Are still together, who twin as 'twere in love
  Unseparable, shall within this hour,
  On a dissension of a doit,° break out   *trivial quarrel*
  To bitterest enmity. So fellest foes,
  Whose passions and whose plots have broke their sleep
20 To take the one the other,[1] by some chance,
  Some trick° not worth an egg, shall grow dear friends   *trifle*
  And interjoin their issues.[2] So with me.
  My birthplace hate I, and my love's upon
  This enemy town. I'll enter. If he slay me,
25 He does fair justice; if he give me way,°   *allows me to proceed*
  I'll do his country service.   *Exit*

4.5

Music plays. Enter a SERVINGMAN

FIRST SERVINGMAN   Wine, wine, wine! What service is here?
  I think our fellows° are asleep.   [*Exit*]   *fellow servants*

Enter [a SECOND] SERVINGMAN

SECOND SERVINGMAN   Where's Cotus? My master calls for him.
  Cotus!   *Exit*

Enter CORIOLANUS [*as before*]

5 CORIOLANUS   A goodly house. The feast
  Smells well, but I appear not like a guest.

Enter the FIRST SERVINGMAN

4.4 Location: Before Aufidius's house in Antium.   2. Unite their causes; marry their children to one another.
1. Whose plots to capture one another have kept them   4.5 Location: Inside Aufidius's house.
awake.

FIRST SERVINGMAN   What would you have, friend? Whence are
you? Here's no place for you. Pray go to the door.   *Exit*

CORIOLANUS   I have deserved no better entertainment
10   In being Coriolanus.
        Enter SECOND [SERVINGMAN]

SECOND SERVINGMAN   Whence are you, sir? Has the porter his
eyes in his head, that he gives entrance to such companions?°   *low persons*
Pray get you out.

CORIOLANUS   Away!

15   SECOND SERVINGMAN   Away? Get you away.

CORIOLANUS   Now thou'rt troublesome.

SECOND SERVINGMAN   Are you so brave?° I'll have you talked   *insolent*
with anon.°   *right away*
        Enter THIRD SERVINGMAN. *The* FIRST *meets him*

THIRD SERVINGMAN   What fellow's this?

20   FIRST SERVINGMAN   A strange one as ever I looked on. I cannot
get him out o'th' house. Prithee, call my master to him.

THIRD SERVINGMAN [*to* CORIOLANUS]   What have you to do° here,   *are you doing*
fellow? Pray you, avoid° the house.   *leave*

CORIOLANUS   Let me but stand. I will not hurt your hearth.

25   THIRD SERVINGMAN   What are you?

CORIOLANUS   A gentleman.

THIRD SERVINGMAN   A marvellous poor one.

CORIOLANUS   True, so I am.

THIRD SERVINGMAN   Pray you, poor gentleman, take up some other
30   station.¹ Here's no place for you. Pray you, avoid. Come.

CORIOLANUS   Follow your function.² Go and batten° on cold   *gorge*
bits.
        [*He*] *pushes him away from him*

THIRD SERVINGMAN   What, you will not?—Prithee tell my master
what a strange guest he has here.

35   SECOND SERVINGMAN   And I shall.   *Exit* SECOND SERVINGMAN

THIRD SERVINGMAN   Where dwell'st thou?

CORIOLANUS   Under the canopy.°   *(of the sky)*

THIRD SERVINGMAN   Under the canopy?

CORIOLANUS   Ay.

40   THIRD SERVINGMAN   Where's that?

CORIOLANUS   I'th' city of kites and crows.°   *(carrion birds)*

THIRD SERVINGMAN   I'th' city of kites and crows? What an ass it
is! Then thou dwell'st with daws,³ too?

CORIOLANUS   No, I serve not thy master.

45   THIRD SERVINGMAN   How, sir? Do you meddle⁴ with my master?

CORIOLANUS   Ay, 'tis an honester service than to meddle with
thy mistress. Thou prat'st and prat'st. Serve with thy trencher.°   *wooden plate*
Hence!
        [*He*] *beats him away.*
        Enter AUFIDIUS, *with the* [SECOND] SERVINGMAN

AUFIDIUS   Where is this fellow?

50   SECOND SERVINGMAN   Here, sir. I'd have beaten him like a dog
but for disturbing the lords within.
        [*The* SERVINGMEN *stand aside*]

---

1. Place to stand (punning on "social rank").
2. Perform your servant's tasks.
3. Jackdaws (proverbially foolish).

4. Busy yourself; but Coriolanus plays on the sense "have
sexual intercourse."

AUFIDIUS Whence com'st thou? What wouldst thou? Thy name?
　　Why speak'st not? Speak, man. What's thy name?
CORIOLANUS [*unmuffling his head*]　　　　　　If, Tullus,
　　Not yet thou know'st me, and seeing me dost not
55　　Think me for the man I am, necessity
　　Commands me name myself.
AUFIDIUS　　　　　　　　　What is thy name?
CORIOLANUS A name unmusical to the Volscians' ears
　　And harsh in sound to thine.
AUFIDIUS　　　　　　　　　Say, what's thy name?
　　Thou hast a grim appearance, and thy face
60　　Bears a command in't. Though thy tackle's torn,
　　Thou show'st° a noble vessel. What's thy name?　　　　*appear to be*
CORIOLANUS Prepare thy brow to frown. Know'st thou me yet?
AUFIDIUS I know thee not. Thy name?
CORIOLANUS My name is Caius Martius, who hath done
65　　To thee particularly, and to all the Volsces,
　　Great hurt and mischief. Thereto witness may
　　My surname Coriolanus. The painful service,
　　The extreme dangers, and the drops of blood
　　Shed for my thankless country, are requited
70　　But with that surname—a good memory°　　　　　　*reminder*
　　And witness of the malice and displeasure
　　Which thou shouldst bear me. Only that name remains.
　　The cruelty and envy of the people,
　　Permitted by our dastard nobles, who
75　　Have all forsook me, hath devoured the rest,
　　And suffered me by th' voice of slaves to be
　　Whooped out of Rome. Now this extremity
　　Hath brought me to thy hearth. Not out of hope—
　　Mistake me not—to save my life, for if
80　　I had feared death, of all the men i'th' world
　　I would have 'voided thee, but in mere° spite　　　　*utter*
　　To be full quit of° those my banishers　　　　*revenged upon; rid of*
　　Stand I before thee here. Then if thou hast
　　A heart of wreak° in thee, that wilt revenge　　　　*vengeance*
85　　Thine own particular wrongs and stop those maims
　　Of shame seen through thy country, speed° thee straight,　　　*hasten*
　　And make my misery serve thy turn. So use it
　　That my revengeful services may prove
　　As benefits to thee; for I will fight
90　　Against my cankered° country with the spleen°　　　*infected / wrath*
　　Of all the under-fiends.° But if so be　　　　*underworld fiends*
　　Thou dar'st not this, and that to prove° more fortunes　　　*try*
　　Thou'rt tired, then, in a word, I also am
　　Longer to live most weary, and present
95　　My throat to thee and to thy ancient° malice,　　　*long-standing*
　　Which not to cut would show thee but a fool,
　　Since I have ever followed thee with hate,
　　Drawn tuns° of blood out of thy country's breast,　　　*huge casks*
　　And cannot live but to thy shame unless
　　It be to do thee service.
100 AUFIDIUS　　　　　　O Martius, Martius!
　　Each word thou hast spoke hath weeded from my heart
　　A root of ancient envy. If Jupiter

Should from yon cloud speak divine things
And say ''Tis true', I'd not believe them more
105 Than thee, all-noble Martius. Let me twine
Mine arms about that body whereagainst
My grainèd ash[5] an hundred times hath broke,
And scarred the moon with splinters.
                         [*He embraces* CORIOLANUS]
                              Here I clip°   embrace
The anvil[6] of my sword, and do contest
110 As hotly and as nobly with thy love
As ever in ambitious strength I did
Contend against thy valour. Know thou first,
I loved the maid I married; never man
Sighed truer breath. But that I see thee here,
115 Thou noble thing, more dances my rapt heart
Than when I first my wedded mistress saw
Bestride my threshold. Why, thou Mars, I tell thee
We have a power on foot,° and I had purpose   army in the field
Once more to hew thy target° from thy brawn,°   shield / arm
120 Or lose mine arm for't. Thou hast beat me out°   outright
Twelve several° times, and I have nightly since   separate
Dreamt of encounters 'twixt thyself and me—
We have been down° together in my sleep,   (on the ground)
Unbuckling helms, fisting° each other's throat—   clutching
125 And waked half dead with nothing. Worthy Martius,
Had we no other quarrel else to Rome but that
Thou art thence banished, we would muster all°   enlist everyone
From twelve to seventy,° and, pouring war   (years old)
Into the bowels of ungrateful Rome,
130 Like a bold flood o'erbear't. O, come, go in,
And take our friendly senators by th' hands
Who now are here taking their leaves of me,
Who am prepared against your territories,
Though not for Rome itself.
CORIOLANUS   You bless me, gods.
135 AUFIDIUS Therefore, most absolute° sir, if thou wilt have   perfect
The leading of thine own revenges, take
Th'one half of my commission° and set down°—   force / determine
As best thou art experienced, since thou know'st
Thy country's strength and weakness—thine own ways:
140 Whether to knock against the gates of Rome,
Or rudely visit° them in parts remote   afflict
To fright them ere destroy. But come in.
Let me commend thee first to those that shall
Say yea to thy desires. A thousand welcomes!
145 And more a friend than ere an enemy;
Yet, Martius, that was much. Your hand. Most welcome!
                                    Exeunt
    [*The*] *two* SERVINGMEN [*come forward*]
FIRST SERVINGMAN Here's a strange alteration!
SECOND SERVINGMAN By my hand, I had thought to have strucken

---

5. Close-grained ashwood spear.
6. Coriolanus's body, on which Aufidius has beaten his sword.

him with a cudgel, and yet my mind gave° me his clothes made   *suggested to*
150 a false report of him.
FIRST SERVINGMAN What an arm he has! He turned me about
with his finger and his thumb as one would set up a top.
SECOND SERVINGMAN Nay, I knew by his face that there was
something in him. He had, sir, a kind of face, methought—I
155 cannot tell how to term it.
FIRST SERVINGMAN He had so, looking, as it were—would I were
hanged but I thought there was more in him than I could
think.
SECOND SERVINGMAN So did I, I'll be sworn. He is simply the
160 rarest man i'th' world.
FIRST SERVINGMAN I think he is yet a greater soldier than he you
wot on.°   *know of*
SECOND SERVINGMAN Who, my master?
FIRST SERVINGMAN Nay, it's no matter for° that.   *no doubt about*
165 SECOND SERVINGMAN Worth six on him.
FIRST SERVINGMAN Nay, not so, neither; but I take him to be the
greater soldier.
SECOND SERVINGMAN Faith, look you, one cannot tell how to
say[7] that. For the defence of a town our general is excellent.
170 FIRST SERVINGMAN Ay, and for an assault too.
            Enter the THIRD SERVINGMAN
THIRD SERVINGMAN O, slaves, I can tell you news—news, you
rascals!
FIRST *and* SECOND SERVINGMEN What, what, what? Let's partake.
THIRD SERVINGMAN I would not be a Roman of all nations. I had
175 as lief° be a condemned man.   *gladly*
FIRST *and* SECOND SERVINGMEN Wherefore? Wherefore?
THIRD SERVINGMAN Why, here's he that was wont to thwack our
general, Caius Martius.
FIRST SERVINGMAN Why do you say 'thwack our general'?
180 THIRD SERVINGMAN I do not say 'thwack our general'; but he was
always good enough for him.
SECOND SERVINGMAN Come, we are fellows and friends. He was
ever too hard for him. I have heard him say so himself.
FIRST SERVINGMAN He was too hard for him directly.° To say the   *simply*
185 truth on't, before Corioles he scotched° him and notched him   *scored*
like a carbonado.[8]
SECOND SERVINGMAN An° he had been cannibally given, he   *If*
might have broiled and eaten him too.
FIRST SERVINGMAN But more of thy news!
190 THIRD SERVINGMAN Why, he is so made on° here within as if he   *made so much of*
were son and heir to Mars; set at upper end o'th' table, no
question asked him by any of the senators but they stand bald°   *hatless*
before him. Our general himself makes a mistress of° him,   *woos*
sanctifies himself with's hand,[9] and turns up the white o'th'
195 eye° to his discourse. But the bottom° of the news is, our gen-   *(in pious devotion) / gist*
eral is cut i'th' middle, and but one half of what he was yester-
day, for the other° has half by the entreaty and grant of the   *(Coriolanus)*
whole table. He'll go, he says, and sowl° the porter of Rome   *drag*

---

7. There's no basis for saying.
8. Piece of meat for broiling.
9. Treats the touch of his hand as holy.

gates by th' ears. He will mow all down before him, and leave
200 his passage polled.°   *stripped*

SECOND SERVINGMAN   And he's as like to do't as any man I can
imagine.

THIRD SERVINGMAN   Do't? He will do't; for look you, sir, he has
as many friends as enemies; which friends, sir, as it were durst
205 not—look you, sir—show themselves, as we term it, his friends
whilst he's in dejectitude.°   *disgraced*

FIRST SERVINGMAN   Dejectitude? What's that?

THIRD SERVINGMAN   But when they shall see, sir, his crest up
again and the man in blood,[1] they will out of their burrows like
210 conies° after rain, and revel all with him.   *rabbits*

FIRST SERVINGMAN   But when goes this forward?

THIRD SERVINGMAN   Tomorrow, today, presently.° You shall have   *at once*
the drum struck up this afternoon. 'Tis as it were a parcel° of   *part*
their feast, and to be executed ere they wipe their lips.

215 SECOND SERVINGMAN   Why, then we shall have a stirring° world   *busy*
again. This peace is nothing but to rust iron, increase tailors,
and breed ballad-makers.[2]

FIRST SERVINGMAN   Let me have war, say I. It exceeds peace as
far as day does night. It's sprightly walking, audible and full of
220 vent.[3] Peace is a very apoplexy, lethargy; mulled,° deaf, sleepy,   *stupefied*
insensible; a getter of more bastard children than war's a
destroyer of men.

SECOND SERVINGMAN   'Tis so, and as war in some sort may be
said to be a ravisher, so it cannot be denied but peace is a great
225 maker of cuckolds.

FIRST SERVINGMAN   Ay, and it makes men hate one another.

THIRD SERVINGMAN   Reason; because they then less need one another. The wars for my money. I hope to see Romans as cheap
as Volscians.

        [A sound within]

230 They are rising, they are rising.°   *(from dinner)*

FIRST *and* SECOND SERVINGMEN   In, in, in, in.   *Exeunt*

4.6

Enter the two tribunes, SICINIUS *and* BRUTUS

SICINIUS   We hear not of him, neither need we fear him.
His remedies are tame[1]—the present peace
And quietness of the people, which before
Were in wild hurry.° Here do we make his friends   *tumult*
5 Blush that the world goes well, who rather had,
Though they themselves did suffer by't, behold
Dissentious numbers pest'ring° streets than see   *obstructing*
Our tradesmen singing in their shops and going
About their functions friendly.

        Enter MENENIUS

10 BRUTUS   We stood to't° in good time. Is this Menenius?   *acted resolutely*

SICINIUS   'Tis he, 'tis he. O, he is grown most kind of late.
Hail, sir.

---

1. In full vigor (usually refers to hounds).
2. Fashionable dress and idle songs flourish in peacetime.
3. *audible . . . vent:* either loud and full of action, or quick of hearing and scent (like a hunting dog).

4.6 Location: A public place in Rome.
1. Those who favor him are unable to act; curing ourselves of him is without violent effects.

MENENIUS   Hail to you both.

SICINIUS   Your Coriolanus is not much missed

15   But with° his friends. The commonwealth doth stand,   by
And so would do were he more angry at it.

MENENIUS   All's well, and might have been much better if
He could have temporized.

SICINIUS   Where is he, hear you?

20   MENENIUS   Nay, I hear nothing.
His mother and his wife hear nothing from him.

Enter three or four CITIZENS

ALL THE CITIZENS [*to the tribunes*]   The gods preserve you both.

SICINIUS   Good e'en, our
neighbours.

BRUTUS   Good e'en to you all, good e'en to you all.

FIRST CITIZEN   Ourselves, our wives and children, on our knees
Are bound to pray for you both.

25   SICINIUS   Live and thrive.

BRUTUS   Farewell, kind neighbours.
We wished Coriolanus had loved you as we did.

ALL THE CITIZENS   Now the gods keep you!

SICINIUS *and* BRUTUS   Farewell, farewell.

Exeunt CITIZENS

SICINIUS   This is a happier and more comely time

30   Than when these fellows ran about the streets
Crying confusion.

BRUTUS   Caius Martius was
A worthy officer i'th' war, but insolent,
O'ercome with pride, ambitious past all thinking,°   *beyond imagination*
Self-loving—

SICINIUS   And affecting one sole throne°   *aspiring to rule alone*
Without assistance.

35   MENENIUS   I think not so.

SICINIUS   We should by this,° to all our lamentation,   *now*
If he had gone forth consul found it so.

BRUTUS   The gods have well prevented it, and Rome
Sits safe and still without him.

Enter an AEDILE

AEDILE   Worthy tribunes,

40   There is a slave whom we have put in prison
Reports the Volsces, with two several powers,°   *separate armies*
Are entered in the Roman territories,
And with the deepest malice of the war
Destroy what lies before 'em.

MENENIUS   'Tis Aufidius,

45   Who, hearing of our Martius' banishment,
Thrusts forth his horns again into the world,
Which were inshelled when Martius stood for Rome,
And durst not once peep out.

SICINIUS   Come, what talk you of Martius?

BRUTUS [*to the* AEDILE]   Go see this rumourer whipped. It cannot be
The Volsces dare break° with us.   *(their treaty)*

50   MENENIUS   Cannot be?
We have record that very well it can,
And three examples of the like hath been
Within my age. But reason° with the fellow,   *discuss*

Before you punish him, where he heard this,
55 Lest you shall chance to whip your information
And beat the messenger who bids beware
Of what is to be dreaded.
SICINIUS   Tell not me.
I know this cannot be.
BRUTUS   Not possible.
        Enter a MESSENGER
MESSENGER   The nobles in great earnestness are going
60 All to the senate-house. Some news is come
That turns° their countenances.   changes
SICINIUS   'Tis this slave.
[*To the* AEDILE] Go whip him fore the people's eyes.—His raising,°   incitement
Nothing but his report.   *Exit* AEDILE
MESSENGER   Yes, worthy sir,
The slave's report is seconded, and more,
More fearful, is delivered.
65 SICINIUS   What more fearful?
MESSENGER   It is spoke freely out of many mouths—
How probable I do not know—that Martius,
Joined with Aufidius, leads a power 'gainst Rome,
And vows revenge as spacious as between
The young'st and oldest thing.
70 SICINIUS   This is most likely!°   (sarcastic)
BRUTUS   Raised only that the weaker sort may wish
Good Martius home again.
SICINIUS   The very trick on't.°   Exactly
MENENIUS   This is unlikely.
75 He and Aufidius can no more atone°   reconcile
Than violent'st contrariety.
        Enter [*another*] MESSENGER
SECOND MESSENGER   You are sent for to the senate.
A fearful army, led by Caius Martius
Associated with Aufidius, rages
80 Upon our territories, and have already
O'erborne their way, consumed with fire and took
What lay before them.
        Enter COMINIUS
COMINIUS   O, you have made good work!
MENENIUS   What news? What news?
85 COMINIUS   You have holp° to ravish your own daughters and   helped
To melt the city leads° upon your pates,°   roof lead / heads
To see your wives dishonoured to° your noses.   in front of
MENENIUS   What's the news? What's the news?
COMINIUS   Your temples burnèd in their cement,° and   to their foundations
90 Your franchises,° whereon you stood,° confined   freedoms / insisted
Into an auger's bore.²
MENENIUS   Pray now, your news?
[*To the tribunes*] You have made fair work, I fear me.
[*To* COMINIUS]   Pray, your news.
If Martius should be joined wi'th' Volscians—
COMINIUS   If? He is their god. He leads them like a thing
95 Made by some other deity than nature,

2. A drill hole (that is, a narrow space).

That shapes man better, and they follow him
Against us brats° with no less confidence   *mere children*
Than boys pursuing summer butterflies,
Or butchers killing flies.
MENENIUS [*to the tribunes*]   You have made good work,
100   You and your apron-men,° you that stood so much   *(artisans wore aprons)*
Upon the voice of occupation° and   *opinion of tradesmen*
The breath of garlic-eaters!
COMINIUS [*to the tribunes*]   He'll shake your Rome about your ears.
MENENIUS   As Hercules did shake down mellow fruit.³
105   [*To the tribunes*] You have made fair work.
BRUTUS   But is this true, sir?
COMINIUS   Ay, and you'll look pale
Before you find it other.° All the regions   *otherwise*
Do smilingly° revolt, and who resists   *gladly*
110   Are mocked for valiant° ignorance,   *steadfast*
And perish constant° fools. Who is't can blame him?   *obstinate*
Your enemies° and his⁴ find something in him.   *(the patricians)*
MENENIUS   We are all undone unless
The noble man have mercy.
COMINIUS   Who shall ask it?
115   The tribunes cannot do't, for shame; the people
Deserve such pity of° him as the wolf   *from*
Does of the shepherds. For his best friends, if they
Should say 'Be good to Rome', they charged° him even   *would direct*
As those should do that had deserved his hate,
And therein showed° like enemies.   *would behave*
120 MENENIUS   'Tis true.
If he were putting to my house the brand°   *fire*
That should consume it, I have not the face°   *shamelessness*
To say 'Beseech you, cease.'
[*To the tribunes*]   You have made fair hands,°   *done well*
You and your crafts! You have crafted fair!
COMINIUS [*to the tribunes*]   You have brought
125   A trembling upon Rome such as was never
S'incapable of help.
SICINIUS *and* BRUTUS   Say not we brought it.
MENENIUS   How? Was't we?
We loved him, but like beasts and cowardly nobles
130   Gave way unto your clusters,° who did hoot   *crowds*
Him out o'th' city.
COMINIUS   But I fear
They'll roar° him in again. Tullus Aufidius,   *(in fear)*
The second name of men,⁵ obeys his points°   *directions*
As if he were his officer. Desperation
135   Is all the policy, strength, and defence
That Rome can make against them.
        Enter a troop of CITIZENS
MENENIUS   Here come the clusters.
[*To the* CITIZENS] And is Aufidius with him? You are they
That made the air unwholesome when you cast

---

3. Hercules' twelfth labor was to gather the apples of
the Hesperides.

4. The Volscians.
5. The second in reputation only to Coriolanus.

Your stinking greasy caps in hooting at
140 Coriolanus' exile. Now he's coming,
And not a hair upon a soldier's head
Which will not prove a whip. As many coxcombs°   *fools*
As you threw caps up will he tumble down,
And pay you for your voices. 'Tis no matter.
145 If he could burn us all into one coal,
We have deserved it.

ALL THE CITIZENS   Faith, we hear fearful news.

FIRST CITIZEN   For mine own part,
When I said 'banish him' I said 'twas pity.

150 SECOND CITIZEN   And so did I.

THIRD CITIZEN   And so did I, and to say the truth so did very
many of us. That° we did, we did for the best, and though we   *What*
willingly consented to his banishment, yet it was against our
will.

COMINIUS   You're goodly things, you voices.

155 MENENIUS   You have made good work,
You and your cry. Shall's to the Capitol?

COMINIUS   O, ay, what else? *Exeunt* [MENENIUS *and* COMINIUS]

SICINIUS   Go, masters, get you home. Be not dismayed.
These are a side° that would be glad to have   *faction*
160 This true which they so seem to fear. Go home,
And show no sign of fear.

FIRST CITIZEN   The gods be good to us! Come, masters, let's home.
I ever said we were i'th' wrong when we banished him.

SECOND CITIZEN   So did we all. But come, let's home.

                                     Exeunt CITIZENS

BRUTUS   I do not like this news.

165 SICINIUS   Nor I.

BRUTUS   Let's to the Capitol. Would half my wealth
Would buy this for a lie.

SICINIUS   Pray let's go.   *Exeunt*

4.7

Enter AUFIDIUS *with his* LIEUTENANT

AUFIDIUS   Do they still fly to th' Roman?

LIEUTENANT   I do not know what witchcraft's in him, but
Your soldiers use him as the grace fore meat,
Their talk at table, and their thanks at end,
5 And you are darkened° in this action, sir,   *overshadowed*
Even by your own.°   *(followers)*

AUFIDIUS   I cannot help it now,
Unless by using means° I lame the foot   *stratagems*
Of our design. He bears himself more proudlier,
Even to my person, than I thought he would
10 When first I did embrace him. Yet his nature
In that's no changeling,° and I must excuse   *waverer*
What cannot be amended.

LIEUTENANT   Yet I wish, sir—
I mean for your particular°—you had not   *own sake*
Joined in commission° with him, but either   *command*
15 Have borne the action of yourself or else
To him had left it solely.

4.7 Location: The Volscian camp near Rome.

AUFIDIUS   I understand thee well, and be thou sure,
When he shall come to his account,[1] he knows not
What I can urge against him. Although it seems—
20 And so he thinks, and is no less apparent
To th' vulgar eye—that he bears all things fairly
And shows good husbandry for the Volscian state,
Fights dragon-like, and does achieve as soon
As draw his sword, yet he hath left undone
25 That which shall break his neck or hazard mine
Whene'er we come to our account.
LIEUTENANT   Sir, I beseech you, think you he'll carry° Rome?   *defeat*
AUFIDIUS   All places yields to him ere he sits down,°   *lays siege*
And the nobility of Rome are his.
30 The senators and patricians love him too.
The tribunes are no soldiers, and their people
Will be as rash in the repeal° as hasty   *recall from exile*
To expel him thence. I think he'll be to Rome
As is the osprey to the fish, who takes it
35 By sovereignty of nature.[2] First he was
A noble servant to them, but he could not
Carry his honours even.° Whether 'twas pride,   *equably*
Which out of daily fortune[3] ever taints
The happy° man; whether defect of judgement,   *fortunate*
40 To fail in the disposing of those chances
Which he was lord of; or whether nature,
Not to be other than one thing, not moving
From th' casque° to th' cushion,° but commanding peace   *helmet / senate seat*
Even with the same austerity and garb°   *stern demeanor*
45 As he controlled the war: but one of these—
As he hath spices° of them all—not all,   *touches*
For I dare so far free him—made him feared,
So hated, and so banished. But he has a merit
To choke it in the utt'rance.[4] So our virtues
50 Lie in th'interpretation of the time,°   *contemporary observers*
And power, unto itself most commendable,
Hath not a tomb so evident as a chair
T'extol what it hath done.[5]
One fire drives out one fire, one nail one nail;
55 Rights by rights falter, strengths by strengths do fail.
Come, let's away. When, Caius, Rome is thine,
Thou art poor'st of all; then shortly art thou mine.   *Exeunt*

5.1

Enter MENENIUS, COMINIUS, SICINIUS, BRUTUS, *the two*
tribunes, with others
MENENIUS   No, I'll not go. You hear what he hath said
Which was sometime his general,° who loved him   *(Cominius)*
In a most dear particular.° He called me father,   *affectionate regard*
But what o' that? [*To the tribunes*] Go, you that banished him.
5 A mile before his tent fall down, and knee°   *crawl*

1. That is, with the Volscian state.
2. Fish were imagined to surrender to ospreys without a struggle.
3. As a result of repeated successes.
4. *he has . . . utt'rance*: his merit is so great that it overwhelms the recital of his faults; alternatively, his merit is of a kind that impedes attempts to praise it.

5. *Hath not . . . done*: a confusing passage, perhaps meaning, Will fall into certain oblivion unless it receives praise from the public rostrum; alternatively, is clearly ruined by public praise. In the first case, power requires reputation; in the second, reputation threatens power.
5.1 Location: A public place in Rome.

The way into his mercy. Nay, if he coyed°   *was reluctant*
To hear Cominius speak, I'll keep at home.
COMINIUS   He would not seem° to know me.   *pretended not*
MENENIUS [*to the tribunes*]   Do you hear?
COMINIUS   Yet one time he did call me by my name.
10   I urged our old acquaintance and the drops
That we have bled together. 'Coriolanus'
He would not answer to, forbade all names.
He was a kind of nothing, titleless,
Till he had forged himself a name o'th' fire
Of burning Rome.
MENENIUS [*to the tribunes*]
15   Why, so! You have made good work.
A pair of tribunes that have wracked° fair Rome   *destroyed*
To make coals cheap—a noble memory!°   *memorial*
COMINIUS   I minded him how royal 'twas to pardon
When it was less expected. He replied
20   It was a bare° petition of a state   *worthless; barefaced*
To one whom they had punished.
MENENIUS   Very well.
Could he say less?
COMINIUS   I offered° to awaken his regard   *tried*
For's private friends. His answer to me was
25   He could not stay to pick them in° a pile   *pick them out from*
Of noisome, musty chaff. He said 'twas folly,
For one poor grain or two, to leave unburnt
And still to nose° th'offence.   *smell*
MENENIUS   For one poor grain or two?
I am one of those. His mother, wife, his child,
30   And this brave fellow too—we are the grains.
[*To the tribunes*] You are the musty chaff, and you are smelt
Above the moon. We must be burnt for you.
SICINIUS   Nay, pray be patient. If you refuse your aid
In this so never-needed help, yet do not
35   Upbraid's with our distress. But sure, if you
Would be your country's pleader, your good tongue,
More than the instant army we can make,[1]
Might stop our countryman.
MENENIUS   No, I'll not meddle.
SICINIUS   Pray you go to him.
MENENIUS   What should I do?
40   BRUTUS   Only make trial what your love can do
For Rome towards Martius.
MENENIUS   Well, and say that Martius return me,
As Cominius is returned, unheard—what then?
But as a discontented friend, grief-shot°   *grief-stricken*
With his unkindness? Say't be so?
45   SICINIUS   Yet your good will
Must have that thanks from Rome after the measure
As° you intended well.   *To the extent that*
MENENIUS   I'll undertake't.
I think he'll hear me. Yet to bite his lip°   *(in anger)*
And 'hmh' at good Cominius much unhearts me.

1. The army we can raise right now.

50   He was not taken well,[2] he had not dined.
      The veins unfilled, our blood is cold, and then
      We pout upon the morning, are unapt
      To give or to forgive; but when we have stuffed
      These pipes and these conveyances° of our blood   *channels*
55   With wine and feeding, we have suppler souls
      Than in our priest-like fasts. Therefore I'll watch him
      Till he be dieted° to my request,   *made amenable by food*
      And then I'll set upon him.
BRUTUS   You know the very road into his kindness,
      And cannot lose your way.
60 MENENIUS   Good faith, I'll prove° him.   *try*
      Speed° how it will, I shall ere long have knowledge   *Turn out*
      Of my success.°   *Exit*   *whether I succeed*
COMINIUS   He'll never hear him.
SICINIUS   Not?
COMINIUS   I tell you, he does sit in gold, his eye
65   Red as 'twould burn Rome, and his injury[3]
      The jailer to his pity. I kneeled before him;
      'Twas very faintly he said 'Rise', dismissed me
      Thus with his speechless hand. What he would do
      He sent in writing after me, what he would not,
70   Bound with an oath to hold to his conditions.
      So that all hope is vain unless his noble mother
      And his wife, who as I hear mean to solicit him
      For mercy to his country. Therefore let's hence,
      And with our fair entreaties haste them on.   *Exeunt*

5.2

Enter MENENIUS to the Watch or guard

FIRST WATCHMAN   Stay. Whence are you?
SECOND WATCHMAN   Stand, and go back.
MENENIUS   You guard like men; 'tis well.
      But, by your leave, I am an officer
5   Of state, and come to speak with Coriolanus.
FIRST WATCHMAN   From whence?
MENENIUS   From Rome.
FIRST WATCHMAN   You may not pass, you must return.
      Our general will no more hear from thence.
SECOND WATCHMAN   You'll see your Rome embraced with fire before
      You'll speak with Coriolanus.
10 MENENIUS   Good my friends,
      If you have heard your general talk of Rome
      And of his friends there, it is lots to blanks°   *the odds are*
      My name hath touched your ears. It is Menenius.
FIRST WATCHMAN   Be it so; go back. The virtue° of your name   *power*
      Is not here passable.[1]
15 MENENIUS   I tell thee, fellow,
      Thy general is my lover.° I have been   *friend*
      The book° of his good acts, whence men have read   *recorder*
      His fame unparalleled happily amplified;

---

2. Not tackled at the right time.
3. The wrong inflicted on him.

5.2 Location: The Volscian camp near Rome.
1. Current (like a coin); effective (as a password).

For I have ever verified[2] my friends,

20 Of whom he's chief, with all the size° that verity   *amplitude*

Would without lapsing suffer.° Nay, sometimes,   *erring allow*

Like to a bowl upon a subtle° ground,   *misleading*

I have tumbled past the throw,[3] and in his praise

Have almost stamped the leasing.[4] Therefore, fellow,

25 I must have leave to pass.

FIRST WATCHMAN   Faith, sir, if you had told as many lies in his
behalf as you have uttered words in your own, you should not
pass here, no, though it were as virtuous to lie as to live
chastely.[5] Therefore go back.

30 MENENIUS   Prithee, fellow, remember my name is Menenius,
always factionary on° the party of your general.   *adherent to*

SECOND WATCHMAN   Howsoever you have been his liar, as you
say you have, I am one that, telling true under him, must say
you cannot pass. Therefore go back.

35 MENENIUS   Has he dined, canst thou tell? For I would not speak
with him till after dinner.

FIRST WATCHMAN   You are a Roman, are you?

MENENIUS   I am as thy general is.

FIRST WATCHMAN   Then you should hate Rome as he does. Can

40 you, when you have pushed out your gates the very defender of
them, and in a violent popular ignorance given your enemy
your shield, think to front° his revenges with the easy[6] groans   *confront*
of old women, the virginal palms of your daughters, or with the
palsied intercession of such a decayed dotant° as you seem to   *old fool*

45 be? Can you think to blow out the intended fire your city is
ready to flame in with such weak breath as this? No, you are
deceived, therefore back to Rome, and prepare for your execution. You are condemned, our general has sworn you out of
reprieve and pardon.

50 MENENIUS   Sirrah, if thy captain knew I were here, he would
use me with estimation.°   *esteem*

FIRST WATCHMAN   Come, my captain knows you not.

MENENIUS   I mean thy general.

FIRST WATCHMAN   My general cares not for you. Back, I say, go,

55 lest I let forth your half pint of blood. Back. That's the utmost
of your having.° Back.   *the most you'll get*

MENENIUS   Nay, but fellow, fellow—

Enter CORIOLANUS *with* AUFIDIUS

CORIOLANUS   What's the matter?

MENENIUS [*to* FIRST WATCHMAN]   Now, you companion,° I'll say   *knave*

60 an errand° for you. You shall know now that I am in estimation.   *deliver a message*
You shall perceive that a jack guardant° cannot office[7] me from   *uncouth guard*
my son Coriolanus. Guess but by my entertainment with him
if thou stand'st not i'th' state of hanging, or of some death more
long in spectatorship and crueller in suffering. Behold now

65 presently, and swoon for what's to come upon thee. [*To* CORIO-
LANUS] The glorious gods sit in hourly synod° about thy particu-   *council*
lar prosperity, and love thee no worse than thy old father
Menenius does! [*Weeping*] O, my son, my son, thou art prepar-

---

2. Testified to the character of.
3. Overshot the mark (from the game of bowls).
4. Authenticated falsehood.

5. Honestly (but playing on "lies with a sexual partner").
6. Easily obtained; insignificant.
7. Officiously keep.

ing fire for us. Look thee, here's water to quench it. I was
70 hardly° moved to come to thee, but being assured none but   *with difficulty*
myself could move thee, I have been blown out of our gates
with sighs, and conjure thee to pardon Rome and thy petition-
ary° countrymen. The good gods assuage thy wrath and turn   *suppliant*
the dregs of it upon this varlet here, this, who like a block° hath   *blockhead; obstruction*
75 denied my access to thee!

CORIOLANUS   Away!

MENENIUS   How? Away?

CORIOLANUS   Wife, mother, child, I know not. My affairs
Are servanted° to others. Though I owe   *subjected*
80 My revenge properly,[8] my remission° lies   *forgiveness*
In Volscian breasts. That we have been familiar,
Ingrate forgetfulness shall poison rather
Than pity note how much.[9] Therefore be gone.
Mine ears against your suits are stronger than
85 Your gates against my force. Yet, for° I loved thee,   *because*
    [*He gives him a letter*]
Take this along. I writ it for thy sake,
And would have sent it. Another word, Menenius,
I will not hear thee speak.—This man, Aufidius,
Was my beloved in Rome; yet thou behold'st.

90 AUFIDIUS   You keep a constant temper.

             Exeunt [CORIOLANUS *and* AUFIDIUS]

FIRST WATCHMAN   Now, sir, is your name Menenius?

SECOND WATCHMAN   'Tis a spell, you see, of much power. You
know the way home again.

FIRST WATCHMAN   Do you hear how we are shent° for keeping   *scolded*
95 your greatness back?

SECOND WATCHMAN   What cause do you think I have to swoon?

MENENIUS   I neither care for th' world nor your general. For
such things as you, I can scarce think there's any, you're so
slight. He that hath a will to die by himself° fears it not from   *at his own hand*
100 another. Let your general do his worst. For you, be that you are
long, and your misery increase with your age. I say to you as I
was said to, 'Away!'   *Exit*

FIRST WATCHMAN   A noble fellow, I warrant him.

SECOND WATCHMAN   The worthy fellow is our general. He's the
105 rock, the oak, not to be wind-shaken.   *Exeunt*

5.3

Enter CORIOLANUS *and* AUFIDIUS [*with Volscian soldiers.*
CORIOLANUS *and* AUFIDIUS *sit*]

CORIOLANUS   We will before the walls of Rome tomorrow
Set down our host.° My partner in this action,   *Lay siege with our forces*
You must report to th' Volscian lords how plainly
I have borne this business.

AUFIDIUS   Only their ends
5 You have respected, stopped your ears against
The general suit of Rome, never admitted

---

8. *owe . . . properly*: possess my own power of revenge.
9. *That we . . . much*: The memory of our friendship shall
be poisoned by Rome's (alternatively, my own) ungrateful
forgetfulness, rather than compassion be awakened by my
awareness of how intimate we were.
5.3 Location: The Volscian camp.

A private whisper, no, not with such friends
That thought them sure of you.

CORIOLANUS   This last old man,
Whom with a cracked heart I have sent to Rome,
10   Loved me above the measure of a father,
Nay, godded° me indeed. Their latest refuge°   *deified/last hope*
Was to send him, for whose old love I have—
Though I showed sourly to him—once more offered
The first conditions, which they did refuse
15   And cannot now accept, to grace him only
That thought he could do more. A very little
I have yielded to. Fresh embassies and suits,
Nor from the state nor private friends, hereafter
Will I lend ear to.
          Shout within
                    Ha, what shout is this?
20   Shall I be tempted to infringe my vow
In the same time 'tis made? I will not.
          Enter VIRGILIA, VOLUMNIA, VALERIA, YOUNG MARTIUS,
          with attendants
My wife comes foremost, then the honoured mould
Wherein this trunk° was framed, and in her hand   *body*
The grandchild to her blood. But out, affection!
25   All bond and privilege of nature break;
Let it be virtuous to be obstinate.
          [VIRGILIA *curtsies*]
What is that curtsy worth? Or those dove's eyes
Which can make gods forsworn? I melt, and am not
Of stronger earth than others.
          [VOLUMNIA *bows*]
                    My mother bows,
30   As if Olympus to a molehill should
In supplication nod; and my young boy
Hath an aspect of intercession° which   *pleading look*
Great nature cries 'Deny not'.—Let the Volsces
Plough Rome and harrow Italy! I'll never
35   Be such a gosling° to obey instinct, but stand   *(foolish) baby goose*
As if a man were author of himself
And knew no other kin.

VIRGILIA   My lord and husband.

CORIOLANUS   These eyes are not the same I wore in Rome.

VIRGILIA   The sorrow that delivers° us thus changed   *presents*
Makes you think so.
40   CORIOLANUS   Like a dull actor now
I have forgot my part, and I am out°   *at a loss*
Even to a full disgrace. [*Rising*] Best of my flesh,
Forgive my tyranny, but do not say
For that 'Forgive our Romans'.
          [VIRGILIA *kisses him*]
                    O, a kiss
45   Long as my exile, sweet as my revenge!
Now, by the jealous queen of heaven,¹ that kiss
I carried from thee, dear, and my true lip

1. Juno, queen of the gods and guardian of marriage.

Hath virgined it e'er since. You gods, I prate,
And the most noble mother of the world

50 Leave unsaluted! Sink, my knee, i'th' earth.
    [*He*] *kneels*
Of thy deep duty more impression° show   *indentation; effect*
Than that of common sons.
VOLUMNIA   O, stand up blest,
    [CORIOLANUS *rises*]
Whilst with no softer cushion than the flint
I kneel before thee, and unproperly°   *against propriety*

55 Show duty as mistaken all this while
Between the child and parent.
    [*She kneels*]
CORIOLANUS   What's this?
Your knees to me? To your corrected² son?
    [*He raises her*]
Then let the pebbles on the hungry beach
Fillip° the stars; then let the mutinous winds   *Strike against*

60 Strike the proud cedars 'gainst the fiery sun,
Murd'ring³ impossibility to make
What cannot be slight work.⁴
VOLUMNIA   Thou art my warrior.
I holp to frame° thee. Do you know this lady?   *helped to make*
CORIOLANUS   The noble sister of Publicola,

65 The moon° of Rome, chaste as the icicle   (*emblem of chastity*)
That's candied° by the frost from purest snow   *crystallized*
And hangs on Dian's⁵ temple—dear Valeria!
VOLUMNIA [*showing* CORIOLANUS *his son*]   This is a poor epitome°   *abridgment*
    of yours,
Which by th' interpretation of full time⁶
May show like all yourself.

70 CORIOLANUS [*to* YOUNG MARTIUS]   The god of soldiers,
With the consent of supreme Jove, inform
Thy thoughts with nobleness, that thou mayst prove
To shame unvulnerable, and stick° i'th' wars   *stand firm*
Like a great sea-mark standing every flaw⁷

75 And saving those that eye thee!
VOLUMNIA [*to* YOUNG MARTIUS]   Your knee, sirrah.
    [YOUNG MARTIUS *kneels*]
CORIOLANUS   That's my brave boy.
VOLUMNIA   Even he, your wife, this lady, and myself
Are suitors to you.
CORIOLANUS   I beseech you, peace.

80 Or if you'd ask, remember this before:
The things I have forsworn to grant may never
Be held by you denials.⁸ Do not bid me
Dismiss my soldiers, or capitulate°   *come to terms*
Again with Rome's mechanics.° Tell me not   *workmen*

85 Wherein I seem unnatural. Desire not t'allay
My rages and revenges with your colder reasons.
VOLUMNIA   O, no more, no more!

---

2. Rebuked (by Volumnia's irony).
3. Putting an end to the idea of.
4. An easy task of what cannot be.
5. Goddess of the moon and of chastity.

6. When time has clarified its full meaning.
7. Like a landmark at sea, withstanding every gust.
8. Be regarded by you as refusals.

You have said you will not grant us anything—
For we have nothing else to ask but that
90 Which you deny already. Yet we will ask,
That, if you fail in our request, the blame
May hang upon your hardness. Therefore hear us.

CORIOLANUS Aufidius and you Volsces, mark, for we'll
Hear naught from Rome in private.
        [He sits]
                                              Your request?

95 VOLUMNIA Should we be silent and not speak, our raiment
And state of bodies would bewray° what life   *divulge*
We have led since thy exile. Think with thyself
How more unfortunate than all living women
Are we come hither, since that thy sight, which should
100 Make our eyes flow with joy, hearts dance with comforts,
Constrains them weep and shake with fear and sorrow,
Making the mother, wife, and child to see
The son, the husband, and the father tearing
His country's bowels out; and to poor we
105 Thine enmity's most capital.° Thou barr'st us   *fatal*
Our prayers to the gods, which is a comfort
That all but we enjoy. For how can we,
Alas, how can we for our country pray,
Whereto we are bound, together with thy victory,
110 Whereto we are bound? Alack, or° we must lose   *either*
The country, our dear nurse, or else thy person,
Our comfort in the country. We must find
An evident° calamity, though we had   *A certain*
Our wish which side should win. For either thou
115 Must as a foreign recreant° be led   *traitor*
With manacles thorough our streets, or else
Triumphantly tread on thy country's ruin,
And bear the palm for having bravely shed
Thy wife and children's blood. For myself, son,
120 I purpose not to wait on fortune till
These wars determine.° If I cannot persuade thee   *conclude*
Rather to show a noble grace to both parts°   *sides*
Than seek the end of one, thou shalt no sooner
March to assault thy country than to tread—
125 Trust to't, thou shalt not—on thy mother's womb
That brought thee to this world.

VIRGILIA   Ay, and mine,
That brought you forth this boy to keep your name
Living to time.

YOUNG MARTIUS A° shall not tread on me.   *He*
I'll run away till I am bigger, but then I'll fight.

130 CORIOLANUS Not of a woman's tenderness to be
Requires nor child nor woman's face to see.[9]
I have sat too long.
        [He rises and turns away]

VOLUMNIA   Nay, go not from us thus.
If it were so that our request did tend
To save the Romans, thereby to destroy

---

9. *Not . . . see:* To avoid having a woman's tenderness, a man must not see a child's or woman's face.

135   The Volsces whom you serve, you might condemn us
      As poisonous of your honour. No, our suit
      Is that you reconcile them: while the Volsces
      May say 'This mercy we have showed', the Romans
      'This we received', and each in either side
140   Give the all-hail to thee and cry 'Be blest
      For making up this peace!' Thou know'st, great son,
      The end of war's uncertain; but this certain,
      That if thou conquer Rome, the benefit
      Which thou shalt thereby reap is such a name
145   Whose repetition will be dogged with curses,
      Whose chronicle thus writ:[1] 'The man was noble,
      But with his last attempt he wiped it out,
      Destroyed his country, and his name remains
      To th' ensuing age abhorred.' Speak to me, son.
150   Thou hast affected° the fine strains° of honour,   *cherished / qualities*
      To imitate the graces of the gods,
      To tear with thunder the wide cheeks o'th' air,
      And yet to charge thy sulphur[2] with a bolt
      That should but rive[3] an oak. Why dost not speak?
155   Think'st thou it honourable for a noble man
      Still° to remember wrongs? Daughter, speak you,   *Perpetually*
      He cares not for your weeping. Speak thou, boy.
      Perhaps thy childishness will move him more
      Than can our reasons. There's no man in the world
160   More bound to's mother, yet here he lets me prate
      Like one i'th' stocks.[4] Thou hast never in thy life
      Showed thy dear mother any courtesy,
      When she, poor hen, fond of° no second brood,   *desiring*
      Has clucked thee to the wars and safely home,
165   Loaden with honour. Say my request's unjust,
      And spurn me back. But if it be not so,
      Thou art not honest, and the gods will plague thee
      That thou restrain'st° from me the duty which   *withhold'st*
      To a mother's part belongs.—He turns away.
170   Down, ladies. Let us shame him with our knees.
      To his surname 'Coriolanus' 'longs° more pride   *belongs*
      Than pity to our prayers.[5] Down! An end.
      This is the last.
            [*The ladies and* YOUNG MARTIUS *kneel*]
                     So we will home to Rome,
      And die among our neighbours.—Nay, behold's.
175   This boy, that cannot tell what he would have,
      But kneels and holds up hands for fellowship,
      Does reason our petition with more strength
      Than thou hast to deny't.—Come, let us go.
      This fellow had a Volscian to his mother.
180   His wife is in Corioles, and this child
      Like him by chance.—Yet give us our dispatch.[6]

1. Whose biography will thus be written.
2. To discharge thy thunder (like Jove, king of the gods, whose tree was the oak).
3. Tear (destroy a tree, not human beings).
4. *prate . . . stocks*: rail pointlessly like a prisoner sentenced to public humiliation in the stocks.
5. Volumnia reinterprets the name as a sign of allegiance to Corioles.
6. Dismissal (with wordplay on "deathblow").

I am hushed until our city be afire,
And then I'll speak a little.
> [*He*] *holds her by the hand, silent*

CORIOLANUS   O mother, mother!
What have you done? Behold, the heavens do ope,
185   The gods look down, and this unnatural scene
They laugh at. O my mother, mother, O!
You have won a happy victory to Rome;
But for your son, believe it, O believe it,
Most dangerously you have with him prevailed,
190   If not most mortal to him. But let it come.
> [*The ladies and* YOUNG MARTIUS *rise*]

Aufidius, though I cannot make true° wars,   *(as I vowed)*
I'll frame convenient° peace. Now, good Aufidius,   *suitable*
Were you in my stead would you have heard
A mother less, or granted less, Aufidius?
AUFIDIUS   I was moved withal.°   *as well*
195 CORIOLANUS   I dare be sworn you were.
And, sir, it is no little thing to make
Mine eyes to sweat compassion. But, good sir,
What peace you'll make, advise me. For my part,
I'll not to Rome; I'll back with you, and pray you
200 Stand to° me in this cause.—O mother! Wife!   *by*
AUFIDIUS [*aside*]   I am glad thou hast set thy mercy and thy honour
At difference in thee. Out of that I'll work
Myself a former fortune.[7]
CORIOLANUS [*to* VOLUMNIA *and* VIRGILIA]   Ay, by and by.
But we will drink together, and you shall bear
205 A better witness back than words, which we
On like conditions will have counter-sealed.
Come, enter with us. Ladies, you deserve
To have a temple built you. All the swords
In Italy, and her confederate arms,
210 Could not have made this peace.   *Exeunt*

5.4

Enter MENENIUS *and* SICINIUS

MENENIUS   See you yon coign° o'th' Capitol, yon cornerstone?   *corner*
SICINIUS   Why, what of that?
MENENIUS   If it be possible for you to displace it with your little
finger, there is some hope the ladies of Rome, especially his
5   mother, may prevail with him. But I say there is no hope in't,
our throats are sentenced and stay upon° execution.   *wait for*
SICINIUS   Is't possible that so short a time can alter the condition°   *character*
of a man?
MENENIUS   There is differency between a grub and a butterfly,
10   yet your butterfly was a grub. This Martius is grown from man
to dragon. He has wings, he's more than a creeping thing.
SICINIUS   He loved his mother dearly.
MENENIUS   So did he me, and he no more remembers his
mother now than° an eight-year old horse. The tartness of his   *than does*
15   face sours ripe grapes. When he walks, he moves like an
engine,° and the ground shrinks before his treading. He is able   *war machine*

---

7. **work . . . fortune**: regain my former preeminence.   **5.4** Location: A public place in Rome.

to pierce a corslet° with his eye, talks like a knell, and his 'hmh!'   *armored shirt*
is a battery.° He sits in his state as a thing made for Alexander.[1]   *bombardment*
What he bids be done is finished with his bidding. He wants°   *lacks*
20   nothing of a god but eternity and a heaven to throne in.
SICINIUS   Yes: mercy, if you report him truly.
MENENIUS   I paint him in the character.° Mark what mercy his   *as he is*
    mother shall bring from him. There is no more mercy in him
    than there is milk in a male tiger. That shall our poor city find;
25   and all this is 'long° of you.   *on account*
SICINIUS   The gods be good unto us!
MENENIUS   No, in such a case the gods will not be good unto
    us. When we banished him we respected not them, and, he
    returning to break our necks, they respect not us.
        Enter a MESSENGER
30   MESSENGER [*to* SICINIUS]   Sir, if you'd save your life, fly to your house.
    The plebeians have got your fellow tribune
    And hale° him up and down, all swearing if   *drag*
    The Roman ladies bring not comfort home
    They'll give him death by inches.°   *little by little*
        Enter another MESSENGER
SICINIUS   What's the news?
35   SECOND MESSENGER   Good news, good news. The ladies have prevailed,
    The Volscians are dislodged,° and Martius gone.   *broken*
    A merrier day did never yet greet Rome,
    No, not th'expulsion of the Tarquins.
SICINIUS   Friend,
    Art thou certain this is true? Is't most certain?
40   SECOND MESSENGER   As certain as I know the sun is fire.
    Where have you lurked that you make doubt of it?
    Ne'er through an arch so hurried the blown° tide   *swollen*
    As the recomforted° through th' gates.   *reinvigorated*
        Trumpets, hautboys,° drums, beat all together   *oboes*
               Why, hark you,
    The trumpets, sackbuts, psalteries,° and fifes,   *trombones, zithers*
45   Tabors° and cymbals and the shouting Romans   *Drums*
    Make the sun dance.
        A shout within
            Hark you!
MENENIUS   This is good news.
    I will go meet the ladies. This Volumnia
    Is worth of consuls, senators, patricians,
    A city full; of tribunes such as you,
50   A sea and land full. You have prayed well today.
    This morning for ten thousand of your throats
    I'd not have given a doit.°   *small coin*
        [*Music*] *sound*[*s*] *still with the shouts*
            Hark how they joy!
SICINIUS [*to the* MESSENGER]   First, the gods bless you for your tidings. Next,
    [*Giving money*] Accept my thankfulness.
55   SECOND MESSENGER   Sir, we have all great cause to give great thanks.
SICINIUS   They are near the city.

---

1. Sits on his throne like a statue of Alexander the Great (who actually postdated Coriolanus).

SECOND MESSENGER   Almost at point to enter.
SICINIUS   We'll meet them, and help the joy.   *Exeunt*

5.5

Enter [at one door] Lords [and CITIZENS; *at another*
door] two SENATORS *with [the] ladies [*VOLUMNIA, VIR-
GILIA, *and* VALERIA,*] passing over the stage*

A SENATOR   Behold our patroness, the life of Rome!
  Call all your tribes together, praise the gods,
  And make triumphant fires.° Strew flowers before them.   *(of sacrifice)*
  Unshout the noise that banished Martius,
5 Repeal¹ him with the welcome of his mother.
  Cry 'Welcome, ladies, welcome!'
ALL   Welcome, ladies, welcome!
              A flourish with drums and trumpets. Exeunt

5.6

Enter Tullus AUFIDIUS *with attendants*
AUFIDIUS   Go tell the lords o'th' city I am here.
  Deliver them this paper. Having read it,
  Bid them repair to th' market-place, where I,
  Even in theirs and in the commons' ears,
5 Will vouch the truth of it. Him I accuse
  The city ports° by this° hath entered, and   *gates / this time*
  Intends t'appear before the people, hoping
  To purge himself with words. Dispatch.   *[Exeunt attendants]*
          Enter three or four CONSPIRATORS *of Aufidius' faction*
                          Most welcome.
FIRST CONSPIRATOR   How is it with our general?
AUFIDIUS   Even so
10 As with a man by his own alms impoisoned,
  And with his charity slain.
SECOND CONSPIRATOR   Most noble sir,
  If you do hold the same intent wherein
  You wished us parties,° we'll deliver you   *allies*
  Of° your great danger.   *From*
AUFIDIUS   Sir, I cannot tell.
15 We must proceed as we do find the people.
THIRD CONSPIRATOR   The people will remain uncertain whilst
  'Twixt you there's difference,° but the fall of either   *disagreement*
  Makes the survivor heir of all.
AUFIDIUS   I know it,
  And my pretext to strike at him admits
20 A good construction.° I raised him, and I pawned   *interpretation*
  Mine honour for his truth; who being so heightened,
  He watered his new plants¹ with dews of flattery,
  Seducing so my friends; and to this end
  He bowed his nature, never known before
25 But to be rough, unswayable, and free.
THIRD CONSPIRATOR   Sir, his stoutness°   *stubbornness*
  When he did stand for consul, which he lost
  By lack of stooping—

5.5 Location: Near the city gates of Rome.   5.6 Location: Corioles.
1. Recall him from banishment.   1. Followers (formerly Aufidius's adherents).

AUFIDIUS   That I would have spoke of.
    Being banished for't, he came unto my hearth,
30   Presented to my knife his throat. I took him,
    Made him joint-servant° with me, gave him way   *partner*
    In all his own desires; nay, let him choose
    Out of my files,° his projects to accomplish,   *troops*
    My best and freshest men; served his designments°   *plans*
35   In mine own person, holp to reap the fame
    Which he did end all his,[2] and took some pride
    To do myself this wrong, till at the last
    I seemed his follower, not partner, and
    He waged° me with his countenance° as if   *paid / appearance*
    I had been mercenary.
40 FIRST CONSPIRATOR   So he did, my lord.
    The army marvelled at it, and in the last,
    When he had carried° Rome and that we looked   *was about to vanquish*
    For no less spoil than glory—
AUFIDIUS   There was it,
    For which my sinews shall be stretched upon him.
45   At a few drops of women's rheum,° which are   *tears*
    As cheap as lies, he sold the blood and labour
    Of our great action; therefore shall he die,
    And I'll renew me in his fall.
           Drums and trumpets sound, with great shouts of the
           people
                 But hark.
FIRST CONSPIRATOR   Your native town you entered like a post,[3]
50   And had no welcomes home; but he returns
    Splitting the air with noise.
SECOND CONSPIRATOR   And patient fools,
    Whose children he hath slain, their base throats tear
    With giving him glory.
THIRD CONSPIRATOR   Therefore, at your vantage,°   *best opportunity*
    Ere he express himself or move the people
55   With what he would say, let him feel your sword,
    Which we will second. When he lies along,°   *prostrate*
    After your way° his tale pronounced shall bury   *In your version*
    His reasons with his body.
           Enter the LORDS *of the city*
AUFIDIUS   Say no more.
    Here come the lords.
60 ALL THE LORDS   You are most welcome home.
AUFIDIUS   I have not deserved it.
    But, worthy lords, have you with heed perused
    What I have written to you?
ALL THE LORDS   We have.
FIRST LORD   And grieve to hear't.
    What faults he made before the last, I think
65   Might have found easy fines.° But there to end   *light penalties*
    Where he was to begin, and give away
    The benefit of our levies,° answering us   *levied troops*

2. Which he did conclude was (or did finally make)   3. Messenger (bearing news of Coriolanus).
entirely his own.

With our own charge,[4] making a treaty where
There was a yielding—this admits no excuse.

70 AUFIDIUS   He approaches. You shall hear him.
          Enter CORIOLANUS *marching with drum and colors, the*
          Commoners being with him
     CORIOLANUS   Hail, lords! I am returned your soldier,
          No more infected with my country's love
          Than when I parted hence, but still subsisting
          Under your great command. You are to know
75   That prosperously[5] I have attempted, and
          With bloody passage led your wars even to
          The gates of Rome. Our spoils we have brought home
          Doth more than counterpoise a full third part[6]
          The charges of the action. We have made peace
80   With no less honour to the Antiates
          Than shame to th' Romans. And we here deliver,
          Subscribed by th' consuls and patricians,
          Together with the seal o'th' senate, what
          We have compounded° on.   agreed
               He gives the LORDS *a paper*
     AUFIDIUS   Read it not, noble lords,
85   But tell the traitor in the highest degree
          He hath abused your powers.
     CORIOLANUS   Traitor? How now?
     AUFIDIUS   Ay, traitor, Martius.
     CORIOLANUS   Martius?
90   AUFIDIUS   Ay, Martius, Caius Martius. Dost thou think
          I'll grace thee with that robbery, thy stol'n name,
          'Coriolanus', in Corioles?
          You lords and heads o'th' state, perfidiously
          He has betrayed your business, and given up,
95   For certain drops of salt,° your city, Rome—   (tears)
          I say your city—to his wife and mother,
          Breaking his oath and resolution like
          A twist° of rotten silk, never admitting   thread
          Counsel o'th' war.[7] But at his nurse's tears
100   He whined and roared away your victory,
          That pages[8] blushed at him, and men of heart°   courage
          Looked wond'ring each at others.
     CORIOLANUS   Hear'st thou, Mars?
     AUFIDIUS   Name not the god, thou boy of tears.
     CORIOLANUS   Ha?
     AUFIDIUS   No more.
     CORIOLANUS   Measureless liar, thou hast made my heart
105   Too great for what contains it. 'Boy'? O slave!—
          Pardon me, lords, 'tis the first time that ever
          I was forced to scold. Your judgements, my grave lords,
          Must give this cur the lie, and his own notion°—   awareness of the truth
          Who wears my stripes° impressed upon him, that   wounds

---

4. *answering . . . charge:* rewarding us with our own costs
(of mounting the campaign); answering accusations by
saying that he acted on our authority.
5. Successfully; with gain of wealth.

6. Outweighs by more than a third.
7. *admitting . . . war:* taking any advice about the war.
8. Youthful servants.

110 Must bear my beating to his grave—shall join
To thrust° the lie unto him.   *turn the accusation of*
FIRST LORD   Peace both, and hear me speak.
CORIOLANUS   Cut me to pieces, Volsces. Men and lads,
Stain all your edges° on me. 'Boy'! False hound,   *sword blades*
If you have writ your annals true, 'tis there
115 That, like an eagle in a dove-cote,° I   *pigeon house*
Fluttered your Volscians in Corioles.
Alone I did it. 'Boy'!
AUFIDIUS   Why, noble lords,
Will you be put in mind of his blind⁹ fortune,
Which was your shame, by this unholy braggart,
Fore your own eyes and ears?
120 ALL THE CONSPIRATORS   Let him die for't.
ALL THE PEOPLE [*shouting dispersedly*]   Tear him to pieces! Do
it presently!°   *immediately*
He killed my son! My daughter! He killed my cousin
Marcus! He killed my father!
SECOND LORD   Peace, ho! No outrage,° peace.   *violence*
The man is noble, and his fame folds in°   *envelops*
125 This orb o'th' earth. His last offences to us
Shall have judicious hearing. Stand,° Aufidius,   *Hold off*
And trouble not the peace.
CORIOLANUS [*drawing his sword*]   O that I had him with six Aufidiuses,
Or more, his tribe, to use my lawful sword!
AUFIDIUS [*drawing his sword*]   Insolent villain!
130 ALL THE CONSPIRATORS   Kill, kill, kill, kill, kill him!
[*Two*] CONSPIRATORS *draw and kill* MARTIUS, *who falls.*
AUFIDIUS [*and* CONSPIRATORS] *stand on him*
LORDS   Hold, hold, hold, hold!
AUFIDIUS   My noble masters, hear me speak.
FIRST LORD   O Tullus!
SECOND LORD [*to* AUFIDIUS]   Thou hast done a deed whereat
Valour will weep.
THIRD LORD [*to* AUFIDIUS *and the* CONSPIRATORS]
Tread not upon him, masters.
All be quiet. Put up your swords.
135 AUFIDIUS   My lords,
When you shall know—as in this rage
Provoked by him you cannot—the great danger
Which this man's life did owe° you, you'll rejoice   *hold in store for*
That he is thus cut off. Please it your honours
140 To call me to your senate, I'll deliver°   *show*
Myself your loyal servant, or endure
Your heaviest censure.
FIRST LORD   Bear from hence his body,
And mourn you for him. Let him be regarded
As the most noble corpse that ever herald
Did follow to his urn.
145 SECOND LORD   His own impatience
Takes from Aufidius a great part of blame.
Let's make the best of it.
AUFIDIUS   My rage is gone,

9. Random (fortune was commonly personified as blind).

And I am struck with sorrow. Take him up.
Help three o'th' chiefest soldiers; I'll be one.
150   Beat thou the drum, that it speak mournfully.
Trail your steel pikes. Though in this city he
Hath widowed and unchilded many a one,
Which to this hour bewail the injury,
Yet he shall have a noble memory.° Assist.   memorial

A dead march sounded. Exeunt
bearing the body of Martius

The Winter's Tale

In his induction to *Bartholomew Fair* (1614), Ben Jonson complained of plays that "make Nature afraid" and "beget Tales, Tempests, and such like Drolleries." His remarks seem aimed directly at his contemporary William Shakespeare, who, in the last years of his theatrical career, had written a number of plays, including *The Winter's Tale* (1609–11) and *The Tempest* (1611), that by some accounts might be said to "make Nature afraid." Jonson implies that such plays, eschewing realism, present fantastic or impossible events that defy the laws of nature. While Jonson found such concoctions unpalatable, most of Shakespeare's contemporaries did not. In prose romances popular throughout the period, characters regularly undertake impossible quests, encounter marvels, and are unexpectedly reunited with lost children. Shakespeare's late plays participate fully in this taste for the marvelous, reveling in, rather than being embarrassed by, the strange and the improbable. In the case of *The Winter's Tale*, we possess a rather full description of the play by Simon Forman, a London astrologer and doctor, who saw it performed on May 15, 1611, and described its complicated plot with no hint that he found either its events absurd or the play defective. On the contrary, Forman's detailed description suggests him to have been fully absorbed by what he saw. Concluding with an account of the deceptive tricks of the play's rogue, Autolycus, Forman moralized: "Beware trusting feigned beggars or fawning fellows."

Modern editors often group *Pericles*, *The Winter's Tale*, *Cymbeline*, and *The Tempest* together under the label "romances," although this is not a category used in the Folio (1623). There Shakespeare's plays are divided into comedies, tragedies, and histories. *Pericles* is not included in the Folio; *Cymbeline* is placed at the end of the tragedies; *The Tempest* appears as the first of the comedies and *The Winter's Tale* as the last. These placements are suggestive of the mixed tragicomic nature of these particular dramas. Like Shakespeare's earlier comedies, they all end happily, with families reunited and marriages in prospect; but the late plays also engage with the tragic dimensions of human life to a degree not customary for the early comedies. Before the characters in these plays reach safe harbor, they encounter tyranny, incest, the loss of wives and children, and the treachery of brothers. The protagonists suffer intensely, both because of fortune's blows and because of their own folly. Only by what is experienced as miracle does tragedy turn to mirth and suffering cease. While the miraculous quality of these reversals binds these plays together as a group, it is also at the heart of Jonson's objections. Improbable occurrences and unexpected transformations of sorrow into joy can affront sober common sense, but they also make romance emotionally and theatrically appealing. In defiance of probability, these plays construct a world in which (at least for some fortunate characters) second chances are possible.

By its very title *The Winter's Tale* signals its affiliations with popular storytelling. Within the play, Mamillius, the King of Sicilia's young son, informs his mother that "a sad tale's best for winter" (2.1.27) and offers to tell her one "of sprites and goblins" (2.1.28). The only sprites and goblins in Shakespeare's play turn out to be the internal demons of jealousy and suspicion that erupt in the mind of its protagonist, King Leontes, but *The Winter's Tale* is permeated by sadness, even during its festive conclusion, and its plot is full of wonders. Its starting point is King Leontes' sudden certainty that his wife, Hermione, is pregnant not with his own child, but with that of his childhood friend, King Polixenes of Bohemia, a visitor at Leontes' Sicilian court. Warned of Leontes' jealousy, Polixenes flees back to Bohemia, leaving the King to vent his wrath on Hermione. Imprisoned, she gives birth to a daughter, Perdita, whom Leontes orders

In the early seventeenth century, popular pamphlet literature circulated sensational stories of parents, especially unmarried women, who murdered or abandoned their children. In this title page from *The Bloudy Mother* (1609), a serving woman and her master bury the illegitimate child she has killed. On the right, for his part in begetting and disposing of the child, the master is consumed by lice and worms.

to be abandoned in the countryside far from Sicilia. Even when the oracle of Apollo subsequently declares Hermione innocent, Leontes continues to insist on her guilt. As he does, the death of his only son, Mamillius, is announced, and Hermione appears to die of grief. The first three acts of *The Winter's Tale* thus enact a miniature tragedy (not unlike Shakespeare's tragedy of the jealous Othello) in which Leontes' actions result in the loss of wife, daughter, and son. His personal tragedy also affects his kingdom. The oracle proclaims: "the King shall live without an heir if that which is lost be not found" (3.2.133–34). A kingdom without an heir to the throne is a kingdom in danger.

But then something extraordinary happens. The character Time appears onstage, informing the audience that sixteen years have passed and that Perdita, abandoned on the seacoast of Bohemia, has survived. Suddenly, instead of the wintry world of Leontes' Sicilian court, the play bursts with the energies of a Bohemian summer. The

Old Shepherd who rescued Perdita is about to hold a sheepshearing festival, and Florizel, King Polixenes' son, has fallen in love with Perdita. A series of extraordinary events returns the young couple to Leontes' court, where Perdita's true status as his child and heir is revealed. More wonders follow. Taken to see what they believe to be a statue of the long-dead Hermione, the King and his newly recovered daughter witness the seeming miracle of the statue's transformation into flesh and blood.

Shakespeare's chief source for this tale was Robert Greene's popular prose romance *Pandosto*, first published in 1588. Greene provided Shakespeare with the story of a jealous King who loses Queen and daughter but eventually has his daughter restored to him. But the differences between Shakespeare's play and Greene's prose tale are as striking as the similarities. For example, Shakespeare carefully changed the names of most of the characters he borrowed from Greene. In *Pandosto*, the King's lost daughter is Fawnia, but Shakespeare names her Perdita, a word that in Latin means "that which is lost." In Shakespeare's hands, Perdita's lover ceases to be Dorastus and becomes, instead, Florizel, which suggests the young prince's connection with the flowers of spring. Greene's protagonist, Pandosto, is transformed into Leontes, evoking the leonine or lionlike nature of his wrath. Shakespeare also reversed the kingdoms ruled by Greene's Kings. In *Pandosto*, the protagonist is King of Bohemia and his childhood friend rules Sicilia. In *The Winter's Tale*, the reverse is true, and one reason may be the association of Sicilia with the myth of Proserpina, the beautiful daughter of Ceres abducted by Dis, the god of the underworld, as she was picking flowers. Her mother attempted to free Proserpina, but she was allowed to return to the upper world only six months of each year. During that period, spring and summer came to the earth, but winter reigned when Proserpina returned to Dis's kingdom. The sixteen years of mourning Leontes undergoes in Perdita's absence provide a counterpart to aspects of this myth.

Shakespeare, however, made much larger changes in Greene's romance. For example, he enhanced the role of Leontes' son, who is barely mentioned by Greene; he added the characters of Paulina, Emilia, Antigonus, Autolycus, Clown, Time, and rustics such as Dorcas and Mopsa (in *Pandosto*, Mopsa was the name of the Old Shepherd's wife; in *The Winter's Tale*, that wife is long dead). The magnificent sheepshearing festival is Shakespeare's invention; nothing like it exists in *Pandosto*. Most importantly, Greene's romance ends on a tragic note. Although the King and his daughter are finally reunited, Pandosto's wife is never restored to him, and overcome with desire for his grown daughter, he attempts incest and later takes his own life.

Shakespeare clearly saw in Greene's grim tale the basis for a much more resonant narrative of loss and redemption. The play is a diptych of winter and summer, hinged by the appearance of Time. It is probably a mistake to account for this structure by using only one interpretive framework, for the play's elegant simplicity resonates with many narratives of renewal. Some have read the play in Christian terms, seeing Leontes as a sinner who, after a period of suffering and repentance, receives the gift of God's grace through the return of his daughter and the Christlike resurrection of his wife. The play loosely traces the liturgical calendar, moving from the hospitality associated with Christmas to the Lenten period of deprivation and repentance to the joyous celebration of Easter and the Maying festivals associated with Whitsuntide, which occurs seven weeks after Easter. Other critics have stressed the mythic qualities of the play, its resemblance, for example, to the myth of Proserpina, or to fertility rites in which the coming of spring and sexual fulfillment depend on the sacrifice of a figure, usually an old King, associated with winter. In *The Winter's Tale*, Leontes does not die, but he does mourn for sixteen years; and his servant Antigonus, who takes the babe to Bohemia and there names her Perdita, becomes Leontes' sacrificial substitute. Once he has deposited Perdita, Antigonus is mauled and eaten by a bear. As the Old Shepherd who rescues Perdita says to his son, who has witnessed this death, "Thou metst with things dying, I with things new-born" (3.3.104–05), the latter event seemingly dependent on the former. Other critics stress the pattern of generational renewal informing the play as the sins of the father, Leontes, give way to the innocent goodness of Florizel and Perdita. In some productions, the actress playing Hermione also plays Perdita (although a double for one of them usually has to be employed in the statue scene when they are both on stage together), deepening the sense that it is through their children that parents have a second life. Resonating with all these interpretive paradigms, *The Winter's Tale* draws richly on the many narratives and structures of belief through which Western culture has produced and sustained its desire for transcendence and renewal.

In modern productions, the symbolic power of the play's diptych structure is often highlighted by contrasts in the costumes and sets used to distinguish Sicilia and Bohemia. Sicilia, for example, is often a snow kingdom, dominated by white clothing and metallic props; Bohemia is a summer kingdom, the stage carpeted in green, the characters at the sheepshearing festival a riot of variegated colors. When the Bohemian party comes to Sicilia, the winter landscape is literally overwritten with the colorful clothes associated with Whitsuntide.

The play, however, is not simply about the triumph of the young, the rebirth of a world of possibility. *The Winter's Tale,* as befits a tragicomedy, moves from sorrow to joy, but that joy is bittersweet. However important the younger generation is to this old tale, the focus in this and the other romances stays resolutely on the older generation. It is Leontes who sins and must repent, Leontes whose family is reconstituted. Crucially, that reconstitution is only partial and imperfect. Mamillius, the young son, dies, the ultimate sacrifice to Leontes' tyrannous actions; and in the play's last scene, the playwright is at pains to stress that the "statue" of Hermione has wrinkles, the mark of time on her body. Traduced while a fertile wife and mother, Hermione returns as a woman past childbearing. Time, whose appearance marks the hinge of the play, may heal old sorrows and bring new births to pass, but it also shuts down possibilities and destroys youth and strength. The ending of Shakespeare's old tale induces wonder and joy, but it cannot make an old man young or erase all the consequences of rash deeds. Shakespeare's late plays achieve their rich emotional effects from the deep strains of melancholia that underwrite their measured celebrations of the return of love and hope to a chastened social order.

Nor, despite the archaic quality that permeates these plays, are they simple enactments of timeless patterns and narratives. The precipitating event of the play—the eruption of Leontes' jealousy—is a symptom of the faultlines in a particular patriarchal culture. Often said to be "irrational," this jealousy in actuality has its roots in the cultural practices that in Jacobean England made men the heads of families, lineages, and kingdoms, but at the same time made them crucially dependent on women's reproductive powers to generate legitimate heirs. As *The Winter's Tale* opens, Leontes asks Polixenes to extend his stay in Sicilia. Polixenes refuses, but when Hermione entreats him, he agrees. This event, and the sight of his pregnant wife conversing with his friend and holding him by the hand, triggers in Leontes so deep a suspicion of his wife's fidelity that he plans to have Polixenes killed and doubts the legitimacy of his son as well. In part, what disturbs Leontes is the unknowability of the biological origins of his children. Men theoretically had dominion over their wives, but as Leontes says, "No barricado for a belly" (1.2.205)—that is, no absolute defense of a woman's chastity but her own honor, and that lies in her control, not her husband's.

A deep ambivalence toward women and sexuality, moreover, surfaces earlier in the same scene when, reminiscing about his boyhood friendship with Leontes, Polixenes describes the two of them as twinned lambs who experienced a fall from paradise only when they felt sexual passion and had their first encounters with women. In this conversation, the two men echo a strand of early modern thought that viewed men's friendships with men as of greater worth than what were seen as men's more dangerous and unpredictable relations with women, an idea examined as early in Shakespeare's work as *The Two Gentlemen of Verona.* Construed as physically imperfect and as intellectually inferior to men, women were supposedly ruled by their passions and could in turn evoke dangerous and degrading emotions in men. Yet men were enjoined to marry these irrational creatures to procreate and to continue family lineage. Leontes' rage at Hermione seems to stem in part from his dependence on her to give him legitimate heirs.

Other tensions permeate the opening scenes. If in their younger days Polixenes and Leontes were like twinned lambs, in adulthood their friendship is tinged with competitiveness, with Hermione gradually becoming the focus of their rivalry. Polixenes' attendant Archidamus opens the play expressing uneasiness about repaying the generous hospitality provided by Leontes and suggesting rivalry as well as friendship between the two kingdoms; in 1.2 Leontes asks Polixenes if he loves *his* son as dearly as Leontes loves Mamillius, again suggesting competitiveness between the two Kings at the level of paternal affection for their sons. In this general context of subterranean rivalry, Leontes' command that Hermione entreat Polixenes to stay not only expresses his ostentatious generosity (he will even share his wife's attentions with his friend), but also calls forth his rivalrous jealousy (perhaps his friend has taken advantage of his generosity and assumed Leontes' place in Hermione's bed).

Once his jealousy has been triggered, Leontes gives the rein to a deadly rage that finds its chief object in Hermione's pregnant body. This anger is played out in part through Leontes' increasing identification with his young son, Mamillius. In Mamillius, Leontes sees himself as he once was, a young boy not yet wearing either the breeches or the sharp phallic dagger associated with adult manhood (1.2.157–58). It is an image of innocence but also of vulnerability. The name Mamillius, another of Shakespeare's brilliant inventions, suggests one source of that vulnerability. *Mamilla* is the word for the nipple on a breast or a diminutive form of *mamma*, the Latin word for the breast itself. His name thus connects Mamillius to the lactating breast and to the world of women, who in early modern culture presided over childbirth and the early years of children's lives. In a culture in which baby formula did not exist, infants depended utterly on women, either wet nurses or mothers, to provide the crucial sustenance, breast milk. As was often true of women from the upper class, Hermione does not herself seem to have nursed Mamillius. As Leontes bitterly exclaims: "I am glad you did not nurse him" (2.1.58). Nonetheless, the young boy's name and his appearance in 2.1 with his pregnant mother and her waiting women clearly associate him with the feminine sphere of birth, lactation, and early childhood. In identifying with Mamillius, a boy so young his nurse's milk is scarcely out of him, Leontes seems to feel both the vulnerability of the infant dependent on the lactating body of woman and the vulnerability of the adult husband dependent on the pregnant body and the chastity of his wife for legitimate offspring. As if to deny these dependencies, Leontes banishes Mamillius from his mother's presence, and he banishes Hermione to prison. Mamillius dies; Leontes appears to lose all that would link him to the future: wife, son, daughter.

The Winter's Tale makes Leontes a dangerous tyrant in Acts 1 to 3 and portrays his anger and paranoia as forces that torture his speech and profoundly isolate him. In the first three acts, Leontes' most characteristic action is to turn away from those who love or attempt to help him. He sends his wife to prison; casts out his infant daughter; refuses the good counsel of his courtiers; rages in misogynistic fury at Paulina, who brings Perdita to him from prison; and finally defies the oracle of Apollo. Lacking trust in his wife and in all those around him, Leontes condemns himself to deathlike isolation. As in Shakespeare's other late plays, much of the language of *The Winter's Tale* is difficult and dense. Normal word order is inverted; speeches begin and end in the middle of a line; figurative language is given elliptical expression. During his period of intense jealousy, Leontes' language becomes even more dense and compressed than is typical of the rest of the play. Looking at his son, he exclaims:

> Can thy dam—may't be?—
> Affection, thy intention stabs the centre.
> Thou dost make possible things not so held,
> Communicat'st with dreams—how can this be?—

With what's unreal thou coactive art,
And fellow'st nothing. Then 'tis very credent
Thou mayst co-join with something, and thou dost—
And that beyond commission; and I find it—
And that to the infection of my brains
And hard'ning of my brows.

(1.2.139–48)

In this difficult passage, Leontes wrestles with the knowledge that his "affection" (the passions of rage, jealousy, and suspicion released in him) wounds him and perhaps leads him to imagine things to be true that are not. On the other hand, his suspicions *may* be justified; he may already be a cuckold. In this horrible state of uncertainty, Leontes' speech verges on incoherence. He interrupts the flow of his own thoughts with questions and ejaculations; his mind darts from boy to mother to his own pain; he realizes he may be wrong, but returns, obsessively, to the coarse and shameful image of his forehead disfigured with the horns of a cuckold.

The inner disorder suggested by this language finds its outward manifestation in Leontes' increasingly tyrannical actions. In the early modern period, the ruler of a king-

In the early modern period, childbirth was largely the affair of women. In this picture from Jakob Rüff's *De conceptu et generatione hominis* (Concerning the conception and birth of man) (1580), several women attend to a woman in labor while, in the background, two men cast the child's horoscope.

dom was often compared to the head of a family. Good order in the commonwealth had its foundation in a well-ordered domestic realm. In *The Winter's Tale*, Leontes oversteps his just authority in both domains, refusing to take counsel from his courtiers, defying the gods, and condemning his wife for adultery with no evidence but his own suspicions. Nowhere, however, does he more certainly exceed his patriarchal authority than when he orders Hermione to stand trial before the proper period of her lying-in has passed. In the Renaissance, childbirth was recognized as an event both important and dangerous. Women gave birth surrounded by other women, usually a hired midwife, as well as by neighbors and female family members. The laboring female body, opened to let the child pass into the world, was considered to be in a particularly vulnerable state, needing to be protected from the unhealthful air that might enter the open womb. Consequently, birthing took place in a closed chamber, and after birth had occurred, women lay in their chambers for an extended period, recovering strength and purging their bodies of the blood and other fluids associated with pregnancy. At the end of this period, often lasting a month but sometimes longer, the woman came out of her house and returned to her normal routines. This occasion was marked by a "churching" ceremony, a rite of purification and celebration in which thanks were given for the safe delivery of a child and the woman's body declared cleansed of the impurities of pregnancy and birth.

When Hermione is made to stand trial, the pathos of her dignified defense of herself is heightened by her weakened state. In many productions, she appears on stage unattended, almost unable to stand. Among the wrongs done her, she accuses Leontes of having "with immodest hatred / The childbed privilege denied, which 'longs / To women of all fashion; lastly, hurried / Here, to this place, i'th' open air, before / I have got strength of limit" (3.2.100–04). Leontes' fury against the maternal body extends to denying that body the privileges of the lying-in period and exposing it to the dangers of the open air of a public place. This is domestic tyranny of a hideous sort.

After such cruelty, what recovery? Bohemia seems to be the place of hope in the play, and that feeling is conveyed in part by the vast expansion of character and event in that pastoral locale. After the claustrophobic focus on Leontes, the action unfolds to encompass the tricks of a wily rogue, Autolycus (whose name links him to the Autolycus of classical mythology, a crafty thief and grandfather of Ulysses; Autolycus's own father, Mercury, was the god of thieves); the sports of a sheepshearing festival; the courtship of Florizel and Perdita; and the intrigues that take many of these players back to Sicilia. The scene depicting the festival at the Old Shepherd's farm, 4.4, is one of the longest in Shakespeare's canon (810 lines), is entirely his own invention, and is a great feast of languages and events. It includes the singing of ballads, a dance of twelve satyrs, Perdita's lyrical catalog of the flowers appropriate to each stage of life, and the painful moment when Polixenes forbids his son's marriage.

As this last moment shows, although Bohemia is a place of healing, it is not a paradise. In Bohemia, "great creating nature" for a time replaces Apollo as the deity who presides over the action. The fertility of the earth and, by extension, the fertility of woman may here seem to be redeemed from the curse laid upon them by Leontes' suspicion of his wife; and Florizel's staunch commitment to Perdita in the face of mounting obstacles to their love augers well. But Polixenes just as staunchly opposes their union, threatening to use his patriarchal power in a way that, as with Leontes, would separate him from his son and from the possibility of future lineage. Bohemia also contains the rogue Autolycus, picking the pockets of country bumpkins and hiding his identity by a series of disguises. Further, Bohemian life is marked by enormous disparities of wealth. The Old Shepherd is rich, in part because of the money he found with Perdita. For the sheepshearing feast, Perdita can afford ingredients—raisins, rice, and spices, for example—that were exotic luxury goods, foodstuffs in excess of the subsistence diet of bread, beer, and cheese that was still the staple for many. It also possible that some of the Old Shepherd's wealth comes from the new profitability of raising sheep. Throughout the sixteenth and seventeenth centuries, land was increasingly enclosed—that is,

In this late seventeenth-century woodcut from the Pepysian collection of early modern ballads, a peddler carries a huge pack and holds several rabbits, or conies, which suggests that he is also a cony-catcher—that is, a con man (like Autolycus), whose victims were popularly called conies.

fenced off for grazing sheep rather than available for communal use in raising food and feeding cattle. These enclosures were popularly blamed for perceived increases in rural poverty and for the creation of masterless men, poor folk who roamed the countryside without fixed places of residence and who were believed to feign sickness or deformity in order to enforce charity from those they met. Autolycus, pretending to have lost his clothes to a highwayman, is a comic version of such a masterless man, yet his presence in the play, juxtaposed to that of the rich shepherd, is a reminder of the social tensions and economic stratifications that permeate the rural landscape with widespread enclosures and other changes in rural life.

Bohemia is also the locale of one of the great set pieces of the play—the debate between Polixenes and Perdita concerning the relative values of art and nature and the relationship between them. This was an ancient debate and one that could give off a decidedly musty odor, even though it was dusted off by a number of Shakespeare's contemporaries. At the heart of this debate lay the question of artifice. Was it a good thing? Did it distort or enhance nature? Given the imperfections of the fallen world and humankind's weaknesses, could art be instrumental in calling into being a better world, or was it merely a temptation to pride or to competition with the divine creator? The refreshing thing about the handling of these issues in *The Winter's Tale* is that the play comes to no abstract resolution concerning them. Rather, it encases the actual debate between Polixenes and Perdita in multiple ironies, and it complexly connects this debate to the actions of characters who seemingly have no involvement with it. For Perdita, product of the pastoral landscape, art is a bad thing. She wants no grafted or hybrid flowers in her garden. Yet even as she speaks her condemnation of art, Perdita is reluctantly dressed as Queen of the sheepshearing feast, a bit of artifice that reveals a truth she herself cannot know: namely, that she is a Queen's daughter. Polixenes, for his part, champions art, declaring that the practice of mixing wild and cultivated plants produces sturdy hybrids and that the art of grafting is itself a gift of nature. Yet when his son wishes to graft himself to a shepherd's daughter, Polixenes finds such a practice abhorrent.

Besides making the obvious point that people don't always act on their stated beliefs, this exchange shows the extreme pressure the play puts on the art-nature dichotomy. In Perdita's case, her "natural" condition as princess is revealed only by means of two kinds of artifice: her dress as Queen of the feast and the role Camillo creates for her as Florizel's Libyan Princess when he devises a way for the two young lovers to return to Leontes' court. Camillo even goes so far as to provide lines for the two to speak. His goal is ameliorative: to satisfy the desires of the young (as well as his own deep longings to again see his homeland) and to heal the breach between the two dissevered kingdoms. The point seems to be not whether in some abstract sense "art" violates "nature," but how artfulness, defined broadly as the representation of the world through painting, statuary, plays, and song, can open new possibilities for imagining what nature is or could be.

This is not an inconsequential point, for in the badly flawed world depicted in *The Winter's Tale* art gradually emerges as one of the resources people can use, either badly or well, to affect the world around them: to correct old mistakes and to forge new realities. Its effects are determined and limited, of course, by the skill and intentions of the artist and by the receptiveness of the audience. Autolycus is a subversive con man who uses disguises and deceptions to fleece money from gulls. By contrast, in the play's final movement, Paulina emerges as the chief representative of the ameliorative artist who uses her skills to make better the world around her. Once reviled by Leontes as a witch, Paulina becomes the King's spiritual guide in the last half of the play (her name linking her to the New Testament evangelist, St. Paul). This strikingly outspoken woman spends sixteen years preparing Leontes to be a fit spectator to the tableau of resurrection and renewal enacted in the last scene. When she had first brought the infant to Leontes from prison, Paulina had seemed to believe in the self-evident nature of truth. Laying the babe at Leontes' feet, she proclaimed that the "good goddess Nature" (2.3.104) had made it an exact copy of the father. Leontes had only to read what nature had written in the face of his child. But distorting jealousy and rage at his wife had bleared the King's vision. He would not or could not see himself in the female child he had fathered. So for sixteen years Paulina worked another way, fueling Leontes' remorse and artfully withholding both from him and from the theater audience the knowledge that Hermione lived. When the disguised Princess returns to Sicilia, Leontes gets a second chance. Looking at Perdita, he is finally able to see—not so much himself as the unslandered image of his wife in the young girl before him. Having admired Perdita, Leontes says to Paulina, "I thought of her [Hermione] / Even in these looks I made" (5.1.226–27). When he can believe in the potential goodness of women, and specifically in the chastity of the young woman who is the simulacrum of his wife, then Leontes can help to create the reality in which Perdita is truly a Princess and his wife a living being rather than the corpse into which his rage and distrust had transformed her.

The statue scene itself is one of the most moving dramatic moments in any of Shakespeare's plays. Like Leontes, the untutored audience does not know that Hermione lives. Consequently, under Paulina's careful guidance, the spectators both onstage and off seem to participate in willing the statue into life. When Hermione descends from her pedestal, the audience can feel itself present at the miraculous resurrection of the dead. In theological terms, this scene touches on controversial matters. Protestants repudiated what they characterized as Catholic idolatry, which involved the veneration of images, including statues of the Virgin Mary. Protestants, by contrast, typically stressed the ear over the eye, words over images, faith over works. In the wake of the Reformation, more radical Protestants went so far as to smash stained-glass windows and the statues of saints that had for many centuries adorned Catholic churches. The final moments of *The Winter's Tale* gesture toward this repudiated world of images and their veneration. While Paulina insists that the audience awaken its faith, she does so in a scene that is visually organized to focus all eyes on a statue that in its chapel setting might well evoke memories of prior Catholic practices. In his characteristic way, Shakespeare seems to have things two ways: drawing on the emotional power of Catholic rituals centered on the image, he simultaneously suggests that there is no statue on the stage at all, only a living woman roused to new vigor by the recovery of a long-lost daughter.

However ambiguous the theological implications of the final scene, ultimately the old tale ends happily, or mostly so. At the end of the play, patriarchy has been reformed, but its potential for abuses has hardly been eradicated. In the final scene, the highly charged image of the pregnant female body is nowhere to be seen. Perdita is not yet a wife; both Paulina and Hermione are probably too old for childbearing. For Perdita and Florizel perhaps the greatest tests of faith and mutuality lie ahead, when Perdita's transformation from maid into wife and mother will present new occasions for jealousy and distrust. Moreover, in *The Winter's Tale* the remembrance of things that were lost and can never be regained intrudes even on the celebration of the return of Perdita and of Hermione. Paulina pointedly recalls her husband, Antigonus, lost in carrying Perdita to Bohemia; Hermione speaks to Perdita of the sixteen long years of their separation; her wrinkles attest to other losses; Mamillius is gone forever. The point of *The Winter's Tale* hardly seems to be that folly has no consequences or that earthly paradise is possible. Those claims would indeed make nature afraid. Rather, the play celebrates the true miracle of partial restorations, of moments of exquisite joy wrested by work, art, and good fortune from the pains of the imperfect world that men and women have made.

JEAN E. HOWARD

TEXTUAL NOTE

The Winter's Tale was first printed in the Folio of 1623 at the end of the group of comedies. Simon Forman, a London doctor, saw a performance at the Globe on May 15, 1611, and it was performed at court on November 11 of that year. Its exact date of composition, however, is unknown. Largely on stylistic evidence and because *The Winter's Tale* is at several points indebted to Plutarch, a principal source for Shakespeare's classical tragedies such as *Coriolanus* (1608), the Oxford editors place the date of composition in 1609, before *Cymbeline*. Other editors believe the play was written late in 1610 or early in 1611 before the May performance witnessed by Forman. In Act 4, Scene 4, working men at the sheepshearing festival perform a satyr dance that resembles a dance in Ben Jonson's *Masque of Oberon,* which was performed at court on January 1, 1611. In Shakespeare's play, the Old Shepherd remarks that three of the performers had "danced before the King" (4.4.324). This reference has been used to suggest that Shakespeare either was writing *The Winter's Tale* in January of 1611 and so incorporated a contemporary court event into his play, or that he composed the bulk of the play after that date. It is also possible that Shakespeare—or someone else—added this dance to *The Winter's Tale* after the play had already been written and was in performance in order to capitalize on the glamour attached to court occasions, especially if, as the Old Shepherd indicates, members of Shakespeare's company performed in Jonson's masque. If so, the dance would have been recorded in the promptbook but not necessarily in Shakespeare's original manuscript.

The Folio text of the play was probably set from a transcript prepared by Ralph Crane, a scrivener who transcribed a number of plays associated with the King's Men. In many of the manuscripts prepared by Crane, and this is true for *The Winter's Tale,* all the characters who appear in certain scenes, regardless of when they actually come on stage, are listed in the opening stage direction. Crane sometimes modified stage directions in the interest of clarity and imposed his own punctuation and spelling on the playscripts, showing a decided preference for the heavy use of parentheses, hyphens, and apostrophes. The changes Crane made while copying the plays make it difficult to recognize what kind of manuscript lay behind his transcriptions: promptbook or foul papers. As with other plays set from Crane's transcriptions, the Folio *Winter's Tale* is a relatively clean text. Act and scene divisions are carefully and consistently noted, although stage directions are sparse. There are only forty-three in the Folio, and they are regularly supplemented in modern editions.

SELECTED BIBLIOGRAPHY

Adelman, Janet. "Masculine Authority and the Maternal Body: The Return to Origins in the Romances." *Suffocating Mothers: Fantasies of Maternal Origin in Shakespeare's Plays, "Hamlet" to "The Tempest."* New York: Routledge, 1992. 193–238. Argues that the romances attempt to redress the loss of the idealized parents enacted in *Hamlet* and that *The Winter's Tale* dramatizes the positive restoration of the sexualized mother in the person of Hermione.

Dolan, Frances. "Finding What Has Been 'Lost': Representations of Infanticide and *The Winter's Tale*." *Dangerous Familiars: Representations of Domestic Crime in England, 1550–1700*. Ithaca, N.Y.: Cornell University Press, 1994. 121–70. Connects *The Winter's Tale* to early modern stories of child abandonment and murder, arguing that the play ultimately forgives the tyrannous father, Leontes, for the exposure of Perdita.

Egan, Robert. "'The Art Itself Is Nature': *The Winter's Tale*." *Drama Within Drama: Shakespeare's Sense of His Art in "King Lear," "The Winter's Tale," and "The Tempest."* New York: Columbia University Press, 1975. 56–89. Discusses the role of art in rectifying the disordered world of *The Winter's Tale*.

Frye, Northrop. "The Triumph of Time." *A Natural Perspective: The Development of Shakespearean Comedy and Romance*. New York: Columbia University Press, 1965. 72–117. Discusses structures of action and conventions common across Shakespeare's comedies and romances.

Hunt, Maurice. "'Bearing Hence' Shakespeare's *The Winter's Tale*." *Studies in English Literature 1500–1900* 44 (2004): 333–46. Explores Shakespeare's creative play with the words "bear" and "bear away" in a play in which a bear appears on stage and is often associated with the tyrannous King Leontes.

Mowat, Barbara A. "Rogues, Shepherds, and the Counterfeit Distressed: Texts and Infracontexts of *The Winter's Tale* 4.3." *Shakespeare Studies* 22 (1994): 58–76. Examines the cultural contexts that help make sense of the figure of Autolycus, rogue and con man, in *The Winter's Tale*.

Newcomb, Lori H. "'If That Which Is Lost Be Not Found': Monumental Bodies, Spectacular Bodies in *The Winter's Tale*." *Ovid and the Renaissance Body*. Ed. Goran V. Stanivukovic. Toronto: University of Toronto Press, 2001. Analyzes the tension between the monumental (stasis and constraint) and the spectacular (metamorphosis and performative freedom) in both the text of *The Winter's Tale* and in its material history as book and as theater piece.

O'Connor, Marion. "'Imagine Me, Gentle Spectators': Iconomachy and *The Winter's Tale*." *A Companion to Shakespeare's Works. IV: The Poems, Problem Comedies, Late Plays*. Ed. Richard Dutton and Jean E. Howard. Malden, Mass.: Blackwell, 2003. 365–88. Discusses the Renaissance theological debate about the value and truth of images as it bears on a number of early modern plays, including *The Winter's Tale*, in which statues are staged. Argues that Shakespeare insists on the collaboration of word and image, eschewing a total embrace of Reformation logocentrism or Catholic image-worship.

Paster, Gail Kern. "Quarreling with the Dug, or 'I Am Glad You Did Not Nurse Him'." *The Body Embarrassed: Drama and the Disciplines of Shame in Early Modern England*. Ithaca, N.Y.: Cornell University Press, 1993. 215–80. Sets *The Winter's Tale* in an array of Shakespearean texts that anxiously explore early modern cultural practices surrounding reproduction and infant care, especially the practice of wet-nursing.

Wilson, Richard. "The Statue of Our Queen: Shakespeare's Open Secret." *Secret Shakespeare: Studies in Theatre, Religion and Resistance*. Manchester: Manchester University Press, 2004. 246–70. Argues for *The Winter's Tale*'s connection to recusant culture, especially the play's emphasis on the importance of secret spaces dominated by women.

FILM

The Winter's Tale. 1999. Dir. Robin Lough. UK. 170 min. A dark and moving Royal Shakespeare Company production with Anthony Sher as a Leontes truly made mad by jealousy and an impressively dignified Alexandra Gilbreath as Hermione. Imaginative staging of the bear and riveting statue scene as Hermione very slowly comes to life.

The Winter's Tale

The Persons of the Play

LEONTES, King of Sicilia
HERMIONE, his wife
MAMILLIUS, his son
PERDITA, his daughter
CAMILLO
ANTIGONUS
CLEOMENES } Lords at Leontes' court
DION
PAULINA, Antigonus's wife
EMILIA, a lady attending on Hermione
A JAILER
A MARINER
Other Lords and Gentlemen, Ladies, Officers, and Servants at
  Leontes' court
POLIXENES, King of Bohemia
FLORIZEL, his son, in love with Perdita; known as Doricles
ARCHIDAMUS, a Bohemian lord
AUTOLYCUS, a rogue, once in the service of Florizel
OLD SHEPHERD
CLOWN, his son
MOPSA
DORCAS } shepherdesses
SERVANT of the Old Shepherd
Other Shepherds and Shepherdesses
Twelve countrymen disguised as satyrs
TIME, as chorus

1.1

Enter CAMILLO *and* ARCHIDAMUS

ARCHIDAMUS If you shall chance, Camillo, to visit Bohemia on
  the like occasion whereon my services are now on foot,[1] you
  shall see, as I have said, great difference betwixt our Bohemia
  and your Sicilia.

5 CAMILLO I think this coming summer the King of Sicilia means
  to pay Bohemia the visitation which he justly owes him.

ARCHIDAMUS Wherein our entertainment shall shame us, we
  will be justified in our loves;[2] for indeed—

CAMILLO Beseech you—

10 ARCHIDAMUS Verily, I speak it in the freedom of my knowledge.
  We cannot with such magnificence—in so rare— I know not
  what to say.—We will give you sleepy drinks,° that your senses, *drinks to make you drowsy*
  unintelligent of our insufficience,[3] may, though they cannot
  praise us, as little accuse us.

15 CAMILLO You pay a great deal too dear for what's given freely.

1.1 Location: Sicilia. The palace of Leontes.
1. On an occasion similar to the one in which I am now engaged (that is, as attendant lord to a visiting King).

2. Insofar as our less elaborate hospitality will put us to shame, we will compensate by (the depth of) our love.
3. Unaware of our inadequacy.

ARCHIDAMUS   Believe me, I speak as my understanding instructs
me, and as mine honesty puts it to utterance.

CAMILLO   Sicilia cannot show himself over-kind to Bohemia.
They were trained together in their childhoods, and there
20 rooted betwixt them then such an affection which cannot
choose but branch⁴ now. Since their more mature dignities
and royal necessities made separation of their society,° their   *forced them apart*
encounters—though not personal— hath been royally attor-
neyed⁵ with interchange of gifts, letters, loving embassies, that°   *so that*
25 they have seemed to be together, though absent; shook hands
as over a vast;° and embraced as it were from the ends of   *wide expanse*
opposed winds.⁶ The heavens continue their loves.

ARCHIDAMUS   I think there is not in the world either malice or
matter to alter it. You have an unspeakable° comfort of° your   *inexpressible / in*
30 young prince, Mamillius. It° is a gentleman of the greatest   *(He)*
promise that ever came into my note.

CAMILLO   I very well agree with you in the hopes of him. It is a
gallant child; one that, indeed, physics the subject,⁷ makes old
hearts fresh. They that went on crutches ere he was born desire
35 yet their life° to see him a man.   *hope to live long enough*

ARCHIDAMUS   Would they else be content to die?

CAMILLO   Yes—if there were no other excuse why they should
desire to live.

ARCHIDAMUS   If the King had no son they would desire to live on
40 crutches till he had one.   *Exeunt*

1.2

Enter LEONTES, HERMIONE, MAMILLIUS, POLIXENES, *and*
CAMILLO¹

POLIXENES   Nine changes of the wat'ry star hath been
The shepherd's note² since we³ have left our throne
Without a burden.° Time as long again   *an occupant*
Would be filled up, my brother, with our thanks,
5 And yet we should for perpetuity
Go hence in debt.⁴ And therefore, like a cipher,
Yet standing in rich place,⁵ I multiply
With one 'We thank you' many thousands more
That go before it.

LEONTES   Stay° your thanks a while,   *Postpone*
And pay them when you part.

10 POLIXENES   Sir, that's tomorrow.
I am questioned by my fears° of what may chance⁶   *I am afraid*
Or breed upon° our absence, that may blow   *develop because of*
No sneaping winds at home to make us say

4. Flourish and spread (as a tree does when it puts
forth branches); divide.
5. Performed by deputies.
6. From opposite ends of the earth. Early modern
atlases often showed the four "corners" of the earth as
the source of the winds.
7. Restores the health of the King's subjects.
1.2 Location: Sicilia. The palace of Leontes.
1. Though listed in the stage direction in F, Camillo has
no part in this scene until line 210, when Leontes says,
"What, Camillo there!" Camillo may be a silent observer
for the first 210 lines, or, as some editors believe, his first
entrance may be marked by Leontes' exclamation.
2. The shepherd has observed nine changes of the
moon (that is, nine months). The moon is "the wat'ry
star" because it governs the tides.
3. Both Kings employ the royal "we," speaking of themselves in the plural.
4. And even then we would depart forever in your debt.
5. Like a zero ("cipher"), which is worthless in itself,
but valuable when it follows another number.
6. Happen by chance.

'This is put forth too truly.'[7] Besides, I have stayed
To tire your royalty.

15 LEONTES   We are tougher, brother,
Than you can put us to't.[8]

POLIXENES   No longer stay.

LEONTES   One sennight° longer.   week

POLIXENES   Very sooth,° tomorrow.   In truth (a mild oath)

LEONTES   We'll part the time° between's, then; and in that   split the difference
I'll no gainsaying.°   allow no contradiction

POLIXENES   Press me not, beseech you, so.

20 There is no tongue that moves, none, none i'th' world
So soon as yours, could win me. So it should now,
Were there necessity in your request, although
'Twere needful I denied it. My affairs
Do even drag me homeward; which to hinder
25 Were, in your love, a whip to me;[9] my stay
To you a charge and trouble. To save both,
Farewell, our brother.

LEONTES   Tongue-tied, our queen? Speak you.

HERMIONE   I had thought, sir, to have held my peace until
You had drawn oaths from him not to stay. You, sir,
30 Charge him too coldly. Tell him you are sure
All in Bohemia's well. This satisfaction
The bygone day proclaimed.[1] Say this to him,
He's beat from his best ward.[2]

LEONTES   Well said, Hermione!

HERMIONE   To tell° he longs to see his son were strong.   assert
35 But let him say so then, and let him go.
But let him swear so and he shall not stay,
We'll thwack him hence with distaffs.[3]
[To POLIXENES] Yet of your royal presence I'll adventure°   risk
The borrow° of a week. When at Bohemia   loan
40 You take my lord, I'll give him my commission°   permission
To let him there a month behind the gest
Prefixed for's parting.[4]—Yet, good deed,° Leontes,   indeed
I love thee not a jar° o'th' clock behind   tick
What lady she her lord.[5]—You'll stay?

POLIXENES   No, madam.

45 HERMIONE   Nay, but you will?

POLIXENES   I may not, verily.

HERMIONE   Verily?
You put me off with limber° vows. But I,   weak
Though you would seek t'unsphere the stars[6] with oaths,
50 Should yet say 'Sir, no going.' Verily
You shall not go. A lady's 'verily' 's
As potent as a lord's. Will you go yet?

---

7. *"that may . . . too truly,"*: an obscure passage. Fearing the worst, Polixenes hopes that no biting ("sneaping") winds may blow (that is, no envious forces be active) at home to make him conclude that his worries were justified.
8. Than any test you put us to.
9. That is, "To hinder me from going home, though lovingly done, would be a punishment ('whip') to me."
1. This good news was announced yesterday.
2. He's forced to relinquish his strongest position. A fencing metaphor.
3. Wooden sticks, usually about 3 feet long, which were used in spinning wool. Proverbially, they were female tools and symbols of female authority.
4. To remain there a month longer than the time ("gest") appointed in advance for his departure.
5. That is, "I love you no less than any noblewoman loves her husband."
6. To disorder the cosmos. Alluding to the idea that the stars move in fixed orbits around the earth.

Force me to keep you as a prisoner,
Not like a guest: so you shall pay your fees
55   When you depart,[7] and save your thanks. How say you?
My prisoner? or my guest? By your dread 'verily',
One of them you shall be.

POLIXENES   Your guest then, madam.
To be your prisoner should import offending,°   *mean I have offended you*
Which is for me less easy to commit
Than you to punish.

60 HERMIONE   Not your jailer then,
But your kind hostess. Come, I'll question you
Of my lord's tricks and yours when you were boys.
You were pretty lordings° then?   *young lords*

POLIXENES   We were, fair Queen,
Two lads that thought there was no more behind°   *(in the future)*
65   But such a day tomorrow as today,
And to be boy eternal.

HERMIONE   Was not my lord
The verier wag° o'th' two?   *greater mischief-maker*

POLIXENES   We were as twinned° lambs that did frisk i'th' sun,   *identical*
70   And bleat the one at th'other. What we changed°   *exchanged*
Was innocence for innocence. We knew not
The doctrine of ill-doing, nor dreamed
That any did. Had we pursued that life,
And our weak spirits ne'er been higher reared
75   With stronger blood,° we should have answered heaven   *With more mature passions*
Boldly, 'Not guilty', the imposition cleared
Hereditary ours.[8]

HERMIONE   By this we gather
You have tripped° since.   *sinned*

POLIXENES   O my most sacred lady,
Temptations have since then been born to's; for
80   In those unfledged[9] days was my wife a girl.
Your precious self had then not crossed the eyes
Of my young playfellow.

HERMIONE   Grace to boot!°   *Heaven help me!*
Of this make no conclusion,[1] lest you say
Your queen and I are devils. Yet go on.
85   Th'offences we have made you do we'll answer,°   *answer for*
If you first sinned with us, and that with us
You did continue fault, and that you slipped not
With any but with us.

LEONTES   Is he won yet?

HERMIONE   He'll stay, my lord.

LEONTES   At my request he would not.
90   Hermione, my dearest, thou never spok'st
To better purpose.

HERMIONE   Never?

LEONTES   Never but once.

HERMIONE   What, have I twice said well? When was't before?

---

7. In early modern England, prisoners were required to pay fees to jailers both for provisions and upon their release.
8. Freed even of the charge of original sin. The doctrine of original sin held that everyone at birth was tainted by sin because the first humans, Adam and Eve,

disobeyed God in the Garden of Eden. Here original sin is linked to the sexual desires that come with maturity.
9. Youthful. An unfledged, or young, bird is one as yet lacking the feathers necessary for flight.
1. Do not follow out this line of reasoning.

I prithee tell me. Cram's° with praise, and make's   *Stuff us; overfeed us*
As fat as tame things. One good deed dying tongueless
95   Slaughters a thousand waiting upon that.[2]
        Our praises are our wages. You may ride's
        With one soft kiss a thousand furlongs ere
        With spur we heat° an acre.[3] But to th' goal.°   *race over / purpose*
        My last good deed was to entreat his stay.
100   What was my first? It has an elder sister,
        Or I mistake you. O, would her name were Grace![4]
        But once before I spoke to th' purpose? When?
        Nay, let me have't. I long.

LEONTES   Why, that was when
        Three crabbèd° months had soured themselves to death   *bitter*
105   Ere I could make thee open thy white hand
        And clap° thyself my love. Then didst thou utter,   *pledge*
        'I am yours for ever.'

HERMIONE   'Tis grace indeed.
        Why lo you now; I have spoke to th' purpose twice.
        The one for ever earned a royal husband;
        Th'other, for some while a friend.[5]
        [*She gives her hand to* POLIXENES.[6]
        They stand aside]

110   LEONTES [*aside*]   Too hot, too hot:
        To mingle friendship farre is mingling bloods.[7]
        I have *tremor cordis*[8] on me. My heart dances,
        But not for joy, not joy. This entertainment°   *hospitality*
        May a free° face put on, derive a liberty   *innocent*
115   From heartiness, from bounty, fertile bosom,°   *generous affection*
        And well become the agent.[9] 'T may, I grant.
        But to be paddling° palms and pinching fingers,[1]   *caressing*
        As now they are, and making practised smiles
        As in a looking-glass; and then to sigh, as 'twere
120   The mort o'th' deer[2]—O, that is entertainment
        My bosom likes not, nor my brows.[3]—Mamillius,
        Art thou my boy?

MAMILLIUS   Ay, my good lord.

LEONTES   I'fecks,°   *In faith (a mild oath)*
        Why, that's my bawcock.° What? Hast smutched° thy nose?   *fine fellow / dirtied*
        They say it is a copy out of mine. Come, captain,
125   We must be neat—not neat,[4] but cleanly, captain.
        And yet the steer, the heifer, and the calf

---

2. If one virtuous act goes unremarked, then the thousand more that might have been inspired by it will not come to be.

3. That is, "You'll go much farther with us if you will treat us kindly," with a pun on "ride" as meaning "enjoy us sexually."

4. Would that my first good act were virtuous (full of God's Grace). Hermione may be countering Polixenes' earlier suggestion that she first caused Leontes to sin. With a possible allusion to the Three Graces (Aglaia, Euphrosyne, and Thalia) of classical mythology. Usually depicted nude and dancing in a circle, the three women represented the epitome of earthly beauty and harmony.

5. "Friend" could also mean "lover," a meaning that Leontes takes up in his next speech.

6. It is not certain when Hermione and Polixenes join hands, but by line 117 Leontes remarks that they are

"paddling palms and pinching fingers." Joined hands—or hands separated from one another—are an important and recurring visual motif in the play, culminating at 5.3.107, when Paulina commands Leontes to "present your hand" to Hermione as she ceases to appear a statue.

7. Uniting in passion; having sexual intercourse.

8. A malady marked by an erratic heart rate.

9. And makes the actor of these deeds (Hermione) appear attractive.

1. Early modern texts often represent hands as erotic body parts. Moist palms were believed to be signs of sexual arousal; finger games may suggest sexual penetration.

2. To sigh as loudly as the horn blast that proclaims the death of a hunted deer.

3. Alluding to the proverbial notion that a cuckold sprouted horns from his brow.

4. Punning on neat as meaning both "clean" and "cattle with horns."

Are all called neat.—Still virginalling
Upon his palm?⁵—How now, you wanton° calf—   *playful*
Art thou my calf?

MAMILLIUS   Yes, if you will, my lord.

130   LEONTES   Thou want'st a rough pash° and the shoots° that I have,   *shaggy head / horns*
To be full° like me. Yet they say we are   *entirely; fully*
Almost as like as eggs. Women say so,
That will say anything. But were they false
As o'er-dyed blacks,⁶ as wind, as waters, false
135   As dice are to be wished by one that fixes
No bourn° 'twixt his and mine, yet were it true   *boundary; limit*
To say this boy were like me. Come, sir page,
Look on me with your welkin° eye. Sweet villain,   *sky blue*
Most dear'st, my collop!⁷ Can thy dam°—may't be?—   *mother*
140   Affection, thy intention stabs the centre.⁸
Thou dost make possible things not so held,°   *things held as impossible*
Communicat'st with dreams—how can this be?—
With what's unreal thou coactive art,°   *you collaborate*
And fellow'st° nothing. Then 'tis very credent°   *are companion to / believable*
145   Thou mayst co-join with something, and thou dost—
And that beyond commission;° and I find it—   *what is permitted*
And that to the infection of my brains
And hard'ning of my brows.°   *(with cuckold's horns)*

POLIXENES   What means Sicilia?
HERMIONE   He something seems° unsettled.   *seems somewhat*
POLIXENES   How, my lord!
LEONTES   What cheer? How is't with you, best brother?
150   HERMIONE   You look
As if you held a brow of much distraction.
Are you moved,° my lord?   *angry*
LEONTES   No, in good earnest.
How sometimes nature will betray its folly,
Its tenderness, and make itself a pastime°   *source of amusement*
155   To harder bosoms! Looking on the lines
Of my boy's face, methoughts I did recoil°   *go back*
Twenty-three years, and saw myself unbreeched,⁹
In my green velvet coat; my dagger muzzled,°   *in its sheath; blunted*
Lest it should bite its master, and so prove,
160   As ornament oft does, too dangerous.
How like, methought, I then was to this kernel,
This squash,° this gentleman.—Mine honest friend,   *unripe peapod*
Will you take eggs for money?¹
MAMILLIUS   No, my lord, I'll fight.
LEONTES   You will? Why, happy man be's dole!²—My brother,

---

5. Still caressing his hand as if playing the virginal, a legless keyboard instrument played on the lap; still acting chastely (like a virgin).
6. Referring to textiles dyed black. Such black cloth was made "false" or weakened by the harsh chemicals in the dye. With a possible reference to Africans, whose dark skin was said to result from overexposure to the sun. It was a commonplace that Africans were prone to licentiousness and were thus sexually "false."
7. That is, "my own flesh." A "collop" is a portion of meat.
8. Passion (probably the passion of jealousy), your

intensity ("intention") pierces my heart or to the core of my being.
9. Not yet old enough to wear men's clothing ("breeches"). Before about the age of six, both girls and boys in early modern England wore a dresslike garment. Giving a boy breeches was a sign of his passage out of childhood and out of the care of women into the world of men.
1. A proverbial expression meaning "Will you accept a trifle in place of something valuable?"
2. Proverbial for "May you have good luck!"

165 Are you so fond of your young prince as we
Do seem to be of ours?

POLIXENES   If at home, sir,
He's all my exercise, my mirth, my matter;°   concern
Now my sworn friend, and then mine enemy;
My parasite, my soldier, statesman, all.
170 He makes a July's day short as December,
And with his varying childness° cures in me   youthful ways
Thoughts that would thick my blood.[3]

LEONTES   So stands this squire
Officed with me.[4] We two will walk, my lord,
And leave you to your graver steps. Hermione,
175 How thou lov'st us show in our brother's welcome.
Let what is dear in Sicily be cheap.
Next to thyself and my young rover, he's
Apparent° to my heart.   Heir apparent

HERMIONE   If you would seek us,
We are yours i'th' garden. Shall's attend you there?
180 LEONTES   To your own bents° dispose you. You'll be found,   inclinations
Be you beneath the sky. [Aside] I am angling° now,   fishing; scheming
Though you perceive me not how I give line.
Go to, go to!
How she holds up the neb, the bill to him,[5]
185 And arms her° with the boldness of a wife   herself
To her allowing° husband!   approving

          [Exeunt POLIXENES and HERMIONE]
          Gone already.
Inch-thick, knee-deep, o'er head and ears a forked° one!—   horned
Go play, boy, play. Thy mother plays,° and I   dallies sexually
Play° too; but so disgraced a part, whose issue[6]   Play a role
190 Will hiss me to my grave. Contempt and clamour
Will be my knell. Go play, boy, play. There have been,
Or I am much deceived, cuckolds ere now,
And many a man there is, even at this present,
Now, while I speak this, holds his wife by th'arm,
195 That little thinks she has been sluiced[7] in's absence,
And his pond[8] fished by his next neighbour, by
Sir Smile, his neighbour.[9] Nay, there's comfort in't,
Whiles other men have gates,[1] and those gates opened,
As mine, against their will. Should all despair
200 That have revolted° wives, the tenth of mankind   rebellious; unfaithful
Would hang themselves. Physic° for't there's none.   Medicine
It is a bawdy planet, that will strike
Where 'tis predominant;[2] and 'tis powerful. Think it:

---

3. Ideas that would make me melancholy, a physical and emotional malady connected with a supposed excess of "thick blood."
4. So this young man performs the same duty for me.
5. How she holds up her face, her mouth to him (to be kissed).
6. Outcome, with puns on "issue" as also meaning "offspring" and "the exit an actor makes from a stage." Leontes' words imply that in playing the part of a cuckold, the result of his role will be disgrace; the illegitimate offspring produced by his wife will bring him disgrace; and his exit from the stage (at death) will be a disgraceful one.
7. Little thinks she has had sexual relations. A sluice

was a trough or channel through which water could be directed. To be sluiced was to have water poured down one's "channel," here probably referring to the vagina where sperm entered.
8. Slang term for the sexual organs of his wife.
9. It is possible that "Sir Smile" is a reference to Polixenes, who may be laughing or smiling in his conversation with Hermione.
1. Another slang term for female genitalia. Leontes imagines the vulva as a gateway that ought to be entered only by a husband.
2. Alluding to the notion that planets control human actions and may exercise malign influences ("strike") when they are in certain "predominant" positions.

From east, west, north, and south, be it concluded,
205 No barricado for a belly.³ Know't,
It will let in and out the enemy
With bag and baggage.⁴ Many thousand on's°   *of us*
Have the disease and feel't not.—How now, boy?

MAMILLIUS   I am like you, they say.

LEONTES   Why, that's some comfort.
What, Camillo there!

210 CAMILLO [*coming forward*]   Ay, my good lord.

LEONTES   Go play, Mamillius, thou'rt an honest man.

[*Exit* MAMILLIUS]

Camillo, this great sir will yet stay longer.

CAMILLO   You had much ado to make his anchor hold.
When you cast out, it still came home.°   *always failed to hold*

LEONTES   Didst note it?

215 CAMILLO   He would not stay at your petitions, made
His business more material.°   *important*

LEONTES   Didst perceive it?
[*Aside*] They're here with me⁵ already, whisp'ring, rounding,°   *murmuring*
'Sicilia is a so-forth'. 'Tis far gone
When I shall gust° it last.—How came't, Camillo,   *perceive; taste*
That he did stay?

220 CAMILLO   At the good Queen's entreaty.

LEONTES   'At the Queen's' be't. 'Good' should be pertinent,
But so° it is, it is not. Was this taken°   *as / perceived*
By any understanding pate but thine?
For thy conceit is soaking,° will draw in   *your wit is quick*
225 More than the common blocks.° Not noted, is't,   *dimwits*
But of° the finer natures? By some severals°   *by / individuals*
Of head-piece° extraordinary? Lower messes⁶   *intellect*
Perchance are to this business purblind?° Say.   *blind*

CAMILLO   Business, my lord? I think most understand
230 Bohemia stays here longer.

LEONTES   Ha?

CAMILLO   Stays here longer.

LEONTES   Ay, but why?

CAMILLO   To satisfy your highness, and the entreaties
Of our most gracious mistress.

235 LEONTES   Satisfy?⁷
Th'entreaties of your mistress? Satisfy?
Let that suffice. I have trusted thee, Camillo,
With all the near'st things to my heart, as well
My chamber-counsels,° wherein, priest-like, thou   *secret matters*
240 Hast cleansed my bosom, I from thee departed
Thy penitent reformed. But we have been
Deceived in thy integrity, deceived
In that which seems so.

CAMILLO   Be it forbid, my lord.

LEONTES   To bide° upon't: thou art not honest; or   *dwell*
245 If thou inclin'st that way, thou art a coward,

Which hoxes honesty behind,[8] restraining
From course required.[9] Or else thou must be counted
A servant grafted in my serious trust[1]
And therein negligent, or else a fool
250   That seest a game played home,° the rich stake drawn,°   *in earnest / won*
And tak'st it all for jest.

CAMILLO   My gracious lord,
I may be negligent, foolish, and fearful.
In every one of these no man is free,°   *guiltless*
But that his negligence, his folly, fear,
255   Among the infinite doings of the world
Sometime puts forth.° In your affairs, my lord,   *reveals itself*
If ever I were wilful-negligent,
It was my folly. If industriously°   *deliberately*
I played the fool, it was my negligence,
260   Not weighing well the end. If ever fearful
To do a thing where I the issue° doubted,   *outcome*
Whereof the execution did cry out
Against the non-performance,[2] 'twas a fear
Which oft infects the wisest. These, my lord,
265   Are such allowed infirmities that honesty
Is never free of. But beseech your grace
Be plainer with me, let me know my trespass
By its own visage. If I then deny it,
'Tis none of mine.

LEONTES   Ha' not you seen, Camillo—
270   But that's past doubt; you have, or your eye-glass°   *the lens of your eye*
Is thicker than a cuckold's horn—or heard—
For, to a vision° so apparent, rumour   *sight*
Cannot be mute—or thought—for cogitation
Resides not in that man that does not think—
275   My wife is slippery? If thou wilt confess—
Or else be impudently negative°   *shamelessly deny*
To have nor eyes, nor ears, nor thought—then say
My wife's a hobby-horse,[3] deserves a name
As rank° as any flax-wench[4] that puts to°   *indecent / has sexual relations*
280   Before her troth-plight.° Say't, and justify't.   *betrothal*

CAMILLO   I would not be a stander-by to hear
My sovereign mistress clouded so without
My present° vengeance taken. 'Shrew° my heart,   *immediate / Curse*
You never spoke what did become you less
285   Than this, which to reiterate° were sin   *repeat*
As deep as that, though true.[5]

LEONTES   Is whispering nothing?
Is leaning cheek to cheek? Is meeting noses?
Kissing with inside lip? Stopping the career°   *full gallop*
Of laughter with a sigh?—a note° infallible   *sign*

---

8. Which ensures that frankness is shackled.
9. Keeping (honesty) from the path it must take (to find out truth).
1. A servant who has grown into my confidence as a cutting is grafted onto a plant.
2. Even when the need to do the deed protested against its nonperformance.
3. Whore. The image is of a woman, who, like a horse,

can be mounted. F has "Holy-Horse," an obscure phrase nearly all modern editors emend to "hobby-horse."
4. A girl or woman, usually of low social status, who worked with flax, a fibrous plant used to make candlewicks, clothing, and linen.
5. That is, "As grave as is the sin that you accuse your wife of, even if it were true (which it is not)."

290	Of breaking honesty.° Horsing foot on foot?[6]	*violating chastity*
	Skulking in corners? Wishing clocks more swift,	
	Hours minutes, noon midnight? And all eyes	
	Blind with the pin and web° but theirs, theirs only,	*cataract disease*
	That would unseen be wicked? Is this nothing?	
295	Why then the world and all that's in't is nothing,	
	The covering sky is nothing, Bohemia nothing,	
	My wife is nothing, nor nothing have these nothings[7]	
	If this be nothing.	

CAMILLO   Good my lord, be cured
Of this diseased opinion, and betimes,°   *quickly*
For 'tis most dangerous.

290 LEONTES   Say it be, 'tis true.
CAMILLO   No, no, my lord.
LEONTES   It is. You lie, you lie.
I say thou liest, Camillo, and I hate thee,
Pronounce thee a gross lout, a mindless slave,
Or else a hovering° temporizer, that   *irresolute*
305 Canst with thine eyes at once see good and evil,
Inclining to them both. Were my wife's liver
Infected as her life, she would not live
The running of one glass.°   *hourglass*
CAMILLO   Who does infect her?
LEONTES   Why, he that wears her like her medal,[8] hanging
310 About his neck, Bohemia, who, if I
Had servants true about me, that bare° eyes   *possessed*
To see alike mine honour as their profits,
Their own particular thrifts,° they would do that   *personal gain*
Which should undo° more doing.° Ay, and thou   *stop / sexual acts*
315 His cupbearer,[9] whom I from meaner form°   *lower rank or place*
Have benched, and reared to worship,[1] who mayst see
Plainly as heaven sees earth and earth sees heaven,
How I am galled,° mightst bespice a cup   *sorely vexed*
To give mine enemy a lasting wink,[2]
Which draught to me were cordial.[3]
320 CAMILLO   Sir, my lord,
I could do this, and that with no rash° potion,   *quick-acting*
But with a ling'ring° dram, that should not work   *slow-working*
Maliciously,° like poison. But I cannot   *Violently*
Believe this crack° to be in my dread mistress,   *flaw*
325 So sovereignly being honourable.
I have loved thee—
LEONTES   Make that thy question,° and go rot!   *concern*
Dost think I am so muddy, so unsettled,
To appoint° myself in this vexation?   *put*
Sully the purity and whiteness of my sheets—
330 Which to preserve is sleep, which being spotted
Is goads, thorns, nettles, tails of wasps—

6. Mounting or rubbing one foot on another. A sexually titillating pastime.
7. Alluding to the proverbial notion that nothing can come of nothing.
8. As though she were a miniature portrait of herself. Ornate lockets containing miniature portraits were popular love tokens among courtiers.
9. In a noble household a male servant whose respon-

sibilities included serving wine to his master.
1. Given authority and elevated to a dignified position. Referring to his "bench" or place at the dining table as a sign of his high rank.
2. To close my enemy's eyes forever.
3. Which drink would be medicinal to me; which drink would cure my heartsickness (perhaps the *"tremor cordis"* to which Leontes referred at 1.2.112).

Give scandal to the blood o'th' prince, my son—
Who I do think is mine, and love as mine—
Without ripe moving° to't? Would I do this?   *good reason*
Could man so blench?°   *stray (from sense)*

335   CAMILLO   I must believe you, sir.
I do, and will fetch off° Bohemia for't,   *kill; rescue*
Provided that when he's removed your highness
Will take again your queen as yours at first,
Even for your son's sake, and thereby for sealing°   *silencing*

340   The injury of tongues in courts and kingdoms
Known and allied to yours.

LEONTES   Thou dost advise me
Even so as I mine own course have set down.
I'll give no blemish to her honour, none.

CAMILLO   My lord, go then, and with a countenance as clear

345   As friendship wears at feasts, keep° with Bohemia   *associate*
And with your queen. I am his cupbearer.
If from me he have wholesome beverage,
Account me not your servant.

LEONTES   This is all.
Do't, and thou hast the one half of my heart;
Do't not, thou splitt'st thine own.

350   CAMILLO   I'll do't, my lord.

LEONTES   I will seem friendly, as thou hast advised me.   *Exit*

CAMILLO   O miserable lady. But for me,
What case stand I in? I must be the poisoner
Of good Polixenes, and my ground to do't

355   Is the obedience to a master—one
Who in rebellion with himself, will have
All that are his so too. To do this deed,
Promotion follows. If I could find example
Of thousands that had struck anointed kings

360   And flourished after, I'd not do't. But since
Nor° brass, nor stone, nor parchment[4] bears not one,   *Neither*
Let villainy itself forswear't.° I must   *swear not to do it*
Forsake the court. To do't, or no, is certain
To me a break-neck.°   *(death)*

      Enter POLIXENES

                     Happy° star reign now!   *Lucky*
Here comes Bohemia.

365   POLIXENES [*aside*]   This is strange. Methinks
My favour here begins to warp. Not speak?—
Good day, Camillo.

CAMILLO   Hail, most royal sir.

POLIXENES   What is the news i'th' court?

CAMILLO   None rare,° my lord.   *noteworthy*

POLIXENES   The King hath on him such a countenance

370   As° he had lost some province, and a region   *As if*
Loved as he loves himself. Even now I met him
With customary compliment, when he,
Wafting his eyes to th' contrary,° and falling   *Shifting his gaze away*
A lip of much contempt,° speeds from me, and   *sneering*

---

4. That is, since no form of historical record (brass monuments, stone markers, or paper manuscripts) shows an example of a man who flourished after killing a King.

375　So leaves me to consider what is breeding
　　　That changes thus his manners.

CAMILLO　　　　　　　　　　I dare not know, my lord.

POLIXENES　How, 'dare not'? Do not? Do you know, and dare not?
　　　Be intelligent° to me. 'Tis thereabouts.[5]　　　　　　　*informative*
　　　For to yourself what you do know you must,°　　　　　　*(know)*
380　And cannot say you 'dare not'. Good Camillo,
　　　Your changed complexions are to me a mirror
　　　Which shows me mine changed, too; for I must be
　　　A party in this alteration,° finding　　　　　　*(of Leontes' manner)*
　　　Myself thus altered with't.

CAMILLO　　　　　　　　　There is a sickness
385　Which puts some of us in distemper, but
　　　I cannot name th' disease, and it is caught
　　　Of you that yet are well.

POLIXENES　　　　　　　　How caught of me?
　　　Make me not sighted like the basilisk.[6]
　　　I have looked on thousands who have sped° the better　　　*fared*
390　By my regard, but killed none so. Camillo,
　　　As you are certainly a gentleman, thereto
　　　Clerk-like experienced,[7] which no less adorns
　　　Our gentry° than our parents' noble names,　　　　　*status as gentlemen*
　　　In whose success we are gentle:[8] I beseech you,
395　If you know aught which does behove my knowledge
　　　Thereof to be informed,[9] imprison't not
　　　In ignorant concealment.[1]

CAMILLO　　　　　　　　　I may not answer.

POLIXENES　A sickness caught of me, and yet I well?
　　　I must be answered. Dost thou hear, Camillo,
400　I conjure thee, by all the parts° of man　　　　　　*duties*
　　　Which honour does acknowledge, whereof the least
　　　Is not this suit of mine, that thou declare
　　　What incidency° thou dost guess of harm　　　　　　*event*
　　　Is creeping toward me; how far off, how near,
405　Which way to be prevented, if to be;
　　　If not, how best to bear it.

CAMILLO　　　　　　　　　Sir, I will tell you,
　　　Since I am charged in honour, and by him
　　　That I think honourable. Therefore mark my counsel,
　　　Which must be e'en as swiftly followed as
410　I mean to utter it; or both yourself and me
　　　Cry lost, and so good night!°　　　　　　*good-bye forever*

POLIXENES　　　　　　　　On, good Camillo.

CAMILLO　I am appointed him to murder you.

POLIXENES　By whom, Camillo?

CAMILLO　　　　　　　　　By the King.

POLIXENES　　　　　　　　　　For what?

CAMILLO　He thinks, nay, with all confidence he swears
415　As he had seen't, or been an instrument
　　　To vice° you to't, that you have touched his queen　　　*force*
　　　Forbiddenly.

---

5. That is, "I'm more or less right (that you are afraid to tell me)."
6. A mythical serpent whose glance was said to be fatal.
7. Also having the experience of an educated man.
8. By succession from whom we are made noble.
9. Which it is necessary for me to know.
1. In concealment that keeps me ignorant; in concealment on the pretense that you are ignorant.

POLIXENES   O, then my best blood turn
To an infected jelly, and my name
Be yoked with his° that did betray the Best!°   *(Judas's) name / Christ*
420 Turn then my freshest reputation to
A savour° that may strike the dullest nostril   *foul odor*
Where I arrive, and my approach be shunned,
Nay hated, too, worse than the great'st infection
That e'er was heard or read.

CAMILLO   Swear his thought over²
425 By each particular star in heaven, and
By all their influences,³ you may as well
Forbid the sea for to obey the moon
As or° by oath remove or counsel shake   *either*
The fabric of his folly, whose foundation
430 Is piled upon his faith, and will continue
The standing of his body.°   *As long as he lives*

POLIXENES   How should this grow?°   *come to be*

CAMILLO   I know not, but I am sure 'tis safer to
Avoid what's grown than question how 'tis born.
If therefore you dare trust my honesty,
435 That lies enclosèd in this trunk° which you   *body*
Shall bear along impawned,⁴ away tonight!
Your followers I will whisper to the business,
And will by twos and threes at several posterns°   *city gates*
Clear them o'th' city. For myself, I'll put
440 My fortunes to your service, which are here
By this discovery° lost. Be not uncertain,   *revelation*
For by the honour of my parents, I
Have uttered truth; which if you seek to prove,
I dare not stand by; nor shall you be safer
445 Than one condemnèd by the King's own mouth,
Thereon his execution sworn.

POLIXENES   I do believe thee,
I saw his heart in's face. Give me thy hand.
Be pilot to me, and thy places° shall   *your position*
Still neighbour° mine. My ships are ready, and   *Always be near*
450 My people did expect my hence departure
Two days ago. This jealousy
Is for a precious creature. As she's rare
Must it be great; and as his person's mighty
Must it be violent; and as he does conceive
455 He is dishonoured by a man which ever
Professed° to him, why, his revenges must   *Professed love*
In that be made more bitter. Fear o'ershades me.
Good expedition° be my friend and comfort   *Let speed (in leaving)*
The gracious Queen, part of his theme, but nothing
460 Of his ill-ta'en suspicion.⁵ Come, Camillo,
I will respect thee as a father if
Thou bear'st my life off hence. Let us avoid.°   *be gone*

---

2. You may swear that his allegations are false.
3. Substances that, according to contemporary astrological theories, were emitted by stars and helped to shape human destiny.

4. Shall carry with you as a pledge (of my faith).
5. And make easier the situation of the virtuous Queen, who is a part of Leontes' accusation, but who is not guilty of his unjustified suspicion.

CAMILLO   It is in mine authority to command
   The keys of all the posterns. Please your highness
465   To take the urgent hour.° Come, sir, away.   *Exeunt*   *seize the moment*

2.1

Enter HERMIONE, MAMILLIUS, [*and*] LADIES

HERMIONE   Take the boy to you. He so troubles me
   'Tis past enduring.
FIRST LADY   Come, my gracious lord,
   Shall I be your play-fellow?
MAMILLIUS   No, I'll none of you.
5   FIRST LADY   Why, my sweet lord?
MAMILLIUS   You'll kiss me hard, and speak to me as if
   I were a baby still. [*To* SECOND LADY] I love you better.
SECOND LADY   And why so, my lord?
MAMILLIUS   Not for because
   Your brows° are blacker—yet black brows they say   *eyebrows*
10   Become some women best, so that there be not
   Too much hair there, but in a semicircle,
   Or a half-moon made with a pen.
SECOND LADY   Who taught° 'this?   *taught you*
MAMILLIUS   I learned it out of women's faces. Pray now,
   What colour are your eyebrows?
FIRST LADY   Blue, my lord.
15   MAMILLIUS   Nay, that's a mock. I have seen a lady's nose
   That has been blue,[1] but not her eyebrows.
FIRST LADY   Hark ye,
   The Queen your mother rounds apace.° We shall   *grows round quickly*
   Present our services to a fine new prince
   One of these days, and then you'd wanton° with us,   *play*
   If we would have you.
20   SECOND LADY   She is spread of late
   Into a goodly bulk, good time encounter her.°   *good fortune be with her*
HERMIONE   What wisdom stirs amongst you? Come sir, now
   I am for you again. Pray you sit by us,
   And tell's a tale.
25   MAMILLIUS   Merry or sad shall't be?
HERMIONE   As merry as you will.
MAMILLIUS   A sad tale's best for winter. I have one
   Of sprites and goblins.
HERMIONE   Let's have that, good sir.
   Come on, sit down, come on, and do your best
30   To fright me with your sprites. You're powerful at it.
MAMILLIUS   There was a man—
HERMIONE   Nay, come sit down, then on.
MAMILLIUS [*sitting*]   Dwelt by a churchyard.—I will tell it softly,
   Yon crickets° shall not hear it.   *(the other women)*
HERMIONE   Come on then, and give't me in mine ear.
   [*Enter apart* LEONTES, ANTIGONUS, *and* LORDS][2]

2.1 Location: Sicilia. The palace of Leontes.
1. It is unclear whether Mamillius is making a joke here or possibly referring to noses made "blue" by the cold or disfigured by venereal disease.
2. As with many scenes in this play, Ralph Crane, the scrivener who probably prepared the manuscript for the printer, massed all the entrances for 2.1 in the initial stage direction, regardless of when individual characters actually appeared on stage. Though it is clear that Leontes, Antigonus, and the other Lords enter only at 2.1.34, in F no entrance is marked for them here, and their names are included in the direction preceding 2.1.1.

35	**LEONTES** Was he met there? His train?° Camillo with him?	*retinue*
	A LORD Behind the tuft of pines I met them. Never	
	Saw I men scour° so on their way. I eyed them	*hurry*
	Even to their ships.	
	LEONTES How blest am I	
	In my just censure,° in my true opinion!	*judgment*
40	Alack, for lesser knowledge°—how accursed	*Would I knew less*
	In being so blest! There may be in the cup	
	A spider steeped, and one may drink, depart,	
	And yet partake no venom, for his knowledge	
	Is not infected;³ but if one present	
45	Th'abhorred ingredient to his eye, make known	
	How he hath drunk, he cracks his gorge,° his sides,	*throat*
	With violent hefts.° I have drunk, and seen the spider.	*retching*
	Camillo was his help in this, his pander.	
	There is a plot against my life, my crown.	
50	All's true that is mistrusted.° That false villain	*suspected*
	Whom I employed was pre-employed by him.	
	He has discovered° my design, and I	*revealed*
	Remain a pinched° thing, yea, a very trick	*tormented*
	For them to play at will. How came the posterns	
	So easily open?	
55	**A LORD** By his great authority,	
	Which often hath no less prevailed than so	
	On your command.	
	LEONTES I know't too well.	
	[*To* HERMIONE] Give me the boy. I am glad you did not nurse him.⁴	
	Though he does bear some signs of me, yet you	
	Have too much blood in him.	
60	**HERMIONE** What is this? Sport?	
	LEONTES [*to a* LORD] Bear the boy hence. He shall not come about her.	
	Away with him, and let her sport herself	
	With that she's big with, [*to* HERMIONE] for 'tis Polixenes	
	Has made thee swell thus. [*Exit one with* MAMILLIUS]	
	HERMIONE But I'd say he had not,	
65	And I'll be sworn you would believe my saying,	
	Howe'er you lean to th' nayward.°	*the contrary*
	LEONTES You, my lords,	
	Look on her, mark her well. Be but about	
	To say she is a goodly lady, and	
	The justice of your hearts will thereto add	
70	''Tis pity she's not honest,° honourable.'	*chaste*
	Praise her but for this her without-door° form—	*external*
	Which on my faith deserves high speech—and straight°	*immediately*
	The shrug, the 'hum' or 'ha', these petty brands°	*expressions; stigmas*
	That calumny° doth use—O, I am out,°	*slander / wrong*
75	That mercy does, for calumny will sear°	*stigmatize*
	Virtue itself⁵—these shrugs, these 'hum's and 'ha's,	
	When you have said she's goodly, come between	
	Ere you can say she's honest. But be't known	

---

3. Alluding to the belief that a spider consumed with food or drink would be poisonous only if its presence were known to the consumer.
4. Women who breast-fed infants were believed to shape an infant's character by substances transmitted in their milk.
5. Leontes seems to mean that calumny (slander) will openly attack virtue, and since Hermione is not virtuous, it is not calumny to attack her. Rather, it is mercy who speaks in indirect "hum's" and "ha's" about her behavior.

From him that has most cause to grieve it should be,
She's an adultress.

80 HERMIONE   Should a villain say so,
The most replenished° villain in the world,   *complete*
He were as much more° villain. You, my lord,   *by so much more a*
Do but mistake.

LEONTES   You have mistook,° my lady—   *erred; improperly taken*
Polixenes for Leontes. O, thou thing,
85 Which I'll not call a creature of thy place,⁶
Lest barbarism,° making me the precedent,   *uncivilized rudeness*
Should a like° language use to all degrees,°   *the same / all ranks*
And mannerly distinguishment° leave out   *proper distinction*
Betwixt the prince and beggar. I have said
90 She's an adultress, I have said with whom.
More, she's a traitor, and Camillo is
A federary° with her, and one that knows   *confederate*
What she should shame to know herself,
But with her most vile principal:° that she's   *partner*
95 A bed-swerver,° even as bad as those   *adultress*
That vulgars give bold'st titles;⁷ ay, and privy
To this their late° escape.   *recent*

HERMIONE   No, by my life,
Privy to none of this. How will this grieve you
When you shall come to clearer knowledge, that
100 You thus have published° me? Gentle my° lord,   *proclaimed / My noble*
You scarce can right me throughly° then to say   *fully do me justice*
You did mistake.

LEONTES   No. If I mistake
In those foundations which I build upon,
The centre° is not big enough to bear   *earth*
105 A schoolboy's top.—Away with her to prison!
He who shall speak for her is afar-off° guilty,   *indirectly*
But that he speaks.°   *Merely for speaking*

HERMIONE   There's some ill planet reigns.
I must be patient till the heavens look
With an aspect more favourable.⁸ Good my° lords,   *My good*
110 I am not prone to weeping, as our sex
Commonly are; the want of which vain dew
Perchance shall dry your pities. But I have
That honourable grief lodged here which burns
Worse than tears drown. Beseech you all, my lords,
115 With thoughts so qualified° as your charities   *tempered*
Shall best instruct you, measure me; and so
The King's will be performed.

LEONTES   Shall I be heard?

HERMIONE   Who is't that goes with me? Beseech your highness
My women may be with me, for you see
120 My plight requires it.—Do not weep, good fools,°   *dear ones*
There is no cause. When you shall know your mistress
Has deserved prison, then abound in tears
As I come out. This action I now go on

---

6. To whom I'll not give the title of your (high) social
position.
7. That common people call by the coarsest names.

8. Another allusion to the belief that planets can have
an evil effect or "aspect" when situated in certain positions.

Is for my better grace.[9]—Adieu, my lord.

125 I never wished to see you sorry; now
I trust I shall. My women, come, you have leave.°   *permission*

LEONTES   Go, do our bidding. Hence!

[Exit HERMIONE, *guarded, with* LADIES]

A LORD   Beseech your highness, call the Queen again.

ANTIGONUS *[to Leontes]*   Be certain what you do, sir, lest your justice

130 Prove violence, in the which three great ones suffer—
Yourself, your queen, your son.

A LORD *[to* LEONTES]   For her, my lord,
I dare my life lay down, and will do't, sir,
Please you t'accept it, that the Queen is spotless
I'th' eyes of heaven and to you—I mean
In this which you accuse her.

135 ANTIGONUS *[to* LEONTES]   If it prove
She's otherwise, I'll keep my stables where
I lodge my wife,[1] I'll go in couples with her;[2]
Than when I feel and see her, no farther trust her.
For every inch of woman in the world,

140 Ay, every dram° of woman's flesh is false   *smallest piece*
If she be.

LEONTES   Hold your peaces.

A LORD   Good my lord—

ANTIGONUS *[to* LEONTES]   It is for you we speak, not for ourselves.
You are abused, and by some putter-on°   *instigator*
That will be damned for't. Would I knew the villain—

145 I would land-damn him.[3] Be she honour-flawed—
I have three daughters: the eldest is eleven;
The second and the third nine and some five;
If this prove true, they'll pay for't. By mine honour,
I'll geld 'em all.[4] Fourteen they shall not see,

150 To bring false generations.° They are co-heirs,   *illegitimate children*
And I had rather glib° myself than they   *castrate*
Should not produce fair issue.°   *legitimate offspring*

LEONTES   Cease, no more!
You smell this business with a sense as cold
As is a dead man's nose. But I do see't and feel't

155 As you feel doing thus;[5] and see withal
The instruments that feel.[6]

ANTIGONUS   If it be so,
We need no grave to bury honesty;°   *chastity*
There's not a grain of it the face to sweeten°   *to sweeten the face*
Of the whole dungy° earth.   *foul*

LEONTES   What? Lack I credit?

160 A LORD   I had rather you did lack than I, my lord,
Upon this ground;° and more it would content me   *In this affair*

---

9. This trial I am enduring is for my greater honor (when vindicated); *or* This suffering I am enduring is to refine and purge me, leading to greater virtue.
1. An obscure passage, meaning that he'll guard his wife's lodgings as vigilantly as he guards his horses *or* that he will treat his wife's lodgings as he does his stables, where mares are separated from stallions.
2. Have her tied to me (as hounds were leashed together for the hunt).
3. A term of abuse whose exact meaning is unclear. It

may be a dialect form of "lamback" or "lambaste," which means "thrash."
4. I'll make them all barren. Literally, I'll cut out their organs of generation.
5. Leontes here probably does some action (touching a courtier or rubbing his hands together) that shows the immediacy of his sensory reactions.
6. I see the fingers ("instruments") with which I touch things; I see the sinners, Hermione and Polixenes, who touch one another.

To have her honour true than your suspicion,
Be blamed for't how you might.

LEONTES   Why, what need we
Commune with you of this, but rather follow
165   Our forceful instigation?° Our prerogative   *Our own powerful impulse*
Calls not your counsels,[7] but our natural goodness
Imparts this;° which, if you—or° stupefied   *this information / either*
Or seeming so in skill°—cannot or will not   *cunningly*
Relish° a truth like us, inform yourselves   *Appreciate*
170   We need no more of your advice. The matter,
The loss, the gain, the ord'ring on't,° is all   *of it*
Properly ours.

ANTIGONUS   And I wish, my liege,
You had only in your silent judgement tried it
Without more overture.°   *public disclosure*

LEONTES   How could that be?
175   Either thou art most ignorant by age
Or thou wert born a fool. Camillo's flight
Added to their familiarity,
Which was as gross as ever touched conjecture
That lacked sight only, naught for approbation
180   But only seeing,[8] all other circumstances
Made up to th' deed°—doth push on this proceeding.[9]   *Pointed to the deed*
Yet for a greater confirmation—
For in an act of this importance 'twere
Most piteous to be wild°—I have dispatched in post°   *rash / haste*
185   To sacred Delphos,[1] to Apollo's temple,
Cleomenes and Dion, whom you know
Of stuffed sufficiency.° Now from the oracle   *ample competence*
They will bring all, whose spiritual counsel had°   *obtained*
Shall stop or spur me. Have I done well?

190   A LORD   Well done, my lord.

LEONTES   Though I am satisfied, and need no more
Than what I know, yet shall the oracle
Give rest to th' minds of others such as he,
Whose ignorant credulity will not
195   Come up to th' truth. So have we thought it good
From our free° person she should be confined,   *openly accessible*
Lest that the treachery of the two fled hence
Be left her to perform. Come, follow us.
We are to speak in public; for this business
Will raise° us all.   *rouse (to action)*

200   ANTIGONUS [*aside*]   To laughter, as I take it,
If the good truth were known.   *Exeunt*

2.2
Enter PAULINA, *a Gentleman[, and attendants]*

PAULINA   The keeper of the prison, call to him.
Let him have knowledge who I am.   [*Exit Gentleman*]

---

7. My privileges as King do not require that I seek your advice.
8. As obvious ("gross") as any suspicion ("conjecture") ever was that only lacked eyewitnesses ("sight" and "seeing") to confirm its truth.
9. Does urge on this course of action.

1. Delos, often called Delphos by Renaissance writers, was the island where Apollo, the sun god, was supposedly buried. It is here conflated with Delphi, the Greek mainland town where the oracle of Apollo could be consulted.
2.2 Location: Sicilia. A prison.

Good lady,
No court in Europe is too good for thee.
What dost thou then in prison?   [*Enter* JAILER *and Gentleman*]
                        Now, good sir,
You know me, do you not?

5 JAILER   For a worthy lady,
And one who much I honour.

PAULINA   Pray you then,
Conduct me to the Queen.

JAILER   I may not, madam. To the contrary
I have express commandment.

10 PAULINA   Here's ado,°   *Here's such a fuss*
To lock up honesty and honour from
Th'access of gentle° visitors. Is't lawful, pray you,   *noble; kind*
To see her women? Any of them? Emilia?

JAILER   So please you, madam,
15 To put apart these your attendants, I
Shall bring Emilia forth.

PAULINA   I pray now call her.—
Withdraw yourselves.   [*Exeunt Gentleman and attendants*]

JAILER   And, madam,
20 I must be present at your conference.

PAULINA   Well, be't so, prithee.   [*Exit* JAILER]
Here's such ado, to make no stain a stain
As passes colouring.[1]
     [*Enter* JAILER *and* EMILIA]
                 Dear gentlewoman,
How fares our gracious lady?

25 EMILIA   As well as one so great and so forlorn
May hold together. On° her frights and griefs,   *Because of*
Which never tender lady hath borne greater,
She is, something° before her time, delivered.   *somewhat*

PAULINA   A boy?

EMILIA   A daughter, and a goodly babe,
30 Lusty,° and like° to live. The Queen receives   *Vigorous / likely*
Much comfort in't; says, 'My poor prisoner,
I am innocent as you.'

PAULINA   I dare be sworn.
These dangerous, unsafe lunes° i'th' King, beshrew them!   *fits of lunacy*
He must be told on't, and he shall. The office°   *job*
35 Becomes a woman best. I'll take't upon me.
If I prove honey-mouthed, let my tongue blister,[2]
And never to my red-looked° anger be   *red-faced*
The trumpet[3] any more. Pray you, Emilia,
Commend° my best obedience to the Queen.   *Send*
40 If she dares trust me with her little babe
I'll show't the King, and undertake to be
Her advocate to th' loud'st. We do not know
How he may soften at the sight o'th' child.

---

1. To make from no stain at all a stain that exceeds what the art of dyeing can do; to make of no sin a sin that surpasses all attempts to justify it.
2. Alluding to the proverb that deceitfulness causes blisters on the tongue.

3. In early modern warfare, a "trumpet" was a soldier who, bearing a trumpet, went before the red-coated herald who carried messages, often angry ones, to the enemy camp.

The silence often of pure innocence
Persuades when speaking fails.

45 EMILIA   Most worthy madam,
Your honour and your goodness is so evident
That your free° undertaking cannot miss   *generous*
A thriving issue.[4] There is no lady living
So meet° for this great errand. Please your ladyship   *suitable*
50 To visit the next room, I'll presently
Acquaint the Queen of your most noble offer,
Who but today hammered of° this design   *mused upon*
But durst not tempt a minister of honour[5]
Lest she should be denied.

PAULINA   Tell her, Emilia,
55 I'll use that tongue I have. If wit flow from't
As boldness from my bosom, let't not be doubted
I shall do good.

EMILIA   Now be you blest for it!
I'll to the Queen. Please you come something° nearer.   *somewhat*

JAILER   Madam, if't please the Queen to send the babe
60 I know not what° I shall incur to pass it,[6]   *what (risk)*
Having no warrant.

PAULINA   You need not fear it, sir.
This child was prisoner to the womb, and is
By law and process of great nature thence
Freed and enfranchised, not a party to
65 The anger of the King, nor guilty of—
If any be—the trespass of the Queen.

JAILER   I do believe it.

PAULINA   Do not you fear. Upon mine honour,
I will stand twixt you and danger.   *Exeunt*

2.3

Enter LEONTES

LEONTES   Nor° night nor day, no rest! It is but weakness   *Neither*
To bear the matter thus, mere weakness. If
The cause were not in being°—part o'th' cause,   *alive*
She, th'adultress; for the harlot° King   *lewd*
5 Is quite beyond mine arm, out of the blank°   *target*
And level° of my brain, plot-proof; but she   *aim*
I can hook to me. Say that she were gone,
Given to the fire,[1] a moiety° of my rest   *portion*
Might come to me again. Who's there?

[*Enter a* SERVANT]

SERVANT   My lord.

LEONTES   How does the boy?

10 SERVANT   He took good rest tonight.
'Tis hoped his sickness is discharged.

LEONTES   To see his nobleness!
Conceiving° the dishonour of his mother   *Realizing*
He straight° declined, drooped, took it deeply,   *immediately*
15 Fastened and fixed the shame on't° in himself;   *of it*

---

4. A successful outcome, with a pun on "issue" as "offspring."
5. But dared not risk asking a person of higher rank.

6. To let it pass (out of the prison).
2.3 Location: Sicilia. The palace of Leontes.
1. Burned at the stake (for treason against the King).

Threw off his spirit, his appetite, his sleep,
And downright languished. Leave me solely.° Go,   *alone*
See how he fares.   [*Exit* SERVANT]
                    Fie, fie, no thought of him.°   *(Polixenes)*
The very thought of my revenges that way
20   Recoil upon me. In himself too mighty,
And in his parties,° his alliance.° Let him be   *supporters / allies*
Until a time may serve. For present vengeance,
Take it on her. Camillo and Polixenes
Laugh at me, make their pastime at my sorrow.
25   They should not laugh if I could reach them, nor
Shall she, within my power.

            Enter PAULINA [*carrying a babe, with* ANTIGONUS,
            LORDS, *and the* SERVANT, *trying to restrain her*]

A LORD   You must not enter.
PAULINA   Nay rather, good my lords, be second to me.°   *help me*
Fear you his tyrannous passion more, alas,
Than the Queen's life?—a gracious, innocent soul,
More free° than he is jealous.   *innocent*
30   ANTIGONUS   That's enough.
SERVANT   Madam, he hath not slept tonight, commanded
None should come at him.
PAULINA   Not so hot, good sir.
I come to bring him sleep. 'Tis such as you,
That creep like shadows by him, and do sigh
35   At each his needless heavings, such as you
Nourish the cause of his awaking.° I   *wakefulness*
Do come with words as medicinal as true,
Honest as either, to purge him of that humour°   *mental disorder*
That presses him from sleep.
LEONTES   What noise there, ho?
40   PAULINA   No noise, my lord, but needful conference
About some gossips² for your highness.
LEONTES   How?
Away with that audacious lady! Antigonus,
I charged thee that she should not come about me.
I knew she would.
ANTIGONUS   I told her so, my lord,
45   On your displeasure's peril° and on mine,   *At the risk of your anger*
She should not visit you.
LEONTES   What, canst not rule her?
PAULINA   From all dishonesty he can. In this,
Unless he take the course that you have done—
Commit° me for committing honour—trust it,   *Imprison*
He shall not rule me.
50   ANTIGONUS   La you now, you hear.
When she will take the rein I let her run,
But she'll not stumble.
PAULINA [*to* LEONTES]   Good my liege, I come—
And I beseech you hear me, who professes
Myself your loyal servant, your physician,
55   Your most obedient counsellor; yet that dares
Less appear so in comforting° your evils   *condoning*

---

2. Godparents or sponsors at a child's baptism.

Than such as most seem yours³—I say, I come
From your good queen.

LEONTES   Good queen?

60 PAULINA   Good queen, my lord, good queen, I say good queen,
And would by combat make her good,⁴ so were I
A man, the worst about° you.   *lowest in rank of*

LEONTES [*to* LORDS]   Force her hence.

PAULINA   Let him that makes but trifles of his eyes
First hand° me. On mine own accord, I'll off.   *touch*

65 But first I'll do my errand. The good Queen—
For she is good—hath brought you forth a daughter—
Here 'tis—commends it to your blessing.

[*She lays down the babe*]

LEONTES   Out!
A mankind° witch! Hence with her, out o'door—   *manlike*
A most intelligencing bawd.°   *spying go-between*

PAULINA   Not so.

70 I am as ignorant in that as you
In so entitling me,° and no less honest   *In calling me that*
Than you are mad, which is enough, I'll warrant,
As this world goes, to pass for honest.

LEONTES [*to* LORDS]   Traitors,
Will you not push her out?

[*To* ANTIGONUS]   Give her the bastard.

75 Thou dotard, thou art woman-tired,⁵ unroosted
By thy Dame Partlet here.⁶ Take up the bastard,
Take't up, I say. Give't to thy crone.°   *old woman*

PAULINA [*to* ANTIGONUS]   For ever
Unvenerable° be thy hands if thou   *Unworthy of respect*
Tak'st up the princess by that forcèd baseness⁷
Which he has put upon't.

80 LEONTES   He dreads° his wife.   *fears*

PAULINA   So I would you did. Then 'twere past all doubt
You'd call your children yours.

LEONTES   A nest of traitors.

ANTIGONUS   I am none, by this good light.

PAULINA   Nor I, nor any
But one that's here, and that's himself, for he

85 The sacred honour of himself, his queen's,
His hopeful son's, his babe's, betrays to slander,
Whose sting is sharper than the sword's; and will not—
For as the case now stands, it is a curse
He cannot be compelled to't—once remove

90 The root of his opinion, which is rotten
As ever oak or stone was sound.

LEONTES [*to* LORDS]   A callat°   *scold; harlot*
Of boundless tongue, who late° hath beat her husband,   *recently*
And now baits° me! This brat is none of mine.   *provokes*
It is the issue° of Polixenes.   *offspring*

---

3. Than those who (wrongly) seem most loyal.
4. Prove her to be innocent. Alluding to the chivalric trials by combat in which knights would establish innocence or guilt by means of duels.
5. You are pecked at by women. A metaphor from fal-

conry referring to tearing of flesh with the beak.
6. Expelled from your "roost" or "perch," the position of domestic authority assigned to men. In medieval tales, "Partlett" is a traditional name for a hen.
7. Under that wrongful name of bastard.

95 Hence with it, and together with the dam
Commit them to the fire.

PAULINA   It is yours,
And might we lay th'old proverb to your charge,°   *apply the proverb to you*
So like you 'tis the worse. Behold, my lords,
Although the print° be little, the whole matter   *copy*
100 And copy of the father: eye, nose, lip,
The trick° of's frown, his forehead, nay, the valley,[8]   *distinctive character*
The pretty dimples of his chin and cheek, his smiles,
The very mould and frame of hand, nail, finger.
And thou good goddess Nature, which hast made it
105 So like to him that got° it, if thou hast   *begot*
The ordering of the mind too, 'mongst all colours
No yellow[9] in't, lest she suspect, as he does,
Her children not her husband's.

LEONTES [*to* ANTIGONUS]   A gross hag!—
And lozel,° thou art worthy to be hanged,   *scoundrel*
That wilt not stay her tongue.
110 ANTIGONUS   Hang all the husbands
That cannot do that feat, you'll leave yourself
Hardly one subject.

LEONTES   Once more, take her hence.

PAULINA   A most unworthy and unnatural lord
Can do no more.

LEONTES   I'll ha' thee burnt.

PAULINA   I care not.
115 It is an heretic that makes the fire,
Not she which burns in't.[1] I'll not call you tyrant;
But this most cruel usage of your queen—
Not able to produce more accusation
Than your own weak-hinged fancy—something savours
120 Of tyranny, and will ignoble make you,
Yea, scandalous to the world.

LEONTES [*to* ANTIGONUS]   On your allegiance,
Out of the chamber with her! Were I a tyrant,
Where were her life? She durst not call me so
If she did know me one. Away with her!
125 PAULINA   I pray you do not push me, I'll be gone.
Look to your babe, my lord; 'tis yours. Jove° send her   *(King of the gods)*
A better guiding spirit. What needs these hands?[2]
You that are thus so tender o'er° his follies   *gentle with*
Will never do him good, not one of you.
130 So, so. Farewell, we are gone.   *Exit*

LEONTES [*to* ANTIGONUS]   Thou, traitor, hast set on thy wife to this.
My child? Away with't! Even thou, that hast
A heart so tender o'er it, take it hence
And see it instantly consumed with fire.
135 Even thou, and none but thou. Take it up straight.°   *at once*
Within this hour bring me word 'tis done,
And by good testimony,° or I'll seize thy life,   *with good evidence*

---

8. Referring to an indentation in the lip or a cleft in the chin.
9. Proverbially, the color of jealousy.
1. The heretic is the one who unjustly makes the fire

(Leontes), not the woman who burns in it (Hermione).
2. Why is it necessary for you to push me out? (spoken to Leontes' attendant lords).

With what thou else call'st thine. If thou refuse
And wilt encounter with my wrath, say so.
140 The bastard brains with these my proper° hands   *own*
Shall I dash out. Go, take it to the fire;
For thou set'st on thy wife.
ANTIGONUS   I did not, sir.
These lords, my noble fellows, if they please
Can clear me in't.
LORDS   We can. My royal liege,
145 He is not guilty of her coming hither.
LEONTES   You're liars all.
A LORD   Beseech your highness, give us better credit.°   *think us more honorable*
We have always truly served you, and beseech
So to esteem of us. And on our knees we beg,
150 As recompense of our dear services
Past and to come, that you do change this purpose
Which, being so horrible, so bloody, must
Lead on to some foul issue. We all kneel.
LEONTES   I am a feather for each wind that blows.
155 Shall I live on, to see this bastard kneel
And call me father? Better burn it now
Than curse it then. But be it. Let it live.
It shall not neither.
[*To* ANTIGONUS]   You, sir, come you hither,
You that have been so tenderly officious
160 With Lady Margery[3] your midwife there,
To save this bastard's life—for 'tis a bastard,
So sure as this beard's grey. What will you adventure°   *risk*
To save this brat's life?
ANTIGONUS   Anything, my lord,
That my ability may undergo,
165 And nobleness impose. At least thus much,
I'll pawn the little blood which I have left[4]
To save the innocent; anything possible.
LEONTES   It shall be possible. Swear by this sword
Thou wilt perform my bidding.
ANTIGONUS   I will, my lord.
170 LEONTES   Mark, and perform it. Seest thou? For the fail°   *failure*
Of any point in't shall not only be
Death to thyself but to thy lewd-tongued wife,
Whom for this time we pardon. We enjoin thee,
As thou art liegeman° to us, that thou carry   *loyal servant*
175 This female bastard hence, and that thou bear it
To some remote and desert place, quite out
Of our dominions; and that there thou leave it,
Without more mercy, to it° own protection   *its*
And favour of the climate. As by strange fortune[5]
180 It came to us, I do in justice charge thee,
On thy soul's peril and thy body's torture,
That thou commend it strangely to some place[6]
Where chance may nurse° or end it. Take it up.   *nurture; help*

---

3. A contemptuous name (like "Dame Partlett") for a
disorderly woman. "Margery-prater" is a slang term for
"hen."
4. Aging was thought to reduce the amount of blood in

the body.
5. Since by some unusual chance; since by the act of a
foreigner (Polixenes).
6. That you take it to some foreign land.

ANTIGONUS　I swear to do this, though a present death
185　Had been more merciful. Come on, poor babe,
　　Some powerful spirit instruct the kites° and ravens　　　　*birds of prey*
　　To be thy nurses. Wolves and bears, they say,
　　Casting their savageness aside, have done
　　Like° offices of pity. Sir, be prosperous　　　　*Similar*
190　In more than this deed does require;[7] [*to the babe*] and blessing
　　Against° this cruelty, fight on thy side,　　　　*To counteract*
　　Poor thing, condemned to loss.°　　　　*Exit [with the babe]*　　　　*ruin*
LEONTES　　　　No, I'll not rear
　　Another's issue.
　　　　Enter a SERVANT
SERVANT　　　　Please your highness, posts°　　　　*messengers*
　　From those you sent to th'oracle are come
195　An hour since. Cleomenes and Dion,
　　Being well arrived from Delphos, are both landed,
　　Hasting to th' court.
A LORD [*to* LEONTES]　So please you, sir, their speed
　　Hath been beyond account.°　　　　*without precedent*
LEONTES　　　　Twenty-three days
　　They have been absent. 'Tis good speed, foretells
200　The great Apollo suddenly° will have　　　　*at once*
　　The truth of this appear. Prepare you, lords.
　　Summon a session,° that we may arraign　　　　*trial*
　　Our most disloyal lady; for as she hath
　　Been publicly accused, so shall she have
205　A just and open trial. While she lives
　　My heart will be a burden to me. Leave me,
　　And think upon my bidding.　　　　*Exeunt [severally]°*　　　　*separately*

3.1

Enter CLEOMENES *and* DION

CLEOMENES　The climate's delicate, the air most sweet;
　　Fertile the isle,[1] the temple much surpassing
　　The common praise it bears.
DION　　　　I shall report,
　　For most it caught° me, the celestial habits—°　　　　*charmed / garments*
5　　Methinks I so should term them—and the reverence
　　Of the grave wearers. O, the sacrifice—
　　How ceremonious, solemn, and unearthly
　　It was i'th' off'ring!
CLEOMENES　　　　But of all, the burst°　　　　*blast (of thunder)*
　　And the ear-deaf'ning voice o'th' oracle,
10　Kin to Jove's thunder, so surprised my sense
　　That I was nothing.
DION　　　　If th'event° o'th' journey　　　　*outcome*
　　Prove as successful to the Queen—O, be't so!—
　　As it hath been to us rare, pleasant, speedy,
　　The time is worth the use on't.[2]
CLEOMENES　　　　Great Apollo

---

7. To a greater extent or in more ways than this action deserves.
3.1 Location: A road in Sicilia.
1. The island of Delphos (Delos), Apollo's birthplace,

here conflated with Delphi, where Apollo's oracle was located. See note to 2.1.185.
2. The time will have been well spent.

15   Turn all to th' best! These proclamations,
        So forcing faults upon Hermione,
        I little like.
    DION   The violent carriage° of it   *rash handling*
        Will clear or end the business. When the oracle,
        Thus by Apollo's great divine° sealed up,   *priest*
20   Shall the contents discover,° something rare   *reveal*
        Even then will rush to knowledge. Go. Fresh horses!
        And gracious be the issue.°   *Exeunt*   *result; the child*

3.2

       Enter LEONTES, LORDS, [*and*] OFFICERS

   LEONTES   This sessions, to our great grief we pronounce,
        Even pushes 'gainst our heart: the party tried
        The daughter of a king, our wife, and one
        Of us° too much beloved. Let us be cleared   *By us*
5   Of being tyrannous since we so openly
        Proceed in justice, which shall have due course
        Even to the guilt or the purgation.°   *acquittal*
        Produce the prisoner.
   OFFICER   It is his highness' pleasure
        That the Queen appear in person here in court.

      [*Enter* HERMIONE *guarded, with* PAULINA *and Ladies*]

10   Silence.[1]
   LEONTES   Read the indictment.
   OFFICER [*reads*]   Hermione, queen to the worthy Leontes, King
        of Sicilia, thou art here accused and arraigned of high treason
        in committing adultery with Polixenes, King of Bohemia, and
15   conspiring with Camillo to take away the life of our sovereign
        lord the King, thy royal husband; the pretence° whereof being   *purpose*
        by circumstances partly laid open, thou, Hermione, contrary to
        the faith and allegiance of a true subject, didst counsel and aid
        them for their better safety to fly away by night.
20   HERMIONE   Since what I am to say must be but° that   *only*
        Which contradicts my accusation, and
        The testimony on my part no other
        But what comes from myself, it shall scarce boot° me   *profit*
        To say 'Not guilty'. Mine integrity
25   Being counted falsehood shall, as I express it,
        Be so received. But thus: if powers divine
        Behold our human actions—as they do—
        I doubt not then but innocence shall make
        False accusation blush, and tyranny
30   Tremble at patience. You, my lord, best know—
        Who least will seem to do so—my past life
        Hath been as continent, as chaste, as true
        As I am now unhappy; which° is more   *which unhappiness*
        Than history can pattern,[2] though devised
35   And played to take° spectators. For behold me,   *captivate*
        A fellow of the royal bed, which owe°   *who owns*
        A moiety° of the throne; a great king's daughter,   *A portion*

3.2 Location: Sicilia. A court of justice.
1. In F, the word "Silence" is printed in italics and set as a stage direction. Here it is treated as an imperative and assigned to the Officer who announces the Queen's entrance.
2. Than story or drama can show a precedent for.

The mother to a hopeful prince, here standing
To prate and talk for life and honour, fore°   *before*
40   Who please to come and hear. For° life, I prize° it   *As for / value*
As I weigh° grief, which I would spare.° For honour,   *value / do without*
'Tis a derivative[3] from me to mine,°   *(my children)*
And only that I stand° for. I appeal   *fight*
To your own conscience, sir, before Polixenes
45   Came to your court how I was in your grace,
How merited to be so; since he came,
With what encounter so uncurrent° I   *conduct so unacceptable*
Have strained° t'appear thus.° If one jot beyond   *transgressed / (on trial)*
The bound of honour, or in act or will
50   That way inclining, hardened be the hearts
Of all that hear me, and my near'st of kin
Cry 'Fie' upon my grave.
LEONTES   I ne'er heard yet
That any of these bolder vices wanted
Less° impudence to gainsay° what they did   *Were more lacking in / deny*
Than to perform it first.
55   HERMIONE   That's true enough,
Though 'tis a saying, sir, not due° to me.   *relevant*
LEONTES   You will not own it.
HERMIONE   More than mistress of
Which comes to me in name of fault, I must not
At all acknowledge.[4] For Polixenes,
60   With whom I am accused, I do confess
I loved him as in honour he required;°   *was his due*
With such a kind of love as might become
A lady like me; with a love, even such,
So, and no other, as yourself commanded;
65   Which not to have done I think had been in me
Both disobedience and ingratitude
To you and toward your friend, whose love had spoke
Even since it could speak, from an infant, freely
That it was yours. Now for conspiracy,
70   I know not how it tastes, though it be dished°   *served*
For me to try how. All I know of it
Is that Camillo was an honest man;
And why he left your court, the gods themselves,
Wotting° no more than I, are ignorant.   *If they know*
75   LEONTES   You knew of his departure, as you know
What you have underta'en to do in's absence.
HERMIONE   Sir,
You speak a language that I understand not.
My life stands in the level of your dreams,[5]
Which I'll lay down.
80   LEONTES   Your actions are my 'dreams'.
You had a bastard by Polixenes,
And I but° dreamed it. As you were past all shame—   *merely*
Those of your fact° are so—so past all truth;   *(guilty) of your crime*

3. Something handed on.
4. I must not answer for ("acknowledge") more than
those faults that I actually possess (am "mistress of").
Hermione is denying she possesses the "bolder vices" of

which Leontes accuses her in line 53.
5. As the target ("level") of your delusions. A metaphor
from archery.

Which to deny concerns more than avails;[6] for as

85 Thy brat hath been cast out, like to itself,°   *as it should be*
No father owning it—which is indeed
More criminal in thee than it—so thou
Shalt feel our justice, in whose easiest passage
Look for no less than death.[7]

HERMIONE   Sir, spare your threats.

90 The bug° which you would fright me with, I seek.   *horrible object*
To me can life be no commodity.°   *profit; comfort*
The crown and comfort of my life, your favour,
I do give° lost, for I do feel it gone   *reckon*
But know not how it went. My second joy,°   *(Mamillius)*

95 And first fruits of my body, from his presence
I am barred, like one infectious. My third comfort,
Starred most unluckily,[8] is from my breast,
The innocent milk in it° most innocent mouth,   *its*
Haled° out to murder; myself on every post[9]   *Dragged*

100 Proclaimed a strumpet, with immodest° hatred   *excessive*
The childbed privilege[1] denied, which 'longs°   *belongs*
To women of all fashion;° lastly, hurried   *ranks*
Here, to this place, i'th' open air,[2] before
I have got strength of limit.[3] Now, my liege,

105 Tell me what blessings I have here alive,
That I should fear to die. Therefore proceed.
But yet hear this—mistake me not—no life,
I prize it not a straw; but for mine honour,
Which I would free:° if I shall be condemned   *vindicate*

110 Upon surmises, all proofs sleeping else°   *except*
But what your jealousies awake, I tell you
'Tis rigour, and not law.[4] Your honours all,
I do refer me° to the oracle.   *appeal*
Apollo be my judge.

A LORD   This your request

115 Is altogether just. Therefore bring forth,
And in Apollo's name, his oracle.   [*Exeunt certain Officers*]

HERMIONE   The Emperor of Russia[5] was my father.
O that he were alive, and here beholding
His daughter's trial; that he did but see

120 The flatness° of my misery—yet with eyes   *boundlessness*
Of pity, not revenge.

[*Enter* OFFICERS *with* CLEOMENES *and* DION]

OFFICER   You here shall swear upon this sword of justice
That you, Cleomenes and Dion, have
Been both at Delphos, and from thence have brought

125 This sealed-up oracle, by the hand delivered

---

6. Your denial of the truth costs you more effort than it's worth.
7. In the mildest course of justice, you can expect death. The implication is that death may well be preceded by torture.
8. Born under most unlucky stars.
9. Alluding to the early modern practice of nailing proclamations to posts in public places.
1. The right to enjoy a period of bedrest and seclusion after childbirth.
2. Exposure to air outside the domestic space was con-sidered unsafe for women weakened by childbirth.
3. Before I have the strength that follows the custom-ary period of confinement.
4. Playing on the expression "the rigor of the law," Hermione implies that judgment against her would be mere tyranny ("rigor") and not law.
5. Possibly a reference to the legendary Czar Ivan the Terrible, who died in 1584. Many London merchants were interested in trade with Russia, especially after the formation of the Muscovy Company in 1553.

Of great Apollo's priest; and that since then
You have not dared to break the holy seal,
Nor read the secrets in't.

CLEOMENES *and* DION   All this we swear.

130 LEONTES   Break up the seals, and read.

OFFICER [*reads*]   Hermione is chaste, Polixenes blameless, Camillo a true subject, Leontes a jealous tyrant, his innocent babe
truly begotten, and the King shall live without an heir if that
which is lost be not found.

LORDS   Now blessèd be the great Apollo!

135 HERMIONE   Praised!

LEONTES   Hast thou read truth?

OFFICER   Ay, my lord, even so as it is here set down.

LEONTES   There is no truth at all i'th' oracle.
The sessions shall proceed. This is mere falsehood.

[*Enter a* SERVANT]

SERVANT   My lord the King! The King!

140 LEONTES   What is the business?

SERVANT   O sir, I shall be hated to report it.
The prince your son, with mere conceit° and fear   thought
Of the Queen's speed,° is gone.   fortune

LEONTES   How, 'gone'?

SERVANT   Is dead.

LEONTES   Apollo's angry, and the heavens themselves
Do strike at my injustice.

[HERMIONE *falls to the ground*]

145   How now there?

PAULINA   This news is mortal to the Queen. Look down
And see what death is doing.

LEONTES   Take her hence.
Her heart is but o'ercharged.° She will recover.   overburdened (*by emotion*)
I have too much believed mine own suspicion.

150 Beseech you, tenderly apply to her
Some remedies for life.

[*Exeunt* PAULINA *and Ladies, carrying* HERMIONE]

                            Apollo, pardon
My great profaneness 'gainst thine oracle.
I'll reconcile me to Polixenes,
New woo my queen, recall the good Camillo,

155 Whom I proclaim a man of truth, of mercy;
For being transported by my jealousies
To bloody thoughts and to revenge, I chose
Camillo for the minister to poison
My friend Polixenes, which had° been done,   would have

160 But that the good mind of Camillo tardied°   delayed
My swift command. Though I with death and with
Reward did threaten and encourage him,
Not doing it, and being done,[6] he, most humane
And filled with honour, to my kingly guest

165 Unclasped my practice,° quit his fortunes here—   Revealed my plot
Which you knew great—and to the certain hazard
Of all incertainties himself commended,°   consigned himself

6. That is, "Though I threatened him with death if he did not do it and encouraged him with the promise of reward
if he did do it."

No richer than his honour.[7] How he glisters
Through my rust![8] And how his piety
Does my deeds make the blacker!
    [*Enter* PAULINA]

170 PAULINA   Woe the while!
O cut my lace,[9] lest my heart, cracking it,
Break too.

A LORD   What fit is this, good lady?

PAULINA [*to* LEONTES]   What studied° torments, tyrant, hast for me?   *expertly devised*
What wheels, racks, fires? What flaying, boiling
175 In leads or oils?[1] What old or newer torture
Must I receive, whose every word deserves
To taste of thy most worst? Thy tyranny,
Together working with thy jealousies—
Fancies too weak for boys, too green and idle°   *immature and foolish*
180 For girls of nine—O think what they have done,
And then run mad indeed, stark mad, for all
Thy bygone fooleries were but spices° of it.   *slight tastes*
That thou betrayed'st Polixenes, 'twas nothing.
That did but show thee, of° a fool, inconstant,   *for*
185 And damnable° ingrateful. Nor was't much   *damnably; cursedly*
Thou wouldst have poisoned good Camillo's honour
To have him kill a king—poor° trespasses,   *minor*
More monstrous standing by,[2] whereof I reckon
The casting forth to crows thy baby daughter
190 To be or° none or little, though a devil   *either*
Would have shed water out of fire ere done't.[3]
Nor is't directly laid to thee the death
Of the young prince, whose honourable thoughts—
Thoughts high for one so tender°—cleft the heart   *young*
195 That could conceive a gross° and foolish sire   *stupid*
Blemished his gracious dam.° This is not, no,   *mother*
Laid to thy answer.[4] But the last—O lords,
When I have said,° cry woe! The Queen, the Queen,   *finished speaking*
The sweet'st, dear'st creature's dead, and vengeance for't
Not dropped down yet.

200 A LORD   The higher powers forbid!

PAULINA   I say she's dead. I'll swear't. If word nor oath
Prevail not, go and see. If you can bring
Tincture° or lustre in her lip, her eye,   *Color*
Heat outwardly or breath within, I'll serve you
205 As I would do the gods. But O thou tyrant,
Do not repent these things, for they are heavier
Than all thy woes° can stir.° Therefore betake thee   *grief / remove*
To nothing but despair. A thousand knees,
Ten thousand years together, naked, fasting,
210 Upon a barren mountain, and still° winter   *always*

---

7. Possessing no fortune but his honor.
8. How he shines ("glisters") in comparison with my rust. The image alludes to polished and rusty armor.
9. It was believed that fainting might be prevented by cutting the stays on the tight bodices characteristic of female dress in this period.
1. A list of early modern forms of torture. The wheel was a device to which a person was tied and his or her limbs broken, usually by beating. The rack typically consisted of a frame with a roller at each end; a person was attached to this frame and his or her limbs stretched by turning the rollers. To "flay" was to strip off someone's skin while he or she was still alive.
2. In comparison with more monstrous ones near at hand.
3. A devil would have shed tears from his fiery eyes (or from hellfires) before he had done it.
4. Presented as a charge you must answer.

In storm perpetual, could not move the gods
To look that way thou wert.°   *in your direction*

LEONTES   Go on, go on.
Thou canst not speak too much. I have deserved
All tongues to talk their bitt'rest.

A LORD [*to* PAULINA]   Say no more.
215   Howe'er the business goes, you have made fault
I'th' boldness of your speech.

PAULINA   I am sorry for't.
All faults I make, when I shall come to know them
I do repent. Alas, I have showed too much
The rashness of a woman. He is touched
220   To th' noble heart. What's gone and what's past help
Should be past grief.
     [*To* LEONTES]   Do not receive affliction
At my petition.° I beseech you, rather   *Because of my injunction*
Let me be punished, that have minded° you   *reminded*
Of what you should forget. Now, good my liege,
225   Sir, royal sir, forgive a foolish woman.
The love I bore your queen—lo, fool again!
I'll speak of her no more, nor of your children.
I'll not remember you of my own lord,
Who is lost too. Take your patience to you,°   *Be patient*
And I'll say nothing.

230   **LEONTES**   Thou didst speak but well
When most the truth, which I receive much better
Than to be pitied of° thee. Prithee bring me   *by*
To the dead bodies of my queen and son.
One grave shall be for both. Upon them shall
235   The causes of their death appear, unto
Our shame perpetual. Once a day I'll visit
The chapel where they lie, and tears shed there
Shall be my recreation.⁵ So long as nature°   *my bodily being*
Will bear up with this exercise, so long
240   I daily vow to use it. Come, and lead me
To these sorrows.   *Exeunt*

3.3

Enter ANTIGONUS, [*carrying the*] *babe,* [*with*] *a* MARINER

ANTIGONUS   Thou art perfect° then our ship hath touched upon   *certain*
The deserts of Bohemia?

MARINER   Ay, my lord, and fear
We have landed in ill time. The skies look grimly
And threaten present blusters.° In my conscience,°   *impending storms / opinion*
5   The heavens with that we have in hand are angry,
And frown upon's.

ANTIGONUS   Their sacred wills be done. Go get aboard.
Look to thy barque.° I'll not be long before   *ship*
I call upon thee.

MARINER   Make your best haste, and go not
10   Too far i'th' land. 'Tis like to be loud° weather.   *stormy*

---

5. My only diversion; my spiritual renewal or recreation.
3.3 Location: Bohemia. The seacoast. This play, as
does Greene's *Pandosto*, credits Bohemia with a coast.

Only for two brief periods in the late Middle Ages may
Bohemia have controlled a small piece of territory on
the Adriatic Sea, but it was otherwise landlocked.

Besides, this place is famous for the creatures
Of prey that keep° upon't.   *live*

ANTIGONUS   Go thou away.
I'll follow instantly.

MARINER   I am glad at heart
To be so rid o'th' business.   *Exit*

ANTIGONUS   Come, poor babe.
15 I have heard, but not believed, the spirits o'th' dead
May walk again. If such thing be, thy mother
Appeared to me last night, for ne'er was dream
So like a waking. To me comes a creature,
Sometimes her head on one side, some another.
20 I never saw a vessel° of like sorrow,   •   *person; receptacle*
So filled and so becoming.[1] In pure white robes
Like very sanctity she did approach
My cabin where I lay, thrice bowed before me,
And, gasping to begin some speech, her eyes
25 Became two spouts. The fury spent, anon°   *soon*
Did this break from her: 'Good Antigonus,
Since fate, against thy better disposition,
Hath made thy person for the thrower-out
Of my poor babe according to thine oath,
30 Places remote enough are in Bohemia.
There weep, and leave it crying; and for° the babe   *because*
Is counted lost for ever, Perdita[2]
I prithee call't. For this ungentle° business   *unkind; ignoble*
Put on thee by my lord, thou ne'er shalt see
35 Thy wife Paulina more.' And so with shrieks
She melted into air. Affrighted much,
I did in time collect myself, and thought
This was so, and no slumber. Dreams are toys,°   *trifles*
Yet for this once, yea superstitiously,
40 I will be squared° by this. I do believe   *ruled*
Hermione hath suffered death, and that
Apollo would—this being indeed the issue°   *child*
Of King Polixenes—it should here be laid,
Either for life or death, upon the earth
45 Of its right father. Blossom, speed° thee well!   *fare*
     [*He lays down the babe and a scroll*]
There lie, and there thy character.[3]
     [*He lays down a box*]
                         There these,[4]
Which may, if fortune please, both breed thee, pretty,
And still rest thine.[5]
     [*Thunder*]
                    The storm begins. Poor wretch,
That for thy mother's fault art thus exposed
50 To loss and what may follow! Weep I cannot,
But my heart bleeds, and most accursed am I
To be by oath enjoined to this. Farewell.

1. So filled with sorrow and so beautiful.
2. Latin for "lost one."
3. The written account of your history and parentage.
4. The gold and jewels with which the Old Shepherd grows rich and which are later used to identify the Princess. See 5.2.29–36.
5. Which may, if you are lucky, be sufficient to pay for your upbringing, pretty child, and still leave you with something besides.

The day frowns more and more. Thou'rt like to have
A lullaby too rough. I never saw
55   The heavens so dim by day. A savage clamour!
Well may I get aboard. This is the chase.°   *hunt*
I am gone for ever!   *Exit, pursued by a bear*[6]
        [*Enter an* OLD SHEPHERD]
OLD SHEPHERD   I would there were no age between ten and
three-and-twenty, or that youth would sleep out the rest; for
60   there is nothing in the between but getting wenches with child,
wronging the ancientry,° stealing, fighting—hark you now,   *elderly people*
would any but these boiled-brains° of nineteen and two-and-   *lunatics*
twenty hunt this weather? They have scared away two of my
best sheep, which I fear the wolf will sooner find than the mas-
65   ter. If anywhere I have them, 'tis by the seaside, browsing of°   *on*
ivy. Good luck, an't° be thy will!   *if it*
        [*He sees the babe*]
What have we here? Mercy on's, a bairn!° A very pretty bairn. *child*
A boy or a child,° I wonder? A pretty one, a very pretty one. *girl*
Sure some scape.[7] Though I am not bookish,° yet I can read   *not familiar with books*
70   'waiting-gentlewoman' in the scape. This has been some stair-
work, some trunk-work, some behind-door-work.[8] They were
warmer that got° this than the poor thing is here. I'll take it up   *begot*
for pity; yet I'll tarry till my son come. He hallooed but even
now. Whoa-ho-hoa!
        Enter CLOWN°   *Bumpkin*
75   CLOWN   Hilloa, loa!
OLD SHEPHERD   What, art so near? If thou'lt see a thing to talk
on° when thou art dead and rotten, come hither. What ail'st   *about*
thou, man?
CLOWN   I have seen two such sights, by sea and by land! But I
80   am not to say it is a sea, for it is now the sky. Betwixt the firmament and it you cannot thrust a bodkin's° point.   *needle's*
OLD SHEPHERD   Why, boy, how is it?
CLOWN   I would you did but see how it chafes, how it rages, how
it takes up the shore. But that's not to the point. O, the most
85   piteous cry of the poor souls! Sometimes to see 'em, and not to
see 'em; now the ship boring° the moon with her mainmast,   *piercing*
and anon swallowed with yeast° and froth, as you'd thrust a cork   *foam*
into a hogshead.° And then for the land-service,[9] to see how the   *cask of liquor*
bear tore out his shoulder-bone, how he cried to me for help,
90   and said his name was Antigonus, a nobleman! But to make an
end of the ship—to see how the sea flap-dragoned it![1] But first,
how the poor souls roared, and the sea mocked them, and how

---

6. One of the most famous stage directions in English drama. A real bear, rather than a man in a bear suit, might have been used in this scene, perhaps discreetly led on a rope by the fleeing Antigonus. There were reports of tame bears in Shakespeare's London, and bearbaiting (setting dogs on chained bears) was a popular Elizabethan sport, sometimes occurring in the same amphitheaters used at other times for stage plays. It is more likely, however, that the bear was impersonated by an actor in a bear costume. Modern productions vary significantly in their representation of the bear. Some strive for realism, having a bearskin-clad actor or a mechanical likeness of a bear pass across a darkened stage illuminated only by the occasional lightning bolt. Others productions are more stylized, suggesting a bear by the obvious artifice of a mask or symbol.
7. Sexual transgression. English ballads and other popular literature of the period offer numerous accounts of female servants who abandon or kill children born out of wedlock.
8. Some secret sexual affair conducted on back stairs, in chests, or behind doors.
9. Punning on the military and culinary meanings of "service" to suggest both "combat on land" and "food to be served up on land."
1. Devoured it as if it were a flapdragon, a raisin floating on flaming brandy.

the poor gentleman roared, and the bear mocked him, both
roaring louder than the sea or weather.

95 OLD SHEPHERD   Name of mercy, when was this, boy?

CLOWN   Now, now. I have not winked° since I saw these sights.   *blinked an eye*
The men are not yet cold under water, nor the bear half dined
on the gentleman. He's at it now.

OLD SHEPHERD   Would I had been by to have helped the old
100 man!

CLOWN   I would you had been by the ship side, to have helped
her. There your charity would have lacked footing.²

OLD SHEPHERD   Heavy° matters, heavy matters. But look thee   *Sad*
here, boy. Now bless thyself. Thou metst with things dying, I
105 with things new-born. Here's a sight for thee. Look thee, a bear-
ing-cloth³ for a squire's child.

[*He points to the box*]

Look thee here, take up, take up, boy. Open't. So, let's see. It
was told me I should be rich by the fairies. This is some
changeling.⁴ Open't. What's within, boy?

110 CLOWN [*opening the box*]   You're a made° old man. If the sins of   *prosperous*
your youth are forgiven you, you're well to live.° Gold, all gold!   *well off; virtuous*

OLD SHEPHERD   This is fairy gold,⁵ boy, and 'twill prove so. Up
with't, keep it close.° Home, home, the next° way. We are   *secret / nearest*
lucky, boy, and to be so still° requires nothing but secrecy. Let   *always*
115 my sheep go. Come, good boy, the next way home.

CLOWN   Go you the next way with your findings. I'll go see if the
bear be gone from the gentleman, and how much he hath
eaten. They are never curst° but when they are hungry. If there   *vicious*
be any of him left, I'll bury it.

120 OLD SHEPHERD   That's a good deed. If thou mayst discern by that
which is left of him what he is,° fetch me to th' sight of him.   *his identity or rank*

CLOWN   Marry⁶ will I; and you shall help to put him i'th' ground.

OLD SHEPHERD   'Tis a lucky day, boy, and we'll do good deeds
on't.   *Exeunt*

4.1

Enter TIME,¹ *the Chorus*

TIME   I that please some, try° all; both joy and terror   *test*
Of good and bad; that makes and unfolds error,
Now take upon me in the name° of Time   *with the authority*
To use my wings. Impute it not a crime
5 To me or my swift passage that I slide
O'er sixteen years and leave the growth untried°   *development unexamined*
Of that wide gap, since it is in my power
To o'erthrow law, and in one self-born° hour   *selfsame*
To plant and o'erwhelm° custom. Let me pass   *establish and overthrow*
10 The same I am ere ancient'st order was

2. There you would not have had a secure place to
stand, with a pun on "footing" as meaning "a foundation" (upon which a charity might be founded).
3. The blanket used to wrap an infant in preparation
for baptism. A squire's child, being of a fairly high
social position, would have a rich bearing-cloth.
4. A child secretly substituted for another by fairies. The
term could apply to the abducted child (usually beautiful)
or to the one (often ugly or deformed) left in its place.
5. Riches left by fairies were unreliable. If not kept
secret, they brought bad luck.

6. A mild oath derived from the name of the Virgin
Mary.
4.1 Location: Scene continues.
1. In early modern texts, Time was conventionally represented as an old bald man with wings, signifying how
swiftly time passes. He often carried an hourglass and
a scythe, symbol of the power of time to destroy life. A
common saying was that Time was the revealer of
Truth, or that Truth was the daughter of Time. Robert
Greene's *Pandosto*, Shakespeare's chief source for *The
Winter's Tale*, was subtitled *The Triumph of Time*.

Or what is now received.[2] I witness to
The times that brought them in; so shall I do
To th' freshest things now reigning, and make stale
The glistering° of this present as my tale   glittering shine
15   Now seems to it.[3] Your patience this allowing,
I turn my glass,° and give my scene such growing   hourglass
As° you had slept between. Leontes leaving   As if
Th'effects of his fond° jealousies, so grieving   foolish
That he shuts up himself, imagine me,
20   Gentle spectators, that I now may be
In fair Bohemia, and remember well
I mentionèd a son o'th' King's, which Florizel
I now name to you; and with speed so pace°   proceed
To speak of Perdita, now grown in grace
25   Equal with wond'ring.[4] What of her ensues
I list not° prophesy, but let Time's news   do not wish to
Be known when 'tis brought forth. A shepherd's daughter
And what to her adheres,° which follows after,   pertains
Is th'argument° of Time. Of this allow,   subject matter
30   If ever you have spent time worse ere now.
If never, yet that Time himself doth say
He wishes earnestly you never may.   *Exit*

4.2

Enter POLIXENES *and* CAMILLO

POLIXENES   I pray thee, good Camillo, be no more importunate.
'Tis a sickness denying° thee anything, a death to grant this.   to deny
CAMILLO   It is sixteen[1] years since I saw my country. Though I
have for the most part been aired abroad,° I desire to lay my   breathed foreign air
5   bones there. Besides, the penitent King, my master, hath sent
for me, to whose feeling° sorrows I might be some allay°—or I   deeply felt / relief
o'erween° to think so—which is another spur to my departure.   am bold enough
POLIXENES   As thou lov'st me, Camillo, wipe not out the rest of
thy services by leaving me now. The need I have of thee thine
10   own goodness hath made. Better not to have had thee than thus
to want° thee. Thou, having made me businesses[2] which none   be without
without thee can sufficiently manage, must either stay to execute them thyself or take away with thee the very services thou
hast done; which if I have not enough considered°—as too   rewarded
15   much I cannot—to be more thankful to thee shall be my study,
and my profit therein, the heaping friendships.[3] Of that fatal° deadly
country Sicilia, prithee speak no more, whose very naming
punishes me with the remembrance of that penitent—as thou
callest him—and reconciled King my brother, whose loss of his
20   most precious queen and children are even now to be afresh°   newly
lamented. Say to me, when sawest thou the Prince Florizel,
my son? Kings are no less unhappy, their issue° not being gra-   children
cious,° than they are in losing them when they have ap-   not proving virtuous
proved° their virtues.   demonstrated

---

2. Let me remain as I have been from before the beginnings of civilization even to the time of present customs.
3. As my tale now seems stale in comparison with the
present.
4. Now grown so gracious as to inspire admiration.
4.2 Location: Bohemia. The palace of Polixenes.

1. F reads "fifteene." At 4.1.6, Time says that sixteen
years have passed. This apparent error may be due to
carelessness on Shakespeare's part or to a misreading of
a Roman numeral by a compositor or scribe.
2. Performed services for me.
3. The accumulation of your kindnesses.

25   CAMILLO   Sir, it is three days since I saw the Prince. What his
           happier affairs may be are to me unknown; but I have missingly
           noted° he is of late much retired from court, and is less fre-   *noted by his absence*
           quent to° his princely exercises than formerly he hath   *less often engaged in*
           appeared.
30   POLIXENES   I have considered so much, Camillo, and with some
           care, so far that I have eyes under my service° which look upon   *spies in my employ*
           his removedness,° from whom I have this intelligence: that he   *retirement (from court)*
           is seldom from the house of a most homely° shepherd, a man,   *simple*
           they say, that from very nothing, and beyond the imagination
35   of his neighbours, is grown into an unspeakable estate.°   *untold wealth*
  CAMILLO   I have heard, sir, of such a man, who hath a daughter
           of most rare note.° The report of her is extended more than can   *quality*
           be thought to begin° from such a cottage.   *originate*
  POLIXENES   That's likewise part of my intelligence; but, I fear,
40   the angle° that plucks our son thither. Thou shalt accompany   *fishhook*
           us to the place, where we will, not appearing what we are, have
           some question with the shepherd; from whose simplicity I
           think it not uneasy° to get the cause of my son's resort thither.   *difficult*
           Prithee, be my present partner in this business, and lay aside
45   the thoughts of Sicilia.
  CAMILLO   I willingly obey your command.
  POLIXENES   My best Camillo! We must disguise ourselves.

Exeunt

4.3

Enter AUTOLYCUS *singing*

AUTOLYCUS
      When daffodils begin to peer,
        With heigh, the doxy° over the dale,   *beggar's wench*
      Why then comes in the sweet° o'the year,   *sweetest part*
        For the red blood reigns in the winter's pale.°   *skin made pale by winter*

5   The white sheet bleaching on the hedge,[1]
        With heigh, the sweet birds, O how they sing!
    Doth set my pugging° tooth on edge,   *thieving*
        For a quart of ale is a dish for a king.

    The lark, that tirra-lirra chants,
10   With heigh, with heigh, the thrush and the jay,
    Are summer songs for me and my aunts[2]
        While we lie tumbling in the hay.

    I have served Prince Florizel, and in my time wore three-pile,[3]
    but now I am out of service.

15   But shall I go mourn for that, my dear?
        The pale moon shines by night,
      And when I wander here and there
        I then do most go right.

      If tinkers[4] may have leave° to live,   *permission*
20   And bear the sow-skin budget,[5]

4.3 Location: Bohemia. Near the cottage where the
Old Shepherd, the Clown, and Perdita live.
1. It was common practice to set clothes out to dry on
hedges.
2. Another slang term for women who take beggars or
vagabonds for lovers.

3. A rich velvet cloth with a thick nap or "pile."
4. Menders of metal pots and kettles. The term was
also applied to itinerant beggars and thieves.
5. Pigskin bag. Bag in which a tinker carried his tools;
hence, a sign of his trade.

Then my account I well may give,
And in the stocks avouch it.°   acknowledge (my crime)
My traffic° is sheets. When the kite builds, look to lesser linen.[6]   trade
My father named me Autolycus,[7] who being, as I am, littered
25   under Mercury,[8] was likewise a snapper-up of unconsidered
trifles. With die and drab° I purchased this caparison, and my   dice and whores
revenue is the silly cheat.[9] Gallows and knock° are too power-   beatings
ful on the highway.[1] Beating and hanging are terrors to me. For°   As for
the life to come, I sleep out the thought of it. A prize, a prize!
         Enter CLOWN
30   CLOWN   Let me see. Every 'leven wether tods,[2] every tod yields
pound and odd° shilling. Fifteen hundred shorn, what comes   one
the wool to?
AUTOLYCUS [*aside*]   If the springe° hold, the cock's[3] mine.   trap
CLOWN   I cannot do't without counters.[4] Let me see, what am I
35   to buy for our sheep-shearing feast?[5] Three pound of sugar, five
pound of currants, rice—what will this sister of mine do with
rice? But my father hath made her mistress of the feast, and she
lays it on. She hath made me four-and-twenty nosegays for the
shearers—three-man-song-men,[6] all, and very good ones—but
40   they are most of them means° and basses, but one Puritan   tenors
amongst them, and he sings psalms to hornpipes.[7] I must have
saffron to colour the warden° pies; mace; dates, none—that's   winter pear
out of my note;° nutmegs, seven; a race° or two of ginger—but   not on my list / root
that I may beg; four pound of prunes, and as many of raisins
45   o'th' sun.°   sun-dried
AUTOLYCUS   [*grovelling on the ground*] O, that ever I was born!
CLOWN   I'th' name of me!
AUTOLYCUS   O help me, help me! Pluck but off these rags, and
then death, death!
50   CLOWN   Alack, poor soul, thou hast need of more rags to lay on
thee rather than have these off.
AUTOLYCUS   O sir, the loathsomeness of them offend me more
than the stripes° I have received, which are mighty ones and   blows
millions.
55   CLOWN   Alas, poor man, a million of beating may come to a
great matter.[8]
AUTOLYCUS   I am robbed, sir, and beaten; my money and apparel
ta'en from me, and these detestable things put upon me.
CLOWN   What, by a horseman, or a footman?°   man on foot
60   AUTOLYCUS   A footman, sweet sir, a footman.
CLOWN   Indeed, he should be a footman, by the garments he has
left with thee. If this be a horseman's coat it hath seen very hot

---

6. The kite, a small bird of prey, supposedly stole small
pieces of linen to make its nest. Autolycus steals sheets,
larger pieces of linen, probably those left to dry on
hedges.
7. In classical mythology, a crafty thief and grandfather
of Ulysses; Autolycus's own father, Mercury, was the
god of thieves.
8. Fathered by Mercury; born when the planet Mercury was ascendant.
9. I was reduced to wearing this garb, and my income
derives from petty swindles.
1. Autolycus fears the penalties meted out to highway-
men. He would rather be a petty thief.
2. Every eleven rams will yield 28 pounds (a "tod") of
wool. The Clown and his father could expect to earn a
substantial amount of money (almost 150 pounds) for

their wool.
3. Woodcock, a bird easily caught and hence proverbial
for its stupidity.
4. Disks used in calculating sums.
5. In rural England, a traditional summer event in
which people of different ranks took part in feasting and
revelry.
6. Men who sing three-part songs.
7. Shrill-sounding musical instruments often played at
country dances and hardly appropriate to accompany
the singing of psalms. Shakespeare may here be satiriz-
ing Puritans, who were notorious for their opposition to
music and dancing.
8. A million blows can be a serious affair, with a pun on
"matter" as "pus," the sign of an infection caused by open
wounds.

service. Lend me thy hand, I'll help thee. Come, lend me thy
hand.
    [*He helps* AUTOLYCUS *up*]
65 AUTOLYCUS O, good sir, tenderly. O!
    CLOWN Alas, poor soul!
    AUTOLYCUS O, good sir, softly,° good sir! I fear, sir, my shoulder-   *gently*
blade is out.
    CLOWN How now? Canst stand?
70 AUTOLYCUS Softly, dear sir. Good sir, softly.
    [*He picks the* CLOWN's *pocket*]⁹
You ha' done me a charitable office.°   *service*
    CLOWN [*reaching for his purse*] Dost lack any money? I have a
little money for thee.
    AUTOLYCUS No, good sweet sir, no, I beseech you, sir.¹ I have a
75 kinsman not past three-quarters of a mile hence, unto whom I
was going. I shall there have money, or anything I want. Offer
me no money, I pray you. That kills° my heart.   *touches*
    CLOWN What manner of fellow was he that robbed you?
    AUTOLYCUS A fellow, sir, that I have known to go about with
80 troll-madams.° I knew him once a servant of the Prince. I can-   *whores*
not tell, good sir, for which of his virtues it was, but he was
certainly whipped out of the court.
    CLOWN His vices, you would say. There's no virtue whipped out
of the court. They cherish it to make it stay there; and yet it
85 will no more but abide.°   *stay there only briefly*
    AUTOLYCUS Vices, I would say, sir. I know this man well. He
hath been since an ape-bearer,² then a process-server—a bai-
liff—then he compassed a motion° of the Prodigal Son,³ and   *devised a puppet show*
married a tinker's wife within a mile where my land and living°   *property*
90 lies, and having flown over many knavish professions, he settled
only in rogue. Some call him Autolycus.
    CLOWN Out upon him! Prig,° for my life, prig! He haunts   *Thief*
wakes,° fairs, and bear-baitings.   *festivals*
    AUTOLYCUS Very true, sir. He, sir, he. That's the rogue that put
95 me into this apparel.
    CLOWN Not a more cowardly rogue in all Bohemia. If you had
but looked big and spit at him, he'd have run.
    AUTOLYCUS I must confess to you, sir, I am no fighter. I am false
of heart° that way, and that he knew, I warrant him.   *without courage*
100 CLOWN How do you now?
    AUTOLYCUS Sweet sir, much better than I was. I can stand, and
walk. I will even take my leave of you, and pace softly towards
my kinsman's.
    CLOWN Shall I bring thee° on the way?   *escort you*
105 AUTOLYCUS No, good-faced sir, no, sweet sir.
    CLOWN Then fare thee well. I must go buy spices for our sheep-
shearing.
    AUTOLYCUS Prosper you, sweet sir.   *Exit* [*the* CLOWN]

9. It is uncertain when Autolycus actually picks the Clown's pocket, but it adds to the humor if Autolycus's next line, "You ha' done me a charitable office," can refer both to the kindness the Clown has knowingly shown Autolycus *and* to the kindness the Clown has unwittingly done him in making available a purse for the wily rogue to steal.
1. Autolycus does not want the Clown to find out he has picked his pocket and so left him with no money. He may here restrain the Clown from putting his hand into his pocket.
2. One who carried about a trained monkey.
3. Alluding to the New Testament story of a spendthrift son who squandered his money only to be forgiven by his father.

　　Your purse is not hot° enough to purchase your spice. I'll be　　　　*full*
110　with you at your sheep-shearing, too. If I make not this cheat°　　　*deception*
　　bring out° another, and the shearers prove sheep, let me be　　　　*lead to*
　　unrolled⁴ and my name put in the book of virtue.
　　[*Sings*]　　　Jog on, jog on, the footpath way,
　　　　　　　　And merrily hent° the stile⁵-a.　　　　　　　*grab (to leap over)*
115　　　　　　　　A merry heart goes all the day,
　　　　　　　　Your sad tires in a mile-a.　　　　　　　*Exit*

4.4

Enter FLORIZEL [*dressed as Doricles a countryman*],
[*and*] PERDITA [*as Queen of the Feast*]¹

FLORIZEL　These your unusual weeds° to each part of you　　　*garments*
　　Does give a life; no shepherdess, but Flora°　　　　*goddess of flowers*
　　Peering in April's front.² This your sheep-shearing
　　Is as a meeting of the petty gods,
　　And you the queen on't.°　　　　　　　　　　　　*of it*
5　PERDITA　　　　　　　　Sir, my gracious lord,
　　To chide at your extremes° it not becomes me—　　　*extravagances*
　　O, pardon that I name them! Your high self,
　　The gracious mark o'th' land,³ you have obscured
　　With a swain's wearing,° and me, poor lowly maid,　　*shepherd's costume*
10　Most goddess-like pranked up.° But that our feasts　　*adorned*
　　In every mess⁴ have folly, and the feeders°　　　　*those who eat*
　　Digest it with a custom,⁵ I should blush
　　To see you so attired; swoon, I think,
　　To show myself a glass.°　　　　　　　　　　　*mirror*
　　FLORIZEL　　　　　　I bless the time
15　When my good falcon made her flight across
　　Thy father's ground.
　　PERDITA　　　　　　　Now Jove afford you cause!
　　To me the difference° forges dread; your greatness　　*(in rank)*
　　Hath not been used to fear. Even now I tremble
　　To think your father by some accident
20　Should pass this way, as you did. O, the fates!
　　How would he look to see his work,° so noble,　　　*offspring; writings*
　　Vilely bound up?⁶ What would he say? Or how
　　Should I, in these my borrowed flaunts,° behold　　*rich garments*
　　The sternness of his presence?
　　FLORIZEL　　　　　　　　Apprehend
25　Nothing but jollity. The gods themselves,
　　Humbling their deities to love, have taken
　　The shapes of beasts upon them. Jupiter
　　Became a bull, and bellowed; the green Neptune
　　A ram, and bleated; and the fire-robed god,
30　Golden Apollo, a poor humble swain,

---

4. Let my name be taken off the list (of thieves and vagabonds).
5. Steps by which people pass over a fence or hedge.
4.4 Location: Bohemia. In front of the cottage where the Old Shepherd, the Clown, and Perdita live.
1. Again, F lists in the initial stage direction all the major characters who appear in this very long scene. Florizel and Perdita seem, however, to have a private conversation before the Old Shepherd, Polixenes, and others enter to them at line 54.
2. Peeping out in early April.
3. The one whose graces make him admired by all.
4. A group of four served at table together. See note to 1.2.227.
5. Tolerate it because they have grown used to it.
6. Outfitted in such an inferior way. A bookbinding metaphor.

As I seem now.[7] Their transformations
Were never for a piece° of beauty rarer,   *person*
Nor in a way so chaste,[8] since my desires
Run not before mine honour, nor my lusts
Burn hotter than my faith.
35 PERDITA   O, but sir,
Your resolution cannot hold when 'tis
Opposed, as it must be, by th' power of the King.
One of these two must be necessities,
Which then will speak that you must change this purpose,
Or I my life.[9]
40 FLORIZEL   Thou dearest Perdita,
With these forced° thoughts I prithee darken not   *unnatural; farfetched*
The mirth o'th' feast. Or° I'll be thine, my fair,   *Either*
Or not my father's. For I cannot be
Mine own, nor anything to any, if
45 I be not thine. To this I am most constant,
Though destiny say no. Be merry, gentle;
Strangle such thoughts as these with anything
That you behold the while. Your guests are coming.
Lift up your countenance as° it were the day   *as if*
50 Of celebration of that nuptial which
We two have sworn shall come.
PERDITA   O Lady Fortune,[1]
Stand you auspicious!
FLORIZEL   See, your guests approach.
Address° yourself to entertain them sprightly,   *Prepare*
And let's be red with mirth.
[*Enter the* OLD SHEPHERD, *with* POLIXENES *and* CA-
MILLO, *disguised, the* CLOWN, MOPSA, DORCAS, *and
others*]
55 OLD SHEPHERD [*to* PERDITA]   Fie, daughter, when my old wife lived, upon
This day she was both pantler,° butler, cook,   *pantry maid*
Both dame° and servant, welcomed all, served all,   *mistress of the house*
Would sing her song and dance her turn, now here
At upper end o'th' table, now i'th' middle,
60 On his° shoulder, and his,° her face afire   *one person's / another's*
With labour, and the thing she took to quench it
She would to each one sip. You are retired
As if you were a feasted one° and not   *a guest*
The hostess of the meeting. Pray you bid
65 These unknown friends to's welcome, for it is
A way to make us better friends, more known.
Come, quench your blushes, and present yourself
That which you are, mistress o'th' feast. Come on,
And bid us welcome to your sheep-shearing,
As your good flock shall prosper.
70 PERDITA [*to* POLIXENES]   Sir, welcome.
It is my father's will I should take on me

7. In classical mythology, Jupiter transformed himself
into a bull and abducted Europa; Neptune took on the
shape of a ram to carry off Theopane; and the sun god
Apollo disguised himself as a shepherd to court Alcestis.
8. Nor ever conducted with so chaste a purpose.

9. One of two things will become necessary: either you
must change your plans, or I must change my life (that
is, risk death).
1. In classical and Renaissance mythology, a woman of
fickle disposition whose favors cannot be relied upon.

The hostess-ship o'th' day.
[*To* CAMILLO]   You're welcome, sir.
Give me those flowers there, Dorcas. Reverend sirs,
For you there's rosemary and rue. These keep°   *retain*
75   Seeming° and savour° all the winter long.   *Color / scent*
Grace and remembrance[2] be to you both,
And welcome to our shearing.
POLIXENES   Shepherdess,
A fair one are you. Well you fit our ages
With flowers of winter.
PERDITA   Sir, the year growing ancient,
80   Not yet on summer's death, nor on the birth
Of trembling winter, the fairest flowers o'th' season
Are our carnations and streaked gillyvors,[3]
Which some call nature's bastards. Of that kind
Our rustic garden's barren, and I care not
To get slips of them.
85   POLIXENES   Wherefore, gentle maiden,
Do you neglect them?
PERDITA   For I have heard it said
There is an art[4] which in their piedness° shares   *streaked color*
With great creating nature.
POLIXENES   Say there be,
Yet nature is made better by no mean°   *means*
90   But nature makes that mean. So over that art
Which you say adds to nature is an art
That nature makes. You see, sweet maid, we marry
A gentler scion to the wildest stock,
And make conceive a bark of baser kind
95   By bud of nobler race.[5] This is an art
Which does mend nature—change it rather; but
The art itself is nature.
PERDITA   So it is.
POLIXENES   Then make your garden rich in gillyvors,
And do not call them bastards.
PERDITA   I'll not put
100   The dibble° in earth to set° one slip of them,   *trowel / plant*
No more than, were I painted,° I would wish   *wearing cosmetics*
This youth should say 'twere well, and only therefore
Desire to breed by me. Here's flowers for you:
Hot[6] lavender, mints, savory, marjoram,
105   The marigold, that goes to bed wi'th' sun,
And with him rises, weeping.[7] These are flowers
Of middle summer, and I think they are given
To men of middle age. You're very welcome.
[*She gives them flowers*]

---

2. Grace ("repentance") and remembrance are qualities associated with rue and rosemary, respectively.
3. Gillyflowers or multicolored carnations. Their variations in color were thought to result from crossbreeding with other flowers, which may be why Perdita calls them "nature's bastards." They were proverbially associated with sexual license.
4. The art of crossbreeding or grafting.
5. We unite a cutting from a highly cultivated plant to the stem of a lesser one and cause the lesser plant to

bring forth a highly cultivated flower, that puns on "gentler scion," "wildest stock," "baser kind," and "nobler race" to suggest a successful union between a highborn heir and a member of the lower social orders.
6. Herbs were divided into "hot" and "cold" varieties based on their supposed temperatures.
7. The marigold, sometimes called "the spouse of the sun," supposedly closed at sunset and opened, filled with dew, in the morning when the sun came up.

CAMILLO   I should leave grazing were I of your flock,
    And only live by gazing.
110 PERDITA   Out, alas,
    You'd be so lean that blasts of January
    Would blow you through and through.
    [*To* FLORIZEL]   Now, my fair'st friend,
    I would I had some flowers o'th' spring that might
    Become your time of day; [*to* MOPSA *and* DORCAS] and yours, and yours,
115   That wear upon your virgin branches yet
    Your maidenheads growing. O Proserpina,[8]
    For the flowers now that, frighted, thou letst fall
    From Dis's wagon!°—daffodils,   *chariot*
    That come before the swallow dares, and take°   *charm*
120   The winds of March with beauty; violets, dim,°   *with hanging head*
    But sweeter than the lids of Juno's eyes
    Or Cytherea's breath;[9] pale primroses,
    That die unmarried ere they can behold
    Bright Phoebus° in his strength—a malady   *the sun god*
125   Most incident to maids;[1] bold oxlips, and
    The crown imperial;[2] lilies of all kinds,
    The flower-de-luce[3] being one. O, these I lack,
    To make you garlands of, and my sweet friend,
    To strew him o'er and o'er.
    FLORIZEL   What, like a corpse?
130 PERDITA   No, like a bank, for love to lie and play on,
    Not like a corpse—or if, not to be buried,
    But quick° and in mine arms. Come, take your flowers. *living*
    Methinks I play as I have seen them do
    In Whitsun pastorals.[4] Sure this robe of mine
    Does change my disposition.
135 FLORIZEL   What you do
    Still° betters what is done. When you speak, sweet, *Always*
    I'd have you do it ever; when you sing,
    I'd have you buy and sell so, so give alms,
    Pray so; and for the ord'ring° your affairs,   *arranging for*
140   To sing them too. When you do dance, I wish you
    A wave o'th' sea, that you might ever do
    Nothing but that, move still, still so,
    And own° no other function. Each your doing,° *have / Each thing you do*
    So singular° in each particular,   *distinctive*
145   Crowns what you are doing in the present deeds,
    That all your acts are queens.
    PERDITA   O Doricles,[5]
    Your praises are too large. But that your youth
    And the true blood which peeps so fairly through't

8. In Ovid's *Metamorphoses*, Proserpina, the daughter of Ceres, is abducted by Dis, or Pluto, as she gathers flowers and is taken in his chariot ("wagon") to his underworld kingdom. Sought out by Ceres, Proserpina is allowed to return to earth for six months each year. Her sojourn on earth coincides with spring and summer, her return to the underworld with fall and winter.
9. Juno was queen of the gods; "Cytherea" was another name for Venus, the goddess of love.
1. Alluding to the superstition that women who died of a kind of anemia known as green sickness would be transformed into primroses. Green sickness was espe-cially associated with young virginal women; vigorous sexual activity was sometimes advocated as a cure.
2. A lily first imported into England from Turkey in the late sixteenth century.
3. Fleur-de-lis, the national flower of France.
4. English rural festivities traditionally held at Whit-suntide, a religious festival occurring in the spring, seven weeks after Easter. The festivities, often orga-nized under a festival King and Queen, included mor-ris dances and Robin Hood plays.
5. The name Florizel has assumed.

Do plainly give you out an unstained shepherd,
150 With wisdom I might fear, my Doricles,
You wooed me the false way.

FLORIZEL   I think you have
As little skill° to fear as I have purpose   *reason*
To put you to't. But come, our dance, I pray;
Your hand, my Perdita. So turtles[6] pair,
That never mean to part.

155 PERDITA   I'll swear for 'em.

POLIXENES [*to* CAMILLO] This is the prettiest low-born lass that ever
Ran on the greensward.° Nothing she does or seems   *grassy turf*
But smacks of something greater than herself,
Too noble for this place.

CAMILLO   He tells her something
160 That makes her blood look out.° Good sooth, she is   *makes her blush*
The queen of curds and cream.[7]

CLOWN   Come on, strike up!

DORCAS Mopsa must be your mistress. Marry, garlic to mend
her kissing with![8]

MOPSA Now, in good time!

165 CLOWN Not a word, a word, we stand upon our manners. Come,
strike up!

[*Music.*] *Here a dance of shepherds and shepherdesses*

POLIXENES Pray, good shepherd, what fair swain is this
Which dances with your daughter?

OLD SHEPHERD They call him Doricles, and boasts himself°   *he boasts*
170 To have a worthy feeding;° but I have it   *good pasture land*
Upon his own report, and I believe it.
He looks like sooth.° He says he loves my daughter.   *appears to be honest*
I think so, too, for never gazed the moon
Upon the water as he'll stand and read,
175 As 'twere, my daughter's eyes; and to be plain,
I think there is not half a kiss to choose
Who loves another° best.   *the other*

POLIXENES   She dances featly.°   *nimbly*

OLD SHEPHERD So she does anything, though I report it
That° should be silent. If young Doricles   *Who*
180 Do light upon her, she shall bring him that
Which he not dreams of.

Enter [a] SERVANT

SERVANT O, master, if you did but hear the pedlar at the door,
you would never dance again after a tabor and pipe.[9] No, the
bagpipe could not move you. He sings several° tunes faster than   *different*
185 you'll tell° money. He utters them as he had eaten ballads,[1]   *count*
and all men's ears grew° to his tunes.   *listened intently*

CLOWN He could never come better.° He shall come in. I love   *at a better time*
a ballad but even too well, if it be doleful matter merrily set
down, or a very pleasant thing indeed, and sung lamentally.

190 SERVANT He hath songs for man or woman, of all sizes. No milli-
ner[2] can so fit his customers with gloves. He has the prettiest

6. Turtledoves, which proverbially mate for life.
7. Referring perhaps to a cream custard known as
"white pot." In some May games, a woman was chosen
as Queen of white-pot cream.
8. To make her breath sweet (said ironically).
9. A small drum and fife used for morris dancing.

1. Alluding to the broadside ballads that were sung
and sold by peddlers who traveled throughout the
country.
2. One who sells fashionable articles of clothing such
as hats and gloves. Originally, the word meant one who
sells items imported from Milan.

love songs for maids, so without bawdry, which is strange, with
such delicate burdens° of dildos and fadings, 'Jump her, and   *refrains*
thump her';[3] and where some stretch-mouthed° rascal would,   *obscene*
195 as it were, mean mischief and break a foul gap into the matter,[4]
he makes the maid to answer, 'Whoop, do me no harm, good
man'; puts him off, slights him, with 'Whoop, do me no harm,
good man!'

POLIXENES   This is a brave° fellow.   *fine*
200 CLOWN   Believe me, thou talkest of an admirable conceited° fel-   *very witty*
low. Has he any unbraided° wares?   *new; not shopworn*

SERVANT   He hath ribbons of all the colours i'th' rainbow; points[5]
more than all the lawyers in Bohemia can learnedly handle,
though they come to him by th' gross; inkles, caddises, cam-
205 brics, lawns[6]—why, he sings 'em over as they were gods or goddesses. You would think a smock° were a she-angel, he so   *a woman's undergarment*
chants to the sleeve-hand° and the work about the square on't.[7]   *wristband*

CLOWN   Prithee bring him in, and let him approach singing.

PERDITA   Forewarn him that he use no scurrilous words in's
210 tunes.   [*Exit* SERVANT]

CLOWN   You have of these° pedlars that have more in them than   *There are some*
you'd think, sister.

PERDITA   Ay, good brother, or go about° to think.   *intend*

        Enter AUTOLYCUS [*wearing a false beard, carrying his
        pack, and*] *singing*

AUTOLYCUS   Lawn as white as driven snow,
215   Cypress[8] black as e'er was crow,
            Gloves as sweet° as damask roses,   *perfumed*
            Masks for faces, and for noses;[9]
            Bugle-bracelet,[1] necklace amber,
            Perfume for a lady's chamber;
220   Golden coifs,° and stomachers[2]   *caps*
            For my lads to give their dears;
            Pins and poking-sticks of steel,[3]
            What maids lack from head to heel
            Come buy of me, come, come buy, come buy,
225   Buy, lads, or else your lasses cry. Come buy!

CLOWN   If I were not in love with Mopsa thou shouldst take no
money of me, but being enthralled as I am, it will also be the
bondage of certain ribbons and gloves.[4]

MOPSA   I was promised them against° the feast, but they come   *in time for*
230 not too late now.

DORCAS   He hath promised you more than that,[5] or there be
liars.

---

3. Though the servant claims that the songs are without bawdiness, the refrains are in fact full of sexual
puns that the servant may not understand. "Dildos" are
artificial penises; "fadings" can mean "orgasms"; and
"jump her and thump her" denotes sexual relations with
a woman.
4. Would interrupt the song with an indecent insertion.
5. Laces for fastening garments, with a pun on "points"
as meaning "legal arguments."
6. "Inkles" were linen tapes; "caddises" were worsted
tapes used for garters; "cambrics" and "lawns" were
heavy and sheer linens.
7. The stitching about the yoke of the garment.
8. A crepe material imported from Cyprus and used for

mourning clothes.
9. Many upper-class English women wore masks to
protect their skin from exposure to the sun. Some
women's noses were eaten away by syphilis, and masks
would also cover this deformity.
1. A bracelet of shiny black beads.
2. Embroidered bodices for dresses.
3. Metal rods used to iron the ruffs or stiff collars worn
by both men and women. The term is also slang for
"penis."
4. Because I am the prisoner of love, certain ribbons
and gloves must also be put in bondage (bound up in a
parcel).
5. (Perhaps he has promised marriage.)

MOPSA He hath paid° you all he promised you. Maybe he has *given; had sex with*
paid you more, which will shame you to give him again.⁶
235 CLOWN Is there no manners left among maids? Will they wear
their plackets where they should bear their faces?⁷ Is there not
milking-time, when you are going to bed, or kiln-hole,° to whis- *fireplace*
tle of these secrets, but you must be tittle-tattling before all our
guests? 'Tis well they are whispering. Clammer your tongues,⁸
240 and not a word more.
MOPSA I have done. Come, you promised me a tawdry-lace⁹ and
a pair of sweet gloves.
CLOWN Have I not told thee how I was cozened by the way,° *cheated on the road*
and lost all my money?
245 AUTOLYCUS And indeed, sir, there are cozeners abroad, therefore
it behoves men to be wary.
CLOWN Fear not thou, man, thou shalt lose nothing here.
AUTOLYCUS I hope so, sir, for I have about me many parcels of
charge.° *valuable goods*
250 CLOWN What hast here? Ballads?
MOPSA Pray now, buy some. I love a ballad in print, alife,° for *on my life*
then we are sure they are true.
AUTOLYCUS Here's one to a very doleful tune, how a usurer's
wife was brought to bed of twenty money-bags at a burden,° and *in one childbirth*
255 how she longed to eat adders' heads and toads carbonadoed.° *cut and grilled*
MOPSA Is it true, think you?
AUTOLYCUS Very true, and but a month old.
DORCAS Bless me from marrying a usurer!
AUTOLYCUS Here's the midwife's name to't, one Mistress Tail-
260 Porter,¹ and five or six honest° wives' that were present. Why *truthful; chaste*
should I carry lies abroad?
MOPSA [to CLOWN] Pray you now, buy it.
CLOWN Come on, lay it by, and let's first see more ballads. We'll
buy the other things anon.
265 AUTOLYCUS Here's another ballad, of a fish that appeared upon
the coast on Wednesday the fourscore° of April, forty thousand *eightieth day*
fathom° above water, and sung this ballad against the hard *measurement of six feet*
hearts of maids. It was thought she was a woman, and was
turned into a cold fish for she would not exchange flesh° with *have sex*
270 one that loved her. The ballad is very pitiful, and as true.
DORCAS Is it true too, think you?
AUTOLYCUS Five justices' hands at it,° and witnesses more than *signatures on it*
my pack will hold.
CLOWN Lay it by, too. Another.
275 AUTOLYCUS This is a merry ballad, but a very pretty one.
MOPSA Let's have some merry ones.
AUTOLYCUS Why, this is a passing° merry one, and goes to the *very*
tune of 'Two Maids Wooing a Man'. There's scarce a maid
westward° but she sings it. 'Tis in request, I can tell you. *in the west*

6. "More" may allude to a pregnancy that will result in an illegitimate child that she will give to the Clown.
7. That is, "Will they reveal their most private affairs in public?" There is a pun on "placket," which refers to both an opening in a petticoat and female genitals.
8. An obscure phrase. The Clown clearly means they are to be quiet. "To clammer" is a term from bell ringing that means to make the jangling sound characteristic of bells before they grow silent. In F, the phrase is printed as "clamor your tongues." Many emendations have been proposed.
9. A cheap, brightly colored scarf associated with St. Audrey's Fair. St. Audrey was the founder of Ely Cathedral; she died of a throat tumor that she believed was a punishment for wearing gay neckerchiefs in her youth.
1. The name punningly suggests one who reports gossip ("tales") as well as one who handles genitalia (slang meaning of "tail").

280 MOPSA   We can both sing it. If thou'lt bear a part² thou shalt
    hear; 'tis in three parts.

DORCAS   We had the tune on't° a month ago.   *of it*

AUTOLYCUS   I can bear my part, you must know, 'tis my occu-
    pation.° Have at it with you.   *job; act of copulation*
        [They sing]

285 AUTOLYCUS   Get you hence, for I must go³
        Where it fits not you to know.

DORCAS   Whither?

MOPSA   O whither?

DORCAS   Whither?

MOPSA   It becomes thy oath full well
        Thou to me thy secrets tell.

290 DORCAS   Me too. Let me go thither.

MOPSA   Or thou go'st to th' grange° or mill,   *farm*

DORCAS   If to either, thou dost ill.

AUTOLYCUS   Neither.

DORCAS   What neither.

AUTOLYCUS   Neither.

DORCAS   Thou hast sworn my love to be.

295 MOPSA   Thou hast sworn it more to me.
            Then whither goest? Say, whither?

CLOWN   We'll have this song out anon by ourselves. My father
    and the gentlemen are in sad° talk, and we'll not trouble them.   *serious*
    Come, bring away thy pack after me. Wenches, I'll buy for you

300 both. Pedlar, let's have the first choice. Follow me, girls.
            [Exit with DORCAS and MOPSA]

AUTOLYCUS   And you shall pay well for 'em.
    [Sings]   Will you buy any tape,
        Or lace for your cape,
        My dainty duck, my dear-a?

305   Any silk, any thread,
        Any toys° for your head,   *small ornaments*
        Of the new'st and fin'st, fin'st wear-a?
        Come to the pedlar,
        Money's a meddler,

310   That doth utter° all men's ware-a.   *Exit*   *put on sale*
        [Enter SERVANT]

SERVANT   Master, there is three carters,° three shepherds, three   *drivers of carts*
    neatherds,° three swineherds that have made themselves all   *keepers of cows*
    men of hair.⁴ They call themselves saultiers,° and they have a   *jumpers*
    dance which the wenches say is a gallimaufry of gambols,°   *jumble of jumps*

315 because they are not in't. But they themselves are o'th' mind,
    if it be not too rough for some that know little but bowling,° it   *(a more sedate sport)*
    will please plentifully.

OLD SHEPHERD   Away. We'll none on't. Here has been too much
    homely° foolery already. *[To POLIXENES]* I know, sir, we weary   *rough*

320 you.

POLIXENES   You weary those that° refresh us. Pray, let's see these   *who*
    four threes° of herdsmen.   *trios*

SERVANT   One three of them, by their own report, sir, hath

---

2. Sing a part in the song; play a role (in a sexual
encounter with the two women).
3. F prints "Song" before this line and "Autolycus"
before the next.

4. Probably they have disguised themselves in animal
skins in order to resemble satyrs—mythical woodland
figures, part man, part beast, having the pointed ears,
legs, and short horns of a goat.

danced before the King,[5] and not the worst of the three but
325   jumps twelve foot and a half by th' square.°   *exactly*

OLD SHEPHERD   Leave your prating. Since these good men are
pleased, let them come in—but quickly, now.

SERVANT   Why, they stay at door, sir.

    Here a dance of twelve satyrs

POLIXENES [*to the* OLD SHEPHERD]   O, father, you'll know more of that hereafter.
330   [*To* CAMILLO] Is it not too far gone? 'Tis time to part them.
He's simple, and tells much.
[*To* FLORIZEL]   How now, fair shepherd,
Your heart is full of something that does take
Your mind from feasting. Sooth, when I was young
And handed love° as you do, I was wont   *pledged love*
335   To load my she with knacks.° I would have ransacked   *small gifts; trifles*
The pedlar's silken treasury, and have poured it
To her acceptance.° You have let him go,   *For her to choose*
And nothing marted° with him. If your lass   *bought from*
Interpretation should abuse,° and call this   *Should misinterpret*
340   Your lack of love or bounty, you were straited°   *hard-pressed*
For a reply, at least if you make a care
Of happy holding her.°   *Of keeping her happy*

FLORIZEL   Old sir, I know
She prizes not such trifles as these are.
The gifts she looks° from me are packed and locked   *expects*
345   Up in my heart, which I have given already,
But not delivered.
[*To* PERDITA]   O, hear me breathe my life°   *make vows of eternal love*
Before this ancient sir, who, it should seem,
Hath sometime loved. I take thy hand, this hand
As soft as dove's down, and as white as it,
350   Or Ethiopian's tooth, or the fanned snow that's bolted°   *sifted*
By th' northern blasts twice o'er.

POLIXENES   What follows this?
How prettily the young swain seems to wash
The hand was° fair before! I have put you out.°   *that was / interrupted you*
But to your protestation. Let me hear
What you profess.
355 FLORIZEL   Do, and be witness to't.

POLIXENES   And this my neighbour too?

FLORIZEL   And he, and more
Than he; and men, the earth, the heavens, and all,
That were I crowned the most imperial monarch,
Thereof most worthy, were I the fairest youth
360   That ever made eye swerve,° had force and knowledge   *commanded attention*
More than was ever man's, I would not prize them
Without her love; for her employ them all,
Commend them and condemn them to her service
Or to their own perdition.[6]

POLIXENES   Fairly offered.

CAMILLO   This shows a sound affection.

---

5. This may be a reference to a court performance of Ben Jonson's *Masque of Oberon*, which included a dance of twelve satyrs. It was first put on in January of 1611.

6. Either dedicate my attributes to her service or sentence them to destruction, with a pun on "perdition" and "Perdita."

365 OLD SHEPHERD   But, my daughter,
    Say you the like to him?
    PERDITA   I cannot speak
    So well, nothing so well, no, nor mean better.
    By th' pattern of mine own thoughts I cut out
    The purity of his.[7]
    OLD SHEPHERD   Take hands, a bargain;
370 And, friends unknown, you shall bear witness to't.
    I give my daughter to him, and will make
    Her portion° equal his.   dowry
    FLORIZEL   O, that must be
    I'th' virtue of your daughter. One° being dead,   Someone
    I shall have more than you can dream of yet,
375 Enough then for your wonder. But come on,
    Contract us fore these witnesses.[8]
    OLD SHEPHERD   Come, your hand;
    And, daughter, yours.
    POLIXENES   Soft,° swain, a while, beseech you.   Go slowly
    Have you a father?
    FLORIZEL   I have. But what of him?
380 POLIXENES   Knows he of this?
    FLORIZEL   He neither does nor shall.
    POLIXENES   Methinks a father
    Is at the nuptial of his son a guest
    That best becomes the table. Pray you once more,
385 Is not your father grown incapable
    Of reasonable affairs?[9] Is he not stupid
    With age and alt'ring rheums?° Can he speak, hear,   debilitating disease
    Know man from man? Dispute° his own estate?°   Discuss / condition
    Lies he not bed-rid, and again does nothing
    But what he did being childish?
390 FLORIZEL   No, good sir.
    He has his health, and ampler strength indeed
    Than most have of his age.
    POLIXENES   By my white beard,
    You offer him, if this be so, a wrong
    Something unfilial.° Reason my son[1]   Somewhat unbecoming a son
395 Should choose himself a wife, but as good reason
    The father, all whose joy is nothing else
    But fair posterity, should hold some counsel
    In such a business.
    FLORIZEL   I yield° all this;   grant
    But for some other reasons, my grave sir,
400 Which 'tis not fit you know, I not acquaint
    My father of this business.
    POLIXENES   Let him know't.
    FLORIZEL   He shall not.
    POLIXENES   Prithee let him.
    FLORIZEL   No, he must not.
    OLD SHEPHERD   Let him, my son. He shall not need to grieve
    At knowing of thy choice.

---

7. By my pure thoughts I recognize the purity of his. A
dressmaking metaphor.
8. A pledge of marriage spoken before two witnesses
was legally binding.

9. Unfit to handle matters requiring reason and good
sense.
1. It is reasonable that my son.

FLORIZEL   Come, come, he must not.
  Mark our contract.
405 POLIXENES [*removing his disguise*]   Mark your divorce, young sir,
  Whom son I dare not call. Thou art too base
  To be acknowledged. Thou a sceptre's heir,
  That thus affects° a sheep-hook?   *desires*
  [*To the* OLD SHEPHERD]   Thou, old traitor,
  I am sorry that by hanging thee I can but
  Shorten thy life one week.
410 [*To* PERDITA]   And thou, fresh piece
  Of excellent witchcraft,² who of force° must know   *of necessity*
  The royal fool thou cop'st° with—   *you deal; you have sex*
OLD SHEPHERD   O, my heart!
POLIXENES   I'll have thy beauty scratched with briers and made
  More homely than thy state.
  [*To* FLORIZEL]   For thee, fond° boy,   *foolish*
415 If I may ever know thou dost but sigh
  That thou no more shalt see this knack,° as never   *worthless thing*
  I mean thou shalt, we'll bar thee from succession,
  Not hold thee of our blood, no, not our kin,
  Farre than Deucalion off.³ Mark thou my words.
  Follow us to the court.
420 [*To the* OLD SHEPHERD]   Thou churl, for this time,
  Though full of our displeasure, yet we free thee
  From the dead° blow of it.   *deadly*
  [*To* PERDITA]   And you, enchantment,
  Worthy enough a herdsman—yea, him° too,   *(Florizel)*
  That makes himself, but for our honour therein,
425 Unworthy thee⁴—if ever henceforth thou
  These rural latches to his entrance open,
  Or hoop° his body more with thy embraces,   *encircle*
  I will devise a death as cruel for thee
  As thou art tender to't.   *Exit*
PERDITA   Even here undone.
430 I was not much afeard, for once or twice
  I was about to speak, and tell him plainly
  The selfsame sun that shines upon his court
  Hides not his visage from our cottage, but
  Looks on alike.° Will't please you, sir, be gone?   *both alike*
435 I told you what would come of this. Beseech you,
  Of your own state take care. This dream of mine
  Being now awake, I'll queen it no inch farther,°   *play the queen no further*
  But milk my ewes and weep.
CAMILLO [*to the* OLD SHEPHERD]   Why, how now, father?
  Speak ere thou diest.
OLD SHEPHERD   I cannot speak, nor think,
  Nor dare to know that which I know.
440 [*To* FLORIZEL]   O sir,
  You have undone a man of fourscore-three,°   *eighty-three*

2. You beautiful young woman skilled in witchcraft. Some people believed that witches could induce love by potions.
3. Less linked in kinship than Deucalion, who according to classical mythology was, along with his wife, the only person to escape a flood sent by Zeus. He thus was the ancestor of humankind and the most distant rela-

tion one might have.
4. A difficult passage. Polixenes seems to mean that Florizel, by his actions, has made himself unworthy of even a shepherd's daughter were it not for the fact that he is a King's son and so would harm his father's honor by such a marriage.

That thought to fill his grave in quiet, yea,
To die upon the bed my father died,
To lie close by his honest bones. But now
445 Some hangman must put on my shroud, and lay me
Where no priest shovels in dust.[5]
[*To* PERDITA]   O cursed wretch,
That knew'st this was the Prince, and wouldst adventure
To mingle faith° with him. Undone, undone!   °exchange vows
If I might die within this hour, I have lived
450 To die when I desire.   *Exit*
FLORIZEL [*to* PERDITA]   Why look you so upon me?
I am but sorry, not afeard; delayed,
But nothing altered. What I was, I am,
More straining on for plucking back,[6] not following
My leash unwillingly.[7]
CAMILLO   Gracious my lord,
455 You know your father's temper. At this time
He will allow no speech—which I do guess
You do not purpose° to him; and as hardly°   °intend / unwillingly
Will he endure your sight as yet, I fear.
Then till the fury of his highness settle,
Come not before him.
460 FLORIZEL   I not purpose it.
I think, Camillo?[8]
CAMILLO   Even he, my lord.
PERDITA [*to* FLORIZEL]   How often have I told you 'twould be thus?
How often said my dignity would last
But° till 'twere known?   °Only
FLORIZEL   It cannot fail but by
465 The violation of my faith, and then
Let nature crush the sides o'th' earth together
And mar the seeds° within. Lift up thy looks.   °sources of life
From my succession wipe me, father! I
Am heir to my affection.
CAMILLO   Be advised.°   °prudent
470 FLORIZEL   I am, and by my fancy.° If my reason   °love
Will thereto be obedient, I have reason.[9]
If not, my senses, better pleased with madness,
Do bid it° welcome.   °(madness)
CAMILLO   This is desperate, sir.
FLORIZEL   So call it. But it does fulfil my vow.
475 I needs must think it honesty. Camillo,
Not for Bohemia, nor the pomp that may
Be thereat gleaned; for all the sun sees, or
The close° earth wombs,° or the profound seas hides   °secret / holds in her womb
In unknown fathoms, will I break my oath
480 To this my fair beloved. Therefore, I pray you,
As you have ever been my father's honoured friend,
When he shall miss me—as, in faith, I mean not
To see him any more—cast your good counsels

5. As a criminal, he would be buried without ritual under the gallows. In regular funeral rites, the priest customarily placed the first shovelful of dirt on the grave.
6. More eager to go forward because of being pulled back.
7. Not following this course of action unwillingly (like a dog dragged by its leash).
8. Camillo may here have taken off his disguise or been recognized by Florizel even with it on.
9. If my reason will obey love, I will embrace reason.

Upon his passion.° Let myself and fortune   *anger*
485 Tug° for the time to come. This you may know,   *Contend*
And so deliver:° I am put to sea   *report*
With her who here I cannot hold on shore;
And most opportune to her need, I have
A vessel rides fast by,° but not prepared   *anchored nearby*
490 For this design. What course I mean to hold
Shall nothing benefit your knowledge, nor
Concern me the reporting.[1]

CAMILLO   O my lord,
I would your spirit were easier for advice,°   *to advise*
Or stronger for your need.

FLORIZEL   Hark, Perdita—
[*To* CAMILLO] I'll hear you by and by.

495 CAMILLO [*aside*]   He's irremovable,°   *unyielding*
Resolved for flight. Now were I happy if
His going I could frame to serve my turn,
Save him from danger, do him love and honour,
Purchase the sight again of dear Sicilia
500 And that unhappy king, my master, whom
I so much thirst to see.

FLORIZEL   Now, good Camillo,
I am so fraught with curious business° that   *matters requiring care*
I leave out ceremony.

CAMILLO   Sir, I think
You have heard of my poor services i'th' love
That I have borne your father?

505 FLORIZEL   Very nobly
Have you deserved. It is my father's music
To speak your deeds, not little of his care
To have them recompensed as thought on.[2]

CAMILLO   Well, my lord,
If you may please to think I love the King,
510 And through him what's nearest to him, which is
Your gracious self, embrace but my direction,°   *simply follow my advice*
If your more ponderous° and settled project   *weighty*
May suffer° alteration. On mine honour,   *permit*
I'll point you where you shall have such receiving
515 As shall become your highness, where you may
Enjoy your mistress—from the whom I see
There's no disjunction° to be made but by,   *separation*
As heavens forfend,° your ruin—marry her,   *forbid*
And with my best endeavours in your absence
520 Your discontenting° father strive to qualify°   *discontented / appease*
And bring him up to liking.°   *to giving approval*

FLORIZEL   How, Camillo,
May this, almost a miracle, be done?—
That I may call thee something more than man,
And after that trust to thee.

CAMILLO   Have you thought on°   *of*
A place whereto you'll go?

525 FLORIZEL   Not any yet.

---

1. Would not benefit you to know nor me to report.
2. And no small matter among his affairs to reward your deeds as fully as he values them.

But as th'unthought-on accident is guilty
To what we wildly do,[3] so we profess
Ourselves to be the slaves of chance, and flies
Of every wind that blows.[4]

CAMILLO   Then list to me.
530   This follows, if you will not change your purpose
        But undergo this flight: make for Sicilia,
        And there present yourself and your fair princess,
        For so I see she must be, fore Leontes.
        She shall be habited° as it becomes   *dressed*
535   The partner of your bed. Methinks I see
        Leontes opening his free° arms and weeping   *generous*
        His welcomes forth; asks thee there 'Son, forgiveness!'
        As 'twere i'th' father's person,[5] kisses the hands
        Of your fresh princess; o'er and o'er divides him
540   'Twixt his unkindness and his kindness.[6] Th'one
        He chides° to hell, and bids the other grow   *rebukes*
        Faster than thought or time.

FLORIZEL   Worthy Camillo,
        What colour° for my visitation shall I   *pretext*
        Hold up before him?

CAMILLO   Sent by the King your father
545   To greet him, and to give him comforts. Sir,
        The manner of your bearing towards him, with
        What you, as from your father, shall deliver—°   *say*
        Things known betwixt us three—I'll write you down,
        The which shall point you forth° at every sitting   *direct you*
550   What you must say, that he shall not perceive
        But that you have your father's bosom° there,   *trust*
        And speak his very heart.

FLORIZEL   I am bound to you.
        There is some sap° in this.   *life*

CAMILLO   A course more promising
        Than a wild dedication of yourselves
555   To unpathed waters, undreamed shores; most certain,
        To miseries enough—no hope to help you,
        But as you shake off one, to take another;
        Nothing so certain° as your anchors, who   *certain (to detain you)*
        Do their best office if they can but stay° you   *keep*
560   Where you'll be loath to be. Besides, you know,
        Prosperity's the very bond of love,
        Whose fresh complexion and whose heart together
        Affliction alters.°   *changes for the worse*

PERDITA   One of these is true.
        I think affliction may subdue the cheek°   *make one pale*
        But not take in° the mind.   *conquer*

565 CAMILLO   Yea, say you so?
        There shall not at your father's house these seven years[7]
        Be born another such.

FLORIZEL   My good Camillo,

---

3. But as the unexpected event (Polixenes' discovery of
our love) is responsible for our rash behavior now.
4. And like flies blown about by the winds.
5. As if he were your father; *or* as if you were your father.

6. That is, he divides his speech between his past
unkindness to your father and the kindness he is eager
to perform now.
7. Proverbial expression meaning "for a long time."

She's as forward of her breeding as
She is i'th' rear our birth.[8]

CAMILLO   I cannot say 'tis pity
570   She lacks instructions,° for she seems a mistress°   *schooling / teacher*
To most that teach.

PERDITA   Your pardon, sir. For this
I'll blush you thanks.

FLORIZEL   My prettiest Perdita!
But O, the thorns we stand upon! Camillo,
Preserver of my father, now of me,
575   The medicine of our house, how shall we do?
We are not furnished° like Bohemia's son,   *dressed; equipped*
Nor shall appear so in Sicilia.

CAMILLO   My lord,
Fear none of this. I think you know my fortunes
580   Do all lie there. It shall be so my care
To have you royally appointed° as if   *outfitted*
The scene you play were mine.° For instance, sir,   *written by me*
That you may know you shall not want—one word.

        [*They speak apart.*]
        Enter AUTOLYCUS

AUTOLYCUS   Ha, ha! What a fool honesty is, and trust—his sworn
585   brother—a very simple gentleman! I have sold all my trumpery;
not a counterfeit stone, not a ribbon, glass, pomander,[9] brooch,
table-book,° ballad, knife, tape, glove, shoe-tie, bracelet, horn-   *notebook*
ring[1] to keep my pack from fasting.° They throng who should   *from going empty*
buy first, as if my trinkets had been hallowed,° and brought a   *blessed; made sacred*
590   benediction to the buyer; by which means I saw whose purse
was best in picture;° and what I saw, to my good use I remem-   *looked best (to steal)*
bered. My clown, who wants but something° to be a reasonable   *lacks only one thing*
man, grew so in love with the wenches' song that he would not
stir his pettitoes° till he had both tune and words, which so   *feet (pigs' toes)*
595   drew the rest of the herd to me that all their other senses stuck
in ears.° You might have pinched a placket, it was sense-   *were devoted to hearing*
less.° 'Twas nothing to geld a codpiece of a purse.[2] I could have   *felt nothing*
filed keys off that hung in chains. No hearing, no feeling but
my sir's song, and admiring the nothing of it.[3] So that in this
600   time of lethargy I picked and cut most of their festival purses,
and had not the old man come in with a hubbub against his
daughter and the King's son, and scared my choughs° from the   *jackdaws (silly birds)*
chaff, I had not left a purse alive in the whole army.

        [CAMILLO, FLORIZEL, *and* PERDITA *come forward*]

CAMILLO   Nay, but my letters by this means being there
605   So soon as you arrive shall clear that doubt.

FLORIZEL   And those that you'll procure from King Leontes—

CAMILLO   Shall satisfy your father.

PERDITA   Happy be you!
All that you speak shows fair.

CAMILLO [*seeing* AUTOLYCUS]   Who have we here?

---

8. That is, "She is as superior to her lowly upbringing
as she is inferior to our noble birth."
9. A mixture of sweet-smelling substances made into a
ball and carried about for ornament or to prevent infection.
1. A ring made from horn, which was said to possess

magical qualities.
2. It was easy to cut a purse loose from a codpiece, the
baglike article of dress attached to the front of a man's
hose and covering his genitals.
3. The silliness of it, with a pun on "nothing" and "noting" (meaning "tune"), which were similarly pronounced.

We'll make an instrument of this, omit

610 Nothing° may give us aid.   *Nothing that*

AUTOLYCUS   [*aside*]   If they have overheard me now—why,
hanging!

CAMILLO   How now, good fellow? Why shakest thou so? Fear
not, man. Here's no harm intended to thee.

615 AUTOLYCUS   I am a poor fellow, sir.

CAMILLO   Why, be so still.° Here's nobody will steal that from   *always*
thee. Yet for the outside of thy poverty,° we must make an   *your ragged clothes*
exchange. Therefore disease° thee instantly— thou must think   *undress*
there's a necessity in't—and change garments with this gentle-

620 man. Though the pennyworth° on his side be the worst, yet   *bargain*
hold thee, [*giving him money*] there's some boot.°   *something more*

AUTOLYCUS   I am a poor fellow, sir. [*Aside*] I know ye well
enough.

CAMILLO   Nay prithee, dispatch°—the gentleman is half flayed[4]   *hurry*

625 already.

AUTOLYCUS   Are you in earnest,[5] sir? [*Aside*] I smell the trick on't.

FLORIZEL   Dispatch, I prithee.

AUTOLYCUS   Indeed, I have had earnest, but I cannot with conscience take it.

630 CAMILLO   Unbuckle, unbuckle.

[FLORIZEL *and* AUTOLYCUS *exchange clothes*]

[*To* PERDITA] Fortunate mistress—let my prophecy
Come home to ye![6]—you must retire yourself
Into some covert,° take your sweetheart's hat   *hiding place*
And pluck it o'er your brows, muffle your face,

635 Dismantle you,° and, as you can, disliken°   *Take off your cloak / disguise*
The truth of your own seeming,° that you may—   *appearance*
For I do fear eyes°—over to shipboard   *spies*
Get undescried.

PERDITA   I see the play so lies
That I must bear a part.

CAMILLO   No remedy.
[*To* FLORIZEL] Have you done there?

640 FLORIZEL   Should I now meet my father
He would not call me son.

CAMILLO   Nay, you shall have no hat.

[*He gives the hat to* PERDITA]
Come, lady, come. Farewell, my friend.

AUTOLYCUS   Adieu, sir.

FLORIZEL   O Perdita, what have we twain forgot!
Pray you, a word.

[*They speak aside*]

645 CAMILLO [*aside*]   What I do next shall be to tell the King
Of this escape, and whither they are bound;
Wherein my hope is I shall so prevail
To force him after, in whose company
I shall re-view Sicilia, for whose sight
I have a woman's longing.[7]

---

4. Half undressed (skinned).
5. "Serious," with a pun on "earnest" as meaning both
"sincere" and "an advance payment." See line 628.

6. Let my prophecy (that she be fortunate) be fulfilled.
7. Women, especially pregnant women, were said to be
vulnerable to irrational and very intense cravings.

650 FLORIZEL   Fortune speed us!
       Thus we set on, Camillo, to th' seaside.
     CAMILLO   The swifter speed the better.
                 Exeunt [FLORIZEL, PERDITA, *and* CAMILLO][8]
     AUTOLYCUS   I understand the business, I hear it. To have an open
       ear, a quick eye, and a nimble hand is necessary for a cutpurse.
655   A good nose is requisite also, to smell out work for th'other
       senses. I see this is the time that the unjust man doth thrive.
       What an exchange had this been without boot!° What a boot[9]   *even without payment*
       is here with this exchange! Sure the gods do this year connive
       at° us, and we may do anything extempore.° The Prince him-   *indulge / spontaneously*
660   self is about a piece of iniquity, stealing away from his father
       with his clog° at his heels. If I thought it were a piece of honesty   *encumbrance (Perdita)*
       to acquaint the King withal,° I would not do't. I hold it the   *with it*
       more knavery to conceal it, and therein am I constant° to my   *faithful*
       profession.
             Enter [*the*] CLOWN *and* [*the* OLD] SHEPHERD[, *carrying a*
             fardel° *and a box*]   *bundle*
665   Aside, aside! Here is more matter for a hot brain. Every lane's
       end, every shop, church, session,° hanging, yields a careful   *court session*
       man work.
     CLOWN   See, see, what a man you are now! There is no other
       way but to tell the King she's a changeling,[1] and none of your
670   flesh and blood.
     OLD SHEPHERD   Nay, but hear me.
     CLOWN   Nay, but hear *me*.
     OLD SHEPHERD   Go to,° then.   *Go ahead*
     CLOWN   She being none of your flesh and blood, your flesh and
675   blood has not offended the King, and so your flesh and blood
       is not to be punished by him. Show those things you found
       about her, those secret things, all but what she has with her.
       This being done, let the law go whistle, I warrant you.
     OLD SHEPHERD   I will tell the King all, every word, yea, and his
680   son's pranks, too, who, I may say, is no honest man, neither to
       his father nor to me, to go about to make me the King's brother-
       in-law.
     CLOWN   Indeed, brother-in-law was the farthest off° you could   *most remote relation*
       have been to him, and then your blood had been the dearer by
685   I know not how much an ounce.
     AUTOLYCUS [*aside*]   Very wisely, puppies.
     OLD SHEPHERD   Well, let us to the King. There is that in this
       fardel will make him scratch his beard.
     AUTOLYCUS [*aside*]   I know not what impediment this complaint
690   may be to the flight of my master.°   *(Florizel)*
     CLOWN   Pray heartily he be at'° palace.   *at the*
     AUTOLYCUS [*aside*]   Though I am not naturally honest, I am so
       sometimes by chance. Let me pocket up my pedlar's excre-
       ment.°   *hair*
             [*He removes his false beard*]
695   —How now, rustics, whither are you bound?
     OLD SHEPHERD   To th' palace, an° it like your worship.   *if*

---

8. F marks a single *"Exit"* here for Camillo, but Florizel
and Perdita undoubtedly exit also, leaving Autolycus
alone on stage to comment on what he has witnessed.

9. Benefit; shoe.
1. A child left or abducted by fairies. See note to
3.3.109.

AUTOLYCUS   Your affairs there? What? With whom? The condi-
tion of that fardel?° The place of your dwelling? Your names?   *nature of that bundle*
Your ages? Of what having,° breeding,° and anything that is   *property / upbringing*
700   fitting to be known, discover.°   *reveal*

CLOWN   We are but plain° fellows, sir.   *simple; smooth*

AUTOLYCUS   A lie, you are rough and hairy. Let me have no
lying. It becomes none but tradesmen, and they often give us
soldiers the lie,[2] but we pay them for it with stamped coin, not
705   stabbing steel, therefore they do not *give* us the lie.[3]

CLOWN   Your worship had like to have given us one° if you had   *(the lie)*
not taken yourself with the manner.[4]

OLD SHEPHERD   Are you a courtier, an't like you, sir?

AUTOLYCUS   Whether it like me or no, I am a courtier. Seest thou
710   not the air of the court in these enfoldings?° Hath not my gait   *garments*
in it the measure° of the court? Receives not thy nose court   *stately walk*
odour from me? Reflect I not on thy baseness court-contempt?
Thinkest thou, for that I insinuate° to toze° from thee thy busi-   *subtly work / tease out*
ness, I am therefore no courtier? I am courtier cap-à-pie,° and   *from head to foot*
715   one that will either push on or pluck back thy business there.
Whereupon I command thee to open° thy affair.   *reveal*

OLD SHEPHERD   My business, sir, is to the King.

AUTOLYCUS   What advocate hast thou to him?

OLD SHEPHERD   I know not, an't like you.

720   CLOWN   [*aside to the* OLD SHEPHERD]   'Advocate' 's the court
word for a pheasant.[5] Say you have none.

OLD SHEPHERD   None, sir. I have no pheasant, cock nor hen.

AUTOLYCUS   [*aside*]   How blessed are we that are not simple men!
Yet nature might have made me as these are,
725   Therefore I will not disdain.

CLOWN   This cannot be but° a great courtier.   *anyone but*

OLD SHEPHERD   His garments are rich, but he wears them not
handsomely.

CLOWN   He seems to be the more noble in being fantastical.° A   *eccentric*
730   great man, I'll warrant. I know by the picking on's teeth.[6]

AUTOLYCUS   The fardel there, what's i'th' fardel? Wherefore that
box?

OLD SHEPHERD   Sir, there lies such secrets in this fardel and box
which none must know but the King, and which he shall know
735   within this hour, if I may come to th' speech of him.

AUTOLYCUS   Age,° thou hast lost thy labour.   *Old man*

OLD SHEPHERD   Why, sir?

AUTOLYCUS   The King is not at the palace, he is gone aboard a
new ship to purge° melancholy and air himself; for if thou   *rid himself of*
740   beest capable of° things serious, thou must know the King is   *can understand*
full of grief.

OLD SHEPHERD   So 'tis said, sir; about his son, that should have
married a shepherd's daughter.

AUTOLYCUS   If that shepherd be not in handfast,° let him fly. The   *arrested*

745   curses he shall have, the tortures he shall feel, will break the
      back of man, the heart of monster.
    CLOWN   Think you so, sir?
    AUTOLYCUS   Not he alone shall suffer what wit can make heavy
      and vengeance bitter, but those that are germane° to him,   *related*
750   though removed fifty times, shall all come under the hangman,
      which, though it be great pity, yet it is necessary. An old sheep-
      whistling rogue,[7] a ram-tender, to offer to have his daughter
      come into grace!° Some say he shall be stoned; but that death   *favor (at court)*
      is too soft for him, say I. Draw our throne into a sheepcote?°   *pen for sheep*
755   All deaths are too few, the sharpest too easy.
    CLOWN   Has the old man e'er a son, sir, do you hear, an't like
      you, sir?
    AUTOLYCUS   He has a son, who shall be flayed alive, then
      'nointed over with honey, set on the head of a wasps' nest, then
760   stand till he be three-quarters-and-a-dram° dead, then recov-   *a tiny bit*
      ered again with aqua-vitae,° or some other hot infusion, then,   *brandy*
      raw as he is, and in the hottest day prognostication° proclaims,   *almanac prediction*
      shall he be set against a brick wall, the sun looking with a
      southward eye upon him, where he is to behold him with flies
765   blown° to death. But what talk we of these traitorly rascals,   *swollen*
      whose miseries are to be smiled at, their offences being so
      capital? Tell me, for you seem to be honest plain men, what
      you have° to the King. Being something gently considered,[8] I'll   *have to say*
      bring you where he is aboard, tender° your persons to his pres-   *deliver*
770   ence, whisper him in your behalfs, and if it be in man, besides
      the King, to effect your suits, here is man shall do it.
    CLOWN [*to the* OLD SHEPHERD]   He seems to be of great author-
      ity. Close° with him, give him gold; and though authority be a   *Make a deal*
      stubborn bear, yet he is oft led by the nose with gold. Show the
775   inside of your purse to the outside of his hand, and no more
      ado. Remember—'stoned', and 'flayed alive'.
    OLD SHEPHERD   An't please you, sir, to undertake the business
      for us, here is that° gold I have. I'll make it as much more, and   *what*
      leave this young man in pawn° till I bring it you.   *as security*
780   AUTOLYCUS   After I have done what I promised?
    OLD SHEPHERD   Ay, sir.
    AUTOLYCUS   Well, give me the moiety.° [*To the* CLOWN] Are you   *half*
      a party in this business?
    CLOWN   In some sort, sir. But though my case° be a pitiful one,   *condition; skin*
785   I hope I shall not be flayed out of it.
    AUTOLYCUS   O, that's the case of the shepherd's son. Hang him,
      he'll be made an example.
    CLOWN [*to the* OLD SHEPHERD]   Comfort, good comfort. We
      must to the King, and show our strange sights. He must
790   know 'tis none of your daughter, nor my sister. We are gone°   *lost (dead)*
      else.° [*To* AUTOLYCUS] Sir, I will give you as much as this old   *otherwise*
      man does when the business is performed, and remain, as he
      says, your pawn till it be brought you.
    AUTOLYCUS   I will trust you. Walk before° toward the seaside. Go   *ahead of me*
795   on the right hand. I will but look upon the hedge,[9] and follow
      you.

---

7. An old rascal who whistles while he tends sheep.   will give me a bribe worthy of my high rank.
8. As I am a highly regarded gentleman at court; if you   9. Slang for "relieve myself."

CLOWN [*to the* OLD SHEPHERD]   We are blessed in this man, as I
may say, even blessed.

OLD SHEPHERD   Let's before, as he bids us. He was provided to
800   do us good.   [*Exit with the* CLOWN]

AUTOLYCUS   If I had a mind to be honest, I see fortune would
not suffer° me. She drops booties° in my mouth. I am courted   *permit / prizes*
now with a double occasion:° gold, and a means to do the   *opportunity*
Prince my master good, which who knows how that may turn
805   back to my advancement? I will bring these two moles, these
blind ones, aboard him.° If he think it fit to shore them[1] again,   *(his ship)*
and that the complaint they have to the King concerns him
nothing, let him call me rogue for being so far officious, for I
am proof against° that title, and what shame else belongs to't.   *impervious to*
810   To him will I present them. There may be matter in it.   *Exit*

5.1

Enter LEONTES, CLEOMENES, DION, [*and*] PAULINA

CLEOMENES [*to* LEONTES]   Sir, you have done enough, and have performed
A saint-like sorrow. No fault could you make
Which you have not redeemed, indeed, paid down
More penitence than done trespass.[1] At the last
5   Do as the heavens have done, forget your evil.
With them, forgive yourself.

LEONTES   Whilst I remember
Her and her virtues I cannot forget
My blemishes in them,° and so still think of   *in relation to them*
The wrong I did myself, which was so much
10   That heirless it hath made my kingdom, and
Destroyed the sweet'st companion that e'er man
Bred his hopes out of. True?

PAULINA   Too true, my lord.
If one by one you wedded all the world,
Or from the all that are took something good
15   To make a perfect woman, she you killed
Would be unparalleled.

LEONTES   I think so. Killed?
She I killed? I did so. But thou strik'st me
Sorely to say I did; it is as bitter
Upon thy tongue as in my thought. Now, good now,°   *if you would*
Say so but seldom.

CLEOMENES   Not at all,° good lady.   *Never (say these things)*
20   You might have spoke a thousand things that would
Have done the time more benefit,[2] and graced°   *showed*
Your kindness better.

PAULINA   You are one of those
Would have him wed again.

DION   If you would not so
25   You pity not the state,° nor the remembrance   *kingdom*
Of his most sovereign name,[3] consider little
What dangers, by his highness' fail of issue,°   *lack of offspring*
May drop upon his kingdom and devour

---

1. Put them ashore.
5.1 Location: Sicilia. The palace of Leontes.
1. Performed more penance than your sin warranted.

2. That would have been more useful in these times.
3. Nor the perpetuation of his royal lineage (through a new child).

Incertain lookers-on.[4] What were more holy

30 Than to rejoice the former queen is well?°   *(in heaven)*
What holier, than for royalty's repair,
For present comfort and for future good,
To bless the bed of majesty again
With a sweet fellow to't?

PAULINA   There is none worthy
35 Respecting° her that's gone. Besides, the gods   *In comparison to*
Will have fulfilled their secret purposes.[5]
For has not the divine Apollo said?
Is't not the tenor of his oracle
That King Leontes shall not have an heir

40 Till his lost child be found? Which that it shall
Is all as monstrous° to our human reason   *incredible*
As my Antigonus to break his grave
And come again to me, who, on my life,
Did perish with the infant. 'Tis your counsel

45 My lord should to the heavens be contrary,
Oppose against their wills.
[*To* LEONTES]   Care not for issue.
The crown will find an heir. Great Alexander
Left his to th' worthiest,[6] so his successor
Was like to be the best.

LEONTES   Good Paulina,
50 Who hast the memory of Hermione,
I know, in honour—O, that ever I
Had squared me° to thy counsel! Then even now   *conformed my actions*
I might have looked upon my queen's full eyes,
Have taken treasure from her lips.

PAULINA   And left them
More rich for what they yielded.

55 LEONTES   Thou speak'st truth.
No more such wives, therefore no wife. One worse,
And better used,° would make her sainted spirit   *treated*
Again possess her° corpse, and on this stage,   *(Hermione's)*
Where we offenders mourn, appear soul-vexed,°   *with troubled soul*
And begin, 'Why° to me?'   *Why offer this insult*

60 PAULINA   Had she such power
She had just cause.

LEONTES   She had, and would incense me
To murder her I married.

PAULINA   I should so.
Were I the ghost that walked I'd bid you mark
Her eye, and tell me for what dull part in't

65 You chose her. Then I'd shriek that even your ears
Should rift° to hear me, and the words that followed   *split*
Should be, 'Remember mine'.°   *(my eyes)*

LEONTES   Stars, stars,
And all eyes else,° dead coals! Fear thou no wife.   *all other eyes*
I'll have no wife, Paulina.

---

4. And destroy those subjects who are bewildered (by the matter of his successor).
5. Will ensure that their secret purposes are fulfilled.
6. Alexander the Great (356–323 B.C.E.), conqueror of Greece, Persia, and Egypt, died before his own son was born and reportedly urged his followers simply to choose the worthiest man as his successor.

	PAULINA	Will you swear
70	Never to marry but by my free leave?	
	LEONTES Never, Paulina, so be blest my spirit.	
	PAULINA Then, good my lords, bear witness to his oath.	
	CLEOMENES You tempt him over-much.	
	PAULINA	Unless another
	As like Hermione as is her picture	
	Affront° his eye—	*Confront*
75	CLEOMENES Good madam, I have done.[7]	
	PAULINA Yet if my lord will marry—if you will, sir;	
	No remedy but you will—give me the office	
	To choose your queen. She shall not be so young	
	As was your former, but she shall be such	
80	As, walked your first queen's ghost,[8] it should take joy	
	To see her in your arms.	
	LEONTES	My true Paulina,
	We shall not marry till thou bidd'st us.	
	PAULINA	That
	Shall be when your first queen's again in breath.°	*alive*
	Never till then.	

Enter a SERVANT

85	SERVANT One that gives out himself° Prince Florizel,	*claims to be*
	Son of Polixenes, with his princess—she	
	The fairest I have yet beheld—desires access	
	To your high presence.	
	LEONTES	What° with him? He comes not	*Who comes*
	Like to° his father's greatness. His approach,	*As befits*
90	So out of circumstance° and sudden, tells us	*informal*
	'Tis not a visitation framed,° but forced	*planned*
	By need and accident. What train?°	*retinue*
	SERVANT	But few,
	And those but mean.°	*of low rank*
	LEONTES	His princess, say you, with him?
	SERVANT Ay, the most peerless piece of earth, I think,	
	That e'er the sun shone bright on.	
95	PAULINA	O, Hermione,
	As every present time doth boast itself	
	Above a better, gone, so must thy grave	
	Give way to what's seen now![9]	
	[*To the* SERVANT]	Sir, you yourself
	Have said and writ so; but your writing now	
100	Is colder than that theme. She had not been	
	Nor was not to be equalled—thus your verse	
	Flowed with her beauty once. 'Tis shrewdly° ebbed	*grievously*
	To say you have seen a better.	
	SERVANT	Pardon, madam.
	The one° I have almost forgot—your pardon!—	*(Hermione)*
105	The other, when she has obtained your eye,	
	Will have your tongue too. This is a creature,	

---

7. Many editors emend this line to assign "I have done" to Paulina, rather than Cleomenes. As it stands, the line suggests Cleomenes' exasperation that Paulina will not listen to him. If emended to assign the last three words to Paulina, the exchange may suggest that Paulina is at least minimally responsive to the pleas of Leontes' courtiers that she mitigate her opposition to his remarriage.
8. If Hermione appeared as a ghost.
9. As each present time boasts itself to be superior to a time better than itself, but gone from view, so you, in your grave, must be superseded by what is now seen.

Would she begin a sect, might quench the zeal
Of all professors else;[1] make proselytes°   *converts*
Of who° she but bid follow.   *Of those who*

PAULINA   How? Not women!

110   SERVANT   Women will love her that she is a woman
More worth° than any man; men, that she is   *worthy*
The rarest of all women.

LEONTES   Go, Cleomenes.
Yourself, assisted with your honoured friends,
Bring them to our embracement.   *Exit* [CLEOMENES]
                         Still 'tis strange
He thus should steal upon us.

115   PAULINA   Had our prince,
Jewel of children, seen this hour, he had paired
Well with this lord. There was not full a month°   *a full month*
Between their births.

LEONTES   Prithee no more, cease. Thou know'st
He dies to me again when talked of. Sure,
120   When I shall see this gentleman thy speeches
Will bring me to consider that which may
Unfurnish me of reason.° They are come.   *Make me go mad*
       Enter FLORIZEL, PERDITA, CLEOMENES, *and others*
Your mother was most true to wedlock, Prince,
For she did print your royal father off,[2]
125   Conceiving you. Were I but twenty-one,
Your father's image is so hit° in you,   *exact*
His very air, that I should call you brother,
As I did him, and speak of something wildly
By us performed before. Most dearly welcome,
130   And your fair princess—goddess! O, alas,
I lost a couple that 'twixt heaven and earth
Might thus have stood, begetting wonder, as
You, gracious couple, do; and then I lost—
All mine own folly—the society,
135   Amity too, of your brave° father, whom,   *stouthearted*
Though bearing misery, I desire my life[3]
Once more to look on him.

FLORIZEL   By his command
Have I here touched Sicilia, and from him
Give you all greetings that a king at friend°   *in friendship*
140   Can send his brother; and but° infirmity,   *were it not that*
Which waits upon worn times,° hath something seized   *accompanies old age*
His wished ability,[4] he had himself
The lands and waters 'twixt your throne and his
Measured° to look upon you, whom he loves—   *Journeyed across*
145   He bade me say so—more than all the sceptres,
And those that bear them, living.

LEONTES   O, my brother!
Good gentleman, the wrongs I have done thee stir
Afresh within me, and these thy offices,°   *greetings*
So rarely° kind, are as interpreters   *extraordinarily*

---

1. Of all those who professed other religions.
2. Made an exact copy of Polixenes, as a printer produces a book.
3. Whom, though I am suffering, I wish to live long enough.
4. Has somewhat deprived him of his desired strength.

150   Of my behindhand slackness.⁵ Welcome hither,
    As is the spring to th'earth! And hath he too
    Exposed this paragon to th' fearful usage—
    At least ungentle—of the dreadful Neptune°   *god of the sea*
    To greet a man not worth her pains, much less
    Th'adventure° of her person?   *risk*
155 FLORIZEL   Good my lord,
    She came from Libya.
    LEONTES   Where the warlike Smalus,⁶
    That noble honoured lord, is feared and loved?
    FLORIZEL   Most royal sir, from thence; from him whose daughter
    His tears proclaimed his, parting with her. Thence,
160 A prosperous south wind friendly, we have crossed,
    To execute the charge my father gave me
    For visiting your highness. My best train
    I have from your Sicilian shores dismissed;
    Who for Bohemia bend,° to signify   *make their way*
165 Not only my success in Libya, sir,
    But my arrival, and my wife's, in safety
    Here where we are.
    LEONTES   The blessèd gods
    Purge all infection from our air whilst you
    Do climate° here! You have a holy father,   *reside*
170 A graceful gentleman, against whose person,
    So sacred as it is, I have done sin,
    For which the heavens, taking angry note,
    Have left me issueless; and your father's blessed,
    As he from heaven merits it, with you,
175 Worthy his goodness. What might I have been,
    Might I a son and daughter now have looked on,
    Such goodly things as you?
         Enter a LORD
    LORD   Most noble sir,
    That which I shall report will bear no credit
    Were not the proof so nigh. Please you, great sir,
180 Bohemia greets you from himself by me;
    Desires you to attach° his son, who has,   *arrest*
    His dignity and duty⁷ both cast off,
    Fled from his father, from his hopes, and with
    A shepherd's daughter.
    LEONTES   Where's Bohemia? Speak.
185 LORD   Here in your city. I now came from him.
    I speak amazedly,° and it becomes°   *confusedly / befits*
    My marvel° and my message. To your court   *astonishment*
    Whiles he was hast'ning—in the chase, it seems,
    Of this fair couple—meets he on the way
190 The father of this seeming° lady and   *apparent; false*
    Her brother, having both their country quitted
    With this young prince.
    FLORIZEL   Camillo has betrayed me,

5. Are reminders of my slowness (in greeting you).   Plutarch.
6. An obscure allusion. The name may be a misprint   7. His royal status and his duty to his father.
for "Synalus," a soldier from Carthage mentioned by

Whose honour and whose honesty till now
Endured all weathers.

LORD   Lay't so to his charge.°   *Accuse him directly*
He's with the King your father.

195 LEONTES   Who, Camillo?

LORD   Camillo, sir. I spake with him, who now
Has these poor men in question. Never saw I
Wretches so quake. They kneel, they kiss the earth,
Forswear° themselves as often as they speak.   *Perjure*

200 Bohemia stops his ears, and threatens them
With divers deaths in death.°   *With diverse tortures*

PERDITA   O, my poor father!
The heaven sets spies upon us, will not have
Our contract celebrated.

LEONTES   You are married?

FLORIZEL   We are not, sir, nor are we like to be.

205 The stars, I see, will kiss the valleys first.
The odds for high and low's alike.[8]

LEONTES   My lord,
Is this the daughter of a king?

FLORIZEL   She is,
When once she is my wife.

LEONTES   That 'once', I see, by your good father's speed

210 Will come on very slowly. I am sorry,
Most sorry, you have broken from his liking
Where you were tied in duty; and as sorry
Your choice is not so rich in worth° as beauty,   *rank*
That you might well enjoy her.

FLORIZEL [*to* PERDITA]   Dear, look up.

215 Though fortune, visible an enemy,
Should chase us with my father, power no jot
Hath she to change our loves.[9]—Beseech you, sir,
Remember since you owed no more to time
Than I do now.° With thought of such affections,   *when you were my age*

220 Step forth mine advocate. At your request
My father will grant precious things as trifles.

LEONTES   Would he do so, I'd beg your precious mistress,
Which he counts but a trifle.

PAULINA   Sir, my liege,
Your eye hath too much youth in't. Not a month

225 Fore your queen died she was more worth such gazes
Than what you look on now.

LEONTES   I thought of her
Even in these looks I made.
[*To* FLORIZEL]   But your petition
Is yet unanswered. I will to your father.
Your honour not o'erthrown by your desires,[1]

230 I am friend to them and you. Upon which errand
I now go toward him. Therefore follow me,
And mark what way I make. Come, good my lord.   *Exeunt*

---

8. That is, "Chance treats those of high and low rank
identically."
9. Even if Lady Fortune were to make herself apparent
as our enemy and join my father in pursuit, she would

remain powerless to change our love.
1. So long as you have not allowed passion to destroy
your virtue.

5.2

Enter AUTOLYCUS *and a* GENTLEMAN

AUTOLYCUS   Beseech you, sir, were you present at this relation?°   *when this was told*

FIRST GENTLEMAN   I was by at the opening of the fardel, heard
the old shepherd deliver the manner how he found it; whereupon, after a little amazedness, we were all commanded out of
5   the chamber. Only this, methought I heard the shepherd say
he found the child.

AUTOLYCUS   I would most gladly know the issue° of it.   *outcome*

FIRST GENTLEMAN   I make a broken delivery° of the business, but   *confused report*
the changes I perceived in the King and Camillo were very
10   notes of admiration.[1] They seemed almost, with staring on one
another, to tear the cases° of their eyes. There was speech in   *burst the sockets*
their dumbness, language in their very gesture. They looked as°   *as if*
they had heard of a world ransomed, or one destroyed. A
notable passion of wonder appeared in them, but the wisest
15   beholder, that knew no more but seeing, could not say if
th'importance were joy or sorrow. But in the extremity of the
one,° it must needs be.   *of the one or the other*

Enter another GENTLEMAN

Here comes a gentleman that happily° knows more. The news,   *perhaps*
Ruggiero!

20 SECOND GENTLEMAN   Nothing but bonfires. The oracle is ful-
filled. The King's daughter is found. Such a deal° of wonder is   *a great quantity*
broken out within this hour, that ballad-makers cannot be able
to express it.[2]

Enter another GENTLEMAN

Here comes the Lady Paulina's steward. He can deliver you
25 more.—How goes it now, sir? This news which is called true is
so like an old tale that the verity of it is in strong suspicion. Has
the King found his heir?

THIRD GENTLEMAN   Most true, if ever truth were pregnant by circumstance.° That which you hear you'll swear you see, there is   *proven by evidence*
30 such unity in the proofs. The mantle of Queen Hermione's,
her jewel about the neck of it, the letters of Antigonus found
with it, which they know to be his character;° the majesty of   *handwriting*
the creature, in resemblance of the mother; the affection of°   *instinct toward*
nobleness which nature shows above° her breeding,° and many   *in excess of / upbringing*
35 other evidences proclaim her with all certainty to be the King's
daughter. Did you see the meeting of the two kings?

SECOND GENTLEMAN   No.

THIRD GENTLEMAN   Then have you lost a sight which was to be
seen, cannot be spoken of. There might you have beheld one
40 joy crown another, so and in such manner that it seemed sorrow wept to take leave of them, for their joy waded in tears.
There was casting up of eyes, holding up of hands, with counte-
nance° of such distraction[3] that they were to be known by gar-   *face*
ment, not by favour.° Our king being ready to leap out of   *features*
45 himself for joy of his found daughter, as if that joy were now
become a loss cries, 'O, thy mother, thy mother!', then asks
Bohemia forgiveness, then embraces his son-in-law, then again

---

5.2 Location: Sicilia. The palace of Leontes.
1. Were the very marks of wonder.
2. Ballads often provided accounts of contemporary

scandals and sensations.
3. So altered by emotion.

worries he° his daughter with clipping° her. Now he thanks the   *he agitates / embracing*
old shepherd, which stands by like a weather-bitten conduit of
50   many kings' reigns.[4] I never heard of such another encounter,
which lames report to follow it,[5] and undoes° description to do°   *defies / express*
it.

SECOND GENTLEMAN   What, pray you, became of Antigonus, that
carried hence the child?

55   THIRD GENTLEMAN   Like an old tale still, which will have matter
to rehearse° though credit° be asleep and not an ear open. He   *relate / belief*
was torn to pieces with a bear. This avouches° the shepherd's   *vows*
son, who has not only his innocence,° which seems much, to   *simplemindedness*
justify him, but a handkerchief and rings of his,° that Paulina   *(of Antigonus)*
60   knows.

FIRST GENTLEMAN   What became of his barque° and his fol-   *ship*
lowers?

THIRD GENTLEMAN   Wrecked the same instant of their master's
death, and in the view of the shepherd; so that all the instru-
65   ments which aided to expose the child were even then lost
when it was found. But O, the noble combat that 'twixt joy and
sorrow was fought in Paulina! She had one eye declined for
the loss of her husband, another elevated[6] that the oracle was
fulfilled. She lifted the Princess from the earth, and so locks
70   her in embracing as if she would pin her to her heart, that she
might no more be in danger of losing.°   *of being lost*

FIRST GENTLEMAN   The dignity of this act was worth the audience of kings and princes, for by such was it acted.

THIRD GENTLEMAN   One of the prettiest touches of all, and that
75   which angled for mine eyes—caught the water,° though not   *(my tears)*
the fish—was when at the relation of the Queen's death, with
the manner how she came to't bravely confessed and lamented
by the King, how attentiveness° wounded his daughter till from   *intent listening*
one sign of dolour° to another she did, with an 'Alas', I would   *grief*
80   fain say bleed tears; for I am sure my heart wept blood. Who
was most marble° there changed colour. Some swooned, all   *unfeeling*
sorrowed. If all the world could have seen't, the woe had been
universal.

FIRST GENTLEMAN   Are they returned to the court?

85   THIRD GENTLEMAN   No. The Princess, hearing of her mother's
statue, which is in the keeping of Paulina, a piece many years
in doing, and now newly performed° by that rare Italian master   *completed*
Giulio Romano,[7] who, had he himself eternity and could put
breath into his work, would beguile° nature of her custom,° so   *cheat / business*
90   perfectly he is her ape.° He so near to Hermione hath done   *imitator*
Hermione that they say one would speak to her and stand in
hope of answer. Thither with all greediness of affection are
they gone, and there they intend to sup.

SECOND GENTLEMAN   I thought she had some great matter there
95   in hand, for she hath privately twice or thrice a day, ever since
the death of Hermione, visited that removed° house. Shall we   *distant; hidden*
thither, and with our company piece° the rejoicing?   *join*

---

4. Who stands by weeping like a waterspout that has
been around for the reigns of many Kings. Some large
buildings had "conduits" or waterpipes in the form of
gargoyles or gnarled human faces.
5. Which makes any account of it seem deficient.
6. That is, Paulina simultaneously cried and laughed.

7. An Italian painter, a follower of Raphael, who died in
1546 and was most famous for a series of erotic draw-
ings illustrating sexual positions, or "postures." It is not
clear whether Shakespeare, in fact, had ever seen any of
his work.

FIRST GENTLEMAN   Who would be thence, that has the benefit
of access? Every wink of an eye some new grace will be born.
100   Our absence makes us unthrifty to our knowledge.[8] Let's
along.   *Exeunt* [GENTLEMEN]

AUTOLYCUS   Now, had I not the dash° of my former life in me,   *stain; touch*
would preferment° drop on my head. I brought the old man   *royal favor*
and his son aboard the° Prince; told him I heard them talk of a   *aboard the ship of the*
105   fardel, and I know not what. But he at that time over-fond of
the shepherd's daughter—so he then took her to be—who
began to be much sea-sick, and himself little better, extremity
of weather continuing, this mystery remained undiscovered.
But 'tis all one to me, for had I been the finder-out of this secret
110   it would not have relished° among my other discredits.   *appeared well*

        Enter [*the* OLD] SHEPHERD *and* [*the*] CLOWN [*dressed as
        gentlemen*]

Here come those I have done good to against my will, and
already appearing in the blossoms of their fortune.

OLD SHEPHERD   Come, boy; I am past more children, but thy
sons and daughters will be all gentlemen born.

115   CLOWN [*to* AUTOLYCUS]   You are well met, sir. You denied to
fight with me this other° day because I was no gentleman born.   *the other*
See you these clothes? Say you see them not, and think me
still no gentleman born. You were best say these robes are not
gentlemen born. Give me the lie,[9] do, and try whether I am
120   not now a gentleman born.

AUTOLYCUS   I know you are now, sir, a gentleman born.

CLOWN   Ay, and have been so any time these four hours.

OLD SHEPHERD   And so have I, boy.

CLOWN   So you have; but I was a gentleman born before my
125   father, for the King's son took me by the hand and called me
brother; and then the two kings called my father brother; and
then the Prince my brother and the Princess my sister called
my father father; and so we wept; and there was the first gentle-
man-like tears that ever we shed.

130   OLD SHEPHERD   We may live, son, to shed many more.

CLOWN   Ay, or else 'twere hard luck, being in so preposterous
estate[1] as we are.

AUTOLYCUS   I humbly beseech you, sir, to pardon me all the
faults I have committed to your worship, and to give me your
135   good report to the Prince my master.

OLD SHEPHERD   Prithee, son, do, for we must be gentle° now we   *act nobly*
are gentlemen.

CLOWN   Thou wilt amend thy life?

AUTOLYCUS   Ay, an it like your good worship.

140   CLOWN   Give me thy hand. I will swear to the Prince thou art as
honest a true fellow as any is in Bohemia.

OLD SHEPHERD   You may say it, but not swear it.

CLOWN   Not swear it now I am a gentleman? Let boors° and   *peasants*
franklins° say it; I'll swear it.   *small farmers*

145   OLD SHEPHERD   How if it be false, son?

CLOWN   If it be ne'er so false,° a true gentleman may swear it in   *Even if it is false*

---

8. Makes us squander an opportunity to add to our
knowledge.
9. Insult me so that I must respond with the challenge
of a duel.
1. The Clown probably means "prosperous," but "preposterous" is a nice blunder for it suggests that their
new status as gentlemen is preposterous in the sense of
(1) contrary to nature or (2) putting last what should be
first—that is, inverting the social order by putting "real"
gentlemen behind "false" gentlemen like themselves.

the behalf of his friend, [*to* AUTOLYCUS] and I'll swear to the
Prince thou art a tall fellow of thy hands° and that thou wilt not   *a brave man of action*
be drunk; but I know thou art no tall fellow of thy hands and
150 that thou wilt be drunk; but I'll swear it, and I would thou
wouldst be a tall fellow of thy hands.

AUTOLYCUS   I will prove so, sir, to my power.°   *as well as I can*

CLOWN   Ay, by any means prove a tall fellow. If I do not wonder
how thou dar'st venture to be drunk, not being a tall fellow,
155 trust me not.

[*Flourish within*]

Hark, the kings and princes, our kindred, are going to see the
Queen's picture.° Come, follow us. We'll be thy good masters.   *likeness*

Exeunt

5.3

Enter LEONTES, POLIXENES, FLORIZEL, PERDITA, CA-
MILLO, PAULINA, LORDS [*and attendants*][1]

LEONTES   O grave and good Paulina, the great comfort
That I have had of thee!

PAULINA   What,° sovereign sir,   *Whatever*
I did not well, I meant well. All my services
You have paid home,° but that you have vouchsafed°   *fully rewarded / vowed*
5 With your crowned brother and these young contracted
Heirs of your kingdoms my poor house to visit,
It is a surplus° of your grace which never   *an additional sign*
My life may last to answer.

LEONTES   O Paulina,
We honour you with trouble.[2] But we came
10 To see the statue of our queen. Your gallery
Have we passed through, not without much content
In many singularities;° but we saw not   *In seeing many rarities*
That which my daughter came to look upon,
The statue of her mother.

PAULINA   As she lived peerless,
15 So her dead likeness I do well believe
Excels what ever yet you looked upon,
Or hand of man hath done. Therefore I keep it
Lonely,° apart. But here it is. Prepare   *Alone*
To see the life as lively mocked° as ever   *realistically imitated*
20 Still° sleep mocked death. Behold, and say 'tis well.   *Quiet*

[*She draws a curtain and reveals the figure of* HERMI-
ONE, *standing like a statue*]

I like your silence; it the more shows off
Your wonder. But yet speak; first you, my liege.
Comes it not something° near?   *somewhat*

LEONTES   Her natural posture.
Chide me, dear stone, that I may say indeed
25 Thou art Hermione; or rather, thou art she
In thy not chiding, for she was as tender

5.3 Location: Sicilia. Paulina's house.
1. In F, the stage direction reads: "*Enter Leontes, Polix-*
enes, Florizell, Perdita, Camillo, Paulina: Hermione (like
a Statue:) Lords, etc." For a reader of the play, this direction suggests that Hermione is a living character pretending to be a statue. For a theatergoer unacquainted

with the play, by contrast, the immobile female figure
seen on stage is probably first assumed to be an actual
statue of the dead Queen.
2. The honor we pay to you demands much of you (by
way of hospitality).

As infancy and grace. But yet, Paulina,
Hermione was not so much wrinkled, nothing°   *not at all*
So agèd as this seems.

POLIXENES   O, not by much.

30 PAULINA   So much the more our carver's excellence,
Which lets go by some sixteen years, and makes her
As° she lived now.   *As if*

LEONTES   As now she might have done,
So much to my good comfort as it is
Now piercing to my soul. O, thus she stood,

35 Even with such life of majesty—warm life,
As now it coldly stands—when first I wooed her.
I am ashamed. Does not the stone rebuke me
For being more stone° than it? O royal piece!°   *hard-hearted / work of art*
There's magic in thy majesty, which has

40 My evils conjured° to remembrance, and   *summoned*
From thy admiring° daughter took the spirits,   *wondering*
Standing like stone with thee.

PERDITA   And give me leave,
And do not say 'tis superstition, that
I kneel and then implore her blessing.³ Lady,

45 Dear Queen, that ended when I but began,
Give me that hand of yours to kiss.

PAULINA   O, patience!
The statue is but newly fixed;° the colour's   *painted*
Not dry.

CAMILLO [*to* LEONTES]   My lord, your sorrow was too sore° laid on,   *painfully*

50 Which sixteen winters cannot blow away,
So many summers dry.⁴ Scarce any joy
Did ever so long live; no sorrow
But killed itself much sooner.

POLIXENES [*to* LEONTES]   Dear my brother,
Let him that was the cause of this have power

55 To take off so much grief from you as he
Will piece up in himself.⁵

PAULINA [*to* LEONTES]   Indeed, my lord,
If I had thought the sight of my poor image
Would thus have wrought you°—for the stone is mine—   *made you distraught*
I'd not have showed it.

            [*She makes to draw the curtain*]

LEONTES   Do not draw the curtain.

60 PAULINA   No longer shall you gaze on't, lest your fancy
May think anon it moves.

LEONTES   Let be, let be!
Would I were dead but that methinks already.⁶
What was he that did make it? See, my lord,
Would you not deem it breathed, and that those veins
Did verily bear blood?

65 POLIXENES   Masterly done.
The very life seems warm upon her lip.

LEONTES   The fixture of her eye has motion in't,⁷

---

3. A possible reference to the Protestant attack on the
Catholic practice of kneeling before images of the Virgin Mary.
4. And an equal number of summers cannot dry up.

5. Will make a part of himself.
6. May I die if I do not think it already moves.
7. The setting ("fixture") of her eye gives the appearance of motion.

As° we are mocked with art.   *In such a way that*

PAULINA   I'll draw the curtain.
My lord's almost so far transported that
He'll think anon it lives.
70 LEONTES   O sweet Paulina,
Make me to think so twenty years together.
No settled senses° of the world can match   *calm state of mind*
The pleasure of that madness. Let't alone.

PAULINA   I am sorry, sir, I have thus far stirred you; but
I could afflict you farther.
75 LEONTES   Do, Paulina,
For this affliction has a taste as sweet
As any cordial° comfort. Still methinks   *restorative*
There is an air comes from her.° What fine chisel   *she seems to breathe*
Could ever yet cut breath? Let no man mock me,
For I will kiss her.
80 PAULINA   Good my lord, forbear.
The ruddiness upon her lip is wet.
You'll mar it if you kiss it, stain your own
With oily painting.° Shall I draw the curtain?   *paint*

LEONTES   No, not these twenty years.

PERDITA   So long could I
Stand by, a looker-on.
85 PAULINA   Either forbear,
Quit presently° the chapel, or resolve you   *immediately*
For more amazement. If you can behold it,
I'll make the statue move indeed, descend,
And take you by the hand. But then you'll think—
90 Which I protest against—I am assisted
By wicked powers.

LEONTES   What you can make her do
I am content to look on; what to speak,
I am content to hear; for 'tis as easy
To make her speak as move.

PAULINA   It is required
95 You do awake your faith. Then, all stand still.
Or those that think it is unlawful business
I am about, let them depart.

LEONTES   Proceed.
No foot shall stir.

PAULINA   Music; awake her; strike!°   *strike up!*
        [*Music*]
[*To* HERMIONE] 'Tis time. Descend. Be stone no more. Approach.
100 Strike all that look upon with marvel. Come,
I'll fill your grave up. Stir. Nay, come away.
Bequeath to death your numbness, for from him°   *(death)*
Dear life redeems you.
[*To* LEONTES]   You perceive she stirs.
        [HERMIONE *slowly descends*]
Start not. Her actions shall be holy as
105 You hear my spell is lawful. Do not shun her
Until you see her die again, for then
You kill her double.[8] Nay, present your hand.
When she was young, you wooed her. Now, in age,

---

8. That is, "If you were to shun her in this new life, you would kill her again."

Is she become the suitor?

LEONTES   O, she's warm!
110 If this be magic, let it be an art
Lawful as eating.

POLIXENES   She embraces him.

CAMILLO   She hangs about his neck.
If she pertain to life,° let her speak too.   *be truly alive*

115 POLIXENES   Ay, and make it manifest where she has lived,
Or how stol'n from the dead.

PAULINA   That she is living,
Were it but told you, should be hooted at
Like an old tale. But it appears she lives,
Though yet she speak not. Mark a little while.
120 [*To* PERDITA] Please you to interpose, fair madam. Kneel,
And pray your mother's blessing.—Turn, good lady,
Our Perdita is found.

HERMIONE   You gods, look down,
And from your sacred vials pour your graces
Upon my daughter's head.—Tell me, mine own,
125 Where hast thou been preserved? Where lived? How found
Thy father's court? For thou shalt hear that I,
Knowing by Paulina that the oracle
Gave hope thou wast in being,° have preserved   *alive*
Myself to see the issue.°   *the outcome; the child*

PAULINA   There's time enough for that,
130 Lest they desire upon this push to trouble
Your joys with like relation.⁹ Go together,
You precious winners all; your exultation
Partake° to everyone. I, an old turtle,¹   *Spread your happiness*
Will wing me to some withered bough, and there
135 My mate, that's never to be found again,
Lament till I am lost.°   *dead*

LEONTES   O peace, Paulina!
Thou shouldst a husband take by my consent,
As I by thine a wife. This is a match,
And made between's by vows. Thou hast found mine,
140 But how is to be questioned, for I saw her,
As I thought, dead, and have in vain said many
A prayer upon her grave. I'll not seek far—
For him, I partly know his mind—to find thee
An honourable husband. Come, Camillo,
145 And take her by the hand, whose worth and honesty
Is richly noted, and here justified°   *testified to*
By us, a pair of kings. Let's from this place.
[*To* HERMIONE] What, look upon my brother. Both your pardons,
That e'er I put between your holy looks
150 My ill suspicion. This'° your son-in-law   *This is*
And son unto the King, whom heavens directing
Is troth-plight° to your daughter. Good Paulina,   *betrothed*
Lead us from hence, where we may leisurely
Each one demand and answer to his part
155 Performed in this wide gap of time since first
We were disservered. Hastily lead away.   *Exeunt*

9. Lest they (bystanders?) desire at this crucial moment to trouble your happiness with similar stories.
1. I.e., turtledove, a symbol of faithful love.

Cymbeline

Toward the end of *Cymbeline*, one of the chief characters, Posthumus Leonatus, awakens from a dream vision to find a tablet on his chest, left there by Jupiter, king of the gods. In the dream, Jupiter had promised that the tablet would explain Posthumus's future fortunes. But when Posthumus reads the writing on the tablet, it is incomprehensible to him:

> 'Tis still a dream, or else such stuff as madmen
> Tongue, . . .
> Or senseless speaking, or a speaking such
> As sense cannot untie.

Yet he concludes: "Be what it is, / The action of my life is like it" (5.5.238–42). By his own estimation, Posthumus's life is a senseless riddle. His immediate circumstances perhaps warrant such a conclusion. When Jupiter appears to him, Posthumus, a Briton crucial to his country's recent defeat of Rome, has subsequently disguised himself as a Roman and been put in a British prison. Posthumus deliberately sought his own capture and death because of the guilt he felt for having wrongly commanded the death of his virtuous wife, Innogen, the British King's daughter, falsely accused of sexual infidelity. Unbeknownst to him, however, Innogen, not dead but also disguised as a Roman boy named Fidele, is likewise among those held captive by the Britons.

Such plot complexities are typical of *Cymbeline*, leading not only Posthumus, but also theatergoers, to find it a baffling muddle. In this play, an inordinate number of characters assume disguises, have more than one name, don't know who their "real" parents are, or find themselves unable to decipher the complicated events around them. In one of the play's most famous (or infamous) scenes, Innogen, traveling in a page's disguise to find Posthumus, wakes up from a drug-induced sleep to find herself lying beside the body of a headless man dressed in her husband's clothing. The man is really Cloten, Posthumus's rival for Innogen's hand and the wicked son of Innogen's evil stepmother. Seeing the headless body, Innogen breaks into a lament for the man she believes to be her husband. Her grief is genuine and affecting, but it is prompted by a profound misreading of the object before her.

The improbabilities and complexities of *Cymbeline*'s plot have given some critics pause, as has the freedom with which times and places are handled. Ostensibly set in Roman Britain at the time of Christ's birth (which, according to the chronicles, occurred during the reign of Cymbeline), the play also contains scenes that appear to take place in contemporary sixteenth-century Italy. It is in this modern Italy, for example, that Posthumus is tricked into believing that Innogen is sexually unfaithful to him. Reacting to the play's unusual features, the eighteenth-century critic Samuel Johnson complained:

> This play has many just sentiments, some natural dialogues, and some pleasing scenes, but they are obtained at the expense of much incongruity. To remark the folly of the fiction, the absurdity of the conduct, the confusion of the names, and manners of different times, and the impossibility of the events in any system of life, were to waste criticism upon unresisting imbecility, upon faults too evident for detection, and too gross for aggravation.

This response, however, may say more about Johnson's neoclassical tastes than about the ultimate value of Shakespeare's play. In *Cymbeline*, the complexity of the action seems deliberate rather than inadvertent or unskillful. It creates in the audience both a longing for clarity and control and an anxiety that the play may afford neither. The pleasure of the final act, therefore, stems from the relief experienced when—after a dizzying whirl of events, reversals, revelations, and disguises—peace descends, all identities revealed and all riddles expounded. The sense of wonder produced by this miraculous untangling of complicated events is one of the signal effects of Shakespeare's late plays: amazement that after astonishing suffering can come new hope, after labyrinthine confusions the solace of questions answered.

This feature of the play is one of the reasons why in modern criticism *Cymbeline* is usually called a romance or sometimes a tragicomedy, even though in the First Folio of 1623 it was grouped with the tragedies, probably because it dramatizes serious historical matter taken from the reign of an early Briton King. Like other plays written late in Shakespeare's career, however, such as *The Winter's Tale, Pericles,* and *The Tempest, Cymbeline* does not end tragically. Rather, it ultimately emphasizes the transformation of suffering into joy. While verging on tragedy, each of these plays wins through to a bittersweet conclusion in which shattered families are reconstituted and plot complexities untangled—but always at a cost. Mistakes have consequences in these plays. Sons die; years are lost in exile and wandering; women suffer from unjust slander. If, in the end, good fortune returns to the sufferers, it does not cancel their former pain but provides a miraculous contrast to it.

The date of *Cymbeline* is uncertain, although it is usually given as 1609 or 1610. Scholars differ as to whether it preceded or followed *The Winter's Tale.* We know that it was in performance by 1611, because Simon Forman, a London doctor and astrologer, wrote about seeing it, probably between April 20 and April 30 of that year. It is not clear whether he saw the play at the Globe, the outdoor theater that Shakespeare's company used after 1599, or at Blackfriars, the indoor theater that they also began to use in 1608. The spectacular scenic effects possible in staging this play, such as the descent of Jupiter on the back of an eagle in Act 5, may have been designed with the more elaborate technical capacities of the Blackfriars venue in mind. Some critics have tried to date the play by relating it to the investiture of Henry, King James's oldest son, as Prince of Wales in 1610, since a number of the key scenes of the play take place in Wales. We have no record of a court performance of the play until 1634, however, when it was played before King Charles, who liked it. Other critics have tried to determine the play's relationship to Beaumont and Fletcher's popular tragicomedy *Philaster,* usually dated 1609, to which *Cymbeline* bears some resemblance. But even though the two plays are related, it is not clear which influenced the other.

Whatever its exact date, *Cymbeline* belongs to Shakespeare's late period, and because of its setting it allowed Shakespeare simultaneously to address his longstanding interests both in British and in Roman history. The play intertwines three plot lines and draws on a variety of source materials. The main plot involves Innogen, the daughter and apparently the only living heir of Cymbeline, King of Britain, and her thwarted attempts to live with her chosen husband, Posthumus. Angry that Innogen loves a man of lesser social rank than herself and that she has not married Cloten, his second wife's son, Cymbeline banishes Posthumus from Britain. Posthumus goes to Italy, where he wagers on his wife's chastity with the villain Giacomo, who ultimately makes Posthumus believe Innogen unfaithful. Whether the love of Innogen and Posthumus can be restored is one of the key questions of this plot. This wager story draws on two sources: Boccacio's *Decameron,* a series of prose tales first translated into English in 1620 but available in a French translation in the sixteenth century, and *Frederick of Jennen,* an English translation of a German version of the same story.

A second plot strand deals with Britain's relationship with Rome, especially Rome's demand that the Britons pay the tribute pledged to Julius Caesar upon his conquest of the isle. For this part of the story, Shakespeare drew primarily on the brief account of Cymbeline's reign in Raphael Holinshed's *Chronicles of England, Scotland, and Ireland* (second edition, 1587). Cymbeline was King when the Roman Emperor Augustus Caesar ushered in the famous time of peace known as the *Pax Romana.* In most of the sources, it was Cymbeline's son Guiderius who refused to pay Rome tribute. Shakespeare modified the story, however, so that Cymbeline, urged on by his Queen and her son, is the one who withholds the tribute and provokes a Roman invasion.

The third plotline has to do with two sons of Cymbeline, stolen from their nursery by a wrongly defamed courtier, Belarius, who raises them in the mountains of Wales. By chance, their sister Innogen, disguised as a boy, stumbles upon their mountain cave on her flight from her father's court in pursuit of Posthumus. Near this cave, Cloten, wearing Posthumus's clothes, is killed by one of these sons; also near this cave, Innogen awakes from her sleep to find herself beside his headless body. For the play to reach its resolution, Cymbeline's sons must be reunited with their father. This reunion occurs, but only after the sons play a decisive role in the final battle against the Roman invaders. Their heroic actions in this battle are modeled on quite another part of Holinshed, *The History of Scotland,* which recounts the story of a farmer named Hay and his two sons, who routed Danish invaders at the Battle of Luncarty in about 976 C.E.

From these complex and diverse materials, Shakespeare wove a play whose rich allusiveness has invited many kinds of topical interpretations. One line of criticism has focused on *Cymbeline*'s relationship to events and ideas connected to the reign of King James I. James was interested in linking imperial Rome and the Roman Emperors to modern Britain and to his own kingship. He had himself painted crowned with laurel leaves, in the Roman manner, and had coins stamped with his laurel-crowned profile. Like Augustus Caesar, James presented himself as the great peacemaker after Elizabeth's

James I liked to present himself as heir to Roman greatness. In this 1613 engraving, Crispin van de Passe portrays him crowned with the laurel wreath worn by Roman emperors.

reluctant involvement in wars in Ireland and in defending the Protestant countries of the Continent against Catholic powers, especially Spain. Moreover, just as Augustus ruled over a vast empire, James aspired to unite Scotland and England (along with the already incorporated Wales) into a single entity with one church and one set of laws. His project failed, but he exerted much effort in promoting this union during the first years of his reign. *Cymbeline* uncannily echoes some of James's preoccupations. Sometimes called Shakespeare's last Roman play, *Cymbeline* dramatizes ancient Britain's attempts to come to terms with imperial Rome. Names of Roman gods—particularly Diana, Apollo, and Jupiter—abound (Jupiter alone is mentioned over thirty times); and figures from Roman mythology and history, such as Tarquin, Philomela, and Aeneas, are often evoked. The play's title character, like James, is a British monarch respectful of Rome, even when asserting his independence in the matter of the tribute. The final word of the play, spoken by the King, is "peace." The analogies between the play and the Stuart court, however, have their limits. Cymbeline is also a King duped by his wicked Queen and her doltish son—hardly a compliment to James and the royal family if events in the play are seen literally to mirror their circumstances.

Other allusions expand the play's possible range of meanings. Much is made, for example, of Milford Haven, the port in southern Wales where the Romans come ashore for their invasion of England. This port was famous to Shakespeare's audience as the place where Henry Richmond landed in 1485 to begin his assault on the forces of Richard III. Having defeated Richard, Richmond was crowned Henry VII, first of the Tudor Kings; Henry's daughter Margaret married James IV of Scotland, grandfather to the James who assumed the English throne in 1603. When the Romans land at Milford Haven, they in effect precipitate a transformation of the kingdom, much as Henry Richmond was to do 1,500 years later. At the time of their arrival, Cymbeline believes his two sons dead, and his daughter and Cloten have both fled the court. Britain is without an heir. But through the battle with the Romans, the lost sons of Cymbeline are discovered and the kingdom renewed. So, too, James fancied himself an agent of renewal, a second Henry VII arriving from Scotland to unite the whole island under his rule.

Wales itself is an important symbolic location in this play. Although officially incorporated into England in the 1530s, Wales remained distinct, often stigmatized as rude and uncivilized. The Welsh language, banned from use in public contexts, was taken to symbolize the barbarity of this borderland region. On the other hand, in some narratives, Wales was also the place from which the legitimate rulers of England sprang. The stories surrounding the mythical King Arthur give him a Welsh origin, and traditionally the eldest son of the British monarch was (and still is) given the title Prince of Wales. In *Cymbeline*, Wales is imagined as a harsh pastoral landscape in which Belarius and the King's sons live in a cave, hunt the food they eat, and have little contact with other human beings. These sons, Guiderius and Arviragus, frequently complain that they know nothing of the world and its customs and manners. But Wales shelters these sons as they grow to manhood and protects them from the vices of court life. In fact, as is traditional in pastoral literature, the Welsh scenes contain a good deal of anticourt satire. In the play's spatial and symbolic economies, Wales is the place where true British manhood is preserved. In part, the Welsh material can be seen as a compliment to Prince Henry, who was a staunch champion of the Protestant cause in Europe and showed every promise of being a more martial figure than his peace-loving father.

There can be little doubt that *Cymbeline* works with material imbued with a new kind of significance under the reign of James. Yet it may be a mistake to tie the play too closely to the royal family or to particular events. The play doesn't just reflect the world around it; it transforms the materials from that world into a powerful imaginative and ideological structure. In the largest sense, *Cymbeline* works to define both Britain and proper British manhood by constructing a complex narrative about national origins. The wager plot, with its story of sexual slander and threatened rape, is central to that narrative, not only because Innogen often seems to stand for Britain itself (she is several times addressed as "Britain," and she bears the name of the wife of Brute, the legendary ancient King of Britain), but also because the realignment of gender relations plays a crucial role in the "renewal" of Britain and in the play's turn from tragedy to comedy.

Strikingly, this play about Britain's past never mentions the word "England." In the history plays written in the 1590s, the reverse tends to be true: "Britain" is seldom employed, "England" is invoked with great frequency. There are several reasons for Shakespeare's choice in this later play. He is, of course, deliberately evoking the world of the ancient Britons, the early inhabitants of the island who provide the starting point for his creation of a fictive national past. At the same time, he is to some extent reflecting, and helping to create, the Stuart monarch's sense of the entity over which he ruled. James, after all, was not an "Englander" in the same way Elizabeth had been. He was a Scotsman who spoke with an accent and aspired to bring the entire island into a new political alignment.

Setting the play in the reign of Cymbeline allowed Shakespeare to imagine a primitive Britain that was also the cosmopolitan heir to the westward movement of empire. The treatment of Rome is particularly interesting in *Cymbeline*. Partly, the Romans are figured as an invading force, threatening the island. Yet the British characters most eager to repel the Romans and to treat them as an enemy are the evil Queen and her evil son. Cymbeline himself, while defending Britain's right to live free and under its own laws, is more disposed to come to terms with his great opponents and invariably treats them with respect. There is, in fact, a pronounced tension in the play between Britain's desires to defeat the Romans and to emulate them. This tension is managed in part through the splitting of the Romans into the noble figure of Lucius and the devilish figure of Giacomo, who in his deceit and misogyny embodies sixteenth-century stereotypes concerning the villainous Italian.

When Giacomo comes to Britain to test Innogen's fidelity, he fails in his initial attempt to portray Posthumus as a philanderer upon whom Innogen should seek sexual revenge. He then proceeds more secretly; he has himself conveyed in a trunk into her bedroom, from which he issues in the dead of night to survey her sleeping body and the contents of her room. His stealthy act is framed by references to infamous acts of rape. As he steps from the trunk, Giacomo compares himself to Tarquin, the Roman tyrant who raped Lucrece (a story told in Shakespeare's lengthy poem *The Rape of Lucrece*, written in the 1590s). Furthermore, the book that Innogen had been reading when she fell asleep is opened to the story of Tereus, who raped Philomela and cut out her tongue. Although

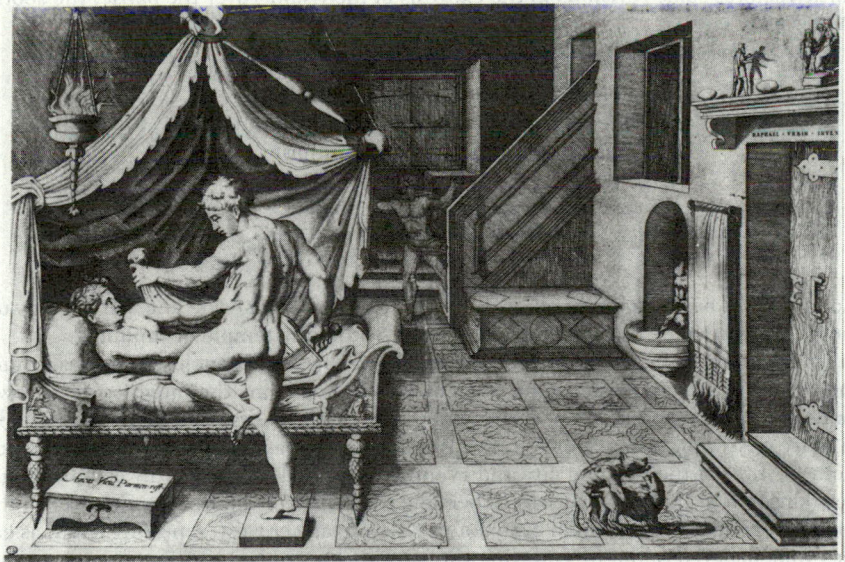

Tarquin's Rape of Lucrece. Sixteenth-century copy of an engraving by Agostino Veneziano.

Giacomo does not literally rape Innogen, he violates the privacy of her body with his peering eyes and rapes her honor by lying successfully to Posthumus about her infidelity. At one level, this incident is about the unjust sufferings of a slandered woman. At another level, Innogen is Britain, threatened by a skillful invader. Giacomo penetrates Innogen's bedchamber, and later he penetrates the ear of Posthumus with his poisonous slander.

In the play's denouement, the threat of foreign penetration is graphically repelled when Belarius and the sons of Cymbeline come from the Welsh mountains, joined by Posthumus disguised as a British peasant, and take a stand "in a narrow lane," putting the Romans to flight and instilling courage in the British. The vulnerable narrow lane is thus barricaded against outsiders by the sons of Cymbeline crying, "Stand, stand" (5.5.28). The moment has gendered and sexual overtones. A vulnerable and feminized Britain is protected from invasion by the swords of virile young men whose cry, "Stand," means both to "hold one's ground" and to "have an erection." This event proves pivotal, lending itself equally well to aphorism and to Posthumus's mocking rhyme: "Two boys, an old man twice a boy, a lane, / Preserved the Britons, was the Romans' bane" (5.5.57–58). In the play's symbolic economy, the threat of penetration initiated by Giacomo is thus repulsed by Innogen's long-lost brothers, and in the final scene Giacomo kneels to Posthumus, asking his forgiveness—the Italian subdued by the Briton.

Something quite different occurs with Lucius, the Roman military leader, who embodies the laudable virtues of ancient Rome rather than the hideous vices of sixteenth-century Italy. Even though the Roman army is defeated, Cymbeline decides to resume paying tribute, and in his final speech the King says: "let / A Roman and a British ensign wave / Friendly together" (5.6.479–81). This rapprochment of warring powers is ratified by one of the play's several mysterious visions. Before the battle, a Roman soothsayer told Lucius what the gods had revealed to him:

> I saw Jove's bird, the Roman eagle, winged
> From the spongy south to this part of the west,
> There vanished in the sunbeams; which portends,
> Unless my sins abuse my divination,
> Success to th' Roman host.
>
> (4.2.350–54)

In this play, not even soothsayers have perfect interpretive skills. The outcome of the battle requires some revisions in the exegesis of the vision. After the battle, the soothsayer says:

> For the Roman eagle,
> From south to west on wing soaring aloft,
> Lessened herself, and in the beams o'th' sun
> So vanished; which foreshowed our princely eagle
> Th'imperial Caesar should again unite
> His favour with the radiant Cymbeline,
> Which shines here in the west.
>
> (5.6.470–76)

Conquest has been transformed into concord as the Roman eagle and the British sun merge and as Cymbeline celebrates this peace within the temple of Jupiter.

In stressing the final union of Britain and Rome, the play's conclusion makes Britain the heir of Rome's imperial legacy even as Britain proclaims the integrity of her own land, laws, and customs. In the early modern period, the course of empire was thought to move westward. When Troy fell, the Trojan hero Aeneas bore his father on his back from the fires of the burning city and eventually fulfilled his destiny by establishing a new kingdom in Italy in what was to become the center of the Roman Empire. In the soothsayer's vision, the Roman eagle journeys even farther west, renewing itself, as eagles were believed to do, by enduring the burning fires of Britain's sun to purge away old feathers in preparation for the growth of new.

The eagle, king of birds and emblem of the Roman god Jupiter; according to myth, it could stare at the sun without blinking and fly into the sun in order to burn off its old feathers. From Joachim Camerarius, *Symbolorum et Emblematum* (1605 ed.).

The play's culminating vision of a Britain separate unto itself but also the cosmopolitan heir of an imperial tradition is anticipated in the actions of Innogen and Posthumus. In the final act, both are partly Roman in their dress and sympathies. Posthumus Leonatus comes to Britain in the company of the Italian gentry, but then dresses as a British peasant and fights with Belarius in the narrow lane before reassuming his Italian garb. Innogen is present at the battle as page to Lucius, the Roman general who had found her weeping over the headless corpse of Cloten. In the final moments of reconciliation, Cymbeline's daughter and her husband stand before the British King in foreign clothes. Innogen, moreover, earlier makes a telling speech about Britain's place in the world when discussing with a trusted servant where she would live after Posthumus had come to believe her unchaste. Her father's court, with Cloten present, she finds unthinkable. She then asks:

> Hath Britain all the sun that shines? Day, night,
> Are they not but in Britain? I'th' world's volume
> Our Britain seems as of it but not in't,
> In a great pool a swan's nest.

(3.4.136–39)

Innogen nicely captures the play's most complex view of Britain. Eschewing an insular patriotism associated with Cloten and the Queen, she recognizes a vast world beyond the shores of Britain. Punning on the double meaning of "volume" as "expanse" or "book," Innogen suggests Britain's partial separation from a larger entity. Britain is a little part of a bigger expanse, a page detached from a large book, or a swan's nest in a great pool. As the image of the swan's nest suggests, Britain remains the special seat of grace and beauty. But it is also connected to something larger than itself. There are other pages in the volume to which, even if detached, Britain belongs.

The play, then, seems to be negotiating a new vision of the nation suited for the Stuart moment, a vision resulting from the richly suggestive concatenation of discursive traditions that Shakespeare brought together in this play. Reaching back into the chronicle materials of ancient Britain, he provides a genealogy for modern Britain that (1) insists on the integrity and freedom of the island kingdom but (2) presents it as purged—largely through the efforts of the King's "Welsh" sons—of the corruptions of modern court life as embodied in figures such as Giacomo or Cloten, and (3) aligns Britain with the cosmopolitan values of Rome, positioning the island kingdom as the appropriate heir of Roman greatness: both warlike and peace-loving.

The renewed Britain has a fourth striking characteristic, and that is its decidedly masculine coloration. The wager plot makes plain the role of gender in configuring British national identity. Consider first the changing fortunes of Innogen. At the beginning of the play, she is a beloved and important figure in her father's court. Cymbeline's only living heir, the Princess is also strong-willed and decisive. She chooses Posthumus for her husband even though he has little money and is not of royal birth. By the end of the play, Innogen has been displaced from the succession by her two rediscovered brothers; she has also been ordered killed by her husband, threatened with rape, knocked unconscious by a drug she believes to be medicine, and struck by her husband when, in her page's attire, she steps forward to reveal her identity to him in the last scene. Though cross-dressed for much of the second half of the play, she does not, like Portia in *The Merchant of Venice* and Rosalind in *As You Like It*, use that disguise aggressively to shape her own destiny. Rather, burdened by the knowledge that her husband unjustly and inexplicably desires her death, Innogen grows less powerful and more passive as the play progresses. Her decline can be summarized in the pun on "heir" and "air." Innogen begins as the former and ends as the latter. The mysterious tablet laid on Posthumus's breast contained a riddling prophecy: "Whenas a lion's whelp shall, to himself unknown, without seeking find, and be embraced by a piece of tender air; and when from a stately cedar shall be lopped branches which, being dead many years, shall after revive, be jointed to the old stock, and freshly grow; then shall Posthumus end his miseries, Britain be fortunate and flourish in peace and plenty" (5.5.232–37). When the soothsayer finally untangles this riddle, he declares Posthumus Leonatus to be the lion's offspring; Cymbeline the cedar tree; his lost sons the lopped branches; and Innogen the tender air, because "tender air" in Latin translates as *mollis aer*, which (by a stretch of the imagination) derives from *mulier*, Latin for "wife." When Posthumus is embraced by the "tender air" (no longer an "heir"), his miseries will cease. Apparently because she is now less important to the succession, Innogen is allowed to live with her chosen husband, his masculinity affirmed by his pivotal role in the British victory over the Roman forces.

Victorian critics loved Innogen, idealizing her as a paragon of selfless and long-suffering womanhood. For example, the Princess never protests her demotion from the position of heir apparent; in fact, she says that she considers finding her brothers worth the loss of the kingdom. To many contemporary critics, however, her role in the play's narrative of nation is a troubling one. Britain renews itself as women are disempowered or disappear. Cymbeline's Queen is an embodiment of hypocritical viciousness (Shakespeare does not even bother to give her a name), and her son, a figure whose father is never mentioned or seen, bears her taint. The play's happy resolution occurs only after all traces of this Queen and her offspring have been erased. When finally united with his children, Cymbeline articulates the fantasy of having himself given birth to all three: "O, what am I? / A mother to the birth of three? Ne'er mother / Rejoiced deliverance more" (5.6.369–71). This is the dream of androgenesis, reproduction without union with women.

Much earlier in the play, Posthumus, believing himself cuckolded by Innogen, voices a similar wish: "Is there no way for men to be, but women / Must be half-workers?" (2.5.1–2). In one of the most deeply misogynist speeches in the Shakespeare canon, Posthumus then blames all the vices of the world on "the woman's part" (line 20)—on woman herself and on that part of woman lodged in man, Eve's mark upon the human race. This mistaken projection onto woman of responsibility for evil may partly explain Cymbeline's fantasy of androgenesis and also why, in the last scene, no persons appareled as women are to be seen (Innogen is still dressed as a page). The happy union of Britain and Rome and Wales is overwhelmingly a union of men.

The play's own counterpoint to its exclusion of women from public power is its demonization of the slanderous Giacomo and its depiction of Posthumus's gradual recovery of faith in Innogen. When Posthumus receives a bloody cloth signifying (falsely) that his order to murder Innogen has been fulfilled, he is overcome with remorse and berates husbands like himself for murdering wives "for wrying but a little" (5.1.5). At this point, Posthumus still believes his wife to have been sexually unfaithful to him, yet he castigates himself for having ordered her punished. His words form a remarkable exception to the more usual patriarchal assumption that female chastity is the primary marker of a woman's value and virtue and that loss of chastity is an unforgivable crime. Critics differ as to how much weight to assign this speech. Posthumus makes it when he believes Innogen to be dead; and generally it is easier to forgive the dead than the living. By the time he is finally reconciled to the living, breathing woman, Giacomo's lies have been exposed and Posthumus takes to himself a wife whose chastity is not in question.

The play, however, overtly punishes violence against women when the evil Cloten, who had fantasized raping Innogen, is beheaded, and it punishes misogynous lies when Giacomo must submit to Posthumus in the final scene. Posthumus, who had formerly himself believed slander against Innogen and had attempted to have her killed, repents and becomes the play's image of the proper husband. After Posthumus's performance in battle and when Innogen is no longer heir apparent, Cymbeline withdraws his objections to Posthumus's union with her. Nevertheless, Innogen's formerly dominant position in that marriage now seems to belong to Posthumus, with Jupiter himself providing the warrant for this reversal. In prison, Posthumus has a dream that not only reconnects him to his familial origins but also provides an image of his own future family. As he sleeps, Posthumus's two warlike brothers and his warlike father appear to him. The father is described as "leading in his hand an ancient matron, his wife, and mother to Posthumus" (stage direction following 5.5.123). After this dream, sent by Jupiter, Posthumus recovers his "true" identity as Innogen's husband and Britain's warrior hero. As he assumes his position in the honored line of Leonati men, the place marked for Innogen is that of Roman / British wife, "led in his hand." In its narratives of nation, *Cymbeline* seems able to reprove the most virulent forms of misogyny only when it simultaneously removes women from public power, transforms them into chaste, domesticated wives, and reaffirms the dominance of husbands.

Samuel Johnson was right when he said that *Cymbeline* is a play with many incongruities of time, place, and circumstance. And yet it is not an incoherent play but rather one that richly interweaves the history of the nation with the stories of the figures who take up their positions in that nation. What is eerie about *Cymbeline* is that its characters often understand so little about what is happening to them, and yet each appears to play out the part assigned to him or her by some higher power: Jupiter, destiny, time. In this regard, *Cymbeline* is of a piece with Shakespeare's other romances, plays in which a higher power often seems to steer all boats to shore and reunite long-severed families. But fictions of inevitability can be deceiving. One should remember that the soothsayer had to revise his interpretation of his vision of the eagle and the sun to make his narrative square with events as they actually happened. And to decipher Posthumus's tablet, he could make the prophecy tally with the facts only by means of a tortuous transformation of "tender air" into "wife." This might suggest that in this play, at least, the higher powers determine less than they appear to do; rather, the forms taken by family, nation, and empire are in some measure the result of human efforts, interventions, and narratives. Shakespeare's play is one such narrative. The resolution of its complex plot may invite relieved assent to its culminating vision, but the very artifice of that resolution also reveals its contingency, suggesting that there is nothing either natural or inevitable about the familial and political arrangements that are repeatedly contested and reordered in this tragicomic play.

JEAN E. HOWARD

TEXTUAL NOTE

Cymbeline was first printed in the First Folio (F) of 1623. Its heavy punctuation suggests that it was prepared for printing by a professional scribe—perhaps by Ralph Crane, who is believed to have prepared five of Shakespeare's other plays for the print shop. While not every feature associated with a Crane manuscript is displayed, the use of parentheses, hyphens, and apostrophes in the Folio text of *Cymbeline* is consistent with Crane's practice. Because the scribe regularized the manuscript he copied, it is hard to determine the exact nature of that manuscript. It may or may not have been a promptbook. Although the Folio text contains almost no stage directions relating to sounds, such as trumpet flourishes to mark ceremonial entrances and exits or the noises associated with battle or with hunting parties, this elision of clues to performance practice is characteristic of "literary" transcripts of the sort associated with Crane.

In this edition, several names have been changed from the versions that appear in F. F's "Iachimo" has been modernized to "Giacomo," the Italian name for "James," on the grounds that a modernized text of Shakespeare should also give personal names in modernized forms. Other editors have proposed "Jackimo" as an alternative modernization. F's "Philario" has also been modernized to "Filario." In this instance, F itself uses the form "Filario" at 1.1.98, though elsewhere it employs "Philario." Finally, the heroine's name, given as "Imogen" in F, is here changed to "Innogen." There are several reasons for this alteration. In Holinshed's *Chronicles,* one of Shakespeare's sources for the play, the wife of Brute (an early King of England) was named Innogen. Many scholars assume that this was Shakespeare's source for the name. In addition, Simon Forman, one of Shakespeare's contemporaries, who described a performance of the play in 1611, gave the name of the Princess as Innogen. Forman could have gotten the name wrong, but he might have been accurately recording a fact of performance lost in the printed text. Finally, in *Much Ado About Nothing,* Leonato has a wife called Innogen (who never makes a stage appearance); that couple might thus anticipate the Innogen and Leonatus of *Cymbeline.* The Oxford editors surmise that the compositors who set type for F misread the word "Innogen," mistaking "nn" for "m" and so printing "Imogen." Other scholars disagree, arguing that Shakespeare might well have changed a name he found in his sources and that Forman may have misheard what he observed on the stage or may have remembered the name from his own reading and mistakenly attributed it to the production.

Act and scene divisions in this text follow those employed in most editions since the eighteenth century, with several exceptions, all in Act 5. In most texts, the culminating battle between the Romans and Britons occurs in 5.2. The Oxford editors divide this battle sequence into three scenes—5.2, 5.3, and 5.4—because at two points the stage is momentarily cleared. On the other hand, most editions separate the action that immediately follows the battle into two scenes: Posthumus's arrest by the Britons after this battle, then the actual depiction of his captivity and the appearance of his family to him in a dream. This edition makes these events into one continuous scene, 5.5, since there is no evidence that Posthumus and his jailers ever leave the stage between these two actions.

SELECTED BIBLIOGRAPHY

Adelman, Janet. "Masculine Authority and the Maternal Body: The Return to Origins in the Romances." *Suffocating Mothers: Fantasies of Maternal Origins in Shakespeare's Plays, "Hamlet" to "The Tempest."* New York: Routledge, 1992. 193–238. Argues that *Cymbeline* recovers the idealized father lost in *Hamlet,* but does so by denigrating maternal authority and the sexualized female body.

Floyd-Wilson, Mary. "'Delving to the root': *Cymbeline,* Scotland, and the English Race," *British Identities and English Renaissance Literature.* Ed. David J. Baker and Willy Maley. Cambridge, Eng.: Cambridge University Press, 2002. 101–15. Partly by associating Cymbeline's evil Queen with Scoto-Britons, Floyd-Wilson argues that *Cymbeline* repudiates the Scottish role in British history, thereby contributing to an Anglocentric historiography.

Hunt, Maurice. "Dismemberment, Corporal Reconstitution, and the Body Politic in *Cymbeline.*" *Studies in Philology* 99.4 (Fall 2002): 404–31. Examines the idea of the body politic—its destruction and reconstitution—in *Cymbeline.*

Jones, Emrys. "Stuart *Cymbeline.*" *Essays in Criticism* 11 (1961): 84–99. Takes an historical approach to the play emphasizing its links to James I's dedication to peace and the role of Milford Haven in Tudor national mythology.

Kahn, Coppélia. "Postscript: *Cymbeline:* Paying Tribute to Rome." *Roman Shakespeare: Warriors, Wounds, and Women.* London: Routledge, 1997. 160–70. Argues that *Cymbeline* shares much with Shakespeare's other Roman plays, including a preoccupation with Roman *virtu* as the root of masculine identity, but an identity constantly made precarious by the woman's part in its formation.

Knight, G. Wilson. "Cymbeline." *The Crown of Life: Essays in Interpretation of Shakespeare's Final Plays.* London: Oxford University Press, 1947. 129–202. Explores national and religious themes in *Cymbeline,* culminating with a sustained analysis of Posthumus's vision of Jupiter.

Mikalachki, Jodi. "Cymbeline and the Masculine Romance of Roman Britain," *The Legacy of Boadicea: Gender and Nation in Early Modern England.* London: Routledge, 1998. 96–114. From a feminist perspective, explores the respective roles of ancient British savagery and Roman civility in the forging of an all-male national community in *Cymbeline.*

Parker, Patricia. "Romance and Empire: Anachronistic *Cymbeline.*" *Unfolded Tales: Essays on Renaissance Romance.* Ed. George M. Logan and Gordon Teskey. Ithaca, N.Y.: Cornell University Press, 1989. 189–207. Examines the pervasive allusions to *The Aeneid* in *Cymbeline,* arguing that the play intimates the passing of Rome's imperial greatness westward to Britain.

Warren, Roger. *Cymbeline.* Shakespeare in Performance series. Manchester: Manchester University Press, 1989. Focuses on performances of the play, especially on striking stage and television versions from the second half of the twentieth century.

Wayne, Valerie. "The Woman's Parts of *Cymbeline.*" *Staged Properties in Early Modern English Drama.* Ed. Jonathan Gil Harris and Natasha Korda. Cambridge, Eng.: Cambridge University Press, 2002. 288–315. Traces the history of three stage properties—manacle, ring, and bloody cloth—as they represent Innogen, and woman more generally, in *Cymbeline.*

FILM

Cymbeline. 1982. Dir. Elijah Moshinsky. UK. 175 min. Boasts such cast luminaries as Richard Johnson (the King), Claire Bloom (the Queen), and Helen Mirren (Innogen), among others.

Cymbeline, King of Britain

THE PERSONS OF THE PLAY

CYMBELINE, King of Britain
Princess INNOGEN, his daughter, later disguised as a man
  named Fidele
GUIDERIUS, known as Polydore   } Cymbeline's sons, stolen by Belarius
ARVIRAGUS, known as Cadwal
QUEEN, Cymbeline's wife, Innogen's stepmother
Lord CLOTEN, her son
BELARIUS, a banished lord, calling himself Morgan
CORNELIUS, a physician
HELEN, a lady attending on Innogen
Two LORDS attending on Cloten
Two GENTLEMEN
Two British CAPTAINS
Two JAILERS
POSTHUMUS Leonatus, a poor gentleman, Innogen's husband
PISANIO, his servant
FILARIO, a friend of Posthumus
GIACOMO, an Italian
A FRENCHMAN   } Filario's friends
A DUTCHMAN
A SPANIARD
Caius LUCIUS, ambassador from Rome, later General of the
  Roman forces
Two Roman SENATORS
Roman TRIBUNES
A Roman CAPTAIN
Philharmonus, a SOOTHSAYER
JUPITER
Ghost of SICILIUS Leonatus, father of Posthumus
Ghost of the MOTHER of Posthumus
Ghosts of the BROTHERS of Posthumus
Lords attending on Cymbeline, ladies attending on the Queen,
  musicians attending on Cloten, messengers, soldiers

1.1

Enter two GENTLEMEN

FIRST GENTLEMAN   You do not meet a man but frowns. Our bloods
  No more obey the heavens than our courtiers
  Still seem as does the King.[1]
SECOND GENTLEMAN   But what's the matter?
FIRST GENTLEMAN   His daughter, and the heir of 's kingdom, whom
5   He purposed to° his wife's sole son—a widow   *intended for*
  That late° he married—hath referred° herself   *recently / given*
  Unto a poor but worthy gentleman. She's wedded,

1.1 Location: Cymbeline's court, Britain.
1. *Our . . . King:* Our dispositions ("bloods") are not more subject to planetary influences than our courtiers'   moods are determined by the King's. (The planets were believed to affect human actions and emotions.)

Her husband banished, she imprisoned. All
Is outward sorrow, though I think the King
Be touched at very heart.

10 SECOND GENTLEMAN   None but the King?

FIRST GENTLEMAN   He° that hath lost her, too. So is the Queen,   *(the Queen's son)*
That most desired the match. But not a courtier—
Although they wear their faces to the bent
Of° the King's looks—hath a heart that is not   *In accordance with*
Glad of the thing they scowl at.

15 SECOND GENTLEMAN   And why so?

FIRST GENTLEMAN   He that hath missed the Princess is a thing
Too bad for bad report, and he that hath her—
I mean that married her—alack, good man,
And therefore banished!—is a creature such
20 As, to seek through the regions of the earth
For one his like, there would be something failing°   *lacking*
In him that should compare.² I do not think
So fair an outward and such stuff° within   *substance; fabric*
Endows a man but he.

SECOND GENTLEMAN   You speak him far.°   *praise him greatly*

25 FIRST GENTLEMAN   I do extend him, sir, within himself;³
Crush him together rather than unfold
His measure duly.⁴

SECOND GENTLEMAN   What's his name and birth?

FIRST GENTLEMAN   I cannot delve him to the root.⁵ His father
Was called Sicilius, who did join his honour°   *prowess (as a soldier)*
30 Against the Romans with Cassibelan
But had his titles by Tenantius,⁶ whom
He served with glory and admired success,
So gained the sur-addition 'Leonatus';⁷
And had, besides this gentleman in question,   *demonstrative*
35 Two other sons who in the wars o'th' time
Died with their swords in hand; for which their father,
Then old and fond of issue,° took such sorrow   *of his offspring*
That he quit being, and his gentle lady,
Big of° this gentleman, our theme, deceased   *Pregnant with*
40 As he was born. The King, he takes the babe
To his protection, calls him Posthumus⁸ Leonatus,
Breeds him,° and makes him of his bedchamber;⁹   *Brings him up*
Puts to him° all the learnings that his time   *Offers him*
Could make him the receiver of, which he took
45 As we do air, fast as 'twas ministered,
And in 's spring became a harvest; lived in court—
Which rare it is to do—most praised, most loved;
A sample° to the youngest, to th' more mature   *An example*
A glass that feated them,¹ and to the graver
50 A child that guided dotards.° To his mistress,   *foolish old men*

---

2. In any man selected for comparison.
3. I set forth his virtues, sir, within the boundaries of his own merit.
4. *rather . . . duly:* rather than reveal what he is really worth. The metaphor picks up on the sense of "stuff" as "fabric" in line 23. Fabric can be crushed together or unfolded and accurately measured.
5. I cannot completely account for his lineage.
6. Tenantius was Cymbeline's father and the brother of Cassibelan, who in 3.1.5 is described as Cymbeline's uncle.
7. The additional name "Leonatus" (born of a lion).
8. In Latin, the word means "after death." As applied to a child, it means "one born after his or her father's death."
9. Makes him a personal servant.
1. A mirror that furnished ("feated") them with images of virtue or elegance.

For whom he now is banished, her own price
Proclaims how she esteemed him and his virtue.[2]
By her election° may be truly read   *choice (of him)*
What kind of man he is.
SECOND GENTLEMAN   I honour him
55   Even out° of your report. But pray you tell me,   *Even beyond the limits*
Is she sole child to th' King?
FIRST GENTLEMAN   His only child.
He had two sons—if this be worth your hearing,
Mark it: the eld'st of them at three years old,
I'th' swathing° clothes the other, from their nursery   *swaddling*
60   Were stol'n, and to this hour no guess in knowledge°   *no informed conjecture*
Which way they went.
SECOND GENTLEMAN   How long is this ago?
FIRST GENTLEMAN   Some twenty years.
SECOND GENTLEMAN   That a king's children should be so conveyed,
65   So slackly guarded, and the search so slow
That could not trace them!
FIRST GENTLEMAN   Howsoe'er 'tis strange,
Or that the negligence may well be laughed at,
Yet is it true, sir.
SECOND GENTLEMAN   I do well believe you.
        Enter the QUEEN, POSTHUMUS, *and* INNOGEN[3]
FIRST GENTLEMAN   We must forbear.° Here comes the gentleman,   *withdraw*
70   The Queen and Princess.   *Exeunt [the two* GENTLEMEN][4]
QUEEN   No, be assured you shall not find me, daughter,
After the slander of[5] most stepmothers,
Evil-eyed unto you. You're my prisoner, but
Your jailer shall deliver you the keys
75   That lock up your restraint. For you, Posthumus,
So soon as I can win th'offended King
I will be known your advocate. Marry,[6] yet
The fire of rage is in him, and 'twere good
You leaned unto° his sentence with what patience   *You obeyed*
Your wisdom may inform° you.   *instill in*
80   POSTHUMUS   Please your highness,
I will from hence today.
QUEEN   You know the peril.
I'll fetch a turn about the garden, pitying
The pangs of barred affections, though the King
Hath charged you should not speak together.   *Exit*
85   INNOGEN   O dissembling courtesy! How fine this tyrant
Can tickle° where she wounds! My dearest husband,   *flatter*
I something° fear my father's wrath, but nothing—   *somewhat*
Always reserved my holy duty—what

---

2. *her . . . virtue:* the price she paid (for loving him) demonstrates how much she valued him and his virtue; her own worth ("price") shows the high esteem in which she held him and his virtues.
3. In F, the name of the Princess is Imogen; but in Holinshed's *Chronicles,* the wife of the ancient English King Brute is called Innogen. A number of scholars have concluded that Shakespeare took the name from Holinshed. For a fuller discussion of the Innogen/Imo-

gen debate, see the Textual Note.
4. F marks *Scena Secunda* (second scene) after the gentlemen exit. Then the Queen, Posthumus, and Innogen enter. There is, however, no change of time or place, and the Queen and the lovers are probably in view at line 69 when the First Gentleman announces their entrance. Most previous editors do not indicate a new scene here.
5. In accordance with the slanderous things said about.
6. A mild oath, from the name of the Virgin Mary.

His rage can do on me.[7] You must be gone,
90 And I shall here abide the hourly shot
Of angry eyes, not comforted to live
But that there is this jewel in the world
That I may see again.

POSTHUMUS   My queen, my mistress!
O lady, weep no more, lest I give cause
95 To be suspected of more tenderness
Than doth become a man. I will remain
The loyal'st husband that did e'er plight troth;°   *pledge marriage*
My residence in Rome at one Filario's,
Who to my father was a friend, to me
100 Known but by letter; thither write, my queen,
And with mine eyes I'll drink the words you send
Though ink be made of gall.°   *bile; bitter liquid*

                Enter QUEEN

QUEEN   Be brief, I pray you.
If the King come, I shall incur I know not
How much of his displeasure. [*Aside*] Yet I'll move him
105 To walk this way. I never do him wrong
But he does buy my injuries, to be friends,[8]
Pays dear for my offences.   [*Exit*]

POSTHUMUS   Should we be taking leave
As long a term° as yet we have to live,   *time*
The loathness° to depart would grow. Adieu.   *unwillingness*

110 INNOGEN   Nay, stay a little.
Were you but riding forth to air yourself
Such parting were too petty. Look here, love:
This diamond was my mother's. Take it, heart;
                [*She gives him a ring*]
But keep it till you woo another wife
When Innogen is dead.

115 POSTHUMUS   How, how? Another?
You gentle gods, give me but this I have,
And cere up[9] my embracements from a next°   *another wife*
With bonds of death! Remain, remain thou here
                [*He puts on the ring*]
While sense° can keep it on; and, sweetest, fairest,   *the ability to feel*
120 As I my poor self did exchange for you
To your so infinite loss, so in our trifles°   *love tokens*
I still win of you.[1] For my sake wear this.
                [*He gives her a bracelet*]
It is a manacle of love. I'll place it
Upon this fairest prisoner.

INNOGEN   O the gods!
When shall we see again?

                Enter CYMBELINE *and lords*

125 POSTHUMUS   Alack, the King!

CYMBELINE   Thou basest° thing, avoid hence,° from my sight!   *most lowborn / be off*

---

7. *but . . . me:* an ambiguous phrase. My holy duty of
obedience to my father excepted (a bond put in jeop-
ardy by Cymbeline's act), I do not at all ("nothing") fear
what Cymbeline's rage can do to me. Or: My holy duty
to my husband excepted (which Cymbeline could dis-
rupt by interfering with the marriage), I do not at all
fear what Cymbeline's rage may do to me.

8. But he does endure the consequences of ("buy") my
injuries in order to be friends.
9. And wrap up (in the cerecloth, or waxed linen, used
in burial shrouds).
1. I still am enriched by you. Posthumus suggests that
he is unequal in rank and wealth to Innogen. Correspondingly, his love token is of less value than hers.

If after this command thou fraught° the court   *burden*
With thy unworthiness, thou diest. Away.
Thou'rt poison to my blood.

POSTHUMUS   The gods protect you,
130   And bless the good remainders of° the court!   *people remaining at*
I am gone.   *Exit*

INNOGEN   There cannot be a pinch° in death   *pain*
More sharp than this is.

CYMBELINE   O disloyal thing,
That shouldst repair° my youth, thou heap'st   *restore*
A year's age on me.

INNOGEN   I beseech you, sir,
135   Harm not yourself with your vexation.
I am senseless of° your wrath. A touch° more rare   *unable to feel / An emotion*
Subdues all pangs, all fears.

CYMBELINE   Past grace,° obedience—   *all sense of duty*

INNOGEN   Past hope and in despair: that way past grace.[2]

CYMBELINE   That mightst have had the sole son of my queen!

140   INNOGEN   O blessèd that I might not! I chose an eagle
And did avoid a puttock.[3]

CYMBELINE   Thou took'st a beggar, wouldst have made my throne
A seat for baseness.

INNOGEN   No, I rather added
A lustre to it.

CYMBELINE   O thou vile one!

INNOGEN   Sir,
145   It is your fault that I have loved Posthumus.
You bred him as my playfellow, and he is
A man worth any woman, over-buys me
Almost the sum he pays.[4]

CYMBELINE   What, art thou mad?

INNOGEN   Almost, sir. Heaven restore me! Would I were
150   A neatherd's° daughter, and my Leonatus   *cowherd's*
Our neighbour shepherd's son.

                    Enter QUEEN

CYMBELINE   Thou foolish thing.
[*To* QUEEN] They were again together; you have done
Not after° our command. [*To lords*] Away with her,   *according to*
And pen her up.

QUEEN   Beseech° your patience, peace,   *I beseech*
155   Dear lady daughter, peace. Sweet sovereign,
Leave us to ourselves, and make yourself some comfort
Out of your best advice.

CYMBELINE   Nay, let her languish
A drop of blood a day,[5] and, being aged,
Die of this folly.   *Exit* [*with lords*]

QUEEN   Fie, you must give way.

                    Enter PISANIO

160   Here is your servant. How now, sir? What news?

_____

2. Redemption. Alluding to the Christian belief that   himself to Innogen in marriage and also pays the price
those who despair distrust God and are beyond the   of banishment.) Innogen insists that Posthumus'
reach of grace.   worth equals her own and that their marriage conse-
3. A kite, or common predatory bird.   quently does not degrade her.
4. *over-buys . . . pays:* pays too much for me by almost   5. Referring to the popular belief that one lost a drop
the amount he gives for me. (Posthumus both gives   of blood with each sigh.

PISANIO   My lord your son drew° on my master.   *drew a sword*

QUEEN   Ha!
No harm, I trust, is done?

PISANIO   There might have been,
But that my master rather played than fought,
And had no help of anger. They were parted
By gentlemen at hand.

165 QUEEN   I am very glad on't.

INNOGEN   Your son's my father's friend; he takes his part
To draw upon an exile°—O brave sir!   *(Posthumus)*
I would they were in Afric° both together,   *Africa*
Myself by with a needle, that I might prick°   *urge on*
The goer-back.° [*To* PISANIO] Why came you from your   *swordsman who retreated*
170   master?

PISANIO   On his command. He would not suffer° me   *allow*
To bring him to the haven, left these notes
Of what commands I should be subject to
When't pleased you to employ me.

QUEEN   This hath been
175 Your faithful servant. I dare lay mine honour
He will remain so.

PISANIO   I humbly thank your highness.

QUEEN   Pray walk a while.   [*Exit*]⁶

INNOGEN   About some half hour hence, pray you speak with me.
180   You shall at least go see my lord aboard.
For this time leave me.   *Exeunt* [*severally*]°   *separately*

1.2

Enter CLOTEN *and two* LORDS

FIRST LORD   Sir, I would advise you to shift° a shirt. The violence   *change*
of action hath made you reek° as a sacrifice. Where air comes   *emit vapors; stink*
out, air comes in. There's none abroad so wholesome as that
you vent.¹

5 CLOTEN   If my shirt were bloody, then to shift it.° Have I hurt   *then I would change it*
him?

SECOND LORD [*aside*]   No, faith, not so much as his patience.

FIRST LORD   Hurt him? His body's a passable° carcass if he be   *pretty good; penetrable*
not hurt. It is a thoroughfare for steel if he be not hurt.

10 SECOND LORD [*aside*]   His steel was in debt—it went o'th' back-
side the town.²

CLOTEN   The villain would not stand° me.   *confront; stay still for*

SECOND LORD [*aside*]   No, but he fled forward still,° toward your   *always*
face.

15 FIRST LORD   Stand you? You have land enough of your own, but
he added to your having, gave you some ground.°   *fell back before you*

SECOND LORD [*aside*]   As many inches as you have oceans.° Pup-   *(i.e., no inches)*
pies!

CLOTEN   I would they had not come between us.

---

6. F does not mark a separate exit for the Queen here,
but Innogen appears to be speaking privately to Pisanio,
and only Pisanio, in the following three lines.
1.2 Location: Cymbeline's court.
1. The First Lord flatters Cloten by saying that the
odorous vapors he is giving off are more healthful than

the outside ("abroad") air that is being exchanged for
them.
2. Cloten's sword, like a debtor avoiding creditors, kept
to the backstreets—that is, avoided the thoroughfare or
main street of Posthumus's body (with a possible allusion to anal penetration).

20 SECOND LORD [*aside*] So would I, till you had measured how
long a fool you were upon the ground.

CLOTEN And that she should love this fellow and refuse me!

SECOND LORD [*aside*] If it be a sin to make a true election,[3] she
is damned.

25 FIRST LORD Sir, as I told you always, her beauty and her brain
go not together. She's a good sign,° but I have seen small   ° she has a good appearance
reflection of her wit.

SECOND LORD [*aside*] She shines not upon fools lest the reflection should hurt her.

30 CLOTEN Come, I'll to my chamber. Would there had been some
hurt done.

SECOND LORD [*aside*] I wish not so, unless it had been the fall
of an ass, which is no great hurt.

CLOTEN [*to* SECOND LORD] You'll go with us?

35 FIRST LORD I'll attend your lordship.

CLOTEN Nay, come, let's go together.

SECOND LORD Well, my lord.   *Exeunt*

1.3

Enter INNOGEN *and* PISANIO

INNOGEN I would thou grew'st unto the shores o'th' haven
And questionedst every sail. If he should write
And I not have it, 'twere a paper lost
As offered mercy is.[1] What was the last
That he spake to thee?

5 PISANIO   It was his queen, his queen.

INNOGEN Then waved his handkerchief?

PISANIO   And kissed it, madam.

INNOGEN Senseless° linen, happier therein than I!   °*Unfeeling*
And that was all?

PISANIO   No, madam. For so long
As he could make me with this eye or ear
10 Distinguish him from others he did keep
The deck, with glove or hat or handkerchief
Still waving, as the fits and stirs of 's mind
Could best express how slow his soul sailed on,
How swift his ship.

INNOGEN   Thou shouldst have made him
15 As little as a crow, or less, ere left
To after-eye him.[2]

PISANIO   Madam, so I did.

INNOGEN I would have broke mine eye-strings,[3] cracked them, but
To look upon him till the diminution
Of space had pointed him sharp as my needle;[4]
20 Nay, followed him till he had melted from
The smallness of a gnat to air, and then
Have turned mine eye and wept. But, good Pisanio,
When shall we hear from him?

---

3. A proper choice; with a pun on the Christian doctrine that certain souls are "elected," or predestined for
salvation.
1.3 Location: Cymbeline's palace.
1. *'twere . . . is:* the lost letter would be a document written in vain, like an offer of mercy that is not accepted or
received (for example, a judge's reprieve that comes too

late or God's mercy to an unrepentant sinner).
2. *ere . . . him:* before ceasing to gaze after him.
3. The muscles of the eye, which were supposed to
break at death or from overuse.
4. *till . . . needle:* until the distance between us had
made him seem as small as the point on my needle.

PISANIO   Be assured, madam,
25   With his next vantage.°   *his first opportunity*

INNOGEN   I did not take my leave of him, but had
    Most pretty things to say. Ere I could tell him
    How I would think on him at certain hours,
    Such thoughts and such, or I could make him swear
30   The shes° of Italy should not betray   *women*
    Mine interest° and his honour, or have charged him   *My entitlement (to him)*
    At the sixth hour of morn, at noon, at midnight
    T'encounter me with orisons⁵—for then
    I am in heaven for him—or ere I could
35   Give him that parting kiss which I had set
    Betwixt two charming words,⁶ comes in my father,
    And, like the tyrannous breathing of the north,°   *north wind*
    Shakes all our buds from growing.

            Enter a LADY

LADY   The Queen, madam,
    Desires your highness' company.

40 INNOGEN [*to* PISANIO]   Those things I bid you do, get them dispatched.
    I will attend the Queen.

PISANIO   Madam, I shall.

        Exeunt [INNOGEN *and* LADY *at one door,* PISANIO *at another*]

1.4

[*A table brought out, with a banquet upon it.*]¹ *Enter*
    FILARIO, GIACOMO, *a* FRENCHMAN, *a* DUTCHMAN, *and a*
    SPANIARD

GIACOMO   Believe it, sir, I have seen him in Britain. He was then
    of a crescent note,° expected to prove so worthy as since he   *growing reputation*
    hath been allowed the name of. But I could then have looked
    on him without the help of admiration,° though the catalogue   *wonder*
5   of his endowments had been tabled° by his side and I to peruse   *listed*
    him by items.°   *part by part*

FILARIO   You speak of him when he was less furnished than now
    he is with that which makes° him both without and within.   *constitutes*

FRENCHMAN   I have seen him in France. We had very many
10   there could behold the sun with as firm eyes as he.²

GIACOMO   This matter of marrying his king's daughter, wherein
    he must be weighed rather by her value than his own, words
    him, I doubt not, a great deal from the matter.³

FRENCHMAN   And then his banishment.

15 GIACOMO   Ay, and the approbation of those that weep this
    lamentable divorce under her colours⁴ are wonderfully to
    extend him,° be it but to fortify her judgement, which else an   *exaggerate his worth*
    easy battery° might lay flat for taking a beggar without less qual-   *a slight assault*

---

5. To join me in prayers ("orisons"); to assail me (as an
object of devotion) with prayers.
6. Between two words carrying a charm to ward off
danger.
1.4 Location: Filario's house, Rome.
1. No banquet—a light meal of fruit, sweetmeats, and
wine following the main meal—is specified in F, but in
other texts, such as Boccacio's *Decameron,* parallel
wager scenes occur during a meal; and at 5.6.155, Gia-

como, retelling the tale of the wager, says it occurred "at
a feast."
2. Alluding to the popular belief that only eagles could
gaze directly on the sun. At 1.1.140, Innogen described
Posthumus as an eagle.
3. *words . . . matter:* causes his reputation, I am sure,
to be amplified beyond what is true.
4. That is, on Innogen's side (with a pun on "colours"
as meaning both "a military banner" and "pretexts").

ity.° But how comes it he is to sojourn with you? How creeps   *of no rank or merit*
20 acquaintance?[5]

FILARIO   His father and I were soldiers together, to whom I have been often bound for no less than my life.

    Enter POSTHUMUS

Here comes the Briton. Let him be so entertained amongst you as suits with gentlemen of your knowing° to a stranger of his   *knowledge*
25 quality.° I beseech you all, be better known to this gentleman,   *foreigner of his rank*
whom I commend to you as a noble friend of mine. How worthy he is I will leave to appear hereafter rather than story° him   *give an account of*
in his own hearing.

FRENCHMAN [*to* POSTHUMUS]   Sir, we have known together° in   *been acquainted*
30 Orléans.

POSTHUMUS   Since when I have been debtor to you for courtesies which I will be ever to pay, and yet pay still.

FRENCHMAN   Sir, you o'er-rate my poor kindness. I was glad I did atone° my countryman and you. It had been pity you should   *reconcile*
35 have been put together° with so mortal° a purpose as then each   *(in a duel) / deadly*
bore, upon importance° of so slight and trivial a nature.   *matters*

POSTHUMUS   By your pardon, sir, I was then a young traveller, rather shunned to go even° with what I heard than[6] in my every   *refused to agree*
action to be guided by others' experiences; but upon my
40 mended° judgement—if I offend not to say it is mended—my   *improved*
quarrel was not altogether slight.

FRENCHMAN   Faith, yes, to be put to the arbitrement of swords,°   *settlement by duel*
and by such two that would by all likelihood have confounded°   *destroyed*
one the other, or have fallen both.

45 GIACOMO   Can we with manners ask what was the difference?

FRENCHMAN   Safely, I think. 'Twas a contention in public, which may without contradiction suffer° the report. It was much like   *permit*
an argument that fell out last night, where each of us fell in praise of our country mistresses,[7] this gentleman at that time
50 vouching—and upon warrant of bloody affirmation°—his to be   *affirming it with blood*
more fair, virtuous, wise, chaste, constant, qualified,° and less   *having notable qualities*
attemptable° than any the rarest of our ladies in France.   *open to seduction*

GIACOMO   That lady is not now living, or this gentleman's opinion by this° worn out.   *by now*

55 POSTHUMUS   She holds her virtue still, and I my mind.

GIACOMO   You must not so far prefer her fore ours of Italy.

POSTHUMUS   Being so far provoked as I was in France I would abate her nothing,[8] though I profess myself her adorer, not her friend.°   *lover; spouse*

60 GIACOMO   As fair and as good—a kind of hand-in-hand comparison[9]—had been something too fair and too good for any lady in Britain. If she went before° others I have seen—as that dia-   *she surpassed*
mond of yours outlustres many I have beheld—I could not but believe she excelled many; but I have not seen the most pre-
65 cious diamond that is, nor you the lady.

POSTHUMUS   I praised her as I rated° her; so do I my stone.   *valued*

GIACOMO   What do you esteem it at?

---

5. How does he claim a connection to you? Giacomo implies that Posthumus cunningly insinuated himself into Filario's friendship.
6. Than to appear.
7. The women of our country.

8. I would subtract nothing from my estimation of her.
9. A comparison claiming equality (not superiority); with a possible pun on the "handfast" by which couples pledged their duty to one another at their betrothal.

POSTHUMUS   More than the world enjoys.°   *possesses*

GIACOMO   Either your unparagoned mistress is dead, or she's
70   outprized° by a trifle.   *exceeded in value*

POSTHUMUS   You are mistaken. The one° may be sold or given,   *(the ring)*
   or if° there were wealth enough for the purchase or merit for   *if either*
   the gift. The other° is not a thing for sale, and only the gift of   *(his mistress)*
   the gods.

75   GIACOMO   Which the gods have given you?

POSTHUMUS   Which, by their graces, I will keep.

GIACOMO   You may wear her in title yours;[1] but, you know,
   strange fowl light upon neighbouring ponds.[2] Your ring[3] may
   be stolen too; so your brace of unprizable estimations,[4] the one
80   is but frail, and the other casual.[5] A cunning thief or a that-way
   accomplished courtier[6] would hazard° the winning both of first   *venture*
   and last.

POSTHUMUS   Your Italy contains none so accomplished a court-
   ier to convince° the honour of my mistress if in the holding or   *overcome*
85   loss of that you term her frail. I do nothing doubt you have
   store° of thieves; notwithstanding, I fear not[7] my ring.   *an abundance*

FILARIO   Let us leave° here, gentlemen.   *stop the conversation*

POSTHUMUS   Sir, with all my heart. This worthy signor, I thank
   him, makes no stranger of me. We are familiar at first.

90   GIACOMO   With five times so much conversation I should get
   ground of[8] your fair mistress, make her go back° even to the   *relent*
   yielding, had I admittance and opportunity to friend.°   *to assist me*

POSTHUMUS   No, no.

GIACOMO   I dare thereupon pawn the moiety° of my estate to   *one half*
95   your ring, which in my opinion o'ervalues it something. But I
   make my wager rather against your confidence than her reputation, and, to bar your offence[9] herein too, I durst attempt it
   against any lady in the world.

POSTHUMUS   You are a great deal abused in too bold a persua-
100   sion,[1] and I doubt not you sustain° what you're worthy of by   *will receive*
   your attempt.

GIACOMO   What's that?

POSTHUMUS   A repulse; though your attempt, as you call it,
   deserve more—a punishment, too.

105   FILARIO   Gentlemen, enough of this. It came in too suddenly.
   Let it die as it was born; and, I pray you, be better acquainted.

GIACOMO   Would I had put my estate and my neighbour's on
   th'approbation° of what I have spoke.   *the proof*

POSTHUMUS   What lady would you choose to assail?

110   GIACOMO   Yours, whom in constancy you think stands so safe. I
   will lay° you ten thousand ducats to your ring that, commend   *wager*
   me to the court where your lady is, with no more advantage
   than the opportunity of a second conference, and I will bring
   from thence that honour of hers which you imagine so
115   reserved.

---

1. You may claim her as your legal possession (with a
pun on "wear" as meaning "enjoy her sexually").
2. *strange . . . ponds:* strangers may come upon your
property (with a pun on "pond" as referring to female
genitals).
3. Punning on "ring" as another slang term for "female
genitals."
4. So of the two ("brace of") objects you deem invaluable.

5. And the other subject to accident (referring to the
ring).
6. A courtier skilled in that way (in the arts of seduction and theft).
7. Am not anxious about.
8. Get the advantage of.
9. To prevent you from feeling personally affronted.
1. A great deal deceived in your too bold belief.

POSTHUMUS   I will wage against your gold, gold to it;° my ring I   *gold equal to it*
hold dear as my finger, 'tis part of it.

GIACOMO   You are a friend, and therein the wiser.[2] If you buy
ladies' flesh at a million a dram,[3] you cannot preserve it from
120   tainting. But I see you have some religion in you, that° you   *since*
fear.

POSTHUMUS   This is but a custom in your tongue.[4] You bear a
graver purpose, I hope.

GIACOMO   I am the master of my speeches, and would undergo°   *undertake*
125   what's spoken, I swear.

POSTHUMUS   Will you? I shall but lend my diamond till your
return. Let there be covenants° drawn between 's. My mistress   *agreements*
exceeds in goodness the hugeness of your unworthy thinking. I
dare you to this match. Here's my ring.

130   FILARIO   I will have it no lay.°   *wager*

GIACOMO   By the gods, it is one. If I bring you no sufficient testimony that I have enjoyed the dearest bodily part of your mistress, my ten thousand ducats are yours; so is your diamond too.
If I come off and leave her in such honour as you have trust in,
135   she your jewel, this your jewel, and my gold are yours, provided
I have your commendation for my more free entertainment.[5]

POSTHUMUS   I embrace these conditions; let us have articles
betwixt us. Only thus far you shall answer: if you make your
voyage upon her and give me directly° to understand you have   *plainly*
140   prevailed, I am no further your enemy; she is not worth our
debate. If she remain unseduced, you not making it appear
otherwise, for your ill opinion and th'assault you have made to
her chastity you shall answer me with your sword.

GIACOMO   Your hand, a covenant. We will have these things set
145   down by lawful counsel, and straight away° for Britain, lest the   *depart at once*
bargain should catch cold and starve.° I will fetch my gold and   *die*
have our two wagers recorded.

POSTHUMUS   Agreed.   [*Exit with* GIACOMO]

FRENCHMAN   Will this hold, think you?

150   FILARIO   Signor Giacomo will not from it. Pray let us follow 'em.
            Exeunt. [*Table is removed*]

1.5

Enter QUEEN, LADIES, *and* CORNELIUS [*a doctor*]

QUEEN   Whiles yet the dew's on ground, gather those flowers.
Make haste. Who has the note° of them?   *list*

A LADY   I, madam.

QUEEN   Dispatch.°   *Exeunt* LADIES   *Make haste*
Now, Master Doctor, have you brought those drugs?

5   CORNELIUS   Pleaseth° your highness, ay. Here they are, madam.   *If it please*
[*He gives her a box*]
But I beseech your grace, without offence—
My conscience bids me ask—wherefore° you have   *why*
Commanded of me these most poisonous compounds,

---

2. Implying that Posthumus's intimacy with Innogen
("friend" means "lover" or "husband") makes him wise
enough not to risk his ring in a wager on her chastity or
wise enough to know the danger of this wager.
3. Even if you pay a large amount of money for a very

small amount (a "dram") of female flesh.
4. This is merely a conventional way for you to speak.
5. Provided I have your introduction (to Innogen) to
ensure a generous reception.
1.5 Location: Cymbeline's court, Britain.

Which are the movers of a languishing death,
But though slow, deadly.

QUEEN   I wonder, doctor,
Thou ask'st me such a question. Have I not been
Thy pupil long? Hast thou not learned° me how   *taught*
To make perfumes, distil, preserve—yea, so
That our great King himself doth woo me oft
For my confections?° Having thus far proceeded,   *medical compounds*
Unless thou think'st me devilish, is't not meet°   *fitting*
That I did amplify my judgement in
Other conclusions?° I will try° the forces   *experiments / test*
Of these thy compounds on such creatures as
We count not worth the hanging, but none human,
To try the vigour of them, and apply
Allayments to their act,[1] and by them° gather   *(these experiments)*
Their several virtues[2] and effects.

CORNELIUS   Your highness
Shall from this practice but make hard your heart.
Besides, the seeing these effects will be
Both noisome° and infectious.   *offensive*

QUEEN   O, content thee.

Enter PISANIO

[*Aside*] Here comes a flattering rascal; upon him
Will I first work. He's factor° for his master,   *an agent*
And enemy to my son. [*Aloud*] How now, Pisanio?—
Doctor, your service for this time is ended.
Take your own way.

CORNELIUS [*aside*]   I do suspect you, madam.
But you shall do no harm.

QUEEN [*to* PISANIO]   Hark thee, a word.

CORNELIUS [*aside*]   I do not like her. She doth think she has
Strange ling'ring poisons. I do know her spirit,
And will not trust one of her malice with
A drug of such damned nature. Those she has
Will stupefy and dull the sense a while,
Which first, perchance, she'll prove° on cats and dogs,   *test*
Then afterward up higher; but there is
No danger in what show of death it makes
More than the locking up the spirits a time,[3]
To be more fresh, reviving. She is fooled
With a most false effect, and I the truer
So to be false with her.

QUEEN   No further service, doctor,
Until I send for thee.

CORNELIUS   I humbly take my leave.   *Exit*

QUEEN [*to* PISANIO]   Weeps she still, sayst thou? Dost thou think in time
She will not quench,° and let instructions° enter   *grow cool / good advice*
Where folly now possesses? Do thou work.
When thou shalt bring me word she loves my son
I'll tell thee on the instant thou art then
As great as is thy master—greater, for
His fortunes all lie speechless, and his name°   *reputation*

---

1. *apply . . . act:* apply antidotes to their operation.
2. Their (the compounds') individual powers.

3. Other than the temporary suspension of the vital functions.

Is at last gasp. Return he cannot, nor
Continue where he is. To shift his being°   *change his abode*
55 Is to exchange one misery with another,
And every day that comes comes to decay°   *destroy*
A day's work in him. What shalt thou expect
To be depender on a thing that leans,[4]
Who cannot be new built nor has no friends
So much as but to prop him?
    [*She drops her box. He takes it up*]
60   Thou tak'st up
Thou know'st not what; but take it for thy labour.
It is a thing I made which hath the King
Five times redeemed from death. I do not know
What is more cordial.° Nay, I prithee take it.   *restorative*
65 It is an earnest° of a farther good   *initial payment*
That I mean to thee. Tell thy mistress how
The case stands with her; do't as from thyself.
Think what a chance thou changest on,[5] but think
Thou hast thy mistress still; to boot,° my son,   *in addition*
70 Who shall take notice of thee.° I'll move the King   *give attention to you*
To any shape of thy preferment,° such   *any kind of advancement*
As thou'lt desire; and then myself, I chiefly,
That set thee on to this desert,° am bound   *action deserving reward*
To load thy merit richly. Call my women.
75 Think on my words.   *Exit* PISANIO
      A sly and constant knave,
Not to be shaked; the agent for his master,
And the remembrancer of her° to hold   *the one who reminds her*
The hand-fast° to her lord. I have given him that[6]   *marriage contract*
Which, if he take, shall quite unpeople her
80 Of liegers for her sweet,[7] and which she after,
Except she bend her humour,[8] shall be assured
To taste of too.
    Enter PISANIO *and* LADIES
     So, so; well done, well done.
The violets, cowslips, and the primroses
Bear to my closet.° Fare thee well, Pisanio.   *private chamber*
Think on my words, Pisanio.
85 PISANIO   And shall do.
      Exeunt QUEEN *and* LADIES
But when to my good lord I prove untrue,
I'll choke myself—there's all I'll do for you.   *Exit*

1.6

Enter INNOGEN
INNOGEN A father cruel and a stepdame false,
A foolish suitor to a wedded lady
That hath her husband banished.[1] O, that husband,
My supreme crown of grief, and those repeated[2]
5 Vexations of it! Had I been thief-stol'n,

---

4. To be dependent on a thing that is about to fall.
5. Consider what opportunity you have to change your service (and become my servant).
6. The box supposedly containing poison.
7. Of ambassadors for her sweetheart.
8. Unless she changes her disposition.
1.6 Location: Cymbeline's court.
1. Who has a banished husband.
2. Those already enumerated. Innogen has already complained of her father, stepmother, and foolish suitor.

As my two brothers, happy;[3] but most miserable
Is the desire that's glorious.[4] Blest be those,
How mean soe'er,[5] that have their honest wills,°   *simple desires*
Which seasons comfort.[6]

          Enter PISANIO *and* GIACOMO

                        Who may this be? Fie!

10   PISANIO   Madam, a noble gentleman of Rome
Comes from my lord with letters.

  GIACOMO   Change you,° madam?   *Do you turn pale*
The worthy Leonatus is in safety,
And greets your highness dearly.

            [*He gives her the letters*]

  INNOGEN   Thanks, good sir.
You're kindly welcome.

            [*She reads the letters*]

15   GIACOMO [*aside*]   All of her that is out of door° most rich!   *is visible*
If she be furnished with a mind so rare
She is alone, th'Arabian bird,[7] and I
Have lost the wager. Boldness be my friend;
Arm me audacity from head to foot,
20 Or, like the Parthian, I shall flying fight;[8]
Rather, directly fly.

  INNOGEN *reads* [*aloud*]   'He is one of the noblest note,° to whose   *reputation*
kindnesses I am most infinitely tied. Reflect° upon him accord-   *Bestow attention*
ingly, as you value

25   Your truest
                           Leonatus.'

[*To Giacomo*] So far I read aloud,
But even the very middle of my heart
Is warmed by th' rest, and takes it thankfully.
30 You are as welcome, worthy sir, as I
Have words to bid you, and shall find it so
In all that I can do.

  GIACOMO   Thanks, fairest lady.
What, are men mad? Hath nature given them eyes
To see this vaulted arch° and the rich crop°
35 Of sea and land, which can distinguish 'twixt   *the sky / harvest*
The fiery orbs above and the twinned° stones   *identical*
Upon th'unnumbered beach,[9] and can we not
Partition make with spectacles[1] so precious
'Twixt fair and foul?

  INNOGEN   What makes your admiration?°   *causes you wonder*
40   GIACOMO   It cannot be i'th' eye—for apes and monkeys,
'Twixt two such shes,° would chatter this way[2] and   *women*
Contemn with mows° the other; nor i'th' judgement,   *Scorn with grimaces*
For idiots in this case of favour° would   *question of preference*
Be wisely definite; nor i'th' appetite—
45 Sluttery,° to such neat° excellence opposed,   *Sluttishness / elegant*

---

3. *happy:* I would have been glad or fortunate.
4. But most wretched is the longing for what is exalted
(in her case, a longing for Posthumus).
5. However low in status.
6. Which adds spice to their comfort.
7. The phoenix, only one of which existed at any given
time. This mythical bird consumed itself in fire every
five hundred years but then rose from its own ashes.
8. The mounted archers of Parthia were famous for
their tactics in warfare, which included shooting arrows
behind them as they retreated.
9. Upon the beach whose grains of sand are uncounted.
1. Make distinction with organs of sight.
2. Would make their preference (for Innogen) clear.

Should make desire vomit emptiness,
Not so allured to feed.[3]

INNOGEN   What is the matter, trow?°   *in truth*

GIACOMO   The cloyèd will,°   *sated sexual desire*
50   That satiate° yet unsatisfied desire, that tub   *glutted*
     Both filled and running,° ravening° first the lamb, *emptying itself / devouring*
     Longs after for the garbage.

INNOGEN   What, dear sir,
     Thus raps° you? Are you well?   *transports*

GIACOMO   Thanks, madam, well. [*To* PISANIO] Beseech° you, sir,   *I ask*
55   Desire° my man's abode where I did leave him.   *Seek out*
     He's strange° and peevish.°   *a foreigner / irritable*

PISANIO   I was going, sir,
     To give him welcome.   *Exit*

INNOGEN   Continues well my lord?
     His health, beseech you?

GIACOMO   Well, madam.

INNOGEN   Is he disposed to mirth? I hope he is.

60   GIACOMO   Exceeding pleasant, none a stranger° there   *none of the foreigners*
     So merry and so gamesome.[4] He is called
     The Briton Reveller.

INNOGEN   When he was here
     He did incline to sadness,° and oft-times   *seriousness*
     Not knowing why.

GIACOMO   I never saw him sad.
65   There is a Frenchman his companion, one
     An eminent monsieur that, it seems, much loves
     A Gallian° girl at home. He furnaces[5]   *French*
     The thick sighs from him, whiles the jolly° Briton—   *lively; lustful*
     Your lord, I mean—laughs from 's free° lungs, cries 'O,   *unconstrained*
70   Can my sides hold, to think that man, who knows
     By history, report or his own proof
     What woman is, yea, what she cannot choose
     But must be, will 's free hours languish°   *pine away*
     For assurèd bondage?'

INNOGEN   Will my lord say so?

75   GIACOMO   Ay, madam, with his eyes in flood with laughter.
     It is a recreation to be by
     And hear him mock the Frenchman. But heavens know
     Some men are much to blame.

INNOGEN   Not he, I hope.

GIACOMO   Not he; but yet heaven's bounty towards him might
80   Be used more thankfully. In himself 'tis much;
     In you, which I count his, beyond all talents.[6]
     Whilst I am bound to wonder, I am bound
     To pity too.

INNOGEN   What do you pity, sir?

GIACOMO   Two creatures heartily.

INNOGEN   Am I one, sir?

---

3. *Should . . . feed*: Should destroy sexual desire, not arouse it (literally, should make desire vomit until it is empty, not tempt it to eat).
4. Sportive; sexually playful.
5. He exhales like a furnace.

6. *In himself . . . talents*: As regards his own qualities, heaven's generosity is considerable. In giving him you, whom I consider his, heaven's generosity surpasses all abundance.

85 You look on me; what wreck° discern you in me   °downfall
    Deserves your pity?
GIACOMO   Lamentable! What,
    To hide me from the radiant sun, and solace°   °take comfort
    I'th' dungeon by a snuff?°   °candle end
INNOGEN   I pray you, sir,
    Deliver with more openness your answers
90 To my demands. Why do you pity me?
GIACOMO   That others do—
    I was about to say enjoy your—but
    It is an office° of the gods to venge° it,   °a duty / °revenge
    Not mine to speak on't.°   °of it
INNOGEN   You do seem to know
95 Something of me, or what concerns me. Pray you,
    Since doubting° things go ill often hurts more   °suspecting
    Than to be sure they do—for certainties
    Either are past remedies, or, timely knowing,
    The remedy then born⁷—discover° to me   °reveal
    What both you spur and stop.⁸
100 GIACOMO   Had I this cheek
    To bathe my lips upon; this hand whose touch,
    Whose every touch, would force the feeler's soul
    To th'oath of loyalty; this object which
    Takes prisoner the wild motion of mine eye,
105 Firing° it only here: should I, damned then,   °Enflaming
    Slaver with lips as common as the stairs
    That mount the Capitol;⁹ join grips with hands
    Made hard with hourly falsehood—falsehood as
    With labour;¹ then by-peeping° in an eye   °glancing coyly
110 Base and illustrous° as the smoky light   °lacking luster
    That's fed with stinking tallow—it were fit
    That all the plagues of hell should at one time
    Encounter° such revolt.°   °Confront / °infidelity
INNOGEN   My lord, I fear,
    Has forgot Britain.
GIACOMO   And himself. Not I
115 Inclined to this intelligence pronounce
    The beggary of his change,² but 'tis your graces
    That from my mutest conscience° to my tongue   °most quiet inner being
    Charms this report out.
INNOGEN   Let me hear no more.
GIACOMO   O dearest soul, your cause doth strike my heart
120 With pity that doth make me sick. A lady   compare
    So fair, and fastened to an empery°   I to whores   °empire
    Would make the great'st king double,° to be partnered   °twice as great
    With tomboys hired with that self exhibition³
    Which your own coffers yield; with diseased ventures°   °prostitutes; vendors
125 That play with all infirmities for gold

---

7. *or . . . born*: or, they being known about in time, the remedy is then brought about.
8. *What you both urge on and restrain (as one commands a horse).*
9. *Slaver . . . Capitol*: Offer drooling kisses to whores who, like the stairs to the Roman Capitol building, are available to everyone.
1. *join . . . labour*: clasp hands made as hard with

hourly lies or sexual infidelities as they might have been made hard with work.
2. *Not . . . change*: It is not because I am disposed to give this information that I report the contemptible nature of his change.
3. With whores ("tomboys") hired with that same payment.

Which rottenness can lend to nature; such boiled stuff[4]
As well might poison poison! Be revenged,
Or she that bore you was no queen, and you
Recoil° from your great stock.   Degenerate

INNOGEN   Revenged?
130   How should I be revenged? If this be true—
As I have such a heart that both mine ears
Must not in haste abuse[5]—if it be true,
How should I be revenged?

GIACOMO   Should he make me
Live like Diana's priest[6] betwixt cold sheets
135   Whiles he is vaulting variable ramps,[7]
In your despite, upon your purse[8]—revenge it.
I dedicate myself to your sweet pleasure,
More noble than that runagate° to your bed,   renegade
And will continue fast° to your affection,   constant
Still close as sure.[9]

140   INNOGEN   What ho, Pisanio!

GIACOMO   Let me my service tender on your lips.

INNOGEN   Away, I do condemn mine ears that have
So long attended thee. If thou wert honourable
Thou wouldst have told this tale for virtue, not
145   For such an end thou seek'st, as base as strange.
Thou wrong'st a gentleman who is as far
From thy report as thou from honour, and
Solicit'st here a lady that disdains
Thee and the devil alike. What ho, Pisanio!
150   The King my father shall be made acquainted
Of thy assault. If he shall think it fit
A saucy stranger in his court to mart°   do business
As in a Romish stew,° and to expound   Roman brothel
His beastly mind to us, he hath a court
155   He little cares for, and a daughter who
He not respects at all. What ho, Pisanio!

GIACOMO   O happy Leonatus! I may say
The credit° that thy lady hath of° thee   trust / in
Deserves thy trust, and thy most perfect goodness
160   Her assured credit.[1] Blessèd live you long,
A lady to the worthiest sir that ever
Country called his;° and you his mistress, only   its own
For the most worthiest fit. Give me your pardon.
I have spoke this to know if your affiance°   faith
165   Were deeply rooted, and shall make your lord
That which he is new o'er;[2] and he is one
The truest mannered,[3] such a holy witch°   a charming person
That he enchants societies into° him;   crowds of people to
Half all men's hearts are his.

4. Such diseased prostitutes. Sweating, usually
induced by the steam from boiling water, was a common treatment for syphilis.
5. *a heart . . . abuse*: a heart that my ears must not
abuse by too hastily accepting what they hear.
6. That is, live chastely. Diana was the Roman goddess
of the hunt known for her chastity and her circle of virgin followers.
7. While he is having sexual intercourse with whores
("ramps") of all kinds.

8. In contempt of you, with your money.
9. Always as secret as I am true.
1. *and . . . credit*: and your most perfect goodness
deserves her absolute trust.
2. *and . . . o'er*: and I (by this news of your fidelity) shall
make your lord feel afresh what he already is (that is,
your lord).
3. *he . . . mannered*: he is above all others the most perfect in conduct.

	INNOGEN	You make amends.	

170 GIACOMO He sits 'mongst men like a descended god.
He hath a kind of honour sets him off
More than a mortal seeming.[4] Be not angry,
Most mighty princess, that I have adventured°   *dared*
To try° your taking of a false report, which hath   *test*
175 Honoured with confirmation your great judgement
In the election of a sir so rare
Which° you know cannot err. The love I bear him   *Whom*
Made me to fan[5] you thus, but the gods made you,
Unlike all others, chaffless.° Pray, your pardon.   *without chaff; perfect*
180 INNOGEN All's well, sir. Take my power i'th' court for yours.
GIACOMO My humble thanks. I had almost forgot
T'entreat your grace but in a small request,
And yet of moment° too, for it concerns   *importance*
Your lord; myself and other noble friends
Are partners in the business.
185 INNOGEN   Pray what is't?
GIACOMO Some dozen Romans of us, and your lord—
Best feather of our wing—have mingled sums
To buy a present for the Emperor,
Which I, the factor° for the rest, have done   *agent*
190 In France. 'Tis plate[6] of rare device, and jewels
Of rich and exquisite form; their value's great,
And I am something curious,° being strange,°   *somewhat anxious / foreign*
To have them in safe stowage. May it please you
To take them in protection?
INNOGEN   Willingly,
195 And pawn mine honour for their safety; since
My lord hath interest° in them, I will keep them   *a stake*
In my bedchamber.
GIACOMO   They are in a trunk
Attended by my men. I will make bold
To send them to you, only for this night.
I must aboard tomorrow.
200 INNOGEN   O, no, no!
GIACOMO Yes, I beseech, or I shall short° my word   *break*
By length'ning my return. From Gallia°   *France*
I crossed the seas on purpose and on promise
To see your grace.
INNOGEN   I thank you for your pains;
But not away tomorrow!
205 GIACOMO   O, I must, madam.
Therefore I shall beseech you, if you please
To greet your lord with writing, do't tonight.
I have outstood° my time, which is material   *overstayed*
To th' tender° of our present.   *the offering*
INNOGEN   I will write.
210 Send your trunk to me, it shall safe be kept,
And truly yielded° you. You're very welcome.   *faithfully returned to*

Exeunt [severally]

---

4. So that he appears more than mortal.
5. Winnow. When grain was harvested, wheat was winnowed from the chaff; metaphorically, the good was

winnowed from the bad.
6. Objects, often tableware, either made of precious
metals or covered ("plated") with them.

2.1

Enter CLOTEN *and the two* LORDS

CLOTEN Was there ever man had such luck? When I kissed the jack[1] upon an upcast,° to be hit away! I had a hundred pound on't, and then a whoreson jackanapes° must take me up[2] for swearing, as if I borrowed mine oaths of him, and might not spend them at my pleasure.　　　　　　　　　*on a final throw*　　*an idiotic bastard*

FIRST LORD What got he by that? You have broke his pate with your bowl.

SECOND LORD [*aside*] If his wit had been like him that broke it, it would have run all out.

CLOTEN When a gentleman is disposed to swear it is not for any standers-by to curtail[3] his oaths, ha?

SECOND LORD No, my lord [*aside*]—nor crop the ears of them.

CLOTEN Whoreson dog! I give him satisfaction? Would he had been one of my rank.[4]

SECOND LORD [*aside*] To have smelled like a fool.

CLOTEN I am not vexed more at anything in th'earth. A pox on't,[5] I had rather not be so noble as I am. They dare not fight with me because of the Queen, my mother. Every jack-slave° hath his bellyful of fighting, and I must go up and down like a cock that nobody can match.°　　　*lowborn fellow*　　*equal; fight with*

SECOND LORD [*aside*] You are cock and capon too an you crow cock with your comb on.[6]

CLOTEN Sayst thou?

SECOND LORD It is not fit your lordship should undertake° every companion° that you give offence to.　　*take on*　*fellow*

CLOTEN No, I know that, but it is fit I should commit offence to[7] my inferiors.

SECOND LORD Ay, it is fit for your lordship only.

CLOTEN Why, so I say.

FIRST LORD Did you hear of a stranger° that's come to court tonight?　　*foreigner*

CLOTEN A stranger, and I not know on't?°　　*of it*

SECOND LORD [*aside*] He's a strange fellow himself and knows it not.

FIRST LORD There's an Italian come, and, 'tis thought, one of Leonatus' friends.

CLOTEN Leonatus? A banished rascal; and he's another, whatso-ever he be. Who told you of this stranger?

FIRST LORD One of your lordship's pages.

CLOTEN Is it fit I went to look upon him? Is there no derogation° in't?　　*loss of dignity*

SECOND LORD You cannot derogate,[8] my lord.

CLOTEN Not easily, I think.

2.1 Location: Cymbeline's court, Britain.
1. In the game of bowls, the jack is the target ball. To "kiss the jack" is to roll one's ball so that it touches the jack.
2. Challenge me; rebuke me.
3. Shorten, as one bobbed the tails (and sometimes the ears) of certain dogs. This leads the Second Lord to talk of cropping the ears of oaths in line 12.
4. Social position. Gentlemen were only supposed to fight ("give satisfaction" to) men of their own rank. The

Second Lord puns on "rank" as meaning "strong smell."
5. A mild oath meaning "a plague on it."
6. And a castrated cock too if you brag ("crow") that you are a cock while wearing a fool's cap (coxcomb). There are puns here on "capon" and "cap on," on "cock's comb" and "coxcomb."
7. I should assault, with the perhaps unintended sec-ondary meaning of "to defecate upon."
8. You cannot forfeit your dignity; you have no dignity to lose.

SECOND LORD [*aside*] You are a fool granted,° therefore your   *an acknowledged fool*
45 issues,° being foolish, do not derogate.   *deeds*

CLOTEN Come, I'll go see this Italian. What I have lost today at
bowls I'll win tonight of him. Come, go.

SECOND LORD I'll attend your lordship.

Exeunt [CLOTEN *and* FIRST LORD]

That such a crafty devil as is his mother
50 Should yield the world this ass!—a woman that
Bears all down° with her brain, and this her son   *Overcomes everyone*
Cannot take two from twenty, for his heart,°   *for the life of him*
And leave eighteen. Alas, poor princess,
Thou divine Innogen, what thou endur'st,
55 Betwixt a father by thy stepdame governed,
A mother hourly coining plots, a wooer
More hateful than the foul expulsion is
Of thy dear husband, than that horrid act
Of the divorce he'd make! The heavens hold firm
60 The walls of thy dear honour, keep unshaked
That temple, thy fair mind, that thou mayst stand
T'enjoy thy banished lord and this great land!   *Exit*

2.2

[A *trunk and arras.*[1] A] *bed* [*is thrust forth with*] INNO-
GEN [*in it, reading a book. Enter to her* HELEN], *a lady*[2]

INNOGEN Who's there? My woman Helen?

HELEN   Please you, madam.

INNOGEN What hour is it?

HELEN   Almost midnight, madam.

INNOGEN I have read three hours then. Mine eyes are weak.
Fold down the leaf where I have left. To bed.
5 Take not away the taper; leave it burning,
And if thou canst awake by four o'th' clock,
I prithee call me. Sleep hath seized me wholly.   [*Exit* HELEN]
To your protection I commend me, gods.
From fairies° and the tempters of the night   *evil beings*
10 Guard me, beseech ye.°   *I entreat you*
[*She*] *sleeps.*

GIACOMO [*comes*] *from the trunk*

GIACOMO The crickets sing, and man's o'er-laboured sense
Repairs itself by rest. Our Tarquin[3] thus
Did softly press the rushes[4] ere he wakened
The chastity he wounded. Cytherea,[5]
15 How bravely° thou becom'st thy bed! Fresh lily,   *splendidly*
And whiter than the sheets! That I might touch,
But kiss, one kiss! Rubies unparagoned,
How dearly they do't![6] 'Tis her breathing that
Perfumes the chamber thus. The flame o'th' taper

2.2 Location: Innogen's chambers.
1. Tapestry wall covering.
2. F's stage direction reads "Enter Imogen, in her Bed, and a Lady." The trunk in which Giacomo is concealed is probably brought onstage as the scene opens, either carried on or raised up through the trapdoor in the stage floor. Beds typically were "thrust forth" from a door at the back of the stage. Giacomo mentions an arras in his ensuing description of Innogen's bedroom. One may

have been hung up at the back of the stage for this scene.
3. The ancient Roman Sextus Tarquinius, whose rape of Lucrece (Lucretia) was the subject of a poem by Shakespeare.
4. Reeds commonly used as a floor covering.
5. A name for Aphrodite, or Venus, the goddess of beauty and love, who first set foot on the island of Cytherea after her birth from sea-foam.
6. How dearly do they (her ruby lips) kiss one another.

20 Bows toward her, and would underpeep her lids,
To see th'enclosèd lights, now canopied
Under these windows,° white and azure-laced   *eyelids*
With blue of heaven's own tinct.° But my design—   *hue*
To note the chamber. I will write all down.
     [*He writes in his tables*]°   *writing tablets*
25 Such and such pictures, there the window, such
Th'adornment of her bed, the arras, figures,
Why, such and such; and the contents o'th' story.[7]
Ah, but some natural notes° about her body   *marks*
Above ten thousand meaner movables[8]
30 Would testify t'enrich mine inventory.
O sleep, thou ape° of death, lie dull° upon her,   *mimic / heavy*
And be her sense but as a monument[9]
Thus in a chapel lying. Come off, come off;
As slippery as the Gordian knot was hard.[1]
     [*He takes the bracelet from her arm*]
35 'Tis mine, and this will witness outwardly,
As strongly as the conscience does within,[2]
To th' madding° of her lord. On her left breast   *maddening*
A mole, cinque-spotted,° like the crimson drops   *with five spots*
I'th' bottom of a cowslip. Here's a voucher°   *piece of evidence*
40 Stronger than ever law could make. This secret
Will force him think I have picked the lock and ta'en
The treasure of her honour.[3] No more. To what end?
Why should I write this down that's riveted,
Screwed to my memory? She hath been reading late,
45 The tale of Tereus.[4] Here the leaf's turned down
Where Philomel gave up. I have enough.
To th' trunk again, and shut the spring of it.
Swift, swift, you dragons of the night, that dawning
May bare the raven's eye![5] I lodge in fear.
50 Though this' a heavenly angel, hell is here.
     Clock strikes
One, two, three. Time, time!
     Exit [*into the trunk. The bed and trunk are removed*]

2.3

     Enter CLOTEN *and* [*the two*] LORDS
FIRST LORD   Your lordship is the most patient man in loss, the
     most coldest° that ever turned up ace.[1]   *least passionate*
CLOTEN   It would make any man cold to lose.

---

7. The design on the tapestry (?). In 2.4.66–91, Giacomo describes in more detail what he saw in Innogen's bedchamber: a tapestry depicting the story of Antony and Cleopatra and a chimneypiece carving of Diana bathing. He could here be referring to the "figures" and "contents" of either the tapestry or chimneypiece.
8. Less important pieces of property, especially furniture or furnishings.
9. And let her senses be like those of an effigy on a tomb.
1. As easy to open as the Gordian knot was difficult to untie. Alluding to the myth of Gordius, King of Phrygia, who tied an impossibly intricate knot and declared that whoever untied it would reign over Asia; with a single thrust of his sword, Alexander the Great cut through it. Giacomo's unclasping of the bracelet has sexual implications. He is metaphorically violating Innogen's chastity and, by stealing Posthumus's love token, is interfering in the marriage bond that links Posthumus and Innogen.
2. As powerfully as does his inward consciousness.
3. Giacomo means his knowledge of the mole will make Posthumus believe he has slept with Innogen. To "pick the lock" is a euphemism for "to have sex."
4. In Greek mythology, Tereus, King of Thrace, raped his wife's sister Philomela and cut out her tongue so she could not reveal what had happened. Philomela later wove the story into a tapestry.
5. May cause the raven to wake. The bird supposedly slept facing east and awakened at dawn.
2.3 Location: A room near Innogen's chambers.
1. *that . . . ace*: who ever threw the lowest score in a game of dice, with a pun on "ass."

FIRST LORD   But not every man patient after° the noble temper   *according to*
5   of your lordship. You are most hot and furious when you win.

CLOTEN   Winning will put any man into courage. If I could get
         this foolish Innogen I should have gold enough. It's almost
         morning, is't not?

FIRST LORD   Day, my lord.

10   CLOTEN   I would this music would come. I am advised to give
         her music o' mornings; they say it will penetrate.[2]

              Enter MUSICIANS

         Come on, tune. If you can penetrate her with your fingering,
         so; we'll try with tongue too.[3] If none will do,° let her remain;   *suffice*
         but I'll never give o'er. First, a very excellent good-conceited°   *ingenious*
15   thing; after, a wonderful sweet air with admirable rich words
         to it; and then let her consider.

              [*Music*]

MUSICIAN [*sings*][4]   Hark, hark, the lark at heaven gate sings,
              And Phoebus gins° arise,[5]   *Apollo (sun god) begins*
              His steeds to water at those springs
20   On chaliced flowers[6] that lies,
              And winking Mary-buds° begin to ope their golden eyes;   *closed marigold buds*
              With everything that pretty is, my lady sweet, arise,
              Arise, arise!

CLOTEN   So, get you gone. If this penetrate I will consider° your   *value*
25   music the better; if it do not, it is a vice° in her ears which   *defect*
         horse hairs and calves' guts[7] nor the voice of unpaved[8] eunuch
         to boot can never amend.   [*Exeunt* MUSICIANS]

              Enter CYMBELINE *and* [*the*] QUEEN

SECOND LORD   Here comes the King.

CLOTEN   I am glad I was up so late, for that's the reason I was up
30   so early. He cannot choose but take this service I have done
         fatherly. Good morrow to your majesty, and to my gracious
         mother.

CYMBELINE   Attend you here the door of our stern daughter?
         Will she not forth?

35   CLOTEN   I have assailed her with musics, but she vouchsafes no
         notice.

CYMBELINE   The exile of her minion° is too new.   *darling*
         She hath not yet forgot him. Some more time
         Must wear the print° of his remembrance out,   *imprint*
         And then she's yours.

40   QUEEN [*to* CLOTEN]   You are most bound to th' King,
              Who lets go by no vantages° that may   *opportunities*
              Prefer° you to his daughter. Frame° yourself   *Recommend / Prepare*
              To° orderly solicits,° and be friended   *With / solicitations*
              With aptness of the season.[9] Make denials
45   Increase your services; so seem as if
              You were inspired to do those duties which
              You tender to her; that you in all obey her,

---

2. Affect her emotions; arouse her sexually.
3. If your instrumental music can move her, that's
good. We'll try to move her with song as well. These
lines also carry an explicitly sexual secondary meaning:
If you can insert your fingers inside her, that's good.
We'll try oral sex as well. It is unclear if Cloten understands the bawdy import of his own words.
4. F does not attribute this song to a particular singer
but simply introduces it as "SONG." It also appears in a

seventeenth-century manuscript located in the
Bodleian Library at Oxford.
5. These lines also echo Shakespeare's sonnet 29, lines
10–12: "my state / Like to the lark at break of day arising / From sullen earth, sings hymns at heaven's gate."
6. Flowers with cuplike blossoms.
7. Both were used as strings for musical instruments.
8. Castrated (lacking stones).
9. And be assisted by appropriate timing.

Save when command to your dismission tends,
And therein you are senseless.[1]

CLOTEN   Senseless? Not so.

       [*Enter a* MESSENGER]

50 MESSENGER [*to* CYMBELINE]   So like you,° sir, ambassadors from Rome;   *If you please*
The one is Caius Lucius.

CYMBELINE   A worthy fellow,
Albeit he comes on angry purpose now:
But that's no fault of his. We must receive him
According to the honour of his sender,
55 And towards himself, his goodness forespent on us,[2]
We must extend our notice. Our dear son,
When you have given good morning to your mistress,
Attend the Queen and us. We shall have need
T'employ you towards this Roman. Come, our queen.

          Exeunt [*all but* CLOTEN]

60 CLOTEN   If she be up, I'll speak with her; if not,
Let her lie still and dream.

       [*He knocks*]

          By your leave, ho!—
I know her women are about her; what
If I do line° one of their hands? 'Tis gold   *fill (with gold)*
Which buys admittance—oft it doth—yea, and makes
65 Diana's rangers false° themselves, yield up   *gamekeepers turn false*
Their deer to th' stand o'th' stealer;[3] and 'tis gold
Which makes the true man killed and saves the thief,
Nay, sometime hangs both thief and true man. What
Can it not do and undo? I will make
70 One of her women lawyer to° me, for   *advocate for*
I yet not understand the case[4] myself.—
By your leave.

       Knocks. Enter a LADY

LADY   Who's there that knocks?

CLOTEN   A gentleman.

LADY   No more?

CLOTEN   Yes, and a gentlewoman's son.

LADY   That's more
75 [*Aside*][5] Than some whose tailors are as dear° as yours   *expensive*
Can justly boast of. [*To him*] What's your lordship's pleasure?

CLOTEN   Your lady's person. Is she ready?°   *dressed; prepared*

LADY   Ay.
[*Aside*] To keep her chamber.

CLOTEN   There is gold for you.
Sell me your good report.

80 LADY   How, my good name?°—or to report of you   *reputation*
What I shall think is good?

       Enter INNOGEN

       The Princess.   [*Exit*]

---

1. *Save . . . senseless:* Except what pertains to your dismissal ("dismission"), which you are incapable of understanding. Cloten, however, takes "senseless" to mean "stupid."
2. *his . . . us:* in view of the virtue he has shown in previous dealings with us.
3. *yield . . . stealer:* surrender their deer to the place where the thief stands to shoot; surrender what is most dear or valuable (their chastity) to the thief's erect penis ("th' stand").
4. *for . . . case:* for I still do not know how to manage the matter (with wordplay on "stand under" as slang for "sexually penetrate" and on "case" as slang for "vagina").
5. The Lady's speaking all or part of this and her next speech in asides explains the outspokenness of her comments; it also follows the pattern of 2.1 and of later scenes in which Cloten's words are slyly subjected to derogatory commentary by those with whom he converses.

CLOTEN Good morrow, fairest. Sister, your sweet hand.

INNOGEN Good morrow, sir. You lay out too much pains
  For purchasing but trouble. The thanks I give
85 Is telling you that I am poor of thanks,
  And scarce can spare them.

CLOTEN   Still I swear I love you.

INNOGEN If you but said so, 'twere as deep° with me.   *solemn; binding*
  If you swear still,° your recompense is still   *always*
  That I regard it not.

CLOTEN   This is no answer.

90 INNOGEN But° that you shall not say I yield being silent,   *Except*
  I would not speak. I pray you, spare me. Faith,
  I shall unfold equal discourtesy[6]
  To your best kindness. One of your great knowing°   *knowledge*
  Should learn, being taught, forbearance.

95 CLOTEN To leave you in your madness, 'twere my sin.
  I will not.

INNOGEN   Fools cure not mad folks.

CLOTEN Do you call me fool?

INNOGEN   As I am mad, I do.
  If you'll be patient, I'll no more be mad;
  That cures us both. I am much sorry, sir,
100 You put me to forget a lady's manners
  By being so verbal;[7] and learn now for all
  That I, which know my heart, do here pronounce
  By th' very truth of it: I care not for you,
  And am so near the lack of charity
105 To accuse myself I hate you,[8] which I had rather
  You felt than make't my boast.°   *than I had to say it*

CLOTEN   You sin against
  Obedience which you owe your father. For°   *As for*
  The contract you pretend° with that base wretch,   *claim*
  One bred of alms and fostered with cold dishes,
110 With scraps o'th' court, it is no contract, none.
  And though it be allowed in meaner° parties—   *socially inferior*
  Yet who than he more mean?—to knit their souls,
  On whom there is no more dependency
  But brats and beggary,[9] in self-figured° knot,   *self-contracted*
115 Yet you are curbed from that enlargement° by   *freedom*
  The consequence o'th' crown,[1] and must not foil°   *defile*
  The precious note° of it with a base slave,   *reputation*
  A hilding for a livery,[2] a squire's cloth,°   *uniform*
  A pantler°—not so eminent.   *pantry servant*

INNOGEN   Profane fellow,
120 Wert thou the son of Jupiter,° and no more   *king of the gods*
  But what thou art besides, thou wert too base
  To be his° groom; thou wert dignified enough,[3]   *(Posthumus's)*
  Even to the point of envy, if 'twere made
  Comparative for your virtues to be styled

---

6. I shall display discourtesy equal.
7. "Verbal" (talkative; plainspoken) may refer either to Cloten or to Innogen.
8. *And . . . you:* And I am so near uncharitableness that I can charge myself with hating you.
9. *On . . . beggary:* Upon whose marriage nothing depends but worthless children and extreme poverty.

1. *by . . . crown:* by the importance of the crown; by the consequences that flow from your inheritance of the crown.
2. A worthless person fit only to wear the uniform ("livery") of his master's household.
3. You were raised in status sufficiently.

125　The under-hangman⁴ of his kingdom, and hated
　　　For being preferred° so well.　　　　　　　　　　　　　*advanced*

CLOTEN　　　　　　　　　　　The south-fog⁵ rot him!

INNOGEN　He never can meet more mischance than come
　　　To be but named of° thee. His meanest garment　　　　　　　*by*
　　　That ever hath but clipped° his body is dearer　　　　　　*encircled*
130　In my respect than all the hairs above thee,°　　　*on your head*
　　　Were they all made such men. How now, Pisanio!

　　　　　Enter PISANIO

CLOTEN　　His garment? Now the devil—

INNOGEN　[*to* PISANIO]　To Dorothy, my woman, hie thee presently.°　　*at once*

CLOTEN　　His garment?

INNOGEN　[*to* PISANIO]　I am sprited with° a fool,　　　*am haunted by*
135　Frighted, and angered worse. Go bid my woman
　　　Search for a jewel that too casually
　　　Hath left mine arm. It was thy master's. 'Shrew me°　　*Beshrew me (plague on me)*
　　　If I would lose it for a revenue
　　　Of any king's in Europe! I do think
140　I saw't this morning; confident I am
　　　Last night 'twas on mine arm; I kissed it.
　　　I hope it be not gone to tell my lord
　　　That I kiss aught but he.

PISANIO　　　　　　　　　　　'Twill not be lost.

INNOGEN　I hope so. Go and search.　　　　　　　[*Exit* PISANIO]

CLOTEN　　　　　　　　　　　　You have abused me.
　　　'His meanest garment'?

145　INNOGEN　　　　　　　　Ay, I said so, sir.
　　　If you will make't an action,° call witness to't.　　　*a lawsuit*

CLOTEN　　I will inform your father.

INNOGEN　　　　　　　　　　Your mother too.
　　　She's my good lady, and will conceive,° I hope,°　　*think / expect*
　　　But the worst of me. So I leave you, sir,
　　　To th' worst of discontent.　　　　　　　　　*Exit*

150　CLOTEN　　　　　　　　I'll be revenged.
　　　'His meanest garment'? Well!　　　　　　　　*Exit*

2.4

　　　　　Enter POSTHUMUS *and* FILARIO

POSTHUMUS　Fear it not, sir. I would I were so sure
　　　To win the King as I am bold her honour
　　　Will remain hers.

FILARIO　　　　　　　What means° do you make to him?　　*intercessions*

POSTHUMUS　Not any; but abide the change of time,
5　Quake in the present winter's state, and wish
　　　That warmer days would come. In these seared° hopes　　*withered*
　　　I barely gratify° your love; they failing,　　　　　　*repay*
　　　I must die much your debtor.

FILARIO　　Your very goodness and your company
10　O'erpays all I can do. By this,° your king　　　　*By now*
　　　Hath heard of great Augustus. Caius Lucius
　　　Will do 's commission throughly.° And I think　　　*thoroughly*

---

4. *if 'twere . . . under-hangman:* if a comparison were made between your virtues and those of Posthumus and you were given the job of assistant hangman; if, in accordance with your virtues, you were given the job of assistant hangman. 5. A damp fog brought by the south wind and supposed to breed infections. 2.4 Location: Filario's house, Rome.

He'll grant the tribute, send th'arrearages,°   *overdue payments*
Ere look upon our Romans, whose remembrance°   *the memory of whom*
Is yet fresh in their grief.[1]
15 POSTHUMUS   I do believe,
   Statist° though I am none, nor like to be,   *Statesman*
   That this will prove a war, and you shall hear
   The legions now in Gallia sooner landed
   In our not-fearing Britain than have tidings
20   Of any penny tribute paid. Our countrymen
   Are men more ordered° than when Julius Caesar   *better disciplined*
   Smiled at their lack of skill but found their courage
   Worthy his frowning at. Their discipline,
   Now wing-led[2] with their courage, will make known
25   To their approvers° they are people such   *those who would test them*
   That mend upon the world.[3]
         Enter GIACOMO
FILARIO   See, Giacomo.
POSTHUMUS [*to* GIACOMO]   The swiftest harts° have posted° you   *deer / conveyed*
   by land,
   And winds of° all the corners° kissed your sails   *from / (of the globe)*
   To make your vessel nimble.
FILARIO [*to* GIACOMO]   Welcome, sir.
30 POSTHUMUS [*to* GIACOMO]   I hope the briefness of your answer made°   *caused*
   The speediness of your return.
GIACOMO   Your lady is
   One of the fair'st that I have looked upon—
POSTHUMUS   And therewithal the best, or let her beauty
   Look through a casement[4] to allure false hearts,
   And be false with them.
35 GIACOMO   Here are letters for you.
POSTHUMUS   Their tenor good, I trust.
GIACOMO   'Tis very like.
       [POSTHUMUS *reads the letters*]
FILARIO   Was Caius Lucius in the Briton court
   When you were there?
GIACOMO   He was expected then,
   But not° approached.   *had not*
POSTHUMUS   All is well yet.
40   Sparkles this stone as it was wont, or is't not
   Too dull for your good wearing?
GIACOMO   If I had lost it
   I should have lost the worth of it in gold.
   I'll make a journey twice as far t'enjoy
   A second night of such sweet shortness which
45   Was mine in Britain; for the ring is won.
POSTHUMUS   The stone's too hard to come by.
GIACOMO   Not a whit,
   Your lady being so easy.
POSTHUMUS   Make not, sir,
   Your loss your sport. I hope you know that we
   Must not continue friends.

---

1. The Britons' grief; the grief inflicted by the Romans.
2. Carried aloft (as if on wings); led on each flank (each "wing"). The Second Folio (F2, printed in 1632) has "mingled," an emendation adopted by some editors.
3. *such . . . world*: who improve in the world's estimation.
4. Look out through a window (alluding to the manner in which prostitutes solicited customers).

GIACOMO   Good sir, we must,

50 If you keep covenant. Had I not brought
The knowledge° of your mistress home I grant   *A sexual account*
We were to question° farther, but I now   *dispute*
Profess myself the winner of her honour,
Together with your ring, and not the wronger
55 Of her or you, having proceeded but
By both your wills.

POSTHUMUS   If you can make't apparent
That you have tasted her in bed, my hand
And ring is yours. If not, the foul opinion
You had of her pure honour gains or loses
60 Your sword or mine,[5] or masterless leaves both°   *both swords*
To who shall find them.

GIACOMO   Sir, my circumstances,°   *detailed evidence*
Being so near the truth as I will make them,
Must first induce you to believe; whose strength
I will confirm with oath, which I doubt not
65 You'll give me leave to spare° when you shall find   *omit*
You need it not.

POSTHUMUS   Proceed.

GIACOMO   First, her bedchamber—
Where I confess I slept not, but profess
Had that was well worth watching°—it was hanged   *staying awake for*
With tapestry of silk and silver; the story
70 Proud Cleopatra when she met her Roman,[6]
And Cydnus[7] swelled above the banks, or for°   *either because of*
The press of boats or pride: a piece of work
So bravely° done, so rich, that it did strive   *splendidly*
In workmanship and value;[8] which I wondered
75 Could be so rarely and exactly wrought,
Such the true life on't was.

POSTHUMUS   This is true,
And this you might have heard of here, by me
Or by some other.

GIACOMO   More particulars
Must justify° my knowledge.   *confirm*

POSTHUMUS   So they must,
Or do your honour injury.

GIACOMO   The chimney°   *fireplace*
80 Is south the chamber, and the chimney-piece[9]
Chaste Dian[1] bathing. Never saw I figures
So likely to report themselves;[2] the cutter
Was as another nature; dumb, outwent her,
Motion and breath left out.[3]

POSTHUMUS   This is a thing
85 Which you might from relation° likewise reap,   *report*

---

5. *gains . . . mine:* makes one of us the winner, the other the loser, of his sword in a duel.
6. Alluding to a meeting, described also in Shakespeare's play *Antony and Cleopatra*, between the Egyptian Queen Cleopatra and Mark Antony, a Roman general who was her lover.
7. A river in Cilicia (now Turkey).
8. *that . . . value:* that craftmanship and monetary worth both competed for preeminence.

9. Ornament above the fireplace.
1. Another reference to the goddess associated in classical mythology with hunting, childbirth, and chastity.
2. So lifelike that they could give an account of themselves.
3. *the cutter . . . out:* the sculptor ("cutter") was like a second nature in creative power. Speechless, the sculpture surpassed nature, apart from its lack of movement and breathing.

Being, as it is, much spoke of.

GIACOMO   The roof o'th' chamber
With golden cherubins is fretted.° Her andirons—   *carved*
I had forgot them—were two winking Cupids[4]
90   Of silver, each on one foot standing, nicely°   *ingeniously*
Depending° on their brands.°   *Leaning / torches*

POSTHUMUS   This is her honour!
Let it be granted you have seen all this—and praise
Be given to your remembrance—the description
Of what is in her chamber nothing saves
The wager you have laid.

95   GIACOMO   Then, if you can
Be pale,° I beg but leave to air this jewel. See!   *Be unmoved*
     [*He shows the bracelet*]
And now 'tis up° again; it must be married   *put away*
To that your diamond. I'll keep them.

POSTHUMUS   Jove!°   *king of the gods*
Once more let me behold it. Is it that
Which I left with her?

100   GIACOMO   Sir, I thank her, that.
She stripped it from her arm. I see her yet.
Her pretty action did outsell° her gift,   *exceed in value*
And yet enriched it too. She gave it me,
And said she prized it once.

POSTHUMUS   Maybe she plucked it off
To send it me.

105   GIACOMO   She writes so to you, doth she?
POSTHUMUS   O, no, no, no—'tis true! Here, take this too.
     [*He gives GIACOMO his ring*]
It is a basilisk[5] unto mine eye,
Kills me to look on't. Let there be no honour
Where there is beauty, truth where semblance,° love   *the mere appearance of it*
110   Where there's another man. The vows° of women   *Let the vows*
Of no more bondage be to where they are made
Than they are° to their virtues, which is nothing!   *Than women are bound*
O, above measure false!

FILARIO   Have patience, sir,
And take your ring again; 'tis not yet won.
115   It may be probable she lost it, or
Who knows if one° her woman, being corrupted,   *one of*
Hath stol'n it from her?

POSTHUMUS   Very true,
And so I hope he came by't. Back my ring.
     [*He takes his ring again*]
Render to me some corporal sign about her
120   More evident° than this; for this was stol'n.   *conclusive*
GIACOMO   By Jupiter,[6] I had it from her arm.
POSTHUMUS   Hark you, he swears, by Jupiter he swears.
'Tis true, nay, keep the ring, 'tis true. I am sure
She would not lose it. Her attendants are
125   All sworn° and honourable. They induced to steal it?   *bound by oaths*

---

4. Two statues of Cupid, the god of love, with eyes
shut. Cupid was often depicted as a beautiful boy with
wings and a torch and wearing a blindfold to signify the
blindness of love.

5. A mythical reptile able with a glance to kill those it
gazed upon.
6. Another reference to the king of the gods. Only the
most solemn vows would be made in his name.

And by a stranger? No, he hath enjoyed her.
The cognizance° of her incontinency   token
Is this. She hath bought the name of whore thus dearly.
     [*He gives* GIACOMO *his ring*]
There, take thy hire,° and all the fiends of hell   fee
Divide themselves between you!

130 FILARIO   Sir, be patient.
This is not strong enough to be believed
Of one persuaded° well of.   thought
POSTHUMUS   Never talk on't.
She hath been colted° by him.   sexually enjoyed
GIACOMO   If you seek
For further satisfying, under her breast—
135 Worthy the pressing—lies a mole, right proud
Of that most delicate lodging. By my life,
I kissed it, and it gave me present° hunger   immediate
To feed again, though full. You do remember
This stain° upon her?   mark
POSTHUMUS   Ay, and it doth confirm
140 Another stain as big as hell can hold,
Were there no more but it.
GIACOMO   Will you hear more?
POSTHUMUS Spare your arithmetic, never count the turns.°   sexual acts
Once, and a million!⁷
GIACOMO   I'll be sworn.
POSTHUMUS   No swearing.
If you will swear you have not done't, you lie,
145 And I will kill thee if thou dost deny
Thou'st made me cuckold.
GIACOMO   I'll deny nothing.
POSTHUMUS O that I had her here to tear her limb-meal!°   limb from limb
I will go there and do't i'th' court, before
Her father. I'll do something.   *Exit*
FILARIO   Quite besides°   beyond
150 The government° of patience! You have won.   control
Let's follow and pervert° the present wrath   turn aside
He hath against himself.
GIACOMO   With all my heart.   *Exeunt*

2.5

Enter POSTHUMUS¹
POSTHUMUS Is there no way for men to be,° but women   to exist
Must be half-workers?° We are bastards all,   be partners
And that most venerable man which I
Did call my father was I know not where
5 When I was stamped.² Some coiner with his tools³
Made me a counterfeit; yet my mother seemed
The Dian of that time: so doth my wife
The nonpareil° of this. O vengeance, vengeance!   one who has no equal

---

7. That is, there is no difference between having been unfaithful once and having done it a million times.
2.5 Location: Scene continues.
1. In F, Posthumus's soliloquy is part of 2.4. He is making a reentry, however, after his departure at line 149,

and most modern editions mark the soliloquy as a separate scene.
2. Conceived, as coins are stamped with images when they are made.
3. With pun on "tool" as meaning "penis."

Me of my lawful pleasure[4] she restrained,

10 And prayed me oft forbearance;[5] did it with

A pudency° so rosy the sweet view on't°   *modesty / of it*

Might well have warmed old Saturn;[6] that I thought her

As chaste as unsunned snow. O all the devils!

This yellow° Giacomo in an hour—was't not?—   *sallow*

15 Or less—at first?° Perchance he spoke not, but   *instantly*

Like a full-acorned boar,[7] a German one,

Cried 'O!' and mounted; found no opposition

But what he looked for should oppose[8] and she

Should from encounter guard. Could I find out

20 The woman's part in me—for there's no motion°   *impulse*

That tends to vice in man but I affirm

It is the woman's part; be it lying, note it,

The woman's; flattering, hers; deceiving, hers;

Lust and rank thoughts, hers, hers; revenges, hers;

25 Ambitions, covetings, change of prides,° disdain,   *varying extravagances*

Nice° longing, slanders, mutability,   *Lustful*

All faults that man can name, nay, that hell knows,

Why, hers in part or all, but rather all—

For even to vice

30 They are not constant, but are changing still

One vice but of a minute old for one

Not half so old as that. I'll write against them,

Detest them, curse them, yet 'tis greater skill°   *cleverness*

In a true hate to pray they have their will.°   *desire*

35 The very devils cannot plague them better.   *Exit*

3.1

[*Flourish.*] *Enter in state* CYMBELINE, [*the*] QUEEN,
CLOTEN, *and lords at one door, and at another,* Caius
LUCIUS *and attendants*

CYMBELINE   Now say, what would Augustus Caesar with us?

LUCIUS   When Julius Caesar—whose remembrance yet

Lives in men's eyes, and will to ears and tongues

Be theme and hearing ever—was in this Britain

5 And conquered it, Cassibelan, thine uncle,

Famous in Caesar's praises no whit less

Than in his feats deserving it, for him

And his succession° granted Rome a tribute,   *heirs*

Yearly three thousand pounds, which by thee lately

Is left untendered.

10 QUEEN   And, to kill the marvel,[1]

Shall be so ever.

CLOTEN   There will be many Caesars

Ere such another Julius. Britain's a world

By itself, and we will nothing pay

For wearing our own noses.[2]

---

4. The sexual pleasure to which marriage entitled him.
5. And often begged me to defer sexual pleasures.
6. The Roman god of agriculture, usually characterized as cold and melancholy.
7. A boar fed full of acorns (with a pun on "boor" as meaning "a German or Dutch peasant").
8. *found . . . oppose:* found no opposition except the body parts he expected to encounter.

3.1 Location: Cymbeline's court, Britain.
1. And, to put a stop to the amazement (which our nonpayment has caused).
2. Perhaps referring to contemporary theories of physiognomy that identified specific physical features, such as noses, with racial types. Roman noses were notoriously prominent.

QUEEN   That opportunity
15 Which then they had to take from 's, to resume°   *take back*
We have again. Remember, sir, my liege,°   *sovereign*
The kings your ancestors, together with
The natural bravery° of your isle, which stands   *splendor*
As Neptune's park,[3] ribbed and paled in°   *enclosed and fenced in*
20 With banks unscalable and roaring waters,
With sands that will not bear your enemies' boats,
But suck them up to th' topmast. A kind of conquest
Caesar made here, but made not here his brag
Of 'came and saw and overcame'.[4] With shame—
25 The first that ever touched him—he was carried
From off our coast, twice beaten; and his shipping,°   *ships*
Poor ignorant° baubles, on our terrible seas   *silly*
Like eggshells moved upon their surges, cracked
As easily 'gainst our rocks; for joy whereof
30 The famed Cassibelan, who was once at point°—   *ready*
O giglot° fortune!—to master Caesar's sword,   *fickle; whorish*
Made Lud's town[5] with rejoicing fires bright,
And Britons strut with courage.
CLOTEN   Come, there's no more tribute to be paid. Our king-
35 dom is stronger than it was at that time, and, as I said, there is
no more such Caesars. Other of them may have crooked noses,
but to owe° such straight° arms, none.   *possess / powerful*
CYMBELINE   Son, let your mother end.
CLOTEN   We have yet many among us can grip as hard as Cassi-
40 belan. I do not say I am one, but I have a hand. Why tribute?
Why should we pay tribute? If Caesar can hide the sun from us
with a blanket, or put the moon in his pocket, we will pay him
tribute for light; else, sir, no more tribute, pray you now.
CYMBELINE [*to* LUCIUS]   You must know,
45 Till the injurious° Romans did extort   *insulting*
This tribute from us we were free. Caesar's ambition,
Which swelled so much that it did almost stretch
The sides o'th' world, against all colour[6] here
Did put the yoke upon 's, which to shake off
50 Becomes a warlike people, whom we reckon
Ourselves to be. We do say then to Caesar,
Our ancestor was that Mulmutius[7] which
Ordained our laws, whose use the sword of Caesar
Hath too much mangled, whose repair and franchise°   *free exercise*
55 Shall by the power we hold be our good deed,
Though Rome be therefore angry. Mulmutius made our laws,
Who was the first of Britain which did put
His brows within a golden crown and called
Himself a king.
LUCIUS   I am sorry, Cymbeline,
60 That I am to pronounce Augustus Caesar—

3. As grounds owned by Neptune, Roman god of the sea.
4. When Julius Caesar, leading an army into Asia, defeated King Pharnaces and his allies, Plutarch reports that Caesar wrote three words to his friend Anitius in Rome: *veni, vidi, vici* ("I came, I saw, I overcame"). See Plutarch's *Life of Julius Caesar* in his *Lives of the Noble Grecians and Romanes* as translated by Thomas North

(1579).
5. London. Contemporary texts such as Holinshed's *Chronicles* erroneously asserted that "London" was derived from "Lud," the name of the mythological British King who was Cymbeline's grandfather.
6. Without any pretense of justice.
7. According to Holinshed, the first King of Britain.

Caesar, that hath more kings his servants than
Thyself domestic officers—thine enemy.
Receive it from me, then: war and confusion°   destruction
In Caesar's name pronounce I 'gainst thee. Look
65   For fury not to be resisted. Thus defied,
I thank thee for myself.
CYMBELINE   Thou art welcome, Caius.
Thy Caesar knighted me; my youth I spent
Much under him; of him I gathered honour,
Which he to seek of me again perforce
70   Behoves me keep at utterance.[8] I am perfect°   fully aware
That the Pannonians and Dalmatians[9] for
Their liberties are now in arms, a precedent
Which not to read would show the Britons cold;°   lacking in spirit
So Caesar shall not find them.
LUCIUS   Let proof° speak.   the result
75   CLOTEN   His majesty bids you welcome. Make pastime with us a
day or two or longer. If you seek us afterwards in other terms,
you shall find us in our salt-water girdle.[1] If you beat us out of
it, it is yours; if you fall in the adventure, our crows shall fare
the better for you; and there's an end.
80   LUCIUS   So, sir.
CYMBELINE   I know your master's pleasure, and he mine.
All the remain° is 'Welcome'.   [Flourish.] Exeunt   All that is left to say

3.2
Enter PISANIO, *reading of a letter*

PISANIO   How? Of adultery? Wherefore write you not
What monster's her accuser? Leonatus,
O master, what a strange infection
Is fall'n into thy ear! What false Italian,
5   As poisonous tongued as handed,[1] hath prevailed
On thy too ready hearing? Disloyal? No.
She's punished for her truth,° and undergoes,   faithfulness
More goddess-like than wife-like, such assaults
As would take in° some virtue. O my master,   overcome
10   Thy mind to° hers is now as low as were   compared to
Thy fortunes. How? That I should murder her,
Upon the love and truth and vows which I
Have made to thy command? I her? Her blood?
If it be so to do good service, never
15   Let me be counted serviceable. How look I,
That I should seem to lack humanity
So much as this fact° comes to? [Reads] 'Do't. The letter   action
That I have sent her, by her own command
Shall give thee opportunity.' O damned paper,[2]
20   Black as the ink that's on thee! Senseless bauble,°   toy; worthless object

---

8. *Which . . . utterance:* His seeking that honor of me
again makes it necessary for me to defend ("keep") it to
the death.
9. Inhabitants of Hungary and Dalmatia, a region on
the Adriatic Sea.
1. In the sea that encircles us (as a girdle does the

body).
3.2 Location: Cymbeline's court.
1. Having as many poisons (lies) in his tongue as in his
hands. Contemporary texts depicted Italians as infinitely skilled in making and administering poisons.
2. O hellish object (referring to the letter).

Art thou a fedary° for this act, and look'st   *an accomplice*
So virgin-like without?°   *on the outside*
    Enter INNOGEN
                Lo, here she comes.
I am ignorant in° what I am commanded.   *will pretend ignorance of*
INNOGEN How now, Pisanio?
25 PISANIO   Madam, here is a letter from my lord.
    INNOGEN Who, thy lord that is my lord, Leonatus?
    O learned indeed were that astronomer°   *astrologer*
    That knew the stars as I his characters°—   *handwriting*
    He'd lay the future open. You good gods,
30   Let what is here contained relish° of love,   *taste*
    Of my lord's health, of his content—yet not
    That we two are asunder; let that grieve him.
    Some griefs are med'cinable;° that is one of them,   *beneficial*
    For it doth physic love[3]—of his content
35   All but in that. Good wax,° thy leave. Blest be   *sealing wax*
    You bees that make these locks of counsel!° Lovers   *for private matters*
    And men in dangerous bonds[4] pray not alike;
    Though forfeiters you cast in prison,[5] yet
    You clasp° young Cupid's tables.° Good news, gods!   *lovingly embrace / tablets*
    [*She opens and reads the letter*]
40   'Justice and your father's wrath, should he take me in his
    dominion, could not be so cruel to me as° you, O the dearest   *but that*
    of creatures, would even renew me° with your eyes. Take   *would revive me*
    notice that I am in Cambria,° at Milford Haven.[6] What your   *Wales*
    own love will out of this advise you, follow. So he wishes you
45   all happiness, that remains loyal to his vow, and your increasing
    in love,
                                Leonatus Posthumus.'
    O for a horse with wings! Hear'st thou, Pisanio?
    He is at Milford Haven. Read, and tell me
50   How far 'tis thither. If one of mean affairs°   *with unimportant business*
    May plod it in a week, why may not I
    Glide thither in a day? Then, true Pisanio,
    Who long'st like me to see thy lord, who long'st—
    O let me bate°—but not like me—yet long'st   *moderate my speech*
55   But in a fainter kind—O, not like me,
    For mine's beyond beyond; say, and speak thick°—   *speak quickly*
    Love's counsellor should fill the bores of hearing,°   *the ears*
    To th' smothering of the sense[7]—how far it is
    To this same blessèd Milford. And by° th' way   *on*
60   Tell me how Wales was made so happy as
    T'inherit such a haven. But first of all,
    How we may steal from hence; and for the gap
    That we shall make in time from our hence-going
    Till our return, to excuse; but first, how get hence.
65   Why should excuse be born or ere begot?[8]

---

3. For it nurtures love; for it keeps love in good health.
4. Men bound by agreements imposing penalties (which are sealed with wax). Innogen is contrasting the fear with which men in legal trouble greet sealed documents to the joy with which lovers receive a sealed love letter.
5. Although you cast those who default on agreements in prison (because sealed bonds lead to indictments).
6. A port in southern Wales that became important in later British history when Henry Tudor landed there in 1485. Defeating the army of Richard III, he crowned Henry VII, bringing to an end the civil strife known as the Wars of the Roses.
7. Until the sense of hearing is overwhelmed.
8. Why should an excuse be born even before it is conceived—that is, be manufactured before it is needed?

We'll talk of that hereafter. Prithee speak,
How many score of° miles may we well ride   set of twenty
'Twixt hour and hour?°   In an hour

PISANIO   One score 'twixt sun and sun,
Madam, 's enough for you, and too much too.

70 INNOGEN Why, one that rode to 's execution, man,
Could never go so slow. I have heard of riding wagers
Where horses have been nimbler than the sands
That run i'th' clock's behalf.[9] But this is fool'ry.
Go bid my woman feign a sickness, say
75 She'll home to her father; and provide me presently°   at once
A riding-suit no costlier than would fit°   suit
A franklin's housewife.[1]

PISANIO   Madam, you're best° consider. you'd better

INNOGEN I see before° me, man. Nor here, nor here,   straight ahead of
Nor what ensues,[2] but have a fog in them
80 That I cannot look through. Away, I prithee,
Do as I bid thee. There's no more to say:
Accessible is none but Milford way.   Exeunt

3.3

Enter BELARIUS, [*followed by*] GUIDERIUS *and* ARVIRA-
GUS [*from a cave in the woods*][1]

BELARIUS A goodly day not to keep house° with such   stay home
Whose roof 's as low as ours. Stoop, boys; this gate
Instructs you how t'adore the heavens, and bows you°   makes you bow down
To a morning's holy office.° The gates of monarchs   a morning prayer
5 Are arched so high that giants may jet° through   swagger
And keep their impious turbans[2] on without
Good morrow to the sun. Hail, thou fair heaven!
We house i'th' rock, yet use thee not so hardly°   badly
As prouder livers° do.   those living more grandly

GUIDERIUS   Hail, heaven!

ARVIRAGUS   Hail, heaven!

10 BELARIUS Now for our mountain sport. Up to yon hill,
Your legs are young; I'll tread these flats.° Consider,   this plain
When you above perceive me like a crow,
That it is place° which lessens and sets off,°   position / enhances
And you may then revolve° what tales I have told you   consider
15 Of courts, of princes, of the tricks in war;
That service is not service, so being done,
But being so allowed.[3] To apprehend thus
Draws us a profit from all things we see,
And often to our comfort shall we find
20 The sharded beetle[4] in a safer hold°   refuge

---

9. *than . . . behalf*: than the sands that run through the hourglass.

1. The wife of a landowning farmer whose social status was lower than that of the gentry. Early modern English sumptuary codes prescribed specific fabrics and styles of dress for people of different ranks.

2. *Nor here . . . ensues*: Neither (what is) on this side, nor on that, nor what, nor what will happen (after Milford Haven is reached).

3.3 Location: The cave of Belarius, Wales.

1. In his account of a performance of the play in 1611, Simon Forman wrote of "the Cave in the woods" and of the "woods" where Innogen's supposedly dead body was laid. It is possible that some form of stage foliage surrounded the entrance to Belarius's cave.

2. The idea of giants wearing turbans may come from romances in which giants were often equated with Saracens, or followers of Islam, who wore turbans and were seen as impious enemies of Christians. See, for example, the Giant Disdain in Edmund Spenser's *Faerie Queene*, who "on his head a roll of linnen plight, / Like to the Mores of Malabar" (6.7.43.5–6).

3. *That service . . . allowed*: That acts of service are not acts of service simply by being done, but rather by being acknowledged as such (by superiors).

4. The beetle who lives in dung. "Shard" means "patch of dung."

Than is the full-winged eagle. O, this life
Is nobler than attending for a check,[5]
Richer than doing nothing for a bauble,
Prouder than rustling in unpaid-for silk;
25 Such gain the cap of him that makes 'em fine,
Yet keeps his book uncrossed.[6] No life to ours.

GUIDERIUS Out of your proof° you speak. We, poor unfledged,[7]   *experience*
Have never winged from view o'th' nest, nor know not
What air's from° home. Haply° this life is best,   *away from / Perhaps*
30 If quiet life be best; sweeter to you
That have a sharper known; well corresponding
With your stiff age, but unto us it is
A cell of ignorance, travelling abed,°   *only while dreaming*
A prison for a debtor, that not dares
To stride a limit.[8]

35 ARVIRAGUS [*to* BELARIUS] What should we speak of
When we are old as you? When we shall hear
The rain and wind beat dark December, how,
In this our pinching cave,[9] shall we discourse
The freezing hours away? We have seen nothing.
40 We are beastly:° subtle as the fox for prey,   *like beasts*
Like° warlike as the wolf for what we eat.   *As*
Our valour is to chase what flies; our cage
We make a choir, as doth the prisoned bird,
And sing our bondage freely.

BELARIUS   How you speak!
45 Did you but know the city's usuries,[1]
And felt them knowingly; the art o'th' court,
As hard to leave as keep,° whose top to climb   *dwell in*
Is certain falling, or so slipp'ry that
The fear's as bad as falling; the toil o'th' war,
50 A pain° that only seems to seek out danger   *labor*
I'th' name of fame and honour, which dies i'th' search
And hath as oft a sland'rous epitaph
As record of fair act; nay, many times
Doth ill deserve° by doing well; what's worse,   *earn ill treatment*
55 Must curtsy at the censure.[2] O boys, this story
The world may read in me. My body's marked
With Roman swords, and my report° was once   *reputation*
First with the best of note.° Cymbeline loved me,   *the most renowned*
And when a soldier was the theme my name
60 Was not far off. Then was I as a tree
Whose boughs did bend with fruit; but in one night
A storm or robbery, call it what you will,
Shook down my mellow hangings,° nay, my leaves,   *ripe fruit*
And left me bare to weather.

GUIDERIUS   Uncertain favour!
65 BELARIUS My fault being nothing, as I have told you oft,
But that two villains, whose false oaths prevailed

5. Than acting as a servant only to be rebuked.
6. *Such . . . uncrossed*: Such men win the deference (shown by removing "the cap") of the tailor who is the source of their grandeur, yet continue to have their debts standing ("uncrossed") in the tailor's account book.
7. Lacking the feathers necessary for flight (spoken of a young bird).

8. *that . . . limit*: who does not dare to leave a place of sanctuary (for fear of being arrested).
9. Our confining cave; our cave that pinches us with cold.
1. Financial practices whereby money was lent at excessive or illegal rates of interest.
2. Must defer to the person who finds fault.

Before my perfect honour, swore to Cymbeline
I was confederate with the Romans. So
Followed my banishment, and this twenty years
70 This rock and these demesnes° have been my world,   *regions*
Where I have lived at honest freedom, paid
More pious debts to heaven than in all
The fore-end° of my time. But up to th' mountains!   *early days*
This is not hunter's language. He that strikes
75 The venison first shall be the lord o'th' feast,
To him the other two shall minister,
And we will fear no poison which attends°   *is always present*
In place of greater state. I'll meet you in the valleys.
                Exeunt [GUIDERIUS *and* ARVIRAGUS]
How hard it is to hide the sparks of nature!
80 These boys know little they are sons to th' King,
Nor Cymbeline dreams that they are alive.
They think they are mine, and though trained up thus meanly°   *in a humble style*
I'th' cave wherein they bow, their thoughts do hit
The roofs of palaces, and nature prompts them
85 In simple and low things to prince it° much   *to act like princes*
Beyond the trick° of others. This Polydore,   *custom*
The heir of Cymbeline and Britain, who
The King his father called Guiderius—Jove,
When on my three-foot stool I sit and tell
90 The warlike feats I have done, his spirits fly out
Into my story: say 'Thus mine enemy fell,
And thus I set my foot on 's neck', even then
The princely blood flows in his cheek, he sweats,
Strains his young nerves,° and puts himself in posture   *sinews*
95 That acts my words. The younger brother, Cadwal,
Once Arviragus, in as like a figure°   *acting the part as aptly*
Strikes life into my speech, and shows much more
His own conceiving.°   *imagination*
     [*A hunting-horn sounds*]
              Hark, the game is roused!
O Cymbeline, heaven and my conscience knows[3]
100 Thou didst unjustly banish me, whereon
At three and two years old I stole these babes,
Thinking to bar thee of succession as
Thou reft'st° me of my lands. Euriphile,   *deprived*
Thou wast their nurse; they took thee for their mother,
105 And every day do honour to her grave.
Myself, Belarius, that am Morgan called,
They take for natural father.
     [*A hunting-horn sounds*]
              The game is up.°   *Exit*   *roused*

3.4

Enter PISANIO, *and* INNOGEN [*in a riding-suit*]
INNOGEN   Thou told'st me when we came from horse° the place   *we dismounted*
Was near at hand. Ne'er longed my mother so

---

3. Editors have conjectured that lines 99–107 are either a non-Shakespearean addition or a section he added in revision. They stand apart from the rest of the speech, providing a hurried summary of information.

Moreover, "the game is roused" (line 98) is repeated in "The game is up" (line 107).
3.4 Location: Wales, near Milford Haven.

To see me first as I have° now. Pisanio, man,   *do*
Where is Posthumus? What is in thy mind
5   That makes thee stare thus? Wherefore breaks that sigh
From th'inward of thee? One but painted thus
Would be interpreted a thing perplexed°   *bewildered*
Beyond self-explication. Put thyself
Into a haviour of less fear,¹ ere wildness°   *madness*
10 Vanquish my staider senses. What's the matter?
        [PISANIO *gives her a letter*]
Why tender'st thou that paper to me with
A look untender? If 't be summer news,
Smile to't before; if winterly, thou need'st
But keep that count'nance still. My husband's hand?
15 That drug-damned Italy² hath out-craftied° him,   *outwitted*
And he's at some hard point.° Speak, man. Thy tongue   *in some crisis*
May take off some extremity° which to read   *reduce the horror*
Would be even mortal° to me.   *fatal*
PISANIO   Please you read,
And you shall find me, wretched man, a thing
20 The most disdained of fortune.
INNOGEN *reads*   'Thy mistress, Pisanio, hath played the strumpet
in my bed, the testimonies whereof lies bleeding in me. I speak
not out of weak surmises but from proof as strong as my grief
and as certain as I expect my revenge. That part thou, Pisanio,
25 must act for me, if thy faith be not tainted with the breach of
hers. Let thine own hands take away her life. I shall give thee
opportunity at Milford Haven. She hath my letter for the purpose, where if thou fear to strike and to make me certain it is
done, thou art the pander to her dishonour and equally to me
30 disloyal.'
PISANIO [*aside*]   What shall I need to draw my sword? The paper
Hath cut her throat already. No, 'tis slander,
Whose edge is sharper than the sword, whose tongue
Outvenoms all the worms of Nile,³ whose breath
35 Rides on the posting° winds and doth belie°   *speeding / deceive*
All corners of the world. Kings, queens, and states,
Maids, matrons, nay, the secrets of the grave
This viperous slander enters. [*To* INNOGEN] What cheer, madam?
INNOGEN   False to his bed? What is it to be false?
40 To lie in watch° there and to think on him?   *wakefulness*
To weep 'twixt clock and clock?° If sleep charge° nature,   *continually / overcome*
To break it with a fearful dream of° him   *a dream fearful for*
And cry myself awake? That's false to 's bed, is it?
PISANIO   Alas, good lady.
45 INNOGEN   I false? Thy conscience witness, Giacomo,
Thou didst accuse him of incontinency.
Thou then lookedst like a villain; now, methinks,
Thy favour's° good enough. Some jay° of Italy,   *appearance is / strumpet*
Whose mother was her painting,⁴ hath betrayed him.

---

1. *Put . . . fear:* Adopt a less fearsome manner.
2. That country notorious for its poisons.
3. Alluding to the poisonous serpents associated with Egypt's Nile River. Slander was often personified as a woman with snakes issuing from her mouth. In early modern England, women frequently brought cases in the ecclesiastical courts against those who defamed or slandered them; overwhelmingly, they were defending their reputations against claims that they had committed a sexual offense and were unchaste. Pisanio rightly assumes that Innogen is the victim of just such slanderous accusations.
4. Whose mother was entirely the product of her cosmetics—i.e., who was false.

50 Poor I am stale,° a garment out of fashion,   *out of date; not new*
    And for I am richer than to hang by th' walls
    I must be ripped.⁵ To pieces with me! O,
    Men's vows are women's traitors. All good seeming,°   *appearance*
    By thy revolt, O husband, shall be thought
55 Put on for villainy; not born where't grows,
    But worn a bait for ladies.

PISANIO   Good madam, hear me.

INNOGEN   True honest men being heard like false Aeneas⁶
    Were in his time thought false, and Sinon's⁷ weeping
    Did scandal° many a holy tear, took pity   *discredit*
60 From most true wretchedness. So thou, Posthumus,
    Wilt lay the leaven on all proper men.⁸
    Goodly° and gallant shall be false and perjured   *Admirable*
    From thy great fail.° [*To* PISANIO] Come, fellow, be thou honest,   *failure*
    Do thou thy master's bidding. When thou seest him,
65 A little witness° my obedience. Look,   *Briefly attest to*
    I draw the sword myself. Take it, and hit
    The innocent mansion of my love, my heart.
    Fear not, 'tis empty of all things but grief.
    Thy master is not there, who was indeed
70 The riches of it. Do his bidding; strike.
    Thou mayst be valiant in a better cause,
    But now thou seem'st a coward.

PISANIO   Hence, vile instrument,
    Thou shalt not damn my hand!

INNOGEN   Why, I must die,
    And if I do not by thy hand thou art
75 No servant of thy master's. Against self-slaughter
    There is a prohibition so divine
    That cravens° my weak hand. Come, here's my heart.   *makes cowardly*
    Something's afore't. Soft,° soft, we'll no defence;   *Gently*
    Obedient as the scabbard. What is here?
    [*She takes letters from her bosom*]
80 The scriptures° of the loyal Leonatus,   *writing; sacred texts*
    All turned to heresy? Away, away,
    Corrupters of my faith, you shall no more
    Be stomachers⁹ to my heart. Thus may poor fools
    Believe false teachers. Though those that are betrayed
85 Do feel the treason sharply, yet the traitor
    Stands in worse case of woe. And thou, Posthumus,
    That didst set up° my disobedience 'gainst the King   *instigate*
    My father, and make me put into contempt the suits
    Of princely fellows,° shalt hereafter find   *those equal to my rank*
90 It is no act of common passage but
    A strain of rareness;¹ and I grieve myself
    To think, when thou shalt be disedged° by her   *surfeited*

---

5. *And . . . ripped:* And because I am too valuable to be discarded (by being hung up and forgotten about), I must be torn apart (so that the material may be reused).
6. Being heard as though they were as false as the hero of Virgil's *Aeneid,* Aeneas, who deserted his love, Dido, the Queen of Carthage.
7. Another deceitful character from the *Aeneid.* Sinon betrayed Troy to the Greeks by inducing the Trojans to

let into the city a wooden horse in which Greek warriors were concealed.
8. Will corrupt the reputations of all faithful men (as a portion of inferior dough spoils the rest).
9. Ornamented chest coverings worn by women under their bodices.
1. *It . . . rareness:* My choice was no commonplace action but the sign of exceptional qualities.

That now thou tirest on,² how thy memory
Will then be panged by° me. [*To* PISANIO] Prithee, dispatch.   *pierced by thoughts of*
95   The lamb entreats the butcher. Where's thy knife?
Thou art too slow to do thy master's bidding
When I desire it too.

PISANIO   O gracious lady,
Since I received command to do this business
I have not slept one wink.

INNOGEN   Do't, and to bed, then.

PISANIO   I'll wake mine eyeballs out first.³

100 INNOGEN   Wherefore then
Didst undertake it? Why hast thou abused
So many miles with a pretence?—this place,
Mine action, and thine own? Our horses' labour,
The time inviting thee? The perturbed court,
105   For my being absent, whereunto I never
Purpose° return? Why hast thou gone so far   *Intend*
To be unbent⁴ when thou hast ta'en thy stand,°   *shooting position*
Th'elected° deer before thee?   *The chosen*

PISANIO   But to win time
To lose so bad employment, in the which
110   I have considered of a course. Good lady,
Hear me with patience.

INNOGEN   Talk thy tongue weary. Speak.
I have heard I am a strumpet, and mine ear,
Therein false struck, can take no greater wound,
Nor tent to bottom that.⁵ But speak.

PISANIO   Then, madam,
I thought you would not back° again.   *go back (to court)*
115 INNOGEN   Most like,
Bringing me here to kill me.

PISANIO   Not so, neither.
But if I were as wise as honest, then
My purpose would prove well. It cannot be
But that my master is abused.° Some villain,   *deceived*
120   Ay, and singular° in his art, hath done you both   *unmatched*
This cursèd injury.

INNOGEN   Some Roman courtesan.

PISANIO   No, on my life.
I'll give but notice you are dead, and send him
125   Some bloody sign of it, for 'tis commanded
I should do so. You shall be missed at court,
And that will well confirm it.

INNOGEN   Why, good fellow,
What shall I do the while, where bide, how live,
Or in my life what comfort when I am
Dead to my husband?

130 PISANIO   If you'll back° to th' court—   *return*

INNOGEN   No court, no father, nor no more ado
With that harsh, churlish, noble, simple nothing,

---

2. Whom now you feed on (in the manner of a bird of   4. To be with bow unready.
prey).   5. Nor probe ("tent") the depths of that wound.
3. I'll stay awake until my eyes drop out before I'll do it.

That Cloten, whose love suit hath been to me
As fearful as a siege.

PISANIO   If not at court,
Then not in Britain must you bide.

135 INNOGEN   Where then?
Hath Britain all the sun that shines? Day, night,
Are they not but° in Britain? I'th' world's volume   *Do they exist only*
Our Britain seems as of it but not in't,[6]
In a great pool a swan's nest. Prithee, think
There's livers out of Britain.[7]

140 PISANIO   I am most glad
You think of other place. Th'ambassador,
Lucius the Roman, comes to Milford Haven
Tomorrow. Now if you could wear a mind
Dark° as your fortune is, and but disguise   *Secret; dismal*
145 That which t'appear itself must not yet be
But by self-danger,[8] you should tread a course
Pretty and full of view;[9] yea, haply° near   *perhaps*
The residence of Posthumus; so nigh, at least,
That though his actions were not visible, yet
150 Report should render° him hourly to your ear   *describe*
As truly as he moves.

INNOGEN   O, for such means,°   *a method of access*
Though peril° to my modesty, not death on't,°   *a danger / of it*
I would adventure.°   *take the risk*

PISANIO   Well then, here's the point:
You must forget to be a woman; change
155 Command[1] into obedience, fear and niceness°—   *daintiness*
The handmaids of all women, or more truly
Woman it pretty self[2]—into a waggish° courage,   *mischievous*
Ready in gibes, quick-answered, saucy and
As quarrelous° as the weasel. Nay, you must   *quarrelsome*
160 Forget that rarest treasure of your cheek,
Exposing it[3]—but O, the harder heart![4]—
Alack, no remedy—to the greedy touch
Of common-kissing Titan,[5] and forget
Your laboursome and dainty trims° wherein   *apparel*
You made great Juno° angry.   *queen of the gods*

165 INNOGEN   Nay, be brief.
I see into thy end,° and am almost   *purpose*
A man already.

PISANIO   First, make yourself but like one.
Forethinking° this, I have already fit°—   *Anticipating / at hand*
'Tis in my cloak-bag—doublet, hat, hose, all
170 That answer to° them. Would you in their serving,[6] *go with*
And with what imitation you can borrow

---

6. Seems part of the world, yet distinct. The metaphor is of the world as a book in which Britain is a page, but one not bound into the volume.
7. *Prithee . . . Britain:* I pray you, believe that there are people living outside Britain.
8. *and but . . . self-danger:* and simply disguise your appearance, which if it were now to show itself for what it is would put you in danger.
9. Advantageous and with good prospects.
1. The commanding ways of a princess.
2. *or . . . self:* or, more accurately, womanhood itself.

3. In early modern England, English women of the upper classes shielded themselves from the sun and cultivated pale complexions, the "treasure" of their cheeks.
4. The "harder heart" probably refers to Innogen, who must harden her heart even as she tans her skin. It may refer to Posthumus's cruelty to Innogen or to Pisanio's cruelty in forcing these harsh facts upon Innogen.
5. The sun god who shines on ("kisses") everyone alike.
6. If you would with their help.

From youth of such a season,° fore° noble Lucius   *an age / before*
Present yourself, desire his service,° tell him   *to serve him*
Wherein you're happy[7]—which will make him know°   *convince him*
175   If that his head have ear in music—doubtless
With joy he will embrace you, for he's honourable,
And, doubling that, most holy. Your means° abroad—   *As for means of support*
You have me, rich, and I will never fail
Beginning nor supplyment.[8]

INNOGEN   Thou art all the comfort
180   The gods will diet° me with. Prithee away.   *feed*
There's more to be considered, but we'll even°   *keep pace with*
All that good time will give us. This attempt
I am soldier to,° and will abide it with   *committed to*
A prince's courage. Away, I prithee.
185 PISANIO   Well, madam, we must take a short farewell
Lest, being missed, I be suspected of
Your carriage° from the court. My noble mistress,   *removal*
Here is a box. I had it from the Queen.
What's in't is precious. If you are sick at sea
190   Or stomach-qualmed° at land, a dram° of this   *nauseous / tiny portion*
Will drive away distemper. To some shade,
And fit you to your manhood.[9] May the gods
Direct you to the best.

INNOGEN   Amen. I thank thee. *Exeunt* [*severally*]

3.5

[*Flourish.*] *Enter* CYMBELINE, [*the*] QUEEN, CLOTEN,
LUCIUS, *and lords*

CYMBELINE [*to* LUCIUS]   Thus far, and so farewell.

LUCIUS   Thanks, royal sir.
My emperor hath wrote I must from hence;
And am right sorry that I must report ye
My master's enemy.

CYMBELINE   Our subjects, sir,
5   Will not endure his yoke, and for ourself
To show less sovereignty than they must needs
Appear unkinglike.

LUCIUS   So, sir, I desire of you
A conduct° over land to Milford Haven.   *An escort*
[*To the* QUEEN] Madam, all joy befall your grace, [*to* CLOTEN] and you.
10 CYMBELINE   My lords, you are appointed for that office.°   *duty*
The due of honour in no point omit.
So farewell, noble Lucius.

LUCIUS   Your hand, my lord.

CLOTEN   Receive it friendly, but from this time forth
I wear it as your enemy.

LUCIUS   Sir, the event°   *outcome*
15   Is yet to name the winner. Fare you well.

CYMBELINE   Leave not the worthy Lucius, good my lords,
Till he have crossed the Severn.[1] Happiness.

Exeunt LUCIUS [*and lords*]

7. In which things you are skilled.
8. In providing the initial amount nor in supplement-
ing it.
9. Dress yourself in accordance with your (pretended)

manhood.
3.5 Location: Cymbeline's court, Britain.
1. River flowing between Wales and England.

QUEEN   He goes hence frowning, but it honours us
    That we have given him cause.

CLOTEN   'Tis all the better.

20   Your valiant Britons have their wishes in it.

CYMBELINE   Lucius hath wrote already to the Emperor
    How it goes here. It fits° us therefore ripely°   *befits / quickly*
    Our chariots and our horsemen be in readiness.
    The powers° that he already hath in Gallia   *military forces*
25   Will soon be drawn to head,[2] from whence he moves
    His war for Britain.

QUEEN   'Tis not sleepy business,
    But must be looked to speedily and strongly.

CYMBELINE   Our expectation that it would be thus
    Hath made us forward.° But, my gentle queen,   *well prepared*
30   Where is our daughter? She hath not appeared
    Before the Roman, nor to us hath tendered
    The duty of the day. She looks us° like   *seems to us*
    A thing more made of malice than of duty.
    We have noted it. Call her before us, for
    We have been too slight in sufferance.°   *[Exit one or more]*   *mild in our tolerance*
35 QUEEN   Royal sir,
    Since the exile of Posthumus most retired
    Hath her life been, the cure whereof, my lord,
    'Tis time must do. Beseech your majesty
    Forbear sharp speeches to her. She's a lady
40   So tender of° rebukes that words are strokes,   *sensitive to*
    And strokes death to her.

              Enter a MESSENGER

CYMBELINE   Where is she, sir? How
    Can her contempt be answered?

MESSENGER   Please you, sir,
    Her chambers are all locked, and there's no answer
    That will be given to th' loud'st of noise we make.

45 QUEEN   My lord, when last I went to visit her
    She prayed me to excuse her keeping close,°   *staying confined*
    Whereto constrained by her infirmity,
    She should that duty leave unpaid to you
    Which daily she was bound to proffer. This
50   She wished me to make known, but our great court°   *court business*
    Made me to blame° in memory.   *at fault*

CYMBELINE   Her doors locked?
    Not seen of late? Grant heavens that which I
    Fear prove false.   *Exit*

QUEEN   Son, I say, follow the King.

CLOTEN   That man of hers, Pisanio, her old servant,
    I have not seen these two days.

55 QUEEN   Go, look after. *Exit* [CLOTEN]
    Pisanio, thou that stand'st so for° Posthumus!   *so much takes the part of*
    He hath a drug of mine. I pray his absence
    Proceed by° swallowing that, for he believes   *Results from*
    It is a thing most precious. But for her,
60   Where is she gone? Haply° despair hath seized her,   *Perhaps*
    Or, winged with fervour of her love, she's flown

---

2. Be gathered to their full strength.

To her desired Posthumus. Gone she is
To death or to dishonour, and my end
Can make good use of either. She being down,
65 I have the placing of the British crown.

Enter CLOTEN

How now, my son?

CLOTEN   'Tis certain she is fled.
Go in and cheer the King. He rages, none
Dare come about him.

QUEEN   All the better. May
This night forestall him of the coming day.³   *Exit*

70 CLOTEN I love and hate her. For° she's fair and royal,   *Because*
And that she hath all courtly parts° more exquisite   *features*
Than lady, ladies, woman—from every one
The best she hath, and she, of all compounded,
Outsells° them all—I love her therefore; but   *Exceeds in value*
75 Disdaining me, and throwing favours on
The low Posthumus, slanders° so her judgement   *discredits*
That what's else° rare is choked; and in that point   *otherwise*
I will conclude to hate her, nay, indeed,
To be revenged upon her. For when fools
Shall—

Enter PISANIO

80   Who is here? What, are you packing,° sirrah?⁴   *scheming*
Come hither. Ah, you precious pander! Villain,
Where is thy lady? In a word, or else
Thou art straightway with the fiends.

PISANIO   O good my lord!

CLOTEN Where is thy lady?—or, by Jupiter,
85 I will not ask again. Close° villain,   *Secretive*
I'll have this secret from thy tongue or rip
Thy heart to find it. Is she with Posthumus,
From whose so many weights° of baseness cannot   *measures*
A dram of worth be drawn?

PISANIO   Alas, my lord,
90 How can she be with him? When was she missed?
He is in Rome.

CLOTEN   Where is she, sir? Come nearer.°   *Be more precise*
No farther halting. Satisfy me home°   *completely*
What is become of her.

PISANIO O my all-worthy lord!

95 CLOTEN All-worthy villain,
Discover° where thy mistress is at once,   *Reveal*
At the next word. No more of 'worthy lord'.
Speak, or thy silence on the instant is
Thy condemnation and thy death.

PISANIO   Then, sir,
100 This paper is the history of my knowledge
Touching her flight.

[He gives CLOTEN *a letter]*

CLOTEN   Let's see't. I will pursue her
Even to Augustus' throne.

PISANIO *[aside]*   Or° this or perish.   *Either*

3. That is, kill him. *forestall:* deprive.   4. Fellow (a common form of address to a social inferior).

She's far enough, and what he learns by this
May prove his travel,[5] not her danger.

CLOTEN   Hum!

105 PISANIO [*aside*] \ I'll write to my lord she's dead. O Innogen,
Safe mayst thou wander, safe return again!

CLOTEN   Sirrah, is this letter true?

PISANIO   Sir, as I think.

CLOTEN   It is Posthumus' hand; I know't. Sirrah, if thou wouldst
not be a villain but do me true service, undergo° those employ-   *undertake*
110   ments wherein I should have cause to use thee with a serious
industry—that is, what villainy soe'er I bid thee do, to perform
it directly and truly—I would think thee an honest man. Thou
shouldst neither want° my means for thy relief nor my voice for   *find lacking*
thy preferment.°   *advancement*

115 PISANIO   Well, my good lord.

CLOTEN   Wilt thou serve me? For since patiently and constantly
thou hast stuck to the bare fortune of that beggar Posthumus,
thou canst not in the course of gratitude but be a diligent follower of mine. Wilt thou serve me?

120 PISANIO   Sir, I will.

CLOTEN   Give me thy hand. Here's my purse. Hast any of thy
late° master's garments in thy possession?   *former*

PISANIO   I have, my lord, at my lodging the same suit he wore
when he took leave of my lady and mistress.

125 CLOTEN   The first service thou dost me, fetch that suit hither.
Let it be thy first service. Go.

PISANIO   I shall, my lord.   *Exit*

CLOTEN   Meet thee at Milford Haven! I forgot to ask him one
thing;[6] I'll remember't anon. Even there, thou villain Posthu-
130   mus, will I kill thee. I would these garments were come. She
said upon a time—the bitterness of it I now belch from my
heart—that she held the very garment of Posthumus in more
respect than my noble and natural person, together with the
adornment of my qualities. With that suit upon my back will I
135   ravish her—first kill him, and in her eyes; there shall she see
my valour, which will then be a torment to her contempt. He
on the ground, my speech of insultment° ended on his dead   *contemptuous triumph*
body, and when my lust hath dined—which, as I say, to vex her
I will execute in the clothes that she so praised—to the court
140   I'll knock° her back, foot° her home again. She hath despised   *beat / kick*
me rejoicingly, and I'll be merry in my revenge.

Enter PISANIO [*with Posthumus' suit*]

Be those the garments?

PISANIO   Ay, my noble lord.

CLOTEN   How long is't since she went to Milford Haven?

PISANIO   She can scarce be there yet.

145 CLOTEN   Bring this apparel to my chamber. That is the second
thing that I have commanded thee. The third is that thou wilt
be a voluntary mute to° my design. Be but duteous, and true   *be quiet about*
preferment shall tender itself to thee. My revenge is now at
Milford. Would I had wings to follow it. Come, and be true.

Exit

5. May turn out to be merely a long journey for him.
6. The "one thing" may be how long a time has passed
since Innogen set out for Milford Haven (see Cloten's
question at line 143).

150 PISANO Thou bidd'st me to my loss,° for true to thee   perdition
       Were to prove false, which I will never be
       To him that is most true. To Milford go,
       And find not her whom thou pursuest. Flow, flow,
       You heavenly blessings, on her. This fool's speed
155   Be crossed° with slowness; labour be his meed.°   *Exit*   thwarted / reward

3.6

Enter INNOGEN [*dressed as a man, before the cave*]

INNOGEN I see a man's life is a tedious one.
       I have tired myself, and for two nights together
       Have made the ground my bed. I should be sick,
       But that my resolution helps me. Milford,
5   When from the mountain-top Pisanio showed thee,
       Thou wast within a ken.° O Jove, I think   within sight
       Foundations[1] fly the wretched—such, I mean,
       Where they should be relieved.[2] Two beggars told me
       I could not miss my way. Will poor folks lie,
10   That have afflictions on them, knowing 'tis
       A punishment or trial?[3] Yes. No wonder,
       When rich ones scarce tell true. To lapse in fullness°   To do wrong when rich
       Is sorer° than to lie for need, and falsehood   worse
       Is worse in kings than beggars. My dear lord,
15   Thou art one o'th' false ones. Now I think on thee
       My hunger's gone, but even before° I was   just a moment ago
       At point° to sink for° food. But what is this?   Ready / for want of
       Here is a path to't. 'Tis some savage hold.°   refuge
       I were best not call; I dare not call; yet famine,
20   Ere clean° it o'erthrow nature, makes it valiant.   completely
       Plenty and peace breeds cowards, hardness° ever   hardship
       Of hardiness is mother. Ho! Who's here?
       If anything that's civil, speak; if savage,
       Take or lend.[4] Ho! No answer? Then I'll enter.
25   Best draw my sword, and if mine enemy
       But fear the sword like me he'll scarcely look on't.
       Such a foe, good heavens![5]   *Exit* [*into the cave*]

Enter BELARIUS, GUIDERIUS, *and* ARVIRAGUS[6]

BELARIUS You, Polydore, have proved best woodman° and   hunter
       Are master of the feast. Cadwal and I
30   Will play the cook and servant; 'tis our match.°   bargain
       The sweat of industry would dry and die
       But for the end it works to. Come, our stomachs
       Will make what's homely° savoury. Weariness   plain
       Can snore upon the flint when resty° sloth   lazy
35   Finds the down pillow hard. Now peace be here,
       Poor house, that keep'st thyself.°   goes untended

GUIDERIUS   I am throughly weary.

ARVIRAGUS I am weak with toil yet strong in appetite.

3.6 Location: Before the cave of Belarius, Wales.
1. Certainties; charitable institutions.
2. *such . . . relieved:* such certainties, I mean, as
should give mental relief to the wretched; such charitable institutions as should give physical relief (food
and rest) to the wretched.

3. *knowing . . . trial:* knowing that poverty is a punishment or a test of one's virtue.
4. Take everything I have, or help me.
5. May it please heaven I meet such a timid foe.
6. F marks a new scene at this point, but the action is
continuous.

GUIDERIUS There is cold meat i'th' cave. We'll browse° on that   *nibble*
   Whilst what we have killed be cooked.

BELARIUS [*looking into the cave*]   Stay, come not in.

40 But° that it eats our victuals I should think   *But for the fact*
   Here were a fairy.

GUIDERIUS   What's the matter, sir?

BELARIUS By Jupiter, an angel—or, if not,
   An earthly paragon. Behold divineness
   No elder than a boy.

   Enter INNOGEN [*from the cave, dressed as a man*]

INNOGEN   Good masters, harm me not.

45 Before I entered here I called, and thought°   *intended*
   To have begged or bought what I have took. Good truth,
   I have stol'n naught, nor would not, though I had found
   Gold strewed i'th' floor. Here's money for my meat.
   I would have left it on the board so° soon   *as*

50 As I had made my meal, and parted
   With prayers for the provider.

GUIDERIUS   Money, youth?

ARVIRAGUS All gold and silver rather turn to dirt,
   As 'tis no better reckoned but of° those   *better thought of but by*
   Who worship dirty gods.

INNOGEN   I see you're angry.

55 Know, if you kill me for my fault, I should
   Have died had I not made it.

BELARIUS   Whither bound?

INNOGEN To Milford Haven.

BELARIUS   What's your name?

INNOGEN Fidele,[7] sir. I have a kinsman who
   Is bound for Italy. He embarked at Milford,

60 To whom being going, almost spent with hunger,
   I am fall'n in° this offence.   *into*

BELARIUS   Prithee, fair youth,
   Think us no churls,° nor measure our good minds   *base fellows*
   By this rude° place we live in. Well encountered.   *wild*
   'Tis almost night. You shall have better cheer°   *provisions*

65 Ere you depart, and thanks to° stay and eat it.   *our gratitude if you*
   Boys, bid him welcome.

GUIDERIUS   Were you a woman, youth,
   I should woo hard but be° your groom in honesty,   *rather than fail to be*
   Ay, bid for you as I'd buy.[8]

ARVIRAGUS   I'll make't my comfort
   He is a man, I'll love him as my brother.

70 [*To* INNOGEN] And such a welcome as I'd give to him
   After long absence, such is yours. Most welcome.
   Be sprightly,° for you fall 'mongst friends.   *cheerful*

INNOGEN   'Mongst friends
   If brothers.[9] [*Aside*] Would it had been so that they
   Had been my father's sons. Then had my price°   *worth*

---

7. In French and Italian, the name means "faithful one."
8. Yes, make an offer for you with every intent to buy (that is, to marry you).
9. *'Mongst . . . brothers:* Yes, certainly I am among friends, if you claim me as a brother.

75 Been less, and so more equal ballasting°   *equal in weight*
    To thee, Posthumus.
                [*The three men speak apart*]
BELARIUS   He wrings° at some distress.   *twists in pain*
GUIDERIUS   Would I could free't.°   *remove it*
ARVIRAGUS   Or I, whate'er it be,
    What° pain it cost, what danger. Gods!   *Whatever*
BELARIUS   Hark, boys.
             [*They whisper*]
INNOGEN [*aside*]   Great men
80   That had a court no bigger than this cave,
    That did attend° themselves and had the virtue   *wait on*
    Which their own conscience sealed° them, laying by°   *assured / disregarding*
    That nothing-gift of differing multitudes,[1]
    Could not outpeer° these twain. Pardon me, gods,   *surpass*
85   I'd change my sex to be companion with them,
    Since Leonatus' false.
BELARIUS   It shall be so.
    Boys, we'll go dress our hunt.° Fair youth, come in.   *game*
    Discourse is heavy, fasting.[2] When we have supped
    We'll mannerly demand thee of thy story,
    So far as thou wilt speak it.
90 GUIDERIUS   Pray draw near.
ARVIRAGUS   The night to th' owl and morn to th' lark less welcome.
INNOGEN   Thanks, sir.
ARVIRAGUS   I pray draw near.   *Exeunt* [*into the cave*]

3.7

Enter two Roman SENATORS, *and* TRIBUNES
FIRST SENATOR   This is the tenor of the Emperor's writ:
    That since the common men are now in action
    'Gainst the Pannonians and Dalmatians,
    And that the legions now in Gallia are
5   Full weak° to undertake our wars against   *Too weak*
    The fall'n-off° Britons, that we do incite   *rebelling*
    The gentry to this business. He creates
    Lucius pro-consul,[1] and to you the tribunes,
    For this immediate levy, he commends°   *entrusts*
10   His absolute commission.° Long live Caesar!   *authority*
A TRIBUNE   Is Lucius general of the forces?
SECOND SENATOR   Ay.
A TRIBUNE   Remaining now in Gallia?
FIRST SENATOR   With those legions
    Which I have spoke of, whereunto your levy
    Must be supplyant.° The words of your commission   *auxiliary*
15   Will tie you to° the numbers and the time   *indicate to you*
    Of their dispatch.
A TRIBUNE   We will discharge our duty.   *Exeunt*

---

1. That worthless gift offered by a public that cannot agree on anything.
2. Conversation is difficult when one is without food.

3.7 Location: A public place, Rome.
1. One who acted as governor or military commander in a Roman province.

4.1

Enter CLOTEN [*in Posthumus' suit*]

CLOTEN   I am near to th' place where they should meet, if
Pisanio have mapped it truly. How fit° his garments serve me!   *aptly*
Why should his mistress, who was made by him that made the
tailor, not be fit° too?—the rather—saving reverence of the   *apt; sexually compatible*
5 word[1]—for 'tis said a woman's fitness comes by fits.[2] Therein I
must play the workman. I dare speak it to myself, for it is not
vainglory for a man and his glass° to confer in his own cham-   *mirror*
ber. I mean the lines of my body are as well drawn as his: no
less young, more strong, not beneath him in fortunes, beyond
10 him in the advantage of the time,[3] above him in birth, alike
conversant in general services, and more remarkable in single
oppositions.[4] Yet this imperceiverant° thing loves him in my   *stupid*
despite.° What mortality[5] is! Posthumus, thy head which now   *to spite me*
is growing upon thy shoulders shall within this hour be off, thy
15 mistress enforced,° thy garments cut to pieces before thy face;   *raped*
and all this done, spurn her home to her father, who may haply
be a little angry for my so rough usage; but my mother, having
power of° his testiness, shall turn all into my commendations.   *over*
My horse is tied up safe. Out, sword, and to a sore purpose!
20 Fortune, put them into my hand. This is the very description
of their meeting-place, and the fellow dares not deceive me.

Exit

4.2

Enter BELARIUS, GUIDERIUS, ARVIRAGUS, *and* INNOGEN
[*dressed as a man,*] *from the cave*

BELARIUS [*to* INNOGEN]   You are not well. Remain here in the cave.
We'll come to you from hunting.

ARVIRAGUS [*to* INNOGEN]   Brother, stay here.
Are we not brothers?

INNOGEN   So man and man should be,
But clay and clay[1] differs in dignity,°   *social position*
5 Whose dust[2] is both alike. I am very sick.

GUIDERIUS [*to* BELARIUS *and* ARVIRAGUS]   Go you to hunting.
I'll abide with him.

INNOGEN   So sick I am not, yet I am not well;
But not so citizen a wanton as
To seem to die ere sick.[3] So please you, leave me.
10 Stick to your journal course.° The breach of custom   *daily routine*
Is breach of all. I am ill, but your being by me
Cannot amend me. Society is no comfort
To one not sociable. I am not very sick,
Since I can reason of° it. Pray you, trust me here.   *talk about*
15 I'll rob none but myself; and let me die,
Stealing so poorly.[4]

4.1 Location: Near the cave of Belarius, Wales.
1. With apologies for my punning.
2. For it is said that a woman's inclination for sexual
intercourse comes intermittently.
3. In the favorable opportunities afforded by the times.
4. *alike . . . oppositions*: similarly acquainted with battle tactics, and superior in single combat or duels (with
puns on "service" and "oppositions" as referring to sexual exploits).

5. Life; humankind.
4.2 Location: Before the cave of Belarius.
1. Yet two humans (alluding to the biblical notion that
humans are formed out of clay).
2. The substance to which all humans return at death.
3. *But . . . sick:* But I am not so city-bred a weakling
("wanton") as to think I am dying even before I am sick.
4. Stealing only from one so poor as myself.

GUIDERIUS   I love thee: I have spoke it;
How much the quantity,° the weight as much,   *As greatly*
As I do love my father.
BELARIUS   What, how, how?
ARVIRAGUS   If it be sin to say so, sir, I yoke me°   *I share*
20   In my good brother's fault. I know not why
I love this youth, and I have heard you say
Love's reason's without reason. The bier⁵ at door
And a demand who is't shall die, I'd say
'My father, not this youth'.
BELARIUS [*aside*]   O noble strain!°   *inherited character*
25   O worthiness of nature, breed of greatness!
Cowards father cowards, and base things sire base.
Nature hath meal and bran,° contempt and grace.   *flour and husks*
I'm not their father, yet who this should be
Doth miracle itself, loved before me.⁶
[*Aloud*] 'Tis the ninth hour o'th' morn.
30 ARVIRAGUS [*to* INNOGEN]   Brother, farewell.
INNOGEN   I wish ye sport.
ARVIRAGUS   You health.—So please you, sir.
INNOGEN [*aside*]   These are kind creatures. Gods, what lies I have heard!
Our courtiers say all's savage but at court.
Experience, O thou disprov'st report!
35   Th'imperious° seas breeds monsters; for the dish   *imperial*
Poor tributary rivers as sweet fish.⁷
I am sick still, heart-sick. Pisanio,
I'll now taste of thy drug.
       [*She swallows the drug. The men speak apart*]
GUIDERIUS   I could not stir him.
He said he was gentle° but unfortunate,   *a gentleman by birth*
40   Dishonestly afflicted but yet honest.
ARVIRAGUS   Thus did he answer me, yet said hereafter
I might know more.
BELARIUS   To th' field, to th' field!
[*To* INNOGEN] We'll leave you for this time. Go in and rest.
ARVIRAGUS [*to* INNOGEN]   We'll not be long away.
BELARIUS [*to* INNOGEN]   Pray be not sick,
For you must be our housewife.
45 INNOGEN   Well or ill,
I am bound° to you.   *Exit*   *indebted*
BELARIUS   And shalt be ever.
This youth, howe'er distressed, appears° hath had   *apparently*
Good ancestors.
ARVIRAGUS   How angel-like he sings!
50 GUIDERIUS   But his neat° cookery!   *dainty*
BELARIUS⁸   He cut our roots in characters,°   *alphabet shapes*
And sauced our broths as° Juno had been sick   *as if*
And he her dieter.°   *cook*
ARVIRAGUS   Nobly he yokes

---

5. The litter, or platform, on which a corpse was carried to the grave.
6. *yet . . . me:* yet who this may be who is loved more than me is a source of great wonder.
7. *for . . . fish:* but when it comes to eating, small tributaries breed fish as sweet as does the sea.

8. F assigns this speech to Arviragus, but he has the next one as well. One editorial solution has been to assign the lines to Guiderius as an extension of his prior speech. Another, as here, is to give the lines to Belarius, who thus joins his adopted sons in praising Innogen/Fidele.

A smiling with a sigh, as if the sigh
55   Was that° it was for not being such a smile;   *Was what*
The smile mocking the sigh that° it would fly   *because*
From so divine a temple to commix°   *join*
With winds that sailors rail at.
GUIDERIUS   I do note
That grief and patience, rooted in him both,
Mingle their spurs° together.   *roots*
60   ARVIRAGUS   Grow patience,
And let the stinking elder,⁹ grief, untwine
His perishing° root with° the increasing vine.   *deadly / from*
BELARIUS   It is great morning.° Come away. Who's there?   *full daylight*
                    Enter CLOTEN [*in Posthumus' suit*]
CLOTEN   I cannot find those runagates.° That villain   *runaways; fugitives*
Hath mocked me. I am faint.
65   BELARIUS [*aside to* ARVIRAGUS *and* GUIDERIUS] 'Those runagates'?
Means he not us? I partly know him; 'tis
Cloten, the son o'th' Queen. I fear some ambush.
I saw him not these many years, and yet
I know 'tis he. We are held as outlaws. Hence!
GUIDERIUS [*aside to* ARVIRAGUS *and* BELARIUS] He is but one.
70   You and my brother search
What companies° are near. Pray you, away.   *companions*
Let me alone with him.   [*Exeunt* ARVIRAGUS *and* BELARIUS]
CLOTEN   Soft, what are you
That fly me thus? Some villain mountaineers?°   *lowborn mountain people*
I have heard of such. What slave art thou?
GUIDERIUS   A thing
75   More slavish did I ne'er than answering
A slave without a knock.°   *without striking him*
CLOTEN   Thou art a robber,
A law-breaker, a villain. Yield thee, thief.
GUIDERIUS   To who? To thee? What art thou? Have not I
An arm as big as thine, a heart as big?
80   Thy words, I grant, are bigger, for I wear not
My dagger in my mouth.¹ Say what thou art,
Why I should yield to thee.
CLOTEN   Thou villain base,
Know'st me not by my clothes?
GUIDERIUS   No, nor thy tailor, rascal,
Who is thy grandfather. He made those clothes,
Which, as it seems, make thee.²
85   CLOTEN   Thou precious varlet,°   *absolute scoundrel*
My tailor made them not.
GUIDERIUS   Hence, then, and thank
The man that gave them thee. Thou art some fool.
I am loath to beat thee.
CLOTEN   Thou injurious° thief,   *insulting*
Hear but my name and tremble.
GUIDERIUS   What's thy name?

---

9. A tree with strong-smelling leaves and flowers on which Judas, the disciple who betrayed Jesus, is said to have hanged himself.

1. *for . . . mouth:* for I don't let words substitute for weapons.

2. Alluding to the proverb "The tailor makes the man."

90 CLOTEN   Cloten, thou villain.
GUIDERIUS   Cloten, thou double villain, be thy name,
   I cannot tremble at it. Were it toad or adder, spider,
   'Twould move me sooner.
CLOTEN   To thy further fear,
   Nay, to thy mere confusion,° thou shalt know   *absolute destruction*
   I am son to th' Queen.
95 GUIDERIUS   I am sorry for't, not seeming
   So worthy as thy birth.
CLOTEN   Art not afeard?
GUIDERIUS   Those that I reverence, those I fear, the wise.
   At fools I laugh, not fear them.
CLOTEN   Die the death.
   When I have slain thee with my proper° hand   *own*
100   I'll follow those that even now fled hence,
   And on the gates of Lud's town° set your heads.[3]   *London*
   Yield, rustic mountaineer.   *Fight and exeunt*
                 Enter BELARIUS *and* ARVIRAGUS
BELARIUS   No company's abroad?°   *about*
ARVIRAGUS   None in the world. You did mistake him, sure.
BELARIUS   I cannot tell. Long is it since I saw him,
105   But time hath nothing blurred those lines of favour°   *facial features*
   Which then he wore. The snatches° in his voice   *hesitations*
   And burst° of speaking were as his. I am absolute°   *sudden rush / sure*
   'Twas very Cloten.°   *Cloten himself*
ARVIRAGUS   In this place we left them.
   I wish my brother make good time with him,[4]
   You say he is so fell.°   *fierce*
110 BELARIUS   Being scarce made up,°   *barely full-grown*
   I mean to man, he had not apprehension°   *had no consciousness*
   Of roaring terrors; for defect of judgement
   Is oft the cause of fear.[5]
                 Enter GUIDERIUS [*with Cloten's head*]
                   But see, thy brother.
GUIDERIUS   This Cloten was a fool, an empty purse,
115   There was no money in't. Not Hercules[6]
   Could have knocked out his brains, for he had none.
   Yet I not doing this,° the fool had borne   *had I not done this*
   My head as I do his.
BELARIUS   What hast thou done?
GUIDERIUS   I am perfect° what: cut off one Cloten's head,   *certain*
120   Son to the Queen after his own report,
   Who called me traitor, mountaineer, and swore
   With his own single hand he'd take us in,°   *capture us*
   Displace our heads where—thanks, ye gods—they grow,
   And set them on Lud's town.
BELARIUS   We are all undone.
125 GUIDERIUS   Why, worthy father, what have we to lose
   But that° he swore to take, our lives? The law   *what*

3. The heads of criminals were frequently displayed on poles on London Bridge and other places throughout the city.
4. I hope my brother is successful with him.
5. *for . . . fear:* an obscure passage. It may mean that Cloten's faulty judgment, which led him to know no fear, caused fear in others. A less likely meaning is that while defects in judgment cause fear, Cloten knew no fear because he had absolutely no judgment, being utterly witless.
6. Mythical hero of enormous strength.

Protects not us: then why should we be tender
To let[7] an arrogant piece of flesh threat us,
Play judge and executioner all himself,
130 For° we do fear the law? What company   *Because*
Discover you abroad?[8]

BELARIUS   No single soul
Can we set eye on, but in all safe reason
He must have some attendants. Though his humour°   *disposition*
Was nothing but mutation,° ay, and that   *changeableness*
135 From one bad thing to worse, not° frenzy,   *neither*
Not° absolute madness, could so far have raved°   *Nor / made him mad enough*
To bring him here alone. Although perhaps
It may be heard at court that such as we
Cave° here, hunt here, are outlaws, and in time   *Live in a cave*
140 May make some stronger head,° the which he hearing—   *raise a stronger force*
As it is like him—might break out, and swear
He'd fetch us in, yet is't not probable
To come° alone, either he so undertaking,   *That he would come*
Or they so suffering.[9] Then on good ground we fear
145 If we do fear this body hath a tail°   *rear end; followers*
More perilous than the head.

ARVIRAGUS   Let ord'nance°   *destiny*
Come as the gods foresay° it; howsoe'er,   *predict*
My brother hath done well.

BELARIUS   I had no mind
To hunt this day. The boy Fidele's sickness
Did make my way long forth.°   *my journey tedious*
150 GUIDERIUS   With his own sword,
Which he did wave against my throat, I have ta'en
His head from him. I'll throw't into the creek
Behind our rock, and let it to the sea
And tell the fishes he's the Queen's son, Cloten.
That's all I reck.°   *Exit [with Cloten's head]*   *care*
155 BELARIUS   I fear 'twill be revenged.
Would, Polydore, thou hadst not done't, though valour
Becomes thee well enough.

ARVIRAGUS   Would I had done't,
So the revenge alone pursued me.° Polydore,   *only pursued me*
I love thee brotherly, but envy much
160 Thou hast robbed me of this deed. I would revenges
That possible strength might meet would seek us through
And put us to our answer.[1]

BELARIUS   Well, 'tis done.
We'll hunt no more today, nor seek for danger
Where there's no profit. I prithee, to our rock.
165 You and Fidele play the cooks. I'll stay
Till hasty Polydore return, and bring him
To dinner presently.

ARVIRAGUS   Poor sick Fidele!
I'll willingly to him. To gain° his colour   *restore*

---

7. *be tender / To let:* be so meek as to allow.
8. *What companions* (of Cloten) did you find here-abouts?
9. *either . . . suffering:* either that he would undertake

it or that they would allow it.
1. *I would . . . answer:* I wish that revenges equal to all the power that we might muster would find us out and test our mettle.

I'd let a parish of such Clotens blood,[2]
And praise myself for charity.   *Exit [into the cave]*

170 BELARIUS   O thou goddess,
Thou divine Nature, how thyself thou blazon'st[3]
In these two princely boys! They are as gentle
As zephyrs° blowing below the violet,   *breezes from the west*
Not wagging his sweet head; and yet as rough,°   *violent*
175 Their royal blood enchafed,° as the rud'st wind   *enflamed*
That by the top doth take the mountain pine
And make him stoop to th' vale. 'Tis wonder
That an invisible instinct should frame° them   *shape*
To royalty unlearned, honour untaught,
180 Civility not seen from other,° valour   *not witnessed in others*
That wildly° grows in them, but yields a crop   *without cultivation*
As if it had been sowed. Yet still it's strange
What Cloten's being here to us portends,
Or what his death will bring us.
          Enter GUIDERIUS

GUIDERIUS   Where's my brother?
185 I have sent Cloten's clotpoll° down the stream   *blockhead*
In embassy to his mother. His body's hostage
For his return.[4]
          Solemn music

BELARIUS   My ingenious° instrument!—   *artfully crafted*
Hark, Polydore, it sounds. But what occasion
Hath Cadwal now to give it motion? Hark!

GUIDERIUS   Is he at home?
190 BELARIUS   He went hence even now.

GUIDERIUS   What does he mean? Since death of my dear'st mother
It did not speak before. All solemn things
Should answer° solemn accidents. The matter?   *correspond to*
Triumphs for nothing and lamenting toys
195 Is jollity for apes and grief for boys.[5]
Is Cadwal mad?
          Enter [from the cave] ARVIRAGUS *with* INNOGEN, *dead,*
          bearing her in his arms

BELARIUS   Look, here he comes,
And brings the dire occasion in his arms
Of what we blame him for.

ARVIRAGUS   The bird is dead
That we have made so much on.° I had rather   *of*
200 Have skipped from sixteen years of age to sixty,
To have turned my leaping time° into a crutch,°   *youth / (old age)*
Than have seen this.

GUIDERIUS [*to* INNOGEN]   O sweetest, fairest lily!
My brother wears thee not one half so well
As when thou grew'st thyself.

BELARIUS   O melancholy,
205 Who ever yet could sound thy bottom,° find   *measure your depths*
The ooze to show what coast thy sluggish crare°   *small ship*
Might easiliest harbour in? Thou blessèd thing,

---

2. I'd draw blood from a whole parish full of fools like Cloten.
3. How you proclaim yourself (as in a coat of arms).
4. *His body's ... return:* I will hold his body hostage

until his head returns (which will be never).
5. *Triumphs ... boys:* Public celebrations for no reason and showing great grief for trivial matters are foolish and unmanly.

Jove knows what man thou mightst have made; but I,°   *I know*
Thou diedst a most rare boy, of melancholy.
[*To* ARVIRAGUS] How found you him?

210 ARVIRAGUS   Stark,° as you see,   *stiff*
Thus smiling as° some fly had tickled slumber,   *as if*
Not as death's dart being laughed at;[6] his right cheek
Reposing on a cushion.

GUIDERIUS   Where?

ARVIRAGUS   O'th' floor,
His arms thus leagued.° I thought he slept, and put   *linked together*
215 My clouted brogues° from off my feet, whose rudeness   *hobnailed boots*
Answered° my steps too loud.   *Rendered*

GUIDERIUS   Why, he but sleeps.
If he be gone he'll make his grave a bed.
With female fairies will his tomb be haunted,
[*To* INNOGEN] And worms will not come to thee.

ARVIRAGUS [*to* INNOGEN]   With fairest flowers
220 Whilst summer lasts and I live here, Fidele,
I'll sweeten thy sad grave. Thou shalt not lack
The flower that's like thy face, pale primrose, nor
The azured harebell,° like thy veins; no, nor   *blue hyacinth*
The leaf of eglantine,° whom not to slander   *honeysuckle*
225 Outsweetened not thy breath. The ruddock would
With charitable bill—O bill sore shaming
Those rich-left heirs that let their fathers lie
Without a monument!—bring thee all this,
Yea, and furred moss besides, when flowers are none,
To winter-gown thy corpse.[7]

230 GUIDERIUS   Prithee, have done,
And do not play in wench-like words[8] with that
Which is so serious. Let us bury him,
And not protract with admiration° what   *wonder*
Is now due debt. To th' grave.

ARVIRAGUS   Say, where shall 's° lay him?   *ought we to*

GUIDERIUS By good Euriphile, our mother.

235 ARVIRAGUS   Be't so,
And let us, Polydore, though now our voices
Have got the mannish crack, sing him to th' ground
As once our mother; use like note° and words,   *a similar tune*
Save that 'Euriphile' must be 'Fidele'.

240 GUIDERIUS Cadwal,
I cannot sing. I'll weep, and word° it with thee,   *speak*
For notes of sorrow out of tune are worse
Than priests and fanes° that lie.   *temples*

ARVIRAGUS   We'll speak it then.

BELARIUS Great griefs, I see, medicine° the less, for Cloten   *cure*
245 Is quite forgot. He was a queen's son, boys,
And though he came our enemy, remember
He was paid° for that. Though mean° and mighty rotting   *punished / lowborn*
Together have one dust, yet reverence,

---

6. Not as if laughing at the approach of death. Death was often depicted carrying a spear ("dart").
7. *The ruddock . . . corpse*: referring to the belief that the robins ("ruddocks") covered dead bodies with flowers and moss. *winter-gown*: clothe for winter.

8. Words appropriate to women. In Shakespeare's plays, speeches about flowers are often delivered by female characters, perhaps most notably in *Hamlet* 4.5.173–82 and *The Winter's Tale* 4.4.73–134.

That angel of the world,[9] doth make distinction
250 Of place 'tween high and low. Our foe was princely,
And though you took his life as being our foe,
Yet bury him as a prince.

GUIDERIUS   Pray you, fetch him hither.
Thersites' body is as good as Ajax'[1]
When neither are alive.

ARVIRAGUS [to BELARIUS]   If you'll go fetch him,
We'll say our song the whilst.   [Exit BELARIUS]
255   Brother, begin.

GUIDERIUS   Nay, Cadwal, we must lay his head to th'east.[2]
My father hath a reason for't.

ARVIRAGUS   'Tis true.

GUIDERIUS   Come on, then, and remove him.

ARVIRAGUS   So, begin.[3]

GUIDERIUS   Fear no more the heat o'th' sun,
260   Nor the furious winter's rages.
Thou thy worldly task hast done,
    Home art gone and ta'en thy wages.
Golden lads and girls all must,
    As° chimney-sweepers, come to dust.   Like

265 ARVIRAGUS   Fear no more the frown o'th' great,
    Thou art past the tyrant's stroke.
Care no more to clothe and eat,
    To thee the reed is as the oak.[4]
The sceptre, learning, physic,° must   medical knowledge
270   All follow this and come to dust.

GUIDERIUS   Fear no more the lightning flash,

ARVIRAGUS   Nor th'all-dreaded thunder-stone.°   thunderbolt

GUIDERIUS   Fear not slander, censure rash.

ARVIRAGUS   Thou hast finished joy and moan.

275 GUIDERIUS and ARVIRAGUS   All lovers young, all lovers must
                        Consign to thee[5] and come to dust.

GUIDERIUS   No exorcisor° harm thee,   conjurer of spirits

ARVIRAGUS   Nor no witchcraft charm thee.

GUIDERIUS   Ghost unlaid forbear thee.[6]

280 ARVIRAGUS   Nothing ill come near thee.

GUIDERIUS and ARVIRAGUS   Quiet consummation° have,   ending
                        And renownèd be thy grave.

Enter BELARIUS with the body of Cloten [in Posthumus'
suit]

GUIDERIUS   We have done our obsequies. Come, lay him down.

BELARIUS   Here's a few flowers, but 'bout midnight more;
285 The herbs that have on them cold dew o'th' night°   of the night
Are strewings fitt'st for graves upon th'earth's face.
You were as flowers, now withered; even so

---

9. Reverence (respect for someone because of his or
her social position) may here be called the "angel of the
world" because social hierarchy was thought by some to
imitate heavenly hierarchy.
1. Alluding to two Greeks present at the siege of Troy:
Thersites, a scurrilous coward, and Ajax, a mighty hero.
Both appear in Shakespeare's *Troilus and Cressida*.
2. An allusion to classical or Celtic burial practices. The
English Christian custom was to lay the head to the
west. This detail reinforces the pagan world of the play.

3. In F, the following duet is introduced as "SONG."
Lines 240–43, in which the brothers say they cannot
sing and must speak the words, may have been added
because the particular actors who played Arviragus and
Guiderius were not good singers.
4. Referring to traditional symbols of weakness and
strength, respectively.
5. Submit to the same terms as you.
6. May spirits who have not been laid to rest leave you
alone.

	These herblets shall,° which we upon you strow.	*shall wither*
	Come on, away; apart upon our knees⁷	
290	[ ]	
	The ground that gave them° first has them again.	*gave them life*
	Their pleasures here are past, so is their pain.	

Exeunt [BELARIUS, ARVIRAGUS, *and* GUIDERIUS]

	INNOGEN *awakes* Yes, sir, to Milford Haven. Which is the way?	
	I thank you. By yon bush? Pray, how far thither?	
295	'Od's pitykins,° can it be six mile yet?	*By God's pity (mild oath)*
	I have gone° all night. 'Faith, I'll lie down and sleep.	*walked*

[*She sees* CLOTEN]

	But soft,° no bedfellow! O gods and goddesses!	*wait*
	These flowers are like the pleasures of the world,	
	This bloody man the care on't.⁸ I hope I dream,	
300	For so° I thought I was a cavekeeper,	*For then*
	And cook to honest creatures. But 'tis not so.	
	'Twas but a bolt° of nothing, shot of° nothing,	*an arrow / from*
	Which the brain makes of fumes.⁹ Our very eyes	
	Are sometimes like our judgements, blind. Good faith,	
305	I tremble still with fear; but if there be	
	Yet left in heaven as small a drop of pity	
	As a wren's eye, feared gods, a part of it!	
	The dream's here still. Even when I wake it is	
	Without me as within me; not imagined, felt.	
310	A headless man? The garments of Posthumus?	
	I know the shape of 's leg; this is his hand,	
	His foot Mercurial, his Martial¹ thigh,	
	The brawns° of Hercules; but his Jovial² face—	*muscles*
	Murder in heaven! How? 'Tis gone. Pisanio,	
315	All curses madded Hecuba³ gave the Greeks,	
	And mine to boot, be darted on thee! Thou,	
	Conspired° with that irregulous° devil Cloten,	*Conspiring / lawless*
	Hath here cut off my lord. To write and read	
	Be henceforth treacherous! Damned Pisanio	
320	Hath with his forgèd letters—damned Pisanio—	
	From this most bravest° vessel of the world	*splendid*
	Struck the main-top!° O Posthumus, alas,	*top of the mast; his head*
	Where is thy head? Where's that? Ay me, where's that?	
	Pisanio might have killed thee at the heart	
325	And left thy head on. How should this be? Pisanio?	
	'Tis he and Cloten. Malice and lucre° in them	*greed*
	Have laid this woe here. O, 'tis pregnant,° pregnant!	*clear*
	The drug he gave me, which he said was precious	
	And cordial° to me, have I not found it	*restorative*
330	Murd'rous to th' senses? That confirms it home.°	*completely*
	This is Pisanio's deed, and Cloten—O,	
	Give colour to my pale cheek with thy blood,	
	That we the horrider° may seem to those	*more terrifying*
	Which chance to find us!	

7. Some other place ("apart"), let us pray (be "upon our knees"). Because the previous two lines rhyme, as do the next two lines, it is probable that a line is missing here. The sense of "apart upon our knees" also seems obscure, probably because the thought is truncated.
8. This bloody man is like the sorrow of the world.
9. "Fumes" (vapors) were thought to rise from the stomach and cause dreams and distortions of the imagination.
1. Fashioned for battle, like that of Mars, the god of war. *Mercurial:* Like that of Mercury, the fleet-footed messenger of the gods.
2. Majestic like the face of Jove, king of the gods.
3. The Queen of Troy, Priam's wife, whose desire for revenge against the Greeks made her insane ("madded").

[*She smears her face with blood*]
O my lord, my lord!
[*She faints.*]
Enter LUCIUS, [*Roman*] *Captains, and a* SOOTHSAYER

A ROMAN CAPTAIN [*to* LUCIUS]   To them° the legions garrisoned   *In addition to them*
335   in Gallia
      After your will⁴ have crossed the sea, attending°   *waiting for*
      You here at Milford Haven with your ships.
      They are hence in readiness.
LUCIUS   But what from Rome?
A ROMAN CAPTAIN   The senate hath stirred up the confiners°   *inhabitants*
340   And gentlemen of Italy, most willing spirits
      That promise noble service, and they come
      Under the conduct of bold Giacomo,
      Siena's° brother.   *The Duke of Siena's*
LUCIUS   When expect you them?
A ROMAN CAPTAIN   With the next benefit o'th' wind.
LUCIUS   This forwardness°   *readiness*
345   Makes our hopes fair. Command our present numbers
      Be mustered; bid the captains look to't.   [*Exit one or more*]
      [*To* SOOTHSAYER]   Now, sir,
      What have you dreamed of late of this war's purpose?°   *outcome*
SOOTHSAYER   Last night the very gods showed me a vision—
      I fast,° and prayed for their intelligence°—thus: *fasted / information*
350   I saw Jove's bird, the Roman eagle, winged
      From the spongy° south to this part of the west,   *damp*
      There vanished in the sunbeams; which portends,
      Unless my sins abuse° my divination,   *falsify*
      Success to th' Roman host.
LUCIUS   Dream often so,
      And never false.°   *dream falsely*
      [*He sees Cloten's body*]
355   Soft, ho, what trunk is here
      Without his top? The ruin speaks that sometime°   *once*
      It was a worthy building. How, a page?
      Or° dead or sleeping on him? But dead rather,   *Either*
      For nature doth abhor to make his bed
360   With the defunct, or sleep upon the dead.
      Let's see the boy's face.
A ROMAN CAPTAIN   He's alive, my lord.
LUCIUS   He'll then instruct us of this body. Young one,
      Inform us of thy fortunes, for it seems
      They crave to be demanded. Who is this
365   Thou mak'st thy bloody pillow? Or who was he
      That, otherwise than noble nature did,⁵
      Hath altered that good picture? What's thy interest
      In this sad wreck?° How came't? Who is't?   *ruin*
      What art thou?
INNOGEN   I am nothing; or if not,
370   Nothing to be were better.⁶ This was my master,
      A very valiant Briton, and a good,
      That here by mountaineers lies slain. Alas,

————————————
4. According to your command.   6. It were better to be nothing.
5. Who, in a manner different from nature's workings.

There is no more such masters. I may wander
From east to occident, cry out for service,
375 Try many, all good; serve truly, never
Find such another master.
LUCIUS   'Lack,° good youth,   Alack
Thou mov'st no less with thy complaining than
Thy master in bleeding. Say his name, good friend.
INNOGEN Richard du Champ.⁷ [Aside] If I do lie and do
380 No harm by it, though the gods hear I hope
They'll pardon it. [Aloud] Say you, sir?
LUCIUS   Thy name?
INNOGEN   Fidele, sir.
LUCIUS Thou dost approve° thyself the very same.   show
Thy name well fits thy faith,° thy faith thy name.   fidelity
Wilt take thy chance with me? I will not say
385 Thou shalt be so well mastered, but be sure,
No less beloved. The Roman Emperor's letters
Sent by a consul to me should not sooner
Than thine own worth prefer° thee. Go with me.   recommend
INNOGEN I'll follow, sir. But first, an't° please the gods,   if it
390 I'll hide my master from the flies as deep
As these poor pickaxes° can dig; and when   (her hands)
With wild-wood leaves and weeds I ha' strewed his grave
And on it said a century of° prayers,   a hundred
Such as I can, twice o'er I'll weep and sigh,
395 And leaving so his service, follow you,
So please you entertain° me.   employ
LUCIUS   Ay, good youth,
And rather father thee than master thee. My friends,
The boy hath taught us manly duties. Let us
Find out the prettiest daisied plot we can,
400 And make him with our pikes and partisans⁸
A grave. Come, arm° him. Boy, he is preferred°   lift / recommended
By thee to us, and he shall be interred
As soldiers can. Be cheerful. Wipe thine eyes.
Some falls are means the happier to arise.⁹
                        Exeunt [with Cloten's body]

4.3
Enter CYMBELINE, LORDS, and PISANIO
CYMBELINE Again, and bring me word how 'tis with her.
                        Exit one or more
A fever with° the absence of her son,   on account of
A madness of which her life's in danger—heavens,
How deeply you at once do touch° me! Innogen,   afflict
5 The great part of my comfort, gone; my queen
Upon a desperate bed,° and in a time   Extremely ill in bed
When fearful wars point at me; her son gone,
So needful for this present!° It strikes me past   So needed now
The hope of comfort. [To PISANIO] But for thee, fellow,

---

7. This French name translates as "Richard of the Field," perhaps an allusion to a well-known London printer named Richard Field, who was born in Stratford-upon-Avon and printed Shakespeare's *Rape of Lucrece* and *Venus and Adonis* in the 1590s.

8. With our spears and our halberds (long-handled weapons with axlike blades).
9. Some falls are means by which good fortune arises.
4.3 Location: Cymbeline's court, Britain.

10   Who needs must know of her departure and
      Dost seem so ignorant, we'll enforce it from thee
      By a sharp torture.
PISANIO   Sir, my life is yours.
      I humbly set it at your will. But for my mistress,
      I nothing know° where she remains, why gone,   *know nothing about*
15   Nor when she purposes° return. Beseech° your highness,   *intends to / I beseech*
      Hold me° your loyal servant.   *Regard me as*
A LORD   Good my liege,
      The day that she was missing he was here.
      I dare be bound he's true, and shall perform
      All parts of his subjection° loyally. For Cloten,   *duty as a subject*
20   There wants° no diligence in seeking him,   *is lacking*
      And will° no doubt be found.   *he will*
CYMBELINE   The time is troublesome.°   *dire*
      [*To* PISANIO] We'll slip you° for a season, but our jealousy   *let you go*
      Does yet depend.[1]
A LORD   So please your majesty,
      The Roman legions, all from Gallia drawn,
25   Are landed on your coast with a supply
      Of Roman gentlemen by the senate sent.
CYMBELINE   Now for° the counsel of my son and queen!   *If only I now had*
      I am amazed° with matter.°   *overwhelmed / business*
A LORD   Good my liege,
      Your preparation can affront no less
30   Than what you hear of.[2] Come more, for more you're ready.
      The want° is but to put those powers in motion   *The only thing needed*
      That long to move.
CYMBELINE   I thank you. Let's withdraw,
      And meet the time as it seeks us. We fear not
      What can from Italy annoy° us, but   *harm*
35   We grieve at chances° here. Away.   *events*

               Exeunt [CYMBELINE *and* LORDS]

PISANIO   I heard no letter from my master since
      I wrote him Innogen was slain. 'Tis strange.
      Nor hear I from my mistress, who did promise
      To yield me often tidings. Neither know I
40   What is betid° to Cloten, but remain   *has happened*
      Perplexed in all. The heavens still must work.
      Wherein I am false I am honest; not true, to be true.
      These present wars shall find I love my country
      Even to the note° o'th' King, or I'll fall in them.   *notice*
45   All other doubts, by time let them be cleared:
      Fortune brings in some boats that are not steered.   *Exit*

                        4.4
      Enter BELARIUS, GUIDERIUS, *and* ARVIRAGUS
GUIDERIUS   The noise is round about us.
BELARIUS   Let us from it.
ARVIRAGUS   What pleasure, sir, find we in life to lock it°   *shut it off*
      From action and adventure?
GUIDERIUS   Nay, what hope

---

1. *but . . . depend*: but our suspicions still hold.   have heard of.
2. *Your . . . of*: Your forces can confront all those you   4.4 Location: Before the cave of Belarius, Wales.

Have we in hiding us? This way° the Romans By this course of action
5 Must or° for Britains slay us, or receive us either
For barbarous and unnatural revolts° rebels
During their use,[1] and slay us after.

BELARIUS Sons,
We'll higher to the mountains; there secure us.
To the King's party there's no going. Newness
10 Of Cloten's death—we being not known, not mustered
Among the bands°—may drive us to a render° troops / an account
Where we have lived, and so extort from 's that
Which we have done, whose answer would be death
Drawn on° with torture. Prolonged

GUIDERIUS This is, sir, a doubt
15 In such a time nothing becoming you
Nor satisfying us.

ARVIRAGUS It is not likely
That when they hear the Roman horses neigh,
Behold their quartered files,° have both their eyes orderly troops
And ears so cloyed importantly[2] as now,
20 That they will waste their time upon our note,° in observing us
To know from whence we are.

BELARIUS O, I am known
Of° many in the army. Many years, By
Though Cloten then° but young, you see, not wore° him was then / did not wear
From my remembrance. And besides, the King
25 Hath not deserved my service nor your loves,
Who find in my exile the want of breeding,
The certainty of this hard life;[3] aye hopeless
To have the courtesy your cradle promised,[4]
But to be still° hot summer's tanlings,[5] and always
The shrinking slaves of winter.

30 **GUIDERIUS** Than be so,
Better to cease to be. Pray, sir, to th'army.
I and my brother are not known; yourself
So out of thought, and thereto° so o'ergrown,[6] in addition
Cannot be questioned.

ARVIRAGUS By this sun that shines,
35 I'll thither. What thing is't[7] that I never
Did see man die, scarce ever looked on blood
But that of coward hares, hot° goats, and venison, lecherous
Never bestrid a horse save one that had
A rider like myself, who ne'er wore rowel[8]
40 Nor iron on his heel! I am ashamed
To look upon the holy sun, to have
The benefit of his blest beams, remaining
So long a poor unknown.

GUIDERIUS By heavens, I'll go.
If you will bless me, sir, and give me leave,
45 I'll take the better care;° but if you will not, be the more careful

---

1. While they have need of us.
2. So completely taken up with important matters.
3. *Who . . . life*: (You) who experience as a result of my exile a lack of proper education, the enduring fact of this hard life.
4. *aye . . . promised*: yes, without hope to have the cultivated existence your noble birth promised.

5. People exposed to the sun. In England at this time, tanned skin denoted low social status.
6. So overgrown with hair or beard; so grown in years; so grown out of memory.
7. What a bad state of affairs it is.
8. Small rotating disk at the end of a spur. Wearing spurs was the privilege of gentlemen.

The hazard therefore due[9] fall on me by
The hands of Romans.

ARVIRAGUS   So say I, amen.

BELARIUS   No reason I, since of your lives you set
So slight a valuation, should reserve
50   My cracked° one to more care. Have with you,° boys!   *weakened / Come then*
If in your country° wars you chance to die,   *country's*
That is my bed, too, lads, and there I'll lie.
Lead, lead. [*Aside*] The time seems long. Their blood thinks scorn°   *disdains itself*
Till it fly out and show them princes born.   *Exeunt*

5.1

Enter POSTHUMUS [*dressed as an Italian*
gentleman, carrying a bloody cloth]

POSTHUMUS   Yea, bloody cloth, I'll keep thee, for I once wished
Thou shouldst be coloured thus. You married ones,
If each of you should take this course, how many
Must murder wives much better than themselves
5   For wrying° but a little! O Pisanio,   *erring*
Every good servant does not all commands,
No bond but° to do just ones. Gods, if you   *No obligation except*
Should have ta'en vengeance on my faults, I never
Had lived to put on this;° so had you saved   *to undertake this deed*
10   The noble Innogen to repent, and struck
Me, wretch, more worth your vengeance. But alack,
You snatch some hence for little faults; that's love,
To have them fall no more.[1] You some permit
To second° ills with ills, each elder° worse,   *reinforce / later fault*
15   And make them dread ill, to the doer's thrift.[2]
But Innogen is your own. Do your blest wills,
And make me blest to obey. I am brought hither
Among th'Italian gentry, and to fight
Against my lady's kingdom. 'Tis enough
20   That, Britain, I have killed thy mistress-piece;[3]
I'll give no wound to thee. Therefore, good heavens,
Hear patiently my purpose. I'll disrobe me
Of these Italian weeds, and suit° myself   *dress*
As does a Briton peasant.

[*He disrobes himself*]

So I'll fight
25   Against the part° I come with; so I'll die   *side*
For thee, O Innogen, even for whom my life
Is every breath a death; and, thus unknown,
Pitied° nor hated, to the face of peril   *Neither pitied*
Myself I'll dedicate. Let me make men know
30   More valour in me than my habits° show.   *garments*
Gods, put the strength o'th' Leonati in me.
To shame the guise° o'th' world, I will begin   *customs; dress*
The fashion—less without and more within.   *Exit*

---

9. May the danger due to me (as a result of my disobedience).
5.1 Location: The Roman camp, Britain.
1. *that's . . . more:* that is a sign of love, to have them no
longer sin.
2. And make them fear punishment, to their own benefit.
3. Punning on "masterpiece." Most editions, following

F, read: "'Tis enough / That, Britain, I have killed thy
mistress; peace." "Mistress-piece," which can be found
in other texts from the period, suggests the extraordinary excellence of Innogen. "Piece" could be spelled
"peace" in the early modern period, and the unfamiliar
compound might have been misread by the person setting type for the play.

5.2

[A march.] Enter LUCIUS, GIACOMO, *and the Roman*
army at one door, and the Briton army at another, Leo-
natus POSTHUMUS *following like a poor soldier. They*
march over and go out. [Alarums.] Then enter again in
skirmish GIACOMO *and* POSTHUMUS: *he vanquisheth and*
disarmeth GIACOMO, *and then leaves him*

GIACOMO   The heaviness and guilt within my bosom
　Takes off° my manhood. I have belied° a lady,　　　　　　*Destroys / slandered*
　The princess of this country, and the air on't°　　　　　　　　　　*of it*
　Revengingly enfeebles me; or° could this carl,°　　　*otherwise / peasant*
5　A very drudge° of nature's, have subdued me　　　　　　　　　　　*slave*
　In my profession? Knighthoods and honours borne
　As I wear mine are titles but° of scorn.　　　　　　　　　　　　*merely*
　If that thy gentry, Britain, go before°　　　　　　　　　　　　*surpass*
　This lout as he exceeds our lords, the odds
10　Is that we scarce are men and you are gods.　　　　*Exit*

5.3[1]

The battle continues. [Alarums. Excursions. The trum-
pets sound a retreat.] The Britons fly, CYMBELINE *is*
taken. Then enter to his rescue BELARIUS, GUIDERIUS,
and ARVIRAGUS

BELARIUS   Stand, stand, we have th'advantage of the ground.
　The lane is guarded. Nothing routs us but
　The villainy of our fears.
GUIDERIUS *and* ARVIRAGUS   Stand, stand, and fight.
　Enter POSTHUMUS [*like a poor soldier*], *and seconds the*
　Britons. They rescue CYMBELINE *and exeunt*

5.4

[The trumpets sound a retreat,] then enter LUCIUS, GIA-
COMO, *and* INNOGEN

LUCIUS [*to* INNOGEN]   Away, boy, from the troops, and save thyself;
　For friends kill friends, and the disorder's such
　As war were hoodwinked.[1]
GIACOMO　　　　　　　　　　　'Tis their fresh supplies.
LUCIUS   It is a day turned strangely. Or betimes
5　Let's reinforce, or fly.[2]　　　　　　　　　　　　*Exeunt*

5.5

Enter POSTHUMUS [*like a poor soldier*], *and a Briton*
　LORD

LORD   Cam'st thou from where they made the stand?
POSTHUMUS　　　　　　　　　　　　　　　　　I did,
　Though you, it seems, come from the fliers.
LORD　　　　　　　　　　　　　　　　　　　Ay.
POSTHUMUS   No blame be to you, sir, for all was lost,
　But° that the heavens fought. The King himself　　　*Had it not been*

5.2 Location: A field between the British and Roman
camps, Britain.
5.3 Location: Scene continues.
1. In F and most modern editions, there is no new
scene marked here or at 5.4, since 5.2, 5.3, and 5.4
form one continuous battle sequence. However, the
stage is temporarily cleared where the Oxford editors

have marked 5.3 and 5.4, and a cleared stage is the
usual signal of a new scene on the Renaissance stage.
5.4 Location: Scene continues.
1. As if war were blindfolded.
2. *Or betimes . . . fly:* Let us either promptly reinforce
our troops or flee.
5.5 Location: Scene continues.

5   Of his wings destitute,[1] the army broken,
And but° the backs of Britons seen, all flying   *only*
Through a strait° lane; the enemy full-hearted,°   *narrow / bold*
Lolling the tongue with slaught'ring,[2] having work
More plentiful than tools to do't, struck down
10   Some mortally, some slightly touched,° some falling   *wounded*
Merely through fear, that the strait pass was dammed°   *clogged*
With dead men hurt behind,[3] and cowards living
To die with lengthened shame.[4]

LORD   Where was this lane?

POSTHUMUS   Close by the battle, ditched, and walled with turf;
15   Which gave advantage to an ancient soldier,
An honest one, I warrant, who deserved
So long a breeding as his white beard came to,[5]
In doing this for 's country. Athwart° the lane   *Across*
He with two striplings—lads more like° to run   *likely*
20   The country base[6] than to commit such slaughter;
With faces fit for masks,[7] or rather fairer
Than those for preservation cased, or shame[8]—
Made good° the passage, cried to those that fled   *Secured*
'Our Britain's harts die flying, not her men.
25   To darkness fleet° souls that fly backwards. Stand,   *rush*
Or we are Romans,[9] and will give you that°   *(death)*
Like beasts which you shun beastly,° and may save   *in cowardly fashion*
But to look back in frown.[1] Stand, stand.' These three,
Three thousand confident,[2] in act as many—
30   For three performers are the file° when all   *entire force*
The rest do nothing—with this word 'Stand, stand',
Accommodated° by the place, more charming[3]   *Assisted*
With their own nobleness, which could have turned
A distaff to a lance,[4] gilded° pale looks;   *brought color to*
35   Part shame, part spirit renewed,[5] that some, turned coward
But by example[6]—O, a sin in war,
Damned in the first beginners![7]—gan° to look   *began*
The way that they° did and to grin[8] like lions   *(the three)*
Upon the pikes o'th' hunters. Then began
40   A stop° i'th' chaser, a retire. Anon°   *halt / Soon*
A rout, confusion thick; forthwith they fly
Chickens the way which they stooped eagles;[9] slaves,
The strides they victors made;[1] and now our cowards,
Like fragments° in hard voyages, became   *scraps of food*

---

1. Deprived of his wings (that is, the troops to either side of the main division of the army).
2. With their tongues hanging out either from the labor of slaughter or from eagerness to commit the slaughter.
3. Hurt on their backs (as they were fleeing).
4. To die later after a life of prolonged shame.
5. *who . . . to:* who deserved to live so long again as his white beard indicated he had already lived.
6. *to run . . . base:* to play a children's game (prisoner's house) that involves running between two bases.
7. Gentlewomen wore masks to protect their complexions from the elements.
8. *fairer . . . shame:* more delicate than those covered with masks for protection ("preservation") or out of modesty.
9. Or we will behave like Romans.
1. *and may . . . frown:* and may prevent only by turning back upon the enemy with threatening face.
2. As confident as if they were three thousand.
3. *more charming:* casting a spell on others.
4. *could . . . lance:* that is, could have made women fight. The distaff, an instrument used in spinning wool, was a proverbial symbol of womanhood.
5. Shame inspired some, courage others.
6. Because of the example set by others.
7. In those who first set the example (of cowardly behavior).
8. To bare their teeth.
9. *forthwith . . . eagles:* straightway they (the Romans) fled like chickens along the passage down which they had just swooped like eagles.
1. *slaves . . . made:* like slaves, they retrace the steps they had made as victors.

45 The life o'th' need.[2] Having found the back door open
Of the unguarded hearts,[3] heavens, how they wound!
Some slain before,[4] some dying, some their friends
O'erborne° i'th' former wave, ten chased by one,   *Overwhelmed*
Are now each one the slaughterman of twenty.
50 Those that would die or ere° resist are grown   *before they would*
The mortal bugs° o'th' field.   *deadly terrors*
LORD   This was strange chance:
A narrow lane, an old man, and two boys.
POSTHUMUS   Nay, do not wonder at it. Yet you are made
55 Rather to wonder at the things you hear
Than to work° any. Will you rhyme upon't,   *perform*
And vent it[5] for a mock'ry? Here is one:
'Two boys, an old man twice a boy,° a lane,   *in his second childhood*
Preserved the Britons, was the Romans' bane.'
LORD   Nay, be not angry, sir.
POSTHUMUS   'Lack,° to what end?   *Alas*
60 Who dares not stand° his foe, I'll be his friend,   *confront*
For if he'll do as he is made° to do,   *inclined*
I know he'll quickly fly my friendship too.
You have put° me into rhyme.   *forced*
LORD   Farewell; you're angry.   *Exit*
POSTHUMUS   Still going?° This a lord? O noble misery,[6]   *Still running away*
65 To be i'th' field and ask 'What news?' of me!
Today how many would have given their honours
To have saved their carcasses—took heel to do't,
And yet died too!° I, in mine own woe charmed,[7]   *anyway*
Could not find death where I did hear him groan,
70 Nor feel him where he struck. Being an ugly monster,
'Tis strange he hides him in fresh cups, soft beds,
Sweet words, or hath more ministers° than we   *other agents*
That draw his knives i'th' war. Well, I will find him;
For being now a favourer to the Briton,[8]
75 No more° a Briton, I have resumed again   *I am no more*
The part° I came in. Fight I will no more,   *role*
But yield me to the veriest hind° that shall   *peasant*
Once touch my shoulder.° Great the slaughter is   *try to arrest me*
Here made by th' Roman; great the answer be°   *great the retaliation*
80 Britons must take. For me, my ransom's death,
On either side I come to spend my breath,°   *give up my life*
Which neither here I'll keep nor bear° again,   *carry away*
But end it by some means for Innogen.
          Enter two [Briton] CAPTAINS, *and soldiers*
FIRST CAPTAIN   Great Jupiter be praised, Lucius is taken.
85 'Tis thought the old man and his sons were angels.
SECOND CAPTAIN   There was a fourth man, in a seely habit,°   *rustic garments*
That gave th'affront with them.
FIRST CAPTAIN   So 'tis reported,
But none of 'em can be found. Stand, who's there?
POSTHUMUS   A Roman,

---

2. Vital in the time of crisis.
3. *Having . . . hearts:* Having found unprotected the weak spot of these undefended souls (that is, the Romans).
4. Some that earlier were as good as dead.

5. And circulate ("vent") your rhymes.
6. What noble wretchedness.
7. In my despair preserved, as if by a charm.
8. Since death is now looking kindly upon Britons.

90   Who had not now been drooping here if seconds°   *supporters*
                Had answered him.°   *followed him*

SECOND CAPTAIN [*to soldiers*] Lay hands on him, a dog!
                A leg of Rome shall not return to tell
                What crows have pecked them here. He brags his service
                As if he were of note.° Bring him to th' King.   *high rank*

                [*Flourish.*] *Enter* CYMBELINE [*and his train*], BELARIUS,
                GUIDERIUS, ARVIRAGUS, PISANIO, *and Roman captives.*
                The CAPTAINS *present* POSTHUMUS *to* CYMBELINE, *who*
                delivers him over to a JAILER. [*Exeunt all but* POSTHU-
                MUS *and two* JAILERS *who lock gyves*° *on his legs*][9]   *fetters*

95   FIRST JAILER You shall not now be stol'n. You have locks upon you,
                So graze as you find pasture.

SECOND JAILER   Ay, or a stomach.   [*Exeunt* JAILERS.]

POSTHUMUS   Most welcome, bondage, for thou art a way,
                I think, to liberty. Yet am I better
                Than one that's sick o'th' gout, since he had rather
100   Groan so in perpetuity than be cured
                By th' sure physician, death, who is the key
                T'unbar these locks. My conscience, thou art fettered
                More than my shanks° and wrists. You good gods give me   *legs*
                The penitent instrument to pick that bolt,
105   Then free for ever.[1] Is't enough I am sorry?
                So children temporal fathers do appease;
                Gods are more full of mercy. Must I repent,
                I cannot do it better than in gyves
                Desired more than constrained.° To satisfy,°   *forced (upon me)* / *atone*
110   If of my freedom 'tis the main part,[2] take
                No stricter render° of me than my all.   *repayment*
                I know you are more clement° than vile men   *merciful*
                Who of their broken° debtors take a third,   *bankrupt*
                A sixth, a tenth, letting them thrive again
115   On their abatement.° That's not my desire.   *reduced amount*
                For Innogen's dear life take mine, and though
                'Tis not so dear,° yet 'tis a life; you coined it.   *valuable*
                'Tween man and man they weigh not every stamp;
                Though light, take pieces for the figure's sake;[3]
120   You rather mine, being yours.[4] And so, great powers,
                If you will make this audit,° take this life,   *settle this account*
                And cancel these cold bonds.[5] O Innogen,
                I'll speak to thee in silence!

---

9. F and most modern editions mark a new scene here. Confusion arises because in F, no exit is marked for any character after Posthumus is handed over to a Jailer. Either everyone exits and Posthumus then reenters with two Jailers, indicating a new scene, or, as here, Posthumus and Jailers stay onstage continuously. The latter option means that Posthumus is fettered in the open fields, giving new point to the First Jailer's injunction to "graze as you find pasture" (5.5.96). Usually, Posthumus is assumed to be fettered inside a British prison.
1. *The . . . ever:* Give me penitence, the instrument to pick that lock (the lock on his conscience, which is fettered by guilt). Then (I am) free forever; then free me

(by death).
2. If it is the most important element in freeing me from guilt.
3. *'Tween . . . sake:* In business dealings between men, they do not weigh every coin ("stamp"). Even though some coins are deficient in weight ("light"), they accept them because of the image (of the King) stamped on them.
4. You should be more inclined to accept my coin (me), since your image is stamped on me. This line refers to the Christian belief that humans are made in the image of God.
5. These old legal agreements; these cruel links with life; these harsh fetters.

[*He sleeps.*] *Solemn music. Enter, as in an apparition,*
SICILIUS *Leonatus (father to Posthumus, an old man),*
attired like a warrior, leading in his hand an ancient
matron, his wife, and MOTHER *to Posthumus, with music*
before them. Then, after other music, follows the two
young Leonati, BROTHERS *to Posthumus, with wounds as*
they died in the wars. They circle POSTHUMUS *round as*
he lies sleeping

SICILIUS   No more, thou thunder-master,[6] show
125   Thy spite on mortal flies.°   *frail creatures*
        With Mars° fall out, with Juno° chide,   *god of war / Jove's wife*
        That° thy adulteries   *Who*
        Rates° and revenges.   *Berates*
        Hath my poor boy done aught but well,
130   Whose face I never saw?
        I died whilst in the womb he stayed,
        Attending nature's law,[7]
        Whose father then—as men report
        Thou orphans' father art—
135   Thou shouldst have been, and shielded him
        From this earth-vexing smart.[8]
MOTHER   Lucina° lent not me her aid,   *goddess of childbirth*
        But took me in my throes,
        That from me was Posthumus ripped,
140   Came crying 'mongst his foes,
        A thing of pity.
SICILIUS   Great nature like his ancestry
        Moulded the stuff° so fair   *substance*
        That he deserved the praise o'th' world
145   As great Sicilius' heir.
FIRST BROTHER   When once he was mature for man,°   *had matured into manhood*
        In Britain where was he
        That could stand up his parallel,
        Or fruitful° object be   *life-giving*
150   In eye of Innogen, that best
        Could deem° his dignity?°   *judge / worth*
MOTHER   With marriage wherefore° was he mocked,   *why*
        To be exiled, and thrown
        From Leonati seat and cast
155   From her his dearest one,
        Sweet Innogen?
SICILIUS   Why did you suffer Giacomo,
        Slight° thing of Italy,   *Worthless*
        To taint his nobler heart and brain
160   With needless jealousy,
        And to become the geck° and scorn   *dupe*
        O'th' other's villainy?
SECOND BROTHER   For this from stiller seats[9] we come,
        Our parents and us twain,
165   That striking in our country's cause
        Fell bravely and were slain,

6. Jupiter, or Jove, the king of the gods, often made himself known to humans through thunder and lightning.
7. Awaiting the decree of nature (for his birth).
8. From this suffering that afflicts all humans.
9. From calmer regions (alluding to the Elysian Fields—in classical mythology the abode of the blessed after death).

Our fealty and Tenantius'° right   *(Cymbeline's father)*
With honour to maintain.

FIRST BROTHER   Like hardiment° Posthumus hath   *Similar bold deeds*
170   To Cymbeline performed.
Then, Jupiter, thou king of gods,
Why hast thou thus adjourned°   *deferred*
The graces for his merits due,
Being all to dolours° turned?   *sorrows*

175 SICILIUS   Thy crystal window ope;° look out;   *open*
No longer exercise
Upon a valiant race thy harsh
And potent injuries.

MOTHER   Since, Jupiter, our son is good,
180   Take off his miseries.

SICILIUS   Peep through thy marble mansion. Help,
Or we poor ghosts will cry
To th' shining synod° of the rest°   *assembly / rest of the gods*
Against thy deity.°   *godhead*

185 BROTHERS   Help, Jupiter, or we appeal,
And from thy justice fly.

JUPITER *descends in thunder and lightning, sitting upon*
an eagle. He throws a thunderbolt. The ghosts fall on
their knees

JUPITER   No more, you petty spirits of region low,
Offend our hearing. Hush! How dare you ghosts
Accuse the thunderer, whose bolt, you know,
190   Sky-planted,° batters all rebelling coasts?   *Rooted in the heavens*
Poor shadows of Elysium, hence, and rest
Upon your never-withering banks of flowers.
Be not with mortal accidents° oppressed;   *events*
No care of yours it is; you know 'tis ours.
195   Whom best I love, I cross,° to make my gift,   *thwart*
The more delayed, delighted.° Be content.   *the more pleasing*
Your low-laid son our godhead will uplift.
His comforts thrive, his trials well are spent.°   *ended*
Our Jovial star° reigned at his birth, and in   *The planet Jupiter*
200   Our temple was he married. Rise, and fade.
He shall be lord of Lady Innogen,
And happier much by his affliction made.
This tablet lay upon his breast, wherein
Our pleasure his full fortune doth confine.[1]
  [*He gives the ghosts a tablet which they lay upon Posthu-*
   mus' breast]
205 And so away. No farther with your din
Express impatience, lest you stir up mine.
Mount, eagle, to my palace crystalline.   [*He*] *ascends* [*into the heavens*]

SICILIUS   He came in thunder. His celestial breath
Was sulphurous to smell.[2] The holy eagle
210   Stooped, as to foot us.[3] His ascension is
More sweet than our blest fields. His royal bird

---

1. *wherein . . . confine:* wherein it is our pleasure his great fortune precisely to set forth.
2. Sulfur was popularly associated with thunder and lightning. As a constituent of gunpowder, its smell may have been detectable in the theater when gunpowder was used.
3. Swooped as if to seize us in its talons.

Preens the immortal wing and claws his beak
As when his god is pleased.

ALL THE GHOSTS   Thanks, Jupiter.

SICILIUS   The marble pavement[4] closes, he is entered
215   His radiant roof. Away, and, to be blest,
Let us with care perform his great behest.   *[The ghosts] vanish*

     [POSTHUMUS *awakes*]

POSTHUMUS   Sleep, thou hast been a grandsire, and begot
A father to me; and thou hast created
A mother and two brothers. But, O scorn,°   *bitter mockery*
220   Gone! They went hence so soon as they were born,
And so I am awake. Poor wretches that depend
On greatness' favour dream as I have done,
Wake and find nothing. But, alas, I swerve.°   *go astray*
Many dream not to find, neither deserve,
225   And yet are steeped in favours; so am I,
That have this golden chance and know not why.
What fairies haunt this ground? A book? O rare one,
Be not, as is our fangled world,[5] a garment
Nobler than that it covers. Let thy effects
230   So follow to° be most unlike our courtiers,   *that they*
As good as promise.

     [He] reads

'Whenas° a lion's whelp shall, to himself unknown, without   *When*
seeking find, and be embraced by a piece of tender air; and
when from a stately cedar shall be lopped branches which,
235   being dead many years, shall after revive, be jointed to the old
stock, and freshly grow; then shall Posthumus end his miseries,
Britain be fortunate and flourish in peace and plenty.'
'Tis still a dream, or else such stuff as madmen
Tongue,° and brain° not; either both, or nothing,   *Speak / understand*
240   Or senseless speaking,° or a speaking such   *Either meaningless speech*
As sense° cannot untie. Be what it is,   *reason*
The action of my life is like it, which I'll keep,
If but for sympathy.[6]

     Enter JAILER

JAILER   Come, sir, are you ready for death?
245 POSTHUMUS   Over-roasted rather; ready long ago.

JAILER   Hanging[7] is the word, sir. If you be ready for that, you
are well cooked.

POSTHUMUS   So, if I prove a good repast to the spectators, the
dish pays the shot.[8]

250 JAILER   A heavy reckoning for you, sir. But the comfort is, you
shall be called to no more payments, fear no more tavern bills,
which are as often the sadness of parting as the procuring of
mirth. You come in faint for want of meat, depart reeling with
too much drink, sorry that you have paid too much and sorry
255 that you are paid too much;[9] purse and brain both empty: the
brain the heavier for being too light,° the purse too light, being   *foolish*

---

4. Referring to the closing of the trapdoor in the ceiling above the stage, which represents the floor ("pavement") of the heavens.
5. Our world so obsessed with fashions.
6. If only because of the similarity.

7. Death by hanging, with a pun on "hanging" as referring to the practice of hanging up raw meat before cooking.
8. The food pays the reckoning; I am worth what it costs to hang me.
9. Subdued by too much drink.

drawn of heaviness.[1] Of this contradiction you shall now be
quit. O, the charity of a penny cord! It sums up thousands in a
trice.° You have no true debitor and creditor[2] but it: of what's   *an instant*
past, is, and to come the discharge.° Your neck, sir, is pen,   *release from debt*
book, and counters;[3] so the acquittance° follows.   *deliverance*

POSTHUMUS I am merrier to die than thou art to live.

JAILER Indeed, sir, he that sleeps feels not the toothache; but a
man that were to° sleep your sleep, and a hangman to help him   *were about to*
to bed, I think he would change places with his officer;° for   *(the hangman)*
look you, sir, you know not which way you shall go.

POSTHUMUS Yes, indeed do I, fellow.

JAILER Your death has eyes in 's head, then. I have not seen him
so pictured.[4] You must either be directed by some that take
upon them° to know, or take upon yourself that which I am   *some who profess*
sure you do not know, or jump° the after-enquiry on your own   *risk*
peril; and how you shall speed° in your journey's end I think   *succeed*
you'll never return to tell on.°   *of*

POSTHUMUS I tell thee, fellow, there are none want° eyes to   *lacking*
direct them the way I am going but such as wink° and will not   *shut their eyes*
use them.

JAILER What an infinite mock is this, that a man should have
the best use of eyes to see the way of blindness!° I am sure   *the way to death*
hanging's the way of winking.

Enter a MESSENGER

MESSENGER Knock off his manacles, bring your prisoner to the
King.

POSTHUMUS Thou bring'st good news, I am called to be made
free.[5]

JAILER I'll be hanged then.

POSTHUMUS Thou shalt be then freer than a jailer; no bolts for
the dead.[6]

JAILER [*aside*] Unless a man would marry a gallows and beget
young gibbets, I never saw one so prone.° Yet, on my con-   *eager*
science, there are verier knaves desire to live, for all° he be a   *even though*
Roman; and there be some of them, too, that die against their
wills; so should I if I were one. I would we were all of one
mind, and one mind good. O, there were desolation° of jailers   *the ruin*
and gallowses! I speak against my present profit, but my wish
hath a preferment[7] in't.   *Exeunt*

5.6

[*Flourish.*] *Enter* CYMBELINE, BELARIUS, GUIDERIUS,
ARVIRAGUS, PISANIO, *and lords*

CYMBELINE [*to* BELARIUS, GUIDERIUS, *and* ARVIRAGUS] Stand by
my side, you whom the gods have made
Preservers of my throne. Woe is my heart

---

1. Being emptied of the money that makes it heavy.
2. Account book.
3. Metal tokens used for making calculations.
4. So depicted (referring to visual representations of
death as a skeleton or skull with no eyes).
5. Posthumus means "set free by death." The Jailer
thinks he means "set free from prison."
6. Most editions, following F2, have everyone leave the
stage here except the Jailer. However, the Jailer himself

has been ordered to bring the prisoner to the King,
which would mean that he must not be separated from
Posthumus. Rather than being a monologue, the ensuing speech may be largely spoken in asides to the audience as the Jailer unlocks Posthumus's fetters and
prepares to take him to Cymbeline.
7. Had a promotion in it (implying that a world without
the need for jailers could offer him better employment).
5.6 Location: The camp of Cymbeline, Britain.

That the poor soldier that so richly fought,
Whose rags shamed gilded arms, whose naked breast
5   Stepped before targs of proof,[1] cannot be found.
He shall be happy that can find him, if
Our grace can make him so.
BELARIUS   I never saw
Such noble fury in so poor a thing,
Such precious deeds in one that promised naught
But beggary and poor looks.
10 CYMBELINE   No tidings of him?
PISANIO   He hath been searched° among the dead and living,   sought
But no trace of him.
CYMBELINE   To my grief I am
The heir of his reward, which I will add
[*To* BELARIUS, GUIDERIUS, *and* ARVIRAGUS] To you, the liver,
heart, and brain of Britain,
15 By whom I grant she lives. 'Tis now the time
To ask of whence you are. Report it.
BELARIUS   Sir,
In Cambria° are we born, and gentlemen.   Wales
Further to boast were neither true nor modest,
Unless I add we are honest.
CYMBELINE   Bow your knees.
[*They kneel. He knights them*]
20 Arise, my knights o'th' battle.[2] I create you
Companions to our person, and will fit° you   supply
With dignities becoming your estates.°   (new) rank
[BELARIUS, GUIDERIUS, *and* ARVIRAGUS *rise.*]
Enter CORNELIUS *and* LADIES
There's business in these faces. Why so sadly
Greet you our victory? You look like Romans,
And not o'th' court of Britain.
25 CORNELIUS   Hail, great King!
To sour your happiness I must report
The Queen is dead.
CYMBELINE   Who worse than a physician
Would this report become? But I consider
By medicine life may be prolonged, yet death
30 Will seize the doctor too. How ended she?
CORNELIUS   With horror, madly dying, like her life,
Which being cruel to the world, concluded
Most cruel to herself. What she confessed
I will report, so please you. These her women
35 Can trip me° if I err, who with wet cheeks   point out my mistakes
Were present when she finished.
CYMBELINE   Prithee, say.
CORNELIUS   First, she confessed she never loved you, only
Affected° greatness got by you, not you;   Desired
Married your royalty, was wife to your place,°   position
Abhorred your person.
40 CYMBELINE   She alone knew this,
And but° she spoke it dying, I would not   except that

1. *targs of proof:* shields whose strength had been tested.
2. A special group of knights who won their titles for extraordinary bravery on the battlefield.

Believe her lips in opening it. Proceed.

CORNELIUS   Your daughter, whom she bore in hand° to love   *she pretended*
    With such integrity, she did confess
45 Was as a scorpion to her sight, whose life,
    But that her flight prevented it, she had
    Ta'en off° by poison.   *Ended*

CYMBELINE   O most delicate° fiend!   *subtle*
    Who is't can read a woman? Is there more?

CORNELIUS   More, sir, and worse. She did confess she had
50 For you a mortal mineral° which, being took,   *a deadly poison*
    Should by the minute feed on life, and, ling'ring,
    By inches waste you. In which time she purposed
    By watching,° weeping, tendance,³ kissing, to   *staying awake*
    O'ercome you with her show;° and in fine,°   *performance / finally*
55 When she had fit you with° her craft, to work   *shaped you by*
    Her son into th'adoption of the crown;⁴
    But failing of her end by his strange absence,
    Grew shameless-desperate, opened° in despite   *revealed*
    Of heaven and men her purposes, repented
60 The evils she hatched were not effected; so
    Despairing died.

CYMBELINE   Heard you all this, her women?

LADIES   We did, so please your highness.

CYMBELINE   Mine eyes
    Were not in fault, for she was beautiful;
    Mine ears that heard her flattery, nor my heart
65 That thought her like her seeming.° It had been vicious°   *appearance / wrong*
    To have mistrusted her. Yet, O my daughter,
    That it was folly in me thou mayst say,
    And prove it in thy feeling.⁵ Heaven mend all!

Enter LUCIUS, GIACOMO, SOOTHSAYER, *and other Roman*
prisoners, POSTHUMUS *behind, and* INNOGEN [*dressed as*
a man, all guarded by Briton soldiers]

    Thou com'st not, Caius, now for tribute. That
70 The Britons have razed out,° though with the loss   *erased*
    Of many a bold one; whose kinsmen have made suit
    That their good souls° may be appeased with slaughter   *(of the dead Britons)*
    Of you, their captives, which ourself have granted.
    So think of your estate.°   *condition*
75 LUCIUS   Consider, sir, the chance of war. The day
    Was yours by accident. Had it gone with us,
    We should not, when the blood was cool, have threatened
    Our prisoners with the sword. But since the gods
    Will have it thus, that nothing but our lives
80 May be called ransom, let it come. Sufficeth
    A Roman with a Roman's heart can suffer.
    Augustus lives to think on't;⁶ and so much
    For my peculiar care.° This one thing only   *concern for myself*
    I will entreat:

        [*He presents* INNOGEN *to* CYMBELINE]
        my boy, a Briton born,

---

3. Showing attention to you.
4. *to work . . . crown:* to work her son into the position
of heir to the crown.

5. And find it true by your experience.
6. Augustus lives and can consider what to do.

85 Let him be ransomed. Never master had
A page so kind, so duteous, diligent,
So tender over his occasions,° true,   *thoughtful of his needs*
So feat,° so nurse-like; let his virtue join   *graceful*
With my request, which I'll make bold your highness
90 Cannot deny. He hath done no Briton harm,
Though he have served a Roman. Save him, sir,
And spare no blood beside.°   *no one else*
CYMBELINE   I have surely seen him.
His favour° is familiar to me. Boy,   *face*
Thou hast looked thyself into my grace,[7]
95 And art mine own. I know not why, wherefore,
To say 'Live, boy'. Ne'er thank thy master. Live,
And ask of Cymbeline what boon° thou wilt   *reward*
Fitting my bounty and thy state,° I'll give it,   *rank*
Yea, though thou do demand a prisoner
The noblest ta'en.
100 INNOGEN   I humbly thank your highness.
LUCIUS   I do not bid thee beg my life, good lad,
And yet I know thou wilt.
INNOGEN   No, no. Alack,
There's other work in hand. I see a thing[8]
Bitter to me as death. Your life, good master,
Must shuffle° for itself.   *shift*
105 LUCIUS   The boy disdains me.
He leaves me, scorns me. Briefly die their joys
That place them on the truth of girls and boys.[9]
Why stands he so perplexed?
CYMBELINE [*to* INNOGEN]   What wouldst thou, boy?
I love thee more and more; think more and more
110 What's best to ask. Know'st him thou look'st on? Speak,
Wilt have him live? Is he thy kin, thy friend?
INNOGEN   He is a Roman, no more kin to me
Than I to your highness, who, being born your vassal,
Am something nearer.
CYMBELINE   Wherefore ey'st him so?
115 INNOGEN   I'll tell you, sir, in private, if you please
To give me hearing.
CYMBELINE   Ay, with all my heart,
And lend my best attention. What's thy name?
INNOGEN   Fidele, sir.
CYMBELINE   Thou'rt my good youth, my page.
I'll be thy master. Walk with me, speak freely.
      [CYMBELINE *and* INNOGEN *speak apart*]
BELARIUS [*aside to* GUIDERIUS *and* ARVIRAGUS]   Is not this boy
   revived from death?
120 ARVIRAGUS   One sand° another   *One grain of sand*
Not more resembles that° sweet rosy lad   *than he resembles that*
Who died, and was Fidele. What think you?
GUIDERIUS   The same dead thing alive.
BELARIUS   Peace, peace, see further. He eyes us not. Forbear.

---

7. You have by your appearance gained my favor.
8. Referring to the ring that she gave to Posthumus and
that is now on Giacomo's finger.

9. *Briefly . . . boys:* Quickly dies the happiness of those
who depend on the fidelity of girls and boys.

125   Creatures may be alike. Were't he, I am sure
      He would have spoke to us.

GUIDERIUS   But we see° him dead.   *saw*

BELARIUS   Be silent; let's see further.

PISANIO [*aside*]   It is my mistress.
      Since she is living, let the time run on
      To good or bad.

CYMBELINE [*to* INNOGEN]   Come, stand thou by our side,

130   Make thy demand aloud. [*To* GIACOMO]   Sir, step you forth.
      Give answer to this boy, and do it freely,
      Or, by our greatness and the grace of it,
      Which is our honour, bitter torture shall
      Winnow° the truth from falsehood.   *Separate*
      [*To* INNOGEN]   On, speak to him.

135 INNOGEN   My boon is that this gentleman may render°   *declare*
      Of whom he had this ring.

POSTHUMUS [*aside*]   What's that to him?

CYMBELINE [*to* GIACOMO]   That diamond upon your finger, say,
      How came it yours?

GIACOMO   Thou'lt torture me to leave° unspoken that   *for leaving*
      Which to be spoke would torture thee.

140 CYMBELINE   How, me?

GIACOMO   I am glad to be constrained to utter that°   *what*
      Torments me to conceal. By villainy
      I got this ring; 'twas Leonatus' jewel,
      Whom thou didst banish; and, which more may grieve thee,

145   As it doth me, a nobler sir ne'er lived
      'Twixt sky and ground. Wilt thou hear more, my lord?

CYMBELINE   All that belongs to this.

GIACOMO   That paragon thy daughter,
      For whom my heart drops blood, and my false spirits
      Quail to remember—give me leave, I faint.

150 CYMBELINE   My daughter? What of her? Renew thy strength.
      I had rather thou shouldst live while nature will°   *as long as nature allows*
      Than die ere I hear more. Strive, man, and speak.

GIACOMO   Upon a time—unhappy was the clock
      That struck the hour—it was in Rome—accursed

155   The mansion where—'twas at a feast—O, would
      Our viands had been poisoned, or at least
      Those which I heaved to head!°—the good Posthumus—   *raised to my mouth*
      What should I say?—he was too good to be
      Where ill men were, and was the best of all

160   Amongst the rar'st of good ones—sitting sadly,
      Hearing us praise our loves of Italy
      For beauty that made barren the swelled boast[1]
      Of him that best could speak; for feature laming
      The shrine of Venus or straight-pitched Minerva,[2]

165   Postures beyond brief nature;[3] for condition,°   *character*
      A shop of all the qualities that man
      Loves woman for; besides that hook of wiving,°   *bait for marriage*
      Fairness which strikes the eye—

---

1. For beauty so great that it rendered hollow even the exaggerated boasts.
2. *for . . . Minerva:* for looks rendering deficient even the body (shrine) of the goddess of love (Venus) or the magisterial goddess of the arts (Minerva). *straight-pitched:* with erect posture.
3. Forms surpassing those of mere mortals.

CYMBELINE   I stand on fire.
         Come to the matter.
GIACOMO   All too soon I shall,
170   Unless thou wouldst grieve quickly. This Posthumus,
         Most like a noble lord in love and one
         That had a royal lover, took his hint,
         And not dispraising whom we praised—therein
         He was as calm as virtue—he began
175   His mistress' picture, which by his tongue being made,
         And then a mind put in't, either our brags
         Were cracked° of kitchen-trulls, or his description   *uttered in defense*
         Proved us unspeaking sots.°   *fools incapable of speech*
CYMBELINE   Nay, nay, to th' purpose.
GIACOMO   Your daughter's chastity—there it begins.
180   He spake of her as° Dian had hot° dreams   *as if / lustful*
         And she alone were cold,° whereat I, wretch,   *chaste*
         Made scruple of° his praise, and wagered with him   *Disputed*
         Pieces of gold 'gainst this which then he wore
         Upon his honoured finger, to attain
185   In suit° the place of 's bed and win this ring   *By urging my suit*
         By hers and mine adultery. He, true knight,
         No lesser of her honour confident
         Than I did truly find her, stakes this ring—
         And would so had it been a carbuncle
190   Of Phoebus' wheel,⁴ and might so safely had it
         Been all the worth of 's car.° Away to Britain   *worth the entire chariot*
         Post° I in this design. Well may you, sir,   *Hasten*
         Remember me at court, where I was taught
         Of° your chaste daughter the wide difference   *By*
195   'Twixt amorous and villainous. Being thus quenched
         Of hope, not longing,° mine Italian brain   *though not of desire*
         Gan° in your duller Britain⁵ operate   *Began*
         Most vilely; for my vantage,° excellent.   *profit*
         And, to be brief, my practice° so prevailed   *deceit*
200   That I returned with simular° proof enough   *pretended; specious*
         To make the noble Leonatus mad
         By wounding his belief in her renown°   *reputation*
         With tokens thus and thus; averring° notes   *confirming*
         Of chamber-hanging, pictures, this her bracelet—
205   O cunning, how I got it!—nay, some marks
         Of secret on her person, that he could not
         But think her bond of chastity quite cracked,
         I having ta'en the forfeit.⁶ Whereupon—
         Methinks I see him now—
POSTHUMUS [*coming forward*] Ay, so thou dost,
210   Italian fiend! Ay me, most credulous fool,
         Egregious murderer, thief, anything
         That's due⁷ to all the villains past, in being,
         To come! O, give me cord, or knife, or poison,
         Some upright justicer!° Thou, King, send out   *judge*
215   For torturers ingenious. It is I

---

4. *had . . . wheel*: even if it had been a precious stone   made its inhabitants sluggish and slow of wit.
from the wheel of the sun god's chariot.   6. Believing I had taken what she gave up (her chastity).
5. Alluding to the belief that England's northern climate   7. *anything / That's due*: any name that's owed.

That all th'abhorrèd things o'th' earth amend[8]
By being worse than they. I am Posthumus,
That killed thy daughter—villain-like, I lie:
That caused a lesser villain than myself,
220 A sacrilegious thief, to do't. The temple
Of virtue was she; yea, and she herself.°   *she was virtue herself*
Spit and throw stones, cast mire upon me, set
The dogs o'th' street to bay me. Every villain
Be called Posthumus Leonatus, and
225 Be 'villain' less than 'twas![9] O Innogen!
My queen, my life, my wife, O Innogen,
Innogen, Innogen!
INNOGEN [*approaching him*]   Peace, my lord. Hear, hear.
POSTHUMUS   Shall 's have a play of this? Thou scornful page,
There lie thy part.°   *Your role is to lie there*
[*He strikes her down*]
PISANIO [*coming forward*]   O gentlemen, help!
230 Mine and your mistress! O my lord Posthumus,
You ne'er killed Innogen till now. Help, help!
[*To* INNOGEN] Mine honoured lady.
CYMBELINE   Does the world go round?
POSTHUMUS   How comes these staggers[1] on me?
PISANIO [*to* INNOGEN]   Wake, my mistress.
CYMBELINE   If this be so, the gods do mean to strike me
235 To death with mortal° joy.   *death-causing*
PISANIO [*to* INNOGEN]   How fares my mistress?
INNOGEN   O, get thee from my sight!
Thou gav'st me poison. Dangerous fellow, hence.
Breathe not where princes are.
CYMBELINE   The tune of Innogen.
240 PISANIO   Lady, the gods throw stones of sulphur° on me if   *thunderbolts*
That box I gave you was not thought by me
A precious thing. I had it from the Queen.
CYMBELINE   New matter still.
INNOGEN   It poisoned me.
CORNELIUS   O gods!
I left out one thing which the Queen confessed
245 [*To* PISANIO] Which must approve° thee honest. 'If Pisanio   *prove*
Have', said she, 'given his mistress that confection°   *compound*
Which I gave him for cordial, she is served
As I would serve a rat.'
CYMBELINE   What's this, Cornelius?
CORNELIUS   The Queen, sir, very oft importuned me
250 To temper° poisons for her, still° pretending   *mix / always*
The satisfaction of her knowledge only
In killing creatures vile, as cats and dogs
Of no esteem.° I, dreading that her purpose   *value*
Was of more danger, did compound for her
255 A certain stuff which, being ta'en, would cease
The present power of life, but in short time

---

8. Who makes all loathsome things seem better.
9. *Every . . . 'twas:* May the word "villain" be less abhorrent than it was, since "Posthumus Leonatus" has replaced it.
1. A disease, usually of horses, that causes an unsteady walk; dizziness.

All offices of nature° should again   *All natural faculties*
Do their due functions. [*To* INNOGEN] Have you ta'en of it?

INNOGEN   Most like° I did, for I was dead.   *likely*

BELARIUS [*aside to* GUIDERIUS *and* ARVIRAGUS]   My boys,
There was our error.

260 GUIDERIUS   This is sure Fidele.

INNOGEN [*to* POSTHUMUS]   Why did you throw your wedded
    lady from you?
Think that you are upon a lock,[2] and now
Throw me again.
        [*She throws her arms about his neck*]

POSTHUMUS   Hang there like fruit, my soul,
Till the tree die.

CYMBELINE [*to* INNOGEN]   How now, my flesh, my child?

265 What, mak'st thou me a dullard° in this act?   *sluggish performer*
Wilt thou not speak to me?

INNOGEN [*kneeling*]   Your blessing, sir.

BELARIUS [*aside to* GUIDERIUS *and* ARVIRAGUS]   Though you did
    love this youth, I blame ye not.
You had a motive° for't.   *reason*

CYMBELINE   My tears that fall
Prove holy water on thee!
        [*He raises her*]
                  Innogen,
Thy mother's dead.

270 INNOGEN   I am sorry for't, my lord.

CYMBELINE   O, she was naught,° and 'long° of her it was   *worthless / because*
That we meet here so strangely.° But her son   *like strangers*
Is gone, we know not how nor where.

PISANIO   My lord,
Now fear is from me I'll speak truth. Lord Cloten,

275 Upon my lady's missing,° came to me   *absence*
With his sword drawn, foamed at the mouth, and swore
If I discovered° not which way she was gone   *revealed*
It was my instant death. By accident°   *chance*
I had a feignèd letter of my master's[3]

280 Then in my pocket, which directed him
To seek her on the mountains near to Milford,
Where in a frenzy, in my master's garments,
Which he enforced from me, away he posts°   *hastens*
With unchaste purpose, and with oath to violate

285 My lady's honour. What became of him
I further know not.

GUIDERIUS   Let me end the story.
I slew him there.

CYMBELINE   Marry, the gods forfend!
I would not thy good deeds° should from my lips   *(on the battlefield)*
Pluck a hard sentence. Prithee, valiant youth,

290 Deny't again.°   *Take it back*

GUIDERIUS   I have spoke it, and I did it.

CYMBELINE   He was a prince.

GUIDERIUS   A most incivil° one. The wrongs he did me   *barbarous*

---

2. You are in a wrestling hold. This is a disputed passage; F here reads "rock."

3. Referring to the letter written by Posthumus to mislead Innogen.

Were nothing prince-like, for he did provoke me
295   With language that would make me spurn the sea
      If it could so roar to me. I cut off 's head,
      And am right glad he is not standing here
      To tell this tale of mine.[4]
CYMBELINE   I am sorrow for thee.
      By thine own tongue thou art condemned, and must
      Endure our law. Thou'rt dead.
300 INNOGEN   That headless man
      I thought had been my lord.
CYMBELINE [to soldiers]   Bind the offender,
      And take him from our presence.
BELARIUS   Stay, sir King.
      This boy is better than the man he slew,
      As well descended as thyself, and hath
305   More of thee merited than a band of Clotens
      Had ever scar for.[5] Let his arms alone;
      They were not born for bondage.
CYMBELINE   Why, old soldier,
      Wilt thou undo the worth thou art unpaid for[6]
      By tasting of our wrath? How of descent
      As good as we?
310 ARVIRAGUS   In that he spake too far.
CYMBELINE [to BELARIUS][7]   And thou shalt die for't.
BELARIUS   We will die all three
      But I will prove° that two on 's° are as good   *Unless I prove / of us*
      As I have given out him. My sons, I must
      For mine own part unfold a dangerous speech,
      Though haply° well for you.   *perhaps*
315 ARVIRAGUS   Your danger's ours.
GUIDERIUS   And our good his.
BELARIUS   Have at it then. By leave,[8]
      Thou hadst, great King, a subject who
      Was called Belarius.
CYMBELINE   What of him? He is
      A banished traitor.
BELARIUS   He it is that hath
320   Assumed° this age. Indeed, a banished man;   *Reached*
      I know not how a traitor.
CYMBELINE [to soldiers]   Take him hence.
      The whole world shall not save him.
BELARIUS   Not too hot.°   *fast*
      First pay me for the nursing of thy sons,
      And let it° be confiscate all so soon   *(the payment)*
      As I have received it.
325 CYMBELINE   Nursing of my sons?
BELARIUS   I am too blunt and saucy. [Kneeling] Here's my knee.
      Ere I arise I will prefer° my sons,   *advance*
      Then spare not the old father. Mighty sir,

---

4. To tell a tale of cutting off my head.
5. *than . . . for:* than an army of Clotens ever earned by their battle scars.
6. The merit you are not yet rewarded for.
7. It is unclear to whom—Arviragus or Belarius—Cymbeline speaks the next line. Arviragus has just

addressed Cymbeline, and one might expect the King's reply to be directed to him. Belarius, however, made the offending remark about Guiderius being of as good birth as Cloten, and the threat of death probably applies to him.
8. Let's begin, then. With your permission.

These two young gentlemen that call me father
330 And think they are my sons are none of mine.
They are the issue° of your loins, my liege,   *offspring*
And blood of your begetting.

CYMBELINE   How, my issue?

BELARIUS   So sure as you your father's. I, old Morgan,⁹
Am that Belarius whom you sometime° banished.   *once*
335 Your pleasure was my mere offence,¹ my punishment
Itself, and all my treason. That I suffered
Was all the harm I did. These gentle princes—
For such and so they are—these twenty years
Have I trained up. Those arts° they have as I   *accomplishments*
340 Could put into them. My breeding was, sir,
As your highness knows. Their nurse Euriphile,
Whom for the theft I wedded, stole these children
Upon my banishment. I moved° her to't,   *persuaded*
Having received the punishment before
345 For that which I did then. Beaten° for loyalty   *Having been beaten*
Excited me to treason. Their dear loss,
The more of you 'twas felt, the more it shaped°   *suited*
Unto° my end° of stealing them. But, gracious sir,   *With / purpose*
Here are your sons again, and I must lose
350 Two of the sweet'st companions in the world.
The benediction of these covering heavens
Fall on their heads like dew, for they are worthy
To inlay heaven with stars.°   *To become constellations*

CYMBELINE   Thou weep'st, and speak'st.
The service that you three have done is more
355 Unlike° than this thou tell'st. I lost my children.   *Improbable*
If these be they, I know not how to wish
A pair of worthier sons.

BELARIUS [*rising*]   Be pleased a while.
This gentleman, whom I call Polydore,
Most worthy prince, as yours, is true Guiderius.
              [GUIDERIUS *kneels*]
360 This gentleman, my Cadwal, Arviragus,
Your younger princely son.
              [ARVIRAGUS *kneels*]
                    He, sir, was lapped°   *wrapped*
In a most curious° mantle wrought by th' hand   *delicately fashioned*
Of his queen mother, which for more probation°   *proof*
I can with ease produce.

CYMBELINE   Guiderius had
365 Upon his neck a mole, a sanguine° star.   *blood-red*
It was a mark of wonder.

BELARIUS   This is he,
Who hath upon him still that natural stamp.
It was wise nature's end in the donation°   *purpose in giving it*
To be his evidence now.

CYMBELINE   O, what am I?
370 A mother to the birth of three? Ne'er mother

9. Morgan was the Welsh name Belarius assumed during the years he spent in Wales.

1. What you pleased (to accuse me of) was my entire
offense.

Rejoiced deliverance more.[2] Blest pray you be,
That, after this strange starting from your orbs,[3]
You may reign in them now!

[GUIDERIUS *and* ARVIRAGUS *rise*]

                          O Innogen,
Thou hast lost by this a kingdom.

INNOGEN   No, my lord,
375 I have got two worlds by't. O my gentle brothers,
Have we thus met? O, never say hereafter
But I am truest speaker. You called me brother
When I was but your sister; I you brothers
When ye were so indeed.

CYMBELINE   Did you e'er meet?

ARVIRAGUS   Ay, my good lord.

380 GUIDERIUS   And at first meeting loved,
Continued so until we thought he died.

CORNELIUS   By the Queen's dram she swallowed.

CYMBELINE   O rare instinct!
When shall I hear all through? This fierce° abridgement   *drastic*
Hath to it circumstantial branches which
385 Distinction should be rich in.[4] Where? How lived you?
And when came you to serve our Roman captive?
How parted with your brothers? How first met them?
Why fled you from the court? And whither? These,
And your three motives° to the battle, with   *the motives of you three*
390 I know not how much more, should be demanded,
And all the other by-dependences,°   *circumstances*
From chance° to chance. But nor° the time nor place   *occurrence / neither*
Will serve our long inter'gatories.° See,   *lengthy questioning*
Posthumus anchors upon Innogen,
395 And she, like harmless lightning, throws her eye
On him, her brothers, me, her master, hitting
Each object with a joy. The counterchange
Is severally in all.[5] Let's quit this ground,
And smoke° the temple with our sacrifices.   *fill with smoke*
400 [*To* BELARIUS] Thou art my brother; so we'll hold thee ever.

INNOGEN [*to* BELARIUS]   You are my father too, and did relieve° me   *save*
To see this gracious season.

CYMBELINE   All o'erjoyed,
Save these in bonds. Let them be joyful too,
For they shall taste our comfort.

INNOGEN [*to* LUCIUS]   My good master,
I will yet do you service.

405 LUCIUS   Happy be you!

CYMBELINE   The forlorn° soldier that so nobly fought,   *wretched*
He would have well becomed this place, and graced
The thankings of a king.

POSTHUMUS   I am, sir,
The soldier that did company these three

---

2. Never did giving birth cause a mother to rejoice more.
3. After this unnatural displacement from your rightful positions. Referring to astrological theories that each heavenly body moved in its proper orb, or circle, around the earth. For a planet to move outside its orb caused disturbances in the heavens.
4. *circumstantial . . . in:* many ramifications that will provide particulars in rich abundance.
5. *The . . . all:* The exchange (of glances) passes from each to each.

410 In poor beseeming.° 'Twas a fitment⁶ for   *appearance*
    The purpose I then followed. That I was he,
    Speak, Giacomo; I had you down, and might
    Have made you finish.°   *die*

GIACOMO [*kneeling*]   I am down again,
    But now my heavy conscience sinks my knee

415 As then your force did. Take that life, beseech you,
    Which I so often owe;° but your ring first,   *owe so many times over*
    And here the bracelet of the truest princess
    That ever swore her faith.

POSTHUMUS [*raising him*]   Kneel not to me.
    The power that I have on you is to spare you,

420 The malice towards you to forgive you. Live,
    And deal with others better.

CYMBELINE   Nobly doomed!°   *sentenced*
    We'll learn our freeness of a son-in-law.
    Pardon's the word to all.

ARVIRAGUS [*to* POSTHUMUS]   You holp° us, sir,   *helped*
    As° you did mean indeed to be our brother.   *As if*

425 Joyed are we that you are.

POSTHUMUS   Your servant, princes. [*To* LUCIUS] Good my lord of Rome,
    Call forth your soothsayer. As I slept, methought
    Great Jupiter, upon his eagle backed,°   *riding on his eagle*
    Appeared to me with other spritely° shows   *ghostly*

430 Of mine own kindred. When I waked I found
    This label° on my bosom, whose containing°   *tablet / contents*
    Is so from sense in hardness that I can
    Make no collection of it.⁷ Let him show
    His skill in the construction.°   *interpretation*

LUCIUS   Philharmonus.

SOOTHSAYER   Here, my good lord.

435 LUCIUS   Read, and declare the meaning.

SOOTHSAYER *reads* [*the tablet*]   'Whenas a lion's whelp shall, to
    himself unknown, without seeking find, and be embraced by a
    piece of tender air; and when from a stately cedar shall be
    lopped branches which, being dead many years, shall after

440 revive, be jointed to the old stock, and freshly grow: then shall
    Posthumus end his miseries, Britain be fortunate and flourish
    in peace and plenty.'
    Thou, Leonatus, art the lion's whelp.
    The fit and apt construction of thy name,

445 Being *leo-natus*,° doth import so much.   *lion-born*
    [*To* CYMBELINE] The piece of tender air thy virtuous daughter,
    Which we call '*mollis aer*';⁸ and '*mollis aer*'
    We term it '*mulier*', [*to* POSTHUMUS] which '*mulier*' I divine
    Is this most constant wife, who even now,

450 Answering the letter of the oracle,⁹
    Unknown to you, unsought, were clipped about°   *embraced*
    With this most tender air.

CYMBELINE   This hath some seeming.

SOOTHSAYER   The lofty cedar, royal Cymbeline,

---

6. A suitable disguise.   8. Latin for "gentle air." An ancient (and erroneous)
7. *Is . . . it:* Is so difficult to make sense of that I can   etymology for *mulier,* Latin for "woman" or "wife."
draw no conclusion from it.   9. Fulfilling the exact terms of the oracle.

Personates° thee, and thy lopped branches point   *Stands for*
455 Thy two sons forth, who, by Belarius stol'n,
For many years thought dead, are now revived,
To the majestic cedar joined, whose issue
Promises Britain peace and plenty.

CYMBELINE   Well,
My peace we will begin; and, Caius Lucius,
460 Although the victor, we submit to Caesar
And to the Roman empire, promising
To pay our wonted tribute, from the which
We were dissuaded by our wicked queen,
Whom° heavens in justice both on her and hers   *On whom*
465 Have laid most heavy hand.

SOOTHSAYER   The fingers of the powers above do tune
The harmony of this peace. The vision,
Which I made known to Lucius ere the stroke
Of this yet scarce-cold battle,[1] at this instant
470 Is full° accomplished. For the Roman eagle,   *entirely*
From south to west on wing soaring aloft,
Lessened herself,[2] and in the beams o'th' sun
So vanished; which foreshowed our princely eagle
Th'imperial Caesar should again unite
475 His favour with the radiant Cymbeline,
Which shines here in the west.

CYMBELINE   Laud we the gods,
And let our crookèd° smokes climb to their nostrils   *curling*
From our blest altars. Publish° we this peace   *Proclaim*
To all our subjects. Set we forward,° let   *Let us go forth*
480 A Roman and a British ensign° wave   *banner*
Friendly together. So through Lud's town march,
And in the temple of great Jupiter
Our peace we'll ratify, seal it with feasts.
Set on there.° Never was a war did cease,   *March forth*
485 Ere bloody hands were washed, with such a peace.

           [Flourish.] Exeunt [in triumph]

---

1. *ere . . . battle:* before the action of this battle, which   2. Made herself small (by flying into the distance).
has only just ceased.

The Tempest

Near the close of *King Lear,* the ruined old king, stripped of the last vestiges of his power, dreams of being locked away happily in prison with his beloved Cordelia. Father and daughter have a more tragic fate in store for them, but Shakespeare returns to the dream in *The Tempest.* The play opens on a remote island of exile where Prospero, deposed from power and thrust out of Milan by his wicked brother, has found shelter with his only daughter, Miranda. Unlike many of Shakespeare's plays, *The Tempest* does not appear to have a single dominant source for its plot, but it is a kind of echo chamber of Shakespearean motifs. Its story of loss and recovery and its air of wonder link it closely to the group of late plays that modern editors generally call "romances" (*Pericles, The Winter's Tale, Cymbeline*), but it resonates as well with issues that haunted Shakespeare's imagination throughout his career: the painful necessity for a father to let his daughter go (*Othello, King Lear*); the treacherous betrayal of a legitimate ruler (*Richard II, Julius Caesar, Hamlet, Macbeth*); the murderous hatred of one brother for another (*Richard III, As You Like It, Hamlet, King Lear*); the passage from court society to the wilderness and the promise of a return (*A Midsummer Night's Dream, As You Like It*); the young heiress, torn from her place in the social hierarchy (*Twelfth Night, Pericles, The Winter's Tale*); the dream of manipulating others by means of art, especially by staging miniature plays within plays (*1 Henry IV, Much Ado About Nothing, Hamlet*); the threat of a radical loss of identity (*The Comedy of Errors, Richard II, King Lear*); the relationship between nature and nurture (*Pericles, The Winter's Tale*); the harnessing of magical powers (*The First Part of the Contention* [*2 Henry VI*], *A Midsummer Night's Dream, Macbeth*).

Though it is the first play printed in the First Folio (1623), *The Tempest* is probably one of the last that Shakespeare wrote. It can be dated fairly precisely: it uses material that was not available until late 1610, and there is a record of a performance before the king on Hallowmas Night, 1611. Since Shakespeare retired soon after to Stratford, *The Tempest* has seemed to many to be his valedictory to the theater. In this view, Prospero's strangely anxious and moving epilogue—"Now my charms are all o'erthrown, / And what strength I have's mine own"—is the expression of Shakespeare's own professional leave-taking. There are reasons to be skeptical: after finishing *The Tempest,* he collaborated on at least two other plays, *All Is True* (*Henry VIII*) and *The Two Noble Kinsmen,* and it is perilous to identify Shakespeare too closely with any of his characters, let alone an exiled, embittered, manipulative princely wizard. Yet the echo-chamber effect is striking, and when Prospero and others speak of his powerful "art," it is difficult not to associate the skill of the great magician with the skill of the great playwright. Near the end of the play, the association is made explicit when Prospero uses his magic powers to produce what he terms "some vanity of mine art" (4.1.41), a betrothal masque performed by spirits whom he calls forth "to enact / My present fancies" (4.1.121–22). The masque, typically a lavish courtly performance with music and dancing, may have seemed particularly appropriate on the occasion of another early performance: *The Tempest* was one of fourteen plays provided as part of the elaborate festivities in honor of the betrothal and marriage of King James's daughter Elizabeth to Frederick, the elector palatine. As Prospero's gift of the beautiful spectacle displays his magnificence and authority, so *The Tempest* and the other plays commanded by the king for his daughter's wedding would have enhanced his own prestige.

The Tempest opens with a spectacular storm that recalls *King Lear* not only in its violence but in its indifference to the ruler's authority: "What cares these roarers for

Magical storm. From Olaus Magnus, *Historia de Gentibus Septentrionalibus* (1555 ed.).

the name of king?" (1.1.15–16), shouts the exasperated Boatswain at the aristocrats who are standing in his way. The Boatswain's outburst seems unanswerable: like the implacable thunder in *King Lear*, the tempest marks the point at which exalted titles are revealed to be absurd pretensions, substanceless in the face of the elemental forces of nature and the desperate struggle for survival. But we soon learn that this tempest is not in fact natural and that it emphatically does hear and respond to human power, a power that is terrifying but, at least by its own account, benign: "The direful spectacle of the wreck," Prospero tells his daughter, "I have with such provision in mine art / So safely ordered" (1.2.26, 28–29) that no one on board has been harmed.

Shakespeare's contemporaries were fascinated by the figure of the magus, the great magician who by dint of deep learning, ascetic discipline, and patient skill could command the secret forces of the natural and supernatural world. Distinct from the village witch and "cunning man," figures engaged in local acts of healing and malice, and distinct, too, from alchemical experimenters bent on turning base metal into gold, the magus, cloaked in a robe covered with mysterious symbols, pronounced his occult charms, called forth spirits, and ranged in his imagination through the heavens and the earth, conjoining contemplative wisdom with virtuous action in order to confer great benefits upon his age. But there was a shiver of fear mingled with the popular admiration: when the person in Shakespeare's time most widely identified as a magus, the wizard John Dee, was away from his house, his library, one of the greatest private collections of books in England, was set on fire and burned to the ground.

Book, costume, powerful language, the ability to enact the fancies of the brain: these are key elements of both magic and theater. "I have bedimmed / The noontide sun," Prospero declares (5.1.41–42), beginning an enumeration of extraordinary accomplishments that culminates with the revelation that

> graves at my command
> Have waked their sleepers, oped, and let 'em forth
> By my so potent art.
>
> (5.1.48–50)

For the playwright who conjured up the ghosts of Caesar and old Hamlet, the claim does not seem extravagant, but for a magician it amounts to an extremely dangerous confession. Necromancy—communing with the spirits of the dead—was the very essence of black magic, the hated practice from which Prospero is careful to distinguish himself throughout the play. Before his exile, the island had been the realm of the "damned witch Sycorax," who was banished there "for mischiefs manifold and sorceries terrible" (1.2.265–66). The legitimacy of Prospero's power, including power over his slave Caliban, Sycorax's son, depends on his claims to moral authority, but for one disturbing moment it is difficult to see the difference between "foul witch" and princely magician. Small wonder that as soon as he has disclosed that he has trafficked with the dead, Prospero declares that he abjures his "rough magic" (5.1.50).

Prospero does not give an explicit reason for this abjuration, but it appears to be a key stage in the complex process that has led, before the time of the play, to his overthrow and will lead, after the play's events are over, to his return to power. This process in its entirety requires years to unfold, but the play depicts only a small, though crucially important, fragment of it. Together with his early *Comedy of Errors, The Tempest* is unusual among Shakespeare's plays in observing what literary critics of the age called the unities of time and place; unlike *Antony and Cleopatra,* for example, which ranges over a huge territory, or *The Winter's Tale,* which covers a huge span of time, the actions of *The Tempest* all take place in a single locale, the island, during the course of a single day. In a long scene of exposition just after the spectacular opening storm, Prospero tells Miranda that he is at a critical moment; everything depends on his seizing the opportunity that fortune has granted him. The whole play, then, is the spectacle of his timing, timing that might be cynically termed political opportunism or theatrical cunning but that Prospero himself associates with the working out of "providence divine" (1.2.160). The opportunity he seizes has its tangled roots in what he calls "the dark backward and abyss of time" (1.2.50). Many years before, when he was Duke of Milan, Prospero's preoccupation with "secret studies" gave his ambitious and unscrupulous brother Antonio the opportunity to topple him from power. Now those same studies, perfected during his long exile, have enabled Prospero to cause

The conjurer. Engraving by Theodore de Bry after a drawing by John White. From Thomas Hariot, *A Briefe and True Report of the New Found Land of Virginia* (1590).

Antonio and his shipmates, sailing back to Italy from Tunis, to be shipwrecked on his island, where they have fallen unwittingly under his control. His magic makes it possible not only to wrest back his dukedom but to avenge himself for the terrible wrong that his brother and his brother's principal ally, Alonso, the King of Naples, have done him: "They now are in my power" (3.3.90). Audiences in Shakespeare's time would have had an all too clear image of how horrendous the vengeance of enraged princes usually was. That Prospero restrains himself from the full exercise of his power to harm his enemies, that he breaks his magic staff and drowns his book, is his highest moral achievement, a triumphant display of self-mastery: "The rarer action is / In virtue than in vengeance" (5.1.27–28).

All of those who are shipwrecked on the island undergo the same shock of terror and unexpected survival, but their experiences, as they cross the yellow sands and make their way toward the interior of the island, differ markedly. The least affected are the mariners, including the feisty Boatswain; after their exhausting labors in the storm, they have sunk into a strange, uneasy sleep, only to be awakened in time to sail the miraculously restored ship back to Italy. The others are put through more complex trials; exposed to varying degrees of anxiety, temptation, grief, fear, and penitence, they are in effect subjects in a psychological experiment carefully conducted by Prospero, who attempts to instill in them moral self-control and work-discipline. The most generously treated is Ferdinand, the only son of the King of Naples, whom Prospero, in what is essentially a carefully planned dynastic alliance, has secretly chosen to be his son-in-law. As Ferdinand bewails what he assumes is his father's death by drowning, he hears strange, haunting music, including the remarkable song of death and metamorphosis, "Full fathom five thy father lies" (1.2.400). Ferdinand is the only one of the shipwrecked company, until the play's final scene, to encounter Prospero directly; the magician makes the experience menacing, humiliating, and frustrating, but this is the modest, salutary price the young man must pay to win the hand of the beautiful Miranda, who seems to him a goddess and who, for her part, has fallen in love with him at first sight.

Prospero directs the experience of the rest as well, but not in person; instead they principally encounter his diligent servant, Ariel. Ariel is not human, although at a crucial moment he is able to imagine what he would feel "were I human" (5.1.20). He is, as the cast of characters describes him, an "airy spirit," capable of moving at immense speed, altering the weather, and producing vivid illusions. We learn that Ariel possesses an inherent moral "delicacy," a delicacy that in the past (that is, before the time depicted in the play) has brought him pain. For, as Prospero reminds him, he had been Sycorax's servant and was, for refusing "to act her earthy and abhorred commands" (1.2.275), imprisoned by the witch for many years in a cloven pine. Prospero freed him from confinement and now demands in return a fixed term of service, which Ariel provides with a mixture of brilliant alacrity and grumbling. Prospero responds in turn with mingled affection and anger, alternating warm praises and dire threats. Although Prospero's "art," through which he commands Ariel and the lesser spirits, seems to foresee and control everything, this control is purchased by constant discipline.

And, for all his godlike powers, there are limits to what Prospero can do. He can make the loathed Antonio and the others know something of the bitterness of loss and isolation; he can produce in them irresistible drowsiness and startled awakenings; he can command Ariel to lay before them a splendid banquet and then make it suddenly vanish; he can drive them to desperation and madness. But in the case of his own brother and Alonso's similarly wicked brother Sebastian, Prospero cannot reshape their inner lives and effect a moral transformation. The most he can do with these men without conscience is to limit through continual vigilance any further harm they might do and to take back what is rightfully his. When, with an obvious effort, Prospero declares that he forgives his brother's "rankest fault" (5.1.134), Antonio is conspicuously silent.

But the higher moral purpose of Prospero's art is not all a failure. With Alonso, the project of provoking repentance by generating intense grief and fear succeeds admirably: Alonso not only gives up his power over the dukedom of Milan but begs Prospero's pardon for the wrong he committed in conspiring to overthrow him. (Both rulers, Alonso and Prospero, can look forward to a unification of their states in the next generation, through the marriage of Ferdinand and Miranda.) Moreover, Prospero's carefully contrived scenarios succeed in confirming the decency, loyalty, and goodness of Alonso's counselor, Gonzalo, who had years before provided the exiled Duke and his daughter with the means necessary for their survival.

It is Gonzalo's goodness that at the end of the play enables him to grasp the dynastic providence in the bewildering tangle of events—"Was Milan thrust from Milan, that his issue / Should become kings of Naples?" (5.1.208–09)—and that earlier inspires him to sense the miraculous nature of their survival. Indifferent to the contemptuous mockery of the cynical Antonio and Sebastian, Gonzalo responds to shipwreck on the strange island by speculating on how he would govern it were he responsible for its "plantation":

> I'th' commonwealth I would by contraries
> Execute all things. For no kind of traffic
> Would I admit, no name of magistrate;
> Letters should not be known; riches, poverty,
> And use of service, none; contract, succession,
> Bourn, bound of land, tilth, vineyard, none;
> No use of metal, corn, or wine, or oil;
> No occupation, all men idle, all.
> (2.1.147–54)

Shakespeare adapted Gonzalo's utopian speculations from a passage in "Of Cannibals" (1580), a remarkably free-spirited essay by the French humanist Michel de Montaigne. The Brazilian Indians, Montaigne admiringly writes (in John Florio's 1603 translation), have "no kind of traffic, no knowledge of letters, no intelligence of numbers, no name

America. Engraving by Theodor Galle after a drawing by Jan van der Straet (c. 1580).

of magistrate nor of politic superiority, no use of service, of riches or of poverty, no contracts, no successions . . . no occupation but idle, no respect of kindred but common, no apparel but natural, no manuring of lands, no use of wine, corn, or metal." For Montaigne, the European adventurers and colonists, confident in their cultural superiority, are the real barbarians, while the American natives, with their cannibalism and free love, live in accordance with nature.

The issues raised by Montaigne, and more generally by New World voyages, may have been particularly interesting to *The Tempest*'s early audiences as news reached London of the extraordinary adventures of the Virginia Company's colony at Jamestown. Shakespeare seems to have read a detailed account of these adventures in a letter written by the colony's secretary, William Strachey; although the letter was not printed until 1625, it was evidently circulating in manuscript in 1610. In 1609, a fleet carrying more than four hundred persons sent out to reinforce the colony was struck by a hurricane near the Virginia coast. Two of the vessels reached their destination, but the third, the ship carrying the governor, Sir Thomas Gates, ran aground on an uninhabited island in the Bermudas. Remarkably enough, all of the passengers and crew survived; but their tribulations were not over. By forcing everyone to labor side by side in order to survive, the violence of the storm had weakened the governor's authority, and both the natural abundance and the isolation of the island where they were shipwrecked weakened it further. Gates ordered the company to build new ships in order to sail to Jamestown, but his command met with ominous grumblings and threats of mutiny. According to Strachey's letter, the main troublemaker directly challenged Gates's authority: "therefore let the Governour (said he) kiss, etc." In response, Gates had the troublemaker shot to death. New ships were built, and in an impressive feat of navigation, the entire company reached Jamestown. The group found the settlement deeply demoralized: illness was rampant, food was scarce, and relations with the neighboring Indians, once amicable, had completely broken down. Only harsh military discipline kept the English colony from falling apart.

With the possible exception of some phrases from Strachey's description of the storm and a few scattered details, *The Tempest* does not directly use any of this vivid narrative. Prospero's island is evidently in the Mediterranean, and the New World is only mentioned as a far-off place, "the still-vexed Bermudas" (1.2.230), where the swift Ariel flies to fetch dew. Yet Shakespeare's play seems constantly to echo precisely the issues raised by the Bermuda shipwreck and its aftermath. What does it take to survive? How do men of different classes and moral character react during a state of emergency? What is the proper relation between theoretical understanding and practical experience or between knowledge and power? Is obedience to authority willing or forced? How can those in power protect themselves from the conspiracies of malcontents? Is it possible to detect a providential design in what looks at first like a succession of accidents? If there are natives to contend with, how should colonists establish friendly and profitable relations with them? What is to be done if relations turn sour? How can those who rule prevent an alliance between hostile natives and the poorer colonists, often disgruntled and themselves exploited? And—Montaigne's more radical questions—what is the justification of one person's rule over another? Who is the civilized man, and who is the barbarian?

The unregenerate nastiness of Antonio and Sebastian, conjoined with the goodness of Gonzalo, might seem indirectly to endorse Montaigne's critique of the Europeans and his praise of the cannibals, were it not for the disturbing presence in *The Tempest* of the character whose name is almost an anagram for "cannibal," Caliban. Caliban, whose god Setebos is mentioned in accounts of Magellan's voyages as a Patagonian deity, is anything but a noble savage. Shakespeare does not shrink from the darkest European fantasies about the Wild Man. Indeed, he exaggerates them: Caliban is deformed, lecherous, evil-smelling, treacherous, naive, drunken, lazy, rebellious, violent, and devil-worshipping. According to Prospero, he is not even human: "A devil, a born devil, on whose nature / Nurture can never stick" (4.1.188–89). When he first came to the island, Prospero recalls, he treated Caliban "with human care" (1.2.349), lodging him in his own cell until the savage tried to rape Miranda. The arrival of the other Europeans brings out still worse qualities. Encountering the basest of the company, Alonso's jester, Trinculo, and drunken butler, Stefano, Caliban falls at their feet in brutish worship and then devises a conspiracy to murder Prospero in his sleep. Were the conspiracy to succeed, Caliban would get neither the girl for whom he lusts nor the freedom for which he shouts—he would become "King" Stefano's "foot-licker" (4.1.218)—but he would satisfy the enormous hatred he feels for Prospero.

Prospero's power, Caliban reasons, derives from his superior knowledge. "Remember / First to possess his books," he urges the louts, "for without them / He's but a sot as I am. . . . Burn but his books" (3.2.86–90). The strategy is a canny one, in recognizing an underlying link between literacy and authority, but the problem is not only that Stefano and Trinculo are hopeless fools but also that Prospero, like all Renaissance princes, has a diligent spy network: the invisible Ariel overhears the conspirators and warns his master of the approaching danger. Prospero's sudden recollection of the warning leads him to break off the betrothal masque with one of the most famous speeches in all of Shakespeare, "Our revels now are ended" (4.1.148ff.). This brooding meditation on the theatrical insubstantiality of the entire world and the dreamlike nature of human existence has seemed to many the pinnacle of the play's visionary wisdom. But it does not subsume in its rich cadences the other voices in *The Tempest;* specifically, it does not silence the surprising power of Caliban's voice.

That voice has been amplified in the centuries that followed the first performances of *The Tempest,* as European colonialism saw its grand political, moral, and economic claims disputed and, after violent struggles, dismantled. During these struggles, many anticolonial writers and critics rewrote Shakespeare's play, casting Prospero as a smugly racist, sexist oppressor, Ariel as a native coopted and corrupted by his colonial master, and Caliban as a victimized hero. "Prospero invaded the islands," declared the Cuban writer Roberto Fernández Retamar, "killed our ancestors, enslaved Caliban, and taught him his language to make himself understood. What else can Caliban do but use that same language—today he has no other—to curse him, to wish that the 'red plague' would fall on him?"

Shakespeare, who wrote when the colonialist project was still in its early stages, could not have anticipated this afterlife, and some scholars have argued that the relevance to *The Tempest* of the New World voyages has been greatly exaggerated. But, as the Barbadian writer George Lamming puts it, "Caliban keeps answering back." Caliban enters the play cursing, grumbling, and, above all, disputing Prospero's authority: "This island's mine, by Sycorax my mother, / Which thou tak'st from me" (1.2.334–35). By the close, his attempt to kill Prospero foiled and his body racked with cramps and bruises, Caliban declares that he will "be wise hereafter, / And seek for grace" (5.1.298–99). Yet it is not his mumbled reformation but his vehement protests that leave an indelible mark on *The Tempest*. The play may depict Caliban, in Prospero's ugly term, as "filth," but it gives him a remarkable, unforgettable eloquence. To Miranda's taunting reminder that she taught him to speak, Caliban retorts, "You taught me language, and my profit on't / Is I know how to curse" (1.2.366–67). It is not only in cursing, however, that Caliban is gifted: in richly sensuous poetry, he speaks of the island's natural resources and of his dreams. Caliban can be beaten into submission, but the master cannot eradicate his slave's desires, his pleasures, and his inconsolable pain. And across the vast gulf that divides the triumphant prince and the defeated savage, there is a momentary, enigmatic glimpse of a hidden bond: "This thing of darkness," Prospero says of Caliban, "I / Acknowledge mine" (5.1.278–79). The words need only be a claim of ownership, but they seem to hint at a deeper, more disturbing link between father and monster, legitimate ruler and savage, judge and criminal. Perhaps the link is only an illusion, a trick of the imagination on a strange island, but as Prospero leaves the island, it is he who begs for pardon.

STEPHEN GREENBLATT

TEXTUAL NOTE

The only authoritative printed text of *The Tempest* is in the First Folio of 1623 (F), where it appears as the first play, at the head of the comedies. The text seems to have been prepared with care. It includes a list of characters *("Names of the Actors")* printed at the end of the play and supplies act and scene divisions that this edition follows. There are also unusually full stage directions, although scholars have argued about whether these were written entirely by Shakespeare or were supplied or elaborated by the person who transcribed the author's manuscript for the compositors. Certain features of this transcription have led scholars to the conclusion that it was done by Ralph Crane, an experienced scribe who was responsible for the preparation of at least four other Shakespeare plays.

Most of the songs in *The Tempest* are preserved in early to mid-seventeenth-century manuscripts. These manuscripts indicate repeats and refrains, which have accordingly been accepted in the text of this edition.

SELECTED BIBLIOGRAPHY

Albanese, Denise. "Admiring Miranda and Enslaving Nature." *New Science, New World*. Durham, N.C.: Duke University Press, 1996. 59–91. Miranda as the feminine locus of the play's exploration of nature and culture.

Barker, Francis, and Peter Hulme. "Nymphs and Reapers Heavily Vanish: The Discursive Con-texts of *The Tempest*." *Alternative Shakespeares*. Vol. I. Ed. John Drakakis. London: Methuen, 1985. 191–205. English colonialism as a discursive context for the play's interest in the usurpation of power.

Brotton, Jerry. " 'This Tunis, sir, was Carthage': Contesting Colonialism in *The Tempest*." *Post-Colonial Shakespeares*. Ed. Ania Loomba and Martin Orkin. London: Routledge, 1998. 23–42. The play's Mediterranean geography exposes a bifurcated interest in both the Old and the New Worlds.

Brown, Paul. " 'This Thing of Darkness I Acknowledge Mine': *The Tempest* and the Discourse of Colonialism." *Political Shakespeare: New Essays in Cultural Materialism*. Ed. Jonathan Dollimore and Alan Sinfield. Ithaca, N.Y.: Cornell University Press, 1985. 48–71. Shakespeare's ambivalent depictions of political, social, and sexual authority read in relation to contemporary colonial practice.

Callaghan, Dympna. "Irish Memories in *The Tempest*." *Shakespeare Without Women: Representing Gender and Race on the Renaissance Stage*. London: Routledge, 2000. 97–138. Using the play's Irish echoes, considers how selective colonial recollection suppresses the cultural memory of the colonized.

Cartelli, Thomas. "Prospero in Africa: *The Tempest* as Colonialist Text and Pretext." *Repositioning Shakespeare: National Formations, Postcolonial Appropriations*. London: Routledge, 1999. 87–104. *The Tempest* can be made to operate both for and against the interests of modern Western ideology.

Greenblatt, Stephen. "Martial Law in the Land of Cockaigne." *Shakespearean Negotiations: The Circulation of Social Energy in Renaissance England*. Berkeley: University of California Press, 1988. 129–63. The play apparently celebrates the restoration of patriarchal order yet also ironically scrutinizes the political manipulation of anxiety.

Hulme, Peter, and William H. Sherman, eds. *"The Tempest" and Its Travels*. Philadelphia: University of Pennsylvania Press, 2000. A range of critical and creative materials, situating the play amid the local and global contexts of its time and beyond.

Orgel, Stephen. *The Illusion of Power: Political Theater in the English Renaissance*. Berkeley: University of California Press, 1975. Compares public and court theater practice, highlighting the masque's role in the allegorized expression of sovereign power.

Vaughan, Virginia Mason, and Alden T. Vaughan. *Critical Essays on Shakespeare's "The Tempest."* New York: Hall, 1998. Eleven essays illustrating the breadth and diversity of critical and cultural engagement with the play.

FILMS

Forbidden Planet. 1956. Dir. Fred M. Wilcox. USA. 98 min. A science-fiction cult classic in which Ariel is a robot and Caliban a monster of the id.

The Tempest. 1960. Dir. George Schaefer. USA. 76 min. A made-for-TV, one-camera film of a solid, though short stage rendition, with Richard Burton standing out as Caliban.

The Tempest. 1979. Dir. Derek Jarman. UK. 95 min. Part Gothic, part punk. Renders Juno's masque as a Broadway musical number.

Tempest. 1982. Dir. Paul Mazursky. USA. 140 min. Disenchanted New York architect escapes to a Greek island to reexamine his life.

Prospero's Books. 1991. Dir. Peter Greenaway. UK. 129 min. Surreal and baroque, focusing on the imagined contents of Prospero's library. John Gielgud stars.

The Tempest

THE PERSONS OF THE PLAY

PROSPERO, the rightful Duke of Milan
MIRANDA, his daughter
ANTONIO, his brother, the usurping Duke of Milan
ALONSO, King of Naples
SEBASTIAN, his brother
FERDINAND, Alonso's son
GONZALO, an honest old counsellor of Naples
ADRIAN
FRANCISCO } lords
ARIEL, an airy spirit attendant upon Prospero
CALIBAN, a savage and deformed native of the island, Prospero's slave
TRINCULO, Alonso's jester
STEFANO, Alonso's drunken butler
The MASTER of a ship
BOATSWAIN
MARINERS
SPIRITS
    The Masque
Spirits appearing as:
IRIS
CERES
JUNO
Nymphs, reapers

1.1

A tempestuous noise of thunder and lightning heard.
Enter a SHIPMASTER *and a* BOATSWAIN[1] [*at separate*
doors]

MASTER   Boatswain!
BOATSWAIN   Here, Master. What cheer?
MASTER   Good,[2] speak to th' mariners. Fall to't yarely,° or we run   *promptly*
    ourselves aground. Bestir, bestir!   *Exit*
    Enter MARINERS
5 BOATSWAIN   Heigh, my hearts!° Cheerly, cheerly, my hearts!   *hearties*
    Yare, yare! Take in the topsail![3] Tend° to th' Master's whistle!—   *Attend*
    Blow till thou burst thy wind, if room enough.[4]
        Enter ALONSO, SEBASTIAN, ANTONIO, FERDINAND, GON-
        ZALO, *and others*
ALONSO   Good Boatswain, have care. Where's the Master?
    [*To the* MARINERS] Play the men!°   *Act like men*
10 BOATSWAIN   I pray now, keep below.
ANTONIO   Where is the Master, Boatswain?

1.1 Location: A ship at sea.
1. The Boatswain probably enters after the shipmaster calls him; the latter is perhaps on the upper stage.
2. Acknowledging the Boatswain's presence; or perhaps short for "good man."

3. To reduce the surface area of the sail, and thereby lessen the force of the wind pushing the ship toward the island.
4. The wind may blow until it splits itself, provided there is enough sea room to maneuver in.

BOATSWAIN   Do you not hear him? You mar our labour. Keep
your cabins; you do assist the storm.

GONZALO   Nay, good,° be patient.   *good man*

15 BOATSWAIN   When the sea is. Hence! What cares these roarers
for the name of king?[5] To cabin! Silence; trouble us not.

GONZALO   Good, yet remember whom thou hast aboard.

BOATSWAIN   None that I more love than myself. You are a councillor;[6] if you can command these elements to silence and work
20 peace of the present,[7] we will not hand° a rope more. Use your   *handle*
authority. If you cannot, give thanks you have lived so long and
make yourself ready in your cabin for the mischance of the
hour, if it so hap.° [*To the* MARINERS] Cheerly, good hearts! [*To*   *happen*
GONZALO] Out of our way, I say!   *Exit*

25 GONZALO   I have great comfort from this fellow. Methinks he
hath no drowning mark[8] upon him; his complexion is perfect
gallows.[9] Stand fast, good Fate, to his hanging. Make the rope
of his destiny our cable,[1] for our own doth little advantage.° If   *use*
he be not born to be hanged, our case is miserable.
                                          Exit [*Courtiers*]
        Enter BOATSWAIN

30 BOATSWAIN   Down with the topmast![2] Yare! Lower, lower! Bring
her to try wi'th' main-course![3]
        A cry within
A plague upon this howling! They are louder than the weather,
or our office.[4]
        Enter SEBASTIAN, ANTONIO, *and* GONZALO
Yet again? What do you here? Shall we give o'er° and drown?   *up*
35 Have you a mind to sink?

SEBASTIAN   A pox o'your throat, you bawling, blasphemous,
incharitable dog!

BOATSWAIN   Work you, then.

ANTONIO   Hang, cur, hang, you whoreson insolent noisemaker.
40 We are less afraid to be drowned than thou art.
                                          [*Exeunt* MARINERS]

GONZALO   I'll warrant him for drowning,[5] though° the ship were   *even if*
no stronger than a nutshell and as leaky as an unstanched°   *a freely menstruating*
wench.

BOATSWAIN   Lay her a-hold, a-hold! Set her two courses![6] Off to
45 sea again! Lay her off!
        Enter MARINERS, *wet*
MARINERS   All lost! To prayers, to prayers! All lost!
                                          [*Exeunt* MARINERS]
BOATSWAIN   What, must our mouths be cold?[7]
GONZALO   The King and Prince at prayers! Let's assist them,
For our case is as theirs.

---

5. "Roarers," referring here to the waves, was also a term for riotous people.
6. Member of the King's council; also an adviser or persuader.
7. Of the present circumstances.
8. Birthmark whose position was held to portend death by drowning. "He that was born to be hanged will never be drowned" was proverbial.
9. His physiognomy, appearance, shows that he will certainly be hanged.
1. Anchor cable (an anchor is actually useless in a storm).

2. To reduce the top weight of the ship and make it more stable.
3. Bring the ship close to the wind sailing only with the mainsail.
4. Duties (in shouting orders).
5. I'll guarantee him against drowning.
6. Set the foresail in addition to the mainsail.
7. To be cold in the mouth—to be dead—was proverbial; may also suggest that the mariners warm their mouths with liquor (line 50).

SEBASTIAN   I'm out of patience.
50 ANTONIO   We are merely° cheated of our lives by drunkards.   *utterly*
    This wide-chopped° rascal—would thou mightst lie drowning   *large-mouthed*
    The washing of ten tides.[8]
    GONZALO   He'll be hanged yet,
    Though every drop of water swear against it
    And gape at wid'st to glut° him.   *its widest to swallow*
        A confused noise within
    MARINERS [*within*]   Mercy on us!
55 We split, we split! Farewell, my wife and children!
    Farewell, brother! We split, we split, we split!
                                [*Exit* BOATSWAIN]
    ANTONIO   Let's all sink wi'th' King.
    SEBASTIAN   Let's take leave of him.
                    Exit [ANTONIO *and* SEBASTIAN]
    GONZALO   Now would I give a thousand furlongs of sea for an
    acre of barren ground: long heath, broom, furze,[9] anything.
60 The wills above be done, but I would fain die a dry death.
                                                        Exit

                        1.2
        Enter PROSPERO [*in his magic cloak, with a staff*], *and*
            MIRANDA
    MIRANDA[1]   If by your art,[2] my dearest father, you have
    Put the wild waters in this roar, allay them.
    The sky, it seems, would pour down stinking pitch,
    But that the sea, mounting to th' welkin's° cheek,   *sky's*
5   Dashes the fire out. O, I have sufferèd
    With those that I saw suffer! A brave° vessel,   *splendid*
    Who had, no doubt, some noble creature in her,
    Dashed all to pieces! O, the cry did knock
    Against my very heart! Poor souls, they perished.
10 Had I been any god of power, I would
    Have sunk the sea within the earth, or ere°   *before*
    It should the good ship so have swallowed and
    The fraughting souls[3] within her.
    PROSPERO[4]   Be collected.
    No more amazement.° Tell your piteous° heart   *consternation / pitying*
    There's no harm done.
    MIRANDA   O woe the day!
15 PROSPERO   No harm.
    I have done nothing but in care of thee,
    Of thee, my dear one, thee, my daughter, who
    Art ignorant of what thou art, naught knowing
    Of whence I am, nor that I am more better°   *higher in rank*

---

8. Pirates were hanged on the shore at low-water mark
and left there for the ebbing and flowing of three tides.
9. Heather, yellow shrubs, and gorse—all shrubs that
grow in poor soil.
1.2 Location: The rest of the play is set in various parts
of Prospero's island.
1. *Miranda* in Latin means "admirable" or "wonder-

ing." Miranda uses the formal "you," contrasting with
Prospero's more familiar "thou."
2. Skill; magic; learning; science.
3. Souls constituting the freight; perhaps also suggesting "burdened."
4. *Prospero* in Italian and Spanish means "fortunate" or
"prosperous."

20   Than Prospero, master of a full poor cell[5]
     And thy no greater father.

MIRANDA   More to know
     Did never meddle with° my thoughts.   *intrude upon*

PROSPERO   'Tis time
     I should inform thee farther. Lend thy hand,
     And pluck my magic garment from me.

        [MIRANDA *removes Prospero's cloak, and he lays it on the*
        ground]

                          So.

25   Lie there, my art.—Wipe thou thine eyes; have comfort.
     The direful spectacle of the wreck, which touched
     The very virtue of compassion in thee,
     I have with such provision° in mine art   *foresight*
     So safely ordered that there is no soul—
30   No, not so much perdition° as an hair   *loss*
     Betid° to any creature in the vessel,   *Happened*
     Which° thou heard'st cry, which thou saw'st sink. Sit down,   *Whom*
     For thou must now know farther.

        [MIRANDA *sits*]

MIRANDA   You have often
     Begun to tell me what I am, but stopped
35   And left me to a bootless inquisition,°   *profitless inquiry*
     Concluding 'Stay; not yet'.

PROSPERO   The hour's now come.
     The very minute bids thee ope° thine ear,   *open*
     Obey, and be attentive. Canst thou remember
     A time before we came unto this cell?
40   I do not think thou canst, for then thou wast not
     Out° three years old.   *Fully*

MIRANDA   Certainly, sir, I can.

PROSPERO   By° what? By any other house or person?   *About*
     Of anything the image tell me that
     Hath kept with thy remembrance.

MIRANDA   'Tis far off,
45   And rather like a dream than an assurance°   *a certainty*
     That my remembrance warrants.° Had I not   *guarantees is true*
     Four or five women once that tended me?

PROSPERO   Thou hadst, and more, Miranda. But how is it
     That this lives in thy mind? What seest thou else
50   In the dark backward° and abyss of time?   *past*
     If thou rememb'rest aught° ere thou cam'st here,   *anything*
     How thou cam'st here thou mayst.

MIRANDA   But that I do not.

PROSPERO   Twelve year since, Miranda, twelve year since,
     Thy father was the Duke of Milan,[6] and
     A prince of power—
55 MIRANDA   Sir, are not you my father?

PROSPERO   Thy mother was a piece° of virtue,° and   *perfect example / chastity*
     She said thou wast my daughter; and thy father
     Was Duke of Milan, and his only heir
     And princess no worse issued.°   *no less nobly born*

---

5. Suggesting a hermit's or a poor man's dwelling. *full:*   6. Pronounced with stress on the first syllable.
very.

MIRANDA   O the heavens!
60   What foul play had we that we came from thence?
      Or blessèd° was't we did?   providential
PROSPERO   Both, both, my girl.
      By foul play, as thou sayst, were we heaved thence,
      But blessedly holp° hither.   helped
MIRANDA   O, my heart bleeds
      To think o'th' teen° that I have turned you to,   sorrow; trouble
65   Which is from° my remembrance. Please you, farther.   out of
PROSPERO   My brother and thy uncle called Antonio—
      I pray thee mark me, that a brother should
      Be so perfidious—he whom next° thyself   after
      Of all the world I loved, and to him put
70   The manage° of my state—as at that time   control
      Through all the signories° it was the first,   lordships
      And Prospero the prime° duke—being so reputed   foremost
      In dignity, and for the liberal arts[7]
      Without a parallel—those being all my study,
75   The government I cast upon my brother,
      And to my state grew stranger, being transported[8]
      And rapt in secret studies. Thy false uncle—
      Dost thou attend me?
MIRANDA   Sir, most heedfully.
PROSPERO   Being once perfected how to grant suits,[9]
80   How to deny them, who t'advance and who
      To trash for over-topping,[1] new created
      The creatures° that were mine, I say—or changed 'em   dependents
      Or else new formed 'em;[2] having both the key°   control
      Of officer and office, set all hearts i'th' state
85   To what tune pleased his ear, that° now he was   so that
      The ivy which had hid my princely trunk
      And sucked my verdure° out on't. Thou attend'st not!   vitality; power
MIRANDA   O good sir, I do.
PROSPERO   I pray thee mark me.
      I, thus neglecting worldly ends, all dedicated
90   To closeness° and the bettering of my mind   seclusion
      With that which but° by being so retired   merely
      O'er-priced all popular rate,[3] in my false brother
      Awaked an evil nature; and my trust,
      Like a good parent,[4] did beget of him
95   A falsehood, in its contrary° as great   inverse qualities
      As my trust was, which had indeed no limit,
      A confidence sans° bound. He being thus lorded   without
      Not only with what my revenue yielded
      But what my power might else exact, like one
100   Who having into° truth, by telling oft,   unto
      Made such a sinner of his memory
      To credit his own lie,[5] he did believe

---

7. As opposed to the "mechanical arts," the "liberal arts" encompassed the trivium (grammar, logic, and rhetoric) and the quadrivium (arithmetic, geometry, music, and astronomy).
8. Enraptured, with suggestions of "conveyed to another place." *grew stranger:* grew alienated from; became a foreigner to.
9. Having mastered handling formal requests.
1. For rising too high. *trash:* restrain, hold back (as by a leash).

2. *changed . . . 'em:* changed the duties and allegiance of existing officials, or created new ones.
3. Became too precious for the people to value, or understand.
4. From the colloquial "Good parents breed bad children."
5. *like one . . . lie:* like someone who comes to believe his own repeatedly stated lie. *To:* So as to.

	He was indeed the Duke. Out o'th'° substitution,	*As a consequence of the*
	And executing° th'outward face° of royalty	*portraying / image*
105	With all prerogative, hence his ambition growing—	
	Dost thou hear?	
	MIRANDA Your tale, sir, would cure deafness.	
	PROSPERO To have no screen between this part he played	
	And him he played it for, he needs will be	
	Absolute Milan.⁶ Me,° poor man—my library	*As for me*
110	Was dukedom large enough—of temporal royalties°	*rule*
	He thinks me now incapable; confederates,°	*(he) plots*
	So dry° he was for sway,° wi'th' King of Naples	*thirsty / power*
	To give him annual tribute, do him homage,	
	Subject his coronet to his crown,⁷ and bend	
115	The dukedom, yet unbowed—alas, poor Milan—	
	To most ignoble stooping.⁸	
	MIRANDA O the heavens!	
	PROSPERO Mark his condition° and th'event,° then tell me	*treaty / outcome*
	If this might be a brother.	
	MIRANDA I should sin	
	To think but° nobly of my grandmother.	*anything but*
	Good wombs have borne bad sons.⁹	
120	PROSPERO Now the condition.	
	This King of Naples, being an enemy	
	To me inveterate, hearkens my brother's suit;	
	Which was that he, in lieu o'th' premises¹	
	Of homage and I know not how much tribute,	
125	Should presently extirpate me and mine	
	Out of the dukedom, and confer fair Milan,	
	With all the honours, on my brother. Whereon,	
	A treacherous army levied, one midnight	
	Fated to th' purpose did Antonio open	
130	The gates of Milan; and, i'th' dead of darkness,	
	The ministers° for th' purpose hurried thence	*agents*
	Me and thy crying self.	
	MIRANDA Alack, for pity!	
	I, not rememb'ring how I cried out then,	
	Will cry it o'er again; it is a hint°	*an occasion*
	That wrings mine eyes to't.	
135	PROSPERO [*sitting*] Hear a little further,	
	And then I'll bring thee to the present business	
	Which now's upon's, without the which this story	
	Were most impertinent.°	*irrelevant*
	MIRANDA Wherefore did they not	
	That hour destroy us?	
	PROSPERO Well demanded, wench;²	
140	My tale provokes that question. Dear, they durst not,	
	So dear the love my people bore me; nor set	
	A mark so bloody on the business, but	
	With colours fairer painted their foul ends.	
	In few,° they hurried us aboard a barque,°	*short / ship*

---

6. *To have . . . Milan:* He wanted to be the Duke of Milan in actual fact, rather than merely exercising power as the Duke's proxy. *screen:* partition, barrier.
7. Subject Antonio's coronet to Alonso's crown. *coronet:* a lesser crown indicating the wearer's inferiority to the sovereign.
8. *and bend . . . stooping:* by making Milan, previously

free, a tributary subject of Naples.
9. Antonio's character need not imply that his mother was a bad parent (see line 94).
1. In return for the conditions agreed upon.
2. A young woman; also term of endearment to wife, daughter, or sweetheart.

145 Bore us some leagues to sea, where they prepared
A rotten carcass of a butt,[3] not rigged,
Nor tackle, sail, nor mast—the very rats
Instinctively have quit it. There they hoist us,
To cry to th' sea that roared to us, to sigh
150 To th' winds, whose pity, sighing back again,
Did us but loving wrong.[4]

MIRANDA   Alack, what trouble
Was I then to you!

PROSPERO   O, a cherubin
Thou wast that did preserve me. Thou didst smile,
Infusèd with a fortitude from heaven,
155 When I have decked° the sea with drops° full salt,   *covered; adorned / tears*
Under my burden groaned;[5] which° raised in me   *(Miranda's smile)*
An undergoing stomach,° to bear up   *A courage to endure*
Against what should ensue.

MIRANDA   How came we ashore?

160 PROSPERO   By providence divine.
Some food we had, and some fresh water, that
A noble Neapolitan, Gonzalo,
Out of his charity—who being then appointed
Master of this design—did give us; with
165 Rich garments, linens, stuffs, and necessaries
Which since have steaded° much. So, of his gentleness,[6]   *been useful*
Knowing I loved my books, he furnished me
From mine own library with volumes that
I prize above my dukedom.

MIRANDA   Would I might
But ever see that man!

170 PROSPERO   Now I arise.[7]
[*He stands and puts on his cloak*][8]
Sit still,° and hear the last of our sea-sorrow.   *Continue to sit*
Here in this island we arrived, and here
Have I thy schoolmaster made thee more profit°   *profit more*
Than other princes[9] can, that have more time
175 For vainer hours and tutors not so careful.°   *caring*

MIRANDA   Heavens thank you for't. And now I pray you, sir—
For still 'tis beating in my mind—your reason
For raising this sea-storm.

PROSPERO   Know thus far forth.
By accident most strange, bountiful Fortune,
180 Now my dear lady,[1] hath mine enemies
Brought to this shore; and by my prescience
I find my zenith[2] doth depend upon
A most auspicious star,[3] whose influence
If now I court not, but omit,° my fortunes   *disregard*

---

3. Cask or tub: here, deprecatory for "boat."
4. The winds, responding sympathetically to our sighs,
only blew us farther out to sea.
5. The secondary sense provides an image of giving birth.
6. Nobility; kindness.
7. Referring to the action of standing; or to Prospero's
rising fortunes (as in lines 179–85). The former might
visually reinforce the latter, especially if Prospero also
resumes his magical powers by putting on his cloak.

8. This direction, necessary before Prospero can charm
Miranda to sleep, follows naturally from the reference to
Prospero's books, his other source of power.
9. *princes*: a generic plural for "princes and princesses."
1. Traditional characterization of Fortune as a woman
changeable in her affections.
2. Highest point, as of a star in the sky.
3. Referring to the belief that celestial bodies had astrological influence on people and events.

185 Will ever after droop. Here cease more questions.
Thou art inclined to sleep; 'tis a good dullness,°   *drowsiness*
And give it way. I know thou canst not choose.
     [MIRANDA *sleeps*]
Come away,° servant, come! I am ready now.   *Come here*
Approach, my Ariel,[4] come!
     Enter ARIEL

190 ARIEL   All hail, great master, grave sir, hail. I come
To answer thy best pleasure. Be't to fly,
To swim, to dive into the fire, to ride
On the curled clouds, to thy strong bidding task
Ariel and all his quality.°   *cohorts; faculties*
PROSPERO   Hast thou, spirit,

195 Performed to point° the tempest that I bade thee?   *in detail*
ARIEL   To every article.
I boarded the King's ship. Now on the beak,°   *prow*
Now in the waste,° the deck,° in every cabin,   *midship / poop*
I flamed amazement.[5] Sometime I'd divide,

200 And burn in many places;[6] on the top-mast,
The yards, and bowsprit, would I flame distinctly;
Then meet and join. Jove's lightning, the precursors
O'th' dreadful thunderclaps, more momentary
And sight-outrunning° were not. The fire and cracks   *quicker than the eye*

205 Of sulphurous[7] roaring the most mighty Neptune
Seem to besiege, and make his bold waves tremble,
Yea, his dread trident shake.
PROSPERO   My brave spirit!
Who was so firm, so constant, that this coil°   *turmoil*
Would not infect his reason?
ARIEL   Not a soul

210 But felt a fever of the mad,° and played   *such as madmen feel*
Some tricks of desperation. All but mariners
Plunged in the foaming brine and quit the vessel,
Then all afire with me. The King's son Ferdinand,
With hair upstaring°—then like reeds, not hair—   *standing on end*

215 Was the first man that leaped; cried 'Hell is empty,
And all the devils are here'.
PROSPERO   Why, that's my spirit!
But was not this nigh shore?
ARIEL   Close by, my master.
PROSPERO   But are they, Ariel, safe?
ARIEL   Not a hair perished.
On their sustaining[8] garments not a blemish,

220 But fresher than before. And, as thou bad'st° me,   *commanded*
In troops° I have dispersed them 'bout the isle.   *groups*
The King's son have I landed by himself,
Whom I left cooling of ° the air with sighs   *cooling*
In an odd angle° of the isle, and sitting,   *corner*
His arms in this sad knot.[9]

---

4. Ariel's name, along with sounding like "airy," also means in Hebrew "lion of God." The name appears as a magical spirit in various occult texts.
5. I appeared as flames, causing terror.
6. The phosphorescent effect of St. Elmo's fire, caused in a thunderstorm by the charge of static electricity that builds up particularly around metal projections.
7. Sulphur was popularly associated with thunder and lightning.
8. Buoying up, and thus suggesting "life-giving."
9. Folded sadly, like this (folded arms implied sorrow).

225 PROSPERO   Of the King's ship,
     The mariners, say how thou hast disposed,
     And all the rest o'th' fleet.
     ARIEL   Safely in harbour
     Is the King's ship, in the deep nook where once
     Thou called'st me up at midnight to fetch dew
230 From the still-vexed° Bermudas, there she's hid;   *ever-stormy*
     The mariners all under hatches stowed,
     Who, with° a charm joined to° their suffered labour,   *by virtue of / with*
     I have left asleep. And for the rest o'th' fleet,
     Which I dispersed, they all have met again,
235 And are upon the Mediterranean float°   *billow; sea*
     Bound sadly home for Naples,
     Supposing that they saw the King's ship wrecked,
     And his great person perish.
     PROSPERO   Ariel, thy charge
     Exactly is performed; but there's more work.
     What is the time o'th' day?
240 ARIEL   Past the mid season.°   *noon*
     PROSPERO   At least two glasses.° The time 'twixt six and now   *hourglasses*
     Must by us both be spent most preciously.
     ARIEL   Is there more toil? Since thou dost give me pains,°   *tasks*
     Let me remember° thee what thou hast promised   *remind*
     Which is not yet performed me.
245 PROSPERO   How now? Moody?
     What is't thou canst demand?
     ARIEL   My liberty.
     PROSPERO   Before the time be out? No more!
     ARIEL   I prithee,
     Remember I have done thee worthy service,
     Told thee no lies, made thee no mistakings, served
250 Without or° grudge or grumblings. Thou did promise   *either*
     To bate° me a full year.   *remit; excuse*
     PROSPERO   Dost thou forget
     From what a torment I did free thee?
     ARIEL   No.
     PROSPERO   Thou dost, and think'st it much to tread the ooze
     Of the salt deep,
255 To run upon the sharp wind of the north,
     To do me business in the veins[1] o'th' earth
     When it is baked° with frost.   *dried and hardened*
     ARIEL   I do not, sir.
     PROSPERO   Thou liest, malignant thing. Hast thou forgot
     The foul witch Sycorax, who with age and envy
260 Was grown into a hoop?° Hast thou forgot her?   *bent over with age*
     ARIEL   No, sir.
     PROSPERO   Thou hast. Where was she born? Speak, tell me!
     ARIEL   Sir, in Algiers.
     PROSPERO   O, was she so! I must
     Once in a month recount what thou hast been,
265 Which thou forget'st. This damned witch Sycorax,
     For mischiefs manifold and sorceries terrible
     To enter human hearing, from Algiers

---

1. Mineral veins or subterranean rivers.

Thou know'st was banished. For one thing she did
They would not take her life.² Is not this true?

270 ARIEL   Ay, sir.

PROSPERO   This blue-eyed³ hag was hither brought with child,
And here was left by th' sailors. Thou, my slave,
As thou report'st thyself, was then her servant;
And for° thou wast a spirit too delicate   because

275 To act her earthy⁴ and abhorred commands,
Refusing her grand hests,° she did confine thee   commands
By help of her more potent ministers,°   agents; slaves
And in her most unmitigable rage,
Into a cloven pine; within which rift

280 Imprisoned thou didst painfully remain
A dozen years, within which space she died
And left thee there, where thou didst vent thy groans
As fast as mill-wheels strike.° Then was this island—   hit the water
Save for the son that she did litter° here,   give birth to

285 A freckled whelp, hag-born—not honoured with
A human shape.

ARIEL   Yes, Caliban her son.

PROSPERO   Dull thing, I say so:⁵ he, that Caliban
Whom now I keep in service. Thou best know'st
What torment I did find thee in. Thy groans

290 Did make wolves howl, and penetrate° the breasts   arouse sympathy in
Of ever-angry bears; it was a torment
To lay upon the damned, which Sycorax
Could not again undo. It was mine art,
When I arrived and heard thee, that made gape
The pine and let thee out.

295 ARIEL   I thank thee, master.

PROSPERO   If thou more murmur'st, I will rend an oak,
And peg thee in his° knotty entrails till   its
Thou hast howled away twelve winters.

ARIEL   Pardon, master.
I will be correspondent° to command,   compliant

300 And do my spriting gently.°   graciously

PROSPERO   Do so, and after two days
I will discharge thee.⁶

ARIEL   That's my noble master!
What shall I do? Say what, what shall I do?

PROSPERO   Go make thyself like to a nymph o'th' sea. Be subject

305 To no sight but thine and mine, invisible
To every eyeball else.⁷ Go take this shape,°   appearance; disguise
And hither come in't. Go; hence with diligence!   Exit [ARIEL]
Awake, dear heart, awake! Thou hast slept well;
Awake.

MIRANDA [awaking] The strangeness of your story put
Heaviness° in me.   Sleepiness

310 PROSPERO   Shake it off. Come on;

---

2. For . . . life: Only because she got pregnant. Capital
sentences were commuted for pregnant women; ordinarily, condemned witches were either hanged or burned
at the stake.
3. Blue eyelids were thought to be a sign of pregnancy.
4. Difficult for Ariel, whose element is air; also, grossly

material, coarse.
5. You dullard, that's just what I said.
6. Prospero reduces this to within two days at line 425
and actually releases Ariel in about four hours' time.
7. Be . . . else: Ariel may wear a conventional costume,
indicating his invisibility to other characters onstage.

We'll visit Caliban my slave, who never
Yields us kind answer.

MIRANDA   'Tis a villain, sir,
I do not love to look on.

PROSPERO   But as 'tis,
We cannot miss° him. He does make our fire,   avoid; do without
315 Fetch in our wood, and serves in offices°   capacities; duties
That profit us.—What ho! Slave, Caliban!
Thou earth, thou, speak!

CALIBAN (within)   There's wood enough within.

PROSPERO   Come forth, I say! There's other business for thee.
Come, thou tortoise! When?
        Enter ARIEL, *like a water-nymph*
320 Fine apparition! My quaint[8] Ariel,
Hark in thine ear.
        [*He whispers*]

ARIEL   My lord, it shall be done.   *Exit*

PROSPERO   Thou poisonous slave, got° by the devil[9] himself   begot
Upon thy wicked dam,° come forth!   harmful, foul mother
        Enter CALIBAN

CALIBAN   As wicked dew as e'er my mother brushed[1]
325 With raven's feather from unwholesome fen°   bog
Drop on you both! A southwest[2] blow on ye,
And blister you all o'er!

PROSPERO   For this be sure tonight thou shalt have cramps,
Side-stitches that shall pen thy breath up. Urchins[3]
330 Shall forth at vast of° night, that they may work   during the boundless
All exercise on thee.[4] Thou shalt be pinched
As thick as honeycomb,[5] each pinch more stinging
Than bees that made 'em.°   (honeycomb cells)

CALIBAN   I must eat my dinner.
This island's mine, by Sycorax my mother,
335 Which thou tak'st from me. When thou cam'st first,
Thou strok'st me and made much of me, wouldst give me
Water with berries in't, and teach me how
To name the bigger light, and how the less,[6]
That burn by day and night; and then I loved thee,
340 And showed thee all the qualities o'th' isle,
The fresh springs, brine-pits, barren place and fertile—
Cursed be I that did so! All the charms°   spells
Of Sycorax, toads, beetles, bats, light on you;
For I am all the subjects that you have,
345 Which first was mine own king, and here you sty me°   pen me up
In this hard rock, whiles you do keep from me
The rest o'th' island.

PROSPERO   Thou most lying slave,
Whom stripes° may move, not kindness! I have used° thee,   lashes / treated

---

8. The term could simultaneously mean "ingenious,"
"curious in appearance," and "elegant."
9. Not merely an insult, but also an allusion to Caliban's
birth from the devil (incubus) and witch.
1. Brushed up, collected. Dew was a common ingredient
of magical potions.
2. A southerly wind was considered plague-bearing.
3. Hedgehogs; but here indicates spirits disguised as
hedgehogs.

4. *that . . . thee*: in order that they may perform their
habitual activity.
5. *Thou . . . honeycomb*: The pinch marks will be as
closely packed as, and of similar texture to, the cells of a
honeycomb.
6. Recalls Genesis 1:16: "God then made two great
lights: the greater light to rule the day, and the less light
to rule the night."

Filth as thou art, with human care, and lodged thee
350 In mine own cell, till thou didst seek to violate
The honour of my child.

CALIBAN   O ho, O ho! Would't had been done!
Thou didst prevent me; I had peopled else
This isle with Calibans.

MIRANDA[7]   Abhorrèd slave,
355 Which any print° of goodness wilt not take,   *impression*
Being capable of° all ill! I pitied thee,   *susceptible to*
Took pains to make thee speak, taught thee each hour
One thing or other. When thou didst not, savage,
Know thine own meaning, but wouldst gabble like
360 A thing most brutish, I endowed thy purposes
With words that made them known. But thy vile race,°   *hereditary nature*
Though thou didst learn, had that in't which good natures
Could not abide to be with; therefore wast thou
Deservedly confined into this rock,
365 Who hadst deserved more than a prison.

CALIBAN   You taught me language, and my profit on't
Is I know how to curse. The red plague rid you[8]
For learning me your language!

PROSPERO   Hag-seed,° hence!   *Offspring of a hag*
Fetch us in fuel. And be quick, thou'rt best,
370 To answer other business.°—Shrug'st thou, malice?   *perform other tasks*
If thou neglect'st or dost unwillingly
What I command, I'll rack thee with old[9] cramps,
Fill all thy bones with aches,[1] make thee roar,
That beasts shall tremble at thy din.

CALIBAN   No, pray thee.
375 [*Aside*] I must obey. His art is of such power
It would control my dam's god Setebos,[2]
And make a vassal of him.

PROSPERO   So, slave, hence!   *Exit* CALIBAN
Enter FERDINAND *and* ARIEL, *invisible, playing and*
singing.[3] [PROSPERO *and* MIRANDA *stand aside*]

Song

ARIEL   Come unto these yellow sands,
                And then take hands;
380   Curtsied when you have and kissed—
                The wild waves whist[4]—
                Foot it featly° here and there,   *Dance nimbly*
                And, sweet sprites, bear°   *sing*
                The burden.° Hark, hark.   *refrain*
385 SPIRITS (*dispersedly* [*within*]) Bow-wow!
ARIEL   The watch-dogs bark.
SPIRITS [*within*] Bow-wow!

7. Many editors assign this speech to Prospero, believing it to be out of character for Miranda.
8. The plague that gives red sores destroy, kill you.
9. As of aged people; long-accustomed.
1. As a noun, this was probably pronounced "aitches."
2. A name found in travel narratives as a god of the Patagonians.

3. This probably does not imply that Ferdinand enters first, even though such a staging is possible if Ferdinand is bewildered as to where this music is coming from. Ariel is invisible to all but Prospero and the audience. He is probably still dressed as a water nymph.
4. Become hushed and attentive.

ARIEL	Hark, hark, I hear	
	The strain of strutting Chanticleer	
390	Cry 'cock-a-diddle-dow'.	
FERDINAND	Where should this music be? I'th' air or th'earth?	
	It sounds no more; and sure it waits° upon	*attends*
	Some god o'th' island. Sitting on a bank,	
	Weeping again the King my father's wreck,	
395	This music crept by me upon the waters,	
	Allaying both their fury and my passion°	*grief*
	With its sweet air.° Thence I have followed it—	*melody*
	Or it hath drawn me rather. But 'tis gone.	
	No, it begins again.	

Song

400	ARIEL	Full fathom five thy father lies.
		Of his bones are coral made;
		Those are pearls that were his eyes;
		Nothing of him that doth fade
		But doth suffer a sea-change
405		Into something rich and strange.
		Sea-nymphs hourly ring his knell:

SPIRITS [*within*]   Ding dong.
ARIEL   Hark, now I hear them.
SPIRITS [*within*]   Ding-dong bell. [*etc.*]

FERDINAND	The ditty does remember⁵ my drowned father.	
410	This is no mortal° business, nor no sound	*human; of death*
	That the earth owes.°	*owns*
	[*Music*]	
	I hear it now above me.	

PROSPERO [*to* MIRANDA]   The fringèd curtains of thine eye advance,°   *raise*
And say what thou seest yon.
MIRANDA   What is't? A spirit?
Lord, how it looks about! Believe me, sir,

415	It carries a brave° form. But 'tis a spirit.	*splendid; gallant*
PROSPERO	No, wench, it eats and sleeps, and hath such senses	
	As we have, such. This gallant° which thou seest	*fine gentleman*
	Was in the wreck, and but° he's something° stained	*except that / somewhat*
	With grief, that's beauty's canker,⁶ thou mightst call him	
420	A goodly person. He hath lost his fellows,	
	And strays about to find 'em.	

MIRANDA   I might call him
A thing divine, for nothing natural
I ever saw so noble.

PROSPERO [*aside*]⁷	It° goes on, I see,	(*My plan*)
	As my soul prompts it. [*To* ARIEL] Spirit, fine spirit, I'll free thee	
425	Within two days for this.	

FERDINAND [*aside*]   Most sure the goddess

	On whom these airs attend.⁸ [*To* MIRANDA] Vouchsafe° my prayer	*Grant*
	May know if you remain° upon this island,	*dwell*

---

5. Commemorate. *ditty:* the words of the song.
6. Cankerworm; caterpillar ("beauty" being seen as a flower); spreading sore.
7. Prospero's asides here and at lines 442, 454, and 497 may be either private utterances or addressed to Ariel. If the former, Ariel may nevertheless hear them; Prospero

speaks to Ariel after all these instances. Their import may well be purposefully enigmatic.
8. *Most . . . attend:* Probably spoken aside, but possibly an invocation. *Most sure the goddess:* Echoes Aeneas's reaction to seeing Venus after his shipwreck, "o dea certe" (*Aeneid* I.328). *airs:* Ariel's melodies.

And that you will some good instruction give
How I may bear me° here. My prime request,   *conduct myself*
430 Which I do last pronounce, is—O you wonder⁹—
If you be maid¹ or no?

MIRANDA   No wonder, sir,
But certainly a maid.

FERDINAND   My language! Heavens!
I am the best² of them that speak this speech,
Were I but where 'tis spoken.

PROSPERO   How, the best?

435 What wert thou if the King of Naples heard thee?

FERDINAND   A single³ thing, as I am now that wonders
To hear thee speak of Naples. He does hear me,⁴
And that he does I weep. Myself am Naples,°   *King of Naples*
Who with mine eyes, never since at ebb,° beheld   *ceasing to flow*
The King my father wrecked.

440 MIRANDA   Alack, for mercy!

FERDINAND   Yes, faith, and all his lords, the Duke of Milan
And his brave son⁵ being twain.

PROSPERO [*aside*]   The Duke of Milan
And his more braver daughter could control⁶ thee,
If now 'twere fit to do't. At the first sight
445 They have changed eyes.⁷—Delicate° Ariel,   *Graceful; artful*
I'll set thee free for this. [*To* FERDINAND] A word, good sir.
I fear you have done yourself some wrong.⁸ A word.

MIRANDA [*aside*]   Why speaks my father so ungently?° This   *discourteously*
Is the third man that e'er I saw, the first
450 That e'er I sighed for. Pity move my father
To be inclined my way.

FERDINAND   O, if a virgin,
And your affection not gone forth,⁹ I'll make you
The Queen of Naples.

PROSPERO   Soft, sir! One word more.
[*Aside*] They are both in either's powers. But this swift business
455 I must uneasy° make, lest too light¹ winning   *difficult*
Make the prize light. [*To* FERDINAND] One word more. I charge thee
That thou attend me. Thou dost here usurp
The name thou ow'st° not; and hast put thyself   *own*
Upon this island as a spy, to win it
From me the lord on't.°   *of it*
460 FERDINAND   No, as I am a man.

MIRANDA   There's nothing ill can dwell in such a temple.²
If the ill spirit have so fair a house,
Good things will strive to dwell with't.

PROSPERO [*to* FERDINAND]   Follow me.
[*To* MIRANDA] Speak not you for him; he's a traitor. [*To* FERDINAND] Come!

---

9. Miracle, punning on the meaning of Miranda's name.
1. Unmarried virgin; made (human).
2. Highest in rank, assuming he has succeeded his father.
3. Weak and helpless; solitary; one and the same.
4. "He" and "me" both refer to Ferdinand. Presuming his father to be dead, Ferdinand takes himself to be the new King of Naples (and as such, he hears himself speaking). Alternatively, Ferdinand thinks his father's spirit hears him.
5. The only instance in which Antonio is mentioned as having a son.
6. Challenge; take to task; exercise power over.
7. Exchanged loving glances; fallen in love at first sight.
8. Euphemistic for "told a lie about yourself."
9. Given over to someone else.
1. Easy; playing on the meanings of "little valued" and also "promiscuous" in line 456.
2. A common metaphor for the body; also a conventional Renaissance notion that moral qualities were physically manifest.

465   I'll manacle thy neck and feet together.
        Sea-water shalt thou drink; thy food shall be
        The fresh-brook mussels,[3] withered roots, and husks
        Wherein the acorn cradled. Follow!
FERDINAND   No.
        I will resist such entertainment° till   *treatment*
        Mine enemy has more power.
           He draws, and is charmed from moving
470 MIRANDA   O dear father,
        Make not too rash a trial of him, for
        He's gentle, and not fearful.[4]
PROSPERO   What, I say,
        My foot° my tutor? Put thy sword up, traitor,   *inferior*
        Who mak'st a show but dar'st not strike, thy conscience
475   Is so possessed with guilt. Come from thy ward,°   *defensive stance*
        For I can here disarm thee with this stick°   *magician's wand*
        And make thy weapon drop.
MIRANDA   Beseech you, father!
PROSPERO   Hence! Hang not on my garments.
MIRANDA   Sir, have pity.
        I'll be his surety.
PROSPERO   Silence! One word more
480   Shall make me chide thee, if not hate thee. What,
        An advocate for an impostor? Hush!
        Thou think'st there is no more such shapes° as he,   *forms; men*
        Having seen but him and Caliban. Foolish wench!
        To° th' most of men this is a Caliban,   *Compared to*
        And they to him are angels.
485 MIRANDA   My affections
        Are then most humble. I have no ambition
        To see a goodlier man.
PROSPERO [*to* FERDINAND]   Come on; obey.
        Thy nerves° are in their infancy again,   *sinews*
        And have no vigour in them.
FERDINAND   So they are.
490   My spirits,° as in a dream, are all bound up.   *mental powers*
        My father's loss, the weakness which I feel,
        The wreck of all my friends, nor this man's threats
        To whom I am subdued, are but light to me,
        Might I but through my prison once a day
495   Behold this maid. All corners else o'th' earth
        Let liberty make use of; space enough
        Have I in such a prison.
PROSPERO [*aside*]   It works. [*To* ARIEL] Come on.—
        Thou hast done well, fine Ariel. [*To* FERDINAND] Follow me.
        [*To* ARIEL] Hark what thou else shalt do me.
MIRANDA [*to* FERDINAND]   Be of comfort.
500   My father's of a better nature, sir,
        Than he appears by speech. This is unwonted°   *unusual*
        Which now came from him.
PROSPERO [*to* ARIEL]   Thou shalt be as free
        As mountain winds; but then° exactly do   *until then*
        All points of my command.

---

3. Freshwater mussels are inedible.   4. He's noble and, therefore, not cowardly. Alternatively,
                                      not fearsome.

505 ARIEL   To th' syllable.
PROSPERO [*to* FERDINAND]   Come, follow. [*To* MIRANDA] Speak
   not for him.   *Exeunt*

<h2 style="text-align:center">2.1</h2>

Enter ALONSO, SEBASTIAN, ANTONIO, GONZALO, ADRIAN,
  and FRANCISCO

GONZALO [*to* ALONSO]   Beseech you, sir, be merry. You have cause,
  So have we all, of joy; for our escape
  Is much beyond our loss. Our hint° of woe   occasion
  Is common; every day some sailor's wife,
5 The masters of some merchant, and the merchant,¹
  Have just° our theme of woe. But for the miracle,   exactly
  I mean our preservation, few in millions
  Can speak like us. Then wisely, good sir, weigh
  Our sorrow with° our comfort.   against
ALONSO   Prithee, peace.²
10 SEBASTIAN [*to* ANTONIO]   He receives comfort like cold porridge.°   broth
ANTONIO   The visitor³ will not give him o'er so.°   leave him alone
SEBASTIAN   Look, he's winding up the watch of his wit. By and
  by it will strike.
GONZALO [*to* ALONSO]   Sir—
15 SEBASTIAN [*to* ANTONIO]   One: tell.°   keep count
GONZALO [*to* ALONSO]   When every grief is entertained° that's   harbored
    offered,
  Comes to th'entertainer⁴—
SEBASTIAN   A dollar.⁵
GONZALO   Dolour° comes to him indeed. You have spoken truer   Sorrow
20   than you purposed.
SEBASTIAN   You have taken it wiselier than I meant you should.
GONZALO [*to* ALONSO]   Therefore my lord—
ANTONIO [*to* SEBASTIAN]   Fie, what a spendthrift is he of his
  tongue!
25 ALONSO [*to* GONZALO]   I prithee, spare.°   spare your words
GONZALO   Well, I have done. But yet—
SEBASTIAN [*to* ANTONIO]   He will be talking.
ANTONIO   Which of he or Adrian, for a good wager, first begins
  to crow?⁶
30 SEBASTIAN   The old cock.
ANTONIO   The cockerel.⁷
SEBASTIAN   Done. The wager?
ANTONIO   A laughter.⁸
SEBASTIAN   A match!
35 ADRIAN [*to* GONZALO]   Though this island seem to be desert°—   uninhabited
ANTONIO [*to* SEBASTIAN]   Ha, ha, ha!
SEBASTIAN   So, you're paid.⁹
ADRIAN   Uninhabitable, and almost inaccessible—
SEBASTIAN [*to* ANTONIO]   Yet—
40 ADRIAN   Yet—

2.1
1. The chief officers of some merchant ship and its
owner.
2. Sebastian takes this as "pease," as in "pease porridge."
3. Antonio compares Gonzalo with one who visits and
comforts the sick and distressed.
4. There comes to the person who accepts that grief.

5. *dollar*: English name for the German thaler.
6. Which of the two will first begin to speak ("crow")?
7. "The young cock crows as the old hears" was proverbial. "Old cock" refers to Gonzalo and "cockerel" to
Adrian.
8. From the proverb "He laughs that wins."
9. Antonio's laugh is his prize.

ANTONIO [*to* SEBASTIAN]   He could not miss't.

ADRIAN   It must needs be of subtle, tender, and delicate[1]
   temperance.°   *climate*

ANTONIO [*to* SEBASTIAN]   Temperance was a delicate wench.[2]

45   SEBASTIAN   Ay, and a subtle, as he most learnedly delivered.[3]

ADRIAN [*to* GONZALO]   The air breathes upon us here most
   sweetly.

SEBASTIAN [*to* ANTONIO]   As if it had lungs, and rotten ones.

ANTONIO   Or as 'twere perfumed by a fen.°   *bog*

50   GONZALO [*to* ADRIAN]   Here is everything advantageous to life.

ANTONIO [*to* SEBASTIAN]   True, save° means to live.   *except*

SEBASTIAN   Of that there's none, or little.

GONZALO [*to* ADRIAN]   How lush and lusty° the grass looks!   *tender and luxuriant*
   How green!

55   ANTONIO   The ground indeed is tawny.

SEBASTIAN   With an eye[4] of green in't.

ANTONIO   He misses not much.

SEBASTIAN   No, he doth but mistake the truth totally.

GONZALO [*to* ADRIAN]   But the rarity[5] of it is, which is indeed
60   almost beyond credit—

SEBASTIAN [*to* ANTONIO]   As many vouched° rarities are.   *alleged, accepted*

GONZALO [*to* ADRIAN]   That our garments being, as they were,
   drenched in the sea, hold notwithstanding their freshness and
   glosses, being rather new-dyed than stained with salt water.

65   ANTONIO [*to* SEBASTIAN]   If but one of his pockets[6] could speak,
   would it not say he lies?

SEBASTIAN   Ay, or very falsely pocket up his report.[7]

GONZALO [*to* ADRIAN]   Methinks our garments are now as fresh
   as when we put them on first in Afric, at the marriage of the
70   King's fair daughter Claribel to the King of Tunis.

SEBASTIAN   'Twas a sweet marriage, and we prosper well in our
   return.

ADRIAN   Tunis was never graced before with such a paragon to°   *for*
   their queen.

75   GONZALO   Not since widow Dido's[8] time.

ANTONIO [*to* SEBASTIAN]   Widow?[9] A pox o'that! How came that
   'widow' in? Widow Dido!

SEBASTIAN   What if he had said 'widower Aeneas' too? Good
   Lord, how you take° it!   *fuss about*

80   ADRIAN [*to* GONZALO]   'Widow Dido' said you? You make me
   study of ° that: she was of Carthage, not of Tunis.   *examine*

GONZALO   This Tunis, sir, was Carthage.[1]

ADRIAN   Carthage?

GONZALO   I assure you, Carthage.

---

1. Exquisite, but in Antonio's usage (line 44), "given to pleasure." *subtle:* fine, but in Sebastian's usage (line 45), "sexually expert" or "crafty."
2. Antonio takes "Temperance" to be the name of a girl. *delicate:* voluptuous, given to pleasure.
3. "Learnedly delivered" was a popular phrase among Puritans who wanted to appear pious.
4. A tinge. In Antonio's reply, an "eye of green" refers to Gonzalo's optimistic capacity to see green.
5. Exceptional quality; but in Sebastian's usage (line 61), "uncommon thing."
6. Seen as the garments' "mouth"; also implying that

Gonzalo's pockets are stained.
7. The evidence of stained pockets would confute Gonzalo's words and reputation for honesty. *pocket up:* suppress, or keep silent; also, receive unprotestingly.
8. Queen of ancient Carthage, whose tragic love affair with Aeneas is related in Virgil's *Aeneid.*
9. Antonio picks on this designation for a woman abandoned by her lover as being either irrelevant or conspicuously prudish. Dido, however, was in fact a widow when she met Aeneas.
1. The city of Tunis was actually built 10 miles from the site of Carthage.

85 ANTONIO [*to* SEBASTIAN]   His word is more than the miraculous harp.[2]

SEBASTIAN   He hath raised the wall, and houses too.

ANTONIO   What impossible matter will he make easy next?

SEBASTIAN   I think he will carry this island home in his pocket,

90 and give it his son for an apple.

ANTONIO   And sowing the kernels° of it in the sea, bring forth   seeds
more islands.

GONZALO [*to* ADRIAN]   Ay.[3]

ANTONIO [*to* SEBASTIAN]   Why, in good time.

95 GONZALO [*to* ALONSO]   Sir, we were talking that our garments
seem now as fresh as when we were at Tunis, at the marriage
of your daughter, who is now queen.

ANTONIO   And the rarest that e'er came there.

SEBASTIAN   Bate,[4] I beseech you, widow Dido.

100 ANTONIO   O, widow Dido? Ay, widow Dido.

GONZALO [*to* ALONSO]   Is not, sir, my doublet as fresh as the first
day I wore it? I mean in a sort.[5]

ANTONIO [*to* SEBASTIAN]   That 'sort' was well fished for.

GONZALO [*to* ALONSO]   When I wore it at your daughter's

105 marriage.

ALONSO   You cram these words into mine ears against
The stomach of my sense.[6] Would I had never
Married my daughter there! For, coming thence,
My son is lost; and, in my rate,° she too,   consideration

110 Who is so far from Italy removed
I ne'er again shall see her. O thou mine heir
Of Naples and of Milan, what strange fish
Hath made his meal on thee?

FRANCISCO   Sir, he may live.
I saw him beat the surges under him

115 And ride upon their backs. He trod the water,
Whose enmity he flung aside, and breasted
The surge, most swoll'n, that met him. His bold head
'Bove the contentious waves he kept, and oared
Himself with his good arms in lusty° stroke   vigorous

120 To th' shore, that o'er his wave-worn basis bowed,[7]
As° stooping to relieve him. I not° doubt   As if / do not
He came alive to land.

ALONSO   No, no; he's gone.

SEBASTIAN [*to* ALONSO]   Sir, you may thank yourself for this great loss,
That would not bless our Europe with your daughter,

125 But rather loose° her to an African,   lose; release
Where she, at least, is banished from your eye,
Who° hath cause to wet the grief° on't.   (Claribel) / weep

ALONSO   Prithee, peace.

SEBASTIAN   You were kneeled to and importuned otherwise[8]
By all of us, and the fair soul herself

130 Weighed between loathness and obedience at

---

2. Referring to Amphion's harp, to the music of which
the walls (but not the houses) of Thebes arose.
3. Affirming his belief that Tunis was Carthage; Antonio
mocks the length of time this took.
4. Except (as a verb); don't mention.
5. Comparatively speaking; Antonio plays on "drawing

lots."
6. *You . . . sense:* The image is of one being force-fed
words against the appetite ("stomach") for hearing them.
7. *that . . . bowed:* that extended out and drooped over
the foot of the cliff, which had been eroded by waves.
8. *otherwise:* to act differently.

Which end o'th' beam should bow.⁹ We have lost your son,
I fear, for ever. Milan and Naples have
More widows in them of this business' making
Than we bring men to comfort them. The fault's your own.

ALONSO   So is the dear'st o'th' loss.¹

135   GONZALO   My lord Sebastian,
The truth you speak doth lack some gentleness
And time to speak it in. You rub the sore²
When you should bring the plaster.

SEBASTIAN [to ANTONIO]   Very well.

140   ANTONIO   And most chirurgeonly.°   surgeonlike

GONZALO [to ALONSO]   It is foul weather in us all, good sir,
When you are cloudy.

SEBASTIAN [to ANTONIO]   Fowl weather?³

ANTONIO   Very foul.

GONZALO [to ALONSO]   Had I plantation⁴ of this isle, my lord—

ANTONIO [to SEBASTIAN]   He'd sow't with nettle-seed.

SEBASTIAN   Or docks,
or mallows.⁵

145   GONZALO   And were the king on't, what would I do?

SEBASTIAN [to ANTONIO]   Scape being drunk, for want of wine.

GONZALO   I'th' commonwealth I would by contraries
Execute all things.⁶ For no kind of traffic°   commerce
Would I admit, no name of magistrate;

150   Letters° should not be known; riches, poverty,   Writing; erudition
And use of service,° none; contract, succession,⁷   servants
Bourn,° bound of land, tilth,° vineyard, none;   Boundary / tillage
No use of metal, corn,° or wine, or oil;   grain
No occupation, all men idle, all;

155   And women too—but innocent and pure;⁸
No sovereignty—

SEBASTIAN [to ANTONIO]   Yet he would be king on't.

ANTONIO   The latter end of his commonwealth forgets the
beginning.

GONZALO [to ALONSO]   All things in common° nature should   for communal use
produce

160   Without sweat or endeavour. Treason, felony,
Sword, pike, knife, gun, or need of any engine,°   weapon
Would I not have; but nature should bring forth
Of it° own kind all foison,° all abundance,   its / plenty
To feed my innocent people.

165   SEBASTIAN [to ANTONIO]   No marrying⁹ 'mong his subjects?

ANTONIO   None, man, all idle: whores and knaves.

GONZALO [to ALONSO]   I would with such perfection govern, sir,
T'excel the Golden Age.¹

---

9. *Weighed . . . bow:* Weighed loathness to marry against
obedience to her father to find out which end of the
scales' beam would sink.
1. That is, the most grievous, or costliest, part of the loss
is also my own.
2. "To rub the sore" was proverbial. *plaster* (line 138): a
soothing remedy.
3. Perhaps recalling lines 28–31.
4. Had I responsibility for colonization of the island, but
also interpreted as "planting" by Antonio and Sebastian.
5. Cited as wild plants prone to grow on uncultivated
land; but dock is a traditional soother of nettle stings, and

mallow roots were used to make soothing ointment.
6. *I would . . . things:* I would advance the opposite to
what would be usual. This speech is based on a passage
in John Florio's translation of Montaigne's essay "Of the
Cannibals."
7. Inheritance of property.
8. Idleness proverbially begets lust.
9. Seen as irrelevant to sexually innocent people; also a
form of contract (line 151).
1. In classical mythology, the earliest of the ages—a time
without strife, labor, or injustice, when abundant food
grew without cultivation.

SEBASTIAN   Save° his majesty!   *God save*

ANTONIO   Long live Gonzalo!

GONZALO [*to* ALONSO]   And—do you mark me, sir?

170   ALONSO   Prithee, no more. Thou dost talk nothing to me.

GONZALO   I do well believe your highness, and did it to minister
      occasion² to these gentlemen, who are of such sensible° and   *sensitive*
      nimble lungs that they always use° to laugh at nothing.   *are accustomed*

ANTONIO   'Twas you we laughed at.

175   GONZALO   Who, in this kind of merry fooling, am nothing to
      you. So you may continue, and laugh at nothing still.

ANTONIO   What a blow was there given!

SEBASTIAN   An it had not fallen flat-long.³

GONZALO   You are gentlemen of brave mettle.⁴ You would lift

180   the moon out of her sphere, if she would continue in it five
      weeks without changing.⁵

                    Enter ARIEL, [*invisible,*] *playing solemn music*

SEBASTIAN   We would so, and then go a-bat-fowling.⁶

ANTONIO [*to* GONZALO]   Nay, good my lord, be not angry.

GONZALO   No, I warrant you, I will not adventure my discretion

185   so weakly.⁷ Will you laugh me asleep? For I am very heavy.°   *tired; serious*

ANTONIO   Go sleep, and hear us.

                    [GONZALO, ADRIAN, *and* FRANCISCO *sleep*]

ALONSO   What, all so soon asleep? I wish mine eyes
      Would, with themselves, shut up my thoughts.—I find
      They are inclined to do so.

SEBASTIAN   Please you, sir,

190   Do not omit° the heavy offer° of it.   *neglect / opportunity*
      It seldom visits sorrow; when it doth,
      It is a comforter.

ANTONIO   We two, my lord,
      Will guard your person while you take your rest,
      And watch your safety.

ALONSO   Thank you. Wondrous heavy.

                    [*He sleeps. Exit* ARIEL]

195   SEBASTIAN   What a strange drowsiness possesses them!

ANTONIO   It is the quality o'th' climate.

SEBASTIAN   Why
      Doth it not then our eyelids sink? I find
      Not myself disposed to sleep.

ANTONIO   Nor I; my spirits are nimble.
      They fell together all, as by consent;°   *consensus*

200   They dropped as by a thunderstroke. What might,
      Worthy Sebastian, O, what might—? No more!—
      And yet methinks I see it in thy face.
      What thou shouldst be th'occasion speaks° thee, and   *opportunity reveals to*
      My strong imagination sees a crown
      Dropping upon thy head.

205   SEBASTIAN   What, art thou waking?°   *awake*

ANTONIO   Do you not hear me speak?

---

2. *minister occasion:* afford opportunity.
3. If it had not fallen on the flat, harmless side of the
sword.
4. Courage; punning on "metal," as of a sword blade.
5. *You would . . . changing:* If the moon were to remain
in her orbit ("sphere") one week longer than usual (five

weeks), you would steal her from her place.
6. Trapping birds by using light to attract them and bats
to strike them down; may also mean swindling and vic-
timizing the simple.
7. I will not put my sound judgment at risk so foolishly.

SEBASTIAN   I do, and surely
    It is a sleepy language, and thou speak'st
    Out of thy sleep. What is it thou didst say?
    This is a strange repose, to be asleep
210   With eyes wide open; standing, speaking, moving,
    And yet so fast asleep.
ANTONIO   Noble Sebastian,
    Thou letst thy fortune sleep, die rather; wink'st°   *shut your eyes*
    Whiles thou art waking.
SEBASTIAN   Thou dost snore distinctly;°   *meaningfully*
    There's meaning in thy snores.
215 ANTONIO   I am more serious than my custom. You
    Must be so too if heed° me, which to do   *if you heed*
    Trebles thee o'er.
SEBASTIAN   Well, I am standing water.[8]
ANTONIO   I'll teach you how to flow.
SEBASTIAN   Do so; to ebb
    Hereditary sloth[9] instructs me.
ANTONIO   O,
220   If you but knew how you the purpose cherish
    Whiles thus you mock it;[1] how in stripping it
    You more invest° it! Ebbing° men, indeed,   *clothe / Declining*
    Most often do so near the bottom run
    By their own fear or sloth.
SEBASTIAN   Prithee, say on.
225   The setting° of thine eye and cheek proclaim   *fixed look*
    A matter° from thee, and a birth, indeed,   *Something important*
    Which throes[2] thee much to yield.
ANTONIO   Thus, sir.
    Although this lord° of weak remembrance,° this,   *(Gonzalo) / memory*
    Who shall be of as little memory°   *remembered*
230   When he is earthed,° hath here almost persuaded—   *buried*
    For he's a spirit of persuasion, only
    Professes[3] to persuade—the King his son's alive,
    'Tis as impossible that he's undrowned
    As he that sleeps here swims.
SEBASTIAN   I have no hope
    That he's undrowned.
235 ANTONIO   O, out of that 'no hope'
    What great hope have you! No hope that way° is   *(that he's not drowned)*
    Another way so high a hope that even
    Ambition cannot pierce a wink° beyond,   *catch a glimpse*
    But doubt discovery there.[4] Will you grant with me
    That Ferdinand is drowned?
SEBASTIAN   He's gone.
240 ANTONIO   Then tell me,
    Who's the next heir of Naples?
SEBASTIAN   Claribel.

---

8. Between tides, and thus open to suggestion; also associated with being slothful. *Trebles thee o'er:* Makes you
three times as great.
9. Inherited laziness, or the slowness to attain prosperity
arising from being born a younger brother.
1. *If . . . it:* If you only understood that your mockery
reveals how great your aspirations really are; also, the

hereditary position you mock is actually to your advantage. *cherish:* hold dear; cultivate.
2. Which puts in agony, as in childbirth.
3. *only / Professes:* his sole vocation is.
4. Doubt that there is anything to achieve beyond the
high hope of the crown.

ANTONIO   She that is Queen of Tunis; she that dwells
Ten leagues beyond man's life;° she that from Naples   *lifetime journey*
Can have no note°—unless the sun were post°—   *information / messenger*
245   The man i'th' moon's too slow—till new-born chins
Be rough and razorable; she that from° whom   *returning from*
We all were sea-swallowed, though some cast again⁵—
And by that destiny, to perform an act
Whereof what's past is prologue, what to come
In yours and my discharge.°   *performance*
250 SEBASTIAN   What stuff is this? How say you?
'Tis true my brother's daughter's Queen of Tunis;
So is she heir of Naples; 'twixt which regions
There is some space.
ANTONIO   A space whose every cubit°   *about 18 to 22 inches*
Seems to cry out 'How shall that Claribel
255   Measure us° back to Naples? Keep° in Tunis,   *(the cubits) / Stay*
And let Sebastian wake.'° Say this were death   *(to his opportunity)*
That now hath seized them; why, they were no worse
Than now they are. There be that° can rule Naples   *those that*
As well as he that sleeps, lords that can prate
260   As amply and unnecessarily
As this Gonzalo; I myself could make
A chough of as deep chat.⁶ O, that you bore
The mind that I do, what a sleep were this
For your advancement! Do you understand me?
SEBASTIAN   Methinks I do.
265 ANTONIO   And how does your content
Tender° your own good fortune?   *Regard; care for*
SEBASTIAN   I remember
You did supplant your brother Prospero.
ANTONIO   True;
And look how well my garments sit upon me,
Much feater° than before. My brother's servants   *more trimly*
270   Were then my fellows; now they are my men.
SEBASTIAN   But for your conscience.
ANTONIO   Ay, sir, where lies that? If 'twere a kibe⁷
'Twould put me to° my slipper; but I feel not   *make me wear*
This deity in my bosom. Twenty consciences
275   That stand 'twixt me and Milan, candied⁸ be they,
And melt ere they molest. Here lies your brother,
No better than the earth he lies upon
If he were that which now he's like—that's dead;
Whom I with this obedient steel,° three inches of it,   *sword*
280   Can lay to bed for ever; whiles you, doing thus,
To the perpetual wink for aye° might put   *sleep forever*
This ancient morsel, this Sir Prudence, who
Should not upbraid our course. For all the rest,
They'll take suggestion° as a cat laps milk;   *prompting to evil*
285   They'll tell the clock° to any business that   *chime; agree*
We say befits the hour.
SEBASTIAN   Thy case, dear friend,

---

5. Regurgitated, cast ashore; also, possibly, theatrical role-playing.
6. *I . . . chat*: I could train a jackdaw (known for imitating speech) to speak as profoundly.
7. Chilblain; sore on the heel.
8. Turned to sugar; crystallized in sugar.

Shall be my precedent. As thou got'st Milan,
I'll come by Naples. Draw thy sword. One stroke
Shall free thee from the tribute which thou payest,
And I the King shall love thee.

290 ANTONIO   Draw together,
And when I rear my hand, do you the like
To fall it on Gonzalo.
           [*They draw*]
SEBASTIAN   O, but one word.
           Enter ARIEL, [*invisible,*] *with music and song*
ARIEL [*to* GONZALO]   My master through his art foresees the danger
That you his friend are in—and sends me forth,
295 For else° his project dies, to keep them⁹ living.   *otherwise*
           [*He*] *sings in Gonzalo's ear*
                     While you here do snoring lie,
                     Open-eyed conspiracy
                          His time° doth take.   *opportunity*
                     If of life you keep a care,
300   Shake off slumber, and beware.
                          Awake, awake!
ANTONIO [*to* SEBASTIAN]   Then let us both be sudden.
GONZALO [*awaking*]   Now good angels
Preserve the King!
ALONSO [*awaking*]   Why, how now? Ho, awake!
           [*The others awake*]
           [*To* ANTONIO *and* SEBASTIAN]   Why are you° drawn?   *your weapons*
           [*To* GONZALO] Wherefore this ghastly° looking?   *fearful*
305 GONZALO   What's the matter?
SEBASTIAN   Whiles we stood here securing° your repose,   *guarding*
Even now we heard a hollow burst of bellowing,
Like bulls, or rather lions. Did't not wake you?
It struck mine ear most terribly.
ALONSO   I heard nothing.
310 ANTONIO   O, 'twas a din to fright a monster's ear,
To make an earthquake! Sure it was the roar
Of a whole herd of lions.
ALONSO   Heard you this, Gonzalo?
GONZALO   Upon mine honour, sir, I heard a humming,
And that a strange one too, which did awake me.
315 I shaked you, sir, and cried.° As mine eyes opened   *called out*
I saw their weapons drawn. There was a noise,
That's verily.° 'Tis best we stand upon our guard,   *the truth*
Or that we quit this place. Let's draw our weapons.
ALONSO   Lead off this ground, and let's make further search
For my poor son.
320 GONZALO   Heavens keep him from these beasts!
For he is sure i'th' island.
ALONSO   Lead away.   [*Exeunt all but* ARIEL]¹
ARIEL   Prospero my lord shall know what I have done.
So, King, go safely on to seek thy son.   *Exit*

---

9. Gonzalo and Alonso.
1. Ariel's following lines are spoken as the other characters depart; he probably exits in another direction.

2.2

Enter CALIBAN, *[wearing a gaberdine,*[1] *and] with a bur-*
den of wood

CALIBAN *[throwing down his burden]*   All the infections that the
sun sucks up
From bogs, fens, flats,° on Prosper fall, and make him   marshes
By inch-meal° a disease!   inch by inch
[*A noise of thunder heard*][2]
                    His spirits hear me,
And yet I needs must curse. But they'll nor pinch,
5   Fright me with urchin-shows,[3] pitch me i'th' mire,
Nor lead me like a fire-brand in the dark
Out of my way, unless he bid 'em. But
For every trifle are they set upon me;
Sometime like apes, that mow° and chatter at me   grimace
10 And after bite me; then like hedgehogs, which
Lie tumbling in my barefoot way and mount
Their pricks at my footfall; sometime am I
All wound with° adders, who with cloven tongues   entwined by
Do hiss me into madness.
                    Enter TRINCULO[4]
                    Lo now, lo!
15 Here comes a spirit of his, and to torment me
For bringing wood in slowly. I'll fall flat.
Perchance he will not mind° me.   notice
[*He lies down*]
TRINCULO   Here's neither bush nor shrub to bear off° any   ward off
weather at all, and another storm brewing. I hear it sing i'th'
20 wind. Yon same black cloud, yon huge one, looks like a foul
bombard[5] that would shed his liquor. If it should thunder as it
did before, I know not where to hide my head. Yon same cloud
cannot choose but fall by pailfuls. [*Seeing* CALIBAN] What have
we here, a man or a fish? Dead or alive?—A fish, he smells
25 like a fish; a very ancient and fish-like smell; a kind of not-of-
the-newest poor-john.[6] A strange fish! Were I in England now,
as once I was, and had but this fish painted,[7] not a holiday-fool
there but would give a piece of silver. There would this monster make a man.[8] Any strange beast there makes a man. When
30 they will not give a doit° to relieve a lame beggar, they will lay   small coin
out ten to see a dead Indian.[9] Legged like a man, and his fins
like arms! Warm, o'my troth! I do now let loose my opinion,
hold it no longer. This is no fish, but an islander that hath
lately suffered by a thunderbolt.
[*Thunder*]
35 Alas, the storm is come again. My best way is to creep under
his gaberdine; there is no other shelter hereabout. Misery
acquaints a man with strange bedfellows. I will here shroud°   take cover
till the dregs[1] of the storm be past.

2.2
1. A loose smock made of coarse material.
2. Caliban takes this as a response to his curse; in F, the
direction comes before Caliban speaks.
3. With the sight of hedgehoglike spirits.
4. Trinculo is probably dressed in traditional fool's motley (many-colored garment).
5. Large leather drinking vessel; stone-throwing military

engine.
6. Dried hake, a poor person's staple.
7. On a sign to attract spectators.
8. Make a fortune for a man; become a man.
9. An allusion to exhibitions of American Indians in
London.
1. Drinks, as from a "bombard" of wine.

[*He hides under Caliban's gaberdine.*]
Enter STEFANO, *singing* [*with a wooden bottle in his hand*]

STEFANO   I shall no more to sea, to sea,
40   Here shall I die ashore—
This is a very scurvy tune to sing at a man's funeral.
Well, here's my comfort.
                    [*He*] *drinks,* [*then*] *sings*
                    The master, the swabber, the boatswain, and I,
                       The gunner and his mate,
45   Loved Mall, Meg, and Marian, and Margery,
                       But none of us cared for Kate.
                          For she had a tongue with a tang,°   sting
                          Would cry to a sailor 'Go hang!'
                    She loved not the savour of tar nor of pitch,
50   Yet a tailor might scratch her where'er she did itch.[2]
                       Then to sea, boys, and let her go hang!
                       Then to sea [*etc.*].
This is a scurvy tune, too. But here's my comfort.
                    [*He*] *drinks*

CALIBAN [*to* TRINCULO]   Do not torment me! O!
55 STEFANO   What's the matter?° Have we devils here? Do you put   *What's going on?*
    tricks upon's with savages and men of Ind,° ha? I have not   *India*
    scaped drowning to be afeard now of your four legs. For it hath
    been said: 'As proper a man as ever went on four legs[3] cannot
    make him give ground.' And it shall be said so again, while
60 Stefano breathes at'° nostrils.   *at the*
CALIBAN   The spirit torments me. O!
STEFANO   This is some monster of the isle with four legs, who
    hath got, as I take it, an ague.° Where the devil should he learn   *a fit of fever*
    our language? I will give him some relief, if it be but for that.
65 If I can recover° him and keep him tame and get to Naples   *cure*
    with him, he's a present for any emperor that ever trod on neat's
    leather.°   *cowhide; shoes*
CALIBAN [*to* TRINCULO]   Do not torment me, prithee! I'll bring
    my wood home faster.
70 STEFANO   He's in his fit now, and does not talk after° the wisest.   *in the manner of*
    He shall taste of my bottle. If he have never drunk wine afore,
    it will go near to° remove his fit. If I can recover him and keep   *almost*
    him tame, I will not take too much for him.[4] He shall pay for
    him that hath° him, and that soundly.   *gets*
75 CALIBAN [*to* TRINCULO]   Thou dost me yet but little hurt. Thou
    wilt anon, I know it by thy trembling. Now Prosper works upon
    thee.
STEFANO   Come on your ways.° Open your mouth. Here is that   *Come on*
    which will give language to you, cat.[5] Open your mouth. This
80 will shake° your shaking, I can tell you, and that soundly. You   *dislodge*
    cannot tell who's your friend. Open your chaps again.
                    [CALIBAN *drinks*]

2. Implying sexual desire and gratification. Tailors were   gesting "on crutches."
often mocked for supposed lack of virility.   4. No sum can be too high for him.
3. Comically varying "on two legs" (upright); also sug-   5. "Ale will make a cat speak" was proverbial.

TRINCULO   I should know that voice. It should be—but he is
drowned, and these are devils. O, defend me!

STEFANO   Four legs and two voices—a most delicate° monster!   *exquisitely made*
His forward voice now is to speak well of his friend; his back-
ward voice is to utter foul speeches and to detract. If all the
wine in my bottle will recover him,[6] I will help his ague.
Come.

[CALIBAN *drinks*]

Amen.° I will pour some in thy other mouth.   *Enough*

TRINCULO   Stefano!

STEFANO   Doth thy other mouth call me? Mercy, mercy! This is
a devil, and no monster. I will leave him. I have no long
spoon.[7]

TRINCULO   Stefano! If thou beest Stefano, touch me and speak
to me, for I am Trinculo. Be not afeard. Thy good friend Trinculo.

STEFANO   If thou beest Trinculo, come forth. I'll pull thee by
the lesser legs. If any be Trinculo's legs, these are they.

[*He pulls out* TRINCULO *by the legs*]

Thou art very° Trinculo indeed! How cam'st thou to be the   *actual*
siege° of this moon-calf?[8] Can he vent° Trinculos?   *excrement / defecate*

TRINCULO [*rising*]   I took him to be killed with a thunderstroke.
But art thou not drowned, Stefano? I hope now thou art not
drowned. Is the storm overblown? I hid me under the dead
moon-calf 's gaberdine for fear of the storm. And art thou living,
Stefano? O Stefano, two Neapolitans scaped!

[*He dances* STEFANO *round*]

STEFANO   Prithee, do not turn me about. My stomach is not
constant.

CALIBAN   These be fine things, an if ° they be not spirits.   *an if = if*
That's a brave° god, and bears celestial liquor.   *an excellent; a fine*
I will kneel to him.

[*He kneels*]

STEFANO [*to* TRINCULO]   How didst thou scape? How cam'st thou
hither? Swear by this bottle how thou cam'st hither. I escaped
upon a butt of sack[9] which the sailors heaved o'erboard, by this
bottle—which I made of the bark of a tree with mine own
hands since I was cast ashore.

CALIBAN   I'll swear upon that bottle to be thy true subject, for
the liquor is not earthly.

STEFANO [*offering* TRINCULO *the bottle*]   Here. Swear then how
thou escapedst.

TRINCULO   Swum ashore, man, like a duck. I can swim like a
duck, I'll be sworn.

STEFANO   Here, kiss the book.[1]

[TRINCULO *drinks*]

Though thou canst swim like a duck, thou art made like a
goose.[2]

6. If it takes all the wine in my bottle to cure him.
7. From the proverbial "He should have a long spoon
that sups with the devil."
8. Deformed creature; miscarriage, owing to the supposed detrimental influence of the moon.
9. Cask of Spanish or Canary wine.

1. Confirming an oath by kissing the Bible; or the proverbial "Kiss the cup" ("Drink").
2. Probably alluding to Trinculo's outstretched neck with
the bottle as a beak; also a byword for giddiness and
unsteadiness on the feet.

125   TRINCULO   O Stefano, hast any more of this?

        STEFANO   The whole butt, man. My cellar is in a rock by th' sea-
        side, where my wine is hid.

               [CALIBAN *rises*]

        How now, moon-calf ? How does thine ague?

        CALIBAN   Hast thou not dropped from heaven?

130   STEFANO   Out o'th' moon, I do assure thee. I was the man i'th'
        moon when time was.°   *once upon a time*

        CALIBAN   I have seen thee in her, and I do adore thee.
        My mistress° showed me thee, and thy dog and thy bush.[3]   *(Miranda)*

        STEFANO   Come, swear to that. Kiss the book. I will furnish it
135   anon with new contents. Swear.

               [CALIBAN *drinks*]

        TRINCULO   By this good light,° this is a very shallow monster! I   *sun*
        afeard of him? A very weak monster! The man i'th' moon? A
        most poor, credulous monster! Well drawn,° monster, in good   *drunk*
        sooth!

140   CALIBAN [*to* STEFANO]   I'll show thee every fertile inch o'th' island,
        And I will kiss thy foot. I prithee, be my god.

        TRINCULO   By this light, a most perfidious and drunken monster!
        When's god's asleep, he'll rob his bottle.

        CALIBAN [*to* STEFANO]   I'll kiss thy foot. I'll swear myself thy subject.

145   STEFANO   Come on then; down, and swear.

               [CALIBAN *kneels*]

        TRINCULO   I shall laugh myself to death at this puppy-headed
        monster. A most scurvy monster! I could find in my heart to
        beat him—

        STEFANO [*to* CALIBAN]   Come, kiss.

              [CALIBAN *kisses his foot*]

150   TRINCULO   But that the poor monster's in drink.° An abominable   *drunk*
        monster!

        CALIBAN   I'll show thee the best springs; I'll pluck thee berries;
        I'll fish for thee, and get thee wood enough.
        A plague upon the tyrant that I serve!

155   I'll bear him no more sticks, but follow thee,
        Thou wondrous man.

        TRINCULO   A most ridiculous monster, to make a wonder of a
        poor drunkard!

        CALIBAN [*to* STEFANO]   I prithee, let me bring thee where crabs°   *crab apples*
        grow,

160   And I with my long nails will dig thee pig-nuts,°   *edible tubers*
        Show thee a jay's nest, and instruct thee how
        To snare the nimble marmoset. I'll bring thee
        To clust'ring filberts, and sometimes I'll get thee
        Young seamews° from the rock. Wilt thou go with me?   *seagulls*

165   STEFANO   I prithee now, lead the way without any more talk-
        ing.—Trinculo, the King and all our company else being
        drowned, we will inherit here.—Here, bear my bottle.[4]—Fel-
        low Trinculo, we'll fill him° by and by again.   *it*

        CALIBAN (*sings drunkenly*)[5]   Farewell, master, farewell, farewell!

170   TRINCULO   A howling monster, a drunken monster!

---

3. A dog and a thornbush were traditional attributes of the man in the moon; cf. *A Midsummer Night's Dream* 5.1.248–49.

4. Probably spoken to Caliban.

5. This stage direction may be misplaced and may actually refer to the following song, "No more dams."

CALIBAN [*sings*]   No more dams I'll make for° fish,   *to trap*
                    Nor fetch in firing°   *firewood*
                    At requiring,
                    Nor scrape trenchering,[6] nor wash dish.
175   'Ban, 'ban, Cacaliban
                    Has a new master.—Get a new man![7]
        Freedom, high-day!° High-day, freedom! Freedom, high-day,   *holiday*
    freedom!

STEFANO   O brave° monster! Lead the way.   *Exeunt*   *excellent; fine*

3.1

Enter FERDINAND, *bearing a log*

FERDINAND   There be some sports are painful, and their labour
    Delight in them sets off.[1] Some kinds of baseness
    Are nobly undergone, and most poor matters
    Point to rich ends. This my mean° task   *lowly*
5   Would be as heavy to me as odious, but°   *except that*
    The mistress which I serve quickens° what's dead,   *enlivens*
    And makes my labours pleasures. O, she is
    Ten times more gentle than her father's crabbed,
    And he's composed of harshness. I must remove
10 Some thousands of these logs and pile them up,
    Upon a sore° injunction. My sweet mistress   *harsh*
    Weeps when she sees me work, and says such baseness
    Had never like executor. I forget,
    But these sweet thoughts do even refresh my labours,
    Most busil'est[2] when I do it.°   *(labor)*

Enter MIRANDA, *and* PROSPERO [*following at a distance*]

15 MIRANDA   Alas now, pray you
    Work not so hard. I would the lightning had
    Burnt up those logs that you are enjoined to pile.
    Pray set it down, and rest you. When this burns
    'Twill weep[3] for having wearied you. My father
20 Is hard at study. Pray now, rest yourself.
    He's safe° for these three hours.   *We are safe from him*
FERDINAND   O most dear mistress,
    The sun will set before I shall discharge
    What I must strive to do.
MIRANDA   If you'll sit down
    I'll bear your logs the while. Pray give me that;
    I'll carry it to the pile.
25 FERDINAND   No, precious creature.
    I had rather crack my sinews, break my back,
    Than you should such dishonour undergo
    While I sit lazy by.
MIRANDA   It would become me
    As well as it does you; and I should do it
30 With much more ease, for my good will is to it,
    And yours it is against.

---

6. Trenchers, or wooden plates.
7. Addressed to the old master, Prospero.
3.1
1. *their . . . off*: the greater effort invested amounts to

more pleasure; the labor of painful activities ("sports") is
offset by whatever delight we take in them.
2. Most busily (giving a double superlative).
3. By exuding drops of resin.

PROSPERO [*aside*]   Poor worm, thou art infected.[4]
This visitation[5] shows it.
MIRANDA [*to* FERDINAND]   You look wearily.
FERDINAND   No, noble mistress, 'tis fresh morning with me
When you are by at night. I do beseech you,
35   Chiefly that I might set it in my prayers,
What is your name?
MIRANDA   Miranda. O my father,
I have broke your hest° to say so!   *disobeyed your command*
FERDINAND   Admired[6] Miranda!
Indeed the top of admiration, worth
What's dearest to the world. Full many a lady
40   I have eyed with best regard, and many a time
Th'harmony of their tongues hath into bondage
Brought my too diligent° ear. For several virtues   *attentive*
Have I liked several° women; never any   *various*
With so full soul but some defect in her
45   Did quarrel with the noblest grace she owed°   *owned*
And put it to the foil.[7] But you, O you,
So perfect and so peerless, are created
Of every creature's best.
MIRANDA   I do not know
One of my sex, no woman's face remember
50   Save from my glass° mine own; nor have I seen   *mirror*
More that I may call men than you, good friend,
And my dear father. How features are abroad[8]
I am skilless° of ; but, by my modesty,°   *ignorant / virginity*
The jewel in my dower,° I would not wish   *dowry*
55   Any companion in the world but you;
Nor can imagination form a shape
Besides° yourself to like of. But I prattle   *Other than*
Something° too wildly, and my father's precepts   *Somewhat*
I therein do forget.
FERDINAND   I am in my condition°   *rank*
60   A prince, Miranda, I do think a king—
I would° not so—and would no more endure   *wish it were*
This wooden slavery[9] than to suffer
The flesh-fly[1] blow my mouth. Hear my soul speak.
The very instant that I saw you did
65   My heart fly to your service; there resides
To make me slave to it. And for your sake
Am I this patient log-man.
MIRANDA   Do you love me?
FERDINAND   O heaven, O earth, bear witness to this sound,
And crown what I profess with kind event°   *favorable outcome*
70   If I speak true! If hollowly,° invert   *falsely*
What best is boded° me to mischief !° I,   *foretold to / misfortune*
Beyond all limit of what° else i'th' world,   *whatsoever*
Do love, prize, honour you.

---

4. Inflicted with lovesickness. *worm:* an expression of tenderness; but a worm was often thought to carry disease.
5. Suggesting a pastoral or charitable visit to the sick; or may indicate a visit by the plague, here lovesickness.
6. Playing on the meaning of Miranda's name.

7. Foiled it, or made it ineffectual; challenged it, as in a fencing match (compare "quarrel" in line 45).
8. What people look like elsewhere.
9. The log as a symbol of Prospero's oppression.
1. Species of fly that deposits its eggs ("blows") in dead flesh.

MIRANDA [*weeping*]   I am a fool
　　To weep at what I am glad of.
PROSPERO [*aside*]   Fair encounter
75　　Of two most rare affections! Heavens rain grace
　　On that which breeds between 'em.
FERDINAND [*to* MIRANDA]   Wherefore weep you?
MIRANDA   At mine unworthiness, that dare not offer
　　What I desire to give, and much less take
　　What I shall die to want.[2] But this is trifling,
80　　And all the more it seeks to hide itself
　　The bigger bulk it shows.[3] Hence, bashful cunning,°   *artful shyness*
　　And prompt me, plain and holy innocence.
　　I am your wife, if you will marry me.
　　If not, I'll die your maid.° To be your fellow°   *virgin; servant / equal*
85　　You may deny me, but I'll be your servant
　　Whether you will or no.
FERDINAND [*kneeling*]   My mistress,° dearest;   *sweetheart*
　　And I thus humble ever.
MIRANDA   My husband then?
FERDINAND   Ay, with a heart as willing°   *desirous*
90　　As bondage e'er of freedom. Here's my hand.[4]
MIRANDA   And mine, with my heart in't. And now farewell
　　Till half an hour hence.
FERDINAND   A thousand thousand.°   *(farewells)*
　　　　Exeunt [severally° MIRANDA *and* FERDINAND]   *separately*
PROSPERO   So glad of this as they I cannot be,
　　Who are surprised with all;° but my rejoicing   *overwhelmed by all*
95　　At nothing can be more. I'll to my book,°   *book of magic*
　　For yet ere supper-time must I perform
　　Much business appertaining.   *Exit*

3.2

Enter CALIBAN, STEFANO, *and* TRINCULO

STEFANO [*to* CALIBAN]   Tell not me. When the butt is out we will
　　drink water, not a drop before. Therefore bear up and board
　　'em.[1] Servant monster, drink to me.
TRINCULO   Servant monster? The folly° of this island! They say   *absurdity*
5　　there's but five upon this isle. We are three of them; if th'other
　　two be brained° like us, the state totters.   *have brains*
STEFANO   Drink, servant monster, when I bid thee. Thy eyes are
　　almost set° in thy head.   *fixed by drunkenness*
TRINCULO   Where should they be set° else? He were a brave   *placed*
10　　monster indeed if they were set in his tail.
STEFANO   My man-monster hath drowned his tongue in sack.
　　For my part, the sea cannot drown me. I swam, ere I could
　　recover the shore, five and thirty leagues,° off and on.[2] By this   *about 100 miles*

---

2. *At . . . want*: Miranda is not at liberty to bestow her
virginity nor to obtain the consummation that she desires
and lacs.
3. *all . . . shows*: an image of secret pregnancy.
4. *I am your wife . . . hand*: Such an exchange could
actually have constituted a marriage ceremony. In
Shakespeare's time, weddings did not need to be wit-

nessed and performed in a church to be valid (compare
4.1.14–19).
3.2
1. Force a way aboard, continuing the naval-warfare
terminology; take onboard (drink). *bear up*: sail to the
attack.
2. Tacking away from and toward the shore.

light, thou shalt be my lieutenant, monster, or my standard.³

15   TRINCULO   Your lieutenant if you list;° he's no standard.   *wish*

    STEFANO   We'll not run, Monsieur Monster.

    TRINCULO   Nor go° neither; but you'll lie⁴ like dogs, and yet say   *walk*
nothing neither.

    STEFANO   Moon-calf, speak once in thy life, if thou beest a good

20   moon-calf.

    CALIBAN   How does thy honour? Let me lick thy shoe.
I'll not serve him; he is not valiant.

    TRINCULO   Thou liest, most ignorant monster! I am in case° to   *prepared*
jostle a constable. Why, thou debauched fish, thou, was there

25   ever man a coward that hath drunk so much sack as I today?
Wilt thou tell a monstrous lie, being but half a fish and half a
monster?

    CALIBAN [*to* STEFANO]   Lo, how he mocks me! Wilt thou let him,
my lord?

30   TRINCULO   'Lord' quoth he? That a monster should be such a
natural!⁵

    CALIBAN [*to* STEFANO]   Lo, lo, again! Bite him to death, I prithee.

    STEFANO   Trinculo, keep a good tongue in your head. If you
prove a mutineer, the next tree.° The poor monster's my sub-   *(for a gallows)*

35   ject, and he shall not suffer indignity.

    CALIBAN   I thank my noble lord. Wilt thou be pleased
To hearken once again to the suit I made to thee?

    STEFANO   Marry, will I. Kneel and repeat it. I will stand, and so
shall Trinculo.

        [CALIBAN *kneels.*]

        Enter ARIEL, *invisible*

40   CALIBAN   As I told thee before, I am subject to a tyrant, a sor-
cerer, that by his cunning hath cheated me of the island.

    ARIEL   Thou liest.

    CALIBAN [*to* TRINCULO]   Thou liest, thou jesting monkey, thou.
I would my valiant master would destroy thee.

45   I do not lie.

    STEFANO   Trinculo, if you trouble him any more in's tale, by this
hand, I will supplant° some of your teeth.   *uproot*

    TRINCULO   Why, I said nothing.

    STEFANO   Mum, then, and no more. [*To* CALIBAN] Proceed.

50   CALIBAN   I say by sorcery he got this isle;
From me he got it. If thy greatness will
Revenge it on him—for I know thou dar'st,
But this thing⁶ dare not—

    STEFANO   That's most certain.

55   CALIBAN   Thou shalt be lord of it, and I'll serve thee.

    STEFANO   How now shall this be compassed?° Canst thou bring   *accomplished*
me to the party?°   *person concerned*

    CALIBAN   Yea, yea, my lord. I'll yield him thee asleep
Where thou mayst knock a nail into his head.⁷

60   ARIEL   Thou liest, thou canst not.

---

3. Standard-bearer, but in Trinculo's reply "one who can
stand up."
4. Lie (down); tell lies; excrete.
5. An idiot, punning on the idea that monsters were

unnatural.
6. Trinculo; or perhaps Caliban himself.
7. As Jael murdered sleeping Sisera in Judges 4:21 and
5:26.

CALIBAN What a pied ninny's° this! [*To* TRINCULO] Thou scurvy   *fool in motley*
    patch!°   *jester; idiot*
    [*To* STEFANO] I do beseech thy greatness give him blows,
    And take his bottle from him. When that's gone
    He shall drink naught but brine, for I'll not show him
65   Where the quick freshes° are.   *fast-flowing springs*
STEFANO Trinculo, run into no further danger. Interrupt the
    monster one word further, and, by this hand, I'll turn my mercy
    out o'doors and make a stockfish of thee.[8]
TRINCULO Why, what did I? I did nothing. I'll go farther off.
70 STEFANO Didst thou not say he lied?
ARIEL Thou liest.
STEFANO Do I so? [*Striking* TRINCULO] Take thou that. As you
    like this, give me the lie° another time.   *call me a liar*
TRINCULO I did not give the lie. Out o'your wits and hearing
75   too? A pox o'your bottle! This can sack and drinking do. A
    murrain° on your monster, and the devil take your fingers.   *plague*
CALIBAN Ha, ha, ha!
STEFANO Now forward with your tale. [*To* TRINCULO] Prithee,
    stand further off.
80 CALIBAN Beat him enough; after a little time
    I'll beat him too.
STEFANO [*to* TRINCULO]
           Stand farther. [*To* CALIBAN] Come, proceed.
CALIBAN Why, as I told thee, 'tis a custom with him
    I'th' afternoon to sleep. There° thou mayst brain him,   *Then*
    Having first seized his books; or with a log
85   Batter his skull, or paunch° him with a stake,   *disembowel*
    Or cut his weasand° with thy knife. Remember   *windpipe*
    First to possess his books, for without them
    He's but a sot° as I am, nor hath not   *stupid fool*
    One spirit to command—they all do hate him
90   As rootedly as I. Burn but his books.
    He has brave utensils,[9] for so he calls them,
    Which when he has a house he'll deck withal.
    And that most deeply to consider is
    The beauty of his daughter. He himself
95   Calls her a nonpareil.° I never saw a woman   *one without equal*
    But only Sycorax my dam and she,
    But she as far surpasseth Sycorax
    As great'st does least.
STEFANO   Is it so brave° a lass?   *excellent; fine*
CALIBAN Ay, lord. She will become thy bed, I warrant,
100   And bring thee forth brave brood.
STEFANO Monster, I will kill this man. His daughter and I will
    be king and queen—save° our graces!—and Trinculo and thy-   *God save*
    self shall be viceroys. Dost thou like the plot, Trinculo?
TRINCULO Excellent.
105 STEFANO Give me thy hand. I am sorry I beat thee. But while
    thou liv'st, keep a good tongue in thy head.

---

8. Proverbial allusion to the beating of dried fish before   9. Perhaps confusing implements for magic and house-
cooking it.   hold goods.

CALIBAN   Within this half hour will he be asleep.
    Wilt thou destroy him then?

STEFANO   Ay, on mine honour.

110 ARIEL [*aside*]   This will I tell my master.

CALIBAN   Thou mak'st me merry; I am full of pleasure.
    Let us be jocund. Will you troll° the catch°   *sing / round; song*
    You taught me but while-ere?°   *a short time ago*

STEFANO   At thy request, monster, I will do reason, any rea-

115 son.°—Come on, Trinculo, let us sing.   *anything reasonable*
    (*Sings*)   Flout 'em and cout[1] 'em,
               And scout° 'em and flout 'em.   *mock*
               Thought is free.

CALIBAN   That's not the tune.

      ARIEL *plays the tune on a tabor and pipe*[2]

120 STEFANO   What is this same?

TRINCULO   This is the tune of our catch, played by the picture
    of Nobody.[3]

STEFANO [*calls towards* ARIEL]   If thou beest a man, show thyself
    in thy likeness. If thou beest a devil, take't as thou list.°   *wish*

125 TRINCULO   O, forgive me my sins!

STEFANO   He that dies pays all debts.[4] [*Calls*] I defy thee.—
    Mercy upon us![5]

CALIBAN   Art thou afeard?

STEFANO   No, monster, not I.

130 CALIBAN   Be not afeard. The isle is full of noises,
    Sounds, and sweet airs,° that give delight and hurt not.   *tunes*
    Sometimes a thousand twangling instruments
    Will hum about mine ears, and sometime voices
    That if I then had waked after long sleep
135 Will make me sleep again; and then in dreaming
    The clouds methought would open and show riches
    Ready to drop upon me, that when I waked
    I cried to dream again.

STEFANO   This will prove a brave kingdom to me, where I shall
140 have my music for nothing.[6]

CALIBAN   When Prospero is destroyed.

STEFANO   That shall be by and by.° I remember the story.   *very soon*
                  [*Exit* ARIEL, *playing music*]

TRINCULO   The sound is going away. Let's follow it, and after do
    our work.

145 STEFANO   Lead, monster; we'll follow.—I would I could see this
    taborer. He lays it on.[7]

TRINCULO [*to* CALIBAN]   Wilt come? I'll follow Stefano.   *Exeunt*

---

1. Probably a dialectal form of "colt" (cheat). The stage direction ("Sings") suggests that the others cannot manage the catch and remain in bewildered silence. But Trinculo, and perhaps Caliban, may attempt to join in.
2. The tabor was a small drum slung on the left-hand side of the body; the tabor pipe was a long narrow pipe played with the left hand. The combination was associated with rustic dances and merrymaking.
3. "Nobody" was a character in a comedy who was depicted on the title page of the printed text. Large

breeches up to his neck made him appear to have no trunk.
4. Varying the proverbial "Death pays all debts."
5. Stefano's defiance comically collapses.
6. James I spent large sums on court music, but not typically of the popular kind Ariel now plays.
7. He sets himself to his music vigorously. Stefano deserts Caliban in order to follow the music. Trinculo and Caliban in turn follow Stefano (line 147).

3.3

Enter ALONSO, SEBASTIAN, ANTONIO, GONZALO, ADRIAN,
and FRANCISCO

GONZALO [*to* ALONSO]   By'r la'kin,[1] I can go no further, sir.
My old bones ache. Here's a maze trod indeed
Through forthrights and meanders.° By your patience,   *direct and winding paths*
I needs must rest me.

ALONSO   Old lord, I cannot blame thee,
5   Who am myself attached° with weariness   *seized*
To th' dulling of my spirits. Sit down and rest.
Even° here I will put off my hope, and keep it   *Exactly*
No longer for° my flatterer. He is drowned   *as*
Whom thus we stray to find, and the sea mocks
10   Our frustrate° search on land. Well, let him go.   *vain*
      [*They sit*]

ANTONIO [*aside to* SEBASTIAN]   I am right glad that he's so out of hope.
Do not for° one repulse forgo the purpose   *on account of*
That you resolved t'effect.

SEBASTIAN [*aside to* ANTONIO] The next advantage
Will we take throughly.°   *thoroughly*

ANTONIO [*aside to* SEBASTIAN] Let it be tonight,
15   For now they are oppressed with travel.° They   *journey; travail*
Will not nor cannot use such vigilance
As when they are fresh.

SEBASTIAN [*aside to* ANTONIO] I say tonight. No more.
            Solemn and strange music. [Enter] PROSPERO *on the
            top,[2] invisible*

ALONSO   What harmony is this? My good friends, hark.

GONZALO   Marvellous sweet music.
            *Enter [spirits, in] several strange shapes, bringing in [a
            table and] a banquet, and dance about it with gentle
            actions of salutations, and, inviting the King and [his
            companions] to eat, they depart*

20 ALONSO   Give us kind keepers,° heavens! What were these?   *guardian angels*

SEBASTIAN   A living drollery.[3] Now I will believe
That there are unicorns; that in Arabia
There is one tree, the phoenix' throne, one phoenix[4]
At this hour reigning there.

ANTONIO   I'll believe both;
25   And what does else want credit° come to me,   *lack belief*
And I'll be sworn 'tis true. Travellers ne'er did lie,[5]
Though fools at home condemn 'em.

GONZALO   If in Naples
I should report this now, would they believe me—
If I should say I saw such islanders?
30   For certes° these are people of the island,   *certainly*
Who though they are of monstrous shape, yet note
Their manners are more gentle-kind than of
Our human generation you shall find
Many, nay, almost any.

3.3
1. Ladykin: a colloquial form of reference to the Virgin
Mary.
2. A small acting area above the upper stage.
3. A puppet show with live actors.

4. The unicorn and phoenix, a bird, were two mythological creatures that sometimes figured in travelers' tales.
Only one pheonix was said to exist in the world at any one
time.
5. Proverbially, "A traveler may lie with authority."

PROSPERO [*aside*]   Honest lord,
35   Thou hast said well, for some of you there present
        Are worse than devils.
ALONSO   I cannot too much muse.°   *marvel*
        Such shapes, such gesture, and such sound, expressing—
        Although they want the use of tongue°—a kind   *language*
        Of excellent dumb discourse.
PROSPERO [*aside*]   Praise in departing.⁶
FRANCISCO   They vanished strangely.
40 SEBASTIAN   No matter, since
        They have left their viands° behind, for we have stomachs.°   *food / good appetites*
        Will't please you taste of what is here?
ALONSO   Not I.
GONZALO   Faith, sir, you need not fear. When we were boys,
        Who would believe that there were mountaineers°   *mountain dwellers*
45   Dewlapped like bulls, whose throats had hanging at 'em
        Wallets° of flesh? Or that there were such men   *Pouches*
        Whose heads stood in their breasts? Which now we find
        Each putter-out of five for one⁷ will bring us
        Good warrant of.
ALONSO [*rising*]   I will stand to and feed,°   *begin eating*
50   Although my last—no matter, since I feel
        The best is past. Brother, my lord the Duke,
        Stand to, and do as we.
        [ALONSO, SEBASTIAN, *and* ANTONIO *approach the table.*]
        Thunder and lightning. Enter ARIEL [*descending*] *like a*
        *harpy,*⁸ *claps his wings upon the table, and, with a*
        quaint device,° *the banquet vanishes*⁹   *an ingenious mechanism*
ARIEL   You are three men of sin, whom destiny—
        That hath to° instrument this lower world   *as its*
55   And what is in't—the never-surfeited sea
        Hath caused to belch up you, and on this island
        Where man doth not inhabit, you 'mongst men
        Being most unfit to live. I have made you mad,
        And even with suchlike valour¹ men hang and drown
        Their proper selves.°   *Themselves*
        [ALONSO, SEBASTIAN, *and* ANTONIO *draw*]²
60   You fools! I and my fellows
        Are ministers of fate. The elements
        Of whom your swords are tempered³ may as well
        Wound the loud winds, or with bemocked-at stabs
        Kill the still-closing⁴ waters, as diminish
65   One dowl° that's in my plume.° My fellow ministers   *featherlet / plumage*
        Are like° invulnerable. If you could hurt,   *similarly*

6. Reserve your praise until the end of the event.
7. A traveler could profit from a voyage by laying down a sum with a broker before departing and undertaking to bring back evidence of having reached his destination; if successful, he was repaid fivefold.
8. A mythological monster with a vulture's wings and claws and a woman's face. Aeneas and his companions encountered these harpies, who stole their meals and threatened to punish them with slow starvation. *Thunder and lightning:* Both spectacular and functional for disguising the mechanics of the "quaint device."
9. The simplest effective staging is by means of a rotating tabletop with the vessels of the banquet fixed to its surface. Leg-to-leg planks supporting the tabletop or a hang-

ing cloth would conceal the vanished banquet. The harpy's wings would hide the mechanics from the audience, and clapping them would provide a visual distraction.
1. *suchlike valour:* fearlessness that comes from madness.
2. Ariel perhaps ascends beyond their reach here. Aeneas's companions, like Alonso here, similarly attempted to kill the harpies with swords.
3. Compounded and hardened. Metal was sometimes thought of as being compounded of earth and fire, here contrasted with winds and waters.
4. Self-healing, since they close immediately once parted.

Your swords are now too massy° for your strengths   *heavy*
And will not be uplifted.
        [ALONSO, SEBASTIAN, *and* ANTONIO *stand amazed*°]   *crazed; bewildered*
                      But remember,
For that's my business to you, that you three
70 From Milan did supplant good Prospero;
Exposed unto the sea, which hath requit it,
Him and his innocent child; for which foul deed,
The powers, delaying not forgetting,[5] have
Incensed the seas and shores, yea, all the creatures,[6]
75 Against your peace. Thee of thy son, Alonso,
They have bereft, and do pronounce by me
Ling'ring perdition[7]—worse than any death
Can be at once—shall step by step attend
You and your ways; whose[8] wraths to guard you from—
80 Which here in this most desolate[9] isle else falls
Upon your heads—is nothing° but heart's sorrow   *there is no alternative*
And a clear life° ensuing.   *a life innocent of sin*
        He [ascends and] vanishes[1] in thunder. Then, to soft
        music, enter the [spirits] again, and dance with mocks
        and mows,° and [they depart,] carrying out the table   *grimaces*
PROSPERO   Bravely the figure of this harpy hast thou
Performed, my Ariel; a grace it had devouring.[2]
85 Of my instruction hast thou nothing bated°   *omitted*
In what thou hadst to say. So with good life[3]
And observation strange[4] my meaner ministers°   *lesser spirits*
Their several kinds° have done.° My high charms work,   *various roles / performed*
And these mine enemies are all knit up
90 In their distractions. They now are in my power;
And in these fits I leave them, while I visit
Young Ferdinand, whom they suppose is drowned,
And his and mine loved darling.   [*Exit*]
        [GONZALO, ADRIAN, *and* FRANCISCO *go towards the*
        others]
GONZALO   I'th' name of something holy, sir, why stand you
    In this strange stare?
95 ALONSO   O, it is monstrous, monstrous!
Methought the billows spoke and told me of it,
The winds did sing it to me, and the thunder,
That deep and dreadful organ-pipe, pronounced
The name of Prosper. It did bass my trespass.[5]
100 Therefor° my son i'th' ooze is bedded, and   *For that*
I'll seek him deeper than e'er plummet sounded,
And with him there lie mudded.   *Exit*
SEBASTIAN   But one fiend at a time,
I'll fight their legions o'er.°   *from beginning to end*

---

5. Related to the proverb "God stays long but strikes at last."
6. Compare Genesis 1:21: "Then God created . . . everything living and moving."
7. Slow starvation; hell on earth of spiritual suffering. The phrase is first the object of "pronounce" and then the subject of "shall . . . attend."
8. Refers to "the powers" in line 73.
9. Joyless, wretched; barren, deserted.

1. Ariel is raised out of sight into the canopy.
2. In clapping his wings, Ariel has created the illusion of having devoured the banquet.
3. Convincingly; with vitality. *So:* In the same way.
4. Remarkable attention to the requirements of their parts, or instructions.
5. The thunder proclaimed my sin ("trespass") in a bass voice, or with a bass background; perhaps wordplay on the "utter baseness" of trespass.

ANTONIO	I'll be thy second.	

Exeunt [SEBASTIAN *and* ANTONIO]

GONZALO   All three of them are desperate.° Their great guilt,   *in despair; reckless*
105   Like poison given to work° a great time after,   *take effect*
Now 'gins to bite the spirits. I do beseech you
That are of suppler joints, follow them swiftly,
And hinder them from what this ecstasy°   *madness*
May now provoke them to.

ADRIAN   Follow, I pray you.   *Exeunt*

4.1

Enter PROSPERO, FERDINAND, *and* MIRANDA

PROSPERO [*to* FERDINAND]   If I have too austerely punished you,
Your compensation makes amends, for I
Have given you here a third[1] of mine own life—
Or that for which I live—who° once again   *whom*
5   I tender° to thy hand. All thy vexations   *offer*
Were but my trials of thy love, and thou
Hast strangely° stood the test. Here, afore heaven,   *wonderfully*
I ratify this my rich gift. O Ferdinand,
Do not smile at me that I boast of her,
10   For thou shalt find she will outstrip all praise,
And make it halt° behind her.   *limp*

FERDINAND   I do believe it
Against an oracle.[2]

PROSPERO   Then, as my gift and thine own acquisition
Worthily purchased,° take my daughter. But   *Gained by effort*
15   If thou dost break her virgin-knot° before   *virginity*
All sanctimonious° ceremonies may   *holy*
With full and holy rite be ministered,
No sweet aspersion° shall the heavens let fall   *shower of grace*
To make this contract grow; but barren hate,
20   Sour-eyed disdain, and discord, shall bestrew
The union of your bed with weeds[3] so loathly
That you shall hate it both. Therefore take heed,
As Hymen's[4] lamps shall light you.

FERDINAND   As I hope
For quiet days, fair issue,° and long life   *children*
25   With such love as 'tis now, the murkiest den,°   *cave*
The most opportune place, the strong'st suggestion°   *temptation*
Our worser genius can,[5] shall never melt
Mine honour into lust to take away
The edge° of that day's celebration;   *unblunted desire*
30   When I shall think or° Phoebus' steeds are foundered[6]   *either*
Or night kept chained below.

PROSPERO   Fairly spoke.

4.1

1. Miranda. The usual poetic conceit was a half; commentators variously conjecture the other third to be his dukedom, his books, or his late wife.
2. *I . . . oracle:* I would believe it even if an oracle said otherwise.
3. Weeds in place of the flowers traditionally strewn on the marriage bed; wordplay on both "marriage bed" and "seed-bed."
4. Classical god of marriage.
5. Is capable of. *worser genius:* evil spirit corresponding to a guardian angel.
6. Collapsed and made lame. *Phoebus' steeds:* the mythological horses that drew the chariot of the sun. Ferdinand anticipates that on his wedding day he will in his impatience think that the night will never come.

Sit, then, and talk with her. She is thine own.
[FERDINAND *and* MIRANDA *sit and talk together*]
What,° Ariel, my industrious servant Ariel!   *Now, then*
    Enter ARIEL

ARIEL   What would my potent master? Here I am.

35   PROSPERO   Thou and thy meaner° fellows your last service   *lesser*
Did worthily perform, and I must use you
In such another trick. Go bring the rabble,[7]
O'er whom I give thee power, here to this place.
Incite them to quick motion, for I must
40   Bestow upon the eyes of this young couple
Some vanity[8] of mine art. It is my promise,
And they expect it from me.

ARIEL   Presently?°   *At once*

PROSPERO   Ay, with a twink.[9]

ARIEL   Before you can say 'Come' and 'Go',
45   And breathe twice, and cry 'So, so',
            Each one tripping on his toe
            Will be here with mop and mow.[1]
            Do you love me, master? No?

PROSPERO   Dearly, my delicate Ariel. Do not approach
Till thou dost hear me call.

50   ARIEL   Well; I conceive.°   *Exit*   *understand*

PROSPERO [*to* FERDINAND]   Look thou be true.[2] Do not give dalliance
Too much the rein.[3] The strongest oaths are straw
To th' fire i'th' blood. Be more abstemious,
Or else, good night your vow.

FERDINAND   I warrant you, sir,
55   The white cold virgin snow upon my heart
Abates the ardour of my liver.[4]

PROSPERO   Well.—
Now come, my Ariel! Bring a corollary°   *surplus*
Rather than want° a spirit. Appear, and pertly.°   *lack / briskly*
    Soft music
[*To* FERDINAND *and* MIRANDA] No tongue, all eyes! Be silent.
    Enter IRIS[5]

60   IRIS   Ceres, most bounteous lady, thy rich leas[6]
Of wheat, rye, barley, vetches,[7] oats, and peas;
Thy turfy mountains where live nibbling sheep,
And flat meads° thatched with stover,[8] them to keep;   *meadows*
Thy banks with peonied and twillèd[9] brims
65   Which spongy° April at thy hest betrims[1]   *wet*
To make cold nymphs chaste crowns; and thy broom-groves,[2]
Whose shadow the dismissèd bachelor° loves,   *rejected suitor*

---

7. Troupe of lesser spirits: *trick:* theatrical device, or clever artifice.
8. Trifle; conceit; illusion; display.
9. In the twinkling of an eye.
1. With derisive and grimacing gestures.
2. Take care that you remain faithful to your promise. Prospero may have caught the lovers just indulging in dalliance.
3. To "give the rein" is to make a horse gallop.
4. *The . . . liver:* Virgin snow lies on his heart because he has remained chaste, never having given in to his ardent liver. The liver was held to be the seat of passion.

5. Goddess of the rainbow and messenger of Juno; her apparel is in the colors of the rainbow, and she wears "saffron wings" (line 78).
6. Arable land. Ceres was the Roman goddess of agriculture and generative nature.
7. Pealike plants grown for fodder.
8. Hay for winter fodder.
9. Reinforced with entwined branches to prevent riverbank erosion. *peonied:* covered with peonies.
1. Adorns with flowers; recalls the colloquial "April showers bring forth May flowers."
2. Thickets of gorse, yellow-flowered shrubs. *cold:* chaste.

Being lass-lorn; thy pole-clipped vineyard,[3]
And thy sea-marge,° sterile and rocky-hard,   *seashore*
70 Where thou thyself dost air:° the Queen o'th' Sky,°   *take fresh air / Juno*
Whose wat'ry arch° and messenger am I,   *rainbow*
Bids thee leave these, and with her sovereign grace
     JUNO [*appears in the air*][4]
Here on this grass-plot,[5] in this very place,
To come and sport.—Her peacocks fly amain.[6]
75 Approach, rich Ceres, her to entertain.
          Enter [ARIEL *as*] CERES[7]
CERES   Hail, many-coloured messenger, that ne'er
Dost disobey the wife of Jupiter;°   *Juno*
Who with thy saffron wings upon my flowers
Diffusest honey-drops, refreshing showers,
80 And with each end of thy blue bow dost crown
My bosky[8] acres and my unshrubbed down,
Rich scarf[9] to my proud earth. Why hath thy queen
Summoned me hither to this short-grassed green?
IRIS   A contract of true love to celebrate,
85 And some donation freely to estate°   *bestow*
On the blest lovers.
CERES   Tell me, heavenly bow,°   *rainbow*
If Venus or her son,[1] as° thou dost know,   *as far as*
Do now attend the Queen. Since they did plot
The means that dusky Dis[2] my daughter got,
90 Her and her blind boy's scandalled° company   *scandalous; notorious*
I have forsworn.
IRIS   Of her society
Be not afraid. I met her deity
Cutting the clouds towards Paphos,[3] and her son
Dove-drawn[4] with her. Here thought they to have done
95 Some wanton charm upon[5] this man and maid,
Whose vows are that no bed-right[6] shall be paid
Till Hymen's torch be lighted[7]—but in vain.
Mars's hot minion° is returned again.   *lover; Venus*
Her waspish-headed[8] son has broke his arrows,
100 Swears he will shoot no more, but play with sparrows,[9]
And be a boy right out.°   *an ordinary boy*
          [*Music.* JUNO *descends to the stage*][1]
CERES   Highest queen of state,
Great Juno, comes; I know her by her gait.°   *majestic bearing*

---

3. Vineyard with vines embracing, twined around, their supporting poles; pruned vineyard. "Vineyard" was pronounced as three syllables. *lass-lorn:* abandoned by the girl he wooed.
4. Juno was queen of the heavens and goddess of women, held to protect marriages and preside over childbirth. Her chair is ornamented with a peacock motif. She descends by a "flight" mechanism to a position suspended in the air above the stage. Music may be played. Juno remains in view aloft until line 101. If, however, F's direction here is misplaced, she may not appear until line 101.
5. Compare "this short-grassed green" (line 83) and "this green land" (line 130): a green carpet on the acting area is indicated.
6. In haste. Peacocks, sacred to Juno, drew her chariot.
7. Her part is probably played by Ariel (see line 167).
8. Covered with bushes and thickets.
9. Ornamental and hung across the body rather than around the neck.
1. Cupid, proverbially blind.
2. King of the underworld in classical mythology. Venus and her son Cupid made him fall in love with Ceres' daughter Proserpine, whom he abducted (Ovid, *Metamorphoses* 5.395ff.).
3. City in Cyprus: associated with Venus.
4. Doves were sacred to Venus and drew her chariot.
5. *done . . . upon:* cast a lustful spell upon.
6. Right to consummate the marriage; also suggesting a rite, as in line 17.
7. Until the wedding ceremony is performed.
8. Peevish, irritable, and with arrows like the wasp's sting.
9. Sparrows were associated with Venus because they were proverbially lustful.
1. This completes Juno's flight to the stage; again, music may be played.

JUNO   How does my bounteous sister? Go with me
　　　To bless this twain, that they may prosperous be,
105　　And honoured in their issue.
　　　　　[CERES *joins* JUNO, *and*] *they sing*[2]
　　JUNO　　　Honour, riches, marriage-blessing,
　　　　　　Long continuance and increasing,
　　　　　　Hourly joys be still° upon you!　　　　　　　　　*always*
　　　　　　Juno sings her blessings on you.
110　CERES　　Earth's increase, and foison° plenty,　　　　　*abundance*
　　　　　　Barns and garners° never empty,　　　　　　　　*granaries*
　　　　　　Vines with clust'ring bunches growing,
　　　　　　Plants with goodly burden bowing;
　　　　　　Spring come to you at the farthest,
115　　　　　In the very end of harvest.[3]
　　　　　　Scarcity and want shall shun you,
　　　　　　Ceres' blessing so is on you.
　FERDINAND   This is a most majestic vision, and
　　　Harmonious charmingly.[4] May I be bold°　　　　　　*Would I be right*
　　　To think these spirits?
120　PROSPERO　　　　　　Spirits, which by mine art
　　　I have from their confines[5] called to enact
　　　My present fancies.
　FERDINAND　　　　　　Let me live here ever!
　　　So rare a wondered° father and a wise　　　　　　　*endowed with wonders*
　　　Makes this place paradise.
　　　　　JUNO *and* CERES *whisper, and send* IRIS *on employment*
　PROSPERO　　　　　　Sweet° now, silence.　　　　　　*Softly*
125　Juno and Ceres whisper seriously.
　　　There's something else to do. Hush, and be mute,
　　　Or else our spell is marred.
　IRIS   You nymphs called naiads of the wind'ring[6] brooks,
　　　With your sedged crowns° and ever-harmless looks,　　*garlands of reeds*
130　Leave your crisp channels, and on this green land
　　　Answer your summons; Juno does command.
　　　Come, temperate nymphs, and help to celebrate
　　　A contract of true love. Be not too late.
　　　　　Enter certain nymphs
　　　You sunburned sicklemen,° of August weary,　　　　*harvesters*
135　Come hither from the furrow and be merry;
　　　Make holiday, your rye-straw hats put on,
　　　And these fresh nymphs encounter every one
　　　In country footing.
　　　　　Enter certain reapers, properly habited.[7] *They join with*
　　　　　the nymphs in a graceful dance; towards the end whereof
　　　　　PROSPERO *starts suddenly, and speaks*
　PROSPERO [*aside*]   I had forgot that foul conspiracy
140　Of the beast Caliban and his confederates
　　　Against my life. The minute of their plot

---

2. Ceres and Juno might be raised together in the flight apparatus and sing suspended above the stage. They would then vanish (line 142 stage direction) by being raised into the heavens.
3. Let spring return immediately after harvest, without any intervening winter. (In Greek mythology, winter was originally caused by Ceres abandoning the earth in search of Proserpine.)
4. Delightfully; magically; harmoniously.
5. Regions of dwelling. Word is accented on the second syllable.
6. Perhaps a conflation of "wandering" and "winding." The naiads were mythical river nymphs.
7. Either properly or finely dressed.

Is almost come. [*To the spirits*] Well done! Avoid;° no more!   *Begone*
    To a strange, hollow, and confused noise, the [*spirits in*
    the pageant] *heavily vanish.*[8]
    [FERDINAND *and* MIRANDA *rise*]

FERDINAND [*to* MIRANDA]   This is strange. Your father's in some passion
    That works° him strongly.   *agitates*

MIRANDA   Never till this day
145 Saw I him touched with anger so distempered.°   *troubled; distracted*

PROSPERO   You do look, my son, in a moved sort,°   *disturbed manner*
    As if you were dismayed. Be cheerful, sir.
    Our revels[9] now are ended. These our actors,
    As I foretold you,° were all spirits, and   *told you before*
150 Are melted into air, into thin air;
    And like the baseless fabric[1] of this vision,
    The cloud-capped towers, the gorgeous palaces,
    The solemn temples, the great globe[2] itself,
    Yea, all which it inherit,[3] shall dissolve;
155 And, like this insubstantial pageant faded,
    Leave not a rack° behind. We are such stuff   *wisp of cloud*
    As dreams are made on,° and our little life   *of*
    Is rounded[4] with a sleep. Sir, I am vexed.
    Bear with my weakness. My old brain is troubled.
160 Be not disturbed with my infirmity.
    If you be pleased, retire into my cell,
    And there repose. A turn or two I'll walk
    To still my beating mind.

FERDINAND *and* MIRANDA   We wish your peace.
                 Exeunt [FERDINAND *and* MIRANDA]

PROSPERO   Come with a thought![5] I thank thee, Ariel. Come!
    Enter ARIEL

ARIEL   Thy thoughts I cleave to. What's thy pleasure?
165 PROSPERO   Spirit,
    We must prepare to meet with Caliban.

ARIEL   Ay, my commander. When I presented[6] Ceres
    I thought to have told thee of it, but I feared
    Lest I might anger thee.

170 PROSPERO   Say again: where didst thou leave these varlets?°   *ruffians*

ARIEL   I told you, sir, they were red-hot with drinking;
    So full of valour that they smote the air
    For breathing in their faces, beat the ground
    For kissing of their feet; yet always bending°   *aiming*
175 Towards their project. Then I beat my tabor,°   *side drum*
    At which like unbacked° colts they pricked their ears,   *never-ridden*
    Advanced° their eyelids, lifted up their noses   *Opened*
    As° they smelt music. So I charmed their ears   *As if*
    That calf-like they my lowing° followed, through   *mooing*
180 Toothed briars, sharp furzes, pricking gorse,° and thorns,   *prickly shrubs*
    Which entered their frail shins. At last I left them
    I'th' filthy-mantled[7] pool beyond your cell,

---

8. Sorrowfully depart (probably not implying a trick of staging).
9. Entertainment, in both festive and theatrical senses.
1. An edifice or substance without foundations; insubstantial, alluding to buildings in masque scenery.
2. World; also with a passing allusion to the Globe Theatre.

3. All who come into possession of it.
4. Rounded off; surrounded; or, possibly, crowned.
5. Come as fast as thought, a colloquial simile.
6. Acted; produced the masque of; introduced while playing Iris.
7. Covered with filthy scum.

There dancing up to th' chins, that° the foul lake   *so that*
O'er-stunk[8] their feet.

PROSPERO   This was well done, my bird.°   *chick; dear*

185   Thy shape invisible retain thou still.
The trumpery° in my house, go bring it hither   *cheap goods*
For stale° to catch these thieves.   *decoy; bait*

ARIEL   I go, I go.   *Exit*

PROSPERO   A devil, a born devil, on whose nature
Nurture can never stick; on whom my pains,

190   Humanely taken, all, all lost, quite lost,
And, as with age his body uglier grows,
So his mind cankers.° I will plague them all,   *festers*
Even to roaring.

       Enter ARIEL, *laden with glistening apparel, etc.*
          Come, hang them on this lime.[9]
   [ARIEL *hangs up the apparel. Exeunt* PROSPERO *and*
                          ARIEL]

     Enter CALIBAN, STEFANO, *and* TRINCULO, *all wet*

CALIBAN   Pray you, tread softly, that the blind mole may

195   Not hear a foot fall. We now are near his cell.

STEFANO   Monster, your fairy, which you say is a harmless fairy,
has done little better than played the Jack° with us.   *knave; will-o'-the-wisp*

TRINCULO   Monster, I do smell° all horse-piss, at which my   *smell of*
nose is in great indignation.

200 STEFANO   So is mine. Do you hear, monster? If I should take a
displeasure against you, look you—

TRINCULO   Thou wert but a lost monster.

CALIBAN   Good my lord, give me thy favour still.
Be patient, for the prize I'll bring thee to

205   Shall hoodwink[1] this mischance. Therefore speak softly.
All's hushed as midnight yet.

TRINCULO   Ay, but to lose our bottles in the pool!

STEFANO   There is not only disgrace and dishonour in that,
monster, but an infinite loss.

210 TRINCULO   That's more to me than my wetting. Yet this is your
harmless fairy, monster.

STEFANO   I will fetch off[2] my bottle, though I be o'er ears° for   *drowned*
my labour.

CALIBAN   Prithee, my king, be quiet. Seest thou here;

215   This is the mouth o'th' cell. No noise, and enter.
Do that good mischief which may make this island
Thine own for ever, and I thy Caliban
For aye° thy foot-licker.   *ever*

STEFANO   Give me thy hand.
I do begin to have bloody thoughts.

220 TRINCULO [*seeing the apparel*] O King Stefano, O peer! O worthy Stefano, look what a wardrobe here is for thee![3]

CALIBAN   Let it alone, thou fool, it is but trash.

TRINCULO [*putting on a gown*] O ho, monster, we know what
belongs to a frippery!° O King Stefano!   *old-clothes shop*

---

8. Made smelly; smelled worse than.
9. Lime tree, indicating a stage property.
1. Blind with a hood, as was done to pacify a hawk—
hence, make harmless; also, put out of sight.

2. Recover; rescue; drink off.
3. Recalling "King Stephen was and a worthy peer, / His
breeches cost him but a crown," a popular ballad about
King Stephen, sung in part in *Othello* 2.3.77ff.

225 STEFANO Put off that gown, Trinculo. By this hand, I'll have that
     gown.

TRINCULO Thy grace shall have it.

CALIBAN The dropsy[4] drown this fool! What do you mean
     To dote thus on such luggage?° Let't alone,   *encumbrances*
230 And do the murder first. If he awake,
     From toe to crown he'll fill our skins with pinches,
     Make us° strange stuff.   *Turn us into*

STEFANO Be you quiet, monster.—Mistress lime, is not this my
     jerkin?° Now is the jerkin under the line.[5] Now, jerkin, you are   *leather jacket*
235 like to lose your hair and prove a bald jerkin.[6]
          [STEFANO *and* TRINCULO *take garments*]

TRINCULO Do, do! We steal by line and level,[7] an't like° your   *if it please*
     grace.

STEFANO I thank thee for that jest. Here's a garment for't. Wit
     shall not go unrewarded while I am king of this country. 'Steal
240 by line and level' is an excellent pass of pate.[8] There's another
     garment for't.

TRINCULO Monster, come, put some lime upon your fingers,[9]
     and away with the rest.

CALIBAN I will have none on't. We shall lose our time,
245 And all be turned to barnacles,[1] or to apes
     With foreheads villainous° low.   *wretchedly*

STEFANO Monster, lay to° your fingers. Help to bear this away   *apply*
     where my hogshead of wine is, or I'll turn you out of my king-
     dom. Go to, carry this.

250 TRINCULO And this.

STEFANO Ay, and this.
          [*They load* CALIBAN *with apparel.*]
          A noise of hunters heard. Enter divers° spirits in shape of   *various*
          dogs and hounds, hunting them about; PROSPERO *and*
          ARIEL *setting them on*

PROSPERO Hey, Mountain, hey!

ARIEL   Silver! There it goes, Silver!

PROSPERO Fury, Fury! There, Tyrant, there! Hark, hark!
          [*Exeunt* STEFANO, TRINCULO, *and* CALIBAN, *pursued by spirits*]
          [*To* ARIEL] Go, charge my goblins that they grind their joints
255 With dry convulsions,[2] shorten up their sinews
     With agèd cramps, and more pinch-spotted[3] make them
     Than pard or cat o'mountain.[4]
          [*Cries within*]

ARIEL   Hark, they roar!

PROSPERO Let them be hunted soundly.° At this hour   *thoroughly*
     Lies at my mercy all mine enemies.

---

4. A disease characterized by the accumulation of fluid
in connective tissue.
5. Below the lime tree; south of the equator; below the
waist. Also a possible allusion to the proverb "Thou hast
stricken the ball under the line," meaning "You have
cheated." Stefano has taken the jerkin from the lime tree.
6. Baldness caused either through tropical disease or by
sailors who customarily shaved the heads of passengers
when they crossed the line of the equator for the first
time. "Under the [waist]line" (line 234) could also be an
allusion to baldness from syphilis.
7. An idiomatic expression for "properly, by the rules"—
literally, "by plumb line and carpenter's level"; also pun-

ning on "lime." *Do, do:* an expression of approval.
8. Thrust of wit (fencing term).
9. Be "lime-fingered," sticky-fingered (alluding to birdlime, a gluey substance used to catch birds).
1. Barnacle geese, also known as "tree geese" and supposed to begin life as barnacle shells.
2. Afflicting "sapless," or old, people.
3. Spotted with bruises from pinches. *agèd cramps:* the
convulsions of old age.
4. Both terms are synonymous with "leopard"; the second
is from Jeremiah 13:23: "May a man of Ind change his
skin, and the cat of the mountain her spots?" (Bishops'
Bible).

260 Shortly shall all my labours end, and thou
     Shalt have the air at freedom. For a little,
     Follow, and do me service.   *Exeunt*

                            5.1
          Enter PROSPERO, *in his magic robes, and* ARIEL
PROSPERO   Now does my project gather to a head.[1]
     My charms crack not, my spirits obey, and time
     Goes upright with his carriage.[2] How's the day?
ARIEL   On the sixth hour; at which time, my lord,
     You said our work should cease.
5 PROSPERO   I did say so
     When first I raised the tempest. Say, my spirit,
     How fares the King and's° followers?   *and his*
ARIEL   Confined together
     In the same fashion as you gave in charge,
     Just as you left them; all prisoners, sir,
10   In the lime-grove which weather-fends[3] your cell.
     They cannot budge till your release.° The King,   *you release them*
     His brother, and yours, abide all three distracted,°   *out of their wits*
     And the remainder mourning over them,
     Brimful of sorrow and dismay; but chiefly
15   Him that you termed, sir, the good old lord Gonzalo:
     His tears run down his beard like winter's drops
     From eaves of reeds.° Your charm so strongly works 'em   *thatched roofs*
     That if you now beheld them your affections°   *feelings*
     Would become tender.
PROSPERO   Dost thou think so, spirit?
ARIEL   Mine would, sir, were I human.
20 PROSPERO   And mine shall.
     Hast thou, which art but air, a touch,° a feeling   *sense*
     Of their afflictions, and shall not myself,
     One of their kind, that relish all as sharply
     Passion as they,[4] be kindlier[5] moved than thou art?
25   Though with their high° wrongs I am struck to th' quick, *great*
     Yet with my nobler reason 'gainst my fury
     Do I take part.° The rarer action is   *side*
     In virtue than in vengeance. They being penitent,
     The sole drift of my purpose doth extend
30   Not a frown further. Go release them, Ariel.
     My charms I'll break, their senses I'll restore,
     And they shall be themselves.
ARIEL   I'll fetch them, sir.   *Exit*
          [PROSPERO *draws a circle with his staff*][6]
PROSPERO[7]   Ye elves of hills, brooks, standing lakes and groves,
     And ye that on the sands with printless foot
35   Do chase the ebbing Neptune, and do fly him
     When he comes back; you demi-puppets[8] that

5.1
1. Draw to its fulfillment. "Project" suggests an alchemical projection or "experiment."
2. Because his carriage, or burden, is now light.
3. Which protects from the weather.
4. *that . . . they*: who feel as much strong emotion as they
do.
5. More tenderly; more naturally.
6. The original text does not indicate when the circle is

drawn. Other possibilities are at the beginning of the
scene or before the entry at line 57.
7. Prospero's speech closely follows Ovid's *Metamorphoses* 7.265–77, in Arthur Golding's translation (1567); the
speaker in Ovid is the sorceress Medea, who uses her
witchcraft to vengeful ends.
8. Puppets; elves; quasi puppets.

By moonshine do the green sour ringlets[9] make
Whereof the ewe not bites; and you whose pastime
Is to make midnight° mushrooms, that rejoice   *springing up overnight*
40 To hear the solemn curfew;[1] by whose aid,
Weak masters[2] though ye be, I have bedimmed
The noontide sun, called forth the mutinous winds,
And 'twixt the green sea and the azured vault°   *the sky*
Set roaring war—to the dread rattling thunder
45 Have I given fire, and rifted° Jove's stout oak   *split*
With his own bolt;° the strong-based promontory   *lightning bolt*
Have I made shake, and by the spurs° plucked up   *roots*
The pine and cedar; graves at my command
Have waked their sleepers, oped, and let 'em forth
50 By my so potent art. But this rough[3] magic
I here abjure. And when I have required°   *summoned*
Some heavenly music—which even now I do—
To work mine end upon their senses that°   *the senses of whom*
This airy[4] charm is for, I'll break my staff,
55 Bury it certain° fathoms in the earth,   *several*
And deeper than did ever plummet sound
I'll drown my book.

> *Solemn music. Here enters [first]* ARIEL *[invisible]; then*
> ALONSO, *with a frantic gesture, attended by* GONZALO;
> SEBASTIAN *and* ANTONIO, *in like manner, attended by*
> ADRIAN *and* FRANCISCO. *They all enter the circle which*
> PROSPERO *had made, and there stand charmed; which*
> PROSPERO *observing, speaks*

[*To* ALONSO][5] A solemn air,° and° the best comforter   *song / which is*
To an unsettled fancy,° cure thy brains,   *imagination*
Now useless, boiled within thy skull.
60 [*To* SEBASTIAN *and* ANTONIO][6]   There stand,
For you are spell-stopped.—
Holy Gonzalo, honourable man,
Mine eyes, ev'n sociable° to the show° of thine,   *sympathetic / appearance*
Fall fellowly drops. [*Aside*] The charm dissolves apace,
65 And as the morning steals upon the night,
Melting the darkness, so their rising senses
Begin to chase the ignorant fumes[7] that mantle°   *envelop*
Their clearer° reason.—O good Gonzalo,   *growing clearer*
My true preserver, and a loyal sir°   *gentleman*
70 To him thou follow'st, I will pay° thy graces   *requite*
Home° both in word and deed.—Most cruelly   *Fully*
Didst thou, Alonso, use me and my daughter.
Thy brother was a furtherer° in the act.—   *an accomplice*
Thou art pinched° for't now, Sebastian.   *tortured; afflicted*
[*To* ANTONIO]   Flesh and blood,
75 You, brother mine, that entertained ambition,
Expelled remorse and nature,[8] whom,° with Sebastian—   *who*

---

9. Fairy rings: distinctive circles of grass supposed to be
caused by dancing fairies but actually caused by mushrooms.
1. The bell rung at nightfall, indicating the time when
spirits are abroad.
2. Ineffectual when acting independently; without supernatural power; subordinate spirits.
3. Violent; discordant; crudely approximate.

4. Wrought by spirits of the air.
5. Prospero remains invisible and inaudible to Alonso
and his party until he greets Alonso at line 108.
6. Or perhaps to all the shipwrecked lords.
7. Fogs of ignorance; the image is of the sun ("rising
senses") dissipating morning mist.
8. Pity and brotherly affection.

Whose inward pinches therefore are most strong,—
Would here have killed your king, I do forgive thee,
Unnatural though thou art. [*Aside*] Their understanding
80   Begins to swell,° and the approaching tide   *(as does a tide)*
Will shortly fill the reasonable shores
That now lie foul and muddy. Not° one of them   *There is not*
That yet looks on me, or would know me.—Ariel,
Fetch me the hat and rapier⁹ in my cell.
85   I will disease° me, and myself present   *undress*
As I was sometime Milan.¹ Quickly, spirit!
Thou shalt ere long be free.

          ARIEL *sings and helps to attire him* [*as Duke of Milan*]

ARIEL   Where the bee sucks, there suck I:
                In a cowslip's bell I lie;
90   There I couch when owls do cry.
                On the bat's back I do fly
                After summer merrily.
                Merrily, merrily shall I live now
                Under the blossom that hangs on the bough.
95   Merrily, merrily shall I live now
                Under the blossom that hangs on the bough.
PROSPERO   Why, that's my dainty Ariel! I shall miss thee,
But yet thou shalt have freedom.—So, so, so.²
To the King's ship, invisible as thou art!
100   There shalt thou find the mariners asleep
Under the hatches. The Master and the Boatswain
Being awake, enforce them to this place,
And presently,° I prithee.   *immediately*
ARIEL   I drink the air before me, and return
105   Or ere° your pulse twice beat.   *Exit*   *Before*
GONZALO   All torment, trouble, wonder, and amazement°   *bewilderment*
Inhabits here. Some heavenly power guide us
Out of this fearful° country!   *fearsome*
PROSPERO   Behold, sir King,
The wrongèd Duke of Milan, Prospero.
110   For more assurance that a living prince
Does now speak to thee, I embrace thy body;
And to thee and thy company I bid
A hearty welcome.
          [*He embraces* ALONSO]
ALONSO   Whe'er° thou beest he or no,   *Whether*
Or some enchanted trifle³ to abuse° me,   *delude; maltreat*
115   As late I have been, I not know. Thy pulse
Beats as of flesh and blood; and since I saw thee
Th'affliction of my mind amends, with which
I fear a madness held me. This must crave°—   *requires, as explanation*
An if this be at all⁴—a most strange story.
120   Thy dukedom⁵ I resign, and do entreat

---

9. Elements of normal aristocratic dress.
1. Formerly, when Duke of Milan.
2. Prospero arranges his attire approvingly.
3. With a suggestion of the old sense of "trifle" as "deception."
4. If this is really happening.
5. Alonso's rights of homage and tribute from it.

Thou pardon me my wrongs. But how should Prospero
Be living and be here?

PROSPERO [*to* GONZALO]   First, noble friend,
Let me embrace thine age,° whose honour cannot   *old body*
Be measured or confined.

       [*He embraces* GONZALO]

GONZALO   Whether this be
Or be not, I'll not swear.

125 PROSPERO   You do yet taste
Some subtleties⁶ o'th' isle that will not let you
Believe things certain.—Welcome, my friends all.

    [*Aside to* SEBASTIAN *and* ANTONIO]

But you, my brace° of lords, were I so minded,   *pair*
I here could pluck his highness' frown upon you
130 And justify° you traitors. At this time   *prove*
I will tell no tales.

SEBASTIAN [*to* ANTONIO] The devil speaks in him.

PROSPERO   No.
[*To* ANTONIO]   For you, most wicked sir, whom° to call brother   *who*
Would even infect my mouth, I do forgive
Thy rankest fault, all of them, and require
135 My dukedom of thee, which perforce° I know   *necessarily*
Thou must restore.

ALONSO   If thou beest Prospero,
Give us particulars of thy preservation,
How thou hast met us here, whom three hours since
Were wrecked upon this shore, where I have lost—
140 How sharp the point of this remembrance is!—
My dear son Ferdinand.

PROSPERO   I am woe° for't, sir.   *I grieve*

ALONSO   Irreparable is the loss, and patience
Says it is past her cure.

PROSPERO   I rather think
You have not sought her help, of° whose soft grace°   *by / mercy*
145 For the like loss I have her sovereign aid,
And rest myself content.

ALONSO   You the like loss?

PROSPERO   As great to me as late;° and supportable   *recent*
To make the dear loss⁷ have I means much weaker
Than you may call to comfort you, for I
Have lost my daughter.⁸

150 ALONSO   A daughter?
O heavens, that they were living both in Naples,
The king and queen there! That they were, I wish
Myself were mudded in that oozy bed
Where my son lies. When did you lose your daughter?

155 PROSPERO   In this last tempest. I perceive these lords
At this encounter do so much admire°   *wonder*
That they devour their reason,⁹ and scarce think
Their eyes do offices of truth,° these words   *function accurately*

---

6. *You . . . subtleties:* You still experience some of the illusions. "Subtleties" were also sweet confections shaped like castles, temples, beasts, allegorical figures, etc., and arranged like a pageant.

7. *supportable . . . loss:* in order to make the heartfelt loss

bearable.

8. Prospero apparently means that Alonso still has a child, his daughter Claribel, to comfort him.

9. "Reason" has the additional sense of "discourse"; hence the phrase is an extension of "swallow their words."

       Are natural breath. But howsoe'er you have
160   Been jostled from your senses, know for certain
       That I am Prospero, and that very Duke
       Which was thrust forth of Milan, who most strangely,
       Upon this shore where you were wrecked, was landed
       To be the lord on't. No more yet of this,
165   For 'tis a chronicle of day by day,
       Not a relation for a breakfast, nor
       Befitting this first meeting. Welcome, sir.
       This cell's my court. Here have I few attendants,
       And subjects none abroad.[1] Pray you, look in.
170   My dukedom since you have given me again,
       I will requite you with as good a thing;
       At least bring forth a wonder to content ye
       As much as me my dukedom.

               Here PROSPERO *discovers*[2] FERDINAND *and* MIRANDA,
               playing at chess

MIRANDA   Sweet lord, you play me false.°   *trick me*
175 FERDINAND   No, my dearest love,
       I would not for the world.
MIRANDA   Yes, for a score of kingdoms you should wrangle,
       An I would call it fair play.[3]
ALONSO   If this prove
       A vision of the island, one dear son
       Shall I twice lose.
180 SEBASTIAN   A most high miracle.
FERDINAND [*coming forward*]   Though the seas threaten, they are merciful.
       I have cursed them without cause.
           [*He kneels*]
ALONSO   Now all the blessings
       Of a glad father compass thee about.°   *surround you*
       Arise and say how thou cam'st here.
           [FERDINAND *rises*]
MIRANDA [*coming forward*]   O wonder!
185   How many goodly creatures are there here!
       How beauteous mankind is! O brave new world
       That has such people in't!
PROSPERO   'Tis new to thee.
ALONSO [*to* FERDINAND]   What is this maid with whom thou
       wast at play?
       Your eld'st° acquaintance cannot be three hours.   *longest*
190   Is she the goddess that hath severed us,
       And brought us thus together?
FERDINAND   Sir, she is mortal;
       But by immortal providence she's mine.
       I chose her when I could not ask my father
       For his advice, nor thought I had one. She
195   Is daughter to this famous Duke of Milan,
       Of whom so often I have heard renown,
       But never saw before; of whom I have

---

1. Elsewhere about the island; beyond the cell.
2. Reveals by drawing back a curtain hanging in front of the discovery space.
3. *for . . . play:* if I would not accuse you of cheating, you would quarrel for twenty kingdoms. Other editions read "And" for "An" (i.e., you could quarrel for twenty kingdoms, and I would still call it fair play.)

Received a second life; and second father
This lady makes him to me.
ALONSO   I am hers.[4]
200   But O, how oddly will it sound, that I
Must ask my child° forgiveness!   (Miranda)
PROSPERO   There, sir, stop.
Let us not burden our remembrance with
A heaviness° that's gone.   sorrow
GONZALO   I have inly wept,
Or should have spoke ere this. Look down, you gods,
205   And on this couple drop a blessèd crown,
For it is you that have chalked forth° the way   marked out
Which brought us hither.
ALONSO   I say amen, Gonzalo.
GONZALO   Was Milan° thrust from Milan, that his issue   the Duke of Milan
Should become kings of Naples? O rejoice
210   Beyond a common joy! And set it down
With gold on lasting pillars:[5] in one voyage
Did Claribel her husband find at Tunis,
And Ferdinand her brother found a wife
Where he himself was lost; Prospero his dukedom
215   In a poor isle; and all of us ourselves,
When no man was his own.[6]
ALONSO [to FERDINAND and MIRANDA] Give me your hands.
Let grief and sorrow still° embrace his heart   always
That° doth not wish you joy.   Who
GONZALO   Be it so! Amen!
      Enter ARIEL, with the MASTER and BOATSWAIN amazedly
      following
O look, sir, look, sir, here is more of us!
220   I prophesied if a gallows were on land
This fellow could not drown. [To the BOATSWAIN] Now,
      blasphemy,°   blasphemer
That swear'st grace o'erboard: not an oath on shore?
Hast thou no mouth by land? What is the news?
BOATSWAIN   The best news is that we have safely found
225   Our King and company. The next, our ship,
Which but three glasses° since we gave out° split, hourglasses / declared
Is tight and yare[7] and bravely rigged, as when
We first put out to sea.
ARIEL [aside to PROSPERO] Sir, all this service
Have I done since I went.
PROSPERO [aside to ARIEL]   My tricksy° spirit!   capricious; neat
230   ALONSO   These are not natural events; they strengthen° increase
From strange to stranger. Say, how came you hither?
BOATSWAIN   If I did think, sir, I were well awake
I'd strive to tell you. We were dead of ° sleep,   with
And—how we know not—all clapped° under hatches, shut up
235   Where but even now, with strange and several° noises various
Of roaring, shrieking, howling, jingling chains,
And more diversity of sounds, all horrible,

4. I will be her second father, Alonso's assent to the betrothal.
5. Suggesting, perhaps, the triumphal arches commissioned to celebrate notable occasions.
6. When we all had lost our senses.
7. Is sound and ready to sail.

We were awaked; straightway at liberty;
Where we in all her trim freshly beheld
240 Our royal, good, and gallant ship, our Master
Cap'ring to eye° her. On° a trice, so please you,   *Dancing to see / In*
Even in a dream, were we divided from them,
And were brought moping° hither.   *dazed*
ARIEL [*aside to* PROSPERO]   Was't well done?
PROSPERO [*aside to* ARIEL]   Bravely, my diligence. Thou shalt be free.
245 ALONSO   This is as strange a maze as e'er men trod,
And there is in this business more than nature
Was ever conduct° of. Some oracle   *conductor*
Must rectify our knowledge.
PROSPERO   Sir, my liege,
Do not infest° your mind with beating on[8]   *trouble*
250 The strangeness of this business. At picked leisure,
Which shall be shortly, single° I'll resolve you,   *in private*
Which to you shall seem probable,° of every   *plausible*
These happened accidents;° till when be cheerful,   *occurrences*
And think of each thing well. [*Aside to* ARIEL] Come hither, spirit.
255 Set Caliban and his companions free.
Untie the spell.   [*Exit* ARIEL]
[*To* ALONSO]   How fares my gracious sir?
There are yet missing of your company
Some few odd lads that you remember not.
      Enter ARIEL, *driving in* CALIBAN, STEFANO, *and* TRIN-
      CULO, *in their stolen apparel*
STEFANO   Every man shift for all the rest, and let no man take
260 care for himself,[9] for all is but fortune. Coragio, bully-monster,[1]
coragio!
TRINCULO   If these° be true spies which I wear in my head, here's   *these eyes*
a goodly sight.
CALIBAN   O Setebos, these be brave spirits indeed!
265 How fine° my master is! I am afraid   *splendidly dressed*
He will chastise me.
SEBASTIAN   Ha, ha! What things are these, my lord Antonio?
Will money buy 'em?
ANTONIO   Very like;° one of them   *likely*
Is a plain° fish, and no doubt marketable.   *mere*
270 PROSPERO   Mark but the badges[2] of these men, my lords,
Then say if they° be true. This misshapen knave,   *(the men); (the badges)*
His mother was a witch, and one so strong
That could control the moon, make flows and ebbs,
And deal in her command without her power.[3]
275 These three have robbed me, and this demi-devil,[4]
For he's a bastard one, had plotted with them
To take my life. Two of these fellows you
Must know and own.[5] This thing of darkness I
Acknowledge mine.
CALIBAN   I shall be pinched to death.
280 ALONSO   Is not this Stefano, my drunken butler?

8. With repeatedly worrying about.
9. Stefano drunkenly confuses the saying "Every man
for himself."
1. Gallant monster. *Coragio:* Take courage (Italian).
2. Livery. Servants often wore their master's emblem,
but Prospero probably refers to the stolen apparel.
3. And wield her (the moon's) power without her
authority, or beyond the reach of her might.
4. Being the offspring of Sycorax and the devil.
5. And acknowledge to be yours.

SEBASTIAN   He is drunk now. Where had he wine?

ALONSO   And Trinculo is reeling ripe.° Where should they   *drunk*
    Find this grand liquor that hath gilded⁶ 'em?
    [*To* TRINCULO] How cam'st thou in this pickle?⁷

285   TRINCULO   I have been in such a pickle since I saw you last that,
    I fear me, will never out of my bones. I shall not fear flyblowing.⁸

SEBASTIAN   Why, how now, Stefano?

STEFANO   O, touch me not! I am not Stefano, but a cramp.

290   PROSPERO   You'd be king o'the isle, sirrah?

STEFANO   I should have been a sore° one, then.   *an inept; severe; pained*

ALONSO   [*pointing to* CALIBAN]   This is a strange thing as e'er I
    looked on.

PROSPERO   He is as disproportioned in his manners⁹

295   As in his shape. [*To* CALIBAN] Go, sirrah, to my cell.
    Take with you your companions. As you look
    To have my pardon, trim° it handsomely.   *tidy; decorate*

CALIBAN   Ay, that I will; and I'll be wise hereafter,
    And seek for grace. What a thrice-double ass

300   Was I to take this drunkard for a god,
    And worship this dull fool!

PROSPERO   Go to, away!   [*Exit* CALIBAN]¹

ALONSO   [*to* STEFANO *and* TRINCULO]
    Hence, and bestow your luggage where you found it.

SEBASTIAN   Or stole it, rather.   [*Exeunt* STEFANO *and* TRINCULO]

PROSPERO   [*to* ALONSO]   Sir, I invite your highness and your train

305   To my poor cell, where you shall take your rest
    For this one night; which part of it° I'll waste°   *part of which / spend*
    With such discourse as I not doubt shall make it
    Go quick away: the story of my life,
    And the particular accidents° gone by   *events*

310   Since I came to this isle. And in the morn
    I'll bring you to your ship, and so to Naples,
    Where I have hope to see the nuptial
    Of these our dear-belovèd solemnized;
    And thence retire me to my Milan, where
    Every third thought shall be my grave.

315   ALONSO   I long
    To hear the story of your life, which must
    Take° the ear strangely.   *Captivate*

PROSPERO   I'll deliver° all,   *relate*
    And promise you calm seas, auspicious gales,
    And sail so expeditious that shall° catch   *it will*

320   Your royal fleet far off. [*Aside to* ARIEL] My Ariel, chick,
    That is thy charge. Then to the elements
    Be free, and fare thou well.   [*Exit* ARIEL]
                       Please you, draw near.°   *go in*
                       Exeunt [*all but* PROSPERO]²

---

6. Probably alluding to the alchemical elixir ("liquor")
known as *aurum potabile* (drinkable gold); hence
"gilded" (flushed).
7. Sorry plight; Trinculo takes up the literal sense of "preserving liquid," recalling both his drunkenness and his
drenching in the lake.
8. Not fear being infested with flies, since he has been

"pickled" (preserved).
9. Behavior; moral character.
1. The Folio does not explicitly say that Caliban leaves
the stage in response to Prospero's command.
2. The general exeunt is through Prospero's cell; Ariel
departs in another direction.

Epilogue

PROSPERO   Now my charms are all o'erthrown,
And what strength I have's mine own,
Which is most faint. Now 'tis true
I must be here confined by you
5   Or sent to Naples. Let me not,
Since I have my dukedom got,
And pardoned the deceiver, dwell
In this bare island° by your spell;   *(the stage)*
But release me from my bands°   *fetters*
10   With the help of your good hands.°   *(applause)*
Gentle breath° of yours my sails   *Favorable comment*
Must fill, or else my project fails,
Which was to please. Now I want°   *lack*
Spirits to enforce, art to enchant;
15   And my ending[1] is despair
Unless I be relieved by prayer,
Which pierces so, that it assaults
Mercy itself, and frees all faults.
As you from crimes would pardoned be,
20   Let your indulgence[2] set me free.
           [*He awaits applause, then*] *exit*

Epilogue
1. Punning on the sense "death."   2. Approval; appeasement; remission for sin.

Cardenio

Many plays acted in Shakespeare's time have failed to survive; they may easily include some that he wrote. The mystery of *Love's Labour's Won* is discussed above. Certain manuscript records of the seventeenth century suggest that at least one other play in which he had a hand may have disappeared. On 9 September 1653 the London publisher Humphrey Moseley entered in the Stationers' Register a batch of plays including '*The History of Cardenio*, by Mr Fletcher and Shakespeare'. Cardenio is a character in Part One of Cervantes' *Don Quixote*, published in English translation in 1612. Two earlier allusions suggest that the King's Men owned a play on this subject at the time that Shakespeare was collaborating with John Fletcher (1579–1625). On 20 May 1613 the Privy Council authorized payment of £20 to John Heminges, as leader of the King's Men, for the presentation at court of six plays, one listed as 'Cardenno'. On 9 July of the same year Heminges received £6 13*s*. 4*d*. for his company's performance of a play 'called Cardenna' before the ambassador of the Duke of Savoy.

No more information about this play survives from the seventeenth century, but in 1728 Lewis Theobald published a play based on the story of Cardenio called *Double Falsehood, or The Distrest Lovers,* which he claimed to have 'revised and adapted' from one 'written originally by W. Shakespeare'. It had been successfully produced at Drury Lane on 13 December 1727, and was given thirteen times up to 1 May 1728. Other performances are recorded in 1740, 1741, 1767 (when it was reprinted), 1770, and 1847. In 1770 a newspaper stated that 'the original manuscript' was 'treasured up in the Museum of Covent Garden Playhouse'; fire destroyed the theatre, including its library, in 1808.

Theobald claimed to own several manuscripts of an original play by Shakespeare, and remarked that some of his contemporaries thought the style was Fletcher's, not Shakespeare's. When he himself came to edit Shakespeare's plays he did not include either *Double Falsehood* or the play on which he claimed to have based it; he simply edited the plays of the First Folio, not adding either *Pericles* or *The Two Noble Kinsmen,* though he believed they were partly by Shakespeare. It is quite possible that *Double Falsehood* is based (however distantly) on a play of Shakespeare's time; if so, the play is likely to have been the one performed by the King's Men and ascribed by Moseley in 1653 to Fletcher and Shakespeare.

Double Falsehood is a tragicomedy; the characters' names differ from those in *Don Quixote;* and the story is varied. Henriquez rapes Violante, then falls in love with Leonora, loved by his friend Julio. Her parents agree to the marriage, but Julio interrupts the ceremony. Leonora (who had intended to kill herself) swoons and later takes sanctuary in a nunnery. Julio goes mad with desire for vengeance on his false friend; and the wronged Violante, disguised as a boy, joins a group of shepherds, and is almost raped by one of them. Henriquez's virtuous brother, Roderick, ignorant of his villainy, helps him to abduct Leonora. Leonora and Violante both denounce Henriquez to Roderick. Finally Henriquez repents and marries Violante, while Julio (now sane) marries Leonora.

Some of the motifs of *Double Falsehood*, such as the disguised heroine wronged by her lover, the hero's descent into madness, and the ultimate restoration of sundered relationships, recall Shakespeare's late plays. But most of the dialogue seems unShakespearean. Theobald's play stands as a tantalizing reminder of what has been lost.

THE OXFORD EDITORS
Revised by Stephen Greenblatt

All Is True (Henry VIII)

All Is True (*Henry VIII*; 1613) is the Shakespearean play that brought down the house. During a performance on June 29, 1613, when it "had beene acted not passinge 2 or 3 times before," "certain Chambers" (small cannons) were shot off. The thatch of the Globe Theatre ignited, and the building burned down. Contemporary accounts disagree about whether the accident occurred early in the play, when King Henry participates in "a Masque at the Cardinal Wolsey's house" and the stage direction reads "Chambers discharged" (1.4.50), or, more improbably, when it "was almost ended." Apparently there was only one injury, to a man who "was scalded with the fire by adventuring in to save a child which otherwise had been burnt." Another version claims that the injured man "had his breeches set on fire, that would perhaps have broyled him, if he had not by the benefit of a provident wit put it out with bottle Ale." (See the Henry Wotton letter, page 1386.)

All Is True does indeed show "a provident wit" and "save a child," though perhaps not in the fashion the two commentators had in mind. In reviewing some of the important events of the reign of Henry VIII, and in parading many of its central historical figures before the audience, the play ultimately reveals the workings of a divine providence that watches over England and assures the birth of the future Queen Elizabeth. It achieves this effect through the mixing of dramatic genres: in *All Is True*, the national history play meets the tragicomic romance. Known as *Henry VIII* at least since 1623, the text is a collaborative effort of Shakespeare and John Fletcher—with Shakespeare apparently the senior partner. It draws on narratives of relatively recent English history—primarily Raphael Holinshed's *Chronicles of England, Scotland, and Ireland* (1587 ed.), Shakespeare's main source for his earlier English history plays, and, for much of Act 5, John Foxe's epic of Protestant propaganda, *Book of Martyrs*. In so doing, the playwrights returned to a genre that Shakespeare had dominated during its heyday in the 1590s. By contrast, tragicomic romance, influenced by late Renaissance elite Italian theater, was very much in vogue in 1613, thanks largely to the recent works of Shakespeare, Francis Beaumont, and Fletcher.

The Shakespearean history play focuses on dynastic instabilities and civil conflicts of the late fourteenth and fifteenth centuries, and especially on the national implications of struggles between aristocratic factions. Shakespearean romance characteristically deploys a fictional plot in which long suffering and separation (often across the sea) are transcended through the virtuous daughter, who redeems her father, and through magical interventions that produce providential outcomes. The synthesis of romance and history in *All Is True* thus emphasizes a providential interpretation of English history. The resulting implication—that the antagonisms of earlier history are justified by the felicity of the present reign—risks chauvinistic sycophancy. Yet *All Is True* also challenges this celebratory interpretation: it is in the tension between these two tendencies that the play's interest lies.

The historical narrative, which combines close reliance on the sources with chronological compression and rearrangement, spans more than fifteen years. Its principal structural unit, first alluded to in the Prologue (lines 25–30), is *de casibus* tragedy, which recounts the fall of illustrious figures and resembles the morality play's abstractly allegorical focus on virtue and vice. The wheel of fortune is the form's dominant, cyclical image: what goes up must come down. Providential romance, however, is more linear and unidirectional: you start in one place and end somewhere else. Moreover, it ends in felicity rather than disaster. *All Is True* reconciles these apparently incompatible movements through an elegant structural trick: it makes a series of local *de casibus* tragedies serve a single overarching providential purpose that does not emerge until the very end. Much of the play accordingly seems to have nothing to do with a transcendently ordered pattern. It does not even concern the ups and downs of monarchs and their rivals, as in Shakespeare's earlier histories. Instead, we witness the successive falls of people close to Henry VIII—Buckingham, Katherine, and Cardinal Wolsey—and the near fall of Cranmer, Archbishop of Canterbury. Each gets a day in court—his or her fifteen minutes of fame—before passing from the scene. These downfalls, like other events in the play, are rendered through stirring speeches and pageantry that recall the spectacle of the contemporary court theatrical form known as the "masque" (see 1.4), which for centuries made the work a success on the stage and which left their mark on film versions of Henry's reign, even those not based on *All Is True* (see the list of films).

Initially, the repetitive *de casibus* structure doesn't seem to be heading anywhere. Yet the linguistic patterning suggests a larger purpose. Beginning with the Prologue's invocation of tears and pity (lines 5–6), the play emphasizes suffering, the burden of life, acquiescence in defeat, forgiveness of one's foes, patience, religious serenity, and an understanding of the fall from power as part of a natural pattern like life itself. Cardinal Wolsey's undoing offers a striking instance of the transformation of conflict into reconciliation. Surrey correctly blames Wolsey for the execution of Buckingham, Surrey's father-in-law. Taunting the Cardinal at the moment of his ruin, he is finally rebuked:

> LORD CHAMBERLAIN   O, my lord,
> Press not a falling man too far. 'Tis virtue.
> His faults lie open to the laws. Let them,
> Not you, correct him. My heart weeps to see him
> So little of his great self.
>   SURREY   I forgive him.
>   (3.2.333–37)

Once the lords have left, Wolsey, in a deviation from Holinshed, gets a moving repentance. Discovering his religious vocation only following the collapse of his secular

Now, to let matters of State ſleep, I will entertain you at the preſent with what hath happened this week at the banks ſide. The Kings Players had a new Play, called *All is true*, repreſenting ſome principall pieces of the raign of *Henry* 8. which was ſet forth with many extraordinary circumſtances of Pomp and Majeſty, even to the matting of the ſtage; the Knights of the Order, with their Georges and Garter, the Guards with their embroidered Coats, and the like: ſufficient in truth within a while to make greatneſs very familiar, if not ridiculous. Now, King *Henry* making a Maſque at the Cardinal *Wolſey's* houſe, and certain Chambers being ſhot off at his entry, ſome of the paper, or other ſtuff wherewith one of them was ſtopped, did light on the thatch, where being thought at firſt but an idle ſmoak, and their eyes more attentive to the ſhow, it kindled inwardly, and ran round like a train, conſuming within leſs then an hour the whole houſe to the very grounds.

This was the fatal period of that vertuous fabrique, wherein yet nothing did periſh, but wood and ſtraw, and a few forſaken cloaks; only one man had his breeches ſet on fire, that would perhaps have broyled him, if he had not by the benefit of a provident wit put it out with bottle Ale. The reſt when we meet: till when, I proteſt every minute is the ſiege of Troy. Gods dear bleſſings till then and ever be with you.

> Your poor Uncle and
> faithful ſervant.
>
> HENRY WOTTON.

One of several accounts of the burning of the Globe Theatre. From a letter of July 2, 1613, in *Letters of Sir Henry Wotton to Sir Edmund Bacon* (1661).

career, the hitherto villainous Cardinal experiences a shift in outlook that aligns him with his victims, Buckingham and Katherine. Asked how he feels, Wolsey replies:

> Why, well—
> Never so truly happy, my good Cromwell.
> I know myself now, and I feel within me
> A peace above all earthly dignities,
> A still and quiet conscience.
>
> (3.2.377–81)

Thus, like Buckingham's and Katherine's precipitous descents, but also like Adam and Eve's, Wolsey's fall is a fortunate one.

The Cardinal considers his former responsibilities "a burden / Too heavy for a man that hopes for heaven" (3.2.385–86). But not too heavy for a woman: the burden is delivered at the end of the play when Queen Anne gives birth to the future Queen Elizabeth—the moment toward which all previous events have been tending. The critic Northrop Frye noted in the play "an invisible but omnipotent and ruthless providence who is ready to tear the whole social and religious structure of England to pieces in order to get Queen Elizabeth born." Buckingham has a serious claim to the crown, so he must be removed. Katherine's defect is that she is not the queen who will bear Elizabeth. Wolsey, who favors a diplomatically useful French alliance for Henry and hence opposes the king's marriage to Anne, unwittingly brings them together at a party he hosts (1.4). The individual tragedies are thus both personally and politically fortunate. Elizabeth's birth promises not only her own reign but also that of her successor, King James I, England's sovereign at the time of *All Is True*. Praise of these two monarchs is accompanied by compliments to James's daughter Elizabeth, who was married in February 1613. Archbishop Cranmer's concluding prophecy makes the link explicit:

> when
> The bird of wonder dies—the maiden phoenix—
> Her ashes new create another heir
> As great in admiration as herself.
>
> (5.4.39–42)

Although Queen Elizabeth is the "maiden phoenix" and James the heir, James's daughter was also compared to the phoenix at the time of her marriage.

This connection also lays to rest Henry's persistent desire for a male heir. That absent royal son earlier justifies Henry's divorce of Katherine:

> methought
> I stood not in the smile of heaven. . . .
> . . . .
> I weighed the danger which my realms stood in
> By this my issue's fail, and that gave to me
> Many a groaning throe.
>
> (2.4.183–96)

Henry assumes the burden himself, experiencing "many a groaning throe" as if he could deliver the son that Katherine cannot. When Anne takes on the burden, Henry reveals his ongoing anxiety:

> KING HENRY   Is the Queen delivered?
>   Say, 'Ay, and of a boy.'
>   OLD LADY   Ay, ay, my liege,
>   And of a lovely boy. The God of heaven
>   Both now and ever bless her! 'Tis a girl
>   Promises boys hereafter.
>
> (5.1.163–67)

Cardinal Wolsey is forced "to render up the great seal" to Norfolk and Suffolk (3.2.230). From George Cavendish, *The Life and Death of Cardinal Wolsey* (1557).

The Old Lady's flattery reveals the truth: Elizabeth *is* "a girl / Promises boys hereafter." In having James succeed her, she fulfills the properly self-effacing function of women in this patriarchal fantasy and delivers to Henry what Anne could not—a male heir.

Providence also enters the play through the standard sea journeys of Shakespearean romance, journeys that typically bring separation, suffering, and a transformation whose association with water links it to baptism. Set entirely in England, *All Is True* seems remote from such concerns. Yet the aquatic and nautical imagery of destruction pervades the play. The "hideous storm" immediately following the conclusion of the Anglo-French treaty is a "tempest" that prophesies the dissolution of the alliance (1.1.90–92). Buckingham metaphorically warns against false friends, who,

> when they once perceive
> The least rub in your fortunes, fall away
> Like water from ye, never found again
> But where they mean to sink ye.
>
> (2.1.129–32)

Henry finds himself "hulling in / The wild sea of my conscience" over his marriage to Katherine (2.4.196–97), who worries about her "shipwrecked" ladies-in-waiting. Wolsey's foes are "rav'nous fishes" who ineffectually attack his "new trimmed" "vessel" (1.2.80–81). Wolsey himself is a "rock" that threatens Buckingham and will protect Henry "against the chiding flood" of danger and rebellion (1.1.113; 3.2.198). He is a boat that "coasts / And hedges" but will "founder" (3.2.38–39, 40). He has swum "far beyond my depth" and is at "the mercy / Of a rude stream that must for ever hide me" (3.2.362, 364–65). He has borne "a load would sink a navy" (3.2.384), but he tells Cromwell that he, who "sounded all the depths and shoals of honour, / Found thee a way, out of his wreck, to rise in" (3.2.437–38). Approaching death, Wolsey is "broken with the storms of state" (4.2.21).

Positive associations with water and the sea are often connected with colonialism, important in the London of 1613 because of western Europe's unprecedented global expansion beginning in the fifteenth century and, in particular, because of the very recent establishment of England's first permanent settlement in the New World. The English nobility in France were so opulently attired that they "made Britain India"

(1.1.21)—an image of fabulous wealth that evokes both the West and East Indies, both the Caribbean and the vast region extending from India to Southeast Asia. "Our King has all the Indies in his arms" (4.1.45) when he embraces Anne, "a very fresh fish" at court (2.3.87). At her public appearance, "such a noise arose / As the shrouds make at sea in a stiff tempest" (4.1.73–74). The perilous journeys and shipwrecks are redeemed by Elizabeth's watery baptism, which has the crowd appeal of "some strange Indian with the great tool" (5.3.32)—a phrase that unites ethnic exoticism and sexual titillation. Speaking of James, Cranmer predicts,

> Wherever the bright sun of heaven shall shine,
> His honour and the greatness of his name
> Shall be, and make new nations.
>
> (5.4.50–52)

The capital of the "new nation" is Jamestown and the nation itself Virginia, named for "the maiden phoenix" who died "yet a virgin" (5.4.40, 60)—James's predecessor, the infant Elizabeth.

Although the providential logic that leads first Elizabeth and then James to the throne often works against human intentions, Henry takes an increasingly active role in securing the destined end. The crucial moment is Cranmer's trial. Just before it begins, the stage direction reads *"Enter* KING [HENRY] . . . *at a window, above"* (5.2.18). There, seeing but unseen, he is quasi-divine, as he himself suggests in angrily observing the council's humiliation of Cranmer: "Is this the honour they do one another? / 'Tis well there's one above 'em yet" (5.2.25–26). The "one above 'em" can be either God or the King, a distinction the scene blurs. This elevated perspective presumably pleased James, who held an absolutist, divine-right view of monarchy. Henry's intervention later in the scene to protect Cranmer preserves the man who later established the doctrinal basis of the English Reformation. As suggested by Cranmer's prophetic promise about Elizabeth's reign—"God shall be truly known" (5.4.36)—this religious outcome is also part of the providential pattern. Yet except in Cranmer's conflict with the Catholic Gardiner, who accuses him of being "a sectary" and Cromwell of being "a favourer / Of this new sect" (5.2.104, 114–15), and in Wolsey's dismissive description of Anne as "a spleeny Lutheran" (3.2.100), little is made of the central event of Henry's reign: the break with Rome. The characters are judged not by their religious sympathies but by their integrity. Accordingly, the outstanding figures are an English Protestant, Cranmer, and a Spanish Catholic, Katherine. The notion of conscience, which is far more prominent here than in Holinshed's *Chronicles* and which Protestants used against the papacy to repudiate blind adherence to any human doctrinal authority, is deployed by the playwrights to judge Catholics and Protestants alike. This impartiality may be more the work of Shakespeare than of Fletcher (see the Textual Note); in any case, the overall result is the characteristic national reconciliation of Shakespeare's history plays.

National reconciliation also transcends class antagonism, an issue largely absent from the sources. Like the other lords, the Duke of Buckingham resents the usurpation of the nobility's traditional power by the proud "beggar" Wolsey, a "butcher's cur" (1.1.122, 120): the Cardinal's father was supposedly a butcher. Despite these humble origins, Wolsey adopts the aristocratic outlook of the position he has risen to. He opposes Henry's marriage to Anne, who came from the gentry rather than the nobility and who had been one of Katherine's ladies-in-waiting: "A knight's daughter / To be her mistress' mistress? The Queen's queen?" (3.2.95–96). But the play also posits a harmony between upper class and lower that can be disturbed only by self-serving intermediaries who mistreat humble folk. Buckingham is betrayed to Wolsey by his surveyor, whom he fired for oppressing his tenants. Katherine gets Henry to repeal a tax levied by Wolsey that is so onerous it drives the poor to rebellion. Interclass unity is affirmed in the popular excitement about the baby Elizabeth, which the play refracts through the lower-class prose of the exasperated Porter (5.3)—a prose noteworthy in a play composed overwhelmingly in blank verse. Similarly, at Anne's earlier coronation, one of the gentlemen, who play the role of a chorus absent from the sources, remarks,

> The citizens,
> I am sure, have shown at full their royal minds—
> As, let 'em have their rights, they are ever forward.
>
> (4.1.7–9)

And, in slightly different fashion, Cranmer renders hereditary class hierarchy a thing of the past. "Those about" Elizabeth "from her shall read the perfect ways of honour, / And by those claim their greatness, not by blood" (5.4.36–38).

Yet as recent productions have emphasized, *All Is True* offers a critical account of Henry's reign. In particular, the play implicitly suggests the costs of the Elizabethan Protestant succession. Even though only Buckingham is executed, *All Is True* makes that execution resonate. The innocent and virtuous Katherine is given a strength of character, consequent impressiveness, and spiritual coronation absent both from Holinshed's portrayal and from her successor, Anne. Yet Henry's "princely commendations" to the dying Katherine are "like a pardon after execution" (4.2.119, 122). As Katherine is succeeded by Anne, so Wolsey is replaced by Sir Thomas More, Cromwell, and Cranmer (3.2.392–460). All four of these successors were later executed, as the audience well knew. Wolsey hopes that More will "do justice / For truth's sake and his conscience" (lines 397–98)—principles that were to cost the Catholic More his life. Anne actually predicts her own fate in lamenting Katherine's mistreatment:

> Much better
> She ne'er had known pomp; though't be temporal,
> Yet if that quarrel, fortune, do divorce
> It from the bearer, 'tis a sufferance panging
> As soul and bodies severing.
>
> (2.3.12–16)

Wolsey advises Cromwell:

> Be just, and fear not.
> Let all the ends thou aim'st at be thy country's,
> Thy God's, and truth's. Then if thou fall'st, O Cromwell,
> Thou fall'st a blessèd martyr.
>
> (3.2.447–50)

Gardiner's anti-Protestant attacks on Cranmer and Cromwell foreshadow his later success in sending both men to their death. Even Elizabeth's christening evokes execution: "Belong to th' gallows, and be hanged" (5.3.5).

Ambivalence extends as well to the centrally providential characters. No man utters anything but praise for the "beauty and honour" of that "angel" Anne Boleyn (2.3.76, 4.1.44). Skepticism about her "honour" is instead voiced by a woman. When Anne denies any desire for political advancement, the Old Lady calls this position "hypocrisy," ridicules Anne's pliant "conscience," and finds her claim "strange" (2.3.26, 32, 36). Yet Anne does become queen, without an explanation of her supposed change of heart but with a suggestive pun on "quean" (whore) characteristic of the entire sexualized exchange and of Anne's earlier banter (1.4.46–49). The scene with the Old Lady, apparently invented by Shakespeare, thus sullies Anne before she becomes a purely ceremonial figure reduced to bearing royal children. Moreover, Elizabeth's conception before Henry and Anne's marriage may be alluded to in the "great-bellied women" at Anne's coronation and the "fry of fornication" at Elizabeth's christening (4.1.78, 5.3.33–34).

As for Henry himself, although he is repeatedly praised by his victims (2.1.87–95, 3.2.381–93, 4.2.161–65), his increasing attention to government raises retrospective questions about his earlier behavior. The Henry of the play, more troubling than Holinshed's, seems oddly abstracted, either culpably unaware or disingenuously disavowing knowledge of foreign affairs, taxation, and treason. He often seems the Teflon king, to whom no blame sticks. The self-destructive zigzags in foreign policy—alliance with

Henry VIII, age fifty-two, in the posthumous portrait engraved by Cornelis Metsys in 1548. Gardiner's unsuccessful attack on Cranmer probably occurred around this time.

France, alliance with Spain, attempted alliance with France—are Wolsey's doings, not his: the buck stops elsewhere. Moreover, his interventions are not fully reassuring. His charges against Wolsey ignore major issues to focus on personal, peripheral concerns. Even his protection of Cranmer is necessary only because Henry allows his biased council to proceed in the first place. Indeed, the play suggests that the law serves the man with power, whether Wolsey or the King.

Explicit skepticism about Henry is produced by his divorce proceedings. *All Is True* shows a man "afflicted" by a "wounded conscience," by "conscience, conscience," by "my conscience" (2.2.62, 74, 142; 2.4.167, 179, 200). But earlier, at Wolsey's banquet, it shows a man attracted to Anne Boleyn: "The fairest hand I ever touched. O beauty, / Till now I never knew thee" (1.4.76–77). This meeting is the play's invention. A disabused view is openly voiced later:

LORD CHAMBERLAIN   It seems the marriage with his brother's wife
    Has crept too near his conscience.
    SUFFOLK   No, his conscience
    Has crept too near another lady.
                                                            (2.2.15–17)

Even apologists for Henry's behavior suspect his motives. Overwhelmed by the sight of Anne, the Second Gentleman remarks, "I cannot blame his conscience" (4.1.47). It is hard to determine whether such criticism undermines the providential pattern or renders the pattern's transcendence of such formidable obstacles all the more miraculous. Like many Shakespearean plays, *All Is True* opposes means and ends, showing and telling, dramatized plot and asserted conclusion, pity and jubilation.

The critique of Henry may have been targeted at James as well, despite the play's closing compliment to him. The satire on French fashion (1.3) ridicules behavior at James's court in which the King participated. Like Henry, James neglected affairs of state, to the dismay of his subjects. His court was riven by factionalism; his absolutist view of monarchy at times resulted in a subordination of law to royal desire. Yet the crucial contemporary parallels lie elsewhere. In urging punishment of Cranmer's Protestantism, Gardiner warns that laxity leads to falling dominoes:

    Commotions, uproars—with a general taint
    Of the whole state, as of late days our neighbours,
    The upper Germany, can dearly witness.
                                                            (5.2.62–64)

The reference is to the Peasants' War in Germany (1524–26), in which the German aristocracy massacred perhaps 100,000 peasants. The danger of popular unrest in England is suggested by the court's fear of "loud rebellion" and the unruly "rabble" (1.2.30,

5.3.65). Similarly, the rowdies at Elizabeth's christening are "your faithful friends o'th' suburbs" (5.3.66). The suburbs were the location of the outdoor "public" theaters, such as the Globe, where *All Is True* was performed. The Porter remarks, "These are the youths that thunder at a playhouse, and fight for bitten apples, that no audience but the tribulation of Tower Hill or the limbs of Limehouse, their dear brothers, are able to endure" (5.3.55–58). The comparison is between the unruly apprentices who come to the theater and the rough crowds who attend public executions or frequent the dockyards. A christening recalls an execution; an ostensibly orthodox play in a suburban theater emphasizes the criminal character of suburb and audience alike.

It is thus the interaction between *All Is True* and its audience that undermines orthodoxy. This interaction is self-reflexive, or metadramatic, in character. That is, while providing a plausibly realistic dramatization of events, the play simultaneously indicates that it is merely a play, just a dramatization, by calling attention to the venue of performance—the "suburbs," the "playhouse," the "audience." As we have seen, however, this self-referentiality is the very opposite of apolitical aesthetic detachment. Furthermore, the Globe, which is surely the playhouse referred to in this scene, is not the only commercial theater that acquires thematic resonance in *All Is True*. By the time of the composition of the play, Shakespeare's acting company, the King's Men, divided its time—in the summer working at the Globe, in the winter at the Blackfriars, a more elite indoor, "private" theater in London itself rather than the suburbs. When Henry decides upon a judicial proceeding to determine whether or not his marriage to Katherine should be annulled, he also specifies a location for the event:

> The most convenient place I can think of
> For such receipt of learning is Blackfriars.
> (2.2.137–38)

Two scenes later, that is where the hearing is held, with the result that the audience of the play sits in judgment in the very place where the decision was actually rendered almost a century earlier, in 1529.

By placing the affluent audience of the Blackfriars in a position where it evaluates the conduct of a king, did *All Is True* undermine aristocratic and royal authority? Perhaps not as much as when the play was performed in the outdoor theater. According to Sir Henry Wotton, a spectator at the fateful performance when the Globe burned down, the work represented "some principall pieces of the raign of *Henry* 8 which was set forth with many extraordinary circumstances of Pomp and Majesty . . . sufficient in truth within a while to make greatness very familiar, if not ridiculous." Rather than dazzling into awestruck submission, the play's pageantry reduced the mystique of monarchy, turning the politically disenfranchised popular audience into moral arbiters of royal power. James's favorite, the Duke of Buckingham, may have felt as much when, in 1628, he commissioned a performance of *All Is True*, only to walk out after his namesake's beheading. In 1649, a Parliament driven by popular pressure emulated the play by staging an execution of its own. This time, however, the victim was James I's own son: the man on the scaffold was the King.

WALTER COHEN

TEXTUAL NOTE

Although the play was initially printed in the First Folio of 1623 (F) under the title *The Famous History of the Life of Henry the Eight* and today is generally known as *Henry VIII*, comments on early performances suggest that it was originally called *All Is True*. Perhaps the compilers of the Folio changed its title to make it conform to the pattern of using monarchs' names for the English history plays: it is placed at the end of this group of plays. Or perhaps John Fletcher, Shakespeare's collaborator on the play, is responsible for the switch (see below). The text is based not on an authorial manuscript but on a scribal copy; either the authorial or the scribal version may have been slightly revised for theatrical performance. F's division into acts and scenes is followed in the present edition; some editors, however, introduce a scene division after 5.2.34.

All Is True probably has links to the marriage on February 14, 1613, of Princess Elizabeth, King James's daughter, to the German Prince Frederick, the Elector Palatine. If so, it might have been written in late 1612. Unlike other plays by Shakespeare, it was not performed at court as part of the wedding festivities, but the text's reference to Blackfriars suggests that it could have been staged during the same period at that theater. But the accidental burning of the Globe Theatre at one of the first performances of the play on June 29, 1613, makes composition following the marriage, with the initial performance at the Globe in June 1613, equally likely. (See the Introduction.)

F attributes the play to Shakespeare. But beginning in the eighteenth century and especially since 1850, many critics have concluded that John Fletcher, who succeeded Shakespeare as the principal dramatist of the King's Men, collaborated on *All Is True*. External evidence for this position is inferential and inconclusive. Toward the end of his career, as perhaps at the beginning, Shakespeare seems to have turned to collaboration— in *Pericles*, the lost *Cardenio*, and *The Two Noble Kinsmen*. In the last two plays, dating from 1612–14, he apparently worked with Fletcher. On the other hand, these plays were all excluded from F by the editors, who were Shakespeare's fellow actors in the King's Men. Even though a minority of scholars continues to believe that Shakespeare was the sole author of *All Is True,* the internal stylistic and linguistic evidence strongly suggests that Fletcher wrote at least one-quarter of the piece—primarily 1.3–4, 3.1, and 5.2–4. (He seems to have written a little more than half of *The Two Noble Kinsmen*.) Yet the problem of attribution is not that simple. Shakespeare may have had some role in 3.1 and especially 5.2–4. Fletcher is likely to have played a part in 2.1–2 and 4.1–2. The unusually full stage directions may also be his work. Fletcher's sections of the play arguably have a more pro-Protestant outlook than Shakespeare's relatively balanced and uncommitted treatment of religious controversy. Finally, scholarly skepticism about the attribution of certain scenes (notably 2.1 and 4.1) to either Shakespeare or Fletcher has led to speculation about a third author. Francis Beaumont, who regularly collaborated with Fletcher, has been proposed, but the suggestion remains conjectural.

In short, both the broad conception of the play and most of the "big" scenes appear to be Shakespeare's.

SELECTED BIBLIOGRAPHY

Bergeron, David M. *Shakespeare's Romances and the Royal Family.* Lawrence: University Press of Kansas, 1985. 203–22. Links the play politically to James I and his family, and generically more to the late romances than to the earlier English history plays.

Frye, Susan. "Queens and the Structure of History in *Henry VIII*." *A Companion to Shakespeare's Works*, Vol. 4: *Poems, Problem Comedies, Late Plays*. Ed. Richard Dutton and Jean E. Howard. Malden, Mass.: Blackwell, 2003. 427–44. Parallels between the courts of Henry VIII and James I, centered on Queens struggling with a succession of male favorites.

Healy, Thomas. "History and Judgement in *Henry VIII*." *Shakespeare's Late Plays: New Readings*. Ed. Jennifer Richards and James Knowles. Edinburgh: Edinburgh University Press, 1999. 158–75. Argues that the play is structured to encourage the audience to respond with judgment rather than emotion to the conflicting possible interpretations of history.

Hodgdon, Barbara. *The End Crowns All: Closure and Contradiction in Shakespeare's History*. Princeton: Princeton University Press, 1991. 212–34. Focuses on Elizabeth as the concluding figure of the play, uniting masquelike and anti-masquelike (or carnivalesque) elements.

Kermode, Frank. "What Is Shakespeare's *Henry VIII* About?" *Shakespeare, The Histories: A Collection of Critical Essays*. Ed. Eugene M. Waith. Englewood Cliffs, N.J.: Prentice-Hall, 1965. 168–79. Henry as God's deputy and the agent of England's future felicity, by means of a morality structure involving the successive falls of the other leading figures.

Knight, G. Wilson. *The Crown of Life: Essays in Interpretation of Shakespeare's Final Plays*. London: Oxford University Press, 1947. 256–336. Sees the play as Shakespeare's culminating work, moving from order through tragic falls to concluding ritual.

McMullan, Gordon, ed. *King Henry VIII (All Is True)*. London: Arden Shakespeare, 2000. Outstanding scholarly edition with a book-length critical introduction.

Noling, Kim H. "Grubbing Up the Stock: Dramatizing Queens in *Henry VIII*." *Shakespeare Quarterly* 39 (1988): 291–306. Katherine's strong stage positions contrasted with Anne's relatively weak role, including dissociation from her daughter, Elizabeth—all in the service of flattering male monarchs, Henry and James.

Shirley, Frances A., ed. *"King John" and "Henry VIII": Critical Essays*. New York: Garland, 1988. Twelve essays on the play from nineteenth- and twentieth-century theatrical and literary criticism.

Wegemer, Gerard. "Henry VIII on Trial: Confronting Malice and Conscience in Shakespeare's *All Is True*." *Renascence* 52 (2000): 111–30. Argues that, in addition to the public trials structuring the play, covert trials of Thomas More and of Henry himself produce a critical view of the monarch.

FILMS

The Private Life of Henry VIII. 1933. Dir. Alexander Korda. UK. 97 min. Unrelated to *All Is True*. Starring Charles Laughton.

A Man for All Seasons. 1966. Dir. Fred Zinnemann. UK. 120 min. Unrelated to *All Is True*. Based on Robert Bolt's play about Sir Thomas More's religious conflict over Henry's decision to divorce Katherine and wed Anne. Stellar cast, including Paul Scofield in the title role; Oscars for Best Actor, Director, Picture.

Anne of the Thousand Days. 1969. Dir. Charles Jarrott. UK. 145 min. Unrelated to *All Is True*. On Anne Boleyn's rise and fall. Distinguished cast, including Geneviève Bujold as Anne and Richard Burton as Henry.

Henry VIII. 1979. Dir. Kevin Billington. UK. 166 min. Highly praised BBC production minimizing the pomp and ceremony in plays or films on Henry and his age, in favor of a contrast between public political life and inwardness and morality, focused on Katherine, played by Claire Bloom.

All Is True

THE PERSONS OF THE PLAY

PROLOGUE
KING HENRY the Eighth
Duke of BUCKINGHAM
Lord ABERGAVENNY } his sons-in-law
Earl of SURREY
Duke of NORFOLK
Duke of SUFFOLK
LORD CHAMBERLAIN
LORD CHANCELLOR
Lord SANDS (also called Sir William SANDS)
Sir Thomas LOVELL
Sir Anthony DENNY
Sir Henry GUILDFORD
CARDINAL WOLSEY
Two SECRETARIES
BUCKINGHAM'S SURVEYOR
CARDINAL CAMPEIUS
GARDINER, the King's new secretary, later Bishop of Winchester
His PAGE
Thomas CROMWELL
CRANMER, Archbishop of Canterbury
QUEEN KATHERINE, later KATHERINE, Princess Dowager
GRIFFITH, her gentleman usher
PATIENCE, her waiting-woman
Other WOMEN
Six spirits, who dance before Katherine in a vision
A MESSENGER
Lord CAPUTIUS
ANNE Boleyn
An OLD LADY
BRANDON } who arrest Buckingham and Abergavenny
SERJEANT-at-arms
Sir Nicholas VAUX ⎫
Tipstaves ⎬ after Buckingham's arraignment
Halberdiers ⎪
Common people ⎭
Two vergers ⎫
Two SCRIBES ⎪
Archbishop of Canterbury ⎪
Bishop of LINCOLN ⎪
Bishop of Ely ⎬ appearing at the Legatine Court
Bishop of Rochester ⎪
Bishop of Saint Asaph ⎪
Two priests ⎪
Serjeant-at-arms ⎪
Two noblemen ⎪
A CRIER ⎭

Three GENTLEMEN
Two judges
Choristers
Lord Mayor of London
Garter King-of-Arms   ⎫
Marquis Dorset   ⎬ appearing in the Coronation
Four Barons of the Cinque Ports
Stokesley, Bishop of London
Old Duchess of Norfolk
Countesses   ⎭

A DOORKEEPER
Doctor BUTTS, the King's physician   ⎫ At Cranmer's trial
Pursuivants, pages, footboys, grooms ⎭

A PORTER
His MAN
Two aldermen
Lord Mayor of London
GARTER King-of-Arms   ⎬ at the Christening
Six noblemen
Old Duchess of Norfolk, godmother
The child, Princess Elizabeth
Marchioness Dorset, godmother

EPILOGUE
Ladies, gentlemen, a SERVANT, guards, attendants, trumpeters

Prologue

[*Enter* PROLOGUE]

PROLOGUE   I come no more to make you laugh. Things now
    That bear a weighty and a serious brow,
    Sad, high, and working,° full of state° and woe—   *full of pathos / grandeur*
    Such noble scenes as draw the eye to flow
5   We now present. Those that can pity here
    May, if they think it well, let fall a tear.
    The subject will deserve it. Such as give
    Their money out of hope they may believe,
    May here find truth, too. Those that come to see
10   Only a show or two, and so agree
    The play may pass, if they be still, and willing,
    I'll undertake may see away their shilling
    Richly in two short hours.[1] Only they
    That come to hear a merry bawdy play,
15   A noise of targets,° or to see a fellow   *shields*
    In a long motley coat guarded[2] with yellow,
    Will be deceived. For, gentle hearers, know
    To rank our chosen truth with such a show
    As fool and fight is, beside forfeiting
20   Our own brains, and the opinion that we bring
    To make that only true we now intend,[3]

Prologue
1. *Those . . . hours:* If those who come only for a spectacle ("show") and approve the play on those terms are quiet and willing, I promise they'll get their shilling's worth (the price of more expensive, genteel seating) in two hours (plays ran two to three hours).
2. Ornamented on its border. The fool's "motley," or patchwork, coat may refer to other plays about Henry's life, including Samuel Rowley's *When You See Me, You Know Me* (1605), which featured Henry's fool, Will Summers, and was reprinted and perhaps revived in 1613.
3. *beside . . . intend:* in addition to wasting our mental labor, and our intention of presenting an entirely truthful representation.

Will leave us never an understanding[4] friend.
Therefore, for goodness' sake, and as you are known
The first and happiest hearers° of the town,   *finest audience*
25 Be sad° as we would make ye. Think ye see   *grave*
The very persons of our noble story
As they were living; think you see them great,°   *of high rank*
And followed with the general throng and sweat
Of thousand friends; then, in a moment, see
30 How soon this mightiness meets misery.
And if you can be merry then, I'll say
A man may weep upon his wedding day.   [*Exit*]

1.1

[*A cloth of state throughout the play.*][1] *Enter the Duke*
of NORFOLK *at one door; at the other* [*door enter*] *the*
Duke of BUCKINGHAM *and the Lord* ABERGAVENNY

BUCKINGHAM [*to* NORFOLK] Good morrow, and well met. How have ye done
Since last we saw° in France?   *met*
NORFOLK   I thank your grace,
Healthful, and ever since a fresh° admirer   *an eager*
Of what I saw there.[2]
BUCKINGHAM   An untimely ague
5 Stayed me a prisoner in my chamber[3] when
Those suns of glory, those two lights of men,
Met in the vale of Ardres.
NORFOLK   'Twixt Guisnes and Ardres.[4]
I was then present, saw them salute on horseback,
Beheld them when they lighted,° how they clung   *got off*
10 In their embracement as° they grew together,   *as if*
Which had they,° what four throned ones could have weighed[5] *if they had*
Such a compounded one?
BUCKINGHAM   All the whole time
I was my chamber's prisoner.
NORFOLK   Then you lost
The view of earthly glory. Men might say
15 Till this time pomp was single, but now married
To one above itself.[6] Each following day
Became the next day's master, till the last
Made former wonders its.[7] Today the French,
All clinquant° all in gold, like heathen gods   *glittering*
20 Shone down the English; and tomorrow they
Made Britain India.[8] Every man that stood
Showed like a mine. Their dwarfish pages were

---

4. Punning reference to the lower-class groundlings, who are literally "understanding" in the sense of "standing under" the raised stage.
1.1. Location: The court at London.
1. A seat under a canopy for the King or Cardinal Wolsey, perhaps onstage throughout the play. The original Globe performances also had "matting" (a woven straw floor-covering) on the stage.
2. The reference is to the rendezvous of Henry VIII and Francis I of France near Calais in June 1520, at the Field of the Cloth of Gold, named for the sumptuous displays by the two Kings.
3. Actually, Buckingham was present, if reluctantly (because of the expense), at the Field of the Cloth of

Gold. The fictional "ague," or fever, allows the dramatist to show Buckingham responding to Norfolk's detailed description.
4. Guisnes belonged to England, Ardres to France.
5. Been as heavy as.
6. *Till . . . itself:* The pomp of each King now joins ("marries") that of the other, making a greater pomp than either alone could display.
7. *Each . . . its:* Each day learned wonders from the previous one, making the last day the most wonderful of all. *master:* standard.
8. *they . . . India:* the English made Britain look as (fabulously) rich as India or the West Indies.

As cherubim, all gilt;[9] the *mesdames*,° too,   *ladies*
Not used to toil, did almost sweat to bear
25   The pride° upon them, that° their very labour   *fancy adornment / so that*
Was to them as a painting.[1] Now this masque
Was cried° incomparable, and th'ensuing night   *said to be*
Made it a fool and beggar. The two kings
Equal in lustre, were now best, now worst,
30   As presence did present them.[2] Him in eye
Still him in praise,[3] and being present both,
'Twas said they saw but one, and no discerner
Durst wag his tongue in censure.[4] When these suns—
For so they phrase 'em—by their heralds challenged
35   The noble spirits to arms, they did perform
Beyond thought's compass, that former fabulous story
Being now seen possible enough, got credit
That *Bevis* was believed.[5]
BUCKINGHAM   O, you go far!
NORFOLK   As I belong to worship,° and affect   *the aristocracy*
40   In honour honesty,[6] the tract of ev'rything
Would by a good discourser lose some life
Which action's self was tongue to.[7] All was royal.
To the disposing° of it naught rebelled.   *arrangement*
Order gave each thing view. The office did
Distinctly his full function.[8]
45   BUCKINGHAM   Who did guide—
I mean, who set the body and the limbs
Of this great sport° together, as you guess?   *show*
NORFOLK   One, certes, that promises no element[9]
In such a business.
BUCKINGHAM   I pray you who, my lord?
50   NORFOLK   All this was ordered by the good discretion
Of the right reverend Cardinal of York.°   *(Wolsey)*
BUCKINGHAM   The devil speed° him! No man's pie is freed   *ruin*
From his ambitious finger. What had he
To do in these fierce° vanities? I wonder   *excessive*
55   That such a keech[1] can, with his very bulk,
Take up the rays o'th' beneficial sun,°   *(Henry)*
And keep it from the earth.
NORFOLK   Surely, sir,
There's in him stuff that puts° him to these ends.   *spurs*
For being not propped by ancestry, whose grace
60   Chalks successors their way,[2] nor called upon
For high feats done to th' crown, neither allied
To eminent assistants,° but spider-like,   *ministers of state*
Out of his self-drawing° web, a° gives us note   *spun from himself / he*

---

9. Gold-plated statues of cherubim, often found in churches.
1. Made them rosy, as if with makeup.
2. According to who was present.
3. *Him . . . praise:* To the King on display at the time went all the acclaim.
4. *no . . . censure:* no one watching dared say one outshone the other.
5. *they did . . . believed:* their performance was such that stories formerly deemed mere fables, now looking possible, gained plausibility. Even *Sir Bevis of Hampton* (Southampton), a popular medieval romance, was believed.
6. *and . . . honesty:* and honorably love truth.
7. *the tract . . . to:* the events surpass their telling.
8. *Order . . . Distinctly:* Careful organization made everything appropriately visible. Each responsible person properly fulfilled his role.
9. One, without doubt, who seems out of place.
1. Hunk of fat from a slaughtered animal. Wolsey was said to be a butcher's son.
2. *ancestry . . . way:* noble ancestors, whose honorable qualities mark the way for future generations.

The force of his own merit makes his way—
65   A gift that heaven gives for him which buys
      A place next to the King.
ABERGAVENNY   I cannot tell
      What heaven hath given him—let some graver eye
      Pierce into that; but I can see his pride
      Peep through each part of him. Whence has he that?°   (such pride)
70   If not from hell, the devil is a niggard°   selfish
      Or has given all before,° and he° begins   already / (Wolsey)
      A new hell in himself.
BUCKINGHAM   Why the devil,
      Upon this French going out,° took he upon him   journey
      Without the privity° o'th' King t'appoint   private sanction
75   Who should attend on him? He makes up the file°   roll
      Of all the gentry, for the most part such
      To whom as great a charge as little honour
      He meant to lay upon;[3] and his own letter,
      The honourable board of council out,
      Must fetch him in, he papers.[4]
80 ABERGAVENNY   I do know
      Kinsmen of mine—three at the least—that have
      By this so sickened° their estates that never   wasted
      They shall abound as formerly.
BUCKINGHAM   O, many
      Have broke their backs with laying manors on 'em[5]
85   For this great journey. What did this vanity
      But minister communication of
      A most poor issue?[6]
NORFOLK   Grievingly I think
      The peace between the French and us not values°   does not merit
      The cost that did conclude it.
BUCKINGHAM   Every man,
90   After the hideous storm that followed, was
      A thing inspired, and, not consulting,° broke   without conferring
      Into a general° prophecy—that this tempest,   collective
      Dashing the garment of this peace, aboded°   prophesied
      The sudden breach on't.°   of it
NORFOLK   Which is budded out°—   has occurred
95   For France hath flawed° the league, and hath attached° betrayed / seized
      Our merchants' goods at Bordeaux.
ABERGAVENNY   Is it therefore°   on this account
      Th'ambassador is silenced?
NORFOLK   Marry is't.°   Of course it is
ABERGAVENNY   A proper title of a° peace, and purchased A fine thing to call
      At a superfluous rate.°   too high a cost
BUCKINGHAM   Why, all this business
      Our reverend Cardinal carried.°   oversaw
100 NORFOLK   Like it° your grace,   May it please
      The state takes notice of the private difference

---

3. *To whom . . . upon:* (Wolsey gave) places of little
honor to the noblemen on whom he laid the greatest
expense for the display.
4. *and . . . papers:* and with the council ignored ("out"),
his own summons ("letter") forces every person he lists
("papers") to comply.
5. *many . . .'em:* many have sold off their estates—and

thus bankrupted themselves—to pay for a costly
wardrobe; with a pun on "manners."
6. *What . . . issue:* What did such wasteful expense do
but bankrupt their own children ("poor issue"); or
encourage talk for a trivial outcome ("poor issue")?

Betwixt you and the Cardinal. I advise you—
And take it from a heart that wishes towards you
Honour and plenteous safety—that you read°   *assess*
105   The Cardinal's malice and his potency
Together; to consider further that
What his high hatred would effect wants° not   *lacks*
A minister° in his power. You know his nature,   *An agent*
That he's revengeful; and I know his sword
110   Hath a sharp edge—it's long, and't may be said
It reaches far; and where 'twill not extend
Thither he darts it. Bosom up° my counsel,   *Keep secret; take to heart*
You'll find it wholesome. Lo, where comes that rock
That I advise your shunning.

    Enter CARDINAL WOLSEY, *the purse*[7] *[containing the
    great seal] borne before him. [Enter with him] certain
    of the guard, and two* SECRETARIES *with papers. The*
    CARDINAL *in his passage fixeth his eye on* BUCKINGHAM
    and BUCKINGHAM *on him, both full of disdain*

CARDINAL WOLSEY [*To a* SECRETARY]   The Duke of Buckingham's
115   surveyor,° ha?   *overseer of an estate*
Where's his examination?°   *testimony*
SECRETARY   Here, so please you.
CARDINAL WOLSEY   Is he in person ready?
SECRETARY   Ay, please your grace.
CARDINAL WOLSEY   Well, we shall then know more, and Buckingham
Shall lessen this big° look.   *pompous*

    Exeunt CARDINAL [WOLSEY] *and his train*

120 BUCKINGHAM   This butcher's cur is venom-mouthed, and I
Have not the power to muzzle him; therefore best
Not wake him in his slumber. A beggar's book°   *learning*
Outworths a noble's blood.°   *inherited privilege*
NORFOLK   What, are you chafed?°   *annoyed*
Ask God for temp'rance; that's th'appliance only°   *the only medicine*
Which your disease requires.
125 BUCKINGHAM   I read in's looks
Matter against me, and his eye reviled
Me as his abject° object. At this instant   *discarded*
He bores° me with some trick. He's gone to th' King—   *pierces; defrauds*
I'll follow, and outstare him.
NORFOLK   Stay, my lord,
130   And let your reason with your choler° question°   *anger/dispute*
What 'tis you go about. To climb steep hills
Requires slow pace at first. Anger is like
A full hot° horse who, being allowed his way,   *feisty*
Self-mettle° tires him. Not a man in England   *His own disposition*
135   Can advise me like you. Be to yourself
As you would to your friend.[8]
BUCKINGHAM   I'll to the King,
And from a mouth of honour[9] quite cry down
This Ipswich° fellow's insolence, or proclaim   *(Wolsey's birthplace)*
There's difference in no persons.°   *Rank no longer matters*

---

7. A special bag that held the "great seal," part of the   a friend to do.
Lord Chancellor's insignia of office.   9. An aristocratic, virtuous mouth.
8. *Be . . . friend:* Don't do anything you wouldn't advise

NORFOLK   Be advised.°   *Be careful*

140   Heat not a furnace for your foe so hot
That it do singe yourself. We may outrun
By violent swiftness that which we run at,°   *toward*
And lose by over-running. Know you not
The fire that mounts° the liquor till't run o'er   *swells (by boiling)*

145   In seeming to augment it wastes it? Be advised.
I say again there is no English soul
More stronger to direct you than yourself,
If with the sap of reason you would quench
Or but allay° the fire of passion.   *abate*

BUCKINGHAM   Sir,
150   I am thankful to you, and I'll go along
By your prescription; but this top-proud° fellow—   *proudest of all*
Whom from the flow of gall I name not, but
From sincere motions[1]—by intelligence,°   *covert information*
And proofs as clear as founts° in July when   *springs*

155   We see each grain of gravel, I do know
To be corrupt and treasonous.

NORFOLK   Say not 'treasonous'.

BUCKINGHAM   To th' King I'll say't, and make my vouch° as strong   *case*
As shore of rock. Attend: this holy fox,
Or wolf, or both—for he is equal° rav'nous   *as*
160   As he is subtle, and as prone to mischief
As able to perform't, his mind and place°   *high position*
Infecting one another, yea, reciprocally—
Only to show his pomp as well in France
As here at home, suggests° the King our master   *tempts*
165   To this last° costly treaty, th'interview°   *latest / the meeting*
That swallowed so much treasure and, like a glass,
Did break i'th' rinsing.

NORFOLK   Faith, and so it did.

BUCKINGHAM   Pray give me favour,° sir. This cunning Cardinal,   *let me continue*
The articles o'th' combination° drew   *terms of the treaty*
170   As himself pleased, and they were ratified
As he cried 'Thus let be', to as much end°   *effect*
As give a crutch to th' dead. But our count-Cardinal[2]
Has done this, and 'tis well for worthy Wolsey,
Who cannot err, he did it. Now this follows—
175   Which, as I take it, is a kind of puppy
To th'old dam,° treason—Charles the Emperor,[3]   *bitch; mother*
Under pretence to see the Queen his aunt°—   *(Katherine)*
For 'twas indeed his colour,° but he came   *alibi*
To whisper° Wolsey—here makes visitation.   *meet covertly with*
180   His fears were that the interview betwixt
England and France might through their amity
Breed him some prejudice, for from this league
Peeped harms that menaced him. Privily° he   *Clandestinely*
Deals with our Cardinal and, as I trow°—   *believe*
185   Which I do well, for I am sure the Emperor
Paid ere he promised, whereby his suit was granted

---

1. *Whom . . . motions:* Whom I name not from a ran-
corous impulse but from pure motives.
2. Church leader assuming secular, aristocratic rank

(compare "King-Cardinal," 2.2.18).
3. Charles V, Holy Roman Emperor and King of Spain.

Ere it was asked—but when the way was made,
And paved with gold, the Emperor thus desired
That he° would please to alter the King's course   *(Wolsey)*
190   And break the foresaid peace. Let the King know,
As soon he shall by me, that thus the Cardinal
Does buy and sell his° honour as he° pleases,   *(Henry's) / (Wolsey)*
And for his own advantage.

NORFOLK   I am sorry
To hear this of him, and could wish he were
Something mistaken° in't.   *Partly misrepresented*
195   BUCKINGHAM   No, not a syllable.
I do pronounce him in that very shape
He shall appear in proof.°   *in practice*
            Enter BRANDON, *a* SERJEANT-*at-arms before him, and*
                two or three of the guard
BRANDON   Your office, serjeant, execute it.
SERJEANT   Sir.
        [*To* BUCKINGHAM] My lord the Duke of Buckingham and Earl
200   Of Hereford, Stafford, and Northampton, I
Arrest thee of high treason in the name
Of our most sovereign King.
BUCKINGHAM [*to* NORFOLK]   Lo° you, my lord,   *Look*
The net has fall'n upon me. I shall perish
Under device and practice.°   *trickery and schemes*
BRANDON   I am sorry
205   To see you ta'en from liberty to look on⁴
The business present. 'Tis his highness' pleasure
You shall to th' Tower.
BUCKINGHAM   It will help me nothing
To plead mine innocence, for that dye is on me
Which makes my whit'st part black. The will of heav'n
210   Be done in this and all things. I obey.
O, my lord Abergavenny, fare you well.
BRANDON   Nay, he must bear you company.
        [*To* ABERGAVENNY]   The King
Is pleased you shall to th' Tower till you know
How he determines further.
ABERGAVENNY   As the Duke said,
215   The will of heaven be done and the King's pleasure
By me obeyed.
BRANDON   Here is a warrant from
The King t'attach° Lord Montague and the bodies   *to seize*
Of the duke's confessor, John de la Car,
One Gilbert Perk, his chancellor—
BUCKINGHAM   So, so;
220   These are the limbs o'th' plot. No more, I hope.
BRANDON   A monk o'th' Chartreux.°   *Carthusian*
BUCKINGHAM   O, Nicholas Hopkins?
BRANDON   He.
BUCKINGHAM   My surveyor is false. The o'er-great Cardinal
Hath showed him gold. My life is spanned° already.   *marked out*
225   I am the shadow of poor Buckingham,

4. *to look on:* and (sorry) to behold.

Whose figure even this instant cloud puts on
By dark'ning my clear sun.[5] [*To* NORFOLK] My lord, farewell.

Exeunt [NORFOLK *at one door,* BUCKINGHAM *and*
ABERGAVENNY *under guard at another*]

1.2

Cornetts. Enter KING HENRY *leaning on Cardinal*
[*Wolsey*]'s *shoulder.* [*Enter with them Wolsey's two* SEC-
RETARIES,] *the nobles, and Sir Thomas* LOVELL. [*The*
KING *ascends to his seat under the cloth of state;*] CAR-
DINAL [WOLSEY] *places himself under the King's feet°*   below the throne
on his right side

KING HENRY [*to* WOLSEY]   My life itself and the best heart° of it   essential core
Thanks you for this great care. I stood i'th' level°   line of fire
Of a full-charged confederacy,° and give thanks   loaded conspiracy
To you that choked it. Let be called before us
5   That gentleman of Buckingham's.° In person   (the surveyor)
I'll hear him his confessions justify,°   verify
And point by point the treasons of his master
He shall again relate.

CRIER (*within*)   Room for the Queen, ushered by the Duke of Norfolk.

Enter QUEEN [KATHERINE, *the Duke of*] NORFOLK, *and*
[*the Duke of*] SUFFOLK. *She kneels.* KING [HENRY]
riseth from his state,° takes her up, and kisses her   throne
10   QUEEN KATHERINE   Nay, we must longer kneel. I am a suitor.
KING HENRY   Arise, and take place by us.
[*He*] *placeth* [*her*] *by him*

                                        Half your suit
Never name to us. You have half our power,
The other moiety° ere you ask is given.   half
Repeat your will° and take it.   State your wish
QUEEN KATHERINE   Thank your majesty.
15   That you would love yourself, and in that love
Not unconsidered leave your honour nor
The dignity of your office, is the point
Of my petition.
KING HENRY   Lady mine, proceed.
QUEEN KATHERINE   I am solicited,° not by a few,   apprised
20   And those of true condition,° that your subjects   loyal character
Are in great grievance. There have been commissions
Sent down among 'em[1] which hath flawed° the heart   broken
Of all their loyalties; wherein, although,
My good lord Cardinal, they vent reproaches
25   Most bitterly on you, as putter-on
Of these exactions,° yet the King our master—   taxes
Whose honour heaven shield from soil°—even he escapes not   blemish
Language unmannerly, yea, such which breaks
The sides[2] of loyalty, and almost appears
In loud rebellion.
30   NORFOLK   Not 'almost appears'—
It doth appear; for upon these taxations

---

5. A cloud having overshadowed my former glory and
come between me and my king ("sun" may refer to
either Buckingham or Henry).
1.2 Location: A council chamber at court.

1. *There . . . 'em:* They have received writs authorizing
the collection of taxes.
2. *which . . . sides:* which oversteps the limits.

The clothiers all, not able to maintain
The many to them 'longing,° have put off°   *they employ / let go*
The spinsters, carders, fullers,[3] weavers, who,
35   Unfit for other life, compelled by hunger
And lack of other means, in desperate manner
Daring th'event to th' teeth,[4] are all in uproar,
And danger serves among them.

KING HENRY   Taxation?
Wherein, and what taxation? My lord Cardinal,
40   You that are blamed for it alike with us,
Know you of this taxation?

CARDINAL WOLSEY   Please you, sir,
I know but of a single° part in aught°   *(his own) / anything*
Pertains to th' state, and front but in that file
Where others tell steps with me.[5]

QUEEN KATHERINE   No, my lord?
45   You know no more than others? But you frame
Things that are known alike, which are not wholesome
To those which would not know them, and yet must
Perforce be their acquaintance.[6] These exactions
Whereof my sovereign would have note,° they are   *knowledge*
50   Most pestilent to th' hearing, and to bear 'em
The back is sacrifice to° th' load. They say   *broken by*
They are devised by you, or else you suffer
Too hard an exclamation.°   *a complaint*

KING HENRY   Still exaction!
The nature of it? In what kind, let's know,
Is this exaction?

55   QUEEN KATHERINE   I am much too venturous
In tempting of your patience, but am boldened
Under your promised pardon. The subjects' grief °   *grievance*
Comes through commissions which compels from each
The sixth part of his substance° to be levied   *wealth*
60   Without delay, and the pretence for this
Is named your wars in France. This makes bold mouths.
Tongues spit their duties out, and cold hearts freeze
Allegiance in them. Their curses now
Live where their prayers did, and it's come to pass
65   This tractable obedience is a slave
To each incensèd will.[7] I would your highness
Would give it quick consideration, for
There is no primer° business.   *more pressing*

KING HENRY   By my life,
This is against our pleasure.

CARDINAL WOLSEY   And for me,
70   I have no further gone in this than by
A single voice,[8] and that not passed me but
By learnèd approbation° of the judges. If I am   *approval*
Traduced° by ignorant tongues, which neither know   *Slandered*

---

3. All involved in wool production: "spinsters" spun the wool; "carders" combed through, extracting impurities; and "fullers" beat the wool to thicken and cleanse it.
4. Refusing adamantly to comply with the result.
5. *front . . . me*: I walk at the front of a line only of those who have power equal to my own (literally, who march in step behind me). Wolsey is denying that he is responsible.

6. *But . . . acquaintance*: But you originate measures that all know, that harm even those who would rather not accept them yet must.
7. *This . . . will*: Each subject's formerly compliant obedience is dominated by his anger.
8. *I . . . voice*: I have only cast my single vote; I have concurred with a unanimous vote.

My faculties° nor person yet will be   *abilities*
75 The chronicles of my doing, let me say
'Tis but the fate of place,° and the rough brake°   *rank / thicket*
That virtue must go through. We must not stint°   *halt*
Our necessary actions in the fear
To cope° malicious censurers, which ever,   *Of facing*
80 As rav'nous fishes, do a vessel follow
That is new trimmed,° but benefit no further   *newly rigged*
Than vainly longing. What we oft do best,
By sick interpreters, once weak ones, is
Not ours or not allowed;[9] what° worst, as oft,   *what we do*
85 Hitting a grosser quality,° is cried up   *Appealing to the base*
For our best act. If we shall stand still,
In fear our motion[1] will be mocked or carped at,
We should take root here where we sit,
Or sit state-statues only.[2]

KING HENRY   Things done well,
90 And with a care, exempt themselves from fear;
Things done without example,° in their issue°   *precedent / effects*
Are to be feared. Have you a precedent
Of this commission? I believe not any.
We must not rend our subjects from our laws
95 And stick them in our will.° Sixth part of each?   *use them at our whim*
A trembling contribution! Why, we take
From every tree lop,° bark, and part o'th' timber,   *branches*
And though we leave it with a root, thus hacked
The air will drink the sap. To every county
100 Where this is questioned° send our letters with   *challenged*
Free pardon to each man that has denied°   *refused*
The force of this commission. Pray look to't—
I put it to your care.

CARDINAL WOLSEY [*to a* SECRETARY]   A word with you.
Let there be letters writ to every shire
Of the King's grace° and pardon.   *mercy*
105 [*Aside to the* SECRETARY]   The grievèd commons
Hardly° conceive of me. Let it be noised°   *Severely / rumored*
That through our intercession this revokement
And pardon comes. I shall anon advise you
Further in the proceeding.   *Exit* SECRETARY
        Enter [BUCKINGHAM'S] SURVEYOR
110 QUEEN KATHERINE [*to the* KING]   I am sorry that the Duke of Buckingham
Is run in° your displeasure.   *Has provoked*
KING HENRY   It grieves many.
The gentleman is learnèd, and a most rare speaker,
To nature none more bound;[3] his training such
That he may furnish and instruct great teachers
115 And never seek for aid out of ° himself. Yet see,   *outside of*
When these so noble benefits shall prove
Not well disposed,° the mind growing once corrupt,   *employed*
They turn to vicious forms ten times more ugly
Than ever they were fair. This man so complete,°   *accomplished*

---

9. *What . . . allowed:* Formerly foolish, now corrupt ("sick") observers never attribute to us or approve in us what we do best.
1. For fear our proposal (or action).
2. Or become nothing but decorative statues of leaders.
3. No man has been given greater gifts by nature.

120   Who was enrolled 'mongst wonders—and when we
       Almost with ravished° list'ning could not find   *spellbound*
       His hour of speech a minute—he, my lady,
       Hath into monstrous habits° put the graces   *shapes; behavior; clothes*
       That once were his, and is become as black
125   As if besmeared in hell. Sit by us. You shall hear—
       This was his gentleman in trust of him—
       Things to strike honour sad.
       [*To* WOLSEY]   Bid him recount
       The fore-recited practices° whereof   *schemes*
       We cannot feel too little, hear too much.
       CARDINAL WOLSEY [*to the* SURVEYOR]   Stand forth, and with bold
130   spirit relate what you
       Most like a careful subject have collected°   *gathered as evidence*
       Out of° the Duke of Buckingham.   *(by observing)*
       KING HENRY [*to the* SURVEYOR]   Speak freely.
       BUCKINGHAM'S SURVEYOR   First, it was usual with him, every day
       It would infect his speech, that if the King
135   Should without issue die, he'll carry it so°   *arrange so as*
       To make the sceptre his. These very words
       I've heard him utter to his son-in-law,
       Lord Abergavenny, to whom by oath he menaced
       Revenge upon the Cardinal.
       CARDINAL WOLSEY [*to the* KING]   Please your highness note
140   His dangerous conception in this point,
       Not friended by his wish to your high person.[4]
       His will is most malignant, and it stretches
       Beyond you to your friends.
       QUEEN KATHERINE   My learned Lord Cardinal,
       Deliver all with charity.
       KING HENRY [*to the* SURVEYOR]   Speak on.
145   How grounded he his title to the crown
       Upon our fail?° To this point hast thou heard him   *childlessness; death*
       At any time speak aught?
       BUCKINGHAM'S SURVEYOR   He was brought to this
       By a vain prophecy of Nicholas Hopkins.
       KING HENRY   What was that Hopkins?
       BUCKINGHAM'S SURVEYOR   Sir, a Chartreux friar,
150   His confessor, who fed him every minute
       With words of sovereignty.
       KING HENRY   How know'st thou this?
       BUCKINGHAM'S SURVEYOR   Not long before your highness sped to France,
       The Duke being at the Rose,[5] within the parish
       Saint Lawrence Poutney, did of me demand
155   What was the speech° among the Londoners   *gossip*
       Concerning the French journey. I replied
       Men feared the French would prove perfidious,
       To the King's danger; presently° the Duke   *at once*
       Said 'twas the fear indeed, and that he doubted°   *suspected*
160   'Twould prove the verity of certain words
       Spoke by a holy monk that oft, says he,
       'Hath sent to me, wishing me to permit

---

4. Since he has not been granted ("friended by") his   5. Manor owned by Buckingham just outside London.
wish that the King die without an heir.

John de la Car, my chaplain, a choice hour°   *a suitable time*
To hear from him a matter of some moment;
165   Whom after under the confession's seal
He solemnly had sworn, that what he spoke
My chaplain to no creature living but
To me should utter, with demure° confidence   *grave*
This pausingly ensued: "neither the King nor's heirs",
170   Tell you the Duke, "shall prosper. Bid him strive
To win the love o'th' commonalty.° The Duke   *common people*
Shall govern England."'

QUEEN KATHERINE   If I know you well,
You were the Duke's surveyor, and lost your office
On the complaint o'th' tenants. Take good heed
175   You charge not in your spleen° a noble person   *spite*
And spoil° your nobler soul. I say, take heed;   *ruin*
Yes, heartily beseech you.

KING HENRY   Let him on.°   *continue*
[*To the* SURVEYOR] Go forward.

BUCKINGHAM'S SURVEYOR   On my soul I'll speak but truth.
I told my lord the Duke, by th' devil's illusions
180   The monk might be deceived, and that 'twas dangerous
To ruminate on this so far until
It forged him some design which, being believed,
It was much like to do.[6] He answered, 'Tush,
It can do me no damage', adding further
185   That had the King in his last sickness failed,°   *died*
The Cardinal's and Sir Thomas Lovell's heads
Should have gone off.

KING HENRY   Ha? What, so rank?° Ah, ha!   *rotten*
There's mischief in this man. Canst thou say further?

BUCKINGHAM'S SURVEYOR   I can, my liege.

KING HENRY   Proceed.

BUCKINGHAM'S SURVEYOR   Being at Greenwich,
190   After your highness had reproved the Duke
About Sir William Bulmer—

KING HENRY   I remember
Such a time, being my sworn servant,
The Duke retained him his.° But on—what hence?   *for his own*

BUCKINGHAM'S SURVEYOR   'If ', quoth he, 'I for this had been committed'—
195   As to the Tower, I thought—'I would have played
The part my father[7] meant to act upon
Th'usurper Richard who, being at Salisbury,
Made suit to come in's presence; which if granted,
As he made semblance of his duty,° would   *seemed to kneel*
Have put his knife into him.'

200   KING HENRY   A giant traitor!

CARDINAL WOLSEY [*to the* QUEEN]   Now, madam, may° his highness   *can*
        live in freedom,
And this man out of prison?

QUEEN KATHERINE   God mend all.

---

6. *until . . . do*: until the Duke's ruminations made him
imagine ("forged him") some scheme that, if he
believed in it (and hence in the Monk's prophecy), he

would probably undertake.
7. The Duke of Buckingham during Richard III's reign.

KING HENRY [*to the* SURVEYOR]   There's something more would
      out of thee—what sayst?
BUCKINGHAM'S SURVEYOR   After 'the Duke his father', with 'the knife',
205   He stretched him,° and with one hand on his dagger,   *stood up straight*
    Another spread on's breast, mounting° his eyes,   *raising up*
    He did discharge a horrible oath whose tenor
    Was, were he evil used,° he would outgo   *poorly treated*
    His father by as much as a performance°   *true performance*
    Does an irresolute purpose.
210 KING HENRY   There's his period°—   *ultimate goal*
    To sheathe his knife in us. He is attached.°   *arrested*
    Call him to present° trial. If he may   *immediate*
    Find mercy in the law, 'tis his; if none,
    Let him not seek't of us. By day and night,
215   He's traitor to th' height.°   [*Flourish.*] *Exeunt*   *to the greatest degree*

1.3

Enter [*the*] LORD CHAMBERLAIN *and Lord* SANDS

LORD CHAMBERLAIN   Is't possible the spells of France should juggle°   *enchant*
    Men into such strange mysteries?°   *outlandish conduct*
SANDS   New customs,
    Though they be never so ridiculous—
    Nay, let 'em be unmanly°—yet are followed.   *effeminate*
5 LORD CHAMBERLAIN   As far as I see, all the good our English
    Have got by the late voyage° is but merely   *(to France)*
    A fit or two o'th' face.° But they are shrewd ones,   *Odd new expressions*
    For when they hold 'em° you would swear directly   *maintain these looks*
    Their very noses had been counsellors
10   To Pépin or Clotharius, they keep state so.[1]
SANDS   They have all new legs,° and lame ones; one would take it,   *new walks and bows*
    That never see 'em pace° before, the spavin   *saw them walk*
    Or spring-halt reigned among 'em.[2]
LORD CHAMBERLAIN   Death,° my lord,   *By God's death*
    Their clothes are after such a pagan cut to't
    That sure they've worn out Christendom.[3]
    Enter Sir Thomas LOVELL
15   How now—
    What news, Sir Thomas Lovell?
LOVELL   Faith, my lord,
    I hear of none but the new proclamation
    That's clapped upon the court gate.
LORD CHAMBERLAIN   What is't for?
LOVELL   The reformation of our travelled gallants
20   That fill the court with quarrels, talk, and tailors.
LORD CHAMBERLAIN   I'm glad 'tis there. Now I would pray our '*messieurs*'
    To think an English courtier may be wise
    And never see the Louvre.°   *French king's palace*
LOVELL   They must either,
    For so run the conditions, leave those remnants

1.3 Location: The court.
1. *To . . . so:* To sixth- and seventh-century kings of France, their noses ("they") have such dignified (but convoluted) postures.
2. *the spavin . . . 'em:* they seem to be lame. *spavin:* swelling in horses' legs. *spring-halt:* spasms in horses'
legs.
3. *Their . . . Christendom:* They have run out of the fashions of Christendom and have moved on to pagan habits. This mockery reflects contemporary anxieties about the "effeminacy" of imported Continental fashions. *are after:* have.

25 Of fool and feather° that they got in France,   *folly and adornment*
With all their honourable points of ignorance[4]
Pertaining thereunto—as fights and fireworks,°   *whoring*
Abusing better men than they can be
Out of a foreign wisdom, renouncing clean
30 The faith they have in tennis and tall stockings,
Short blistered breeches, and those types of travel[5]—
And understand again like honest men,
Or pack° to their old playfellows. There, I take it,   *return*
They may, *cum privilegio, 'oui'* away
35 The lag end of their lewdness[6] and be laughed at.

SANDS   'Tis time to give 'em physic,° their diseases   *medicine*
Are grown so catching.

LORD CHAMBERLAIN   What a loss our ladies
Will have of these trim vanities!°   *well-dressed fops*

LOVELL   Ay, marry,°   *indeed*
There will be woe indeed, lords. The sly whoresons
40 Have got a speeding° trick to lay down° ladies.   *an expeditious / seduce*
A French song and a fiddle has no fellow.°   *equal*

SANDS   The devil fiddle 'em! I am glad they are going,
For sure there's no converting of 'em.° Now   *changing their ways*
An honest country lord, as I am, beaten
45 A long time out of play,° may bring his plainsong°   *love / unadorned tune*
And have an hour of hearing, and, by'r Lady,
Held current° music, too.   *modern; stylish*

LORD CHAMBERLAIN   Well said, Lord Sands.
Your colt's tooth is not cast yet?[7]

SANDS   No, my lord,
Nor shall not while I have a stump.°   *(of a tooth—sexual)*

LORD CHAMBERLAIN [*to* LOVELL]   Sir Thomas,
Whither were you a-going?

50 LOVELL   To the Cardinal's.
Your lordship is a guest too.

LORD CHAMBERLAIN   O, 'tis true.
This night he makes° a supper, and a great one,   *holds*
To many lords and ladies. There will be
The beauty of this kingdom, I'll assure you.

55 LOVELL   That churchman bears a bounteous mind indeed,
A hand as fruitful° as the land that feeds us.   *benevolent*
His dews° fall everywhere.   *(pun on "dues," taxes)*

LORD CHAMBERLAIN   No doubt he's noble.
He had a black mouth that said other of him.[8]

SANDS   He may, my lord; he's wherewithal.° In him   *he can afford to*
60 Sparing° would show a worse sin than ill doctrine.°   *Stinginess / heresy*
Men of his way° should be most liberal.   *profession*
They are set here for examples.

LORD CHAMBERLAIN   True, they are so,
But few now give so great ones.° My barge stays.°   *examples / waits*
Your lordship shall along.° [*To* LOVELL] Come, good Sir Thomas,   *join me*

---

4. Which, in their ignorance, they consider honorable.
5. *Abusing . . . travel:* They must stop "abusing" their betters out of a misplaced faith in French wisdom, and start "renouncing" French habits like tennis, tall stockings, puffed breeches, and such marks of travel (which were affected by Henry VIII and James I, as well as James's courtiers).

6. *They . . . lewdness:* They may, with immunity ("*cum privilegio*"), indulge their remaining decadence by copying the French. *oui:* yes.
7. You haven't abandoned your youthful lasciviousness ("colt's tooth") yet?
8. Anyone who denies this generosity must have an evil mouth.

65 We shall be late else, which I would not be,
For I was spoke to,° with Sir Henry Guildford,   invited
This night to be comptrollers.°   stewards
SANDS   I am your lordship's. *Exeunt*

1.4

Hautboys.[1] *[Enter servants with] a small table for* CAR-
DINAL *[*WOLSEY *which they place] under the [cloth of]
state, [and] a longer table for the guests. Then enter at
one door* ANNE *Boleyn and divers other ladies and gentlemen as guests, [and] at another door enter Sir Henry*
GUILDFORD

GUILDFORD   Ladies, a general welcome from his grace
Salutes ye all. This night he dedicates
To fair content and you. None here, he hopes,
In all this noble bevy,° has brought with her   company
5 One care abroad. He would have all as merry
As feast, good company, good wine, good welcome
Can make good people.
                    Enter [the] LORD CHAMBERLAIN, *Lord* SANDS, *and [Sir
                    Thomas]* LOVELL
[*To the* LORD CHAMBERLAIN] O, my lord, you're tardy.
The very thought of this fair company
Clapped wings to me.
LORD CHAMBERLAIN   You are young, Sir Harry Guildford.
10 SANDS   Sir Thomas Lovell, had the Cardinal
But half my lay° thoughts in him, some of these   secular
Should find a running banquet,[2] ere they rested,
I think would better please 'em. By my life,
They are a sweet society of fair ones.
15 LOVELL   O, that your lordship were but now confessor
To one or two of these.
SANDS   I would I were.
They should find easy penance.
LOVELL   Faith, how easy?
SANDS   As easy as a down bed would afford it.
LORD CHAMBERLAIN   Sweet ladies, will it please you sit?
[*To* GUILDFORD]   Sir Harry,
20 Place you° that side, I'll take the charge of this.   Arrange seating on
                    [*They sit about the longer table. A noise within*]
His grace is ent'ring. Nay, you must not freeze—
Two women placed together makes cold weather—
My lord Sands, you are one will keep 'em waking.°   spirited
Pray sit between these ladies.
SANDS   By my faith,
And thank your lordship.
                    [*He sits between* ANNE *and another*]
25   By your leave, sweet ladies.
If I chance to talk a little wild, forgive me.
I had it from my father.
ANNE   Was he mad, sir?

1.4 Location: Westminster, a hall in York Place.   2. Light refreshments; furtive, stolen pleasures.
1. Early reeded wind instrument, ancestor of the oboe.

SANDS   O, very mad; exceeding mad—in love, too.
But he would bite° none. Just as I do now,   (sign of madness)
He would kiss you twenty with a breath.³
　　[He kisses her]

30 LORD CHAMBERLAIN   Well said,° my lord.   done
So now you're fairly seated. Gentlemen,
The penance lies on you if these fair ladies
Pass away frowning.

SANDS   For my little cure,°   duty; (of souls)
35 Let me alone.
　　　Hautboys. Enter CARDINAL WOLSEY [who] takes his
　　　[seat at the small table under the] state°   chair of state

CARDINAL WOLSEY   You're welcome, my fair guests. That noble lady
Or gentleman that is not freely merry
Is not my friend. This, to confirm my welcome,
And to you all, good health!
　　[He drinks]

SANDS   Your grace is noble.
40 Let me have such a bowl may° hold my thanks,   as may
And save me so much talking.

CARDINAL WOLSEY   My lord Sands,
I am beholden to you. Cheer° your neighbours.   Amuse
Ladies, you are not merry! Gentlemen,
Whose fault is this?

SANDS   The red wine first must rise
45 In their fair cheeks, my lord, then we shall have 'em
Talk us to silence.

ANNE   You are a merry gamester,°   fellow; gambler
My lord Sands.

SANDS   Yes, if I make my play.⁴
Here's to your ladyship; and pledge it,° madam,   drink to it
For 'tis to such a thing—

ANNE   You cannot show me.°   (sexual)

SANDS [to WOLSEY]   I told your grace they would talk anon.
　　　Drum and trumpet. Chambers discharged⁵

50 CARDINAL WOLSEY   What's that?

LORD CHAMBERLAIN [to the SERVANTS]
Look out there, some of ye.   [Exit a SERVANT]

CARDINAL WOLSEY   What warlike voice,
And to what end is this? Nay, ladies, fear not.
By all the laws of war you're privileged.°   safe from harm
　　　Enter [the] SERVANT

LORD CHAMBERLAIN   How now—what is't?

SERVANT   A noble troop of strangers,
55 For so they seem. They've left their barge and landed,
And hither make as° great ambassadors   come like
From foreign princes.

CARDINAL WOLSEY   Good Lord Chamberlain,
Go give 'em welcome—you can speak the French tongue.
And pray receive 'em nobly, and conduct 'em

---

3. He would kiss you twenty times with a single breath.
4. If I win my hand (at cards or love).
5. Small cannon fired. The firing of this cannon in a

June 29, 1613, performance of the play probably
caused the fire that destroyed the Globe Theatre. See
the Introduction.

60 Into our presence where this heaven of beauty
Shall shine at full upon them. Some attend him.

[Exit CHAMBERLAIN, *attended]*
All rise, and [some servants] remove [the] tables

You have now a broken banquet, but we'll mend it.
A good digestion to you all, and once more
I shower a welcome on ye—welcome all.

Hautboys. Enter, ushered by the LORD CHAMBERLAIN,
King [HENRY] *and others as masquers habited like shep-*
herds. They pass directly before CARDINAL [WOLSEY]
and gracefully salute him

65 A noble company. What are their pleasures?
LORD CHAMBERLAIN   Because they speak no English, thus they prayed
To tell your grace, that, having heard by fame°   *rumor*
Of this so noble and so fair assembly
This night to meet here, they could do no less,
70 Out of the great respect they bear to beauty,
But leave their flocks, and, under your fair conduct,°   *if you'll permit me*
Crave leave to view these ladies, and entreat
An hour of revels⁶ with 'em.
CARDINAL WOLSEY   Say, Lord Chamberlain,
They have done my poor house grace, for which I pay 'em
75 A thousand thanks, and pray 'em take their pleasures.

[The masquers] choose ladies. [The] KING [*chooses]*
ANNE *Boleyn*

KING HENRY [*to* ANNE]   The fairest hand I ever touched. O beauty,
Till now I never knew thee.
Music. [They] dance
CARDINAL WOLSEY [*to the* LORD CHAMBERLAIN]   My lord.
LORD CHAMBERLAIN   Your grace.
80 CARDINAL WOLSEY   Pray tell 'em thus much from me.
There should be one amongst 'em by his person
More worthy this place° than myself, to whom,   *chair of state*
If I but knew him, with my love and duty
I would surrender it.
LORD CHAMBERLAIN   I will, my lord.
[He] whisper[s with the masquers]
CARDINAL WOLSEY   What say they?
85 LORD CHAMBERLAIN   Such a one they all confess
There is indeed, which they would have your grace
Find out, and he will take it.°   *(the place of honor)*
CARDINAL WOLSEY [*standing]*   Let me see then.
By all your good leaves, gentlemen, here I'll make
My royal choice.
[He bows before the KING]
KING HENRY [*unmasking]*   Ye have found him, Cardinal.
90 You hold a fair assembly. You do well, lord.
You are a churchman, or I'll tell you, Cardinal,
I should judge now unhappily.⁷
CARDINAL WOLSEY   I am glad
Your grace is grown so pleasant.°   *merry*
KING HENRY   My Lord Chamberlain,
Prithee come hither.

6. Entertainment; perhaps, more specifically, the danc-   7. I would judge such ostentatiousness unfavorably.
ing with the audience of the actors in a court masque.

[*Gesturing towards* ANNE] What fair lady's that?

LORD CHAMBERLAIN   An't° please your grace, Sir Thomas   *If it*
95   Boleyn's daughter—
    The Viscount Rochford—one of her highness' women.

KING HENRY   By heaven, she is a dainty one. [*To* ANNE] Sweetheart,
    I were unmannerly to take you out°   *(to dance)*
    And not to kiss you [*kisses her*]. A health,° gentlemen;   *toast*
    [*He drinks*]
100   Let it go round.

CARDINAL WOLSEY   Sir Thomas Lovell, is the banquet ready
    I'th' privy chamber?

LOVELL   Yes, my lord.

CARDINAL WOLSEY [*to the* KING]   Your grace
    I fear with dancing is a little heated.

KING HENRY   I fear too much.

105   CARDINAL WOLSEY   There's fresher air, my lord,
    In the next chamber.

KING HENRY   Lead in your ladies, every one. [*To* ANNE] Sweet partner,
    I must not yet forsake you. [*To* WOLSEY] Let's be merry,
    Good my lord Cardinal. I have half a dozen healths
110   To drink to these fair ladies, and a measure°   *majestic dance*
    To lead 'em once again, and then let's dream
    Who's best in favour.⁸ Let the music knock it.°   *strike it up*

                              Exeunt with trumpets

                              2.1

                Enter two GENTLEMEN, *at several*° *doors*   *separate*
    FIRST GENTLEMAN   Whither away so fast?

    SECOND GENTLEMAN   O, God save ye.
    Ev'n to the hall° to hear what shall become   *Westminster Hall*
    Of the great Duke of Buckingham.

FIRST GENTLEMAN   I'll save you
    That labour, sir. All's now done but the ceremony
    Of bringing back the prisoner.

5   SECOND GENTLEMAN   Were you there?

    FIRST GENTLEMAN   Yes, indeed was I.

    SECOND GENTLEMAN   Pray speak what has happened.

    FIRST GENTLEMAN   You may guess quickly what.

    SECOND GENTLEMAN   Is he found guilty?

    FIRST GENTLEMAN   Yes, truly is he, and condemned upon't.

    SECOND GENTLEMAN   I am sorry for't.

10   FIRST GENTLEMAN   So are a number more.

    SECOND GENTLEMAN   But pray, how passed it?°   *how did the trial go*

    FIRST GENTLEMAN   I'll tell you in a little.° The great Duke   *concisely*
    Came to the bar, where to his accusations
    He pleaded still not guilty, and allegèd°   *offered up*
15   Many sharp reasons to defeat the law.°   *the crown's case*
    The King's attorney, on the contrary,
    Urged on the examinations,° proofs,° confessions,   *depositions / statements*
    Of divers witnesses, which the Duke desired
    To him brought *viva voce*° to his face—   *in person*
20   At which appeared against him his surveyor,
    Sir Gilbert Perk his chancellor, and John Car,

---

8. Who's most popular with the ladies; who's best looking.   2.1 Location: A street in Westminster.

Confessor to him, with that devil-monk,
Hopkins, that made this mischief.
SECOND GENTLEMAN   That was he
That fed him with his prophecies.
FIRST GENTLEMAN   The same.
25   All these accused him strongly, which he fain[1]
Would have flung from him, but indeed he could not.
And so his peers, upon this evidence,
Have found him guilty of high treason. Much
He spoke, and learnèdly, for life, but all
30   Was either pitied in him or forgotten.[2]
SECOND GENTLEMAN   After all this, how did he bear himself?
FIRST GENTLEMAN   When he was brought again to th' bar to hear
His knell rung out, his judgement,° he was stirred   sentence
With such an agony he sweat extremely,
35   And something spoke in choler,° ill and hasty;   anger
But he fell to° himself again, and sweetly   got control of
In all the rest showed a most noble patience.
SECOND GENTLEMAN   I do not think he fears death.
FIRST GENTLEMAN   Sure he does not.
He never was so womanish. The cause
He may a little grieve at.
40   SECOND GENTLEMAN   Certainly
The Cardinal is the end° of this.   source
FIRST GENTLEMAN   'Tis likely
By all conjectures: first, Kildare's attainder,
Then deputy of Ireland,[3] who, removed,
Earl Surrey was sent thither—and in haste, too,
Lest he should help his father.°   father-in-law
45   SECOND GENTLEMAN   That trick of state
Was a deep envious° one.   deeply spiteful
FIRST GENTLEMAN   At his return
No doubt he will requite it. This is noted,
And generally:° whoever the King favours,   by all
The Card'nal instantly will find employment—
And far enough from court, too.
50   SECOND GENTLEMAN   All the commons
Hate him perniciously° and, o' my conscience,   want him dead
Wish him ten fathom deep. This Duke as much
They love and dote on, call him 'bounteous Buckingham,
The mirror° of all courtesy[4]—   exemplar
        Enter [the Duke of] BUCKINGHAM from his arraign-
        ment, tipstaves before him, the axe with the edge
        towards him, halberd[ier]s on each side, accompanied
        with Sir Thomas LOVELL, Sir Nicholas VAUX, Sir
        [William] SANDS,[5] and common people
FIRST GENTLEMAN   Stay there, sir,
55   And see the noble ruined man you speak of.

1. Which accusations he gladly.
2. all . . . forgotten: (Buckingham's defense) either was fruitless or brought only pity.
3. Thomas Fitzgerald, Earl of Kildare, Lord Lieutenant of Ireland, lost his estates and position ("attainder") and was sentenced to death by Wolsey.
4. Polished manners, but also courtliness more generally.
5. tipstaves: court-appointed officers who carried

tipstaves, staffs tipped with metal. halberdiers: guards who carried halberds, long-handled weapons with both spear tips and battle-ax blades. "Sir William Sands" is called "Lord Sands" in the stage directions at the beginning of 1.3 and at 1.4.7. The discrepancy occurs because the play violates chronology here: Henry and Anne actually met years after Buckingham's trial, and Sands became a baron in the interim.

SECOND GENTLEMAN   Let's stand close° and behold him.   *aside; silent*
       [They stand apart]
    BUCKINGHAM *[to the common people]*   All good people,
        You that thus far have come to pity me,
        Hear what I say, and then go home and lose° me.   *forget*
        I have this day received a traitor's judgement,°   *sentence*
60   And by that name must die. Yet, heaven bear witness,
        And if I have a conscience let it sink° me,   *destroy*
        Even as the axe falls, if I be not faithful.
        The law I bear no malice for my death.
        'T has done, upon the premises,° but justice.   *evidence*
65   But those that sought it I could wish more° Christians.   *truer*
        Be what they will, I heartily forgive 'em.
        Yet let 'em look° they glory not in mischief,   *beware*
        Nor build their evils on the graves of great men,[6]
        For then my guiltless blood must cry against 'em.
70   For further life in this world I ne'er hope,
        Nor will I sue, although the King have mercies
        More than I dare make faults.° You few that loved me,   *commit misdeeds*
        And dare be bold to weep for Buckingham,
        His noble friends and fellows, whom to leave
75   Is only bitter to him, only dying,[7]
        Go with me like good angels to my end,
        And, as the long divorce° of steel falls on me,   *(of body and soul)*
        Make of your prayers one sweet sacrifice,°   *offering*
        And lift my soul to heaven. *[To the guard]* Lead on, i' God's name.
80   LOVELL   I do beseech your grace, for charity,
        If ever any malice in your heart
        Were hid against me, now to forgive me frankly.
    BUCKINGHAM   Sir Thomas Lovell, I as free forgive you
        As I would be forgiven. I forgive all.
85   There cannot be those numberless offences
        'Gainst me that I cannot take° peace with. No black envy°   *make / spite*
        Shall mark my grave. Commend me to his grace,
        And if he speak of Buckingham, pray tell him
        You met him half in heaven. My vows and prayers
90   Yet are the King's, and, till my soul forsake,°   *depart (my body)*
        Shall cry for blessings on him. May he live
        Longer than I have time to tell° his years;   *count*
        Ever beloved and loving may his rule be;
        And, when old time° shall lead him to his end,   *old age*
95   Goodness and he fill up one monument.°   *share one tomb*
    LOVELL   To th' waterside I must conduct your grace,
        Then give my charge up to Sir Nicholas Vaux,
        Who undertakes° you to your end.   *leads*
    VAUX *[to an attendant]*   Prepare there—
        The Duke is coming. See the barge be ready,
100   And fit it with such furniture° as suits   *trappings*
        The greatness of his person.
    BUCKINGHAM   Nay, Sir Nicholas,
        Let it alone. My state[8] now will but mock me.
        When I came hither I was Lord High Constable

---

6. Nor advance their evil designs through plotting the downfall of noblemen.
7. *His . . . dying:* Leaving his friends is the only bitter part of Buckingham's sentence, the only death.
8. status; "furniture" (line 100).

And Duke of Buckingham; now, poor Edward Bohun.[9]

105 Yet I am richer than my base accusers,
That never knew what truth meant. I now seal it,°   *attest to truth*
And with that blood will make 'em one day groan for't.
My noble father, Henry of Buckingham,
Who first raised head° against usurping Richard,   *an army*
110 Flying for succour to his servant Banister,
Being distressed, was by that wretch betrayed,
And without trial fell. God's peace be with him.
Henry the Seventh succeeding, truly pitying
My father's loss, like a most royal prince,
115 Restored me to my honours, and out of ruins
Made my name once more noble. Now his son,
Henry the Eighth, life, honour, name, and all
That made me happy, at one stroke has taken
For ever from the world. I had my trial,
120 And must needs say a noble one; which makes me
A little happier than my wretched father.
Yet thus far we are one in fortunes: both
Fell by our servants, by those men we loved most—
A most unnatural and faithless service.
125 Heaven has an end° in all. Yet, you that hear me,   *a purpose*
This from a dying man receive as certain—
Where you are liberal of your loves and counsels,
Be sure you be not loose;° for those you make friends   *unrestrained*
And give your hearts to, when they once perceive
130 The least rub° in your fortunes, fall away   *obstacle*
Like water from ye, never found again
But where they mean to sink° ye. All good people   *destroy*
Pray for me. I must now forsake ye. The last hour
Of my long weary life is come upon me.
135 Farewell, and when you would say something that is sad,
Speak how I fell. I have done, and God forgive me.

Exeunt [*the*] *Duke* [*of* BUCKINGHAM] *and train*
[*The two* GENTLEMEN *come forward*]

FIRST GENTLEMAN   O, this is full of pity, sir; it calls,
I fear, too many curses on their heads
That were the authors.

SECOND GENTLEMAN   If the Duke be guiltless,
140 'Tis full of woe. Yet I can give you inkling°   *forewarning*
Of an ensuing evil, if it fall,°   *should occur*
Greater than this.

FIRST GENTLEMAN   Good angels keep it from us.
What may it be? You do not doubt my faith,[1] sir?

SECOND GENTLEMAN   This secret is so weighty, 'twill require
A strong faith to conceal it.

145 FIRST GENTLEMAN   Let me have it—
I do not talk much.

SECOND GENTLEMAN   I am confident;°   *I trust you*
You shall, sir. Did you not of late days hear
A buzzing° of a separation   *gossip*
Between the King and Katherine?

FIRST GENTLEMAN   Yes, but it held not.°   *did not persist*

9. Actually Edward Stafford; Shakespeare copies Holinshed's mistake.
1. "Faith" (here and in line 145) picks up the religious language of "curses" (line 138) and "angels" (line 142), while suggesting fidelity, loyalty, trustworthiness, and, as line 146 suggests, discretion.

150   For when the King once heard it, out of anger
    He sent command to the Lord Mayor straight
    To stop the rumour and allay° those tongues   *suppress*
    That durst disperse it.

SECOND GENTLEMAN   But that slander, sir,
    Is found a truth now, for it grows again
155   Fresher than e'er it was, and held° for certain   *believed*
    The King will venture at it. Either the Cardinal
    Or some about him near° have, out of malice   *his confidants*
    To the good Queen, possessed him with a scruple°   *doubt*
    That will undo her. To confirm this, too,
160   Cardinal Campeius[2] is arrived, and lately,
    As all think, for this business.

FIRST GENTLEMAN   'Tis the Cardinal;
    And merely to revenge him on the Emperor[3]
    For not bestowing on him at his asking
    The Archbishopric of Toledo this is purposed.

SECOND GENTLEMAN   I think you have hit the mark.° But is't not   *guessed correctly*
165   cruel
    That she should feel the smart° of this? The Cardinal   *pain*
    Will have his will, and she must fall.

FIRST GENTLEMAN   'Tis woeful.
    We are too open° here to argue this.   *exposed*
    Let's think in private more.   *Exeunt*

2.2

Enter [the] LORD CHAMBERLAIN *[with a] letter*

LORD CHAMBERLAIN *[reads]* 'My lord, the horses your lordship
sent for, with all the care I had, I saw well chosen, ridden, and
furnished.° They were young and handsome, and of the best *trained and equipped*
breed in the north. When they were ready to set out for Lon-
5 don, a man of my lord Cardinal's, by commission and main
power,[1] took 'em from me with this reason—his master would be
served before a subject, if not before the King; which stopped
our mouths, sir.'
    I fear he will indeed. Well, let him have them.
10 He will have all, I think.

Enter to the LORD CHAMBERLAIN *the Dukes of* NORFOLK
and SUFFOLK

NORFOLK   Well met, my Lord Chamberlain.

LORD CHAMBERLAIN   Good day to both your graces.

SUFFOLK   How is the King employed?

LORD CHAMBERLAIN   I left him private,°   *alone*
    Full of sad° thoughts and troubles.   *grave*

NORFOLK   What's the cause?

15 LORD CHAMBERLAIN   It seems the marriage with his brother's wife
    Has crept too near his conscience.

SUFFOLK   No, his conscience
    Has crept too near another lady.

---

2. Henry had to get a special dispensation from the
Pope before marrying Katherine, because her previous
husband was Prince Arthur, Henry's brother, who died
a year after the marriage took place. Wolsey had Cardinal Laurence Campeius (Lorenzo Campeggio) come to
London as a papal legate in 1528 to reopen debate

about the marriage and to aid his plot to have it
annulled.
3. Charles V, Holy Roman Emperor and King of Spain,
was Katherine's nephew.
2.2 Location: The court at London.
1. By warrant and superior strength.

NORFOLK   'Tis so.
This is the Cardinal's doing. The King-Cardinal,
That blind priest, like the eldest son of fortune,
20 Turns what he list.² The King will know him° one day.   *(for what he is)*
SUFFOLK   Pray God he do. He'll never know himself else.
NORFOLK   How holily he° works in all his business,   *(Wolsey)*
And with what zeal! For now he has cracked the league
Between us and the Emperor, the Queen's great-nephew,³
25 He dives into the King's soul and there scatters
Dangers, doubts, wringing° of the conscience,   *affliction*
Fears, and despairs—and all these for his marriage.
And out of all these, to restore the King,
He counsels a divorce—a loss of her
30 That like a jewel has hung twenty years
About his neck, yet never lost her lustre;
Of her that loves him with that excellence°   *great virtue*
That angels love good men with; even of her
That, when the greatest stroke° of fortune falls,   *severest blow*
35 Will bless the King⁴—and is not this course° pious?°   *(of action)* / *(ironic)*
LORD CHAMBERLAIN   Heaven keep me from such counsel! 'Tis most true—
These news are everywhere, every tongue speaks 'em,
And every true heart weeps for't. All that dare
Look into these affairs see this main end°—   *ultimate aim*
40 The French king's sister.⁵ Heaven will one day open
The King's eyes, that so long have slept, upon
This bold bad man.
SUFFOLK   And free us from his slavery.
NORFOLK   We had need pray,
45 And heartily, for our deliverance,
Or this imperious man will work us all
From princes into pages. All men's honours
Lie like one lump° before him, to be fashioned   *(of clay)*
Into what pitch° he please.   *stature*
SUFFOLK   For me, my lords,
50 I love him not, nor fear him—there's my creed.
As I am made without him, so I'll stand,⁶
If the King please. His curses and his blessings
Touch me alike; they're breath I° not believe in.   *I do*
I knew him, and I know him; so I leave him
To him that made him proud—the Pope.
55 NORFOLK   Let's in,
And with some other business put the King
From these sad thoughts that work too much upon him.
[*To the* LORD CHAMBERLAIN] My lord, you'll bear us company?
LORD CHAMBERLAIN   Excuse me,
The King has sent me otherwhere. Besides,
60 You'll find a most unfit time to disturb him.
Health to your lordships.

2. *The King-Cardinal . . . list:* Like Fortune, his mother, Wolsey blindly turns the wheel of fortune as he likes ("list").
3. Wolsey has now broken the alliance between Henry and Charles V to get additional revenge on Charles: see 2.1.161–64. Previously (1.1.176–93), to gain favor with Charles, he engineered the breaking of the treaty with France sealed at the Field of the Cloth of Gold.

4. Prophetic: Katherine does later "bless the King" who has repudiated her (4.2.164).
5. Henry's marriage to the Duchess of Alençon will reunite the English and French Kings, thus still further injuring Charles V. See 3.2.86–87.
6. Since not Wolsey but the King granted my nobility of rank, I'll remain firm in my position.

NORFOLK	Thanks, my good Lord Chamberlain.	

Exit [the] LORD CHAMBERLAIN

KING [HENRY] *draws the curtain,*[7] *and sits reading pensively*

SUFFOLK	How sad° he looks! Sure he is much afflicted.°	*grave / distressed*
KING HENRY	Who's there? Ha?	
NORFOLK	Pray God he be not angry.	
KING HENRY	Who's there, I say? How dare you thrust yourselves	

65   Into my private meditations!
    Who am I? Ha?

NORFOLK	A gracious king that pardons all offences	

    Malice ne'er meant. Our breach of duty this way°   *in this respect*
    Is business of estate,° in which we come   *state*
    To know your royal pleasure.

70 KING HENRY   Ye are too bold.
    Go to, I'll make ye know your times of business.
    Is this an hour for temporal affairs? Ha?

Enter [CARDINAL] WOLSEY *and* [CARDINAL] CAMPEIUS,
[*the latter*] *with a commission*

    Who's there? My good lord Cardinal? O, my Wolsey,
    The quiet° of my wounded conscience,   *ease*
    Thou art a cure° fit for a king.   *balm; curate (priest)*

75   [*To* CAMPEIUS]   You're welcome,
    Most learnèd reverend sir, into our kingdom.
    Use us, and it. [*To* WOLSEY] My good lord, have great care
    I be not found a talker.[8]

CARDINAL WOLSEY	Sir, you cannot.	

    I would your grace would give us but an hour
    Of private conference.

80 KING HENRY [*to* NORFOLK *and* SUFFOLK]   We are busy; go.

[NORFOLK *and* SUFFOLK *speak privately to one another
as they depart*]

NORFOLK	This priest has no pride in him!°	*(more irony)*
SUFFOLK	Not to speak of.	

    I would not be so sick, though, for his place[9]—
    But this cannot continue.

NORFOLK	If it do	

    I'll venture one have-at-him.°   *thrust (in fencing)*

SUFFOLK	I another.	

Exeunt NORFOLK *and* SUFFOLK

CARDINAL WOLSEY [*to the* KING]   Your grace has given a precedent°   *model*
85   of wisdom
    Above all princes in committing freely
    Your scruple to the voice of Christendom.[1]
    Who can be angry now? What envy reach you?
    The Spaniard,° tied by blood and favour to her,   *Charles V*
90   Must now confess, if they have any goodness,
    The trial just and noble. All the clerks°—   *clerics*
    I mean the learnèd ones in Christian kingdoms—
    Have their free voices.° Rome, the nurse of judgement,   *may vote freely*

---

7. Almost certainly drawn by an attendant. The King's chamber is upstage in the discovery space, a curtained-off, perhaps recessed area at the back of the stage.
8. *have . . . talker:* make sure my offer of hospitality counts for more than mere words.

9. I would not want to be afflicted with such pride, even for his exalted position.
1. *voice of Christendom:* the papal legate Campeius and the representatives of the great European universities who have come to England to hear the case.

Invited by your noble self, hath sent
One general tongue° unto us: this good man,   *representative voice*
This just and learnèd priest, Card'nal Campeius,
Whom once more I present unto your highness.

KING HENRY [*embracing* CAMPEIUS]   And once more in mine
   arms I bid him welcome,
And thank the holy conclave° for their loves.   *College of Cardinals*
They have sent me such a man I would have wished for.

CARDINAL CAMPEIUS   Your grace must needs deserve all strangers'° loves,   *foreigners'*
You are so noble. To your highness' hand
I tender my commission,
   [*He gives the commission to the* KING]
[*to* WOLSEY]   by whose virtue,
The Court of Rome commanding, you, my lord
Cardinal of York, are joined with me their servant
In the unpartial° judging of this business.   *impartial*

KING HENRY   Two equal° men. The Queen shall be acquainted°   *fair / apprised*
Forthwith for what you come. Where's Gardiner?

CARDINAL WOLSEY   I know your majesty has always loved her
So dear in heart not to deny her that°   *that which*
A woman of less place° might ask by law—   *rank*
Scholars allowed freely to argue for her.

KING HENRY   Ay, and the best she shall have, and my favour
To him that does best, God forbid else. Cardinal,
Prithee call Gardiner to me, my new secretary.[2]
   [CARDINAL WOLSEY *goes to the door and calls* GARDINER]
I find him a fit fellow.
               Enter GARDINER

CARDINAL WOLSEY [*aside to* GARDINER]   Give me your hand. Much joy
   and favour to you.
You are the King's now.

GARDINER [*aside to* WOLSEY]   But to be commanded
For ever by your grace, whose hand has raised me.

KING HENRY   Come hither, Gardiner.
   [*The* KING] *walks* [*with* GARDINER] *and whispers* [*with*
   him]

CARDINAL CAMPEIUS [*to* WOLSEY]   My lord of York, was not one
   Doctor Pace[3]
In this man's place before him?

CARDINAL WOLSEY   Yes, he was.

CARDINAL CAMPEIUS   Was he not held a learnèd man?

CARDINAL WOLSEY   Yes, surely.

CARDINAL CAMPEIUS   Believe me, there's an ill opinion spread then,
Even of yourself, lord Cardinal.

CARDINAL WOLSEY   How? Of me?

CARDINAL CAMPEIUS   They will not stick° to say you envied him,   *scruple*
And fearing he would rise, he was so virtuous,
Kept him a foreign man still,° which so grieved him   *always abroad*
That he ran mad and died.

CARDINAL WOLSEY   Heav'n's peace be with him—
That's Christian care enough. For living murmurers°   *malcontents*

2. Stephen Gardiner, former secretary to Wolsey, became Henry's secretary in July 1529 through Wolsey's preferment, and Bishop of Winchester in 1531.
3. Richard Pace, the King's former secretary, was now sent frequently abroad by Wolsey on diplomatic business, apparently as punishment for becoming too close to the King.

There's places of rebuke. He was a fool,
For he would needs be virtuous.
[*Gesturing towards* GARDINER]   That good fellow,
If I command him, follows my appointment.°   *orders*
I will have none so near⁴ else. Learn this, brother:
135   We live not to be griped° by meaner persons.   *grasped; brought down*

KING HENRY [*to* GARDINER]   Deliver this with modesty° to th'   *Announce this mildly*
          Queen.   *Exit* GARDINER
The most convenient place that I can think of
For such receipt of⁵ learning is Blackfriars;
There ye shall meet about this weighty business.
140   My Wolsey, see it furnished.° O, my lord,   *fitted out properly*
Would it not grieve an able° man to leave   *a (sexually) vigorous*
So sweet a bedfellow? But conscience, conscience—
O, 'tis a tender place,° and I must leave her.   *Exeunt*   *(conscience); (sexual)*

2.3
Enter ANNE *Boleyn and an* OLD LADY

ANNE   Not for that neither. Here's the pang that pinches°—   *pain that torments*
His highness having lived so long with her, and she
So good a lady that no tongue could ever
Pronounce dishonour of her—by my life,
5   She never knew harm-doing—O now, after
So many courses of the sun° enthronèd,   *years*
Still° growing in a majesty and pomp the which   *Ever*
To leave a thousandfold more bitter than
'Tis sweet at first t'acquire—after this process,
10   To give her the avaunt,° it is a pity   *boot*
Would move a monster.

OLD LADY   Hearts of most hard temper°   *constitution*
Melt and lament for her.

ANNE   O, God's will! Much better
She ne'er had known pomp; though't be temporal,°   *only of this world*
Yet if that quarrel,° fortune, do divorce   *quarreler*
15   It from the bearer, 'tis a sufferance panging°   *as painful*
As soul and bodies severing.

OLD LADY   Alas, poor lady!
She's a stranger° now again.   *foreigner*

ANNE   So much the more
Must pity drop upon her. Verily,
I swear, 'tis better to be lowly born
20   And range with humble livers in content
Than to be perked up in a glist'ring grief¹
And wear a golden sorrow.

OLD LADY   Our content
Is our best having.°   *possession*

ANNE   By my troth° and maidenhead,   *faith*
I would not be a queen.

OLD LADY   Beshrew me,° I would—   *Devil take me*
25   And venture maidenhead for't; and so would you,
For all this spice° of your hypocrisy.   *sample*
You, that have so fair parts° of woman on you,   *qualities; beauty*

4. I want no one else on such intimate terms with the King.
5. For hearing such scholarly disputation, or such scholars.

2.3 Location: The Queen's apartments at court.
1. *'tis . . . grief*: it's better to be born poor and to occupy a lowly rank happily than to be unhappy despite one's riches (literally, to be dressed up in a glittering sadness).

Have, too, a woman's heart which ever yet
Affected° eminence, wealth, sovereignty;   *Craved*
30   Which, to say sooth,° are blessings; and which gifts,   *truth*
Saving your mincing,° the capacity   *Despite your affectation*
Of your soft cheveril° conscience would receive   *kid leather (pliant)*
If you might please to stretch it.

ANNE   Nay, good troth.[2]

OLD LADY   Yes, troth and troth. You would not be a queen?

35   ANNE   No, not for all the riches under heaven.

OLD LADY   'Tis strange. A threepence bowed would hire me,
Old as I am, to queen it.[3] But I pray you,
What think you of a duchess? Have you limbs
To bear that load of title?

ANNE   No, in truth.

40   OLD LADY   Then you are weakly made. Pluck off[4] a little;
I would not be a young count in your way
For more than blushing comes to.[5] If your back
Cannot vouchsafe this burden,[6] 'tis too weak
Ever to get a boy.

ANNE   How you do talk!
45   I swear again, I would not be a queen
For all the world.

OLD LADY   In faith, for little England
You'd venture an emballing;[7] I myself
Would for Caernarfonshire,[8] although there 'longed°   *belonged*
No more to th' crown but that. Lo, who comes here?

Enter [the] LORD CHAMBERLAIN

50   LORD CHAMBERLAIN   Good morrow, ladies. What were't worth to know
The secret of your conference?°   *conversation*

ANNE   My good lord,
Not your demand; it values not° your asking.   *does not merit*
Our mistress' sorrows we were pitying.

LORD CHAMBERLAIN   It was a gentle business, and becoming
55   The action of good women. There is hope
All will be well.

ANNE   Now I pray God, amen.

LORD CHAMBERLAIN   You bear a gentle mind, and heav'nly blessings
Follow such creatures. That you may, fair lady,
Perceive I speak sincerely, and high note's
60   Ta'en of your many virtues, the King's majesty
Commends his good opinion of you,° and   *Sends his compliments*
Does purpose° honour to you no less flowing°   *intend / copious*
Than Marchioness of Pembroke; to which title
A thousand pound a year annual support
Out of his grace he adds.

65   ANNE   I do not know
What kind of my obedience I should tender.

---

2. Faith (exclamatory); perhaps a pun on "trot," a demeaning term for an old woman.
3. *A threepence . . . it:* A bent ("bowed") and hence worthless coin would convince me to be a Queen. Sexual puns ("queen"—"quean," or whore; "bowed"—bawd) continue through the scene.
4. Come lower in rank; undress.
5. *I . . . to:* Perhaps: If you persist in this "way" (path; being unable to bear the load of being duchess; condi-

tion of virginity), a "count" (an earl, the rank below duke) will get no more from you than blushes. Also: I would give up being a young virginal cunt ("count") like you with no more than a blush.
6. Cannot bear these honors. "Burden," like "bear" (line 39), suggests both intercourse and childbearing.
7. *for . . . emballing:* for England you'd accept investiture with the royal emblem of ball and scepter (you'd get laid).
8. Particularly poor Welsh county.

More than my all is nothing; nor my prayers
Are not° words duly hallowed, nor my wishes   *no more than*
More worth than empty vanities; yet prayers and wishes
70 Are all I can return. Beseech your lordship,
Vouchsafe° to speak my thanks and my obedience,   *Condescend*
As from a blushing handmaid to his highness,
Whose health and royalty I pray for.

LORD CHAMBERLAIN   Lady,
I shall not fail t'approve° the fair conceit°   *endorse / opinion*
75 The King hath of you. [*Aside*] I have perused her well.
Beauty and honour in her are so mingled
That they have caught the King, and who knows yet
But from this lady may proceed a gem
To lighten⁹ all this isle. [*To* ANNE] I'll to the King
80 And say I spoke with you.

ANNE   My honoured lord.

Exit [*the*] LORD CHAMBERLAIN

OLD LADY   Why, this it is—see, see!
I have been begging sixteen years in court,
Am yet a courtier beggarly,° nor could   *still begging*
85 Come pat betwixt too early and too late
For any suit of pounds;¹ and you—O, fate!—
A very fresh fish here—fie, fie upon
This compelled° fortune!—have your mouth filled up   *forced upon you*
Before you open it.

ANNE   This is strange to me.
90 OLD LADY   How tastes it? Is it bitter? Forty pence, no.²
There was a lady once—'tis an old story—
That would not be a queen, that would she not,
For all the mud in Egypt.³ Have you heard it?

ANNE   Come, you are pleasant.°   *merry; joking*
OLD LADY   With your theme I could
95 O'ermount the lark. The Marchioness of Pembroke?
A thousand pounds a year, for pure° respect?   *mere*
No other obligation? By my life,
That promises more thousands. Honour's train
Is longer than his foreskirt.⁴ By this time
100 I know your back will bear a duchess. Say,
Are you not stronger than you were?

ANNE   Good lady,
Make yourself mirth with your particular fancy,°   *private fantasies*
And leave me out on't. Would I had no being,
If this salute° my blood a jot. It faints me°   *agitates / I faint*
105 To think what follows.⁵
The Queen is comfortless, and we forgetful
In our long absence. Pray do not deliver
What here you've heard to her.

OLD LADY   What do you think me—

Exeunt

9. To bring light to (alluding to Elizabeth), with religious connotations. Gems were believed to emit light.
1. *nor . . . pounds:* nor could I arrive at just the right
moment to succeed in any petition for money.
2. I'll bet a small sum (conventionally, 40 pence) that
it isn't.
3. For all the wealth (in this case, the fertile land, or

"mud") of Egypt.
4. *That . . . foreskirt:* Future rewards will exceed present ones, just as a noblewoman's dress is longer in back
than in front.
5. "What follows," ultimately, is Anne's execution at
Henry's order in 1536, on the charge of adultery.

2.4

Trumpets: sennet.° [Then] cornetts. Enter two vergers¹   *fanfare*
with short silver wands; next them two SCRIBES *in the*
habit of doctors;² after them the [Arch]bishop of Can-
terbury alone; after him the Bishops of LINCOLN, *Ely,*
Rochester, and Saint Asaph; next them, with some small
distance, follows a gentleman bearing [both] the purse
[containing] the great seal and a cardinal's hat; then
two priests bearing each a silver cross; then a gentleman
usher, bare-headed, accompanied with a serjeant-at-
arms bearing a silver mace;° then two gentlemen bear-   *ceremonial staff*
ing two great silver pillars; after them, side by side, the
*two cardinals, [*WOLSEY *and* CAMPEIUS; *then] two noble-*
men with the sword and mace. The KING *[ascends to his*
seat] under the cloth of state; the two cardinals sit
under him as judges; the QUEEN *[attended by* GRIFFITH
her gentleman usher] takes place some distance from
the KING; *the Bishops place themselves on each side the*
court in [the] manner of a consistory,° below them,   *church court*
the SCRIBES. *The lords sit next the Bishops. The rest of*
the attendants stand in convenient order about the stage

CARDINAL WOLSEY   Whilst our commission from Rome is read
  Let silence be commanded.

KING HENRY   What's the need?
  It hath already publicly been read,
  And on all sides th'authority allowed.°   *accepted*
  You may then spare that time.

5   CARDINAL WOLSEY   Be't so. Proceed.

SCRIBE [*to the* CRIER]   Say, 'Henry, King of England, come into the court'.

CRIER   Henry, King of England, come into the court.

KING HENRY   Here.

SCRIBE [*to the* CRIER]   Say, 'Katherine, Queen of England, come
        into the court'.

10   CRIER   Katherine, Queen of England, come into the court.
    The QUEEN *makes no answer, [but] rises out of her chair,*
    goes about the court, comes to the KING, *and kneels at*
    his feet. Then [she] speaks

QUEEN KATHERINE   Sir, I desire you do me right and justice,
  And to bestow your pity on me; for
  I am a most poor woman, and a stranger,°   *foreigner*
  Born out of your dominions, having here
15 No judge indifferent,° nor no more assurance   *impartial*
  Of equal° friendship and proceeding.° Alas, sir,   *just / legal order*
  In what have I offended you? What cause
  Hath my behaviour given to your displeasure
  That thus you should proceed to put me off,°   *abandon me*
20 And take your good grace° from me? Heaven witness *good will; yourself*
  I have been to you a true and humble wife,
  At all times to your will conformable,

2.4 Location: A hall in Blackfriars.
1. Officials who carry the verge (a staff symbolizing the authority of office) before a bishop or other dignitary.
2. Furred black gown and flat caps of doctors of law.

Ever in fear to kindle your dislike,
Yea, subject to your countenance, glad or sorry
25 As I saw it inclined. When was the hour
I ever contradicted your desire,
Or made it not mine too? Or which of your friends
Have I not strove to love, although I knew
He were mine enemy? What friend of mine
30 That had to him derived° your anger did I   incurred
Continue in my liking? Nay, gave notice
He was from thence discharged? Sir, call to mind
That I have been your wife in this obedience
Upward of twenty years, and have been blessed
35 With many children by you.³ If, in the course
And process of this time, you can report—
And prove it, too—against mine honour aught,°   anything
My bond to wedlock, or my love and duty
Against° your sacred person, in God's name   Toward
40 Turn me away, and let the foul'st contempt
Shut door upon me, and so give me up
To the sharp'st kind of justice. Please you, sir,
The King your father was reputed for
A prince most prudent, of an excellent
45 And unmatched wit° and judgement. Ferdinand   wisdom
My father, King of Spain, was reckoned one
The wisest⁴ prince that there had reigned by many
A year before. It is not to be questioned
That they had gathered a wise council to them
50 Of every realm, that did debate this business,
Who deemed our marriage lawful. Wherefore I humbly
Beseech you, sir, to spare me till I may
Be by my friends in Spain advised, whose counsel
I will implore. If not, i'th' name of God,
Your pleasure be fulfilled.
55 CARDINAL WOLSEY   You have here, lady,
And of your choice, these reverend fathers, men
Of singular integrity and learning,
Yea, the elect o'th' land, who are assembled
To plead your cause. It shall be therefore bootless°   pointless
60 That longer you desire° the court, as well   beg (for a delay)
For your own quiet,° as to rectify   peace of mind
What is unsettled in the King.
CARDINAL CAMPEIUS   His grace
Hath spoken well and justly. Therefore, madam,
It's fit this royal session do proceed,
65 And that without delay their arguments
Be now produced and heard.
QUEEN KATHERINE [to WOLSEY]   Lord Cardinal,
To you I speak.
CARDINAL WOLSEY   Your pleasure, madam.
QUEEN KATHERINE   Sir,
I am about to weep, but thinking that
We are a queen, or long have dreamed so, certain°   without doubt

---

3. Queen Katherine bore five of Henry's children. All   4. was . . . wisest: was judged the very wisest.
but one, later Queen Mary, died at birth or in infancy.

70 The daughter of a king, my drops of tears
I'll turn to sparks of fire.

CARDINAL WOLSEY   Be patient yet.

QUEEN KATHERINE   I will when you are humble! Nay, before,
Or God will punish me. I do believe,
Induced° by potent circumstances, that   *Convinced*
75 You are mine enemy, and make my challenge°   *legal objection that*
You shall not be my judge. For it is you
Have blown this coal betwixt my lord and me,
Which God's dew quench. Therefore I say again,
I utterly abhor,° yea, from my soul,   *loathe; reject*
80 Refuse you for my judge, whom yet once more
I hold my most malicious foe, and think not
At all a friend to truth.

CARDINAL WOLSEY   I do profess°   *declare*
You speak not like yourself, who ever yet°   *always*
Have stood to° charity, and displayed th'effects   *upheld*
85 Of disposition gentle and of wisdom
O'er-topping woman's power. Madam, you do me wrong.
I have no spleen° against you, nor injustice   *malevolence*
For you or any. How far I have proceeded,
Or how far further shall, is warranted
90 By a commission from the consistory,°   *College of Cardinals*
Yea, the whole consistory of Rome. You charge me
That I 'have blown this coal'. I do deny it.
The King is present. If it be known to him
That I gainsay my deed,° how may he wound,   *deny what took place*
95 And worthily,° my falsehood—yea, as much   *justly*
As you have done my truth. If he know
That I am free of your report, he knows
I am not of your wrong.⁵ Therefore in him
It lies to cure° me, and the cure is to   *absolve*
100 Remove these thoughts from you. The which before
His highness shall speak in,° I do beseech   *about*
You, gracious madam, to unthink your speaking,
And to say so no more.

QUEEN KATHERINE   My lord, my lord—
I am a simple woman, much too weak
105 T'oppose your cunning. You're meek and humble-mouthed;
You sign your place and calling, in full seeming,
With meekness and humility⁶—but your heart
Is crammed with arrogancy, spleen,° and pride.   *malice*
You have by fortune and his highness' favours
110 Gone slightly° o'er low steps, and now are mounted   *effortlessly*
Where powers are your retainers, and your words,
Domestics to you, serve your will as't please
Yourself pronounce their office.⁷ I must tell you,
You tender more° your person's honour than   *have more regard for*
115 Your high profession spiritual, that again
I do refuse you for my judge, and here,

5. *If . . . wrong*: If he agrees that I am innocent ("free") of your accusation, then he knows that I have done you no wrong; and that I have no part in the wrong you do me by thus accusing me.
6. *You . . . humility*: You mark your office and role with

great outward display of meekness and humility.
7. *and now . . . office*: and now have attained a place where men of authority ("powers") serve you, and your words are like attendants ("domestics"), which transform into deeds anything you pronounce as your will.

Before you all, appeal unto the Pope,
To bring my whole cause 'fore his holiness,
And to be judged by him.

She curtsies to the KING *and [begins] to depart*

CARDINAL CAMPEIUS   The Queen is obstinate,
120   Stubborn° to justice, apt to accuse it, and   *Impervious*
Disdainful to be tried by't. 'Tis not well.
She's going away.

KING HENRY [*to the* CRIER]   Call her again.

CRIER   Katherine, Queen of England, come into the court.

GRIFFITH [*to the* QUEEN]   Madam, you are called back.

QUEEN KATHERINE   What° need you note it? Pray you keep your   *Why*
125   way.°   *keep going*
When *you* are called, return. Now the Lord help.
They vex me past my patience. Pray you, pass on.
I will not tarry; no, nor ever more
Upon this business my appearance make
In any of their courts.

Exeunt QUEEN [KATHERINE] *and her attendants*

130   KING HENRY   Go thy ways, Kate.
That man i'th' world who shall report he has
A better wife, let him in naught be trusted
For speaking false in that. Thou art alone—
If thy rare qualities, sweet gentleness,
135   Thy meekness saint-like, wife-like government,°   *restraint*
Obeying in commanding,[8] and thy parts°   *qualities*
Sovereign and pious else° could speak thee out°—   *besides / describe you*
The queen of earthly queens. She's noble born,
And like her true nobility she has
Carried° herself towards me.   *Conducted*

140   CARDINAL WOLSEY   Most gracious sir,
In humblest manner I require° your highness   *entreat*
That it shall please you to declare in hearing
Of all these ears—for where I am robbed and bound,
There must I be unloosed, although not there
145   At once and fully satisfied°—whether ever I   *given recompense*
Did broach this business to your highness, or
Laid any scruple in your way which might
Induce you to the question on't,° or ever   *of it*
Have to you, but with thanks to God for such
150   A royal lady, spake one the least° word that might   *the very least*
Be to the prejudice of her present state,
Or touch° of her good person?   *censure*

KING HENRY   My lord Cardinal,
I do excuse you;° yea, upon mine honour,   *forgive you fully*
I free you from't. You are not° to be taught   *do not require*
155   That you have many enemies that know not
Why they are so, but, like to village curs,
Bark when their fellows do. By some of these
The Queen is put in anger. You're excused.
But will you be more justified?° You ever   *vindicated*
160   Have wished the sleeping of this business, never desired
It to be stirred, but oft have hindered, oft,

---

8. Acting like an obedient wife even as you rule like a Queen.

The passages° made toward it. On my honour   *proceedings*
I speak my good lord Card'nal to this point,
And thus far clear him.⁹ Now, what moved me to't,°   *convinced me of it*
165   I will be bold with time and your attention.
Then mark th'inducement.° Thus it came—give heed to't.   *what influenced me*
My conscience first received a tenderness,°   *sensitivity*
Scruple, and prick, on° certain speeches uttered   *from*
By th' Bishop of Bayonne, then French Ambassador,
170   Who had been hither sent on the debating
A marriage 'twixt the Duke of Orléans¹ and
Our daughter Mary. I'th' progress of this business,
Ere a determinate resolution,° he—   *decisive settlement*
I mean the Bishop—did require a respite
175   Wherein he might the King his lord advertise°   *make aware*
Whether our daughter were legitimate,
Respecting this our marriage with the dowager,
Sometimes° our brother's wife. This respite shook   *Formerly*
The bosom of my conscience, entered me,
180   Yea, with a spitting° power, and made to tremble   *piercing*
The region of my breast; which forced such way
That many mazed considerings did throng
And prest in with this caution.² First, methought
I stood not in the smile of heaven, who had
185   Commanded nature that my lady's womb,
If it conceived a male child by me, should
Do no more offices of life to't than
The grave does yield to th' dead. For her male issue
Or° died where they were made, or shortly after   *Either*
190   This world had aired them.° Hence I took a thought   *given life to; shown*
This was a judgement on me that my kingdom,
Well worthy the best heir³ o'th' world, should not
Be gladded° in't by me. Then follows that   *made joyful*
I weighed the danger which my realms stood in
195   By this my issue's fail,° and that gave to me   *lack; death*
Many a groaning throe.° Thus hulling in⁴   *pang (of pregnancy)*
The wild sea of my conscience, I did steer
Toward this remedy, whereupon we are
Now present here together—that's to say
200   I meant to rectify my conscience, which
I then did feel full sick, and yet° not well,   *still*
By all the reverend fathers of the land
And doctors learned. First I began in private
With you, my lord of Lincoln.⁵ You remember
205   How under my oppression I did reek°   *sweat*
When I first moved° you.   *appealed to*
LINCOLN   Very well, my liege.
KING HENRY   I have spoke long. Be pleased yourself to say
How far you satisfied me.

---

9. *I speak . . . Him:* Here the King speaks to the court as a whole, announcing that up to this point he exonerates the Cardinal of any wrongdoing.
1. Second son of King Francis I of France, he later became Henry II of France.
2. *many . . . caution:* many confused thoughts crowded

in at this warning.
3. Pun on "aired" (line 190).
4. Floating aimlessly, like a ship adrift in the current that is not making use of its sails.
5. The Bishop of Lincoln, according to Holinshed, was the King's confessor.

LINCOLN   So please your highness,
The question did at first so stagger me,
210 Bearing a state of mighty moment° in't   *so weighty, urgent a matter*
And consequence of dread,° that I committed   *dire consequences*
The daring'st counsel which I had to doubt,[6]
And did entreat your highness to this course
Which you are running here.
KING HENRY [*to Canterbury*]   I then moved you,
215 My lord of Canterbury, and got your leave
To make this present summons. Unsolicited
I left no reverend person in this court,
But by particular consent proceeded
Under your hands and seals.[7] Therefore, go on,
220 For no dislike i'th' world against the person
Of the good Queen, but the sharp thorny points
Of my allegèd° reasons, drives this forward.   *advanced by me*
Prove but our marriage lawful, by my life
And kingly dignity, we are contented
225 To wear our mortal state to come with her,
Katherine, our queen, before the primest° creature   *most perfect*
That's paragoned o'°th' world.   *considered a model by*
CARDINAL CAMPEIUS   So please your highness,
The Queen being absent, 'tis a needful fitness°   *only appropriate*
That we adjourn this court till further° day.   *a later*
230 Meanwhile must be an earnest motion°   *plea*
Made to the Queen to call back her appeal
She intends unto his holiness.
KING HENRY [*aside*]   I may perceive
These cardinals trifle with me. I abhor
This dilatory sloth and tricks of Rome.
235 My learned and well-belovèd servant, Cranmer,
Prithee return.[8] With thy approach I know
My comfort comes along. [*Aloud*] Break up the court.
I say, set on.°   *Exeunt in manner as they entered*   *proceed*

3.1
Enter QUEEN [KATHERINE] *and her women, as at work*
QUEEN KATHERINE   Take thy lute, wench. My soul grows sad with troubles.
Sing, and disperse 'em if thou canst. Leave° working.   *Cease*
GENTLEWOMAN [*sings*]   Orpheus[1] with his lute made trees,
And the mountain tops that freeze,
5   Bow themselves when he did sing.
To his music plants and flowers
Ever sprung, as° sun and showers   *as if*
There had made a lasting spring.
Everything that heard him play,
10   Even the billows of the sea,
Hung their heads, and then lay by.°   *were still*

6. *I committed . . . doubt:* I distrusted even the boldest
advice I myself could offer.
7. With your written agreement.
8. The King here apostrophizes Thomas Cranmer, who
is not present but is traveling on the Continent collect-
ing opinions on the status of Henry and Katherine's

marriage. See 3.2.401–02 for mention of his return and
his elevation to the position of Archbishop of Canterbury.
3.1 Location: The Queen's apartments at court.
1. In Greek mythology, he was famous for the power of
his music.

                In sweet music is such art,
                Killing care and grief of heart
                Fall asleep, or hearing, die.
             Enter [GRIFFITH,] *a gentleman*

15 QUEEN KATHERINE How now?
GRIFFITH An't please your grace, the two great cardinals
  Wait in the presence.°   *reception chamber*
QUEEN KATHERINE   Would they speak with me?
GRIFFITH They willed me say so, madam.
QUEEN KATHERINE   Pray their graces
  To come near.   [*Exit* GRIFFITH]
            What can be their business
20   With me, a poor weak woman, fall'n from favour?
  I do not like their coming, now I think on't;
  They should be good men, their affairs as righteous—
  But all hoods make not monks.²
            Enter the two cardinals, WOLSEY *and* CAMPEIUS [*ushered*
            by GRIFFITH]
CARDINAL WOLSEY   Peace to your highness.
QUEEN KATHERINE Your graces find me here part of a housewife—
25   I would be all,³ against° the worst may happen.   *in case*
  What are your pleasures with me, reverend lords?
CARDINAL WOLSEY May it please you, noble madam, to withdraw
  Into your private chamber, we shall give you
  The full cause of our coming.
QUEEN KATHERINE   Speak it here.
30   There's nothing I have done yet, o' my conscience,
  Deserves a corner.° Would all other women   *subterfuge*
  Could speak this with as free° a soul as I do.   *innocent*
  My lords, I care not—so much I am happy°   *favored*
  Above a number°—if my actions   *many*
35   Were tried by ev'ry tongue, ev'ry eye saw 'em,
  Envy and base opinion° set against 'em,   *Spite and base gossip*
  I know my life so even.° If your business   *uniformly virtuous*
  Seek me out and that way I am wife in,⁴
  Out with it boldly. Truth loves open dealing.
40 CARDINAL WOLSEY *Tanta est erga te mentis integritas, Regina serenissima*⁵—
QUEEN KATHERINE O, good my lord, no Latin.
  I am not such a truant° since my coming°   *so idle* / (*to England*)
  As not to know the language I have lived in.
  A strange° tongue makes my cause more strange° suspicious— *foreign* / *unusually*
45   Pray, speak in English. Here are some will thank you,
  If you speak truth, for their poor mistress' sake.
  Believe me, she has had much wrong. Lord Cardinal,
  The willing'st° sin I ever yet committed   *most premeditated*
  May be absolved in English.
CARDINAL WOLSEY   Noble lady,
50   I am sorry my integrity should breed—
  And service to his majesty and you—
  So deep suspicion, where all faith° was meant.   *loyalty*
  We come not by the way° of accusation,   *for the sake*

---

2. Proverbial: religious trappings do not ensure piety.
3. I would like to be not just partly but completely a housewife.
4. *If . . . in:* If your business concerns me and my behavior as wife.
5. So great is the integrity of (my) mind toward you, most serene Queen (Latin).

To taint that honour every good tongue blesses,
55 Nor to betray you any way° to sorrow—   *by any means*
You have too much, good lady—but to know
How you stand minded° in the weighty difference   *Your deliberation*
Between the King and you, and to deliver,°   *recount*
Like free° and honest men, our just opinions   *unprejudiced*
And comforts to your cause.
60 CARDINAL CAMPEIUS   Most honoured madam,
My lord of York, out of his noble nature,
Zeal, and obedience he still bore° your grace,   *has always borne*
Forgetting, like a good man, your late censure
Both of his truth and him—which was° too far—   *went*
65 Offers, as I do, in a sign of peace,
His service and his counsel.
QUEEN KATHERINE [*aside*]   To betray me.
[*Aloud*] My lords, I thank you both for your good wills.
Ye speak like honest men—pray God ye prove so.
But how to make ye suddenly° an answer   *without deliberation*
70 In such a point of weight, so near° mine honour—   *bound up with*
More near my life, I fear—with my weak wit,°   *comprehension*
And to such men of gravity and learning,
In truth I know not. I was set° at work   *sitting*
Among my maids, full little—God knows—looking
75 Either for such men or such business.
For her sake that I have been⁶—for I feel
The last fit° of my greatness—good your graces,   *spell*
Let me have time and counsel for my cause.
Alas, I am a woman friendless, hopeless.
80 CARDINAL WOLSEY   Madam, you wrong the King's love with these fears.
Your hopes and friends are infinite.
QUEEN KATHERINE   In England
But little for my profit.° Can you think, lords,   *of little use to me*
That any Englishman dare give me counsel,
Or be a known friend 'gainst his highness' pleasure—
85 Though he be grown so desperate° to be honest—   *rash enough*
And live a subject?° Nay, forsooth, my friends,   *survive in this land*
They that must weigh out° my afflictions,   *offset*
They that my trust must grow to, live not here.
They are, as all my other comforts, far hence,
In mine own country, lords.
90 CARDINAL CAMPEIUS   I would your grace
Would leave your griefs and take my counsel.
QUEEN KATHERINE   How, sir?
CARDINAL CAMPEIUS   Put your main cause into the King's protection.
He's loving and most gracious. 'Twill be much
Both for your honour better and your cause,
95 For if the trial of the law o'ertake ye
You'll part away° disgraced.   *leave*
CARDINAL WOLSEY [*to the* QUEEN]   He tells you rightly.
QUEEN KATHERINE   Ye tell me what ye wish for both—my ruin.
Is this your Christian counsel? Out upon ye!
Heaven is above all yet—there sits a judge
That no king can corrupt.

6. For the sake of the woman—the Queen—I once was.

100	CARDINAL CAMPEIUS Your rage mistakes° us.	*misrepresents*
	QUEEN KATHERINE The more shame for ye! Holy men I thought ye,	
	Upon my soul, two reverend cardinal virtues[7]—	
	But cardinal sins and hollow hearts I fear ye.	
	Mend° 'em, for shame, my lords! Is this your comfort?	*Reform*
105	The cordial° that ye bring a wretched lady,	*restoring medicine*
	A woman lost° among ye, laughed at, scorned?	*ruined*
	I will not wish ye half my miseries—	
	I have more charity. But say I warned ye.	
	Take heed, for heaven's sake take heed, lest at once°	*all at once*
110	The burden of my sorrows fall upon ye.	
	CARDINAL WOLSEY Madam, this is a mere distraction.°	*utter madness; evasion*
	You turn the good we offer into envy.°	*malevolence*
	QUEEN KATHERINE Ye turn me into nothing. Woe upon ye,	
	And all such false professors.° Would you have me—	*(of religion)*
115	If you have any justice, any pity,	
	If ye be anything but churchmen's habits°—	*vestments*
	Put my sick cause into his hands that hates me?	
	Alas, he's banished me his bed already—	
	His love, too, long ago. I am old, my lords,	
120	And all the fellowship I hold now with him	
	Is only my obedience. What can happen	
	To me above° this wretchedness? All your studies	*beyond*
	Make me accursed like this.[8]	*immediate*
	CARDINAL CAMPEIUS Your fears are worse.°	*(than reality)*
	QUEEN KATHERINE Have I lived thus long—let me speak° myself,	*represent*
125	Since virtue finds no friends—a wife, a true one?	
	A woman, I dare say, without vainglory,°	*conceit*
	Never yet branded with suspicion?	
	Have I with all my full affections	
	Still° met the King, loved him next° heav'n, obeyed him,	*Always / next to*
130	Been out of fondness superstitious° to him,	*overly devoted*
	Almost forgot my prayers to content him?	
	And am I thus rewarded? 'Tis not well, lords.	
	Bring me a constant woman to her husband,	
	One that ne'er dreamed a joy beyond his pleasure,	
135	And to that woman when she has done most,	
	Yet will I add an° honour, a great patience.	*another*
	CARDINAL WOLSEY Madam, you wander from° the good we aim at.	*misinterpret*
	QUEEN KATHERINE My lord, I dare not make myself so guilty	
	To give up willingly that noble title	
140	Your master wed me to. Nothing but death	
	Shall e'er divorce my dignities.	
	CARDINAL WOLSEY Pray, hear me.	
	QUEEN KATHERINE Would I had never trod this English earth,	
	Or felt the flatteries that grow upon it.	
	Ye have angels' faces, but heaven knows your hearts.	
145	What will become of me now, wretched lady?	
	I am the most unhappy woman living.	
	[*To her women*] Alas, poor wenches, where are now your forturnes?	

7. The cardinal virtues (justice, temperance, prudence, and fortitude, with a play on their rank), which,
along with the three theological virtues (faith, hope,
and charity), constitute the seven virtues. These oppose
the seven deadly ("cardinal," punning on "carnal") sins

referred to in the next line.
8. *All . . . this:* All your endeavors (and inquiries) bring
me only these miseries; I defy you, with all your clerical learning, to imagine a more terrible fate than this.

Shipwrecked upon a kingdom where no pity,
No friends, no hope, no kindred weep for me?
150 Almost no grave allowed me? Like the lily,
That once was mistress of the field and flourished,
I'll hang my head and perish.

CARDINAL WOLSEY   If your grace
Could but be brought to know our ends° are honest,   *intentions*
You'd feel more comfort. Why should we, good lady,
155 Upon what cause, wrong you? Alas, our places,°   *official duties*
The way of our profession, is against it.
We are to cure such sorrows, not to sow 'em.
For goodness' sake, consider what you do,
How you may hurt yourself, ay, utterly
160 Grow from the King's acquaintance by this carriage.°   *behavior*
The hearts of princes kiss obedience,
So much they love it, but to stubborn spirits
They swell and grow as terrible as storms.
I know you have a gentle noble temper,°   *temperament*
165 A soul as even° as a calm. Pray, think us   *unwavering*
Those we profess—peacemakers, friends, and servants.

CARDINAL CAMPEIUS   Madam, you'll find it so. You wrong your virtues
With these weak women's fears. A noble spirit,
As yours was put° into you, ever casts   *given*
170 Such doubts as false coin from it. The King loves you.
Beware you lose it not. For° us, if you please   *As for*
To trust us in your business, we are ready
To use our utmost studies in your service.

QUEEN KATHERINE   Do what ye will, my lords, and pray forgive me.
175 If I have used° myself unmannerly,   *behaved*
You know I am a woman, lacking wit°   *understanding*
To make a seemly answer to such persons.
Pray do my service° to his majesty.   *give my respects*
He has my heart yet, and shall have my prayers
180 While I shall have my life. Come, reverend fathers,
Bestow your counsels on me. She now begs
That° little thought, when she set footing here,°   *Who / (in England)*
She should have bought her dignities so dear.   *Exeunt*

3.2
Enter the Duke of NORFOLK, [*the*] *Duke of* SUFFOLK,
Lord SURREY, *and* [*the*] LORD CHAMBERLAIN

NORFOLK   If you will now unite in your complaints,
And force them with a constancy,° the Cardinal   *persevere in them*
Cannot stand under them. If you omit°   *neglect*
The offer of this time,° I cannot promise   *This opportunity*
5 But that you shall sustain more new disgraces
With these you bear already.

SURREY   I am joyful
To meet the least occasion that may give me
Remembrance of my father-in-law the Duke,°   *(of Buckingham)*
To be revenged on him.°   *(Wolsey)*

SUFFOLK   Which of the peers
10 Have uncontemned gone° by him, or at least   *not been disdained*
Strangely neglected?° When did he regard   *snubbed as a stranger*

3.2 Location: The court.

The stamp of nobleness in any person
Out of° himself?   *Aside from*

LORD CHAMBERLAIN   My lords, you speak your pleasures.
What he deserves of you and me I know;

15   What we can do to him—though now the time
Gives way to° us—I much fear. If you cannot   *Favors*
Bar his access to th'King, never attempt
Anything on° him, for he hath a witchcraft   *against*
Over the King in's tongue.

NORFOLK   O, fear him not.

20   His spell in that is out.° The King hath found   *past*
Matter against him that for ever mars
The honey of his language. No, he's settled,
Not to come off, in his displeasure.[1]

SURREY   Sir,
I should be glad to hear such news as this
Once every hour.

25   NORFOLK   Believe it, this is true.
In the divorce his contrary proceedings°   *double-dealing*
Are all unfolded,° wherein he appears   *exposed*
As I would wish mine enemy.

SURREY   How came
His practices° to light?   *schemes*

SUFFOLK   Most strangely.

SURREY   O, how, how?

30   SUFFOLK   The Cardinal's letters to the Pope miscarried,°   *went astray; got diverted*
And came to th'eye o'th'King, wherein was read
How that the Cardinal did entreat his holiness
To stay° the judgement o'th'divorce, for if   *delay*
It did take place, 'I do', quoth he, 'perceive

35   My king is tangled in affection to
A creature° of the Queen's, Lady Anne Boleyn'.   *servant*

SURREY   Has the King this?

SUFFOLK   Believe it.

SURREY   Will this work?

LORD CHAMBERLAIN   The King in this perceives him how he coasts°   *sails indirectly*
And hedges° his own way. But in this point   *moves secretly*

40   All his tricks founder, and he brings his physic°   *medicine*
After his patient's death. The King already
Hath married the fair lady.

SURREY   Would he had.

SUFFOLK   May you be happy in your wish, my lord,
For I profess you have it.

SURREY   Now all my joy
Trace the conjunction.°   *Follow the union*

SUFFOLK   My amen to't.

45   NORFOLK   All men's.

SUFFOLK   There's order given for her coronation.
Marry, this is yet but young,° and may be left   *recent*
To some ears unrecounted. But, my lords,
She is a gallant° creature, and complete°   *an excellent / perfect*

50   In mind and feature. I persuade me,° from her   *am sure*
Will fall some blessing to this land which shall
In it be memorized.[2]

1. No, Wolsey is stuck, with no way out, in Henry's displeasure. Or: No, Henry is firm, with no possibility of
changing, in his displeasure toward Wolsey.
2. Be made memorable (alluding to Elizabeth).

SURREY   But will the King
Digest° this letter of the Cardinal's?   *Tolerate*
The Lord forbid!

NORFOLK   Marry, amen.

SUFFOLK   No, no—
55 There be more wasps that buzz about his nose
Will make this sting the sooner. Cardinal Campeius
Is stol'n away to Rome; hath ta'en no leave;
Has left the cause o'th' King unhandled,° and   *unsettled*
Is posted° as the agent of our Cardinal   *Has rushed*
60 To second all his plot. I do assure you
The King cried 'Ha!'³ at this.

LORD CHAMBERLAIN   Now God incense him,
And let him cry 'Ha!' louder.

NORFOLK   But, my lord,
When returns Cranmer?

SUFFOLK   He is returned in his opinions, which
65 Have satisfied the King for his divorce,
Together with all famous colleges,
Almost, in Christendom.⁴ Shortly, I believe,
His second marriage shall be published,° and   *announced publicly*
Her coronation. Katherine no more
70 Shall be called 'Queen', but 'Princess Dowager',
And 'widow to Prince Arthur'.

NORFOLK   This same Cranmer's
A worthy fellow, and hath ta'en much pain°   *great pains*
In the King's business.

SUFFOLK   He has, and we shall see him
For it an archbishop.

NORFOLK   So I hear.

SUFFOLK   'Tis so.
Enter [CARDINAL] WOLSEY *and* CROMWELL
The Cardinal.

75 NORFOLK   Observe, observe—he's moody.
[*They stand apart and observe* WOLSEY *and* CROMWELL]

CARDINAL WOLSEY [*to* CROMWELL]   The packet,° Cromwell—   *parcel of letters*
gave't you the King?

CROMWELL   To his own hand, in's bedchamber.

CARDINAL WOLSEY   Looked he
O'th' inside of the paper?°   *wrapper*

CROMWELL   Presently°   *Immediately*
He did unseal them, and the first he viewed
80 He did it with a serious mind; a heed°   *concerned look*
Was in his countenance. You he bade
Attend him here this morning.

CARDINAL WOLSEY   Is he ready
To come abroad?

CROMWELL   I think by this° he is.   *by this time*

85 CARDINAL WOLSEY   Leave me a while.   *Exit* CROMWELL
[*Aside*] It shall be to the Duchess of Alençon,
The French King's sister—he shall marry her.

---

3. Henry's characteristic expression of impatience and
part of his legend in the Renaissance. See, for instance,
1.2.187 and 2.2.63, 66.
4. *He . . . Christendom:* Cranmer has sent ahead the
opinions concerning the King's marriage that he collected on the Continent, and the results have satisfied
both the King and most learned clerics.

Anne Boleyn? No, I'll no Anne Boleyns for him.
There's more in't than fair visage. Boleyn?
90 No, we'll no Boleyns. Speedily I wish
To hear from Rome. The Marchioness of Pembroke?
    [*The nobles speak among themselves*]
NORFOLK   He's discontented.
SUFFOLK   Maybe he hears the King
Does whet his anger to° him.   *against*
SURREY   Sharp enough,
Lord, for thy justice.
CARDINAL WOLSEY [*aside*]   The late° Queen's gentlewoman? A   *former*
95   knight's daughter
To be her mistress' mistress? The Queen's queen?
This candle burns not clear;° 'tis I must snuff it,   *bright*
Then out it goes. What though I know her virtuous
And well deserving? Yet I know her for
100 A spleeny Lutheran,⁵ and not wholesome° to   *beneficial*
Our cause, that she should lie i'th' bosom of
Our hard-ruled° King. Again, there is sprung up   *hard-to-advise*
An heretic, an arch-one, Cranmer, one°   *one who*
Hath crawled into the favour of the King
And is his oracle.⁶
    [*The nobles speak among themselves*]
105 NORFOLK   He is vexed at something.
    Enter KING [HENRY] *reading a schedule°* [*and* LOVELL   *scroll*
    with him]
SURREY   I would 'twere something that would fret the string,
The master-cord on's heart!⁷
SUFFOLK   The King, the King!
KING HENRY [*aside*]   What piles of wealth hath he accumulated
To his own portion?° And what expense by th' hour   *share*
110 Seems to flow from him? How i'th' name of thrift
Does he rake this together? [*To the nobles*] Now, my lords,
Saw you the Cardinal?
NORFOLK   My lord, we have
Stood here observing him. Some strange commotion°   *rebellion*
Is in his brain. He bites his lip, and starts,
115 Stops on a sudden, looks upon the ground,
Then lays his finger on his temple, straight°   *immediately*
Springs out into fast gait, then stops again,
Strikes his breast hard, and anon he casts
His eye against the moon. In most strange postures
We have seen him set himself.
120 KING HENRY   It may well be
There is a mutiny in's mind. This morning
Papers of state he sent me to peruse
As I required, and wot° you what I found   *know*
There, on my conscience put unwittingly?
125 Forsooth, an inventory thus importing°   *delineating*
The several parcels of his plate,⁸ his treasure,

---

5. *Passionate Lutheran*. It is possible that Wolsey objected to Henry's marriage to Anne on religious grounds, as well as on the class grounds that he outlines in this speech.
6. *is his oracle*: is considered by Henry to be divinely inspired.

7. *would . . . heart*: would eat through ("fret") the heartstrings (tying Henry to Wolsey), with a musical allusion: "fret" (fingering bar), "string," and "cord" (chord).
8. *plate*: gold and silver functional household equipment that also stored and displayed wealth.

Rich stuffs, and ornaments of household which
I find at such proud rate° that it outspeaks   *high value*
Possession of a subject.[9]

NORFOLK   It's heaven's will.
130 Some spirit put this paper in the packet
To bless your eye withal.°   *with*

KING HENRY   If we did think
His contemplation were above the earth
And fixed on spiritual object, he should still
Dwell in his musings. But I am afraid
135 His thinkings are below the moon,° not worth   *mundane*
His serious considering.

[The] KING *takes his seat [and] whispers [with]* LOVELL,
    who [then] goes to the CARDINAL

CARDINAL WOLSEY   Heaven forgive me!
[To the KING*]* Ever God bless your highness!

KING HENRY   Good my lord,
You are full of heavenly stuff,[1] and bear the inventory
Of your best graces in your mind, the which
140 You were now running o'er. You have scarce time
To steal from spiritual leisure a brief span
To keep your earthly audit. Sure, in that,
I deem you an ill husband, and am glad
To have you therein my companion.[2]

CARDINAL WOLSEY   Sir,
145 For holy offices I have a time; a time
To think upon the part of business which
I bear i'th' state; and nature does require
Her times of preservation which, perforce,
I, her frail son, amongst my brethren mortal,
Must give my tendance to.°   *take care of*
150 KING HENRY   You have said well.

CARDINAL WOLSEY   And ever may your highness yoke together,
As I will lend you cause, my doing well
With my well-saying.

KING HENRY   'Tis well said again,
And 'tis a kind of good deed to say well—
155 And yet words are no deeds. My father loved you.
He said he did, and with his deed did crown°   *make good*
His word upon you. Since I had my office,
I have kept you next° my heart, have not alone   *nearest to*
Employed you where high profits might come home,
160 But pared my present havings° to bestow   *given up possessions*
My bounties upon you.

CARDINAL WOLSEY *[aside]*   What should this mean?
SURREY *[aside]*   The Lord increase this business!
KING HENRY   Have I not made you
The prime° man of the state? I pray you tell me   *principal*
If what I now pronounce you have found true,

---

9. *a . . . subject:* it inventories more wealth than is fit
for a subject.
1. Godly qualities, but Henry's ironic language ("stuff,"
"steal," "audit") refers to both worldly and spiritual
matters.
2. Henry jokes that both he and Wolsey are "ill husbands," Wolsey because he cannot manage ("husband")

his household resources (ostensibly, he is otherworldly,
but really he is a greedy spendthrift) and because he
now opposes Henry's remarriage, and perhaps Henry
because he has literally been a poor husband to Katherine. Henry is being ironic, however, and may merely
mean that he has husbanded his resources badly in
trusting them to Wolsey.

165 And, if you may confess it, say withal
If you are bound to us or no. What say you?
CARDINAL WOLSEY   My sovereign, I confess your royal graces°   *favors*
Showered on me daily have been more than could
My studied purposes requite,° which went   *conscious efforts repay*
170 Beyond all man's endeavours. My endeavours
Have ever come too short of my desires,°   *aspirations*
Yet filed° with my abilities. Mine own ends°   *matched / aims*
Have been mine so that° evermore they pointed   *only insofar as*
To th' good of your most sacred person and
175 The profit of the state. For your great graces
Heaped upon me, poor undeserver, I
Can nothing render but allegiant° thanks,   *loyal*
My prayers to heaven for you, my loyalty,
Which ever has and ever shall be growing,
Till death, that winter, kill it.
180 KING HENRY   Fairly answered.
A loyal and obedient subject is
Therein illustrated. The honour of it
Does pay the act of it, as, i'th' contrary,
The foulness is the punishment.[3] I presume
185 That as my hand has opened° bounty to you,   *freely offered*
My heart dropped love, my power rained honour, more
On you than any, so your hand and heart,
Your brain, and every function of your power,
Should, notwithstanding that° your bond of duty,°   *despite / (to Rome)*
190 As 'twere in love's particular,° be more   *peculiar intimacy*
To me, your friend, than any.
CARDINAL WOLSEY   I do profess
That for your highness' good I ever laboured
More than mine own; that am, have,° and will be—   *have been*
Though all the world should crack° their duty to you,   *forswear*
195 And throw it from their soul, though perils did
Abound, as thick as thought could make 'em, and
Appear in forms more horrid—yet, my duty,
As doth a rock against the chiding° flood,   *roaring*
Should the approach of this wild river break,°   *check*
And stand unshaken yours.
200 KING HENRY   'Tis nobly spoken.
Take notice, lords, he has a loyal breast,
For you have seen him open't. [*To* WOLSEY] Read o'er this,
      [*He gives him a paper*]
And after this [*giving him another paper*], and then to breakfast with
What appetite you have.
                              Exit KING [HENRY], *frowning upon the*
                              CARDINAL. *The nobles throng after*
                              [*the* KING], *smiling and whispering*
CARDINAL WOLSEY   What should this mean?
205 What sudden anger's this? How have I reaped° it?   *acquired*
He parted frowning from me, as if ruin
Leaped from his eyes. So looks the chafèd° lion   *angry*
Upon the daring huntsman that has galled° him,   *wounded*

---

3. *The honour . . . punishment:* The reward for loyalty and obedience is the honor they bring. Similarly, disloyalty and corruption are their own punishment, causing the subject dishonor.

Then makes him nothing.° I must read this paper—   *slaughters the hunter*
I fear, the story of his anger.
              [*He reads one of the papers*]
210   'Tis so.
This paper has undone° me. 'Tis th'account   *ruined*
Of all that world° of wealth I have drawn together   *vast quantity*
For mine own ends—indeed, to gain the popedom,
And fee° my friends in Rome. O negligence,   *pay off*
215 Fit for a fool to fall by! What cross° devil   *perverse*
Made me put this main° secret in the packet   *most important*
I sent the King? Is there no way to cure this?
No new device to beat this from his brains?
I know 'twill stir him strongly. Yet I know
220 A way, if it take right,° in spite of fortune   *if it succeed*
Will bring me off° again. What's this?   *save me*
              [*He reads the other paper*]
                    'To th' Pope'?
The letter, as I live, with all the business
I writ to's holiness. Nay then, farewell.
I have touched the highest point of all my greatness,
225 And from that full meridian° of my glory   *a star's highest point*
I haste now to my setting. I shall fall
Like a bright exhalation° in the evening,   *shooting star*
And no man see me more.
        Enter to [CARDINAL] WOLSEY *the Dukes of* NORFOLK
        and SUFFOLK, *the Earl of* SURREY, *and the* LORD CHAM-
        BERLAIN
NORFOLK   Hear the King's pleasure, Cardinal, who commands you
230 To render up the great seal presently°   *immediately*
Into our hands, and to confine yourself
To Asher House, my lord of Winchester's,
Till you hear further from his highness.
CARDINAL WOLSEY   Stay—
Where's your commission,° lords? Words cannot carry   *written warrant*
Authority so weighty.
235 SUFFOLK   Who dare cross° 'em   *challenge*
Bearing the King's will from his mouth expressly?
CARDINAL WOLSEY   Till I find more than will or words to do it—
I mean your malice—know, officious lords,
I dare and must deny it. Now I feel
240 Of what coarse metal° ye are moulded—envy.°⁴   *(also) mettle*
How eagerly ye follow my disgraces
As if it fed ye, and how sleek° and wanton°   *obsequious / impetuous*
Ye appear in everything may bring my ruin!
Follow your envious courses, men of malice.
245 You have Christian warrant for 'em, and no doubt
In time will find their fit rewards.⁵ That seal
You ask with such a violence,° the King,   *vehemence*
Mine and your master, with his own hand gave me,
Bade me enjoy it, with the place° and honours,   *position*
250 During my life; and, to confirm his goodness,
Tied it by letters patents.° Now, who'll take it?   *open letters*
SURREY   The King that gave it.

---

4. Malice; jealousy.
5. *You . . . rewards:* You emulate other, equally unjust Christians and will reap their "rewards" (punishments).

CARDINAL WOLSEY   It must be himself then.

SURREY   Thou art a proud traitor, priest.

CARDINAL WOLSEY   Proud lord, thou liest.

Within these forty hours Surrey durst better

Have burnt that tongue than said so.

255 **SURREY**   Thy ambition,

Thou scarlet sin,⁶ robbed this bewailing land

Of noble Buckingham, my father-in-law.

The heads of all thy brother cardinals

With thee and all thy best parts° bound together   *attributes*

260 Weighed° not a hair of his. Plague of° your policy,°   *Equaled / on / scheming*

You sent me deputy for Ireland,

Far from his succour, from the King, from all

That might have mercy on the fault thou gav'st him;°   *charged him wtih*

Whilst your great goodness, out of holy pity,

Absolved him with an axe.

265 **CARDINAL WOLSEY**   This, and all else

This talking lord can lay upon my credit,°   *good reputation*

I answer is most false. The Duke by law

Found his deserts. How innocent I was

From° any private malice in his end,   *Of*

270 His noble jury and foul cause can witness.

If I loved many words, lord, I should tell you

You have as little honesty as honour,

That° in the way of loyalty and truth   *I who*

Toward the King, my ever royal master,

275 Dare mate° a sounder man than Surrey can be,   *rival*

And all that love his follies.

SURREY   By my soul,

Your long coat, priest, protects you; thou shouldst feel

My sword i'th' life-blood of thee else. My lords,

Can ye endure to hear this arrogance,

280 And from this fellow?° If we live thus tamely,   *(contemptuous)*

To be thus jaded° by a piece of scarlet,   *cowed*

Farewell nobility. Let his grace go forward

And dare us with his cap, like larks.⁷

CARDINAL WOLSEY   All goodness

Is poison to thy stomach.

SURREY   Yes, that goodness

285 Of gleaning all the land's wealth into one,

Into your own hands, Card'nal, by extortion;

The goodness of your intercepted packets

You writ to th' Pope against the King; your goodness—

Since you provoke me—shall be most notorious.

290 My lord of Norfolk, as you are truly noble,

As you respect the common good, the state

Of our despised nobility, our issues°—   *sons*

Whom if he° live will scarce be gentlemen—   *(Wolsey)*

Produce the grand sum of his sins, the articles°   *charges against him*

295 Collected from his life. [*To* WOLSEY] I'll startle you

---

6. *scarlet*: referring to the cardinal's robes; see line 281 and 3.1.103. *scarlet sin*: egregious sin in the Bible; see Isaiah 1:18.

7. And befuddle us with his scarlet cap, as larks are caught by dazzling them with scarlet cloth.

Worse than the sacring-bell when the brown wench
Lay kissing in your arms,[8] lord Cardinal.
CARDINAL WOLSEY [*aside*]   How much, methinks, I could despise this man,
But that I am bound in charity against it.

300 NORFOLK [*to* SURREY]   Those articles, my lord, are in the King's hand;°   *possession*
But thus° much—they are foul ones.   *I'll tell you this*
CARDINAL WOLSEY   So much fairer
And spotless shall mine innocence arise
When the King knows my truth.°   *loyalty*
SURREY   This cannot save you.
I thank my memory I yet remember
305 Some of these articles, and out they shall.
Now, if you can blush and cry 'Guilty', Cardinal,
You'll show a little honesty.
CARDINAL WOLSEY   Speak on, sir;
I dare your worst objections.° If I blush,   *accusations*
It is to see a nobleman want° manners.   *lack*
310 SURREY   I had rather want those than my head. Have at you!°   *(a challenge)*
First, that without the King's assent or knowledge
You wrought to be a legate,[9] by which power
You maimed the jurisdiction of all bishops.
NORFOLK [*to* WOLSEY]   Then, that in all you writ to Rome, or else
315 To foreign princes, *'Ego et Rex meus'*[1]
Was still° inscribed—in which you brought the King   *always*
To be your servant.
SUFFOLK [*to* WOLSEY]   Then, that without the knowledge
Either of King or Council, when you went
Ambassador to the Emperor,° you made bold   *Charles V*
320 To carry into Flanders the great seal.
SURREY [*to* WOLSEY]   Item,° you sent a large commission°   *Next / delegation*
To Gregory de Cassado, to conclude,
Without the King's will or the state's allowance,°   *consent*
A league between his highness and Ferrara.
325 SUFFOLK [*to* WOLSEY]   That out of mere° ambition you have caused   *pure*
Your holy hat to be stamped on the King's coin.[2]
SURREY [*to* WOLSEY]   Then, that you have sent innumerable substance°—   *untold riches*
By what means got, I leave to your own conscience—
To furnish° Rome, and to prepare the ways   *supply; bribe*
330 You have for dignities to the mere undoing°   *complete destruction*
Of all the kingdom. Many more there are,
Which since they are of you, and odious,
I will not taint my mouth with.
LORD CHAMBERLAIN   O, my lord,
Press° not a falling man too far. 'Tis virtue.°   *Oppress / (not to)*
335 His faults lie open to° the laws. Let them,   *exposed before*
Not you, correct him. My heart weeps to see him
So little of his great self.
SURREY   I forgive him.

---

8. *I'll . . . arms*: The small "sacring bell" was rung at Mass when the priest elevated the consecrated Host. Surrey imagines Wolsey surprised with a country girl ("brown" because tanned or dirty from working, or perhaps ugly or promiscuous) when he should have been at Mass.
9. You schemed to be a papal representative.
1. I and my King. Norfolk accuses Wolsey of putting himself before the King and of making the King his dependent. Technically, however, the Latin word order is correct and means "my King and I," thus making it less offensive.
2. Allowed to produce half groats and half pennies with his insignia in his home diocese of York, Wolsey had his cardinal's hat stamped on a groat, thereby usurping the King's monopoly on coins of larger denominations.

SUFFOLK   Lord Cardinal, the King's further pleasure is—
Because all those things you have done of late,
340   By your power legantine within this kingdom,
Fall into th' compass of a praemunire³—
That therefore such a writ be sued° against you,   served
To forfeit all your goods, lands, tenements,
Chattels,° and whatsoever, and to be   Personal property
345   Out of the King's protection. This is my charge.
NORFOLK [to WOLSEY]   And so we'll leave you to your meditations
How to live better. For your stubborn answer
About the giving back the great seal to us,
The King shall know it and, no doubt, shall thank you.
350   So fare you well, my little good lord Cardinal. Exeunt all but WOLSEY
CARDINAL WOLSEY   So farewell—to the little good you bear me.
Farewell, a long farewell, to all my greatness!
This is the state of man. Today he puts forth
The tender leaves of hopes; tomorrow blossoms,
355   And bears his blushing° honours thick upon him;   resplendent
The third day comes a frost, a killing frost,
And when he thinks, good easy° man, full surely   trusting
His greatness is a-ripening, nips his root,
And then he falls, as I do. I have ventured,
360   Like little wanton boys that swim on bladders,⁴
This many summers in a sea of glory,
But far beyond my depth; my high-blown pride
At length broke under me, and now has left me
Weary, and old with service, to the mercy
365   Of a rude stream° that must for ever hide me.   turbulent current
Vain pomp and glory of this world, I hate ye!
I feel my heart new opened. O, how wretched
Is that poor man that hangs on princes' favours!
There is betwixt that smile we would aspire to,
370   That sweet aspect of princes, and their ruin,⁵
More pangs and fears than wars or women have,
And when he falls, he falls like Lucifer,°   (from heaven to hell)
Never to hope again.
               Enter CROMWELL, [who then] stand[s] amazed
                              Why, how now, Cromwell?
CROMWELL   I have no power to speak, sir.
CARDINAL WOLSEY   What, amazed
375   At my misfortunes? Can thy spirit wonder
A great man should decline?°   fall from power
               [CROMWELL begins to weep]
                              Nay, an° you weep   if
I am fall'n indeed.
CROMWELL   How does your grace?
CARDINAL WOLSEY   Why, well—
Never so truly happy, my good Cromwell.
I know myself now, and I feel within me

3. Having made himself a papal legate, Wolsey is subject to punishment because he has broken the law of
praemunire—that is, he has appealed to an outside
(here, papal) court when the offense fell under the
jurisdiction of English courts. Wolsey is thus charged

with elevating the Pope's authority over his sovereign's.
4. Like frolicsome little boys who stay afloat (only by)
using inflated membranes from an animal's body.
5. their ruin: the destruction they cause.

380   A peace above all earthly dignities,
      A still and quiet conscience. The King has cured me.
      I humbly thank his grace, and from these shoulders,
      These ruined pillars,⁶ out of pity, taken
      A load would sink a navy—too much honour.
385   O, 'tis a burden, Cromwell, 'tis a burden
      Too heavy for a man that hopes for heaven.

CROMWELL   I am glad your grace has made that right use of it.

CARDINAL WOLSEY   I hope I have. I am able now, methinks,
      Out of a fortitude of soul I feel,
390   To endure more miseries and greater far
      Than my weak-hearted enemies dare offer.
      What news abroad?

CROMWELL   The heaviest and the worst
      Is your displeasure° with the King.   *disgrace*

CARDINAL WOLSEY   God bless him.

CROMWELL   The next is that Sir Thomas More is chosen
      Lord Chancellor in your place.

395   CARDINAL WOLSEY   That's somewhat sudden.
      But he's a learnèd man. May he continue
      Long in his highness' favour, and do justice
      For truth's sake and his conscience, that his bones,
      When he has run his course and sleeps in blessings,
400   May have a tomb of orphans' tears wept on him.⁷
      What more?

CROMWELL   That Cranmer is returned° with welcome,   *(from the Continent)*
      Installed lord Archbishop of Canterbury.⁸

CARDINAL WOLSEY   That's news indeed.

CROMWELL   Last, that the Lady Anne,
      Whom the King hath in secrecy long married,
405   This day was viewed in open as his queen,
      Going to chapel, and the voice° is now   *gossip*
      Only about her coronation.

CARDINAL WOLSEY   There was the weight that pulled me down.
      O, Cromwell,
      The King has gone beyond° me. All my glories   *overreached*
410   In° that one woman I have lost for ever.   *Due to*
      No sun shall ever usher forth mine honours,
      Or gild again the noble troops° that waited   *retainers*
      Upon my smiles. Go, get thee from me, Cromwell.
      I am a poor fall'n man, unworthy now
415   To be thy lord and master. Seek the King—
      That sun I pray may never set—I have told him
      What and how true thou art. He will advance thee.
      Some little memory of me will stir him.
      I know his noble nature not to let
420   Thy hopeful service perish too. Good Cromwell,
      Neglect him not. Make use° now, and provide   *Seize your chance*
      For thine own future safety.

CROMWELL [*weeping*]   O, my lord,
      Must I then leave you? Must I needs forgo°   *renounce*

---

6. Perhaps the pillars carried during Wolsey's triumphal entrance in 2.4.
7. The Lord Chancellor's duties included guardianship of all children under twenty-one, particularly

orphans. Henry had More beheaded in 1535 for his
Catholicism.
8. In 1533; Cranmer was beheaded by Henry's oldest
daughter, Queen Mary, in 1556 for his Protestantism.

So good, so noble, and so true a master?
425 Bear witness, all that have not hearts of iron,
With what a sorrow Cromwell leaves his lord.
The King shall have my service, but my prayers
For ever and for ever shall be yours.
CARDINAL WOLSEY [*weeping*]   Cromwell, I did not think to shed a tear
430 In all my miseries, but thou hast forced me,
Out of thy honest truth, to play the woman.°   *to weep*
Let's dry our eyes, and thus far hear me, Cromwell,
And when I am forgotten, as I shall be,
And sleep in dull cold marble, where no mention
435 Of me more must be heard of, say I taught thee—
Say Wolsey, that once trod the ways of glory,
And sounded° all the depths and shoals of honour,   *fathomed*
Found thee a way, out of his wreck,° to rise in,   *shipwreck*
A sure and safe one, though thy master missed it.
440 Mark but my fall, and that that ruined me.
Cromwell, I charge thee, fling away ambition.⁹
By that sin fell the angels. How can man, then,
The image of his maker, hope to win° by it?   *profit*
Love thyself last. Cherish those hearts that hate thee.
445 Corruption wins not more than honesty.
Still° in thy right hand carry gentle peace   *Ever*
To silence envious tongues. Be just, and fear not.
Let all the ends thou aim'st at be thy country's,
Thy God's, and truth's. Then if thou fall'st, O Cromwell,
450 Thou fall'st a blessèd martyr.¹
Serve the King. And prithee, lead me in—
There take an inventory of all I have:
To the last penny 'tis the King's. My robe,
And my integrity to heaven, is all
455 I dare now call mine own. O Cromwell, Cromwell,
Had I but served my God with half the zeal
I served my King, He would not in mine age
Have left me naked° to mine enemies.   *utterly exposed*
CROMWELL   Good sir, have patience.
CARDINAL WOLSEY   So I have. Farewell
460 The hopes of court; my hopes in heaven do dwell.   *Exeunt*

4.1

Enter [the] two GENTLEMEN *meeting one another. [The
first holds a paper]*
FIRST GENTLEMAN   You're well met once again.¹
SECOND GENTLEMAN   So are you.
FIRST GENTLEMAN   You come to take your stand here and behold
The Lady Anne pass from her coronation?
SECOND GENTLEMAN   'Tis all my business. At our last encounter
5 The Duke of Buckingham came from his trial.
FIRST GENTLEMAN   'Tis very true. But that time offered sorrow,
This, general joy.
SECOND GENTLEMAN   'Tis well. The citizens,

9. Cromwell did not take Wolsey's advice; Henry had   Shakespeare's time.
him beheaded in 1540 for treason and heresy after an   4.1 Location: A street in Westminster.
even more rapid rise and fall than Wolsey's.   1. See 2.1.
1. As Cromwell was sometimes thought to be in

I am sure, have shown at full their royal minds°— *royalist allegiance*
As, let 'em have their rights, they are ever forward²—
10   In celebration of this day with shows,
Pageants, and sights of honour.
FIRST GENTLEMAN   Never greater,
Nor, I'll assure you, better taken,° sir. *received*
SECOND GENTLEMAN   May I be bold to ask what that contains,
That paper in your hand?
FIRST GENTLEMAN   Yes, 'tis the list
15   Of those that claim their offices this day
By custom of the coronation.
The Duke of Suffolk is the first, and claims
To be High Steward; next, the Duke of Norfolk,
He to be Earl Marshal. You may read the rest.
[He gives him the paper]
20   SECOND GENTLEMAN   I thank you, sir. Had I not known those customs,
I should have been beholden to your paper.
But I beseech you, what's become of Katherine,
The Princess Dowager? How goes her business?
FIRST GENTLEMAN   That I can tell you too. The Archbishop
25   Of Canterbury, accompanied with other
Learnèd and reverend fathers of his order,
Held a late° court at Dunstable, six miles off *Recently held a*
From Ampthill, where the Princess lay;° to which *resided*
She was often cited° by them, but appeared not. *summoned*
30   And, to be short, for not appearance, and
The King's late scruple, by the main assent° *consensus*
Of all these learnèd men, she was divorced,
And the late marriage made of none effect,° *null*
Since which she was removed to Kimbolton,
Where she remains now sick.
35   SECOND GENTLEMAN   Alas, good lady!
[Flourish of trumpets within]
The trumpets sound. Stand close.° The Queen is coming. *aside*
[Enter the coronation procession, which] pass[es] over
the stage in order and state. Hautboys [within,
play during the procession]

THE ORDER OF THE CORONATION

1. *[First, enter] trumpet[ers, who play] a lively flourish.*
2. *Then, [enter] two judges.*
3. *[Then, enter the]* LORD CHANCELLOR, *with [both the]*
purse [containing the great seal] and [the] mace [borne]
before him.
4. *[Then, enter] choristers singing; [with them,]*
music[ians playing.]
5. *[Then, enter the Lord] Mayor of London bearing the*
mace, [followed by] Garter [King-of-Arms° wearing] his *chief herald*
coat of arms and a gilt copper crown.
6. *[Then, enter] Marquis Dorset bearing a sceptre of*
gold, [and wearing,] on his head, a demi-coronal of
gold [and, about his neck, a collar of esses].³ With him

2. As, to give them their due, they are always eager to
demonstrate.

3. Heavy gold chain made of S-shaped links worn
around the neck by men of high office.

[enter] the Earl of SURREY bearing the rod of silver with
the dove, crowned with an earl's coronet, [and also wearing a] collar of esses.
7. [Next, enter the] Duke of SUFFOLK as High Steward,
in his robe of estate, [with] his coronet on his head,
[and] bearing a long white wand. With him, [enter] the
Duke of NORFOLK with the rod of marshalship [and] a
coronet on his head. [Each wears a] collar of esses.
8. [Then,] under a canopy borne by four [barons] of
the Cinque Ports,⁴ [enter] ANNE, the [new] Queen, in
her robe. Her hair, [which hangs loose,° is] richly   *a bridal custom*
adorned with pearl. [She wears a] crown. [Accompany-
ing] her on [either] side [are] the Bishops of London
and Winchester.
9. [Next, enter] the old Duchess of Norfolk, in a coronal
of gold wrought with flowers, bearing the Queen's train.
10. [Finally, enter] certain ladies or countesses, with
plain circlets of gold without flowers.
[The two GENTLEMEN comment on the procession as it
passes over the stage]

SECOND GENTLEMAN   A royal train,° believe me. These I know.   *procession*
  Who's that that bears the sceptre?
FIRST GENTLEMAN   Marquis Dorset.
  And that, the Earl of Surrey with the rod.
40 SECOND GENTLEMAN   A bold brave gentleman. That should be
  The Duke of Suffolk?
FIRST GENTLEMAN   'Tis the same: High Steward.
SECOND GENTLEMAN   And that, my lord of Norfolk?
FIRST GENTLEMAN   Yes.
SECOND GENTLEMAN [seeing ANNE]   Heaven bless thee!
  Thou hast the sweetest face I ever looked on.
  Sir, as I have a soul, she is an angel.
45 Our King has all the Indies⁵ in his arms,
  And more, and richer, when he strains° that lady.   *embraces*
  I cannot blame his conscience.
FIRST GENTLEMAN   They that bear
  The cloth of honour° over her are four barons   *canopy*
  Of the Cinque Ports.
50 SECOND GENTLEMAN   Those men are happy,
  And so are all° are near her.   *all who*
  I take it she that carries up the train
  Is that old noble lady, Duchess of Norfolk.
FIRST GENTLEMAN   It is. And all the rest are countesses.
55 SECOND GENTLEMAN   Their coronets say so. These are stars indeed—
FIRST GENTLEMAN   And sometimes falling ones.°   *meteors; (sexual)*
SECOND GENTLEMAN   No more of that.
              Exit [the last of the procession,] and then
                  a great flourish of trumpets [within]
        Enter a third GENTLEMAN [in a sweat]
FIRST GENTLEMAN   God save you, sir. Where have you been broiling?°   *overheating*
THIRD GENTLEMAN   Among the crowd i'th' Abbey, where a finger

---

4. By traditional prerogative, the barons of the Cinque
Ports (Hastings, Sandwich, Dover, Romney, and Hythe
on the southeast coast of England) carried a canopy
over the sovereign at state occasions.
5. The East and West Indies were considered sources
of great wealth. See 1.1.21.

Could not be wedged in more. I am stifled

60   With the mere rankness° of their joy.   *exuberance; odor*

SECOND GENTLEMAN   You saw the ceremony?

THIRD GENTLEMAN   That I did.

FIRST GENTLEMAN   How was it?

THIRD GENTLEMAN   Well worth the seeing.

SECOND GENTLEMAN   Good sir, speak° it to us.   *describe*

THIRD GENTLEMAN   As well as I am able. The rich stream

65   Of lords and ladies, having brought the Queen

To a prepared place in the choir,° fell off°   *company / drew back*

A distance from her, while her grace sat down

To rest a while—some half an hour or so—

In a rich chair of state, opposing° freely   *displaying*

70   The beauty of her person to the people.

Believe me, sir, she is the goodliest° woman   *fairest*

That ever lay by man; which when the people

Had the full view of, such a noise arose

As the shrouds° make at sea in a stiff tempest,   *ship's rigging*

75   As loud and to as many tunes. Hats, cloaks—

Doublets,° I think—flew up, and had their faces   *Short jackets*

Been loose, this day they had been lost. Such joy

I never saw before. Great-bellied women,

That had not half a week to go, like rams°   *battering rams*

80   In the old time of war, would shake the press,°   *crowd*

And make 'em reel before 'em. No man living

Could say 'This is my wife' there, all were woven

So strangely in one piece.

SECOND GENTLEMAN   But what followed?

THIRD GENTLEMAN   At length her grace rose, and with modest paces

85   Came to the altar, where she kneeled, and saint-like

Cast her fair eyes to heaven, and prayed devoutly,

Then rose again, and bowed her to the people,

When by the Archbishop of Canterbury

She had all the royal makings° of a queen,   *essential trappings*

90   As holy oil, Edward Confessor's crown,

The rod and bird of peace, and all such emblems

Laid nobly on her. Which performed, the choir,

With all the choicest music° of the kingdom,   *musicians*

Together sung *Te Deum*.[6] So she parted,°   *departed*

95   And with the same full state° paced back again   *ceremony*

To York Place, where the feast is held.

FIRST GENTLEMAN   Sir,

You must no more call it York Place—that's past,

For since the Cardinal fell, that title's lost.

'Tis now the King's, and called Whitehall.

THIRD GENTLEMAN   I know it,

100   But 'tis so lately altered that the old name

Is fresh about me.

SECOND GENTLEMAN   What two reverend bishops

Were those that went on each side of the Queen?

THIRD GENTLEMAN   Stokesley and Gardiner, the one of Winchester—

---

6. Hymn of praise and thanksgiving beginning *"Te Deum laudamus,"* "We praise thee, O Lord."

Newly preferred° from the King's secretary— *promoted*
The other London.[7]

105 SECOND GENTLEMAN   He of Winchester
Is held no great good lover of the Archbishop's,
The virtuous Cranmer.

THIRD GENTLEMAN   All the land knows that.
However, yet there is no great breach. When it comes,
Cranmer will find a friend will not° shrink from him. *who will not*

SECOND GENTLEMAN   Who may that be, I pray you?

110 THIRD GENTLEMAN   Thomas Cromwell,
A man in much esteem with th' King, and truly
A worthy friend. The King has made him
Master o'th' Jewel House,
And one already of the Privy Council.

SECOND GENTLEMAN   He will deserve more.

115 THIRD GENTLEMAN   Yes, without all doubt.
Come, gentlemen, ye shall go my way,
Which is to th' court, and there ye shall be my guests.
Something° I can command. As I walk thither *Some influence*
I'll tell ye more.

FIRST *and* SECOND GENTLEMEN   You may command us, sir.

Exeunt

4.2

[Three chairs.] Enter KATHERINE *Dowager, sick, led*
between GRIFFITH *her gentleman usher, and* PATIENCE
her woman

GRIFFITH   How does your grace?

KATHERINE   O Griffith, sick to death.
My legs, like loaden° branches, bow to th' earth, *heavily laden*
Willing to leave their burden. Reach a chair.
[A chair is brought to her. She sits]
So now, methinks, I feel a little ease.

5 Didst thou not tell me, Griffith, as thou led'st me,
That the great child of honour,° Cardinal Wolsey, *(ironic)*
Was dead?

GRIFFITH   Yes, madam, but I think your grace,
Out of the pain you suffered, gave no ear to't.

KATHERINE   Prithee, good Griffith, tell me how he died.

10 If well, he stepped before me happily° *aptly*
For my example.

GRIFFITH   Well, the voice° goes, madam. *talk*
For after the stout Earl Northumberland
Arrested him at York, and brought him forward,
As a man sorely tainted,° to his answer,° *disgraced / hearing*

15 He fell sick, suddenly, and grew so ill
He could not sit his mule.

KATHERINE   Alas, poor man.

GRIFFITH   At last, with easy roads,° he came to Leicester, *stages of a journey*
Lodged in the abbey, where the reverend abbot,
With all his convent,° honourably received him, *monastery*

---

7. John Stokesley was Bishop of London; already secretary to the King, Gardiner also became Bishop of
Winchester following Wolsey's demise.
4.2 Location: Katherine's apartments in Kimbolton.

20   To whom he gave these words: 'O father abbot,
    An old man broken with the storms of state
    Is come to lay his weary bones among ye.
    Give him a little earth,° for charity.'   *a resting place*
    So went to bed, where eagerly his sickness
25   Pursued him still, and three nights after this,
    About the hour of eight, which he himself
    Foretold should be his last, full of repentance,
    Continual meditations, tears, and sorrows,
    He gave his honours to the world again,
30   His blessèd part° to heaven, and slept in peace.   *soul*
   KATHERINE   So may he rest, his faults lie gently on him.
    Yet thus far, Griffith, give me leave to speak° him,   *describe*
    And yet with charity. He was a man
    Of an unbounded stomach,° ever ranking   *ambition*
35   Himself with princes; one that by suggestion°   *underhanded dealing*
    Tied° all the kingdom. Simony[1] was fair play.   *Shackled*
    His own opinion was his law. I'th' presence°   *King's chamber*
    He would say untruths, and be ever double°   *duplicitious*
    Both in his words and meaning. He was never,
40   But where he meant to ruin, pitiful.°   *merciful*
    His promises were, as he then was, mighty;
    But his performance, as he is now, nothing.
    Of his own body he was ill,° and gave   *sexually immoral*
    The clergy ill example.
   GRIFFITH   Noble madam,
45   Men's evil manners live in brass, their virtues
    We write in water.[2] May it please your highness
    To hear me speak his good now?
   KATHERINE   Yes, good Griffith,
    I were malicious else.
   GRIFFITH   This cardinal,
    Though from an humble stock, undoubtedly
50   Was fashioned to much honour. From his cradle
    He was a scholar, and a ripe and good one,
    Exceeding wise, fair-spoken, and persuading;°   *persuasive*
    Lofty and sour to them that loved him not,
    But to those men that sought him,° sweet as summer.   *befriended him*
55   And though he were unsatisfied° in getting°—   *insatiable / (riches)*
    Which was a sin—yet in bestowing, madam,
    He was most princely: ever witness for him
    Those twins of learning that he raised° in you,   *set up*
    Ipswich and Oxford[3]—one of which fell with him,
60   Unwilling to outlive the good that did it;
    The other, though unfinished, yet so famous,
    So excellent in art,° and still so rising,   *scholarship*
    That Christendom shall ever speak his virtue.
    His overthrow heaped happiness upon him,
65   For then, and not till then, he felt° himself,   *recognized*
    And found the blessèdness of being little.°   *humble*

---

1. Trading, for money or favors, in ecclesiastical offices.
2. *Men's . . . water*: Evil deeds are long remembered, good ones soon forgotten (proverbial).
3. Wolsey founded colleges at Ipswich and Oxford; the latter survives as Christ Church.

And to add greater honours to his age
Than man could give him, he died fearing God.

KATHERINE   After my death I wish no other herald,
70   No other speaker of my living actions
To keep mine honour from corruption
But such an honest chronicler as Griffith.
Whom I most hated living,° thou hast made me,   *while alive*
With thy religious truth and modesty,°   *equanimity*
75   Now in his ashes honour. Peace be with him.
[*To her woman*] Patience, be near me still, and set me lower.
I have not long to trouble thee. Good Griffith,
Cause the musicians play me that sad note°   *melody*
I named my knell, whilst I sit meditating
80   On that celestial harmony I go to.[4]
            Sad and solemn music. [KATHERINE *sleeps*]
    GRIFFITH [*to the woman*]   She is asleep. Good wench, let's sit down quiet
For fear we wake her. Softly, gentle Patience.
        [*They sit*]

                    THE VISION

Enter, solemnly tripping one after another, six person-
ages clad in white robes, wearing on their heads gar-
lands of bays, and golden visors on their faces.[5] [*They*]
carry] branches of bays or palm in their hands. They first   *bow*
congé° unto [KATHERINE], *then dance; and, at certain*
changes,° the first two hold a spare garland over her   *dance movements*
head at which the other four make reverent curtsies.
Then the two that held the garland deliver the same to
the other next two, who observe the same order in their
changes and holding the garland over her head. Which
done, they deliver the same garland to the last two who
likewise observe the same order. At which, as it were by
inspiration, she makes in her sleep signs of rejoicing, and
holdeth up her hands to heaven. And so in their dancing
vanish, carrying the garland with them. The music con-
tinues

KATHERINE [*waking*]   Spirits of peace, where are ye? Are ye all gone,
And leave me here in wretchedness behind ye?
        [GRIFFITH *and* PATIENCE *rise and come forward*]
    GRIFFITH   Madam, we are here.
85   KATHERINE   It is not you I call for.
Saw ye none enter since I slept?
GRIFFITH   None, madam.
KATHERINE   No? Saw you not even now a blessèd troop
Invite me to a banquet, whose bright faces
Cast thousand beams upon me, like the sun?
90   They promised me eternal happiness,
And brought me garlands, Griffith, which I feel
I am not worthy yet to wear. I shall,
Assuredly.

---

4. After death, the soul supposedly could hear the music of the spheres (the heavenly bodies) as they revolved around the earth.

5. White to signify purity; bay leaves ("bays") to indicate triumph or joy; golden masks ("visors") perhaps to suggest they are spirits.

GRIFFITH   I am most joyful, madam, such good dreams
      Possess your fancy.°   *Fill your imagination*
95 KATHERINE   Bid the music° leave.   *musicians*
      They are harsh and heavy° to me.   *tiresome*
          Music ceases
    PATIENCE [*to* GRIFFITH]   Do you note
      How much her grace is altered on the sudden?
      How long her face is drawn? How pale she looks,
      And of an earthy colour? Mark her eyes?
    GRIFFITH   She is going, wench. Pray, pray.
100 PATIENCE   Heaven comfort her.
          Enter a MESSENGER
    MESSENGER [*to* KATHERINE]
      An't like° your grace—   *If it please*
    KATHERINE   You are a saucy fellow—
      Deserve we no more reverence?
    GRIFFITH [*to the* MESSENGER]   You are to blame,
      Knowing she will not lose her wonted° greatness,   *forgo her usual*
      To use so rude behaviour. Go to, kneel.
    MESSENGER [*kneeling before* KATHERINE]   I humbly do entreat
105   your highness' pardon.
      My haste made me unmannerly. There is staying°   *waiting*
      A gentleman sent from the King to see you.
    KATHERINE   Admit him entrance, Griffith. But this fellow
      Let me ne'er see again.   *Exit* MESSENGER
          Enter Lord CAPUTIUS [*ushered by* GRIFFITH]
          If my sight fail not,
110   You should be lord ambassador from the Emperor,°   *Charles V*
      My royal nephew, and your name Caputius.
    CAPUTIUS   Madam, the same, [*bowing*] your servant.
    KATHERINE   O, my lord,
      The times and titles now are altered strangely
      With me since first you knew me. But I pray you,
      What is your pleasure with me?
115 CAPUTIUS   Noble lady,
      First mine own service to your grace; the next,
      The King's request that I would visit you,
      Who grieves much for your weakness, and by me
      Sends you his princely commendations,°   *compliments*
120   And heartily entreats you take good comfort.
    KATHERINE   O, my good lord, that comfort comes too late,
      'Tis like a pardon after execution.
      That gentle physic,° given in time, had cured me;   *medicine*
      But now I am past all comforts here but prayers.
      How does his highness?
125 CAPUTIUS   Madam, in good health.
    KATHERINE   So may he ever do, and ever flourish
      When I shall dwell with worms, and my poor name
      Banished the kingdom. [*To her woman*] Patience, is that letter
      I caused you write yet sent away?
    PATIENCE   No, madam.
130 KATHERINE [*to* CAPUTIUS]   Sir, I most humbly pray you to deliver
      This to my lord the King.
          [*The letter is given to* CAPUTIUS]

CAPUTIUS   Most willing,° madam.   *willingly*

KATHERINE   In which I have commended to his goodness
The model° of our chaste loves, his young daughter[6]—   *image*
The dews of heaven fall thick in blessings on her—
135   Beseeching him to give her virtuous breeding.°   *raise her virtuously*
She is young, and of a noble modest nature.
I hope she will deserve well—and a little
To love her for her mother's sake, that loved him,
Heaven knows how dearly. My next poor petition
140   Is that his noble grace would have some pity
Upon my wretched women, that so long
Have followed both my fortunes° faithfully;   *(good and bad)*
Of which there is not one, I dare avow—
And now I should not lie[7]—but will deserve,
145   For virtue and true beauty of the soul,
For honesty° and decent carriage,°   *chastity / conduct*
A right good husband. Let him be a noble,
And sure those men are happy that shall have 'em.
The last is for my men—they are the poorest,
150   But poverty could never draw 'em from me—
That they may have their wages duly paid 'em,
And something over to remember me by.
If heaven had pleased to have given me longer life,
And able° means, we had not parted thus.   *sufficient*
155   These are the whole contents; and, good my lord,
By that you love the dearest in this world,
As you wish Christian peace to souls departed,
Stand these poor people's friend and urge the King
To do me this last rite.°   *(also) right*

CAPUTIUS   By heaven I will,
160   Or let me lose the fashion of a man.°   *forfeit my humanity*

KATHERINE   I thank you, honest lord. Remember me
In all humility unto his highness.
Say his long trouble now is passing
Out of this world. Tell him, in death I blessed him,
165   For so I will. Mine eyes grow dim. Farewell,
My lord. Griffith, farewell.
[*To her woman*]   Nay, Patience,
You must not leave me yet. I must to bed.
Call in more women. When I am dead, good wench,
Let me be used° with honour. Strew me over   *treated*
170   With maiden° flowers, that all the world may know   *(signifying chastity)*
I was a chaste wife to my grave. Embalm me,
Then lay me forth.° Although unqueened, yet like   *prepare me for burial*
A queen and daughter to a king inter me.
I can° no more.   *can say or do*

Exeunt [CAPUTIUS *and* GRIFFITH *at one door;*
PATIENCE] *leading* KATHERINE [*at another*]

---

6. Mary was Katherine and Henry's only child who survived infancy (see 2.4.35 and note). She was Queen for
five years (1553–58) before Elizabeth, her half sister.

7. Now, on the point of death, I would not (ought not
to) lie. It was generally thought that people spoke truth
on their deathbeds.

5.1

Enter [at one door] GARDINER, *Bishop of Winchester;*
before him, a PAGE *with a torch*

GARDINER   It's one o'clock, boy, is't not?

PAGE   It hath struck.

GARDINER   These should be hours for necessities,
Not for delights; times to repair° our nature   °restore
With comforting repose, and not for us
To waste these times.

            [Enter at another door] Sir Thomas LOVELL *[meeting*
            them]

5   Good hour of night, Sir Thomas!
Whither so late?

LOVELL   Came you from the King, my lord?

GARDINER   I did, Sir Thomas, and left him at primero°   °*a card game*
With the Duke of Suffolk.

LOVELL   I must to him too,
Before he go to bed. I'll take my leave.

10 GARDINER   Not yet, Sir Thomas Lovell—what's the matter?
It seems you are in haste. An if there be
No great offence° belongs to't, give your friend   °*inappropriateness*
Some touch° of your late business. Affairs that walk,   °*hint*
As they say spirits do, at midnight, have
15 In them a wilder nature than the business
That seeks dispatch° by day.   °*to be done*

LOVELL   My lord, I love you,
And durst commend° a secret to your ear   °*entrust*
Much weightier than this work.° The Queen's in labour—   °*my affairs*
They say in great extremity—and feared°   °*it is feared that*
She'll with the labour end.

20 GARDINER   The fruit she goes with
I pray for heartily, that it may find
Good time,° and live. But, for the stock,° Sir Thomas,   °*Fortune / trunk (Anne)*
I wish it grubbed up° now.   °*rooted out*

LOVELL   Methinks I could
Cry the amen,° and yet my conscience says   °*Agree*
25 She's a good creature and, sweet lady, does
Deserve our better wishes.

GARDINER   But sir, sir,
Hear me, Sir Thomas. You're a gentleman
Of mine own way.[1] I know you wise, religious.
And let me tell you, it will ne'er be well—
30 'Twill not, Sir Thomas Lovell, take't of me—
Till Cranmer, Cromwell—her two hands—and she,
Sleep in their graves.

LOVELL   Now, sir, you speak of two
The most remarked° i'th' kingdom. As for Cromwell,   °*regarded*
Beside that of the Jewel House is made Master
35 O'th' Rolls and the King's secretary. Further, sir,
Stands in the gap and trade° of more preferments   °*open road*
With which the time will load him. Th'Archbishop

5.1 Location: London, a gallery at court.
1. Of my religious persuasion (Catholicism, as opposed to Anne's Lutheranism).

Is the King's hand and tongue, and who dare speak
One syllable against him?
GARDINER   Yes, yes, Sir Thomas—
40   There are that dare, and I myself have ventured
To speak my mind of him, and, indeed, this day,
Sir—I may tell it you, I think—I have
Incensed° the lords o'th' Council that he is—   *Angered*
For so I know he is, they know he is—
45   A most arch heretic, a pestilence
That does infect the land; with which they, moved,°   *angered*
Have broken with° the King, who hath so far   *revealed to*
Given ear to our complaint, of his great grace
And princely care, foreseeing those fell mischiefs
50   Our reasons laid before him, hath° commanded   *that he has*
Tomorrow morning to the Council board
He be convented.° He's a rank° weed, Sir Thomas,   *summoned / rotten*
And we must root him out. From your affairs
I hinder you too long. Good night, Sir Thomas.
55   LOVELL   Many good nights, my lord; I rest° your servant.   *remain*
                    Exeunt GARDINER *and* PAGE [*at one door*]
          Enter KING [HENRY] *and* SUFFOLK [*at another door*]
KING HENRY [*to* SUFFOLK]   Charles, I will play no more tonight.
My mind's not on't. You are too hard° for me.   *skillful*
SUFFOLK   Sir, I did never win of you before.
KING HENRY   But little, Charles,
60   Nor shall not when my fancy's° on my play.   *attention is*
Now, Lovell, from the Queen what is the news?
LOVELL   I could not personally deliver to her
What you commanded me, but by her woman
I sent your message, who returned her thanks
65   In the great'st humbleness, and desired your highness
Most heartily to pray for her.
KING HENRY   What sayst thou? Ha?
To pray for her? What, is she crying out?
LOVELL   So said her woman, and that her suffrance° made   *suffering*
Almost each pang a death.
KING HENRY   Alas, good lady.
70   SUFFOLK   God safely quit° her of her burden, and   *release*
With gentle travail,° to the gladding° of   *labor / making joyful*
Your highness with an heir.
KING HENRY   'Tis midnight, Charles.
Prithee to bed, and in thy prayers remember
Th'estate° of my poor queen. Leave me alone,   *condition*
75   For I must think of that which company
Would not be friendly to.[2]
SUFFOLK   I wish your highness
A quiet night, and my good mistress will°   *I will*
Remember in my prayers.
KING HENRY   Charles, good night. *Exit* SUFFOLK
          Enter Sir Anthony DENNY
Well, sir, what follows?
80   DENNY   Sir, I have brought my lord the Archbishop,
As you commanded me.

---

2. *which . . . to:* which requires privacy.

KING HENRY   Ha, Canterbury?

DENNY   Ay, my good lord.

KING HENRY   'Tis true—where is he, Denny?

DENNY   He attends your highness' pleasure.

KING HENRY   Bring him to us.

                              [*Exit* DENNY]

LOVELL [*aside*]   This is about that which the Bishop° spake.   *Gardiner*

85   I am happily° come hither.   *fortunately*

       Enter CRANMER [*the Archbishop, ushered by*] DENNY

KING HENRY [*to* LOVELL *and* DENNY]   Avoid° the gallery.   *Quit*

    [DENNY *begins to depart.*] LOVELL *seems to stay*

Ha? I have said. Be gone.

What?   *Exeunt* LOVELL *and* DENNY

CRANMER [*aside*]   I am fearful. Wherefore° frowns he thus?   *Why*

'Tis his aspect° of terror. All's not well.   *countenance*

90   KING HENRY   How now, my lord? You do desire to know

Wherefore I sent for you.

CRANMER [*kneeling*]   It is my duty

T'attend your highness' pleasure.

KING HENRY   Pray you, arise,

My good and gracious Lord of Canterbury.

Come, you and I must walk a turn together.

95   I have news to tell you. Come, come—give me your hand.

       [CRANMER *rises. They walk*]

Ah, my good lord, I grieve at what I speak,

And am right sorry to repeat what follows.

I have, and most unwillingly, of late

Heard many grievous°—I do say, my lord,   *serious*

100   Grievous—complaints of you, which, being considered,

Have moved us and our Council that you shall

This morning come before us, where I know

You cannot with such freedom purge° yourself   *with ease clear*

But that, till further trial in those charges

105   Which will require your answer, you must take

Your patience to you,³ and be well contented

To make your house our Tower. You a brother of us,°   *a fellow councillor*

It fits we thus proceed, or else no witness

Would come against you.

CRANMER [*kneeling*]   I humbly thank your highness,

110   And am right glad to catch this good occasion

Most throughly to be winnowed, where my chaff

And corn shall fly asunder.⁴ For I know

There's none stands under° more calumnious tongues   *is subject to*

Than I myself, poor man.

KING HENRY   Stand up, good Canterbury.

115   Thy truth and thy integrity is rooted

In us, thy friend. Give me thy hand. Stand up.

Prithee, let's walk.

       [CRANMER *rises. They walk*]

            Now, by my halidom,°   *by our Lady*

What manner of man are you? My lord, I looked°   *predicted*

---

3. *must . . . you:* must be patient.
4. *And am . . . asunder:* And I am glad to have the occasion thoroughly to see the bad ("chaff") separated from the good ("corn," or wheat) in my character. See Matthew 3:12 and Luke 3:17.

You would have given me your petition that
I should have ta'en some pains to bring together
Yourself and your accusers, and to have heard you
Without indurance° further.   *imprisonment*

CRANMER   Most dread liege,
The good° I stand on is my truth and honesty.   *virtue*
If they shall fail, I with mine enemies
Will triumph o'er my person, which I weigh not,
Being of those virtues vacant.⁵ I fear nothing°   *not at all*
What can be said against me.

KING HENRY   Know you not
How your state stands i'th' world, with the whole world?
Your enemies are many, and not small;° their practices *insignificant*
Must bear the same proportion, and not ever
The justice and the truth o'th' question carries
The dew o'th' verdict with it.⁶ At what ease°   *How easily*
Might corrupt minds procure knaves as corrupt
To swear against you? Such things have been done.
You are potently° opposed, and with a malice   *powerfully*
Of as great size. Ween you of ° better luck,   *Do you anticipate*
I mean in perjured witness,° than your master,°   *evidence / Christ*
Whose minister you are, whiles here he lived
Upon this naughty° earth? Go to, go to.   *wicked*
You take a precipice for no leap of danger,
And woo your own destruction.

CRANMER   God and your majesty
Protect mine innocence, or I fall into
The trap is° laid for me.   *that is*

KING HENRY   Be of good cheer.
They shall no more prevail than we give way to.°   *let them*
Keep comfort to you, and this morning see
You do appear before them. If they shall chance,
In charging you with matters, to commit° you,   *imprison*
The best persuasions to the contrary
Fail not to use, and with what vehemency
Th'occasion shall instruct you. If entreaties
Will render you no remedy, [*giving his ring*] this ring
Deliver them, and your appeal to us
There make before them.

                    [CRANMER *weeps*]
                              Look, the good man weeps.
He's honest, on mine honour. God's blest mother,
I swear he is true-hearted, and a soul
None better in my kingdom. Get you gone,
And do as I have bid you.   *Exit* CRANMER
                              He has strangled
His language in his tears.
               Enter [*the*] OLD LADY
LOVELL (*within*)   Come back! What mean you?
          [*Enter* LOVELL, *following her*]
OLD LADY   I'll not come back. The tidings that I bring

---

5. *If . . . vacant:* If I lack truth and honesty, I will agree
with my enemies in condemning myself, whom I do not
value in the absence of truth and honesty.
6. *their . . . it:* their schemes are equally numerous and

powerful, and justice and truth do not always prevail.
"Dew" suggests fecundity or generosity; there may also
be a sense of "due," implying justness.

160   Will make my boldness manners.° [*To the* KING] Now good angels   *into manners*
           Fly o'er thy royal head, and shade thy person
           Under their blessèd wings.
     KING HENRY   Now by thy looks
           I guess thy message. Is the Queen delivered?
           Say, 'Ay, and of a boy.'
     OLD LADY   Ay, ay, my liege,
165   And of a lovely boy. The God of heaven
           Both now and ever bless her! 'Tis a girl°   *Anne; Elizabeth*
           Promises boys hereafter. Sir, your queen
           Desires your visitation, and° to be   *and for you*
           Acquainted with this stranger. 'Tis as like you
           As cherry is to cherry.
     KING HENRY   Lovell—
170   LOVELL   Sir?
     KING HENRY   Give her an hundred marks.° I'll to the Queen.   *roughly 65 pounds*
                                            Exit
     OLD LADY   An hundred marks? By this light, I'll ha' more.
           An ordinary groom is for° such payment.   *deserves*
           I will have more, or scold it out of him.
175   Said I for this the girl was like to him? I'll
           Have more, or else unsay't; and now, while 'tis hot,
           I'll put it to the issue.   *Exeunt*

5.2

Enter [pursuivants,° pages, footboys, and grooms. Then   *messengers*
enter] CRANMER, *Archbishop of Canterbury*
     CRANMER   I hope I am not too late, and yet the gentleman
           That was sent to me from the council prayed me
           To make great haste. All fast?° What means this? [*Calling at*   *The doors closed*
           the door] Ho!
           Who waits there?
           Enter [a DOOR]KEEPER
                 Sure you know me?
     DOORKEEPER   Yes, my lord,
           But yet I cannot help you.
5   CRANMER   Why?
           Enter Doctor BUTTS [*passing over the stage*]
     DOORKEEPER   Your grace must wait till you be called for.
     CRANMER   So.
     BUTTS [*aside*]   This is a piece of malice. I am glad
           I came this way so happily.° The King   *fortunately*
           Shall understand it presently.°   *Exit*   *immediately*
     CRANMER [*aside*]   'Tis Butts,
10   The King's physician. As he passed along
           How earnestly he cast his eyes upon me!
           Pray heaven he sound° not my disgrace. For certain   *fathom; publicize*
           This is of purpose laid° by some that hate me—   *carried out*
           God turn their hearts, I never sought their malice—
15   To quench° mine honour. They would shame to make me   *destroy*
           Wait else at door, a fellow Councillor,
           'Mong boys, grooms, and lackeys. But their pleasures
           Must be fulfilled, and I attend with patience.

5.2 Location: Anteroom and council chamber at court.

Enter KING [HENRY] *and* [*Doctor*] BUTTS *at a window,*
above

BUTTS I'll show your grace the strangest sight—

KING HENRY   What's that, Butts?

20 BUTTS I think your highness saw this many a day.

KING HENRY Body o'me, where is it?

BUTTS [*pointing at* CRANMER, *below*] There, my lord.
The high promotion of his grace of Canterbury,
Who holds his state° at door, 'mongst pursuivants,   *waits with dignity*
Pages, and footboys.

KING HENRY   Ha? 'Tis he indeed.

25 Is this the honour they do one another?
'Tis well there's one above 'em[1] yet. I had thought
They had parted° so much honesty among 'em—   *shared*
At least good manners—as not thus to suffer
A man of his place° and so near our favour   *rank*

30 To dance attendance on their lordships' pleasures,
And at the door, too, like a post with packets!°   *courier with letters*
By holy Mary, Butts, there's knavery!
Let 'em alone, and draw the curtain close.
We shall hear more anon.

[CRANMER *and the* DOORKEEPER *stand to one side.*
Exeunt the lackeys]
[*Above,* BUTTS *partly draws the curtain close. Below,*][2] *a*
council table [*is*] *brought in* [*along*] *with chairs and*
stools, and placed under the [*cloth of*] *state. Enter* [*the*]
LORD CHANCELLOR, [*who*] *places himself at the upper*
end of the table, on the left hand, [*leaving*] *a seat void*
above him [*at the table's head*] *as*° *for Canterbury's seat.*   *as if*
[*The*] *Duke of* SUFFOLK, [*the*] *Duke of* NORFOLK, [*the*
Earl of] SURREY, [*the*] LORD CHAMBERLAIN, [*and*] GARDI-
NER, [*the Bishop of Winchester,*] *seat themselves in order*
on each side [*of the table*]. CROMWELL [*sits*] *at* [*the*]
lower end, [*and acts*] *as secretary*

35 LORD CHANCELLOR [*to* CROMWELL] Speak to the business, master secretary.
Why are we met in council?

CROMWELL   Please your honours,
The chief cause concerns his grace of Canterbury.

GARDINER Has he had° knowledge of it?   *been given*

CROMWELL   Yes.

NORFOLK [*to the* DOORKEEPER]   Who waits there?

DOORKEEPER [*coming forward*]
Without,° my noble lords?   *Outside*

GARDINER   Yes.

DOORKEEPER   My lord Archbishop;

40 And has done half an hour, to know your pleasures.

LORD CHANCELLOR Let him come in.

DOORKEEPER [*to* CRANMER]   Your grace may enter now.

CRANMER *approaches the Council table*

LORD CHANCELLOR My good lord Archbishop, I'm very sorry
To sit here at this present° and behold   *moment*

---

1. Both God and King, here implicitly linked.
2. Some editions begin a new scene here. But Cranmer
should be visible throughout, and the King and Butts

stay sequestered in the gallery above the stage until the
King's abrupt entrance.

That chair stand empty, but we all are men
45   In our own natures frail, and capable°   *prone to failings*
Of our flesh; few are angels; out of which frailty
And want° of wisdom, you, that best should teach us,   *lack*
Have misdemeaned yourself,° and not a little,   *behaved badly*
Toward the King first, then his laws, in filling
50   The whole realm, by your teaching and your chaplains'—
For so we are informed—with new opinions,
Diverse and dangerous, which are heresies,
And, not reformed, may prove pernicious.°   *lethal*
GARDINER   Which reformation must be sudden too,
55   My noble lords; for those that tame wild horses
Pace 'em not in their hands to make 'em gentle,[3]
But stop their mouths with stubborn bits and spur 'em
Till they obey the manège.° If we suffer,°   *training / allow*
Out of our easiness° and childish pity   *leniency*
60   To one man's honour, this contagious sickness,
Farewell all physic°—and what follows then?   *remedies*
Commotions, uproars—with a general taint
Of the whole state, as of late days our neighbours,
The upper Germany, can dearly witness,[4]
65   Yet freshly pitied in our memories.
CRANMER   My good lords, hitherto in all the progress
Both of my life and office, I have laboured,
And with no little study,° that my teaching   *effort*
And the strong course of my authority
70   Might go one way, and safely; and the end
Was ever to do well. Nor is there living—
I speak it with a single° heart, my lords—   *pure*
A man that more detests, more stirs against,°   *actively resists*
Both in his private conscience and his place,°   *office*
75   Defacers° of a public peace than I do.   *Destroyers*
Pray heaven the King may never find a heart
With less allegiance in it. Men that make
Envy and crooked malice nourishment
Dare bite the best. I do beseech your lordships
80   That, in this case of justice, my accusers,
Be what they will,° may stand forth face to face,   *Whoever they are*
And freely urge against° me.   *openly accuse*
SUFFOLK   Nay, my lord,
That cannot be. You are a Councillor,
And by that virtue° no man dare accuse you.   *by virtue of that*
GARDINER [*to* CRANMER]   My lord, because we have business of
85   more moment,°   *import*
We will be short° with you. 'Tis his highness' pleasure   *brief*
And our consent, for better trial of you,
From hence you be committed to the Tower
Where, being but a private man again,
90   You shall know many dare accuse you boldly,
More than, I fear, you are provided for.°   *ready for*
CRANMER   Ah, my good lord of Winchester, I thank you.
You are always my good friend. If your will pass,°   *is approved*

---

3. Do not put them through their paces with only a hand for restraint.
4. Alluding to Protestant sects in Germany who fomented uprisings in urban centers in the 1520s and 1530s (the Peasants' War, 1524–26, and perhaps the killing of the Münster Anabaptists in 1535).

I shall both find your lordship judge and juror,[5]

95   You are so merciful. I see your end°—   *aim*

'Tis my undoing. Love and meekness, lord,

Become a churchman better than ambition.

Win straying souls with modesty again;

Cast none away. That I shall clear myself,

100   Lay all the weight ye can upon my patience,

I make as little doubt as you do conscience[6]

In doing daily wrongs. I could say more,

But reverence to your calling makes me modest.°   *temperate*

GARDINER   My lord, my lord—you are a sectary,°   *Protestant*

105   That's the plain truth. Your painted gloss discovers,

To men that understand you, words and weakness.[7]

CROMWELL [*to* GARDINER]   My lord of Winchester, you're a little,

By your good favour,° too sharp. Men so noble,   *If you'll excuse me*

However faulty, yet should find° respect   *be offered*

110   For what they have been. 'Tis a cruelty

To load° a falling man.   *burden further*

GARDINER   Good master secretary,

I cry your honour mercy.[8] You may worst°   *least justifiably*

Of all this table say so.

CROMWELL   Why, my lord?

GARDINER   Do not I know you for a favourer

Of this new sect? Ye are not sound.°   *loyal; orthodox*

115 CROMWELL   Not sound?

GARDINER   Not sound, I say.

CROMWELL   Would you were half so honest!

Men's prayers then would seek you, not their fears.

GARDINER   I shall remember this bold language.

CROMWELL   Do.

Remember your bold life, too.

LORD CHANCELLOR   This is too much.

Forbear, for shame, my lords.

GARDINER   I have done.

120 CROMWELL   And I.

LORD CHANCELLOR [*to* CRANMER]   Then thus for you, my lord. It

       stands agreed,

I take it, by all voices,° that forthwith   *votes*

You be conveyed to th' Tower a prisoner,

There to remain till the King's further pleasure

125   Be known unto us. Are you all agreed, lords?

ALL THE COUNCIL   We are.

CRANMER   Is there no other way of mercy,

But I must needs to° th' Tower, my lords?   *must go to*

GARDINER   What other

Would you expect? You are strangely° troublesome.   *extraordinarily*

Let some o'th' guard be ready there.

       Enter the guard

CRANMER   For me?

Must I go like a traitor thither?

130 GARDINER [*to the guard*]   Receive° him,   *Take*

And see him safe i'th' Tower.

---

5. Gardiner would both try (as "judge") and pass judgment (as "juror")—to Cranmer, an injustice.
6. I doubt no more than you act ethically.
7. *Your . . . weakness*: Your false exterior (or, perhaps, your specious language) exposes, to men who can see through you, empty words and human frailty.
8. I beg your pardon.

CRANMER   Stay, good my lords.
I have a little yet to say. Look there, my lords—
        [*He shows the King's ring*]
      By virtue of that ring I take my cause
      Out of the grips° of cruel men, and give it   clutches
135   To a most noble judge, the King my master.
LORD CHAMBERLAIN   This is the King's ring.
SURREY   'Tis no counterfeit.
SUFFOLK   'Tis the right ring, by heav'n. I told ye all
      When we first put this dangerous stone a-rolling
      'Twould fall upon ourselves.
NORFOLK   Do you think, my lords,
140   The King will suffer but the little finger
      Of this man to be vexed?
LORD CHAMBERLAIN   'Tis now too certain.
      How much more is his life in value with him!°   esteemed by the King
      Would I were fairly out on't.°   out of (the plot)
                  [*Exit* KING *with* BUTTS *above*]
CROMWELL   My mind gave me,°   I suspected
      In seeking tales and informations
145   Against this man, whose honesty the devil
      And his disciples only envy at,°   covet; despise
      Ye blew the fire that burns ye. Now have at ye!°   be on guard
                  Enter [*below*,] KING [HENRY] *frowning on them*.
                  [*He*] *takes his seat*
GARDINER   Dread sovereign, how much are we bound to heaven
      In daily thanks, that gave us such a prince,
150   Not only good and wise, but most religious.
      One that in all obedience makes the church
      The chief aim of his honour, and, to strengthen
      That holy duty, out of dear respect,°   sincere piety
      His royal self in judgement comes to hear
155   The cause betwixt her° and this great offender.   (the Church)
KING HENRY   You were ever good at sudden commendations,°   extempore flattery
      Bishop of Winchester. But know I come not
      To hear such flattery now; and in my presence
      They are too thin and base to hide offences.
160   To me you cannot reach. You play the spaniel,
      And think with wagging of your tongue to win me.
      But whatsoe'er thou tak'st me for, I'm sure
      Thou hast a cruel nature and a bloody.
      [*To* CRANMER] Good man, sit down.
                  [CRANMER *takes his seat at the head of the Council*
                  table]
                                  Now let me see the proudest,
165   He° that dares most, but wag his finger at thee.   The man
      By all that's holy, he had better starve°   die
      Than but once think this place becomes thee not.
SURREY   May it please your grace—
KING HENRY   No, sir, it does not please me!
      I had thought I had had men of some understanding
170   And wisdom of° my Council, but I find none.   in
      Was it discretion, lords, to let this man,
      This good man—few of you deserve that title—
      This honest man, wait like a lousy footboy

At chamber door? And one as great as you are?
175 Why, what a shame° was this! Did my commission   *shameful act*
Bid ye so far forget yourselves? I gave ye
Power as he was a Councillor to try him,
Not as a groom. There's some of ye, I see,
More out of malice than integrity,
180 Would try him to the utmost, had ye mean;°   *the means*
Which ye shall never have while I live.
LORD CHANCELLOR   Thus far,
My most dread sovereign, may it like° your grace   *please*
To let my tongue excuse all. What was purposed°   *intended*
Concerning his imprisonment was rather—
185 If there be faith in men—meant for his trial
And fair purgation° to the world than malice,   *acquittal of suspicion*
I'm sure, in me.
KING HENRY   Well, well, my lords—respect him.
Take him and use him well, he's worthy of it.
I will say thus much for him—if a prince
190 May be beholden to a subject, I
Am for his love and service so to him.
Make me no more ado, but all embrace him.
Be friends, for shame, my lords. (*To* CRANMER) My lord of Canterbury,
I have a suit which you must not deny me:
195 That is a fair young maid that yet wants baptism—
You must be godfather, and answer for her.
CRANMER   The greatest monarch now alive may glory
In such an honour; how may I deserve it,
That am a poor and humble subject to you?
200 KING HENRY   Come, come, my lord—you'd spare your spoons.⁹
You shall have two noble partners with you—the old Duchess
of Norfolk and Lady Marquis Dorset. Will these please you?
[*To* GARDINER] Once more, my lord of Winchester, I charge you
Embrace and love this man.
GARDINER   With a true heart
And brother-love I do it.
       [GARDINER *and* CRANMER *embrace*]
205 CRANMER [*weeping*]   And let heaven
Witness how dear I hold this confirmation.
KING HENRY   Good man, those joyful tears show thy true heart.
The common voice,° I see, is verified   *opinion*
Of thee which says thus, 'Do my lord of Canterbury
210 A shrewd turn,° and he's your friend for ever.'   *An act of malice*
Come, lords, we trifle time away. I long
To have this young one made a Christian.
As I have made ye one, lords, one remain—
So I grow stronger, you more honour gain.   *Exeunt*

5.3

Noise and tumult within.° Enter PORTER [*with rushes*]   *offstage*
       and his MAN [*with a broken cudgel*]
PORTER [*to those within*]   You'll leave° your noise anon, ye rascals.   *stop*
       Do you take

---

9. The King teases Cranmer that he hesitates only because   spoons, the customary gift from a godparent to a child.
he wants to spare himself the expense of christening   **5.3** Location: The palace yard.

The court for Paris Garden,[1] ye rude slaves?
Leave your gaping.°   *yelling*
ONE (*within*)   Good master porter, I belong to th' larder.°   *serve in the pantry*
5   PORTER   Belong to th' gallows, and be hanged, ye rogue!
Is this a place to roar in?
[*To his* MAN] Fetch me a dozen crab-tree staves, and strong ones,
[*Raising his rushes*] These are but switches to 'em.
[*To those within*]   I'll scratch your heads.
You must be seeing christenings? Do you look
10   For ale and cakes here, you rude rascals?
MAN   Pray, sir, be patient. 'Tis as much impossible,
Unless we sweep 'em from the door with cannons,
To scatter 'em as 'tis to make 'em sleep
On May-day morning[2]—which will never be.
15   We may as well push against Paul's° as stir 'em.   *St. Paul's Cathedral*
PORTER   How got they in, and be hanged?°   *(a curse or expletive)*
MAN   Alas, I know not. How gets the tide in?
As much as one sound cudgel° of four foot—   *club*
[*He raises his cudgel*]
You see the poor remainder°—could distribute,   *what's left of it*
I made no spare,° sir.   *spared no one*
20   PORTER   You did nothing, sir.
MAN   I am not Samson, nor Sir Guy, nor Colbrand,[3]
To mow 'em down before me; but if I spared any
That had a head to hit, either young or old,
He or she, cuckold or cuckold-maker,
25   Let me ne'er hope to see a chine° again—   *cut of beef*
And that I would not for a cow,° God save her!   *for anything*
ONE (*within*)   Do you hear, master porter?
PORTER   I shall be with you presently,
Good master puppy. [*To his* MAN] Keep the door close, sirrah.
MAN   What would you have me do?
30   PORTER   What should you do,
but knock 'em down by th' dozens? Is this Moorfields[4] to muster in? Or have we some strange Indian with the great tool
come to court,[5] the women so besiege us? Bless me, what a fry
of fornication[6] is at door! On my Christian conscience, this one
35   christening will beget a thousand. Here will be father, godfather, and all together.
MAN   The spoons° will be the bigger, sir. There is a fellow some-   *(for christening)*
what near the door, he should be a brazier° by his face, for o'   *brass worker*
my conscience twenty of the dog-days° now reign in's nose. All   *hottest summer days*
40   that stand about him are under the line[7]—they need no other
penance. That fire-drake° did I hit three times on the head, and   *fiery dragon*
three times was his nose discharged against me. He stands there
like a mortar-piece, to blow us.[8] There was a haberdasher's wife
of small wit near him, that railed upon me till her pinked por-

1. A park for bear- and bullbaiting located in Southwark, a London suburb, where the Globe Theatre also stood.
2. On May Day, revelers rose before dawn for festivities to greet spring.
3. Figures of legendary physical powers. In the Bible, Samson is renowned for his strength; in the romance tradition, Sir Guy of Warwick, who killed the Danish giant Colebrand, was also known for his prowess.
4. Parkland outside London's walls where citizen militias may have trained.
5. Indians brought to England and exhibited at court excited popular fascination, here about their genitalia.
6. Crowd of would-be fornicators or bastards.
7. All those near him seem to be standing at the equator, his face is so red.
8. Like a cannon, ready to blow us up; ready to blow his nose at us.

45   ringer[9] fell off her head, for kindling such a combustion° in the   *tumult*
     state. I missed the meteor° once, and hit that woman, who cried   *brazier*
     out 'Clubs!',[1] when I might see from far some forty truncheon-
     ers° draw to her succour, which were the hope o'th' Strand,[2]   *men with cudgels*
     where she was quartered.° They fell on.° I made good my place.   *lived / attacked*
50   At length they came to th' broomstaff to° me. I defied 'em still,   *right next to*
     when suddenly a file of boys behind 'em, loose shot,[3] delivered
     such a shower of pebbles that I was fain° to draw mine honour   *obliged*
     in and let 'em win the work.° The devil was amongst 'em, I   *fort*
     think, surely.
55   PORTER   These are the youths° that thunder at a playhouse, and   *apprentices*
     fight for bitten apples, that no audience but the tribulation of
     Tower Hill or the limbs of Limehouse,[4] their dear brothers, are
     able to endure. I have some of 'em in *limbo patrum*,[5] and there
     they are like to dance these three days, besides the running
60   banquet of two beadles that is to come.[6]
                  Enter [the] LORD CHAMBERLAIN
     LORD CHAMBERLAIN   Mercy o' me, what a multitude are here!
     They grow still, too—from all parts they are coming,
     As if we kept a fair here! Where are these porters,
     These lazy knaves? [*To the* PORTER *and his* MAN] You've made
          a fine hand,° fellows!   *nice work (ironic)*
65   There's a trim° rabble let in—are all these   *an elegant (ironic)*
     Your faithful friends o'th' suburbs?[7] we shall have
     Great store of room, no doubt, left for the ladies
     When they pass back from the christening!
     PORTER   An't° please your honour,   *If it*
     We are but men, and what so many may do,
70   Not being torn a-pieces, we have done.
     An army cannot rule 'em.°   *keep them in order*
     LORD CHAMBERLAIN   As I live,
     If the King blame me for't, I'll lay ye all
     By th' heels,° and suddenly—and on your heads   *In the stocks*
     Clap round° fines for neglect. You're lazy knaves,   *large*
75   And here ye lie baiting of bombards° when   *you lie drinking*
     Ye should do service.
                  [*Flourish of trumpets within*]
                               Hark, the trumpets sound.
     They're come, already, from the christening.
     Go break among the press,° and find a way out   *crowd*
     To let the troop pass fairly,° or I'll find   *fittingly*
80   A Marshalsea shall hold ye play[8] these two months.
                  [*As they leave, the* PORTER *and his* MAN *call within*]
     PORTER   Make way there for the Princess!

---

9. Perforated small cap.
1. London apprentices would shout this when about to begin or end a street fight.
2. Fashionable shopping and residential part of London.
3. Marksmen (here, throwers) unattached to a company.
4. The tough crowds at the Tower for executions; or further east in Limehouse, a rough part of London near the docks.
5. In prison (literally, limbo of the fathers). Jewish patriarchs, because they predated Christ, at death went not to Christian heaven but to limbo, near hell, where

they remained until Judgment Day. With echoes of "limbs of Limehouse" (line 57).
6. *dance . . . come*: festive celebration ("dance") with dessert ("running banquet"); public whipping of prisoners (like a "running banquet," or dessert) after imprisonment (the main course) by minor law-enforcement officials ("beadles").
7. From the suburbs, areas outside London's city walls, beyond the city's legal jurisdiction, and hence considered lawless.
8. *I'll . . . play*: I'll shut you in the Marshalsea, a prison in Southwark.

MAN   You great fellow,[9]

Stand close up,° or I'll make your head ache.   *Move aside*

PORTER   You i'th' camlet,° get up o'th' rail—   *rough cloth*

I'll peck you o'er the pales else.[1]   *Exeunt*

5.4

Enter trumpet[er]s, sounding. Then [enter] two alder-
men, [the] Lord Mayor [of London], GARTER [King-of-
Arms], CRANMER [the Archbishop of Canterbury, the]
Duke of NORFOLK with his marshal's staff, [the] Duke of
SUFFOLK, two noblemen bearing great standing bowls for
the christening gifts; then [enter] four noblemen bearing
a canopy, under which [is] the Duchess of Norfolk, god-
mother, bearing the child [Elizabeth] richly habited in a
mantle, [whose] train [is] borne by a lady. Then follows
the Marchioness Dorset, the other godmother, and
ladies. The troop pass once about the stage and GARTER
speaks

GARTER   Heaven, from thy endless goodness send prosperous
life, long, and ever happy, to the high and mighty Princess of
England, Elizabeth.[1]

Flourish. Enter KING [HENRY] and guard

CRANMER *[kneeling]*   And to your royal grace, and the good Queen!

5   My noble partners° and myself thus pray   *fellow godparents*
All comfort, joy, in this most gracious lady,
Heaven ever laid up to make parents happy,
May hourly fall upon ye.

KING HENRY   Thank you, good lord Archbishop.
What is her name?

CRANMER   Elizabeth.

KING HENRY   Stand up, lord.

[CRANMER rises]

[To the child] With this kiss take my blessing—

[He kisses the child]

10   God protect thee,
Into whose hand I give thy life.

CRANMER   Amen.

KING HENRY *[to CRANMER, old duchess, and Marchioness]*
My noble gossips,° you've been too prodigal.°   *godparents / generous*
I thank ye heartily. So shall this lady,
When she has so much English.

CRANMER   Let me speak, sir,

15   For heaven now bids me, and the words I utter
Let none think flattery, for they'll find 'em truth.
This royal infant—heaven still° move about her—   *always*
Though in her cradle, yet now promises
Upon this land a thousand thousand blessings

20   Which time shall bring to ripeness. She shall be—
But few now living can behold that goodness—
A pattern to all princes living with her,

9. Addressed to someone either onstage or in the audience.
1. *get . . . else:* get off the rail (the railing running
around the edge of the stage), or I'll throw you off.
5.4 Location: The court.
1. This formulaic speech is similar to one given at the 1613

wedding of King James I's daughter Elizabeth to Prince
Frederick, the Elector Palatine. This scene parallels the
christening celebration of one Princess Elizabeth, in
the play, to the wedding celebration of another, at the
time of the play's first production.

And all that shall succeed. Saba[2] was never
More covetous° of wisdom and fair virtue   *desirous*
25 Than this pure soul shall be. All princely graces
That mould up° such a mighty piece° as this is,   *produce / masterpiece*
With all the virtues that attend the good,
Shall still be doubled on her. Truth shall nurse her,
Holy and heavenly thoughts still counsel her.
30 She shall be loved and feared. Her own° shall bless her;   *own people*
Her foes shake like a field of beaten° corn,   *windswept*
And hang their heads with sorrow. Good grows with her.
In her days every man shall eat in safety
Under his own vine what he plants, and sing
35 The merry songs of peace to all his neighbours.
God shall be truly known,° and those about her   *(via Protestantism)*
From her shall read° the perfect ways of honour,   *learn*
And by those claim their greatness, not by blood.
Nor shall this peace sleep with her, but, as when
40 The bird of wonder dies—the maiden phoenix[3]—
Her ashes new create another heir
As great in admiration° as herself,   *deserving of wonder*
So shall she leave her blessèdness to one,°   *(James I)*
When heaven shall call her from this cloud of darkness,°   *earthly state*
45 Who from the sacred ashes of her honour
Shall star-like rise as great in fame as she was,
And so stand fixed. Peace, plenty, love, truth, terror,
That were the servants to this chosen infant,
Shall then be his, and, like a vine, grow to him.
50 Wherever the bright sun of heaven shall shine,
His honour and the greatness of his name
Shall be, and make new nations.[4] He shall flourish,
And like a mountain cedar reach his branches
To all the plains about him. Our children's children
Shall see this, and bless heaven.
55 KING HENRY   Thou speakest wonders.
CRANMER   She shall be, to the happiness of England,
An agèd princess. Many days shall see her,
And yet no day without a deed° to crown it.   *an accomplishment*
Would I had known no more. But she must die—
60 She must, the saints must have her—yet a virgin,
A most unspotted lily shall she pass
To th' ground, and all the world shall mourn her.
KING HENRY   O lord Archbishop,
Thou hast made me now a man. Never before
65 This happy child did I get° anything.   *beget; achieve*
This oracle of comfort has so pleased me
That when I am in heaven I shall desire
To see what this child does, and praise my maker.
I thank ye all. To you, my good Lord Mayor,

---

2. The Queen of Sheba visited Solomon in Jerusalem in order to benefit from his wisdom, and thus became a model for wise (but presumably deferential) women. See 1 Kings 10:1–10.

3. Mythical Arabian bird, the only one of its kind, who, when it dies after a long life, regenerates itself from its own ashes. James I inherits the spirit of the phoenix, Queen Elizabeth—a spirit now, perhaps, being passed on to his daughter Princess Elizabeth.

4. See Genesis 17:4: "A father of many nations have I made thee." The passage was frequently invoked in relation to Princess Elizabeth's marriage. The play here also compliments James on the "new nation" he has established in America, appropriately named Virginia after the "virgin" Queen Elizabeth (line 60).

70   And your good brethren, I am much beholden.
      I have received much honour by your presence,
      And ye shall find me thankful. Lead the way, lords.
      Ye must all see the Queen, and she must thank ye.
      She will be sick° else. This day, no man think   *unhappy*
75   He's business at his house, for all shall stay°—   *stop work*
      This little one shall make it holiday.   [*Flourish.*] *Exeunt*

Epilogue

          [*Enter* EPILOGUE]
      EPILOGUE   'Tis ten to one this play can never please
          All that are here. Some come to take their ease,
          And sleep an act or two; but those, we fear,
          We've frighted with our trumpets; so, 'tis clear,
5   They'll say 'tis naught.° Others to hear the city   *worth nothing*
          Abused extremely, and to cry 'That's witty!'[1]—
          Which we have not done neither; that,° I fear,   *such that*
          All the expected good° we're like to hear   *anticipated praise*
          For this play at this time is only in
10   The merciful construction of ° good women,   *interpretation by*
          For such a one we showed 'em. If they smile,
          And say ''Twill do', I know within a while
          All the best men are ours—for 'tis ill hap°   *luck*
          If they hold° when their ladies bid 'em clap.   [*Exit*]   *refrain*

Epilogue
1. "The city," both London and its citizens, was sati-
rized in "city comedies" at the private theaters (as
opposed to public playhouses like the Globe, whose
leading dramatist here retaliates).

And your good brethren, I am much beholden.
I have received much honour by your presence,
And ye shall find me thankful. Lead the way, lords.
Ye must all see the Queen, and she must thank ye,
She will be sick else. This day, no man think
Has business at his house, for all shall stay—
This little one shall make it holiday.

[Flourish.] Exeunt

Epilogue

[Enter Epilogue.]

EPILOGUE   'Tis ten to one this play can never please
All that are here. Some come to take their ease
And sleep an act or two; but those, we fear,
We've frighted with our trumpets; so, 'tis clear,
They'll say 'tis naught. Others to hear the city
Abused extremely, and to cry 'That's witty!'—
Which we have not done neither; that, I fear,
All the expected good we're like to hear
For this play at this time is only in
The merciful construction of good women,
For such a one we showed 'em. If they smile,
And say 'twill do, I know within a while
All the best men are ours; for 'tis ill hap
If they hold when their ladies bid 'em clap.

[Exit]

The Two Noble Kinsmen

When Prospero proclaims near the end of *The Tempest* (1611), "But this rough magic / I here abjure" (5.1.50–51), audiences often think they are hearing Shakespeare's farewell to the theater. But the final passage Shakespeare wrote for the stage is more likely to be found at the conclusion of *The Two Noble Kinsmen* (1613–14). Theseus, Duke of Athens, the play's highest-ranking character, attempts to grasp the ironic, paradoxical twists of fate he has witnessed:

> Never fortune
> Did play a subtler game—the conquered triumphs,
> The victor has the loss. Yet in the passage
> The gods have been most equal.
> . . . .
> Let us be thankful
> For that which is, and with you [the gods] leave dispute
> That are above our question. Let's go off
> And bear us like the time.
>
> (5.6.112–37)

It is thus tempting to interpret Theseus's resigned disillusionment as Shakespeare's last word—perhaps on life, certainly on *The Two Noble Kinsmen*. The message of the play is not that easy to determine, however. Theseus's emphasis on the gods, his confidence in their justice (they "have been most equal"), and his counsel of an ambivalent mixture of joy and sorrow ("bear us like the time") underestimate the grim cynicism that accompanies the undeniable pathos of the play. Chivalric military and sexual norms give a touching nobility to the action; but, arguably, they also generate the misery and destruction to which the bewildered Theseus attempts to respond.

The problem of determining the work's tone is related to the question of authorship. Shakespeare probably wrote *The Two Noble Kinsmen* with John Fletcher, a younger contemporary who succeeded him as the leading dramatist of Shakespeare's acting company, the King's Men. Several of Shakespeare's very early and very late plays may have involved collaboration. In his final years, he worked with Fletcher—on the lost *Cardenio* (1612–13; probably based on an episode of Part One of Cervantes's *Don Quixote*, 1605; translated 1612), on *All Is True* (*Henry VIII*; 1613), and on *The Two Noble Kinsmen*. For this last play, Shakespeare seems to have written most of the first and last acts plus a few other scenes, while his colleague composed the rest and, hence, slightly more than half of the work as a whole. (There may also be a third hand involved; see the Textual Note). The two main dramatists differ in style, presentation, and outlook. The rhetorically knotty, ritualistic, near-tragic grandeur in Shakespeare's share contrasts with the syntactically simpler, dramatically more dynamic, near-absurd deflation in Fletcher's. The play as a whole is, therefore, neither simply Shakespearean nor simply Fletcherian. It is the product of their collaboration and is accordingly marked by dissonance as well as unity.

Broadly speaking, *The Two Noble Kinsmen* represents a moment of transition from the more popular theater of Shakespeare's time to the more elite drama of Fletcher's. In many respects, it is typical of the very last phase of Shakespeare's career, and it offers a particularly illuminating comparison to other tragicomic romances written separately by Shakespeare and Fletcher in the preceding six or seven years. Among Shakespeare's leading works in this genre—*Pericles, The Winter's Tale, Cymbeline,* and *The Tempest*—one finds parallels to *The Two Noble Kinsmen*'s medieval source, pseudo-historical ancient Greek setting, emphasis on spectacle and ceremony, defense of innocence in the midst of corruption, striving for self-mastery, and transcendence of self-interest. There are further similarities in the insistence on death as a necessary price of the survivors' happiness, successful supplication to the gods for aid, and consequent sense of a controlling metaphysical presence that orders events in a way that is beyond human control. Although *The Two Noble Kinsmen* occurs exclusively on dry land, the work replicates even the trademark maritime imagery of Shakespearean romance, with its focus on peril and destruction: the dying Arcite "such a vessel 'tis that floats but for / The surge that next approaches" (5.6.83–84).

Yet *The Two Noble Kinsmen* has a very different feel from other romances of the time. As the Prologue explains, "Chaucer, of all admired, the story gives" (line 13). The main plot is taken—with greater freedom by Shakespeare than by Fletcher—from *The Knight's Tale,* which immediately follows *The General Prologue* in *The Canterbury Tales* (late fourteenth century). Its subject is the mortal rivalry between Palamon and Arcite, the two cousins referred to in the title, for the hand of Emilia. But the play's atypicality stems only partly from its resulting stylized chivalric ethos and accompanying acts of courtesy, acts that go beyond even what is found in Chaucer. What sets *The Two Noble Kinsmen* apart is its unusually somber resolution to the impossible dilemmas of the plot. Despite Theseus's assertions, the behavior of the gods does not restore confidence in a benevolent Providence. Indeed, Mars, whose intercession Arcite requests, and Venus, to whom Palamon prays, emblematize the chaos reigning in human affairs. The play is also structurally distinctive. Shakespearean romance reveals the passage from suffering to serenity, the redemption of the older generation by the younger (and particularly by the virtuous daughter). But Shakespeare and Fletcher's play has no interest in the restorative workings of time. All relationships occur within a single generation, and the young woman (Emilia) incites violence rather than reconciliation.

For these reasons, *The Two Noble Kinsmen* is sometimes viewed as an antiromance. As such, it bears comparison both to Shakespeare's other collaborations with Fletcher, noted earlier, and to a number of Shakespeare's earlier plays, which are pervasively echoed particularly in Fletcher's scenes. Palamon and Arcite's initial resignation in prison recalls *Richard II;* their conflict over Emilia, *The Two Gentlemen of Verona;* Emilia's comparison of pictures, *Hamlet.* When Arcite asks for a sign before his decisive battle with Palamon, he correctly takes Mars's answering thunder as a promise of victory. But this reassurance is no less duplicitous than the guarantee that "none of woman born / Shall harm Macbeth" (*Macbeth,* 4.1.96–97), with the important difference that Macbeth is a usurping mass murderer whereas Arcite is guilty only of desiring a woman his cousin saw first. The divine poetic justice often thought to be operating, however deviously, in *Macbeth* seems like little more than a dirty trick in *The Two Noble Kinsmen.*

A similar indebtedness to previous Shakespearean plays marks the subplot, which has no known source and which dramatizes the unrequited love of the Jailer's Daughter for Palamon. It is mainly the work of Fletcher, who borrowed the morris dance before Theseus and Hippolyta in 3.5 not from Shakespeare but from a masque (an aristocratic theatrical event emphasizing song, dance, and spectacle) that Francis Beaumont had composed for court performance in February 1613. (The morris dance itself is a rural folk form often performed on May Day by dancers in outlandish costumes who employ stock characters to partly mime traditional stories.) Otherwise, the Shakespearean legacy is pronounced. The Daughter's fall into madness when ignored by Palamon is modeled on Ophelia's in *Hamlet,* complete with an attempted suicide. Her willow song (4.1.79–80) was earlier sung by Desdemona in *Othello*. The Doctor who prescribes her cure previously ministered to King Lear and rather more unsuccessfully to Lady Macbeth. When the Daughter joins the people whom "ruder tongues distinguish 'villager'" (3.5.106) in the morris dance, the allusion is to another play indebted to *The Knight's Tale*: in *A Midsummer Night's Dream*, "rude mechanicals" (artisans, 3.2.9) also perform before Theseus and Hippolyta on the occasion of their wedding, and unrequited lovers wander through the forest.

But *The Two Noble Kinsmen* is *A Midsummer Night's Dream* with a difference. One of Shakespeare's previous romances, *The Winter's Tale*, might be understood as the tragic jealousy of *Othello* lightened and redeemed by the pastoral experience of a romantic comedy, *As You Like It*. By contrast, in *The Two Noble Kinsmen*, the comic tone of *A Midsummer Night's Dream* is darkened by the intervening experience of *Measure for Measure*, *All's Well That Ends Well*, and especially *Troilus and Cressida*, a work also drawing on Chaucerian narrative to depict a combination of chivalry and sensuality that leads to self-destructive violence and an indifference to the desires of the idealized woman. Indeed, Theseus's final words, quoted earlier, have been likened to Gloucester's metaphysical despair in *King Lear*:

> As flies to wanton boys are we to th' gods;
> They kill us for their sport.
> (Folio, 4.1.37–38)

A geographical and legendary legacy lies behind this outlook. Although the opening scene and the vast majority of the remainder of the play are set in and around Athens, the darker influence of Thebes is immediately felt. In an episode greatly expanded from the source, three widowed queens beg Theseus to come to their aid against Thebes, thus introducing the military dimension of chivalric conduct. Theseus reluctantly yields to Hippolyta's and Emilia's entreaties to defer his own pleasure (marriage to Hippolyta) to help dowagers in distress. His intervention pits him against Palamon and Arcite, who conclude that they must fight for their home city despite their hatred of its ruler, Creon. This initial sequence implicitly invokes Thebes' history of intrafamilial violence. According to ancient Greek narratives, Cadmus sows the soil with serpent's teeth, from which armed men grow; these men slaughter each other and, together with Cadmus, the few survivors found Thebes. Later, Oedipus unwittingly murders his father, and as the play opens, his two sons have killed each other in a battle for the throne that has also widowed the three queens.

The two cousins, imprisoned following Theseus's victory over Thebes, are compelled to repeat this history. When Theseus catches them fighting each other over Emilia, he orders their death, only to reverse his decision at Hippolyta's and Emilia's request. He ultimately proposes a chivalric combat in which each cousin is to be aided by three knights and all members of the losing side are to be executed. This plan increases the expected death toll beyond what is necessary and, indeed, beyond what is found in Chaucer. It is thwarted by the accidental death of Arcite, a death that is hard to see as providential but that undeniably makes Theseus's strategy look bad by comparison. Earlier, Palamon laments "Mars's so-scorned altar" and yearns for war "to get the soldier work, that peace might purge / For her repletion" (1.2.20, 23–24). This image of war as the virtuous means of purging the excesses of peace is echoed in Arcite's prayer to Mars, who

> heal'st with blood
> The earth when it is sick, and cur'st the world
> O'th' plurisy of people.
> (5.1.63–65)

Yet *The Two Noble Kinsmen* sees in war and chivalric combat less a cure for society than a loss of life.

A compulsive sexuality bears much of the blame for the havoc that is wreaked. As Theseus says, "Being sensually subdued / We lose our human title" (1.1.231–32). Arcite and especially Palamon are willing to kill and die for a woman about whom they know nothing except her appearance, and even that only at a distance. Arcite seems partly motivated by competitive emulation, by a desire to spite Palamon. He tells his cousin that when he sees Emilia, he will "pitch between her arms to anger thee" (2.2.221). The kinsmen claim rights to Emilia while serving life sentences in prison and without her being aware of their existence, much less expressing any interest in them. Her feelings don't matter to them. From this perspective, chivalric combat seems an appropriate mechanism for determining which cousin deserves her. In the event, this stance is validated by their society through the intervention of Theseus. Emilia really doesn't have the choice of rejecting them both. When, bowing to the inevitable, she temporarily is attracted to them, she is unable to decide between "two such young handsome men" (4.2.3). She, too, looks only to looks.

Palamon's prayer to Venus unwittingly reveals a simultaneous approval and denigration of sexuality:

> I knew a man
> Of eighty winters, this I told them, who
> A lass of fourteen brided—'twas thy power
> To put life into dust. The agèd cramp
> Had screwed his square foot round,
> The gout had knit his fingers into knots,
> Torturing convulsions from his globy eyes
> Had almost drawn their spheres, that what was life
> In him seemed torture. This anatomy
> Had by his young fair fere a boy, and I
> Believed it was his, for she swore it was,
> And who would not believe her?
>
> (5.2.39–50)

The power of love is thus exalted through deliberately repellent description. The reference to the "boy" anticipates imagery of sexuality and reproduction at the conclusion—

The beginning of *The Knight's Tale*, from *The Workes of Our Ancient and Learned English Poet, Geffrey Chaucer* (1602 ed.).

"consummation," "miscarry," "conceives," "deliver" (5.5.94, 101, 137, 138)—that is unremittingly associated with loss. And the account ends with an apparently rhetorical but actually open question that undermines both Venus's sovereignty and female chastity. The very celebration of love has the effect of raising anxieties about women's fidelity and childbirth.

Heterosexual desire is rendered even more unappealing in *The Two Noble Kinsmen* by the extended representation of what it destroys. This positive alternative is same-sex attachment, whether understood as the Renaissance ideal of male friendship, as girlish intimacy, or as homoerotic attraction. In a romantic comedy such as *Much Ado About Nothing*, the rejection of heterosexual bonding is seen as an immature

The imprisoned Palamon and Arcite gazing at Emilia in the garden below. From a French translation of about 1455 of Giovanni Boccaccio's *Teseida* (the source of Chaucer's *Knight's Tale*), by René of Anjou.

foible to be overcome. Here, however, the movement from same-sex innocence to heterosexual experience is figured primarily as loss—comically in the Prologue, with its comparison of "new plays and maidenheads" (line 1), more grimly thereafter. Although in no other respect an Amazon, Emilia emphatically does prefer virginity and the company of females to the prospect of marriage. She tells Theseus that if he does not grant her petition, she will not "be so hardy / Ever to take a husband" (1.1.203–4). In her sexual joking with her Woman, she says that "men are mad things" (2.2.126) and praises the rose above all other flowers because "it is the very emblem of a maid" (2.2.137). Even after coming to admire the cousins, she still prays to Diana either that the more loving and deserving win her or that she be allowed to continue a virgin "in thy band" (5.3.26). When Theseus tells her, "If you can love, end this difference" by choosing one of the kinsmen, she evasively replies, "I cannot, sir. They are both too excellent" (3.6.277, 285).

This stance is explained by Emilia's earlier touching recollection of her intimacy with Flavina, who died when each was eleven. Her account of two girls who "loved for [simply because] we did" (1.3.61) culminates in this exchange:

> EMILIA   . . . the true love 'tween maid and maid may be
>   More than in sex dividual.
> HIPPOLYTA   You're out of breath,
>   And this high-speeded pace is but to say
>   That you shall never, like the maid Flavina,
>   Love any that's called man.
> EMILIA   I am sure I shall not.
>   (1.3.81–86)

Female friendship thus stands against the absolute monarch's commitment to enforced marriage. Neither she nor the play repudiates this position.

Palamon and Arcite do so, however, choosing to kill and die—and hence to ruin the most precious thing in their lives, their love for each other—out of desire for Emilia. This resolution of the standard Renaissance debate over the respective claims of love and friendship has a paradoxical effect. The very depreciation of the cousins' attachment, which is not emphasized in Chaucer, only highlights its value. When they are first imprisoned, though they regret that life imprisonment precludes marriage and family, their thoughts quickly turn to each other. Arcite recommends "the enjoying of our griefs together" (2.2.60) and misogynistically notes the danger of freedom, which "might, like women / Woo us to wander from" "the ways of honour" (lines 75–76, 73). "Were we at liberty / A wife might part us lawfully," but in prison "we are one another's wife, ever begetting / New births of love" (lines 88–89, 80–81).

As they boast of their loving friendship, Palamon's first sight of Emilia undermines their resolution. She is talking to her Woman about the narcissus flower. This leads her to reflect upon the myth of Narcissus, who fell in love with his own beautiful reflection in a pool and died pining for it: "That was a fair boy, certain, but a fool / To love himself. Were there not maids enough?" (2.2.120–21). This implicit connection between Palamon and Narcissus is made explicit when Emilia remarks that Palamon shows

> not a smile.
> Yet these that we count errors may become him:
> Narcissus was a sad boy, but a heavenly.
> (4.2.30–32)

Palamon's suggested autoeroticism and preference for males over females is anticipated in Emilia's immediately preceding, unequivocally homosexual description of Arcite:

> Just such another wanton Ganymede
> Set Jove afire once, and enforced the god
> Snatch up the goodly boy and set him by him.
> (4.2.15–17)

Similarly, as the cousins prepare to arm and then battle each other, Arcite admiringly remarks, "Defy me in these fair terms, and you show / More than a mistress to me" (3.6.25–26). And most strikingly of all, when Arcite is released from prison, Palamon imagines what would happen if the roles were reversed:

> Were I at liberty I would do things
> Of such a virtuous greatness that this lady,
> This blushing virgin, should take manhood to her
> And seek to ravish me.
> (2.2.260–63)

Even the thought of the woman he loves becomes a fantasy of homosexual rape.

If the play anywhere offers an ideal balance between same-sex and other-sex bonding, it is in Theseus, whose friendship with Pirithous coexists comfortably with his impending marriage to Hippolyta. As suggested earlier, however, Theseus's conduct is open to question. Moreover, it is at least suggested that marriage to Hippolyta will never measure up to friendship with Pirithous. Most important, the catastrophic experience of Emilia and the kinsmen carries far more weight than Theseus's greater success in negotiating potentially antagonistic emotional and sexual attachments. Nonetheless, the figure of Theseus may be crucial to an extended allusion to the Jacobean court in *The Two Noble Kinsmen*. Theseus is perhaps an idealized image of King James, who combined marriage with homosexual behavior. In this interpretation, Arcite's death corresponds to the death of James's oldest son, Prince Henry, in the fall of 1612. The concluding, bittersweet union of Emilia with Palamon similarly parallels the marriage a few months later of James's daughter Elizabeth with the Elector Palatine. The probable revivals of 1619–20 and 1625–26, as well as the publication of the First Quarto in 1634, may also have res-

onated with court life. On the other hand, the evidence is not overwhelming for a direct
connection of the play to the Jacobean court, whose members in any case might not have
been flattered by the comparison. Such questions could not much matter to subsequent
audiences, however, and with the exception of an adaptation in the late 1660s, *The Two
Noble Kinsmen* seems to have remained unstaged until 1928. Since then, performances
have tended to be effective when they have eschewed realism for ritual. But an interesting alternative is provided by a 1979 production, where the decision to employ an all-male
cast emphasized the work's homoerotic motifs.

A joust celebrating the marriage of Henry IV of England to Joan of Navarre. From the
Beauchamp Pageant (1485–90).

In general, however, beginning with the late seventeenth-century adaptation, the most consistently successful feature of the staging has been the Jailer's Daughter, who, though isolated and powerless, often emerges as the drama's central figure. Her four successive soliloquies in the middle of the play (2.4, 2.6, 3.2, 3.4), three of them probably—and the fourth perhaps—by Fletcher, are marked by exclamations, questions, and a consequent intimacy with the audience denied the other characters. The Daughter's special stage position thus helps win sympathy for her. In Shakespeare's plays, this position is characteristically reserved for a lower-class male character, especially the clown or fool, with whom the groundlings might identify. Here, however, we see a meshing of Shakespeare's interest in the folk with Fletcher's in strong women.

The Daughter stands at the center of a subplot that interacts with and critically reflects on the main action. Immediately following some frank sexual talk by the morris dancers in 2.3, she delivers her first soliloquy and then frees Palamon from prison in the hope that he will satisfy her sexual desire for him. Even though the genders are reversed, the situation is the same as in the main plot: the person in love knows little of the beloved, who, in turn, is almost completely oblivious of the lover. When the Daughter later joins the morris dance, she is appropriately cast as the "She-fool" (3.5.138 stage direction). In a dramaturgical sense, she *is* the female equivalent of the fool, for by this time Palamon's indifference has driven her mad. Her illness is cured pragmatically and amorally. On the advice of the Doctor and over the principled objections of her father (the Jailer), the Wooer pretends to be Palamon and makes love with her. Tricked into losing a virginity she was not trying to preserve, "she's well restored / And to be married shortly" (5.6.27–28) to the man who is socially and emotionally right for her. (Earlier, he foils her attempted suicide.) This outcome makes perfect sense in light of Renaissance medicine, which believed hysteria was caused by a wandering womb that could be returned to its proper place by intercourse. More cynically, however, one might conclude that the only thing women really need is sex and that any man will do.

The Daughter thinks she is marrying one man only to end up with another. Similarly, as Emilia settles into her fate, fate forces her to resettle her affections. Neither woman is given a choice—which is just as well, since neither is capable of making distinctions. The generic names in the subplot—Daughter, Jailer, Wooer, Doctor, Brother, Friends—highlight lack of individuality while pointing toward a similar absence in the main plot. The critical effort to discriminate between Palamon and Arcite inadvertently reaffirms what it seeks to deny: that it takes an effort to tell the cousins apart.

Even the Daughter's madness is arguably no more deviant and certainly much less destructive than the suicidal and homicidal behavior of Palamon and Arcite. Yet the two noble kinsmen are taken seriously in a way that she is not. Either because she is a woman or because she is from the lower class or both, she has no right to expect her feelings to be reciprocated, even though she has done more for Palamon than either of the cousins has for Emilia. It is unclear, however, whether the play aims to call attention to this obvious double standard. Ironically, her service to Palamon leads to Arcite's death after earlier bringing Palamon within a hair's breadth of the executioner's ax. Palamon meets the Jailer on his way to the block, graciously acknowledges his gratitude to "your gentle daughter" (5.6.24), and "gives his purse" (5.6.32 stage direction) as part of the dowry for her impending marriage. His generosity infects the other knights slated to die with him:

> FIRST KNIGHT   Nay, let's be offerers all.
> SECOND KNIGHT   Is it a maid?
> PALAMON   Verily, I think so—
>   (5.6.32–33)

Thus, with the play's characteristic irony, "they give their purses" (5.6.35 stage direction) on a doubly false assumption—that they are doomed and that they are contributing to a virgin's dowry. But in another sense, the Daughter is bought off. Palamon speaks with greater accuracy than he knows in saying she is "more to me deserving / Than I can quit [requite] or speak of" (5.6.34–35).

Long before this, the Daughter's sequence of soliloquies has come to an end. In the second half of the play, having moved from one form of folly to another, she appears only in dialogue scenes and hence partly loses her unique contact with the audience. Yet even here, her vigorous language and stage presence produce an immediacy that effectively combines with the pathos of her predicament. It is, finally, a pathos she shares with the characters in the main plot, who watch in bewildered incomprehension as their most cherished ideals fail them when it matters most.

WALTER COHEN

TEXTUAL NOTE

The Two Noble Kinsmen dates from between February 20, 1613, and October 31, 1614. The mention of "our losses" in the Prologue (line 32) has sometimes been taken as a reference to the burning of the Globe Theatre on June 29, 1613. If so, this is Shakespeare's final play, perhaps performed at Blackfriars, the King's Men's indoor theater, in the fall of 1613 or winter of 1614, or at the opening of the rebuilt Globe, their outdoor theater, a year after the fire. Both the only substantive text, the Quarto of 1634 (Q), and an entry from earlier the same year in the Stationers' Register (a listing of books approved for publication), which calls the play a "TragiComedy," attribute it to John Fletcher and Shakespeare. The exclusion of *The Two Noble Kinsmen* from the First Folio of 1623 (F) has sometimes led to doubts about Shakespeare's authorship, but most scholars accept the attribution, which is supported by other internal and external evidence.

Although the exact division of labor between the two playwrights cannot be determined with certainty, Shakespeare probably wrote a little less than half the play: 1.1–2.1 (although some scholars give Fletcher 1.4–1.5), perhaps 2.3, 3.1, perhaps 3.2, perhaps 4.3, 5.1.34–5.3 (although 5.2 is sometimes attributed to Fletcher), and 5.5–5.6. These attributions are necessarily tentative, given the likelihood that the plan of the play changed a bit in the course of composition and that Fletcher undertook some revision to bring the play to its final form—perhaps of Shakespeare's text, perhaps of his own in light of Shakespeare's sections. A further complication is the possible presence of a third, less central, author—either Francis Beaumont, a major collaborator with Fletcher, or, more likely, Nathan Field, who also collaborated with Fletcher at this time and might have been one of the leading actors in the performance of the play.

Q is based either on the authors' manuscript or on a scribal transcript. The latter is the more likely alternative. The manuscript apparently underwent some revision, possibly by an author, perhaps in the Prologue, more probably in 4.2, and especially in 4.3. Whether authorial or scribal, it was annotated with stage directions and other indications (for instance, about props) in preparation for performance, perhaps more than once—for the original production and again for a revival in 1625–26 by Edward Knight, who worked for the King's Men at the time.

Two compositors probably set the type for Q, alternating work quite frequently. The printed text is a good one, but it contains two scenes headed 2.4 (followed by 2.6); editors routinely convert the second 2.4 to 2.5. Q also follows 3.4 with 3.6 and 3.7, perhaps a sign of an original 3.5 that was cut without the subsequent scenes being renumbered, as they are here (as 3.5 and 3.6). In addition, it missets verse as prose and, more often (2.1, 4.3), prose as verse. Some editors have ignored Q's scene break between 2.1 and 2.2 on the grounds that the scene is continuous. As the notes explain, the present edition proposes a staging for the two scenes that justifies the scene division. On the other hand, though again for reasons of staging, this edition expands Q's

5.1 into three scenes: the final three scenes in the play are, therefore, converted from 5.2–4 to 5.4–6.

SELECTED BIBLIOGRAPHY

Berggren, Paula S. "'For what we lack / We laugh': Incompletion and *The Two Noble Kinsmen*." *Modern Language Studies* 14.4 (1984): 3–17. Sees the play as an anti-romance marked by frustrated attempts at action, intensified through the imagery, and by lack of either divine justice or redemptive reconciliation.

Briggs, Julia. "Tears at the Wedding: Shakespeare's Last Phase." *Shakespeare's Late Plays: New Readings.* Ed. Jennifer Richards and James Knowles. Edinburgh: Edinburgh University Press, 1999. 210–27. *The Two Noble Kinsmen* as typical of Shakespeare's late collaborations with Fletcher in its grim posing of irreconcilable choices in the absence of metaphysical consolation.

Bruster, Douglas. "The Jailer's Daughter and the Politics of Madwomen's Language." *Shakespeare Quarterly* 46 (1995): 277–300. Sees the Daughter as powerless and isolated but nonetheless central to the play, her unique language marked by class and gender, her madness constituting a form of resistance; more generally, her depiction understood as the intersection of Shakespeare's interest in the folk and Fletcher's in strong women characters, and also as indicative of a transition to a less popular drama.

Finkelpearl, Philip J. "Two Distincts, Division None: Shakespeare's and Fletcher's *The Two Noble Kinsmen* of 1613." *Elizabethan Theater: Essays in Honor of S. Schoenbaum.* Ed. R. B. Parker and S. P. Zitner. Newark: University of Delaware Press, 1996. 184–99. Shakespearean cosmological concerns versus Fletcher's more worldly and irreverent approach, united by a critical independence from views of honor and chivalry associated with the royal family.

Frey, Charles, ed. *Shakespeare, Fletcher, and "The Two Noble Kinsmen."* Columbia: University of Missouri Press, 1989. A collection of modern criticism together with a review of scholarship on the play.

Herman, Peter C. "'Is This Winning?': Prince Henry's Death and the Problem of Chivalry in *The Two Noble Kinsmen*." *South Atlantic Review* 62 (1997): 1–31. The death of King James's son and heir as a blow to chivalry, generating in the play a skepticism about its martial and erotic implications.

Potter, Lois, ed. *The Two Noble Kinsmen.* 3rd ed. Walton-on-Thames, Surrey: Thomas Nelson, 1997. Outstanding scholarly edition with a lengthy critical introduction.

Shannon, Laurie J. "Emilia's Argument: Friendship and 'Human Title' in *The Two Noble Kinsmen*." *English Literary Renaissance* 64 (1997): 657–682. Emilia as Amazonian rational advocate of female friendship (understood as chastity, homoeroticism, and conscience) against irrational absolute power (understood as imposing the obligation to marry).

Spencer, Theodore. "*The Two Noble Kinsmen*." *Modern Philology* 36 (1939): 255–76. Contrasts the ritualistic action and convoluted rhetoric of Shakespeare's scenes with the greater emotional intensity but slighter thematic depth of Fletcher's.

Stewart, Alan. "'Near Akin': The Trials of Friendship in *The Two Noble Kinsmen*." *Shakespeare's Late Plays: New Readings.* Ed. Jennifer Richards and James Knowles. Edinburgh: Edinburgh University Press, 1999. 57–71. The main plot as the failure of idealized male friendship and especially kinship, showing the incompatibility of classical and chivalric ideals with Jacobean social reality.

The Two Noble Kinsmen

THE PERSONS OF THE PLAY

PROLOGUE
THESEUS, Duke of Athens
HIPPOLYTA, Queen of the Amazons, later wife of Theseus
EMILIA, her sister
PIRITHOUS, friend of Theseus
PALAMON ⎱ the two noble kinsmen, cousins, nephews of
ARCITE ⎰ Creon, the King of Thebes
Hymen, god of marriage
A BOY, who sings
ARTESIUS, an Athenian soldier
Three QUEENS, widows of kings killed in the siege of Thebes
VALERIUS, a Theban
A HERALD
WOMAN, attending Emilia
An Athenian GENTLEMAN
MESSENGERS
Six KNIGHTS, three attending Arcite and three Palamon
A SERVANT
A JAILER in charge of Theseus' prison
The JAILER'S DAUGHTER
The JAILER'S BROTHER
The WOOER of the Jailer's daughter
Two FRIENDS of the Jailer
A DOCTOR
Six COUNTRYMEN, one dressed as a babion, or baboon
Gerald, a SCHOOLMASTER
NELL, a country wench
Four other country wenches: Friz, Madeline, Luce, and
   Barbara
Timothy, a TABORER
EPILOGUE
Nymphs, attendants, maids, executioner, guard

Prologue

Flourish.° [*Enter* PROLOGUE]   *Trumpet call*

PROLOGUE   New plays and maidenheads are near akin:
   Much followed both, for both much money giv'n
   If they stand sound and well.[1] And a good play,
5 Whose modest scenes blush on his marriage day
   And shake to lose his honour,[2] is like her
   That after holy tie° and first night's stir   *marriage*
   Yet still is modesty, and still retains

Prologue
1. *stand sound and well:* sexual wordplay about virility and lack of venereal disease.
2. *Whose . . . honour:* Whose previously unwatched scenes are "modest" and shy (they "blush") on opening night and "shake" with fear at the thought of being viewed (losing their virginity).

More of the maid to sight than husband's pains.[3]
We pray our play may be so,° for I am sure   (modest)
10   It has a noble breeder° and a pure,   begetter
A learnèd, and a poet never went
More famous yet 'twixt Po and silver Trent.[4]
Chaucer, of° all admired, the story gives: by
There° constant to eternity it lives.   In his words
15   If we let fall° the nobleness of this°   demean / (the poem)
And the first sound this child° hear be a hiss,   play
How will it shake the bones of that good man,°   (Chaucer)
And make him cry from under ground, 'O fan
From me the witless chaff of such a writer,
20   That blasts my bays and my famed works makes lighter
Than Robin Hood'?[5] This is the fear we bring,
For to say truth, it were an endless° thing   never-ending; pointless
And too ambitious to aspire to him,°   (Chaucer)
Weak as we are, and almost breathless swim
25   In this deep water. Do but you hold out
Your helping hands and we shall tack about
And something do to save us.[6] You shall hear
Scenes, though below his art, may yet appear
Worth two hours' travail.[7] To his bones, sweet sleep;
30   Content to you. If this play do not keep
A little dull time from us,[8] we perceive
Our losses fall so thick we must needs leave.[9]   *Flourish.* [*Exit*]

1.1

Music. Enter Hymen° with a torch burning, a BOY *in a*   god of marriage
white robe before, singing and strewing flowers. After
Hymen, a nymph encompassed in her tresses, bearing a
wheaten garland.[1] *Then* THESEUS *between two other*
nymphs with wheaten chaplets° on their heads. Then   wreaths
HIPPOLYTA,[2] *the bride, led by* [PIRITHOUS] *and another*
holding a garland over her head, her tresses likewise
hanging. After her, EMILIA *holding up her train.* [*Then*
ARTESIUS *and other attendants*]

BOY [*sings during procession*]
     Roses, their sharp spines being gone,
     Not royal in their smells alone,
          But in their hue;

3. *still . . . pains:* still looks more like a virgin ("maid") than like a married woman who has experienced her husband's sexual exertions.
4. *a poet . . . Trent:* there has never been a more famous poet from Italy to England. The Po is a river in Italy, the Trent an English waterway.
5. *That . . . Hood:* Who disgraces my fame as a poet (garlands of bay or laurel were awarded to great poets, hence the name "poet laureate") and makes my renowned creations seem more trivial than a popular tale or ballad (such as Robin Hood).
6. *Do but . . . us:* Help us by applauding, and we will turn like a sailboat in the breeze produced by your clapping hands, thereby saving our reputation.
7. *two hours' travail:* the actors' labor ("travail") for two hours in performing the play (standard length was two to three hours); also, since Q reads "travel," the audience will take part in a two-hour imaginative journey

while watching the play. "Travail" continues the metaphor of childbirth and rearing begun in line 10, which itself develops from the image of the loss of virginity on the marriage night.
8. *keep . . . us:* keep us amused.
9. Our losses will be so great that we will need to quit the theater. The "losses" refer to the decline in reputation from a poorly received play and perhaps also to the burning of the Globe Theatre on June 29, 1613, during a performance of *All Is True (Henry VIII).*
1.1 Location: Athens, near the temple where Hippolyta and Theseus are to be married.
1. The young woman's hair hangs loose, indicating virginity; her garland signifies fertility.
2. According to legend, Hippolyta was Queen of the Amazons before Theseus conquered her race of women warriors and brought her to Thebes as his captive and bride.

   Maiden pinks, of odour faint,

5 Daisies smell-less, yet most quaint,°   *fine*
   And sweet thyme true;

   Primrose, first-born child of Ver,°   *spring*
   Merry springtime's harbinger,
    With harebells dim;°   *dark hyacinths*
10 Oxlips,° in their cradles growing,   *Flowering herbs*
   Marigolds, on deathbeds blowing,°   *flowering on graves*
    Lark's-heels trim;°   *Fine larkspur*
   All dear nature's children sweet,
   Lie fore bride and bridegroom's feet,
   [He] strew[s] flowers
15   Blessing their sense.
   Not an angel of the air,°   *bird*
   Bird melodious, or bird fair,
    Is absent hence.

20 The crow, the sland'rous³ cuckoo, nor
   The boding° raven, nor chough hoar,⁴   *ominous*
    Nor chatt'ring pie,°   *magpie*
   May on our bridehouse° perch or sing,   *wedding venue*
   Or with them any discord bring,
    But from it fly.

 Enter three QUEENS *in black, with veils stained,° with* *dyed black*
 imperial crowns. The FIRST QUEEN *falls down at the*
 foot of THESEUS; *the* SECOND *falls down at the foot of*
25 HIPPOLYTA; *the* THIRD, *before* EMILIA

FIRST QUEEN [*to* THESEUS] For pity's sake and true gentility's,
 Hear and respect° me.   *attend to*
SECOND QUEEN [*to* HIPPOLYTA] For your mother's sake,
 And as you wish your womb may thrive with fair ones,
 Hear and respect me.
THIRD QUEEN [*to* EMILIA] Now for the love of him whom Jove
30 hath marked°   *singled out for*
 The honour of your bed, and for the sake
 Of clear° virginity, be advocate   *unspotted*
 For us and our distresses. This good deed
 Shall raze you out o'th' Book of Trespasses
 All you are set down there.⁵
THESEUS [*to* FIRST QUEEN] Sad lady, rise.
35 HIPPOLYTA [*to* SECOND QUEEN]   Stand up.
 EMILIA [*to* THIRD QUEEN]   No knees to me.
 What woman I may stead° that is distressed   *assist*
 Does bind me to her.
THESEUS [*to* FIRST QUEEN] What's your request? Deliver° you *Speak*
  for all.
FIRST QUEEN [*kneeling still*] We are three queens whose sovereigns
  fell before
40 The wrath of cruel Creon;⁶ who° endured *(the sovereigns)*

---

3. Because it yelled out "cuckold" (husband of an adulterous wife), impugning faithful wives.
4. A jackdaw—a small, rare, gray-headed ("hoar"), red-
beaked, cliff-dwelling member of the crow family.
5. *Shall . . . there:* Will expunge your sins from the
divine ledger.
6. Brother to Jocasta and, hence, both brother-in-law

and uncle to Oedipus, Creon succeeded Oedipus's son
Eteocles as King of Thebes following the siege known
as the "Seven Against Thebes," in which both Eteocles
and all the attackers, led by Eteocles' brother Polynices,
were killed. Creon refused to bury any of the seven,
including the husbands of the Three Queens.

The beaks of ravens, talons of the kites,
And pecks of crows in the foul fields° of Thebes.   *battlefields*
He will not suffer us to burn their bones,
To urn their ashes, nor to take th'offence
45 Of mortal loathsomeness from the blest eye
Of holy Phoebus,° but infects the winds   *the sun*
With stench of our slain lords. O pity, Duke!
Thou purger of the earth,[7] draw thy feared sword
That does good turns to'th' world; give us the bones
50 Of our dead kings that we may chapel° them;   *entomb*
And of° thy boundless goodness take some note   *in*
That for our crownèd heads we have no roof,
Save this,° which is the lion's and the bear's,   *(the sky)*
And vault° to everything.   *ceiling*

THESEUS   Pray you, kneel not:
55 I was transported with° your speech, and suffered   *moved by*
Your knees to wrong themselves.° I have heard the fortunes   *(by kneeling)*
Of your dead lords, which gives me such lamenting
As wakes my vengeance and revenge for 'em.
King Capaneus was your lord: the day
60 That he should° marry you—at such a season   *was about to*
As now it is with me—I met your groom
By Mars's altar. You were that time fair,
Not Juno's mantle fairer than your tresses,
Nor in more bounty spread her.[8] Your wheaten wreath
65 Was then nor° threshed nor blasted;° fortune at you   *neither / withered*
Dimpled her cheek with smiles; Hercules our kinsman—
Then weaker than° your eyes—laid by his club.   *overwhelmed by*
He tumbled down upon his Nemean hide
And swore his sinews thawed.[9] O grief and time,
70 Fearful° consumers, you will all devour.   *Terrifying*

FIRST QUEEN [*kneeling still*]   O, I hope some god,
Some god hath put his mercy in your manhood,
Whereto he'll infuse power and press you forth
Our undertaker.°   *champion*

THESEUS   O no knees, none, widow:

[*The* FIRST QUEEN *rises*]

75 Unto the helmeted Bellona° use them   *Roman goddess of war*
And pray for me, your soldier. Troubled I am.

[*He*] *turns away*

SECOND QUEEN [*kneeling still*]   Honoured Hippolyta,
Most dreaded Amazonian, that hast slain
The scythe-tusked boar,[1] that with thy arm, as strong
80 As it is white, wast near to° make the male   *almost managed to*
To thy sex captive, but that this, thy lord—
Born to uphold creation in that honour
First nature styled it in[2]—shrunk thee into

7. Like his cousin Hercules (see 1.1.66, 3.6.175), Theseus was known for ridding the world of monsters and
evildoers.
8. Nor is Juno (goddess of marriage) more luxuriantly
wrapped in her mantle than you were in your hanging
tresses.
9. *He . . . thawed:* He (Hercules) flopped down on the
hide of the Nemean lion (which he wore after killing it
as one of his twelve labors) and swore his muscles were
turned to water by your beauty. Most powerful of Greek

mythological heroes, performer of "twelve strong
labours" set for him by his cousin (3.6.175), Hercules
was typically portrayed armed with a club.
1. *Honored . . . boar:* Hippolyta is here confused with
Atalanta, another Amazon, who participated with
Meleager in the hunt for the Calydonian boar. See note
to 3.5.18.
2. *Born . . . in:* Born to sustain the natural order of
creation—the order of man over woman.

The bound thou wast o'erflowing,[3] at once subduing
85 Thy force and thy affection; soldieress,
That equally canst poise° sternness with pity,   *balance*
Whom now I know hast much more power on° him   *over*
Than ever he had on thee, who ow'st° his strength,   *owns*
And his love too, who is a servant for
90 The tenor of thy speech;[4] dear glass of° ladies,   *mirror for*
Bid him that we, whom flaming war doth scorch,
Under the shadow of his sword may cool us.
Require him he° advance it o'er our heads.   *Ask him to*
Speak't in a woman's key, like such a woman
95 As any of us three. Weep ere you fail.
Lend us a knee:[5]
But touch the ground for us no longer time
Than a dove's motion when the head's plucked off.
Tell him, if he i'th' blood-sized° field lay swoll'n,   *blood-soaked*
100 Showing the sun his teeth, grinning at the moon,
What you would do.

HIPPOLYTA   Poor lady, say no more.
I had as lief trace[6] this good action with you
As that° whereto I am going, and never yet   *(marriage)*
Went I so willing way. My lord is taken°   *affected*
105 Heart-deep with your distress. Let him consider.
I'll speak anon.°   *soon*
        [*The* SECOND QUEEN *rises*]

THIRD QUEEN (*kneel*[*ing still*] *to* EMILIA)   O, my petition was
Set down in ice,[7] which by hot grief uncandied°   *thawed*
Melts into drops; so sorrow, wanting form,
Is pressed with deeper matter.[8]

EMILIA   Pray stand up:
Your grief is written in your cheek.

110 THIRD QUEEN   O woe,
You cannot read it there; there,° through my tears,   *in my eye*
Like wrinkled pebbles in a glassy stream,
You may behold 'em.°   *(my sorrows)*
        [*The* THIRD QUEEN *rises*]
                    Lady, lady, alack—
He that will all the treasure know o'th' earth
115 Must know° the centre too; he that will fish   *dig deep throughout*
For my least minnow, let him lead° his line   *weight with lead*
To catch one at my heart. O, pardon me:
Extremity, that sharpens sundry wits,
Makes me a fool.[9]

EMILIA   Pray you, say nothing, pray you.
120 Who cannot feel nor see the rain, being in't,
Knows neither wet nor dry. If that you were
The ground-piece of some painter,[1] I would buy you
T'instruct me 'gainst a capital° grief, indeed   *deadly*

---

3. *shrunk . . . o'erflowing:* returned you to the limits of
your sex, which you had previously exceeded.
4. *who is . . . speech:* who, like a good lover, obeys your
every spoken desire.
5. *Speak't . . . knee:* Don't speak like an Amazon. Use
tears to avoid defeat. Join us in kneeling.
6. I would as willingly follow through.
7. *my . . . ice:* my former speech was cold and formal.

8. *so . . . matter:* so sorrow, lacking a way to express
itself, is made yet more oppressive by its inarticulateness;
or, perhaps, receives the stamp of "deeper" impulses.
9. *Extremity . . . fool:* Extreme suffering, which makes
some minds more clear, has made me speak inappro-
priately.
1. *If . . . painter:* If you were merely the subject
(model; preliminary sketch?) of a painting.

Such heart-pierced° demonstration; but, alas,   *heartrending*
125 Being a natural sister of our sex,[2]
Your sorrow beats so ardently° upon me   *burningly*
That it shall make a counter-reflect 'gainst[3]
My brother's° heart, and warm it to some pity,   *brother-in-law's*
Though it were made of stone. Pray have good comfort.

130 THESEUS   Forward to th' temple.° Leave not out a jot   *(for the wedding)*
O'th' sacred ceremony.

FIRST QUEEN   O, this celebration
Will longer last and be more costly than
Your suppliants' war. Remember that your fame
Knolls° in the ear o'th' world: what you do quickly   *Tolls like a bell*
135 Is not done rashly; your first thought is more
Than others' laboured meditance;° your premeditating   *careful meditation*
More than their actions. But, O Jove, your actions,
Soon as they move, as ospreys do the fish,[4]
Subdue before they touch. Think, dear Duke, think
What beds our slain kings have.

140 SECOND QUEEN   What griefs our beds,
That our dear lords have none.

THIRD QUEEN   None fit for th' dead.
Those that with cords, knives, drams,° precipitance,°   *poisons / leaps*
Weary of this world's light, have to themselves
Been death's most horrid agents, human grace°   *mercy*
Affords them dust and shadow.

145 FIRST QUEEN   But our lords
Lie blist'ring fore the visitating° sun,   *inspecting*
And were good kings, when living.

THESEUS   It is true,
And I will give you comfort to give° your dead lords graves,   *by giving*
The which to do must make some work with Creon.

150 FIRST QUEEN   And that work presents itself to th' doing.[5]
Now 'twill take form, the heats are gone tomorrow.[6]
Then, bootless° toil must recompense itself   *fruitless*
With its own sweat; now he's secure,°   *unaware of danger*
Not dreams we stand before your puissance°   *power*
155 Rinsing our holy begging in our eyes
To make petition clear.°   *pure; manifest*

SECOND QUEEN   Now you may take him,
Drunk with his victory.

THIRD QUEEN   And his army full
Of bread and sloth.

THESEUS   Artesius, that best knowest
How to draw out,° fit to this enterprise   *select*
160 The prim'st° for this proceeding and the number   *best soldiers*
To carry° such a business: forth and levy   *conduct; win*
Our worthiest instruments, whilst we dispatch
This grand act of our life, this daring deed
Of fate[7] in wedlock.

---

2. Since you are actually a live woman (rather than a
representation of a grieving wife).
3. That, like a mirror, I'll reflect your (sunlike) sorrow
back toward.
4. According to popular legend, ospreys had the power
to compel fish to rise to the surface and turn over, making themselves available for capture.

5. And that work needs to be done as soon as possible.
6. While the plan, like molten metal, is still hot, it can
be transformed into something—once it grows cold, it
can no longer be shaped.
7. *this daring deed / Of fate*: this act (marriage) that
challenges fate.

FIRST QUEEN [*to the other two* QUEENS]   Dowagers,° take hands;   *Widows*

165   Let us be widows to our woes; delay
    Commends us to a famishing hope.⁸

ALL THREE QUEENS   Farewell.

SECOND QUEEN   We come unseasonably,° but when could grief   *at a bad time*
    Cull forth,° as unpanged° judgement can, fitt'st time   *Choose / untormented*
    For best solicitation?

THESEUS   Why, good ladies,

170   This is a service whereto I am going
    Greater than any war—it more imports me°   *means more to me*
    Than all the actions that I have foregone,°   *done to date*
    Or futurely can cope.°   *achieve*

FIRST QUEEN   The more proclaiming°   *Clearly showing that*
    Our suit shall be neglected when her arms,

175   Able to lock Jove from a synod,⁹ shall
    By warranting° moonlight corslet thee!¹ O when   *authorizing*
    Her twinning cherries° shall their sweetness fall°   *lips / let fall*
    Upon thy tasteful° lips, what wilt thou think   *tasting*
    Of rotten kings or blubbered° queens? What care   *tear-soaked*

180   For what thou feel'st not, what thou feel'st being able
    To make Mars spurn his drum?° O, if thou couch   *(battle signal)*
    But one night with her, every hour in't will
    Take hostage of thee° for a hundred,° and   *Commit you / (more)*
    Thou shalt remember nothing more than what
    That banquet bids° thee to.   *appetizer invites*

185 HIPPOLYTA [*to* THESEUS]   Though much unlike
    You should be so transported, as much sorry
    I should be such a suitor²—yet I think
    Did I not by th'abstaining of my joy,
    Which breeds a deeper longing, cure their surfeit°   *excess of grief*

190   That craves a present medicine,° I should pluck   *an immediate relief*
    All ladies' scandal° on me. [*Kneels*] Therefore, sir,   *reproach*
    As I shall here make trial of my prayers,
    Either presuming them to have some force,
    Or sentencing for aye their vigour dumb,³

195   Prorogue° this business we are going about, and hang   *Delay*
    Your shield afore your heart—about that neck
    Which is my fee,° and which I freely lend   *property*
    To do these poor queens service.

ALL THREE QUEENS [*to* EMILIA]   O, help now,
    Our cause cries for your knee.

EMILIA [*kneels to* THESEUS]   If you grant not

200   My sister her petition in that force°   *with that energy*
    With that celerity and nature° which   *spontaneous speed*
    She makes it in, from henceforth I'll not dare
    To ask you anything, nor be so hardy°   *bold*
    Ever to take a husband.

THESEUS   Pray stand up.

---

8. *Let . . . hope*: Let us mourn our misfortunes as we mourned our husbands (or, let us, widowlike, part from our woes), since by delaying the battle until his marriage is completed, Theseus consigns us to failure.
9. Able to keep Jupiter from a meeting of the gods.
1. Encircle you like a "corslet," close-fitting defensive armor. Theseus has traded arms (armor) for arms (embraces).

2. *Though . . . suitor*: Although it's highly unlikely you'd be so carried away, and just as unlikely I'd now request you to postpone the wedding.
3. Or forever "sentencing" my prayers to silence, than which they are no more effectual.

[*They rise*]

205 I am entreating of myself to do
That which you kneel to have me.°—Pirithous,   *have me do*
Lead on the bride: get you° and pray the gods   *go*
For success and return; omit not anything
In the pretended° celebration.—Queens,   *intended*
210 Follow your soldier.° [*To* ARTESIUS] As before, hence you,   *Theseus*
And at the banks of Aulis[4] meet us with
The forces you can raise, where we shall find
The moiety of a number for a business
More bigger looked.[5]   [*Exit* ARTESIUS]
[*To* HIPPOLYTA]   Since that our theme is haste,
215 I stamp this kiss upon thy current lip—
Sweet, keep it as my token.[6] [*To the wedding party*] Set you
    forward,
For I will see you gone.
[*To* EMILIA] Farewell, my beauteous sister.—Pirithous,
Keep the feast full:° bate° not an hour on't.°   *fully / abate / of it*
PIRITHOUS   Sir,
220 I'll follow you at heels. The feast's solemnity°   *ceremonial splendor*
Shall want° till your return.   *be lacking*
THESEUS   Cousin,° I charge you   *Friend*
Budge not from Athens. We shall be returning
Ere you can end this feast, of which, I pray you,
Make no abatement.°—Once more, farewell all.   *reduction*
      Exeunt [HIPPOLYTA, EMILIA, PIRITHOUS, *and train*]
                       towards the temple
FIRST QUEEN   Thus dost thou still make good the tongue o'th'
225   world.[7]
SECOND QUEEN   And earn'st a deity equal with Mars—
THIRD QUEEN   If not above him, for
Thou being but mortal mak'st affections° bend   *sexual urges*
To godlike honours;[8] they themselves, some say,
Groan under such a mast'ry.[9]
230 THESEUS   As we are men,
Thus should we do; being sensually subdued°   *overcome by appetites*
We lose our human title.° Good cheer, ladies.   *claim to humanity*
Now turn we towards your comforts.   *Flourish. Exeunt*

1.2

      Enter PALAMON *and* ARCITE
ARCITE   Dear Palamon, dearer in love than blood,
And our prime cousin,° yet unhardened in   *nearest kin*
The crimes of nature,[1] let us leave the city,

---

4. Port where the Greek troops assembled before sailing for Troy.
5. *where . . . looked:* where we shall find part of an army already assembled for a larger campaign than this one.
6. *I . . . token:* puns on coining and engraving. *stamp:* press (a kiss); make a coin by impressing an image on metal. *current:* flowing away (like a stream); red (currant); genuine, not counterfeit. *token:* memento (often of love); metal stamped and used as a coin.
7. In this way, you (Theseus) prove true everything the world says of you.
8. *mak'st . . . honours:* subordinate your human passions to godlike deeds.

9. *they . . . mast'ry:* the gods themselves complain of such self-restraint; suffer because their passions master them.
1.2 Location: Thebes.
1. *unhardened . . . nature:* inexperienced in the natural vices of man. In this scene, a number of the most important themes of the play are introduced: that maturity and experience necessitate a loss of innocence; that friendship constitutes a stronger tie than either marriage / love relations or blood; and that duty to the knightly virtue of honor is stronger than duty to human laws and sovereigns (except in times of war).

	Thebes, and the temptings° in't, before we further	*temptations*
5	Sully our gloss of° youth.	*Tarnish our pristine*
	And here to keep in abstinence we shame	
	As in incontinence;[2] for not to swim	
	I'th' aid o'th' current° were almost to sink—	*With the flow*
	At least to frustrate striving;[3] and to follow	
10	The common stream 'twould bring us to an eddy	
	Where we should turn° or drown; if labour through,	*spin endlessly*
	Our gain but life and weakness.[4]	

PALAMON   Your advice

	Is cried up with example.[5] What strange ruins°	*ruined men*
	Since first we went to school may we perceive	
15	Walking in Thebes? Scars and bare weeds°	*tattered clothes*
	The gain o'th' martialist° who did propound	*soldier*
	To his bold ends[6] honour and golden ingots,	
	Which though he won, he had not;[7] and now flirted°	*(is) mocked*
	By peace for whom he fought. Who then shall offer	
20	To Mars's so-scorned altar? I do bleed	
	When such I meet, and wish great Juno[8] would	
	Resume her ancient° fit of jealousy	*former*
	To get the soldier work, that peace might purge	
	For her repletion[9] and retain° anew	*take into service*
25	Her° charitable heart, now hard and harsher	*(Juno's); (peace's)*
	Than strife or war could be.	

ARCITE   Are you not out?°   *off the point*

	Meet you no ruin but the soldier in	
	The cranks and turns° of Thebes? You did begin	*winding streets*
	As if you met decays of many kinds.	
30	Perceive you none that do arouse your pity	
	But th'unconsidered° soldier?	*neglected*

PALAMON   Yes, I pity

	Decays where'er I find them, but such most	
	That, sweating in an honourable toil,	
	Are paid with ice° to cool 'em.	*treated coldly*

ARCITE   'Tis not this

35	I did begin to speak of. This is virtue,	
	Of no respect in Thebes. I spake of Thebes,	
	How dangerous, if we will keep our honours,	
	It is for our residing where every evil	
	Hath a good colour,° where every seeming good's	*appearance*
40	A certain evil, where not to be ev'n jump	
	As they are here were to be strangers, and	
	Such things to be, mere monsters.[1]	

PALAMON   'Tis in our power,

	Unless we fear that apes can tutor's,° to	*that we're mere mimics*
	Be masters of our manners. What need I	
45	Affect another's gait, which is not catching°	*infectious; attractive*

2. *here . . . incontinence:* we incur as much shame here (in a corrupt city) by remaining innocent as we would elsewhere by debauching ourselves.
3. And at least renders our exertions (on behalf of goodness) pointless.
4. *if . . . weakness:* if we were to pass through such a whirlpool ("eddy"), we would gain only our lives in a weakened state.
5. Is borne out by numerous examples.
6. *propound . . . ends:* propose as recompense for his

courage.
7. Which, though victorious in battle, he didn't receive.
8. Juno's jealousy led to the Trojan War and other conflicts.
9. *purge / For her repletion:* take medicine to alleviate her (peace's) overeating (the indulgent life of peacetime).
1. *where . . . monsters:* where failure to conform exactly ("jump") makes you a foreigner and perfect conformity makes you a monster.

Where there is faith?[2] Or to be fond° upon		*to dote*
Another's way of speech, when by mine own		
I may be reasonably conceived°—saved, too—		*understood*
Speaking it° truly? Why am I bound		*If I speak*
50 By any generous° bond to follow him		*noble*
Follows° his tailor, haply° so long until		*Who heeds / at least*
The followed make pursuit?° Or let me know		*(for unpaid bills)*
Why mine own barber is unblest—with him		
My poor chin, too—for 'tis not scissored just		
55 To such a favourite's glass?° What canon° is there		*image / law*
That does command my rapier from my hip		
To dangle't in my hand? Or to go tiptoe		
Before the street be foul?[3] Either I am		
The fore-horse in the team or I am none		
60 That draw i'th' sequent trace.[4] These poor slight sores		
Need not a plantain.[5] That which rips my bosom		
Almost to th' heart's—		

ARCITE   Our uncle Creon.

PALAMON   He,

A most unbounded° tyrant, whose successes		*unrestrained*
Makes heaven unfeared and villainy assured°		*assured that*
65 Beyond its power there's nothing; almost puts		
Faith in a fever,[6] and deifies alone		
Voluble chance;° who only attributes		*Variable fortune*
The faculties of other instruments		
To his own nerves and act;[7] commands men's service,		
70 And what they win in't, boot° and glory; one		*booty; gain*
That fears not to do harm, good dares not.° Let		*dares not do good*
The blood of mine that's sib° to him be sucked		*related*
From me with leeches. Let them break° and fall		*burst*
Off me with that° corruption.		*(Creon's)*

ARCITE   Clear-spirited° cousin,   *Noble-spirited*

75 Let's leave his court that we may nothing share		
Of his loud° infamy: for our milk		*well-known*
Will relish of the pasture,[8] and we must		
Be vile or disobedient; not his kinsmen		
In blood unless in quality.[9]		

PALAMON   Nothing truer.

80 I think the echoes of his shames have deafed		
The ears of heav'nly justice. Widows' cries		
Descend again into their throats and have not		

Enter VALERIUS

Due audience of° the gods—Valerius.		*Proper notice from*

VALERIUS   The King calls for you; yet be leaden-footed°   *go slowly*

85 Till his great rage be off him. Phoebus, when		
He broke his whipstock and exclaimed against		
The horses of the sun,[1] but whispered to°		*compared to*

2. Self-reliance. Palamon's speech echoes familiar criticisms of the contrived, "effeminate" manners of courtiers and men of fashion, here contrasted with implicit religious norms ("faith"; "saved," line 48; "canon," line 55).
3. *go . . . foul*: tiptoe on a clean street.
4. *Either . . . trace*: I will not pull behind the lead ("fore-") horse (follow fashion).
5. Herb used for treating wounds.
6. *puts . . . fever*: undermines religion.

7. *attributes . . . act*: takes credit for others' successes.
8. Like cows whose milk absorbs the taste of whatever they eat.
9. *not . . . quality*: we ought not to act like his kinsmen unless we're willing to act like him; we're not his kinsmen unless we act like him.
1. After his son Phaeton died driving the horses of the sun, Phoebus (the sun) vented his grief at the horses—hence the broken whip handle ("whipstock").

The loudness of his fury.

PALAMON　　　　　　　　　　　Small winds shake him.
But what's the matter?

90　VALERIUS　Theseus, who where he threats, appals, hath sent
Deadly defiance to him° and pronounces　　　　　　　*(Creon)*
Ruin to Thebes, who° is at hand to seal　　　　　　　*(Theseus)*
The promise of his wrath.[2]

ARCITE　　　　　　　　　　　Let him approach.
But that we fear the gods in him,° he brings not　　*justness of his cause*
95　A jot of terror to us. Yet what man
Thirds his own worth—the case is each of ours—
When that his action's dregged with mind assured
'Tis bad he goes about.[3]

PALAMON　　　　　　　Leave that unreasoned.°　　　　*Forget that*
Our services stand now for Thebes, not Creon,
100　Yet to be neutral to him were dishonour,
Rebellious° to oppose. Therefore we must　　　　　　*Treasonable*
With him stand to the mercy of° our fate,　　　　　　*submit to*
Who hath bounded our last minute.[4]

ARCITE　　　　　　　　　　　So we must.
Is't said this war's afoot? Or it shall be
On fail of° some condition?　　　　　　　　　　　　*If Thebes rejects*

105　VALERIUS　　　　　　　　　'Tis in motion,
The intelligence of state° came in the instant　　　*official announcement*
With the defier.°　　　　　　　　　　　　　　　　　*herald of Theseus*

PALAMON　　　　　　Let's to the King, who, were he
A quarter carrier of that honour which
His enemy come in, the blood we venture
110　Should be as for our health,[5] which were not spent,°　*wasted*
Rather laid out for purchase.° But, alas,　　　　　　*invested for profit*
Our hands advanced before° our hearts, what will　　*beyond*
The fall o'th' stroke do damage?[6]

ARCITE　　　　　　　　　　Let th'event°—　　　　*outcome*
That never-erring arbitrator—tell us
115　When we know all ourselves,[7] and let us follow
The becking° of our chance.　　　*Exeunt*　　　　　*calling*

1.3

Enter PIRITHOUS, HIPPOLYTA, *and* EMILIA

PIRITHOUS　　No further.

HIPPOLYTA　　　　　　　　Sir, farewell. Repeat my wishes
To our great lord, of whose success I dare not
Make any timorous question; yet I wish him
Excess and overflow of power, an't might be,°　　　*if possible*
5　To dure° ill-dealing fortune. Speed to him;　　　*endure*
Store[1] never hurts good governors.

PIRITHOUS　　　　　　　　　Though I know
His ocean needs not my poor drops, yet they
Must yield their tribute there. [*To* EMILIA] My precious maid,

---

2. *seal . . . wrath:* turn anger to action.
3. *Yet . . . about:* Yet any man reduces his worth by two-thirds—when he knows the action he undertakes is unworthy.
4. *Who . . . minute:* Which has determined when we die.
5. *the blood . . . health:* our loss of blood in combat

would be equivalent to a therapeutic bloodletting.
6. *what . . . damage:* what harm will "the fall o'th' stroke" do?
7. *tell . . . ourselves:* speak for itself.
1.3 Location: The outskirts of Athens.
1. Abundant resources (here, good men like Pirithous).

Those best affections° that the heavens infuse   *inclinations*
10 In their best-tempered pieces° keep enthroned   *greatest creations*
In your dear heart.

EMILIA   Thanks, sir. Remember me
To our all-royal brother, for whose speed°   *success*
The great Bellona I'll solicit; and
Since in our terrene state° petitions are not   *earthly condition*
15 Without gifts understood, I'll offer to her
What I shall be advised she likes. Our hearts
Are in his army, in his tent.

HIPPOLYTA   In's bosom.
We have been soldiers,° and we cannot weep   *(as Amazons)*
When our friends don their helms,° or put to sea,   *helmets*
20 Or tell of babes broached° on the lance, or women   *speared*
That have sod° their infants in—and after eat them—   *boiled*
The brine they wept at killing 'em:² then if
You stay to see of us such spinsters, we
Should hold you here forever.³

PIRITHOUS   Peace be to you
25 As I pursue this war, which° shall be then   *(peace)*
Beyond further requiring.°   *Exit* PIRITHOUS   *In no need of prayer*

EMILIA   How his longing
Follows his friend! Since his depart,° his sports,   *Theseus's departure*
Though craving° seriousness and skill, passed slightly   *requiring*
His careless execution,⁴ where nor° gain   *neither*
30 Made him regard or loss consider, but
Playing one business in his hand, another
Directing in his head, his mind nurse equal
To these so diff'ring twins.⁵ Have you observed him
Since our great lord departed?

HIPPOLYTA   With much labour;°   *diligence*
35 And I did love him for't. They two have cabined°   *shared quarters*
In many as dangerous as poor a corner,
Peril and want contending;⁶ they have skiffed°   *sailed across*
Torrents whose roaring tyranny and power
I'th' least of these° was dreadful, and they have   *At the weakest point*
40 Fought out together where death's self was lodged;⁷
Yet fate hath brought them off. Their knot of love,
Tied, weaved, entangled with so true, so long,
And with a finger of so deep a cunning,°   *skill*
May be outworn,° never undone. I think   *worn out (in death)*
45 Theseus cannot be umpire to himself,
Cleaving his conscience into twain and doing
Each side like° justice, which⁸ he loves best.   *equal*

EMILIA   Doubtless
There is a best, and reason has no manners
To say it is not you. I was acquainted
50 Once with a time when I enjoyed a playfellow;
You were at wars when she the grave enriched,

---

2. Miriam killed, cooked, and ate her son during the Roman siege of Jerusalem, adding her own tears for sauce.
3. *then if . . . forever*: if you wait long enough for us to turn into spinners (housewives), you'll wait forever.
4. *passed . . . execution*: were pursued carelessly.

5. *his . . . twins*: his attention divided equally between sports and Theseus.
6. Contending for which was the greater hardship.
7. *where . . . lodged*: the underworld, to rescue Proserpina.
8. Pirithous or Hippolyta.

Who made too proud the bed;° took leave o'th' moon[9]—   *grave*
Which then looked pale at parting—when our count°   *age*
Was each eleven.

HIPPOLYTA   'Twas Flavina.

EMILIA   Yes.

55 You talk of Pirithous' and Theseus' love:
Theirs has more ground,° is more maturely seasoned,   *a stronger base*
More buckled° with strong judgement, and their needs   *joined together*
The one of th'other may be said to water
Their intertangled roots of love; but I
60 And she I sigh and spoke of were things innocent,
Loved for° we did, and like the elements,[1]   *simply because*
That know not what, nor why, yet do effect°   *create*
Rare issues° by their operance, our souls   *Amazing results*
Did so to one another. What she liked
65 Was then of° me approved; what not, condemned—   *by*
No more arraignment.° The flower that I would pluck   *inquiry*
And put between my breasts—O then but beginning
To swell about the blossom—she would long°   *desire*
Till she had such another, and commit it
70 To the like innocent cradle, where, phoenix-like,
They died in perfume.[2] On my head no toy°   *trifle*
But was her pattern.° Her affections—pretty,   *model*
Though happily her careless wear—I followed
For my most serious decking.[3] Had mine ear
75 Stol'n some new air,° or at adventure° hummed one,   *tune / by chance*
From musical coinage,° why, it was a note   *improvisation*
Whereon her spirits would sojourn—rather dwell on—
And sing it in her slumbers. This rehearsal—
Which, seely innocence wots well, comes in
80 Like old emportment's bastard[4]—has this end:
That the true love 'tween maid and maid may be
More than in sex dividual.[5]

HIPPOLYTA   You're out of breath,
And this high-speeded pace is but to say
That you shall never, like the maid Flavina,
85 Love any that's called man.

EMILIA   I am sure I shall not.

HIPPOLYTA   Now alack, weak sister,
I must no more believe thee in this point—
Though in't I know thou dost believe thyself—
90 Than I will trust a sickly appetite
That loathes even as it longs. But sure, my sister,
If I were ripe for your persuasion,° you   *open to your views*
Have said enough to shake me from the arm

9. Diana (the moon goddess), who watched over virgins and Amazons; hence Emilia's (equivocal) patron.
1. Air, fire, earth, and water—constituents of all matter.
2. The phoenix died by being burned on aromatic
wood, only to be reborn from its own ashes.
3. *Her affections . . . decking:* Whatever she wore—
even though she wasn't aware of how appealing it
was—I'd imitate with utmost seriousness. For "happily"
Q has "happely," which could also mean "haply" (by
chance).

4. *This . . . bastard:* This narrative, which, as any happy
innocent well knows, is an illegitimate descendant
(poor likeness) of my former passion (or, the former significance of the relationship). For "seely innocence" Q
has "fury-innocent" (innocent passionate love), which
may be correct.
5. *in sex dividual:* between two sexes. Q has "individuall," which in the seventeenth century could mean the
indivisible unity of male and female, and hence may be
correct.

Of the all-noble Theseus, for whose fortunes
95 I will now in and kneel, with great assurance
That we more than his Pirithous possess
The high throne in his heart.
EMILIA   I am not
Against your faith, yet I continue mine.   *Exeunt*

1.4

Cornetts. A battle struck within. Then a retreat.
Flourish.[1] Then enter THESEUS, *victor. The three* QUEENS
meet him and fall on their faces before him. [Also enter
a HERALD, *and attendants bearing]* PALAMON *and*
ARCITE [*on*] *two hearses*°   biers
FIRST QUEEN [*to* THESEUS]   To thee no star be dark.°   unfavorable
SECOND QUEEN [*to* THESEUS]   Both heaven and earth
Friend thee for ever.
THIRD QUEEN [*to* THESEUS]   All the good that may
Be wished upon thy head, I cry 'Amen' to't.
THESEUS   Th'impartial gods, who from the mounted° heavens   high
5 View us their mortal herd, behold who err
And in their time chastise. Go and find out
The bones of your dead lords and honour them
With treble ceremony: rather than a gap
Should be in their dear° rites we would supply't.   valued
10 But those we will depute which shall invest°   clothe
You in your dignities, and even° each thing   rectify
Our haste does leave imperfect. So adieu,
And heaven's good eyes look on you.   *Exeunt* [*the*] QUEENS
                                    What are those?
HERALD   Men of great quality,° as may be judged   rank
15 By their appointment.° Some of Thebes have told's   armor and weapons
They are sisters' children, nephews to the King.
THESEUS   By th' helm° of Mars I saw them in the war,   helmet
Like to a pair of lions smeared with prey,
Make lanes in troops aghast. I fixed my note°   attention
20 Constantly on them, for they were a mark°   striking sight
Worth a god's view. What prisoner was't told me
When I enquired their names?
HERALD   Wi' leave, they're called
Arcite and Palamon.
THESEUS   'Tis right: those, those.
They are not dead?
25 HERALD   Nor in a state of life. Had they been taken
When their last hurts were given, 'twas possible
They might have been recovered.° Yet they breathe,   healed
And have the name of men.
THESEUS   Then like men use 'em.
The very lees of such, millions of rates
30 Exceed the wine of others.[2] All our surgeons
Convent° in their behoof;° our richest balms,   Assemble / behalf
Rather than niggard,° waste. Their lives concern us   use stingily

---

1.4 Location: On the outskirts of Thebes.
1. Small horns sound offstage, signaling the start of
battle, a retreat, and then a triumphal entrance.

2. *The very . . . others:* The dregs of such men far
exceed the best that others can offer.

Much more than Thebes is worth. Rather than have 'em
Freed of this plight and in their morning° state—— *former (healthy)*
35 Sound and at liberty——I would 'em dead;
But forty-thousandfold we had rather have 'em
Prisoners to us, than death. Bear 'em speedily
From our kind air, to them unkind,[3] and minister
What man to man may do——for our sake, more,
40 Since I have known frights, fury, friends' behests,
Love's provocations, zeal, a mistress' task,
Desire of liberty, a fever, madness,
Hath set a mark which nature could not reach to
Without some imposition, sickness in will
45 O'er-wrestling strength in reason.[4] For our love
And great Apollo's° mercy, all our best *god of healing*
Their best skill tender.——Lead into the city
Where, having bound things scattered,° we will post° *reimposed order / hurry*
To Athens fore our army.   *Flourish. Exeunt*

1.5

Music. Enter the [three] QUEENS *with the hearses of*
their [lords] in a funeral solemnity [with attendants]
                                Song
Urns and odours, bring away,
Vapours, sighs, darken the day;
    Our dole° more deadly looks than dying. *mourning*
Balms and gums[1] and heavy cheers,° *sad countenances*
5 Sacred vials filled with tears,
    And clamours through the wild air flying:

Come all sad and solemn shows,
That are quick-eyed pleasure's foes.
We convent naught else but woes,
10 We convent naught else but woes.

THIRD QUEEN This funeral path brings° to your household's *leads*
    grave——
Joy seize on you again, peace sleep with him.
SECOND QUEEN And this to yours.
FIRST QUEEN   Yours this way. Heavens lend
A thousand differing ways to one sure end.° *death*
15 THIRD QUEEN This world's a city full of straying streets,
And death's the market-place where each one meets.
                                Exeunt severally° *separately*

2.1

Enter [the] JAILER *and [the]* WOOER
JAILER I may depart with° little, while I live; something I may *may spare*
cast° to you, not much. Alas, the prison I keep, though it be for *give (as a dowry)*
great ones, yet they seldom come; before one salmon you shall
take a number of minnows. I am given out to be better lined° *said to be richer*
5 than it can appear to me report° is a true speaker. I would I *rumor*

---

3. Fresh air was thought dangerous to wounds.
4. *Since . . . reason:* Since compelling incentives can
impel men to perform beyond their normal abilities,
whereas otherwise weak will triumphs over strong reason. *mark:* target. *imposition:* command.
1.5 Scene continues.

1. Aromatic substances used in mourning rituals.
2.1 Location: The palace garden in Athens, perhaps
with the second, or higher, gallery above representing
the window of the cell where Palamon and Arcite are
being held.

were really that° I am delivered° to be. Marry¹, what I have—   *what / reported*
be it what it will—I will assure upon° my daughter at the day   *bequeath to*
of my death.

10 WOOER   Sir, I demand no more than your own offer, and I will
estate° your daughter in what I have promised.   *settle*

JAILER   Well, we will talk more of this when the solemnity² is
past. But have you a full promise of° her?   *from*
       Enter [the JAILER'S] DAUGHTER [*with rushes*]°   *(as floor coverings)*
When that shall be seen, I tender my consent.

WOOER   I have, sir. Here she comes.

15 JAILER [*to* DAUGHTER]   Your friend and I have chanced to name
you here, upon the old business—but no more of that now. So
soon as the court hurry is over we will have an end of it. I'th'
mean time, look tenderly° to the two prisoners. I can tell you   *carefully*
they are princes.

20 JAILER'S DAUGHTER   These strewings° are for their chamber. 'Tis   *rushes*
pity they are in prison, and 'twere pity they should be out. I do
think they have patience to make any adversity ashamed; the
prison itself is proud of 'em, and they have all the world in
their chamber.³

25 JAILER   They are famed° to be a pair of absolute° men.   *reputed / perfect*

JAILER'S DAUGHTER   By my troth, I think fame but stammers°   *underrates*
'em—they stand a grece° above the reach of report.   *step*

JAILER   I heard them reported in the battle to be the only doers.°   *supreme achievers*

JAILER'S DAUGHTER   Nay, most likely, for they are noble sufferers.⁴
30 I marvel how they would have looked had they been victors, that
with such a constant nobility enforce a freedom out of bondage,
making misery their mirth, and affliction a toy° to jest at.   *trifle*

JAILER   Do they so?

JAILER'S DAUGHTER   It seems to me they have no more sense of
35 their captivity than I of ruling Athens. They eat well, look merrily, discourse of many things, but° nothing of their own   *but say*
restraint° and disasters. Yet sometime a divided° sigh—martyred   *captivity / half-audible*
as 'twere i'th' deliverance—will break from one of them, when
the other presently° gives it so sweet a rebuke that I could wish   *immediately*
40 myself a sigh to be so chid, or at least a sigher to be comforted.

WOOER   I never saw 'em.

JAILER   The Duke himself came privately in the night,
       PALAMON *and* ARCITE [*appear at a window*] *above*
and so did they.⁵ What the reason of it is I know not. Look,
yonder they are. That's Arcite looks out.

45 JAILER'S DAUGHTER   No, sir, no—that's Palamon. Arcite is the
lower° of the twain—[*pointing at* ARCITE] you may perceive a   *shorter*
part of him.

JAILER   Go to,° leave your pointing. They would not make us   *Come now*
their object.⁶ Out of their sight.

50 JAILER'S DAUGHTER   It is a holiday to look on them. Lord, the difference of° men!   *Exeunt*   *between*

---

1. To be sure (originally, by the Virgin Mary).
2. Theseus and Hippolyta's wedding.
3. They have everything they need in their prison cell,
because they have each other. See 2.2.60.
4. For they endure nobly what others do to them. To do

and to suffer are antithetical.
5. Theseus brought them secretly at night.
6. They would not be so rude as to point at us; they
don't want to look at us.

2.2

Enter PALAMON *and* ARCITE *in prison [in shackles, above]*

PALAMON How do you, noble cousin?

ARCITE   How do you, sir?

PALAMON Why, strong enough to laugh at misery
And bear the chance° of war. Yet we are prisoners,   °uncertainties
I fear, for ever, cousin.

ARCITE   I believe it,
And to that destiny have patiently
5 Laid up my hour to come.°   °Consigned my future

PALAMON   O, cousin Arcite,
Where is Thebes now?[1] Where is our noble country?
Where are our friends and kindreds? Never more
Must we behold those comforts, never see
The hardy youths strive for° the games of honour,   °in
10 Hung with the painted favours° of their ladies,   °love tokens
Like tall ships under sail; then start amongst 'em
And, as an east wind, leave 'em all behind us,
Like lazy clouds, whilst Palamon and Arcite,
Even in the wagging of a wanton leg,[2]
15 Outstripped the people's praises, won the garlands
Ere they have time to wish 'em ours. O never
Shall we two exercise, like twins of honour,
Our arms again and feel our fiery horses
Like proud seas under us. Our good swords, now—
20 Better° the red-eyed god of war ne'er wore—   °Better swords
Ravished° our sides, like age must run to rust   °Torn from
And deck the temples of those gods that hate us.
These hands shall never draw 'em out like lightning
To blast° whole armies more.   °annihilate

ARCITE   No, Palamon,
25 Those hopes are prisoners with us. Here we are,
And here the graces of our youths must wither,
Like a too-timely° spring. Here age must find us   °buds in a premature
And, which is heaviest,° Palamon, unmarried—   °what is saddest
The sweet embraces of a loving wife
30 Loaden with kisses, armed with thousand Cupids,
Shall never clasp our necks; no issue° know us;   °offspring
No figures° of ourselves shall we e'er see   °images
To glad our age, and, like young eagles, teach 'em
Boldly to gaze against bright arms[3] and say,
35 'Remember what your fathers were, and conquer.'
The fair-eyed maids shall weep our banishments,
And in their songs curse ever-blinded fortune,
Till she for shame see what a wrong she has done
To youth and nature. This is all our world.
40 We shall know nothing here but one another,

2.2 Location: The prison in Athens, perhaps represented by the principal upper stage, located on the first,
or lower, gallery; as in 2.1, the garden is located on the
main stage. The shift of Palamon and Arcite from the
higher to the lower gallery is implied by the stage directions and start of a new scene here in Q.

1. The kinsmen's view of Thebes in 1.2 is very different, perhaps because Shakespeare probably wrote the
earlier scene and Fletcher this one.
2. *Even . . . leg*: Effortlessly.
3. Eagles supposedly could gaze at the sun without
being blinded.

Hear nothing but the clock that tells° our woes.   *counts*
The vine shall grow, but we shall never see it;
Summer shall come, and with her all delights,
45 But dead-cold winter must inhabit here still.
PALAMON   'Tis too true, Arcite. To our Theban hounds
That shook the agèd forest with their echoes,
No more now must we holler; no more shake
Our pointed javelins whilst the angry swine°   *the wild boar*
50 Flies like a Parthian quiver⁴ from our rages,
Struck with our well-steeled darts. All valiant uses°—   *activities*
The food and nourishment of noble minds—
In us two here shall perish; we shall die—
Which is the curse of honour—lastly,°   *at last*
Children of grief and ignorance.°   *Sad and unknown*
55 ARCITE   Yet, cousin,
Even from the bottom of these miseries,
From all that fortune can inflict upon us,
I see two comforts rising—two mere° blessings,   *pure*
If the gods please, to hold here a brave patience
60 And the enjoying of our griefs together.
Whilst Palamon is with me, let me perish
If I think this our prison.
PALMON   Certainly
'Tis a main° goodness, cousin, that our fortunes   *the greatest*
Were twined together. 'Tis most true, two souls
65 Put in two noble bodies, let 'em suffer
The gall of hazard,° so° they grow together,   *bitterest luck / if*
Will never sink;° they must not, say° they could.   *succumb / even if*
A willing man dies sleeping⁵ and all's done.
ARCITE   Shall we make worthy uses of this place
That all men hate so much?
70 PALAMON   How, gentle cousin?
ARCITE   Let's think this prison holy sanctuary,
To keep us from corruption of worse men.
We are young, and yet desire the ways of honour
That liberty and common conversation,°   *worldly acquaintances*
75 The poison of pure spirits, might, like women,
Woo us to wander from. What worthy blessing
Can be, but our imaginations
May make it ours? And here being thus together,
We are an endless mine° to one another: *resource*
80 We are one another's wife, ever begetting
New births of love; we are father, friends, acquaintance;
We are in one another, families—
I am your heir, and you are mine; this place
Is our inheritance: no hard oppressor
85 Dare take this from us. Here, with a little patience,
We shall live long and loving. No surfeits° seek us—   *diseases from excess*
The hand of war hurts none here, nor the seas
Swallow their youth. Were we at liberty

---

4. During the era of ancient Rome's supremacy, the   5. A man resigned to his fate dies in peace, as if merely
Parthians were renowned archers, famous for shooting   falling asleep.
behind them at their enemies as they pretended to flee.

A wife might part us lawfully, or business;
90   Quarrels consume us; envy of ill men
Crave our acquaintance.⁶ I might sicken, cousin,
Where you should never know it, and so perish
Without your noble hand to close mine eyes,
Or prayers to the gods. A thousand chances,
Were we from hence, would sever us.

95 PALAMON   You have made me—
I thank you, cousin Arcite—almost wanton°   *frolicsome*
With my captivity. What a misery
It is to live abroad,° and everywhere!   *out of captivity*
'Tis like a beast, methinks. I find the court here;
100   I am sure, a more content;° and all those pleasures   *greater happiness*
That woo the wills of men to vanity
I see through now, and am sufficient
To tell the world 'tis but a gaudy shadow,
That old Time, as he passes by, takes with him.
105   What had we been, old° in the court of Creon,   *grown old*
Where sin is justice, lust and ignorance
The virtues of the great ones? Cousin Arcite,
Had not the loving gods found this place for us,
We had died as they do, ill° old men, unwept,   *wicked*
110   And had° their epitaphs, the people's curses.   *had for*
Shall I say more?

ARCITE   I would hear you still.°   *forever*

PALAMON
Is there record of any two that loved
Better than we do, Arcite?

ARCITE   Sure there cannot.

PALAMON   I do not think it possible our friendship
Should ever leave us.

115 ARCITE   Till our deaths it cannot,
    Enter EMILIA *and her* WOMAN [*below.*° PALAMON *sees*   *(in the garden)*
    EMILIA *and is silent*]
And after death our spirits shall be led
To those that love eternally.° Speak on, sir.   *(in Elysium)*

EMILIA [*to her* WOMAN]   This garden has a world of pleasure in't.
What flower is this?

WOMAN   'Tis called narcissus, madam.

120 EMILIA   That was a fair boy, certain, but a fool
To love himself.⁷ Were there not maids enough?

ARCITE [*to* PALAMON]   Pray forward.°   *go on speaking*

PALAMON   Yes.

EMILIA [*to her* WOMAN]   Or were they all hard-hearted?

WOMAN   They could not be to one so fair.

EMILIA   Thou wouldst not.

WOMAN   I think I should not, madam.

EMILIA   That's a good wench—
But take heed to your kindness, though.

125 WOMAN   Why, madam?

EMILIA   Men are mad things.

---

6. *envy . . . acquaintance:* the malice (or, our envy) of
evil men might infect us.
7. Narcissus fell in love with his own reflection in a

pool and drowned trying to embrace it. After his death,
he was turned into a flower.

ARCITE [*to* PALAMON]   Will ye go forward, cousin?

EMILIA [*to her* WOMAN]   Canst not thou work° such flowers in   °*embroider*
    silk, wench?

WOMAN   Yes.

EMILIA   I'll have a gown full of 'em, and of these.
    This is a pretty colour—will't not do
    Rarely° upon a skirt, wench?   °*Beautifully*

130 WOMAN   Dainty,° madam.   °*Very nicely*

ARCITE [*to* PALAMON]   Cousin, cousin, how do you, sir? Why,
    Palamon!

PALAMON   Never till now was I in prison, Arcite.

ARCITE   Why, what's the matter, man?

PALAMON   Behold and wonder!
    [ARCITE *sees* EMILIA]
    By heaven, she is a goddess!

ARCITE   Ha!

PALAMON   Do reverence.
    She is a goddess, Arcite.

135 EMILIA [*to her* WOMAN]   Of all flowers
    Methinks a rose is best.

WOMAN   Why, gentle madam?

EMILIA   It is the very emblem of a maid—
    For when the west wind courts her gently,
    How modestly she blows,° and paints the sun⁸   °*blooms*
140   With her chaste blushes! When the north° comes near her,   °*north wind*
    Rude and impatient, then, like chastity,
    She locks her beauties in her bud again,
    And leaves him to base briers.°   °*thorns*

WOMAN   Yet, good madam,
    Sometimes her modesty will blow° so far   °*open*
145 She falls for't°—a maid,   °*because of it*
    If she have any honour, would be loath
    To take example by her.

EMILIA   Thou art wanton.

ARCITE [*to* PALAMON]   She is wondrous fair.

PALAMON   She is all the beauty extant.

EMILIA [*to her* WOMAN]   The sun grows high—let's walk in.
    Keep these flowers.
150   We'll see how close art can come near their colours.
    I am wondrous merry-hearted—I could laugh now.

WOMAN   I could lie down, I am sure.⁹

EMILIA   And take one° with you?   °*(a rose); (a lover)*

WOMAN   That's as we bargain, madam.

EMILIA   Well, agree° then.   °*let's bargain*
    Exeunt EMILIA *and* [*her*] WOMAN

PALAMON   What think you of this beauty?

ARCITE   'Tis a rare one.

PALAMON   Is't but a rare one?

155 ARCITE   Yes, a matchless beauty.

PALAMON   Might not a man well lose himself and love her?

ARCITE   I cannot tell what you have done; I have,
    Beshrew mine eyes° for't. Now I feel my shackles.   °*Curse me (an oath)*

---

8. Tints the sunlight pink; the inside of a rose looks like
an image of the sun.

9. "Laugh and lie down" was an Elizabethan card
game; sexual allusion.

PALAMON You love her then?

160 ARCITE Who would not?

PALAMON And desire her?

ARCITE Before my liberty.

PALAMON I saw her first.

ARCITE   That's nothing.

PALAMON   But it shall be.

ARCITE I saw her too.

PALAMON   Yes, but you must not love her.

165 ARCITE I will not, as you do, to worship her
    As she is heavenly and a blessèd goddess!
    I love her as a woman, to enjoy her—
    So both may love.

PALAMON   You shall not love at all.

ARCITE Not love at all—who shall deny me?

170 PALAMON I that first saw her, I that took possession
    First with mine eye of all those beauties
    In her revealed to mankind. If thou[1] lov'st her,
    Or entertain'st a hope to blast my wishes,
    Thou art a traitor, Arcite, and a fellow°   *(contemptuous)*

175   False as thy title to° her. Friendship, blood,   *claim to possess*
    And all the ties between us I disclaim,
    If thou once think upon her.

ARCITE   Yes, I love her—
    And if the lives of all my name lay° on it,   *my family depended*
    I must do so. I love her with my soul—

180   If that will lose ye, farewell, Palamon!
    I say again,
    I love her, and in loving her maintain
    I am as worthy and as free° a lover,   *noble*
    And have as just a title to her beauty,

185   As any Palamon, or any living
    That is a man's son.

PALAMON   Have I called thee friend?

ARCITE Yes, and have found me so. Why are you moved° thus?   *incensed*
    Let me deal coldly° with you. Am not I   *dispassionately*
    Part of your blood, part of your soul? You have told me
    That I was Palamon and you were Arcite.

190 PALAMON   Yes.

ARCITE Am not I liable to those affections,°   *passions*
    Those joys, griefs, angers, fears, my friend shall suffer?

PALAMON Ye may be.

ARCITE   Why then would you deal so cunningly,
    So strangely, so unlike a noble kinsman,

195   To love alone? Speak truly. Do you think me
    Unworthy of her sight?

PALAMON   No, but unjust
    If thou pursue that sight.

ARCITE   Because another
    First sees the enemy, shall I stand still,
    And let mine honour down, and never charge?

PALAMON Yes, if he be but one.°   *be alone*

---

1. The contemptuous "thou" replaces the more polite "you." Arcite follows suit at line 218.

200 ARCITE   But say that one
　　Had rather combat me?
　PALAMON   Let that one say so,
　　And use thy freedom; else, if thou pursuest her,
　　Be as that cursèd man that hates his country,
　　A branded villain.
　ARCITE   You are mad.
　PALAMON   I must be.
205　Till thou art worthy, Arcite, it concerns me;
　　And in this madness if I hazard° thee   *endanger*
　　And take thy life, I deal but truly.°   *fairly*
　ARCITE   Fie, sir.
　　You play the child extremely. I will love her,
　　I must, I ought to do so, and I dare—
　　And all this justly.
210　PALAMON   O, that now, that now
　　Thy false self and thy friend had but this fortune—
　　To be one hour at liberty and grasp
　　Our good swords in our hands! I would quickly teach thee
　　What 'twere to filch affection from another.
215　Thou art baser in it than a cutpurse.°   *thief*
　　Put but thy head out of this window more
　　And, as I have a soul, I'll nail thy life to't.°   *to the window frame*
　ARCITE   Thou dar'st not, fool; thou canst not; thou art feeble.
　　Put my head out? I'll throw my body out
220　And leap° the garden when I see her next,   *jump down to*
　　　　　Enter [the JAILER above]
　　And pitch° between her arms to anger thee.   *hurl myself*
　PALAMON   No more—the keeper's coming. I shall live
　　To knock thy brains out with my shackles.
　ARCITE   Do.
　JAILER   By your leave, gentlemen.
　PALAMON   Now, honest keeper?
225　JAILER   Lord Arcite, you must presently to th' Duke.
　　The cause I know not yet.
　ARCITE   I am ready, keeper.
　JAILER   Prince Palamon, I must a while bereave you
　　Of your fair cousin's company.
　　　　　　　　Exeunt ARCITE and [the JAILER]
　PALAMON   And me, too,
　　Even when you please, of life. Why is he sent for?
230　It may be he shall marry her—he's goodly,°   *handsome*
　　And like enough the Duke hath taken notice
　　Both of his blood° and body. But his falsehood!   *noble family*
　　Why should a friend be treacherous? If that
　　Get him a wife so noble and so fair,
235　Let honest men ne'er love again. Once more
　　I would but see this fair one. Blessèd garden,
　　And fruit and flowers more blessèd, that still° blossom *perpetually*
　　As her bright eyes shine on ye! Would I were,
　　For all the fortune of my life hereafter,
240　Yon little tree, yon blooming apricot—
　　How I would spread and fling my wanton arms
　　In at her window! I would bring her fruit
　　Fit for the gods to feed on; youth and pleasure

Still as° she tasted should be doubled on her;   *Whenever*
245 And if she be not heavenly, I would make her
So near the gods in nature they should fear her—
              Enter [*the* JAILER *above*]
And then I am sure she would love me. How now, keeper,
Where's Arcite?

JAILER   Banishèd—Prince Pirithous
Obtained his liberty;[2] but never more,
250 Upon his oath and life, must he set foot
Upon this kingdom.

PALAMON [*aside*]   He's a blessèd man.
He shall see Thebes again, and call to arms
The bold young men that, when he bids 'em charge,
Fall on like fire. Arcite shall have a fortune,°   *chance*
255 If he dare make himself a worthy lover,
Yet in the field to strike a battle for her;
And if he lose her then, he's a cold coward.
How bravely may he bear himself to win her
If he be noble Arcite; thousand ways!
260 Were I at liberty I would do things
Of such a virtuous greatness that this lady,
This blushing virgin, should take manhood to her
And seek to ravish me.

JAILER   My lord, for you
I have this charge° to—   *order*

PALAMON   To discharge my life.
265 JAILER No, but from this place to remove your lordship—
The windows are too open.

PALAMON   Devils take 'em
That are so envious° to me—prithee kill me.   *spiteful*

JAILER And hang for't afterward?

PALAMON   By this good light,
Had I a sword I would kill thee.

JAILER   Why, my lord?

270 PALAMON Thou bring'st such pelting° scurvy news continually,   *paltry*
Thou art not worthy life. I will not go.

JAILER Indeed you must, my lord.

PALAMON   May I° see the garden?   *Will I be able to*

JAILER No.

PALAMON Then I am resolved—I will not go.

JAILER I must constrain you, then; and for° you are dangerous,   *because*
I'll clap more irons on you.

275 PALAMON   Do, good keeper.
I'll shake 'em so ye shall not sleep:
I'll make ye a new morris.[3] Must I go?

JAILER There is no remedy.

PALAMON   Farewell, kind window.
May rude wind never hurt thee. O, my lady,
280 If ever thou hast felt what sorrow was,
Dream how I suffer. Come, now bury me.[4]
              Exeunt PALAMON *and* [*the* JAILER]

---

2. The motives behind Pirithous's intercession are not
explained.
3. Morris dancers wore bells on their clothes.

4. Palamon's new cell will be like a grave because he
will be banished from Emilia.

2.3

Exeunt ARCITE

ARCITE Banished the kingdom? 'Tis a benefit,
A mercy I must thank 'em for; but banished
The free enjoying of that face I die for—
O, 'twas a studied° punishment, a death   *deliberate*
5   Beyond imagination; such a vengeance
That, were I old and wicked, all my sins
Could never pluck upon me. Palamon,
Thou hast the start° now—thou shalt stay and see   *advantage*
Her bright eyes break° each morning 'gainst thy window,   *(like dawn)*
10 And let in life into thee. Thou shalt feed
Upon the sweetness of a noble beauty
That nature ne'er exceeded, nor ne'er shall.
Good gods! What happiness has Palamon!
Twenty to one he'll come to speak to her,
15 And if she be as gentle as she's fair,
I know she's his—he has a tongue will tame
Tempests and make the wild rocks wanton.°   *full of joy*
Come what can come,
The worst is death. I will not leave the kingdom.
20 I know mine own° is but a heap of ruins,   *(Thebes)*
And no redress there. If I go he has her.
I am resolved another shape° shall make me,   *a disguise*
Or end my fortunes. Either way I am happy—
I'll see her and be near her, or no more.°   *or die*

Enter four COUNTRY [MEN], *one [of whom carries] a
garland before them.* [ARCITE *stands apart*]

25 FIRST COUNTRYMAN My masters, I'll be there—that's certain.
SECOND COUNTRYMAN And I'll be there.
THIRD COUNTRYMAN And I.
FOURTH COUNTRYMAN Why then, have with ye,° boys! 'Tis but *I'll come too*
a chiding[1]—
Let the plough play° today, I'll tickle't out   *be idle*
Of the jades' tails tomorrow.[2]
30 FIRST COUNTRYMAN   I am sure
To have my wife as jealous as a turkey[3]—
But that's all one. I'll go through, let her mumble.°   *grumble*
SECOND COUNTRYMAN Clap her aboard tomorrow night and
stow her,[4]
And all's made up again.
THIRD COUNTRYMAN   Ay, do but put
35 A fescue° in her fist and you shall see her   *teacher's pointer*
Take a new lesson out° and be a good wench.   *Learn a new lesson*
Do we all hold against the maying?[5]
FOURTH COUNTRYMAN Hold? What should ail us?°   *prevent us*
THIRD COUNTRYMAN   Arcas will be there.
SECOND COUNTRYMAN And Sennois, and Rycas, and three bet-
40 ter lads ne'er danced under green tree; and ye know what
wenches, ha? But will the dainty dominie,° the schoolmaster, *fussy teacher*

2.3 Location: The countryside outside Athens.
1. The worst punishment I'll get (for not working) is a scolding.
2. *I'll . . . tomorrow*: I'll whip extra work out of the horses ("jades") tomorrow.
3. Thought to be jealously territorial.
4. Sexual metaphor: board her (like a ship) and fill up her cargo hold.
5. Are we still going to participate in the May Day celebrations (of fertility and the coming of spring)?

keep touch,° do you think? For he does all,[6] ye know.　　　*keep this promise*

THIRD COUNTRYMAN　He'll eat a hornbook[7] ere he fail. Go to, the
matter's too far driven° between him and the tanner's daughter　　*affair's gone too far*
45　　to let slip now, and she must see the Duke, and she must dance too.

FOURTH COUNTRYMAN　Shall we be lusty?°　　　　　　　　　*lively*

SECOND COUNTRYMAN　All the boys in Athens blow wind i'th'
breech on's![8] And here I'll be and there I'll be, for our town,
and here again and there again—ha, boys, hey for the weavers![9]

50　FIRST COUNTRYMAN　This must be done i'th' woods.

FOURTH COUNTRYMAN　O, pardon me.

SECOND COUNTRYMAN　By any° means, our thing of learning°　　*all / our teacher*
said so; where he himself will edify the Duke most parlously°　　*cleverly*
in our behalfs— he's excellent i'th' woods, bring him to th'
55　　plains, his learning makes no cry.°　　　　　　　　　*falls silent*

THIRD COUNTRYMAN　We'll see the sports, then every man to's
tackle°—and, sweet companions, let's rehearse, by any means,　　*morris-dancing gear*
before the ladies see us, and do sweetly, and God knows what
may come on't.

60　FOURTH COUNTRYMAN　Content—the sports once ended, we'll
perform. Away boys, and hold.°　　　　　　　　　　　*keep your word*

ARCITE [*coming forward*]　By your leaves, honest friends, pray
you whither go you?

FOURTH COUNTRYMAN　Whither? Why, what a° question's that?　　*what sort of a*

ARCITE　Yet 'tis a question
To me that know not.

65　THIRD COUNTRYMAN　To the games, my friend.

SECOND COUNTRYMAN　Where were you bred, you know it not?

ARCITE　　　　　　　　　　　　　　　　　　Not far, sir—
Are there such games today?

FIRST COUNTRYMAN　　　　　　　Yes, marry, are there,
And such as you never saw. The Duke himself
Will be in person there.

ARCITE　　　　　　　What pastimes are they?

SECOND COUNTRYMAN　Wrestling and running. [*To the others*]
70　　'Tis a pretty fellow.

THIRD COUNTRYMAN [*to* ARCITE]
Thou wilt not go along?

ARCITE　　　　　　　Not yet, sir.

FOURTH COUNTRYMAN　　　　　　Well, sir,
Take your own time. [*To the others*] Come, boys.

FIRST COUNTRYMAN　　　　　　　My mind misgives me—
This fellow has a vengeance trick o'th' hip:[1]
Mark how his body's made for't.

SECOND COUNTRYMAN　　　　　I'll be hanged though
75　If he dare venture; hang him, plum porridge![2]
He wrestle? He roast eggs![3] Come, let's be gone, lads.

Exeunt [*the*] *four* [COUNTRYMEN]

ARCITE　This is an offered° opportunity　　　　　　　*unsought*
I durst not° wish for. Well I could have wrestled[4]—　　*would not have dared*

6. For he arranges everything.
7. A primer or tablet, protected by a translucent plate of horn, inscribed with the alphabet.
8. Will try—and fail—to keep up with us.
9. Hooray for the weavers (the profession to which the speaker apparently belongs).
1. *My . . . hip:* I fear that this man may be a skillful wrestler.
2. Contemptuous, suggesting that Arcite is out of shape. Plum porridge was a heavy dessert of stewed dried fruits eaten at Christmas.
3. He'd be a better cook than wrestler (?); he probably can't cook an egg (?).
4. I knew how to wrestle.

The best men called it excellent—and run
80 Swifter than wind upon a field of corn,°   *wheat*
Curling the wealthy° ears, never° flew. I'll venture,   *abundant / ever*
And in some poor disguise be there. Who knows
Whether my brows may not be girt with garlands,
And happiness prefer° me to a place   *good fortune promote*
85 Where I may ever dwell in sight of her?   *Exit*

2.4

Enter [the] JAILER'S DAUGHTER

JAILER'S DAUGHTER   Why should I love this gentleman? 'Tis
   odds°   *Chances are*
He never will affect° me. I am base,   *love*
My father the mean° keeper of his prison,   *lowly*
And he a prince. To marry him is hopeless,
5 To be his whore[1] is witless. Out upon't,°   *(Expressing abhorrence)*
What pushes° are we wenches driven to   *extremities*
When fifteen° once has found us? First, I saw him;   *(the age)*
I, seeing, thought he was a goodly man;
He has as much to please a woman in him—
10 If he please to bestow it so—as ever
These eyes yet looked on. Next, I pitied him,
And so would any young wench, o'my conscience,
That ever dreamed or vowed her maidenhead
To a young handsome man. Then, I loved him,
15 Extremely loved him, infinitely loved him—
And yet he had a cousin fair as he, too.
But in my heart was Palamon, and there,
Lord, what a coil he keeps!° To hear him   *turmoil he makes*
Sing in an evening, what a heaven it is!
20 And yet his songs are sad ones. Fairer spoken
Was never gentleman. When I come in
To bring him water in a morning, first
He bows his noble body, then salutes° me, thus: *greets*
'Fair, gentle maid, good morrow. May thy goodness
25 Get thee a happy husband.' Once he kissed me—
I loved my lips the better ten days after.
Would he would do so every day! He grieves much,
And me as much to see his misery.
What should I do to make him know I love him?
30 For I would fain° enjoy him. Say I ventured   *eagerly*
To set him free? What says the law then? Thus much
For law or kindred! I will do it,
And this night; ere tomorrow he shall love me.   *Exit*

2.5

Short flourish of cornetts and shouts within. Enter THE-
SEUS, HIPPOLYTA, PIRITHOUS, EMILIA, ARCITE *[disguised]*
with a garland [and attendants]

THESEUS   You have done worthily. I have not seen
Since Hercules a man of tougher sinews.°   *muscles*
Whate'er you are, you run the best and wrestle°   *wrestle the best*
That these times can allow.°   *show*

2.4 Location: The prison in Athens.
1. Premarital sex, not prostitution.

2.5 Location: Athens, near the site of the athletic
games.

ARCITE   I am proud to please you.
THESEUS   What country bred you?
5 ARCITE   This—but far off, prince.
THESEUS   Are you a gentleman?
ARCITE   My father said so,
    And to those gentle uses gave me life.[1]
THESEUS   Are you his heir?
ARCITE   His youngest, sir.
THESEUS   Your father
    Sure is a happy sire, then. What proves you?°   *(a gentleman)*
10 ARCITE   A little of all noble qualities.°   *accomplishments*
    I could have kept° a hawk and well have hollered   *I knew how to keep*
    To a deep° cry of dogs; I dare not praise   *loud*
    My feat in horsemanship, yet they that knew me
    Would say it was my best piece;° last and greatest,   *attribute*
    I would° be thought a soldier.   *used to*
15 THESEUS   You are perfect.
PIRITHOUS   Upon my soul, a proper° man.   *handsome*
EMILIA   He is so.
PIRITHOUS [*to* HIPPOLYTA]   How do you like him, lady?
HIPPOLYTA   I admire° him.   *am amazed at*
    I have not seen so young a man so noble—
    If he say true—of his sort.°   *rank*
EMILIA   Believe°   *Be sure*
20 His mother was a wondrous handsome woman—
    His face methinks goes that way.°   *demonstrates that*
HIPPOLYTA   But his body
    And fiery mind illustrate° a brave father.   *indicate; copy*
PIRITHOUS   Mark how his virtue,° like a hidden sun,   *excellence*
    Breaks through his baser garments.
HIPPOLYTA   He's well got,° sure.   *wellborn*
THESEUS [*to* ARCITE]   What made you seek this place, sir?
25 ARCITE   Noble Theseus,
    To purchase name° and do my ablest service   *get a reputation*
    To such a well-found° wonder as thy worth,   *well-deserved*
    For only in thy court of all the world
    Dwells fair-eyed honour.
PIRITHOUS   All his words are worthy.
30 THESEUS [*to* ARCITE]   Sir, we are much indebted to your travel,°   *journey; effort*
    Nor shall you lose your wish.—Pirithous,
    Dispose of° this fair gentleman.   *Place*
PIRITHOUS   Thanks, Theseus.
    [*To* ARCITE] Whate'er you are, you're mine, and I shall give you
    To a most noble service, to this lady,
35 This bright young virgin; pray observe° her goodness.   *respect*
    You have honoured her fair birthday with your virtues,
    And as your due you're hers. Kiss her fair hand, sir.
ARCITE   Sir, you're a noble giver. [*To* EMILIA] Dearest beauty,
    Thus let me seal my vowed faith.
        [*He kisses her hand*]
                                    When your servant,
    Your most unworthy creature, but offends you,
40 Command him die, he shall.

---

1. And raised me for those genteel pursuits.

EMILIA   That were too cruel.
    If you deserve well, sir, I shall soon see't.
    You're mine, and somewhat better than your rank° I'll use you.   *position*
PIRITHOUS [*to* ARCITE]   I'll see you furnished,° and, because you   *equipped*
    say
45   You are a horseman, I must needs entreat you
    This afternoon to ride—but 'tis a rough one.°   *(horse)*
ARCITE   I like him better, prince—I shall not then
    Freeze in my saddle.
THESEUS [*to* HIPPOLYTA]   Sweet, you must be ready—
    And you, Emilia, [*to* PIRITHOUS] and you, friend—and all,
50   Tomorrow by the sun,° to do observance   *by sunrise*
    To flow'ry May in Dian's wood. [*To* ARCITE] Wait well, sir,
    Upon your mistress.—Emily, I hope
    He shall not go afoot.
EMILIA   That were a shame, sir,
    While I have horses. [*To* ARCITE] Take your choice, and what
55   You want,° at any time, let me but know it.   *lack*
    If you serve faithfully, I dare assure you,
    You'll find a loving mistress.
ARCITE   If I do not,
    Let me find that° my father ever hated—   *that which*
    Disgrace and blows.
THESEUS   Go, lead the way—you have won it.[2]
60   It shall be so: you shall receive all dues
    Fit for the honour you have won. 'Twere wrong else.
    [*To* EMILIA] Sister, beshrew my heart, you have a servant
    That, if I were a woman, would be master.
    But you are wise.
EMILIA   I hope too wise for that, sir. *Flourish. Exeunt*

2.6

Enter [the] JAILER'S DAUGHTER

JAILER'S DAUGHTER   Let all the dukes and all the devils roar—
    He is at liberty! I have ventured° for him,   *taken a risk*
    And out I have brought him. To a little wood
    A mile hence I have sent him, where a cedar
    Higher than all the rest spreads like a plane,°   *plane tree*
    Fast° by a brook—and there he shall keep close°   *Close / shall hide*
5   Till I provide him files and food, for yet
    His iron bracelets° are not off. O Love,°   *shackles / Cupid*
    What a stout-hearted child thou art! My father
    Durst better have endured cold iron than done it.[1]
    I love him beyond love and beyond reason
10   Or wit° or safety. I have made him know it—   *sense*
    I care not, I am desperate. If the law
    Find me and then condemn me for't, some wenches,
    Some honest-hearted maids, will sing my dirge
    And tell to memory my death was noble,
15   Dying almost a martyr. That way he takes,
    I purpose, is my way too. Sure, he cannot

---

2. Won the honor of leading the procession.
2.6 Location: Near the prison in Athens.

1. *My . . . it:* My father would sooner have been run through than have freed a prisoner.

Be so unmanly as to leave me here.
20 If he do, maids will not so easily
Trust men again. And yet, he has not thanked me
For what I have done—no, not so much as kissed me—
And that, methinks, is not so well. Nor scarcely
Could I persuade him to become a free man,
25 He made such scruples of the wrong he did
To me and to my father. Yet, I hope
When he considers more, this love of mine
Will take more root within him. Let him do
What he will with me—so he use me kindly.[2]
30 For use me,° so he shall, or I'll proclaim him,   (sexually)
And to his face, no man.° I'll presently   (sexually)
Provide him necessaries and pack my clothes up,
And where there is a patch of ground I'll venture,
So he be with me. By him, like a shadow,
35 I'll ever dwell. Within this hour the hubbub
Will be all o'er the prison—I am then
Kissing the man they look for. Farewell, father:
Get° many more such prisoners and such daughters,   Catch; beget
And shortly you may keep yourself.[3] Now to him.   [Exit]

3.1

[A bush in place.] Cornetts in sundry° places. Noise and   various (offstage)
hollering as [of] people a-Maying.[1]
Enter ARCITE
ARCITE   The Duke has lost Hippolyta—each took°   went to
A several laund.° This is a solemn rite   A different clearing
They owe bloomed May, and the Athenians pay° it   observe
To th' heart of° ceremony. O, Queen Emilia,   With the utmost
5 Fresher than May, sweeter
Than her gold buttons° on the boughs, or all   buds
Th'enamelled knacks° o'th' mead° or garden—yea,   flowers / meadow
We challenge too the bank of any nymph
That makes the stream seem flowers;[2] thou, O jewel
10 O'th' wood, o'th' world, hast likewise blessed a pace°   path through the woods
With thy sole presence in thy [
                                    ][3] rumination.
That I, poor man, might eftsoons come between
And chop on some cold thought.[4] Thrice blessèd chance
15 To drop on° such a mistress, expectation   run into
Most guiltless on't!° Tell me, O Lady Fortune,   unexpectedly
Next after Emily my sovereign, how far
I may be proud. She takes strong note of me,
Hath made me near her, and this beauteous morn,

2. Provided that he treat me gently; naturally; nobly, in a manner befitting a man of his kind.
3. You yourself may use the jail, since everyone else will either have escaped or been freed.
3.1 Location: All of Act 3 takes place in a forest near Athens.
1. May Day celebrations included feasts, hunting, music, entertainments (such as the morris dance of 3.5.139), and dancing around the maypole. See note to 2.3.37.

2. We . . . flowers: Emilia surpasses in beauty even a nymph's flowered riverbank, whose reflection makes the river itself seem covered with flowers.
3. Q has a comma after "presence" and lacks this gap. Editors often strengthen the punctuation by starting a new sentence with "In thy rumination." It is unclear how Arcite could "come between" (line 13) a "rumination," however—hence the hypothesis of a missing line.
4. might . . . thought: might suddenly come upon you and seize some chaste thought.

20	The prim'st° of all the year, presents me with	best
	A brace° of horses—two such steeds might well	pair
	Be by a pair of kings backed,° in a field	ridden
	That their crowns' titles tried.⁵ Alas, alas,	
	Poor cousin Palamon, poor prisoner—thou	
25	So little dream'st upon my fortune that	
	Thou think'st thyself the happier thing to be	
	So near Emilia. Me thou deem'st at Thebes,	
	And therein wretched, although free. But if	
	Thou knew'st my mistress breathed on me, and that	
30	I eared her language,° lived in her eye—O, coz,	listened to her
	What passion would enclose° thee!	rage would possess

Enter PALAMON *as out of a bush with his shackles. [He]*
bends° his fist at ARCITE   *shakes*

PALAMON   Traitor kinsman,
Thou shouldst perceive my passion if these signs
Of prisonment⁶ were off me, and this hand
But owner of a sword. By all oaths in one,

35	I and the justice of my love would make thee	
	A confessed traitor. O thou most perfidious	
	That ever gently looked,° the void'st of honour	seemed gentlemanly
	That e'er bore gentle token,° falsest cousin	wore noble emblems
	That ever blood made kin—call'st thou her thine?	
40	I'll prove it in my shackles, with these hands,	
	Void of appointment,° that thou liest and art	Devoid of weapons
	A very thief in love, a chaffy° lord	worthless
	Not worth the name of villain. Had I a sword	
	And these house-clogs° away—	fetters

ARCITE   Dear cousin Palamon—

| 45 | PALAMON   Cozener° Arcite, give me language such | Cheater (punning) |
| | As thou hast showed me feat.⁷ | |

ARCITE   Not finding in
The circuit of my breast any gross stuff
To form me like your blazon holds me to
This gentleness of answer⁸—'tis your passion

50	That thus mistakes, the which, to you being enemy,	
	Cannot to me be kind.⁹ Honour and honesty	
	I cherish and depend on, howsoe'er	
	You skip° them in me, and with them, fair coz,	ignore
	I'll maintain my proceedings. Pray be pleased	
55	To show in generous° terms your griefs,° since that	genteel / grievances
	Your question's° with your equal, who professes	dispute is
	To clear his own way¹ with the mind and sword	
	Of a true gentleman.	

PALAMON   That thou durst,° Arcite!   *You wouldn't dare*

ARCITE   My coz, my coz, you have been well advised°   *informed*

| 60 | How much I dare; you've seen me use my sword | |
| | Against th'advice° of fear. Sure, of° another | warning / by |

---

5. *in . . . tried:* on a battlefield where they were fighting
for each other's kingdoms.
6. *signs / Of prisonment:* shackles.
7. *give . . . feat:* use words that accord better with your
(perfidious) actions.
8. *Not . . . answer:* Since I find nothing in me that fits
your description of me, I answer gently. *blazon:* (descrip-

tion of a) coat of arms.
9. *'tis . . . kind:* your anger ("passion") is your enemy
(distorts your judgment) and thus to me cannot be kind
(because you are my kinsman—"kind" also means
"kin"—and friend, and hence we share all enemies).
1. To justify; to make his own way.

You would not hear me doubted, but your silence
Should break out, though i'th' sanctuary.²

PALAMON   Sir,
I have seen you move in such a place° which well   *battle; tournament*
65   Might justify your manhood; you were called
A good knight and a bold. But the whole week's not fair
If any day it rain: their valiant temper°   *attitude*
Men lose when they incline to treachery,
And then they fight like compelled bears³—would fly
Were they not tied.

70   ARCITE   Kinsman, you might as well
Speak this and act it in your glass° as to   *mirror*
His ear which now disdains you.

PALAMON   Come up to me,
Quit° me of these cold gyves,° give me a sword,   *Free / chains*
Though it be rusty, and the charity
75   Of one meal lend me. Come before me then,
A good sword in thy hand, and do but say
That Emily is thine—I will forgive
The trespass° thou hast done me, yea, my life,   *wrong*
If then thou carry't;° and brave souls in shades°   *beat me / Hades*
80   That have died manly, which will seek of me
Some news from earth, they shall get none but this—
That thou art brave and noble.

ARCITE   Be content,
Again betake you to° your hawthorn house.   *go back into*
With counsel of the night⁴ I will be here
85   With wholesome viands.° These impediments°   *food / shackles*
Will I file off. You shall have garments and
Perfumes to kill the smell o'th' prison. After,
When you shall stretch yourself and say but 'Arcite,
I am in plight',° there shall be at your choice   *I am ready*
Both sword and armour.

90   PALAMON   O, you heavens, dares any
So noble bear a guilty business!° None   *act shamefully*
But only Arcite, therefore none but Arcite
In this kind is so bold.

ARCITE   Sweet Palamon.

PALAMON   I do embrace you and your offer—for
95   Your offer do't I only, sir; your person,
Without hypocrisy, I may not wish
            Wind° horns [within]   *Sound*
More than my sword's edge on't.

ARCITE   You hear the horns—
Enter your muset° lest this match between's   *gap in a thicket*
Be crossed ere met.° Give me your hand, farewell. *prevented before begun*
100 I'll bring you every needful thing—I pray you,
Take comfort and be strong.

PALAMON   Pray hold your promise,
And do the deed with a bent brow.° Most certain   *stern countenance*
You love me not—be rough with me and pour

2. *your . . . sanctuary:* you would speak to defend me
even if you were hiding in a safe place (or in a church).
3. In bearbaiting competitions (a popular pastime with
connections to the theater), bears were tied to a stake.
4. With darkness to assist (and hide) me.

	This oil° out of your language. By this air,	smoothness; flattery
105	I could for each word give a cuff, my stomach°	anger
	Not reconciled by reason.	

ARCITE   Plainly spoken,
  Yet—pardon me—hard language: when I spur

Wind horns [within]

  My horse I chide him not. Content and anger
  In me have but one face.° Hark, sir, they call   *the same expression*
110 The scattered to the banquet. You must guess
  I have an office° there.   *assigned duty*

PALAMON   Sir, your attendance
  Cannot please heaven, and I know your office
  Unjustly is achieved.°   *Was earned unfairly*

ARCITE   'Tis a good title.°   *It was won justly*
  I am persuaded this question, sick between's,
115 By bleeding must be cured.[5] I am a suitor°   *I beg*
  That to your sword you will bequeath this plea°   *lawsuit*
  And talk of it no more.

PALAMON   But this one word:
  You are going now to gaze upon my mistress—
  For note you, mine she is—

ARCITE   Nay then—

PALAMON   Nay, pray you—
120 You talk of feeding me to breed me strength—
  You are going now to look upon a sun
  That strengthens what it looks on. There you have
  A vantage° o'er me, but enjoy it till   *advantage*
  I may enforce my remedy. Farewell.

Exeunt [severally, PALAMON as into the bush]

3.2

Enter [the] JAILER'S DAUGHTER [with a file]

JAILER'S DAUGHTER He has mistook the brake° I meant, is gone   *thicket*
  After[1] his fancy. 'Tis now wellnigh morning.
  No matter—would it were perpetual night,
  And darkness lord o'th' world. Hark, 'tis a wolf!
5 In me hath grief slain fear, and, but for one thing,
  I care for nothing—and that's Palamon.
  I reck° not if the wolves would jaw° me, so°   *care / gnaw / if*
  He had this file. What if I hollered for him?
  I cannot holler. If I whooped, what then?
10 If he not answered, I should call a wolf
  And do him but that service.[2] I have heard
  Strange howls this livelong night—why may't not be
  They have made prey of him? He has no weapons;
  He cannot run; the jangling of his gyves°   *fetters*
15 Might call fell° things to listen, who have in them   *wild*
  A sense to know a man unarmed, and can
  Smell where resistance is. I'll set it down°   *take it as fact*
  He's torn to pieces: they howled many together

---

5. *I am . . . cured:* I am convinced that the dispute
between us (here, imagined as a sick person) can only
be settled (cured) by a bloodletting.

3.2
1. *is gone / After:* is led by (only).
2. I would at least serve him by calling a wolf to attack
him (ironic).

And then they fed on him. So much for that.
20 Be bold to ring the bell.° How stand I then?   *ring his death knell*
All's chared° when he is gone. No, no, I lie: *My work is all done*
My father's to be hanged for his escape,
Myself to beg, if I prized life so much
As to deny my act—but that I would not,
25 Should I try death by dozens.³ I am moped°—   *dazed*
Food took I none these two days,
Sipped some water. I have not closed mine eyes
Save when my lids scoured off their brine.⁴ Alas,
Dissolve, my life; let not my sense unsettle,°   *reason come unhinged*
30 Lest I should drown or stab or hang myself.
O state of nature,° fail together° in me,   *life / entirely*
Since thy best props° are warped. So which way now?   *supports*
The best way is the next° way to a grave,   *nearest*
Each errant step beside⁵ is torment. Lo,
35 The moon is down, the crickets chirp, the screech-owl
Calls in the dawn. All offices are done
Save what I fail in:⁶ but the point is this,
An end,° and that is all.   *Exit*   *A death*

3.3

Enter ARCITE *with [a bundle containing] meat, wine,*
and files

ARCITE   I should be near the place. Ho, cousin Palamon!
Enter PALAMON [*as from the bush*]
PALAMON   Arcite.
ARCITE   The same. I have brought you food and files.
Come forth and fear not, here's no Theseus.
PALAMON   Nor none so honest, Arcite.
ARCITE   That's no matter—
5 We'll argue that hereafter. Come, take courage—
You shall not die thus beastly.° Here, sir, drink;   *like an animal*
I know you are faint. Then I'll talk further with you.
PALAMON   Arcite, thou mightst now poison me.
ARCITE   I might—
But I must° fear you first. Sit down and, good now,   *should need to*
10 No more of these vain parleys.° Let us not,   *pointless comments*
Having our ancient¹ reputation with us,
Make talk for² fools and cowards. To your health, sir.
PALAMON   Do.°   *You drink first*
[ARCITE *drinks*]
ARCITE   Pray sit down, then, and let me entreat you,
By all the honesty and honour in you,
15 No mention of this woman—'twill disturb us.
We shall have time enough.
PALAMON   Well, sir, I'll pledge you.°   *drink your health*
[PALAMON *drinks*]
ARCITE   Drink a good hearty draught; it breeds good blood,° man.   *makes you strong*

---

3. Even if I had to die dozens of times (ways).
4. Except when I blinked to clear my eyes of tears.
5. Each step that wanders from the direct path to the grave.
6. *All . . . in:* All tasks are done, except the one I've failed to complete (either giving the file to Palamon or killing herself).
3.3
1. Of long standing; former (now reestablished through escape).
2. Talk as though we were; make ourselves the talk of.

Do not you feel it thaw you?

PALAMON   Stay, I'll tell you
After a draught or two more.
> [PALAMON *drinks*]

ARCITE   Spare it not—
The Duke has more, coz. Eat now.

PALAMON   Yes.
> [PALAMON *eats*]

20 ARCITE   I am glad
You have so good a stomach.°   *an appetite; an anger*

PALAMON   I am gladder
I have so good meat° to't.   *(to feed my anger)*

ARCITE   Is't not mad,° lodging   *strange; maddening*
Here in the wild woods,[3] cousin?

PALAMON   Yes, for them
That have wild° consciences.   *uncivilized*

ARCITE   How tastes your victuals?
Your hunger needs no sauce, I see.

25 PALAMON   Not much.
But if it did, yours is too tart,[4] sweet cousin.
What is this?

ARCITE   Venison.

PALAMON   'Tis a lusty° meat—   *hearty*
Give me more wine. Here, Arcite, to the wenches
We have known in our days. [*Drinking*] The lord steward's
   daughter.
Do you remember her?

30 ARCITE   After you,[5] coz.

PALAMON   She loved a black-haired man.

ARCITE   She did so; well, sir.

PALAMON   And I have heard some call him Arcite, and—

ARCITE   Out with't, faith.

PALAMON   She met him in an arbour—
What did she there, coz? Play o'th' virginals?[6]

ARCITE   Something° she did, sir—   *To some extent*

35 PALAMON   Made her groan a month for't—
Or two, or three, or ten.°   *(in pregnancy)*

ARCITE   The marshal's sister
Had her share too, as I remember, cousin,
Else there be tales° abroad. You'll pledge her? *false rumors*

PALAMON   Yes.
> [*They drink*]

ARCITE   A pretty brown° wench 'tis. There was a time *brunette*
40 When young men went a-hunting, and a wood,
And a broad beech, and thereby hangs a tale—
Heigh-ho!°   *(a sigh)*

PALAMON   For Emily, upon my life! Fool,
Away with this strained mirth. I say again,
That sigh was breathed for Emily. Base cousin,
Dar'st thou break[7] first?

ARCITE   You are wide.°   *wide of the mark*

---

3. *woods*: Pun on "wode" (mad).
4. Your insolence ("sauce," line 25) is too bitter ("tart").
5. Finish your toast first, before I propose mine.
6. Small keyboard instrument; (sexual).
7. Break our agreement (not to refer to Emilia).

45 PALAMON   By heaven and earth,
    There's nothing in thee honest.
    ARCITE   Then I'll leave you—
    You are a beast° now.   *behaving savagely*
    PALAMON   As thou mak'st me, traitor.
    ARCITE [*pointing to the bundle*]   There's all things needful: files
            and shirts and perfumes—
    I'll come again some two hours hence and bring
    That that shall quiet° all.   *silence*
50 PALAMON   A sword and armour.
    ARCITE   Fear° me not. You are now too foul.° Farewell.   *Doubt / beastly*
    Get off your trinkets:° you shall want naught.   *shackles*
    PALAMON   Sirrah°—   *(an insult)*
    ARCITE   I'll hear no more.   *Exit*
    PALAMON   If he keep touch°, he dies for't.   *keeps his promise*
                                    Exit [*as into the bush*]

                              ## 3.4

                    Enter [*the*] JAILER'S DAUGHTER
    JAILER'S DAUGHTER   I am very cold, and all the stars are out too,
    The little stars and all, that look like aglets°—   *shiny ornaments*
    The sun has seen my folly. Palamon!
    Alas, no, he's in heaven. Where am I now?
5   Yonder's the sea and there's a ship—how't tumbles!
    And there's a rock lies watching under water—
    Now, now, it° beats upon it—now, now, now,   *(the ship)*
    There's a leak sprung, a sound° one—how they cry!   *large*
    Open her¹ before the wind—you'll lose all else.
10 Up with a course° or two and tack° about, boys.   *lower sail / turn*
    Good night, good night, you're gone. I am very hungry.
    Would I could find a fine frog—he would tell me
    News from all parts o'th' world, then would I make
    A carrack° of a cockle-shell, and sail   *cargo ship*
15 By east and north-east to the King of Pygmies,
    For he tells fortunes rarely.° Now my father,   *wonderfully*
    Twenty to one, is trussed up in a trice°   *to be hanged quickly*
    Tomorrow morning. I'll say never a word.
    [*She*] sing[*s*]
    For I'll cut my green coat, a foot above my knee,
20 And I'll clip my yellow locks, an inch below mine eye,
        Hey nonny, nonny, nonny,
    He s'buy° me a white cut,² forth for to ride,   *He shall buy*
    And I'll go seek him, through the world that is so wide,
        Hey nonny, nonny, nonny.
25 O for a prick now, like a nightingale,
    To put my breast against.³ I shall sleep like a top° else.   *Exit*   *soundly*

3.4
1. Open her sails (so she can run).
2. Horse (called a "cut" because it was a gelding or had
a cropped tail).

3. *O . . . against*: nightingales supposedly pricked themselves to stay awake at night. "Prick" also carries a sexual meaning; compare the sexual punning here with
that in Ophelia's "mad" speeches in *Hamlet*.

3.5

Enter [Gerald] a SCHOOLMASTER, *[five]* COUNTRYMEN,
[one of whom is dressed as a] BABION, *[five]* Wenches,
[and Timothy,] a TABORER. *[All are attired as morris
dancers]*[1]

SCHOOLMASTER Fie, fie,
  What tediosity and disinsanity[2]
  Is here among ye! Have my rudiments°   *lessons; rehearsals*
  Been laboured so long with ye, milked unto ye,
5 And, by a figure,° even the very plum-broth   *figure of speech*
  And marrow[3] of my understanding laid upon ye?
  And do you still cry 'where?' and 'how?' and 'wherefore?'
  You most coarse frieze capacities, ye jean judgements,[4]
  Have I said, 'thus let be', and 'there let be',
10 And 'then let be', and no man understand me?
  Proh deum, medius fidius[5]—ye are all dunces.
  Forwhy, here stand I. Here the Duke comes. There are you,
  Close° in the thicket. The Duke appears. I meet him,   *Hidden*
  And unto him I utter learnèd things
15 And many figures. He hears, and nods, and hums,°   *murmurs approval*
  And then cries, 'Rare!', and I go forward.° At length   *continue*
  I fling my cap up—mark there—then do you,
  As once did Meleager and the boar,[6]
  Break comely out° before him, like true lovers,[7]   *Appear decorously*
20 Cast yourselves in a body decently,[8]
  And sweetly, by a figure, trace° and turn, boys.   *follow the steps*
FIRST COUNTRYMAN And sweetly we will do it, master Gerald.
SECOND COUNTRYMAN Draw up the company. Where's the
    taborer?
THIRD COUNTRYMAN Why, Timothy!
TABORER   Here, my mad boys, have at ye!°   *go ahead; I'm ready*
SCHOOLMASTER But I say, where's these women?
25 FOURTH COUNTRYMAN   Here's Friz and Madeline.
SECOND COUNTRYMAN And little Luce with the white legs, and
    bouncing° Barbara.   *robust*
FIRST COUNTRYMAN And freckled Nell, that never failed her
    master.°   *(with sexual overtone)*
SCHOOLMASTER Where be your ribbons,[9] maids? Swim° with *Dance gracefully*
    your bodies
  And carry it° sweetly and deliverly,°   *move / nimbly*
30 And now and then a favour° and a frisk.°   *kiss; bow / leap*
NELL Let us alone,° sir.   *Leave it to us*
SCHOOLMASTER   Where's the rest o'th' music?°   *musicians*
THIRD COUNTRYMAN Dispersed° as you commanded.   *Placed here and there*
SCHOOLMASTER   Couple,° then,   *Pair up*
  And see what's wanting.° Where's the babion?   *who's missing*

3.5
1. The morris dance was a rural folk dance of north
English origin, performed in costume. *babion:* one morris dancer, who took the part of the fool, always wore
the costume of an ape or a baboon. *taborer:* drummer.
2. What tedium and folly (pedantic).
3. "Plum-broth" (hearty stew of dried fruits and suet)
and "marrow" both suggest essence or fortifying sustenance.
4. *You . . . judgements:* You people of rudimentary
intellects. "Frieze" and "jean" were coarse fabrics worn

by laborers.
5. O God, heaven help me (Latin).
6. Meleager was a Greek warrior who killed the great
Calydonian boar and brought its head to the Amazon
warrior Atalanta.
7. Like loving subjects of Theseus; in couples, as lovers
do.
8. Position yourselves appropriately for the dance.
9. Morris dancers carried ribbons or streamers as
props.

[*To the* BABION] My friend, carry your tail without offence°   *sexual offense*

35 Or scandal to the ladies; and be sure

You tumble with audacity and manhood,°   *bravery*

And when you bark,[1] do it with judgement.

BABION   Yes, sir.

SCHOOLMASTER   *Quousque tandem?*[2] Here is a woman wanting!

FOURTH COUNTRYMAN   We may go whistle—all the fat's i'th'
    fire.[3]

40 SCHOOLMASTER   We have,

As learnèd authors utter, washed a tile;°   *worked in vain*

We have been *fatuus*,° and laboured vainly.   *foolish*

SECOND COUNTRYMAN   This is that scornful piece, that scurvy

hilding°   *worthless woman*

That gave her promise faithfully she would be here—

45 Cicely, the seamstress' daughter.

The next gloves that I give her shall be dogskin.°   *cheap leather*

Nay, an° she fail me once—you can tell, Arcas,   *if*

She swore by wine and bread she would not break.°   *(her solemn oath)*

SCHOOLMASTER   An eel and woman,

50 A learnèd poet says, unless by th' tail

And with thy teeth thou hold, will either° fail—   *both*

In manners this was false position.[4]

FIRST COUNTRYMAN   A fire-ill take her!° Does she flinch now?   *A pox infect her*

THIRD COUNTRYMAN   What

Shall we determine,° sir?   *decide to do*

SCHOOLMASTER   Nothing;

55 Our business is become a nullity,

Yea, and a woeful and a piteous nullity.

FOURTH COUNTRYMAN   Now, when the credit of our town lay on it,

Now to be frampold, now to piss o'th' nettle![5]

Go thy ways—I'll remember thee, I'll fit thee!°   *get even with you*

Enter [the] JAILER'S DAUGHTER

JAILER'S DAUGHTER [*sings*]

60 The *George Alow*[6] came from the south,

    From the coast of Barbary-a;

And there he met with brave gallants of war,°   *warships*

    By one, by two, by three-a.

'Well hailed, well hailed, you jolly gallants,

65   And whither now are you bound-a?

O let me have your company

    Till I come to the sound-a.'

There was three fools fell out about an owlet—

    The one he said it was an owl,

70   The other he said nay,

    The third he said it was a hawk,

        And her bells were cut away.[7]

---

1. Baboons were considered half man, half dog.
2. How much longer (must I wait)? (Latin, as throughout the scene.) Expression of impatience that opens the ancient Roman writer Cicero's first oration against Catiline but here indicates the Schoolmaster's pomposity.
3. We may as well give up, since all our work has produced nothing. Both phrases were proverbial, although the second has a different meaning today.

4. A false (pro)position is a logical fallacy. The Schoolmaster compares Cicely's flawed manners to faulty logic.
5. Now to be temperamental, to lose her temper.
6. Probably taken from "The George Aloe and the Sweepstake," a ballad published in 1611. The *George Aloe* was a ship.
7. Hawks used for falconry wore bells in order to make them easier to catch.

THIRD COUNTRYMAN   There's a dainty° madwoman, master,   *fine*
   Comes i'th' nick,° as mad as a March hare.   *nick (of time)*
75 If we can get her dance, we are made again.°   *all will be well*
   I warrant her, she'll do the rarest gambols.°   *finest capers*
FIRST COUNTRYMAN   A madwoman? We are made, boys.
SCHOOLMASTER [*to the* JAILER'S DAUGHTER]   And are you mad,
   good woman?
JAILER'S DAUGHTER   I would be sorry else.
   Give me your hand.
SCHOOLMASTER   Why?
JAILER'S DAUGHTER   I can tell your fortune.
   [*She examines his hand*]
80 You are a fool. Tell ten—I have posed him.[8] Buzz!°   *Silence*
   Friend, you must eat no white bread—if you do,
   Your teeth will bleed extremely. Shall we dance, ho?
   I know you—you're a tinker.° Sirrah tinker,   *mender of kettles*
   Stop no more holes but what you should.°   *(sexual)*
SCHOOLMASTER   *Dii boni*°—   *Good gods*
   A tinker, damsel?
85 JAILER'S DAUGHTER   Or a conjurer°—   *magician*
   Raise me a devil now and let him play
   Qui passa o'th' bells and bones.[9]
SCHOOLMASTER   Go, take her,
   And fluently persuade her to a peace.°   *to do what we want*
   Et opus exegi, quod nec Iovis ira, nec ignis[1]—
   Strike up, and lead her in.
90 SECOND COUNTRYMAN   Come, lass, let's trip it.°   *let's dance*
JAILER'S DAUGHTER   I'll lead.
THIRD COUNTRYMAN   Do, do.
SCHOOLMASTER   Persuasively and cunningly°—   *skillfully*
   Wind horns [*within*]   away, boys,
   I hear the horns. Give me some meditation,°   *time to think*
   And mark° your cue.   *don't forget*
     Exeunt all but [*Gerald the*] SCHOOLMASTER
95   Pallas° inspire me.   *goddess of wisdom*
   Enter THESEUS, PIRITHOUS, HIPPOLYTA, EMILIA, ARCITE,
   and train
THESEUS   This way the stag took.
SCHOOLMASTER   Stay and edify.°   *be edified*
THESEUS   What have we here?
PIRITHOUS   Some country sport, upon my life, sir.
THESEUS [*to the* SCHOOLMASTER]   Well, sir, go forward—we will
100 edify.
   Ladies, sit down—we'll stay it.°   *stay to watch*
   [*They sit:* THESEUS *in a chair, the others on stools*]
SCHOOLMASTER   Thou doughty Duke, all hail! All hail, sweet
   ladies.
THESEUS   This is a cold° beginning.   *(punning on "hail")*

---

8. *Tell . . . him:* Count to ten (a common test for insanity or idiocy)—I have stumped ("posed") him. The Jailer's Daughter tests the Schoolmaster for idiocy and fails him.
9. *Chi passa* (Italian: who passes) were the first words of a common dance tune. Bones were used as percus-

sion instruments, along with bells.
1. "And I have created a work which neither Jove's anger nor fire [can destroy]." Slightly misquoted from Ovid's *Metamorphoses* 15.871.

SCHOOLMASTER   If you but favour,[2] our country pastime made is.

105 We are a few of those collected here,
     That ruder tongues distinguish° 'villager';   *call*
     And to say verity, and not to fable,
     We are a merry rout, or else a rabble,
     Or company, or, by a figure,° chorus,   *figure of speech*
110 That fore thy dignity will dance a morris.
     And I, that am the rectifier° of all,   *director; connector*
     By title *pedagogus*,° that let fall   *teacher*
     The birch upon the breeches of the small ones,
     And humble with a ferula° the tall ones,   *cane*
115 Do here present this machine, or this frame;[3]
     And dainty Duke, whose doughty dismal° fame   *awe-inspiring*
     From Dis to Daedalus,[4] from post to pillar,
     Is blown abroad, help me, thy poor well-willer,°   *well-wisher*
     And with thy twinkling eyes, look right and straight
120 Upon this mighty 'Moor'—of mickle° weight—   *much*
     'Ice' now comes in,[5] which, being glued together,
     Makes 'morris', and the cause that we came hither.
     The body of our sport, of no small study,[6]
     I first appear, though rude, and raw, and muddy,
125 To speak, before thy noble grace, this tenor[7]
     At whose great feet I offer up my penner.°   *pen case*
     The next,° the Lord of May and Lady bright;   *next to appear*
     The Chambermaid and Servingman, by night
     That seek out silent hanging;[8] then mine Host
130 And his fat Spouse, that welcomes, to their cost,
     The gallèd° traveller, and with a beck'ning   *tired*
     Informs the tapster° to inflame the reck'ning;°   *bartender / overcharge*
     Then the beest-eating Clown;[9] and next, the Fool;
     The babion with long tail and eke long tool,°   *penis*
135 *Cum multis aliis*° that make a dance—   *With many others*
     Say 'ay', and all shall presently° advance.   *at once*
THESEUS   Ay, ay, by any means, dear dominie.°   *teacher*
PIRITHOUS   Produce.°   *Put on (your show)*
SCHOOLMASTER   (knock[s] for the dance)
     Intrate filii,[1] come forth and foot it.
     [*He flings up his cap.*] *Music.*
     [*The* SCHOOLMASTER *ushers in*
     May Lord,   May Lady.
     Servingman,   Chambermaid.
     A Country Clown,
     or Shepherd,   Country Wench.

---

2. Approve. Compare Quince's speech to Theseus in *A Midsummer Night's Dream* 5.1.126–50.
3. Both "machine" and "frame" mean "structure" or "production."
4. Dis was god of the underworld; Daedalus was creator of the Cretan labyrinth and inventor of wings for human flight. Theseus triumphed over both the underworld and the labyrinth. Daedalus is invoked for the sake of alliteration and, because of his association with flight and hence the heavens, for contrast to Dis.
5. The Schoolmaster displays the word "morris" from two placards, possibly held by the dancers. In Q, the word is split into two syllables, "Morr" and "Is" (here emended to "Moor" and "Ice"). They may have been

spelled out, or perhaps pictograms were used, with the first placard depicting a Moor and the second the allegorical figure Winter.
6. The main part in our entertainment, carefully prepared.
7. Argument; tenner (ten-syllable line).
8. Curtain behind which they can make love.
9. Clown or country shepherd (see stage direction at line 138) who likes "beest," the thick milk produced by a cow for the first few days after calving.
1. Come in, my sons (children). The masculine *filii* is especially appropriate, since the women's parts were played by boy actors.

An Host,	Hostess.
A He-babion,	She-babion.
A He-fool,	The JAILER'S DAUGHTER as She-fool.

All these persons apparelled to the life,° the men issuing   in lifelike costume
out of one door and the wenches from the other. They
dance a morris]

     Ladies, if we have been merry,
140   And have pleased ye with a derry,
     And a derry, and a down,°   (song refrain words)
     Say the schoolmaster's no clown.
     Duke, if we have pleased thee too,
     And have done as good boys should do,
145   Give us but a tree or twain
     For a maypole, and again,
     Ere another year run out,
     We'll make thee laugh, and all this rout.°   company

THESEUS   Take twenty, dominie. [*To* HIPPOLYTA] How does my
     sweetheart?
HIPPOLYTA   Never so pleased, sir.
150 EMILIA   'Twas an excellent dance,
     And for a preface,° I never heard a better.   as for the prologue
THESEUS   Schoolmaster, I thank you. One see 'em all rewarded.
PIRITHOUS   And here's something to paint your pole withal.
     [*He gives them money*]
THESEUS   Now to our sports again.
SCHOOLMASTER
155   May the stag thou hunt'st stand long,°   give a good chase
     And thy dogs be swift and strong;
     May they kill him without lets,°   obstacles
     And the ladies eat his dowsets.°   testicles (a delicacy)
     [*Exeunt* THESEUS *and train.*] *Wind horns* [*within*]
     Come, we are all made. *Dii deaeque omnes,*°   Gods and goddesses all
160   Ye have danced rarely, wenches.   *Exeunt*

3.6

Enter PALAMON *from the bush*

PALAMON   About this hour my cousin gave his faith°   word
     To visit me again, and with him bring
     Two swords and two good armours;° if he fail,   suits of armor
     He's neither man nor soldier. When he left me,
5   I did not think a week could have restored
     My lost strength to me, I was grown so low
     And crest-fall'n with my wants. I thank thee, Arcite,
     Thou art yet a fair foe, and I feel myself,
     With this refreshing, able once again
10   To out-dure° danger. To delay it longer   endure; outlast
     Would make the world think, when it comes to hearing,°   when word gets out
     That I lay fatting, like a swine, to fight,
     And not a soldier.[1] Therefore this blest morning

3.6
1. *fatting . . . soldier:* being fattened like a swine for the slaughter, rather than preparing myself like a warrior for the fight.

Shall be the last; and that sword he refuses,°   *(in choosing first)*
15   If it but hold,° I kill him with; 'tis justice.   *Unless it breaks*
     So, love and fortune for me!
               Enter ARCITE *with [two] armours and [two] swords*
                    O, good morrow.
ARCITE   Good morrow, noble kinsman.
PALAMON   I have put you
     To too much pains, sir.
ARCITE   That too much, fair cousin,
     Is but a debt to honour, and my duty.
20   PALAMON   Would you were so in all, sir—I could wish ye
     As kind a kinsman, as you force me find
     A beneficial foe, that my embraces
     Might thank ye, not my blows.
ARCITE   I shall think either,
     Well done, a noble recompense.
PALAMON   Then I shall quit° you.   *repay*
25   ARCITE   Defy me in these fair terms, and you show°   *show youself to be*
     More than a mistress to me—no more anger,
     As you love anything that's honourable.
     We were not bred to talk, man. When we are armed
     And both upon our guards, then let our fury,
30   Like meeting of two tides, fly strongly from us;
     And then to whom the birthright° of this beauty   *rightful possession*
     Truly pertains°—without upbraidings, scorns,   *belongs*
     Despisings of our persons, and such poutings
     Fitter for girls and schoolboys—will be seen,
35   And quickly, yours or mine. Will't please you arm, sir?
     Or, if you feel yourself not fitting° yet,   *ready*
     And furnished with your old strength, I'll stay,° cousin,   *wait*
     And every day discourse you into health,
     As I am spared.° Your person I am friends with,   *In my spare time*
40   And I could wish I had not said I loved her,
     Though I had died;[2] but loving such a lady,
     And justifying° my love, I must not fly from't.   *affirming*
PALAMON   Arcite, thou art so brave an enemy
     That no man but thy cousin's fit to kill thee.
     I am well and lusty°—choose your arms.   *eager to do battle*
45   ARCITE   Choose you, sir.
PALAMON   Wilt thou exceed in all,[3] or dost thou do it
     To make me spare thee?
ARCITE   If you think so, cousin,
     You are deceived, for as I am a soldier,
     I will not spare you.
PALAMON   That's well said.
ARCITE   You'll find it.°   *find it so*
50   PALAMON   Then as I am an honest man, and love
     With all the justice of affection,[4]
     I'll pay thee soundly.°   *punish you properly*
               [He chooses one armour]
                    This I'll take.

---

2. Although it would have killed me to keep silent.
3. Will you always outdo me in courtesy (as here, by letting me choose my arms first)?
4. Palamon's love of Emilia is just; Palamon will deal justly (honorably) with Arcite because he loves him.

ARCITE [*indicating the remaining armour*]   That's mine, then.
   I'll arm you first.
PALAMON   Do.
         [ARCITE *arms* PALAMON]
                 Pray thee tell me, cousin,
   Where gott'st thou this good armour?
ARCITE   'Tis the Duke's,
   And to say true, I stole it. Do I pinch you?
55 PALAMON   No.
ARCITE   Is't not too heavy?
PALAMON   I have worn a lighter—
   But I shall make it serve.
ARCITE   I'll buckle't close.°   *tightly*
PALAMON   By any means.
ARCITE   You care not for a grand guard?[5]
PALAMON   No, no, we'll use no horses. I perceive
   You would fain be at that fight.°   *rather fight mounted*
60 ARCITE   I am indifferent.
PALAMON   Faith, so am I. Good cousin, thrust the buckle
   Through far enough.
ARCITE   I warrant you.°   *Trust me*
PALAMON   My casque° now.   *helmet*
ARCITE   Will you fight bare-armed?
PALAMON   We shall be the nimbler.
ARCITE   But use your gauntlets, though—those are o'th' least.° *too small*
   Prithee take mine, good cousin.
65 PALAMON   Thank you, Arcite.
   How do I look? Am I fall'n much away?°   *much thinner*
ARCITE   Faith, very little—love has used you kindly.
PALAMON   I'll warrant thee, I'll strike home.
ARCITE   Do, and spare not—
   I'll give you cause, sweet cousin.
PALAMON   Now to you, sir.
        [PALAMON *arms* ARCITE]
70 Methinks this armour's very like that, Arcite,
   Thou wor'st that day the three kings fell, but lighter.
ARCITE   That was a very good one, and that day,
   I well remember, you outdid me, cousin.
   I never saw such valour. When you charged
75 Upon the left wing of the enemy,
   I spurred hard to come up,° and under me   *keep up with you*
   I had a right good horse.
PALAMON   You had indeed—
   A bright bay, I remember.
ARCITE   Yes. But all
   Was vainly laboured in me—you outwent me,
80 Nor could my wishes reach you.[6] Yet a little
   I did by imitation.
PALAMON   More by virtue°—   *valor*
   You are modest, cousin.
ARCITE   When I saw you charge first,
   Methought I heard a dreadful clap of thunder
   Break from the troop.

---

5. Chest plate for fighting on horseback.   6. My wishes to keep up with you were not answered.

PALAMON   But still before that flew

85   The lightning of your valour. Stay a little,

    Is not this piece too strait?°   *tight*

ARCITE   No, no, 'tis well.

PALAMON   I would have nothing hurt thee but my sword—

    A bruise would be dishonour.

ARCITE   Now I am perfect°.   *ready*

PALAMON   Stand off,° then.   *Step back*

ARCITE   Take my sword; I hold° it better.   *consider*

90   PALAMON   I thank ye. No, keep it—your life lies° on it.   *depends*

    Here's one—if it but hold,° I ask no more   *holds together*

    For all my hopes. My cause and honour guard me.

ARCITE   And me, my love.

           They bow several ways,[7] *then advance and stand*

                      Is there aught else to say?

PALAMON   This only, and no more. Thou art mine aunt's son,

95   And that blood we desire to shed is mutual:

    In me, thine, and in thee, mine. My sword

    Is in my hand, and if thou kill'st me,

    The gods and I forgive thee. If there be

    A place prepared for those that sleep in honour,

100   I wish his weary soul that falls may win it.

    Fight bravely, cousin. Give me thy noble hand.

ARCITE   Here, Palamon. This hand shall never more

    Come near thee with such friendship.

PALAMON   I commend thee.°   *(to God)*

ARCITE   If I fall, curse me, and say I was a coward—

105   For none but such dare die in these just trials.

    Once more farewell, my cousin.

PALAMON   Farewell, Arcite.

      Fight. Horns within; they stand

ARCITE   Lo, cousin, lo, our folly has undone us.

PALAMON   Why?

ARCITE   This is the Duke a-hunting, as I told you.

    If we be found, we are wretched. O, retire,

110   For honour's sake, and safely, presently,

    Into your bush again. Sir, we shall find

    Too many° hours to die. In, gentle cousin—   *More than enough*

    If you be seen, you perish instantly

    For breaking prison, and I, if you reveal me,

115   For my contempt.[8] Then all the world will scorn us,

    And say we had a noble difference,

    But base disposers of it.°   *settled it ignobly*

PALAMON   No, no, cousin,

    I will no more be hidden, nor put off

    This great adventure° to a second trial.   *undertaking*

120   I know your cunning and I know your cause°—   *motive (for delay)*

    He that faints° now, shame take him! Put thyself   *is fainthearted*

    Upon thy present guard°—   *At once on guard*

ARCITE   You are not mad?

PALAMON   Or° I will make th'advantage of this hour   *Either I'm mad or*

---

7. They make ceremonial bows in various directions, as if they were jousting in a tournament.

8. For my disobedience to Theseus's order that I be banished.

Mine own, and what to come shall threaten me
125 I fear less than my fortune.° Know, weak cousin, *(in this fight)*
I love Emilia, and in that I'll bury
Thee and all crosses else.° *all other obstacles*

ARCITE   Then come what can come,
Thou shalt know, Palamon, I dare as well
Die as discourse or sleep. Only this fears° me, *frightens*
130 The law will have the honour of our ends.⁹
Have at thy life!

PALAMON   Look to thine own well, Arcite!
    [*They*] *fight again.*
    Horns. Enter THESEUS, HIPPOLYTA, EMILIA, PIRITHOUS,
    and train. [THESEUS *separates* PALAMON *and* ARCITE]

THESEUS   What ignorant and mad malicious° traitors *evil-minded*
Are you, that 'gainst the tenor° of my laws *purport*
Are making battle, thus like knights appointed,° *armed*
135 Without my leave and officers of arms?¹
By Castor,² both shall die.

PALAMON   Hold° thy word, Theseus. *Keep*
We are certainly both traitors, both despisers° *disobedient*
Of thee and of thy goodness. I am Palamon,
That cannot love thee, he that broke thy prison—
140 Think well what that deserves. And this is Arcite;
A bolder traitor never trod thy ground,
A falser ne'er seemed friend. This is the man
Was begged° and banished; this is he contemns thee, *petitioned for*
And what thou dar'st do; and in this disguise,
145 Against thine own edict, follows thy sister,° *sister-in-law*
That fortunate bright° star, the fair Emilia, *luck-bringing*
Whose servant°—if there be a right in seeing *courtly lover*
And first bequeathing of the soul to—justly
I am; and, which is more, dares think her his.
150 This treachery, like a most trusty lover,
I called him now to answer. If thou be'st
As thou art spoken,° great and virtuous, *reported to be*
The true decider of all injuries,
Say, 'Fight again', and thou shalt see me, Theseus,
155 Do such a justice thou thyself wilt envy.
Then take my life—I'll woo thee to't.

PIRITHOUS   O heaven,
What more than man is this!

THESEUS   I have sworn.

ARCITE   We seek not
Thy breath of mercy, Theseus. 'Tis to me
A thing as soon to die as thee to say it,
160 And no more moved. Where this man calls me traitor
Let me say thus much—if in love be treason,
In service of so excellent a beauty,
As I love most, and in that faith will perish,
As I have brought my life here to confirm it,
165 As I have served her truest, worthiest,
As I dare kill this cousin that denies it,

---

9. We will die by execution rather than combat.
1. Overseers of chivalric combat.

2. Common Roman oath. Castor and Pollux, twins, were sons of Jupiter.

So let me be most traitor and ye please me.
For° scorning thy edict, Duke, ask that lady   *As for*
Why she is fair, and why her eyes command me
170   Stay here to love her, and if she say, 'Traitor',
I am a villain fit to lie unburied.
PALAMON   Thou shalt have pity of° us both, O Theseus,   *on*
If unto neither thou show mercy. Stop,
As thou art just, thy noble ear against us;
175   As thou art valiant, for thy cousin's° soul,   *(Hercules')*
Whose twelve strong labours crown his memory,
Let's die together, at one instant, Duke.
Only a little let him fall before me,
That I may tell my soul he shall not have her.
180   THESEUS   I grant your wish; for to say true, your cousin
Has ten times more offended, for I gave him
More mercy than you found, sir, your offences
Being no more than his. None here speak for 'em,
For ere the sun set both shall sleep for ever.
185   HIPPOLYTA *[to* EMILIA*]*   Alas, the pity! Now or never, sister,
Speak, not to be denied. That face of yours
Will bear the curses else of after ages
For these lost cousins.
EMILIA   In my face, dear sister,
I find no anger to 'em, nor no ruin.
190   The misadventure of their own eyes kill° 'em.   *kills*
Yet that° I will be woman and have pity,   *to show that*
    [She kneels]
My knees shall grow to th' ground, but° I'll get mercy.   *unless*
Help me, dear sister—in a deed so virtuous
The powers of all women will be with us.
    *[*HIPPOLYTA *kneels]*
Most royal brother—
HIPPOLYTA   Sir, by our tie of marriage—
EMILIA   By your own spotless honour—
195   HIPPOLYTA   By that faith,
That fair hand, and that honest heart you gave me—
EMILIA   By that you would have pity in another,[3]
By your own virtues infinite—
HIPPOLYTA   By valour,
By all the chaste° nights I have ever pleased you—   *faithful only to you*
THESEUS   These are strange conjurings.°   *incantations*
200   PIRITHOUS   Nay, then, I'll in too.
    [He kneels]
By all our friendship, sir, by all our dangers,
By all you love most: wars, and this sweet lady—
EMILIA   By that° you would have trembled to deny   *(chivalric aid)*
A blushing maid—
HIPPOLYTA   By your own eyes, by strength—
In which you swore I went beyond° all women,   *I excelled*
205   Almost all men—and yet I yielded, Theseus—
PIRITHOUS   To crown all this, by your most noble soul,
Which cannot want° due mercy, I beg first—   *lack*

---

3. By whatever you would expect someone else to pity.

HIPPOLYTA   Next hear my prayers—
210 EMILIA   Last let me entreat, sir—
PIRITHOUS   For mercy.
HIPPOLYTA   Mercy.
EMILIA   Mercy on these princes.
THESEUS   Ye make my faith reel.[4] Say I felt
    Compassion to 'em both, how would you place° it?   have me bestow
        [*They rise*]
EMILIA   Upon their lives—but with their banishments.
215 THESEUS   You are a right° woman, sister: you have pity,   typical
    But want the understanding where to use it.
    If you desire their lives, invent a way
    Safer than banishment. Can these two live,
    And have the agony of love about 'em,
220   And not kill one another? Every day
    They'd fight about you, hourly bring your honour
    In public question with their swords.[5] Be wise, then,
    And here forget 'em. It concerns your credit°   reputation
    And my oath equally. I have said—they die.
225   Better they fall by th' law than one another.
    Bow not my honour.[6]
EMILIA   O my noble brother,
    That oath was rashly° made, and in your anger.   impulsively
    Your reason will not hold° it. If such vows   sustain
    Stand for express will,° all the world must perish.   steadfast resolve
230   Beside, I have another oath 'gainst yours,
    Of more authority, I am sure more love—
    Not made in passion, neither, but good heed.°   thoughtfulness
THESEUS   What is it, sister?
PIRITHOUS [*to* EMILIA]   Urge it home, brave lady.
EMILIA   That you would ne'er deny me anything
235   Fit for my modest suit and your free granting.
    I tie you to your word now; if ye fail in't,
    Think how you maim your honour—
    For now I am set a-begging, sir. I am deaf
    To all but your compassion—how their lives
240   Might breed the ruin of my name, opinion.°   my reputation
    Shall anything that loves me perish for° me?   because of
    That were a cruel wisdom: do men prune
    The straight young boughs that blush with thousand blossoms
    Because they may be° rotten? O, Duke Theseus,   become
245   The goodly mothers that have groaned for these,°   (in childbirth)
    And all the longing maids that ever loved,
    If your vow stand,° shall curse me and my beauty,   holds
    And in their funeral songs for these two cousins
    Despise my cruelty and cry woe worth° me,   befall
250   Till I am nothing but the scorn of women.
    For heaven's sake, save their lives and banish 'em.
THESEUS   On what conditions?
EMILIA   Swear 'em° never more   Have them swear
    To make me their contention, or to know me,°   think of me

---

4. You make my constancy to my own oath (to kill the kinsmen) waver.
5. *They'd . . . swords:* They'd fight publicly over you, thus compromising your honor.
6. Don't force me to lower (bend) my standards of honor.

To tread upon thy dukedom; and to be,
255 Wherever they shall travel, ever strangers
To one another.

PALAMON   I'll be cut a-pieces
Before I take this oath—forget I love her?
O all ye gods, despise me, then. Thy banishment
I not mislike, so we may fairly carry
260 Our swords and cause along—else, never trifle,
But take our lives, Duke. I must love, and will;
And for that love must and dare kill this cousin
On any piece° the earth has.   *spot of ground*

THESEUS   Will you, Arcite,
Take these conditions?

PALAMON   He's a villain then.

PIRITHOUS   These are men!

265 ARCITE   No, never, Duke. 'Tis worse to me than begging,
To take° my life so basely. Though I think   *value*
I never shall enjoy her, yet I'll preserve
The honour of affection and die for her,
Make death a devil.°   *Even horribly*

270 THESEUS   What may be done? For now I feel compassion.

PIRITHOUS   Let it not fall° again, sir.   *diminish*

THESEUS   Say, Emilia,
If one of them were dead—as one must—are you
Content to take the other to your husband?
They cannot both enjoy you. They are princes
275 As goodly as your own eyes, and as noble
As ever fame yet spoke of. Look upon 'em,
And if you can love, end this difference.
I give consent. [*To* PALAMON *and* ARCITE] Are you content too,
        princes?

PALAMON *and* ARCITE   With all our souls.

THESEUS   He that she refuses
Must die, then.

280 PALAMON *and* ARCITE   Any death thou canst invent, Duke.

PALAMON   If I fall from that mouth,° I fall with favour,   *(because of her decision)*
And lovers yet unborn shall bless my ashes.

ARCITE   If she refuse me, yet my grave will wed me,
And soldiers sing my epitaph.

THESEUS [*to* EMILIA]   Make choice, then.

285 EMILIA   I cannot, sir. They are both too excellent.
For° me, a hair shall never fall of these men.   *On account of*

HIPPOLYTA [*to* THESEUS]   What will become of 'em?

THESEUS   Thus I ordain it,
And by mine honour once again it stands,
Or both shall die. [*To* PALAMON *and* ARCITE] You shall both to your country,
290 And each within this month, accompanied
With three fair knights, appear again in this place,
In which I'll plant° a pyramid; and whether,°   *fix / whichever*
Before us that are here, can force his cousin,
By fair and knightly strength, to touch the pillar,
295 He shall enjoy her; the other lose his head,
And all his friends; nor shall he grudge to fall,[7]

---

7. And all his friends will die with him; nor should he consider his execution unjust.

Nor think he dies with interest in° this lady.   *a rightful claim to*
Will this content ye?
PALAMON   Yes. Here, cousin Arcite,
I am friends again till that hour.
ARCITE   I embrace ye.
THESEUS [*to* EMILIA]   Are you content, sister?
300 EMILIA   Yes, I must, sir,
Else both miscarry.°   *perish*
THESEUS [*to* PALAMON *and* ARCITE]
                    Come, shake hands again, then,
And take heed, as you are gentlemen, this quarrel
Sleep till the hour prefixed, and hold your course.°   *keep your resolve*
PALAMON   We dare not fail thee, Theseus.
THESEUS   Come, I'll give ye
305 Now usage like to princes and to friends.
When ye return, who wins I'll settle here,°   *set up in Athens*
Who loses, yet I'll weep upon his bier.
                    Exeunt. [*In the act-time the bush is removed*]

4.1

Enter [*the*] JAILER *and his* FRIEND

JAILER   Hear you no more? Was nothing said of me
Concerning the escape of Palamon?
Good sir, remember.
FRIEND   Nothing that I heard,
For I came home before the business
5 Was fully ended. Yet I might perceive,
Ere I departed, a great likelihood
Of both their pardons: for Hippolyta
And fair-eyed Emily upon their knees
Begged with such handsome pity that the Duke,
10 Methought, stood staggering° whether he should follow   *wavering as to*
His rash oath or the sweet compassion
Of those two ladies; and to second them
That truly noble prince, Pirithous—
Half his own heart[1]—set in too, that° I hope   *so that*
15 All shall be well. Neither heard I one question
Of your name or his scape.
                    Enter [*the*] SECOND FRIEND
JAILER   Pray heaven it hold° so.   *continue*
SECOND FRIEND   Be of good comfort, man. I bring you news,
Good news.
JAILER   They are welcome.
SECOND FRIEND   Palamon has cleared you,
And got your pardon, and discovered° how   *exposed*
20 And by whose means he scaped—which was your daughter's,
Whose pardon is procured too; and the prisoner,
Not to be held ungrateful to her goodness,
Has given a sum of money to her marriage—
A large one, I'll assure you.
JAILER   Ye are a good man,
And ever bring good news.
25 FIRST FRIEND   How was it ended?

4.1 Location: The prison   1. Hippolyta is (has) the other half.

SECOND FRIEND   Why, as it should be: they that ne'er begged,
But° they prevailed, had their suits fairly granted—   *Still*
The prisoners have their lives.
FIRST FRIEND   I knew 'twould be so.
SECOND FRIEND   But there be new conditions which you'll hear of
At better time.
JAILER   I hope they are good.
30   SECOND FRIEND   They are honourable—
How good they'll prove I know not.
                    Enter [the] WOOER
FIRST FRIEND   'Twill be known.
WOOER   Alas, sir, where's your daughter?
JAILER   Why do you ask?
WOOER   O, sir, when did you see her?
SECOND FRIEND   How he looks!
JAILER   This morning.
WOOER   Was she well? Was she in health?
Sir, when did she sleep?
35   FIRST FRIEND   These are strange questions.
JAILER   I do not think she was very well: for now
You make me mind° her, but this very day   *remind me of*
I asked her questions and she answered me
So far from what she was,° so childishly,   *her usual manner*
40   So sillily, as if she were a fool,
An innocent—and I was very angry.
But what of her, sir?
WOOER   Nothing, but my pity²—
But you must know it, and as good by me
As by another that less loves her—
JAILER   Well, sir?
FIRST FRIEND   Not right?°   *in her right mind*
WOOER   No, sir, not well.
45   SECOND FRIEND   Not well?
WOOER   'Tis too true—she is mad.
FIRST FRIEND   It cannot be.
WOOER   Believe, you'll find it so.
JAILER   I half suspected
What you told me—the gods comfort her!
Either this was her love to Palamon,
50   Or fear of my miscarrying on³ his scape,
Or both.
WOOER   'Tis likely.
JAILER   But why all this haste, sir?
WOOER   I'll tell you quickly. As I late was angling°   *fishing*
In the great lake that lies behind the palace,
From the far shore, thick set with reeds and sedges,
55   As patiently I was attending sport,°   *awaiting a fish*
I heard a voice—a shrill one—and attentive
I gave my ear, when I might well perceive
'Twas one that sung, and by the smallness° of it   *high pitch*
A boy or woman. I then left my angle°   *fishing rod*
60   To his own skill,° came near, but yet perceived not   *To fish by itself*
Who made the sound, the rushes and the reeds

2. My pity for you and her makes me speak.   3. My being punished because of.

Had so encompassed it.° I laid me down   *overgrown the place*
And listened to the words she sung, for then,
Through a small glade cut by the fishermen,
I saw it was your daughter.
65 JAILER   Pray go on, sir.
WOOER   She sung much, but no sense; only I heard her
Repeat this often—'Palamon is gone,
Is gone to th' wood to gather mulberries;
I'll find him out tomorrow.'
FIRST FRIEND   Pretty soul!
70 WOOER   'His shackles will betray him—he'll be taken,
And what shall I do then? I'll bring a bevy,°   *company*
A hundred black-eyed maids that love as I do,
With chaplets° on their heads of daffodillies,   *wreaths*
With cherry lips and cheeks of damask roses,
75 And all we'll dance an antic° fore the Duke   *a grotesque dance*
And beg his pardon.'⁴ Then she talked of you, sir—
That you must lose your head tomorrow morning,
And she must gather flowers to bury you,
And see the house made handsome.° Then she sung   *neat*
80 Nothing but 'willow, willow, willow',⁵ and between
Ever was 'Palamon, fair Palamon',
And 'Palamon was a tall° young man'. The place   *valiant*
Was knee-deep° where she sat; her careless tresses   *(in rushes)*
A wreath of bull-rush rounded;° about her stuck   *encircled*
85 Thousand freshwater flowers of several° colours—   *various*
That° she appeared, methought, like the fair nymph   *Such that*
That feeds the lake with waters, or as Iris⁶
Newly dropped down from heaven. Rings she made
Of rushes that grew by,⁷ and to 'em spoke
90 The prettiest posies⁸—'Thus our true love's tied',
'This you may lose, not me', and many a one.
And then she wept, and sung again, and sighed—
And with the same breath smiled and kissed her hand.
SECOND FRIEND   Alas, what pity it is!
WOOER   I made in to° her: *approached*
95 She saw me and straight sought the flood°—I saved her, *at once jumped in*
And set her safe to land, when presently
She slipped away and to the city made,
With such a cry and swiftness that, believe me,
She left me far behind her. Three or four
100 I saw from far off cross° her—one of 'em   *intercept*
I knew to be your brother, where she stayed°   *stopped*
And fell, scarce to be got away. I left them with her,
Enter [the JAILER'S*] BROTHER, [the* JAILER'S*] DAUGHTER,*
and others
And hither came to tell you—here they are.
JAILER'S DAUGHTER [*sings*]   'May you never more enjoy the
light . . .'°—   *(unknown song)*
Is not this a fine song?
105 JAILER'S BROTHER   O, a very fine one.

---

4. Beg Duke Theseus to pardon Palamon.
5. Refrain of a popular song, also sung by Desdemona in *Othello* 4.3.
6. Goddess of the rainbow and Juno's messenger.
7. *Rings . . . by*: sometimes used as wedding rings in rural (or mock) wedding ceremonies.
8. Mottoes and aphorisms, sometimes engraved on the inside of rings.

JAILER'S DAUGHTER I can sing twenty more.

JAILER'S BROTHER I think you can.

JAILER'S DAUGHTER Yes, truly can I—I can sing 'The Broom'
And 'Bonny Robin'⁹—are not you a tailor?

JAILER'S BROTHER Yes.

JAILER'S DAUGHTER Where's my wedding gown?

JAILER'S BROTHER I'll bring it tomorrow.

110 JAILER'S DAUGHTER Do, very rarely°—I must be abroad else,°   *early / or I'll be out*
To call the maids and pay the minstrels,
For I must lose my maidenhead by cocklight,°   *before dawn*
'Twill never thrive else.¹ (*Sings*) 'O fair, O sweet . . .'²

JAILER'S BROTHER [*to the* JAILER] You must e'en take it
patiently.

JAILER 'Tis true.

JAILER'S DAUGHTER Good ev'n, good men. Pray, did you ever
115 hear
Of one young Palamon?

JAILER Yes, wench, we know him.

JAILER'S DAUGHTER Is't not a fine young gentleman?

JAILER 'Tis, love.

JAILER'S BROTHER By no mean cross her, she is then distempered
Far worse than now she shows.³

FIRST FRIEND [*to the* JAILER'S DAUGHTER] Yes, he's a fine man.

JAILER'S DAUGHTER O, is he so? You have a sister.

120 FIRST FRIEND Yes.

JAILER'S DAUGHTER But she shall never have him, tell her so,
For° a trick that I know. You'd best look to her,   *Because of*
For if she see him once, she's gone—she's done
And undone in an hour. All the young maids
125 Of our town are in love with him, but I laugh at 'em
And let 'em all alone. Is't not a wise course?

FIRST FRIEND Yes.

JAILER'S DAUGHTER There is at least two hundred now with
child by him,
There must be four;° yet I keep close⁴ for all this,   *four hundred*
Close as a cockle;° and all these° must be boys—   *clam / (the offspring)*
130 He has the trick on't°—and at ten years old   *of producing boys*
They must be all gelt for musicians⁵
And sing the wars of Theseus.

SECOND FRIEND This is strange.

JAILER'S BROTHER As ever you heard, but say nothing.

FIRST FRIEND No.

JAILER'S DAUGHTER They come from all parts of the dukedom
to him.
135 I'll warrant ye, he had not so few last night
As twenty to dispatch. He'll tickle't up°   *do the (sexual) job*
In two hours, if his hand be in.°   *if he's in good shape*

JAILER She's lost
Past all cure.

---

9. "The Broom" and "Bonny Robin" were popular songs (Ophelia sings a line of the latter in *Hamlet* 4.5). "Robin" could mean "penis."
1. Otherwise things (or possibly the marriage) won't prosper for me.
2. A song adapted from the seventh of Sir Philip Sid-

ney's *Certain Sonnets* (1598).
3. *By . . . shows:* Don't contradict her in any way, or she'll become far more deranged than she is now.
4. Keep my mouth (and thighs) closed.
5. They must all be castrated so that their voices do not break and they can become singers.

JAILER'S BROTHER Heaven forbid, man!

JAILER'S DAUGHTER [to the JAILER] Come hither—you are a
    wise man.

FIRST FRIEND Does she know him?°   *recognize her father*

SECOND FRIEND No—would she did.

140 JAILER'S DAUGHTER   You are master of a ship?

JAILER Yes.

JAILER'S DAUGHTER Where's your compass?

JAILER   Here.

JAILER'S DAUGHTER   Set it to th' north.

And now direct your course to th' wood where Palamon

Lies longing for me. For the tackling,°   *rigging*

Let me alone.° Come, weigh,° my hearts, cheerly all.   *I'll do it / (anchor)*

145 Uff, uff, uff !⁶ 'Tis up.° The wind's fair. Top° the bowline.   *(the anchor) / Tighten*

Out with the mainsail. Where's your whistle, master?

JAILER'S BROTHER Let's get her in.°   *inside (an aside)*

JAILER Up to the top,° boy!   *top of the mast*

JAILER'S BROTHER   Where's the pilot?

FIRST FRIEND   Here.

JAILER'S DAUGHTER What kenn'st thou?°   *What do you see*

SECOND FRIEND   A fair wood.

JAILER'S DAUGHTER   Bear for° it, master. *Steer toward*

150 Tack about!

    (Sings) 'When Cynthia° with her borrowed light . . .'⁷   *the moon*

                                Exeunt

4.2

Enter EMILIA, *with two pictures*°   *(Palamon and Arcite)*

EMILIA Yet I may bind those wounds up that must open

And bleed to death for my sake else—I'll choose,

And end their strife. Two such young handsome men

Shall never fall for° me; their weeping mothers   *die because of*

5 Following the dead cold ashes of their sons,

Shall never curse my cruelty. Good heaven,

What a sweet face has Arcite! If wise nature,

With all her best endowments, all those beauties

She sows into the births of noble bodies,

10 Were here a mortal woman and had in her

The coy° denials of young maids, yet doubtless   *modest*

She would run mad for this man. What an eye,

Of what a fiery sparkle and quick° sweetness   *lively*

Has this young prince! Here° love himself sits smiling!   *In his eye*

15 Just such another wanton Ganymede

Set Jove afire once, and enforced the god

Snatch up the goodly boy and set him by him,

A shining constellation.¹ What a brow,

Of what a spacious majesty, he carries!

20 Arched like the great-eyed Juno's, but far sweeter,

Smoother than Pelops' shoulder!° Fame and honour,   *(made of ivory)*

---

6. Grunts of exertion; possibly the sound of the wind in
the sails.
7. Line from an unknown song.

4.2 Location: Theseus's palace in Athens.
1. Ganymede was a beautiful youth whom Jupiter
became enamored of and carried off to be his cupbearer
on Mt. Olympus. In the end, Ganymede was transformed into the constellation Aquarius.

Methinks, from hence,° as from a promontory *his brow*
Pointed° in heaven, should clap their wings and sing *Reaching its peak*
To all the under world° the loves and fights *the earth*
25 Of gods, and such men near 'em.° Palamon *men most like gods*
Is but his foil;[2] to him a mere dull shadow;
He's swart and meagre,° of an eye as heavy° *dark and thin / sad*
As if he had lost his mother; a still temper,° *lethargic disposition*
No stirring in him, no alacrity,
30 Of all this° sprightly sharpness, not a smile.° *(Arcite's) / trace*
Yet these° that we count errors may become him: *these qualities*
Narcissus was a sad° boy, but a heavenly.° *serious / beautiful*
O, who can find the bent of woman's fancy?[3]
I am a fool, my reason is lost in me,
35 I have no choice,[4] and I have lied so lewdly° *wickedly*
That women ought to beat me. On my knees
I ask thy pardon, Palamon, thou art alone° *uniquely*
And only beautiful, and these the eyes,
These the bright lamps of beauty, that command
40 And threaten love—and what young maid dare cross° 'em? *oppose*
What a bold gravity, and yet inviting,
Has this brown manly face? O, love, this only
From this hour is complexion.[5] Lie there, Arcite,
Thou art a changeling to him, a mere gypsy,[6]
45 And this the noble body. I am sotted,° *made stupid*
Utterly lost—my virgin's faith[7] has fled me.
For if my brother, but even now, had asked me
Whether I loved, I had run mad for Arcite;
Now if my sister, more for Palamon.
50 Stand both together.° Now come ask me, brother— *(comparing portraits)*
Alas, I know not; ask me now, sweet sister—
I may go look.° What a mere child is fancy, *seek further*
That having two fair gauds° of equal sweetness, *toys*
Cannot distinguish,° but must cry for both! *choose*
    Enter [a] GENTLEMAN
How now, sir?
55 GENTLEMAN   From the noble Duke your brother,
Madam, I bring you news. The knights are come.
EMILIA   To end the quarrel?
GENTLEMAN   Yes.
EMILIA   Would I might end first!
What sins have I committed, chaste Diana,[8]
That my unspotted youth must now be soiled° *defiled*
60 With blood of princes, and my chastity
Be made the altar where the lives of lovers—
Two greater and two better never yet
Made mothers joy—must be the sacrifice
To my unhappy beauty?

---

2. Piece of thin, reflective metal in which a jewel was set, enhancing the jewel's brilliance (setting it off by contrast).
3. Who can discern which way a woman's affections will tend?
4. I am incapable of choosing.
5. *this only . . . complexion:* the only "complexion" I'll appreciate from now on is a dark one.
6. A changeling was an ugly or deformed child left by fairies in exchange for one they stole. Gypsies were also thought to steal children; otherwise the meaning is unclear, since the word generally referred to a swarthy person and Palamon has the dark complexion. Perhaps if a dark complexion is "fair," Arcite's fair skin will be considered the "gypsy" one.
7. My prior oath (1.3.86ff.) to remain a virgin.
8. Virgin goddess of the moon and of the Amazons. See 1.3.52 and note.

Enter THESEUS, HIPPOLYTA, PIRITHOUS, *and attendants*

THESEUS   Bring 'em in

65   Quickly, by any means, I long to see 'em.   [*Exit one or more*]

     [*To* EMILIA] Your two contending lovers are returned,
     And with them their fair knights. Now, my fair sister,
     You must love one of them.

EMILIA   I had rather both,

     So° neither for my sake should fall untimely.°   *So that / prematurely*

Enter [*a*] MESSENGER

THESEUS   Who saw 'em?

PIRITHOUS   I a while.

70   GENTLEMAN   And I.

THESEUS [*to the* MESSENGER]
     From whence come you, sir?

MESSENGER   From the knights.

THESEUS   Pray speak,
     You that have seen them, what they are.

MESSENGER   I will, sir,
     And truly what I think. Six braver spirits
     Than these they have brought, if we judge by the outside,

75   I never saw nor read of.[9] He that stands
     In the first place with Arcite, by his seeming,°   *appearance*
     Should be a stout° man; by his face, a prince.   *brave*
     His very looks so say° him: his complexion,   *declare*
     Nearer a brown than black, stern and yet noble,

80   Which shows him hardy, fearless, proud° of dangers.   *scornful*
     The circles of his eyes show fire within him,
     And, as a heated° lion, so he looks.   *an angry*
     His hair hangs long behind him, black and shining,
     Like ravens' wings. His shoulders, broad and strong;

85   Armed long and round;[1] and on his thigh a sword
     Hung by a curious baldric, when he frowns
     To seal his will with.[2] Better,° o' my conscience,   *A better sword*
     Was never soldier's friend.

THESEUS   Thou hast well described him.

90   PIRITHOUS   Yet a great deal short,
     Methinks, of him that's first with Palamon.

THESEUS   Pray speak° him, friend.   *describe*

PIRITHOUS   I guess he is a prince too,
     And, if it may be, greater—for his show°   *appearance*
     Has all the ornament of honour in't.

95   He's somewhat bigger than the knight he° spoke of,   *(the messenger)*
     But of a face far sweeter. His complexion
     Is as a ripe grape, ruddy. He has felt,
     Without doubt, what he fights for,° and so apter   *(love)*
     To make this cause his own. In's face appears

100   All the fair hopes of ° what he undertakes,   *confidence about*
     And when he's angry, then a settled° valour,   *steady*
     Not tainted with extremes, runs through his body
     And guides his arm to brave things. Fear he cannot—

---

9. *nor read of:* possibly a joke on the playwright's part; the following descriptions closely follow Chaucer's *Knight's Tale* 2129–78.
1. With long, well-muscled arms.

2. *Hung . . . with:* Hung from an artfully crafted ("curious") sword belt ("baldric"), which he uses to carry out his will when he is angry.

	He shows no such soft temper. His head's yellow,	
105	Hard-haired[3] and curled, thick twined: like ivy tods,°	*bushes*
	Not to undo with° thunder. In his face	*Not destroyed by*
	The livery of the warlike maid[4] appears,	
	Pure red and white—for yet no beard has blessed him—	
	And in his rolling° eyes sits victory,	*passionate*
110	As if she ever° meant to court his valour.	*(victory) always*
	His nose stands high, a character° of honour;	*distinguishing mark*
	His red lips, after fights, are fit for ladies.	

EMILIA Must these men die too?

PIRITHOUS   When he speaks, his tongue

	Sounds like a trumpet. All his lineaments°	*body parts*
115	Are as a man would wish 'em—strong and clean.°	*perfectly shaped*
	He wears a well-steeled° axe, the staff ° of gold.	*well-honed / handle*
	His age, some five-and-twenty.	

MESSENGER   There's another—

A little man, but of a tough soul, seeming

	As great° as any. Fairer promises	*noble*
120	In such a body yet I never looked on.	

PIRITHOUS O, he that's freckle-faced?

MESSENGER   The same, my lord.

	Are they° not sweet ones?	*(the freckles)*

PIRITHOUS   Yes, they are well.

MESSENGER   Methinks,

	Being so few and well disposed,° they show	*arranged*
	Great and fine art in nature. He's white-haired°—	*blond*
125	Not wanton white,° but such a manly colour	*effeminately fair*
	Next to an auburn, tough and nimble set,°	*and lithe*
	Which shows an active soul. His arms are brawny,	
	Lined with strong sinews—to the shoulder piece	
	Gently they swell, like women new-conceived,°	*starting pregnancy*
130	Which speaks him prone to labour, never fainting	
	Under the weight of arms; stout-hearted, still,°	*when motionless*
	But when he stirs, a tiger. He's grey-eyed,[5]	
	Which yields compassion where he conquers; sharp	
	To spy advantages, and where he finds 'em,	
135	He's swift to make 'em his. He does no wrongs,	
	Nor takes none.° He's round-faced, and when he smiles	*tolerates any*
	He shows° a lover; when he frowns, a soldier.	*looks like*
	About his head he wears the winner's oak,[6]	
	And in it stuck the favour of his lady.	
140	His age, some six-and-thirty. In his hand	
	He bears a charging staff ° embossed with silver.	*lance*

THESEUS Are they all thus?

PIRITHOUS   They are all the sons of honour.

THESEUS Now as I have a soul, I long to see 'em.

[*To* HIPPOLYTA] Lady, you shall see men fight now.

HIPPOLYTA   I wish it,

145	But not the cause, my lord. They would show	

---

3. Perhaps influenced by Thomas Speght's 1602 edition of Chaucer's *Knight's Tale*, where King Emetrius's hair "was of yron" (was made of iron) instead of "yronne" (curled).
4. *The . . . maid*: His allegiance to Bellona, goddess of war (or possibly to Athena, also associated with warlike

powers).
5. With eyes of blue or blue-gray. Eyes of this color supposedly implied compassion.
6. Valiant soldiers received a wreath of oak leaves, particularly if they saved their friends in battle.

Bravely about the titles of two kingdoms[7]—
'Tis pity love should be so tyrannous.
[*To* EMILIA] O my soft-hearted sister, what think you?
Weep not till they weep blood. Wench, it must be.

THESEUS [*to* EMILIA]
You have steeled 'em° with your beauty.   *made them determined*

150 [*To* PIRITHOUS]   Honoured friend,
To you I give the field:° pray order it   *charge of the combat*
Fitting the persons that must use it.

PIRITHOUS   Yes, sir.

THESEUS   Come, I'll go visit 'em—I cannot stay,°   *wait*
Their fame° has fired me so. Till they appear,   *This account of them*
Good friend, be royal.°   *treat them royally*

155 PIRITHOUS   There shall want no bravery.°   *splendor*

EMILIA [*aside*]   Poor wench, go weep—for whosoever wins
Loses a noble cousin for thy sins.   *Exeunt*

4.3

Enter [the] JAILER, *[the]* WOOER, *[and the]* DOCTOR

DOCTOR   Her distraction is more at some time of the moon than
at other some,° is it not?   *at others*

JAILER   She is continually in a harmless distemper:° sleeps little;   *state of confusion*
altogether without appetite, save often drinking; dreaming of
5   another world, and a better; and what broken piece of matter
soe'er she's about, the name 'Palamon' lards it,[1] that she
farces° every business   *stuffs*

Enter [the JAILER'S] DAUGHTER

withal,° fits it to every question. Look where she comes—you   *with it*
shall perceive her behaviour.

[*They stand apart*]

10 JAILER'S DAUGHTER   I have forgot it quite—the burden on't° was   *refrain of the song*
'Down-a, down-a', and penned by no worse man than Giraldo,
Emilia's schoolmaster. He's as fantastical,° too, as ever he may   *fanciful*
go upon's legs°— for in the next world will Dido see Palamon,   *as any man*
and then will she be out of love with Aeneas.[2]

15 DOCTOR   What stuff's here? Poor soul.

JAILER   E'en thus all day long.

JAILER'S DAUGHTER   Now for this charm that I told you of—you
must bring a piece of silver on the tip of your tongue, or no
ferry:[3] then, if it be your chance to come where the blessed
20   spirits are—there's a sight now! We maids that have our livers
perished,[4] cracked to pieces with love, we shall come there and
do nothing all day long but pick flowers with Proserpine.[5] Then
will I make Palamon a nosegay, then let him mark me,° then—   *notice me*

DOCTOR   How prettily she's amiss! Note her a little further.

25 JAILER'S DAUGHTER   Faith, I'll tell you: sometime we go to barley-

---

7. *They . . . kingdoms:* It would be more appropriate if
they were fighting for each other's kingdoms.
4.3 Location: The prison.
1. Whatever disjointed piece of business she tries to
do (or discuss), Palamon's name is inserted into it (like
a piece of fat into lean meat in order to make it cook
better).
2. Presumably the Schoolmaster has written a song
about Dido and her lover, Aeneas, who abandons her in
Virgil's *Aeneid*. The Jailer's Daughter imagines a new
ending in which Dido falls in love with Palamon rather

than Aeneas in the afterworld.
3. Charon demanded payment for ferrying dead souls
across the river Styx to the underworld. Hence the custom of placing a coin on the tongues of the dead.
4. Shrivel up from unrequited love. The liver was supposed to be the seat of the passions.
5. One day while she was picking flowers, Proserpine
was spotted by Pluto, who carried her off to the underworld to be his queen. Her mother, Demeter, got Zeus
to allow her to spend six months on earth each year.

break,[6] we of the blessed. Alas, 'tis a sore life they have i'th'
other place—such burning, frying, boiling, hissing, howling,
chattering, cursing—O they have shrewd measure°—take   *harsh retribution*
heed! If one be mad or hang or drown themselves, thither they
30 go, Jupiter bless us, and there shall we be put in a cauldron of
lead and usurers' grease,[7] amongst a whole million of cutpurses, and there boil like a gammon° of bacon that will never   *side*
be enough.°   *cooked enough*
DOCTOR   How her brain coins!°   *invents*
35 JAILER'S DAUGHTER   Lords and courtiers that have got maids with
child—they are in this place. They shall stand in fire up to the
navel and in ice up to th' heart, and there th'offending part
burns, and the deceiving part freezes—in truth a very grievous
punishment as one would think for such a trifle. Believe me,
40 one would marry a leprous witch to be rid on't, I'll assure you.
DOCTOR   How she continues this fancy! 'Tis not an engrafted
madness, but a most thick and profound melancholy.[8]
JAILER'S DAUGHTER   To hear there a proud° lady and a proud city   *an aristocratic*
wife° howl together! I were a beast an° I'd call it good sport.   *merchant's wife / if*
45 One cries, 'O this smoke!', th'other, 'This fire!'; one cries, 'O
that ever I did it behind the arras!',° and then howls—th'other   *wall hanging*
curses a suing fellow and her garden-house.[9]
(*Sings*) 'I will be true, my stars, my fate . . .'°   *Exit* DAUGHTER   *(unknown song)*
JAILER [*to the* DOCTOR]   What think you of her, sir?
50 DOCTOR   I think she has a perturbed mind, which I cannot
minister to.
JAILER   Alas, what then?
DOCTOR   Understand you she ever affected° any man ere she   *loved*
beheld Palamon?
55 JAILER   I was once, sir, in great hope she had fixed her liking on
this gentleman, my friend.
WOOER   I did think so too, and would account I had a great pen-
n'orth° on't to give half my state° that both she and I, at this   *bargain / property*
present, stood unfeignedly on the same terms.
60 DOCTOR   That intemperate surfeit of her eye hath distempered
the other senses.[1] They may return and settle again to execute
their preordained faculties, but they are now in a most extravagant vagary.° This you must do: confine her to a place where   *errant wandering*
the light may rather seem to steal in than be permitted; take
65 upon you, young sir her friend, the name of Palamon; say you
come to eat with her and to commune of love. This will catch
her attention, for this her mind beats upon°—other objects that   *is obsessed with*
are inserted 'tween her mind and eye become the pranks and
friskins° of her madness. Sing to her such green songs[2] of love   *tricks and frolics*
70 as she says Palamon hath sung in prison; come to her stuck in°   *decorated with*
as sweet flowers as the season is mistress of, and thereto make
an addition of some other compounded odours° which are   *blended perfumes*

6. A game played with male-female couples: one
couple assigned to a place in the field called "hell"
attempted to entrap the other couples.
7. The traditional punishment for avarice was boiling
in oil (here, imagined as the sweat, "grease," given off
by usurers).
8. It is not a rooted ("an engrafted"), true madness,
but a deep depression (what today might be called love

sickness).
9. *a suing . . . garden-house*: the persuasive Wooer who
lured her into a garden house, a site notorious for
amorous trysts.
1. Her excessive gazing at Palamon has thrown her
other senses off.
2. Songs typical of youth.

grateful° to the sense. All this shall become° Palamon, for   *pleasant / befit*
Palamon can sing, and Palamon is sweet and every good thing.
75 Desire to eat with her, carve° her, drink to her, and still among³   *carve for*
intermingle your petition of grace and acceptance into her
favour. Learn what maids have been her companions and play
feres,° and let them repair to her, with Palamon in their mouths,   *playmates*
and appear with tokens as if they suggested° for him. It is a   *interceded*
80 falsehood° she is in, which is with falsehoods to be combated.   *delusion*
This may bring° her to eat, to sleep, and reduce what's now out   *induce*
of square° in her into their former law and regiment.° I have   *disordered / rule*
seen it approved,⁴ how many times I know not, but to make the
number more I have great hope in this. I will between the
85 passages° of this project come in with my appliance.⁵ Let us   *stages*
put it in execution, and hasten the success,° which doubt not   *outcome*
will bring forth comfort.   *Exeunt*

5.1

[*An altar prepared.*] *Flourish. Enter* THESEUS, PIRI-
THOUS, HIPPOLYTA, *attendants*

THESEUS   Now let 'em enter and before the gods
Tender their holy prayers. Let the temples
Burn bright with sacred fires, and the altars
In hallowed clouds commend° their swelling incense   *deliver*
5 To those above us. Let no due° be wanting.   *proper ritual*
                              Flourish of cornetts
They have a noble work in hand, will° honour   *which will*
The very powers that love 'em.
        Enter PALAMON [*with his three*] *Knights* [*at one door*],
        and ARCITE [*with his three Knights at the other door*]
PIRITHOUS   Sir, they enter.
THESEUS   You valiant and strong-hearted enemies,
You royal german° foes that this day come   *closely related*
10 To blow that nearness° out that flames between ye,   *close kinship*
Lay by your anger for an hour and, dove-like,
Before the holy altars of your helpers,
The all-feared gods, bow down your stubborn bodies.
Your ire° is more than mortal—so° your help be;   *anger / so may*
15 And as the gods regard° ye, fight with justice.   *are watching*
I'll leave you to your prayers, and betwixt ye
I part my wishes.°   *divide my hopes*
PIRITHOUS   Honour crown the worthiest.
                              Exit THESEUS *and his train*
PALAMON [*to* ARCITE]   The glass° is running now that cannot   *hourglass*
        finish
Till one of us expire. Think you but thus,
20 That were there aught in me which strove to show°   *to expose itself as*
Mine enemy in this business, were't one eye
Against another, arm oppressed by arm,
I would destroy th'offender—coz, I would,

3. Among these pastimes.
4. I have seen this type of treatment successfully carried out.
5. My final mode of treatment (see 5.4).
5.1 Location: The forest. A single altar is probably visible upstage, perhaps on the inner stage, for this scene

(at least from line 34) and the next two. Here, it is dedicated to Mars. Q treats these first three scenes as a single one. This makes sense if there are three altars onstage, rather than, as assumed here, only one, which successively represents three different altars, presumably in different locations.

Though parcel° of myself. Then from this gather		*it were a piece*
How I should tender° you.		*treat*

25 ARCITE   I am in labour

To push your name, your ancient love, our kindred,°	*kinship*
Out of my memory, and i'th' selfsame place	
To seat something I would confound.° So hoist we	*destroy*
The sails that must these vessels port even where°	*carry wherever*
The heavenly limiter° pleases.	*(of life)*

30 PALAMON   You speak well.

Before I turn,° let me embrace thee, cousin—	*turn away*
This I shall never do again.	

ARCITE   One farewell.

PALAMON   Why, let it be so—farewell, coz.

ARCITE   Farewell, sir.

Exeunt PALAMON *and his [three] Knights*

Knights, kinsmen, lovers—yea, my sacrifices,[1]	
35	True worshippers of Mars, whose spirit in you	
Expels the seeds of fear and th'apprehension	
Which still is father of it,[2] go with me	
Before the god of our profession.° There	*god we worship*
Require° of him the hearts of lions and	*Request*
40	The breath° of tigers, yea, the fierceness too,	*endurance*
Yea, the speed also—to go on,° I mean,	*go forward*
Else° wish we to be snails. You know my prize	*Otherwise (in retreat)*
Must be dragged out of blood—force and great feat	
Must put my garland on me, where she sticks,	
45	The queen of flowers.[3] Our intercession, then,	
Must be to him° that makes the camp a cistern	*(Mars)*
Brimmed with the blood of men—give me your aid,	
And bend your spirits towards him.	

They kneel [before the altar, fall on their faces, then on their knees again]

[*Praying to Mars*]   Thou mighty one,

That with thy power hast turned green Neptune° into purple;[4]	*god of the sea*
50	Whose havoc in vast field comets prewarn,°	*forecast*
Unearthèd° skulls proclaim; whose breath blows down	*As yet unburied*
The teeming Ceres' foison;[5] who dost pluck°	*pull down*
With hand armipotent° from forth blue clouds	*powerful in arms*
The masoned° turrets, that both mak'st and break'st	*stone*
55	The stony girths° of cities; me thy pupil,	*walls*
Youngest follower of thy drum, instruct this day	
With military skill, that to thy laud°	*praise*
I may advance my streamer,° and by thee	*banner*
Be styled° the lord o'th' day. Give me, great Mars,	*named*
60 | Some token of thy pleasure. | |

Here they fall on their faces, as formerly, and there is heard clanging of armour, with a short thunder, as the burst of a battle, whereupon they all rise and bow to the altar

---

1. The three knights may literally become human sacrifices from Arcite to Mars if Arcite loses the battle.
2. *th'apprehension . . . it:* the anticipation of a daunting situation, which always breeds fear.
3. *Must put . . . flowers:* Will win for my head (where Emilia already resides) the victor's laurels, of which she, as the most beautiful of flowers, is part.
4. Red with blood.
5. *whose breath . . . foison:* whose breath (wind) destroys the plenty of the fields produced by Ceres, goddess of agriculture.

O great corrector of enormous° times,   *disordered*
Shaker of o'er-rank° states, thou grand decider   *overripe*
Of dusty and old titles, that heal'st with blood°   *through bloodletting*
The earth when it is sick, and cur'st the world
65 O'th' plurisy° of people, I do take   *excess*
Thy signs auspiciously, and in thy name,
To my design, march boldly. [*To his Knights*] Let us go.

Exeunt

5.2

Enter PALAMON *and his Knights with the former*
observance

PALAMON [*to his Knights*]   Our stars must glister° with new fire,   *fortunes must glisten*
    or be
Today extinct.° Our argument is love,   *extinguished*
Which if the goddess of it grant, she gives
Victory too. Then blend your spirits with mine,
5 You whose free nobleness° do make my cause   *generous nobility*
Your personal hazard. To the goddess Venus
Commend° we our proceeding, and implore   *Commit*
Her power unto our party.
        Here they kneel [*before the altar, fall on their faces then*
        on their knees again]
    [*Praying to Venus*] Hail, sovereign queen of secrets,¹ who hast
        power
10 To call the fiercest tyrant from his rage
And weep unto a girl;² that hast the might,
Even with an eye-glance, to choke° Mars's drum   *silence*
And turn th'alarum° to whispers; that canst make   *call to arms*
A cripple flourish with° his crutch, and cure him   *brandish*
15 Before Apollo;³ that mayst force the king
To be his subject's vassal, and induce
Stale gravity° to dance; the polled° bachelor   *old men / bald*
Whose youth, like wanton boys through bonfires,
Have skipped° thy flame, at seventy thou canst catch   *Has escaped*
20 And make him to the scorn° of his hoarse throat   *(by listeners)*
Abuse young lays of love.⁴ What godlike power
Hast thou not power upon? To Phoebus° thou   *the sun*
Add'st flames hotter than his—the heavenly fires
Did scorch his mortal son,⁵ thine him. The huntress,
25 All moist and cold, some say, began to throw
Her bow away and sigh.⁶ Take to thy grace
Me, thy vowed soldier, who do bear thy yoke
As 'twere a wreath of roses, yet is° heavier   *though the yoke is*
Than lead itself, stings more than nettles.
30 I have never been foul-mouthed against thy law;
Ne'er revealed secret, for I knew none; would not,
Had I kenned° all that were. I never practised   *known*
Upon⁷ man's wife, nor would the libels° read   *(against love)*

5.2 Location: The altar, here dedicated to Venus.
1. As the rest of the speech (lines 31ff.) indicates,
secrecy and discretion were essential components of
the chivalric love code.
2. Make him weep for a girl (or, weep so much that he
becomes like a girl).
3. Even more quickly than Apollo, the god of medicine.

4. Botch young lovers' love songs.
5. See note to 1.2.85–87.
6. *The huntress . . . sigh*: Diana, notwithstanding her
vow of chastity, fell in love with the shepherd
Endymion. *cold*: chaste.
7. *practised / Upon*: wooed.

Of liberal° wits. I never at great feasts   *licentious*
35 Sought to betray° a beauty, but have blushed   *expose the affairs of*
At simp'ring sirs that did. I have been harsh
To large confessors,[8] and have hotly asked them
If they had mothers—I had one, a woman,
And women 'twere they wronged. I knew a man
40 Of eighty winters, this I told them, who
A lass of fourteen brided°—'twas thy° power   *wedded / Venus's*
To put life into dust. The agèd cramp°   *cramp of old age*
Had screwed° his square foot round,   *twisted*
The gout had knit his fingers into knots,
45 Torturing convulsions from his globy eyes°   *swollen sockets*
Had almost drawn their spheres,° that° what was life   *eyeballs / so that*
In him seemed torture. This anatomy°   *skeleton*
Had by his young fair fere° a boy, and I   *mate*
Believed it was his, for she swore it was,
50 And who would not believe her? Brief °—I am   *In short*
To those that prate and have done,[9] no companion;
To those that boast and have not,° a defier;   *have done nothing*
To those that would and cannot, a rejoicer.
Yea, him I do not love that tells close offices°   *secret matters*
55 The foulest way, nor names concealments[1] in
The boldest language. Such a one I am,
And vow that lover never yet made sigh
Truer than I. O, then, most soft sweet goddess,
Give me the victory of this question,° which   *conflict*
60 Is true love's merit,° and bless me with a sign   *just deserts*
Of thy great pleasure.

     Here music is heard, doves° are seen to flutter. They fall   *(sacred to Venus)*
     again upon their faces, then on their knees

O thou that from eleven to ninety reign'st
In mortal bosoms, whose chase° is this world   *hunting ground*
And we in herds thy game, I give thee thanks
65 For this fair token, which, being laid unto°   *added to*
Mine innocent true heart, arms in assurance
My body to this business. [*To his Knights*] Let us rise
And bow before the goddess.

     They [rise and] bow
          Time comes on.   *Exeunt*

5.3

     Still° music of record[er]s. Enter EMILIA *in white, her*   *Soft*
     hair about her shoulders, [with] a wheaten wreath; one
     in white holding up her train, her hair stuck with flow-
     ers; one before her carrying a silver hind° in which is   *(sacred to Diana)*
     conveyed incense and sweet odours, which being set
     upon the altar, her maids standing [apart], she sets fire
     to it. Then they curtsy and kneel

EMILIA [*praying to Diana*]   O sacred, shadowy, cold,[1] and con-
     stant queen,
     Abandoner of revels, mute contemplative,

---

8. To those who boast of their love conquests.
9. To those who talk of deeds they have actually done.
1. Nor exposes what should remain hidden.
5.3 Location: The altar, here dedicated to Diana.

1. *shadowy:* a goddess of the moon, Diana was associated with the night. *cold:* chaste. See 1.3.52, 4.2.58,
and notes to these lines.

Sweet, solitary, white as chaste, and pure
As wind-fanned° snow, who to thy female knights   *windblown*
5   Allow'st no more blood° than will make a blush,   *sexual desire*
Which is their order's robe: I here, thy priest,
Am humbled fore thine altar. O, vouchsafe
With that thy rare green eye, which never yet
Beheld thing maculate,° look on thy virgin;   *tainted*
10   And, sacred silver mistress, lend thine ear—
Which ne'er heard scurril° term, into whose port°   *scurrilous / opening*
Ne'er entered wanton° sound—to my petition,   *lewd*
Seasoned with holy fear.° This is my last   *pious awe*
Of vestal office.² I am bride-habited,°   *dressed as a bride*
15   But maiden-hearted. A husband I have 'pointed,° *have been assigned*
But do not know him. Out of two, I should
Choose one and pray for his success, but I
Am guiltless of election.³ Of mine eyes
Were I to lose one, they are equal precious—
20   I could doom neither: that which perished should
Go to't unsentenced. Therefore, most modest queen,
He of the two pretenders° that best loves me   *suitors*
And has the truest title in't,° let him   *claim to me*
Take off my wheaten garland,° or else grant   *Take my virginity*
25   The file and quality I hold I may
Continue in thy band.⁴

     Here the hind vanishes under the altar and in the place
     ascends a rose tree having one rose° upon it   *(symbol of virginity)*

[*To her women*] See what our general of ebbs and flows⁵
Out from the bowels of her holy altar,
With sacred act, advances—but one rose!
30   If well inspired,⁶ this battle shall confound°   *destroy*
Both these brave knights, and I a virgin flower
Must grow alone, unplucked.

     Here is heard a sudden twang of instruments and the
     rose falls from the tree

The flower is fall'n, the tree descends. [*To Diana*] O mistress,
Thou here dischargest me—I shall be gathered.⁷
35   I think so, but I know not thine own will.
Unclasp thy mystery.° [*To her women*] I hope she's pleased; *Reveal your meaning*
Her signs were gracious.   *They curtsy and exeunt*

5.4

     Enter [the] DOCTOR, *[the]* JAILER, *and [the]* WOOER *in*
     [the] habit of° Palamon   *dressed as*

DOCTOR   Has this advice I told you done any good upon her?
WOOER   O, very much. The maids that kept her company have
half persuaded her that I am Palamon. Within this half-hour
she came smiling to me, and asked me what I would eat, and
5   when I would kiss her. I told her presently,° and kissed her   *at once*
twice.

---

2. *my . . . office*: my last duty as your virginal devotee.
3. Am not guilty of having made a choice (and hence
of having betrayed my vows).
4. *grant . . . band*: grant that I may continue to hold the
rank and condition (of virginity) as one of your devotees.

5. Our ruler of the moon and, hence, of tides.
6. If this is a true omen.
7. I shall be married; I shall lose my virginity.
5.4 Location: The prison.

DOCTOR 'Twas well done—twenty times had been far better,
For there° the cure lies mainly.   *(in kissing)*
WOOER   Then she told me
She would watch° with me tonight, for well she knew   *stay up*
What hour my fit° would take me.   *urgent inclination*

10 DOCTOR   Let her do so,
And when your fit comes, fit her home,[1]
And presently.
WOOER   She would have me sing.
DOCTOR You did so?
WOOER   No.
DOCTOR   'Twas very ill done, then.
You should observe° her every way.   *accommodate*
WOOER   Alas,
15 I have no voice, sir, to confirm° her that way.   *assure*
DOCTOR That's all one,° if ye make a noise.   *That doesn't matter*
If she entreat° again, do anything—   *beg*
Lie with her if she ask you.
JAILER   Ho there, Doctor.
DOCTOR Yes, in the way of cure.
JAILER   But first, by your leave,
I'th' way of honesty.°   *(after marriage)*
20 DOCTOR   That's but a niceness°—   *an excessive scruple*
Ne'er cast your child away for honesty.[2]
Cure her first this way, then if she will° be honest,   *wants to*
She has the path° before her.   *(of marriage)*
JAILER   Thank ye, Doctor.
DOCTOR Pray bring her in and let's see how she is.
25 JAILER I will, and tell her her Palamon stays° for her.   *waits*
But, Doctor, methinks you are i'th' wrong still.   *Exit* JAILER
DOCTOR Go, go. You fathers are fine fools—her honesty?
An we should give her physic till we find that[3]—
WOOER Why, do you think she is not honest, sir?
DOCTOR How old is she?
WOOER   She's eighteen.
30 DOCTOR   She may be—
But that's all one. 'Tis nothing to our purpose.°   *It makes no difference*
Whate'er her father says, if you perceive
Her mood inclining that way that I spoke of,
Videlicet,° the way of flesh—you have me?   *Namely*
WOOER Yes, very well, sir.
35 DOCTOR   Please her appetite,
And do it home°—it cures her, *ipso facto,*[4]   *completely*
The melancholy humour° that infects her.   *mood (medical)*
WOOER I am of your mind, Doctor.
          Enter [the] JAILER *and [his]* DAUGHTER *[mad]*
DOCTOR You'll find it so—she comes: pray humour her.
          [The DOCTOR *and the* WOOER *stand apart]*
JAILER *[to his* DAUGHTER*]* Come, your love Palamon stays for
40 you, child,

1. Fully serve her needs (have sex with her).
2. A paradox: don't lose your daughter (to her madness) in order to keep her (honest).
3. If we were to treat her until we could be sure of her virginity (the obvious continuation of the unfinished thought being, we'd be treating her forever).
4. By the very act (*ipso facto*) of having sex, she'll be cured. The Doctor assumes, correctly in the event, that the Daughter suffers from hysteria, thought to be caused by a wandering womb and cured by intercourse.

And has done this long hour, to visit you.

JAILER'S DAUGHTER   I thank him for his gentle patience.
He's a kind gentleman, and I am much bound° to him.   *obliged*
Did you ne'er see the horse he gave me?

JAILER   Yes.

JAILER'S DAUGHTER   How do you like him?

45 JAILER   He's a very fair° one.   *beautiful*

JAILER'S DAUGHTER   You never saw him dance?

JAILER   No.

JAILER'S DAUGHTER   I have, often.
He dances very finely, very comely,
And, for a jig, come cut and long-tail to him,[5]
He turns ye like a top.

JAILER   That's fine, indeed.

50 JAILER'S DAUGHTER   He'll dance the morris twenty mile an hour,
And that will founder the best hobbyhorse,[6]
If I have any skill,° in all the parish—   *judgment*
And gallops to the tune of 'Light o' love'.[7]
What think you of this horse?

JAILER   Having these virtues
55 I think he might be brought° to play at tennis.   *taught*

JAILER'S DAUGHTER   Alas, that's nothing.

JAILER   Can he write and read too?

JAILER'S DAUGHTER   A very fair hand, and casts himself th'accounts[8]
Of all his hay and provender. That ostler
Must rise betime that cozens° him. You know   *get up early to cheat*
The chestnut mare the Duke has?

60 JAILER   Very well.

JAILER'S DAUGHTER   She is horribly in love with him, poor beast,
But he is like his master—coy° and scornful.   *aloof*

JAILER What dowry has she?

JAILER'S DAUGHTER   Some two hundred bottles°   *bales of hay*
And twenty strike° of oats, but he'll ne'er have her.   *bushels*
65 He lisps in's neighing, able to entice
A miller's mare.[9] He'll be the death of her.

DOCTOR   What stuff she utters!

JAILER   Make curtsy—here your love comes.

WOOER [*coming forward*]   Pretty soul,
How do ye?
        [*She curtsies*]
70   That's a fine maid, there's a curtsy.

JAILER'S DAUGHTER   Yours to command, i'th' way of honesty—
How far is't now to th' end o'th' world, my masters?

DOCTOR   Why, a day's journey, wench.

JAILER'S DAUGHTER [*to* WOOER]   Will you go with me?

WOOER   What shall we do there, wench?

---

5. *He . . . him:* He dances finely no matter what horse he is compared with. *cut:* a horse with a docked tail (see note to 3.4.22). There is sexual wordplay throughout this scene.
6. That will lame ("founder") the best morris dancer. *hobbyhorse:* one extremely agile morris dancer was dressed as a horse and imitated its movements.
7. Popular ballad, also referred to in *Much Ado About*

Nothing 3.4.39 and *The Two Gentlemen of Verona* 1.2.83. The title means "inconstant in love."
8. He has beautiful penmanship and reckons his own expenses.
9. *He . . . mare:* He's such a smooth talker he could seduce even a miller's mare—a workhorse renowned for its steadfast, circular plodding and, hence, least likely to be distracted.

JAILER'S DAUGHTER   Why, play at stool-ball¹—
　　What is there else to do?

75　WOOER   I am content
　　If we shall keep our wedding° there.　　　　　　　　　　*As long as we marry*
JAILER'S DAUGHTER   'Tis true—
　　For there, I will assure you, we shall find
　　Some blind priest for the purpose that will venture
　　To marry us, for here they are nice,° and foolish.　　　　*too scrupulous*
80　Besides, my father must be hanged tomorrow,
　　And that would be a blot i'th' business.
　　Are not you Palamon?
WOOER   Do not you know me?
JAILER'S DAUGHTER   Yes, but you care not for me. I have nothing
　　But this poor petticoat and two coarse smocks.°　　　　*undergarments*
WOOER   That's all one—I will have you.
85　JAILER'S DAUGHTER   Will you surely?
WOOER   Yes, by this fair hand, will I.
JAILER'S DAUGHTER   We'll to bed then.
WOOER   E'en when you will.°　　　　　　　　　　　*Whenever you like*
　　　　[*He kisses her*]
JAILER'S DAUGHTER [*rubbing off the kiss*]
　　　　　　　　　　　　O, sir, you would fain be nibbling.
WOOER   Why do you rub my kiss off?
JAILER'S DAUGHTER   'Tis a sweet one,
　　And will perfume me finely against° the wedding.　　　*in preparation for*
　　[*Indicating the* DOCTOR] Is not this your cousin Arcite?
90　DOCTOR   Yes, sweetheart,
　　And I am glad my cousin Palamon
　　Has made so fair a choice.
JAILER'S DAUGHTER   Do you think he'll have me?
DOCTOR   Yes, without doubt.
JAILER'S DAUGHTER [*to the* JAILER]   Do you think so too?
JAILER   Yes.
JAILER'S DAUGHTER   We shall have many children. [*To the* DOCTOR]
　　Lord, how you're grown!
95　My Palamon, I hope, will grow too,² finely,
　　Now he's at liberty. Alas, poor chicken,
　　He was kept down with hard meat° and ill lodging,　　　*coarse food*
　　But I'll kiss him up again.
　　　　Enter a MESSENGER
MESSENGER   What do you here? You'll lose the noblest sight
　　That e'er was seen.
JAILER   Are they i'th' field?
100　MESSENGER   They are—
　　You bear a charge° there too.　　　　　　　　　　*have a duty*
JAILER   I'll away straight.
　　[*To the others*] I must e'en leave you here.
DOCTOR   Nay, we'll go with you—
　　I will not lose the sight.
JAILER   How did you like her?
DOCTOR   I'll warrant you, within these three or four days

---

1. A game, somewhat like cricket, played with ball and
bat by women or by men and women together.　　2. Get fat; have an erection.

I'll make her right again.

[*Exit the* JAILER *with the* MESSENGER]

105 [*To the* WOOER]   You must not from her,
But still preserve° her in this way.   *keep treating*

WOOER   I will.

DOCTOR   Let's get her in.

WOOER   [*to the* JAILER'S DAUGHTER]
                              Come, sweet, we'll go to dinner,
And then we'll play at cards.

JAILER'S DAUGHTER   And shall we kiss too?

WOOER   A hundred times.

JAILER'S DAUGHTER   And twenty.

WOOER   Ay, and twenty.

JAILER'S DAUGHTER   And then we'll sleep together.

110 DOCTOR [*to the* WOOER]   Take her offer.

WOOER [*to the* JAILER'S DAUGHTER]
Yes, marry, will we.

JAILER'S DAUGHTER   But you shall not hurt me.

WOOER   I will not, sweet.

JAILER'S DAUGHTER   If you do, love, I'll cry.   *Exeunt*

5.5

Flourish. Enter THESEUS, HIPPOLYTA, EMILIA,
PIRITHOUS, *and some attendants*

EMILIA   I'll no step further.

PIRITHOUS   Will you lose this sight?

EMILIA   I had rather see a wren hawk at° a fly   *attack in midair*
Than this decision. Every blow that falls
Threats a brave life; each stroke laments
5   The place whereon it falls, and sounds more like
A bell° than blade. I will stay here.   *death knell*
It is enough my hearing shall be punished
With what shall happen, 'gainst the which there is
No deafing, but to hear;[1] not taint mine eye
With dread sights it may shun.

10 PIRITHOUS [*to* THESEUS]   Sir, my good lord,
Your sister will no further.

THESEUS   O, she must.
She shall see deeds of honour in their kind,°   *true nature*
Which sometime show well pencilled.° Nature now   *even when just drawn*
Shall make and act° the story, the belief   *invent and perform*
Both sealed with eye and ear.[2] [*To* EMILIA] You must be
15   present—
You are the victor's meed,° the price and garland   *reward*
To crown the question's title.[3]

EMILIA   Pardon me,
If I were there I'd wink.°   *keep my eyes closed*

THESEUS   You must be there—
This trial is, as 'twere, i'th' night, and you
The only star to shine.

20 EMILIA   I am extinct.°   *extinguished*

5.5 Location: The forest, near the tournament field.
1. *there . . . hear*: there is no way to block out the noise
in order not to hear.
2. *the belief . . . ear*: the story will be rendered credible

by all that is seen and heard.
3. To crown the rightful victor in the dispute.

There is but envy° in that light which shows   *malice*
The one the other. Darkness, which ever was
The dam° of horror, who does stand accursed   *mother*
Of many mortal millions, may even now,
25 By casting her black mantle over both,
That° neither could find other, get herself   *So that*
Some part of a good name, and many a murder
Set off whereto° she's guilty.   *Atone for of which*
HIPPOLYTA   You must go.
EMILIA In faith, I will not.
THESEUS   Why, the knights must kindle
30 Their valour at your eye. Know, of this war
You are the treasure, and must needs be by°   *nearby*
To give the service pay.°   *reward the winner*
EMILIA   Sir, pardon me—
The title of a kingdom may be tried
Out of itself.°   *Outside the kingdom*
THESEUS   Well, well—then at your pleasure.
35 Those that remain with you could wish their office
To any of their enemies.
HIPPOLYTA   Farewell, sister.
I am like to know your husband fore yourself,
By some small start of time. He whom the gods
Do of the two know° best, I pray them he   *know to be*
40 Be made your lot.   *Exeunt [all but* EMILIA]
  [EMILIA *takes out two pictures, one from her right side,*
  and one from her left]
EMILIA Arcite is gently visaged,° yet his eye   *has a gentle expression*
Is like an engine bent[4] or a sharp weapon
In a soft sheath. Mercy and manly courage
Are bedfellows in his visage. Palamon
45 Has a most menacing aspect. His brow
Is graved° and seems to bury what it frowns on,   *frowned*
Yet sometime 'tis not so, but alters to°   *according to*
The quality° of his thoughts. Long time his eye   *nature*
Will dwell upon his object. Melancholy
50 Becomes° him nobly—so does Arcite's mirth,   *Suits*
But Palamon's sadness is a kind of mirth,
So mingled as if mirth did make him sad
And sadness merry. Those darker humours° that   *moods*
Stick misbecomingly° on others, on them   *Seem misplaced*
55 Live in fair dwelling.[5]
    Cornetts. Trumpets sound as to a charge
Hark, how yon spurs to spirit° do incite   *bravery*
The princes to their proof.° Arcite may win me,   *to prove themselves*
And yet may Palamon wound Arcite to
The spoiling of his figure.° O, what pity   *(so as to disfigure him)*
60 Enough for such a chance![6] If I were by°   *near*
I might do hurt, for they would glance their eyes
Toward my seat, and in that motion might
Omit a ward or forfeit an offence

---

4. Is like a weapon, such as a bow, ready to be released. 6. Would be sufficient for such a (sad) turn of events.
5. *on them . . . dwelling:* suit them well.

Which craved that very time.[7] It is much better
　　　Cornetts. A great cry and noise within, crying,
　　　'A Palamon'
65　I am not there. O better never born,
　　Than minister to such harm.
　　　Enter SERVANT
　　　　　　　　　　　　What is the chance?°　　　　　　　*Who won*
SERVANT　The cry's 'A Palamon'.
EMILIA　Then he has won. 'Twas ever likely—
　　He looked all grace and success, and he is
70　Doubtless the prim'st° of men. I prithee run　　　*most perfect*
　　And tell me how it goes.
　　　Shout and cornetts, crying, 'A Palamon'
SERVANT　　　　　　　　　　Still 'Palamon'.
EMILIA　Run and enquire.　　　　　　　　[*Exit* SERVANT]
　　[*She speaks to the picture in her right hand*]
　　　　　　　　　Poor servant,° thou hast lost.　　　*lover (Arcite)*
　　Upon my right side still I° wore thy picture,　　　*I always*
　　Palamon's on the left. Why so, I know not.
75　I had no end° in't, else chance would have it so.　　　*purpose*
　　　Another cry and shout within and cornetts
　　On the sinister side the heart lies—Palamon
　　Had the best-boding chance.[8] This burst of clamour
　　Is sure the end o'th' combat.
　　　Enter SERVANT
SERVANT　They said that Palamon had Arcite's body
80　Within an inch o'th' pyramid—that the cry
　　Was general 'A Palamon'. But anon
　　Th'assistants° made a brave redemption,° and　　　*knights / rescue*
　　The two bold titlers° at this instant are　　　*fighters for the title*
　　Hand to hand at it.
EMILIA　　　　　　　Were they° metamorphosed　　　*I wish they were*
85　Both into one! O why? There were no woman
　　Worth so composed a man:[9] their single share,
　　Their nobleness peculiar to them, gives
　　The prejudice of disparity, value's shortness,
　　To any lady breathing[1]—
　　　Cornetts. Cry within, 'Arcite, Arcite'
　　　　　　　　　More exulting?
　　'Palamon' still?
90　SERVANT　　　　　Nay, now the sound is 'Arcite'.
EMILIA　I prithee, lay attention to the cry.
　　　Cornetts. A great shout and cry, 'Arcite, victory!'
　　Set both thine ears to th' business.
SERVANT　　　　　　　　　　The cry is
　　'Arcite' and 'Victory'—hark, 'Arcite, victory!'
　　The combat's consummation° is proclaimed　　　*conclusion*
　　By the wind instruments.
95　EMILIA　　　　　　　Half sights saw°　　　*Mere glimpses showed*
　　That Arcite was no babe. God's lid,° his richness　　　*By God's eyelid*

7. *might . . . time:* might miss the perfect moment for a defensive parry or an offensive move.
8. *On . . . chance:* The location of Palamon's picture—on Emilia's left ("sinister") side, where her heart is—portended victory, since the contest is about love.
9. *There . . . man:* No woman could be worthy of this composite man made up of both Palamon and Arcite.
1. *their single . . . breathing:* no woman could have as much nobility as either one of them. *their single share:* each one's value.

And costliness of spirit looked through him—it could
No more be hid in him than fire in flax,°   *straw*
Than humble banks can go to law with° waters   *can battle*
100   That drift° winds force to raging. I did think   *driving*
Good Palamon would miscarry, yet I knew not
Why I did think so. Our reasons are not prophets
When oft our fancies are. They are coming off°—   *leaving the field*
Alas, poor Palamon.
         [*She puts away the pictures.*]
         Cornetts. Enter THESEUS, HIPPOLYTA, PIRITHOUS, ARCITE
         as victor, and attendants
105   THESEUS   Lo, where our sister is in expectation,
Yet quaking and unsettled. Fairest Emily,
The gods by their divine arbitrament
Have given you this knight. He is a good one
As ever struck at head. [*To* ARCITE *and* EMILIA] Give me your
     hands.
[*To* ARCITE] Receive you her, [*to* EMILIA] you him: [*to both*]
110   be plighted with
A love that grows as you decay.
ARCITE   Emilia,
To buy you I have lost what's dearest to me
Save what is bought,° and yet I purchase cheaply   *(Emilia)*
As I do rate your value.
THESEUS [*to* EMILIA]   O lovèd sister,
115   He speaks now of as brave a knight as e'er
Did spur a noble steed. Surely the gods
Would have him die a bachelor lest his race
Should show i'th' world too godlike. His behaviour
So charmed me that, methought, Alcides° was   *Hercules*
120   To him a sow[2] of lead. If I could praise
Each part of him to th'all I have spoke,[3] your Arcite
Did° not lose by't; for he that was thus good,   *Would*
Encountered yet his better. I have heard
Two emulous Philomels[4] beat the ear o'th' night
125   With their contentious throats, now one the higher,
Anon the other, then again the first,
And by and by out-breasted, that the sense[5]
Could not be judge between 'em—so it fared
Good space° between these kinsmen, till heavens did   *For a good while*
130   Make hardly° one the winner. [*To* ARCITE] Wear the garland   *Barely make*
With joy that you have won.—For the subdued,°   *losers*
Give them our present° justice, since I know   *immediate*
Their lives but pinch° 'em. Let it here be done.   *torment*
The scene's not for our seeing; go we hence
135   Right joyful, with some sorrow. [*To* ARCITE] Arm° your prize;   *Give your arm to*
I know you will not lose her. Hippolyta,
I see one eye of yours conceives a tear,
The which it will deliver.
         Flourish

---

2. Smelted metal taken from a furnace.
3. *to . . . spoke:* in the same way I have praised Palamon as a whole.
4. Two rival nightingales. In Greek mythology,
Philomela was raped by her sister's husband, who cut

out her tongue so she couldn't accuse him. By weaving
the story into cloth, she nonetheless informed her sister, who fed her husband their son. The gods turned the
sister into a nightingale and Philomela into a swallow.
5. And by and by outsung, so that the sense of hearing.

EMILIA   Is this winning?
          O all you heavenly powers, where is your mercy?
140   But that your wills have said it must be so,
          And charge me live to comfort this unfriended,°   *deprived of his friend*
          This miserable prince, that cuts away
          A life more worthy from him than all women,
          I should and would die too.
HIPPOLYTA   Infinite pity
145   That four such eyes should be so fixed on one°   *one woman*
          That two must needs be blind for't.⁶
THESEUS   So it is.   Exeunt

5.6

Enter [guarded] PALAMON *and his [three]* KNIGHTS *pin-*
ioned; [enter with them the] JAILER *[and an] execu-*
tioner [with block and axe]

PALAMON   There's many a man alive that hath outlived
          The love o'th' people; yea, i'th' selfsame state
          Stands many a father with his child: some comfort
          We have by so considering. We expire,
5   And not without men's pity; to live still,
          Have their good wishes.¹ We prevent°   *avoid*
          The loathsome misery of age, beguile°   *cheat*
          The gout and rheum° that in lag° hours attend   *coughing / final*
          For grey approachers;° we come towards the gods   *(to death)*
10   Young and unwappered,° not halting° under crimes   *untired / limping morally*
          Many and stale°—that sure shall please the gods   *long gone*
          Sooner than such,° to give us nectar with 'em,   *(sinful old men)*
          For we are more clear° spirits. My dear kinsmen,   *innocent*
          Whose lives for this poor comfort are laid down,
          You have sold 'em° too too cheap.   *(your lives)*
15   FIRST KNIGHT   What ending could be
          Of more content? O'er us the victors have
          Fortune, whose title° is as momentary   *claim*
          As to us death is certain—a grain of honour
          They not o'erweigh us.²
SECOND KNIGHT   Let us bid farewell,
20   And with our patience anger tott'ring° fortune,   *unstable*
          Who at her certain'st reels.³
THIRD KNIGHT   Come, who begins?
PALAMON   E'en he that led you to this banquet shall
          Taste to you all.⁴ [*To the* JAILER] Aha, my friend, my friend,
          Your gentle daughter gave me freedom once;
25   You'll see't done° now for ever. Pray, how does she?   *see me set free*
          I heard she was not well; her kind of ill°   *illness*
          Gave me some sorrow.
JAILER   Sir, she's well restored
          And to be married shortly.
PALAMON   By my short life,

---

6. That two eyes must be blinded (in death); that two
men could be so blind as to fight to the death for one
woman.
5.6 Location: Scene continues.
1. *We expire . . . wishes:* Even though we are to die, we
have men's good wishes that we might go on living.

2. *a grain . . . us:* they have no more honor than we do.
3. Who, when she seems most certain, suddenly
changes direction.
4. Taste (death) first, like the servant at a state banquet
who was required to taste the food before the king and
guests to make sure it wasn't poisoned.

      I am most glad on't. 'Tis the latest° thing   *last*
30 I shall be glad of. Prithee, tell her so;
      Commend me to her, and to piece her portion°   *increase her dowry*
      Tender her this.

               [*He gives his purse*]

FIRST KNIGHT   Nay, let's be offerers all.

SECOND KNIGHT Is it a maid?°   *virgin*

PALAMON   Verily, I think so—
      A right good creature more to me° deserving   *from me*
      Than I can quit° or speak of.   *requite*

35 ALL THREE KNIGHTS   Commend us to her.

        They give their purses

JAILER   The gods requite you all, and make her thankful.

PALAMON   Adieu, and let my life be now as short
      As my leave-taking.

         [*He*] *lies on the block*

FIRST KNIGHT   Lead, courageous cousin.

SECOND AND THIRD KNIGHTS   We'll follow cheerfully.

      A great noise within: crying, 'Run! Save! Hold!'
      Enter in haste a MESSENGER

40 MESSENGER   Hold! Hold! O, hold! Hold! Hold!

      Enter PIRITHOUS *in haste*

PIRITHOUS   Hold, ho! It is a cursèd haste you made
      If you have done° so quickly! Noble Palamon,   *finished*
      The gods will show their glory in a life
      That thou art yet to lead.

PALAMON   Can that be,
45 When Venus, I have said, is false? How do things fare?

PIRITHOUS   Arise, great sir, and give the tidings ear
      That are most rarely sweet and bitter.

PALAMON   What
      Hath waked us from our dream?

PIRITHOUS   List,° then: your cousin,   *Listen*
      Mounted upon a steed that Emily
50 Did first bestow on him, a black one owing°   *owning*
      Not a hair-worth of white—which some will say
      Weakens his price[5] and many will not buy
      His goodness with this note;° which superstition   *distinctive mark*
      Here finds allowance°—on this horse is Arcite   *gains support*
55 Trotting the stones of Athens, which the calkins
      Did rather tell than trample;[6] for the horse
      Would make his length° a mile, if 't pleased his rider *length of stride*
      To put pride in him. As he thus went counting
      The flinty pavement, dancing, as 'twere, to th' music
60 His own hooves made—for, as they say, from iron
      Came music's origin[7]—what envious flint,°   *cobblestone*
      Cold as old Saturn[8] and like him possessed
      With fire malevolent, darted a spark,

---

5. Makes him less valuable, because dark horses were considered vicious or ill omened.
6. *which . . . trample:* the horse's gait was so long and light that its feet seemed more to count ("tell") the cobbles one by one than to trample them. *calkins:* turned-down edges of a horseshoe.
7. Pythagoras is supposed to have discovered music when walking through a blacksmith's forge.
8. According to Chaucer's *Knight's Tale*, Saturn, father of Jupiter, was responsible for the reversal of fortune described here, because he had promised Venus that Palamon would win Emilia. Shakespeare and Fletcher limit Saturn's responsibility to a simile.

Or what fierce sulphur else, to this end made,[9]

65 I comment not—the hot horse, hot as fire,

Took toy° at this and fell to what disorder   *a capricious dislike*

His power could give his will; bounds; comes on end;

Forgets school-doing,° being therein trained   *school training*

And of kind manège;° pig-like he whines   *well disciplined*

70 At the sharp rowel,° which he frets at rather   *spur*

Than any jot obeys; seeks all foul means

Of boist'rous and rough jad'ry° to disseat   *behavior like a nag*

His lord, that kept it° bravely. When naught served,   *who kept his seat*

When neither curb would crack, girth break, nor diff'ring°   *various*

plunges

75 Disroot his rider whence he grew,° but that   *was fixed*

He kept him 'tween his legs, on his hind hooves—

On end he stands—

That Arcite's legs, being higher than his head,

Seemed with strange art to hang. His victor's wreath

80 Even then fell off his head; and presently

Backward the jade comes o'er and his full poise°   *weight*

Becomes the rider's load. Yet is he living;

But such a vessel 'tis that floats but for

The surge that next approaches.[1] He much desires

85 To have some speech with you—lo, he appears.

Enter THESEUS, HIPPOLYTA, EMILIA, [*and*] ARCITE *in a
chair* [*borne by attendants*]

PALAMON   O miserable end of our alliance!

The gods are mighty. Arcite, if thy heart,

Thy worthy manly heart, be yet unbroken,

Give me thy last words. I am Palamon,

One that yet loves thee dying.

90 ARCITE   Take Emilia,

And with her all the world's joy. Reach° thy hand—   *Give me*

Farewell—I have told° my last hour. I was false,   *counted*

Yet never treacherous.[2] Forgive me, cousin—

One kiss from fair Emilia—[*they kiss*] 'tis done.

Take her; I die.   [*He dies*]

95 PALAMON   Thy brave soul seek Elysium.

EMILIA [*to Arcite's body*]   I'll close thine eyes, Prince. Blessèd
souls be with thee.

Thou art a right good man, and, while I live,

This day I give to tears.

PALAMON   And I to honour.

THESEUS   In this place first you fought, e'en very here

100 I sundered you.° Acknowledge to the gods   *separated your fight*

Our thanks that you are living.

His part is played, and, though it were too short,

He did it well. Your day is lengthened and

The blissful dew of heaven does arrouse° you.   *sprinkle*

105 The powerful Venus well hath graced her altar,

And given you your love; our master, Mars,

9. Or some spark of hellfire made for this purpose.
1. *But such . . . approaches:* But he can live only until
the next onslaught (like a boat that can stay afloat only
until the next wave hits).

2. *I was . . . treacherous:* I was "false" to our friendship
(because Palamon did see Emilia first) but "never
treacherous" in vying for Emilia's love.

Hath vouched° his oracle, and to Arcite gave   *made good on*
The grace of the contention.° So the deities   *victory in the battle*
Have showed due justice.—Bear this hence.

        [*Exeunt attendants with Arcite's body*]

PALAMON   O cousin,
110 That we should things desire which do cost us
The loss of our desire! That naught could buy
Dear love, but loss of dear love!

THESEUS   Never fortune
Did play a subtler game—the conquered triumphs,
The victor has the loss. Yet in the passage°   *proceedings*
115 The gods have been most equal.° Palamon,   *impartial*
Your kinsman hath confessed the right o'th' lady°   *the right to Emilia*
Did lie in you,° for you first saw her and   *Was yours*
Even then proclaimed your fancy. He restored her
As your stol'n jewel, and desired your spirit
120 To send him hence forgiven. The gods my justice
Take from my hand, and they themselves become
The executioners.° Lead your lady off,   *executors of justice*
And call your lovers from the stage of death,°   *friends from the scaffold*
Whom I adopt my friends. A day or two
125 Let us look sadly and give grace unto
The funeral of Arcite, in whose end°   *after which*
The visages of bridegrooms we'll put on
And smile with Palamon, for whom an hour,
But one hour since, I was as dearly sorry
130 As glad of Arcite, and am now as glad
As for him sorry. O you heavenly charmers,°   *gods who enchant us*
What things you make of us! For what we lack
We laugh, for what we have, are sorry; still
Are children in some kind. Let us be thankful
135 For that which is, and with you leave dispute
That are above our question.[3] Let's go off
And bear us like° the time.   *Flourish. Exeunt*   *act in accordance with*

Epilogue

[*Enter* EPILOGUE]

EPILOGUE   I would now ask ye how ye like the play,
But, as it is with schoolboys, cannot say.°   *speak*
I am cruel fearful.° Pray yet stay awhile,[1]   *horribly afraid*
And let me look upon ye. No man smile?
5 Then it goes hard, I see. He that has
Loved a young handsome wench, then, show his face—
'Tis strange if none be here—and, if he will,
Against his conscience let him hiss and kill
Our market.° 'Tis in vain, I see, to stay ye.   *Our chance of success*
10 Have at the worst can come,° then! Now, what say ye?   *Do your worst*
And yet mistake me not—I am not bold—
We have no such cause.° If the tale we have told—   *purpose*
For 'tis no other—any way content° ye,   *please*
For to that honest purpose it was meant ye,°   *intended for you*

---

3. *with . . . question:* cease to dispute with you, who
are beyond our questioning.

Epilogue
1. Don't hiss or applaud yet.

15   We have our end;° and ye shall have ere long,   *achieved our aim*
      I dare say, many a better to prolong
      Your old loves to us. We and all our might°   *all we can do*
      Rest at your service. Gentlemen, good night.   *Flourish.* [*Exit*]

APPENDICES

APPENDICES

Early Modern Map Culture

In the early modern period, maps were often considered rare and precious objects, and seeing a map could be an important and life-changing event. This was so for Richard Hakluyt, whose book *The Principal Navigations, Voiages, Traffiques and Discoveries of the English Nation* (1598–1600) was the first major collection of narratives describing England's overseas trading ventures. Hakluyt tells how, as a boy still at school in London, he visited his uncle's law chambers and saw a book of cosmography lying open there. Perceiving his nephew's interest in the maps it contained, the uncle turned to a modern map and "pointed with his wand to all the knowen Seas, Gulfs, Bayes, Straights, Capes, Rivers, Empires, Kingdomes, Dukedomes, and Territories of ech part, with declaration also of their speciall commodities and particular wants, which by the benefit of traffike, and entercourse of merchants, are plentifully supplied. From the Mappe he brought me to the Bible, and turning to the 107 Psalme, directed mee to the 23 and 24 verses, where I read, that they which go downe to the sea in ships, and occupy [work] by the great waters, they see the works of the Lord, and his woonders in the deepe." This event, Hakluyt records, made so deep an impression upon him, that he vowed he would devote his life to the study of this kind of knowledge. *The Principal Navigations* was the result, a book that mixes a concern with the profit to be made from trade and from geographical knowledge with praise for the Christian god who made the "great waters" and, in Hakluyt's view, looked with special favor on the English merchants and sailors who voyaged over them.

In the early modern period, access to maps was far less easy than it is today. Before the advent of printing in the late fifteenth century, maps were drawn and decorated by hand. Because they were rare and expensive, these medieval maps were for the most part owned by the wealthy and the powerful. Sometimes adorned with pictures of fabulous sea monsters and exotic creatures, maps often revealed the Christian worldview of those who composed them. Jerusalem appeared squarely in the middle of many maps (called T and O maps), with Asia, Africa, and Europe, representing the rest of the known world, arranged symmetrically around the Holy City. Because they had not yet been discovered by Europeans, North and South America were not depicted.

Mapping practices changed markedly during the late fifteenth and sixteenth centuries both because of the advent of print and also because European nations such as Portugal and Spain began sending ships on long sea voyages to open new trade routes to the East and, eventually, to the Americas. During this period, monarchs competed to have the best cartographers supply them with accurate maps of their realms and especially of lands in Africa, Asia, or the Americas, where they hoped to trade or plant settlements. Such knowledge was precious and jealously guarded. The value of such maps and the secrecy that surrounded them are indicated by a story published in Hakluyt's *The Principal Navigations*. An English ship had captured a Portuguese vessel in the Azores, and a map was discovered among the ship's valuable cargo, which included spices, silks, carpets, porcelain, and other exotic commercial objects. The map was "inclosed in a case of sweete Cedar wood, and lapped up almost an hundred fold in fine calicut-cloth, as though it had been some incomparable jewell." The value of the map and what explains the careful way in which it was packed lay in the particular information it afforded the English about Portuguese trading routes. More than beautiful objects, maps like this one were crucial to the international race to find safe sea routes to the most profitable trading centers in the East.

In the sixteenth century, books of maps began to be printed, making them more affordable for ordinary people, though some of these books, published as big folio volumes, remained too dear for any but wealthy patrons to buy. Yet maps were increasingly a part of daily life, and printing made many of them more accessible. Playgoers in Shakespeare's audiences must have understood in general the value and uses of maps, for they appear as props in a number of his plays. Most famously, at the beginning of *King Lear,* the old king has a map brought onstage showing the extent of his kingdom. He then points on the map to the three separate parts into which he is dividing his realm to share among his daughters. The map, often unfurled with a flourish on a table or held up for view by members of Lear's retinue, signals the crucial relationship of the land to the monarch. He is his domains, and the map signifies his possession of them. To divide the kingdom, in essence to tear apart the map, would have been judged foolish and destructive by early modern political theorists. Similarly, in *1 Henry IV,* when rebels against the sitting monarch, Henry IV, plot to overthrow him, they bring a map onstage in order to decide what part of the kingdom will be given to each rebel leader. Their proposed dismemberment of the realm signifies the danger they pose. Treasonously, they would rend in pieces the body of the commonwealth.

Maps, of course, had other uses besides signifying royal domains. In some instances, they were used pragmatically to help people find their way from one place to another. A very common kind of map, a portolan chart, depicted in minute detail the coastline of a particular body of water. Used by sailors, these maps frequently were made by people native to the region they described. Many world or regional maps, because they were beautifully decorated and embellished with vivid colors, were used for decorative purposes. John Dee, a learned adviser to Queen Elizabeth and a great book collector, wrote that some people used maps "to beautifie their Halls, Parlers, Chambers, Galeries, Studies, or Libraries." He also spoke of more scholarly uses for these objects. They could, for example, be useful aids in the study of history or geography, enabling people to locate "thinges past, as battels fought, earthquakes, heavenly fyringes, and such occurents in histories mentioned." Today we make similar use of maps, like those included in this volume, when, in reading Shakespeare's plays, we resort to a map to find out where the Battle of Agincourt took place or where Othello sailed when he left Venice for Cyprus.

This edition of the *Norton Shakespeare* includes six maps. Three of them are modern maps drawn specifically to show the location of places important to Shakespeare's plays. They depict London, the British Isles and France, and the eastern Mediterranean. This edition also includes three early modern maps that indicate some of the different kinds of printed maps that people might have seen in Shakespeare's lifetime. The earliest is a map of London that appeared in a 1574 edition of a famous German atlas, *Civitates Orbis Terrarum (Cities of the World),* compiled by George Braun with engravings by Franz Hogenberg. This remarkable atlas includes maps and information on cities throughout Europe, Asia, and North Africa; the first of its six volumes appeared in 1572, the last in 1617. Being included in the volume indicated a city's status as a recognized metropolitan center. In a charming touch, Braun added to his city maps pictures of figures in local dress. At the bottom of the map of London, for example, there are four figures who appear to represent the city's prosperous citizens. In the center, a man in a long robe holds the hand of soberly dressed matron. On either side of them are younger and more ornately dressed figures. The young man sports a long sword and a short cloak, the woman a dress with elaborate skirts. In the atlas, the map is colored, and the clothes of the two young people echo one another in shades of green and red.

At the time the map was made, London was a rapidly expanding metropolis. In 1550, it contained about 55,000 people; by 1600, it would contain nearly 200,000. The map shows the densely populated old walled city north of the Thames River, in the middle of which was Eastcheap, the commercial district where, in Shakespeare's plays about the reign of Henry IV, Falstaff holds court in a tavern. The map also shows that by 1570 London was spreading westward beyond the wall toward Westminster Palace. This medieval structure, which appears on the extreme left side of the map, was where English monarchs resided when in London and where, at the end of *2 Henry IV,* the king dies in the fabled Jerusalem Chamber of the Westminster complex. On the far right of the map, one can see the Tower of London, where Edward IV's young sons were imprisoned by Richard III, an event depicted in Shakespeare's *The Tragedy of King Richard the Third*. The map also indicates the centrality of the Thames to London's commercial life. It shows the river full of boats, some of those on the east side of London Bridge large oceangoing vessels with several masts. South of the river, where many of the most famous London theaters, including Shakespeare's Globe, were to be constructed in the 1590s, there are relatively few buildings. By 1600, this would change, as Southwark, as it was known, came to be an increasingly busy entertainment, residential, and commercial district.

The map of the Christian Holy Lands at the eastern tip of the Mediterranean Sea had extremely wide distribution because it was included in the many editions of the Geneva Bible, an English translation of the Scriptures put together by a group of Puritan scholars working in Geneva in the 1550s. Moderately sized and priced, the Geneva Bible became the most popular Bible in English until the King James version was produced in 1611. Even after that date, many ordinary Protestant readers continued to use the popular Geneva Bible, which underwent refinements, changes, and additions throughout the second half of the sixteenth century, including in 1576 a new translation of the New Testament heavily indebted to the scholarship of the French theologian Théodore de Bèze.

The map included here is from a 1592 edition of this Bible, printed in London by Christopher Barker. The map was placed before Matthew, the first book of the New Testament, and it shows places mentioned in the first four Gospels (Matthew, Mark, Luke, and John), which collectively tell of the life and deeds of Jesus. It indicates, for example, the location of Bethlehem, where he was born; Nazareth, where he spent his youth; and Cana of Galilee, where he turned water into wine at a marriage. It suggests that, to the English reader, this particular territory was overwritten by and completely intertwined with Christian history. Yet in the Mediterranean Sea, on the left of the map, several large ships are visible, and they are reminders of another fact about this region: it was a vigorous trading arena where European Christian merchants did business with local merchants—Christian, Jew, and Muslim—and with traders bringing luxury goods by overland routes from the East. A number of Shakespeare's plays are set in this complex eastern Mediterranean region where several religious traditions laid claim to its territories and many commercial powers competed for preeminence. *Pericles,* for example, has a hero who is the ruler of Tyre, a city on the upper right side of the map. In the course of his wanderings, Pericles visits many cities along the eastern coasts of the Mediterranean. The conclusion of the play, in which the hero is reunited both with his long-lost daughter and the wife he believes dead, has seemed to many critics to share in a sense of Christian miracle, despite the fact of its ostensibly pagan setting. *The Comedy of Errors* and parts of *Othello* and of *Antony and Cleopatra* are also set in the eastern Mediterranean. One of Shakespeare's earliest plays, *The Comedy of Errors,* is an urban comedy in which the protagonists are merchants deeply involved in commercial transactions. It is also the first play in which Shakespeare mentions the Americas in an extended joke in which he compares parts of a serving woman's body to the countries on a map including Ireland, France, and the Americas. In *Othello,* the eastern Mediterranean island of Cyprus is represented as a tense Christian outpost defending Venetian interests against the Muslim Turks. In *Antony and Cleopatra,* Egypt figures as the site of Eastern luxury and also of imperial conquest, an extension of the Roman Empire. Clearly, this region was to Shakespeare and his audiences one of the most complex and most highly charged areas of the world: a site of religious, commercial, and imperial significance.

The map of Great Britain and Ireland comes from a 1612 edition of John Speed's *The Theatre of the Empire of Great Britaine,* an innovative atlas containing individual maps of counties and towns in England and Wales, as well as larger maps that include Scotland and Ireland. Speed was by trade a tailor who increasingly devoted his time to the study of history and cartography. Befriended by the antiquarian scholar William Camden, he eventually won patronage from Sir Fulke Greville, who gave him a pension that allowed him to devote full time to his scholarly endeavors. *The Theatre* was one product of this newfound freedom. The map included here is one of his most ambitious. It shows the entire British Isles, nominated by Speed as "The Kingdome of Great Britaine and Ireland," though at this time Ireland was far from under the control of the English crown and Scotland was still an independent kingdom, despite the fact that James I, a Scot by birth, had tried hard to forge a formal union between England and Scotland. This problem of the relationship of the parts of the British Isles to one another, and England's assertion of power over the others, is treated in *Henry V,* in which officers from Wales, Ireland, and Scotland are sharply delineated yet all depicted as loyal subjects of the English king.

One striking aspect of Speed's map is the balance it strikes between the two capital cities, London on the left, prominently featuring the Thames and London Bridge, and Edinburgh on the right. This would have pleased James, whose interest in his native country Shakespeare played to in his writing of *Macbeth,* based on material from Scottish history. Speed's map acknowledges the claims of the monarch to the territory it depicts. In the upper left corner, the British lion and the Scottish unicorn support a roundel topped with a crown. When James became king of England in 1603, he created this merged symbol of Scottish-English unity. The motto of the Royal Order of the Garter, "Honi soit qui mal y pense" (Shamed be he who thinks ill of it), is inscribed around the circumference. In the bottom left corner of the map, another locus of authority is established. Two cherubs, one holding a compass, the other a globe, sit beneath a banner on which is inscribed the words: "Performed by John Speede." If the territory is the monarch's, the craft that depicts it belongs to the tailor turned cartographer.

Today, maps are readily available from any gasoline station or on the Internet, but in early modern England they were still rare and valuable objects that could generate great excitement in those who owned or beheld them. Along with other precious items, maps were sometimes put on display in libraries and sitting rooms, but they had functions beyond the ornamental. They helped to explain and order the world, indicating who claimed certain domains, showing where the familiar stories of the Bible or of English history occurred, helping merchants find their way to distant markets. As John Dee, the early modern map enthusiast concluded, "Some, for one purpose: and some, for an other, liketh, loveth, getteth, and useth, Mappes, Chartes, and Geographicall Globes."

JEAN E. HOWARD

Ireland, Scotland, Wales, England, and Western France: Places Important to Shakespeare's Plays.

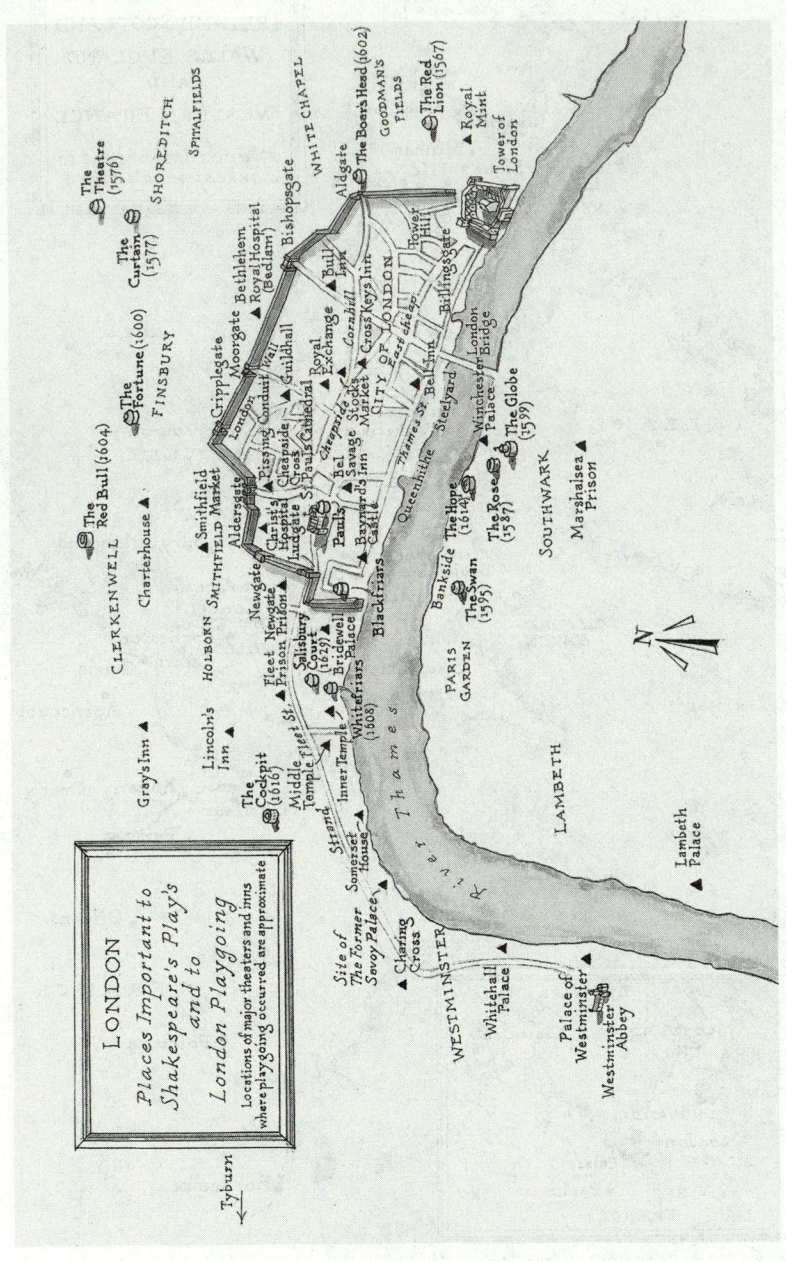

London: Places Important to Shakespeare's Plays and London Playgoing.

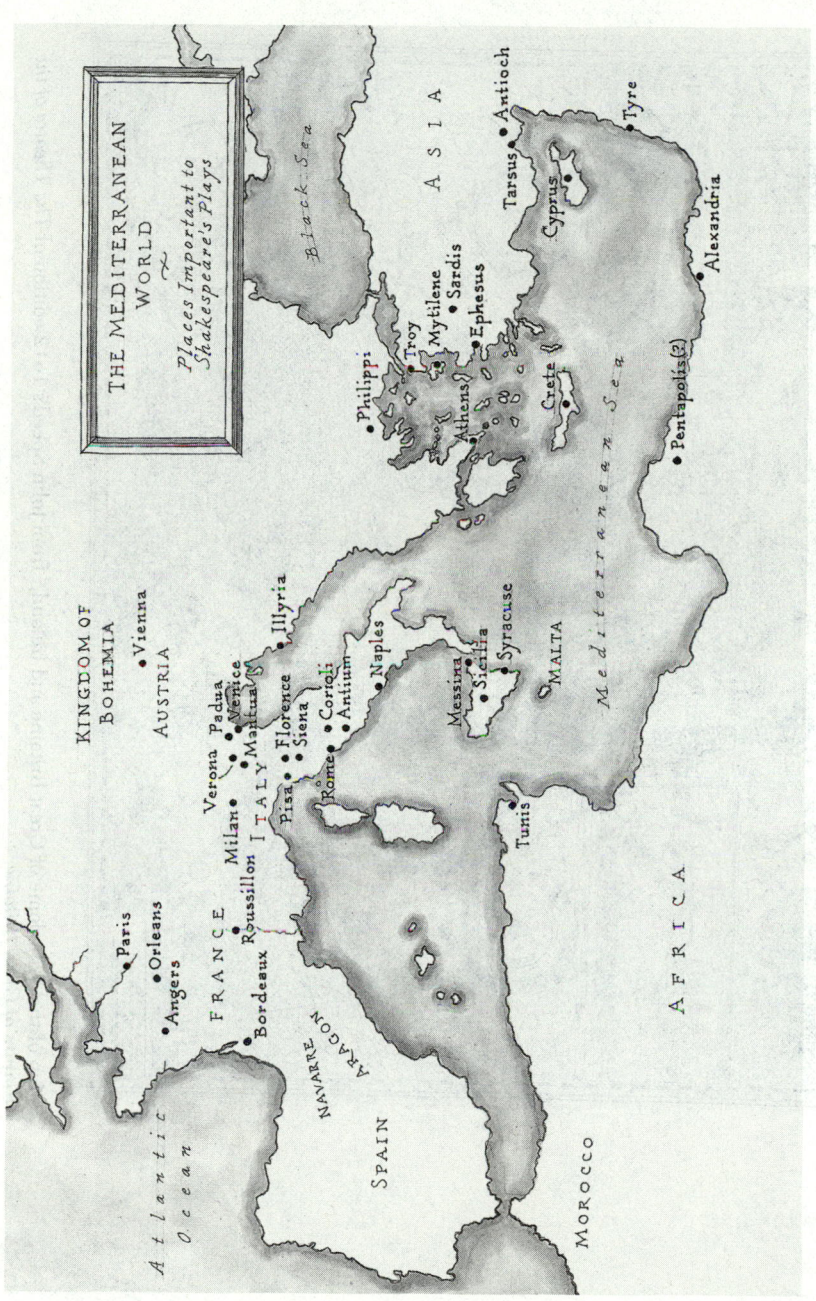

The Mediterranean World: Places Important to Shakespeare's Plays.

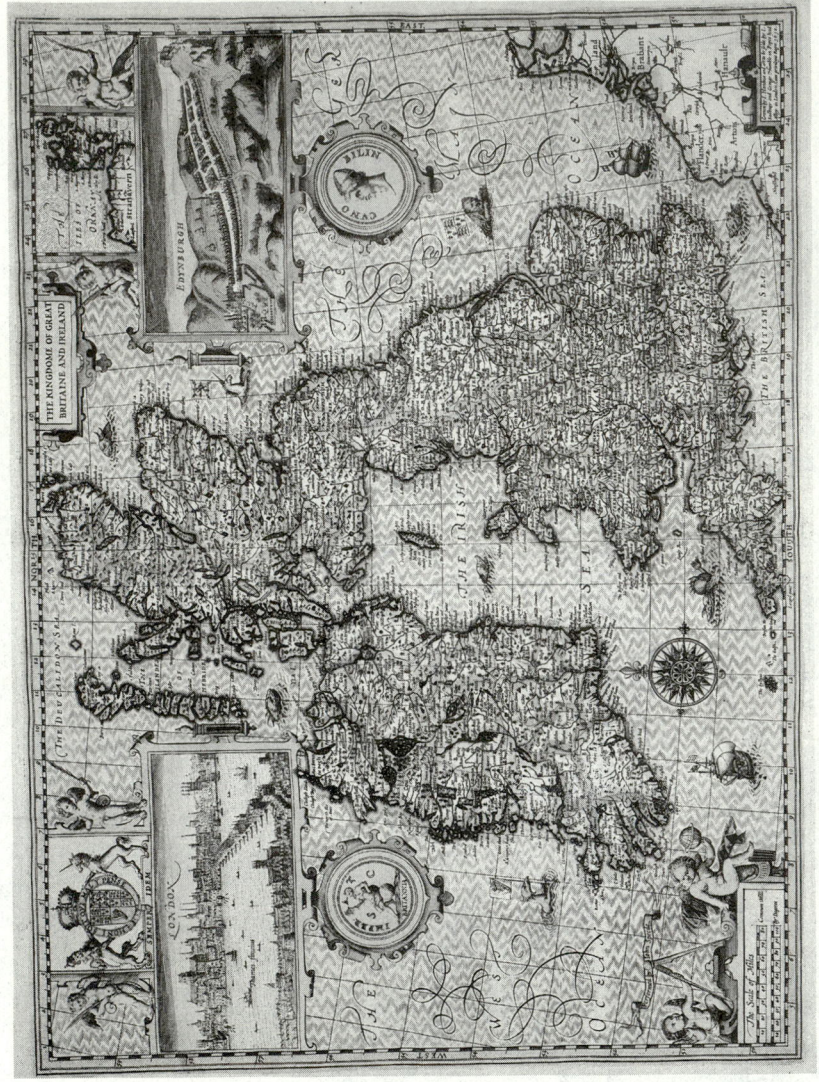

Map of the "Kingdome of Great Britaine and Ireland," from John Speed's 1612 edition of *The Theatre of the Empire of Great Britaine.*

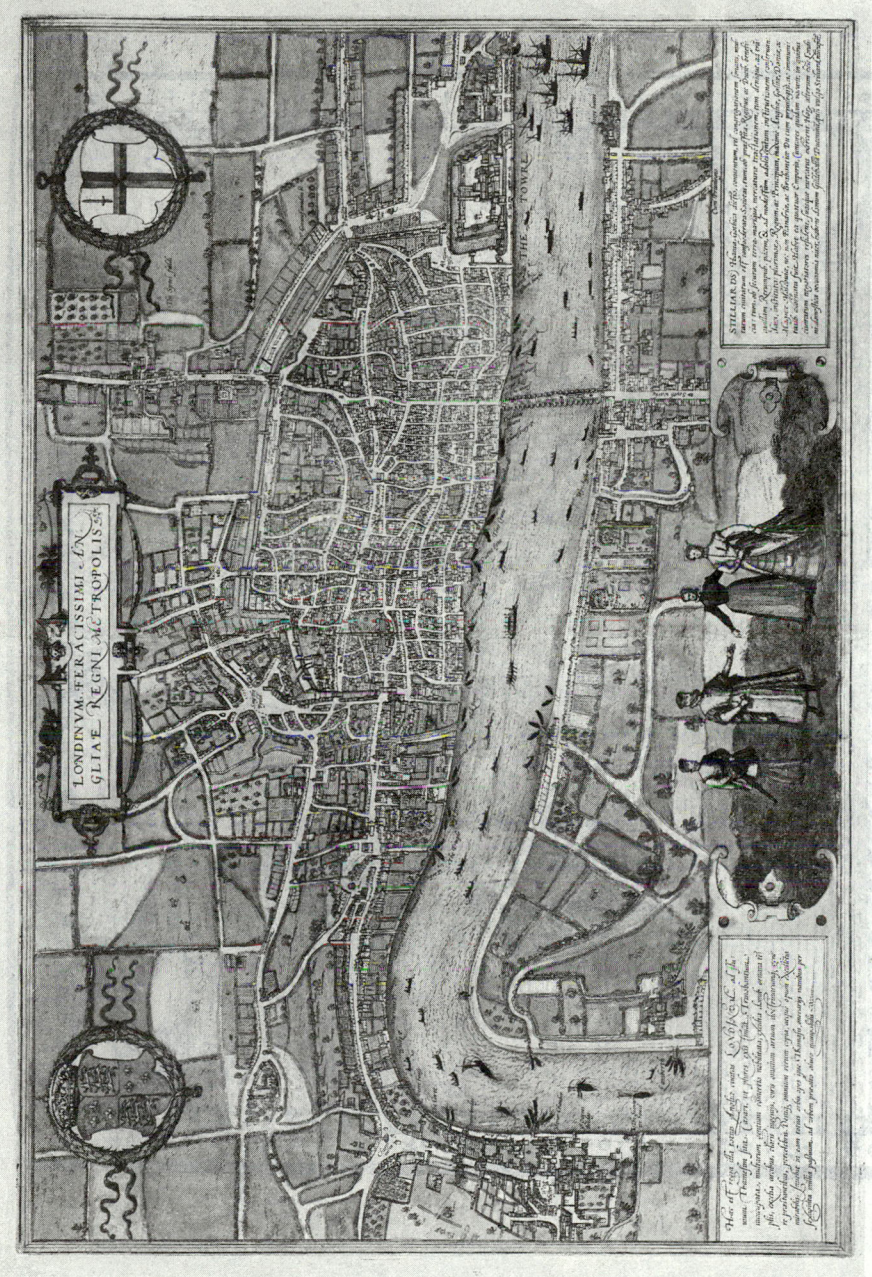

Printed map of London, 1574, taken from a German atlas of European cities by George Braun and Franz Hogenberg.

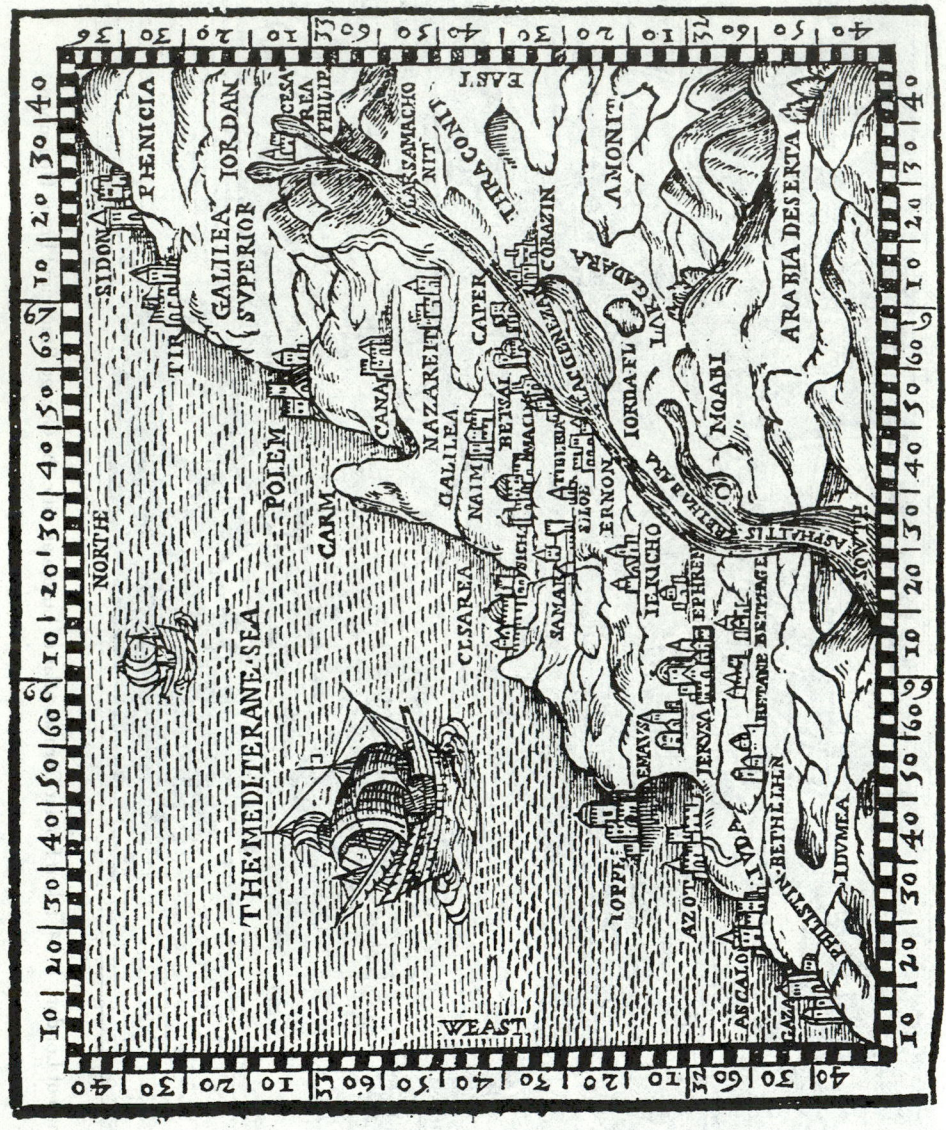

Map of the Holy Land, from the Théodore de Bèze Bible, printed in London, 1592.

Documents

This selection of documents provides a range of contemporary testimony about Shakespeare's character, his work, and the social and institutional conditions under which it was produced. In the absence of newspapers and reviewers, few references to the theater survive. The availability of such hints and fragments as are presented here serves as a mark of Shakespeare's distinction, for the theater was perceived by much of the literate population as ephemeral popular entertainment. The reports of spectators whose accounts we have are more like reviews than any other texts the period has to offer; hence the importance even of brief notes such as Nashe's or Platter's, and the particular value of extended accounts such as those of Simon Forman. The government documents included here offer a vivid glimpse of the institutional procedures by which the theater was regulated. The legal documents—a contract for the construction of a theater modeled on the Globe, and Shakespeare's will—provide the most detailed account available of the material conditions of his life and work. The extracts from criticism and other literary texts show the diversity of contemporary response to his art.

The source for each text is given at the end of the introductory headnote. Additional documents can be found at wwnorton.com/shakespeare.

WS: E. K. Chambers, *William Shakespeare: A Study of Facts and Problems*, 2 vols. (Oxford: Clarendon Press, 1930).
ES: E. K. Chambers, *The Elizabethan Stage*, 4 vols. (Oxford: Clarendon Press, 1923).

Robert Greene on Shakespeare (1592)

[Robert Greene (1560–1592), a prolific author of plays, romances, and pamphlets, attacked Shakespeare in his *Greenes, Groats-worth of Witte, bought with a million of Repentance.* Greene had studied at Cambridge, and his "M.A." was prominently displayed on his title pages. Shakespeare's lack of a university education is clearly one motive for the professional resentment of the following excerpt. Another is probably that Greene was poor and very ill and felt forsaken while writing the *Groats-worth of Witte;* the preface refers to it as his "Swanne-like song," and the narrative is framed as the repentance of a dying man. (Some scholars have held that the posthumously published work contains fabrications by a publisher attempting to capitalize on Greene's name.) The three colleagues Greene addresses are likely to be Christopher Marlowe, Thomas Nashe, and George Peele. The text is that of 1596, as printed in Alexander B. Grosart's *Life and Complete Works in Prose and Verse of Robert Greene*, vol. 12 (New York: Russell and Russell).]

> *To those Gentlemen his Quondam acquaintance,*
> *that spend their wits in making Plaies,* R. G.
> *wisheth a better exercise, and wisdome*
> *to prevent his extremities.* . . .

Base minded men al three of you, if by my miserie ye be not warned: for unto none of you (like me) fought those burres to cleave: those Puppits (I meane) that speake from our mouthes, those Anticks garnisht in our colours. Is it not strange that I, to whom they al have beene beholding: is it not like that you, to whome they all have beene beholding, shall (were ye in that case that I am now) be both at once of them forsaken? Yes trust them not: for there is an upstart Crow, beautified with our feathers, that with his *Tygers heart wrapt in a Players hide*,[1] *supposes he is as well able to bumbast out a blanke verse as the best of you: and being an absolute Johannes fac totum*,[2] is in his owne conceit the onely Shake-scene in a countrie. O that I might intreate your rare wits to be imployed in more profitable courses: & let those Apes imitate your past excellence, and never more acquaint them with your admired inventions. I know the best husband[3] of you all will never prove an Usurer, and the kindest of them / all will never proove a kinde nurse: yet whilst you may, seeke you better Maisters; for it is pittie men of such rare wits, should be subject to the pleasures of such rude groomes.

Thomas Nashe on *1 Henry VI* (1592)

[Thomas Nashe (1567–1601), Greene's fellow playwright and pamphleteer, protests the attribution to himself of the *Groats-worth of Witte* in the preface to the 1592 edition of a pamphlet of his own, *Pierce Penilisse; His Supplication to the Devil*. The satire of *Pierce Penilisse* is more general and political than that of the *Groats-worth,* attacking the manners of the middle class. The allusion to the Talbot scenes of *1 Henry VI* (4.2–7) comes in a section subtitled "The defence of Playes." Talbot is supposed to have been played by Richard Burbage, later the leading actor of the Lord Chamberlain's and King's Men. The text is from Ronald B. McKerrow's 1904 edition of Nashe's *Works,* vol. 1 (London: Bullen).]

How would it have joyed brave *Talbot* (the terror of the French) to thinke that after he had lyne two hundred yeares in his Tombe, hee should triumphe againe on the Stage, and have his bones newe embalmed with the teares of ten thousand spectators at least (at severall times), who, in the Tragedian that represents his person, imagine they behold him fresh bleeding.

Francis Meres on Shakespeare (1598)

[Francis Meres (1565–1647) was educated at Cambridge and was active in London literary circles in 1597–98, after which he became a rector and schoolmaster in the country. The descriptions of Shakespeare are taken from a section on poetry in *Palladis Tamia, Wits Treasury,* a work largely consisting of translated classical quotations and exempla. Unlike the main body of the work, the subsections on poetry, painting, and music include comparisons of English artists to figures of antiquity. Meres goes on after the extract below to list Shakespeare among the best English writers for lyric, tragedy, comedy, elegy, and love poetry. The text is from Don Cameron Allen's 1933 edition of the section "Poetrie" (Urbana: University of Illinois).]

From XI

As the Greeke tongue is made famous and eloquent by *Homer, Hesiod, Euripedes, Aeschilus, Sophocles, Pindarus, Phocylides* and *Aristophanes*; and the Latine tongue by *Virgill, Ovid, Horace, Silius Italicus, Lucanus, Lucretius, Ausonius* and *Claudianus*: so the English tongue is mightily enriched, and gorgeouslie invested

---

1. A parody of *Richard Duke of York (3 Henry VI)* 1.4.138: "O tiger's heart wrapped in a woman's hide!" This obvious allusion and the following pun on Shakespeare's name make it certain that Shakespeare is the

"crow" described here.
2. Jack-of-all-trades. *conceit:* imagination.
3. Steward.

in rare ornaments and resplendent abiliments by Sir *Philip Sidney, Spencer, Daniel, Drayton, Warner, Shakespeare, Marlow* and *Chapman*.

From XIV

As the soule of *Euphorbus* was thought to live in *Pythagoras*: so the sweete wittie soule of Ovid lives in mellifluous & honytongued *Shakespeare*, witnes his *Venus* and *Adonis*, his *Lucrece*, his sugred Sonnets.

From XV

As *Plautus* and *Seneca* are accounted the best for Comedy and Tragedy among the Latines: so *Shakespeare* among ye English is the most excellent in both kinds for the stage; for Comedy, witnes his *Gētlemē of Verona*, his *Errors*, his *Love labors lost*, his *Love labours wonne*,[1] his *Midsummers night dreame*, & his *Merchant of Venice*: for Tragedy his *Richard the 2. Richard the 3. Henry the 4. King John, Titus Andronicus* and his *Romeo* and *Juliet*.

As *Epius Stolo* said, that the Muses would speake with *Plautus* tongue, if they would speak Latin: so I say that the Muses would speak with *Shakespeares* fine filed phrase, if they would speake English.

Thomas Platter on *Julius Caesar* (September 21, 1599)

[Thomas Platter (b. 1574), a Swiss traveler, recorded his experience at the Globe playhouse in an account of his travels. The German text is printed in WS 2:322.]

Den 21 Septembris nach dem Imbissessen, etwan umb zwey vhren, bin ich mitt meiner geselschaft v̄ber daz wasser gefahren, haben in dem streüwinen Dachhaus die Tragedy vom ersten Keyser Julio Caesare mitt ohngefahr 15 personen sehen gar artlich agieren; zu endt der Comedien dantzeten sie ihrem gebraucht nach gar v̄berausz zierlich, ye zwen in mannes vndt 2 in weiber kleideren angethan, wunderbahrlich mitt einanderen.

On the 21st of September after lunch, about two o'clock, I crossed the water [the Thames] with my party, and we saw the tragedy of the first emperor Julius Caesar acted very prettily in the house with the thatched roof, with about fifteen characters; at the end of the comedy, according to their custom, they danced with exceeding elegance, two each in men's and two in women's clothes, wonderfully together.

[Translated by Noah Heringman]

Gabriel Harvey on *Hamlet, Venus and Adonis,* and *The Rape of Lucrece* (1598–1603)

[Gabriel Harvey (c. 1550–1631), a scholar perhaps best remembered as the particular friend of Spenser, gave the following account of Shakespeare and other contemporaries in a long manuscript note in his copy of Speght's 1598 edition of Chaucer. The date of the note is uncertain, but internal evidence makes it highly unlikely to be later than 1603. The references to Shakespeare are brief but suggestive, and the note is useful both in providing a context for the appreciation of Shakespeare and for its characteris-

---

1. The play—or at least the title—has not survived; a bookseller's record of the title does survive, however.

tically keen assessment of the state of modern literature. The text is from G. C. Moore Smith's edition of *Gabriel Harvey's Marginalia* (Stratford-upon-Avon: Shakespeare Head Press, 1913).]

And now translated Petrarch, Ariosto, Tasso, & Bartas himself deserve curious comparison with Chaucer, Lidgate, & owre best Inglish, aunciect & moderne. Amongst which, the Countesse of Pembrokes Arcadia, & the Faerie Queene ar now freshest in request: & Astrophil, & Amyntas ar none of the idlest pastimes of sum fine humanists. The Earle of Essex much commendes Albions England:[1] and not unworthily for diverse notable pageants, before, & in the Chronicle. Sum Inglish, & other Histories nowhere more sensibly described, or more inwardly discovered. The Lord Mountjoy makes the like account of Daniels peece of the Chronicle,[2] touching the Usurpation of Henrie of Bullingbrooke, which in deede is a fine, sententious, & politique peece of Poetrie: as proffitable, as pleasurable. The younger sort takes much delight in Shakespeares Venus, & Adonis: but his Lucrece, & his tragedie of Hamlet, Prince of Denmarke, have it in them, to please the wiser sort. Or such poets: or better: or none.

> Vilia miretur vulgus: mihi flavus Apollo
> Pocula Castaliæ plena ministret aquæ:[3]

quoth Sir Edward Dier, betwene jest, & earnest. Whose written devises farr excell most of the sonets, and cantos in print. His Amaryllis, & Sir Walter Raleighs Cynthia, how fine & sweet inventions? Excellent matter of emulation for Spencer, Constable, France, Watson, Daniel, Warner, Chapman, Silvester, Shakespeare, & the rest of owr florishing metricians. I looke for much, aswell in verse, as in prose, from mie two Oxford frends, Doctor Gager, & M. Hackluit: both rarely furnished for the purpose: & I have a phansie to Owens new Epigrams, as pithie as elegant, as plesant as sharp, & sumtime as weightie as breife: & amongst so manie gentle, noble, & royall spirits meethinkes I see sum heroical thing in the clowdes: mie soveraine hope. Axiophilus[4] shall forgett himself, or will remember to leave sum memorials behinde him: & to make an use of so manie rhapsodies, cantos, hymnes, odes, epigrams, sonets, & discourses, as at idle howers, or at flowing fitts he hath compiled. God knowes what is good for the world, & fitting for this age.

Contract for the Building of the Fortune Theatre (1600)

[This contract was drawn up between Philip Henslowe and Edward Alleyn, partners in the venture, and Peter Street, the carpenter (or general contractor) in charge of the construction. In fact, Alleyn seems to have put up all the money, £440 for the work specified in the contract in addition to £80 for decoration and considerable sums to acquire the lot and surrounding properties. Alleyn faced opposition from residents of the neighborhood, but he had secured the favor of key supporters, so that he was able to proceed with the construction. As the new home of the Lord Admiral's Men, the Fortune did in fact become a center of disturbances, with complaints coming to the Middlesex Bench of assaults, petty thefts, and riotous behavior. Alleyn had been the leading actor of the Lord Admiral's Men, chief competitors of the Lord Chamberlain's Men, and the Fortune was conceived to compete with the Globe, meanwhile replacing the decaying and poorly situated Rose Theatre. The contract's

---

1. By William Warner (1586).
2. *The Ciuile Wars Between the Two Houses of Lancaster and Yorke* (1595).
3. "Let what is cheap excite the marvel of the crowd; for me may golden Apollo minister full cups from the

Castalian fount" (Ovid, *Amores* 1.15.35–36, Loeb translation). These lines also appear on the title page of Shakespeare's *Venus and Adonis* (1592–93).
4. Probably Harvey himself.

descriptions and frequent references to the Globe, given this background, can be seen as providing some of our best evidence on the nature of the Globe itself. The text is reprinted in *ES,* vol. 2.]

'This Indenture made the Eighte daie of Januarye 1599,[1] and in the Twoe and Fortyth yeare of the Reigne of our sovereigne Ladie Elizabeth, by the grace of god Queene of Englande, Fraunce and Irelande, defender of the Faythe, &c. betwene Phillipp Henslowe and Edwarde Allen of the parishe of S[te] Saviours in Southwark in the Countie of Surrey, gentlemen, on thone parte, and Peeter Streete, Cittizen and Carpenter of London, on thother parte witnesseth That whereas the saide Phillipp Henslowe & Edward Allen, the daie of the date hereof, have bargayned, compounded & agreed with the saide Peter Streete ffor the erectinge, buildinge & settinge upp of a new howse and Stadge for a Plaiehouse in and uppon a certeine plott or parcell of grounde appoynted oute for that purpose, scytuate and beinge nere Goldinge lane in the parishe of S[te] Giles withoute Cripplegate of London,[2] to be by him the saide Peeter Streete or somme other sufficyent woorkmen of his provideinge and appoyntemente and att his propper costes & chardges, for the consideracion hereafter in theis pres-entes expressed, made, erected, builded and sett upp in manner & forme followinge (that is to saie); The frame of the saide howse to be sett square[3] and to conteine ffow-erscore foote of lawfull assize everye waie square withoutt and fiftie five foote of like assize square everye waie within, with a good suer and stronge foundacion of pyles, brick, lyme and sand bothe without & within, to be wroughte one foote of assize att the leiste above the grounde; And the saide fframe to conteine three Stories in heighth, the first or lower Storie to conteine Twelve foote of lawfull assize in heighth, the second Storie Eleaven foote of lawfull assize in heigth, and the third or upper Sto-rie to conteine Nyne foote of lawfull assize in heigth; All which Stories shall conteine Twelve foote and a halfe of lawfull assize in breadth througheoute, besides a juttey forwardes in either of the saide twoe upper Stories of Tenne ynches of lawfull assize, with ffower convenient divisions for gentlemens roomes,[4] and other sufficient and convenient divisions for Twoe pennie roomes, with necessarie seates to be placed and sett, aswell in those roomes as througheoute all the rest of the galleries of the saide howse, and with suchelike steares, conveyances & divisions withoute & within, as are made & contryved in and to the late erected Plaiehowse on the Banck in the saide parishe of S[te] Saviours called the Globe; With a Stadge and Tyreinge howse[5] to be made, erected & settupp within the saide fframe, with a shadowe or cover[6] over the saide Stadge, which Stadge shalbe placed & sett, as alsoe the stearecases of the saide fframe, in suche sorte as is prefigured in a plott[7] thereof drawen, and which Stadge shall conteine in length Fortie and Three foote of lawfull assize and in breadth to extende to the middle of the yarde[8] of the saide howse; The same Stadge to be paled in belowe with good, stronge and sufficyent newe oken bourdes, and likewise the lower Storie of the saide fframe withinside, and the same lower storie to be alsoe laide over and fenced with stronge yron pykes; And the saide Stadge to be in all other pro-porcions contryved and fashioned like unto the Stadge of the saide Plaie howse called the Globe; With convenient windowes and lightes glazed to the saide Tyreinge howse; And the saide fframe, Stadge and Stearecases to be covered with Tyle, and to have a sufficient gutter of lead to carrie & convey the water frome the coveringe of the saide Stadge to fall backwardes; And also all the saide fframe and the Stairecases thereof

1. 1600 (New Style).
2. *nere . . . London*: an area then in the northwest suburbs, literally outside Cripplegate and, like the Globe across the water, outside the jurisdiction of a City Council often inimical to the theater.
3. This square shape was unusual; the outlines of comparable theaters of the period were round or polygonal (with more than four sides).
4. Something like the VIP boxes of the present day.

5. "Attiring house," a dressing room and backstage area extending onto the rear of the stage.
6. A roof (known as "the heavens") partially covering the stage, supported by the pillars that also served as versatile pieces of scenery.
7. Plan.
8. *in breadth . . . yarde*: the stage would then extend about 27 feet into the yard, specified earlier as 55 feet square.

to be sufficyently enclosed withoute with lathe, lyme & haire, and the gentlemens roomes and Twoe pennie roomes to be seeled[9] with lathe, lyme & haire, and all the fflowers of the saide Galleries, Stories and Stadge to be bourded with good & sufficyent newe deale bourdes of the whole thicknes, wheare need shalbe; And the saide howse and other thinges beforemencioned to be made & doen to be in all other contrivitions, conveyances, fashions, thinge and thinges effected, finished and doen accordinge to the manner and fashion of the saide howse called the Globe, saveinge only that all the princypall and maine postes of the saide fframe and Stadge forwarde shalbe square and wroughte palasterwise,[1] with carved proporcions called Satiers[2] to be placed & sett on the topp of every of the same postes, and saveinge alsoe that the said Peeter Streete shall not be chardged with anie manner of pay[ntin]ge in or aboute the saide fframe howse or Stadge or anie parte thereof, nor rendringe[3] the walls within, nor seeling anie more or other roomes then the gentlemens roomes, Twoe pennie roomes and Stadge before remembred. Nowe theiruppon the saide Peeter Streete dothe covenant, promise and graunte ffor himself, his executours and administratours, to and with the saide Phillipp Henslowe and Edward Allen and either of them, and thexecutours and administratours of them and either of them, by theis presentes in manner & forme followeinge (that is to saie); That he the saide Peeter Streete, his executours or assignes, shall & will att his or their owne propper costes & chardges well, woorkmanlike & substancyallie make, erect, sett upp and fully finishe in and by all thinges, accordinge to the true meaninge of theis presentes, with good, stronge and substancyall newe tymber and other necessarie stuff, all the saide fframe and other woorkes whatsoever in and uppon the saide plott or parcell of grounde (beinge not by anie aucthoretie restrayned, and haveinge ingres, egres & regres to doe the same) before the ffyve & twentith daie of Julie next commeinge after the date hereof; And shall alsoe at his or theire like costes and chardges provide and finde all manner of woorkmen, tymber, joystes, rafters, boordes, dores, boltes, hinges, brick, tyle, lathe, lyme, haire, sande, nailes, lade, iron, glasse, woorkmanshipp and other thinges whatsoever, which shalbe needefull, convenyent & necessarie for the saide fframe & woorkes & everie parte thereof; And shall alsoe make all the saide fframe in every poynte for Scantlinges[4] lardger and bigger in assize then the Scantlinges of the timber of the saide newe erected howse called the Globe; And alsoe that he the saide Peeter Streete shall furthwith, aswell by himself as by suche other and soemanie woorkmen as shalbe convenient & necessarie, enter into and uppon the saide buildinges and woorkes, and shall in reasonable manner proceede therein withoute anie wilfull detraccion untill the same shalbe fully effected and finished. In consideracion of all which buildinges and of all stuff & woorkemanshipp thereto belonginge, the saide Phillipp Henslowe & Edward Allen and either of them, ffor themselves, theire, and either of theire executours & administratours, doe joynctlie & severallie covenante & graunte to & with the saide Peeter Streete, his executours & administratours by theis presentes, that they the saide Phillipp Henslowe & Edward Allen or one of them, or the executours administratours or assignes of them or one of them, shall & will well & truelie paie or cawse to be paide unto the saide Peeter Streete, his executours or assignes, att the place aforesaid appoynted for the erectinge of the saide fframe, the full somme of Fower hundred & Fortie Poundes of lawfull money of Englande in manner & forme followeinge (that is to saie), att suche tyme and when as the Tymberwoork of the saide fframe shalbe rayzed & sett upp by the saide Peeter Streete his executours or assignes, or within seaven daies then next followeinge, Twoe hundred & Twentie poundes, and att suche time and when as the saide fframe & woorkes shalbe fullie effected & ffynished as is aforesaide, or within seaven daies then next followeinge, thother Twoe hundred and Twentie poundes,

9. Coated both on the "ceiling" (a related word) and the walls.
1. Finished in the form of pilasters, ornamental columns in the classical style.
2. Satyrs. *proporcions:* figures.
3. Plastering.
4. Prescribed dimensions of the beams.

withoute fraude or coven.[5] Provided allwaies, and it is agreed betwene the saide parties, that whatsoever somme or sommes of money the saide Phillipp Henslowe &
Edward Allen or either of them, or thexecutours or assignes of them or either of them,
shall lend or deliver unto the saide Peter Streete his executours or assignes, or anie
other by his appoyntemente or consent, ffor or concerninge the saide woorkes or anie
parte thereof or anie stuff thereto belonginge, before the raizeinge & settinge upp of
the saide fframe, shalbe reputed, accepted, taken & accoumpted in parte of the firste
paymente aforesaid of the saide some of Fower hundred & Fortie poundes, and all
suche somme & sommes of money, as they or anie of them shall as aforesaid lend or
deliver betwene the razeinge of the saide fframe & finishinge thereof and of all the
rest of the saide woorkes, shalbe reputed, accepted, taken & accoumpted in parte of
the laste pamente aforesaid of the same somme of Fower hundred & Fortie poundes,
anie thinge abovesaid to the contrary notwithstandinge. In witnes whereof the parties abovesaid to theis presente Indentures Interchaungeably have sett theire handes
and seales. Geoven[6] the daie and yeare ffirste abovewritten.

P S

Sealed and delivered by the saide Peter Streete in the presence of me William Harris Pub[lic] Scr[ivener] And me Frauncis Smyth appr[entice] to the said Scr[ivener]
[*Endorsed:*] Peater Streat ffor The Building of the Fortune.

Augustine Phillips, Francis Bacon, et al. on *Richard II* (1601)

[These extracts from testimony submitted at the Earl of Essex's trial for treason, and
related documents, show that some of Essex's supporters had contracted with the Lord
Chamberlain's Men to revive *Richard II*, apparently in order to provide a model for the justified deposition of a monarch and thus propitiate the coup in which Essex planned to
depose Elizabeth. The play was performed on February 7, and "it was on the same day,"
according to E. K. Chambers, "that Essex received a summons to appear before the Privy
Council. This interrupted his plans for securing possession of the Queen's person and
arresting her ministers, and precipitated his futile outbreak of February 8." Augustine
Phillips was one of Shakespeare's colleagues in the Lord Chamberlain's Men. Sir Edward
Coke was, for a time, chief justice under King James. The last excerpt is a contemporary
record of a conversation between the queen and her archivist several months after Essex
was executed. The texts are from *WS*, vol. 2.]

From the Abstract of Evidence

The Erle of Essex is charged with high Treason, namely, That he plotted and
practised with the Pope and king of Spaine for the disposing and settling to himself Aswell the Crowne of England, as of the kingdom of Ireland.

From the Examination of Augustine Phillips, February 18, 1601

The Examination of Augustyne Phillypps servant unto the L Chamberlyne and
one of hys players taken the xviij[th] of Februarij 1600 upon hys oth
He sayeth that on Fryday last was sennyght or Thursday S[r] Charles Percy S[r]
Josclyne Percy and the L. Montegle with some thre more spak to some of the play-

---

ers in the presans of thys examinate to have the play of the deposyng and kyllyng of
Kyng Rychard the second to be played the Saterday next promysyng to gete them xls.
more then their ordynary to play yt. Wher thys Examinate and hys fellowes were
determyned to have played some other play, holdyng that play of Kyng Richard to be
so old & so long out of use as that they shold have small or no Company at yt. But
at their request this Examinate and his fellowes were Content to play yt the Saterday and had their xls. more then their ordynary for yt and so played yt accordyngly

Augustine Phillipps

From the speech of Sir Edward Coke at Essex's trial, February 19

I protest upon my soul and conscience I doe beleeve she should not have long
lived after she had been in your power. Note but the precedents of former ages,
how long lived Richard the Second after he was surprised in the same manner? The
pretence was alike for the removing of certain counsellors, but yet shortly after it
cost him his life.

From [Francis Bacon's] "A Declaration of the . . . Treasons . . . by Robert late Earle of Essex"

The afternoone before the rebellion, Merricke,[1] with a great company of others, that afterwards were all in the action, had procured to bee played before them,
the play of deposing King Richard the second. Neither was it casuall, but a play
bespoken by Merrick. And not so onely, but when it was told him by one of the
players, that the play was olde, and they should have losse in playing it, because
fewe would come to it: there was fourty shillings extraordinarie given to play it, and
so thereupon playd it was. So earnest hee was to satisfie his eyes with the sight of
that tragedie which hee thought soone after his lord should bring from the stage
to the state, but that God turned it upon their owne heads.

From a Memorandum in the Lambard family manuscript, August 4

. . . so her Majestie fell upon[2] the reign of King Richard II. saying, 'I am Richard II. know ye not that?'

W.L. 'Such a wicked imagination was determined and attempted by a most
unkind Gent. the most adorned creature that ever your Majestie made.'

Her Majestie. 'He that will forget God, will also forget his benefactors; this tragedy was played 40[tie] times in open streets and houses.'

John Manningham on *Twelfth Night* and *Richard III* (1602)

[John Manningham (d. 1622) kept a diary during his time as a law student at the
Middle Temple, recording the witticisms of his colleagues and a rich variety of anecdotes. The vibrant and boisterous life of the Inns of Court is also illustrated by the *Gesta
Grayorum* (see above). The February entry describes the festivities organized for Can-
dlemas Day at the Middle Temple, while the second recounts an anecdote related to
Manningham by one Mr. Touse (this name is difficult to read in the manuscript). As
with all the documents in this section, any date before March 25 is assigned to the following year according to our calendar, so that 1601 here becomes 1602 (New Style).

1. Sir Gilly Merrick, one of Essex's supporters, was later tried separately for treason.
2. Came across (in reading). The memorandum describes a scene in which the queen is reading over the archives that have been in the keeping of her interlocutor, William Lambard.

The text is from the 1976 edition of Robert Sorlien (Hanover, N.H.: University Press of New England).]

Febr. 1601

2. At our feast wee had a play called "Twelve night, or what you will"; much like the commedy of errores, or Menechmi[1] in Plautus, but most like and neere to that in Italian called Inganni.[2] A good practise in it to make the steward beleeve his Lady widdowe[3] was in Love with him, by counterfayting a letter, as from his Lady, in generall termes, telling him what shee liked best in him, and prescribing his gesture in smiling, his apparraile, &c., and then when he came to practise, making him beleeve they tooke him to be mad.

Marche. 1601

13. . . . Upon a tyme when Burbidge played Rich[ard] 3. there was a Citizen grewe soe farr in liking with him, that before shee went from the play shee appointed him to come that night unto hir by the name of Ri[chard] the 3. Shakespeare, overhearing their conclusion, went before, was intertained, and at his game ere Burbidge came. Then message being brought that Richard the 3ᵈ. was at the dore, Shakespeare caused returne to be made that William the Conquerour was before Rich[ard] the 3. Shakespeare's name William. (Mr. Touse.)

Letters Patent Formalizing the Adoption of the Lord Chamberlain's Men as the King's Men (May 19, 1603)

[James I issued the warrant ordering this patent shortly after his coronation, enhancing the status of Shakespeare's company. As retainers of the royal household with the title of Grooms of the Chamber, they performed at the court with increasing frequency (177 times between 1603 and 1616) and assisted occasionally with other court functions; but, more important, they acted throughout the kingdom under the authority of the royal patent, whose scope the forceful wording below makes clear. The patent, bearing the Great Seal, was issued May 19 as ordered in the warrant of May 17. There is some evidence to suggest that James was particularly taken with Shakespeare's poetry, and the playwright's valorization of James's ancestry (as originating with Banquo) in *Macbeth* certainly suggests that Shakespeare cultivated his esteem. The text is from *ES,* vol. 2.]

Commissio specialis pro Laurencio Fletcher & Willelmo Shackespeare et aliis[2]

James by the grace of god &c. To all Justices, Maiors, Sheriffes, Constables, hedborowes,[1] and other our Officers and lovinge Subjectes greeting. Knowe yee that Wee of our speciall grace, certeine knowledge, & mere motion[3] have licenced and aucthorized and by theise presentes[4] doe licence and aucthorize theise our Servauntes Lawrence Fletcher, William Shakespeare, Richard Burbage, Augustyne Phillippes, John Heninges, Henrie Condell, William Sly, Robert Armyn, Richard Cowly, and the rest of theire Assosiates freely to use and exercise the Arte and faculty of playinge

---

1. Source for *The Comedy of Errors.*
2. The two plays with this exact title (1562 and 1592) seem less likely to be "most like" *Twelfth Night* than another Italian play, *Ingannati* (1537), which has characters named Fabio and Malevolti and makes reference to Twelfth Night (Epiphany).
3. Olivia is not a widow in the version of Shakespeare's play that has come down to us, though she is

so described in one of Shakespeare's principal sources for the play.
1. A parish officer similar to a petty constable.
2. *Commissio . . . aliis:* By special commission on behalf of . . . and others.
3. Inclination, desire.
4. The present document.

Comedies, Tragedies, histories, Enterludes, moralls,[5] pastoralls, Stageplaies, and Suche others like as theie have alreadie studied or hereafter shall use or studie, aswell for the recreation of our lovinge Subjectes, as for our Solace and pleasure when wee shall thincke good to see them, duringe our pleasure. And the said Commedies, tragedies, histories, Enterludes, Morralles, Pastoralls, Stageplayes, and suche like to shewe and exercise publiquely to theire best Commoditie,[6] when the infection of the plague shall decrease, aswell within theire nowe usual howse called the Globe within our County of Surrey, as alsoe within anie towne halls or Moute halls[7] or other conveniente places within the liberties and freedome of anie other Cittie, universitie, towne, or Boroughe whatsoever within our said Realmes and domynions. Willinge and Commaundinge you and everie of you, as you tender our pleasure, not onelie to permitt and suffer them herein without anie your lettes hindrances or molestacions during our said pleasure, but alsoe to be aidinge and assistinge to them, yf anie wronge be to them offered, And to allowe them such former Curtesies as hath bene given to men of theire place and quallitie,[8] and alsoe what further favour you shall shewe to theise our Servauntes for our sake wee shall take kindlie at your handes. In wytnesse whereof &c. witnesse our selfe at Westminster the nyntenth day of May

per breve de privato sigillo[9] &c.

Master of the Wardrobe's Account (March 1604)

[This entry offers us a rare glimpse of the players in the entourage of King James, sporting festive regalia in their capacity as Grooms of the Chamber. The royal procession took place March 15, 1604. The text is from *WS*, vol. 2.]

Red Clothe bought of sondrie persons and given by his Majestie to diverse persons against[1] his Majesties sayd royall proceeding through the Citie of London, viz.:— . . .

The Chamber . . .	
Fawkeners[2] &c. &c.	Red cloth
William Shakespeare	iiii yardes di.
Augustine Phillipps	"
Lawrence Fletcher	"
John Hemminges	"
Richard Burbidge	"
William Slye	"
Robert Armyn	"
Henry Cundell	"
Richard Cowley	"

Simon Forman on *Macbeth, Cymbeline,* and *The Winter's Tale* (1611)

[Simon Forman (1552–1611) was a largely self-educated physician and astrologer who rose from humble beginnings to establish a successful London practice. A large parcel of his manuscripts, including scientific and autobiographical material as well as the diary from which this account of the plays is taken, has survived, making his life one of the best-documented Elizabethan lives. These manuscripts provide

5. Morality plays.
6. Advantage.
7. Council chambers.
8. Profession.
9. In sum, from the privy seal.

1. For.
2. Obsolete form of "falconers," very likely the men who trained the falcons used for James's fowl-hunting expeditions. The falconers might owe their place in the retinue to James's well-known passion for hunting.

detailed information about Forman's many sidelines, such as the manufacture of talismans, alchemy, and necromancy, as well about his sex life. The text is from *WS*, vol. 2.]

The Bocke of Plaies and Notes therof per formane for Common Pollicie[1]

In Mackbeth at the Glob, 1610 ⟨1611⟩, the 20 of Aprill ♄ (Saturday), ther was to be observed, firste, howe Mackbeth and Bancko, 2 noble men of Scotland, Ridinge thorowe a wod, the ⟨r⟩ stode before them 3 women feiries or Nimphes, And saluted Mackbeth, sayinge, 3 tyms unto him, haille Mackbeth, king of Codon;[2] for thou shalt be a kinge, but shalt beget No kinges, &c. Then said Bancko, What all to Mackbeth And nothing to me. Yes, said the nimphes, haille to thee Bancko, thou shalt beget kinges, yet be no kinge. And so they departed & cam to the Courte of Scotland to Dunkin king of Scotes, and yt was in the dais of Edward the Confessor. And Dunkin bad them both kindly wellcome, And made Mackbeth forth with Prince of Northumberland,[3] and sent him hom to his own castell, and appointed Mackbeth to provid for him, for he would sup with him the next dai at night, & did soe. And Mackebeth contrived to kill Dunkin, & thorowe the persuasion of his wife did that night Murder the kinge in his own Castell, beinge his guest. And ther were many prodigies seen that night & the dai before. And when Mack Beth had murdred the kinge, the blod on his handes could not be washed of by Any meanes, nor from his wives handes, which handled the bloddi daggers in hiding them, By which means they became both moch amazed & Affronted. The murder being knowen, Dunkins 2 sonns fled, the on to England, the ⟨other to⟩ Walles, to save them selves, they being fled, they were supposed guilty of the murder of their father, which was nothinge so. Then was Mackbeth crowned kinge, and then he for feare of Banko, his old companion, that he should beget kinges but be no kinge him selfe, he contrived the death of Banko, and caused him to be Murdred on the way as he Rode. The next night, beinge at supper with his noble men whom he had bid to a feaste to the which also Banco should have com, he began to speake of Noble Banco, and to wish that he wer ther. And as he thus did, standing up to drincke a Carouse to him, the ghoste of Banco came and sate down in his cheier behind him. And he turninge About to sit down Again sawe the goste of Banco, which fronted him so, that he fell into a great passion of fear and fury, Utterynge many wordes about his murder, by which, when they hard that Banco was Murdred they Suspected Mackbet.

Then MackDove fled to England to the kinges sonn, And soe they Raised an Army, And cam into Scotland, and at Dunston Anyse overthrue Mackbet. In the meantyme whille Macdovee was in England, Mackbet slewe Mackdoves wife & children, and after in the battelle Mackdove slewe Mackbet.

Observe Also howe Mackbetes quen did Rise in the night in her slepe, & walke and talked and confessed all, & the docter noted her wordes.

Of Cimbalin king of England.

Remember also the storri of Cymbalin king of England, in Lucius tyme, howe Lucius Cam from Octavus Cesar for Tribut, and being denied, after sent Lucius with a greate Arme of Souldiars who landed at Milford haven, and Affter wer vanquished by Cimbalin, and Lucius taken prisoner, and all by means of 3 outlawes, of the which 2 of them were the sonns of Cimbalim, stolen from him when they were but 2 yers old by an old man whom Cymbalin banished, and he kept them as his own sonns 20 yers with him in A cave. And howe ⟨one⟩ of them slewe Clotan, that was the quens sonn, goinge to Milford haven to sek the love of Innogen the

---

1. *Common Pollicie:* practical use. Forman's title for his notes on plays is not printed in Chambers, but interpolated here from G. Blakemore Evans's transcription in the *Riverside Shakespeare.*

2. Cawdor.
3. Probably Forman's error; Duncan gives Macbeth the title Thane of Cawdor. Duncan's son Malcolm is the Prince of Northumberland.

kinges daughter, whom he had banished also for lovinge his daughter,[4] and howe the Italian that cam from her love conveied him selfe into A Cheste, and said yt was a chest of plate sent from her love & others, to be presented to the kinge. And in the depest of the night, she being aslepe, he opened the cheste, & cam forth of yt, And vewed her in her bed, and the markes of her body, & toke awai her braslet, & after Accused her of adultery to her love, &c. And in thend howe he came with the Romains into England & was taken prisoner, and after Reveled to Innogen, Who had turned her self into mans apparrell & fled to mete her love at Milford haven, & chanchsed to fall on the Cave in the wodes wher her 2 brothers were, & howe by eating a sleping Dram they thought she had bin deed, & laid her in the wodes, & the body of Cloten by her, in her loves apparrell that he left behind him, & howe she was found by Lucius, &c.

In the Winters Talle at the glob 1611 the 15 of maye ☿ ⟨Wednesday⟩.

Observe ther howe Lyontes the kinge of Cicillia was overcom with Jelosy of his wife with the kinge of Bohemia his frind that came to see him, and howe he contrived his death and wold have had his cup berer to have poisoned, who gave the king of Bohemia warning therof & fled with him to Bohemia.

Remember also howe he sent to the Orakell of Appollo & the Annswer of Apollo, that she was giltles and that the king was jelouse &c. and howe Except the child was found Again that was loste the kinge should die without yssue, for the child was caried into Bohemia & ther laid in a forrest & brought up by a sheppard And the kinge of Bohemia his sonn maried that wentch & howe they fled into Cicillia to Leontes, and the sheppard having showed the letter of the nobleman by whom Leontes sent a was ⟨away?⟩ that child and the jewells found about her, she was knowen to be Leontes daughter and was then 16 yers old.

Remember also the Rog[5] that cam in all tottered like coll pixci[6] and howe he feyned him sicke & to have bin Robbed of all that he had and howe he cosened the por man of all his money, and after cam to the shep sher[7] with a pedlers packe & ther cosened them Again of all their money And howe he changed apparrell with the kinge of Bomia his sonn, and then howe he turned Courtier &c. Beware of trustinge feined beggars or fawninge fellouss.

Sir Henry Wotton on *All Is True* (*Henry VIII*) and the Burning of the Globe (1613)

[Sir Henry Wotton (1568–1639), a highly educated poet and essayist, distinguished diplomat, and finally provost of Eton College, wrote to his nephew Sir Edmund Bacon shortly after the burning of the Globe. Chambers includes several other accounts of this incident in *The Elizabethan Stage,* vol. 2, pp. 419ff. The event is also recorded in John Stow's chronicles and was lamented by poets, including (several years later) Ben Jonson, and held up by Puritan divines like Prynne as an intimation of God's wrath. The excerpt below is from the earliest extant text, *Letters of Sir Henry Wotton to Sir Edmund Bacon* (London, 1661), p. 29.]

Now, to let matters of State sleep, I will entertain you at the present with what hath happened this week at the banks side. The Kings Players had a new Play, called *All is true,* representing some principall pieces of the raign of *Henry* 8, which was set forth with many extraordinary circumstances of Pomp and Majesty, even to the matting of the stage; the Knights of the Order, with their Georges and Garter, the Guards with their embroidered Coats, and the like: sufficient in truth within a while to make

---

4. Morgan/Belarius is not banished in the version of the play that comes down to us.
5. Rogue (Autolycus).

6. Probably "colt-pixie," a mischievous sprite or fairy.
7. Sheep shearing.

greatness very familiar, if not ridiculous. Now, King *Henry* making a Masque at the Cardinal, *Wolsey*'s house, and certain Chambers[1] being shot off at his entry, some of the paper, or other stuff wherewith one of them was stopped, did light on the thatch, where being thought at first but an idle smoak, and their eyes more attentive to the show, it kindled inwardly, and ran round like a train, consuming within less then an hour the whole house to the very grounds.

This was the fatal period of that vertuous fabrique, wherein yet nothing did perish, but wood and straw, and a few forsaken cloaks; only one man had his breeches set on fire, that would perhaps have broyled him, if he had not by the benefit of a provident wit put it out with bottle Ale. The rest when we meet.

Ben Jonson on *The Tempest* (and *Titus Andronicus*) (1614)

[This extract from *Bartholomew Fair* contains one of several allusions to Shakespeare in the plays of his associate and sometime rival. The first paragraph alludes to the fashion for revenge plays such as Shakespeare's *Titus Andronicus* and Kyd's *Spanish Tragedy*, at its height roughly twenty-five years before *Bartholomew Fair* was written. The second paragraph refers disapprovingly to *The Tempest* (1613), first produced shortly before *Bartholomew Fair*. The text is that reprinted in *WS*, vol. 2, from the 1631 edition of Jonson's play (from the play's Induction).]

Hee that will sweare, *Jeronimo*, or *Andronicus* are the best playes, yet, shall passe unexcepted at,[1] heere, as a man whose Judgement shewes it is constant, and hath stood still, these five and twentie, or thirtie yeeres. . . .

If there bee never a *Servant-monster* i' the Fayre; who can helpe it? he[2] sayes; nor a nest of Antiques?[3] Hee is loth to make Nature afraid[4] in his *Playes*, like those that beget *Tales, Tempests,* and such like *Drolleries,* to mixe his head with other mens heeles; let the concupisence of *Jigges* and *Dances,* raigne as strong as it will amongst you.[5]

Shakespeare's Will (March 25, 1616)

[Shakespeare probably dictated this will sometime around January 1616. The first draft seems to have been dated in January, and 1616 is the most likely inference for the year (see note 1). The final revision was certainly made on the date given, but no clean copy was prepared, so the manuscript contains a substantial number of insertions and deletions. The text here has been silently emended to assist in ease of reading. Deleted passages have been eliminated; the most significant of these is reproduced in the notes, where significant interlineations are also identified. Most of the altered passages, as Chambers writes, simply "correct slips, make the legal terminology more precise, or incorporate afterthoughts." The revision of the will was occasioned chiefly by the February marriage of Shakespeare's daughter Judith. Our text is adapted from E. A. J. Honigmann and Susan Brock, eds., *Playhouse Wills, 1558–1642* (Manchester: Manchester University Press, 1993). For a facsimile and thorough discussion of the will, see *WS* 2:169–80.]

1. Small pieces of artillery, used for firing salutes.
1. Uncriticized.
2. The author.
3. Variant spelling of "antics," grotesque or ludicrous representations, or the actors (such as the clowns in *The Tempest*) playing such parts.
4. Make nature afraid by inexact imitation or too much fantasy.
5. *concupisence . . . you:* a reference to the dance generally incorporated into theatrical performance (see, for example, Platter's account above). Jonson suggests he is refusing to cater to the vulgar taste for more dancing in plays.

Testamentum willelmij Shackspeare
Vicesimo Quinto die martij Anno Regni Domini nostri Jacobi nunc Regis Anglie &c
decimo quarto & Scotie xlixo Annoque domini 1616[1]
In the name of god Amen I William Shackspeare of Stratford upon Avon in the countie of warrwick gentleman in perfect health & memorie god be praysed doe make &
Ordayne this my last will & testament in manner & forme followeing That ys to saye
ffirst I Comend my Soule into the handes of god my Creator hoping & assuredlie
beleeving through thonelie merittes of Jesus Christe my Saviour to be made partaker
of lyfe everlastinge And my bodye to the Earth whereof yt ys made Item I Gyve &
bequeath unto my Daughter Judyth One Hundred & ffyftie poundes of lawfull English money to be paied unto her in manner & forme followeing That ys to saye One
Hundred Poundes in discharge of her marriage porcion[2] within one yeare after my
Deceas with consideracion[3] after the Rate of twoe shillinges in the pound for soe
long tyme as the same shalbe unpaied unto her after my deceas & the ffyftie poundes
Residewe thereof upon her Surrendring of or gyving of such sufficient securitie as
the overseers of this my Will shall like of to Surrender or graunnte All her[4] estate &
Right that shall discend or come unto her after my deceas or that shee nowe hath of
in or to one Copiehold tenemente with thappurtenaunces lyeing & being in Stratford upon Avon aforesaied in the saied countie of warrwick being parcell or holden
of the mannour of Rowington unto my Daughter Susanna Hall & her heires for ever
Item I Gyve & bequeath unto my saied Daughter Judith One Hundred & ffyftie
Poundes more if shee or Anie issue of her bodie be Lyvinge att thend of three Yeares
next ensueing the daie of the Date of this my Will during which tyme my executours
to paie her consideracion from my deceas according to the Rate afore saied And if
she dye within the saied terme without issue of her bodye then my will ys & I doe
gyve & bequeath One Hundred Poundes thereof to my Neece Elizabeth Hall & the
ffiftie Poundes to be sett fourth by my executours during the lief of my Sister Johane
Harte & the use & proffitt thereof Cominge shalbe payed to my saied Sister Jone &
after her deceas the saied l li[5] shall Remaine Amongst the children of my saied Sister Equallie to be Devided Amongst them But if my saied Daughter Judith be lyving
att thend of the saied three Yeares or anie yssue of her bodye then my Will ys & soe
I devise & bequeath the saied Hundred & ffyftie poundes to be sett out by my executours & overseers for the best benefitt of her & her issue & the stock[6] not to be paied
unto her soe long as she shalbe marryed & Covert Baron[7] but my will ys that she shall
have the consideracon yearelie paied unto her during her lief & after her deceas the
saied stock and consideracion to bee paied to her children if she have Anie & if not
to her executours or assignes she lyving the saied terme after my deceas Provided that
if such husbond as she shall att thend of the saied three Yeares be marryed unto
or attaine after doe sufficientle Assure unto her & thissue of her bodie landes
Awnswereable to the porcion by this my will gyven unto her & to be adjudged soe by
my executours & overseers then my will ys that the saied Cl li[8] shalbe paied to such
husbond as shall make such assurance to his owne use Item I gyve & bequeath unto
my saied sister Jone xx li & all my wearing Apparrell to be paied & Delivered within
one yeare after my deceas And I doe Will & devise unto her the house with thappurtenaunces in Stratford wherein she dwelleth for her naturall lief under the yearelie Rent of xii d. Itm I gyve & bequeath unto her three sonns William Harte[9]

1. *Testamentum . . . 1616:* The Will of William
Shakespeare (marginal heading). On the twenty-fifth
day of March, in the fourteenth year of the reign of
our lord James now King of England, etc., and of Scotland the forty-ninth, in the year of our Lord 1616.
(The abbreviation for "January" is crossed out in the
manuscript, "March" having been substituted at the
time the will was revised.)
2. The phrase "in discharge of her marriage porcion"
was inserted during the course of revision.
3. Compensation, or interest.
4. Susanna Hall's. (The preceding "All" marks the
beginning of a new sentence.)
5. *l li:* £50.
6. Principal.
7. *Covert Baron:* under the protection of a husband.
8. *Cl li:* £150.
9. A blank in the manuscript. Shakespeare appears to
have forgotten the name of one of his nephews,
Thomas.

hart & Michaell Harte ffyve poundes A peece to be payed within one Yeare after my deceas[1] Item I gyve & bequeath unto her the saied Elizabeth Hall All my Plate (except my brod silver & gilt bole)[2] that I nowe have att the Date of this my Will Itm I gyve & bequeath unto the Poore of Stratford aforesaied tenn poundes to mr Thomas Combe my Sword to Thomas Russell Esquier ffyve poundes & to ffrauncis Collins of the Borough of Warrwick in the countie of Warrwick gentleman thirteene poundes Six shillinges & Eight pence to be paied within one Yeare after my Deceas Itm I gyve & bequeath to Hamlett Sadler xxvi s viii d[3] to buy him A Ringe to William Raynoldes gentleman xxvi s viii d to buy him A Ringe to my godson William Walker xx s in gold to Anthonye Nashe gentleman xxvi s viii d & to mr John Nashe xx vi s viii d & to my fellows John Hemynnges Richard Burbage & Henry Cundell xxvi s viii d A peece to buy them Ringes[4] Item I Gyve Will bequeath & Devise unto my Daughter Susanna Hall for better enabling of her to performe this my will & towardes the performans thereof All that Capitall messuage or tenemente[5] with thappurtenaunces in Stratford aforesaied Called the newe place Wherein I nowe Dwell & twoe messuages or tenementes with thappurtenaunces scituat lyeing & being in Henley streete within the borough of Stratford aforesaied And all my barnes stables Orchardes gardens landes tenementes & hereditamentes[6] Whatsoever scituat lyeing & being or to be had Receyved perceyved or taken within the townes Hamlettes villages ffieldes & groundes of Stratford upon Avon Oldstratford Bushopton & Welcombe or in anie of them in the saied countie of warrwick And alsoe All that Messuage or tenemente with thappurtenaunces wherein one John Robinson dwelleth scituat lyeing & being in the blackfriers in London nere the Wardrobe & all other my landes tenementes & hereditamentes Whatsoever To Have & to hold All & singuler the saied premisses with their Appurtenaunces unto the saied Susanna Hall for & During the terme of her naturall lief & after her Deceas to the first sonne of her bodie lawfullie Issueing & to the heires males of the bodie of the saied first Sonne lawfullie Issueinge & for defalt of such issue to the second Sonne of her bodie lawfullie issueinge & to the heires males of the bodie of the saied Second Sonne lawfullie issueinge & for defalt of such heires to the third Sonne of the bodie of the saied Susanna Lawfullie issueing & of the heries males of the bodie of the saied third sonne lawfullie issueing And for defalt of such issue the same soe to be & Remaine to the ffourth ffyfth sixte & Seaventh sonnes of her bodie lawfullie issueing one after Another & to the heires[7] Males of the bodies of the saied ffourth fifth Sixte & Seaventh sonnes lawfullie issueing in such manner as yt ys before Lymitted to be & Remaine to the first second & third Sonns of her bodie & to their heires males And for defalt of such issue the saied premisses to be & Remaine to my sayed Neece Hall[8] & the heires Males of her bodie Lawfullie yssueing for Defalt of such issue to my Daughter Judith & the heires Males of her bodie lawfullie issueinge And for Defalt of such issue to the Right heires of me the saied William

---

1. *unto . . . deceas:* this passage was inserted at the top of the second page, probably when the will was revised. The following lines, with which the page originally began, are crossed out in the original: "to be sett out for her within one Yeare after my Deceas by my executours with thadvise & direccions of my overseers for her best proffitt untill her Marriage & then the same with the increase thereof to be paied unto her." These lines evidently referred to Judith Shakespeare as unmarried.
2. This parenthetical clause is an insertion, and has sparked some debate about Shakespeare's opinion of Judith's marriage.
3. The "s" stands for "shillings," the "d" for "pence."
4. *to my fellows . . . Ringes:* Shakespeare's "fellows," or colleagues, Heminges, Burbage, and Condell, had worked with him in the Lord Chamberlain's Men and King's Men for many years. Many other wills and documents of the period provide evidence of the practice of wearing mourning rings alluded to here.
5. Residence. *messuage:* dwelling house with its outbuildings or adjoining lands.
6. Heritable property.
7. In addition to the signature near the end, Shakespeare signed the will here, in the bottom right-hand corner of the second page.
8. Susanna Hall's daughter Elizabeth, actually Shakespeare's granddaughter (the sense of "niece" is less restricted in early modern usage). Elizabeth proved to be Susanna's only surviving child, and since Susanna was already thirty-three in 1616, the hypothetical series of seven sons preceding this mention of Elizabeth is doubly remarkable.

Shackspere for ever Itm I gyve unto my wief my second best bed[9] with the furniture Item I gyve & bequeath to my saied Daughter Judith my broad silver gilt bole
All the Rest of my goodes Chattelles Leases plate Jewels & household stuffe
Whatsoever after my dettes and Legasies paied & my funerall expences discharged
I gyve Devise & bequeath to my Sonne in Lawe John Hall gentleman & my Daughter Susanna his wief Whom I ordaine & make executours of this my Last Will &
testament And I doe intreat & Appoint the saied Thomas Russell Esquier &
ffrauncis Collins gentleman to be overseers hereof And doe Revoke All former
wills & publishe this to be my last Will & testament In Witnes Whereof I have here
unto put my hand the Daie & Yeare first above Written. /   By me
William Shakespeare witnes to the publishing hereof Fra: Collyns Julyus Shawe
John Robinson Hamnet Sadler Robert Whattcott[1]

Front Matter from the First Folio of Shakespeare's Plays (1623)

[John Heminges and Henry Condell, friends and colleagues of Shakespeare, organized
this first publication of his collected (thirty-six) plays. Eighteen of the plays had not
appeared in print before, and for these the First Folio is the sole surviving source. Only
Pericles, The Two Noble Kinsmen, and Sir Thomas More are not included in the volume.
Four of the first twelve (printed) pages of the Folio are reproduced below in reduced facsimile, with a minimum of explanatory notes. They include Jonson's brief address "To
the Reader," Droeshout's portrait of Shakespeare, a table of contents, and a list of
actors.]

---

9. This bequest to Shakespeare's wife, Anne, was
inserted in the course of his revision of the will. She
is not mentioned elsewhere in the will at least partly
because, as Shakespeare's widow, she would be guaranteed a certain portion of the estate by law. The
appearance of this inserted bequest is nevertheless

strange enough to have evoked much speculation.
1. After Shakespeare's death, the will was endorsed
here at the bottom of the third page with a Latin
inscription indicating that the will had gone to pro-
bate before a magistrate on June 22, 1616.

To the Reader.

This Figure, that thou here ſeeſt put,
    It was for gentle Shakeſpeare cut;
Wherein the Grauer had a ſtrife
    with Nature, to out-doo the life :
O, could he but haue drawne his wit
    As well in braſſe, as he hath hit
His face ; the Print would then ſurpaſſe
    All, that was euer writ in braſſe.
But, ſince he cannot, Reader, looke
    Not on his Picture, but his Booke.

                                    B. I.

Mr. WILLIAM

SHAKESPEARES

COMEDIES,
HISTORIES, &
TRAGEDIES.

Published according to the True Originall Copies.

Martin Droeshout sculpsit London.

LONDON
Printed by Isaac Iaggard, and Ed. Blount. 1623.

A CATALOGVE

of the ſeuerall Comedies, Hiſtories, and Tragedies contained in this Volume.

The Workes of William Shakespeare,

containing all his Comedies, Histories, and
Tragedies: Truely set forth, according to their first
ORIGINALL.

The Names of the Principall Actors
in all these Playes.

 Illiam Shakespeare.

Richard Burbadge.

John Hemmings.

Augustine Phillips.

William Kempt.

Thomas Poope.

George Bryan.

Henry Condell.

William Slye.

Richard Cowly.

John Lowine.

Samuell Crosse.

Alexander Cooke.

Samuel Gilburne.

Robert Armin.

William Ostler.

Nathan Field.

John Underwood.

Nicholas Tooley.

William Ecclestone.

Joseph Taylor.

Robert Benfield.

Robert Goughe.

Richard Robinson.

Iohn Shancke.

Iohn Rice.

John Milton on Shakespeare (1630)

[John Milton (1608–1674) was born in London and as a boy might conceivably have seen Shakespeare's company act. This poem first appeared prefixed to the Second Folio of Shakespeare's works in 1632 and again in the 1640 *Poems* of Shakespeare. The text is from the 1645 edition of Milton's *Poems,* as reprinted in *WS,* vol. 2, but the title given is from the Second Folio version.]

An Epitaph on the admirable Dramaticke Poet, W. Shakespeare

> What needs my *Shakespear* for his honour'd Bones,
> The labour of an age in piled Stones,
> Or that his hallow'd reliques should be hid
> Under a star-ypointing[1] *Pyramid?*
> Dear son of memory, great heir of Fame,
> What need'st thou such weak witnes of thy name?
> Thou in our wonder and astonishment
> Hast built thy self a live-long Monument.
> For whilst toth' shame of slow-endeavouring art,
> They easie numbers flow, and that each heart
> Hath from the leaves of thy unvalu'd[2] Book,
> Those Delphick[3] lines with deep impression took,
> Then thou our fancy of itself bereaving,[4]
> Dost make us Marble with too much conceaving;
> And so Sepulcher'd in such pomp dost lie,
> That Kings for such a Tomb would wish to die.

Ben Jonson on Shakespeare (1623–37)

[In addition to numerous allusions to Shakespeare in his plays, Ben Jonson (1573–1637) writes explicitly about his friend, colleague, and rival in a number of places, most significantly in the two commendatory poems prefixed to the First Folio (see above) and in the published extracts from his notebooks entitled *Timber: or, Discoveries; Made upon Men and Matter,* first published in his *Works* of 1640. It is impossible to date the original entries precisely; Chambers's conjecture is that the following entry on Shakespeare was made after 1630. The text is from the authoritative edition by C. H. Herford and Percy Simpson, vol. 8 (Oxford: Clarendon Press, 1952).]

Indeed, the multitude commend Writers, as they doe Fencers, or Wrastlers; who if they come in robustiously, and put for it, with a deale of violence, are received for the *braver-fellowes:* when many times their owne rudenesse is a cause of their disgrace; and a slight touch of their Adversary, gives all that boisterous force the foyle. But in these things, the unskilfull are naturally deceiv'd, and judging wholly by the bulke, thinke rude things greater then polish'd; and scatter'd more numerous, then compos'd: Nor thinke this only to be true in the sordid multitude, but the neater sort of our *Gallants:* for all are the multitude; only they differ in cloaths, not in judgement or understanding.

I remember, the Players have often mentioned it as an honour to *Shakespeare,*

---

1. Pointing to the stars.
2. Invaluable.
3. Reference to Apollo, god of poetry, whose most famous shrine was at Delphi.

4. *our . . . bereaving:* "our imaginations are rapt 'out of ourselves,' leaving behind our soulless bodies like statues"—Isabel MacCaffrey.

that in his writing, (whatsoever he penn'd) hee never blotted out line.[1] My answer hath beene, Would he had blotted a thousand. Which they thought a malevolent speech. [I had not told posterity this,] but for their ignorance, who choose that circumstance to commend their friend by, wherein he most faulted. And to justifie mine owne candor, (for I lov'd the man, and doe honour his memory (on this side Idolatry) as much as any.) Hee was (indeed) honest, and of an open, and free nature: had an excellent *Phantsie*[2]; brave notions, and gentle expressions: wherein hee flow'd with that facility, that sometime it was necessary he should be stop'd: *Sufflaminandus erat*;[3] as *Augustus* said of *Haterius*.[4] His wit was in his owne power; would the rule of it had beene so too. Many times hee fell into those things, could not escape laughter: As when hee said in the person of *Cæsar*, one speaking to him; *Cæsar, thou dost me wrong*. Hee replyed: *Cæsar did never wrong, but with just cause*[5]: and such like; which were ridiculous. But hee redeemed his vices, with his vertues. There was ever more in him to be praysed, then to be pardoned.

John Aubrey on Shakespeare (1681)

[What Chambers calls "the Shakespeare-mythos" was already well under way by the time John Aubrey (1626–1697) collected these anecdotes for the biographies in his *Brief Lives*, first anthologized in 1692. Aubrey's chief sources were prominent figures of the Restoration stage, which had seen increasingly popular revivals and adaptations of *Hamlet, The Tempest,* and many other plays of Shakespeare. Numerous actors and critics in the latter part of the seventeenth century helped to "rehabilitate" Shakespeare; if at the time of the Restoration his plays had seemed terribly musty and old-fashioned, by the 1680s his reputation as an author of lasting value was well established, thanks to the enthusiasm of Restoration playgoers. Aubrey's first source, Christopher Beeston, was the son of a one-time member of Shakespeare's company. William Davenant was a formidable entrepreneur as well as a dramatist, and Thomas Shadwell a prolific playwright perhaps best remembered as Dryden's King of Dullness. The text is from Chambers's transcription (*WS*, vol. 2), with a few silent emendations for ease of reading. Some of the material is from the published version of *Brief Lives,* and some of it from manuscript notes apparently used in writing the *Lives.*]

> the more to be admired q[uia][1] he was not a company keeper[2]
> lived in Shoreditch, wouldnt be debauched, & if invited to
> writ; he was in paine.[3]
>
> W. Shakespeare.

M[r]. William Shakespear. [*bay-wreath in margin*] was borne at Stratford upon Avon, in the County of Warwick; his father was a Butcher, & I have been told heretofore by some of the neighbours, that when he was a boy he exercised his father's Trade, but when he kill'd a Calfe, he would doe it in a *high style,* & make a Speech. There was at that time another Butcher's son in this Towne, that was held not at all inferior to him for a naturall witt, his acquaintance & coetanean,[4] but dyed young. This Wm. being inclined naturally to Poetry and acting, came to London I guesse about 18. and was an Actor at one of the Play-houses and did act

---

1. Compare Heminges and Condell's address to the reader in the First Folio: "And what he thought, he uttered with that easinesse, that wee have scarse received from him a blot in his papers."
2. Imagination.
3. "He needed the drag-chain" (adapted from Marcus Seneca's *Controversiae* 4, Preface).
4. Quintus Haterius, Roman rhetorician (d. 26 C.E.).
5. See *Julius Caesar* 3.1.47.

1. Because.
2. "Company keeper" can mean "libertine" or "reveler"; the general sense of the passage is that Shakespeare is "the more to be admired" for his temperance and modesty.
3. The embarrassment ("paine") at being asked to write is presumably due to the same alleged modesty.
4. Contemporary.

exceedingly well: now B. Johnson was never a good Actor, but an excellent Instructor. He began early to make essayes at Dramatique Poetry, which at that time was very lowe; and his Playes tooke well: He was a handsome well shap't man: very good company, and of a very readie and pleasant smooth Witt. The Humour[5] of . . . the Constable in a Midsomersnight's Dreame, he happened to take at Grendon [*In margin,* 'I thinke it was Midsomer night that he happened to lye there'.] in Bucks[6] which is the roade from London to Stratford, and there was living that Constable about 1642 when I first came to Oxon.[7] M[r]. Jos. Howe is of that parish and knew him. Ben Johnson and he did gather Humours of men dayly where ever they came. One time as he was at the Tavern at Stratford super[8] Avon, one Combes an old rich Usurer was to be buryed, he makes there this extemporary[9] Epitaph

> Ten in the Hundred[1] the Devill allowes
> But *Combes* will have twelve, he sweares & vowes:
> If any one askes who lies in this Tombe:
> Hoh! quoth the Devill, 'Tis my John o' Combe.

He was wont to goe to his native Country once a yeare. I thinke I have been told that he left 2 or 300[li] per annum[2] there and therabout: to a sister. [*In margin,* 'V.[3] his Epitaph in Dugdales Warwickshire'.] I have heard S[r] Wm. Davenant and M[r]. Thomas Shadwell (who is counted the best Comœdian we have now) say, that he had a most prodigious Witt, and did admire his naturall parts beyond all other Dramaticall writers. He was wont to say, That he never blotted out a line in his life: sayd Ben: Johnson, I wish he had blotted out a thousand. [*In margin,* 'B. Johnsons Underwoods'.] His Comœdies will remaine witt, as long as the English tongue is understood; for that he handles mores hominum;[4] now our present writers reflect so much upon particular persons, and coxcombeities, that 20 yeares hence, they will not be understood. Though as Ben: Johnson sayes of him, that he had but little Latine and lesse Greek, He understood Latine pretty well: for he had been in his younger yeares a Schoolmaster in the Countrey. [*In margin,* 'from M[r] —— Beeston'.]

S[r] William Davenant Knight Poet Laureate was borne in _____ street in the City of Oxford, at the Crowne Tavern. His father was John Davenant a Vintner there, a very grave and discreet Citizen: his mother was a very beautifull woman, & of a very good witt and of conversation extremely agreable. . . . M[r] William Shakespeare was wont to goe into Warwickshire once a yeare, and did commonly in his journey lye at this house in Oxon: where he was exceedingly respected. I have heard parson Robert D[avenant] say that here M[r] W. Shakespeare here gave him a hundred kisses. Now S[r] Wm. would sometimes when he was pleasant over a glasse of wine with his most intimate friends e.g. Sam: Butler (author of Hudibras) &c. say, that it seemed to him that he writt with the very spirit that Shakespeare,[5] and seemed contented enough to be thought his Son: he would tell them the story as above. in which way his mother had a very light report, whereby she was called a whore.

---

5. Character, personality.
6. Buckinghamshire.
7. Oxford.
8. Upon.
9. Extemporaneous.
1. 10-percent interest. (Combe is damned because he charges 12 percent on his loans, 2 percent above the maximum allowed for usury not to be a mortal sin.)
2. £300 a year.
3. See.
4. *for that . . . hominum:* because he treats of (general) human manners or customs.
5. A word such as "had" seems to be missing.

TIMELINE

TEXT	CONTEXT
	1558 Queen Mary I, a Roman Catholic, dies; her sister Elizabeth, raised Protestant, is proclaimed queen.
	1559 Church of England is reestablished under the authority of the sovereign with the passage of the Act of Uniformity and the Act of Supremacy.
1562 *The Tragedy of Gorboduc*, by Thomas Norton and Thomas Sackville, is performed; it is the first English play in blank verse.	**1563** The Church of England adopts the Thirty-nine Articles of Religion, detailing its points of doctrine and clarifying its differences both from Roman Catholicism and from more extreme forms of Protestantism.
	1564 William Shakespeare is born in Stratford to John and Mary Arden Shakespeare; he is christened a few days later, on April 23.
	1565 John Shakespeare is made an alderman of Stratford.
	1567 Mary Queen of Scots is imprisoned on suspicion of the murder of her husband, Lord Darnley. Their infant son, Charles James, is crowned James VI of Scotland.
	1568 John Shakespeare is elected Bailiff of Stratford, the town's highest office. Performances in Stratford by the Queen's Players and the Earl of Worcester's men.
	1572 An act is passed that severely punishes vagrants and wanderers, including actors not affiliated with a patron. Performances in Stratford by the Earl of Leicester's men.
	1574 The Earl of Warwick's and Earl of Worcester's men perform in Stratford.
	1576 James Burbage, father of Richard, later the leading actor in Shakespeare's company, builds the Theatre in Shoreditch, a suburb of London.
	1577 The Curtain Theatre opens in Shoreditch.

TEXT	CONTEXT
	1577–1580 Sir Francis Drake circumnavigates the globe.
	1578 Mary Shakespeare pawns her lands, suggesting that the family is in financial distress. Lord Strange's Men and Lord Essex's Men perform at Stratford.
	1580 A Jesuit mission is established in England with the aim of reconverting the nation to Roman Catholicism.
	1582 Shakespeare marries Anne Hathaway.
	1583 The birth of Shakespeare's older daughter, Susanna.
	1584 Sir Walter Ralegh establishes the first English colony in the New World at Roanoke Island in modern North Carolina; the colony fails.
	1585 The birth of Shakespeare's twin son and daughter, Hamnet and Judith. John Shakespeare is fined for not going to church.
	1586 Sir Philip Sidney dies from battle wounds.
1587 Thomas Kyd's *The Spanish Tragedy* (pub. c. 1592) and Christopher Marlowe's *Tamburlaine* (pub. 1590) are performed.	**1587** Mary Queen of Scots is executed for treason against Elizabeth I. Francis Drake defeats the Spanish fleet at Cádiz. John Shakespeare loses his position as an alderman. Philip Henslowe builds the Rose theater at Bankside, on the Thames.
	1588 The Spanish Armada attempts an invasion of England but is defeated.
1589 Robert Greene, *Friar Bacon and Friar Bungay.* Thomas Kyd, *Hamlet* (not extant; perhaps a source for Shakespeare's *Hamlet*). Christopher Marlowe, *The Jew of Malta.*	**1589** Shakespeare is probably affiliated with the amalgamated Lord Strange's and Lord Admiral's Men from about this time until 1594.
1590 Anonymous, *The True Chronicle History of King Leir, and his Three Daughters.*	**1590** James VI of Scotland marries Anne of Denmark, but believes himself to be bewitched on his honeymoon when he cannot consummate the marriage. Witch trials in Scotland.
1591 Shakespeare's *1, 2,* and *3 Henry VI* performed.	**1592** The theatrical manager of the Admiral's Men, Philip Henslowe, begins his diary, continued until 1604, recording his business

TEXT	CONTEXT
	transactions, an important source for theater historians.
1592–1593 *Richard III.* *Venus and Adonis.* *The Comedy of Errors.* *Titus Andronicus.* *The Taming of the Shrew.*	From June 1592 to June 1594, London theaters are shut down because of the plague; acting companies tour the provinces.
1594 Shakespeare dedicates *The Rape of Lucrece* to Henry Wriothesley, Earl of Southampton.	1594 Roderigo Lopez, Portuguese physician and a Jewish convert to Christianity, is executed on slight evidence for having plotted to poison Elizabeth I.
1594–1596 *A Midsummer Night's Dream.* *Richard II.* *Romeo and Juliet.*	The birth of James VI's first son, Henry. 1595 Shakespeare lives in St. Helen's Parish, Bishopsgate, London. Shakespeare apparently becomes a sharer in (provides capital for) the newly re-formed Lord Chamberlain's Men. The Swan Theatre is built in Bankside. Hugh O'Neill, Earl of Tyrone, rebels against English rule in Ireland. Walter Ralegh explores Guiana, on the north coast of South America.
1596 *King John.* *The Merchant of Venice.* *1 Henry IV.*	1596 John Shakespeare is granted a coat of arms; hence the title of "gentleman." William Shakespeare's son Hamnet dies.
1597 *The Merry Wives of Windsor.*	1597 James Burbage builds the second Blackfriars Theatre. But the Lord Chamberlain's Men are not permitted to play in it, so they rent it to boys' companies for a number of years. The landlord refuses to renew the lease on the land under the Theatre in Shoreditch.
1598 *2 Henry IV.* *Much Ado About Nothing.* Ben Jonson, *Every Man in His Humor,* which lists Shakespeare as one of the actors.	1598 The Edict of Nantes ends the French civil wars, granting toleration to Protestants. Materials from the demolished Theatre in Shoreditch are transported across the Thames to be used in building the Globe Theatre.
1599 *Henry V.* *Julius Caesar.* *As You Like it.*	1599 The queen's favorite, Robert Devereux, Earl of Essex, leads an expedition to Ireland in March but returns home without permission in October and is imprisoned. Satires and other offensive books are prohibited by ecclesiastical order. Extant copies are gathered and burned. Two notorious satirists, Thomas Nashe and Gabriel Harvey, are forbidden to publish.

TEXT	CONTEXT
1600 *Hamlet.* Michael Drayton and several collaborators, who object to Shakespeare's depiction of Oldcastle-Falstaff in the *Henry IV* plays, write *The First Part of the True and Honorable History of the Life of Sir John Oldcastle, the Good Lord Cobham.*	**1600** The Earl of Essex is suspended from some of his offices and confined to house arrest. The birth of James VI's second son, Charles. The founding of the East India Company. Edward Alleyn and Philip Henslowe build the Fortune Theatre for the Lord Admiral's Men, competing with the Lord Chamberlain's Men at the Globe.
1601 "The Phoenix and the Turtle" published in Robert Chester's *Love's Martyr.* *Twelfth Night.* In the "War of the Theaters," Ben Jonson, John Marston, and Thomas Dekker write a series of satiric plays mocking one another.	**1601** The Earl of Essex leads some gentlemen against Elizabeth I, but the rising is quickly quelled. A few of the rebels, including Shakespeare's patron, the Earl of Southampton, arrange a staging of *Richard II* at the Globe, apparently to incite rebellion. Essex is convicted of treason and beheaded. Shakespeare's father dies.
1602 *Troilus and Cressida.*	**1602** Shakespeare makes substantial real-estate purchases in Stratford. The opening of the Bodleian Library in Oxford.
	1603 Queen Elizabeth dies; she is succeeded by her cousin, James VI of Scotland (now James I of England). Shakespeare's name appears for the last time in Ben Jonson's lists of actors, as a "principal tragedian" in *Sejanus.* Plague closes the London theaters from mid-1603 to April 1604. Hugh O'Neill surrenders in Ireland.
1604 *Measure for Measure.* *Othello.*	**1604** The conclusion of a peace with Spain makes travel across the Atlantic safer, encouraging plans for English colonies in the Americas.
1605 *All's Well That Ends Well.* *King Lear.*	**1605** The discovery of the Gunpowder Plot by some radical Catholics to blow up the Houses of Parliament during its opening ceremonies, when the royal family, Lords, and Commons are assembled in one place. The Red Bull Theatre built.
1606 *Macbeth.* *Antony and Cleopatra.* Ben Jonson, *Volpone.* Anonymous, *The Revenger's Tragedy.*	**1606** The London and Plymouth Companies receive charters to colonize Virginia. Parliament passes "An Act to Restrain Abuses of Players," prohibiting oaths or blasphemy onstage.
1607 *Timon of Athens.* *Pericles.*	**1607** An English colony is established in Jamestown, Virginia. Shakespeare's daughter Susanna marries John Hall. Shakespeare's brother Edmund (described as a player) dies.

TEXT	CONTEXT
1608 *Coriolanus.*	**1608** The King's Men obtain permission to play at the second Blackfriars Theatre, a smaller indoor venue.
1609 *Cymbeline.* Unauthorized publication of the sonnets.	
1610 *The Winter's Tale.* Ben Jonson, *The Alchemist.*	**1610** Henry is made Prince of Wales. Shakespeare probably returns to Stratford and settles there.
1611 *The Tempest.* Francis Beaumont and John Fletcher, *A King and No King.* Publication of the Authorized (King James) Bible.	**1611** Plantation of Ulster in Ireland, a colony of English and Scottish Protestants settled on land confiscated from Irish rebels.
1612 *All Is True (Henry VIII)*, with John Fletcher. John Webster, *The White Devil.*	**1612** Prince Henry dies.
1613 *The Two Noble Kinsmen*, with John Fletcher.	**1613** Princess Elizabeth marries Frederick V, Elector Palatine. The Globe Theatre burns down during a performance of *All Is True.*
1614 Ben Jonson, *Bartholomew Fair.* John Webster, *The Duchess of Malfi.*	**1614** Philip Henslowe and Jacob Meade build the Hope Theatre, used both for play performances and as a bearbaiting arena. The Globe Theatre reopens.
1616 Ben Jonson publishes *The Works of Benjamin Jonson,* the first collection of plays by an English author.	**1616** William Harvey describes the circulation of the blood. Shakespeare's daughter Judith marries. Shakespeare dies on April 23.
1623 Members of the King's Men publish the First Folio of Shakespeare's plays.	

Textual Variants

THE TRAGEDY OF HAMLET, PRINCE OF DENMARK

CONTROL TEXT: F

F: The Folio of 1623

Fa, Fb: Successive states of F incorporating various print-shop corrections and changes

Q1: The Quarto of 1603 ("bad")

Q2: The Quarto of 1604 ("good")

Q2a, Q2b: Successive states of Q2 incorporating various print-shop corrections and changes

Q3: The Quarto of 1611

s.p. KING CLAUDIUS [F's use of *King* has been standardized throughout.]

s.p. QUEEN GERTRUDE [F's use of *Queen* has been standardized throughout.]

s.p. PLAYER KING [F's use of *King* has been standardized throughout.]

s.p. PLAYER QUEEN [F's use of *Baptista* and *Queen* has been standardized throughout.]

s.p. FIRST CLOWN [F's use of *Clown* has been standardized throughout.]

s.p. SECOND CLOWN [F's use of *Other* has been changed throughout.]

Title: *The Tragedie of Hamlet Prince of Denmarke* [Q2 (head title, running titles), F (head title), Q1 (running titles)] THE Tragicall Historie of HAMLET, *Prince of Denmarke* [Q2 (title page)] *The Tragedie of Hamlet* [F (running titles, table of contents)] THE Tragicall Historie of HAMLET *Prince of Denmarke* [Q1 (title page, head title)]

1.1.60 he [Q1, Q2; not in F] 62 Polacks Pollax 93 designed designe 106.8 tenantless tennatlesse [Q2] 106.10 At As [Q2] 106.14 feared feare [Q2] 106.18 climature climatures [Q2] 131 morn [Q2] day 139 say [Q1, Q2] sayes 144 takes [Q1, Q2] talkes 155 Let's [Q1, Q2] Let

1.2.8 sometime [Q2] sometimes 21 Coleaguèd Coleagued [Q2] Colleagued 34 Valtemand [Q2] *Voltemond* 35 bearers [Q1, Q2] bearing 58–60 wrung . . . consent [Q2; not in F] wrung from me a forced graunt [Q1; Oxford editor G. R. Hibbard argues that the "forced graunt" recollected by the Q1 reporter suggests that he was aware of Laertes' "laboursome petition" as it appears in Q2.

The omission is therefore most likely an accident, not an authorial cut.] 77 good-mother good Mother 119 pray thee [Q2] prythee 132 canon cannon 134 Seem [Q2] Seemes 135 ah [Q2] Oh 141 beteem [Q2] beteene 150 God [Q1, Q2] Heauen 164 Marcellus. [Q2; F (text) indents, like a speech prefix; F (c.w.) is *"Mar-."*] 167 Wittenberg [Q2] *Wittemberge* 176 prithee [Q2] pray thee 186 A [Q2] He 195 God's [Q1, Q2] Heauens 204 distilled [Q1, Q2] bestil'd 209 Where, as [Q1] Whereas 237 s.p. BARNARDO *and* MARCELLUS *Both.* [Q2] *All.* [F] 242 walk [Q1, Q2] wake

1.3.1 inbarqued [Q1, Q2] imbark't 5 favour [Q2] fauours 8 Forward [Q2] Froward 9 perfume and [Q2; not in F] 16 will [Q2] feare 21 sanity and sanctity and whole [Q2] weole 40 their [Q2] the 46 watchman [Q2] watchmen 57 thee [Q1, Q2] you 65 new-hatched [Q2] vnhatch't 74 all a 109 Running Roaming 117 Lends [Q1, Q2] Giues 120 From [Q2] For 128 dye [Q2] eye 129 imploratators implorators 130 bawds bonds

1.4.1 it is [Q2] is it 10 wassail [Q1, Q2] wassels 18.1 revel [Q3] reueale [Q2] 18.11 the their [Q2] 18.20 evil eale [Q2] 18.21 over of a [Q2] daub doubt [Q2] 23 intents [Q1, Q2] euents 26 O [Q1] Oh, oh 37 the [Q1, Q2] thee 51 summit [Q2] Sonnet 53 assume [Q1, Q2] assumes 59 artere Artire

1.5.1 Whither [Q1, Q2] Where 19 on [Q1] an 20 porcupine Porpentine 22 List, Hamlet, list, O list! list *Hamlet*, oh list 24 God [Q1, Q2] Heauen 35 'Tis [Q1, Q2] It's 43 wit wits with traitorous gifts— [Q2] hath Traitorous guifts. 45 to his [Q1, Q2] to to this 69 eager Aygre 71 barked bak'd 75 of queen [Q1, Q2] and Queene 93 Hold, hold [Q2] hold 117 s.p. HAMLET *Marcellus* 120 is't [Q1, Q2] ist't 137 whirling [Q1, Q2] hurling 140 Horatio [Q1, Q2] my Lord 158 our [Q1, Q2] for 164 earth [Q1, Q2] ground 175 this headshake [Q1, Q2] thus, head shake 178 they [Q1, Q2] there

2.1.1 this [Q1, Q2] his 3 marv'lous maruels 4 to [Q2] you enquire [Q2] inquiry 14 As [Q2] And 47 and the addition Addition 49 does a this—a does— [Q2] he this? / He does: 50 By the mass [Q2; not in F] 58 a [Q2] he 62 carp [Q2] Cape 69 b'wi' [Q2] buy 69 Fare ye [Q2] fare you 77 i'th' name of God [Q2] in the name of Heauen 92 a [Q2] he 98 shoulder [Q1, Q2] shoulders 102 Come, [Q2; not in F] 113 feared [Q2] feare 115 By heaven [Q1, Q2] It seemes

2.2.17 Whether . . . thus [Q2; not in F] 20 is [Q2] are 29 But we [Q2] We 31 service [Q2] Seruices 39 Ay [Q2; not in F] 45 and [Q1, Q2] one 48 it hath [Q2] I haue 52 fruit [Q2] Newes 58 my [Q2; not in F] 59 Valtemand [Q2] Voltumand 99 'tis 'tis [Q2] it is 126 solicitings [Q2] soliciting 150 wherein [Q2] whereon 162 does [Q2] ha's 168 But [Q2] And 180 ten [Q1, Q2] two 188 a said [Q2] he said 189 A is [Q2] he is 195 read [Q1, Q2] meane 199 lack [Q2] locke 200 most [Q2; not in F] 210–11 My Lord, I will take [Q1, Q2] My Honourable Lord, I will most humbly / Take 213 except my life, my life, my life except my life, my life 216 the [Q2] my 221 Ah [Q2] Oh 272 of [Q1, Q2; not in F] 286 discovery, and [Q2] discovery of 289 heavily [Q2] heauenly 302 then, when [Q1, Q2] when 328 berattle [Q2] be-ratled 334 like most will like most 350 'Sblood [Q2; not in F] 367 Haply [Q2] Happily 373 was [Q1, Q2; not in F] 378 came [Q2] can 382 individable [Q2] indiuible 403 pious chanson [Q2] Pons Chanson 407 valanced [Q2] valiant 415 good [Q1, Q2; not in F] 418 caviare [Q1, Q2] Cauiarie 419 judgements [Q1, Q2] iudgement 425–26 as wholesome as sweet, and . . . fine [Q2; not in F] 426 One [Q2] One cheefe 437 total [Q1, Q2] to take 445 So, proceed you [Q2; not in F] so goe on [Q1; probably an accidental omission. See variant at 1.2.58–60.] 449 antique anticke [probably punning on "antic"] 470 armour [Q2] Armours 479 to the [Q1, Q2] to'th 482 mobbled [Q1, Q2] inobled 484 mobbled [Q1] Inobled 485 flames [Q2] flame 499 whe'er [Q2] whether 500 Prithee [Q2] Pray you 506 live [Q1, Q2] liued 508 much [Q2; not in F] 516 s.p. PLAYERS Play⟨ers⟩. 526 b'wi' [F, Q2] buy 531 wanned [Q2] warm'd 553 'Swounds [Q2] Why 556 'a' [Q1, Q2] haue 557 offal. Bloody, bawdy [Q2] Offall, bloudy: a Bawdy 560 Why, [Q2] Who? 561 the dear murderèd Deere 574 a [Q2] he

3.1.32 here [Q2] there 45 please you [Q2] please ye 50 sugar [Q2] surge 51 too true [Q2] true 73 Th' [Q2] The proud [Q2] poore 76 th' [Q2] the 89 awry [Q2] away 99 you know [Q1, Q2] I know 101 Their perfume lost then perfume left 112 with [Q1, Q2] your 133 nowhere [Q1, Q2] no way 142 paintings, too [Q1] pratlings too 143 hath [Q1, Q2] has face [Q1, Q2] pace selves [Q1, Q2] selfe 154 And [Q2] Haue

3.2.4 with [Q1, Q2; not in F] 6 your [Q2; not in F] 8 hear [Q1, Q2] see 11 would [Q1, Q2] could 17 o'erstep [Q2] ore-stop 28–29 nor no man or Norman 53 tongue lick [Q2] tongue, like 55 feigning faining 56 her [Q2] my 72 thy [Q2] my 77 stithy [Q2] Stythe heedful [Q2] needfull 81 a [Q2] he 89 mine now. My Lord, you mine. Now my Lord, you 120 a must [Q2] he must 121 a suffer [Q2] he suffer 124 malhecho Malicho 127 this fellow [Q1, Q2] these Fellowes 129 a [Q2] they 148 former [Q2] forme 156 their [Q2] my 178 either [Q2] other 179 enactures [Q2] enactors 186 favourite [Q2] fauourites 198 me give [Q2] giue me 199.2 An And [Q2] 221 wince [Q2] winch 222 unwrung [Q2] vnrung 224 as good as a [Q1, Q2] a good 228 mine [Q2] my 230 mis-take [Q2] mistake your [Q1, Q2; not in F] 239 A [Q2] He 248 s.p. COURTIERS All. 249 stricken [F] strucken 268 Ah ha! [Q2] Oh, ha? 296 as you [Q2] you 298 struck stroke 330 fingers [Q2] finger 339 it speak. [Q2] it S'blood [Q2] Why I [Q1, Q2] that I 345 yonder [Q1, Q2] that of [Q1, Q2] like 347 mass [Q2] Misse and 'tis, [Q2] and it's

3.3.14 weal [Q2] spirit 18 summit Somnet 73 a [Q2] he 74 a [Q2] he 77 sole [Q2] soule 80 A [Q2] He 81 flush [Q2] fresh 88 hint hent

3.4.1 A [Q2] He 12 a wicked [Q2] an idle 31 better [Q2] Betters 36 brassed braz'd 41 off [Q2] of 43 sets [Q2] makes 54 this [Q2] his 64 brother [Q2] breath 78 And [Q2] As 108 you do [Q2] you 109 th'incorporal [Q2] their corporall 122 whom [Q2] who 142 o'er or 143 ranker [Q2] ranke 144 these this 151.1–2 eat, / Of habits devilish eate / Of habits deuill [Q2] 151.5 Refrain tonight [F] to refraine night [Q2] 151.9 either in either [Q2] 166 bloat [Q2] blunt 172 mad [Q2] made 185.6 and't an't [Q2]

4.1.1 matter [Q2] matters 6 sea [Q1, Q2] Seas 11 O [Q2] On 21 let [Q2] let's 26 a [Q2] He 34 mother's closet [Q2] Mother Clossets 39.1 So envious slander [Q2]

4.2.16 like an ape an apple like an Ape

4.3.7 never [Q2] neerer 20 a [Q2] he 21 politic [Q1, Q2; not in F] 23 ourselves [Q2] our selfe 26–28 s.p. KING CLAUDIUS Alas . . . that worm [Q2; not in F] 38 A will [Q2] He will 44 is [Q2] at 50 them [Q2] him

4.4.9.16 now [not in Q2]

4.5.12 might [Q2] would 41 God'ield God dil'd 65 thus [Q2] this 74 sorrows come [Q2] sorrowes comes 75 battalions [Q2] Battaliaes 85 Feeds [Q2] Keepes this [Q2] his 88 Wherein [Q2] Where in 93 is [Q2]

are **96 impetuous** impittious **114 that's** calm [Q2] that calmes **124 Where is** [Q2] Where's **138 is't** [Q2] if **139 sweepstake** Soop-stake **144 pelican** [Q2] Politician **148 sensibly** [Q2] sensible **151 s.p.** VOICES [not in F] **165 rained** [Q2] *raines* **166 Fare you well, my dove.** [F italicizes as part of the song.] **174 pansies** [Q2] Paconcies **181 a made** [Q2] he made **185–86 a . . . a** [Q2] *he . . . he* **194 God 'a' mercy** [Q1, Q2] *Gramercy* **196 O God** [Q2] you Gods **197 commune** common **212 call't** [Q2] call

4.6.8 A [Q2] Hee **9 ambassador** [Q2] Ambassadours **11 Horatio** [Q2; not in F] **21 thine** [Q2] *your*

4.7.11 they're [Q2] they are **21 guilts** Gyues **24 aimed** [Q2] arm'd **27 Who has** Who was **48 abuse, and** [Q2] abuse? Or **66 since** [Q2] hence **69 can** [Q2] ran **77 Lamord** [Q2] *Lamound* **79 the** [Q2] our **made** [Q2] mad **84.1 Th'escrimers** the Scrimures [Q2] **84 Sir, this** [Q2] Sir. This **88 What** [Q2] Why **97 in deed** indeed **114 that, but dip** [Q2] I but dipt **127 cunnings** [Q2] commings **129 that** [Q2] the **133 How now, sweet Queen?** how sweet Queene. **135 they** [Q2] they'l **139 Therewith** [Q2] There with **make** [Q2] come **143 crownet** Coronet **152 their** [Q1, Q2] her **153 lay** [Q2] buy

5.1.4 coroner [Q2] Crowner **11 to act** [Q2] an Act **23 o'** [Q2] of **31 A** [Q2] He **60 there-a-was nothing-a** [Q2] *there was nothing* **61 a** [Q2] he **71 'twere** [Q2] it / were **72 This** [Q2] It **73 would** [Q2] could **78 a** [Q2] he **83 an** [Q2] if **90 of** [Q1] of of **101–2 th'inheritor** [Q2] the Inheritor **108 sirrah** [Q2] Sir **129 heel** [Q1, Q2] heeles **129–30 the courtier** [Q1, Q2] our Courtier **139–40 a . . . A . . . a . . .** [Q2] he . . . hee . . . he **140 'tis** [Q2] it's **142 him there. There** [Q2] him, there **149 sexton** [Q2] sixteene **152 a . . . a** [Q2] he . . . he **154 a will** [Q2] he will **166 This same skull, sir** [Q2] This same Scull Sir, this same Scull sir **173 now, how** [Q1, Q2] how **177 Not** [Q2] No **grinning** [Q2] Ieering **185 Pah** puh **188 a** [Q2] he **202 rites** rights **204 of** [Q2; not in F] **212 prayers** [Q2] praier **230 treble woer** [Q2] terrible woer **237 To o'ertop** [Q2] To o'retop **238 grief** [Q2] griefes **240 Conjures** [Q2] Conuire **246 For** [Q1, Q2] Sir **250 ALL THE LORDS Gentlemen!** [not in F] **s.p. HORATIO** [Q2] *Gen.* **259 'Swounds** [Q2] Come **260 woot fast** [Q2; not in F] **272 couplets** [Q2] Cuplet **279 your** [Q2] you

5.2.7 praised [Q2] praise **8 sometime** [Q2] sometimes **9 pall** paule **21 reasons** [Q2] reason **30 villainies** villaines **38 Th'** [Q2] The **effect** [Q2] effects **41 like** [Q2] as

49 ordinant [Q2] ordinate **52 the form of** th' forme of the **55 sequent** [Q2] sement **59 defeat** [Q2] debate **79 court** count **88 chuff** Chowgh **89 say** [Q2] saw **92 sir** [Q2; not in F] **100 a** [Q2] he **102 Nay, good my Lord** [Q2] Nay, in good faith, **102.2 gentleman** gentlemen [Q2] **102.4 feelingly** [Q3] sellingly [Q2a] fellingly [Q2b] **102.8 dizzy** [Q3] dazzie [Q2] **102.9 yaw** [Q2a] raw [Q2b] **102.20 to't** [Q2a] doo't [Q2b] **rarely** really [Q2] **102.34 his** this [Q2] **108 King, sir** [Q2] sir King **hath wagered** [Q2] ha's wag'd **110 hanger** [Q2] Hangers **120 bet** [Q2] but **122 laid, sir** [Q2] laid **124 on't** one **nine** [Q2] mine it [Q2] that **132 and** [Q2] if **138 turn** [Q2] tongue **140 A** [Q2] He a [Q2] hee **141 has** [Q2] had **many** [Q2] mine **144 fanned** fond **145 trial** [Q2] tryalls **150 it** [Q2; not in F] **181 brother** [Q1, Q2] Mother **187 ungored** [Q2] vngorg'd **213 trumpet speak** [Q2] Trumpets speake **219 my lord** [Q2] on sir **227 Set it** [Q1, Q2] set **231 Here, Hamlet, take my** Heere's a **249 mine own** [Q2] mine **254 Ho!** [Q2] How? **265 s.p. ALL THE COURTIERS** [Q2] *All.* **281 cause aright** [Q2] causes right **285 ha't** [Q2] haue't **286 God** [Q2] good **299 th'occurrents** [Q2] the occurents **302 cracks** [Q2] cracke **308 This** [Q2] His **310 shot** [Q2] shoote **329 th'inventors'** [Q2] the Inuentors **333 rights** [Q1, Q2] Rites **334 now** [Q1, Q2] are **335 also** [Q2] always

TROILUS AND CRESSIDA

CONTROL TEXT: F; OCCASIONALLY, AS NOTED BELOW, Q

F: The Folio of 1623

Q: The Quarto of 1609

Qa, Qb, Fa, Fb: The "b" texts of both Q and F are corrected versions. The change from Qa to Qb is significant: Qb adds a prefatory epistle not found in Qa or in either state of F. See the Introduction and the Textual Note.

Title: *Troilus and Cressida* [F most running titles] The booke of Troilus and Cresseda [Stationers' Register, 1603], THE history of Troylus and Cressida [Stationers' Register, 1609], THE Historie of Troylus and Cresseida [Qa title page], THE Famous Historie of Troylus *and* Cresseid [Qb title page], The history of *Troylus* and *Cresseida* [Q head title; running titles, all italic], THE TRAGEDIE OF Troylus and Cressida [F title page; initial running titles, all italic]

s.p. PROLOGUE [It is unclear whether the lines of the Prologue in F are actually attributed to a character called "Prologue," as they are in this edition.]

s.p. BASTARD [As in F, Margareton is referred to in the s.p.'s and s.d.'s of 5.8 as *Bastard*. In F, he is mistakenly referred to in dialogue (at 5.5.7) as *Margarelon*.]

s.p. PANDARUS [F's occasional use of *Pandar* in s.p.'s and s.d.'s may be deliberate, but it has been standardized to "Pandarus" throughout.]

s.p. ALEXANDER [F refers to Cressida's servant in 1.2 as *Her Man* or simply as *Man,* while Pandarus refers to him in dialogue as *Alexander*. His name has been standardized to "Alexander" throughout that scene.]

s.p. MAN [Reserved in this edition for the servant of Troilus, who is referred to in the s.p.'s of 3.2 (in this edition as in F) as "Man."]

s.p. SERVANT [Reserved in 3.1 for the servant of Paris and in 5.5 for the servant of Diomedes, both of whom are also referred to in F as *Servant*]

Pro.   12 barques *Barke* **13 freightage** *frautage* **17 Antenorides** Antenonidus **18 full-filling** fulfilling **19 Spar** *Stirre*

1.1.0–1.2.215 Enter . . . Hector's, and how he [F in these lines simply reprints Q with a few errors; therefore its readings and press variants are here treated as without substantive authority. Q is taken as control text; thus variants from Q rather than from F will be noted for these lines. Rejected Q readings are labeled "[Q]" to avoid confusion. See below also 2.2.103–209, 3.3.1–95, and 4.6.0–64.] **29 So, traitor!** 'When she comes'? When is she thence? so traitor then she comes when she is thence [Q] **35 askance** a scorne [Q] **68 on of you** [F] of you [Q] **72 not kin** [Fb] kin [Q] **73 care I** [F] I [Q] **97 resides** [F] reides [Q]

1.2.17 they [F] the [Q] **22 farced** sauced [Q] **108 lift** [F] liste [Q] **120 the** thee [Q] **136 pot** [F] por [Q] **137 or** [not in Q] **176 a man** [F] man [Q] **188 man's** [F] mans man [Q] **215 looks and how** [At this point, F regains its independent authority and becomes the control text again.] **220 an eye** [Q] money **221 comes** [Q] come **234 season** [Q] seasons **237 date is** [Q] dates **243 lie at a** [Q] lye at, at a **267 price** [Q] prize **272 Then** [Q] That

1.3.7 Infects [Q] Infect **18 shames** [Q] shame **50 flee** fled **53 Retorts** Retires **58 th'** [Q] the **62 As, Agamemnon, every hand** As *Agamemnon* and the hand **66 On** [Q] In **83 masque** Maske [ ] [The conjectural missing line is not in Q or F. Some contrast with "Th'unworthiest" (line 83) seems

required.] **87 Infixture** Insisture **101 fixture** fixure **106 primogenity** [Q] primogenitiue **117 resides** recides **118 their** [Q] her **127 it is** [Q] is it **156 scaffoldage** Scaffolage **159 a-mending** a mending **161 seem** [Q] seemes **202 calls** [Q] call **207 swinge** [Q] swing **209 finesse** [Q] finenesse **221 heart** head **236 great** [Q; not in F] **acorn** accord **240 that the** [Q] that he **241 what, repining, the** what the repining **260 resty** [Q] rusty **262 among** [Q] among'st **298 prove** [Q] pawne **348 e'en** in

2.1.6 then [Q; not in F] **13 thou** [Q] you **unsifted** whinid'st **18 o' thy** ath thy **27 foot.** An foot, and **42–43 in thy skull** [not in F] **45 thrash** [Q] thresh **53 ye thus** you this **87 bade the** [Q] bad the bad thee **96 an** [Q] and if **97 a knock** he knocke **A were** [Q] he were **101 your** their **106 wit** [not in F] **109 peace** [Q; not in F] **brach** Brooch

2.2.9 toucheth [Q] touches **34 reason** [Q] reasons **44–45 And . . . reason** [Q; lines transposed in F] **47 hare** [Q] hard **49 Make** [Q] Makes **55 mad** [Q] madde made **70 sewer** same **89 never fortune** [Q] Fortune neuer **103–209 old . . . shriek** [F shows no sign of access to manuscript copy in these lines; Q therefore again becomes the control text for this passage.] **110 Ah . . . ah** a . . . a [Q] **119 the** [not in Q] **163 But** and [Q] **209** [After "shriek," F again becomes the control text.]

2.3.10 ye [Q] thou **14 their** [Q] the **16 Neapolitan** [Q; not in F] **21 could ha'** [Q] could haue **30 prayer** [Q] a prayer **32 s.p. PATROCLUS** Amen [Q; not in F] **41 Thersites** [Q] thy selfe **65 whore and a cuckold** [Q] Cuckold and a Whore **66 emulous** [Q] emulations **72 faced** sent **74 so, lest** so, least [Q] of, so [F] **80 you will** [Q] will 'tis it is **97–98 his legs . . . flexure** [Q] his legge . . . flight **110   on**   [Q]   of **112 unwholesome** [Q] vnholdsome **114 come** [Q] came **118 tend** [Q] tends **122 lunes** lines **128 Bring** [Fb] ring [Fa] **132 second** [Fb]; fecond [Fa] **161 worth** [Q] wroth **165 himself** [Q] it selfe **208 s.p. AJAX** Ulis⟨ses⟩. **209 s.p. ULYSSES** Aia⟨x⟩. **211 Farce** Force **216 does** [Q] do's doth **228 Famed** [Q] Fame **230 thine** [Q] thy **245 great** [Q; not in F] **247 today to Troy** to *Troy* **252 sail . . . hulks** [Q] may saile . . . bulkes

3.1.6 notable [Q] noble **16 titles** [Q] title **27 thou** [Q] thou art **31 visible** inuisible **33 not you** [Q] you not **36 Cressid** [Q] *Cressida* **39 s.d. HELEN** [Q] *Helena* **52 Will you** well, you **66 Ay, faith** I faith **77 sweet** [Q] sweere **80 I'll lay my life** [Q; not in F] **80, 82 dispenser** disposer **83 make 's** makes [Q] make [F] **85 dispenser's** disposer's **104–05 s.p. PANDARUS In . . . so.** [*Sings*]

Love [Fb] In . . . so. *Pan⟨darus⟩: Love* [Fa] [In Fa, Paris continues to speak until the beginning of the song. The song itself is then attributed to Pandarus.] **105 still love, still more** [Q] *still more* **111, 113 O! O!** *oh ho* **115, 116 O! O!** *O ho* **118 ay, faith** [Q] I faith *yfaith* **141 these** [Q] this **148 s.p. PARIS** [not in F. The line is attributed to Helen.]

3.2.12 Pandar [Q] *Pandarus* **20 repurèd** [Q] reputed **22 tuned** [Q] and **30 spirit** [Q] spirite sprite **31 as short** [Q] so short **64 fears** teares **66 safer** [Q] safe **71 Nor** [Q] Not **109 till now not** [Q] not till now **111 grown** [Q] grone grow **121 Cunning . . . in my Comming** . . . from my **139 speak so** [Q] speakes so **157 truth** [Q] truths **179 wind or** [Q] as Wind, as **180 or** [Q] as **186 pain** [Q] paines **193–94 with a bed** [not in F] **197 pander** [Q] and Pander

3.3.1–95 Now . . . virtues [F shows no clear evidence of manuscript authority until "shining" (3.3.95). Q thus becomes the control text in the interim.] **1 you** [F; not in Q] **3 your** [F; not in Q] **4 come** loue [Q] **5 profession** possession [Q] **67 use** us'd [Q] **95 shining** [F] ayming [Q; here F regains its status as control text, though (as elsewhere) some of the variants it retrieved from the manuscript were themselves errors.] **97 givers** [Q] giuer **100–101 To . . . behold itself** [Q; not in F] **105 mirrored** married **107 at** [Q] it at **110 man** [Q] may **111 be** [Q] is **115 they're** th'are [Q] they are [F] **132 fasting** [Q] feasting **156 abject rear** abiect, neere **162 Welcome** the welcome **163 Farewell** [Q] farewels **172 give** goe **177 sooner** [Q] begin to **178 once** [Q] out **192 aught** thought **193 infant** [not in F] **203 his island** her Iland **218 air** [Q] ayre ayrie ayre **237 as** [not in F] **244 a** [Q] he **247 this** [Q] his **260 his presence** [Q] hit presence **make** [Q] make his **286 ye** [Q] you **290 am feared** am sure

4.1.9 wherein [Q] within **10 e'en** in **17 meet** [Q] meetes **37 'twas** [Q] it was **45 wherefore** [Q] whereof **67 nor less** [Q] no lesse **80 but** not

4.2.4 lull kill **6 As to** As **12 joys** [Q] eyes **26 Here** [Q] heere Heare **33 Ah . . . capocchia** a *Chipochia* **53 It's** [Q] 'tis **56 Whoa** Who **57 you are** [Q] y'are **67 Diomedes'** [Q] *Diomeds* **68 so concluded** [Q] concluded so **74 secrecies** secrets

4.3.5 Ah, ah [Q] Ah, ha **26 force** orce **30 I'll** [Q] Ile I will

4.4.3 us [not in F] **9 own** [Q; not in F]

4.5.4 violenteth [Q] no lesse **9 dross** [Q] crosse **11 Ah** a **ducks** [Q] ducke **14 you** [not in F] **23 strained** [Q] strange **40 one** [Q] our **47 Distasted** [Q] Distasting **48**

s.p. AENEAS *Aeneas within* **56 When** [Q] *Troy⟨lus⟩*. When [F attributes the line to Troilus rather than, as here, to Cressida.] **77 gifts . . . flowing** guift . . . Flawing **79 novelty** [Q] nouelties **82 afeard** [Q] affraid **119 usage** vsage [Q] visage [F] **122 zeal** seale **thee** [Q; not in F] **123 In** [Q] I **132 you** [Q] my **144 s.p. DEIPHOBUS** *Dio⟨medes⟩*.

4.6.0–64 Enter . . . game. [F in this passage shows no sign of manuscript influence and repeats several suspicious or erroneous Q readings. F is therefore here regarded as a mere reprint, and Q is taken as control text.] **38 s.p. MENELAUS** *Patr⟨oclus⟩*. [Q] **44 not** [F] nor [Q] **49 too** then [Q] **60 accosting** a coasting [Q] **64 Exeunt** *Exennt* [F; not in Q. F here regains its access to manuscript authority and hence its status as control text.] **71 they** [Q; not in F] **75 s.p. ACHILLES** *Aga⟨memnon⟩*. **94 breath** [Q] breach

4.7.28 could [Q] could'st **72 th'advancèd** [Q] thy aduanced **147 have** [Q; not in F] **168 you** [Q] thee

5.1.5 botch batch **24 cur, no** [Q] curre **58 sprites** [Q] spirits **68 sewer** sure **84 it: that** it, that it

5.2.3 your [Q] you **10 sing** [Q] finde **11 clef** [Q] Cliff life **13 s.p. CRESSIDA** *Cal⟨chas⟩*. **22 forsworn** [Q] a forsworne **27 do** [Q] doe not **40 prithee** [Q] pray thee **41 all hell's** [Q] hell **57 la lo 72 ha't** [Q] haue't **83–84 s.p. DIOMEDES** As . . . thee. **CRESSIDA** Nay . . . withal As . . . thee. *Dio⟨medes⟩*: Nay . . . me. *Cres⟨sida⟩*: He . . . withal [F makes "As I kiss thee" the end of Cressida's preceding speech and attributes "Nay . . . me" to Diomedes and "He . . . withal" to Cressida. Here, "As I kiss thee" is attributed to Diomedes, and both "Nay . . . me" and the succeeding line, "He . . . withal," to Cressida.] **84 doth take** [Q] rakes **90 one's** [Q] on's one **103 s.p. TROILUS** *Ther⟨sites⟩*: **you** [Q] me **114 said** [Q] say **122 th'attest** [Q] that test **136 a** [Q] he **139 be sanctimonies** [Q] are sanctimonie **144 Bifold** [Q] By foule **161 e'en** be be **167 as I** I **Cressid** [Q] *Cressida* **173 sun** [Q] Fenne

5.3.4 in [Q] gone **5 all** [Q; not in F] **21 give much, to use** count giue much to as **47 mother** [Q] Mothers **75 sire** sir **85 do** [Q] doth **87 dolours** [Q] dolour **92 Yet** [Q] yes **106 o' these** o'th's

5.4.8 stale [Q] stole **10 proved not** not proou'd

5.5.6 Polydamas [Q] *Polidamus* **7 Margareton** *Margarelon* **11 Cedius** *Cedus* **12 Thoas** *Thous* **17 Go** [Q] Coe **24 strawy** [Q] straying **47 brave** [not in F]

5.6.7 the thy **13 Ha** [Q; not in F]
5.7.6 arms [Q] arme
5.8.3 horned Spartan *hen'd* sparrow **8–9 am bastard begot** [Q] am a Bastard begot
5.9.7 dark'ning [Q] darking **13 and** [Q; not in F] **15 retire** [Q] retreat **16 sound** [Q] sounds **20 bait** [Q] bed
5.11.7 smite smile **12 fear of** [Q] feare, of **17 their** [Q] there **20 Cold** Coole

SIR THOMAS MORE

CONTROL TEXT: BRITISH LIBRARY MS HARLEY 7368: ADD.II.D. (FOLS. 8ᴿ— 9ᴿ); ADD.III (FOL. 11*ᵛ)

Add.II.D s.d. [John . . . aloof] *Enter Lincoln. Doll. Clown. Georg betts williamson others And a sergaunt at armes* **27 now? Prentices 'simple'?** now prenty prentisses symple **34 s.p. SHERWIN** [Hand D, crossed out] williamson [Hand C] **42 s.p. SOME** all **43 s.p. OTHERS** [Hand D, crossed out] **54 s.p. SOME** all **55 s.p. OTHERS** all **89 order** orderd (?) **153 s.p. ONE** all
Add.III 18 stings state

MEASURE FOR MEASURE

CONTROL TEXT: F

F: The Folio of 1623

s.p. MISTRESS OVERDONE [F's use of *Bawd* has been changed throughout.]
s.p. POMPEY [F's use of *Clown* has been changed throughout.]

1.1.8 But this But that **51 leavened** a leauen'd
1.2.17 wast was't **31 pil'd . . . pilled** pil'd . . . pil'd **75 you?** [In F, a short exchange follows between Pompey and Mistress Overdone, which the preceding dialogue apparently was meant to replace: printed in this edition as Additional Passage A.] **102 bonds** words **113 morality** mortality **145 fourteen** ninteene **166 thy** the
1.3.10 a witless witlesse **27 More mocked becomes** More mock'd **43 T'allow in** To do in
1.4.5. sisterhood Sisterstood
2.1.12 your our **21–23 What . . . on thieves?/What's . . . seizes.** what's . . . ceizes;/What . . . on theeves? **21 law** Lawes **34 execute** executed **39 vice** Ice **205 spay** splay
2.2.25 God save 'Save **98 raw** now **101 ere** here **119 Split'st** splits **164 prayer is crossed** prayers crosse **166 God save** 'Save

2.3.42 law Loue
2.4.4 God heauen **9 seared** feard **12 in** for **17 now the** not the **45 God's** heauens **48 moulds** meanes **53 or** and **75 craftily** crafty **76 me be** be **94 all-binding law** all-building-Law **112 Ignominy** Ignomie
3.1.29 sire fire **38 in** yet in **51 me . . . them** them . . . me **67 Though** Through **89 enew** emmew **92, 95 precise** prenzie **121 dilated** delighted **130 penury** perjury **169 falsify** satisfie **265 on** and **280 eat, array** eate away **294 Free from** From **or** as **356 ungenerative** generatiue **413 not** now **450 it** as it **451 inconstant** constant **494 Make my** Making
4.1.1 s.p. BOY Song. **6 though** but **51 and so** and **58 their** these **72 tilth's** Tithes **93–94 s.p. PROVOST** *Duke.*
4.2.81 unlisting vnsisting **100 s.p. DUKE** *Pro⟨vost⟩.* **111 s.p. PROVOST** The letter [centered on a separate line]
4.3.13 Forthright Forthlight **81 yonder** yond
4.4.4 redeliver reliver
4.5.6 Flavio's Flavia's **8 Valentinus** Valencius
5.1.13 me your we your **167 her face** your face **237 even to** to **367 wast** was't **415 confiscation** confutation **532 that's meet** that meete

Additional Passage Very well met Very well met, and well come

THE TRAGEDY OF OTHELLO THE MOOR OF VENICE

CONTROL TEXT: F

F: The Folio of 1623
Q: The Quarto of 1622
Fa, Fb, Qc, Qd: Successive states of F or Q incorporating various print-shop corrections and changes
Title: *The Tragedy of* Othello *the Moore of Venice* [Q] *Tragoedy* [Q title page] THE TRAGEDIE OF Othello, the Moore of Venice [F, Stationers' Register entry]
1.1.1 Tush [Q; not in F] **4 'Sblood** [Q; not in F] **24 togaed** [Q] Tongued **28 other** [Q] others **32 God** [Q; not in F] **53 'em** [Q] them **66 full** [Q] fall **79 thieves, thieves thieves** [Q] Theeues, Theeues **86 'Swounds, sir** [Q] Sir **101 bravery** [Q] knauerie **110 'Swounds, sir** [Q] Sir **118 now** [Q; not in F] **183 night** [Q] might
1.2.34 Duke [Q] Dukes **46 sent** [Q] hath sent **55 comes another** [Q] come another [Fa] come sanother [Fb] **59 Roderigo? Come** [Q, Fa] *Rodorigoc?* Cme [Fb] **60 'em** [Q] them **69 darlings** [Q] Deareling **88 I** [Q; not in F]

1.3.1 There is [Q] There's **these** [Q] this **53
nor** [Q] hor **73 s.p. SENATORS** *All.* **90 tale**
[Q] u Tale **106 upon** [Q] vp on **s.p. DUKE**
[Q *(Du⟨ke⟩)*; not in F] **107 overt** [Q] over
129 battles [Q] Battaile **fortunes** [Q] Fortune **139 antres** [Q *(Antrees)*] Antars **140
and hills whose heads** [Q] Hills, whose
head **142 other** [Q] others **143 Anthro-**
pophagi [Q] *Antropophague* **144 Do grow**
[Q] Grew **146 thence** [Q] hence **154
intentiuely** [Q] instinctiuely **188 b'wi'you**
[Q (bu'y)] be with you **197 'em** [Q] them
200 Into your favour [Q; not in F] **218 ear**
[Q] eares **228 couch** [Q] Coach **247 I did**
[Q] I **263 me** my **269 instruments** [Q]
Instrument **277 DESDEMONA . . . This night**
[Q; not in F] **299 the** [Q] the the **309 ha'**
[Q] haue **322 beam** braine **326 our unbit-**
ted [Q] or vnbitted **343 error** [Q] errors
347 a super-subtle [Q] super-subtle **349
pox o'** [Q] pox of **367 a** [Q; not in F] **370
He has** She ha's **385 ha't** [Q] haue't

2.1.7 ha' [Q] hath **13 mane** [Q (mayne)]
Maine **27 Veronessa** [Q] *Verennessa* **34
prays** [Q] praye **41 s.p. THIRD GENTLEMAN**
[Q *(3 Gent.)*] *Gent.* **43 arrivance** [Q] Arri-
uancie **44 this** [Q] the **52 s.p. / s.d. VOICES**
(within) Within [s.p.] **83 And bring all
Cyprus comfort** [Q; not in F] **89 me** [Q;
not in F] **95 VOICES** *(within)* A sail, a sail!
Within., A Saile, a Saile. [after line 96] **97
their** [Q] this **108 ha'** [Q] haue **111 ha'**
[Q] haue **115 hussies** Huswiues **123 essay**
assay **174 an** [Q] and **211 hither** [Q]
thither **222 again** [Q] a game **235 has** [Q]
he's **251 mutualities** [Q] mutabilities **293
rank** [Q] right

2.2.5 addiction addition **9 Heaven bless** [Q]
Blesse

2.3.33 ha' [Q] haue **53 to put** [Q] put to **57
God** [Q] heauen **66 God** [Q] Heauen **70
Englishman** [Q] Englishmen **84 Then** [Q]
And **86 Fore God** [Q] Why **89 God's** [Q]
heau'ns **96 ha'** [Q] haue **97 God forgive**
[Q] Forgiue **124 engraffed** ingraft **129
VOICES** *(within)* Help, help! [Q *(Helpe,*
helpe, within.); not in F] **130 'Swounds, you**
[Q] You **141 God's will** [Q] Alas **142 Sir!
Montano! Sir!** [Q] *Sir Montano:* **145 God's
will** [Q] Fie, fie **hold** [Q; not in F] **147
'Swounds** [Q; not in F] **151 Hold, hold** [Q]
hold **173 be** [Q] to be **190 'Swounds, if I**
[Q] If I once **201 leagued** [Q] league **204
ha'** [Q] haue **216 the** [Q] then **236 now** [Q;
not in F] **245 God** [Q] Heauen **246 ha'** [Q]
haue **247 ha'** [Q] haue **249 thought** [Q]
had thought **269 O God** [Q] Oh **291 I'll** [Q]
I **294 denotement** deuotement **306 here**
[Q; not in F] **317 were't** [Q] were **339 ha'**
[Q] haue **343 ha'** [Q] haue **348 hast** [Q]
hath **351 By the mass** [Q] Introth

3.1.3 ha' [Q] haue **8–9 tail . . . tale** tale . . .
tale **17 ha'** [Q] haue **20 my** [Q] me, mine
23 general's wife Cenerals wife [Q] Generall **28 CASSIO Do, good my friend** [Q; not in
F] **29 ha'** [Q] haue **30 ha'** [Q] haue **47 To
take the saf'st occasion by the front** [Q;
not in F]

3.3.16 circumstance [Q] Circumstances **53
Yes, faith** [Q] I sooth **61 or** [Q] on **75 By'r
Lady** [Q] Trust me **96 you** [Q] he **110 By
heaven** [Q] Alas **116 In** [Q] Of **140 free to**
[Q] free **144 But some** [Q] Wherein **152
oft** [Q] of **153 that your wisdom then** I
intreate you then [Q] that your wisedome
166 By heaven [Q; not in F] **174 fondly**
soundly **179 God** [Q] Heauen **184 once**
[Q; not in F] **189 well** [Q; not in F] **206
God** [Q] Heauen **208 keep't** kept **219
I'faith** [Q] Trust me **221 my** [Q] your **253
hold** [Q; not in F] **263 qualities** [Q] Quantities **277 of** [Q] to **282 O then heaven
mocks** [Q] Heauen mock'd **289 Faith** [Q]
Why **300 ha'** [Q] haue **316 faith** [Q] but
319 with it [Q] with't **343 of** [Q] in **396 sir**
[Q; not in F] **400 supervisor** [Q] supervision **413 ha't** [Q] haue't **428 lay** laid
434 s.p. IAGO [Q *(Iag⟨o⟩.)*. Prefixed to line
435 *(Iago.)*: in other words, F gives line 434
to Othello.] **445 that was it was 458
knows** keepes **463 s.d.** *He kneels* [Q; not in
F]

3.4.53 faith [Q] indeed **73 I'faith** [Q] Indeed?
75 God [Q] Heauen seen it [Q] seene't **79
Heaven bless** [Q] Blesse **84 sir** [Q; not in F]
89–90 DESDEMONA I pray, talk me of Cas-
sio. / OTHELLO The handkerchief. [Q; not in
F] **94 I'faith** [Q] Insooth **95 'Swounds** [Q]
Away **166 I'faith** [Q] Indeed **182 by my
faith** [Q] in good troth

4.1.32 Faith [Q] Why **35 'Swounds,** [Q; not
in F] **49 No, forbear** [Q; not in F] **75
unsuiting** [Qd] vnfitting [Qc] resulting **77
'scuse** [Q] scuses **92 hussy** huswife **99
conster** [Q] conserue **101 now** [Q; not in F]
105 power [Q] dowre **109 a woman** [Q]
woman **110 i'faith** [Q] indeed **120 Faith**
[Q] Why **123 Ha'** [Q] Haue **127 beckons**
[Q] becomes **129 the sea-** [Fb] the the Sea-
[Fa] **145 whole** [Q; not in F] **153 An . . .
An** [Q] If . . . if **156 Faith** [Q; not in F]
158 Faith [Q] Yes **179 so** [Fb] fo [Fa] **207
God save the** [Q] Save you **227 the letter**
[Q] thle etter [Fa] thLetter [Fb] **230 By my
troth** [Q] Trust me **243 an** [Q; not in F]
276 denote [Q] deonte [Fa] deuote [Fb]

4.2.5 'em [Q] them **16 ha'** [Q] haue **24 ha'**
[Q] haue **32 nay** [Q] May **33 knees** [Q]
knee **35 But not the words** [Q; not in F]
49 God Heauen **50 He** [Q] they **71 ne'er**
[Q] neuer **97 ha'** [Q] haue **105 ha'** [Q]
haue **116 ha'** [Q] haue **120 hearts** [Fb]

heart [Fa] **145 heaven** [Q] Heauens **152 O God** O Good [Q] Alas **159 them in** them: or **171 And he does chide with you** [Q; not in F] **186 Faith** [Q; not in F] **I have heard too much, for your words, and** [Q] And hell gnaw his bones, [Fa] I haue heard too much: and your words and [Fb] **192 'em** [Q] them **224 takes** [Q] taketh **228 of** [Q; not in F]

4.3.12 He [Q] And **20 in them** [Q; not in F] **22 faith** [Q] Father **23 thee** [Q; not in F] **37 nether** [Fb] neither [Fa] **38 soul sat** [Fb] *Sonle set* [Fa] **sighing** *sining* [Fa] singing [Fb] **73 Ud's pity** [Q] why **102 God** [Q] Heauen

5.1.1 bulk [Q] Barke **22 hear** [Q] heard **34 dear** [Q] deere **36 Forth** [Q] For **51 heaven's** heauen **62 'em** [Q] them **91 O heaven** [Q] yes, 'tis **106 out** [Q; not in F] **109 an** [Q] if **116 dead** [Q] quite dead **125 Fough** [Q; not in F]

5.2.37 so [Q; not in F] **62 Then Lord** [Q] O Heauen **82 'em** [Q] them **88 an** [Q] if **93 DESDEMONA O Lord, Lord, Lord!** [Q; not in F] **96 that am** [Fb] am that [Fa] **106 ha'** [Q] haue **110 Should** [Q] Did **127 O Lord,** [Q] Alas! **136 heard** [Q] heare **166 worst** [Q] wotst **224 God! O heavenly God!** [Q] Heauen! oh heauenly Powres! **225 'Swounds** [Q] come **227 'em** [Q] them **247 here** [Q; not in F] **260 ice-brook's** Isebrookes [Q] Ice brookes **356 Indian** [Q] Iudean

ALL'S WELL THAT ENDS WELL

COPY TEXT: F

F: The Folio of 1623

s.p. COUNTESS [also called *Mother, Lady, Old Lady*]
s.p. HELEN [occasionally called *Hellena* in F, although *Hellen* is the more common form]
s.p. LAVATCH [changed from *Clowne*]
s.p. REYNALDO [changed from *Steward*]
s.p. LAFEU [occasionally called *old Lafew*]
s.p. BERTRAM [standardized from *Bertram, Count,* and *Rossillion*]
s.p. FIRST and SECOND LORD DUMAINE [standardized from F's *French E.* and *French G., Captaine E.* and *Captaine G., Lord E.,* and *1 Lord E*]

1.1.50 not [not in F] **63 Farewell.** Farwell **121 got** goe
1.2.18 Roussillon *Rosignoll*
1.3.37 madam— Madam **46 Poisson** *Poysam* **78 ere** ore **100 Dian no** [not in F] **155 loneliness** louelinesse **161 to** th'other

tooth to th'other **186 intenable** intemible **200 to find not** not to finde
2.1.3 gain all, gaine, all: **41 with his cicatrice** his sicatrice, with **60 fee** see **61 bought** brought **139–40 denied** [. . .] denied. **143 fits** shifts **154 impostor** Impostrue **161 coacher** torcher **172 nay** ne **191 heaven** helpe
2.2.26 beyond below **35 I pray you** La⟨dy⟩. I pray you **53 An end, sir!** To And end sir to
2.3.59 these those **62 s.p. ALL** [but HELEN] *All.* **89 her** heere **92 s.p. HELEN** La⟨dy⟩. **121 when** whence **126 it is** is is **133 word's a slave** words, a slaue **134 grave** graue: **276 detested** detected
2.4.14 fortunes fortune **31 s.p. PAROLES** In myself, knave. [not in F]
2.5.25 End And **43 wit** [not in F] **46 not** [not in F]
3.1.17 nation nature **23 to the** to'th the
3.2.8 sold hold **19 s.p. COUNTESS** [*reads the letter aloud*] A Letter. **41 heard** heare **110 cleave** moue **still-piecing** still-peering
3.4.4 s.p. REYNALDO [not in F, which has *"Letter."*] **18 s.p. COUNTESS** [not in F]
3.5.5 greatest great'st **17 their** these **30 you** [not in F] **63 warr'nt** write **82 those places** these places
3.6.32 his this **33 ore** ours **98 s.p. SECOND LORD DUMAINE** *Cap⟨tain⟩.* G. **101, 108 s.p. FIRST LORD DUMAINE** *Cap⟨tain⟩.* E.
3.7.19 Resolved Resolue **46 wicked act** lawfull act
4.1.1 s.p. SECOND LORD DUMAINE *1. Lord* E. **38 mute** Mule **59 SOLDIERS** [*severally*] *All.* **83 art** are
4.2.39 toys e'en such a surance rope's in such a scarre
4.3.80 FIRST LORD DUMAINE *Ber⟨tram⟩.* **84 apiece;** a peece, **114 s.p. FIRST LORD DUMAINE** [not in F] **115 s.p. SECOND LORD DUMAINE** *Cap⟨tain⟩.* G. **122 s.p. SECOND LORD DUMAINE** *Cap⟨tain⟩.* G. **134 s.p. FIRST LORD DUMAINE** [not in F] **155 die** liue **157 Guillaume** *Guiltan* **188 lordship** Lord **242–43 bedclothes; but they about him** bed-cloathes about him: but they **262 quart d'écu** Cardceue
4.4.16 you, mistress your Mistris **31 that** the
4.5.3 Else [not in F] **7 a** I **16 grass** hearbes **33 name** maine **41 since** sure **42 the nobility** his Nobilitie
5.2.21 similes smiles **27 under her** vnder **34 one** [not in F]
5.3.27 s.p. ATTENDANT *Gent⟨leman⟩.* **51 Stained** Scorn'd **60 grace-sender** great sender, **72 s.p. COUNTESS** [not in F] **102 Plutus** *Platus* **115 conjectural** connecturall **141 s.p. KING** [not in F] **156 since** sir, **184 them.** Fairer them fairer: **198**

gem; Iemme **218 inf'nite cunning** insuite comming **220 my** any **310 are** is

THE LIFE OF TIMON OF ATHENS

CONTROL TEXT: F

F: The Folio of 1623

s.p. ISIDORE' S SERVANT [F's use of *Isid.* has been changed throughout.]

s.p. VARRO' S SERVANT [F's use of *Var.* has been changed throughout.]

s.p. VARRO' S SECOND SERVANT [F's use of *2. Var.* has been changed throughout.]

s.p. LUCIUS' SERVANT [F's use of *Luci.* has been changed throughout.]

s.p. FIRST LORD, SECOND LORD [F's use of *1, 2* has been changed throughout.]

s.p. FIRST STRANGER, SECOND STRANGER, THIRD STRANGER [F's use of *1, 2, 3* has been changed throughout.]

s.p. FIRST THIEF [F's use of *1* has been changed throughout.]

1.1.21 gum which oozes Gowne, which vses **25 chafes** chases **40 man** men **47 tax** wax **56 service** services **88 hands** hand **fall** sit **212 cost** cast **235 augury but** angry wit **250 'mongst** amongst **272 Come** Comes **273 taste** raste **283 s.p. FIRST LORD** [not in F]

1.2.28 ever verie **79 thou** then thou **119 smell, all** all **123 s.p. FIRST LORD** *Luc.* **144 s.p. LADY** *Lord.* **147 'tends** attends **165 Accept** Accept it

2.1.33 Take I go sir? / Take **34 in count** in. Come

2.2.4 resumes resume **37 broken** debt, broken **59, 61, 65, 88, 92 s.p. ALL SERVANTS** *Al., All.* **69 mistress'** Masters **123 proposed** propose **130 summed** sound **181 s.p. ALL SERVANTS** *Ser.* **199 treasure** Treature

3.1.51 this hour his Honor

3.2.19 not mistook mistooke **23 s.p. LUCIUS** *Lucil⟨ius⟩.* **43 before** a before for a **44 I, I** I **59 spirit** sport

3.3.21 I 'mongst lords 'mong'st Lords

3.4.59 If If't **77 an answer** answer **85 s.p. HORTENSIUS' SERVANT** *1 Var⟨ro⟩.* **86 s.p. VARRO'S FIRST** *and* **SECOND SERVANTS** *2. Var⟨ro⟩.*

3.5.8 Sempronius—all luxors, *Sempronius Ullorxa:* **11 There is** There's

3.6.1 lords Lord **17 An** And **22 behave his** behoove his **49 felon** fellow **61 Why, I** Why **65 'em** him **100 your** our

3.7.73 foes Fees **74 tag** legge **83 with your flattery** you with Flatteries **99 the** rhe **104 s.p. THIRD** 2 **105 s.p. SECOND** 3

4.1.6 steads steeds **13 Son** Some **21 let** yet
4.2.41 does do
4.3.9–10, 11–13 It . . . lean. / **Raise . . . honour.** Raise . . . Honor. / It . . . leaue: **11 demit** deny't **12 senator** Senators **15 say** fay **39 wappered** wappen'd **41 at, this** at. This **73–75 If thou wilt promise . . . If thou dost not perform** If thou wilt not promise . . . if thou do'st performe **87 tub-fast** Fubfast **116 bars** Barne **121 thy** the **132, 148, 166 s.p. PHYRNIA** *and* **TIMANDRA** *Both.* **134 wholesomeness** Whores **143 pain-sick paines** six **155 scolds** scold'st **185 thy** the **204 fortune** future **223 mossed** moyst **255 command** command'st **285 my** thy **375 son and sire** Sunne and fire **391 them** then **402 s.p. OTHER THIEVES** *All.* **427 villainy** villaine **441 Steal no** Steal **446 us,** vs **467 grant'st thou'rt man,** grunt'st, th'art a man. **484 mild** wilde **501 A** If not a

5.1.5 Phrynia Phrinica **Timandra** Timandylo **50 worship** worshipt **68 men** man **105 apart** a part

5.2.1 is in is **11 chance** chanc'd **32 sense** since

5.3.1 s.p. THIRD SENATOR 1 **4 s.p. FOURTH SENATOR** 2 **14 s.p. FIRST SENATOR** 3

5.4.2 this? this? / *Tymon* is dead, who hath out-stretcht his span, / Some beast read this; There do's not liue a Man.

5.5.37 revenges Reuenge **55 Descend** Defend **66 s.p. SOLDIER** *Mes⟨senger⟩.*

THE HISTORY OF KING LEAR

CONTROL TEXT: Q1

F: The Folio of 1623
F2: The Folio of 1632
Q1: The Quarto of 1608
Q2: The Quarto of 1619
Qa, Qb: Successive printings of Q1 incorporating various printshop corrections and changes
Title: The Historie of King Lear [Q running title] M. William Shak-speare / HIS / Historie, of King Lear. [Q head title, Stationers' Register] M. William Shak-speare: / HIS / True Chronicle Historie of the life and / death of King LEAR and his three / Daughters. / *With the vnfortunate life of* Edgar, *sonne* / and heire to the Earle of Gloster, and his / sullen and assumed humor of / TOM of Bedlam: [Q title page]

s.p. EDMUND [Q's use of *Bastard* has been standardized throughout.]

s.p. OSWALD [Q's use of *Oswald, Gentleman,* and *Steward* has been standardized throughout.]

s.p. ALBANY [Q's use of *Duke* and *Albany* has been standardized throughout.]

s.p. CORNWALL [Q's use of *Duke* and *Cornwall* has been standardized throughout.]

s.p. FIRST GENTLEMAN, SECOND GENTLEMAN [Q only uses *Gentleman.*]

s.p. SECOND CAPTAIN, THIRD CAPTAIN [Q only uses *Captain.*]

1.37 off of 51 as [F] a 100 mysteries [F2] mistresse night [F] might 117 dowers [F] dower 128 crownet Coronet 135 mad [Q2, F] man 163 next tenth 208 your [F] you 215 acknow may know 219 the for 230 a [F] and 244 my [F] thy 255 Ye The 267 the worst the worth

2.13 dull-eyed dull lyed 14 creating [F] creating of 15 then [F] the 35 s.p. EDMUND *Ba⟨stard⟩.* [Qb; not in Qa] 73 ay I 103 honesty [F] honest 109 spherical [F] spirituall 119 on's cue out out 120 sigh sithe

4.2 diffuse defuse 60 these this 79 if you have you haue 94 my any 95 off of 98 Lady the brach Ladie oth'e brach 99 gall [F] gull 136 ladies [Qb] lodes [Qa] 159 learn to [Qb] learne [Qa] 171 Now [Qb] thou [Qa] 186 it [F; not in Q] 207 lethargied [F] lethergie 223 more like to more like 237 my any 241 are [F] and 260 thwart thourt disnatured [F] disuetur'd 262 cadent [F] accent 277 And [not in Q] 278 Untented [Qb] vntender [Qa] 279 Pierce [Qb] peruse [Qa] thee! the 281 cast you [F] you cast 294 thee [F; not in Q] 308 And after [Qa] & hasten [Qb] retinue returne 309 milky [Qb] mildie [Qa] 311 ataxed alapt [Qa] attaskt [Qb] for want [Qb] want [Qa] 312 praised [F] praise

5.6 were [Q2] where 16 stands [Q2] stande

6.18 Wit [not in Q] 27 you your 29 cunning [F] crauing 36 Ho no 47 fine [F] a fine 51 lanced lancht 54 ghasted gasted 55 Or . . . I know not [not in Q] 65 pitched pight 95 tend tends 100 the spoil and waste these—and wast [Qa, Q2] his [Qb] this his [Qa] 118 This Thus 119 poise [Qb] prise [Qa] 122 differences [Qb] defences [Qa] least [Qb] best [Qa] 123 home [Qb, F] hand [Qa]

7.58 Z Zedd 62 have you you haue 69 entrenched intrench unloose, [F] inloose 71 fire [F] stir 74 dogs [F] dayes 76 Smile Smoile 78 Camelot [F] Camulet 87 Than [Q2, F] That 90 roughness [F] ruffines 101 flickering flitkring 102 dialect [F] dialogue 114 fleshment [F] flechuent 117 ancient [F] ausrent [Qa] miscreant [Qb] 123 Stocking [F] Stobing [Qa] Stopping [Qb] 129 speaks [Q2, F] speake 133 contemnèd temnest [Qb] 146 out [Q2, F] ont

150 say [Qa] saw [Qb] 155 miracles [F] my rackles [Qa] my wracke [Qb] 157 now not [Qa] most [Qb] 159 For From 160 their [Qb] and [Qa] overwatched [Q2, F] ouerwatch 161 Take [Qb] Late [Qa] 163 heard [F] heare 167 Does [F] Dost 172 elf [F] else 177 and [Qb; not in Qa] 178 Pins [Qb] Pies [Qa] 179 farms [F] seruice 182 Tuelygod [Qa] *Turlygod* [Qb] 184 home [F] hence 189 cruel [F] crewell 190 heads [F] heeles 201 propose purpose 210 meiny [Qb] men 222 *Histerica Historica* 246 pardie perdy 250 insolence Iustice 259 father [Qb] fate [Qa] 260 his [Qb] the [Qa] commands [Qb] come and [Qa] tends [Qa] her [Qb] 261 'Fiery'? The The fierie [Qa] Fierie [Qb] 265 commands [Q2] Cōmand 287 divorce [Qb] deuose [Qa] shrine, tombe 293 deplored deptoued [Qa] depriued [Qb] 294 you [F; not in Q] 299 in [F] on 317 s.p. LEAR [Q2; not in Q1, which does indent the line as though it were the beginning of a speech] 323 Thy [F] The 342 your [F] you 361–62 To be . . . air [In Q, the lines appear in the opposite order: "To be . . . owle" after "To wage . . . Ayre."] 366 beg [Q2, F] bag 375 boil bile 417 need [F] deed 420 life is [F] life as 428 so [F] to 429 tamely [F] lamely 438 into [F] in flaws [F] flowes

8.9 outstorm outscorne 36 am [F; not in Q] 45 In which endeavor [not in Q]

9.2 cataracts [F] caterickes hurricanoes [F] Hicanios 8 germens Germains 15 tax [F] taske 34 but [Qb] hut [Qa] 43 wanderers [F] wanderer 59 than [F] their 65 you [F] me 71 your [F] you 74 tiny tine

10.3 took [Q2, F] tooke me 23 The [F] then

11.2 The [Qb] the/the [Qa] 4 here [F; not in Q] 6 contentious [F] crulentious [Qa] tempestious [Qb] 10 roaring [Qb, F] raging [Qa] 12 This [Qb] the [Qa] 14 beats [Qb, F] beares [Qa] 22 own one 51 starblasting [F] starre-blusting 53 there, and [Q2] there, and / and 54 has his [F2] his 69 word words 84 no nonny [F] no on ny 92 lendings [Qb] leadings [Qa] on, be true [Qa] on [Qb] 95 on 's [F] in 97 Flibbertigibbet [F] fliberdegibek 98 gives [Qb] gins [Qa] and the [Qb] the [Qa] 99 pin, squinies pin- / queues [Qa] pin, / squemes [Qb] hare [Qb] harte [Qa] 101 Swithin Swithald wold old 102 A [Qa] he [Qb] met the [Qb] nellthu [Qa] mare [Qb] more [Qa] foal fold 103 her alight [F] her, O light 105 witch [Qb] with [Qa] 110 tadpole tod pole wall-newt [Qb] wall-wort [Qa] 119 Smolking snulbug 122 Mahu [F] ma hu 158 tower [F] towne

12.10 were not [F] were

13.5 discern deserue **6 Frateretto** [F] *Fretereto* **16 justicer** Iustice **19 troll** tral **20 burn** broome **28 cushions** cushings **29 the** their **30 robèd** robbed **41 she** [Q2; not in Q1] **44 join-stool** ioyne stoole **46 on** an **58 mongrel** mungril **58–59 grim, / Hound** [F] grim-hound **84 Take up, take up** [F] Take vp to keepe [Qa] take vp the King [Qb]

14.5 revenges [F] reuenge **8 festinate** [F2] festuent **posts** [F] post **14 questants** questrits **55 anointed** [Qb] aurynted [Qa] **56 as** [F] of [Qa] on [Qb] **bowed** lou'd [Qa] lowd [Qb] **57 bouyed** [F] layd [Qa] bod [Qb] **58 stellèd** [Qb, F] steeled [Qa] **60 howled** [F] heard **62 I'll subscribe** else subscrib'd **70 you** [Q2, F; not in Q1] **83 enkindle** [F] vnbridle **84 quite** quit **96 s.p. SECOND** [not in Q] **97 s.p. THIRD** 2 **100 s.p. SECOND** I **101 roguish** [Qa; not in Qb]

15.4 esperance [F] experience **7 parti-eyed** [Qb] poorlie, leed [Qa] **35 to** [F] are toth' **36 kill** [F] bitt **37 play fool** [F] play the / foole **41 hence** [F] here **55 thee** the **57 as . . . lust,** Of lust, as *Obidicut,* **58 Flibbertiggibet** *Stiberdigebit* **mocking** Mobing, **59 mowing** *Mohing* **67 undo** [F] vnder **71 saucily** firmly

16.10 defy desire **12 terror** [Qb, F] curre [Qa, Q2] **15 Edmund** [Q2, F] *Edgar* **21 command** [Qb, F] coward [Qa, Q2] **27 a** [Qb; not in Qa] **28 My foot usurps my body** [Qa] A Foole vsurps my bed [Qb] **29 whistling** [Qb] whistle [Qa] **44 benefacted** beniflicted [Qa] benifited [Qb] **46 these** [Qb] the [Qa] **48 Humanity** [Qb] Humanly [Qa] **51 discerning** [F] deseruing **55 noiseless** [Qb] noystles [Qa] **56 flaxen biggin threats** thy flayer begin threats [Qa] thy state begins thereat [Qb] **59 shows** [Qb] seemes [Qa] **64 dislocate** dislecate **67 mew** [Qb] now [Qa] **77 You** [Qb] your [Qa] **justicers** [Qb] Iustices [Qa]

17.9 Maréchal Marshall **12 sir** say **17 strove** streme **21 seemed** seeme **30 Let piety not be believed** Let pitie not be beleeft **32 mastered** moystened her

18.2 racked vent **3 fumitor** femiter **4 burdocks** hor-docks **6 The centuries** a centurie is **send** [F] sent **28 incite** [Q2] in sight

19.4 Lord [F] Lady **11 Edmund** [F] and now **15 after** after him **letters, madam.** letters **27 I, madam?** [F] I Madam.

20.2 up it now [F] it vpnow **39 snuff** [Q2] snurff **40 bless him** [F] blesse **42 may** [Q2, F] my **53 a-length** at each **57 summit** [F] sommons **65 how now** how **68 beggar** [Q2, F] bagger **81 ne'er** neare **91 Ha!** hagh **102 ague-proof** [F] argue-proofe **104 every** [Q2, F] euer **109 Does** [F] doe **115 does** [F] do **116 To** [F; not in Q] **117**

The [F] to **129 Shall** [F] should **133 of 't** oft **149 An** And **150 dog's obeyed** [F] dogge, so bade **153 Thy blood as** thy bloud **155 tattered** tottered **158 No tears, now** no now **170 shoe** [F] shoot **171 felt** [F] fell **181 a man a man** [F] a man **183 s.p. FIRST GENTLEMAN** Good Sir— [not in Q1] **191 speaking** speaking of **201 speedy foot** [F] speed fort **descriers** descryes **202 Stands** [F] Standst **214 bounty** [Qb, Q2, F] bornet [Qa] **the benison** [Qb, Q2, F] beniz [Qa] **215 send thee** saue thee [Qa; not in Qb] **boot to boot** [Qb, Q2; not in Qa] **216 first** [Qb, Q2, F; not in Qa] **228 vortnight** [Qb, Q2, F] fortnight [Qa] **229 costard** [Qb, Q2, F] coster [Qa] **230 baton** bat- / tero [Qa] bat [Qb] **257 venture** *Venter*

21.19–21 s.p. FIRST GENTLEMAN . . . DOCTOR *Doct⟨or⟩. . . . Gent⟨leman⟩.* **33 perdu** Per du **34 injurer's** iniurious **mean'st** [not in Q]

22.3 abdication [Qa] alteration [Qb] **28 Yet Not** bold's bolds **32 poor** dore **56 Here** [F] Hard **59 sisters** [Q2, F] sister **60 stung** [F] sting

24.24 goodyear good **45 send** [Qb, Q2, F] saue [Qa] **46 and appointed guard,** [Qb, Q2; not in Q1] **48 common** coren? **bosom** [Qa] bossome [Qb] **on** [F] of **54 We** [Qb] mee **56 sharpness** [Qb] sharpes **83 bar** bare **85 banns** banes **119 ere** are **128 fortune** [F] fortun'd **131 Conspirant** [F] Conspicuate **135 are** [F] As **139 tongue** [F] being **140 My** by **142 hated lie** [F] hatedly o'erturn oreturnd **146 s.p. ALL** *Alb⟨any⟩.* **163 ignobly** [not in Q] **165 vices** [F] vertues, **209 him** me **264 you** [Q2, F] your **278 you** [F; not in Q] **282 from your first** [F] from your life **285 fordone** [F] foredoome **291 great** [F; not in Q] **295 honours** [Q2, F] honor **300 have** [Q2, F] of

THE TRAGEDY OF KING LEAR

CONTROL TEXT: F

F1: The Folio of 1623
F2: The Folio of 1632
Q1: The Quarto of 1608
Q2: The Quarto of 1619
Qa, Qb, Fa, Fb: Successive printings of Q1 and F incorporating various printshop corrections and changes

s.p. EDMOND [F's use of *Edmond* and *Bastard* are standardized throughout.]
s.p. OSWALD [F only uses *Steward.*]
s.p. FIRST GENTLEMAN [F uses only *Gentleman.*]
s.p. LEAR [F uses *Kear* once.]
s.p. KENT [F uses *Lent* once.]

1.1.53 words [Q] word **72 possesses** [Q] professes **98 Haply** Happily **108 mysteries** [F2] miseries **137 crownet** Coronet **153** a [Q, F2; not in F1] **154 ne'er feared** nere feare **159 s.p.** ALBANY *and* CORDELIA Alb⟨any⟩. Cor⟨delia⟩. **167 sentence** [Q] sentences **173 seventh** tenth **213 best** [Q; not in F] **dear'st** deerest **223 well** [Q] will **228 the** for **265 Ye** The **278 pleated** plighted **279 covert** couers
1.2.119 Fut! [Q; not in F]
1.4.1 well [Q] will **2 diffuse** defuse **18 thou'rt** [Q1] thou art **28 canst** [Q1] canst thou **44 Daughter** [Q] daughters **48** A [Q1] he **61 these** this **96 off** of **122 know** [Q1] thou know **129 crown** [Q] crownes **130 o'th'** [Q1] on thy **144 fools** [Q] foole **145 Prithee** [Q] Pry'thy **163 nor crumb,** [Q] not crum **249-50 that she may feel—** / That she may feel That she may feele, **306 You** [F1] your [F2] **attasked** [Qb] at task
1.5.21 a may [Q1] he may
2.1.2 you [Q] your **36 Ho** no **39 stand 's** [Q1] stand **54 ghasted** gasted **69 I should** [Q] should I **70 ay,** [Q; not in F] **78 why** [Q] wher **86 strange news** [Q] strangenesse **94 tend** tended **99 spoil** [Qb] wast **120 poise** [Qb] prize **123 least** [Qb] best **thought** [Q] though
2.2.20 clamorous [Q] clamours **59 you'll** [Q1] you will **68 holy** [Fb] holly [Fa] **72 Renege** [Q] Reuenge **77 an** [Q1] if **93 take't** [Q1] take it **101 flick'ring** flicking **114 dread** [Q] dead **121 respect** [Q] respects **136 good** [Q1; not in F] **137 Duke's** [Q] Duke **144 to** [Q1] too **145 say** [Qa] saw **152 now** most **154 For** From **161 unusual** [Q1] vnusall **175 sheepcotes** [Q] sheeps-coates **176 Sometime** [Q] sometimes **177 Tuelygod** [Qa] *Turly-god* **180 messenger** [Q] Messengers **186 man's** [Q] man **204 whose** [Q] those **216 wild** wil'd **226** *Histerica* Historica **231 the** [Q] the the **242 gives** [Q, Fb] giue [Fa] **have** [Q] hause **246 begin** [Q1] begins **293 you** [Q] your **295 mother's** [Q] Mother **shrine** tombe **336 tender-hafted** tenderhefted **351 sickly** fickly a [Q1] he **374-75 To be a comrade with the wolf and owl,** / **To wage against the enmity o'th' air** To wage against the enmity oth'ayre, / To be a Comrade with the Wolfe, and Owle, **377 hot-blooded** [Fa] hot-bloodied [Fb] **451 mad** [Q, Fb] mads [Fa] **471 to** [Q1] too **472 wild** [Q] wil'd
3.1.2 s.p. FIRST GENTLEMAN Gen⟨tleman⟩. [The stage direction calls for "a Gentleman," and F uses this combination to mean this specific character who reappears in 5.3.196-249.]
3.2.3 drowned [Q] drown **49 pother** pudder **84-85 Then . . . confusion.** [in F, after 3.2.91]

3.3.15 for't [Q1] for it
3.4.10 thy [Q] they **12 This** [Qb] the **31 looped** lop'd **44 Thorough** [Q1] through **45 cold** [Q; not in F] **47 two** [Q; not in F] **50 led through** [Q] led though **ford** [Q] Sword **55 Bless** Blisse **82 deeply** [Q2] deerely **89 Dauphin** Dolphin *cessez Sesey* **103 fiend** [Q; not in F] **104 till the** [Q] at **107 Swithin** *Swithold* wold old **108 A** [Qa] he **nine foal,** nine-fold **120 had** [Q; not in F] **150 a** [Q1] he **156 in t'** [Q1] into th'
3.5.22 dearer [Q] deere
3.6.25 Bobtail [Q] Or Bobtaile **tyke** [Q] tight **trundle** [Q2] Troudle **32 makes** [Q] make
3.7.8 festinate festiuate **63 cruels I'll subscribe** Cruels else subscribe
4.1.10 parti-eyed [Qb] poorly led **32** A [Q1] He
4.2.30 whistling [Qb] whistle **36 shows** [Qb] seemes **43 thereat enraged** [Q, F2] threat-enrag'd **47 justicers** [Qb] Iustices
4.3.3 fumitor [Q] Fenitar **4 burdocks** Hardokes **18 distress** [Q] desires **good man's** [Q] Goodmans
4.4.6 letters [Q1] Letter **15 after, madam** after him, Madam **39 him** [Q, F2; not in F1]
4.5.7 speak'st [Q2] speakest **17 walk** [Q] walk'd **53 a-length** at each **69 methoughts** [Q1] me thought **119 They're** [Q1] they are **154 Through** [Q] Tho- / rough [F's unmetrical substitution straddles a page break in a passage set as justified prose; "Through" could not be split, and the compositor almost certainly added the "o" for reasons of page makeup.] **155 Plate sin** Place sinnes **178 s.p.** FIRST GENTLEMAN Gent. ⟨leman⟩. **195 speaking** speaking of **201-2 hears that /** That [Q] heares that, which **206 in** on **225 Durst** [Q1] Dar'st **228 'cagion** [Q] 'casion **231 swaggered** [Q1] zwaggerd **232 so** [Q1] zo **234 baton** Ballow **I'll** [Q1] chill **236 sir** [Q1] zir **249 sorrow** [Q1] sorry **261 and for you her own for venture,** [Q1; not in F]

The Tragedy of Macbeth

Control text: F

F: The Folio of 1623

Fa, Fb: Successive states of F incorporating various print-shop corrections and changes

s.p. FIRST WITCH, SECOND WITCH, THIRD WITCH [F's use of *1, 2,* and *3* has been standardized throughout.]
s.p. KING DUNCAN [F's use of *King* has been standardized throughout.]
s.p. LADY MACBETH [F's use of *Lady* has been standardized throughout.]
s.p. FIRST MURDERER [F's use of *1 Murderer, 1,* and *Murderer* has been standardized throughout.]

s.p. SECOND MURDERER [F's use of *2 Murderer* and 2 has been standardized throughout.]

s.p. THIRD MURDERER [F's use of 3 has been standardized throughout.]

s.p. ALL THE WITCHES [F's use of *All.* has been standardized throughout.]

s.p. FIRST APPARITION, SECOND APPARITION, THIRD APPARITION [F's use of *1 Apparition, 2 Apparition,* and *3 Apparition* has been standardized throughout.]

s.p. LADY MACDUFF [F's use of *Wife* has been standardized throughout.]

s.p. MACDUFF'S SON [F's use of *Son* has been standardized throughout.]

s.p. A MURDERER [F's use of *Murderer* has been standardized throughout.]

s.p. A SOLDIER [F's use of *Soldier* has been standardized throughout.]

1.1.9–11 s.p. SECOND WITCH Paddock calls. / THIRD WITCH Anon. / ALL Fair . . . air. *All. Padock calls anon: faire . . . ayre.*

1.2.13 galloglasses Gallowgrosses **26 break** [not in F] **31 Norwegian** Norweyan **46 haste** a haste **61 Colum's** Colmes

1.3.30 weird weyward **37 Forres** Soris **95 hail** Tale **96 Came** Can

1.4.1 Are Or

1.5.21 'Thus . . . do' [not in F] **29, 32 s.p. SERVANT** *Mess.* **63 the innocent** th'innocent

1.6.4 martlet Barlet **9 most** must

1.7.6 shoal Schoole **47 do** no

2.1.55 strides sides **56 sure** sowre **57 way they** they may

2.3.77 horror. horror. Ring the Bell. **108 Outran** Out-run

3.1.2, 3.4.132, 4.1.152 weird weyard **23 talk** take **76 s.p. MURDERERS** [F uses *Murth.* three times in 3.1, and each time it would be appropriate for both to speak. See also 3.1.116 and 3.1.140.]

3.3.7 and end

3.4.77 time times **88 of** o' **143 in deed** indeed

3.5.34–35 s.p. SPIRITS . . . away. [not in F; see Textual Note] **38–73 s.p. SPIRITS . . . reach.** [not in F; see Textual Note]

3.6.24 son Sonnes

4.1.44–60 s.p. HECATE . . . out. [not in F; see Textual Note] **75 germens** Germaine **109 Dunsinane** Dunsmane **114 on's high place** our high plac'd

4.2.22 none moue **83 shag-haired** shagge-ear'd

4.3.134 thy they **155 with** [Fb] my with [Fa] **161 not** nor **237 tune** time

5.3.41 Cure her Cure **46 fraught** stufft

5.4.11 gone giuen

5.5.40 pall pull

5.11.25 s.p. ALL BUT MALCOLM *All.*

THE TRAGEDY OF ANTONY AND CLEOPATRA

CONTROL TEXT: F

F: THE FOLIO OF 1623

FA, FB: FA IS THE UNCORRECTED VERSION, FB THE CORRECTED VERSION OF F

Title: Anthony & Cleopatra [Stationers' Register entry] *Anthony and Cleopater* [F table of contents] *The Tragedie of Anthonie, and Cleopatra* [F head title] *The Tragedie of Anthony and Cleopatra* [F running title]

s.p. SILIUS [F's use of *Romaine* in 3.1 (where Silius is referred to by name in dialogue) is standardized throughout.]

s.p. BOY [Not in F's speech prefixes or stage directions, although Enobarbus refers to the boy in dialogue. See 2.7.]

s.p. WATCH, GUARD, SERVANTS, SOLDIERS [F refers to these characters either by category (*Soldier, 3. Watch,* etc.) or by number (*I, 2,* etc.). This edition never uses numbers alone, preferring prefixes such as "First Servant," "Third Soldier," etc.]

1.1.52 how who

1.2.0 s.d. Enter . . . attendants *Enter Enobarbus, Lamprius, a Southsayer, Rannius, Lucillius, Charmian, Iras, Mardian the Eunuch, and Alexas.* [Rannius and Lucillius are ghost characters; so is Lamprius, unless he is the soothsayer. As these three are not mentioned again, their names are irrelevant and hence omitted.] **5 charge** change **34 fertile fore- / tell 55 Alexas—come** *Alexas.* Come [F attributes the rest of the speech, beginning with "Come," to Alexas, taking the name as a speech prefix rather than an address.] **70 Saw you** Saue you **102 ho** how **103 s.p. SECOND MESSENGER The . . . Sicyon— / s.p. ANTHONY Is . . . one?** *I. Mes.* (First Messenger) *The Scicion,* / Is . . . one? [The First Messenger speaks the entire line in F.] **125 occasion** an occasion **163 leave** loue **168 Hath** Haue **177 hair** heire **179 place is under us, requires** places under us, require

1.3.11 Iwis I wish **82 my** [not in F]

1.4.3 Our One **8 vouchsafed** vouchsafe **9 the abstract** th'abstracts **44 deared** fear'd **46 lackeying** lacking **56 wassails** Vassailes **57 Modena** Medena **58 Pansa** Pausa **76 we me** 76 council counsell

1.5.3 mandragora *Mandragoru* **47 arm-jaunced** Arme-gaunt **49 dumbed** dumbe **60 man** mans

2.1.2, 5, 16, 18, 38 s.p. MENECRATES . . . MENECRATES . . . MENAS . . . MENAS . . . MENAS *Mene⟨crates⟩.* [Menecrates throughout in F] **21 waned** wand **38 ne'er** neere **41 warred** wan'd

2.2.49 the your **126 not so, Agrippa** not, say *Agrippa* **127 reproof** proofe **210 glow** gloue **212 gentlewomen** Gentlewoman **238 breathless, pour breath** breathlesse powre breath

2.3.12 Gone thither thither **20 afeard** a feare **28 away,** alway

2.4.6 at the at **9 s.p. MAECENAS** *and* **AGRIPPA** *Both.*

2.5.2 s.p. CHARMIAN, IRAS, *and* **ALEXAS** *Omnes.* **12 finned** fine **43 is** 'tis **52 But** Bur **104 act** art

2.6.16 the [not in F] **19 is** his **39 s.p. CAESAR, ANTONY,** *and* **LEPIDUS** *Omnes.* **53 There is** ther's **67 meanings** meaning **71 o'** [not in F] **83 s.p. CAESAR, ANTONY,** *and* **LEPIDUS** *All.*

2.7.1–13 s.p. FIRST SERVANT . . . SECOND SERVANT . . . FIRST SERVANT *I . . . 2 . . . I* **86 part then** is part, then he is **108 s.p. BOY** [*sings*] The Song. **110 vats** Fattes **115 off** of **119 speaks. The** [Fa] speakest: he [Fb] **123 father's** Father **125 s.p. MENAS** [Not in F; Enobarbus continues speaking until the second half of 1.129, which is spoken by Menas in F, as in this edition.] **127 hear** [Fb] heare a [Fa] **a loud** aloud

3.1.5, 27, 34 s.p. SILIUS *Romaine.* [variously spelled] **14 to** [Fa] too [Fb] **37 there** [Fa] their [Fb]

3.2.3 are [Fb] art [Fa] **10 s.p. AGRIPPA** *Ant⟨ony⟩.* **16 figures** Figure **26 bond** Band **49 at** at the **full of** [Fa]; of full [Fb] **60 wept** weepe

3.3.17 gait? gate, **18 looked'st** look'st

3.4.8 them, then **9 took't** look't **24 yours** your **30 Your** You **38 has** he's

3.5.12 world, thou hast a pair of chops, would thou hadst a pair of chaps **14 one the** [not in F]

3.6.13 he there **. . . kings of kings** hither . . . King of Kings **61 obstruct** abstract **72 Malchus** *Mauchus* **74 Comagene;** Pole-mon Comageat, *Polemen* **75 Lycaonia** Licoania **88 their** his

3.7.4 it is it it **5 Is't not** If not, **21 Brundis-ium** Brandusium **23 Toryne** Troine **51 Actium** Action **69 leader's led** Leaders leade **72 s.p. CAMIDIUS** *Ven⟨tidius⟩.* **78 Taurus** *Towrus* **80 in** with

3.10.10 riband-red ribaudred **14 June** Inne **27 he** his

3.11.6 s.p. ATTENDANTS *Omnes.* **19 that** them **47 seize** cease **58 tow** stowe **59 Thy** The

3.12.0 s.d. DOLABELLA *Dollabello* **13 lessens** Lessons **29 As** From

3.13.10 mooted meered **25 caparisons** Com-parisons **54 Caesar** *Caesars* **55 embraced** embrace **74 deputation** disputation

76–77 kneel / Till kneele. / Tell him, **103 This** the **149 abyss** Abisme **165 smite** smile **168 discandying** discandering **171 sits** sets **201 on** in

4.2.1 Domitius *Domitian* **19 s.p. SERVITORS** *Omnes.*

4.3.7 s.p. THIRD SOLDIER *I.*

4.4.5–6 too. / . . . **for? s.p. ANTONY** too, *Antony.* / . . . for? [In F, Cleopatra's speech includes lines 6–7 and thus continues uninterrupted from line 5 to line 8.] **13 doff't** daft **24 s.p. CAPTAIN** *Alex⟨as⟩.* **25 s.p. SOLDIERS** *All.*

4.5.1, 3, 7 s.p. SOLDIER *Eros.*

4.6.15 Camidius *Camindius* **19 more** mote

4.8 [Most editions continue 4.7, even though the stage is cleared. The new scene affects the numbering of the remaining scenes in the act.]

4.9.2 gests guests **18 My** Mine

4.13.4 augurs Auguries **21 spanieled** pan-nelled

4.15.4 towered toward **10 distains** dislimes **19 Caesar** *Caesars* **107, 132 s.p. ALL THE GUARDS** *All.* **110 s.p. DECRETAS** *Dercetus.* **122 sent word** sent you word

4.16.42 s.p. ALL THE LOOKERS-ON *All.* **46 hussy** huswife **75 e'en** in **77 chores** chares **89 do it** doo't

5.1.0 s.d. MAECENAS *Menas* **2 but** [not in F] **15 rivèd** round **18 that** the **27 a** [not in F] **28, 31 s.p. AGRIPPA** *Dola⟨bella⟩.* **36 lance** launch **59 live** leaue **70 s.p. ALL BUT CAESAR** *All.*

5.2.80 O [not in F] **86 autumn 'twas** *Anthony* it was **95 or** nor **103 smites** suites **212 Ballad** Ballads o' a **219 my** mine **224 Cydnus** *Cidrus* **304 vile** wilde **308 awry** away

PERICLES, PRINCE OF TYRE

CONTROL TEXT: Q1

Q1: The Quarto of 1609
Q2: The Quarto of 1609
Q3: The Quarto of 1611
Q4: The Quarto of 1619
Q5: The Quarto of 1630
Q6: The Quarto of 1635
Qa, Qb: Successive states of Q1 incorporating various print-shop corrections and changes
PA: George Wilkins, THE Painfull Aduentures of *Pericles* Prince of Tyre. *Being* The true History of the Play of *Pericles*, as it was lately presented by the worthy and ancient Poet *Iohn Gower*

Title: Pericles, Prynce of Tyre [Stationers' Register entry] THE LATE, / And much admired Play, / Called / Pericles, Prince of

Tyre. / With the true Relation of the whole Historie, / aduentures, and fortunes of the said Prince: / As also, / The no lesse strange, and worthy accidents, / in the Birth and Life, of his Daughter / MARIANA. [Q1 title page] The Play of Pericles / Prince of Tyre. &c. [Q1 head title] *The Play of Pericles Prince of Tyre* [Q1 running titles]
Scene 1 [not in Q1; see note to Scene 1] **6 holy-ales** Holydayes **11 these** [Q2] those **17 This'** This **21 fere** Peere **29 By** But **30 account'** account'd **39 a wight** of wight **42 s.d.** *lords and peers in their richest ornaments* [PA] *fellowers* **50 Fit for th'** For **54 In her their best perfections to knit** To knit in her, their best perfections **60 razed** racte **67 boundless** bondlesse **73 heav'n-like face** face like Heauen **79 semblants** semblance **bloodless** pale **83 From** For **99 s.p.** ANTIOCHUS [not in Q1] **s.d.** *He . . . riddle* [not in Q1] which the tyrant receiuing with an angry brow, threw downe the Riddle [PA] **102 'sayed** sayd **107 s.d.** *He . . . riddle* [not in Q1] which the Prince taking vp, read aloude [PA] **113 this** [PA] they **139 like** is like **152 He's** he ha's **154 our** your **156 cancel** counsell **163 your worth and our degree** our honour and your worth **170 you're** you **171 uncomely** vntimely **179 'schew** shew **186 the which** which **194–95 And . . . your** And our minde pertakes her priuat actions, / To your secrecie; and for your **202 s.d.** *hastily* [PA; not in Q1] **204 Your majesty** My Lord **205 after;** like after, and like **208 it be to say** thou say **209 Your majesty** [not in Q1] **210–11 If . . . highness** My Lord, if I can get him within my Pistols length, Ile make him sure enough, so farewell to your highnesse. [prose] **212 s.p.** ANTIOCHUS [Q4; not in Q1]
Scene 2 [not in Q1] **s.d.** *distempered* [not in Q1] Princes distemperature [PA] **3 Be my** By me **7 feared,** 's fearde is **10 care's author's** the others **20 honour him** honour **25 th'ostent** the stint **30 am** once **33 s.d.** *among them old* HELICANUS [not in Q1] olde [PA, describing Helicanus] **37–42 You . . . contradict it** [not in Q1] he did not wel so to abuse himselfe, to waste his body there with pyning sorrow, vpon whose safety depended the liues and proserity of a whole kingdome, that it was ill in him to doe it, and no lesse in his counsell to suffer him, without contradicting it [PA; Helicanus to Pericles] **55 wind** sparke **49 a** [not in Q1] **55 Helicane** *Hellicans* **59 brows** face **63 you but** [Q4] but you **64 s.d.** *lifting him up* [PA; not in Q1] **65 for it** [Q4] fort **the heav'ns** heauē **68 mak'st** makes **70 you** you **your selfe** **75 Where, as** [Q2] Whereas **78 As children are heav'n's blessings: to par-**

ents, objects [not in Q1] **86 of** of a **88 me** [not in Q1] **89 fears** feare **91 doubt—as doubt no doubt** doo't, as no doubt **105 grieve** griue for **113 Or** or til the **117 in my absence wrong thy liberties** wrong my liberties in my absence **120 Tarsus** *Tharsus* **126 sure crack** cracke **127 we'll** will
Scene 3 [not in Q1] **2–3 and am caught . . . but if I do it** [not in Q1] **10–40 You . . . Tyre** [prose in Q1] **11 question** question mee **21 lest that he** lest hee **27 King's ears** it Kings seas **28 on the seas** at the Sea **30 Lord Thaliart am I, of Antioch** [not in Q1] **31 s.p.** HELICANUS [Q4; not in Q1] of Antioch from *Antiochus* **32 King Antiochus** him **35 lord's** Lord has **betoke** [Q2] betake **36 Now my** now **37 enquire** desire
Scene 4 [not in Q1] **8 they're** they are **midges'** mischiefs **13 our sorrows** and sorrowes **15 lungs** toungs **17 helps** helpers **20 As you think best** Ile doe my best **22 o'er** on **23 the** [Q3] her **34 Those** These **36 they** [Q2] thy **39 two summers** [PA] too sauers **47 Here weeping stands a lord, there lies a lady dying** Heere stands a Lord, and there a Ladie weeping; heere standes one weeping, and there lies another dying [PA] **54 heed** heare **55 s.d.** *fainting . . . slowly* a fainting messenger came slowely into them [PA] **57 thou** [Q4] thee **58 t'expect** to expect **64 neighbour** [PA] neighbouring **66 Hath** That **these** the **68 men** mee **72 not** not as **73 him's** himnes **77 grave's** grounds **79 whence he comes.** whence he comes, and what he craues? **82 s.d.** the LORD *again conducting* [not in Q1] he demaunded of the fellow where the Gouernour was, and foorthwith to be conducted to him [PA] **87–88 Since entering your unshut gates have witnessed / The widowed desolation** And seene the desolation; Pericles . . . no sooner entred into their unshut gates, but his princely eies were partaking witnesses of their widowed desolation [PA] **89 hearts** teares **92 fraught** stuft; fraughted [PA] **93 importing** expecting **96 s.p.** ALL OF TARSUS *Omnes.* **s.d.** *falling . . . weeping* [not in Q1] the feeble soules . . . fell on their knees, and wept [PA] **99 me,** my our selfe, our **104 ne'er** neare
Scene 5 [not in Q1] **4 Prove** That Will prove **11 Tarsus** *Tharstill* **12 speken** spoken **14 His statue build** Build his Statue **17 Helicane** [Q3] *Helicon* **19 for that** for though **22 Sent word** Sau'd one **24 hid intent to murden** hid in Tent to murdred [Qa] had intent to murder [Qb] **25 Tarsus** *Tharsis* **27 deeming** doing **36 aught** ought **51 s.d.** *two poor* three; pore Fishermen [PA; in this edition, the Third Fisherman enters after the first two.] **52 s.p.** MASTER I.; the maister Fisher-

man [*PA;* changed throughout, except at line 80, where "I." is changed to "THIRD FISHER-MAN"] **What ho, Pilch** What, to pelch **54 s.d.** *He . . . repair* [not in Q1] certayne *Fishermen . . .* were come out from their homely cottages to dry and repaire their nettes [*PA*] **56–72, 74–75, 77–81, 83–84, 90–92, 93–94, 99–101, 123, 136–37, 139–40, 144–47, 152–54, 195–97** [verse in Q1] **70 devours** deuowre **77 s.p.** THIRD FISHERMAN [Q4] 3. FISHER-MAN I. **110 crave** aske **112 pray** [Q4] pray you **113 quotha** ke-tha an and **114 s.d.** *To . . . ground* the chiefe of these fishermen . . . lifting him vp from the ground [*PA*] **116 holidays** all day **117 moreo'er** more; or **123 an** and **124 all your** you **128–30 beadle.** MASTER Thine office, knave— SECOND FISHERMAN Is to draw up the other nets. I'll go Beadle: But Maister, Ile goe draw vp the Net; goe dragge vp some other nettes [*PA;* the Master commanding his servants—hence, this edition introduces an interjection by the Master into the Second Fisherman's speech.] **133 s.d.** *seating . . . Pericles* [not in Q1] the maister . . . seated himselfe by him [*PA*] **136 is** [Q2] I **141–42 from his subjects / He gains** he gaines from / His subjects **144 some half** [*PA*] halfe **148 Were but** [*PA*] Were **answerable** [*PA*] equall **151 get himself** get **for with** for **153 s.d.** *Before . . . prize* [not in Q1] before helpe came, vp came the Fish expected, but prooued indeede to be a rusty armour. [*PA*] **155 pray** [Qb] pary [Qa] **156 thy** [not in Q1] all her crosses [*PA*] **157 losses** selfe **164 forfend, the same may** protect thee, Fame may **169 in 's** [Q4] in his **176 with't** with it **180 learned** [*PA*] borne **185 this** them **187 I'm** I am **188 rapture** rupture **191 delightsome** delight **193 friends** friend **198 equal** a Goale

Scene 6 [not in Q1] **s.d.** *and sit on two thrones* [not in Q1] They thus seated [*PA*] **4 daughter** daughter heere **8 my** my royall **13 renown** Renownes **14 office** honour **16 s.d.** *richly . . .* THAISA [not in Q1] richly armed, their Pages before them bearing their Deuices on their shields being by the knights Page deliuered to the Lady [*PA;* repeated for each knight in this edition] **21 s.d.** *She . . .* KING [not in Q1] from her presented to the King her father [*PA;* repeated for each knight in this edition] **22 s.d.** [See note to 6.16.] **26 An armèd** Is an Armed **27 thus** thus in Spanish **Piùe per dolcezza che per forza** *Pue Per doleera kee per forsa* **s.d.** [See note to 6.21.] **28 You . . . force** [not in Q1] more by lenitie than by force [*PA*] **s.d.** [See note to 6.16.] **29 what's** [Q4] with **31 pompae** Pompey; *pompa* [*PA*] **s.d.** [See note to 6.21.]

32–33 Desire . . . enterprise [not in Q1] desire of renowne drew him to this enterprise [*PA*] **33 s.d.** [See note to 6.16.] **34 A knight of Athens bearing** [not in Q1] The fift of *Athens,* and his Deuice was [*PA*] **36 s.d.** [See note to 6.21.] **37 this** his **38 s.d.** [See note to 6.16.] **39 And who the fifth?** [not in Q1] **39–40 a prince of Corinth / Presents** [not in Q1] a prince of *Corinth* [*PA*] **43 So . . . into** [*PA;* not in Q1] **s.d.** PERICLES . . . THAISA [not in Q1] The sixt and last was *Pericles,* Prince of *Tyre,* who hauing neither Page to deliuer his shield, nor shield to deliuer . . . Himselfe with a most gracefull curtesie presented it vnto her . . . being himselfe in a rusty Armour [*PA*] **45 delivereth** deliuered **49 From** A pretty morrall frõ **54 T'have** To haue **56 Unto** To **60 for** by

Scene 7 [not in Q1] **s.d.** *A stately banquet is brought in* [not in Q1] a most stately banquet [*PA*] *a* MARSHAL *conducting* [not in Q1] by the Kings Marshall conducted [*PA*] **1 to the** KNIGHTS To say Knights, to say **2 To I 7 You're** You are **11 yours** [Q4] your **13 artists** an Artist **15 You are** And you are **24 Envied** Enuies **25 s.d.** PERICLES . . . THAISA placed directly ouer-against where the king and his daughter sate [*PA* (said of Pericles)] **27 distaste** resist **but not 29 I am amazed** [not in Q1] **34 broke** broken **36 Yon** [Q2] You **37 me** [Q4; not in Q1] what that **42 son's** sonne a **like a 48 s.p.** THE OTHER KNIGHTS *Knights* **49 stored** stur'd **50 you do** [Q4] do you **full fill 51 s.p.** THE OTHER KNIGHTS *Knight.* **59 so doing** doing so **like like to 61 entertain** entraunce **62 bear** say wee drinke **69 Furthermore** And furthermore **know** know of him **71–72** THAISA The King . . . Wishing *Tha.* The king my father (sir) has drunke to you / *Peri.* I thanke him / *Tha.* Wishing **79 unconstant** [not in Q1] and vnconstant [*PA*] **79–80 bereft / Unfortunately both** reft [Q1] most vnfortunately bereft both [*PA*] **83–84 seeking adventures / Was** [not in Q1] **83–84 A gentleman . . . seas** A Gentleman of *Tyre:* who onely by misfortune of the seas **84 solely** onely **86 mishaps** misfortune **87 s.d.–95** SIMONIDES . . . *accept* [not in Q1] Which mishaps of his the king vnderstanding of, hee was strucke with present pitty to him, and rising from his state, he came foorthwith and imbraced him, bade him be cheered, and tolde him, that whatsoeuer misfortune had impayred him of, fortune, by his helpe, could repayre to him, for both himselfe and Countrey should be his friendes, and presently calling for a goodly milke white Steede, and a payre of golden spurres, them first hee bestowed vppon him, telling him, they were the prises due to his merite, and ordained for that dayes enterprise: which kingly curtesie Pericles as thankefully accepting. Much time beeing spent in dauncing and other reuells [*PA*] **99 Your limbs will** Will **104 Come** Come sir **105 sir, that the** you **112 Lights, pages, to** Pages and lights to **114 should** [not in Q1] **116 s.p. KING SIMONIDES** [Q3; not in Q1, where the speech continues as Pericles']

Scene 8 [not in Q1] **4 hold** with-hold **9 both apparelled all in jewels** [*PA*; not in Q1] **11 Their** those **13 hands** hand **29 step** breath **33 death indeed's** death in deed, **34 this— kingdoms** this Kingdome is **36 utter** [not in Q1] **38 unto** as vnto our **40 By** Try **44 But . . . love** [follows line 48 in Q1] **45 longer then let me** longer, let me **46 Further to bear** To forbeare **49 seek your noble prince** search like nobles, **55 us** [not in Q1] **56–57 If . . . out / If . . . there** [after line 29 in Q1]

Scene 8a [not in Q1] Prince *Pericles* hauing had (as before is mentioned) his lodging directed next adioyning to the kings bedchamber, whereas all the other Princes vppon their comming to their lodgings betooke themselues to their pillowes, and to the nourishment of a quiet sleepe, he of the Gentlemen that attended him, (for it is to be noted, that vpon the grace that the king had bestowed on him, there was of his Officers toward him no attendance wanting) hee desired that hee might be left priuate, onely that for his instant solace they would pleasure him with some delightfull Instrument, with which, and his former practise hee intended to passe away the tediousnesse of the night insteade of more fitting slumbers. His wil was presently obeyed in all things since their master had commaunded he should be disobeyed in nothing: the Instrument is brought him, and as hee had formerly wished, the Chamber is disfurnished of any other company but himselfe [*PA*, from which this scene is reconstructed] **8 s.d.** *a stringed instrument* [implied by *PA*, which refers to the "fingering" of the instrument and describes Pericles singing as he plays] **9–10 Now . . . sleep** all the other Princes . . . betooke themselues to their pillowes [*PA*] **10 s.d. PERICLES** *plays and sings* [*PA* elaborately describes the performance.] **11–13 Day . . . on.** But day that hath still that soueraigntie to drawe backe the empire of the night, though a while shee in darkenesse vsurpe, brought the morning on [*PA*] **14–15 I . . . me** euen in the instant came in *Pericles*, to giue his Grace that salu-

tation which the morning required of him [*PA*]

Scene 9 [not in Q1] **5 none can** by no meanes can I **6 have** get **7–8 It . . . chamber** she hath so strictly / Tyed her to her Chamber, that t'is impossible **15 light** light / T'is well Mistris, your choyce agrees with mine **18 Mistress, 'tis well** Well, your her **20–21 that / In show, I have determined on in heart** it; the king intending to dissemble that in shew, which hee had determined on in heart [*PA*] **24–25 night. My ears, / I do protest** night: / I do protest, my eares **30 think you of my daughter** do you thinke of my Daughter, sir **31 And** And she is **33 My daughter, sir** Sir, my Daughter **34 So well indeed** I so well **39 s.d.** *He . . . feet* [not in Q1] foorthwith prostrating himselfe at the kings feete [*PA*] **43 her** her. / *king*. Thou has bewicht my daughter, / And thou art a villaine. / *Peri*. By the Gods I haue not **47 Thou liest like a traitor** Traytor, thou lyest **48–50 That . . . child** [not in Q1] I, traytour, quoth the king, that thus disguised, art stolne into my Court, with the witchcraft of thy actions to bewitch, the yeelding spirit of my tender Childe [*PA*] **51–52 Who calls me traitor, unless it be the King, / Ev'n in his bosom I will write the lie** Even in his throat, vnless it be the King, / That cals me Traytor, I returne the lye [Q1] were it any in his Court, except himselfe, durst call him traytor, even in his bosome he would write the lie [*PA*] **54 blood** thoughts **56 in search of honour** [*PA*] for Honours cause **57 your state** her state [Q1] his State [*PA*] **60–62 I . . . witness** No? heere comes my Daughter, she can witnesse it [Q1] answered, he should prooue it otherwise, since by his daughters hand, it there was euident, both his practise and her consent therein [*PA*] **64–65 By what . . . fulfilled** [not in Q1] demaunded of her by the hope she had of heauen, or the desire she had to haue her best wished fulfilled heere in the worlde [*PA*] **68 made** that made **71 How, minion** [*PA*] Yea Mistris **72–96 I am glad on't . . . only child** I am glad on't with all my heart [Q1] How minion, quoth her Father (taking her off at the very word, who dare be displeased withalle) Is this a fit match for you? a stragling *Theseus* borne we knowe not where, one that hath neither bloud nor merite for thee to hope for, or himselfe to challenge euen the least allowaunce of thy perfections, when she humbling her princely knees before her Father, besought him to consider, that suppose his birth were base (when his life shewed him not to be so) yet hee had vertue, which is the very ground of all nobilitie, enough to make him noble: she intreated him to remember that she was in loue, the power of which loue was not to be confined by the power of his will. And my most royall Father, quoth shee, what with my penne I haue in secret written vnto you, with my tongue now I openly confirme, which is, that I haue no life but his loue, neither any being but in the enioying of his worth. But daughter (quoth *Symonides*) equalles to equalls, good to good is ioyned, this not being so, the bauine of your minde in rashnesse kindled, must againe be quenched, or purchase our displeasure, And for you sir (speaking to prince *Pericles*) first learne to know, I banish you my Court, and yet scorning that our kingly inragement should stoope so lowe, for that your ambition sir, Ile haue your life. Be constant quoth *Thaysa*, for euerie droppe of blood hee sheades of yours, he shall draw an other from his onely childe [*PA*] 97 **yea** [not in Q1] 102 **s.d.** *He . . . hand* [not in Q1] catching them both rashly by the handes [*PA*] 103 **s.d.** *He . . . hand* [not in Q1; see note to line 102 s.d.] 105 **I shall** Ile **s.d.** *He . . . together* [not in Q1] heclapt them hand in hand [*PA*] 106 **s.d.** PERICLES *and* THAISA *kiss* [not in Q1] while they as louingly ioyned lip to lip [*PA*] 108 **your further** further **you** you both 112 **s.p.** PERICLES *and* THAISA *Ambo.* 113 **Then** And then

Scene 10 [not in Q1] 2 **the house** about about the house 6 **fore** from 7 **crickets** Cricket 8 **As** Are 10 **Where by** [Q2] Whereby 13 **eche** each 14 **s.d.** *comes hastily in to meetes;* came hastily in to them [*PA*] 17 **coigns** Crignes 21 **stead** steed 29 **mutiny there he** mutanie, hee there t'appease t'oppresse 46 **fortune's mood** fortune mou'd 60 **sea-tossed** seas tost **speke** speake

Scene 11 [not in Q1] 7 **Thou stormest** then storme 8 **spit** speat 11 **patroness** [Q4] patrioness **midwife** my wife 27 **s.d.** *She . . . infant* [not in Q1] vp comes *Lycorida* the Nurse . . . and into his armies deliuers his Sea-borne Babe [*PA*] **s.d.** PERICLES *. . . weeps* [not in Q1] *Pericles* looking mournfully vpon it, shooke his head, and wept [*PA*] 34 **Poor inch of nature** [*PA*; not in Q1] 36 **partage** portage 37 **s.d.** *the* MASTER *and a* SAILOR *two* Saylers 38, 43, 47, 51 **s.p.** MASTER 1. *Sayl.* 40 **its worst** the worst 43–53 [verse in Q1] 43 **Slack** Slacke [Qb] Slake [Qa] **bow-lines** bolins 45 **s.p.** SAILOR 2. *Sayl.* **an** and 50 **but** [not in Q1] 52 **custom** easterne 52–54 **yield 'er . . . queen!** yeeld'er, / *Per.* As you thinke meet; for she must ouer board straight: / Most wretched Queene. 59 **ooze** oare 61 **And** The **ayeremaining** ayre remayning 64 **paper** [Q2]

Taper 66 **coffer** coffin 69 **s.p.** SAILOR 2. 72, 74 **s.p.** MASTER 2. 73 **from** for 74 **Make** O make

Scene 12 [not in Q1] **s.d.** *poor man and a some that came to him both for helpe for themselues, and reliefe for others* [*PA*] 2 **those** these 4 **seen** been in 5 **ne'er** neare 7 **in to** 8 **to th'** to the 19–20 **lordship should, / Having . . . you,** at Lordship, / Hauing . . . you, should at 20 **this hour** these early howers 22 **to should** 23 **held** hold 26 **dispend** [*PA*] expend 34 **so** [not in Q1] 36 **and cause** in course 39 **glad** please 42 **alone** [not in Q1] 46 48, 53 **s.p.** PHILEMON *Seru⟨ant⟩* [variously abbreviated] 49 **The sea tossed up** did the sea tosse vp 52–53 **Did . . . sir** [Question and answer occur after "bitumed" at line 58 in Q1.] 54 **Or a more eager** as tost it vpon shore **s.p.** CERIMON [not in Q1; see last note to line 58] 56 **by** [not in Q1] **queasy** [not in Q1] 58 **bitumed** bottomed **soft** *Cer.* Wrench it open soft. 62 **and crowned** [not in Q1] crowned [*PA*] 65 **i'th'** in the 75 **even** [Q4] euer 77 **rash** rough 82 **have heard** heard 83 **nine hours dead** that had 9. howers lien dead 84 **appliances** applyaunce 84 **s.d.** PHILEMON *one* 86 **still** rough 87 **vial** Violl 90–91 **warmth / Breathes** warmth breath 94 **set** sets 104 **gentle** my gentle

Scene 13 [not in Q1] 5 **strokes** shakes 6 **hurt** hant 7 **woundingly** wondringly 8 **you'd** you had 9 **T'have** to haue 10 **Should** Could 14 **and leave** leauing 25 **th'** the 29 **Unscissored** vncisserd [*PA*] vnsisterd 29 **hair** heyre 32 **s.p.** DIONYZA I [Q1] *Cler.* I [Q1 catchword] 35 **s.p.** CLEON *Cler.* 36 **th'** masted** the mask'd

Scene 14 [not in Q1] **s.d.** THAISA *Tharsa* 2 **are** all are 5 **eaning** learning 6 **th'** the 11 **s.p.** CERIMON *Cler.* 13 **till your date expire** you may abide you may abide till your date expire 16 **s.p.** THAISA [Q4] *Thin.*

Scene 15 [not in Q1] 8 **music** Musicks 10 **her** hie **the heart** the art 14 **Seeks** Seeke 15 **has** hath 16 **lass** wench 17 **ripe** [Q2] **right rite** sight 26 **bird** bed 32 **With dove of Paphos might the** The Doue of *Paphos* might with the 38 **murder** murderer 42 **s.d.** *A tomb is revealed* a monument in remembrance [*PA*] 47 **carry** carried 55 **i'th'** in the 57–58 **or fanning love thy bosom / Unflame** in flaming, thy loue bosome, enflame 63 **weeping** weeping for **nurse's** Mistresse 66 **grave** greene 68 **tomb** graue 71 **but** [not in Q1] **ceaseless** lasting 76–77 **favour / Is changed** fauours / Changd 78 **Give me your flowers. Come** Come giue me your flowers **o'er** ere **margin** marre it 79 **is piercing** is quicke 80 **And quick; it sharps** And it perces and sharpens 81 **th'** the

81–151 No . . . slain [prose in Q1; many of the following emendations help create metrical verse lines] **90 resume** reserue **94 truly** yet **95 Nay** Come, come **99 Pray you** pray **104 mariners** Saylers **105 with** [not in Q1] **111 Once** and **114 stem** stern **120 The** for the **121 would** will **128 once on a worm** vpon a worme **129 for it** [Q4] fort **131 danger** any danger **139 s.d.** *drawing out his sword* [*PA*] **140 s.d.** *running* [*PA*] **144 s.d.** PIRATES *carrying* MARINA the pyrates who had thus rescued *Marina*, carried her to their shippes [*PA*] LEONINE *steals back Enter Leonine*; he secretly stole back [*PA*] **146 An** and **147 she'll** shee will

Scene 16 [not in Q1] **4 lose** lost **too much** [Q2] too much much **4 wenchless** too wenchlesse **17 They're too** ther's two **33 mystery** trade **37 s.p. A** PIRATE *Sayler.* **45 hundred sesterces** [*PA*] thousand peeces **58 had but** had not **59 To** for to **66 like** [Q4; not in Q1] **80 must stir** [Q4] stir **88 watered as** watred, and **92 Veroles** Verollus **98 of** in **100 all** [not in Q1] **103 to despise** despise **111 s.p.** BAWD *Mari⟨na⟩* **123–24 reapest the harvest out of thine own setting forth** hast the haruest out of thine owne report **133 with me** with vs

Scene 17 [not in Q1] **s.d.** *in mourning garments* mourning garments [*PA*] **1 are** ere **5–47 Were . . . done** [prose in Q1] **6 A lady** O Ladie **12 fact** face **13 demands** shall demaund **15 is not** it, not **17 pious** [*PA*] impious **25 cowed** coward **27 prime** prince **28 sources** courses **31 distain** disdaine **33 Marina's** [Q2] *Marianas* **34 malkin** Mawkin **48 angel** Angells **49 in thine eagle talons** with thine Eagles talents

Scene 18 [not in Q1] **1 make we** make **3 take** take our **7 scene** sceanes **8 i'th'** with **10 the** [Q2] thy **14 govern,** gouerne it, **16 Tyre** time **18 his** this **19 go on** grone **24 true-owed** true olde **29 puts** put **34 sweetest, best** *sweetest, and best* **36–37 In . . . good** [*PA*; not in Q1. For the eight lines from Q1 omitted here, see Additional Passage.] **42 scene** Steare

Scene 19 [not in Q1] **2 s.p.** SECOND GENTLEMAN [Qa, Qb, Qb catchword] *Gower.* [Qa catchword] **13 the whole of** a whole **24 loon** Lowne **25 custom** customers **27 tobless** to blesse **34 deed** deedes **41 dignifies** dignities **42 noble** number **52 honourably** know worthilie note **63 hers** her **64–139 Fair . . . Away** [prose in Q1; many of the following emendations help create metrical verse lines] **64 Fair** Now prittie **66 I Why** I **name it but** name but **71 or** or at **73 Proclaimeth you** proclaimes you to be **74 And** [not in Q1] **75 into it** intoo't **76 blood** parts **77 whole province** place **78 What** Why **informed**

made knowne vnto **80 seeds of shame, roots of** seeds and rootes of shame and **s.d.** MARINA *weeps* [not in Q1] teares [*PA*] **81 you've** you haue **82 off aloof for a** aloft for **84–89 can . . . ling'ring** shall not see thee, or else looke friendly vpon thee; vrging her, that he was the Gouernour, whose authoritie coulde wincke at those blemishes, her selfe, and that sinnefull house could cast vppon her, or his displeasure punish at his owne pleasure, which displeasure of mine, thy beauty shall not priuiledge thee from, nor my affection, which hath drawen me vnto this place abate, if thou with further lingering withstand me [*PA*] **85 or can on faults look friendly** or else looke friendly vpon thee [not in *PA*] **91–93 Let . . . yourself** [not in Q1] If as you say (my Lorde) you are the Gouernour, let not your authoritie, which should teach you to rule others, be the meanes to make you misgouerne your selfe [*PA*] **96–106 What . . . impoverish me** [not in Q1] What reason is there in your Justice, who hath power ouer all, to vndoe any? If you take from mee mine honour, you are like him, that makes a gappe into forbidden ground, after whome too many enter, and you are guiltie of all their euilles: my life is yet vnspotted, my chastitie vnstained in thought. Then if your violence deface this building, the workemanship of heauen, made vp for good, and not to be the exercise of sinnes intemperaunce, you do kill your owne honour, abuse your owne iustice, and impouerish me. . . . Is there a necessitie (my yet good Lord) if there be fire before me, that I must strait then thither flie and burne my selfe? Or if suppose this house, (which too many feele such houses are) should be the Doctors patrimony, and Surgeons feeding; folowes it therefore, that I must needs infect my self to giue them maintenaunce? [*PA*] **114 s.d.** *kneeling* [not in Q1] which wordes (being spoken vpon her knees) [*PA*] **115 franked plac't** **119 s.d.** *moved* [*PA*; not in Q1] **120 s.d.** *He . . . hands* [not in Q1] hee lift her vp with his hands [*PA*] **121 Though** Had **122 hath** had **s.d.** *He . . . eyes* [not in Q1] in steede of willing her to drie her eyes, he wiped the wet himselfe off [*PA*] **and my foul thoughts** [not in Q1] I hither came with thoughte intemperate, foule and deformed [*PA*] **123 Thy . . . white** [not in Q1] the which your paines so well hath laued, that they are now white [*PA*] **124–26 I . . . honesty** holde, heeres golde for thee [Q1] and for my parte, who hither came but to haue payd the price, a peece of golde for your virginitie, now giue you twenty to releeue your honesty [*PA*] **127 Persever still** perseuer **128 The** For me be you thoughten, that I came with no ill intent, for to me the **131 The . . . made**

[*PA*; not in Q1] **132 not** not but **noble** noble, hold, heeres more golde for thee **134 honour. Hold, here's more gold. /** If goodnes, if [A shorter version of the words omitted at line 132 is reintroduced here.] **135 s.d.** *Enter . . . out* [not in Q1] the bawde standing ready at the doore, as hee should go out, making his obeysaunce vnto him as hee should returne [*PA*] **146 executioner shall do** hãg-man shal execute **We'll come your way, weele 152 She** He **158 s.p.** PANDER *Bawd.* **159 ice** glass **167 s.d.** *catching . . . hand* [*PA*; not in Q1] **176–84** *Neither . . . lungs* [prose in Q1; many of the following emendations help create metrical verse lines] **176 can be** are **178 place** place for which **179 change with thee** change **180 Thou** Thou art the **182 To th'** To the **ev'ry** euery **190 sew'rs** shores **190 public** common **191 these** these wayes **193 dear** deere, that the gods wold safely deliuer me from this place **Here's** here, heers **194 make gain** gaine **197 I will** will **206 women** [Q4] woman

Scene 20 [not in Q1] **8 twin** Twine **13 We Where** wee **Waves there him tossed** wee there him left **14 Whence** Where **tofore** before **20 fervour** [Qb] former [Qa] **22 the** his

Scene 21 [not in Q1] **1 s.p.** SAILOR OF TYRE 1 *Say.* **1–53** *Where . . . prevented* [prose in Q1] **1 Lord Helicanus can resolve you, sir** Where is Lord *Helicanus?* hee can resolue you, O here he is Sir **3 In it** and in it is **6 s.p.** SAILOR OF TYRE 2 *Say.* **6 Ho** Ho Gentlemen **What is your lordship's pleasure** Doeth your Lordship call **7 some** there is some **8 you** [not in Q1] **9 s.p.** SAILOR OF MYTILENE *Hell.* [Qa] 1 *Say* [Qb] **This** Sir, this **aught** ought you would **11 sir** [not in Q1] **12–16 You wish me well. / I . . . Mytilene; / Being . . . are** Li⟨simachus⟩ You wish mee well, beeing . . . are. *Hell⟨icanus⟩* First what is your place? *Ly⟨simachus⟩* I . . . this place you lie before [Helicanus's question in Q1 is omitted, and an emended version of Lysimachus's reply ("I . . . before") is moved to an earlier position, after "You wish me well."] **17 Our** Syr our **our king** the King **21 grew** is **22 tell it ouer** repeat **23 precious** [not in Q1] **25 See him, sir, you may** You may **26 sight. He** [Qb] sight see [Qa] **27 any.** LYSIMACHUS Let me yet any, yet let me [speech continued by Helicanus in Q1, with different word order] **28 s.p.** HELICANUS [Q4] *Lys⟨imachus⟩* **s.d.** *lying . . . sack-cloth* [not in Q1] so attired from the ordinary habite of other men, as with a long ouer-growne beard, diffused hayre, vndecent nayles on his fingers, and himselfe lying vppon his cowch groueling on his face [*PA*; when Pericles first learns of Marina's death, *PA* reports that "hee

apparrelles himselfe in sacke-cloth."] **28–29 person, /** Till [Q4] person. / *Hell⟨icanus⟩* Till [In this edition, Helicanus is already speaking.] **29 of that night** wight **30 all hail** all haile, the Gods preserue you **s.d.** PERICLES . . . *pillow* hee shruncke himselfe downe vppon his pillow [*PA*] **35 choice** chosen **alarum** allure **36 deafened ports** defend parts **37 in all** is all **38 among** and **39 Dwells now i'th'** now vpon the **40 Go fetch her hither** [not in Q1] **47 gods** God **51 it** it to you **54 presence** present **57 of** of a **or** and **I'd** [Q4] I do **58 to** and **wed** [Q4] to wed **59 one** on **bounty** beautie **60 feat** fate **64–140** *Sir . . . end here* [prose in Q1; many of the following emendations help to create metrical verse lines] **65 recure** recouerie **67 Let** Come, let **68 prosper her** make her prosperous **Marked** [Q4] Marke **69 s.p.** MAID *Mar⟨ina⟩* **84 Stay** go not **88 My lord** [after "said," line 87, in Q1] **90–91 what . . . shores?** what Countrey women heare of these shewes? **93 seem** appeare **95 such** sucha one **99 cased** caste **109 palace** *Pallas* **111 make my senses** [Q4] makes senses **112 Thou show'st** for thou lookest **114 say** stay **121 circumstance** thoughts **123 thousandth** thousand **128 lost thou them?** Thy name lost thou thy name **130 sir,** [not in Q1] **142 Motion as well?** Motion well **146 when** the minute **147 recounted** deliuered **153 You will scarce believe me** You scorne, beleeue me **159 wooed** hauing wood **160 the deed** it **162 To Mytilene they brought me** Brought me to *Metaline* **163 What will you of me** whither wil you haue me? **164 impostor** imposture **167 s.p.** PERICLES *Hell⟨icanus⟩* **174 would never** neuer would **192 rest** rest you sayd **193 So prove but true in that, thou art my daughter** [not in Q1] **194 life** like **196 name?** name was *Thaisa* **199 Thou art** [Q4] th'art **s.d.** *He kisses her* he falls on hir necke, and kisses her [*PA*] **201 Not** shee is not **207 sir** [not in Q1] **211 doubt** doat **217–18** LYSIMACHUS **Music, my lord? /** PERICLES I hear most *Lys.* Musicke my Lord? I heare. / *Per.* Most **219 raps** nips **220 eyelids** eyes **s.d.** *He sleeps* he fell into a slumber [*PA*] **221 A . . . head. Companion** A Pillow for his head, so leaue him all. / Well my companion **223 So leave him all** [after "head" (line 222) in Q1] **227–28 At large . . . voice** [not in Q1] **231 life** like **232 Perform** or performe **233 rest** [not in Q1] **238 Th'** The

Scene 22 [not in Q1] **9 well** [not in Q1] **23 espouse** [*PA*] wed **24 The fair Thaisa . . . at Pentapolis** at *Pentapolis,* the faire *Thaisa* **s.d.** THAISA *starts* At the naming of whome, she her selfe being by, could not choose but starte [*PA*] **26 who** whom **28 whom** who

30 Bore brought **31 our barque** vs **35 nun** mum **39 same** verie **42 one** in **48 upon him** [not in Q1] **70** s.d. *embracing* MARINA [not in Q1] giuing his daughter to her armes to embrace her as a child [*PA*] **72** s.p. PERI-CLES [Q4] *Hell⟨icanus⟩* **82 is the** [not in Q1] **90 And told how in this temple she came placed** How shee came plac'ste heere in the Temple [Q1] for in this Temple was she placed [*PA*] **91 Diana** *Dian* **92 I** [not in Q1] **93 Nightly** Night **Beloved** [not in Q1] **95 At Pentapolis shall marry her** shall marrie her at *Pentapolis* **101 from Pentapolis** [not in Q1] **102 Heav'n** Heauens [Q1] Heauen [Q1 catchword] **112 preserved** preferd **113 Led** [Q2] Led **119 their** [Q4] his **deed to th' deede, the 123 that** [not in Q1]

THE TRAGEDY OF CORIOLANUS

CONTROL TEXT: F

F: The Folio of 1623

s.p. NICANOR *Roman*.
s.p. ADRIAN *Vol⟨scian⟩*.

1.1.23–24 s.p. THIRD CITIZEN Against . . . first. / s.p. fourth citizen He's . . . com-monalty. *All*. Against . . . comonality. **29** s.p. FIFTH CITIZEN *All*. **49** s.p. FIRST CITI-ZEN 2 *Cit⟨izen⟩*; likewise for the remainder of 1.1. **82 stale't** scale't **99 tauntingly** taint-ingly **161 geese. You are no** Geese you are: No **190 all most** almost **205 Junius** *Annius* **207 unroofed** vnroo'st **230 Lartius** *Lucius* **232, 236** s.p. LARTIUS Tit⟨us⟩.
1.3.33 that's that **40 Grecian sword,** con-temning. Tell Grecian sword. *Contenning*, tell **77** s.p. VIRGILIA *Vlug*. **79 Ithaca** *Athica*
1.5.13 trenches. Follow Trenches followes **18** s.p. THIRD SOLDIER *All*. **19** s.p. LARTIUS *Tit⟨us⟩*. s.p. FOURTH SOLDIER *All*. **25 art lost,** art left, **28 Cato's** *Calues*
1.6.4 honours hours
1.7.53 Antiates Antients **70 Lesser** Lessen **76 O'** Oh **84 I** foure
1.10.40 upheld beheld **67, 78, 81** s.p. CORI-OLANUS *Martius*. **82 And** at At **89** s.p. CORIOLANUS *Martius*.
1.11.17 valour, poisoned *valors poison'd*
2.1.16 with all withall **22 how are** ho ware **51 cannot** can **95** s.p. VIRGILIA and VALE-RIA 2. *Ladies*. **151 Coriolanus** *Martius Caius Coriolanus* **166** s.p. CORIOLANUS *Com⟨inius⟩*. **171 begnaw** at begin at **172 You** Yon **203 guarded** gawded **241 touch** teach
2.2.63, 119, 127 s.p. FIRST SENATOR *Senat⟨or⟩*.

2.3.47 tongue tougne **62 but not** but **80, 83** s.p. FOURTH CITIZEN 1. **95** s.p. FIFTH CITI-ZEN 2. **97** s.p. FOURTH CITIZEN 1. **104 hire** higher **105 womanish toge** Wooluish tongue **108 do't** doo't? **122** s.p. SIXTH CIT-IZEN 1. *Cit⟨izen⟩*. **232 And . . . surnamed** [not in F] **243** s.p. A CITIZEN We . . . s.p. ANOTHER CITIZEN Almost *All*. We . . . almost
3.1.33 s.p. FIRST SENATOR *Senat*. **50** s.p. CORIOLANUS *Com⟨inius⟩*. **61 abused, set on.** abus': set on, **94 good God!** **101 impo-tence** Ignorance **146 Where one** Whereon **180** s.p. ALL THE PATRICIANS *All*. **185** s.p. ALL THE CITIZENS *All*. **186** s.p. CITIZENS AND PATRICIANS [not in F] **193, 199** s.p. ALL THE CITIZENS *All*. **198** s.p. FIRST SENA-TOR *Sena⟨tor⟩*. **203** s.p. CORIOLANUS *Com⟨inius⟩*. **220 poisons** poysonous **228** s.p. ALL THE CITIZENS *All*. **229 your** our **231** s.p. CORIOLANUS *Com⟨inius⟩*. **236** s.p. COMINIUS *Corio⟨lanus⟩*. **237** s.p. CORI-OLANUS *Mene⟨nius⟩*. **239** s.p. MENENIUS Be Be **272, 282** s.p. ALL THE CITIZENS All. **289 our** one **307** s.p. SICINIUS *Menen⟨ius⟩*. **326 bring him** bring him in peace
3.2.20 taxings things **25** s.p. FIRST SENATOR *Sen*. **31 herd** heart **78 With** Which **101 bear?** Well beare well? **102 plot to lose,** Plot, to loose
3.3.33 for th' fourth **37 Throng** Through **56 accents** Actions **99 Inveighed** Enui'd **114 for** from **143 despite.** despight
4.1.38 s.p. VIRGILIA *Corio⟨lanus⟩*.
4.3.9 approved appear'd
4.4.13 seem seems **23 hate** haue
4.5.130 o'erbear't o're-beate **161 is yet** is: but **188 broiled** boyld **206, 207 dejecti-tude** Directitude **220 sleepy** sleepe **221 war's** Warres
4.6.36 lamentation Lamention **60 come** comming **145 one** oue
4.7.37 'twas 'was **39 defect** detect **49 virtues** Vertue, **55 falter** fouler
5.1.16 fair for **69 hold to his** yeeld to his
5.2.62 but by but **71 our** your
5.3.48 prate pray **63 holp** hope **66 candied** curdied **81 things** thing **116 thorough** through **150 fine** fiue **153 charge** change **170 him with** him with him with **180 this** his
5.6.116 Fluttered Flatter'd

THE WINTER'S TALE

CONTROL TEXT: F

F: THE FOLIO OF 1623

s.p. OLD SHEPHERD [F's use of *"Shep⟨heard⟩."* has been changed throughout.]

s.p. FIRST LADY [F's use of *"Lady"* has been changed at 2.1.2, 5, 14, 16.]

s.p. A LORD [F's use of *"Lord"* has been changed throughout 2.1; at 2.3.26, 147, and 197; and at 3.2.114, 172, 200, and 214.]

1.2.106 And A **160 ornament** Ornaments **209 they** [not in F] **278 hobby-horse** Holy-Horse

2.2.56 let't le't **69 twixt** betwixt

2.3.39 What Who

3.2.10 Silence. [italicized and set as stage direction in F] **31 Who** Whom **166 certain** [not in F]

3.3.67 bairn Barne **73 hallooed** hallow'd **110 made** mad

4.2.3 sixteen fifteene

4.3.10 With heigh, with heigh, *With heigh,*

4.4.12 it [not in F] **13 swoon** sworne **98 your** you **148 so** [not in F] **160 out** on't **237 kiln-hole** kill-hole **239 Clammer** clamor **298 gentlemen** Gent. **347 who** whom **407 acknowledged** acknowledge **411 who** whom **416 see** neuer see **427 hoop** hope **455 your** my **577 so** [not in F] **597 could** would **685 know not** know **713 to** at

5.1.21 spoke spoken **58–59 stage,** / **Where . . . mourn, appear** Stage / (Where . . . now appeare) **61 just** iust **78 your** you a

5.3.5 young contracted your contracted **18 Lonely** Louely **67 fixture** fixure **96 Or those** On: those **150 This'** This

CYMBELINE, KING OF BRITAIN

CONTROL TEXT: F

F: The Folio of 1623

Fa, Fb: Successive states of F incorporating various print-shop corrections and changes

Title: *Cymbeline King of Britaine* [F table of contents] *The Tragedie of Cymbeline* [F head title]

s.p. INNOGEN [F's use of *Imogen* is changed throughout.]

s.p. GIACOMO [F's use of *Iachimo* is modernized throughout.]

s.p. HELEN [In 2.2, F's use of *La.* is changed throughout.]

s.p. FILARIO [F's use of *Philario* is modernized throughout.]

s.p. A ROMAN CAPTAIN [F's *Captain* is changed at 4.2.335, 339, 344, and 361.]

s.p. A LORD [F's use of *Lord* is changed at 4.3.16, 23, 28.]

s.p. FIRST JAILER [F's use of *Gao* is changed at 5.5.95.]

1.1.3 King Kings **15 of** at **30 Cassibelan** *Cassibulan* **98 Filario's** *Filorio's*

1.2.9 steel if he Steele if it

1.3.9 this his

1.4.40 not to to **62 Britain** Britanie **63 not** but not **72 purchase** purchases **90 five** [Fb] fine [Fa] **111 thousand** thousands

1.5.28 factor for for **85 words, Pisanio** words

1.6.7 desire desires **25 truest** *trust.* **29 takes** take **37 th'unnumbered** the number'd **81 count** account **126 lend to** lend **163 me** [Fb] ma [Fa] **169 men's** men **170 descended** defended **187 Best** The best

2.1.21 an and **24 your** you **31 tonight** night **58 husband, than** husband then.

2.2.2 hour houre [Fb] houe [Fa] **43 riveted** riueted [Fb] riuete [Fa] **49 bare** beare

2.3.6 s.p. CLOTEN [not in text] **17 s.p. MUSICIAN** [not in F] **heaven** Heauens **24 s.p. CLOTEN** [not in F] **25 vice** voyce **27 amend** amed **39 out** on't **43 solicits** solicity **96 cure** are **116 foil** foyle **132 garment** Garments **149 you** your

2.4.6 seared hopes fear'd hope **14 Ere** Or **18 legions** Legion **24 courage** courages **34 through** thorough **37 s.p. FILARIO** *Post.* **41 had** haue **47 not** note **57 you** yon **60 leaves** leaue **76 Such** since **116 her woman** her women **135 the** her **151 follow** follow him

2.5.2 bastards all all Bastards **16 German one** Iarmen on **27 man can name** name

3.1.5 Cassibelan *Cassibulan* **11 There will** There **20 banks** Oakes **30, 39–40 Cassibelan** *Cassibulan*

3.2.2 accuser accuse **10 to hers** to her **14 to do good** [Fb] to go do od [Fa] **22 here** [Fb] her [Fa] **64 Till** And **67 score** store **ride** rid **78 Nor here, nor** nor heere, not

3.3.2 Stoop Sleepe **15–16 war;** / That Warre. / This **23 bauble** Babe **25 'em** him **28 know** knowes **33 travelling abed** trauailing a bed **34 prison for** Prison, or **83 wherein they bow** whereon the Bowe **86 Polydore** Poladour **106 Morgan** *Mergan*

3.4.78 afore't a-foot **88 make** makes **100 out** [not in F] **132 churlish, noble** noble

3.5.32 looks looke **40 strokes,** stroke; **44 loud'st** lowd of **86 tongue** heart

3.6.68 Ay I **I'd** I do **74 price** prize

3.7.9 commends commands

4.2.2 from after **47 hath** he hath **51 s.p. BELARIUS** *Arui⟨ragus⟩.* **59 him** them **60 patience** patient **123 thanks, ye** thanks the **133 humour** Honor **171 how** thou **187 ingenious** ingenuous **203 not** not the **206 crare** care **207 Might** Might'st **225 rud-**

dock Raddocke 230 **winter-gown** winter-
ground 238 **once** once to 258 **begin.** begin.
/ SONG. 286 **th'earth's** face their Faces
288 **strow** strew 292 **is** are 325 **thy** this
338 **are** hence are heere 392 **wild-wood
leaves** wild wood-leaues 401 **he is** hee's
4.3.40 **betid** betide
4.4.2 **find we** we finde 17 **the** their 18 **files**
Fires 27 **hard** heard
5.1.1 **once wished** am wisht 15 **dread ill**
dread it 16 **blest** best 20 **mistress-piece**
Mistris: Peace
5.5.2 **Ay I did** 24 **harts** hearts **her** our 42
stooped stopt 43 **they** the 53 **Yet you** you
64 **This** This is 121 **make** take 161 **geck**
geeke 163 **come** came 175 **look** looke /
looke 212 **Preens** Prunes **claws** cloyes
252 **are** as are 257 **Of** Oh, of 260 **sir** Sis
270 **or take** or to take 273 **on** one
5.6.54 **and in fine** and in time 55 **fit** fitted 62
s.p. LADIES La. 64 **heard** heare 134 **On**
One 142 **Torments** Which torments 205
got it got 225 **villain** villany 261 **from** fro
262 **lock** Rocke 303 **boy** man 335 **mere**
neere 352 **like** liks 379 **you** we 387
brothers Brother 393 **inter'gatories** Inter-
rogatories 406 **so** no 469 **this yet** yet this

THE TEMPEST

CONTROL TEXT: F

F: The Folio of 1623
Fa, Fb: Successive states of F incorporating
various print-shop corrections and changes

1.1.18–19 **councillor** Councellor 19–20
work peace worke the peace 31 **wi'th'** with
54 **s.p.** MARINERS [not in F] 57 **wi'th'** with'
59 **broom** Browne **furze** firrs
1.2.100 **oft** of it. 112 **wi'th'** with 153 **wast**
was't 174 **princes** Princesse 201
bowsprit Bore-spritt 230 **Bermudas**
Bermoothes 262 **Algiers** Argier 284 **she**
he 304 **to** [not in F] 330 **forth at** for that
349 **human** humane 383 **sprites** Sprights
385–88 **s.p.** SPIRITS . . . ARIEL . . . SPIR-
ITS [Only the last refrain, "Hark, hark, I
hear," is assigned to Ar⟨iel⟩. in F.] 390
cock-a-diddle-dow cockadiddle-dowe 407
s.p. SPIRITS . . . *dong* Burthen ding dong
408 **s.p.** SPIRITS [*within*] [not in F] 470
power pow'r
2.1.37 **s.p.** ANTONIO. . . Sebastian *Seb⟨ast-
ian⟩. . . . Ant⟨onio⟩.* 133 **More** Mo 140
chirurgeonly Chirurgeonly 253 **every** eu'ry
2.2.52 **Then to sea** [*etc.*] [not in F] 108 **spirits** sprights 120 **Swum** Swom 164
seamews Scamels
3.1.2 **sets** set 15 **busil'est** busie lest 47 **peerless** peetlesse

3.2.24 **debauched** debosh'd 30 **s.p.** TRIN-
CULO [F (text)] *Cal⟨iban⟩.* [F (catchword)]
3.3.2 **ache** akes 15 **travel** trauaile 29
islanders Islands 33 **human** humaine 65
plume plumbe 99 **bass** base
4.1.9 **of her** her of 13 **gift** guest 17 **rite** right
52 **rein** raigne 53 **abstemious** abstenious
61 **vetches** Fetches **peas** Pease 64 **peonied**
pioned 74 **Her** here 81 **bosky** boskie 83
short-grassed short gras'd 110 **s.p.** CERES
[not in F] **and** [not in F] 123 **wise** wife 136
holiday holly day 180 **gorse** gosse 193
them on on them **lime** line 229 **Let't alone**
let's alone
5.1.10 **lime-grove** *Line-groue* 16 **run** runs
60 **boiled** boile 72 **Didst** [F (catchword)]
Did [F (text)] 75 **entertained** entertaine
81 **shores** shore 93–96 **Merrily . . . bough**
[In F, these lines are not repeated.] 113
Whe'er Where 126 **not** nor 158 **these**
Their 178 **An** And 202 **remembrance**
remembrances 230 **events** [Fb] euens [Fa]
237 **more** mo 239 **her** our 288 **Why** [Fb]
Who [Fa]

ALL IS TRUE (HENRY VIII)

CONTROL TEXT: F

F: The Folio of 1623

Title: The Famous History of the Life of King
HENRY the Eight [main Title] *The Life of
King Henry the Eight* [running title; see the
Introduction]

s.p. PROLOGUE, EPILOGUE [Though treated
in this edition as characters, F's
THE PROLOGVE and THE EPILOGVE
could be either speech prefixes or section
headings.]
s.p. KING HENRY [F's *King* has been expanded
throughout.]
s.p. LORD CHAMBERLAIN [F uses *Chamberlain* and *Lord Chamberlain*; standardized
throughout.]
s.p. LORD CHANCELLOR [F's *Chancellor* has
been expanded throughout.]
s.p. SANDS [F uses *Sands* and *Lord Sands*;
standardized throughout. See note to
2.1.54 stage direction.]
s.p. GUILDFORD [F's *Sir Henry Guilford* has
been shortened throughout.]
s.p. CARDINAL WOLSEY [F uses *Cardinal* and
Wolsey. The latter occurs primarily when
Cardinal Campeius is also onstage,
although even then Cardinal Wolsey is usually referred to in the dialogue as "Cardinal"; standardized throughout.]

s.p. BUCKINGHAM'S SURVEYOR [F's *Surveyor* has been expanded throughout.]

s.p. CARDINAL CAMPEIUS [F uses *Campeius*, presumably in part to distinguish him from Cardinal Wolsey; expanded throughout.]

s.p. PAGE [F's *Boy* has been changed throughout.]

Epilogue

s.p. QUEEN KATHERINE, KATHERINE [F uses *Queen* until she becomes the princess dowager (4.2), at which point it switches to *Katherine*. Similarly, this edition switches from "Queen Katherine" to "Katherine" at 4.2.]

s.p. GRIFFITH [F's *Gentleman Usher* (2.4), *Gentleman* (3.1), and *Griffith* have been standardized throughout. See notes below for more information.]

s.p. ANNE Boleyn [F uses *Anne* and *Anne Bullen*; standardized throughout.]

s.p. OLD LADY [F uses *Old Lady* more frequently than *Lady*; standardized throughout.]

s.p. LINCOLN [F uses *Lincoln* and *Bishop of Lincoln*; standardized throughout.]

s.p. GENTLEMEN [F's "1," "2," and "3" have been expanded to "First Gentleman," etc.]

Prologue s.d. / s.p. *Enter* PROLOGUE / PROLOGUE *THE PROLOGVE.* **11 pass, if** *passe: If*

1.1.7 Ardres . . . Guisnes . . . Ardres *Andren . . . Guynes . . . Arde* **23** *mesdames* Madams **42–48 to. All . . . function. s.p.** BUCKINGHAM **Who . . . together, as you guess? s.p.** NORFOLK **too. /** *Buc⟨kingham⟩. All . . . Function: who . . . together? / Nor⟨folk⟩.* As you guesse: [In F, Buckingham begins speaking at "All was Royal" (line 42) and continues through "together" (line 47). Norfolk then begins the following speech with the phrase "As you guesse" (line 47).] **63 web, a** Web. O **116, 117 s.p.** SECRETARY *Secr⟨etary⟩.* [We cannot be certain which secretary speaks which lines, since two enter with Wolsey and they are not distinguished by speech prefix.] **120 venom-mouthed** *venom'd-mouth'd* **154 July** *Inly* **167 rinsing** *wrenching* **183 Privily he** *Priuily* **200 Hereford** *Hertford* **211 Abergavenny** *Aburgany* **219 Perk, his chancellor** *Pecke,* his Councellour. [The emendation derives from Holinshed.] **221 Nicholas** *Michaell* [The emendation derives from Holinshed.] **227 lord** Lords

1.2.9 s.p. CRIER ⟨*within*⟩ **Room . . . Norfolk.** *A noyse within crying roome . . . Duke of Norfolke.* [In F, this entire sentence is a stage direction, and there is no speech prefix.] **68 business** *basenesse* **140 His** This **148, 149 Hopkins** *Henton.* [The emendation derives

from Holinshed. At 1.1.221, the name is presented correctly.] **157 feared** *feare* **165 confession's** Commissions [The emendation derives from Holinshed.] **171 win** [not in F] **181 To** For this to **191 Bulmer** *Blumer* [The emendation derives from Holinshed.] **191 remember** remember of

1.3.13 Or A 21 'messieurs' *Monsieurs* **34** *'oui'* wee **59 he's** Ha's

1.4.6 feast first

2.1.21 Perk *Pecke.* **54 s.d.** *William Walter* [The emendation derives from Holinshed.] **79 i'** a **87 mark** make

2.2.1 s.p. LORD CHAMBERLAIN [*reads*] [not in F]

2.3.59 note's notes **61 of you** of you, to you **87 fie, fie** fye, fye, fye

2.4.7, 10 come into the court &c. **11 s.p.** QUEEN KATHERINE [not in F] **124 s.p.** GRIFFITH *Gent⟨leman⟩ Vsh⟨er⟩.* [It seems reasonable to suppose that this gentleman is the same as the *Gentleman* who attends the queen at 3.1.14. s.d. and is referred to as *Gent⟨leman⟩* at 3.1.16, 18 s.p., later identified as *Griffith, her Gentleman Vsher* at 4.2.0 s.d. **171 A And 188 does yield to** th' does to th' **196 throe** throw

3.1.3 s.p. GENTLEWOMAN [*sings*] SONG. [In F, no speech prefix precedes the song.] **16, 18 s.p.** GRIFFITH *Gent⟨leman⟩.* **60 your** our **118 he's** ha's **123 accursed** a Curse

3.2.58 Has Ha's **143 glad** gald **172 filed** fill'd **340 legantine** Legatiue **344 Chattels** Castles

4.1.20 s.p. SECOND GENTLEMAN I **56 s.p.** FIRST GENTLEMAN [not in F, which gives all of lines 55–56 to "2." Here, FIRST GENTLEMAN speaks the beginning of line 56.] **103 Stokesley** *Stokeley* [The emendation derives from Holinshed.] **119 s.p.** FIRST *and* SECOND GENTLEMEN *Both.*

4.2.5 led'st lead'st **7 think** thanke **99 colour** cold **109 s.d.** CAPUTIUS *Capuchius*

5.1.37 time Lime **140 precipice** Precepit **158 s.p.** LOVELL ⟨*within*⟩ *Gent⟨leman⟩ within.*

5.2.7 piece Peere **119, 121 s.p.** LORD CHANCELLOR ⟨*Lord*⟩ *Cham⟨berlain⟩.* **126 s.p.** ALL THE COUNCIL *All.* **167 this** his **207 heart** hearts

5.3.2 Paris Parish **4, 27 s.p.** ONE ⟨*within*⟩ *Within.* **78** *a way* away

5.4.37 ways way **70 your** you **75 He's** 'Has

Epilogue s.d. / s.p. *Enter* EPILOGUE / EPILOGUE *THE EPILOGVE.*

THE TWO NOBLE KINSMEN

Control text: Q

Q: The Quarto of 1634

Qa, Qb: The uncorrected (Qa) and corrected (Qb) states of Q

Title: *The Two Noble Kinsmen* [Q] a Tragi-Comedy called the two noble kinsmen [Stationers' Register]

s.p. PROLOGUE , EPILOGUE [Q simply titles each section "PROLOGVE" and "EPILOGVE," which could be interpreted either as speech prefixes or as section headings.]

s.p. JAILER [Q alternates between *Jailer* and *Keeper.* Standardized throughout.]

s.p. JAILER'S DAUGHTER [Q's consistent use of *Daughter* is expanded throughout.]

s.p. JAILER'S BROTHER [Q's consistent use of *Brother* is expanded throughout.]

s.p. COUNTRYMEN [Q uses only numbers to refer to the Countrymen, except in 3.5, when one of the Countrymen, who is dressed as a baboon, is referred to as *Baum* or *Bavian* ("babion," old form of "baboon") in Q and "babion" in this edition.]

Prologue s.d. *Enter* PROLOGUE / **s.p.** PROLOGUE PROLOGVE. **26 tack** take

1.1. s.d. PIRITHOUS Theseus **1 s.p. BOY** The Song. [In Q, the song is not assigned to a particular character. It is clear from the preceding stage direction, however, that it is the boy who sings.] **7 born** borne **9 harebells** her bels **13–14 children sweet,** / **Lie** *children: sweete-* / *Ly* **20 chough hoar** *Clough hee* **68 Nemean** Nenuan **90 thy** the **112 glassy** glasse **132 longer** long **138 move** mooves **155 Rinsing** Wrinching **158 Artesius** *Artesuis* **166 s.p. ALL THREE QUEENS** *All.* **171 war** was **177 twinning** twyning. ["Twined" remains a possible alternative modernization. Compare 2.2.64.] **211 Aulis** Anly

1.2.55 canon Cannon **69 men's service** men service **70 glory; one** glory on

1.3.31 one ore **54 eleven** a eleven **54 Flavina** Flauia **73 happily** happely **73 wear** were **75 one** on **79 seely innocence** fury-innocent **82 dividual** individuall **82 out** ont

1.4.18 smeared [Qb] succard [Qa] **22 Wi'leave** We leave **45 O'erwrestling** Or wrastling **49 fore** for

1.5. s.d. Song [not in Q] **9–10 woes,** / **We . . . woes.** woes. *We convent, &c.*

2.2.21 wore were **22 Ravished** Bravishd **64 twined** twyn'd **118–19 s.p. EMILIA This . . . in't.** / **What** This . . . in't. / *Emil.* What [In Q, Arcite continues speaking until the end of line 118.] **132 was I** I was **150 close** neere **182 love her** love **189 your blood** you blood **264 to** too **272 you** yon

2.3.6 sins [Qb] fins [Qa] **24 s.d. garland** garlond [Qb] *Garlon* [Qa] **40 ye** yet **53 said** sees **64 Yet** Yes

2.4.33 night; ere tomorrow night, or to-morrow

2.5 Scaena 4 28 For Fo

2.6.33 patch path

3.1.2 laund land **11–12 With . . . rumination** [Q prints as one line with no lacuna marked.] **37 looked, the void'st** lookd the voydes **43 Not** Nor **96 s.d. within** of *Cornets.* [In Q's *"Winde hornes of Cornets," "Cornets"* may be a playhouse addition; *"of"* could mean "off," or "offstage," here rendered as "within."] **98 muset** Musicke **108 not** nor **113 'Tis** If **123 enjoy it** enjoy't

3.2.1 mistook the brake mistooke; the Beake **7 reck** wreake **19 fed** feed **28 brine** bine

3.3.12 sir &c. **23 them** then **52 Sirrah—** Sir ha:

3.4.9 Open Vpon **10 tack** take **19 a foot** *afoote*

3.5 Scaena 6 s.d. BABION Baum **8 jean** jave **25 these** their **33, 134 babion** *Bavian* **67 I** [not in Q] **68 There . . . owlet—** *There . . . howlet* [Q's italics appear to derive from the compositor mistakenly interpreting this line as part of the song.] **69 he** [not in Q] **100 s.p. THESEUS** *Per.* [Pirithous] **120 'Moor'** Morr **121 'Ice'** Is **125 tenor** tenner **133 beest-eating** beast eating **138 s.p. SCHOOLMASTER** [not in Q] **139–48 Ladies . . . rout** [italics in Q. The compositor possibly misinterpreted this speech as a song.] **140 ye** *thee* **143 thee** *three* **152 you** yon

3.6 Scaena 7 145 thine this **236 fail** fall **272 must** muff **273 the other** th'other **279, 280 s.p. PALAMON** *and* ARCITE *Both.*

4.1.11 oath o'th **20 he scaped** he escapt **45 WOOER No, Sir, not well. SECOND FRIEND Not well?** 2 *Fr.* Not well?—*Wooer,* No Sir not well. **63 sung** song **84 wreath** wreake **86 she appeared, methought,** me thought she appeard **104 light . . .'** *light, &c.* [Here and at 4.1.113 and 151 and 4.3.48, Q's "&c." suggests that more than the single line of the song printed in the text was sung.] **113 sweet . . .'** *sweete, &c.* **119 Far** For **133 s.p. JAILER'S BROTHER** *Daugh.* [Jailer's Daughter] **140 s.p. SECOND FRIEND** *I. Fr.* [First Friend] **144–45 Cheerly all.** / **Uff** cheerely. / *All.* Owgh [In Q, the *"All"* pretend to join in.] **150 Tack** Take **151 light . . .'** *light, &c.*

4.2.16 Jove afire once Loue a fire with **54–55 both!** / **s.d.** *Enter* [a] GENTLEMAN How both. / s.d. *Enter Emil⟨ia⟩ and Gent⟨leman⟩:* **s.p.** *Emil⟨ia⟩.* How [Q's superfluous references to Emilia in the s.d. and s.p. are omitted.] **76 first** fitst **81 fire** faire **105 tods** tops **110 court** corect

4.3.20 spirits are spirits, as **27 i'th' other** i'th / Thother **41 engrafted** engraffed **45 th'other** another **46 behind** [Qb] behold [Qa] **48 fate . . .'** *fate, &c.* **75 carve** crave

5.1.37 father of farther off **44 me** [not in Q] **49–50 purple;** / **Whose havoc in vast field comets prewarn,** purple. / Comets pre-

warne, whose havocke in vaste Feild **53
armipotent** armenypotent
5.2, 5.3 [Q continues as part of 5.1]
5.4 Scaena 2 34 Yes, Yet **38 s.d.** *mad Maide* **39
humour** honour **53 tune** turne **103 lose the
sight** loose the Fight
5.5 Scaena 3 78 the end th'end **111 Emilia**
Emily **139 your** you

5.6 Scaena 4 1 s.p. PALAMON [not in Q] **39
s.p.** SECOND *and* THIRD KNIGHTS I.2.
K⟨nights⟩. **47 rarely** early **79 victor's** [Qb]
victoros [Qa] **107 Hath** Hast
Epilogue s.d. *Enter* EPILOGUE / **s.p.** EPI-
LOGUE EPILOGVE.

General Bibliography*

There is a huge and ever-expanding scholarly literature about Shakespeare and his culture. This general list and the lists that accompany the individual plays and the poems in this volume are only a small sampling of the available resources. Journals devoted to Shakespeare studies include *Shakespeare Bulletin, Shakespeare Jahrbuch* (Germany), *Shakespeare Quarterly, Shakespeare Studies,* and *Shakespeare Survey* (England); other journals, such as *English Literary History, English Literary Renaissance, Renaissance Quarterly, Representations,* or *Studies in English Literature,* also frequently publish essays on Shakespeare's works. The categories below are only approximate; many of the texts could properly belong in more than one category.

Guides and Companions to Shakespeare Studies

Callaghan, Dympna, ed. *A Feminist Companion to Shakespeare*. Malden, Mass.: Blackwell, 2000.

de Grazia, Margreta, and Stanley Wells, eds. *The Cambridge Companion to Shakespeare*. Cambridge, Eng.: Cambridge University Press, 2001.

Drakakis, John, ed. *Alternative Shakespeares*. 2nd ed. London: Routledge, 1985.

Dutton, Richard, and Jean E. Howard, eds. *A Companion to Shakespeare's Works*, I: *The Tragedies*. Malden, Mass.: Blackwell, 2003.

———, eds. *A Companion to Shakespeare's Works*, II: *The Histories*. Malden, Mass.: Blackwell, 2003.

———, eds. *A Companion to Shakespeare's Works*, III: *The Comedies*. Malden, Mass.: Blackwell, 2003.

———, eds. *A Companion to Shakespeare's Works*, IV: *Poems, Problem Comedies, Late Plays*. Malden, Mass.: Blackwell, 2003.

Hattaway, Michael, ed. *The Cambridge Companion to Shakespeare's History Plays*. Cambridge, Eng.: Cambridge University Press, 2002.

Hawkes, Terence, ed. *Alternative Shakespeares, Volume 2*. London: Routledge, 1996.

Hodgdon, Barbara, and W. B. Worthen, eds. *A Companion to Shakespeare and Performance*. Malden, Mass.: Blackwell, 2005.

Jackson, Russell, ed. *The Cambridge Companion to Shakespeare on Film*. 2nd ed. Cambridge, Eng.: Cambridge University Press, 2007.

Kasten, David Scott, ed. *A Companion to Shakespeare*. Malden, Mass.: Blackwell, 1999.

Kinney, Arthur F. *Shakespeare by Stages: An Historical Introduction*. Malden, Mass.: Blackwell, 2003.

Leggatt, Alexander, ed. *The Cambridge Companion to Shakespearean Comedy*. Cambridge, Eng.: Cambridge University Press, 2002.

McDonald, Russ, ed. *The Bedford Companion to Shakespeare: An Introduction with Documents*. 2nd ed. Houndmills, Basingstoke: Palgrave Macmillan, 2001.

———, ed. *Shakespeare: An Anthology of Criticism and Theory, 1945–2000*. Malden, Mass.: Blackwell, 2004.

McEachern, Claire, ed. *The Cambridge Companion to Shakespearean Tragedy*. Cambridge, Eng.: Cambridge University Press, 2002.

*Edited by Holger Schott Syme, Department of English, University of Toronto.

Schoenfeldt, Michael. *A Companion to Shakespeare's Sonnets*. Malden, Mass.: Blackwell, 2006.

Smith, Emma, ed. *Shakespeare's Comedies: A Guide to Criticism*. Malden, Mass.: Blackwell, 2003.

———, ed. *Shakespeare's Histories: A Guide to Criticism*. Malden, Mass.: Blackwell, 2003.

———, ed. *Shakespeare's Tragedies: A Guide to Criticism*. Malden, Mass.: Blackwell, 2003.

Wells, Stanley, and Lena Cowen Orlin, eds. *Shakespeare: An Oxford Guide*. Oxford: Oxford University Press, 2003.

Wells, Stanley, and Sarah Stanton, eds. *The Cambridge Companion to Shakespeare on Stage*. New York: Cambridge University Press, 2002.

Shakespeare's World

Social, Political, and Economic History

Amussen, Susan Dwyer. *An Ordered Society: Gender and Class in Early Modern England*. New York: Columbia University Press, 1993.

Archer, Ian W. *The Pursuit of Stability: Social Relations in Elizabethan London*. New York: Cambridge University Press, 1991.

Ariès, Philippe, and Georges Duby, general eds. *A History of Private Life*, Volume III: *Passions of the Renaissance*. Ed. Roger Chartier. Trans. Arthur Goldhammer. Cambridge, Mass.: Belknap Press, 1989.

Armitage, David, and Michael J. Braddick, eds. *The British Atlantic World, 1500–1800*. New York: Palgrave Macmillan, 2002.

Barry, Jonathan, ed. *The Tudor and Stuart Town: A Reader in English Urban History, 1530–1688*. London: Longman, 1990.

Barry, Jonathan, and Christopher Brooks. *The Middling Sort of People: Culture, Society and Politics in England, 1550–1800*. Houndmills, Basingstoke: Palgrave Macmillan, 1994.

Barthelmey, Anthony Gerard. *Black Face, Maligned Race: The Representation of Blacks in English Drama from Shakespeare to Southerne*. Baton Rouge: Louisiana State University Press, 1987.

Beier, A. L. *Masterless Men: The Vagrancy Problem in England, 1560–1640*. New York: Methuen, 1985.

Beier, A. L., and Roger Finlay, eds. *London 1500–1700: The Making of the Metropolis*. New York: Longman, 1986.

Ben-Amos, Ilana Krausman. *Adolescence and Youth in Early Modern England*. New Haven: Yale University Press, 1994.

Bridenbaugh, Carl. *Vexed and Troubled Englishmen, 1590–1642*. New York: Oxford University Press, 1976.

Brigden, Susan. *New Worlds, Lost Worlds: The Rule of the Tudors, 1485–1603*. New York: Viking, 2001.

Burgess, Glenn. *The Politics of the Ancient Constitution: An Introduction to English Political Thought, 1603–1642*. University Park: Pennsylvania State University Press, 1993.

Capp, Bernard S. *When Gossips Meet: Women, Family, and Neighbourhood in Early Modern England*. Oxford: Oxford University Press, 2003.

Clark, Alice. *Working Life of Women in the Seventeenth Century*. Introduction by Amy Louise Erickson. 1968. New York: Routledge, 1992.

Clay, C. G. A. *Economic Expansion and Social Change: England 1500–1700*. 2 vols. New York: Cambridge University Press, 1984.

Cressy, David. *Birth, Marriage, and Death: Ritual, Religion, and the Life-Cycle in Tudor and Stuart England*. Oxford: Oxford University Press, 1997.

Cruickshank, Charles Greig. *Elizabeth's Army*. 2nd ed. Oxford: Clarendon, 1966.

Elliot, John Huxtable. *The Old World and the New, 1492–1650*. New York: Cambridge University Press, 1970.

Ellis, Steven G. *Tudor Ireland: Crown, Community, and the Conflict of Cultures, 1470–1603*. London: Longman, 1985.

Elton, G. R. *England Under the Tudors*. 3rd ed. New York: Routledge, 1991.

———. *The Tudor Revolution in Government: Administrative Changes in the Reign of Henry VIII*. Cambridge, Eng.: Cambridge University Press, 1959.

Emmison, F. G. *Elizabethan Life*. Chelmsford: Essex County Council, 1970.

Erickson, Amy Louise. *Women and Property in Early Modern England*. New York: Routledge, 1993.

Finlay, Roger. *Population and Metropolis: The Demography of London, 1580–1650*. Cambridge, Eng.: Cambridge University Press, 1981.

Fletcher, Anthony. *Gender, Sex, and Subordination in England, 1500–1800*. New Haven: Yale University Press, 1995.

Fletcher, Anthony, and John Stevenson, eds. *Order and Disorder in Early Modern England*. New York: Cambridge University Press, 1985.

Gaskill, Malcolm. *Crime and Mentalities in Early Modern England*. New York: Cambridge University Press, 2000.

Gittings, Clare. *Death, Burial and the Individual in Early Modern England*. London: Croom Helm, 1984.

Gowing, Laura. *Common Bodies: Women, Touch and Power in Seventeenth-Century England*. New Haven: Yale University Press, 2003.

Griffiths, Paul. *Youth and Authority: Formative Experiences in England, 1560–1640*. Oxford: Clarendon, 1996.

Griffiths, Paul, Adam Fox, and Steve Hindle, eds. *The Experience of Authority in Early Modern England*. New York: St. Martin's, 1996.

Guy, John A. *Queen of Scots: The True Life of Mary Stuart*. Boston: Houghton Mifflin, 2004.

———, ed. *The Reign of Elizabeth I: Court and Culture in the Last Decade*. Cambridge, Eng.: Cambridge University Press, 1995.

———. *Tudor England*. New York: Oxford University Press, 1988.

Heal, Felicity, and Clive Holmes. *The Gentry in England and Wales, 1500–1700*. Basingstoke: Macmillan, 1994.

Herrup, Cynthia B. *The Common Peace: Participation and the Criminal Law in Seventeenth-Century England*. New York: Cambridge University Press, 1987.

Hindle, Steve. *The State and Social Change in Early Modern England, c.1550–1640*. New York: St. Martin's, 2000.

Hirst, Derek. *Authority and Conflict: England, 1603–1658*. Cambridge, Mass.: Harvard University Press, 1986.

Ingram, Martin. *Church Courts, Sex, and Marriage in England, 1570–1640*. New York: Cambridge University Press, 1987.

James, Mervyn. *Society, Politics and Culture: Studies in Early Modern England*. New York: Cambridge University Press, 1986.

King, John N. *Tudor Royal Iconography: Literature and Art in an Age of Religious Crisis*. Princeton: Princeton University Press, 1989.

Kishlansky, Mark A. *A Monarchy Transformed: Britain 1603–1714*. New York: Penguin Books, 1996.

Klein, Joan Larsen. *Daughters, Wives, and Widows: Writings by Men about Women and Marriage in England, 1500–1640*. Urbana: University of Illinois Press, 1992.

Lake, Peter, with Michael Questier. *The Anti-Christ's Lewd Hat: Protestants, Papists and Players in Post-Reformation England*. New Haven: Yale University Press, 2002.

Laslett, Peter. *The World We Have Lost: Further Explored*. 3rd ed. New York: Scribner, 1984.

Levin, Carole. *The Heart and Stomach of a King: Elizabeth I and the Politics of Sex and Power*. Philadelphia: University of Pennsylvania Press, 1994.

Lockyer, Roger. *The Early Stuarts: A Political History of England, 1603–1642.* 2nd ed. London: Longman, 1999.

MacCaffrey, Wallace T. *Elizabeth I: War and Politics, 1588–1603.* Princeton: Princeton University Press, 1992.

Manning, Roger B. *Village Revolts: Social Protest and Popular Disturbances in England, 1509–1640.* Oxford: Clarendon, 1988.

Matar, Nabil I. *Islam in Britain, 1558–1685.* New York: Cambridge University Press, 1998.

———. *Turks, Moors, and Englishmen in the Age of Discovery.* New York: Columbia University Press, 1999.

Mendelson, Sara Heller, and Patricia Crawford. *Women in Early Modern England, 1550–1720.* Oxford: Clarendon, 1998.

Moody, T. W., F. X. Martin, and F. J. Byrne, eds. *A New History of Ireland,* Volume 3: *Early Modern Ireland, 1534–1691.* Oxford: Oxford University Press, 2001.

Mukerji, Chandra. *From Graven Images: Patterns of Modern Materialism.* New York: Columbia University Press, 1983.

Neale, J. E. *Elizabeth I and Her Parliaments, 1559–1581.* London: Cape, 1971.

———. *Queen Elizabeth I.* London: Pimlico, 1998.

Nichols, John, ed. *The Progresses and Public Processions of Queen Elizabeth.* 3 vols. London: J. Nichols, 1823.

Palliser, D. M. *The Age of Elizabeth: England under the Later Tudors, 1547–1603.* 2nd ed. New York: Longman, 1992.

Parry, J. H. *The Age of Reconnaissance: Discovery, Exploration, and Settlement, 1450 to 1650.* New York: Praeger, 1969.

Pearson, Lu Emily Hess. *Elizabethans at Home.* Stanford: Stanford University Press, 1967.

Peck, Linda Levy. *Court Patronage and Corruption in Early Stuart England.* Boston: Unwin Hyman, 1990.

Peters, Christine. *Women in Early Modern Britain, 1450–1640.* New York: Palgrave Macmillan, 2004.

Pocock, J. G. A. *The Ancient Constitution and the Feudal Law: Study of English Historical Thought in the Seventeenth Century—A Reissue with a Retrospect.* Rev. ed. New York: Cambridge University Press, 1987.

Rappaport, Steve. *Worlds within Worlds: Structures of Life in Sixteenth-Century London.* New York: Cambridge University Press, 1989.

Sharpe, J. A. *Crime in Early Modern England, 1550–1750.* 2nd ed. New York: Longman, 1999.

———. *Early Modern England: A Social History, 1550–1760.* 2nd ed. London: Arnold, 1997.

Slack, Paul. *The Impact of Plague in Tudor and Stuart England.* Boston: Routledge and Kegan Paul, 1985.

———. *Poverty and Policy in Tudor and Stuart England.* New York: Longman, 1988.

———, ed. *Rebellion, Popular Protest, and the Social Order in Early Modern England.* New York: Cambridge University Press, 1984.

Stone, Lawrence. *The Causes of the English Revolution, 1529–1642.* New York: Routledge, 2002.

———. *The Crisis of the Aristocracy, 1558–1641.* Oxford: Clarendon, 1965.

———. *The Family, Sex and Marriage in England, 1500–1800.* New York: Harper & Row, 1979.

Thirsk, Joan. *Economic Policy and Projects: The Development of a Consumer Society in Early Modern England.* Oxford: Clarendon, 1978.

Thomas, Keith. *Religion and the Decline of Magic: Studies in Popular Beliefs in Sixteenth and Seventeenth Century England.* New York: Scribner, 1971.

Underdown, David. *Fire from Heaven: Life in an English Town in the Seventeenth Century.* London: HarperCollins, 1992.

———. *Revel, Riot, and Rebellion: Popular Politics and Culture in England, 1603–1660.* Oxford: Clarendon, 1985.

Williams, Penry. *The Later Tudors: England, 1547–1603*. New York: Oxford University Press, 1995.

Wrightson, Keith. *Earthly Necessities: Economic Lives in Early Modern Britain*. New Haven: Yale University Press, 2000.

———. *English Society, 1580–1680*. London: Hutchinson, 1982.

Yates, Frances Amelia. *Astraea: The Imperial Theme in the Sixteenth Century*. London: Routledge and Kegan Paul, 1975.

Zagorin, Perez. *Rebels and Rulers, 1500–1660*. 2 vols. New York: Cambridge University Press, 1982.

Intellectual and Religious History

Armitage, David. *The Ideological Origins of the British Empire*. New York: Cambridge University Press, 2000.

Baker, Herschel Clay. *The Race of Time: Three Lectures on Renaissance Historiography*. Toronto: University of Toronto Press, 1967.

Barkan, Leonard. *Nature's Work of Art: The Human Body as Image of the World*. New Haven: Yale University Press, 1975.

Bossy, John. *Christianity in the West, 1400–1700*. New York: Oxford University Press, 1985.

Bouwsma, William James. *John Calvin: A Sixteenth-Century Portrait*. New York: Oxford University Press, 1988.

Cassirer, Ernst. *The Individual and the Cosmos in Renaissance Philosophy*. Trans. Mario Domandi. Philadelphia: University of Pennsylvania Press, 1972.

Clark, Stuart. *Thinking with Demons: The Idea of Witchcraft in Early Modern Europe*. New York: Oxford University Press, 1997.

Collinson, Patrick. *The Birthpangs of Protestant England: Religion and Cultural Change in the Sixteenth and Seventeenth Centuries*. New York: St. Martin's, 1988.

———. *The Elizabethan Puritan Movement*. New York: Oxford University Press, 1990.

———. *The Religion of Protestants: The Church in English Society, 1559–1625*. Oxford: Clarendon, 1982.

Doran, Susan, and Christopher Durston. *Princes, Pastors, and People: The Church and Religion in England, 1500–1700*. Rev. ed. New York: Routledge, 2003.

Duffy, Eamon. *The Stripping of the Altars: Traditional Religion in England, c. 1400–c. 1580*. 2nd ed. New Haven: Yale University Press, 1992.

Gadd, Ian, and Alexandra Gillespie, eds. *John Stow (1525–1605) and the Making of the English Past*. London: British Library, 2004.

Haigh, Christopher. *English Reformations: Religion, Politics, and Society under the Tudors*. New York: Oxford University Press, 1993.

Hill, Christopher. *Society and Puritanism in Pre-Revolutionary England*. New York: Schocken Books, 1964.

Houlbrooke, Ralph A. *Death, Religion, and the Family in England, 1480–1700*. New York: Oxford University Press, 1998.

Kelly, Henry Ansgar. *Divine Providence in the England of Shakespeare's Histories*. Cambridge, Mass.: Harvard University Press, 1970.

Kilroy, Gerard. *Edmund Campion. Memory and Transcription*. Aldershot, Eng.: Ashgate, 2005.

Klaits, Joseph. *Servants of Satan: The Age of the Witch Hunts*. Bloomington: Indiana University Press, 1985.

Kristeller, Paul Oskar. *Renaissance Thought: The Classic, Scholastic, and Humanistic Strains*. New York: Harper & Row, 1961.

Levao, Ronald. *Renaissance Minds and Their Fictions: Cusanus, Sidney, Shakespeare*. Berkeley: University of California Press, 1985.

Levin, Harry. *The Myth of the Golden Age in the Renaissance*. Bloomington: University of Indiana Press, 1969.

Levy, Fred Jacob. *Tudor Historical Thought*. San Marino, Calif.: Huntington Library Press, 1967.

MacCulloch, Diarmaid. *The Later Reformation in England, 1547–1603*. 2nd ed. New York: Palgrave, 2001.

———. *The Reformation*. New York: Viking, 2004.

Mack, Peter, ed. *Renaissance Rhetoric*. New York: St. Martin's, 1994.

Marotti, Arthur F. *Religious Ideology and Cultural Fantasy: Catholic and Anti-Catholic Discourses in Early Modern England*. Notre Dame, Ind.: University of Notre Dame Press, 2005.

Marshall, Peter. *Beliefs and the Dead in Reformation England*. London: Oxford University Press, 2002.

Oldridge, Darren, ed. *The Witchcraft Reader*. London: Routledge, 2001.

Patterson, Annabel M. *Reading Holinshed's Chronicles*. Chicago: University of Chicago Press, 1994.

Popkin, Richard H. *The History of Skepticism from Erasmus to Spinoza*. Berkeley: University of California Press, 1979.

Sharpe, James. *Instruments of Darkness: Witchcraft in England 1550–1750*. New York: Penguin Books, 1996.

Shuger, Debora Kuller. *Habits of Thought in the English Renaissance: Religion, Politics, and the Dominant Culture*. Berkeley: University of California Press, 1990.

Sonnino, Lee A. *A Handbook to Sixteenth-Century Rhetoric*. London: Routledge and Kegan Paul, 1968.

Strong, Roy. *The Cult of Elizabeth: Elizabethan Portraiture and Pageantry*. London: Thames and Hudson, 1977.

———. *The English Icon: Elizabethan & Jacobean Portraiture*. New York: Pantheon Books, 1969.

Walsham, Alexandra. *Providence in Early Modern England*. New York: Oxford University Press, 1999.

Watt, Tessa. *Cheap Print and Popular Piety, 1560–1649*. New York: Cambridge University Press, 1991.

Wind, Edgar. *Pagan Mysteries in the Renaissance*. Rev. and enl. ed. London: Oxford University Press, 1980.

Woolf, D. R. *Reading History in Early Modern England*. New York: Cambridge University Press, 2000.

———. *The Social Circulation of the Past: English Historical Culture, 1500–1730*. New York: Oxford University Press, 2003.

Cultural History and Early Modern Cultural Studies

Aers, David, Bob Hodge, and Gunther Kress. *Literature, Language, and Society in England, 1589–1680*. Totowa, N.J.: Barnes & Noble Books, 1981.

Agnew, Jean-Christophe. *Worlds Apart: The Market and the Theater in Anglo-American Thought, 1550–1750*. New York: Cambridge University Press, 1986.

Andersen, Jennifer, and Elizabeth Sauer, eds. *Books and Readers in Early Modern England: Material Studies*. Philadelphia: University of Pennsylvania Press, 2001.

Bakhtin, Mikhail. *Rabelais and His World*. Trans. Hélène Iswolsky. Rev. ed. Bloomington: Indiana University Press, 1984.

Baldwin, Thomas Whitfield. *William Shakespere's Small Latine & Lesse Greeke*. Urbana: University of Illinois Press, 1944.

Barkan, Leonard. *The Gods Made Flesh: Metamorphosis & the Pursuit of Paganism*. New Haven: Yale University Press, 1986.

Barker, Francis. *The Tremulous Private Body: Essays on Subjection*. New York: Methuen, 1984.

Baron, Sabrina Alcorn, ed. *The Reader Revealed*. Washington, D.C.: Folger Shakespeare Library, 2001.

Bartels, Emily Carroll. *Spectacles of Strangeness: Imperialism, Alienation, and Marlowe*. Philadelphia: University of Pennsylvania Press, 1993.

Beilin, Elaine V. *Redeeming Eve: Women Writers of the English Renaissance*. Princeton: Princeton University Press, 1987.

Blank, Paula. *Broken English: Dialects and the Politics of Language in Renaissance Literature*. New York: Routledge, 1996.

Bloom, Gina. *Voice in Motion: Staging Gender, Shaping Sound in Early Modern England*. Philadelphia: Pennsylvania University Press, 2007.

Bray, Alan. *Homosexuality in Renaissance England*. Rev. ed. New York: Columbia University Press, 1995.

Brayman Hackel, Heidi. *Reading Material in Early Modern England: Print, Gender, and Literacy*. New York: Cambridge University Press, 2005.

Briggs, Julia. *This Stage-Play World: Texts and Contexts, 1580–1625*. 2nd ed. New York: Oxford University Press, 1997.

Bristol, Michael D. *Carnival and Theater: Plebeian Culture and the Structure of Authority in Renaissance England*. New York: Methuen, 1985.

Brotton, Jerry. *Trading Territories: Mapping the Early Modern World*. London: Reaktion Books, 1997.

Brown, Pamela Allen. *Better a Shrew than a Sheep: Women, Drama, and the Culture of Jest in Early Modern England*. Ithaca, N.Y.: Cornell University Press, 2003.

Burke, Peter. *Popular Culture in Early Modern Europe*. New York: New York University Press, 1978.

Burt, Richard, and John Michael Archer, eds. *Enclosure Acts: Sexuality, Property, and Culture in Early Modern England*. Ithaca, N.Y.: Cornell University Press, 1994.

Bushnell, Rebecca W. *A Culture of Teaching: Early Modern Humanism in Theory and Practice*. Ithaca, N.Y.: Cornell University Press, 1996.

Buxton, John. *Elizabethan Taste*. London: Macmillan, 1963.

Caldwell, John. *The Oxford History of English Music*. New York: Oxford University Press, 1991.

Carroll, William C. *Fat King, Lean Beggar: Representations of Poverty in the Age of Shakespeare*. Ithaca, N.Y.: Cornell University Press, 1996.

Clegg, Cyndia Susan. *Press Censorship in Elizabethan England*. New York: Cambridge University Press, 1997.

———. *Press Censorship in Jacobean England*. New York: Cambridge University Press, 2001.

Cox, John D. *The Devil and the Sacred in English Drama, 1350–1642*. New York: Cambridge University Press, 2000.

Crane, Mary Thomas. *Framing Authority: Sayings, Self, and Society in Sixteenth-Century England*. Princeton: Princeton University Press, 1993.

Crawford, Julie. *Marvelous Protestantism: Monstrous Births in Post-Reformation England*. Baltimore: Johns Hopkins University Press, 2005.

Cressy, David. *Literacy and the Social Order: Reading and Writing in Tudor and Stuart England*. New York: Cambridge University Press, 1980.

De Grazia, Margreta, Maureen Quilligan, and Peter Stallybrass, eds. *Subject and Object in Renaissance Culture*. New York: Cambridge University Press, 1996.

Diehl, Huston. *Staging Reform, Reforming the Stage: Protestantism and Popular Theater in Early Modern England*. Ithaca, N.Y.: Cornell University Press, 1997.

Dolan, Frances E. *Dangerous Familiars: Representations of Domestic Crime in England, 1550–1700*. Ithaca, N.Y.: Cornell University Press, 1994.

———. *Whores of Babylon: Catholicism, Gender, and Seventeenth-Century Print Culture*. Ithaca, N.Y.: Cornell University Press, 1999.

Eisenstein, Elizabeth L. *The Printing Press as an Agent of Change: Communications and Cultural Transformations in Early-Modern Europe*. 2 vols. New York: Cambridge University Press, 1979.

Ferguson, Margaret W. *Dido's Daughters: Literacy, Gender, and Empire in Early Modern England and France*. Chicago: University of Chicago Press, 2003.

Ferguson, Margaret W., Maureen Quilligan, and Nancy J. Vickers, eds. *Rewriting the Renaissance: The Discourses of Sexual Difference in Early Modern Europe*. Chicago: University of Chicago Press, 1986.

Fisher, Will. *Materializing Gender in Early Modern English Literature and Culture*. New York: Cambridge University Press, 2006.

Fleming, Juliet. *Graffiti and the Writing Arts of Early Modern England*. Philadelphia: University of Pennsylvania Press, 2001.

Frye, Susan. *Elizabeth I: The Competition for Representation*. New York: Oxford University Press, 1993.

Fumerton, Patricia. *Cultural Aesthetics: Renaissance Literature and the Practice of Social Ornament*. Chicago: University of Chicago Press, 1991.

———. *Unsettled: The Culture of Mobility and the Working Poor in Early Modern England*. Chicago: University of Chicago Press, 2006.

Gillies, John. *Shakespeare and the Geography of Difference*. New York: Cambridge University Press, 1994.

Goldberg, Jonathan. *James I and the Politics of Literature: Jonson, Shakespeare, Donne, and Their Contemporaries*. Baltimore: Johns Hopkins University Press, 1983.

———. *Writing Matter: From the Hands of the English Renaissance*. Stanford: Stanford University Press, 1990.

———, ed. *Queering the Renaissance*. Durham, N.C.: Duke University Press, 1994.

Greenblatt, Stephen. *Learning to Curse: Essays in Early Modern Culture*. New York: Routledge, 1990.

———. *Renaissance Self-Fashioning: From More to Shakespeare*. Chicago: University of Chicago Press, 1980.

———, ed. *New World Encounters*. Berkeley: University of California Press, 1993.

———, ed. *Representing the English Renaissance*. Berkeley: University of California Press, 1988.

Grout, Donald Jay, and Hermine Weigel Williams. *A Short History of Opera*. 4th ed. New York: Columbia University Press, 2003.

Hall, Kim F. *Things of Darkness: Economies of Race and Gender in Early Modern England*. Ithaca, N.Y.: Cornell University Press, 1995.

Harris, Jonathan Gil. *Foreign Bodies and the Body Politic: Discourses of Social Pathology in Early Modern England*. New York: Cambridge University Press, 1998.

Harvey, Elizabeth D., ed. *Sensible Flesh: On Touch in Early Modern Culture*. Philadelphia: University of Pennsylvania Press, 2003.

Haselkorn, Anne M., and Betty S. Travitsky, eds. *The Renaissance Englishwoman in Print: Counterbalancing the Canon*. Amherst: University of Massachusetts Press, 1990.

Helgerson, Richard. *Forms of Nationhood: The Elizabethan Writing of England*. Chicago: University of Chicago Press, 1992.

Henderson, Katherine Usher, and Barbara F. McManus. *Half Humankind: Contexts and Texts of the Controversy About Women in England, 1540–1640*. Urbana: University of Illinois Press, 1985.

Hendricks, Margo, and Patricia Parker, eds. *Women, "Race," and Writing in the Early Modern Period*. New York: Routledge, 1994.

Hillman, David, and Carla Mazzio, eds. *The Body in Parts: Fantasies of Corporeality in Early Modern Europe*. New York: Routledge, 1997.

Hoeniger, F. David. *Medicine and Shakespeare in the English Renaissance*. Newark: University of Delaware Press, 1992.

Huizinga, Johan. *The Autumn of the Middle Ages*. Trans. Rodney J. Payton and Ulrich Mammitzsch. Chicago: University of Chicago Press, 1996.

Hull, Suzanne W. *Chaste, Silent & Obedient: English Books for Women, 1475–1640*. San Marino, Calif.: Huntington Library, 1982.

Hutson, Lorna. *The Usurer's Daughter: Male Friendship and Fictions of Women in Sixteenth-Century England*. New York: Routledge, 1994.

Javitch, Daniel. *Poetry and Courtliness in Renaissance England*. Princeton: Princeton University Press, 1978.

Jones, Ann Rosalind, and Peter Stallybrass. *Renaissance Clothing and the Materials of Memory*. New York: Cambridge University Press, 2000.

Jordan, Constance. *Renaissance Feminism: Literary Texts and Political Models*. Ithaca, N.Y.: Cornell University Press, 1990.

Knapp, Jeffrey. *Shakespeare's Tribe: Church, Nation, and Theater in Renaissance England*. Chicago: University of Chicago Press, 2002.

Laqueur, Thomas Walter. *Making Sex: Body and Gender from the Greeks to Freud*. Cambridge, Mass.: Harvard University Press, 1990.

MacDonald, Joyce Green. *Women and Race in Early Modern Texts*. New York: Cambridge University Press, 2002.

Magnusson, Lynne. *Shakespeare and Social Dialogue: Dramatic Language and Elizabethan Letters*. New York: Cambridge University Press, 1999.

Manley, Lawrence. *Literature and Culture in Early Modern London*. New York: Cambridge University Press, 1995.

Marcus, Leah S. *The Politics of Mirth: Jonson, Herrick, Milton, Marvell, and the Defense of Old Holiday Pastimes*. Chicago: University of Chicago Press, 1986.

McJannet, Linda. *The Sultan Speaks: Dialogue in English Plays and Histories about the Ottoman Turks*. New York: Palgrave Macmillan, 2006.

Meron, Theodor. *Bloody Constraint: War and Chivalry in Shakespeare*. New York: Oxford University Press, 1998.

Miller, David Lee, Sharon O'Dair, and Harold Weber, eds. *The Production of English Renaissance Culture*. Ithaca, N.Y.: Cornell University Press, 1994.

Montrose, Louis. *The Subject of Elizabeth: Authority, Gender, and Representation*. Chicago: University of Chicago Press, 2006.

Neill, Michael. *Issues of Death: Mortality and Identity in English Renaissance Tragedy*. Oxford: Clarendon, 1997.

Netzloff, Mark. *England's Internal Colonies: Class, Capital, and the Literature of Early Modern English Colonialism*. New York: Palgrave Macmillan, 2003.

Orlin, Lena Cowen. *Private Matters and Public Culture in Post-Reformation England*. Ithaca, N.Y.: Cornell University Press, 1994.

———, ed. *Material London, ca. 1600*. Philadelphia: University of Pennsylvania Press, 2000.

Parry, Graham. *The Golden Age Restor'd: The Culture of the Stuart Court, 1603–42*. New York: St. Martin's, 1981.

Paster, Gail Kern. *The Body Embarrassed: Drama and the Disciplines of Shame in Early Modern England*. Ithaca, N.Y.: Cornell University Press, 1993.

———. *Humoring the Body: Emotions and the Shakespearean Stage*. Chicago: University of Chicago Press, 2004.

Paster, Gail Kern, Katherine Rowe, and Mary Floyd-Wilson, eds. *Reading the Early Modern Passions: Essays in the Cultural History of Emotion*. Philadelphia: University of Pennsylvania Press, 2004.

Patterson, Annabel M. *Censorship and Interpretation: The Conditions of Writing and Reading in Early Modern England*. Madison: University of Wisconsin Press, 1984.

Peck, Linda Levy. *Consuming Splendor: Society and Culture in Seventeenth-Century England*. New York: Cambridge University Press, 2005.

Platt, Peter G. *Reason Diminished: Shakespeare and the Marvelous*. Lincoln: University of Nebraska Press, 1997.

Pollard, Tanya. *Drugs and Theater in Early Modern England*. New York: Oxford University Press, 2005.

Sanders, Eve Rachele. *Gender and Literacy on Stage in Early Modern England*. New York: Cambridge University Press, 1998.

Sawday, Jonathan. *The Body Emblazoned: Dissection and the Human Body in Renaissance Culture*. New York: Routledge, 1995.

Schoenfeldt, Michael C. *Bodies and Selves in Early Modern England: Physiology and Inwardness in Spenser, Shakespeare, Herbert, and Milton*. New York: Cambridge University Press, 1999.

Schwyzer, Philip. *Literature, Nationalism, and Memory in Early Modern England and Wales*. New York: Cambridge University Press, 2004.

Shapiro, James. *Shakespeare and the Jews*. New York: Columbia University Press, 1996.

Sharpe, Kevin, and Peter Lake, eds. *Culture and Politics in Early Stuart England*. Stanford: Stanford University Press, 1993.

Sherman, William H. *John Dee: The Politics of Reading and Writing in the English Renaissance*. Amherst: University of Massachusetts Press, 1995.

Shuger, Debora. *Censorship and Cultural Sensibility: The Regulation of Language in Tudor-Stuart England*. Philadelphia: University of Pennsylvania Press, 2006.

Simon, Joan. *Education and Society in Tudor England*. Cambridge, Eng.: Cambridge University Press, 1966.

Singh, Jyotsna G. *Colonial Narratives/Cultural Dialogues: 'Discoveries' of India in the Language of Colonialism*. New York: Routledge, 1996.

Smith, Bruce R. *The Acoustic World of Early Modern England: Attending to the O-Factor*. Chicago: University of Chicago Press, 1999.

———. *Homosexual Desire in Shakespeare's England: A Cultural Poetics*. Chicago: University of Chicago Press, 1994.

Smuts, R. Malcolm. *Court Culture and the Origins of a Royalist Tradition in Early Stuart England*. Philadelphia: University of Pennsylvania Press, 1987.

Stallybrass, Peter, and Allon White. *The Politics and Poetics of Transgression*. Ithaca, N.Y.: Cornell University Press, 1986.

Traub, Valerie, M. Lindsay Kaplan, and Dympna Callaghan, eds. *Feminist Readings of Early Modern Culture: Emerging Subjects*. New York: Cambridge University Press, 1996.

Turner, Henry S. *The English Renaissance Stage: Geometry, Poetics, and the Practical Spatial Arts 1580–1630*. New York: Oxford University Press, 2006.

Turner, James Grantham, ed. *Sexuality and Gender in Early Modern Europe: Institutions, Texts, Images*. New York: Cambridge University Press, 1993.

Wall, Wendy. *Staging Domesticity: Household Work and English Identity in Early Modern Drama*. New York: Cambridge University Press, 2002.

Watson, Robert N. *The Rest Is Silence: Death as Annihilation in the English Renaissance*. Berkeley: University of California Press, 1994.

Whigham, Frank. *Ambition and Privilege: The Social Tropes of Elizabethan Courtesy Theory*. Berkeley: University of California Press, 1984.

Woodbridge, Linda. *Vagrancy, Homelessness, and English Renaissance Literature*. Urbana: University of Illinois Press, 2001.

———. *Women and the English Renaissance: Literature and the Nature of Womankind, 1540 to 1620*. Urbana: University of Illinois Press, 1984.

Shakespeare's Generic, Literary, and Theatrical Contexts

Alpers, Paul. *What Is Pastoral?* Chicago: University of Chicago Press, 1996.

Altman, Joel. *The Tudor Play of Mind: Rhetorical Inquiry and the Development of Elizabethan Drama*. Berkeley: University of California Press, 1978.

Barish, Jonas. *The Antitheatrical Prejudice*. Berkeley: University of California Press, 1981.

Bate, Jonathan. *Shakespeare and Ovid*. Oxford: Clarendon, 1993.

Bates, Catherine. *The Rhetoric of Courtship in Elizabethan Language and Literature*. New York: Cambridge University Press, 1992.

Beckwith, Sarah. *Signifying God: Social Relation and Symbolic Act in the York Corpus Christi Plays*. Chicago: University of Chicago Press, 2001.

Belsey, Catherine. *The Subject of Tragedy: Identity and Difference in Renaissance Drama*. New York: Methuen, 1985.

Bevington, David M. *From "Mankind" to Marlowe: Growth of Structure in the Popular Drama of Tudor England*. Cambridge, Mass.: Harvard University Press, 1962.

———. *Tudor Drama and Politics: A Critical Approach to Topical Meaning*. Cambridge, Mass.: Harvard University Press, 1968.

Bly, Mary. *Queer Virgins and Virgin Queans on the Early Modern Stage*. New York: Oxford University Press, 2000.

Bowers, Fredson Thayer. *Elizabethan Revenge Tragedy, 1587–1642*. Princeton: Princeton University Press, 1940.

Braden, Gordon. *Renaissance Tragedy and the Senecan Tradition: Anger's Privilege*. New Haven: Yale University Press, 1985.

Bruster, Douglas. *Drama and the Market in the Age of Shakespeare*. New York: Cambridge University Press, 1992.

Bullough, Geoffrey, ed. *Narrative and Dramatic Sources of Shakespeare*. 8 vols. New York: Columbia University Press, 1957–75.

Butler, Martin. *Theatre and Crisis, 1632–1642*. New York: Cambridge University Press, 1984.

Carroll, William C. *The Metamorphoses of Shakespearean Comedy*. Princeton: Princeton University Press, 1985.

Cartwright, Kent. *Theatre and Humanism: English Drama in the Sixteenth Century*. New York: Cambridge University Press, 1999.

Clubb, Louise George. *Italian Drama in Shakespeare's Time*. New Haven: Yale University Press, 1989.

Cohen, Walter. *Drama of a Nation: Public Theater in Renaissance England and Spain*. Ithaca, N.Y.: Cornell University Press, 1985.

Crewe, Jonathan. *Trials of Authorship: Anterior Forms and Poetic Reconstruction from Wyatt to Shakespeare*. Berkeley: University of California Press, 1990.

Danson, Lawrence. *Shakespeare's Dramatic Genres*. New York: Oxford University Press, 2000.

Dawson, Anthony B., and Paul Yachnin. *The Culture of Playgoing in Shakespeare's England: A Collaborative Debate*. New York: Cambridge University Press, 2001.

Dillon, Janette. *Language and Stage in Medieval and Renaissance England*. New York: Cambridge University Press, 1998.

Felperin, Howard. *Shakespearean Romance*. Princeton: Princeton University Press, 1972.

Finkelpearl, Philip J. *John Marston of the Middle Temple: An Elizabethan Dramatist in His Social Setting*. Cambridge, Mass.: Harvard University Press, 1969.

Gardiner, Harold C. *Mysteries' End: An Investigation of the Last Days of the Medieval Religious Stage*. New Haven: Yale University Press, 1946.

Halasz, Alexandra. *The Marketplace of Print: Pamphlets and the Public Sphere in Early Modern England*. New York: Cambridge University Press, 1997.

Harbage, Alfred. *Shakespeare and the Rival Traditions*. New York: Macmillan, 1952.

Hardison, O. B. *Christian Rite and Christian Drama in the Middle Ages: Essays in the Origin and Early History of Modern Drama*. Baltimore: Johns Hopkins University Press, 1965.

Heinemann, Margot. *Puritanism and Theatre: Thomas Middleton and Opposition Drama under the Early Stuarts*. New York: Cambridge University Press, 1980.

Honan, Park. *Christopher Marlowe: Poet & Spy*. New York: Oxford University Press, 2005.

Honigmann, E. A. J., ed. *Shakespeare and His Contemporaries: Essays in Comparison*. Manchester: Manchester University Press, 1986.

———, ed. *Shakespeare's Impact on His Contemporaries*. London: Macmillan, 1982.

Howard, Jean E. *Theater of a City: The Places of London Comedy, 1598–1642*. Philadelphia: University of Pennsylvania Press, 2007.

Hunter, G. K. *John Lyly: The Humanist as Courtier*. Cambridge, Mass.: Harvard University Press, 1962.

Jones, Emrys. *The Origins of Shakespeare*. Oxford: Clarendon, 1977.

———. *Scenic Form in Shakespeare*. Oxford: Clarendon, 1971.

Kastan, David Scott, and Peter Stallybrass, eds. *Staging the Renaissance: Reinterpretations of Elizabethan and Jacobean Drama*. New York: Routledge, 1991.

Kermode, Lloyd Edward, Jason Scott-Warren, and Martine van Elk, eds. *Tudor Drama Before Shakespeare, 1485–1590: New Directions for Research, Criticism, and Pedagogy*. New York: Palgrave Macmillan, 2004.

Kolve, V. A. *The Play Called Corpus Christi*. Stanford: Stanford University Press, 1966.

Leggatt, Alexander. *Citizen Comedy in the Age of Shakespeare*. Toronto: University of Toronto Press, 1973.

———. *Introduction to English Renaissance Comedy*. Manchester: Manchester University Press, 1999.

Levin, Harry. *Shakespeare and the Revolution of the Times: Perspectives and Commentaries*. New York: Oxford University Press, 1976.

Levith, Murray J. *Shakespeare's Italian Settings and Plays*. Basingstoke: Macmillan, 1989.

Lomax, Marion. *Stage Images and Traditions: Shakespeare to Ford*. New York: Cambridge University Press, 1987.

Martindale, Charles, and A. B. Taylor, eds. *Shakespeare and the Classics*. New York: Cambridge University Press, 2004.

Masten, Jeffrey. *Textual Intercourse: Collaboration, Authorship, and Sexualities in Renaissance Drama*. New York: Cambridge University Press, 1997.

McLuskie, Kathleen. *Renaissance Dramatists*. New York: Harvester Wheatsheaf, 1989.

McMillin, Scott. *The Elizabethan Theatre and the Book of Sir Thomas More*. Ithaca, N.Y.: Cornell University Press, 1987.

McMillin, Scott, and Sally-Beth MacLean. *The Queen's Men and Their Plays*. New York: Cambridge University Press, 1998.

McMullan, Gordon, and Jonathan Hope, eds. *The Politics of Tragicomedy: Shakespeare and After*. New York: Routledge, 1991.

Miola, Robert S. *Shakespeare's Reading*. New York: Oxford University Press, 2000.

———. *Shakespeare's Rome*. New York: Cambridge University Press, 1983.

Newcomb, Lori Humphrey. *Reading Popular Romance in Early Modern England*. New York: Columbia University Press, 2002.

Norbrook, David. *Poetry and Politics in the English Renaissance*. London: Routledge and Kegan Paul, 1984.

Orgel, Stephen. *The Illusion of Power: Political Theater in the English Renaissance*. Berkeley: University of California Press, 1975.

Peters, Julie Stone. *Theatre of the Book, 1480–1880: Print, Text, and Performance in Europe*. New York: Oxford University Press, 2000.

Riggs, David. *Ben Jonson: A Life*. Cambridge, Mass.: Harvard University Press, 1989.

———. *The World of Christopher Marlowe*. London: Faber and Faber, 2004.

Rose, Mark. *Shakespearean Design*. Cambridge, Mass.: Belknap Press, 1972.

Rose, Mary Beth. *The Expense of Spirit: Love and Sexuality in English Renaissance Drama*. Ithaca, N.Y.: Cornell University Press, 1988.

Salingar, Leo. *Dramatic Form in Shakespeare and the Jacobeans: Essays*. New York: Cambridge University Press, 1986.

———. *Shakespeare and the Traditions of Comedy*. New York: Cambridge University Press, 1974.

Schwyzer, Philip. *Archaeologies of English Renaissance Literature*. New York: Oxford University Press, 2007.

Shapiro, James. *Rival Playwrights: Marlowe, Jonson, Shakespeare*. New York: Columbia University Press, 1991.

Snyder, Susan. *The Comic Matrix of Shakespeare's Tragedies:* Romeo and Juliet, Hamlet, Othello, *and* King Lear. Princeton: Princeton University Press, 1979.

Spivack, Bernard. *Shakespeare and the Allegory of Evil: The History of a Metaphor in Relation to His Major Villains.* New York: Columbia University Press, 1958.

Thomas, Vivian. *The Moral Universe of Shakespeare's Problem Plays.* New York: Routledge, 1991.

Vickers, Brian, ed. *English Renaissance Literary Criticism.* New York: Oxford University Press, 1999.

Vitkus, Daniel. *Turning Turk: English Theater and the Multicultural Mediterranean, 1570–1630.* New York: Palgrave Macmillan, 2003.

Weimann, Robert. *Shakespeare and the Popular Tradition in the Theater: Studies in the Social Dimension of Dramatic Form and Function.* Ed. Robert Schwartz. Baltimore: Johns Hopkins University Press, 1978.

Whitney, Charles. *Early Responses to Renaissance Drama.* New York: Cambridge University Press, 2006.

Woolf, Rosemary. *The English Mystery Plays.* Berkeley: University of California Press, 1972.

The Playing Field: Theaters, Actors, Patrons, and the State

Astington, John H. *English Court Theatre, 1558–1642.* Cambridge, Eng.: Cambridge University Press, 1999.

———, ed. *The Development of Shakespeare's Theater.* New York: AMS Press, 1992.

Barroll, J. Leeds. *Politics, Plague, and Shakespeare's Theater: The Stuart Years.* Ithaca, N.Y.: Cornell University Press, 1991.

Beckerman, Bernard. *Shakespeare at the Globe, 1599–1609.* New York: Macmillan, 1962.

Bentley, Gerald Eades. *The Jacobean and Caroline Stage.* 7 vols. Oxford: Clarendon, 1941–68.

———. *The Profession of Dramatist in Shakespeare's Time, 1590–1642.* Princeton: Princeton University Press, 1971.

———. *The Profession of Player in Shakespeare's Time, 1590–1642.* Princeton: Princeton University Press, 1984.

Berry, Herbert. *Shakespeare's Playhouses.* Illustrated by C. Walter Hodges. New York: AMS Press, 1987.

Bradbrook, M. C. *The Rise of the Common Player: A Study of Actor and Society in Shakespeare's England.* Cambridge, Mass.: Harvard University Press, 1962.

Chambers, E. K. *The Elizabethan Stage.* 4 vols. Oxford: Clarendon, 1923.

———. *The Mediaeval Stage.* 2 vols. Oxford: Clarendon, 1903.

Clare, Janet. *Art Made Tongue-Tied by Authority: Elizabethan and Jacobean Dramatic Censorship.* 2nd ed. Manchester: Manchester University Press, 1999.

Cook, Ann Jennalie. *The Privileged Playgoers of Shakespeare's London: 1576–1642.* Princeton: Princeton University Press, 1981.

Cox, John D., and David Scott Kastan, eds. *A New History of Early English Drama.* New York: Columbia University Press, 1997.

Dessen, Alan C. *Elizabethan Stage Conventions and Modern Interpreters.* Cambridge, Eng.: Cambridge University Press, 1984.

———. *Recovering Shakespeare's Theatrical Vocabulary.* New York: Cambridge University Press, 1995.

Dessen, Alan C., and Leslie Thomson. *A Dictionary of Stage Directions in English Drama, 1580–1642.* New York: Cambridge University Press, 1999.

Dillon, Janette. *The Cambridge Introduction to Early English Theatre.* New York: Cambridge University Press, 2006.

Dutton, Richard. *Licensing, Censorship and Authorship in Early Modern England: Buggeswords.* Houndmills, Basingstoke: Palgrave Macmillan, 2000.

————. *Mastering the Revels: The Regulation and Censorship of English Renaissance Drama*. London: Macmillan, 1991.

Dutton, Richard, Alison Findlay, and Richard Wilson, eds. *Region, Religion, and Patronage: Lancastrian Shakespeare*. Manchester: Manchester University Press, 2003.

Erne, Lukas. *Shakespeare as Literary Dramatist*. New York: Cambridge University Press, 2003.

Foakes, R. A. *Illustrations of the English Stage, 1580–1642*. Stanford: Stanford University Press, 1985.

Gair, W. Reavley. *The Children of Paul's: The Story of a Theatre Company, 1553–1608*. New York: Cambridge University Press, 1982.

Greg, W. W., ed. *Dramatic Documents from the Elizabethan Playhouses: Stage Plots: Actor's Parts: Prompt Books*. 2 vols. Oxford: Clarendon, 1931.

Gurr, Andrew. *Playgoing in Shakespeare's London*. 3rd ed. New York: Cambridge University Press, 2004.

————. *The Shakespeare Company, 1594–1642*. New York: Cambridge University Press, 2004.

————. *The Shakespearian Playing Companies*. Oxford: Clarendon, 1996.

————. *The Shakespearean Stage, 1574–1642*. 3rd ed. New York: Cambridge University Press, 1992.

Gurr, Andrew, and John Orrell. *Rebuilding Shakespeare's Globe*. London: Weidenfeld & Nicolson, 1989.

Harris, Jonathan Gil, and Natasha Korda, eds. *Staged Properties in Early Modern Drama*. New York: Cambridge University Press, 2002.

Hattaway, Michael. *Elizabethan Popular Theatre: Plays in Performance*. London: Routledge and Kegan Paul, 1982.

Henslowe, Philip. *Henslowe's Diary*. Ed. R. A. Foakes. 2nd ed. New York: Cambridge University Press, 2002.

Hodges, C. Walter. *The Globe Restored: A Study of the Elizabethan Theatre*. New York: Norton, 1973.

Holland, Peter, and Stephen Orgel, eds. *From Performance to Print in Shakespeare's England*. New York: Palgrave Macmillan, 2006.

————, eds. *From Script to Stage in Early Modern England*. Houndmills, Basingstoke: Palgrave Macmillan, 2004.

Ingram, William. *The Business of Playing: The Beginnings of Adult Professional Theater in Elizabethan London*. Ithaca, N.Y.: Cornell University Press, 1992.

Kernan, Alvin. *Shakespeare, the King's Playwright: Theater in the Stuart Court, 1603–1613*. New Haven: Yale University Press, 1995.

King, T. J. *Shakespearean Staging, 1599–1642*. Cambridge, Mass.: Harvard University Press, 1971.

Knutson, Roslyn Lander. *Playing Companies and Commerce in Shakespeare's Time*. Cambridge, Eng.: Cambridge University Press, 2001.

————. *The Repertory of Shakespeare's Company, 1594–1613*. Fayetteville: University of Arkansas Press, 1991.

Laroque, François. *Shakespeare's Festive World: Elizabethan Seasonal Entertainment and the Professional Stage*. New York: Cambridge University Press, 1991.

Lopez, Jeremy. *Theatrical Convention and Audience Response in Early Modern Drama*. New York: Cambridge University Press, 2002.

MacIntyre, Jean. *Costumes and Scripts in the Elizabethan Theatres*. Edmonton: University of Alberta Press, 1992.

Milling, Jane, and Peter Thomson, eds. *The Cambridge History of British Theatre*, Vol. 1: *Origins to 1660*. New York: Cambridge University Press, 2004.

Mulryne, J. R., and Margaret Shewring, eds. *Shakespeare's Globe Rebuilt*. New York: Cambridge University Press, 1997.

Munro, Lucy. *Children of the Queen's Revels: A Jacobean Theatre Repertory*. New York: Cambridge University Press, 2005.

Palfrey, Simon, and Tiffany Stern. *Shakespeare in Parts*. Oxford: Oxford University Press, 2007.

Shapiro, Michael. *Children of the Revels: The Boy Companies of Shakespeare's Time and Their Plays*. New York: Columbia University Press, 1977.

Smith, Irwin. *Shakespeare's Blackfriars Playhouse: Its History and Its Design*. New York: New York University Press, 1964.

Stern, Tiffany. *Making Shakespeare: From Stage to Page*. New York: Routledge, 2004.

———. *Rehearsal from Shakespeare to Sheridan*. Oxford: Clarendon, 2000.

White, Paul Whitfield, and Suzanne Westfall, eds. *Shakespeare and Theatrical Patronage in Early Modern England*. New York: Cambridge University Press, 2002.

Wickham, Glynne. *Early English Stages, 1300 to 1660*. 4 vols. New York: Routledge, 2002.

Wickham, Glynne, Herbert Berry, and William Ingram, eds. *English Professional Theatre, 1530–1660*. New York: Cambridge University Press, 2000.

Shakespeare's Life

Alexander, Peter. *Shakespeare's Life and Art*. New ed. New York: New York University Press, 1961.

Bate, Jonathan. *The Genius of Shakespeare*. London: Picador, 1997.

Bradbrook, M. C. *Shakespeare: The Poet in His World*. New York: Columbia University Press, 1978.

Chambers, E. K. *William Shakespeare: A Study of Facts and Problems*. 2 vols. Oxford: Clarendon, 1930.

Duncan-Jones, Katherine. *Ungentle Shakespeare: Scenes from His Life*. London: Arden Shakespeare, 2001.

Eccles, Mark. *Shakespeare in Warwickshire*. Madison: University of Wisconsin Press, 1961.

Edwards, Philip. *Shakespeare: A Writer's Progress*. New York: Oxford University Press, 1986.

Fraser, Russell A. *Shakespeare, The Later Years*. New York: Columbia University Press, 1992.

———. *Young Shakespeare*. New York: Columbia University Press, 1988.

Greenblatt, Stephen. *Will in the World: How Shakespeare Became Shakespeare*. New York: Norton, 2004.

Greer, Germaine. *Shakespeare*. New York: Oxford University Press, 1986.

Honan, Park. *Shakespeare: A Life*. New York: Oxford University Press, 1998.

Honigmann, E. A. J. *Shakespeare: The Lost Years*. 2nd ed. Manchester: Manchester University Press, 1998.

Hotson, Leslie. *Shakespeare Versus Shallow*. Boston: Little, Brown, and Company, 1931.

Levi, Peter. *The Life and Times of William Shakespeare*. New York: Macmillan, 1988.

Matus, Irvin Leigh. *Shakespeare, The Living Record*. Houndmills, Basingstoke: Macmillan, 1991.

Reese, M. M. *Shakespeare: His World and His Work*. Rev. ed. London: Edward Arnold, 1980.

Sams, Eric. *The Real Shakespeare: Retrieving the Early Years, 1564–1594*. New Haven: Yale University Press, 1995.

Schmidgall, Gary. *Shakespeare and the Poet's Life*. Lexington: University Press of Kentucky, 1990.

Schoenbaum, Samuel. *Shakespeare's Lives*. New ed. New York: Oxford University Press, 1991.

———. *William Shakespeare: A Compact Documentary Life*. Rev. ed. New York: Oxford University Press, 1987.

Shapiro, James. *A Year in the Life of William Shakespeare: 1599*. New York: Harper-Collins, 2005.

Taylor, Gary. *Reinventing Shakespeare: A Cultural History, from the Restoration to the Present*. New York: Weidenfeld & Nicolson, 1989.

Thomson, Peter. *Shakespeare's Professional Career*. New York: Cambridge University Press, 1992.

Wells, Stanley. *Shakespeare: A Life in Drama*. New York: Norton, 1995.

———. *Shakespeare: For All Time*. London: Macmillan, 2002.

Wood, Michael. *In Search of Shakespeare*. London: BBC, 2003.

Critical Approaches

Classics of Shakespeare Criticism

Barber, C. L. *Shakespeare's Festive Comedy: A Study of Dramatic Form and Its Relation to Social Custom*. Princeton: Princeton University Press, 1959.

Bradley, A. C. *Shakespearean Tragedy: Lectures on* Hamlet, Othello, King Lear, Macbeth. 3rd ed. New York: St. Martin's Press, 1992.

Coleridge, Samuel Taylor. *Coleridge on Shakespeare: The Text of the Lectures of 1811–12*. Ed. R. A. Foakes. Charlottesville: University Press of Virginia, 1971.

———. *Shakespearean Criticism*. 2 vols. Ed. T. M. Raysor. 2nd ed. New York: Dutton, 1969.

Eliot, T. S. "Shakespeare and the Stoicism of Seneca." *Selected Essays, 1917–1932*. New ed. New York: Harcourt, Brace, 1950.

Empson, William. *The Structure of Complex Words*. 3rd ed. London: Chatto & Windus, 1977.

Frye, Northrop. *Fools of Time: Studies in Shakespearean Tragedy*. Toronto: University of Toronto Press, 1967.

———. *A Natural Perspective: The Development of Shakespearean Comedy and Romance*. New York: Columbia University Press, 1965.

Hazlitt, William. *Characters of Shakespear's Plays*. London, 1817.

Johnson, Samuel. *Samuel Johnson on Shakespeare*. Ed. H. R. Woudhuysen. New York: Penguin, 1989.

Jones, Ernest. *Hamlet and Oedipus*. New York: Norton, 1949.

Kermode, Frank, ed. *Four Centuries of Shakespearian Criticism*. 1965. New York: Avon, 1965.

Knight, G. Wilson. *The Wheel of Fire: Interpretations of Shakespearean Tragedy, with Three New Essays*. 4th ed. New York: Harper & Row, 1977.

Kott, Jan. *Shakespeare Our Contemporary*. Trans. Boleslaw Taborski. Garden City, N.Y.: Anchor Books, 1966.

Morgann, Maurice. *Shakespearean Criticism*. Ed. Daniel A. Fineman. Oxford: Clarendon, 1972.

Spurgeon, Caroline F. E. *Shakespeare's Imagery, and What It Tells Us*. New York: Macmillan, 1935.

Tillyard, E. M. W. *Shakespeare's History Plays*. London: Chatto and Windus, 1944.

Vickers, Brian, ed. *Shakespeare: The Critical Heritage*. 6 vols. London: Routledge and Kegan Paul, 1974–1981.

General Studies

Barton, Anne. *Essays, Mainly Shakespearean*. New York: Cambridge University Press, 1994.

Bloom, Harold. *Shakespeare: The Invention of the Human*. New York: Riverhead Books, 1998.

Burckhardt, Sigurd. *Shakespearean Meanings*. Princeton: Princeton University Press, 1968.

Garber, Marjorie. *Shakespeare After All*. New York: Pantheon, 2004.

Hibbard, G. R. *The Making of Shakespeare's Dramatic Poetry*. Toronto: University of Toronto Press, 1981.

Honigmann, E. A. J. *Myriad-Minded Shakespeare: Essays on the Tragedies, Problem Comedies, and Shakespeare the Man*. 2nd ed. New York: St. Martin's Press, 1998.

Jones, John. *Shakespeare at Work*. New York: Oxford University Press, 1995.

Nuttall, A. D. *Shakespeare the Thinker*. New Haven: Yale University Press, 2007.

Ryan, Kiernan. *Shakespeare*. 3rd ed. New York: Palgrave Macmillan, 2001.

Language and Style

Baxter, John. *Shakespeare's Poetic Styles: Verse into Drama*. London: Routledge and Kegan Paul, 1980.

Blake, N. F. *Shakespeare's Language: An Introduction*. New York: St. Martin's Press, 1983.

Cercignani, Fausto. *Shakespeare's Works and Elizabethan Pronunciation*. New York: Oxford University Press, 1981.

Clemen, Wolfgang. *Shakespeare's Soliloquies*. Trans. Charity Scott Stokes. New York: Methuen, 1987.

———. *The Development of Shakespeare's Imagery*. New York: Hill and Wang, 1962.

Danson, Lawrence. *Tragic Alphabet: Shakespeare's Drama of Language*. New Haven: Yale University Press, 1974.

Donawerth, Jane. *Shakespeare and the Sixteenth-Century Study of Language*. Urbana: University of Illinois Press, 1984.

Edwards, Philip, Inga-Stina Ewbank, and G. K. Hunter, eds. *Shakespeare's Styles: Essays in Honour of Kenneth Muir*. New York: Cambridge University Press, 1980.

Gross, Kenneth. *Shakespeare's Noise*. Chicago: University of Chicago Press, 2001.

Hope, Jonathan. *Shakespeare's Grammar*. London: Arden Shakespeare, 2003.

Houston, John Porter. *Shakespearean Sentences: A Study in Style and Syntax*. Baton Rouge: Louisiana State University Press, 1988.

Hussey, S. S. *The Literary Language of Shakespeare*. 2nd ed. New York: Longman, 1992.

Kökeritz, Helge. *Shakespeare's Pronunciation*. New Haven: Yale University Press, 1953.

Mahood, M. M. *Shakespeare's Wordplay*. London: Methuen, 1957.

McDonald, Russ. *Shakespeare and the Arts of Language*. New York: Oxford University Press, 2001.

———. *Shakespeare's Late Style*. New York: Cambridge University Press, 2006.

Miriam Joseph, Sister. *Shakespeare's Use of the Arts of Language*. New York: Columbia University Press, 1947.

Palfrey, Simon. *Late Shakespeare: A New World of Words*. Oxford: Clarendon, 1997.

Parker, Patricia. *Literary Fat Ladies: Rhetoric, Gender, Property*. New York: Methuen, 1987.

———. *Shakespeare from the Margins: Language, Culture, Context*. Chicago: University of Chicago Press, 1996.

Partridge, Eric. *Shakespeare's Bawdy: A Literary & Psychological Essay and a Comprehensive Glossary*. 3rd ed. New York: Routledge, 1991.

Trousdale, Marion. *Shakespeare and the Rhetoricians*. Chapel Hill: University of North Carolina Press, 1982.

Vickers, Brian. *The Artistry of Shakespeare's Prose*. London: Methuen, 1968.

———. "Shakespeare's Use of Rhetoric." *A New Companion to Shakespeare Studies*. Ed. Kenneth Muir and S. Schoenbaum. Cambridge, Eng.: Cambridge University Press, 1971. 83–98.

Wright, George T. *Shakespeare's Metrical Art*. Berkeley: University of California Press, 1988.

Young, David. *The Action to the Word: Structure and Style in Shakespearean Tragedy.*
New Haven: Yale University Press, 1990.

Psychoanalytic Criticism

Adelman, Janet. *Suffocating Mothers: Fantasies of Maternal Origin in Shakespeare's
Plays,* Hamlet to The Tempest. New York: Routledge, 1992.

Armstrong, Philip. *Shakespeare in Psychoanalysis.* New York: Routledge, 2001.

Berger, Harry Jr. *Making Trifles of Terrors: Redistributing Complicities in Shakespeare.*
Stanford: Stanford University Press, 1997.

Charnes, Linda. *Notorious Identity: Materializing the Subject in Shakespeare.* Cambridge, Mass.: Harvard University Press, 1993.

Enterline, Lynn. *The Rhetoric of the Body from Ovid to Shakespeare.* Cambridge, Eng.:
Cambridge University Press, 2000.

Fineman, Joel. *Shakespeare's Perjured Eye: The Invention of Poetic Subjectivity in the
Sonnets.* Berkeley: University of California Press, 1986.

Freedman, Barbara. *Staging the Gaze: Postmodernism, Psychoanalysis, and Shakespearean Comedy.* Ithaca, N.Y.: Cornell University Press, 1991.

Garber, Marjorie. *Coming of Age in Shakespeare.* New York: Methuen, 1981.

————. *Shakespeare's Ghost Writers: Literature as Uncanny Causality.* New York:
Methuen, 1987.

Girard, René. *A Theater of Envy: William Shakespeare.* New York: Oxford University
Press, 1991.

Holland, Norman N. *Psychoanalysis and Shakespeare.* New York: Octagon, 1966.

Lupton, Julia Reinhard, and Kenneth Reinhard. *After Oedipus: Shakespeare in Psychoanalysis.* Ithaca, N.Y.: Cornell University Press, 1993.

Marshall, Cynthia. *The Shattering of the Self: Violence, Subjectivity, and Early Modern
Texts.* Baltimore: Johns Hopkins University Press, 2002.

Mazzio, Carla, and Douglas Trevor, eds. *Historicism, Psychoanalysis, and Early Modern
Culture.* New York: Routledge, 2000.

Pye, Christopher. *The Regal Phantasm: Shakespeare and the Politics of Spectacle.* New
York: Routledge, 1990.

————. *The Vanishing: Shakespeare, the Subject, and Early Modern Culture.* Durham,
N.C.: Duke University Press, 2000.

Schwartz, Murray M., and Coppélia Kahn, eds. *Representing Shakespeare: New Psychoanalytic Essays.* Baltimore: Johns Hopkins University Press, 1982.

Skura, Meredith Anne. *The Literary Use of the Psychoanalytic Process.* New Haven: Yale
University Press, 1981.

————. *Shakespeare the Actor and the Purposes of Playing.* Chicago: University of Chicago Press, 1993.

Wheeler, Richard P. *Shakespeare's Development and the Problem Comedies: Turn and
Counter-Turn.* Berkeley: University of California Press, 1981.

Zimmerman, Susan, ed. *Erotic Politics: Desire on the Renaissance Stage.* New York:
Routledge, 1992.

Feminism, Gender Studies, and Queer Studies

Bamber, Linda. *Comic Women, Tragic Men: A Study of Gender and Genre in Shakespeare.* Stanford: Stanford University Press, 1982.

Barker, Deborah, and Ivo Kamps, eds. *Shakespeare and Gender: A History.* New York:
Verso, 1995.

Boose, Lynda E. "The Father and the Bride in Shakespeare." *PMLA* 97 (1982): 325–47.

Callaghan, Dympna. *Shakespeare Without Women: Representing Gender and Race on
the Renaissance Stage.* New York: Routledge, 2000.

————. *Women and Gender in Renaissance Tragedy: A Study of* King Lear, Othello, The Duchess of Malfi, *and* The White Devil. Atlantic Highlands, N.J.: Humanities Press International, 1989.

Chedgzoy, Kate, ed. *Shakespeare, Feminism and Gender.* Houndmills, Basingstoke: Palgrave Macmillan, 2001.

Dash, Irene G. *Wooing, Wedding, and Power: Women in Shakespeare's Plays.* New York: Columbia University Press, 1981.

DiGangi, Mario. *The Homoerotics of Early Modern Drama.* New York: Cambridge University Press, 1997.

Dusinberre, Juliet. *Shakespeare and the Nature of Women.* 3rd ed. New York: Palgrave Macmillan, 2003.

Erickson, Peter. *Patriarchal Structures in Shakespeare's Drama.* Berkeley: University of California Press, 1985.

French, Marilyn. *Shakespeare's Division of Experience.* New York: Summit Books, 1981.

Garner, Shirley Nelson, and Madelon Sprengnether, eds. *Shakespearean Tragedy and Gender.* Bloomington: Indiana University Press, 1996.

Goldberg, Jonathan. *Sodometries: Renaissance Texts, Modern Sexualities.* Stanford: Stanford University Press, 1992.

Howard, Jean E., and Phyllis Rackin. *Engendering a Nation: A Feminist Account of Shakespeare's English Histories.* New York: Routledge, 1997.

Jardine, Lisa. *Still Harping on Daughters: Women and Drama in the Age of Shakespeare.* 2nd ed. New York: Columbia University Press, 1989.

Kahn, Coppèlia. *Man's Estate: Masculine Identity in Shakespeare.* Berkeley: University of California Press, 1981.

————. *Roman Shakespeare: Warriors, Wounds, and Women.* New York: Routledge, 1997.

Korda, Natasha. *Shakespeare's Domestic Economies: Gender and Property in Early Modern England.* Philadelphia: University of Pennsylvania Press, 2002.

Lenz, Carolyn, Ruth Swift, Gayle Greene, and Carol Thomas Neely, eds. *The Woman's Part: Feminist Criticism of Shakespeare.* Urbana: University of Illinois Press, 1980.

Neely, Carol Thomas. *Broken Nuptials in Shakespeare's Plays.* New Haven: Yale University Press, 1985.

————. *Distracted Subjects: Madness and Gender in Shakespeare and Early Modern Culture.* Ithaca, N.Y.: Cornell University Press, 2004.

Newman, Karen. *Fashioning Femininity and English Renaissance Drama.* Chicago: University of Chicago Press, 1991.

Novy, Marianne. *Love's Argument: Gender Relations in Shakespeare.* Chapel Hill: University of North Carolina Press, 1984.

————, ed. *Women's Re-Visions of Shakespeare: On the Responses of Dickinson, Woolf, Rich, H.D., George Eliot, and Others.* Urbana: University of Illinois Press, 1990.

Orgel, Stephen. *Impersonations: The Performance of Gender in Shakespeare's England.* New York: Cambridge University Press, 1996.

Shapiro, Michael. *Gender in Play on the Shakespearean Stage: Boy Heroines and Female Pages.* Ann Arbor: University of Michigan Press, 1994.

Shepherd, Simon. *Amazons and Warrior Women: Varieties of Feminism in Seventeenth Century Drama.* New York: St. Martin's, 1981.

Traub, Valerie. *Desire and Anxiety: Circulations of Sexuality in Shakespearean Drama.* New York: Routledge, 1992.

————. *The Renaissance of Lesbianism in Eary Modern England.* New York: Cambridge University Press, 2002.

Wayne, Valerie, ed. *The Matter of Difference: Materialist Feminist Criticism of Shakespeare.* Ithaca, N.Y.: Cornell University Press, 1991.

Historical Approaches: Materialism, New Historicism, and Cultural Materialism

Archer, John Michael. *Citizen Shakespeare: Freemen and Aliens in the Language of the Plays*. New York: Palgrave Macmillan, 2005.

Arnold, Oliver. *The Third Citizen: Shakespeare's Theater and the Early Modern House of Commons*. Baltimore: Johns Hopkins University Press, 2007.

Belsey, Catherine. *Shakespeare and the Loss of Eden: The Construction of Family Values in Early Modern Culture*. New Brunswick, N.J.: Rutgers University Press, 1999.

Berry, Ralph. *Shakespeare and Social Class*. Atlantic Highlands, N.J.: Humanities Press International, 1988.

Bristol, Michael D. *Shakespeare's America, America's Shakespeare*. New York: Routledge, 1990.

Bruster, Douglas. *Shakespeare and the Question of Culture: Early Modern Literature and the Cultural Turn*. New York: Palgrave Macmillan, 2003.

Cox, John D. *Shakespeare and the Dramaturgy of Power*. Princeton: Princeton University Press, 1989.

Dollimore, Jonathan. *Radical Tragedy: Religion, Ideology, and Power in the Drama of Shakespeare and His Contemporaries*. 3rd ed. New York: Palgrave Macmillan, 2004.

Dollimore, Jonathan, and Alan Sinfield, eds. *Political Shakespeare: Essays in Cultural Materialism*. 2nd ed. Ithaca, N.Y.: Cornell University Press, 1994.

Dubrow, Heather, and Richard Strier, eds. *The Historical Renaissance: New Essays on Tudor and Stuart Literature and Culture*. Chicago: University of Chicago Press, 1988.

Eagleton, Terry. *William Shakespeare*. Malden, Mass.: Blackwell, 1986.

Greenblatt, Stephen. *Hamlet in Purgatory*. Princeton: Princeton University Press, 2001.

————. *Shakespearean Negotiations: The Circulation of Social Energy in Renaissance England*. Berkeley: University of California Press, 1988.

Hadfield, Andrew. *Shakespeare and Republicanism*. New York: Cambridge University Press, 2005.

Hawkes, Terence. *Meaning by Shakespeare*. New York: Routledge, 1992.

————. *That Shakespeherian Rag: Essays on a Critical Process*. New York: Methuen, 1986.

Holderness, Graham, ed. *The Shakespeare Myth*. Manchester: Manchester University Press, 1988.

————, ed. *Shakespeare's History Plays: Richard II to Henry V*. Houndmills, Basingstoke: Palgrave Macmillan, 1992.

Howard, Jean E. *The Stage and Social Struggle in Early Modern England*. New York: Routledge, 1994.

Howard, Jean E., and Scott Cutler Shershow, eds. *Marxist Shakespeares*. New York: Routledge, 2001.

Howard, Jean E., and Marion F. O'Connor, eds. *Shakespeare Reproduced: The Text in History and Ideology*. New York: Methuen, 1987.

Jardine, Lisa. *Reading Shakespeare Historically*. New York: Routledge, 1996.

Jordan, Constance. *Shakespeare's Monarchies: Ruler and Subject in the Romances*. Ithaca, N.Y.: Cornell University Press, 1997.

Kamps, Ivo, ed. *Materialist Shakespeare: A History*. New York: Verso, 1995.

Kastan, David Scott. *Shakespeare After Theory*. London: Routledge, 1999.

————. *Shakespeare and the Shapes of Time*. Hanover, N.H.: University Press of New England, 1982.

Mallin, Eric S. *Inscribing the Time: Shakespeare and the End of Elizabethan England*. Berkeley: University of California Press, 1995.

Marcus, Leah S. *Puzzling Shakespeare: Local Reading and Its Discontents*. Berkeley: University of California Press, 1988.

Maus, Katharine Eisaman. *Inwardness and Theater in the English Renaissance*. Chicago: University of Chicago Press, 1995.

Montrose, Louis. *The Purpose of Playing: Shakespeare and the Cultural Politics of the Elizabethan Theatre*. Chicago: University of Chicago Press, 1996.

Mullaney, Steven. *The Place of the Stage: License, Play, and Power in Renaissance England*. Chicago: University of Chicago Press, 1988.

Orgel, Stephen. *The Authentic Shakespear: and Other Problems of the Early Modern Stage*. New York: Routledge, 2002.

Patterson, Annabel. *Shakespeare and the Popular Voice*. Malden, Mass.: Blackwell, 1989.

Rackin, Phyllis. *Stages of History: Shakespeare's English Chronicles*. Ithaca, N.Y.: Cornell University Press, 1990.

Siemon, James R. *Word Against Word: Shakespearean Utterance*. Amherst: University of Massachusetts Press, 2002.

Sinfield, Alan. *Shakespeare, Authority, Sexuality: Unfinished Business in Cultural Materialism*. New York: Routledge, 2006.

Tennenhouse, Leonard. *Power on Display: The Politics of Shakespeare's Genres*. New York: Methuen, 1986.

Weimann, Robert. *Author's Pen and Actor's Voice: Playing and Writing in Shakespeare's Theatre*. Ed. Helen Higbee and William West. New York: Cambridge University Press, 2000.

Wells, Robin Headlam. *Shakespeare, Politics, and the State*. Houndmills, Basingstoke: Palgrave Macmillan, 1986.

Wilson, Richard. *Secret Shakespeare: Studies in Theatre, Religion and Resistance*. Manchester: Manchester University Press, 2004.

———. *Will Power: Essays on Shakespearean Authority*. Detroit: Wayne State University Press, 1993.

Postcolonial Criticism, Race, and Ethnicity

Alexander, Catherine M. S., and Stanley Wells, eds. *Shakespeare and Race*. New York: Cambridge University Press, 2000.

Cartelli, Thomas. *Repositioning Shakespeare: National Formations, Postcolonial Appropriations*. New York: Routledge, 1999.

de Sousa, Geraldo U. *Shakespeare's Cross-Cultural Encounters*. Houndmills, Basingstoke: Palgrave Macmillan, 2002.

Floyd-Wilson, Mary. *English Ethnicity and Race in Early Modern Drama*. New York: Cambridge University Press, 2003.

Hendricks, Margo. " 'Obscured by dreams:' Race, Empire, and Shakespeare's *A Midsummer Night's Dream*." *Shakespeare Quarterly* 47 (1996): 37–60.

Hulme, Peter. *Colonial Encounters: Europe and the Native Caribbean, 1492–1797*. New York: Methuen, 1986.

Knapp, Jeffrey. *An Empire Nowhere: England, America, and Literature from* Utopia *to* The Tempest. Berkeley: University of California Press, 1992.

Loomba, Ania. *Gender, Race, Renaissance Drama*. Manchester: Manchester University Press, 1989.

Loomba, Ania, and Martin Orkin, eds. *Post-colonial Shakespeares*. New York: Routledge, 1998.

Maley, Willy. *Nation, State, and Empire in English Renaissance Literature: Shakespeare to Milton*. New York: Palgrave Macmillan, 2003.

Vaughan, Virginia Mason. *Performing Blackness on English Stages, 1500–1800*. New York: Cambridge University Press, 2005.

Other Philosophical and Theoretical Approaches

Booth, Stephen. *King Lear, Macbeth, Indefinition, and Tragedy*. New Haven: Yale University Press, 1983.

Cavell, Stanley. *Disowning Knowledge in Seven Plays of Shakespeare.* Updated ed. New York: Cambridge University Press, 2003.

Engle, Lars. *Shakespearean Pragmatism: Market of His Time.* Chicago: University of Chicago Press, 1993.

Evans, Malcolm. *Signifying Nothing: Truth's True Contents in Shakespeare's Text.* Athens: University of Georgia Press, 1986.

Felperin, Howard. *The Uses of the Canon: Elizabethan Literature and Contemporary Theory.* New York: Oxford University Press, 1990.

Goldberg, Jonathan. *Shakespeare's Hand.* Minneapolis: University of Minnesota Press, 2003.

Grady, Hugh. *The Modernist Shakespeare: Critical Texts in a Material World.* Oxford: Clarendon, 1991.

———. *Shakespeare, Machiavelli, and Montaigne: Power and Subjectivity from* Richard II *to* Hamlet. Oxford: Oxford University Press, 2002.

Grady, Hugh, and Terence Hawkes, eds. *Presentist Shakespeares.* New York: Routledge, 2006.

Hawkes, Terence. *Shakespeare in the Present.* New York: Routledge, 2002.

Knapp, Robert S. *Shakespeare—The Theater and the Book.* Princeton: Princeton University Press, 1989.

Lukacher, Ned. *Daemonic Figures: Shakespeare and the Question of Conscience.* Ithaca, N.Y.: Cornell University Press, 1994.

Lupton, Julia Reinhard. *Citizen-Saints: Shakespeare and Political Theology.* Chicago: University of Chicago Press, 2005.

Parker, Patricia, and Geoffrey Hartman, eds. *Shakespeare and the Question of Theory.* New York: Methuen, 1985.

Pechter, Edward. *What Was Shakespeare?: Renaissance Plays and Changing Critical Practice.* Ithaca, N.Y.: Cornell University Press, 1995.

Rabkin, Norman. *Shakespeare and the Problem of Meaning.* Chicago: University of Chicago Press, 1981.

Schalkwyk, David. *Speech and Performance in Shakespeare's Sonnets and Plays.* Cambridge, Eng.: Cambridge University Press, 2002.

Textual Criticism and Bibliography

Allen, Michael J. B., and Kenneth Muir, eds. *Shakespeare's Plays in Quarto: A Facsimile Edition of Copies Primarily from the Henry E. Huntington Library.* Berkeley: University of California Press, 1981.

Blayney, Peter W. M. *The First Folio of Shakespeare.* Washington, D.C.: Folger Library Publications, 1991.

———. *The Texts of* King Lear *and Their Origins.* Vol. 1: *Nicholas Okes and the First Quarto.* New York: Cambridge University Press, 1982.

Bowers, Fredson. *On Editing Shakespeare.* Charlottesville: University Press of Virginia, 1966.

Brooks, Douglas A. *From Playhouse to Printing House: Drama and Authorship in Early Modern England.* New York: Cambridge University Press, 2000.

De Grazia, Margreta. "Homonyms Before and After Lexical Standardization." *Deutsche Shakespeare-Gesellschaft West* (Jahrbuch 1990): 143–56.

———. *Shakespeare Verbatim: The Reproduction of Authenticity and the 1790 Apparatus.* New York: Oxford University Press, 1991.

De Grazia, Margreta, and Peter Stallybrass. "The Materiality of the Shakespearean Text." *Shakespeare Quarterly* 44 (1993): 255–83.

Erne, Lukas, and Margaret Jane Kidnie, eds. *Textual Performances: The Modern Reproduction of Shakespeare's Drama.* New York: Cambridge University Press, 2004.

Franklin, Colin. *Shakespeare Domesticated: The Eighteenth-Century Editions.* Brookfield, Vt.: Gower Publishing Company, 1991.

Hinman, Charlton, ed. *The First Folio of Shakespeare.* 2nd ed. New York: Norton, 1996.

———. *The Printing and Proof-Reading of the First Folio of Shakespeare.* 2 vols. Oxford: Clarendon, 1963.

Honigmann, E. A. J. *The Stability of Shakespeare's Text.* London: E. Arnold, 1965.

Ioppolo, Grace. *Dramatists and Their Manuscripts in the Age of Shakespeare, Jonson, Middleton and Heywood: Authorship, Authority and the Playhouse.* New York: Routledge, 2006.

———. *Revising Shakespeare.* Cambridge, Mass.: Harvard University Press, 1991.

Irace, Kathleen O. *Reforming the "Bad" Quartos: Performance and Provenance of Six Shakespearean First Editions.* Newark: University of Delaware Press, 1994.

Jackson, MacDonald P. *Defining Shakespeare: Pericles as Test Case.* New York: Oxford University Press, 2003.

Kastan, David Scott. *Shakespeare and the Book.* New York: Cambridge University Press, 2001.

Lesser, Zachary. *Renaissance Drama and the Politics of Publication: Readings in the English Book Trade.* New York: Cambridge University Press, 2004.

Maguire, Laurie E. *Shakespearean Suspect Texts: The "Bad" Quartos and Their Contexts.* New York: Cambridge University Press, 1996.

Maguire, Laurie E., and Thomas L. Berger, eds. *Textual Formations and Reformations.* Newark: University of Delaware Press, 1998.

Marcus, Leah S. *Unediting the Renaissance: Shakespeare, Marlowe, Milton.* New York: Routledge, 1996.

McKerrow, Ronald B. *Prolegomena for the Oxford Shakespeare: A Study in Editorial Method.* Oxford: Clarendon, 1939.

McLeod, Randall, ed. *Crisis in Editing: Texts of the English Renaissance.* New York: AMS Press, 1994.

———. "UN *Editing* Shak-speare." *SubStance* 33/34 (1982): 26–55.

———[as Random Cloud]. "The Psychopathology of Everyday Art." *The Elizabethan Theatre IX.* Ed. G. R. Hibbard. Port Credit, Ontario: P. D. Meany, 1986. 100–68.

Murphy, Andrew. *Shakespeare in Print: A History and Chronology of Shakespeare Publishing.* New York: Cambridge University Press, 2003.

———, ed. *The Renaissance Text: Theory, Editing, Textuality.* Manchester: Manchester University Press, 2000.

Pollard, Alfred W. *Shakespeare's Folios and Quartos: A Study in the Bibliography of Shakespeare's Plays, 1594–1685.* London: Methuen, 1909.

Seary, Peter. *Lewis Theobald and the Editing of Shakespeare.* Oxford: Clarendon, 1990.

Taylor, Gary, and Michael Warren, eds. *The Division of the Kingdoms: Shakespeare's Two Versions of* King Lear. Oxford: Clarendon, 1986.

Urkowitz, Steven. *Shakespeare's Revision of* King Lear. Princeton: Princeton University Press, 1980.

Vickers, Brian. *Shakespeare, Co-Author: A Historical Study of Five Collaborative Plays.* New York: Oxford University Press, 2002.

Walker, Alice. *Textual Problems of the First Folio:* Richard III, King Lear, Troilus & Cressida, 2 Henry IV, Hamlet, Othello. Cambridge, Eng.: Cambridge University Press, 1953.

Wells, Stanley. *Re-Editing Shakespeare for the Modern Reader.* New York: Oxford University Press, 1984.

Wells, Stanley, and Gary Taylor. *Modernizing Shakespeare's Spelling.* Oxford: Clarendon, 1979.

———. *William Shakespeare: A Textual Companion.* Oxford: Clarendon, 1987.

Werstine, Paul. "A Century of 'Bad' Shakespeare Quartos." *Shakespeare Quarterly* 50 (1999): 310–33.

———. "Narratives about Printed Shakespeare Texts: 'Foul Papers' and 'Bad' Quartos." *Shakespeare Quarterly* 41 (1990): 65–86.

Williams, George Walton. *The Craft of Printing and the Publication of Shakespeare's Works.* Washington, D.C.: Folger Shakespeare Library, 1985.

Wilson, J. Dover. *The Manuscript of Shakespeare's "Hamlet" and the Problems of Its Transmission: An Essay in Critical Bibliography.* 2 vols. New York: Macmillan, 1934.

Shakespeare and Performance

Aebischer, Pascale. *Shakespeare's Violated Bodies: Stage and Screen Performance.* New York: Cambridge University Press, 2003.

Aebischer, Pascale, Edward J. Esche, and Nigel Wheale, eds. *Remaking Shakespeare: Performance Across Media, Genres, and Cultures.* New York: Palgrave Macmillan, 2003.

Bartholomeusz, Dennis. *"Macbeth" and the Players.* Cambridge, Eng.: Cambridge University Press, 1969.

Barton, John. *Playing Shakespeare.* London: Methuen, 1984.

Bate, Jonathan, and Russell Jackson, eds. *Shakespeare: An Illustrated Stage History.* New York: Oxford University Press, 1996.

Berger, Harry Jr. *Imaginary Audition: Shakespeare on Stage and Page.* Berkeley: University of California Press, 1989.

Berry, Francis. *The Shakespeare Inset: Word and Picture.* London: Routledge and Kegan Paul, 1965.

Berry, Ralph. *Changing Styles in Shakespeare.* Boston: Allen & Unwin, 1981.

Bevington, David M. *Action Is Eloquence: Shakespeare's Language of Gesture.* Cambridge, Mass.: Harvard University Press, 1984.

———. *This Wide and Universal Theater: Shakespeare in Performance, Then and Now.* Chicago: University of Chicago Press, 2007.

Branam, George Curtis. *Eighteenth-Century Adaptations of Shakespearean Tragedy.* Berkeley: University of California Press, 1956.

Bratton, Jacky, and Julie Hankey, gen. eds. The Shakespeare in Production Series. Cambridge, Eng.: Cambridge University Press, 1996–.

Brennan, Anthony. *Onstage and Offstage Worlds in Shakespeare's Plays.* New York: Routledge, 1989.

———. *Shakespeare's Dramatic Structures.* Boston: Routledge and Kegan Paul, 1986.

Brown, Ivor. *Shakespeare and the Actors.* London: Bodley Head, 1970.

Brown, John Russell. *Shakespeare and the Theatrical Event.* Houndmills, Basingstoke: Palgrave Macmillan, 2002.

———. *Shakespeare's Dramatic Style:* Romeo and Juliet, As You Like It, Julius Caesar, Twelfth Night, Macbeth. London: Heinemann, 1970.

Bulman, James C., ed. *Shakespeare, Theory, and Performance.* New York: Routledge, 1996.

Calderwood, James. *Shakespearean Metadrama: The Argument of the Play in* Titus Andronicus, Love's Labour's Lost, Romeo and Juliet, A Midsummer Night's Dream, *and* Richard II. Minneapolis: University of Minnesota Press, 1971.

Carlisle, Carol Jones. *Shakespeare from the Greenroom: Actors' Criticisms of Four Major Tragedies.* Chapel Hill: University of North Carolina Press, 1969.

Cohn, Ruby. *Modern Shakespeare Offshoots.* Princeton: Princeton University Press, 1976.

Dean, Winton. "Shakespeare in the Opera House." *Shakespeare Survey* 18 (1965): 75–93.

Dobson, Michael. *The Making of the National Poet: Shakespeare, Adaptation and Authorship, 1660–1769.* Oxford: Clarendon, 1992.

————, ed. *Performing Shakespeare's Tragedies Today: The Actor's Perspective.* New York: Cambridge University Press, 2006.

Downer, Alan S. *The Eminent Tragedian William Charles Macready.* Cambridge, Mass.: Harvard University Press, 1966.

Duffin, Ross W. *Shakespeare's Songbook.* New York: Norton, 2004.

Foulkes, Richard, ed. *Shakespeare and the Victorian Stage.* New York: Cambridge University Press, 1986.

Goldman, Michael. *Acting and Action in Shakespearean Tragedy.* Princeton: Princeton University Press, 1985.

Hirsch, James E. *The Structure of Shakespearean Scenes.* New Haven: Yale University Press, 1981.

Hogan, Charles Beecher, ed. *Shakespeare in the Theatre, 1701–1800.* 2 vols. Oxford: Clarendon, 1952–57.

Holland, Peter. *English Shakespeares: Shakespeare on the English Stage in the 1990's.* New York: Cambridge University Press, 1997.

Homan, Sidney, ed. *Shakespeare's "More Than Words Can Witness": Essays on Visual and Nonverbal Enactment in the Plays.* Lewisburg, Pa.: Bucknell University Press, 1980.

————, ed. *When the Theater Turns to Itself: The Aesthetic Metaphor in Shakespeare.* Lewiston, Pa.: Bucknell University Press, 1981.

Hoenselaars, Ton, ed. *Shakespeare's History Plays: Performance, Translation and Adaptation in Britain and Abroad.* Cambridge, Eng.: Cambridge University Press, 2004.

Howard, Jean E. *Shakespeare's Art of Orchestration: Stage Technique and Audience Response.* Urbana: University of Illinois Press, 1984.

Jones, Emrys. *Scenic Form in Shakespeare.* Oxford: Clarendon, 1971.

Kennedy, Dennis. *Looking at Shakespeare: A Visual History of Twentieth-Century Performance.* 2nd ed. New York: Cambridge University Press, 2001.

————, ed. *Foreign Shakespeare: Contemporary Performance.* New York: Cambridge University Press, 1993.

Marshall, Gail, and Adrian Poole, eds. *Victorian Shakespeare.* New York: Palgrave Macmillan, 2003.

McGuire, Philip C. *Speechless Dialect: Shakespeare's Open Silences.* Berkeley: University of California Press, 1985.

McGuire, Philip C., and David A. Samuelson. *Shakespeare: The Theatrical Dimension.* New York: AMS Press, 1979.

Mooney, Michael E. *Shakespeare's Dramatic Transactions.* Durham, N.C.: Duke University Press, 1990.

Mowat, Barbara A. *The Dramaturgy of Shakespeare's Romances.* Athens: University of Georgia Press, 1976.

Odell, George Clinton Densmore. *Shakespeare from Betterton to Irving.* 2 vols. New York: Scribner, 1920.

Parsons, Keith, and Pamela Mason, eds. *Shakespeare in Performance.* London: Salamander, 1995.

Poel, William. *Shakespeare in the Theater.* London: Sidgwick and Jackson, 1913.

Rosenberg, Marvin. *The Masks of King Lear.* Berkeley: University of California Press, 1972.

Rosenberg, Marvin, et al. *Clamorous Voices: Shakespeare's Women Today.* London: Women's Press, 1988.

Rutter, Carol, gen. ed. The Shakespeare in Performance Series. Manchester: Manchester University Press, 1982–.

Shattuck, Charles H. *Shakespeare on the American Stage,* vol. 1: *From the Hallams to Edwin Booth.* Washington, D.C.: Folger Shakespeare Library, 1976.

————. *Shakespeare on the American Stage,* vol. 2: *From Booth and Barrett to Sothern and Marlowe.* Washington, D.C.: Folger Shakespeare Library, 1987.

————. *The Shakespeare Promptbooks: A Descriptive Catalogue.* Urbana: University of Illinois Press, 1965.

Slater, Ann. *Shakespeare, the Director.* Totowa, N.J.: Barnes & Noble Books, 1982.

Smallwood, Robert, ed. *Players of Shakespeare.* 6 vols. New York: Cambridge University Press, 1985–2004.

————, gen. ed. The Shakespeare at Stratford series. London: Arden Shakespeare, 2002– .

Speaight, Robert. *Shakespeare on the Stage: An Illustrated History of Shakespearian Performance.* London: Collins, 1973.

————. *William Poel and the Elizabethan Revival.* Cambridge, Mass.: Harvard University Press, 1954.

Spencer, Hazelton. *Shakespeare Improved: The Restoration Versions in Quarto and On the Stage.* Cambridge, Mass.: Harvard University Press, 1927.

Styan, J. L. *The Shakespeare Revolution: Criticism and Performance in the Twentieth Century.* New York: Cambridge University Press, 1977.

————. *Shakespeare's Stagecraft.* Cambridge, Eng.: Cambridge University Press, 1967.

————. "Sight and Space: The Perception of Shakespeare on Stage and Screen." *Shakespeare, Pattern of Excelling Nature: Shakespeare Criticism in Honor of America's Bicentennial.* Ed. David Bevington and Jay L. Halio. Newark: University of Delaware Press, 1978.

Thompson, Marvin and Ruth, eds. *Shakespeare and the Sense of Performance.* Newark: University of Delaware Press, 1989.

Trewin, J. C. *Shakespeare on the English Stage, 1900–1964.* London: Barrie and Rockliff, 1964.

Wells, Stanley. *Royal Shakespeare: Four Major Productions at Stratford-upon-Avon.* Manchester: Manchester University Press, 1977.

————, ed. *Shakespeare in the Theatre: An Anthology of Criticism.* New York: Oxford University Press, 1997.

Worthen, William B. *Shakespeare and the Authority of Performance.* New York: Cambridge University Press, 1997.

————. *Shakespeare and the Force of Modern Performance.* New York: Cambridge University Press, 2003.

Shakespeare on Film

Ball, Robert Hamilton. *Shakespeare on Silent Film: A Strange Eventful History.* London: Allen & Unwin, 1968.

Burt, Richard, and Lynda E. Boose, eds. *Shakespeare the Movie: Popularizing the Plays on Film, TV, and Video.* New York: Routledge, 1997.

————. *Shakespeare the Movie II: Popularizing the Plays on Film, TV, Video, and DVD.* New York: Routledge, 2003.

Bristol, Michael D. *Big-Time Shakespeare.* New York: Routledge, 1996.

Buchanan, Judith. *Shakespeare on Film.* New York: Pearson Longman, 2005.

Buchman, Lorne Michael. *Still in Movement: Shakespeare on Screen.* New York: Oxford University Press, 1991.

Bulman, J. C., and H. R. Coursen, eds. *Shakespeare on Television: An Anthology of Essays and Reviews.* Hanover, N.H.: University Press of New England, 1988.

Burnett, Mark Thornton, and Ramona Wray, eds. *Shakespeare, Film, Fin de Siècle.* New York: St. Martin's, 2000.

Burt, Richard. *Shakespeare After Mass Media.* New York: Palgrave Macmillan, 2002.

Cartelli, Thomas, and Katherine Rowe, eds. *New Wave Shakespeare on Screen.* Malden, Mass.: Polity Press, 2007.

Crowl, Samuel. *Shakespeare at the Cineplex: The Kenneth Branagh Era.* Athens: Ohio University Press, 2003.

————. *Shakespeare and Film*. New York: Norton, 2008.

Davies, Anthony, and Stanley Wells, eds. *Shakespeare and the Moving Image: The Plays on Film and Television*. New York: Cambridge University Press, 1994.

Donaldson, Peter S. *Shakespearean Films/Shakespearean Directors*. Boston: Unwin Hyman, 1990.

Henderson, Diana E. *Collaborations with the Past: Reshaping Shakespeare Across Time and Media*. Ithaca, N.Y.: Cornell University Press, 2006.

————. *A Concise Companion to Shakespeare on Screen*. Malden, Mass.: Blackwell, 2007.

Hindle, Maurice. *Studying Shakespeare on Film*. New York: Palgrave Macmillan, 2007.

Kliman, Bernice W. *Hamlet: Film, Television, and Audio Performance*. Madison, N.J.: Fairleigh Dickinson University Press, 1988.

Lehmann, Courtney. *Shakespeare Remains: Theater to Film, Early Modern to Postmodern*. Ithaca, N.Y.: Cornell, 2002.

Lehmann, Courtney, and Lisa S. Starks, eds. *Spectacular Shakespeare: Critical Theory and Popular Cinema*. Madison, N.J.: Fairleigh Dickinson University Press, 2002.

Rothwell, Kenneth S. *A History of Shakespeare on Screen: A Century of Film and Television*. 2nd ed. Cambridge, Eng.: Cambridge University Press, 2004.

Glossary

STAGE TERMS

"Above" The gallery on the upper level of the *frons scenae*. In open-air theaters, such as the Globe, this space contained the lords' rooms. The central section of the gallery was sometimes used by the players for short scenes. Indoor theaters such as Blackfriars featured a curtained alcove for musicians above the stage.

"Aloft" See *"Above."*

Amphitheater An open-air theater, such as the Globe.

Arras See *Curtain.*

Cellerage See *Trap.*

Chorus In the works of Shakespeare and other Elizabethan playwrights, a single individual (not, as in Greek tragedy, a group) who speaks before the play (and often before each act), describing events not shown on stage as well as commenting on the action witnessed by the audience.

Curtain Curtains, or arras (hanging tapestries), covered a part of the *frons scenae,* thus concealing the discovery space, and may also have been draped around the edge of the stage to conceal the open area underneath.

Discovery space A central opening or alcove concealed behind a curtain in the center of the *frons scenae.* The curtain could be drawn aside to "discover" tableaux such as Portia's caskets, the body of Polonius, or the statue of Hermione. Shakespeare appears to have used this stage device only sparingly.

Doubling The common practice of having one actor play multiple roles, so that a play with a large cast of characters might be performed by a relatively small company.

Dumb shows Mimed scenes performed before a play (or before each act), summarizing or foreshadowing the plot. Dumb shows were popular in early Elizabethan drama; although they already seemed old-fashioned in Shakespeare's time, they were employed by writers up to the 1640s.

Epilogue A brief speech or poem addressed to the audience by an actor after the play. In some cases, as in *2 Henry IV,* the epilogue could be combined with, or could merge into, the jig.

Forestage The front of the stage, closest to the audience.

Frons scenae The wall at the back of the stage, behind which lay the players' tiring-house. The *frons scenae* of the Globe featured two doors flanking the central discovery space, with a gallery "above."

Gallery Covered seating areas surrounding the open yard of the public amphitheaters. There were three levels of galleries at the Globe; admission to these seats cost an extra penny (in addition to the basic admission fee of one penny to the yard), and seating in the higher galleries another penny yet. In indoor theaters such as Blackfriars, where there was no standing room, gallery seating was less expensive than seating in the pit; indeed, seats nearest the stage were the most expensive.

Gatherers Persons employed by the playing company to take money at the entrances to the theater.

Groundlings Audience members who paid the minimum price of admission (one penny) to stand in the yard of the open-air theaters; also referred to as "understanders."

Heavens The canopied roof over the stage in the open-air theaters, protecting the players and their costumes from rain. The "heavens" would be brightly decorated with sun, moon, and stars, and perhaps the signs of the zodiac.

Hut A structure on the top of the cover over the stage, where stagehands produced the effects of thunder and lightning and operated the machinery by which gods, such as Jupiter in *Cymbeline,* descended through the trapdoor in the "heavens."

Jig A song-and-dance performance by the clown and other members of the company at the conclusion of a play. These performances were frequently bawdy and were officially banned in 1612.

Lords' rooms Partitioned sections of the gallery "above," where the most prestigious and expensive seats in the public playhouses were located. These rooms were designed not to provide the best view of the action on the stage below, but to make their privileged occupants conspicuous to the rest of the audience.

Open-air theaters Unroofed public playhouses in the suburbs of London, such as The Theatre, the Rose, and the Globe.

Part The character played by an actor. In Shakespeare's theater, actors were given a roll of paper called a "part" containing all of the speeches and all of the cues belonging to their character. The term "role," synonymous with "part," is derived from such rolls of paper.

Patrons Important nobles and members of the royal family under whose protection the theatrical companies of London operated; players not in the service of patrons were punishable as vagabonds. The companies were referred to as their patrons' "Men" or "Servants." Thus the name of the company to which Shakespeare belonged for most of his career was first the Lord Chamberlain's Men, then was changed to the King's Men in 1603, when James I became their patron.

Pillars The "heavens" were supported by two tall painted pillars or posts near the front of the stage. These occasionally played a role in stage action, allowing a character to "hide" while remaining in full view of the audience.

Pit The area in front of the stage in indoor theaters such as Blackfriars, where the most expensive and prestigious bench seating was to be had.

Posts See *Pillars.*

Proscenium The space of the transparent "fourth wall," which divides the actors from the orchestra and audience in the standard modern theater. The stages on which Shakespeare's plays were first performed had no proscenium.

Rearstage The back of the stage, farthest from the audience.

Repertory The stock of plays a company had ready for performance at a given time. Companies generally performed a different play each day, often more than a dozen plays in a month and more than thirty in the course of the season.

Role See *Part*.

Sharers Senior actors holding shares in a joint-stock theatrical company; they paid for costumes, hired hands, and new plays, and they shared profits and losses equally. Shakespeare was not only a longtime "sharer" of the Lord Chamberlain's Men but, from 1599, a "housekeeper," the holder of a one-eighth share in the Globe playhouse.

Tiring-house The players' dressing (attiring) room, a structure located at the back of the stage and connected to the stage by two or more doors in the *frons scenae*.

Trap A trapdoor near the front of the stage that allowed access to the "cellarage" beneath and was frequently associated with hell's mouth. Another trapdoor in the "heavens" opened for the descent of gods to the stage below.

"Within" The tiring-house, from which offstage sound effects such as shouts, drums, and trumpets were produced.

Yard The central space in open-air theaters such as the Globe, into which the stage projected and in which audience members stood. Admission to the yard in the public theaters cost a penny, the cheapest admission available.

TEXTUAL TERMS

Aside See *Stage direction*.

Autograph Text written in the author's own hand. With the possible exception of a few pages of the collaborative play *Sir Thomas More*, no dramatic works or poems written in Shakespeare's hand are known to survive.

Canonical Of an author, the writings generally accepted as authentic. In the case of Shakespeare's dramatic works, only two plays that are not among the thirty-six plays contained in the First Folio, *Pericles* and *The Two Noble Kinsmen*, have won widespread acceptance into the Shakespearean canon. (This sense of "canonical" should not be confused with the use of "the canon" to denote the entire body of literary works, including but not limited to Shakespeare's, that have traditionally been regarded as fit objects of admiration and study.)

Catchword A word printed below the text at the bottom of a page, matching the first word on the following page. The catchword enabled the printer to keep the pages in their proper sequence. Where the catchword fails to match the word at the top of the next page, there is reason to suspect that something has been lost or misplaced.

Compositor A person employed in a print shop to set type. To speed the printing process, most of Shakespeare's plays were set by more than one compositor. Compositors frequently followed their own standards in spelling and punctuation. They inevitably introduced some errors into the text, often by selecting the wrong piece from the type case or by setting the correct letter upside down.

Conflation A version of a play created by combining readings from more than one substantive edition. Since the early eighteenth century, for example, most versions of *King Lear* and of several other plays by Shakespeare have been conflations of quarto and First Folio texts.

Control text   The text upon which a modern edition is based.

Dramatis personae   A list of the characters appearing in the play. In the First Folio such lists were printed at the end of some but not all of the plays. The editor Nicholas Rowe (1709) first provided lists of dramatis personae for all of Shakespeare's dramatic works.

Exeunt / Exit   See *Stage direction*.

Fair copy   A transcript of the "foul papers" made either by a scribe or by the playwright.

Folio   A bookmaking format in which each large sheet of paper is folded once, making two leaves (four pages front and back). This format produced large volumes, generally handsome and expensive. The First Folio of Shakespeare's plays was printed in 1623.

Foul papers   An author's first completed draft of a play, typically full of blotted-out passages and revisions. None of Shakespeare's foul papers is known to survive.

Licensing   By an order of 1581, new plays could not be performed until they had received a license from the Master of the Revels. A separate license, granted by the Court of High Commission, was required for publication, though in practice plays were often printed without license. From 1610, the Master of the Revels had the authority to license plays for publication as well as for performance.

Manent / Manet   See *Stage direction*.

Memorial reconstruction   The conjectured practice of reconstructing the text of a play from memory. Companies touring in the provinces without access to promptbooks may have resorted to memorial reconstruction. This practice also provides a plausible explanation for the existence of the so-called bad Quartos.

Octavo   A bookmaking format in which each large sheet of paper is folded three times, making eight leaves (sixteen pages front and back). Only one of Shakespeare's plays, *Richard Duke of York* (*3 Henry VI*, 1595), was published in octavo format.

Playbook   See *Promptbook*.

Press variants   Minor textual variations among books of the same edition, resulting from corrections made in the course of printing or from damaged or slipped type.

Promptbook   A manuscript of a play (either foul papers or fair copy) annotated and adapted for performance by the theatrical company. The promptbook incorporated stage directions, notes on properties and special effects, and revisions, sometimes including those required by the Master of the Revels. Promptbooks are usually identifiable by the replacement of characters' names with actors' names.

Quarto   A bookmaking format in which each large sheet of paper is folded twice, making four leaves (eight pages front and back). Quarto volumes were smaller and less expensive than books printed in the folio format.

Scribal copy   A transcript of a play produced by a professional scribe (or "scrivener"). Scribes tended to employ their own preferred spellings and abbreviations and could be responsible for introducing a variety of errors.

Speech prefix (s.p.)   The indication of the identity of the speaker of the following line or lines. Early editions of Shakespeare's plays often use different prefixes at different points to designate the same person. On occasion, the name of the actor who was to play the role appears in place of the name of the character.

Stage direction (s.d.)   The part of the text that is not spoken by any character but that indicates actions to be performed onstage. Stage directions in the earliest editions of Shakespeare's plays are sparse and are sometimes grouped together at the beginning of a scene rather than next to the spoken lines they should precede, accompany, or follow. By convention, the most basic stage directions were written in Latin. "Exit" indicates the departure of a single actor from the stage, "exeunt" the departure of more than one. "Manet" indicates that a single actor remains onstage, "manent" that more than one remains. Lines accompanied by the stage direction "aside" are spoken so as not to be heard by the others onstage. This stage direction appeared in some early editions of Shakespeare plays, but other means were also used to indicate such speech (such as placing the words within parentheses), and sometimes no indication was provided.

Stationers' Register   The account books of the Company of Stationers (of which all printers were legally required to be members), recording the fees paid for permission to print new works as well as the fines exacted for printing without permission. The Stationers' Register thus provides a valuable if incomplete record of publication in England.

Substantive text   The text of an edition based upon access to a manuscript, as opposed to a derivative text based only on an earlier edition.

Variorum editions   Comprehensive editions of a work or works in which the various views of previous editors and commentators are compiled.

ILLUSTRATION ACKNOWLEDGMENTS

Early Modern Map Culture Speed: © British Library/HIP/Art Resource, NY • Braun and Hogenberg: HIP/Art Resource, NY. Museum of London, London, Great Britain
Contemporary Documents
First Folio front matter: *The Norton Facsimile of the First Folio of Shakespeare,* 2nd ed. (1996)

Index of Plays